PERSONOLOGY

The Precision Approach to Charting Your
Life, Career, and Relationships

* * *BY GARY GOLDSCHNEIDER * * *

RUNNING PRESS
PHILADELPHIA · LONDON

9   8   7   6   5   4   3   2
Digit on the right indicates the number of this printing

Library of Congress Control Number: 2005902521

ISBN 0-7624-2229-7

ECHO CHERNIK provided illustrations for the cover,
for each of the planet chapter opening pages, and the
spot illustrations on pages 28, 110, and 112.
www.echo-x.com

RON TANOVITZ provided the 48 symbols that link
the Personology periods in the chapters on the Sun, Moon,
and each of the eight planets.

Designed by **GWEN GALEONE**

Edited by **DEBORAH GRANDINETTI**

This book may be ordered by mail from the publisher.
Please include $2.50 for postage and handling.
But try your bookstore first!

Visit us on the web!
www.runningpress.com
www.goldschneider.com

C O N T E N T S

INTRODUCTION

FORECASTING
CHARTS USING THE
PERSONOLOGY SYSTEM

P *ersonology* gives you the tools you need to become your own astrologer. In a few easy steps, without any special knowledge at all, you can create a "Personology" birthday (or natal) chart for yourself—or anyone you know—and interpret it accurately. You can also construct a chart for any upcoming day to help you know what you can expect on that day. This can be useful if you have a special presentation coming up, an important job interview, or are planning a wedding or other special affair.

Personology offers a more nuanced "reading" than one that you would get from traditional astrology. Traditional astrology subdivides the zodiac into twelve constellations or "sun" signs. My system subdivides the zodiac into forty-eight "personology periods" instead of the traditional twelve. That allows for forty-eight different positions for the sun alone, each of them dependent upon your date of birth. Someone considered an "Aries" under traditional astrology may find their personality more accurately described within my personology system, under one of the following sun sign types: *Pisces-Aries Cusp* (The Cusp of Rebirth), *Aries I* (The Week of the Child), *Aries II* (The Week of the Star), or *Aries III* (The Week of the Pioneer), or *Aries-Taurus Cusp* (The Week of Power).

Every one of the twelve sun signs is similarly segmented. Although there are five possible designations for each sun sign, the last cusp becomes the first personology period in the new "sun" sign, making for forty-eight classifications in all. The Aries-Taurus Cusp, for instance, applies to individuals born between April 19-24—the last days of Aries and the first days of Taurus.

My system also places the Moon, Mercury, Venus, Mars, Jupiter, Saturn, Uranus, Neptune, and Pluto in one of forty-eight personology periods, which creates forty-eight possible interpretations for each of the ten planets. Thus, Personology yields more specific information about each planet than does conventional astrology.

ABOUT MY
PERSONOLOGY SYSTEM

I am often asked how I created the personology system. It is important to emphasize that it really developed more as a result of my hobby of collecting birthdays than directly from my study of astrology. Over the years I asked many people their birthdays, collected them and made observations about what types of people seemed to be born at what times of the year. My ability to ascribe characteristics to people born on any given day and eventually to all the 366 days was the result of some forty years of research on my part. Like any scientist collecting data, I formed certain conclusions from my data and then made them into a theory. Once the theory was created, I was able to make remarkably accurate predictions on the basis of it.

Only much later did I realize the importance of the two equinoxes and two solstices in forming the grand cross whose circular track we have been treading for many hundreds of thousands of years. Also, although the signs of the zodiac had become very important to me as an astrologer, the cusps or overlapping areas between the signs seemed to me even more important. It was a very important moment when I realized what should have been obvious from the start, that the solstices and equinoxes were cusps themselves, and therefore of even more significance to us here on earth than the heavenly astrological constellations and the signs derived from them.

Finally, I had enough data to describe the forty-eight personology periods (thirty-six "weeks" and twelve cusps) and at a later stage to delineate each of the 366 possible days of the year. Whereas astrologers used degrees of the zodiac signs to delineate the position of the Sun at one's birth, I preferred to use the day itself, since people experience days as dates rather than as degrees of the zodiac. Thus personology speaks directly to people about their position in both the earthly and the heavenly scheme of things. In this book, *Personology*, the reader is able to place all of their ten planets in the forty-eight personology periods and form a picture of their astrological chart in a pragmatic, specific, and earth-oriented manner. Furthermore, they can do the same not only for other people, but also for many dates past, present and future, which might have significance in their lives. Doing such a personology chart can prove helpful in understanding ourselves and the times in which we live.

CREATE YOUR OWN CHART

Use the Fill-In Chart and Wheel below to create your own astrological reading using the Personology system.
Make multiple copies of this page so you can make readings for various people and dates.

FILL-IN CHART

Date & Time	SUN	MOON	MERCURY	VENUS	MARS	JUPITER	SATURN	URANUS	NEPTUNE	PLUTO

⊙	Sun
☽	Moon
☿	Mercury
♀	Venus
♂	Mars
♃	Jupiter
♄	Saturn
♅	Uranus
♆	Neptune
♇	Pluto

FILL-IN WHEEL

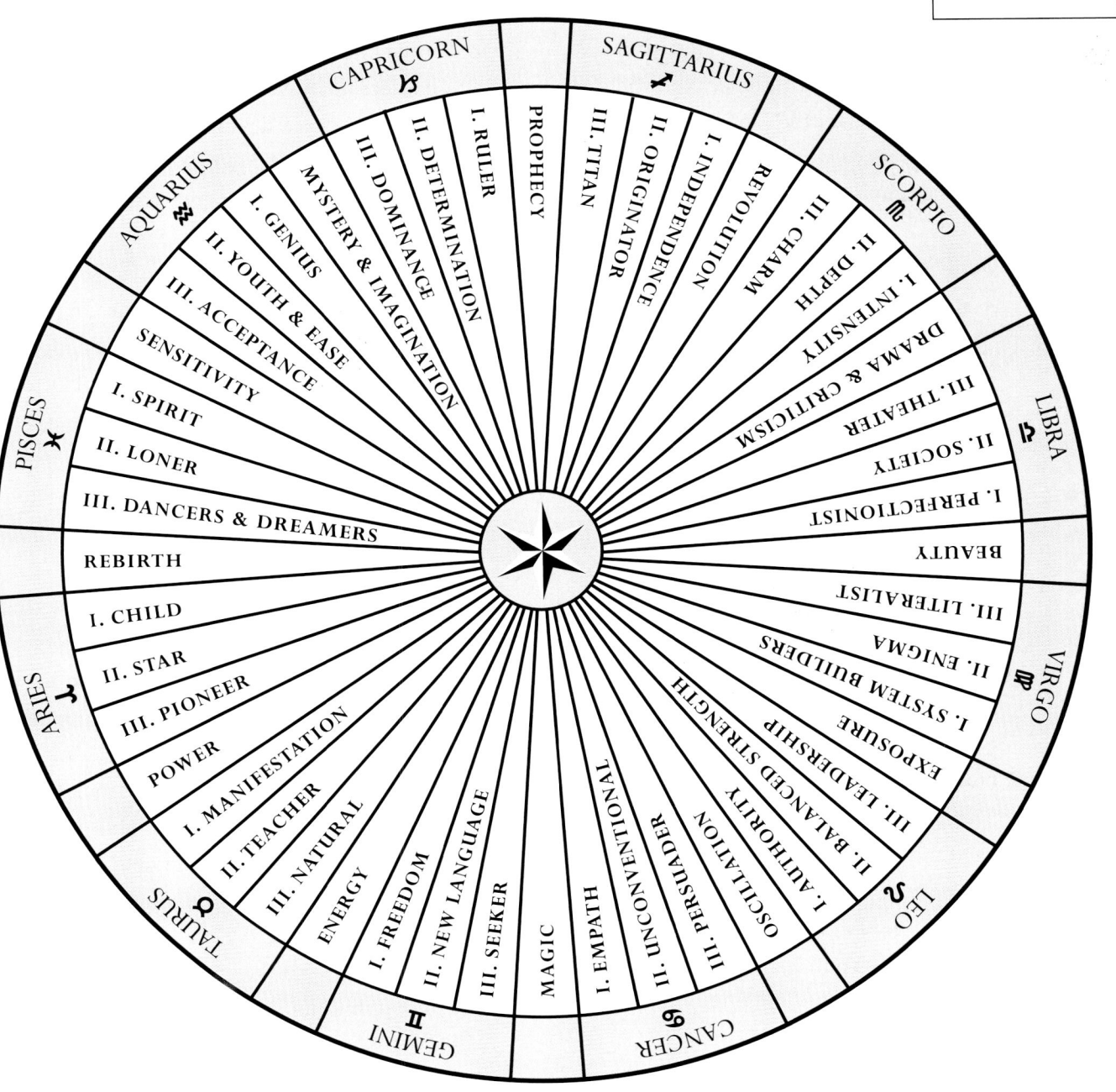

CREATING A PERSONOLOGY BIRTHDAY PROFILE

Thanks to the extensive tables in the back of this book, creating a personology natal chart and interpreting it is very easy. The tables in the back of the book cover the years from 1900 to 2025. You can get information on any day within this 125-year period by looking up your birth date in the tables in the back of the book. Simply look up the year and date of your birth.

The numbers in the tables correspond to the numbered paragraphs in each of the chapters in the main text. If you look at the Sun chapter, for instance, you will find forty-eight different positions for the sun, each of which is numbered. These numbers correspond to the numbers in the table. Here is an example:

✳ 1 ✳
SUN ON THE CUSP
OF REBIRTH
(PISCES-ARIES CUSP) MARCH 19-24

Often direct in their attitudes and opinions, their more aggressive outward side masks an inner sensitivity. This latter trait can keep them from moving forward in the world and achieving outright success. They are frequently misunderstood and must take the time to explain themselves fully. Above all, they need to maintain a positive approach and not fall prey to depression.

Notice the number "1," the phrase (Pisces-Aries Cusp), and the dates. The number "1" corresponds to the numbers in the tables in the back of the book, and the phrase "Pisces-Aries Cusp" tells you where anyone born on these dates is situated in my personology system. The phrase "Pisces-Aries" cusp, also tells you where to find this placement on the personology wheel.

To put together a birthday profile for any day between January 1, 1900 and December 31, 2025, simply:

1. Copy the Personology Fill-In Chart and Wheel on page 5 onto a separate piece of paper.
2. Turn to the tables in the back of the book and find the year, month, and date.
3. Look up the number for the Sun, and write it in your Personology Fill-In Chart.
4. You may need to do some simple calculations to help you select the right column for the moon. (The tables give you a choice of three.) First, obtain the time of birth. Then consider whether it falls within Eastern Standard Time, in the United States. If it does not, convert it to Eastern Standard Time. Then consider whether the date falls within Daylight Savings Time. (Daylight Savings Time begins for most of the United States at 2 a.m. on the first Sunday of April. Time reverts to standard time at 2 a.m. on the last Sunday of October. In the U.S., each time zone switches at a different time.) If the time falls within Daylight Savings Time, subtract one hour. Please don't forget to convert Daylight Savings Time within Eastern Standard Time if you were born when Daylight Savings Time was in effect.

Use this birth time to choose the correct moon column, and take the number from that column. Again, you only need one number for the moon. To choose the column that is correct for you, determine whether the time of your birth was between 12:01 a.m. and 8 a.m., in which case you'd use the number in the first column. If it falls between or 8:01 a.m. and 4 p.m., use the number in the second column; and if it falls between 4:01 p.m. and 12:00 a.m., use the number in the third moon column.

The reason that there are three possible choices for the moon, but not the other planets, is that the moon changes astrological signs every two and a half days and changes personology periods approximately every 15 hours. The Sun and the eight planets do not change astrological signs as frequently.

5. Copy the relevant numbers for the Moon, and the eight planets into the top box on your copy of the Personology Fill-In Chart.

6. Once you have all ten numbers filled in, turn to the interpretive chapters in the front of the book. Start with the sun. Look up the numbered paragraph that corresponds to the number you found in the Sun column in the tables.

7. The top line of the numbered paragraph will give you the specific personology period. Let's say you were born on October 17, 1963. The table would direct you to look up the 28th paragraph in the Sun chapter. That paragraph tells you that individuals born on this date fall within the period I have designated as Libra III, or "Sun in the Week of Theater," which covers the period from October 11-18th.

8. You can now find the segment of the wheel dedicated to Libra III. You may either write the word "sun" in that segment, or use the special glyph for the sun. (You will find a key showing you the glyphs for the sun, moon and each of the planets on the same page as the "Personology Fill-In Chart and Wheel."

9. Copy the interpretive paragraph on the back of that sheet.

10. Repeat the process for the Moon, and each of the eight planets. When you are done, you will have a complete personology chart, and a complete ten-paragraph birthday (or special day) profile.

Let's do a practice chart together, using the date October 17, 1963. Let's assume the time of birth was 3 a.m.

1. Turn to page 522 and find the line for October 17, 1963 on the right hand side of the page.

ATTRIBUTES OF THE TEN PLANETS

In astrology, the Sun and Moon are considered planets. As you read the interpretative paragraphs, keep in mind that each planet represents one or more specific aspects of the person. In brief:

The Sun represents
your self, ego structure, personality.
∗
The Moon represents
your feelings, unconscious, dreams.
∗
Mercury represents
logic and communication.
∗
Venus represents
love, romance, social interactions,
and the feminine side.
∗
Mars represents
aggression, forcefulness,
the masculine side.
∗
Jupiter represents
optimism, expansive attitudes,
luck, the big picture.
∗
Saturn represents
responsibility, limitation, and realism.
∗
Uranus represents
psychic powers, unpredictability,
and higher thought.
∗
Neptune represents
spirituality, religion, and fantasy.
∗
Pluto represents
money, sexuality, and the dark side.

2. Determine that 3 a.m. falls within the first moon column, since 3 a.m. is after 12:01 a.m. but *before* 8 a.m. Therefore, the relevant numbers are:

> **Sun:** 28
>
> **Moon:** 28
>
> **Mercury:** 26
>
> **Venus:** 30
>
> **Mars:** 32
>
> **Jupiter:** 3
>
> **Saturn:** 43
>
> **Uranus:** 22
>
> **Neptune:** 31
>
> **Pluto:** 23

3. Copy the "Personology Fill-In Chart and Wheel." Log these numbers on the chart.

Date & Time	SUN	MOON 1	MERCURY	VENUS	MARS	JUPITER	SATURN	URANUS	NEPTUNE	PLUTO
OCT. 17	28	28	26	30	32	3	43	22	31	23

4. Use this chart to look up each of the ten interpretative paragraphs. Let's start with the Sun. Turn to page 35 and find the 28th paragraph. It says:

★28★
SUN IN THE WEEK OF THEATER
(LIBRA III) OCTOBER 11–18

These capable, forceful individuals usually have little doubt about what they think and are not shy about expressing their opinions either. Yet they can have a terrible time making choices and even making up their minds about what course to take. This is because they can see the value of the other guy's point of view and want to keep options open whenever possible.

---

5. Find the segment marked "Libra III" in the personology wheel on the copy you've made of the "Personology Fill-In Chart and Wheel." Write the word "Sun" on the wheel, or draw in the symbol (☉).

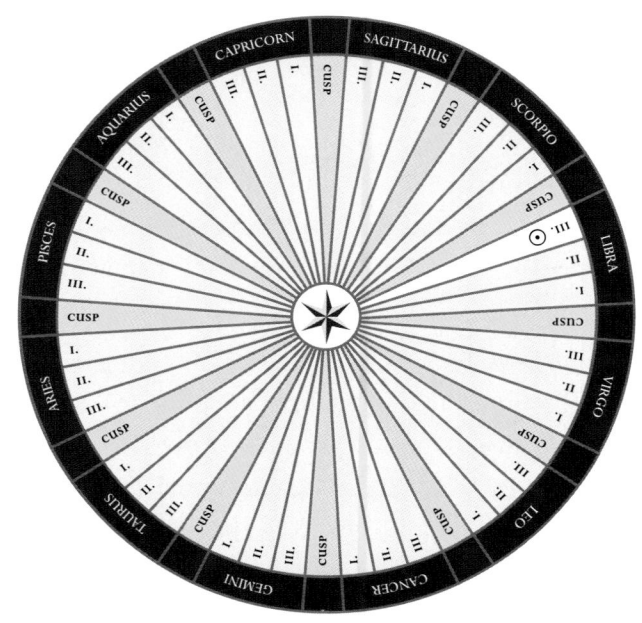

6. Copy the contents of the paragraph down. You can use a separate sheet of lined paper, or write on the back of the "Personology Fill-In Chart and Wheel" copy you've already made.

7. Repeat the process for the Moon, and each of the other planets. Your composite portrait should read just like this one:

NATAL PORTRAIT
FOR INDIVIDUAL BORN OCTOBER 17, 1963, AT 3 A.M.

> **Sun:** Libra III
>
> **Moon:** Libra III
>
> **Mercury:** Libra I
>
> **Venus:** Scorpio I
>
> **Mars:** Scorpio III
>
> **Jupiter:** Aries II
>
> **Saturn:** Aquarius II
>
> **Uranus:** Virgo I
>
> **Neptune:** Scorpio II
>
> **Pluto:** Virgo II

NATAL PORTRAIT FOR INDIVIDUAL BORN OCTOBER 17, 1963, AT 3 A.M.

★28★
SUN IN THE WEEK OF THEATER
(LIBRA III) OCTOBER 11-18

These capable, forceful individuals usually have little doubt about what they think and are not shy about expressing their opinions either. Yet they can have a terrible time making choices and even making up their minds about what course to take. This is because they can see the value of the other guy's point of view and want to keep options open whenever possible.

★28★
MOON IN THE WEEK OF THEATER
(LIBRA III)

A natural tendency toward exhibitionism appears here and if such individuals are quiet or shy it usually indicates repression, often due to judgmental attitudes from family members or teachers early in life. For enthusiastic individuals who are not blocked emotionally, they can be the life of any party. Sometimes they go too far and need to be reined in.

★26★
MERCURY IN THE WEEK OF THE PERFECTIONIST
(LIBRA I)

Mercury tends to be highly critical here and so those with that planet in this position are difficult to please. Always looking for something better, they never seem satisfied with what they have. They should make an effort to control their pickiness and learn to accept things as they are without trying to alter or fix them.

★30★
VENUS IN THE WEEK OF INTENSITY
(SCORPIO I)

Seduction figures prominently here. Masters in attracting and controlling the opposite sex, those with Venus in this week are born flirts and specialists in the arts of love. Because of the intensity with which they love they are not easily forgotten. They must learn, however, to back off and allow the other person to express their true feelings or risk losing them.

★32★
MARS IN THE WEEK OF CHARM
(SCORPIO III)

Mars is given an extra seductive attraction in this position. If encouraged, these folks are likely to take over the lives of weaker family members and friends. Thus they are capable of making most or even all of the important decisions for the other person. In doing so they create dependencies that might not be so healthy for either party in the future.

★3★
JUPITER IN THE WEEK OF THE STAR
(ARIES II)

Self-expression is demanded here, even if the personality involved is a quiet one. Working behind the scenes will achieve as much success as being in the spotlight. The important thing is maintaining the central position, whether the principal player or not. Good luck comes easily here and cannot really be earned with hard work. Serendipity plays a role.

★43★
SATURN IN THE WEEK OF YOUTH AND EASE
(AQUARIUS II)

Either Saturn can enjoy himself and take a bit of a vacation from heavy responsibilities or one's abilities to relax can be impaired by thoughts concerning what needs doing. In either case, a balance should be sought between pleasure and work. This is quite possible and can lead to a more healthy personality that can function well on the job and on vacation.

★22★
URANUS IN THE WEEK OF SYSTEM BUILDERS
(VIRGO I)

Uranus has much to learn in this week from the methodical Virgo I energies. However, because the planet is opposed to orderly activities he may wind up undermining them. The result can be a messy bedroom or work station. Breaking structures apart rather than building them up is Uranus's specialty, so his destructive bent may be aroused and directed against strict regimens and ingrained habits.

★31★
NEPTUNE IN THE WEEK OF DEPTH
(SCORPIO II)

If isolation and nursing private resentments and grudges manifest here, Neptune in this week can lead to serious depressions. Opening up avenues of true communication with others is advised, in order to avoid getting bottled up in one's own private world. Particularly in the professional sphere, making slow, gradual progress is advised rather than expecting sudden miracles to surface.

★23★
PLUTO IN THE WEEK OF THE ENIGMA
(VIRGO II)

Cultivating an air of mystery, these folks are not easy to understand nor do they wish to be understood, in many respects. Yet this quality often has the effect of attracting people to them rather than keeping them away. More personally than socially oriented, they tend to value a quiet evening with a few close friends rather than seeking out wider social interaction.

HERE IS HOW THE PERSONOLOGY WHEEL SHOULD LOOK:

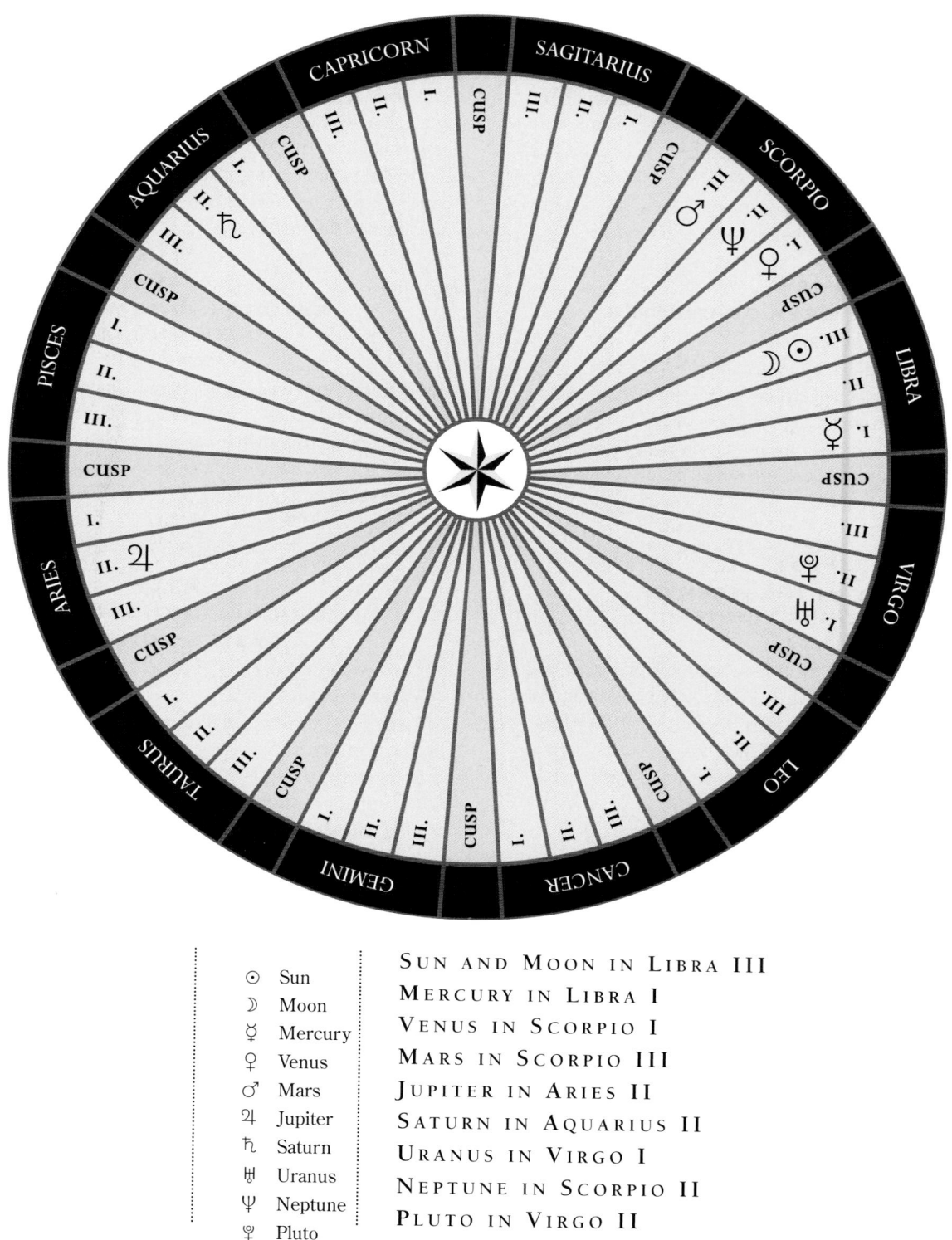

☉	Sun	**SUN AND MOON IN LIBRA III**
☽	Moon	**MERCURY IN LIBRA I**
☿	Mercury	**VENUS IN SCORPIO I**
♀	Venus	**MARS IN SCORPIO III**
♂	Mars	**JUPITER IN ARIES II**
♃	Jupiter	**SATURN IN AQUARIUS II**
♄	Saturn	**URANUS IN VIRGO I**
♅	Uranus	**NEPTUNE IN SCORPIO II**
♆	Neptune	**PLUTO IN VIRGO II**
♇	Pluto	

That's it. You're finished. Does your chart and wheel look the same? If not, double check the tables and you will see where you made your error.

Now try the same with your own birth date. Be sure to keep your birthday chart, and the interpretation because you will use it as the baseline for any astrological forecasts you do for yourself. I will explain how to do those a little later on.

THE YEAR MAKES A BIG DIFFERENCE

One of the terrific features of this book is that it allows you to be precise to the year. Here's an example of how much difference this can make. Let's say the individual in question was born on the same date, but in 1960 Here's how the reading would differ. Notice that the Sun is the same, but everything else is different:

1960	1963
Sun: 28	**Sun:** 28
Moon: 23	**Moon:** 28
Mercury: 31	**Mercury:** 26
Venus: 32	**Venus:** 30
Mars: 15	**Mars:** 32
Jupiter: 37	**Jupiter:** 3
Saturn: 39	**Saturn:** 43
Uranus: 20	**Uranus:** 22
Neptune: 30	**Neptune:** 31
Pluto: 22	**Pluto:** 23

And here is how the Natal Portrait would read:

NATAL PORTRAIT

FOR INDIVIDUAL BORN OCTOBER 17, 1960, AT 3 A.M.

Sun: Libra III
Moon: Virgo II
Mercury: Scorpio II
Venus: Scorpio III
Mars: Cancer II
Jupiter: Sagittarius-Capricorn Cusp
Saturn: Capricorn II
Uranus: Leo III
Neptune: Scorpio I
Pluto: Virgo I

✷28✷
SUN IN THE WEEK OF THEATER
(LIBRA III) OCTOBER 11-18

These capable, forceful individuals usually have little doubt about what they think and are not shy about expressing their opinions either. Yet they can have a terrible time making choices and even making up their minds about what course to take. This is because they can see the value of the other guy's point of view and want to keep options open whenever possible.

✷23✷
MOON IN THE WEEK OF THE ENIGMA
(VIRGO II)

An air of mystery shrouds the emotions of those born on this day. It will be difficult to read the feelings of such individuals and even more difficult to understand their actions. They themselves do not specialize in self-knowledge either, and must learn to plumb their depths and confront themselves emotionally if they are to further their own inner development.

✷31✷
MERCURY IN THE WEEK OF DEPTH
(SCORPIO II)

Deep thought is the natural state here. However, this does not imply that such thoughts can be easily communicated to others. Those with this Mercury position do not specialize in talking about themselves or sharing their private ruminations. Unfortunately, thinking frequently turns to worry and worry to self-induced stress. In order to avoid anxiety or depression, positive thinking must predominate.

✷32✷
VENUS IN THE WEEK OF CHARM
(SCORPIO III)

The darker aspects of sex, love and romance have a magnetic pull on these folks. Consequently, it will be important to their mental health to keep it light, but also to at least give more conventional approaches to love a chance. Marriage is often a means to straighten out their more wayward impulses. Remaining true to their life partner is a major challenge.

✷15✷
MARS IN THE WEEK OF THE UNCONVENTIONAL
(CANCER II)

Mars is decidedly uncomfortable in this watery week. His tendency toward action and aggressive behavior is undercut and often individuals with this position find it difficult to be taken seriously. Bizarre thoughts and behavior frequently cause mistrust on both sides. It is best for these folks to proceed slowly and carefully, taking one step at a time and avoiding sudden moves.

NATAL PORTRAIT FOR INDIVIDUAL BORN OCTOBER 17, 1960, AT 1 A.M.

✴37✴
JUPITER ON THE CUSP OF PROPHECY
(SAGITTARIUS-CAPRICORN CUSP)

A need is found here to balance the optimistic, free and expansive attitudes of Jupiter with the more serious, limited and responsible attitudes of Saturn. Good luck can follow this position only if both are taken into account and can be balanced one against the other. A talent for predicting the future can result in gains on the stock market or in taking calculated gambles in life.

✴39✴
SATURN IN THE WEEK OF DETERMINATION
(CAPRICORN II)

Care will have to be taken to keep one's heart open. Too often Capricorn's presence here can lead to certain ruthlessness and disregard for the feelings of others. Should this occur it could result in cutting such an individual off from the world and fixing them in a lonely stance. Such isolation is detrimental and can be combated by a more caring and empathic attitude.

✴20✴
URANUS IN THE WEEK OF LEADERSHIP
(LEO III)

Although Uranus may fancy himself a leader, he really isn't. His attempts to take the reins of power are not likely to succeed, therefore. If he can reconcile himself to a secondary role, which is unlikely, the group to which this individual belongs will be spared a lot of agony. Incompatible energies here are likely to upset the old apple cart.

✴30✴
NEPTUNE IN THE WEEK OF INTENSITY
(SCORPIO I)

Sexual fantasies may periodically overcome those with this Neptune placement. If there are real outlets for this energy, involving a loving person, many good results can be expected both in the relationship and in other aspects of daily life. However, should narcissism or other extreme forms of self-stimulation result, frustration can build to intolerable levels. Frequent reality checks are advised.

✴22✴
PLUTO IN THE WEEK OF SYSTEM BUILDERS
(VIRGO I)

Investments often thrive in the hands of these individuals. If they are inclined to save rather than spend, they are capable of making outstanding decisions as to what to do with their money. They can also give good advice on this subject to others, both as amateurs and professionals. Because they recognize the importance of sound finances, they make realistic plans for the future.

ADDING NUANCE: FAVORABLE AND UNFAVORABLE PLANETARY ASPECTS

You can supplement the information available in a basic chart, and make the reading even more accurate by considering the "favorable and unfavorable planetary aspects." Any two planets can form certain aspects to each other, that is, occupy a configuration within the 360 degree zodiac circle which is either conjunct (next to each other), opposite (180 degrees away), square (90 degrees away) or trine (120 degrees away). This is true whether they are both found in the same birth chart or each in separate charts you are comparing (like your chart and your partner's, or your chart and that of a specific day you are consulting).

Generally speaking, astrologers have historically considered conjunctions and trines favorable and squares and oppositions unfavorable. However, nowadays this has taken on a less severe and more constructive cast, in which conjunctions and trines are thought of as more relaxed and pleasurable while squares and oppositions are considered more dynamic and action-oriented.

There are many ways in which these aspects can be used, and in fact they form a large part of the methods used by professional astrologers. For example, if your Venus is trine the Venus of someone else (the two planets are approximately 120 degrees apart), this could indicate a sensuous or favorable possibility for a love relationship. On the other hand, if the two Venus positions are square (90 degrees apart), it could indicate a stressful or negative influence, but also a dynamic one in which arguments arise but there is rarely a dull moment.

Here is a simple method for calculating whether two planets are conjunct, trine, square or opposite each other, using the personology system in this book.

(1) **A conjunction:** The two planets must be in the same personology period. That means that when you look them up in their table, they will have the same number.

(2) **A trine:** The two planets must be exactly four signs or four cusps apart. For example, if one planet is in Aries I and another planet is in Leo I or Sagittarius I, then they

are trine. If three planets are each four signs distant from each other, then we have a so-called grand trine, which can be viewed as favorable, relaxed and satisfied.

(3) **A square:** The planets are exactly three signs or three cusps apart. For example, if one planet is on the Gemini-Cancer cusp and the other on the Virgo-Libra Cusp, then they are square to each other. The two equinoxes (spring, Pisces-Aries Cusp, and fall, Virgo-Libra Cusp) and the two solstices (summer, Gemini-Cancer Cusp, and winter, Sagittarius-Capricorn Cusp) form a grand cross, in which there are four squares. This is a highly stressed and tense configuration, which can be viewed as problematic or difficult, but also as highly active and exciting.

(4) **An opposition:** These are easy to spot in a chart since they will be directly 180 degrees opposite to each other. For example, Taurus II is directly opposite Scorpio II, and Virgo I directly opposite Pisces I. Such oppositions can be viewed as being in conflict with each other, but also can compliment each other through their differences. For example, someone with Sun in Pisces II is very different from someone in Virgo II, but through these differences they may stay together longer than two people whose Suns are trine to each other. They find each other more interesting—opposites attract!

AN EXAMPLE OF A BASIC CHART, FURTHER DEFINED:

NATAL PORTRAIT
FOR INDIVIDUAL BORN MARCH 20, 1952

Sun: Pisces-Aries Cusp

Moon: Capricorn II

Mercury: Aries II

Venus: Pisces I

Mars: Scorpio II

Jupiter: Aries III

Saturn: Libra II

Uranus: Cancer I

Neptune: Libra III

Pluto: Leo III

✴1✴
SUN ON THE CUSP OF REBIRTH
(PISCES-ARIES CUSP)

Often direct in their attitudes and opinions, their more aggressive outward side masks an inner sensitivity. This latter trait can keep them from moving forward in the world and achieving outright success. They are frequently misunderstood and must take the time to explain themselves fully. Above all, they need to maintain a positive approach and not fall prey to depression.

✴39✴
MOON IN THE WEEK OF DETERMINATION
(CAPRICORN II)

A fear exists in such individuals of others using their feelings against them, and so they are likely to build an emotional barrier between themselves and others. Often, however, one individual will be given the key to their inner sanctum. They can become very dependent on such a person for love and understanding. Because of the importance of career here, feelings and emotions may be mistrusted.

✴3✴
MERCURY IN THE WEEK OF THE STAR
(ARIES II)

A bit of a tendency to show off how smart one is here. These know-it-alls have something to say on practically any subject. Their desire to shock with the originality and directness of their latest idea is pronounced. Learning to temper such thrusts is important if they wish to avoid being summarily rejected by others and gain a fair hearing for their ideas.

✴46✴
VENUS IN THE WEEK OF SPIRIT
(PISCES I)

Platonic love is important to Venus in this personology period. All forms of friendship are favored here, and such relationships usually come to achieve greater importance in the life of the individual than sexual or overtly passionate ones. Being on the same wavelength as their partner has profound significance for them and so emotional understanding is highly valued.

✴31✴
MARS IN THE WEEK OF DEPTH
(SCORPIO II)

Aggression can be aroused in these individuals, but they are usually slow to react. More often than not, they can repress Mars and as a result wind up with a headache, stomachache or full-blown depressions. Lethargic periods are often the result. Their passion for food and sex is legendary, at times leaving them slaves to the table and bed.

✴4✴
JUPITER IN THE WEEK OF THE PIONEER
(ARIES III)

Taking the lead in one's family or social group, at least ideologically, is favored here. However, some can lead professional endeavors into financial difficulties with this Jupiter position, through lack of good business sense. Aries III has strong initiative and impulses, though,, which can get many a favorable domestic or neighborhood project up and running, with a successful outcome.

★27★
SATURN IN THE WEEK OF SOCIETY
(LIBRA II)

This Saturn position can impair one's social skills and in extreme cases make the individual a bit reclusive or antisocial. The upside of this is a strong sense of social responsibility, making for a personality that can be trusted with putting the good of the group first. This can, however, lead to a neglect of one's own personal development, and this must be guarded against.

★28★
NEPTUNE IN THE WEEK OF THEATER
(LIBRA III)

Neptune can lead these folks to live in an unreal world, populated by film and TV stars, and with dramatic public figures. They see a connection between themselves and such notables, frequently fantasizing about possible relationships, sexual or otherwise. Their real challenge is to discover the true drama in everyday life and to invest more real energy in events around them.

★14★
URANUS IN THE WEEK OF THE EMPATH
(CANCER I)

The lightning quick Uranus may be baffled by the emotional orientation of this week. Thus, the forcefulness and communicative abilities of this planet may get blunted here, resulting in some confusion. Garbled and mixed messages can be the result. In order to avoid confusion, a connection should be sought between emotional and psychic understanding. Patience will be required in such an effort.

★20★
PLUTO IN THE WEEK OF LEADERSHIP
(LEO III)

Strongly dictatorial tendencies can surface here. Those with this Pluto position are frequently at the mercy of their ambitious drives and too likely to sacrifice the well being of their friends and colleagues to their own desire for recognition. At the same time, they are able to hide their true feelings and have difficulty accessing or understanding them.

SUN ON PISCES-ARIES CUSP
MOON IN CAPRICORN II
MERCURY IN ARIES II
VENUS IN PISCES I
MARS IN SCORPIO II
JUPITER IN ARIES III
SATURN IN LIBRA II
URANUS IN CANCER I
NEPTUNE IN LIBRA III
PLUTO IN LEO III

⊙ Sun
☽ Moon
☿ Mercury
♀ Venus
♂ Mars
♃ Jupiter
♄ Saturn
♅ Uranus
♆ Neptune
♇ Pluto

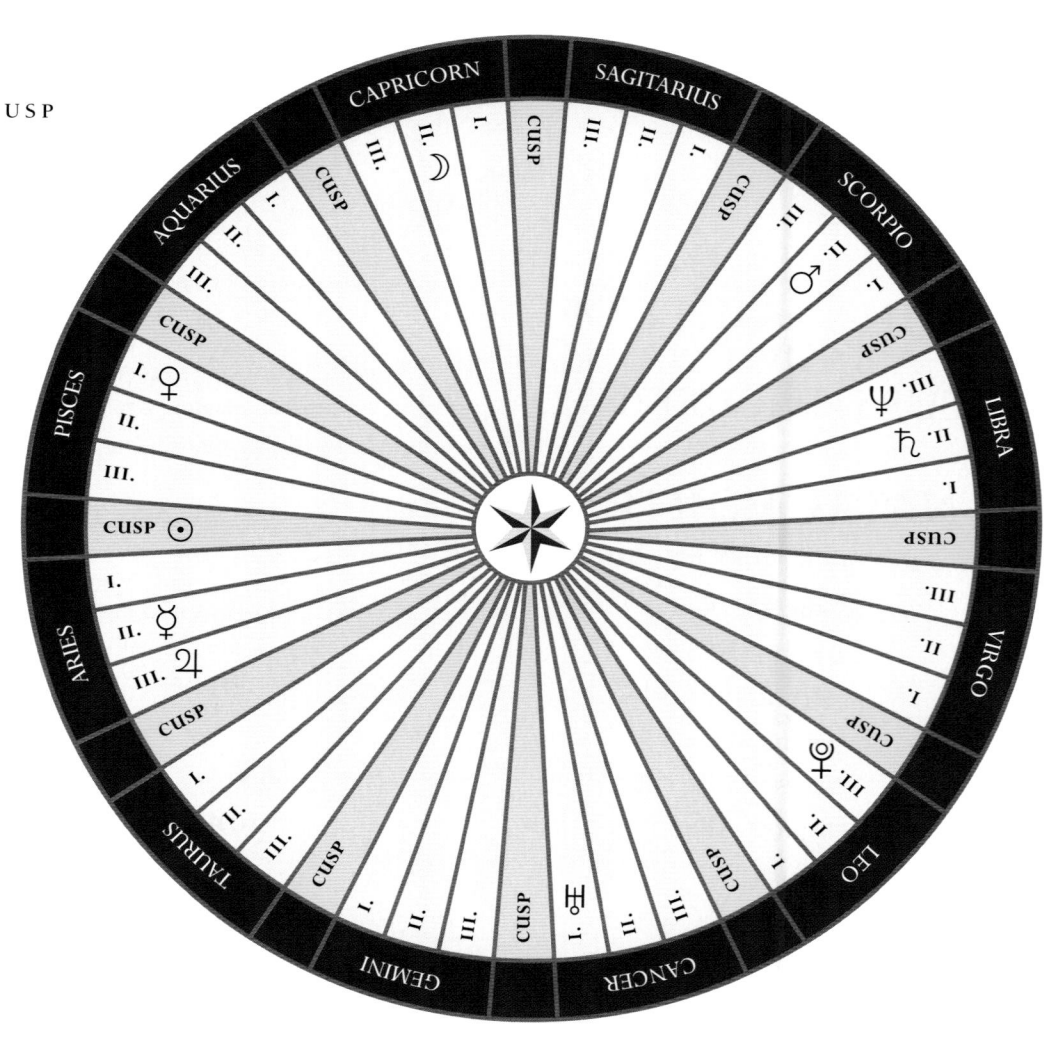

Using the Aspects to Add Detail to the Basic Natal Portrait

Here is an example of how planets in conjunctions, oppositions, trines, and squares can add further detail to the birthday forecast. The individual above, born on March 20, 1952, on the Cusp of Rebirth in my personology system, is subject to these influences:

Jupiter opposite Neptune: He must beware of allowing himself to get carried away by fantasies and illusions. Yet, paradoxically, much of his luck will depend on his belief in himself and having the courage to follow his dreams. Thus it is often a matter of finding a point of balance and not getting swept away.

Venus trine Uranus: Likely to fall in love easily, this person can just as easily fall out of it, to the bewilderment of his partner. Sudden emotional changes are in general characteristic across the board, making commitment extremely difficult. Such individuals can be highly attractive, leading to much heartaches and heartbreaks on both sides.

Jupiter trine Pluto: Indicates talent in the money sector and accompanying luck in financial matters. This individual can move ahead through savvy financial investments as well as being able to advise his company, family or friends as to good deals and worthwhile projects.

Mercury opposite Saturn: Headaches and worry are likely through taking on too much responsibility. Also the individual's thinking can be adversely affected in such situations, which can lead to making incorrect decisions.

Moon square Saturn: A very hard aspect. Extremely powerful emotionally. Emotional problems, particularly when young. Challenge to get one's act together emotionally through self-knowledge and determination.

Moon square Mercury: Head warring against the heart. Try not to always mistrust your own dreams or those of others. Keep your critical faculties under control and avoid sarcasm or cynicism. Learning to relax and express feelings rather than always relying on logic are essential to achieve happiness. Strive for a balance between common sense and romance, giving both their due.

CREATING AND INTERPRETING A CHART FOR ANY DAY

Say an important day is coming up when you are scheduling a job interview, a presentation, or even planning to get engaged or married. In order to cast a chart for that day, you would simply consult the tables for each of the ten planets and place them in the proper numbered segment of the chart, just as you did for the birthday earlier. Reading all ten of the corresponding paragraphs for the ten planets will give you a picture of what that day's energies will be like and what you might expect in terms of positive and negative influences. This will help you deal with such energies on the spot, and also plan ahead in order to be prepared. You may even decide to change the date of your scheduled event to another one that is more auspicious.

Since each of the planets deals with a specific area of life, it is also possible to quickly consult any date for only the influence of one particular planet. For example, if love is your main interest on a particular day, then consult Venus; if it is money, consult Pluto; if communication, consult Mercury, as indicated earlier in *Attributes of the Ten Planets*.

These methods will yield objective information about a given day or a specific life area of that day, but it is also possible to use this book to personalize such a search to your own birth chart. Once you get to know your chart well, by reading the ten paragraphs corresponding to the planetary positions in the forty-eight personology periods, you can then form an overall picture of such a person (yourself) and see how you would fare on the day under discussion. In other words, form a picture of the energies of that day by reading the info on each of the planets; then do the same for your own birth chart and compare the two to see how to proceed, given the nature of the day and your own astrological profile. This method could also be used for a friend, parent, child, or colleague.

Let's explore how to do this using the chart of the individual born on October 17, 1963, at 3 a.m. Let's say he would like to peer ahead into the afternoon of January 1, 2010.

COMPARING THE INFLUENCE OF THE SUN

The Sun's influence on his birthday:

SUN IN THE WEEK OF THEATER
(LIBRA III) OCTOBER 11-18

These capable, forceful individuals usually have little doubt about what they think and are not shy about expressing their opinions either. Yet they can have a terrible time making choices and even making up their minds about what course to take. This is because they can see the value of the other guy's point of view and want to keep options open whenever possible.

The Sun's influence on January 1, 2010:

SUN IN THE WEEK OF THE RULER
(CAPRICORN I) DECEMBER 26-JANUARY 2

Those born in this week know how to control their living and working situations. True rulers, they regard their home as their castle and like to see it running smoothly. Allergic to chaos, they run the risk of becoming control freaks. Unless they give up their tendency to make up other people's minds for them, they are likely to arouse resentments.

Interpretation

The Libra III person would face a kind of ultimate challenge in the Week of the Ruler, being forced to make up their mind and also to assume a strong leadership role. If they are sensitive to the points of view of others, they could be highly successful in leading them forward.

COMPARING THE INFLUENCE OF THE MOON

The Moon's influence on his birthday:

MOON IN THE WEEK OF THEATER
(LIBRA III)

A natural tendency toward exhibitionism appears here and if such individuals are quiet or shy it usually indicates repression, often due to judgmental attitudes from family members or teachers early in life. For enthusiastic individuals who are not blocked emotionally, they can be the life of any party. Sometimes they go too far and need to be reined in.

The Moon's influence on January 1, 2010:

MOON IN THE WEEK OF THE PERSUADER
(CANCER III)

Too often emotionally manipulative, those with moon in Cancer III indulge in a wild fantasy life that frequently proves more satisfying than reality. So strong are their powers of projection that others are forced to act out the imagined roles assigned to them. By learning to accept things as they come without influencing them unduly, these individuals can lead a healthier life. The individual with Moon in Cancer III faces special difficulties and challenges on January 1, 2010, since the two moon positions (Libra III for the person and Cancer III for the day) are directly square to one another. Great care will have to be taken not to get swept away by fantasy and imagination, and lose all sense of reality.

Interpretation

The individual with Moon in Cancer III faces special difficulties and challenges on January 1, 2010, since the two moon positions (Libra III for the person and Cancer III for the day) are directly square to one another. Great care will have to be taken not to get swept away by fantasy and imagination, and lose all sense of reality.

COMPARING THE INFLUENCE OF MERCURY

Mercury's influence on his birthday:

MERCURY IN THE WEEK OF THE PERFECTIONIST

(LIBRA I)

Mercury tends to be highly critical here and so those with that planet in this position are difficult to please. Always looking for something better, they never seem satisfied with what they have. They should make an effort to control their pickiness and learn to accept things as they are without trying to alter or fix them.

Mercury's influence on January 1, 2010:

MERCURY IN THE WEEK OF DETERMINATION

(CAPRICORN II)

Mercury is not usually characterized by the dogged plodding typical of this week. It feels restrained by practicality here and responsibilities weigh heavily on its freedom-loving spirit. Mercury wants to fly, while Capricorn II insists on a step-by-step, cautious approach. These seemingly irreconcilable energies can work in synch as long as they agree to reconcile extremes and to be open to compromise.

Interpretation

With Mercury in the Week of the Perfectionist such an individual can make tangible gains on this day. Mercury in the Week of Determination demands the patience and attention to detail that the Perfectionist Mercury may be able to give.

COMPARING THE INFLUENCE OF VENUS

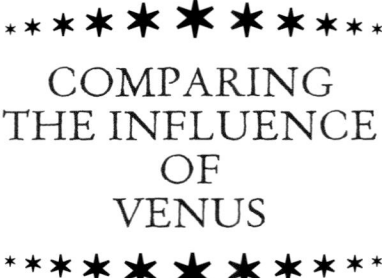

Venus' influence on his birthday:

VENUS IN THE WEEK OF INTENSITY

(SCORPIO I)

Seduction figures prominently here. Masters in attracting and controlling the opposite sex, those with Venus in this week are born flirts and specialists in the arts of love. Because of the intensity with which they love they are not easily forgotten. They must learn, however, to back off and allow the other person to express their true feelings or risk losing them.

Venus' influence on January 1, 2010:

VENUS IN THE WEEK OF THE RULER

(CAPRICORN I)

Venus feels constricted in this position and therefore these folks may find it difficult to express love easily or openly. Furthermore, they know instinctively how to withhold their affections and can even use silence as a weapon to gain an advantage over family members and partners alike. Learning from a loving mate how to express affection is quite possible here, but passion comes more naturally than sensuous expression.

Interpretation

The individual's seductive powers and even the ability to love can be cramped by Capricorn I energies.

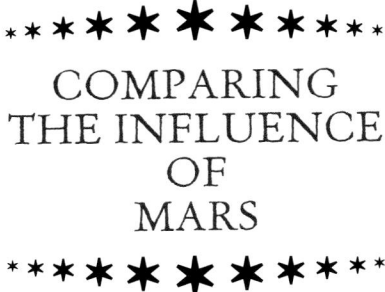

COMPARING
THE INFLUENCE
OF
MARS

Mars' influence on his birthday:

MARS IN THE WEEK OF CHARM

(SCORPIO III)

Mars is given an extra seductive attraction in this position. If encouraged, these folks are likely to take over the lives of weaker family members and friends. Thus they are capable of making most or even all of the important decisions for the other person. In doing so they create dependencies that might not be so healthy for either party in the future.

Mars' influence on January 1, 2010:

MARS IN THE WEEK OF BALANCED STRENGTH

(LEO II)

Mars is comfortable here and very efficacious in getting the job done. Depression is the only problem, since it may seem to these individuals that they haven't accomplished as much as they could. Self-judgments can lower confidence, undermining their ability to get results in the future. It is important to keep one's heart open and avoid succumbing to negativity or pessimism. Keep believing that you can do it.

Interpretation

The individual's seductive powers are again inhibited. However, they can use their power to get results from others as long as they stay positive and avoid depression.

COMPARING
THE INFLUENCE
OF
JUPITER

Jupiter's influence on his birthday:

JUPITER IN THE WEEK OF THE STAR

(ARIES II)

Self-expression is demanded here, even if the personality involved is a quiet one. Working behind the scenes will achieve as much success as being in the spotlight. The important thing is maintaining the central position, whether the principal player or not. Good luck comes easily here and cannot really be earned with hard work. Serendipity plays an important role.

Jupiter's influence on January 1, 2010:

JUPITER IN THE WEEK OF ACCEPTANCE

(AQUARIUS III)

A talent to see the other guy's point of view even when we don't share it can result in success in relationships and also with one's colleagues. People find such an attitude disarming and are more likely to go along with ideas advanced by such an individual. By not putting up barriers to others, a more receptive audience can be found in the future.

Interpretation

As long as the individual remains sensitive and open to the wishes of others they can use their innate good luck to advance the cause of all concerned by trusting to fate and remaining open to taking chances.

COMPARING THE INFLUENCE OF SATURN

Saturn's influence on his birthday

SATURN IN THE WEEK OF YOUTH AND EASE

(AQUARIUS II)

Either Saturn can enjoy himself and take a bit of a vacation from heavy responsibilities or one's abilities to relax can be impaired by thoughts concerning what needs doing. In either case, a balance should be sought between pleasure and work. This is quite possible and can lead to a more healthy personality that can function well on the job and on vacation.

Saturn's influence on January 1, 2010:

SATURN IN THE WEEK OF THE PERFECTIONIST

(LIBRA I)

Care should be taken that critical attitudes do not become overly judgmental ones. Because standards are so high, Saturn tends to come down with its full weight on those who do not come up to the mark. When such attitudes are internalized they can result in enormous stress, even leading to periodic breakdowns. Riding a bit looser in the saddle is essential.

Interpretation

The individual must bring his more fun-loving and lighter energies to alleviate the stress of this Perfectionistic day.

COMPARING THE INFLUENCE OF URANUS

Uranus' influence on his birthday:

URANUS IN THE WEEK OF SYSTEM BUILDERS

(VIRGO I)

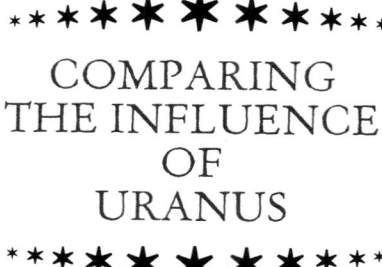

Uranus has much to learn in this week from the methodical Virgo I energies. However, because the planet is opposed to orderly activities he may wind up undermining them. The result can be a messy bedroom or work station. Breaking structures apart rather than building them up is Uranus's specialty, so his destructive bent may be aroused and directed against strict regimens and ingrained habits.

Uranus' influence on January 1, 2010:

URANUS IN THE WEEK OF DANCERS AND DREAMERS

(PISCES III)

No project is too far out, no concept too abstract or philosophical for these nimble-witted people to consider and perhaps embrace. Like butterflies, they are likely to flit from one intellectual concept to the next. If not intellectuals, they still demand a great deal of variety in their work and private lives. They can also specialize in several areas at once.

Interpretation

The individual's chaotic side may undermine the little innate stability that exists on such a day. Extreme disorder can result.

COMPARING THE INFLUENCE OF NEPTUNE

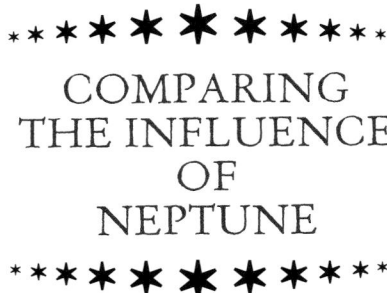

Neptune's influence on his birthday:

NEPTUNE IN THE WEEK OF DEPTH

(SCORPIO II)

If isolation and nursing private resentments and grudges manifest here, Neptune in this week can lead to serious depressions. Opening up avenues of true communication with others is advised, in order to avoid getting bottled up in one's own private world. Particularly in the professional sphere, making slow, gradual progress is advised rather than expecting sudden miracles to surface.

Neptune's influence on January 1, 2010:

NEPTUNE IN THE WEEK OF ACCEPTANCE

(AQUARIUS III)

Far-out individuals who share many New Age and advanced points of view, these people are up for new, exciting projects which come their way. They react strongly against conservative points of view and become true revolutionaries in the face of despotism. Gentle toward children and small animals, these kind folks are there to help their friends when in need.

Interpretation

Because the individual's Neptune in Aquarius III causes him to get bottled up he may not be able to take advantage of the new and exciting project which is coming along. The only hope for success lies in building bridges to others.

COMPARING THE INFLUENCE OF PLUTO

Pluto's influence on his birthday:

PLUTO IN THE WEEK OF THE STAR

(ARIES II)

Requiring undue amounts of attention is characteristic here. An insatiable desire to be at the center of everything is characteristic, making such individuals appear egotistical and self-serving. Once they learn the joy of true service they are more likely to correct this impression and to put their energies toward helping others. They may actually succeed in being recognized more once they take this important step.

Pluto's influence on January 1, 2010:

PLUTO ON THE CUSP OF PROPHECY

(SAGITTARIUS-CAPRICORN CUSP)

The nature of the future in an uncertain world is the prime topic during this Pluto placement. Discussions range from the environment to politics to an apocalypse. A feeling grows that the future is not set in stone but that we can do something about it. Procrastination is recognized as the enemy and the need to act sooner rather than later is in the forefront for individuals born here.

Interpretation

It is necessary for the individual to forget about himself and concentrate more on issues of importance for all.

THE COMPLETE INTERPRETATION

SUN: The Libra III person would face a real challenge in the Week of the Ruler, being forced to make up his or her mind and also to assume a strong leadership role. By using sensitivity to the points of view of others, the Libra III person could be highly successful in leading them forward.

MOON: The individual with Moon in Cancer III faces special difficulties and challenges on January 1, 2010, since the two moon positions (Libra III for the person and Cancer III for the day) are directly square to one another. Great care will have to be taken not to get swept away by fantasy and imagination, and lose all sense of reality.

MERCURY: With Mercury in the Week of the Perfectionist such an individual can make tangible gains on this day. Mercury in the Week of Determination demands the patience and attention to detail that the Perfectionist Mercury may be able to give.

VENUS: The individual's seductive powers and even the ability to love can be cramped by Capricorn I energies.

MARS: The individual's seductive powers are again inhibited. However, they can use their power to get results from others as long as they stay positive and avoid depression.

JUPITER: As long as the individual remains sensitive and open to the wishes of others, he or she can use their innate good luck to advance the cause of those concerned by trusting to fate and remaining open to taking chances.

SATURN: The individual must bring his more fun-loving and lighter energies to alleviate the stress of this Perfectionistic day.

URANUS: The individual's chaotic side may undermine the little innate stability which exists on such a day. Extreme disorder can result.

NEPTUNE: Because the individual's Neptune in Aquarius III causes him to get bottled up he may not be able to take advantage of the new and exciting project which is coming along. The only hope for success lies in building bridges to others.

PLUTO: It is necessary for the individual to forget about himself and concentrate more on issues of importance for all.

In **SUMMATION**, professional and career activities are favored, in general, while personal interactions are not. The impairment of the ability to express love is a constant theme, as is the danger of forgetting about the feelings of others. A lot of chaos could result on this day, unless an extreme effort is made to be orderly, taking things one step at a time while not flying off on unrealistic tangents. In business matters solid, albeit unspectacular gains can be made by exerting great dedication and patience. In general, this person needs to keep things light on January 1, 2010, and go with the flow.

Solar Returns:
A New Possibility
Each Year

Of course, your birth chart is applicable through your entire life, but each year on your birthday the planets occupy different positions from when you were born. This chart, called your solar return, creates a picture of what the following year will be like for you. For example, if you are born on June 23rd 1984, you can create your birth chart, interpret it and use it throughout your life, but in any upcoming year, say 2006, you can also cast a chart for June 23rd 2006 and this will be specific to the upcoming year, between June 23rd 2006 and June 23rd 2007.

Furthermore, you can make comparisons between the solar return chart and your birthday chart to find out whether this year will be especially favorable or unfavorable for you, particularly in certain areas. You might also wish to examine one particular area of your life that is of interest, such as love, communication, etc. By using the system of conjunctions, trines, squares and oppositions described in the preceding section, you can compare any or all of your birth chart and solar return planets with each other.

COMPARING CHARTS

Copy these side-by-side Fill-In Charts and Wheels and use any time you want to compare your birthday chart with the birthday chart of someone important to you; or to see how the planetary line up on an upcoming day compares with the alignment at your birth. Read page 18 for more information on comparing charts. Don't forget to check for conjunctions, trines, squares and/or oppositions.

FILL-IN CHART

Date & Time	SUN	MOON	MERCURY	VENUS	MARS	JUPITER	SATURN	URANUS	NEPTUNE	PLUTO

FILL-IN WHEEL

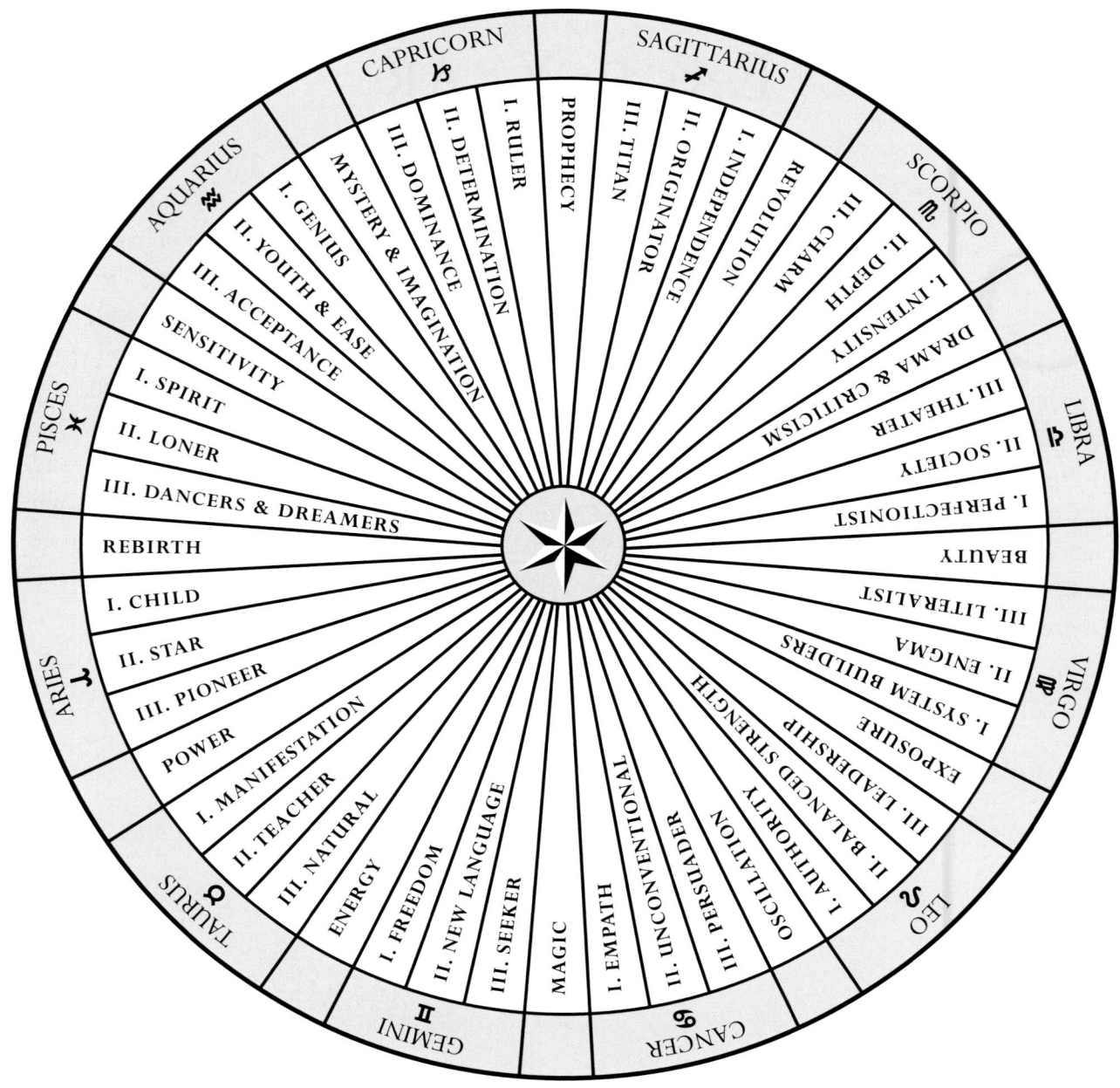

KEY

- ☉ Sun
- ☽ Moon
- ☿ Mercury
- ♀ Venus
- ♂ Mars
- ♃ Jupiter
- ♄ Saturn
- ♅ Uranus
- ♆ Neptune
- ♇ Pluto

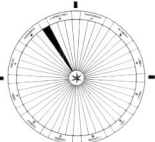

Conjunction:
Two planets
in the same
Personology period

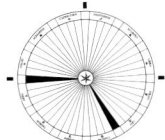

Trine:
Two planets
exactly four signs
or cusps apart

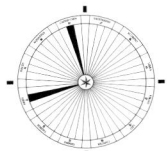

Square:
Two planets
exactly three signs
or cusps apart

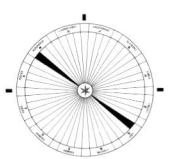

Opposition:
Two planets 180
degrees—or directly—
opposite each other

FILL-IN CHART

Date & Time	SUN	MOON	MERCURY	VENUS	MARS	JUPITER	SATURN	URANUS	NEPTUNE	PLUTO

FILL-IN WHEEL

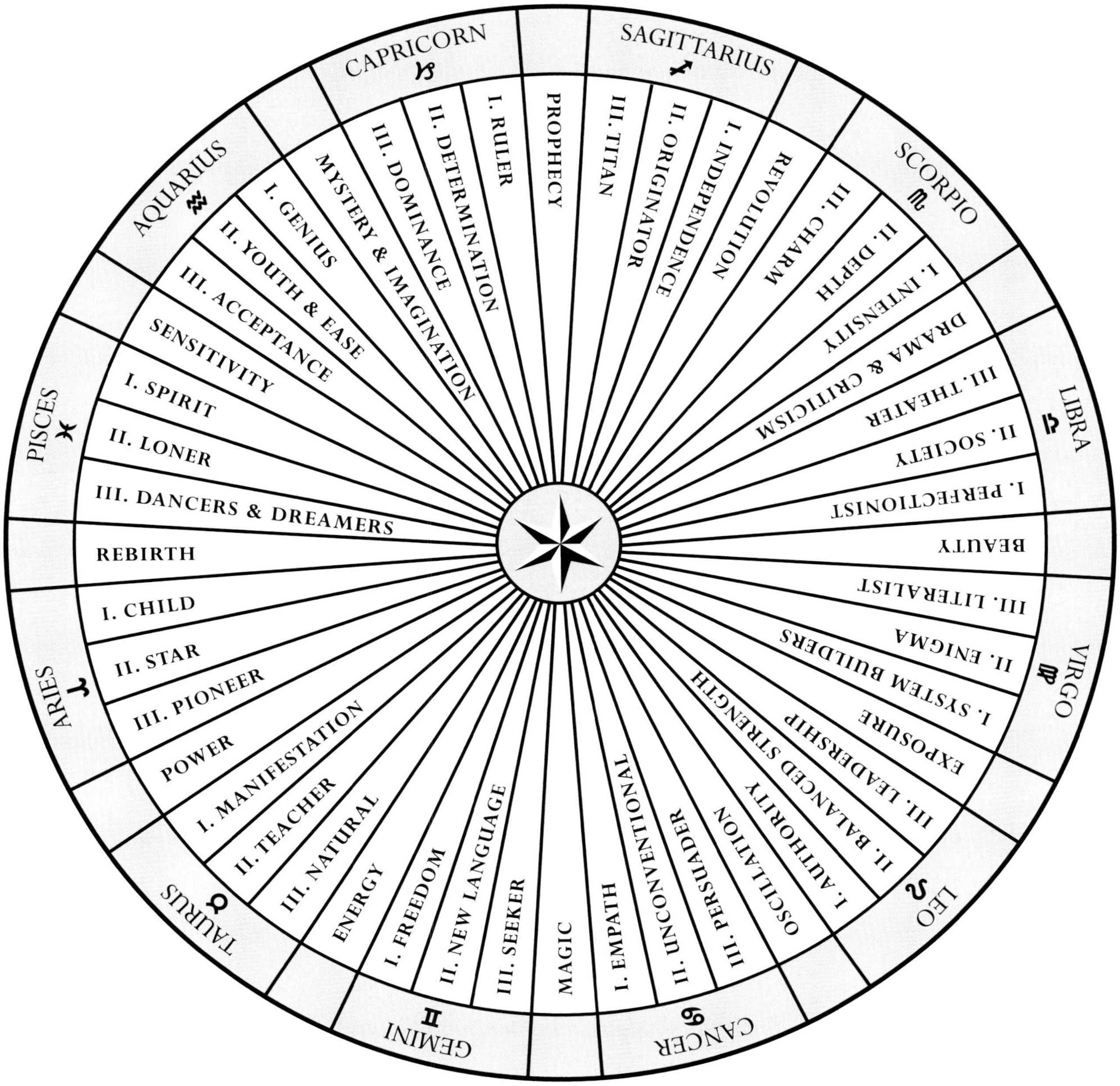

(A circular zodiac wheel divided into the twelve signs, each with numbered Personology periods:)

- **CAPRICORN ♑** — I. RULER, II. DETERMINATION, III. DOMINANCE, MYSTERY & IMAGINATION
- **SAGITTARIUS ♐** — PROPHECY, III. TITAN, II. ORIGINATOR, I. INDEPENDENCE, REVOLUTION
- **SCORPIO ♏** — III. CHARM, II. DEPTH, I. INTENSITY, DRAMA & CRITICISM
- **LIBRA ♎** — III. THEATER, II. SOCIETY, I. PERFECTIONIST, BEAUTY
- **VIRGO ♍** — III. LITERALIST, II. ENIGMA, I. SYSTEM BUILDERS, EXPOSURE
- **LEO ♌** — III. LEADERSHIP, II. BALANCED STRENGTH, I. AUTHORITY, OSCILLATION
- **CANCER ♋** — III. PERSUADER, II. UNCONVENTIONAL, I. EMPATH, MAGIC
- **GEMINI ♊** — III. SEEKER, II. NEW LANGUAGE, I. FREEDOM, ENERGY
- **TAURUS ♉** — III. NATURAL, II. TEACHER, I. MANIFESTATION, POWER
- **ARIES ♈** — III. PIONEER, II. STAR, I. CHILD, REBIRTH
- **PISCES ♓** — III. DANCERS & DREAMERS, II. LONER, I. SPIRIT, SENSITIVITY
- **AQUARIUS ♒** — III. ACCEPTANCE, II. YOUTH & EASE, I. GENIUS

INTERPRETING THE POSITION OF THE PLANETS

THE SUN

THE SUN REPRESENTS YOUR SELF, EGO STRUCTURE, PERSONALITY.

NOTE FROM THE ARTIST ABOUT THE ILLUSTRATION ON THE FACING PAGE: In this illustration and all that follow, the outermost border is a stylized representation of the solar system. The background shows aspects of the planet through flat art or aspects of the god associated with the planet. The foreground shows the planet itself. The woman represents you, the reader, as well as the spirit of that planet, and the interaction between the reader and these specific planetary energies. She wears a mask designed to represent the attributes associated with that planet.

In this illustration of the Sun, the sun's strong, masculine force is portrayed in the background. The female figure shines brightly, evoking the sun's aspect as a giver of life. The sun represents the will to live and the creative force. Thus, the female Sun goddess holds in her hand the dawn (the spark of creativity). She is blowing a hot wind—representative of the "solar wind" which flows throughout the universe.

THE SUN

IN THE 48 PERSONOLOGY PERIODS

✳1✳
SUN ON THE
CUSP OF REBIRTH

(PISCES-ARIES CUSP) MARCH 19-24

Often direct in their attitudes and opinions, their more aggressive outward side masks an inner sensitivity. This latter trait can keep them from moving forward in the world and achieving outright success. They are frequently misunderstood and must take the time to explain themselves fully. Above all, they need to maintain a positive approach and not fall prey to depression.

✳2✳
SUN IN THE WEEK
OF THE CHILD

(ARIES I) MARCH 25-APRIL 2

These serious individuals value acceptance more than anything else. They do not like to be analyzed and insist that what you see is what you get. They are observers who take a measured view of the world, but prize their close friends and family who allow them to have fun. Because of their open attitudes they can be easily hurt emotionally.

✳3✳
SUN IN THE WEEK
OF THE STAR

(ARIES I)I APRIL 3-10

Not all of these people know they are a star. Many take years to shine in their own right. Others consider it sufficient to be at the center of whatever is going on, rather than making a theatrical splash. Although they may be swept away by their own ego drives, they can also be extremely helpful and giving. They can be highly competitive.

✳4✳
SUN IN THE WEEK
OF THE PIONEER

(ARIES III) APRIL 11-18

Less self-centered than other Aries, these individuals are more social in their makeup and can be true leaders. Highly inspirational, they follow their ideals and rarely compromise. They tend to make rules (their own) but also to break them (other people's). Highly protective, they are often seen defending and serving the needy. Their idealism at times makes them insensitive to other people's feelings.

✳5✳
SUN ON THE CUSP
OF POWER

(ARIES-TAURUS CUSP) APRIL 19-24

These forceful individuals know how to get their way. Because of their powerful nature they find it hard to admit failure. They only give when it suits them and do not like being obligated to anyone. Frequently lavish in their approach to life, their love of the pleasures of table and bed are a frequent temptation for excessive indulgence.

✳6✳
SUN IN THE WEEK OF
MANIFESTATION

(TAURUS I) APRIL 25-MAY 2

For those born in this week, having an idea is not sufficient – it must also be put into practice. Their pragmatic attitudes can lead them to be extremely hard-headed and stubborn. These are not people to be opposed head on but rather approached peacefully and with warmth. They hate constant conflict and long to be left alone to do their own thing.

✶ 7 ✶
SUN IN THE WEEK OF
THE TEACHER
(TAURUS II) MAY 3-10

Whether student or instructor, these individuals know the true value of learning. Although mental activity is essential to their makeup, they are also strongly physical people who enjoy sports and dance. Their powers of attraction, which result in many admirers, often belie a strong need to be alone. Although fair, they can also be quite demanding and judgmental.

✶ 8 ✶
SUN IN THE WEEK OF
THE NATURAL
(TAURUS III) MAY 11-18

Personal self-expression is so important to these people that they react very badly to being suppressed. If hemmed in they will inevitably break out of their restrictive environment, often in an unforgettable manner. Their love of nature is best expressed through living in the country or visiting it frequently. Their rebelliousness must be curbed at times and they must learn self-control.

✶ 9 ✶
SUN ON THE CUSP
OF ENERGY
(TAURUS-GEMINI CUSP) MAY 19-24

These prolific and versatile individuals usually cover a wide field of endeavor. Because of their obsessive tendencies, they are also likely to produce a large volume of work. They must be extremely careful not to let their energies get out of control or allow too many attractive detours to claim their attention. Having an appreciative audience to communicate with is essential to their mental health.

✶ 10 ✶
SUN IN THE WEEK
OF FREEDOM
(GEMINI I) MAY 25-JUNE 2

Those born in this week are usually happiest when self-employed. Technically gifted, they are most fulfilled when solving problems and figuring out solutions to difficulties. Because of their wit and seductive charm, they attract all manner of admirers. However, they can be tyrannical and deny others the freedom they demand for themselves. Their highly charged nervous system needs to be kept calm.

✶ 11 ✶
SUN IN THE WEEK OF
NEW LANGUAGE
(GEMINI II) JUNE 3-10

Gemini II's have an unusual way of expressing themselves. Because being understood is so important to them, they experience great frustration when others do not comprehend them. Therefore, they need to work hard on being clear about what they say and do. Their liveliness and positive outlook has a telling impact on their relationships with family and friends.

✶ 12 ✶
SUN IN THE WEEK OF
THE SEEKER
(GEMINI III) JUNE 11-18

To go beyond ordinary human limitations toward the unknown—this is often the goal of those born in this week. They usually understand that achieving mastery on the physical plane is the first step in such a process. However, their own emotional instability can lay all kinds of traps for them, unless they are able to balance and temper their feelings.

✶ 13 ✶
SUN ON THE CUSP
OF MAGIC
(GEMINI-CANCER CUSP) JUNE 19-24

The most romantic of all Personology periods, this magical cusp lends a compelling intimacy to contacts with these individuals. Private, but not shy, they are likely to lead a life hidden from the prying eyes of the world in which love plays an important role. Summer solstice people, they radiate conscious energies and can be highly developed both mentally and emotionally.

✶ 14 ✶
SUN IN THE WEEK OF
THE EMPATH
(CANCER I) JUNE 25-JULY 2

Those born in this week arouse strong feelings in others. Also, they are so tuned in to the emotional state of those they meet, often at an unconscious level, that they tend to experience feelings of other people. True psychological mirrors, they must realize when they are picking up on what the other guy is projecting.

✶ 15 ✶
SUN IN THE WEEK OF
THE UNCONVENTIONAL
(CANCER II) JULY 3-10

Not always easy to understand, Cancer II's have their own unique thought patterns and odd ways of doing things. Frequently misunderstood, those born in this week must learn to explain themselves patiently and clearly. Their frequently bizarre approach to life is not always appreciated, yet they will continue to explore the more unusual byways of existence. Eye-catching colors and bizarre sounds have special fascination for them.

✱ 16 ✱
SUN IN THE WEEK OF
THE PERSUADER
(CANCER III) JULY 11-18

Dominant individuals, those born in this week are likely to exert a strong influence on their immediate surroundings. Because of their highly persuasive nature and their need to control, they most frequently get their way, sooner or later. Using a blend of cajoling, personal magnetism and reward, they are able to soften the hardest of hearts and convince the hardest of heads.

✱ 17 ✱
SUN ON THE CUSP
OF OSCILLATION
(CANCER-LEO CUSP) JULY 19-25

Wide mood swings characterize these individuals. Sometimes up, sometimes down, they must learn to seek the middle ground and even out their lives. Because of the influence of the Sun (outer world) and the Moon (inner world), they have access to both a sparkling persona and a deep unconscious. Both their intuition and sensitivity are usually well developed.

✱ 18 ✱
SUN IN THE WEEK
OF AUTHORITY
(LEO I) JULY 26-AUGUST 2

Noble and regal, these proud individuals expect the very best that life has to offer. Unfortunately, since they are not geared for failure they are frequently unable to handle the disappointment of setbacks. Their frustration level tends to be low and also their patience. In order to achieve happiness they will have to become more accepting while being less demanding.

✱ 19 ✱
SUN IN THE WEEK OF
BALANCED STRENGTH
(LEO II) AUGUST 3-10

Leo II's are faithful, hard-working folks with an ability to make a commitment to their projects and to hang in there. Although their equilibrium is generally high, when they are knocked off their balance they can present a woesome sight. Unhappiness is likely to take hold of them too easily and result in acute depression. By lightening up a bit they can avoid much suffering in life.

✱ 20 ✱
SUN IN THE WEEK
OF LEADERSHIP
(LEO III) AUGUST 11-18

Arrogance is the Achilles heel of these dynamic, driving individuals. Too often they are likely to overestimate their abilities. Their occasional lack of sensitivity serves them well in that they are not really bothered by failure. However, by not recognizing or acknowledging their own failures they can easily lose touch with reality. It is necessary for them to learn to keep their pride under control.

✱ 21 ✱
SUN ON THE CUSP
OF EXPOSURE
(LEO-VIRGO CUSP) AUGUST 19-25

Hard to know at a deep level, these secretive individuals seem to reveal a lot but in fact keep even more hidden. Like the tip of an iceberg, there is a lot which doesn't meet the eye. Moreover, they only choose to reveal themselves at the right time and place, and only to very few people. Their trust factor is not high, making them very discriminating.

✱ 22 ✱
SUN IN THE WEEK OF
SYSTEM BUILDERS
(VIRGO I) AUGUST 26-SEPTEMBER 2

A feeling for structure and order dominates the lives of those born in this week. Yet, paradoxically, chaotic elements threaten them constantly and therefore they run the risk of adopting a rigid stance against perceived threats and intrusions. Virgo I's are mentally oriented and try to use logic to find their way in life. Many are repressed emotionally and must learn to loosen up.

✱ 23 ✱
SUN IN THE WEEK OF
THE ENIGMA
(VIRGO II) SEPTEMBER 3-10

Keeping secrets is a specialty of those born in this week. Since many born here cultivate an air of mystery, they may be seen as puzzling individuals. Even the most normal of Virgo II's have strange quirks and idiosyncrasies. For the most part, they must be left alone to do things their own, special way without fear of blame.

✱ 24 ✱
SUN IN THE WEEK OF
THE LITERALIST
(VIRGO III) SEPTEMBER 11-18

Quite practical and pragmatic, Virgo III's will demand that you keep your word once a promise is made. They tend to judge others quite severely when they do not live up to their expectations. Their extreme capability in most areas marks them as highly dependable and trustworthy. Yet their dramatic flair makes them anything but dull in their approach to life.

✶ 25 ✶
SUN ON THE CUSP
OF BEAUTY
(VIRGO-LIBRA CUSP)
SEPTEMBER 19-24

In love with physical, sensuous beauty, these aesthetic individuals can't get enough of it, whether in paintings or people. Not necessarily sensualists themselves, they may be content to look and not touch. A certain detachment and objectivity pervades their approach toward life, and they are unparalleled as observers and admirers. Highly discriminating, they are selective in their choice of friends.

✶ 26 ✶
SUN IN THE WEEK OF
THE PERFECTIONIST
(LIBRA I) SEPTEMBER 25-OCTOBER 2

In their endless search to get things or make things right, Libra I's are intensely demanding individuals. Too often they put themselves and those around them under stress. Learning that it is all right to relax is an important lesson for them to learn. Their technical abilities are pronounced, but they must also learn the adage, "if it ain't broke, don't fix it."

✶ 27 ✶
SUN IN THE WEEK
OF SOCIETY
(LIBRA II) OCTOBER 3-10

Whether or not these individuals choose to be with others most of the time, their karma is inexorably bound up with the lives of other people. Frequently loners, they cannot deny their psychological skills and their human understanding. Often charming to a fault, they do not always attract the energies which are good for them. Learning to draw boundaries can be a real challenge for them.

✶ 28 ✶
SUN IN THE WEEK
OF THEATER
(LIBRA III) OCTOBER 11-18

These capable, forceful individuals usually have little doubt about what they think and are not shy about expressing their opinions either. Yet they can have a terrible time making choices and even making up their minds about what course to take. This is because they can see the value of the other guy's point of view and want to keep options open whenever possible.

✶ 29 ✶
SUN ON THE CUSP OF
DRAMA AND CRITICISM
(LIBRA-SCORPIO CUSP)
OCTOBER 19-25

Most born on this cusp have a strong opinion on almost any matter, one which they do not hesitate in making known. Hard to fool, you must present a sound and cogent argument to have them agree with your point of view. Lovers of excitement, travel and challenge, they lend individuality and passion to all of their endeavors.

✶ 30 ✶
SUN IN THE WEEK
OF INTENSITY
(SCORPIO I)
OCTOBER 26-NOVEMBER 2

These highly focused individuals usually know what they want and don't give up easily until they get it. They may go through periods of their life, however, in which they either lack direction or let themselves drift. In judging others, they place more emphasis on intention than success. They must learn to keep their highly critical tendencies under control.

✶ 31 ✶
SUN IN THE WEEK OF DEPTH
(SCORPIO II) NOVEMBER 3-11

Deep, serious people, Scorpio II's are not easy to reach emotionally. No matter how successful or involved they are in affairs of the world, they must retreat regularly to their own inner sanctum where they are not disturbed. Their home is usually set up to provide this kind of refuge. They must never be frontally attacked; otherwise, expect the worst.

✶ 32 ✶
SUN IN THE WEEK
OF CHARM
(SCORPIO III) NOVEMBER 12-18

These highly capable individuals are particularly good at running a family or business. Moreover, since their powers of persuasion are high they exert a magnetic and often seductive influence on those around them. It is a matter of pride for them not to ask for help, but they must remember to allow others to give to as well as take from them.

✶ 33 ✶
SUN ON THE CUSP
OF REVOLUTION
(SCORPIO-SAGITTARIUS CUSP)
NOVEMBER 19-24

Scorpio-Sagittarians must learn to keep their combative instincts under control. Feisty individuals, they will rarely back down from a fight. Moreover, they will discover sooner or later that by allowing others to push their buttons at will they are buying into such people controlling them. These are wonderful individuals to work with on projects–highly energetic, dependable, creative.

✴ 34 ✴
SUN IN THE WEEK
OF INDEPENDENCE
(SAGITTARIUS I)
NOVEMBER 25-DECEMBER 2

Those born in this week must do things their own way. They find it difficult to take orders and have to be self-motivated if they are to accomplish their objectives. Often highly idealistic, they must learn to compromise in their personal interactions and to listen to what others have to say. A good sense of humor is an important ingredient of their psychological makeup.

✴ 35 ✴
SUN IN THE WEEK OF
THE ORIGINATOR
(SAGITTARIUS II) DECEMBER 3-10

Highly inventive in their approach to life, these unusual individuals find their own solutions to problems which come their way. Because they may be seen as different, even peculiar, they learn from an early age that they are not everyone's cup of tea and do best with those who accept and understand their quirks. Frequently their creativity is pronounced and their creations striking.

✴ 36 ✴
SUN IN THE WEEK
OF THE TITAN
(SAGITTARIUS III) DECEMBER 11-18

These people think big. They are the most expansive of the Sagittarians and the influence of Jupiter is seen clearly in the grandeur of their ideas and their ideals. Powerful people, they tend to overwork and to put those around them under pressure through their hard-driving style. Their optimism is usually pronounced and they can have a hard time dealing with negative attitudes.

✴ 37 ✴
SUN ON THE CUSP
OF PROPHECY
(SAGITTARIUS-CAPRICORN CUSP)
DECEMBER 19-25

These are serious individuals who must be reckoned with. They do not specialize in getting out of the way easily and are frequently able to get their point across in very few words. Their emotional depth is undeniable but they can also be difficult to reach emotionally. Good at seeing into the future, they also know how to attain their goals.

✴ 38 ✴
SUN IN THE WEEK
OF THE RULER
(CAPRICORN I)
DECEMBER 26-JANUARY 2

Those born in this week know how to control their living and working situations. True rulers, they regard their home as their castle and like to see it running smoothly. Allergic to chaos, they run the risk of becoming control freaks. Unless they give up their tendency to make up other people's minds for them, they are likely to arouse resentments.

✴ 39 ✴
SUN IN THE WEEK
OF DETERMINATION
(CAPRICORN II) JANUARY 3-9

Ambition surfaces in these well-directed individuals sooner or later in life. There is only one direction they are interested in moving – and that is up! It is best not to get in the way of their career drives unless you enjoy being trampled. In their personal lives they are equally intense, but not always as lucky as in their careers.

✴ 40 ✴
SUN IN THE WEEK
OF DOMINANCE
(CAPRICORN III) JANUARY 10-16

As long as these individuals can dominate their work and living spaces they are content to leave others alone. Also, they are less interested in dreams of advancement and more concerned with present realities. Among the most realistic and pragmatic people in the year, they usually get their way through steadfastness and persistence. Loyal, they are unlikely to let their loved ones down.

✴ 41 ✴
SUN ON THE CUSP OF
MYSTERY AND IMAGINATION
(CAPRICORN-AQUARIUS CUSP)
JANUARY 17-22

These vivid, exciting individuals are really in touch with their own fantasy world. Imaginative to the extreme, they lend an air of excitement to any gathering they attend or relationship they enter into. Holding on to them for very long may be difficult but well worth the effort. Better left to go their own way, they can prove good friends and partners as long as the choices are left to them.

✴ 42 ✴
SUN IN THE WEEK
OF GENIUS
(AQUARIUS I) JANUARY 23-30

Those born in this week are extremely quick in picking things up. Often precocious in their early youth, they are often highly perceptive and mentally gifted. In order to avoid superficiality, they are advised to dig a bit deeper and indeed often seek out more profound partners in relationships. Learning to listen to what others have to say is an important lesson for them to learn.

✶ 43 ✶
SUN IN THE WEEK OF
YOUTH AND EASE
(AQUARIUS II)
JANUARY 31-FEBRUARY 7

Aquarius II's do not like trouble and will do almost anything to avoid it. They love it when things run smoothly, without problems. Because happiness is so important to them, they will often refuse to become involved with troublesome people or projects. These are individuals who really enjoy the good things which life has to offer without feeling any guilt at all.

✶ 44 ✶
SUN IN THE WEEK
OF ACCEPTANCE
(AQUARIUS III) FEBRUARY 8-15

Acceptance is an important theme in the lives of those born in this week. Some of them prove to be highly accepting people, others have problems with acceptance and are challenged to become more open and tolerant. Usually idealistic, they nevertheless have a strong reality factor built into their personalities which can help keep them grounded. Rarely will they sacrifice their principles for the sake of gain.

✶ 45 ✶
SUN ON THE CUSP
OF SENSITIVITY
(AQUARIUS-PISCES CUSP)
FEBRUARY 16-22

Classically a position for those who were extremely sensitive to the criticism of others during their childhood and formative years. By building a wall around themselves, they manage to protect their unusually sensitive natures. Dismantling this psychological barrier in adulthood can become their major task in the personal sphere. Learning the joys of trust and sharing becomes their reward.

✶ 46 ✶
SUN IN THE WEEK OF SPIRIT
(PISCES I) FEBRUARY 23-MARCH 2

Those born in this week have an innate feeling for the non-material side of life. Matters dealing with aesthetics, religion, music and dance come easily to them. They can also be very successful with money, understanding the fluid and changeable nature of economics. Because they do not put up rigid defenses they are more likely to withstand great shocks in life.

✶ 47 ✶
SUN IN THE WEEK
OF THE LONER
(PISCES II) MARCH 3-MARCH10

Pisces II's would much rather be alone than have to share time and space with those they don't like. Yet they can be remarkably social and have a circle of dear and devoted friends, as long as things are carried out with consideration of their personal wishes. Usually those born in this week only ask to be accepted as they are.

✶ 48 ✶
SUN IN THE WEEK OF
DANCERS AND DREAMERS
(PISCES III) MARCH 11-18

In some ways the most highly evolved individuals of the year, these spiritually advanced people rely heavily on their intuitive gifts. They are often baffled by ignorance and insensitivity and will take the time to explain to others clearly where they are coming from and how their ideas could prove helpful. Persuasive, they usually exert a strong influence on their family, professional and social sphere.

THE MOON

THE MOON REPRESENTS YOUR FEELINGS, UNCONSCIOUS, DREAMS.

NOTE FROM THE ARTIST ABOUT THE ILLUSTRATION ON THE FACING PAGE: The female figure wears a starry veil, which can be seen as a reflection of how the moon looks behind the clouds on some nights, and also as a   wedding veil of sorts, in a way that suggests the moon's 'marriage' to the earth. The phases of the moon are reflected in the starry border behind the female figure. The moon, itself, is sensual and bright. In astrological lore, the moon reflects our subconscious, basic habits, and reactions.

THE MOON

IN THE 48 PERSONOLOGY PERIODS

✶1✶
MOON ON THE
CUSP OF REBIRTH

(PISCES-ARIES CUSP)

This moon position demands a lot of understanding. Such individuals go very deep and are not at all easy to figure out. Because of their emotional sensitivity they are easily hurt, particularly when it comes to rejection. Moreover, they are not easy to reach emotionally and are likely to keep many secrets and not share their true feelings with others.

✶2✶
MOON IN THE WEEK
OF THE CHILD

(ARIES I)

Feelings here tend to be bottled up tightly inside. Those with their moon in this position distrust being analyzed and mistrust those who try to practice psychological analysis on them. Their dream life can be very active but they may have trouble remembering their dreams. Waking fantasies or daydreams can occupy a good part of their day.

✶3✶
MOON IN THE WEEK
OF THE STAR

(ARIES II)

The moon often causes these individuals to project their inner repressed feelings out on the world. They frequently fall in love with their own inner opposite, the man within (animus for women) or woman within (anima for men) projected out on the world. Because of their need to identify with an ideal person, they tend to put themselves down in favor of the one they adore.

✶4✶
MOON IN THE WEEK
OF THE PIONEER

(ARIES III)

These individuals really need to get to know themselves. The trick is for them to realize that self-knowledge can be as great a reward as any external form of discovery or recognition. Usually cut off from their own feelings, they too often lock themselves up tight as a drum inside, thus guaranteeing a great deal of frustration. Learning to relax and to meditate is important.

✶5✶
MOON ON THE CUSP
OF POWER

(ARIES-TAURUS CUSP)

The moon here makes an individual too controlling of others. They tend to view any act of personal expression in their environment as an attempt to rebel against their rule. Because of their need to repress the true feelings of others, they often prefer when someone is dishonest but agreeable, polite but duplicitous. The real challenge for such folks is to learn to handle emotional honesty.

✶6✶
MOON IN THE WEEK OF
MANIFESTATION

(TAURUS I)

Nurturers, those with the moon in this position love to take care of others. The emotional satisfaction they gain from giving is extraordinary, and yet they find it just as difficult to accept what others have to give. Mostly they hate feeling obligated, and therefore the lesson they must learn is to be able to ask for help when they need it.

✴ 7 ✴
MOON IN THE WEEK OF
THE TEACHER
(TAURUS II)

Too often those with the moon here think they have it all figured out. They think they are expert psychologists when it comes to matters of human feeling and have many opinions on the subject which they are willing to give away free of charge. Although they are frequently right about others, they do have a classic blind spot when it comes to themselves.

✴ 8 ✴
MOON IN THE WEEK OF
THE NATURAL
(TAURUS III)

The moon in this position can make an individual astonishingly frank. Blurting out whatever is on their mind is typical here. Often they have no thought for how such remarks may push the buttons of those around them. We can admire such individuals for their lack of inhibition, but they really must learn something about tact and consideration for others.

✴ 9 ✴
MOON ON THE CUSP
OF ENERGY
(TAURUS-GEMINI CUSP)

Tremendous sexual energy characterizes this position. Those who have little to do with sex can be sure to be suffering under terrible repression. Frequently such individuals live in a fantasy world, in which only they can satisfy their urges. Learning to normalize such urges and express them in a healthier manner can become the work of a lifetime.

✴ 10 ✴
MOON IN THE WEEK
OF FREEDOM
(GEMINI I)

Flitting from one object of desire to the next may be the lot of those with their moon in Gemini I. Inconstancy in emotional matters can lead these butterflies to drive their partners crazy. Because of the changeability of their feelings, they too often arouse unhappiness and mistrust in others, but can be very attractive to those who are drawn to danger and uncertainty.

✴ 11 ✴
MOON IN THE WEEK OF
NEW LANGUAGE
(GEMINI II)

We find out a lot about these fascinating individuals not only by what they say but how they say it. Their body language is usually a dead giveaway to what they are feeling. Unable to hide much inside, they tend to wear their heart on their sleeve. Although often accused of emotional superficiality, they feel pain deeply, however briefly.

✴ 12 ✴
MOON IN THE WEEK OF
THE SEEKER
(GEMINI III)

When it comes to new emotional experiences, these folks are up for almost anything. Challenged by an unattainable love, they are likely to be led astray by their desires and left with a whole lot of unhappiness. Until they get a grip on their feelings, they will continue to make poor partner choices. Falling in love with love will provide continual ecstatic highs, but inevitably depressions also.

✴ 13 ✴
MOON ON THE CUSP
OF MAGIC
(GEMINI-CANCER CUSP)

Because their powers of attraction are so great, those with this moon position will never want for admirers. Unfortunately, they also attract a lot of weirdos and will have to get better at not sending out too many mixed signals. Often unaware of their own magnetism, they may see themselves as unattractive. Their self image must be brought into sync with reality before they can achieve happiness.

✴ 14 ✴
MOON IN THE WEEK OF
THE EMPATH
(CANCER I)

The moon is very comfortable here. Swimming around in a sea of emotions is normal for these folks. They must learn to objectify a bit and also to distinguish between their feelings and those of the other person. Falling deeply in love with a supposed soul mate can cause untold hurt. They must learn not only how to give but also benefit from their relationships.

✴ 15 ✴
MOON IN THE WEEK OF
THE UNCONVENTIONAL
(CANCER II)

Suffering the pangs of rejection is too often the fate of these sensitive creatures. Sooner or later they must face the hard fact that they are just asking and sometimes even begging to be rejected. Secret insecurities must be rooted out and a firm ego built, brick by brick. Moon in Cancer II's must toughen up a bit and learn to draw emotional boundaries.

✴ 16 ✴
MOON IN THE WEEK OF
THE PERSUADER
(CANCER III)

Too often emotionally manipulative, those with moon in Cancer III indulge in a wild fantasy life which frequently proves more satisfying than reality. So strong are their powers of projection that others are forced to act out the imagined roles assigned to them. By learning to accept things as they come without influencing them unduly, these individuals can lead a healthier life.

✴ 17 ✴
MOON ON THE CUSP
OF OSCILLATION
(CANCER-LEO CUSP)

The moon feels a bit unbalanced in this position and so imparts a restless instability to its natives. Moreover, since emotions can take a nosedive at almost any moment, those with their moon here tend to suffer periodically from bouts of depression. Manic phases can also arise, giving a see-saw effect to the feelings. Stimulants should be avoided by these folks.

✴ 18 ✴
MOON IN THE WEEK
OF AUTHORITY
(LEO I)

Such individuals are not likely to know themselves well. Frequently, they cannot remember their dreams or really get in touch with their deepest feelings. They are too likely to burst out in anger or aggression at unexpected moments and to be at the mercy of their feelings once or twice a year. Learning to know themselves better is essential for good health.

✴ 19 ✴
MOON IN THE WEEK OF
BALANCED STRENGTH
(LEO II)

Feelings here are likely to be both ignored and overvalued. A kind of rough approach to the emotions of others in their daily life, one which decries sentimentality or overt displays of feeling, hides a hidden insecurity. In matters of love they can ride roughshod over their mates and be too strongly dominant. Developing kindness and sympathy are their real challenge in life.

✴ 20 ✴
MOON IN THE WEEK
OF LEADERSHIP
(LEO III)

Somewhat charismatic, those with the Moon in Leo III can inspire trust and even worship in others. However, too often their selfishness leads them to use others for their own purposes. This dangerous approach can backfire on them, when the other person's resentments spill over. Chilling out and developing their hedonistic side will help moderate their intensity levels.

✴ 21 ✴
MOON ON THE CUSP
OF EXPOSURE
(LEO-VIRGO CUSP)

The temptation to live a hidden life is very strong here. Too often, such individuals can cut themselves off from society and live in a dream or fantasy world. Usually their dream life is very active and can have a powerful impact on their daily existence. Occasional episodes of exhibitionism help take some of the pressure off their self-repressive attitudes.

✴ 22 ✴
MOON IN THE WEEK OF
SYSTEM BUILDERS
(VIRGO I)

Feelings are likely to be tightly locked up inside and quite under control most of the time. However, this control pays as its price a kind of nervousness and an inability to express oneself evenly, usually resulting in periodic flare-ups. Those born in this week need to value their hearts more and their heads less if they are to find happiness.

✴ 23 ✴
MOON IN THE WEEK OF
THE ENIGMA
(VIRGO II)

An air of mystery shrouds the emotions of those born on this day. It will be difficult to read the feelings of such individuals and even more difficult to understand their actions. They themselves do not specialize in self-knowledge either, and must learn to plumb their depths and confront themselves emotionally if they are to further their own inner development.

✴ 24 ✴
MOON IN THE WEEK OF
THE LITERALIST
(VIRGO III)

Those with their moon in Virgo III can be extremely detached and cool when they are confronted by more emotional types. The more the other person rages, the cooler they become. These are good people to talk to if you want an objective evaluation of someone's emotional state. Surprisingly, they often lead a highly active and exciting dream life.

✳ 25 ✳
MOON ON THE CUSP OF BEAUTY
(VIRGO-LIBRA CUSP)

Such individuals usually reserve their feelings for only those they consider worthy of them. Their ideal of beauty usually leads them to worship the one they love and to put him/her up on a pedestal, where they can do no wrong. Likely to be highly sensuous, they must beware of living too much in their fantasies at the expense of reality.

✳ 26 ✳
MOON IN THE WEEK OF THE PERFECTIONIST
(LIBRA I)

The moon is not so much at home here because of the mental orientation of this position and its critical attitudes. These people tend to be a bit nervous and jumpy, finding it difficult to sit still for very long. Often they are out of touch with their emotions and driven by forces they do not understand. They can be magnetic, however, and usually are viewed as attractive personalities.

✳ 27 ✳
MOON IN THE WEEK OF SOCIETY
(LIBRA II)

Moon in Libra II people reflect the world around them. They are reactive and sensitive to the input from their environments and find it difficult to isolate themselves for long periods of time. Good at enjoying good times with friends, they seek refuge from their own inner demons in the arms of the world. Being appreciated by others is especially important to them.

✳ 28 ✳
MOON IN THE WEEK OF THEATER
(LIBRA III)

A natural tendency toward exhibitionism appears here and if such individuals are quiet or shy it usually indicates repression, often due to judgmental attitudes from family members or teachers early in life. For enthusiastic individuals who are not blocked emotionally, they can be the life of any party. Sometimes they go too far and need to be reined in.

✳ 29 ✳
MOON ON THE CUSP OF DRAMA AND CRITICISM
(LIBRA-SCORPIO CUSP)

Extremely discriminating when it comes to emotional matters, these individuals are suspicious of any display of sentimentality or self-dramatization. Yet they are prone to such behavior themselves, usually without being aware of it. Too often they can be at the mercy of their impetuous and danger-loving urges, which more often than not land them in hot water.

✳ 30 ✳
MOON IN THE WEEK OF INTENSITY
(SCORPIO I)

Not everyone is prepared for the torrents of emotion in which such individuals may engulf others. Moreover, these people know how to get to your weak spots and thus make formidable adversaries. When they turn their aggression or anger inward, it too often results in fits of depression, which are beyond their abilities to control. Developing a sense of humor will help them.

✳ 31 ✳
MOON IN THE WEEK OF DEPTH
(SCORPIO II)

A very profound position for the moon. Deep thoughts and feelings, however, should not turn to endless rumination and worry. A tendency to withdraw and brood is all too apparent here. Also, a suspicion of anything too glib or superficial. Such individuals must not undervalue love and happiness or ignore their need for it on a regular basis.

✳ 32 ✳
MOON IN THE WEEK OF CHARM
(SCORPIO III)

Extremely persuasive, those with this moon position can be highly manipulative and controlling in gaining their goals. Once identified as a love object by such people, it will not be easy to escape them. In relationships with such individuals it is easy to leave emotional choices to them, and in fact to rely on their feelings more than on your own.

✳ 33 ✳
MOON ON THE CUSP OF REVOLUTION
(SCORPIO-SAGITTARIUS CUSP)

Those with their moon here must beware of letting their emotions run out of control. Frequently their anger and irritation build and boil over, much to the consternation of family, friends and colleagues. By allowing themselves to lose their temper and be easily provoked, they can end up letting others control them. It is important for them to learn to acquire equanimity and detachment.

✳ 34 ✳
MOON IN THE WEEK
OF INDEPENDENCE
(SAGITTARIUS I)

A rather nervous setting for the Moon. Emotional change and, in some cases, instability and unreliability is likely to accompany these individuals. Even though their feelings are so subject to change—and sometimes even because of it—they can hold out a fascinating lure for many. Magnetic individuals, they can be heartbreakers, but rarely intentionally.

✳ 35 ✳
MOON IN THE WEEK OF
THE ORIGINATOR
(SAGITTARIUS II)

Too often these individuals can isolate themselves in a fantasy world. Difficult to fathom, they are likely to spend long periods of time alone with their own thoughts and feelings. Because they do not easily fit into a category, they can be misunderstood and be seen to send out mixed signals. Knowing when to approach and when to avoid them is key to gaining their friendship.

✳ 36 ✳
MOON IN THE WEEK
OF THE TITAN
(SAGITTARIUS III)

Such individuals may find it difficult to keep up with their own dreams and visions, which far outstrip their everyday progress. Dissatisfaction and boredom with daily routines usually surface here. Being easily bored, they often seek sources of constant stimulation and are never happier than when they have found a new friend or love interest. Keeping a handle on reality is their constant challenge.

✳ 37 ✳
MOON ON THE CUSP
OF PROPHECY
(SAGITTARIUS-CAPRICORN CUSP)

Because of the depth and darkness of this cusp located on the winter solstice, the moon takes on a profound character. Still waters run deep and this position is no exception. The fantasy life is well-developed. They're in danger of existing too much in unreality, but emotions are strong and vivid. Those with their moon here can be strong, silent types.

✳ 38 ✳
MOON IN THE WEEK
OF THE RULER
(CAPRICORN I)

Powerful in influencing and controlling the feelings of others, people with their Moon in Capricorn I are likely to prevent others from viewing or influencing what they feel. Losing control over their feelings is a nightmare. Yet this can happen from time to time; to avoid lashing out, control is not the answer but instead they need to to express themselves regularly and to feel appreciated.

✳ 39 ✳
MOON IN THE WEEK
OF DETERMINATION
(CAPRICORN II)

A fear exists in such individuals of others using their feelings against them, and so they are likely to build an emotional barrier between themselves and others. Often, however, one individual will be given the key to their inner sanctum. They can become very dependent on such a person for love and understanding. Because of the importance of career here, feelings and emotions may be mistrusted.

✳ 40 ✳
MOON IN THE WEEK
OF DOMINANCE
(CAPRICORN III)

Such individuals as parents, bosses or professional advisors come to play a dominant role in the lives of others. Fostering dependencies is characteristic of those with Capricorn III Moons. Great care should be taken by these folks to leave enough time for themselves and not to overstress themselves with awesome responsibilities. Their disapproval can be devastating, their judgments severe.

✳ 41 ✳
MOON ON THE CUSP OF
MYSTERY AND IMAGINATION
(CAPRICORN-AQUARIUS CUSP)

A wealth of fantasies and dreams come crowding in on these people during both waking and sleeping hours. Often prey to such visions, they may at times be overwhelmed by the intensity of their inner life. Keeping their feet on the ground while tending to the normal tasks of everyday life can be quite challenging, but is essential to their mental health.

✳ 42 ✳
MOON IN THE WEEK
OF GENIUS
(AQUARIUS I) JANUARY 23-30

A somewhat jittery position for the moon. Because of the extreme mental orientation of this week, the moon feels a bit neglected here. Those with Moon in Aquarius I can have difficulty making commitments in relationships. Also, they may give the impression of being a tad superficial in the sense of their feelings not going very deep.

✳ 43 ✳
MOON IN THE WEEK OF
YOUTH AND EASE
(AQUARIUS II)

Lovers of comfort, these individuals avoid conflict and emotional strain. If their feelings are disturbed or too violently aroused, they are likely to go completely off track. They are happiest when on an even emotional keel and affection is often more rewarding than passion. Keeping their internal state quiet is essential to their well-being. They should avoid chaotic individuals, despite their fascination with them.

✳ 44 ✳
MOON IN THE WEEK
OF ACCEPTANCE
(AQUARIUS III)

Peculiar likes and dislikes and idiosyncrasy in general may be the bane of those with this Moon position. Irrational prejudices can surface, causing difficulties for all in their immediate environment. If they can become more emotionally accepting, they will have accomplished one of their chief tasks in life. However, they must still remember to maintain ego boundaries and not go overboard in giving their feelings away.

✳ 45 ✳
MOON ON THE CUSP
OF SENSITIVITY
(AQUARIUS-PISCES CUSP)

Such individuals are constantly being bombarded by upsetting stimuli in their immediate environment. They have to get a handle on their feelings and if their buttons are pushed, they simply learn to develop a whole new set of buttons which cannot be so easily reached. These people are likely to be in touch with their inner world and are expressive by nature.

✳ 46 ✳
MOON IN THE WEEK
OF SPIRIT
(PISCES I)

A highly creative Moon position. The artistic powers of the individual are heightened and also their appreciation of art, music, film and literature. A special interest in spiritual matters may surface here, particularly matters dealing with reincarnation, diet and meditation. Such persons should not forget to attend to the more practical aspects of life. Physical exercise is recommended.

✳ 47 ✳
MOON IN THE WEEK
OF THE LONER
(PISCES II)

The danger of becoming isolated and living in a dream world is pronounced here, even the possibility of getting fantasy and reality mixed up. It will be important to maintain a degree of objectivity and also to have a few close friends who can act as touchstones for the outside world. Keeping in touch with the unconscious but not being dominated by it is essential.

✳ 48 ✳
MOON IN THE WEEK OF
DANCERS AND DREAMERS
(PISCES III)

Vivid individuals who are not afraid to flaunt their differences, those with their Moon in this position must be careful not to have an overpowering effect on those around them. Extremely influential, they know how to manipulate others emotionally. Because this will ultimately arouse anger and resentment, they must learn how to back off and curb their controlling attitudes.

MERCURY

MERCURY REPRESENTS LOGIC AND COMMUNICATION.

NOTE FROM THE ARTIST ABOUT THE ILLUSTRATION ON THE FACING PAGE: The planet Mercury is named after the messenger of the gods, Mercury. The female figure's winged mask evokes Mercury's legendary fleetness of foot. In astrological lore, Mercury rules communication. Mercury is said to be curious, unemotional, and opportunistic. Mercury's curiosity and mode of expression is reflected in the way the female figure holds—and gazes a— the planet. The rays come out from behind the planet, reflecting the earth's view of Mercury.

MERCURY

IN THE 48 PERSONOLOGY PERIODS

✱1✱
MERCURY ON THE CUSP OF REBIRTH
(PISCES-ARIES CUSP)

A lively position, but not always an easy one to deal with. People with their Mercury on this cusp stir up the pot and are not always appreciated at more peaceful or laid-back gatherings. Constantly questioning and probing, they are a valuable asset to any professional group. In their private lives it is important for them to keep their critical tendencies under control.

✱2✱
MERCURY IN THE WEEK OF THE CHILD
(ARIES I)

Mercury asserts an influence on speech and indeed all forms of expression, making these individuals direct, honest and open. They frequently do not pay enough attention to what they say or really care what others think of them. Their thoughts are usually well examined, however, and they are open to other points of view, even those which contradict their own ideas.

✱3✱
MERCURY IN THE WEEK OF THE STAR
(ARIES II)

A bit of a tendency here to show off how smart one is. These know-it-alls have something to say on practically any subject. Their desire to shock with the originality and directness of their latest idea is pronounced. Learning to temper such thrusts is important if they wish to avoid being summarily rejected by others and to gain a fair hearing for their ideas.

✱4✱
MERCURY IN THE WEEK OF THE PIONEER
(ARIES III)

Public speaking can be a special talent for such individuals. If this talent has not yet been explored, it should be initiated at family gatherings and within informal professional settings. Influential in speech, such individuals need to communicate their ideas to others and to watch their effect to change people's lives. Isolation is difficult to bear for those with their Mercury in this week.

✱5✱
MERCURY ON THE CUSP OF POWER
(ARIES-TAURUS CUSP)

Those with Mercury on this cusp can convey their message in few words. Particularly when it comes to warning people to back off, a simple glance will usually do the trick. Often more fluent and expressive in writing than in speech, these individuals can organize their thoughts well, given enough time and space. They usually hit the nail right on the head with their telling observations.

✱6✱
MERCURY IN THE WEEK OF MANIFESTATION
(TAURUS I)

Translating their thoughts into reality is a specialty of these individuals. This may not happen quickly and, in fact, may take years of planning. Such people have the ability to wait as long as it takes for the right moment to come along. Happy to be of service to the social or family group to which they belong, they often provide the brains behind the group's decisions.

✳ 7 ✳
MERCURY IN THE WEEK OF
THE TEACHER
(TAURUS II)

Too often didactic in speech, those with Mercury in this period can appear to be omniscient or at the very least self-assured. They usually have no doubt that what they are advocating is right for all those around them. In order to arouse less resentment, they should learn to curb what appears as a know-it-all approach.

✳ 8 ✳
MERCURY IN THE WEEK OF
THE NATURAL
(TAURUS III)

Happy to indulge in conversation, these individuals may overwhelm you with their easy approach. Rarely do they seek to cause problems, but in fact they do arouse opposition from others who resent their free and easy manner. Usually forthright in what they say, these folks do not mince words when it comes to their likes and dislikes.

✳ 9 ✳
MERCURY ON THE CUSP
OF ENERGY
(TAURUS-GEMINI CUSP)

Few can withstand the verbal assaults of those with Mercury in this position. Aggressive in speech, they must learn to tone down their rhetoric and also to soften the intensity of their delivery. Through writing, rather than speaking, they can learn the value of editing the length of their message and cutting to only the essentials.

✳ 10 ✳
MERCURY IN THE WEEK
OF FREEDOM
(GEMINI I)

Frequently branded as troublemakers, those born in this week usually work to undermine authority and encourage others to think as freely as they themselves do. Since they often lack structure in their lives, it will be useful to work in circumstances where limits are put on their thinking and demands are made to support their ideas with hard facts.

✳ 11 ✳
MERCURY IN THE WEEK OF
NEW LANGUAGE
(GEMINI II)

Not everyone can understand the unusual verbal expression of these individuals. Therefore, those born in this week must take the time to explain themselves clearly and fully, in plain and simple language. Often good at public speaking, they may be encouraged to develop an often hidden talent for speaking to groups or representing the organizations of which they are a member.

✳ 12 ✳
MERCURY IN THE WEEK
OF THE SEEKER
(GEMINI III)

Curiosity is paramount here and a need to explore, for such people need to fully investigate their immediate environment. In doing this they should be careful not to be branded as busybodies who stick their noses into other people's business. It is important to them not only to seek new exploits, but also to tell about them, so they are prone to spin tall tales and engage in gossip.

✳ 13 ✳
MERCURY ON THE CUSP
OF MAGIC
(GEMINI-CANCER CUSP)

This position grants the charisma to attract others and bewitch them with your verbal expression. Of course, attracting unstable individuals can have a deleterious effect and undermine the stability of any given situation. Best to harness this energy for positive ends and not to abuse it. Also, to learn to be selective when choosing lasting friendships.

✳ 14 ✳
MERCURY IN THE WEEK OF
THE EMPATH
(CANCER I)

Mercury's logic is likely to be clouded in this week. Feeling the emotions of others is not conducive to keeping a steady hand on the wheel and consequently the periodic influx of emotion will make it difficult to bring one's rational faculties into play. Using the mind to differentiate between one's personal feelings and those of the other person will help bolster Mercury's energies here.

✳ 15 ✳
MERCURY IN THE WEEK OF
THE UNCONVENTIONAL
(CANCER II)

Care must be taken not to let the mind wander along strange and hidden byways. Losing focus is the danger here, resulting in an inability to concentrate on matters at hand. Bizarre thought patterns are likely to predominate, bringing with them the pleasures of fantasy but also the blows that hard reality can dish out in abundance. Keeping to strict schedules can help.

✷ 16 ✷
MERCURY IN THE WEEK OF
THE PERSUADER
(CANCER III)

A definite talent to convince others through speech and logical argument accompanies this position. In order to follow through on promises, however, it will be necessary to adopt a more pragmatic approach. This can be difficult if emphasis is placed more on convincing others than on satisfying them. These individuals risk incurring the wrath of those sent off on the wrong track.

✷ 17 ✷
MERCURY ON THE CUSP
OF OSCILLATION
(CANCER-LEO CUSP)

It is difficult for Mercury to achieve consistency here. Flashes of brilliance can alternate with muddled thought, thereby making it difficult to arouse the confidence of other people. Trying to even out the highs and lows of mental processes is advised and also settling for a lower, but more consistent, standard in the quality of one's output.

✷ 18 ✷
MERCURY IN THE WEEK
OF AUTHORITY
(LEO I)

Giving others the impression that you know what you are talking about can prove a strength here, but also leave one open to blame when things don't go well. It is best to abandon an omniscient attitude in favor of simply giving advice in a straightforward and humble manner. Telling others to take it or leave it is better than promising the moon.

✷ 19 ✷
MERCURY IN THE WEEK OF
BALANCED STRENGTH
(LEO II)

This Mercury position can guarantee a responsible standing in the family or professional sphere. Those with Mercury here can be extremely valuable to the group in a crisis situation in which keeping a level head is essential. The only danger here is that of becoming indispensable and thereby creating dependencies on the part of less capable individuals.

✷ 20 ✷
MERCURY IN THE WEEK
OF LEADERSHIP
(LEO III)

Those with Mercury in this week have powerful ideas which can attract many followers. Others are likely to be so convinced of your arguments that they can follow you without thinking for themselves. A tremendous responsibility accompanies this position and you should think carefully about the results of leading others astray. Do not betray the trust of those who believe in you.

✷ 21 ✷
MERCURY ON THE CUSP
OF EXPOSURE
(LEO-VIRGO CUSP)

A sense of mystery accompanies this position, since these individuals tend to keep their thoughts to themselves. It will be difficult to unearth their motives or gain a sense of what logic they follow. Such people may be quiet and only speak their mind at the most necessary or opportune times. Their silence can be powerful and their disapproval strong.

✷ 22 ✷
MERCURY IN THE WEEK OF
SYSTEM BUILDERS
(VIRGO I)

The power of logic is prominent here and with it the ability to structure daily life in a highly rational manner. Mercury is right at home in this position, bestowing his razor-sharp mental abilities. Care must be taken, however, not to neglect the feelings of others in the name of telling the truth or bringing critical attitudes to bear.

✷ 23 ✷
MERCURY IN THE WEEK OF
THE ENIGMA
(VIRGO II)

A delight in solving mysteries and puzzles of all sorts surfaces here. These individuals like nothing better than ferreting out secret motives or uncovering heretofore neglected facts. A talent for research is likely to manifest, accompanied by the ability to order material effectively. The ability to write telling reports is especially favored and this talent should be practiced in one's profession.

✷ 24 ✷
MERCURY IN THE WEEK
OF THE LITERALIST
(VIRGO III)

Care must be taken that this Mercury position does not lead to a rigidity of thought. Remembering every promise made or holding others to agreements which allow little or no flexibility will only cause problems. Trying to adopt a more accepting approach will make things a lot easier for all concerned. The importance of expressing one's true feelings should not be forgotten.

✳ 25 ✳
MERCURY ON THE CUSP
OF BEAUTY
(VIRGO-LIBRA CUSP)

Those with Mercury on this cusp are easily upset by disharmony of any sort, particularly that associated with loud noises, unpalatable tastes, noxious smells and ugly color combinations. They are best able to think clearly in a pleasing or at least neutral environment, where they can concentrate fully. Distractions, real or imagined, can prey on their minds.

✳ 26 ✳
MERCURY IN THE WEEK OF
THE PERFECTIONIST
(LIBRA I)

Mercury tends to be highly critical here and so those with that planet in this position are difficult to please. Always looking for something better, they never seem satisfied with what they have. They should make an effort to control their pickiness and learn to accept things as they are without trying to alter or fix them.

✳ 27 ✳
MERCURY IN THE WEEK
OF SOCIETY
(LIBRA II)

Quick wits usually accompany this position. Also, an insight into the way human, and particularly, group psychology, works. Astute observers of the world around them, their telling comments usually drive their point home effectively. Others respect their judgment and seek their counsel in times of need. They can benefit by turning more attention to their own personal problems.

✳ 28 ✳
MERCURY IN THE WEEK
OF THEATER
(LIBRA III)

A tendency to show off mental abilities is characteristic of this Mercury placement. Such individuals can be acutely embarrassed when they are proven wrong, but usually snap back with vigor. Their irrepressible side makes it difficult for them to be silent in a group and, indeed, they are usually expected to be the life of the party by friends and family.

✳ 29 ✳
MERCURY ON THE CUSP OF
DRAMA AND CRITICISM
(LIBRA-SCORPIO CUSP)

Such individuals must be careful that constant and merciless criticism on their part does not drag them down or lead others to reject their ideas as unconstructive and negative. They have a great deal to offer. It is not their message which needs improvement but their delivery. Taking the feelings of others into account is important for them to learn.

✳ 30 ✳
MERCURY IN THE WEEK
OF INTENSITY
(SCORPIO I)

Whether of the book-learning variety or simply reflected in patience of observation, study comes easily to those with Mercury here. Sitting for hours absorbed in such activities comes naturally to them. Keeping it light and not laying heavy trips on others will be important to their happiness and that of their loved ones. Stress is highly detrimental to their health.

✳ 31 ✳
MERCURY IN THE WEEK
OF DEPTH
(SCORPIO II)

Deep thought is the natural state here. However, this does not imply that such thoughts can be easily communicated to others. Those with this Mercury position do not specialize in talking about themselves or sharing private ruminations. Unfortunately, thinking frequently turns to worry and worry to self-induced stress. In order to avoid anxiety or depression, positive thinking must predominate.

✳ 32 ✳
MERCURY IN THE WEEK
OF CHARM
(SCORPIO III)

The kind of smooth talk that can lead to pleasant seduction is the gift bestowed by Mercury in this week. Even mild flirtation is given extra pizzazz here. Such individuals have a way with words that can soften the hardest heart or convince the most confirmed skeptics. Although these people can talk themselves out of trouble, they must be careful not to talk themselves into it either.

✳ 33 ✳
MERCURY ON THE CUSP
OF REVOLUTION
(SCORPIO-SAGITTARIUS CUSP)

Such individuals must not allow their inflammatory statements to incite others to action or otherwise unduly influence them. Fond of stirring up the soup, those with Mercury on this cusp usually can't keep their opinions to themselves. Because they often speak out against fixed ideas or the status quo, they may gain an unfavorable reputation as a troublemaker and make others wary of their ideas.

✴ 34 ✴
MERCURY IN THE WEEK OF INDEPENDENCE
(SAGITTARIUS I)

Quite outspoken, those with Mercury in this position speak their mind straight out. Not much for being analyzed or having their statements dissected, they rarely have ulterior motives in mind. Freedom of speech has a special significance to them and they would be more unhappy than most to be deprived of this inalienable right. Engaging in lively debate is particularly satisfying to them.

✴ 35 ✴
MERCURY IN THE WEEK OF THE ORIGINATOR
(SAGITTARIUS II)

A creative and at times bizarre use of language characterizes these individuals. Because of this idiosyncratic way of expressing themselves, their original verbal style is easily recognizable. Indeed, it can become their hallmark and serve to identify them more than their appearance or their actions. Those who truly understand them occupy a special place in their heart.

✴ 36 ✴
MERCURY IN THE WEEK OF THE TITAN
(SAGITTARIUS III)

Because expansive thought is already an important part of this Personology period, the presence of Mercury is doubly stimulating as far as seeing the big picture is concerned and communicating important ideas. Those with this Mercury position should be careful not to overlook the details or to trip over their shoelaces while taking in the panoramic view ahead.

✴ 37 ✴
MERCURY ON THE CUSP OF PROPHECY
(SAGITTARIUS-CAPRICORN CUSP)

A deep and probing mind which is able to see in the life of things is usually denoted by this Mercury position. Not necessarily intelligent, but highly intuitive, such individuals use their mind power to best advantage. They are able to convince others through the focus and intensity of their arguments. Others often rely on them for sage advice.

✴ 38 ✴
MERCURY IN THE WEEK OF THE RULER
(CAPRICORN I)

Sharp verbal and written skills make such individuals difficult to oppose and their colleagues are usually happy to have them as members of the group. They can, however, get into trouble when they are placed in executive positions, frequently arousing rebellion through autocratic attitudes. Their success usually depends on the trust of those working under them.

✴ 39 ✴
MERCURY IN THE WEEK OF DETERMINATION
(CAPRICORN II)

Mercury is not usually characterized by the dogged plodding typical of this week. It feels restrained by practicality here and responsibilities weigh heavily on its freedom-loving spirit. Mercury wants to fly, while Capricorn II insists on a step-by-step, cautious approach. These seemingly irreconcilable energies can work in synch as long as they agree to reconcile extremes and to be open to compromise.

✴ 40 ✴
MERCURY IN THE WEEK OF DOMINANCE
(CAPRICORN III)

Mercury can serve the purpose of this week by bringing structure and logic to the activities of daily life. With this position, the intellect is easily put in the service of pragmatism, allowing a high degree of control. Dominance here usually means dominating one's material rather than one's friends. In the workplace, it could denote a tidy agenda and an orderly work flow; at home, a spotless kitchen and everything in its place.

✴ 41 ✴
MERCURY ON THE CUSP OF MYSTERY AND IMAGINATION
(CAPRICORN-AQUARIUS CUSP)

Although Mercury is happy with the mental orientation of this cusp, too much energy may spill over into the realms of dreams, cutting one off from present realities. The creative side of this orientation benefits while the practical side suffers. Those with Mercury on this cusp must strive to keep mentally balanced and not allow their fantasies to run riot.

✴ 42 ✴
MERCURY IN THE WEEK OF GENIUS
(AQUARIUS I) JANUARY 23-30

This Mercury position is most favorable. Intelligence is high, meaning quick comprehension, penetrating analysis and accurate computation. Such individuals can get easily frustrated with the slower thought processes of others, but also with their own difficulties in putting their complex ideas into language which others can understand. Above all, they must not assume that others know what they are thinking or talking about and must take time to explain.

✱ 43 ✱
MERCURY IN THE WEEK OF
YOUTH AND EASE
(AQUARIUS II)

Worry is anathema to those with Mercury in this week. It can cause enormous stress, leading to illness. The mind needs to be constantly reassured that everything is all right and will turn out for the best. These individuals should harness their abundant mental skills to more productive endeavors than endlessly ruminating on things. Puzzles, games and riddles are good outlets for these active minds.

✱ 44 ✱
MERCURY IN THE WEEK
OF ACCEPTANCE
(AQUARIUS III)

Because strongly critical attitudes are conveyed by Mercury in this position, efforts must be made to be more accepting. A tendency toward cynicism, disbelief and mistrust is apparent here, a refusal to believe anything which does not pass the strict standards set by logic. If one's own beliefs are examined with equal scrutiny, however, they may also need to be improved.

✱ 45 ✱
MERCURY ON THE CUSP
OF SENSITIVITY
(AQUARIUS-PISCES CUSP)

Unless an attempt is made to objectify, Mercury can find itself too reactive to inner feelings. Thus, emotion swaying logic may prove to be a problem throughout life. In order to think effectively, it will be necessary to acquire a certain detachment from one's emotional state and to keep a cool head in times of stress. Not taking everything so seriously and keeping a good sense of humor will help in this respect.

✱ 46 ✱
MERCURY IN THE WEEK
OF SPIRIT
(PISCES I)

The challenge here is to bring the spiritual and intellectual aspects of one's nature into a harmonious balance. This can be very difficult, as much as bringing an atheist and an orthodox believer to an understanding and cooperative relationship. Indeed, much spirituality depends heavily on a clear mental orientation and intellectual curiosity is often fed by the enthusiasm of the true believer.

✱ 47 ✱
MERCURY IN THE WEEK
OF THE LONER
(PISCES II)

Living in one's own little dream world can be a problem here, particularly if Mercury is satisfied with the internal challenges raised and obsessed with countless individual details. Self-obsession can lead to true neurosis, so a strong effort should me made to share one's ideas with others and also to express these ideas regularly to family and friends.

✱ 48 ✱
MERCURY IN THE WEEK OF
DANCERS AND DREAMERS
(PISCES III)

Thought goes far indeed with Mercury in this position. The mind is likely to roam the cosmos and the worlds of imagination and intellect in search of the true, the good and the beautiful. At home in the most far-out areas of thought, one may come to live in a highly rarified atmosphere. The danger, of course, is being unable to return at will from such distant outposts.

VENUS

VENUS REPRESENTS LOVE, ROMANCE, SOCIAL INTERACTIONS, AND THE FEMININE SIDE

NOTE FROM THE ARTIST ABOUT THE ILLUSTRATION ON THE FACING PAGE: Venus is the goddess of love and money. Doves are one of the signs of the goddess Venus, as are flower garlands. The planet is known as the 'morning star' and the 'evening star' which is reflected by the two stars the female figure holds in her hands. In astrological lore, Venus is associated with the heart and what gives us pleasure.

VENUS

IN THE 48 PERSONOLOGY PERIODS

✷ 1 ✷
VENUS ON THE
CUSP OF REBIRTH
(PISCES-ARIES CUSP)

Although forthright in matters of love, those with Venus on this cusp can keep their deepest feelings hidden. Thus, their actions are open to interpretation and their real motives are not always clear. Frequently unaware of their own feelings, they are likely to get in trouble through excessive emotionality.

✷ 2 ✷
VENUS IN THE WEEK
OF THE CHILD
(ARIES I)

Not easy to reach emotionally, these people often build barriers between themselves and the outside world. Not comfortable in this week, Venus can create difficulties in relationships and make a long-standing romantic partnership difficult to sustain. In matters of love, such individuals can be too passive at one moment, too active at another. They need to cultivate a better feeling for kairos (the right time for doing something).

✷ 3 ✷
VENUS IN THE WEEK
OF THE STAR
(ARIES II)

Usually suckers for admiration, those with Venus here need to be adored. At the same time, they are suspicious of flatterers and at times refuse to believe anything good which others say about them. A deep seated feeling of inferiority can be present, even though they may be outwardly extremely attractive. Their self-image can use a reality check and a bit of sprucing up.

✷ 4 ✷
VENUS IN THE WEEK
OF THE PIONEER
(ARIES III)

Often more in love with love than with a person, these romantic souls constantly search for challenging relationships, often with the most unlikely people. The thrill of being in love is paramount for them; rejection is not necessarily an obstacle since they don't give up easily and also tend to live in a bit of a fantasy world when it comes to the love object.

✷ 5 ✷
VENUS ON THE CUSP
OF POWER
(ARIES-TAURUS CUSP)

These individuals enjoy using their powers of seduction to the highest degree. Behind these actions is a real need to control, particularly in love relationships. By calling the shots, those with Venus on this cusp are usually the ones who break off the relationship and dish out the hurt. Unfortunately, when that "real thing" comes along, they are likely to suffer greatly when they are ignored or rejected.

✷ 6 ✷
VENUS IN THE WEEK OF
MANIFESTATION
(TAURUS I)

Fatally in love with sensuous beauty, those born on this cusp can get hopelessly lost in adoration for their lover and in outright addiction to sensual or sexual bonds. Difficult to get rid of, those with this Venus position can hang in there for years in a relationship which is less than desirable for their partner. Once their mind is made up, it is hard to make them see the truth.

✳7✳
VENUS IN THE WEEK OF
THE TEACHER
(TAURUS II)

High ideals in love make those with this Venus position very demanding of their partners. Living up to their expectations is not easy, and the demands of being put on a pedestal as the loved one are high. Usually these folks are able to see only what they want to see, imbuing their world with their own strong point of view.

✳8✳
VENUS IN THE WEEK OF
THE NATURAL
(TAURUS III)

A shamelessly honest approach to love characterizes Venus in Taurus III. They are not only outwardly demonstrative but also refuse to fake it or appear to have feelings or attitudes which are not true. These individuals hate pretense above all. Their approach is so straightforward that they can be accused occasionally of being too rough in their refusal to coddle their sweethearts.

✳9✳
VENUS ON THE CUSP
OF ENERGY
(TAURUS-GEMINI CUSP)

Those with Venus here are usually fated to have many friendships, love affairs and even several live-in relationships during their lifetime. Moreover, their choice of partners is likely to be broad and diverse, encompassing many different personality types. A love of variety is present, and with it a need for change, particularly when things are not going well.

✳10✳
VENUS IN THE WEEK
OF FREEDOM
(GEMINI I)

A refusal to be held down to fixed responsibilities in relationships characterizes this Venus position. Often at the first sign of ownership attitudes on the part of their mate, they withdraw and sometimes even leave. The trick in handling these mercurial feelings is allowing their owners to have the freedom they need and to allow, rather than compelling them to express themselves.

✳11✳
VENUS IN THE WEEK OF
NEW LANGUAGE
(GEMINI II)

Often the emotions of these individuals do not easily translate into words which can be understood. For example, when they try to tell you they love you they may leave exactly the opposite impression. Being sensitive to what they say and the true meaning behind it will require effort on the part of their lovers and friends. Often it is best not to take their statements too seriously.

✳12✳
VENUS IN THE WEEK OF
THE SEEKER
(GEMINI III)

These individuals don't like to be handed love on a platter. Challenge-oriented, they consider the hunt and the chase as important elements in the whole romantic package. Gemini IIIs love the process of exploration, so they not only enjoy discovering a loved one's psyche, but also plumbing its depths. They must beware of getting too involved in the process itself and neglecting the feelings of those they are involved with.

✳13✳
VENUS ON THE CUSP
OF MAGIC
(GEMINI-CANCER CUSP)

The naturally enchanting qualities of both Venus and of this cusp are mutually enhanced by their contact. Since this is a highly romantic position, those with their Venus here can be swept away by a flood of emotion. Love is an irresistible force, one before which all bulwarks of reason or common sense are doomed to fall.

✳14✳
VENUS IN THE WEEK OF
THE EMPATH
(CANCER I)

Those with Venus in this week usually know when someone has romantic feelings for them. However, having antennae out for the emotional orientation of others means that they sense both the personal likes and dislikes of others easily. They will usually back off quickly if they do not share a mutual interest with the other person and can become unusually upset when faced with unwanted aggression.

✳15✳
VENUS IN THE WEEK OF
THE UNCONVENTIONAL
(CANCER II)

The popularity of these individuals is usually due to their highly individual approach to social interaction. Thus, they attract the attention of others through their unusual behavior and are able to hold that interest through a personality that never ceases to fascinate. Although they often shirk formal social responsibilities, they do choose to help out in their own way.

✴ 16 ✴
VENUS IN THE WEEK OF
THE PERSUADER
(CANCER III)

It is difficult to withstand the amorous assaults of those with Venus in this week, particularly once they have set their sights on you. Should they convince themselves they are in love with you, they are likely to convince you to reciprocate. Most often they remain in control, guiding the relationship according to their deepest desires, which are difficult or impossible to resist.

✴ 17 ✴
VENUS ON THE CUSP
OF OSCILLATION
(CANCER-LEO CUSP)

Ups and downs in the love life are inevitable here. Remaining constant in one's expression of love can be a real challenge, since so many seductive byways beckon. Likewise, in matters of friendship, although loyalty is the rule, old friends may be miffed when new friends appear with frightening regularity. Avoiding the excesses of romance and unreality in general is essential to good mental health.

✴ 18 ✴
VENUS IN THE WEEK
OF AUTHORITY
(LEO I)

Venus' willfulness emerges here and also its passion. Likely to bolt or revolt at the first hint of an authoritative attitude, those with this Venus position need to temper their fiery, reactive instincts. They also need to temper their desire, which could easily lead to unhappiness and burnout. Trying to understand the other person in any relationship is essential, particularly listening carefully to what they have to say.

✴ 19 ✴
VENUS IN THE WEEK OF
BALANCED STRENGTH
(LEO II)

Usually loyal and trustworthy in matters of love, these folks can also be very long-suffering. By hanging in there they frequently expose themselves to trying and painful situations without too much protest. The strain will eventually show, however, and can lead to breakdowns. Better that they learn to express their personal feelings to their partners directly.

✴ 20 ✴
VENUS IN THE WEEK
OF LEADERSHIP
(LEO III)

This week lends a certain dignity and high idealism to matters of love. People with this Venus position are likely to idealize their relationship, but not necessarily their partner. Realists, they see the other person's illusions but will do everything they can to keep the relationship going, as long as they believe in it. They must be careful about loosing touch with reality.

✴ 21 ✴
VENUS ON THE CUSP
OF EXPOSURE
(LEO-VIRGO CUSP)

Hidden love is a theme associated with this Venus position. Not only can thoughts of the loved one be hidden, but amorous activities also. Such secrecy can be practiced for years with few if any others finding out about them. When such activities are finally revealed, it may be with spectacular effect, taking friends and family by surprise.

✴ 22 ✴
VENUS IN THE WEEK OF
SYSTEM BUILDERS
(VIRGO I)

Straightforward in their approach to love, those with Venus here are quite matter-of-fact in even their most romantic relationships. Their feeling for structure enables them to schedule even the most passionate of meetings with sense and order. When they are interested in extending a relationship or making it permanent, they usually proceed in a series of conscious and well-defined steps to attain their object.

✴ 23 ✴
VENUS IN THE WEEK OF
THE ENIGMA
(VIRGO II)

The romantic feelings of these individuals are often complex, difficult for others to figure out but for themselves as well. They can express interest in and affection for another person in the strangest ways. Negative, sarcastic, or offhand statements can be evidence of deeper emotion. Because of their indirect and cryptic manner of expression, they frequently send mixed signals.

✴ 24 ✴
VENUS IN THE WEEK OF
THE LITERALIST
(VIRGO III)

These highly passionate individuals often present a cool exterior when it comes to matters of romance. Their brains never stop working, even when their bodies are most active. Generally calculating the situation to their own best advantage, they will rarely if ever put themselves at the mercy of another person's feelings. Because of their detachment, they are formidable adversaries in battles of love.

✷ 25 ✷
VENUS ON THE CUSP
OF BEAUTY

(VIRGO-LIBRA CUSP)

Venus feels very much at home on this cusp. Consequently, those with this Venus position usually have marked aesthetic tendencies. Their love of beauty is enhanced far beyond the average and they are often at the mercy of it. Falling in love with love or with an ideal can become a real problem for them.

✷ 26 ✷
VENUS IN THE WEEK OF
THE PERFECTIONIST

(LIBRA I)

Standards for one's mate, partner or friend may be impossibly high. Judgmental attitudes, standards and even checklists can abound, making it sometimes difficult to relate to these demands. Those with this Venus position should aim to accept people as they are and not to subject them to such evaluations. Remembering that we are all only human is vitally important.

✷ 27 ✷
VENUS IN THE WEEK
OF SOCIETY

(LIBRA II)

Those with Venus here usually have an easy manner with people. Because of their advanced social instincts they are often highly valued for their talents in dealing with groups. They should be careful not to lose sight of their own individual needs and wants, nor their own personal development. The tendency to lose oneself in the crowd is often found here.

✷ 28 ✷
VENUS IN THE WEEK
OF THEATER

(LIBRA III)

An acute consciousness of one's personal appearance and its effect on others is apparent with this Venus position. The theatrical nature of the personality is enhanced; often life is seen as a kind of stage on which personal dramas can be acted out. This can lead to alienating friends and family alike, so attention should be paid to the other person as well.

✷ 29 ✷
VENUS ON THE CUSP OF
DRAMA AND CRITICISM

(LIBRA-SCORPIO CUSP)

Interest in the byways of love, both platonic and sexual, are often evident here, making such individuals quite unusual in their tastes. Eschewing the ordinary for the bizarre, they are attracted to new experiences which hold the promise of richer reward, both mental and physical. They should be careful not to let their amorous desires get out of hand and control other more normal aspects of their lives.

✷ 30 ✷
VENUS IN THE WEEK
OF INTENSITY

(SCORPIO I)

Seduction figures prominently here. Masters in attracting and controlling the opposite sex, those with Venus in this week are born flirts and specialists in the arts of love. Because of the intensity with which they love, they are not easily forgotten. They must learn, however, to back off and allow the other person to express their true feelings or risk losing them.

✷ 31 ✷
VENUS IN THE WEEK
OF DEPTH

(SCORPIO II)

The danger of becoming unduly attached or obsessed with the loved one is always present for these passionate individuals. Sex and love addictions are not at all uncommon with this position, making love affairs and even deep friendships alternately ecstatic and painful. Depression may easily surface in cases of loss or rejection, and learning to be less dependent on feelings is essential.

✷ 32 ✷
VENUS IN THE WEEK
OF CHARM

(SCORPIO III)

The darker aspects of sex, love and romance have a magnetic pull on these folks. Consequently, it will be important to their mental health to keep it light, but also to at least give more conventional approaches to love a chance. Marriage is often a means to straighten out their more wayward impulses. Remaining true to their life partner is a major challenge.

✷ 33 ✷
VENUS ON THE CUSP
OF REVOLUTION

(SCORPIO-SAGITTARIUS CUSP)

Stormy scenes frequently punctuate the love lives of those with this Venus position. Very outspoken in their views about their partners, they are not long-suffering types and will not allow themselves to be trodden upon without protest and, ultimately, without separation and even divorce. Not unlike a combination of nitroglycerine and dynamite, their package bears the words "Handle with Extreme Care."

✱ 34 ✱
VENUS IN THE WEEK
OF INDEPENDENCE
(SAGITTARIUS I)

Those who have Venus in this week would rather be alone than with someone who is not really the right person for them. In general, their lack of true dependency makes them ideal mates for those who prefer spunk and honesty to a more passive submissiveness. Frequently their deepest affection is given to pets and children, rather than to their lovers or mates.

✱ 35 ✱
VENUS IN THE WEEK OF
THE ORIGINATOR
(SAGITTARIUS II)

Such individuals are more attracted to unconventional relationships. Uncomfortable with the usual dynamics of relationship, they may not jump at the chance of marriage and indeed even feel hemmed in by the normal responsibilities of carrying on a friendship. They often, however, wind up with more ordinary folks who give them the stability they so sorely need and may secretly crave.

✱ 36 ✱
VENUS IN THE WEEK
OF THE TITAN
(SAGITTARIUS III)

Those with this Venus position usually are willing to overlook differences in their close relationships. When they fall in love, their hearts soar higher than most and they may crash to the ground with greater force during a breakup. Because they're optimistic and can see the big picture, these folks are usually willing to give their loved one a second chance and to try again.

✱ 37 ✱
VENUS ON THE CUSP
OF PROPHECY
(SAGITTARIUS-CAPRICORN CUSP)

A fascination and even obsession with the dark side of human relationships can manifest here. In matters of love, the sexual element is extremely strong and a deeply passionate orientation usually dominates the emotional landscape. Strong in silence, these individuals know how to control their emotions and use this control to their benefit. They are formidable opponents in the arena of love.

✱ 38 ✱
VENUS IN THE WEEK
OF THE RULER
(CAPRICORN I)

Venus feels constricted in this position and therefore these folks may find it difficult to express love easily or openly. Furthermore, they know instinctively how to withhold their affections and can even use silence as a weapon to gain an advantage over family members and partners alike. Learning from a loving mate how to express affection is quite possible here, but passion comes more naturally than sensuous expression.

✱ 39 ✱
VENUS IN THE WEEK
OF DETERMINATION
(CAPRICORN II)

"I'll make you love me" is too often the thought or spoken intention of these individuals. However, sooner or later they usually learn that if they begin to give up their need to control and go with the flow they can achieve much greater happiness and contentment. They will fight for the one they love against all comers and do not run away from pitched battles.

✱ 40 ✱
VENUS IN THE WEEK
OF DOMINANCE
(CAPRICORN III)

Venus is not comfortable in this period, which can have a hardening influence on the romantic orientation of the individual. The trick here is to turn the equation around and allow Venus to work her charms on the Capricorn III qualities, and thus to melt what could be an embittered or hardened heart. By tickling Capricorn's funny bone, Venus can lighten the mood considerably.

✱ 41 ✱
VENUS ON THE CUSP OF
MYSTERY AND IMAGINATION
(CAPRICORN-AQUARIUS CUSP)

Exciting love affairs and romantic infatuations are the order of the day here. Vivid imaginations can conjure up the wildest fantasies, rarely equaled in intensity by real life experiences. One might say that these individuals can go pretty far without even having a real-life love object. They must convince their lovers that they really care for them and not just their own fantasies.

✱ 42 ✱
VENUS IN THE WEEK
OF GENIUS
(AQUARIUS I) JANUARY 23-30

Intelligent people are not necessarily all brain power. Exuding an interest in sexuality in all forms, those with this Venus position use their fertile minds to explore all aspects of sex and even to try out as many as they can. Open to almost any form of experimentation, they are likely to prove exciting and inventive lovers.

✱ 43 ✱
VENUS IN THE WEEK OF
YOUTH AND EASE
(AQUARIUS II)

Highly sensuous, those with this Venus position often prefer more relaxed romantic situations, ones that are not overly demanding. Candlelight, good wine and food, and perhaps a skillful massage or luxurious bath is what really turns them on. Violent or passionate scenes are not really their cup of tea. These folks like their love life problem-free.

✱ 44 ✱
VENUS IN THE WEEK
OF ACCEPTANCE
(AQUARIUS III)

Those with Venus in this period are not interested in judging or criticizing their mates. Although they know what they want, they can be remarkably tolerant of the weakness or failings of those they love. Frequently they make links between their ideology and their partners, favoring shared beliefs. In their relationships, the perfect combination is a healthy balance of the mental and physical.

✱ 45 ✱
VENUS ON THE CUSP
OF SENSITIVITY
(AQUARIUS-PISCES CUSP)

Rejection is the hardest thing for these individuals to deal with. Often they go too far in acquiescing to their partner's demands in order to avoid rejection. It is perhaps their greatest challenge in life to learn to be honest about their feelings and to express them without fear of rejection. Building a stronger ego can improve the quality of their relationships.

✱ 46 ✱
VENUS IN THE WEEK
OF SPIRIT
(PISCES I)

Platonic love is important to Venus in this Personology period. All forms of friendship are favored here, and such relationships usually come to achieve greater importance in the life of the individual than sexual or overtly passionate ones. Being on the same wavelength as their partner has profound significance for them and so they highly value emotional understanding.

✱ 47 ✱
VENUS IN THE WEEK
OF THE LONER
(PISCES II)

Such individuals may only have one—or at most two—deep loves in a lifetime. Venus feels a bit cut off from social interaction here, although those with this Venus position usually have several good friends with whom regular one-on-one interactions are important. They must beware of isolating themselves from their fellow human beings and leading too private a life.

✱ 48 ✱
VENUS IN THE WEEK OF
DANCERS AND DREAMERS
(PISCES III)

A joyful attitude toward life characterizes Venus's presence in this week. Playful attitudes toward romance and sexuality can lend a special charm to these individuals, who do not usually go out of their way to cause trouble for their mates or make things overly serious. Thus, relationships with these folks can carry many tangible rewards, as long as their partners do not make too many demands on them.

MARS

MARS REPRESENTS AGGRESSION, FORCEFULNESS, THE MASCULINE SIDE.

NOTE FROM THE ARTIST ABOUT THE ILLUSTRATION ON THE FACING PAGE: Mars is the god of war. Mars, the planet, is associated with raw energy, action and sexual desire. The roman helmet-like mask on the female figure relates to the Mercury, and her demeanor is of that of a woman who takes what she wants in a passionate way. She reflects strong drives and desires. I've used strong complementary colors to evoke the clash of two strong people, or ideas, coming together.

MARS

IN THE 48 PERSONOLOGY PERIODS

✱ 1 ✱
MARS ON THE
CUSP OF REBIRTH
(PISCES-ARIES CUSP)

Those with this Mars position usually have great energy for starting up new projects. Not always able to finish them, they at least provide the innovation and impetus for getting projects started. Appreciated for their positive and often inspiring attitudes, these folks can always be relied upon to come up with innovative ideas.

✱ 2 ✱
MARS IN THE WEEK
OF THE CHILD
(ARIES I)

Mars is quite happy in this period. Its exuberance is felt here by everyone who comes in contact with such a person. Perhaps a tad insensitive to the wishes of others, these people can steamroll anyone or anything which stands in their way. Being more reflective about what they do is advised, and perhaps being more thoughtful before they act.

✱ 3 ✱
MARS IN THE WEEK
OF THE STAR
(ARIES II)

Ego issues usually surface here, since these individuals must shine brightly and have lots of fans who adore them, whether friends, family, colleagues or their social circle at large. Because of their preoccupation with themselves, relationships with such individuals may be pretty much a one-way street. Putting their energies in the service of others is recommended.

✱ 4 ✱
MARS IN THE WEEK
OF THE PIONEER
(ARIES III)

Rugged individualists, those with this Mars position usually have highly developed leadership qualities. They are not ones to hang back either, but will proceed on their own whether or not they have anyone to follow them. Blazing new trails is their specialty. It is usually impossible to stop them from moving ahead, or even to slow them down.

✱ 5 ✱
MARS ON THE CUSP
OF POWER
(ARIES-TAURUS CUSP)

Because of their overly aggressive attitudes, others may back off when they see these people advancing. Combative attitudes and also arousing resistance can be problems for all concerned. Learning to chill out and maintain detachment while at the same time trying to register and acknowledge the wishes of others is essential here. They also need to learn to be more understanding.

✱ 6 ✱
MARS IN THE WEEK OF
MANIFESTATION
(TAURUS I)

Those with their Mars here can be the absolute immovable object. There is little chance that they will change their mind or exhibit much flexibility. It is not so much aggression that characterizes these individuals, but rather a determined defensive position. Although they will usually not attack first, it is best not to wave red flags in front of them unless you are ready for a full-blown response.

✷ 7 ✷
MARS IN THE WEEK OF
THE TEACHER
(TAURUS II)

The idealistic and protective aspects of Mars in this position urge these individuals to stick up for what they believe is right and to fight for it. Not likely to back down, they will defend their beliefs to the bitter end. Moreover, they are likely to set a good example for others to follow but must beware of a tendency to become martyrs for their cause.

✷ 8 ✷
MARS IN THE WEEK OF
THE NATURAL
(TAURUS III)

A perfect position for an environmentalist. Passionate defenders of nature, these folks are likely to give their support to projects designed to save the earth or, at the very least, to improve conditions for all. Rarely concerned with what other people think of them, they should be careful not to actively insult others with their frank attitudes and opinions.

✷ 9 ✷
MARS ON THE CUSP
OF ENERGY
(TAURUS-GEMINI CUSP)

Watch out! These people are likely to bowl others over with their high voltage. Burnout is the downside here and anyone with this Mars position will have to be careful not to stress themselves out. The trick is leaving time to recharge and in spending this time doing something both relaxing and pleasurable. The comforts of table and bed are particularly recommended.

✷ 10 ✷
MARS IN THE WEEK
OF FREEDOM
(GEMINI I)

Not easily contained, these people will tend to break any restrictions placed on them. The more they are held down, the harder they will fight to break free. At some point they must learn to accept restrictions and work within them, keeping their aggressive energies under control and put to better use than in attempting to break their bonds, real or imagined.

✷ 11 ✷
MARS IN THE WEEK OF
NEW LANGUAGE
(GEMINI II)

Aggressive in speech, those with this Mars position will have to learn to tone down the rhetoric. Born salespeople and promoters, whether pushing a product or a person, even themselves, they are likely to make a strong impression. However, they can also alienate others with their pitch, particularly those who misunderstand where they are coming from.

✷ 12 ✷
MARS IN THE WEEK OF
THE SEEKER
(GEMINI III)

Very outwardly directed in this period, Mars urges exploration despite danger and also at certain times because of it. They readily embrace challenges, but reaching the goal is often not nearly so important as the struggle to get there. Travel can be a real learning experience for these individuals, who, oddly enough, are likely to learn more about themselves through what they encounter along the way.

✷ 13 ✷
MARS ON THE CUSP
OF MAGIC
(GEMINI-CANCER CUSP)

Mars' directness is redirected here. Those with this Mars position are frequently in possession of extra-sensory powers of which they may be completely unaware. Very influential without realizing it, they are at their best when they just let things take their course and do not try to control the flow or push too hard. They must come to trust more in the natural forces around them.

✷ 14 ✷
MARS IN THE WEEK OF
THE EMPATH
(CANCER I)

The charisma which is manifested here is felt by all those who come in touch with these individuals. Not necessarily tuned in to the feelings of others on a personal level, they are able to inspire others and arouse their deepest emotions. Because of this, a great responsibility is placed on their shoulders, which they must take seriously. Otherwise, irresponsible or even unethical behavior can result.

✷ 15 ✷
MARS IN THE WEEK OF
THE UNCONVENTIONAL
(CANCER II)

Mars is decidedly uncomfortable in this watery week. His tendency toward action and aggressive behavior is undercut and often individuals with this position find it difficult to be taken seriously. Bizarre thoughts and behavior frequently cause mistrust on both sides. It is best for these folks to proceed slowly and carefully, taking one step at a time and avoiding sudden moves.

✷ 16 ✷
MARS IN THE WEEK OF
THE PERSUADER
(CANCER III)

Natural salespeople, those born in this week channel their aggression into convincing others of the reliability of their products or their work. Often highly pragmatic, they are able to provide the data and documentation necessary to support their sales pitch. Often it is best to buy into what they show, at least at a modest level, since they may not leave you alone until you acquiesce.

✷ 17 ✷
MARS ON THE CUSP
OF OSCILLATION
(CANCER-LEO CUSP)

Unbalanced energies can topple even the most stable structures and therefore it is important to keep things under control. An inability to follow through on plans and schedules accompanies this position, due to an erratic energy flow. Evening out highs and lows will result in forward motion. Above all, be objective. Aim for attainable goals.

✷ 18 ✷
MARS IN THE WEEK
OF AUTHORITY
(LEO I)

The danger here is that a feeling of moral authority, even omniscience, may propel these individuals with unstoppable force, cutting a swath of destruction through life and wreaking havoc on more sensitive souls. Keeping the ego under control is important here and getting rid of a superiority complex. Respect others for their gifts as well as their judgments.

✷ 19 ✷
MARS IN THE WEEK OF
BALANCED STRENGTH
(LEO II)

Mars is comfortable here and very efficacious in getting the job done. Depression is the only problem, since it may seem to these individuals that they haven't accomplished as much as they could. Self-judgments can lower confidence, undermining their ability to get results in the future. It is important to keep one's heart open and avoid succumbing to negativity or pessimism. Keep believing that you can do it.

✷ 20 ✷
MARS IN THE WEEK
OF LEADERSHIP
(LEO III)

A powerful Mars position, it urges these individuals to take the lead in family, social or business circles. Such people can be relied on year after year to stand in the forefront of their group and take on seemingly crushing responsibilities and really enjoy it. Learning to delegate authority is key here, leaving the leader free to make new plans for the future.

✷ 21 ✷
MARS ON THE CUSP
OF EXPOSURE
(LEO-VIRGO CUSP)

This is an internalized and highly personal position for the Red Planet. These folks are likely to try to hide their light under a bushel, often in vain. Their standout energies will usually attract attention anyway, in spite of their efforts to conceal them. Because they may appear to be strong silent types, their enormous energies can be hidden at times but are accessible when needed.

✷ 22 ✷
MARS IN THE WEEK OF
SYSTEM BUILDERS
(VIRGO I)

These people are most effective when they are able to use their energies in a logical way, according to plan, and to take things as they come, one at a time. Their greatest strength is being able to use their energies sensibly; their deficiency is a periodic succumbing to lethargy, which blunts their purpose. Keeping their hearts open and not just proceeding in a matter-of-fact way is important.

✷ 23 ✷
MARS IN THE WEEK OF
THE ENIGMA
(VIRGO II)

Such individuals have to be left alone to get the job done in their own peculiar fashion. Many may not understand what they are about, but their devotion to their tasks should not be doubted. They will do what is required of them and more as long as they are given enough latitude to feel comfortable with their tasks. Their dependability is beyond question.

✷ 24 ✷
MARS IN THE WEEK OF
THE LITERALIST
(VIRGO III)

Although they may seem quite down to earth, a love of excitement characterizes these individuals. Prone to attracting wayward energies, they specialize in grounding unsettled individuals with whom they come in contact, helping to put their lives in good order. Life for them is a fine blend of pragmatism and inspiration. They must beware of their tendency to lash out when neglected or criticized.

✷ 25 ✷
MARS ON THE CUSP
OF BEAUTY
(VIRGO-LIBRA CUSP)

The natural ferocity of Mars is tempered on this cusp. Characterized by a drive toward things aesthetic, this Mars position exhibits great enthusiasm for creative endeavors of all sorts. A lifelong love for favorite recordings, paintings, films and novels from childhood to young adulthood is often carried through one's more mature years. Thus, nostalgia is characteristic here.

✷ 26 ✷
MARS IN THE WEEK OF
THE PERFECTIONIST
(LIBRA I)

Being aggressive in one's perfectionistic demands does not usually earn friends. This stressful position can drive everyone concerned a bit crazy, unless they can learn to be a bit more laid back. In dealing with technical matters, Mars in this period does guarantee perseverance and usually produces results. Great care must be taken to avoid neglecting the emotional and social spheres. Scheduling regular yoga, meditation or prayer sessions is advised.

✷ 27 ✷
MARS IN THE WEEK
OF SOCIETY
(LIBRA II)

Mars is decidedly uncomfortable here in Venus territory and would like nothing better than to challenge the group's mores or just run off to some more adventuresome activity. Learning to put one's energies in service of the social or family group can yield extremely positive results once Mars accepts that we are here primarily to serve each other.

✷ 28 ✷
MARS IN THE WEEK
OF THEATER
(LIBRA III)

The more outgoing side of Mars wants to be as outrageous as possible here. By flaunting flamboyance in public displays of emotion, real or mock aggression, or in unconventional behavior, these individuals give shock value a high priority. Playing a role so fully and consummately that others tend to believe in its reality is the goal.

✷ 29 ✷
MARS ON THE CUSP OF
DRAMA AND CRITICISM
(LIBRA-SCORPIO CUSP)

Aggressive attitudes are likely to fly out of hand. This Mars position is characterized by a sharp tongue. Care must be taken not to offend others or to undermine their self-worth. Insights into the other person's character must be presented in a respectful and helpful manner. By arousing antagonism and opposition you make things more difficult.

✷ 30 ✷
MARS IN THE WEEK
OF INTENSITY
(SCORPIO I)

More likely to become angry and belligerent when attacked, these individuals do not usually indulge in a first strike. Defensive, they usually are well-protected and have their bases covered. They are likely to get extremely upset when those near and dear to them are threatened in any way; this brings out their fighting instincts like no other event.

✷ 31 ✷
MARS IN THE WEEK
OF DEPTH
(SCORPIO II)

Aggression can be aroused in these individuals, but they are usually slow to react. More often than not, they can repress Mars and, as a result, wind up with a headache, stomachache or full-blown depressions. Lethargic periods are often the result. Their passion for food and sex is legendary, at times leaving them slaves to the table and bed.

✷ 32 ✷
MARS IN THE WEEK
OF CHARM
(SCORPIO III)

Mars is given an extra seductive attraction in this position. If encouraged, these folks are likely to take over the lives of weaker family members and friends. Thus they are capable of making most or even all of the important decisions for the other person. In doing so they create dependencies which might not be so healthy for either party in the future.

✷ 33 ✷
MARS ON THE CUSP
OF REVOLUTION
(SCORPIO-SAGITTARIUS CUSP)

Hell-raisers, these spirited individuals must not let their feisty energies run away with them. Subtler forms of interaction than constant confrontation will bring them a lot further in their attempts to change the status quo and institute meaningful reforms. They are protective toward others and you want to have them on your side in a good fight.

✴ 34 ✴
MARS IN THE WEEK OF INDEPENDENCE
(SAGITTARIUS I)

Quick and impulsive movement character-ize this Mars position. Unlikely to keep still for very long, these active individuals fly from one project to the next, from one idea or topic to the other. They do have a thoughtful side, however, and can spend a great deal of time and energy working on themselves, whether in physical, intellectual, or spiritual realms.

✴ 35 ✴
MARS IN THE WEEK OF THE ORIGINATOR
(SAGITTARIUS II)

Those with Mars here tend to stand out from others and are not good at hiding themselves away. Their unusual nature is often reflected in their clothes, their manner of speech, even in their unpredictable, sudden changes of mood and movement. Irrepressible, there is never a dull moment when they are around; they are highly prized as interesting people by friends and family.

✴ 36 ✴
MARS IN THE WEEK OF THE TITAN
(SAGITTARIUS III)

When these irresistible forces move, immovable objects are likely to fly. Powerfully aggressive in this position, Mars usually sweeps all obstacles aside. However, over time this directly confrontational approach becomes less effective and these folks must figure out a more reasonable way to proceed in life. Their success is often dependent on this process.

✴ 37 ✴
MARS ON THE CUSP OF PROPHECY
(SAGITTARIUS-CAPRICORN CUSP)

Frustration and anger are too often driven down deep inside, resulting in heavy depressions which can go on for days and weeks. Learning to lighten up a bit and not take everything so seriously will help mod-erate the inversion of Mars' influences. It is important to find both small daily tasks and larger projects to which the Red Planet's energies can be harnessed.

✴ 38 ✴
MARS IN THE WEEK OF THE RULER
(CAPRICORN I)

Mars is at his most regal here. Happy with taking command at the head of any team, such individuals can put all of their energies in constructive service of the group. Usually not so interested in furthering their own personal ambitions, they often nevertheless succeed in enhancing their social standing through the success of group endeavors which they lead.

✴ 39 ✴
MARS IN THE WEEK OF DETERMINATION
(CAPRICORN II)

Strength of purpose is reinforced by Mars in this period. A never say die and never give up attitude is present and with it a desire to see things through to the (sometimes bitter) end. Learning flexibility is important but is a difficult lesson for these folks. Their con-centration may develop into a monomania, making them highly obsessive.

✴ 40 ✴
MARS IN THE WEEK OF DOMINANCE
(CAPRICORN III)

These people really need to mull things over. Possessed of an iron will, they cling to the status quo and even frequently embody it in their family or social position. Because of their opposition to change, they run afoul of more innovative and liberal-minded thinkers. They need to learn that giving up power may be the most empowering act of their lives.

✴ 41 ✴
MARS ON THE CUSP OF MYSTERY AND IMAGINATION
(CAPRICORN-AQUARIUS CUSP)

Extreme willfulness and a penchant for sud-den impulsive behavior characterize this Mars position. Because of a tendency to invest lots of energy into vivid and highly personal fantasies, these people need to get out there and make their fantasies work for them. At some point they will have to devote less time to fantasy and more to real-ity if they wish to stay mentally healthy.

✴ 42 ✴
MARS IN THE WEEK OF GENIUS
(AQUARIUS I) JANUARY 23-30

Puzzles, games, wordplay, abstract thinking – all of these things fascinate those with this Mars position. Much of their leisure time is spent with such activities, often to the cha-grin of their mates who want to spend some quality time with them. Those with Mars here must be careful of coming to live in their own fascinating but selfish world.

✱ 43 ✱
MARS IN THE WEEK OF
YOUTH AND EASE
(AQUARIUS II)

Those with Mars in this period can spend incredible amounts of energy and time getting things just they way they want them. Because comfort, happiness and contentment rule their lives, Mars energies can be blunted in professional areas or in providing service to others. They are happiest when fixing up their living space, rearranging things or just making everything more convenient for themselves.

✱ 44 ✱
MARS IN THE WEEK
OF ACCEPTANCE
(AQUARIUS III)

Too often Mars here lends intolerance to one's outlook. The inability to accept things as they are often leads these folks to try to change people and, if that fails, to judge and reject them. Learning acceptance is obviously their most important lesson or, at the very least, just learning to back off and leave people alone.

✱ 45 ✱
MARS ON THE CUSP
OF SENSITIVITY
(AQUARIUS-PISCES CUSP)

Overreactive, these folks must not let people push their buttons so easily. Moreover, they must learn that there is not so much to be afraid of and to modify or even drop their sometimes paranoid stance. By toughening up a bit and being more sure of themselves they won't get so upset by the attitudes of others toward them.

✱ 46 ✱
MARS IN THE WEEK
OF SPIRIT
(PISCES I)

Mars is softened here and often its energies can be redirected to spiritual matters and non-physical pursuits. Putting their energies in service of introspection and meditation can have wonderful results and do a great deal to tone down and even eliminate stresses in their lives. They should be careful, however, of a tendency to try to convert others to their point of view.

✱ 47 ✱
MARS IN THE WEEK
OF THE LONER
(PISCES II)

A tendency to push others away with a "leave me alone" attitude can leave these folks isolated and unhappy. Redirecting their energies outward in more social pursuits is their greatest challenge and one that can indeed be met. Inviting others to enter their world and share with them is important for improving their mental health and overcoming their fears.

✱ 48 ✱
MARS IN THE WEEK OF
DANCERS AND DREAMERS
(PISCES III)

These individuals are likely to put their principal energies to work in the most abstruse and far-out areas and activities. Being understood or appreciated is not of primary interest to them. What is most important is actively pursuing their dreams and ideals no matter what anyone else thinks. Their unusual plans are often appreciated by others in their social circle.

JUPITER

JUPITER REPRESENTS OPTIMISM, EXPANSIVE ATTITUDES, LUCK, THE BIG PICTURE.

NOTE FROM THE ARTIST ABOUT THE ILLUSTRATION ON THE FACING PAGE: Jupiter is the king of the gods, also known as Zeus. His symbol—the lightning bolt—can be seen on the mosaic with his image. The female figure wears a mask with an eagle—the messenger of Jupiter. This symbolizes the reader's interactions with Jupiter's energies. The female figure actively 'speaks' through her exhalation. The pattern on her dress depicts the asteroid belt situated between Mars and Jupiter. Her necklace shows the largest four moons. Her red cloak represents of the great storm. Jupiter is associated with optimism, growth, good luck, and bounty.

JUPITER

IN THE 48 PERSONOLOGY PERIODS

★ 1 ★
JUPITER ON THE
CUSP OF REBIRTH
(PISCES-ARIES CUSP)

This Jupiter position grants luck when starting up new projects. Using a good blend of feeling and intuition is key to success here. Partners should be found who are strong in seeing a project through until it yields results, and other helpers who can maintain such work year after year. Then new projects can be attempted and ongoing ones sustained.

★ 2 ★
JUPITER IN THE WEEK
OF THE CHILD
(ARIES I)

Jupiter is happy in this Personology period, since his optimistic outlook can be given free rein. However, he is also easily disappointed and this can lead to quite severe depressions. In order to guarantee luck with this Jupiter position, one must be realistic enough to see the world as it really is, not just as one would want it to be.

★ 3 ★
JUPITER IN THE WEEK
OF THE STAR
(ARIES II)

Self-expression is demanded here, even if the personality involved is a quiet one. Working behind the scenes will achieve as much success as being in the spotlight. The important thing is maintaining the central position, whether the principal player or not. Good luck comes easily here and cannot really be earned with hard work. Serendipity plays an important role.

★ 4 ★
JUPITER IN THE WEEK
OF THE PIONEER
(ARIES III)

Taking the lead in one's family or social group, at least ideologically, is favored here. Professional endeavors, however, can be tainted with financial difficulties by someone with this Jupiter position, through lack of good business sense. However, impulse and initiative are bestowed, which can get many a favorable domestic or neighborhood project up and running, with a successful outcome.

★ 5 ★
JUPITER ON THE CUSP
OF POWER
(ARIES-TAURUS CUSP)

Luck here comes through forceful expression of the will. Such a Jupiter position will usually persevere when accompanied by focused determination. Care must be taken, however, not to arouse antagonism through overly forceful assertions or deeply entrenched prejudices or even assumptions. Keep plans as practical and down to earth as possible to achieve the greatest success in life.

★ 6 ★
JUPITER IN THE WEEK OF
MANIFESTATION
(TAURUS I)

When plans are well worked out beforehand, and many problems anticipated and even solved, the resulting projects stand a good chance of succeeding. Good luck is something that these people do not necessarily believe in but achieve in their own minds through thorough preparation and hard work. This pragmatic view of luck can take them far.

✴ 7 ✴
JUPITER IN THE WEEK OF
THE TEACHER
(TAURUS II)

Because of the high idealism and even intellectual character of this week, Jupiter is at its most studious here, constantly investigating new and challenging fields of information. For those with this Jupiter position who read a great deal, they are likely to stumble accidentally on all sorts of interesting facts and observations, which can bring luck in their careers and private lives.

✴ 8 ✴
JUPITER IN THE WEEK OF
THE NATURAL
(TAURUS III)

A great love of the outdoors and wildlife accompanies this position of Jupiter. Happiness is usually difficult for these folks to achieve unless they are able to indulge in long walks in natural settings, jogging, gardening and keeping in contact with the elements. Their souls soar once in contact with the glories of Mother Nature.

✴ 9 ✴
JUPITER ON THE CUSP
OF ENERGY
(TAURUS-GEMINI CUSP)

Diversity favors one's chances for success. By seeking good fortune in many places and activities, the luck factor is increased; by getting tied down to a single pursuit, one only increases the likelihood of boredom and lack of enthusiasm. Each of many projects is likely to have a beneficial influence on the other. In this way it is possible to learn from one's own experience.

✴ 10 ✴
JUPITER IN THE WEEK
OF FREEDOM
(GEMINI I)

Jupiter feels a bit constricted during this week and so periodic wild outbursts can result in an attempt to free up the personality. Attention to detail even to the point of obsession interferes with Jupiter's broad point of view. Creating a balance between seeing both the proverbial forest and the trees clearly is required here.

✴ 11 ✴
JUPITER IN THE WEEK OF
NEW LANGUAGE
(GEMINI II)

Telling tall stories and spinning yarns is characteristic of this Jupiter position. Such individuals find it easier to embellish the truth than to blandly state it as it is. Trust is an important issue here, for many refuse to believe what these expressive individuals have to say, not wanting to get burned a second time. Building a trustworthy persona can be a major challenge.

✴ 12 ✴
JUPITER IN THE WEEK OF
THE SEEKER
(GEMINI III)

Exploration can be immensely satisfying to these folks but too often they go a bit beyond their limits and lose themselves, or just simply get lost in strange surroundings. Creating limits for themselves and accomplishing the probable rather than the impossible can become a major challenge. By attempting the very ordinary and sticking with it, they give periodic adventures new meaning and new life.

✴ 13 ✴
JUPITER ON THE CUSP
OF MAGIC
(GEMINI-CANCER CUSP)

The good fortune accompanying this period is usually of the serendipitous variety. All kinds of strange and unexpected circumstances send Lady Luck one's way. Because of an ability to be open to or expect the unexpected, it is not a big surprise when it does occur, but it is precisely this openness which is the catalyst for good things to come to pass.

✴ 14 ✴
JUPITER IN THE WEEK OF
THE EMPATH
(CANCER I)

Luck in life here is very much tied up with an acute sensitivity to the needs and wishes of others. In both the personal and professional spheres, a reputation as an understanding person augments one's social standing. Because people feel they can relate to such an empathic attitude they tend to be more trusting and open.

✴ 15 ✴
JUPITER IN THE WEEK OF
THE UNCONVENTIONAL
(CANCER II)

Taking risks and finding unusual solutions to problems is characteristic of the luck found in this Jupiter position. Outright gambling for profit is also possible here, whether at the casino or in friendly card games with friends. Good fortune is not usually found on the straight and narrow path but through all kinds of alluring byways and hidden detours.

✴ 16 ✴
JUPITER IN THE WEEK OF
THE PERSUADER
(CANCER III)

Being a salesperson comes naturally and brings success. Not only in one's career but also in one's personal life, the ability to persuade others to a point of view is often the direct reason for good fortune in the realms of finance or love. Outright seduction can be operative here, but also the gentle nudge which can get things moving in the right direction.

✴ 17 ✴
JUPITER ON THE CUSP
OF OSCILLATION
(CANCER-LEO CUSP)

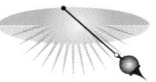

The secret to success here is flexibility. Rolling with the punches and going with the flow will lend an advantage over others who are more fixed in their ways. The problem is maintaining stability, but that can be accomplished by keeping a calm center as a fixed reference point, which can always be counted on in times of challenge and adversity.

✴ 18 ✴
JUPITER IN THE WEEK
OF AUTHORITY
(LEO I)

Good luck is guaranteed in all sorts of endeavors by following a fixed star in the firmament, whether a teacher, a belief, or an outlook on life. This inspirational orientation will carry you far through life. Should the belief be in your own powers, so much the better. However, in this latter case, be careful that self-delusion does not become part of the equation.

✴ 19 ✴
JUPITER IN THE WEEK OF
BALANCED STRENGTH
(LEO II)

Success is most likely to be the reward of honesty and steadfastness of purpose. This position finds Jupiter in its most noble, upright and courageous state. Underhanded methods of any sort will not be rewarded in the long run and can result in ruin. It is not necessary, however, to keep to the straight and narrow since exploration and travel usually figure here also.

✴ 20 ✴
JUPITER IN THE WEEK
OF LEADERSHIP
(LEO III)

Even if this person is not a born leader, they can achieve great success at the helm of a family or professional group. This may very well be only a temporary leadership position, perhaps adopted in times of need and stress. Quiet individuals who are able to rise to the occasion are frequently found here. Once the crisis is past they can return to more humble activities.

✴ 21 ✴
JUPITER ON THE CUSP
OF EXPOSURE
(LEO-VIRGO CUSP)

Jupiter doesn't like being hidden away and just trotted out on occasion. Thus, those with Jupiter on this cusp must be careful not to repress the very energies which can lead to their success. However, investing in themselves and allowing their talents to ripen slowly can work in their favor. Time will usually tell them when to let others into their private world.

✴ 22 ✴
JUPITER IN THE WEEK OF
SYSTEM BUILDERS
(VIRGO I)

With this Jupiter position, good luck comes through structuring the daily life in a methodical and sensible fashion. Although care should be taken not to get locked into fixed attitudes which entirely preclude unexpected happenings, chaos management will generally prove beneficial. Working with organizations can also lead to success. Once structures are set up, risks may be taken and visions implemented.

✴ 23✴
JUPITER IN THE WEEK OF
THE ENIGMA
(VIRGO II)

Expecting the unexpected and being open to all sorts of chance happenings will forward Jupiter's purpose here. Chances for success are augmented by keeping to oneself and periodically withdrawing completely from the world in order to develop private plans. Not reacting to criticism but keeping true to strongly held principles are favored. However, compromise and flexibility will also help.

✴ 24 ✴
JUPITER IN THE WEEK OF
THE LITERALIST
(VIRGO III)

It is important to distinguish between wants and needs. Therefore, self-knowledge is essential if we are to avoid confusing the two. Although satisfying desires is important to avoid frustration, this activity may not bring success. Better to determine what is needed at a deep level and work to satisfy these needs. Through this activity it is more likely that success can be achieved.

✴ 25 ✴
JUPITER ON THE CUSP
OF BEAUTY
(VIRGO-LIBRA CUSP)

Success is likely to be achieved through activities involving the senses. Thus, computer graphics, website design, music-making, culinary pursuits and art appreciation are all favored activities. Through these and other cultural pursuits, like-minded individuals can be contacted and through these connections successful personal and professional bonds can be forged. What seems to be a hobby could have practical applications.

✴ 26 ✴
JUPITER IN THE WEEK OF
THE PERFECTIONIST
(LIBRA I)

Jupiter's rewards can be realized through the pursuit of technical endeavors. If you can avoid undue mental strain, successes will be booked through an ability to analyze the faults of a system or organization and come up with a reasonable solution to problems. However, it is not necessary to correct every detail and it is also important to remember the adage, "If it ain't broke, don't fix it."

✴ 27 ✴
JUPITER IN THE WEEK
OF SOCIETY
(LIBRA II)

It is unlikely that success will be gained through private or personal pursuits. Jupiter loves company here and even if people are not really the most important thing, they will have to be consulted and networked in order to achieve maximum results. A talent for organizing is often found here and a team can relieve one of many responsibilities, leaving time for individual initiative.

✴ 28 ✴
JUPITER IN THE WEEK
OF THEATER
(LIBRA III)

The more dramatic aspects of life exert a strong pull here, favoring colorful behavior and even an interest in betting and gambling. A daredevil aspect of Jupiter surfaces here, granting luck through risk-taking and daring to fail. Those who crash from lofty positions with this aspect are able to get up, dust themselves off and start anew.

✴ 29 ✴
JUPITER ON THE CUSP OF
DRAMA AND CRITICISM
(LIBRA-SCORPIO CUSP)

Although Jupiter does not feel comfortable with criticism, this position tends to make success more a matter of diligent attention to detail than to sheer luck. This position of the jovial planet favors the use of mental powers and concise expression. By conserving energy rather than spreading it too thin, success can be achieved in a conservative, straightforward fashion.

✴ 30 ✴
JUPITER IN THE WEEK
OF INTENSITY
(SCORPIO I)

Here Jupiter is urged to focus his prodigious energies and to find good fortune through a laser-like focus on the job at hand. Although driving oneself too hard can result in a sudden breakdown, it is this very intense approach which also leads to results and, ultimately, success. Relaxation should be factored into the equation and chance happenings during the timeouts can contribute their share, too.

✴ 31 ✴
JUPITER IN THE WEEK
OF DEPTH
(SCORPIO II)

This position of Jupiter demands adequate research and preparation in order to achieve success. Digging deep into the content of the subject at hand and mulling over all the ramifications of one's actions will yield positive results. This is not a Jupiter position which favors flying by the seat of one's pants. The need to focus is apparent here and with it an ability to resist alluring distractions.

✴ 32 ✴
JUPITER IN THE WEEK
OF CHARM
(SCORPIO III)

To advance in business projects, it is important to pay as much attention to the wrapping of the package as to its contents. Thus, the way in which content is offered may very well determine the outcome of the presentation or deal. The element of seduction plays an undeniable role here. To augment good fortune, choose the right time, place and setting for meetings.

✴ 33 ✴
JUPITER ON THE CUSP
OF REVOLUTION
(SCORPIO-SAGITTARIUS CUSP)

Speaking one's mind can alienate people but also win their respect. Generally speaking, good luck is increased by stirring the pot, even if there is some initial shock or resistance. Others will respect an honest attitude, particularly if it can achieve results. The spirit of reform is strong here, and reorganization is likely to achieve significant results for any company or family.

* 34 *
JUPITER IN THE WEEK
OF INDEPENDENCE
(SAGITTARIUS I)

Success is more likely to be achieved in areas of self-employment and self-teaching than in company endeavors or scholastic efforts. Making one's own decisions without needing the permission or approval of others has the best chance of yielding rewards. Furthermore, being able to maintain a balanced psychological state free from carping criticism will facilitate positive results.

* 35 *
JUPITER IN THE WEEK OF
THE ORIGINATOR
(SAGITTARIUS II)

Good luck is furthered through unusual thoughts and ideas. Conservative thinking is not favored here, but rather the ability to be adroit, flexible and positive in outlook. No idea is too far out, no plan too daring to be implemented. With this Jupiter position, the future belongs to those who dare to take chances and ultimately to those who dare to fail.

* 36 *
JUPITER IN THE WEEK
OF THE TITAN
(SAGITTARIUS III)

Jupiter is perhaps more at home here than in any other Personology period. Expansive thoughts, far-reaching plans, seeing the big picture—all of these are favored. Even if one falls flat on one's face occasionally, a significant percentage of these visionary projects are likely to work out. However, it is important to pay more attention to the details, too.

* 37 *
JUPITER ON THE CUSP
OF PROPHECY
(SAGITTARIUS-CAPRICORN CUSP)

A need is found here to balance the optimistic, free and expansive attitudes of Jupiter with the more serious, limited and responsible attitudes of Saturn. Good luck can follow this position only if both are taken into account and can be balanced one against the other. A talent for predicting the future can result in gains on the stock market or in taking calculated gambles in life.

* 38 *
JUPITER IN THE WEEK
OF THE RULER
(CAPRICORN I)

A take-charge attitude can be effective in leading almost any group – social, familial, or professional. An honorable, upright and conscientious attitude will most often result in success for all concerned. Running away from responsibilities will yield only negative results. Through taking the helm, the best qualities emerge, as long as dictatorial attitudes are not invoked.

* 39 *
JUPITER IN THE WEEK
OF DETERMINATION
(CAPRICORN II)

Here Jupiter's vision is harnessed to a practical attitude and a desire to move ahead. Not only is a far-reaching goal sought but no rest is granted until it is reached. However, the question to be answered is: Success at what price? Stress can cause physical problems, lack of sound sleep, and psychological difficulties. Therefore, an ability to pace oneself and get enough rest is essential.

* 40 *
JUPITER IN THE WEEK
OF DOMINANCE
(CAPRICORN III)

Megalomania may be a problem here. Delusions of grandeur can only be avoided through attention to the details of everyday life, performing humble tasks and being dedicated to a kind and caring attitude to one's fellow human beings. Through learning to serve others, the dominant energies of Jupiter here can be put to work for truly altruistic ends.

* 41 *
JUPITER ON THE CUSP OF
MYSTERY AND IMAGINATION
(CAPRICORN-AQUARIUS CUSP)

In this Personology period, Jupiter is happy to follow the promptings of the imagination. Putting fantasy to work will often result in financial results, as long as things do not get out of control. Giving that oddball twist or little unusual touch to one's projects is likely to attract attention and make such projects something special to any boss, investor or potential client.

* 42 *
JUPITER IN THE WEEK
OF GENIUS
(AQUARIUS I) JANUARY 23-30

A quick mind allows immediate comprehension of the matter at hand. Although problems can be encountered in the emotional sphere, a grasp of logic and the ability to order one's thinking will give an advantage to those with this Jupiter position. Although long-term memory can suffer later on in life, an alert and highly conscious orientation to everyday affairs can bring good luck.

✳ 43 ✳
JUPITER IN THE WEEK OF
YOUTH AND EASE
(AQUARIUS II)

Jupiter is at its most relaxed in this position—perhaps too relaxed. Thus, a real threat posed to one's drive toward success may be feeling too comfortable with where one is in life. Although this attitude reduces stress, it can also promote lethargy, leading to overweight and a contentment which undermines one's chances to succeed in personal or career matters.

✳ 44 ✳
JUPITER IN THE WEEK
OF ACCEPTANCE
(AQUARIUS III)

A talent to see the other guy's point of view even when we don't share it can result in success in relationships and also with one's colleagues. People find such an attitude disarming and are more likely to go along with ideas advanced by such an individual. By not putting up barriers to others, a more receptive audience can be found in the future.

✳ 45 ✳
JUPITER ON THE CUSP
OF SENSITIVITY
(AQUARIUS-PISCES CUSP)

Because of antennae which pick up the smallest stimuli, those with this Jupiter position are more likely to pick up clues that can lead them to good fortune. As long as they can separate the wheat from the chaff, those with Jupiter here can find valuable bargains, locate good jobs and find reasonable places to live.

✳ 46 ✳
JUPITER IN THE WEEK
OF SPIRIT
(PISCES I)

A positive attitude promotes success here in one's drive toward self-development. Usually gains will not be actively sought in financial realms but in the enthusiastic involvement with one particular area in life. Paradoxically, this area, even a hobby, can prove to be a moneymaker that leads to unexpected rewards. Jupiter's optimism here shines through even the darkest clouds, bringing hope.

✳ 47 ✳
JUPITER IN THE WEEK
OF THE LONER
(PISCES II)

An unusual personality frequently accompanies this Jupiter position, often one which others find intriguing. Thus, those with Jupiter here succeed in attracting those they are interested in and can find success through involvements with a few close friends or business colleagues, Such individuals are discriminating and they know what the genuine article is. They are happy to spend limited time each week as a team member.

✳ 48 ✳
JUPITER IN THE WEEK OF
DANCERS AND DREAMERS
(PISCES III)

Jupiter soars here. Giving rein to far-reaching plans and following one's star will bring such an individual far on the road of success. Through high idealism, many mundane pursuits can be illuminated and made special. However, a tendency toward gullibility requires one to avoid becoming an easy mark for unscrupulous individuals. Cultivating some practicality won't hurt at all.

SATURN

SATURN REPRESENTS RESPONSIBILITY, LIMITATION, AND REALISM.

NOTE FROM THE ARTIST ABOUT THE ILLUSTRATION ON THE FACING PAGE: Saturn is the Greek father of the titans and the father of Jupiter. Saturn is associated with restriction and limitation, and also with time. The female figure holds the stream of smoke with control and restraint. It is very linear, representing a timeline. Saturn is the god of agriculture as well, as reflected in her mask. Saturn reminds us of our boundaries, responsibilities and commitments.

S A T U R N

IN THE 48 PERSONOLOGY PERIODS

★1★
SATURN ON THE CUSP OF REBIRTH
(PISCES-ARIES CUSP)

There can be a bit of a struggle here between one's dreams and present realities. Saturn looks askance at the more imaginative aspects of this Personology period and demands a more down to earth attitude. Hence, disapproval of more far-out thoughts from parents and other authority figures can be expected throughout life. It is necessary to toughen up and continue to pursue one's goals.

★2★
SATURN IN THE WEEK OF THE CHILD
(ARIES I)

Although Saturn may approve of the open and frank approach here, he condemns childish behavior in any form. Therefore, this Saturn position can lend restrictions to one's enthusiasm and tend to bottle up various positive expressions of feeling. Often one has the feeling of being judged here and that one's more extroverted behavior is not fully appreciated by others, particularly in career matters.

★3★
SATURN IN THE WEEK OF THE STAR
(ARIES II)

Saturn can lend approval to more responsible behavior here, i.e., being at the center of a group or project and providing solid and practical support to such groups and endeavors. This is particularly true in the family sphere. However, any sign of being a show-off or having an ego in need of excessive attention will meet with sharp disapproval. In extreme cases, Saturn here can produce an introverted and fearful individual.

★4★
SATURN IN THE WEEK OF THE PIONEER
(ARIES III)

This Saturn position can impart a discomfort with assuming a leadership role. The suspicions of the ringed planet are aroused for any fanciful ideas or a need to impose them on others. Strangely, such individuals can have a significant effect on those around them, but these influences usually arise in the most unexpected manner. Intentions to take over any group are often met with strong resistance.

★5★
SATURN ON THE CUSP OF POWER
(ARIES-TAURUS CUSP)

A misuse of power is likely to surface here. Paradoxically, this can occur when feelings of insecurity or low self-esteem surface, as if this individual has to overcompensate for inner fears by imposing his or her will on others. Great care should be taken to avoid being carried away by illusions about one's personal powers, or a destructive need to implement them.

★6★
SATURN IN THE WEEK OF MANIFESTATION
(TAURUS I)

The ability to manifest ideas is impaired here by Saturn's presence. Consequently, plans can be aborted and many jobs left unfinished. Derailment of work in progress is common, often through a self-destructive impulse which is unrecognized by the individuals themselves. Working carefully, step by step, is advised here, with frequent checks and a realistic goal kept in sight.

★7★
SATURN IN THE WEEK OF THE TEACHER
(TAURUS II)

Saturn lends dogmatism here. Such individuals will be convinced they are right, even to the extreme of omniscience. They may stubbornly resist any attempts to prove them wrong or to disagree. Although they may have much to teach, they must learn to get it across in a more human and less intimidating fashion. Excessive seriousness should be tempered.

★8★
SATURN IN THE WEEK OF THE NATURAL
(TAURUS III)

By opposing the natural tendency of this week, Saturn tends to inhibit expression and to manifest as shame or guilt. Fighting this tendency is possible, and through friendship and love (ultimately, finding individuals who can be trusted) real strides can be made to heal old wounds and allow self-consciousness to fall away or even disappear.

★9★
SATURN ON THE CUSP OF ENERGY
(TAURUS-GEMINI CUSP)

The lack of energy found here often manifests as laziness, complacency or lack of ambition. Such individuals will enjoy talking about something more than doing it. They try to convince themselves and others of their plans but do not succeed in producing tangible results. Often they fritter away what energies they have on a number of different, unrelated pursuits.

★10★
SATURN IN THE WEEK OF FREEDOM
(GEMINI I)

Saturn is not comfortable with the energies of this week. Either of two possibilities usually surfaces, one for the worse and the other for the better. The negative scenario urges the individual to be less free and may produce a fearful or uptight personality. The happier scenario can create a truer kind of liberation than mere freedom, a sort that involves taking responsibility for one's actions.

★11★
SATURN IN THE WEEK OF NEW LANGUAGE
(GEMINI II)

A block in communication, either permanent or simply during times of stress, can manifest with this Saturn position. Colleagues and family may find it difficult to understand the ideas of this individual and so more emphasis should be placed on uttering clear and cogent statements, regardless of how simple they may be. Taking time to explain is important to being understood.

★12★
SATURN IN THE WEEK OF THE SEEKER
(GEMINI III)

Saturn disapproves of far-reaching visions that are not based on hard facts. Thus, although inhibiting factors may tend to keep these people at home, at the same time they will be forced to substantiate their plans and make them more practical. This can produce a more balanced personality who will take chances when the odds seem in their favor.

★13★
SATURN ON THE CUSP OF MAGIC
(GEMINI-CANCER CUSP)

This position of Saturn can be a powerfully persuasive one, allowing the individual to have a charismatic influence over others, both in the personal and professional sphere. The coupling of pragmatism and clairvoyance grants great powers, providing the two are well integrated. A shaman or sorcerer with practical abilities and goals is indeed a formidable opponent.

★14★
SATURN IN THE WEEK OF THE EMPATH
(CANCER I)

Emotional blocks may inhibit one's sympathies for the plight of others and prevent one from feeling compassion. Opening the heart chakra and letting love in is essential here. Saturn can actually benefit from this position by allowing one's business attitudes to take the personal feelings of others more into account. In any event, Saturn's sternness should be tempered, if possible.

★15★
SATURN IN THE WEEK OF THE UNCONVENTIONAL
(CANCER II)

The conservatism of Saturn here usually condemns kooky or bizarre outlooks, both in others and in oneself. On the other hand, this position allows the serious Saturn to lighten up a little bit, have fun and not take things so seriously. If the pragmatism of Saturn can be combined with a more unusual outlook on life, positive benefits will accrue.

★ 16 ★
SATURN IN THE WEEK OF
THE PERSUADER
(CANCER III)

Two possibilities here: One is that the ability to convince others will be undermined, the other is that it will be strengthened. Everything depends on attitude and developing the self-confidence to trust one's powers. Maintaining a flexible approach is important, since Saturn tends to tighten up and use one unchanging approach each time. It is important to listen to objections to and criticism of one's ideas.

★ 17 ★
SATURN ON THE CUSP
OF OSCILLATION
(CANCER-LEO CUSP)

Saturn can have a positive effect here, evening out the swings of this cusp and granting the power to put both introvert and extrovert tendencies to good use. Thus, episodes of depression can serve as a window to self-knowledge; more manic phases can bring fun and vibrancy to one's life if modulated and not allowed to get out of control. Thus, more stability can be granted.

★ 18 ★
SATURN IN THE WEEK
OF AUTHORITY
(LEO I)

A healthy respect for authority may surface here, but at its extreme this influence can produce a dictatorial personality or at the very least one which is over-awed by those in power. In less dramatic cases, the individual may be inhibited in their own creative expression by a worship of authorities in their field and a lack of confidence in their own efforts.

★ 19 ★
SATURN IN THE WEEK OF
BALANCED STRENGTH
(LEO II)

Since an energy imbalance is the greatest threat to this week, it is possible for Saturn to uncover underlying insecurities. This can work positively, since they may have been unknown and therefore untreatable. On the other hand, if one gets fixated on such difficulties they can work like self-fulfilling prophecies to produce a failure scenario. Putting self-knowledge to positive uses is key.

★ 20 ★
SATURN IN THE WEEK
OF LEADERSHIP
(LEO III)

It is possible for this Saturn to position to weaken or strengthen the individual's ability to assume a leadership role in their family or profession. It is best to avoid extremes when possible here and simply to exert a steady and helpful influence. Dictatorial tendencies should be fought, but also a tendency to give up on group activities and retire into one's own private world.

★ 21 ★
SATURN ON THE CUSP
OF EXPOSURE
(LEO-VIRGO CUSP)

Inhibitions of all types can surface here, ranging from hang-ups over one's appearance to self-consciousness about speech or intelligence. Because of repression of true feelings, a severely introverted personality may result. Learning to trust and share is key in overcoming such inhibitions. Positive steps taken in this direction usually result in success. Self-pity should be avoided like the plague.

★ 22 ★
SATURN IN THE WEEK OF
SYSTEM BUILDERS
(VIRGO I)

A desire to control and order one's environment can result in an obsessive or compulsive personality. If responsibilities can be taken in a free and easy manner, Saturn's position here can aid desires to serve others. It is crucial to avoid a tendency to hover or to overly influence others with critical opinions—better to back off and let things work themselves out.

★ 23 ★
SATURN IN THE WEEK OF
THE ENIGMA
(VIRGO II)

If these individuals get too serious about themselves, they are likely to fixate on their peculiarities and not be able or even wish to change. They must beware of feeling that the world is against them and relinquish a protective, even paranoid stance. Once they learn that the world is not out to get them, they will be able to relax and accept constructive criticism and help.

★ 24 ★
SATURN IN THE WEEK OF
THE LITERALIST
(VIRGO III)

Overly stern and judgmental attitudes come to the fore with this Saturn position. Once promises are made, they are written in stone for these folks and so they are not very forgiving when someone retracts an offer or promise. Thus, memory can create unhappiness; it is crucial for such individuals to forget the past and live in the here and now.

✴ 25 ✴
SATURN ON THE CUSP
OF BEAUTY
(VIRGO-LIBRA CUSP)

Shyness or extreme modesty may be the result of this Saturn placement. Such attitudes could make this individual more attractive, in fact, but easily overlooked by the average person. Like an unusual flower growing by the wayside that not everyone sees, this person is there only for the few who recognize their beauty. Learning to be just a bit more assertive will help them in life.

✴ 26 ✴
SATURN IN THE WEEK OF
THE PERFECTIONIST
(LIBRA I)

Care should be taken that critical attitudes do not become overly judgmental ones. Because standards are so high, Saturn tends to come down with its full weight on those who do not come up to the mark. When such attitudes are internalized they can result in enormous stress, even leading to periodic breakdowns. Riding a bit looser in the saddle is essential.

✴ 27 ✴
SATURN IN THE WEEK
OF SOCIETY
(LIBRA II)

This Saturn position can impair one's social skills and in extreme cases make the individual a bit reclusive or antisocial. The upside of this is a strong sense of social responsibility, making for a personality which can be trusted with putting the good of the group first. However, such altruism can lead to neglect of one's own personal development, and this must be guarded against.

✴ 28 ✴
SATURN IN THE WEEK
OF THEATER
(LIBRA III)

Problems may be encountered in forming an ego structure which can function well enough in personal and professional spheres. Because self-confidence is not high, there is a tendency with this Saturn position to put oneself down. Although modesty is considered a virtue by many, those with Saturn in this week must learn to put themselves first when necessary.

✴ 29 ✴
SATURN ON THE CUSP OF
DRAMA AND CRITICISM
(LIBRA-SCORPIO CUSP)

Stress here can lead to a periodic need to isolate oneself and also to indulge in binges of all sorts. Those involving drugs can prove particularly destructive and should be monitored carefully. Also, such individuals can get themselves in hot water fast with their stern judgmental attitudes. Timeouts on a daily basis are essential for reducing pressures, both in family and career activities.

✴ 30 ✴
SATURN IN THE WEEK
OF INTENSITY
(SCORPIO I)

Saturn can have a negative effect on the ability to concentrate one's efforts on what is most important. In fact, attention can get fixated on certain areas which are not really relevant and divert one's energy from necessary pursuits. Moreover, if attitudes become too serious they may make matters too heavy for anyone to handle.

✴ 31 ✴
SATURN IN THE WEEK
OF DEPTH
(SCORPIO II)

Pessimism and depression may be the outcome of such a Saturn position. Falling into a deep hole and not being able to drag oneself out is typical here. An effort should be made to lighten up and have more fun. If emotional blocks are present, a serious attempt should be made to free up feelings, perhaps with professional help.

✴ 32 ✴
SATURN IN THE WEEK
OF CHARM
(SCORPIO III)

Controlling attitudes are likely to come to forefront here. Attraction can be positive, both toward others and oneself, but too often it can result in attachments which are difficult to break. Further, outright addictive behavior may surface, ramping up one's needs and raising the threshold necessary for stimulation. Particularly in matters of love, the addictive element may get out of hand and ultimately prove destructive.

✴ 33 ✴
SATURN ON THE CUSP
OF REVOLUTION
(SCORPIO-SAGITTARIUS CUSP)

A serious desire to change the status quo manifests itself here. The problem is that rebelliousness may be carried too far and Saturn, in reaction, can substitute repression in its place. Thus, these energies may arouse the very opposite of what they seem to portend. Instead of becoming freer, this individual may wind up more restricted through the reactions of others.

✲ 34 ✲
SATURN IN THE WEEK
OF INDEPENDENCE
(SAGITTARIUS I)

Saturn will allow independent thought and behavior in this Personology position, as long as it is carried out in a responsible manner. Thus, it is not total freedom which is the birthright here but rather a sensible application of individuality—well thought out and sure. In the best case scenario, the combination of Jupiter's rulership of Sagittarius and Saturn's presence can be an auspicious one.

✲ 35 ✲
SATURN IN THE WEEK OF
THE ORIGINATOR
(SAGITTARIUS II)

As long as new ideas can be put to pragmatic ends, this can be a favorable position. However, the possibility also exists that this individual can be highly criticized for having far-out ideas, and be severely judged should they fail or cause problems for others. Inventions and concepts of a more practical nature are favored, ones which can work to enhance the daily quality of life.

✲ 36 ✲
SATURN IN THE WEEK
OF THE TITAN
(SAGITTARIUS III)

Saturn is not comfortable here in the most expansive and the most Jupiterian of weeks. Consequently, there can be major conflicts between visionary attitudes and pragmatic ones. This can result in a personality which expects to be judged harshly for any big ideas or overly optimistic attitudes. This individual may even go so far as to become a reactionary who refuses to listen to new proposals.

✲ 37 ✲
SATURN ON THE CUSP
OF PROPHECY
(SAGITTARIUS-CAPRICORN CUSP)

Individuals with this Saturn position may take themselves too seriously, particularly in the area of making predictions about the future. Their obsession with what is coming up for each individual they speak to leads them to often give unwanted advice and to restrict the more open attitudes of others. It is best if they leave the innocence and naiveté of others uncensored.

✲ 38 ✲
SATURN IN THE WEEK
OF THE RULER
(CAPRICORN I)

Saturn is happy to enter Capricorn, the sign which it rules. Feeling at home here, the ringed planet may hang loose and confident in the saddle as long as the individual with this Personology position is calling the shots. However, a threat to their authority may arouse reactions which prove unpleasant to all concerned. Self-confidence is key to maintain calm and stability.

✲ 39 ✲
SATURN IN THE WEEK
OF DETERMINATION
(CAPRICORN II)

Care will have to be taken to keep one's heart open. Too often Capricorn's presence here can lead to a certain ruthlessness and disregard for the feelings of others. Should this occur it can result in cutting such an individual off from the world and fixing them in a lonely stance. Such isolation is detrimental and can be combated by a more caring and empathic attitude.

✲ 40 ✲
SATURN IN THE WEEK
OF DOMINANCE
(CAPRICORN III)

The danger here is that Saturn will promote dictatorial attitudes which smother the free expression of others. A desire to control many aspects of the lives of one's family and friends and to be the sole arbiter in professional areas can arouse resentment and ultimately rebellion. Learning to work as part of a team and give up controlling attitudes will lead to greater happiness for all.

✲ 41 ✲
SATURN ON THE CUSP OF
MYSTERY AND IMAGINATION
(CAPRICORN-AQUARIUS CUSP)

This Saturn position can work out well by grounding some of this cusp's imaginative qualities. Actually, the combination of fantasy and practicality which results can lead to success or, at the very least, supply a more pragmatic base for both plans and implementation. In extreme cases, Saturn may inhibit the creative process here and its critical and restrictive faculties will have to be controlled.

✲ 42 ✲
SATURN IN THE WEEK
OF GENIUS
(AQUARIUS I) JANUARY 23-30

Saturn's presence here can lead to an overemphasis on mental considerations. Since serious thought is given top priority, this could result in headaches and increased stress in general. Worry emerges as a major problem in this case and great care should be taken that a fearful personality does not result. A know-it-all or omniscient attitude should also be guarded against.

✸ 43 ✸
SATURN IN THE WEEK OF
YOUTH AND EASE
(AQUARIUS II)

Either Saturn can enjoy himself and take a bit of a vacation from heavy responsibilities or one's abilities to relax can be impaired by thoughts concerning what needs doing. In either case, a balance should be sought between pleasure and work. This is quite possible and can lead to a more healthy personality which can function well on the job and on vacation.

✸ 44 ✸
SATURN IN THE WEEK
OF ACCEPTANCE
(AQUARIUS III)

If Saturn pushes the individual to be suspicious and not overly receptive to the ideas and personalities of others, problems could result. A closed personality and closed heart can create physical as well as social difficulties, which can only be overcome through dedication and hard work on oneself. Opening up to the world should be the principal goal in this process.

✸ 45 ✸
SATURN ON THE CUSP
OF SENSITIVITY
(AQUARIUS-PISCES CUSP)

Extreme introversion is the greatest danger when Saturn is found in this Personology period. Because of hurtful attitudes, perhaps in childhood, feelings may have been repressed out of fear of censure. This may have resulted in bouts of depression. Emotional expression is what is sorely needed and this may be accomplished through the trust gained in love relationships and friendships.

✸ 46 ✸
SATURN IN THE WEEK
OF SPIRIT
(PISCES I)

As long as Saturn's skepticism and suspicion do not cloud one's belief system, it can have a positive influence here. The clash between a material and spiritual outlook is not at all necessary, and in fact reconciling the two and harnessing their mutual energies can bring success to the most far-out endeavors. A steady cash flow will ease the expenses of study.

✸ 47 ✸
SATURN IN THE WEEK
OF THE LONER
(PISCES II)

A serious cast to one's inner thoughts is frequently the result here. Such an attitude enables the individual to work on themselves and proceed further in their self-development. Deep introversion can be a problem here in extreme cases. Often such an individual takes their few friendships seriously and makes an excellent companion or associate. Holding on to failed relationships can be a problem, however.

✸ 48 ✸
SATURN IN THE WEEK OF
DANCERS AND DREAMERS
(PISCES III)

A talent for money and financial investment can manifest here. Such individuals are generally good in generating an income for themselves, even under the most difficult circumstances. When things are going well they must be careful to put something aside to cover lean periods ahead. By providing a solid investment base they can help provide a more secure future for themselves and their dear ones.

URANUS

URANUS REPRESENTS PSYCHIC POWERS, UNPREDICTABILITY, AND HIGHER THOUGHT.

NOTE FROM THE ARTIST ABOUT THE ILLUSTRATION ON THE FACING PAGE: Uranus is the only planet tipped on its side. It has a small ring like Saturn's, but vertical. This is why the female figure is shown in a semi-reclining pose. In astrological lore, Uranus is associated with enlightenment, progressiveness, individuality, novelty, and technology. It is also associated with Aquarius, the water bearer, which is why I've included a water jug and given a blue color to the female figure's hair. The twelve titans appear in the background. The titans are the sons of Uranus. One sun is Saturn, which makes Uranus the grandfather of Jupiter.

URANUS

IN THE 48 PERSONOLOGY PERIODS

✴1✴
URANUS ON THE CUSP OF REBIRTH
(PISCES-ARIES CUSP)

Impulsive behavior is pronounced here. Such a Uranus position is highly unpredictable, often giving the impression of an unstable personality. These people can be highly reliable over the long haul, but like to make their short range plans from moment to moment. They do best when responsibilities placed upon them are not made too heavy or constraining.

✴2✴
URANUS IN THE WEEK OF THE CHILD
(ARIES I)

Sudden changes of mood are likely here, even sometimes from one second to the next. Such an individual can move quickly from exhilaration to despair with no gradations in between. This makes them unpredictable and often people do not know what to expect. Also, sudden outbursts of temper alternating with equally sudden bouts of depression are common here.

✴3✴
URANUS IN THE WEEK OF THE STAR
(ARIES II)

Uranus strives for recognition and attention, sometimes using rather spectacular means to get it. If ignored, such individuals may use the element of surprise to garner attention, saving up their energy and unleashing it on a gathering at the most opportune, albeit awkward, moment. Such unforgettable and regrettable displays may earn them a reputation for theatrical behavior.

✴4✴
URANUS IN THE WEEK OF THE PIONEER
(ARIES III)

Forging ahead, these determined individuals could lead armies into the jaws of hell if necessary. Heedless of their own personal safety, they dynamically forge ahead into the unknown, preferably going where no one has trodden before. They must be aware of not leading others astray, however, and realize that we are not all meant to be on the same path.

✴5✴
URANUS ON THE CUSP OF POWER
(ARIES-TAURUS CUSP)

With the force of an express train, these individuals may shatter barriers and knock others out of their way. Like battering rams, they make their way through life often showing little consideration for the feelings of others. When they are made aware that such behavior is not often appreciated, they may learn to harness their prodigious energies in a subtle and efficacious manner.

✴6✴
URANUS IN THE WEEK OF MANIFESTATION
(TAURUS I)

Uranus is given a steadying influence here. Its habit of bringing sudden change is tempered severely, making its energies more suitable and predictable. Individuals with this position are powerful persuaders whose highly cogent arguments usually speak for themselves. Often such people can make their wishes known unambiguously through their body language. They are the type you usually want on your side in any fight.

✶ 7 ✶
URANUS IN THE WEEK OF
THE TEACHER
(TAURUS II)

The more intellectual and idealistic side of Uranus emerges here. A high level of thought is favored and with it the ability to transmit and share ideas. Such individuals are sent as universal teachers to their families, professional groups and community at large. They may be unaware of their role and yet function in this capacity unknowingly as unofficial advisors.

✶ 8 ✶
URANUS IN THE WEEK OF
THE NATURAL
(TAURUS III)

Free and open attitudes rule this week with Uranus here, but with them also a need to express somewhat outlandish behavior. Letting it all hang out is one thing, but such individuals revel in displaying themselves. Care should be taken not to insult more conservative minded individuals or drive them to take reprisals against this behavior. Enjoyment need not be at the cost of other people's feelings.

✶ 9 ✶
URANUS ON THE CUSP
OF ENERGY
(TAURUS-GEMINI CUSP)

The explosive energies of Uranus can get out of hand here, engulfing everyone in the immediate vicinity. Keeping these under control and harnessing them to perform useful tasks is the idea. Also, these individuals need to guard against the potential to use up these energies in a single burst and instead make an effort to distribute them more evenly.

✶ 10 ✶
URANUS IN THE WEEK
OF FREEDOM
(GEMINI I)

Breaking free of restrictions is the keynote here. Also, such individuals can serve as an inspiration to others through the example of their own struggle for liberation. Uranus is likely to be rebellious against authority here, but care must be taken not to assume the very authoritarian roles one is in the act of opposing! Revolution should become a metaphor for an ongoing process of self-discovery.

✶ 11 ✶
URANUS IN THE WEEK OF
NEW LANGUAGE
(GEMINI II)

Non-verbal and telepathic communication will be more and more important in the Aquarian Age. Uranus is right at home here, fostering and promoting all new forms of communication. An interest in long-distance communication through Internet, telephone and television will give way to psychic communication in the long run as the years go by. The brain as transmitter is the central symbol here.

✶ 12 ✶
URANUS IN THE WEEK OF
THE SEEKER
(GEMINI III)

Penetrating into the unknown, those with this Uranus position expect to come up against barriers and obstacles, and to smash them out of their way. Easy tasks do not really interest such individuals much. It is the big challenge and even the impossibilities lying ahead which lure them on. The will to overcome is strong here and with it a desire to achieve significant breakthroughs.

✶ 13 ✶
URANUS ON THE CUSP
OF MAGIC
(GEMINI-CANCER CUSP)

Uranus the magician is right at home here. Although such an individual is likely to be possessed of charismatic and enchanting qualities, they will have to be careful not to disappear in their own world of illusion. Keeping a grip on reality is important here. Therefore, attending to small daily tasks can act as an important grounding influence.

✶ 14 ✶
URANUS IN THE WEEK OF
THE EMPATH
(CANCER I)

The lightning quick Uranus may be baffled by the emotional orientation of this week. Thus, the forcefulness and communicative abilities of this planet may get blunted here, resulting in some confusion. Garbled and mixed messages can be the result. In order to avoid confusion, a connection should be sought between emotional and psychic understanding. Patience will be required in such an effort.

✶ 15 ✶
URANUS IN THE WEEK OF
THE UNCONVENTIONAL
(CANCER II)

The quirky qualities of Uranus and of this week make for a strong bond. Such an individual is truly one of a kind and must not be made self-conscious about it by the world's judgments. Pride should be taken in their thoughts and appearance, and such strong idiosyncrasies should be put to work to attract more friends, lovers and work of an interesting nature.

✹ 16 ✹
URANUS IN THE WEEK OF
THE PERSUADER
(CANCER III)

It is less in the nature of Uranus to persuade and more to simply blast opponents out of the way. Therefore, Uranus is made nervous by the tact and diplomacy required here. This can result in an inability or unwillingness to win others over through patiently seductive tactics and a kind of gruff impatience which just doesn't work to convince them.

✹ 17 ✹
URANUS ON THE CUSP
OF OSCILLATION
(CANCER-LEO CUSP)

Extreme instability can be the result of such a Uranus position. Bouncing around from one philosophical position to another, being inconsistent in thought and action, and having difficulty keeping to one course or purpose can plague this individual. Family members may despair of bringing such a reactive individual back into the fold. Better just to accept them as the maverick they are.

✹ 18 ✹
URANUS IN THE WEEK
OF AUTHORITY
(LEO I)

Intrigued by the power inherent in this week, Uranus is likely to adopt a stance here that wants to set rules rather than break them. A drive toward exerting power over others may prove tyrannical and engender tremendous opposition. Uranus' response is likely to be pretty ferocious and if disaster is to be avoided both parties must learn to back off a bit and chill out.

✹ 19 ✹
URANUS IN THE WEEK OF
BALANCED STRENGTH
(LEO II)

If there is anything Uranus finds it difficult to achieve, it is balance. Because the energies of this week are at their worst when they are not centered, the influence of Uranus here can be decidedly negative. On the other hand, Leo II may have a salutary effect on the erratic planet and provide it with some of the stability it needs. Dynamism and constructive efforts can result.

✹ 20 ✹
URANUS IN THE WEEK
OF LEADERSHIP
(LEO III)

Although Uranus may fancy himself a leader, he really isn't. His attempts to take the reins of power are not likely to succeed, therefore. If he can reconcile himself to a secondary role, which is unlikely, the group to which this individual belongs will be spared a lot of agony. Incompatible energies here are likely to upset the old apple cart.

✹ 21 ✹
URANUS ON THE CUSP
OF EXPOSURE
(LEO-VIRGO CUSP)

The magical and exhibitionistic character of Uranus is likely to shine here. On the other hand, the needs inherent in this week to keep many activities and thoughts secret are not at all favored. Chances are that the individual may pick all the wrong moments to reveal their true selves. A feeling for kairos, the right time for doing things, must be cultivated.

✹ 22 ✹
URANUS IN THE WEEK OF
SYSTEM BUILDERS
(VIRGO I)

Uranus has much to learn in this week from the methodical Virgo I energies. However, because the planet is opposed to orderly activities he may wind up undermining them. The result can be a messy bedroom or work station. Breaking structures apart rather than building them up is Uranus's specialty, so his destructive bent may be aroused and directed against strict regimens and ingrained habits.

✹ 23 ✹
URANUS IN THE WEEK OF
THE ENIGMA
(VIRGO II)

An interest in all things strange and unusual is characteristic of this Uranus position. Extreme curiosity manifests here and with it a desire to ferret out secrets and search through every nook and cranny for interesting tidbits of information. Such an individual should not be left alone for long in your house. They are likely to uncover material that not even you knew about.

✹ 24 ✹
URANUS IN THE WEEK OF
THE LITERALIST
(VIRGO III)

Because Uranus is so likely to proceed on impulse, the planet cannot be bothered to keep to its promises. Hence, conflicts will arise between the kinds of consistency required by this week and Uranus's erratic nature. It may therefore be difficult to trust such an individual, although in fact their instincts may keep them on the right track. Trust must be built through solid results.

✴ 25 ✴
URANUS ON THE CUSP OF BEAUTY
(VIRGO-LIBRA CUSP)

The kind of beauty which appeals to Uranus here is that which relates to technology, particularly that concerned with communication. Thus, a love of online browsing, email use, and all matters concerning the media surfaces here. Such individuals are just as likely to be attracted to a virtual image as to a real one, sometimes even more so.

✴ 26 ✴
URANUS IN THE WEEK OF THE PERFECTIONIST
(LIBRA I)

The demands of Uranus can be quite severe in this week when it comes to communication. Those with this Uranus position demand that others make themselves perfectly clear and unambiguous in their verbal and written statements. Unfortunately, they may not apply the same exacting rules to themselves, resulting in a double standard that can prove maddening to the other person involved.

✴ 27 ✴
URANUS IN THE WEEK OF SOCIETY
(LIBRA II)

Outlandish behavior could lead to being socially ostracized here. Yet the person with this Uranus position has an acute need for their shenanigans to be observed and even in some cases to be accepted. At the very least, their shock effect must be felt. Like the boy who cried wolf too often, others are likely to become bored with such antics.

✴ 28 ✴
URANUS IN THE WEEK OF THEATER
(LIBRA III)

A love of excitement is the keynote here, pushing such individuals to higher and higher levels of expression and stimulation. All matters relating to change of appearance—sudden new hairstyles, makeup, clothing, etc.—are to be expected. The frequently upsetting results can make others suspicious of Libra III's sanity on occasion, should such behavior be carried to extremes.

✴ 29 ✴
URANUS ON THE CUSP OF DRAMA AND CRITICISM
(LIBRA-SCORPIO CUSP)

The destructive powers of Uranus can be felt here. These folks must learn not only how devastating their criticism can be, but also that such judgment does not usually bring positive results to the lives of those around them. Characterized by a cutting tongue and often mercilessly persistent approach, those with this Uranus placement can wreak havoc on the personalities of more susceptible family members and colleagues.

✴ 30 ✴
URANUS IN THE WEEK OF INTENSITY
(SCORPIO I)

The normally acute focus of this week can be undermined by Uranus's unpredictability and need for sudden, extreme change. An inability to concentrate can surface here, often during the most stressful of times. The result may be pursuing detours and byways which only take attention away from the principal matter at hand. An unexciting, methodical approach should be employed whenever this occurs.

✴ 31 ✴
URANUS IN THE WEEK OF DEPTH
(SCORPIO II)

Uranus can have a beneficial influence here, making such an individual less serious and self-preoccupied. Bringing fun and play to their daily life could be the result. However, if carried too far, such an influence could result in a refusal to take people seriously or to recognize pressing problems as being truly important. A balance should be found between lighter and heavier moods and attitudes.

✴ 32 ✴
URANUS IN THE WEEK OF CHARM
(SCORPIO III)

A sparkling and intriguing personality may be the result of this Uranus placement. Such individuals can dazzle others with their charm and melt even the hardest heart. Because of these magical qualities, they are often highly sought after in their social set. Furthermore, they can put these abilities to good use in the professional sphere when dealing with colleagues and clients alike.

✴ 33 ✴
URANUS ON THE CUSP OF REVOLUTION
(SCORPIO-SAGITTARIUS CUSP)

Revolution is something that is close to the very essence of the planet Uranus. Conceived and discovered at the time of the French Revolution, it carries an energy which opposes established systems and seeks to overthrow them. These energies should not be allowed to get out of control here or this individual may become very unpopular with those around them.

✴ 34 ✴
URANUS IN THE WEEK OF INDEPENDENCE
(SAGITTARIUS I)

Uranus is happy in this week. However, should irresponsible behavior be expressed to too great a degree, chaos can result. Uranus must also learn the lesson of cooperation and the need to function well in group endeavors and in society in general. Harnessing energies to benefit the group could lead to independent actions to produce significant social change.

✴ 35 ✴
URANUS IN THE WEEK OF THE ORIGINATOR
(SAGITTARIUS II)

Uranus the inventor emerges here. A love of all sorts of gadgets and of inventing bizarre solutions to the most simple problems is evident. A direct approach is almost impossible for such individuals to adopt, often leading to roundabout ways of doing things which can be staggering in their complexity. Such individuals can always think of a "better" way of proceeding with a technical challenge.

✴ 36 ✴
URANUS IN THE WEEK OF THE TITAN
(SAGITTARIUS III)

The energies of Uranus and Jupiter are likely to collide here. The joviality and optimism of Jupiter is undermined by Saturn's dissatisfaction with the status quo and need for change. Should the energies of these planets be coupled, however, they can lead to great success in the most far-reaching endeavors. Grounding such projects in reality is essential to their progress.

✴ 37 ✴
URANUS ON THE CUSP OF PROPHECY
(SAGITTARIUS-CAPRICORN CUSP)

Uranus is more than happy to use his psychic qualities to look into the crystal ball and divine the future. Individuals with Uranus on this cusp can make accurate predictive statements and their warnings should be heeded. They must, however, learn to trust their intuitions more, since they have probably encountered resistance to their paranormal qualities when growing up.

✴ 38 ✴
URANUS IN THE WEEK OF THE RULER
(CAPRICORN I)

There is little of the rebel present here. Uranus has a good healthy respect for the dominant qualities of this week and admiration for someone who can give direction to work projects and family endeavors. Uranian energies are likely to provide the kind of impulse which a ruler needs to succeed in life, but should only beware of arousing resistance.

✴ 39 ✴
URANUS IN THE WEEK OF DETERMINATION
(CAPRICORN II)

The determination of Uranus to follow a project through to the bitter end and never give up is typical here. Obstacles are simply circumvented or, when necessary, blasted out of the way. Surrender or admissions of failure are not an option. The force of Uranus may assume irresistible proportions here and revel in moving even the most immovable of objects.

✴ 40 ✴
URANUS IN THE WEEK OF DOMINANCE
(CAPRICORN III)

Uranus has a tyrannical as well as a rebellious side, much like the exponents of the French Revolution who later became dictatorial and meted out punishment mercilessly. Such individuals will hold on to their power and never give it up or allow others to take it away. They should at some point learn the value of letting go and moving on.

✴ 41 ✴
URANUS ON THE CUSP OF MYSTERY AND IMAGINATION
(CAPRICORN-AQUARIUS CUSP)

Great care should be taken here that the more violent aspects of Uranus do not get out of control. Occasionally the wild fantasy life of these individuals can burst into their everyday routines and cause problems for all concerned. Using the imagination in a creative, not destructive, manner is key here. Such individuals can be highly prized by society and actively sought out for their vision.

✴ 42 ✴
URANUS IN THE WEEK OF GENIUS
(AQUARIUS I) JANUARY 23-30

A mental predominance manifests here, which can cause problems to emerge in the emotional and physical spheres. Brain power is accentuated by this Uranus position, but not necessarily that of logic or even common sense. It is the kind of blinding and brilliant thought patterns which are likely to emerge from time to time, often at the most unexpected moments.

✴ 43 ✴
URANUS IN THE WEEK OF
YOUTH AND EASE
(AQUARIUS II)

Uranus is perhaps at his most relaxed point in the Zodiac here. Even his dynamic and electric energies enjoy a rest from time to time, and here he can fully stretch out, kick back and enjoy himself. During such periods of enjoyment he is quite likely to become inspired to new feats of daring. With fully charged batteries he is ready to leap into the fray once more.

✴ 44 ✴
URANUS IN THE WEEK
OF ACCEPTANCE
(AQUARIUS III)

Certainly the most "New Age-y" of Uranus positions, such individuals value the concepts of universal love, brother and sisterhood, and world peace above all others. Truly Aquarian, these folks are happiest when part of a group seeking to be granted a fair hearing about its ideas, no matter how far out they are. A strong ideal for them is living in a community of individuals.

✴ 45 ✴
URANUS ON THE CUSP
OF SENSITIVITY
(AQUARIUS-PISCES CUSP)

Overreactive, such individuals are made very jumpy by even slightly unpleasant sensory stimuli, particularly those involving sound and smell. Since their buttons can be easily pushed, they must learn to grow a whole set which cannot be pushed so easily. Perhaps their greatest lesson is learning not to let others control them through their predictable responses.

✴ 46 ✴
URANUS IN THE WEEK
OF SPIRIT
(PISCES I)

Psychic phenomena and spirituality do not always get along, but in this position it is possible. Thus, a practice like meditation can serve to both link an individual to others telepathically but also to the divinity within. Religious orientations are common here, particularly those which substitute a highly personal God for one promulgated by a major belief system.

✴ 47 ✴
URANUS IN THE WEEK
OF THE LONER
(PISCES II)

Isolation in action can lead such individuals to continually act on their own without seeking the advice of others. Their work may be solitary and of a highly personal nature, but such people can be very dramatic when bringing it out in the open. They should be encouraged, however, to touch base with groups if only to voice their ideas to a wider public.

✴ 48 ✴
URANUS IN THE WEEK OF
DANCERS AND DREAMERS
(PISCES III)

No project is too far out, no concept too abstract or philosophical for these nimble-witted people to consider and perhaps embrace. Like butterflies, they are likely to flit from one intellectual concept to the next. If not intellectuals, they still demand a great deal of variety in their work and private lives. They can also specialize in several areas at once.

NEPTUNE

NEPTUNE REPRESENTS SPIRITUALITY, RELIGION, AND FANTASY.

NOTE FROM THE ARTIST ABOUT THE ILLUSTRATION ON THE FACING PAGE: Neptune is the ruler of Pisces, as reflected in her mask. The mask can be seen as the two fish in the Pisces sign or as the dolphins of Neptune. Because Pisces is a water sign, and Neptune is its ruler, I've colored the planet a watery blue. In the background, you can see the god, Neptune, and his trident, in the lower left corner of the mosaic. In the foreground, the female figure holds aloft the largest of Neptune's moons. The light behind her fingers evokes the planet's association with enlightenment and intuition. In astrological lore, Neptune is also associated with mercy and compassion.

N E P T U N E

IN THE 48 PERSONOLOGY PERIODS

✳ 1 ✳
NEPTUNE ON THE CUSP OF REBIRTH
(PISCES-ARIES CUSP)

The watery influence of Neptune is felt strongly on the Pisces-Aries Cusp. Hence, new beginnings are likely to be blunted or clouded in hopes and expectations rather than resulting in solid action. Undermining one's own efforts is the danger here. Great care must be taken that self-destructive energies do not spiral out of control. Start with small things and build slowly.

✳ 2 ✳
NEPTUNE IN THE WEEK OF THE CHILD
(ARIES I)

"What-if" thinking tends to dominate here. Beginning sentences with the words "I wish" indicates a lack of self-confidence. Too often this Neptune position indicates a child with unfulfilled desires and one who is content to do nothing but await the arrival of some magical Santa. Rather than engaging in solid hard work, dreams and fantasies abound. Set rigorous schedules to make progress.

✳ 3 ✳
NEPTUNE IN THE WEEK OF THE STAR
(ARIES II)

Delusions of self-grandeur are likely with Neptune here. At the very least, the personality can become immersed in self-congratulatory admiration of one's self and one's efforts, and it is possible to go as far as megalomaniac obsession with grand projects. In order to remain healthy, these illusory states must be scaled back and replaced with a quiet and more realistic self-confidence which promotes true growth and personal development.

✳ 4 ✳
NEPTUNE IN THE WEEK OF THE PIONEER
(ARIES III)

Forging ahead, these determined individuals could lead armies into the jaws of hell if necessary. Heedless of their own personal safety, they dynamically forge ahead into the unknown, preferably going where no one has trodden before. They must be aware of not leading others astray, however, and realize that we are not all meant to be on the same path.

✳ 5 ✳
NEPTUNE ON THE CUSP OF POWER
(ARIES-TAURUS CUSP)

Like a tidal wave, Neptune in this position is likely to sweep others away with emotional and idealistic expressions. Nothing can withstand the vast pressure and ultimately such energy will wear away even the most stubborn rock. Individuals with this position must be careful not to exert undue influence on others and to keep an ear open to what they have to say.

✳ 6 ✳
NEPTUNE IN THE WEEK OF MANIFESTATION
(TAURUS I)

Neptune tends to undermine the stability of this week. Those with this position may find it difficult to carry through their ideas or to implement them satisfactorily. Ideas tend to remain in the theoretical stage, providing much pleasure but few results. Grounding influences which enhance Taurus I's powers should be actively sought out.

★7★
NEPTUNE IN THE WEEK OF THE TEACHER
(TAURUS II)

Charisma in spades here can urge others to follow the ideas and example of these seductive individuals. Their inspiring words light up the lives of those around them, certainly when they are of a positive nature. However, their subtle criticism can also erode the self-confidence of others, leaving them prey to their own subjective fears and doubts.

★8★
NEPTUNE IN THE WEEK OF THE NATURAL
(TAURUS III)

A great love of Nature, particularly its watery aspects, abounds here. All sports related to water, such as swimming and boating, are likely to emerge, but vacations by the sea, lakes and rivers are usually favored, as well. An appreciation of the flux and flow of life is characteristic, and of going with the stream of things, rather than fighting to control.

★9★
NEPTUNE ON THE CUSP OF ENERGY
(TAURUS-GEMINI CUSP)

Neptune lends an irresistibly watery character to the energies of this cusp. Difficult to withstand, such individuals are able to lend an unstoppable character to projects in which they become involved. Hard to shut out of one's heart, they are also emotionally persistent. They will usually not stop until their partner or lover accedes to their wishes and demands.

★10★
NEPTUNE IN THE WEEK OF FREEDOM
(GEMINI I)

A loss of focus caused by Neptune's presence here can allow the efforts of those with this position to easily lose momentum and spin out of control. A wild character is frequently evidenced here, as well as an inability to concentrate, making it difficult to keep on a direct path. Some may see such an individual as distracted, others as having lost it at crucial moments.

★11★
NEPTUNE IN THE WEEK OF NEW LANGUAGE
(GEMINI II)

A hesitant and often vague manner of expression, particularly in speech, often manifests here. Because of the rambling character of their statements, these folks tend to alternately confuse or bore others. They must tighten up their language, cutting away the fat and fighting its tendency to drift. A real danger exists that others will not really understand or even listen to them.

★12★
NEPTUNE IN THE WEEK OF THE SEEKER
(GEMINI III)

Far reaching dreams and visions are characteristic here. These folks are usually way out there in planning and assessing future possibilities. Often enough, they do succeed in their endeavors and therefore can inspire others to follow them. However, they are more interested in going it alone than attracting disciples, since their plans are individualistic, unique and at times peculiar.

★13★
NEPTUNE ON THE CUSP OF MAGIC
(GEMINI-CANCER CUSP)

Neptune can be at its most bewitching here. Those with this position are able to bring others under their spell practically at will. As their life progresses, so does their conscious realization of the extent of their powers. So that all is not surface glitz and glitter, they should work hard on developing their more profound attributes and building a personality of substance.

★14★
NEPTUNE IN THE WEEK OF THE EMPATH
(CANCER I)

An extreme receptivity to unspoken signals and wishes characterizes this Neptune position. Emotional sensitivity is pronounced and with it a comforting air which others seek out in times of stress. Sympathy for the plight of others should not lead an individual to neglect their own self-interest. A clearer focus on the hard realities of life is needed.

★15★
NEPTUNE IN THE WEEK OF THE UNCONVENTIONAL
(CANCER II)

Matters of style take center stage. Neptune lends an imaginative slant here, fostering an unusual approach to this individual's personal appearance (hair, clothing, lifestyle). Such people are not shy about flaunting their differences, but in fact are not really interested in impressing or creating a shock effect. Their flair comes quite naturally and is rarely calculated.

✴ 16 ✴
NEPTUNE IN THE WEEK OF
THE PERSUADER
(CANCER III)

It is hard to resist the wishes of these convincing individuals. Because of their ability to touch the hearts of those around them, they have few problems getting their way. A dependency can spring up easily on either side, however, and they must beware of the highly dependent relationships that can result. Attracting people is not as difficult in the long run as cutting them loose.

✴ 17 ✴
NEPTUNE ON THE CUSP
OF OSCILLATION
(CANCER-LEO CUSP)

This cusp carries passive-aggressive tendencies and it is the passive ones which are underlined here. Such individuals are likely to hang back and on occasion let themselves be taken advantage of. Learning to toughen up and stand up for themselves is a difficult but necessary lesson. Keeping to a set course will be difficult for these flexible people. Therefore, writing down a schedule of fixed obligations is recommended.

✴ 18 ✴
NEPTUNE IN THE WEEK
OF AUTHORITY
(LEO I)

The watery planet Neptune is not comfortable in this hot week. Because of its aversion to fixed ideas, no matter how effective or brilliant, Neptune tends to exert a dissolving effect on authority here, encouraging those with this position to undermine any omniscient attitudes. They may have difficulty exerting direct influences in their family life.

✴ 19 ✴
NEPTUNE IN THE WEEK OF
BALANCED STRENGTH
(LEO II)

The balance inherent in this week can be severely upset by Neptune's position here. The strength inherent in Neptune is not usually a direct, forceful one but rather involves a more subtle, indirect and devious power. Therefore, those with this Neptune position must learn to get their way through other patterns of behavior, particularly seductive ones.

✴ 20 ✴
NEPTUNE IN THE WEEK
OF LEADERSHIP
(LEO III)

Those with Neptune in this week can galvanize support behind them. Through becoming the projection or embodiment of the dreams of others they can be highly influential in heading up families, business organizations and social groups. They arouse the belief of others through their fiery stimulus and so guarantee their position of powerful command.

✴ 21 ✴
NEPTUNE ON THE CUSP
OF EXPOSURE
(LEO-VIRGO CUSP)

Extremely persuasive, these individuals may be found working behind the scenes in a quiet, unobtrusive manner. By keeping out of the way of others, they spare themselves many confrontational problems. Although agreeable to compromise, they will only give way up to a point and after that hold firm to their principles and ideals. They resist being taken advantage of.

✴ 22 ✴
NEPTUNE IN THE WEEK OF
SYSTEM BUILDERS
(VIRGO I)

If one's ability to structure thoughts and activities works hand in hand with imaginative powers, this Neptune position can be extremely productive. Certainly all artistic activities are favored here, as long as they are ordered and well-planned. Care must be taken, however, that the desire to control creative impulses does not dampen creativity or lead to repetitive or compulsive behavior.

✴ 23 ✴
NEPTUNE IN THE WEEK OF
THE ENIGMA
(VIRGO II)

Mystery and allure color the personalities of those with this Neptune placement. Hidden personalities, they may indulge in all sorts of secretive behavior, thereby stimulating others to investigate and also to get involved. These people may even invite danger and precarious relationships which challenge the status quo. Their loves are unusual and their methods for achieving fulfillment may take bizarre forms.

✴ 24 ✴
NEPTUNE IN THE WEEK OF
THE LITERALIST
(VIRGO III)

Neptune is not comfortable in this week, since the rational demands made on it are so high. The vague character of the watery planet is not easy to pin down with fixed responsibilities and expectations. Consequently, such individuals may experience real conflict between pragmatism and fantasy. When this dichotomy reaches critical mass, the personality could be torn to shreds by the conflict.

✴ 25 ✴
NEPTUNE ON THE CUSP OF BEAUTY
(VIRGO-LIBRA CUSP)

An idealization of beauty accompanies this position. Such individuals are paralyzed by sensuous, visual and auditory forms of lush, rich attraction. They are also likely to pay attention to their own appearance, mixing fantasy and reality in an attractive blend. Too often they neglect the substance of things, and feel little or no need to dig beneath the surface.

✴ 26 ✴
NEPTUNE IN THE WEEK OF THE PERFECTIONIST
(LIBRA I)

A preoccupation with computer software, technical intricacies, cars and websites is characteristic here. Such individuals do well as consultants and troubleshooters, ferreting out problems and solving them. Usually strong in design concepts, they are never happier than when dreaming up a new plan for any group or organization. Being appreciated for their services is important to them in all aspects of life.

✴ 27 ✴
NEPTUNE IN THE WEEK OF SOCIETY
(LIBRA II)

Such individuals tend to idealize their friendships. They are not usually realistic toward those they really care for and are likely to overlook faults and trust those who do not deserve it. They danger is that they may sacrifice themselves in the process and allow themselves to be taken advantage of. Their fear of rejection is intense, leading them to be overly accommodating.

✴ 28 ✴
NEPTUNE IN THE WEEK OF THEATER
(LIBRA III)

Neptune can lead these folks to live in an unreal world, populated by film and TV stars, and with dramatic public figures. They see a connection between themselves and such notables, frequently fantasizing about possible relationships, sexual or otherwise. Their real challenge is to discover the true drama in everyday life and to invest more real energy in events around them.

✴ 29 ✴
NEPTUNE ON THE CUSP OF DRAMA AND CRITICISM
(LIBRA-SCORPIO CUSP)

Drugs of all sorts should be avoided by such individuals and, if medically prescribed, handled with extreme care. They are likely to rave about their physician or therapist and get overly enthusiastic about their treatment. Also, they are prone to accumulating masses of evidence to rationally support their position, making it difficult or impossible to argue with them.

✴ 30 ✴
NEPTUNE IN THE WEEK OF INTENSITY
(SCORPIO I)

Sexual fantasies may periodically overcome those with this Neptune placement. If there are real outlets for this energy, involving a loving person, many good results can be expected both in the relationship and in other aspects of daily life. However, should narcissism or other extreme forms of self-stimulation result, frustration can build to intolerable levels. Frequent reality checks are advised.

✴ 31 ✴
NEPTUNE IN THE WEEK OF DEPTH
(SCORPIO II)

If isolation and nursing private resentments and grudges manifest here, Neptune in this week can lead to serious depressions. Opening up avenues of true communication with others is advised, in order to avoid getting bottled up in one's own private world. Particularly in the professional sphere, making slow, gradual progress is advised rather than expecting sudden miracles to surface.

✴ 32 ✴
NEPTUNE IN THE WEEK OF CHARM
(SCORPIO III)

Those with this Neptune position are likely to have magnetically attractive personalities, but this does not always work to produce the best results. By sending out mixed signals, these folks may give the wrong idea to others and put themselves in a position of being repeatedly misunderstood. In order to provide a more realistic picture of their true feelings, they will have to keep their magnetism under control.

✴ 33 ✴
NEPTUNE ON THE CUSP OF REVOLUTION
(SCORPIO-SAGITTARIUS CUSP)

Such individuals are good at undermining the status quo. Not big on all-out confrontation, they are more likely to change things through delicate and highly subtle maneuvering, usually behind the scenes. In order to effect change, they are meticulous in their preparation and efficient in execution. They can also act as catalysts for change, simply by their presence alone.

✷ 34 ✷
NEPTUNE IN THE WEEK
OF INDEPENDENCE
(SAGITTARIUS I)

Often appearing to be amoral, those with this Neptune position are likely to simply go off and do their own thing, without regard for the wishes of others or for obligations and responsibilities. Not to be stopped, these feisty individuals do as they please, despite threats of punishment or reprisal. Yet they have a caring side as well and will frequently choose to help family and friends.

✷ 35 ✷
NEPTUNE IN THE WEEK OF
THE ORIGINATOR
(SAGITTARIUS II)

Few people outdo Sagittarius II in the scope of their imagination and depth of fantasy. These colorful individuals definitely dream in Technicolor. Those who are able to bring unconscious elements into their work are likely to achieve recognition for their highly idiosyncratic world view and for their artistic vision. Giving structure to such vision is usually their greatest challenge.

✷ 36 ✷
NEPTUNE IN THE WEEK
OF THE TITAN
(SAGITTARIUS III)

Because of their expansiveness of thought, these individuals are likely to get out of touch with reality easily. Those with this Neptune position do not acknowledge boundaries nor heed warning signals of having gone too far. Grounding and actualizing their ideas is their major problem, since these individuals often prefer to enjoy their latest fantasy. A touch of pragmatism will help implement their ideas.

✷ 37 ✷
NEPTUNE ON THE CUSP
OF PROPHECY
(SAGITTARIUS-CAPRICORN CUSP)

Religion plays an important role with this position, including all sorts of beliefs in pagan ceremonies, so-called "primitive" rituals and esoteric matters. Those with Neptune here are deep thinkers and take seriously the non-rational areas of human thought. Not averse to making predictions about the future, they are also effective in quietly winning others over to their cause.

✷ 38 ✷
NEPTUNE IN THE WEEK
OF THE RULER
(CAPRICORN I)

Dogmatic beliefs characterize Neptune in this Personology period. Such individuals can be autocratic in their attitudes and often insist that others follow their strict and often stern points of view. Their belief in themselves is high, enabling them to go far in implementing their ideas, but they can also arouse great resistance and antagonism by refusing to listen.

✷ 39 ✷
NEPTUNE IN THE WEEK
OF DETERMINATION
(CAPRICORN II)

The determination characteristic of this week can be severely undermined by Neptune's dissolving influence. Such individuals can seem to make up their minds about something but then find that the will to carry out their decisions slowly fades away. Thus they often promise much but deliver little. It is important for them to limit their expectations and those of others, and to keep their active imaginations under control.

✷ 40 ✷
NEPTUNE IN THE WEEK
OF DOMINANCE
(CAPRICORN III)

Flooding those around them with controlling influences often accomplishes more harm than good here. These individuals will be more effective if they can limit themselves to proceeding in one direction at a time and accomplishing things on a step-by-step basis. Learning to keep a handle on their need to control and allow others a chance to help out will be important to their self-development.

✷ 41 ✷
NEPTUNE ON THE CUSP OF
MYSTERY AND IMAGINATION
(CAPRICORN-AQUARIUS CUSP)

One of the most imaginative and far-reaching positions of the year for Neptune. Those with this position have extremely vivid dream and fantasy lives, which usually spill over into their day-to-day existence. It may be difficult for those they live with to accept their often bizarre and strange points of view. Violent tendencies, when opposed or misunderstood, must be kept under control.

✷ 42 ✷
NEPTUNE IN THE WEEK
OF GENIUS
(AQUARIUS I) JANUARY 23-30

Conflicts can arise in the minds of such individuals between right- and left-brains, that is, between their logical and rational side and the creative, imaginative side. Thus, these folks can proceed in a sensible fashion and suddenly be swept away by a flood of emotion. They are not particularly good about keeping their cool under stress.

✶ 43 ✶
NEPTUNE IN THE WEEK OF YOUTH AND EASE
(AQUARIUS II)

Those with this Neptune position are so relaxed that they frequently cannot get much done when placed under stress. Going with the flow is their forte, and if they simply let things happen at their own pace they can achieve great success. They are particularly good with money because they adopt a free-and-easy approach and avoid undue worry about financial problems.

✶ 44 ✶
NEPTUNE IN THE WEEK OF ACCEPTANCE
(AQUARIUS III)

Far-out individuals who share many New Age and advanced points of view, these people are up for new, exciting projects which come their way. They react strongly against conservative points of view and become true revolutionaries in the face of despotism. Gentle toward children and small animals, these kind folks are there to help their friends when in need.

✶ 45 ✶
NEPTUNE ON THE CUSP OF SENSITIVITY
(AQUARIUS-PISCES CUSP)

Extremely responsive to the feelings of others, these folks are sympathetic to the plight of the underdog. Particularly susceptible to needy individuals, those with this Neptune position can be an easy touch for the more unscrupulous. Toughening up a tad and working on not being so emotionally reactive will help them greatly. Their fear of rejection should not lead them to be overly accommodating.

✶ 46 ✶
NEPTUNE IN THE WEEK OF SPIRIT
(PISCES I)

One of the most spiritual positions of Neptune, the higher causes of humanity are usually espoused and the most noble truths followed. These individuals are more likely than most to see beyond the petty problems of everyday life and to look toward the high ideals and beliefs of mankind. Following a love of truth and compassion usually characterizes their life's work.

✶ 47 ✶
NEPTUNE IN THE WEEK OF THE LONER
(PISCES II)

A highly creative Neptune placement. The watery planet feels totally at home here and is at its most expressive. Such individuals are remarkably gifted in the arts, particularly the visual arts or music, or at the very least highly appreciative of such creativity. In their personal lives they must beware of a tendency to feel hurt and neglected.

✶ 48 ✶
NEPTUNE IN THE WEEK OF DANCERS AND DREAMERS
(PISCES III)

Such individuals are highly advanced universal thinkers, usually able to put their high ideals to use in the service of humankind. Whether in family, business or social settings, these folks lend an air of magic and mystery to all their activities and are able to achieve a great deal with little effort. By plugging into universal energies they take others far along into uncharted waters.

PLUTO

PLUTO REPRESENTS MONEY, SEXUALITY,
AND THE DARK SIDE.

NOTE FROM THE ARTIST ABOUT THE ILLUSTRATION ON THE FACING PAGE: Pluto is the farthest planet from the Sun. The view in the illustration is similar to what the sun would look like from Pluto. Charon is Pluto's one moon, half the size of the planet. Pluto, the god of the underworld, wears a mask that makes him invisible. Pluto represents subconscious forces, money and seduction. The female figure wears an icy drape that trails like a comet's tail, and a pomegranate red mask that references the ancient Greek tale of Demeter and Persephone.

PLUTO

IN THE 48 PERSONOLOGY PERIODS

✱1✱
PLUTO ON THE
CUSP OF REBIRTH
(PISCES-ARIES CUSP)

A highly dominant position for the dark planet, Pluto. Those with this placement are difficult to oppose, and the full force of their power is felt once they set their mind to something. Although their judgment is not always the best, when they are on the right track they can achieve positive results. They must beware of a tendency to steamroll others with their prodigious energies.

✱2✱
PLUTO IN THE WEEK
OF THE CHILD
(ARIES I)

Those with Pluto here must be careful of letting their temper get out of control. Capable of full-blown tantrums, they either let off steam or stuff their anger down inside and get depressed. They must become more contemplative in order to deal honestly and effectively with Pluto's dark force. Putting unhappy elements of childhood behind them is required to move on.

✱3✱
PLUTO IN THE WEEK
OF THE STAR
(ARIES II)

Requiring undue amounts of attention is characteristic here. An insatiable desire to be at the center of everything is characteristic, making such individuals appear egotistical and self-serving. Once they learn the joy of true service they are more likely to correct this impression and to put their energies toward helping others. They may actually succeed in being recognized more once they take this important step.

✱4✱
PLUTO IN THE WEEK
OF THE PIONEER
(ARIES III)

Although these individuals are not necessarily good at keeping track of money, they are lucky in having it come their way, usually unexpectedly. Not averse to sharing with others, they can support family and friends in times of need. They will have to work hard to hold on to it, however; the best solution is usually making good investments, particularly in real estate.

✱5✱
PLUTO ON THE CUSP
OF POWER
(ARIES-TAURUS CUSP)

The danger here is misuse of power. Whether in professional or family settings, these folks are likely to be carried away by power drives, and seek to control or dominate those around them. Dark forces are likely to emerge and destructive behavior result. Pluto's energies should be put to work for more altruistic ends, since such energies could be harnessed for the common good.

✱6✱
PLUTO IN THE WEEK OF
MANIFESTATION
(TAURUS I)

Strong sensuous and sexual feelings are likely to arise with this position. Furthermore, a preoccupation with money, investment and tax issues are usually present as well. These individuals are only interested in results, and too often are unconcerned with how they accomplish their goals. By trampling on the feelings of others they are likely to arouse resentment.

★7★
PLUTO IN THE WEEK OF
THE TEACHER
(TAURUS II)

Severe and judgmental attitudes surface here. The unforgiving side of such individuals can cause them to remember slights or imagined insults for years and at times to be dominated by a desire for reprisal. Learning to let go of such attitudes will be an important step in their self-development. The financial instincts of such people are usually well-developed and can lead to profitable outcomes.

★8★
PLUTO IN THE WEEK OF
THE NATURAL
(TAURUS III)

Emotional outbursts, occasional but serious, are likely to prove a disruptive force in the lives of such people. Not only their own feelings can easily spin out of control, but also the feelings of those with whom they come in contact. Because of their susceptibility to the effects of dark forces, they should practice meditation, yoga or other forms of spiritual training.

★9★
PLUTO ON THE CUSP
OF ENERGY
(TAURUS-GEMINI CUSP)

With such powerful and abundant energies present, the main question is to what ends they are directed – good or bad. It is necessary to adopt a strong ethical position in this respect and also to take the feelings of others into account. A tendency to take advantage of business colleagues and family members should be countered by a more philosophical and humane view of things.

★10★
PLUTO IN THE WEEK
OF FREEDOM
(GEMINI I)

If Pluto's dark energies get out of control here, highly destructive behavior can result. In particular, jealousy, anger and feelings of revenge will have to be guarded against. Fortunately, these emotions are often transitory in nature and are unlikely to stick around very long. When such individuals establish themselves in one location, they are more likely to achieve success.

★11★
PLUTO IN THE WEEK OF
NEW LANGUAGE
(GEMINI II)

Hidden meanings in the verbal and written statements of those with this Pluto position can lead to misunderstandings. Too often ambiguous and likely to send mixed messages, they will have to work hard to make themselves clear to others. By being more direct, they are more likely to arouse trust instead of suspicion.

★12★
PLUTO IN THE WEEK OF
THE SEEKER
(GEMINI III)

A need to burrow deeply into everyday matters characterizes these people. Not content to leave things alone or simply deal with appearances, they may go too far in their investigations and arouse animosity in family members and friends. Their investigative energies are better put to use in objective pursuits, particularly those which do not involve people in their social group.

★13★
PLUTO ON THE CUSP
OF MAGIC
(GEMINI-CANCER CUSP)

Those with this Pluto position are highly seductive individuals, able to get their way in most situations. Their sexual magnetism is high, allowing them to control others and bind them to their desires. Problems with sex and love addictions are likely to surface on both sides. More objectivity will have to be employed if both parties are not to fall victim to possessive feelings.

★14★
PLUTO IN THE WEEK OF
THE EMPATH
(CANCER I)

Emotional manipulation is likely to be a constant theme with Pluto here. An ability to control the feelings of others and a need to do so may lead such people to manipulative behavior, which will ultimately arouse resentment and dependency. Such individuals should detach themselves from the feelings of others and assert a more independent stance by concentrating on their own well-being.

★15★
PLUTO IN THE WEEK OF
THE UNCONVENTIONAL
(CANCER II)

A tendency to secretive behavior and nursing personal grudges can manifest here. Such individuals can despair of ever being understood or accepted, but by going their own way and having the courage of their own convictions, they can be remarkably successful. The sooner they leave the house of their parents in young adulthood, the better, as they cannot develop until they are off on their own.

✴ 16 ✴
PLUTO IN THE WEEK OF
THE PERSUADER
(CANCER III)

The problem here is usually for the other person, since those with Pluto in this position will not be denied. They may be forceful or gently seductive but are able to win the hearts and minds of those they fix their sights on. Able to quickly adjust their tactics to their quarry, chances of escape are usually quite slim, the capture swift and often quite pleasurable.

✴ 17 ✴
PLUTO ON THE CUSP
OF OSCILLATION
(CANCER-LEO CUSP)

Pluto can have a stabilizing effect on this highly volatile cusp. As long as the eruptive forces of the dark planet do not get out of control during manic episodes, these folks can be surprisingly calm and able to go with the flow. Vibrant individuals, they lend liveliness to many proceedings but are also tuned in to the more serious aspects of life.

✴ 18 ✴
PLUTO IN THE WEEK
OF AUTHORITY
(LEO I)

A healthy respect for elders and those in positions of power is characteristic here. Furthermore, those with this Pluto position are not unhappy working as part of a team, in organizations and taking direct orders from superiors. Perhaps this is why they are able to assume command themselves and rise to the top, usually earning the respect of their fellow workers.

✴ 19 ✴
PLUTO IN THE WEEK OF
BALANCED STRENGTH
(LEO II)

Somber moods and depressions should be guarded against here. A tendency to take things too seriously demands a mate or friend who can keep things light and provide the opportunity to have fun. Also, being able to let off steam in physical or athletic pursuits will help them avoid negativity. Prone to worry, these folks need to learn to forget their troubles and to smile at life's ironies.

✴ 20 ✴
PLUTO IN THE WEEK
OF LEADERSHIP
(LEO III)

Strongly dictatorial tendencies can surface here. Those with this Pluto position are frequently at the mercy of their ambitious drives and too likely to sacrifice the well-being of their friends and colleagues to their desire for recognition. At the same time, they are able to hide their true feelings and have difficulty accessing or understanding them.

✴ 21 ✴
PLUTO ON THE CUSP
OF EXPOSURE
(LEO-VIRGO CUSP)

The alternating tendencies of this cusp to hide and reveal are enhanced many-fold by the presence of Pluto here. Truly exhibitionistic tendencies may be followed by periods of secretive behavior and vice-versa. It is as if these people can't make up their minds whether they want to be noticed by others. Learning to seek the middle ground will have a stabilizing effect on their mental health.

✴ 22 ✴
PLUTO IN THE WEEK OF
SYSTEM BUILDERS
(VIRGO I)

Investments often thrive in the hands of these individuals. If they are inclined to save rather than spend, they are capable of making outstanding decisions as to what to do with their money. They can also give good advice on this subject to others, both as amateurs and professionals. Because they recognize the importance of sound finances, they make realistic plans for the future.

✴ 23 ✴
PLUTO IN THE WEEK OF
THE ENIGMA
(VIRGO II)

Cultivating an air of mystery, these folks are not easy to understand nor do they wish to be understood, in many respects. Yet this quality often has the effect of attracting people to them rather than keeping them away. More personally than socially oriented, they tend to value a quiet evening with a few close friends rather than seeking out wider social interaction.

✴ 24 ✴
PLUTO IN THE WEEK OF
THE LITERALIST
(VIRGO III)

Inflexibility is frequently a problem here, which can be reflected in mental or physical symptoms as these individuals get older. Arthritic, back, neck and muscular problems are all too common. Pleasurable forms of exercise and walking in the open air are recommended. Furthermore, remaining open to new ideas and suggestions will aid them in their quest for a healthy lifestyle.

✴ 25 ✴
PLUTO ON THE CUSP OF BEAUTY
(VIRGO-LIBRA CUSP)

A strong attraction to all media is present here. The desire to watch attractive images on television and film and listen to sound recordings is pronounced. Perusal of glossy magazines also has special allure. Such individuals must be careful not to be so swept up in the glamour world of stars and models that they forsake the realities of everyday life.

✴ 26 ✴
PLUTO IN THE WEEK OF THE PERFECTIONIST
(LIBRA I)

Special interest will be bestowed here on projects involving the use of technical equipment to make money or to manage it in one's business endeavors. Bringing critical and logical abilities to bear on financial matters is likely to bring gain to any individual or group involved. Taking human considerations into account is important to provide the counterweight to such activities.

✴ 27 ✴
PLUTO IN THE WEEK OF SOCIETY
(LIBRA II)

The need of these individuals to isolate themselves should be countered by an attempt to take a more active role in the social life around them. A conscious effort will have to be made, however, because if given their preference such people might just as soon decide to stay at home. Joining community organizations and taking an active role in school, church and sporting activities is recommended.

✴ 28 ✴
PLUTO IN THE WEEK OF THEATER
(LIBRA III)

An interest in the darker aspects of life, particularly those connected with conflicts, wars and battles of all sorts is evident in these individuals. They can even encounter problems that do not exist by summoning them up with their active imaginations. Expectation of excitement is characteristic here and does not allow for a dull moment in their lives.

✴ 29 ✴
PLUTO ON THE CUSP OF DRAMA AND CRITICISM
(LIBRA-SCORPIO CUSP)

An interest in political and intellectual matters is characteristic of this Pluto position. Newspapers, radio and TV are frequently consulted for breaking stories, which provide the grist for the mills of rumor, controversy and gossip. Keeping their ears to the ground and adjusting to new directions when warranted is customary here. Neither spiritual matters nor self-development should not be neglected.

✴ 30 ✴
PLUTO IN THE WEEK OF INTENSITY
(SCORPIO I)

These folks have an intense need to investigate and plumb any given subject to its depths. Not one to treat things lightly, such people are curious about almost everything, but are able to focus their energies on one pursuit at a time. Their aggressions and adversarial instincts should not be allowed to get out of hand, however, and they must keep their belligerence in check.

✴ 31 ✴
PLUTO IN THE WEEK OF DEPTH
(SCORPIO II)

The high seriousness accompanying this Pluto position should not be allowed to dominate the entire personality. A feeling of responsibility for the environment, world hunger, and opposition to dictatorial regimes usually surfaces, particularly when helpless animals or human populations are threatened. A love of gardening, swimming, walking in natural settings and consuming fresh food is also characteristic here.

✴ 32 ✴
PLUTO IN THE WEEK OF CHARM
(SCORPIO III)

Care will have to be taken that the seductive powers of such individuals do not get out of hand. Outlandish dress, free sexual behavior, provocative verbal and physical expression are all part of the package. Parents will necessarily have problems with children having this Pluto position if they seek to oppose them directly and not take the time to understand them.

✴ 33 ✴
PLUTO ON THE CUSP OF REVOLUTION
(SCORPIO-SAGITTARIUS CUSP)

All forms of fixed authority invite the rebellion of such individuals, which is likely to be swift and violent. Destructive impulses will not be denied here, although the resulting structures which come into being will probably have their own inherent problems. Group protests are also characteristic here, as the individual's need to protest is subsumed into the larger opposition of the group.

✴ 34 ✴
PLUTO IN THE WEEK
OF INDEPENDENCE
(SAGITTARIUS I)

A feeling of optimism is pervasive here and with it the energy needed to accomplish great tasks. The more explosive aspects of Pluto are tempered and his energies can be effectively harnessed. Still there is a feeling that forces beyond one's control are operating here and that respect should be given to the mighty impersonal forces operating in the universe.

✴ 35 ✴
PLUTO IN THE WEEK OF
THE ORIGINATOR
(SAGITTARIUS II)

A feeling of hopelessness in controlling destructive forces is characteristic here. The darker and difficult side of Pluto makes him recalcitrant and difficult or impossible to bargain with. Unpredictability and a refusal of events to obey historical precedents makes the swirling and explosive energies here unique. Not a time to seek or expect stability. Each unique happening must be dealt with in a special way.

✴ 36 ✴
PLUTO IN THE WEEK
OF THE TITAN
(SAGITTARIUS III)

Individuals with this Pluto position feel insecure and unable to handle earth-shaking events around them. However, many view this as a challenge and will rise to the occasion, showing great bravery. Overcoming fear is crucial to this process and with it a belief that the individual and small dedicated groups can make a difference in the world's destiny.

✴ 37 ✴
PLUTO ON THE CUSP
OF PROPHECY
(SAGITTARIUS-CAPRICORN CUSP)

The nature of the future in an uncertain world is the prime topic during this Pluto placement. Discussions range from the environment to politics to an apocalypse. A feeling grows that the future is not set in stone but that we can do something about it. Procrastination is recognized as the enemy and the need to act sooner rather than later is in the forefront for individuals born here.

✴ 38 ✴
PLUTO IN THE WEEK
OF THE RULER
(CAPRICORN I)

The more severe aspects of Pluto are brought out here. A certain insensitivity to the plight of the needy is apparent and with it a need to control and impose one's will on others. Efforts must be made to understand that the well-being of others is essential to one's own welfare and that we all share the human condition. Insistence on dictatorial attitudes can only yield negative results.

✴ 39 ✴
PLUTO IN THE WEEK
OF DETERMINATION
(CAPRICORN II)

It is not easy to oppose Pluto's pursuits in this position. Such individuals are very prone to the workings of fate and the more forceful of them are relentlessly advancing their own projects. Free will does not seem to play a part here, since such individuals are clearly driven by forces beyond their control. Kindness and sympathy must be achieved through struggle.

✴ 40 ✴
PLUTO IN THE WEEK
OF DOMINANCE
(CAPRICORN III)

One of the most unforgiving and inflexible of Pluto positions. The dark force is ever-present here, seeking to control and subjugate. Fighting such tendencies is possible, but involves great courage, self-awareness, and a strong desire to evolve spiritually. One option is putting the severe Pluto energies in service of highly responsible and effective projects to improve the conditions of life.

✴ 41 ✴
PLUTO ON THE CUSP OF
MYSTERY AND IMAGINATION
(CAPRICORN-AQUARIUS CUSP)

An exciting and vibrant position for Pluto, one which seeks out adventure and new opportunities. Sexual energies are high, but not necessarily leading to biological reproduction. If such energies are overpowering they can be sublimated in sports, martial-arts, body-building, running, swimming and other physical endeavors. Such individuals must find an outlet for their energies or else suffer major frustrations and depressions.

✴ 42 ✴
PLUTO IN THE WEEK
OF GENIUS
(AQUARIUS I) JANUARY 23-30

The powers of Pluto in this week lead to explosive behavior. Lighting-fast decisions and impulsive implementation of such decisions is characteristic here. The energies surrounding this Pluto position are unpredictable and irresistibly powerful, both in constructive and destructive directions. Care must be taken to give serious thought before acting to avoid disaster. True intuition is more productive than sheer impulse.

✴ 43 ✴
PLUTO IN THE WEEK OF
YOUTH AND EASE
(AQUARIUS II)

Pluto shows his lazier and pleasure-loving side here. The joys of the table and bed, as well as all sorts of luxurious cravings and pleasures, surface here. A tendency to put on weight is inevitable, perhaps accompanied by a certain amount of debilitation. Getting work done is difficult, but making money effortlessly is favored. Strong self-discipline is required to keep in shape.

✴ 44 ✴
PLUTO IN THE WEEK
OF ACCEPTANCE
(AQUARIUS III)

A dark, forbidding and mistrustful attitude is strong here, making acceptance of the ideas and personalities of others extremely difficult. Although this can serve the positive end of eliminating unnecessary complications and thinking more practically, one must develop a more open attitude to further self-development. Step-by-step, as the years go by, progress can be made and great lessons learned through becoming more accepting. Learning to share and to give and take are essential to this process.

✴ 45 ✴
PLUTO ON THE CUSP
OF SENSITIVITY
(AQUARIUS-PISCES CUSP)

Cutting oneself off from the world is an ever-present danger here. Through rejections and frustrations in childhood, such individuals may isolate themselves behind an impenetrable barrier. Pluto is powerful in opposition, but the ability to give and receive love must be fostered if full human development is to take place. Learning to show weakness and admit failure is important here.

✴ 46 ✴
PLUTO IN THE WEEK
OF SPIRIT
(PISCES I)

A very advanced position for the dark planet. Interests in philosophy, religion and mystical thought are all abundant here. These energies may lead to advanced spiritual development and also to the development of special powers and abilities. Forsaking practicality, such individuals seek the highest levels of truth and understanding, and investigate hitherto unknown sources of cosmic power.

✴ 47 ✴
PLUTO IN THE WEEK
OF THE LONER
(PISCES II)

Pluto's energies here can lead to great self-understanding and ultimately to self-growth. A need to withdraw from the world and give oneself over to the joys of contemplation and meditation manifests. Such a period could serve as an important time out in the life of an individual or in human history. Through reflection and understanding the active side of life can be renewed in the future.

✴ 48 ✴
PLUTO IN THE WEEK OF
DANCERS AND DREAMERS
(PISCES III)

Pluto's underground and volcanic energies are tempered here and put to positive use in the pursuit of truly cosmic and universal goals. Whether space exploration, investigating higher avenues of thought, or the highest of artistic goals, many miraculous discoveries await the individual and mankind in general with this Pluto position. Full rein should be given to imaginative projects and personal endeavors.

ABOUT THE MOON

Since the moon changes astrological signs every two and a half days and changes Personology periods approximately every 15 hours, you will also have to know your time of birth to find your correct moon position. All times are given in Eastern Standard Time, so you should convert your birthday time to EST. Also remember to convert daylight savings time within Eastern Standard Time if you were born when Daylight Standard Time was in effect.

The tables give you three possibilities for the moon. To choose the column that is correct for you, determine whether the time of your birth was between 12:01 A.M. and 8 A.M., in which case you'd use the number in the first column. If it falls between or 8:01 A.M. and 4 P.M., use the number in the second column; and if it falls between 4:01 P.M. and 12:00 A.M., use the number in the third moon column.

Date & Time	MOON 1 ◖	MOON 2 ◐	MOON 3 ●
APR. 1	2 30	31	31

◖ **MOON 1:**	Between 12:01 A.M. and 8:00 A.M.
◐ **MOON 2:**	Between 8:01 A.M. and 4:00 P.M.
● **MOON 3:**	Between 4:01 P.M. and 12:00 A.M.

HOW TO CONVERT TO EASTERN STANDARD TIME

The times given in the chart are based on American Eastern Standard Time. If you were born in a different time zone, you will need to convert local time to Eastern Standard Time, to get the correct moon position.

If you were born in a locale that uses Pacific Standard Time, Mountain Standard Time or Central Standard Time, you can convert the time to Eastern Standard Time by adding three hours, two hours, or one hour respectively to your time of birth. You need to convert the time before you look up your moon position in the tables that follow.

If you were born elsewhere in the world, you must also convert your time zone to Eastern Standard Time and NOT Greenwich Mean Time.

Don't forget to take Daylight Savings Time into account. Daylight Savings Time is begins for most of the United States at 2 a.m. on the first Sunday of April. Time reverts to standard time at 2 a.m. on the last Sunday of October. In the U.S., each time zone switches at a different time.

What happens if you convert the time and the date gets pushed to the day before, or the day after your actual birthday? Ignore it for everything but the moon position. In other words, use the personology periods for the actual DAY of your birthday, regardless of where the time conversion places the date. In my personology system, someone's birthday is his or her birthday, whereever they are in the world, and it carries that energy.

Again, you only need to do the time conversion so you can get the correct Moon position.

YOU ONLY NEED TO DO
THE TIME CONVERSION SO
YOU CAN GET THE CORRECT
MOON POSITION.

1900-1909

1900s

Greta Garbo

✴ ✴ ✴ BORN SEPTEMBER 18, 1905 ✴ ✴ ✴

> **Brief Bio:** Born Greta Gustafson in Sweden, she was the epitome of the glamorous Hollywood leading lady in the 1930s and '40s, and in her later years, became quite a recluse.

Personology Profile:

SUN IN THE WEEK OF THE LITERALIST
(VIRGO III)

✴

Quite practical and pragmatic, Virgo III's will demand that you keep your word once a promise is made. They tend to judge others quite severely when they do not live up to their expectations. Their extreme capability in most areas marks them as highly dependable and trustworthy. Yet their dramatic flair makes them anything but dull in their approach to life.

MOON IN THE WEEK OF THE TEACHER
(TAURUS II)

✴

Too often those with the moon here think they have it all figured out. They think they are expert psychologists when it comes to matters of human feeling and have many opinions on the subject which they are willing to give away free of charge. Although they are frequently right about others, they do have a classic blind spot when it comes to themselves.

MERCURY IN THE WEEK OF SYSTEM BUILDERS
(VIRGO I)

✴

The power of logic is prominent here and with it the ability to structure daily life in a highly rational manner. Mercury is right at home in this position, bestowing his razor-sharp mental abilities. Care must be taken, however, not to neglect the feelings of others in the name of telling the truth or bringing critical attitudes to bear.

VENUS IN THE WEEK OF LEADERSHIP
(LEO III)

✴

This week lends a certain dignity and high idealism to matters of love. People with this Venus position are likely to idealize their relationship, but not necessarily their partner. Realists, they have a distorted, illusory view of the other person but will do everything they can to keep the relationship going, as long as they believe in it. They must be careful of getting out of touch with reality.

MARS IN THE WEEK OF ORIGINALITY
(SAGITTARIUS II)

✴

Those with Mars here tend to stand out from others and are not good at hiding themselves away. Their unusual nature is often reflected in their clothes, their manner of speech, even in their unpredictable, sudden changes of mood and movement. Irrepressible, there is never a dull moment when they are around; they are highly prized as interesting people by friends and family

JUPITER IN THE WEEK OF FREEDOM
(GEMINI I)

✴

Jupiter feels a bit constricted during this week and so periodic wild outbursts can result in an attempt to free up the personality. Attention to detail even to the point of obsession interferes with Jupiter's broad point of view. Creating a balance between seeing both the proverbial forest and the trees clearly is required here.

SATURN ON THE CUSP OF SENSITIVITY
(AQUARIUS-PISCES CUSP)

*

Extreme introversion is the greatest danger when Saturn is found in this Personology period. Because of hurtful attitudes, perhaps in childhood, feelings may have been repressed out of fear of censure. This may have resulted in bouts of depression. Emotional expression is what is sorely needed and this may be accomplished through the trust gained in love relationships and friendships

URANUS ON THE CUSP OF PROPHECY
(SAGITTARIUS-CAPRICORN CUSP)

*

Uranus is more than happy to use his psychic qualities to look into the crystal ball and divine the future. Individuals with Uranus on this cusp can make accurate predictive statements and their warnings should be heeded. They must, however, learn to trust their intuitions more, since they have probably encountered resistance to their paranormal qualities when growing up.

NEPTUNE IN THE WEEK OF THE EMPATH
(CANCER I)

*

An extreme receptivity to unspoken signals and wishes characterizes this Neptune position. Emotional sensitivity is pronounced and with it a comforting air which others seek out in times of stress. Sympathy for the plight of others should not lead an individual to neglect their own self-interest. A clearer focus on the hard realities of life is needed.

PLUTO IN THE WEEK OF THE SEEKER
(GEMINI III)

*

A need to burrow deeply into everyday matters characterizes these people. Not content to leave things alone or simply deal with appearances, they may go too far in their investigations and arouse animosity in family members and friends. Their investigative energies are better put to use in objective pursuits, particularly those that do not involve people in their social group.

Some Highlights of the Decade 1900-1909

- THE GREAT PARIS EXHIBITION, THE WORLD'S FAIR, OPENS IN PARIS.

- CARRIE NATION, TEMPERANCE ACTIVIST, USES A HATCHET TO SMASH A BAR AT THE CAREY HOTEL IN WICHITA, KANSAS.

- THE GREATEST NATURAL DISASTER IN US HISTORY OCCURS IN GALVESTON, TEXAS, FLOODING THE CITY UNDER 15 FEET OF WATER.

- IN RESPONSE TO A CALL FOR AN OPEN DOOR POLICY, THOUSANDS OF CHINESE LAY SIEGE TO FOREIGN MISSION COMPOUNDS IN BEIJING, IN WHAT BECAME KNOWN AS THE "BOXER REBELLION." IT WAS AN ATTEMPT TO EXPEL "FOREIGN DEVILS."

- SIGMUND FREUD'S *THE INTERPRETATION OF DREAMS* IS PUBLISHED IN 1911.

1900

January

February

Date & Time	SUN	MOON 1	MOON 2	MOON 3	MERCURY	VENUS	MARS	JUPITER	SATURN	URANUS	NEPTUNE	PLUTO
JAN. 1	38	38	38	39	36	42	39	33	37	34	12	11
JAN. 2	38	40	40	41	36	42	39	33	37	34	12	11
JAN. 3	39	42	42	43	36	42	39	33	37	34	12	11
JAN. 4	39	44	44	45	36	42	39	33	37	34	12	11
JAN. 5	39	46	46	47	36	43	39	33	37	34	12	11
JAN. 6	39	47	48	1	36	43	39	33	37	34	12	11
JAN. 7	39	1	2	3	37	43	39	33	37	34	12	11
JAN. 8	39	3	4	4	37	43	40	33	37	34	12	11
JAN. 9	39	5	6	6	37	43	40	33	37	34	12	11
JAN. 10	40	7	7	8	37	43	40	33	37	34	12	11
JAN. 11	40	9	9	10	37	44	40	33	37	34	12	11
JAN. 12	40	10	11	11	38	44	40	33	37	34	12	11
JAN. 13	40	12	13	13	38	44	40	33	37	34	12	11
JAN. 14	40	14	14	15	38	44	40	33	37	34	12	11
JAN. 15	40	15	16	16	38	44	40	33	37	34	12	11
JAN. 16	40	17	18	18	38	44	40	33	37	34	12	11
JAN. 17	41	19	19	20	39	44	40	34	37	34	12	11
JAN. 18	41	20	21	21	39	45	41	34	37	34	12	11
JAN. 19	41	22	22	23	39	45	41	34	37	34	12	11
JAN. 20	41	23	24	24	39	45	41	34	37	34	12	11
JAN. 21	41	25	25	26	39	45	41	34	37	34	12	11
JAN. 22	41	27	27	28	40	45	41	34	37	34	12	11
JAN. 23	42	28	29	29	40	45	41	34	37	34	12	11
JAN. 24	42	30	30	31	40	46	41	34	37	34	12	11
JAN. 25	42	31	32	33	40	46	41	34	37	34	12	11
JAN. 26	42	33	34	34	40	46	41	34	37	34	12	11
JAN. 27	42	35	36	36	41	46	42	34	37	34	12	11
JAN. 28	42	37	37	38	41	46	42	34	37	34	12	11
JAN. 29	42	39	39	40	41	46	42	34	37	34	12	11
JAN. 30	42	41	41	42	41	47	42	34	37	35	12	11
JAN. 31	43	43	43	44	42	47	42	34	37	35	12	11

Date & Time	SUN	MOON 1	MOON 2	MOON 3	MERCURY	VENUS	MARS	JUPITER	SATURN	URANUS	NEPTUNE	PLUTO
FEB. 1	43	45	45	46	42	47	42	34	37	35	12	11
FEB. 2	43	47	47	48	42	47	42	34	37	35	12	11
FEB. 3	43	1	1	2	42	47	42	34	37	35	12	11
FEB. 4	43	3	3	4	42	47	42	34	37	35	12	11
FEB. 5	43	5	5	6	43	48	42	34	37	35	12	11
FEB. 6	43	6	7	8	43	48	43	34	37	35	12	11
FEB. 7	43	8	9	9	43	48	43	34	37	35	12	11
FEB. 8	44	10	11	11	43	48	43	34	37	35	12	11
FEB. 9	44	12	12	13	44	48	43	34	37	35	12	11
FEB. 10	44	13	14	14	44	48	43	34	37	35	12	11
FEB. 11	44	15	15	16	44	1	43	34	37	35	12	11
FEB. 12	44	17	17	18	44	1	43	34	37	35	12	11
FEB. 13	44	18	19	19	45	1	43	34	37	35	12	11
FEB. 14	44	20	20	21	45	1	43	34	37	35	12	11
FEB. 15	44	21	22	22	45	1	44	34	37	35	12	11
FEB. 16	45	23	23	24	45	1	44	34	37	35	12	11
FEB. 17	45	25	25	26	46	2	44	34	37	35	12	11
FEB. 18	45	26	27	27	46	2	44	34	37	35	12	11
FEB. 19	45	28	28	29	46	2	44	34	37	35	12	11
FEB. 20	45	29	30	30	46	2	44	34	37	35	12	11
FEB. 21	45	31	32	32	47	2	44	34	37	35	12	11
FEB. 22	45	33	33	34	47	2	44	34	37	35	12	11
FEB. 23	46	34	35	36	47	3	44	34	37	35	12	11
FEB. 24	46	36	37	37	47	3	44	34	37	35	12	11
FEB. 25	46	38	39	39	47	3	45	34	37	35	12	11
FEB. 26	46	40	40	41	48	3	45	34	37	35	12	11
FEB. 27	46	42	42	43	48	3	45	34	37	35	12	11
FEB. 28	46	44	44	45	48	3	45	34	37	35	12	11

MOON 1 ☾ 12:01 A.M. TO 8:00 A.M.   **MOON 2** ◑ 8:01 A.M. TO 4:00 P.M.   **MOON 3** ● 4:01 P.M. TO 12:00 A.M.
Use only one "moon" number. Choose the column closest to your time of birth. If your place of birth is not on Eastern Standard Time, be sure to read "How to Convert to Eastern Standard Time" at the beginning of this section.

Date & Time	SUN	MOON 1	MOON 2	MOON 3	MERCURY	VENUS	MARS	JUPITER	SATURN	URANUS	NEPTUNE	PLUTO
MAY 1	6	27	27	28	4	6	21	39	39	35	13	11
MAY 2	6	28	29	29	5	6	21	39	39	35	13	11
MAY 3	7	30	30	31	5	7	21	39	39	35	13	11
MAY 4	7	31	32	32	5	7	21	39	39	35	13	11
MAY 5	7	33	33	34	5	7	21	39	39	35	13	11
MAY 6	7	35	35	36	6	7	21	39	39	35	13	11
MAY 7	7	36	37	37	6	7	21	39	39	35	13	11
MAY 8	7	38	38	39	6	7	21	39	39	35	13	11
MAY 9	7	39	40	41	6	8	21	39	39	35	13	11
MAY 10	7	41	42	42	7	8	21	39	39	35	13	11
MAY 11	8	43	44	44	7	8	21	39	39	35	13	11
MAY 12	8	45	45	46	7	8	21	39	39	35	13	11
MAY 13	8	47	47	48	8	8	21	39	39	35	13	11
MAY 14	8	1	1	2	8	8	21	39	39	35	13	11
MAY 15	8	2	3	4	8	9	21	39	39	35	13	11
MAY 16	8	4	5	6	8	9	21	39	39	35	13	11
MAY 17	8	6	7	8	9	9	21	39	39	35	13	11
MAY 18	8	8	9	10	9	9	21	39	39	35	13	11
MAY 19	9	10	11	12	9	9	21	39	39	35	13	11
MAY 20	9	12	13	14	10	9	21	39	39	35	13	11
MAY 21	9	14	15	16	10	10	21	39	39	35	13	11
MAY 22	9	16	17	17	10	10	22	39	39	35	13	11
MAY 23	9	18	19	19	10	10	22	39	39	35	13	11
MAY 24	9	20	20	21	11	10	22	39	39	35	13	11
MAY 25	10	21	22	22	11	10	22	39	39	35	13	11
MAY 26	10	23	24	24	11	10	22	39	39	35	13	11
MAY 27	10	25	25	26	12	11	22	39	39	35	13	11
MAY 28	10	26	27	27	12	11	22	39	39	35	13	11
MAY 29	10	28	28	29	12	11	22	39	39	35	13	11
MAY 30	10	29	30	30	12	11	22	39	39	35	13	11
MAY 31	10	31	31	32	13	11	22	39	39	35	13	11

Date & Time	SUN	MOON 1	MOON 2	MOON 3	MERCURY	VENUS	MARS	JUPITER	SATURN	URANUS	NEPTUNE	PLUTO
JUN. 1	10	33	33	34	13	11	22	39	39	35	13	11
JUN. 2	10	34	35	35	13	12	22	38	39	35	13	11
JUN. 3	11	36	36	37	13	12	22	38	39	35	13	11
JUN. 4	11	37	38	39	13	12	22	38	39	35	13	11
JUN. 5	11	39	40	40	14	12	22	38	39	35	13	11
JUN. 6	11	41	41	42	14	12	22	38	39	35	13	11
JUN. 7	11	43	43	44	14	12	22	38	39	35	13	11
JUN. 8	11	44	45	46	14	13	22	38	39	35	13	11
JUN. 9	11	46	47	47	14	13	23	38	39	35	13	11
JUN. 10	11	48	1	1	15	13	23	38	39	35	13	11
JUN. 11	12	2	2	3	15	13	23	38	39	35	13	11
JUN. 12	12	4	4	5	15	13	23	38	39	35	13	11
JUN. 13	12	6	6	7	15	13	23	38	39	35	13	11
JUN. 14	12	8	8	9	15	14	23	38	39	35	13	11
JUN. 15	12	10	10	11	15	14	23	38	39	35	13	11
JUN. 16	12	12	12	13	15	14	23	38	39	35	13	11
JUN. 17	12	13	14	15	16	14	23	38	39	35	13	11
JUN. 18	12	15	16	17	16	14	23	38	39	35	13	11
JUN. 19	13	17	18	18	16	14	23	38	39	35	13	11
JUN. 20	13	19	20	20	16	15	23	38	39	35	13	11
JUN. 21	13	21	21	22	16	15	23	38	39	35	13	11
JUN. 22	13	22	23	24	16	15	23	38	39	35	13	11
JUN. 23	13	24	25	25	16	15	23	38	39	35	13	11
JUN. 24	13	26	26	27	16	15	24	38	39	35	13	11
JUN. 25	14	27	28	28	16	15	24	38	39	35	13	11
JUN. 26	14	29	29	30	16	16	24	38	39	35	13	11
JUN. 27	14	30	31	32	16	16	24	38	39	35	13	11
JUN. 28	14	32	33	33	16	16	24	38	39	35	13	11
JUN. 29	14	34	34	35	16	16	24	38	39	35	13	11
JUN. 30	14	35	36	36	16	16	24	38	39	35	13	11

MOON 1 ◖ 12:01 A.M. TO 8:00 A.M. **MOON 2** ◑ 8:01 A.M. TO 4:00 P.M. **MOON 3** ● 4:01 P.M. TO 12:00 A.M.
Use only one "moon" number. Choose the column closest to your time of birth. If your place of birth is not on
Eastern Standard Time, be sure to read "How to Convert to Eastern Standard Time" at the beginning of this section.

1900

May

June

Date & Time	SUN	MOON 1	MOON 2	MOON 3	MERCURY	VENUS	MARS	JUPITER	SATURN	URANUS	NEPTUNE	PLUTO
MAY 1	6	10	10	11	3	12	3	34	38	35	12	11
MAY 2	6	12	12	13	3	13	3	34	38	35	12	11
MAY 3	7	13	14	15	3	13	4	34	38	35	12	11
MAY 4	7	15	16	16	4	13	4	34	38	35	12	11
MAY 5	7	17	17	18	4	13	4	34	38	35	12	11
MAY 6	7	18	19	20	4	13	4	34	38	35	12	11
MAY 7	7	20	21	21	4	13	4	34	38	34	12	11
MAY 8	7	22	22	23	4	13	4	34	38	34	12	11
MAY 9	7	23	24	24	5	13	4	34	38	34	12	11
MAY 10	7	25	25	26	5	14	4	34	38	34	12	11
MAY 11	8	26	27	27	5	14	4	34	38	34	12	11
MAY 12	8	28	29	29	5	14	4	34	38	34	12	11
MAY 13	8	30	30	31	5	14	5	34	38	34	12	11
MAY 14	8	31	32	32	6	14	5	34	38	34	12	11
MAY 15	8	33	34	34	6	14	5	34	38	34	12	11
MAY 16	8	35	35	36	6	14	5	34	38	34	12	11
MAY 17	8	37	37	38	6	14	5	34	38	34	12	11
MAY 18	8	38	39	39	7	14	5	34	38	34	12	11
MAY 19	9	40	41	41	7	14	5	34	38	34	12	11
MAY 20	9	42	43	43	7	15	5	34	38	34	12	11
MAY 21	9	44	44	45	7	15	5	34	37	34	12	11
MAY 22	9	46	46	47	8	15	6	34	37	34	12	11
MAY 23	9	48	48	1	8	15	6	34	37	34	12	11
MAY 24	9	1	2	3	8	15	6	34	37	34	12	11
MAY 25	10	3	4	5	9	15	6	34	37	34	12	11
MAY 26	10	5	6	7	9	15	6	34	37	34	12	11
MAY 27	10	7	8	8	9	15	6	34	37	34	12	11
MAY 28	10	9	10	10	9	15	6	34	37	34	12	11
MAY 29	10	11	12	12	10	15	6	34	37	34	12	11
MAY 30	10	13	13	14	10	15	6	34	37	34	12	11
MAY 31	10	15	15	16	10	16	6	34	37	34	12	11

Date & Time	SUN	MOON 1	MOON 2	MOON 3	MERCURY	VENUS	MARS	JUPITER	SATURN	URANUS	NEPTUNE	PLUTO
JUN. 1	10	16	17	17	11	16	6	34	37	34	12	11
JUN. 2	10	18	18	19	11	16	7	34	37	34	12	11
JUN. 3	11	20	20	21	11	16	7	34	37	34	12	11
JUN. 4	11	21	22	22	12	16	7	34	37	34	12	11
JUN. 5	11	23	23	24	12	16	7	34	37	34	12	11
JUN. 6	11	24	25	25	12	16	7	34	37	34	12	11
JUN. 7	11	26	26	27	12	16	7	34	37	34	12	11
JUN. 8	11	27	28	29	13	16	7	34	37	34	12	11
JUN. 9	11	29	30	30	13	16	7	34	37	34	12	11
JUN. 10	11	31	31	32	13	16	7	34	37	34	12	11
JUN. 11	12	32	33	33	13	16	7	34	37	34	12	11
JUN. 12	12	34	35	35	14	16	8	34	37	34	12	11
JUN. 13	12	36	37	37	14	16	8	33	37	34	13	11
JUN. 14	12	38	38	39	14	16	8	33	37	34	13	11
JUN. 15	12	40	40	41	14	16	8	33	37	34	13	11
JUN. 16	12	41	42	43	15	16	8	33	37	34	13	11
JUN. 17	12	43	44	45	15	16	8	33	37	34	13	11
JUN. 18	12	45	46	47	15	16	8	33	37	34	13	11
JUN. 19	13	47	48	48	15	16	8	33	37	34	13	11
JUN. 20	13	1	2	2	16	16	8	33	37	34	13	11
JUN. 21	13	3	4	4	16	16	8	33	37	34	13	11
JUN. 22	13	5	5	6	16	16	8	33	37	34	13	11
JUN. 23	13	7	7	8	16	16	9	33	37	34	13	11
JUN. 24	13	9	9	10	16	16	9	33	37	34	13	11
JUN. 25	14	10	11	12	17	16	9	33	37	34	13	11
JUN. 26	14	12	13	13	17	16	9	33	37	34	13	11
JUN. 27	14	14	14	15	17	16	9	33	37	34	13	11
JUN. 28	14	16	16	17	17	16	9	33	37	34	13	11
JUN. 29	14	17	18	18	17	16	9	33	37	34	13	11
JUN. 30	14	19	19	20	17	16	9	33	37	34	13	11

MOON 1 ◗ 12:01 A.M. TO 8:00 A.M.   **MOON 2** ◑ 8:01 A.M. TO 4:00 P.M.   **MOON 3** ● 4:01 P.M. TO 12:00 A.M.
Use only one "moon" number. Choose the column closest to your time of birth. If your place of birth is not on Eastern Standard Time, be sure to read "How to Convert to Eastern Standard Time" at the beginning of this section.

Date & Time	SUN	MOON 1	MOON 2	MOON 3	MERCURY	VENUS	MARS	JUPITER	SATURN	URANUS	NEPTUNE	PLUTO
JUL. 1	14	21	21	22	18	16	9	33	37	34	13	11
JUL. 2	14	22	23	23	18	16	9	33	37	34	13	11
JUL. 3	15	24	24	25	18	15	10	33	37	34	13	11
JUL. 4	15	25	26	26	18	15	10	33	37	34	13	11
JUL. 5	15	27	27	28	18	15	10	33	37	34	13	11
JUL. 6	15	29	29	30	18	15	10	33	37	34	13	11
JUL. 7	15	30	31	31	18	15	10	33	37	34	13	11
JUL. 8	15	32	32	33	18	15	10	33	37	34	13	11
JUL. 9	15	34	34	35	19	15	10	33	37	34	13	11
JUL. 10	15	35	36	36	19	15	10	33	37	34	13	11
JUL. 11	16	37	38	38	19	15	10	33	37	34	13	11
JUL. 12	16	39	40	40	19	15	10	33	37	34	13	11
JUL. 13	16	41	41	42	19	15	10	33	37	34	13	11
JUL. 14	16	43	43	44	19	15	11	33	37	34	13	11
JUL. 15	16	45	45	46	19	15	11	33	37	34	13	11
JUL. 16	16	47	47	48	19	14	11	33	37	34	13	11
JUL. 17	16	1	1	2	19	14	11	33	37	34	13	11
JUL. 18	16	3	3	4	19	14	11	33	37	34	13	11
JUL. 19	17	4	5	6	19	14	11	33	37	34	13	11
JUL. 20	17	6	7	7	19	14	11	33	37	34	13	11
JUL. 21	17	8	9	9	19	14	11	33	37	34	13	11
JUL. 22	17	10	10	11	19	14	11	33	37	34	13	11
JUL. 23	17	12	12	13	19	14	11	33	37	34	13	11
JUL. 24	17	13	14	15	19	14	11	33	37	34	13	11
JUL. 25	17	15	16	16	19	14	12	33	37	34	13	11
JUL. 26	18	17	17	18	19	14	12	33	37	34	13	11
JUL. 27	18	18	19	20	19	14	12	33	37	34	13	11
JUL. 28	18	20	21	21	19	14	12	33	37	34	13	11
JUL. 29	18	22	22	23	18	14	12	33	37	34	13	11
JUL. 30	18	23	24	24	18	14	12	33	37	34	13	11
JUL. 31	18	25	25	26	18	14	12	33	37	34	13	11

Date & Time	SUN	MOON 1	MOON 2	MOON 3	MERCURY	VENUS	MARS	JUPITER	SATURN	URANUS	NEPTUNE	PLUTO
AUG. 1	18	26	27	28	18	14	12	33	37	34	13	11
AUG. 2	18	28	29	29	18	14	12	33	37	34	13	11
AUG. 3	19	30	30	31	18	14	12	33	37	34	13	11
AUG. 4	19	31	32	32	18	14	12	33	37	34	13	11
AUG. 5	19	33	33	34	18	14	13	33	37	34	13	11
AUG. 6	19	35	35	36	18	14	13	33	37	34	13	11
AUG. 7	19	36	37	38	18	14	13	33	37	34	13	11
AUG. 8	19	38	39	39	18	14	13	33	37	34	13	11
AUG. 9	19	40	41	41	18	14	13	33	37	34	13	11
AUG. 10	19	42	43	43	17	14	13	33	37	34	13	11
AUG. 11	20	44	45	45	17	14	13	33	37	34	13	11
AUG. 12	20	46	47	47	17	14	13	33	37	34	13	11
AUG. 13	20	48	1	1	17	14	13	33	37	34	13	11
AUG. 14	20	2	3	3	18	14	13	33	37	34	13	11
AUG. 15	20	4	5	5	18	15	13	33	37	34	13	11
AUG. 16	20	6	6	7	18	15	14	33	37	34	13	11
AUG. 17	20	8	8	9	18	15	14	33	37	34	13	11
AUG. 18	20	9	10	11	18	15	14	33	37	34	13	11
AUG. 19	21	11	12	12	18	15	14	33	37	34	13	11
AUG. 20	21	13	14	14	18	15	14	33	37	34	13	11
AUG. 21	21	15	15	16	18	15	14	33	37	34	13	11
AUG. 22	21	16	17	17	18	15	14	33	37	34	13	11
AUG. 23	21	18	19	19	19	15	14	33	37	34	13	11
AUG. 24	21	20	20	21	19	15	14	33	37	34	13	11
AUG. 25	21	21	22	22	19	15	14	33	37	34	13	11
AUG. 26	22	23	23	24	19	15	14	33	37	34	13	11
AUG. 27	22	24	25	25	19	16	14	33	37	34	13	11
AUG. 28	22	26	27	27	20	16	15	33	37	34	13	11
AUG. 29	22	28	28	29	20	16	15	33	37	34	13	11
AUG. 30	22	29	30	30	20	16	15	33	37	34	13	11
AUG. 31	22	31	31	32	20	16	15	33	37	34	13	11

MOON 1 ☽ 12:01 A.M. TO 8:00 A.M.   **MOON 2** ◑ 8:01 A.M. TO 4:00 P.M.   **MOON 3** ● 4:01 P.M. TO 12:00 A.M.

Use only one "moon" number. Choose the column closest to your time of birth. If your place of birth is not on Eastern Standard Time, be sure to read "How to Convert to Eastern Standard Time" at the beginning of this section.

1900

September

Date & Time	SUN	MOON 1	MOON 2	MOON 3	MERCURY	VENUS	MARS	JUPITER	SATURN	URANUS	NEPTUNE	PLUTO
SEP. 1	22	32	33	33	21	16	15	33	37	34	13	11
SEP. 2	22	34	35	35	21	16	15	33	37	34	13	11
SEP. 3	23	36	36	37	21	16	15	33	37	34	13	11
SEP. 4	23	37	38	39	21	16	15	33	37	34	13	11
SEP. 5	23	39	40	41	22	17	15	33	37	34	13	11
SEP. 6	23	41	42	42	22	17	15	33	37	34	13	11
SEP. 7	23	43	44	44	22	17	15	33	37	34	13	11
SEP. 8	23	45	46	46	22	17	15	33	37	34	13	11
SEP. 9	23	47	48	48	23	17	16	33	37	34	13	11
SEP. 10	23	1	2	2	23	17	16	33	37	34	13	11
SEP. 11	24	3	4	4	23	17	16	33	37	34	13	11
SEP. 12	24	5	6	6	23	17	16	33	37	34	13	11
SEP. 13	24	7	8	8	24	17	16	34	37	34	13	11
SEP. 14	24	9	10	10	24	18	16	34	37	34	13	11
SEP. 15	24	11	11	12	24	18	16	34	37	34	13	11
SEP. 16	24	13	13	14	24	18	16	34	37	34	13	11
SEP. 17	24	14	15	15	25	18	16	34	37	34	13	11
SEP. 18	24	16	17	17	25	18	16	34	37	34	13	11
SEP. 19	25	18	18	19	25	18	16	34	37	34	13	11
SEP. 20	25	19	20	20	25	18	16	34	37	34	13	11
SEP. 21	25	21	21	22	25	19	17	34	37	34	13	11
SEP. 22	25	22	23	23	26	19	17	34	37	34	13	11
SEP. 23	25	24	25	25	26	19	17	34	37	34	13	11
SEP. 24	25	26	26	27	26	19	17	34	37	34	13	11
SEP. 25	26	27	28	28	26	19	17	34	37	34	13	11
SEP. 26	26	29	29	30	27	19	17	34	37	34	13	11
SEP. 27	26	30	31	31	27	19	17	34	37	34	13	11
SEP. 28	26	32	32	33	27	19	17	34	37	34	13	11
SEP. 29	26	34	34	35	27	20	17	34	37	34	13	11
SEP. 30	26	35	36	36	27	20	17	34	37	34	13	11

October

Date & Time	SUN	MOON 1	MOON 2	MOON 3	MERCURY	VENUS	MARS	JUPITER	SATURN	URANUS	NEPTUNE	PLUTO
OCT. 1	26	37	37	38	28	20	17	34	37	34	13	11
OCT. 2	26	39	39	40	28	20	17	34	37	34	13	11
OCT. 3	27	40	41	42	28	20	17	34	37	34	13	11
OCT. 4	27	42	43	44	28	20	18	34	37	34	13	11
OCT. 5	27	44	45	46	29	20	18	34	37	34	13	11
OCT. 6	27	46	47	48	29	21	18	34	37	34	13	11
OCT. 7	27	48	1	2	29	21	18	34	37	34	13	11
OCT. 8	27	2	3	4	29	21	18	34	37	34	13	11
OCT. 9	27	4	5	6	29	21	18	34	37	34	13	11
OCT. 10	27	6	7	8	30	21	18	34	37	34	13	11
OCT. 11	28	8	9	10	30	21	18	34	37	34	13	11
OCT. 12	28	10	11	11	30	22	18	34	37	34	13	11
OCT. 13	28	12	13	13	30	22	18	34	37	34	13	11
OCT. 14	28	14	14	15	30	22	18	34	37	34	13	11
OCT. 15	28	16	16	17	30	22	18	34	37	34	13	11
OCT. 16	28	17	18	18	31	22	18	34	37	34	13	11
OCT. 17	28	19	19	20	31	22	19	34	37	34	13	11
OCT. 18	28	20	21	22	31	22	19	34	37	34	13	11
OCT. 19	29	22	23	23	31	23	19	34	37	34	13	11
OCT. 20	29	24	24	25	31	23	19	34	37	34	13	11
OCT. 21	29	25	26	26	32	23	19	34	37	34	13	11
OCT. 22	29	27	27	28	32	23	19	34	37	34	13	11
OCT. 23	29	28	29	29	32	23	19	34	37	34	13	11
OCT. 24	29	30	30	31	32	23	19	34	37	34	13	11
OCT. 25	29	32	32	33	32	23	19	34	37	34	13	11
OCT. 26	30	33	34	34	32	24	19	34	37	34	13	11
OCT. 27	30	35	35	36	32	24	19	34	37	34	13	11
OCT. 28	30	36	37	38	33	24	19	35	37	34	13	11
OCT. 29	30	38	39	39	33	24	19	35	37	34	13	11
OCT. 30	30	40	41	41	33	24	19	35	37	34	13	11
OCT. 31	30	42	42	43	33	24	20	35	37	34	13	11

MOON 1 ◐ 12:01 A.M. TO 8:00 A.M.   **MOON 2** ◑ 8:01 A.M. TO 4:00 P.M.   **MOON 3** ● 4:01 P.M. TO 12:00 A.M.

Use only one "moon" number. Choose the column closest to your time of birth. If your place of birth is not on Eastern Standard Time, be sure to read "How to Convert to Eastern Standard Time" at the beginning of this section.

1900

November

Date & Time	SUN ☉	MOON 1 ◗	MOON 2 ◑	MOON 3 ●	MERCURY	VENUS	MARS	JUPITER	SATURN	URANUS	NEPTUNE	PLUTO
NOV. 1	30	44	44	45	33	25	20	35	37	34	13	11
NOV. 2	30	45	46	47	33	25	20	35	37	34	13	11
NOV. 3	31	47	48	1	33	25	20	35	37	34	13	11
NOV. 4	31	1	2	3	34	25	20	35	37	34	13	11
NOV. 5	31	3	4	5	34	25	20	35	37	34	13	11
NOV. 6	31	5	6	7	34	25	20	35	37	34	13	11
NOV. 7	31	7	8	9	34	25	20	35	37	34	13	11
NOV. 8	31	9	10	11	34	26	20	35	37	34	13	11
NOV. 9	31	11	12	12	34	26	20	35	37	34	13	11
NOV. 10	31	13	14	14	34	26	20	35	37	34	13	11
NOV. 11	31	15	15	16	34	26	20	35	37	34	13	11
NOV. 12	32	17	17	18	34	26	20	35	37	34	13	11
NOV. 13	32	18	19	19	34	26	20	35	37	34	13	11
NOV. 14	32	20	21	21	34	27	20	35	37	34	13	11
NOV. 15	32	22	22	23	34	27	20	35	37	34	13	11
NOV. 16	32	23	24	24	33	27	21	35	37	35	13	11
NOV. 17	32	25	25	26	33	27	21	35	37	35	13	11
NOV. 18	32	26	27	27	33	27	21	35	37	35	13	11
NOV. 19	33	28	28	29	33	27	21	35	37	35	13	11
NOV. 20	33	30	30	31	33	28	21	35	37	35	13	11
NOV. 21	33	31	32	32	33	28	21	35	37	35	13	11
NOV. 22	33	33	33	34	32	28	21	35	37	35	13	11
NOV. 23	33	34	35	36	32	28	21	35	37	35	13	11
NOV. 24	33	36	37	37	32	28	21	35	37	35	13	11
NOV. 25	34	38	38	39	32	28	21	35	37	35	13	11
NOV. 26	34	40	40	41	32	29	21	35	37	35	13	11
NOV. 27	34	41	42	42	32	29	21	35	37	35	13	11
NOV. 28	34	43	44	44	32	29	21	35	37	35	13	11
NOV. 29	34	45	46	46	32	29	21	35	37	35	13	11
NOV. 30	34	47	47	48	32	29	21	35	38	35	13	11

December

Date & Time	SUN ☉	MOON 1 ◗	MOON 2 ◑	MOON 3 ●	MERCURY	VENUS	MARS	JUPITER	SATURN	URANUS	NEPTUNE	PLUTO
DEC. 1	34	1	1	2	32	29	21	35	38	35	13	11
DEC. 2	34	3	3	4	32	30	21	36	38	35	13	11
DEC. 3	35	5	5	6	32	30	21	36	38	35	13	11
DEC. 4	35	7	7	8	32	30	22	36	38	35	13	11
DEC. 5	35	8	9	10	32	30	22	36	38	35	13	11
DEC. 6	35	10	11	12	32	30	22	36	38	35	13	11
DEC. 7	35	12	13	14	32	30	22	36	38	35	13	11
DEC. 8	35	14	15	15	32	30	22	36	38	35	13	11
DEC. 9	35	16	17	17	32	31	22	36	38	35	13	11
DEC. 10	35	18	18	19	33	31	22	36	38	35	13	11
DEC. 11	36	19	20	20	33	31	22	36	38	35	13	11
DEC. 12	36	21	22	22	33	31	22	36	38	35	13	11
DEC. 13	36	23	23	24	33	31	22	36	38	35	13	11
DEC. 14	36	24	25	25	33	31	22	36	38	35	13	11
DEC. 15	36	26	26	27	33	32	22	36	38	35	13	11
DEC. 16	36	27	28	28	34	32	22	36	38	35	13	11
DEC. 17	36	29	30	30	34	32	22	36	38	35	13	11
DEC. 18	36	31	31	32	34	32	22	36	38	35	13	11
DEC. 19	37	32	33	33	34	32	22	36	38	35	13	11
DEC. 20	37	34	34	35	34	32	22	36	38	35	13	11
DEC. 21	37	36	36	37	35	33	22	36	38	35	13	11
DEC. 22	37	37	38	38	35	33	22	36	38	35	13	11
DEC. 23	37	39	40	40	35	33	22	36	38	35	13	11
DEC. 24	37	41	41	42	35	33	22	36	38	35	13	11
DEC. 25	37	43	43	44	35	33	22	36	38	35	13	11
DEC. 26	38	45	45	46	35	33	22	36	38	35	13	11
DEC. 27	38	46	47	48	36	34	22	36	38	35	13	11
DEC. 28	38	48	1	2	36	34	22	36	38	35	13	11
DEC. 29	38	2	3	3	36	34	22	36	38	35	13	11
DEC. 30	38	4	5	5	36	34	22	36	38	35	13	11
DEC. 31	38	6	7	7	36	34	23	36	38	35	13	11

MOON 1 ◗ 12:01 A.M. TO 8:00 A.M.   **MOON 2** ◑ 8:01 A.M. TO 4:00 P.M.   **MOON 3** ● 4:01 P.M. TO 12:00 A.M.

Use only one "moon" number. Choose the column closest to your time of birth. If your place of birth is not on Eastern Standard Time, be sure to read "How to Convert to Eastern Standard Time" at the beginning of this section.

1901

January ☆ ★ ☆

Date & Time	SUN	MOON 1	MOON 2	MOON 3	MERCURY	VENUS	MARS	JUPITER	SATURN	URANUS	NEPTUNE	PLUTO
JAN. 1	38	8	8	9	37	34	23	36	38	35	13	11
JAN. 2	38	10	10	11	37	35	23	36	38	35	13	11
JAN. 3	39	12	12	13	37	35	23	36	38	35	13	11
JAN. 4	39	13	14	15	37	35	23	37	38	35	13	11
JAN. 5	39	15	16	16	38	35	23	37	38	35	13	11
JAN. 6	39	17	18	18	38	35	23	37	38	35	13	11
JAN. 7	39	19	19	20	38	35	23	37	38	35	13	11
JAN. 8	39	20	21	22	38	36	23	37	38	35	13	11
JAN. 9	39	22	23	23	38	36	23	37	38	35	13	11
JAN. 10	40	24	24	25	39	36	23	37	38	35	13	11
JAN. 11	40	25	26	26	39	36	23	37	38	35	13	11
JAN. 12	40	27	27	28	39	36	23	37	38	35	13	11
JAN. 13	40	28	29	30	39	36	23	37	38	35	13	11
JAN. 14	40	30	31	31	39	37	23	37	38	35	13	11
JAN. 15	40	32	32	33	40	37	23	37	38	35	13	11
JAN. 16	40	33	34	34	40	37	23	37	38	35	13	11
JAN. 17	41	35	35	36	40	37	23	37	38	35	13	11
JAN. 18	41	37	37	38	40	37	23	37	38	35	13	11
JAN. 19	41	38	39	40	41	37	23	37	38	35	13	11
JAN. 20	41	40	41	41	41	38	23	37	38	35	13	11
JAN. 21	41	42	43	43	41	38	23	37	38	35	13	11
JAN. 22	41	44	45	45	41	38	23	37	38	35	13	11
JAN. 23	42	46	47	47	41	38	23	37	38	35	13	11
JAN. 24	42	48	48	1	42	38	23	37	38	35	13	11
JAN. 25	42	2	2	3	42	38	23	37	38	35	13	11
JAN. 26	42	4	4	5	42	39	22	37	38	35	13	11
JAN. 27	42	5	6	7	42	39	22	37	38	35	13	11
JAN. 28	42	7	8	9	43	39	22	37	38	35	13	11
JAN. 29	42	9	10	10	43	39	22	37	38	35	13	11
JAN. 30	42	11	12	12	43	39	22	37	38	35	13	11
JAN. 31	43	13	13	14	43	39	22	37	38	35	13	11

February ☆ ★ ☆

Date & Time	SUN	MOON 1	MOON 2	MOON 3	MERCURY	VENUS	MARS	JUPITER	SATURN	URANUS	NEPTUNE	PLUTO
FEB. 1	43	15	15	16	43	40	22	37	38	35	13	11
FEB. 2	43	16	17	18	44	40	22	37	38	35	13	11
FEB. 3	43	18	19	19	44	40	22	37	38	35	13	11
FEB. 4	43	20	20	21	44	40	22	37	39	35	13	11
FEB. 5	43	21	22	23	44	40	22	37	39	35	13	11
FEB. 6	43	23	24	24	45	40	22	37	39	35	13	11
FEB. 7	43	25	25	26	45	41	22	37	39	35	13	11
FEB. 8	44	26	27	27	45	41	22	38	39	35	13	11
FEB. 9	44	28	28	29	45	41	22	38	39	35	13	11
FEB. 10	44	29	30	31	46	41	22	38	39	35	13	11
FEB. 11	44	31	32	32	46	41	22	38	39	35	13	11
FEB. 12	44	33	33	34	46	41	22	38	39	35	13	11
FEB. 13	44	34	35	35	46	42	22	38	39	35	13	11
FEB. 14	44	36	37	37	46	42	22	38	39	35	13	11
FEB. 15	44	38	38	39	47	42	22	38	39	35	13	11
FEB. 16	45	39	40	41	47	42	22	38	39	35	13	11
FEB. 17	45	41	42	43	47	42	22	38	39	35	13	11
FEB. 18	45	43	44	44	47	42	22	38	39	35	13	11
FEB. 19	45	45	46	46	47	43	22	38	39	35	13	11
FEB. 20	45	47	48	48	47	43	21	38	39	35	13	11
FEB. 21	45	1	2	2	48	43	21	38	39	35	13	11
FEB. 22	45	3	4	4	48	43	21	38	39	35	12	11
FEB. 23	46	5	6	6	48	43	21	38	39	35	12	11
FEB. 24	46	7	8	8	48	43	21	38	39	35	12	11
FEB. 25	46	9	9	10	48	44	21	38	39	35	12	11
FEB. 26	46	11	11	12	48	44	21	38	39	35	12	11
FEB. 27	46	12	13	14	48	44	21	38	39	35	12	11
FEB. 28	46	14	15	15	48	44	21	38	39	35	12	11

MOON 1 ◖ 12:01 A.M. TO 8:00 A.M.   **MOON 2** ◑ 8:01 A.M. TO 4:00 P.M.   **MOON 3** ● 4:01 P.M. TO 12:00 A.M.

Use only one "moon" number. Choose the column closest to your time of birth. If your place of birth is not on Eastern Standard Time, be sure to read "How to Convert to Eastern Standard Time" at the beginning of this section.

Date & Time	SUN	MOON 1	MOON 2	MOON 3	MERCURY	VENUS	MARS	JUPITER	SATURN	URANUS	NEPTUNE	PLUTO
MAR. 1	46	16	17	17	48	44	21	38	39	35	12	11
MAR. 2	46	18	18	19	48	44	21	38	39	35	12	11
MAR. 3	47	19	20	20	48	45	21	38	39	35	12	11
MAR. 4	47	21	22	22	48	45	21	38	39	35	12	11
MAR. 5	47	23	23	24	47	45	21	38	39	35	12	11
MAR. 6	47	24	25	25	47	45	21	38	39	35	12	11
MAR. 7	47	26	26	27	47	45	21	38	39	35	12	11
MAR. 8	47	27	28	28	47	45	21	38	39	35	12	11
MAR. 9	47	29	30	30	47	46	21	38	39	35	12	11
MAR. 10	47	31	31	32	47	46	21	38	39	35	12	11
MAR. 11	48	32	33	33	47	46	21	38	39	35	12	11
MAR. 12	48	34	34	35	47	46	20	38	39	35	12	11
MAR. 13	48	35	36	36	46	46	20	38	39	35	12	11
MAR. 14	48	37	38	38	46	46	20	38	39	35	12	11
MAR. 15	48	39	39	40	46	47	20	38	39	35	12	11
MAR. 16	48	41	41	42	46	47	20	38	39	35	12	11
MAR. 17	48	42	43	44	46	47	20	38	39	35	12	11
MAR. 18	48	44	45	46	46	47	20	38	39	35	12	11
MAR. 19	1	46	47	48	46	47	20	38	39	35	12	11
MAR. 20	1	48	1	2	46	47	20	38	39	35	12	11
MAR. 21	1	2	3	4	46	48	20	38	39	35	12	11
MAR. 22	1	4	5	6	46	48	20	38	39	35	12	11
MAR. 23	1	6	7	8	46	48	20	38	39	35	13	11
MAR. 24	1	8	9	10	46	48	20	38	39	35	13	11
MAR. 25	2	10	11	11	46	48	20	38	39	35	13	11
MAR. 26	2	12	13	13	46	48	20	38	39	35	13	11
MAR. 27	2	14	14	15	46	1	20	38	39	35	13	11
MAR. 28	2	16	16	17	46	1	20	38	39	35	13	11
MAR. 29	2	17	18	18	46	1	20	38	39	35	13	11
MAR. 30	2	19	19	20	47	1	20	39	39	35	13	11
MAR. 31	2	21	21	22	47	1	20	39	39	35	13	11
APR. 1	2	22	23	23	47	1	20	39	39	35	13	11
APR. 2	2	24	24	25	47	2	20	39	39	35	13	11
APR. 3	3	25	26	26	47	2	20	39	39	35	13	11
APR. 4	3	27	28	28	47	2	20	39	39	35	13	11
APR. 5	3	29	29	30	47	2	20	39	39	35	13	11
APR. 6	3	30	31	31	47	2	20	39	39	35	13	11
APR. 7	3	32	32	33	48	2	20	39	39	35	13	11
APR. 8	3	33	34	34	48	3	20	39	39	35	13	11
APR. 9	3	35	35	36	48	3	20	39	39	35	13	11
APR. 10	3	37	37	38	48	3	20	39	39	35	13	11
APR. 11	4	38	39	39	48	3	20	39	39	35	13	11
APR. 12	4	40	40	41	48	3	20	39	39	35	13	11
APR. 13	4	42	42	43	1	3	20	39	39	35	13	11
APR. 14	4	43	44	45	1	4	20	39	39	35	13	11
APR. 15	4	45	46	47	1	4	20	39	39	35	13	11
APR. 16	4	47	48	1	1	4	20	39	39	35	13	11
APR. 17	4	1	2	3	1	4	20	39	39	35	13	11
APR. 18	4	3	4	5	1	4	20	39	39	35	13	11
APR. 19	5	5	6	7	2	4	20	39	39	35	13	11
APR. 20	5	7	8	9	2	5	20	39	39	35	13	11
APR. 21	5	9	10	11	2	5	20	39	39	35	13	11
APR. 22	5	11	12	13	2	5	20	39	39	35	13	11
APR. 23	5	13	14	14	2	5	20	39	39	35	13	11
APR. 24	5	15	16	16	3	5	20	39	39	35	13	11
APR. 25	6	17	17	18	3	5	20	39	39	35	13	11
APR. 26	6	19	19	20	3	5	20	39	39	35	13	11
APR. 27	6	20	21	21	3	6	20	39	39	35	13	11
APR. 28	6	22	22	23	4	6	20	39	39	35	13	11
APR. 29	6	23	24	25	4	6	20	39	39	35	13	11
APR. 30	6	25	26	26	4	6	21	39	39	35	13	11

MOON 1 ☽ 12:01 A.M. TO 8:00 A.M.　　**MOON 2** ☽ 8:01 A.M. TO 4:00 P.M.　　**MOON 3** ● 4:01 P.M. TO 12:00 A.M.

Use only one "moon" number. Choose the column closest to your time of birth. If your place of birth is not on Eastern Standard Time, be sure to read "How to Convert to Eastern Standard Time" at the beginning of this section.

1901

May

June

Date & Time	SUN	MOON 1	MOON 2	MOON 3	MERCURY	VENUS	MARS	JUPITER	SATURN	URANUS	NEPTUNE	PLUTO
MAY 1	6	27	27	28	4	6	21	39	39	35	13	11
MAY 2	6	28	29	29	5	6	21	39	39	35	13	11
MAY 3	7	30	30	31	5	7	21	39	39	35	13	11
MAY 4	7	31	32	32	5	7	21	39	39	35	13	11
MAY 5	7	33	33	34	5	7	21	39	39	35	13	11
MAY 6	7	35	35	36	6	7	21	39	39	35	13	11
MAY 7	7	36	37	37	6	7	21	39	39	35	13	11
MAY 8	7	38	38	39	6	7	21	39	39	35	13	11
MAY 9	7	39	40	41	6	8	21	39	39	35	13	11
MAY 10	7	41	42	42	7	8	21	39	39	35	13	11
MAY 11	8	43	44	44	7	8	21	39	39	35	13	11
MAY 12	8	45	45	46	7	8	21	39	39	35	13	11
MAY 13	8	47	47	48	8	8	21	39	39	35	13	11
MAY 14	8	1	1	2	8	8	21	39	39	35	13	11
MAY 15	8	2	3	4	8	9	21	39	39	35	13	11
MAY 16	8	4	5	6	8	9	21	39	39	35	13	11
MAY 17	8	6	7	8	9	9	21	39	39	35	13	11
MAY 18	8	8	9	10	9	9	21	39	39	35	13	11
MAY 19	9	10	11	12	9	9	21	39	39	35	13	11
MAY 20	9	12	13	14	10	9	21	39	39	35	13	11
MAY 21	9	14	15	16	10	10	21	39	39	35	13	11
MAY 22	9	16	17	17	10	10	22	39	39	35	13	11
MAY 23	9	18	19	19	10	10	22	39	39	35	13	11
MAY 24	9	20	20	21	11	10	22	39	39	35	13	11
MAY 25	10	21	22	22	11	10	22	39	39	35	13	11
MAY 26	10	23	24	24	11	10	22	39	39	35	13	11
MAY 27	10	25	25	26	12	11	22	39	39	35	13	11
MAY 28	10	26	27	27	12	11	22	39	39	35	13	11
MAY 29	10	28	28	29	12	11	22	39	39	35	13	11
MAY 30	10	29	30	30	12	11	22	39	39	35	13	11
MAY 31	10	31	31	32	13	11	22	39	39	35	13	11

Date & Time	SUN	MOON 1	MOON 2	MOON 3	MERCURY	VENUS	MARS	JUPITER	SATURN	URANUS	NEPTUNE	PLUTO
JUN. 1	10	33	33	34	13	11	22	39	39	35	13	11
JUN. 2	10	34	35	35	13	12	22	38	39	35	13	11
JUN. 3	11	36	36	37	13	12	22	38	39	35	13	11
JUN. 4	11	37	38	39	13	12	22	38	39	35	13	11
JUN. 5	11	39	40	40	14	12	22	38	39	35	13	11
JUN. 6	11	41	41	42	14	12	22	38	39	35	13	11
JUN. 7	11	43	43	44	14	12	22	38	39	35	13	11
JUN. 8	11	44	45	46	14	13	22	38	39	35	13	11
JUN. 9	11	46	47	47	14	13	23	38	39	35	13	11
JUN. 10	11	48	1	1	15	13	23	38	39	35	13	11
JUN. 11	12	2	2	3	15	13	23	38	39	35	13	11
JUN. 12	12	4	4	5	15	13	23	38	39	35	13	11
JUN. 13	12	6	6	7	15	13	23	38	39	35	13	11
JUN. 14	12	8	8	9	15	14	23	38	39	35	13	11
JUN. 15	12	10	10	11	15	14	23	38	39	35	13	11
JUN. 16	12	12	12	13	15	14	23	38	39	35	13	11
JUN. 17	12	13	14	15	16	14	23	38	39	35	13	11
JUN. 18	12	15	16	17	16	14	23	38	39	35	13	11
JUN. 19	13	17	18	18	16	14	23	38	39	35	13	11
JUN. 20	13	19	20	20	16	15	23	38	39	35	13	11
JUN. 21	13	21	21	22	16	15	23	38	39	35	13	11
JUN. 22	13	22	23	24	16	15	23	38	39	35	13	11
JUN. 23	13	24	25	25	16	15	23	38	39	35	13	11
JUN. 24	13	26	26	27	16	15	24	38	39	35	13	11
JUN. 25	14	27	28	28	16	15	24	38	39	35	13	11
JUN. 26	14	29	29	30	16	15	24	38	39	35	13	11
JUN. 27	14	30	31	32	16	16	24	38	39	35	13	11
JUN. 28	14	32	33	33	16	16	24	38	39	35	13	11
JUN. 29	14	34	34	35	16	16	24	38	39	35	13	11
JUN. 30	14	35	36	36	16	16	24	38	39	35	13	11

MOON 1 ◐ 12:01 A.M. TO 8:00 A.M.   **MOON 2** ◑ 8:01 A.M. TO 4:00 P.M.   **MOON 3** ● 4:01 P.M. TO 12:00 A.M.

Use only one "moon" number. Choose the column closest to your time of birth. If your place of birth is not on Eastern Standard Time, be sure to read "How to Convert to Eastern Standard Time" at the beginning of this section.

1901

July

August

Date & Time	SUN	MOON 1	MOON 2	MOON 3	MERCURY	VENUS	MARS	JUPITER	SATURN	URANUS	NEPTUNE	PLUTO
JUL. 1	14	37	37	38	16	16	24	38	39	35	13	11
JUL. 2	14	39	39	40	16	16	24	38	39	35	13	11
JUL. 3	15	40	41	42	16	17	24	38	39	35	13	11
JUL. 4	15	42	43	43	16	17	24	38	39	35	13	11
JUL. 5	15	44	44	45	16	17	24	38	39	35	13	11
JUL. 6	15	46	46	47	16	17	24	38	39	35	13	11
JUL. 7	15	48	48	1	16	17	24	38	39	35	13	11
JUL. 8	15	1	2	3	16	17	25	38	39	35	13	11
JUL. 9	15	3	4	5	16	18	25	38	39	35	13	11
JUL. 10	15	5	6	6	16	18	25	38	39	35	13	11
JUL. 11	16	7	8	8	16	18	25	38	39	35	13	11
JUL. 12	16	9	10	10	16	18	25	38	39	35	13	11
JUL. 13	16	11	12	12	16	18	25	38	39	35	13	11
JUL. 14	16	13	13	14	16	18	25	38	39	35	13	11
JUL. 15	16	15	15	16	16	19	25	38	39	35	13	11
JUL. 16	16	17	17	18	15	19	25	38	39	35	13	11
JUL. 17	16	18	19	20	15	19	25	38	39	35	13	11
JUL. 18	16	20	21	21	15	19	25	38	39	35	13	11
JUL. 19	17	22	22	23	15	19	25	38	39	35	13	11
JUL. 20	17	24	24	25	15	19	25	38	39	35	13	11
JUL. 21	17	25	26	26	15	20	26	38	39	35	13	11
JUL. 22	17	27	27	28	15	20	26	38	39	35	13	11
JUL. 23	17	28	29	29	15	20	26	38	39	35	13	11
JUL. 24	17	30	30	31	15	20	26	38	39	35	13	11
JUL. 25	17	32	32	33	15	20	26	38	39	35	13	11
JUL. 26	18	33	34	34	15	20	26	38	39	35	13	11
JUL. 27	18	35	35	36	15	21	26	38	39	35	13	11
JUL. 28	18	36	37	37	15	21	26	38	39	35	13	11
JUL. 29	18	38	39	39	15	21	26	38	38	35	13	11
JUL. 30	18	40	40	41	15	21	26	38	38	35	13	11
JUL. 31	18	42	42	43	15	21	26	38	38	35	13	11

Date & Time	SUN	MOON 1	MOON 2	MOON 3	MERCURY	VENUS	MARS	JUPITER	SATURN	URANUS	NEPTUNE	PLUTO
AUG. 1	18	43	44	45	16	21	26	38	38	35	13	11
AUG. 2	18	45	46	46	16	22	26	38	38	35	13	11
AUG. 3	19	47	48	48	16	22	27	38	38	35	13	11
AUG. 4	19	1	2	2	16	22	27	38	38	35	13	11
AUG. 5	19	3	3	4	16	22	27	38	38	35	13	11
AUG. 6	19	5	5	6	16	22	27	38	38	35	13	11
AUG. 7	19	7	7	8	16	22	27	38	38	35	13	11
AUG. 8	19	8	9	10	17	22	27	38	38	35	13	11
AUG. 9	19	10	11	12	17	23	27	37	38	35	13	11
AUG. 10	19	12	13	13	17	23	27	37	38	35	13	11
AUG. 11	20	14	15	15	17	23	27	37	38	35	13	11
AUG. 12	20	16	17	17	17	23	27	37	38	35	13	11
AUG. 13	20	18	18	19	18	23	27	37	38	35	13	11
AUG. 14	20	19	20	21	18	23	28	37	38	35	13	11
AUG. 15	20	21	22	22	18	24	28	37	38	35	13	11
AUG. 16	20	23	23	24	18	24	28	37	38	35	13	11
AUG. 17	20	25	25	26	19	24	28	37	38	35	13	11
AUG. 18	20	26	27	27	19	24	28	37	38	35	13	11
AUG. 19	21	28	28	29	19	24	28	37	38	35	13	11
AUG. 20	21	29	30	30	19	24	28	37	38	35	13	11
AUG. 21	21	31	32	32	20	25	28	37	38	35	13	11
AUG. 22	21	33	33	34	20	25	28	37	38	35	13	11
AUG. 23	21	34	35	35	20	25	28	37	38	35	13	11
AUG. 24	21	36	36	37	21	25	28	37	38	35	13	11
AUG. 25	21	37	38	39	21	25	28	37	38	35	13	11
AUG. 26	22	39	40	40	21	25	28	37	38	35	13	11
AUG. 27	22	41	41	42	21	26	29	37	38	35	13	11
AUG. 28	22	43	43	44	22	26	29	37	38	35	13	11
AUG. 29	22	45	45	46	22	26	29	37	38	35	13	11
AUG. 30	22	46	47	48	22	26	29	37	38	35	13	11
AUG. 31	22	48	1	2	22	26	29	37	38	35	13	11

MOON 1 ◗ 12:01 A.M. TO 8:00 A.M.   **MOON 2** ◑ 8:01 A.M. TO 4:00 P.M.   **MOON 3** ● 4:01 P.M. TO 12:00 A.M.
Use only one "moon" number. Choose the column closest to your time of birth. If your place of birth is not on Eastern Standard Time, be sure to read "How to Convert to Eastern Standard Time" at the beginning of this section.

1901

September

Date & Time	SUN �	MOON 1 ◗	MOON 2 ◑	MOON 3 ●	MERCURY	VENUS	MARS	JUPITER	SATURN	URANUS	NEPTUNE	PLUTO
SEP. 1	22	2	3	4	23	26	29	37	38	35	13	11
SEP. 2	22	4	5	6	23	27	29	37	38	35	13	11
SEP. 3	23	6	7	7	23	27	29	37	38	35	13	11
SEP. 4	23	8	9	9	23	27	29	37	38	35	13	11
SEP. 5	23	10	11	11	24	27	29	37	38	35	13	11
SEP. 6	23	12	12	13	24	27	29	37	38	35	13	11
SEP. 7	23	14	14	15	24	27	30	37	38	35	13	11
SEP. 8	23	15	16	17	24	27	30	37	38	35	13	11
SEP. 9	23	17	18	18	25	28	30	37	38	35	13	11
SEP. 10	23	19	20	20	25	28	30	37	38	35	13	11
SEP. 11	24	21	21	22	25	28	30	37	38	35	13	11
SEP. 12	24	22	23	24	25	28	30	37	38	35	13	11
SEP. 13	24	24	25	25	25	28	30	37	38	35	13	11
SEP. 14	24	26	26	27	26	28	30	37	38	35	13	11
SEP. 15	24	27	28	28	26	29	30	37	38	35	13	11
SEP. 16	24	29	29	30	26	29	30	37	38	35	13	11
SEP. 17	24	31	31	32	26	29	30	37	38	35	13	11
SEP. 18	24	32	33	33	26	29	31	37	38	35	13	11
SEP. 19	25	34	34	35	27	29	31	37	38	35	13	11
SEP. 20	25	35	36	36	27	29	31	37	38	35	13	11
SEP. 21	25	37	37	38	27	30	31	37	38	35	13	11
SEP. 22	25	38	39	40	27	30	31	38	38	35	13	11
SEP. 23	25	40	41	41	27	30	31	38	38	35	13	11
SEP. 24	25	42	43	43	28	30	31	38	38	35	13	11
SEP. 25	26	44	44	45	28	30	31	38	38	35	13	11
SEP. 26	26	46	46	47	28	30	31	38	38	35	13	11
SEP. 27	26	48	48	1	28	31	31	38	38	35	13	11
SEP. 28	26	2	2	3	28	31	31	38	38	35	13	11
SEP. 29	26	3	4	5	29	31	32	38	38	35	13	11
SEP. 30	26	5	6	7	29	31	32	38	38	35	13	11

October

Date & Time	SUN ☉	MOON 1 ◗	MOON 2 ◑	MOON 3 ●	MERCURY	VENUS	MARS	JUPITER	SATURN	URANUS	NEPTUNE	PLUTO
OCT. 1	26	7	8	9	29	31	32	38	38	35	13	11
OCT. 2	26	9	10	11	29	31	32	38	38	35	13	11
OCT. 3	27	11	12	13	29	31	32	38	38	35	13	11
OCT. 4	27	13	14	14	29	32	32	38	38	35	13	11
OCT. 5	27	15	16	16	30	32	32	38	38	35	13	11
OCT. 6	27	17	17	18	30	32	32	38	38	35	13	11
OCT. 7	27	19	19	20	30	32	32	38	38	35	13	11
OCT. 8	27	20	21	21	30	32	32	38	38	35	13	11
OCT. 9	27	22	23	23	30	32	32	38	38	35	13	11
OCT. 10	27	24	24	25	30	33	33	38	38	35	13	11
OCT. 11	28	25	26	26	31	33	33	38	38	35	13	11
OCT. 12	28	27	27	28	31	33	33	38	38	35	13	11
OCT. 13	28	28	29	30	31	33	33	38	38	35	13	11
OCT. 14	28	30	31	31	31	33	33	38	38	35	13	11
OCT. 15	28	32	32	33	31	33	33	38	38	35	13	11
OCT. 16	28	33	34	34	31	33	33	38	38	35	13	11
OCT. 17	28	35	35	36	31	34	33	38	38	35	13	11
OCT. 18	28	36	37	37	31	34	33	38	38	35	13	11
OCT. 19	29	38	39	39	31	34	33	38	38	35	13	11
OCT. 20	29	40	40	41	32	34	34	38	38	35	13	11
OCT. 21	29	41	42	42	32	34	34	38	38	35	13	11
OCT. 22	29	43	44	44	32	34	34	38	38	35	13	11
OCT. 23	29	45	45	46	32	35	34	38	38	35	13	11
OCT. 24	29	47	47	48	32	35	34	38	38	35	13	11
OCT. 25	29	1	1	2	32	35	34	38	38	35	13	11
OCT. 26	30	3	3	4	32	35	34	38	38	35	13	11
OCT. 27	30	5	5	6	32	35	34	38	38	35	13	11
OCT. 28	30	7	7	8	32	35	34	38	38	35	13	11
OCT. 29	30	9	9	10	31	36	34	38	38	35	13	11
OCT. 30	30	11	11	12	31	36	34	38	38	35	13	11
OCT. 31	30	13	13	14	31	36	35	38	39	35	13	11

MOON 1 ◗ 12:01 A.M. TO 8:00 A.M.   **MOON 2 ◑ 8:01 A.M. TO 4:00 P.M.**   **MOON 3 ● 4:01 P.M. TO 12:00 A.M.**
Use only one "moon" number. Choose the column closest to your time of birth. If your place of birth is not on Eastern Standard Time, be sure to read "How to Convert to Eastern Standard Time" at the beginning of this section.

Date & Time	SUN	MOON 1	MOON 2	MOON 3	MERCURY	VENUS	MARS	JUPITER	SATURN	URANUS	NEPTUNE	PLUTO
NOV. 1	30	14	15	16	31	36	35	38	39	35	13	11
NOV. 2	30	16	17	18	31	36	35	38	39	35	13	11
NOV. 3	31	18	19	19	31	36	35	38	39	35	13	11
NOV. 4	31	20	20	21	31	36	35	38	39	35	13	11
NOV. 5	31	22	22	23	30	37	35	38	39	35	13	11
NOV. 6	31	23	24	24	30	37	35	38	39	35	13	11
NOV. 7	31	25	25	26	30	37	35	38	39	35	13	11
NOV. 8	31	26	27	28	30	37	35	38	39	35	13	11
NOV. 9	31	28	29	29	30	37	35	38	39	35	13	11
NOV. 10	31	30	30	31	30	37	36	38	39	35	13	11
NOV. 11	31	31	32	32	30	37	36	38	39	35	13	11
NOV. 12	32	33	33	34	30	38	36	38	39	35	13	11
NOV. 13	32	34	35	35	30	38	36	38	39	35	13	11
NOV. 14	32	36	36	37	30	38	36	38	39	35	13	11
NOV. 15	32	38	38	39	30	38	36	39	39	35	13	11
NOV. 16	32	39	40	40	30	38	36	39	39	35	13	11
NOV. 17	32	41	41	42	30	38	36	39	39	35	13	11
NOV. 18	32	43	43	44	30	39	36	39	39	35	13	11
NOV. 19	33	44	45	45	30	39	36	39	39	35	13	11
NOV. 20	33	46	47	47	30	39	37	39	39	35	13	11
NOV. 21	33	48	48	1	30	39	37	39	39	35	13	11
NOV. 22	33	2	2	3	30	39	37	39	39	35	13	11
NOV. 23	33	4	4	5	30	39	37	39	39	35	13	11
NOV. 24	33	6	6	7	31	39	37	39	39	35	13	11
NOV. 25	34	8	8	9	31	40	37	39	39	35	13	11
NOV. 26	34	10	10	11	31	40	37	39	39	35	13	11
NOV. 27	34	12	12	13	31	40	37	39	39	35	13	11
NOV. 28	34	14	14	15	31	40	37	39	39	35	13	11
NOV. 29	34	16	16	17	31	40	37	39	39	35	13	11
NOV. 30	34	18	18	19	32	40	38	39	39	35	13	11

Date & Time	SUN	MOON 1	MOON 2	MOON 3	MERCURY	VENUS	MARS	JUPITER	SATURN	URANUS	NEPTUNE	PLUTO
DEC. 1	34	19	20	21	32	40	38	39	39	35	13	11
DEC. 2	34	21	22	22	32	41	38	39	39	35	13	11
DEC. 3	35	23	23	24	32	41	38	39	39	35	13	11
DEC. 4	35	24	25	26	32	41	38	39	39	35	13	11
DEC. 5	35	26	27	27	33	41	38	39	39	35	13	11
DEC. 6	35	28	28	29	33	41	38	39	39	35	13	11
DEC. 7	35	29	30	30	33	41	38	39	39	35	13	11
DEC. 8	35	31	31	32	33	41	38	39	39	35	13	11
DEC. 9	35	32	33	33	33	41	38	39	39	35	13	11
DEC. 10	35	34	34	35	34	42	39	39	39	35	13	11
DEC. 11	36	36	36	37	34	42	39	39	39	35	13	11
DEC. 12	36	37	38	38	34	42	39	39	39	35	13	11
DEC. 13	36	39	39	40	34	42	39	39	39	35	13	11
DEC. 14	36	40	41	42	34	42	39	39	39	35	13	11
DEC. 15	36	42	43	43	35	42	39	39	39	35	13	11
DEC. 16	36	44	44	45	35	42	39	39	39	35	13	11
DEC. 17	36	46	46	47	35	42	39	39	39	35	13	11
DEC. 18	36	47	48	1	35	43	39	39	39	35	13	11
DEC. 19	37	1	2	2	35	43	40	39	39	35	13	11
DEC. 20	37	3	4	4	36	43	40	39	39	35	13	11
DEC. 21	37	5	5	6	36	43	40	39	39	35	13	11
DEC. 22	37	7	7	8	36	43	40	40	39	35	13	11
DEC. 23	37	9	9	10	36	43	40	40	39	35	13	11
DEC. 24	37	11	11	12	37	43	40	40	39	35	13	11
DEC. 25	37	13	13	14	37	43	40	40	39	35	13	11
DEC. 26	38	15	15	16	37	44	40	40	39	35	13	11
DEC. 27	38	17	17	18	37	44	40	40	39	35	13	11
DEC. 28	38	19	19	20	37	44	40	40	39	35	13	11
DEC. 29	38	20	21	22	38	44	41	40	39	35	13	11
DEC. 30	38	22	23	23	38	44	41	40	39	35	13	11
DEC. 31	38	24	24	25	38	44	41	40	39	35	13	11

MOON 1 ◑ 12:01 A.M. TO 8:00 A.M.   **MOON 2** ◑ 8:01 A.M. TO 4:00 P.M.   **MOON 3** ● 4:01 P.M. TO 12:00 A.M.

Use only one "moon" number. Choose the column closest to your time of birth. If your place of birth is not on Eastern Standard Time, be sure to read "How to Convert to Eastern Standard Time" at the beginning of this section.

1902

January

Date & Time	SUN	MOON 1	MOON 2	MOON 3	MERCURY	VENUS	MARS	JUPITER	SATURN	URANUS	NEPTUNE	PLUTO
JAN. 1	38	26	26	27	38	44	41	40	39	35	13	11
JAN. 2	38	27	28	28	38	44	41	40	39	35	13	11
JAN. 3	39	29	29	30	39	44	41	40	39	35	13	11
JAN. 4	39	30	31	31	39	44	41	40	39	35	13	11
JAN. 5	39	32	32	33	39	44	41	40	39	35	13	11
JAN. 6	39	34	34	35	39	45	41	40	39	35	13	11
JAN. 7	39	35	36	36	39	45	42	40	39	35	13	11
JAN. 8	39	37	37	38	40	45	42	40	39	35	13	11
JAN. 9	39	38	39	39	40	45	42	40	39	35	13	11
JAN. 10	40	40	41	41	40	45	42	40	39	35	13	11
JAN. 11	40	42	42	43	40	45	42	40	39	36	13	11
JAN. 12	40	43	44	45	41	45	42	40	40	36	13	11
JAN. 13	40	45	46	46	41	45	42	40	40	36	13	11
JAN. 14	40	47	47	48	41	45	42	40	40	36	13	11
JAN. 15	40	1	1	2	41	45	42	40	40	36	13	11
JAN. 16	40	2	3	4	42	45	42	40	40	36	13	11
JAN. 17	41	4	5	6	42	45	43	40	40	36	13	11
JAN. 18	41	6	7	7	42	45	43	40	40	36	13	11
JAN. 19	41	8	9	9	42	45	43	40	40	36	13	11
JAN. 20	41	10	11	11	42	45	43	40	40	36	13	11
JAN. 21	41	12	13	13	43	45	43	40	40	36	13	11
JAN. 22	41	14	15	15	43	45	43	40	40	36	13	11
JAN. 23	42	16	16	17	43	45	43	41	40	36	13	11
JAN. 24	42	18	18	19	43	45	43	41	40	36	13	11
JAN. 25	42	20	20	21	44	45	43	41	40	36	13	11
JAN. 26	42	21	22	23	44	45	44	41	40	36	13	11
JAN. 27	42	23	24	24	44	45	44	41	40	36	13	11
JAN. 28	42	25	26	26	44	45	44	41	40	36	13	11
JAN. 29	42	27	27	28	44	45	44	41	40	36	13	11
JAN. 30	42	28	29	29	45	45	44	41	40	36	13	11
JAN. 31	43	30	30	31	45	45	44	41	40	36	13	11

February

Date & Time	SUN	MOON 1	MOON 2	MOON 3	MERCURY	VENUS	MARS	JUPITER	SATURN	URANUS	NEPTUNE	PLUTO
FEB. 1	43	31	32	32	45	45	44	41	40	36	13	11
FEB. 2	43	33	34	34	45	45	44	41	40	36	13	11
FEB. 3	43	35	35	36	45	45	44	41	40	36	13	11
FEB. 4	43	36	37	37	45	45	44	41	40	36	13	11
FEB. 5	43	38	38	39	45	45	45	41	40	36	13	11
FEB. 6	43	39	40	41	45	45	45	41	40	36	13	11
FEB. 7	43	41	42	42	45	45	45	41	40	36	13	11
FEB. 8	44	43	43	44	46	45	45	41	40	36	13	11
FEB. 9	44	45	45	46	46	45	45	41	40	36	13	11
FEB. 10	44	46	47	48	46	45	45	41	40	36	13	11
FEB. 11	44	48	1	1	46	45	45	41	40	36	13	11
FEB. 12	44	2	3	3	46	45	45	41	40	36	13	11
FEB. 13	44	4	5	5	46	44	45	41	40	36	13	11
FEB. 14	44	6	6	7	45	44	46	41	40	36	13	11
FEB. 15	44	8	8	9	45	44	46	41	40	36	13	11
FEB. 16	45	10	10	11	45	44	46	41	40	36	13	11
FEB. 17	45	11	12	13	45	44	46	41	40	36	13	11
FEB. 18	45	13	14	15	44	44	46	41	40	36	13	11
FEB. 19	45	15	16	16	44	44	46	41	40	36	13	11
FEB. 20	45	17	18	18	44	44	46	41	40	36	13	11
FEB. 21	45	19	20	20	45	44	46	41	40	36	13	11
FEB. 22	45	21	21	22	44	44	46	41	40	36	13	11
FEB. 23	46	23	23	24	44	44	46	41	40	36	13	11
FEB. 24	46	24	25	25	44	44	47	41	40	36	13	11
FEB. 25	46	26	27	27	44	44	47	42	40	36	13	11
FEB. 26	46	28	28	29	44	44	47	42	40	36	13	11
FEB. 27	46	29	30	30	44	43	47	42	40	36	13	11
FEB. 28	46	31	31	32	44	43	47	42	40	36	13	11

MOON 1 ☽ 12:01 A.M. TO 8:00 A.M.   **MOON 2** ☾ 8:01 A.M. TO 4:00 P.M.   **MOON 3** ● 4:01 P.M. TO 12:00 A.M.

Use only one "moon" number. Choose the column closest to your time of birth. If your place of birth is not on Eastern Standard Time, be sure to read "How to Convert to Eastern Standard Time" at the beginning of this section.

1902

March

April

Date & Time	SUN	MOON 1	MOON 2	MOON 3	MERCURY	VENUS	MARS	JUPITER	SATURN	URANUS	NEPTUNE	PLUTO
MAR. 1	46	32	33	34	44	43	47	42	40	36	13	11
MAR. 2	46	34	35	35	44	43	47	42	40	36	13	11
MAR. 3	47	36	36	37	44	43	47	42	40	36	13	11
MAR. 4	47	37	38	38	44	43	47	42	40	36	13	11
MAR. 5	47	39	39	40	44	43	48	42	40	36	13	11
MAR. 6	47	41	41	42	44	43	48	42	40	36	13	11
MAR. 7	47	42	43	43	44	43	48	42	40	36	13	11
MAR. 8	47	44	45	45	44	43	48	42	40	36	13	11
MAR. 9	47	46	46	47	44	43	48	42	40	36	13	11
MAR. 10	47	48	48	1	44	43	48	42	40	36	13	11
MAR. 11	48	1	2	3	44	43	48	42	40	36	13	11
MAR. 12	48	3	4	5	44	43	48	42	40	36	13	11
MAR. 13	48	5	6	7	44	43	48	42	40	36	13	11
MAR. 14	48	7	8	8	44	43	48	42	40	36	13	11
MAR. 15	48	9	10	10	44	43	1	42	40	36	13	11
MAR. 16	48	11	12	12	45	43	1	42	40	36	13	11
MAR. 17	48	13	14	14	45	44	1	42	40	36	13	11
MAR. 18	48	15	15	16	45	44	1	42	40	36	13	11
MAR. 19	1	17	17	18	45	44	1	42	40	36	13	11
MAR. 20	1	18	19	20	45	44	1	42	40	36	13	11
MAR. 21	1	20	21	21	45	44	1	42	40	36	13	11
MAR. 22	1	22	23	23	45	44	1	42	40	36	13	11
MAR. 23	1	24	24	25	46	44	1	42	40	36	13	11
MAR. 24	1	25	26	27	46	44	1	42	40	36	13	11
MAR. 25	2	27	28	28	46	44	2	42	40	36	13	11
MAR. 26	2	29	29	30	46	44	2	42	40	36	13	11
MAR. 27	2	30	31	31	46	44	2	42	40	36	13	11
MAR. 28	2	32	32	33	46	44	2	42	40	36	13	11
MAR. 29	2	34	34	35	47	44	2	42	41	36	13	11
MAR. 30	2	35	36	36	47	44	2	42	41	36	13	11
MAR. 31	2	37	37	38	47	45	2	42	41	36	13	11

Date & Time	SUN	MOON 1	MOON 2	MOON 3	MERCURY	VENUS	MARS	JUPITER	SATURN	URANUS	NEPTUNE	PLUTO
APR. 1	2	38	39	39	47	45	2	42	41	36	13	11
APR. 2	2	40	40	41	47	45	2	42	41	36	13	11
APR. 3	3	42	42	43	48	45	3	42	41	36	13	11
APR. 4	3	43	44	44	48	45	3	43	41	36	13	11
APR. 5	3	45	46	46	48	45	3	43	41	36	13	11
APR. 6	3	47	47	48	48	45	3	43	41	36	13	11
APR. 7	3	1	1	2	48	45	3	43	41	36	13	11
APR. 8	3	3	3	4	1	45	3	43	41	36	13	11
APR. 9	3	5	5	6	1	45	3	43	41	36	13	11
APR. 10	3	7	7	8	1	46	3	43	41	36	13	11
APR. 11	4	9	9	10	1	46	3	43	41	36	13	11
APR. 12	4	10	11	12	2	46	3	43	41	36	13	11
APR. 13	4	12	13	14	2	46	4	43	41	36	13	11
APR. 14	4	14	15	16	2	46	4	43	41	36	13	11
APR. 15	4	16	17	17	2	46	4	43	41	36	13	11
APR. 16	4	18	19	19	3	46	4	43	41	36	13	11
APR. 17	4	20	20	21	3	46	4	43	41	36	13	11
APR. 18	4	22	22	23	3	46	4	43	41	36	13	11
APR. 19	5	23	24	24	3	47	4	43	41	36	13	11
APR. 20	5	25	26	26	4	47	4	43	41	36	13	11
APR. 21	5	27	27	28	4	47	4	43	41	36	13	11
APR. 22	5	28	29	29	4	47	4	43	41	36	13	11
APR. 23	5	30	30	31	4	47	5	43	41	36	13	11
APR. 24	5	31	32	33	5	47	5	43	41	36	13	11
APR. 25	6	33	34	34	5	47	5	43	41	36	13	11
APR. 26	6	35	35	36	5	47	5	43	41	36	13	11
APR. 27	6	36	37	37	5	48	5	43	41	36	13	11
APR. 28	6	38	38	39	6	48	5	43	41	36	13	11
APR. 29	6	39	40	40	6	48	5	43	41	36	13	11
APR. 30	6	41	42	42	6	48	5	43	41	36	13	11

MOON 1 ◗ 12:01 A.M. TO 8:00 A.M.　　**MOON 2** ◑ 8:01 A.M. TO 4:00 P.M.　　**MOON 3** ● 4:01 P.M. TO 12:00 A.M.
Use only one "moon" number. Choose the column closest to your time of birth. If your place of birth is not on Eastern Standard Time, be sure to read "How to Convert to Eastern Standard Time" at the beginning of this section.

1902

May

June

Date & Time	SUN	MOON 1	MOON 2	MOON 3	MERCURY	VENUS	MARS	JUPITER	SATURN	URANUS	NEPTUNE	PLUTO
MAY 1	6	43	43	44	7	48	5	43	41	36	13	11
MAY 2	6	44	45	46	7	48	5	43	41	36	13	11
MAY 3	7	46	47	47	7	48	6	43	41	36	13	11
MAY 4	7	48	1	1	7	1	6	43	41	36	13	11
MAY 5	7	2	2	3	8	1	6	43	41	36	13	11
MAY 6	7	4	4	5	8	1	6	43	41	36	13	11
MAY 7	7	6	6	7	8	1	6	43	41	36	13	11
MAY 8	7	8	8	9	9	1	6	43	41	36	13	11
MAY 9	7	10	10	11	9	1	6	43	41	36	13	11
MAY 10	7	12	12	13	9	1	6	43	41	36	13	11
MAY 11	8	14	14	15	9	2	6	43	41	36	13	11
MAY 12	8	16	16	17	10	2	6	43	41	36	13	11
MAY 13	8	18	18	19	10	2	7	43	41	36	13	11
MAY 14	8	19	20	21	10	2	7	43	41	36	13	11
MAY 15	8	21	22	22	10	2	7	43	41	36	13	11
MAY 16	8	23	23	24	11	2	7	43	41	36	13	11
MAY 17	8	25	25	26	11	2	7	43	41	36	13	11
MAY 18	8	26	27	27	11	3	7	43	41	36	13	11
MAY 19	9	28	28	29	11	3	7	43	41	36	13	11
MAY 20	9	29	30	31	11	3	7	43	41	36	13	11
MAY 21	9	31	32	32	12	3	7	43	41	36	13	11
MAY 22	9	33	33	34	12	3	7	43	41	36	13	11
MAY 23	9	34	35	35	12	3	8	43	41	36	13	11
MAY 24	9	36	36	37	12	4	8	43	41	36	13	11
MAY 25	10	37	38	38	12	4	8	43	41	36	13	11
MAY 26	10	39	40	40	13	4	8	43	41	36	13	11
MAY 27	10	41	41	42	13	4	8	43	41	36	13	11
MAY 28	10	42	43	43	13	4	8	43	41	36	13	11
MAY 29	10	44	44	45	13	4	8	43	41	36	13	11
MAY 30	10	46	46	47	13	4	8	43	41	36	13	11
MAY 31	10	47	48	48	13	4	8	43	41	36	13	11

Date & Time	SUN	MOON 1	MOON 2	MOON 3	MERCURY	VENUS	MARS	JUPITER	SATURN	URANUS	NEPTUNE	PLUTO
JUN. 1	10	1	2	2	13	5	8	43	41	36	13	11
JUN. 2	10	3	4	4	13	5	8	43	41	36	13	11
JUN. 3	11	5	5	6	13	5	9	43	41	36	13	11
JUN. 4	11	7	7	8	14	5	9	43	41	36	13	11
JUN. 5	11	9	9	10	14	5	9	43	41	36	13	11
JUN. 6	11	11	11	12	14	5	9	43	41	36	13	11
JUN. 7	11	13	14	14	14	5	9	43	41	36	13	11
JUN. 8	11	15	16	16	14	6	9	43	41	36	13	11
JUN. 9	11	17	17	18	14	6	9	43	41	36	13	11
JUN. 10	11	19	19	20	14	6	9	43	41	36	13	11
JUN. 11	12	21	21	22	14	6	9	43	41	36	13	11
JUN. 12	12	22	23	24	14	6	9	43	41	36	13	11
JUN. 13	12	24	25	25	14	6	10	43	41	36	13	11
JUN. 14	12	26	26	27	14	7	10	43	41	36	13	11
JUN. 15	12	27	28	29	14	7	10	43	41	36	13	11
JUN. 16	12	29	30	30	14	7	10	43	41	36	13	11
JUN. 17	12	31	31	32	14	7	10	43	41	36	13	11
JUN. 18	12	32	33	33	14	7	10	43	41	36	13	11
JUN. 19	13	34	34	35	13	7	10	43	40	35	13	11
JUN. 20	13	35	36	36	13	7	10	43	40	35	13	11
JUN. 21	13	37	38	38	13	8	10	43	40	35	13	11
JUN. 22	13	39	39	40	13	8	10	43	40	35	13	11
JUN. 23	13	40	41	41	13	8	10	43	40	35	13	11
JUN. 24	13	42	42	43	13	8	11	43	40	35	13	11
JUN. 25	14	43	44	45	13	8	11	43	40	35	13	11
JUN. 26	14	45	46	46	13	8	11	43	40	35	13	11
JUN. 27	14	47	47	48	13	8	11	43	40	35	13	11
JUN. 28	14	1	1	2	13	9	11	43	40	35	13	11
JUN. 29	14	2	3	4	13	9	11	43	40	35	13	11
JUN. 30	14	4	5	5	13	9	11	43	40	35	13	11

MOON 1 ☽ **12:01 A.M. TO 8:00 A.M.**   **MOON 2** ◑ **8:01 A.M. TO 4:00 P.M.**   **MOON 3** ● **4:01 P.M. TO 12:00 A.M.**
Use only one "moon" number. Choose the column closest to your time of birth. If your place of birth is not on
Eastern Standard Time, be sure to read "How to Convert to Eastern Standard Time" at the beginning of this section.

1902

July

August

Date & Time	SUN	MOON 1	MOON 2	MOON 3	MERCURY	VENUS	MARS	JUPITER	SATURN	URANUS	NEPTUNE	PLUTO
JUL. 1	14	6	7	7	13	9	11	43	40	35	13	11
JUL. 2	14	8	9	9	13	9	11	43	40	35	13	11
JUL. 3	15	10	11	11	13	9	11	43	40	35	13	11
JUL. 4	15	12	13	13	13	10	11	43	40	35	13	11
JUL. 5	15	14	15	15	13	10	12	43	40	35	13	11
JUL. 6	15	16	17	17	13	10	12	43	40	35	13	11
JUL. 7	15	18	19	19	13	10	12	43	40	35	13	11
JUL. 8	15	20	21	21	13	10	12	43	40	35	13	11
JUL. 9	15	22	22	23	13	10	12	43	40	35	13	11
JUL. 10	15	24	24	25	13	11	12	43	40	35	13	11
JUL. 11	16	25	26	26	13	11	12	43	40	35	13	11
JUL. 12	16	27	28	28	13	11	12	43	40	35	13	11
JUL. 13	16	29	29	30	13	11	12	43	40	35	13	11
JUL. 14	16	30	31	31	13	11	12	43	40	35	13	11
JUL. 15	16	32	32	33	13	11	12	43	40	35	13	11
JUL. 16	16	33	34	34	13	11	13	43	40	35	13	11
JUL. 17	16	35	36	36	13	12	13	43	40	35	13	11
JUL. 18	16	37	37	38	14	12	13	43	40	35	13	12
JUL. 19	17	38	39	39	14	12	13	43	40	35	13	12
JUL. 20	17	40	40	41	14	12	13	43	40	35	13	12
JUL. 21	17	41	42	43	14	12	13	43	40	35	13	12
JUL. 22	17	43	44	44	14	12	13	43	40	35	13	12
JUL. 23	17	45	45	46	14	13	13	43	40	35	13	12
JUL. 24	17	46	47	48	15	13	13	43	40	35	13	12
JUL. 25	17	48	1	1	15	13	13	43	40	35	13	12
JUL. 26	18	2	2	3	15	13	13	43	40	35	13	12
JUL. 27	18	4	4	5	15	13	14	43	40	35	13	12
JUL. 28	18	6	6	7	16	13	14	43	40	35	13	12
JUL. 29	18	7	8	9	16	14	14	43	40	35	13	12
JUL. 30	18	9	10	11	16	14	14	43	40	35	13	12
JUL. 31	18	11	12	13	16	14	14	43	40	35	13	12

Date & Time	SUN	MOON 1	MOON 2	MOON 3	MERCURY	VENUS	MARS	JUPITER	SATURN	URANUS	NEPTUNE	PLUTO
AUG. 1	18	13	14	14	17	14	14	43	40	35	13	12
AUG. 2	18	15	16	16	17	14	14	43	40	35	13	12
AUG. 3	19	17	18	18	17	14	14	43	40	35	13	12
AUG. 4	19	19	20	20	17	14	14	43	40	35	13	12
AUG. 5	19	21	22	22	18	15	14	43	40	35	13	12
AUG. 6	19	23	23	24	18	15	14	43	40	35	13	12
AUG. 7	19	25	25	26	18	15	15	43	40	35	13	12
AUG. 8	19	26	27	28	18	15	15	43	40	35	13	12
AUG. 9	19	28	29	29	19	15	15	43	40	35	13	12
AUG. 10	19	30	30	31	19	15	15	43	40	35	13	12
AUG. 11	20	31	32	32	19	16	15	43	40	35	13	12
AUG. 12	20	33	33	34	20	16	15	42	40	35	13	12
AUG. 13	20	35	35	36	20	16	15	42	40	35	13	12
AUG. 14	20	36	37	37	20	16	15	42	40	35	13	12
AUG. 15	20	38	38	39	20	16	15	42	40	35	13	12
AUG. 16	20	39	40	40	21	16	15	42	40	35	13	12
AUG. 17	20	41	41	42	21	17	15	42	40	35	13	12
AUG. 18	20	43	43	44	21	17	15	42	40	35	13	12
AUG. 19	21	44	45	45	21	17	16	42	40	35	13	12
AUG. 20	21	46	47	47	22	17	16	42	40	35	13	12
AUG. 21	21	48	48	1	22	17	16	42	40	35	13	12
AUG. 22	21	1	2	3	22	17	16	42	40	35	13	12
AUG. 23	21	3	4	4	22	18	16	42	40	35	13	12
AUG. 24	21	5	6	6	23	18	16	42	40	35	13	12
AUG. 25	21	7	8	8	23	18	16	42	40	35	13	12
AUG. 26	22	9	9	10	23	18	16	42	40	35	13	12
AUG. 27	22	11	11	12	23	18	16	42	40	35	13	12
AUG. 28	22	13	13	14	23	18	16	42	40	35	13	12
AUG. 29	22	15	15	16	24	18	16	42	40	35	13	12
AUG. 30	22	16	17	18	24	19	17	42	40	35	13	12
AUG. 31	22	18	19	20	24	19	17	42	40	35	13	12

MOON 1 ☽ 12:01 A.M. TO 8:00 A.M.   **MOON 2** ◑ 8:01 A.M. TO 4:00 P.M.   **MOON 3** ● 4:01 P.M. TO 12:00 A.M.

Use only one "moon" number. Choose the column closest to your time of birth. If your place of birth is not on
Eastern Standard Time, be sure to read "How to Convert to Eastern Standard Time" at the beginning of this section.

1902

September

Date & Time	☉ SUN	☽ MOON 1	☽ MOON 2	● MOON 3	MERCURY	VENUS	MARS	JUPITER	SATURN	URANUS	NEPTUNE	PLUTO
SEP. 1	22	20	21	21	24	19	17	42	40	35	13	12
SEP. 2	22	22	23	23	25	19	17	42	40	35	13	12
SEP. 3	23	24	25	25	25	19	17	42	40	35	13	12
SEP. 4	23	26	26	27	25	19	17	42	40	35	13	12
SEP. 5	23	27	28	29	25	20	17	42	40	35	13	12
SEP. 6	23	29	30	30	25	20	17	42	40	35	13	12
SEP. 7	23	31	31	32	26	20	17	42	40	35	13	12
SEP. 8	23	32	33	33	26	20	17	42	40	35	13	12
SEP. 9	23	34	35	35	26	20	17	42	40	35	13	12
SEP. 10	23	36	36	37	26	20	17	42	40	35	13	12
SEP. 11	24	37	38	38	26	21	18	42	40	35	13	12
SEP. 12	24	39	39	40	27	21	18	42	40	35	13	12
SEP. 13	24	40	41	41	27	21	18	42	40	35	13	12
SEP. 14	24	42	43	43	27	21	18	42	40	35	13	12
SEP. 15	24	44	44	45	27	21	18	42	40	35	13	12
SEP. 16	24	45	46	47	27	21	18	42	40	35	13	12
SEP. 17	24	47	48	48	27	22	18	42	40	35	13	12
SEP. 18	24	1	2	2	28	22	18	42	40	35	13	12
SEP. 19	25	3	3	4	28	22	18	42	40	35	13	12
SEP. 20	25	5	5	6	28	22	18	42	40	35	13	12
SEP. 21	25	6	7	8	28	22	18	42	40	35	13	12
SEP. 22	25	8	9	10	28	22	18	42	40	35	13	12
SEP. 23	25	10	11	12	28	23	19	42	40	35	13	12
SEP. 24	25	12	13	13	28	23	19	42	40	35	13	12
SEP. 25	26	14	15	15	29	23	19	42	40	35	13	12
SEP. 26	26	16	17	17	29	23	19	42	40	35	13	12
SEP. 27	26	18	18	19	29	23	19	42	40	35	13	12
SEP. 28	26	20	20	21	29	24	19	42	40	35	13	12
SEP. 29	26	22	22	23	29	24	19	42	40	35	13	12
SEP. 30	26	23	24	25	29	24	19	42	40	35	13	12

October

Date & Time	☉ SUN	☽ MOON 1	☽ MOON 2	● MOON 3	MERCURY	VENUS	MARS	JUPITER	SATURN	URANUS	NEPTUNE	PLUTO
OCT. 1	26	25	26	26	29	24	19	42	40	35	13	12
OCT. 2	26	27	27	28	29	24	19	42	40	35	13	12
OCT. 3	27	29	29	30	29	24	19	42	40	35	13	12
OCT. 4	27	30	31	31	29	24	19	42	40	35	13	12
OCT. 5	27	32	32	33	29	25	19	42	40	35	13	12
OCT. 6	27	33	34	35	30	25	20	42	40	35	13	12
OCT. 7	27	35	36	36	30	25	20	42	40	35	13	12
OCT. 8	27	37	37	38	30	25	20	42	40	35	13	12
OCT. 9	27	38	39	39	30	25	20	42	40	35	13	12
OCT. 10	27	40	40	41	30	25	20	42	40	35	13	12
OCT. 11	28	41	42	43	29	26	20	42	40	35	13	12
OCT. 12	28	43	44	44	29	26	20	42	40	35	13	12
OCT. 13	28	45	45	46	29	26	20	42	40	35	13	12
OCT. 14	28	46	47	48	29	26	20	42	40	35	13	12
OCT. 15	28	48	1	1	29	26	20	42	40	35	13	12
OCT. 16	28	2	3	3	29	26	20	42	40	35	13	12
OCT. 17	28	4	5	5	29	27	20	42	40	35	13	12
OCT. 18	28	6	6	7	29	27	21	42	40	35	13	12
OCT. 19	29	8	8	9	28	27	21	42	40	35	13	12
OCT. 20	29	10	10	11	28	27	21	42	40	35	13	12
OCT. 21	29	12	12	13	28	27	21	42	40	35	13	12
OCT. 22	29	14	14	15	28	27	21	42	40	35	13	12
OCT. 23	29	16	16	17	28	28	21	42	40	35	13	12
OCT. 24	29	17	18	19	28	28	21	42	40	35	13	12
OCT. 25	29	19	20	20	28	28	21	42	40	35	13	12
OCT. 26	30	21	22	22	28	28	21	42	40	35	13	12
OCT. 27	30	23	23	24	27	28	21	42	40	35	13	12
OCT. 28	30	25	25	26	27	28	21	42	40	35	13	12
OCT. 29	30	26	27	27	27	29	21	42	40	35	13	12
OCT. 30	30	28	29	29	27	29	21	42	40	35	13	12
OCT. 31	30	30	30	31	28	29	22	42	40	35	13	12

MOON 1 ☽ 12:01 A.M. TO 8:00 A.M.   **MOON 2** ☾ 8:01 A.M. TO 4:00 P.M.   **MOON 3** ● 4:01 P.M. TO 12:00 A.M.

Use only one "moon" number. Choose the column closest to your time of birth. If your place of birth is not on Eastern Standard Time, be sure to read "How to Convert to Eastern Standard Time" at the beginning of this section.

1902

November

Date & Time	SUN	MOON 1	MOON 2	MOON 3	MERCURY	VENUS	MARS	JUPITER	SATURN	URANUS	NEPTUNE	PLUTO
NOV. 1	30	31	32	32	28	29	22	42	40	36	13	12
NOV. 2	30	33	33	34	28	29	22	42	40	36	13	12
NOV. 3	31	35	35	36	28	29	22	42	40	36	13	12
NOV. 4	31	36	37	37	28	30	22	42	40	36	13	12
NOV. 5	31	38	38	39	28	30	22	42	40	36	13	12
NOV. 6	31	39	40	40	28	30	22	42	40	36	13	12
NOV. 7	31	41	41	42	28	30	22	42	40	36	13	12
NOV. 8	31	42	43	44	29	30	22	42	40	36	13	12
NOV. 9	31	44	45	45	29	30	22	42	40	36	13	12
NOV. 10	31	46	46	47	29	31	22	42	40	36	13	12
NOV. 11	31	48	48	1	29	31	22	42	40	36	13	12
NOV. 12	32	1	2	3	29	31	22	42	40	36	13	12
NOV. 13	32	3	4	4	29	31	22	42	40	36	13	12
NOV. 14	32	5	6	6	30	31	23	42	40	36	13	12
NOV. 15	32	7	8	8	30	31	23	42	40	36	13	12
NOV. 16	32	9	10	10	30	32	23	42	40	36	13	12
NOV. 17	32	11	12	12	30	32	23	42	40	36	13	12
NOV. 18	32	13	14	14	30	32	23	42	40	36	13	12
NOV. 19	33	15	16	16	31	32	23	42	40	36	13	12
NOV. 20	33	17	18	18	31	32	23	42	40	36	13	12
NOV. 21	33	19	19	20	31	32	23	42	40	36	13	12
NOV. 22	33	21	21	22	31	33	23	42	40	36	13	12
NOV. 23	33	22	23	24	32	33	23	42	40	36	13	12
NOV. 24	33	24	25	25	32	33	23	42	40	36	13	12
NOV. 25	34	26	26	27	32	33	23	43	40	36	13	11
NOV. 26	34	28	28	29	32	33	23	43	40	36	13	11
NOV. 27	34	29	30	30	32	33	23	43	40	36	13	11
NOV. 28	34	31	31	32	33	34	24	43	40	36	13	11
NOV. 29	34	32	33	34	33	34	24	43	40	36	13	11
NOV. 30	34	34	35	35	33	34	24	43	40	36	13	11

December

Date & Time	SUN	MOON 1	MOON 2	MOON 3	MERCURY	VENUS	MARS	JUPITER	SATURN	URANUS	NEPTUNE	PLUTO
DEC. 1	34	36	36	37	33	34	24	43	40	36	13	11
DEC. 2	34	37	38	38	33	34	24	43	40	36	13	11
DEC. 3	35	39	39	40	34	34	24	43	40	36	13	11
DEC. 4	35	40	41	41	34	35	24	43	40	36	13	11
DEC. 5	35	42	43	43	34	35	24	43	40	36	13	11
DEC. 6	35	44	44	45	34	35	24	43	40	36	13	11
DEC. 7	35	45	46	46	34	35	24	43	40	36	13	11
DEC. 8	35	47	47	48	35	35	24	43	40	36	13	11
DEC. 9	35	1	1	2	35	35	24	43	40	36	13	11
DEC. 10	35	2	3	4	35	36	24	43	40	36	13	11
DEC. 11	36	4	5	5	35	36	24	43	40	36	13	11
DEC. 12	36	6	7	7	36	36	24	43	40	36	13	11
DEC. 13	36	8	9	9	36	36	25	43	40	36	13	11
DEC. 14	36	10	11	11	36	36	25	43	40	36	13	11
DEC. 15	36	12	13	13	36	36	25	43	40	36	13	11
DEC. 16	36	14	15	15	36	37	25	43	40	36	13	11
DEC. 17	36	16	17	17	37	37	25	43	40	36	13	11
DEC. 18	36	18	19	19	37	37	25	43	40	36	13	11
DEC. 19	37	20	21	21	37	37	25	43	40	36	13	11
DEC. 20	37	22	23	23	37	37	25	43	40	36	13	11
DEC. 21	37	24	24	25	37	37	25	43	41	36	13	11
DEC. 22	37	25	26	27	38	38	25	43	41	36	13	11
DEC. 23	37	27	28	28	38	38	25	43	41	36	13	11
DEC. 24	37	29	30	30	38	38	25	43	41	36	13	11
DEC. 25	37	30	31	32	38	38	25	43	41	36	13	11
DEC. 26	38	32	33	33	38	38	25	43	41	36	13	11
DEC. 27	38	34	34	35	39	38	25	43	41	36	13	11
DEC. 28	38	35	36	36	39	39	25	43	41	36	13	11
DEC. 29	38	37	37	38	39	39	25	43	41	36	13	11
DEC. 30	38	38	39	39	39	39	26	43	41	36	13	11
DEC. 31	38	40	41	41	40	39	26	43	41	36	13	11

MOON 1 ☽ 12:01 A.M. TO 8:00 A.M. **MOON 2** ☽ 8:01 A.M. TO 4:00 P.M. **MOON 3** ● 4:01 P.M. TO 12:00 A.M.

Use only one "moon" number. Choose the column closest to your time of birth. If your place of birth is not on Eastern Standard Time, be sure to read "How to Convert to Eastern Standard Time" at the beginning of this section.

1903

January

Date & Time	SUN	MOON 1	MOON 2	MOON 3	MERCURY	VENUS	MARS	JUPITER	SATURN	URANUS	NEPTUNE	PLUTO
JAN. 1	38	42	42	43	40	39	26	43	41	36	13	11
JAN. 2	38	43	44	44	40	39	26	43	41	36	13	11
JAN. 3	39	45	45	46	40	40	26	43	41	36	13	11
JAN. 4	39	46	47	48	40	40	26	44	41	36	13	11
JAN. 5	39	48	1	1	41	40	26	44	41	36	13	11
JAN. 6	39	2	2	3	41	40	26	44	41	36	13	11
JAN. 7	39	4	4	5	41	40	26	44	41	36	13	11
JAN. 8	39	5	6	7	41	40	26	44	41	36	13	11
JAN. 9	39	7	8	8	41	41	26	44	41	36	13	11
JAN. 10	40	9	10	10	42	41	26	44	41	36	13	11
JAN. 11	40	11	12	12	42	41	26	44	41	36	13	11
JAN. 12	40	13	14	14	42	41	26	44	41	36	13	11
JAN. 13	40	15	16	17	42	41	26	44	41	36	13	11
JAN. 14	40	17	18	19	42	41	26	44	41	36	13	11
JAN. 15	40	19	20	21	43	42	26	44	41	36	13	11
JAN. 16	40	21	22	22	43	42	26	44	41	36	13	11
JAN. 17	41	23	24	24	43	42	26	44	41	36	13	11
JAN. 18	41	25	26	26	43	42	26	44	41	36	13	11
JAN. 19	41	27	27	28	43	42	26	44	41	36	13	11
JAN. 20	41	28	29	30	43	42	27	44	41	36	13	11
JAN. 21	41	30	31	31	43	43	27	44	41	36	13	11
JAN. 22	41	32	32	33	43	43	27	44	41	36	13	11
JAN. 23	42	33	34	34	43	43	27	44	41	36	13	11
JAN. 24	42	35	35	37	44	43	27	44	41	36	13	11
JAN. 25	42	36	37	37	43	43	27	44	41	36	13	11
JAN. 26	42	38	39	39	43	43	27	44	41	36	13	11
JAN. 27	42	40	40	41	44	44	27	44	41	36	13	11
JAN. 28	42	41	42	42	43	44	27	44	41	36	13	11
JAN. 29	42	43	43	44	43	44	27	44	41	36	13	11
JAN. 30	42	44	45	46	43	44	27	44	41	36	13	11
JAN. 31	43	46	47	47	43	44	27	44	41	36	13	11

February

Date & Time	SUN	MOON 1	MOON 2	MOON 3	MERCURY	VENUS	MARS	JUPITER	SATURN	URANUS	NEPTUNE	PLUTO
FEB. 1	43	48	48	1	43	44	27	44	41	36	13	11
FEB. 2	43	1	2	3	43	45	27	44	41	36	13	11
FEB. 3	43	3	4	4	43	45	27	44	41	36	13	11
FEB. 4	43	5	5	6	42	45	27	44	41	36	13	11
FEB. 5	43	7	7	8	42	45	27	44	41	36	13	11
FEB. 6	43	8	9	10	42	45	27	45	41	36	13	11
FEB. 7	43	10	11	12	42	45	27	45	41	36	13	11
FEB. 8	44	12	13	14	42	46	27	45	41	36	13	11
FEB. 9	44	14	15	16	42	46	27	45	41	36	13	11
FEB. 10	44	16	17	18	42	46	27	45	41	36	13	11
FEB. 11	44	18	19	20	42	46	27	45	41	36	13	11
FEB. 12	44	20	21	22	41	46	27	45	41	36	13	11
FEB. 13	44	22	23	23	41	46	27	45	41	36	13	11
FEB. 14	44	24	25	25	41	47	27	45	41	36	13	11
FEB. 15	44	26	27	27	41	47	27	45	41	36	13	11
FEB. 16	45	28	28	29	41	47	27	45	41	36	13	11
FEB. 17	45	29	30	31	41	47	27	45	41	36	13	11
FEB. 18	45	31	32	32	42	47	27	45	41	36	13	11
FEB. 19	45	33	33	34	42	47	27	45	41	36	13	11
FEB. 20	45	34	35	35	42	48	27	45	41	36	13	11
FEB. 21	45	36	37	37	42	48	27	45	41	36	13	11
FEB. 22	45	38	38	39	42	48	27	45	41	36	13	11
FEB. 23	46	39	40	40	42	48	27	45	41	36	13	11
FEB. 24	46	41	41	42	42	48	27	45	42	36	13	11
FEB. 25	46	42	43	43	42	48	27	45	42	36	13	11
FEB. 26	46	44	45	45	42	1	27	45	42	36	13	11
FEB. 27	46	46	46	47	42	1	27	45	42	36	13	11
FEB. 28	46	47	48	48	42	1	27	45	42	36	13	.11

MOON 1 ◑ 12:01 A.M. TO 8:00 A.M.   **MOON 2** ◑ 8:01 A.M. TO 4:00 P.M.   **MOON 3** ● 4:01 P.M. TO 12:00 A.M.
Use only one "moon" number. Choose the column closest to your time of birth. If your place of birth is not on Eastern Standard Time, be sure to read "How to Convert to Eastern Standard Time" at the beginning of this section.

March

April

Date & Time	SUN	MOON 1	MOON 2	MOON 3	MERCURY	VENUS	MARS	JUPITER	SATURN	URANUS	NEPTUNE	PLUTO
MAR. 1	46	1	2	2	43	1	27	45	42	36	13	11
MAR. 2	46	3	3	4	43	1	27	45	42	36	13	11
MAR. 3	47	4	5	6	43	1	27	45	42	36	13	11
MAR. 4	47	6	7	7	43	2	27	45	42	36	13	11
MAR. 5	47	8	9	9	43	2	27	45	42	36	13	11
MAR. 6	47	10	10	11	43	2	27	45	42	36	13	11
MAR. 7	47	12	12	13	44	2	27	45	42	36	13	11
MAR. 8	47	14	14	15	44	2	27	45	42	36	13	11
MAR. 9	47	16	16	17	44	2	27	46	42	36	13	11
MAR. 10	47	18	18	19	44	3	27	46	42	36	13	11
MAR. 11	48	19	20	21	44	3	27	46	42	36	13	11
MAR. 12	48	21	22	23	44	3	27	46	42	36	13	11
MAR. 13	48	23	24	25	45	3	27	46	42	36	13	11
MAR. 14	48	25	26	26	45	3	27	46	42	36	13	11
MAR. 15	48	27	28	28	45	3	27	46	42	36	13	11
MAR. 16	48	29	29	30	45	4	27	46	42	36	13	11
MAR. 17	48	31	31	32	45	4	27	46	42	36	13	11
MAR. 18	48	32	33	33	46	4	27	46	42	36	13	11
MAR. 19	1	34	34	35	46	4	26	46	42	36	13	11
MAR. 20	1	35	36	37	46	4	26	46	42	36	13	11
MAR. 21	1	37	38	38	46	4	26	46	42	36	13	11
MAR. 22	1	39	39	40	46	5	26	46	42	36	13	11
MAR. 23	1	40	41	41	47	5	26	46	42	36	13	11
MAR. 24	1	42	42	43	47	5	26	46	42	36	13	11
MAR. 25	2	43	44	45	47	5	26	46	42	36	13	11
MAR. 26	2	45	46	47	48	5	26	46	42	36	13	11
MAR. 27	2	47	47	48	48	5	26	46	42	36	13	11
MAR. 28	2	48	1	2	48	6	26	46	42	36	13	11
MAR. 29	2	2	3	3	48	6	26	46	42	36	13	11
MAR. 30	2	4	5	5	48	6	26	46	42	36	13	11
MAR. 31	2	6	6	7	1	6	26	46	42	36	13	11

Date & Time	SUN	MOON 1	MOON 2	MOON 3	MERCURY	VENUS	MARS	JUPITER	SATURN	URANUS	NEPTUNE	PLUTO
APR. 1	2	8	8	9	1	6	26	46	42	36	13	11
APR. 2	2	9	10	11	1	6	26	46	42	36	13	11
APR. 3	3	11	12	13	1	7	26	46	42	36	13	11
APR. 4	3	13	14	14	2	7	26	46	42	36	13	11
APR. 5	3	15	16	16	2	7	26	46	42	36	13	11
APR. 6	3	17	18	18	2	7	26	46	42	36	13	11
APR. 7	3	19	20	20	2	7	25	46	42	36	13	11
APR. 8	3	21	21	22	3	7	25	46	42	36	13	11
APR. 9	3	23	23	24	3	8	25	46	42	36	13	11
APR. 10	3	24	25	26	3	8	25	46	42	36	13	11
APR. 11	4	26	27	28	3	8	25	47	42	36	13	11
APR. 12	4	28	29	29	4	8	25	47	42	36	13	11
APR. 13	4	30	30	31	4	8	25	47	42	36	13	11
APR. 14	4	32	32	33	4	8	25	47	42	36	13	11
APR. 15	4	33	34	34	4	8	25	47	42	36	13	11
APR. 16	4	35	35	36	5	9	25	47	42	36	13	11
APR. 17	4	37	37	38	5	9	25	47	42	36	13	11
APR. 18	4	38	39	39	5	9	25	47	42	36	13	11
APR. 19	5	40	40	41	5	9	25	47	42	36	13	11
APR. 20	5	41	42	42	6	9	25	47	42	36	13	11
APR. 21	5	43	43	44	6	9	25	47	42	36	13	11
APR. 22	5	44	45	46	6	10	25	47	42	36	13	11
APR. 23	5	46	47	47	7	10	25	47	42	36	13	11
APR. 24	5	48	48	1	7	10	25	47	42	36	13	11
APR. 25	6	2	2	3	7	10	25	47	42	36	13	11
APR. 26	6	3	4	5	8	10	25	47	42	36	13	11
APR. 27	6	5	6	6	8	10	25	47	42	36	13	11
APR. 28	6	7	8	8	11	11	25	47	42	36	13	11
APR. 29	6	9	10	10	8	11	25	47	42	36	13	11
APR. 30	6	11	11	12	8	11	25	47	42	36	13	11

MOON 1 ☽ 12:01 A.M. TO 8:00 A.M.   **MOON 2** ☽ 8:01 A.M. TO 4:00 P.M.   **MOON 3** ● 4:01 P.M. TO 12:00 A.M.

Use only one "moon" number. Choose the column closest to your time of birth. If your place of birth is not on Eastern Standard Time, be sure to read "How to Convert to Eastern Standard Time" at the beginning of this section.

1903

May

Date & Time	SUN	MOON 1	MOON 2	MOON 3	MERCURY	VENUS	MARS	JUPITER	SATURN	URANUS	NEPTUNE	PLUTO
MAY 1	6	13	13	14	9	11	25	47	42	36	13	11
MAY 2	6	15	15	16	9	11	25	47	42	36	13	11
MAY 3	7	17	17	18	9	11	25	47	42	36	13	11
MAY 4	7	18	19	20	9	11	25	47	42	36	13	11
MAY 5	7	20	21	22	9	12	25	47	42	36	13	11
MAY 6	7	22	23	23	10	12	25	47	42	36	13	11
MAY 7	7	24	25	25	10	12	25	47	42	36	13	11
MAY 8	7	26	26	27	10	12	25	47	42	36	13	11
MAY 9	7	28	28	29	10	12	25	47	42	36	13	11
MAY 10	7	29	30	30	10	12	25	47	42	36	13	11
MAY 11	8	31	32	32	10	13	25	47	42	36	13	11
MAY 12	8	33	33	34	11	13	25	47	42	36	13	11
MAY 13	8	34	35	35	11	13	25	47	42	36	13	11
MAY 14	8	36	37	37	11	13	25	47	42	36	13	11
MAY 15	8	38	38	39	11	13	25	47	42	36	13	11
MAY 16	8	39	40	40	11	13	25	47	42	36	13	11
MAY 17	8	41	41	42	11	14	25	47	42	36	13	11
MAY 18	8	42	43	43	11	14	25	47	42	36	13	11
MAY 19	9	44	44	45	11	14	25	47	42	36	13	11
MAY 20	9	46	46	47	11	14	25	47	42	36	13	11
MAY 21	9	47	48	48	11	14	25	47	42	36	13	11
MAY 22	9	1	1	2	11	14	25	48	42	36	13	11
MAY 23	9	3	3	4	11	14	25	48	42	36	13	11
MAY 24	9	4	5	6	11	15	25	48	42	36	13	11
MAY 25	10	6	7	7	11	15	25	48	42	36	13	11
MAY 26	10	8	9	9	11	15	25	48	42	36	13	11
MAY 27	10	10	11	11	11	15	25	48	42	36	13	11
MAY 28	10	12	13	13	11	15	25	48	42	36	13	11
MAY 29	10	14	15	15	11	15	25	48	42	36	13	11
MAY 30	10	16	17	17	11	15	25	48	42	36	13	11
MAY 31	10	18	19	19	11	16	25	48	42	36	13	11

June

Date & Time	SUN	MOON 1	MOON 2	MOON 3	MERCURY	VENUS	MARS	JUPITER	SATURN	URANUS	NEPTUNE	PLUTO
JUN. 1	10	20	21	21	11	16	25	48	42	36	13	11
JUN. 2	10	22	22	23	11	16	25	48	42	36	13	11
JUN. 3	11	24	24	25	11	16	25	48	42	36	13	11
JUN. 4	11	25	26	27	11	16	25	48	42	36	13	11
JUN. 5	11	27	28	28	10	16	25	48	42	36	13	12
JUN. 6	11	29	29	30	10	17	25	48	42	36	13	12
JUN. 7	11	31	31	32	10	17	25	48	42	36	13	12
JUN. 8	11	32	33	33	10	17	25	48	42	36	13	12
JUN. 9	11	34	34	35	10	17	25	48	42	36	13	12
JUN. 10	11	36	36	37	10	17	25	48	42	36	13	12
JUN. 11	12	37	38	38	10	17	25	48	42	36	13	12
JUN. 12	12	39	39	40	10	17	25	48	42	36	13	12
JUN. 13	12	40	41	41	10	18	25	48	42	36	13	12
JUN. 14	12	42	42	43	10	18	26	48	42	36	13	12
JUN. 15	12	43	44	45	10	18	26	48	42	36	13	12
JUN. 16	12	45	46	46	10	18	26	48	42	36	13	12
JUN. 17	12	47	47	48	10	18	26	48	42	36	13	12
JUN. 18	12	48	1	1	10	18	26	48	42	36	13	12
JUN. 19	13	2	3	3	10	18	26	48	42	36	13	12
JUN. 20	13	4	4	5	10	18	26	48	42	36	13	12
JUN. 21	13	5	6	7	10	19	26	48	42	36	13	12
JUN. 22	13	7	8	9	10	19	26	48	42	36	13	12
JUN. 23	13	9	10	11	10	19	26	48	42	36	13	12
JUN. 24	13	11	12	13	10	19	26	48	42	36	13	12
JUN. 25	14	13	14	15	10	19	26	48	42	36	13	12
JUN. 26	14	15	16	17	10	19	26	48	42	36	13	12
JUN. 27	14	17	18	19	10	20	26	48	42	36	13	12
JUN. 28	14	19	20	21	10	20	26	48	42	36	13	12
JUN. 29	14	21	22	22	11	20	26	48	42	36	13	12
JUN. 30	14	23	24	24	11	20	26	48	42	36	13	12

MOON 1 ◐ 12:01 A.M. TO 8:00 A.M.   **MOON 2** ◑ 8:01 A.M. TO 4:00 P.M.   **MOON 3** ● 4:01 P.M. TO 12:00 A.M.
Use only one "moon" number. Choose the column closest to your time of birth. If your place of birth is not on Eastern Standard Time, be sure to read "How to Convert to Eastern Standard Time" at the beginning of this section.

1903

July

August

Date & Time	SUN	MOON 1 ☽	MOON 2 ☽	MOON 3 ●	MERCURY	VENUS	MARS	JUPITER	SATURN	URANUS	NEPTUNE	PLUTO
JUL. 1	14	25	26	26	11	20	26	48	42	36	13	12
JUL. 2	14	27	27	28	11	20	26	48	42	36	13	12
JUL. 3	15	28	29	30	11	20	27	48	42	36	13	12
JUL. 4	15	30	31	31	12	20	27	48	42	36	13	12
JUL. 5	15	32	32	33	12	21	27	48	42	36	13	12
JUL. 6	15	33	34	35	12	21	27	48	42	36	13	12
JUL. 7	15	35	36	36	12	21	27	48	42	36	13	12
JUL. 8	15	37	37	38	12	21	27	48	42	36	13	12
JUL. 9	15	38	39	39	13	21	27	48	42	36	13	12
JUL. 10	15	40	40	41	13	21	27	48	42	36	13	12
JUL. 11	16	41	42	42	13	21	27	48	42	36	14	12
JUL. 12	16	43	44	44	13	22	27	48	42	36	14	12
JUL. 13	16	45	45	46	14	22	27	48	42	36	14	12
JUL. 14	16	46	47	47	14	22	27	48	42	36	14	12
JUL. 15	16	48	48	1	14	22	27	48	42	36	14	12
JUL. 16	16	1	2	3	14	22	27	48	42	36	14	12
JUL. 17	16	3	4	4	15	22	27	48	42	36	14	12
JUL. 18	16	5	5	6	15	22	28	48	42	36	14	12
JUL. 19	17	7	7	8	15	22	28	48	42	36	14	12
JUL. 20	17	8	9	10	15	22	28	48	42	36	14	12
JUL. 21	17	10	11	12	16	23	28	48	42	36	14	12
JUL. 22	17	12	13	14	16	23	28	48	42	36	14	12
JUL. 23	17	14	15	16	16	23	28	48	42	36	14	12
JUL. 24	17	16	17	18	17	23	28	48	42	36	14	12
JUL. 25	17	18	19	20	17	23	28	48	42	36	14	12
JUL. 26	18	20	21	22	17	23	28	48	42	36	14	12
JUL. 27	18	22	23	24	17	23	28	48	42	36	14	12
JUL. 28	18	24	25	26	18	23	28	48	42	36	14	12
JUL. 29	18	26	27	27	18	23	28	48	42	36	14	12
JUL. 30	18	28	29	29	18	24	28	48	42	36	14	12
JUL. 31	18	30	30	31	19	24	28	48	42	36	14	12

Date & Time	SUN	MOON 1 ☽	MOON 2 ☽	MOON 3 ●	MERCURY	VENUS	MARS	JUPITER	SATURN	URANUS	NEPTUNE	PLUTO
AUG. 1	18	31	32	33	19	24	29	48	42	36	14	12
AUG. 2	18	33	34	34	19	24	29	48	42	36	14	12
AUG. 3	19	35	35	36	19	24	29	48	42	36	14	12
AUG. 4	19	36	37	37	20	24	29	48	42	36	14	12
AUG. 5	19	38	38	39	20	24	29	48	42	36	14	12
AUG. 6	19	39	40	41	20	24	29	48	42	36	14	12
AUG. 7	19	41	42	42	20	24	29	48	42	36	14	12
AUG. 8	19	43	43	44	21	24	29	48	42	36	14	12
AUG. 9	19	44	45	45	21	24	29	48	42	36	14	12
AUG. 10	19	46	46	47	21	25	29	48	42	36	14	12
AUG. 11	20	47	48	1	21	25	29	48	42	36	14	12
AUG. 12	20	1	2	2	22	25	29	48	42	36	14	12
AUG. 13	20	3	3	4	22	25	29	48	42	36	14	12
AUG. 14	20	4	5	6	22	25	30	48	42	36	14	12
AUG. 15	20	6	7	7	22	25	30	48	42	36	14	12
AUG. 16	20	8	8	9	23	25	30	48	42	36	14	12
AUG. 17	20	10	10	11	23	25	30	48	42	36	14	12
AUG. 18	20	12	12	13	23	25	30	48	42	36	14	12
AUG. 19	21	14	14	15	23	25	30	48	42	36	14	12
AUG. 20	21	15	16	17	23	25	30	48	42	36	14	12
AUG. 21	21	18	18	19	23	25	30	48	42	36	14	12
AUG. 22	21	20	20	21	24	25	30	48	42	36	14	12
AUG. 23	21	22	22	23	24	25	30	48	42	36	14	12
AUG. 24	21	24	24	25	24	25	30	48	42	36	14	12
AUG. 25	21	25	26	27	24	25	30	48	42	36	14	12
AUG. 26	22	27	28	29	24	25	31	48	42	36	14	12
AUG. 27	22	29	30	30	25	25	31	48	42	36	14	12
AUG. 28	22	31	31	32	25	25	31	48	41	36	14	12
AUG. 29	22	33	33	34	25	25	31	48	41	36	14	12
AUG. 30	22	34	35	35	25	25	31	48	41	36	14	12
AUG. 31	22	36	36	37	25	25	31	48	41	36	14	12

MOON 1 ☽ 12:01 A.M. TO 8:00 A.M.   **MOON 2** ☽ 8:01 A.M. TO 4:00 P.M.   **MOON 3** ● 4:01 P.M. TO 12:00 A.M.

Use only one "moon" number. Choose the column closest to your time of birth. If your place of birth is not on Eastern Standard Time, be sure to read "How to Convert to Eastern Standard Time" at the beginning of this section.

1903

September

Date & Time	SUN	MOON 1	MOON 2	MOON 3	MERCURY	VENUS	MARS	JUPITER	SATURN	URANUS	NEPTUNE	PLUTO
SEP. 1	22	37	38	39	25	25	31	48	41	36	14	12
SEP. 2	22	39	40	40	26	25	31	48	41	36	14	12
SEP. 3	23	41	41	42	26	25	31	48	41	36	14	12
SEP. 4	23	42	43	43	26	25	31	48	41	36	14	12
SEP. 5	23	44	44	45	26	25	31	48	41	36	14	12
SEP. 6	23	45	46	47	26	25	31	48	41	36	14	12
SEP. 7	23	47	48	48	26	25	32	47	41	36	14	12
SEP. 8	23	1	1	2	26	25	32	47	41	36	14	12
SEP. 9	23	2	3	3	27	25	32	47	41	36	14	12
SEP. 10	23	4	5	5	27	25	32	47	41	36	14	12
SEP. 11	24	6	6	7	27	25	32	47	41	36	14	12
SEP. 12	24	7	8	9	27	25	32	47	41	36	14	12
SEP. 13	24	9	10	10	27	25	32	47	41	36	14	12
SEP. 14	24	11	12	12	27	24	32	47	41	36	14	12
SEP. 15	24	13	14	14	27	24	32	47	41	36	14	12
SEP. 16	24	15	15	16	27	24	32	47	41	36	14	12
SEP. 17	24	17	17	18	27	24	32	47	41	36	14	12
SEP. 18	24	19	19	20	27	24	33	47	41	36	14	12
SEP. 19	25	21	21	22	27	24	33	47	41	36	14	12
SEP. 20	25	23	23	24	27	24	33	47	41	36	14	12
SEP. 21	25	25	25	26	27	24	33	47	41	36	14	12
SEP. 22	25	27	27	28	27	24	33	47	41	36	14	12
SEP. 23	25	28	29	30	27	24	33	47	41	36	14	12
SEP. 24	25	30	31	31	27	24	33	47	41	36	14	12
SEP. 25	26	32	33	33	27	24	33	47	41	36	14	12
SEP. 26	26	34	34	35	27	24	33	47	41	36	14	12
SEP. 27	26	35	36	36	27	23	33	47	41	36	14	12
SEP. 28	26	37	38	38	27	23	33	47	41	36	14	12
SEP. 29	26	39	39	40	27	23	34	47	41	36	14	12
SEP. 30	26	40	41	41	27	23	34	47	41	36	14	12

October

Date & Time	SUN	MOON 1	MOON 2	MOON 3	MERCURY	VENUS	MARS	JUPITER	SATURN	URANUS	NEPTUNE	PLUTO
OCT. 1	26	42	42	43	27	23	34	47	41	36	14	12
OCT. 2	26	43	44	44	26	23	34	47	41	36	14	12
OCT. 3	27	45	45	46	26	23	34	47	41	36	14	12
OCT. 4	27	47	47	48	26	23	34	47	41	36	14	12
OCT. 5	27	48	1	1	26	23	34	47	41	36	14	12
OCT. 6	27	2	2	3	26	23	34	47	41	36	14	12
OCT. 7	27	4	4	5	26	23	34	47	41	36	14	12
OCT. 8	27	5	6	6	26	23	34	47	41	36	14	12
OCT. 9	27	7	8	8	25	23	35	47	41	36	14	12
OCT. 10	27	9	9	10	25	23	35	47	41	36	14	12
OCT. 11	28	11	11	12	25	23	35	47	41	36	14	12
OCT. 12	28	13	13	14	25	23	35	47	41	36	14	12
OCT. 13	28	14	15	16	25	23	35	47	41	36	14	12
OCT. 14	28	16	17	18	25	23	35	47	41	36	14	12
OCT. 15	28	18	19	19	25	23	35	47	41	36	14	12
OCT. 16	28	20	21	21	26	23	35	47	41	36	14	12
OCT. 17	28	22	23	23	26	23	35	47	41	36	14	12
OCT. 18	28	24	25	25	26	23	35	47	41	36	14	12
OCT. 19	29	26	26	27	26	23	35	47	41	36	14	12
OCT. 20	29	28	28	29	26	23	36	47	41	36	14	12
OCT. 21	29	29	30	31	26	23	36	47	41	36	14	12
OCT. 22	29	31	32	32	26	23	36	47	41	36	14	12
OCT. 23	29	33	34	34	26	24	36	47	41	36	14	12
OCT. 24	29	35	36	36	27	24	36	47	41	36	14	12
OCT. 25	29	36	37	37	27	24	36	47	41	36	14	12
OCT. 26	30	38	39	39	27	24	36	47	41	36	14	12
OCT. 27	30	40	40	41	27	24	36	47	41	36	14	12
OCT. 28	30	41	42	42	27	24	36	47	41	36	14	12
OCT. 29	30	43	43	44	28	24	36	47	41	36	14	12
OCT. 30	30	44	45	45	28	24	37	47	41	36	14	12
OCT. 31	30	46	47	47	28	24	37	47	41	36	14	12

MOON 1 ◑ 12:01 A.M. TO 8:00 A.M.   **MOON 2** ◐ 8:01 A.M. TO 4:00 P.M.   **MOON 3** ● 4:01 P.M. TO 12:00 A.M.

Use only one "moon" number. Choose the column closest to your time of birth. If your place of birth is not on Eastern Standard Time, be sure to read "How to Convert to Eastern Standard Time" at the beginning of this section.

1903

November

Date & Time	SUN	MOON 1	MOON 2	MOON 3	MERCURY	VENUS	MARS	JUPITER	SATURN	URANUS	NEPTUNE	PLUTO
NOV. 1	30	48	48	1	28	24	37	47	41	36	14	12
NOV. 2	30	1	2	2	29	24	37	47	41	36	14	12
NOV. 3	31	3	4	4	29	24	37	47	41	36	14	12
NOV. 4	31	5	5	6	29	25	37	47	41	36	14	12
NOV. 5	31	6	7	8	29	25	37	47	41	36	14	12
NOV. 6	31	8	9	10	29	25	37	47	41	36	14	12
NOV. 7	31	10	11	11	30	25	37	47	41	36	14	12
NOV. 8	31	12	13	13	30	25	37	47	41	36	14	12
NOV. 9	31	14	15	15	30	25	38	47	41	36	14	12
NOV. 10	31	16	16	17	30	25	38	47	41	36	14	12
NOV. 11	31	18	18	19	30	25	38	47	41	36	14	12
NOV. 12	32	20	20	21	31	25	38	47	41	36	14	12
NOV. 13	32	21	22	23	31	25	38	47	41	36	14	12
NOV. 14	32	23	24	25	31	26	38	47	41	36	14	12
NOV. 15	32	25	26	26	31	26	38	47	41	36	14	12
NOV. 16	32	27	28	28	32	26	38	47	41	36	14	12
NOV. 17	32	29	29	30	32	26	38	47	41	36	14	12
NOV. 18	32	31	31	32	32	26	38	47	42	36	14	12
NOV. 19	33	32	33	34	32	26	39	47	42	36	14	12
NOV. 20	33	34	35	35	32	26	39	47	42	36	14	12
NOV. 21	33	36	36	37	33	26	39	47	42	36	14	12
NOV. 22	33	37	38	39	33	27	39	47	42	36	14	12
NOV. 23	33	39	40	40	33	27	39	47	42	36	14	12
NOV. 24	33	41	41	42	33	27	39	47	42	36	14	12
NOV. 25	34	42	43	43	33	27	39	47	42	36	14	12
NOV. 26	34	44	44	45	34	27	39	47	42	36	14	12
NOV. 27	34	45	46	46	34	27	39	47	42	36	14	12
NOV. 28	34	47	48	48	34	27	39	47	42	36	14	12
NOV. 29	34	1	1	2	34	28	40	47	42	36	14	12
NOV. 30	34	2	3	3	35	28	40	47	42	36	14	12

December

Date & Time	SUN	MOON 1	MOON 2	MOON 3	MERCURY	VENUS	MARS	JUPITER	SATURN	URANUS	NEPTUNE	PLUTO
DEC. 1	34	4	5	5	35	28	40	47	42	36	14	12
DEC. 2	34	6	6	7	35	28	40	47	42	36	14	12
DEC. 3	35	8	8	9	35	28	40	47	42	36	14	12
DEC. 4	35	9	10	11	35	28	40	47	42	36	14	12
DEC. 5	35	11	12	13	36	28	40	47	42	36	14	12
DEC. 6	35	13	14	15	36	28	40	47	42	36	14	12
DEC. 7	35	15	16	17	36	29	40	47	42	36	14	12
DEC. 8	35	17	18	19	36	29	41	47	42	36	14	12
DEC. 9	35	19	20	20	36	29	41	47	42	36	14	12
DEC. 10	35	21	22	22	37	29	41	47	42	36	14	12
DEC. 11	36	23	24	24	37	29	41	47	42	36	14	12
DEC. 12	36	25	25	26	37	29	41	47	42	36	14	12
DEC. 13	36	27	27	28	37	29	41	47	42	36	14	12
DEC. 14	36	28	29	30	37	30	41	47	42	36	14	12
DEC. 15	36	30	31	31	38	30	41	47	42	36	14	12
DEC. 16	36	32	32	33	38	30	41	47	42	36	14	12
DEC. 17	36	34	34	35	38	30	41	47	42	36	14	12
DEC. 18	36	35	36	36	38	30	42	47	42	36	14	12
DEC. 19	37	37	37	38	38	30	42	47	42	36	14	12
DEC. 20	37	39	39	40	39	31	42	47	42	36	14	12
DEC. 21	37	40	41	41	39	31	42	47	42	36	14	12
DEC. 22	37	42	42	43	39	31	42	47	42	36	14	12
DEC. 23	37	43	44	44	39	31	42	47	42	36	14	12
DEC. 24	37	45	45	46	39	31	42	47	42	36	14	12
DEC. 25	37	47	47	48	40	31	42	47	42	36	14	12
DEC. 26	38	48	1	1	40	31	42	47	42	36	14	12
DEC. 27	38	2	2	3	40	32	43	47	42	36	14	12
DEC. 28	38	3	4	4	40	32	43	47	42	36	14	12
DEC. 29	38	5	6	6	40	32	43	47	42	36	14	12
DEC. 30	38	7	7	8	41	32	43	47	42	36	14	12
DEC. 31	38	9	9	10	41	32	43	47	42	37	14	12

MOON 1 ☽ 12:01 A.M. TO 8:00 A.M. **MOON 2** ☽ 8:01 A.M. TO 4:00 P.M. **MOON 3** ● 4:01 P.M. TO 12:00 A.M.
Use only one "moon" number. Choose the column closest to your time of birth. If your place of birth is not on Eastern Standard Time, be sure to read "How to Convert to Eastern Standard Time" at the beginning of this section.

1904

January

Date & Time	SUN	MOON 1	MOON 2	MOON 3	MERCURY	VENUS	MARS	JUPITER	SATURN	URANUS	NEPTUNE	PLUTO
JAN. 1	38	10	11	12	41	32	43	47	42	37	14	12
JAN. 2	38	12	13	14	41	33	43	47	42	37	14	12
JAN. 3	39	14	15	16	41	33	43	47	42	37	14	12
JAN. 4	39	16	17	18	41	33	43	47	42	37	14	12
JAN. 5	39	18	19	20	41	33	43	47	42	37	14	12
JAN. 6	39	20	21	22	41	33	44	47	42	37	14	12
JAN. 7	39	22	23	24	41	33	44	47	42	37	14	12
JAN. 8	39	24	25	26	41	33	44	47	42	37	14	12
JAN. 9	39	26	27	27	41	34	44	48	42	37	14	12
JAN. 10	40	28	29	29	41	34	44	48	42	37	14	12
JAN. 11	40	30	30	31	41	34	44	48	42	37	14	12
JAN. 12	40	31	32	33	41	34	44	48	42	37	14	12
JAN. 13	40	33	34	34	41	34	44	48	42	37	14	12
JAN. 14	40	35	35	36	41	34	44	48	42	37	14	12
JAN. 15	40	36	37	38	41	35	45	48	42	37	14	12
JAN. 16	40	38	39	39	41	35	45	48	42	37	14	12
JAN. 17	41	40	40	41	41	35	45	48	42	37	13	12
JAN. 18	41	41	42	42	40	35	45	48	42	37	13	12
JAN. 19	41	43	43	44	40	35	45	48	42	37	13	12
JAN. 20	41	44	45	46	40	35	45	48	42	37	13	12
JAN. 21	41	46	47	47	40	35	45	48	42	37	13	11
JAN. 22	41	48	48	1	40	36	45	48	42	37	13	11
JAN. 23	42	1	2	2	40	36	45	48	42	37	13	11
JAN. 24	42	3	3	4	39	36	45	48	42	37	13	11
JAN. 25	42	4	5	6	39	36	46	48	42	37	13	11
JAN. 26	42	6	7	7	39	36	46	48	42	37	13	11
JAN. 27	42	8	8	9	39	36	46	48	42	37	13	11
JAN. 28	42	10	10	11	39	37	46	48	42	37	13	11
JAN. 29	42	12	12	13	39	37	46	48	42	37	13	11
JAN. 30	42	13	14	15	39	37	46	48	42	37	13	11
JAN. 31	43	15	16	17	39	37	46	48	43	37	13	11

February

Date & Time	SUN	MOON 1	MOON 2	MOON 3	MERCURY	VENUS	MARS	JUPITER	SATURN	URANUS	NEPTUNE	PLUTO
FEB. 1	43	18	18	19	39	37	46	48	43	37	13	11
FEB. 2	43	20	20	21	39	37	46	48	43	37	13	11
FEB. 3	43	22	22	23	39	38	46	48	43	37	13	11
FEB. 4	43	24	24	25	40	38	47	48	43	37	13	11
FEB. 5	43	26	26	27	40	38	47	48	43	37	13	11
FEB. 6	43	27	28	29	40	38	47	48	43	37	13	11
FEB. 7	43	29	30	30	40	38	47	48	43	37	13	11
FEB. 8	44	31	32	32	40	38	47	48	43	37	13	11
FEB. 9	44	33	33	34	40	39	47	48	43	37	13	11
FEB. 10	44	34	35	36	40	39	47	48	43	37	13	11
FEB. 11	44	36	37	37	40	39	47	48	43	37	13	11
FEB. 12	44	38	38	39	40	39	47	48	43	37	13	11
FEB. 13	44	39	40	40	41	39	48	48	43	37	13	11
FEB. 14	44	41	41	42	41	39	48	48	43	37	13	11
FEB. 15	44	43	43	44	41	40	48	1	43	37	13	11
FEB. 16	45	44	44	45	41	40	48	1	43	37	13	11
FEB. 17	45	46	46	47	41	40	48	1	43	37	13	11
FEB. 18	45	47	48	48	41	40	48	1	43	37	13	11
FEB. 19	45	1	1	2	42	40	48	1	43	37	13	11
FEB. 20	45	2	3	3	42	40	48	1	43	37	13	11
FEB. 21	45	4	5	5	42	40	48	1	43	37	13	11
FEB. 22	45	6	6	7	42	41	48	1	43	37	13	11
FEB. 23	46	7	8	9	42	41	1	1	43	37	13	11
FEB. 24	46	9	10	10	42	41	1	1	43	37	13	11
FEB. 25	46	11	11	12	43	41	1	1	43	37	13	11
FEB. 26	46	13	14	14	43	41	1	1	43	37	13	11
FEB. 27	46	15	15	16	43	41	1	1	43	37	13	11
FEB. 28	46	17	17	18	43	42	1	1	43	37	13	11
FEB. 29	46	19	19	20	43	42	1	1	43	37	13	11

MOON 1 ☾ 12:01 A.M. TO 8:00 A.M.   **MOON 2** ☽ 8:01 A.M. TO 4:00 P.M.   **MOON 3** ● 4:01 P.M. TO 12:00 A.M.
Use only one "moon" number. Choose the column closest to your time of birth. If your place of birth is not on Eastern Standard Time, be sure to read "How to Convert to Eastern Standard Time" at the beginning of this section.

1904

March

Date & Time	SUN	MOON 1	MOON 2	MOON 3	MERCURY	VENUS	MARS	JUPITER	SATURN	URANUS	NEPTUNE	PLUTO
MAR. 1	46	21	21	22	44	42	1	1	43	37	13	11
MAR. 2	46	23	23	24	44	42	1	1	43	37	13	11
MAR. 3	47	25	25	26	44	42	1	1	43	37	13	11
MAR. 4	47	27	27	28	44	42	2	1	43	37	13	11
MAR. 5	47	29	29	30	45	43	2	1	43	37	13	11
MAR. 6	47	30	31	32	45	43	2	1	43	37	13	11
MAR. 7	47	32	33	33	45	43	2	1	43	37	13	11
MAR. 8	47	34	35	35	45	43	2	1	43	37	13	11
MAR. 9	47	36	36	37	45	43	2	1	43	37	13	11
MAR. 10	47	37	38	38	46	43	2	1	43	37	13	11
MAR. 11	48	39	39	40	46	44	2	1	43	37	13	11
MAR. 12	48	41	41	42	46	44	2	1	43	37	13	11
MAR. 13	48	42	43	43	46	44	3	1	43	37	13	11
MAR. 14	48	44	44	45	47	44	3	1	43	37	13	11
MAR. 15	48	45	46	46	47	44	3	1	43	37	13	11
MAR. 16	48	47	47	48	47	44	3	1	43	37	13	11
MAR. 17	48	48	1	1	47	45	3	1	43	37	13	11
MAR. 18	48	2	3	3	47	45	3	2	43	37	13	11
MAR. 19	1	4	4	5	48	45	3	2	43	37	13	11
MAR. 20	1	5	6	6	48	45	3	2	43	37	13	11
MAR. 21	1	7	8	8	48	45	3	2	43	37	13	11
MAR. 22	1	9	9	10	1	45	3	2	43	37	13	11
MAR. 23	1	10	11	12	1	46	4	2	43	37	13	11
MAR. 24	1	12	13	13	1	46	4	2	43	37	13	11
MAR. 25	2	14	15	15	1	46	4	2	43	37	13	11
MAR. 26	2	16	17	17	2	46	4	2	43	37	13	11
MAR. 27	2	18	18	19	2	46	4	2	43	37	13	11
MAR. 28	2	20	20	21	2	46	4	2	43	37	13	11
MAR. 29	2	22	22	23	2	47	4	2	43	37	13	11
MAR. 30	2	24	24	25	3	47	4	2	43	37	13	11
MAR. 31	2	26	26	27	3	47	4	2	43	37	13	11

April

Date & Time	SUN	MOON 1	MOON 2	MOON 3	MERCURY	VENUS	MARS	JUPITER	SATURN	URANUS	NEPTUNE	PLUTO
APR. 1	2	28	28	29	3	47	4	2	43	37	13	11
APR. 2	2	30	30	31	3	47	5	2	43	37	13	11
APR. 3	3	31	32	33	4	47	5	2	43	37	13	11
APR. 4	3	33	34	34	4	48	5	2	43	37	13	11
APR. 5	3	35	36	36	4	48	5	2	43	37	13	11
APR. 6	3	37	37	38	5	48	5	2	43	37	13	11
APR. 7	3	38	39	40	5	48	5	2	43	37	13	11
APR. 8	3	40	41	41	5	48	5	2	43	37	13	11
APR. 9	3	42	42	43	5	48	5	2	43	37	13	11
APR. 10	3	43	44	44	6	48	5	2	43	37	13	11
APR. 11	4	45	45	46	6	1	5	2	43	37	13	11
APR. 12	4	46	47	47	6	1	6	2	44	37	13	11
APR. 13	4	48	48	1	6	1	6	2	44	37	13	11
APR. 14	4	2	2	3	6	1	6	2	44	37	13	11
APR. 15	4	3	4	4	7	1	6	2	44	37	13	12
APR. 16	4	5	5	6	7	1	6	2	44	37	13	12
APR. 17	4	7	7	8	7	2	6	2	44	37	13	12
APR. 18	4	8	9	9	7	2	6	2	44	37	13	12
APR. 19	5	10	11	11	7	2	6	3	44	37	13	12
APR. 20	5	12	12	13	8	2	6	3	44	37	13	12
APR. 21	5	14	14	15	8	2	6	3	44	37	13	12
APR. 22	5	15	16	17	8	2	6	3	44	37	13	12
APR. 23	5	17	18	19	8	3	7	3	44	37	13	12
APR. 24	5	19	20	20	8	3	7	3	44	37	13	12
APR. 25	6	21	22	22	8	3	7	3	44	37	13	12
APR. 26	6	23	24	24	8	3	7	3	44	37	13	12
APR. 27	6	25	26	26	8	3	7	3	44	37	13	12
APR. 28	6	27	28	28	8	3	7	3	44	37	13	12
APR. 29	6	29	29	30	8	4	7	3	44	37	13	12
APR. 30	6	31	31	32	8	4	7	3	44	37	13	12

MOON 1 ☽ 12:01 A.M. TO 8:00 A.M.   **MOON 2** ☽ 8:01 A.M. TO 4:00 P.M.   **MOON 3** ● 4:01 P.M. TO 12:00 A.M.
Use only one "moon" number. Choose the column closest to your time of birth. If your place of birth is not on Eastern Standard Time, be sure to read "How to Convert to Eastern Standard Time" at the beginning of this section.

Date & Time	SUN	MOON 1	MOON 2	MOON 3	MERCURY	VENUS	MARS	JUPITER	SATURN	URANUS	NEPTUNE	PLUTO
MAY 1	6	33	33	34	8	4	7	3	44	37	13	12
MAY 2	6	34	35	36	8	4	7	3	44	37	13	12
MAY 3	7	36	37	37	8	4	8	3	44	37	13	12
MAY 4	7	38	38	39	8	4	8	3	44	37	13	12
MAY 5	7	39	40	41	8	5	8	3	44	37	13	12
MAY 6	7	41	42	42	8	5	8	3	44	37	13	12
MAY 7	7	43	43	44	8	5	8	3	44	37	13	12
MAY 8	7	44	45	45	8	5	8	3	44	37	13	12
MAY 9	7	46	46	47	8	5	8	3	44	37	13	12
MAY 10	7	47	48	1	8	5	8	3	44	37	13	12
MAY 11	8	1	2	2	8	6	8	3	44	37	14	12
MAY 12	8	3	3	4	8	6	8	3	44	37	14	12
MAY 13	8	4	5	5	8	6	9	3	44	37	14	12
MAY 14	8	6	7	7	8	6	9	3	44	37	14	12
MAY 15	8	8	8	9	8	6	9	3	44	37	14	12
MAY 16	8	10	10	11	8	6	9	3	44	37	14	12
MAY 17	8	11	12	13	8	7	9	3	44	37	14	12
MAY 18	8	13	14	14	8	7	9	3	44	37	14	12
MAY 19	9	15	16	16	8	7	9	3	44	37	14	12
MAY 20	9	17	18	18	7	7	9	3	44	37	14	12
MAY 21	9	19	19	20	7	7	9	3	44	37	14	12
MAY 22	9	21	21	22	7	7	9	4	44	37	14	12
MAY 23	9	23	23	24	7	8	9	4	44	37	14	12
MAY 24	9	24	25	26	8	8	10	4	44	37	14	12
MAY 25	10	26	27	28	7	8	10	4	44	37	14	12
MAY 26	10	28	29	29	7	8	10	4	44	37	14	12
MAY 27	10	30	31	31	7	8	10	4	44	37	14	12
MAY 28	10	32	32	33	7	8	10	4	44	37	14	12
MAY 29	10	34	34	35	7	8	10	4	44	37	14	12
MAY 30	10	35	36	37	7	9	10	4	44	37	14	12
MAY 31	10	37	38	38	7	9	10	4	44	37	14	12

Date & Time	SUN	MOON 1	MOON 2	MOON 3	MERCURY	VENUS	MARS	JUPITER	SATURN	URANUS	NEPTUNE	PLUTO
JUN. 1	10	39	39	40	7	9	10	4	44	37	14	12
JUN. 2	10	41	41	42	8	9	10	4	44	37	14	12
JUN. 3	11	42	43	43	8	9	10	4	44	37	14	12
JUN. 4	11	44	44	45	8	9	11	4	44	37	14	12
JUN. 5	11	45	46	46	8	10	11	4	44	37	14	12
JUN. 6	11	47	47	48	8	10	11	4	44	37	14	12
JUN. 7	11	1	1	2	8	10	11	4	44	37	14	12
JUN. 8	11	2	3	3	8	10	11	4	44	37	14	12
JUN. 9	11	4	4	5	8	10	11	4	44	37	14	12
JUN. 10	11	5	6	7	8	10	11	4	44	37	14	12
JUN. 11	12	7	8	8	8	11	11	4	44	37	14	12
JUN. 12	12	9	9	10	9	11	11	4	44	37	14	12
JUN. 13	12	11	11	12	9	11	11	4	44	37	14	12
JUN. 14	12	13	13	14	9	11	11	4	44	37	14	12
JUN. 15	12	14	15	15	9	11	12	4	44	37	14	12
JUN. 16	12	16	17	18	9	11	12	4	44	37	14	12
JUN. 17	12	18	19	20	9	12	12	4	44	37	14	12
JUN. 18	12	20	21	21	10	12	12	4	44	37	14	12
JUN. 19	13	22	23	23	10	12	12	4	44	37	14	12
JUN. 20	13	24	25	25	10	12	12	4	44	37	14	12
JUN. 21	13	26	27	27	10	12	12	4	44	37	14	12
JUN. 22	13	28	28	29	11	12	12	4	44	37	14	12
JUN. 23	13	30	30	31	11	13	12	4	44	37	14	12
JUN. 24	13	31	32	33	11	13	12	4	44	37	14	12
JUN. 25	14	33	34	34	11	13	12	4	44	37	14	12
JUN. 26	14	35	35	36	11	13	13	4	44	37	14	12
JUN. 27	14	37	37	38	12	13	13	4	44	37	14	12
JUN. 28	14	38	39	39	12	13	13	4	44	37	14	12
JUN. 29	14	40	41	41	12	13	13	4	44	37	14	12
JUN. 30	14	42	42	43	12	14	13	4	44	37	14	12

MOON 1 ◖ **12:01 A.M. TO 8:00 A.M.**   **MOON 2** ◑ **8:01 A.M. TO 4:00 P.M.**   **MOON 3** ● **4:01 P.M. TO 12:00 A.M.**
Use only one "moon" number. Choose the column closest to your time of birth. If your place of birth is not on Eastern Standard Time, be sure to read "How to Convert to Eastern Standard Time" at the beginning of this section.

Date & Time	SUN	MOON 1	MOON 2	MOON 3	MERCURY	VENUS	MARS	JUPITER	SATURN	URANUS	NEPTUNE	PLUTO
JUL. 1	14	43	44	44	13	14	13	4	44	37	14	12
JUL. 2	14	45	45	46	13	14	13	5	44	37	14	12
JUL. 3	15	46	47	47	13	14	13	5	44	37	14	12
JUL. 4	15	48	1	1	14	14	13	5	44	37	14	12
JUL. 5	15	2	2	3	14	15	13	5	44	37	14	12
JUL. 6	15	3	4	4	14	15	13	5	44	37	14	12
JUL. 7	15	5	5	6	14	15	14	5	44	37	14	12
JUL. 8	15	6	7	8	15	15	14	5	44	37	14	12
JUL. 9	15	8	9	9	15	15	14	5	44	37	14	12
JUL. 10	15	10	11	11	15	15	14	5	44	37	14	12
JUL. 11	16	12	12	13	16	16	14	5	44	37	14	12
JUL. 12	16	14	14	15	16	16	14	5	44	37	14	12
JUL. 13	16	16	16	17	16	16	14	5	44	37	14	12
JUL. 14	16	18	18	19	16	16	14	5	44	37	14	12
JUL. 15	16	20	20	21	17	16	14	5	44	37	14	12
JUL. 16	16	22	22	23	17	16	14	5	44	37	14	12
JUL. 17	16	24	24	25	17	17	14	5	44	37	14	12
JUL. 18	16	25	26	27	18	17	15	5	44	37	14	12
JUL. 19	17	27	28	29	18	17	15	5	44	37	14	12
JUL. 20	17	29	30	30	18	17	15	5	44	37	14	12
JUL. 21	17	31	32	32	18	17	15	5	44	37	14	12
JUL. 22	17	33	33	34	19	17	15	5	44	37	14	12
JUL. 23	17	34	35	36	19	18	15	5	44	37	14	12
JUL. 24	17	36	37	37	19	18	15	5	43	37	14	12
JUL. 25	17	38	38	39	19	18	15	5	43	37	14	12
JUL. 26	18	40	40	41	20	18	15	5	43	37	14	12
JUL. 27	18	41	42	42	20	18	15	5	43	37	14	12
JUL. 28	18	43	43	44	20	18	15	5	43	37	14	12
JUL. 29	18	44	45	45	20	18	15	5	43	37	14	12
JUL. 30	18	46	46	47	20	19	16	5	43	36	14	12
JUL. 31	18	48	48	1	21	19	16	5	43	36	14	12

Date & Time	SUN	MOON 1	MOON 2	MOON 3	MERCURY	VENUS	MARS	JUPITER	SATURN	URANUS	NEPTUNE	PLUTO
AUG. 1	18	1	2	2	21	19	16	5	43	36	14	12
AUG. 2	18	3	3	4	21	19	16	5	43	36	14	12
AUG. 3	19	4	5	5	21	19	16	5	43	36	14	12
AUG. 4	19	6	6	7	22	19	16	5	43	36	14	12
AUG. 5	19	8	8	9	22	20	16	5	43	36	14	12
AUG. 6	19	9	10	10	22	20	16	5	43	36	14	12
AUG. 7	19	11	12	12	22	20	16	5	43	36	14	12
AUG. 8	19	13	14	14	22	20	16	5	43	36	14	12
AUG. 9	19	15	15	16	22	20	16	5	43	36	14	12
AUG. 10	19	17	17	18	23	20	17	5	43	36	14	12
AUG. 11	20	19	19	20	23	21	17	5	43	36	14	12
AUG. 12	20	21	21	22	23	21	17	5	43	36	14	12
AUG. 13	20	23	23	24	23	21	17	5	43	36	14	12
AUG. 14	20	25	25	26	23	21	17	5	43	36	14	12
AUG. 15	20	27	27	28	23	21	17	5	43	36	14	12
AUG. 16	20	29	29	30	24	21	17	5	43	36	14	12
AUG. 17	20	30	31	32	24	22	17	5	43	36	14	12
AUG. 18	20	32	33	33	24	22	17	5	43	36	14	12
AUG. 19	21	34	35	35	24	22	17	5	43	36	14	12
AUG. 20	21	36	36	37	24	22	17	5	43	36	14	12
AUG. 21	21	37	38	39	24	22	17	5	43	36	14	12
AUG. 22	21	39	40	40	24	22	18	5	43	36	14	12
AUG. 23	21	41	41	42	25	23	18	5	43	36	14	12
AUG. 24	21	42	43	43	25	23	18	5	43	36	14	12
AUG. 25	21	44	44	45	25	23	18	5	43	36	14	12
AUG. 26	22	46	46	47	25	23	18	5	43	36	14	12
AUG. 27	22	47	48	48	25	23	18	5	43	36	14	12
AUG. 28	22	1	1	2	25	23	18	5	43	36	14	12
AUG. 29	22	2	3	3	25	24	18	5	43	36	14	12
AUG. 30	22	4	4	5	25	24	18	5	43	36	14	12
AUG. 31	22	5	6	7	25	24	18	5	43	36	14	12

MOON 1 ◖ 12:01 A.M. TO 8:00 A.M.   **MOON 2** ◑ 8:01 A.M. TO 4:00 P.M.   **MOON 3** ● 4:01 P.M. TO 12:00 A.M.

Use only one "moon" number. Choose the column closest to your time of birth. If your place of birth is not on Eastern Standard Time, be sure to read "How to Convert to Eastern Standard Time" at the beginning of this section.

September

Date & Time	SUN	MOON 1	MOON 2	MOON 3	MERCURY	VENUS	MARS	JUPITER	SATURN	URANUS	NEPTUNE	PLUTO
SEP. 1	22	7	8	8	25	24	18	5	43	36	14	12
SEP. 2	22	9	9	10	25	24	19	5	43	36	14	12
SEP. 3	23	10	11	12	25	24	19	5	43	36	14	12
SEP. 4	23	12	13	13	25	25	19	5	43	36	14	12
SEP. 5	23	14	15	15	25	25	19	5	43	36	14	12
SEP. 6	23	16	17	17	25	25	19	5	43	36	14	12
SEP. 7	23	18	19	19	25	25	19	5	43	36	14	12
SEP. 8	23	20	21	21	25	25	19	5	43	36	14	12
SEP. 9	23	22	23	23	25	25	19	5	43	36	14	12
SEP. 10	23	24	25	25	25	26	19	5	43	36	14	12
SEP. 11	24	26	27	27	25	26	19	5	43	36	14	12
SEP. 12	24	28	29	29	25	26	19	5	43	36	14	12
SEP. 13	24	30	30	31	24	26	19	5	43	36	14	12
SEP. 14	24	32	32	33	24	26	20	5	43	36	14	12
SEP. 15	24	34	34	35	24	26	20	5	43	36	14	12
SEP. 16	24	35	36	36	24	27	20	5	43	36	14	12
SEP. 17	24	37	38	38	24	27	20	5	43	36	14	12
SEP. 18	24	39	39	40	24	27	20	5	43	36	14	12
SEP. 19	25	40	41	41	24	27	20	5	43	36	14	12
SEP. 20	25	42	43	43	23	27	20	5	43	36	14	12
SEP. 21	25	44	44	45	23	27	20	5	43	36	14	12
SEP. 22	25	45	46	46	23	28	20	5	43	36	14	12
SEP. 23	25	47	47	48	23	28	20	5	43	36	14	12
SEP. 24	25	48	1	1	23	28	20	5	43	36	14	12
SEP. 25	26	2	2	3	23	28	20	5	43	36	14	12
SEP. 26	26	3	4	5	23	28	21	5	43	36	14	12
SEP. 27	26	5	6	6	23	28	21	5	43	36	14	12
SEP. 28	26	7	7	8	23	29	21	5	43	36	14	12
SEP. 29	26	8	9	9	23	29	21	5	43	36	14	12
SEP. 30	26	10	11	11	23	29	21	5	43	36	14	12

October

Date & Time	SUN	MOON 1	MOON 2	MOON 3	MERCURY	VENUS	MARS	JUPITER	SATURN	URANUS	NEPTUNE	PLUTO
OCT. 1	26	12	12	13	24	29	21	5	43	36	14	12
OCT. 2	26	13	14	15	24	29	21	5	43	36	14	12
OCT. 3	27	15	16	17	24	29	21	5	43	36	14	12
OCT. 4	27	17	18	18	24	30	21	5	43	36	14	12
OCT. 5	27	19	20	20	24	30	21	5	43	36	14	12
OCT. 6	27	21	22	22	24	30	21	5	43	36	14	12
OCT. 7	27	23	24	24	25	30	21	5	43	36	14	12
OCT. 8	27	25	26	26	25	30	22	5	43	36	14	12
OCT. 9	27	27	28	28	25	30	22	4	43	36	14	12
OCT. 10	27	29	30	30	25	31	22	4	43	36	14	12
OCT. 11	28	31	32	32	25	31	22	4	43	37	14	12
OCT. 12	28	33	33	34	26	31	22	4	43	37	14	12
OCT. 13	28	35	35	36	26	31	22	4	43	37	14	12
OCT. 14	28	36	37	38	26	31	22	4	43	37	14	12
OCT. 15	28	38	39	39	26	31	22	4	43	37	14	12
OCT. 16	28	40	40	41	27	31	22	4	43	37	14	12
OCT. 17	28	42	42	43	27	32	22	4	43	37	14	12
OCT. 18	28	43	44	44	27	32	22	4	43	37	14	12
OCT. 19	29	45	45	46	27	32	22	4	43	37	14	12
OCT. 20	29	46	47	47	27	32	22	4	43	37	14	12
OCT. 21	29	48	48	1	28	32	23	4	43	37	14	12
OCT. 22	29	1	2	2	28	32	23	4	43	37	14	12
OCT. 23	29	3	4	4	28	33	23	4	43	37	14	12
OCT. 24	29	5	5	6	28	33	23	4	43	37	14	12
OCT. 25	29	6	7	7	29	33	23	4	43	37	14	12
OCT. 26	30	8	9	9	29	33	23	4	43	37	14	12
OCT. 27	30	10	10	11	29	33	23	4	43	37	14	12
OCT. 28	30	11	12	13	29	33	23	4	43	37	14	12
OCT. 29	30	13	14	14	29	34	23	4	43	37	14	12
OCT. 30	30	15	15	16	30	34	23	4	43	37	14	12
OCT. 31	30	17	17	18	30	34	23	4	43	37	14	12

MOON 1 ☽ 12:01 A.M. TO 8:00 A.M.   **MOON 2** ☽ 8:01 A.M. TO 4:00 P.M.   **MOON 3** ● 4:01 P.M. TO 12:00 A.M.

Use only one "moon" number. Choose the column closest to your time of birth. If your place of birth is not on Eastern Standard Time, be sure to read "How to Convert to Eastern Standard Time" at the beginning of this section.

1904

November

Date & Time	SUN ☉	MOON 1 ☽	MOON 2 ☽	MOON 3 ●	MERCURY	VENUS	MARS	JUPITER	SATURN	URANUS	NEPTUNE	PLUTO
NOV. 1	30	18	19	20	30	34	23	4	43	37	14	12
NOV. 2	30	20	21	22	30	34	24	4	43	37	14	12
NOV. 3	31	22	23	24	31	34	24	4	43	37	14	12
NOV. 4	31	24	25	26	31	35	24	4	43	37	14	12
NOV. 5	31	26	27	27	31	35	24	4	43	37	14	12
NOV. 6	31	28	29	29	31	35	24	4	43	37	14	12
NOV. 7	31	30	31	31	31	35	24	4	43	37	14	12
NOV. 8	31	32	33	33	32	35	24	4	43	37	14	12
NOV. 9	31	34	35	35	32	35	24	4	43	37	14	12
NOV. 10	31	36	36	37	32	36	24	4	43	37	14	12
NOV. 11	31	38	38	39	32	36	24	4	43	37	14	12
NOV. 12	32	39	40	40	32	36	24	4	43	37	14	12
NOV. 13	32	41	42	42	33	36	24	4	43	37	14	12
NOV. 14	32	43	43	44	33	36	24	4	43	37	14	12
NOV. 15	32	44	45	45	33	36	25	4	43	37	14	12
NOV. 16	32	46	46	47	33	37	25	4	43	37	14	12
NOV. 17	32	47	48	48	34	37	25	4	43	37	14	12
NOV. 18	32	1	1	2	34	37	25	4	43	37	14	12
NOV. 19	33	3	3	4	34	37	25	4	43	37	14	12
NOV. 20	33	4	5	5	34	37	25	4	43	37	14	12
NOV. 21	33	6	6	7	34	37	25	4	43	37	14	12
NOV. 22	33	7	8	9	35	38	25	4	43	37	14	12
NOV. 23	33	9	10	10	35	38	25	4	43	37	14	12
NOV. 24	33	11	11	12	35	38	25	4	43	37	14	12
NOV. 25	34	13	13	14	35	38	25	4	43	37	14	12
NOV. 26	34	14	15	16	35	38	25	4	43	37	14	12
NOV. 27	34	16	17	17	36	38	26	4	43	37	14	12
NOV. 28	34	18	19	19	36	39	26	4	43	37	14	12
NOV. 29	34	20	21	21	36	39	26	4	43	37	14	12
NOV. 30	34	22	22	23	36	39	26	4	43	37	14	12

December

Date & Time	SUN ☉	MOON 1 ☽	MOON 2 ☽	MOON 3 ●	MERCURY	VENUS	MARS	JUPITER	SATURN	URANUS	NEPTUNE	PLUTO
DEC. 1	34	24	24	25	36	39	26	4	43	37	14	12
DEC. 2	34	26	26	27	37	39	26	4	43	37	14	12
DEC. 3	35	27	28	29	37	39	26	4	43	37	14	12
DEC. 4	35	29	30	31	37	39	26	4	43	37	14	12
DEC. 5	35	31	32	33	37	40	26	4	43	37	14	12
DEC. 6	35	33	34	34	37	40	26	4	43	37	14	12
DEC. 7	35	35	36	36	37	40	26	4	43	37	14	12
DEC. 8	35	37	37	38	38	40	26	4	43	37	14	12
DEC. 9	35	39	39	40	38	40	26	4	43	37	14	12
DEC. 10	35	40	41	41	38	40	26	4	43	37	14	12
DEC. 11	36	42	43	43	38	41	27	4	43	37	14	12
DEC. 12	36	44	44	45	38	41	27	4	43	37	14	12
DEC. 13	36	45	46	46	38	41	27	4	43	37	14	12
DEC. 14	36	47	47	48	39	41	27	4	43	37	14	12
DEC. 15	36	48	1	1	39	41	27	4	43	37	14	12
DEC. 16	36	2	3	3	39	41	27	4	43	37	14	12
DEC. 17	36	4	4	5	39	42	27	4	43	37	14	12
DEC. 18	36	5	6	6	39	42	27	4	43	37	14	12
DEC. 19	37	7	7	8	39	42	27	4	43	37	14	12
DEC. 20	37	9	9	10	39	42	27	4	43	37	14	12
DEC. 21	37	10	11	11	39	42	27	4	43	37	14	12
DEC. 22	37	12	13	13	39	42	27	4	43	37	14	12
DEC. 23	37	14	14	15	39	43	27	4	43	37	14	12
DEC. 24	37	16	16	17	39	43	28	4	43	37	14	12
DEC. 25	37	18	18	19	39	43	28	4	43	37	14	12
DEC. 26	38	19	20	21	39	43	28	4	43	37	14	12
DEC. 27	38	21	22	23	39	43	28	4	43	37	14	12
DEC. 28	38	23	24	25	39	43	28	4	43	37	14	12
DEC. 29	38	25	26	26	39	43	28	4	43	37	14	12
DEC. 30	38	27	28	28	39	44	28	4	43	37	14	12
DEC. 31	38	29	29	30	38	44	28	4	43	37	14	12

MOON 1 ☽ 12:01 A.M. TO 8:00 A.M.   **MOON 2 ☽ 8:01 A.M. TO 4:00 P.M.**   **MOON 3 ● 4:01 P.M. TO 12:00 A.M.**
Use only one "moon" number. Choose the column closest to your time of birth. If your place of birth is not on
Eastern Standard Time, be sure to read "How to Convert to Eastern Standard Time" at the beginning of this section.

Date & Time	SUN	MOON 1	MOON 2	MOON 3	MERCURY	VENUS	MARS	JUPITER	SATURN	URANUS	NEPTUNE	PLUTO
JAN. 1	38	31	31	32	38	44	28	4	43	37	14	12
JAN. 2	38	33	33	34	38	44	28	4	43	37	14	12
JAN. 3	39	34	35	36	38	44	28	4	43	37	14	12
JAN. 4	39	36	37	37	38	44	28	4	43	37	14	12
JAN. 5	39	38	39	39	37	45	28	4	43	37	14	12
JAN. 6	39	40	40	41	37	45	28	4	44	37	14	12
JAN. 7	39	41	42	43	37	45	28	4	44	37	14	12
JAN. 8	39	43	44	44	37	45	29	4	44	37	14	12
JAN. 9	39	45	45	46	37	45	29	4	44	37	14	12
JAN. 10	40	46	47	47	37	45	29	4	44	37	14	12
JAN. 11	40	48	48	1	37	46	29	4	44	37	14	12
JAN. 12	40	1	2	2	37	46	29	4	44	37	14	12
JAN. 13	40	3	4	4	37	46	29	4	44	37	14	12
JAN. 14	40	5	5	6	37	46	29	4	44	37	14	12
JAN. 15	40	6	7	7	37	46	29	4	44	37	14	12
JAN. 16	40	8	8	9	37	46	29	4	44	37	14	12
JAN. 17	41	10	10	11	37	46	29	4	44	37	14	12
JAN. 18	41	11	12	12	37	47	29	4	44	37	14	12
JAN. 19	41	13	14	14	38	47	29	4	44	37	14	12
JAN. 20	41	15	16	16	38	47	29	4	44	37	14	12
JAN. 21	41	17	18	18	38	47	29	4	44	37	14	12
JAN. 22	41	19	19	20	38	47	30	4	44	37	14	12
JAN. 23	42	21	21	22	38	47	30	4	44	37	14	12
JAN. 24	42	23	23	24	38	48	30	4	44	37	14	12
JAN. 25	42	25	25	26	38	48	30	4	44	37	14	12
JAN. 26	42	27	27	28	38	48	30	4	44	37	14	12
JAN. 27	42	28	29	30	39	48	30	4	44	37	14	12
JAN. 28	42	30	31	32	39	48	30	4	44	37	14	12
JAN. 29	42	32	33	33	39	48	30	4	44	37	14	12
JAN. 30	42	34	35	35	39	48	30	4	44	37	14	12
JAN. 31	43	36	36	37	39	1	30	4	44	37	14	12

Date & Time	SUN	MOON 1	MOON 2	MOON 3	MERCURY	VENUS	MARS	JUPITER	SATURN	URANUS	NEPTUNE	PLUTO
FEB. 1	43	37	38	39	39	1	30	4	44	37	14	12
FEB. 2	43	39	40	40	40	1	30	4	44	37	14	12
FEB. 3	43	41	41	42	40	1	30	4	44	37	14	12
FEB. 4	43	43	43	44	40	1	30	4	44	37	14	12
FEB. 5	43	44	45	45	40	1	30	4	44	37	14	12
FEB. 6	43	46	46	47	40	1	30	4	44	37	14	12
FEB. 7	43	47	48	48	41	2	30	4	44	37	14	12
FEB. 8	44	1	1	2	41	2	31	4	44	37	14	12
FEB. 9	44	3	3	4	41	2	31	4	44	37	14	12
FEB. 10	44	4	5	5	41	2	31	4	44	37	14	12
FEB. 11	44	6	6	7	41	2	31	4	44	37	14	12
FEB. 12	44	7	8	8	42	2	31	4	44	37	14	12
FEB. 13	44	9	10	10	42	2	31	4	44	37	14	12
FEB. 14	44	11	11	12	42	3	31	4	44	37	14	12
FEB. 15	44	12	13	14	42	3	31	4	44	37	14	12
FEB. 16	45	14	15	15	42	3	31	4	44	37	14	12
FEB. 17	45	16	17	17	43	3	31	4	44	37	14	12
FEB. 18	45	18	19	19	43	3	31	5	44	37	14	12
FEB. 19	45	20	21	21	43	3	31	5	44	37	14	12
FEB. 20	45	22	23	23	43	3	31	5	44	37	14	12
FEB. 21	45	24	25	25	43	3	31	5	44	37	14	12
FEB. 22	45	26	27	27	44	4	31	5	44	37	14	12
FEB. 23	46	28	29	29	44	4	31	5	44	37	14	12
FEB. 24	46	30	30	31	44	4	31	5	44	37	14	12
FEB. 25	46	32	32	33	44	4	31	5	44	37	14	12
FEB. 26	46	34	34	35	45	4	31	5	44	37	14	12
FEB. 27	46	35	36	37	45	4	31	5	44	37	14	12
FEB. 28	46	37	38	38	45	4	32	5	44	37	14	12

MOON 1 ◗ 12:01 A.M. TO 8:00 A.M.   **MOON 2** ◑ 8:01 A.M. TO 4:00 P.M.   **MOON 3** ● 4:01 P.M. TO 12:00 A.M.
Use only one "moon" number. Choose the column closest to your time of birth. If your place of birth is not on Eastern Standard Time, be sure to read "How to Convert to Eastern Standard Time" at the beginning of this section.

1905

March

Date & Time	SUN ☉	MOON 1 ☽	MOON 2 ◑	MOON 3 ●	MERCURY	VENUS	MARS	JUPITER	SATURN	URANUS	NEPTUNE	PLUTO
MAR. 1	46	39	39	40	45	4	32	5	44	37	14	12
MAR. 2	46	40	41	42	46	5	32	5	44	37	14	12
MAR. 3	47	42	43	43	46	5	32	5	44	37	14	12
MAR. 4	47	44	44	45	46	5	32	5	44	37	14	12
MAR. 5	47	45	46	46	46	5	32	5	44	37	14	12
MAR. 6	47	47	47	48	46	5	32	5	44	37	14	12
MAR. 7	47	1	1	2	47	5	32	5	44	37	14	12
MAR. 8	47	2	3	3	47	5	32	5	44	37	14	12
MAR. 9	47	4	4	5	47	5	32	5	44	37	14	12
MAR. 10	47	5	6	6	47	5	32	5	44	37	14	12
MAR. 11	48	7	7	8	48	5	32	5	45	37	14	12
MAR. 12	48	8	9	10	48	6	32	5	45	37	14	12
MAR. 13	48	10	11	11	48	6	32	5	45	37	14	12
MAR. 14	48	12	12	13	1	6	32	5	45	37	14	12
MAR. 15	48	13	14	15	1	6	32	5	45	37	14	12
MAR. 16	48	15	16	16	1	6	32	5	45	37	14	12
MAR. 17	48	17	18	18	1	6	32	5	45	38	14	12
MAR. 18	48	19	20	20	2	6	32	5	45	38	14	12
MAR. 19	1	21	22	22	2	6	32	5	45	38	14	12
MAR. 20	1	23	24	24	2	6	32	5	45	38	14	12
MAR. 21	1	25	26	26	2	6	32	5	45	38	14	12
MAR. 22	1	27	28	28	3	6	32	5	45	38	14	12
MAR. 23	1	29	30	30	3	6	32	5	45	38	14	12
MAR. 24	1	31	32	32	3	7	32	5	45	38	14	12
MAR. 25	2	33	34	34	3	7	32	5	45	38	14	12
MAR. 26	2	35	35	36	4	7	32	5	45	38	14	12
MAR. 27	2	37	37	38	4	7	32	5	45	38	14	12
MAR. 28	2	38	39	40	4	7	32	6	45	38	14	12
MAR. 29	2	40	41	41	4	7	32	6	45	38	14	12
MAR. 30	2	42	42	43	5	7	32	6	45	38	14	12
MAR. 31	2	43	44	44	5	7	32	6	45	38	14	12

April

Date & Time	SUN ☉	MOON 1 ☽	MOON 2 ◑	MOON 3 ●	MERCURY	VENUS	MARS	JUPITER	SATURN	URANUS	NEPTUNE	PLUTO
APR. 1	2	45	45	46	5	7	32	6	45	38	14	12
APR. 2	2	47	47	48	5	7	32	6	45	38	14	12
APR. 3	3	48	1	1	5	7	32	6	45	38	14	12
APR. 4	3	2	2	3	5	7	32	6	45	38	14	12
APR. 5	3	3	4	4	5	7	32	6	45	38	14	12
APR. 6	3	5	5	6	5	7	32	6	45	38	14	12
APR. 7	3	6	7	8	5	7	32	6	45	38	14	12
APR. 8	3	8	9	9	6	7	32	6	45	38	14	12
APR. 9	3	10	10	11	6	7	32	6	45	38	14	12
APR. 10	3	11	12	12	6	7	32	6	45	38	14	12
APR. 11	4	13	14	14	6	7	32	6	45	38	14	12
APR. 12	4	15	15	16	6	7	32	6	45	38	14	12
APR. 13	4	16	17	18	6	7	32	6	45	38	14	12
APR. 14	4	18	19	20	6	7	32	6	45	38	14	12
APR. 15	4	20	21	21	6	7	32	6	45	38	14	12
APR. 16	4	22	23	23	6	7	32	6	45	38	14	12
APR. 17	4	24	25	25	6	7	32	6	45	38	14	12
APR. 18	4	26	27	27	6	7	32	6	45	38	14	12
APR. 19	5	28	29	29	6	6	32	6	45	38	14	12
APR. 20	5	30	31	31	6	6	32	6	45	38	14	12
APR. 21	5	32	33	33	6	6	32	6	45	38	14	12
APR. 22	5	34	35	35	6	6	32	6	45	38	14	12
APR. 23	5	36	37	37	5	6	32	6	45	38	14	12
APR. 24	5	38	38	39	5	6	32	6	45	38	14	12
APR. 25	6	40	40	41	5	6	32	6	45	38	14	12
APR. 26	6	41	42	42	5	6	32	6	45	38	14	12
APR. 27	6	43	43	44	5	6	32	6	45	38	14	12
APR. 28	6	45	45	46	5	6	32	7	45	38	14	12
APR. 29	6	46	47	47	5	6	32	7	45	38	14	12
APR. 30	6	48	48	1	5	6	32	7	45	38	14	12

MOON 1 ☽ 12:01 A.M. TO 8:00 A.M.   **MOON 2** ◑ 8:01 A.M. TO 4:00 P.M.   **MOON 3** ● 4:01 P.M. TO 12:00 A.M.

Use only one "moon" number. Choose the column closest to your time of birth. If your place of birth is not on Eastern Standard Time, be sure to read "How to Convert to Eastern Standard Time" at the beginning of this section.

1905

May

June

Date & Time	SUN	MOON 1	MOON 2	MOON 3	MERCURY	VENUS	MARS	JUPITER	SATURN	URANUS	NEPTUNE	PLUTO
MAY 1	6	1	2	2	5	6	32	7	45	38	14	12
MAY 2	6	3	3	4	5	5	32	7	45	38	14	12
MAY 3	7	4	5	6	5	5	32	7	45	37	14	12
MAY 4	7	6	7	7	5	5	32	7	45	37	14	12
MAY 5	7	8	8	9	5	5	31	7	45	37	14	12
MAY 6	7	9	10	10	5	5	31	7	45	37	14	12
MAY 7	7	11	11	12	5	5	31	7	45	37	14	12
MAY 8	7	13	13	14	5	5	31	7	45	37	14	12
MAY 9	7	14	15	15	5	5	31	7	45	37	14	12
MAY 10	7	16	17	17	5	5	31	7	45	37	14	12
MAY 11	8	18	18	19	5	5	31	7	45	37	14	12
MAY 12	8	20	20	21	5	5	31	7	45	37	14	12
MAY 13	8	21	22	23	5	5	31	7	45	37	14	12
MAY 14	8	23	24	25	5	5	31	7	45	37	14	12
MAY 15	8	25	26	27	5	5	31	7	45	37	14	12
MAY 16	8	27	28	29	5	5	31	7	45	37	14	12
MAY 17	8	29	30	31	5	5	31	7	45	37	14	12
MAY 18	8	31	32	33	5	5	31	7	45	37	14	12
MAY 19	9	33	34	35	5	5	31	7	45	37	14	12
MAY 20	9	35	36	36	5	5	31	7	45	37	14	12
MAY 21	9	37	38	38	6	5	31	7	45	37	14	12
MAY 22	9	39	39	40	6	5	31	7	45	37	14	12
MAY 23	9	41	41	42	6	5	31	7	45	37	14	12
MAY 24	9	42	43	43	6	5	31	7	45	37	14	12
MAY 25	10	44	45	45	6	5	31	7	45	37	14	12
MAY 26	10	46	46	47	6	5	31	7	45	37	14	12
MAY 27	10	47	48	48	6	5	30	7	45	37	14	12
MAY 28	10	1	1	2	7	5	30	7	45	37	14	12
MAY 29	10	2	3	3	7	5	30	7	45	37	14	12
MAY 30	10	4	5	5	7	5	30	8	45	37	14	12
MAY 31	10	6	6	7	7	5	30	8	45	37	14	12

Date & Time	SUN	MOON 1	MOON 2	MOON 3	MERCURY	VENUS	MARS	JUPITER	SATURN	URANUS	NEPTUNE	PLUTO
JUN. 1	10	7	8	8	7	5	30	8	45	37	14	12
JUN. 2	10	9	9	10	8	5	30	8	45	37	14	12
JUN. 3	11	10	11	12	8	5	30	8	45	37	14	12
JUN. 4	11	12	13	13	8	5	30	8	45	37	14	12
JUN. 5	11	14	14	15	8	5	30	8	45	37	14	12
JUN. 6	11	16	16	17	8	6	30	8	45	37	14	12
JUN. 7	11	17	18	19	9	6	30	8	45	37	14	12
JUN. 8	11	19	20	20	9	6	30	8	45	37	14	12
JUN. 9	11	21	22	22	9	6	30	8	45	37	14	12
JUN. 10	11	23	23	24	9	6	30	8	45	37	14	12
JUN. 11	12	25	25	26	10	6	30	8	45	37	14	12
JUN. 12	12	27	27	28	10	6	30	8	45	37	14	12
JUN. 13	12	29	29	30	10	6	30	8	45	37	14	12
JUN. 14	12	31	31	32	10	6	30	8	45	37	14	12
JUN. 15	12	32	33	34	11	6	30	8	45	37	14	12
JUN. 16	12	34	35	36	11	6	30	8	45	37	14	12
JUN. 17	12	36	37	38	11	6	30	8	45	37	14	12
JUN. 18	12	38	39	39	11	7	30	8	45	37	14	12
JUN. 19	13	40	41	41	12	7	30	8	45	37	14	12
JUN. 20	13	42	42	43	12	7	30	8	45	37	14	12
JUN. 21	13	43	44	45	12	7	30	8	45	37	14	12
JUN. 22	13	45	46	46	13	7	30	8	45	37	14	12
JUN. 23	13	47	47	48	13	7	30	8	45	37	14	12
JUN. 24	13	48	1	1	13	7	30	8	45	37	14	12
JUN. 25	14	2	2	3	13	7	30	8	45	37	14	12
JUN. 26	14	3	4	5	14	7	30	8	45	37	14	12
JUN. 27	14	5	6	6	14	8	30	8	45	37	14	12
JUN. 28	14	7	7	8	14	8	30	8	45	37	14	12
JUN. 29	14	8	9	9	15	8	30	8	45	37	14	12
JUN. 30	14	10	11	11	15	8	30	8	45	37	14	12

MOON 1 ◖ 12:01 A.M. TO 8:00 A.M.　　**MOON 2** ◑ 8:01 A.M. TO 4:00 P.M.　　**MOON 3** ● 4:01 P.M. TO 12:00 A.M.

Use only one "moon" number. Choose the column closest to your time of birth. If your place of birth is not on Eastern Standard Time, be sure to read "How to Convert to Eastern Standard Time" at the beginning of this section.

1905

July

August

Date & Time	SUN	MOON 1	MOON 2	MOON 3	MERCURY	VENUS	MARS	JUPITER	SATURN	URANUS	NEPTUNE	PLUTO
JUL. 1	14	12	12	13	15	8	30	8	45	37	14	12
JUL. 2	14	13	14	15	15	8	30	8	45	37	14	12
JUL. 3	15	15	16	16	16	8	30	9	45	37	14	12
JUL. 4	15	17	18	18	16	8	30	9	45	37	14	12
JUL. 5	15	19	19	20	16	9	30	9	45	37	14	12
JUL. 6	15	21	21	22	17	9	30	9	45	37	14	12
JUL. 7	15	22	23	24	17	9	30	9	45	37	14	12
JUL. 8	15	24	25	26	17	9	30	9	45	37	14	12
JUL. 9	15	26	27	27	17	9	30	9	45	37	14	12
JUL. 10	15	28	29	29	18	9	31	9	45	37	14	12
JUL. 11	16	30	31	31	18	9	31	9	45	37	14	12
JUL. 12	16	32	33	33	18	9	31	9	45	37	14	12
JUL. 13	16	34	34	35	18	10	31	9	45	37	14	12
JUL. 14	16	36	36	37	18	10	31	9	45	37	14	12
JUL. 15	16	37	38	39	19	10	31	9	45	37	14	12
JUL. 16	16	39	40	40	19	10	31	9	45	37	14	12
JUL. 17	16	41	42	42	19	10	31	9	45	37	14	12
JUL. 18	16	43	43	44	19	10	31	9	45	37	14	12
JUL. 19	17	45	45	46	20	10	31	9	45	37	14	12
JUL. 20	17	46	47	47	20	11	31	9	45	37	14	12
JUL. 21	17	48	48	1	20	11	31	9	45	37	14	12
JUL. 22	17	1	2	2	20	11	31	9	45	37	14	12
JUL. 23	17	3	3	4	20	11	31	9	45	37	14	12
JUL. 24	17	5	5	6	20	11	31	9	45	37	14	12
JUL. 25	17	6	7	7	21	11	31	9	45	37	14	12
JUL. 26	18	8	8	9	21	11	31	9	45	37	14	12
JUL. 27	18	9	10	10	21	12	31	9	45	37	14	12
JUL. 28	18	11	12	12	21	12	31	9	45	37	14	12
JUL. 29	18	13	13	14	21	12	31	9	45	37	14	12
JUL. 30	18	15	15	16	21	12	31	9	45	37	14	12
JUL. 31	18	16	17	18	22	12	32	9	45	37	14	12

Date & Time	SUN	MOON 1	MOON 2	MOON 3	MERCURY	VENUS	MARS	JUPITER	SATURN	URANUS	NEPTUNE	PLUTO
AUG. 1	18	18	19	19	22	12	32	9	45	37	14	12
AUG. 2	18	20	21	21	22	12	32	9	45	37	14	12
AUG. 3	19	22	23	23	22	13	32	9	45	37	14	12
AUG. 4	19	24	24	25	22	13	32	9	45	37	14	12
AUG. 5	19	26	26	27	22	13	32	9	45	37	14	12
AUG. 6	19	28	28	29	22	13	32	9	45	37	14	12
AUG. 7	19	30	30	31	22	13	32	9	45	37	14	12
AUG. 8	19	31	32	33	22	13	32	9	45	37	14	12
AUG. 9	19	33	34	35	23	13	32	9	45	37	14	12
AUG. 10	19	35	36	36	23	14	32	9	45	37	14	12
AUG. 11	20	37	38	38	23	14	32	9	45	37	14	12
AUG. 12	20	39	39	40	23	14	32	9	45	37	14	12
AUG. 13	20	41	41	42	23	14	32	9	45	37	14	12
AUG. 14	20	42	43	43	23	14	32	9	45	37	14	12
AUG. 15	20	44	45	45	23	14	32	9	45	37	14	12
AUG. 16	20	46	46	47	23	14	33	9	45	37	14	12
AUG. 17	20	47	48	48	23	15	33	10	45	37	14	12
AUG. 18	20	1	1	2	23	15	33	10	45	37	14	12
AUG. 19	21	2	3	4	23	15	33	10	45	37	14	12
AUG. 20	21	4	5	5	23	15	33	10	45	37	14	12
AUG. 21	21	6	6	7	23	15	33	10	45	37	14	12
AUG. 22	21	7	8	8	23	15	33	10	45	37	14	12
AUG. 23	21	9	9	10	23	15	33	10	45	37	14	12
AUG. 24	21	10	11	12	22	16	33	10	45	37	14	12
AUG. 25	21	12	13	13	22	16	33	10	45	37	14	12
AUG. 26	22	14	14	15	22	16	33	10	45	37	14	12
AUG. 27	22	16	16	17	22	16	33	10	45	37	14	12
AUG. 28	22	17	18	19	22	16	33	10	45	37	14	12
AUG. 29	22	19	20	21	22	16	34	10	45	37	14	12
AUG. 30	22	21	22	22	22	17	34	10	45	37	14	12
AUG. 31	22	23	24	24	22	17	34	10	45	37	14	12

MOON 1 ◔ 12:01 A.M. TO 8:00 A.M.   **MOON 2** ◑ 8:01 A.M. TO 4:00 P.M.   **MOON 3** ● 4:01 P.M. TO 12:00 A.M.

Use only one "moon" number. Choose the column closest to your time of birth. If your place of birth is not on Eastern Standard Time, be sure to read "How to Convert to Eastern Standard Time" at the beginning of this section.

September

October

Date & Time	SUN	MOON 1	MOON 2	MOON 3	MERCURY	VENUS	MARS	JUPITER	SATURN	URANUS	NEPTUNE	PLUTO
SEP. 1	22	25	26	26	22	17	34	10	45	37	14	12
SEP. 2	22	27	28	28	21	17	34	10	45	37	14	12
SEP. 3	23	29	30	30	21	17	34	10	45	37	14	12
SEP. 4	23	31	32	32	21	17	34	10	45	37	14	12
SEP. 5	23	33	34	34	21	17	34	10	45	37	14	12
SEP. 6	23	35	35	36	21	18	34	10	45	37	14	12
SEP. 7	23	37	37	38	21	18	34	10	45	37	14	12
SEP. 8	23	38	39	40	21	18	34	10	45	37	14	12
SEP. 9	23	40	41	41	21	18	34	10	45	37	14	12
SEP. 10	23	42	42	43	21	18	35	10	45	37	14	12
SEP. 11	24	43	44	45	21	18	35	10	45	37	14	12
SEP. 12	24	45	46	46	21	19	35	10	45	37	14	12
SEP. 13	24	47	47	48	21	19	35	10	45	37	14	12
SEP. 14	24	48	1	1	21	19	35	10	45	37	14	12
SEP. 15	24	2	3	3	21	19	35	10	45	37	14	12
SEP. 16	24	4	4	5	22	19	35	10	45	37	14	12
SEP. 17	24	5	6	6	22	19	35	10	45	37	14	12
SEP. 18	24	7	7	8	22	20	35	10	45	37	14	12
SEP. 19	25	8	9	9	22	20	35	10	45	37	14	12
SEP. 20	25	10	10	11	22	20	35	10	45	37	14	12
SEP. 21	25	12	12	13	22	20	35	10	45	37	14	12
SEP. 22	25	13	14	14	23	20	36	10	45	37	14	12
SEP. 23	25	15	15	16	23	20	36	10	45	37	14	12
SEP. 24	25	17	17	18	23	20	36	10	45	37	14	12
SEP. 25	26	18	19	20	23	21	36	10	45	37	14	12
SEP. 26	26	20	21	22	24	21	36	10	45	37	14	12
SEP. 27	26	22	23	24	24	21	36	10	45	37	14	12
SEP. 28	26	24	25	26	24	21	36	10	45	37	14	12
SEP. 29	26	26	27	28	24	21	36	10	45	37	14	12
SEP. 30	26	28	29	30	25	21	36	10	45	37	14	12

Date & Time	SUN	MOON 1	MOON 2	MOON 3	MERCURY	VENUS	MARS	JUPITER	SATURN	URANUS	NEPTUNE	PLUTO
OCT. 1	26	30	31	32	25	22	36	10	45	37	14	12
OCT. 2	26	32	33	34	25	22	36	10	45	37	14	12
OCT. 3	27	34	35	35	25	22	37	10	45	37	14	12
OCT. 4	27	36	37	37	26	22	37	10	45	37	14	12
OCT. 5	27	38	39	39	26	22	37	10	45	37	14	12
OCT. 6	27	40	40	41	26	22	37	10	45	37	14	12
OCT. 7	27	41	42	43	26	23	37	10	45	37	14	12
OCT. 8	27	43	44	44	26	23	37	10	45	37	14	12
OCT. 9	27	45	45	46	27	23	37	10	45	37	14	12
OCT. 10	27	46	47	47	27	23	37	10	45	37	14	12
OCT. 11	28	48	1	1	27	23	37	10	45	37	14	12
OCT. 12	28	2	2	3	27	23	37	10	45	37	14	12
OCT. 13	28	3	4	4	28	24	37	10	44	37	14	12
OCT. 14	28	5	5	6	28	24	38	10	44	37	14	12
OCT. 15	28	6	7	7	28	24	38	10	44	37	14	12
OCT. 16	28	8	8	9	28	24	38	10	44	37	14	12
OCT. 17	28	10	10	11	29	24	38	10	44	37	14	12
OCT. 18	28	11	12	12	29	24	38	10	44	37	14	12
OCT. 19	29	13	13	14	29	25	38	10	44	37	14	12
OCT. 20	29	14	15	16	29	25	38	10	44	37	14	12
OCT. 21	29	16	17	17	29	25	38	10	44	37	14	12
OCT. 22	29	18	18	19	30	25	38	10	44	37	14	12
OCT. 23	29	20	20	21	30	25	38	10	44	37	14	12
OCT. 24	29	21	22	23	30	25	39	10	44	37	14	12
OCT. 25	29	23	24	25	30	26	39	10	44	37	14	12
OCT. 26	30	25	26	27	30	26	39	10	44	37	14	12
OCT. 27	30	27	28	29	31	26	39	10	44	37	14	12
OCT. 28	30	29	30	31	31	26	39	10	44	37	14	12
OCT. 29	30	31	32	33	31	26	39	10	44	37	14	12
OCT. 30	30	33	34	35	31	26	39	10	44	37	14	12
OCT. 31	30	35	36	37	31	27	39	10	44	37	14	12

MOON 1 ◗ 12:01 A.M. TO 8:00 A.M.　　**MOON 2** ◑ 8:01 A.M. TO 4:00 P.M.　　**MOON 3** ● 4:01 P.M. TO 12:00 A.M.
Use only one "moon" number. Choose the column closest to your time of birth. If your place of birth is not on
Eastern Standard Time, be sure to read "How to Convert to Eastern Standard Time" at the beginning of this section.

1905

November

Date & Time	SUN	MOON 1	MOON 2	MOON 3	MERCURY	VENUS	MARS	JUPITER	SATURN	URANUS	NEPTUNE	PLUTO
NOV. 1	30	37	38	39	32	27	39	10	44	37	14	12
NOV. 2	30	39	40	40	32	27	39	10	44	37	14	12
NOV. 3	31	41	42	42	32	27	39	10	44	37	14	12
NOV. 4	31	43	43	44	32	27	40	10	44	37	14	12
NOV. 5	31	44	45	45	32	27	40	9	44	37	14	12
NOV. 6	31	46	47	47	33	28	40	9	44	37	14	12
NOV. 7	31	48	48	1	33	28	40	9	44	37	14	12
NOV. 8	31	1	2	2	33	28	40	9	44	37	14	12
NOV. 9	31	3	3	4	33	28	40	9	44	37	14	12
NOV. 10	31	4	5	5	33	28	40	9	44	37	14	12
NOV. 11	31	6	6	7	34	28	40	9	44	37	14	12
NOV. 12	32	8	8	9	34	29	40	9	44	37	14	12
NOV. 13	32	9	10	10	34	29	40	9	44	37	14	12
NOV. 14	32	11	11	12	34	29	41	9	44	37	14	12
NOV. 15	32	12	13	13	34	29	41	9	44	37	14	12
NOV. 16	32	14	15	15	35	29	41	9	44	37	14	12
NOV. 17	32	16	16	17	35	29	41	9	44	37	14	12
NOV. 18	32	17	18	18	35	30	41	9	44	37	14	12
NOV. 19	33	19	20	20	35	30	41	9	45	37	14	12
NOV. 20	33	21	21	22	35	30	41	9	45	37	14	12
NOV. 21	33	23	23	24	35	30	41	9	45	37	14	12
NOV. 22	33	25	25	26	36	30	41	9	45	37	14	12
NOV. 23	33	26	27	28	36	30	41	9	45	37	14	12
NOV. 24	33	28	29	30	36	31	42	9	45	37	14	12
NOV. 25	34	30	31	32	36	31	42	9	45	37	14	12
NOV. 26	34	32	33	34	36	31	42	9	45	37	14	12
NOV. 27	34	34	35	36	36	31	42	9	45	37	14	12
NOV. 28	34	36	37	38	37	31	42	9	45	37	14	12
NOV. 29	34	38	39	40	37	31	42	9	45	37	14	12
NOV. 30	34	40	41	41	37	32	42	9	45	37	14	12

December

Date & Time	SUN	MOON 1	MOON 2	MOON 3	MERCURY	VENUS	MARS	JUPITER	SATURN	URANUS	NEPTUNE	PLUTO
DEC. 1	34	42	43	43	37	32	42	9	45	37	14	12
DEC. 2	34	44	44	45	37	32	42	9	45	37	14	12
DEC. 3	35	45	46	47	37	32	42	9	45	37	14	12
DEC. 4	35	47	48	48	37	32	43	9	45	37	14	12
DEC. 5	35	1	1	2	37	32	43	9	45	37	14	12
DEC. 6	35	2	3	3	37	33	43	9	45	37	14	12
DEC. 7	35	4	4	5	37	33	43	9	45	37	14	12
DEC. 8	35	5	6	7	37	33	43	9	45	37	14	12
DEC. 9	35	7	8	8	37	33	43	9	45	37	14	12
DEC. 10	35	9	9	10	37	33	43	9	45	37	14	12
DEC. 11	36	10	11	11	37	33	43	9	45	37	14	12
DEC. 12	36	12	12	13	37	34	43	9	45	37	14	12
DEC. 13	36	14	14	15	37	34	44	9	45	37	14	12
DEC. 14	36	15	16	16	36	34	44	9	45	37	14	12
DEC. 15	36	17	18	18	36	34	44	9	45	37	14	12
DEC. 16	36	19	19	20	36	34	44	9	45	37	14	12
DEC. 17	36	20	21	22	36	34	44	9	45	37	14	12
DEC. 18	36	22	23	23	36	35	44	9	45	37	14	12
DEC. 19	37	24	25	25	36	35	44	9	45	37	14	12
DEC. 20	37	26	26	27	35	35	44	9	45	37	14	12
DEC. 21	37	28	28	29	35	35	44	9	45	38	14	12
DEC. 22	37	30	30	31	35	35	44	9	45	38	14	12
DEC. 23	37	32	32	33	35	35	45	9	45	38	14	12
DEC. 24	37	34	34	35	35	36	45	9	45	38	14	12
DEC. 25	37	36	36	37	35	36	45	9	45	38	14	12
DEC. 26	38	38	38	39	35	36	45	9	45	38	14	12
DEC. 27	38	39	40	41	35	36	45	9	45	38	14	12
DEC. 28	38	41	42	43	35	36	45	9	45	38	14	12
DEC. 29	38	43	44	44	35	36	45	9	45	38	14	12
DEC. 30	38	45	45	46	35	37	45	9	45	38	14	12
DEC. 31	38	47	47	48	35	37	45	9	45	38	14	12

MOON 1 ☽ 12:01 A.M. TO 8:00 A.M.   **MOON 2** ◑ 8:01 A.M. TO 4:00 P.M.   **MOON 3** ● 4:01 P.M. TO 12:00 A.M.
Use only one "moon" number. Choose the column closest to your time of birth. If your place of birth is not on Eastern Standard Time, be sure to read "How to Convert to Eastern Standard Time" at the beginning of this section.

1906

January

Date & Time	SUN	MOON 1	MOON 2	MOON 3	MERCURY	VENUS	MARS	JUPITER	SATURN	URANUS	NEPTUNE	PLUTO
JAN. 1	38	48	1	1	35	37	45	9	45	38	14	12
JAN. 2	38	2	2	3	35	37	46	9	45	38	14	12
JAN. 3	39	3	4	4	36	37	46	9	45	38	14	12
JAN. 4	39	5	6	6	36	37	46	9	45	38	14	12
JAN. 5	39	7	7	8	36	38	46	9	45	38	14	12
JAN. 6	39	8	9	9	36	38	46	9	45	38	14	12
JAN. 7	39	10	10	11	36	38	46	9	45	38	14	12
JAN. 8	39	11	12	13	36	38	46	9	45	38	14	12
JAN. 9	39	13	14	14	36	38	46	9	45	38	14	12
JAN. 10	40	15	15	16	37	38	46	9	45	38	14	12
JAN. 11	40	16	17	18	37	39	46	9	45	38	14	12
JAN. 12	40	18	19	19	37	39	47	9	45	38	14	12
JAN. 13	40	20	21	21	37	39	47	9	45	38	14	12
JAN. 14	40	22	22	23	37	39	47	9	45	38	14	12
JAN. 15	40	24	24	25	37	39	47	9	45	38	14	12
JAN. 16	40	25	26	27	38	39	47	9	45	38	14	12
JAN. 17	41	27	28	29	38	40	47	8	45	38	14	12
JAN. 18	41	29	30	30	38	40	47	8	45	38	14	12
JAN. 19	41	31	32	32	38	40	47	8	45	38	14	12
JAN. 20	41	33	34	34	38	40	47	8	45	38	14	12
JAN. 21	41	35	36	36	38	40	47	8	45	38	14	12
JAN. 22	41	37	37	38	39	40	48	8	45	38	14	12
JAN. 23	42	39	39	40	39	41	48	8	45	38	14	12
JAN. 24	42	41	41	42	39	41	48	8	45	38	14	12
JAN. 25	42	42	43	44	39	41	48	8	45	38	14	12
JAN. 26	42	44	45	45	39	41	48	8	45	38	14	12
JAN. 27	42	46	46	47	40	41	48	9	45	38	14	12
JAN. 28	42	48	48	1	40	41	48	9	45	38	14	12
JAN. 29	42	1	2	2	40	42	48	9	45	38	14	12
JAN. 30	42	3	3	4	40	42	48	9	45	38	14	12
JAN. 31	43	4	5	6	40	42	48	9	45	38	14	12

February

Date & Time	SUN	MOON 1	MOON 2	MOON 3	MERCURY	VENUS	MARS	JUPITER	SATURN	URANUS	NEPTUNE	PLUTO
FEB. 1	43	6	7	7	41	42	1	9	45	38	14	12
FEB. 2	43	8	8	9	41	42	1	9	45	38	14	12
FEB. 3	43	9	10	10	41	42	1	9	45	38	14	12
FEB. 4	43	11	11	12	41	43	1	9	45	38	14	12
FEB. 5	43	12	13	14	42	43	1	9	45	38	14	12
FEB. 6	43	14	15	15	42	43	1	9	45	38	14	12
FEB. 7	43	16	16	17	42	43	1	9	45	38	14	12
FEB. 8	44	18	18	19	42	43	1	9	45	38	14	12
FEB. 9	44	19	20	21	42	43	1	9	45	38	14	12
FEB. 10	44	21	22	22	43	44	1	9	45	38	14	12
FEB. 11	44	23	24	24	43	44	2	9	45	38	14	12
FEB. 12	44	25	26	26	43	44	2	9	45	38	14	12
FEB. 13	44	27	27	28	43	44	2	9	46	38	14	12
FEB. 14	44	29	29	30	44	44	2	9	46	38	14	12
FEB. 15	44	31	31	32	44	44	2	9	46	38	14	12
FEB. 16	45	33	33	34	44	45	2	9	46	38	14	12
FEB. 17	45	34	35	36	44	45	2	9	46	38	14	12
FEB. 18	45	36	37	38	44	45	2	9	46	38	14	12
FEB. 19	45	38	39	39	45	45	2	9	46	38	14	12
FEB. 20	45	40	41	41	45	45	2	9	46	38	14	12
FEB. 21	45	42	42	43	45	46	3	9	46	38	14	12
FEB. 22	45	44	44	45	45	46	3	9	46	38	14	12
FEB. 23	46	45	46	46	46	46	3	9	46	38	14	12
FEB. 24	46	47	48	48	46	46	3	9	46	38	14	12
FEB. 25	46	1	1	2	46	46	3	9	46	38	14	12
FEB. 26	46	2	3	3	46	46	3	9	46	38	14	12
FEB. 27	46	4	4	5	47	46	3	9	46	38	14	12
FEB. 28	46	6	6	7	47	47	3	9	46	38	14	12

MOON 1 ☽ 12:01 A.M. TO 8:00 A.M.   **MOON 2** ☽ 8:01 A.M. TO 4:00 P.M.   **MOON 3** ● 4:01 P.M. TO 12:00 A.M.

Use only one "moon" number. Choose the column closest to your time of birth. If your place of birth is not on Eastern Standard Time, be sure to read "How to Convert to Eastern Standard Time" at the beginning of this section.

1906

March

April

Date & Time	SUN	MOON 1	MOON 2	MOON 3	MERCURY	VENUS	MARS	JUPITER	SATURN	URANUS	NEPTUNE	PLUTO
MAR. 1	46	7	8	8	47	47	3	9	46	38	14	12
MAR. 2	46	9	9	10	47	47	3	9	46	38	14	12
MAR. 3	47	10	11	11	48	47	4	9	46	38	14	12
MAR. 4	47	12	12	13	48	47	4	9	46	38	14	12
MAR. 5	47	13	14	15	48	47	4	9	46	38	14	12
MAR. 6	47	15	16	16	1	48	4	9	46	38	14	12
MAR. 7	47	17	17	18	1	48	4	9	46	38	14	12
MAR. 8	47	19	19	20	1	48	4	9	46	38	14	12
MAR. 9	47	20	21	22	1	48	4	9	46	38	14	12
MAR. 10	47	22	23	24	1	48	4	9	46	38	14	12
MAR. 11	48	24	25	26	2	48	4	9	46	38	14	12
MAR. 12	48	26	27	28	2	1	4	9	46	38	14	12
MAR. 13	48	28	29	29	2	1	5	9	46	38	14	12
MAR. 14	48	30	31	31	2	1	5	9	46	38	14	12
MAR. 15	48	32	33	33	2	1	5	9	46	38	14	12
MAR. 16	48	34	35	35	3	1	5	9	46	38	14	12
MAR. 17	48	36	37	37	3	1	5	9	46	38	14	12
MAR. 18	48	38	38	39	3	2	5	9	46	38	14	12
MAR. 19	1	40	40	41	3	2	5	9	46	38	14	12
MAR. 20	1	41	42	42	3	2	5	9	46	38	14	12
MAR. 21	1	43	44	44	3	2	5	9	46	38	14	12
MAR. 22	1	45	45	46	3	2	5	9	46	38	14	12
MAR. 23	1	46	47	48	3	2	6	9	46	38	14	12
MAR. 24	1	48	1	1	4	3	6	9	46	38	14	12
MAR. 25	2	2	2	3	4	3	6	9	46	38	14	12
MAR. 26	2	3	4	4	4	3	6	9	46	38	14	12
MAR. 27	2	5	6	6	4	3	6	9	46	38	14	12
MAR. 28	2	7	7	8	4	3	6	9	46	38	14	12
MAR. 29	2	8	9	9	3	3	6	9	46	38	14	12
MAR. 30	2	10	10	11	3	4	6	9	46	38	14	12
MAR. 31	2	11	12	12	3	4	6	9	46	38	14	12

Date & Time	SUN	MOON 1	MOON 2	MOON 3	MERCURY	VENUS	MARS	JUPITER	SATURN	URANUS	NEPTUNE	PLUTO
APR. 1	2	13	13	14	3	4	6	9	46	38	14	12
APR. 2	2	15	15	16	3	4	6	9	46	38	14	12
APR. 3	3	16	17	17	3	4	7	9	46	38	14	12
APR. 4	3	18	19	19	3	4	7	10	46	38	14	12
APR. 5	3	20	20	21	3	5	7	10	46	38	14	12
APR. 6	3	22	22	23	3	5	7	10	46	38	14	12
APR. 7	3	23	24	25	3	5	7	10	46	38	14	12
APR. 8	3	25	26	27	3	5	7	10	46	38	14	12
APR. 9	3	27	28	29	2	5	7	10	46	38	14	12
APR. 10	3	29	30	31	2	5	7	10	46	38	14	12
APR. 11	4	31	32	33	2	6	7	10	46	38	14	12
APR. 12	4	33	34	35	2	6	7	10	46	38	14	12
APR. 13	4	35	36	37	2	6	8	10	46	38	14	12
APR. 14	4	37	38	38	2	6	8	10	46	38	14	12
APR. 15	4	39	40	40	2	6	8	10	46	38	14	12
APR. 16	4	41	42	42	2	6	8	10	46	38	14	12
APR. 17	4	43	43	44	2	7	8	10	46	38	14	12
APR. 18	4	44	45	46	2	7	8	10	46	38	14	12
APR. 19	5	46	47	47	2	7	8	10	46	38	14	12
APR. 20	5	48	48	1	2	7	8	10	47	38	14	12
APR. 21	5	1	2	2	2	7	8	10	47	38	14	12
APR. 22	5	3	4	4	2	7	8	10	47	38	14	12
APR. 23	5	5	5	6	2	8	8	10	47	38	14	12
APR. 24	5	6	7	7	2	8	9	10	47	38	14	12
APR. 25	6	8	8	9	2	8	9	10	47	38	14	12
APR. 26	6	9	10	10	2	8	9	10	47	38	14	12
APR. 27	6	11	11	12	2	8	9	10	47	38	14	12
APR. 28	6	12	13	14	2	8	9	10	47	38	14	12
APR. 29	6	14	15	15	3	8	9	10	47	38	14	12
APR. 30	6	16	16	17	3	9	9	10	47	38	14	12

MOON 1 ◐ 12:01 A.M. TO 8:00 A.M.   **MOON 2** ◑ 8:01 A.M. TO 4:00 P.M.   **MOON 3** ● 4:01 P.M. TO 12:00 A.M.

Use only one "moon" number. Choose the column closest to your time of birth. If your place of birth is not on Eastern Standard Time, be sure to read "How to Convert to Eastern Standard Time" at the beginning of this section.

May

June

Date & Time	SUN	MOON 1	MOON 2	MOON 3	MERCURY	VENUS	MARS	JUPITER	SATURN	URANUS	NEPTUNE	PLUTO
MAY 1	6	17	18	18	3	9	9	10	47	38	14	12
MAY 2	6	19	20	20	3	9	9	10	47	38	14	12
MAY 3	7	21	21	22	3	9	9	10	47	38	14	12
MAY 4	7	23	23	24	3	9	9	10	47	38	14	12
MAY 5	7	24	25	26	3	9	10	10	47	38	14	12
MAY 6	7	26	27	28	3	10	10	10	47	38	14	12
MAY 7	7	28	29	30	4	10	10	10	47	38	14	12
MAY 8	7	30	31	32	4	10	10	10	47	38	14	12
MAY 9	7	33	33	34	4	10	10	10	47	38	14	12
MAY 10	7	35	35	36	4	10	10	11	47	38	14	12
MAY 11	8	37	37	38	4	10	10	11	47	38	14	12
MAY 12	8	38	39	40	4	11	10	11	47	38	14	12
MAY 13	8	40	41	42	5	11	10	11	47	38	14	12
MAY 14	8	42	43	43	5	11	10	11	47	38	14	12
MAY 15	8	44	45	45	5	11	10	11	47	38	14	12
MAY 16	8	46	46	47	5	11	11	11	47	38	14	12
MAY 17	8	47	48	48	5	11	11	11	47	38	14	12
MAY 18	8	1	2	2	6	12	11	11	47	38	14	12
MAY 19	9	3	3	4	6	12	11	11	47	38	14	12
MAY 20	9	4	5	5	6	12	11	11	47	38	14	12
MAY 21	9	6	6	7	6	12	11	11	47	38	14	12
MAY 22	9	7	8	8	6	12	11	11	47	38	14	12
MAY 23	9	9	9	10	7	12	11	11	47	38	14	12
MAY 24	9	11	11	12	7	13	11	11	47	38	14	12
MAY 25	10	12	13	13	7	13	11	11	47	38	14	12
MAY 26	10	14	14	15	7	13	11	11	47	38	14	12
MAY 27	10	15	16	16	8	13	11	11	47	38	14	12
MAY 28	10	17	18	18	8	13	12	11	47	38	14	12
MAY 29	10	19	19	20	8	13	12	11	47	38	14	12
MAY 30	10	20	21	21	8	14	12	11	47	38	14	12
MAY 31	10	22	23	23	9	14	12	11	47	38	14	12

Date & Time	SUN	MOON 1	MOON 2	MOON 3	MERCURY	VENUS	MARS	JUPITER	SATURN	URANUS	NEPTUNE	PLUTO
JUN. 1	10	24	24	25	9	14	12	11	47	38	14	12
JUN. 2	10	26	26	27	9	14	12	11	47	38	14	12
JUN. 3	11	28	28	29	10	14	12	11	47	38	14	12
JUN. 4	11	30	30	31	10	14	12	11	47	38	14	12
JUN. 5	11	32	32	33	10	14	12	11	47	38	14	12
JUN. 6	11	34	34	35	10	15	12	11	47	38	14	12
JUN. 7	11	36	36	37	11	15	13	11	47	38	14	12
JUN. 8	11	38	38	39	11	15	13	11	47	38	14	12
JUN. 9	11	40	40	41	11	15	13	11	47	38	14	12
JUN. 10	11	42	42	43	12	15	13	11	47	38	14	12
JUN. 11	12	43	44	45	12	15	13	11	47	38	14	12
JUN. 12	12	45	46	46	12	16	13	12	47	38	14	12
JUN. 13	12	47	47	48	13	16	13	12	47	38	14	12
JUN. 14	12	1	1	2	13	16	13	12	47	38	14	12
JUN. 15	12	2	3	3	13	16	13	12	47	38	14	12
JUN. 16	12	4	4	5	13	16	13	12	47	38	14	12
JUN. 17	12	5	6	6	14	16	13	12	47	38	14	12
JUN. 18	12	7	7	8	14	17	14	12	47	38	14	12
JUN. 19	13	9	9	10	14	17	14	12	47	38	14	12
JUN. 20	13	10	11	11	14	17	14	12	47	38	14	12
JUN. 21	13	12	12	13	15	17	14	12	47	38	14	12
JUN. 22	13	13	14	14	15	17	14	12	47	38	14	12
JUN. 23	13	15	15	16	15	17	14	12	47	38	14	12
JUN. 24	13	17	17	18	15	18	14	12	47	38	14	12
JUN. 25	14	18	19	19	16	18	14	12	47	38	14	12
JUN. 26	14	20	20	21	16	18	14	12	47	38	14	12
JUN. 27	14	22	22	23	16	18	14	12	47	38	14	12
JUN. 28	14	23	24	25	16	18	14	12	47	38	14	12
JUN. 29	14	25	26	26	17	18	15	12	47	38	14	12
JUN. 30	14	27	28	28	17	18	15	12	47	38	14	12

MOON 1 ◐ 12:01 A.M. TO 8:00 A.M.   **MOON 2** ◑ 8:01 A.M. TO 4:00 P.M.   **MOON 3** ● 4:01 P.M. TO 12:00 A.M.

Use only one "moon" number. Choose the column closest to your time of birth. If your place of birth is not on Eastern Standard Time, be sure to read "How to Convert to Eastern Standard Time" at the beginning of this section.

1906

July

August

Date & Time	SUN	MOON 1	MOON 2	MOON 3	MERCURY	VENUS	MARS	JUPITER	SATURN	URANUS	NEPTUNE	PLUTO
JUL. 1	14	29	30	30	17	19	15	12	47	38	14	12
JUL. 2	14	31	31	32	17	19	15	12	47	38	14	12
JUL. 3	15	33	33	34	17	19	15	12	47	38	14	12
JUL. 4	15	35	35	36	18	19	15	12	47	38	14	12
JUL. 5	15	37	37	38	18	19	15	12	47	38	14	12
JUL. 6	15	39	39	40	18	19	15	12	47	38	14	12
JUL. 7	15	41	41	42	18	20	15	12	47	38	14	12
JUL. 8	15	43	43	44	18	20	15	12	47	38	14	12
JUL. 9	15	44	45	46	19	20	15	12	47	38	14	12
JUL. 10	15	46	47	47	19	20	15	12	47	38	14	12
JUL. 11	16	48	1	1	19	20	16	12	47	38	14	12
JUL. 12	16	2	2	3	19	20	16	12	47	38	14	12
JUL. 13	16	3	4	4	19	21	16	12	47	38	14	12
JUL. 14	16	5	5	6	19	21	16	12	47	38	14	12
JUL. 15	16	6	7	8	19	21	16	13	47	38	14	12
JUL. 16	16	8	9	9	20	21	16	13	47	38	14	12
JUL. 17	16	10	10	11	20	21	16	13	47	38	14	12
JUL. 18	16	11	12	12	20	21	16	13	47	38	14	12
JUL. 19	17	13	13	14	20	21	16	13	47	38	14	12
JUL. 20	17	14	15	16	20	22	16	13	47	38	14	12
JUL. 21	17	16	17	17	20	22	16	13	47	38	14	12
JUL. 22	17	18	18	19	20	22	17	13	47	38	14	12
JUL. 23	17	19	20	21	20	22	17	13	47	38	14	12
JUL. 24	17	21	22	22	20	22	17	13	47	38	14	12
JUL. 25	17	23	24	24	20	22	17	13	47	38	14	12
JUL. 26	18	25	25	26	20	23	17	13	47	38	14	12
JUL. 27	18	27	27	28	20	23	17	13	47	38	14	12
JUL. 28	18	28	29	30	20	23	17	13	47	38	14	12
JUL. 29	18	30	31	32	20	23	17	13	47	38	14	12
JUL. 30	18	32	33	34	20	23	17	13	47	38	14	12
JUL. 31	18	34	35	35	20	23	17	13	47	38	14	12

Date & Time	SUN	MOON 1	MOON 2	MOON 3	MERCURY	VENUS	MARS	JUPITER	SATURN	URANUS	NEPTUNE	PLUTO
AUG. 1	18	36	37	37	20	23	17	13	47	38	14	12
AUG. 2	18	38	39	39	20	24	17	13	47	38	14	12
AUG. 3	19	40	41	41	20	24	18	13	47	38	14	12
AUG. 4	19	42	42	43	20	24	18	13	47	38	14	12
AUG. 5	19	44	44	45	20	24	18	13	47	38	14	12
AUG. 6	19	46	46	47	20	24	18	13	47	38	14	12
AUG. 7	19	47	48	48	20	24	18	13	47	38	14	12
AUG. 8	19	1	2	2	20	25	18	13	47	38	14	12
AUG. 9	19	3	3	4	20	25	18	13	47	38	14	12
AUG. 10	19	4	5	5	20	25	18	13	47	38	14	12
AUG. 11	20	6	7	7	20	25	18	13	47	38	15	12
AUG. 12	20	8	8	9	20	25	18	13	47	38	15	12
AUG. 13	20	9	10	10	19	25	18	13	47	38	15	12
AUG. 14	20	11	11	12	19	25	18	13	47	38	15	12
AUG. 15	20	12	13	13	19	26	19	13	47	38	15	12
AUG. 16	20	14	14	15	19	26	19	13	47	38	15	12
AUG. 17	20	16	16	17	19	26	19	13	47	38	15	12
AUG. 18	20	17	18	18	19	26	19	13	47	38	15	12
AUG. 19	21	19	20	20	19	26	19	13	47	38	15	12
AUG. 20	21	21	21	22	19	26	19	13	47	38	15	12
AUG. 21	21	22	23	24	19	26	19	14	47	38	15	12
AUG. 22	21	24	25	26	19	27	19	14	47	38	15	12
AUG. 23	21	26	27	27	19	27	19	14	47	38	15	12
AUG. 24	21	28	29	29	19	27	19	14	47	38	15	12
AUG. 25	21	30	31	31	19	27	19	14	47	38	15	12
AUG. 26	22	32	32	33	19	27	19	14	47	38	15	12
AUG. 27	22	34	34	35	19	27	20	14	47	38	15	12
AUG. 28	22	36	36	37	19	27	20	14	47	38	15	12
AUG. 29	22	37	38	39	19	28	20	14	47	38	15	12
AUG. 30	22	39	40	41	19	28	20	14	47	38	15	12
AUG. 31	22	41	42	42	19	28	20	14	47	38	15	12

MOON 1 ◗ 12:01 A.M. TO 8:00 A.M.   **MOON 2** ◖ 8:01 A.M. TO 4:00 P.M.   **MOON 3** ● 4:01 P.M. TO 12:00 A.M.
Use only one "moon" number. Choose the column closest to your time of birth. If your place of birth is not on Eastern Standard Time, be sure to read "How to Convert to Eastern Standard Time" at the beginning of this section.

1906

September

Date & Time	SUN	MOON 1	MOON 2	MOON 3	MERCURY	VENUS	MARS	JUPITER	SATURN	URANUS	NEPTUNE	PLUTO
SEP. 1	22	43	44	44	20	28	20	14	47	38	15	12
SEP. 2	22	45	45	46	20	28	20	14	47	38	15	12
SEP. 3	23	47	47	48	20	28	20	14	47	38	15	12
SEP. 4	23	48	1	2	20	28	20	14	47	38	15	12
SEP. 5	23	2	3	3	20	29	20	14	47	38	15	12
SEP. 6	23	4	4	5	21	29	20	14	47	38	15	12
SEP. 7	23	5	6	6	21	29	21	14	46	38	15	12
SEP. 8	23	7	8	8	21	29	21	14	46	38	15	12
SEP. 9	23	9	9	10	21	29	21	14	46	38	15	12
SEP. 10	23	10	11	11	22	29	21	14	46	38	15	12
SEP. 11	24	12	12	13	22	29	21	14	46	38	15	12
SEP. 12	24	13	14	14	22	30	21	14	46	38	15	12
SEP. 13	24	15	16	16	22	30	21	14	46	38	15	12
SEP. 14	24	17	17	18	22	30	21	14	46	38	15	12
SEP. 15	24	18	19	19	23	30	21	14	46	38	15	12
SEP. 16	24	20	21	21	23	30	21	14	46	38	15	12
SEP. 17	24	22	22	23	23	30	21	14	46	38	15	12
SEP. 18	24	24	24	25	24	30	21	14	46	38	15	12
SEP. 19	25	26	26	27	24	31	22	14	46	38	15	12
SEP. 20	25	27	28	29	24	31	22	14	46	38	15	12
SEP. 21	25	29	30	31	24	31	22	14	46	38	15	12
SEP. 22	25	31	32	33	24	31	22	14	46	38	15	12
SEP. 23	25	33	34	35	25	31	22	14	46	38	15	12
SEP. 24	25	35	36	36	25	31	22	14	46	38	15	12
SEP. 25	26	37	38	38	25	31	22	14	46	38	15	12
SEP. 26	26	39	40	40	25	31	22	14	46	38	15	12
SEP. 27	26	41	41	42	26	32	22	14	46	38	15	12
SEP. 28	26	43	43	44	26	32	22	14	46	38	15	12
SEP. 29	26	44	45	46	26	32	22	14	46	38	15	12
SEP. 30	26	46	47	47	26	32	22	14	46	38	15	12

October

Date & Time	SUN	MOON 1	MOON 2	MOON 3	MERCURY	VENUS	MARS	JUPITER	SATURN	URANUS	NEPTUNE	PLUTO
OCT. 1	26	48	48	1	27	32	23	14	46	38	15	12
OCT. 2	26	2	2	3	27	32	23	14	46	38	15	12
OCT. 3	27	3	4	4	27	32	23	14	46	38	15	12
OCT. 4	27	5	5	6	27	32	23	14	46	38	15	12
OCT. 5	27	7	7	8	28	33	23	14	46	38	15	12
OCT. 6	27	8	9	9	28	33	23	14	46	38	15	12
OCT. 7	27	10	10	11	28	33	23	14	46	38	15	12
OCT. 8	27	11	12	12	28	33	23	14	46	38	15	12
OCT. 9	27	13	13	14	28	33	23	14	46	38	15	12
OCT. 10	27	14	15	16	29	33	23	14	46	38	15	12
OCT. 11	28	16	17	17	29	33	23	14	46	38	15	12
OCT. 12	28	18	18	19	29	33	23	14	46	38	15	12
OCT. 13	28	19	20	21	29	33	24	14	46	38	15	12
OCT. 14	28	21	22	22	29	33	24	14	46	38	15	12
OCT. 15	28	23	24	24	30	34	24	14	46	38	15	12
OCT. 16	28	25	25	26	30	34	24	14	46	38	15	12
OCT. 17	28	27	27	28	30	34	24	14	46	38	15	12
OCT. 18	28	29	29	30	30	34	24	14	46	38	15	12
OCT. 19	29	31	31	32	30	34	24	14	46	38	15	12
OCT. 20	29	33	33	34	31	34	24	14	46	38	15	12
OCT. 21	29	35	35	36	31	34	24	14	46	38	15	12
OCT. 22	29	37	37	38	31	34	24	14	46	38	15	12
OCT. 23	29	38	39	40	31	34	24	14	46	38	15	12
OCT. 24	29	40	41	42	31	34	24	14	46	38	15	12
OCT. 25	29	42	43	43	32	34	25	14	46	38	15	12
OCT. 26	30	44	45	45	32	34	25	14	46	38	15	12
OCT. 27	30	46	46	47	32	34	25	14	46	38	15	12
OCT. 28	30	47	48	1	32	35	25	14	46	38	15	12
OCT. 29	30	1	2	2	32	35	25	14	46	38	15	12
OCT. 30	30	3	3	4	33	35	25	14	46	38	15	12
OCT. 31	30	4	5	5	33	35	25	14	46	38	15	12

MOON 1 ◑ 12:01 A.M. TO 8:00 A.M.   **MOON 2** ◐ 8:01 A.M. TO 4:00 P.M.   **MOON 3** ● 4:01 P.M. TO 12:00 A.M.
Use only one "moon" number. Choose the column closest to your time of birth. If your place of birth is not on Eastern Standard Time, be sure to read "How to Convert to Eastern Standard Time" at the beginning of this section.

1906

November

December

Date & Time	SUN	MOON 1	MOON 2	MOON 3	MERCURY	VENUS	MARS	JUPITER	SATURN	URANUS	NEPTUNE	PLUTO
NOV. 1	30	6	7	7	33	35	25	14	46	38	15	12
NOV. 2	30	8	8	9	33	35	25	14	46	38	15	12
NOV. 3	31	9	10	10	33	35	25	14	46	38	15	12
NOV. 4	31	11	11	12	33	35	25	14	46	38	15	12
NOV. 5	31	12	13	13	34	35	25	14	46	38	15	12
NOV. 6	31	14	14	15	34	35	26	14	46	38	15	12
NOV. 7	31	16	16	17	34	35	26	14	46	38	15	12
NOV. 8	31	17	18	18	34	35	26	14	46	38	15	12
NOV. 9	31	19	19	20	34	35	26	14	46	38	15	12
NOV. 10	31	20	21	22	34	35	26	14	46	38	15	12
NOV. 11	31	22	23	23	34	35	26	14	46	38	15	12
NOV. 12	32	24	25	25	35	35	26	14	46	38	15	12
NOV. 13	32	26	26	27	35	35	26	14	46	38	15	12
NOV. 14	32	28	28	29	35	35	26	14	46	38	15	12
NOV. 15	32	30	30	31	35	35	26	14	46	38	15	12
NOV. 16	32	32	32	33	35	35	26	14	46	38	15	12
NOV. 17	32	34	34	35	35	35	26	14	46	38	15	12
NOV. 18	32	36	36	37	35	35	27	14	46	38	15	12
NOV. 19	33	38	38	39	35	35	27	14	46	38	15	12
NOV. 20	33	40	40	41	35	35	27	14	46	38	15	12
NOV. 21	33	42	42	43	35	35	27	14	46	38	15	12
NOV. 22	33	43	44	45	35	35	27	14	46	38	15	12
NOV. 23	33	45	46	46	35	34	27	14	46	38	15	12
NOV. 24	33	47	48	48	35	34	27	14	46	38	15	12
NOV. 25	34	1	1	2	35	34	27	14	46	38	15	12
NOV. 26	34	2	3	3	35	34	27	14	46	38	15	12
NOV. 27	34	4	5	5	34	34	27	14	46	38	15	12
NOV. 28	34	6	6	7	34	34	27	14	46	38	15	12
NOV. 29	34	7	8	8	34	34	27	14	46	38	15	12
NOV. 30	34	9	9	10	34	34	28	14	46	38	15	12

Date & Time	SUN	MOON 1	MOON 2	MOON 3	MERCURY	VENUS	MARS	JUPITER	SATURN	URANUS	NEPTUNE	PLUTO
DEC. 1	34	10	11	11	34	34	28	14	46	38	15	12
DEC. 2	34	12	13	13	34	34	28	14	46	38	15	12
DEC. 3	35	14	14	15	33	34	28	14	46	38	15	12
DEC. 4	35	15	16	16	33	34	28	14	46	38	15	12
DEC. 5	35	17	17	18	33	34	28	14	46	38	15	12
DEC. 6	35	18	19	19	33	33	28	14	46	38	15	12
DEC. 7	35	20	21	21	33	33	28	14	46	38	15	12
DEC. 8	35	22	22	23	33	33	28	14	46	38	15	12
DEC. 9	35	23	24	25	33	33	28	14	46	38	15	12
DEC. 10	35	25	26	26	33	33	28	14	46	38	15	12
DEC. 11	36	27	28	28	33	33	28	14	46	38	15	12
DEC. 12	36	29	29	30	33	33	29	14	46	38	15	12
DEC. 13	36	31	31	32	33	33	29	14	46	38	15	12
DEC. 14	36	33	33	34	33	33	29	14	46	38	15	12
DEC. 15	36	35	36	36	33	33	29	14	46	38	15	12
DEC. 16	36	37	38	38	33	33	29	14	46	38	15	12
DEC. 17	36	39	40	40	33	33	29	14	46	38	15	12
DEC. 18	36	41	42	42	33	33	29	14	46	38	15	12
DEC. 19	37	43	43	44	34	33	29	14	46	38	15	12
DEC. 20	37	45	45	46	34	33	29	14	46	38	15	12
DEC. 21	37	46	47	48	34	33	29	14	46	38	15	12
DEC. 22	37	48	1	1	34	33	29	14	46	38	15	12
DEC. 23	37	2	2	3	34	33	29	14	46	38	15	12
DEC. 24	37	4	4	5	34	33	30	14	46	38	15	12
DEC. 25	37	5	6	6	35	33	30	14	46	38	14	12
DEC. 26	38	7	7	8	35	33	30	14	46	38	14	12
DEC. 27	38	8	9	9	35	33	30	14	46	38	14	12
DEC. 28	38	10	11	11	35	33	30	14	46	38	14	12
DEC. 29	38	12	12	13	35	33	30	14	46	38	14	12
DEC. 30	38	13	14	14	35	33	30	14	46	38	14	12
DEC. 31	38	15	15	16	36	33	30	14	46	38	14	12

MOON 1 ◐ 12:01 A.M. TO 8:00 A.M.   **MOON 2** ◑ 8:01 A.M. TO 4:00 P.M.   **MOON 3** ● 4:01 P.M. TO 12:00 A.M.

Use only one "moon" number. Choose the column closest to your time of birth. If your place of birth is not on Eastern Standard Time, be sure to read "How to Convert to Eastern Standard Time" at the beginning of this section.

1907

January

Date & Time	SUN	MOON 1	MOON 2	MOON 3	MERCURY	VENUS	MARS	JUPITER	SATURN	URANUS	NEPTUNE	PLUTO
JAN. 1	38	16	17	17	36	33	30	14	46	38	14	12
JAN. 2	38	18	18	19	36	33	30	14	46	38	14	12
JAN. 3	39	20	20	21	36	33	30	14	46	38	14	12
JAN. 4	39	21	22	22	36	33	30	14	46	38	14	12
JAN. 5	39	23	23	24	37	33	30	14	46	38	14	12
JAN. 6	39	25	25	26	37	34	31	14	46	38	14	12
JAN. 7	39	26	27	28	37	34	31	14	46	38	14	12
JAN. 8	39	28	29	29	37	34	31	14	46	38	14	12
JAN. 9	39	30	31	31	37	34	31	14	46	38	14	12
JAN. 10	40	32	33	33	38	34	31	14	46	38	14	12
JAN. 11	40	34	35	35	38	34	31	14	46	38	14	12
JAN. 12	40	36	37	37	38	34	31	14	46	38	14	12
JAN. 13	40	38	39	39	38	34	31	13	46	38	14	12
JAN. 14	40	40	41	41	38	34	31	13	47	38	14	12
JAN. 15	40	42	43	43	39	34	31	13	47	38	14	12
JAN. 16	40	44	45	45	39	34	31	13	47	38	14	12
JAN. 17	41	46	46	47	39	35	31	13	47	38	14	12
JAN. 18	41	48	48	1	39	35	32	13	47	38	14	12
JAN. 19	41	1	2	3	39	35	32	13	47	38	14	12
JAN. 20	41	3	4	4	40	35	32	13	47	38	14	12
JAN. 21	41	5	5	6	40	35	32	13	47	38	14	12
JAN. 22	41	6	7	7	40	35	32	13	47	38	14	12
JAN. 23	42	8	8	9	40	35	32	13	47	38	14	12
JAN. 24	42	10	10	11	41	35	32	13	47	38	14	12
JAN. 25	42	11	12	12	41	35	32	13	47	38	14	12
JAN. 26	42	13	13	14	41	36	32	13	47	38	14	12
JAN. 27	42	14	15	15	41	36	32	13	47	38	14	12
JAN. 28	42	16	16	17	41	36	32	13	47	38	14	12
JAN. 29	42	18	18	19	42	36	32	13	47	38	14	12
JAN. 30	42	19	20	20	42	36	32	13	47	38	14	12
JAN. 31	43	21	21	22	42	36	33	13	47	38	14	12

February

Date & Time	SUN	MOON 1	MOON 2	MOON 3	MERCURY	VENUS	MARS	JUPITER	SATURN	URANUS	NEPTUNE	PLUTO
FEB. 1	43	23	23	24	42	36	33	13	47	38	14	12
FEB. 2	43	24	25	25	43	36	33	13	47	38	14	12
FEB. 3	43	26	27	27	43	37	33	13	47	38	14	12
FEB. 4	43	28	28	29	43	37	33	13	47	38	14	12
FEB. 5	43	30	30	31	43	37	33	13	47	38	14	12
FEB. 6	43	31	32	33	43	37	33	13	47	38	14	12
FEB. 7	43	33	34	35	44	37	33	13	47	38	14	12
FEB. 8	44	35	36	37	44	37	33	13	47	38	14	12
FEB. 9	44	37	38	38	44	37	33	13	47	38	14	12
FEB. 10	44	39	40	40	44	37	33	13	47	38	14	12
FEB. 11	44	41	42	42	45	38	33	13	47	38	14	12
FEB. 12	44	43	44	44	45	38	33	13	47	38	14	12
FEB. 13	44	45	46	46	45	38	34	13	47	38	14	12
FEB. 14	44	47	47	48	45	38	34	13	47	38	14	12
FEB. 15	44	1	1	2	46	38	34	13	47	38	14	12
FEB. 16	45	2	3	4	46	38	34	13	47	38	14	12
FEB. 17	45	4	5	5	46	38	34	13	47	38	14	12
FEB. 18	45	6	6	7	46	39	34	13	47	38	14	12
FEB. 19	45	7	8	9	47	39	34	13	47	38	14	12
FEB. 20	45	9	10	10	47	39	34	13	47	38	14	12
FEB. 21	45	11	11	12	47	39	34	13	47	38	14	12
FEB. 22	45	12	13	13	47	39	34	13	47	38	14	12
FEB. 23	46	14	14	15	48	39	34	13	47	38	14	12
FEB. 24	46	15	16	16	48	39	34	13	47	38	14	12
FEB. 25	46	17	18	18	48	40	34	13	47	39	14	12
FEB. 26	46	19	19	20	48	40	35	13	47	39	14	12
FEB. 27	46	20	21	21	48	40	35	13	47	39	14	12
FEB. 28	46	22	23	23	48	40	35	13	47	39	14	12

MOON 1 ☽ 12:01 A.M. TO 8:00 A.M.   **MOON 2** ◑ 8:01 A.M. TO 4:00 P.M.   **MOON 3** ● 4:01 P.M. TO 12:00 A.M.

Use only one "moon" number. Choose the column closest to your time of birth. If your place of birth is not on Eastern Standard Time, be sure to read "How to Convert to Eastern Standard Time" at the beginning of this section.

1907

March — April

Date & Time	SUN	MOON 1	MOON 2	MOON 3	MERCURY	VENUS	MARS	JUPITER	SATURN	URANUS	NEPTUNE	PLUTO
MAR. 1	46	24	24	25	1	40	35	13	47	39	14	12
MAR. 2	46	26	26	27	1	40	35	13	47	39	14	12
MAR. 3	47	27	28	29	1	40	35	13	47	39	14	12
MAR. 4	47	29	30	30	1	41	35	13	47	39	14	12
MAR. 5	47	31	32	32	1	41	35	13	47	39	14	12
MAR. 6	47	33	34	34	1	41	35	13	47	39	14	12
MAR. 7	47	35	35	36	1	41	35	13	47	39	14	12
MAR. 8	47	37	37	38	1	41	35	13	47	39	14	12
MAR. 9	47	39	39	40	1	41	35	13	47	39	14	12
MAR. 10	47	40	41	42	1	41	35	13	47	39	14	12
MAR. 11	48	42	43	44	1	42	36	13	47	39	14	12
MAR. 12	48	44	45	45	1	42	36	13	47	39	14	12
MAR. 13	48	46	47	47	1	42	36	13	47	39	14	12
MAR. 14	48	48	48	1	1	42	36	13	47	39	14	12
MAR. 15	48	2	2	3	1	42	36	13	47	39	14	12
MAR. 16	48	3	4	5	1	42	36	13	47	39	14	12
MAR. 17	48	5	6	6	1	43	36	13	47	39	14	12
MAR. 18	48	7	7	8	1	43	36	13	47	39	14	12
MAR. 19	1	8	9	10	48	43	36	13	47	39	14	12
MAR. 20	1	10	11	11	48	43	36	13	47	39	14	12
MAR. 21	1	12	12	13	48	43	36	13	48	39	14	12
MAR. 22	1	13	14	14	48	43	36	13	48	39	14	12
MAR. 23	1	15	15	16	48	43	36	13	48	39	14	12
MAR. 24	1	16	17	17	48	44	36	13	48	39	14	12
MAR. 25	2	18	19	19	48	44	36	13	48	39	14	12
MAR. 26	2	20	20	21	48	44	37	13	48	39	14	12
MAR. 27	2	21	22	23	48	44	37	13	48	39	14	12
MAR. 28	2	23	24	24	48	44	37	13	48	39	14	12
MAR. 29	2	25	26	26	48	44	37	13	48	39	14	12
MAR. 30	2	27	27	28	47	45	37	13	48	39	14	12
MAR. 31	2	29	29	30	47	45	37	13	48	39	14	12
APR. 1	2	31	31	32	47	45	37	13	48	39	14	12
APR. 2	2	32	33	34	47	45	37	13	48	39	14	12
APR. 3	3	34	35	36	47	45	37	13	48	39	14	12
APR. 4	3	36	37	37	48	45	37	13	48	39	14	12
APR. 5	3	38	39	39	48	45	37	13	48	39	14	12
APR. 6	3	40	41	41	48	46	37	13	48	39	14	12
APR. 7	3	42	42	43	48	46	37	13	48	39	14	12
APR. 8	3	44	44	45	48	46	37	13	48	39	14	12
APR. 9	3	46	46	47	48	46	37	13	48	39	14	12
APR. 10	3	47	48	1	48	46	37	13	48	39	14	12
APR. 11	4	1	2	2	48	46	38	14	48	39	14	12
APR. 12	4	3	3	4	48	47	38	14	48	39	14	12
APR. 13	4	5	5	6	48	47	38	14	48	39	14	12
APR. 14	4	6	7	7	48	47	38	14	48	39	14	12
APR. 15	4	8	8	9	1	47	38	14	48	39	14	12
APR. 16	4	10	10	11	1	47	38	14	48	39	14	12
APR. 17	4	11	12	12	1	47	38	14	48	39	14	12
APR. 18	4	13	13	14	1	47	38	14	48	39	14	12
APR. 19	5	14	15	15	1	48	38	14	48	39	14	12
APR. 20	5	16	16	17	1	48	38	14	48	39	14	12
APR. 21	5	17	18	19	1	48	38	14	48	39	14	12
APR. 22	5	19	20	20	1	48	38	14	48	39	14	12
APR. 23	5	21	21	22	2	48	38	14	48	39	14	12
APR. 24	5	22	23	24	2	48	38	14	48	39	14	12
APR. 25	6	24	25	25	2	1	38	14	48	39	14	12
APR. 26	6	26	27	27	2	1	38	14	48	39	14	12
APR. 27	6	28	29	29	2	1	38	14	48	39	14	12
APR. 28	6	30	30	31	3	1	38	14	48	39	14	12
APR. 29	6	32	32	33	3	1	39	14	48	39	14	12
APR. 30	6	34	34	35	3	1	39	14	48	39	14	12

MOON 1 ☽ 12:01 A.M. TO 8:00 A.M.   **MOON 2** ☽ 8:01 A.M. TO 4:00 P.M.   **MOON 3** ● 4:01 P.M. TO 12:00 A.M.
Use only one "moon" number. Choose the column closest to your time of birth. If your place of birth is not on
Eastern Standard Time, be sure to read "How to Convert to Eastern Standard Time" at the beginning of this section.

1907

May

June

Date & Time	SUN	MOON 1	MOON 2	MOON 3	MERCURY	VENUS	MARS	JUPITER	SATURN	URANUS	NEPTUNE	PLUTO
MAY 1	6	36	36	37	3	2	39	14	48	39	14	12
MAY 2	6	38	38	39	4	2	39	14	48	39	14	12
MAY 3	7	40	40	41	4	2	39	14	48	39	14	12
MAY 4	7	41	42	43	4	2	39	14	48	39	14	12
MAY 5	7	43	44	44	4	2	39	14	48	39	14	12
MAY 6	7	45	46	46	4	2	39	14	48	39	14	12
MAY 7	7	47	47	48	5	3	39	14	48	39	14	12
MAY 8	7	1	1	2	5	3	39	14	48	39	14	12
MAY 9	7	2	3	4	5	3	39	14	48	39	14	12
MAY 10	7	4	5	5	5	3	39	14	48	39	14	12
MAY 11	8	6	6	7	6	3	39	14	48	39	14	12
MAY 12	8	7	8	9	6	3	39	14	48	39	14	12
MAY 13	8	9	10	10	6	3	39	14	48	39	14	12
MAY 14	8	11	11	12	6	4	39	14	48	39	14	12
MAY 15	8	12	13	13	7	4	39	14	48	39	14	12
MAY 16	8	14	14	15	7	4	39	14	48	39	14	12
MAY 17	8	15	16	16	7	4	39	14	48	39	14	12
MAY 18	8	17	18	18	7	4	39	14	48	39	14	12
MAY 19	9	19	19	20	8	4	39	14	48	39	14	12
MAY 20	9	20	21	21	8	5	39	14	48	39	14	12
MAY 21	9	22	22	23	8	5	39	14	48	39	14	12
MAY 22	9	24	24	25	9	5	39	14	48	39	14	12
MAY 23	9	25	26	26	9	5	39	14	48	39	14	12
MAY 24	9	27	28	28	9	5	39	14	48	39	14	12
MAY 25	10	29	30	30	9	5	39	14	48	39	14	12
MAY 26	10	31	32	32	10	6	39	15	48	39	14	12
MAY 27	10	33	34	34	10	6	39	15	48	39	14	12
MAY 28	10	35	36	36	10	6	39	15	48	39	14	12
MAY 29	10	37	38	38	11	6	39	15	48	39	14	12
MAY 30	10	39	40	40	11	6	39	15	48	39	14	12
MAY 31	10	41	41	42	11	6	39	15	48	39	14	12

Date & Time	SUN	MOON 1	MOON 2	MOON 3	MERCURY	VENUS	MARS	JUPITER	SATURN	URANUS	NEPTUNE	PLUTO
JUN. 1	10	43	43	44	12	6	39	15	48	39	14	12
JUN. 2	10	45	45	46	12	7	39	15	48	39	14	12
JUN. 3	11	46	47	48	12	7	39	15	48	39	14	12
JUN. 4	11	48	1	1	12	7	39	15	48	39	14	12
JUN. 5	11	2	3	3	13	7	39	15	48	39	14	12
JUN. 6	11	4	4	5	13	7	39	15	1	39	14	12
JUN. 7	11	5	6	6	13	7	39	15	1	39	14	12
JUN. 8	11	7	8	8	13	8	39	15	1	39	14	12
JUN. 9	11	9	9	10	14	8	39	15	1	39	14	12
JUN. 10	11	10	11	11	14	8	39	15	1	39	14	12
JUN. 11	12	12	12	13	14	8	39	15	1	39	14	12
JUN. 12	12	13	14	14	14	8	39	15	1	39	15	12
JUN. 13	12	15	16	16	15	8	39	15	1	39	15	12
JUN. 14	12	17	17	18	15	9	39	15	1	38	15	12
JUN. 15	12	18	19	19	15	9	39	15	1	38	15	12
JUN. 16	12	20	20	21	15	9	39	15	1	38	15	12
JUN. 17	12	21	22	22	15	9	39	15	1	38	15	12
JUN. 18	12	23	24	24	16	9	39	15	1	38	15	12
JUN. 19	13	25	25	26	16	9	39	15	1	38	15	12
JUN. 20	13	26	27	28	16	10	39	15	1	38	15	12
JUN. 21	13	28	29	29	16	10	39	15	1	38	15	12
JUN. 22	13	30	31	31	16	10	39	15	1	38	15	12
JUN. 23	13	32	33	33	16	10	39	15	1	38	15	12
JUN. 24	13	34	35	35	17	10	39	15	1	38	15	12
JUN. 25	14	36	37	37	17	10	39	15	1	38	15	12
JUN. 26	14	38	39	39	17	11	39	15	1	38	15	12
JUN. 27	14	40	41	41	17	11	39	15	1	38	15	12
JUN. 28	14	42	43	43	17	11	39	15	1	38	15	12
JUN. 29	14	44	45	45	17	11	39	15	1	38	15	12
JUN. 30	14	46	47	47	17	11	39	16	1	38	15	12

MOON 1 ☽ 12:01 A.M. TO 8:00 A.M.   **MOON 2** ◑ 8:01 A.M. TO 4:00 P.M.   **MOON 3** ● 4:01 P.M. TO 12:00 A.M.

Use only one "moon" number. Choose the column closest to your time of birth. If your place of birth is not on Eastern Standard Time, be sure to read "How to Convert to Eastern Standard Time" at the beginning of this section.

1907

July

August

Date & Time	SUN	MOON 1	MOON 2	MOON 3	MERCURY	VENUS	MARS	JUPITER	SATURN	URANUS	NEPTUNE	PLUTO
JUL. 1	14	48	48	1	17	11	39	16	1	38	15	12
JUL. 2	14	2	2	3	18	11	39	16	1	38	15	12
JUL. 3	15	3	4	4	18	12	39	16	1	38	15	12
JUL. 4	15	5	6	6	18	12	39	16	1	38	15	12
JUL. 5	15	7	7	8	18	12	39	16	1	38	15	12
JUL. 6	15	8	9	9	18	12	39	16	1	38	15	12
JUL. 7	15	10	10	11	18	12	39	16	1	38	15	12
JUL. 8	15	11	12	12	18	12	39	16	1	38	15	12
JUL. 9	15	13	14	14	18	13	39	16	1	38	15	12
JUL. 10	15	15	15	16	18	13	39	16	1	38	15	12
JUL. 11	16	16	17	17	18	13	39	16	1	38	15	12
JUL. 12	16	18	18	19	18	13	39	16	1	38	15	12
JUL. 13	16	19	20	20	18	13	38	16	1	38	15	12
JUL. 14	16	21	21	22	18	13	38	16	1	38	15	12
JUL. 15	16	23	23	24	18	14	38	16	1	38	15	12
JUL. 16	16	24	25	25	18	14	38	16	1	38	15	12
JUL. 17	16	26	26	27	18	14	38	16	1	38	15	12
JUL. 18	16	28	28	29	18	14	38	16	1	38	15	12
JUL. 19	17	29	30	31	18	14	38	16	1	38	15	12
JUL. 20	17	31	32	33	18	14	38	16	1	38	15	12
JUL. 21	17	33	34	34	17	15	38	16	1	38	15	12
JUL. 22	17	35	36	36	17	15	38	16	1	38	15	12
JUL. 23	17	37	38	38	17	15	38	16	1	38	15	12
JUL. 24	17	39	40	40	17	15	38	16	1	38	15	12
JUL. 25	17	41	42	42	17	15	38	16	1	38	15	12
JUL. 26	18	43	44	44	17	15	38	16	1	38	15	12
JUL. 27	18	45	46	46	17	16	38	16	1	38	15	12
JUL. 28	18	47	48	48	17	16	38	16	1	38	15	12
JUL. 29	18	1	2	2	17	16	38	16	1	38	15	12
JUL. 30	18	3	3	4	17	16	38	16	1	38	15	12
JUL. 31	18	4	5	6	17	16	38	16	1	38	15	12

Date & Time	SUN	MOON 1	MOON 2	MOON 3	MERCURY	VENUS	MARS	JUPITER	SATURN	URANUS	NEPTUNE	PLUTO
AUG. 1	18	6	7	7	17	16	38	16	1	38	15	12
AUG. 2	18	8	8	9	17	17	38	16	1	38	15	12
AUG. 3	19	9	10	11	17	17	38	17	1	38	15	12
AUG. 4	19	11	12	12	16	17	38	17	1	38	15	12
AUG. 5	19	13	13	14	16	17	38	17	1	38	15	12
AUG. 6	19	14	15	15	17	17	38	17	1	38	15	12
AUG. 7	19	16	16	17	17	17	38	17	1	38	15	12
AUG. 8	19	17	18	18	17	18	38	17	1	38	15	12
AUG. 9	19	19	19	20	17	18	38	17	1	38	15	12
AUG. 10	19	21	21	22	17	18	38	17	1	38	15	12
AUG. 11	20	22	23	23	17	18	38	17	1	38	15	12
AUG. 12	20	24	24	25	17	18	38	17	1	38	15	12
AUG. 13	20	26	26	27	17	18	38	17	1	38	15	12
AUG. 14	20	27	28	28	17	19	38	17	48	38	15	12
AUG. 15	20	29	30	30	17	19	38	17	48	38	15	12
AUG. 16	20	31	31	32	17	19	38	17	48	38	15	12
AUG. 17	20	33	33	34	18	19	38	17	48	38	15	12
AUG. 18	20	34	35	36	18	19	38	17	48	38	15	12
AUG. 19	21	36	37	38	18	19	38	17	48	38	15	12
AUG. 20	21	38	39	40	18	19	38	17	48	38	15	12
AUG. 21	21	40	41	42	18	20	38	17	48	38	15	12
AUG. 22	21	42	43	44	18	20	38	17	48	38	15	12
AUG. 23	21	44	45	46	19	20	38	17	48	38	15	12
AUG. 24	21	46	47	48	19	20	38	17	48	38	15	12
AUG. 25	21	48	1	1	19	20	38	17	48	38	15	12
AUG. 26	22	2	3	3	20	20	38	17	48	38	15	12
AUG. 27	22	4	4	5	20	21	38	17	48	38	15	12
AUG. 28	22	6	6	7	20	21	38	17	48	38	15	12
AUG. 29	22	7	8	8	20	21	38	17	48	38	15	12
AUG. 30	22	9	9	10	21	21	38	17	48	38	15	12
AUG. 31	22	11	11	12	21	21	38	17	48	38	15	12

MOON 1 ☽ 12:01 A.M. TO 8:00 A.M.   **MOON 2** ◗ 8:01 A.M. TO 4:00 P.M.   **MOON 3** ● 4:01 P.M. TO 12:00 A.M.

Use only one "moon" number. Choose the column closest to your time of birth. If your place of birth is not on Eastern Standard Time, be sure to read "How to Convert to Eastern Standard Time" at the beginning of this section.

1907

September

Date & Time	SUN	MOON 1	MOON 2	MOON 3	MERCURY	VENUS	MARS	JUPITER	SATURN	URANUS	NEPTUNE	PLUTO
SEP. 1	22	12	13	13	21	21	38	17	48	38	15	12
SEP. 2	22	14	14	15	21	22	38	17	48	38	15	12
SEP. 3	23	15	16	16	22	22	38	17	48	38	15	12
SEP. 4	23	17	17	18	22	22	38	17	48	38	15	12
SEP. 5	23	18	19	20	22	22	39	17	48	38	15	12
SEP. 6	23	20	21	21	23	22	39	17	48	38	15	12
SEP. 7	23	22	22	23	23	22	39	17	48	38	15	12
SEP. 8	23	23	24	25	23	23	39	18	48	38	15	12
SEP. 9	23	25	26	26	23	23	39	18	48	38	15	12
SEP. 10	23	27	27	28	24	23	39	18	48	38	15	12
SEP. 11	24	29	29	30	24	23	39	18	48	38	15	12
SEP. 12	24	30	31	32	24	23	39	18	48	38	15	12
SEP. 13	24	32	33	33	24	23	39	18	48	38	15	12
SEP. 14	24	34	35	35	24	24	39	18	48	38	15	12
SEP. 15	24	36	37	37	25	24	39	18	48	38	15	12
SEP. 16	24	38	38	39	25	24	39	18	48	38	15	12
SEP. 17	24	40	40	41	25	24	39	18	48	38	15	12
SEP. 18	24	42	42	43	25	24	39	18	48	38	15	12
SEP. 19	25	44	44	45	26	24	39	18	48	38	15	12
SEP. 20	25	45	46	47	26	25	39	18	48	38	15	12
SEP. 21	25	47	48	1	26	25	39	18	48	38	15	12
SEP. 22	25	1	2	2	26	25	39	18	48	38	15	12
SEP. 23	25	3	4	4	27	25	40	18	48	38	15	12
SEP. 24	25	5	5	6	27	25	40	18	48	38	15	12
SEP. 25	26	7	7	8	27	25	40	18	48	38	15	12
SEP. 26	26	8	9	9	27	26	40	18	48	38	15	12
SEP. 27	26	10	11	11	27	26	40	18	48	38	15	12
SEP. 28	26	12	12	13	28	26	40	18	48	38	15	12
SEP. 29	26	13	14	14	28	26	40	18	48	38	15	12
SEP. 30	26	15	15	16	28	26	40	18	48	38	15	12

October

Date & Time	SUN	MOON 1	MOON 2	MOON 3	MERCURY	VENUS	MARS	JUPITER	SATURN	URANUS	NEPTUNE	PLUTO
OCT. 1	26	16	17	17	28	26	40	18	48	38	15	12
OCT. 2	26	18	18	19	28	27	40	18	48	38	15	12
OCT. 3	27	20	20	21	29	27	40	18	48	38	15	12
OCT. 4	27	21	22	22	29	27	40	18	48	38	15	12
OCT. 5	27	23	23	24	29	27	40	18	48	38	15	12
OCT. 6	27	25	25	26	29	27	40	18	48	38	15	12
OCT. 7	27	26	27	27	29	27	40	18	48	38	15	12
OCT. 8	27	28	29	29	30	28	41	18	48	38	15	12
OCT. 9	27	30	31	31	30	28	41	18	48	38	15	12
OCT. 10	27	32	32	33	30	28	41	18	48	38	15	12
OCT. 11	28	34	34	35	30	28	41	18	48	38	15	12
OCT. 12	28	35	36	37	30	28	41	18	48	38	15	12
OCT. 13	28	37	38	39	30	28	41	18	48	38	15	12
OCT. 14	28	39	40	40	31	29	41	18	48	38	15	12
OCT. 15	28	41	42	42	31	29	41	18	48	38	15	12
OCT. 16	28	43	44	44	31	29	41	18	48	38	15	12
OCT. 17	28	45	45	46	31	29	41	18	48	38	15	12
OCT. 18	28	47	47	48	31	29	41	18	48	38	15	12
OCT. 19	29	1	1	2	31	29	41	18	48	38	15	12
OCT. 20	29	2	3	4	32	30	41	18	48	38	15	12
OCT. 21	29	4	5	5	32	30	42	18	48	38	15	12
OCT. 22	29	6	7	7	32	30	42	18	48	38	15	12
OCT. 23	29	8	8	9	32	30	42	18	48	38	15	12
OCT. 24	29	9	10	11	32	30	42	18	48	38	15	12
OCT. 25	29	11	12	12	32	30	42	18	48	38	15	12
OCT. 26	30	13	13	14	32	31	42	19	48	38	15	12
OCT. 27	30	14	15	15	32	31	42	19	48	38	15	12
OCT. 28	30	16	16	17	33	31	42	19	48	38	15	12
OCT. 29	30	17	18	18	33	31	42	19	48	38	15	12
OCT. 30	30	19	20	20	33	31	42	19	48	38	15	12
OCT. 31	30	21	21	22	33	31	42	19	48	38	15	12

MOON 1 ◐ 12:01 A.M. TO 8:00 A.M.   **MOON 2** ◑ 8:01 A.M. TO 4:00 P.M.   **MOON 3** ● 4:01 P.M. TO 12:00 A.M.

Use only one "moon" number. Choose the column closest to your time of birth. If your place of birth is not on Eastern Standard Time, be sure to read "How to Convert to Eastern Standard Time" at the beginning of this section.

1907

November

Date & Time	SUN ☀	MOON 1 ◗	MOON 2 ◖	MOON 3 ●	MERCURY	VENUS	MARS	JUPITER	SATURN	URANUS	NEPTUNE	PLUTO
NOV. 1	30	22	23	23	33	32	42	19	48	38	15	12
NOV. 2	30	24	24	25	33	32	43	19	48	38	15	12
NOV. 3	31	26	26	27	33	32	43	19	48	38	15	12
NOV. 4	31	27	28	29	33	32	43	19	48	38	15	12
NOV. 5	31	29	30	30	33	32	43	19	48	38	15	12
NOV. 6	31	31	32	32	33	32	43	19	48	38	15	12
NOV. 7	31	33	34	34	33	33	43	19	48	38	15	12
NOV. 8	31	35	36	36	33	33	43	19	48	38	15	12
NOV. 9	31	37	37	38	33	33	43	19	48	38	15	12
NOV. 10	31	39	39	40	32	33	43	19	48	38	15	12
NOV. 11	31	41	41	42	32	33	43	19	48	38	15	12
NOV. 12	32	43	43	44	32	33	43	19	48	38	15	12
NOV. 13	32	44	45	46	32	34	44	19	48	38	15	12
NOV. 14	32	46	47	48	32	34	44	19	48	38	15	12
NOV. 15	32	48	1	1	32	34	44	19	48	38	15	12
NOV. 16	32	2	3	3	31	34	44	19	48	38	15	12
NOV. 17	32	4	4	5	31	34	44	19	48	38	15	12
NOV. 18	32	5	6	7	31	34	44	19	48	38	15	12
NOV. 19	33	7	8	8	31	35	44	19	48	38	15	12
NOV. 20	33	9	9	10	31	35	44	19	48	38	15	12
NOV. 21	33	11	11	12	31	35	44	19	48	38	15	12
NOV. 22	33	12	13	13	31	35	44	19	48	38	15	12
NOV. 23	33	14	14	15	31	35	44	19	48	38	15	12
NOV. 24	33	15	16	16	31	35	45	19	48	38	15	12
NOV. 25	34	17	17	18	31	36	45	19	48	38	15	12
NOV. 26	34	18	19	20	31	36	45	19	48	38	15	12
NOV. 27	34	20	21	21	31	36	45	19	48	38	15	12
NOV. 28	34	22	22	23	31	36	45	19	48	38	15	12
NOV. 29	34	23	24	24	31	36	45	19	48	38	15	12
NOV. 30	34	25	26	26	31	36	45	19	48	38	15	12

December

Date & Time	SUN ☀	MOON 1 ◗	MOON 2 ◖	MOON 3 ●	MERCURY	VENUS	MARS	JUPITER	SATURN	URANUS	NEPTUNE	PLUTO
DEC. 1	34	27	27	28	31	37	45	19	48	38	15	12
DEC. 2	34	28	29	30	31	37	45	19	48	38	15	12
DEC. 3	35	30	31	32	32	37	45	19	48	38	15	12
DEC. 4	35	32	33	33	32	37	45	19	48	38	15	12
DEC. 5	35	34	35	35	32	37	46	19	48	38	15	12
DEC. 6	35	36	37	37	32	37	46	19	48	38	15	12
DEC. 7	35	38	39	39	32	38	46	19	48	38	15	12
DEC. 8	35	40	41	41	32	38	46	19	48	38	15	12
DEC. 9	35	42	43	43	33	38	46	19	48	38	15	12
DEC. 10	35	44	45	45	33	38	46	19	48	38	15	12
DEC. 11	36	46	46	47	33	38	46	19	48	38	15	12
DEC. 12	36	48	48	1	33	38	46	19	48	38	15	12
DEC. 13	36	2	2	3	33	39	46	19	48	39	15	12
DEC. 14	36	3	4	4	34	39	46	19	48	39	15	12
DEC. 15	36	5	6	6	34	39	46	19	48	39	15	12
DEC. 16	36	7	7	8	34	39	47	19	48	39	15	12
DEC. 17	36	8	9	9	34	39	47	19	48	39	15	12
DEC. 18	36	10	11	11	34	39	47	19	48	39	15	12
DEC. 19	37	12	12	13	35	40	47	19	48	39	15	12
DEC. 20	37	13	14	14	35	40	47	19	48	39	15	12
DEC. 21	37	15	15	16	35	40	47	19	48	39	15	12
DEC. 22	37	16	17	17	35	40	47	19	48	39	15	12
DEC. 23	37	18	19	19	35	40	47	19	48	39	15	12
DEC. 24	37	20	20	21	36	40	47	19	48	39	15	12
DEC. 25	37	21	22	22	36	41	47	19	48	39	15	12
DEC. 26	38	23	23	24	36	41	47	19	48	39	15	12
DEC. 27	38	24	25	25	36	41	48	19	48	39	15	12
DEC. 28	38	26	27	27	36	41	48	19	48	39	15	12
DEC. 29	38	28	28	29	37	41	48	19	48	39	15	12
DEC. 30	38	30	30	31	37	41	48	19	48	39	15	12
DEC. 31	38	31	32	33	37	42	48	19	48	39	15	12

MOON 1 ◗ 12:01 A.M. TO 8:00 A.M.   **MOON 2** ◖ 8:01 A.M. TO 4:00 P.M.   **MOON 3** ● 4:01 P.M. TO 12:00 A.M.

Use only one "moon" number. Choose the column closest to your time of birth. If your place of birth is not on Eastern Standard Time, be sure to read "How to Convert to Eastern Standard Time" at the beginning of this section.

1908

January

Date & Time	SUN	MOON 1	MOON 2	MOON 3	MERCURY	VENUS	MARS	JUPITER	SATURN	URANUS	NEPTUNE	PLUTO
JAN. 1	38	33	34	35	37	42	48	19	48	39	15	12
JAN. 2	38	35	36	37	37	42	48	19	48	39	15	12
JAN. 3	39	37	38	39	38	42	48	19	48	39	15	12
JAN. 4	39	39	40	41	38	42	48	19	48	39	15	12
JAN. 5	39	41	42	43	38	42	48	19	48	39	15	12
JAN. 6	39	43	44	45	38	43	48	19	48	39	15	12
JAN. 7	39	45	46	46	38	43	1	18	48	39	15	12
JAN. 8	39	47	48	48	39	43	1	18	48	39	15	12
JAN. 9	39	1	2	2	39	43	1	18	48	39	15	12
JAN. 10	40	3	3	4	39	43	1	18	48	39	15	12
JAN. 11	40	5	5	6	39	43	1	18	48	39	15	12
JAN. 12	40	6	7	7	40	44	1	18	48	39	15	12
JAN. 13	40	8	9	9	40	44	1	18	48	39	15	12
JAN. 14	40	10	10	11	40	44	1	18	48	39	15	12
JAN. 15	40	11	12	12	40	44	1	18	48	39	15	12
JAN. 16	40	13	13	14	40	44	1	18	48	39	15	12
JAN. 17	41	14	15	15	41	44	2	18	48	39	15	12
JAN. 18	41	16	17	17	41	45	2	18	48	39	15	12
JAN. 19	41	18	18	19	41	45	2	18	48	39	15	12
JAN. 20	41	19	20	20	41	45	2	18	48	39	15	12
JAN. 21	41	21	21	22	42	45	2	18	48	39	15	12
JAN. 22	41	22	23	23	42	45	2	18	48	39	15	12
JAN. 23	42	24	24	25	42	45	2	18	48	39	15	12
JAN. 24	42	26	26	27	42	46	2	18	48	39	15	12
JAN. 25	42	27	28	28	42	46	2	18	48	39	15	12
JAN. 26	42	29	30	30	43	46	2	18	48	39	15	12
JAN. 27	42	31	31	32	43	46	2	18	48	39	15	12
JAN. 28	42	32	33	34	43	46	3	18	48	39	15	12
JAN. 29	42	34	35	36	43	46	3	18	48	39	15	12
JAN. 30	42	36	37	38	44	47	3	18	48	39	15	12
JAN. 31	43	38	39	40	44	47	3	18	48	39	15	12

February

Date & Time	SUN	MOON 1	MOON 2	MOON 3	MERCURY	VENUS	MARS	JUPITER	SATURN	URANUS	NEPTUNE	PLUTO
FEB. 1	43	40	41	42	44	47	3	18	48	39	15	12
FEB. 2	43	42	43	44	44	47	3	18	48	39	15	12
FEB. 3	43	44	45	46	45	47	3	18	48	39	15	12
FEB. 4	43	46	47	48	45	47	3	18	48	39	15	12
FEB. 5	43	48	1	2	45	48	3	18	48	39	15	12
FEB. 6	43	2	3	3	45	48	3	18	48	39	15	12
FEB. 7	43	4	5	5	45	48	3	18	48	39	15	12
FEB. 8	44	6	6	7	46	48	4	18	48	39	15	12
FEB. 9	44	8	8	9	46	48	4	18	48	39	15	12
FEB. 10	44	9	10	10	46	48	4	18	48	39	15	12
FEB. 11	44	11	11	12	46	48	4	18	48	39	15	12
FEB. 12	44	12	13	14	46	1	4	18	48	39	15	12
FEB. 13	44	14	15	15	46	1	4	18	48	39	15	12
FEB. 14	44	16	16	17	47	1	4	18	48	39	15	12
FEB. 15	44	17	18	18	47	1	4	18	48	39	15	12
FEB. 16	45	19	19	20	47	1	4	18	48	39	15	12
FEB. 17	45	20	21	21	47	1	4	18	48	39	15	12
FEB. 18	45	22	22	23	47	2	5	18	48	39	15	12
FEB. 19	45	24	24	25	47	2	5	18	48	39	15	12
FEB. 20	45	25	26	26	47	2	5	18	1	39	15	12
FEB. 21	45	27	27	28	47	2	5	18	1	39	15	12
FEB. 22	45	29	29	30	47	2	5	18	1	39	15	12
FEB. 23	46	30	31	31	47	2	5	18	1	39	15	12
FEB. 24	46	32	33	33	47	3	5	18	1	39	15	12
FEB. 25	46	34	34	35	47	3	5	18	1	39	15	12
FEB. 26	46	36	36	37	47	3	5	18	1	39	15	12
FEB. 27	46	37	38	39	46	3	5	18	1	39	15	12
FEB. 28	46	39	40	41	46	3	5	18	1	39	15	12
FEB. 29	46	41	42	43	46	3	6	18	1	39	15	12

MOON 1 ◗ 12:01 A.M. TO 8:00 A.M.   **MOON 2** ◖ 8:01 A.M. TO 4:00 P.M.   **MOON 3** ● 4:01 P.M. TO 12:00 A.M.

Use only one "moon" number. Choose the column closest to your time of birth. If your place of birth is not on Eastern Standard Time, be sure to read "How to Convert to Eastern Standard Time" at the beginning of this section.

1908

March

April

Date & Time	SUN ☉	MOON 1 ◔	MOON 2 ◑	MOON 3 ●	MERCURY	VENUS	MARS	JUPITER	SATURN	URANUS	NEPTUNE	PLUTO
MAR. 1	46	43	44	45	46	4	6	18	1	39	15	12
MAR. 2	46	45	46	47	46	4	6	18	1	39	15	12
MAR. 3	47	47	48	1	46	4	6	18	1	39	15	12
MAR. 4	47	1	2	3	46	4	6	18	1	39	15	12
MAR. 5	47	3	4	5	46	4	6	18	1	39	15	12
MAR. 6	47	5	6	6	46	4	6	18	1	39	15	12
MAR. 7	47	7	8	8	45	4	6	18	1	39	15	12
MAR. 8	47	9	9	10	45	5	6	18	1	39	15	12
MAR. 9	47	10	11	11	45	5	6	18	1	39	15	12
MAR. 10	47	12	13	13	45	5	6	18	1	39	15	12
MAR. 11	48	14	14	15	45	5	7	18	1	39	15	12
MAR. 12	48	15	16	16	45	5	7	18	1	39	15	12
MAR. 13	48	17	17	18	45	5	7	18	1	39	15	12
MAR. 14	48	18	19	19	45	6	7	17	1	39	15	12
MAR. 15	48	20	20	21	45	6	7	17	1	39	15	12
MAR. 16	48	21	22	23	45	6	7	17	1	39	15	12
MAR. 17	48	23	24	24	45	6	7	17	1	39	15	12
MAR. 18	48	25	25	26	45	6	7	17	1	39	15	12
MAR. 19	1	26	27	28	45	6	7	17	1	39	15	12
MAR. 20	1	28	29	29	45	6	7	17	1	39	15	12
MAR. 21	1	30	30	31	45	7	7	17	1	39	15	12
MAR. 22	1	32	32	33	46	7	8	17	1	39	15	12
MAR. 23	1	33	34	35	46	7	8	17	1	39	15	12
MAR. 24	1	35	36	36	46	7	8	17	1	39	15	12
MAR. 25	2	37	38	38	46	7	8	17	1	39	15	12
MAR. 26	2	39	39	40	46	7	8	17	1	39	15	12
MAR. 27	2	41	41	42	46	8	8	17	1	39	15	12
MAR. 28	2	43	43	44	46	8	8	17	1	39	15	12
MAR. 29	2	45	45	46	46	8	8	17	1	39	15	12
MAR. 30	2	47	47	48	47	8	8	17	1	39	15	12
MAR. 31	2	1	1	2	47	8	8	17	1	39	15	12

Date & Time	SUN ☉	MOON 1 ◔	MOON 2 ◑	MOON 3 ●	MERCURY	VENUS	MARS	JUPITER	SATURN	URANUS	NEPTUNE	PLUTO
APR. 1	2	2	3	4	47	8	8	17	1	39	15	12
APR. 2	2	4	5	6	47	8	9	17	1	39	15	12
APR. 3	3	6	7	7	47	9	9	17	1	39	15	12
APR. 4	3	8	9	9	47	9	9	17	1	39	15	12
APR. 5	3	10	10	11	47	9	9	17	1	39	15	12
APR. 6	3	11	12	13	48	9	9	17	1	39	15	12
APR. 7	3	13	14	14	48	9	9	17	1	39	15	12
APR. 8	3	15	15	16	48	9	9	17	1	39	15	12
APR. 9	3	16	17	17	48	9	9	17	1	39	15	12
APR. 10	3	18	18	19	48	10	9	17	1	39	15	12
APR. 11	4	19	20	20	1	10	9	17	1	39	15	12
APR. 12	4	21	22	22	1	10	9	17	1	39	15	12
APR. 13	4	23	23	24	1	10	10	17	1	39	15	12
APR. 14	4	24	25	25	1	10	10	17	1	39	15	12
APR. 15	4	26	26	27	1	10	10	17	1	39	15	12
APR. 16	4	28	28	29	2	10	10	17	1	39	15	12
APR. 17	4	29	30	31	2	11	10	18	1	39	15	12
APR. 18	4	31	32	32	2	11	10	18	1	39	15	12
APR. 19	5	33	34	34	2	11	10	18	1	39	15	12
APR. 20	5	35	35	36	3	11	10	18	1	39	15	12
APR. 21	5	37	37	38	3	11	10	18	1	39	15	12
APR. 22	5	38	39	40	3	11	10	18	2	39	15	12
APR. 23	5	40	41	42	3	11	10	18	2	39	15	12
APR. 24	5	42	43	43	4	12	10	18	2	39	15	12
APR. 25	6	44	45	45	4	12	11	18	2	39	15	12
APR. 26	6	46	47	47	4	12	11	18	2	39	15	12
APR. 27	6	48	48	1	4	12	11	18	2	39	15	12
APR. 28	6	2	2	3	5	12	11	18	2	39	15	12
APR. 29	6	4	4	5	5	12	11	18	2	39	15	12
APR. 30	6	5	6	7	5	12	11	18	2	39	15	12

MOON 1 ◔ 12:01 A.M. TO 8:00 A.M.   **MOON 2** ◑ 8:01 A.M. TO 4:00 P.M.   **MOON 3** ● 4:01 P.M. TO 12:00 A.M.

Use only one "moon" number. Choose the column closest to your time of birth. If your place of birth is not on Eastern Standard Time, be sure to read "How to Convert to Eastern Standard Time" at the beginning of this section.

1908

May

Date & Time	SUN	MOON 1	MOON 2	MOON 3	MERCURY	VENUS	MARS	JUPITER	SATURN	URANUS	NEPTUNE	PLUTO
MAY 1	6	7	8	8	5	12	11	18	2	39	15	12
MAY 2	6	9	10	10	6	13	11	18	2	39	15	12
MAY 3	7	11	11	12	6	13	11	18	2	39	15	12
MAY 4	7	12	13	14	6	13	11	18	2	39	15	12
MAY 5	7	14	15	15	6	13	11	18	2	39	15	12
MAY 6	7	16	16	17	7	13	12	18	2	39	15	12
MAY 7	7	17	18	18	7	13	12	18	2	39	15	12
MAY 8	7	19	19	20	7	13	12	18	2	39	15	12
MAY 9	7	20	21	22	8	13	12	18	2	39	15	12
MAY 10	7	22	23	23	8	13	12	18	2	39	15	12
MAY 11	8	24	24	25	8	14	12	18	2	39	15	12
MAY 12	8	25	26	26	8	14	12	18	2	39	15	12
MAY 13	8	27	28	28	9	14	12	18	2	39	15	12
MAY 14	8	29	29	30	9	14	12	18	2	39	15	12
MAY 15	8	31	31	32	9	14	12	18	2	39	15	12
MAY 16	8	32	33	34	10	14	12	18	2	39	15	12
MAY 17	8	34	35	35	10	14	12	18	2	39	15	12
MAY 18	8	36	37	37	10	14	13	18	2	39	15	12
MAY 19	9	38	39	39	10	14	13	18	2	39	15	12
MAY 20	9	40	40	41	11	15	13	18	2	39	15	12
MAY 21	9	42	42	43	11	15	13	18	2	39	15	12
MAY 22	9	44	44	45	11	15	13	18	2	39	15	12
MAY 23	9	46	46	47	11	15	13	18	2	39	15	12
MAY 24	9	47	48	1	12	15	13	18	2	39	15	12
MAY 25	10	1	2	3	12	15	13	18	2	39	15	12
MAY 26	10	3	4	4	12	15	13	18	2	39	15	12
MAY 27	10	5	6	6	12	15	13	18	2	39	15	12
MAY 28	10	7	7	8	13	15	13	18	2	39	15	12
MAY 29	10	8	9	10	13	15	14	18	2	39	15	12
MAY 30	10	10	11	11	13	15	14	18	2	39	15	12
MAY 31	10	12	12	13	13	15	14	18	2	39	15	12

June

Date & Time	SUN	MOON 1	MOON 2	MOON 3	MERCURY	VENUS	MARS	JUPITER	SATURN	URANUS	NEPTUNE	PLUTO
JUN. 1	10	14	14	15	13	15	14	18	2	39	15	12
JUN. 2	10	15	16	16	14	16	14	18	2	39	15	12
JUN. 3	11	17	17	18	14	16	14	18	2	39	15	12
JUN. 4	11	18	19	19	14	16	14	18	2	39	15	12
JUN. 5	11	20	20	21	14	16	14	18	2	39	15	12
JUN. 6	11	22	22	23	14	16	14	18	2	39	15	12
JUN. 7	11	23	24	24	14	16	14	18	2	39	15	12
JUN. 8	11	25	25	26	14	16	14	18	2	39	15	12
JUN. 9	11	26	27	27	15	16	14	18	2	39	15	12
JUN. 10	11	28	29	29	15	16	15	18	2	39	15	12
JUN. 11	12	30	30	31	15	16	15	18	2	39	15	12
JUN. 12	12	32	32	33	15	16	15	18	2	39	15	12
JUN. 13	12	33	34	35	15	16	15	18	2	39	15	12
JUN. 14	12	35	36	37	15	16	15	18	2	39	15	12
JUN. 15	12	37	38	39	15	16	15	18	2	39	15	12
JUN. 16	12	39	40	41	15	16	15	19	2	39	15	12
JUN. 17	12	41	42	42	15	16	15	19	2	39	15	12
JUN. 18	12	43	44	44	15	16	15	19	2	39	15	12
JUN. 19	13	45	46	46	15	16	15	19	2	39	15	12
JUN. 20	13	47	48	48	15	16	15	19	2	39	15	12
JUN. 21	13	1	1	2	15	16	16	19	2	39	15	12
JUN. 22	13	3	3	4	15	16	16	19	2	39	15	12
JUN. 23	13	5	5	6	15	16	16	19	2	39	15	12
JUN. 24	13	6	7	7	15	16	16	19	2	39	15	12
JUN. 25	14	8	9	9	15	16	16	19	2	39	15	12
JUN. 26	14	10	10	11	15	16	16	19	2	39	15	12
JUN. 27	14	11	12	13	15	15	16	19	2	39	15	12
JUN. 28	14	13	14	14	15	15	16	19	2	39	15	12
JUN. 29	14	15	15	16	15	15	16	19	2	39	15	12
JUN. 30	14	16	17	17	15	15	16	19	2	39	15	12

MOON 1 ☽ 12:01 A.M. TO 8:00 A.M.　　**MOON 2** ◑ 8:01 A.M. TO 4:00 P.M.　　**MOON 3** ● 4:01 P.M. TO 12:00 A.M.

Use only one "moon" number. Choose the column closest to your time of birth. If your place of birth is not on Eastern Standard Time, be sure to read "How to Convert to Eastern Standard Time" at the beginning of this section.

1908

July

August

Date & Time	SUN	MOON 1	MOON 2	MOON 3	MERCURY	VENUS	MARS	JUPITER	SATURN	URANUS	NEPTUNE	PLUTO
JUL. 1	14	18	18	19	15	15	16	19	2	39	15	12
JUL. 2	14	19	20	21	15	15	16	19	2	39	15	12
JUL. 3	15	21	22	22	15	15	17	19	2	39	15	12
JUL. 4	15	23	23	24	15	15	17	19	2	39	15	12
JUL. 5	15	24	25	25	15	15	17	19	2	39	15	12
JUL. 6	15	26	26	27	15	15	17	19	2	39	15	12
JUL. 7	15	27	28	29	14	15	17	19	2	39	15	12
JUL. 8	15	29	30	30	14	15	17	19	2	39	15	12
JUL. 9	15	31	31	32	14	15	17	19	2	39	15	12
JUL. 10	15	33	33	34	14	14	17	19	2	39	15	12
JUL. 11	16	35	35	36	14	14	17	19	2	39	15	12
JUL. 12	16	36	37	38	14	14	17	19	2	39	15	12
JUL. 13	16	38	39	40	14	14	17	19	2	39	15	12
JUL. 14	16	40	41	42	14	14	17	19	2	39	15	12
JUL. 15	16	42	43	44	14	14	18	19	2	39	15	12
JUL. 16	16	44	45	46	14	14	18	19	2	39	15	12
JUL. 17	16	46	47	48	14	14	18	19	2	39	15	12
JUL. 18	16	48	1	2	14	14	18	19	2	39	15	12
JUL. 19	17	2	3	3	14	14	18	19	2	39	15	12
JUL. 20	17	4	5	5	14	14	18	19	2	39	15	12
JUL. 21	17	6	6	7	14	14	18	19	2	39	15	12
JUL. 22	17	8	8	8	14	14	18	19	2	39	15	12
JUL. 23	17	9	10	10	14	14	18	19	2	39	15	12
JUL. 24	17	11	12	12	14	14	18	20	2	39	15	12
JUL. 25	17	13	13	14	15	14	18	20	2	39	15	12
JUL. 26	18	14	15	15	15	14	19	20	2	39	15	12
JUL. 27	18	16	16	17	15	14	19	20	2	39	15	12
JUL. 28	18	17	18	19	15	14	19	20	2	39	15	12
JUL. 29	18	19	20	20	15	14	19	20	2	39	15	12
JUL. 30	18	21	21	22	15	14	19	20	2	39	15	12
JUL. 31	18	22	23	23	15	14	19	20	2	39	15	12

Date & Time	SUN	MOON 1	MOON 2	MOON 3	MERCURY	VENUS	MARS	JUPITER	SATURN	URANUS	NEPTUNE	PLUTO
AUG. 1	18	24	24	25	16	14	19	20	2	39	15	12
AUG. 2	18	25	26	26	16	14	19	20	2	39	15	12
AUG. 3	19	27	28	28	16	14	19	20	2	39	15	12
AUG. 4	19	29	29	30	16	14	19	20	2	39	15	12
AUG. 5	19	30	31	31	17	14	19	20	2	39	15	12
AUG. 6	19	32	33	33	17	14	19	20	2	39	15	12
AUG. 7	19	34	34	35	17	14	20	20	2	39	15	12
AUG. 8	19	36	36	37	17	14	20	20	2	39	15	12
AUG. 9	19	38	38	39	18	14	20	20	2	39	15	12
AUG. 10	19	39	40	41	18	14	20	20	2	39	15	12
AUG. 11	20	41	42	43	18	14	20	20	2	39	15	12
AUG. 12	20	44	44	45	18	14	20	20	2	39	15	12
AUG. 13	20	46	46	47	19	14	20	20	2	39	15	12
AUG. 14	20	48	48	1	19	14	20	20	2	39	15	12
AUG. 15	20	2	2	3	19	14	20	20	2	39	15	12
AUG. 16	20	3	4	5	19	15	20	20	2	39	15	12
AUG. 17	20	5	6	7	20	15	20	20	2	39	15	12
AUG. 18	20	7	8	8	20	15	20	20	2	39	15	12
AUG. 19	21	9	9	10	20	15	21	20	2	39	15	12
AUG. 20	21	11	11	12	20	15	21	20	2	39	15	12
AUG. 21	21	12	13	13	21	15	21	20	2	39	15	12
AUG. 22	21	14	14	15	21	15	21	20	2	39	15	12
AUG. 23	21	15	16	17	21	15	21	20	2	39	15	12
AUG. 24	21	17	18	18	22	15	21	20	2	39	15	12
AUG. 25	21	19	19	20	22	15	21	20	2	39	15	12
AUG. 26	22	20	21	21	22	15	21	20	2	39	15	12
AUG. 27	22	22	22	23	22	16	21	21	2	39	15	12
AUG. 28	22	23	24	24	23	16	21	21	2	39	15	12
AUG. 29	22	25	26	26	23	16	21	21	2	39	15	12
AUG. 30	22	27	27	28	23	16	21	21	2	39	15	12
AUG. 31	22	28	29	29	23	16	22	21	2	39	15	12

MOON 1 ☽ 12:01 A.M. TO 8:00 A.M.   **MOON 2** ☽ 8:01 A.M. TO 4:00 P.M.   **MOON 3** ● 4:01 P.M. TO 12:00 A.M.
Use only one "moon" number. Choose the column closest to your time of birth. If your place of birth is not on
Eastern Standard Time, be sure to read "How to Convert to Eastern Standard Time" at the beginning of this section.

1908

September

Date & Time	SUN	MOON 1	MOON 2	MOON 3	MERCURY	VENUS	MARS	JUPITER	SATURN	URANUS	NEPTUNE	PLUTO
SEP. 1	22	30	30	31	23	16	22	21	2	39	15	12
SEP. 2	22	32	32	33	24	16	22	21	2	39	15	12
SEP. 3	23	33	34	34	24	16	22	21	2	39	15	12
SEP. 4	23	35	36	36	24	16	22	21	2	39	15	12
SEP. 5	23	37	37	38	24	17	22	21	2	39	15	12
SEP. 6	23	39	39	40	25	17	22	21	2	39	15	12
SEP. 7	23	41	41	42	25	17	22	21	2	39	15	12
SEP. 8	23	43	43	44	25	17	22	21	2	39	15	12
SEP. 9	23	45	45	46	25	17	22	21	2	39	15	12
SEP. 10	23	47	47	48	25	17	22	21	2	39	15	12
SEP. 11	24	1	1	2	26	17	22	21	2	39	15	12
SEP. 12	24	3	3	4	26	17	23	21	2	39	15	12
SEP. 13	24	5	5	6	26	18	23	21	2	39	15	12
SEP. 14	24	7	7	8	26	18	23	21	2	39	15	12
SEP. 15	24	8	9	10	27	18	23	21	2	39	15	12
SEP. 16	24	10	11	11	27	18	23	21	2	39	15	12
SEP. 17	24	12	12	13	27	18	23	21	2	39	15	12
SEP. 18	24	13	14	15	27	18	23	21	2	39	15	12
SEP. 19	25	15	16	16	27	18	23	21	2	39	15	12
SEP. 20	25	17	17	18	27	18	23	21	2	39	15	12
SEP. 21	25	18	19	19	28	19	23	21	2	39	15	12
SEP. 22	25	20	20	21	28	19	23	21	2	39	15	12
SEP. 23	25	21	22	22	28	19	24	21	2	39	15	12
SEP. 24	25	23	24	24	28	19	24	21	2	39	15	12
SEP. 25	26	25	25	26	28	19	24	21	2	39	15	12
SEP. 26	26	26	27	27	29	19	24	21	2	39	15	12
SEP. 27	26	28	28	29	29	19	24	21	2	39	15	12
SEP. 28	26	29	30	31	29	20	24	21	2	39	15	12
SEP. 29	26	31	32	32	29	20	24	21	2	39	15	12
SEP. 30	26	33	33	34	29	20	24	21	2	39	15	12

October

Date & Time	SUN	MOON 1	MOON 2	MOON 3	MERCURY	VENUS	MARS	JUPITER	SATURN	URANUS	NEPTUNE	PLUTO
OCT. 1	26	35	35	36	29	20	24	21	2	39	15	12
OCT. 2	26	36	37	38	29	20	24	22	2	39	15	12
OCT. 3	27	38	39	39	30	20	24	22	2	39	15	12
OCT. 4	27	40	41	41	30	20	24	22	2	39	15	12
OCT. 5	27	42	43	43	30	21	25	22	2	39	15	12
OCT. 6	27	44	44	45	30	21	25	22	2	39	15	12
OCT. 7	27	46	46	47	30	21	25	22	2	39	15	12
OCT. 8	27	48	48	1	30	21	25	22	2	39	15	12
OCT. 9	27	2	2	3	30	21	25	22	2	39	15	12
OCT. 10	27	4	5	5	30	21	25	22	2	39	15	12
OCT. 11	28	6	6	7	31	21	25	22	2	39	15	12
OCT. 12	28	8	8	9	31	22	25	22	2	39	15	12
OCT. 13	28	9	10	11	31	22	25	22	2	39	15	12
OCT. 14	28	11	12	12	31	22	25	22	2	39	15	12
OCT. 15	28	13	13	14	31	22	25	22	2	39	15	12
OCT. 16	28	15	15	16	31	22	25	22	2	39	15	12
OCT. 17	28	16	17	17	31	22	26	22	2	39	15	12
OCT. 18	28	18	18	19	31	22	26	22	2	39	15	12
OCT. 19	29	19	20	20	31	23	26	22	2	39	15	12
OCT. 20	29	21	21	22	31	23	26	22	2	39	15	12
OCT. 21	29	23	23	24	31	23	26	22	2	39	15	12
OCT. 22	29	24	25	25	31	23	26	22	2	39	15	12
OCT. 23	29	26	26	27	30	23	26	22	2	39	15	12
OCT. 24	29	27	28	28	30	23	26	22	2	39	15	12
OCT. 25	29	29	30	30	30	24	26	22	2	39	15	12
OCT. 26	30	31	31	32	30	24	26	22	2	39	15	12
OCT. 27	30	32	33	34	30	24	26	22	2	39	15	12
OCT. 28	30	34	35	35	30	24	27	22	2	39	15	12
OCT. 29	30	36	37	37	30	24	27	22	2	39	15	12
OCT. 30	30	38	38	39	30	24	27	22	2	39	15	12
OCT. 31	30	40	40	41	29	24	27	22	2	39	15	12

MOON 1 ☽ 12:01 A.M. TO 8:00 A.M.   **MOON 2** ◑ 8:01 A.M. TO 4:00 P.M.   **MOON 3** ● 4:01 P.M. TO 12:00 A.M.
Use only one "moon" number. Choose the column closest to your time of birth. If your place of birth is not on Eastern Standard Time, be sure to read "How to Convert to Eastern Standard Time" at the beginning of this section.

1908

November

Date & Time	SUN ☉	MOON 1 ◗	MOON 2 ◑	MOON 3 ●	MERCURY	VENUS	MARS	JUPITER	SATURN	URANUS	NEPTUNE	PLUTO
NOV. 1	30	41	42	43	29	25	27	22	2	39	15	12
NOV. 2	30	43	44	45	29	25	27	22	2	39	15	12
NOV. 3	31	45	46	46	29	25	27	22	2	39	15	12
NOV. 4	31	47	48	48	29	25	27	22	2	39	15	12
NOV. 5	31	1	2	2	29	25	27	22	2	39	15	12
NOV. 6	31	3	4	4	29	25	27	22	2	39	15	12
NOV. 7	31	5	6	6	29	26	27	22	2	39	15	12
NOV. 8	31	7	7	8	29	26	27	22	2	39	15	12
NOV. 9	31	9	9	10	29	26	28	22	2	39	15	12
NOV. 10	31	10	11	12	29	26	28	22	1	39	15	12
NOV. 11	31	12	13	13	29	26	28	22	1	39	15	12
NOV. 12	32	14	14	15	29	26	28	22	1	39	15	12
NOV. 13	32	16	16	17	29	27	28	22	1	39	15	12
NOV. 14	32	17	18	18	29	27	28	22	1	39	15	12
NOV. 15	32	19	19	20	29	27	28	22	1	39	15	12
NOV. 16	32	20	21	21	30	27	28	23	1	39	15	12
NOV. 17	32	22	23	23	30	27	28	23	1	39	15	12
NOV. 18	32	24	24	25	30	27	28	23	1	39	15	12
NOV. 19	33	25	26	26	30	27	28	23	1	39	15	12
NOV. 20	33	27	27	28	30	28	28	23	1	39	15	12
NOV. 21	33	28	29	30	30	28	29	23	1	39	15	12
NOV. 22	33	30	31	31	31	28	29	23	1	39	15	12
NOV. 23	33	32	32	33	31	28	29	23	1	39	15	12
NOV. 24	33	34	34	35	31	28	29	23	1	39	15	12
NOV. 25	34	35	36	37	31	28	29	23	1	39	15	12
NOV. 26	34	37	38	39	31	29	29	23	1	39	15	12
NOV. 27	34	39	40	40	32	29	29	23	1	39	15	12
NOV. 28	34	41	42	42	32	29	29	23	1	39	15	12
NOV. 29	34	43	43	44	32	29	29	23	1	39	15	12
NOV. 30	34	45	45	46	32	29	29	23	1	39	15	12

December

Date & Time	SUN ☉	MOON 1 ◗	MOON 2 ◑	MOON 3 ●	MERCURY	VENUS	MARS	JUPITER	SATURN	URANUS	NEPTUNE	PLUTO
DEC. 1	34	47	47	48	32	29	29	23	1	39	15	12
DEC. 2	34	1	1	2	33	30	30	23	1	39	15	12
DEC. 3	35	2	3	4	33	30	30	23	1	39	15	12
DEC. 4	35	4	5	6	33	30	30	23	1	39	15	12
DEC. 5	35	6	7	7	33	30	30	23	1	39	15	12
DEC. 6	35	8	9	9	33	30	30	23	1	39	15	12
DEC. 7	35	10	10	11	34	30	30	23	1	39	15	12
DEC. 8	35	12	12	13	34	31	30	23	1	39	15	12
DEC. 9	35	13	14	14	34	31	30	23	1	39	15	12
DEC. 10	35	15	16	16	34	31	30	23	1	39	15	12
DEC. 11	36	17	17	18	35	31	30	23	1	39	15	12
DEC. 12	36	18	19	19	35	31	30	23	1	39	15	12
DEC. 13	36	20	20	21	35	31	31	23	1	39	15	12
DEC. 14	36	21	22	23	35	32	31	23	1	39	15	12
DEC. 15	36	23	24	24	35	32	31	23	1	39	15	12
DEC. 16	36	25	25	26	36	32	31	23	1	39	15	12
DEC. 17	36	26	27	27	36	32	31	23	1	39	15	12
DEC. 18	36	28	28	29	36	32	31	23	1	39	15	12
DEC. 19	37	30	30	31	36	32	31	23	1	39	15	12
DEC. 20	37	31	32	32	36	33	31	23	1	39	15	12
DEC. 21	37	33	34	34	37	33	31	23	1	39	15	12
DEC. 22	37	35	35	36	37	33	31	23	1	39	15	12
DEC. 23	37	37	37	38	37	33	31	23	1	39	15	12
DEC. 24	37	38	39	40	37	33	31	23	1	39	15	12
DEC. 25	37	40	41	42	37	33	32	23	1	39	15	12
DEC. 26	38	42	43	44	38	34	32	23	1	39	15	12
DEC. 27	38	44	45	46	38	34	32	23	1	39	15	12
DEC. 28	38	46	47	47	38	34	32	23	1	39	15	12
DEC. 29	38	48	1	1	38	34	32	23	1	39	15	12
DEC. 30	38	2	3	3	39	34	32	23	1	39	15	12
DEC. 31	38	4	4	5	39	34	32	23	1	39	15	12

MOON 1 ◗ 12:01 A.M. TO 8:00 A.M.   **MOON 2** ◑ 8:01 A.M. TO 4:00 P.M.   **MOON 3** ● 4:01 P.M. TO 12:00 A.M.

Use only one "moon" number. Choose the column closest to your time of birth. If your place of birth is not on Eastern Standard Time, be sure to read "How to Convert to Eastern Standard Time" at the beginning of this section.

January

Date & Time	SUN	MOON 1	MOON 2	MOON 3	MERCURY	VENUS	MARS	JUPITER	SATURN	URANUS	NEPTUNE	PLUTO
JAN. 1	38	6	6	7	39	35	32	23	1	39	15	12
JAN. 2	38	7	8	9	39	35	32	23	1	39	15	12
JAN. 3	39	9	10	10	39	35	32	23	2	39	15	12
JAN. 4	39	11	12	12	40	35	32	23	2	39	15	12
JAN. 5	39	13	13	14	40	35	33	23	2	39	15	12
JAN. 6	39	14	15	16	40	35	33	23	2	39	15	12
JAN. 7	39	16	17	17	40	36	33	23	2	39	15	12
JAN. 8	39	18	18	19	40	36	33	23	2	39	15	12
JAN. 9	39	19	20	20	41	36	33	23	2	39	15	12
JAN. 10	40	21	21	22	41	36	33	23	2	39	15	12
JAN. 11	40	23	23	24	41	36	33	23	2	39	15	12
JAN. 12	40	24	25	25	42	36	33	23	2	39	15	12
JAN. 13	40	26	26	27	42	37	33	23	2	39	15	12
JAN. 14	40	27	28	28	42	37	33	23	2	39	15	12
JAN. 15	40	29	29	30	42	37	33	23	2	39	15	12
JAN. 16	40	31	31	32	42	37	34	23	2	39	15	12
JAN. 17	41	32	33	33	42	37	34	23	2	39	15	12
JAN. 18	41	34	35	35	43	37	34	23	2	39	15	12
JAN. 19	41	36	36	37	43	38	34	23	2	39	15	12
JAN. 20	41	38	38	39	43	38	34	23	2	39	15	12
JAN. 21	41	40	40	41	43	38	34	23	2	39	15	12
JAN. 22	41	42	42	43	43	38	34	23	2	39	15	12
JAN. 23	42	44	44	45	44	38	34	23	2	39	15	12
JAN. 24	42	46	46	47	44	38	34	23	2	39	15	12
JAN. 25	42	48	48	1	44	39	34	23	2	39	15	12
JAN. 26	42	1	2	3	44	39	34	23	2	39	15	12
JAN. 27	42	3	4	5	44	39	34	23	2	39	15	12
JAN. 28	42	5	6	6	44	39	35	23	2	39	15	12
JAN. 29	42	7	8	8	45	39	35	23	2	39	15	12
JAN. 30	42	9	9	10	45	39	35	23	2	39	15	12
JAN. 31	43	11	11	12	45	39	35	23	2	39	15	12

February

Date & Time	SUN	MOON 1	MOON 2	MOON 3	MERCURY	VENUS	MARS	JUPITER	SATURN	URANUS	NEPTUNE	PLUTO
FEB. 1	43	12	13	13	45	40	35	23	2	39	15	12
FEB. 2	43	14	15	15	45	40	35	23	2	39	15	12
FEB. 3	43	16	16	17	45	40	35	23	2	39	15	12
FEB. 4	43	17	18	18	45	40	35	23	2	39	15	12
FEB. 5	43	19	19	20	45	40	35	23	2	39	15	12
FEB. 6	43	20	21	22	45	40	35	23	2	39	15	12
FEB. 7	43	22	23	23	45	41	35	23	2	39	15	12
FEB. 8	44	24	24	25	44	41	36	23	2	39	15	12
FEB. 9	44	25	26	26	44	41	36	23	2	39	15	12
FEB. 10	44	27	27	28	44	41	36	23	2	39	15	12
FEB. 11	44	28	29	29	44	41	36	23	2	39	15	12
FEB. 12	44	30	31	31	44	41	36	23	2	40	15	12
FEB. 13	44	32	32	33	44	42	36	23	2	40	15	12
FEB. 14	44	33	34	34	44	42	36	22	2	40	15	12
FEB. 15	44	35	36	36	43	42	36	22	2	40	15	12
FEB. 16	45	37	37	38	43	42	36	22	2	40	15	12
FEB. 17	45	39	39	40	43	42	36	22	2	40	15	12
FEB. 18	45	41	41	42	43	42	36	22	2	40	15	12
FEB. 19	45	43	43	44	43	43	37	22	2	40	15	12
FEB. 20	45	45	45	46	43	43	37	22	2	40	15	12
FEB. 21	45	47	47	48	43	43	37	22	2	40	15	12
FEB. 22	45	1	1	2	43	43	37	22	2	40	15	12
FEB. 23	46	3	3	4	43	43	37	22	2	40	15	12
FEB. 24	46	5	5	6	43	43	37	22	2	40	15	12
FEB. 25	46	7	7	8	43	44	37	22	2	40	15	12
FEB. 26	46	8	9	10	43	44	37	22	2	40	15	12
FEB. 27	46	10	11	11	43	44	37	22	2	40	15	12
FEB. 28	46	12	12	13	43	44	37	22	2	40	15	12

MOON 1 ☽ 12:01 A.M. TO 8:00 A.M.   **MOON 2** ☽ 8:01 A.M. TO 4:00 P.M.   **MOON 3** ● 4:01 P.M. TO 12:00 A.M.

Use only one "moon" number. Choose the column closest to your time of birth. If your place of birth is not on Eastern Standard Time, be sure to read "How to Convert to Eastern Standard Time" at the beginning of this section.

1909

March

Date & Time	SUN	MOON 1	MOON 2	MOON 3	MERCURY	VENUS	MARS	JUPITER	SATURN	URANUS	NEPTUNE	PLUTO
MAR. 1	46	14	14	15	43	44	37	22	2	40	15	12
MAR. 2	46	15	16	16	43	44	38	22	2	40	15	12
MAR. 3	47	17	17	18	43	45	38	22	2	40	15	12
MAR. 4	47	18	19	20	43	45	38	22	2	40	15	12
MAR. 5	47	20	21	21	43	45	38	22	2	40	15	12
MAR. 6	47	22	22	23	43	45	38	22	2	40	15	12
MAR. 7	47	23	24	24	43	45	38	22	2	40	15	12
MAR. 8	47	25	25	26	44	45	38	22	2	40	15	12
MAR. 9	47	26	27	27	44	46	38	22	2	40	15	12
MAR. 10	47	28	29	29	44	46	38	22	2	40	15	12
MAR. 11	48	30	30	31	44	46	38	22	2	40	15	12
MAR. 12	48	31	32	32	44	46	38	22	2	40	15	12
MAR. 13	48	33	33	34	44	46	38	22	2	40	15	12
MAR. 14	48	35	35	36	44	46	39	22	2	40	15	12
MAR. 15	48	36	37	37	45	47	39	22	2	40	15	12
MAR. 16	48	38	39	39	45	47	39	22	2	40	15	12
MAR. 17	48	40	40	41	45	47	39	22	2	40	15	12
MAR. 18	48	42	42	43	45	47	39	22	2	40	15	12
MAR. 19	1	44	44	45	45	47	39	22	2	40	15	12
MAR. 20	1	46	46	47	45	47	39	22	2	40	15	12
MAR. 21	1	48	48	1	46	48	39	22	2	40	15	12
MAR. 22	1	2	3	3	46	48	39	22	3	40	15	12
MAR. 23	1	4	4	5	46	48	39	22	3	40	15	12
MAR. 24	1	6	6	7	46	48	39	22	3	40	15	12
MAR. 25	2	8	8	9	46	48	40	22	3	40	15	12
MAR. 26	2	10	10	11	47	48	40	22	3	40	15	12
MAR. 27	2	11	12	13	47	1	40	22	3	40	15	12
MAR. 28	2	13	14	14	47	1	40	22	3	40	15	12
MAR. 29	2	15	15	16	47	1	40	22	3	40	15	12
MAR. 30	2	16	17	18	47	1	40	22	3	40	15	12
MAR. 31	2	18	19	19	48	1	40	22	3	40	15	12

April

Date & Time	SUN	MOON 1	MOON 2	MOON 3	MERCURY	VENUS	MARS	JUPITER	SATURN	URANUS	NEPTUNE	PLUTO
APR. 1	2	20	20	21	48	1	40	22	3	40	15	12
APR. 2	2	21	22	22	48	2	40	22	3	40	15	12
APR. 3	3	23	23	24	48	2	40	22	3	40	15	12
APR. 4	3	24	25	25	1	2	40	22	3	40	15	12
APR. 5	3	26	27	27	1	2	41	22	3	40	15	12
APR. 6	3	28	28	29	1	2	41	22	3	40	15	12
APR. 7	3	29	30	30	1	2	41	22	3	40	15	12
APR. 8	3	31	31	32	1	3	41	22	3	40	15	12
APR. 9	3	32	33	34	2	3	41	22	3	40	15	12
APR. 10	3	34	35	35	2	3	41	22	3	40	15	12
APR. 11	4	36	36	37	2	3	41	22	3	40	15	12
APR. 12	4	38	38	39	2	3	41	22	3	40	15	12
APR. 13	4	39	40	41	3	3	41	22	3	40	15	12
APR. 14	4	41	42	42	3	4	41	22	3	40	15	12
APR. 15	4	43	44	44	3	4	41	22	3	40	15	12
APR. 16	4	45	46	46	4	4	42	22	3	40	15	12
APR. 17	4	47	48	48	4	4	42	22	3	40	15	12
APR. 18	4	1	2	2	4	4	42	22	3	40	15	12
APR. 19	5	3	4	4	4	5	42	22	3	40	15	12
APR. 20	5	5	6	6	5	5	42	22	3	40	15	12
APR. 21	5	7	8	8	5	5	42	22	3	40	15	12
APR. 22	5	9	9	10	5	5	42	22	3	40	15	12
APR. 23	5	11	11	12	5	5	42	22	3	40	15	12
APR. 24	5	12	13	14	6	5	42	22	3	40	15	12
APR. 25	6	14	15	15	6	5	42	22	3	40	15	12
APR. 26	6	16	16	17	6	6	42	22	3	40	15	12
APR. 27	6	18	18	19	7	6	43	22	3	40	15	12
APR. 28	6	19	20	20	7	6	43	22	3	40	15	12
APR. 29	6	21	21	22	7	6	43	22	3	40	15	12
APR. 30	6	22	23	23	7	6	43	22	3	40	15	12

MOON 1 ◯ 12:01 A.M. TO 8:00 A.M.   **MOON 2** ◑ 8:01 A.M. TO 4:00 P.M.   **MOON 3** ● 4:01 P.M. TO 12:00 A.M.

Use only one "moon" number. Choose the column closest to your time of birth. If your place of birth is not on Eastern Standard Time, be sure to read "How to Convert to Eastern Standard Time" at the beginning of this section.

1909

May

June

Date & Time	SUN	MOON 1	MOON 2	MOON 3	MERCURY	VENUS	MARS	JUPITER	SATURN	URANUS	NEPTUNE	PLUTO
MAY 1	6	24	24	25	8	6	43	22	3	40	15	12
MAY 2	6	26	26	27	8	7	43	22	3	40	15	12
MAY 3	7	27	28	28	8	7	43	22	3	40	15	12
MAY 4	7	29	29	30	9	7	43	22	3	40	15	12
MAY 5	7	30	31	31	9	7	43	22	3	40	15	12
MAY 6	7	32	33	33	9	7	43	22	3	40	15	12
MAY 7	7	34	34	35	9	7	43	22	3	40	15	12
MAY 8	7	35	36	37	10	8	43	22	3	40	15	12
MAY 9	7	37	38	38	10	8	44	22	3	40	15	12
MAY 10	7	39	40	40	10	8	44	22	3	40	15	12
MAY 11	8	41	41	42	10	8	44	22	3	40	15	12
MAY 12	8	43	43	44	10	8	44	22	3	40	15	12
MAY 13	8	44	45	46	11	8	44	22	3	40	15	12
MAY 14	8	46	47	48	11	9	44	22	3	40	15	12
MAY 15	8	48	1	2	11	9	44	22	3	40	15	12
MAY 16	8	2	3	3	11	9	44	22	3	40	15	12
MAY 17	8	4	5	5	11	9	44	22	3	40	15	12
MAY 18	8	6	7	7	11	9	44	22	3	40	15	12
MAY 19	9	8	9	9	12	9	44	22	3	40	15	12
MAY 20	9	10	11	11	12	10	44	22	3	40	15	12
MAY 21	9	12	12	13	12	10	45	22	3	40	15	12
MAY 22	9	14	14	15	12	10	45	22	3	40	15	12
MAY 23	9	15	16	16	12	10	45	22	3	40	15	12
MAY 24	9	17	18	18	12	10	45	22	4	40	15	12
MAY 25	10	19	19	20	12	10	45	22	4	40	15	12
MAY 26	10	20	21	21	12	11	45	22	4	40	15	12
MAY 27	10	22	22	23	12	11	45	22	4	40	15	12
MAY 28	10	23	24	25	13	11	45	22	4	40	15	12
MAY 29	10	25	26	26	13	11	45	22	4	40	15	12
MAY 30	10	27	27	28	13	11	45	22	4	40	15	12
MAY 31	10	28	29	29	13	11	45	22	4	40	15	12

Date & Time	SUN	MOON 1	MOON 2	MOON 3	MERCURY	VENUS	MARS	JUPITER	SATURN	URANUS	NEPTUNE	PLUTO
JUN. 1	10	30	30	31	13	11	45	22	4	40	15	12
JUN. 2	10	32	32	33	13	12	46	22	4	40	15	12
JUN. 3	11	33	34	34	13	12	46	22	4	40	15	12
JUN. 4	11	35	36	36	13	12	46	22	4	40	15	12
JUN. 5	11	37	37	38	13	12	46	22	4	40	15	12
JUN. 6	11	38	39	40	13	12	46	22	4	40	15	12
JUN. 7	11	40	41	41	13	12	46	22	4	40	15	12
JUN. 8	11	42	43	43	13	13	46	22	4	40	15	12
JUN. 9	11	44	45	45	12	13	46	22	4	40	15	12
JUN. 10	11	46	46	47	12	13	46	22	4	40	15	12
JUN. 11	12	48	48	1	12	13	46	22	4	40	15	12
JUN. 12	12	2	2	3	12	13	46	22	4	40	15	12
JUN. 13	12	4	4	5	12	13	46	22	4	40	15	12
JUN. 14	12	5	6	7	12	14	47	22	4	40	15	12
JUN. 15	12	7	8	9	12	14	47	22	4	40	15	12
JUN. 16	12	9	10	10	12	14	47	22	4	40	15	12
JUN. 17	12	11	12	12	12	14	47	22	4	40	15	12
JUN. 18	12	13	13	14	12	14	47	22	4	40	15	12
JUN. 19	13	15	15	16	12	14	47	22	4	40	15	12
JUN. 20	13	16	17	17	12	15	47	22	4	40	15	12
JUN. 21	13	18	19	19	12	15	47	22	4	40	15	12
JUN. 22	13	20	20	21	12	15	47	22	4	40	15	12
JUN. 23	13	21	22	22	12	15	47	22	4	40	15	12
JUN. 24	13	23	23	24	12	15	47	22	4	40	15	12
JUN. 25	14	25	25	26	12	15	47	22	4	40	15	12
JUN. 26	14	26	27	27	12	16	47	22	4	40	15	12
JUN. 27	14	28	28	29	12	16	47	22	4	40	15	12
JUN. 28	14	29	30	30	12	16	48	22	4	40	15	12
JUN. 29	14	31	31	32	12	16	48	22	4	40	15	12
JUN. 30	14	33	33	34	12	16	48	22	4	40	15	12

MOON 1 ◖ 12:01 A.M. TO 8:00 A.M. **MOON 2** ◑ 8:01 A.M. TO 4:00 P.M. **MOON 3** ● 4:01 P.M. TO 12:00 A.M.

Use only one "moon" number. Choose the column closest to your time of birth. If your place of birth is not on Eastern Standard Time, be sure to read "How to Convert to Eastern Standard Time" at the beginning of this section.

1909

July

Date & Time	SUN ☉	MOON 1 ◐	MOON 2 ◑	MOON 3 ●	MERCURY	VENUS	MARS	JUPITER	SATURN	URANUS	NEPTUNE	PLUTO
JUL. 1	14	34	35	35	12	16	48	22	4	40	15	12
JUL. 2	14	36	37	37	12	17	48	22	4	40	15	12
JUL. 3	15	38	38	39	12	17	48	22	4	40	15	12
JUL. 4	15	40	40	41	12	17	48	22	4	40	15	12
JUL. 5	15	42	42	43	12	17	48	22	4	40	15	12
JUL. 6	15	43	44	45	12	17	48	22	4	40	15	12
JUL. 7	15	45	46	47	12	17	48	22	4	40	15	12
JUL. 8	15	47	48	1	12	18	48	22	4	40	15	12
JUL. 9	15	1	2	2	12	18	48	22	4	40	15	12
JUL. 10	15	3	4	4	12	18	48	22	4	40	15	12
JUL. 11	16	5	6	6	13	18	48	22	4	40	15	12
JUL. 12	16	7	7	8	13	18	48	22	4	40	15	12
JUL. 13	16	9	9	10	13	18	1	22	4	40	15	12
JUL. 14	16	11	11	12	13	19	1	23	4	40	15	12
JUL. 15	16	12	13	13	13	19	1	23	4	39	15	12
JUL. 16	16	14	15	15	14	19	1	23	4	39	15	12
JUL. 17	16	16	16	17	14	19	1	23	4	39	15	12
JUL. 18	16	17	18	19	14	19	1	23	4	39	15	12
JUL. 19	17	19	20	20	14	19	1	23	4	39	15	12
JUL. 20	17	21	21	22	14	19	1	23	4	39	15	12
JUL. 21	17	22	23	23	15	20	1	23	4	39	15	12
JUL. 22	17	24	25	25	15	20	1	23	4	39	15	12
JUL. 23	17	26	26	27	15	20	1	23	4	39	15	12
JUL. 24	17	27	28	28	15	20	1	23	4	39	15	12
JUL. 25	17	29	29	30	16	20	1	23	4	39	15	12
JUL. 26	18	30	31	31	16	20	1	23	4	39	15	12
JUL. 27	18	32	33	33	16	21	1	23	4	39	15	12
JUL. 28	18	34	34	35	16	21	1	23	4	39	15	12
JUL. 29	18	35	36	37	17	21	1	23	4	39	15	12
JUL. 30	18	37	38	38	17	21	1	23	4	39	15	12
JUL. 31	18	39	40	40	17	21	1	23	4	39	15	12

August

Date & Time	SUN ☉	MOON 1 ◐	MOON 2 ◑	MOON 3 ●	MERCURY	VENUS	MARS	JUPITER	SATURN	URANUS	NEPTUNE	PLUTO
AUG. 1	18	41	41	42	18	21	1	23	4	39	15	12
AUG. 2	18	43	43	44	18	22	1	23	4	39	15	12
AUG. 3	19	45	45	46	18	22	2	23	4	39	15	12
AUG. 4	19	47	47	48	18	22	2	23	4	39	15	12
AUG. 5	19	1	1	2	19	22	2	23	4	39	15	12
AUG. 6	19	3	3	4	19	22	2	23	4	39	15	12
AUG. 7	19	5	5	6	19	22	2	23	4	39	15	12
AUG. 8	19	6	7	8	19	23	2	23	4	39	15	12
AUG. 9	19	8	9	9	20	23	2	23	4	39	15	12
AUG. 10	19	10	11	11	20	23	2	23	4	39	15	12
AUG. 11	20	12	12	13	20	23	2	23	4	39	15	12
AUG. 12	20	14	14	15	21	23	2	23	4	39	15	13
AUG. 13	20	15	16	16	21	23	2	23	4	39	15	13
AUG. 14	20	17	18	18	21	24	2	23	4	39	15	13
AUG. 15	20	19	19	20	21	24	2	23	4	39	15	13
AUG. 16	20	20	21	21	22	24	2	23	4	39	15	13
AUG. 17	20	22	22	23	22	24	2	23	4	39	15	13
AUG. 18	20	24	24	25	22	24	2	23	4	39	15	13
AUG. 19	21	25	26	26	22	24	2	23	4	39	15	13
AUG. 20	21	27	27	28	22	25	2	23	4	39	15	13
AUG. 21	21	28	29	29	23	25	2	23	4	39	15	13
AUG. 22	21	30	30	31	23	25	2	24	4	39	15	13
AUG. 23	21	31	32	33	23	25	2	24	4	39	15	13
AUG. 24	21	33	34	34	23	25	2	24	4	39	15	13
AUG. 25	21	35	35	36	24	25	2	24	4	39	15	13
AUG. 26	22	36	37	38	24	25	2	24	4	39	15	13
AUG. 27	22	38	39	39	24	26	2	24	4	39	15	13
AUG. 28	22	40	41	41	24	26	2	24	4	39	15	13
AUG. 29	22	42	43	43	24	26	2	24	4	39	15	13
AUG. 30	22	44	45	45	25	26	2	24	4	39	15	13
AUG. 31	22	46	47	47	25	26	2	24	4	39	15	13

MOON 1 ◐ 12:01 A.M. TO 8:00 A.M.   **MOON 2** ◑ 8:01 A.M. TO 4:00 P.M.   **MOON 3** ● 4:01 P.M. TO 12:00 A.M.

Use only one "moon" number. Choose the column closest to your time of birth. If your place of birth is not on Eastern Standard Time, be sure to read "How to Convert to Eastern Standard Time" at the beginning of this section.

1909

September

Date & Time	SUN	MOON 1	MOON 2	MOON 3	MERCURY	VENUS	MARS	JUPITER	SATURN	URANUS	NEPTUNE	PLUTO
SEP. 1	22	48	1	1	25	26	2	24	4	39	15	13
SEP. 2	22	2	3	3	25	27	2	24	4	39	15	13
SEP. 3	23	4	5	5	25	27	2	24	4	39	15	13
SEP. 4	23	6	7	7	26	27	2	24	4	39	15	13
SEP. 5	23	8	8	9	26	27	2	24	4	39	15	13
SEP. 6	23	10	10	11	26	27	2	24	4	39	15	13
SEP. 7	23	11	12	13	26	27	2	24	4	39	15	13
SEP. 8	23	13	14	14	26	28	2	24	4	39	15	13
SEP. 9	23	15	15	16	26	28	2	24	4	39	15	13
SEP. 10	23	17	17	18	27	28	2	24	4	39	15	13
SEP. 11	24	18	19	19	27	28	2	24	4	39	15	13
SEP. 12	24	20	20	21	27	28	2	24	4	39	15	13
SEP. 13	24	22	22	23	27	28	1	24	4	39	15	13
SEP. 14	24	23	24	24	27	29	1	24	4	39	15	13
SEP. 15	24	25	25	26	27	29	1	24	4	39	15	13
SEP. 16	24	26	27	27	28	29	1	24	4	39	15	13
SEP. 17	24	28	28	29	28	29	1	24	4	39	15	13
SEP. 18	24	29	30	30	28	29	1	24	4	39	16	13
SEP. 19	25	31	32	32	28	29	1	24	4	39	16	13
SEP. 20	25	33	33	34	28	29	1	24	4	39	16	13
SEP. 21	25	34	35	35	28	30	1	24	4	39	16	13
SEP. 22	25	36	36	37	28	30	1	24	4	39	16	13
SEP. 23	25	38	38	39	28	30	1	24	4	39	16	13
SEP. 24	25	39	40	41	28	30	1	24	4	39	16	13
SEP. 25	26	41	42	42	28	30	1	24	4	39	16	13
SEP. 26	26	43	44	44	29	30	1	25	4	39	16	13
SEP. 27	26	45	46	46	29	31	1	25	4	39	16	13
SEP. 28	26	47	48	48	29	31	1	25	4	39	16	13
SEP. 29	26	1	2	2	29	31	1	25	4	39	16	13
SEP. 30	26	3	4	4	29	31	1	25	4	39	16	13

October

Date & Time	SUN	MOON 1	MOON 2	MOON 3	MERCURY	VENUS	MARS	JUPITER	SATURN	URANUS	NEPTUNE	PLUTO
OCT. 1	26	5	6	6	29	31	1	25	4	39	16	13
OCT. 2	26	7	8	8	29	31	1	25	4	39	16	13
OCT. 3	27	9	10	10	29	32	1	25	4	39	16	13
OCT. 4	27	11	12	12	29	32	1	25	4	39	16	13
OCT. 5	27	13	13	14	29	32	1	25	4	39	16	13
OCT. 6	27	14	15	16	29	32	1	25	4	39	16	13
OCT. 7	27	16	17	17	28	32	1	25	4	39	16	13
OCT. 8	27	18	18	19	28	32	1	25	4	39	16	13
OCT. 9	27	20	20	21	28	32	1	25	4	39	16	13
OCT. 10	27	21	22	22	28	33	1	25	4	39	16	13
OCT. 11	28	23	23	24	28	33	1	25	4	39	16	13
OCT. 12	28	24	25	25	28	33	48	25	4	39	16	13
OCT. 13	28	26	26	27	27	33	48	25	4	39	16	13
OCT. 14	28	27	28	29	27	33	48	25	4	39	16	13
OCT. 15	28	29	30	30	27	33	48	25	4	39	16	13
OCT. 16	28	31	31	32	27	34	48	25	4	39	16	13
OCT. 17	28	32	33	33	27	34	48	25	4	39	16	13
OCT. 18	28	34	34	35	27	34	48	25	4	39	16	13
OCT. 19	29	35	36	37	27	34	48	25	4	39	16	13
OCT. 20	29	37	38	38	27	34	48	25	4	39	16	13
OCT. 21	29	39	39	40	27	34	48	25	4	39	16	13
OCT. 22	29	41	41	42	27	34	48	25	4	39	16	13
OCT. 23	29	42	43	44	27	35	48	25	4	39	16	13
OCT. 24	29	44	45	46	27	35	48	25	3	39	16	13
OCT. 25	29	46	47	47	27	35	48	25	3	39	16	13
OCT. 26	30	48	1	1	27	35	48	25	3	39	16	13
OCT. 27	30	2	3	3	27	35	48	25	3	39	16	13
OCT. 28	30	4	5	6	27	35	48	25	3	39	16	13
OCT. 29	30	6	7	8	27	36	48	25	3	39	16	13
OCT. 30	30	8	9	10	27	36	48	25	3	39	16	13
OCT. 31	30	10	11	11	28	36	48	25	3	39	16	13

MOON 1 ☽ 12:01 A.M. TO 8:00 A.M.　　**MOON 2** ◑ 8:01 A.M. TO 4:00 P.M.　　**MOON 3** ● 4:01 P.M. TO 12:00 A.M.

Use only one "moon" number. Choose the column closest to your time of birth. If your place of birth is not on Eastern Standard Time, be sure to read "How to Convert to Eastern Standard Time" at the beginning of this section.

1909

November

Date & Time	SUN	MOON 1	MOON 2	MOON 3	MERCURY	VENUS	MARS	JUPITER	SATURN	URANUS	NEPTUNE	PLUTO
NOV. 1	30	12	13	13	28	36	48	26	3	39	16	13
NOV. 2	30	14	14	15	28	36	48	26	3	39	16	13
NOV. 3	31	16	16	17	28	36	48	26	3	39	16	13
NOV. 4	31	17	18	19	28	36	48	26	3	39	16	13
NOV. 5	31	19	20	20	28	37	48	26	3	39	16	13
NOV. 6	31	21	21	22	29	37	1	26	3	39	16	13
NOV. 7	31	22	23	23	29	37	1	26	3	39	16	13
NOV. 8	31	24	24	25	29	37	1	26	3	39	16	13
NOV. 9	31	25	26	27	29	37	1	26	3	39	16	13
NOV. 10	31	27	28	28	29	37	1	26	3	39	16	13
NOV. 11	31	29	29	30	30	38	1	26	3	39	16	13
NOV. 12	32	30	31	31	30	38	1	26	3	39	16	13
NOV. 13	32	32	32	33	30	38	1	26	3	39	16	13
NOV. 14	32	33	34	35	30	38	1	26	3	39	16	12
NOV. 15	32	35	36	36	31	38	1	26	3	39	16	12
NOV. 16	32	37	37	38	31	38	1	26	3	39	16	12
NOV. 17	32	38	39	40	31	38	1	26	3	39	16	12
NOV. 18	32	40	41	41	31	39	1	26	3	39	16	12
NOV. 19	33	42	43	43	31	39	1	26	3	39	16	12
NOV. 20	33	44	44	45	32	39	1	26	3	39	16	12
NOV. 21	33	46	46	47	32	39	1	26	3	39	16	12
NOV. 22	33	47	48	1	32	39	1	26	3	39	16	12
NOV. 23	33	1	2	3	32	39	1	26	3	39	16	12
NOV. 24	33	3	4	5	32	39	1	26	3	39	16	12
NOV. 25	34	5	6	7	33	40	1	26	3	39	16	12
NOV. 26	34	7	8	9	33	40	1	26	3	39	16	12
NOV. 27	34	9	10	11	33	40	1	26	3	39	16	12
NOV. 28	34	11	12	12	33	40	1	26	3	39	15	12
NOV. 29	34	13	14	14	34	40	1	26	3	39	15	12
NOV. 30	34	15	16	16	34	40	1	26	3	39	15	12

December

Date & Time	SUN	MOON 1	MOON 2	MOON 3	MERCURY	VENUS	MARS	JUPITER	SATURN	URANUS	NEPTUNE	PLUTO
DEC. 1	34	17	17	18	34	40	1	26	3	39	15	12
DEC. 2	34	18	19	20	34	41	1	26	3	39	15	12
DEC. 3	35	20	21	21	34	41	2	26	3	39	15	12
DEC. 4	35	22	22	23	35	41	2	26	3	39	15	12
DEC. 5	35	23	24	24	35	41	2	26	3	40	15	12
DEC. 6	35	25	26	26	35	41	2	26	3	40	15	12
DEC. 7	35	27	27	28	35	41	2	26	3	40	15	12
DEC. 8	35	28	29	29	35	41	2	26	3	40	15	12
DEC. 9	35	30	30	31	36	41	2	26	3	40	15	12
DEC. 10	35	31	32	32	36	42	2	26	3	40	15	12
DEC. 11	36	33	34	34	36	42	2	26	3	40	15	12
DEC. 12	36	35	35	36	36	42	2	26	3	40	15	12
DEC. 13	36	36	37	37	36	42	2	26	3	40	15	12
DEC. 14	36	38	39	39	37	42	2	26	3	40	15	12
DEC. 15	36	40	40	41	37	42	2	26	3	40	15	12
DEC. 16	36	42	42	43	37	42	2	27	3	40	15	12
DEC. 17	36	43	44	45	37	42	2	27	3	40	15	12
DEC. 18	36	45	46	46	37	43	2	27	3	40	15	12
DEC. 19	37	47	48	48	38	43	2	27	3	40	15	12
DEC. 20	37	1	1	2	38	43	3	27	3	40	15	12
DEC. 21	37	3	3	4	38	43	3	27	3	40	15	12
DEC. 22	37	5	5	6	38	43	3	27	3	40	15	12
DEC. 23	37	7	7	8	39	43	3	27	3	40	15	12
DEC. 24	37	8	9	10	39	43	3	27	3	40	15	12
DEC. 25	37	10	11	12	39	43	3	27	3	40	15	12
DEC. 26	38	12	13	14	39	43	3	27	3	40	15	12
DEC. 27	38	14	15	15	39	44	3	27	3	40	15	12
DEC. 28	38	16	17	17	40	44	3	27	3	40	15	12
DEC. 29	38	18	18	19	40	44	3	27	3	40	15	12
DEC. 30	38	19	20	21	40	44	3	27	3	40	15	12
DEC. 31	38	21	22	22	40	44	3	27	3	40	15	12

MOON 1 ◐ 12:01 A.M. TO 8:00 A.M. **MOON 2** ◑ 8:01 A.M. TO 4:00 P.M. **MOON 3** ● 4:01 P.M. TO 12:00 A.M.
Use only one "moon" number. Choose the column closest to your time of birth. If your place of birth is not on
Eastern Standard Time, be sure to read "How to Convert to Eastern Standard Time" at the beginning of this section.

1910-1919

1910s

Nelson Mandela

★ ★ ★ BORN JULY 18, 1918 ★ ★ ★

Brief Bio: Nelson Mandela was a statesman and president of South Africa who was jailed for 27 years on Robben Island during apartheid rule in South Africa.

Personology Profile:

SUN IN THE WEEK OF THE PERSUADER
(CANCER III)

※

Dominant individuals, those born in this week are likely to exert a strong influence on their immediate surroundings. Because of their highly persuasive nature and their need to control, they most frequently get their way, sooner or later. Using a blend of cajoling, personal magnetism and reward, they are able to soften the hardest of hearts and convince the hardest of heads

MOON IN THE WEEK OF CHARM
(SCORPIO III)

※

Extremely persuasive, those with this moon position can be highly manipulative and controlling in gaining their goals. Once identified as a love object by such people, it will not be easy to escape them. In relationships with such individuals it is easy to leave emotional choices to them, and in fact to rely on their feelings more than on your own.

MERCURY IN THE WEEK OF BALANCED STRENGTH
(LEO II)

※

This Mercury position can guarantee a responsible standing in the family or professional sphere. Those with Mercury here can be extremely valuable to the group in a crisis situation in which keeping a level head is essential. The only danger here is that of becoming indispensable and thereby creating dependencies on the part of less capable individuals.

VENUS IN THE WEEK OF THE SEEKER
(GEMINI III)

※

These individuals don't like to be handed love on a platter. Challenge-oriented, they consider the hunt and the chase as important elements in the whole romantic package. Gemini IIIs love the process of exploration, so they not only enjoy discovering a loved one's psyche, but also plumbing its depths. They must beware of getting too involved in the process itself and neglecting the feelings of those they are involved with.

MARS IN THE WEEK OF SOCIETY
(LIBRA II)

※

Mars is decidedly uncomfortable here in Venus territory and would like nothing better than to challenge the group's mores or just run off to some more adventuresome activity. Learning to put one's energies in service of the social or family group can yield extremely positive results once Mars accepts that we are here primarily to serve each other.

JUPITER ON THE CUSP OF MAGIC
(GEMINI-CANCER CUSP)

※

The good fortune accompanying this period is usually of the serendipitous variety. All kinds of strange and unexpected circumstances send Lady Luck one's way. Because of an ability to be open to or expect the unexpected, it is not a big surprise when it does occur, but it is precisely this openness which is the catalyst for good things to come to pass.

SATURN IN THE WEEK OF BALANCED STRENGTH
(LEO II)

✳

Since an energy imbalance is the greatest threat to this week, it is possible for Saturn to uncover underlying insecurities. This can work positively, since they may have been unknown and therefore untreatable. On the other hand, if one gets fixated on such difficulties they can work like self-fulfilling prophecies to produce a failure scenario. Putting self-knowledge to positive uses is key.

URANUS ON THE CUSP OF SENSITIVITY
(AQUARIUS-PISCES CUSP)

✳

Overreactive, such individuals are made very jumpy by even slightly unpleasant sensory stimuli, particularly those involving sound and smell. Since their buttons can be easily pushed, they must learn to grow a whole set which cannot be pushed so easily. Perhaps their greatest lesson is learning not to let others control them through their predictable responses.

NEPTUNE IN THE WEEK OF AUTHORITY
(LEO I)

✳

The watery planet Neptune is not comfortable in this hot week. Because of its aversion to fixed ideas, no matter how effective or brilliant, Neptune tends to exert a dissolving effect on authority here, encouraging those with this position to undermine any omniscient attitudes. They may have difficulty exerting direct influences in their family life.

PLUTO IN THE WEEK OF THE EMPATH
(CANCER I)

✳

Emotional manipulation is likely to be a constant theme with Pluto here. An ability to control the feelings of others and a need to do so may lead such people to manipulative behavior, which will ultimately arouse resentment and dependency. Such individuals should detach themselves from the feelings of others and assert a more independent stance by concentrating on their own well-being.

Some Highlights of the Decade 1910-1919

- THE TREATY OF VERSAILLES IS SIGNED IN FRANCE, ENDING WORLD WAR I.
- THE BOLSHEVIKS, HEADED BY LENIN, SEIZE POWER IN RUSSIA.
- SWEDISH-BORN ENGINEER GIDEON SUNDBACK RECEIVES A PATENT FOR THE ZIPPER WHILE EMPLOYED AT THE AUTOMATIC HOOK AND EYE CO. OF HOBOKEN, NEW JERSEY.
- THE MAIDEN VOYAGE OF THE TITANIC ENDS TRAGICALLY WHEN IT HITS AN ICEBERG OFF THE COAST OF NEWFOUNDLAND, KILLING 1,500 PASSENGERS.
- THE "STAR SPANGLED BANNER" IS SUNG AT THE BEGINNING OF A BASEBALL GAME FOR THE FIRST TIME IN COOPERSTOWN, NEW YORK.
- D. W. GRIFFITH'S EPIC FILM ABOUT THE CIVIL WAR, *BIRTH OF A NATION*, ENJOYED ITS PREMIERE.

1910

January

Date & Time	SUN	MOON 1	MOON 2	MOON 3	MERCURY	VENUS	MARS	JUPITER	SATURN	URANUS	NEPTUNE	PLUTO
JAN. 1	38	23	23	24	40	44	3	27	3	40	15	12
JAN. 2	38	24	25	26	41	44	3	27	3	40	15	12
JAN. 3	39	26	27	27	41	44	4	27	3	40	15	12
JAN. 4	39	28	28	29	41	44	4	27	3	40	15	12
JAN. 5	39	29	30	30	41	44	4	27	3	40	15	12
JAN. 6	39	31	31	32	41	44	4	27	3	40	15	12
JAN. 7	39	32	33	33	42	45	4	27	3	40	15	12
JAN. 8	39	34	35	35	42	45	4	27	3	40	15	12
JAN. 9	39	36	36	37	42	45	4	27	3	40	15	12
JAN. 10	40	37	38	39	42	45	4	27	3	40	15	12
JAN. 11	40	39	40	40	42	45	4	27	3	40	15	12
JAN. 12	40	41	42	42	42	45	4	27	3	40	15	12
JAN. 13	40	43	43	44	42	45	4	27	3	40	15	12
JAN. 14	40	45	45	46	42	45	4	27	3	40	15	12
JAN. 15	40	47	47	48	43	45	4	27	3	40	15	12
JAN. 16	40	48	1	2	43	45	4	27	3	40	15	12
JAN. 17	41	2	3	4	43	45	5	27	3	40	15	12
JAN. 18	41	4	5	5	43	45	5	27	3	40	15	12
JAN. 19	41	6	7	7	43	45	5	27	3	40	15	12
JAN. 20	41	8	9	9	43	45	5	27	3	40	15	12
JAN. 21	41	10	10	11	42	45	5	27	3	40	15	12
JAN. 22	41	12	12	13	42	45	5	27	3	40	15	12
JAN. 23	42	13	14	15	42	45	5	27	3	40	15	12
JAN. 24	42	15	16	16	42	45	5	27	3	40	15	12
JAN. 25	42	17	18	18	42	45	5	27	3	40	15	12
JAN. 26	42	19	19	20	42	45	5	27	3	40	15	12
JAN. 27	42	21	21	22	42	45	5	27	3	40	15	12
JAN. 28	42	22	23	23	41	45	5	27	3	40	15	12
JAN. 29	42	24	24	25	41	45	5	27	3	40	15	12
JAN. 30	42	25	26	27	41	45	6	27	3	40	15	12
JAN. 31	43	27	28	28	41	45	6	27	3	40	15	12

February

Date & Time	SUN	MOON 1	MOON 2	MOON 3	MERCURY	VENUS	MARS	JUPITER	SATURN	URANUS	NEPTUNE	PLUTO
FEB. 1	43	29	29	30	41	45	6	27	3	40	15	12
FEB. 2	43	30	31	31	41	45	6	27	3	40	15	12
FEB. 3	43	32	32	33	41	45	6	27	3	40	15	12
FEB. 4	43	33	34	35	41	45	6	27	3	40	15	12
FEB. 5	43	35	36	36	41	45	6	27	3	40	15	12
FEB. 6	43	37	37	38	41	45	6	27	3	40	15	12
FEB. 7	43	38	39	40	41	44	6	27	3	40	15	12
FEB. 8	44	40	41	41	41	44	6	27	3	40	15	12
FEB. 9	44	42	43	43	41	44	6	27	3	40	15	12
FEB. 10	44	44	45	45	41	44	6	27	3	40	15	12
FEB. 11	44	46	47	47	41	44	6	27	3	40	15	12
FEB. 12	44	48	1	1	41	44	7	27	3	40	15	12
FEB. 13	44	2	2	3	41	44	7	27	4	40	15	12
FEB. 14	44	4	4	5	41	44	7	27	4	40	15	12
FEB. 15	44	6	6	7	41	44	7	27	4	40	15	12
FEB. 16	45	8	8	9	41	44	7	27	4	40	15	12
FEB. 17	45	9	10	11	41	44	7	27	4	40	15	12
FEB. 18	45	11	12	12	41	44	7	27	4	40	15	12
FEB. 19	45	13	14	14	41	43	7	27	4	40	15	12
FEB. 20	45	15	15	16	42	43	7	27	4	40	15	12
FEB. 21	45	17	17	18	42	43	7	27	4	40	15	12
FEB. 22	45	18	19	19	42	43	7	27	4	40	15	12
FEB. 23	46	20	21	21	42	43	7	27	4	40	15	12
FEB. 24	46	22	22	23	42	43	7	27	4	40	15	12
FEB. 25	46	23	24	24	42	43	8	27	4	40	15	12
FEB. 26	46	25	26	26	42	43	8	27	4	40	15	12
FEB. 27	46	27	27	28	43	43	8	27	4	40	15	12
FEB. 28	46	28	29	29	43	43	8	27	4	40	15	12

MOON 1 ◐ 12:01 A.M. TO 8:00 A.M.   **MOON 2** ◑ 8:01 A.M. TO 4:00 P.M.   **MOON 3** ● 4:01 P.M. TO 12:00 A.M.

Use only one "moon" number. Choose the column closest to your time of birth. If your place of birth is not on Eastern Standard Time, be sure to read "How to Convert to Eastern Standard Time" at the beginning of this section.

1910

March

Date & Time	SUN	MOON 1	MOON 2	MOON 3	MERCURY	VENUS	MARS	JUPITER	SATURN	URANUS	NEPTUNE	PLUTO
MAR. 1	46	30	30	31	43	43	8	27	4	40	15	12
MAR. 2	46	31	32	32	43	43	8	27	4	40	15	12
MAR. 3	47	33	33	34	43	43	8	27	4	40	15	12
MAR. 4	47	34	35	36	43	43	8	27	4	40	15	12
MAR. 5	47	36	37	37	44	43	8	27	4	40	15	12
MAR. 6	47	38	38	39	44	43	8	27	4	40	15	12
MAR. 7	47	40	40	41	44	43	8	27	4	40	15	12
MAR. 8	47	41	42	43	44	43	8	27	4	40	15	12
MAR. 9	47	43	44	44	44	43	9	27	4	40	15	12
MAR. 10	47	45	46	46	45	43	9	27	4	40	15	12
MAR. 11	48	47	48	48	45	43	9	27	4	40	15	12
MAR. 12	48	1	2	2	45	43	9	27	4	40	15	12
MAR. 13	48	3	4	4	45	43	9	27	4	40	15	12
MAR. 14	48	5	6	6	45	43	9	27	4	40	15	12
MAR. 15	48	7	8	8	46	43	9	27	4	40	15	12
MAR. 16	48	9	10	10	46	43	9	27	4	40	15	12
MAR. 17	48	11	11	12	46	43	9	26	4	40	15	12
MAR. 18	48	13	13	14	46	43	9	26	4	40	15	12
MAR. 19	1	14	15	16	47	43	9	26	4	40	15	12
MAR. 20	1	16	17	17	47	44	9	26	4	40	15	12
MAR. 21	1	18	18	19	47	44	10	26	4	40	15	12
MAR. 22	1	20	20	21	47	44	10	26	4	40	15	12
MAR. 23	1	21	22	22	47	44	10	26	4	40	15	12
MAR. 24	1	23	23	24	48	44	10	26	4	40	15	12
MAR. 25	2	25	25	26	48	44	10	26	4	40	15	12
MAR. 26	2	26	27	27	48	44	10	26	4	40	15	12
MAR. 27	2	28	28	29	48	44	10	26	4	40	15	12
MAR. 28	2	29	30	30	1	44	10	26	4	40	15	12
MAR. 29	2	31	31	32	1	44	10	26	4	40	15	12
MAR. 30	2	32	33	33	1	44	10	26	4	40	15	12
MAR. 31	2	34	35	35	1	44	10	26	4	40	15	12

April

Date & Time	SUN	MOON 1	MOON 2	MOON 3	MERCURY	VENUS	MARS	JUPITER	SATURN	URANUS	NEPTUNE	PLUTO
APR. 1	2	36	36	37	2	45	10	26	4	40	15	12
APR. 2	2	37	38	38	2	45	11	26	4	40	15	12
APR. 3	3	39	39	40	2	45	11	26	4	40	15	12
APR. 4	3	41	41	42	3	45	11	26	4	40	15	12
APR. 5	3	42	43	44	3	45	11	26	4	40	15	12
APR. 6	3	44	45	46	3	45	11	26	4	40	15	12
APR. 7	3	46	47	47	3	45	11	26	4	40	15	12
APR. 8	3	48	1	1	4	45	11	26	4	40	15	12
APR. 9	3	2	3	3	4	45	11	26	4	40	15	12
APR. 10	3	4	5	6	4	45	11	26	4	40	15	12
APR. 11	4	6	7	8	4	46	11	26	4	40	15	12
APR. 12	4	8	9	10	5	46	11	26	4	40	15	12
APR. 13	4	10	11	11	5	46	11	26	4	40	15	12
APR. 14	4	12	13	13	5	46	12	26	4	40	15	12
APR. 15	4	14	15	15	6	46	12	26	4	40	15	12
APR. 16	4	16	16	17	6	46	12	26	4	40	15	12
APR. 17	4	17	18	19	6	46	12	26	4	40	15	12
APR. 18	4	19	20	20	6	46	12	26	4	40	15	12
APR. 19	5	21	21	22	7	47	12	26	5	40	15	12
APR. 20	5	22	23	24	7	47	12	26	5	40	15	12
APR. 21	5	24	25	25	7	47	12	26	5	40	15	12
APR. 22	5	26	26	27	7	47	12	26	5	40	15	12
APR. 23	5	27	28	28	8	47	12	26	5	40	15	12
APR. 24	5	29	29	30	8	47	12	26	5	40	15	12
APR. 25	6	30	31	32	8	47	12	26	5	40	15	12
APR. 26	6	32	33	33	8	47	12	26	5	40	15	12
APR. 27	6	34	34	35	8	48	13	26	5	40	15	12
APR. 28	6	35	36	36	9	48	13	26	5	40	15	12
APR. 29	6	37	37	38	9	48	13	26	5	40	15	12
APR. 30	6	38	39	40	9	48	13	26	5	40	15	12

MOON 1 ◐ 12:01 A.M. TO 8:00 A.M.   **MOON 2** ◑ 8:01 A.M. TO 4:00 P.M.   **MOON 3** ● 4:01 P.M. TO 12:00 A.M.

Use only one "moon" number. Choose the column closest to your time of birth. If your place of birth is not on Eastern Standard Time, be sure to read "How to Convert to Eastern Standard Time" at the beginning of this section.

Date & Time	SUN	MOON 1	MOON 2	MOON 3	MERCURY	VENUS	MARS	JUPITER	SATURN	URANUS	NEPTUNE	PLUTO
MAY 1	6	40	41	41	9	48	13	26	5	40	15	12
MAY 2	6	42	42	43	9	48	13	26	5	40	15	12
MAY 3	7	44	44	45	9	48	13	26	5	40	15	12
MAY 4	7	45	46	47	9	1	13	26	5	40	15	12
MAY 5	7	47	48	1	10	1	13	26	5	40	15	12
MAY 6	7	1	2	3	10	1	13	26	5	40	15	12
MAY 7	7	3	4	5	10	1	13	26	5	40	15	12
MAY 8	7	5	6	7	10	1	13	26	5	40	15	12
MAY 9	7	7	8	9	10	1	14	26	5	40	15	12
MAY 10	7	9	10	11	10	1	14	26	5	40	15	12
MAY 11	8	11	12	13	10	2	14	26	5	40	15	12
MAY 12	8	13	14	14	10	2	14	26	5	40	15	12
MAY 13	8	15	16	16	10	2	14	26	5	40	15	12
MAY 14	8	17	18	18	10	2	14	26	5	40	15	12
MAY 15	8	19	19	20	10	2	14	26	5	40	15	12
MAY 16	8	20	21	22	10	2	14	26	5	40	15	12
MAY 17	8	22	23	23	10	2	14	26	5	40	15	12
MAY 18	8	24	24	25	10	3	14	26	5	40	15	12
MAY 19	9	25	26	26	10	3	14	26	5	40	15	12
MAY 20	9	27	27	28	10	3	14	26	5	40	15	12
MAY 21	9	28	29	30	10	3	15	26	5	40	15	12
MAY 22	9	30	31	31	10	3	15	26	5	40	15	12
MAY 23	9	32	32	33	10	3	15	26	5	40	15	12
MAY 24	9	33	34	34	10	3	15	26	5	40	15	12
MAY 25	10	35	35	36	9	4	15	26	5	40	15	12
MAY 26	10	36	37	38	9	4	15	26	5	40	15	12
MAY 27	10	38	39	39	9	4	15	26	5	40	15	12
MAY 28	10	40	40	41	9	4	15	26	5	40	15	12
MAY 29	10	41	42	43	9	4	15	26	5	40	15	12
MAY 30	10	43	44	44	9	4	15	26	5	40	15	12
MAY 31	10	45	46	46	9	4	15	26	5	40	15	12

Date & Time	SUN	MOON 1	MOON 2	MOON 3	MERCURY	VENUS	MARS	JUPITER	SATURN	URANUS	NEPTUNE	PLUTO
JUN. 1	10	47	47	48	9	5	15	26	5	40	15	12
JUN. 2	10	1	1	2	9	5	16	26	5	40	15	12
JUN. 3	11	3	3	4	9	5	16	26	5	40	15	12
JUN. 4	11	4	5	6	9	5	16	26	5	40	15	12
JUN. 5	11	6	7	8	9	5	16	26	5	40	15	12
JUN. 6	11	8	9	10	9	5	16	26	5	40	15	12
JUN. 7	11	10	11	12	9	6	16	26	5	40	15	12
JUN. 8	11	12	13	14	9	6	16	26	5	40	15	12
JUN. 9	11	14	15	16	9	6	16	26	5	40	15	12
JUN. 10	11	16	17	17	9	6	16	26	5	40	15	12
JUN. 11	12	18	19	19	9	6	16	26	5	40	15	12
JUN. 12	12	20	20	21	9	6	16	26	5	40	15	12
JUN. 13	12	22	22	23	9	6	16	26	5	40	15	12
JUN. 14	12	23	24	24	9	7	17	26	5	40	15	12
JUN. 15	12	25	25	26	9	7	17	26	5	40	15	12
JUN. 16	12	26	27	28	9	7	17	26	5	40	15	12
JUN. 17	12	28	29	29	9	7	17	26	5	40	15	12
JUN. 18	12	30	30	31	9	7	17	26	5	40	15	12
JUN. 19	13	31	32	32	10	7	17	26	5	40	15	12
JUN. 20	13	33	33	34	10	7	17	26	5	40	15	12
JUN. 21	13	34	35	35	10	8	17	26	5	40	15	12
JUN. 22	13	36	37	37	10	8	17	26	5	40	15	12
JUN. 23	13	38	38	39	10	8	17	26	5	40	15	12
JUN. 24	13	39	40	40	10	8	17	26	5	40	15	13
JUN. 25	14	41	42	42	10	8	17	26	6	40	15	13
JUN. 26	14	43	43	44	11	8	18	26	6	40	15	13
JUN. 27	14	45	45	46	11	9	18	26	6	40	15	13
JUN. 28	14	46	47	48	11	9	18	26	6	40	15	13
JUN. 29	14	48	1	1	11	9	18	26	6	40	15	13
JUN. 30	14	2	3	3	11	9	18	26	6	40	15	13

MOON 1 ☾ 12:01 A.M. TO 8:00 A.M.   **MOON 2** ☽ 8:01 A.M. TO 4:00 P.M.   **MOON 3** ● 4:01 P.M. TO 12:00 A.M.
Use only one "moon" number. Choose the column closest to your time of birth. If your place of birth is not on
Eastern Standard Time, be sure to read "How to Convert to Eastern Standard Time" at the beginning of this section.

1910

July

August

Date & Time	SUN	MOON 1	MOON 2	MOON 3	MERCURY	VENUS	MARS	JUPITER	SATURN	URANUS	NEPTUNE	PLUTO
JUL. 1	14	4	5	5	12	9	18	26	6	40	15	13
JUL. 2	14	6	6	7	12	9	18	26	6	40	15	13
JUL. 3	15	8	8	9	12	9	18	26	6	40	15	13
JUL. 4	15	10	10	11	12	10	18	26	6	40	15	13
JUL. 5	15	12	12	13	12	10	18	26	6	40	15	13
JUL. 6	15	14	14	15	13	10	18	26	6	40	15	13
JUL. 7	15	15	16	17	13	10	18	26	6	40	15	13
JUL. 8	15	17	18	19	13	10	19	26	6	40	15	13
JUL. 9	15	19	20	20	14	10	19	26	6	40	15	13
JUL. 10	15	21	21	22	14	11	19	26	6	40	15	13
JUL. 11	16	23	23	24	14	11	19	26	6	40	16	13
JUL. 12	16	24	25	25	14	11	19	26	6	40	16	13
JUL. 13	16	26	26	27	15	11	19	26	6	40	16	13
JUL. 14	16	28	28	29	15	11	19	26	6	40	16	13
JUL. 15	16	29	30	30	15	11	19	26	6	40	16	13
JUL. 16	16	31	31	32	15	12	19	26	6	40	16	13
JUL. 17	16	32	33	33	16	12	19	26	6	40	16	13
JUL. 18	16	34	34	35	16	12	19	26	6	40	16	13
JUL. 19	17	35	36	37	16	12	19	26	6	40	16	13
JUL. 20	17	37	38	38	17	12	20	26	6	40	16	13
JUL. 21	17	39	39	40	17	12	20	26	6	40	16	13
JUL. 22	17	41	41	42	17	12	20	26	6	40	16	13
JUL. 23	17	42	43	43	17	13	20	26	6	40	16	13
JUL. 24	17	44	45	45	18	13	20	26	6	40	16	13
JUL. 25	17	46	46	47	18	13	20	26	6	40	16	13
JUL. 26	18	48	48	1	18	13	20	26	6	40	16	13
JUL. 27	18	2	2	3	19	13	20	26	6	40	16	13
JUL. 28	18	3	4	5	19	13	20	26	6	40	16	13
JUL. 29	18	5	6	7	19	14	20	26	6	40	16	13
JUL. 30	18	7	8	8	19	14	20	26	6	40	16	13
JUL. 31	18	9	10	10	20	14	20	26	6	40	16	13

Date & Time	SUN	MOON 1	MOON 2	MOON 3	MERCURY	VENUS	MARS	JUPITER	SATURN	URANUS	NEPTUNE	PLUTO
AUG. 1	18	11	12	12	20	14	21	26	6	40	16	13
AUG. 2	18	13	14	14	20	14	21	26	6	40	16	13
AUG. 3	19	15	15	16	20	14	21	26	6	40	16	13
AUG. 4	19	17	17	18	21	15	21	26	6	40	16	13
AUG. 5	19	18	19	20	21	15	21	26	6	40	16	13
AUG. 6	19	20	21	21	21	15	21	26	6	40	16	13
AUG. 7	19	22	23	23	21	15	21	26	6	40	16	13
AUG. 8	19	24	24	25	21	15	21	26	6	40	16	13
AUG. 9	19	25	26	26	22	15	21	26	6	40	16	13
AUG. 10	19	27	28	28	22	16	21	26	6	40	16	13
AUG. 11	20	29	29	30	22	16	21	26	6	40	16	13
AUG. 12	20	30	31	31	22	16	21	26	6	40	16	13
AUG. 13	20	32	32	33	22	16	22	26	6	40	16	13
AUG. 14	20	33	34	34	23	16	22	27	6	40	16	13
AUG. 15	20	35	35	36	23	16	22	27	6	40	16	13
AUG. 16	20	37	37	38	23	16	22	27	6	40	16	13
AUG. 17	20	38	39	39	23	17	22	27	6	40	16	13
AUG. 18	20	40	40	41	23	17	22	27	6	40	16	13
AUG. 19	21	42	42	43	24	17	22	27	6	40	16	13
AUG. 20	21	43	44	45	24	17	22	27	6	40	16	13
AUG. 21	21	45	46	47	24	17	22	27	6	40	16	13
AUG. 22	21	47	48	48	24	17	22	27	6	40	16	13
AUG. 23	21	1	2	2	24	18	22	27	6	40	16	13
AUG. 24	21	3	4	4	24	18	23	27	6	40	16	13
AUG. 25	21	5	6	6	25	18	23	27	6	40	16	13
AUG. 26	22	7	7	8	25	18	23	27	6	40	16	13
AUG. 27	22	9	9	10	25	18	23	27	6	40	16	13
AUG. 28	22	11	11	12	25	18	23	27	6	40	16	13
AUG. 29	22	12	13	14	25	19	23	27	6	40	16	13
AUG. 30	22	14	15	15	25	19	23	27	6	40	16	13
AUG. 31	22	16	17	17	26	19	23	27	6	40	16	13

MOON 1 ☽ 12:01 A.M. TO 8:00 A.M.   **MOON 2** ☽ 8:01 A.M. TO 4:00 P.M.   **MOON 3** ● 4:01 P.M. TO 12:00 A.M.

Use only one "moon" number. Choose the column closest to your time of birth. If your place of birth is not on Eastern Standard Time, be sure to read "How to Convert to Eastern Standard Time" at the beginning of this section.

1910

September

Date & Time	SUN	MOON 1	MOON 2	MOON 3	MERCURY	VENUS	MARS	JUPITER	SATURN	URANUS	NEPTUNE	PLUTO
SEP. 1	22	18	18	19	26	19	23	27	6	40	16	13
SEP. 2	22	20	20	21	26	19	23	27	6	40	16	13
SEP. 3	23	21	22	23	26	19	23	27	6	40	16	13
SEP. 4	23	23	24	24	26	20	23	27	6	40	16	13
SEP. 5	23	25	25	26	26	20	24	27	6	40	16	13
SEP. 6	23	26	27	28	26	20	24	27	6	40	16	13
SEP. 7	23	28	29	29	26	20	24	27	6	40	16	13
SEP. 8	23	30	30	31	26	20	24	27	6	40	16	13
SEP. 9	23	31	32	32	26	20	24	27	6	40	16	13
SEP. 10	23	33	33	34	26	21	24	27	6	40	16	13
SEP. 11	24	34	35	35	26	21	24	27	6	40	16	13
SEP. 12	24	36	37	37	26	21	24	27	6	40	16	13
SEP. 13	24	38	38	39	26	21	24	27	6	40	16	13
SEP. 14	24	39	40	40	26	21	24	27	6	40	16	13
SEP. 15	24	41	42	42	26	21	24	27	6	40	16	13
SEP. 16	24	43	43	44	26	22	24	27	6	40	16	13
SEP. 17	24	45	45	46	26	22	25	27	6	40	16	13
SEP. 18	24	46	47	48	26	22	25	27	6	40	16	13
SEP. 19	25	48	1	2	26	22	25	27	6	40	16	13
SEP. 20	25	2	3	4	26	22	25	27	6	40	16	13
SEP. 21	25	4	5	6	26	22	25	27	6	40	16	13
SEP. 22	25	6	7	8	26	23	25	28	6	40	16	13
SEP. 23	25	8	9	9	26	23	25	28	6	40	16	13
SEP. 24	25	10	11	11	26	23	25	28	6	40	16	13
SEP. 25	26	12	13	13	25	23	25	28	6	40	16	13
SEP. 26	26	14	14	15	25	23	25	28	6	40	16	13
SEP. 27	26	16	16	17	25	23	25	28	6	40	16	13
SEP. 28	26	17	18	19	25	24	26	28	6	40	16	13
SEP. 29	26	19	20	20	25	24	26	28	6	40	16	13
SEP. 30	26	21	22	22	25	24	26	28	6	40	16	13

October

Date & Time	SUN	MOON 1	MOON 2	MOON 3	MERCURY	VENUS	MARS	JUPITER	SATURN	URANUS	NEPTUNE	PLUTO
OCT. 1	26	23	23	24	25	24	26	28	6	40	16	13
OCT. 2	26	24	25	25	25	24	26	28	6	40	16	13
OCT. 3	27	26	27	27	25	24	26	28	6	40	16	13
OCT. 4	27	28	28	29	24	25	26	28	6	40	16	13
OCT. 5	27	29	30	30	24	25	26	28	6	40	16	13
OCT. 6	27	31	31	32	24	25	26	28	6	40	16	13
OCT. 7	27	32	33	33	25	25	26	28	6	40	16	13
OCT. 8	27	34	34	35	25	25	26	28	6	40	16	13
OCT. 9	27	35	36	37	25	25	26	28	6	40	16	13
OCT. 10	27	37	38	38	25	26	27	28	6	40	16	13
OCT. 11	28	39	39	40	25	26	27	28	6	40	16	13
OCT. 12	28	40	41	41	25	26	27	28	6	40	16	13
OCT. 13	28	42	43	43	25	26	27	28	6	40	16	13
OCT. 14	28	44	44	45	25	26	27	28	6	40	16	13
OCT. 15	28	46	46	47	25	26	27	28	6	40	16	13
OCT. 16	28	48	48	1	26	27	27	28	5	40	16	13
OCT. 17	28	1	2	3	26	27	27	28	5	40	16	13
OCT. 18	28	3	4	5	26	27	27	28	5	40	16	13
OCT. 19	29	5	6	7	26	27	27	28	5	40	16	13
OCT. 20	29	7	8	9	26	27	27	28	5	40	16	13
OCT. 21	29	9	10	11	27	27	28	28	5	40	16	13
OCT. 22	29	11	12	13	27	28	28	28	5	40	16	13
OCT. 23	29	13	14	15	27	28	28	28	5	40	16	13
OCT. 24	29	15	16	16	27	28	28	28	5	40	16	13
OCT. 25	29	17	18	18	28	28	28	28	5	40	16	13
OCT. 26	30	19	19	20	28	28	28	28	5	40	16	13
OCT. 27	30	21	22	22	28	29	28	28	5	40	16	13
OCT. 28	30	22	23	23	28	29	29	29	5	40	16	13
OCT. 29	30	24	24	25	28	29	29	29	5	40	16	13
OCT. 30	30	26	26	27	29	29	28	29	5	40	16	13
OCT. 31	30	27	28	28	29	29	29	29	5	40	16	13

MOON 1 ◐ 12:01 A.M. TO 8:00 A.M.   **MOON 2** ◑ 8:01 A.M. TO 4:00 P.M.   **MOON 3** ● 4:01 P.M. TO 12:00 A.M.

Use only one "moon" number. Choose the column closest to your time of birth. If your place of birth is not on Eastern Standard Time, be sure to read "How to Convert to Eastern Standard Time" at the beginning of this section.

November

Date & Time	SUN	MOON 1	MOON 2	MOON 3	MERCURY	VENUS	MARS	JUPITER	SATURN	URANUS	NEPTUNE	PLUTO
NOV. 1	30	29	29	30	29	29	28	29	5	40	16	13
NOV. 2	30	30	31	31	29	29	29	29	5	40	16	13
NOV. 3	31	32	32	33	30	30	29	29	5	40	16	13
NOV. 4	31	33	34	35	30	30	29	29	5	40	16	13
NOV. 5	31	35	36	36	30	30	29	29	5	40	16	13
NOV. 6	31	37	37	38	30	30	29	29	5	40	16	13
NOV. 7	31	38	39	39	30	30	29	29	5	40	16	13
NOV. 8	31	40	40	41	31	30	29	29	5	40	16	13
NOV. 9	31	41	42	43	31	31	29	29	5	40	16	13
NOV. 10	31	43	44	44	31	31	29	29	5	40	16	13
NOV. 11	31	45	46	46	31	31	29	29	5	40	16	13
NOV. 12	32	47	47	48	31	31	29	29	5	40	16	13
NOV. 13	32	1	1	2	32	31	30	29	5	40	16	13
NOV. 14	32	3	3	4	32	31	30	29	5	40	16	13
NOV. 15	32	4	5	6	32	32	30	29	5	40	16	13
NOV. 16	32	6	7	8	32	32	30	29	5	40	16	13
NOV. 17	32	9	9	10	33	32	30	29	5	40	16	13
NOV. 18	32	11	11	12	33	32	30	29	5	40	16	13
NOV. 19	33	13	13	14	33	32	30	29	5	40	16	13
NOV. 20	33	15	15	16	33	32	30	29	5	40	16	13
NOV. 21	33	16	17	18	33	33	30	29	5	40	16	13
NOV. 22	33	18	19	19	34	33	30	29	5	40	16	13
NOV. 23	33	20	21	21	34	33	30	29	5	40	16	13
NOV. 24	33	22	22	23	34	33	31	29	5	40	16	13
NOV. 25	34	24	24	25	34	33	31	29	5	40	16	13
NOV. 26	34	25	26	26	34	33	31	29	5	40	16	13
NOV. 27	34	27	27	28	35	34	31	29	5	40	16	13
NOV. 28	34	28	29	29	35	34	31	29	5	40	16	13
NOV. 29	34	30	30	31	35	34	31	29	5	40	16	13
NOV. 30	34	32	32	33	35	34	31	29	5	40	16	13

December

Date & Time	SUN	MOON 1	MOON 2	MOON 3	MERCURY	VENUS	MARS	JUPITER	SATURN	URANUS	NEPTUNE	PLUTO
DEC. 1	34	33	34	34	35	34	31	30	5	40	16	13
DEC. 2	34	35	35	36	36	34	31	30	5	40	16	13
DEC. 3	35	36	37	37	36	35	31	30	5	40	16	13
DEC. 4	35	38	38	39	36	35	31	30	5	40	16	13
DEC. 5	35	39	40	41	36	35	32	30	5	40	16	13
DEC. 6	35	41	42	42	36	35	32	30	5	40	16	13
DEC. 7	35	43	43	44	37	35	32	30	5	40	16	13
DEC. 8	35	44	45	46	37	35	32	30	5	40	16	13
DEC. 9	35	46	47	47	37	36	32	30	5	40	16	13
DEC. 10	35	48	1	1	37	36	32	30	5	40	16	13
DEC. 11	36	2	2	3	37	36	32	30	5	40	16	13
DEC. 12	36	4	4	5	38	36	32	30	5	40	16	13
DEC. 13	36	6	6	7	38	36	32	30	5	40	16	13
DEC. 14	36	8	8	9	38	36	32	30	5	40	16	13
DEC. 15	36	10	10	11	38	37	32	30	5	40	16	13
DEC. 16	36	12	12	13	38	37	33	30	5	40	16	13
DEC. 17	36	14	14	15	39	37	33	30	5	40	16	13
DEC. 18	36	16	16	17	39	37	33	30	5	40	16	13
DEC. 19	37	18	18	19	39	37	33	30	5	40	16	13
DEC. 20	37	19	20	21	39	37	33	30	5	40	16	13
DEC. 21	37	21	22	22	39	38	33	30	5	40	16	13
DEC. 22	37	23	24	24	40	38	33	30	5	40	16	13
DEC. 23	37	25	25	26	40	38	33	30	5	40	16	13
DEC. 24	37	26	27	27	40	38	33	30	5	40	16	13
DEC. 25	37	28	28	29	40	38	33	30	5	40	16	13
DEC. 26	38	30	30	31	40	38	33	30	5	40	16	13
DEC. 27	38	31	32	32	40	39	34	30	5	40	16	13
DEC. 28	38	33	33	34	40	39	34	30	5	40	16	13
DEC. 29	38	34	35	35	40	39	34	30	5	40	16	13
DEC. 30	38	36	36	37	40	39	34	30	5	40	16	13
DEC. 31	38	37	38	38	40	39	34	30	5	40	16	13

MOON 1 ☽ 12:01 A.M. TO 8:00 A.M.   **MOON 2** ☽ 8:01 A.M. TO 4:00 P.M.   **MOON 3** ● 4:01 P.M. TO 12:00 A.M.
Use only one "moon" number. Choose the column closest to your time of birth. If your place of birth is not on
Eastern Standard Time, be sure to read "How to Convert to Eastern Standard Time" at the beginning of this section.

1911

January

Date & Time	SUN	MOON 1	MOON 2	MOON 3	MERCURY	VENUS	MARS	JUPITER	SATURN	URANUS	NEPTUNE	PLUTO
JAN. 1	38	39	40	40	40	39	34	30	5	40	16	13
JAN. 2	38	41	41	42	40	40	34	30	5	40	16	13
JAN. 3	39	42	43	43	40	40	34	30	5	40	16	13
JAN. 4	39	44	45	45	40	40	34	30	5	40	16	13
JAN. 5	39	46	46	47	40	40	34	30	5	40	16	13
JAN. 6	39	48	48	1	40	40	35	30	5	40	16	13
JAN. 7	39	1	2	3	40	40	35	30	5	40	16	13
JAN. 8	39	3	4	4	40	41	35	30	5	40	16	13
JAN. 9	39	5	6	6	40	41	35	30	5	40	16	13
JAN. 10	40	7	7	8	40	41	35	30	5	40	16	13
JAN. 11	40	9	9	10	39	41	35	30	5	40	16	12
JAN. 12	40	11	11	12	39	41	35	30	5	40	16	12
JAN. 13	40	13	13	14	39	41	35	30	5	40	16	12
JAN. 14	40	15	15	16	39	42	35	30	5	40	16	12
JAN. 15	40	17	17	18	39	42	35	31	5	40	16	12
JAN. 16	40	19	19	20	39	42	35	31	5	40	16	12
JAN. 17	41	20	21	22	39	42	36	31	5	40	16	12
JAN. 18	41	22	23	23	38	42	36	31	5	40	16	12
JAN. 19	41	24	25	25	38	42	36	31	5	40	16	12
JAN. 20	41	26	26	27	38	43	36	31	5	40	16	12
JAN. 21	41	27	28	28	38	43	36	31	5	40	16	12
JAN. 22	41	29	30	30	38	43	36	31	5	40	16	12
JAN. 23	42	31	31	32	38	43	36	31	5	40	16	12
JAN. 24	42	32	33	33	38	43	36	31	5	40	16	12
JAN. 25	42	34	34	35	38	43	36	31	5	40	16	12
JAN. 26	42	35	36	36	38	44	36	31	5	40	16	12
JAN. 27	42	37	37	38	39	44	37	31	5	40	16	12
JAN. 28	42	39	39	40	39	44	37	31	5	40	16	12
JAN. 29	42	40	41	41	39	44	37	31	5	40	16	12
JAN. 30	42	42	42	43	39	44	37	31	5	40	16	12
JAN. 31	43	44	44	45	39	44	37	31	5	40	16	12

February

Date & Time	SUN	MOON 1	MOON 2	MOON 3	MERCURY	VENUS	MARS	JUPITER	SATURN	URANUS	NEPTUNE	PLUTO
FEB. 1	43	45	46	47	39	45	37	31	5	40	16	12
FEB. 2	43	47	48	48	39	45	37	31	5	40	16	12
FEB. 3	43	1	1	2	39	45	37	31	5	40	16	12
FEB. 4	43	3	3	4	40	45	37	31	5	40	16	12
FEB. 5	43	5	5	6	40	45	37	31	5	40	16	12
FEB. 6	43	6	7	8	40	45	37	31	5	40	16	12
FEB. 7	43	8	9	10	40	46	38	31	5	41	16	12
FEB. 8	44	10	11	11	40	46	38	31	5	41	16	12
FEB. 9	44	12	13	13	40	46	38	31	5	41	16	12
FEB. 10	44	14	15	15	40	46	38	31	5	41	16	12
FEB. 11	44	16	17	17	41	46	38	31	5	41	16	12
FEB. 12	44	18	18	19	41	46	38	31	5	41	16	12
FEB. 13	44	20	20	21	41	47	38	31	5	41	16	12
FEB. 14	44	22	22	23	41	47	38	31	5	41	16	12
FEB. 15	44	23	24	25	41	47	38	31	5	41	16	12
FEB. 16	45	25	26	26	42	47	38	31	5	41	16	12
FEB. 17	45	27	27	28	42	47	39	31	5	41	16	12
FEB. 18	45	28	29	30	42	47	39	31	5	41	16	12
FEB. 19	45	30	31	31	42	48	39	31	5	41	16	12
FEB. 20	45	32	32	33	42	48	39	31	5	41	16	12
FEB. 21	45	33	34	34	42	48	39	31	5	41	16	12
FEB. 22	45	35	35	36	42	48	39	31	5	41	16	12
FEB. 23	46	36	37	37	43	48	39	31	5	41	16	12
FEB. 24	46	38	39	39	43	48	39	31	5	41	16	12
FEB. 25	46	40	40	41	43	1	39	31	5	41	16	12
FEB. 26	46	41	42	42	44	1	39	31	5	41	16	12
FEB. 27	46	43	44	44	44	1	40	31	5	41	16	12
FEB. 28	46	45	45	46	44	1	40	31	5	41	16	12

MOON 1 ◐ 12:01 A.M. TO 8:00 A.M.   **MOON 2** ◑ 8:01 A.M. TO 4:00 P.M.   **MOON 3** ● 4:01 P.M. TO 12:00 A.M.

Use only one "moon" number. Choose the column closest to your time of birth. If your place of birth is not on Eastern Standard Time, be sure to read "How to Convert to Eastern Standard Time" at the beginning of this section.

1911

March

April

Date & Time	SUN ☉	MOON 1 ☽	MOON 2 ◑	MOON 3 ●	MERCURY	VENUS	MARS	JUPITER	SATURN	URANUS	NEPTUNE	PLUTO
MAR. 1	46	47	47	48	44	1	40	31	5	41	16	12
MAR. 2	46	48	1	2	44	1	40	31	5	41	15	12
MAR. 3	47	2	3	3	45	2	40	31	5	41	15	12
MAR. 4	47	4	5	5	45	2	40	31	5	41	15	12
MAR. 5	47	6	7	7	45	2	40	31	5	41	15	12
MAR. 6	47	8	8	9	45	2	40	31	5	41	15	12
MAR. 7	47	10	10	11	45	2	40	31	5	41	15	12
MAR. 8	47	12	12	13	46	2	40	31	5	41	15	12
MAR. 9	47	13	14	15	46	3	40	31	5	41	15	12
MAR. 10	47	15	16	17	46	3	41	31	5	41	15	12
MAR. 11	48	17	18	18	46	3	41	31	5	41	15	12
MAR. 12	48	19	20	20	47	3	41	31	5	41	15	12
MAR. 13	48	21	21	22	47	3	41	31	5	41	15	12
MAR. 14	48	23	23	24	47	3	41	31	5	41	15	12
MAR. 15	48	24	25	26	47	4	41	31	6	41	15	12
MAR. 16	48	26	27	27	48	4	41	31	6	41	15	12
MAR. 17	48	28	28	29	48	4	41	31	6	41	15	12
MAR. 18	48	29	30	31	48	4	41	31	6	41	15	12
MAR. 19	1	31	32	32	48	4	41	31	6	41	15	12
MAR. 20	1	33	33	34	1	4	42	31	6	41	15	12
MAR. 21	1	34	35	35	1	5	42	31	6	41	15	12
MAR. 22	1	36	36	37	1	5	42	31	6	41	15	12
MAR. 23	1	37	38	39	2	5	42	31	6	41	15	12
MAR. 24	1	39	40	40	2	5	42	31	6	41	15	12
MAR. 25	2	41	41	42	2	5	42	31	6	41	15	12
MAR. 26	2	42	43	43	2	5	42	31	6	41	15	12
MAR. 27	2	44	45	45	2	5	42	31	6	41	15	12
MAR. 28	2	46	46	47	3	6	42	31	6	41	15	12
MAR. 29	2	48	48	1	3	6	42	31	6	41	15	12
MAR. 30	2	2	2	3	3	6	43	31	6	41	15	12
MAR. 31	2	3	4	5	4	6	43	31	6	41	15	12

Date & Time	SUN ☉	MOON 1 ☽	MOON 2 ◑	MOON 3 ●	MERCURY	VENUS	MARS	JUPITER	SATURN	URANUS	NEPTUNE	PLUTO
APR. 1	2	5	6	7	4	6	43	31	6	41	15	12
APR. 2	2	7	8	9	4	6	43	31	6	41	15	12
APR. 3	3	9	10	11	4	7	43	31	6	41	15	12
APR. 4	3	11	12	12	5	7	43	31	6	41	15	12
APR. 5	3	13	14	14	5	7	43	31	6	41	15	12
APR. 6	3	15	16	16	5	7	43	31	6	41	15	12
APR. 7	3	17	17	18	5	7	43	31	6	41	15	12
APR. 8	3	19	19	20	6	7	43	31	6	41	15	12
APR. 9	3	20	21	22	6	8	44	31	6	41	15	12
APR. 10	3	22	23	23	6	8	44	31	6	41	15	12
APR. 11	4	24	24	25	6	8	44	31	6	41	15	12
APR. 12	4	26	26	27	6	8	44	31	6	41	15	12
APR. 13	4	27	28	28	7	8	44	31	6	41	15	12
APR. 14	4	29	30	30	7	8	44	31	6	41	15	12
APR. 15	4	31	31	32	7	9	44	31	6	41	15	12
APR. 16	4	32	33	33	7	9	44	31	6	41	15	12
APR. 17	4	34	34	35	7	9	44	30	6	41	15	12
APR. 18	4	35	36	36	7	9	44	30	6	41	15	12
APR. 19	5	37	37	38	7	9	45	30	6	41	15	12
APR. 20	5	39	39	40	7	9	45	30	6	41	15	12
APR. 21	5	40	41	41	7	10	45	30	6	41	15	12
APR. 22	5	42	42	43	7	10	45	30	6	41	15	12
APR. 23	5	43	44	45	7	10	45	30	6	41	15	12
APR. 24	5	45	46	46	7	10	45	30	6	41	15	12
APR. 25	6	47	48	48	7	10	45	30	6	41	15	12
APR. 26	6	1	1	2	7	10	45	30	6	41	15	12
APR. 27	6	3	3	4	7	10	45	30	6	41	15	12
APR. 28	6	5	5	6	7	11	45	30	6	41	15	12
APR. 29	6	7	7	8	7	11	46	30	6	41	15	12
APR. 30	6	8	9	10	7	11	46	30	6	41	16	12

MOON 1 ☽ 12:01 A.M. TO 8:00 A.M.   **MOON 2** ◑ 8:01 A.M. TO 4:00 P.M.   **MOON 3** ● 4:01 P.M. TO 12:00 A.M.

Use only one "moon" number. Choose the column closest to your time of birth. If your place of birth is not on Eastern Standard Time, be sure to read "How to Convert to Eastern Standard Time" at the beginning of this section.

1911

May

June

Date & Time	SUN	MOON 1	MOON 2	MOON 3	MERCURY	VENUS	MARS	JUPITER	SATURN	URANUS	NEPTUNE	PLUTO
MAY 1	6	10	11	12	7	11	46	30	6	41	16	12
MAY 2	6	12	13	14	7	11	46	30	6	41	16	12
MAY 3	7	14	15	16	7	11	46	30	6	41	16	12
MAY 4	7	16	17	18	7	12	46	30	6	41	16	12
MAY 5	7	18	19	19	7	12	46	30	6	41	16	12
MAY 6	7	20	21	21	7	12	46	30	6	41	16	12
MAY 7	7	22	22	23	7	12	46	30	6	41	16	12
MAY 8	7	24	24	25	7	12	46	30	6	41	16	12
MAY 9	7	25	26	26	7	12	47	30	6	41	16	13
MAY 10	7	27	27	28	6	12	47	30	6	41	16	13
MAY 11	8	29	29	30	6	13	47	30	6	41	16	13
MAY 12	8	30	31	31	6	13	47	30	6	41	16	13
MAY 13	8	32	32	33	6	13	47	30	6	41	16	13
MAY 14	8	33	34	34	6	13	47	30	6	41	16	13
MAY 15	8	35	35	36	6	13	47	30	7	41	16	13
MAY 16	8	36	37	38	6	13	47	30	7	41	16	13
MAY 17	8	38	39	39	6	14	47	30	7	41	16	13
MAY 18	8	40	40	41	6	14	47	30	7	41	16	13
MAY 19	9	41	42	42	6	14	48	30	7	41	16	13
MAY 20	9	43	43	44	6	14	48	30	7	41	16	13
MAY 21	9	45	45	46	6	14	48	30	7	41	16	13
MAY 22	9	46	47	47	6	14	48	30	7	41	16	13
MAY 23	9	48	1	1	6	14	48	30	7	41	16	13
MAY 24	9	2	2	3	6	15	48	30	7	41	16	13
MAY 25	10	4	4	5	6	15	48	30	7	41	16	13
MAY 26	10	6	6	7	6	15	48	30	7	41	16	13
MAY 27	10	8	8	9	6	15	48	30	7	41	16	13
MAY 28	10	10	10	11	7	15	48	30	7	41	16	13
MAY 29	10	12	12	13	7	15	1	30	7	41	16	13
MAY 30	10	14	14	15	7	16	1	30	7	41	16	13
MAY 31	10	16	16	17	7	16	1	30	7	41	16	13

Date & Time	SUN	MOON 1	MOON 2	MOON 3	MERCURY	VENUS	MARS	JUPITER	SATURN	URANUS	NEPTUNE	PLUTO
JUN. 1	10	18	18	19	7	16	1	30	7	41	16	13
JUN. 2	10	19	20	21	7	16	1	30	7	41	16	13
JUN. 3	11	21	22	23	7	16	1	30	7	41	16	13
JUN. 4	11	23	24	24	7	16	1	30	7	41	16	13
JUN. 5	11	25	25	26	8	16	1	30	7	41	16	13
JUN. 6	11	26	27	28	8	17	1	30	7	41	16	13
JUN. 7	11	28	29	29	8	17	1	30	7	41	16	13
JUN. 8	11	30	30	31	8	17	1	30	7	41	16	13
JUN. 9	11	31	32	32	8	17	2	30	7	41	16	13
JUN. 10	11	33	33	34	8	17	2	30	7	41	16	13
JUN. 11	12	35	35	36	9	17	2	30	7	41	16	13
JUN. 12	12	36	37	37	9	17	2	30	7	41	16	13
JUN. 13	12	38	38	39	9	18	2	30	7	41	16	13
JUN. 14	12	39	40	40	9	18	2	30	7	41	16	13
JUN. 15	12	41	41	42	9	18	2	30	7	41	16	13
JUN. 16	12	42	43	44	10	18	2	30	7	41	16	13
JUN. 17	12	44	45	45	10	18	2	30	7	41	16	13
JUN. 18	12	46	46	47	10	18	2	30	7	41	16	13
JUN. 19	13	47	48	1	10	18	3	30	7	41	16	13
JUN. 20	13	1	2	2	11	19	3	30	7	41	16	13
JUN. 21	13	3	4	4	11	19	3	30	7	41	16	13
JUN. 22	13	5	5	6	11	19	3	30	7	41	16	13
JUN. 23	13	7	7	8	11	19	3	30	7	41	16	13
JUN. 24	13	9	9	10	12	19	3	30	7	41	16	13
JUN. 25	14	11	11	12	12	19	3	30	7	41	16	13
JUN. 26	14	13	13	14	12	19	3	30	7	41	16	13
JUN. 27	14	15	15	16	12	20	3	30	7	41	16	13
JUN. 28	14	17	17	18	13	20	3	30	7	41	16	13
JUN. 29	14	19	19	20	13	20	3	30	7	41	16	13
JUN. 30	14	21	21	22	13	20	4	30	7	41	16	13

MOON 1 ◖ 12:01 A.M. TO 8:00 A.M.   **MOON 2** ◑ 8:01 A.M. TO 4:00 P.M.   **MOON 3** ● 4:01 P.M. TO 12:00 A.M.

Use only one "moon" number. Choose the column closest to your time of birth. If your place of birth is not on Eastern Standard Time, be sure to read "How to Convert to Eastern Standard Time" at the beginning of this section.

1911

July

Date & Time	SUN	MOON 1	MOON 2	MOON 3	MERCURY	VENUS	MARS	JUPITER	SATURN	URANUS	NEPTUNE	PLUTO
JUL. 1	14	23	23	24	14	20	4	30	7	41	16	13
JUL. 2	14	24	25	25	14	20	4	30	7	41	16	13
JUL. 3	15	26	27	27	14	20	4	30	7	41	16	13
JUL. 4	15	28	28	29	14	21	4	30	7	41	16	13
JUL. 5	15	29	30	30	15	21	4	30	7	41	16	13
JUL. 6	15	31	31	32	15	21	4	30	7	41	16	13
JUL. 7	15	33	33	34	15	21	4	30	7	41	16	13
JUL. 8	15	34	35	35	16	21	4	30	7	41	16	13
JUL. 9	15	36	36	37	16	21	4	30	7	41	16	13
JUL. 10	15	37	38	38	16	21	4	30	7	41	16	13
JUL. 11	16	39	39	40	16	21	5	30	7	41	16	13
JUL. 12	16	40	41	42	17	22	5	30	7	41	16	13
JUL. 13	16	42	43	43	17	22	5	30	7	41	16	13
JUL. 14	16	44	44	45	17	22	5	30	7	41	16	13
JUL. 15	16	45	46	47	18	22	5	30	7	41	16	13
JUL. 16	16	47	48	48	18	22	5	30	7	41	16	13
JUL. 17	16	1	1	2	18	22	5	30	7	41	16	13
JUL. 18	16	3	3	4	18	22	5	30	7	41	16	13
JUL. 19	17	4	5	6	18	22	5	30	7	41	16	13
JUL. 20	17	6	7	7	19	22	5	30	7	41	16	13
JUL. 21	17	8	9	9	19	23	5	30	7	41	16	13
JUL. 22	17	10	11	11	19	23	6	30	7	41	16	13
JUL. 23	17	12	13	13	19	23	6	30	7	41	16	13
JUL. 24	17	14	15	15	20	23	6	30	7	41	16	13
JUL. 25	17	16	17	17	20	23	6	30	7	41	16	13
JUL. 26	18	18	19	19	20	23	6	30	7	41	16	13
JUL. 27	18	20	21	21	20	23	6	30	7	41	16	13
JUL. 28	18	22	22	23	20	23	6	30	8	41	16	13
JUL. 29	18	24	24	25	21	23	6	30	8	41	16	13
JUL. 30	18	25	26	27	21	23	6	30	8	41	16	13
JUL. 31	18	27	28	28	21	24	6	30	8	41	16	13

August

Date & Time	SUN	MOON 1	MOON 2	MOON 3	MERCURY	VENUS	MARS	JUPITER	SATURN	URANUS	NEPTUNE	PLUTO
AUG. 1	18	29	29	30	21	24	6	30	8	41	16	13
AUG. 2	18	30	31	32	21	24	6	30	8	41	16	13
AUG. 3	19	32	33	33	22	24	7	30	8	41	16	13
AUG. 4	19	34	34	35	22	24	7	30	8	41	16	13
AUG. 5	19	35	36	36	22	24	7	30	8	41	16	13
AUG. 6	19	37	37	38	22	24	7	30	8	41	16	13
AUG. 7	19	38	39	39	22	24	7	30	8	41	16	13
AUG. 8	19	40	41	41	22	24	7	30	8	41	16	13
AUG. 9	19	42	42	43	23	24	7	30	8	41	16	13
AUG. 10	19	43	44	44	23	24	7	30	8	41	16	13
AUG. 11	20	45	46	46	23	24	7	30	8	41	16	13
AUG. 12	20	47	47	48	23	24	7	30	8	41	16	13
AUG. 13	20	48	1	2	23	25	7	30	8	40	16	13
AUG. 14	20	2	3	3	23	25	7	30	8	40	16	13
AUG. 15	20	4	5	5	23	25	7	30	8	40	16	13
AUG. 16	20	6	6	7	24	25	8	30	8	40	16	13
AUG. 17	20	8	8	9	24	25	8	30	8	40	16	13
AUG. 18	20	9	10	11	24	25	8	30	8	40	16	13
AUG. 19	21	11	12	13	24	25	8	30	8	40	16	13
AUG. 20	21	13	14	15	24	25	8	30	8	40	16	13
AUG. 21	21	15	16	16	24	25	8	30	8	40	16	13
AUG. 22	21	17	18	18	24	25	8	30	8	40	16	13
AUG. 23	21	19	20	20	24	25	8	30	8	40	16	13
AUG. 24	21	21	22	22	24	25	8	30	8	40	16	13
AUG. 25	21	23	24	24	24	25	8	30	8	40	16	13
AUG. 26	22	25	25	26	24	25	8	30	8	40	16	13
AUG. 27	22	27	27	28	24	25	8	30	8	40	16	13
AUG. 28	22	28	29	29	24	25	8	30	8	40	16	13
AUG. 29	22	30	30	31	24	25	8	30	8	40	16	13
AUG. 30	22	32	32	33	24	25	9	30	8	40	16	13
AUG. 31	22	33	34	34	24	25	9	30	8	40	16	13

MOON 1 ◐ 12:01 A.M. TO 8:00 A.M.　　**MOON 2** ◑ 8:01 A.M. TO 4:00 P.M.　　**MOON 3** ● 4:01 P.M. TO 12:00 A.M.

Use only one "moon" number. Choose the column closest to your time of birth. If your place of birth is not on Eastern Standard Time, be sure to read "How to Convert to Eastern Standard Time" at the beginning of this section.

1911

September

Date & Time	SUN	MOON 1	MOON 2	MOON 3	MERCURY	VENUS	MARS	JUPITER	SATURN	URANUS	NEPTUNE	PLUTO
SEP. 1	22	35	35	36	24	25	9	30	8	40	16	13
SEP. 2	22	36	37	37	24	25	9	30	8	40	16	13
SEP. 3	23	38	38	39	24	25	9	30	8	40	16	13
SEP. 4	23	40	40	41	24	25	9	30	8	40	16	13
SEP. 5	23	41	42	42	24	25	9	30	8	40	16	13
SEP. 6	23	43	43	44	24	25	9	30	8	40	16	13
SEP. 7	23	44	45	46	23	24	9	30	8	40	16	13
SEP. 8	23	46	47	47	23	24	9	30	8	40	16	13
SEP. 9	23	48	48	1	23	24	9	30	8	40	16	13
SEP. 10	23	2	2	3	23	24	9	30	8	40	16	13
SEP. 11	24	3	4	5	23	24	9	30	8	40	16	13
SEP. 12	24	5	6	7	23	24	9	30	8	40	16	13
SEP. 13	24	7	8	8	23	24	9	31	8	40	16	13
SEP. 14	24	9	10	10	23	24	9	31	8	40	16	13
SEP. 15	24	11	11	12	22	24	10	31	8	40	16	13
SEP. 16	24	13	13	14	22	24	10	31	8	40	16	13
SEP. 17	24	15	15	16	22	24	10	31	8	40	16	13
SEP. 18	24	17	17	18	22	24	10	31	8	40	16	13
SEP. 19	25	18	19	20	22	24	10	31	8	40	16	13
SEP. 20	25	20	21	22	22	23	10	31	8	40	16	13
SEP. 21	25	22	23	23	22	23	10	31	8	40	16	13
SEP. 22	25	24	25	25	22	23	10	31	8	40	16	13
SEP. 23	25	26	26	27	23	23	10	31	8	40	16	13
SEP. 24	25	28	28	29	23	23	10	31	8	40	16	13
SEP. 25	26	29	30	30	23	23	10	31	8	40	16	13
SEP. 26	26	31	32	32	23	23	10	31	8	40	16	13
SEP. 27	26	33	33	34	23	23	10	31	8	40	16	13
SEP. 28	26	34	35	35	23	23	10	31	8	40	16	13
SEP. 29	26	36	36	37	23	23	10	31	8	40	16	13
SEP. 30	26	37	38	38	24	23	10	31	8	40	16	13

October

Date & Time	SUN	MOON 1	MOON 2	MOON 3	MERCURY	VENUS	MARS	JUPITER	SATURN	URANUS	NEPTUNE	PLUTO
OCT. 1	26	39	40	40	24	23	10	31	8	40	16	13
OCT. 2	26	41	41	42	24	23	10	31	8	40	16	13
OCT. 3	27	42	43	43	24	23	10	31	8	40	16	13
OCT. 4	27	44	44	45	24	23	10	31	8	40	16	13
OCT. 5	27	46	46	47	25	23	10	31	8	40	16	13
OCT. 6	27	47	48	48	25	23	10	31	8	40	16	13
OCT. 7	27	1	2	2	25	23	10	31	8	40	16	13
OCT. 8	27	3	3	4	25	23	10	31	8	40	16	13
OCT. 9	27	5	5	6	26	23	10	31	8	40	16	13
OCT. 10	27	7	7	8	26	23	10	31	8	40	16	13
OCT. 11	28	8	9	10	26	23	10	31	7	40	16	13
OCT. 12	28	10	11	12	26	23	10	31	7	40	16	13
OCT. 13	28	12	13	14	26	23	10	31	7	40	16	13
OCT. 14	28	14	15	15	27	23	10	31	7	40	16	13
OCT. 15	28	16	17	17	27	23	10	31	7	40	16	13
OCT. 16	28	18	19	19	27	23	10	31	7	40	16	13
OCT. 17	28	20	20	21	27	23	10	31	7	40	16	13
OCT. 18	28	22	22	23	28	23	10	31	7	40	16	13
OCT. 19	29	23	24	25	28	23	10	31	7	40	16	13
OCT. 20	29	25	26	26	28	23	10	31	7	40	16	13
OCT. 21	29	27	28	28	28	23	10	31	7	40	16	13
OCT. 22	29	29	30	30	29	23	10	32	7	40	16	13
OCT. 23	29	30	31	31	29	23	10	32	7	40	16	13
OCT. 24	29	32	33	33	29	23	10	32	7	40	16	13
OCT. 25	29	34	34	35	29	24	10	32	7	40	16	13
OCT. 26	30	35	36	36	29	24	10	32	7	40	16	13
OCT. 27	30	37	37	38	29	24	10	32	7	40	16	13
OCT. 28	30	38	39	39	30	24	10	32	7	40	16	13
OCT. 29	30	40	41	41	30	24	10	32	7	40	16	13
OCT. 30	30	42	42	43	30	24	10	32	7	40	16	13
OCT. 31	30	43	44	44	30	24	10	32	7	40	16	13

MOON 1 ◖ 12:01 A.M. TO 8:00 A.M.   **MOON 2** ◗ 8:01 A.M. TO 4:00 P.M.   **MOON 3** ● 4:01 P.M. TO 12:00 A.M.

Use only one "moon" number. Choose the column closest to your time of birth. If your place of birth is not on Eastern Standard Time, be sure to read "How to Convert to Eastern Standard Time" at the beginning of this section.

1911

November

Date & Time	SUN	MOON 1	MOON 2	MOON 3	MERCURY	VENUS	MARS	JUPITER	SATURN	URANUS	NEPTUNE	PLUTO
NOV. 1	30	45	45	46	31	24	10	32	7	40	16	13
NOV. 2	30	47	47	48	31	24	10	32	7	40	16	13
NOV. 3	31	48	1	2	31	24	10	32	7	40	16	13
NOV. 4	31	2	3	3	31	24	10	32	7	40	16	13
NOV. 5	31	4	5	5	32	25	10	32	7	40	16	13
NOV. 6	31	6	6	7	32	25	10	32	7	40	16	13
NOV. 7	31	8	8	9	32	25	10	32	7	40	16	13
NOV. 8	31	10	10	11	32	25	10	32	7	40	16	13
NOV. 9	31	12	12	13	32	25	10	32	7	40	16	13
NOV. 10	31	14	14	15	33	25	10	32	7	40	16	13
NOV. 11	31	16	16	17	33	25	10	32	7	40	16	13
NOV. 12	32	18	18	19	33	25	10	32	7	40	16	13
NOV. 13	32	19	20	21	33	25	10	32	7	40	16	13
NOV. 14	32	21	22	22	33	26	10	32	7	40	16	13
NOV. 15	32	23	24	24	34	26	10	32	7	40	16	13
NOV. 16	32	25	25	26	34	26	10	32	7	40	16	13
NOV. 17	32	27	27	28	34	26	10	32	7	40	16	13
NOV. 18	32	28	29	29	34	26	10	32	7	40	16	13
NOV. 19	33	30	30	31	34	26	10	32	7	40	16	13
NOV. 20	33	32	32	33	35	26	9	32	7	40	16	13
NOV. 21	33	33	34	34	35	26	9	32	7	40	16	13
NOV. 22	33	35	35	36	35	27	9	32	7	40	16	13
NOV. 23	33	36	37	37	35	27	9	32	7	40	16	13
NOV. 24	33	38	38	39	35	27	9	32	7	40	16	13
NOV. 25	34	40	40	41	36	27	9	33	7	40	16	13
NOV. 26	34	41	42	42	36	27	9	33	7	40	16	13
NOV. 27	34	43	43	44	36	27	9	33	7	41	16	13
NOV. 28	34	44	45	45	36	27	9	33	7	41	16	13
NOV. 29	34	46	47	47	36	28	9	33	7	41	16	13
NOV. 30	34	48	48	1	36	28	9	33	7	41	16	13

December

Date & Time	SUN	MOON 1	MOON 2	MOON 3	MERCURY	VENUS	MARS	JUPITER	SATURN	URANUS	NEPTUNE	PLUTO
DEC. 1	34	1	2	3	37	28	9	33	7	41	16	13
DEC. 2	34	3	4	4	37	28	9	33	7	41	16	13
DEC. 3	35	5	6	6	37	28	9	33	7	41	16	13
DEC. 4	35	7	8	8	37	28	9	33	7	41	16	13
DEC. 5	35	9	10	10	37	28	9	33	7	41	16	13
DEC. 6	35	11	12	12	37	29	9	33	7	41	16	13
DEC. 7	35	13	14	14	38	29	9	33	7	41	16	13
DEC. 8	35	15	16	16	38	29	9	33	7	41	16	13
DEC. 9	35	17	18	18	38	29	9	33	7	41	16	13
DEC. 10	35	19	20	20	38	29	9	33	7	41	16	13
DEC. 11	36	21	21	22	38	29	9	33	7	41	16	13
DEC. 12	36	23	23	24	38	29	8	33	7	41	16	13
DEC. 13	36	24	25	26	38	30	8	33	7	41	16	13
DEC. 14	36	26	27	27	38	30	8	33	7	41	16	13
DEC. 15	36	28	28	29	38	30	8	33	7	41	16	13
DEC. 16	36	30	30	31	38	30	8	33	7	41	16	13
DEC. 17	36	31	32	32	38	30	8	33	7	41	16	13
DEC. 18	36	33	33	34	38	30	8	33	7	41	16	13
DEC. 19	37	34	35	35	38	30	8	33	7	41	16	13
DEC. 20	37	36	36	37	38	31	8	33	7	41	16	13
DEC. 21	37	38	38	39	38	31	8	33	7	41	16	13
DEC. 22	37	39	40	40	38	31	8	33	7	41	16	13
DEC. 23	37	41	41	42	38	31	8	33	7	41	16	13
DEC. 24	37	42	43	43	38	31	8	33	7	41	16	13
DEC. 25	37	44	44	45	37	31	8	33	7	41	16	13
DEC. 26	38	45	46	47	37	31	8	33	7	41	16	13
DEC. 27	38	47	48	48	37	32	8	33	7	41	16	13
DEC. 28	38	1	1	2	37	32	8	33	7	41	16	13
DEC. 29	38	2	3	4	37	32	8	33	7	41	16	13
DEC. 30	38	4	5	5	37	32	8	34	7	41	16	13
DEC. 31	38	6	7	7	36	32	8	34	7	41	16	13

MOON 1 ☽ 12:01 A.M. TO 8:00 A.M.   **MOON 2** ☽ 8:01 A.M. TO 4:00 P.M.   **MOON 3** ● 4:01 P.M. TO 12:00 A.M.
Use only one "moon" number. Choose the column closest to your time of birth. If your place of birth is not on
Eastern Standard Time, be sure to read "How to Convert to Eastern Standard Time" at the beginning of this section.

1912

January

Date & Time	SUN	MOON 1	MOON 2	MOON 3	MERCURY	VENUS	MARS	JUPITER	SATURN	URANUS	NEPTUNE	PLUTO
JAN. 1	38	8	9	9	36	32	8	34	7	41	16	13
JAN. 2	38	10	11	11	36	33	8	34	7	41	16	13
JAN. 3	39	12	13	13	36	33	8	34	7	41	16	13
JAN. 4	39	14	15	15	36	33	8	34	7	41	16	13
JAN. 5	39	16	17	17	36	33	8	34	7	41	16	13
JAN. 6	39	18	19	19	36	33	8	34	7	41	16	13
JAN. 7	39	20	21	21	36	33	8	34	7	41	16	13
JAN. 8	39	22	23	23	36	34	8	34	7	41	16	13
JAN. 9	39	24	24	25	36	34	8	34	7	41	16	13
JAN. 10	40	26	26	27	36	34	8	34	7	41	16	13
JAN. 11	40	27	28	29	37	34	8	34	7	41	16	13
JAN. 12	40	29	30	30	37	34	8	34	7	41	16	13
JAN. 13	40	31	31	32	37	34	8	34	7	41	16	13
JAN. 14	40	32	33	33	37	34	8	34	7	41	16	13
JAN. 15	40	34	34	35	37	35	8	34	7	41	16	13
JAN. 16	40	36	36	37	37	35	8	34	7	41	16	13
JAN. 17	41	37	38	38	37	35	8	34	7	41	16	13
JAN. 18	41	39	39	40	37	35	8	34	7	41	16	13
JAN. 19	41	40	41	41	38	35	9	34	7	41	16	13
JAN. 20	41	42	42	43	38	35	9	34	7	41	16	13
JAN. 21	41	43	44	45	38	36	9	34	7	41	16	13
JAN. 22	41	45	46	46	38	36	9	34	7	41	16	13
JAN. 23	42	47	47	48	38	36	9	34	7	41	16	13
JAN. 24	42	48	1	1	38	36	9	34	7	41	16	13
JAN. 25	42	2	3	3	39	36	9	34	7	41	16	13
JAN. 26	42	4	4	5	39	36	9	34	7	41	16	13
JAN. 27	42	5	6	7	39	37	9	34	7	41	16	13
JAN. 28	42	7	8	9	39	37	9	34	7	41	16	13
JAN. 29	42	9	10	10	39	37	9	34	7	41	16	13
JAN. 30	42	11	12	12	39	37	9	34	7	41	16	13
JAN. 31	43	13	14	14	40	37	9	34	7	41	16	13

February

Date & Time	SUN	MOON 1	MOON 2	MOON 3	MERCURY	VENUS	MARS	JUPITER	SATURN	URANUS	NEPTUNE	PLUTO
FEB. 1	43	15	16	16	40	37	9	34	7	41	16	13
FEB. 2	43	17	18	18	40	37	9	34	7	41	16	13
FEB. 3	43	19	20	20	40	38	9	34	7	41	16	13
FEB. 4	43	21	22	22	40	38	9	34	7	41	16	13
FEB. 5	43	23	24	24	41	38	9	34	7	41	16	13
FEB. 6	43	25	26	26	41	38	9	34	7	41	16	13
FEB. 7	43	27	27	28	41	38	9	34	7	41	16	13
FEB. 8	44	29	29	30	41	38	9	34	7	41	16	13
FEB. 9	44	30	31	31	41	39	9	34	7	41	16	13
FEB. 10	44	32	32	33	42	39	9	35	7	41	16	13
FEB. 11	44	34	34	35	42	39	10	35	7	41	16	13
FEB. 12	44	35	36	36	42	39	10	35	7	41	16	13
FEB. 13	44	37	37	38	42	39	10	35	7	41	16	13
FEB. 14	44	38	39	39	42	39	10	35	7	41	16	13
FEB. 15	44	40	40	41	43	40	10	35	7	41	16	13
FEB. 16	45	41	42	43	43	40	10	35	7	41	16	13
FEB. 17	45	43	44	44	43	40	10	35	7	41	16	13
FEB. 18	45	45	45	46	43	40	10	35	7	41	16	13
FEB. 19	45	46	47	47	44	40	10	35	7	41	16	13
FEB. 20	45	48	1	1	44	40	10	35	7	41	16	13
FEB. 21	45	2	2	3	44	41	10	35	7	41	16	13
FEB. 22	45	3	4	5	44	41	10	35	7	41	16	13
FEB. 23	46	5	6	6	44	41	10	35	7	41	16	13
FEB. 24	46	7	7	8	45	41	10	35	7	41	16	13
FEB. 25	46	9	9	10	45	41	10	35	7	41	16	13
FEB. 26	46	10	11	12	45	41	10	35	7	41	16	13
FEB. 27	46	12	13	14	45	42	10	35	7	41	16	13
FEB. 28	46	14	15	16	46	42	10	35	7	41	16	13
FEB. 29	46	16	17	18	46	42	11	35	7	41	16	13

MOON 1 ◑ 12:01 A.M. TO 8:00 A.M.   **MOON 2** ◑ 8:01 A.M. TO 4:00 P.M.   **MOON 3** ● 4:01 P.M. TO 12:00 A.M.

Use only one "moon" number. Choose the column closest to your time of birth. If your place of birth is not on Eastern Standard Time, be sure to read "How to Convert to Eastern Standard Time" at the beginning of this section.

Date & Time	SUN ☉	MOON 1 ☽	MOON 2 ◐	MOON 3 ●	MERCURY	VENUS	MARS	JUPITER	SATURN	URANUS	NEPTUNE	PLUTO
MAR. 1	46	18	19	20	46	42	11	35	7	41	16	13
MAR. 2	46	20	21	22	46	42	11	35	7	41	16	13
MAR. 3	47	22	23	23	47	42	11	35	7	41	16	13
MAR. 4	47	24	25	25	47	43	11	35	7	41	16	13
MAR. 5	47	26	27	27	47	43	11	35	7	41	16	13
MAR. 6	47	28	28	29	47	43	11	35	7	41	16	13
MAR. 7	47	30	30	31	48	43	11	35	7	41	16	13
MAR. 8	47	31	32	32	48	43	11	35	7	41	16	13
MAR. 9	47	33	34	34	48	43	11	35	7	41	16	13
MAR. 10	47	35	35	36	48	44	11	35	7	41	16	13
MAR. 11	48	36	37	37	1	44	11	35	7	41	16	13
MAR. 12	48	38	38	39	1	44	11	35	7	41	16	13
MAR. 13	48	39	40	40	1	44	11	35	7	41	16	13
MAR. 14	48	41	42	42	2	44	11	35	7	41	16	13
MAR. 15	48	43	43	44	2	44	11	35	7	41	16	13
MAR. 16	48	44	45	45	2	44	12	35	7	41	16	13
MAR. 17	48	46	46	47	2	45	12	35	7	41	16	13
MAR. 18	48	47	48	1	3	45	12	35	7	41	16	13
MAR. 19	1	1	2	2	3	45	12	35	7	41	16	13
MAR. 20	1	3	3	4	3	45	12	35	7	41	16	13
MAR. 21	1	5	5	6	3	45	12	35	7	41	16	13
MAR. 22	1	6	7	8	3	45	12	35	7	41	16	13
MAR. 23	1	8	9	9	4	46	12	35	7	41	16	13
MAR. 24	1	10	11	11	4	46	12	35	7	41	16	13
MAR. 25	2	12	13	13	4	46	12	35	7	41	16	13
MAR. 26	2	14	14	15	4	46	12	35	7	41	16	13
MAR. 27	2	16	16	17	4	46	12	35	7	41	16	13
MAR. 28	2	18	18	19	4	46	12	35	7	41	16	13
MAR. 29	2	20	20	21	5	47	12	35	7	41	16	13
MAR. 30	2	21	22	23	5	47	13	35	7	41	16	13
MAR. 31	2	23	24	25	5	47	13	35	7	41	16	13

Date & Time	SUN ☉	MOON 1 ☽	MOON 2 ◐	MOON 3 ●	MERCURY	VENUS	MARS	JUPITER	SATURN	URANUS	NEPTUNE	PLUTO
APR. 1	2	25	26	26	5	47	13	35	7	41	16	13
APR. 2	2	27	28	28	5	47	13	35	7	41	16	13
APR. 3	3	29	29	30	5	47	13	35	7	41	16	13
APR. 4	3	31	31	32	5	48	13	35	7	41	16	13
APR. 5	3	32	33	33	5	48	13	35	7	41	16	13
APR. 6	3	34	35	35	5	48	13	35	7	41	16	13
APR. 7	3	36	36	37	5	48	13	35	7	41	16	13
APR. 8	3	37	38	38	5	48	13	35	7	41	16	13
APR. 9	3	39	39	40	5	48	13	35	8	41	16	13
APR. 10	3	40	41	42	5	1	13	35	8	41	16	13
APR. 11	4	42	43	43	5	1	13	35	8	41	16	13
APR. 12	4	44	44	45	5	1	13	35	8	41	16	13
APR. 13	4	45	46	46	5	1	14	35	8	41	16	13
APR. 14	4	47	47	48	4	1	14	35	8	41	16	13
APR. 15	4	1	1	2	4	1	14	35	8	41	16	13
APR. 16	4	2	3	3	4	2	14	35	8	41	16	13
APR. 17	4	4	5	5	4	2	14	35	8	41	16	13
APR. 18	4	6	6	7	4	2	14	35	8	41	16	13
APR. 19	5	8	8	9	4	2	14	35	8	41	16	13
APR. 20	5	10	10	11	4	2	14	35	8	41	16	13
APR. 21	5	11	12	13	4	2	14	35	8	41	16	13
APR. 22	5	13	14	15	4	3	14	35	8	41	16	13
APR. 23	5	15	16	17	4	3	14	35	8	41	16	13
APR. 24	5	17	18	18	4	3	14	35	8	41	16	13
APR. 25	6	19	20	20	4	3	14	35	8	41	16	13
APR. 26	6	21	22	22	4	3	14	35	8	41	16	13
APR. 27	6	23	23	24	4	3	15	35	8	41	16	13
APR. 28	6	25	25	26	4	4	15	35	8	41	16	13
APR. 29	6	26	27	28	3	4	15	35	8	41	16	13
APR. 30	6	28	29	29	3	4	15	35	8	41	16	13

MOON 1 ☽ 12:01 A.M. TO 8:00 A.M.　　**MOON 2** ◐ 8:01 A.M. TO 4:00 P.M.　　**MOON 3** ● 4:01 P.M. TO 12:00 A.M.

Use only one "moon" number. Choose the column closest to your time of birth. If your place of birth is not on Eastern Standard Time, be sure to read "How to Convert to Eastern Standard Time" at the beginning of this section.

Date & Time	SUN	MOON 1	MOON 2	MOON 3	MERCURY	VENUS	MARS	JUPITER	SATURN	URANUS	NEPTUNE	PLUTO
MAY 1	6	30	31	31	4	4	15	35	8	41	16	13
MAY 2	6	32	32	33	4	4	15	35	8	41	16	13
MAY 3	7	33	34	35	4	4	15	35	8	41	16	13
MAY 4	7	35	36	36	4	4	15	35	8	41	16	13
MAY 5	7	37	37	38	4	5	15	35	8	41	16	13
MAY 6	7	38	39	39	4	5	15	35	8	41	16	13
MAY 7	7	40	40	41	4	5	15	35	8	41	16	13
MAY 8	7	42	42	43	4	5	15	35	8	41	16	13
MAY 9	7	43	44	44	4	5	15	35	8	41	16	13
MAY 10	7	45	45	46	4	5	16	35	8	41	16	13
MAY 11	8	46	47	47	4	6	16	35	8	41	16	13
MAY 12	8	48	1	1	4	6	16	35	8	41	16	13
MAY 13	8	2	2	3	4	6	16	35	8	41	16	13
MAY 14	8	3	4	5	5	6	16	35	8	41	16	13
MAY 15	8	5	6	6	5	6	16	35	8	41	16	13
MAY 16	8	7	8	8	5	6	16	35	8	41	16	13
MAY 17	8	9	10	10	5	7	16	35	8	41	16	13
MAY 18	8	11	11	12	5	7	16	35	8	41	16	13
MAY 19	9	13	13	14	5	7	16	35	8	41	16	13
MAY 20	9	15	15	16	6	7	16	35	8	41	16	13
MAY 21	9	17	17	18	6	7	16	35	8	41	16	13
MAY 22	9	19	19	20	6	7	16	35	8	41	16	13
MAY 23	9	21	21	22	6	8	17	35	8	41	16	13
MAY 24	9	22	23	24	6	8	17	35	8	41	16	13
MAY 25	10	24	25	25	6	8	17	34	8	41	16	13
MAY 26	10	26	27	27	7	8	17	34	8	41	16	13
MAY 27	10	28	28	29	7	8	17	34	8	41	16	13
MAY 28	10	30	30	31	7	8	17	34	8	41	16	13
MAY 29	10	31	32	32	7	9	17	34	8	41	16	13
MAY 30	10	33	33	34	8	9	17	34	8	41	16	13
MAY 31	10	35	35	36	8	9	17	34	8	41	16	13

Date & Time	SUN	MOON 1	MOON 2	MOON 3	MERCURY	VENUS	MARS	JUPITER	SATURN	URANUS	NEPTUNE	PLUTO
JUN. 1	10	36	37	37	8	9	17	34	8	41	16	13
JUN. 2	10	38	38	39	8	9	17	34	8	41	16	13
JUN. 3	11	39	40	40	8	9	17	34	8	41	16	13
JUN. 4	11	41	42	42	9	10	18	34	8	41	16	13
JUN. 5	11	43	43	44	9	10	18	34	8	41	16	13
JUN. 6	11	44	45	45	9	10	18	34	8	41	16	13
JUN. 7	11	46	46	47	9	10	18	34	9	41	16	13
JUN. 8	11	47	48	48	10	10	18	34	9	41	16	13
JUN. 9	11	1	2	2	10	10	18	34	9	41	16	13
JUN. 10	11	3	3	4	10	11	18	34	9	41	16	13
JUN. 11	12	4	5	6	11	11	18	34	9	41	16	13
JUN. 12	12	6	7	8	11	11	18	34	9	41	16	13
JUN. 13	12	8	9	9	11	11	18	34	9	41	16	13
JUN. 14	12	10	11	11	11	11	18	34	9	41	16	13
JUN. 15	12	12	13	13	12	11	18	34	9	41	16	13
JUN. 16	12	14	15	15	12	12	18	34	9	41	16	13
JUN. 17	12	16	17	17	12	12	19	34	9	41	16	13
JUN. 18	12	18	19	19	12	12	19	34	9	41	16	13
JUN. 19	13	20	21	21	12	12	19	34	9	41	16	13
JUN. 20	13	22	23	23	12	12	19	34	9	41	16	13
JUN. 21	13	24	24	25	12	12	19	34	9	41	16	13
JUN. 22	13	26	26	27	14	13	19	34	9	41	16	13
JUN. 23	13	27	28	29	14	13	19	34	9	41	16	13
JUN. 24	13	29	30	30	14	13	19	34	9	41	16	13
JUN. 25	14	31	31	32	15	13	19	34	9	41	16	13
JUN. 26	14	32	33	34	15	13	19	34	9	41	16	13
JUN. 27	14	34	35	35	15	13	19	34	9	41	16	13
JUN. 28	14	36	36	37	15	13	19	34	9	41	16	13
JUN. 29	14	37	38	38	16	14	20	34	9	41	16	13
JUN. 30	14	39	40	40	16	14	20	34	9	41	16	13

MOON 1 ◐ 12:01 A.M. TO 8:00 A.M.　　**MOON 2** ◑ 8:01 A.M. TO 4:00 P.M.　　**MOON 3** ● 4:01 P.M. TO 12:00 A.M.

Use only one "moon" number. Choose the column closest to your time of birth. If your place of birth is not on Eastern Standard Time, be sure to read "How to Convert to Eastern Standard Time" at the beginning of this section.

1912

July

Date & Time	SUN	MOON 1	MOON 2	MOON 3	MERCURY	VENUS	MARS	JUPITER	SATURN	URANUS	NEPTUNE	PLUTO
JUL. 1	14	41	41	42	16	14	20	34	9	41	16	13
JUL. 2	14	42	43	43	16	14	20	34	9	41	16	13
JUL. 3	15	44	44	45	17	14	20	34	9	41	16	13
JUL. 4	15	45	46	46	17	14	20	34	9	41	16	13
JUL. 5	15	47	47	48	17	15	20	34	9	41	16	13
JUL. 6	15	1	1	2	17	15	20	34	9	41	16	13
JUL. 7	15	2	3	3	18	15	20	34	9	41	16	13
JUL. 8	15	4	4	5	18	15	20	34	9	41	16	13
JUL. 9	15	6	6	7	18	15	20	34	9	41	16	13
JUL. 10	15	7	8	9	18	15	20	34	9	41	16	13
JUL. 11	16	9	10	11	18	16	20	34	9	41	16	13
JUL. 12	16	11	12	12	19	16	21	34	9	41	16	13
JUL. 13	16	13	14	14	19	16	21	34	9	41	16	13
JUL. 14	16	15	16	17	19	16	21	34	9	41	16	13
JUL. 15	16	17	18	19	19	16	21	34	9	41	16	13
JUL. 16	16	19	20	21	19	16	21	34	9	41	16	13
JUL. 17	16	21	22	23	20	17	21	34	9	41	16	13
JUL. 18	16	23	24	24	20	17	21	34	9	41	16	13
JUL. 19	17	25	26	26	20	17	21	34	9	41	16	13
JUL. 20	17	27	28	28	20	17	21	34	9	41	16	13
JUL. 21	17	29	29	30	20	17	21	34	9	41	16	13
JUL. 22	17	30	31	32	20	17	21	34	9	41	16	13
JUL. 23	17	32	33	33	21	18	21	34	9	41	16	13
JUL. 24	17	34	34	35	21	18	22	34	9	41	16	13
JUL. 25	17	35	36	36	21	18	22	34	9	41	16	13
JUL. 26	18	37	38	38	21	18	22	34	9	41	16	13
JUL. 27	18	39	39	40	21	18	22	34	9	41	16	13
JUL. 28	18	40	41	41	21	18	22	34	9	41	16	13
JUL. 29	18	42	42	43	21	19	22	34	9	41	16	13
JUL. 30	18	43	44	44	21	19	22	34	9	41	16	13
JUL. 31	18	45	45	46	21	19	22	34	9	41	16	13

August

Date & Time	SUN	MOON 1	MOON 2	MOON 3	MERCURY	VENUS	MARS	JUPITER	SATURN	URANUS	NEPTUNE	PLUTO
AUG. 1	18	47	47	48	22	19	22	34	9	41	16	13
AUG. 2	18	48	1	1	22	19	22	34	9	41	16	13
AUG. 3	19	2	2	3	22	19	22	34	9	41	16	13
AUG. 4	19	3	4	4	22	20	22	34	9	41	16	13
AUG. 5	19	5	6	6	22	20	23	34	9	41	16	13
AUG. 6	19	7	7	8	22	20	23	34	9	41	16	13
AUG. 7	19	9	9	10	22	20	23	34	9	41	16	13
AUG. 8	19	10	11	12	22	20	23	34	9	41	16	13
AUG. 9	19	12	13	14	22	20	23	34	9	41	16	13
AUG. 10	19	14	15	16	22	21	23	34	9	41	16	13
AUG. 11	20	16	17	18	22	21	23	34	9	41	16	13
AUG. 12	20	18	19	20	22	21	23	34	9	41	16	13
AUG. 13	20	20	21	22	21	21	23	34	9	41	16	13
AUG. 14	20	22	23	24	22	21	23	34	9	41	16	13
AUG. 15	20	24	25	26	22	21	23	34	9	41	16	13
AUG. 16	20	26	27	27	21	22	23	34	9	41	16	13
AUG. 17	20	28	29	29	21	22	24	34	9	41	16	13
AUG. 18	20	30	30	31	21	22	24	34	9	41	16	13
AUG. 19	21	32	32	33	21	22	24	34	9	41	16	13
AUG. 20	21	33	34	34	21	22	24	34	9	41	16	13
AUG. 21	21	35	36	36	21	22	24	34	9	41	16	13
AUG. 22	21	37	37	38	21	23	24	34	9	41	16	13
AUG. 23	21	38	39	39	21	23	24	34	9	41	16	13
AUG. 24	21	40	41	41	21	23	24	34	9	41	16	13
AUG. 25	21	41	42	42	21	23	24	34	9	41	16	13
AUG. 26	22	43	43	44	20	23	24	34	9	41	16	13
AUG. 27	22	45	45	46	20	23	24	34	9	41	16	13
AUG. 28	22	46	47	47	20	24	24	34	9	41	16	13
AUG. 29	22	48	48	1	20	24	25	34	9	41	16	13
AUG. 30	22	1	2	2	20	24	25	34	9	41	16	13
AUG. 31	22	3	4	4	20	24	25	34	9	41	16	13

MOON 1 ☽ 12:01 A.M. TO 8:00 A.M.   **MOON 2** ☽ 8:01 A.M. TO 4:00 P.M.   **MOON 3** ● 4:01 P.M. TO 12:00 A.M.

Use only one "moon" number. Choose the column closest to your time of birth. If your place of birth is not on Eastern Standard Time, be sure to read "How to Convert to Eastern Standard Time" at the beginning of this section.

1912

September

Date & Time	SUN	MOON 1	MOON 2	MOON 3	MERCURY	VENUS	MARS	JUPITER	SATURN	URANUS	NEPTUNE	PLUTO
SEP. 1	22	5	5	6	20	24	25	34	9	41	16	13
SEP. 2	22	6	7	8	20	24	25	34	9	41	16	13
SEP. 3	23	8	9	9	20	25	25	34	9	41	16	13
SEP. 4	23	10	10	11	20	25	25	34	9	41	16	13
SEP. 5	23	12	12	13	20	25	25	34	9	41	16	13
SEP. 6	23	14	14	15	20	25	25	34	10	41	16	13
SEP. 7	23	16	16	17	20	25	25	34	10	41	16	13
SEP. 8	23	17	18	19	21	25	25	34	10	41	16	13
SEP. 9	23	19	20	21	21	25	26	34	10	41	16	13
SEP. 10	23	21	22	23	21	26	26	34	10	41	16	13
SEP. 11	24	23	24	25	21	26	26	34	10	41	16	13
SEP. 12	24	25	26	27	21	26	26	34	10	41	16	13
SEP. 13	24	27	28	29	21	26	26	34	10	41	16	13
SEP. 14	24	29	30	30	22	26	26	34	10	41	16	13
SEP. 15	24	31	32	32	22	26	26	34	10	41	16	13
SEP. 16	24	33	33	34	22	27	26	34	10	41	16	13
SEP. 17	24	34	35	36	22	27	26	34	10	41	16	13
SEP. 18	24	36	37	37	23	27	26	34	10	41	16	13
SEP. 19	25	38	38	39	23	27	26	34	10	41	16	13
SEP. 20	25	39	40	40	23	27	26	34	10	41	16	13
SEP. 21	25	41	41	42	23	27	27	34	10	41	16	13
SEP. 22	25	42	43	44	23	28	27	34	10	41	16	13
SEP. 23	25	44	45	45	24	28	27	34	10	41	16	13
SEP. 24	25	46	46	47	24	28	27	34	10	41	16	13
SEP. 25	26	47	48	48	24	28	27	34	10	41	16	13
SEP. 26	26	1	1	2	24	28	27	34	10	41	16	13
SEP. 27	26	3	3	4	25	28	27	34	10	41	16	13
SEP. 28	26	4	5	5	25	29	27	34	9	41	16	13
SEP. 29	26	6	7	7	25	29	27	34	9	41	16	13
SEP. 30	26	8	8	9	25	29	27	34	9	41	16	13

October

Date & Time	SUN	MOON 1	MOON 2	MOON 3	MERCURY	VENUS	MARS	JUPITER	SATURN	URANUS	NEPTUNE	PLUTO
OCT. 1	26	9	10	11	26	29	27	34	9	41	16	13
OCT. 2	26	11	12	12	26	29	28	34	9	41	16	13
OCT. 3	27	13	14	14	26	29	28	34	9	41	16	13
OCT. 4	27	15	16	16	26	30	28	34	9	41	16	13
OCT. 5	27	17	18	18	27	30	28	34	9	41	16	13
OCT. 6	27	19	19	20	27	30	28	34	9	41	16	13
OCT. 7	27	21	21	22	27	30	28	35	9	41	16	13
OCT. 8	27	23	23	24	27	30	28	35	9	41	16	13
OCT. 9	27	25	25	26	28	30	28	35	9	41	16	13
OCT. 10	27	27	27	28	28	31	28	35	9	41	16	13
OCT. 11	28	28	29	30	28	31	28	35	9	41	16	13
OCT. 12	28	30	31	31	28	31	28	35	9	41	16	13
OCT. 13	28	32	33	33	28	31	29	35	9	41	16	13
OCT. 14	28	34	34	35	29	31	29	35	9	41	16	13
OCT. 15	28	36	36	37	29	31	29	35	9	41	16	13
OCT. 16	28	37	38	38	29	32	29	35	9	41	16	13
OCT. 17	28	39	39	40	29	32	29	35	9	41	16	13
OCT. 18	28	40	41	41	29	32	29	35	9	41	16	13
OCT. 19	29	42	43	43	30	32	29	35	9	41	16	13
OCT. 20	29	44	44	45	30	32	29	35	9	41	16	13
OCT. 21	29	45	46	46	30	32	29	35	9	41	16	13
OCT. 22	29	47	47	48	30	33	29	35	9	41	16	13
OCT. 23	29	48	1	1	31	33	29	35	9	41	16	13
OCT. 24	29	2	3	3	31	33	30	35	9	41	16	13
OCT. 25	29	4	4	5	31	33	30	35	9	41	16	13
OCT. 26	30	5	6	7	31	33	30	35	9	41	16	13
OCT. 27	30	7	8	8	31	33	30	35	9	41	16	13
OCT. 28	30	9	10	10	32	34	30	35	9	41	16	13
OCT. 29	30	11	11	12	32	34	30	35	9	41	16	13
OCT. 30	30	13	13	14	32	34	30	35	9	41	16	13
OCT. 31	30	15	15	16	32	34	30	35	9	41	16	13

MOON 1 ◐ 12:01 A.M. TO 8:00 A.M.   **MOON 2** ◑ 8:01 A.M. TO 4:00 P.M.   **MOON 3** ● 4:01 P.M. TO 12:00 A.M.

Use only one "moon" number. Choose the column closest to your time of birth. If your place of birth is not on Eastern Standard Time, be sure to read "How to Convert to Eastern Standard Time" at the beginning of this section.

1912

November

Date & Time	SUN	MOON 1	MOON 2	MOON 3	MERCURY	VENUS	MARS	JUPITER	SATURN	URANUS	NEPTUNE	PLUTO
NOV. 1	30	16	17	18	32	34	30	35	9	41	16	13
NOV. 2	30	18	19	20	33	34	30	35	9	41	16	13
NOV. 3	31	20	21	21	33	35	30	35	9	41	16	13
NOV. 4	31	22	23	23	33	35	31	35	9	41	16	13
NOV. 5	31	24	25	25	33	35	31	35	9	41	16	13
NOV. 6	31	26	26	27	33	35	31	35	9	41	16	13
NOV. 7	31	28	28	29	33	35	31	35	9	41	16	13
NOV. 8	31	30	30	31	34	35	31	35	9	41	16	13
NOV. 9	31	31	32	33	34	35	31	35	9	41	16	13
NOV. 10	31	33	34	34	34	36	31	35	9	41	16	13
NOV. 11	31	35	36	36	34	36	31	35	9	41	16	13
NOV. 12	32	37	37	38	34	36	31	35	9	41	16	13
NOV. 13	32	38	39	39	35	36	31	35	9	41	16	13
NOV. 14	32	40	40	41	35	36	31	35	9	41	16	13
NOV. 15	32	41	42	43	35	36	32	36	9	41	16	13
NOV. 16	32	43	44	44	35	37	32	36	9	41	16	13
NOV. 17	32	45	45	46	35	37	32	36	9	41	16	13
NOV. 18	32	46	47	47	35	37	32	36	9	41	16	13
NOV. 19	33	48	48	1	35	37	32	36	9	41	16	13
NOV. 20	33	1	2	3	36	37	32	36	9	41	16	13
NOV. 21	33	3	4	4	36	37	32	36	9	41	16	13
NOV. 22	33	5	5	6	36	38	32	36	9	41	16	13
NOV. 23	33	7	7	8	36	38	32	36	9	41	16	13
NOV. 24	33	8	9	10	36	38	32	36	9	41	16	13
NOV. 25	34	10	11	11	36	38	32	36	9	41	16	13
NOV. 26	34	12	13	13	36	38	33	36	9	41	16	13
NOV. 27	34	14	15	15	36	38	33	36	9	41	16	13
NOV. 28	34	16	17	17	36	39	33	36	9	41	16	13
NOV. 29	34	18	19	19	36	39	33	36	9	41	16	13
NOV. 30	34	20	20	21	36	39	33	36	9	41	16	13

December

Date & Time	SUN	MOON 1	MOON 2	MOON 3	MERCURY	VENUS	MARS	JUPITER	SATURN	URANUS	NEPTUNE	PLUTO
DEC. 1	34	22	22	23	36	39	33	36	9	41	16	13
DEC. 2	34	24	24	25	36	39	33	36	9	41	16	13
DEC. 3	35	25	26	27	36	39	33	36	9	41	16	13
DEC. 4	35	27	28	28	36	40	33	36	9	41	16	13
DEC. 5	35	29	30	30	36	40	33	36	9	41	16	13
DEC. 6	35	31	31	32	36	40	34	36	9	41	16	13
DEC. 7	35	33	33	34	36	40	34	36	9	41	16	13
DEC. 8	35	34	35	35	35	40	34	36	9	41	16	13
DEC. 9	35	36	37	37	35	40	34	36	9	41	16	13
DEC. 10	35	38	38	39	35	41	34	36	9	41	16	13
DEC. 11	36	39	40	40	35	41	34	36	9	41	16	13
DEC. 12	36	41	41	42	35	41	34	36	9	41	16	13
DEC. 13	36	43	43	44	34	41	34	36	9	41	16	13
DEC. 14	36	44	45	45	34	41	34	36	9	41	16	13
DEC. 15	36	46	46	47	34	41	34	36	9	41	16	13
DEC. 16	36	47	48	48	34	41	34	36	9	41	16	13
DEC. 17	36	1	1	2	34	42	35	36	9	41	16	13
DEC. 18	36	2	3	4	34	42	35	36	9	41	16	13
DEC. 19	37	4	5	5	34	42	35	37	9	41	16	13
DEC. 20	37	6	6	7	34	42	35	37	9	41	16	13
DEC. 21	37	8	8	9	34	42	35	37	9	41	16	13
DEC. 22	37	9	10	11	34	42	35	37	9	41	16	13
DEC. 23	37	11	12	13	34	43	35	37	9	41	16	13
DEC. 24	37	13	14	15	34	43	35	37	9	41	16	13
DEC. 25	37	15	16	17	34	43	35	37	9	41	16	13
DEC. 26	38	17	18	19	35	43	35	37	9	41	16	13
DEC. 27	38	19	20	21	35	43	36	37	9	41	16	13
DEC. 28	38	21	22	22	35	43	36	37	9	41	16	13
DEC. 29	38	23	24	24	35	44	36	37	9	41	16	13
DEC. 30	38	25	26	26	35	44	36	37	9	41	16	13
DEC. 31	38	27	27	28	35	44	36	37	9	41	16	13

MOON 1 ☽ 12:01 A.M. TO 8:00 A.M.   **MOON 2** ☽ 8:01 A.M. TO 4:00 P.M.   **MOON 3** ● 4:01 P.M. TO 12:00 A.M.

Use only one "moon" number. Choose the column closest to your time of birth. If your place of birth is not on Eastern Standard Time, be sure to read "How to Convert to Eastern Standard Time" at the beginning of this section.

1913

January

Date & Time	SUN	MOON 1	MOON 2	MOON 3	MERCURY	VENUS	MARS	JUPITER	SATURN	URANUS	NEPTUNE	PLUTO
JAN. 1	38	29	29	30	35	44	36	37	9	41	16	13
JAN. 2	38	30	31	32	36	44	36	37	9	41	16	13
JAN. 3	39	32	33	33	36	44	36	37	9	41	16	13
JAN. 4	39	34	34	35	36	44	36	37	9	41	16	13
JAN. 5	39	35	36	37	36	45	36	37	9	41	16	13
JAN. 6	39	37	38	38	36	45	37	37	9	41	16	13
JAN. 7	39	39	39	40	36	45	37	37	9	41	16	13
JAN. 8	39	40	41	41	37	45	37	37	9	41	16	13
JAN. 9	39	42	43	43	37	45	37	37	9	41	16	13
JAN. 10	40	44	44	45	37	45	37	37	9	41	16	13
JAN. 11	40	45	46	46	37	46	37	37	9	41	16	13
JAN. 12	40	47	47	48	37	46	37	37	9	41	16	13
JAN. 13	40	48	1	1	38	46	37	37	9	41	16	13
JAN. 14	40	2	2	3	38	46	37	37	9	41	16	13
JAN. 15	40	4	4	5	38	46	37	37	9	41	16	13
JAN. 16	40	5	6	6	38	46	38	37	9	41	16	13
JAN. 17	41	7	7	8	38	46	38	37	9	41	16	13
JAN. 18	41	9	9	10	39	47	38	37	9	41	16	13
JAN. 19	41	10	11	12	39	47	38	37	9	41	16	13
JAN. 20	41	12	13	14	39	47	38	37	9	41	16	13
JAN. 21	41	14	15	16	39	47	38	38	9	41	16	13
JAN. 22	41	16	17	18	39	47	38	38	9	41	16	13
JAN. 23	42	18	19	20	40	47	38	38	9	41	16	13
JAN. 24	42	20	21	22	40	48	38	38	9	41	16	13
JAN. 25	42	22	23	24	40	48	38	38	9	41	16	13
JAN. 26	42	24	25	26	40	48	39	38	9	41	16	13
JAN. 27	42	26	27	28	40	48	39	38	9	41	16	13
JAN. 28	42	28	29	29	41	48	39	38	9	41	16	13
JAN. 29	42	30	31	31	41	48	39	38	9	41	16	13
JAN. 30	42	32	32	33	41	48	39	38	9	41	16	13
JAN. 31	43	33	34	35	41	1	39	38	9	41	16	13

February

Date & Time	SUN	MOON 1	MOON 2	MOON 3	MERCURY	VENUS	MARS	JUPITER	SATURN	URANUS	NEPTUNE	PLUTO
FEB. 1	43	35	36	36	41	1	39	38	9	41	16	13
FEB. 2	43	37	37	38	42	1	39	38	9	42	16	13
FEB. 3	43	38	39	39	42	1	39	38	9	42	16	13
FEB. 4	43	40	41	41	42	1	39	38	9	42	16	13
FEB. 5	43	42	42	43	42	1	40	38	9	42	16	13
FEB. 6	43	43	43	44	43	1	40	38	9	42	16	13
FEB. 7	43	45	45	46	43	2	40	38	9	42	16	13
FEB. 8	44	46	47	47	43	2	40	38	9	42	16	13
FEB. 9	44	48	48	1	43	2	40	38	9	42	16	13
FEB. 10	44	1	2	3	43	2	40	38	9	42	16	13
FEB. 11	44	3	4	4	44	2	40	38	9	42	16	13
FEB. 12	44	5	5	6	44	2	40	38	9	42	16	13
FEB. 13	44	6	7	7	44	2	40	38	9	42	16	13
FEB. 14	44	8	9	9	44	3	40	38	9	42	16	13
FEB. 15	44	10	10	11	45	3	41	38	9	42	16	13
FEB. 16	45	12	12	13	45	3	41	38	9	42	16	13
FEB. 17	45	13	14	15	45	3	41	38	9	42	16	13
FEB. 18	45	15	16	17	45	3	41	38	9	42	16	13
FEB. 19	45	17	18	19	46	3	41	38	9	42	16	13
FEB. 20	45	19	20	21	46	3	41	38	9	42	16	13
FEB. 21	45	21	22	23	46	3	41	38	9	42	16	13
FEB. 22	45	23	24	25	46	4	41	38	9	42	16	13
FEB. 23	46	25	26	27	47	4	41	38	9	42	16	13
FEB. 24	46	27	28	29	47	4	41	38	9	42	16	13
FEB. 25	46	29	30	31	47	4	42	38	9	42	16	13
FEB. 26	46	31	32	32	47	4	42	38	9	42	16	13
FEB. 27	46	33	34	34	48	4	42	38	9	42	16	13
FEB. 28	46	35	35	36	48	4	42	39	9	42	16	13

MOON 1 ☽ 12:01 A.M. TO 8:00 A.M.   **MOON 2** ☽ 8:01 A.M. TO 4:00 P.M.   **MOON 3** ● 4:01 P.M. TO 12:00 A.M.

Use only one "moon" number. Choose the column closest to your time of birth. If your place of birth is not on Eastern Standard Time, be sure to read "How to Convert to Eastern Standard Time" at the beginning of this section.

1913

March

April

Date & Time	SUN	MOON 1	MOON 2	MOON 3	MERCURY	VENUS	MARS	JUPITER	SATURN	URANUS	NEPTUNE	PLUTO
MAR. 1	46	36	37	37	48	4	42	39	9	42	16	13
MAR. 2	46	38	39	39	48	4	42	39	9	42	16	13
MAR. 3	47	40	40	41	1	5	42	39	9	42	16	13
MAR. 4	47	41	42	42	1	5	42	39	9	42	16	13
MAR. 5	47	43	43	44	1	5	42	39	9	42	16	13
MAR. 6	47	44	45	45	1	5	42	39	9	42	16	13
MAR. 7	47	46	46	47	1	5	43	39	9	42	16	13
MAR. 8	47	48	48	1	2	5	43	39	9	42	16	13
MAR. 9	47	1	2	2	2	5	43	39	9	42	16	13
MAR. 10	47	3	3	4	2	5	43	39	9	42	16	13
MAR. 11	48	4	5	5	2	5	43	39	9	42	16	13
MAR. 12	48	6	7	7	2	5	43	39	9	42	16	13
MAR. 13	48	8	9	9	2	6	43	39	9	42	16	13
MAR. 14	48	9	10	10	2	6	43	39	9	42	16	13
MAR. 15	48	11	12	12	2	6	43	39	9	42	16	13
MAR. 16	48	13	13	14	3	6	44	39	9	42	16	13
MAR. 17	48	15	15	16	3	6	44	39	9	42	16	13
MAR. 18	48	17	17	18	3	6	44	39	9	42	16	13
MAR. 19	1	19	19	20	3	6	44	39	9	42	16	13
MAR. 20	1	21	21	22	3	6	44	39	9	42	16	13
MAR. 21	1	23	23	24	2	6	44	39	9	42	16	13
MAR. 22	1	25	25	26	2	6	44	39	9	42	16	13
MAR. 23	1	27	27	28	2	6	44	39	9	42	16	13
MAR. 24	1	29	29	30	2	6	44	39	9	42	16	13
MAR. 25	2	30	31	32	2	6	44	39	9	42	16	13
MAR. 26	2	32	33	33	2	6	45	39	9	42	16	13
MAR. 27	2	34	35	35	2	6	45	39	9	42	16	13
MAR. 28	2	36	36	37	2	7	45	39	9	42	16	13
MAR. 29	2	38	38	39	2	7	45	39	9	42	16	13
MAR. 30	2	39	40	40	2	7	45	39	9	42	16	13
MAR. 31	2	41	41	42	2	7	45	39	9	42	16	13

Date & Time	SUN	MOON 1	MOON 2	MOON 3	MERCURY	VENUS	MARS	JUPITER	SATURN	URANUS	NEPTUNE	PLUTO
APR. 1	2	42	43	43	1	7	45	39	9	42	16	13
APR. 2	2	44	44	45	1	7	45	39	9	42	16	13
APR. 3	3	46	46	47	1	7	45	39	9	42	16	13
APR. 4	3	47	48	48	1	7	45	39	9	42	16	13
APR. 5	3	1	1	2	1	7	46	39	9	42	16	13
APR. 6	3	2	3	3	1	7	46	39	9	42	16	13
APR. 7	3	4	4	5	1	7	46	39	9	42	16	13
APR. 8	3	6	6	7	1	7	46	39	9	42	16	13
APR. 9	3	7	8	8	1	7	46	39	9	42	16	13
APR. 10	3	9	10	10	1	7	46	39	9	42	16	13
APR. 11	4	11	11	12	1	6	46	39	9	42	16	13
APR. 12	4	12	13	14	1	6	46	39	9	42	16	13
APR. 13	4	14	15	15	1	6	46	39	9	42	16	13
APR. 14	4	16	17	17	1	6	47	39	9	42	16	13
APR. 15	4	18	19	19	1	6	47	39	9	42	16	13
APR. 16	4	20	20	21	1	6	47	39	9	42	16	13
APR. 17	4	22	22	23	1	6	47	39	9	42	16	13
APR. 18	4	24	24	25	1	6	47	39	9	42	16	13
APR. 19	5	26	26	27	1	6	47	39	9	42	16	13
APR. 20	5	28	28	29	1	6	47	39	9	42	16	13
APR. 21	5	30	30	31	1	6	47	39	9	42	16	13
APR. 22	5	31	32	33	2	6	47	39	9	42	16	13
APR. 23	5	33	34	35	2	6	47	39	9	42	16	13
APR. 24	5	35	36	36	2	6	48	39	9	42	16	13
APR. 25	6	37	37	38	2	6	48	39	9	42	16	13
APR. 26	6	39	39	40	2	5	48	39	9	42	16	13
APR. 27	6	40	41	41	2	5	48	39	9	42	16	13
APR. 28	6	42	42	43	2	5	48	39	9	42	16	13
APR. 29	6	43	44	45	3	5	48	39	9	42	16	13
APR. 30	6	45	46	46	3	5	48	39	9	42	16	13

MOON 1 ◖ 12:01 A.M. TO 8:00 A.M. **MOON 2** ◑ 8:01 A.M. TO 4:00 P.M. **MOON 3** ● 4:01 P.M. TO 12:00 A.M.

Use only one "moon" number. Choose the column closest to your time of birth. If your place of birth is not on Eastern Standard Time, be sure to read "How to Convert to Eastern Standard Time" at the beginning of this section.

1913

May

June

Date & Time	SUN	MOON 1	MOON 2	MOON 3	MERCURY	VENUS	MARS	JUPITER	SATURN	URANUS	NEPTUNE	PLUTO
MAY 1	6	47	47	48	3	5	48	39	9	42	16	13
MAY 2	6	48	1	1	3	5	48	39	10	42	16	13
MAY 3	7	2	2	3	3	5	48	39	10	42	16	13
MAY 4	7	3	4	5	3	5	1	39	10	42	16	13
MAY 5	7	5	6	6	4	5	1	39	10	42	16	13
MAY 6	7	7	7	8	4	5	1	39	10	42	16	13
MAY 7	7	8	9	10	4	5	1	39	10	42	16	13
MAY 8	7	10	11	11	4	5	1	39	10	42	16	13
MAY 9	7	12	13	13	4	5	1	39	10	42	16	13
MAY 10	7	14	14	15	5	5	1	39	10	42	16	13
MAY 11	8	16	16	17	5	5	1	39	10	42	16	13
MAY 12	8	18	18	19	5	4	1	39	10	42	16	13
MAY 13	8	19	20	21	5	4	1	39	10	42	16	13
MAY 14	8	21	22	23	5	4	2	39	10	42	16	13
MAY 15	8	23	24	24	6	4	2	39	10	42	16	13
MAY 16	8	25	26	26	6	4	2	39	10	42	16	13
MAY 17	8	27	28	28	6	4	2	39	10	42	16	13
MAY 18	8	29	29	30	6	4	2	39	10	42	16	13
MAY 19	9	31	31	32	7	4	2	39	10	42	16	13
MAY 20	9	33	33	34	7	4	2	39	10	42	16	13
MAY 21	9	34	35	36	7	5	2	39	10	42	16	13
MAY 22	9	36	37	37	7	5	2	39	10	42	16	13
MAY 23	9	38	39	39	8	5	2	39	10	42	16	13
MAY 24	9	40	40	41	8	5	3	39	10	42	16	13
MAY 25	10	41	42	43	8	5	3	39	10	42	16	13
MAY 26	10	43	43	44	8	5	3	39	10	42	16	13
MAY 27	10	45	45	46	9	5	3	39	10	42	16	13
MAY 28	10	46	47	47	9	5	3	39	10	42	16	13
MAY 29	10	48	48	1	9	5	3	39	10	42	16	13
MAY 30	10	1	2	2	10	5	3	39	10	42	16	13
MAY 31	10	3	3	4	10	5	3	39	10	42	16	13

Date & Time	SUN	MOON 1	MOON 2	MOON 3	MERCURY	VENUS	MARS	JUPITER	SATURN	URANUS	NEPTUNE	PLUTO
JUN. 1	10	4	5	6	10	5	3	39	10	42	16	13
JUN. 2	10	6	7	7	10	5	4	39	10	42	16	13
JUN. 3	11	8	8	9	11	5	4	39	10	42	16	13
JUN. 4	11	10	10	11	11	5	4	39	10	42	16	13
JUN. 5	11	11	12	13	11	5	4	39	10	42	16	13
JUN. 6	11	13	14	15	12	5	4	39	10	42	16	13
JUN. 7	11	15	16	16	12	5	4	39	10	42	16	13
JUN. 8	11	17	18	18	12	6	4	39	10	42	16	13
JUN. 9	11	19	20	20	12	6	4	39	10	42	16	13
JUN. 10	11	21	21	22	13	6	4	39	10	42	16	13
JUN. 11	12	23	23	24	13	6	4	39	10	42	16	13
JUN. 12	12	25	25	26	13	6	4	39	10	42	16	13
JUN. 13	12	26	27	28	14	6	5	39	10	42	16	13
JUN. 14	12	28	29	30	14	6	5	39	10	42	16	13
JUN. 15	12	30	31	31	14	6	5	39	10	42	16	13
JUN. 16	12	32	33	33	14	6	5	39	10	42	16	13
JUN. 17	12	34	34	35	15	6	5	39	10	42	16	13
JUN. 18	12	36	36	37	15	7	5	39	10	42	16	13
JUN. 19	13	37	38	38	15	7	5	39	10	42	16	13
JUN. 20	13	39	40	40	15	7	5	39	10	42	16	13
JUN. 21	13	41	41	42	16	7	5	39	10	42	16	13
JUN. 22	13	42	43	43	16	7	5	39	10	42	16	13
JUN. 23	13	44	45	45	16	7	6	39	10	42	16	13
JUN. 24	13	46	46	47	16	7	6	39	10	42	16	13
JUN. 25	14	47	48	48	16	7	6	39	10	42	16	13
JUN. 26	14	1	1	2	17	7	6	39	10	42	16	13
JUN. 27	14	2	3	3	17	8	6	39	10	42	16	13
JUN. 28	14	4	4	5	17	8	6	39	10	42	16	13
JUN. 29	14	6	6	7	17	8	6	39	10	42	16	13
JUN. 30	14	7	8	8	17	8	6	39	11	42	16	13

MOON 1 ☽ 12:01 A.M. TO 8:00 A.M.   **MOON 2** ◑ 8:01 A.M. TO 4:00 P.M.   **MOON 3** ● 4:01 P.M. TO 12:00 A.M.

Use only one "moon" number. Choose the column closest to your time of birth. If your place of birth is not on Eastern Standard Time, be sure to read "How to Convert to Eastern Standard Time" at the beginning of this section.

1913

July

August

Date & Time	SUN	MOON 1	MOON 2	MOON 3	MERCURY	VENUS	MARS	JUPITER	SATURN	URANUS	NEPTUNE	PLUTO
JUL. 1	14	9	10	10	17	8	6	39	11	42	16	13
JUL. 2	14	11	11	12	18	8	6	39	11	42	16	13
JUL. 3	15	13	13	14	18	8	7	39	11	42	16	13
JUL. 4	15	15	15	16	18	8	7	39	11	42	16	13
JUL. 5	15	16	17	18	18	9	7	39	11	42	16	13
JUL. 6	15	18	19	20	19	9	7	39	11	42	16	13
JUL. 7	15	20	21	22	19	9	7	39	11	42	16	13
JUL. 8	15	22	23	24	19	9	7	39	11	42	16	13
JUL. 9	15	24	25	25	19	9	7	39	11	42	16	13
JUL. 10	15	26	27	27	19	9	7	39	11	42	16	13
JUL. 11	16	28	29	29	19	9	7	39	11	42	16	13
JUL. 12	16	30	30	31	19	9	7	39	11	42	16	13
JUL. 13	16	32	32	33	19	10	7	39	11	42	16	13
JUL. 14	16	33	34	35	19	10	8	39	11	42	16	13
JUL. 15	16	35	36	36	19	10	8	39	11	42	16	13
JUL. 16	16	37	37	38	19	10	8	39	11	42	16	13
JUL. 17	16	39	39	40	19	10	8	38	11	42	16	13
JUL. 18	16	40	41	41	19	10	8	38	11	42	16	13
JUL. 19	17	42	42	43	19	10	8	38	11	42	16	13
JUL. 20	17	43	44	45	19	11	8	38	11	42	16	13
JUL. 21	17	45	46	46	19	11	8	38	11	42	16	13
JUL. 22	17	47	47	48	19	11	8	38	11	42	16	13
JUL. 23	17	48	1	1	19	11	8	38	11	42	16	13
JUL. 24	17	2	2	3	19	11	8	38	11	42	16	13
JUL. 25	17	3	4	4	19	11	9	38	11	42	16	13
JUL. 26	18	5	6	6	19	11	9	38	11	42	16	13
JUL. 27	18	7	7	8	19	12	9	38	11	42	16	13
JUL. 28	18	8	9	9	19	12	9	38	11	42	16	13
JUL. 29	18	10	11	11	19	12	9	38	11	42	16	13
JUL. 30	18	12	12	13	19	12	9	38	11	42	16	13
JUL. 31	18	14	14	15	19	12	9	38	11	42	16	13

Date & Time	SUN	MOON 1	MOON 2	MOON 3	MERCURY	VENUS	MARS	JUPITER	SATURN	URANUS	NEPTUNE	PLUTO
AUG. 1	18	16	16	17	19	12	9	38	11	42	16	13
AUG. 2	18	18	18	19	19	12	9	38	11	42	16	13
AUG. 3	19	20	20	21	19	13	9	38	11	42	16	13
AUG. 4	19	22	22	23	19	13	9	38	11	42	16	13
AUG. 5	19	24	24	25	18	13	10	38	11	42	16	13
AUG. 6	19	26	26	27	18	13	10	38	11	42	16	13
AUG. 7	19	27	28	29	18	13	10	38	11	42	16	13
AUG. 8	19	29	30	31	18	13	10	38	11	42	16	13
AUG. 9	19	31	32	32	18	13	10	38	11	42	17	13
AUG. 10	19	33	34	34	18	14	10	38	11	42	17	13
AUG. 11	20	35	35	36	18	14	10	38	11	42	17	13
AUG. 12	20	36	37	38	18	14	10	38	11	42	17	13
AUG. 13	20	38	39	39	18	14	10	38	11	42	17	13
AUG. 14	20	40	40	41	18	14	10	38	11	42	17	13
AUG. 15	20	41	42	43	18	14	10	38	11	42	17	13
AUG. 16	20	43	44	44	18	14	11	38	11	42	17	13
AUG. 17	20	45	45	46	18	15	11	38	11	42	17	13
AUG. 18	20	46	47	47	18	15	11	38	11	42	17	13
AUG. 19	21	48	48	1	18	15	11	38	11	42	17	13
AUG. 20	21	1	2	2	18	15	11	38	11	42	17	13
AUG. 21	21	3	3	4	18	15	11	38	11	42	17	13
AUG. 22	21	5	5	6	18	15	11	38	11	42	17	13
AUG. 23	21	6	7	7	18	16	11	38	11	42	17	13
AUG. 24	21	8	8	9	19	16	11	38	11	42	17	13
AUG. 25	21	9	10	11	19	16	11	38	11	42	17	13
AUG. 26	22	11	12	12	19	16	11	38	11	42	17	13
AUG. 27	22	13	14	14	19	16	11	38	11	42	17	13
AUG. 28	22	15	15	16	19	16	12	38	11	42	17	13
AUG. 29	22	17	17	18	20	16	12	38	11	42	17	13
AUG. 30	22	19	19	20	20	17	12	38	11	42	17	13
AUG. 31	22	21	21	22	20	17	12	38	11	42	17	13

MOON 1 ◑ 12:01 A.M. TO 8:00 A.M.   **MOON 2** ◑ 8:01 A.M. TO 4:00 P.M.   **MOON 3** ● 4:01 P.M. TO 12:00 A.M.
Use only one "moon" number. Choose the column closest to your time of birth. If your place of birth is not on Eastern Standard Time, be sure to read "How to Convert to Eastern Standard Time" at the beginning of this section.

1913

September

Date & Time	SUN	MOON 1	MOON 2	MOON 3	MERCURY	VENUS	MARS	JUPITER	SATURN	URANUS	NEPTUNE	PLUTO
SEP. 1	22	23	23	24	20	17	12	38	11	42	17	13
SEP. 2	22	25	25	26	20	17	12	38	11	42	17	13
SEP. 3	23	27	27	28	21	17	12	38	11	42	17	13
SEP. 4	23	29	29	30	21	17	12	38	11	42	17	13
SEP. 5	23	31	31	32	21	18	12	38	11	42	17	13
SEP. 6	23	32	33	34	21	18	12	38	11	42	17	13
SEP. 7	23	34	35	35	22	18	12	38	11	42	17	13
SEP. 8	23	36	37	37	22	18	12	38	11	42	17	13
SEP. 9	23	38	38	39	22	18	12	38	11	42	17	13
SEP. 10	23	39	40	40	22	18	13	38	11	42	17	13
SEP. 11	24	41	42	42	23	19	13	38	11	42	17	13
SEP. 12	24	43	43	44	23	19	13	38	11	42	17	13
SEP. 13	24	44	45	45	23	19	13	38	11	41	17	13
SEP. 14	24	46	46	47	23	19	13	38	11	41	17	13
SEP. 15	24	47	48	48	24	19	13	38	11	41	17	13
SEP. 16	24	1	1	2	24	19	13	38	11	41	17	13
SEP. 17	24	3	3	4	24	19	13	38	11	41	17	13
SEP. 18	24	4	5	5	24	20	13	38	11	41	17	13
SEP. 19	25	6	6	7	25	20	13	38	11	41	17	13
SEP. 20	25	7	8	8	25	20	13	38	11	41	17	13
SEP. 21	25	9	10	10	25	20	13	38	11	41	17	13
SEP. 22	25	11	11	12	25	20	13	38	11	41	17	13
SEP. 23	25	12	13	14	26	20	14	38	11	41	17	13
SEP. 24	25	14	15	16	26	21	14	38	11	41	17	13
SEP. 25	26	16	17	17	26	21	14	38	11	41	17	13
SEP. 26	26	18	19	19	26	21	14	38	11	41	17	13
SEP. 27	26	20	20	21	27	21	14	38	11	41	17	13
SEP. 28	26	22	22	23	27	21	14	38	11	41	17	13
SEP. 29	26	24	24	25	27	21	14	38	11	41	17	13
SEP. 30	26	26	27	27	27	22	14	38	11	41	17	13

October

Date & Time	SUN	MOON 1	MOON 2	MOON 3	MERCURY	VENUS	MARS	JUPITER	SATURN	URANUS	NEPTUNE	PLUTO
OCT. 1	26	28	29	29	27	22	14	38	11	41	17	13
OCT. 2	26	30	30	31	28	22	14	38	11	41	17	13
OCT. 3	27	32	32	33	28	22	14	38	11	41	17	13
OCT. 4	27	34	34	35	28	22	14	38	11	41	17	13
OCT. 5	27	35	36	37	28	22	14	38	11	41	17	13
OCT. 6	27	37	38	38	28	23	14	38	11	41	17	13
OCT. 7	27	39	40	40	29	23	14	38	11	41	17	13
OCT. 8	27	41	41	42	29	23	14	38	11	41	17	13
OCT. 9	27	42	43	43	29	23	15	38	11	41	17	13
OCT. 10	27	44	44	45	29	23	15	38	11	41	17	13
OCT. 11	28	45	46	46	29	23	15	38	11	41	17	13
OCT. 12	28	47	48	48	30	23	15	38	11	41	17	13
OCT. 13	28	1	1	2	30	24	15	38	11	41	17	13
OCT. 14	28	2	3	3	30	24	15	38	11	41	17	13
OCT. 15	28	4	4	5	30	24	15	38	11	41	17	13
OCT. 16	28	5	6	6	30	24	15	38	11	41	17	13
OCT. 17	28	7	8	8	31	24	15	38	11	41	17	13
OCT. 18	28	9	9	10	31	24	15	38	11	41	17	13
OCT. 19	29	10	11	11	31	25	15	38	11	41	17	13
OCT. 20	29	12	13	13	31	25	15	38	11	41	17	13
OCT. 21	29	14	14	15	31	25	15	38	11	41	17	13
OCT. 22	29	15	16	17	32	25	15	38	11	41	17	13
OCT. 23	29	17	18	19	32	25	15	39	11	41	17	13
OCT. 24	29	19	20	20	32	25	15	39	11	41	17	13
OCT. 25	29	21	22	22	32	26	15	39	11	41	17	13
OCT. 26	30	23	24	24	32	26	15	39	11	41	17	13
OCT. 27	30	25	26	26	32	26	16	39	11	41	17	13
OCT. 28	30	27	28	28	33	26	16	39	11	41	17	13
OCT. 29	30	29	30	30	33	26	16	39	11	41	17	13
OCT. 30	30	31	32	32	33	26	16	39	11	41	17	13
OCT. 31	30	33	33	34	33	27	16	39	11	41	17	13

MOON 1 ☽ 12:01 A.M. TO 8:00 A.M. **MOON 2** ◑ 8:01 A.M. TO 4:00 P.M. **MOON 3** ● 4:01 P.M. TO 12:00 A.M.

Use only one "moon" number. Choose the column closest to your time of birth. If your place of birth is not on Eastern Standard Time, be sure to read "How to Convert to Eastern Standard Time" at the beginning of this section.

1913

November

Date & Time	SUN	MOON 1	MOON 2	MOON 3	MERCURY	VENUS	MARS	JUPITER	SATURN	URANUS	NEPTUNE	PLUTO
NOV. 1	30	35	35	36	33	27	16	39	11	41	17	13
NOV. 2	30	37	37	38	33	27	16	39	11	41	17	13
NOV. 3	31	38	39	40	33	27	16	39	11	41	17	13
NOV. 4	31	40	41	41	34	27	16	39	11	41	17	13
NOV. 5	31	42	42	43	34	27	16	39	11	41	17	13
NOV. 6	31	43	44	44	34	28	16	39	11	41	17	13
NOV. 7	31	45	45	46	34	28	16	39	11	41	17	13
NOV. 8	31	47	47	48	34	28	16	39	11	41	17	13
NOV. 9	31	48	1	1	34	28	16	39	11	41	17	13
NOV. 10	31	2	2	3	34	28	16	39	11	41	17	13
NOV. 11	31	3	4	4	34	28	16	39	11	41	17	13
NOV. 12	32	5	5	6	34	29	16	39	11	41	17	13
NOV. 13	32	7	7	8	34	29	16	39	11	41	17	13
NOV. 14	32	8	9	9	34	29	16	39	11	42	17	13
NOV. 15	32	10	10	11	34	29	16	39	11	42	17	13
NOV. 16	32	12	12	13	34	29	16	39	11	42	17	13
NOV. 17	32	13	14	14	34	29	16	39	11	42	17	13
NOV. 18	32	15	16	16	34	30	16	39	11	42	17	13
NOV. 19	33	17	17	18	34	30	16	39	11	42	17	13
NOV. 20	33	19	19	20	34	30	16	39	11	42	17	13
NOV. 21	33	21	21	22	33	30	16	39	11	42	17	13
NOV. 22	33	22	23	24	33	30	16	39	11	42	17	13
NOV. 23	33	24	25	26	33	30	16	39	11	42	17	13
NOV. 24	33	26	27	27	33	31	16	39	11	42	17	13
NOV. 25	34	28	29	29	33	31	16	39	11	42	17	13
NOV. 26	34	30	31	31	33	31	16	39	11	42	17	13
NOV. 27	34	32	33	33	32	31	16	39	11	42	17	13
NOV. 28	34	34	35	35	32	31	16	39	11	42	17	13
NOV. 29	34	36	36	37	32	31	16	39	11	42	17	13
NOV. 30	34	38	38	39	32	32	16	39	11	42	17	13

December

Date & Time	SUN	MOON 1	MOON 2	MOON 3	MERCURY	VENUS	MARS	JUPITER	SATURN	URANUS	NEPTUNE	PLUTO
DEC. 1	34	39	40	41	32	32	16	39	11	42	17	13
DEC. 2	34	41	42	42	32	32	16	39	11	42	17	13
DEC. 3	35	43	43	44	32	32	16	39	11	42	17	13
DEC. 4	35	44	45	45	32	32	16	40	11	42	17	13
DEC. 5	35	46	47	47	32	32	16	40	11	42	17	13
DEC. 6	35	48	48	1	32	33	16	40	11	42	17	13
DEC. 7	35	1	2	2	32	33	16	40	11	42	17	13
DEC. 8	35	3	3	4	32	33	16	40	11	42	17	13
DEC. 9	35	4	5	5	32	33	16	40	11	42	17	13
DEC. 10	35	6	7	7	33	33	16	40	11	42	17	13
DEC. 11	36	8	8	9	33	33	16	40	11	42	17	13
DEC. 12	36	9	10	10	33	34	16	40	11	42	17	13
DEC. 13	36	11	12	12	33	34	16	40	11	42	17	13
DEC. 14	36	13	13	14	33	34	16	40	11	42	17	13
DEC. 15	36	15	15	16	33	34	16	40	11	42	17	13
DEC. 16	36	16	17	18	33	34	16	40	11	42	17	13
DEC. 17	36	18	19	19	34	34	16	40	11	42	17	13
DEC. 18	36	20	21	21	34	35	16	40	11	42	17	13
DEC. 19	37	22	23	23	34	35	16	40	11	42	17	13
DEC. 20	37	24	24	25	34	35	16	40	11	42	17	13
DEC. 21	37	26	26	27	34	35	16	40	11	42	17	13
DEC. 22	37	28	28	29	34	35	16	40	11	42	17	13
DEC. 23	37	29	30	31	35	35	16	40	11	42	17	13
DEC. 24	37	31	32	33	35	36	16	40	11	42	17	13
DEC. 25	37	33	34	34	35	36	16	40	11	42	17	13
DEC. 26	38	35	36	36	35	36	15	40	11	42	17	13
DEC. 27	38	37	38	38	35	36	15	40	11	42	17	13
DEC. 28	38	39	39	40	36	36	15	40	11	42	17	13
DEC. 29	38	40	41	42	36	36	15	40	11	42	17	13
DEC. 30	38	42	43	43	36	37	15	40	11	42	17	13
DEC. 31	38	44	44	45	36	37	15	40	11	42	17	13

MOON 1 ☽ 12:01 A.M. TO 8:00 A.M.　　**MOON 2** ◑ 8:01 A.M. TO 4:00 P.M.　　**MOON 3** ● 4:01 P.M. TO 12:00 A.M.

Use only one "moon" number. Choose the column closest to your time of birth. If your place of birth is not on Eastern Standard Time, be sure to read "How to Convert to Eastern Standard Time" at the beginning of this section.

1914

January

February

Date & Time	SUN	MOON 1	MOON 2	MOON 3	MERCURY	VENUS	MARS	JUPITER	SATURN	URANUS	NEPTUNE	PLUTO
JAN. 1	38	45	46	47	36	37	15	40	11	42	17	13
JAN. 2	38	47	48	48	37	37	15	40	11	42	17	13
JAN. 3	39	1	1	2	37	37	15	40	11	42	17	13
JAN. 4	39	2	3	3	37	37	15	40	11	42	17	13
JAN. 5	39	4	4	5	37	38	15	40	11	42	17	13
JAN. 6	39	5	6	6	37	38	15	40	11	42	17	13
JAN. 7	39	7	8	8	38	38	15	41	11	42	17	13
JAN. 8	39	9	9	10	38	38	15	41	11	42	17	13
JAN. 9	39	10	11	12	38	38	15	41	11	42	17	13
JAN. 10	40	12	13	13	38	38	15	41	11	42	17	13
JAN. 11	40	14	15	15	38	39	15	41	11	42	17	13
JAN. 12	40	16	16	17	39	39	15	41	11	42	17	13
JAN. 13	40	18	18	19	39	39	15	41	11	42	17	13
JAN. 14	40	20	20	21	39	39	14	41	11	42	17	13
JAN. 15	40	21	22	23	39	39	14	41	11	42	17	13
JAN. 16	40	23	24	25	40	39	14	41	11	42	17	13
JAN. 17	41	25	26	27	40	40	14	41	11	42	17	13
JAN. 18	41	27	28	28	40	40	14	41	11	42	17	13
JAN. 19	41	29	30	30	40	40	14	41	11	42	17	13
JAN. 20	41	31	32	32	40	40	14	41	11	42	17	13
JAN. 21	41	33	33	34	41	40	14	41	11	42	17	13
JAN. 22	41	35	35	36	41	40	14	41	11	42	17	13
JAN. 23	42	36	37	38	41	41	14	41	11	42	17	13
JAN. 24	42	38	39	39	41	41	14	41	11	42	17	13
JAN. 25	42	40	40	41	42	41	14	41	11	42	17	13
JAN. 26	42	42	42	43	42	41	14	41	10	42	17	13
JAN. 27	42	43	44	44	42	41	14	41	10	42	17	13
JAN. 28	42	45	45	46	42	41	14	41	10	42	17	13
JAN. 29	42	47	47	48	42	42	14	41	10	42	17	13
JAN. 30	42	48	1	1	43	42	14	41	10	42	16	13
JAN. 31	43	2	2	3	43	42	14	41	10	42	16	13

Date & Time	SUN	MOON 1	MOON 2	MOON 3	MERCURY	VENUS	MARS	JUPITER	SATURN	URANUS	NEPTUNE	PLUTO
FEB. 1	43	3	4	4	43	42	14	41	10	42	16	13
FEB. 2	43	5	5	6	43	42	14	41	10	42	16	13
FEB. 3	43	6	7	8	44	42	14	41	10	42	16	13
FEB. 4	43	8	9	9	44	43	14	41	10	42	16	13
FEB. 5	43	10	10	11	44	43	14	41	10	42	16	13
FEB. 6	43	11	12	13	44	43	14	41	10	42	16	13
FEB. 7	43	13	14	14	45	43	14	41	10	42	16	13
FEB. 8	44	15	16	16	45	43	14	42	10	42	16	13
FEB. 9	44	17	17	18	45	43	14	42	10	42	16	13
FEB. 10	44	19	19	20	45	44	14	42	10	42	16	13
FEB. 11	44	21	21	22	46	44	14	42	10	42	16	13
FEB. 12	44	23	23	24	46	44	14	42	10	42	16	13
FEB. 13	44	25	25	26	46	44	14	42	10	42	16	13
FEB. 14	44	27	27	28	46	44	14	42	10	42	16	13
FEB. 15	44	29	29	30	46	44	14	42	10	42	16	13
FEB. 16	45	30	31	32	47	45	14	42	10	42	16	13
FEB. 17	45	32	33	34	47	45	14	42	10	42	16	13
FEB. 18	45	34	35	35	47	45	14	42	10	42	16	13
FEB. 19	45	36	37	37	47	45	14	42	10	42	16	13
FEB. 20	45	38	38	39	47	45	14	42	10	42	16	13
FEB. 21	45	39	40	41	48	46	14	42	10	42	16	13
FEB. 22	45	41	42	42	48	46	14	42	10	42	16	13
FEB. 23	46	43	43	44	48	46	14	42	10	42	16	13
FEB. 24	46	44	45	46	48	46	14	42	10	42	16	13
FEB. 25	46	46	47	47	48	46	14	42	10	42	16	13
FEB. 26	46	48	48	1	48	46	14	42	10	42	16	13
FEB. 27	46	1	2	2	48	47	14	42	10	42	16	13
FEB. 28	46	3	3	4	48	47	14	42	10	42	16	13

MOON 1 ☽ 12:01 A.M. TO 8:00 A.M.   **MOON 2** ◑ 8:01 A.M. TO 4:00 P.M.   **MOON 3** ● 4:01 P.M. TO 12:00 A.M.

Use only one "moon" number. Choose the column closest to your time of birth. If your place of birth is not on Eastern Standard Time, be sure to read "How to Convert to Eastern Standard Time" at the beginning of this section.

March

April

Date & Time	SUN	MOON 1	MOON 2	MOON 3	MERCURY	VENUS	MARS	JUPITER	SATURN	URANUS	NEPTUNE	PLUTO
MAR. 1	46	4	5	5	48	47	14	42	10	42	16	13
MAR. 2	46	6	6	7	48	47	14	42	11	42	16	13
MAR. 3	47	8	8	9	48	47	14	42	11	42	16	13
MAR. 4	47	9	10	10	48	47	14	42	11	42	16	13
MAR. 5	47	11	11	12	48	48	14	42	11	42	16	13
MAR. 6	47	12	13	14	48	48	14	42	11	42	16	13
MAR. 7	47	14	15	15	48	48	14	42	11	42	16	13
MAR. 8	47	16	17	17	48	48	14	42	11	42	16	13
MAR. 9	47	18	19	19	48	48	14	42	11	42	16	13
MAR. 10	47	20	20	21	48	48	14	42	11	42	16	13
MAR. 11	48	22	22	23	47	48	14	42	11	42	16	13
MAR. 12	48	24	24	25	47	1	14	42	11	42	16	13
MAR. 13	48	26	26	27	47	1	14	42	11	42	16	13
MAR. 14	48	28	28	29	47	1	14	43	11	42	16	13
MAR. 15	48	30	30	31	47	1	14	43	11	42	16	13
MAR. 16	48	32	32	33	47	1	14	43	11	42	16	13
MAR. 17	48	34	34	35	47	1	14	43	11	42	16	13
MAR. 18	48	36	36	37	47	2	14	43	11	42	16	13
MAR. 19	1	37	38	38	47	2	15	43	11	42	16	13
MAR. 20	1	39	40	40	47	2	15	43	11	42	16	13
MAR. 21	1	41	41	42	46	2	15	43	11	42	16	13
MAR. 22	1	42	43	43	46	2	15	43	11	42	16	13
MAR. 23	1	44	45	45	46	2	15	43	11	42	16	13
MAR. 24	1	46	46	47	46	3	15	43	11	42	16	13
MAR. 25	2	47	48	48	46	3	15	43	11	42	16	13
MAR. 26	2	1	1	2	46	3	15	43	11	42	16	13
MAR. 27	2	2	3	3	46	3	15	43	11	42	16	13
MAR. 28	2	4	4	5	47	3	15	43	11	42	16	13
MAR. 29	2	6	6	7	47	3	15	43	11	42	16	13
MAR. 30	2	7	8	8	47	4	15	43	11	42	16	13
MAR. 31	2	9	9	10	47	4	15	43	11	42	16	13

Date & Time	SUN	MOON 1	MOON 2	MOON 3	MERCURY	VENUS	MARS	JUPITER	SATURN	URANUS	NEPTUNE	PLUTO
APR. 1	2	10	11	11	47	4	15	43	11	42	16	13
APR. 2	2	12	13	13	47	4	15	43	11	42	16	13
APR. 3	3	14	14	15	47	4	15	43	11	42	16	13
APR. 4	3	15	16	17	47	4	15	43	11	42	16	13
APR. 5	3	17	18	18	47	5	15	43	11	42	16	13
APR. 6	3	19	20	20	47	5	15	43	11	42	16	13
APR. 7	3	21	22	22	47	5	15	43	11	42	16	13
APR. 8	3	23	24	24	48	5	16	43	11	42	16	13
APR. 9	3	25	26	26	48	5	16	43	11	42	16	13
APR. 10	3	27	28	28	48	5	16	43	11	42	16	13
APR. 11	4	29	30	30	48	6	16	43	11	42	16	13
APR. 12	4	31	32	32	48	6	16	43	11	42	16	13
APR. 13	4	33	34	34	48	6	16	43	11	42	16	13
APR. 14	4	35	35	36	1	6	16	43	11	42	16	13
APR. 15	4	37	37	38	1	6	16	43	11	42	16	13
APR. 16	4	39	39	40	1	6	16	43	11	42	16	13
APR. 17	4	40	41	41	1	7	16	43	11	42	16	13
APR. 18	4	42	43	43	1	7	16	43	11	42	16	13
APR. 19	5	44	44	45	1	7	16	43	11	42	16	13
APR. 20	5	45	46	46	2	7	16	43	11	42	16	13
APR. 21	5	47	47	48	2	7	16	43	11	42	16	13
APR. 22	5	48	1	1	2	7	16	43	11	42	16	13
APR. 23	5	2	3	3	2	8	16	43	11	42	16	13
APR. 24	5	4	4	5	2	8	16	43	11	42	16	13
APR. 25	6	5	6	6	3	8	17	43	11	42	16	13
APR. 26	6	7	7	8	3	8	17	44	11	42	16	13
APR. 27	6	8	9	9	3	8	17	44	11	42	16	13
APR. 28	6	10	10	11	3	8	17	44	11	42	16	13
APR. 29	6	12	12	13	4	9	17	44	11	42	16	13
APR. 30	6	13	14	14	4	9	17	44	11	43	16	13

MOON 1 ☽ 12:01 A.M. TO 8:00 A.M.   **MOON 2** ◑ 8:01 A.M. TO 4:00 P.M.   **MOON 3** ● 4:01 P.M. TO 12:00 A.M.

Use only one "moon" number. Choose the column closest to your time of birth. If your place of birth is not on Eastern Standard Time, be sure to read "How to Convert to Eastern Standard Time" at the beginning of this section.

May

June

Date & Time	SUN	MOON 1	MOON 2	MOON 3	MERCURY	VENUS	MARS	JUPITER	SATURN	URANUS	NEPTUNE	PLUTO
MAY 1	6	15	16	16	4	9	17	44	11	43	16	13
MAY 2	6	17	17	18	4	9	17	44	11	43	16	13
MAY 3	7	18	19	20	5	9	17	44	11	43	16	13
MAY 4	7	20	21	22	5	9	17	44	11	43	16	13
MAY 5	7	22	23	23	5	10	17	44	11	43	16	13
MAY 6	7	24	25	25	5	10	17	44	11	43	16	13
MAY 7	7	26	27	27	6	10	17	44	11	43	16	13
MAY 8	7	28	29	29	6	10	17	44	11	43	16	13
MAY 9	7	30	31	31	6	10	17	44	11	43	16	13
MAY 10	7	32	33	33	6	10	18	44	11	43	16	13
MAY 11	8	34	35	35	7	11	18	44	11	43	16	13
MAY 12	8	36	37	37	7	11	18	44	11	43	16	13
MAY 13	8	38	38	39	7	11	18	44	11	43	16	13
MAY 14	8	40	40	41	7	11	18	44	11	43	16	13
MAY 15	8	41	42	43	8	11	18	44	11	43	16	13
MAY 16	8	43	44	44	8	11	18	44	11	43	16	13
MAY 17	8	45	45	46	8	12	18	44	11	43	16	13
MAY 18	8	46	47	47	9	12	18	44	11	43	16	13
MAY 19	9	48	1	1	9	12	18	44	11	43	16	13
MAY 20	9	2	2	3	9	12	18	44	11	43	16	13
MAY 21	9	3	4	4	9	12	18	44	11	43	16	13
MAY 22	9	5	5	6	10	12	18	44	11	43	16	13
MAY 23	9	6	7	7	10	12	18	44	11	43	16	13
MAY 24	9	8	8	9	10	13	19	44	12	43	16	13
MAY 25	10	10	10	11	11	13	19	44	12	43	16	13
MAY 26	10	11	12	12	11	13	19	44	12	43	16	13
MAY 27	10	13	13	14	11	13	19	44	12	43	16	13
MAY 28	10	15	15	16	11	13	19	44	12	43	16	13
MAY 29	10	16	17	17	12	13	19	44	12	43	16	13
MAY 30	10	18	19	19	12	14	19	44	12	43	16	13
MAY 31	10	20	20	21	12	14	19	44	12	43	16	13

Date & Time	SUN	MOON 1	MOON 2	MOON 3	MERCURY	VENUS	MARS	JUPITER	SATURN	URANUS	NEPTUNE	PLUTO
JUN. 1	10	22	22	23	12	14	19	44	12	43	16	13
JUN. 2	10	23	24	25	13	14	19	44	12	43	16	13
JUN. 3	11	25	26	27	13	14	19	44	12	43	16	13
JUN. 4	11	27	28	29	13	14	19	44	12	42	16	13
JUN. 5	11	29	30	31	13	15	19	44	12	42	16	13
JUN. 6	11	31	32	33	14	15	19	44	12	42	16	13
JUN. 7	11	33	34	35	14	15	20	44	12	42	16	13
JUN. 8	11	35	36	36	14	15	20	44	12	42	16	13
JUN. 9	11	37	38	38	14	15	20	44	12	42	16	13
JUN. 10	11	39	40	40	14	15	20	44	12	42	17	13
JUN. 11	12	41	41	42	15	16	20	44	12	42	17	13
JUN. 12	12	43	43	44	15	16	20	44	12	42	17	13
JUN. 13	12	44	45	45	15	16	20	44	12	42	17	13
JUN. 14	12	46	46	47	15	16	20	44	12	42	17	13
JUN. 15	12	47	48	1	15	16	20	44	12	42	17	13
JUN. 16	12	1	2	2	15	16	20	44	12	42	17	13
JUN. 17	12	3	3	4	16	16	20	44	12	42	17	13
JUN. 18	12	4	5	5	16	17	20	44	12	42	17	13
JUN. 19	13	6	6	7	16	17	20	44	12	42	17	13
JUN. 20	13	7	8	9	16	17	21	44	12	42	17	13
JUN. 21	13	9	10	10	16	17	21	44	12	42	17	13
JUN. 22	13	11	11	12	16	17	21	44	12	42	17	13
JUN. 23	13	12	13	14	16	17	21	44	12	42	17	13
JUN. 24	13	14	15	15	17	18	21	44	12	42	17	13
JUN. 25	14	16	16	17	17	18	21	44	12	42	17	13
JUN. 26	14	18	18	19	17	18	21	44	12	42	17	13
JUN. 27	14	19	20	21	17	18	21	44	12	42	17	13
JUN. 28	14	21	22	22	17	18	21	44	12	42	17	13
JUN. 29	14	23	24	24	17	18	21	44	12	42	17	13
JUN. 30	14	25	26	26	17	19	21	44	12	42	17	13

MOON 1 ◗ 12:01 A.M. TO 8:00 A.M.   **MOON 2** ◖ 8:01 A.M. TO 4:00 P.M.   **MOON 3** ● 4:01 P.M. TO 12:00 A.M.

Use only one "moon" number. Choose the column closest to your time of birth. If your place of birth is not on Eastern Standard Time, be sure to read "How to Convert to Eastern Standard Time" at the beginning of this section.

1914

July

Date & Time	SUN	MOON 1	MOON 2	MOON 3	MERCURY	VENUS	MARS	JUPITER	SATURN	URANUS	NEPTUNE	PLUTO
JUL. 1	14	27	27	28	17	19	21	44	12	42	17	13
JUL. 2	14	29	29	30	17	19	21	44	12	42	17	13
JUL. 3	15	31	31	32	17	19	22	44	12	42	17	13
JUL. 4	15	33	33	34	17	19	22	44	12	42	17	13
JUL. 5	15	34	35	36	17	19	22	44	12	42	17	13
JUL. 6	15	36	37	38	17	20	22	44	12	42	17	13
JUL. 7	15	38	39	39	17	20	22	44	12	42	17	13
JUL. 8	15	40	41	41	17	20	22	44	12	42	17	13
JUL. 9	15	42	42	43	17	20	22	44	12	42	17	13
JUL. 10	15	44	44	45	17	20	22	44	12	42	17	13
JUL. 11	16	45	46	46	17	20	22	44	12	42	17	13
JUL. 12	16	47	47	48	16	20	22	44	12	42	17	13
JUL. 13	16	1	1	2	16	21	22	44	12	42	17	13
JUL. 14	16	2	3	3	16	21	22	44	12	42	17	13
JUL. 15	16	4	4	5	16	21	22	44	12	42	17	13
JUL. 16	16	5	6	6	16	21	23	44	12	42	17	13
JUL. 17	16	7	7	8	16	21	23	44	12	42	17	13
JUL. 18	16	9	9	10	16	21	23	44	12	42	17	13
JUL. 19	17	10	11	11	16	22	23	44	12	42	17	13
JUL. 20	17	12	12	13	16	22	23	44	12	42	17	13
JUL. 21	17	14	14	15	16	22	23	44	12	42	17	13
JUL. 22	17	15	15	16	16	22	23	43	13	42	17	13
JUL. 23	17	17	18	16	16	22	23	44	13	42	17	13
JUL. 24	17	19	19	20	16	22	23	44	13	42	17	13
JUL. 25	17	21	21	22	16	22	23	44	13	42	17	13
JUL. 26	18	23	23	24	15	23	23	44	13	42	17	13
JUL. 27	18	24	25	26	15	23	23	44	13	42	17	13
JUL. 28	18	26	27	28	15	23	24	44	13	42	17	13
JUL. 29	18	28	29	30	16	23	24	43	13	42	17	13
JUL. 30	18	30	31	31	16	23	24	43	13	42	17	13
JUL. 31	18	32	33	33	16	23	24	43	13	42	17	13

August

Date & Time	SUN	MOON 1	MOON 2	MOON 3	MERCURY	VENUS	MARS	JUPITER	SATURN	URANUS	NEPTUNE	PLUTO
AUG. 1	18	34	35	35	16	24	24	43	13	42	17	13
AUG. 2	18	36	36	37	16	24	24	43	13	42	17	13
AUG. 3	19	38	38	39	16	24	24	43	13	42	17	13
AUG. 4	19	39	40	41	16	24	24	43	13	42	17	13
AUG. 5	19	41	42	42	16	24	24	43	13	42	17	13
AUG. 6	19	43	44	44	16	24	24	43	13	42	17	13
AUG. 7	19	45	45	46	16	24	24	43	13	42	17	13
AUG. 8	19	46	47	47	16	25	24	43	13	42	17	13
AUG. 9	19	48	1	1	17	25	25	43	13	42	17	13
AUG. 10	19	2	2	3	17	25	25	43	13	42	17	13
AUG. 11	20	3	4	4	17	25	25	43	13	42	17	13
AUG. 12	20	5	5	6	17	25	25	43	13	42	17	13
AUG. 13	20	6	7	7	17	25	25	43	13	42	17	13
AUG. 14	20	8	8	9	18	25	25	43	13	42	17	13
AUG. 15	20	10	10	11	18	26	25	43	13	42	17	13
AUG. 16	20	11	12	12	18	26	25	43	13	42	17	13
AUG. 17	20	13	13	14	18	26	25	43	13	42	17	13
AUG. 18	20	15	15	16	19	26	25	43	13	42	17	13
AUG. 19	21	16	17	17	19	26	25	43	13	42	17	13
AUG. 20	21	18	19	19	19	26	25	43	13	42	17	13
AUG. 21	21	20	21	21	19	27	26	43	13	42	17	13
AUG. 22	21	22	23	23	20	27	26	43	13	42	17	13
AUG. 23	21	24	25	25	20	27	26	43	13	42	17	13
AUG. 24	21	26	26	27	20	27	26	43	13	42	17	13
AUG. 25	21	28	28	29	20	27	26	43	13	42	17	13
AUG. 26	22	30	30	31	21	27	26	43	13	42	17	13
AUG. 27	22	32	32	33	21	27	26	43	13	42	17	13
AUG. 28	22	34	34	35	21	28	26	43	13	42	17	13
AUG. 29	22	35	36	37	21	28	26	43	13	42	17	13
AUG. 30	22	37	38	38	22	28	26	43	13	42	17	13
AUG. 31	22	39	40	40	22	28	26	43	13	42	17	13

MOON 1 ☾ 12:01 A.M. TO 8:00 A.M.   **MOON 2** ☽ 8:01 A.M. TO 4:00 P.M.   **MOON 3** ● 4:01 P.M. TO 12:00 A.M.
Use only one "moon" number. Choose the column closest to your time of birth. If your place of birth is not on Eastern Standard Time, be sure to read "How to Convert to Eastern Standard Time" at the beginning of this section.

1914

September

October

Date & Time	SUN	MOON 1	MOON 2	MOON 3	MERCURY	VENUS	MARS	JUPITER	SATURN	URANUS	NEPTUNE	PLUTO
SEP. 1	22	41	41	42	22	28	26	43	13	42	17	13
SEP. 2	22	42	43	44	22	28	27	43	13	42	17	13
SEP. 3	23	44	45	45	23	28	27	43	13	42	17	13
SEP. 4	23	46	46	47	23	29	27	43	13	42	17	13
SEP. 5	23	47	48	1	23	29	27	43	13	42	17	13
SEP. 6	23	1	2	2	23	29	27	43	13	42	17	13
SEP. 7	23	3	3	4	24	29	27	43	13	42	17	13
SEP. 8	23	4	5	5	24	29	27	43	13	42	17	13
SEP. 9	23	6	6	7	24	29	27	43	13	42	17	13
SEP. 10	23	7	8	9	24	29	27	43	13	42	17	13
SEP. 11	24	9	10	10	25	29	27	43	13	42	17	13
SEP. 12	24	11	11	12	25	30	27	43	13	42	17	13
SEP. 13	24	12	13	13	25	30	28	43	13	42	17	13
SEP. 14	24	14	15	15	25	30	28	43	13	42	17	13
SEP. 15	24	16	16	17	26	30	28	43	13	42	17	13
SEP. 16	24	17	18	19	26	30	28	43	13	42	17	13
SEP. 17	24	19	20	21	26	30	28	43	13	42	17	13
SEP. 18	24	21	22	22	26	30	28	43	13	42	17	13
SEP. 19	25	23	24	24	26	31	28	43	13	42	17	13
SEP. 20	25	25	26	26	27	31	28	43	13	42	17	13
SEP. 21	25	27	28	28	27	31	28	43	13	42	17	13
SEP. 22	25	29	30	30	27	31	28	43	13	42	17	13
SEP. 23	25	31	32	32	27	31	28	43	13	42	17	13
SEP. 24	25	33	34	34	27	31	28	43	13	42	17	13
SEP. 25	26	35	36	36	28	31	29	43	13	42	17	13
SEP. 26	26	37	37	38	28	31	29	43	13	42	17	13
SEP. 27	26	39	39	40	28	32	29	43	13	42	17	13
SEP. 28	26	40	41	41	28	32	29	43	13	42	17	13
SEP. 29	26	42	43	43	28	32	29	43	13	42	17	13
SEP. 30	26	44	44	45	29	32	29	43	13	42	17	13

Date & Time	SUN	MOON 1	MOON 2	MOON 3	MERCURY	VENUS	MARS	JUPITER	SATURN	URANUS	NEPTUNE	PLUTO
OCT. 1	26	45	46	47	29	32	29	43	13	42	17	13
OCT. 2	26	47	48	48	29	32	29	43	13	42	17	13
OCT. 3	27	1	1	2	29	32	29	43	13	42	17	13
OCT. 4	27	2	3	3	29	32	29	43	13	42	17	13
OCT. 5	27	4	4	5	29	32	29	43	13	42	17	13
OCT. 6	27	5	6	6	30	33	30	43	13	42	17	13
OCT. 7	27	7	8	8	30	33	30	43	13	42	17	13
OCT. 8	27	9	9	10	30	33	30	43	13	42	17	13
OCT. 9	27	10	11	11	30	33	30	43	13	42	17	13
OCT. 10	27	12	12	13	30	33	30	43	13	42	17	13
OCT. 11	28	13	14	15	30	33	30	43	13	42	17	13
OCT. 12	28	15	16	16	31	33	30	43	13	42	17	13
OCT. 13	28	17	17	18	31	33	30	43	13	42	17	13
OCT. 14	28	19	19	20	31	33	30	43	13	42	17	13
OCT. 15	28	20	21	22	31	33	30	43	13	42	17	13
OCT. 16	28	22	23	24	31	34	30	43	13	42	17	13
OCT. 17	28	24	25	25	31	34	31	43	13	42	17	13
OCT. 18	28	26	27	27	31	34	31	43	13	42	17	13
OCT. 19	29	28	29	30	32	34	31	43	13	42	17	13
OCT. 20	29	30	31	32	32	34	31	43	13	42	17	13
OCT. 21	29	32	33	34	32	34	31	43	13	42	17	13
OCT. 22	29	34	35	36	32	34	31	43	13	42	17	13
OCT. 23	29	36	37	37	32	34	31	43	13	42	17	13
OCT. 24	29	38	39	39	32	34	31	43	13	42	17	13
OCT. 25	29	40	40	41	32	34	31	43	13	42	17	13
OCT. 26	30	42	42	43	32	34	31	43	13	42	17	13
OCT. 27	30	43	44	44	32	34	32	43	13	42	17	13
OCT. 28	30	45	46	46	32	34	32	43	13	42	17	13
OCT. 29	30	47	47	48	32	34	32	43	13	42	17	13
OCT. 30	30	48	1	1	32	34	32	43	13	42	17	13
OCT. 31	30	2	2	3	32	34	32	43	13	42	17	13

MOON 1 ☽ 12:01 A.M. TO 8:00 A.M.   **MOON 2** ◑ 8:01 A.M. TO 4:00 P.M.   **MOON 3** ● 4:01 P.M. TO 12:00 A.M.

Use only one "moon" number. Choose the column closest to your time of birth. If your place of birth is not on Eastern Standard Time, be sure to read "How to Convert to Eastern Standard Time" at the beginning of this section.

1914

November

Date & Time	SUN	MOON 1	MOON 2	MOON 3	MERCURY	VENUS	MARS	JUPITER	SATURN	URANUS	NEPTUNE	PLUTO
NOV. 1	30	3	4	4	32	35	32	43	13	42	17	13
NOV. 2	30	5	6	6	32	35	32	43	13	42	17	13
NOV. 3	31	7	7	8	32	35	32	43	13	42	17	13
NOV. 4	31	8	9	9	31	35	32	43	13	42	17	13
NOV. 5	31	10	10	11	31	35	32	43	13	42	17	13
NOV. 6	31	11	12	12	31	35	32	43	13	42	17	13
NOV. 7	31	13	14	14	31	35	33	43	13	42	17	13
NOV. 8	31	15	15	16	31	35	33	43	13	42	17	13
NOV. 9	31	16	17	17	31	35	33	43	13	42	17	13
NOV. 10	31	18	19	19	30	35	33	43	13	42	17	13
NOV. 11	31	20	20	21	30	35	33	43	13	42	17	13
NOV. 12	32	22	22	23	30	35	33	43	13	42	17	13
NOV. 13	32	23	24	25	30	35	33	43	13	42	17	13
NOV. 14	32	25	26	27	30	34	33	43	13	42	17	13
NOV. 15	32	27	28	29	30	34	33	43	13	42	17	13
NOV. 16	32	29	30	31	30	34	33	43	13	42	17	13
NOV. 17	32	31	32	33	30	34	34	43	13	42	17	13
NOV. 18	32	33	34	35	30	34	34	43	13	42	17	13
NOV. 19	33	35	36	37	30	34	34	43	13	42	17	13
NOV. 20	33	37	38	39	30	34	34	43	13	42	17	13
NOV. 21	33	39	40	40	30	34	34	43	13	42	17	13
NOV. 22	33	41	42	42	30	34	34	43	13	42	17	13
NOV. 23	33	43	43	44	30	34	34	43	13	42	17	13
NOV. 24	33	45	45	46	30	34	34	43	13	42	17	13
NOV. 25	34	46	47	47	31	34	34	43	13	42	17	13
NOV. 26	34	48	48	1	31	34	34	43	13	42	17	13
NOV. 27	34	1	2	3	31	34	34	43	13	42	17	13
NOV. 28	34	3	4	4	31	34	35	43	13	42	17	13
NOV. 29	34	5	5	6	31	33	35	43	13	42	17	13
NOV. 30	34	6	7	7	31	33	35	43	13	42	17	13

December

Date & Time	SUN	MOON 1	MOON 2	MOON 3	MERCURY	VENUS	MARS	JUPITER	SATURN	URANUS	NEPTUNE	PLUTO
DEC. 1	34	8	8	9	32	33	35	43	13	42	17	13
DEC. 2	34	9	10	10	32	33	35	43	13	42	17	13
DEC. 3	35	11	12	12	32	33	35	43	13	42	17	13
DEC. 4	35	13	13	14	32	33	35	43	13	42	17	13
DEC. 5	35	14	15	15	32	33	35	43	13	42	17	13
DEC. 6	35	16	16	17	33	33	35	43	13	42	17	13
DEC. 7	35	18	18	19	33	33	35	43	13	42	17	13
DEC. 8	35	19	20	20	33	33	36	43	13	42	17	13
DEC. 9	35	21	22	22	33	33	36	43	13	42	17	13
DEC. 10	35	23	23	24	33	33	36	43	13	42	17	13
DEC. 11	36	25	25	26	34	33	36	43	13	42	17	13
DEC. 12	36	27	27	28	34	33	36	43	13	42	17	13
DEC. 13	36	28	29	30	34	33	36	43	13	42	17	13
DEC. 14	36	30	31	32	34	33	36	43	13	42	17	13
DEC. 15	36	32	33	34	34	33	36	44	13	42	17	13
DEC. 16	36	34	35	36	35	33	36	44	13	42	17	13
DEC. 17	36	36	37	38	35	33	36	44	13	42	17	13
DEC. 18	36	38	39	40	35	33	37	44	13	42	17	13
DEC. 19	37	40	41	42	35	33	37	44	13	42	17	13
DEC. 20	37	42	43	43	35	33	37	44	13	42	17	13
DEC. 21	37	44	45	45	36	33	37	44	13	42	17	13
DEC. 22	37	46	46	47	36	33	37	44	13	42	17	13
DEC. 23	37	47	48	48	36	33	37	44	13	42	17	13
DEC. 24	37	1	2	2	36	33	37	44	13	42	17	13
DEC. 25	37	3	3	4	36	33	37	44	13	42	17	13
DEC. 26	38	4	5	5	37	33	37	44	13	42	17	13
DEC. 27	38	6	6	7	37	33	37	44	13	42	17	13
DEC. 28	38	7	8	8	37	33	38	44	13	42	17	13
DEC. 29	38	9	9	10	37	33	38	44	13	42	17	13
DEC. 30	38	11	11	12	37	33	38	44	13	42	17	13
DEC. 31	38	12	13	13	38	33	38	44	13	42	17	13

MOON 1 ☽ 12:01 A.M. TO 8:00 A.M.   **MOON 2** ☽ 8:01 A.M. TO 4:00 P.M.   **MOON 3** ● 4:01 P.M. TO 12:00 A.M.

Use only one "moon" number. Choose the column closest to your time of birth. If your place of birth is not on Eastern Standard Time, be sure to read "How to Convert to Eastern Standard Time" at the beginning of this section.

1915

January

February

Date & Time	SUN	MOON 1	MOON 2	MOON 3	MERCURY	VENUS	MARS	JUPITER	SATURN	URANUS	NEPTUNE	PLUTO
JAN. 1	38	14	14	15	38	33	38	44	13	42	17	13
JAN. 2	38	15	16	17	38	33	38	44	13	42	17	13
JAN. 3	39	17	18	18	38	33	38	44	13	42	17	13
JAN. 4	39	19	19	20	39	33	38	44	13	42	17	13
JAN. 5	39	21	21	22	39	33	38	44	13	42	17	13
JAN. 6	39	22	23	24	39	33	38	44	13	42	17	13
JAN. 7	39	24	25	25	39	33	39	44	13	42	17	13
JAN. 8	39	26	27	27	39	34	39	44	13	42	17	13
JAN. 9	39	28	29	29	40	34	39	44	13	42	17	13
JAN. 10	40	30	30	31	40	34	39	44	13	42	17	13
JAN. 11	40	32	32	33	40	34	39	44	13	42	17	13
JAN. 12	40	34	34	35	40	34	39	44	13	42	17	13
JAN. 13	40	36	36	37	41	34	39	44	13	42	17	13
JAN. 14	40	38	38	39	41	34	39	44	13	42	17	13
JAN. 15	40	39	40	41	41	34	39	44	13	42	17	13
JAN. 16	40	41	42	43	41	34	40	44	13	42	17	13
JAN. 17	41	43	44	44	41	34	40	44	13	42	17	13
JAN. 18	41	45	46	46	42	35	40	44	13	42	17	13
JAN. 19	41	47	47	48	42	35	40	44	13	42	17	13
JAN. 20	41	48	1	1	42	35	40	45	13	42	17	13
JAN. 21	41	2	3	3	42	35	40	45	13	42	17	13
JAN. 22	41	4	4	5	43	35	40	45	12	42	17	13
JAN. 23	42	5	6	6	43	35	40	45	12	42	17	13
JAN. 24	42	7	7	8	43	35	40	45	12	42	17	13
JAN. 25	42	8	9	9	43	35	40	45	12	42	17	13
JAN. 26	42	10	11	11	43	35	41	45	12	42	17	13
JAN. 27	42	12	12	13	44	36	41	45	12	42	17	13
JAN. 28	42	13	14	14	44	36	41	45	12	42	17	13
JAN. 29	42	15	15	16	44	36	41	45	12	42	17	13
JAN. 30	42	17	17	18	44	36	41	45	12	42	17	13
JAN. 31	43	18	19	20	45	36	41	45	12	43	17	13

Date & Time	SUN	MOON 1	MOON 2	MOON 3	MERCURY	VENUS	MARS	JUPITER	SATURN	URANUS	NEPTUNE	PLUTO
FEB. 1	43	20	21	21	45	36	41	45	12	43	17	13
FEB. 2	43	22	23	23	45	36	41	45	12	43	17	13
FEB. 3	43	24	24	25	45	37	41	45	12	43	17	13
FEB. 4	43	26	26	27	45	37	41	45	12	43	17	13
FEB. 5	43	27	28	29	45	37	42	45	12	43	17	13
FEB. 6	43	29	30	31	46	37	42	45	12	43	17	13
FEB. 7	43	31	32	33	46	37	42	45	12	43	17	13
FEB. 8	44	33	34	34	46	37	42	45	12	43	17	13
FEB. 9	44	35	36	36	46	37	42	45	12	43	17	13
FEB. 10	44	37	38	38	46	37	42	45	12	43	17	13
FEB. 11	44	39	39	40	46	38	42	45	12	43	17	13
FEB. 12	44	41	41	42	46	38	42	45	12	43	17	13
FEB. 13	44	42	43	44	46	38	42	45	12	43	17	13
FEB. 14	44	44	45	45	46	38	43	45	12	43	17	13
FEB. 15	44	46	47	47	46	38	43	45	12	43	17	13
FEB. 16	45	48	48	1	46	38	43	45	12	43	17	13
FEB. 17	45	1	2	2	46	38	43	45	12	43	17	13
FEB. 18	45	3	4	4	46	39	43	45	12	43	17	13
FEB. 19	45	5	5	6	46	39	43	45	12	43	17	13
FEB. 20	45	6	7	7	45	39	43	45	12	43	17	13
FEB. 21	45	8	8	9	45	39	43	46	12	43	17	13
FEB. 22	45	9	10	10	45	39	43	46	12	43	17	13
FEB. 23	46	11	12	12	45	39	44	46	12	43	17	13
FEB. 24	46	13	13	14	45	39	44	46	12	43	17	13
FEB. 25	46	14	15	15	45	40	44	46	12	43	17	13
FEB. 26	46	16	17	17	45	40	44	46	12	43	17	13
FEB. 27	46	18	18	19	44	40	44	46	12	43	17	13
FEB. 28	46	19	20	21	44	40	44	46	12	43	17	13

MOON 1 ☽ 12:01 A.M. TO 8:00 A.M.   **MOON 2** ☽ 8:01 A.M. TO 4:00 P.M.   **MOON 3** ● 4:01 P.M. TO 12:00 A.M.

Use only one "moon" number. Choose the column closest to your time of birth. If your place of birth is not on Eastern Standard Time, be sure to read "How to Convert to Eastern Standard Time" at the beginning of this section.

1915

March

Date & Time	SUN	MOON 1	MOON 2	MOON 3	MERCURY	VENUS	MARS	JUPITER	SATURN	URANUS	NEPTUNE	PLUTO
MAR. 1	46	21	22	23	44	40	44	46	12	43	17	13
MAR. 2	46	23	24	24	44	40	44	46	12	43	17	13
MAR. 3	47	25	26	26	44	40	44	46	12	43	17	13
MAR. 4	47	27	28	28	44	41	44	46	12	43	17	13
MAR. 5	47	29	30	30	44	41	45	46	12	43	17	13
MAR. 6	47	31	31	32	44	41	45	46	12	43	17	13
MAR. 7	47	33	33	34	44	41	45	46	12	43	17	13
MAR. 8	47	35	35	36	44	41	45	46	12	43	17	13
MAR. 9	47	37	37	38	44	41	45	46	12	43	17	13
MAR. 10	47	38	39	40	44	42	45	46	12	43	17	13
MAR. 11	48	40	41	41	44	42	45	46	12	43	17	13
MAR. 12	48	42	43	43	44	42	45	46	12	43	17	13
MAR. 13	48	44	44	45	44	42	45	46	12	43	17	13
MAR. 14	48	45	46	47	44	42	45	46	12	43	17	13
MAR. 15	48	47	48	48	44	42	46	46	12	43	17	13
MAR. 16	48	1	1	2	45	42	46	46	12	43	17	13
MAR. 17	48	2	3	4	45	43	46	46	12	43	17	13
MAR. 18	48	4	5	5	45	43	46	46	12	43	17	13
MAR. 19	1	6	6	7	45	43	46	46	12	43	17	13
MAR. 20	1	7	8	8	45	43	46	46	12	43	17	13
MAR. 21	1	9	9	10	45	43	46	46	12	43	17	13
MAR. 22	1	10	11	12	45	43	46	46	12	43	17	13
MAR. 23	1	12	13	13	45	44	46	46	12	43	17	13
MAR. 24	1	14	14	15	46	44	47	47	12	43	17	13
MAR. 25	2	15	16	16	46	44	47	47	12	43	17	13
MAR. 26	2	17	18	18	46	44	47	47	12	43	17	13
MAR. 27	2	19	19	20	46	44	47	47	12	43	17	13
MAR. 28	2	20	21	22	46	44	47	47	12	43	17	13
MAR. 29	2	22	23	24	46	44	47	47	12	43	17	13
MAR. 30	2	24	25	26	47	45	47	47	12	43	17	13
MAR. 31	2	26	27	27	47	45	47	47	12	43	17	13

April

Date & Time	SUN	MOON 1	MOON 2	MOON 3	MERCURY	VENUS	MARS	JUPITER	SATURN	URANUS	NEPTUNE	PLUTO
APR. 1	2	28	29	29	47	45	47	47	12	43	17	13
APR. 2	2	30	31	31	47	45	47	47	12	43	17	13
APR. 3	3	32	33	33	47	45	48	47	13	43	17	13
APR. 4	3	34	35	35	48	45	48	47	13	43	17	13
APR. 5	3	36	37	37	48	46	48	47	13	43	17	13
APR. 6	3	38	39	39	48	46	48	47	13	43	17	13
APR. 7	3	40	40	41	48	46	48	47	13	43	17	13
APR. 8	3	42	42	43	48	46	48	47	13	43	17	13
APR. 9	3	43	44	44	1	46	48	47	13	43	17	13
APR. 10	3	45	46	46	1	46	48	47	13	43	17	13
APR. 11	4	47	47	48	1	46	48	47	13	43	17	13
APR. 12	4	48	1	1	1	47	48	47	13	43	17	13
APR. 13	4	2	3	3	2	47	1	47	13	43	17	13
APR. 14	4	4	4	5	2	47	1	47	13	43	17	13
APR. 15	4	5	6	6	2	47	1	47	13	43	17	13
APR. 16	4	7	7	8	2	47	1	47	13	43	17	13
APR. 17	4	8	9	9	2	47	1	47	13	43	17	13
APR. 18	4	10	11	11	3	48	1	47	13	43	17	13
APR. 19	5	12	12	13	3	48	1	47	13	43	17	13
APR. 20	5	13	14	14	3	48	1	47	13	43	17	13
APR. 21	5	15	15	16	3	48	1	47	13	43	17	13
APR. 22	5	16	17	18	4	48	2	47	13	43	17	13
APR. 23	5	18	19	19	4	48	2	47	13	43	17	13
APR. 24	5	20	20	21	4	1	2	47	13	43	17	13
APR. 25	6	22	22	23	5	1	2	47	13	43	17	13
APR. 26	6	23	24	25	5	1	2	47	13	43	17	13
APR. 27	6	25	26	27	5	1	2	48	13	43	17	13
APR. 28	6	27	28	29	5	1	2	48	13	43	17	13
APR. 29	6	29	30	31	6	1	2	48	13	43	17	13
APR. 30	6	31	32	33	6	1	2	48	13	43	17	13

MOON 1 ◗ 12:01 A.M. TO 8:00 A.M.   **MOON 2** ◑ 8:01 A.M. TO 4:00 P.M.   **MOON 3** ● 4:01 P.M. TO 12:00 A.M.

Use only one "moon" number. Choose the column closest to your time of birth. If your place of birth is not on Eastern Standard Time, be sure to read "How to Convert to Eastern Standard Time" at the beginning of this section.

1915

May

Date & Time	☉ SUN	☽ MOON 1	◑ MOON 2	● MOON 3	MERCURY	VENUS	MARS	JUPITER	SATURN	URANUS	NEPTUNE	PLUTO
MAY 1	6	33	34	35	6	2	2	48	13	43	17	13
MAY 2	6	35	36	37	6	2	3	48	13	43	17	13
MAY 3	7	37	38	39	7	2	3	48	13	43	17	13
MAY 4	7	39	40	40	7	2	3	48	13	43	17	13
MAY 5	7	41	42	42	7	2	3	48	13	43	17	13
MAY 6	7	43	43	44	8	2	3	48	13	43	17	13
MAY 7	7	45	45	46	8	3	3	48	13	43	17	13
MAY 8	7	46	47	47	8	3	3	48	13	43	17	13
MAY 9	7	48	1	1	8	3	3	48	13	43	17	13
MAY 10	7	2	2	3	9	3	3	48	13	43	17	13
MAY 11	8	3	4	4	9	3	3	48	13	43	17	13
MAY 12	8	5	5	6	9	3	4	48	13	43	17	13
MAY 13	8	6	7	8	10	4	4	48	13	43	17	13
MAY 14	8	8	9	9	10	4	4	48	13	43	17	13
MAY 15	8	10	10	11	10	4	4	48	13	43	17	13
MAY 16	8	11	12	12	10	4	4	48	13	43	17	13
MAY 17	8	13	13	14	11	4	4	48	13	43	17	13
MAY 18	8	14	15	15	11	4	4	48	13	43	17	13
MAY 19	9	16	17	17	11	5	4	48	13	43	17	13
MAY 20	9	18	18	19	11	5	4	48	13	43	17	13
MAY 21	9	19	20	20	11	5	4	48	13	43	17	13
MAY 22	9	21	22	22	12	5	5	48	13	43	17	13
MAY 23	9	23	23	24	12	5	5	48	13	43	17	13
MAY 24	9	25	25	26	12	5	5	48	13	43	17	13
MAY 25	10	26	27	28	12	5	5	48	13	43	17	13
MAY 26	10	28	29	30	12	5	5	48	13	43	17	13
MAY 27	10	30	31	32	13	5	5	48	13	43	17	13
MAY 28	10	32	33	34	13	5	5	48	13	43	17	13
MAY 29	10	34	35	36	13	5	5	48	13	43	17	13
MAY 30	10	36	37	38	13	6	5	48	13	43	17	13
MAY 31	10	38	39	40	13	6	5	48	13	43	17	13

June

Date & Time	☉ SUN	☽ MOON 1	◑ MOON 2	● MOON 3	MERCURY	VENUS	MARS	JUPITER	SATURN	URANUS	NEPTUNE	PLUTO
JUN. 1	10	40	41	42	13	7	6	48	13	43	17	13
JUN. 2	10	42	43	44	13	7	6	48	13	43	17	13
JUN. 3	11	44	45	45	14	7	6	48	13	43	17	13
JUN. 4	11	46	46	47	14	7	6	48	13	43	17	13
JUN. 5	11	48	48	1	14	7	6	48	13	43	17	13
JUN. 6	11	1	2	2	14	7	6	48	13	43	17	13
JUN. 7	11	3	3	4	14	8	6	48	13	43	17	13
JUN. 8	11	4	5	6	14	8	6	48	13	43	17	13
JUN. 9	11	6	7	7	14	8	6	48	13	43	17	13
JUN. 10	11	8	8	9	14	8	6	48	13	43	17	13
JUN. 11	12	9	10	10	14	8	7	48	13	43	17	13
JUN. 12	12	11	11	12	14	8	7	48	13	43	17	13
JUN. 13	12	12	13	13	14	9	7	48	13	43	17	13
JUN. 14	12	14	15	15	14	9	7	1	14	43	17	13
JUN. 15	12	16	16	17	14	9	7	1	14	43	17	13
JUN. 16	12	17	18	18	14	9	7	1	14	43	17	13
JUN. 17	12	19	19	20	14	9	7	1	14	43	17	13
JUN. 18	12	21	21	22	14	9	7	1	14	43	17	13
JUN. 19	13	22	23	23	14	9	7	1	14	43	17	13
JUN. 20	13	24	25	25	14	10	7	1	14	43	17	13
JUN. 21	13	26	26	27	14	10	8	1	14	43	17	13
JUN. 22	13	28	28	29	14	10	8	1	14	43	17	13
JUN. 23	13	30	30	31	14	10	8	1	14	43	17	13
JUN. 24	13	32	32	33	14	10	8	1	14	43	17	13
JUN. 25	14	34	34	35	14	10	8	1	14	43	17	13
JUN. 26	14	36	36	37	14	11	8	1	14	43	17	13
JUN. 27	14	38	38	39	14	11	8	1	14	43	17	13
JUN. 28	14	40	40	41	13	11	8	1	14	43	17	13
JUN. 29	14	42	42	43	13	11	8	1	14	43	17	13
JUN. 30	14	43	44	45	13	11	8	1	14	43	17	13

MOON 1 ☽ 12:01 A.M. TO 8:00 A.M. **MOON 2** ◑ 8:01 A.M. TO 4:00 P.M. **MOON 3** ● 4:01 P.M. TO 12:00 A.M.
Use only one "moon" number. Choose the column closest to your time of birth. If your place of birth is not on Eastern Standard Time, be sure to read "How to Convert to Eastern Standard Time" at the beginning of this section.

1915

July · August

Date & Time	SUN	MOON 1	MOON 2	MOON 3	MERCURY	VENUS	MARS	JUPITER	SATURN	URANUS	NEPTUNE	PLUTO
JUL. 1	14	45	46	46	13	11	8	1	14	43	17	13
JUL. 2	14	47	48	48	13	12	9	1	14	43	17	13
JUL. 3	15	1	1	2	13	12	9	1	14	43	17	13
JUL. 4	15	2	3	3	13	12	9	1	14	43	17	13
JUL. 5	15	4	5	5	13	12	9	1	14	43	17	13
JUL. 6	15	6	6	7	13	12	9	1	14	43	17	13
JUL. 7	15	7	8	8	13	12	9	1	14	43	17	13
JUL. 8	15	9	9	10	13	13	9	1	14	43	17	13
JUL. 9	15	10	11	11	13	13	9	1	14	43	17	13
JUL. 10	15	12	13	13	13	13	9	1	14	43	17	13
JUL. 11	16	14	15	15	13	13	9	1	14	43	17	13
JUL. 12	16	15	16	16	13	13	10	1	14	43	17	13
JUL. 13	16	17	17	18	13	13	10	1	14	43	17	13
JUL. 14	16	18	19	20	13	14	10	1	14	43	17	13
JUL. 15	16	20	21	21	13	14	10	1	14	43	17	13
JUL. 16	16	22	22	23	13	14	10	1	14	43	17	13
JUL. 17	16	24	24	25	13	14	10	1	14	43	17	13
JUL. 18	16	25	26	27	14	14	10	1	14	43	17	13
JUL. 19	17	27	28	28	14	14	10	1	14	43	17	13
JUL. 20	17	29	30	30	14	15	10	1	14	43	17	13
JUL. 21	17	31	32	32	14	15	10	1	14	43	17	13
JUL. 22	17	33	34	34	14	15	10	1	14	43	17	13
JUL. 23	17	35	35	36	14	15	11	1	14	43	17	13
JUL. 24	17	37	37	38	14	15	11	1	14	43	17	13
JUL. 25	17	39	39	40	15	15	11	1	14	43	17	13
JUL. 26	18	41	41	42	15	15	11	1	14	43	17	13
JUL. 27	18	43	43	44	15	16	11	1	14	43	17	13
JUL. 28	18	45	45	46	15	16	11	1	14	43	17	13
JUL. 29	18	46	47	48	15	16	11	1	14	43	17	13
JUL. 30	18	48	1	1	16	16	11	1	14	43	17	13
JUL. 31	18	2	2	3	16	16	11	1	14	43	17	13

Date & Time	SUN	MOON 1	MOON 2	MOON 3	MERCURY	VENUS	MARS	JUPITER	SATURN	URANUS	NEPTUNE	PLUTO
AUG. 1	18	3	4	5	16	16	11	1	14	43	17	13
AUG. 2	18	5	6	6	16	17	11	1	14	43	17	13
AUG. 3	19	7	7	8	17	17	12	1	14	43	17	13
AUG. 4	19	8	9	9	17	17	12	1	14	43	17	13
AUG. 5	19	10	10	11	17	17	12	1	14	43	17	13
AUG. 6	19	11	12	13	17	17	12	1	14	43	17	13
AUG. 7	19	13	14	14	18	17	12	1	14	43	17	13
AUG. 8	19	15	15	16	18	18	12	1	14	43	17	13
AUG. 9	19	16	17	17	18	18	12	1	14	43	17	13
AUG. 10	19	18	19	19	19	18	12	1	14	43	17	13
AUG. 11	20	20	20	21	19	18	12	1	14	43	17	13
AUG. 12	20	21	22	23	19	18	12	1	14	43	17	13
AUG. 13	20	23	24	24	19	18	12	1	15	43	17	13
AUG. 14	20	25	26	26	20	19	13	1	15	43	17	13
AUG. 15	20	27	27	28	20	19	13	1	15	43	17	13
AUG. 16	20	29	29	30	20	19	13	1	15	43	17	13
AUG. 17	20	31	31	32	20	19	13	1	15	43	17	13
AUG. 18	20	32	33	34	21	19	13	1	15	43	17	13
AUG. 19	21	34	35	36	21	19	13	1	15	43	17	13
AUG. 20	21	36	37	37	21	20	13	1	15	43	17	13
AUG. 21	21	38	39	39	21	20	13	1	15	43	17	13
AUG. 22	21	40	41	41	22	20	13	1	15	43	17	13
AUG. 23	21	42	43	43	22	20	13	1	15	43	17	13
AUG. 24	21	44	44	45	22	20	13	1	15	43	17	13
AUG. 25	21	46	46	47	22	20	13	48	15	43	17	13
AUG. 26	22	47	48	1	23	21	14	48	15	43	17	13
AUG. 27	22	1	2	2	23	21	14	48	15	43	17	13
AUG. 28	22	3	3	4	23	21	14	48	15	43	17	13
AUG. 29	22	5	5	6	23	21	14	48	15	43	17	13
AUG. 30	22	6	7	7	24	21	14	48	15	43	17	13
AUG. 31	22	8	8	9	24	21	14	48	15	43	17	13

MOON 1 ☽ 12:01 A.M. TO 8:00 A.M. **MOON 2** ☽ 8:01 A.M. TO 4:00 P.M. **MOON 3** ● 4:01 P.M. TO 12:00 A.M.
Use only one "moon" number. Choose the column closest to your time of birth. If your place of birth is not on Eastern Standard Time, be sure to read "How to Convert to Eastern Standard Time" at the beginning of this section.

1915

September

Date & Time	SUN	MOON 1	MOON 2	MOON 3	MERCURY	VENUS	MARS	JUPITER	SATURN	URANUS	NEPTUNE	PLUTO
SEP. 1	22	9	10	10	24	22	14	48	15	43	17	13
SEP. 2	22	11	11	12	24	22	14	48	15	43	17	13
SEP. 3	23	13	13	14	25	22	14	48	15	43	17	13
SEP. 4	23	14	15	15	25	22	14	48	15	43	17	13
SEP. 5	23	16	16	17	25	22	14	48	15	43	17	13
SEP. 6	23	17	18	19	25	22	14	48	15	43	17	13
SEP. 7	23	19	20	20	25	23	15	48	15	43	17	13
SEP. 8	23	21	21	22	26	23	15	48	15	43	17	13
SEP. 9	23	23	23	24	26	23	15	48	15	43	17	13
SEP. 10	23	24	25	26	26	23	15	48	15	43	17	13
SEP. 11	24	26	27	28	26	23	15	48	15	43	17	13
SEP. 12	24	28	29	29	26	23	15	48	15	43	17	13
SEP. 13	24	30	31	31	27	24	15	48	15	43	17	13
SEP. 14	24	32	33	33	27	24	15	48	15	43	17	13
SEP. 15	24	34	34	35	27	24	15	48	15	43	17	13
SEP. 16	24	36	36	37	27	24	15	48	15	43	17	13
SEP. 17	24	38	38	39	27	24	15	48	15	43	17	13
SEP. 18	24	40	40	41	27	24	15	48	15	43	17	13
SEP. 19	25	41	42	43	28	25	16	48	15	43	17	13
SEP. 20	25	43	44	44	28	25	16	48	15	43	17	13
SEP. 21	25	45	46	46	28	25	16	48	15	43	17	13
SEP. 22	25	47	47	48	28	25	16	48	15	43	17	13
SEP. 23	25	1	1	2	28	25	16	48	15	43	17	13
SEP. 24	25	2	3	3	28	25	16	48	15	43	17	13
SEP. 25	26	4	5	5	29	25	16	48	15	43	17	13
SEP. 26	26	6	6	7	29	26	16	48	15	43	17	13
SEP. 27	26	7	8	8	29	26	16	48	15	43	17	13
SEP. 28	26	9	9	10	29	26	16	48	15	43	17	13
SEP. 29	26	10	11	11	29	26	16	48	15	43	17	13
SEP. 30	26	12	13	13	29	26	16	48	15	43	17	13

October

Date & Time	SUN	MOON 1	MOON 2	MOON 3	MERCURY	VENUS	MARS	JUPITER	SATURN	URANUS	NEPTUNE	PLUTO
OCT. 1	26	14	14	15	29	27	16	48	15	43	17	13
OCT. 2	26	15	16	16	29	27	17	48	15	43	17	13
OCT. 3	27	17	17	18	30	27	17	48	15	43	17	13
OCT. 4	27	18	19	20	30	27	17	48	15	43	17	13
OCT. 5	27	20	21	21	30	27	17	48	15	43	17	13
OCT. 6	27	22	23	23	30	27	17	48	15	43	17	13
OCT. 7	27	24	24	25	30	28	17	48	15	43	17	13
OCT. 8	27	26	26	27	30	28	17	48	15	43	17	13
OCT. 9	27	27	28	29	30	28	17	48	15	43	17	13
OCT. 10	27	29	30	31	30	28	17	48	15	43	17	13
OCT. 11	28	31	32	33	30	28	17	48	15	43	17	13
OCT. 12	28	33	34	35	30	28	17	48	15	43	17	13
OCT. 13	28	35	36	37	30	29	17	48	15	43	17	13
OCT. 14	28	37	38	38	30	29	17	48	15	43	17	13
OCT. 15	28	39	40	40	30	29	17	48	15	43	17	13
OCT. 16	28	41	42	42	30	29	18	48	15	43	17	13
OCT. 17	28	43	43	44	30	29	18	48	15	43	17	13
OCT. 18	28	45	45	46	29	29	18	48	15	43	17	13
OCT. 19	29	46	47	47	29	30	18	48	15	43	17	13
OCT. 20	29	48	1	1	29	30	18	48	15	43	17	13
OCT. 21	29	2	2	3	29	30	18	48	15	43	17	13
OCT. 22	29	3	4	4	29	30	18	48	15	43	17	13
OCT. 23	29	5	6	6	29	30	18	48	15	43	17	13
OCT. 24	29	7	7	8	28	30	18	48	15	43	17	13
OCT. 25	29	8	9	9	28	31	18	48	15	43	17	13
OCT. 26	30	10	10	11	28	31	18	48	15	43	17	13
OCT. 27	30	12	12	13	28	31	18	48	15	43	17	13
OCT. 28	30	13	14	14	28	31	18	48	15	43	17	13
OCT. 29	30	15	15	16	28	31	18	48	15	43	17	13
OCT. 30	30	16	17	17	28	31	19	48	15	43	17	13
OCT. 31	30	18	18	19	28	32	19	47	15	43	17	13

MOON 1 ◐ 12:01 A.M. TO 8:00 A.M. **MOON 2** ◐ 8:01 A.M. TO 4:00 P.M. **MOON 3** ● 4:01 P.M. TO 12:00 A.M.
Use only one "moon" number. Choose the column closest to your time of birth. If your place of birth is not on Eastern Standard Time, be sure to read "How to Convert to Eastern Standard Time" at the beginning of this section.

November

Date & Time	SUN	MOON 1	MOON 2	MOON 3	MERCURY	VENUS	MARS	JUPITER	SATURN	URANUS	NEPTUNE	PLUTO
NOV. 1	30	20	20	21	28	32	19	47	15	43	17	13
NOV. 2	30	21	22	22	28	32	19	47	15	43	17	13
NOV. 3	31	23	24	24	28	32	19	47	15	43	17	13
NOV. 4	31	25	25	26	28	32	19	47	15	43	17	13
NOV. 5	31	27	27	28	28	32	19	47	15	43	17	13
NOV. 6	31	29	29	30	28	33	19	47	15	43	17	13
NOV. 7	31	31	31	32	28	33	19	47	15	43	17	13
NOV. 8	31	33	33	34	28	33	19	47	15	43	17	13
NOV. 9	31	35	35	36	29	33	19	47	15	43	17	13
NOV. 10	31	37	37	38	29	33	19	47	15	43	17	13
NOV. 11	31	39	39	40	29	33	19	47	15	43	17	13
NOV. 12	32	40	41	42	29	34	19	47	15	43	17	13
NOV. 13	32	42	43	44	29	34	19	47	15	43	17	13
NOV. 14	32	44	45	45	29	34	19	47	15	43	17	13
NOV. 15	32	46	46	47	30	34	19	47	15	43	17	13
NOV. 16	32	48	48	1	30	34	20	47	15	43	17	13
NOV. 17	32	1	2	2	30	34	20	47	15	43	17	13
NOV. 18	32	3	4	4	30	35	20	47	15	43	17	13
NOV. 19	33	5	5	6	30	35	20	47	15	43	17	13
NOV. 20	33	6	7	7	31	35	20	47	15	43	17	13
NOV. 21	33	8	8	9	31	35	20	47	15	43	17	13
NOV. 22	33	10	10	11	31	35	20	47	15	43	17	13
NOV. 23	33	11	12	12	31	35	20	47	15	43	17	13
NOV. 24	33	13	13	14	31	36	20	47	15	43	17	13
NOV. 25	34	14	15	15	32	36	20	47	15	43	17	13
NOV. 26	34	16	16	17	32	36	20	47	15	43	17	13
NOV. 27	34	17	18	18	32	36	20	47	15	43	17	13
NOV. 28	34	19	20	20	32	36	20	47	15	43	17	13
NOV. 29	34	21	21	22	33	36	20	47	15	43	17	13
NOV. 30	34	22	23	23	33	37	20	48	15	43	17	13

December

Date & Time	SUN	MOON 1	MOON 2	MOON 3	MERCURY	VENUS	MARS	JUPITER	SATURN	URANUS	NEPTUNE	PLUTO
DEC. 1	34	24	25	25	33	37	20	48	15	43	17	13
DEC. 2	34	26	26	27	33	37	20	48	15	43	17	13
DEC. 3	35	28	28	29	33	37	20	48	15	43	17	13
DEC. 4	35	30	30	31	34	37	20	48	15	43	17	13
DEC. 5	35	32	32	33	34	37	20	48	15	43	17	13
DEC. 6	35	34	34	35	34	38	20	48	15	43	17	13
DEC. 7	35	36	36	37	34	38	20	48	15	43	17	13
DEC. 8	35	38	38	39	34	38	20	48	15	43	17	13
DEC. 9	35	40	40	41	35	38	21	48	15	43	17	13
DEC. 10	35	42	42	43	35	38	21	48	15	43	17	13
DEC. 11	36	44	44	45	35	38	21	48	15	43	17	13
DEC. 12	36	45	46	47	35	39	21	48	15	43	17	13
DEC. 13	36	47	48	48	35	39	21	48	15	43	17	13
DEC. 14	36	1	1	2	36	39	21	48	15	43	17	13
DEC. 15	36	3	3	4	36	39	21	48	15	43	17	13
DEC. 16	36	4	5	5	36	39	21	48	15	43	17	13
DEC. 17	36	6	6	7	36	39	21	48	15	43	17	13
DEC. 18	36	8	8	9	36	40	21	48	15	43	17	13
DEC. 19	37	9	10	10	37	40	21	48	15	43	17	13
DEC. 20	37	11	11	12	37	40	21	48	15	43	17	13
DEC. 21	37	12	13	13	37	40	21	48	15	43	17	13
DEC. 22	37	14	14	15	37	40	21	48	15	43	17	13
DEC. 23	37	15	16	16	38	40	21	48	15	43	17	13
DEC. 24	37	17	18	18	38	41	21	48	15	43	17	13
DEC. 25	37	19	19	20	38	41	21	48	15	43	17	13
DEC. 26	38	20	21	21	38	41	21	48	15	43	17	13
DEC. 27	38	22	22	23	38	41	21	48	15	43	17	13
DEC. 28	38	24	24	25	39	41	21	48	15	43	17	13
DEC. 29	38	25	26	26	39	41	21	48	15	43	17	13
DEC. 30	38	27	28	28	39	42	21	48	15	43	17	13
DEC. 31	38	29	30	30	39	42	21	48	15	43	17	13

MOON 1 ☽ 12:01 A.M. TO 8:00 A.M.   **MOON 2** ☽ 8:01 A.M. TO 4:00 P.M.   **MOON 3** ● 4:01 P.M. TO 12:00 A.M.

Use only one "moon" number. Choose the column closest to your time of birth. If your place of birth is not on Eastern Standard Time, be sure to read "How to Convert to Eastern Standard Time" at the beginning of this section.

1916

January

Date & Time	SUN	MOON 1	MOON 2	MOON 3	MERCURY	VENUS	MARS	JUPITER	SATURN	URANUS	NEPTUNE	PLUTO
JAN. 1	38	31	31	32	39	42	21	48	15	43	17	13
JAN. 2	38	33	33	34	40	42	21	48	15	43	17	13
JAN. 3	39	35	35	36	40	42	21	48	15	43	17	13
JAN. 4	39	37	37	38	40	42	21	48	15	43	17	13
JAN. 5	39	39	39	40	40	43	21	48	15	43	17	13
JAN. 6	39	41	41	42	41	43	21	48	15	43	17	13
JAN. 7	39	43	43	44	41	43	21	48	15	43	17	13
JAN. 8	39	45	45	46	41	43	21	48	15	43	17	13
JAN. 9	39	47	47	48	41	43	21	48	15	43	17	13
JAN. 10	40	48	1	2	41	43	21	48	15	43	17	13
JAN. 11	40	2	3	3	42	44	21	48	15	43	17	13
JAN. 12	40	4	4	5	42	44	21	48	15	43	17	13
JAN. 13	40	5	6	7	42	44	21	48	15	43	17	13
JAN. 14	40	7	8	8	42	44	21	48	15	43	17	13
JAN. 15	40	9	9	10	42	44	21	48	15	43	17	13
JAN. 16	40	10	11	11	43	44	21	48	15	43	17	13
JAN. 17	41	12	12	13	43	44	21	48	15	43	17	13
JAN. 18	41	13	14	14	43	45	21	48	15	43	17	13
JAN. 19	41	15	16	16	43	45	21	48	15	43	17	13
JAN. 20	41	17	17	18	43	45	21	48	15	43	17	13
JAN. 21	41	18	19	19	43	45	21	48	15	43	17	13
JAN. 22	41	20	20	21	44	45	21	48	15	43	17	13
JAN. 23	42	21	22	23	44	45	21	48	15	43	17	13
JAN. 24	42	23	24	24	44	46	20	48	14	43	17	13
JAN. 25	42	25	25	26	44	46	20	48	14	43	17	13
JAN. 26	42	27	27	28	44	46	20	48	14	43	17	13
JAN. 27	42	28	29	30	44	46	20	1	14	43	17	13
JAN. 28	42	30	31	31	44	46	20	1	14	43	17	13
JAN. 29	42	32	33	33	44	46	20	1	14	43	17	13
JAN. 30	42	34	35	35	44	47	20	1	14	43	17	13
JAN. 31	43	36	37	37	44	47	20	1	14	43	17	13

February

Date & Time	SUN	MOON 1	MOON 2	MOON 3	MERCURY	VENUS	MARS	JUPITER	SATURN	URANUS	NEPTUNE	PLUTO
FEB. 1	43	38	39	39	44	47	20	1	14	43	17	13
FEB. 2	43	40	41	41	43	47	20	1	14	43	17	13
FEB. 3	43	42	43	43	43	47	20	1	14	43	17	13
FEB. 4	43	44	44	45	43	47	20	1	14	43	17	13
FEB. 5	43	46	46	47	43	48	20	1	14	43	17	13
FEB. 6	43	48	48	1	43	48	20	1	14	43	17	13
FEB. 7	43	1	2	3	43	48	20	1	14	43	17	13
FEB. 8	44	3	4	4	43	48	20	1	14	43	17	13
FEB. 9	44	5	5	6	42	48	20	1	14	43	17	13
FEB. 10	44	7	7	8	42	48	20	1	14	43	17	13
FEB. 11	44	8	9	9	42	1	20	1	14	43	17	13
FEB. 12	44	10	10	11	42	1	20	1	14	43	17	13
FEB. 13	44	11	12	12	42	1	19	1	14	43	17	13
FEB. 14	44	13	13	14	42	1	19	1	14	43	17	13
FEB. 15	44	15	15	16	42	1	19	1	14	43	17	13
FEB. 16	45	16	17	17	42	1	19	1	14	43	17	13
FEB. 17	45	18	18	19	42	2	19	1	14	43	17	13
FEB. 18	45	19	20	20	42	2	19	1	14	43	17	13
FEB. 19	45	21	22	22	42	2	19	1	14	43	17	13
FEB. 20	45	23	23	24	42	2	19	1	14	43	17	13
FEB. 21	45	24	25	26	42	2	19	1	14	43	17	13
FEB. 22	45	26	27	27	42	2	19	1	14	43	17	13
FEB. 23	46	28	29	29	42	2	19	1	14	43	17	13
FEB. 24	46	30	30	31	42	3	19	1	14	43	17	13
FEB. 25	46	32	32	33	42	3	19	1	14	43	17	13
FEB. 26	46	33	34	35	42	3	19	1	14	43	17	13
FEB. 27	46	35	36	37	42	3	19	1	14	43	17	13
FEB. 28	46	37	38	39	42	3	19	1	14	43	17	13
FEB. 29	46	39	40	40	43	3	19	1	14	43	17	13

MOON 1 ◗ 12:01 A.M. TO 8:00 A.M.   **MOON 2** ◐ 8:01 A.M. TO 4:00 P.M.   **MOON 3** ● 4:01 P.M. TO 12:00 A.M.
Use only one "moon" number. Choose the column closest to your time of birth. If your place of birth is not on
Eastern Standard Time, be sure to read "How to Convert to Eastern Standard Time" at the beginning of this section.

1916

March

April

Date & Time	SUN	MOON 1	MOON 2	MOON 3	MERCURY	VENUS	MARS	JUPITER	SATURN	URANUS	NEPTUNE	PLUTO
MAR. 1	46	41	42	42	43	4	19	2	14	43	17	13
MAR. 2	46	43	44	44	43	4	19	2	14	43	17	13
MAR. 3	47	45	46	46	43	4	19	2	14	43	17	13
MAR. 4	47	47	47	48	43	4	19	2	14	43	17	13
MAR. 5	47	1	1	2	43	4	19	2	14	43	17	13
MAR. 6	47	2	3	4	43	4	19	2	14	43	17	13
MAR. 7	47	4	5	5	44	5	19	2	14	43	17	13
MAR. 8	47	6	7	7	44	5	18	2	14	43	17	13
MAR. 9	47	8	8	9	44	5	18	2	14	43	17	13
MAR. 10	47	9	10	10	44	5	18	2	14	43	17	13
MAR. 11	48	11	11	12	44	5	18	2	14	43	17	13
MAR. 12	48	12	13	13	44	5	18	2	14	43	17	13
MAR. 13	48	14	15	15	45	5	18	2	14	43	17	13
MAR. 14	48	16	16	17	45	6	18	2	14	43	17	13
MAR. 15	48	17	18	18	45	6	18	2	14	43	17	13
MAR. 16	48	19	19	20	45	6	18	2	14	43	17	13
MAR. 17	48	20	21	22	45	6	18	2	14	43	17	13
MAR. 18	48	22	23	23	46	6	18	2	14	43	17	13
MAR. 19	1	24	24	25	46	6	18	2	14	43	17	13
MAR. 20	1	26	26	27	46	7	18	2	14	43	17	13
MAR. 21	1	27	28	29	46	7	18	2	14	43	17	13
MAR. 22	1	29	30	31	46	7	18	2	14	43	17	13
MAR. 23	1	31	32	32	47	7	18	2	14	43	17	13
MAR. 24	1	33	34	34	47	7	18	2	14	43	17	13
MAR. 25	2	35	36	36	47	7	18	2	14	43	17	13
MAR. 26	2	37	37	38	47	7	18	2	14	43	17	13
MAR. 27	2	39	39	40	47	8	18	2	14	43	17	13
MAR. 28	2	41	41	42	48	8	18	2	14	43	17	13
MAR. 29	2	42	43	44	48	8	18	2	14	43	17	13
MAR. 30	2	44	45	46	48	8	18	2	14	43	17	13
MAR. 31	2	46	47	47	48	8	18	2	14	43	17	13

Date & Time	SUN	MOON 1	MOON 2	MOON 3	MERCURY	VENUS	MARS	JUPITER	SATURN	URANUS	NEPTUNE	PLUTO
APR. 1	2	48	1	1	1	8	18	2	14	43	17	13
APR. 2	2	2	2	3	1	8	18	3	14	43	17	13
APR. 3	3	4	4	5	1	9	18	3	14	43	17	13
APR. 4	3	5	6	6	1	9	18	3	14	43	17	13
APR. 5	3	7	8	8	2	9	19	3	14	43	17	13
APR. 6	3	9	9	10	2	9	19	3	14	43	17	13
APR. 7	3	10	11	11	2	9	19	3	14	43	17	13
APR. 8	3	12	12	13	2	9	19	3	14	43	17	13
APR. 9	3	13	14	15	3	9	19	3	14	43	17	13
APR. 10	3	15	16	16	3	10	19	3	14	43	17	13
APR. 11	4	17	17	18	3	10	19	3	14	43	17	13
APR. 12	4	18	19	19	4	10	19	3	14	43	17	13
APR. 13	4	20	20	21	4	10	19	3	14	44	17	13
APR. 14	4	22	22	23	4	10	19	3	14	44	17	13
APR. 15	4	23	24	24	4	10	19	3	14	44	17	13
APR. 16	4	25	26	26	5	10	19	3	14	44	17	13
APR. 17	4	27	27	28	5	11	19	3	14	44	17	13
APR. 18	4	29	29	30	5	11	19	3	14	44	17	13
APR. 19	5	31	31	32	5	11	19	3	14	44	17	13
APR. 20	5	32	33	34	6	11	19	3	14	44	17	13
APR. 21	5	34	35	36	6	11	19	3	14	44	17	13
APR. 22	5	36	37	38	6	11	19	3	14	44	17	13
APR. 23	5	38	39	40	7	11	19	3	14	44	17	13
APR. 24	5	40	41	41	7	12	19	3	14	44	17	13
APR. 25	6	42	43	43	7	12	19	3	14	44	17	13
APR. 26	6	44	45	45	7	12	19	3	14	44	17	13
APR. 27	6	46	46	47	8	12	19	3	14	44	17	13
APR. 28	6	48	48	1	8	12	19	3	15	44	17	13
APR. 29	6	1	2	2	8	12	19	3	15	44	17	13
APR. 30	6	3	4	4	8	12	19	3	15	44	17	13

MOON 1 ☽ 12:01 A.M. TO 8:00 A.M.   **MOON 2** ☽ 8:01 A.M. TO 4:00 P.M.   **MOON 3** ● 4:01 P.M. TO 12:00 A.M.

Use only one "moon" number. Choose the column closest to your time of birth. If your place of birth is not on Eastern Standard Time, be sure to read "How to Convert to Eastern Standard Time" at the beginning of this section.

1916

May

Date & Time	SUN	MOON 1	MOON 2	MOON 3	MERCURY	VENUS	MARS	JUPITER	SATURN	URANUS	NEPTUNE	PLUTO
MAY 1	6	5	5	6	9	12	19	3	15	44	17	13
MAY 2	6	6	7	8	9	13	19	3	15	44	17	13
MAY 3	7	8	9	9	9	13	20	4	15	44	17	13
MAY 4	7	10	10	11	9	13	20	4	15	44	17	13
MAY 5	7	11	12	12	9	13	20	4	15	44	17	13
MAY 6	7	13	14	14	10	13	20	4	15	44	17	13
MAY 7	7	15	15	16	10	13	20	4	15	44	17	13
MAY 8	7	16	17	17	10	13	20	4	15	44	17	13
MAY 9	7	18	18	19	10	13	20	4	15	44	17	13
MAY 10	7	19	20	20	10	13	20	4	15	44	17	13
MAY 11	8	21	21	22	11	14	20	4	15	44	17	13
MAY 12	8	23	23	24	11	14	20	4	15	44	17	13
MAY 13	8	24	25	25	11	14	20	4	15	44	17	13
MAY 14	8	26	27	27	11	14	20	4	15	44	17	13
MAY 15	8	28	29	29	11	14	20	4	15	44	17	13
MAY 16	8	30	30	31	11	14	20	4	15	44	17	13
MAY 17	8	32	32	33	11	14	20	4	15	44	17	13
MAY 18	8	34	34	35	11	14	20	4	15	44	17	13
MAY 19	9	36	36	37	11	14	20	4	15	44	17	13
MAY 20	9	38	38	39	11	14	20	4	15	44	17	13
MAY 21	9	40	40	41	11	15	21	4	15	44	17	13
MAY 22	9	42	42	43	11	15	21	4	15	44	17	13
MAY 23	9	43	44	45	12	15	21	4	15	44	17	13
MAY 24	9	45	46	47	12	15	21	4	15	44	17	13
MAY 25	10	47	48	48	12	15	21	4	15	44	17	13
MAY 26	10	1	1	2	12	15	21	4	15	44	17	13
MAY 27	10	3	3	4	12	15	21	4	15	44	17	13
MAY 28	10	4	5	5	12	15	21	4	15	44	17	13
MAY 29	10	6	7	7	11	15	21	4	15	44	17	13
MAY 30	10	8	8	9	11	15	21	4	15	44	17	13
MAY 31	10	9	10	10	11	15	21	4	15	44	17	13

June

Date & Time	SUN	MOON 1	MOON 2	MOON 3	MERCURY	VENUS	MARS	JUPITER	SATURN	URANUS	NEPTUNE	PLUTO
JUN. 1	10	11	11	12	11	15	21	4	15	44	17	13
JUN. 2	10	13	13	14	11	15	21	4	15	44	17	13
JUN. 3	11	14	15	15	11	15	21	4	15	44	17	13
JUN. 4	11	16	16	17	11	15	21	4	15	44	17	13
JUN. 5	11	17	18	18	11	15	21	4	15	44	17	13
JUN. 6	11	19	19	20	11	15	22	5	15	44	17	13
JUN. 7	11	20	21	21	11	16	22	5	15	44	17	13
JUN. 8	11	22	23	23	11	16	22	5	15	44	17	13
JUN. 9	11	24	24	25	11	16	22	5	15	44	17	13
JUN. 10	11	25	26	27	11	16	22	5	15	44	17	13
JUN. 11	12	27	28	28	11	16	22	5	15	44	17	13
JUN. 12	12	29	30	30	11	16	22	5	15	44	17	13
JUN. 13	12	31	32	32	11	16	22	5	15	44	17	13
JUN. 14	12	33	33	34	10	16	22	5	15	44	17	13
JUN. 15	12	35	35	36	10	16	22	5	15	44	17	13
JUN. 16	12	37	38	38	10	16	22	5	15	44	17	13
JUN. 17	12	39	40	40	10	16	22	5	15	44	17	13
JUN. 18	12	41	42	42	10	16	22	5	15	44	17	13
JUN. 19	13	43	43	44	10	15	22	5	15	44	17	13
JUN. 20	13	45	45	46	10	15	22	5	15	44	17	13
JUN. 21	13	47	47	48	10	15	23	5	15	44	17	13
JUN. 22	13	48	1	2	10	15	23	5	15	44	17	13
JUN. 23	13	2	3	3	11	15	23	5	15	44	17	13
JUN. 24	13	4	5	5	11	15	23	5	15	44	17	13
JUN. 25	14	6	6	7	11	15	23	5	15	44	17	13
JUN. 26	14	7	8	8	11	15	23	5	15	44	17	13
JUN. 27	14	9	9	10	11	15	23	5	15	44	17	13
JUN. 28	14	11	11	12	11	15	23	5	15	44	17	13
JUN. 29	14	12	13	13	11	15	23	5	15	44	17	13
JUN. 30	14	14	14	15	11	15	23	5	15	44	17	13

MOON 1 ◯ 12:01 A.M. TO 8:00 A.M.   **MOON 2** ◑ 8:01 A.M. TO 4:00 P.M.   **MOON 3** ● 4:01 P.M. TO 12:00 A.M.
Use only one "moon" number. Choose the column closest to your time of birth. If your place of birth is not on Eastern Standard Time, be sure to read "How to Convert to Eastern Standard Time" at the beginning of this section.

1916

July

Date & Time	SUN	MOON 1	MOON 2	MOON 3	MERCURY	VENUS	MARS	JUPITER	SATURN	URANUS	NEPTUNE	PLUTO
JUL. 1	14	15	16	16	11	15	23	5	15	44	17	13
JUL. 2	14	17	17	18	11	15	23	5	15	44	17	13
JUL. 3	15	18	19	19	12	15	23	5	15	44	17	13
JUL. 4	15	20	21	21	12	14	23	5	15	44	17	13
JUL. 5	15	22	22	23	12	14	24	5	16	44	17	13
JUL. 6	15	23	24	24	12	14	24	5	16	44	17	13
JUL. 7	15	25	25	26	12	14	24	5	16	43	17	13
JUL. 8	15	27	27	28	12	14	24	5	16	43	17	13
JUL. 9	15	28	29	30	13	14	24	5	16	43	17	13
JUL. 10	15	30	31	31	13	14	24	5	16	43	17	13
JUL. 11	16	32	33	33	13	14	24	5	16	43	17	13
JUL. 12	16	34	35	35	13	14	24	5	16	43	17	13
JUL. 13	16	36	37	37	14	14	24	5	16	43	17	13
JUL. 14	16	38	39	39	14	14	24	5	16	43	17	13
JUL. 15	16	40	41	41	14	14	24	5	16	43	17	13
JUL. 16	16	42	43	43	14	14	24	5	16	43	17	13
JUL. 17	16	44	45	45	15	14	24	5	16	43	17	13
JUL. 18	16	46	47	47	15	14	25	5	16	43	17	13
JUL. 19	17	48	48	1	15	13	25	5	16	43	17	13
JUL. 20	17	2	2	3	15	13	25	5	16	43	17	13
JUL. 21	17	3	4	5	16	13	25	5	16	43	17	13
JUL. 22	17	5	6	6	16	13	25	5	16	43	17	13
JUL. 23	17	7	7	8	16	13	25	5	16	43	17	13
JUL. 24	17	9	9	10	16	13	25	5	16	43	17	13
JUL. 25	17	10	11	11	17	13	25	5	16	43	17	13
JUL. 26	18	12	12	13	17	13	25	5	16	43	17	13
JUL. 27	18	13	14	14	17	13	25	6	16	43	17	13
JUL. 28	18	15	15	16	18	13	25	6	16	43	17	13
JUL. 29	18	16	17	17	18	13	25	6	16	43	17	13
JUL. 30	18	18	19	19	18	13	26	6	16	43	17	13
JUL. 31	18	20	20	21	18	13	26	6	16	43	17	13

August

Date & Time	SUN	MOON 1	MOON 2	MOON 3	MERCURY	VENUS	MARS	JUPITER	SATURN	URANUS	NEPTUNE	PLUTO
AUG. 1	18	21	22	22	19	14	26	6	16	43	17	13
AUG. 2	18	23	23	24	19	14	26	6	16	43	17	13
AUG. 3	19	24	25	26	19	14	26	6	16	43	17	13
AUG. 4	19	26	27	27	19	14	26	6	16	43	17	13
AUG. 5	19	28	28	29	20	14	26	6	16	43	17	13
AUG. 6	19	30	30	31	20	14	26	6	16	43	17	13
AUG. 7	19	31	32	33	20	14	26	6	16	43	17	13
AUG. 8	19	33	34	35	20	14	26	6	16	43	17	13
AUG. 9	19	35	36	36	21	14	26	6	16	43	17	13
AUG. 10	19	37	38	38	21	14	26	6	16	43	17	13
AUG. 11	20	39	40	40	21	14	27	6	16	43	17	13
AUG. 12	20	41	42	42	21	14	27	6	16	43	17	13
AUG. 13	20	43	44	44	22	14	27	6	16	43	17	13
AUG. 14	20	45	46	46	22	14	27	6	16	43	17	13
AUG. 15	20	47	48	48	22	14	27	6	16	43	17	13
AUG. 16	20	1	2	2	22	14	27	6	16	43	17	13
AUG. 17	20	3	3	4	23	14	27	6	16	43	17	13
AUG. 18	20	5	5	6	23	15	27	6	16	43	17	14
AUG. 19	21	6	7	7	23	15	27	6	16	43	17	14
AUG. 20	21	8	9	9	23	15	27	6	16	43	17	14
AUG. 21	21	10	10	11	23	15	27	6	16	43	17	14
AUG. 22	21	11	12	12	24	15	27	6	16	43	17	14
AUG. 23	21	13	14	14	24	15	28	6	16	43	17	14
AUG. 24	21	14	15	15	24	15	28	6	16	43	17	14
AUG. 25	21	16	17	17	24	15	28	6	16	43	17	14
AUG. 26	22	18	18	19	24	15	28	6	16	43	17	14
AUG. 27	22	19	20	20	25	15	28	6	16	43	17	14
AUG. 28	22	21	21	22	25	16	28	6	16	43	17	14
AUG. 29	22	22	23	24	25	16	28	6	16	43	17	14
AUG. 30	22	24	25	25	25	16	28	6	16	43	17	14
AUG. 31	22	26	26	27	25	16	28	6	16	43	17	14

MOON 1 ◗ 12:01 A.M. TO 8:00 A.M.   **MOON 2** ◑ 8:01 A.M. TO 4:00 P.M.   **MOON 3** ● 4:01 P.M. TO 12:00 A.M.
Use only one "moon" number. Choose the column closest to your time of birth. If your place of birth is not on Eastern Standard Time, be sure to read "How to Convert to Eastern Standard Time" at the beginning of this section.

1916

September

October

Date & Time	SUN	MOON 1	MOON 2	MOON 3	MERCURY	VENUS	MARS	JUPITER	SATURN	URANUS	NEPTUNE	PLUTO
SEP. 1	22	27	28	29	25	16	28	6	16	43	17	14
SEP. 2	22	29	30	30	26	16	28	6	16	43	17	14
SEP. 3	23	31	32	32	26	16	28	6	16	43	17	14
SEP. 4	23	33	33	34	26	16	29	6	17	43	17	14
SEP. 5	23	35	35	36	26	17	29	6	17	43	17	14
SEP. 6	23	37	37	38	26	17	29	6	17	43	17	14
SEP. 7	23	38	39	40	26	17	29	6	17	43	17	14
SEP. 8	23	40	41	42	27	17	29	6	17	43	17	14
SEP. 9	23	42	43	44	27	17	29	6	17	43	17	14
SEP. 10	23	44	45	46	27	17	29	6	17	43	17	14
SEP. 11	24	46	47	48	27	17	29	6	17	43	18	14
SEP. 12	24	48	1	1	27	17	29	6	17	43	18	14
SEP. 13	24	2	3	3	27	18	29	6	17	43	18	14
SEP. 14	24	4	5	5	27	18	29	6	17	43	18	14
SEP. 15	24	6	6	7	27	18	30	6	17	43	18	14
SEP. 16	24	7	8	9	27	18	30	6	17	43	18	14
SEP. 17	24	9	10	10	28	18	30	6	17	43	18	14
SEP. 18	24	11	11	12	28	18	30	6	17	43	18	14
SEP. 19	25	12	13	13	28	18	30	6	17	43	18	14
SEP. 20	25	14	14	15	28	18	30	6	17	43	18	14
SEP. 21	25	16	16	17	28	19	30	6	17	43	18	14
SEP. 22	25	17	18	18	28	19	30	6	17	43	18	14
SEP. 23	25	19	19	20	28	19	30	6	17	43	18	14
SEP. 24	25	20	21	21	28	19	30	5	17	43	18	14
SEP. 25	26	22	22	23	28	19	30	5	17	43	18	14
SEP. 26	26	24	24	25	28	19	31	5	17	43	18	14
SEP. 27	26	25	26	26	28	19	31	5	17	43	18	14
SEP. 28	26	27	28	28	28	20	31	5	17	43	18	14
SEP. 29	26	29	29	30	27	20	31	5	17	43	18	14
SEP. 30	26	31	31	32	27	20	31	5	17	43	18	14

Date & Time	SUN	MOON 1	MOON 2	MOON 3	MERCURY	VENUS	MARS	JUPITER	SATURN	URANUS	NEPTUNE	PLUTO
OCT. 1	26	32	33	34	27	20	31	5	17	43	18	14
OCT. 2	26	34	35	35	27	20	31	5	17	43	18	14
OCT. 3	27	36	37	37	27	20	31	5	17	43	18	14
OCT. 4	27	38	39	39	27	20	31	5	17	43	18	14
OCT. 5	27	40	40	41	27	21	31	5	17	43	18	14
OCT. 6	27	42	42	43	26	21	31	5	17	43	18	14
OCT. 7	27	44	44	45	26	21	32	5	17	43	18	14
OCT. 8	27	46	46	47	26	21	32	5	17	43	18	14
OCT. 9	27	47	48	1	26	21	32	5	17	43	18	14
OCT. 10	27	1	2	3	26	21	32	5	17	43	18	14
OCT. 11	28	3	4	4	26	21	32	5	17	43	18	14
OCT. 12	28	5	6	6	26	22	32	5	17	43	18	14
OCT. 13	28	7	7	8	26	22	32	5	17	43	18	14
OCT. 14	28	8	9	10	26	22	32	5	17	43	18	14
OCT. 15	28	10	11	11	26	22	32	5	17	43	18	14
OCT. 16	28	12	12	13	26	22	32	5	17	43	18	14
OCT. 17	28	13	14	14	26	22	32	5	17	43	18	14
OCT. 18	28	15	16	16	26	23	33	5	17	43	18	14
OCT. 19	29	17	17	18	26	23	33	5	17	43	18	14
OCT. 20	29	18	19	19	26	23	33	5	17	43	18	14
OCT. 21	29	20	20	21	26	23	33	5	17	43	18	14
OCT. 22	29	21	22	22	26	23	33	5	17	43	18	14
OCT. 23	29	23	24	27	27	23	33	5	17	43	18	14
OCT. 24	29	25	25	26	27	23	33	5	17	43	18	14
OCT. 25	29	26	27	28	27	24	33	5	17	43	18	14
OCT. 26	30	28	29	29	27	24	33	5	17	43	18	14
OCT. 27	30	30	31	31	27	24	33	5	17	43	18	14
OCT. 28	30	32	32	33	27	24	34	5	17	43	18	14
OCT. 29	30	34	34	35	28	24	34	5	17	43	18	14
OCT. 30	30	36	36	37	28	24	34	5	17	43	18	14
OCT. 31	30	38	38	39	28	25	34	5	17	43	18	14

MOON 1 ◐ 12:01 A.M. TO 8:00 A.M.   **MOON 2** ◑ 8:01 A.M. TO 4:00 P.M.   **MOON 3** ● 4:01 P.M. TO 12:00 A.M.

Use only one "moon" number. Choose the column closest to your time of birth. If your place of birth is not on Eastern Standard Time, be sure to read "How to Convert to Eastern Standard Time" at the beginning of this section.

1916

November

Date & Time	SUN	MOON 1	MOON 2	MOON 3	MERCURY	VENUS	MARS	JUPITER	SATURN	URANUS	NEPTUNE	PLUTO
NOV. 1	30	39	40	41	28	25	34	5	17	43	18	14
NOV. 2	30	41	42	43	28	25	34	5	17	43	18	14
NOV. 3	31	43	44	44	29	25	34	5	17	43	18	14
NOV. 4	31	45	46	46	29	25	34	5	17	43	18	14
NOV. 5	31	47	48	48	29	25	34	5	17	43	18	14
NOV. 6	31	1	1	2	29	25	34	5	17	43	18	14
NOV. 7	31	3	3	4	30	26	35	5	17	43	18	14
NOV. 8	31	4	5	6	30	26	35	5	17	43	18	14
NOV. 9	31	6	7	7	30	26	35	5	17	43	18	14
NOV. 10	31	8	8	9	30	26	35	5	17	43	18	14
NOV. 11	31	10	10	11	30	26	35	5	17	43	18	14
NOV. 12	32	11	12	12	31	26	35	5	17	43	18	14
NOV. 13	32	13	13	14	31	27	35	5	17	43	18	14
NOV. 14	32	14	15	16	31	27	35	5	17	43	18	14
NOV. 15	32	16	17	17	31	27	35	5	17	43	18	14
NOV. 16	32	18	18	19	31	27	35	5	17	43	18	14
NOV. 17	32	19	20	20	32	27	36	5	17	43	18	14
NOV. 18	32	21	21	22	32	27	36	5	17	43	18	14
NOV. 19	33	22	23	23	32	28	36	5	17	43	18	14
NOV. 20	33	24	25	25	32	28	36	5	17	43	18	14
NOV. 21	33	26	26	27	33	28	36	5	17	43	18	14
NOV. 22	33	27	28	29	33	28	36	5	17	43	18	14
NOV. 23	33	29	30	31	33	28	36	5	17	43	18	13
NOV. 24	33	31	32	32	33	28	36	5	17	43	18	13
NOV. 25	34	33	34	34	33	29	36	5	17	43	18	13
NOV. 26	34	35	36	36	34	29	36	4	17	43	18	13
NOV. 27	34	37	38	38	34	29	37	4	17	43	18	13
NOV. 28	34	39	40	40	34	29	37	4	17	43	18	13
NOV. 29	34	41	41	42	34	29	37	4	17	43	18	13
NOV. 30	34	43	43	44	34	29	37	4	17	43	18	13

December

Date & Time	SUN	MOON 1	MOON 2	MOON 3	MERCURY	VENUS	MARS	JUPITER	SATURN	URANUS	NEPTUNE	PLUTO
DEC. 1	34	45	45	46	35	29	37	4	17	43	18	13
DEC. 2	34	46	47	48	35	30	37	4	17	43	18	13
DEC. 3	35	48	1	2	35	30	37	4	17	43	18	13
DEC. 4	35	2	3	3	35	30	37	4	17	43	18	13
DEC. 5	35	4	4	5	35	30	37	4	17	43	18	13
DEC. 6	35	6	6	7	36	30	37	4	17	43	18	13
DEC. 7	35	7	8	8	36	30	38	4	17	43	18	13
DEC. 8	35	9	10	10	36	31	38	4	17	43	18	13
DEC. 9	35	11	11	12	36	31	38	4	17	43	18	13
DEC. 10	35	12	13	13	37	31	38	4	17	43	18	13
DEC. 11	36	14	15	15	37	31	38	4	17	43	18	13
DEC. 12	36	16	16	17	37	31	38	4	17	43	18	13
DEC. 13	36	17	18	18	37	31	38	4	17	43	18	13
DEC. 14	36	19	19	20	37	32	38	4	17	43	18	13
DEC. 15	36	20	21	21	38	32	38	4	17	43	18	13
DEC. 16	36	22	22	23	38	32	38	4	17	43	18	13
DEC. 17	36	23	24	25	38	32	39	4	17	43	18	13
DEC. 18	36	25	26	26	38	32	39	4	17	43	18	13
DEC. 19	37	27	27	28	38	32	39	4	17	43	18	13
DEC. 20	37	29	29	30	39	33	39	4	17	43	18	13
DEC. 21	37	30	31	32	39	33	39	4	17	43	18	13
DEC. 22	37	32	33	33	39	33	39	4	17	43	18	13
DEC. 23	37	34	35	35	39	33	39	4	17	43	18	13
DEC. 24	37	36	37	37	39	33	39	4	17	43	18	13
DEC. 25	37	38	39	39	40	33	39	4	17	43	18	13
DEC. 26	38	40	41	41	40	34	39	4	17	43	18	13
DEC. 27	38	42	43	43	40	34	40	4	17	43	18	13
DEC. 28	38	44	45	45	40	34	40	4	17	43	18	13
DEC. 29	38	46	47	47	40	34	40	4	17	43	18	13
DEC. 30	38	48	48	1	41	34	40	4	17	43	18	13
DEC. 31	38	2	2	3	41	34	40	4	17	43	18	13

MOON 1 ◗ 12:01 A.M. TO 8:00 A.M.   **MOON 2** ◑ 8:01 A.M. TO 4:00 P.M.   **MOON 3** ● 4:01 P.M. TO 12:00 A.M.

Use only one "moon" number. Choose the column closest to your time of birth. If your place of birth is not on Eastern Standard Time, be sure to read "How to Convert to Eastern Standard Time" at the beginning of this section.

1917

January

Date & Time	SUN	MOON 1	MOON 2	MOON 3	MERCURY	VENUS	MARS	JUPITER	SATURN	URANUS	NEPTUNE	PLUTO
JAN. 1	38	3	4	5	41	35	40	4	17	43	18	13
JAN. 2	38	5	6	6	41	35	40	4	17	43	18	13
JAN. 3	39	7	8	8	41	35	40	4	17	43	18	13
JAN. 4	39	9	9	10	41	35	40	4	17	43	18	13
JAN. 5	39	10	11	11	41	35	41	4	17	43	18	13
JAN. 6	39	12	12	12	42	35	41	4	17	43	17	13
JAN. 7	39	14	14	15	42	36	41	4	17	43	17	13
JAN. 8	39	15	16	16	42	36	41	4	17	43	17	13
JAN. 9	39	17	17	18	42	36	41	4	17	43	17	13
JAN. 10	40	18	19	19	42	36	41	4	17	43	17	13
JAN. 11	40	20	20	21	42	36	41	4	17	43	17	13
JAN. 12	40	21	22	22	42	36	41	4	17	43	17	13
JAN. 13	40	23	24	24	42	37	41	4	17	43	17	13
JAN. 14	40	25	25	26	42	37	41	4	17	43	17	13
JAN. 15	40	26	27	27	41	37	42	5	17	43	17	13
JAN. 16	40	28	28	29	41	37	42	5	17	43	17	13
JAN. 17	41	30	30	31	41	37	42	5	17	43	17	13
JAN. 18	41	31	32	33	41	37	42	5	17	43	17	13
JAN. 19	41	33	34	35	41	38	42	5	17	43	17	13
JAN. 20	41	35	36	36	41	38	42	5	17	43	17	13
JAN. 21	41	37	38	38	40	38	42	5	17	43	17	13
JAN. 22	41	39	40	40	40	38	42	5	17	43	17	13
JAN. 23	42	41	42	42	40	38	42	5	17	43	17	13
JAN. 24	42	43	44	44	40	38	43	5	17	43	17	13
JAN. 25	42	45	46	46	40	39	43	5	17	43	17	13
JAN. 26	42	47	48	48	40	39	43	5	16	43	17	13
JAN. 27	42	1	2	2	40	39	43	5	16	43	17	13
JAN. 28	42	3	4	4	40	39	43	5	16	44	17	13
JAN. 29	42	5	5	6	40	39	43	5	16	44	17	13
JAN. 30	42	7	7	8	40	39	43	5	16	44	17	13
JAN. 31	43	8	9	9	40	40	43	5	16	44	17	13

February

Date & Time	SUN	MOON 1	MOON 2	MOON 3	MERCURY	VENUS	MARS	JUPITER	SATURN	URANUS	NEPTUNE	PLUTO
FEB. 1	43	10	10	11	40	40	43	5	16	44	17	13
FEB. 2	43	12	12	13	40	40	43	5	16	44	17	13
FEB. 3	43	13	14	14	40	40	44	5	16	44	17	13
FEB. 4	43	15	15	16	40	40	44	5	16	44	17	13
FEB. 5	43	16	17	17	40	40	44	5	16	44	17	13
FEB. 6	43	18	18	19	40	41	44	5	16	44	17	13
FEB. 7	43	19	20	20	40	41	44	5	16	44	17	13
FEB. 8	44	21	22	22	40	41	44	5	16	44	17	13
FEB. 9	44	23	23	24	40	41	44	5	16	44	17	13
FEB. 10	44	24	25	25	40	41	44	5	16	44	17	13
FEB. 11	44	26	26	27	40	41	44	5	16	44	17	13
FEB. 12	44	27	28	29	41	42	45	5	16	44	17	13
FEB. 13	44	29	30	30	41	42	45	5	16	44	17	13
FEB. 14	44	31	31	32	41	42	45	5	16	44	17	13
FEB. 15	44	33	33	34	41	42	45	5	16	44	17	13
FEB. 16	45	34	35	36	41	42	45	5	16	44	17	13
FEB. 17	45	36	37	38	41	42	45	5	16	44	17	13
FEB. 18	45	38	39	40	41	43	45	5	16	44	17	13
FEB. 19	45	40	41	42	42	43	45	5	16	44	17	13
FEB. 20	45	42	43	44	42	43	45	5	16	44	17	13
FEB. 21	45	44	45	46	42	43	45	5	16	44	17	13
FEB. 22	45	46	47	48	42	43	46	5	16	44	17	13
FEB. 23	46	48	1	2	42	43	46	5	16	44	17	13
FEB. 24	46	2	3	3	42	44	46	5	16	44	17	13
FEB. 25	46	4	5	5	43	44	46	5	16	44	17	13
FEB. 26	46	6	7	7	43	44	46	5	16	44	17	13
FEB. 27	46	8	8	9	43	44	46	5	16	44	17	13
FEB. 28	46	9	10	11	43	44	46	5	16	44	17	13

MOON 1 ◐ 12:01 A.M. TO 8:00 A.M.   **MOON 2** ◑ 8:01 A.M. TO 4:00 P.M.   **MOON 3** ● 4:01 P.M. TO 12:00 A.M.
Use only one "moon" number. Choose the column closest to your time of birth. If your place of birth is not on
Eastern Standard Time, be sure to read "How to Convert to Eastern Standard Time" at the beginning of this section.

1917

March

Date & Time	SUN ☉	MOON 1 ◗	MOON 2 ◑	MOON 3 ●	MERCURY	VENUS	MARS	JUPITER	SATURN	URANUS	NEPTUNE	PLUTO
MAR. 1	46	11	12	12	43	44	46	5	16	44	17	13
MAR. 2	46	13	13	14	44	45	46	5	16	44	17	13
MAR. 3	47	14	15	15	44	45	47	5	16	44	17	13
MAR. 4	47	16	16	17	44	45	47	5	16	44	17	13
MAR. 5	47	17	18	18	44	45	47	5	16	44	17	13
MAR. 6	47	19	20	20	44	45	47	5	16	44	17	13
MAR. 7	47	21	21	22	45	45	47	5	16	44	17	13
MAR. 8	47	22	23	23	45	46	47	6	16	44	17	13
MAR. 9	47	24	24	25	45	46	47	6	16	44	17	13
MAR. 10	47	25	26	27	45	46	47	6	16	44	17	13
MAR. 11	48	27	28	28	46	46	47	6	16	44	17	13
MAR. 12	48	29	29	30	46	46	47	6	16	44	17	13
MAR. 13	48	30	31	32	46	46	48	6	16	44	17	13
MAR. 14	48	32	33	33	46	47	48	6	16	44	17	13
MAR. 15	48	34	35	35	46	47	48	6	16	44	17	13
MAR. 16	48	36	36	37	47	47	48	6	16	44	17	13
MAR. 17	48	38	38	39	47	47	48	6	16	44	17	13
MAR. 18	48	39	40	41	47	47	48	6	16	44	17	13
MAR. 19	1	41	42	43	47	47	48	6	16	44	17	13
MAR. 20	1	43	44	45	48	48	48	6	16	44	17	13
MAR. 21	1	45	46	47	48	48	48	6	16	44	17	13
MAR. 22	1	47	48	1	48	48	48	6	16	44	17	13
MAR. 23	1	1	2	3	48	48	1	6	16	44	17	13
MAR. 24	1	3	4	5	1	48	1	6	16	44	17	13
MAR. 25	2	5	6	6	1	48	1	6	16	44	17	13
MAR. 26	2	7	8	8	1	1	1	6	16	44	17	13
MAR. 27	2	9	9	10	1	1	1	6	16	44	17	13
MAR. 28	2	11	11	12	2	1	1	6	16	44	17	13
MAR. 29	2	12	13	13	2	1	1	6	16	44	17	13
MAR. 30	2	14	14	15	2	1	1	6	16	44	17	13
MAR. 31	2	15	16	16	2	1	1	6	16	44	17	13

April

Date & Time	SUN ☉	MOON 1 ◗	MOON 2 ◑	MOON 3 ●	MERCURY	VENUS	MARS	JUPITER	SATURN	URANUS	NEPTUNE	PLUTO
APR. 1	2	17	18	18	3	2	2	6	16	44	17	13
APR. 2	2	19	19	20	3	2	2	6	16	44	17	13
APR. 3	3	20	21	21	3	2	2	6	16	44	17	13
APR. 4	3	22	22	23	4	2	2	6	16	44	17	13
APR. 5	3	23	24	24	4	2	2	6	16	44	17	13
APR. 6	3	25	26	26	4	2	2	6	16	44	17	13
APR. 7	3	27	27	28	4	3	2	6	16	44	17	13
APR. 8	3	28	29	29	5	3	2	6	16	44	17	13
APR. 9	3	30	31	31	5	3	2	6	16	44	17	13
APR. 10	3	32	32	33	5	3	2	6	16	44	17	13
APR. 11	4	34	34	35	5	3	3	7	16	44	17	13
APR. 12	4	35	36	37	6	3	3	7	16	44	17	13
APR. 13	4	37	38	38	6	4	3	7	16	44	17	13
APR. 14	4	39	40	40	6	4	3	7	16	44	17	13
APR. 15	4	41	42	42	6	4	3	7	16	44	17	13
APR. 16	4	43	43	44	7	4	3	7	16	44	17	13
APR. 17	4	45	45	46	7	4	3	7	16	44	17	13
APR. 18	4	47	47	48	7	4	3	7	16	44	17	13
APR. 19	5	1	1	2	7	5	3	7	16	44	17	13
APR. 20	5	2	3	4	7	5	3	7	16	44	17	13
APR. 21	5	4	5	6	8	5	4	7	16	44	17	13
APR. 22	5	6	7	7	8	5	4	7	16	44	17	13
APR. 23	5	8	9	9	8	5	4	7	16	44	17	13
APR. 24	5	10	10	11	8	5	4	7	16	44	17	13
APR. 25	6	12	12	13	8	6	4	7	16	44	17	13
APR. 26	6	13	14	14	9	6	4	7	16	44	17	13
APR. 27	6	15	15	16	8	6	4	7	16	44	17	13
APR. 28	6	16	17	18	9	6	4	7	16	44	17	13
APR. 29	6	18	19	19	9	6	4	7	16	44	17	13
APR. 30	6	20	20	21	9	6	4	7	16	44	17	13

MOON 1 ◗ 12:01 A.M. TO 8:00 A.M.　　**MOON 2** ◑ 8:01 A.M. TO 4:00 P.M.　　**MOON 3** ● 4:01 P.M. TO 12:00 A.M.

Use only one "moon" number. Choose the column closest to your time of birth. If your place of birth is not on Eastern Standard Time, be sure to read "How to Convert to Eastern Standard Time" at the beginning of this section.

1917

May

June

Date & Time	SUN	MOON 1	MOON 2	MOON 3	MERCURY	VENUS	MARS	JUPITER	SATURN	URANUS	NEPTUNE	PLUTO
MAY 1	6	21	22	22	9	7	5	7	16	44	17	13
MAY 2	6	23	23	24	9	7	5	7	16	44	17	13
MAY 3	7	24	25	26	9	7	5	7	16	44	17	13
MAY 4	7	26	27	27	9	7	5	7	16	44	17	13
MAY 5	7	28	28	29	9	7	5	7	16	44	17	13
MAY 6	7	30	30	31	9	7	5	7	16	44	17	13
MAY 7	7	31	32	32	9	7	5	7	16	44	17	13
MAY 8	7	33	34	34	9	8	5	7	16	44	17	13
MAY 9	7	35	36	36	9	8	5	7	16	44	17	13
MAY 10	7	37	37	38	9	8	5	7	16	44	17	13
MAY 11	8	39	39	40	9	8	6	7	16	44	17	13
MAY 12	8	40	41	42	9	8	6	7	16	44	17	13
MAY 13	8	42	43	44	9	8	6	8	16	44	17	13
MAY 14	8	44	45	46	9	9	6	8	16	44	17	13
MAY 15	8	46	47	47	8	9	6	8	16	44	17	13
MAY 16	8	48	1	1	8	9	6	8	16	44	17	13
MAY 17	8	2	3	3	8	9	6	8	16	44	17	13
MAY 18	8	4	4	5	8	9	6	8	16	44	17	13
MAY 19	9	6	6	7	8	9	6	8	16	44	17	13
MAY 20	9	7	8	9	8	10	6	8	16	44	17	13
MAY 21	9	9	10	10	8	10	7	8	16	44	17	13
MAY 22	9	11	12	12	8	10	7	8	16	44	17	13
MAY 23	9	13	13	14	8	10	7	8	17	44	17	13
MAY 24	9	14	15	15	8	10	7	8	17	44	17	13
MAY 25	10	16	16	17	8	10	7	8	17	44	17	13
MAY 26	10	18	18	19	8	11	7	8	17	44	17	13
MAY 27	10	19	20	20	8	11	7	8	17	44	17	13
MAY 28	10	21	21	22	8	11	7	8	17	44	17	13
MAY 29	10	22	23	23	8	11	7	8	17	44	17	13
MAY 30	10	24	24	25	8	11	7	8	17	44	17	13
MAY 31	10	25	26	27	8	11	8	8	17	44	17	13

Date & Time	SUN	MOON 1	MOON 2	MOON 3	MERCURY	VENUS	MARS	JUPITER	SATURN	URANUS	NEPTUNE	PLUTO
JUN. 1	10	27	28	28	8	12	8	8	17	44	17	13
JUN. 2	10	29	29	30	8	12	8	8	17	44	17	13
JUN. 3	11	31	31	32	8	12	8	8	17	44	17	13
JUN. 4	11	32	33	34	8	12	8	8	17	44	17	13
JUN. 5	11	34	35	35	8	12	8	8	17	44	17	13
JUN. 6	11	36	37	37	8	12	8	8	17	44	17	13
JUN. 7	11	38	39	39	8	13	8	8	17	44	17	13
JUN. 8	11	40	41	41	8	13	8	8	17	44	17	13
JUN. 9	11	42	43	43	8	13	8	8	17	44	17	13
JUN. 10	11	44	44	45	8	13	8	8	17	44	17	13
JUN. 11	12	46	46	47	8	13	8	8	17	44	17	13
JUN. 12	12	48	48	1	9	13	8	8	17	44	17	13
JUN. 13	12	1	2	3	9	14	9	8	17	44	17	13
JUN. 14	12	3	4	5	9	14	9	8	17	44	17	13
JUN. 15	12	5	6	6	9	14	9	9	17	44	17	13
JUN. 16	12	7	8	8	9	14	9	9	17	44	17	13
JUN. 17	12	9	9	10	9	14	9	9	17	44	17	13
JUN. 18	12	10	11	12	10	14	9	9	17	44	17	13
JUN. 19	13	12	13	13	10	15	9	9	17	44	17	13
JUN. 20	13	14	14	15	10	15	9	9	17	44	17	13
JUN. 21	13	15	16	16	10	15	9	9	17	44	17	13
JUN. 22	13	17	18	18	10	15	9	9	17	44	17	13
JUN. 23	13	19	19	20	10	15	10	9	17	44	17	13
JUN. 24	13	20	21	21	11	15	10	9	17	44	17	13
JUN. 25	14	22	22	23	11	16	10	9	17	44	17	13
JUN. 26	14	23	24	24	11	16	10	9	17	44	17	13
JUN. 27	14	25	25	26	11	16	10	9	17	44	17	13
JUN. 28	14	27	27	28	12	16	10	9	17	44	17	13
JUN. 29	14	28	29	29	12	16	10	9	17	44	17	13
JUN. 30	14	30	31	31	12	16	10	9	17	44	17	14

MOON 1 ◖ 12:01 A.M. TO 8:00 A.M.   **MOON 2** ◑ 8:01 A.M. TO 4:00 P.M.   **MOON 3** ● 4:01 P.M. TO 12:00 A.M.

Use only one "moon" number. Choose the column closest to your time of birth. If your place of birth is not on Eastern Standard Time, be sure to read "How to Convert to Eastern Standard Time" at the beginning of this section.

1917

July   August

Date & Time	SUN	MOON 1	MOON 2	MOON 3	MERCURY	VENUS	MARS	JUPITER	SATURN	URANUS	NEPTUNE	PLUTO
JUL. 1	14	32	32	33	12	16	11	9	17	44	17	14
JUL. 2	14	33	34	35	13	17	11	9	17	44	17	14
JUL. 3	15	35	36	37	13	17	11	9	17	44	17	14
JUL. 4	15	37	38	39	13	17	11	9	17	44	17	14
JUL. 5	15	39	40	41	13	17	11	9	17	44	17	14
JUL. 6	15	41	42	43	14	17	11	9	17	44	17	14
JUL. 7	15	43	44	44	14	17	11	9	17	44	17	14
JUL. 8	15	45	46	46	14	18	11	9	17	44	17	14
JUL. 9	15	47	48	48	15	18	11	9	17	44	17	14
JUL. 10	15	1	2	2	15	18	11	9	17	44	17	14
JUL. 11	16	3	4	4	15	18	11	9	17	44	17	14
JUL. 12	16	5	5	6	15	18	12	9	17	44	18	14
JUL. 13	16	7	7	8	16	18	12	9	17	44	18	14
JUL. 14	16	8	9	9	16	19	12	9	17	44	18	14
JUL. 15	16	10	11	11	16	19	12	9	17	44	18	14
JUL. 16	16	12	12	13	17	19	12	9	17	44	18	14
JUL. 17	16	13	14	14	17	19	12	9	17	44	18	14
JUL. 18	16	15	15	16	17	19	12	9	17	44	18	14
JUL. 19	17	17	17	18	17	19	12	9	17	44	18	14
JUL. 20	17	18	19	19	18	20	12	9	17	44	18	14
JUL. 21	17	20	20	21	18	20	12	10	17	44	18	14
JUL. 22	17	21	22	22	18	20	12	10	17	44	18	14
JUL. 23	17	23	23	24	18	20	13	10	17	44	18	14
JUL. 24	17	24	25	26	19	20	13	10	17	44	18	14
JUL. 25	17	26	27	27	19	20	13	10	17	44	18	14
JUL. 26	18	28	28	29	19	21	13	10	17	44	18	14
JUL. 27	18	29	30	30	19	21	13	10	18	44	18	14
JUL. 28	18	31	32	32	20	21	13	10	18	44	18	14
JUL. 29	18	33	33	34	20	21	13	10	18	44	18	14
JUL. 30	18	35	35	36	20	21	13	10	18	44	18	14
JUL. 31	18	36	37	38	20	21	13	10	18	44	18	14

Date & Time	SUN	MOON 1	MOON 2	MOON 3	MERCURY	VENUS	MARS	JUPITER	SATURN	URANUS	NEPTUNE	PLUTO
AUG. 1	18	38	39	40	21	22	13	10	18	44	18	14
AUG. 2	18	40	41	42	21	22	13	10	18	44	18	14
AUG. 3	19	42	43	44	21	22	14	10	18	44	18	14
AUG. 4	19	44	45	46	21	22	14	10	18	44	18	14
AUG. 5	19	46	47	48	21	22	14	10	18	44	18	14
AUG. 6	19	48	1	2	22	22	14	10	18	44	18	14
AUG. 7	19	2	3	4	22	22	14	10	18	44	18	14
AUG. 8	19	4	5	5	22	23	14	10	18	44	18	14
AUG. 9	19	6	7	7	22	23	14	10	18	44	18	14
AUG. 10	19	8	8	9	22	23	14	10	18	44	18	14
AUG. 11	20	10	10	11	23	23	14	10	18	44	18	14
AUG. 12	20	11	12	12	23	23	14	10	18	44	18	14
AUG. 13	20	13	13	14	23	23	14	10	18	44	18	14
AUG. 14	20	15	15	16	23	24	14	10	18	44	18	14
AUG. 15	20	16	17	17	23	24	15	10	18	44	18	14
AUG. 16	20	18	18	19	24	24	15	10	18	44	18	14
AUG. 17	20	19	20	20	24	24	15	10	18	44	18	14
AUG. 18	20	21	21	22	24	24	15	10	18	44	18	14
AUG. 19	21	22	23	24	24	24	15	10	18	44	18	14
AUG. 20	21	24	25	25	24	25	15	10	18	44	18	14
AUG. 21	21	26	26	27	24	25	15	10	18	44	18	14
AUG. 22	21	27	28	28	24	25	15	10	18	44	18	14
AUG. 23	21	29	30	30	25	25	15	10	18	44	18	14
AUG. 24	21	31	31	32	25	25	15	10	18	44	18	14
AUG. 25	21	32	33	33	25	25	15	10	18	44	18	14
AUG. 26	22	34	35	35	25	26	16	10	18	44	18	14
AUG. 27	22	36	36	37	25	26	16	10	18	44	18	14
AUG. 28	22	38	38	39	25	26	16	10	18	44	18	14
AUG. 29	22	39	40	41	25	26	16	10	18	44	18	14
AUG. 30	22	41	42	43	25	26	16	10	18	44	18	14
AUG. 31	22	43	44	45	25	26	16	10	18	44	18	14

MOON 1 ◗ 12:01 A.M. TO 8:00 A.M.   **MOON 2** ◐ 8:01 A.M. TO 4:00 P.M.   **MOON 3** ● 4:01 P.M. TO 12:00 A.M.

Use only one "moon" number. Choose the column closest to your time of birth. If your place of birth is not on Eastern Standard Time, be sure to read "How to Convert to Eastern Standard Time" at the beginning of this section.

1917

September

Date & Time	SUN	MOON 1	MOON 2	MOON 3	MERCURY	VENUS	MARS	JUPITER	SATURN	URANUS	NEPTUNE	PLUTO
SEP. 1	22	45	46	47	25	27	16	10	18	44	18	14
SEP. 2	22	48	48	1	25	27	16	10	18	44	18	14
SEP. 3	23	2	2	3	25	27	16	10	18	44	18	14
SEP. 4	23	4	4	5	25	27	16	10	18	44	18	14
SEP. 5	23	5	6	7	26	27	16	10	18	44	18	14
SEP. 6	23	7	8	8	26	27	16	10	18	44	18	14
SEP. 7	23	9	10	10	25	27	17	10	18	44	18	14
SEP. 8	23	11	11	12	25	28	17	10	18	44	18	14
SEP. 9	23	13	13	14	25	28	17	10	18	44	18	14
SEP. 10	23	14	15	15	25	28	17	10	18	44	18	14
SEP. 11	24	16	16	17	25	28	17	10	18	44	18	14
SEP. 12	24	17	18	18	25	28	17	10	18	44	18	14
SEP. 13	24	19	19	20	25	28	17	10	18	44	18	14
SEP. 14	24	21	21	22	25	29	17	10	18	44	18	14
SEP. 15	24	22	23	23	25	29	17	10	18	44	18	14
SEP. 16	24	24	24	25	25	29	17	10	18	44	18	14
SEP. 17	24	25	26	26	25	29	17	10	18	44	18	14
SEP. 18	24	27	27	28	25	29	17	10	18	44	18	14
SEP. 19	25	28	29	30	24	29	18	10	18	44	18	14
SEP. 20	25	30	31	31	24	30	18	10	18	44	18	14
SEP. 21	25	32	32	33	24	30	18	10	18	44	18	14
SEP. 22	25	33	34	35	24	30	18	10	18	44	18	14
SEP. 23	25	35	36	36	24	30	18	10	18	44	18	14
SEP. 24	25	37	38	38	24	30	18	10	18	44	18	14
SEP. 25	26	39	39	40	24	30	18	10	18	44	18	14
SEP. 26	26	41	41	42	24	30	18	10	18	44	18	14
SEP. 27	26	43	43	44	24	31	18	10	18	44	18	14
SEP. 28	26	45	45	46	24	31	18	11	19	44	18	14
SEP. 29	26	47	47	48	24	31	18	11	19	44	18	14
SEP. 30	26	1	1	2	24	31	18	11	19	44	18	14

October

Date & Time	SUN	MOON 1	MOON 2	MOON 3	MERCURY	VENUS	MARS	JUPITER	SATURN	URANUS	NEPTUNE	PLUTO
OCT. 1	26	3	3	4	24	31	18	11	19	44	18	14
OCT. 2	26	5	5	6	24	31	19	11	19	44	18	14
OCT. 3	27	7	7	8	24	32	19	11	19	44	18	14
OCT. 4	27	8	9	10	24	32	19	10	19	44	18	14
OCT. 5	27	10	11	11	24	32	19	10	19	44	18	14
OCT. 6	27	12	13	13	24	32	19	10	19	44	18	14
OCT. 7	27	14	14	15	24	32	19	10	19	44	18	14
OCT. 8	27	15	16	16	25	32	19	10	19	44	18	14
OCT. 9	27	17	17	18	25	33	19	10	19	44	18	14
OCT. 10	27	19	19	20	25	33	19	10	19	44	18	14
OCT. 11	28	20	21	21	25	33	19	10	19	44	18	14
OCT. 12	28	22	22	23	25	33	19	10	19	44	18	14
OCT. 13	28	23	24	24	26	33	19	10	19	44	18	14
OCT. 14	28	25	25	26	26	33	20	10	19	44	18	14
OCT. 15	28	26	27	28	26	33	20	10	19	44	18	14
OCT. 16	28	28	29	29	26	34	20	10	19	44	18	14
OCT. 17	28	30	30	31	26	34	20	10	19	44	18	14
OCT. 18	28	31	32	33	27	34	20	10	19	44	18	14
OCT. 19	29	33	34	34	27	34	20	10	19	44	18	14
OCT. 20	29	35	35	36	27	34	20	10	19	44	18	14
OCT. 21	29	37	37	38	27	34	20	10	19	44	18	14
OCT. 22	29	38	39	40	28	35	20	10	19	44	18	14
OCT. 23	29	40	41	41	28	35	20	10	19	44	18	14
OCT. 24	29	42	43	43	28	35	20	10	19	44	18	14
OCT. 25	29	44	45	45	28	35	20	10	19	44	18	14
OCT. 26	30	46	47	47	29	35	20	10	19	44	18	14
OCT. 27	30	48	48	1	29	35	21	10	19	44	18	14
OCT. 28	30	2	2	3	29	35	21	10	19	44	18	14
OCT. 29	30	4	4	5	29	36	21	10	19	44	18	14
OCT. 30	30	6	6	7	29	36	21	10	19	44	18	14
OCT. 31	30	8	8	9	30	36	21	10	19	44	18	14

MOON 1 ◗ 12:01 A.M. TO 8:00 A.M. **MOON 2** ◑ 8:01 A.M. TO 4:00 P.M. **MOON 3** ● 4:01 P.M. TO 12:00 A.M.

Use only one "moon" number. Choose the column closest to your time of birth. If your place of birth is not on Eastern Standard Time, be sure to read "How to Convert to Eastern Standard Time" at the beginning of this section.

1917

November

Date & Time	SUN	MOON 1	MOON 2	MOON 3	MERCURY	VENUS	MARS	JUPITER	SATURN	URANUS	NEPTUNE	PLUTO
NOV. 1	30	9	10	11	30	36	21	10	19	44	18	14
NOV. 2	30	11	12	12	30	36	21	10	19	44	18	14
NOV. 3	31	13	14	14	30	36	21	10	19	44	18	14
NOV. 4	31	15	15	16	30	37	21	10	19	44	18	14
NOV. 5	31	16	17	17	31	37	21	10	19	44	18	14
NOV. 6	31	18	19	19	31	37	21	10	19	44	18	14
NOV. 7	31	20	20	21	31	37	21	10	19	44	18	14
NOV. 8	31	21	22	22	31	37	21	10	19	44	18	14
NOV. 9	31	23	23	24	32	37	21	10	19	44	18	14
NOV. 10	31	24	25	25	32	37	22	10	19	44	18	14
NOV. 11	31	26	26	27	32	38	22	10	19	44	18	14
NOV. 12	32	28	28	29	32	38	22	10	19	44	18	14
NOV. 13	32	29	30	30	32	38	22	10	19	44	18	14
NOV. 14	32	31	31	32	33	38	22	10	19	44	18	14
NOV. 15	32	33	33	34	33	38	22	10	19	44	18	14
NOV. 16	32	34	35	36	33	38	22	10	19	44	18	14
NOV. 17	32	36	37	37	33	38	22	10	19	44	18	14
NOV. 18	32	38	39	39	33	39	22	10	19	44	18	14
NOV. 19	33	40	40	41	34	39	22	10	19	44	18	14
NOV. 20	33	42	42	43	34	39	22	10	19	44	18	14
NOV. 21	33	43	44	45	34	39	22	10	19	44	18	14
NOV. 22	33	45	46	47	34	39	22	10	19	44	18	14
NOV. 23	33	47	48	1	34	39	22	10	19	44	18	14
NOV. 24	33	1	2	2	35	39	22	10	19	44	18	14
NOV. 25	34	3	4	4	35	40	23	10	19	44	18	14
NOV. 26	34	5	6	6	35	40	23	10	19	44	18	14
NOV. 27	34	7	7	8	35	40	23	10	19	44	18	14
NOV. 28	34	9	9	10	35	40	23	10	19	44	18	14
NOV. 29	34	11	11	12	36	40	23	10	19	44	18	14
NOV. 30	34	12	13	13	36	40	23	10	19	44	18	14

December

Date & Time	SUN	MOON 1	MOON 2	MOON 3	MERCURY	VENUS	MARS	JUPITER	SATURN	URANUS	NEPTUNE	PLUTO
DEC. 1	34	14	15	15	36	40	23	10	19	44	18	14
DEC. 2	34	16	16	17	36	41	23	10	19	44	18	14
DEC. 3	35	17	18	18	36	41	23	10	19	44	18	14
DEC. 4	35	19	20	20	37	41	23	10	19	44	18	14
DEC. 5	35	21	21	22	37	41	23	10	19	44	18	14
DEC. 6	35	22	23	23	37	41	23	10	19	44	18	14
DEC. 7	35	24	24	25	37	41	23	10	19	44	18	14
DEC. 8	35	25	26	26	37	41	23	10	19	44	18	14
DEC. 9	35	27	28	28	38	41	23	10	19	44	18	14
DEC. 10	35	29	29	30	38	42	23	10	19	44	18	14
DEC. 11	36	30	31	31	38	42	24	10	19	44	18	14
DEC. 12	36	32	33	33	38	42	24	10	19	44	18	14
DEC. 13	36	34	34	35	38	42	24	10	19	44	18	14
DEC. 14	36	36	36	37	39	42	24	10	19	44	18	14
DEC. 15	36	37	38	39	39	42	24	10	19	44	18	14
DEC. 16	36	39	40	40	39	42	24	10	19	44	18	14
DEC. 17	36	41	42	42	39	42	24	10	19	44	18	14
DEC. 18	36	43	44	44	39	43	24	9	19	44	18	14
DEC. 19	37	45	46	46	39	43	24	9	19	44	18	14
DEC. 20	37	47	47	48	39	43	24	9	19	44	18	14
DEC. 21	37	1	1	2	39	43	24	9	19	44	18	14
DEC. 22	37	3	3	4	39	43	24	9	19	44	18	14
DEC. 23	37	4	5	6	40	43	24	9	19	44	18	14
DEC. 24	37	6	7	8	40	43	24	9	19	44	18	14
DEC. 25	37	8	9	9	40	43	24	9	19	44	18	14
DEC. 26	38	10	11	11	40	43	24	9	19	44	18	14
DEC. 27	38	12	12	13	40	43	24	9	19	44	18	14
DEC. 28	38	13	14	15	39	43	24	9	19	44	18	14
DEC. 29	38	15	16	16	39	44	24	9	19	44	18	14
DEC. 30	38	17	17	18	39	44	24	9	19	44	18	14
DEC. 31	38	18	19	20	39	44	25	9	19	44	18	14

MOON 1 ◗ 12:01 A.M. TO 8:00 A.M.   **MOON 2** ◑ 8:01 A.M. TO 4:00 P.M.   **MOON 3** ● 4:01 P.M. TO 12:00 A.M.

Use only one "moon" number. Choose the column closest to your time of birth. If your place of birth is not on Eastern Standard Time, be sure to read "How to Convert to Eastern Standard Time" at the beginning of this section.

1918

January

Date & Time	SUN	MOON 1	MOON 2	MOON 3	MERCURY	VENUS	MARS	JUPITER	SATURN	URANUS	NEPTUNE	PLUTO
JAN. 1	38	20	21	21	39	44	25	9	19	44	18	14
JAN. 2	38	22	22	23	39	44	25	9	19	44	18	14
JAN. 3	39	23	24	24	39	44	25	9	19	44	18	14
JAN. 4	39	25	25	26	38	44	25	9	19	44	18	14
JAN. 5	39	26	27	27	38	44	25	9	19	44	18	14
JAN. 6	39	28	29	29	38	44	25	9	19	44	18	14
JAN. 7	39	30	30	31	38	44	25	9	19	44	18	14
JAN. 8	39	31	32	32	38	44	25	9	19	44	18	14
JAN. 9	39	33	34	34	38	44	25	9	19	44	18	14
JAN. 10	40	35	35	36	38	45	25	9	19	44	18	14
JAN. 11	40	37	37	38	38	45	25	9	19	44	18	14
JAN. 12	40	38	39	40	37	45	25	9	19	44	18	14
JAN. 13	40	40	41	42	37	45	25	9	19	44	18	14
JAN. 14	40	42	43	44	37	45	25	9	19	44	18	14
JAN. 15	40	44	45	46	37	45	25	9	19	44	18	14
JAN. 16	40	46	47	48	37	45	25	9	19	44	18	14
JAN. 17	41	48	1	2	38	45	25	9	19	44	18	14
JAN. 18	41	2	3	3	38	45	25	9	19	44	18	14
JAN. 19	41	4	5	5	38	45	25	9	19	44	18	14
JAN. 20	41	6	7	7	38	45	25	9	19	44	18	14
JAN. 21	41	8	8	9	38	45	25	9	19	44	18	13
JAN. 22	41	9	10	11	38	45	25	9	19	44	18	13
JAN. 23	42	11	12	12	38	45	25	9	19	44	18	13
JAN. 24	42	13	14	14	38	45	25	9	19	44	18	13
JAN. 25	42	15	15	16	38	45	25	9	19	44	18	13
JAN. 26	42	16	17	17	38	45	25	9	19	44	18	13
JAN. 27	42	18	18	19	39	45	25	9	18	44	18	13
JAN. 28	42	20	20	21	39	45	25	9	18	44	18	13
JAN. 29	42	21	22	22	39	45	25	9	18	44	18	13
JAN. 30	42	23	23	24	39	44	25	9	18	44	18	13
JAN. 31	43	24	25	25	39	44	25	9	18	44	18	13

February

Date & Time	SUN	MOON 1	MOON 2	MOON 3	MERCURY	VENUS	MARS	JUPITER	SATURN	URANUS	NEPTUNE	PLUTO
FEB. 1	43	26	26	27	39	44	25	9	18	44	18	13
FEB. 2	43	28	28	29	39	44	25	9	18	44	18	13
FEB. 3	43	29	30	30	40	44	25	9	18	44	18	13
FEB. 4	43	31	31	32	40	44	25	9	18	44	18	13
FEB. 5	43	32	33	34	40	44	25	9	18	44	18	13
FEB. 6	43	34	35	35	40	44	25	9	18	44	18	13
FEB. 7	43	36	36	37	40	44	25	9	18	44	18	13
FEB. 8	44	38	38	39	41	44	25	9	18	44	18	13
FEB. 9	44	40	40	41	41	44	25	9	18	44	18	13
FEB. 10	44	41	42	43	41	44	25	9	18	44	18	13
FEB. 11	44	43	44	45	41	44	25	9	18	44	18	13
FEB. 12	44	45	46	47	41	44	25	9	18	44	18	13
FEB. 13	44	47	48	1	42	43	25	9	18	44	18	13
FEB. 14	44	2	2	3	42	43	25	9	18	44	18	13
FEB. 15	44	3	4	5	42	43	25	9	18	44	18	13
FEB. 16	45	5	6	7	42	43	25	9	18	44	18	13
FEB. 17	45	7	8	8	42	43	25	9	18	44	18	13
FEB. 18	45	9	10	10	43	43	25	9	18	44	18	13
FEB. 19	45	11	11	12	43	43	25	9	18	44	18	13
FEB. 20	45	13	13	14	43	43	25	9	18	44	18	13
FEB. 21	45	14	15	15	43	43	25	9	18	44	18	13
FEB. 22	45	16	16	17	43	43	25	9	18	44	18	13
FEB. 23	46	18	18	19	44	43	25	9	18	44	18	13
FEB. 24	46	19	20	20	44	43	25	9	18	44	18	13
FEB. 25	46	21	21	22	44	43	25	9	18	44	18	13
FEB. 26	46	22	23	23	44	43	25	9	18	44	18	13
FEB. 27	46	24	24	25	44	43	25	9	18	44	18	13
FEB. 28	46	25	26	27	45	43	25	9	18	44	18	13

MOON 1 ◗ 12:01 A.M. TO 8:00 A.M.   **MOON 2** ◖ 8:01 A.M. TO 4:00 P.M.   **MOON 3** ● 4:01 P.M. TO 12:00 A.M.
Use only one "moon" number. Choose the column closest to your time of birth. If your place of birth is not on Eastern Standard Time, be sure to read "How to Convert to Eastern Standard Time" at the beginning of this section.

1918

March

Date & Time	SUN	MOON 1	MOON 2	MOON 3	MERCURY	VENUS	MARS	JUPITER	SATURN	URANUS	NEPTUNE	PLUTO
MAR. 1	46	27	28	28	45	43	25	9	18	44	18	13
MAR. 2	46	29	29	30	45	43	25	9	18	44	18	13
MAR. 3	47	30	31	31	45	43	25	9	18	44	18	13
MAR. 4	47	32	32	33	46	43	25	9	18	44	18	13
MAR. 5	47	34	34	35	46	43	25	9	18	44	18	13
MAR. 6	47	35	36	36	46	43	25	9	18	44	18	13
MAR. 7	47	37	38	38	46	43	25	9	18	44	18	13
MAR. 8	47	39	39	40	47	43	25	10	18	44	18	13
MAR. 9	47	41	41	42	47	43	24	10	18	44	18	13
MAR. 10	47	43	43	44	47	43	24	10	18	44	18	13
MAR. 11	48	45	45	46	47	43	24	10	18	44	18	13
MAR. 12	48	47	47	48	48	43	24	10	18	44	18	13
MAR. 13	48	1	1	2	48	43	24	10	18	44	18	13
MAR. 14	48	3	3	4	48	43	24	10	18	44	18	13
MAR. 15	48	5	5	6	48	43	24	10	18	44	18	13
MAR. 16	48	7	7	8	1	43	24	10	18	44	18	13
MAR. 17	48	9	9	10	1	43	24	10	18	44	18	13
MAR. 18	48	10	11	12	1	43	24	10	18	44	18	13
MAR. 19	1	12	13	13	1	43	24	10	18	44	18	13
MAR. 20	1	14	14	15	2	43	24	10	18	44	18	13
MAR. 21	1	15	16	17	2	43	24	10	18	44	18	13
MAR. 22	1	17	18	18	2	44	24	10	18	44	18	13
MAR. 23	1	19	19	20	3	44	24	10	18	44	18	13
MAR. 24	1	20	21	21	3	44	24	10	18	44	18	13
MAR. 25	2	22	22	23	3	44	24	10	18	44	18	13
MAR. 26	2	24	24	25	3	44	24	10	18	44	18	13
MAR. 27	2	25	26	26	4	44	24	10	18	44	18	13
MAR. 28	2	27	27	28	4	44	24	10	18	44	18	13
MAR. 29	2	28	29	29	4	44	23	10	18	44	18	13
MAR. 30	2	30	30	31	4	44	23	10	18	44	18	13
MAR. 31	2	31	32	33	4	44	23	10	18	44	18	13

April

Date & Time	SUN	MOON 1	MOON 2	MOON 3	MERCURY	VENUS	MARS	JUPITER	SATURN	URANUS	NEPTUNE	PLUTO
APR. 1	2	33	34	34	5	44	23	10	18	44	18	13
APR. 2	2	35	35	36	5	45	23	10	18	44	18	13
APR. 3	3	36	37	38	5	45	23	10	18	44	18	13
APR. 4	3	38	39	39	5	45	23	10	18	44	18	13
APR. 5	3	40	41	41	5	45	23	10	18	44	18	13
APR. 6	3	42	42	43	6	45	23	10	18	44	18	13
APR. 7	3	44	44	45	6	45	23	10	18	44	18	13
APR. 8	3	46	46	47	6	45	23	10	18	45	18	13
APR. 9	3	48	48	1	6	45	23	10	18	45	18	13
APR. 10	3	2	2	3	6	45	23	10	18	45	18	13
APR. 11	4	4	4	5	6	46	23	10	18	45	18	13
APR. 12	4	6	6	7	6	46	23	10	18	45	18	13
APR. 13	4	8	8	9	6	46	23	10	18	45	18	13
APR. 14	4	10	10	11	6	46	23	10	18	45	18	13
APR. 15	4	11	12	13	6	46	23	10	18	45	18	13
APR. 16	4	13	14	14	6	46	23	10	18	45	18	13
APR. 17	4	15	16	16	6	46	23	10	18	45	18	13
APR. 18	4	17	17	18	6	46	23	10	18	45	18	13
APR. 19	5	18	19	19	6	47	23	10	18	45	18	13
APR. 20	5	20	20	21	6	47	23	10	18	45	18	13
APR. 21	5	22	22	23	6	47	23	10	18	45	18	13
APR. 22	5	23	24	24	6	47	23	11	18	45	18	13
APR. 23	5	25	25	26	6	47	23	11	18	45	18	13
APR. 24	5	26	27	27	6	47	23	11	18	45	18	13
APR. 25	6	28	28	29	6	47	23	11	18	45	18	13
APR. 26	6	29	30	31	6	47	23	11	18	45	18	13
APR. 27	6	31	32	32	6	48	23	11	18	45	18	13
APR. 28	6	33	33	34	6	48	23	11	18	45	18	13
APR. 29	6	34	35	36	6	48	23	11	18	45	18	13
APR. 30	6	36	37	37	6	48	23	11	18	45	18	13

MOON 1 ◗ 12:01 A.M. TO 8:00 A.M.   **MOON 2** ◑ 8:01 A.M. TO 4:00 P.M.   **MOON 3** ● 4:01 P.M. TO 12:00 A.M.

Use only one "moon" number. Choose the column closest to your time of birth. If your place of birth is not on Eastern Standard Time, be sure to read "How to Convert to Eastern Standard Time" at the beginning of this section.

1918

May

June

Date & Time	SUN	MOON 1	MOON 2	MOON 3	MERCURY	VENUS	MARS	JUPITER	SATURN	URANUS	NEPTUNE	PLUTO
MAY 1	6	38	38	39	5	48	23	11	18	45	18	13
MAY 2	6	40	40	41	5	48	23	11	18	45	18	13
MAY 3	7	41	42	43	5	48	23	11	18	45	18	13
MAY 4	7	43	44	44	5	1	23	11	18	45	18	13
MAY 5	7	45	46	46	5	1	23	11	18	45	18	13
MAY 6	7	47	48	48	5	1	23	11	18	45	18	13
MAY 7	7	1	2	2	5	1	23	11	18	45	18	13
MAY 8	7	3	4	4	5	1	23	11	18	45	18	13
MAY 9	7	5	6	6	5	1	23	11	18	45	18	13
MAY 10	7	7	8	8	5	1	23	11	18	45	18	13
MAY 11	8	9	9	10	5	2	23	11	18	45	18	13
MAY 12	8	11	11	12	5	2	23	11	18	45	18	13
MAY 13	8	13	13	14	5	2	23	11	18	45	18	14
MAY 14	8	14	15	16	5	2	23	11	18	45	18	14
MAY 15	8	16	17	17	5	2	23	11	18	45	18	14
MAY 16	8	18	18	19	5	2	23	11	18	45	18	14
MAY 17	8	19	20	20	5	2	23	11	18	45	18	14
MAY 18	8	21	22	22	5	3	23	11	18	45	18	14
MAY 19	9	23	23	24	5	3	23	11	18	45	18	14
MAY 20	9	24	25	25	5	3	23	11	18	45	18	14
MAY 21	9	26	26	27	6	3	23	11	18	45	18	14
MAY 22	9	27	28	28	6	3	23	11	18	45	18	14
MAY 23	9	29	30	30	6	3	23	11	18	45	18	14
MAY 24	9	31	31	32	6	3	23	11	18	45	18	14
MAY 25	10	32	33	33	6	4	23	11	18	45	18	14
MAY 26	10	34	35	35	6	4	23	12	18	45	18	14
MAY 27	10	36	36	37	6	4	24	12	18	45	18	14
MAY 28	10	37	38	39	6	4	24	12	18	45	18	14
MAY 29	10	39	40	40	7	4	24	12	18	45	18	14
MAY 30	10	41	42	42	7	4	24	12	18	45	18	14
MAY 31	10	43	43	44	7	5	24	12	18	45	18	14

Date & Time	SUN	MOON 1	MOON 2	MOON 3	MERCURY	VENUS	MARS	JUPITER	SATURN	URANUS	NEPTUNE	PLUTO
JUN. 1	10	45	45	46	7	5	24	12	18	45	18	14
JUN. 2	10	46	47	48	7	5	24	12	18	45	18	14
JUN. 3	11	48	1	2	8	5	24	12	18	45	18	14
JUN. 4	11	2	3	4	8	5	24	12	18	45	18	14
JUN. 5	11	4	5	5	8	5	24	12	18	45	18	14
JUN. 6	11	6	7	7	8	5	24	12	18	45	18	14
JUN. 7	11	8	9	8	8	6	24	12	18	45	18	14
JUN. 8	11	10	11	11	9	6	24	12	18	45	18	14
JUN. 9	11	12	12	13	9	6	24	12	18	45	18	14
JUN. 10	11	14	14	15	9	6	24	12	18	45	18	14
JUN. 11	12	15	16	17	9	6	24	12	18	45	18	14
JUN. 12	12	17	18	19	9	6	24	12	18	45	18	14
JUN. 13	12	19	19	20	10	6	24	12	18	45	18	14
JUN. 14	12	20	21	22	10	7	24	12	18	45	18	14
JUN. 15	12	22	23	23	10	7	24	12	18	45	18	14
JUN. 16	12	24	24	25	10	7	25	12	18	45	18	14
JUN. 17	12	25	26	26	11	7	25	12	18	45	18	14
JUN. 18	12	27	27	28	11	7	25	12	19	45	18	14
JUN. 19	13	28	29	30	11	7	25	12	19	45	18	14
JUN. 20	13	30	31	31	12	8	25	12	19	45	18	14
JUN. 21	13	32	32	33	12	8	25	12	19	45	18	14
JUN. 22	13	33	34	35	12	8	25	12	19	45	18	14
JUN. 23	13	35	36	36	12	8	25	12	19	45	18	14
JUN. 24	13	37	37	38	13	8	25	12	19	45	18	14
JUN. 25	14	39	39	40	13	8	25	12	19	45	18	14
JUN. 26	14	40	41	42	13	8	25	12	19	45	18	14
JUN. 27	14	42	43	44	14	9	25	12	19	45	18	14
JUN. 28	14	44	45	45	14	9	25	13	19	45	18	14
JUN. 29	14	46	47	47	14	9	25	13	19	45	18	14
JUN. 30	14	48	1	1	14	9	25	13	19	45	18	14

MOON 1 ◑ 12:01 A.M. TO 8:00 A.M.　　**MOON 2** ◑ 8:01 A.M. TO 4:00 P.M.　　**MOON 3** ● 4:01 P.M. TO 12:00 A.M.

Use only one "moon" number. Choose the column closest to your time of birth. If your place of birth is not on Eastern Standard Time, be sure to read "How to Convert to Eastern Standard Time" at the beginning of this section.

1918

July

August

Date & Time	SUN	MOON 1	MOON 2	MOON 3	MERCURY	VENUS	MARS	JUPITER	SATURN	URANUS	NEPTUNE	PLUTO
JUL. 1	14	2	2	3	15	9	25	13	19	45	18	14
JUL. 2	14	4	4	5	15	9	26	13	19	45	18	14
JUL. 3	15	6	6	7	15	10	26	13	19	45	18	14
JUL. 4	15	7	8	9	16	10	26	13	19	45	18	14
JUL. 5	15	9	10	11	16	10	26	13	19	45	18	14
JUL. 6	15	11	12	12	16	10	26	13	19	45	18	14
JUL. 7	15	13	14	14	16	10	26	13	19	45	18	14
JUL. 8	15	15	15	16	17	10	26	13	19	45	18	14
JUL. 9	15	17	17	18	17	11	26	13	19	45	18	14
JUL. 10	15	18	19	19	17	11	26	13	19	45	18	14
JUL. 11	16	20	20	21	17	11	26	13	19	45	18	14
JUL. 12	16	22	22	23	18	11	26	13	19	45	18	14
JUL. 13	16	23	24	24	18	11	26	13	19	45	18	14
JUL. 14	16	25	25	26	18	11	26	13	19	45	18	14
JUL. 15	16	26	27	27	18	11	26	13	19	45	18	14
JUL. 16	16	28	28	29	19	12	26	13	19	45	18	14
JUL. 17	16	30	30	31	19	12	27	13	19	45	18	14
JUL. 18	16	31	32	32	19	12	27	13	19	45	18	14
JUL. 19	17	33	33	34	19	12	27	13	19	45	18	14
JUL. 20	17	34	35	36	19	12	27	13	19	45	18	14
JUL. 21	17	36	37	37	20	12	27	13	19	45	18	14
JUL. 22	17	38	39	39	20	13	27	13	19	45	18	14
JUL. 23	17	40	40	41	20	13	27	13	19	45	18	14
JUL. 24	17	42	42	43	20	13	27	13	19	45	18	14
JUL. 25	17	44	44	45	20	13	27	13	19	45	18	14
JUL. 26	18	45	46	47	21	13	27	13	19	45	18	14
JUL. 27	18	47	48	1	21	13	27	13	19	45	18	14
JUL. 28	18	1	2	3	21	14	27	13	19	45	18	14
JUL. 29	18	3	4	5	21	14	27	13	19	45	18	14
JUL. 30	18	5	6	6	21	14	28	13	19	45	18	14
JUL. 31	18	7	8	8	21	14	28	13	19	44	18	14

Date & Time	SUN	MOON 1	MOON 2	MOON 3	MERCURY	VENUS	MARS	JUPITER	SATURN	URANUS	NEPTUNE	PLUTO
AUG. 1	18	9	10	10	22	14	28	14	19	44	18	14
AUG. 2	18	11	11	12	22	14	28	14	19	44	18	14
AUG. 3	19	12	13	14	22	14	28	14	19	44	18	14
AUG. 4	19	14	15	15	22	15	28	14	19	44	18	14
AUG. 5	19	16	17	17	22	15	28	14	19	44	18	14
AUG. 6	19	18	18	19	22	15	28	14	19	44	18	14
AUG. 7	19	19	20	20	22	15	28	14	19	44	18	14
AUG. 8	19	21	22	22	23	15	28	14	19	44	18	14
AUG. 9	19	23	23	24	23	15	28	14	19	44	18	14
AUG. 10	19	24	25	25	23	16	28	14	19	44	18	14
AUG. 11	20	26	26	27	23	16	28	14	19	44	18	14
AUG. 12	20	27	28	28	23	16	29	14	19	44	18	14
AUG. 13	20	29	30	30	23	16	29	14	19	44	18	14
AUG. 14	20	31	31	32	23	16	29	14	19	44	18	14
AUG. 15	20	32	33	33	23	16	29	14	19	44	18	14
AUG. 16	20	34	34	35	23	17	29	14	19	44	18	14
AUG. 17	20	36	36	37	23	17	29	14	19	44	18	14
AUG. 18	20	37	38	38	23	17	29	14	19	44	18	14
AUG. 19	21	39	40	40	23	17	29	14	20	44	18	14
AUG. 20	21	41	42	42	23	17	29	14	20	44	18	14
AUG. 21	21	43	43	44	23	17	29	14	20	44	18	14
AUG. 22	21	45	45	46	23	18	29	14	20	44	18	14
AUG. 23	21	47	47	48	23	18	29	14	20	44	18	14
AUG. 24	21	1	1	2	23	18	30	14	20	44	18	14
AUG. 25	21	3	3	4	23	18	30	14	20	44	18	14
AUG. 26	22	5	5	6	23	18	30	14	20	44	18	14
AUG. 27	22	7	7	8	23	18	30	14	20	44	18	14
AUG. 28	22	8	9	10	23	19	30	14	20	44	18	14
AUG. 29	22	10	11	12	23	19	30	14	20	44	18	14
AUG. 30	22	12	13	13	22	19	30	14	20	44	18	14
AUG. 31	22	14	14	15	22	19	30	14	20	44	18	14

MOON 1 ◗ 12:01 A.M. TO 8:00 A.M.   **MOON 2** ◖ 8:01 A.M. TO 4:00 P.M.   **MOON 3** ● 4:01 P.M. TO 12:00 A.M.

Use only one "moon" number. Choose the column closest to your time of birth. If your place of birth is not on Eastern Standard Time, be sure to read "How to Convert to Eastern Standard Time" at the beginning of this section.

September

October

Date & Time	SUN	MOON 1	MOON 2	MOON 3	MERCURY	VENUS	MARS	JUPITER	SATURN	URANUS	NEPTUNE	PLUTO
SEP. 1	22	16	16	17	22	19	30	14	20	44	18	14
SEP. 2	22	17	18	18	22	19	30	14	20	44	18	14
SEP. 3	23	19	19	20	22	19	30	14	20	44	18	14
SEP. 4	23	21	21	22	22	20	31	14	20	44	18	14
SEP. 5	23	22	23	23	22	20	31	14	20	44	18	14
SEP. 6	23	24	24	25	22	20	31	14	20	44	18	14
SEP. 7	23	25	26	26	22	20	31	14	20	44	18	14
SEP. 8	23	27	28	28	22	20	31	14	20	44	18	14
SEP. 9	23	29	29	30	21	20	31	14	20	44	18	14
SEP. 10	23	30	31	31	21	21	31	14	20	44	18	14
SEP. 11	24	32	32	33	21	21	31	15	20	44	18	14
SEP. 12	24	33	34	34	21	21	31	15	20	44	18	14
SEP. 13	24	35	35	36	21	21	31	15	20	44	18	14
SEP. 14	24	37	37	38	21	21	31	15	20	44	18	14
SEP. 15	24	38	39	40	22	21	31	15	20	44	18	14
SEP. 16	24	40	41	41	22	22	32	15	20	44	18	14
SEP. 17	24	42	43	43	22	22	32	15	20	44	18	14
SEP. 18	24	44	45	45	22	22	32	15	20	44	18	14
SEP. 19	25	46	47	47	22	22	32	15	20	44	18	14
SEP. 20	25	48	1	1	22	22	32	15	20	44	18	14
SEP. 21	25	2	3	3	22	22	32	15	20	44	18	14
SEP. 22	25	4	5	5	22	23	32	15	20	44	18	14
SEP. 23	25	6	7	7	23	23	32	15	20	44	18	14
SEP. 24	25	8	9	9	23	23	32	15	20	44	18	14
SEP. 25	26	10	10	11	23	23	32	15	20	44	18	14
SEP. 26	26	12	12	13	23	23	32	15	20	44	18	14
SEP. 27	26	13	14	15	24	23	33	15	20	44	18	14
SEP. 28	26	15	16	16	24	24	33	15	20	44	18	14
SEP. 29	26	17	17	18	24	24	33	15	20	44	18	14
SEP. 30	26	19	19	20	24	24	33	15	20	44	18	14

Date & Time	SUN	MOON 1	MOON 2	MOON 3	MERCURY	VENUS	MARS	JUPITER	SATURN	URANUS	NEPTUNE	PLUTO
OCT. 1	26	20	21	21	24	24	33	15	20	44	18	14
OCT. 2	26	22	22	23	25	24	33	15	20	44	18	14
OCT. 3	27	23	24	24	25	24	33	15	20	44	18	14
OCT. 4	27	25	26	26	25	25	33	15	20	44	18	14
OCT. 5	27	27	27	28	25	25	33	15	20	44	18	14
OCT. 6	27	28	29	29	26	25	33	15	20	44	18	14
OCT. 7	27	30	30	31	26	25	34	15	20	44	18	14
OCT. 8	27	31	32	32	26	25	34	15	20	44	18	14
OCT. 9	27	33	33	34	26	25	34	15	20	44	18	14
OCT. 10	27	35	35	36	27	26	34	15	20	44	18	14
OCT. 11	28	36	37	37	27	26	34	15	20	44	18	14
OCT. 12	28	38	38	39	27	26	34	15	20	44	18	14
OCT. 13	28	40	40	41	27	26	34	15	20	44	18	14
OCT. 14	28	41	42	42	28	26	34	15	20	44	18	14
OCT. 15	28	43	44	44	28	26	34	15	20	44	18	14
OCT. 16	28	45	46	46	28	27	34	15	20	44	18	14
OCT. 17	28	47	48	48	28	27	34	15	20	44	18	14
OCT. 18	28	1	2	2	28	27	35	15	20	44	18	14
OCT. 19	29	3	4	4	29	27	35	15	20	44	18	14
OCT. 20	29	5	6	6	29	27	35	15	20	44	18	14
OCT. 21	29	7	8	8	29	27	35	15	20	44	18	14
OCT. 22	29	9	10	10	29	28	35	15	20	44	18	14
OCT. 23	29	11	12	12	30	28	35	15	20	44	18	14
OCT. 24	29	13	13	14	30	28	35	15	20	44	18	14
OCT. 25	29	15	15	16	30	28	35	15	20	44	18	14
OCT. 26	30	16	17	18	30	28	35	15	20	44	18	14
OCT. 27	30	18	19	19	30	28	35	15	21	44	18	14
OCT. 28	30	20	20	21	31	29	36	15	21	44	18	14
OCT. 29	30	21	22	22	31	29	36	15	21	44	18	14
OCT. 30	30	23	24	24	31	29	36	15	21	44	18	14
OCT. 31	30	25	25	26	31	29	36	15	21	44	18	14

MOON 1 ☽ 12:01 A.M. TO 8:00 A.M.   **MOON 2** ☽ 8:01 A.M. TO 4:00 P.M.   **MOON 3** ● 4:01 P.M. TO 12:00 A.M.

Use only one "moon" number. Choose the column closest to your time of birth. If your place of birth is not on Eastern Standard Time, be sure to read "How to Convert to Eastern Standard Time" at the beginning of this section.

1918

November

Date & Time	SUN	MOON 1	MOON 2	MOON 3	MERCURY	VENUS	MARS	JUPITER	SATURN	URANUS	NEPTUNE	PLUTO
NOV. 1	30	26	27	27	31	29	36	15	21	44	18	14
NOV. 2	30	28	28	29	32	29	36	15	21	44	18	14
NOV. 3	31	29	30	30	32	30	36	15	21	44	18	14
NOV. 4	31	31	31	32	32	30	36	15	21	44	18	14
NOV. 5	31	33	33	34	32	30	36	15	21	44	18	14
NOV. 6	31	34	35	35	32	30	36	15	21	44	18	14
NOV. 7	31	36	36	37	33	30	37	15	21	44	18	14
NOV. 8	31	37	38	39	33	30	37	15	21	44	18	14
NOV. 9	31	39	40	40	33	31	37	15	21	44	18	14
NOV. 10	31	41	41	42	33	31	37	15	21	44	18	14
NOV. 11	31	43	43	44	33	31	37	15	21	44	18	14
NOV. 12	32	44	45	46	34	31	37	15	21	44	18	14
NOV. 13	32	46	47	47	34	31	37	15	21	44	18	14
NOV. 14	32	48	1	1	34	31	37	15	21	44	18	14
NOV. 15	32	2	3	3	34	32	37	15	21	44	18	14
NOV. 16	32	4	5	5	34	32	37	15	21	44	18	14
NOV. 17	32	6	7	7	35	32	38	15	21	44	18	14
NOV. 18	32	8	9	9	35	32	38	15	21	44	18	14
NOV. 19	33	10	11	11	35	32	38	15	21	44	18	14
NOV. 20	33	12	13	13	35	32	38	15	21	44	18	14
NOV. 21	33	14	15	15	35	33	38	15	21	44	18	14
NOV. 22	33	16	16	17	35	33	38	15	21	44	18	14
NOV. 23	33	18	18	19	36	33	38	15	21	44	18	14
NOV. 24	33	19	20	20	36	33	38	15	21	44	18	14
NOV. 25	34	21	21	22	36	33	38	15	21	44	18	14
NOV. 26	34	23	23	24	36	33	38	15	21	44	18	14
NOV. 27	34	24	25	25	36	34	39	15	21	44	18	14
NOV. 28	34	26	26	27	36	34	39	15	21	44	18	14
NOV. 29	34	27	28	28	37	34	39	15	21	44	18	14
NOV. 30	34	29	29	30	37	34	39	15	21	44	18	14

December

Date & Time	SUN	MOON 1	MOON 2	MOON 3	MERCURY	VENUS	MARS	JUPITER	SATURN	URANUS	NEPTUNE	PLUTO
DEC. 1	34	30	31	32	37	34	39	15	21	44	18	14
DEC. 2	34	32	33	33	37	34	39	15	21	44	18	14
DEC. 3	35	34	34	35	37	35	39	15	21	44	18	14
DEC. 4	35	35	36	36	37	35	39	15	21	44	18	14
DEC. 5	35	37	38	38	37	35	39	15	21	44	18	14
DEC. 6	35	39	39	40	37	35	39	15	21	44	18	14
DEC. 7	35	40	41	42	37	35	40	15	21	44	18	14
DEC. 8	35	42	43	43	37	35	40	15	21	44	18	14
DEC. 9	35	44	45	45	37	36	40	15	21	44	18	14
DEC. 10	35	46	46	47	37	36	40	15	21	44	18	14
DEC. 11	36	48	48	1	37	36	40	15	21	44	18	14
DEC. 12	36	1	2	3	37	36	40	15	21	44	18	14
DEC. 13	36	3	4	5	37	36	40	15	21	44	18	14
DEC. 14	36	5	6	7	37	36	40	15	21	44	18	14
DEC. 15	36	7	8	9	37	37	40	15	21	44	18	14
DEC. 16	36	9	10	11	37	37	41	15	21	44	18	14
DEC. 17	36	11	12	12	37	37	41	15	21	44	18	14
DEC. 18	36	13	14	14	37	37	41	15	21	44	18	14
DEC. 19	37	15	16	16	37	37	41	15	21	44	18	14
DEC. 20	37	17	17	18	36	37	41	15	21	44	18	14
DEC. 21	37	19	19	20	36	38	41	15	21	44	18	14
DEC. 22	37	20	21	21	36	38	41	15	21	44	18	14
DEC. 23	37	22	23	23	36	38	41	15	21	44	18	14
DEC. 24	37	24	24	25	36	38	41	15	21	44	18	14
DEC. 25	37	25	26	26	35	38	41	15	21	44	18	14
DEC. 26	38	27	27	28	35	38	42	15	21	44	18	14
DEC. 27	38	28	29	29	35	39	42	15	21	44	18	14
DEC. 28	38	30	30	31	35	39	42	14	21	44	18	14
DEC. 29	38	32	32	33	35	39	42	14	21	44	18	14
DEC. 30	38	33	34	34	35	39	42	14	21	44	18	14
DEC. 31	38	35	35	36	35	39	42	14	21	44	18	14

MOON 1 ☽ 12:01 A.M. TO 8:00 A.M.   **MOON 2** ☽ 8:01 A.M. TO 4:00 P.M.   **MOON 3** ● 4:01 P.M. TO 12:00 A.M.

Use only one "moon" number. Choose the column closest to your time of birth. If your place of birth is not on Eastern Standard Time, be sure to read "How to Convert to Eastern Standard Time" at the beginning of this section.

1919

January

February

Date & Time	SUN	MOON 1	MOON 2	MOON 3	MERCURY	VENUS	MARS	JUPITER	SATURN	URANUS	NEPTUNE	PLUTO
JAN. 1	38	36	37	38	35	39	42	14	21	44	18	14
JAN. 2	38	38	39	39	35	40	42	14	21	44	18	14
JAN. 3	39	40	41	42	36	40	42	14	21	44	18	14
JAN. 4	39	42	42	43	36	40	43	14	21	44	18	14
JAN. 5	39	43	44	45	36	40	43	14	21	44	18	14
JAN. 6	39	45	46	47	36	40	43	14	21	44	18	14
JAN. 7	39	47	48	48	36	40	43	14	21	44	18	14
JAN. 8	39	1	2	2	36	41	43	14	21	44	18	14
JAN. 9	39	3	4	4	36	41	43	14	21	44	18	14
JAN. 10	40	5	5	6	36	41	43	14	21	44	18	14
JAN. 11	40	7	7	8	37	41	43	14	21	44	18	14
JAN. 12	40	9	9	10	37	41	43	14	21	44	18	14
JAN. 13	40	10	11	12	37	42	43	14	21	44	18	14
JAN. 14	40	12	13	14	37	42	44	14	21	44	18	14
JAN. 15	40	14	15	15	37	42	44	14	21	44	18	14
JAN. 16	40	16	17	17	37	42	44	14	21	44	18	14
JAN. 17	41	18	18	19	38	42	44	14	21	44	18	14
JAN. 18	41	20	20	21	38	42	44	14	21	44	18	14
JAN. 19	41	21	22	22	38	43	44	14	21	44	18	14
JAN. 20	41	23	24	24	38	43	44	14	21	44	18	14
JAN. 21	41	25	25	26	38	43	44	14	21	44	18	14
JAN. 22	41	26	27	27	38	43	44	14	21	44	18	14
JAN. 23	42	28	28	29	39	43	45	14	21	44	18	14
JAN. 24	42	29	30	30	39	43	45	14	20	44	18	14
JAN. 25	42	31	32	32	39	44	45	14	20	44	18	14
JAN. 26	42	33	33	34	39	44	45	14	20	44	18	14
JAN. 27	42	34	35	35	39	44	45	14	20	44	18	14
JAN. 28	42	36	36	37	40	44	45	14	20	45	18	14
JAN. 29	42	38	38	39	40	44	45	14	20	45	18	14
JAN. 30	42	39	40	40	40	44	45	14	20	45	18	14
JAN. 31	43	41	42	42	40	45	45	14	20	45	18	14

Date & Time	SUN	MOON 1	MOON 2	MOON 3	MERCURY	VENUS	MARS	JUPITER	SATURN	URANUS	NEPTUNE	PLUTO
FEB. 1	43	43	44	44	40	45	45	14	20	45	18	14
FEB. 2	43	45	45	46	41	45	46	14	20	45	18	14
FEB. 3	43	47	47	48	41	45	46	14	20	45	18	14
FEB. 4	43	1	1	2	41	45	46	14	20	45	18	14
FEB. 5	43	2	3	4	41	45	46	14	20	45	18	14
FEB. 6	43	4	5	6	41	46	46	14	20	45	18	14
FEB. 7	43	6	7	8	42	46	46	14	20	45	18	14
FEB. 8	44	8	9	9	42	46	46	14	20	45	18	14
FEB. 9	44	10	11	11	42	46	46	14	20	45	18	14
FEB. 10	44	12	12	13	42	46	46	14	20	45	18	14
FEB. 11	44	14	14	15	43	46	47	14	20	45	18	14
FEB. 12	44	15	16	17	43	47	47	14	20	45	18	14
FEB. 13	44	17	18	18	43	47	47	14	20	45	18	14
FEB. 14	44	19	20	20	43	47	47	14	20	45	18	14
FEB. 15	44	21	21	22	43	47	47	14	20	45	18	14
FEB. 16	45	22	23	24	44	47	47	14	20	45	18	14
FEB. 17	45	24	25	25	44	47	47	14	20	45	18	14
FEB. 18	45	26	26	27	44	48	47	14	20	45	18	14
FEB. 19	45	27	28	28	44	48	47	14	20	45	18	14
FEB. 20	45	29	29	30	45	48	47	14	20	45	18	14
FEB. 21	45	30	31	32	45	48	48	14	20	45	18	14
FEB. 22	45	32	33	33	45	48	48	14	20	45	18	14
FEB. 23	46	34	34	35	45	48	48	14	20	45	18	14
FEB. 24	46	35	36	36	46	48	48	14	20	45	18	14
FEB. 25	46	37	37	38	46	1	48	14	20	45	18	14
FEB. 26	46	39	39	40	46	1	48	14	20	45	18	14
FEB. 27	46	40	41	42	46	1	48	14	20	45	18	14
FEB. 28	46	42	43	43	47	1	48	14	20	45	18	14

MOON 1 ◐ 12:01 A.M. TO 8:00 A.M.   **MOON 2** ◑ 8:01 A.M. TO 4:00 P.M.   **MOON 3** ● 4:01 P.M. TO 12:00 A.M.

Use only one "moon" number. Choose the column closest to your time of birth. If your place of birth is not on Eastern Standard Time, be sure to read "How to Convert to Eastern Standard Time" at the beginning of this section.

1919

March

April

Date & Time	SUN	MOON 1 ◗	MOON 2 ◑	MOON 3 ●	MERCURY	VENUS	MARS	JUPITER	SATURN	URANUS	NEPTUNE	PLUTO
MAR. 1	46	44	45	45	47	1	48	14	20	45	18	14
MAR. 2	46	46	47	47	47	1	48	14	20	45	18	14
MAR. 3	47	48	1	1	47	2	1	14	20	45	18	14
MAR. 4	47	2	2	3	48	2	1	14	20	45	18	14
MAR. 5	47	4	4	5	48	2	1	14	20	45	18	14
MAR. 6	47	6	6	7	48	2	1	14	20	45	18	14
MAR. 7	47	8	8	9	48	2	1	14	20	45	18	14
MAR. 8	47	10	10	11	1	2	1	14	20	45	18	14
MAR. 9	47	11	12	13	1	3	1	14	20	45	18	14
MAR. 10	47	13	14	14	1	3	1	14	20	45	18	14
MAR. 11	48	15	16	16	1	3	1	14	20	45	18	14
MAR. 12	48	17	17	18	2	3	2	14	20	45	18	14
MAR. 13	48	19	19	20	2	3	2	14	20	45	18	14
MAR. 14	48	20	21	21	2	3	2	14	20	45	18	14
MAR. 15	48	22	22	23	2	4	2	14	20	45	18	14
MAR. 16	48	24	24	25	3	4	2	14	20	45	18	14
MAR. 17	48	25	26	26	3	4	2	14	20	45	18	14
MAR. 18	48	27	27	28	3	4	2	14	20	45	18	14
MAR. 19	1	28	29	29	3	4	2	14	20	45	18	14
MAR. 20	1	30	31	31	3	4	2	14	20	45	18	14
MAR. 21	1	32	32	33	3	5	2	14	20	45	18	14
MAR. 22	1	33	34	34	3	5	3	14	20	45	18	14
MAR. 23	1	35	35	36	4	5	3	14	20	45	18	14
MAR. 24	1	36	37	37	4	5	3	14	20	45	18	14
MAR. 25	2	38	39	39	4	5	3	14	20	45	18	14
MAR. 26	2	40	40	41	4	5	3	14	20	45	18	14
MAR. 27	2	41	42	43	4	6	3	14	20	45	18	14
MAR. 28	2	43	44	44	4	6	3	14	20	45	18	14
MAR. 29	2	45	46	46	4	6	3	14	20	45	18	14
MAR. 30	2	47	48	48	4	6	3	14	20	45	18	14
MAR. 31	2	1	2	2	4	6	3	14	20	45	18	14

Date & Time	SUN	MOON 1 ◗	MOON 2 ◑	MOON 3 ●	MERCURY	VENUS	MARS	JUPITER	SATURN	URANUS	NEPTUNE	PLUTO
APR. 1	2	3	4	4	4	6	4	14	20	45	18	14
APR. 2	2	5	6	6	4	7	4	14	20	45	18	14
APR. 3	3	7	8	8	4	7	4	14	20	45	18	14
APR. 4	3	9	10	10	4	7	4	14	20	45	18	14
APR. 5	3	11	12	12	4	7	4	14	20	45	18	14
APR. 6	3	13	13	14	3	7	4	14	20	45	18	14
APR. 7	3	15	15	16	3	7	4	14	20	45	18	14
APR. 8	3	16	17	18	3	8	4	14	20	45	18	14
APR. 9	3	18	19	19	3	8	4	14	20	45	18	14
APR. 10	3	20	20	21	3	8	4	14	20	45	18	14
APR. 11	4	22	22	23	3	8	5	14	20	45	18	14
APR. 12	4	23	24	24	3	8	5	14	20	45	18	14
APR. 13	4	25	25	26	3	8	5	14	20	45	18	14
APR. 14	4	26	27	27	3	8	5	14	20	45	18	14
APR. 15	4	28	29	29	3	9	5	14	20	45	18	14
APR. 16	4	30	30	31	3	9	5	14	20	45	18	14
APR. 17	4	31	32	32	3	9	5	14	20	45	18	14
APR. 18	4	33	33	34	2	9	5	14	20	45	18	14
APR. 19	5	34	35	35	2	9	5	14	20	45	18	14
APR. 20	5	36	36	37	2	9	5	14	20	45	18	14
APR. 21	5	37	38	39	2	10	6	14	20	45	18	14
APR. 22	5	39	40	40	2	10	6	14	20	45	18	14
APR. 23	5	41	41	42	2	10	6	14	20	45	18	14
APR. 24	5	43	43	44	2	10	6	14	20	45	18	14
APR. 25	6	44	45	46	2	10	6	14	20	45	18	14
APR. 26	6	46	47	47	2	10	6	14	20	45	18	14
APR. 27	6	48	1	1	3	11	6	14	20	45	18	14
APR. 28	6	2	3	3	3	11	6	14	20	45	18	14
APR. 29	6	4	5	5	3	11	6	14	20	45	18	14
APR. 30	6	6	7	7	3	11	6	14	20	45	18	14

MOON 1 ◗ 12:01 A.M. TO 8:00 A.M.　　**MOON 2** ◑ 8:01 A.M. TO 4:00 P.M.　　**MOON 3** ● 4:01 P.M. TO 12:00 A.M.
Use only one "moon" number. Choose the column closest to your time of birth. If your place of birth is not on Eastern Standard Time, be sure to read "How to Convert to Eastern Standard Time" at the beginning of this section.

1919

May

June

Date & Time	SUN	MOON 1	MOON 2	MOON 3	MERCURY	VENUS	MARS	JUPITER	SATURN	URANUS	NEPTUNE	PLUTO
MAY 1	6	8	9	9	3	11	7	14	20	45	18	14
MAY 2	6	10	11	11	3	11	7	14	20	45	18	14
MAY 3	7	12	13	13	3	11	7	14	20	45	18	14
MAY 4	7	14	15	15	3	12	7	14	20	45	18	14
MAY 5	7	16	16	17	3	12	7	15	20	45	18	14
MAY 6	7	18	18	19	3	12	7	15	20	45	18	14
MAY 7	7	19	20	21	4	12	7	15	20	45	18	14
MAY 8	7	21	22	22	4	12	7	15	20	45	18	14
MAY 9	7	23	23	24	4	12	7	15	20	45	18	14
MAY 10	7	24	25	25	4	13	7	15	20	45	18	14
MAY 11	8	26	27	27	4	13	8	15	20	45	18	14
MAY 12	8	28	28	29	4	13	8	15	20	45	18	14
MAY 13	8	29	30	30	4	13	8	15	20	45	18	14
MAY 14	8	31	31	32	5	13	8	15	20	45	18	14
MAY 15	8	32	33	33	5	13	8	15	20	45	18	14
MAY 16	8	34	34	35	5	13	8	15	20	45	18	14
MAY 17	8	35	36	37	5	14	8	15	20	45	18	14
MAY 18	8	37	38	38	5	14	8	15	20	45	18	14
MAY 19	9	39	39	40	6	14	8	15	20	45	18	14
MAY 20	9	40	41	42	6	14	8	15	20	45	18	14
MAY 21	9	42	43	43	6	14	8	15	20	45	18	14
MAY 22	9	44	44	45	6	14	9	15	20	45	18	14
MAY 23	9	46	46	47	6	15	9	15	20	45	18	14
MAY 24	9	47	48	1	7	15	9	15	20	45	18	14
MAY 25	10	1	2	3	7	15	9	15	20	45	18	14
MAY 26	10	3	4	5	7	15	9	15	20	45	18	14
MAY 27	10	5	6	7	7	15	9	15	20	45	18	14
MAY 28	10	7	8	9	8	15	9	15	20	45	18	14
MAY 29	10	9	10	11	8	15	9	15	20	45	18	14
MAY 30	10	11	12	13	8	16	9	15	20	45	18	14
MAY 31	10	13	14	14	8	16	9	15	20	45	18	14

Date & Time	SUN	MOON 1	MOON 2	MOON 3	MERCURY	VENUS	MARS	JUPITER	SATURN	URANUS	NEPTUNE	PLUTO
JUN. 1	10	15	16	16	9	16	10	15	20	45	18	14
JUN. 2	10	17	18	18	9	16	10	15	20	45	18	14
JUN. 3	11	19	19	20	9	16	10	15	20	45	18	14
JUN. 4	11	21	21	22	9	16	10	15	20	45	18	14
JUN. 5	11	22	23	23	10	16	10	15	20	45	18	14
JUN. 6	11	24	24	25	10	17	10	15	20	45	18	14
JUN. 7	11	26	26	27	10	17	10	15	20	45	18	14
JUN. 8	11	27	28	28	11	17	10	15	20	45	18	14
JUN. 9	11	29	29	30	11	17	10	15	20	45	18	14
JUN. 10	11	30	31	31	11	17	10	15	20	45	18	14
JUN. 11	12	32	32	33	11	17	10	15	20	45	18	14
JUN. 12	12	33	34	35	12	18	11	15	20	45	18	14
JUN. 13	12	35	36	36	12	18	11	15	20	45	18	14
JUN. 14	12	37	37	38	12	18	11	16	20	45	18	14
JUN. 15	12	38	39	39	13	18	11	16	20	45	18	14
JUN. 16	12	40	41	41	13	18	11	16	20	45	18	14
JUN. 17	12	42	42	43	13	18	11	16	20	45	18	14
JUN. 18	12	43	44	45	13	18	11	16	20	45	18	14
JUN. 19	13	45	46	46	14	19	11	16	20	45	18	14
JUN. 20	13	47	48	48	14	19	11	16	20	45	18	14
JUN. 21	13	1	1	2	14	19	11	16	20	45	18	14
JUN. 22	13	3	3	4	15	19	11	16	20	45	18	14
JUN. 23	13	5	5	6	15	19	12	16	20	45	18	14
JUN. 24	13	6	7	8	15	19	12	16	20	45	18	14
JUN. 25	14	8	9	10	15	19	12	16	20	45	18	14
JUN. 26	14	10	11	12	16	19	12	16	20	45	18	14
JUN. 27	14	12	13	14	16	20	12	16	20	45	18	14
JUN. 28	14	14	15	16	16	20	12	16	20	45	18	14
JUN. 29	14	16	17	17	16	20	12	16	20	45	18	14
JUN. 30	14	18	19	19	17	20	12	16	20	45	18	14

MOON 1 ◖ 12:01 A.M. TO 8:00 A.M.   **MOON 2** ◐ 8:01 A.M. TO 4:00 P.M.   **MOON 3** ● 4:01 P.M. TO 12:00 A.M.

Use only one "moon" number. Choose the column closest to your time of birth. If your place of birth is not on Eastern Standard Time, be sure to read "How to Convert to Eastern Standard Time" at the beginning of this section.

July

August

Date & Time	SUN ☉	MOON 1 ☽	MOON 2 ☽	MOON 3 ●	MERCURY	VENUS	MARS	JUPITER	SATURN	URANUS	NEPTUNE	PLUTO
JUL. 1	14	20	21	21	17	20	12	16	20	45	18	14
JUL. 2	14	22	22	23	17	20	12	16	20	45	18	14
JUL. 3	15	23	24	25	17	20	12	16	20	45	18	14
JUL. 4	15	25	26	26	17	21	13	16	20	45	18	14
JUL. 5	15	27	27	28	18	21	13	16	20	45	18	14
JUL. 6	15	28	29	29	18	21	13	16	20	45	18	14
JUL. 7	15	30	30	31	18	21	13	16	20	45	18	14
JUL. 8	15	31	32	32	18	21	13	16	20	45	18	14
JUL. 9	15	33	34	34	18	21	13	16	20	45	18	14
JUL. 10	15	35	35	36	19	21	13	16	20	45	18	14
JUL. 11	16	36	37	37	19	21	13	16	20	45	18	14
JUL. 12	16	38	38	39	19	22	13	16	20	45	18	14
JUL. 13	16	40	40	41	19	22	13	16	20	45	18	14
JUL. 14	16	41	42	42	19	22	13	16	20	45	18	14
JUL. 15	16	43	44	44	19	22	14	16	21	45	18	14
JUL. 16	16	45	45	46	20	22	14	16	21	45	18	14
JUL. 17	16	47	47	48	20	22	14	16	21	45	18	14
JUL. 18	16	48	1	2	20	22	14	17	21	45	18	14
JUL. 19	17	2	3	3	20	22	14	17	21	45	18	14
JUL. 20	17	4	5	5	20	22	14	17	21	45	18	14
JUL. 21	17	6	7	7	20	23	14	17	21	45	18	14
JUL. 22	17	8	9	9	20	23	14	17	21	45	18	14
JUL. 23	17	10	10	11	20	23	14	17	21	45	18	14
JUL. 24	17	12	12	13	20	23	14	17	21	45	18	14
JUL. 25	17	14	14	15	21	23	14	17	21	45	18	14
JUL. 26	18	15	16	17	21	23	15	17	21	45	18	14
JUL. 27	18	17	18	19	21	23	15	17	21	45	18	14
JUL. 28	18	19	20	20	21	23	15	17	21	45	18	14
JUL. 29	18	21	22	22	21	23	15	17	21	45	18	14
JUL. 30	18	23	23	24	21	23	15	17	21	45	18	14
JUL. 31	18	24	25	26	21	24	15	17	21	45	18	14

Date & Time	SUN ☉	MOON 1 ☽	MOON 2 ☽	MOON 3 ●	MERCURY	VENUS	MARS	JUPITER	SATURN	URANUS	NEPTUNE	PLUTO
AUG. 1	18	26	27	27	21	24	15	17	21	45	18	14
AUG. 2	18	28	28	29	21	24	15	17	21	45	18	14
AUG. 3	19	29	30	30	21	24	15	17	21	45	18	14
AUG. 4	19	31	31	32	21	24	15	17	21	45	18	14
AUG. 5	19	33	33	34	21	24	15	17	21	45	18	14
AUG. 6	19	34	35	35	21	24	15	17	21	45	18	14
AUG. 7	19	36	36	37	21	24	16	17	21	45	18	14
AUG. 8	19	37	38	38	21	24	16	17	21	45	18	14
AUG. 9	19	39	40	40	21	24	16	17	21	45	18	14
AUG. 10	19	41	41	42	20	24	16	17	21	45	18	14
AUG. 11	20	42	43	44	20	24	16	17	21	45	18	14
AUG. 12	20	44	45	45	20	24	16	17	21	45	18	14
AUG. 13	20	46	47	47	20	24	16	17	21	45	18	14
AUG. 14	20	48	1	1	20	24	16	17	21	45	18	14
AUG. 15	20	2	2	3	20	24	16	17	21	45	18	14
AUG. 16	20	4	4	5	20	24	16	17	21	45	18	14
AUG. 17	20	6	6	7	20	25	16	17	21	45	18	14
AUG. 18	20	7	8	9	20	25	17	17	21	45	18	14
AUG. 19	21	9	10	11	19	25	17	17	21	45	18	14
AUG. 20	21	11	12	12	19	25	17	17	21	45	18	14
AUG. 21	21	13	14	14	19	25	17	18	21	45	18	14
AUG. 22	21	15	16	16	19	25	17	18	21	45	18	14
AUG. 23	21	17	17	18	19	25	17	18	21	45	18	14
AUG. 24	21	19	19	20	19	25	17	18	21	45	18	14
AUG. 25	21	20	21	22	19	25	17	18	21	45	18	14
AUG. 26	22	22	23	23	19	25	17	18	21	45	18	14
AUG. 27	22	24	24	25	19	25	17	18	21	45	18	14
AUG. 28	22	26	26	27	19	25	17	18	21	45	18	14
AUG. 29	22	27	28	28	19	24	17	18	21	45	18	14
AUG. 30	22	29	29	30	19	24	18	18	21	45	18	14
AUG. 31	22	30	31	31	19	24	18	18	21	45	18	14

MOON 1 ☽ 12:01 A.M. TO 8:00 A.M.   **MOON 2** ☽ 8:01 A.M. TO 4:00 P.M.   **MOON 3** ● 4:01 P.M. TO 12:00 A.M.

Use only one "moon" number. Choose the column closest to your time of birth. If your place of birth is not on Eastern Standard Time, be sure to read "How to Convert to Eastern Standard Time" at the beginning of this section.

1919

September

October

Date & Time	SUN	MOON 1	MOON 2	MOON 3	MERCURY	VENUS	MARS	JUPITER	SATURN	URANUS	NEPTUNE	PLUTO
SEP. 1	22	32	33	33	20	24	18	18	21	45	18	14
SEP. 2	22	34	34	35	20	24	18	18	21	45	18	14
SEP. 3	23	35	36	36	20	24	18	18	21	45	18	14
SEP. 4	23	37	37	38	20	24	18	18	21	45	18	14
SEP. 5	23	38	39	39	20	24	18	18	21	45	18	14
SEP. 6	23	40	41	41	20	24	18	18	21	45	18	14
SEP. 7	23	42	42	43	21	24	18	18	21	45	18	14
SEP. 8	23	44	44	45	21	24	18	18	21	45	18	14
SEP. 9	23	45	46	47	21	24	18	18	21	45	18	14
SEP. 10	23	47	48	1	21	24	18	18	21	45	18	14
SEP. 11	24	1	2	2	21	24	19	18	21	45	18	14
SEP. 12	24	3	4	4	22	24	19	18	21	45	18	14
SEP. 13	24	5	6	6	22	24	19	18	21	45	18	14
SEP. 14	24	7	8	8	22	23	19	18	22	45	18	14
SEP. 15	24	9	9	10	22	23	19	18	22	45	18	14
SEP. 16	24	11	11	12	23	23	19	18	22	45	18	14
SEP. 17	24	13	13	14	23	23	19	18	22	45	18	14
SEP. 18	24	14	15	16	23	23	19	18	22	45	18	14
SEP. 19	25	16	17	17	23	23	19	18	22	45	18	14
SEP. 20	25	18	19	19	24	23	19	18	22	45	18	14
SEP. 21	25	20	20	21	24	23	19	18	22	45	18	14
SEP. 22	25	22	22	23	24	23	19	18	22	45	18	14
SEP. 23	25	23	24	24	24	23	20	18	22	45	18	14
SEP. 24	25	25	26	26	25	23	20	18	22	45	18	14
SEP. 25	26	27	27	28	25	23	20	18	22	45	18	14
SEP. 26	26	28	29	29	25	23	20	18	22	45	18	14
SEP. 27	26	30	30	31	25	23	20	18	22	45	18	14
SEP. 28	26	31	32	33	26	23	20	18	22	45	18	14
SEP. 29	26	33	34	34	26	23	19	19	22	45	18	14
SEP. 30	26	35	35	36	26	22	20	19	22	45	18	14

Date & Time	SUN	MOON 1	MOON 2	MOON 3	MERCURY	VENUS	MARS	JUPITER	SATURN	URANUS	NEPTUNE	PLUTO
OCT. 1	26	36	37	37	26	22	20	19	22	45	18	14
OCT. 2	26	38	38	39	27	22	20	19	22	45	18	14
OCT. 3	27	39	40	41	27	22	20	19	22	45	18	14
OCT. 4	27	41	42	42	27	22	20	19	22	45	18	14
OCT. 5	27	43	43	44	27	22	21	19	22	45	18	14
OCT. 6	27	45	45	46	27	22	21	19	22	45	18	14
OCT. 7	27	46	47	48	28	22	21	19	22	45	18	14
OCT. 8	27	48	1	2	28	22	21	19	22	45	18	14
OCT. 9	27	2	3	4	28	23	21	19	22	45	18	14
OCT. 10	27	4	5	6	28	23	21	19	22	45	18	14
OCT. 11	28	6	7	8	29	23	21	19	22	45	18	14
OCT. 12	28	8	9	10	29	23	21	19	22	45	18	14
OCT. 13	28	10	11	11	29	23	21	19	22	45	18	14
OCT. 14	28	12	13	13	29	23	21	19	22	45	18	14
OCT. 15	28	14	15	15	29	23	21	19	22	45	18	14
OCT. 16	28	16	16	17	30	23	21	19	22	45	18	14
OCT. 17	28	18	18	19	30	23	22	19	22	45	18	14
OCT. 18	28	19	20	21	30	23	22	19	22	45	18	14
OCT. 19	29	21	22	22	30	23	22	19	22	45	18	14
OCT. 20	29	23	23	24	30	24	22	19	22	45	18	14
OCT. 21	29	25	25	26	31	23	22	19	22	45	18	14
OCT. 22	29	26	27	27	31	23	22	19	22	45	18	14
OCT. 23	29	28	28	29	31	23	22	19	22	45	18	14
OCT. 24	29	29	30	31	31	23	22	19	22	45	18	14
OCT. 25	29	31	32	32	31	23	22	19	22	45	18	14
OCT. 26	30	33	33	34	32	24	22	19	22	45	18	14
OCT. 27	30	34	35	35	32	24	22	19	22	45	18	14
OCT. 28	30	36	36	37	32	24	22	19	22	45	18	14
OCT. 29	30	37	38	38	32	24	22	19	22	45	18	14
OCT. 30	30	39	39	40	32	24	23	19	22	45	18	14
OCT. 31	30	41	41	42	32	24	23	19	22	45	18	14

MOON 1 ◗ 12:01 A.M. TO 8:00 A.M.   **MOON 2** ◖ 8:01 A.M. TO 4:00 P.M.   **MOON 3** ● 4:01 P.M. TO 12:00 A.M.
Use only one "moon" number. Choose the column closest to your time of birth. If your place of birth is not on Eastern Standard Time, be sure to read "How to Convert to Eastern Standard Time" at the beginning of this section.

1919

November

Date & Time	SUN ☉	MOON 1 ☽	MOON 2 ☽	MOON 3 ●	MERCURY	VENUS	MARS	JUPITER	SATURN	URANUS	NEPTUNE	PLUTO
NOV. 1	30	42	43	43	33	24	23	19	22	45	18	14
NOV. 2	30	44	45	45	33	24	23	19	22	45	18	14
NOV. 3	31	46	46	47	33	24	23	19	22	45	19	14
NOV. 4	31	48	48	1	33	24	23	19	22	45	19	14
NOV. 5	31	1	2	3	33	24	23	19	22	45	19	14
NOV. 6	31	3	4	5	34	25	23	19	22	45	19	14
NOV. 7	31	5	6	7	34	25	23	19	22	45	19	14
NOV. 8	31	7	8	9	34	25	23	19	22	45	19	14
NOV. 9	31	9	10	11	34	25	23	19	22	45	19	14
NOV. 10	31	11	12	13	34	25	23	19	22	45	19	14
NOV. 11	31	13	14	15	34	25	24	19	22	45	19	14
NOV. 12	32	15	16	17	34	25	24	19	22	45	19	14
NOV. 13	32	17	18	18	35	25	24	19	22	45	19	14
NOV. 14	32	19	20	20	35	26	24	19	22	45	19	14
NOV. 15	32	21	21	22	35	26	24	19	22	45	19	14
NOV. 16	32	22	23	24	35	26	24	19	22	45	19	14
NOV. 17	32	24	25	25	35	26	24	19	22	45	19	14
NOV. 18	32	26	26	27	35	26	24	19	22	45	19	14
NOV. 19	33	27	28	29	35	26	24	19	22	45	19	14
NOV. 20	33	29	30	30	35	26	24	19	22	45	19	14
NOV. 21	33	31	31	32	35	26	24	19	22	45	19	14
NOV. 22	33	32	33	33	35	27	24	19	22	45	19	14
NOV. 23	33	34	34	35	35	27	24	19	22	45	19	14
NOV. 24	33	35	36	36	35	27	24	19	22	45	19	14
NOV. 25	34	37	37	38	35	27	25	19	22	45	19	14
NOV. 26	34	39	39	40	35	27	25	19	22	45	19	14
NOV. 27	34	40	41	41	35	27	25	19	22	45	19	14
NOV. 28	34	42	42	43	35	27	25	19	22	45	18	14
NOV. 29	34	43	44	45	35	28	25	19	22	45	18	14
NOV. 30	34	45	46	46	35	28	25	19	22	45	18	14

December

Date & Time	SUN ☉	MOON 1 ☽	MOON 2 ☽	MOON 3 ●	MERCURY	VENUS	MARS	JUPITER	SATURN	URANUS	NEPTUNE	PLUTO
DEC. 1	34	47	47	48	35	28	25	19	22	45	18	14
DEC. 2	34	1	1	2	34	28	25	19	22	45	18	14
DEC. 3	35	3	3	4	34	28	25	19	22	45	18	14
DEC. 4	35	4	5	6	34	28	25	19	22	45	18	14
DEC. 5	35	6	7	8	34	28	25	19	22	45	18	14
DEC. 6	35	8	9	10	34	29	25	19	22	45	18	14
DEC. 7	35	10	11	12	34	29	25	19	22	45	18	14
DEC. 8	35	12	13	14	33	29	26	19	22	45	18	14
DEC. 9	35	14	15	16	33	29	26	19	22	45	18	14
DEC. 10	35	16	17	18	33	29	26	19	23	45	18	14
DEC. 11	36	18	19	20	33	29	26	19	23	45	18	14
DEC. 12	36	20	21	21	33	29	26	19	23	45	18	14
DEC. 13	36	22	23	23	33	30	26	19	23	45	18	14
DEC. 14	36	24	24	25	33	30	26	19	23	45	18	14
DEC. 15	36	25	26	26	33	30	26	19	23	45	18	14
DEC. 16	36	27	28	28	33	30	26	19	23	45	18	14
DEC. 17	36	29	29	30	33	30	26	19	23	45	18	14
DEC. 18	36	30	31	31	34	30	26	19	23	45	18	14
DEC. 19	37	32	32	33	34	30	26	19	23	45	18	14
DEC. 20	37	33	34	34	34	31	26	19	23	45	18	14
DEC. 21	37	35	35	36	34	31	26	19	23	45	18	14
DEC. 22	37	37	37	38	34	31	27	19	23	45	18	14
DEC. 23	37	38	39	39	34	31	27	19	23	45	18	14
DEC. 24	37	40	40	41	34	31	27	19	23	45	18	14
DEC. 25	37	41	42	42	34	31	27	19	23	45	18	14
DEC. 26	38	43	44	44	35	32	27	19	23	45	18	14
DEC. 27	38	45	45	46	35	32	27	19	23	45	18	14
DEC. 28	38	46	47	48	35	32	27	19	23	45	18	14
DEC. 29	38	48	1	1	35	32	27	19	23	45	18	14
DEC. 30	38	2	3	3	35	32	27	19	23	45	18	14
DEC. 31	38	4	4	5	35	32	27	19	23	45	18	14

MOON 1 ☽ 12:01 A.M. TO 8:00 A.M.   **MOON 2** ☽ 8:01 A.M. TO 4:00 P.M.   **MOON 3** ● 4:01 P.M. TO 12:00 A.M.
Use only one "moon" number. Choose the column closest to your time of birth. If your place of birth is not on
Eastern Standard Time, be sure to read "How to Convert to Eastern Standard Time" at the beginning of this section.

1920-1929

1920s

Martin Luther King

✦ ✦ ✦ BORN JANUARY 15, 1929 ✦ ✦ ✦

Brief Bio: Orator, civil rights activist and advocate for nonviolence, Martin Luther King delivered his famous
"I Have a Dream" speech on the steps of the Lincoln Memorial.

Personology Profile:

SUN IN THE WEEK OF DOMINANCE
(CAPRICORN III)

✳

As long as these individuals can dominate their work and living spaces they are content to leave others alone. Also, they are less interested in dreams of advancement and more concerned with present realities. Among the most realistic and pragmatic people in the year, they usually get their way through steadfastness and persistence. Loyal, they are unlikely to let their loved ones down.

MERCURY IN THE WEEK OF THE RULER
(CAPRICORN I)

✳

Sharp verbal and written skills make such individuals difficult to oppose and their colleagues are usually happy to have them as members of the group. They can, however, get into trouble when they are placed in executive positions, frequently arousing rebellion through autocratic attitudes. Their success usually depends on the trust of those working under them.

MARS IN THE WEEK OF THEATER
(LIBRA III)

✳

The more outgoing side of Mars wants to be as outrageous as possible here. By flaunting flamboyance in public displays of emotion, real or mock aggression, or in unconventional behavior, these individuals give shock value a high priority. Playing a role so fully and consummately that others tend to believe in its reality is the goal.

MOON IN THE WEEK OF CHARM
(SCORPIO III)

✳

Extremely persuasive, those with this moon position can be highly manipulative and controlling in gaining their goals. Once identified as a love object by such people, it will not be easy to escape them. In relationships with such individuals it is easy to leave emotional choices to them, and in fact to rely on their feelings more than on your own.

VENUS IN THE WEEK OF ORIGINALITY
(SAGITTARIUS II)

✳

Such individuals are more attracted to unconventional relationships. Uncomfortable with the usual dynamics of relationship, they may not jump at the chance of marriage and indeed even feel hemmed in by the normal responsibilities of carrying on a friendship. They often, however, wind up with more ordinary folks who give them the stability they so sorely need and may secretly crave.

JUPITER IN THE WEEK OF BALANCED STRENGTH
(LEO II)

✳

Success is most likely to be the reward of honesty and steadfastness of purpose. This position finds Jupiter in its most noble, upright and courageous state. Underhanded methods of any sort will not be rewarded in the long run and can result in ruin. It is not necessary, however, to keep to the straight and narrow since exploration and travel usually figure here also.

SATURN IN THE WEEK OF SYSTEM BUILDERS
(VIRGO I)

✳

A desire to control and order one's environment can result in an obsessive or compulsive personality. If responsibilities can be taken in a free and easy manner, Saturn's position here can aid desires to serve others. It is crucial to avoid a tendency to hover or to overly influence others with critical opinions—better to back off and let things work themselves out.

URANUS ON THE CUSP OF SENSITIVITY
(AQUARIUS-PISCES CUSP)

✳

Overreactive, such individuals are made very jumpy by even slightly unpleasant sensory stimuli, particularly those involving sound and smell. Since their buttons can be easily pushed, they must learn to grow a whole set which cannot be pushed so easily. Perhaps their greatest lesson is learning not to let others control them through their predictable responses.

NEPTUNE IN THE WEEK OF AUTHORITY
(LEO I)

✳

The watery planet Neptune is not comfortable in this hot week. Because of its aversion to fixed ideas, no matter how effective or brilliant, Neptune tends to exert a dissolving effect on authority here, encouraging those with this position to undermine any omniscient attitudes. They may have difficulty exerting direct influences in their family life.

PLUTO IN THE WEEK OF THE EMPATH
(CANCER I)

✳

Emotional manipulation is likely to be a constant theme with Pluto here. An ability to control the feelings of others and a need to do so may lead such people to manipulative behavior, which will ultimately arouse resentment and dependency. Such individuals should detach themselves from the feelings of others and assert a more independent stance by concentrating on their own well-being.

Some Highlights of the Decade 1920-1929

- US CONGRESS RATIFIES 19TH AMENDMENT, GUARANTEEING WOMEN THE RIGHT TO VOTE.

- THE FIRST LEAGUE OF NATIONS SESSION OPENS IN GENEVA, SWITZERLAND.

- THE BRITISH EMPIRE REACHES AN ACCORD WITH SINN FEIN THAT ALLOWS IRELAND TO BECOME A FREE STATE.

- WINNIE-THE-POOH, BY A. A. MILNE, IS PUBLISHED IN LONDON, INTRODUCING THE CHARACTERS OF POOH, CHRISTOPHER ROBIN AND TIGGER.

- THE US STOCK MARKET CRASHES ON "BLACK FRIDAY," SETTING OFF THE GREAT DEPRESSION.

- CHARLES LINDBERGH, FLYING THE SPIRIT OF ST. LOUIS, COMPLETES THE FIRST SOLO NONSTOP FLIGHT ACROSS THE ATLANTIC.

1920

January

Date & Time	SUN	MOON 1	MOON 2	MOON 3	MERCURY	VENUS	MARS	JUPITER	SATURN	URANUS	NEPTUNE	PLUTO
JAN. 1	38	6	6	7	36	32	27	19	23	45	18	14
JAN. 2	38	8	8	9	36	33	27	19	23	45	18	14
JAN. 3	39	10	10	11	36	33	27	19	23	45	18	14
JAN. 4	39	12	12	13	36	33	27	19	23	45	18	14
JAN. 5	39	14	14	15	36	33	27	19	23	45	18	14
JAN. 6	39	16	16	17	37	33	28	19	23	45	18	14
JAN. 7	39	17	18	19	37	33	28	19	22	45	18	14
JAN. 8	39	19	20	21	37	34	28	19	22	45	18	14
JAN. 9	39	21	22	23	37	34	28	19	22	45	18	14
JAN. 10	40	23	24	24	37	34	28	19	22	45	18	14
JAN. 11	40	25	25	26	38	34	28	19	22	45	18	14
JAN. 12	40	27	27	28	38	34	28	19	22	45	18	14
JAN. 13	40	28	29	29	38	34	28	19	22	45	18	14
JAN. 14	40	30	30	31	38	35	28	19	22	45	18	14
JAN. 15	40	31	32	32	38	35	28	19	22	45	18	14
JAN. 16	40	33	33	34	39	35	28	19	22	45	18	14
JAN. 17	41	34	35	36	39	35	28	19	22	45	18	14
JAN. 18	41	36	37	37	39	35	28	19	22	45	18	14
JAN. 19	41	38	38	39	39	35	28	19	22	45	18	14
JAN. 20	41	39	40	40	39	35	28	19	22	45	18	14
JAN. 21	41	41	41	42	40	36	28	19	22	45	18	14
JAN. 22	41	43	43	44	40	36	28	19	22	45	18	14
JAN. 23	42	44	45	45	40	36	29	19	22	45	18	14
JAN. 24	42	46	47	47	40	36	29	19	22	45	18	14
JAN. 25	42	48	48	1	40	36	29	19	22	45	18	14
JAN. 26	42	2	2	3	41	36	29	19	22	45	18	14
JAN. 27	42	3	4	5	41	37	29	19	22	45	18	14
JAN. 28	42	5	6	6	41	37	29	19	22	45	18	14
JAN. 29	42	7	8	8	41	37	29	19	22	45	18	14
JAN. 30	42	9	10	10	42	37	29	19	22	45	18	14
JAN. 31	43	11	11	12	42	37	29	19	22	45	18	14

February

Date & Time	SUN	MOON 1	MOON 2	MOON 3	MERCURY	VENUS	MARS	JUPITER	SATURN	URANUS	NEPTUNE	PLUTO
FEB. 1	43	13	13	14	42	37	29	19	22	45	18	14
FEB. 2	43	15	15	16	42	38	29	19	22	45	18	14
FEB. 3	43	17	17	18	42	38	29	19	22	45	18	14
FEB. 4	43	19	19	20	43	38	29	19	22	45	18	14
FEB. 5	43	20	21	22	43	38	29	19	22	45	18	14
FEB. 6	43	22	23	24	43	38	29	19	22	45	18	14
FEB. 7	43	24	25	25	43	38	29	19	22	45	18	14
FEB. 8	44	26	26	27	44	39	29	19	22	45	18	14
FEB. 9	44	28	28	29	44	39	29	19	22	45	18	14
FEB. 10	44	29	30	30	44	39	29	19	22	45	18	14
FEB. 11	44	31	31	32	44	39	29	19	22	45	18	14
FEB. 12	44	32	33	33	45	39	29	19	22	45	18	14
FEB. 13	44	34	35	35	45	39	30	19	22	45	18	14
FEB. 14	44	36	36	37	45	40	30	19	22	45	18	14
FEB. 15	44	37	38	38	45	40	30	19	22	45	18	14
FEB. 16	45	39	39	40	46	40	30	18	22	45	18	14
FEB. 17	45	40	41	41	46	40	30	18	22	45	18	14
FEB. 18	45	42	43	43	46	40	30	18	22	45	18	14
FEB. 19	45	44	44	45	46	40	30	18	22	45	18	14
FEB. 20	45	46	46	47	47	40	30	18	22	45	18	14
FEB. 21	45	47	48	48	47	41	30	18	22	45	18	14
FEB. 22	45	1	2	2	47	41	30	18	22	45	18	14
FEB. 23	46	3	4	4	47	41	30	18	22	45	18	14
FEB. 24	46	5	5	6	47	41	30	18	22	45	18	14
FEB. 25	46	7	7	8	48	41	30	18	22	45	18	14
FEB. 26	46	8	9	10	48	41	30	18	22	45	18	14
FEB. 27	46	10	11	12	48	42	30	18	22	45	18	14
FEB. 28	46	12	13	13	48	42	30	18	22	45	18	14
FEB. 29	46	14	15	15	1	42	30	18	22	45	18	14

MOON 1 ◐ 12:01 A.M. TO 8:00 A.M. **MOON 2** ◑ 8:01 A.M. TO 4:00 P.M. **MOON 3** ● 4:01 P.M. TO 12:00 A.M.

Use only one "moon" number. Choose the column closest to your time of birth. If your place of birth is not on Eastern Standard Time, be sure to read "How to Convert to Eastern Standard Time" at the beginning of this section.

Date & Time	SUN ☉	MOON 1 ◗	MOON 2 ◖	MOON 3 ●	MERCURY	VENUS	MARS	JUPITER	SATURN	URANUS	NEPTUNE	PLUTO
MAR. 1	46	16	17	17	1	42	30	18	22	45	18	14
MAR. 2	46	18	19	19	1	42	30	18	22	45	18	14
MAR. 3	47	20	20	21	1	42	30	18	22	45	18	14
MAR. 4	47	22	22	23	1	43	30	18	22	45	18	14
MAR. 5	47	23	24	25	1	43	30	18	22	45	18	14
MAR. 6	47	25	26	26	1	43	30	18	22	45	18	14
MAR. 7	47	27	27	28	1	43	30	18	22	45	18	14
MAR. 8	47	29	29	30	2	43	30	18	22	45	18	14
MAR. 9	47	30	31	31	2	43	30	18	22	45	18	14
MAR. 10	47	32	32	33	2	44	30	18	22	45	18	14
MAR. 11	48	33	34	35	2	44	30	18	22	45	18	14
MAR. 12	48	35	36	36	2	44	30	18	22	45	18	14
MAR. 13	48	37	37	38	2	44	30	18	22	45	18	14
MAR. 14	48	38	39	39	1	44	30	18	22	45	18	14
MAR. 15	48	40	40	41	1	44	30	18	22	45	18	14
MAR. 16	48	41	42	43	1	45	30	18	22	45	18	14
MAR. 17	48	43	44	44	1	45	30	18	22	45	18	14
MAR. 18	48	45	45	46	1	45	30	18	22	45	18	14
MAR. 19	1	47	47	48	1	45	30	18	22	45	18	14
MAR. 20	1	48	1	2	1	45	30	18	22	45	18	14
MAR. 21	1	2	3	4	1	45	30	18	22	45	18	14
MAR. 22	1	4	5	5	1	46	30	18	22	45	18	14
MAR. 23	1	6	7	7	1	46	30	18	22	45	18	14
MAR. 24	1	8	9	9	48	46	30	18	22	45	18	14
MAR. 25	2	10	11	11	48	46	30	18	22	45	18	14
MAR. 26	2	12	12	13	48	46	30	18	22	45	18	14
MAR. 27	2	14	14	15	48	46	30	18	22	45	18	14
MAR. 28	2	16	16	17	48	47	30	18	22	45	18	14
MAR. 29	2	17	18	19	48	47	30	18	22	45	18	14
MAR. 30	2	19	20	20	48	47	30	18	22	45	18	14
MAR. 31	2	21	22	22	48	47	30	18	22	45	18	14

Date & Time	SUN ☉	MOON 1 ◗	MOON 2 ◖	MOON 3 ●	MERCURY	VENUS	MARS	JUPITER	SATURN	URANUS	NEPTUNE	PLUTO
APR. 1	2	23	23	24	48	47	30	18	22	45	18	14
APR. 2	2	25	25	26	48	47	30	18	22	45	18	14
APR. 3	3	26	27	27	48	48	30	18	22	45	18	14
APR. 4	3	28	29	29	48	48	30	18	22	45	18	14
APR. 5	3	30	30	31	48	48	30	18	22	46	18	14
APR. 6	3	31	32	32	48	48	30	18	22	46	18	14
APR. 7	3	33	33	34	48	48	30	18	22	46	18	14
APR. 8	3	35	35	36	48	48	30	18	22	46	18	14
APR. 9	3	36	37	37	48	48	30	18	22	46	18	14
APR. 10	3	38	38	39	48	1	30	18	22	46	18	14
APR. 11	4	39	40	40	48	1	30	18	22	46	18	14
APR. 12	4	41	41	42	48	1	30	18	22	46	18	14
APR. 13	4	43	43	44	48	1	29	18	22	46	18	14
APR. 14	4	44	45	45	1	1	29	18	22	46	18	14
APR. 15	4	46	47	47	1	1	29	18	22	46	18	14
APR. 16	4	48	48	1	1	2	29	18	22	46	18	14
APR. 17	4	2	2	3	1	2	29	18	22	46	18	14
APR. 18	4	3	4	5	1	2	29	18	22	46	18	14
APR. 19	5	5	6	7	1	2	29	18	22	46	18	14
APR. 20	5	7	8	9	1	2	29	18	22	46	18	14
APR. 21	5	9	10	11	1	2	29	18	22	46	18	14
APR. 22	5	11	12	13	2	3	29	18	22	46	18	14
APR. 23	5	13	14	14	2	3	29	18	22	46	18	14
APR. 24	5	15	16	16	2	3	29	18	22	46	18	14
APR. 25	6	17	18	18	2	3	29	18	22	46	18	14
APR. 26	6	19	19	20	2	3	29	18	22	46	18	14
APR. 27	6	21	21	22	2	3	29	18	22	46	18	14
APR. 28	6	22	23	24	3	4	29	18	22	46	18	14
APR. 29	6	24	25	25	3	4	29	18	22	46	18	14
APR. 30	6	26	26	27	3	4	29	18	22	46	18	14

MOON 1 ◗ 12:01 A.M. TO 8:00 A.M.   **MOON 2** ◖ 8:01 A.M. TO 4:00 P.M.   **MOON 3** ● 4:01 P.M. TO 12:00 A.M.

Use only one "moon" number. Choose the column closest to your time of birth. If your place of birth is not on Eastern Standard Time, be sure to read "How to Convert to Eastern Standard Time" at the beginning of this section.

1920

May

June

Date & Time	SUN	MOON 1	MOON 2	MOON 3	MERCURY	VENUS	MARS	JUPITER	SATURN	URANUS	NEPTUNE	PLUTO
MAY 1	6	28	28	29	3	4	29	18	22	46	18	14
MAY 2	6	29	30	30	3	4	29	18	22	46	18	14
MAY 3	7	31	31	32	4	4	29	18	22	46	18	14
MAY 4	7	32	33	33	4	5	28	18	22	46	18	14
MAY 5	7	34	35	35	4	5	28	18	22	46	18	14
MAY 6	7	36	36	37	4	5	28	18	22	46	18	14
MAY 7	7	37	38	38	5	5	28	18	22	46	18	14
MAY 8	7	39	39	40	5	5	28	18	22	46	18	14
MAY 9	7	40	41	41	5	5	28	18	22	46	18	14
MAY 10	7	42	43	43	5	6	28	18	22	46	18	14
MAY 11	8	44	44	45	5	6	28	18	22	46	18	14
MAY 12	8	45	46	46	6	6	28	18	22	46	18	14
MAY 13	8	47	48	48	6	6	28	18	22	46	18	14
MAY 14	8	1	1	2	6	6	28	18	22	46	18	14
MAY 15	8	3	3	4	7	6	28	18	22	46	18	14
MAY 16	8	5	5	6	7	7	28	18	22	46	18	14
MAY 17	8	6	7	8	7	7	28	18	22	46	18	14
MAY 18	8	8	9	10	7	7	28	18	22	46	18	14
MAY 19	9	10	11	12	7	7	28	18	22	46	18	14
MAY 20	9	12	13	14	8	7	28	18	22	46	18	14
MAY 21	9	14	15	16	8	7	28	18	22	46	18	14
MAY 22	9	16	17	18	8	8	28	18	22	46	18	14
MAY 23	9	18	19	20	8	8	28	19	22	46	18	14
MAY 24	9	20	21	21	9	8	28	19	22	46	18	14
MAY 25	10	22	23	23	9	8	28	19	22	46	18	14
MAY 26	10	24	24	25	10	8	28	19	22	46	18	14
MAY 27	10	25	26	27	10	8	28	19	22	46	18	14
MAY 28	10	27	28	28	10	9	28	19	22	46	18	14
MAY 29	10	29	29	30	10	9	28	19	22	46	18	14
MAY 30	10	30	31	31	11	9	28	19	22	46	18	14
MAY 31	10	32	33	33	11	9	28	19	22	46	18	14

Date & Time	SUN	MOON 1	MOON 2	MOON 3	MERCURY	VENUS	MARS	JUPITER	SATURN	URANUS	NEPTUNE	PLUTO
JUN. 1	10	34	34	35	11	9	28	19	22	46	18	14
JUN. 2	10	35	36	36	12	9	28	19	22	46	18	14
JUN. 3	11	37	37	38	12	9	28	19	22	46	18	14
JUN. 4	11	38	39	39	12	10	28	19	22	46	18	14
JUN. 5	11	40	40	41	12	10	28	19	22	46	18	14
JUN. 6	11	42	42	43	13	10	28	19	22	46	18	14
JUN. 7	11	43	44	44	13	10	28	19	22	46	18	14
JUN. 8	11	45	45	46	13	10	28	19	22	46	18	14
JUN. 9	11	46	47	48	13	10	28	19	22	46	18	14
JUN. 10	11	48	1	1	14	11	28	19	22	46	18	14
JUN. 11	12	2	3	3	14	11	28	19	22	46	18	14
JUN. 12	12	4	4	5	14	11	28	19	22	46	18	14
JUN. 13	12	6	6	7	14	11	28	19	22	46	18	14
JUN. 14	12	8	8	9	15	11	28	19	22	46	18	14
JUN. 15	12	10	10	11	15	11	28	19	22	46	18	14
JUN. 16	12	12	12	13	15	12	28	19	22	46	18	14
JUN. 17	12	14	14	15	15	12	28	19	22	46	18	14
JUN. 18	12	16	16	17	16	12	28	19	22	46	18	14
JUN. 19	13	18	18	19	16	12	28	19	22	46	18	14
JUN. 20	13	20	20	21	16	12	28	19	22	46	18	14
JUN. 21	13	21	22	23	16	12	28	19	22	46	18	14
JUN. 22	13	23	24	24	16	13	28	19	22	46	18	14
JUN. 23	13	25	26	26	16	13	28	19	22	46	18	14
JUN. 24	13	27	27	28	17	13	28	19	22	46	18	14
JUN. 25	14	28	29	29	17	13	28	19	22	46	18	14
JUN. 26	14	30	31	31	17	13	28	19	22	46	18	14
JUN. 27	14	32	32	33	17	13	28	19	22	46	18	14
JUN. 28	14	33	34	34	17	14	28	19	22	46	18	14
JUN. 29	14	35	35	36	17	14	28	19	22	46	18	14
JUN. 30	14	36	37	37	17	14	28	19	22	46	18	14

MOON 1 ◗ 12:01 A.M. TO 8:00 A.M.　　**MOON 2** ◖ 8:01 A.M. TO 4:00 P.M.　　**MOON 3** ● 4:01 P.M. TO 12:00 A.M.

Use only one "moon" number. Choose the column closest to your time of birth. If your place of birth is not on Eastern Standard Time, be sure to read "How to Convert to Eastern Standard Time" at the beginning of this section.

Date & Time	SUN	MOON 1 ◖	MOON 2 ◗	MOON 3 ●	MERCURY	VENUS	MARS	JUPITER	SATURN	URANUS	NEPTUNE	PLUTO
JUL. 1	14	38	38	39	18	14	29	19	22	46	18	14
JUL. 2	14	40	40	41	18	14	29	19	22	46	18	14
JUL. 3	15	41	42	42	18	14	29	19	22	46	18	14
JUL. 4	15	43	43	44	18	15	29	19	22	46	18	14
JUL. 5	15	44	45	45	18	15	29	19	22	46	18	14
JUL. 6	15	46	47	47	18	15	29	19	22	46	18	14
JUL. 7	15	48	48	1	18	15	29	20	22	46	18	14
JUL. 8	15	1	2	3	18	15	29	20	22	46	18	14
JUL. 9	15	3	4	4	18	15	29	20	22	46	18	14
JUL. 10	15	5	6	6	18	16	29	20	22	46	18	14
JUL. 11	16	7	7	8	18	16	29	20	22	46	18	14
JUL. 12	16	9	9	10	18	16	29	20	22	46	18	14
JUL. 13	16	11	11	12	18	16	29	20	22	46	18	14
JUL. 14	16	13	13	14	18	16	29	20	22	46	18	14
JUL. 15	16	15	15	16	18	16	29	20	22	46	18	14
JUL. 16	16	17	17	18	18	17	29	20	22	46	18	14
JUL. 17	16	19	19	20	18	17	29	20	22	46	18	14
JUL. 18	16	21	21	22	18	17	29	20	22	46	18	14
JUL. 19	17	23	23	24	18	17	29	20	22	46	18	14
JUL. 20	17	24	25	26	18	17	30	20	22	46	18	14
JUL. 21	17	26	27	27	18	17	30	20	22	46	18	14
JUL. 22	17	28	28	29	18	18	30	20	22	46	18	14
JUL. 23	17	30	30	31	18	18	30	20	22	46	18	14
JUL. 24	17	31	32	32	18	18	30	20	22	46	18	14
JUL. 25	17	33	33	34	18	18	30	20	22	46	18	14
JUL. 26	18	34	35	35	18	18	30	20	22	46	18	14
JUL. 27	18	36	36	37	18	18	30	20	22	46	18	14
JUL. 28	18	38	38	39	17	19	30	20	22	46	18	14
JUL. 29	18	39	40	40	17	19	30	20	22	46	18	14
JUL. 30	18	41	41	42	17	19	30	20	22	46	18	14
JUL. 31	18	42	43	43	17	19	30	20	22	46	18	14

Date & Time	SUN	MOON 1 ◖	MOON 2 ◗	MOON 3 ●	MERCURY	VENUS	MARS	JUPITER	SATURN	URANUS	NEPTUNE	PLUTO
AUG. 1	18	44	45	45	17	19	30	20	22	46	18	14
AUG. 2	18	46	46	47	17	19	30	20	22	46	18	14
AUG. 3	19	47	48	48	17	19	30	20	22	46	18	14
AUG. 4	19	1	2	2	17	20	30	20	22	46	18	14
AUG. 5	19	3	3	4	17	20	31	20	22	46	18	14
AUG. 6	19	5	5	6	17	20	31	20	22	46	18	14
AUG. 7	19	6	7	7	17	20	31	20	22	46	18	14
AUG. 8	19	8	9	9	17	20	31	20	22	46	18	14
AUG. 9	19	10	11	11	17	20	31	20	22	46	18	14
AUG. 10	19	12	13	13	17	21	31	20	22	46	19	14
AUG. 11	20	14	15	15	17	21	31	21	23	46	19	14
AUG. 12	20	16	17	17	17	21	31	21	23	46	19	14
AUG. 13	20	18	19	19	17	21	31	21	23	46	19	14
AUG. 14	20	20	21	21	17	21	31	21	23	46	19	14
AUG. 15	20	22	22	23	17	21	31	21	23	46	19	14
AUG. 16	20	24	24	25	18	22	31	21	23	46	19	14
AUG. 17	20	26	26	27	18	22	31	21	23	46	19	14
AUG. 18	20	27	28	28	18	22	32	21	23	46	19	14
AUG. 19	21	29	30	30	18	22	32	21	23	46	19	14
AUG. 20	21	31	31	32	18	22	32	21	23	45	19	14
AUG. 21	21	32	33	33	18	22	32	21	23	45	19	14
AUG. 22	21	34	34	35	19	23	32	21	23	45	19	14
AUG. 23	21	35	36	37	19	23	32	21	23	45	19	14
AUG. 24	21	37	38	38	19	23	32	21	23	45	19	14
AUG. 25	21	39	39	40	19	23	32	21	23	45	19	14
AUG. 26	22	40	41	41	20	23	32	21	23	45	19	14
AUG. 27	22	42	42	43	20	23	32	21	23	45	19	14
AUG. 28	22	44	44	45	20	24	32	21	23	45	19	14
AUG. 29	22	45	46	46	20	24	32	21	23	45	19	14
AUG. 30	22	47	47	48	21	24	32	21	23	45	19	14
AUG. 31	22	1	1	2	21	24	33	21	23	45	19	14

MOON 1 ◖ 12:01 A.M. TO 8:00 A.M.   **MOON 2** ◗ 8:01 A.M. TO 4:00 P.M.   **MOON 3** ● 4:01 P.M. TO 12:00 A.M.

Use only one "moon" number. Choose the column closest to your time of birth. If your place of birth is not on Eastern Standard Time, be sure to read "How to Convert to Eastern Standard Time" at the beginning of this section.

1920

September

Date & Time	SUN	MOON 1	MOON 2	MOON 3	MERCURY	VENUS	MARS	JUPITER	SATURN	URANUS	NEPTUNE	PLUTO
SEP. 1	22	2	3	4	21	24	33	21	23	45	19	14
SEP. 2	22	4	5	5	21	24	33	21	23	45	19	14
SEP. 3	23	6	7	7	22	25	33	21	23	45	19	14
SEP. 4	23	8	8	9	22	25	33	21	23	45	19	14
SEP. 5	23	10	10	11	22	25	33	21	23	45	19	14
SEP. 6	23	11	12	13	22	25	33	21	23	45	19	14
SEP. 7	23	13	14	15	23	25	33	21	23	45	19	14
SEP. 8	23	15	16	17	23	25	33	21	23	45	19	14
SEP. 9	23	17	18	18	23	26	33	21	23	45	19	14
SEP. 10	23	19	20	20	23	26	33	21	23	45	19	14
SEP. 11	24	21	22	22	24	26	34	21	23	45	19	14
SEP. 12	24	23	24	24	24	26	34	21	23	45	19	14
SEP. 13	24	25	25	26	24	26	34	21	23	45	19	14
SEP. 14	24	27	27	28	24	26	34	21	23	45	19	14
SEP. 15	24	28	29	30	25	27	34	22	23	45	19	14
SEP. 16	24	30	31	31	25	27	34	22	23	45	19	14
SEP. 17	24	32	32	33	25	27	34	22	23	45	19	14
SEP. 18	24	33	34	34	25	27	34	22	23	45	19	14
SEP. 19	25	35	36	36	26	27	34	22	23	45	19	14
SEP. 20	25	37	37	38	26	27	34	22	23	45	19	14
SEP. 21	25	38	39	39	26	28	34	22	23	45	19	14
SEP. 22	25	40	40	41	26	28	34	22	23	45	19	14
SEP. 23	25	41	42	42	26	28	35	22	23	45	19	14
SEP. 24	25	43	44	44	27	28	35	22	23	45	19	14
SEP. 25	26	45	45	46	27	28	35	22	23	45	19	14
SEP. 26	26	46	47	47	27	28	35	22	23	45	19	14
SEP. 27	26	48	1	1	27	29	35	22	23	45	19	14
SEP. 28	26	2	2	3	28	29	35	22	23	45	19	14
SEP. 29	26	4	4	5	28	29	35	22	23	45	19	14
SEP. 30	26	5	6	7	28	29	35	22	23	45	19	14

October

Date & Time	SUN	MOON 1	MOON 2	MOON 3	MERCURY	VENUS	MARS	JUPITER	SATURN	URANUS	NEPTUNE	PLUTO
OCT. 1	26	7	8	9	28	29	35	22	23	45	19	14
OCT. 2	26	9	10	10	28	29	35	22	23	45	19	14
OCT. 3	27	11	12	12	29	30	36	22	23	45	19	14
OCT. 4	27	13	14	14	29	30	36	22	23	45	19	14
OCT. 5	27	15	15	16	29	30	36	22	23	45	19	14
OCT. 6	27	17	17	18	29	30	36	22	23	45	19	14
OCT. 7	27	19	19	20	29	30	36	22	23	45	19	14
OCT. 8	27	20	21	22	30	30	36	22	23	45	19	14
OCT. 9	27	22	23	24	30	31	36	22	23	45	19	14
OCT. 10	27	24	25	25	30	31	36	22	23	45	19	14
OCT. 11	28	26	27	27	30	31	36	22	24	45	19	14
OCT. 12	28	28	28	29	30	31	36	22	24	45	19	14
OCT. 13	28	29	30	31	30	31	36	22	24	45	19	14
OCT. 14	28	31	32	32	31	31	37	22	24	45	19	14
OCT. 15	28	33	33	34	31	31	37	22	24	45	19	14
OCT. 16	28	34	35	35	31	32	37	22	24	45	19	14
OCT. 17	28	36	37	37	31	32	37	22	24	45	19	14
OCT. 18	28	38	38	39	31	32	37	22	24	45	19	14
OCT. 19	29	39	40	40	31	32	37	22	24	45	19	14
OCT. 20	29	41	41	42	32	32	37	22	24	45	19	14
OCT. 21	29	42	43	43	32	32	37	22	24	45	19	14
OCT. 22	29	44	45	45	32	33	37	22	24	45	19	14
OCT. 23	29	46	46	47	32	33	37	23	24	45	19	14
OCT. 24	29	47	48	1	32	33	38	23	24	45	19	14
OCT. 25	29	1	2	2	32	33	38	23	24	45	19	14
OCT. 26	30	3	4	4	32	33	38	23	24	45	19	14
OCT. 27	30	5	5	6	33	33	38	23	24	45	19	14
OCT. 28	30	7	7	8	33	34	38	23	24	45	19	14
OCT. 29	30	9	9	10	33	34	38	23	24	45	19	14
OCT. 30	30	10	11	12	33	34	38	23	24	45	19	14
OCT. 31	30	12	13	14	33	34	38	23	24	45	19	14

MOON 1 ◗ 12:01 A.M. TO 8:00 A.M.   **MOON 2** ◖ 8:01 A.M. TO 4:00 P.M.   **MOON 3** ● 4:01 P.M. TO 12:00 A.M.

Use only one "moon" number. Choose the column closest to your time of birth. If your place of birth is not on Eastern Standard Time, be sure to read "How to Convert to Eastern Standard Time" at the beginning of this section.

1920

November

Date & Time	SUN	MOON 1	MOON 2	MOON 3	MERCURY	VENUS	MARS	JUPITER	SATURN	URANUS	NEPTUNE	PLUTO
NOV. 1	30	14	15	16	33	34	38	23	24	45	19	14
NOV. 2	30	16	17	18	33	34	38	23	24	45	19	14
NOV. 3	31	18	19	19	33	35	39	23	24	45	19	14
NOV. 4	31	20	21	21	33	35	39	23	24	45	19	14
NOV. 5	31	22	22	23	33	35	39	23	24	45	19	14
NOV. 6	31	24	24	25	33	35	39	23	24	45	19	14
NOV. 7	31	25	26	27	33	35	39	23	24	45	19	14
NOV. 8	31	27	28	28	33	35	39	23	24	45	19	14
NOV. 9	31	29	29	30	33	36	39	23	24	45	19	14
NOV. 10	31	31	31	32	33	36	39	23	24	45	19	14
NOV. 11	31	32	33	33	33	36	39	23	24	45	19	14
NOV. 12	32	34	34	35	33	36	39	23	24	45	19	14
NOV. 13	32	36	36	37	33	36	40	23	24	45	19	14
NOV. 14	32	37	38	38	32	36	40	23	24	45	19	14
NOV. 15	32	39	39	40	32	37	40	23	24	45	19	14
NOV. 16	32	40	41	41	32	37	40	23	24	45	19	14
NOV. 17	32	42	42	43	32	37	40	23	24	45	19	14
NOV. 18	32	43	44	45	32	37	40	23	24	45	19	14
NOV. 19	33	45	46	46	32	37	40	23	24	45	19	14
NOV. 20	33	47	47	48	31	37	40	23	24	45	19	14
NOV. 21	33	48	1	2	31	38	40	23	24	45	19	14
NOV. 22	33	2	3	3	31	38	40	23	24	45	19	14
NOV. 23	33	4	5	5	31	38	41	23	24	45	19	14
NOV. 24	33	6	6	7	31	38	41	23	24	45	19	14
NOV. 25	34	8	8	9	31	38	41	23	24	45	19	14
NOV. 26	34	10	10	11	31	38	41	23	24	45	19	14
NOV. 27	34	12	12	13	31	39	41	23	24	45	19	14
NOV. 28	34	14	14	15	31	39	41	23	24	45	19	14
NOV. 29	34	16	16	17	31	39	41	23	24	45	19	14
NOV. 30	34	18	18	19	31	39	41	23	24	45	19	14

December

Date & Time	SUN	MOON 1	MOON 2	MOON 3	MERCURY	VENUS	MARS	JUPITER	SATURN	URANUS	NEPTUNE	PLUTO
DEC. 1	34	20	20	21	31	39	41	23	24	45	19	14
DEC. 2	34	21	22	23	32	39	41	23	24	45	19	14
DEC. 3	35	23	24	24	32	39	42	23	24	45	19	14
DEC. 4	35	25	26	26	32	40	42	23	24	45	19	14
DEC. 5	35	27	27	28	32	40	42	23	24	45	19	14
DEC. 6	35	28	29	30	32	40	42	23	24	45	19	14
DEC. 7	35	30	31	31	32	40	42	23	24	45	19	14
DEC. 8	35	32	32	33	32	40	42	23	24	45	19	14
DEC. 9	35	33	34	35	33	40	42	23	24	45	19	14
DEC. 10	35	35	36	36	33	41	42	23	24	45	19	14
DEC. 11	36	37	37	38	33	41	42	23	24	45	19	14
DEC. 12	36	38	39	39	33	41	42	23	24	45	19	14
DEC. 13	36	40	40	41	33	41	43	23	24	45	19	14
DEC. 14	36	41	42	42	34	41	43	23	24	45	19	14
DEC. 15	36	43	43	44	34	41	43	23	24	45	19	14
DEC. 16	36	45	45	46	34	42	43	23	24	45	19	14
DEC. 17	36	46	47	47	34	42	43	23	24	45	19	14
DEC. 18	36	48	48	1	34	42	43	23	24	45	19	14
DEC. 19	37	1	2	3	34	42	43	23	24	45	19	14
DEC. 20	37	3	4	4	35	42	43	23	24	45	19	14
DEC. 21	37	5	6	6	35	42	43	23	24	45	19	14
DEC. 22	37	7	7	8	35	43	44	23	24	45	19	14
DEC. 23	37	9	9	10	35	43	44	23	24	45	19	14
DEC. 24	37	11	11	12	35	43	44	23	24	45	19	14
DEC. 25	37	13	13	14	36	43	44	23	24	45	19	14
DEC. 26	38	15	16	16	36	43	44	23	24	45	19	14
DEC. 27	38	17	18	18	36	43	44	23	24	45	19	14
DEC. 28	38	19	20	20	36	43	44	23	24	45	19	14
DEC. 29	38	21	21	22	37	44	44	23	24	45	19	14
DEC. 30	38	23	23	24	37	44	44	23	24	45	19	14
DEC. 31	38	25	25	26	37	44	44	23	24	45	19	14

MOON 1 ◗ 12:01 A.M. TO 8:00 A.M.　　**MOON 2** ◑ 8:01 A.M. TO 4:00 P.M.　　**MOON 3** ● 4:01 P.M. TO 12:00 A.M.
Use only one "moon" number. Choose the column closest to your time of birth. If your place of birth is not on
Eastern Standard Time, be sure to read "How to Convert to Eastern Standard Time" at the beginning of this section.

1921

January

Date & Time	SUN	MOON 1	MOON 2	MOON 3	MERCURY	VENUS	MARS	JUPITER	SATURN	URANUS	NEPTUNE	PLUTO
JAN. 1	38	26	27	28	37	44	45	23	24	45	19	14
JAN. 2	38	28	29	29	37	44	45	23	24	45	19	14
JAN. 3	39	30	30	31	38	44	45	23	24	45	19	14
JAN. 4	39	31	32	32	38	45	45	23	24	45	19	14
JAN. 5	39	33	34	34	38	45	45	23	24	45	19	14
JAN. 6	39	35	35	36	38	45	45	23	24	45	19	14
JAN. 7	39	36	37	37	38	45	45	23	24	45	19	14
JAN. 8	39	38	38	39	39	45	45	23	24	45	19	14
JAN. 9	39	39	40	40	39	45	45	23	24	45	19	14
JAN. 10	40	41	42	42	39	45	45	23	24	45	19	14
JAN. 11	40	43	43	44	39	46	46	23	24	45	19	14
JAN. 12	40	44	45	45	39	46	46	23	24	45	19	14
JAN. 13	40	46	46	47	40	46	46	23	24	45	19	14
JAN. 14	40	47	48	48	40	46	46	23	24	45	19	14
JAN. 15	40	1	2	2	40	46	46	23	24	45	19	14
JAN. 16	40	3	3	4	40	46	46	23	24	45	19	14
JAN. 17	41	4	5	6	41	47	46	23	24	45	19	14
JAN. 18	41	6	7	7	41	47	46	23	24	45	19	14
JAN. 19	41	8	9	9	41	47	46	23	24	45	19	14
JAN. 20	41	10	11	11	41	47	47	23	24	45	19	14
JAN. 21	41	12	13	13	41	47	47	23	24	45	19	14
JAN. 22	41	14	15	15	42	47	47	23	24	45	19	14
JAN. 23	42	16	17	17	42	47	47	23	24	45	19	14
JAN. 24	42	18	19	19	42	48	47	23	24	45	19	14
JAN. 25	42	20	21	21	42	48	47	23	24	45	19	14
JAN. 26	42	22	23	23	43	48	47	23	24	45	19	14
JAN. 27	42	24	25	25	43	48	47	23	24	45	19	14
JAN. 28	42	26	26	27	43	48	47	23	24	46	19	14
JAN. 29	42	28	28	29	43	48	47	23	24	46	19	14
JAN. 30	42	29	30	30	44	48	48	23	24	46	19	14
JAN. 31	43	31	32	32	44	1	48	23	24	46	19	14

February

Date & Time	SUN	MOON 1	MOON 2	MOON 3	MERCURY	VENUS	MARS	JUPITER	SATURN	URANUS	NEPTUNE	PLUTO
FEB. 1	43	33	33	34	44	1	48	23	24	46	19	14
FEB. 2	43	34	35	35	44	1	48	23	24	46	19	14
FEB. 3	43	36	36	37	44	1	48	23	24	46	19	14
FEB. 4	43	37	38	38	45	1	48	23	24	46	19	14
FEB. 5	43	39	40	40	45	1	48	23	24	46	19	14
FEB. 6	43	41	41	42	45	1	48	23	24	46	19	14
FEB. 7	43	42	43	43	45	2	48	23	24	46	19	14
FEB. 8	44	44	44	45	46	2	48	23	24	46	19	14
FEB. 9	44	45	46	46	46	2	1	23	24	46	19	14
FEB. 10	44	47	48	48	46	2	1	23	24	46	19	14
FEB. 11	44	1	1	2	46	2	1	23	24	46	19	14
FEB. 12	44	2	3	3	46	2	1	23	24	46	19	14
FEB. 13	44	4	5	5	47	2	1	23	24	46	19	14
FEB. 14	44	6	6	7	47	3	1	23	24	46	19	14
FEB. 15	44	7	8	9	47	3	1	23	24	46	19	14
FEB. 16	45	9	10	11	47	3	1	23	24	46	19	14
FEB. 17	45	11	12	12	47	3	1	23	24	46	19	14
FEB. 18	45	13	14	14	47	3	1	23	24	46	19	14
FEB. 19	45	15	16	16	47	3	2	23	24	46	19	14
FEB. 20	45	17	18	18	47	3	2	23	24	46	19	14
FEB. 21	45	19	20	20	47	3	2	23	24	46	19	14
FEB. 22	45	21	22	22	47	4	2	23	24	46	19	14
FEB. 23	46	23	24	24	47	4	2	23	24	46	19	14
FEB. 24	46	25	26	26	47	4	2	23	24	46	19	14
FEB. 25	46	27	27	28	47	4	2	23	24	46	19	14
FEB. 26	46	29	29	30	47	4	2	23	24	46	19	14
FEB. 27	46	30	31	32	47	4	2	23	24	46	19	14
FEB. 28	46	32	33	33	47	4	2	23	24	46	19	14

MOON 1 ◐ 12:01 A.M. TO 8:00 A.M.　　**MOON 2** ◑ 8:01 A.M. TO 4:00 P.M.　　**MOON 3** ● 4:01 P.M. TO 12:00 A.M.
Use only one "moon" number. Choose the column closest to your time of birth. If your place of birth is not on Eastern Standard Time, be sure to read "How to Convert to Eastern Standard Time" at the beginning of this section.

1921

March

April

Date & Time	☉ SUN	☽ MOON 1	◑ MOON 2	● MOON 3	MERCURY	VENUS	MARS	JUPITER	SATURN	URANUS	NEPTUNE	PLUTO
MAR. 1	46	34	34	35	47	4	3	23	24	46	19	14
MAR. 2	46	35	36	36	47	4	3	23	24	46	19	14
MAR. 3	47	37	37	38	47	5	3	23	24	46	19	14
MAR. 4	47	39	39	40	46	5	3	23	24	46	19	14
MAR. 5	47	40	41	41	46	5	3	23	24	46	19	14
MAR. 6	47	42	42	43	46	5	3	23	24	46	19	14
MAR. 7	47	43	44	44	46	5	3	23	24	46	19	14
MAR. 8	47	45	45	46	46	5	3	23	24	46	18	14
MAR. 9	47	47	47	48	46	5	3	23	24	46	18	14
MAR. 10	47	48	1	1	46	5	3	23	24	46	18	14
MAR. 11	48	2	2	3	46	5	4	23	24	46	18	14
MAR. 12	48	4	4	5	46	5	4	23	24	46	18	14
MAR. 13	48	5	6	6	45	5	4	23	24	46	18	14
MAR. 14	48	7	8	8	45	6	4	23	24	46	18	14
MAR. 15	48	9	9	10	45	6	4	23	24	46	18	14
MAR. 16	48	11	11	12	45	6	4	23	24	46	18	14
MAR. 17	48	13	13	14	45	6	4	23	24	46	18	14
MAR. 18	48	14	15	16	45	6	4	23	24	46	18	14
MAR. 19	1	16	17	18	45	6	4	23	24	46	18	14
MAR. 20	1	18	19	20	46	6	4	23	24	46	18	14
MAR. 21	1	20	21	22	46	6	5	23	24	46	18	14
MAR. 22	1	22	23	23	46	6	5	23	24	46	18	14
MAR. 23	1	24	25	25	46	6	5	23	24	46	18	14
MAR. 24	1	26	27	27	46	6	5	23	24	46	18	14
MAR. 25	2	28	28	29	46	6	5	22	24	46	18	14
MAR. 26	2	30	30	31	46	6	5	22	24	46	18	14
MAR. 27	2	31	32	33	46	6	5	22	24	46	18	14
MAR. 28	2	33	34	34	46	6	5	22	24	46	18	14
MAR. 29	2	35	35	36	46	6	5	22	24	46	18	14
MAR. 30	2	36	37	38	46	6	5	22	24	46	18	14
MAR. 31	2	38	39	39	47	6	6	22	24	46	18	14

Date & Time	☉ SUN	☽ MOON 1	◑ MOON 2	● MOON 3	MERCURY	VENUS	MARS	JUPITER	SATURN	URANUS	NEPTUNE	PLUTO
APR. 1	2	40	40	41	47	6	6	22	24	46	18	14
APR. 2	2	41	42	42	47	6	6	22	24	46	18	14
APR. 3	3	43	43	44	47	6	6	22	24	46	18	14
APR. 4	3	44	45	45	47	6	6	22	24	46	18	14
APR. 5	3	46	47	47	47	6	6	22	24	46	18	14
APR. 6	3	48	48	1	48	6	6	22	24	46	18	14
APR. 7	3	1	2	2	48	6	6	22	24	46	18	14
APR. 8	3	3	4	4	48	6	6	22	24	46	18	14
APR. 9	3	5	5	6	48	6	6	22	24	46	18	14
APR. 10	3	7	7	8	48	6	7	22	24	46	18	14
APR. 11	4	8	9	10	48	6	7	22	24	46	18	14
APR. 12	4	10	11	11	1	6	7	22	24	46	18	14
APR. 13	4	12	13	13	1	6	7	22	24	46	18	14
APR. 14	4	14	15	15	1	6	7	22	24	46	18	14
APR. 15	4	16	17	17	1	6	7	22	24	46	18	14
APR. 16	4	18	18	19	1	6	7	22	23	46	18	14
APR. 17	4	20	20	21	2	6	7	22	23	46	18	14
APR. 18	4	22	22	23	2	6	7	22	23	46	18	14
APR. 19	5	23	24	25	2	6	7	22	23	46	18	14
APR. 20	5	25	26	27	2	5	7	22	23	46	18	14
APR. 21	5	27	28	28	2	5	8	22	23	46	18	14
APR. 22	5	29	30	30	3	5	8	22	23	46	18	14
APR. 23	5	31	31	32	3	5	8	22	23	46	18	14
APR. 24	5	32	33	34	3	5	8	22	23	46	18	14
APR. 25	6	34	35	35	3	5	8	22	23	46	18	14
APR. 26	6	36	36	37	4	5	8	22	23	46	18	14
APR. 27	6	37	38	39	4	5	8	22	23	46	18	14
APR. 28	6	39	40	40	4	5	8	22	23	46	18	14
APR. 29	6	41	41	42	4	5	8	22	23	46	18	14
APR. 30	6	42	43	43	5	5	8	22	23	46	18	14

MOON 1 ☽ 12:01 A.M. TO 8:00 A.M.   **MOON 2** ◑ 8:01 A.M. TO 4:00 P.M.   **MOON 3** ● 4:01 P.M. TO 12:00 A.M.
Use only one "moon" number. Choose the column closest to your time of birth. If your place of birth is not on Eastern Standard Time, be sure to read "How to Convert to Eastern Standard Time" at the beginning of this section.

1921

May

June

Date & Time	SUN	MOON 1	MOON 2	MOON 3	MERCURY	VENUS	MARS	JUPITER	SATURN	URANUS	NEPTUNE	PLUTO
MAY 1	6	44	44	45	5	5	9	22	23	46	18	14
MAY 2	6	45	46	47	5	5	9	22	23	46	18	14
MAY 3	7	47	48	48	6	4	9	22	23	46	18	14
MAY 4	7	1	1	2	6	4	9	22	23	46	18	14
MAY 5	7	2	3	4	6	4	9	22	23	46	18	14
MAY 6	7	4	5	5	6	4	9	22	23	46	18	14
MAY 7	7	6	7	7	6	4	9	22	23	46	18	14
MAY 8	7	8	8	9	7	4	9	22	23	46	18	14
MAY 9	7	10	10	11	7	4	9	22	23	46	18	14
MAY 10	7	12	12	13	7	4	9	22	23	46	18	14
MAY 11	8	14	14	15	8	4	9	22	23	46	18	14
MAY 12	8	15	16	17	8	4	10	22	23	46	18	14
MAY 13	8	17	18	19	8	4	10	22	23	46	18	14
MAY 14	8	19	20	21	9	4	10	22	23	46	18	14
MAY 15	8	21	22	22	9	4	10	22	23	46	18	14
MAY 16	8	23	24	24	9	4	10	22	23	46	18	14
MAY 17	8	25	25	26	9	4	10	22	23	46	18	14
MAY 18	8	27	27	28	10	4	10	22	23	46	18	14
MAY 19	9	28	29	30	10	4	10	22	23	46	18	14
MAY 20	9	30	31	31	10	4	10	22	23	46	18	14
MAY 21	9	32	32	33	11	4	10	22	23	46	18	14
MAY 22	9	34	34	35	11	4	10	22	23	46	18	14
MAY 23	9	35	36	36	11	4	11	22	23	46	18	14
MAY 24	9	37	37	38	11	4	11	22	23	46	18	14
MAY 25	10	39	39	40	12	4	11	22	23	46	18	14
MAY 26	10	40	41	41	12	5	11	22	23	46	18	14
MAY 27	10	42	42	43	12	5	11	22	23	46	18	14
MAY 28	10	43	44	44	12	5	11	22	23	46	18	14
MAY 29	10	45	45	46	13	5	11	22	23	46	18	14
MAY 30	10	47	47	48	13	5	11	22	23	46	18	14
MAY 31	10	48	1	1	13	5	11	22	23	46	18	14

Date & Time	SUN	MOON 1	MOON 2	MOON 3	MERCURY	VENUS	MARS	JUPITER	SATURN	URANUS	NEPTUNE	PLUTO
JUN. 1	10	2	2	3	13	5	11	22	23	46	18	14
JUN. 2	10	4	4	5	13	5	11	22	23	46	18	14
JUN. 3	11	5	6	6	14	5	12	22	23	46	18	14
JUN. 4	11	7	8	8	14	5	12	22	23	46	18	14
JUN. 5	11	9	10	10	14	5	12	22	23	46	18	14
JUN. 6	11	11	12	12	14	5	12	22	23	46	19	14
JUN. 7	11	13	13	14	14	5	12	22	23	46	19	14
JUN. 8	11	15	15	16	14	5	12	22	23	46	19	14
JUN. 9	11	17	17	18	15	6	12	22	23	46	19	14
JUN. 10	11	19	19	20	15	6	12	22	23	46	19	14
JUN. 11	12	21	21	22	15	6	12	22	23	46	19	14
JUN. 12	12	23	23	24	15	6	12	22	23	46	19	14
JUN. 13	12	24	25	26	15	6	12	22	23	46	19	14
JUN. 14	12	26	27	27	15	6	13	22	23	46	19	14
JUN. 15	12	28	29	29	15	6	13	22	23	46	19	14
JUN. 16	12	30	30	31	15	6	13	22	23	46	19	14
JUN. 17	12	31	32	33	15	6	13	22	23	46	19	14
JUN. 18	12	33	34	34	16	7	13	23	23	46	19	14
JUN. 19	13	35	35	36	16	7	13	23	23	46	19	14
JUN. 20	13	36	37	38	16	7	13	23	23	46	19	14
JUN. 21	13	38	39	39	16	7	13	23	23	46	19	14
JUN. 22	13	40	40	41	16	7	13	23	23	46	19	14
JUN. 23	13	41	42	42	16	7	13	23	23	46	19	14
JUN. 24	13	43	43	44	16	7	13	23	23	46	19	14
JUN. 25	14	44	45	45	16	7	14	23	24	46	19	14
JUN. 26	14	46	47	47	16	7	14	23	24	46	19	14
JUN. 27	14	48	48	1	16	8	14	23	24	46	19	14
JUN. 28	14	1	2	2	16	8	14	23	24	46	19	14
JUN. 29	14	3	3	4	16	8	14	23	24	46	19	14
JUN. 30	14	5	5	6	16	8	14	23	24	46	19	14

MOON 1 ☽ 12:01 A.M. TO 8:00 A.M.   **MOON 2** ☽ 8:01 A.M. TO 4:00 P.M.   **MOON 3** ● 4:01 P.M. TO 12:00 A.M.

Use only one "moon" number. Choose the column closest to your time of birth. If your place of birth is not on Eastern Standard Time, be sure to read "How to Convert to Eastern Standard Time" at the beginning of this section.

1921

July

August

Date & Time	SUN	MOON 1	MOON 2	MOON 3	MERCURY	VENUS	MARS	JUPITER	SATURN	URANUS	NEPTUNE	PLUTO
JUL. 1	14	6	7	8	16	8	14	23	24	46	19	14
JUL. 2	14	8	9	9	16	8	14	23	24	46	19	14
JUL. 3	15	10	11	11	15	8	14	23	24	46	19	14
JUL. 4	15	12	13	13	15	8	14	23	24	46	19	14
JUL. 5	15	14	15	15	15	9	14	23	24	46	19	14
JUL. 6	15	16	17	17	15	9	15	23	24	46	19	14
JUL. 7	15	18	19	19	15	9	15	23	24	46	19	14
JUL. 8	15	20	21	21	15	9	15	23	24	46	19	14
JUL. 9	15	22	23	23	15	9	15	23	24	46	19	14
JUL. 10	15	24	25	25	15	9	15	23	24	46	19	14
JUL. 11	16	26	26	27	15	9	15	23	24	46	19	14
JUL. 12	16	28	28	29	15	9	15	23	24	46	19	14
JUL. 13	16	29	30	31	15	10	15	23	24	46	19	14
JUL. 14	16	31	32	32	15	10	15	23	24	46	19	14
JUL. 15	16	33	33	34	15	10	15	23	24	46	19	14
JUL. 16	16	34	35	35	15	10	15	23	24	46	19	14
JUL. 17	16	36	37	37	14	10	15	23	24	46	19	14
JUL. 18	16	38	38	39	14	10	16	23	24	46	19	14
JUL. 19	17	39	40	40	14	10	16	23	24	46	19	14
JUL. 20	17	41	41	42	14	11	16	23	24	46	19	14
JUL. 21	17	42	43	43	14	11	16	23	24	46	19	14
JUL. 22	17	44	45	45	15	11	16	23	24	46	19	14
JUL. 23	17	46	46	47	15	11	16	23	24	46	19	14
JUL. 24	17	47	48	48	15	11	16	23	24	46	19	14
JUL. 25	17	1	1	2	15	11	16	23	24	46	19	14
JUL. 26	18	2	3	4	15	11	16	23	24	46	19	14
JUL. 27	18	4	5	5	15	12	16	23	24	46	19	14
JUL. 28	18	6	6	7	15	12	16	23	24	46	19	14
JUL. 29	18	7	8	9	15	12	17	23	24	46	19	14
JUL. 30	18	9	10	11	15	12	17	23	24	46	19	14
JUL. 31	18	11	12	12	15	12	17	23	24	46	19	14

Date & Time	SUN	MOON 1	MOON 2	MOON 3	MERCURY	VENUS	MARS	JUPITER	SATURN	URANUS	NEPTUNE	PLUTO
AUG. 1	18	13	14	14	16	12	17	23	24	46	19	14
AUG. 2	18	15	16	16	16	12	17	23	24	46	19	14
AUG. 3	19	17	18	18	16	13	17	23	24	46	19	14
AUG. 4	19	19	20	21	16	13	17	24	24	46	19	14
AUG. 5	19	21	22	23	16	13	17	24	24	46	19	14
AUG. 6	19	23	24	24	16	13	17	24	24	46	19	14
AUG. 7	19	25	26	26	17	13	17	24	24	46	19	14
AUG. 8	19	27	28	28	17	13	17	24	24	46	19	14
AUG. 9	19	29	29	30	17	14	17	24	24	46	19	14
AUG. 10	19	31	31	32	17	14	18	24	24	46	19	14
AUG. 11	20	32	33	33	18	14	18	24	24	46	19	14
AUG. 12	20	34	35	35	18	14	18	24	24	46	19	14
AUG. 13	20	36	36	37	18	14	18	24	24	46	19	14
AUG. 14	20	37	38	38	18	14	18	24	24	46	19	14
AUG. 15	20	39	39	40	19	14	18	24	24	46	19	14
AUG. 16	20	40	41	42	19	15	18	24	24	46	19	14
AUG. 17	20	42	43	43	19	15	18	24	24	46	19	14
AUG. 18	20	44	44	45	20	15	18	24	24	46	19	14
AUG. 19	21	45	46	46	20	15	18	24	24	46	19	14
AUG. 20	21	47	47	48	20	15	18	24	24	46	19	14
AUG. 21	21	48	1	1	20	15	18	24	24	46	19	14
AUG. 22	21	2	3	3	21	15	19	24	24	46	19	14
AUG. 23	21	4	4	5	21	16	19	24	24	46	19	14
AUG. 24	21	5	6	6	21	16	19	24	24	46	19	14
AUG. 25	21	7	8	8	21	16	19	24	24	46	19	14
AUG. 26	22	9	9	10	22	16	19	24	24	46	19	14
AUG. 27	22	11	11	12	22	16	19	24	24	46	19	14
AUG. 28	22	12	13	14	22	16	19	24	24	46	19	14
AUG. 29	22	14	15	16	22	17	19	24	24	46	19	14
AUG. 30	22	16	17	18	23	17	19	24	24	46	19	14
AUG. 31	22	18	19	20	23	17	19	24	24	46	19	14

MOON 1 ◗ 12:01 A.M. TO 8:00 A.M.   **MOON 2** ◖ 8:01 A.M. TO 4:00 P.M.   **MOON 3** ● 4:01 P.M. TO 12:00 A.M.
Use only one "moon" number. Choose the column closest to your time of birth. If your place of birth is not on Eastern Standard Time, be sure to read "How to Convert to Eastern Standard Time" at the beginning of this section.

1921

September

Date & Time	SUN	MOON 1	MOON 2	MOON 3	MERCURY	VENUS	MARS	JUPITER	SATURN	URANUS	NEPTUNE	PLUTO
SEP. 1	22	20	21	22	23	17	19	24	24	46	19	14
SEP. 2	22	22	23	24	23	17	20	24	24	46	19	14
SEP. 3	23	24	25	26	24	17	20	24	24	46	19	14
SEP. 4	23	26	27	28	24	17	20	24	24	46	19	14
SEP. 5	23	28	29	29	24	18	20	24	24	46	19	14
SEP. 6	23	30	31	31	24	18	20	24	24	46	19	14
SEP. 7	23	32	32	33	25	18	20	24	24	46	19	14
SEP. 8	23	34	34	35	25	18	20	24	24	46	19	14
SEP. 9	23	35	36	36	25	18	20	24	24	46	19	14
SEP. 10	23	37	37	38	25	18	20	25	25	46	19	14
SEP. 11	24	38	39	40	25	19	20	25	25	46	19	14
SEP. 12	24	40	41	41	26	19	20	25	25	46	19	14
SEP. 13	24	42	42	43	26	19	20	25	25	46	19	14
SEP. 14	24	43	44	44	26	19	21	25	25	46	19	14
SEP. 15	24	45	45	46	26	19	21	25	25	46	19	14
SEP. 16	24	46	47	47	26	19	21	25	25	46	19	14
SEP. 17	24	48	1	1	27	20	21	25	25	46	19	14
SEP. 18	24	2	2	3	27	20	21	25	25	46	19	14
SEP. 19	25	3	4	4	27	20	21	25	25	46	19	14
SEP. 20	25	5	5	6	27	20	21	25	25	46	19	14
SEP. 21	25	7	7	8	27	20	21	25	25	46	19	14
SEP. 22	25	8	9	10	28	20	21	25	25	46	19	14
SEP. 23	25	10	11	11	28	20	21	25	25	46	19	14
SEP. 24	25	12	12	13	28	21	21	25	25	46	19	14
SEP. 25	26	14	14	15	28	21	21	25	25	46	19	14
SEP. 26	26	16	16	17	28	21	22	25	25	46	19	14
SEP. 27	26	18	18	19	29	21	22	25	25	46	19	14
SEP. 28	26	19	20	21	29	21	22	25	25	46	19	14
SEP. 29	26	21	22	23	29	21	22	25	25	46	19	14
SEP. 30	26	23	24	25	29	22	22	25	25	46	19	14

October

Date & Time	SUN	MOON 1	MOON 2	MOON 3	MERCURY	VENUS	MARS	JUPITER	SATURN	URANUS	NEPTUNE	PLUTO
OCT. 1	26	25	26	27	29	22	22	25	25	46	19	14
OCT. 2	26	27	28	29	29	22	22	25	25	46	19	14
OCT. 3	27	29	30	30	30	22	22	25	25	46	19	14
OCT. 4	27	31	32	32	30	22	22	25	25	46	19	14
OCT. 5	27	33	33	34	30	22	22	25	25	46	19	14
OCT. 6	27	35	35	36	30	23	22	25	25	46	19	14
OCT. 7	27	36	37	37	30	23	22	25	25	46	19	14
OCT. 8	27	38	38	39	30	23	23	25	25	46	19	14
OCT. 9	27	40	40	41	30	23	23	25	25	46	19	14
OCT. 10	27	41	42	42	30	23	23	25	25	46	19	14
OCT. 11	28	43	43	44	31	23	23	25	25	46	19	14
OCT. 12	28	44	45	45	31	24	23	25	25	46	19	14
OCT. 13	28	46	46	47	31	24	23	25	25	46	19	14
OCT. 14	28	48	48	1	31	24	23	26	25	46	19	14
OCT. 15	28	1	2	2	31	24	23	26	25	46	19	14
OCT. 16	28	3	3	4	31	24	23	26	25	46	19	14
OCT. 17	28	4	5	6	31	24	23	26	25	46	19	14
OCT. 18	28	6	7	7	31	25	23	26	25	46	19	14
OCT. 19	29	8	8	9	31	25	23	26	25	46	19	14
OCT. 20	29	10	10	11	31	25	24	26	25	46	19	14
OCT. 21	29	11	12	13	31	25	24	26	25	46	19	14
OCT. 22	29	13	14	15	31	25	24	26	25	46	19	14
OCT. 23	29	15	16	16	31	25	24	26	25	46	19	14
OCT. 24	29	17	18	18	31	26	24	26	25	46	19	14
OCT. 25	29	19	20	20	31	26	24	26	25	46	19	14
OCT. 26	30	21	21	22	31	26	24	25	25	46	19	14
OCT. 27	30	23	23	24	31	26	24	26	25	46	19	14
OCT. 28	30	25	25	26	31	26	24	26	25	46	19	14
OCT. 29	30	27	27	28	30	26	24	26	25	46	19	14
OCT. 30	30	28	29	30	30	27	24	26	25	46	19	14
OCT. 31	30	30	31	32	30	27	24	26	25	46	19	14

MOON 1 ☽ 12:01 A.M. TO 8:00 A.M. **MOON 2** ☽ 8:01 A.M. TO 4:00 P.M. **MOON 3** ● 4:01 P.M. TO 12:00 A.M.

Use only one "moon" number. Choose the column closest to your time of birth. If your place of birth is not on Eastern Standard Time, be sure to read "How to Convert to Eastern Standard Time" at the beginning of this section.

1921

November

Date & Time	SUN	MOON 1	MOON 2	MOON 3	MERCURY	VENUS	MARS	JUPITER	SATURN	URANUS	NEPTUNE	PLUTO
NOV. 1	30	32	33	33	30	27	25	26	25	46	19	14
NOV. 2	30	34	34	35	30	27	25	26	25	46	19	14
NOV. 3	31	36	36	37	30	27	25	26	25	46	19	14
NOV. 4	31	37	38	38	29	27	25	26	25	46	19	14
NOV. 5	31	39	40	40	29	28	25	26	25	46	19	14
NOV. 6	31	41	41	42	29	28	25	26	25	46	19	14
NOV. 7	31	42	43	43	29	28	25	26	25	46	19	14
NOV. 8	31	44	44	45	29	28	25	26	25	46	19	14
NOV. 9	31	45	46	46	29	28	25	26	25	46	19	14
NOV. 10	31	47	47	48	29	28	25	26	25	46	19	14
NOV. 11	31	1	1	2	29	29	25	26	25	46	19	14
NOV. 12	32	2	3	3	29	29	25	26	25	46	19	14
NOV. 13	32	4	4	5	29	29	26	26	26	46	19	14
NOV. 14	32	6	6	7	29	29	26	26	26	46	19	14
NOV. 15	32	7	8	9	29	29	26	26	26	46	19	14
NOV. 16	32	9	10	10	30	29	26	26	26	46	19	14
NOV. 17	32	11	12	12	30	30	26	26	26	46	19	14
NOV. 18	32	13	13	14	30	30	26	26	26	46	19	14
NOV. 19	33	15	15	16	30	30	26	26	26	46	19	14
NOV. 20	33	17	17	18	30	30	26	26	26	46	19	14
NOV. 21	33	19	19	20	30	30	26	26	26	46	19	14
NOV. 22	33	20	21	22	30	30	26	26	26	46	19	14
NOV. 23	33	22	23	24	31	31	26	27	26	46	19	14
NOV. 24	33	24	25	25	31	31	26	27	26	46	19	14
NOV. 25	34	26	27	27	31	31	26	27	26	46	19	14
NOV. 26	34	28	28	29	31	31	27	27	26	46	19	14
NOV. 27	34	30	30	31	31	31	27	27	26	46	19	14
NOV. 28	34	31	32	33	32	31	27	27	26	46	19	14
NOV. 29	34	33	34	34	32	32	27	27	26	46	19	14
NOV. 30	34	35	36	36	32	32	27	27	26	46	19	14

December

Date & Time	SUN	MOON 1	MOON 2	MOON 3	MERCURY	VENUS	MARS	JUPITER	SATURN	URANUS	NEPTUNE	PLUTO
DEC. 1	34	37	37	38	32	32	27	27	26	46	19	14
DEC. 2	34	38	39	39	32	32	27	27	26	46	19	14
DEC. 3	35	40	41	41	33	32	27	27	26	46	19	14
DEC. 4	35	42	42	43	33	32	27	27	26	46	19	14
DEC. 5	35	43	44	44	33	33	27	27	26	46	19	14
DEC. 6	35	45	45	46	33	33	27	27	26	46	19	14
DEC. 7	35	46	47	47	33	33	27	27	26	46	19	14
DEC. 8	35	48	1	1	34	33	28	27	26	46	19	14
DEC. 9	35	2	2	3	34	33	28	27	26	46	19	14
DEC. 10	35	3	4	4	34	33	28	27	26	46	19	14
DEC. 11	36	5	5	6	34	34	28	27	26	46	19	14
DEC. 12	36	7	7	8	34	34	28	27	26	46	19	14
DEC. 13	36	8	9	10	35	34	28	27	26	46	19	14
DEC. 14	36	10	11	12	35	34	28	27	26	46	19	14
DEC. 15	36	12	13	13	35	34	28	27	26	46	19	14
DEC. 16	36	14	15	15	35	34	28	27	26	46	19	14
DEC. 17	36	16	17	17	35	35	28	27	26	46	19	14
DEC. 18	36	18	19	19	36	35	28	27	26	46	19	14
DEC. 19	37	20	21	21	36	35	28	27	26	46	19	14
DEC. 20	37	22	22	23	36	35	28	27	26	46	19	14
DEC. 21	37	24	24	25	36	35	29	27	26	46	19	14
DEC. 22	37	26	26	27	35	35	29	27	26	46	19	14
DEC. 23	37	27	28	29	37	36	29	27	26	46	19	14
DEC. 24	37	29	30	30	37	36	29	27	26	46	19	14
DEC. 25	37	31	32	32	37	36	29	27	26	46	19	14
DEC. 26	38	33	33	34	37	36	29	27	26	46	19	14
DEC. 27	38	34	35	36	38	36	29	27	26	46	19	14
DEC. 28	38	36	37	37	38	36	29	27	26	46	19	14
DEC. 29	38	38	38	39	38	37	29	27	26	46	19	14
DEC. 30	38	40	40	41	38	37	29	27	26	46	19	14
DEC. 31	38	41	42	42	38	37	29	27	26	46	19	14

MOON 1 ☽ 12:01 A.M. TO 8:00 A.M.   **MOON 2** ◑ 8:01 A.M. TO 4:00 P.M.   **MOON 3** ● 4:01 P.M. TO 12:00 A.M.

Use only one "moon" number. Choose the column closest to your time of birth. If your place of birth is not on Eastern Standard Time, be sure to read "How to Convert to Eastern Standard Time" at the beginning of this section.

1922

January

Date & Time	SUN	MOON 1	MOON 2	MOON 3	MERCURY	VENUS	MARS	JUPITER	SATURN	URANUS	NEPTUNE	PLUTO
JAN. 1	38	43	43	44	39	37	29	27	26	46	19	14
JAN. 2	38	44	45	45	39	37	29	27	26	46	19	14
JAN. 3	39	46	46	47	39	37	30	27	26	46	19	14
JAN. 4	39	47	48	1	39	38	30	27	26	46	19	14
JAN. 5	39	1	2	2	40	38	30	27	26	46	19	14
JAN. 6	39	3	3	4	40	38	30	27	26	46	19	14
JAN. 7	39	4	5	5	40	38	30	27	26	46	19	14
JAN. 8	39	6	7	7	40	38	30	27	26	46	19	14
JAN. 9	39	8	8	9	40	38	30	27	26	46	19	14
JAN. 10	40	9	10	11	41	39	30	27	26	46	19	14
JAN. 11	40	11	12	13	41	39	30	27	26	46	19	14
JAN. 12	40	13	14	15	41	39	30	27	26	46	19	14
JAN. 13	40	15	16	17	41	39	30	27	26	46	19	14
JAN. 14	40	17	18	19	42	39	30	27	26	46	19	14
JAN. 15	40	19	20	21	42	39	30	27	26	46	19	14
JAN. 16	40	21	22	23	42	40	31	27	26	46	19	14
JAN. 17	41	23	24	24	42	40	31	27	26	46	19	14
JAN. 18	41	25	26	26	42	40	31	27	26	46	19	14
JAN. 19	41	27	28	28	43	40	31	27	26	46	19	14
JAN. 20	41	29	29	30	43	40	31	27	26	46	19	14
JAN. 21	41	31	31	32	43	40	31	27	26	46	19	14
JAN. 22	41	32	33	33	43	41	31	27	26	46	19	14
JAN. 23	42	34	35	35	43	41	31	27	26	46	19	14
JAN. 24	42	36	36	37	44	41	31	27	26	46	19	14
JAN. 25	42	37	38	39	44	41	31	27	26	46	19	14
JAN. 26	42	39	40	40	44	41	31	27	26	46	19	14
JAN. 27	42	41	41	42	44	41	31	27	26	46	19	14
JAN. 28	42	42	43	43	44	42	31	27	26	46	19	14
JAN. 29	42	44	44	45	45	42	32	27	26	46	19	14
JAN. 30	42	45	46	47	45	42	32	27	26	46	19	14
JAN. 31	43	47	48	48	45	42	32	27	26	46	19	14

February

Date & Time	SUN	MOON 1	MOON 2	MOON 3	MERCURY	VENUS	MARS	JUPITER	SATURN	URANUS	NEPTUNE	PLUTO
FEB. 1	43	1	1	2	45	42	32	27	26	46	19	14
FEB. 2	43	2	3	3	45	42	32	27	26	46	19	14
FEB. 3	43	4	4	5	45	43	32	27	26	46	19	14
FEB. 4	43	5	6	7	45	43	32	27	26	46	19	14
FEB. 5	43	7	8	8	45	43	32	27	26	46	19	14
FEB. 6	43	9	9	10	45	43	32	27	26	46	19	14
FEB. 7	43	11	11	12	45	43	32	27	26	46	19	14
FEB. 8	44	12	13	14	45	43	32	27	26	46	19	14
FEB. 9	44	14	15	16	45	44	32	27	26	46	19	14
FEB. 10	44	16	17	18	45	44	32	27	26	46	19	14
FEB. 11	44	18	19	20	45	44	32	27	26	46	19	14
FEB. 12	44	20	21	22	45	44	33	27	26	46	19	14
FEB. 13	44	22	23	24	44	44	33	27	26	46	19	14
FEB. 14	44	24	25	26	44	44	33	27	26	46	19	14
FEB. 15	44	26	27	28	44	45	33	27	26	46	19	14
FEB. 16	45	28	29	29	44	45	33	27	26	46	19	14
FEB. 17	45	30	31	31	44	45	33	27	26	46	19	14
FEB. 18	45	32	32	33	44	45	33	27	26	46	19	14
FEB. 19	45	34	34	35	44	45	33	27	26	46	19	14
FEB. 20	45	35	36	36	43	45	33	27	26	46	19	14
FEB. 21	45	37	38	38	43	46	33	27	26	46	19	14
FEB. 22	45	39	39	40	43	46	33	27	26	46	19	14
FEB. 23	46	40	41	41	43	46	33	27	26	46	19	14
FEB. 24	46	42	42	43	43	46	33	27	26	46	19	14
FEB. 25	46	43	44	45	43	46	33	27	26	46	19	14
FEB. 26	46	45	46	46	43	46	33	27	26	46	19	14
FEB. 27	46	47	47	48	43	47	34	27	26	46	19	14
FEB. 28	46	48	1	1	43	47	34	27	26	46	19	14

MOON 1 ◐ 12:01 A.M. TO 8:00 A.M.   **MOON 2** ◑ 8:01 A.M. TO 4:00 P.M.   **MOON 3** ● 4:01 P.M. TO 12:00 A.M.
Use only one "moon" number. Choose the column closest to your time of birth. If your place of birth is not on Eastern Standard Time, be sure to read "How to Convert to Eastern Standard Time" at the beginning of this section.

1922

March

Date & Time	SUN	MOON 1	MOON 2	MOON 3	MERCURY	VENUS	MARS	JUPITER	SATURN	URANUS	NEPTUNE	PLUTO
MAR. 1	46	2	2	3	43	47	34	27	26	46	19	14
MAR. 2	46	3	4	4	43	47	34	27	26	46	19	14
MAR. 3	47	5	6	6	43	47	34	27	26	46	19	14
MAR. 4	47	7	7	8	43	47	34	27	26	46	19	14
MAR. 5	47	8	9	9	43	48	34	27	26	46	19	14
MAR. 6	47	10	11	11	43	48	34	27	26	46	19	14
MAR. 7	47	12	12	13	44	48	34	27	26	46	19	14
MAR. 8	47	14	14	15	44	48	34	27	26	46	19	14
MAR. 9	47	15	16	17	44	48	34	27	26	46	19	14
MAR. 10	47	17	18	19	44	48	34	27	26	46	19	14
MAR. 11	48	19	20	21	44	1	34	27	26	46	19	14
MAR. 12	48	21	22	23	44	1	34	27	26	46	19	14
MAR. 13	48	23	24	25	44	1	34	27	26	46	19	14
MAR. 14	48	25	26	27	44	1	34	27	26	46	19	14
MAR. 15	48	27	28	29	44	1	35	27	26	46	19	14
MAR. 16	48	29	30	31	45	1	35	27	26	46	19	14
MAR. 17	48	31	32	32	45	2	35	27	26	46	19	14
MAR. 18	48	33	34	34	45	2	35	27	26	46	19	14
MAR. 19	1	35	35	36	45	2	35	27	26	46	19	14
MAR. 20	1	37	37	38	45	2	35	27	26	46	19	14
MAR. 21	1	38	39	39	45	2	35	27	26	46	19	14
MAR. 22	1	40	40	41	46	2	35	27	26	46	19	14
MAR. 23	1	41	42	43	46	3	35	27	26	46	19	14
MAR. 24	1	43	44	46	46	3	35	27	26	46	19	14
MAR. 25	2	45	45	46	46	3	35	27	26	46	19	14
MAR. 26	2	46	47	46	46	3	35	27	26	46	19	14
MAR. 27	2	48	48	1	47	3	35	27	26	46	19	14
MAR. 28	2	1	2	2	47	3	35	27	26	46	19	14
MAR. 29	2	3	4	4	47	4	35	27	25	46	19	14
MAR. 30	2	5	5	6	47	4	35	27	25	46	19	14
MAR. 31	2	6	7	7	47	4	35	27	25	46	19	14

April

Date & Time	SUN	MOON 1	MOON 2	MOON 3	MERCURY	VENUS	MARS	JUPITER	SATURN	URANUS	NEPTUNE	PLUTO
APR. 1	2	8	8	9	48	4	35	27	25	46	19	14
APR. 2	2	10	10	11	48	4	35	27	25	46	19	14
APR. 3	3	11	12	12	48	4	35	27	25	46	19	14
APR. 4	3	13	14	14	48	5	36	27	25	46	19	14
APR. 5	3	15	15	16	48	5	36	27	25	47	19	14
APR. 6	3	17	17	18	1	5	36	27	25	47	19	14
APR. 7	3	19	19	20	1	5	36	27	25	47	19	14
APR. 8	3	21	21	22	1	5	36	27	25	47	19	14
APR. 9	3	23	23	24	1	5	36	27	25	47	19	14
APR. 10	3	25	25	26	2	6	36	27	25	47	19	14
APR. 11	4	26	27	28	2	6	36	27	25	47	19	14
APR. 12	4	28	29	30	2	6	36	27	25	47	19	14
APR. 13	4	30	31	32	2	6	36	27	25	47	19	14
APR. 14	4	32	33	34	3	6	36	27	25	47	19	14
APR. 15	4	34	35	35	3	6	36	27	25	47	19	14
APR. 16	4	36	37	37	3	7	36	27	25	47	19	14
APR. 17	4	38	38	39	3	7	36	27	25	47	19	14
APR. 18	4	39	40	40	4	7	36	27	25	47	19	14
APR. 19	5	41	42	42	4	7	36	27	25	47	19	14
APR. 20	5	43	43	44	4	7	36	27	25	47	19	14
APR. 21	5	44	45	45	4	7	36	27	25	47	19	14
APR. 22	5	46	46	47	5	8	36	27	25	47	19	14
APR. 23	5	47	48	48	5	8	36	27	25	47	19	14
APR. 24	5	1	1	2	5	8	36	27	25	47	19	14
APR. 25	6	3	3	4	6	8	36	26	25	47	19	14
APR. 26	6	4	5	5	6	8	36	26	25	47	19	14
APR. 27	6	6	6	7	6	8	36	26	25	47	19	14
APR. 28	6	7	8	9	6	9	36	26	25	47	19	14
APR. 29	6	9	10	10	7	9	36	26	25	47	19	14
APR. 30	6	11	11	12	9	9	36	26	25	47	19	14

MOON 1 ◐ 12:01 A.M. TO 8:00 A.M.   **MOON 2** ◑ 8:01 A.M. TO 4:00 P.M.   **MOON 3** ● 4:01 P.M. TO 12:00 A.M.

Use only one "moon" number. Choose the column closest to your time of birth. If your place of birth is not on Eastern Standard Time, be sure to read "How to Convert to Eastern Standard Time" at the beginning of this section.

1922

May

June

Date & Time	SUN ☉	MOON 1 ◐	MOON 2 ◑	MOON 3 ●	MERCURY	VENUS	MARS	JUPITER	SATURN	URANUS	NEPTUNE	PLUTO
MAY 1	6	13	13	14	7	9	36	26	25	47	19	14
MAY 2	6	14	15	16	8	9	36	26	25	47	19	14
MAY 3	7	16	17	17	8	9	36	26	25	47	19	14
MAY 4	7	18	19	19	8	9	36	26	25	47	19	14
MAY 5	7	20	21	21	8	10	36	26	25	47	19	14
MAY 6	7	22	23	23	9	10	36	26	25	47	19	14
MAY 7	7	24	24	25	9	10	36	26	25	47	19	14
MAY 8	7	26	26	27	9	10	36	26	25	47	19	14
MAY 9	7	28	28	29	9	10	36	26	25	47	19	14
MAY 10	7	30	30	31	10	10	36	26	25	47	19	14
MAY 11	8	32	32	33	10	11	36	26	25	47	19	14
MAY 12	8	33	34	35	10	11	36	26	25	47	19	14
MAY 13	8	35	36	36	10	11	36	26	25	47	19	14
MAY 14	8	37	38	38	11	11	36	26	25	47	19	14
MAY 15	8	39	39	40	11	11	36	26	25	47	19	14
MAY 16	8	40	41	42	11	11	36	26	25	47	19	14
MAY 17	8	42	43	43	11	12	36	26	25	47	19	14
MAY 18	8	44	44	45	11	12	36	26	25	47	19	14
MAY 19	9	45	46	46	12	12	36	26	25	47	19	14
MAY 20	9	47	47	48	12	12	36	26	25	47	19	14
MAY 21	9	48	1	1	12	12	36	26	25	47	19	14
MAY 22	9	2	3	3	12	12	36	26	25	47	19	14
MAY 23	9	4	4	5	12	13	36	26	25	47	19	14
MAY 24	9	5	6	6	12	13	36	26	25	47	19	14
MAY 25	10	7	7	8	12	13	36	26	25	47	19	14
MAY 26	10	9	9	10	13	13	36	26	25	47	19	14
MAY 27	10	10	11	12	13	13	36	26	25	47	19	14
MAY 28	10	12	13	13	13	13	36	26	25	47	19	14
MAY 29	10	14	15	15	13	14	36	26	25	47	19	14
MAY 30	10	16	16	17	13	14	36	26	25	47	19	14
MAY 31	10	18	18	19	13	14	36	26	25	47	19	14

Date & Time	SUN ☉	MOON 1 ◐	MOON 2 ◑	MOON 3 ●	MERCURY	VENUS	MARS	JUPITER	SATURN	URANUS	NEPTUNE	PLUTO
JUN. 1	10	20	20	21	13	14	36	26	25	47	19	14
JUN. 2	10	21	22	23	13	14	36	26	25	47	19	14
JUN. 3	11	23	24	25	13	14	36	26	25	47	19	14
JUN. 4	11	25	26	26	13	14	36	26	25	47	19	14
JUN. 5	11	27	28	28	13	15	36	26	25	47	19	14
JUN. 6	11	29	30	30	13	15	36	26	25	47	19	14
JUN. 7	11	31	31	32	13	15	36	26	25	47	19	14
JUN. 8	11	33	33	34	13	15	36	26	25	47	19	14
JUN. 9	11	35	35	36	13	15	36	26	25	47	19	14
JUN. 10	11	36	37	38	13	15	36	26	25	47	19	14
JUN. 11	12	38	39	39	13	16	35	26	25	47	19	14
JUN. 12	12	40	40	41	13	16	35	26	25	47	19	14
JUN. 13	12	41	42	43	13	16	35	26	25	47	19	14
JUN. 14	12	43	44	44	13	16	35	26	25	47	19	14
JUN. 15	12	45	45	46	13	16	35	26	25	47	19	14
JUN. 16	12	46	47	48	13	16	35	26	25	47	19	14
JUN. 17	12	48	48	1	13	17	35	26	25	47	19	14
JUN. 18	12	1	2	3	12	17	35	26	25	47	19	14
JUN. 19	13	3	4	4	12	17	35	26	25	47	19	14
JUN. 20	13	5	5	6	12	17	35	26	25	47	19	14
JUN. 21	13	6	7	7	12	17	35	26	25	47	19	14
JUN. 22	13	8	9	9	12	17	35	26	25	47	19	14
JUN. 23	13	10	10	11	12	18	35	26	25	47	19	14
JUN. 24	13	12	12	13	12	18	35	26	25	47	19	14
JUN. 25	14	13	14	15	12	18	35	26	25	47	19	14
JUN. 26	14	15	16	17	12	18	35	26	25	47	19	14
JUN. 27	14	17	18	18	12	18	35	26	25	47	19	14
JUN. 28	14	19	20	20	12	18	35	26	25	47	19	14
JUN. 29	14	21	22	22	12	18	35	26	25	47	19	14
JUN. 30	14	23	24	24	12	19	35	26	25	47	19	14

MOON 1 ◐ 12:01 A.M. TO 8:00 A.M.   **MOON 2** ◑ 8:01 A.M. TO 4:00 P.M.   **MOON 3** ● 4:01 P.M. TO 12:00 A.M.
Use only one "moon" number. Choose the column closest to your time of birth. If your place of birth is not on
Eastern Standard Time, be sure to read "How to Convert to Eastern Standard Time" at the beginning of this section.

1922

July

August

Date & Time	SUN	MOON 1	MOON 2	MOON 3	MERCURY	VENUS	MARS	JUPITER	SATURN	URANUS	NEPTUNE	PLUTO
JUL. 1	14	25	25	26	12	19	35	26	25	47	19	14
JUL. 2	14	27	27	28	12	19	35	26	25	47	19	14
JUL. 3	15	29	29	30	12	19	35	26	25	47	19	14
JUL. 4	15	30	31	32	12	19	35	26	25	47	19	14
JUL. 5	15	32	33	33	12	19	35	26	25	47	19	14
JUL. 6	15	34	35	35	12	20	35	26	25	47	19	14
JUL. 7	15	36	36	37	12	20	35	26	25	47	19	14
JUL. 8	15	38	38	39	12	20	35	26	25	47	19	14
JUL. 9	15	39	40	40	12	20	35	26	25	47	19	14
JUL. 10	15	41	41	42	12	20	34	26	25	47	19	14
JUL. 11	16	43	43	44	13	20	34	26	25	47	19	14
JUL. 12	16	44	45	45	13	21	34	26	25	47	19	14
JUL. 13	16	46	46	47	13	21	34	26	25	47	19	14
JUL. 14	16	47	48	48	13	21	34	26	25	47	19	14
JUL. 15	16	1	1	2	13	21	34	26	25	47	19	14
JUL. 16	16	3	3	4	13	21	34	26	25	47	19	14
JUL. 17	16	4	5	5	14	21	34	26	25	47	19	14
JUL. 18	16	6	6	7	14	21	34	26	25	47	19	14
JUL. 19	17	7	8	9	14	22	34	27	25	47	19	14
JUL. 20	17	9	10	10	14	22	34	27	25	47	19	14
JUL. 21	17	11	11	12	14	22	34	27	25	47	19	14
JUL. 22	17	13	13	14	15	22	34	27	25	47	19	14
JUL. 23	17	15	15	16	15	22	34	27	25	47	19	14
JUL. 24	17	16	17	18	15	22	34	27	25	47	19	14
JUL. 25	18	18	19	20	16	23	35	27	25	47	19	14
JUL. 26	18	20	21	22	16	23	35	27	25	47	19	14
JUL. 27	18	22	23	24	16	23	35	27	25	47	19	14
JUL. 28	18	24	25	26	16	23	35	27	25	47	19	14
JUL. 29	18	26	27	27	16	23	35	27	25	47	19	14
JUL. 30	18	28	29	29	17	23	35	27	25	47	19	14
JUL. 31	18	30	31	31	17	23	35	27	25	47	19	14

Date & Time	SUN	MOON 1	MOON 2	MOON 3	MERCURY	VENUS	MARS	JUPITER	SATURN	URANUS	NEPTUNE	PLUTO
AUG. 1	18	32	32	33	17	24	35	27	25	47	19	14
AUG. 2	18	34	34	35	17	24	35	27	25	47	19	14
AUG. 3	19	35	36	37	18	24	35	27	25	47	19	14
AUG. 4	19	37	38	38	18	24	35	27	25	47	19	14
AUG. 5	19	39	39	40	18	24	35	27	25	47	19	14
AUG. 6	19	40	41	42	18	24	35	27	25	47	19	14
AUG. 7	19	42	43	43	19	25	35	27	25	47	19	14
AUG. 8	19	44	44	45	19	25	35	27	26	47	19	14
AUG. 9	19	45	46	46	19	25	35	27	26	47	19	14
AUG. 10	19	47	47	48	20	25	35	27	26	47	19	14
AUG. 11	20	1	1	2	20	25	35	27	26	47	19	14
AUG. 12	20	2	3	3	20	25	35	27	26	47	19	14
AUG. 13	20	4	4	5	20	25	35	27	26	47	19	14
AUG. 14	20	5	6	6	21	26	35	27	26	47	19	14
AUG. 15	20	7	7	8	21	26	35	27	26	47	19	14
AUG. 16	20	8	9	10	21	26	35	27	26	47	19	14
AUG. 17	20	10	11	11	21	26	35	27	26	47	19	14
AUG. 18	20	12	13	13	22	26	35	27	26	47	19	14
AUG. 19	21	14	14	15	22	26	35	27	26	47	19	14
AUG. 20	21	16	16	17	22	26	35	27	26	47	19	14
AUG. 21	21	18	18	19	22	27	35	27	26	47	19	14
AUG. 22	21	20	20	21	23	27	36	27	26	47	19	14
AUG. 23	21	22	22	23	23	27	36	27	26	47	19	14
AUG. 24	21	24	24	25	23	27	36	27	26	47	19	14
AUG. 25	21	26	26	27	23	27	36	27	26	47	19	14
AUG. 26	22	28	28	29	24	27	36	27	26	47	19	14
AUG. 27	22	29	30	31	24	27	36	27	26	47	19	14
AUG. 28	22	31	32	33	24	28	36	27	26	47	19	14
AUG. 29	22	33	34	34	24	28	36	27	26	47	19	14
AUG. 30	22	35	36	36	24	28	36	27	26	47	19	14
AUG. 31	22	37	37	38	25	28	36	27	26	47	19	14

MOON 1 ◖ 12:01 A.M. TO 8:00 A.M.   **MOON 2** ◑ 8:01 A.M. TO 4:00 P.M.   **MOON 3** ● 4:01 P.M. TO 12:00 A.M.

Use only one "moon" number. Choose the column closest to your time of birth. If your place of birth is not on Eastern Standard Time, be sure to read "How to Convert to Eastern Standard Time" at the beginning of this section.

1922

September

October

Date & Time	SUN	MOON 1	MOON 2	MOON 3	MERCURY	VENUS	MARS	JUPITER	SATURN	URANUS	NEPTUNE	PLUTO
SEP. 1	22	38	39	40	25	28	36	27	26	47	19	14
SEP. 2	22	40	41	41	25	28	36	27	26	47	19	14
SEP. 3	23	42	42	43	25	28	36	27	26	47	19	14
SEP. 4	23	43	44	44	25	29	36	27	26	47	19	14
SEP. 5	23	45	45	46	26	29	36	28	26	47	19	14
SEP. 6	23	47	47	48	26	29	36	28	26	47	19	14
SEP. 7	23	48	1	1	26	29	37	28	26	47	19	14
SEP. 8	23	2	2	3	26	29	37	28	26	46	19	14
SEP. 9	23	3	4	4	26	29	37	28	26	46	19	14
SEP. 10	23	5	5	6	26	29	37	28	26	46	19	14
SEP. 11	24	6	7	7	27	29	37	28	26	46	19	14
SEP. 12	24	8	9	9	27	30	37	28	26	46	19	14
SEP. 13	24	10	10	11	27	30	37	28	26	46	19	14
SEP. 14	24	11	12	13	27	30	37	28	26	46	19	14
SEP. 15	24	13	14	14	27	30	37	28	26	46	19	14
SEP. 16	24	15	16	16	27	30	37	28	26	46	19	14
SEP. 17	24	17	17	18	28	30	37	28	26	46	19	14
SEP. 18	24	19	19	20	28	30	37	28	26	46	19	14
SEP. 19	25	21	21	22	28	31	37	28	26	46	19	14
SEP. 20	25	23	23	24	28	31	37	28	26	46	19	14
SEP. 21	25	25	25	26	28	31	38	28	26	46	19	14
SEP. 22	25	27	27	28	28	31	38	28	26	46	19	14
SEP. 23	25	29	29	30	28	31	38	28	26	46	19	14
SEP. 24	25	31	31	32	28	31	38	28	26	46	19	14
SEP. 25	26	33	33	34	29	31	38	28	26	46	19	14
SEP. 26	26	34	35	36	29	31	38	28	26	46	19	14
SEP. 27	26	36	37	37	29	32	38	28	26	46	19	14
SEP. 28	26	38	39	39	29	32	38	28	26	46	19	14
SEP. 29	26	40	40	41	29	32	38	28	26	46	19	14
SEP. 30	26	41	42	42	29	32	38	28	26	46	19	14

Date & Time	SUN	MOON 1	MOON 2	MOON 3	MERCURY	VENUS	MARS	JUPITER	SATURN	URANUS	NEPTUNE	PLUTO
OCT. 1	26	43	43	44	29	32	38	28	26	46	19	14
OCT. 2	26	45	45	46	29	32	38	28	26	46	19	14
OCT. 3	27	46	47	47	29	32	39	28	26	46	19	14
OCT. 4	27	48	48	1	29	32	39	28	26	46	19	14
OCT. 5	27	1	2	2	29	32	39	28	26	46	19	14
OCT. 6	27	3	3	4	29	33	39	28	26	46	19	14
OCT. 7	27	4	5	5	29	33	39	28	26	46	19	14
OCT. 8	27	6	7	7	29	33	39	28	26	46	19	14
OCT. 9	27	8	8	9	29	33	39	28	26	46	19	14
OCT. 10	27	9	10	10	29	33	39	28	26	46	19	14
OCT. 11	28	11	11	12	28	33	39	29	26	46	19	14
OCT. 12	28	13	13	14	28	33	39	29	27	46	19	14
OCT. 13	28	14	15	16	28	33	39	29	27	46	19	14
OCT. 14	28	16	17	17	28	33	39	29	27	46	19	14
OCT. 15	28	18	19	19	28	33	40	29	27	46	19	14
OCT. 16	28	20	20	21	28	33	40	29	27	46	19	14
OCT. 17	28	22	22	23	28	34	40	29	27	46	19	14
OCT. 18	28	24	24	25	27	34	40	29	27	46	19	14
OCT. 19	29	26	26	27	27	34	40	29	27	46	19	14
OCT. 20	29	28	28	29	27	34	40	29	27	46	19	14
OCT. 21	29	30	30	31	27	34	40	29	27	46	19	14
OCT. 22	29	32	32	33	27	34	40	29	27	46	19	14
OCT. 23	29	34	34	35	27	34	40	29	27	46	19	14
OCT. 24	29	36	36	37	27	34	40	29	27	46	19	14
OCT. 25	29	37	38	39	27	34	40	29	27	46	19	14
OCT. 26	30	39	40	40	27	34	41	29	27	46	19	14
OCT. 27	30	41	41	42	27	34	41	29	27	46	19	14
OCT. 28	30	42	43	44	27	34	41	29	27	46	19	14
OCT. 29	30	44	45	45	27	34	41	29	27	46	19	14
OCT. 30	30	46	46	47	27	34	41	29	27	46	19	14
OCT. 31	30	47	48	48	27	34	41	29	27	46	19	14

MOON 1 ◖ 12:01 A.M. TO 8:00 A.M. **MOON 2** ◑ 8:01 A.M. TO 4:00 P.M. **MOON 3** ● 4:01 P.M. TO 12:00 A.M.
Use only one "moon" number. Choose the column closest to your time of birth. If your place of birth is not on Eastern Standard Time, be sure to read "How to Convert to Eastern Standard Time" at the beginning of this section.

1922

November

Date & Time	SUN	MOON 1	MOON 2	MOON 3	MERCURY	VENUS	MARS	JUPITER	SATURN	URANUS	NEPTUNE	PLUTO
NOV. 1	30	1	1	2	28	34	41	29	27	46	19	14
NOV. 2	30	2	3	3	28	34	41	29	27	46	19	14
NOV. 3	31	4	5	5	28	34	41	29	27	46	19	14
NOV. 4	31	6	6	7	28	34	41	29	27	46	19	14
NOV. 5	31	7	8	8	28	34	41	29	27	46	19	14
NOV. 6	31	9	9	10	28	34	42	29	27	46	19	14
NOV. 7	31	11	11	12	29	34	42	29	27	46	19	14
NOV. 8	31	12	13	13	29	34	42	29	27	46	19	14
NOV. 9	31	14	15	15	29	34	42	29	27	46	19	14
NOV. 10	31	16	16	17	29	34	42	29	27	46	19	14
NOV. 11	31	17	18	19	29	34	42	29	27	46	19	14
NOV. 12	32	19	20	21	30	34	42	29	27	46	19	14
NOV. 13	32	21	22	22	30	34	42	29	27	46	19	14
NOV. 14	32	23	24	24	30	34	42	29	27	46	19	14
NOV. 15	32	25	26	26	30	34	42	30	27	46	19	14
NOV. 16	32	27	28	28	30	34	43	30	27	46	19	14
NOV. 17	32	29	30	30	31	34	43	30	27	46	19	14
NOV. 18	32	31	32	32	31	34	43	30	27	46	19	14
NOV. 19	33	33	33	34	31	34	43	30	27	46	19	14
NOV. 20	33	35	35	36	31	34	43	30	27	46	19	14
NOV. 21	33	37	37	38	32	34	43	30	27	46	19	14
NOV. 22	33	38	39	40	32	34	43	30	27	46	19	14
NOV. 23	33	40	41	41	32	33	43	30	27	46	19	14
NOV. 24	33	42	42	43	32	33	43	30	27	46	19	14
NOV. 25	34	44	44	45	32	33	43	30	27	46	19	14
NOV. 26	34	45	46	46	33	33	43	30	27	46	19	14
NOV. 27	34	47	47	48	33	33	44	30	27	46	19	14
NOV. 28	34	48	1	1	33	33	44	30	27	46	19	14
NOV. 29	34	2	2	3	33	33	44	30	27	46	19	14
NOV. 30	34	4	4	5	33	33	44	30	27	46	19	14

December

Date & Time	SUN	MOON 1	MOON 2	MOON 3	MERCURY	VENUS	MARS	JUPITER	SATURN	URANUS	NEPTUNE	PLUTO
DEC. 1	34	5	6	6	34	33	44	30	27	46	19	14
DEC. 2	34	7	7	8	34	33	44	30	27	46	19	14
DEC. 3	35	8	9	9	34	33	44	30	27	46	19	14
DEC. 4	35	10	11	11	34	33	44	30	27	46	19	14
DEC. 5	35	12	12	13	34	33	44	30	27	46	19	14
DEC. 6	35	14	14	15	35	32	44	30	27	46	19	14
DEC. 7	35	15	16	16	35	32	45	30	27	46	19	14
DEC. 8	35	17	18	18	35	32	45	30	27	46	19	14
DEC. 9	35	19	20	20	35	32	45	30	27	46	19	14
DEC. 10	35	21	21	22	36	32	45	30	27	46	19	14
DEC. 11	36	23	23	24	36	32	45	30	27	46	19	14
DEC. 12	36	24	25	26	36	32	45	30	27	46	19	14
DEC. 13	36	26	27	28	36	32	45	30	27	46	19	14
DEC. 14	36	28	29	30	36	32	45	30	27	46	19	14
DEC. 15	36	30	31	31	37	32	45	30	27	46	19	14
DEC. 16	36	32	33	33	37	32	45	30	27	46	19	14
DEC. 17	36	34	35	35	37	32	45	30	27	46	19	14
DEC. 18	36	36	36	37	37	32	46	30	27	46	19	14
DEC. 19	37	38	38	39	37	32	46	30	27	46	19	14
DEC. 20	37	39	40	41	38	32	46	30	27	46	19	14
DEC. 21	37	41	42	42	38	32	46	30	27	46	19	14
DEC. 22	37	43	44	44	38	32	46	31	27	46	19	14
DEC. 23	37	45	45	46	38	32	46	31	27	46	19	14
DEC. 24	37	46	47	47	38	32	46	31	27	46	19	14
DEC. 25	37	48	48	1	39	32	46	31	28	46	19	14
DEC. 26	38	1	2	2	39	33	46	31	28	46	19	14
DEC. 27	38	3	3	4	39	33	47	31	28	46	19	14
DEC. 28	38	5	5	6	39	33	47	31	28	46	19	14
DEC. 29	38	6	7	7	40	33	47	31	28	46	19	14
DEC. 30	38	8	8	9	40	33	47	31	28	46	19	14
DEC. 31	38	9	10	11	40	33	47	31	28	46	19	14

MOON 1 ☾ 12:01 A.M. TO 8:00 A.M.   **MOON 2** ☽ 8:01 A.M. TO 4:00 P.M.   **MOON 3** ● 4:01 P.M. TO 12:00 A.M.
Use only one "moon" number. Choose the column closest to your time of birth. If your place of birth is not on Eastern Standard Time, be sure to read "How to Convert to Eastern Standard Time" at the beginning of this section.

1923

January

Date & Time	SUN	MOON 1	MOON 2	MOON 3	MERCURY	VENUS	MARS	JUPITER	SATURN	URANUS	NEPTUNE	PLUTO
JAN. 1	38	11	12	12	40	33	47	31	28	46	19	14
JAN. 2	38	13	14	14	40	33	47	31	28	46	19	14
JAN. 3	39	15	15	16	41	33	47	31	28	46	19	14
JAN. 4	39	17	17	18	41	33	47	31	28	46	19	14
JAN. 5	39	18	19	20	41	33	47	31	28	46	19	14
JAN. 6	39	20	21	22	41	33	47	31	28	46	19	14
JAN. 7	39	22	23	23	41	33	48	31	28	46	19	14
JAN. 8	39	24	25	25	42	33	48	31	28	46	19	14
JAN. 9	39	26	27	27	42	34	48	31	28	46	19	14
JAN. 10	40	28	28	29	42	34	48	31	28	46	19	14
JAN. 11	40	30	30	31	42	34	48	31	28	46	19	14
JAN. 12	40	32	32	33	42	34	48	31	28	46	19	14
JAN. 13	40	33	34	35	42	34	48	31	28	46	19	14
JAN. 14	40	35	36	36	43	34	48	31	28	46	19	14
JAN. 15	40	37	38	38	43	34	48	31	28	46	19	14
JAN. 16	40	39	39	40	43	34	48	31	28	46	19	14
JAN. 17	41	41	41	42	43	34	1	31	28	46	19	14
JAN. 18	41	42	43	43	43	35	1	31	28	46	19	14
JAN. 19	41	44	45	45	43	35	1	31	28	46	19	14
JAN. 20	41	46	46	48	43	35	1	31	28	46	19	14
JAN. 21	41	47	48	48	43	35	1	31	28	46	19	14
JAN. 22	41	1	1	2	43	35	1	31	28	46	19	14
JAN. 23	42	2	3	3	43	35	1	31	28	46	19	14
JAN. 24	42	4	5	5	43	35	1	31	28	46	19	14
JAN. 25	42	6	6	7	43	35	1	31	28	46	19	14
JAN. 26	42	7	8	8	43	35	1	31	28	46	19	14
JAN. 27	42	9	9	10	42	36	2	31	28	47	19	14
JAN. 28	42	10	11	12	42	36	2	31	28	47	19	14
JAN. 29	42	12	13	13	42	36	2	31	28	47	19	14
JAN. 30	42	14	15	15	42	36	2	31	28	47	19	14
JAN. 31	43	16	16	17	42	36	2	31	28	47	19	14

February

Date & Time	SUN	MOON 1	MOON 2	MOON 3	MERCURY	VENUS	MARS	JUPITER	SATURN	URANUS	NEPTUNE	PLUTO
FEB. 1	43	18	18	19	42	36	2	31	28	47	19	14
FEB. 2	43	20	20	21	41	36	2	31	28	47	19	14
FEB. 3	43	22	22	23	41	37	2	31	28	47	19	14
FEB. 4	43	23	24	25	41	37	2	31	28	47	19	14
FEB. 5	43	25	26	27	41	37	2	31	28	47	19	14
FEB. 6	43	27	28	29	41	37	2	31	28	47	19	14
FEB. 7	43	29	30	30	41	37	3	31	28	47	19	14
FEB. 8	44	31	32	32	41	37	3	31	28	47	19	14
FEB. 9	44	33	34	34	41	37	3	31	28	47	19	14
FEB. 10	44	35	35	36	41	37	3	31	28	47	19	14
FEB. 11	44	37	37	38	38	3	31	28	47	19	14	
FEB. 12	44	38	39	40	41	38	3	31	28	47	19	14
FEB. 13	44	40	41	41	41	38	3	31	28	47	19	14
FEB. 14	44	42	42	43	41	38	3	31	28	47	19	14
FEB. 15	44	43	44	45	41	38	3	31	28	47	19	14
FEB. 16	45	45	46	46	41	38	3	31	28	47	19	14
FEB. 17	45	47	47	48	41	38	4	31	28	47	19	14
FEB. 18	45	48	1	1	41	39	4	31	28	47	19	14
FEB. 19	45	2	2	3	41	39	4	31	28	47	19	14
FEB. 20	45	4	4	5	42	39	4	31	28	47	19	14
FEB. 21	45	5	6	6	42	39	4	31	28	47	19	14
FEB. 22	45	7	7	8	42	39	4	31	28	47	19	14
FEB. 23	46	8	9	9	42	39	4	31	28	47	19	14
FEB. 24	46	10	10	11	42	39	4	31	28	47	19	14
FEB. 25	46	12	12	13	42	40	4	31	28	47	19	14
FEB. 26	46	13	14	14	42	40	4	31	28	47	19	14
FEB. 27	46	15	16	16	42	40	5	31	28	47	19	14
FEB. 28	46	17	17	18	43	40	5	31	28	47	19	14

MOON 1 ◗ 12:01 A.M. TO 8:00 A.M. **MOON 2** ◑ 8:01 A.M. TO 4:00 P.M. **MOON 3** ● 4:01 P.M. TO 12:00 A.M.
Use only one "moon" number. Choose the column closest to your time of birth. If your place of birth is not on Eastern Standard Time, be sure to read "How to Convert to Eastern Standard Time" at the beginning of this section.

1923

March

Date & Time	SUN	MOON 1	MOON 2	MOON 3	MERCURY	VENUS	MARS	JUPITER	SATURN	URANUS	NEPTUNE	PLUTO
MAR. 1	46	19	19	20	43	40	5	31	28	47	19	14
MAR. 2	46	21	21	22	43	40	5	31	28	47	19	14
MAR. 3	47	23	23	24	43	41	5	31	28	47	19	14
MAR. 4	47	25	25	26	43	41	5	31	28	47	19	14
MAR. 5	47	27	27	28	43	41	5	31	28	47	19	14
MAR. 6	47	29	29	30	44	41	5	31	28	47	19	14
MAR. 7	47	31	31	32	44	41	5	31	27	47	19	14
MAR. 8	47	32	33	34	44	41	5	31	27	47	19	14
MAR. 9	47	34	35	36	44	41	5	31	27	47	19	14
MAR. 10	47	36	37	37	44	42	6	31	27	47	19	14
MAR. 11	48	38	39	39	45	42	6	31	27	47	19	14
MAR. 12	48	40	40	41	45	42	6	31	27	47	19	14
MAR. 13	48	41	42	42	45	42	6	31	27	47	19	14
MAR. 14	48	43	44	44	45	42	6	31	27	47	19	14
MAR. 15	48	45	45	46	45	42	6	31	27	47	19	14
MAR. 16	48	46	47	46	46	42	6	31	27	47	19	14
MAR. 17	48	48	48	1	46	43	6	31	27	47	19	14
MAR. 18	48	1	2	3	46	43	6	31	27	47	19	14
MAR. 19	1	3	4	4	46	43	6	31	27	47	19	14
MAR. 20	1	5	5	6	46	43	6	31	27	47	19	14
MAR. 21	1	6	7	7	47	43	7	31	27	47	19	14
MAR. 22	1	8	8	9	47	43	7	31	27	47	19	14
MAR. 23	1	9	10	10	47	44	7	31	27	47	19	14
MAR. 24	1	11	12	12	47	44	7	31	27	47	19	14
MAR. 25	2	13	13	14	48	44	7	31	27	47	19	14
MAR. 26	2	14	15	16	48	44	7	31	27	47	19	14
MAR. 27	2	16	17	17	48	44	7	31	27	47	19	14
MAR. 28	2	18	19	19	48	44	7	31	27	47	19	14
MAR. 29	2	20	20	21	1	44	7	31	27	47	19	14
MAR. 30	2	22	22	23	1	45	7	31	27	47	19	14
MAR. 31	2	24	24	25	1	45	8	31	27	47	19	14

April

Date & Time	SUN	MOON 1	MOON 2	MOON 3	MERCURY	VENUS	MARS	JUPITER	SATURN	URANUS	NEPTUNE	PLUTO
APR. 1	2	26	26	27	1	45	8	31	27	47	19	14
APR. 2	2	28	28	29	2	45	8	31	27	47	19	14
APR. 3	3	30	30	31	2	45	8	31	27	47	19	14
APR. 4	3	32	32	33	2	45	8	31	27	47	19	14
APR. 5	3	34	34	35	2	46	8	31	27	47	19	14
APR. 6	3	36	36	37	3	46	8	31	27	47	19	14
APR. 7	3	37	38	39	3	46	8	31	27	47	19	14
APR. 8	3	39	40	40	3	46	8	31	27	47	19	14
APR. 9	3	41	42	42	3	46	8	31	27	47	19	14
APR. 10	3	43	43	44	4	46	8	31	27	47	19	14
APR. 11	4	44	45	45	4	47	9	31	27	47	19	14
APR. 12	4	46	46	47	4	47	9	31	27	47	19	14
APR. 13	4	48	48	1	5	47	9	31	27	47	19	14
APR. 14	4	1	2	2	5	47	9	31	27	47	19	14
APR. 15	4	3	3	4	5	47	9	31	27	47	19	14
APR. 16	4	4	5	5	5	47	9	31	27	47	19	14
APR. 17	4	6	6	7	6	47	9	31	27	47	19	14
APR. 18	4	7	8	8	6	48	9	31	27	47	19	14
APR. 19	5	9	10	10	6	48	9	31	27	47	19	14
APR. 20	5	11	11	12	7	48	9	31	27	47	19	14
APR. 21	5	12	13	13	7	48	9	31	27	47	19	14
APR. 22	5	14	14	15	7	48	10	31	27	47	19	14
APR. 23	5	16	16	17	7	48	10	31	27	47	19	14
APR. 24	5	17	18	19	8	1	10	31	27	47	19	14
APR. 25	6	19	20	20	8	1	10	31	27	47	19	14
APR. 26	6	21	22	22	8	1	10	31	27	47	19	14
APR. 27	6	23	24	24	8	1	10	31	27	47	19	14
APR. 28	6	25	25	26	8	1	10	31	27	47	19	14
APR. 29	6	27	27	28	9	1	10	31	27	47	19	14
APR. 30	6	29	30	30	9	2	10	31	27	47	19	14

MOON 1 ☽ 12:01 A.M. TO 8:00 A.M.   **MOON 2** ◑ 8:01 A.M. TO 4:00 P.M.   **MOON 3** ● 4:01 P.M. TO 12:00 A.M.
Use only one "moon" number. Choose the column closest to your time of birth. If your place of birth is not on Eastern Standard Time, be sure to read "How to Convert to Eastern Standard Time" at the beginning of this section.

Date & Time	SUN	MOON 1	MOON 2	MOON 3	MERCURY	VENUS	MARS	JUPITER	SATURN	URANUS	NEPTUNE	PLUTO
MAY 1	6	31	32	32	9	2	10	31	27	47	19	14
MAY 2	6	33	34	34	9	2	10	31	27	47	19	14
MAY 3	7	35	36	36	9	2	11	31	27	47	19	14
MAY 4	7	37	37	38	9	2	11	31	27	47	19	14
MAY 5	7	39	39	40	10	2	11	31	27	47	19	14
MAY 6	7	40	41	42	10	3	11	31	27	47	19	14
MAY 7	7	42	43	43	10	3	11	31	27	47	19	14
MAY 8	7	44	44	45	10	3	11	31	27	47	19	14
MAY 9	7	46	46	47	10	3	11	31	27	47	19	14
MAY 10	7	47	48	48	10	3	11	31	27	47	19	14
MAY 11	8	1	1	2	10	3	11	31	27	47	19	14
MAY 12	8	2	3	3	10	3	11	31	27	47	19	14
MAY 13	8	4	4	5	10	4	11	31	27	47	19	14
MAY 14	8	5	6	6	10	4	11	31	27	47	19	14
MAY 15	8	7	8	8	10	4	12	31	27	47	19	14
MAY 16	8	9	9	10	10	4	12	31	27	47	19	14
MAY 17	8	10	11	11	10	4	12	31	27	47	19	14
MAY 18	8	12	12	13	10	4	12	31	27	47	19	14
MAY 19	9	14	14	15	10	5	12	31	27	47	19	14
MAY 20	9	15	16	16	10	5	12	31	27	47	19	14
MAY 21	9	17	17	18	10	5	12	31	27	47	19	14
MAY 22	9	19	19	20	10	5	12	31	27	47	19	14
MAY 23	9	20	21	22	10	5	12	31	27	47	19	14
MAY 24	9	22	23	24	10	5	12	31	27	47	19	14
MAY 25	10	24	25	25	10	6	12	31	27	47	19	14
MAY 26	10	26	27	27	10	6	13	31	27	47	19	14
MAY 27	10	28	29	29	10	6	13	30	27	47	19	14
MAY 28	10	30	31	31	10	6	13	30	27	47	19	14
MAY 29	10	32	33	33	10	6	13	30	27	47	19	14
MAY 30	10	34	35	35	10	6	13	30	27	47	19	14
MAY 31	10	36	37	37	10	7	13	30	27	47	19	14

Date & Time	SUN	MOON 1	MOON 2	MOON 3	MERCURY	VENUS	MARS	JUPITER	SATURN	URANUS	NEPTUNE	PLUTO
JUN. 1	10	38	39	39	10	7	13	30	27	47	19	14
JUN. 2	10	40	40	41	10	7	13	30	27	47	19	14
JUN. 3	11	42	42	43	10	7	13	30	27	47	19	14
JUN. 4	11	43	44	44	9	7	13	30	27	47	19	14
JUN. 5	11	45	46	46	9	7	13	30	27	47	19	14
JUN. 6	11	47	47	48	9	7	14	30	27	47	19	14
JUN. 7	11	48	1	1	9	8	14	30	27	47	19	14
JUN. 8	11	2	2	3	9	8	14	30	27	47	19	14
JUN. 9	11	3	4	4	9	8	14	30	27	47	19	14
JUN. 10	11	5	5	6	9	8	14	30	27	47	19	14
JUN. 11	12	7	7	8	9	8	14	30	27	47	19	14
JUN. 12	12	8	9	9	9	8	14	30	27	47	19	14
JUN. 13	12	10	10	11	9	9	14	30	27	47	19	14
JUN. 14	12	11	12	13	9	9	14	30	27	47	19	14
JUN. 15	12	13	14	14	9	9	14	30	27	47	19	14
JUN. 16	12	15	15	16	9	9	14	30	27	47	19	14
JUN. 17	12	17	17	18	10	9	14	30	27	47	19	14
JUN. 18	12	18	19	19	10	9	15	30	27	47	19	14
JUN. 19	13	20	21	21	10	10	15	30	27	47	19	14
JUN. 20	13	22	22	23	10	10	15	30	27	47	19	14
JUN. 21	13	24	24	25	10	10	15	30	27	47	19	14
JUN. 22	13	26	26	27	10	10	15	30	27	47	19	14
JUN. 23	13	27	28	29	10	10	15	30	27	47	19	14
JUN. 24	13	29	30	31	10	10	15	30	27	47	19	14
JUN. 25	14	31	32	33	10	11	15	30	27	47	19	14
JUN. 26	14	33	34	35	11	11	15	30	27	47	19	14
JUN. 27	14	35	36	36	11	11	15	30	27	47	19	14
JUN. 28	14	37	38	38	11	11	15	30	27	47	19	14
JUN. 29	14	39	40	40	11	11	16	30	27	47	19	14
JUN. 30	14	41	41	42	11	11	16	30	27	47	19	14

MOON 1 ☽ 12:01 A.M. TO 8:00 A.M.   **MOON 2** ◑ 8:01 A.M. TO 4:00 P.M.   **MOON 3** ● 4:01 P.M. TO 12:00 A.M.

Use only one "moon" number. Choose the column closest to your time of birth. If your place of birth is not on Eastern Standard Time, be sure to read "How to Convert to Eastern Standard Time" at the beginning of this section.

July

August

Date & Time	SUN ☉	MOON 1 ◐	MOON 2 ◑	MOON 3 ●	MERCURY	VENUS	MARS	JUPITER	SATURN	URANUS	NEPTUNE	PLUTO
JUL. 1	14	43	43	44	11	12	16	30	27	47	19	14
JUL. 2	14	44	45	45	12	12	16	30	27	47	19	14
JUL. 3	15	46	47	47	12	12	16	30	27	47	19	14
JUL. 4	15	48	48	1	12	12	16	30	27	47	19	14
JUL. 5	15	1	2	2	12	12	16	30	27	47	19	14
JUL. 6	15	3	3	4	12	12	16	30	27	47	19	14
JUL. 7	15	4	5	6	13	12	16	30	27	47	19	14
JUL. 8	15	6	7	7	13	13	16	30	27	47	19	14
JUL. 9	15	8	8	9	13	13	16	30	27	47	19	14
JUL. 10	15	9	10	10	13	13	16	30	27	47	19	14
JUL. 11	16	11	11	11	14	13	17	30	27	47	19	14
JUL. 12	16	13	13	14	14	13	17	30	27	47	19	14
JUL. 13	16	14	15	15	14	13	17	30	27	47	19	14
JUL. 14	16	16	17	17	14	14	17	30	27	47	19	14
JUL. 15	16	18	18	19	15	14	17	30	27	47	19	14
JUL. 16	16	20	20	21	15	14	17	30	27	47	19	14
JUL. 17	16	21	22	23	15	14	17	30	27	47	19	14
JUL. 18	16	23	24	24	16	14	17	30	27	47	19	14
JUL. 19	17	25	26	26	16	14	17	30	27	47	19	14
JUL. 20	17	27	28	28	16	15	17	30	27	47	19	14
JUL. 21	17	29	30	30	16	15	17	30	27	47	19	14
JUL. 22	17	31	31	32	17	15	17	30	27	47	19	14
JUL. 23	17	33	33	34	17	15	18	30	27	47	19	14
JUL. 24	17	35	35	36	17	15	18	30	27	47	19	14
JUL. 25	17	36	37	38	18	15	18	30	27	47	19	14
JUL. 26	18	38	39	40	18	16	18	30	27	47	19	14
JUL. 27	18	40	41	41	18	16	18	30	27	47	19	14
JUL. 28	18	42	43	43	18	16	18	30	27	47	19	14
JUL. 29	18	44	44	45	19	16	18	30	27	47	19	14
JUL. 30	18	45	46	47	19	16	18	30	27	47	19	14
JUL. 31	18	47	48	48	19	16	18	30	27	47	19	14

Date & Time	SUN ☉	MOON 1 ◐	MOON 2 ◑	MOON 3 ●	MERCURY	VENUS	MARS	JUPITER	SATURN	URANUS	NEPTUNE	PLUTO
AUG. 1	18	1	1	2	19	17	18	30	27	47	19	14
AUG. 2	18	2	3	3	20	17	18	30	27	47	19	14
AUG. 3	19	4	4	5	20	17	19	30	27	47	19	14
AUG. 4	19	6	6	7	20	17	19	30	27	47	19	14
AUG. 5	19	7	8	8	20	17	19	30	27	47	19	15
AUG. 6	19	9	9	10	21	17	19	30	27	47	19	15
AUG. 7	19	10	11	11	21	18	19	30	27	47	19	15
AUG. 8	19	12	13	13	21	18	19	30	27	47	19	15
AUG. 9	19	14	14	15	21	18	19	30	27	47	19	15
AUG. 10	19	15	16	17	22	18	19	30	27	47	19	15
AUG. 11	20	17	18	18	22	18	19	30	27	47	19	15
AUG. 12	20	19	20	20	22	18	19	30	27	47	19	15
AUG. 13	20	21	21	22	22	19	19	30	27	47	19	15
AUG. 14	20	23	23	24	22	19	19	30	27	47	19	15
AUG. 15	20	25	25	26	23	19	20	30	27	47	19	15
AUG. 16	20	27	27	28	23	19	20	30	27	47	19	15
AUG. 17	20	28	29	30	23	19	20	30	27	47	19	15
AUG. 18	20	30	31	32	23	19	20	31	27	47	19	15
AUG. 19	21	32	33	33	23	20	20	31	27	47	19	15
AUG. 20	21	34	35	35	24	20	20	31	27	47	19	15
AUG. 21	21	36	37	37	24	20	20	31	27	47	19	15
AUG. 22	21	38	38	39	24	20	20	31	27	47	19	15
AUG. 23	21	40	40	41	24	20	20	31	27	47	19	15
AUG. 24	21	41	42	43	24	20	20	31	27	47	19	15
AUG. 25	21	43	44	44	25	21	20	31	27	47	19	15
AUG. 26	22	45	45	46	25	21	20	31	27	47	19	15
AUG. 27	22	47	47	48	25	21	21	31	27	47	19	15
AUG. 28	22	48	1	1	25	21	21	31	27	47	19	15
AUG. 29	22	2	2	3	25	21	21	31	27	47	19	15
AUG. 30	22	3	4	4	25	21	21	31	27	47	19	15
AUG. 31	22	5	6	6	25	21	21	31	27	47	19	15

MOON 1 ◐ 12:01 A.M. TO 8:00 A.M.   **MOON 2** ◑ 8:01 A.M. TO 4:00 P.M.   **MOON 3** ● 4:01 P.M. TO 12:00 A.M.
Use only one "moon" number. Choose the column closest to your time of birth. If your place of birth is not on
Eastern Standard Time, be sure to read "How to Convert to Eastern Standard Time" at the beginning of this section.

1923

September

Date & Time	SUN	MOON 1	MOON 2	MOON 3	MERCURY	VENUS	MARS	JUPITER	SATURN	URANUS	NEPTUNE	PLUTO
SEP. 1	22	7	7	8	26	22	21	31	27	47	19	15
SEP. 2	22	8	9	9	26	22	21	31	27	47	19	15
SEP. 3	23	10	10	11	26	22	21	31	27	47	19	15
SEP. 4	23	11	12	12	26	22	21	31	27	47	19	15
SEP. 5	23	13	14	14	26	22	21	31	27	47	19	15
SEP. 6	23	15	15	16	26	22	21	31	27	47	19	15
SEP. 7	23	16	17	18	26	23	21	31	27	47	19	15
SEP. 8	23	18	19	19	26	23	22	31	27	47	19	15
SEP. 9	23	20	21	21	26	23	22	31	27	47	19	15
SEP. 10	23	22	23	23	27	23	22	31	27	47	19	15
SEP. 11	24	24	25	25	27	23	22	31	27	47	20	15
SEP. 12	24	26	27	27	27	23	22	31	27	47	20	15
SEP. 13	24	28	28	29	27	24	22	31	27	47	20	15
SEP. 14	24	30	30	31	27	24	22	31	28	47	20	15
SEP. 15	24	32	32	33	27	24	22	31	28	47	20	15
SEP. 16	24	34	34	35	27	24	22	31	28	47	20	15
SEP. 17	24	36	36	37	27	24	22	31	28	47	20	15
SEP. 18	24	37	38	39	27	24	22	31	28	47	20	15
SEP. 19	25	39	40	40	27	25	23	31	28	47	20	15
SEP. 20	25	41	42	42	27	25	23	31	28	47	20	15
SEP. 21	25	43	43	44	27	25	23	31	28	47	20	15
SEP. 22	25	44	45	46	27	25	23	31	28	47	20	15
SEP. 23	25	46	47	47	26	25	23	31	28	47	20	15
SEP. 24	25	48	48	1	26	25	23	31	28	47	20	15
SEP. 25	26	1	2	2	26	26	23	31	28	47	20	15
SEP. 26	26	3	3	4	26	26	23	31	28	47	20	15
SEP. 27	26	5	5	6	26	26	23	31	28	47	20	15
SEP. 28	26	6	7	7	26	26	23	31	28	47	20	15
SEP. 29	26	8	9	9	26	26	23	31	28	47	20	15
SEP. 30	26	9	10	10	25	26	23	31	28	47	20	15

October

Date & Time	SUN	MOON 1	MOON 2	MOON 3	MERCURY	VENUS	MARS	JUPITER	SATURN	URANUS	NEPTUNE	PLUTO
OCT. 1	26	11	11	12	25	27	24	31	28	47	20	15
OCT. 2	26	12	13	14	25	27	24	31	28	47	20	15
OCT. 3	27	14	15	15	25	27	24	31	28	47	20	15
OCT. 4	27	16	16	17	25	27	24	32	28	47	20	15
OCT. 5	27	18	18	19	25	27	24	32	28	47	20	15
OCT. 6	27	19	20	20	25	28	24	32	28	47	20	15
OCT. 7	27	21	22	22	25	28	24	32	28	47	20	15
OCT. 8	27	23	24	24	25	28	24	32	28	47	20	15
OCT. 9	27	25	26	26	25	28	24	32	28	47	20	15
OCT. 10	27	27	28	28	25	28	24	32	28	47	20	15
OCT. 11	28	29	30	30	25	28	24	32	28	47	20	15
OCT. 12	28	31	32	32	25	28	24	32	28	47	20	15
OCT. 13	28	33	34	34	25	29	25	32	28	47	20	15
OCT. 14	28	35	36	36	25	29	25	32	28	47	20	15
OCT. 15	28	37	38	38	25	29	25	32	28	47	20	15
OCT. 16	28	39	39	40	25	29	25	32	28	47	20	15
OCT. 17	28	41	41	42	25	29	25	32	28	47	20	15
OCT. 18	28	42	43	43	26	29	25	32	28	47	20	15
OCT. 19	29	44	45	45	26	30	25	32	28	47	20	15
OCT. 20	29	46	46	47	26	30	25	32	28	47	20	15
OCT. 21	29	47	48	48	26	30	25	32	28	47	20	15
OCT. 22	29	1	1	2	27	30	25	32	28	47	20	15
OCT. 23	29	3	3	4	27	30	25	32	28	47	20	15
OCT. 24	29	4	5	5	27	30	25	32	28	47	20	15
OCT. 25	29	6	6	7	27	31	26	32	28	47	20	15
OCT. 26	30	7	8	8	27	31	26	32	28	47	20	15
OCT. 27	30	9	9	10	27	31	26	32	28	47	20	15
OCT. 28	30	10	11	12	28	31	26	32	28	47	20	15
OCT. 29	30	12	13	13	28	31	26	32	28	47	20	15
OCT. 30	30	14	14	15	28	31	26	32	28	47	20	15
OCT. 31	30	15	16	16	29	32	26	32	28	47	20	15

MOON 1 ☽ 12:01 A.M. TO 8:00 A.M.   **MOON 2** ☽ 8:01 A.M. TO 4:00 P.M.   **MOON 3** ● 4:01 P.M. TO 12:00 A.M.

Use only one "moon" number. Choose the column closest to your time of birth. If your place of birth is not on Eastern Standard Time, be sure to read "How to Convert to Eastern Standard Time" at the beginning of this section.

Date & Time	SUN	MOON 1 ◖	MOON 2 ◗	MOON 3 ●	MERCURY	VENUS	MARS	JUPITER	SATURN	URANUS	NEPTUNE	PLUTO
NOV. 1	30	17	18	18	29	32	26	32	28	47	20	15
NOV. 2	30	19	19	20	29	32	26	32	28	47	20	15
NOV. 3	31	20	21	22	29	32	26	32	28	47	20	15
NOV. 4	31	22	23	23	29	32	26	32	28	47	20	15
NOV. 5	31	24	25	25	30	32	27	32	28	47	20	15
NOV. 6	31	26	27	27	30	33	27	32	28	47	20	15
NOV. 7	31	28	29	29	30	33	27	32	28	47	20	15
NOV. 8	31	30	31	31	30	33	27	32	28	47	20	15
NOV. 9	31	32	33	34	31	33	27	33	28	47	20	15
NOV. 10	31	34	35	36	31	33	27	33	28	47	20	15
NOV. 11	31	36	37	37	31	33	27	33	28	47	20	15
NOV. 12	32	38	39	39	31	34	27	33	28	47	20	15
NOV. 13	32	40	41	41	31	34	27	33	28	47	20	15
NOV. 14	32	42	42	43	32	34	27	33	28	47	20	15
NOV. 15	32	44	44	45	32	34	27	33	28	47	20	15
NOV. 16	32	45	46	46	32	34	27	33	29	47	20	15
NOV. 17	32	47	47	48	32	34	28	33	29	47	20	15
NOV. 18	32	1	1	2	32	35	28	33	29	47	20	15
NOV. 19	33	2	3	3	33	35	28	33	29	47	20	15
NOV. 20	33	4	4	5	33	35	28	33	29	47	20	15
NOV. 21	33	5	6	6	33	35	28	33	29	47	20	15
NOV. 22	33	7	7	8	33	35	28	33	29	47	20	15
NOV. 23	33	8	9	10	33	35	28	33	29	47	20	15
NOV. 24	33	10	11	11	34	36	28	33	29	47	20	15
NOV. 25	34	12	12	13	34	36	28	33	29	47	20	15
NOV. 26	34	13	14	14	34	36	28	33	29	47	20	15
NOV. 27	34	15	15	16	34	36	28	33	29	47	20	15
NOV. 28	34	17	17	18	35	36	28	33	29	47	20	15
NOV. 29	34	18	19	19	35	36	29	33	29	47	20	15
NOV. 30	34	20	21	21	35	37	29	33	29	47	20	15

Date & Time	SUN	MOON 1 ◖	MOON 2 ◗	MOON 3 ●	MERCURY	VENUS	MARS	JUPITER	SATURN	URANUS	NEPTUNE	PLUTO
DEC. 1	34	22	22	23	35	37	29	33	29	47	20	15
DEC. 2	34	23	24	25	35	37	29	33	29	47	20	15
DEC. 3	35	25	26	27	36	37	29	33	29	47	20	15
DEC. 4	35	27	28	29	36	37	29	33	29	47	20	15
DEC. 5	35	29	30	31	36	37	29	33	29	47	20	15
DEC. 6	35	31	32	33	36	38	29	33	29	47	20	15
DEC. 7	35	33	34	35	36	38	29	33	29	47	20	15
DEC. 8	35	35	36	37	37	38	29	33	29	47	20	15
DEC. 9	35	37	38	39	37	38	29	33	29	47	20	15
DEC. 10	35	39	40	40	37	38	29	33	29	47	20	15
DEC. 11	36	41	42	42	37	38	30	33	29	47	20	15
DEC. 12	36	43	44	44	37	39	30	33	29	47	20	15
DEC. 13	36	45	45	46	38	39	30	34	29	47	20	15
DEC. 14	36	46	47	48	38	39	30	34	29	47	20	15
DEC. 15	36	48	1	1	38	39	30	34	29	47	20	15
DEC. 16	36	2	2	3	38	39	30	34	29	47	20	15
DEC. 17	36	3	4	4	38	39	30	34	29	47	20	15
DEC. 18	36	5	5	6	39	40	30	34	29	47	20	15
DEC. 19	37	6	7	8	39	40	30	34	29	47	20	15
DEC. 20	37	8	9	9	39	40	30	34	29	47	20	15
DEC. 21	37	10	10	11	39	40	30	34	29	47	20	15
DEC. 22	37	11	12	12	39	40	31	34	29	47	20	15
DEC. 23	37	13	13	14	40	40	31	34	29	47	20	15
DEC. 24	37	14	15	16	40	41	31	34	29	47	20	15
DEC. 25	37	16	17	17	40	41	31	34	29	47	20	14
DEC. 26	38	18	18	19	40	41	31	34	29	47	20	14
DEC. 27	38	20	20	21	40	41	31	34	29	47	20	14
DEC. 28	38	21	22	22	40	41	31	34	29	47	20	14
DEC. 29	38	23	24	24	40	41	31	34	29	47	20	14
DEC. 30	38	25	25	26	41	42	31	34	29	47	20	14
DEC. 31	38	27	27	28	41	42	31	34	29	47	20	14

MOON 1 ◖ 12:01 A.M. TO 8:00 A.M.   **MOON 2** ◗ 8:01 A.M. TO 4:00 P.M.   **MOON 3** ● 4:01 P.M. TO 12:00 A.M.
Use only one "moon" number. Choose the column closest to your time of birth. If your place of birth is not on
Eastern Standard Time, be sure to read "How to Convert to Eastern Standard Time" at the beginning of this section.

1924

January

Date & Time	SUN	MOON 1	MOON 2	MOON 3	MERCURY	VENUS	MARS	JUPITER	SATURN	URANUS	NEPTUNE	PLUTO
JAN. 1	38	29	29	30	41	42	31	34	29	47	20	14
JAN. 2	38	30	31	32	41	42	31	34	29	47	20	14
JAN. 3	39	32	33	34	41	42	32	34	29	47	20	14
JAN. 4	39	34	35	36	41	42	32	34	29	47	20	14
JAN. 5	39	36	37	38	41	43	32	34	29	47	20	14
JAN. 6	39	38	39	40	41	43	32	34	29	47	20	14
JAN. 7	39	40	41	42	41	43	32	34	29	47	20	14
JAN. 8	39	42	43	43	41	43	32	34	29	47	20	14
JAN. 9	39	44	45	45	40	43	32	34	29	47	20	14
JAN. 10	40	46	46	47	40	43	32	34	29	47	20	14
JAN. 11	40	47	48	1	40	44	32	34	29	47	20	14
JAN. 12	40	1	2	2	40	44	32	34	29	47	20	14
JAN. 13	40	3	3	4	40	44	32	34	29	47	20	14
JAN. 14	40	4	5	5	40	44	32	34	29	47	20	14
JAN. 15	40	6	6	7	40	44	33	34	29	47	20	14
JAN. 16	40	8	8	9	39	44	33	34	29	47	20	14
JAN. 17	41	9	10	10	39	45	33	34	29	47	20	14
JAN. 18	41	11	11	12	39	45	33	35	29	47	20	14
JAN. 19	41	12	13	13	39	45	33	35	29	47	20	14
JAN. 20	41	14	15	15	39	45	33	35	29	47	20	14
JAN. 21	41	16	16	17	39	45	33	35	29	47	20	14
JAN. 22	41	17	18	19	39	45	33	35	29	47	20	14
JAN. 23	42	19	20	20	39	46	33	35	29	47	20	14
JAN. 24	42	21	21	22	39	46	33	35	29	47	20	14
JAN. 25	42	23	23	24	39	46	33	35	29	47	20	14
JAN. 26	42	24	25	26	39	46	34	35	29	47	20	14
JAN. 27	42	26	27	27	39	46	34	35	29	47	20	14
JAN. 28	42	28	29	29	39	46	34	35	29	47	20	14
JAN. 29	42	30	31	31	39	47	34	35	29	47	20	14
JAN. 30	42	32	33	33	39	47	34	35	29	47	20	14
JAN. 31	43	34	34	35	39	47	34	35	29	47	20	14

February

Date & Time	SUN	MOON 1	MOON 2	MOON 3	MERCURY	VENUS	MARS	JUPITER	SATURN	URANUS	NEPTUNE	PLUTO
FEB. 1	43	36	36	37	39	47	34	35	29	47	20	14
FEB. 2	43	38	38	39	39	47	34	35	29	47	20	14
FEB. 3	43	40	40	41	39	47	34	35	29	47	20	14
FEB. 4	43	41	42	43	39	48	34	35	29	47	20	14
FEB. 5	43	43	44	44	40	48	34	35	29	47	20	14
FEB. 6	43	45	46	46	40	48	34	35	29	47	20	14
FEB. 7	43	47	47	48	40	48	35	35	29	47	20	14
FEB. 8	44	1	1	2	40	48	35	35	29	47	20	14
FEB. 9	44	2	3	3	40	48	35	35	29	47	20	14
FEB. 10	44	4	4	5	40	48	35	35	29	47	19	14
FEB. 11	44	5	6	6	40	1	35	35	29	47	19	14
FEB. 12	44	7	8	8	41	1	35	35	29	47	19	14
FEB. 13	44	9	9	10	41	1	35	35	29	47	19	14
FEB. 14	44	10	11	11	41	1	35	35	29	47	19	14
FEB. 15	44	12	12	13	41	1	35	35	29	47	19	14
FEB. 16	45	13	14	15	41	1	35	35	29	47	19	14
FEB. 17	45	15	16	16	42	2	35	35	29	47	19	14
FEB. 18	45	17	17	18	42	2	35	35	29	47	19	14
FEB. 19	45	18	19	20	42	2	36	35	29	47	19	14
FEB. 20	45	20	21	21	42	2	36	35	29	47	19	14
FEB. 21	45	22	23	23	42	2	36	35	29	47	19	14
FEB. 22	45	24	25	25	42	2	36	35	29	47	19	14
FEB. 23	46	26	26	27	43	3	36	35	29	47	19	14
FEB. 24	46	28	28	29	43	3	36	35	29	47	19	14
FEB. 25	46	30	30	31	43	3	36	35	29	47	19	14
FEB. 26	46	31	32	33	43	3	36	35	29	47	19	14
FEB. 27	46	33	34	35	43	3	36	35	29	47	19	14
FEB. 28	46	35	36	36	44	3	36	35	29	47	19	14
FEB. 29	46	37	38	38	44	4	36	35	29	47	19	14

MOON 1 ◗ 12:01 A.M. TO 8:00 A.M.   **MOON 2** ◑ 8:01 A.M. TO 4:00 P.M.   **MOON 3** ● 4:01 P.M. TO 12:00 A.M.

Use only one "moon" number. Choose the column closest to your time of birth. If your place of birth is not on Eastern Standard Time, be sure to read "How to Convert to Eastern Standard Time" at the beginning of this section.

March

Date & Time	SUN	MOON 1	MOON 2	MOON 3	MERCURY	VENUS	MARS	JUPITER	SATURN	URANUS	NEPTUNE	PLUTO
MAR. 1	46	39	40	40	44	4	36	35	29	47	19	14
MAR. 2	46	41	41	42	44	4	37	35	29	47	19	14
MAR. 3	47	43	43	44	45	4	37	35	29	47	19	14
MAR. 4	47	44	45	46	45	4	37	35	29	47	19	14
MAR. 5	47	46	47	47	45	4	37	35	29	47	19	14
MAR. 6	47	48	48	1	45	4	37	35	29	47	19	14
MAR. 7	47	2	2	3	45	5	37	35	29	47	19	14
MAR. 8	47	3	4	4	46	5	37	35	29	47	19	14
MAR. 9	47	5	5	6	46	5	37	35	29	47	19	14
MAR. 10	47	6	7	8	46	5	37	35	29	47	19	14
MAR. 11	48	8	9	9	46	5	37	35	29	47	19	14
MAR. 12	48	10	10	11	47	5	37	35	29	47	19	14
MAR. 13	48	11	12	12	47	6	38	36	29	47	19	14
MAR. 14	48	13	13	14	47	6	38	36	29	47	19	14
MAR. 15	48	14	15	16	47	6	38	36	29	47	19	14
MAR. 16	48	16	17	17	48	6	38	36	29	47	19	14
MAR. 17	48	18	18	19	48	6	38	36	29	47	19	14
MAR. 18	48	20	20	21	48	6	38	36	29	47	19	14
MAR. 19	1	21	22	23	48	6	38	36	29	47	19	14
MAR. 20	1	23	24	24	1	7	38	36	29	47	19	14
MAR. 21	1	25	26	26	1	7	38	36	29	47	19	14
MAR. 22	1	27	28	28	1	7	38	36	29	47	19	14
MAR. 23	1	29	30	30	1	7	38	36	29	47	19	14
MAR. 24	1	31	32	32	2	7	38	36	29	47	19	14
MAR. 25	2	33	33	34	2	7	39	36	29	47	19	14
MAR. 26	2	35	35	36	2	7	39	36	29	47	19	14
MAR. 27	2	37	37	38	2	8	39	36	29	47	19	14
MAR. 28	2	39	39	40	3	8	39	36	29	47	19	14
MAR. 29	2	40	41	42	3	8	39	36	29	47	19	14
MAR. 30	2	42	43	43	3	8	39	36	29	47	19	14
MAR. 31	2	44	45	45	4	8	39	36	29	47	19	14

April

Date & Time	SUN	MOON 1	MOON 2	MOON 3	MERCURY	VENUS	MARS	JUPITER	SATURN	URANUS	NEPTUNE	PLUTO
APR. 1	2	46	46	47	4	8	39	36	29	47	19	14
APR. 2	2	47	48	48	4	9	39	36	29	47	19	14
APR. 3	3	1	2	2	4	9	39	36	29	47	19	14
APR. 4	3	3	3	4	5	9	39	36	29	48	19	14
APR. 5	3	4	5	5	5	9	39	36	29	48	19	14
APR. 6	3	6	6	7	5	9	39	36	29	48	19	14
APR. 7	3	8	8	9	5	9	40	36	29	48	19	14
APR. 8	3	9	10	10	6	9	40	36	29	48	19	14
APR. 9	3	11	11	12	6	10	40	36	29	48	19	14
APR. 10	3	12	13	13	6	10	40	36	29	48	19	14
APR. 11	4	14	14	15	6	10	40	36	29	48	19	14
APR. 12	4	16	16	17	6	10	40	36	29	48	19	14
APR. 13	4	17	18	18	7	10	40	36	29	48	19	14
APR. 14	4	19	19	20	7	10	40	36	29	48	19	14
APR. 15	4	21	21	22	7	10	40	36	29	48	19	14
APR. 16	4	22	23	24	7	10	40	36	29	48	19	14
APR. 17	4	24	25	25	7	11	40	36	29	48	19	14
APR. 18	4	26	27	27	7	11	40	36	29	48	19	14
APR. 19	5	28	29	29	7	11	41	36	29	48	19	14
APR. 20	5	30	31	31	8	11	41	36	29	48	19	14
APR. 21	5	32	33	33	8	11	41	36	29	48	19	14
APR. 22	5	34	35	35	8	11	41	36	29	48	19	14
APR. 23	5	36	37	37	8	11	41	36	29	48	19	14
APR. 24	5	38	39	39	8	12	41	36	29	48	19	14
APR. 25	6	40	41	41	8	12	41	36	29	48	19	14
APR. 26	6	42	42	43	8	12	41	36	29	48	19	14
APR. 27	6	44	44	45	8	12	41	36	29	48	19	14
APR. 28	6	45	46	46	8	12	41	36	29	48	19	14
APR. 29	6	47	48	48	8	12	41	36	29	48	19	14
APR. 30	6	1	1	2	8	12	41	36	29	48	19	14

MOON 1 ◗ 12:01 A.M. TO 8:00 A.M.   **MOON 2** ◑ 8:01 A.M. TO 4:00 P.M.   **MOON 3** ● 4:01 P.M. TO 12:00 A.M.
Use only one "moon" number. Choose the column closest to your time of birth. If your place of birth is not on Eastern Standard Time, be sure to read "How to Convert to Eastern Standard Time" at the beginning of this section.

1924

May

June

Date & Time	SUN	MOON 1	MOON 2	MOON 3	MERCURY	VENUS	MARS	JUPITER	SATURN	URANUS	NEPTUNE	PLUTO
MAY 1	6	2	3	3	8	12	41	35	29	48	19	14
MAY 2	6	4	4	5	8	13	42	35	29	48	19	14
MAY 3	7	6	6	7	8	13	42	35	29	48	19	14
MAY 4	7	7	8	8	8	13	42	35	29	48	19	14
MAY 5	7	9	9	10	7	13	42	35	29	48	19	14
MAY 6	7	10	11	11	7	13	42	35	29	48	19	14
MAY 7	7	12	12	13	7	13	42	35	29	48	19	14
MAY 8	7	13	14	15	7	13	42	35	29	48	19	14
MAY 9	7	15	16	16	7	13	42	35	29	48	19	14
MAY 10	7	17	17	18	7	13	42	35	29	48	19	14
MAY 11	8	18	19	19	7	14	42	35	29	48	19	14
MAY 12	8	20	21	21	7	14	42	35	29	48	19	14
MAY 13	8	22	22	23	7	14	42	35	29	48	19	14
MAY 14	8	23	24	25	7	14	42	35	29	48	19	14
MAY 15	8	25	26	27	7	14	43	35	29	48	19	14
MAY 16	8	27	28	29	7	14	43	35	29	48	19	14
MAY 17	8	29	30	31	7	14	43	35	29	48	19	14
MAY 18	8	31	32	33	7	14	43	35	29	48	19	14
MAY 19	9	33	34	35	7	14	43	35	29	48	19	14
MAY 20	9	35	36	37	7	14	43	35	29	48	19	14
MAY 21	9	37	38	39	7	14	43	35	29	48	19	14
MAY 22	9	39	40	41	7	15	43	35	29	48	19	14
MAY 23	9	41	42	42	7	15	43	35	29	48	19	14
MAY 24	9	43	44	44	7	15	43	35	29	48	19	14
MAY 25	10	45	45	46	7	15	43	35	29	48	19	14
MAY 26	10	47	47	48	7	15	43	35	29	48	19	14
MAY 27	10	48	1	1	7	15	43	35	28	48	19	14
MAY 28	10	2	2	3	7	15	43	35	28	48	19	14
MAY 29	10	4	4	5	7	15	43	35	28	48	19	14
MAY 30	10	5	6	6	7	15	44	35	28	48	19	14
MAY 31	10	7	7	8	7	15	44	35	28	48	19	14

Date & Time	SUN	MOON 1	MOON 2	MOON 3	MERCURY	VENUS	MARS	JUPITER	SATURN	URANUS	NEPTUNE	PLUTO
JUN. 1	10	8	9	9	7	15	44	35	28	48	19	14
JUN. 2	10	10	10	11	7	15	44	35	28	48	19	14
JUN. 3	11	11	12	13	7	15	44	35	28	48	19	14
JUN. 4	11	13	14	14	8	15	44	35	28	48	19	14
JUN. 5	11	15	15	16	8	15	44	35	28	48	19	14
JUN. 6	11	16	17	17	8	15	44	35	28	48	19	14
JUN. 7	11	18	18	19	8	15	44	35	28	48	19	14
JUN. 8	11	20	20	21	8	15	44	35	28	48	19	14
JUN. 9	11	21	22	22	8	15	44	35	28	48	19	14
JUN. 10	11	23	24	24	8	15	44	35	28	48	19	14
JUN. 11	12	25	25	26	9	15	44	35	28	48	19	14
JUN. 12	12	27	27	28	9	15	44	35	28	48	19	14
JUN. 13	12	28	29	30	9	15	44	35	28	48	19	14
JUN. 14	12	30	31	32	9	15	44	35	28	48	19	14
JUN. 15	12	32	33	34	9	15	45	35	28	48	19	14
JUN. 16	12	34	35	36	10	15	45	35	28	48	19	14
JUN. 17	12	36	37	38	10	15	45	35	28	48	19	14
JUN. 18	12	38	39	40	10	15	45	35	28	48	19	14
JUN. 19	13	40	41	42	10	15	45	35	28	48	19	15
JUN. 20	13	42	43	44	11	15	45	35	28	48	19	15
JUN. 21	13	44	45	45	11	15	45	35	28	48	19	15
JUN. 22	13	46	47	47	11	15	45	35	28	48	19	15
JUN. 23	13	48	48	1	11	15	45	35	28	48	19	15
JUN. 24	13	1	2	3	12	15	45	35	28	48	19	15
JUN. 25	14	3	4	4	12	15	45	35	28	48	19	15
JUN. 26	14	5	5	6	12	15	45	35	28	48	19	15
JUN. 27	14	6	7	7	12	15	45	35	28	48	19	15
JUN. 28	14	8	8	9	13	14	45	35	28	48	19	15
JUN. 29	14	10	10	11	13	14	45	35	28	48	19	15
JUN. 30	14	11	12	12	13	14	45	35	28	48	19	15

MOON 1 ◐ 12:01 A.M. TO 8:00 A.M.   **MOON 2** ◑ 8:01 A.M. TO 4:00 P.M.   **MOON 3** ● 4:01 P.M. TO 12:00 A.M.
Use only one "moon" number. Choose the column closest to your time of birth. If your place of birth is not on
Eastern Standard Time, be sure to read "How to Convert to Eastern Standard Time" at the beginning of this section.

July

August

Date & Time	SUN	MOON 1	MOON 2	MOON 3	MERCURY	VENUS	MARS	JUPITER	SATURN	URANUS	NEPTUNE	PLUTO
JUL. 1	14	13	13	14	13	14	45	35	28	48	19	15
JUL. 2	14	14	15	15	14	14	45	35	28	48	19	15
JUL. 3	15	16	16	17	14	14	45	35	28	48	19	15
JUL. 4	15	17	18	19	14	14	45	35	28	48	19	15
JUL. 5	15	19	20	20	15	14	45	35	28	48	19	15
JUL. 6	15	21	21	22	15	14	45	35	28	48	19	15
JUL. 7	15	23	23	24	15	14	45	34	28	48	19	15
JUL. 8	15	24	25	25	15	14	45	34	28	48	19	15
JUL. 9	15	26	27	27	16	14	45	34	28	48	19	15
JUL. 10	15	28	28	29	16	14	46	34	28	48	19	15
JUL. 11	16	30	30	31	16	13	46	34	28	48	19	15
JUL. 12	16	32	32	33	17	13	46	34	28	48	19	15
JUL. 13	16	34	34	35	17	13	46	34	28	48	20	15
JUL. 14	16	36	36	37	17	13	46	34	28	48	20	15
JUL. 15	16	38	38	39	17	13	46	34	28	48	20	15
JUL. 16	16	40	40	41	18	13	46	34	28	48	20	15
JUL. 17	16	42	42	43	18	13	46	34	28	48	20	15
JUL. 18	16	43	44	45	18	13	46	34	28	48	20	15
JUL. 19	17	45	46	47	18	13	46	34	28	48	20	15
JUL. 20	17	47	48	48	19	13	46	34	28	48	20	15
JUL. 21	17	1	1	2	19	13	46	34	28	48	20	15
JUL. 22	17	3	3	4	19	13	46	34	28	48	20	15
JUL. 23	17	4	5	5	19	13	46	34	28	48	20	15
JUL. 24	17	6	6	7	20	13	46	34	28	48	20	15
JUL. 25	17	7	8	9	20	13	46	34	28	48	20	15
JUL. 26	18	9	10	10	20	13	46	34	28	48	20	15
JUL. 27	18	11	11	12	20	13	46	34	28	48	20	15
JUL. 28	18	12	13	13	20	13	46	34	28	48	20	15
JUL. 29	18	14	14	15	21	13	46	34	28	48	20	15
JUL. 30	18	15	16	17	21	13	46	34	28	48	20	15
JUL. 31	18	17	18	18	21	13	46	34	28	48	20	15

Date & Time	SUN	MOON 1	MOON 2	MOON 3	MERCURY	VENUS	MARS	JUPITER	SATURN	URANUS	NEPTUNE	PLUTO
AUG. 1	18	19	19	20	21	13	46	34	29	48	20	15
AUG. 2	18	20	21	22	21	13	46	34	29	48	20	15
AUG. 3	19	22	23	23	22	13	46	34	29	48	20	15
AUG. 4	19	24	24	25	22	13	46	34	29	48	20	15
AUG. 5	19	26	26	27	22	14	46	34	29	48	20	15
AUG. 6	19	27	28	29	22	14	46	34	29	48	20	15
AUG. 7	19	29	30	30	22	14	46	34	29	48	20	15
AUG. 8	19	31	32	32	23	14	45	34	29	48	20	15
AUG. 9	19	33	34	34	23	14	45	34	29	48	20	15
AUG. 10	19	35	36	36	23	14	45	34	29	48	20	15
AUG. 11	20	37	38	38	23	14	45	34	29	48	20	15
AUG. 12	20	39	39	40	23	14	45	34	29	48	20	15
AUG. 13	20	41	41	42	23	14	45	34	29	48	20	15
AUG. 14	20	43	43	44	23	14	45	34	29	48	20	15
AUG. 15	20	45	45	46	24	14	45	34	29	48	20	15
AUG. 16	20	46	47	48	24	14	45	34	29	48	20	15
AUG. 17	20	48	1	1	24	14	45	34	29	48	20	15
AUG. 18	20	2	3	3	24	15	45	34	29	48	20	15
AUG. 19	21	4	4	5	24	15	45	34	29	48	20	15
AUG. 20	21	5	6	6	24	15	45	34	29	48	20	15
AUG. 21	21	7	7	8	24	15	45	34	29	48	20	15
AUG. 22	21	9	9	10	24	15	45	34	29	48	20	15
AUG. 23	21	10	11	11	24	15	45	34	29	48	20	15
AUG. 24	21	12	12	13	24	15	45	34	29	48	20	15
AUG. 25	21	13	14	14	24	15	45	34	29	48	20	15
AUG. 26	22	15	15	16	25	15	45	34	29	48	20	15
AUG. 27	22	17	17	18	25	16	45	34	29	48	20	15
AUG. 28	22	18	19	19	25	16	45	34	29	48	20	15
AUG. 29	22	20	20	21	25	16	45	34	29	48	20	15
AUG. 30	22	22	22	23	25	16	45	34	29	48	20	15
AUG. 31	22	23	24	25	25	16	45	34	29	48	20	15

MOON 1 ☽ 12:01 A.M. TO 8:00 A.M. **MOON 2** ☾ 8:01 A.M. TO 4:00 P.M. **MOON 3** ● 4:01 P.M. TO 12:00 A.M.
Use only one "moon" number. Choose the column closest to your time of birth. If your place of birth is not on Eastern Standard Time, be sure to read "How to Convert to Eastern Standard Time" at the beginning of this section.

1924

September

Date & Time	SUN	MOON 1	MOON 2	MOON 3	MERCURY	VENUS	MARS	JUPITER	SATURN	URANUS	NEPTUNE	PLUTO
SEP. 1	22	25	26	26	24	16	45	34	29	48	20	15
SEP. 2	22	27	28	28	24	16	45	34	29	48	20	15
SEP. 3	23	29	29	30	24	16	45	34	29	48	20	15
SEP. 4	23	31	31	32	24	16	45	34	29	48	20	15
SEP. 5	23	33	33	34	24	17	45	34	29	48	20	15
SEP. 6	23	34	35	36	24	17	45	34	29	48	20	15
SEP. 7	23	36	37	38	24	17	45	34	29	48	20	15
SEP. 8	23	38	39	40	24	17	45	35	29	48	20	15
SEP. 9	23	40	41	41	24	17	44	35	29	48	20	15
SEP. 10	23	42	43	43	24	17	44	35	29	48	20	15
SEP. 11	24	44	44	45	23	17	44	35	29	48	20	15
SEP. 12	24	46	46	47	23	17	44	35	29	48	20	15
SEP. 13	24	48	48	1	23	18	44	35	29	48	20	15
SEP. 14	24	1	2	2	23	18	44	35	29	48	20	15
SEP. 15	24	3	4	4	23	18	44	35	29	48	20	15
SEP. 16	24	5	5	6	23	18	44	35	29	48	20	15
SEP. 17	24	6	7	7	23	18	44	35	29	48	20	15
SEP. 18	24	8	9	9	23	18	44	35	29	48	20	15
SEP. 19	25	10	10	11	23	18	44	35	29	48	20	15
SEP. 20	25	11	12	12	23	18	44	35	29	48	20	15
SEP. 21	25	13	13	14	23	19	44	35	29	48	20	15
SEP. 22	25	14	15	15	23	19	44	35	29	48	20	15
SEP. 23	25	16	17	17	23	19	44	35	29	48	20	15
SEP. 24	25	18	18	19	23	19	44	35	29	48	20	15
SEP. 25	26	19	20	20	23	19	44	35	29	48	20	15
SEP. 26	26	21	22	22	23	19	44	35	29	47	20	15
SEP. 27	26	23	23	24	23	19	44	35	29	47	20	15
SEP. 28	26	25	25	26	24	20	44	35	29	47	20	15
SEP. 29	26	26	27	28	23	20	44	35	29	47	20	15
SEP. 30	26	28	29	30	24	20	44	35	29	47	20	15

October

Date & Time	SUN	MOON 1	MOON 2	MOON 3	MERCURY	VENUS	MARS	JUPITER	SATURN	URANUS	NEPTUNE	PLUTO
OCT. 1	26	30	31	31	24	20	44	35	29	47	20	15
OCT. 2	26	32	33	33	24	20	44	35	29	47	20	15
OCT. 3	27	34	35	35	24	20	44	35	29	47	20	15
OCT. 4	27	36	37	37	24	20	44	35	29	47	20	15
OCT. 5	27	38	38	39	25	21	44	35	29	47	20	15
OCT. 6	27	40	40	41	25	21	45	35	29	47	20	15
OCT. 7	27	42	42	43	25	21	45	35	29	47	20	15
OCT. 8	27	43	44	45	25	21	45	35	29	47	20	15
OCT. 9	27	45	46	46	25	21	45	35	29	47	20	15
OCT. 10	27	47	48	48	26	21	45	35	29	47	20	15
OCT. 11	28	1	1	2	26	22	45	35	29	47	20	15
OCT. 12	28	2	3	4	26	22	45	35	29	47	20	15
OCT. 13	28	4	5	5	26	22	45	35	29	47	20	15
OCT. 14	28	6	6	7	27	22	45	35	29	47	20	15
OCT. 15	28	7	8	9	27	22	45	35	29	47	20	15
OCT. 16	28	9	10	10	27	22	45	35	29	47	20	15
OCT. 17	28	11	11	12	27	22	45	35	29	47	20	15
OCT. 18	28	12	13	13	28	23	45	35	29	47	20	15
OCT. 19	29	14	14	15	28	23	45	35	29	47	20	15
OCT. 20	29	15	16	16	28	23	45	35	30	47	20	15
OCT. 21	29	17	18	18	28	23	45	35	30	47	20	15
OCT. 22	29	19	19	20	28	23	45	35	30	47	20	15
OCT. 23	29	20	21	21	29	23	45	35	30	47	20	15
OCT. 24	29	22	23	23	29	24	45	35	30	47	20	15
OCT. 25	29	24	24	25	29	24	45	35	30	47	20	15
OCT. 26	30	26	26	27	29	24	45	35	30	47	20	15
OCT. 27	30	27	28	29	30	24	45	35	30	47	20	15
OCT. 28	30	29	30	31	30	24	45	35	30	47	20	15
OCT. 29	30	31	32	33	30	24	45	36	30	47	20	15
OCT. 30	30	33	34	35	30	24	45	36	30	47	20	15
OCT. 31	30	35	36	37	30	25	46	36	30	47	20	15

MOON 1 ◗ 12:01 A.M. TO 8:00 A.M.   **MOON 2** ◖ 8:01 A.M. TO 4:00 P.M.   **MOON 3** ● 4:01 P.M. TO 12:00 A.M.

Use only one "moon" number. Choose the column closest to your time of birth. If your place of birth is not on Eastern Standard Time, be sure to read "How to Convert to Eastern Standard Time" at the beginning of this section.

1924
November — December

Date & Time	SUN	MOON 1	MOON 2	MOON 3	MERCURY	VENUS	MARS	JUPITER	SATURN	URANUS	NEPTUNE	PLUTO
NOV. 1	30	37	38	39	31	25	46	36	30	47	20	15
NOV. 2	30	39	40	41	31	25	46	36	30	47	20	15
NOV. 3	31	41	42	42	31	25	46	36	30	47	20	15
NOV. 4	31	43	44	44	31	25	46	36	30	47	20	15
NOV. 5	31	45	45	46	31	25	46	36	30	47	20	15
NOV. 6	31	47	47	48	32	26	46	36	30	47	20	15
NOV. 7	31	48	1	1	32	26	46	36	30	47	20	15
NOV. 8	31	2	3	3	32	26	46	36	30	47	20	15
NOV. 9	31	4	4	5	32	26	46	36	30	47	20	15
NOV. 10	31	5	6	6	32	26	46	36	30	47	20	15
NOV. 11	31	7	8	8	33	26	46	36	30	47	20	15
NOV. 12	32	9	9	10	33	26	46	36	30	47	20	15
NOV. 13	32	10	11	11	33	27	46	36	30	47	20	15
NOV. 14	32	12	12	13	33	27	46	36	30	47	20	15
NOV. 15	32	13	14	14	34	27	46	36	30	47	20	15
NOV. 16	32	15	15	16	34	27	47	36	30	47	20	15
NOV. 17	32	17	17	18	34	27	47	36	30	47	20	15
NOV. 18	32	18	19	19	34	27	47	36	30	47	20	15
NOV. 19	33	20	20	21	34	28	47	36	30	47	20	15
NOV. 20	33	21	22	22	35	28	47	36	30	47	20	15
NOV. 21	33	23	24	24	35	28	47	36	30	47	20	15
NOV. 22	33	25	25	26	35	28	47	36	30	47	20	15
NOV. 23	33	27	27	28	35	28	47	36	30	47	20	15
NOV. 24	33	29	29	30	35	28	47	36	30	47	20	15
NOV. 25	34	30	31	32	36	29	47	36	30	47	20	15
NOV. 26	34	32	33	34	36	29	47	36	30	47	20	15
NOV. 27	34	35	35	36	36	29	47	36	30	47	20	15
NOV. 28	34	37	37	38	36	29	47	36	30	47	20	15
NOV. 29	34	39	39	40	36	29	47	36	30	47	20	15
NOV. 30	34	41	41	42	36	29	47	36	30	47	20	15

Date & Time	SUN	MOON 1	MOON 2	MOON 3	MERCURY	VENUS	MARS	JUPITER	SATURN	URANUS	NEPTUNE	PLUTO
DEC. 1	34	42	43	44	37	30	48	36	30	47	20	15
DEC. 2	34	44	45	46	37	30	48	36	30	47	20	15
DEC. 3	35	46	47	47	37	30	48	37	30	47	20	15
DEC. 4	35	48	48	1	37	30	48	37	30	47	20	15
DEC. 5	35	2	2	3	37	30	48	37	30	47	20	15
DEC. 6	35	3	4	4	38	30	48	37	30	47	20	15
DEC. 7	35	5	5	6	38	31	48	37	30	47	20	15
DEC. 8	35	7	7	8	38	31	48	37	30	47	20	15
DEC. 9	35	8	9	9	38	31	48	37	30	47	20	15
DEC. 10	35	10	10	11	38	31	48	37	30	47	20	15
DEC. 11	36	11	12	12	38	31	48	37	30	47	20	15
DEC. 12	36	13	13	14	38	31	48	37	30	47	20	15
DEC. 13	36	15	15	16	38	32	48	37	30	47	20	15
DEC. 14	36	16	17	17	39	32	1	37	30	47	20	15
DEC. 15	36	18	18	19	39	32	1	37	30	47	20	15
DEC. 16	36	19	20	20	39	32	1	37	30	47	20	15
DEC. 17	36	21	21	23	39	32	1	37	30	47	20	15
DEC. 18	36	23	23	24	39	32	1	37	30	47	20	15
DEC. 19	37	24	25	25	39	33	1	37	30	47	20	15
DEC. 20	37	26	27	27	39	33	1	37	30	47	20	15
DEC. 21	37	28	28	29	39	33	1	37	30	47	20	15
DEC. 22	37	30	30	31	38	33	1	37	30	47	20	15
DEC. 23	37	32	32	33	38	33	1	37	30	47	20	15
DEC. 24	37	34	34	35	38	33	1	37	30	47	20	15
DEC. 25	37	36	36	37	38	34	1	37	30	47	20	15
DEC. 26	38	38	38	39	38	34	2	37	31	47	20	15
DEC. 27	38	40	40	41	38	34	2	37	31	47	20	15
DEC. 28	38	42	42	43	38	34	2	37	31	47	20	15
DEC. 29	38	44	44	45	37	34	2	37	31	47	20	15
DEC. 30	38	46	46	47	37	34	2	37	31	47	20	15
DEC. 31	38	47	48	1	37	35	2	37	31	47	20	15

MOON 1 ☽ 12:01 A.M. TO 8:00 A.M.   **MOON 2** ◐ 8:01 A.M. TO 4:00 P.M.   **MOON 3** ● 4:01 P.M. TO 12:00 A.M.
Use only one "moon" number. Choose the column closest to your time of birth. If your place of birth is not on
Eastern Standard Time, be sure to read "How to Convert to Eastern Standard Time" at the beginning of this section.

1925

January

Date & Time	SUN	MOON 1	MOON 2	MOON 3	MERCURY	VENUS	MARS	JUPITER	SATURN	URANUS	NEPTUNE	PLUTO
JAN. 1	38	1	2	2	37	35	2	37	31	47	20	15
JAN. 2	38	3	3	4	37	35	2	37	31	47	20	15
JAN. 3	39	5	5	6	37	35	2	37	31	47	20	15
JAN. 4	39	6	7	7	37	35	2	37	31	47	20	15
JAN. 5	39	8	8	9	37	35	2	38	31	47	20	15
JAN. 6	39	9	10	10	37	36	2	38	31	47	20	15
JAN. 7	39	11	11	12	37	36	2	38	31	47	20	15
JAN. 8	39	13	13	14	37	36	3	38	31	47	20	15
JAN. 9	39	14	15	15	37	36	3	38	31	47	20	15
JAN. 10	40	16	16	17	37	36	3	38	31	47	20	15
JAN. 11	40	17	18	18	37	36	3	38	31	47	20	15
JAN. 12	40	19	19	20	37	37	3	38	31	47	20	15
JAN. 13	40	20	21	22	37	37	3	38	31	47	20	15
JAN. 14	40	22	23	23	37	37	3	38	31	47	20	15
JAN. 15	40	24	24	25	37	37	3	38	31	47	20	15
JAN. 16	40	25	26	27	37	37	3	38	31	47	20	15
JAN. 17	41	27	28	28	37	38	3	38	31	47	20	15
JAN. 18	41	29	30	30	37	38	3	38	31	47	20	15
JAN. 19	41	31	31	32	38	38	4	38	31	47	20	15
JAN. 20	41	33	33	34	38	38	4	38	31	47	20	15
JAN. 21	41	35	35	36	38	38	4	38	31	47	20	15
JAN. 22	41	37	37	38	38	38	4	38	31	47	20	15
JAN. 23	42	39	39	40	38	38	4	38	31	47	20	15
JAN. 24	42	41	41	42	38	39	4	38	31	47	20	15
JAN. 25	42	43	43	44	38	39	4	38	31	48	20	15
JAN. 26	42	45	45	46	39	39	4	38	31	48	20	15
JAN. 27	42	47	47	48	39	39	4	38	31	48	20	15
JAN. 28	42	48	1	2	39	39	4	38	31	48	20	15
JAN. 29	42	2	3	3	39	39	4	38	31	48	20	15
JAN. 30	42	4	5	5	39	40	4	38	31	48	20	15
JAN. 31	43	6	6	7	40	40	5	38	31	48	20	15

February

Date & Time	SUN	MOON 1	MOON 2	MOON 3	MERCURY	VENUS	MARS	JUPITER	SATURN	URANUS	NEPTUNE	PLUTO
FEB. 1	43	7	8	8	40	40	5	38	31	48	20	15
FEB. 2	43	9	9	10	40	40	5	38	31	48	20	15
FEB. 3	43	11	11	12	40	40	5	38	31	48	20	15
FEB. 4	43	12	13	13	40	40	5	38	31	48	20	15
FEB. 5	43	14	14	15	41	41	5	38	31	48	20	15
FEB. 6	43	15	16	16	41	41	5	38	31	48	20	15
FEB. 7	43	17	17	18	41	41	5	38	31	48	20	15
FEB. 8	44	18	19	20	41	41	5	39	31	48	20	15
FEB. 9	44	20	21	21	41	41	5	39	31	48	20	15
FEB. 10	44	22	22	23	42	41	5	39	31	48	20	15
FEB. 11	44	23	24	25	42	42	5	39	31	48	20	15
FEB. 12	44	25	26	26	42	42	6	39	31	48	20	15
FEB. 13	44	27	27	28	42	42	6	39	31	48	20	15
FEB. 14	44	29	29	30	42	42	6	39	31	48	20	15
FEB. 15	44	30	31	32	43	42	6	39	31	48	20	15
FEB. 16	45	32	33	33	43	42	6	39	31	48	20	15
FEB. 17	45	34	35	35	43	43	6	39	31	48	20	15
FEB. 18	45	36	37	37	43	43	6	39	31	48	20	15
FEB. 19	45	38	39	39	43	43	6	39	31	48	20	15
FEB. 20	45	40	41	41	44	43	6	39	31	48	20	15
FEB. 21	45	42	42	43	44	43	6	39	31	48	20	15
FEB. 22	45	44	44	45	44	43	6	39	31	48	20	15
FEB. 23	46	46	46	47	44	44	6	39	31	48	20	15
FEB. 24	46	48	48	1	45	44	7	39	31	48	20	15
FEB. 25	46	1	2	3	45	44	7	39	31	48	20	15
FEB. 26	46	3	4	4	45	44	7	39	31	48	20	15
FEB. 27	46	5	6	6	45	44	7	39	31	48	20	15
FEB. 28	46	7	7	8	46	44	7	39	31	48	20	15

MOON 1 ◔ 12:01 A.M. TO 8:00 A.M.   **MOON 2** ◑ 8:01 A.M. TO 4:00 P.M.   **MOON 3** ● 4:01 P.M. TO 12:00 A.M.

Use only one "moon" number. Choose the column closest to your time of birth. If your place of birth is not on Eastern Standard Time, be sure to read "How to Convert to Eastern Standard Time" at the beginning of this section.

1925

March

April

Date & Time	SUN	MOON 1	MOON 2	MOON 3	MERCURY	VENUS	MARS	JUPITER	SATURN	URANUS	NEPTUNE	PLUTO
MAR. 1	46	8	9	9	46	45	7	39	31	48	20	15
MAR. 2	46	10	11	11	46	45	7	39	31	48	20	15
MAR. 3	47	12	12	13	46	45	7	39	31	48	20	15
MAR. 4	47	13	14	14	47	45	7	39	31	48	20	14
MAR. 5	47	15	15	16	47	45	7	39	31	48	20	14
MAR. 6	47	16	17	17	47	45	7	39	31	48	20	14
MAR. 7	47	18	18	19	47	45	8	39	31	48	20	14
MAR. 8	47	20	20	21	48	46	8	39	31	48	20	14
MAR. 9	47	21	22	22	48	46	8	39	31	48	20	14
MAR. 10	47	23	23	24	48	46	8	39	31	48	20	14
MAR. 11	48	25	25	26	48	46	8	39	31	48	20	14
MAR. 12	48	26	27	28	1	46	8	39	31	48	20	14
MAR. 13	48	28	29	29	1	46	8	39	31	48	20	14
MAR. 14	48	30	31	31	1	47	8	39	31	48	20	14
MAR. 15	48	32	32	33	1	47	8	39	31	48	20	14
MAR. 16	48	34	34	35	2	47	8	39	31	48	20	14
MAR. 17	48	36	36	37	2	47	8	39	31	48	20	14
MAR. 18	48	37	38	39	2	47	8	39	31	48	20	14
MAR. 19	1	39	40	41	2	47	9	39	31	48	20	14
MAR. 20	1	41	42	42	3	48	9	39	31	48	20	14
MAR. 21	1	43	44	44	3	48	9	39	31	48	20	14
MAR. 22	1	45	46	46	3	48	9	39	31	48	20	14
MAR. 23	1	47	47	48	3	48	9	40	31	48	20	14
MAR. 24	1	1	1	2	4	48	9	40	31	48	20	14
MAR. 25	2	3	3	4	4	48	9	40	31	48	20	14
MAR. 26	2	4	5	6	4	1	9	40	31	48	20	14
MAR. 27	2	6	7	7	4	1	9	40	31	48	20	14
MAR. 28	2	8	8	9	4	1	9	40	31	48	20	14
MAR. 29	2	9	10	11	5	1	9	40	31	48	20	14
MAR. 30	2	11	12	12	5	1	9	40	31	48	20	14
MAR. 31	2	13	13	14	5	1	10	40	31	48	20	14

Date & Time	SUN	MOON 1	MOON 2	MOON 3	MERCURY	VENUS	MARS	JUPITER	SATURN	URANUS	NEPTUNE	PLUTO
APR. 1	2	14	15	15	5	2	10	40	31	48	20	14
APR. 2	2	16	16	17	5	2	10	40	31	48	20	14
APR. 3	3	17	18	18	5	2	10	40	31	48	20	14
APR. 4	3	19	20	20	5	2	10	40	31	48	20	14
APR. 5	3	21	21	22	5	2	10	40	31	48	20	14
APR. 6	3	22	23	23	5	2	10	40	31	48	20	14
APR. 7	3	24	25	25	5	3	10	40	31	48	20	14
APR. 8	3	26	26	27	5	3	10	40	31	48	20	14
APR. 9	3	28	28	29	5	3	10	40	31	48	20	14
APR. 10	3	29	30	31	5	3	10	40	31	48	20	14
APR. 11	4	31	32	33	5	3	11	40	31	48	20	14
APR. 12	4	33	34	34	5	3	11	40	31	48	20	14
APR. 13	4	35	36	36	5	4	11	40	31	48	20	14
APR. 14	4	37	38	38	5	4	11	40	31	48	20	14
APR. 15	4	39	40	40	5	4	11	40	31	48	20	14
APR. 16	4	41	41	42	5	4	11	40	31	48	20	14
APR. 17	4	43	43	44	5	4	11	40	31	48	20	15
APR. 18	4	45	45	46	5	4	11	40	31	48	20	15
APR. 19	5	46	47	48	5	5	11	40	31	48	20	15
APR. 20	5	48	1	1	5	5	11	40	31	48	20	15
APR. 21	5	2	3	3	4	5	11	40	31	48	20	15
APR. 22	5	4	4	5	4	5	11	40	31	48	20	15
APR. 23	5	5	6	7	4	5	12	40	31	48	20	15
APR. 24	5	7	8	8	4	5	12	40	31	48	20	15
APR. 25	6	9	9	10	4	6	12	40	31	48	20	15
APR. 26	6	11	11	12	4	6	12	40	30	48	20	15
APR. 27	6	12	13	13	4	6	12	40	30	48	20	15
APR. 28	6	14	14	15	4	6	12	40	30	48	20	15
APR. 29	6	15	16	16	4	6	12	40	30	48	20	15
APR. 30	6	17	17	18	4	6	12	40	30	48	20	15

MOON 1 ◗ 12:01 A.M. TO 8:00 A.M. **MOON 2** ◖ 8:01 A.M. TO 4:00 P.M. **MOON 3** ● 4:01 P.M. TO 12:00 A.M.

Use only one "moon" number. Choose the column closest to your time of birth. If your place of birth is not on Eastern Standard Time, be sure to read "How to Convert to Eastern Standard Time" at the beginning of this section.

May

June

Date & Time	SUN	MOON 1	MOON 2	MOON 3	MERCURY	VENUS	MARS	JUPITER	SATURN	URANUS	NEPTUNE	PLUTO
MAY 1	6	18	19	20	4	7	12	40	30	48	20	15
MAY 2	6	20	21	21	4	7	12	40	30	48	20	15
MAY 3	7	22	22	23	4	7	12	40	30	48	20	15
MAY 4	7	23	24	24	4	7	12	40	30	48	20	15
MAY 5	7	25	26	26	4	7	13	40	30	48	20	15
MAY 6	7	27	27	28	4	7	13	40	30	48	20	15
MAY 7	7	29	29	30	4	8	13	40	30	48	20	15
MAY 8	7	31	31	32	4	8	13	40	30	48	20	15
MAY 9	7	33	33	34	4	8	13	40	30	48	20	15
MAY 10	7	34	35	36	4	8	13	40	30	48	20	15
MAY 11	8	36	37	38	4	8	13	40	30	48	20	15
MAY 12	8	38	39	40	4	8	13	40	30	48	20	15
MAY 13	8	40	41	42	5	9	13	40	30	48	20	15
MAY 14	8	42	43	43	5	9	13	40	30	48	20	15
MAY 15	8	44	45	45	5	9	13	40	30	48	20	15
MAY 16	8	46	47	47	5	9	13	40	30	48	20	15
MAY 17	8	48	48	1	5	9	14	40	30	48	20	15
MAY 18	8	2	2	3	5	9	14	40	30	48	20	15
MAY 19	9	3	4	4	5	10	14	40	30	48	20	15
MAY 20	9	5	6	6	5	10	14	40	30	48	20	15
MAY 21	9	7	7	8	6	10	14	40	30	48	20	15
MAY 22	9	8	9	9	6	10	14	40	30	48	20	15
MAY 23	9	10	11	11	6	10	14	40	30	48	20	15
MAY 24	9	12	12	13	6	10	14	40	30	48	20	15
MAY 25	10	13	14	14	6	11	14	40	30	48	20	15
MAY 26	10	15	15	16	6	11	14	40	30	48	20	15
MAY 27	10	16	17	17	7	11	14	40	30	48	20	15
MAY 28	10	18	18	19	7	11	14	40	30	48	20	15
MAY 29	10	20	20	21	7	11	15	40	30	48	20	15
MAY 30	10	21	22	22	7	11	15	40	30	48	20	15
MAY 31	10	23	23	24	7	12	15	40	30	48	20	15

Date & Time	SUN	MOON 1	MOON 2	MOON 3	MERCURY	VENUS	MARS	JUPITER	SATURN	URANUS	NEPTUNE	PLUTO
JUN. 1	10	24	25	26	8	12	15	40	30	48	20	15
JUN. 2	10	26	27	27	8	12	15	40	30	48	20	15
JUN. 3	11	28	29	29	8	12	15	40	30	48	20	15
JUN. 4	11	30	30	31	8	12	15	40	30	48	20	15
JUN. 5	11	32	32	33	9	12	15	40	30	48	20	15
JUN. 6	11	34	34	35	9	12	15	40	30	48	20	15
JUN. 7	11	36	36	37	9	13	15	40	30	48	20	15
JUN. 8	11	38	38	39	9	13	15	40	30	48	20	15
JUN. 9	11	40	40	41	10	13	16	40	30	48	20	15
JUN. 10	11	42	42	43	10	13	16	40	30	48	20	15
JUN. 11	12	44	44	45	10	13	16	40	30	48	20	15
JUN. 12	12	45	46	47	10	13	16	40	30	48	20	15
JUN. 13	12	47	48	1	11	14	16	40	30	48	20	15
JUN. 14	12	1	2	2	11	14	16	40	30	48	20	15
JUN. 15	12	3	3	4	11	14	16	40	30	48	20	15
JUN. 16	12	5	5	6	12	14	16	40	30	48	20	15
JUN. 17	12	6	7	7	12	14	16	40	30	48	20	15
JUN. 18	12	8	9	9	12	14	16	40	30	48	20	15
JUN. 19	13	10	10	11	12	15	16	40	30	48	20	15
JUN. 20	13	11	12	12	13	15	16	40	30	48	20	15
JUN. 21	13	13	13	14	13	15	17	40	30	48	20	15
JUN. 22	13	14	15	15	13	15	17	40	30	48	20	15
JUN. 23	13	16	16	17	14	15	17	40	30	48	20	15
JUN. 24	13	18	18	19	14	15	17	40	30	48	20	15
JUN. 25	14	19	20	20	14	16	17	40	30	48	20	15
JUN. 26	14	21	21	22	14	16	17	40	30	48	20	15
JUN. 27	14	22	23	23	15	16	17	40	30	48	20	15
JUN. 28	14	24	24	25	15	16	17	40	30	48	20	15
JUN. 29	14	26	26	27	15	16	17	40	30	48	20	15
JUN. 30	14	27	28	28	16	16	17	39	30	48	20	15

MOON 1 ◖ 12:01 A.M. TO 8:00 A.M.   **MOON 2** ◗ 8:01 A.M. TO 4:00 P.M.   **MOON 3** ● 4:01 P.M. TO 12:00 A.M.

Use only one "moon" number. Choose the column closest to your time of birth. If your place of birth is not on Eastern Standard Time, be sure to read "How to Convert to Eastern Standard Time" at the beginning of this section.

1925

July

Date & Time	SUN	MOON 1	MOON 2	MOON 3	MERCURY	VENUS	MARS	JUPITER	SATURN	URANUS	NEPTUNE	PLUTO
JUL. 1	14	29	30	30	16	17	17	39	30	48	20	15
JUL. 2	14	31	32	32	16	17	17	39	30	48	20	15
JUL. 3	15	33	33	34	16	17	18	39	30	48	20	15
JUL. 4	15	35	35	36	17	17	18	39	30	48	20	15
JUL. 5	15	37	37	38	17	18	18	39	30	48	20	15
JUL. 6	15	39	39	40	17	18	18	39	30	48	20	15
JUL. 7	15	41	41	42	17	18	18	39	30	48	20	15
JUL. 8	15	43	43	44	18	18	18	39	30	48	20	15
JUL. 9	15	45	45	46	18	18	18	39	30	48	20	15
JUL. 10	15	47	47	48	18	18	18	39	30	48	20	15
JUL. 11	16	1	1	2	18	18	18	39	30	48	20	15
JUL. 12	16	2	3	4	18	18	18	39	30	48	20	15
JUL. 13	16	4	5	5	19	19	18	39	30	48	20	15
JUL. 14	16	6	6	7	19	19	18	39	30	48	20	15
JUL. 15	16	8	8	9	19	19	19	39	30	48	20	15
JUL. 16	16	9	10	10	19	19	19	39	30	48	20	15
JUL. 17	16	11	11	12	19	19	19	39	30	48	20	15
JUL. 18	16	12	13	13	20	19	19	39	30	48	20	15
JUL. 19	17	14	15	15	20	20	19	39	30	48	20	15
JUL. 20	17	16	16	17	20	20	19	39	30	48	20	15
JUL. 21	17	17	18	18	20	20	19	39	30	48	20	15
JUL. 22	17	19	19	20	20	20	19	39	30	48	20	15
JUL. 23	17	20	21	21	20	20	19	39	30	48	20	15
JUL. 24	17	22	22	23	21	20	19	39	30	48	20	15
JUL. 25	17	23	24	25	21	20	19	39	30	48	20	15
JUL. 26	18	25	26	26	21	21	19	39	30	48	20	15
JUL. 27	18	27	27	28	21	21	20	39	30	48	20	15
JUL. 28	18	29	29	30	21	21	20	39	30	48	20	15
JUL. 29	18	30	31	32	21	21	20	39	30	48	20	15
JUL. 30	18	32	33	33	21	21	20	39	30	48	20	15
JUL. 31	18	34	35	35	22	21	20	39	30	48	20	15

August

Date & Time	SUN	MOON 1	MOON 2	MOON 3	MERCURY	VENUS	MARS	JUPITER	SATURN	URANUS	NEPTUNE	PLUTO
AUG. 1	18	36	37	37	22	22	20	39	30	48	20	15
AUG. 2	18	38	39	39	22	22	20	39	30	48	20	15
AUG. 3	19	40	41	41	22	22	20	39	30	48	20	15
AUG. 4	19	42	43	43	22	22	20	39	30	48	20	15
AUG. 5	19	44	45	45	22	22	20	39	30	48	20	15
AUG. 6	19	46	47	47	22	22	20	39	30	48	20	15
AUG. 7	19	48	1	1	22	23	20	39	30	48	20	15
AUG. 8	19	2	2	3	22	23	21	39	30	48	20	15
AUG. 9	19	4	4	5	22	23	21	39	30	48	20	15
AUG. 10	19	5	6	7	22	23	21	39	30	48	20	15
AUG. 11	20	7	8	8	22	23	21	39	30	48	20	15
AUG. 12	20	9	9	10	22	23	21	39	30	48	20	15
AUG. 13	20	10	11	11	22	24	21	39	30	48	20	15
AUG. 14	20	12	13	13	22	24	21	39	30	48	20	15
AUG. 15	20	14	14	15	22	24	21	39	30	48	20	15
AUG. 16	20	15	16	16	22	24	21	39	30	48	20	15
AUG. 17	20	17	17	18	22	24	21	39	30	48	20	15
AUG. 18	20	18	19	19	22	24	21	39	30	48	20	15
AUG. 19	21	20	20	21	22	25	22	39	30	48	20	15
AUG. 20	21	21	22	23	22	25	22	39	30	48	20	15
AUG. 21	21	23	24	24	22	25	22	39	30	48	20	15
AUG. 22	21	25	25	26	22	25	22	39	30	48	20	15
AUG. 23	21	26	27	28	21	25	22	39	30	48	20	15
AUG. 24	21	28	29	29	21	25	22	39	30	48	20	15
AUG. 25	21	30	30	31	21	25	22	39	30	48	20	15
AUG. 26	22	32	32	33	21	26	22	39	30	48	20	15
AUG. 27	22	33	34	35	21	26	22	39	30	48	20	15
AUG. 28	22	35	36	37	21	26	22	39	30	48	20	15
AUG. 29	22	37	38	38	21	26	22	39	30	48	20	15
AUG. 30	22	39	40	40	21	26	22	39	30	48	20	15
AUG. 31	22	41	42	42	21	26	23	39	30	48	20	15

MOON 1 ◐ 12:01 A.M. TO 8:00 A.M.   **MOON 2** ◑ 8:01 A.M. TO 4:00 P.M.   **MOON 3** ● 4:01 P.M. TO 12:00 A.M.

Use only one "moon" number. Choose the column closest to your time of birth. If your place of birth is not on Eastern Standard Time, be sure to read "How to Convert to Eastern Standard Time" at the beginning of this section.

1925

September — October

Date & Time	SUN	MOON 1	MOON 2	MOON 3	MERCURY	VENUS	MARS	JUPITER	SATURN	URANUS	NEPTUNE	PLUTO
SEP. 1	22	43	44	44	21	27	23	39	30	48	20	15
SEP. 2	22	45	46	46	21	27	23	39	30	48	20	15
SEP. 3	23	47	48	48	20	27	23	39	30	48	20	15
SEP. 4	23	1	2	2	20	27	23	39	30	48	20	15
SEP. 5	23	3	3	4	20	27	23	39	30	48	20	15
SEP. 6	23	5	5	6	21	27	23	39	30	48	20	15
SEP. 7	23	6	7	8	21	28	23	39	30	48	20	15
SEP. 8	23	8	9	9	21	28	23	39	30	48	20	15
SEP. 9	23	10	10	11	21	28	23	39	30	48	20	15
SEP. 10	23	12	12	13	21	28	23	39	30	48	20	15
SEP. 11	24	13	14	14	21	28	23	39	30	48	20	15
SEP. 12	24	15	15	16	21	28	24	39	30	48	20	15
SEP. 13	24	16	17	17	21	29	24	39	30	48	20	15
SEP. 14	24	18	18	19	21	29	24	39	30	48	20	15
SEP. 15	24	19	20	21	22	29	24	39	30	48	20	15
SEP. 16	24	21	22	22	22	29	24	39	30	48	20	15
SEP. 17	24	23	23	24	22	29	24	39	30	48	20	15
SEP. 18	24	24	25	25	22	29	24	39	30	48	20	15
SEP. 19	25	26	27	27	22	29	24	39	30	48	20	15
SEP. 20	25	28	28	29	23	30	24	39	30	48	20	15
SEP. 21	25	29	30	31	23	30	24	39	30	48	20	15
SEP. 22	25	31	32	32	23	30	24	39	31	48	20	15
SEP. 23	25	33	34	34	23	30	24	39	31	48	20	15
SEP. 24	25	35	35	36	24	30	25	39	31	48	20	15
SEP. 25	26	37	37	38	24	30	25	39	31	48	20	15
SEP. 26	26	39	39	40	24	31	25	39	31	48	20	15
SEP. 27	26	40	41	42	24	31	25	39	31	48	20	15
SEP. 28	26	42	43	44	25	31	25	39	31	48	20	15
SEP. 29	26	44	45	46	25	31	25	39	31	48	20	15
SEP. 30	26	46	47	48	25	31	25	39	31	48	20	15
OCT. 1	26	48	1	1	25	31	25	39	31	48	20	15
OCT. 2	26	2	3	3	26	32	25	39	31	48	20	15
OCT. 3	27	4	5	5	26	32	25	39	31	48	20	15
OCT. 4	27	6	6	7	26	32	25	39	31	48	20	15
OCT. 5	27	8	8	9	26	32	26	39	31	48	20	15
OCT. 6	27	9	10	10	27	32	26	39	31	48	20	15
OCT. 7	27	11	12	12	27	32	26	39	31	48	20	15
OCT. 8	27	13	13	14	27	32	26	39	31	48	20	15
OCT. 9	27	14	15	15	27	33	26	39	31	48	20	15
OCT. 10	27	16	16	17	27	33	26	39	31	48	20	15
OCT. 11	28	17	17	18	28	33	26	39	31	48	20	15
OCT. 12	28	19	19	20	28	33	26	39	31	48	20	15
OCT. 13	28	21	21	22	28	33	26	39	31	48	20	15
OCT. 14	28	22	23	23	28	33	26	39	31	48	20	15
OCT. 15	28	24	24	25	29	34	26	39	31	48	20	15
OCT. 16	28	25	26	27	29	34	26	39	31	48	20	15
OCT. 17	28	27	28	28	29	34	27	39	31	48	20	15
OCT. 18	28	29	30	30	29	34	27	39	31	48	20	15
OCT. 19	29	31	31	32	29	34	27	39	31	48	20	15
OCT. 20	29	33	33	34	30	34	27	39	31	48	20	15
OCT. 21	29	34	35	36	30	34	27	39	31	48	20	15
OCT. 22	29	36	37	38	30	35	27	39	31	48	20	15
OCT. 23	29	38	39	39	30	35	27	39	31	48	20	15
OCT. 24	29	40	41	41	30	35	27	39	31	48	20	15
OCT. 25	29	42	43	43	31	35	27	39	31	48	20	15
OCT. 26	30	44	44	45	31	35	27	39	31	48	20	15
OCT. 27	30	46	46	47	31	35	27	39	31	48	20	15
OCT. 28	30	48	48	1	31	36	28	39	31	48	20	15
OCT. 29	30	1	2	3	31	36	28	39	31	48	20	15
OCT. 30	30	3	4	4	32	36	28	39	31	48	20	15
OCT. 31	30	5	6	6	32	36	28	39	31	48	20	15

MOON 1 ☽ 12:01 A.M. TO 8:00 A.M.   **MOON 2** ◑ 8:01 A.M. TO 4:00 P.M.   **MOON 3** ● 4:01 P.M. TO 12:00 A.M.

Use only one "moon" number. Choose the column closest to your time of birth. If your place of birth is not on Eastern Standard Time, be sure to read "How to Convert to Eastern Standard Time" at the beginning of this section.

1925

November

Date & Time	SUN	MOON 1	MOON 2	MOON 3	MERCURY	VENUS	MARS	JUPITER	SATURN	URANUS	NEPTUNE	PLUTO
NOV. 1	30	7	7	8	32	36	28	39	31	48	20	15
NOV. 2	30	9	9	10	32	36	28	39	31	48	20	15
NOV. 3	31	10	11	11	32	36	28	39	31	48	20	15
NOV. 4	31	12	13	13	33	37	28	39	31	48	20	15
NOV. 5	31	14	14	15	33	37	28	39	31	48	20	15
NOV. 6	31	15	16	16	33	37	28	39	31	48	20	15
NOV. 7	31	17	17	18	33	37	28	39	31	48	20	15
NOV. 8	31	18	19	19	33	37	28	39	31	48	20	15
NOV. 9	31	20	20	21	34	37	29	39	31	48	20	15
NOV. 10	31	22	22	23	34	37	29	39	31	48	20	15
NOV. 11	31	23	24	24	34	38	29	39	31	48	20	15
NOV. 12	32	25	25	26	34	38	29	39	31	48	20	15
NOV. 13	32	27	27	28	34	38	29	39	31	48	20	15
NOV. 14	32	28	29	29	35	38	29	39	31	48	20	15
NOV. 15	32	30	31	31	35	38	29	40	31	48	20	15
NOV. 16	32	32	33	33	35	38	29	40	31	48	20	15
NOV. 17	32	34	34	35	35	38	29	40	31	48	20	15
NOV. 18	32	36	36	37	35	39	29	40	31	48	20	15
NOV. 19	33	38	38	39	35	39	29	40	31	48	20	15
NOV. 20	33	40	40	41	36	39	30	40	31	48	20	15
NOV. 21	33	41	42	43	36	39	30	40	31	48	20	15
NOV. 22	33	43	44	45	36	39	30	40	31	48	20	15
NOV. 23	33	45	46	46	36	39	30	40	31	48	20	15
NOV. 24	33	47	48	48	36	39	30	40	31	48	20	15
NOV. 25	34	1	2	2	36	40	30	40	31	48	20	15
NOV. 26	34	3	3	4	36	40	30	40	31	48	20	15
NOV. 27	34	5	5	6	36	40	30	40	32	48	20	15
NOV. 28	34	6	7	7	36	40	30	40	32	48	20	15
NOV. 29	34	8	9	9	37	40	30	40	32	48	20	15
NOV. 30	34	10	10	11	37	40	30	40	32	48	20	15

December

Date & Time	SUN	MOON 1	MOON 2	MOON 3	MERCURY	VENUS	MARS	JUPITER	SATURN	URANUS	NEPTUNE	PLUTO
DEC. 1	34	11	12	13	37	40	31	40	32	48	20	15
DEC. 2	34	13	14	14	37	41	31	40	32	48	20	15
DEC. 3	35	15	15	16	37	41	31	40	32	48	20	15
DEC. 4	35	16	17	17	37	41	31	40	32	48	20	15
DEC. 5	35	18	18	19	36	41	31	40	32	48	20	15
DEC. 6	35	19	20	20	36	41	31	40	32	48	20	15
DEC. 7	35	21	22	22	36	41	31	40	32	48	20	15
DEC. 8	35	23	23	24	36	41	31	40	32	48	20	15
DEC. 9	35	24	25	25	36	41	31	40	32	48	20	15
DEC. 10	35	26	26	27	36	42	31	40	32	48	20	15
DEC. 11	36	28	28	29	36	42	31	40	32	48	20	15
DEC. 12	36	29	30	31	35	42	32	40	32	48	20	15
DEC. 13	36	31	32	32	35	42	32	40	32	48	20	15
DEC. 14	36	33	34	34	35	42	32	40	32	48	20	15
DEC. 15	36	35	36	36	35	42	32	40	32	48	20	15
DEC. 16	36	37	38	38	35	42	32	40	32	48	20	15
DEC. 17	36	39	40	40	35	42	32	40	32	48	20	15
DEC. 18	36	41	41	42	35	42	32	40	32	48	20	15
DEC. 19	37	43	43	44	34	43	32	40	32	48	20	15
DEC. 20	37	45	45	46	34	43	32	40	32	48	20	15
DEC. 21	37	47	47	48	34	43	32	40	32	48	20	15
DEC. 22	37	1	1	2	34	43	32	41	32	48	20	15
DEC. 23	37	2	3	4	34	43	33	41	32	48	20	15
DEC. 24	37	4	5	5	34	43	33	41	32	48	20	15
DEC. 25	37	6	6	7	35	43	33	41	32	48	20	15
DEC. 26	38	8	8	9	35	43	33	41	32	48	20	15
DEC. 27	38	9	10	10	35	43	33	41	32	48	20	15
DEC. 28	38	11	12	12	35	43	33	41	32	48	20	15
DEC. 29	38	13	13	14	35	44	33	41	32	48	20	15
DEC. 30	38	14	15	15	35	44	33	41	32	48	20	15
DEC. 31	38	16	16	17	35	44	33	41	32	48	20	15

MOON 1 ◗ 12:01 A.M. TO 8:00 A.M.   **MOON 2** ◑ 8:01 A.M. TO 4:00 P.M.   **MOON 3** ● 4:01 P.M. TO 12:00 A.M.

Use only one "moon" number. Choose the column closest to your time of birth. If your place of birth is not on Eastern Standard Time, be sure to read "How to Convert to Eastern Standard Time" at the beginning of this section.

1926

January

Date & Time	SUN	MOON 1	MOON 2	MOON 3	MERCURY	VENUS	MARS	JUPITER	SATURN	URANUS	NEPTUNE	PLUTO
JAN. 1	38	17	18	18	35	44	33	41	32	48	20	15
JAN. 2	38	19	19	20	35	44	33	41	32	48	20	15
JAN. 3	39	21	21	22	36	44	34	41	32	48	20	15
JAN. 4	39	22	23	23	36	44	34	41	32	48	20	15
JAN. 5	39	24	24	25	36	44	34	41	32	48	20	15
JAN. 6	39	25	26	26	36	44	34	41	32	48	20	15
JAN. 7	39	27	28	28	36	44	34	41	32	48	20	15
JAN. 8	39	29	29	30	36	44	34	41	32	48	20	15
JAN. 9	39	30	31	32	37	44	34	41	32	48	20	15
JAN. 10	40	32	33	33	37	44	34	41	32	48	20	15
JAN. 11	40	34	35	35	37	44	34	41	32	48	20	15
JAN. 12	40	36	37	37	37	44	34	41	32	48	20	15
JAN. 13	40	38	39	39	37	44	34	41	32	48	20	15
JAN. 14	40	40	41	41	38	44	35	41	32	48	20	15
JAN. 15	40	42	43	43	38	44	35	41	32	48	20	15
JAN. 16	40	44	45	45	38	44	35	41	32	48	20	15
JAN. 17	41	46	47	47	38	44	35	41	32	48	20	15
JAN. 18	41	48	1	1	38	44	35	41	32	48	20	15
JAN. 19	41	2	2	3	38	44	35	41	32	48	20	15
JAN. 20	41	4	4	5	39	44	35	41	32	48	20	15
JAN. 21	41	5	6	7	39	44	35	41	32	48	20	15
JAN. 22	41	7	8	8	39	44	35	41	32	48	20	15
JAN. 23	42	9	9	10	39	44	35	42	32	48	20	15
JAN. 24	42	11	11	12	39	44	35	42	32	48	20	15
JAN. 25	42	12	13	13	40	44	36	42	32	48	20	15
JAN. 26	42	14	14	15	40	44	36	42	32	48	20	15
JAN. 27	42	15	16	16	40	44	36	42	32	48	20	15
JAN. 28	42	17	18	18	40	44	36	42	32	48	20	15
JAN. 29	42	19	19	20	40	44	36	42	32	48	20	15
JAN. 30	42	20	21	21	41	44	36	42	32	48	20	15
JAN. 31	43	22	22	23	41	44	36	42	32	48	20	15

February

Date & Time	SUN	MOON 1	MOON 2	MOON 3	MERCURY	VENUS	MARS	JUPITER	SATURN	URANUS	NEPTUNE	PLUTO
FEB. 1	43	23	24	24	41	44	36	42	32	48	20	15
FEB. 2	43	25	25	26	41	44	36	42	32	48	20	15
FEB. 3	43	27	27	28	42	44	36	42	32	48	20	15
FEB. 4	43	28	29	29	42	44	37	42	32	48	20	15
FEB. 5	43	30	30	31	42	44	37	42	32	48	20	15
FEB. 6	43	32	32	33	42	43	37	42	32	48	20	15
FEB. 7	43	33	34	35	42	43	37	42	32	48	20	15
FEB. 8	44	35	36	36	43	43	37	42	32	48	20	15
FEB. 9	44	37	38	38	43	43	37	42	32	48	20	15
FEB. 10	44	39	40	40	43	43	37	42	32	48	20	15
FEB. 11	44	41	42	42	43	43	37	42	32	48	20	15
FEB. 12	44	43	44	44	44	43	37	42	32	48	20	15
FEB. 13	44	45	46	46	44	43	37	42	32	48	20	15
FEB. 14	44	47	48	48	44	43	37	42	32	48	20	15
FEB. 15	44	1	2	2	44	43	38	42	32	48	20	15
FEB. 16	45	3	4	4	45	43	38	42	32	48	20	15
FEB. 17	45	5	5	6	45	43	38	42	32	48	20	15
FEB. 18	45	7	7	8	45	43	38	42	32	48	20	15
FEB. 19	45	8	9	10	45	43	38	42	32	48	20	15
FEB. 20	45	10	11	11	46	43	38	42	32	48	20	15
FEB. 21	45	12	12	13	46	42	38	42	32	48	20	15
FEB. 22	45	13	14	14	46	42	38	42	32	48	20	15
FEB. 23	46	15	16	16	46	42	38	42	32	48	20	15
FEB. 24	46	17	17	18	47	42	38	43	32	48	20	15
FEB. 25	46	18	19	19	47	42	38	43	32	48	20	15
FEB. 26	46	20	20	21	47	42	39	43	32	48	20	15
FEB. 27	46	21	22	22	47	42	39	43	32	48	20	15
FEB. 28	46	23	23	24	48	42	39	43	32	48	20	15

MOON 1 ◖ 12:01 A.M. TO 8:00 A.M.   **MOON 2** ◑ 8:01 A.M. TO 4:00 P.M.   **MOON 3** ● 4:01 P.M. TO 12:00 A.M.
Use only one "moon" number. Choose the column closest to your time of birth. If your place of birth is not on Eastern Standard Time, be sure to read "How to Convert to Eastern Standard Time" at the beginning of this section.

1926

March

Date & Time	SUN	MOON 1	MOON 2	MOON 3	MERCURY	VENUS	MARS	JUPITER	SATURN	URANUS	NEPTUNE	PLUTO
MAR. 1	46	24	25	26	48	42	39	43	32	48	20	15
MAR. 2	46	26	27	27	48	42	39	43	32	48	20	15
MAR. 3	47	28	28	29	48	42	39	43	32	48	20	15
MAR. 4	47	29	30	31	1	42	39	43	32	48	20	15
MAR. 5	47	31	32	32	1	42	39	43	32	48	20	15
MAR. 6	47	33	33	34	1	42	39	43	32	48	20	15
MAR. 7	47	35	35	36	1	42	39	43	32	48	20	15
MAR. 8	47	36	37	38	1	43	40	43	32	48	20	15
MAR. 9	47	38	39	40	2	43	40	43	32	48	20	15
MAR. 10	47	40	41	41	2	43	40	43	32	48	20	15
MAR. 11	48	42	43	43	2	43	40	43	32	48	20	15
MAR. 12	48	44	45	45	2	43	40	43	32	48	20	15
MAR. 13	48	46	47	47	2	43	40	43	32	48	20	15
MAR. 14	48	48	1	1	2	43	40	43	32	48	20	15
MAR. 15	48	2	3	3	3	43	40	43	32	48	20	15
MAR. 16	48	4	5	5	3	43	40	43	32	48	20	15
MAR. 17	48	6	7	7	3	43	40	43	32	48	20	15
MAR. 18	48	8	8	9	3	43	40	43	32	48	20	15
MAR. 19	1	10	10	11	3	43	41	43	32	48	20	15
MAR. 20	1	11	12	12	3	43	41	43	32	48	20	15
MAR. 21	1	13	13	14	3	43	41	43	32	48	20	15
MAR. 22	1	15	15	16	3	43	41	43	32	48	20	15
MAR. 23	1	16	17	17	3	44	41	43	32	48	20	15
MAR. 24	1	18	18	19	3	44	41	43	32	48	20	15
MAR. 25	2	19	20	20	3	44	41	43	32	48	20	15
MAR. 26	2	21	21	22	3	44	41	43	32	48	20	15
MAR. 27	2	22	23	24	3	44	41	43	32	48	20	15
MAR. 28	2	24	25	25	3	44	41	43	32	48	20	15
MAR. 29	2	26	26	27	2	44	42	43	32	48	20	15
MAR. 30	2	27	28	28	2	44	42	43	32	48	20	15
MAR. 31	2	29	30	30	2	44	42	43	32	48	20	15

April

Date & Time	SUN	MOON 1	MOON 2	MOON 3	MERCURY	VENUS	MARS	JUPITER	SATURN	URANUS	NEPTUNE	PLUTO
APR. 1	2	31	31	32	2	44	42	44	32	48	20	15
APR. 2	2	32	33	34	2	45	42	44	32	48	20	15
APR. 3	3	34	35	35	2	45	42	44	32	48	20	15
APR. 4	3	36	37	37	2	45	42	44	32	48	20	15
APR. 5	3	38	38	39	2	45	42	44	32	1	20	15
APR. 6	3	40	40	41	2	45	42	44	32	1	20	15
APR. 7	3	42	42	43	2	45	42	44	32	1	20	15
APR. 8	3	43	44	45	1	45	43	44	32	1	20	15
APR. 9	3	45	46	47	1	45	43	44	32	1	20	15
APR. 10	3	47	48	1	1	45	43	44	32	1	20	15
APR. 11	4	1	2	3	1	46	43	44	32	1	20	15
APR. 12	4	3	4	5	1	46	43	44	32	1	20	15
APR. 13	4	5	6	6	1	46	43	44	32	1	20	15
APR. 14	4	7	8	8	1	46	43	44	32	1	20	15
APR. 15	4	9	9	10	1	46	43	44	32	1	20	15
APR. 16	4	11	11	12	1	46	43	44	32	1	20	15
APR. 17	4	12	13	13	1	46	43	44	32	1	20	15
APR. 18	4	14	15	15	1	46	43	44	32	1	20	15
APR. 19	5	16	16	17	1	47	44	44	32	1	20	15
APR. 20	5	17	18	18	2	47	44	44	32	1	20	15
APR. 21	5	19	19	20	2	47	44	44	32	1	20	15
APR. 22	5	20	21	21	2	47	44	44	32	1	20	15
APR. 23	5	22	22	23	2	47	44	44	32	1	20	15
APR. 24	5	24	24	25	2	47	44	44	32	1	20	15
APR. 25	6	25	26	26	2	47	44	44	32	1	20	15
APR. 26	6	27	27	28	2	48	44	44	32	1	20	15
APR. 27	6	29	29	30	2	48	44	44	32	1	20	15
APR. 28	6	30	31	31	2	48	44	44	32	1	20	15
APR. 29	6	32	33	33	2	48	45	44	32	1	20	15
APR. 30	6	34	34	35	2	48	45	44	32	1	20	15

MOON 1 ◖ 12:01 A.M. TO 8:00 A.M. **MOON 2** ◑ 8:01 A.M. TO 4:00 P.M. **MOON 3** ● 4:01 P.M. TO 12:00 A.M.
Use only one "moon" number. Choose the column closest to your time of birth. If your place of birth is not on Eastern Standard Time, be sure to read "How to Convert to Eastern Standard Time" at the beginning of this section.

1926

May

June

Date & Time	SUN	MOON 1	MOON 2	MOON 3	MERCURY	VENUS	MARS	JUPITER	SATURN	URANUS	NEPTUNE	PLUTO
MAY 1	6	36	36	37	3	48	45	44	32	1	20	15
MAY 2	6	37	38	39	3	48	45	44	32	1	20	15
MAY 3	7	39	40	40	3	48	45	44	32	1	20	15
MAY 4	7	41	42	42	3	1	45	44	32	1	20	15
MAY 5	7	43	44	44	3	1	45	44	32	1	20	15
MAY 6	7	45	45	46	4	1	45	44	32	1	20	15
MAY 7	7	47	47	48	4	1	45	44	32	1	20	15
MAY 8	7	1	1	2	4	1	45	44	32	1	20	15
MAY 9	7	3	3	4	4	1	45	44	32	1	20	15
MAY 10	7	4	5	6	4	1	46	44	32	1	20	15
MAY 11	8	6	7	8	5	2	46	44	32	1	20	15
MAY 12	8	8	9	9	5	2	46	44	32	1	20	15
MAY 13	8	10	11	11	5	2	46	44	32	1	20	15
MAY 14	8	12	12	13	5	2	46	44	32	1	20	15
MAY 15	8	13	14	15	5	2	46	44	32	1	20	15
MAY 16	8	15	16	16	6	2	46	44	32	1	20	15
MAY 17	8	17	17	18	6	2	46	44	32	1	20	15
MAY 18	8	18	19	19	6	3	46	44	32	1	20	15
MAY 19	9	20	20	21	6	3	46	44	32	1	20	15
MAY 20	9	21	22	22	6	3	47	44	32	1	20	15
MAY 21	9	23	24	24	7	3	47	44	32	1	20	15
MAY 22	9	25	25	26	7	3	47	44	32	1	20	15
MAY 23	9	26	27	27	7	3	47	44	32	1	20	15
MAY 24	9	28	28	29	8	4	47	44	32	1	20	15
MAY 25	10	30	30	31	8	4	47	44	32	1	20	15
MAY 26	10	31	32	33	8	4	47	44	32	1	20	15
MAY 27	10	33	34	34	8	4	47	45	32	1	20	15
MAY 28	10	35	36	36	8	4	47	45	32	1	20	15
MAY 29	10	37	37	38	9	4	47	45	32	1	20	15
MAY 30	10	39	39	40	9	4	47	45	32	1	20	15
MAY 31	10	41	41	42	9	5	48	45	32	1	20	15

Date & Time	SUN	MOON 1	MOON 2	MOON 3	MERCURY	VENUS	MARS	JUPITER	SATURN	URANUS	NEPTUNE	PLUTO
JUN. 1	10	43	43	44	10	5	48	45	32	1	20	15
JUN. 2	10	44	45	46	10	5	48	45	32	1	20	15
JUN. 3	11	46	47	48	10	5	48	45	32	1	20	15
JUN. 4	11	48	1	1	11	5	48	45	32	1	20	15
JUN. 5	11	2	3	3	11	5	48	45	32	1	20	15
JUN. 6	11	4	5	5	11	5	48	45	32	1	20	15
JUN. 7	11	6	6	7	11	6	48	45	32	1	20	15
JUN. 8	11	8	8	9	12	6	48	45	32	1	20	15
JUN. 9	11	9	10	11	12	6	48	45	32	1	20	15
JUN. 10	11	11	12	12	12	6	1	45	32	1	20	15
JUN. 11	12	13	13	14	13	6	1	45	32	1	20	15
JUN. 12	12	14	15	16	13	6	1	45	32	1	20	15
JUN. 13	12	16	17	17	13	7	1	45	32	1	20	15
JUN. 14	12	18	18	19	13	7	1	45	32	1	20	15
JUN. 15	12	19	20	20	14	7	1	45	32	1	20	15
JUN. 16	12	21	21	22	14	7	1	45	32	1	20	15
JUN. 17	12	22	23	24	14	7	1	45	32	1	20	15
JUN. 18	12	24	25	25	15	7	1	45	32	1	20	15
JUN. 19	13	26	26	27	15	7	1	45	32	1	20	15
JUN. 20	13	27	28	28	15	8	1	45	32	1	20	15
JUN. 21	13	29	30	30	15	8	2	45	32	1	20	15
JUN. 22	13	31	31	32	15	8	2	45	32	1	20	15
JUN. 23	13	32	33	34	16	8	2	45	32	1	20	15
JUN. 24	13	34	35	36	16	8	2	45	32	1	20	15
JUN. 25	14	36	37	37	16	8	2	45	32	1	20	15
JUN. 26	14	38	39	39	16	9	2	45	32	1	20	15
JUN. 27	14	40	41	41	17	9	2	45	32	1	20	15
JUN. 28	14	42	43	43	17	9	2	45	32	1	20	15
JUN. 29	14	44	45	45	17	9	2	45	32	1	20	15
JUN. 30	14	46	46	47	17	9	2	45	32	1	20	15

MOON 1 ☽ 12:01 A.M. TO 8:00 A.M.   **MOON 2** ◑ 8:01 A.M. TO 4:00 P.M.   **MOON 3** ● 4:01 P.M. TO 12:00 A.M.

Use only one "moon" number. Choose the column closest to your time of birth. If your place of birth is not on Eastern Standard Time, be sure to read "How to Convert to Eastern Standard Time" at the beginning of this section.

1926

July

Date & Time	SUN	MOON 1	MOON 2	MOON 3	MERCURY	VENUS	MARS	JUPITER	SATURN	URANUS	NEPTUNE	PLUTO
JUL. 1	14	48	48	1	17	9	2	45	32	1	20	15
JUL. 2	14	2	2	3	18	9	3	45	32	1	20	15
JUL. 3	15	4	4	5	18	10	3	45	32	1	20	15
JUL. 4	15	5	6	7	18	10	3	45	32	1	20	15
JUL. 5	15	7	8	8	18	10	3	45	32	1	20	15
JUL. 6	15	9	9	10	18	10	3	45	32	1	20	15
JUL. 7	15	11	11	12	18	10	3	44	32	1	20	15
JUL. 8	15	12	13	13	18	10	3	44	32	1	20	15
JUL. 9	15	14	15	15	19	11	3	44	32	1	20	15
JUL. 10	15	16	16	17	19	11	3	44	32	1	20	15
JUL. 11	16	17	18	19	19	11	3	44	32	1	20	15
JUL. 12	16	19	19	20	19	11	3	44	32	1	20	15
JUL. 13	16	20	21	21	19	11	3	44	32	1	20	15
JUL. 14	16	22	23	23	19	11	4	44	32	1	20	15
JUL. 15	16	24	24	25	19	12	4	44	32	1	20	15
JUL. 16	16	25	26	26	19	12	4	44	32	1	20	15
JUL. 17	16	27	27	28	20	12	4	44	32	1	20	15
JUL. 18	16	28	29	30	20	12	4	44	32	1	20	15
JUL. 19	17	30	31	31	20	12	4	44	32	1	20	15
JUL. 20	17	32	32	33	20	12	4	44	32	1	20	15
JUL. 21	17	34	34	35	20	12	4	44	32	1	20	15
JUL. 22	17	35	36	37	20	13	4	44	32	1	20	15
JUL. 23	17	37	38	39	20	13	4	44	32	1	20	15
JUL. 24	17	39	40	40	20	13	4	44	32	1	20	15
JUL. 25	17	41	42	42	20	13	4	44	32	1	20	15
JUL. 26	18	43	44	44	20	13	5	44	32	1	20	15
JUL. 27	18	45	46	46	20	13	5	44	32	1	20	15
JUL. 28	18	47	48	48	20	14	5	44	32	1	20	15
JUL. 29	18	1	2	2	20	14	5	44	32	1	20	15
JUL. 30	18	3	4	4	20	14	5	44	32	1	20	15
JUL. 31	18	5	6	6	20	14	5	44	32	1	20	15

August

Date & Time	SUN	MOON 1	MOON 2	MOON 3	MERCURY	VENUS	MARS	JUPITER	SATURN	URANUS	NEPTUNE	PLUTO
AUG. 1	18	7	7	8	19	14	5	44	32	1	20	15
AUG. 2	18	9	9	10	19	14	5	44	32	1	20	15
AUG. 3	19	10	11	11	19	15	5	44	32	1	20	15
AUG. 4	19	12	12	13	19	15	5	44	32	1	20	15
AUG. 5	19	14	14	15	19	15	5	44	32	1	20	15
AUG. 6	19	15	16	16	19	15	5	44	32	1	20	15
AUG. 7	19	17	17	18	19	15	5	44	32	1	20	15
AUG. 8	19	18	19	19	19	15	5	44	32	1	20	15
AUG. 9	19	20	21	21	19	16	6	44	32	1	20	15
AUG. 10	19	22	22	23	19	16	6	44	32	1	20	15
AUG. 11	20	23	24	24	19	16	6	44	32	1	20	15
AUG. 12	20	25	25	26	18	16	6	44	32	1	20	15
AUG. 13	20	26	27	27	18	16	6	44	32	1	20	15
AUG. 14	20	28	28	29	18	16	6	44	32	1	20	15
AUG. 15	20	30	30	31	18	16	6	44	32	1	20	15
AUG. 16	20	31	32	32	18	17	6	44	32	1	20	15
AUG. 17	20	33	33	34	18	17	6	44	32	1	20	15
AUG. 18	20	35	35	36	18	17	6	44	32	1	20	15
AUG. 19	21	36	37	38	18	17	6	44	32	1	20	15
AUG. 20	21	38	39	40	18	17	6	44	32	1	20	15
AUG. 21	21	40	41	42	18	17	6	44	32	1	20	15
AUG. 22	21	42	43	44	18	18	6	44	32	1	20	15
AUG. 23	21	44	45	46	18	18	6	44	32	1	20	15
AUG. 24	21	46	47	48	19	18	6	44	32	1	20	15
AUG. 25	21	48	1	2	19	18	7	44	32	1	20	15
AUG. 26	22	2	3	4	19	18	7	44	32	1	20	15
AUG. 27	22	4	5	6	19	18	7	44	32	1	20	15
AUG. 28	22	6	7	7	19	19	7	44	32	1	20	15
AUG. 29	22	8	9	9	19	19	7	44	32	1	20	15
AUG. 30	22	10	10	11	19	19	7	44	32	1	20	15
AUG. 31	22	12	12	13	20	19	7	44	32	1	20	15

MOON 1 ◗ 12:01 A.M. TO 8:00 A.M.   **MOON 2** ◖ 8:01 A.M. TO 4:00 P.M.   **MOON 3** ● 4:01 P.M. TO 12:00 A.M.
Use only one "moon" number. Choose the column closest to your time of birth. If your place of birth is not on Eastern Standard Time, be sure to read "How to Convert to Eastern Standard Time" at the beginning of this section.

1926

September

Date & Time	SUN	MOON 1	MOON 2	MOON 3	MERCURY	VENUS	MARS	JUPITER	SATURN	URANUS	NEPTUNE	PLUTO
SEP. 1	22	13	14	14	20	19	7	44	32	1	20	15
SEP. 2	22	15	15	16	20	19	7	44	32	1	20	15
SEP. 3	23	16	17	17	20	20	7	44	32	1	20	15
SEP. 4	23	18	19	19	21	20	7	44	32	1	20	15
SEP. 5	23	20	20	21	21	20	7	44	32	1	20	15
SEP. 6	23	21	22	22	21	20	7	44	32	1	20	15
SEP. 7	23	23	23	24	21	20	7	44	32	1	20	15
SEP. 8	23	24	25	25	22	20	7	44	32	1	20	15
SEP. 9	23	26	26	27	22	21	7	44	32	1	20	15
SEP. 10	23	28	28	29	22	21	7	44	32	1	20	15
SEP. 11	24	29	30	30	22	21	7	44	32	1	20	15
SEP. 12	24	31	31	32	23	21	7	43	32	1	20	15
SEP. 13	24	32	33	34	23	21	7	43	32	1	20	15
SEP. 14	24	34	35	35	23	21	7	43	32	1	20	15
SEP. 15	24	36	36	37	23	22	7	43	32	1	20	15
SEP. 16	24	38	38	39	24	22	7	43	32	1	20	15
SEP. 17	24	40	40	41	24	22	7	43	32	1	20	15
SEP. 18	24	41	42	43	24	22	7	43	32	1	20	15
SEP. 19	25	43	44	45	24	22	7	43	32	1	20	15
SEP. 20	25	45	46	47	25	22	7	43	32	1	20	15
SEP. 21	25	47	48	1	25	23	7	43	32	1	20	15
SEP. 22	25	1	2	3	25	23	8	43	32	1	20	15
SEP. 23	25	3	4	5	25	23	8	43	32	1	20	15
SEP. 24	25	5	6	7	26	23	8	43	32	1	20	15
SEP. 25	26	7	8	9	26	23	8	43	32	1	20	15
SEP. 26	26	9	10	10	26	23	8	43	32	1	20	15
SEP. 27	26	11	12	12	26	24	8	43	32	1	20	15
SEP. 28	26	13	13	14	26	24	8	43	32	1	20	15
SEP. 29	26	14	15	15	27	24	8	43	32	1	20	15
SEP. 30	26	16	17	17	27	24	8	43	32	1	20	15

October

Date & Time	SUN	MOON 1	MOON 2	MOON 3	MERCURY	VENUS	MARS	JUPITER	SATURN	URANUS	NEPTUNE	PLUTO
OCT. 1	26	18	18	19	27	24	8	43	32	1	20	15
OCT. 2	26	19	20	20	27	24	8	43	32	1	20	15
OCT. 3	27	21	21	22	28	25	8	43	32	1	20	15
OCT. 4	27	22	23	23	28	25	8	43	32	1	20	15
OCT. 5	27	24	24	25	28	25	8	43	32	1	20	15
OCT. 6	27	26	26	27	28	25	8	43	32	1	20	15
OCT. 7	27	27	28	28	28	25	7	43	32	1	20	15
OCT. 8	27	29	29	30	29	25	7	43	32	1	20	15
OCT. 9	27	30	31	32	29	26	7	43	32	1	20	15
OCT. 10	27	32	33	33	29	26	7	43	32	1	20	15
OCT. 11	28	34	34	35	29	26	7	43	32	1	20	15
OCT. 12	28	35	36	37	29	26	7	43	32	1	20	15
OCT. 13	28	37	38	38	30	26	7	43	32	1	20	15
OCT. 14	28	39	40	40	30	26	7	43	32	1	20	15
OCT. 15	28	41	41	42	30	27	7	43	32	1	20	15
OCT. 16	28	43	43	44	30	27	7	43	32	48	20	15
OCT. 17	28	45	45	46	30	27	7	43	32	48	20	15
OCT. 18	28	47	47	48	31	27	7	43	32	48	20	15
OCT. 19	29	1	1	2	31	27	7	43	32	48	21	15
OCT. 20	29	3	3	4	31	27	7	43	32	48	21	15
OCT. 21	29	5	5	6	31	28	7	43	32	48	21	15
OCT. 22	29	7	7	8	31	28	7	43	32	48	21	15
OCT. 23	29	8	9	10	32	28	7	43	32	48	21	15
OCT. 24	29	10	11	11	32	28	7	43	32	48	21	15
OCT. 25	29	12	13	13	32	28	7	43	32	48	21	15
OCT. 26	30	14	14	15	32	28	7	43	32	48	21	15
OCT. 27	30	15	16	17	32	29	7	43	32	48	21	15
OCT. 28	30	17	18	18	32	29	7	43	32	48	21	15
OCT. 29	30	19	19	20	33	29	7	43	32	48	21	15
OCT. 30	30	20	21	21	33	29	7	43	32	48	21	15
OCT. 31	30	22	22	23	33	29	7	43	32	48	21	15

MOON 1 ☽ 12:01 A.M. TO 8:00 A.M.   **MOON 2** ◑ 8:01 A.M. TO 4:00 P.M.   **MOON 3** ● 4:01 P.M. TO 12:00 A.M.

Use only one "moon" number. Choose the column closest to your time of birth. If your place of birth is not on Eastern Standard Time, be sure to read "How to Convert to Eastern Standard Time" at the beginning of this section.

Date & Time	SUN	MOON 1	MOON 2	MOON 3	MERCURY	VENUS	MARS	JUPITER	SATURN	URANUS	NEPTUNE	PLUTO
NOV. 1	30	23	24	25	33	29	7	43	32	48	21	15
NOV. 2	30	25	26	26	33	30	7	43	32	48	21	15
NOV. 3	31	27	27	28	33	30	7	43	32	48	21	15
NOV. 4	31	28	29	29	34	30	6	43	33	48	21	15
NOV. 5	31	30	31	31	34	30	6	43	33	48	21	15
NOV. 6	31	32	32	33	34	30	6	43	33	48	21	15
NOV. 7	31	33	34	34	34	30	6	43	33	48	21	15
NOV. 8	31	35	36	36	34	31	6	43	33	48	21	15
NOV. 9	31	37	37	38	34	31	6	43	33	48	21	15
NOV. 10	31	39	39	40	34	31	6	43	33	48	21	15
NOV. 11	31	40	41	42	34	31	6	43	33	48	21	15
NOV. 12	32	42	43	43	34	31	6	43	33	48	21	15
NOV. 13	32	44	45	45	34	31	6	43	33	48	21	15
NOV. 14	32	46	47	47	34	32	6	43	33	48	21	15
NOV. 15	32	48	1	1	34	32	6	43	33	48	21	15
NOV. 16	32	2	2	3	34	32	6	44	33	48	21	15
NOV. 17	32	4	4	5	34	32	6	44	33	48	21	15
NOV. 18	32	6	6	7	34	32	6	44	33	48	21	15
NOV. 19	33	8	8	9	34	32	6	44	33	48	21	15
NOV. 20	33	9	10	11	34	33	6	44	33	48	21	15
NOV. 21	33	11	12	13	34	33	6	44	33	48	21	15
NOV. 22	33	13	14	14	34	33	6	44	33	48	21	15
NOV. 23	33	15	15	16	34	33	6	44	33	48	21	15
NOV. 24	33	17	17	18	34	33	6	44	33	48	21	15
NOV. 25	34	18	19	19	33	34	6	44	33	48	21	15
NOV. 26	34	20	20	21	33	34	6	44	33	48	21	15
NOV. 27	34	21	22	22	33	34	6	44	33	48	21	15
NOV. 28	34	23	23	24	33	34	6	44	33	48	21	15
NOV. 29	34	25	25	26	33	34	6	44	33	48	21	15
NOV. 30	34	26	27	27	33	34	6	44	33	48	21	15

Date & Time	SUN	MOON 1	MOON 2	MOON 3	MERCURY	VENUS	MARS	JUPITER	SATURN	URANUS	NEPTUNE	PLUTO
DEC. 1	34	28	28	29	33	34	6	44	33	48	21	15
DEC. 2	34	29	30	31	32	35	6	44	33	48	21	15
DEC. 3	35	31	32	32	32	35	6	44	33	48	21	15
DEC. 4	35	33	33	34	32	35	6	44	33	48	21	15
DEC. 5	35	35	35	36	32	35	6	44	33	48	21	15
DEC. 6	35	36	37	38	32	35	6	44	33	48	21	15
DEC. 7	35	38	39	39	32	35	6	44	33	48	21	15
DEC. 8	35	40	41	41	32	36	6	44	33	48	21	15
DEC. 9	35	42	42	43	32	36	6	44	33	48	21	15
DEC. 10	35	44	44	45	33	36	6	44	33	48	21	15
DEC. 11	36	46	46	47	33	36	6	44	33	48	21	15
DEC. 12	36	47	48	1	33	36	6	44	33	48	21	15
DEC. 13	36	1	2	3	33	36	6	44	33	48	21	15
DEC. 14	36	3	4	4	33	37	6	44	33	48	21	15
DEC. 15	36	5	6	6	33	37	6	44	33	48	21	15
DEC. 16	36	7	8	8	33	37	6	44	33	48	21	15
DEC. 17	36	9	9	10	33	37	6	44	33	48	21	15
DEC. 18	36	11	11	12	34	37	6	44	33	48	21	15
DEC. 19	37	12	13	14	34	37	6	44	33	48	21	15
DEC. 20	37	14	15	15	34	38	6	44	33	48	21	15
DEC. 21	37	16	16	17	34	38	6	44	33	48	21	15
DEC. 22	37	18	18	19	34	38	6	44	33	48	21	15
DEC. 23	37	19	20	20	34	38	6	44	33	48	21	15
DEC. 24	37	21	21	22	35	38	6	44	33	48	21	15
DEC. 25	37	22	23	23	35	38	6	44	33	48	21	15
DEC. 26	38	24	25	25	35	39	6	44	33	48	21	15
DEC. 27	38	26	26	27	35	39	6	44	33	48	21	15
DEC. 28	38	27	28	28	35	39	6	44	33	48	21	15
DEC. 29	38	29	29	30	36	39	6	44	33	48	21	15
DEC. 30	38	30	31	32	36	39	6	44	33	48	21	15
DEC. 31	38	32	33	33	36	39	6	44	33	48	21	15

MOON 1 ☽ 12:01 A.M. TO 8:00 A.M.   **MOON 2** ◑ 8:01 A.M. TO 4:00 P.M.   **MOON 3** ● 4:01 P.M. TO 12:00 A.M.
Use only one "moon" number. Choose the column closest to your time of birth. If your place of birth is not on Eastern Standard Time, be sure to read "How to Convert to Eastern Standard Time" at the beginning of this section.

1927

January

Date & Time	SUN	MOON 1	MOON 2	MOON 3	MERCURY	VENUS	MARS	JUPITER	SATURN	URANUS	NEPTUNE	PLUTO
JAN. 1	38	34	34	35	36	40	6	44	33	48	21	15
JAN. 2	38	36	36	37	36	40	6	45	33	48	21	15
JAN. 3	39	37	38	39	37	40	6	45	33	48	21	15
JAN. 4	39	39	40	41	37	40	6	45	33	48	21	15
JAN. 5	39	41	42	42	37	40	6	45	33	48	21	15
JAN. 6	39	43	44	44	37	40	6	45	33	48	21	15
JAN. 7	39	45	46	46	37	41	6	45	33	48	21	15
JAN. 8	39	47	48	48	38	41	6	45	33	48	21	15
JAN. 9	39	1	2	2	38	41	6	45	34	48	21	15
JAN. 10	40	3	3	4	38	41	6	45	34	48	21	15
JAN. 11	40	5	5	6	38	41	6	45	34	48	21	15
JAN. 12	40	7	7	8	38	41	7	45	34	48	20	15
JAN. 13	40	8	9	10	39	42	7	45	34	48	20	15
JAN. 14	40	10	11	11	39	42	7	45	34	48	20	15
JAN. 15	40	12	12	13	39	42	7	45	34	48	20	15
JAN. 16	40	14	14	15	39	42	7	45	34	48	20	15
JAN. 17	41	15	16	16	39	42	7	45	34	48	20	15
JAN. 18	41	17	18	18	40	42	7	45	34	48	20	15
JAN. 19	41	19	19	20	40	43	7	45	34	48	20	15
JAN. 20	41	20	21	21	40	43	7	45	34	48	20	15
JAN. 21	41	22	22	23	40	43	7	45	34	48	20	15
JAN. 22	41	23	24	25	41	43	7	45	34	48	20	15
JAN. 23	42	25	26	26	41	43	7	45	34	1	20	15
JAN. 24	42	27	27	28	41	43	7	45	34	1	20	15
JAN. 25	42	28	29	29	41	44	7	45	34	1	20	15
JAN. 26	42	30	30	31	41	44	7	45	34	1	20	15
JAN. 27	42	31	32	33	42	44	7	45	34	1	20	15
JAN. 28	42	33	34	34	42	44	7	45	34	1	20	15
JAN. 29	42	35	35	36	42	44	7	45	34	1	20	15
JAN. 30	42	37	37	38	42	44	7	45	34	1	20	15
JAN. 31	43	38	39	40	43	45	8	45	34	1	20	15

February

Date & Time	SUN	MOON 1	MOON 2	MOON 3	MERCURY	VENUS	MARS	JUPITER	SATURN	URANUS	NEPTUNE	PLUTO
FEB. 1	43	40	41	42	43	45	8	45	34	1	20	15
FEB. 2	43	42	43	44	43	45	8	45	34	1	20	15
FEB. 3	43	44	45	46	43	45	8	45	34	1	20	15
FEB. 4	43	46	47	48	44	45	8	45	34	1	20	15
FEB. 5	43	48	1	2	44	45	8	45	34	1	20	15
FEB. 6	43	2	3	4	44	46	8	46	34	1	20	15
FEB. 7	43	4	5	5	44	46	8	46	34	1	20	15
FEB. 8	44	6	7	7	44	46	8	46	34	1	20	15
FEB. 9	44	8	9	9	45	46	8	46	34	1	20	15
FEB. 10	44	10	10	11	45	46	8	46	34	1	20	15
FEB. 11	44	11	12	13	45	46	8	46	34	1	20	15
FEB. 12	44	13	14	14	45	47	8	46	34	1	20	15
FEB. 13	44	15	15	16	46	47	8	46	34	1	20	15
FEB. 14	44	17	17	18	46	47	8	46	34	1	20	15
FEB. 15	44	18	19	19	46	47	9	46	34	1	20	15
FEB. 16	45	20	20	21	46	47	9	46	34	1	20	15
FEB. 17	45	21	22	22	47	47	9	46	34	1	20	15
FEB. 18	45	23	24	24	47	48	9	46	34	1	20	15
FEB. 19	45	25	25	26	47	48	9	46	34	1	20	15
FEB. 20	45	26	27	27	47	48	9	46	34	1	20	15
FEB. 21	45	28	28	29	47	48	9	46	34	1	20	15
FEB. 22	45	29	30	30	48	48	9	46	34	1	20	15
FEB. 23	46	31	31	32	48	48	9	46	34	1	20	15
FEB. 24	46	33	33	34	48	1	9	46	34	1	20	15
FEB. 25	46	34	35	35	48	1	9	46	34	1	20	15
FEB. 26	46	36	37	37	48	1	9	46	34	1	20	15
FEB. 27	46	38	38	39	48	1	9	46	34	1	20	15
FEB. 28	46	40	40	41	48	1	9	46	34	1	20	15

MOON 1 ☽ 12:01 A.M. TO 8:00 A.M.　　**MOON 2** ☽ 8:01 A.M. TO 4:00 P.M.　　**MOON 3** ● 4:01 P.M. TO 12:00 A.M.
Use only one "moon" number. Choose the column closest to your time of birth. If your place of birth is not on Eastern Standard Time, be sure to read "How to Convert to Eastern Standard Time" at the beginning of this section.

Date & Time	SUN	MOON 1	MOON 2	MOON 3	MERCURY	VENUS	MARS	JUPITER	SATURN	URANUS	NEPTUNE	PLUTO
MAR. 1	46	41	42	43	1	1	9	46	34	1	20	15
MAR. 2	46	43	44	45	1	2	10	46	34	1	20	15
MAR. 3	47	45	46	47	1	2	10	46	34	1	20	15
MAR. 4	47	47	48	1	1	2	10	46	34	1	20	15
MAR. 5	47	1	2	3	1	2	10	46	34	1	20	15
MAR. 6	47	3	4	5	1	2	10	46	34	1	20	15
MAR. 7	47	5	6	7	1	2	10	46	34	1	20	15
MAR. 8	47	7	8	9	48	3	10	46	34	1	20	15
MAR. 9	47	9	10	10	48	3	10	47	34	1	20	15
MAR. 10	47	11	12	12	48	3	10	47	34	1	20	15
MAR. 11	48	13	13	14	48	3	10	47	34	1	20	15
MAR. 12	48	14	15	16	48	3	10	47	34	1	20	15
MAR. 13	48	16	17	17	48	3	10	47	34	1	20	15
MAR. 14	48	18	18	19	48	4	10	47	34	1	20	15
MAR. 15	48	19	20	20	48	4	10	47	34	1	20	15
MAR. 16	48	21	22	22	48	4	11	47	34	1	20	15
MAR. 17	48	23	23	24	47	4	11	47	34	1	20	15
MAR. 18	48	24	25	25	47	4	11	47	34	1	20	15
MAR. 19	1	26	26	27	47	4	11	47	34	1	20	15
MAR. 20	1	27	28	28	47	5	11	47	34	1	20	15
MAR. 21	1	29	29	30	47	5	11	47	34	1	20	15
MAR. 22	1	31	31	32	47	5	11	47	34	1	20	15
MAR. 23	1	32	33	33	47	5	11	47	34	1	20	15
MAR. 24	1	34	34	35	47	5	11	47	34	1	20	15
MAR. 25	2	35	36	37	47	5	11	47	34	1	20	15
MAR. 26	2	37	38	38	47	5	11	47	34	1	20	15
MAR. 27	2	39	39	40	47	6	11	47	34	1	20	15
MAR. 28	2	41	41	42	47	6	11	47	34	1	20	15
MAR. 29	2	43	43	44	47	6	12	47	34	1	20	15
MAR. 30	2	44	45	46	47	6	12	47	34	1	20	15
MAR. 31	2	46	47	48	47	6	12	47	34	1	20	15

Date & Time	SUN	MOON 1	MOON 2	MOON 3	MERCURY	VENUS	MARS	JUPITER	SATURN	URANUS	NEPTUNE	PLUTO
APR. 1	2	48	1	2	47	6	12	47	34	1	20	15
APR. 2	2	3	3	4	47	7	12	47	34	1	20	15
APR. 3	3	5	5	6	47	7	12	47	34	1	20	15
APR. 4	3	7	7	8	47	7	12	47	34	1	20	15
APR. 5	3	9	9	10	47	7	12	47	34	1	20	15
APR. 6	3	10	11	12	47	7	12	47	34	1	20	15
APR. 7	3	12	13	13	47	7	12	47	34	1	20	15
APR. 8	3	14	15	15	48	8	12	47	34	1	20	15
APR. 9	3	16	16	17	48	8	12	48	34	1	20	15
APR. 10	3	17	18	18	48	8	12	48	34	1	20	15
APR. 11	4	19	20	20	48	8	13	48	34	1	20	15
APR. 12	4	21	21	22	48	8	13	48	34	1	20	15
APR. 13	4	22	23	23	48	8	13	48	34	1	20	15
APR. 14	4	24	24	25	48	9	13	48	34	1	20	15
APR. 15	4	25	26	26	1	9	13	48	34	1	20	15
APR. 16	4	27	27	28	1	9	13	48	34	1	20	15
APR. 17	4	29	29	30	1	9	13	48	34	1	20	15
APR. 18	4	30	31	31	1	9	13	48	34	1	20	15
APR. 19	5	32	32	33	1	9	13	48	34	1	20	15
APR. 20	5	33	34	34	1	10	13	48	34	1	20	15
APR. 21	5	35	36	36	1	10	13	48	34	1	20	15
APR. 22	5	37	37	38	2	10	13	48	34	1	20	15
APR. 23	5	38	39	40	2	10	13	48	34	1	20	15
APR. 24	5	40	41	41	2	10	14	48	34	1	20	15
APR. 25	6	42	43	43	2	10	14	48	34	1	20	15
APR. 26	6	44	44	45	3	10	14	48	34	1	20	15
APR. 27	6	46	46	47	3	11	14	48	34	1	20	15
APR. 28	6	48	48	1	3	11	14	48	34	1	20	15
APR. 29	6	2	2	3	3	11	14	48	34	1	20	15
APR. 30	6	4	4	5	3	11	14	48	34	1	20	15

MOON 1 ☽ **12:01 A.M. TO 8:00 A.M.**   **MOON 2** ☽ **8:01 A.M. TO 4:00 P.M.**   **MOON 3** ● **4:01 P.M. TO 12:00 A.M.**
Use only one "moon" number. Choose the column closest to your time of birth. If your place of birth is not on Eastern Standard Time, be sure to read "How to Convert to Eastern Standard Time" at the beginning of this section.

1927

May

Date & Time	SUN	MOON 1	MOON 2	MOON 3	MERCURY	VENUS	MARS	JUPITER	SATURN	URANUS	NEPTUNE	PLUTO
MAY 1	6	6	6	7	4	11	14	48	34	1	20	15
MAY 2	6	8	8	9	4	11	14	48	34	1	20	15
MAY 3	7	10	10	11	4	12	14	48	34	1	20	15
MAY 4	7	12	12	13	4	12	14	48	34	1	20	15
MAY 5	7	13	14	15	5	12	14	48	34	1	20	15
MAY 6	7	15	16	16	5	12	14	48	34	1	20	15
MAY 7	7	17	17	18	5	12	15	48	34	1	20	15
MAY 8	7	19	19	20	5	12	15	48	34	1	20	15
MAY 9	7	20	21	21	6	12	15	48	34	1	20	15
MAY 10	7	22	22	23	6	13	15	48	34	1	20	15
MAY 11	8	23	24	24	6	13	15	48	34	1	20	15
MAY 12	8	25	25	26	6	13	15	48	34	1	20	15
MAY 13	8	27	27	28	7	13	15	48	34	1	20	15
MAY 14	8	28	29	29	7	13	15	48	34	1	20	15
MAY 15	8	30	30	31	7	13	15	48	34	1	20	15
MAY 16	8	31	32	32	8	14	15	1	34	1	20	15
MAY 17	8	33	34	34	8	14	15	1	34	1	20	15
MAY 18	8	35	35	36	8	14	15	1	34	1	20	15
MAY 19	9	36	37	37	8	14	15	1	34	1	20	15
MAY 20	9	38	39	39	9	14	16	1	34	1	20	15
MAY 21	9	40	40	41	9	14	16	1	34	1	20	15
MAY 22	9	42	42	43	9	14	16	1	34	1	20	15
MAY 23	9	43	44	45	10	15	16	1	34	1	20	15
MAY 24	9	45	46	46	10	15	16	1	34	1	20	15
MAY 25	10	47	48	48	10	15	16	1	34	1	20	15
MAY 26	10	1	2	2	10	15	16	1	34	1	20	15
MAY 27	10	3	4	4	11	15	16	1	34	1	20	15
MAY 28	10	5	6	6	11	15	16	1	34	1	20	15
MAY 29	10	7	8	8	11	16	16	1	34	1	20	15
MAY 30	10	9	9	10	12	16	16	1	34	1	20	15
MAY 31	10	11	11	12	12	16	16	1	34	1	20	15

June

Date & Time	SUN	MOON 1	MOON 2	MOON 3	MERCURY	VENUS	MARS	JUPITER	SATURN	URANUS	NEPTUNE	PLUTO
JUN. 1	10	13	13	14	12	16	17	1	33	1	20	15
JUN. 2	10	14	15	16	12	16	17	1	33	1	20	15
JUN. 3	11	16	17	17	13	16	17	1	33	1	20	15
JUN. 4	11	18	18	19	13	16	17	1	33	1	20	15
JUN. 5	11	20	20	21	13	17	17	1	33	1	20	15
JUN. 6	11	21	22	22	13	17	17	1	33	1	20	15
JUN. 7	11	23	23	24	14	17	17	1	33	1	20	15
JUN. 8	11	24	25	26	14	17	17	1	33	1	20	15
JUN. 9	11	26	27	27	14	17	17	1	33	1	20	15
JUN. 10	11	28	28	29	14	17	17	1	33	1	20	15
JUN. 11	12	29	30	30	14	17	17	1	33	1	20	15
JUN. 12	12	31	31	32	15	18	17	1	33	1	20	15
JUN. 13	12	32	33	34	15	18	18	1	33	1	20	15
JUN. 14	12	34	35	35	15	18	18	1	33	1	20	15
JUN. 15	12	36	36	37	15	18	18	1	33	1	20	15
JUN. 16	12	38	38	39	15	18	18	1	33	1	20	15
JUN. 17	12	39	40	41	16	18	18	1	33	1	20	15
JUN. 18	12	41	42	42	16	18	18	1	33	1	20	15
JUN. 19	13	43	44	44	16	19	18	1	33	1	20	15
JUN. 20	13	45	45	46	16	19	18	1	33	1	20	15
JUN. 21	13	47	47	48	16	19	18	1	33	1	20	15
JUN. 22	13	1	1	2	16	19	18	1	33	1	20	15
JUN. 23	13	2	3	4	16	19	18	1	33	1	20	15
JUN. 24	13	4	5	6	17	19	18	1	33	1	20	15
JUN. 25	14	6	7	8	17	19	18	1	33	1	20	15
JUN. 26	14	8	9	9	17	19	19	1	33	1	20	15
JUN. 27	14	10	11	11	17	20	19	1	33	1	20	15
JUN. 28	14	12	13	13	17	20	19	1	33	1	20	15
JUN. 29	14	14	14	15	17	20	19	1	33	1	20	15
JUN. 30	14	16	16	17	18	20	19	1	33	1	20	15

MOON 1 ◑ 12:01 A.M. TO 8:00 A.M.   **MOON 2** ◑ 8:01 A.M. TO 4:00 P.M.   **MOON 3** ● 4:01 P.M. TO 12:00 A.M.

Use only one "moon" number. Choose the column closest to your time of birth. If your place of birth is not on Eastern Standard Time, be sure to read "How to Convert to Eastern Standard Time" at the beginning of this section.

1927

July

Date & Time	SUN ☉	MOON 1 ◖	MOON 2 ◑	MOON 3 ●	MERCURY	VENUS	MARS	JUPITER	SATURN	URANUS	NEPTUNE	PLUTO
JUL. 1	14	17	18	18	17	20	19	1	33	1	20	15
JUL. 2	14	19	20	20	17	20	19	1	33	1	20	15
JUL. 3	15	21	21	22	17	20	19	1	33	1	20	15
JUL. 4	15	22	23	23	17	21	19	1	33	1	20	15
JUL. 5	15	24	24	25	17	21	19	1	33	1	20	15
JUL. 6	15	26	26	27	17	21	19	1	33	1	20	15
JUL. 7	15	27	28	28	17	21	19	1	33	1	20	15
JUL. 8	15	29	29	30	17	21	20	1	33	1	20	15
JUL. 9	15	30	31	31	17	21	20	1	33	1	20	15
JUL. 10	15	32	32	33	17	21	20	1	33	1	20	15
JUL. 11	16	34	34	35	17	21	20	1	33	1	20	15
JUL. 12	16	35	36	36	17	21	20	1	33	1	20	15
JUL. 13	16	37	38	38	17	22	20	1	33	1	20	15
JUL. 14	16	39	39	40	17	22	20	1	33	1	20	15
JUL. 15	16	41	41	42	17	22	20	1	33	1	20	15
JUL. 16	16	42	43	44	17	22	20	1	33	1	20	15
JUL. 17	16	44	45	46	17	22	20	1	33	1	20	15
JUL. 18	16	46	47	47	17	22	20	1	33	1	20	15
JUL. 19	17	48	1	1	17	22	20	1	33	1	20	15
JUL. 20	17	2	3	3	16	22	21	1	33	1	20	15
JUL. 21	17	4	5	5	16	22	21	1	33	1	20	15
JUL. 22	17	6	6	7	16	23	21	1	33	1	20	15
JUL. 23	17	8	9	9	16	23	21	1	33	1	20	15
JUL. 24	17	10	10	11	16	23	21	1	33	1	20	15
JUL. 25	17	11	12	13	16	23	21	1	33	1	20	15
JUL. 26	18	13	14	14	16	23	21	1	33	1	20	15
JUL. 27	18	15	16	16	16	23	21	1	33	1	20	15
JUL. 28	18	17	17	18	16	23	21	1	33	1	20	15
JUL. 29	18	18	19	20	16	23	21	1	33	1	20	15
JUL. 30	18	20	21	21	16	23	21	1	33	1	20	15
JUL. 31	18	22	22	23	16	23	21	1	33	1	20	15

August

Date & Time	SUN ☉	MOON 1 ◖	MOON 2 ◑	MOON 3 ●	MERCURY	VENUS	MARS	JUPITER	SATURN	URANUS	NEPTUNE	PLUTO
AUG. 1	18	23	24	24	16	23	22	1	33	1	20	15
AUG. 2	18	25	26	26	16	24	22	1	33	1	20	15
AUG. 3	19	27	27	28	16	24	22	1	33	1	20	15
AUG. 4	19	28	29	29	16	24	22	1	33	1	20	15
AUG. 5	19	30	30	31	16	24	22	1	33	1	20	15
AUG. 6	19	31	32	32	16	24	22	1	33	1	20	15
AUG. 7	19	33	33	34	16	24	22	1	33	1	20	15
AUG. 8	19	35	35	36	16	24	22	1	33	1	20	15
AUG. 9	19	36	37	37	17	24	22	1	33	1	20	15
AUG. 10	19	38	39	39	17	24	22	1	33	1	20	15
AUG. 11	20	40	40	41	17	24	22	1	33	1	20	15
AUG. 12	20	42	42	43	17	24	22	1	33	1	20	15
AUG. 13	20	44	44	45	17	24	23	1	33	1	20	15
AUG. 14	20	46	46	47	17	24	23	1	33	1	20	15
AUG. 15	20	47	48	1	18	24	23	1	33	1	21	15
AUG. 16	20	1	2	3	18	24	23	1	33	1	21	15
AUG. 17	20	3	4	5	18	24	23	1	33	1	21	15
AUG. 18	20	5	6	7	18	24	23	1	33	1	21	15
AUG. 19	21	7	8	8	18	24	23	1	33	1	21	15
AUG. 20	21	9	10	10	19	24	23	1	33	1	21	15
AUG. 21	21	11	12	12	19	24	23	1	33	1	21	15
AUG. 22	21	13	14	14	19	24	23	1	33	1	21	15
AUG. 23	21	14	15	16	19	24	23	1	33	1	21	15
AUG. 24	21	16	17	17	20	24	23	1	33	1	21	15
AUG. 25	21	18	18	19	20	24	24	1	33	1	21	15
AUG. 26	22	20	20	21	20	24	24	1	33	1	21	15
AUG. 27	22	21	22	22	21	24	24	1	33	1	21	15
AUG. 28	22	23	23	24	21	24	24	1	33	1	21	15
AUG. 29	22	24	25	26	21	24	24	1	33	1	21	15
AUG. 30	22	26	27	27	21	24	24	1	33	1	21	15
AUG. 31	22	28	28	29	22	24	24	1	33	1	21	15

MOON 1 ◖ 12:01 A.M. TO 8:00 A.M.   **MOON 2** ◑ 8:01 A.M. TO 4:00 P.M.   **MOON 3** ● 4:01 P.M. TO 12:00 A.M.

Use only one "moon" number. Choose the column closest to your time of birth. If your place of birth is not on Eastern Standard Time, be sure to read "How to Convert to Eastern Standard Time" at the beginning of this section.

September

October

Date & Time	SUN	MOON 1	MOON 2	MOON 3	MERCURY	VENUS	MARS	JUPITER	SATURN	URANUS	NEPTUNE	PLUTO
SEP. 1	22	29	30	30	22	24	24	1	33	1	21	15
SEP. 2	22	31	31	32	22	24	24	1	33	1	21	15
SEP. 3	23	32	33	33	22	24	24	1	33	1	21	15
SEP. 4	23	34	35	35	23	24	24	1	33	1	21	15
SEP. 5	23	36	36	37	23	24	25	1	33	1	21	15
SEP. 6	23	37	38	39	23	24	25	1	33	1	21	15
SEP. 7	23	39	40	40	23	24	25	1	33	1	21	15
SEP. 8	23	41	42	42	24	23	25	1	33	1	21	15
SEP. 9	23	43	43	44	24	23	25	1	33	1	21	15
SEP. 10	23	45	45	46	24	23	25	1	33	1	21	15
SEP. 11	24	47	47	48	24	23	25	1	33	1	21	15
SEP. 12	24	1	1	2	25	23	25	1	33	1	21	15
SEP. 13	24	3	3	4	25	23	25	1	33	1	21	15
SEP. 14	24	5	5	6	25	23	25	1	33	1	21	15
SEP. 15	24	7	7	8	25	23	25	1	33	1	21	15
SEP. 16	24	9	9	10	25	23	25	1	33	1	21	15
SEP. 17	24	10	11	12	26	23	25	1	33	1	21	15
SEP. 18	24	12	13	13	26	23	26	1	33	1	21	15
SEP. 19	25	14	15	15	26	23	26	1	33	1	21	15
SEP. 20	25	16	16	17	26	23	26	1	33	1	21	15
SEP. 21	25	18	18	19	27	22	26	1	33	1	21	15
SEP. 22	25	19	20	20	27	22	26	1	33	1	21	15
SEP. 23	25	21	21	22	27	22	26	1	33	1	21	15
SEP. 24	25	22	23	24	27	22	26	1	33	1	21	15
SEP. 25	26	24	25	25	27	22	26	1	33	1	21	15
SEP. 26	26	26	26	27	28	22	26	1	33	1	21	15
SEP. 27	26	27	28	28	28	22	26	1	33	1	21	15
SEP. 28	26	29	29	30	28	22	26	1	33	1	21	15
SEP. 29	26	30	31	31	28	22	27	1	33	1	21	15
SEP. 30	26	32	33	33	28	22	27	1	33	1	21	15

Date & Time	SUN	MOON 1	MOON 2	MOON 3	MERCURY	VENUS	MARS	JUPITER	SATURN	URANUS	NEPTUNE	PLUTO
OCT. 1	26	34	34	35	29	22	27	1	33	1	21	15
OCT. 2	26	35	36	36	29	22	27	1	33	1	21	15
OCT. 3	27	37	37	38	29	22	27	1	33	1	21	15
OCT. 4	27	38	39	40	29	22	27	1	33	1	21	15
OCT. 5	27	40	41	41	29	22	27	1	33	1	21	15
OCT. 6	27	42	43	43	29	22	27	1	33	1	21	15
OCT. 7	27	44	44	45	30	22	27	1	33	1	21	15
OCT. 8	27	46	46	47	30	22	27	48	34	1	21	15
OCT. 9	27	48	48	1	30	22	27	48	34	1	21	15
OCT. 10	27	2	2	3	30	22	28	48	34	1	21	15
OCT. 11	28	4	5	5	30	22	28	48	34	1	21	15
OCT. 12	28	6	7	7	31	22	28	48	34	1	21	15
OCT. 13	28	8	9	9	31	22	28	48	34	1	21	15
OCT. 14	28	10	10	11	31	23	28	48	34	1	21	15
OCT. 15	28	12	12	13	31	23	28	48	34	1	21	15
OCT. 16	28	14	14	15	31	23	28	48	34	1	21	15
OCT. 17	28	15	16	17	31	23	28	48	34	1	21	15
OCT. 18	28	17	18	18	31	23	28	48	34	1	21	15
OCT. 19	29	19	19	20	32	23	28	48	34	1	21	15
OCT. 20	29	20	21	22	32	23	28	48	34	1	21	15
OCT. 21	29	22	23	23	32	23	28	48	34	1	21	15
OCT. 22	29	24	24	25	32	23	29	48	34	1	21	15
OCT. 23	29	25	26	26	32	23	29	48	34	1	21	15
OCT. 24	29	27	27	28	32	23	29	48	34	1	21	15
OCT. 25	29	28	29	29	32	23	29	48	34	1	21	15
OCT. 26	30	30	31	31	32	23	29	48	34	1	21	15
OCT. 27	30	32	32	33	32	24	29	48	34	1	21	15
OCT. 28	30	33	34	34	32	24	29	48	34	1	21	15
OCT. 29	30	35	35	36	32	24	29	48	34	1	21	15
OCT. 30	30	36	37	37	32	24	29	48	34	1	21	15
OCT. 31	30	38	39	39	32	24	29	48	34	1	21	15

MOON 1 ◐ 12:01 A.M. TO 8:00 A.M.   **MOON 2** ◑ 8:01 A.M. TO 4:00 P.M.   **MOON 3** ● 4:01 P.M. TO 12:00 A.M.

Use only one "moon" number. Choose the column closest to your time of birth. If your place of birth is not on Eastern Standard Time, be sure to read "How to Convert to Eastern Standard Time" at the beginning of this section.

Date & Time	SUN	MOON 1	MOON 2	MOON 3	MERCURY	VENUS	MARS	JUPITER	SATURN	URANUS	NEPTUNE	PLUTO
NOV. 1	30	40	40	41	32	24	30	48	34	1	21	15
NOV. 2	30	41	42	43	32	24	30	48	34	1	21	15
NOV. 3	31	43	44	44	32	24	30	48	34	1	21	15
NOV. 4	31	45	46	46	32	24	30	48	34	1	21	15
NOV. 5	31	47	48	48	32	24	30	48	34	1	21	15
NOV. 6	31	1	2	2	32	25	30	48	34	1	21	15
NOV. 7	31	3	4	4	32	25	30	48	34	1	21	15
NOV. 8	31	5	6	6	32	25	30	48	34	1	21	15
NOV. 9	31	7	8	8	31	25	30	48	34	1	21	15
NOV. 10	31	9	10	10	31	25	30	48	34	1	21	15
NOV. 11	31	11	12	12	31	25	30	48	34	1	21	15
NOV. 12	32	13	13	14	31	25	31	48	34	1	21	15
NOV. 13	32	15	15	16	31	25	31	48	34	1	21	15
NOV. 14	32	17	17	18	31	26	31	48	34	1	21	15
NOV. 15	32	18	19	19	30	26	31	48	34	1	21	15
NOV. 16	32	20	21	21	30	26	31	48	34	1	21	15
NOV. 17	32	22	22	23	30	26	31	48	34	1	21	15
NOV. 18	32	23	24	24	30	26	31	48	34	1	21	15
NOV. 19	33	25	25	26	30	26	31	48	34	1	21	15
NOV. 20	33	26	27	27	30	26	31	48	34	1	21	15
NOV. 21	33	28	29	29	30	26	31	48	34	1	21	15
NOV. 22	33	30	30	31	30	27	31	48	34	1	21	15
NOV. 23	33	31	32	32	30	27	32	48	34	1	21	15
NOV. 24	33	33	33	34	30	27	32	48	34	1	21	15
NOV. 25	34	34	35	35	31	27	32	48	34	1	21	15
NOV. 26	34	36	37	37	31	27	32	48	34	1	21	15
NOV. 27	34	38	38	39	31	27	32	48	34	1	21	15
NOV. 28	34	39	40	40	31	27	32	48	34	1	21	15
NOV. 29	34	41	42	42	31	28	32	48	34	1	21	15
NOV. 30	34	43	43	44	31	28	32	48	34	1	21	15

Date & Time	SUN	MOON 1	MOON 2	MOON 3	MERCURY	VENUS	MARS	JUPITER	SATURN	URANUS	NEPTUNE	PLUTO
DEC. 1	34	45	45	46	31	28	32	48	34	1	21	15
DEC. 2	34	46	47	48	32	28	32	48	34	1	21	15
DEC. 3	35	48	1	1	32	28	32	48	34	1	21	15
DEC. 4	35	2	3	3	32	28	33	48	34	1	21	15
DEC. 5	35	4	5	5	32	28	33	48	34	1	21	15
DEC. 6	35	6	7	7	32	29	33	48	34	1	21	15
DEC. 7	35	8	9	9	33	29	33	48	34	1	21	15
DEC. 8	35	10	11	11	33	29	33	48	34	1	21	15
DEC. 9	35	12	13	13	33	29	33	48	34	1	21	15
DEC. 10	35	14	15	15	33	29	33	48	34	1	21	15
DEC. 11	36	16	16	17	33	29	33	48	34	1	21	15
DEC. 12	36	18	18	19	34	29	33	48	34	1	21	15
DEC. 13	36	19	20	21	34	30	33	48	34	1	21	15
DEC. 14	36	21	22	22	34	30	34	48	34	1	21	15
DEC. 15	36	23	23	24	34	30	34	48	35	1	21	15
DEC. 16	36	24	25	25	34	30	34	48	35	1	21	15
DEC. 17	36	26	26	27	35	30	34	48	35	1	21	15
DEC. 18	36	28	28	29	35	30	34	48	35	1	21	15
DEC. 19	37	29	30	30	35	31	34	48	35	1	21	15
DEC. 20	37	31	31	32	35	31	34	48	35	1	21	15
DEC. 21	37	32	33	33	35	31	34	48	35	1	21	15
DEC. 22	37	34	34	35	36	31	34	48	35	1	21	15
DEC. 23	37	36	36	37	36	31	34	48	35	1	21	15
DEC. 24	37	37	38	38	36	31	34	48	35	1	21	15
DEC. 25	37	39	39	40	36	31	35	48	35	1	21	15
DEC. 26	38	41	41	42	36	32	35	48	35	1	21	15
DEC. 27	38	42	43	44	37	32	35	48	35	1	21	15
DEC. 28	38	44	45	45	37	32	35	48	35	1	21	15
DEC. 29	38	46	47	47	37	32	35	48	35	1	21	15
DEC. 30	38	48	48	1	37	32	35	48	35	1	21	15
DEC. 31	38	2	2	3	37	32	35	48	35	1	21	15

MOON 1 ◗ 12:01 A.M. TO 8:00 A.M.   **MOON 2** ◑ 8:01 A.M. TO 4:00 P.M.   **MOON 3** ● 4:01 P.M. TO 12:00 A.M.

Use only one "moon" number. Choose the column closest to your time of birth. If your place of birth is not on Eastern Standard Time, be sure to read "How to Convert to Eastern Standard Time" at the beginning of this section.

1928

January

Date & Time	SUN	MOON 1	MOON 2	MOON 3	MERCURY	VENUS	MARS	JUPITER	SATURN	URANUS	NEPTUNE	PLUTO
JAN. 1	38	4	4	5	38	33	35	1	35	1	21	15
JAN. 2	38	5	6	7	38	33	35	1	35	1	21	15
JAN. 3	39	7	8	9	38	33	35	1	35	1	21	15
JAN. 4	39	9	10	11	38	33	36	1	35	1	21	15
JAN. 5	39	11	12	12	38	33	36	1	35	1	21	15
JAN. 6	39	13	14	14	39	33	36	1	35	1	21	15
JAN. 7	39	15	16	16	39	33	36	1	35	1	21	15
JAN. 8	39	17	17	18	39	34	36	1	35	1	21	15
JAN. 9	39	19	19	20	39	34	36	1	35	1	21	15
JAN. 10	40	20	21	22	40	34	36	1	35	1	21	15
JAN. 11	40	22	23	23	40	34	36	1	35	1	21	15
JAN. 12	40	24	24	25	40	34	36	1	35	1	21	15
JAN. 13	40	25	26	26	40	34	36	1	35	1	21	15
JAN. 14	40	27	28	28	40	35	36	1	35	1	21	15
JAN. 15	40	29	29	30	41	35	37	1	35	1	21	15
JAN. 16	40	30	31	31	41	35	37	1	35	1	21	15
JAN. 17	41	32	32	33	41	35	37	1	35	1	21	15
JAN. 18	41	33	34	34	41	35	37	1	35	1	21	15
JAN. 19	41	35	36	36	42	35	37	1	35	1	21	15
JAN. 20	41	37	37	38	42	36	37	1	35	1	21	15
JAN. 21	41	38	39	39	42	36	37	1	35	1	21	15
JAN. 22	41	40	41	41	42	36	37	1	35	1	21	15
JAN. 23	42	42	42	43	42	36	37	1	35	1	21	15
JAN. 24	42	44	44	45	43	36	37	1	35	1	21	15
JAN. 25	42	45	46	47	43	36	38	1	35	1	21	15
JAN. 26	42	47	48	1	43	37	38	1	35	1	21	15
JAN. 27	42	1	2	2	43	37	38	1	35	1	21	15
JAN. 28	42	3	4	4	44	37	38	1	35	1	21	15
JAN. 29	42	5	6	6	44	37	38	1	35	1	21	15
JAN. 30	42	7	7	8	44	37	38	1	35	1	21	15
JAN. 31	43	9	9	10	44	37	38	1	35	1	21	15

February

Date & Time	SUN	MOON 1	MOON 2	MOON 3	MERCURY	VENUS	MARS	JUPITER	SATURN	URANUS	NEPTUNE	PLUTO
FEB. 1	43	11	11	12	45	37	38	1	35	1	21	15
FEB. 2	43	12	13	14	45	38	38	1	35	1	21	15
FEB. 3	43	14	15	16	45	38	38	1	35	1	21	15
FEB. 4	43	16	17	17	45	38	39	1	35	1	21	15
FEB. 5	43	18	19	19	45	38	39	1	35	1	21	15
FEB. 6	43	20	20	21	45	38	39	1	35	1	21	15
FEB. 7	43	21	22	23	46	38	39	1	35	1	21	15
FEB. 8	44	23	24	24	46	39	39	1	35	1	21	15
FEB. 9	44	25	25	26	46	39	39	1	35	1	21	15
FEB. 10	44	26	27	28	46	39	39	1	35	1	21	15
FEB. 11	44	28	29	29	46	39	39	1	35	1	21	15
FEB. 12	44	30	30	31	46	39	39	1	35	1	21	15
FEB. 13	44	31	32	32	46	39	39	2	35	1	21	15
FEB. 14	44	33	33	34	46	40	40	2	35	1	21	15
FEB. 15	44	34	35	35	46	40	40	2	35	1	21	15
FEB. 16	45	36	37	37	46	40	40	2	35	1	21	15
FEB. 17	45	38	38	39	46	40	40	2	35	1	21	15
FEB. 18	45	39	40	41	46	40	40	2	35	1	21	15
FEB. 19	45	41	42	42	46	40	40	2	35	1	21	15
FEB. 20	45	43	44	44	46	41	40	2	35	1	21	15
FEB. 21	45	45	45	46	46	41	40	2	35	1	21	15
FEB. 22	45	47	47	48	46	41	40	2	35	1	21	15
FEB. 23	46	1	1	2	46	41	40	2	35	1	21	15
FEB. 24	46	3	3	4	46	41	41	2	35	1	21	15
FEB. 25	46	5	5	6	46	41	41	2	35	1	21	15
FEB. 26	46	6	7	8	45	42	41	2	35	1	21	15
FEB. 27	46	8	9	10	45	42	41	2	35	1	21	15
FEB. 28	46	10	11	11	45	42	41	2	35	1	21	15
FEB. 29	46	12	13	13	45	42	41	2	35	1	21	15

MOON 1 ◐ 12:01 A.M. TO 8:00 A.M.   **MOON 2** ◑ 8:01 A.M. TO 4:00 P.M.   **MOON 3** ● 4:01 P.M. TO 12:00 A.M.
Use only one "moon" number. Choose the column closest to your time of birth. If your place of birth is not on Eastern Standard Time, be sure to read "How to Convert to Eastern Standard Time" at the beginning of this section.

1928

March

April

Date & Time	SUN	MOON 1	MOON 2	MOON 3	MERCURY	VENUS	MARS	JUPITER	SATURN	URANUS	NEPTUNE	PLUTO
MAR. 1	46	14	14	15	45	42	41	2	35	1	21	15
MAR. 2	46	16	16	17	45	42	41	2	35	1	21	15
MAR. 3	47	17	18	19	45	43	41	2	35	1	21	15
MAR. 4	47	19	20	20	45	43	41	2	35	1	21	15
MAR. 5	47	21	21	22	45	43	42	2	35	1	21	15
MAR. 6	47	23	23	24	44	43	42	2	35	1	21	15
MAR. 7	47	24	25	25	44	43	42	2	35	1	21	15
MAR. 8	47	26	26	27	44	43	42	2	35	1	21	15
MAR. 9	47	28	28	29	44	44	42	2	35	1	21	15
MAR. 10	47	29	30	30	44	44	42	2	35	1	21	15
MAR. 11	48	31	31	32	44	44	42	2	35	1	21	15
MAR. 12	48	32	33	33	45	44	42	2	35	1	21	15
MAR. 13	48	34	34	35	45	44	42	2	35	1	21	15
MAR. 14	48	35	36	37	45	44	42	2	35	1	21	15
MAR. 15	48	37	38	38	45	44	43	2	35	1	21	15
MAR. 16	48	39	39	40	45	45	43	2	35	1	21	15
MAR. 17	48	40	41	42	45	45	43	3	36	1	21	15
MAR. 18	48	42	43	43	45	45	43	3	36	1	21	15
MAR. 19	1	44	45	45	45	45	43	3	36	1	21	15
MAR. 20	1	46	47	47	45	45	43	3	36	1	21	15
MAR. 21	1	48	48	1	45	45	43	3	36	1	21	15
MAR. 22	1	2	2	3	45	46	43	3	36	1	21	15
MAR. 23	1	4	4	5	46	46	43	3	36	1	21	15
MAR. 24	1	6	6	7	46	46	43	3	36	1	21	15
MAR. 25	2	8	8	9	46	46	44	3	36	1	21	15
MAR. 26	2	10	10	11	46	46	44	3	36	1	21	15
MAR. 27	2	12	12	13	46	46	44	3	36	1	21	15
MAR. 28	2	13	14	15	46	47	44	3	36	1	21	15
MAR. 29	2	15	16	16	46	47	44	3	36	1	21	15
MAR. 30	2	17	18	18	47	47	44	3	36	1	21	15
MAR. 31	2	19	19	20	47	47	44	3	36	1	21	15

Date & Time	SUN	MOON 1	MOON 2	MOON 3	MERCURY	VENUS	MARS	JUPITER	SATURN	URANUS	NEPTUNE	PLUTO
APR. 1	2	20	21	22	47	47	44	3	36	1	21	15
APR. 2	2	22	23	23	47	47	44	3	36	1	21	15
APR. 3	3	24	24	25	47	48	45	3	36	1	21	15
APR. 4	3	25	26	27	48	48	45	3	36	1	21	15
APR. 5	3	27	28	28	48	48	45	3	36	2	21	15
APR. 6	3	29	29	30	48	48	45	3	36	2	21	15
APR. 7	3	30	31	31	48	48	45	3	36	2	21	15
APR. 8	3	32	32	33	48	48	45	3	36	2	21	15
APR. 9	3	33	34	34	1	1	45	3	36	2	21	15
APR. 10	3	35	36	36	1	1	45	3	36	2	21	15
APR. 11	4	37	37	38	1	1	45	3	35	2	21	15
APR. 12	4	38	39	39	1	1	45	3	35	2	21	15
APR. 13	4	40	40	41	1	1	46	3	35	2	21	15
APR. 14	4	42	42	43	2	1	46	3	35	2	21	15
APR. 15	4	43	44	44	2	2	46	3	35	2	21	15
APR. 16	4	45	46	46	2	2	46	3	35	2	21	15
APR. 17	4	47	48	48	2	2	46	4	35	2	21	15
APR. 18	4	1	2	2	3	2	46	4	35	2	20	15
APR. 19	5	3	4	4	3	2	46	4	35	2	20	15
APR. 20	5	5	6	6	3	2	46	4	35	2	20	15
APR. 21	5	7	8	8	3	3	46	4	35	2	20	15
APR. 22	5	9	10	10	4	3	46	4	35	2	20	15
APR. 23	5	11	12	12	4	3	47	4	35	2	20	15
APR. 24	5	13	14	14	4	3	47	4	35	2	20	15
APR. 25	6	15	15	16	4	3	47	4	35	2	20	15
APR. 26	6	17	17	18	5	3	47	4	35	2	20	15
APR. 27	6	18	19	20	5	4	47	4	35	2	20	15
APR. 28	6	20	21	21	5	4	47	4	35	2	20	15
APR. 29	6	22	22	23	5	4	47	4	35	2	20	15
APR. 30	6	23	24	25	6	4	47	4	35	2	20	15

MOON 1 ☽ 12:01 A.M. TO 8:00 A.M.   **MOON 2** ☽ 8:01 A.M. TO 4:00 P.M.   **MOON 3** ● 4:01 P.M. TO 12:00 A.M.
Use only one "moon" number. Choose the column closest to your time of birth. If your place of birth is not on
Eastern Standard Time, be sure to read "How to Convert to Eastern Standard Time" at the beginning of this section.

May

Date & Time	SUN	MOON 1	MOON 2	MOON 3	MERCURY	VENUS	MARS	JUPITER	SATURN	URANUS	NEPTUNE	PLUTO
MAY 1	6	25	26	26	6	4	47	4	35	2	20	15
MAY 2	6	27	27	28	6	4	47	4	35	2	20	15
MAY 3	7	28	29	29	7	5	48	4	35	2	20	15
MAY 4	7	30	30	31	7	5	48	4	35	2	20	15
MAY 5	7	31	32	32	7	5	48	4	35	2	20	15
MAY 6	7	33	34	34	7	5	48	4	35	2	20	15
MAY 7	7	35	35	36	8	5	48	4	35	2	20	15
MAY 8	7	36	37	37	8	5	48	4	35	2	20	15
MAY 9	7	38	38	39	8	5	48	4	35	2	20	15
MAY 10	7	39	40	40	9	6	48	4	35	2	20	15
MAY 11	8	41	42	42	9	6	48	4	35	2	20	15
MAY 12	8	43	43	44	9	6	48	4	35	2	20	15
MAY 13	8	44	45	46	9	6	1	4	35	2	20	15
MAY 14	8	46	47	48	10	6	1	4	35	2	20	15
MAY 15	8	48	1	1	10	6	1	4	35	2	20	15
MAY 16	8	2	3	3	10	7	1	4	35	2	20	15
MAY 17	8	4	5	5	10	7	1	4	35	2	20	15
MAY 18	8	6	7	7	11	7	1	4	35	2	20	15
MAY 19	9	8	9	9	11	7	1	5	35	2	20	15
MAY 20	9	10	11	11	11	7	1	5	35	2	20	15
MAY 21	9	12	13	13	11	7	1	5	35	2	20	15
MAY 22	9	14	15	15	12	8	2	5	35	2	20	15
MAY 23	9	16	17	17	12	8	2	5	35	2	20	15
MAY 24	9	18	18	19	12	8	2	5	35	2	20	15
MAY 25	10	20	20	21	12	8	2	5	35	2	20	15
MAY 26	10	21	22	22	12	8	2	5	35	2	20	15
MAY 27	10	23	24	24	12	8	2	5	35	2	20	15
MAY 28	10	25	25	26	13	9	2	5	35	2	21	15
MAY 29	10	26	27	27	13	9	2	5	35	2	21	15
MAY 30	10	28	28	29	13	9	2	5	35	2	21	15
MAY 31	10	29	30	30	13	9	2	5	35	2	21	15

June

Date & Time	SUN	MOON 1	MOON 2	MOON 3	MERCURY	VENUS	MARS	JUPITER	SATURN	URANUS	NEPTUNE	PLUTO
JUN. 1	10	31	32	32	13	9	3	5	35	2	21	15
JUN. 2	10	33	33	34	14	9	3	5	35	2	21	15
JUN. 3	11	34	35	35	14	10	3	5	35	2	21	15
JUN. 4	11	36	36	37	14	10	3	5	35	2	21	15
JUN. 5	11	37	38	38	14	10	3	5	35	2	21	15
JUN. 6	11	39	40	40	14	10	3	5	35	2	21	15
JUN. 7	11	41	41	42	14	10	3	5	35	2	21	15
JUN. 8	11	42	43	43	14	10	3	5	35	2	21	15
JUN. 9	11	44	45	45	14	11	3	5	35	2	21	15
JUN. 10	11	46	46	47	14	11	3	5	35	2	21	15
JUN. 11	12	48	48	1	14	11	3	5	35	2	21	15
JUN. 12	12	1	2	3	15	11	4	5	35	2	21	15
JUN. 13	12	3	4	5	15	11	4	5	35	2	21	15
JUN. 14	12	5	6	7	15	11	4	5	35	2	21	15
JUN. 15	12	7	8	9	15	12	4	5	35	2	21	15
JUN. 16	12	9	10	11	15	12	4	5	35	2	21	15
JUN. 17	12	11	12	13	15	12	4	5	35	2	21	15
JUN. 18	12	13	14	14	15	12	4	5	35	2	21	15
JUN. 19	13	15	16	16	15	12	4	5	35	2	21	15
JUN. 20	13	17	18	18	15	12	4	5	35	2	21	15
JUN. 21	13	19	20	20	15	13	4	5	35	2	21	15
JUN. 22	13	21	21	22	14	13	5	5	35	2	21	15
JUN. 23	13	22	23	24	14	13	5	5	35	2	21	15
JUN. 24	13	24	25	25	14	13	5	5	35	2	21	15
JUN. 25	14	26	26	27	14	13	6	5	35	2	21	15
JUN. 26	14	27	28	28	14	13	6	5	35	2	21	15
JUN. 27	14	29	30	30	14	14	6	5	35	2	21	15
JUN. 28	14	31	31	32	14	14	6	5	35	2	21	15
JUN. 29	14	32	33	33	14	14	6	5	35	2	21	15
JUN. 30	14	34	34	35	14	14	6	5	35	2	21	15

MOON 1 ◐ 12:01 A.M. TO 8:00 A.M.   **MOON 2** ◑ 8:01 A.M. TO 4:00 P.M.   **MOON 3** ● 4:01 P.M. TO 12:00 A.M.
Use only one "moon" number. Choose the column closest to your time of birth. If your place of birth is not on Eastern Standard Time, be sure to read "How to Convert to Eastern Standard Time" at the beginning of this section.

1928

July · August

Date & Time	SUN	MOON 1	MOON 2	MOON 3	MERCURY	VENUS	MARS	JUPITER	SATURN	URANUS	NEPTUNE	PLUTO
JUL. 1	14	35	36	36	14	14	5	6	35	2	21	15
JUL. 2	14	37	37	38	14	14	6	6	35	2	21	15
JUL. 3	15	39	39	40	14	14	6	6	35	2	21	15
JUL. 4	15	40	41	41	14	15	6	6	35	2	21	15
JUL. 5	15	42	42	43	14	15	6	6	35	2	21	15
JUL. 6	15	44	44	45	14	15	6	6	35	2	21	15
JUL. 7	15	45	46	47	13	15	6	6	35	2	21	15
JUL. 8	15	47	48	48	13	15	6	6	35	2	21	15
JUL. 9	15	1	2	2	13	15	6	6	35	2	21	15
JUL. 10	15	3	3	4	13	16	6	6	35	2	21	15
JUL. 11	16	5	5	6	13	16	6	6	35	2	21	15
JUL. 12	16	7	7	8	13	16	6	6	35	2	21	15
JUL. 13	16	8	9	10	13	16	7	6	35	2	21	15
JUL. 14	16	10	11	12	13	16	7	6	35	2	21	15
JUL. 15	16	12	13	14	14	16	7	6	35	2	21	15
JUL. 16	16	14	15	16	14	17	7	6	35	2	21	15
JUL. 17	16	16	17	18	14	17	7	6	35	2	21	15
JUL. 18	16	18	19	19	14	17	7	6	35	2	21	15
JUL. 19	17	20	21	21	14	17	7	6	35	2	21	15
JUL. 20	17	22	22	23	14	17	7	6	35	2	21	15
JUL. 21	17	24	24	25	14	17	7	6	35	2	21	15
JUL. 22	17	25	26	26	14	18	7	6	35	2	21	15
JUL. 23	17	27	27	28	14	18	7	6	35	2	21	15
JUL. 24	17	29	29	30	14	18	8	6	35	2	21	15
JUL. 25	17	30	31	31	15	18	8	6	35	2	21	15
JUL. 26	18	32	32	33	15	18	8	6	35	2	21	15
JUL. 27	18	33	34	34	15	18	8	6	35	2	21	15
JUL. 28	18	35	35	36	15	19	8	6	35	2	21	15
JUL. 29	18	36	37	38	15	19	8	6	35	2	21	15
JUL. 30	18	38	39	39	16	19	8	6	35	2	21	15
JUL. 31	18	40	40	41	16	19	8	6	35	2	21	15

Date & Time	SUN	MOON 1	MOON 2	MOON 3	MERCURY	VENUS	MARS	JUPITER	SATURN	URANUS	NEPTUNE	PLUTO
AUG. 1	18	41	42	43	16	19	8	6	35	2	21	15
AUG. 2	18	43	44	44	16	19	8	6	35	2	21	15
AUG. 3	19	45	46	46	17	20	8	6	35	2	21	15
AUG. 4	19	47	47	48	17	20	9	6	35	2	21	15
AUG. 5	19	1	1	2	17	20	9	6	35	2	21	15
AUG. 6	19	2	3	4	17	20	9	6	35	2	21	15
AUG. 7	19	4	5	5	18	20	9	6	35	2	21	15
AUG. 8	19	6	7	7	18	20	9	6	35	2	21	15
AUG. 9	19	8	9	9	18	21	9	6	35	2	21	15
AUG. 10	19	10	11	11	18	21	9	6	35	2	21	15
AUG. 11	20	12	12	13	19	21	9	6	35	2	21	15
AUG. 12	20	14	14	15	19	21	9	6	35	2	21	15
AUG. 13	20	16	16	17	19	21	9	6	35	2	21	15
AUG. 14	20	17	18	19	20	21	9	6	35	2	21	15
AUG. 15	20	19	20	21	20	22	9	6	35	2	21	15
AUG. 16	20	21	22	22	20	22	10	6	35	2	21	15
AUG. 17	20	23	23	24	20	22	10	6	35	2	21	15
AUG. 18	20	25	25	26	21	22	10	6	35	2	21	15
AUG. 19	21	26	27	27	21	22	10	6	35	2	21	15
AUG. 20	21	28	28	29	21	22	10	6	35	2	21	15
AUG. 21	21	30	30	31	21	23	10	6	35	2	21	15
AUG. 22	21	31	32	32	22	23	10	6	35	2	21	15
AUG. 23	21	33	33	34	22	23	10	6	35	2	21	15
AUG. 24	21	34	35	35	22	23	10	6	35	2	21	15
AUG. 25	21	36	36	37	22	23	10	6	35	2	21	15
AUG. 26	22	38	38	39	23	23	10	6	35	2	21	15
AUG. 27	22	39	40	40	23	24	10	6	35	2	21	15
AUG. 28	22	41	41	42	23	24	11	6	35	2	21	15
AUG. 29	22	43	43	44	23	24	11	6	35	2	21	15
AUG. 30	22	44	45	46	24	24	11	6	35	2	21	15
AUG. 31	22	46	47	47	24	24	11	6	35	2	21	15

MOON 1 ☽ 12:01 A.M. TO 8:00 A.M. **MOON 2** ☽ 8:01 A.M. TO 4:00 P.M. **MOON 3** ● 4:01 P.M. TO 12:00 A.M.

Use only one "moon" number. Choose the column closest to your time of birth. If your place of birth is not on Eastern Standard Time, be sure to read "How to Convert to Eastern Standard Time" at the beginning of this section.

September

Date & Time	SUN	MOON 1	MOON 2	MOON 3	MERCURY	VENUS	MARS	JUPITER	SATURN	URANUS	NEPTUNE	PLUTO
SEP. 1	22	48	1	1	24	24	11	6	35	2	21	15
SEP. 2	22	2	3	3	24	25	11	6	35	2	21	15
SEP. 3	23	4	4	5	24	25	11	6	35	2	21	15
SEP. 4	23	6	6	7	25	25	11	6	35	2	21	15
SEP. 5	23	8	8	9	25	25	11	6	35	2	21	15
SEP. 6	23	9	10	11	25	25	11	6	35	2	21	15
SEP. 7	23	11	12	13	25	25	11	6	35	2	21	15
SEP. 8	23	13	14	14	25	26	11	6	35	2	21	15
SEP. 9	23	15	16	16	26	26	11	6	35	2	21	15
SEP. 10	23	17	18	18	26	26	12	6	35	2	21	15
SEP. 11	24	19	19	20	26	26	12	6	35	2	21	15
SEP. 12	24	21	21	22	26	26	12	6	35	2	21	15
SEP. 13	24	22	23	23	26	26	12	6	35	2	21	15
SEP. 14	24	24	25	25	27	26	12	6	35	2	21	15
SEP. 15	24	26	26	27	27	27	12	6	35	2	21	15
SEP. 16	24	27	28	28	27	27	12	6	35	2	21	15
SEP. 17	24	29	30	30	27	27	12	6	35	2	21	15
SEP. 18	24	31	31	32	27	27	12	6	35	2	21	15
SEP. 19	25	32	33	33	28	27	12	6	35	2	21	15
SEP. 20	25	34	34	35	28	27	12	6	35	2	21	15
SEP. 21	25	35	36	36	28	28	12	6	35	2	21	15
SEP. 22	25	37	37	38	28	28	12	6	35	2	21	15
SEP. 23	25	39	39	40	28	28	12	6	35	2	21	15
SEP. 24	25	40	41	41	28	28	12	6	35	2	21	15
SEP. 25	26	42	42	43	29	28	13	6	35	2	21	15
SEP. 26	26	44	44	45	29	28	13	6	35	2	21	15
SEP. 27	26	45	46	47	29	29	13	6	35	2	21	15
SEP. 28	26	47	48	1	29	29	13	6	35	2	21	15
SEP. 29	26	1	2	2	29	29	13	6	35	2	21	15
SEP. 30	26	3	4	4	29	29	13	6	35	2	21	15

October

Date & Time	SUN	MOON 1	MOON 2	MOON 3	MERCURY	VENUS	MARS	JUPITER	SATURN	URANUS	NEPTUNE	PLUTO
OCT. 1	26	5	6	6	29	29	13	6	35	2	21	15
OCT. 2	26	7	8	8	30	29	13	6	35	2	21	15
OCT. 3	27	9	10	10	30	30	13	6	35	2	21	15
OCT. 4	27	11	12	12	30	30	13	6	35	2	21	15
OCT. 5	27	13	13	14	30	30	13	6	35	2	21	15
OCT. 6	27	15	15	16	30	30	13	6	35	2	21	15
OCT. 7	27	16	17	18	30	30	13	6	35	2	21	15
OCT. 8	27	18	19	19	30	30	13	6	35	2	21	15
OCT. 9	27	20	21	21	30	31	13	6	35	2	21	15
OCT. 10	27	22	22	23	30	31	13	6	35	2	21	15
OCT. 11	28	24	24	25	30	31	13	6	35	2	21	15
OCT. 12	28	25	26	26	30	31	13	6	35	2	21	15
OCT. 13	28	27	27	28	30	31	13	6	35	2	21	15
OCT. 14	28	29	29	30	30	31	14	6	35	2	21	15
OCT. 15	28	30	31	31	30	32	14	6	35	2	21	15
OCT. 16	28	32	32	33	30	32	14	6	35	2	21	15
OCT. 17	28	33	34	34	30	32	14	6	35	2	21	15
OCT. 18	28	35	35	36	30	32	14	6	35	2	21	15
OCT. 19	29	36	37	38	30	32	14	6	35	2	21	15
OCT. 20	29	38	39	39	30	32	14	6	35	2	21	15
OCT. 21	29	40	40	41	30	33	14	6	35	2	21	15
OCT. 22	29	41	42	42	29	33	14	6	35	2	21	15
OCT. 23	29	43	44	44	29	33	14	6	35	2	21	15
OCT. 24	29	45	45	46	29	33	14	6	35	2	21	15
OCT. 25	29	46	47	48	29	33	14	6	35	2	21	15
OCT. 26	30	48	1	2	29	33	14	6	35	2	21	15
OCT. 27	30	2	3	4	29	34	14	6	35	2	21	15
OCT. 28	30	4	5	6	28	34	14	6	35	2	21	15
OCT. 29	30	6	7	8	28	34	14	6	35	2	21	15
OCT. 30	30	8	9	10	28	34	14	6	35	2	21	15
OCT. 31	30	10	11	12	28	34	14	6	35	2	21	15

MOON 1 ☽ 12:01 A.M. TO 8:00 A.M.   **MOON 2** ◑ 8:01 A.M. TO 4:00 P.M.   **MOON 3** ● 4:01 P.M. TO 12:00 A.M.

Use only one "moon" number. Choose the column closest to your time of birth. If your place of birth is not on Eastern Standard Time, be sure to read "How to Convert to Eastern Standard Time" at the beginning of this section.

1928

November

Date & Time	SUN	MOON 1	MOON 2	MOON 3	MERCURY	VENUS	MARS	JUPITER	SATURN	URANUS	NEPTUNE	PLUTO
NOV. 1	30	12	13	13	28	34	14	6	35	2	21	15
NOV. 2	30	14	15	15	28	35	14	6	35	2	21	15
NOV. 3	31	16	17	17	28	35	14	6	35	2	21	15
NOV. 4	31	18	18	19	28	35	14	6	35	2	21	15
NOV. 5	31	20	20	21	28	35	14	6	35	2	21	15
NOV. 6	31	21	22	23	28	35	14	6	35	2	21	15
NOV. 7	31	23	24	24	28	35	14	6	35	1	21	15
NOV. 8	31	25	25	26	29	35	14	5	35	1	21	15
NOV. 9	31	26	27	28	29	36	14	5	35	1	21	15
NOV. 10	31	28	29	29	29	36	14	5	35	1	21	15
NOV. 11	31	30	30	31	29	36	14	5	35	1	21	15
NOV. 12	32	31	32	32	29	36	14	5	35	1	21	15
NOV. 13	32	33	33	34	29	36	14	5	35	1	21	15
NOV. 14	32	34	35	35	29	36	14	5	35	1	21	15
NOV. 15	32	36	37	37	30	37	14	5	35	1	21	15
NOV. 16	32	38	38	39	30	37	14	5	35	1	21	15
NOV. 17	32	39	40	40	30	37	14	5	35	1	21	15
NOV. 18	32	41	41	42	30	37	14	5	35	1	21	15
NOV. 19	33	42	43	44	30	37	14	5	35	1	21	15
NOV. 20	33	44	45	45	31	37	14	5	35	1	21	15
NOV. 21	33	46	46	47	31	37	14	5	35	1	21	15
NOV. 22	33	48	48	1	31	38	14	5	36	1	21	15
NOV. 23	33	1	2	3	31	38	14	5	36	1	21	15
NOV. 24	33	3	4	5	31	38	14	5	36	1	21	15
NOV. 25	34	5	6	7	32	38	14	5	36	1	21	15
NOV. 26	34	7	8	9	32	38	14	5	36	1	21	15
NOV. 27	34	9	10	11	32	39	14	5	36	1	21	15
NOV. 28	34	11	12	13	32	39	14	5	36	1	21	15
NOV. 29	34	13	14	15	32	39	14	5	36	1	21	15
NOV. 30	34	15	16	17	33	39	14	5	36	1	21	15

December

Date & Time	SUN	MOON 1	MOON 2	MOON 3	MERCURY	VENUS	MARS	JUPITER	SATURN	URANUS	NEPTUNE	PLUTO
DEC. 1	34	17	18	19	33	39	14	5	36	1	21	15
DEC. 2	34	19	20	20	33	39	14	5	36	1	21	15
DEC. 3	35	21	22	22	33	40	14	5	36	1	21	15
DEC. 4	35	23	23	24	33	40	14	5	36	1	21	15
DEC. 5	35	24	25	26	34	40	14	5	36	1	21	15
DEC. 6	35	26	27	27	34	40	14	5	36	1	21	15
DEC. 7	35	28	28	29	34	40	14	5	36	1	21	15
DEC. 8	35	29	30	30	34	40	14	5	36	1	21	15
DEC. 9	35	31	31	32	35	41	14	5	36	1	21	15
DEC. 10	35	32	33	34	35	41	13	5	36	1	21	15
DEC. 11	36	34	35	35	35	41	13	5	36	1	21	15
DEC. 12	36	36	36	37	35	41	13	5	36	1	21	15
DEC. 13	36	37	38	38	35	41	13	5	36	1	21	15
DEC. 14	36	39	39	40	36	41	13	5	36	1	21	15
DEC. 15	36	40	41	41	36	41	13	5	36	1	21	15
DEC. 16	36	42	43	43	36	42	13	5	36	1	21	15
DEC. 17	36	44	44	45	36	42	13	5	36	1	21	15
DEC. 18	36	45	46	46	36	42	13	5	36	1	21	15
DEC. 19	37	47	48	48	37	42	13	5	36	1	21	15
DEC. 20	37	1	1	2	37	42	13	5	36	1	21	15
DEC. 21	37	3	3	4	37	42	13	5	36	1	21	15
DEC. 22	37	4	5	6	37	43	13	5	36	1	21	15
DEC. 23	37	6	7	8	37	43	13	5	36	1	21	15
DEC. 24	37	8	9	10	38	43	13	5	36	1	21	15
DEC. 25	37	10	11	12	38	43	13	5	36	1	21	15
DEC. 26	38	12	13	14	38	43	13	5	36	1	21	15
DEC. 27	38	14	15	16	38	43	13	5	36	1	21	15
DEC. 28	38	16	17	18	39	44	13	5	36	1	21	15
DEC. 29	38	18	19	20	39	44	13	5	36	1	21	15
DEC. 30	38	20	21	21	39	44	12	5	36	1	21	15
DEC. 31	38	22	23	23	39	44	12	5	36	1	21	15

MOON 1 ◐ 12:01 A.M. TO 8:00 A.M.　　**MOON 2** ◑ 8:01 A.M. TO 4:00 P.M.　　**MOON 3** ● 4:01 P.M. TO 12:00 A.M.
Use only one "moon" number. Choose the column closest to your time of birth. If your place of birth is not on Eastern Standard Time, be sure to read "How to Convert to Eastern Standard Time" at the beginning of this section.

1929

January

Date & Time	SUN	MOON 1	MOON 2	MOON 3	MERCURY	VENUS	MARS	JUPITER	SATURN	URANUS	NEPTUNE	PLUTO
JAN. 1	38	24	24	25	39	44	12	5	36	1	21	15
JAN. 2	38	26	26	27	40	44	12	5	36	1	21	15
JAN. 3	39	27	28	28	40	44	12	5	36	1	21	15
JAN. 4	39	29	29	30	40	45	12	5	36	1	21	15
JAN. 5	39	30	31	32	40	45	12	5	36	1	21	15
JAN. 6	39	32	33	33	41	45	12	5	36	1	21	15
JAN. 7	39	34	34	35	41	45	12	5	36	1	21	15
JAN. 8	39	35	36	36	41	45	12	5	36	1	21	15
JAN. 9	39	37	37	38	41	45	12	5	36	1	21	15
JAN. 10	40	38	39	39	41	46	12	5	36	1	21	15
JAN. 11	40	40	41	41	42	46	12	5	36	1	21	15
JAN. 12	40	42	42	43	42	46	12	5	36	1	21	15
JAN. 13	40	43	44	44	42	46	12	5	36	1	21	15
JAN. 14	40	45	46	46	42	46	12	5	36	1	21	15
JAN. 15	40	47	47	48	42	46	12	5	36	1	21	15
JAN. 16	40	48	1	2	43	46	12	5	36	1	21	15
JAN. 17	41	2	3	3	43	47	12	5	36	1	21	15
JAN. 18	41	4	5	5	43	47	12	5	36	2	21	15
JAN. 19	41	6	7	7	43	47	12	5	36	2	21	15
JAN. 20	41	8	8	9	43	47	12	5	36	2	21	15
JAN. 21	41	10	10	11	44	47	12	5	36	2	21	15
JAN. 22	41	11	12	13	44	47	12	5	36	2	21	15
JAN. 23	42	13	14	15	44	47	12	5	36	2	21	15
JAN. 24	42	15	16	17	44	48	12	5	36	2	21	15
JAN. 25	42	17	18	19	44	48	12	5	36	2	21	15
JAN. 26	42	19	20	21	44	48	12	5	36	2	21	15
JAN. 27	42	21	22	23	44	48	12	5	37	2	21	15
JAN. 28	42	23	24	24	44	48	12	5	37	2	21	15
JAN. 29	42	25	26	26	44	48	12	5	37	2	21	15
JAN. 30	42	27	27	28	44	48	12	5	37	2	21	15
JAN. 31	43	28	29	29	44	1	12	5	37	2	21	15

February

Date & Time	SUN	MOON 1	MOON 2	MOON 3	MERCURY	VENUS	MARS	JUPITER	SATURN	URANUS	NEPTUNE	PLUTO
FEB. 1	43	30	31	31	44	1	12	5	37	2	21	15
FEB. 2	43	32	32	33	44	1	12	5	37	2	21	15
FEB. 3	43	33	34	34	44	1	12	5	37	2	21	15
FEB. 4	43	35	35	36	44	1	12	5	37	2	21	15
FEB. 5	43	36	37	37	44	1	12	5	37	2	21	15
FEB. 6	43	38	38	39	44	1	12	5	37	2	21	15
FEB. 7	43	40	40	41	43	2	12	5	37	2	21	15
FEB. 8	44	41	42	42	43	2	12	5	37	2	21	15
FEB. 9	44	43	43	44	43	2	12	5	37	2	21	15
FEB. 10	44	44	45	46	43	2	12	5	37	2	21	15
FEB. 11	44	46	47	47	43	2	12	6	37	2	21	15
FEB. 12	44	48	1	1	43	2	12	6	37	2	21	15
FEB. 13	44	2	2	3	42	2	12	6	37	2	21	15
FEB. 14	44	4	4	5	42	3	12	6	37	2	21	15
FEB. 15	44	5	6	7	42	3	12	6	37	2	21	15
FEB. 16	45	7	8	8	42	3	12	6	37	2	21	15
FEB. 17	45	9	10	10	42	3	12	6	37	2	21	15
FEB. 18	45	11	12	12	42	3	12	6	37	2	21	15
FEB. 19	45	13	13	14	42	3	12	6	37	2	21	15
FEB. 20	45	15	15	16	42	3	12	6	37	2	21	15
FEB. 21	45	17	17	18	42	3	12	6	37	2	21	15
FEB. 22	45	19	19	20	42	4	12	6	37	2	21	15
FEB. 23	46	20	21	22	42	4	12	6	37	2	21	15
FEB. 24	46	22	23	24	42	4	12	6	37	2	21	15
FEB. 25	46	24	25	25	42	4	12	6	37	2	21	15
FEB. 26	46	26	27	27	42	4	12	6	37	2	21	15
FEB. 27	46	28	28	29	43	4	12	6	37	2	21	15
FEB. 28	46	29	30	30	43	4	12	6	37	2	21	15

MOON 1 ☾ 12:01 A.M. TO 8:00 A.M.   **MOON 2** ☽ 8:01 A.M. TO 4:00 P.M.   **MOON 3** ● 4:01 P.M. TO 12:00 A.M.

Use only one "moon" number. Choose the column closest to your time of birth. If your place of birth is not on Eastern Standard Time, be sure to read "How to Convert to Eastern Standard Time" at the beginning of this section.

1929

March

Date & Time	SUN ☉	MOON 1 ☽	MOON 2 ◐	MOON 3 ●	MERCURY	VENUS	MARS	JUPITER	SATURN	URANUS	NEPTUNE	PLUTO
MAR. 1	46	31	32	32	43	4	13	6	37	2	21	15
MAR. 2	46	33	33	34	43	4	13	6	37	2	21	15
MAR. 3	47	34	35	35	43	4	13	6	37	2	21	15
MAR. 4	47	36	36	37	43	5	13	6	37	2	21	15
MAR. 5	47	37	38	38	43	5	13	6	37	2	21	15
MAR. 6	47	39	39	40	43	5	13	6	37	2	21	15
MAR. 7	47	41	41	42	44	5	13	6	37	2	21	15
MAR. 8	47	42	43	43	44	5	13	6	37	2	21	15
MAR. 9	47	44	44	45	44	5	13	6	37	2	21	15
MAR. 10	47	46	46	47	44	5	13	6	37	2	21	15
MAR. 11	48	47	48	1	44	5	13	6	37	2	21	15
MAR. 12	48	1	2	2	44	5	13	6	37	2	21	15
MAR. 13	48	3	4	4	44	5	13	6	37	2	21	15
MAR. 14	48	5	6	6	45	5	13	6	37	2	21	15
MAR. 15	48	7	7	8	45	6	13	6	37	2	21	15
MAR. 16	48	9	9	10	45	6	13	6	37	2	21	15
MAR. 17	48	11	11	12	45	6	13	6	37	2	21	15
MAR. 18	48	12	13	14	45	6	13	6	37	2	21	15
MAR. 19	1	14	15	16	46	6	13	6	37	2	21	15
MAR. 20	1	16	17	17	46	6	13	6	37	2	21	15
MAR. 21	1	18	19	19	46	6	14	6	37	2	21	15
MAR. 22	1	20	20	21	46	6	14	6	37	2	21	15
MAR. 23	1	22	22	23	46	6	14	6	37	2	21	15
MAR. 24	1	24	24	25	47	6	14	6	37	2	21	15
MAR. 25	2	25	26	26	47	6	14	7	37	2	21	15
MAR. 26	2	27	28	28	47	6	14	7	37	2	21	15
MAR. 27	2	29	29	30	47	6	14	7	37	2	21	15
MAR. 28	2	30	31	32	47	6	14	7	37	2	21	15
MAR. 29	2	32	33	33	48	6	14	7	37	2	21	15
MAR. 30	2	34	34	35	48	6	14	7	37	2	21	15
MAR. 31	2	35	36	36	48	6	14	7	37	2	21	15

April

Date & Time	SUN ☉	MOON 1 ☽	MOON 2 ◐	MOON 3 ●	MERCURY	VENUS	MARS	JUPITER	SATURN	URANUS	NEPTUNE	PLUTO
APR. 1	2	37	37	38	48	6	14	7	37	2	21	15
APR. 2	2	38	39	39	1	6	14	7	37	2	21	15
APR. 3	3	40	41	41	1	6	14	7	37	2	21	15
APR. 4	3	42	42	43	1	6	14	7	37	2	21	15
APR. 5	3	43	44	44	1	6	14	7	37	2	21	15
APR. 6	3	45	46	46	2	6	14	7	37	2	21	15
APR. 7	3	47	47	48	2	6	15	7	37	2	21	15
APR. 8	3	1	1	2	2	6	15	7	37	2	21	15
APR. 9	3	2	3	4	2	6	15	7	37	2	21	15
APR. 10	3	4	5	6	3	6	15	7	37	2	21	15
APR. 11	4	6	7	7	3	6	15	7	37	2	21	15
APR. 12	4	8	9	9	3	6	15	7	37	2	21	15
APR. 13	4	10	11	11	3	6	15	7	37	2	21	15
APR. 14	4	12	13	13	4	5	15	7	37	2	21	15
APR. 15	4	14	14	15	4	5	15	7	37	2	21	15
APR. 16	4	16	16	17	4	5	15	7	37	2	21	15
APR. 17	4	18	18	19	4	5	15	7	37	2	21	15
APR. 18	4	19	20	21	5	5	15	7	37	2	21	15
APR. 19	5	21	22	22	5	5	15	7	37	2	21	15
APR. 20	5	23	24	24	5	5	15	7	37	2	21	15
APR. 21	5	25	25	26	6	5	15	7	37	2	21	15
APR. 22	5	27	27	28	6	5	15	7	37	2	21	15
APR. 23	5	28	29	29	6	5	16	7	37	2	21	15
APR. 24	5	30	30	31	6	5	16	7	37	2	21	15
APR. 25	6	32	32	33	7	5	16	7	37	2	21	15
APR. 26	6	33	34	34	7	4	16	7	37	2	21	15
APR. 27	6	35	35	36	7	4	16	8	37	2	21	15
APR. 28	6	36	37	37	8	4	16	8	37	2	21	15
APR. 29	6	38	38	39	8	4	16	8	37	2	21	15
APR. 30	6	39	40	41	8	4	16	8	37	2	21	15

MOON 1 ☽ 12:01 A.M. TO 8:00 A.M.　　**MOON 2** ◐ 8:01 A.M. TO 4:00 P.M.　　**MOON 3** ● 4:01 P.M. TO 12:00 A.M.

Use only one "moon" number. Choose the column closest to your time of birth. If your place of birth is not on Eastern Standard Time, be sure to read "How to Convert to Eastern Standard Time" at the beginning of this section.

May

June

Date & Time	SUN ☉	MOON 1 ☽	MOON 2 ◐	MOON 3 ●	MERCURY	VENUS	MARS	JUPITER	SATURN	URANUS	NEPTUNE	PLUTO
MAY 1	6	41	42	42	8	4	16	8	37	2	21	15
MAY 2	6	43	43	44	9	4	16	8	37	2	21	15
MAY 3	7	44	45	45	9	4	16	8	37	2	21	15
MAY 4	7	46	47	47	9	4	16	8	37	2	21	15
MAY 5	7	48	48	1	9	4	16	8	37	2	21	15
MAY 6	7	2	2	3	9	4	16	8	37	2	21	15
MAY 7	7	3	4	5	10	4	17	8	37	2	21	15
MAY 8	7	5	6	7	10	4	17	8	37	2	21	15
MAY 9	7	7	8	9	10	4	17	8	37	2	21	15
MAY 10	7	9	10	11	10	4	17	8	37	2	21	15
MAY 11	8	11	12	13	10	4	17	8	37	2	21	15
MAY 12	8	13	14	15	11	4	17	8	37	2	21	15
MAY 13	8	15	16	16	11	4	17	8	37	2	21	15
MAY 14	8	17	18	18	11	4	17	8	37	2	21	15
MAY 15	8	19	20	20	11	4	17	8	37	2	21	15
MAY 16	8	21	21	22	11	4	17	8	37	2	21	15
MAY 17	8	23	23	24	11	4	17	8	37	2	21	15
MAY 18	8	24	25	26	11	4	17	8	37	2	21	15
MAY 19	9	26	27	27	12	4	17	8	37	2	21	15
MAY 20	9	28	28	29	12	4	17	8	37	2	21	15
MAY 21	9	29	30	31	12	4	18	8	37	2	21	15
MAY 22	9	31	32	32	12	4	18	8	37	2	21	15
MAY 23	9	33	33	34	12	4	18	8	37	2	21	15
MAY 24	9	34	35	35	12	4	18	8	37	2	21	15
MAY 25	10	36	36	37	12	4	18	8	37	2	21	15
MAY 26	10	37	38	39	12	4	18	8	37	2	21	15
MAY 27	10	39	40	40	12	4	18	8	37	2	21	15
MAY 28	10	41	41	42	12	4	18	8	37	2	21	15
MAY 29	10	42	43	43	12	5	18	9	37	2	21	15
MAY 30	10	44	44	45	12	5	18	9	37	2	21	15
MAY 31	10	45	46	47	12	5	18	9	37	2	21	15

Date & Time	SUN ☉	MOON 1 ☽	MOON 2 ◐	MOON 3 ●	MERCURY	VENUS	MARS	JUPITER	SATURN	URANUS	NEPTUNE	PLUTO
JUN. 1	10	47	48	48	12	5	18	9	37	2	21	15
JUN. 2	10	1	1	2	12	5	18	9	37	2	21	15
JUN. 3	11	3	3	4	12	5	19	9	37	2	21	15
JUN. 4	11	5	5	6	12	5	19	9	37	2	21	15
JUN. 5	11	6	7	8	12	5	19	9	37	2	21	15
JUN. 6	11	8	9	10	12	5	19	9	37	2	21	15
JUN. 7	11	10	11	12	12	5	19	9	37	2	21	15
JUN. 8	11	12	13	14	11	5	19	9	37	2	21	15
JUN. 9	11	14	15	16	11	6	19	9	37	2	21	15
JUN. 10	11	16	17	18	11	6	19	9	37	2	21	15
JUN. 11	12	18	19	20	11	6	19	9	37	2	21	15
JUN. 12	12	20	21	22	11	6	19	9	37	2	21	15
JUN. 13	12	22	23	23	11	6	19	9	37	2	21	15
JUN. 14	12	24	25	25	11	6	19	9	37	2	21	15
JUN. 15	12	26	26	27	11	6	19	9	37	2	21	15
JUN. 16	12	27	28	29	11	6	20	9	37	2	21	15
JUN. 17	12	29	30	30	11	6	20	9	37	2	21	15
JUN. 18	12	31	31	32	11	6	20	9	37	2	21	15
JUN. 19	13	32	33	33	11	7	20	9	37	2	21	15
JUN. 20	13	34	34	35	11	7	20	9	37	2	21	15
JUN. 21	13	35	36	37	11	7	20	9	37	2	21	15
JUN. 22	13	37	38	38	11	7	20	9	37	2	21	15
JUN. 23	13	39	39	40	11	7	20	9	37	2	21	15
JUN. 24	13	40	41	41	11	7	20	9	37	2	21	15
JUN. 25	14	42	42	43	11	7	20	9	37	2	21	15
JUN. 26	14	43	44	44	11	7	20	9	37	2	21	15
JUN. 27	14	45	46	46	11	8	20	9	37	2	21	15
JUN. 28	14	47	47	48	11	8	20	9	37	2	21	15
JUN. 29	14	48	1	2	11	8	21	9	36	2	21	15
JUN. 30	14	2	3	3	11	8	21	9	36	2	21	15

MOON 1 ☽ 12:01 A.M. TO 8:00 A.M.   **MOON 2 ◐ 8:01 A.M. TO 4:00 P.M.**   **MOON 3 ● 4:01 P.M. TO 12:00 A.M.**
Use only one "moon" number. Choose the column closest to your time of birth. If your place of birth is not on Eastern Standard Time, be sure to read "How to Convert to Eastern Standard Time" at the beginning of this section.

1929

July

Date & Time	SUN	MOON 1	MOON 2	MOON 3	MERCURY	VENUS	MARS	JUPITER	SATURN	URANUS	NEPTUNE	PLUTO
JUL. 1	14	4	4	5	11	8	21	10	36	2	21	15
JUL. 2	14	6	6	7	11	8	21	10	36	2	21	15
JUL. 3	15	8	8	9	12	8	21	10	36	2	21	15
JUL. 4	15	10	10	11	12	8	21	10	36	2	21	15
JUL. 5	15	12	12	13	12	9	21	10	36	2	21	15
JUL. 6	15	14	14	15	12	9	21	10	36	2	21	15
JUL. 7	15	16	16	17	12	9	21	10	36	2	21	15
JUL. 8	15	18	18	19	12	9	21	10	36	2	21	15
JUL. 9	15	20	20	21	12	9	21	10	36	2	21	15
JUL. 10	15	22	22	23	13	9	21	10	36	2	21	15
JUL. 11	16	23	24	25	13	9	22	10	36	2	21	15
JUL. 12	16	25	26	26	13	10	22	10	36	2	21	15
JUL. 13	16	27	28	28	13	10	22	10	36	2	21	15
JUL. 14	16	29	29	30	13	10	22	10	36	2	21	15
JUL. 15	16	30	31	31	14	10	22	10	36	2	21	15
JUL. 16	16	32	32	33	14	10	22	10	36	2	21	15
JUL. 17	16	33	34	35	14	10	22	10	36	2	21	15
JUL. 18	16	35	36	36	14	10	22	10	36	2	21	15
JUL. 19	17	37	37	38	15	10	22	10	36	2	21	15
JUL. 20	17	38	39	39	15	11	22	10	36	2	21	15
JUL. 21	17	40	40	41	15	11	22	10	36	2	21	15
JUL. 22	17	41	42	42	15	11	22	10	36	2	21	15
JUL. 23	17	43	44	44	16	11	22	10	36	2	21	15
JUL. 24	17	45	45	46	16	11	23	10	36	2	21	15
JUL. 25	17	46	47	47	16	11	23	10	36	2	21	15
JUL. 26	18	48	1	1	17	11	23	10	36	2	21	15
JUL. 27	18	2	3	3	17	12	23	10	36	2	21	15
JUL. 28	18	3	4	5	17	12	23	10	36	2	21	15
JUL. 29	18	5	6	6	17	12	23	10	36	2	21	15
JUL. 30	18	7	8	8	18	12	23	10	36	2	21	15
JUL. 31	18	9	9	10	18	12	23	10	36	2	21	15

August

Date & Time	SUN	MOON 1	MOON 2	MOON 3	MERCURY	VENUS	MARS	JUPITER	SATURN	URANUS	NEPTUNE	PLUTO
AUG. 1	18	11	11	12	18	12	23	10	36	2	21	15
AUG. 2	18	13	13	14	19	13	23	10	36	2	21	15
AUG. 3	19	15	15	16	19	13	23	10	36	2	21	15
AUG. 4	19	17	17	18	19	13	23	10	36	2	21	15
AUG. 5	19	19	19	20	19	13	24	10	36	2	21	15
AUG. 6	19	21	21	22	20	13	24	10	36	2	21	15
AUG. 7	19	23	23	24	20	13	24	10	36	2	21	15
AUG. 8	19	25	25	26	20	13	24	10	36	2	21	15
AUG. 9	19	26	27	28	20	14	24	10	36	2	21	15
AUG. 10	19	28	29	29	21	14	24	11	36	2	21	15
AUG. 11	20	30	30	31	21	14	24	11	36	2	21	15
AUG. 12	20	31	32	33	21	14	24	11	36	2	21	15
AUG. 13	20	33	34	34	21	14	24	11	36	2	21	15
AUG. 14	20	35	35	36	22	14	24	11	36	2	21	15
AUG. 15	20	36	37	37	22	14	24	11	36	2	21	15
AUG. 16	20	38	38	39	22	15	24	11	36	2	21	15
AUG. 17	20	39	40	40	22	15	25	11	36	2	21	15
AUG. 18	20	41	42	42	23	15	25	11	36	2	21	15
AUG. 19	21	43	43	44	23	15	25	11	36	2	21	15
AUG. 20	21	44	45	45	23	15	25	11	36	2	21	15
AUG. 21	21	46	46	47	23	15	25	11	36	2	21	15
AUG. 22	21	48	48	1	23	16	25	11	36	2	21	15
AUG. 23	21	1	2	2	24	16	25	11	36	2	21	15
AUG. 24	21	3	4	4	24	16	25	11	36	2	21	15
AUG. 25	21	5	5	6	24	16	25	11	36	2	21	16
AUG. 26	22	7	7	8	24	16	25	11	36	2	21	16
AUG. 27	22	8	9	10	24	16	25	11	36	2	21	16
AUG. 28	22	10	11	11	25	16	26	11	36	2	21	16
AUG. 29	22	12	13	13	25	17	26	11	36	2	21	16
AUG. 30	22	14	15	15	25	17	26	11	36	2	21	16
AUG. 31	22	16	17	17	25	17	26	11	36	2	21	16

MOON 1 ☽ 12:01 A.M. TO 8:00 A.M.   **MOON 2** ☾ 8:01 A.M. TO 4:00 P.M.   **MOON 3** ● 4:01 P.M. TO 12:00 A.M.

Use only one "moon" number. Choose the column closest to your time of birth. If your place of birth is not on Eastern Standard Time, be sure to read "How to Convert to Eastern Standard Time" at the beginning of this section.

1929

September · October

Date & Time	SUN	MOON 1	MOON 2	MOON 3	MERCURY	VENUS	MARS	JUPITER	SATURN	URANUS	NEPTUNE	PLUTO
SEP. 1	22	18	19	19	25	17	26	11	36	2	21	16
SEP. 2	22	20	21	21	25	17	26	11	36	2	21	16
SEP. 3	23	22	22	23	26	17	26	11	36	2	21	16
SEP. 4	23	24	24	25	26	18	26	11	36	2	21	16
SEP. 5	23	26	26	27	26	18	26	11	36	2	21	16
SEP. 6	23	27	28	29	26	18	26	11	36	2	21	16
SEP. 7	23	29	30	30	26	18	26	11	36	2	21	16
SEP. 8	23	31	31	32	26	18	26	11	36	2	21	16
SEP. 9	23	33	33	34	27	18	27	11	36	2	21	16
SEP. 10	23	34	35	35	27	18	27	11	36	2	21	16
SEP. 11	24	36	36	37	27	19	27	11	36	2	21	16
SEP. 12	24	37	38	38	27	19	27	11	36	2	21	16
SEP. 13	24	39	39	40	27	19	27	11	36	2	21	16
SEP. 14	24	40	41	42	27	19	27	11	36	2	21	16
SEP. 15	24	42	43	43	27	19	27	11	36	2	21	16
SEP. 16	24	44	44	45	28	19	27	11	36	2	21	16
SEP. 17	24	45	46	46	28	20	27	11	36	2	21	16
SEP. 18	24	47	48	48	28	20	27	11	36	2	21	16
SEP. 19	25	1	1	2	28	20	27	11	36	2	21	16
SEP. 20	25	3	3	4	28	20	28	11	36	2	21	16
SEP. 21	25	4	5	6	28	20	28	11	36	2	21	16
SEP. 22	25	6	7	7	28	20	28	11	36	2	21	16
SEP. 23	25	8	9	9	28	21	28	11	36	2	21	16
SEP. 24	25	10	10	11	28	21	28	11	36	2	21	16
SEP. 25	26	12	12	13	28	21	28	11	36	2	21	16
SEP. 26	26	14	14	15	28	21	28	11	36	2	21	16
SEP. 27	26	15	16	17	28	21	28	11	36	2	21	16
SEP. 28	26	17	18	19	28	21	28	11	36	2	21	16
SEP. 29	26	19	20	21	28	22	28	11	36	2	21	16
SEP. 30	26	21	22	22	28	22	28	11	36	2	21	16

Date & Time	SUN	MOON 1	MOON 2	MOON 3	MERCURY	VENUS	MARS	JUPITER	SATURN	URANUS	NEPTUNE	PLUTO
OCT. 1	26	23	24	24	28	22	28	11	36	2	21	16
OCT. 2	26	25	25	26	28	22	29	11	36	2	21	16
OCT. 3	27	27	27	28	28	22	29	11	36	2	21	16
OCT. 4	27	28	29	30	28	22	29	11	36	2	21	16
OCT. 5	27	30	31	31	27	23	29	11	36	2	21	16
OCT. 6	27	32	32	33	27	23	29	11	36	2	21	16
OCT. 7	27	34	34	35	27	23	29	11	36	2	21	16
OCT. 8	27	35	36	36	27	23	29	11	36	2	21	16
OCT. 9	27	37	37	38	27	23	29	11	36	2	21	16
OCT. 10	27	38	39	39	27	23	29	11	36	2	21	16
OCT. 11	28	40	40	41	26	23	29	11	36	2	21	16
OCT. 12	28	42	42	43	26	24	29	11	36	2	21	16
OCT. 13	28	43	44	44	26	24	30	11	36	2	21	16
OCT. 14	28	45	45	46	26	24	30	11	36	2	21	16
OCT. 15	28	46	47	48	26	24	30	11	36	2	21	16
OCT. 16	28	48	1	1	26	24	30	11	36	2	21	16
OCT. 17	28	2	3	3	26	24	30	11	36	2	21	16
OCT. 18	28	4	4	5	26	25	30	11	36	2	21	16
OCT. 19	29	6	6	7	26	25	30	11	36	2	21	16
OCT. 20	29	7	8	9	26	25	30	11	36	2	21	16
OCT. 21	29	9	10	11	26	25	30	11	36	2	21	16
OCT. 22	29	11	12	12	26	25	30	11	36	2	21	16
OCT. 23	29	13	14	14	26	25	30	11	36	2	21	16
OCT. 24	29	15	16	16	27	26	31	11	36	2	21	16
OCT. 25	29	17	18	18	27	26	31	11	36	2	21	16
OCT. 26	30	19	19	20	27	26	31	11	37	2	21	16
OCT. 27	30	21	21	22	27	26	31	11	37	2	21	16
OCT. 28	30	22	23	24	27	26	31	11	37	2	21	16
OCT. 29	30	24	25	26	27	26	31	11	37	2	21	16
OCT. 30	30	26	27	27	28	27	31	11	37	2	21	16
OCT. 31	30	28	28	29	28	27	31	11	37	2	21	16

MOON 1 ☽ 12:01 A.M. TO 8:00 A.M.   **MOON 2** ☽ 8:01 A.M. TO 4:00 P.M.   **MOON 3** ● 4:01 P.M. TO 12:00 A.M.
Use only one "moon" number. Choose the column closest to your time of birth. If your place of birth is not on Eastern Standard Time, be sure to read "How to Convert to Eastern Standard Time" at the beginning of this section.

November

Date & Time	SUN	MOON 1	MOON 2	MOON 3	MERCURY	VENUS	MARS	JUPITER	SATURN	URANUS	NEPTUNE	PLUTO
NOV. 1	30	30	30	31	28	27	31	11	37	2	21	16
NOV. 2	30	31	32	32	28	27	31	11	37	2	21	16
NOV. 3	31	33	34	34	28	27	32	11	37	2	21	16
NOV. 4	31	35	35	36	29	27	32	11	37	2	21	16
NOV. 5	31	36	37	37	29	28	32	11	37	2	21	16
NOV. 6	31	38	38	39	29	28	32	11	37	2	21	16
NOV. 7	31	39	40	40	29	28	32	11	37	2	21	16
NOV. 8	31	41	42	42	29	28	32	11	37	2	21	16
NOV. 9	31	43	43	44	30	28	32	11	37	2	21	16
NOV. 10	31	44	45	45	30	28	32	11	37	2	21	16
NOV. 11	31	46	46	47	30	29	32	11	37	2	21	16
NOV. 12	32	47	48	1	30	29	32	11	37	2	21	16
NOV. 13	32	1	2	2	31	29	32	11	37	2	21	16
NOV. 14	32	3	4	4	31	29	33	11	37	2	21	16
NOV. 15	32	5	5	6	31	29	33	11	37	2	21	16
NOV. 16	32	7	7	8	31	29	33	11	37	2	21	16
NOV. 17	32	9	9	10	31	30	33	11	37	2	21	16
NOV. 18	32	11	11	12	32	30	33	11	37	2	21	16
NOV. 19	33	12	13	14	32	30	33	11	37	2	21	16
NOV. 20	33	14	15	16	32	30	33	11	37	2	21	16
NOV. 21	33	16	17	18	32	30	33	11	37	2	21	16
NOV. 22	33	18	19	20	32	30	33	11	37	2	21	16
NOV. 23	33	20	21	21	33	31	33	11	37	2	21	16
NOV. 24	33	22	23	23	33	31	34	11	37	2	21	16
NOV. 25	34	24	24	25	33	31	34	11	37	2	21	16
NOV. 26	34	26	26	27	33	31	34	11	37	2	21	16
NOV. 27	34	27	28	29	34	31	34	11	37	2	21	16
NOV. 28	34	29	30	30	34	31	34	11	37	2	21	16
NOV. 29	34	31	31	32	34	32	34	11	37	2	21	16
NOV. 30	34	32	33	34	34	32	34	11	37	2	21	16

December

Date & Time	SUN	MOON 1	MOON 2	MOON 3	MERCURY	VENUS	MARS	JUPITER	SATURN	URANUS	NEPTUNE	PLUTO
DEC. 1	34	34	35	35	34	32	34	11	37	2	21	16
DEC. 2	34	36	36	37	35	32	34	11	37	2	21	16
DEC. 3	35	37	38	38	35	32	34	10	37	2	21	16
DEC. 4	35	39	39	40	35	32	34	10	37	2	21	16
DEC. 5	35	41	41	42	35	33	35	10	37	2	21	16
DEC. 6	35	42	43	43	35	33	35	10	37	2	21	16
DEC. 7	35	44	44	45	36	33	35	10	37	2	21	16
DEC. 8	35	45	46	46	36	33	35	10	37	2	21	16
DEC. 9	35	47	47	48	36	33	35	10	37	2	21	16
DEC. 10	35	1	1	2	36	33	35	10	37	2	21	16
DEC. 11	36	2	3	3	36	34	35	10	37	2	21	16
DEC. 12	36	4	5	5	37	34	35	10	37	2	21	16
DEC. 13	36	6	6	7	37	34	35	10	37	2	21	16
DEC. 14	36	8	8	9	37	34	35	10	37	2	21	16
DEC. 15	36	10	10	11	37	34	36	10	37	2	21	16
DEC. 16	36	12	12	13	38	34	36	10	37	2	21	16
DEC. 17	36	14	14	15	38	35	36	10	37	2	21	16
DEC. 18	36	16	16	17	38	35	36	10	37	2	21	16
DEC. 19	37	18	18	19	38	35	36	10	37	2	21	15
DEC. 20	37	20	20	21	38	35	36	10	37	2	21	15
DEC. 21	37	22	22	23	39	35	36	10	37	2	21	15
DEC. 22	37	23	24	25	39	35	36	10	37	2	21	15
DEC. 23	37	25	26	26	39	36	36	10	37	2	21	15
DEC. 24	37	27	28	28	39	36	36	10	37	2	21	15
DEC. 25	37	29	29	30	39	36	37	10	37	2	21	15
DEC. 26	38	30	31	32	40	36	37	10	37	2	21	15
DEC. 27	38	32	33	33	40	36	37	10	37	2	21	15
DEC. 28	38	34	34	35	40	36	37	10	37	2	21	15
DEC. 29	38	35	36	36	40	37	37	10	37	2	21	15
DEC. 30	38	37	37	38	40	37	37	10	37	2	21	15
DEC. 31	38	38	39	40	41	37	37	10	37	2	21	15

MOON 1 ☽ 12:01 A.M. TO 8:00 A.M.   **MOON 2** ☽ 8:01 A.M. TO 4:00 P.M.   **MOON 3** ● 4:01 P.M. TO 12:00 A.M.
Use only one "moon" number. Choose the column closest to your time of birth. If your place of birth is not on
Eastern Standard Time, be sure to read "How to Convert to Eastern Standard Time" at the beginning of this section.

1930-1939

1930s

Mickey Mantle

* * * BORN OCTOBER 21, 1931 * * *

Brief Bio: Mickey Mantle was a legendary New York Yankees player who won seven World Championships and set many World Series records.

Personology Profile:

SUN ON THE CUSP OF DRAMA AND CRITICISM
(LIBRA-SCORPIO CUSP) OCTOBER 19-25

*

Most born on this cusp have a strong opinion on almost any matter, one which they do not hesitate in making known. Hard to fool, you must present a sound and cogent argument to have them agree with your point of view. Lovers of excitement, travel and challenge, they lend individuality and passion to all of their endeavors.

MERCURY ON THE CUSP OF DRAMA AND CRITICISM
(LIBRA-SCORPIO CUSP)

*

Such individuals must be careful that constant and merciless criticism on their part does not drag them down or lead others to reject their ideas as unconstructive and negative. They have a great deal to offer but it is not their message which needs improvement but their delivery. Taking the feelings of others into account is important for them to learn.

MARS IN THE WEEK OF CHARM
(SCORPIO III)

*

Mars is given an extra seductive attraction in this position. If encouraged, these folks are likely to take over the lives of weaker family members and friends. Thus they are capable of making most or even all of the important decisions for the other person. In doing so they create dependencies which might not be so healthy for either party in the future.

MOON IN THE WEEK OF ACCEPTANCE
(AQUARIUS III)

*

Peculiar likes and dislikes and idiosyncrasy in general may be the bane of those with this Moon position. Irrational prejudices can surface, causing difficulties for all in their immediate environment. If they can become more emotionally accepting, they will have accomplished one of their chief tasks in life. However, they must still remember to maintain ego boundaries and not go overboard in giving their feelings away.

VENUS IN THE WEEK OF INTENSITY
(SCORPIO I)

*

Seduction figures prominently here. Masters in attracting and controlling the opposite sex, those with Venus in this week are born flirts and specialists in the arts of love. Because of the intensity with which they love they are not easily forgotten. They must learn, however, to back off and allow the other person to express their true feelings or risk losing them.

JUPITER IN THE WEEK OF BALANCED STRENGTH
(LEO II)

*

Success is most likely to be the reward of honesty and steadfastness of purpose. This position finds Jupiter in its most noble, upright and courageous state. Underhanded methods of any sort will not be rewarded in the long run and can result in ruin. It is not necessary, however, to keep to the straight and narrow since exploration and travel usually figure here also.

SATURN IN THE WEEK OF DETERMINATION
(CAPRICORN II)

✱

Care will have to be taken to keep one's heart open. Too often Capricorn's presence here can lead to a certain ruthlessness and disregard for the feelings of others. Should this occur, it can result in cutting such an individual off from the world and fixing them in a lonely stance. Such isolation is detrimental and can be combated by a more caring and empathic attitude.

URANUS IN THE WEEK OF THE STAR
(ARIES II)

✱

Uranus strives for recognition and attention, sometimes using rather spectacular means to get it. If ignored, such individuals may use the element of surprise to garner attention, saving up their energy and unleashing it on a gathering at the most opportune, albeit awkward, moment. Such unforgettable and regrettable displays may earn them a reputation for theatrical behavior.

NEPTUNE IN THE WEEK OF SYSTEM BUILDERS
(VIRGO I)

✱

If one's ability to structure thoughts and activities works hand in hand with imaginative powers, this Neptune position can be extremely productive. Certainly all artistic activities are favored here, as long as they are ordered and well-planned. Care must be taken, however, that the desire to control creative impulses does not dampen creativity or lead to repetitive or compulsive behavior.

PLUTO IN THE WEEK OF THE PERSUADER
(CANCER III)

✱

The problem here is usually for the other person, since those with Pluto in this position will not be denied. They may be forceful or gently seductive but are able to win the hearts and minds of those they fix their sights on. Able to quickly adjust their tactics to their quarry, chances of escape are usually quite slim, the capture swift and often quite pleasurable.

Some Highlights of the Decade 1930-1939

- ENGLAND'S KING EDWARD VIII ABDICATES THE THRONE TO MARRY AN AMERICAN, MRS. WALLIS SIMPSON, AND THE COUPLE IS EXILED FROM BRITAIN.

- AVIATOR AMELIA EARHART DEPARTS FROM MIAMI, FLORIDA, IN AN ATTEMPT TO BE THE FIRST WOMAN TO FLY AROUND THE WORLD; HER PLANE MYSTERIOUSLY DISAPPEARS AND THE MOST EXTENSIVE RESCUE SEARCH MISSION IN US HISTORY IS LAUNCHED.

- GERMAN DIRIGIBLE HINDENBERG, THE LARGEST AIRCRAFT EVER TO FLY, BURST INTO FLAMES AS IT TRIED TO LAND IN LAKEHURST, NEW JERSEY, AFTER A FLIGHT FROM FRANKFURT, GERMANY.

- THE PULITZER PRIZE WAS AWARDED TO PLAYWRIGHT THORNTON WILDER FOR *OUR TOWN*.

- LEGENDARY BLUES GUITARIST AND "KING OF THE MISSISSIPPI DELTA BLUES" ROBERT JOHNSON DIES IN MISSISSIPPI, AFTER BEING POISONED.

- ORSON WELLES BROADCASTS "WAR OF THE WORLDS," PANICKING RADIO LISTENERS, WHO BELIEVE THAT THE SIMULATED MARTIAN INVASION OF NEW JERSEY IS REAL.

1930

January

Date & Time	SUN	MOON 1	MOON 2	MOON 3	MERCURY	VENUS	MARS	JUPITER	SATURN	URANUS	NEPTUNE	PLUTO
JAN. 1	38	40	41	41	41	37	37	10	37	2	21	15
JAN. 2	38	42	42	43	41	37	37	10	37	2	21	15
JAN. 3	39	43	44	44	41	37	37	10	37	2	21	15
JAN. 4	39	45	45	46	41	38	38	10	38	2	21	15
JAN. 5	39	46	47	48	41	38	38	10	38	2	21	15
JAN. 6	39	48	1	1	42	38	38	10	38	2	21	15
JAN. 7	39	2	2	3	42	38	38	10	38	2	21	15
JAN. 8	39	3	4	5	42	38	38	10	38	2	21	15
JAN. 9	39	5	6	6	42	38	38	10	38	2	21	15
JAN. 10	40	7	8	8	42	39	38	10	38	2	21	15
JAN. 11	40	9	9	10	42	39	38	10	38	2	21	15
JAN. 12	40	11	11	12	42	39	38	10	38	2	21	15
JAN. 13	40	13	13	14	42	39	38	10	38	2	21	15
JAN. 14	40	15	15	16	42	39	39	10	38	2	21	15
JAN. 15	40	17	17	18	42	39	39	10	38	2	21	15
JAN. 16	40	19	19	20	42	40	39	10	38	2	21	15
JAN. 17	41	21	21	22	42	40	39	10	38	2	21	15
JAN. 18	41	23	23	24	42	40	39	10	38	2	21	15
JAN. 19	41	25	25	26	42	40	39	10	38	2	21	15
JAN. 20	41	27	27	28	41	40	39	10	38	2	21	15
JAN. 21	41	28	29	29	41	41	39	10	38	2	21	15
JAN. 22	41	30	31	31	41	41	39	10	38	2	21	15
JAN. 23	42	32	32	33	41	41	39	10	38	2	21	15
JAN. 24	42	33	34	34	41	41	40	10	38	2	21	15
JAN. 25	42	35	35	36	41	41	40	10	38	2	21	15
JAN. 26	42	37	37	38	40	41	40	10	38	2	21	15
JAN. 27	42	38	39	39	40	42	40	10	38	2	21	15
JAN. 28	42	40	40	41	40	42	40	10	38	2	21	15
JAN. 29	42	41	42	42	40	42	40	10	38	2	21	15
JAN. 30	42	43	43	44	40	42	40	10	38	2	21	15
JAN. 31	43	44	45	46	40	42	40	10	38	2	21	15

February

Date & Time	SUN	MOON 1	MOON 2	MOON 3	MERCURY	VENUS	MARS	JUPITER	SATURN	URANUS	NEPTUNE	PLUTO
FEB. 1	43	46	47	47	40	42	40	10	38	2	21	15
FEB. 2	43	48	48	1	40	43	40	10	38	2	21	15
FEB. 3	43	1	2	2	40	43	41	10	38	2	21	15
FEB. 4	43	3	3	4	40	43	41	10	38	2	21	15
FEB. 5	43	5	5	6	40	43	41	10	38	2	21	15
FEB. 6	43	6	7	8	40	43	41	10	38	2	21	15
FEB. 7	43	8	9	9	40	43	41	10	38	2	21	15
FEB. 8	44	10	11	11	40	44	41	10	38	2	21	15
FEB. 9	44	12	12	13	40	44	41	10	38	2	21	15
FEB. 10	44	14	14	15	40	44	41	10	38	2	21	15
FEB. 11	44	16	16	17	40	44	41	10	38	2	21	15
FEB. 12	44	18	18	19	41	44	42	10	38	2	21	15
FEB. 13	44	20	21	21	41	44	42	10	38	2	21	15
FEB. 14	44	22	23	23	41	45	42	10	38	2	21	15
FEB. 15	44	24	24	25	41	45	42	10	38	2	21	15
FEB. 16	45	26	26	27	41	45	42	10	38	2	21	15
FEB. 17	45	28	28	29	41	45	42	10	38	2	21	15
FEB. 18	45	29	30	31	41	45	42	10	38	2	21	15
FEB. 19	45	31	32	32	41	45	42	10	38	2	21	15
FEB. 20	45	33	33	34	42	46	42	10	38	2	21	15
FEB. 21	45	34	35	36	42	46	42	10	38	2	21	15
FEB. 22	45	36	37	37	42	46	43	10	38	2	21	15
FEB. 23	46	38	38	39	42	46	43	10	38	2	21	15
FEB. 24	46	39	40	40	42	46	43	10	38	2	21	15
FEB. 25	46	41	41	42	42	46	43	10	38	2	21	15
FEB. 26	46	42	43	43	43	47	43	10	38	2	21	15
FEB. 27	46	44	45	45	43	47	43	10	38	2	21	15
FEB. 28	46	46	46	47	43	47	43	10	38	2	21	15

MOON 1 ☽ 12:01 A.M. TO 8:00 A.M.　　**MOON 2** ☽ 8:01 A.M. TO 4:00 P.M.　　**MOON 3** ● 4:01 P.M. TO 12:00 A.M.
Use only one "moon" number. Choose the column closest to your time of birth. If your place of birth is not on Eastern Standard Time, be sure to read "How to Convert to Eastern Standard Time" at the beginning of this section.

March

Date & Time	SUN ☉	MOON 1 ◗	MOON 2 ◐	MOON 3 ●	MERCURY	VENUS	MARS	JUPITER	SATURN	URANUS	NEPTUNE	PLUTO
MAR. 1	46	47	48	48	43	47	43	10	38	2	21	15
MAR. 2	46	1	1	2	43	47	43	10	38	2	21	15
MAR. 3	47	3	3	4	44	47	44	10	38	2	21	15
MAR. 4	47	4	5	5	44	48	44	10	38	2	21	15
MAR. 5	47	6	7	7	44	48	44	10	38	2	21	15
MAR. 6	47	8	8	9	44	48	44	10	38	2	21	15
MAR. 7	47	9	10	11	44	48	44	10	38	2	21	15
MAR. 8	47	11	12	13	45	48	44	10	38	2	21	15
MAR. 9	47	13	14	14	45	48	44	10	38	2	21	15
MAR. 10	47	15	16	16	45	1	44	10	38	2	21	15
MAR. 11	48	17	18	18	45	1	44	10	38	2	21	15
MAR. 12	48	19	20	20	45	1	44	10	38	2	21	15
MAR. 13	48	21	22	22	46	1	45	10	38	2	21	15
MAR. 14	48	23	24	24	46	1	45	10	38	2	21	15
MAR. 15	48	25	26	26	46	1	45	10	38	2	21	15
MAR. 16	48	27	27	28	46	2	45	10	38	2	21	15
MAR. 17	48	29	29	30	47	2	45	10	38	2	21	15
MAR. 18	48	30	31	32	47	2	45	10	38	2	21	15
MAR. 19	1	32	33	33	47	2	45	10	38	2	21	15
MAR. 20	1	34	34	35	47	2	45	10	38	2	21	15
MAR. 21	1	36	36	37	48	2	45	10	38	2	21	15
MAR. 22	1	37	38	38	48	3	45	10	38	2	21	15
MAR. 23	1	39	39	40	48	3	46	10	38	2	21	15
MAR. 24	1	40	41	41	48	3	46	10	38	2	21	15
MAR. 25	2	42	42	43	1	3	46	10	38	2	21	15
MAR. 26	2	44	44	45	1	3	46	10	38	2	21	15
MAR. 27	2	45	46	46	1	3	46	10	38	2	21	15
MAR. 28	2	47	47	48	1	3	46	10	38	2	21	15
MAR. 29	2	48	1	2	2	4	46	10	38	2	21	15
MAR. 30	2	2	3	3	2	4	46	10	38	2	21	15
MAR. 31	2	4	4	5	2	4	46	11	39	2	21	15

April

Date & Time	SUN ☉	MOON 1 ◗	MOON 2 ◐	MOON 3 ●	MERCURY	VENUS	MARS	JUPITER	SATURN	URANUS	NEPTUNE	PLUTO
APR. 1	2	6	6	7	2	4	47	11	39	2	21	15
APR. 2	2	7	8	8	3	4	47	11	39	2	21	15
APR. 3	3	9	10	10	3	4	47	11	39	2	21	15
APR. 4	3	11	11	12	3	5	47	11	39	2	21	15
APR. 5	3	13	13	14	3	5	47	11	39	3	21	15
APR. 6	3	15	15	16	4	5	47	11	39	3	21	15
APR. 7	3	16	17	18	4	5	47	11	39	3	21	15
APR. 8	3	18	19	20	4	5	47	11	39	3	21	15
APR. 9	3	20	21	22	5	5	47	11	39	3	21	15
APR. 10	3	22	23	24	5	6	47	11	39	3	21	15
APR. 11	4	24	25	25	5	6	48	11	39	3	21	15
APR. 12	4	26	27	27	5	6	48	11	39	3	21	15
APR. 13	4	28	29	29	6	6	48	11	39	3	21	15
APR. 14	4	30	30	31	6	6	48	11	39	3	21	15
APR. 15	4	32	32	33	6	6	48	11	39	3	21	15
APR. 16	4	33	34	34	6	7	48	11	39	3	21	15
APR. 17	4	35	36	36	7	7	48	11	39	3	21	15
APR. 18	4	37	37	38	7	7	48	11	39	3	21	15
APR. 19	5	38	39	39	7	7	48	11	39	3	21	15
APR. 20	5	40	40	41	7	7	48	11	39	3	21	15
APR. 21	5	41	42	42	7	7	1	11	39	3	21	15
APR. 22	5	43	44	44	8	8	1	11	39	3	21	15
APR. 23	5	45	45	46	8	8	1	11	39	3	21	15
APR. 24	5	46	47	47	8	8	1	11	39	3	21	15
APR. 25	6	48	48	1	8	8	1	11	39	3	21	15
APR. 26	6	2	2	3	8	8	1	11	39	3	21	15
APR. 27	6	3	4	4	9	8	1	11	39	3	21	15
APR. 28	6	5	6	6	9	9	1	11	39	3	21	15
APR. 29	6	7	7	8	9	9	1	11	39	3	21	15
APR. 30	6	9	9	10	9	9	2	11	39	3	21	15

MOON 1 ◗ 12:01 A.M. TO 8:00 A.M.   **MOON 2** ◐ 8:01 A.M. TO 4:00 P.M.   **MOON 3** ● 4:01 P.M. TO 12:00 A.M.

Use only one "moon" number. Choose the column closest to your time of birth. If your place of birth is not on Eastern Standard Time, be sure to read "How to Convert to Eastern Standard Time" at the beginning of this section.

1930

May

June

Date & Time	SUN	MOON 1	MOON 2	MOON 3	MERCURY	VENUS	MARS	JUPITER	SATURN	URANUS	NEPTUNE	PLUTO
MAY 1	6	10	11	12	9	9	2	11	39	3	21	15
MAY 2	6	12	13	14	9	9	2	11	39	3	21	15
MAY 3	7	14	15	15	9	9	2	11	39	3	21	15
MAY 4	7	16	17	17	9	10	2	11	39	3	21	15
MAY 5	7	18	19	19	9	10	2	11	39	3	21	15
MAY 6	7	20	20	21	9	10	2	11	39	3	21	15
MAY 7	7	22	22	23	9	10	2	11	39	3	21	15
MAY 8	7	24	24	25	9	10	2	11	39	3	21	15
MAY 9	7	25	26	27	9	10	2	12	39	3	21	15
MAY 10	7	27	28	29	9	11	3	12	39	3	21	15
MAY 11	8	29	30	30	9	11	3	12	39	3	21	15
MAY 12	8	31	31	32	9	11	3	12	39	3	21	15
MAY 13	8	33	33	34	9	11	3	12	39	3	21	15
MAY 14	8	34	35	35	9	11	3	12	38	3	21	15
MAY 15	8	36	37	37	9	11	3	12	38	3	21	15
MAY 16	8	38	38	39	9	12	3	12	38	3	21	15
MAY 17	8	39	40	40	9	12	3	12	38	3	21	15
MAY 18	8	41	41	42	9	12	3	12	38	3	21	15
MAY 19	9	42	43	44	9	12	3	12	38	3	21	15
MAY 20	9	44	45	45	9	12	4	12	38	3	21	15
MAY 21	9	46	46	47	9	12	4	12	38	3	21	15
MAY 22	9	47	48	48	9	12	4	12	38	3	21	15
MAY 23	9	1	1	2	9	13	4	12	38	3	21	15
MAY 24	9	3	3	4	9	13	4	12	38	3	21	15
MAY 25	10	4	5	5	8	13	4	12	38	3	21	15
MAY 26	10	6	7	7	8	13	4	12	38	3	21	15
MAY 27	10	8	8	9	8	13	4	12	38	3	21	15
MAY 28	10	10	10	11	8	13	4	12	38	3	21	15
MAY 29	10	12	12	13	8	14	4	12	38	3	21	15
MAY 30	10	14	14	15	8	14	5	12	38	3	21	15
MAY 31	10	16	16	17	8	14	5	12	38	3	21	15

Date & Time	SUN	MOON 1	MOON 2	MOON 3	MERCURY	VENUS	MARS	JUPITER	SATURN	URANUS	NEPTUNE	PLUTO
JUN. 1	10	17	18	19	8	14	5	12	38	3	21	15
JUN. 2	10	19	20	21	8	14	5	12	38	3	21	15
JUN. 3	11	21	22	23	8	14	5	12	38	3	21	15
JUN. 4	11	23	24	24	8	15	5	12	38	3	21	15
JUN. 5	11	25	26	26	8	15	5	12	38	3	21	15
JUN. 6	11	27	27	28	8	15	5	12	38	3	21	15
JUN. 7	11	29	29	30	8	15	5	12	38	3	21	15
JUN. 8	11	30	31	32	8	15	5	12	38	3	21	15
JUN. 9	11	32	33	33	8	15	6	12	38	3	21	15
JUN. 10	11	34	34	35	8	16	6	12	38	3	21	15
JUN. 11	12	35	36	37	9	16	6	13	38	3	21	15
JUN. 12	12	37	38	38	9	16	6	13	38	3	21	15
JUN. 13	12	39	39	40	9	16	6	13	38	3	21	15
JUN. 14	12	40	41	41	9	16	6	13	38	3	21	15
JUN. 15	12	42	43	43	9	16	6	13	38	3	21	15
JUN. 16	12	44	44	45	9	16	6	13	38	3	21	15
JUN. 17	12	45	46	46	9	17	6	13	38	3	21	15
JUN. 18	12	47	47	48	9	17	6	13	38	3	21	15
JUN. 19	13	48	1	1	10	17	7	13	38	3	21	15
JUN. 20	13	2	3	3	10	17	7	13	38	3	21	15
JUN. 21	13	4	4	5	10	17	7	13	38	3	21	15
JUN. 22	13	5	6	7	10	17	7	13	38	3	21	15
JUN. 23	13	7	8	8	10	18	7	13	38	3	21	15
JUN. 24	13	9	10	10	10	18	7	13	38	3	21	15
JUN. 25	14	11	12	12	11	18	7	13	38	3	21	15
JUN. 26	14	13	13	14	11	18	7	13	38	3	21	15
JUN. 27	14	15	15	16	11	18	7	13	38	3	21	15
JUN. 28	14	17	17	18	11	18	7	13	38	3	21	15
JUN. 29	14	19	19	20	12	19	8	13	38	3	21	15
JUN. 30	14	21	21	22	12	19	8	13	38	3	21	15

MOON 1 ☽ 12:01 A.M. TO 8:00 A.M.   **MOON 2** ◑ 8:01 A.M. TO 4:00 P.M.   **MOON 3** ● 4:01 P.M. TO 12:00 A.M.

Use only one "moon" number. Choose the column closest to your time of birth. If your place of birth is not on Eastern Standard Time, be sure to read "How to Convert to Eastern Standard Time" at the beginning of this section.

1930

July

August

Date & Time	SUN	MOON 1	MOON 2	MOON 3	MERCURY	VENUS	MARS	JUPITER	SATURN	URANUS	NEPTUNE	PLUTO
JUL. 1	14	23	23	24	12	19	8	13	38	3	21	15
JUL. 2	14	25	25	26	12	19	8	13	38	3	21	15
JUL. 3	15	26	27	28	13	19	8	13	38	3	21	15
JUL. 4	15	28	29	29	13	19	8	13	38	3	21	15
JUL. 5	15	30	31	31	13	19	8	13	38	3	21	15
JUL. 6	15	32	32	33	13	20	8	13	38	3	21	15
JUL. 7	15	33	34	35	14	20	8	13	38	3	21	16
JUL. 8	15	35	36	36	14	20	8	13	38	3	21	16
JUL. 9	15	37	37	38	14	20	8	13	38	3	21	16
JUL. 10	15	38	39	39	14	20	9	13	38	3	21	16
JUL. 11	16	40	40	41	15	20	9	13	38	3	21	16
JUL. 12	16	42	42	43	15	21	9	13	38	3	21	16
JUL. 13	16	43	44	44	15	21	9	13	38	3	21	16
JUL. 14	16	45	45	46	16	21	9	13	38	3	21	16
JUL. 15	16	46	47	47	16	21	9	14	38	3	21	16
JUL. 16	16	48	48	1	16	21	9	14	38	3	21	16
JUL. 17	16	1	2	3	16	21	9	14	38	3	21	16
JUL. 18	16	3	4	4	17	22	9	14	38	3	21	16
JUL. 19	17	5	5	6	17	22	9	14	38	3	21	16
JUL. 20	17	6	7	8	17	22	9	14	38	3	21	16
JUL. 21	17	8	9	9	18	22	10	14	38	3	21	16
JUL. 22	17	10	11	11	18	22	10	14	38	3	21	16
JUL. 23	17	12	13	13	18	22	10	14	38	3	21	16
JUL. 24	17	14	15	15	18	22	10	14	38	3	21	16
JUL. 25	17	16	17	17	19	23	10	14	38	3	21	16
JUL. 26	18	18	19	19	19	23	10	14	38	3	21	16
JUL. 27	18	20	21	21	19	23	10	14	38	3	21	16
JUL. 28	18	22	23	23	19	23	10	14	38	3	21	16
JUL. 29	18	24	25	25	20	23	10	14	38	3	21	16
JUL. 30	18	26	27	27	20	23	10	14	38	3	21	16
JUL. 31	18	28	28	29	20	23	10	14	38	3	21	16

Date & Time	SUN	MOON 1	MOON 2	MOON 3	MERCURY	VENUS	MARS	JUPITER	SATURN	URANUS	NEPTUNE	PLUTO
AUG. 1	18	30	30	31	20	24	11	14	38	3	21	16
AUG. 2	18	31	32	32	21	24	11	14	38	3	21	16
AUG. 3	19	33	34	34	21	24	11	14	38	3	21	16
AUG. 4	19	35	35	36	21	24	11	14	38	3	21	16
AUG. 5	19	36	37	37	21	24	11	14	38	3	21	16
AUG. 6	19	38	38	39	21	24	11	14	38	3	21	16
AUG. 7	19	40	40	41	22	25	11	14	38	3	21	16
AUG. 8	19	41	42	42	22	25	11	14	38	3	21	16
AUG. 9	19	43	43	44	22	25	11	14	38	3	21	16
AUG. 10	19	44	45	45	22	25	11	14	38	3	21	16
AUG. 11	20	46	46	47	22	25	11	14	38	3	21	16
AUG. 12	20	47	48	1	23	25	12	14	38	3	21	16
AUG. 13	20	1	2	2	23	25	12	14	38	3	21	16
AUG. 14	20	3	3	4	23	26	12	14	38	3	21	16
AUG. 15	20	4	5	5	23	26	12	14	38	3	21	16
AUG. 16	20	6	7	7	23	26	12	14	38	3	21	16
AUG. 17	20	8	8	9	24	26	12	14	38	3	21	16
AUG. 18	20	9	10	11	24	26	12	14	38	3	21	16
AUG. 19	21	11	12	12	24	26	12	14	38	3	21	16
AUG. 20	21	13	14	14	24	26	12	15	38	3	21	16
AUG. 21	21	15	16	16	24	27	12	15	38	3	21	16
AUG. 22	21	17	18	18	24	27	12	15	38	3	21	16
AUG. 23	21	19	20	20	24	27	13	15	38	3	21	16
AUG. 24	21	21	22	22	25	27	13	15	38	3	21	16
AUG. 25	21	23	24	24	25	27	13	15	38	3	21	16
AUG. 26	22	25	26	26	25	27	13	15	38	3	21	16
AUG. 27	22	27	28	28	25	27	13	15	38	3	21	16
AUG. 28	22	29	30	30	25	28	13	15	38	3	21	16
AUG. 29	22	31	31	32	25	28	13	15	38	3	21	16
AUG. 30	22	33	33	34	25	28	13	15	38	3	21	16
AUG. 31	22	34	35	35	25	28	13	15	38	3	21	16

MOON 1 ◗ 12:01 A.M. TO 8:00 A.M.　　**MOON 2** ◐ 8:01 A.M. TO 4:00 P.M.　　**MOON 3** ● 4:01 P.M. TO 12:00 A.M.
Use only one "moon" number. Choose the column closest to your time of birth. If your place of birth is not on
Eastern Standard Time, be sure to read "How to Convert to Eastern Standard Time" at the beginning of this section.

1930

September

Date & Time	SUN	MOON 1	MOON 2	MOON 3	MERCURY	VENUS	MARS	JUPITER	SATURN	URANUS	NEPTUNE	PLUTO
SEP. 1	22	36	36	37	26	28	13	15	38	3	21	16
SEP. 2	22	38	38	39	26	28	13	15	38	3	21	16
SEP. 3	23	39	40	40	26	28	13	15	38	3	21	16
SEP. 4	23	41	41	42	26	29	14	15	38	3	21	16
SEP. 5	23	42	43	43	26	29	14	15	38	3	21	16
SEP. 6	23	44	44	45	26	29	14	15	38	3	21	16
SEP. 7	23	45	46	47	26	29	14	15	38	3	21	16
SEP. 8	23	47	48	48	26	29	14	15	38	3	21	16
SEP. 9	23	1	1	2	26	29	14	15	38	3	21	16
SEP. 10	23	2	3	3	26	29	14	15	38	3	21	16
SEP. 11	24	4	4	5	26	30	14	15	38	3	21	16
SEP. 12	24	6	6	7	26	30	14	15	38	3	21	16
SEP. 13	24	7	8	8	26	30	14	15	38	3	21	16
SEP. 14	24	9	10	10	26	30	14	15	38	3	21	16
SEP. 15	24	11	11	12	26	30	14	15	38	3	22	16
SEP. 16	24	13	13	14	25	30	14	15	38	3	22	16
SEP. 17	24	14	15	16	25	30	15	15	38	3	22	16
SEP. 18	24	16	17	18	25	30	15	15	38	3	22	16
SEP. 19	25	18	19	20	25	31	15	15	38	3	22	16
SEP. 20	25	20	21	22	25	31	15	15	38	3	22	16
SEP. 21	25	22	23	24	25	31	15	15	38	3	22	16
SEP. 22	25	24	25	26	25	31	15	15	38	3	22	16
SEP. 23	25	26	27	28	25	31	15	15	38	3	22	16
SEP. 24	25	28	29	29	24	31	15	15	38	3	22	16
SEP. 25	26	30	31	31	24	31	15	15	38	3	22	16
SEP. 26	26	32	32	33	24	31	15	15	38	3	22	16
SEP. 27	26	34	34	35	24	31	15	15	38	3	22	16
SEP. 28	26	35	36	36	24	32	15	15	38	3	22	16
SEP. 29	26	37	38	38	24	32	15	15	38	3	22	16
SEP. 30	26	39	39	40	24	32	16	15	38	3	22	16

October

Date & Time	SUN	MOON 1	MOON 2	MOON 3	MERCURY	VENUS	MARS	JUPITER	SATURN	URANUS	NEPTUNE	PLUTO
OCT. 1	26	40	41	41	24	32	16	15	38	3	22	16
OCT. 2	26	42	42	43	24	32	16	15	38	3	22	16
OCT. 3	27	43	44	45	24	32	16	15	38	3	22	16
OCT. 4	27	45	46	46	24	32	16	15	38	3	22	16
OCT. 5	27	47	47	48	24	32	16	15	38	3	22	16
OCT. 6	27	48	1	1	24	32	16	15	38	3	22	16
OCT. 7	27	2	2	3	24	33	16	15	38	3	22	16
OCT. 8	27	3	4	5	24	33	16	15	38	3	22	16
OCT. 9	27	5	6	6	25	33	16	16	38	3	22	16
OCT. 10	27	7	7	8	25	33	16	16	38	3	22	16
OCT. 11	28	9	9	10	25	33	16	16	38	3	22	16
OCT. 12	28	10	11	12	25	33	16	16	38	3	22	16
OCT. 13	28	12	13	13	25	33	16	16	38	3	22	16
OCT. 14	28	14	15	15	26	33	17	16	38	3	22	16
OCT. 15	28	16	16	17	26	33	17	16	38	3	22	16
OCT. 16	28	18	18	19	26	33	17	16	38	3	22	16
OCT. 17	28	20	20	21	26	33	17	16	38	3	22	16
OCT. 18	28	21	22	23	26	33	17	16	38	3	22	16
OCT. 19	29	23	24	25	27	33	17	16	38	3	22	16
OCT. 20	29	25	26	27	27	34	17	16	38	3	22	16
OCT. 21	29	27	28	29	27	34	17	16	38	3	22	16
OCT. 22	29	29	30	30	27	34	17	16	38	3	22	16
OCT. 23	29	31	32	32	28	34	17	16	38	3	22	16
OCT. 24	29	33	34	34	28	34	17	16	38	3	22	16
OCT. 25	29	35	35	36	28	34	17	16	38	3	22	16
OCT. 26	30	36	37	38	28	34	17	16	38	3	22	16
OCT. 27	30	38	39	39	28	34	17	16	38	3	22	16
OCT. 28	30	40	40	41	29	34	17	16	38	3	22	16
OCT. 29	30	41	42	42	29	34	17	16	38	3	22	16
OCT. 30	30	43	43	44	29	34	18	16	38	3	22	16
OCT. 31	30	45	45	46	29	34	18	16	38	3	22	16

MOON 1 ◐ 12:01 A.M. TO 8:00 A.M.   **MOON 2** ◑ 8:01 A.M. TO 4:00 P.M.   **MOON 3** ● 4:01 P.M. TO 12:00 A.M.

Use only one "moon" number. Choose the column closest to your time of birth. If your place of birth is not on Eastern Standard Time, be sure to read "How to Convert to Eastern Standard Time" at the beginning of this section.

1930

November

Date & Time	SUN	MOON 1	MOON 2	MOON 3	MERCURY	VENUS	MARS	JUPITER	SATURN	URANUS	NEPTUNE	PLUTO
NOV. 1	30	46	47	47	30	34	18	16	38	3	22	16
NOV. 2	30	48	48	1	30	34	18	16	38	3	22	16
NOV. 3	31	1	2	2	30	34	18	16	38	3	22	16
NOV. 4	31	3	4	4	30	34	18	16	38	3	22	16
NOV. 5	31	5	5	6	30	34	18	16	38	3	22	16
NOV. 6	31	6	7	8	31	34	18	16	38	3	22	16
NOV. 7	31	8	9	9	31	34	18	16	38	3	22	16
NOV. 8	31	10	10	11	31	34	18	16	38	3	22	16
NOV. 9	31	12	12	13	31	34	18	16	38	3	22	16
NOV. 10	31	13	14	15	31	34	18	16	38	3	22	16
NOV. 11	31	15	16	17	32	34	18	16	38	3	22	16
NOV. 12	32	17	18	18	32	34	18	16	38	3	22	16
NOV. 13	32	19	20	20	32	34	18	16	38	3	22	16
NOV. 14	32	21	22	22	32	34	18	16	38	3	22	16
NOV. 15	32	23	24	24	33	34	18	16	38	3	22	16
NOV. 16	32	25	25	26	33	33	18	16	38	3	22	16
NOV. 17	32	27	27	28	33	33	18	16	38	3	22	16
NOV. 18	32	29	29	30	33	33	19	16	38	3	22	16
NOV. 19	33	30	31	32	33	33	19	16	38	3	22	16
NOV. 20	33	32	33	33	34	33	19	16	38	3	22	16
NOV. 21	33	34	35	35	34	33	19	16	38	3	22	16
NOV. 22	33	36	36	37	34	33	19	16	38	3	22	16
NOV. 23	33	37	38	39	34	33	19	16	38	3	22	16
NOV. 24	33	39	40	40	34	33	19	16	38	3	22	16
NOV. 25	34	41	41	42	35	33	19	16	38	3	22	16
NOV. 26	34	42	43	43	35	33	19	16	38	3	22	16
NOV. 27	34	44	45	45	35	33	19	16	38	3	22	16
NOV. 28	34	46	46	47	35	33	19	16	38	3	22	16
NOV. 29	34	47	48	48	35	32	19	16	38	3	22	16
NOV. 30	34	1	1	2	36	32	19	16	38	3	22	16

December

Date & Time	SUN	MOON 1	MOON 2	MOON 3	MERCURY	VENUS	MARS	JUPITER	SATURN	URANUS	NEPTUNE	PLUTO
DEC. 1	34	2	3	3	36	32	19	16	38	3	22	16
DEC. 2	34	4	5	5	36	32	19	16	38	3	22	16
DEC. 3	35	6	6	7	36	32	19	16	38	3	22	16
DEC. 4	35	7	8	9	36	32	19	16	38	3	22	16
DEC. 5	35	9	10	10	37	32	19	16	38	3	22	16
DEC. 6	35	11	12	12	37	32	19	16	38	3	22	16
DEC. 7	35	13	14	14	37	32	19	16	38	3	22	16
DEC. 8	35	15	15	16	37	32	19	16	38	3	22	16
DEC. 9	35	17	17	18	37	32	19	15	38	3	22	16
DEC. 10	35	19	19	20	38	32	19	15	38	2	22	16
DEC. 11	36	21	21	22	38	32	19	15	38	2	22	16
DEC. 12	36	22	23	24	38	32	19	15	38	2	22	16
DEC. 13	36	24	25	26	38	32	19	15	39	2	22	16
DEC. 14	36	26	27	27	38	32	19	15	39	2	22	16
DEC. 15	36	28	29	29	39	32	19	15	39	2	22	16
DEC. 16	36	30	30	31	39	32	19	15	39	2	22	16
DEC. 17	36	32	32	33	39	32	19	15	39	2	22	16
DEC. 18	36	33	34	35	39	32	19	15	39	2	22	16
DEC. 19	37	35	36	36	39	32	19	15	39	2	22	16
DEC. 20	37	37	37	38	39	32	19	15	39	2	22	16
DEC. 21	37	39	39	40	39	32	19	15	39	2	22	16
DEC. 22	37	40	41	41	40	32	19	15	39	2	22	16
DEC. 23	37	42	42	43	40	32	19	15	39	2	22	16
DEC. 24	37	43	44	45	40	32	19	15	39	2	22	16
DEC. 25	37	45	46	46	40	32	19	15	39	2	22	16
DEC. 26	38	47	47	48	40	32	19	15	39	2	22	16
DEC. 27	38	48	1	1	40	32	19	15	39	2	22	16
DEC. 28	38	2	2	3	40	32	19	15	39	2	22	16
DEC. 29	38	3	4	4	40	33	19	15	39	2	22	16
DEC. 30	38	5	6	6	40	33	19	15	39	2	22	16
DEC. 31	38	7	7	8	40	33	19	15	39	2	22	16

MOON 1 ◐ 12:01 A.M. TO 8:00 A.M.　　**MOON 2** ◑ 8:01 A.M. TO 4:00 P.M.　　**MOON 3** ● 4:01 P.M. TO 12:00 A.M.
Use only one "moon" number. Choose the column closest to your time of birth. If your place of birth is not on
Eastern Standard Time, be sure to read "How to Convert to Eastern Standard Time" at the beginning of this section.

1931

January

Date & Time	SUN	MOON 1	MOON 2	MOON 3	MERCURY	VENUS	MARS	JUPITER	SATURN	URANUS	NEPTUNE	PLUTO
JAN. 1	38	8	9	10	40	33	19	15	39	2	22	16
JAN. 2	38	10	11	12	40	33	19	15	39	3	22	16
JAN. 3	39	12	13	13	39	33	19	15	39	3	22	16
JAN. 4	39	14	15	15	39	33	19	15	39	3	22	16
JAN. 5	39	16	17	17	39	33	19	15	39	3	22	16
JAN. 6	39	18	19	19	39	33	19	15	39	3	22	16
JAN. 7	39	20	21	21	39	33	19	15	39	3	22	16
JAN. 8	39	22	23	23	39	33	19	15	39	3	22	16
JAN. 9	39	24	25	25	38	33	19	15	39	3	22	16
JAN. 10	40	26	26	27	38	34	19	15	39	3	22	16
JAN. 11	40	28	28	29	38	34	19	15	39	3	22	16
JAN. 12	40	29	30	31	38	34	19	15	39	3	22	16
JAN. 13	40	31	32	32	38	34	19	15	39	3	22	16
JAN. 14	40	33	34	34	38	34	19	15	39	3	22	16
JAN. 15	40	35	35	36	38	34	19	15	39	3	22	16
JAN. 16	40	36	37	38	38	34	18	15	39	3	22	16
JAN. 17	41	38	39	39	38	34	18	15	39	3	22	16
JAN. 18	41	40	40	41	38	34	18	15	39	3	22	16
JAN. 19	41	41	42	42	38	35	18	15	39	3	22	16
JAN. 20	41	43	44	44	38	35	18	15	39	3	22	16
JAN. 21	41	45	45	46	38	35	18	15	39	3	22	16
JAN. 22	41	46	47	47	38	35	18	15	39	3	22	16
JAN. 23	42	48	48	1	38	35	18	15	39	3	22	16
JAN. 24	42	1	2	2	38	35	18	15	39	3	22	16
JAN. 25	42	3	3	4	38	35	18	15	39	3	22	16
JAN. 26	42	4	5	6	38	35	18	15	39	3	22	16
JAN. 27	42	6	7	7	38	36	18	15	39	3	22	16
JAN. 28	42	8	9	8	39	36	18	15	39	3	22	16
JAN. 29	42	10	10	11	39	36	18	15	39	3	22	16
JAN. 30	42	11	12	13	39	36	18	15	39	3	22	16
JAN. 31	43	13	14	14	39	36	18	15	39	3	22	16

February

Date & Time	SUN	MOON 1	MOON 2	MOON 3	MERCURY	VENUS	MARS	JUPITER	SATURN	URANUS	NEPTUNE	PLUTO
FEB. 1	43	15	16	16	39	36	18	15	39	3	22	16
FEB. 2	43	17	18	18	39	36	18	15	39	3	22	16
FEB. 3	43	19	20	20	40	37	18	15	39	3	22	16
FEB. 4	43	21	22	22	40	37	18	15	39	3	22	16
FEB. 5	43	23	24	24	40	37	17	15	39	3	22	16
FEB. 6	43	25	26	26	40	37	17	15	39	3	22	16
FEB. 7	43	27	28	28	40	37	17	15	39	3	22	16
FEB. 8	44	29	30	30	40	37	17	15	39	3	22	16
FEB. 9	44	31	31	32	41	37	17	15	39	3	22	16
FEB. 10	44	33	33	34	41	37	17	14	39	3	22	16
FEB. 11	44	34	35	35	41	38	17	14	39	3	22	16
FEB. 12	44	36	37	37	41	38	17	14	39	3	22	16
FEB. 13	44	38	38	39	41	38	17	14	39	3	22	16
FEB. 14	44	39	40	40	41	38	17	14	39	3	22	16
FEB. 15	44	41	41	42	42	38	17	14	39	3	22	16
FEB. 16	45	43	43	44	42	38	17	14	39	3	22	16
FEB. 17	45	44	45	45	42	38	17	14	40	3	22	16
FEB. 18	45	46	46	47	42	39	17	14	40	3	22	16
FEB. 19	45	47	48	48	42	39	17	14	40	3	22	16
FEB. 20	45	1	1	2	43	39	17	14	40	3	22	16
FEB. 21	45	2	3	4	43	39	17	14	40	3	22	16
FEB. 22	45	4	5	5	43	39	17	14	40	3	22	15
FEB. 23	46	6	6	7	43	39	17	14	40	3	22	15
FEB. 24	46	7	8	8	44	40	17	14	40	3	22	15
FEB. 25	46	9	10	10	44	40	17	14	40	3	22	15
FEB. 26	46	11	11	12	44	40	17	14	40	3	22	15
FEB. 27	46	12	13	14	44	40	17	14	40	3	22	15
FEB. 28	46	14	15	16	44	40	17	14	40	3	22	15

MOON 1 ☾ 12:01 A.M. TO 8:00 A.M.   **MOON 2** ☽ 8:01 A.M. TO 4:00 P.M.   **MOON 3** ● 4:01 P.M. TO 12:00 A.M.
Use only one "moon" number. Choose the column closest to your time of birth. If your place of birth is not on Eastern Standard Time, be sure to read "How to Convert to Eastern Standard Time" at the beginning of this section.

Date & Time	SUN	MOON 1	MOON 2	MOON 3	MERCURY	VENUS	MARS	JUPITER	SATURN	URANUS	NEPTUNE	PLUTO
MAR. 1	46	16	17	18	45	40	17	14	40	3	22	15
MAR. 2	46	18	19	20	45	40	17	14	40	3	22	15
MAR. 3	47	20	21	22	45	41	17	14	40	3	22	15
MAR. 4	47	22	23	24	45	41	17	14	40	3	22	15
MAR. 5	47	24	25	26	46	41	17	14	40	3	22	15
MAR. 6	47	26	27	28	46	41	17	14	40	3	22	15
MAR. 7	47	28	29	30	46	41	17	14	40	3	22	15
MAR. 8	47	30	31	31	46	41	17	14	40	3	22	15
MAR. 9	47	32	33	33	47	41	17	14	40	3	22	15
MAR. 10	47	34	34	35	47	42	17	14	40	3	22	15
MAR. 11	48	36	36	37	47	42	17	14	40	3	21	15
MAR. 12	48	37	38	38	47	42	17	14	40	3	21	15
MAR. 13	48	39	39	40	48	42	17	14	40	3	21	15
MAR. 14	48	41	41	42	48	42	17	14	40	3	21	15
MAR. 15	48	42	43	43	48	42	17	14	40	3	21	15
MAR. 16	48	44	44	44	48	43	17	14	40	3	21	15
MAR. 17	48	45	46	46	1	43	17	14	40	3	21	15
MAR. 18	48	47	47	48	1	43	17	14	40	3	21	15
MAR. 19	1	48	1	2	1	43	17	14	40	3	21	15
MAR. 20	1	2	3	3	1	43	17	14	40	3	21	15
MAR. 21	1	4	4	5	2	43	17	14	40	3	21	15
MAR. 22	1	5	6	6	2	43	17	14	40	3	21	15
MAR. 23	1	7	7	8	2	44	17	14	40	3	21	15
MAR. 24	1	9	9	10	2	44	17	14	40	3	21	15
MAR. 25	2	10	11	11	3	44	17	14	40	3	21	15
MAR. 26	2	12	13	13	3	44	17	14	40	3	21	15
MAR. 27	2	14	14	14	3	44	17	14	40	3	21	15
MAR. 28	2	16	16	17	3	44	17	14	40	3	21	15
MAR. 29	2	17	18	19	4	45	17	14	40	3	21	15
MAR. 30	2	19	20	21	4	45	17	14	40	3	21	15
MAR. 31	2	21	22	23	4	45	17	14	40	3	21	15
APR. 1	2	23	24	25	4	45	17	14	40	3	21	15
APR. 2	2	25	26	27	5	45	17	15	40	3	21	15
APR. 3	3	27	28	29	5	45	17	15	40	3	21	15
APR. 4	3	29	30	31	5	46	17	15	40	3	21	15
APR. 5	3	31	32	33	5	46	17	15	40	3	21	15
APR. 6	3	33	34	34	5	46	17	15	40	3	21	15
APR. 7	3	35	36	36	6	46	17	15	40	3	21	15
APR. 8	3	37	37	38	6	46	17	15	40	3	21	15
APR. 9	3	38	39	40	6	46	17	15	40	3	21	15
APR. 10	3	40	41	41	6	46	17	15	40	3	21	15
APR. 11	4	42	42	43	6	47	17	15	40	3	21	15
APR. 12	4	43	44	44	6	47	17	15	40	3	21	15
APR. 13	4	45	45	46	6	47	17	15	40	3	21	15
APR. 14	4	46	47	48	7	47	18	15	40	3	21	15
APR. 15	4	48	1	1	7	47	18	15	40	3	21	15
APR. 16	4	2	2	3	7	47	18	15	40	3	21	15
APR. 17	4	3	4	4	7	48	18	15	40	3	21	15
APR. 18	4	5	5	6	7	48	18	15	40	3	21	15
APR. 19	5	6	7	8	7	48	18	15	40	3	21	15
APR. 20	5	8	9	9	7	48	18	15	40	3	21	15
APR. 21	5	10	10	11	7	48	18	15	40	3	21	15
APR. 22	5	12	12	13	7	48	18	15	40	3	21	15
APR. 23	5	13	14	14	7	1	18	15	40	3	21	15
APR. 24	5	15	16	16	7	1	18	15	40	3	21	15
APR. 25	6	17	18	18	7	1	18	15	40	3	21	15
APR. 26	6	19	19	20	7	1	18	15	40	3	21	15
APR. 27	6	21	21	22	6	1	18	15	40	3	21	15
APR. 28	6	23	23	24	6	1	18	15	40	3	21	15
APR. 29	6	25	25	26	6	1	18	15	40	3	21	15
APR. 30	6	26	27	28	6	2	18	15	40	3	21	15

MOON 1 ◐ 12:01 A.M. TO 8:00 A.M.   **MOON 2** ◑ 8:01 A.M. TO 4:00 P.M.   **MOON 3** ● 4:01 P.M. TO 12:00 A.M.

Use only one "moon" number. Choose the column closest to your time of birth. If your place of birth is not on Eastern Standard Time, be sure to read "How to Convert to Eastern Standard Time" at the beginning of this section.

1931

May

June

Date & Time	SUN	MOON 1	MOON 2	MOON 3	MERCURY	VENUS	MARS	JUPITER	SATURN	URANUS	NEPTUNE	PLUTO
MAY 1	6	28	29	30	6	2	18	15	40	3	21	15
MAY 2	6	30	31	32	6	2	18	15	40	3	21	15
MAY 3	7	32	33	34	6	2	18	15	40	3	21	15
MAY 4	7	34	35	35	6	2	19	15	40	3	21	15
MAY 5	7	36	37	37	6	2	19	15	40	3	21	15
MAY 6	7	38	38	39	6	3	19	15	40	3	21	15
MAY 7	7	40	40	41	6	3	19	15	40	3	21	15
MAY 8	7	41	42	42	6	3	19	15	40	3	21	15
MAY 9	7	43	43	44	6	3	19	15	40	3	21	15
MAY 10	7	44	45	45	6	3	19	15	40	3	21	15
MAY 11	8	46	47	47	6	3	19	15	40	3	21	15
MAY 12	8	48	48	1	5	4	19	15	40	3	21	16
MAY 13	8	1	2	2	5	4	19	15	40	3	21	16
MAY 14	8	3	4	4	5	4	19	15	40	3	21	16
MAY 15	8	4	5	5	5	4	19	15	40	3	21	16
MAY 16	8	6	7	7	5	4	19	15	40	3	21	16
MAY 17	8	8	8	9	6	4	19	15	40	3	21	16
MAY 18	8	9	10	11	6	5	19	15	40	3	21	16
MAY 19	9	11	12	12	6	5	19	15	40	3	21	16
MAY 20	9	13	13	14	6	5	20	15	40	3	21	16
MAY 21	9	15	15	16	6	5	20	15	40	3	21	16
MAY 22	9	16	17	18	6	5	20	15	40	3	21	16
MAY 23	9	18	19	20	6	5	20	15	40	3	21	16
MAY 24	9	20	21	21	6	5	20	15	40	3	21	16
MAY 25	10	22	23	23	6	6	20	15	40	3	21	16
MAY 26	10	24	25	25	6	6	20	16	40	3	21	16
MAY 27	10	26	26	27	6	6	20	16	40	3	21	16
MAY 28	10	28	28	29	6	6	20	16	40	3	21	16
MAY 29	10	30	30	31	7	6	20	16	40	3	21	16
MAY 30	10	32	32	33	7	6	20	16	40	3	21	16
MAY 31	10	33	34	35	7	7	20	16	40	3	21	16

Date & Time	SUN	MOON 1	MOON 2	MOON 3	MERCURY	VENUS	MARS	JUPITER	SATURN	URANUS	NEPTUNE	PLUTO
JUN. 1	10	35	36	37	7	7	20	16	40	3	21	16
JUN. 2	10	37	38	38	7	7	20	16	40	3	21	16
JUN. 3	11	39	39	40	7	7	20	16	40	3	21	16
JUN. 4	11	41	41	42	8	7	21	16	40	3	21	16
JUN. 5	11	42	43	43	8	7	21	16	40	3	21	16
JUN. 6	11	44	44	45	8	8	21	16	40	3	21	16
JUN. 7	11	45	46	47	8	8	21	16	40	3	21	16
JUN. 8	11	47	48	48	8	8	21	16	40	3	21	16
JUN. 9	11	1	1	2	9	8	21	16	40	3	21	16
JUN. 10	11	2	3	3	9	8	21	16	40	3	21	16
JUN. 11	12	4	4	5	9	8	21	16	40	3	21	16
JUN. 12	12	5	6	7	9	9	21	16	40	3	21	16
JUN. 13	12	7	8	8	9	9	21	16	40	3	21	16
JUN. 14	12	9	9	10	10	9	21	16	40	3	21	16
JUN. 15	12	11	11	12	10	9	21	16	40	3	21	16
JUN. 16	12	12	13	14	10	9	21	16	40	3	21	16
JUN. 17	12	14	15	15	10	9	21	16	40	3	21	16
JUN. 18	12	16	17	17	11	9	22	16	40	3	21	16
JUN. 19	13	18	18	19	11	10	22	16	40	3	21	16
JUN. 20	13	20	20	21	11	10	22	16	40	3	21	16
JUN. 21	13	22	22	23	11	10	22	16	40	3	21	16
JUN. 22	13	24	24	25	12	10	22	16	40	3	21	16
JUN. 23	13	25	26	27	12	10	22	16	40	3	21	16
JUN. 24	13	27	28	29	12	10	22	16	40	3	21	16
JUN. 25	14	29	30	30	13	11	22	16	40	3	21	16
JUN. 26	14	31	32	32	13	11	22	16	40	4	21	16
JUN. 27	14	33	33	34	13	11	22	16	40	4	21	16
JUN. 28	14	35	35	36	13	11	22	16	40	4	21	16
JUN. 29	14	36	37	38	14	11	22	16	40	4	21	16
JUN. 30	14	38	39	39	14	11	22	16	40	4	21	16

MOON 1 ◖ 12:01 A.M. TO 8:00 A.M.   **MOON 2** ◑ 8:01 A.M. TO 4:00 P.M.   **MOON 3** ● 4:01 P.M. TO 12:00 A.M.
Use only one "moon" number. Choose the column closest to your time of birth. If your place of birth is not on Eastern Standard Time, be sure to read "How to Convert to Eastern Standard Time" at the beginning of this section.

1931

July

Date & Time	SUN	MOON 1	MOON 2	MOON 3	MERCURY	VENUS	MARS	JUPITER	SATURN	URANUS	NEPTUNE	PLUTO
JUL. 1	14	40	41	41	14	12	22	16	40	4	21	16
JUL. 2	14	42	42	43	15	12	23	17	40	4	21	16
JUL. 3	15	43	44	44	15	12	23	17	40	4	21	16
JUL. 4	15	45	45	46	15	12	23	17	40	4	21	16
JUL. 5	15	47	47	48	15	12	23	17	40	4	21	16
JUL. 6	15	48	1	1	15	12	23	17	40	4	21	16
JUL. 7	15	2	2	3	16	13	23	17	40	4	21	16
JUL. 8	15	3	4	4	16	13	23	17	40	4	21	16
JUL. 9	15	5	5	6	17	13	23	17	40	4	21	16
JUL. 10	15	7	7	8	17	13	23	17	40	4	21	16
JUL. 11	16	8	9	9	17	13	23	17	40	4	21	16
JUL. 12	16	10	10	11	17	13	23	17	40	4	21	16
JUL. 13	16	12	12	13	18	14	23	17	40	4	21	16
JUL. 14	16	13	14	15	18	14	23	17	40	4	21	16
JUL. 15	16	15	16	17	18	14	24	17	40	4	21	16
JUL. 16	16	17	18	19	18	14	24	17	40	4	21	16
JUL. 17	16	19	20	20	19	14	24	17	40	4	22	16
JUL. 18	16	21	22	22	19	14	24	17	40	4	22	16
JUL. 19	17	23	24	24	19	15	24	17	40	4	22	16
JUL. 20	17	25	26	26	19	15	24	17	40	4	22	16
JUL. 21	17	27	28	28	19	15	24	17	40	4	22	16
JUL. 22	17	29	29	30	20	15	24	17	40	4	22	16
JUL. 23	17	31	31	32	20	15	24	17	40	4	22	16
JUL. 24	17	32	33	34	20	15	24	17	40	4	22	16
JUL. 25	17	34	35	35	20	16	24	17	40	4	22	16
JUL. 26	18	36	37	37	20	16	24	17	40	4	22	16
JUL. 27	18	38	38	39	21	16	25	17	39	4	22	16
JUL. 28	18	39	40	41	21	16	25	17	39	4	22	16
JUL. 29	18	41	42	42	21	16	25	17	39	4	22	16
JUL. 30	18	43	43	44	21	16	25	17	39	4	22	16
JUL. 31	18	44	45	46	21	16	25	17	39	4	22	16

August

Date & Time	SUN	MOON 1	MOON 2	MOON 3	MERCURY	VENUS	MARS	JUPITER	SATURN	URANUS	NEPTUNE	PLUTO
AUG. 1	18	46	47	47	22	17	25	17	39	4	22	16
AUG. 2	18	48	48	1	22	17	25	17	39	4	22	16
AUG. 3	19	1	2	2	22	17	25	17	39	4	22	16
AUG. 4	19	3	3	4	22	17	25	17	39	4	22	16
AUG. 5	19	4	5	5	22	17	25	18	39	4	22	16
AUG. 6	19	6	6	7	22	17	25	18	39	4	22	16
AUG. 7	19	8	8	9	22	18	25	18	39	4	22	16
AUG. 8	19	9	10	10	23	18	26	18	39	4	22	16
AUG. 9	19	11	12	12	23	18	26	18	39	4	22	16
AUG. 10	19	13	13	14	23	18	26	18	39	4	22	16
AUG. 11	20	15	15	16	23	18	26	18	39	4	22	16
AUG. 12	20	16	17	18	23	18	26	18	39	4	22	16
AUG. 13	20	18	19	20	23	19	26	18	39	4	22	16
AUG. 14	20	20	21	22	23	19	26	18	39	4	22	16
AUG. 15	20	22	23	24	23	19	26	18	39	4	22	16
AUG. 16	20	24	25	26	23	19	26	18	39	4	22	16
AUG. 17	20	26	27	28	23	19	26	18	39	4	22	16
AUG. 18	20	28	29	30	23	19	26	18	39	4	22	16
AUG. 19	21	30	31	31	24	20	26	18	39	4	22	16
AUG. 20	21	32	33	33	24	20	27	18	39	4	22	16
AUG. 21	21	34	34	35	24	20	27	18	39	4	22	16
AUG. 22	21	36	36	37	24	20	27	18	39	4	22	16
AUG. 23	21	37	38	38	24	20	27	18	39	4	22	16
AUG. 24	21	39	40	40	24	20	27	18	39	4	22	16
AUG. 25	21	41	41	42	24	21	27	18	39	4	22	16
AUG. 26	22	42	43	43	23	21	27	18	39	3	22	16
AUG. 27	22	44	45	45	23	21	27	18	39	3	22	16
AUG. 28	22	46	46	47	23	21	27	18	39	3	22	16
AUG. 29	22	47	48	48	23	21	27	18	39	3	22	16
AUG. 30	22	1	1	2	23	21	27	18	39	3	22	16
AUG. 31	22	2	3	3	23	22	27	18	39	3	22	16

MOON 1 ◖ 12:01 A.M. TO 8:00 A.M.　　**MOON 2** ◑ 8:01 A.M. TO 4:00 P.M.　　**MOON 3** ● 4:01 P.M. TO 12:00 A.M.

Use only one "moon" number. Choose the column closest to your time of birth. If your place of birth is not on Eastern Standard Time, be sure to read "How to Convert to Eastern Standard Time" at the beginning of this section.

1931

September

Date & Time	SUN	MOON 1	MOON 2	MOON 3	MERCURY	VENUS	MARS	JUPITER	SATURN	URANUS	NEPTUNE	PLUTO
SEP. 1	22	4	4	5	23	22	28	18	39	3	22	16
SEP. 2	22	5	6	7	23	22	28	18	39	3	22	16
SEP. 3	23	7	8	8	23	22	28	18	39	3	22	16
SEP. 4	23	9	9	10	23	22	28	18	39	3	22	16
SEP. 5	23	10	11	12	22	22	28	18	39	3	22	16
SEP. 6	23	12	13	13	22	23	28	18	39	3	22	16
SEP. 7	23	14	14	15	22	23	28	18	39	3	22	16
SEP. 8	23	16	16	17	22	23	28	18	39	3	22	16
SEP. 9	23	18	18	19	22	23	28	19	39	3	22	16
SEP. 10	23	19	20	21	22	23	28	19	39	3	22	16
SEP. 11	24	21	22	23	22	23	28	19	39	3	22	16
SEP. 12	24	23	24	25	22	24	29	19	39	3	22	16
SEP. 13	24	25	26	27	22	24	29	19	39	3	22	16
SEP. 14	24	28	28	29	22	24	29	19	39	3	22	16
SEP. 15	24	29	30	31	22	24	29	19	39	3	22	16
SEP. 16	24	31	32	33	22	24	29	19	39	3	22	16
SEP. 17	24	33	34	35	22	24	29	19	39	3	22	16
SEP. 18	24	35	36	36	22	25	29	19	39	3	22	16
SEP. 19	25	37	37	38	22	25	29	19	39	3	22	16
SEP. 20	25	39	39	40	22	25	29	19	39	3	22	16
SEP. 21	25	40	41	41	22	25	29	19	39	3	22	16
SEP. 22	25	42	43	43	22	25	29	19	39	3	22	16
SEP. 23	25	44	44	45	23	25	29	19	39	3	22	16
SEP. 24	25	45	46	46	23	26	30	19	39	3	22	16
SEP. 25	26	47	47	48	23	26	30	19	39	3	22	16
SEP. 26	26	48	1	1	23	26	30	19	39	3	22	16
SEP. 27	26	2	2	3	23	26	30	19	39	3	22	16
SEP. 28	26	4	4	5	23	26	30	19	39	3	22	16
SEP. 29	26	5	6	6	24	26	30	19	39	3	22	16
SEP. 30	26	7	7	8	24	27	30	19	39	3	22	16

October

Date & Time	SUN	MOON 1	MOON 2	MOON 3	MERCURY	VENUS	MARS	JUPITER	SATURN	URANUS	NEPTUNE	PLUTO
OCT. 1	26	8	9	9	24	27	30	19	39	3	22	16
OCT. 2	26	10	10	11	24	27	30	19	39	3	22	16
OCT. 3	27	12	12	13	25	27	30	19	39	3	22	16
OCT. 4	27	13	14	14	25	27	30	19	39	3	22	16
OCT. 5	27	15	16	16	25	27	31	19	39	3	22	16
OCT. 6	27	17	17	18	25	28	31	19	39	3	22	16
OCT. 7	27	19	19	20	26	28	31	19	39	3	22	16
OCT. 8	27	21	21	22	26	28	31	19	39	3	22	16
OCT. 9	27	23	23	24	26	28	31	19	39	3	22	16
OCT. 10	27	25	25	26	26	28	31	19	39	3	22	16
OCT. 11	28	27	27	28	26	28	31	19	39	3	22	16
OCT. 12	28	29	29	30	27	29	31	19	39	3	22	16
OCT. 13	28	31	31	32	27	29	31	19	39	3	22	16
OCT. 14	28	33	33	34	27	29	31	19	39	3	22	16
OCT. 15	28	34	35	36	27	29	32	19	39	3	22	16
OCT. 16	28	36	37	38	28	29	32	19	39	3	22	16
OCT. 17	28	38	39	39	28	29	32	19	39	3	22	16
OCT. 18	28	40	40	41	28	30	32	19	39	3	22	16
OCT. 19	29	42	42	43	28	30	32	19	39	3	22	16
OCT. 20	29	43	44	44	29	30	32	19	39	3	22	16
OCT. 21	29	45	45	46	29	30	32	19	39	3	22	16
OCT. 22	29	46	47	47	29	30	32	20	39	3	22	16
OCT. 23	29	48	48	1	29	30	32	20	39	3	22	16
OCT. 24	29	2	2	3	29	31	32	20	39	3	22	16
OCT. 25	29	3	4	4	30	31	32	20	39	3	22	16
OCT. 26	30	5	5	6	30	31	33	20	39	3	22	16
OCT. 27	30	6	7	7	30	31	33	20	39	3	22	16
OCT. 28	30	8	8	9	30	31	33	20	39	3	22	16
OCT. 29	30	10	10	11	31	31	33	20	39	3	22	16
OCT. 30	30	11	12	12	31	32	33	20	39	3	22	16
OCT. 31	30	13	13	14	31	32	33	20	39	3	22	16

MOON 1 ☽ 12:01 A.M. TO 8:00 A.M.　　**MOON 2** ☾ 8:01 A.M. TO 4:00 P.M.　　**MOON 3** ● 4:01 P.M. TO 12:00 A.M.

Use only one "moon" number. Choose the column closest to your time of birth. If your place of birth is not on Eastern Standard Time, be sure to read "How to Convert to Eastern Standard Time" at the beginning of this section.

1931

November

Date & Time	SUN	MOON 1	MOON 2	MOON 3	MERCURY	VENUS	MARS	JUPITER	SATURN	URANUS	NEPTUNE	PLUTO
NOV. 1	30	15	15	16	31	32	33	20	39	3	22	16
NOV. 2	30	16	17	18	31	32	33	20	39	3	22	16
NOV. 3	31	18	19	19	32	32	33	20	39	3	22	16
NOV. 4	31	20	21	21	32	32	33	20	39	3	22	16
NOV. 5	31	22	22	23	32	33	34	20	39	3	22	16
NOV. 6	31	24	24	25	32	33	34	20	39	3	22	16
NOV. 7	31	26	26	27	32	33	34	20	39	3	22	16
NOV. 8	31	28	28	29	33	33	34	20	39	3	22	16
NOV. 9	31	30	30	31	33	33	34	20	39	3	22	16
NOV. 10	31	32	32	33	33	33	34	20	39	3	22	16
NOV. 11	31	34	34	35	33	34	34	20	39	3	22	16
NOV. 12	32	36	36	37	33	34	34	20	39	3	22	16
NOV. 13	32	37	38	39	34	34	34	20	39	3	22	16
NOV. 14	32	39	40	40	34	34	34	20	39	3	22	16
NOV. 15	32	41	42	42	34	34	34	20	39	3	22	16
NOV. 16	32	43	43	44	34	34	35	20	40	3	22	16
NOV. 17	32	44	45	45	34	35	35	20	40	3	22	16
NOV. 18	32	46	46	47	35	35	35	20	40	3	22	16
NOV. 19	33	48	48	1	35	35	35	20	40	3	22	16
NOV. 20	33	1	2	2	35	35	35	20	40	3	22	16
NOV. 21	33	3	3	4	35	35	35	20	40	3	22	16
NOV. 22	33	4	5	5	35	35	35	20	40	3	22	16
NOV. 23	33	6	6	7	35	36	35	20	40	3	22	16
NOV. 24	33	7	8	9	36	36	35	20	40	3	22	16
NOV. 25	34	9	10	10	36	36	35	20	40	3	22	16
NOV. 26	34	11	11	12	36	36	36	20	40	3	22	16
NOV. 27	34	12	13	14	36	36	36	20	40	3	22	16
NOV. 28	34	14	15	15	36	36	36	20	40	3	22	16
NOV. 29	34	16	17	17	37	37	36	20	40	3	22	16
NOV. 30	34	18	18	19	37	37	36	20	40	3	22	16

December

Date & Time	SUN	MOON 1	MOON 2	MOON 3	MERCURY	VENUS	MARS	JUPITER	SATURN	URANUS	NEPTUNE	PLUTO
DEC. 1	34	20	20	21	37	37	36	20	40	3	22	16
DEC. 2	34	21	22	23	37	37	36	20	40	3	22	16
DEC. 3	35	23	24	24	37	37	36	20	40	3	22	16
DEC. 4	35	25	26	26	37	37	36	20	40	3	22	16
DEC. 5	35	27	28	28	37	38	36	20	40	3	22	16
DEC. 6	35	29	30	30	37	38	37	20	40	3	22	16
DEC. 7	35	31	32	32	38	38	37	20	40	3	22	16
DEC. 8	35	33	33	34	38	38	37	20	40	3	22	16
DEC. 9	35	35	35	36	38	38	37	20	40	3	22	16
DEC. 10	35	37	37	38	38	38	37	20	40	3	22	16
DEC. 11	36	38	39	40	38	39	37	20	40	3	22	16
DEC. 12	36	40	41	41	38	39	37	20	40	3	22	16
DEC. 13	36	42	43	43	38	39	37	20	40	3	22	16
DEC. 14	36	44	44	45	38	39	37	20	40	3	22	16
DEC. 15	36	45	46	46	38	39	37	20	40	3	22	16
DEC. 16	36	47	48	48	38	39	38	20	40	3	22	16
DEC. 17	36	1	1	2	37	40	38	20	40	3	22	16
DEC. 18	36	2	3	3	37	40	38	20	40	3	22	16
DEC. 19	37	4	4	5	37	40	38	20	40	3	22	16
DEC. 20	37	5	6	6	37	40	38	20	40	3	22	16
DEC. 21	37	7	7	8	37	40	38	20	40	3	22	16
DEC. 22	37	9	9	10	37	40	38	20	40	3	22	16
DEC. 23	37	10	11	11	36	41	38	20	40	3	22	16
DEC. 24	37	12	13	13	36	41	38	20	40	3	22	16
DEC. 25	37	14	14	15	36	41	39	20	40	3	22	16
DEC. 26	38	15	16	17	36	41	39	20	40	3	22	16
DEC. 27	38	17	18	18	36	41	39	20	40	3	22	16
DEC. 28	38	19	20	20	36	41	39	20	40	3	22	16
DEC. 29	38	21	22	22	36	42	39	20	40	3	22	16
DEC. 30	38	23	23	24	36	42	39	20	40	3	22	16
DEC. 31	38	25	25	26	36	42	39	20	40	3	22	16

MOON 1 ☽ 12:01 A.M. TO 8:00 A.M.   **MOON 2** ☽ 8:01 A.M. TO 4:00 P.M.   **MOON 3** ● 4:01 P.M. TO 12:00 A.M.

Use only one "moon" number. Choose the column closest to your time of birth. If your place of birth is not on Eastern Standard Time, be sure to read "How to Convert to Eastern Standard Time" at the beginning of this section.

1932

January

Date & Time	SUN	MOON 1	MOON 2	MOON 3	MERCURY	VENUS	MARS	JUPITER	SATURN	URANUS	NEPTUNE	PLUTO
JAN. 1	38	27	27	28	36	42	39	20	40	3	22	16
JAN. 2	38	28	29	30	36	42	39	20	40	3	22	16
JAN. 3	39	30	31	32	36	42	39	20	40	3	22	16
JAN. 4	39	32	33	33	36	43	40	20	40	3	22	16
JAN. 5	39	34	35	35	36	43	40	20	40	3	22	16
JAN. 6	39	36	37	37	36	43	40	20	40	3	22	16
JAN. 7	39	38	38	39	36	43	40	20	40	3	22	16
JAN. 8	39	40	40	41	36	43	40	20	40	3	22	16
JAN. 9	39	41	42	43	36	43	40	20	40	3	22	16
JAN. 10	40	43	44	44	36	44	40	20	40	3	22	16
JAN. 11	40	45	45	46	36	44	40	20	40	3	22	16
JAN. 12	40	46	47	47	37	44	40	20	40	3	22	16
JAN. 13	40	48	1	1	37	44	40	20	40	3	22	16
JAN. 14	40	2	2	3	37	44	41	20	40	3	22	16
JAN. 15	40	3	4	4	37	44	41	20	40	3	22	16
JAN. 16	40	5	5	6	37	44	41	20	40	3	22	16
JAN. 17	41	6	7	7	37	45	41	20	40	3	22	16
JAN. 18	41	8	9	9	38	45	41	20	40	3	22	16
JAN. 19	41	10	10	11	38	45	41	20	40	3	22	16
JAN. 20	41	11	12	12	38	45	41	20	40	3	22	16
JAN. 21	41	13	14	14	38	45	41	20	40	3	22	16
JAN. 22	41	15	15	16	38	45	41	20	40	3	22	16
JAN. 23	42	17	17	18	38	46	42	20	40	3	22	16
JAN. 24	42	18	19	20	39	46	42	20	40	3	22	16
JAN. 25	42	20	21	22	39	46	42	20	41	3	22	16
JAN. 26	42	22	23	24	39	46	42	20	41	3	22	16
JAN. 27	42	24	25	25	39	46	42	20	41	3	22	16
JAN. 28	42	26	27	27	39	46	42	20	41	3	22	16
JAN. 29	42	28	29	29	40	47	42	19	41	3	22	16
JAN. 30	42	30	30	31	40	47	42	19	41	3	22	16
JAN. 31	43	32	32	33	40	47	42	19	41	3	22	16

February

Date & Time	SUN	MOON 1	MOON 2	MOON 3	MERCURY	VENUS	MARS	JUPITER	SATURN	URANUS	NEPTUNE	PLUTO
FEB. 1	43	34	34	35	40	47	42	19	41	3	22	16
FEB. 2	43	35	36	37	40	47	43	19	41	3	22	16
FEB. 3	43	37	38	38	41	47	43	19	41	3	22	16
FEB. 4	43	39	40	40	41	48	43	19	41	3	22	16
FEB. 5	43	41	41	42	41	48	43	19	41	3	22	16
FEB. 6	43	42	43	44	41	48	43	19	41	3	22	16
FEB. 7	43	44	45	45	41	48	43	19	41	3	22	16
FEB. 8	44	46	46	47	42	48	43	19	41	3	22	16
FEB. 9	44	47	48	1	42	48	43	19	41	3	22	16
FEB. 10	44	1	2	2	42	48	43	19	41	3	22	16
FEB. 11	44	3	3	4	42	1	43	19	41	3	22	16
FEB. 12	44	4	5	5	42	1	44	19	41	3	22	16
FEB. 13	44	6	6	7	43	1	44	19	41	3	22	16
FEB. 14	44	7	8	8	43	1	44	19	41	3	22	16
FEB. 15	44	9	10	10	43	1	44	19	41	3	22	16
FEB. 16	45	11	11	12	43	2	44	19	41	3	22	16
FEB. 17	45	12	13	13	44	2	44	19	41	3	22	16
FEB. 18	45	14	15	15	44	2	44	19	41	3	22	16
FEB. 19	45	16	16	17	44	2	44	19	41	3	22	16
FEB. 20	45	18	18	19	44	2	44	19	41	3	22	16
FEB. 21	45	20	20	21	45	2	45	19	41	3	22	16
FEB. 22	45	22	22	23	45	2	45	19	41	3	22	16
FEB. 23	46	23	24	25	45	3	45	19	41	3	22	16
FEB. 24	46	25	26	27	45	3	45	19	41	3	22	16
FEB. 25	46	27	28	29	45	3	45	19	41	3	22	16
FEB. 26	46	29	30	31	46	3	45	19	41	3	22	16
FEB. 27	46	31	32	33	46	3	45	19	41	3	22	16
FEB. 28	46	33	34	34	46	3	45	19	41	3	22	16
FEB. 29	46	35	36	36	46	4	45	19	41	3	22	16

MOON 1 ◗ 12:01 A.M. TO 8:00 A.M.   **MOON 2** ◑ 8:01 A.M. TO 4:00 P.M.   **MOON 3** ● 4:01 P.M. TO 12:00 A.M.

Use only one "moon" number. Choose the column closest to your time of birth. If your place of birth is not on Eastern Standard Time, be sure to read "How to Convert to Eastern Standard Time" at the beginning of this section.

1932

March

April

Date & Time	SUN ☼	MOON 1 ◗	MOON 2 ◑	MOON 3 ●	MERCURY	VENUS	MARS	JUPITER	SATURN	URANUS	NEPTUNE	PLUTO
MAR. 1	46	37	37	38	47	4	46	19	41	3	22	16
MAR. 2	46	39	39	40	47	4	46	19	41	3	22	16
MAR. 3	47	40	41	41	47	4	46	19	41	3	22	16
MAR. 4	47	42	43	43	48	4	46	19	41	3	22	16
MAR. 5	47	44	44	45	48	4	46	19	41	3	22	16
MAR. 6	47	45	46	46	48	5	46	19	41	3	22	16
MAR. 7	47	47	48	48	48	5	46	19	41	3	22	16
MAR. 8	47	1	1	2	1	5	46	19	41	3	22	16
MAR. 9	47	2	3	3	1	5	46	19	41	3	22	16
MAR. 10	47	4	4	5	1	5	46	19	41	3	22	16
MAR. 11	48	5	6	6	1	5	47	19	41	3	22	16
MAR. 12	48	7	7	8	2	5	47	19	41	3	22	16
MAR. 13	48	8	9	10	2	6	47	19	41	3	22	16
MAR. 14	48	10	11	11	2	6	47	19	41	3	22	16
MAR. 15	48	12	12	13	2	6	47	19	41	3	22	16
MAR. 16	48	13	14	15	2	6	47	19	41	3	22	16
MAR. 17	48	15	16	16	3	6	47	19	41	3	22	16
MAR. 18	48	17	18	18	3	6	47	19	41	3	22	16
MAR. 19	1	19	19	20	3	7	47	19	41	3	22	16
MAR. 20	1	21	21	22	3	7	47	19	41	3	22	16
MAR. 21	1	23	23	24	3	7	48	19	41	3	22	16
MAR. 22	1	25	25	26	4	7	48	19	41	3	22	16
MAR. 23	1	27	27	28	4	7	48	19	41	3	22	16
MAR. 24	1	29	29	30	4	7	48	19	41	3	22	16
MAR. 25	2	31	31	32	4	7	48	19	41	3	22	16
MAR. 26	2	33	33	34	4	8	48	19	41	3	22	16
MAR. 27	2	34	35	36	4	8	48	19	41	3	22	16
MAR. 28	2	36	37	38	4	8	48	19	41	3	22	16
MAR. 29	2	38	39	39	4	8	48	19	41	3	22	16
MAR. 30	2	40	41	41	4	8	1	19	41	3	22	16
MAR. 31	2	42	42	43	4	8	1	19	41	3	22	16

Date & Time	SUN ☼	MOON 1 ◗	MOON 2 ◑	MOON 3 ●	MERCURY	VENUS	MARS	JUPITER	SATURN	URANUS	NEPTUNE	PLUTO
APR. 1	2	43	44	44	4	8	1	19	41	3	22	16
APR. 2	2	45	46	46	4	9	1	19	41	3	22	16
APR. 3	3	47	47	48	4	9	1	19	41	3	22	16
APR. 4	3	48	1	1	4	9	1	19	41	4	22	16
APR. 5	3	2	2	3	4	9	1	19	41	4	22	16
APR. 6	3	3	4	4	4	9	1	19	41	4	22	16
APR. 7	3	5	5	6	4	9	1	19	41	4	22	16
APR. 8	3	6	7	8	4	9	1	19	41	4	22	16
APR. 9	3	8	9	9	4	10	2	19	41	4	22	16
APR. 10	3	10	10	11	4	10	2	19	41	4	22	16
APR. 11	4	11	12	12	4	10	2	19	41	4	22	16
APR. 12	4	13	13	14	4	10	2	19	41	4	22	16
APR. 13	4	15	15	16	3	10	2	19	41	4	22	16
APR. 14	4	16	17	17	3	10	2	19	42	4	22	16
APR. 15	4	18	19	19	3	10	2	19	42	4	22	16
APR. 16	4	20	20	21	3	11	2	19	42	4	22	16
APR. 17	4	22	22	23	3	11	2	19	42	4	22	16
APR. 18	4	24	24	25	3	11	3	19	42	4	22	16
APR. 19	5	26	26	27	3	11	3	19	42	4	22	16
APR. 20	5	28	28	29	3	11	3	19	42	4	22	16
APR. 21	5	30	30	31	3	11	3	19	42	4	22	16
APR. 22	5	32	32	33	3	11	3	19	42	4	22	16
APR. 23	5	34	34	35	3	11	3	19	42	4	22	16
APR. 24	5	36	36	37	3	12	3	19	42	4	22	16
APR. 25	6	38	38	39	3	12	3	19	42	4	22	16
APR. 26	6	39	40	41	3	12	3	19	42	4	22	16
APR. 27	6	41	42	42	3	12	3	19	42	4	22	16
APR. 28	6	43	43	44	3	12	4	19	42	4	22	16
APR. 29	6	45	45	46	3	12	4	19	42	4	22	16
APR. 30	6	46	47	47	3	12	4	19	42	4	22	16

MOON 1 ◗ 12:01 A.M. TO 8:00 A.M.　　**MOON 2** ◑ 8:01 A.M. TO 4:00 P.M.　　**MOON 3** ● 4:01 P.M. TO 12:00 A.M.

Use only one "moon" number. Choose the column closest to your time of birth. If your place of birth is not on Eastern Standard Time, be sure to read "How to Convert to Eastern Standard Time" at the beginning of this section.

1932

May   **June**

Date & Time	SUN	MOON 1	MOON 2	MOON 3	MERCURY	VENUS	MARS	JUPITER	SATURN	URANUS	NEPTUNE	PLUTO
MAY 1	6	48	48	1	3	12	4	19	42	4	22	16
MAY 2	6	1	2	2	3	13	4	19	42	4	22	16
MAY 3	7	3	3	4	3	13	4	19	42	4	22	16
MAY 4	7	5	5	6	3	13	4	19	42	4	22	16
MAY 5	7	6	7	7	3	13	4	19	42	4	22	16
MAY 6	7	8	8	9	4	13	4	19	42	4	22	16
MAY 7	7	9	10	10	4	13	4	19	42	4	22	16
MAY 8	7	11	11	12	4	13	5	19	42	4	22	16
MAY 9	7	13	13	14	4	13	5	19	42	4	22	16
MAY 10	7	14	15	15	4	13	5	19	42	4	22	16
MAY 11	8	16	16	17	4	13	5	19	42	4	22	16
MAY 12	8	18	18	19	4	14	5	19	42	4	22	16
MAY 13	8	19	20	20	5	14	5	19	42	4	22	16
MAY 14	8	21	22	22	5	14	5	19	42	4	22	16
MAY 15	8	23	24	24	5	14	5	19	42	4	22	16
MAY 16	8	25	25	26	5	14	5	19	42	4	22	16
MAY 17	8	27	27	28	5	14	5	19	42	4	22	16
MAY 18	8	29	29	30	5	14	6	19	42	4	22	16
MAY 19	9	31	31	32	6	14	6	19	42	4	22	16
MAY 20	9	33	33	34	6	14	6	19	42	4	22	16
MAY 21	9	35	35	36	6	14	6	19	42	4	22	16
MAY 22	9	37	37	38	6	14	6	19	42	4	22	16
MAY 23	9	39	39	40	6	14	6	19	42	4	22	16
MAY 24	9	41	41	42	7	15	6	19	42	4	22	16
MAY 25	10	42	43	43	7	15	6	19	42	4	22	16
MAY 26	10	44	45	45	7	15	6	19	42	4	22	16
MAY 27	10	46	46	47	7	15	6	19	42	4	22	16
MAY 28	10	47	48	48	8	15	7	19	42	4	22	16
MAY 29	10	1	1	2	8	15	7	19	42	4	22	16
MAY 30	10	3	3	4	8	15	7	19	42	4	22	16
MAY 31	10	4	5	5	8	15	7	19	42	4	22	16

Date & Time	SUN	MOON 1	MOON 2	MOON 3	MERCURY	VENUS	MARS	JUPITER	SATURN	URANUS	NEPTUNE	PLUTO
JUN. 1	10	6	6	7	9	15	7	19	42	4	22	16
JUN. 2	10	7	8	8	9	15	7	19	42	4	22	16
JUN. 3	11	9	9	10	9	15	7	19	42	4	22	16
JUN. 4	11	10	11	12	9	15	7	19	42	4	22	16
JUN. 5	11	12	13	13	10	15	7	19	42	4	22	16
JUN. 6	11	14	14	15	10	15	7	19	42	4	22	16
JUN. 7	11	15	16	17	10	15	8	19	42	4	22	16
JUN. 8	11	17	18	18	10	15	8	19	42	4	22	16
JUN. 9	11	19	19	20	11	15	8	19	42	4	22	16
JUN. 10	11	21	21	22	11	15	8	19	42	4	22	16
JUN. 11	12	22	23	24	11	15	8	19	42	4	22	16
JUN. 12	12	24	25	26	12	15	8	19	42	4	22	16
JUN. 13	12	26	27	27	12	15	8	19	42	4	22	16
JUN. 14	12	28	29	29	12	15	8	19	42	4	22	16
JUN. 15	12	30	31	31	12	15	8	19	41	4	22	16
JUN. 16	12	32	33	33	13	15	8	19	41	4	22	16
JUN. 17	12	34	35	35	13	15	8	20	41	4	22	16
JUN. 18	12	36	37	37	13	15	9	20	41	4	22	16
JUN. 19	13	38	39	39	14	15	9	20	41	4	22	16
JUN. 20	13	40	40	41	14	15	9	20	41	4	22	16
JUN. 21	13	42	42	43	14	15	9	20	41	4	22	16
JUN. 22	13	43	44	45	14	14	9	20	41	4	22	16
JUN. 23	13	45	46	46	15	14	9	20	41	4	22	16
JUN. 24	13	47	47	48	15	14	9	20	41	4	22	16
JUN. 25	14	48	1	2	15	14	9	20	41	4	22	16
JUN. 26	14	2	3	5	15	14	9	20	41	4	22	16
JUN. 27	14	4	4	5	16	14	9	20	41	4	22	16
JUN. 28	14	5	6	6	16	14	10	20	41	4	22	16
JUN. 29	14	7	7	8	16	14	10	20	41	4	22	16
JUN. 30	14	8	9	9	16	14	10	20	41	4	22	16

MOON 1 ☽ 12:01 A.M. TO 8:00 A.M.   **MOON 2** ☽ 8:01 A.M. TO 4:00 P.M.   **MOON 3** ● 4:01 P.M. TO 12:00 A.M.

Use only one "moon" number. Choose the column closest to your time of birth. If your place of birth is not on Eastern Standard Time, be sure to read "How to Convert to Eastern Standard Time" at the beginning of this section.

Date & Time	SUN ☉	MOON 1 ◗	MOON 2 ◑	MOON 3 ●	MERCURY	VENUS	MARS	JUPITER	SATURN	URANUS	NEPTUNE	PLUTO
JUL. 1	14	10	11	11	17	14	10	20	41	4	22	16
JUL. 2	14	12	12	13	17	14	10	20	41	4	22	16
JUL. 3	15	13	14	14	17	14	10	20	41	4	22	16
JUL. 4	15	15	16	16	17	14	10	20	41	4	22	16
JUL. 5	15	17	17	18	18	13	10	20	41	4	22	16
JUL. 6	15	18	19	20	18	13	10	20	41	4	22	16
JUL. 7	15	20	21	21	18	13	10	20	41	4	22	16
JUL. 8	15	22	23	23	18	13	10	20	41	4	22	16
JUL. 9	15	24	24	25	18	13	11	20	41	4	22	16
JUL. 10	15	26	26	27	19	13	11	20	41	4	22	16
JUL. 11	16	28	28	29	19	13	11	20	41	4	22	16
JUL. 12	16	29	30	31	19	13	11	20	41	4	22	16
JUL. 13	16	31	32	33	19	13	11	20	41	4	22	16
JUL. 14	16	33	34	35	19	13	11	20	41	4	22	16
JUL. 15	16	35	36	37	19	13	11	20	41	4	22	16
JUL. 16	16	37	38	38	20	13	11	20	41	4	22	16
JUL. 17	16	39	40	40	20	13	11	20	41	4	22	16
JUL. 18	16	41	42	42	20	13	11	20	41	4	22	16
JUL. 19	17	43	43	44	20	13	11	20	41	4	22	16
JUL. 20	17	44	45	46	20	13	12	20	41	4	22	16
JUL. 21	17	46	47	47	20	13	12	20	41	4	22	16
JUL. 22	17	48	48	1	20	13	12	20	41	4	22	16
JUL. 23	17	2	2	3	21	13	12	20	41	4	22	16
JUL. 24	17	3	4	4	21	13	12	20	41	4	22	16
JUL. 25	17	5	5	6	21	13	12	20	41	4	22	16
JUL. 26	18	6	7	7	21	13	12	21	41	4	22	16
JUL. 27	18	8	8	9	21	13	12	21	41	4	22	16
JUL. 28	18	9	10	11	21	13	12	21	41	4	22	16
JUL. 29	18	11	12	12	21	13	12	21	41	4	22	16
JUL. 30	18	13	13	14	21	13	12	21	41	4	22	16
JUL. 31	18	14	15	16	21	13	13	21	41	4	22	16

Date & Time	SUN ☉	MOON 1 ◗	MOON 2 ◑	MOON 3 ●	MERCURY	VENUS	MARS	JUPITER	SATURN	URANUS	NEPTUNE	PLUTO
AUG. 1	18	16	17	17	21	13	13	21	41	4	22	16
AUG. 2	18	18	19	19	21	13	13	21	41	4	22	16
AUG. 3	19	20	20	21	21	13	13	21	41	4	22	16
AUG. 4	19	22	22	23	21	13	13	21	41	4	22	16
AUG. 5	19	23	24	25	21	13	13	21	41	4	22	16
AUG. 6	19	25	26	27	21	13	13	21	41	4	22	16
AUG. 7	19	27	28	28	21	14	13	21	41	4	22	16
AUG. 8	19	29	30	30	21	14	13	21	41	4	22	16
AUG. 9	19	31	32	32	21	14	13	21	41	4	22	16
AUG. 10	19	33	33	34	21	14	13	21	41	4	22	16
AUG. 11	20	35	35	36	21	14	14	21	41	4	22	16
AUG. 12	20	37	37	38	21	14	14	21	41	4	22	16
AUG. 13	20	38	39	40	21	14	14	21	41	4	22	16
AUG. 14	20	40	41	42	21	14	14	21	41	4	22	16
AUG. 15	20	42	43	43	20	14	14	21	41	4	22	16
AUG. 16	20	44	44	45	20	14	14	21	41	4	22	16
AUG. 17	20	46	46	47	20	14	14	21	41	4	22	16
AUG. 18	20	47	48	48	20	14	14	21	41	4	22	16
AUG. 19	21	1	1	2	20	15	14	21	41	4	22	16
AUG. 20	21	3	3	4	20	15	14	21	41	4	22	16
AUG. 21	21	4	5	5	20	15	14	21	41	4	22	16
AUG. 22	21	6	6	7	20	15	14	21	41	4	22	16
AUG. 23	21	7	8	8	20	15	15	21	41	4	22	16
AUG. 24	21	9	9	10	20	15	15	21	41	4	22	16
AUG. 25	21	11	11	12	20	15	15	21	41	4	22	16
AUG. 26	22	12	13	13	20	15	15	21	41	4	22	16
AUG. 27	22	14	14	15	20	15	15	21	41	4	22	16
AUG. 28	22	16	16	17	20	16	15	21	41	4	22	16
AUG. 29	22	17	18	18	20	16	15	21	41	4	22	16
AUG. 30	22	19	20	20	20	16	15	22	41	4	22	16
AUG. 31	22	21	22	22	20	16	15	22	41	4	22	16

MOON 1 ◗ 12:01 A.M. TO 8:00 A.M.　　**MOON 2** ◑ 8:01 A.M. TO 4:00 P.M.　　**MOON 3** ● 4:01 P.M. TO 12:00 A.M.

Use only one "moon" number. Choose the column closest to your time of birth. If your place of birth is not on Eastern Standard Time, be sure to read "How to Convert to Eastern Standard Time" at the beginning of this section.

1932

September

Date & Time	SUN ☉	MOON 1 ◖	MOON 2 ◑	MOON 3 ●	MERCURY	VENUS	MARS	JUPITER	SATURN	URANUS	NEPTUNE	PLUTO
SEP. 1	22	23	23	24	20	16	15	22	41	4	22	16
SEP. 2	22	25	25	26	20	16	15	22	41	4	22	16
SEP. 3	23	27	27	28	20	16	16	22	41	4	22	16
SEP. 4	23	29	29	30	20	16	16	22	41	4	22	16
SEP. 5	23	30	31	32	20	17	16	22	41	4	22	16
SEP. 6	23	32	33	34	20	17	16	22	41	4	22	16
SEP. 7	23	34	35	36	21	17	16	22	41	4	22	16
SEP. 8	23	36	37	37	21	17	16	22	41	4	22	16
SEP. 9	23	38	39	39	21	17	16	22	41	4	22	16
SEP. 10	23	40	40	41	21	17	16	22	41	4	22	16
SEP. 11	24	42	42	43	21	17	16	22	41	4	22	16
SEP. 12	24	43	44	45	22	17	16	22	41	4	22	16
SEP. 13	24	45	46	46	22	18	16	22	41	4	22	16
SEP. 14	24	47	47	48	22	18	16	22	41	4	22	16
SEP. 15	24	48	1	2	22	18	17	22	41	4	22	16
SEP. 16	24	2	3	3	23	18	17	22	41	4	22	16
SEP. 17	24	4	4	5	23	18	17	22	41	4	22	16
SEP. 18	24	5	6	6	23	18	17	22	41	4	22	16
SEP. 19	25	7	7	8	23	18	17	22	41	4	22	16
SEP. 20	25	8	9	9	24	19	17	22	41	4	22	16
SEP. 21	25	10	11	11	24	19	17	22	41	4	22	16
SEP. 22	25	12	12	13	24	19	17	22	41	4	22	16
SEP. 23	25	13	14	14	24	19	17	22	41	4	22	16
SEP. 24	25	15	15	16	25	19	17	22	41	4	22	16
SEP. 25	26	17	17	18	25	19	17	22	41	4	22	16
SEP. 26	26	18	19	20	25	19	17	22	41	4	22	16
SEP. 27	26	20	21	21	25	19	17	22	41	4	22	16
SEP. 28	26	22	23	23	25	20	18	22	41	4	22	16
SEP. 29	26	24	25	25	26	20	18	22	41	4	22	16
SEP. 30	26	26	26	27	26	20	18	22	41	4	22	16

October

Date & Time	SUN ☉	MOON 1 ◖	MOON 2 ◑	MOON 3 ●	MERCURY	VENUS	MARS	JUPITER	SATURN	URANUS	NEPTUNE	PLUTO
OCT. 1	26	28	28	29	26	20	18	22	41	4	22	16
OCT. 2	26	30	30	31	26	20	18	22	41	4	22	16
OCT. 3	27	32	32	33	27	20	18	22	41	4	22	16
OCT. 4	27	34	34	35	27	21	18	23	41	4	22	16
OCT. 5	27	36	36	37	27	21	18	23	41	4	22	16
OCT. 6	27	38	38	39	27	21	18	23	41	4	22	16
OCT. 7	27	39	40	41	28	21	18	23	41	4	22	16
OCT. 8	27	41	42	42	28	21	18	23	41	4	22	16
OCT. 9	27	43	44	44	28	21	18	23	41	4	22	16
OCT. 10	27	45	45	46	28	21	18	23	41	4	22	16
OCT. 11	28	46	47	47	28	22	19	23	41	4	22	16
OCT. 12	28	48	1	1	29	22	19	23	41	4	22	16
OCT. 13	28	2	2	3	29	22	19	23	41	4	22	16
OCT. 14	28	3	4	4	29	22	19	23	41	4	22	16
OCT. 15	28	5	5	6	29	22	19	23	41	4	22	16
OCT. 16	28	6	7	7	30	22	19	23	41	4	22	16
OCT. 17	28	8	9	9	30	22	19	23	41	4	22	16
OCT. 18	28	10	10	11	30	23	19	23	41	4	22	16
OCT. 19	29	11	12	12	30	23	19	23	41	4	22	16
OCT. 20	29	13	13	14	30	23	19	23	41	4	22	16
OCT. 21	29	14	15	15	31	23	19	23	41	4	22	16
OCT. 22	29	16	17	17	31	23	19	23	41	4	22	16
OCT. 23	29	18	18	19	31	23	19	23	41	4	22	16
OCT. 24	29	19	20	21	31	24	20	23	41	4	22	16
OCT. 25	29	21	22	22	31	24	20	23	41	4	22	16
OCT. 26	30	23	24	32	32	24	20	23	41	4	22	16
OCT. 27	30	25	26	26	32	24	20	23	41	4	22	16
OCT. 28	30	27	28	28	32	24	20	23	41	4	22	16
OCT. 29	30	29	30	30	32	24	20	23	41	4	22	16
OCT. 30	30	31	32	32	32	24	20	23	41	4	22	16
OCT. 31	30	33	34	34	32	25	20	23	41	4	22	16

MOON 1 ◖ 12:01 A.M. TO 8:00 A.M.   **MOON 2** ◑ 8:01 A.M. TO 4:00 P.M.   **MOON 3** ● 4:01 P.M. TO 12:00 A.M.

Use only one "moon" number. Choose the column closest to your time of birth. If your place of birth is not on Eastern Standard Time, be sure to read "How to Convert to Eastern Standard Time" at the beginning of this section.

1932

November

December

Date & Time	SUN	MOON 1	MOON 2	MOON 3	MERCURY	VENUS	MARS	JUPITER	SATURN	URANUS	NEPTUNE	PLUTO
NOV. 1	30	35	36	36	33	25	20	23	41	4	22	16
NOV. 2	30	37	38	38	33	25	20	23	41	4	22	16
NOV. 3	31	39	40	40	33	25	20	23	41	4	22	16
NOV. 4	31	41	41	42	33	25	20	23	41	4	22	16
NOV. 5	31	43	43	44	33	25	20	23	41	4	22	16
NOV. 6	31	44	45	45	34	25	20	23	41	4	22	16
NOV. 7	31	46	46	47	34	26	21	23	41	4	22	16
NOV. 8	31	48	48	1	34	26	21	23	41	4	22	16
NOV. 9	31	1	2	2	34	26	21	23	41	4	22	16
NOV. 10	31	3	3	4	34	26	21	23	41	4	22	16
NOV. 11	31	4	5	5	34	26	21	23	41	4	22	16
NOV. 12	32	6	7	7	35	27	21	23	41	4	22	16
NOV. 13	32	8	8	9	35	27	21	23	41	4	22	16
NOV. 14	32	9	10	10	35	27	21	23	41	4	22	16
NOV. 15	32	11	11	12	35	27	21	24	41	4	22	16
NOV. 16	32	12	13	13	35	27	21	24	41	4	22	16
NOV. 17	32	14	14	15	35	27	21	24	41	4	22	16
NOV. 18	32	16	16	17	35	28	21	24	41	4	22	16
NOV. 19	33	17	18	18	35	28	21	24	41	4	22	16
NOV. 20	33	19	19	20	36	28	21	24	41	4	22	16
NOV. 21	33	21	21	22	36	28	21	24	41	4	22	16
NOV. 22	33	22	23	24	36	28	21	24	41	4	22	16
NOV. 23	33	24	25	25	36	28	22	24	41	4	22	16
NOV. 24	33	26	27	27	36	29	22	24	41	4	22	16
NOV. 25	34	28	29	29	36	29	22	24	41	4	22	16
NOV. 26	34	30	31	31	36	29	22	24	41	4	22	16
NOV. 27	34	32	33	33	36	29	22	24	41	4	22	16
NOV. 28	34	34	35	35	36	29	22	24	41	4	22	16
NOV. 29	34	36	37	37	35	29	22	24	41	4	22	16
NOV. 30	34	38	39	39	35	29	22	24	41	4	22	16

Date & Time	SUN	MOON 1	MOON 2	MOON 3	MERCURY	VENUS	MARS	JUPITER	SATURN	URANUS	NEPTUNE	PLUTO
DEC. 1	34	40	41	41	35	30	22	24	41	4	22	16
DEC. 2	34	42	43	43	35	30	22	24	41	4	22	16
DEC. 3	35	44	44	45	35	30	22	24	41	4	22	16
DEC. 4	35	45	46	47	35	30	22	24	41	4	22	16
DEC. 5	35	47	48	48	35	30	22	24	41	4	22	16
DEC. 6	35	1	1	2	34	30	22	24	41	4	22	16
DEC. 7	35	2	3	3	34	31	22	24	41	4	22	16
DEC. 8	35	4	5	5	34	31	22	24	41	4	22	16
DEC. 9	35	6	6	7	34	31	22	24	41	4	22	16
DEC. 10	35	7	8	8	34	31	22	24	41	4	22	16
DEC. 11	36	9	9	10	34	31	23	24	41	4	22	16
DEC. 12	36	10	11	11	34	31	23	24	41	4	22	16
DEC. 13	36	12	12	13	34	32	23	24	41	4	22	16
DEC. 14	36	14	14	15	34	32	23	24	41	4	22	16
DEC. 15	36	15	16	16	34	32	23	24	41	4	22	16
DEC. 16	36	17	17	18	34	32	23	24	41	4	22	16
DEC. 17	36	18	19	20	34	32	23	24	41	4	22	16
DEC. 18	36	20	21	21	34	32	23	24	41	4	22	16
DEC. 19	37	22	22	23	34	33	23	24	41	4	22	16
DEC. 20	37	24	24	25	34	33	23	24	41	4	22	16
DEC. 21	37	25	26	27	34	33	23	24	41	4	22	16
DEC. 22	37	27	28	29	34	33	23	24	41	4	22	16
DEC. 23	37	29	30	31	34	33	23	24	41	4	22	16
DEC. 24	37	31	32	32	34	33	23	24	41	4	22	16
DEC. 25	37	33	34	34	34	34	23	24	41	4	22	16
DEC. 26	38	35	36	37	35	34	23	24	41	4	22	16
DEC. 27	38	37	38	38	35	34	23	24	41	4	22	16
DEC. 28	38	39	40	40	35	34	23	24	41	4	22	16
DEC. 29	38	41	42	42	35	34	23	24	41	4	22	16
DEC. 30	38	43	44	44	35	34	23	24	41	4	22	16
DEC. 31	38	45	45	46	35	35	23	24	41	4	22	16

MOON 1 ☽ 12:01 A.M. TO 8:00 A.M.　　**MOON 2** ☽ 8:01 A.M. TO 4:00 P.M.　　**MOON 3** ● 4:01 P.M. TO 12:00 A.M.

Use only one "moon" number. Choose the column closest to your time of birth. If your place of birth is not on Eastern Standard Time, be sure to read "How to Convert to Eastern Standard Time" at the beginning of this section.

1933

January

Date & Time	SUN	MOON 1	MOON 2	MOON 3	MERCURY	VENUS	MARS	JUPITER	SATURN	URANUS	NEPTUNE	PLUTO
JAN. 1	38	47	47	48	36	35	23	24	42	4	22	16
JAN. 2	38	48	1	1	36	35	23	24	42	4	22	16
JAN. 3	39	2	2	3	36	35	23	24	42	4	22	16
JAN. 4	39	4	4	5	36	35	23	24	42	4	22	16
JAN. 5	39	5	6	6	36	35	23	24	42	4	22	16
JAN. 6	39	7	7	8	37	36	23	24	42	4	22	16
JAN. 7	39	8	9	9	37	36	24	24	42	4	22	16
JAN. 8	39	10	10	11	37	36	24	24	42	4	22	16
JAN. 9	39	11	12	13	37	36	24	24	42	4	22	16
JAN. 10	40	13	14	14	37	36	24	24	42	4	22	16
JAN. 11	40	15	15	15	38	36	24	24	42	4	22	16
JAN. 12	40	16	17	17	38	37	24	24	42	4	22	16
JAN. 13	40	18	19	19	38	37	24	24	42	4	22	16
JAN. 14	40	20	20	21	38	37	24	24	42	4	22	16
JAN. 15	40	21	22	23	38	37	24	24	42	4	22	16
JAN. 16	40	23	24	24	39	37	24	24	42	4	22	16
JAN. 17	41	25	26	26	39	37	24	24	42	4	22	16
JAN. 18	41	27	27	28	39	38	24	24	42	4	22	16
JAN. 19	41	29	29	30	39	38	24	24	42	4	22	16
JAN. 20	41	31	31	32	39	38	24	24	42	4	22	16
JAN. 21	41	32	33	34	40	38	24	24	42	4	22	16
JAN. 22	41	34	35	36	40	38	24	24	42	4	22	16
JAN. 23	42	36	37	38	40	38	24	24	42	4	22	16
JAN. 24	42	38	39	40	40	39	24	24	42	4	22	16
JAN. 25	42	40	41	42	40	39	24	24	42	4	22	16
JAN. 26	42	42	43	43	41	39	24	24	42	4	22	16
JAN. 27	42	44	45	45	41	39	24	24	42	4	22	16
JAN. 28	42	46	46	47	41	39	24	24	42	4	22	16
JAN. 29	42	48	48	1	41	39	24	24	42	4	22	16
JAN. 30	42	1	2	2	41	40	24	24	42	4	22	16
JAN. 31	43	3	4	4	42	40	24	24	42	4	22	16

February

Date & Time	SUN	MOON 1	MOON 2	MOON 3	MERCURY	VENUS	MARS	JUPITER	SATURN	URANUS	NEPTUNE	PLUTO
FEB. 1	43	5	5	6	42	40	24	24	42	4	22	16
FEB. 2	43	6	7	7	42	40	24	24	42	4	22	16
FEB. 3	43	8	8	9	42	40	24	24	42	4	22	16
FEB. 4	43	9	10	10	43	40	23	24	42	4	22	16
FEB. 5	43	11	11	12	43	41	23	24	42	4	22	16
FEB. 6	43	13	13	14	43	41	23	24	42	4	22	16
FEB. 7	43	14	15	15	43	41	23	24	42	4	22	16
FEB. 8	44	16	16	17	44	41	23	24	42	4	22	16
FEB. 9	44	18	18	19	44	41	23	24	42	4	22	16
FEB. 10	44	19	20	20	44	41	23	24	42	4	22	16
FEB. 11	44	21	22	22	44	42	23	24	42	4	22	16
FEB. 12	44	23	23	24	44	42	23	24	42	4	22	16
FEB. 13	44	25	25	26	45	42	23	24	42	4	22	16
FEB. 14	44	26	27	28	45	42	23	24	42	4	22	16
FEB. 15	44	28	29	30	45	42	23	24	42	4	22	16
FEB. 16	45	30	31	31	45	42	23	24	42	4	22	16
FEB. 17	45	32	33	33	46	43	23	24	42	4	22	16
FEB. 18	45	34	35	35	46	43	23	24	42	4	22	16
FEB. 19	45	36	36	37	46	43	23	24	42	4	22	16
FEB. 20	45	38	38	39	46	43	23	24	42	4	22	16
FEB. 21	45	40	40	41	47	43	23	24	42	4	22	16
FEB. 22	45	41	42	43	47	43	23	24	42	4	22	16
FEB. 23	46	43	44	45	47	44	23	24	42	4	22	16
FEB. 24	46	45	46	46	47	44	23	24	42	4	22	16
FEB. 25	46	47	47	48	48	44	23	24	42	4	22	16
FEB. 26	46	1	1	2	48	44	23	24	42	4	22	16
FEB. 27	46	2	3	3	48	44	23	24	42	4	22	16
FEB. 28	46	4	5	5	48	44	22	24	42	4	22	16

MOON 1 ◖ 12:01 A.M. TO 8:00 A.M.　　**MOON 2** ◑ 8:01 A.M. TO 4:00 P.M.　　**MOON 3** ● 4:01 P.M. TO 12:00 A.M.

Use only one "moon" number. Choose the column closest to your time of birth. If your place of birth is not on Eastern Standard Time, be sure to read "How to Convert to Eastern Standard Time" at the beginning of this section.

1933

March

April

Date & Time	SUN	MOON 1	MOON 2	MOON 3	MERCURY	VENUS	MARS	JUPITER	SATURN	URANUS	NEPTUNE	PLUTO
MAR. 1	46	6	6	7	1	45	22	24	42	4	22	16
MAR. 2	46	7	8	8	1	45	22	24	42	4	22	16
MAR. 3	47	9	9	10	1	45	22	24	42	4	22	16
MAR. 4	47	10	11	11	1	45	22	24	42	4	22	16
MAR. 5	47	12	13	13	1	45	22	23	42	4	22	16
MAR. 6	47	14	14	15	1	45	22	23	42	4	22	16
MAR. 7	47	15	16	16	2	46	22	23	43	4	22	16
MAR. 8	47	17	17	18	2	46	22	23	43	4	22	16
MAR. 9	47	19	19	20	2	46	22	23	43	4	22	16
MAR. 10	47	20	21	22	2	46	22	23	43	4	22	16
MAR. 11	48	22	23	23	2	46	22	23	43	4	22	16
MAR. 12	48	24	25	25	2	46	22	23	43	4	22	16
MAR. 13	48	26	26	27	2	47	22	23	43	4	22	16
MAR. 14	48	28	28	29	2	47	22	23	43	4	22	16
MAR. 15	48	30	30	31	2	47	22	23	43	4	22	16
MAR. 16	48	32	32	33	2	47	22	23	43	4	22	16
MAR. 17	48	34	34	35	2	47	22	23	43	4	22	16
MAR. 18	48	35	36	37	2	47	22	23	43	4	22	16
MAR. 19	1	37	38	39	2	48	22	23	43	4	22	16
MAR. 20	1	39	40	40	2	48	22	23	43	4	22	16
MAR. 21	1	41	42	42	2	48	21	23	43	4	22	16
MAR. 22	1	43	44	44	1	48	21	23	43	4	22	16
MAR. 23	1	45	45	46	1	48	21	23	43	4	22	16
MAR. 24	1	46	47	47	1	48	21	23	43	4	22	16
MAR. 25	2	48	1	1	1	1	21	23	43	4	22	16
MAR. 26	2	2	2	3	1	1	21	23	43	4	22	16
MAR. 27	2	3	4	5	1	1	21	23	43	4	22	16
MAR. 28	2	5	6	6	1	1	21	23	43	4	22	16
MAR. 29	2	7	7	8	1	1	21	23	43	4	22	16
MAR. 30	2	8	9	9	1	1	21	23	43	4	22	16
MAR. 31	2	10	10	11	48	2	21	23	43	4	22	16

Date & Time	SUN	MOON 1	MOON 2	MOON 3	MERCURY	VENUS	MARS	JUPITER	SATURN	URANUS	NEPTUNE	PLUTO
APR. 1	2	11	12	13	48	2	21	23	43	4	22	16
APR. 2	2	13	14	14	48	2	21	23	43	4	22	16
APR. 3	3	15	15	16	48	2	21	23	43	4	22	16
APR. 4	3	16	17	17	48	2	21	23	43	4	22	16
APR. 5	3	18	18	19	48	2	21	23	43	4	22	16
APR. 6	3	20	20	21	48	3	21	23	43	4	22	16
APR. 7	3	21	22	23	48	3	21	23	43	4	22	16
APR. 8	3	23	24	24	48	3	21	23	43	4	22	16
APR. 9	3	25	26	26	48	3	21	23	43	4	22	16
APR. 10	3	27	28	28	48	3	21	23	43	4	22	16
APR. 11	4	29	30	30	48	3	21	23	43	4	22	16
APR. 12	4	31	32	32	48	4	21	23	43	4	22	16
APR. 13	4	33	34	34	1	4	21	23	43	4	22	16
APR. 14	4	35	36	36	1	4	21	23	43	4	22	16
APR. 15	4	37	37	38	1	4	21	23	43	4	22	16
APR. 16	4	39	39	40	1	4	21	23	43	4	22	16
APR. 17	4	41	41	42	1	4	21	23	43	4	22	16
APR. 18	4	42	43	44	1	5	21	23	43	4	22	16
APR. 19	5	44	45	45	1	5	21	23	43	4	22	16
APR. 20	5	46	46	47	1	5	21	23	43	4	22	16
APR. 21	5	48	48	1	1	5	21	23	43	4	22	16
APR. 22	5	1	2	2	2	5	21	23	43	4	22	16
APR. 23	5	3	4	4	2	5	21	23	43	4	22	16
APR. 24	5	5	5	6	2	6	21	23	43	4	22	16
APR. 25	6	6	7	7	2	6	21	23	43	4	22	16
APR. 26	6	8	8	9	2	6	21	23	43	4	22	16
APR. 27	6	9	10	10	2	6	21	23	43	4	22	16
APR. 28	6	11	12	12	3	6	21	23	43	4	22	16
APR. 29	6	13	13	14	3	6	21	23	43	4	22	16
APR. 30	6	14	15	15	3	7	21	23	43	4	22	16

MOON 1 ◐ 12:01 A.M. TO 8:00 A.M.   **MOON 2** ◑ 8:01 A.M. TO 4:00 P.M.   **MOON 3** ● 4:01 P.M. TO 12:00 A.M.

Use only one "moon" number. Choose the column closest to your time of birth. If your place of birth is not on Eastern Standard Time, be sure to read "How to Convert to Eastern Standard Time" at the beginning of this section.

1933

May

Date & Time	SUN	MOON 1	MOON 2	MOON 3	MERCURY	VENUS	MARS	JUPITER	SATURN	URANUS	NEPTUNE	PLUTO
MAY 1	6	16	16	17	3	7	21	23	43	4	22	16
MAY 2	6	17	18	18	3	7	21	23	43	4	22	16
MAY 3	7	19	20	20	3	7	21	23	43	4	22	16
MAY 4	7	21	21	22	4	7	21	23	43	4	22	16
MAY 5	7	22	23	24	4	7	21	23	43	4	22	16
MAY 6	7	24	25	25	4	8	21	23	43	4	22	16
MAY 7	7	26	27	27	4	8	22	23	43	4	22	16
MAY 8	7	28	29	29	4	8	22	23	43	4	22	16
MAY 9	7	30	31	31	5	8	22	23	43	4	22	16
MAY 10	7	32	33	33	5	8	22	23	43	4	22	16
MAY 11	8	34	35	35	5	8	22	23	43	4	22	16
MAY 12	8	36	37	37	5	8	22	23	43	4	22	16
MAY 13	8	38	39	39	6	9	22	23	43	4	22	16
MAY 14	8	40	41	41	6	9	22	23	43	4	22	16
MAY 15	8	42	43	43	6	9	22	23	43	4	22	16
MAY 16	8	44	44	45	6	9	22	23	43	4	22	16
MAY 17	8	46	46	47	7	9	22	23	43	4	22	16
MAY 18	8	47	48	48	7	9	22	23	43	4	22	16
MAY 19	9	1	1	2	7	10	22	23	43	4	22	16
MAY 20	9	3	3	4	7	10	22	23	43	4	22	16
MAY 21	9	4	5	5	8	10	22	23	43	4	22	16
MAY 22	9	6	6	7	8	10	22	23	43	4	22	16
MAY 23	9	7	8	8	8	10	22	23	43	4	22	16
MAY 24	9	9	10	10	9	10	22	23	43	4	22	16
MAY 25	10	11	11	12	9	11	22	23	43	4	22	16
MAY 26	10	12	13	13	9	11	22	23	43	4	22	16
MAY 27	10	14	14	15	9	11	22	23	43	4	22	16
MAY 28	10	15	16	16	10	11	22	23	43	4	22	16
MAY 29	10	17	17	18	10	11	23	23	43	4	22	16
MAY 30	10	19	19	20	10	11	23	23	43	4	22	16
MAY 31	10	20	21	21	11	12	23	23	43	4	22	16

June

Date & Time	SUN	MOON 1	MOON 2	MOON 3	MERCURY	VENUS	MARS	JUPITER	SATURN	URANUS	NEPTUNE	PLUTO
JUN. 1	10	22	22	23	11	12	23	23	43	4	22	16
JUN. 2	10	24	24	25	11	12	23	23	43	4	22	16
JUN. 3	11	25	26	27	11	12	23	23	43	4	22	16
JUN. 4	11	27	28	29	12	12	23	23	43	4	22	16
JUN. 5	11	29	30	30	12	12	23	23	43	4	22	16
JUN. 6	11	31	32	32	12	13	23	23	43	4	22	16
JUN. 7	11	33	34	35	13	13	23	23	43	4	22	16
JUN. 8	11	35	36	37	13	13	23	23	43	4	22	16
JUN. 9	11	37	38	39	13	13	23	23	43	4	22	16
JUN. 10	11	39	40	41	13	13	23	23	43	4	22	16
JUN. 11	12	41	42	43	14	13	23	23	43	4	22	16
JUN. 12	12	43	44	44	14	14	23	23	43	4	22	16
JUN. 13	12	45	46	46	14	14	23	23	43	4	22	16
JUN. 14	12	47	47	48	14	14	23	23	43	4	22	16
JUN. 15	12	48	1	2	15	14	23	23	43	4	22	16
JUN. 16	12	2	3	3	15	14	24	23	43	5	22	16
JUN. 17	12	4	4	5	15	14	24	23	43	5	22	16
JUN. 18	12	5	6	6	15	15	24	23	43	5	22	16
JUN. 19	13	7	8	8	15	15	24	23	43	5	22	16
JUN. 20	13	9	9	10	16	15	24	23	43	5	22	16
JUN. 21	13	10	11	11	16	15	24	23	43	5	22	16
JUN. 22	13	12	12	13	16	15	24	23	43	5	22	16
JUN. 23	13	13	14	14	16	15	24	23	43	5	22	16
JUN. 24	13	15	15	16	16	16	24	23	43	5	22	16
JUN. 25	14	17	17	18	17	16	24	23	43	5	22	16
JUN. 26	14	18	19	19	17	16	24	23	43	5	22	16
JUN. 27	14	20	20	21	17	16	24	23	43	5	22	16
JUN. 28	14	21	22	23	17	16	24	23	43	5	22	16
JUN. 29	14	23	24	24	17	16	24	23	43	5	22	16
JUN. 30	14	25	25	26	17	17	24	23	43	5	22	16

MOON 1 ◗ 12:01 A.M. TO 8:00 A.M.   **MOON 2** ◑ 8:01 A.M. TO 4:00 P.M.   **MOON 3** ● 4:01 P.M. TO 12:00 A.M.
Use only one "moon" number. Choose the column closest to your time of birth. If your place of birth is not on Eastern Standard Time, be sure to read "How to Convert to Eastern Standard Time" at the beginning of this section.

Date & Time	SUN ☉	MOON 1 ◐	MOON 2 ◑	MOON 3 ●	MERCURY	VENUS	MARS	JUPITER	SATURN	URANUS	NEPTUNE	PLUTO
JUL. 1	14	27	27	28	18	17	25	23	43	5	22	16
JUL. 2	14	29	29	30	18	17	25	23	43	5	22	16
JUL. 3	15	30	31	32	18	17	25	23	43	5	22	16
JUL. 4	15	32	33	34	18	17	25	23	43	5	22	16
JUL. 5	15	34	35	36	18	17	25	23	43	5	22	16
JUL. 6	15	36	37	38	18	17	25	23	43	5	22	16
JUL. 7	15	38	39	40	18	18	25	23	43	5	22	16
JUL. 8	15	40	41	42	18	18	25	23	43	5	22	16
JUL. 9	15	42	43	44	18	18	25	23	43	5	22	16
JUL. 10	15	44	45	46	19	18	25	23	43	5	22	16
JUL. 11	16	46	47	47	19	18	25	23	43	5	22	16
JUL. 12	16	48	48	1	19	18	25	23	43	5	22	16
JUL. 13	16	2	2	3	19	19	25	23	43	5	22	16
JUL. 14	16	3	4	4	19	19	25	23	43	5	22	16
JUL. 15	16	5	6	6	19	19	26	24	43	5	22	16
JUL. 16	16	7	7	8	19	19	26	24	43	5	22	16
JUL. 17	16	8	9	9	19	19	26	24	43	5	22	16
JUL. 18	16	10	10	11	19	19	26	24	43	5	22	16
JUL. 19	17	11	12	12	19	20	26	24	43	5	22	16
JUL. 20	17	13	13	14	19	20	26	24	43	5	22	16
JUL. 21	17	15	15	16	19	20	26	24	43	5	22	16
JUL. 22	17	16	17	17	19	20	26	24	43	5	22	16
JUL. 23	17	18	18	19	19	20	26	24	43	5	22	16
JUL. 24	17	19	20	21	18	20	26	24	43	5	22	16
JUL. 25	17	21	22	22	18	21	26	24	43	5	22	16
JUL. 26	18	23	23	24	18	21	26	24	43	5	22	16
JUL. 27	18	24	25	25	18	21	26	24	43	5	22	16
JUL. 28	18	26	27	27	18	21	27	24	43	5	22	16
JUL. 29	18	28	29	29	18	21	27	24	43	5	22	16
JUL. 30	18	30	30	31	18	21	27	24	43	5	22	16
JUL. 31	18	32	32	33	18	22	27	24	43	5	22	16

Date & Time	SUN ☉	MOON 1 ◐	MOON 2 ◑	MOON 3 ●	MERCURY	VENUS	MARS	JUPITER	SATURN	URANUS	NEPTUNE	PLUTO
AUG. 1	18	34	34	35	18	22	27	24	43	5	22	16
AUG. 2	18	36	36	37	18	22	27	24	43	5	22	16
AUG. 3	19	38	38	39	18	22	27	24	43	5	22	16
AUG. 4	19	40	40	41	17	22	27	24	43	5	22	16
AUG. 5	19	42	42	43	17	22	27	24	43	5	22	16
AUG. 6	19	43	44	45	17	23	27	24	43	5	22	16
AUG. 7	19	45	46	47	17	23	27	24	43	5	22	16
AUG. 8	19	47	48	48	17	23	27	24	43	5	22	16
AUG. 9	19	1	2	2	17	23	28	24	43	5	22	16
AUG. 10	19	3	3	4	17	23	28	24	43	5	22	16
AUG. 11	20	4	5	6	17	23	28	24	43	5	22	16
AUG. 12	20	6	7	7	17	23	28	24	43	5	22	16
AUG. 13	20	8	8	9	17	24	28	24	43	5	22	16
AUG. 14	20	9	10	10	17	24	28	24	43	5	22	16
AUG. 15	20	11	11	12	17	24	28	24	43	5	22	16
AUG. 16	20	12	13	14	18	24	28	24	43	5	22	16
AUG. 17	20	14	15	15	18	24	28	24	43	5	22	16
AUG. 18	20	16	16	17	18	24	28	24	43	5	22	16
AUG. 19	21	17	18	18	18	25	28	24	43	5	22	16
AUG. 20	21	19	19	20	18	25	28	24	43	5	22	16
AUG. 21	21	21	21	22	18	25	29	24	43	5	22	16
AUG. 22	21	22	23	23	18	25	29	24	43	5	22	16
AUG. 23	21	24	25	25	19	25	29	24	43	5	22	16
AUG. 24	21	26	26	27	19	25	29	24	43	5	22	16
AUG. 25	21	28	28	29	19	26	29	25	43	5	22	16
AUG. 26	22	29	30	31	19	26	29	25	43	5	22	16
AUG. 27	22	31	32	33	19	26	29	25	43	5	22	16
AUG. 28	22	33	34	34	20	26	29	25	42	5	22	16
AUG. 29	22	35	36	36	20	26	29	25	42	5	22	16
AUG. 30	22	37	38	38	20	26	29	25	42	5	22	16
AUG. 31	22	39	40	40	20	27	29	25	42	5	22	16

MOON 1 ◐ 12:01 A.M. TO 8:00 A.M.   **MOON 2** ◑ 8:01 A.M. TO 4:00 P.M.   **MOON 3** ● 4:01 P.M. TO 12:00 A.M.
Use only one "moon" number. Choose the column closest to your time of birth. If your place of birth is not on
Eastern Standard Time, be sure to read "How to Convert to Eastern Standard Time" at the beginning of this section.

1933

September

Date & Time	SUN	MOON 1	MOON 2	MOON 3	MERCURY	VENUS	MARS	JUPITER	SATURN	URANUS	NEPTUNE	PLUTO
SEP. 1	22	41	41	42	21	27	29	25	42	5	22	16
SEP. 2	22	43	43	44	21	27	30	25	42	5	22	16
SEP. 3	23	45	45	46	21	27	30	25	42	5	22	16
SEP. 4	23	46	47	48	21	27	30	25	42	5	22	16
SEP. 5	23	48	1	1	22	27	30	25	42	5	22	16
SEP. 6	23	2	3	3	22	27	30	25	42	5	22	16
SEP. 7	23	4	4	5	22	28	30	25	42	5	22	16
SEP. 8	23	5	6	7	23	28	30	25	42	5	22	16
SEP. 9	23	7	8	8	23	28	30	25	42	5	22	16
SEP. 10	23	9	9	10	23	28	30	25	42	5	22	16
SEP. 11	24	10	11	11	23	28	30	25	42	5	22	16
SEP. 12	24	12	12	13	24	28	30	25	42	5	22	16
SEP. 13	24	14	14	15	24	29	31	25	42	5	22	16
SEP. 14	24	15	16	16	24	29	31	25	42	5	22	16
SEP. 15	24	17	17	18	24	29	31	25	42	5	22	16
SEP. 16	24	18	19	19	25	29	31	25	42	5	22	16
SEP. 17	24	20	21	21	25	29	31	25	42	5	22	16
SEP. 18	24	22	22	23	25	29	31	25	42	5	22	16
SEP. 19	25	23	24	25	25	30	31	25	42	5	22	16
SEP. 20	25	25	26	26	25	30	31	25	42	5	22	16
SEP. 21	25	27	28	28	26	30	31	25	42	4	22	16
SEP. 22	25	29	30	30	26	30	31	25	42	4	22	16
SEP. 23	25	31	31	32	26	30	31	25	42	4	22	16
SEP. 24	25	33	33	34	26	30	32	25	42	4	22	16
SEP. 25	26	35	35	36	27	30	32	25	42	4	22	16
SEP. 26	26	37	37	38	27	31	32	25	42	4	22	16
SEP. 27	26	38	39	40	27	31	32	25	42	4	22	16
SEP. 28	26	40	41	42	27	31	32	25	42	4	22	16
SEP. 29	26	42	43	43	27	31	32	26	42	4	22	16
SEP. 30	26	44	45	45	28	31	32	26	42	4	22	16

October

Date & Time	SUN	MOON 1	MOON 2	MOON 3	MERCURY	VENUS	MARS	JUPITER	SATURN	URANUS	NEPTUNE	PLUTO
OCT. 1	26	46	46	47	28	31	32	26	42	4	22	16
OCT. 2	26	48	48	1	28	32	32	26	42	4	22	16
OCT. 3	27	1	2	3	28	32	32	26	42	4	22	16
OCT. 4	27	3	4	4	28	32	32	26	42	4	22	16
OCT. 5	27	5	5	6	29	32	33	26	42	4	22	16
OCT. 6	27	7	7	9	29	32	33	26	42	4	22	16
OCT. 7	27	8	9	9	29	32	33	26	42	4	22	16
OCT. 8	27	10	10	11	29	33	33	26	42	4	22	16
OCT. 9	27	11	12	12	29	33	33	26	42	4	22	16
OCT. 10	27	13	14	14	30	33	33	26	42	4	22	16
OCT. 11	28	15	15	16	30	33	33	26	42	4	22	16
OCT. 12	28	16	17	17	30	33	33	26	42	4	22	16
OCT. 13	28	18	18	19	30	33	33	26	42	4	22	16
OCT. 14	28	19	20	21	30	33	33	26	42	4	22	16
OCT. 15	28	21	22	22	31	34	34	26	42	4	22	16
OCT. 16	28	23	23	24	31	34	34	26	42	4	22	16
OCT. 17	28	25	25	26	31	34	34	26	42	4	22	16
OCT. 18	28	26	27	28	31	34	34	26	42	4	22	16
OCT. 19	29	28	29	30	31	34	34	26	42	4	23	16
OCT. 20	29	30	31	32	31	34	34	26	42	4	23	16
OCT. 21	29	32	33	33	32	35	34	26	42	4	23	16
OCT. 22	29	34	35	35	32	35	34	26	42	4	23	16
OCT. 23	29	36	37	37	32	35	34	26	42	4	23	16
OCT. 24	29	38	39	39	32	35	34	26	42	4	23	16
OCT. 25	29	40	41	41	32	35	34	26	42	4	23	16
OCT. 26	30	42	42	43	32	35	35	26	42	4	23	16
OCT. 27	30	44	44	45	33	35	35	26	42	4	23	16
OCT. 28	30	45	46	47	33	36	35	26	42	4	23	16
OCT. 29	30	47	48	48	33	36	35	26	42	4	23	16
OCT. 30	30	1	1	2	33	36	35	26	42	4	23	16
OCT. 31	30	3	3	4	33	36	35	26	42	4	23	16

MOON 1 ◗ 12:01 A.M. TO 8:00 A.M.   **MOON 2** ◐ 8:01 A.M. TO 4:00 P.M.   **MOON 3** ● 4:01 P.M. TO 12:00 A.M.
Use only one "moon" number. Choose the column closest to your time of birth. If your place of birth is not on Eastern Standard Time, be sure to read "How to Convert to Eastern Standard Time" at the beginning of this section.

November

Date & Time	SUN	MOON 1	MOON 2	MOON 3	MERCURY	VENUS	MARS	JUPITER	SATURN	URANUS	NEPTUNE	PLUTO
NOV. 1	30	4	5	5	33	36	35	26	42	4	23	16
NOV. 2	30	6	7	7	33	36	35	26	42	4	23	16
NOV. 3	31	8	8	9	33	36	35	26	42	4	23	16
NOV. 4	31	9	10	10	33	37	35	27	42	4	23	16
NOV. 5	31	11	11	12	34	37	36	27	42	4	23	16
NOV. 6	31	13	13	14	34	37	36	27	42	4	23	16
NOV. 7	31	14	15	15	34	37	36	27	42	4	23	16
NOV. 8	31	16	16	17	34	37	36	27	42	4	23	16
NOV. 9	31	17	18	18	34	37	36	27	42	4	23	16
NOV. 10	31	19	19	20	34	37	36	27	42	4	23	16
NOV. 11	31	20	21	22	34	38	36	27	42	4	23	16
NOV. 12	32	22	23	23	33	38	36	27	42	4	23	16
NOV. 13	32	24	24	25	33	38	36	27	42	4	23	16
NOV. 14	32	26	26	27	33	38	36	27	42	4	23	16
NOV. 15	32	27	28	29	33	38	37	27	42	4	23	16
NOV. 16	32	29	30	31	33	38	37	27	42	4	23	16
NOV. 17	32	31	32	33	33	38	37	27	42	4	23	16
NOV. 18	32	33	34	35	33	39	37	27	42	4	23	16
NOV. 19	33	35	36	37	32	39	37	27	42	4	23	16
NOV. 20	33	37	38	39	32	39	37	27	42	4	23	16
NOV. 21	33	39	40	41	32	39	37	27	42	4	23	16
NOV. 22	33	41	42	43	32	39	37	27	42	4	23	16
NOV. 23	33	43	44	44	32	39	37	27	42	4	23	16
NOV. 24	33	45	46	46	32	39	37	27	42	4	23	16
NOV. 25	34	47	47	48	32	40	38	27	42	4	23	16
NOV. 26	34	1	1	2	32	40	38	27	42	4	23	16
NOV. 27	34	2	2	3	31	40	38	27	42	4	23	16
NOV. 28	34	4	4	5	31	40	38	27	42	4	23	16
NOV. 29	34	6	6	7	31	40	38	27	42	4	23	16
NOV. 30	34	7	8	8	31	40	38	27	42	4	23	16

December

Date & Time	SUN	MOON 1	MOON 2	MOON 3	MERCURY	VENUS	MARS	JUPITER	SATURN	URANUS	NEPTUNE	PLUTO
DEC. 1	34	9	9	10	32	40	38	27	43	4	23	16
DEC. 2	34	10	11	12	32	41	38	27	43	4	23	16
DEC. 3	35	12	13	13	32	41	38	27	43	4	23	16
DEC. 4	35	14	14	15	32	41	38	27	43	4	23	16
DEC. 5	35	15	16	16	32	41	39	27	43	4	23	16
DEC. 6	35	17	17	18	32	41	39	27	43	4	23	16
DEC. 7	35	18	19	19	32	41	39	27	43	4	23	16
DEC. 8	35	20	20	21	32	41	39	27	43	4	23	16
DEC. 9	35	22	22	23	32	41	39	27	43	4	23	16
DEC. 10	35	23	24	24	33	42	39	27	43	4	23	16
DEC. 11	36	25	26	26	33	42	39	27	43	4	23	16
DEC. 12	36	27	27	28	33	42	39	27	43	4	23	16
DEC. 13	36	29	29	30	33	42	39	27	43	4	23	16
DEC. 14	36	30	31	32	33	42	40	27	43	4	23	16
DEC. 15	36	32	33	34	34	42	40	27	43	4	23	16
DEC. 16	36	34	35	36	34	42	40	28	43	4	23	16
DEC. 17	36	36	37	38	34	42	40	28	43	4	23	16
DEC. 18	36	38	39	40	34	42	40	28	43	4	23	16
DEC. 19	37	41	41	42	34	43	40	28	43	4	23	16
DEC. 20	37	42	43	44	34	43	40	28	43	4	23	16
DEC. 21	37	44	45	46	35	43	40	28	43	4	23	16
DEC. 22	37	46	47	47	35	43	40	28	43	4	23	16
DEC. 23	37	48	1	1	35	43	40	28	43	4	23	16
DEC. 24	37	2	2	3	35	43	41	28	43	4	23	16
DEC. 25	37	4	4	5	35	43	41	28	43	4	23	16
DEC. 26	38	5	6	6	36	43	41	28	43	4	23	16
DEC. 27	38	7	7	8	36	43	41	28	43	4	23	16
DEC. 28	38	8	9	10	36	43	41	28	43	4	23	16
DEC. 29	38	10	11	11	36	43	41	28	43	4	23	16
DEC. 30	38	12	12	13	36	43	41	28	43	4	23	16
DEC. 31	38	13	14	14	37	44	41	28	43	4	23	16

MOON 1 ◔ 12:01 A.M. TO 8:00 A.M.   **MOON 2** ◑ 8:01 A.M. TO 4:00 P.M.   **MOON 3** ● 4:01 P.M. TO 12:00 A.M.

Use only one "moon" number. Choose the column closest to your time of birth. If your place of birth is not on Eastern Standard Time, be sure to read "How to Convert to Eastern Standard Time" at the beginning of this section.

1934

January

February

Date & Time	SUN	MOON 1	MOON 2	MOON 3	MERCURY	VENUS	MARS	JUPITER	SATURN	URANUS	NEPTUNE	PLUTO
JAN. 1	38	15	15	16	37	44	41	28	43	4	23	16
JAN. 2	38	16	17	17	37	44	41	28	43	4	23	16
JAN. 3	39	18	18	19	37	44	42	28	43	4	23	16
JAN. 4	39	20	20	21	37	44	42	28	43	4	23	16
JAN. 5	39	21	22	22	38	44	42	28	43	4	23	16
JAN. 6	39	23	23	24	38	44	42	28	43	4	23	16
JAN. 7	39	24	25	26	38	44	42	28	43	4	23	16
JAN. 8	39	26	27	27	38	44	42	28	43	4	23	16
JAN. 9	39	28	29	29	39	44	42	28	43	4	23	16
JAN. 10	40	30	30	31	39	44	42	28	43	4	23	16
JAN. 11	40	32	32	33	39	44	42	28	43	4	23	16
JAN. 12	40	34	34	35	39	44	43	28	43	4	23	16
JAN. 13	40	35	36	37	39	44	43	28	43	4	23	16
JAN. 14	40	38	38	39	40	44	43	28	43	4	23	16
JAN. 15	40	40	40	41	40	44	43	28	43	4	23	16
JAN. 16	40	42	42	43	40	44	43	28	43	4	23	16
JAN. 17	41	44	44	45	40	44	43	28	43	4	23	16
JAN. 18	41	46	46	47	40	44	43	28	43	4	23	16
JAN. 19	41	47	48	1	41	44	43	28	43	4	23	16
JAN. 20	41	1	2	2	41	44	43	28	43	4	23	16
JAN. 21	41	3	4	4	41	44	43	28	43	4	23	16
JAN. 22	41	5	5	6	41	44	44	28	43	4	23	16
JAN. 23	42	6	7	7	42	44	44	28	43	4	23	16
JAN. 24	42	8	9	9	42	44	44	28	43	4	23	16
JAN. 25	42	10	10	11	42	44	44	28	43	4	23	16
JAN. 26	42	11	12	12	42	44	44	28	43	4	23	16
JAN. 27	42	13	13	14	42	44	44	28	43	4	23	16
JAN. 28	42	14	15	15	43	44	44	28	43	4	23	16
JAN. 29	42	16	16	17	43	44	44	28	43	4	23	16
JAN. 30	42	18	18	19	43	44	44	28	43	4	23	16
JAN. 31	43	19	20	20	43	43	45	28	43	4	23	16

Date & Time	SUN	MOON 1	MOON 2	MOON 3	MERCURY	VENUS	MARS	JUPITER	SATURN	URANUS	NEPTUNE	PLUTO
FEB. 1	43	21	21	22	44	43	45	28	43	4	23	16
FEB. 2	43	22	23	24	44	43	45	28	43	4	23	16
FEB. 3	43	24	25	25	44	43	45	28	43	4	23	16
FEB. 4	43	26	26	27	44	43	45	28	43	4	23	16
FEB. 5	43	27	28	29	45	43	45	28	43	4	23	16
FEB. 6	43	29	30	30	45	43	45	28	43	4	23	16
FEB. 7	43	31	32	32	45	43	45	28	43	4	23	16
FEB. 8	44	33	33	34	45	43	45	28	43	4	23	16
FEB. 9	44	35	35	36	46	43	45	28	43	4	23	16
FEB. 10	44	37	37	38	46	43	46	28	44	4	23	16
FEB. 11	44	39	39	40	46	43	46	28	44	4	23	16
FEB. 12	44	41	41	42	46	43	46	28	44	4	23	16
FEB. 13	44	43	43	44	46	42	46	28	44	4	22	16
FEB. 14	44	45	45	46	47	42	46	28	44	4	22	16
FEB. 15	44	47	47	48	47	42	46	28	44	4	22	16
FEB. 16	45	48	1	2	47	42	46	28	44	4	22	16
FEB. 17	45	2	3	3	47	42	46	28	44	4	22	16
FEB. 18	45	4	5	5	47	42	46	28	44	4	22	16
FEB. 19	45	6	6	7	47	42	47	28	44	4	22	16
FEB. 20	45	8	8	9	47	42	47	28	44	4	22	16
FEB. 21	45	9	10	10	48	42	47	28	44	4	22	16
FEB. 22	45	11	11	12	48	42	47	28	44	4	22	16
FEB. 23	46	12	13	13	48	42	47	28	44	4	22	16
FEB. 24	46	14	14	15	48	42	47	28	44	4	22	16
FEB. 25	46	16	16	17	48	42	47	28	44	4	22	16
FEB. 26	46	17	18	18	48	42	47	28	44	4	22	16
FEB. 27	46	19	19	20	48	42	47	28	44	4	22	16
FEB. 28	46	20	21	21	48	42	47	28	44	4	22	16

MOON 1 ◐ 12:01 A.M. TO 8:00 A.M.   **MOON 2** ◑ 8:01 A.M. TO 4:00 P.M.   **MOON 3** ● 4:01 P.M. TO 12:00 A.M.
Use only one "moon" number. Choose the column closest to your time of birth. If your place of birth is not on Eastern Standard Time, be sure to read "How to Convert to Eastern Standard Time" at the beginning of this section.

1934

March

Date & Time	SUN	MOON 1	MOON 2	MOON 3	MERCURY	VENUS	MARS	JUPITER	SATURN	URANUS	NEPTUNE	PLUTO
MAR. 1	46	22	22	23	47	42	48	28	44	4	22	16
MAR. 2	46	24	24	25	47	42	48	28	44	4	22	16
MAR. 3	47	25	26	26	47	42	48	28	44	4	22	16
MAR. 4	47	27	28	28	47	42	48	28	44	4	22	16
MAR. 5	47	29	29	30	47	42	48	28	44	4	22	16
MAR. 6	47	31	31	32	47	42	48	28	44	4	22	16
MAR. 7	47	32	33	34	47	42	48	28	44	4	22	16
MAR. 8	47	34	35	36	47	42	48	28	44	4	22	16
MAR. 9	47	36	37	37	47	42	48	28	44	4	22	16
MAR. 10	47	38	39	39	46	42	1	28	44	4	22	16
MAR. 11	48	40	41	41	46	42	1	28	44	4	22	16
MAR. 12	48	42	43	43	46	43	1	28	44	4	22	16
MAR. 13	48	44	44	45	46	43	1	28	44	4	22	16
MAR. 14	48	46	46	47	46	43	1	28	44	4	22	16
MAR. 15	48	48	48	1	46	43	1	28	44	4	22	16
MAR. 16	48	2	2	3	46	43	1	28	44	4	22	16
MAR. 17	48	3	4	5	46	43	1	28	44	4	22	16
MAR. 18	48	5	6	6	46	43	1	28	44	4	22	16
MAR. 19	1	7	7	8	46	43	1	28	44	4	22	16
MAR. 20	1	9	9	10	46	43	2	28	44	4	22	16
MAR. 21	1	10	11	11	46	43	2	28	44	4	22	16
MAR. 22	1	12	12	13	46	43	2	28	44	4	22	16
MAR. 23	1	13	14	14	46	43	2	28	44	4	22	16
MAR. 24	1	15	16	16	46	44	2	28	44	4	22	16
MAR. 25	2	17	17	18	46	44	2	28	44	4	22	16
MAR. 26	2	18	19	19	46	44	2	28	44	4	22	16
MAR. 27	2	20	20	21	46	44	2	28	44	4	22	16
MAR. 28	2	21	22	23	46	44	2	28	44	4	22	16
MAR. 29	2	23	24	24	46	44	2	28	44	4	22	16
MAR. 30	2	25	25	26	46	44	3	28	44	4	22	16
MAR. 31	2	27	27	28	47	44	3	28	44	4	22	16

April

Date & Time	SUN	MOON 1	MOON 2	MOON 3	MERCURY	VENUS	MARS	JUPITER	SATURN	URANUS	NEPTUNE	PLUTO
APR. 1	2	28	29	30	47	44	3	28	44	4	22	16
APR. 2	2	30	31	31	47	44	3	28	44	4	22	16
APR. 3	3	32	33	33	47	45	3	28	44	5	22	16
APR. 4	3	34	34	35	47	45	3	27	44	5	22	16
APR. 5	3	36	36	37	47	45	3	27	44	5	22	16
APR. 6	3	38	38	39	47	45	3	27	44	5	22	16
APR. 7	3	39	40	41	48	45	3	27	44	5	22	16
APR. 8	3	41	42	43	48	45	4	27	44	5	22	16
APR. 9	3	43	44	45	48	45	4	27	44	5	22	16
APR. 10	3	45	46	46	48	45	4	27	44	5	22	16
APR. 11	4	47	48	48	48	46	4	27	44	5	22	16
APR. 12	4	1	1	2	48	46	4	27	44	5	22	16
APR. 13	4	3	3	4	1	46	4	27	44	5	22	16
APR. 14	4	4	5	6	1	46	4	27	44	5	22	16
APR. 15	4	6	7	7	1	46	4	27	44	5	22	16
APR. 16	4	8	8	9	1	46	4	27	44	5	22	16
APR. 17	4	10	10	11	1	46	4	27	44	5	22	16
APR. 18	4	11	12	12	2	46	5	27	44	5	22	16
APR. 19	5	13	13	14	2	47	5	27	44	5	22	16
APR. 20	5	14	15	16	2	47	5	27	44	5	22	16
APR. 21	5	16	17	17	2	47	5	27	44	5	22	16
APR. 22	5	18	18	19	2	47	5	27	44	5	22	16
APR. 23	5	19	20	20	3	47	5	27	44	5	22	16
APR. 24	5	21	21	22	3	47	5	27	45	5	22	16
APR. 25	6	22	23	24	3	47	5	27	45	5	22	16
APR. 26	6	24	25	25	3	48	5	27	45	5	22	16
APR. 27	6	26	26	27	4	48	5	27	45	5	22	16
APR. 28	6	28	28	29	4	48	5	27	45	5	22	16
APR. 29	6	29	30	31	4	48	6	27	45	5	22	16
APR. 30	6	31	32	33	4	48	6	27	45	5	22	16

MOON 1 ◖ 12:01 A.M. TO 8:00 A.M.   **MOON 2** ◑ 8:01 A.M. TO 4:00 P.M.   **MOON 3** ● 4:01 P.M. TO 12:00 A.M.

Use only one "moon" number. Choose the column closest to your time of birth. If your place of birth is not on Eastern Standard Time, be sure to read "How to Convert to Eastern Standard Time" at the beginning of this section.

1934

May

June

Date & Time	SUN	MOON 1	MOON 2	MOON 3	MERCURY	VENUS	MARS	JUPITER	SATURN	URANUS	NEPTUNE	PLUTO
MAY 1	6	33	34	35	5	48	6	27	45	5	22	16
MAY 2	6	35	36	36	5	48	6	27	45	5	22	16
MAY 3	7	37	38	38	5	1	6	27	45	5	22	16
MAY 4	7	39	40	40	5	1	6	27	45	5	22	16
MAY 5	7	41	42	42	6	1	6	27	45	5	22	16
MAY 6	7	43	43	44	6	1	6	27	45	5	22	16
MAY 7	7	45	45	46	6	1	6	27	45	5	22	16
MAY 8	7	47	47	48	6	1	7	27	45	5	22	16
MAY 9	7	48	1	2	7	1	7	27	45	5	22	16
MAY 10	7	2	3	3	7	2	7	27	45	5	22	16
MAY 11	8	4	5	6	7	2	7	27	45	5	22	16
MAY 12	8	6	6	7	8	2	7	27	45	5	22	16
MAY 13	8	7	8	9	8	2	7	27	45	5	22	16
MAY 14	8	9	10	10	8	2	7	27	45	5	22	16
MAY 15	8	11	11	12	8	2	7	27	45	5	22	16
MAY 16	8	12	13	13	9	2	7	27	45	5	22	16
MAY 17	8	14	14	15	9	3	7	27	45	5	22	16
MAY 18	8	16	16	17	9	3	7	27	45	5	22	16
MAY 19	9	17	18	18	10	3	8	27	45	5	22	16
MAY 20	9	19	19	20	10	3	8	27	45	5	22	16
MAY 21	9	20	21	21	10	3	8	27	45	5	22	16
MAY 22	9	22	22	23	10	3	8	27	45	5	22	16
MAY 23	9	24	24	25	11	3	8	27	45	5	22	16
MAY 24	9	25	26	26	11	4	8	27	45	5	22	16
MAY 25	10	27	28	28	11	4	8	27	45	5	22	16
MAY 26	10	29	29	30	12	4	8	27	45	5	22	16
MAY 27	10	31	31	32	12	4	8	27	45	5	22	16
MAY 28	10	33	33	34	12	4	8	27	45	5	22	16
MAY 29	10	34	35	36	12	4	9	27	45	5	22	16
MAY 30	10	36	37	38	12	4	9	27	45	5	22	16
MAY 31	10	38	39	40	13	5	9	27	45	5	22	16

Date & Time	SUN	MOON 1	MOON 2	MOON 3	MERCURY	VENUS	MARS	JUPITER	SATURN	URANUS	NEPTUNE	PLUTO
JUN. 1	10	40	41	42	13	5	9	27	45	5	22	16
JUN. 2	10	42	43	44	13	5	9	27	45	5	22	16
JUN. 3	11	44	45	46	13	5	9	27	45	5	22	16
JUN. 4	11	46	47	47	14	5	9	27	45	5	22	16
JUN. 5	11	48	1	1	14	5	9	27	45	5	22	16
JUN. 6	11	2	2	3	14	6	9	27	45	5	22	16
JUN. 7	11	4	4	5	14	6	9	27	45	5	22	16
JUN. 8	11	5	6	6	14	6	9	27	45	5	22	16
JUN. 9	11	7	7	8	14	6	10	27	45	5	22	16
JUN. 10	11	9	9	10	15	6	10	27	45	5	22	16
JUN. 11	12	10	11	11	15	6	10	27	45	5	22	16
JUN. 12	12	12	12	13	15	6	10	27	45	5	22	16
JUN. 13	12	13	14	15	15	7	10	27	45	5	22	16
JUN. 14	12	15	16	16	15	7	10	27	45	5	22	16
JUN. 15	12	17	17	18	15	7	10	27	45	5	22	16
JUN. 16	12	18	19	19	15	7	10	27	45	5	22	16
JUN. 17	12	20	20	21	16	7	10	27	45	5	22	16
JUN. 18	12	21	22	22	16	7	10	27	45	5	22	16
JUN. 19	13	23	24	24	16	8	11	27	45	5	22	16
JUN. 20	13	25	25	26	16	8	11	27	45	5	22	16
JUN. 21	13	26	27	27	16	8	11	27	45	5	22	16
JUN. 22	13	28	29	29	16	8	11	27	45	5	22	16
JUN. 23	13	30	30	31	16	8	11	27	45	5	22	16
JUN. 24	13	32	32	33	16	8	11	27	45	5	22	16
JUN. 25	14	34	34	35	16	8	11	27	45	5	22	16
JUN. 26	14	36	36	37	16	9	11	27	45	5	22	16
JUN. 27	14	38	38	39	16	9	11	27	45	5	22	16
JUN. 28	14	40	40	41	16	9	11	27	45	5	22	16
JUN. 29	14	42	42	43	16	9	11	27	45	5	22	16
JUN. 30	14	44	44	45	16	9	12	27	45	5	22	16

MOON 1 ☽ 12:01 A.M. TO 8:00 A.M.   **MOON 2** ☽ 8:01 A.M. TO 4:00 P.M.   **MOON 3** ● 4:01 P.M. TO 12:00 A.M.

Use only one "moon" number. Choose the column closest to your time of birth. If your place of birth is not on Eastern Standard Time, be sure to read "How to Convert to Eastern Standard Time" at the beginning of this section.

1934

July

August

Date & Time	SUN ☉	MOON 1 ☽	MOON 2 ☽	MOON 3 ●	MERCURY	VENUS	MARS	JUPITER	SATURN	URANUS	NEPTUNE	PLUTO
JUL. 1	14	46	46	47	16	9	12	27	45	5	22	16
JUL. 2	14	47	48	1	16	10	12	27	45	5	22	16
JUL. 3	15	1	2	2	16	10	12	27	45	5	22	16
JUL. 4	15	3	4	4	16	10	12	27	45	5	22	16
JUL. 5	15	5	5	6	16	10	12	27	45	5	22	16
JUL. 6	15	7	7	8	16	10	12	27	45	5	22	16
JUL. 7	15	8	9	9	16	10	12	27	45	5	22	16
JUL. 8	15	10	10	11	16	11	12	27	45	5	22	16
JUL. 9	15	11	12	13	16	11	12	27	45	5	22	16
JUL. 10	15	13	14	14	16	11	12	27	45	5	22	16
JUL. 11	16	15	15	16	15	11	13	27	45	5	22	16
JUL. 12	16	16	17	17	15	11	13	27	45	5	22	16
JUL. 13	16	18	18	19	15	11	13	27	45	5	22	16
JUL. 14	16	19	20	20	15	11	13	27	45	5	22	16
JUL. 15	16	21	21	22	15	12	13	27	45	5	22	16
JUL. 16	16	23	23	24	15	12	13	27	45	5	22	16
JUL. 17	16	24	25	25	15	12	13	27	45	5	22	16
JUL. 18	16	26	26	27	15	12	13	27	45	5	22	16
JUL. 19	17	27	28	29	15	12	13	27	45	5	22	16
JUL. 20	17	29	30	30	15	12	13	27	45	5	22	16
JUL. 21	17	31	32	32	15	13	13	27	45	5	22	16
JUL. 22	17	33	33	34	15	13	14	27	45	5	22	16
JUL. 23	17	35	35	36	15	13	14	27	45	5	22	16
JUL. 24	17	37	37	38	15	13	14	27	45	5	22	16
JUL. 25	17	39	39	40	15	13	14	27	45	5	22	16
JUL. 26	18	41	41	42	15	13	14	27	44	5	22	16
JUL. 27	18	43	43	44	15	14	14	27	44	5	22	16
JUL. 28	18	45	45	46	15	14	14	27	44	5	22	16
JUL. 29	18	47	47	48	15	14	14	27	44	5	22	16
JUL. 30	18	1	1	2	15	14	14	27	44	5	22	16
JUL. 31	18	3	3	4	15	14	14	27	44	5	22	16

Date & Time	SUN ☉	MOON 1 ☽	MOON 2 ☽	MOON 3 ●	MERCURY	VENUS	MARS	JUPITER	SATURN	URANUS	NEPTUNE	PLUTO
AUG. 1	18	4	5	6	15	14	14	27	44	5	22	16
AUG. 2	18	6	7	7	16	14	15	27	44	5	22	16
AUG. 3	19	8	8	9	16	15	15	27	44	5	22	16
AUG. 4	19	9	10	11	16	15	15	27	44	5	22	16
AUG. 5	19	11	12	12	16	15	15	27	44	5	22	16
AUG. 6	19	13	13	14	16	15	15	27	44	5	22	16
AUG. 7	19	14	15	15	16	15	15	27	44	5	22	16
AUG. 8	19	16	16	17	17	15	15	27	44	5	22	16
AUG. 9	19	17	18	18	17	16	15	27	44	5	22	16
AUG. 10	19	19	20	20	17	16	15	27	44	5	22	16
AUG. 11	20	21	21	22	17	16	15	27	44	5	22	16
AUG. 12	20	22	23	23	18	16	15	27	44	5	22	16
AUG. 13	20	24	24	25	18	16	15	27	44	5	22	16
AUG. 14	20	25	26	27	18	16	16	27	44	5	22	16
AUG. 15	20	27	28	28	18	17	16	28	44	5	22	16
AUG. 16	20	29	29	30	19	17	16	28	44	5	22	16
AUG. 17	20	30	31	32	19	17	16	28	44	5	22	16
AUG. 18	20	32	33	33	19	17	16	28	44	5	22	16
AUG. 19	21	34	35	35	19	17	16	28	44	5	22	16
AUG. 20	21	36	37	37	20	17	16	28	44	5	23	16
AUG. 21	21	38	39	39	20	18	16	28	44	5	23	16
AUG. 22	21	40	41	41	20	18	16	28	44	5	23	16
AUG. 23	21	42	43	43	20	18	16	28	44	5	23	16
AUG. 24	21	44	45	45	21	18	16	28	44	5	23	16
AUG. 25	21	46	47	47	21	18	17	28	44	5	23	16
AUG. 26	22	48	1	1	21	18	17	28	44	5	23	16
AUG. 27	22	2	2	3	22	19	17	28	44	5	23	16
AUG. 28	22	4	4	5	22	19	17	28	44	5	23	16
AUG. 29	22	5	6	7	22	19	17	28	44	5	23	16
AUG. 30	22	7	8	8	22	19	17	28	44	5	23	16
AUG. 31	22	9	10	10	23	19	17	28	44	5	23	16

MOON 1 ☽ **12:01 A.M. TO 8:00 A.M.**   **MOON 2** ☽ **8:01 A.M. TO 4:00 P.M.**   **MOON 3** ● **4:01 P.M. TO 12:00 A.M.**
Use only one "moon" number. Choose the column closest to your time of birth. If your place of birth is not on
Eastern Standard Time, be sure to read "How to Convert to Eastern Standard Time" at the beginning of this section.

September

Date & Time	SUN	MOON 1	MOON 2	MOON 3	MERCURY	VENUS	MARS	JUPITER	SATURN	URANUS	NEPTUNE	PLUTO
SEP. 1	22	11	11	12	23	19	17	28	44	5	23	16
SEP. 2	22	12	13	13	23	19	17	28	44	5	23	16
SEP. 3	23	14	14	15	23	20	17	28	44	5	23	16
SEP. 4	23	15	16	16	24	20	17	28	44	5	23	16
SEP. 5	23	17	18	18	24	20	17	28	44	5	23	16
SEP. 6	23	19	19	20	24	20	18	28	44	5	23	16
SEP. 7	23	20	21	21	24	20	18	28	44	5	23	16
SEP. 8	23	22	22	23	24	20	18	28	44	5	23	16
SEP. 9	23	23	24	24	25	21	18	28	44	5	23	16
SEP. 10	23	25	26	26	25	21	18	28	44	5	23	16
SEP. 11	24	27	27	28	25	21	18	28	44	5	23	16
SEP. 12	24	28	29	30	25	21	18	28	44	5	23	16
SEP. 13	24	30	31	31	26	21	18	28	44	5	23	16
SEP. 14	24	32	32	33	26	21	18	28	44	5	23	16
SEP. 15	24	34	34	35	26	22	18	28	44	5	23	16
SEP. 16	24	35	36	37	26	22	18	28	44	5	23	16
SEP. 17	24	37	38	39	26	22	18	28	44	5	23	16
SEP. 18	24	39	40	40	27	22	18	28	44	5	23	16
SEP. 19	25	41	42	42	27	22	19	28	44	5	23	16
SEP. 20	25	43	44	44	27	22	19	28	44	5	23	16
SEP. 21	25	45	46	46	27	23	19	28	44	5	23	16
SEP. 22	25	47	48	48	27	23	19	28	44	5	23	16
SEP. 23	25	1	2	2	28	23	19	28	44	5	23	16
SEP. 24	25	3	4	4	28	23	19	28	44	5	23	16
SEP. 25	26	5	5	6	28	23	19	29	44	5	23	16
SEP. 26	26	7	7	8	28	23	19	29	44	5	23	16
SEP. 27	26	8	9	9	28	24	19	29	44	5	23	16
SEP. 28	26	10	11	11	29	24	19	29	44	5	23	16
SEP. 29	26	12	12	13	29	24	19	29	44	5	23	16
SEP. 30	26	13	14	14	29	24	20	29	44	5	23	16

October

Date & Time	SUN	MOON 1	MOON 2	MOON 3	MERCURY	VENUS	MARS	JUPITER	SATURN	URANUS	NEPTUNE	PLUTO
OCT. 1	26	15	15	16	29	24	20	29	44	5	23	16
OCT. 2	26	17	17	18	29	24	20	29	44	5	23	16
OCT. 3	27	18	19	19	29	25	20	29	44	5	23	16
OCT. 4	27	20	20	21	30	25	20	29	44	5	23	16
OCT. 5	27	21	22	22	30	25	20	29	44	5	23	16
OCT. 6	27	23	23	24	30	25	20	29	44	5	23	16
OCT. 7	27	25	25	26	30	25	20	29	44	5	23	16
OCT. 8	27	26	27	27	30	25	20	29	44	5	23	16
OCT. 9	27	28	28	29	30	26	20	29	44	5	23	16
OCT. 10	27	30	30	31	30	26	20	29	44	5	23	16
OCT. 11	28	31	32	33	31	26	20	29	44	5	23	16
OCT. 12	28	33	34	34	31	26	20	29	44	5	23	16
OCT. 13	28	35	36	36	31	26	21	29	44	5	23	16
OCT. 14	28	37	38	38	31	26	21	29	44	5	23	16
OCT. 15	28	39	39	40	31	27	21	29	44	5	23	16
OCT. 16	28	41	41	42	31	27	21	29	44	5	23	16
OCT. 17	28	42	43	44	31	27	21	29	44	5	23	16
OCT. 18	28	44	45	46	31	27	21	29	44	5	23	16
OCT. 19	29	46	47	48	31	27	21	29	44	5	23	16
OCT. 20	29	48	1	1	31	27	21	29	44	5	23	16
OCT. 21	29	2	3	3	31	28	21	29	44	5	23	16
OCT. 22	29	4	5	5	31	28	21	29	44	5	23	16
OCT. 23	29	6	6	7	31	28	21	29	44	5	23	16
OCT. 24	29	8	8	9	31	28	21	29	44	5	23	16
OCT. 25	29	9	10	11	31	28	22	29	44	5	23	16
OCT. 26	30	11	12	12	31	28	22	29	44	5	23	16
OCT. 27	30	13	13	14	31	29	22	29	44	5	23	16
OCT. 28	30	14	15	15	31	29	22	29	44	5	23	16
OCT. 29	30	16	17	17	31	29	22	29	44	5	23	16
OCT. 30	30	18	18	19	31	29	22	30	44	5	23	16
OCT. 31	30	19	20	20	31	29	22	30	44	5	23	16

MOON 1 ☽ 12:01 A.M. TO 8:00 A.M.   **MOON 2** ☽ 8:01 A.M. TO 4:00 P.M.   **MOON 3** ● 4:01 P.M. TO 12:00 A.M.
Use only one "moon" number. Choose the column closest to your time of birth. If your place of birth is not on Eastern Standard Time, be sure to read "How to Convert to Eastern Standard Time" at the beginning of this section.

1934

November

Date & Time	SUN ☉	MOON 1 ☽	MOON 2 ☽	MOON 3 ●	MERCURY	VENUS	MARS	JUPITER	SATURN	URANUS	NEPTUNE	PLUTO
NOV. 1	30	21	21	22	31	29	22	30	44	5	23	16
NOV. 2	30	22	23	23	30	30	22	30	44	5	23	16
NOV. 3	31	24	25	25	30	30	22	30	44	5	23	16
NOV. 4	31	26	26	27	30	30	22	30	44	5	23	16
NOV. 5	31	27	28	28	30	30	22	30	44	5	23	16
NOV. 6	31	29	30	30	30	30	22	30	44	5	23	16
NOV. 7	31	31	31	32	30	30	23	30	44	5	23	16
NOV. 8	31	33	33	34	30	31	23	30	44	5	23	16
NOV. 9	31	35	35	36	29	31	23	30	44	5	23	16
NOV. 10	31	36	37	38	29	31	23	30	44	5	23	16
NOV. 11	31	38	39	40	29	31	23	30	44	5	23	16
NOV. 12	32	40	41	41	29	31	23	30	44	5	23	16
NOV. 13	32	42	43	43	29	31	23	30	44	5	23	16
NOV. 14	32	44	45	45	29	32	23	30	44	5	23	16
NOV. 15	32	46	46	47	29	32	23	30	44	5	23	16
NOV. 16	32	48	48	1	30	32	23	30	44	5	23	16
NOV. 17	32	2	2	3	30	32	23	30	44	5	23	16
NOV. 18	32	3	4	5	30	32	23	30	44	5	23	16
NOV. 19	33	5	6	6	30	32	23	30	44	5	23	16
NOV. 20	33	7	8	8	30	33	23	30	44	5	23	16
NOV. 21	33	9	9	10	30	33	24	30	44	5	23	16
NOV. 22	33	10	11	12	30	33	24	30	44	5	23	16
NOV. 23	33	12	13	13	30	33	24	30	44	5	23	16
NOV. 24	33	14	14	15	31	33	24	30	44	5	23	16
NOV. 25	34	15	16	17	31	33	24	30	44	5	23	16
NOV. 26	34	17	18	18	31	34	24	30	44	5	23	16
NOV. 27	34	19	19	20	31	34	24	30	44	5	23	16
NOV. 28	34	20	21	21	31	34	24	30	44	5	23	16
NOV. 29	34	22	22	23	32	34	24	30	44	5	23	16
NOV. 30	34	23	24	24	32	34	24	30	44	5	23	16

December

Date & Time	SUN ☉	MOON 1 ☽	MOON 2 ☽	MOON 3 ●	MERCURY	VENUS	MARS	JUPITER	SATURN	URANUS	NEPTUNE	PLUTO
DEC. 1	34	25	26	26	32	34	24	30	44	5	23	16
DEC. 2	34	27	27	28	32	35	24	30	44	5	23	16
DEC. 3	35	28	29	30	32	35	24	30	44	5	23	16
DEC. 4	35	30	31	31	33	35	24	31	44	5	23	16
DEC. 5	35	32	33	33	33	35	25	31	44	5	23	16
DEC. 6	35	34	34	35	33	35	25	31	44	5	23	16
DEC. 7	35	36	36	37	33	35	25	31	44	5	23	16
DEC. 8	35	38	38	39	33	36	25	31	44	5	23	16
DEC. 9	35	40	40	41	34	36	25	31	44	5	23	16
DEC. 10	35	42	42	43	34	36	25	31	44	5	23	16
DEC. 11	36	43	44	45	34	36	25	31	44	5	23	16
DEC. 12	36	45	46	47	34	36	25	31	44	5	23	16
DEC. 13	36	47	48	1	34	36	25	31	44	5	23	16
DEC. 14	36	1	2	2	35	37	25	31	44	5	23	16
DEC. 15	36	3	4	4	35	37	25	31	44	5	23	16
DEC. 16	36	5	5	6	35	37	25	31	44	5	23	16
DEC. 17	36	7	7	8	35	37	25	31	44	5	23	16
DEC. 18	36	8	9	9	35	37	25	31	44	5	23	16
DEC. 19	37	10	11	11	36	37	25	31	44	5	23	16
DEC. 20	37	12	12	13	36	38	26	31	44	5	23	16
DEC. 21	37	13	14	14	36	38	26	31	44	5	23	16
DEC. 22	37	15	15	16	36	38	26	31	44	5	23	16
DEC. 23	37	17	17	18	36	38	26	31	44	5	23	16
DEC. 24	37	18	19	19	37	38	26	31	44	5	23	16
DEC. 25	37	20	20	21	37	38	26	31	44	5	23	16
DEC. 26	38	21	22	22	37	39	26	31	44	5	23	16
DEC. 27	38	23	23	24	37	39	26	31	44	5	23	16
DEC. 28	38	24	25	26	38	39	26	31	44	5	23	16
DEC. 29	38	26	27	27	38	39	26	31	44	5	23	16
DEC. 30	38	28	28	29	38	39	26	31	44	5	23	16
DEC. 31	38	29	30	31	38	40	26	31	44	5	23	16

MOON 1 ☽ 12:01 A.M. TO 8:00 A.M. • **MOON 2 ☽ 8:01 A.M. TO 4:00 P.M.** • **MOON 3 ● 4:01 P.M. TO 12:00 A.M.**
Use only one "moon" number. Choose the column closest to your time of birth. If your place of birth is not on Eastern Standard Time, be sure to read "How to Convert to Eastern Standard Time" at the beginning of this section.

1935

January

Date & Time	SUN	MOON 1	MOON 2	MOON 3	MERCURY	VENUS	MARS	JUPITER	SATURN	URANUS	NEPTUNE	PLUTO
JAN. 1	38	31	32	32	38	40	26	31	44	5	23	16
JAN. 2	38	33	34	34	39	40	26	31	44	5	23	16
JAN. 3	39	35	36	36	39	40	26	31	44	5	23	16
JAN. 4	39	37	37	38	39	40	26	31	44	5	23	16
JAN. 5	39	39	39	40	39	40	27	31	44	5	23	16
JAN. 6	39	41	41	42	39	41	27	31	44	5	23	16
JAN. 7	39	43	43	44	39	41	27	31	44	5	23	16
JAN. 8	39	45	45	46	40	41	27	31	44	5	23	16
JAN. 9	39	47	47	48	40	41	27	31	44	5	23	16
JAN. 10	40	1	1	2	40	41	27	31	44	5	23	16
JAN. 11	40	3	3	4	41	41	27	31	44	5	23	16
JAN. 12	40	4	5	6	41	42	27	31	44	5	23	16
JAN. 13	40	6	7	7	41	42	27	31	44	5	23	16
JAN. 14	40	8	8	9	41	42	27	31	44	5	23	16
JAN. 15	40	10	10	11	41	42	27	32	44	5	23	16
JAN. 16	40	11	12	12	42	42	27	32	45	5	23	16
JAN. 17	41	13	13	14	42	42	27	32	45	5	23	16
JAN. 18	41	14	15	16	42	42	27	32	45	5	23	16
JAN. 19	41	16	17	17	42	43	27	32	45	5	23	16
JAN. 20	41	18	18	19	42	43	27	32	45	5	23	16
JAN. 21	41	19	20	20	43	43	27	32	45	5	23	16
JAN. 22	41	21	21	22	43	43	27	32	45	5	23	16
JAN. 23	42	22	23	23	43	43	27	32	45	5	23	16
JAN. 24	42	24	25	25	43	44	27	32	45	5	23	16
JAN. 25	42	26	26	27	44	44	27	32	45	5	23	16
JAN. 26	42	27	28	28	44	44	28	32	45	5	23	16
JAN. 27	42	29	29	30	44	44	28	32	45	5	23	16
JAN. 28	42	31	31	32	44	44	28	32	45	5	23	16
JAN. 29	42	32	33	33	44	44	28	32	45	5	23	16
JAN. 30	42	34	35	35	45	45	28	32	45	5	23	16
JAN. 31	43	36	37	37	45	45	28	32	45	5	23	16

February

Date & Time	SUN	MOON 1	MOON 2	MOON 3	MERCURY	VENUS	MARS	JUPITER	SATURN	URANUS	NEPTUNE	PLUTO
FEB. 1	43	38	39	39	45	45	28	32	45	5	23	16
FEB. 2	43	40	41	41	45	45	28	32	45	5	23	16
FEB. 3	43	42	43	43	45	45	28	32	45	5	23	16
FEB. 4	43	44	45	45	45	45	28	32	45	5	23	16
FEB. 5	43	46	47	47	45	46	28	32	45	5	23	16
FEB. 6	43	48	1	1	45	46	28	32	45	5	23	16
FEB. 7	43	2	3	3	45	46	28	32	45	5	23	16
FEB. 8	44	4	4	5	45	46	28	32	45	5	23	16
FEB. 9	44	6	6	7	45	46	28	32	45	5	23	16
FEB. 10	44	7	8	9	45	46	28	32	45	5	23	16
FEB. 11	44	9	10	10	45	47	28	32	45	5	23	16
FEB. 12	44	11	11	12	45	47	28	32	45	5	23	16
FEB. 13	44	12	13	14	45	47	28	32	45	5	23	16
FEB. 14	44	14	15	15	45	47	28	32	45	5	23	16
FEB. 15	44	16	16	17	45	47	28	32	45	5	23	16
FEB. 16	45	17	18	18	45	47	28	32	45	5	23	16
FEB. 17	45	19	19	20	45	48	28	32	45	5	23	16
FEB. 18	45	20	21	21	45	48	28	32	45	5	23	16
FEB. 19	45	22	23	23	44	48	28	32	45	5	23	16
FEB. 20	45	24	24	25	44	48	28	32	45	5	23	16
FEB. 21	45	25	26	26	44	48	28	32	45	5	23	16
FEB. 22	45	27	27	28	44	48	28	32	45	5	23	16
FEB. 23	46	28	29	30	44	1	28	32	45	5	23	16
FEB. 24	46	30	31	31	44	1	28	32	45	5	23	16
FEB. 25	46	32	32	33	44	1	28	32	45	5	23	16
FEB. 26	46	34	34	35	44	1	28	32	45	5	23	16
FEB. 27	46	35	36	36	44	1	28	32	45	5	23	16
FEB. 28	46	37	38	38	43	1	28	32	45	5	23	16

MOON 1 ◐ 12:01 A.M. TO 8:00 A.M.   **MOON 2** ◑ 8:01 A.M. TO 4:00 P.M.   **MOON 3** ● 4:01 P.M. TO 12:00 A.M.
Use only one "moon" number. Choose the column closest to your time of birth. If your place of birth is not on Eastern Standard Time, be sure to read "How to Convert to Eastern Standard Time" at the beginning of this section.

1935

March / April

Date & Time	SUN	MOON 1	MOON 2	MOON 3	MERCURY	VENUS	MARS	JUPITER	SATURN	URANUS	NEPTUNE	PLUTO
MAR. 1	46	39	40	40	43	1	28	32	45	5	23	16
MAR. 2	46	41	42	42	43	2	28	32	45	5	23	16
MAR. 3	47	43	44	44	43	2	28	32	45	5	23	16
MAR. 4	47	45	46	46	44	2	28	32	45	5	23	16
MAR. 5	47	47	48	48	44	2	28	32	45	5	23	16
MAR. 6	47	1	2	2	44	2	28	32	45	5	23	16
MAR. 7	47	3	4	4	44	2	28	32	45	5	23	16
MAR. 8	47	5	6	6	44	3	28	32	45	5	23	16
MAR. 9	47	7	7	8	44	3	28	32	45	5	23	16
MAR. 10	47	9	9	10	44	3	28	32	45	5	23	16
MAR. 11	48	10	11	11	44	3	28	32	45	5	23	16
MAR. 12	48	12	13	13	44	3	28	32	45	5	23	16
MAR. 13	48	14	14	15	44	3	28	32	45	5	23	16
MAR. 14	48	15	16	16	44	4	28	32	45	5	23	16
MAR. 15	48	17	17	18	44	4	28	32	45	5	23	16
MAR. 16	48	18	19	19	45	4	28	32	45	5	23	16
MAR. 17	48	20	21	21	45	4	28	32	45	5	23	16
MAR. 18	48	22	22	23	45	4	28	32	45	5	23	16
MAR. 19	1	23	24	24	45	4	28	32	45	5	23	16
MAR. 20	1	25	25	26	45	5	28	32	46	5	23	16
MAR. 21	1	26	27	27	45	5	28	32	46	5	23	16
MAR. 22	1	28	29	29	45	5	28	32	46	5	23	16
MAR. 23	1	30	30	31	46	5	28	32	46	5	23	16
MAR. 24	1	31	32	33	46	5	28	32	46	5	23	16
MAR. 25	2	33	34	34	46	5	28	32	46	5	23	16
MAR. 26	2	35	35	36	46	6	28	32	46	5	23	16
MAR. 27	2	37	37	38	46	6	28	32	46	5	23	16
MAR. 28	2	38	39	40	47	6	28	32	46	5	23	16
MAR. 29	2	40	41	42	47	6	28	32	46	5	23	16
MAR. 30	2	42	43	43	47	6	27	32	46	5	23	16
MAR. 31	2	44	45	45	47	6	27	32	46	5	23	16

Date & Time	SUN	MOON 1	MOON 2	MOON 3	MERCURY	VENUS	MARS	JUPITER	SATURN	URANUS	NEPTUNE	PLUTO
APR. 1	2	46	47	47	47	7	27	32	46	5	23	16
APR. 2	2	48	1	1	48	7	27	32	46	5	23	16
APR. 3	3	2	3	3	48	7	27	32	46	5	23	16
APR. 4	3	4	5	5	48	7	27	32	46	5	23	16
APR. 5	3	6	7	7	48	7	27	32	46	5	23	16
APR. 6	3	8	8	9	48	7	27	32	46	5	23	16
APR. 7	3	10	10	11	1	8	27	32	46	5	23	16
APR. 8	3	11	12	13	1	8	27	32	46	5	23	16
APR. 9	3	13	14	14	1	8	27	32	46	5	23	16
APR. 10	3	15	15	16	1	8	27	32	46	5	23	16
APR. 11	4	16	17	17	2	8	27	32	46	5	23	16
APR. 12	4	18	18	19	2	8	27	32	46	5	23	16
APR. 13	4	20	20	21	2	8	27	32	46	5	23	16
APR. 14	4	21	22	22	2	9	27	32	46	5	23	16
APR. 15	4	23	23	24	3	9	27	32	46	5	23	16
APR. 16	4	24	25	25	3	9	27	32	46	5	23	16
APR. 17	4	26	26	27	3	9	27	32	46	5	23	16
APR. 18	4	28	28	29	3	9	27	32	46	5	23	16
APR. 19	5	29	30	30	4	9	26	32	46	5	23	16
APR. 20	5	31	32	32	4	10	26	32	46	5	23	16
APR. 21	5	33	33	34	4	10	26	32	46	5	23	16
APR. 22	5	34	35	36	4	10	26	32	46	5	23	16
APR. 23	5	36	37	37	5	10	26	32	46	5	23	16
APR. 24	5	38	39	39	5	10	26	32	46	5	23	16
APR. 25	6	40	40	41	5	10	26	32	46	5	23	16
APR. 26	6	42	42	43	5	11	26	32	46	5	23	16
APR. 27	6	44	44	45	5	11	26	32	46	5	23	16
APR. 28	6	45	46	47	6	11	26	32	46	5	23	16
APR. 29	6	47	48	1	6	11	26	32	46	5	23	16
APR. 30	6	1	2	3	7	11	26	32	46	5	23	16

MOON 1 ◖ 12:01 A.M. TO 8:00 A.M.   **MOON 2** ◐ 8:01 A.M. TO 4:00 P.M.   **MOON 3** ● 4:01 P.M. TO 12:00 A.M.
Use only one "moon" number. Choose the column closest to your time of birth. If your place of birth is not on
Eastern Standard Time, be sure to read "How to Convert to Eastern Standard Time" at the beginning of this section.

1935

May

June

Date & Time	SUN	MOON 1	MOON 2	MOON 3	MERCURY	VENUS	MARS	JUPITER	SATURN	URANUS	NEPTUNE	PLUTO
MAY 1	6	3	4	5	7	11	26	32	46	5	23	16
MAY 2	6	5	6	6	7	11	26	32	46	5	23	16
MAY 3	7	7	8	8	7	12	26	32	46	5	23	16
MAY 4	7	9	10	10	8	12	26	32	46	5	23	16
MAY 5	7	11	11	12	8	12	26	32	46	5	23	16
MAY 6	7	12	13	14	8	12	26	31	46	5	23	16
MAY 7	7	14	15	15	9	12	26	31	46	5	23	16
MAY 8	7	16	16	17	9	12	26	31	46	5	23	16
MAY 9	7	17	18	19	9	13	26	31	46	5	23	16
MAY 10	7	19	20	20	9	13	26	31	46	5	23	16
MAY 11	8	21	21	22	9	13	26	31	46	5	23	16
MAY 12	8	22	23	23	10	13	26	31	46	5	23	16
MAY 13	8	24	24	25	10	13	26	31	46	5	23	16
MAY 14	8	25	26	26	10	13	26	31	46	5	23	16
MAY 15	8	27	28	28	11	13	26	31	46	5	23	16
MAY 16	8	29	29	30	11	14	26	31	46	5	23	16
MAY 17	8	30	31	32	11	14	26	31	46	5	23	16
MAY 18	8	32	33	33	11	14	26	31	46	5	23	16
MAY 19	9	34	35	35	11	14	26	31	46	5	23	16
MAY 20	9	36	36	37	12	14	26	31	46	5	23	16
MAY 21	9	38	38	39	12	14	26	31	46	5	23	16
MAY 22	9	39	40	41	12	15	26	31	46	5	23	16
MAY 23	9	41	42	43	12	15	26	31	46	5	23	16
MAY 24	9	43	44	44	12	15	26	31	46	5	23	16
MAY 25	10	45	46	46	12	15	26	31	46	5	23	16
MAY 26	10	47	48	48	13	15	26	31	46	5	23	16
MAY 27	10	1	1	2	13	15	26	31	46	5	23	16
MAY 28	10	3	3	4	13	15	26	31	46	5	23	16
MAY 29	10	5	5	6	13	16	26	31	46	5	23	16
MAY 30	10	6	7	8	13	16	26	31	46	5	23	16
MAY 31	10	8	9	9	13	16	26	31	46	5	23	16

Date & Time	SUN	MOON 1	MOON 2	MOON 3	MERCURY	VENUS	MARS	JUPITER	SATURN	URANUS	NEPTUNE	PLUTO
JUN. 1	10	10	11	11	13	16	26	31	46	5	23	16
JUN. 2	10	12	12	13	13	16	26	31	46	5	23	16
JUN. 3	11	14	14	15	13	16	26	31	46	5	23	16
JUN. 4	11	15	16	16	13	16	26	31	46	5	23	16
JUN. 5	11	17	17	18	13	17	26	31	46	5	23	16
JUN. 6	11	18	19	20	13	17	26	31	46	5	23	16
JUN. 7	11	20	21	21	13	17	26	31	46	5	23	16
JUN. 8	11	22	22	23	14	17	26	31	46	5	23	16
JUN. 9	11	23	24	24	14	17	26	31	46	5	23	16
JUN. 10	11	25	25	24	14	17	26	31	46	5	23	16
JUN. 11	12	26	27	28	13	17	26	31	46	6	23	16
JUN. 12	12	28	29	29	13	18	26	31	46	6	23	16
JUN. 13	12	30	30	31	13	18	26	31	46	6	23	16
JUN. 14	12	31	32	33	13	18	26	31	46	6	23	16
JUN. 15	12	33	34	34	13	18	26	31	46	6	23	16
JUN. 16	12	35	36	36	13	18	26	31	46	6	23	16
JUN. 17	12	37	38	38	13	18	26	31	46	6	23	16
JUN. 18	12	39	39	40	13	18	27	31	46	6	23	16
JUN. 19	13	41	41	42	13	19	27	31	46	6	23	16
JUN. 20	13	43	43	44	13	19	27	31	46	6	23	16
JUN. 21	13	45	45	46	13	19	27	31	46	6	23	16
JUN. 22	13	46	47	48	13	19	27	31	46	6	23	16
JUN. 23	13	48	1	2	13	19	27	31	46	6	23	16
JUN. 24	13	2	3	4	13	19	27	31	46	6	23	16
JUN. 25	14	4	5	5	13	19	27	31	46	6	23	16
JUN. 26	14	6	7	7	13	20	27	31	46	6	23	16
JUN. 27	14	8	9	9	13	20	27	31	46	6	23	16
JUN. 28	14	10	10	11	12	20	27	31	46	6	23	16
JUN. 29	14	11	12	12	12	20	27	31	46	6	23	16
JUN. 30	14	13	14	14	12	20	27	31	46	6	23	16

MOON 1 ◗ 12:01 A.M. TO 8:00 A.M.　**MOON 2** ◑ 8:01 A.M. TO 4:00 P.M.　**MOON 3** ● 4:01 P.M. TO 12:00 A.M.
Use only one "moon" number. Choose the column closest to your time of birth. If your place of birth is not on Eastern Standard Time, be sure to read "How to Convert to Eastern Standard Time" at the beginning of this section.

1935

July

August

Date & Time	SUN	MOON 1	MOON 2	MOON 3	MERCURY	VENUS	MARS	JUPITER	SATURN	URANUS	NEPTUNE	PLUTO
JUL. 1	14	15	15	16	12	20	27	31	46	6	23	16
JUL. 2	14	16	17	17	12	20	27	31	46	6	23	16
JUL. 3	15	18	19	19	12	20	27	31	46	6	23	16
JUL. 4	15	20	20	21	12	21	27	31	46	6	23	16
JUL. 5	15	21	22	22	12	21	27	31	46	6	23	16
JUL. 6	15	23	23	24	12	21	27	31	46	6	23	16
JUL. 7	15	24	25	25	12	21	27	31	46	6	23	16
JUL. 8	15	26	26	27	12	21	28	31	46	6	23	16
JUL. 9	15	28	28	29	13	21	28	31	46	6	23	16
JUL. 10	15	29	30	30	13	21	28	31	46	6	23	16
JUL. 11	16	31	31	32	13	21	28	31	46	6	23	16
JUL. 12	16	33	33	34	13	21	28	31	46	6	23	16
JUL. 13	16	34	35	36	13	22	28	31	46	6	23	16
JUL. 14	16	36	37	37	13	22	28	31	46	6	23	16
JUL. 15	16	38	39	39	13	22	28	31	46	6	23	16
JUL. 16	16	40	41	41	13	22	28	31	46	6	23	16
JUL. 17	16	42	43	43	13	22	28	31	46	6	23	16
JUL. 18	16	44	45	45	14	22	28	31	46	6	23	16
JUL. 19	17	46	47	47	14	22	28	31	46	6	23	16
JUL. 20	17	48	1	1	14	22	28	31	46	6	23	16
JUL. 21	17	2	3	3	14	22	28	31	46	6	23	16
JUL. 22	17	4	4	5	14	23	28	31	46	6	23	16
JUL. 23	17	6	6	7	15	23	29	31	46	6	23	16
JUL. 24	17	7	8	9	15	23	29	31	46	6	23	16
JUL. 25	17	9	10	10	15	23	29	31	46	6	23	16
JUL. 26	18	11	11	12	15	23	29	31	46	6	23	16
JUL. 27	18	13	13	14	15	23	29	31	46	6	23	16
JUL. 28	18	14	15	15	16	23	29	31	46	6	23	16
JUL. 29	18	16	16	17	16	23	29	31	46	6	23	16
JUL. 30	18	18	18	19	16	23	29	31	46	6	23	16
JUL. 31	18	19	20	20	16	23	29	31	46	6	23	16

Date & Time	SUN	MOON 1	MOON 2	MOON 3	MERCURY	VENUS	MARS	JUPITER	SATURN	URANUS	NEPTUNE	PLUTO
AUG. 1	18	21	21	22	17	23	29	31	46	6	23	16
AUG. 2	18	22	23	23	17	23	29	31	46	6	23	16
AUG. 3	19	24	24	25	17	23	29	31	46	6	23	16
AUG. 4	19	25	26	26	18	24	29	31	46	6	23	16
AUG. 5	19	27	28	28	18	24	29	31	46	6	23	16
AUG. 6	19	29	29	30	18	24	30	31	46	6	23	16
AUG. 7	19	30	31	31	18	24	30	31	46	6	23	16
AUG. 8	19	32	33	33	19	24	30	31	46	6	23	16
AUG. 9	19	34	34	35	19	24	30	31	46	6	23	16
AUG. 10	19	35	36	37	19	24	30	31	46	6	23	16
AUG. 11	20	37	38	39	19	24	30	31	46	6	23	16
AUG. 12	20	39	40	40	20	24	30	31	46	6	23	16
AUG. 13	20	41	42	42	20	24	30	31	46	6	23	16
AUG. 14	20	43	44	44	20	24	30	31	46	6	23	16
AUG. 15	20	45	46	46	21	24	30	31	46	6	23	16
AUG. 16	20	47	48	48	21	24	30	31	46	6	23	16
AUG. 17	20	1	2	2	21	24	30	31	46	6	23	16
AUG. 18	20	3	4	4	21	24	30	31	46	6	23	16
AUG. 19	21	5	6	6	22	24	31	31	46	6	23	16
AUG. 20	21	7	8	8	22	24	31	31	46	6	23	16
AUG. 21	21	9	9	10	22	24	31	31	46	6	23	16
AUG. 22	21	10	11	12	22	24	31	31	46	6	23	17
AUG. 23	21	12	13	13	23	24	31	31	46	6	23	17
AUG. 24	21	14	14	15	23	24	31	31	46	6	23	17
AUG. 25	21	15	16	17	23	24	31	31	46	6	23	17
AUG. 26	22	17	18	18	23	24	31	31	46	6	23	17
AUG. 27	22	19	19	20	23	24	31	31	46	6	23	17
AUG. 28	22	20	21	21	24	24	31	31	46	6	23	17
AUG. 29	22	22	22	23	24	24	31	31	46	6	23	17
AUG. 30	22	23	24	24	24	24	31	31	46	6	23	17
AUG. 31	22	25	26	26	24	24	32	31	46	6	23	17

MOON 1 ◖ 12:01 A.M. TO 8:00 A.M.   **MOON 2** ◑ 8:01 A.M. TO 4:00 P.M.   **MOON 3** ● 4:01 P.M. TO 12:00 A.M.

Use only one "moon" number. Choose the column closest to your time of birth. If your place of birth is not on Eastern Standard Time, be sure to read "How to Convert to Eastern Standard Time" at the beginning of this section.

1935

September   October

Date & Time	SUN	MOON 1	MOON 2	MOON 3	MERCURY	VENUS	MARS	JUPITER	SATURN	URANUS	NEPTUNE	PLUTO
SEP. 1	22	27	27	28	25	23	32	31	46	6	23	17
SEP. 2	22	28	29	29	25	23	32	31	46	6	23	17
SEP. 3	23	30	30	31	25	23	32	31	46	6	23	17
SEP. 4	23	31	32	33	25	23	32	31	46	6	23	17
SEP. 5	23	33	34	34	25	23	32	31	46	6	23	17
SEP. 6	23	35	35	36	26	23	32	31	46	6	23	17
SEP. 7	23	37	37	38	26	23	32	31	46	6	23	17
SEP. 8	23	38	39	40	26	23	32	31	46	6	23	17
SEP. 9	23	40	41	42	26	23	32	31	46	6	23	17
SEP. 10	23	42	43	44	26	23	32	31	46	6	23	17
SEP. 11	24	44	45	46	26	23	32	31	46	6	23	17
SEP. 12	24	46	47	48	27	23	33	31	46	6	23	17
SEP. 13	24	48	1	2	27	23	33	31	46	6	23	17
SEP. 14	24	2	3	4	27	22	33	32	46	6	23	17
SEP. 15	24	4	5	6	27	22	33	32	46	6	23	17
SEP. 16	24	6	7	8	27	22	33	32	46	6	23	17
SEP. 17	24	8	9	9	27	22	33	32	46	6	23	17
SEP. 18	24	10	11	11	28	22	33	32	46	6	23	17
SEP. 19	25	12	12	13	28	22	33	32	46	6	23	17
SEP. 20	25	13	14	15	28	22	33	32	46	6	23	17
SEP. 21	25	15	16	16	28	22	33	32	46	6	23	17
SEP. 22	25	17	17	18	28	22	33	32	46	6	23	17
SEP. 23	25	18	19	19	28	22	34	32	46	6	23	17
SEP. 24	25	20	20	21	28	22	34	32	46	6	23	17
SEP. 25	26	21	22	23	29	22	34	32	46	6	23	17
SEP. 26	26	23	24	24	29	22	34	32	46	6	23	17
SEP. 27	26	25	25	26	29	22	34	32	46	6	23	17
SEP. 28	26	26	27	27	29	22	34	32	46	6	23	17
SEP. 29	26	28	28	29	29	22	34	32	46	6	23	17
SEP. 30	26	29	30	31	29	22	34	32	46	6	23	17

Date & Time	SUN	MOON 1	MOON 2	MOON 3	MERCURY	VENUS	MARS	JUPITER	SATURN	URANUS	NEPTUNE	PLUTO
OCT. 1	26	31	32	32	29	22	34	32	46	6	23	17
OCT. 2	26	33	33	34	29	22	34	32	46	6	23	17
OCT. 3	27	34	35	36	29	22	34	32	46	6	23	17
OCT. 4	27	36	37	37	29	22	35	32	46	6	23	17
OCT. 5	27	38	38	39	29	22	35	32	46	6	23	17
OCT. 6	27	40	40	41	29	22	35	32	46	6	23	17
OCT. 7	27	41	42	43	29	22	35	32	46	6	23	17
OCT. 8	27	43	44	45	29	22	35	32	46	6	23	17
OCT. 9	27	45	46	47	29	22	35	32	46	6	23	17
OCT. 10	27	47	48	1	29	22	35	32	46	6	23	17
OCT. 11	28	1	2	3	29	22	35	32	46	6	23	17
OCT. 12	28	3	4	5	29	22	35	32	46	6	23	17
OCT. 13	28	5	6	7	29	22	35	32	46	6	23	17
OCT. 14	28	7	8	9	29	22	36	32	46	6	23	17
OCT. 15	28	9	10	10	29	22	36	32	45	6	23	17
OCT. 16	28	11	12	12	29	22	36	32	45	5	23	17
OCT. 17	28	13	13	14	28	23	36	32	45	5	23	17
OCT. 18	28	15	15	16	28	23	36	32	45	5	23	17
OCT. 19	29	16	17	17	28	23	36	32	45	5	23	17
OCT. 20	29	18	18	19	28	23	36	32	45	5	23	17
OCT. 21	29	19	20	21	28	23	36	32	45	5	23	17
OCT. 22	29	21	22	22	28	23	36	32	45	5	23	17
OCT. 23	29	23	23	24	27	23	36	32	45	5	23	17
OCT. 24	29	24	25	25	27	23	37	33	45	5	23	17
OCT. 25	29	26	26	27	27	23	37	33	45	5	23	17
OCT. 26	30	27	28	28	27	23	37	33	45	5	23	17
OCT. 27	30	29	30	30	27	23	37	33	45	5	23	17
OCT. 28	30	31	31	32	27	24	37	33	45	5	23	17
OCT. 29	30	32	33	33	27	24	37	33	45	5	23	17
OCT. 30	30	34	35	35	27	24	37	33	45	5	23	17
OCT. 31	30	36	36	37	27	24	37	33	45	5	23	17

MOON 1 ☽ 12:01 A.M. TO 8:00 A.M.   **MOON 2** ◑ 8:01 A.M. TO 4:00 P.M.   **MOON 3** ● 4:01 P.M. TO 12:00 A.M.
Use only one "moon" number. Choose the column closest to your time of birth. If your place of birth is not on Eastern Standard Time, be sure to read "How to Convert to Eastern Standard Time" at the beginning of this section.

1935

November

Date & Time	SUN	MOON 1	MOON 2	MOON 3	MERCURY	VENUS	MARS	JUPITER	SATURN	URANUS	NEPTUNE	PLUTO
NOV. 1	30	37	38	39	28	24	37	33	45	5	23	17
NOV. 2	30	39	40	40	28	24	37	33	45	5	23	17
NOV. 3	31	41	42	42	28	24	38	33	45	5	23	17
NOV. 4	31	43	43	44	28	24	38	33	45	5	23	17
NOV. 5	31	45	45	46	28	24	38	33	45	5	23	17
NOV. 6	31	47	47	48	28	25	38	33	45	5	23	17
NOV. 7	31	1	1	2	28	25	38	33	45	5	23	17
NOV. 8	31	3	3	4	29	25	38	33	45	5	23	17
NOV. 9	31	5	5	6	29	25	38	33	45	5	23	17
NOV. 10	31	6	7	8	29	25	38	33	45	5	23	17
NOV. 11	31	8	9	10	29	25	38	33	45	5	23	17
NOV. 12	32	10	11	12	29	25	38	33	45	5	23	17
NOV. 13	32	12	13	13	30	25	39	33	45	5	23	17
NOV. 14	32	14	15	15	30	26	39	33	45	5	23	17
NOV. 15	32	16	16	17	30	26	39	33	45	5	23	17
NOV. 16	32	17	18	18	30	26	39	33	45	5	23	17
NOV. 17	32	19	19	20	30	26	39	33	45	5	23	17
NOV. 18	32	21	21	22	31	26	39	33	45	5	23	17
NOV. 19	33	22	23	23	31	26	39	33	45	5	23	17
NOV. 20	33	24	24	25	31	26	39	33	45	5	23	17
NOV. 21	33	25	26	26	31	26	39	33	45	5	23	17
NOV. 22	33	27	27	28	31	27	39	33	45	5	23	17
NOV. 23	33	29	29	30	32	27	40	33	45	5	23	17
NOV. 24	33	30	31	31	32	27	40	33	45	5	23	17
NOV. 25	34	32	32	33	32	27	40	33	45	5	23	17
NOV. 26	34	34	34	35	32	27	40	33	45	5	23	17
NOV. 27	34	35	36	36	33	27	40	34	45	5	23	17
NOV. 28	34	37	38	38	33	27	40	34	45	5	23	17
NOV. 29	34	39	39	40	33	28	40	34	45	5	23	17
NOV. 30	34	41	41	42	33	28	40	34	45	5	23	17

December

Date & Time	SUN	MOON 1	MOON 2	MOON 3	MERCURY	VENUS	MARS	JUPITER	SATURN	URANUS	NEPTUNE	PLUTO
DEC. 1	34	42	43	44	33	28	40	34	45	5	23	17
DEC. 2	34	44	45	46	34	28	40	34	46	5	23	17
DEC. 3	35	46	47	47	34	28	41	34	46	5	23	17
DEC. 4	35	48	1	1	34	28	41	34	46	5	23	17
DEC. 5	35	2	3	3	34	28	41	34	46	5	23	17
DEC. 6	35	4	4	5	34	29	41	34	46	5	23	17
DEC. 7	35	6	6	7	35	29	41	34	46	5	23	17
DEC. 8	35	8	8	9	35	29	41	34	46	5	23	17
DEC. 9	35	10	10	11	35	29	41	34	46	5	23	17
DEC. 10	35	11	12	13	35	29	41	34	46	5	23	17
DEC. 11	36	13	14	14	35	29	41	34	46	5	23	17
DEC. 12	36	15	16	16	36	30	41	34	46	5	23	17
DEC. 13	36	17	17	18	36	30	42	34	46	5	23	17
DEC. 14	36	18	19	19	36	30	42	34	46	5	23	17
DEC. 15	36	20	21	21	36	30	42	34	46	5	23	17
DEC. 16	36	22	22	23	37	30	42	34	46	5	23	17
DEC. 17	36	23	24	24	37	30	42	34	46	5	23	17
DEC. 18	36	25	25	26	37	30	42	34	46	5	23	17
DEC. 19	37	26	27	27	37	31	42	34	46	5	23	17
DEC. 20	37	28	28	29	37	31	42	34	46	5	23	17
DEC. 21	37	30	30	31	38	31	42	34	46	5	23	17
DEC. 22	37	31	32	32	38	31	43	34	46	5	23	17
DEC. 23	37	33	33	34	38	31	43	34	46	5	23	17
DEC. 24	37	35	35	36	38	31	43	34	46	5	23	17
DEC. 25	37	36	37	38	38	31	43	34	46	5	23	17
DEC. 26	38	38	39	39	39	32	43	34	46	5	23	17
DEC. 27	38	40	41	41	39	32	43	34	46	5	23	17
DEC. 28	38	42	43	43	39	32	43	34	46	5	23	17
DEC. 29	38	44	44	45	39	32	43	34	46	5	23	17
DEC. 30	38	46	46	47	39	32	43	34	46	5	23	17
DEC. 31	38	48	48	1	40	32	43	34	46	5	23	17

MOON 1 ◐ 12:01 A.M. TO 8:00 A.M.   **MOON 2** ◑ 8:01 A.M. TO 4:00 P.M.   **MOON 3** ● 4:01 P.M. TO 12:00 A.M.
Use only one "moon" number. Choose the column closest to your time of birth. If your place of birth is not on
Eastern Standard Time, be sure to read "How to Convert to Eastern Standard Time" at the beginning of this section.

1936

January

Date & Time	SUN	MOON 1	MOON 2	MOON 3	MERCURY	VENUS	MARS	JUPITER	SATURN	URANUS	NEPTUNE	PLUTO
JAN. 1	38	1	2	3	40	33	44	35	46	5	23	17
JAN. 2	38	3	4	5	40	33	44	35	46	5	23	17
JAN. 3	39	5	6	7	40	33	44	35	46	5	23	17
JAN. 4	39	7	8	8	41	33	44	35	46	5	23	17
JAN. 5	39	9	10	10	41	33	44	35	46	5	23	17
JAN. 6	39	11	11	12	41	33	44	35	46	5	23	17
JAN. 7	39	13	13	14	41	34	44	35	46	5	23	17
JAN. 8	39	14	15	15	41	34	44	35	46	5	23	17
JAN. 9	39	16	17	17	42	34	44	35	46	5	23	16
JAN. 10	40	18	18	19	42	34	45	35	46	5	23	16
JAN. 11	40	19	20	20	42	34	45	35	46	5	23	16
JAN. 12	40	21	22	22	42	34	45	35	46	5	23	16
JAN. 13	40	23	23	24	42	34	45	35	46	5	23	16
JAN. 14	40	24	25	25	42	35	45	35	46	5	23	16
JAN. 15	40	26	26	27	43	35	45	35	46	5	23	16
JAN. 16	40	27	28	28	43	35	45	35	46	5	23	16
JAN. 17	41	29	30	30	43	35	45	35	46	5	23	16
JAN. 18	41	31	31	32	43	35	45	35	46	5	23	16
JAN. 19	41	32	33	33	43	35	45	35	46	5	23	16
JAN. 20	41	34	35	35	43	36	46	35	46	5	23	16
JAN. 21	41	36	36	37	43	36	46	35	46	5	23	16
JAN. 22	41	37	38	39	43	36	46	35	46	5	23	16
JAN. 23	42	39	40	41	43	36	46	35	46	5	23	16
JAN. 24	42	41	42	42	43	36	46	35	46	5	23	16
JAN. 25	42	43	44	44	43	36	46	35	46	5	23	16
JAN. 26	42	45	46	46	43	37	46	35	46	5	23	16
JAN. 27	42	47	48	48	43	37	46	35	46	5	23	16
JAN. 28	42	1	2	2	43	37	46	35	46	5	23	16
JAN. 29	42	3	4	4	43	37	46	35	46	5	23	16
JAN. 30	42	5	5	6	43	37	47	35	46	5	23	16
JAN. 31	43	7	7	8	43	37	47	35	46	5	23	16

February

Date & Time	SUN	MOON 1	MOON 2	MOON 3	MERCURY	VENUS	MARS	JUPITER	SATURN	URANUS	NEPTUNE	PLUTO
FEB. 1	43	9	9	10	42	38	47	35	46	5	23	16
FEB. 2	43	10	11	12	42	38	47	35	46	5	23	16
FEB. 3	43	12	13	13	42	38	47	35	46	5	23	16
FEB. 4	43	14	14	15	42	38	47	35	46	5	23	16
FEB. 5	43	16	16	17	42	38	47	35	46	5	23	16
FEB. 6	43	17	18	18	42	38	47	35	46	5	23	16
FEB. 7	43	19	19	20	42	39	47	35	46	5	23	16
FEB. 8	44	21	21	22	41	39	48	35	46	5	23	16
FEB. 9	44	22	23	23	41	39	48	36	46	5	23	16
FEB. 10	44	24	24	25	41	39	48	36	46	5	23	16
FEB. 11	44	25	26	26	41	39	48	36	46	5	23	16
FEB. 12	44	27	27	28	41	39	48	36	46	5	23	16
FEB. 13	44	28	29	30	41	40	48	36	46	5	23	16
FEB. 14	44	30	31	31	41	40	48	36	46	5	23	16
FEB. 15	44	32	32	33	41	40	48	36	46	5	23	16
FEB. 16	45	33	34	34	41	40	48	36	46	5	23	16
FEB. 17	45	35	36	36	41	40	48	36	46	5	23	16
FEB. 18	45	37	37	38	41	40	1	36	46	5	23	16
FEB. 19	45	39	39	40	41	40	1	36	46	5	23	16
FEB. 20	45	40	41	42	42	41	1	36	46	5	23	16
FEB. 21	45	42	43	44	42	41	1	36	46	5	23	16
FEB. 22	45	44	45	46	42	41	1	36	47	5	23	16
FEB. 23	46	46	47	48	42	41	1	36	47	5	23	16
FEB. 24	46	48	1	2	42	41	1	36	47	5	23	16
FEB. 25	46	2	3	4	42	41	1	36	47	5	23	16
FEB. 26	46	4	5	6	42	42	1	36	47	5	23	16
FEB. 27	46	6	7	7	42	42	1	36	47	5	23	16
FEB. 28	46	8	9	9	43	42	2	36	47	5	23	16
FEB. 29	46	10	11	11	43	42	2	36	47	5	23	16

MOON 1 ◗ 12:01 A.M. TO 8:00 A.M.   **MOON 2** ◖ 8:01 A.M. TO 4:00 P.M.   **MOON 3** ● 4:01 P.M. TO 12:00 A.M.

Use only one "moon" number. Choose the column closest to your time of birth. If your place of birth is not on Eastern Standard Time, be sure to read "How to Convert to Eastern Standard Time" at the beginning of this section.

Date & Time	SUN	MOON 1	MOON 2	MOON 3	MERCURY	VENUS	MARS	JUPITER	SATURN	URANUS	NEPTUNE	PLUTO
MAR. 1	46	12	12	13	43	42	2	36	47	5	23	16
MAR. 2	46	13	14	15	43	42	2	36	47	5	23	16
MAR. 3	47	15	16	16	43	43	2	36	47	5	23	16
MAR. 4	47	17	17	18	43	43	2	36	47	5	23	16
MAR. 5	47	18	19	20	43	43	2	36	47	5	23	16
MAR. 6	47	20	21	21	44	43	2	36	47	5	23	16
MAR. 7	47	22	22	23	44	43	2	36	47	5	23	16
MAR. 8	47	23	24	24	44	43	2	36	47	5	23	16
MAR. 9	47	25	25	26	44	44	3	36	47	5	23	16
MAR. 10	47	26	27	28	44	44	3	36	47	5	23	16
MAR. 11	48	28	29	29	45	44	3	36	47	5	23	16
MAR. 12	48	30	30	31	45	44	3	36	47	5	23	16
MAR. 13	48	31	32	32	45	44	3	36	47	5	23	16
MAR. 14	48	33	33	34	45	44	3	36	47	5	23	16
MAR. 15	48	34	35	36	45	45	3	36	47	5	23	16
MAR. 16	48	36	37	37	46	45	3	36	47	5	23	16
MAR. 17	48	38	38	39	46	45	3	36	47	5	23	16
MAR. 18	48	40	40	41	46	45	4	36	47	5	23	16
MAR. 19	1	41	42	43	46	45	4	36	47	5	23	16
MAR. 20	1	43	44	45	46	45	4	36	47	5	23	16
MAR. 21	1	45	46	47	47	46	4	36	47	5	23	16
MAR. 22	1	47	48	1	47	46	4	36	47	5	23	16
MAR. 23	1	1	2	3	47	46	4	36	47	5	23	16
MAR. 24	1	3	4	5	47	46	4	36	47	5	23	16
MAR. 25	2	5	6	7	48	46	4	36	47	5	23	16
MAR. 26	2	7	8	9	48	46	4	36	47	5	23	16
MAR. 27	2	9	10	11	48	47	4	36	47	5	23	16
MAR. 28	2	11	12	12	48	47	5	36	47	5	23	16
MAR. 29	2	13	14	14	48	47	5	36	47	5	23	16
MAR. 30	2	15	15	16	1	47	5	36	47	5	23	16
MAR. 31	2	16	17	18	1	47	5	36	47	6	23	16

Date & Time	SUN	MOON 1	MOON 2	MOON 3	MERCURY	VENUS	MARS	JUPITER	SATURN	URANUS	NEPTUNE	PLUTO
APR. 1	2	18	19	19	1	47	5	36	47	6	23	16
APR. 2	2	20	20	21	1	48	5	36	47	6	23	16
APR. 3	3	21	22	22	2	48	5	36	47	6	23	16
APR. 4	3	23	23	24	2	48	5	36	47	6	23	16
APR. 5	3	24	25	26	2	48	5	36	47	6	23	16
APR. 6	3	26	27	27	3	48	5	36	47	6	23	16
APR. 7	3	28	28	29	3	48	5	36	47	6	23	16
APR. 8	3	29	30	30	3	1	6	36	47	6	23	16
APR. 9	3	31	31	32	3	1	6	36	47	6	23	16
APR. 10	3	32	33	34	4	1	6	36	47	6	23	16
APR. 11	4	34	35	35	4	1	6	36	47	6	23	16
APR. 12	4	36	36	37	4	1	6	36	47	6	23	16
APR. 13	4	37	38	38	4	1	6	36	47	6	23	16
APR. 14	4	39	40	40	5	1	6	36	47	6	23	16
APR. 15	4	41	41	42	5	2	6	36	47	6	23	16
APR. 16	4	43	43	44	5	2	6	36	47	6	23	16
APR. 17	4	45	45	46	6	2	6	36	47	6	23	16
APR. 18	4	46	47	48	6	2	7	36	47	6	23	16
APR. 19	5	48	1	2	6	2	7	36	47	6	23	16
APR. 20	5	2	3	4	6	2	7	36	47	6	23	16
APR. 21	5	4	5	6	7	3	7	36	47	6	23	16
APR. 22	5	7	7	8	7	3	7	36	47	6	23	16
APR. 23	5	9	9	10	7	3	7	36	47	6	23	16
APR. 24	5	10	11	12	7	3	7	36	47	6	23	16
APR. 25	6	12	13	14	8	3	7	36	47	6	23	16
APR. 26	6	14	15	15	8	3	7	36	47	6	23	16
APR. 27	6	16	16	17	8	4	7	36	48	6	23	16
APR. 28	6	18	18	19	8	4	8	36	48	6	23	16
APR. 29	6	19	20	20	9	4	8	36	48	6	23	16
APR. 30	6	21	21	22	9	4	8	36	48	6	23	16

MOON 1 ◑ 12:01 A.M. TO 8:00 A.M. **MOON 2** ◐ 8:01 A.M. TO 4:00 P.M. **MOON 3** ● 4:01 P.M. TO 12:00 A.M.
Use only one "moon" number. Choose the column closest to your time of birth. If your place of birth is not on Eastern Standard Time, be sure to read "How to Convert to Eastern Standard Time" at the beginning of this section.

1936

May

Date & Time	SUN	MOON 1	MOON 2	MOON 3	MERCURY	VENUS	MARS	JUPITER	SATURN	URANUS	NEPTUNE	PLUTO
MAY 1	6	22	23	24	9	4	8	36	48	6	23	16
MAY 2	6	24	25	25	9	4	8	36	48	6	23	16
MAY 3	7	26	26	27	9	5	8	36	48	6	23	16
MAY 4	7	27	28	28	10	5	8	36	48	6	23	16
MAY 5	7	29	29	30	10	5	8	36	48	6	23	16
MAY 6	7	30	31	31	10	5	8	36	48	6	23	16
MAY 7	7	32	33	33	10	5	8	36	48	6	23	16
MAY 8	7	34	34	35	10	5	8	36	48	6	23	16
MAY 9	7	35	36	36	10	6	9	36	48	6	23	16
MAY 10	7	37	38	38	10	6	9	36	48	6	23	16
MAY 11	8	39	39	40	11	6	9	36	48	6	23	16
MAY 12	8	40	41	42	11	6	9	36	48	6	23	16
MAY 13	8	42	43	43	11	6	9	36	48	6	23	16
MAY 14	8	44	45	45	11	6	9	36	48	6	23	16
MAY 15	8	46	46	47	11	7	9	36	48	6	23	16
MAY 16	8	48	48	1	11	7	9	36	48	6	23	16
MAY 17	8	2	2	3	11	7	9	36	48	6	23	16
MAY 18	8	4	4	5	11	7	9	36	48	6	23	16
MAY 19	9	6	6	7	11	7	10	36	48	6	23	16
MAY 20	9	8	8	9	11	7	10	36	48	6	23	16
MAY 21	9	10	10	11	11	8	10	36	48	6	23	16
MAY 22	9	12	12	13	11	8	10	36	48	6	23	16
MAY 23	9	13	14	15	11	8	10	36	48	6	23	16
MAY 24	9	15	16	16	11	8	10	36	48	6	23	16
MAY 25	10	17	18	18	11	8	10	36	48	6	23	16
MAY 26	10	19	19	20	11	8	10	36	48	6	23	16
MAY 27	10	20	21	21	11	8	10	36	48	6	23	16
MAY 28	10	22	23	23	11	8	10	36	48	6	23	16
MAY 29	10	24	24	25	10	9	10	36	48	6	23	16
MAY 30	10	25	26	26	10	9	11	36	48	6	23	16
MAY 31	10	27	27	28	10	9	11	36	48	6	23	16

June

Date & Time	SUN	MOON 1	MOON 2	MOON 3	MERCURY	VENUS	MARS	JUPITER	SATURN	URANUS	NEPTUNE	PLUTO
JUN. 1	10	28	29	29	10	9	11	36	48	6	23	16
JUN. 2	10	30	30	31	10	10	11	36	48	6	23	16
JUN. 3	11	32	32	33	10	10	11	36	48	6	23	16
JUN. 4	11	33	34	34	10	10	11	36	48	6	23	16
JUN. 5	11	35	35	36	10	10	11	36	48	6	23	16
JUN. 6	11	37	37	38	10	10	11	36	48	6	23	16
JUN. 7	11	38	39	39	10	10	11	36	48	6	23	16
JUN. 8	11	40	41	41	10	10	11	36	48	6	23	16
JUN. 9	11	42	42	43	10	11	11	36	48	6	23	16
JUN. 10	11	44	44	45	10	11	12	36	48	6	23	16
JUN. 11	12	45	46	47	10	11	12	36	48	6	23	16
JUN. 12	12	47	48	1	10	11	12	36	48	6	23	16
JUN. 13	12	1	2	2	10	11	12	36	48	6	23	16
JUN. 14	12	3	4	4	10	11	12	36	48	6	23	16
JUN. 15	12	5	6	6	10	12	12	35	48	6	23	16
JUN. 16	12	7	8	8	10	12	12	35	48	6	23	16
JUN. 17	12	9	9	10	10	12	12	35	48	6	23	16
JUN. 18	12	11	11	12	10	12	12	35	48	6	23	16
JUN. 19	13	13	13	14	10	12	12	35	48	6	23	16
JUN. 20	13	14	15	16	10	12	12	35	48	6	23	16
JUN. 21	13	16	17	17	10	13	13	35	48	6	23	16
JUN. 22	13	18	19	19	10	13	13	35	48	6	23	16
JUN. 23	13	20	20	21	10	13	13	35	48	6	23	16
JUN. 24	13	21	22	23	10	13	13	35	48	6	23	16
JUN. 25	14	23	24	24	10	13	13	35	48	6	23	16
JUN. 26	14	25	25	26	11	13	13	35	48	6	23	16
JUN. 27	14	26	27	27	11	14	13	35	48	6	23	16
JUN. 28	14	28	28	29	11	14	13	35	48	6	23	16
JUN. 29	14	29	30	31	11	14	13	35	48	6	23	16
JUN. 30	14	31	32	32	11	14	13	35	48	6	23	16

MOON 1 ☾ 12:01 A.M. TO 8:00 A.M. **MOON 2** ◑ 8:01 A.M. TO 4:00 P.M. **MOON 3** ● 4:01 P.M. TO 12:00 A.M.

Use only one "moon" number. Choose the column closest to your time of birth. If your place of birth is not on Eastern Standard Time, be sure to read "How to Convert to Eastern Standard Time" at the beginning of this section.

1936

July   August

Date & Time	SUN	MOON 1	MOON 2	MOON 3	MERCURY	VENUS	MARS	JUPITER	SATURN	URANUS	NEPTUNE	PLUTO
JUL. 1	14	33	33	34	11	14	13	35	48	6	23	16
JUL. 2	14	34	35	35	12	14	14	35	48	6	23	16
JUL. 3	15	36	37	37	12	15	14	35	48	6	23	17
JUL. 4	15	38	38	39	12	15	14	35	48	6	23	17
JUL. 5	15	39	40	41	12	15	14	35	48	6	23	17
JUL. 6	15	41	42	42	12	15	14	35	48	6	23	17
JUL. 7	15	43	44	44	13	15	14	35	48	6	23	17
JUL. 8	15	45	46	46	13	15	14	35	48	6	23	17
JUL. 9	15	47	47	48	13	16	14	35	48	6	23	17
JUL. 10	15	1	1	2	13	16	14	35	48	6	23	17
JUL. 11	16	3	3	4	14	16	14	35	48	6	23	17
JUL. 12	16	5	5	6	14	16	14	35	48	6	23	17
JUL. 13	16	6	7	8	14	16	15	35	48	6	23	17
JUL. 14	16	8	9	10	14	16	15	35	48	6	23	17
JUL. 15	16	10	11	11	15	17	15	35	48	6	23	17
JUL. 16	16	12	13	13	15	17	15	35	48	6	23	17
JUL. 17	16	14	14	15	15	17	15	35	48	6	23	17
JUL. 18	16	16	16	17	15	17	15	35	48	6	23	17
JUL. 19	17	17	18	19	16	17	15	35	48	6	23	17
JUL. 20	17	19	20	20	16	17	15	35	48	6	23	17
JUL. 21	17	21	21	22	16	18	15	35	48	6	23	17
JUL. 22	17	22	23	24	17	18	15	35	48	6	23	17
JUL. 23	17	24	25	25	17	18	15	35	48	6	23	17
JUL. 24	17	26	26	27	17	18	15	35	48	6	23	17
JUL. 25	17	27	28	28	17	18	16	35	48	6	23	17
JUL. 26	18	29	29	30	18	18	16	35	48	6	23	17
JUL. 27	18	30	31	32	18	19	16	35	48	6	23	17
JUL. 28	18	32	33	33	18	19	16	35	48	6	23	17
JUL. 29	18	34	34	35	19	19	16	35	48	6	23	17
JUL. 30	18	35	36	37	19	19	16	35	48	6	23	17
JUL. 31	18	37	38	38	19	19	16	35	48	6	23	17

Date & Time	SUN	MOON 1	MOON 2	MOON 3	MERCURY	VENUS	MARS	JUPITER	SATURN	URANUS	NEPTUNE	PLUTO
AUG. 1	18	39	39	40	19	19	16	35	48	6	23	17
AUG. 2	18	41	41	42	20	20	16	35	48	6	23	17
AUG. 3	19	42	43	44	20	20	16	35	48	6	23	17
AUG. 4	19	44	45	46	20	20	16	35	48	6	23	17
AUG. 5	19	46	47	48	20	20	17	35	48	6	23	17
AUG. 6	19	48	1	2	21	20	17	35	48	6	23	17
AUG. 7	19	2	3	3	21	20	17	35	48	6	23	17
AUG. 8	19	4	5	5	21	20	17	35	48	6	23	17
AUG. 9	19	6	7	7	21	21	17	35	48	6	23	17
AUG. 10	19	8	8	9	21	21	17	35	48	6	23	17
AUG. 11	20	10	10	11	22	21	17	35	48	6	23	17
AUG. 12	20	12	12	13	22	21	17	35	48	6	23	17
AUG. 13	20	13	14	15	22	21	17	35	48	6	23	17
AUG. 14	20	15	16	16	22	21	17	35	48	6	23	17
AUG. 15	20	17	17	18	23	22	17	35	48	6	23	17
AUG. 16	20	19	19	20	23	22	17	35	48	6	23	17
AUG. 17	20	20	21	21	23	22	18	35	48	6	23	17
AUG. 18	20	22	23	23	23	22	18	35	48	6	23	17
AUG. 19	21	24	24	25	23	22	18	35	48	6	23	17
AUG. 20	21	25	26	26	24	22	18	35	48	6	23	17
AUG. 21	21	27	27	28	24	23	18	35	48	6	23	17
AUG. 22	21	28	29	29	24	23	18	35	48	6	23	17
AUG. 23	21	30	31	31	24	23	18	35	48	6	23	17
AUG. 24	21	32	33	33	24	23	18	35	48	6	23	17
AUG. 25	21	33	34	34	25	23	18	35	48	6	23	17
AUG. 26	22	35	35	36	25	23	18	35	48	6	23	17
AUG. 27	22	36	37	38	25	24	18	35	48	6	23	17
AUG. 28	22	38	39	39	25	24	18	35	48	6	23	17
AUG. 29	22	40	40	41	25	24	19	35	48	6	23	17
AUG. 30	22	42	42	43	25	24	19	35	48	6	23	17
AUG. 31	22	44	44	45	26	24	19	35	48	6	23	17

MOON 1 ◐ 12:01 A.M. TO 8:00 A.M.   **MOON 2** ◑ 8:01 A.M. TO 4:00 P.M.   **MOON 3** ● 4:01 P.M. TO 12:00 A.M.

Use only one "moon" number. Choose the column closest to your time of birth. If your place of birth is not on Eastern Standard Time, be sure to read "How to Convert to Eastern Standard Time" at the beginning of this section.

1936

September

Date & Time	SUN	MOON 1	MOON 2	MOON 3	MERCURY	VENUS	MARS	JUPITER	SATURN	URANUS	NEPTUNE	PLUTO
SEP. 1	22	46	46	47	26	24	19	35	48	6	23	17
SEP. 2	22	47	48	1	26	25	19	35	48	6	23	17
SEP. 3	23	1	2	3	26	25	19	35	48	6	23	17
SEP. 4	23	3	4	5	26	25	19	35	48	6	23	17
SEP. 5	23	5	6	7	26	25	19	35	48	6	23	17
SEP. 6	23	7	8	9	26	25	19	35	48	6	23	17
SEP. 7	23	9	10	11	26	25	19	35	48	6	23	17
SEP. 8	23	11	12	12	27	26	19	35	48	6	23	17
SEP. 9	23	13	14	14	27	26	20	35	48	6	23	17
SEP. 10	23	15	15	16	27	26	20	35	48	6	23	17
SEP. 11	24	16	17	18	27	26	20	35	48	6	23	17
SEP. 12	24	18	19	19	27	26	20	35	48	6	23	17
SEP. 13	24	20	20	21	27	26	20	35	48	6	23	17
SEP. 14	24	21	22	23	27	27	20	35	47	6	23	17
SEP. 15	24	23	24	24	27	27	20	35	47	6	23	17
SEP. 16	24	25	25	26	27	27	20	35	47	6	23	17
SEP. 17	24	26	27	27	27	27	20	35	47	6	23	17
SEP. 18	24	28	28	29	27	27	20	35	47	6	23	17
SEP. 19	25	30	30	31	27	27	20	35	47	6	23	17
SEP. 20	25	31	32	32	27	28	20	35	47	6	23	17
SEP. 21	25	33	33	34	27	28	21	35	47	6	23	17
SEP. 22	25	34	35	35	27	28	21	35	47	6	23	17
SEP. 23	25	36	36	37	27	28	21	35	47	6	23	17
SEP. 24	25	38	38	39	27	28	21	35	47	6	23	17
SEP. 25	26	39	40	40	27	28	21	35	47	6	23	17
SEP. 26	26	41	42	42	27	29	21	35	47	6	23	17
SEP. 27	26	43	43	44	27	29	21	35	47	6	23	17
SEP. 28	26	45	45	46	26	29	21	35	47	6	23	17
SEP. 29	26	47	47	48	26	29	21	35	47	6	23	17
SEP. 30	26	1	1	2	26	29	21	35	47	6	23	17

October

Date & Time	SUN	MOON 1	MOON 2	MOON 3	MERCURY	VENUS	MARS	JUPITER	SATURN	URANUS	NEPTUNE	PLUTO
OCT. 1	26	3	3	4	26	29	21	35	47	6	23	17
OCT. 2	26	5	5	6	26	30	21	35	47	6	23	17
OCT. 3	27	7	7	8	26	30	22	35	47	6	23	17
OCT. 4	27	9	9	10	26	30	22	35	47	6	23	17
OCT. 5	27	11	11	12	25	30	22	35	47	6	23	17
OCT. 6	27	12	13	14	25	30	22	35	47	6	23	17
OCT. 7	27	14	15	15	25	30	22	36	47	6	23	17
OCT. 8	27	16	17	17	25	31	22	36	47	6	23	17
OCT. 9	27	18	18	19	25	31	22	36	47	6	23	17
OCT. 10	27	19	20	21	25	31	22	36	47	6	23	17
OCT. 11	28	21	22	22	25	31	22	36	47	6	23	17
OCT. 12	28	23	23	24	25	31	22	36	47	6	23	17
OCT. 13	28	24	25	25	25	31	22	36	47	6	23	17
OCT. 14	28	26	26	27	25	31	22	36	47	6	23	17
OCT. 15	28	28	28	29	25	32	23	36	47	6	23	17
OCT. 16	28	29	30	30	26	32	23	36	47	6	23	17
OCT. 17	28	31	31	32	26	32	23	36	47	6	23	17
OCT. 18	28	32	33	33	26	32	23	36	47	6	23	17
OCT. 19	29	34	34	35	26	32	23	36	47	6	23	17
OCT. 20	29	35	36	37	26	33	23	36	47	6	23	17
OCT. 21	29	37	38	38	26	33	23	36	47	6	23	17
OCT. 22	29	39	39	40	27	33	23	36	47	6	23	17
OCT. 23	29	40	41	42	27	33	23	36	47	6	23	17
OCT. 24	29	42	43	43	27	33	23	36	47	6	23	17
OCT. 25	29	44	45	45	27	33	23	36	47	6	23	17
OCT. 26	30	46	46	47	27	33	23	36	47	6	23	17
OCT. 27	30	48	48	1	28	34	23	36	47	6	23	17
OCT. 28	30	2	2	3	28	34	24	36	47	6	23	17
OCT. 29	30	4	4	5	28	34	24	36	47	6	23	17
OCT. 30	30	6	6	7	28	34	24	36	47	6	23	17
OCT. 31	30	8	8	9	28	34	24	36	47	6	23	17

MOON 1 ◐ 12:01 A.M. TO 8:00 A.M.   **MOON 2** ◑ 8:01 A.M. TO 4:00 P.M.   **MOON 3** ● 4:01 P.M. TO 12:00 A.M.
Use only one "moon" number. Choose the column closest to your time of birth. If your place of birth is not on Eastern Standard Time, be sure to read "How to Convert to Eastern Standard Time" at the beginning of this section.

1936

November

Date & Time	SUN	MOON 1	MOON 2	MOON 3	MERCURY	VENUS	MARS	JUPITER	SATURN	URANUS	NEPTUNE	PLUTO
NOV. 1	30	10	10	11	29	34	24	36	47	6	23	17
NOV. 2	30	12	12	13	29	35	24	36	47	6	23	17
NOV. 3	31	14	14	15	29	35	24	36	47	6	23	17
NOV. 4	31	16	16	17	29	35	24	36	47	6	23	17
NOV. 5	31	17	18	18	30	35	24	36	47	6	23	17
NOV. 6	31	19	20	20	30	35	24	36	47	6	23	17
NOV. 7	31	21	21	22	30	35	24	36	47	6	23	17
NOV. 8	31	22	23	23	30	36	24	36	47	6	23	17
NOV. 9	31	24	24	25	30	36	25	36	47	6	23	17
NOV. 10	31	26	26	27	31	36	25	36	47	6	23	17
NOV. 11	31	27	28	28	31	36	25	36	47	6	23	17
NOV. 12	32	29	29	30	31	36	25	36	47	6	23	17
NOV. 13	32	30	31	31	31	36	25	36	47	6	23	17
NOV. 14	32	32	32	33	32	37	25	36	47	6	23	17
NOV. 15	32	33	34	35	32	37	25	36	47	6	23	17
NOV. 16	32	35	36	36	32	37	25	37	47	6	23	17
NOV. 17	32	37	37	38	32	37	25	37	47	6	23	17
NOV. 18	32	38	39	39	32	37	25	37	47	6	23	17
NOV. 19	33	40	41	41	33	37	25	37	47	6	23	17
NOV. 20	33	42	42	43	33	38	25	37	47	6	23	17
NOV. 21	33	43	44	45	33	38	25	37	47	6	23	17
NOV. 22	33	45	46	46	33	38	26	37	47	6	23	17
NOV. 23	33	47	48	48	33	38	26	37	47	6	23	17
NOV. 24	33	1	2	2	34	38	26	37	47	6	23	17
NOV. 25	34	3	4	4	34	38	26	37	47	6	23	17
NOV. 26	34	5	6	6	34	38	26	37	47	6	23	17
NOV. 27	34	7	8	8	34	39	26	37	47	6	23	17
NOV. 28	34	9	10	10	34	39	26	37	47	6	23	17
NOV. 29	34	11	12	12	35	39	26	37	47	6	23	17
NOV. 30	34	13	13	14	35	39	26	37	47	6	23	17

December

Date & Time	SUN	MOON 1	MOON 2	MOON 3	MERCURY	VENUS	MARS	JUPITER	SATURN	URANUS	NEPTUNE	PLUTO
DEC. 1	34	15	15	16	35	39	26	37	47	6	23	17
DEC. 2	34	17	17	18	35	39	26	37	47	6	23	17
DEC. 3	35	18	19	20	36	40	26	37	47	6	23	17
DEC. 4	35	20	21	21	36	40	27	37	47	6	23	17
DEC. 5	35	22	22	23	36	40	27	37	47	6	23	17
DEC. 6	35	23	24	25	36	40	27	37	47	6	23	17
DEC. 7	35	25	26	26	36	40	27	37	47	6	23	17
DEC. 8	35	27	27	28	37	40	27	37	47	6	23	17
DEC. 9	35	28	29	29	37	41	27	37	47	6	23	17
DEC. 10	35	30	30	31	37	41	27	37	47	6	23	17
DEC. 11	36	31	32	32	37	41	27	37	47	6	23	17
DEC. 12	36	33	34	34	37	41	27	37	47	6	23	17
DEC. 13	36	35	35	36	38	41	27	37	47	6	23	17
DEC. 14	36	36	37	37	38	41	27	37	47	6	23	17
DEC. 15	36	38	38	39	38	42	27	37	47	6	23	17
DEC. 16	36	40	40	41	38	42	27	37	47	6	23	17
DEC. 17	36	41	42	42	38	42	28	37	47	6	23	17
DEC. 18	36	43	44	44	39	42	28	37	47	6	23	17
DEC. 19	37	45	45	46	39	42	28	37	47	6	23	17
DEC. 20	37	47	47	48	39	42	28	38	47	6	23	17
DEC. 21	37	48	1	2	39	42	28	38	47	6	23	17
DEC. 22	37	2	3	4	39	43	28	38	47	6	23	17
DEC. 23	37	4	5	5	40	43	28	38	47	6	23	17
DEC. 24	37	6	7	7	40	43	28	38	47	6	23	17
DEC. 25	37	8	9	9	40	43	28	38	47	6	23	17
DEC. 26	38	10	11	11	40	43	28	38	47	6	23	17
DEC. 27	38	12	13	13	40	43	28	38	47	6	23	17
DEC. 28	38	14	15	15	40	44	28	38	47	6	23	17
DEC. 29	38	16	16	17	41	44	28	38	47	6	23	17
DEC. 30	38	18	18	19	41	44	28	38	47	6	23	17
DEC. 31	38	19	20	21	41	44	29	38	47	6	23	17

MOON 1 ◖ 12:01 A.M. TO 8:00 A.M.   **MOON 2** ◗ 8:01 A.M. TO 4:00 P.M.   **MOON 3** ● 4:01 P.M. TO 12:00 A.M.

Use only one "moon" number. Choose the column closest to your time of birth. If your place of birth is not on Eastern Standard Time, be sure to read "How to Convert to Eastern Standard Time" at the beginning of this section.

1937

January

Date & Time	SUN	MOON 1	MOON 2	MOON 3	MERCURY	VENUS	MARS	JUPITER	SATURN	URANUS	NEPTUNE	PLUTO
JAN. 1	38	21	22	22	41	44	29	38	47	6	23	17
JAN. 2	38	23	23	24	41	44	29	38	47	6	23	17
JAN. 3	39	25	25	26	41	45	29	38	47	6	23	17
JAN. 4	39	26	27	27	41	45	29	38	47	6	23	17
JAN. 5	39	28	28	29	41	45	29	38	47	6	23	17
JAN. 6	39	29	30	30	41	45	29	38	47	6	23	17
JAN. 7	39	31	31	32	41	45	29	38	47	6	23	17
JAN. 8	39	33	33	34	41	45	29	38	47	6	23	17
JAN. 9	39	34	35	35	41	45	29	38	47	6	23	17
JAN. 10	40	36	36	37	41	46	29	38	47	6	23	17
JAN. 11	40	37	38	39	41	46	29	38	47	6	23	17
JAN. 12	40	39	40	40	41	46	29	38	47	6	23	17
JAN. 13	40	41	41	42	41	46	29	38	47	6	23	17
JAN. 14	40	43	43	44	40	46	30	38	47	6	23	17
JAN. 15	40	44	45	46	40	46	30	38	47	6	23	17
JAN. 16	40	46	47	47	40	46	30	38	47	6	23	17
JAN. 17	41	48	1	1	40	47	30	38	47	6	23	17
JAN. 18	41	2	2	3	40	47	30	38	47	6	23	17
JAN. 19	41	4	4	5	40	47	30	38	47	6	23	17
JAN. 20	41	6	6	7	39	47	30	38	47	6	23	17
JAN. 21	41	7	8	9	39	47	30	38	47	6	23	17
JAN. 22	41	9	10	11	39	47	30	39	48	6	23	17
JAN. 23	42	11	12	13	39	48	30	39	48	6	23	17
JAN. 24	42	13	14	14	39	48	30	39	48	6	23	17
JAN. 25	42	15	16	17	39	48	30	39	48	6	23	17
JAN. 26	42	17	17	18	39	48	30	39	48	6	23	17
JAN. 27	42	19	19	20	39	48	30	39	48	6	23	17
JAN. 28	42	20	21	22	39	48	31	39	48	6	23	17
JAN. 29	42	22	23	23	39	48	31	39	48	6	23	17
JAN. 30	42	24	24	25	39	1	31	39	48	6	23	17
JAN. 31	43	26	26	27	39	1	31	39	48	6	23	17

February

Date & Time	SUN	MOON 1	MOON 2	MOON 3	MERCURY	VENUS	MARS	JUPITER	SATURN	URANUS	NEPTUNE	PLUTO
FEB. 1	43	27	28	28	39	1	31	39	48	6	23	17
FEB. 2	43	29	29	30	39	1	31	39	48	6	23	17
FEB. 3	43	30	31	31	39	1	31	39	48	6	23	17
FEB. 4	43	32	33	33	40	1	31	39	48	6	23	17
FEB. 5	43	34	34	35	40	1	31	39	48	6	23	17
FEB. 6	43	35	36	36	40	1	31	39	48	6	23	17
FEB. 7	43	37	37	38	40	2	31	39	48	6	23	17
FEB. 8	44	38	39	40	40	2	31	39	48	6	23	17
FEB. 9	44	40	41	41	40	2	31	39	48	6	23	17
FEB. 10	44	42	43	43	40	2	31	39	48	6	23	17
FEB. 11	44	44	44	45	41	2	31	39	48	6	23	17
FEB. 12	44	46	46	47	41	2	31	39	48	6	23	17
FEB. 13	44	47	48	1	41	2	32	39	48	6	23	17
FEB. 14	44	1	2	3	41	3	32	39	48	6	23	17
FEB. 15	44	3	4	5	41	3	32	39	48	6	23	17
FEB. 16	45	5	6	6	41	3	32	39	48	6	23	17
FEB. 17	45	7	8	8	42	3	32	39	48	6	23	17
FEB. 18	45	9	10	10	42	3	32	39	48	6	23	17
FEB. 19	45	11	11	12	42	3	32	39	48	6	23	17
FEB. 20	45	13	13	14	42	3	32	39	48	6	23	17
FEB. 21	45	14	15	16	42	3	32	39	48	6	23	17
FEB. 22	45	16	17	18	42	3	32	39	48	6	23	17
FEB. 23	46	18	19	19	43	4	32	39	48	6	23	17
FEB. 24	46	20	20	21	43	4	32	39	48	6	23	17
FEB. 25	46	22	22	23	43	4	32	39	48	6	23	17
FEB. 26	46	23	24	24	43	4	32	39	48	6	23	17
FEB. 27	46	25	26	26	43	4	32	40	48	6	23	17
FEB. 28	46	27	27	28	44	4	32	40	48	6	23	17

MOON 1 ◖ 12:01 A.M. TO 8:00 A.M.   **MOON 2** ◑ 8:01 A.M. TO 4:00 P.M.   **MOON 3** ● 4:01 P.M. TO 12:00 A.M.

Use only one "moon" number. Choose the column closest to your time of birth. If your place of birth is not on Eastern Standard Time, be sure to read "How to Convert to Eastern Standard Time" at the beginning of this section.

1937

March

April

Date & Time	SUN	MOON 1	MOON 2	MOON 3	MERCURY	VENUS	MARS	JUPITER	SATURN	URANUS	NEPTUNE	PLUTO
MAR. 1	46	28	29	29	44	4	32	40	48	6	23	17
MAR. 2	46	30	30	31	44	4	32	40	48	6	23	17
MAR. 3	47	31	32	32	44	4	33	40	48	6	23	17
MAR. 4	47	33	34	34	44	5	33	40	48	6	23	17
MAR. 5	47	35	35	36	45	5	33	40	48	6	23	17
MAR. 6	47	36	37	37	45	5	33	40	48	6	23	17
MAR. 7	47	38	38	39	45	5	33	40	48	6	23	17
MAR. 8	47	39	40	41	45	5	33	40	48	6	23	17
MAR. 9	47	41	42	42	46	5	33	40	48	6	23	17
MAR. 10	47	43	44	44	46	5	33	40	48	6	23	17
MAR. 11	48	45	45	46	46	5	33	40	48	6	23	17
MAR. 12	48	47	47	48	46	5	33	40	48	6	23	17
MAR. 13	48	1	1	2	46	5	33	40	48	6	23	17
MAR. 14	48	3	3	4	47	5	33	40	48	6	23	17
MAR. 15	48	5	5	6	47	5	33	40	48	6	23	17
MAR. 16	48	7	7	8	47	5	33	40	48	6	23	17
MAR. 17	48	8	9	10	47	5	33	40	48	6	23	17
MAR. 18	48	10	11	12	48	6	33	40	48	6	23	17
MAR. 19	1	12	13	13	48	6	33	40	48	6	23	17
MAR. 20	1	14	15	15	48	6	33	40	48	6	23	17
MAR. 21	1	16	16	17	48	6	33	40	48	6	23	17
MAR. 22	1	18	18	19	1	6	33	40	48	6	23	17
MAR. 23	1	19	20	21	1	6	33	40	48	6	23	17
MAR. 24	1	21	22	22	1	6	33	40	48	6	23	17
MAR. 25	2	23	23	24	2	6	33	40	48	6	23	17
MAR. 26	2	24	25	26	2	6	33	40	48	6	23	17
MAR. 27	2	26	27	27	2	6	33	40	1	6	23	17
MAR. 28	2	28	28	29	2	6	33	40	1	6	23	17
MAR. 29	2	29	30	30	3	6	33	40	1	6	23	17
MAR. 30	2	31	31	32	3	6	34	40	1	6	23	17
MAR. 31	2	33	33	34	3	6	34	40	1	6	23	17

Date & Time	SUN	MOON 1	MOON 2	MOON 3	MERCURY	VENUS	MARS	JUPITER	SATURN	URANUS	NEPTUNE	PLUTO
APR. 1	2	34	35	35	3	6	34	40	1	6	23	17
APR. 2	2	36	36	37	4	6	34	40	1	6	23	17
APR. 3	3	37	38	38	4	6	34	40	1	6	23	17
APR. 4	3	39	39	40	4	6	34	40	1	6	23	17
APR. 5	3	41	41	42	4	6	34	40	1	6	23	16
APR. 6	3	42	43	43	5	6	34	40	1	6	23	16
APR. 7	3	44	45	45	5	5	34	40	1	6	23	16
APR. 8	3	46	47	47	5	5	34	40	1	6	23	16
APR. 9	3	48	48	1	6	5	34	40	1	6	23	16
APR. 10	3	2	2	3	6	5	34	40	1	6	23	16
APR. 11	4	4	4	5	6	5	34	40	1	6	23	16
APR. 12	4	6	6	7	6	5	34	40	1	6	23	16
APR. 13	4	8	8	9	6	5	34	40	1	6	23	16
APR. 14	4	10	10	11	7	5	34	40	1	6	23	16
APR. 15	4	12	12	13	7	5	34	40	1	6	23	17
APR. 16	4	14	14	15	7	5	34	40	1	6	23	17
APR. 17	4	15	16	17	7	5	34	40	1	6	23	17
APR. 18	4	17	18	18	7	5	34	40	1	6	23	17
APR. 19	5	19	20	20	7	5	34	40	1	6	23	17
APR. 20	5	21	21	22	8	4	34	40	1	6	23	17
APR. 21	5	22	23	24	8	4	34	40	1	6	23	17
APR. 22	5	24	25	25	8	4	34	40	1	6	23	17
APR. 23	5	26	26	27	8	4	34	41	1	6	23	17
APR. 24	5	27	28	28	8	4	34	41	1	6	23	17
APR. 25	6	29	29	30	8	4	34	41	1	6	23	17
APR. 26	6	31	31	32	8	4	34	41	1	6	23	17
APR. 27	6	32	33	33	8	4	34	41	1	6	23	17
APR. 28	6	34	34	35	4	4	34	41	1	6	23	17
APR. 29	6	35	36	36	4	4	34	41	1	6	23	17
APR. 30	6	37	37	38	8	4	34	41	1	6	23	17

MOON 1 ◑ 12:01 A.M. TO 8:00 A.M.   **MOON 2** ◑ 8:01 A.M. TO 4:00 P.M.   **MOON 3** ● 4:01 P.M. TO 12:00 A.M.

Use only one "moon" number. Choose the column closest to your time of birth. If your place of birth is not on Eastern Standard Time, be sure to read "How to Convert to Eastern Standard Time" at the beginning of this section.

Date & Time	SUN ☉	MOON 1 ◔	MOON 2 ◑	MOON 3 ●	MERCURY	VENUS	MARS	JUPITER	SATURN	URANUS	NEPTUNE	PLUTO
MAY 1	6	38	39	40	8	4	33	41	1	6	23	17
MAY 2	6	40	41	41	8	4	33	41	1	6	23	17
MAY 3	7	42	42	43	8	4	33	41	1	6	23	17
MAY 4	7	43	44	45	8	4	33	41	1	6	23	17
MAY 5	7	45	46	46	8	4	33	41	1	6	23	17
MAY 6	7	47	48	48	8	4	33	41	1	6	23	17
MAY 7	7	1	2	2	8	4	33	41	1	6	23	17
MAY 8	7	3	4	4	8	4	33	41	1	6	23	17
MAY 9	7	5	6	6	8	4	33	41	1	6	23	17
MAY 10	7	7	8	8	8	4	33	41	1	6	23	17
MAY 11	8	9	10	10	8	4	33	41	1	6	23	17
MAY 12	8	11	12	12	8	4	33	41	1	6	23	17
MAY 13	8	13	14	14	8	4	33	41	1	6	23	17
MAY 14	8	15	15	16	7	4	33	41	1	6	23	17
MAY 15	8	17	17	18	7	4	33	41	1	6	23	17
MAY 16	8	19	19	20	7	4	33	41	1	6	23	17
MAY 17	8	20	21	21	7	4	33	41	1	6	23	17
MAY 18	8	22	23	23	7	4	33	41	1	6	23	17
MAY 19	9	24	24	25	7	4	33	41	1	6	23	17
MAY 20	9	25	26	26	7	4	33	41	1	6	23	17
MAY 21	9	27	27	28	7	4	33	41	1	6	23	17
MAY 22	9	29	29	30	7	4	33	41	1	6	23	17
MAY 23	9	30	31	31	7	4	33	41	1	6	23	17
MAY 24	9	32	32	33	7	4	33	41	1	6	23	17
MAY 25	10	33	34	34	7	4	32	41	1	6	23	17
MAY 26	10	35	35	36	7	4	32	41	1	6	23	17
MAY 27	10	36	37	38	7	4	32	41	1	6	23	17
MAY 28	10	38	39	39	7	4	32	41	1	6	23	17
MAY 29	10	40	40	41	7	4	32	41	1	6	23	17
MAY 30	10	41	42	42	7	5	32	41	1	6	23	17
MAY 31	10	43	44	44	7	5	32	41	1	6	23	17
JUN. 1	10	45	45	46	7	5	32	41	1	6	23	17
JUN. 2	10	46	47	48	7	5	32	41	1	6	23	17
JUN. 3	11	48	1	1	7	5	32	41	1	6	23	17
JUN. 4	11	2	3	3	8	5	32	41	1	7	23	17
JUN. 5	11	4	5	5	8	5	32	41	1	7	23	17
JUN. 6	11	6	7	7	8	5	32	41	1	7	23	17
JUN. 7	11	8	9	9	8	5	32	41	1	7	23	17
JUN. 8	11	10	11	11	8	5	32	40	1	7	23	17
JUN. 9	11	12	13	13	8	5	32	40	1	7	23	17
JUN. 10	11	14	15	15	8	6	32	40	2	7	23	17
JUN. 11	12	16	17	17	9	6	32	40	2	7	23	17
JUN. 12	12	18	18	19	9	6	32	40	2	7	23	17
JUN. 13	12	20	20	21	9	6	32	40	2	7	23	17
JUN. 14	12	21	22	23	9	6	32	40	2	7	23	17
JUN. 15	12	23	24	24	9	6	32	40	2	7	23	17
JUN. 16	12	25	25	26	9	6	32	40	2	7	23	17
JUN. 17	12	27	27	28	10	6	32	40	2	7	23	17
JUN. 18	12	28	29	29	10	6	32	40	2	7	23	17
JUN. 19	13	30	30	31	10	7	32	40	2	7	23	17
JUN. 20	13	31	32	32	10	7	32	40	2	7	23	17
JUN. 21	13	33	33	34	10	7	32	40	2	7	23	17
JUN. 22	13	34	35	36	11	7	32	40	2	7	23	17
JUN. 23	13	36	37	37	11	7	32	40	2	7	23	17
JUN. 24	13	38	38	39	11	7	32	40	2	7	23	17
JUN. 25	14	39	40	40	11	7	32	40	2	7	23	17
JUN. 26	14	41	41	42	12	7	32	40	2	7	23	17
JUN. 27	14	43	43	44	12	8	32	40	2	7	23	17
JUN. 28	14	44	45	45	12	8	32	40	2	7	23	17
JUN. 29	14	46	47	47	12	8	32	40	2	7	23	17
JUN. 30	14	48	48	1	13	8	32	40	2	7	23	17

MOON 1 ◔ 12:01 A.M. TO 8:00 A.M.   **MOON 2** ◑ 8:01 A.M. TO 4:00 P.M.   **MOON 3** ● 4:01 P.M. TO 12:00 A.M.

Use only one "moon" number. Choose the column closest to your time of birth. If your place of birth is not on Eastern Standard Time, be sure to read "How to Convert to Eastern Standard Time" at the beginning of this section.

1937

July

Date & Time	SUN	MOON 1	MOON 2	MOON 3	MERCURY	VENUS	MARS	JUPITER	SATURN	URANUS	NEPTUNE	PLUTO
JUL. 1	14	2	2	3	13	8	32	40	2	7	23	17
JUL. 2	14	3	4	5	13	8	32	40	2	7	23	17
JUL. 3	15	5	6	7	14	8	32	40	2	7	23	17
JUL. 4	15	7	8	9	14	8	32	40	2	7	23	17
JUL. 5	15	9	10	11	14	9	32	40	2	7	23	17
JUL. 6	15	11	12	12	14	9	32	40	2	7	23	17
JUL. 7	15	13	14	14	15	9	32	40	2	7	23	17
JUL. 8	15	15	16	16	15	9	32	40	2	7	23	17
JUL. 9	15	17	18	18	15	9	32	40	2	7	23	17
JUL. 10	15	19	20	20	16	9	32	40	2	7	23	17
JUL. 11	16	21	21	22	16	9	32	40	2	7	23	17
JUL. 12	16	23	23	24	16	10	32	40	2	7	23	17
JUL. 13	16	24	25	25	16	10	32	40	2	7	23	17
JUL. 14	16	26	27	27	17	10	32	40	2	7	23	17
JUL. 15	16	28	28	29	17	10	32	40	2	7	23	17
JUL. 16	16	29	30	30	17	10	32	40	2	7	23	17
JUL. 17	16	31	31	32	18	10	32	40	2	7	23	17
JUL. 18	16	32	33	33	18	10	32	40	2	7	23	17
JUL. 19	17	34	35	35	18	11	32	40	2	7	23	17
JUL. 20	17	36	36	37	18	11	32	40	2	7	23	17
JUL. 21	17	37	38	38	18	11	32	40	2	7	23	17
JUL. 22	17	39	39	40	19	11	32	40	2	7	23	17
JUL. 23	17	40	41	42	19	11	32	40	2	7	23	17
JUL. 24	17	42	43	43	19	11	32	40	2	7	23	17
JUL. 25	17	44	44	45	19	11	32	40	2	7	23	17
JUL. 26	18	46	46	47	20	12	32	40	2	7	23	17
JUL. 27	18	47	48	1	20	12	32	40	2	7	23	17
JUL. 28	18	1	2	2	20	12	32	40	2	7	23	17
JUL. 29	18	3	4	4	20	12	32	40	2	7	23	17
JUL. 30	18	5	5	6	20	12	32	40	2	7	23	17
JUL. 31	18	7	7	8	21	12	32	40	2	7	23	17

August

Date & Time	SUN	MOON 1	MOON 2	MOON 3	MERCURY	VENUS	MARS	JUPITER	SATURN	URANUS	NEPTUNE	PLUTO
AUG. 1	18	9	9	10	21	12	33	40	2	7	23	17
AUG. 2	18	11	11	12	21	13	33	40	2	7	23	17
AUG. 3	19	12	13	14	21	13	33	40	2	7	23	17
AUG. 4	19	14	15	16	22	13	33	40	2	7	23	17
AUG. 5	19	16	17	18	22	13	33	40	2	7	23	17
AUG. 6	19	18	19	19	22	13	33	40	2	7	23	17
AUG. 7	19	20	21	21	22	13	33	40	2	7	23	17
AUG. 8	19	22	22	23	22	13	33	40	2	7	23	17
AUG. 9	19	24	24	25	23	14	33	40	2	7	23	17
AUG. 10	19	25	26	27	23	14	33	40	2	7	23	17
AUG. 11	20	27	28	28	23	14	33	40	2	7	23	17
AUG. 12	20	29	29	30	23	14	33	40	2	7	23	17
AUG. 13	20	30	31	31	23	14	33	40	2	7	23	17
AUG. 14	20	32	32	33	23	14	33	39	2	7	23	17
AUG. 15	20	33	34	35	24	15	33	39	2	7	23	17
AUG. 16	20	35	36	36	24	15	33	39	2	7	23	17
AUG. 17	20	37	37	38	24	15	33	39	2	7	23	17
AUG. 18	20	38	39	39	24	15	34	39	2	7	23	17
AUG. 19	21	40	40	41	24	15	34	39	2	7	23	17
AUG. 20	21	42	42	43	24	15	34	39	2	7	23	17
AUG. 21	21	43	44	44	24	15	34	39	2	7	23	17
AUG. 22	21	45	46	46	24	16	34	39	2	7	23	17
AUG. 23	21	47	47	48	24	16	34	39	2	7	23	17
AUG. 24	21	1	1	2	25	16	34	39	1	7	23	17
AUG. 25	21	3	3	4	25	16	34	39	1	7	23	17
AUG. 26	22	4	5	6	25	16	34	39	1	7	23	17
AUG. 27	22	6	7	8	25	16	34	39	1	7	23	17
AUG. 28	22	8	9	9	25	17	34	39	1	7	23	17
AUG. 29	22	10	11	11	25	17	34	39	1	7	23	17
AUG. 30	22	12	13	13	25	17	34	39	1	7	23	17
AUG. 31	22	14	14	15	25	17	34	39	1	7	23	17

MOON 1 ☽ 12:01 A.M. TO 8:00 A.M.   **MOON 2** ☽ 8:01 A.M. TO 4:00 P.M.   **MOON 3** ● 4:01 P.M. TO 12:00 A.M.

Use only one "moon" number. Choose the column closest to your time of birth. If your place of birth is not on Eastern Standard Time, be sure to read "How to Convert to Eastern Standard Time" at the beginning of this section.

1937

September

Date & Time	SUN ☉	MOON 1 ☽	MOON 2 ◑	MOON 3 ●	MERCURY	VENUS	MARS	JUPITER	SATURN	URANUS	NEPTUNE	PLUTO
SEP. 1	22	16	16	17	25	17	35	39	1	7	23	17
SEP. 2	22	18	18	19	25	17	35	39	1	7	23	17
SEP. 3	23	19	20	21	25	17	35	39	1	7	23	17
SEP. 4	23	21	22	22	25	18	35	39	1	7	23	17
SEP. 5	23	23	24	24	25	18	35	39	1	7	23	17
SEP. 6	23	25	25	26	25	18	35	39	1	7	23	17
SEP. 7	23	26	27	28	25	18	35	39	1	7	23	17
SEP. 8	23	28	29	29	25	18	35	39	1	7	23	17
SEP. 9	23	30	30	31	24	18	35	39	1	7	23	17
SEP. 10	23	31	32	32	24	19	35	39	1	7	23	17
SEP. 11	24	33	33	34	24	19	35	39	1	7	23	17
SEP. 12	24	35	35	36	24	19	35	39	1	7	23	17
SEP. 13	24	36	37	37	24	19	35	39	1	7	23	17
SEP. 14	24	38	38	39	24	19	36	39	1	7	23	17
SEP. 15	24	39	40	40	24	19	36	39	1	7	23	17
SEP. 16	24	41	42	42	24	20	36	39	1	7	23	17
SEP. 17	24	43	43	44	23	20	36	39	1	7	23	17
SEP. 18	24	44	45	46	23	20	36	39	1	7	23	17
SEP. 19	25	46	47	47	23	20	36	39	1	7	23	17
SEP. 20	25	48	1	1	23	20	36	39	1	7	24	17
SEP. 21	25	2	3	3	23	20	36	39	1	7	24	17
SEP. 22	25	4	5	5	23	20	36	39	1	7	24	17
SEP. 23	25	6	6	7	23	21	36	39	1	7	24	17
SEP. 24	25	8	8	9	23	21	36	39	1	7	24	17
SEP. 25	26	10	10	11	23	21	37	39	1	7	24	17
SEP. 26	26	12	12	13	23	21	37	39	1	7	24	17
SEP. 27	26	13	14	15	23	21	37	39	1	7	24	17
SEP. 28	26	15	16	16	23	21	37	39	1	7	24	17
SEP. 29	26	17	18	18	23	22	37	39	1	7	24	17
SEP. 30	26	19	20	20	23	22	37	39	1	7	24	17

October

Date & Time	SUN ☉	MOON 1 ☽	MOON 2 ◑	MOON 3 ●	MERCURY	VENUS	MARS	JUPITER	SATURN	URANUS	NEPTUNE	PLUTO
OCT. 1	26	21	21	22	24	22	37	39	1	7	24	17
OCT. 2	26	22	23	24	24	22	37	39	1	7	24	17
OCT. 3	27	24	25	25	24	22	37	39	1	7	24	17
OCT. 4	27	26	26	27	24	22	37	39	1	7	24	17
OCT. 5	27	28	28	29	24	23	37	39	1	7	24	17
OCT. 6	27	29	30	30	25	23	37	39	1	7	24	17
OCT. 7	27	31	31	32	25	23	38	39	1	7	24	17
OCT. 8	27	32	33	34	25	23	38	39	1	7	24	17
OCT. 9	27	34	35	35	25	23	38	39	1	7	24	17
OCT. 10	27	36	36	37	25	23	38	39	1	7	24	17
OCT. 11	28	37	38	38	26	24	38	39	1	7	24	17
OCT. 12	28	39	39	40	26	24	38	39	1	7	24	17
OCT. 13	28	40	41	41	26	24	38	39	1	7	24	17
OCT. 14	28	42	43	43	26	24	38	39	1	7	24	17
OCT. 15	28	44	44	45	26	24	38	40	1	7	24	17
OCT. 16	28	45	46	47	27	24	38	40	1	7	24	17
OCT. 17	28	47	48	1	27	25	39	40	1	7	24	17
OCT. 18	28	1	2	2	27	25	39	40	1	7	24	17
OCT. 19	29	3	4	4	27	25	39	40	1	7	24	17
OCT. 20	29	5	6	6	28	25	39	40	1	7	24	17
OCT. 21	29	7	8	8	28	25	39	40	1	7	24	17
OCT. 22	29	9	10	10	28	25	39	40	1	7	24	17
OCT. 23	29	11	12	12	28	26	39	40	1	7	24	17
OCT. 24	29	13	14	14	29	26	39	40	1	7	24	17
OCT. 25	29	15	15	16	29	26	39	40	1	7	24	17
OCT. 26	30	17	17	18	29	26	39	40	1	7	24	17
OCT. 27	30	19	19	20	29	26	39	40	1	7	24	17
OCT. 28	30	20	21	21	29	26	40	40	1	7	24	17
OCT. 29	30	22	23	23	30	27	40	40	1	7	24	17
OCT. 30	30	24	24	25	30	27	40	40	1	7	24	17
OCT. 31	30	25	26	27	30	27	40	40	1	7	24	17

MOON 1 ☽ 12:01 A.M. TO 8:00 A.M.   **MOON 2** ◑ 8:01 A.M. TO 4:00 P.M.   **MOON 3** ● 4:01 P.M. TO 12:00 A.M.
Use only one "moon" number. Choose the column closest to your time of birth. If your place of birth is not on Eastern Standard Time, be sure to read "How to Convert to Eastern Standard Time" at the beginning of this section.

1937

November

Date & Time	SUN	MOON 1	MOON 2	MOON 3	MERCURY	VENUS	MARS	JUPITER	SATURN	URANUS	NEPTUNE	PLUTO
NOV. 1	30	27	28	28	30	27	40	40	1	7	24	17
NOV. 2	30	29	29	30	31	27	40	40	1	7	24	17
NOV. 3	31	30	31	31	31	27	40	40	1	7	24	17
NOV. 4	31	32	33	33	31	28	40	40	1	7	24	17
NOV. 5	31	34	34	35	31	28	40	40	1	7	24	17
NOV. 6	31	35	36	36	31	28	40	40	1	7	24	17
NOV. 7	31	37	37	38	32	28	41	40	1	7	24	17
NOV. 8	31	38	39	39	32	28	41	40	1	7	24	17
NOV. 9	31	40	40	41	32	28	41	40	1	6	24	17
NOV. 10	31	41	42	43	32	29	41	40	1	6	24	17
NOV. 11	31	43	44	44	32	29	41	40	1	6	24	17
NOV. 12	32	45	45	46	33	29	41	40	1	6	24	17
NOV. 13	32	47	47	48	33	29	41	40	1	6	24	17
NOV. 14	32	48	1	2	33	29	41	40	1	6	24	17
NOV. 15	32	2	3	3	33	29	41	40	1	6	24	17
NOV. 16	32	4	5	5	33	30	41	40	1	6	24	17
NOV. 17	32	6	7	7	34	30	42	40	1	6	24	17
NOV. 18	32	8	9	9	34	30	42	40	1	6	24	17
NOV. 19	33	10	11	11	34	30	42	40	1	6	24	17
NOV. 20	33	12	13	13	34	30	42	40	1	6	24	17
NOV. 21	33	14	15	15	34	30	42	40	1	6	24	17
NOV. 22	33	16	17	17	35	31	42	40	1	6	24	17
NOV. 23	33	18	19	19	35	31	42	40	1	6	24	17
NOV. 24	33	20	20	21	35	31	42	40	1	6	24	17
NOV. 25	34	22	22	23	35	31	42	40	1	6	24	17
NOV. 26	34	23	24	25	35	31	42	40	1	6	24	17
NOV. 27	34	25	26	26	36	31	42	40	1	6	24	17
NOV. 28	34	27	27	28	36	32	43	40	1	6	24	17
NOV. 29	34	28	29	29	36	32	43	40	1	6	24	17
NOV. 30	34	30	31	31	36	32	43	40	1	6	24	17

December

Date & Time	SUN	MOON 1	MOON 2	MOON 3	MERCURY	VENUS	MARS	JUPITER	SATURN	URANUS	NEPTUNE	PLUTO
DEC. 1	34	32	32	33	36	32	43	40	1	6	24	17
DEC. 2	34	33	34	34	37	32	43	40	1	6	24	17
DEC. 3	35	35	35	36	37	32	43	40	1	6	24	17
DEC. 4	35	36	37	37	37	33	43	41	1	6	24	17
DEC. 5	35	38	38	39	37	33	43	41	1	6	24	17
DEC. 6	35	39	40	41	37	33	43	41	1	6	24	17
DEC. 7	35	41	42	42	38	33	44	41	1	6	24	17
DEC. 8	35	43	43	44	38	33	44	41	1	6	24	17
DEC. 9	35	44	45	45	38	33	44	41	1	6	24	17
DEC. 10	35	46	47	47	38	34	44	41	1	6	24	17
DEC. 11	36	48	48	1	38	34	44	41	1	6	24	17
DEC. 12	36	1	2	3	38	34	44	41	1	6	24	17
DEC. 13	36	3	4	5	38	34	44	41	1	6	24	17
DEC. 14	36	5	6	7	39	34	44	41	1	6	24	17
DEC. 15	36	7	8	8	39	34	44	41	1	6	24	17
DEC. 16	36	9	10	11	39	35	44	41	1	6	24	17
DEC. 17	36	11	12	13	39	35	45	41	1	6	24	17
DEC. 18	36	13	14	15	39	35	45	41	1	6	24	17
DEC. 19	37	15	16	17	39	35	45	41	1	6	24	17
DEC. 20	37	17	18	19	39	35	45	41	1	6	24	17
DEC. 21	37	19	20	20	39	35	45	41	1	6	24	17
DEC. 22	37	21	22	22	39	36	45	41	1	6	24	17
DEC. 23	37	23	23	24	39	36	45	41	1	6	24	17
DEC. 24	37	25	25	26	39	36	45	41	1	6	24	17
DEC. 25	37	26	27	27	39	36	45	41	1	6	24	17
DEC. 26	38	28	29	29	39	36	45	41	1	6	24	17
DEC. 27	38	30	30	31	39	36	46	41	1	6	24	17
DEC. 28	38	31	32	32	38	37	46	41	1	6	24	17
DEC. 29	38	33	33	34	38	37	46	41	1	6	24	17
DEC. 30	38	34	35	35	38	37	46	41	1	6	24	17
DEC. 31	38	36	36	37	38	37	46	41	1	6	24	17

MOON 1 ◗ 12:01 A.M. TO 8:00 A.M.　　**MOON 2** ◑ 8:01 A.M. TO 4:00 P.M.　　**MOON 3** ● 4:01 P.M. TO 12:00 A.M.

Use only one "moon" number. Choose the column closest to your time of birth. If your place of birth is not on Eastern Standard Time, be sure to read "How to Convert to Eastern Standard Time" at the beginning of this section.

1938

January

Date & Time	SUN	MOON 1	MOON 2	MOON 3	MERCURY	VENUS	MARS	JUPITER	SATURN	URANUS	NEPTUNE	PLUTO
JAN. 1	38	37	38	39	38	37	46	41	1	6	24	17
JAN. 2	38	39	40	40	37	37	46	41	1	6	24	17
JAN. 3	39	41	41	42	37	38	46	41	1	6	24	17
JAN. 4	39	42	43	43	37	38	46	41	1	6	24	17
JAN. 5	39	44	44	45	37	38	46	41	1	6	24	17
JAN. 6	39	46	46	47	37	38	47	41	1	6	24	17
JAN. 7	39	47	48	48	37	38	47	42	1	6	24	17
JAN. 8	39	1	2	2	37	38	47	42	1	6	24	17
JAN. 9	39	3	3	4	37	39	47	42	1	6	24	17
JAN. 10	40	5	6	6	37	39	47	42	1	6	24	17
JAN. 11	40	6	7	8	37	39	47	42	1	6	24	17
JAN. 12	40	8	9	10	37	39	47	42	1	6	24	17
JAN. 13	40	10	11	12	37	39	47	42	1	6	24	17
JAN. 14	40	12	13	14	37	39	47	42	1	6	24	17
JAN. 15	40	14	15	16	37	40	47	42	1	6	24	17
JAN. 16	40	16	17	18	37	40	48	42	1	6	24	17
JAN. 17	41	18	19	20	37	40	48	42	1	6	24	17
JAN. 18	41	20	21	22	37	40	48	42	1	6	24	17
JAN. 19	41	22	23	23	38	40	48	42	1	6	24	17
JAN. 20	41	24	25	25	38	40	48	42	1	6	24	17
JAN. 21	41	26	26	27	38	41	48	42	1	6	24	17
JAN. 22	41	27	28	29	38	41	48	42	1	6	24	17
JAN. 23	42	29	30	30	38	41	48	42	1	6	24	17
JAN. 24	42	31	31	32	38	41	48	42	1	6	24	17
JAN. 25	42	32	33	33	38	41	48	42	1	6	24	17
JAN. 26	42	34	34	35	39	41	1	42	1	6	24	17
JAN. 27	42	35	36	37	39	42	1	42	1	6	24	17
JAN. 28	42	37	38	38	39	42	1	42	1	6	24	17
JAN. 29	42	39	39	40	39	42	1	42	1	6	24	17
JAN. 30	42	40	41	41	39	42	1	42	1	6	24	17
JAN. 31	43	42	42	43	39	42	1	42	1	6	24	17

February

Date & Time	SUN	MOON 1	MOON 2	MOON 3	MERCURY	VENUS	MARS	JUPITER	SATURN	URANUS	NEPTUNE	PLUTO
FEB. 1	43	44	44	45	40	42	1	42	1	6	24	17
FEB. 2	43	45	46	46	40	43	1	42	1	6	24	17
FEB. 3	43	47	47	48	40	43	1	42	1	6	24	17
FEB. 4	43	1	1	2	40	43	1	42	1	6	24	17
FEB. 5	43	2	3	4	40	43	2	42	1	6	24	17
FEB. 6	43	4	5	5	41	43	2	42	1	6	24	17
FEB. 7	43	6	7	7	41	43	2	42	1	6	24	17
FEB. 8	44	8	8	9	41	44	2	43	1	6	24	17
FEB. 9	44	10	10	11	41	44	2	43	1	6	24	17
FEB. 10	44	12	12	13	41	44	2	43	1	6	24	17
FEB. 11	44	13	14	15	41	44	2	43	1	6	24	17
FEB. 12	44	15	16	17	42	44	2	43	1	6	24	17
FEB. 13	44	17	18	19	42	44	2	43	1	6	24	17
FEB. 14	44	19	20	21	42	45	2	43	1	6	24	17
FEB. 15	44	21	22	23	42	45	3	43	1	6	24	17
FEB. 16	45	23	24	24	43	45	3	43	1	6	24	17
FEB. 17	45	25	26	26	43	45	3	43	1	6	24	17
FEB. 18	45	27	27	28	43	45	3	43	1	6	24	17
FEB. 19	45	29	29	30	43	45	3	43	1	6	24	17
FEB. 20	45	30	31	31	43	46	3	43	1	6	24	17
FEB. 21	45	32	32	33	44	46	3	43	1	6	24	17
FEB. 22	45	33	34	34	44	46	3	43	1	6	24	17
FEB. 23	46	35	35	36	44	46	3	43	1	6	24	17
FEB. 24	46	37	37	38	44	46	3	43	1	6	24	17
FEB. 25	46	38	39	39	45	46	4	43	2	6	24	17
FEB. 26	46	40	40	41	45	47	4	43	2	6	24	17
FEB. 27	46	41	42	42	45	47	4	43	2	6	24	17
FEB. 28	46	43	44	44	45	47	4	43	2	6	24	17

MOON 1 ☽ 12:01 A.M. TO 8:00 A.M.   **MOON 2** ☽ 8:01 A.M. TO 4:00 P.M.   **MOON 3** ● 4:01 P.M. TO 12:00 A.M.
Use only one "moon" number. Choose the column closest to your time of birth. If your place of birth is not on Eastern Standard Time, be sure to read "How to Convert to Eastern Standard Time" at the beginning of this section.

1938

March

April

Date & Time	SUN	MOON 1	MOON 2	MOON 3	MERCURY	VENUS	MARS	JUPITER	SATURN	URANUS	NEPTUNE	PLUTO
MAR. 1	46	45	45	46	45	47	4	43	2	6	24	17
MAR. 2	46	46	47	48	46	47	4	43	2	6	24	17
MAR. 3	47	48	1	1	46	47	4	43	2	6	24	17
MAR. 4	47	2	3	3	46	48	4	43	2	6	24	17
MAR. 5	47	4	4	5	46	48	4	43	2	6	24	17
MAR. 6	47	6	6	7	47	48	4	43	2	6	24	17
MAR. 7	47	7	8	9	47	48	4	43	2	6	24	17
MAR. 8	47	9	10	10	47	48	5	43	2	6	24	17
MAR. 9	47	11	12	12	47	48	5	43	2	6	24	17
MAR. 10	47	13	14	14	48	1	5	43	2	6	24	17
MAR. 11	48	15	16	16	48	1	5	43	2	6	24	17
MAR. 12	48	17	17	18	48	1	5	43	2	6	24	17
MAR. 13	48	19	19	20	48	1	5	44	2	6	24	17
MAR. 14	48	21	21	22	1	1	5	44	2	6	24	17
MAR. 15	48	22	23	24	1	1	5	44	2	6	24	17
MAR. 16	48	24	25	25	1	2	5	44	2	6	24	17
MAR. 17	48	26	27	27	2	2	5	44	2	6	24	17
MAR. 18	48	28	28	29	2	2	6	44	2	6	24	17
MAR. 19	1	30	30	31	2	2	6	44	2	6	24	17
MAR. 20	1	31	32	32	2	2	6	44	2	6	24	17
MAR. 21	1	33	33	34	3	2	6	44	2	6	24	17
MAR. 22	1	34	35	35	3	3	6	44	2	6	24	17
MAR. 23	1	36	37	37	3	3	6	44	2	6	24	17
MAR. 24	1	38	38	39	3	3	6	44	2	6	24	17
MAR. 25	2	39	40	40	4	3	6	44	2	6	24	17
MAR. 26	2	41	41	42	4	3	6	44	2	7	24	17
MAR. 27	2	42	43	44	4	3	6	44	2	7	24	17
MAR. 28	2	44	45	45	4	4	6	44	2	7	24	17
MAR. 29	2	46	46	47	4	4	7	44	2	7	24	17
MAR. 30	2	48	48	1	5	4	7	44	2	7	24	17
MAR. 31	2	1	2	3	5	4	7	44	2	7	24	17

Date & Time	SUN	MOON 1	MOON 2	MOON 3	MERCURY	VENUS	MARS	JUPITER	SATURN	URANUS	NEPTUNE	PLUTO
APR. 1	2	3	4	4	5	4	7	44	2	7	24	17
APR. 2	2	5	6	6	5	4	7	44	2	7	24	17
APR. 3	3	7	8	8	5	5	7	44	2	7	24	17
APR. 4	3	9	9	10	5	5	7	44	2	7	24	17
APR. 5	3	11	11	12	5	5	7	44	2	7	24	17
APR. 6	3	13	13	14	5	5	7	44	2	7	24	17
APR. 7	3	14	15	16	5	5	7	44	2	7	24	17
APR. 8	3	16	17	18	6	5	8	44	2	7	24	17
APR. 9	3	18	19	19	6	6	8	44	2	7	24	17
APR. 10	3	20	21	21	6	6	8	44	2	7	23	17
APR. 11	4	22	22	23	6	6	8	44	2	7	23	17
APR. 12	4	24	24	25	6	6	8	44	2	7	23	17
APR. 13	4	25	26	27	6	6	8	44	2	7	23	17
APR. 14	4	27	28	28	6	6	8	44	2	7	23	17
APR. 15	4	29	30	30	6	7	8	44	2	7	23	17
APR. 16	4	31	31	32	6	7	8	44	2	7	23	17
APR. 17	4	32	33	33	6	7	8	44	2	7	23	17
APR. 18	4	34	34	35	5	7	8	44	2	7	23	17
APR. 19	5	35	36	37	5	7	9	44	2	7	23	17
APR. 20	5	37	38	38	5	7	9	45	2	7	23	17
APR. 21	5	39	39	40	5	8	9	45	2	7	23	17
APR. 22	5	40	41	41	5	8	9	45	2	7	23	17
APR. 23	5	42	42	43	5	8	9	45	2	7	23	17
APR. 24	5	43	44	45	5	8	9	45	2	7	23	17
APR. 25	6	45	46	46	5	8	9	45	2	7	23	17
APR. 26	6	47	47	48	5	8	9	45	2	7	23	17
APR. 27	6	1	1	2	5	9	9	45	3	7	23	17
APR. 28	6	2	3	4	5	9	9	45	3	7	23	17
APR. 29	6	4	5	6	5	9	9	45	3	7	23	17
APR. 30	6	6	7	7	4	9	10	45	3	7	23	17

MOON 1 ◐ 12:01 A.M. TO 8:00 A.M.   **MOON 2** ◑ 8:01 A.M. TO 4:00 P.M.   **MOON 3** ● 4:01 P.M. TO 12:00 A.M.

Use only one "moon" number. Choose the column closest to your time of birth. If your place of birth is not on Eastern Standard Time, be sure to read "How to Convert to Eastern Standard Time" at the beginning of this section.

1938

May

June

Date & Time	SUN	MOON 1	MOON 2	MOON 3	MERCURY	VENUS	MARS	JUPITER	SATURN	URANUS	NEPTUNE	PLUTO
MAY 1	6	8	9	9	4	9	10	45	3	7	23	17
MAY 2	6	10	11	11	4	9	10	45	3	7	23	17
MAY 3	7	12	13	13	4	9	10	45	3	7	23	17
MAY 4	7	14	15	15	4	10	10	45	3	7	23	17
MAY 5	7	16	17	17	4	10	10	45	3	7	23	17
MAY 6	7	18	18	19	4	10	10	45	3	7	23	17
MAY 7	7	20	20	21	4	10	10	45	3	7	23	17
MAY 8	7	21	22	23	4	10	10	45	3	7	23	17
MAY 9	7	23	24	24	4	10	10	45	3	7	23	17
MAY 10	7	25	26	26	4	11	10	45	3	7	23	17
MAY 11	8	27	27	28	5	11	11	45	3	7	23	17
MAY 12	8	28	29	30	5	11	11	45	3	7	23	17
MAY 13	8	30	31	31	5	11	11	45	3	7	23	17
MAY 14	8	32	32	33	5	11	11	45	3	7	23	17
MAY 15	8	33	34	34	5	11	11	45	3	7	23	17
MAY 16	8	35	36	36	5	12	11	45	3	7	23	17
MAY 17	8	37	37	38	5	12	11	45	3	7	23	17
MAY 18	8	38	39	39	5	12	11	45	3	7	23	17
MAY 19	9	40	40	41	5	12	11	45	3	7	23	17
MAY 20	9	41	42	42	5	12	11	45	3	7	23	17
MAY 21	9	43	43	44	6	12	11	45	3	7	23	17
MAY 22	9	45	45	46	6	13	12	45	3	7	23	17
MAY 23	9	46	47	47	6	13	12	45	3	7	23	17
MAY 24	9	48	48	1	6	13	12	45	3	7	23	17
MAY 25	10	2	2	3	6	13	12	45	3	7	23	17
MAY 26	10	3	4	5	6	13	12	45	3	7	23	17
MAY 27	10	5	6	7	6	13	12	45	3	7	23	17
MAY 28	10	7	8	9	7	14	12	45	3	7	23	17
MAY 29	10	9	10	11	7	14	12	45	3	7	23	17
MAY 30	10	11	12	13	7	14	12	45	3	7	23	17
MAY 31	10	13	14	15	7	14	12	45	3	7	23	17

Date & Time	SUN	MOON 1	MOON 2	MOON 3	MERCURY	VENUS	MARS	JUPITER	SATURN	URANUS	NEPTUNE	PLUTO
JUN. 1	10	15	16	17	7	14	12	45	3	7	23	17
JUN. 2	10	17	18	18	8	14	13	45	3	7	23	17
JUN. 3	11	19	20	20	8	14	13	45	3	7	23	17
JUN. 4	11	21	22	22	8	15	13	45	3	7	23	17
JUN. 5	11	23	23	24	8	15	13	45	3	7	23	17
JUN. 6	11	25	25	26	9	15	13	45	3	7	23	17
JUN. 7	11	26	27	28	9	15	13	45	3	7	23	17
JUN. 8	11	28	29	29	9	15	13	45	3	7	23	17
JUN. 9	11	30	30	31	9	15	13	45	3	7	23	17
JUN. 10	11	31	32	32	10	16	13	45	3	7	23	17
JUN. 11	12	33	34	34	10	16	13	45	3	7	23	17
JUN. 12	12	35	35	36	10	16	13	45	3	7	23	17
JUN. 13	12	36	37	37	10	16	14	45	3	7	23	17
JUN. 14	12	38	38	39	11	16	14	45	3	7	23	17
JUN. 15	12	39	40	40	11	16	14	45	3	7	23	17
JUN. 16	12	41	41	42	11	17	14	45	3	7	23	17
JUN. 17	12	42	43	44	11	17	14	45	3	7	23	17
JUN. 18	12	44	45	45	12	17	14	45	3	7	23	17
JUN. 19	13	46	46	47	12	17	14	45	3	7	23	17
JUN. 20	13	47	48	48	12	17	14	45	3	7	23	17
JUN. 21	13	1	2	2	13	17	14	45	3	7	23	17
JUN. 22	13	3	3	4	13	18	14	45	3	7	23	17
JUN. 23	13	5	5	6	13	18	14	45	3	7	23	17
JUN. 24	13	6	7	8	13	18	14	45	3	7	23	17
JUN. 25	14	8	9	10	14	18	15	45	3	7	23	17
JUN. 26	14	10	11	12	14	18	15	45	3	7	23	17
JUN. 27	14	12	13	14	14	18	15	45	3	7	23	17
JUN. 28	14	14	15	16	15	18	15	45	3	7	23	17
JUN. 29	14	16	17	18	15	19	15	45	3	7	23	17
JUN. 30	14	18	19	20	15	19	15	45	3	7	23	17

MOON 1 ☽ 12:01 A.M. TO 8:00 A.M.　　**MOON 2** ◑ 8:01 A.M. TO 4:00 P.M.　　**MOON 3** ● 4:01 P.M. TO 12:00 A.M.
Use only one "moon" number. Choose the column closest to your time of birth. If your place of birth is not on Eastern Standard Time, be sure to read "How to Convert to Eastern Standard Time" at the beginning of this section.

1938

July   August

Date & Time	SUN ☉	MOON 1 ◖	MOON 2 ◑	MOON 3 ●	MERCURY	VENUS	MARS	JUPITER	SATURN	URANUS	NEPTUNE	PLUTO
JUL. 1	14	20	21	22	15	19	15	45	3	7	23	17
JUL. 2	14	22	23	24	16	19	15	45	3	7	23	17
JUL. 3	15	24	25	25	16	19	15	45	3	7	23	17
JUL. 4	15	26	26	27	16	19	15	45	3	7	23	17
JUL. 5	15	28	28	29	16	20	15	45	3	7	23	17
JUL. 6	15	29	30	30	16	20	16	45	3	7	23	17
JUL. 7	15	31	32	32	17	20	16	45	3	7	23	17
JUL. 8	15	33	33	34	17	20	16	45	3	7	23	17
JUL. 9	15	34	35	35	17	20	16	45	3	7	23	17
JUL. 10	15	36	36	37	18	20	16	45	3	7	23	17
JUL. 11	16	37	38	38	18	20	16	45	3	7	23	17
JUL. 12	16	39	39	40	18	21	16	45	3	7	23	17
JUL. 13	16	40	41	42	18	21	16	45	3	7	23	17
JUL. 14	16	42	43	43	19	21	16	45	3	7	23	17
JUL. 15	16	44	44	45	19	21	16	45	3	7	23	17
JUL. 16	16	45	46	46	19	21	16	45	3	7	23	17
JUL. 17	16	47	48	48	19	21	16	45	3	7	23	17
JUL. 18	16	1	1	2	19	22	17	45	3	7	23	17
JUL. 19	17	2	3	3	20	22	17	45	3	7	24	17
JUL. 20	17	4	5	5	20	22	17	45	3	7	24	17
JUL. 21	17	6	6	7	20	22	17	45	3	7	24	17
JUL. 22	17	8	8	9	20	22	17	45	3	7	24	17
JUL. 23	17	10	10	11	20	22	17	45	3	7	24	17
JUL. 24	17	11	12	13	21	22	17	45	3	7	24	17
JUL. 25	17	13	14	15	21	23	17	45	3	7	24	17
JUL. 26	18	15	16	17	21	23	17	45	3	7	24	17
JUL. 27	18	18	18	19	21	23	17	45	3	7	24	17
JUL. 28	18	20	20	21	21	23	17	45	3	7	24	17
JUL. 29	18	22	22	23	21	23	18	45	3	7	24	17
JUL. 30	18	23	24	25	21	23	18	45	3	7	24	17
JUL. 31	18	25	26	27	22	24	18	45	3	7	24	17
AUG. 1	18	27	28	28	22	24	18	45	3	7	24	17
AUG. 2	18	29	29	30	22	24	18	45	3	7	24	17
AUG. 3	19	31	31	32	22	24	18	45	3	7	24	17
AUG. 4	19	32	33	33	22	24	18	45	3	7	24	17
AUG. 5	19	34	34	35	22	24	18	45	3	7	24	17
AUG. 6	19	35	36	36	22	24	18	45	3	7	24	17
AUG. 7	19	37	37	38	22	24	18	45	3	7	24	17
AUG. 8	19	39	39	40	22	25	18	45	3	7	24	17
AUG. 9	19	40	41	41	22	25	18	45	3	7	24	17
AUG. 10	19	42	42	43	22	25	19	45	3	7	24	17
AUG. 11	20	43	44	44	23	25	19	45	3	7	24	17
AUG. 12	20	45	45	46	23	25	19	45	3	7	24	17
AUG. 13	20	47	47	48	23	25	19	45	3	7	24	17
AUG. 14	20	48	1	1	23	26	19	45	3	7	24	17
AUG. 15	20	2	2	3	23	26	19	45	3	7	24	17
AUG. 16	20	4	4	5	23	26	19	45	3	7	24	17
AUG. 17	20	5	6	7	23	26	19	45	3	7	24	17
AUG. 18	20	7	8	8	23	26	19	45	3	7	24	17
AUG. 19	21	9	10	10	22	26	19	45	3	7	24	17
AUG. 20	21	11	11	12	22	26	19	45	3	7	24	17
AUG. 21	21	13	13	14	22	27	19	45	3	7	24	17
AUG. 22	21	15	15	16	22	27	20	45	3	7	24	17
AUG. 23	21	17	17	18	22	27	20	45	3	7	24	17
AUG. 24	21	19	19	20	22	27	20	45	3	7	24	17
AUG. 25	21	21	21	22	22	27	20	45	3	7	24	17
AUG. 26	22	23	23	24	22	27	20	45	3	7	24	17
AUG. 27	22	25	25	26	22	27	20	44	3	7	24	17
AUG. 28	22	26	27	28	22	28	20	44	3	7	24	17
AUG. 29	22	28	29	29	21	28	20	44	3	7	24	17
AUG. 30	22	30	31	31	21	28	20	44	3	7	24	17
AUG. 31	22	32	32	33	21	28	20	44	3	7	24	17

MOON 1 ◖ 12:01 A.M. TO 8:00 A.M.   **MOON 2** ◑ 8:01 A.M. TO 4:00 P.M.   **MOON 3** ● 4:01 P.M. TO 12:00 A.M.
Use only one "moon" number. Choose the column closest to your time of birth. If your place of birth is not on Eastern Standard Time, be sure to read "How to Convert to Eastern Standard Time" at the beginning of this section.

1938

September / October

Date & Time	SUN	MOON 1	MOON 2	MOON 3	MERCURY	VENUS	MARS	JUPITER	SATURN	URANUS	NEPTUNE	PLUTO
SEP. 1	22	33	34	34	21	28	20	44	3	7	24	17
SEP. 2	22	35	35	36	21	28	20	44	3	7	24	17
SEP. 3	23	36	37	38	21	28	21	44	3	7	24	17
SEP. 4	23	38	39	39	21	29	21	44	3	7	24	17
SEP. 5	23	40	40	41	21	29	21	44	3	7	24	17
SEP. 6	23	41	42	42	21	29	21	44	3	7	24	17
SEP. 7	23	43	43	44	21	29	21	44	3	7	24	17
SEP. 8	23	44	45	46	21	29	21	44	3	7	24	17
SEP. 9	23	46	47	47	21	29	21	44	3	7	24	17
SEP. 10	23	48	48	1	21	29	21	44	3	7	24	17
SEP. 11	24	1	2	3	21	30	21	44	3	7	24	17
SEP. 12	24	3	4	4	21	30	21	44	3	7	24	17
SEP. 13	24	5	6	6	21	30	21	44	3	7	24	17
SEP. 14	24	7	7	8	21	30	22	44	3	7	24	17
SEP. 15	24	9	9	10	21	30	22	44	3	7	24	17
SEP. 16	24	10	11	12	22	30	22	44	3	7	24	17
SEP. 17	24	12	13	14	22	30	22	44	3	7	24	17
SEP. 18	24	14	15	15	22	30	22	44	3	7	24	17
SEP. 19	25	16	17	17	22	31	22	44	3	7	24	17
SEP. 20	25	18	19	19	22	31	22	44	3	7	24	17
SEP. 21	25	20	21	21	23	31	22	44	3	7	24	17
SEP. 22	25	22	22	23	23	31	22	44	3	7	24	17
SEP. 23	25	24	24	25	23	31	22	44	3	7	24	17
SEP. 24	25	26	26	27	23	31	22	44	3	7	24	17
SEP. 25	26	27	28	29	24	31	22	44	3	7	24	17
SEP. 26	26	29	30	30	24	31	23	44	3	7	24	17
SEP. 27	26	31	32	32	24	31	23	44	3	7	24	17
SEP. 28	26	33	33	34	24	32	23	44	3	7	24	17
SEP. 29	26	34	35	35	24	32	23	44	3	7	24	17
SEP. 30	26	36	36	37	25	32	23	44	3	7	24	17
OCT. 1	26	38	38	39	25	32	23	44	3	7	24	17
OCT. 2	26	39	40	40	25	32	23	44	3	7	24	17
OCT. 3	27	41	41	42	25	32	23	44	3	7	24	17
OCT. 4	27	42	43	43	26	32	23	44	3	7	24	17
OCT. 5	27	44	44	45	26	32	23	44	3	7	24	17
OCT. 6	27	46	46	47	26	32	23	44	3	7	24	17
OCT. 7	27	47	48	48	26	32	23	44	3	7	24	17
OCT. 8	27	1	2	2	27	33	24	44	3	7	24	17
OCT. 9	27	3	3	4	27	33	24	44	3	7	24	17
OCT. 10	27	4	5	6	27	33	24	44	3	7	24	17
OCT. 11	28	6	7	7	27	33	24	44	3	7	24	17
OCT. 12	28	8	9	9	28	33	24	44	3	7	24	17
OCT. 13	28	10	11	11	28	33	24	44	3	7	24	17
OCT. 14	28	12	12	13	28	33	24	44	3	7	24	17
OCT. 15	28	14	14	15	28	33	24	44	3	7	24	17
OCT. 16	28	16	16	17	28	33	24	44	3	7	24	17
OCT. 17	28	17	18	19	29	33	24	44	3	7	24	17
OCT. 18	28	19	20	21	29	33	24	44	3	7	24	17
OCT. 19	29	21	22	23	29	33	24	44	3	7	24	17
OCT. 20	29	23	24	24	29	33	25	44	3	7	24	17
OCT. 21	29	25	26	26	30	33	25	44	3	7	24	17
OCT. 22	29	27	27	28	30	33	25	44	3	7	24	17
OCT. 23	29	29	29	30	30	33	25	44	3	7	24	17
OCT. 24	29	30	31	31	30	34	25	44	3	7	24	17
OCT. 25	29	32	33	33	30	34	25	44	3	7	24	17
OCT. 26	30	34	34	35	31	34	25	44	3	7	24	17
OCT. 27	30	35	36	36	31	34	25	44	3	7	24	17
OCT. 28	30	37	38	38	31	34	25	44	3	7	24	17
OCT. 29	30	39	39	40	31	34	25	44	3	7	24	17
OCT. 30	30	40	41	41	31	34	25	44	3	7	24	17
OCT. 31	30	42	42	43	32	34	25	44	3	7	24	17

MOON 1 ◖ 12:01 A.M. TO 8:00 A.M.　　**MOON 2** ◑ 8:01 A.M. TO 4:00 P.M.　　**MOON 3** ● 4:01 P.M. TO 12:00 A.M.

Use only one "moon" number. Choose the column closest to your time of birth. If your place of birth is not on Eastern Standard Time, be sure to read "How to Convert to Eastern Standard Time" at the beginning of this section.

1938

November

Date & Time	SUN	MOON 1	MOON 2	MOON 3	MERCURY	VENUS	MARS	JUPITER	SATURN	URANUS	NEPTUNE	PLUTO
NOV. 1	30	43	44	44	32	34	26	44	3	7	24	17
NOV. 2	30	45	46	46	32	34	26	44	3	7	24	17
NOV. 3	31	47	47	48	32	34	26	44	3	7	24	17
NOV. 4	31	48	1	1	32	34	26	44	3	7	24	17
NOV. 5	31	2	3	3	33	34	26	44	3	7	24	17
NOV. 6	31	4	4	5	33	34	26	44	3	7	24	17
NOV. 7	31	6	6	7	33	33	26	44	3	7	24	17
NOV. 8	31	7	8	9	33	33	26	44	3	7	24	17
NOV. 9	31	9	10	11	33	33	26	44	3	7	24	17
NOV. 10	31	11	12	13	34	33	26	44	3	7	24	17
NOV. 11	31	13	14	14	34	33	26	44	3	7	24	17
NOV. 12	32	15	16	16	34	33	26	44	3	7	24	17
NOV. 13	32	17	18	18	34	33	27	44	3	7	24	17
NOV. 14	32	19	20	20	34	33	27	44	3	7	24	17
NOV. 15	32	21	21	22	35	33	27	44	3	7	24	17
NOV. 16	32	23	23	24	35	33	27	44	3	7	24	17
NOV. 17	32	25	25	26	35	33	27	44	3	7	24	17
NOV. 18	32	26	27	27	35	33	27	44	3	7	24	17
NOV. 19	33	28	29	29	35	33	27	44	3	7	24	17
NOV. 20	33	30	30	31	35	33	27	44	3	7	24	17
NOV. 21	33	32	32	33	36	33	27	44	3	7	24	17
NOV. 22	33	33	34	34	36	32	27	44	3	7	24	17
NOV. 23	33	35	35	36	36	32	27	44	3	7	24	17
NOV. 24	33	36	37	38	36	32	27	44	3	7	24	17
NOV. 25	34	38	39	39	36	32	28	44	3	7	24	17
NOV. 26	34	40	40	41	36	32	28	44	3	7	24	17
NOV. 27	34	41	42	42	36	32	28	44	3	7	24	17
NOV. 28	34	43	43	44	37	32	28	44	2	7	24	17
NOV. 29	34	44	45	45	37	32	28	44	2	7	24	17
NOV. 30	34	46	47	47	37	32	28	44	2	7	24	17

December

Date & Time	SUN	MOON 1	MOON 2	MOON 3	MERCURY	VENUS	MARS	JUPITER	SATURN	URANUS	NEPTUNE	PLUTO
DEC. 1	34	48	48	1	37	32	28	44	2	7	24	17
DEC. 2	34	1	2	2	37	32	28	44	2	7	24	17
DEC. 3	35	3	4	4	37	32	28	44	2	7	24	17
DEC. 4	35	5	5	6	37	32	28	44	2	7	24	17
DEC. 5	35	7	7	8	37	32	28	44	2	7	24	17
DEC. 6	35	9	9	10	37	32	28	44	2	7	24	17
DEC. 7	35	10	11	12	37	32	29	44	2	7	24	17
DEC. 8	35	12	13	14	37	32	29	44	2	7	24	17
DEC. 9	35	14	15	16	37	32	29	44	2	7	24	17
DEC. 10	35	16	17	18	37	32	29	45	2	7	24	17
DEC. 11	36	18	19	20	36	32	29	45	2	7	24	17
DEC. 12	36	20	21	22	36	32	29	45	2	7	24	17
DEC. 13	36	22	23	23	36	32	29	45	2	7	24	17
DEC. 14	36	24	25	25	36	32	29	45	2	7	24	17
DEC. 15	36	26	26	27	36	32	29	45	2	7	24	17
DEC. 16	36	28	28	29	36	32	29	45	2	7	24	17
DEC. 17	36	29	30	31	36	32	29	45	2	7	24	17
DEC. 18	36	31	32	32	35	32	29	45	2	7	24	17
DEC. 19	37	33	33	34	35	32	30	45	2	7	24	17
DEC. 20	37	34	35	35	35	32	30	45	2	7	24	17
DEC. 21	37	36	37	37	35	32	30	45	2	7	24	17
DEC. 22	37	38	38	39	35	32	30	45	2	7	24	17
DEC. 23	37	39	40	40	35	32	30	45	2	7	24	17
DEC. 24	37	41	41	42	35	32	30	45	2	7	24	17
DEC. 25	37	42	43	43	35	32	30	45	2	7	24	17
DEC. 26	38	44	44	45	35	32	30	45	2	7	24	17
DEC. 27	38	46	46	47	35	32	30	45	2	7	24	17
DEC. 28	38	47	48	48	35	32	30	45	2	7	24	17
DEC. 29	38	1	1	2	35	32	30	45	2	7	24	17
DEC. 30	38	2	3	4	35	32	30	45	2	7	24	17
DEC. 31	38	4	5	5	35	33	31	45	2	7	24	17

MOON 1 ◗ 12:01 A.M. TO 8:00 A.M.   **MOON 2** ◑ 8:01 A.M. TO 4:00 P.M.   **MOON 3** ● 4:01 P.M. TO 12:00 A.M.

Use only one "moon" number. Choose the column closest to your time of birth. If your place of birth is not on Eastern Standard Time, be sure to read "How to Convert to Eastern Standard Time" at the beginning of this section.

1939

January

Date & Time	SUN	MOON 1	MOON 2	MOON 3	MERCURY	VENUS	MARS	JUPITER	SATURN	URANUS	NEPTUNE	PLUTO
JAN. 1	38	6	6	7	35	33	31	45	3	7	24	17
JAN. 2	38	8	8	9	35	33	31	45	3	7	24	17
JAN. 3	39	10	10	11	36	33	31	45	3	7	24	17
JAN. 4	39	12	12	13	36	33	31	45	3	7	24	17
JAN. 5	39	14	14	15	36	33	31	45	3	7	24	17
JAN. 6	39	16	16	17	36	33	31	45	3	7	24	17
JAN. 7	39	18	18	19	36	33	31	45	3	7	24	17
JAN. 8	39	20	20	21	36	33	31	45	3	7	24	17
JAN. 9	39	22	22	23	36	33	31	45	3	7	24	17
JAN. 10	40	24	24	25	37	34	31	45	3	7	24	17
JAN. 11	40	25	26	27	37	34	31	45	3	7	24	17
JAN. 12	40	27	28	28	37	34	32	45	3	7	24	17
JAN. 13	40	29	30	30	37	34	32	45	3	7	24	17
JAN. 14	40	31	31	32	37	34	32	45	3	7	24	17
JAN. 15	40	32	33	33	37	34	32	45	3	7	24	17
JAN. 16	40	34	35	35	38	34	32	45	3	7	24	17
JAN. 17	41	36	36	37	38	34	32	45	3	7	24	17
JAN. 18	41	37	38	38	38	34	32	45	3	7	24	17
JAN. 19	41	39	39	40	38	35	32	46	3	7	24	17
JAN. 20	41	40	41	41	38	35	32	46	3	7	24	17
JAN. 21	41	42	42	43	39	35	32	46	3	7	24	17
JAN. 22	41	44	44	45	39	35	32	46	3	7	24	17
JAN. 23	42	45	46	46	39	35	32	46	3	7	24	17
JAN. 24	42	47	47	48	39	35	33	46	3	7	24	17
JAN. 25	42	48	1	1	39	35	33	46	3	7	24	17
JAN. 26	42	2	2	3	40	35	33	46	3	7	24	17
JAN. 27	42	4	4	5	40	35	33	46	3	7	24	17
JAN. 28	42	5	6	6	40	36	33	46	3	7	24	17
JAN. 29	42	7	8	8	40	36	33	46	3	7	24	17
JAN. 30	42	9	9	10	40	36	33	46	3	7	24	17
JAN. 31	43	11	11	12	41	36	33	46	3	7	24	17

February

Date & Time	SUN	MOON 1	MOON 2	MOON 3	MERCURY	VENUS	MARS	JUPITER	SATURN	URANUS	NEPTUNE	PLUTO
FEB. 1	43	13	13	14	41	36	33	46	3	7	24	17
FEB. 2	43	15	15	16	41	36	33	46	3	7	24	17
FEB. 3	43	17	17	18	41	37	33	46	3	7	24	17
FEB. 4	43	19	19	20	41	37	33	46	3	7	24	17
FEB. 5	43	21	21	22	42	37	34	46	3	7	24	17
FEB. 6	43	23	23	24	42	37	34	46	3	7	24	17
FEB. 7	43	25	25	26	42	37	34	46	3	7	24	17
FEB. 8	44	27	27	28	42	37	34	46	3	7	24	17
FEB. 9	44	28	29	30	43	37	34	46	3	7	24	17
FEB. 10	44	30	31	31	43	38	34	46	3	7	24	17
FEB. 11	44	32	32	33	43	38	34	46	3	7	24	17
FEB. 12	44	34	34	35	43	38	34	46	3	7	24	17
FEB. 13	44	35	36	36	44	38	34	46	3	7	24	17
FEB. 14	44	37	37	38	44	38	34	46	3	7	24	17
FEB. 15	44	38	39	39	44	38	34	46	3	7	24	17
FEB. 16	45	40	40	41	44	38	34	46	3	7	24	17
FEB. 17	45	42	42	43	44	39	34	46	3	7	24	17
FEB. 18	45	43	44	44	45	39	35	46	3	7	24	17
FEB. 19	45	45	45	46	45	39	35	46	3	7	24	17
FEB. 20	45	46	47	47	45	39	35	47	3	7	24	17
FEB. 21	45	48	48	1	45	39	35	47	3	7	24	17
FEB. 22	45	2	2	3	46	39	35	47	3	7	24	17
FEB. 23	46	3	4	4	46	39	35	47	3	7	24	17
FEB. 24	46	5	5	6	46	40	35	47	3	7	24	17
FEB. 25	46	7	7	8	46	40	35	47	3	7	24	17
FEB. 26	46	8	9	10	47	40	35	47	3	7	24	17
FEB. 27	46	10	11	11	47	40	35	47	3	7	24	17
FEB. 28	46	12	13	13	47	40	35	47	3	7	24	17

MOON 1 ☽ 12:01 A.M. TO 8:00 A.M.   **MOON 2** ☽ 8:01 A.M. TO 4:00 P.M.   **MOON 3** ● 4:01 P.M. TO 12:00 A.M.
Use only one "moon" number. Choose the column closest to your time of birth. If your place of birth is not on Eastern Standard Time, be sure to read "How to Convert to Eastern Standard Time" at the beginning of this section.

March

Date & Time	SUN ☉	MOON 1 ☽	MOON 2 ◑	MOON 3 ●	MERCURY	VENUS	MARS	JUPITER	SATURN	URANUS	NEPTUNE	PLUTO
MAR. 1	46	14	14	15	47	40	35	47	3	7	24	17
MAR. 2	46	16	16	17	48	40	36	47	3	7	24	17
MAR. 3	47	18	18	19	48	41	36	47	3	7	24	17
MAR. 4	47	20	20	21	48	41	36	47	3	7	24	17
MAR. 5	47	22	22	23	48	41	36	47	3	7	24	17
MAR. 6	47	24	24	25	1	41	36	47	3	7	24	17
MAR. 7	47	26	26	27	1	41	36	47	3	7	24	17
MAR. 8	47	28	28	29	1	41	36	47	3	7	24	17
MAR. 9	47	29	30	31	1	42	36	47	3	7	24	17
MAR. 10	47	31	32	32	2	42	36	47	3	7	24	17
MAR. 11	48	33	34	34	2	42	36	47	3	7	24	17
MAR. 12	48	35	35	36	2	42	36	47	3	7	24	17
MAR. 13	48	36	37	37	2	42	36	47	3	7	24	17
MAR. 14	48	38	38	39	2	42	36	47	3	7	24	17
MAR. 15	48	40	40	41	3	42	37	47	3	7	24	17
MAR. 16	48	41	42	42	3	43	37	47	3	7	24	17
MAR. 17	48	43	43	44	3	43	37	47	3	7	24	17
MAR. 18	48	44	45	45	3	43	37	47	3	7	24	17
MAR. 19	1	46	46	47	3	43	37	47	3	7	24	17
MAR. 20	1	47	48	1	3	43	37	47	3	7	24	17
MAR. 21	1	1	2	2	3	43	37	47	3	7	24	17
MAR. 22	1	3	5	4	3	44	37	47	3	7	24	17
MAR. 23	1	4	5	6	3	44	37	48	3	7	24	17
MAR. 24	1	6	7	7	3	44	37	48	3	7	24	17
MAR. 25	2	8	9	9	3	44	37	48	3	7	24	17
MAR. 26	2	10	10	11	3	44	37	48	3	7	24	17
MAR. 27	2	11	12	13	3	44	37	48	4	7	24	17
MAR. 28	2	13	14	15	3	44	37	48	4	7	24	17
MAR. 29	2	15	16	16	3	45	38	48	4	7	24	17
MAR. 30	2	17	18	18	3	45	38	48	4	7	24	17
MAR. 31	2	19	20	20	3	45	38	48	4	7	24	17

April

Date & Time	SUN ☉	MOON 1 ☽	MOON 2 ◑	MOON 3 ●	MERCURY	VENUS	MARS	JUPITER	SATURN	URANUS	NEPTUNE	PLUTO
APR. 1	2	21	22	22	3	45	38	48	4	7	24	17
APR. 2	2	23	24	24	3	45	38	48	4	7	24	17
APR. 3	3	25	26	26	3	45	38	48	4	7	24	17
APR. 4	3	27	27	28	3	46	38	48	4	7	24	17
APR. 5	3	29	29	30	2	46	38	48	4	7	24	17
APR. 6	3	31	31	32	2	46	38	48	4	7	24	17
APR. 7	3	32	33	33	2	46	38	48	4	7	24	17
APR. 8	3	34	35	35	2	46	38	48	4	7	24	17
APR. 9	3	36	36	37	2	46	38	48	4	7	24	17
APR. 10	3	37	38	38	2	47	38	48	4	7	24	17
APR. 11	4	39	40	40	2	47	38	48	4	7	24	17
APR. 12	4	41	41	42	2	47	39	48	4	7	24	17
APR. 13	4	42	43	43	2	47	39	48	4	7	24	17
APR. 14	4	44	44	45	2	47	39	48	4	7	24	17
APR. 15	4	45	46	46	2	47	39	48	4	7	24	17
APR. 16	4	47	48	48	2	47	39	48	4	7	24	17
APR. 17	4	1	1	2	2	48	39	48	4	7	24	17
APR. 18	4	2	3	3	2	48	39	48	4	7	24	17
APR. 19	5	4	5	5	2	48	39	48	4	7	24	17
APR. 20	5	6	6	7	2	48	39	48	4	7	24	17
APR. 21	5	7	8	9	2	48	39	48	4	7	24	17
APR. 22	5	9	10	10	2	48	39	48	4	7	24	17
APR. 23	5	11	12	12	2	1	39	48	4	7	24	17
APR. 24	5	13	14	14	2	1	39	48	4	7	24	17
APR. 25	6	15	15	16	2	1	39	1	4	7	24	17
APR. 26	6	17	17	18	2	1	39	1	4	7	24	17
APR. 27	6	19	19	20	2	1	40	1	4	7	24	17
APR. 28	6	20	21	22	2	1	40	1	4	7	24	17
APR. 29	6	22	23	24	2	2	40	1	4	7	24	17
APR. 30	6	24	25	26	3	2	40	1	4	7	24	17

MOON 1 ☽ 12:01 A.M. TO 8:00 A.M.   **MOON 2 ◑ 8:01 A.M. TO 4:00 P.M.**   **MOON 3 ● 4:01 P.M. TO 12:00 A.M.**

Use only one "moon" number. Choose the column closest to your time of birth. If your place of birth is not on Eastern Standard Time, be sure to read "How to Convert to Eastern Standard Time" at the beginning of this section.

May

Date & Time	SUN	MOON 1	MOON 2	MOON 3	MERCURY	VENUS	MARS	JUPITER	SATURN	URANUS	NEPTUNE	PLUTO
MAY 1	6	26	27	27	3	2	40	1	4	7	24	17
MAY 2	6	28	29	29	3	2	40	1	4	7	24	17
MAY 3	7	30	30	31	3	2	40	1	4	7	24	17
MAY 4	7	32	32	33	3	2	40	1	4	7	24	17
MAY 5	7	33	34	35	3	3	40	1	4	7	24	17
MAY 6	7	35	36	36	3	3	40	1	4	7	24	17
MAY 7	7	37	37	38	4	3	40	1	4	7	24	17
MAY 8	7	38	39	40	4	3	40	1	4	7	24	17
MAY 9	7	40	41	41	4	3	40	1	4	7	24	17
MAY 10	7	42	42	43	4	3	40	1	4	7	24	17
MAY 11	8	43	44	44	4	4	40	1	4	7	24	17
MAY 12	8	45	45	46	5	4	40	1	4	7	24	17
MAY 13	8	46	47	47	5	4	40	1	4	7	24	17
MAY 14	8	48	1	1	5	4	40	1	4	7	24	17
MAY 15	8	2	2	3	5	4	41	1	4	7	24	17
MAY 16	8	3	4	4	5	4	41	1	4	7	24	17
MAY 17	8	5	6	6	6	4	41	1	4	7	24	17
MAY 18	8	7	7	8	6	5	41	1	4	7	24	17
MAY 19	9	9	9	10	6	5	41	1	4	7	24	17
MAY 20	9	11	11	12	6	5	41	1	4	7	24	17
MAY 21	9	12	13	14	7	5	41	1	4	7	24	17
MAY 22	9	14	15	16	7	5	41	1	4	7	24	17
MAY 23	9	16	17	17	7	5	41	1	4	7	24	17
MAY 24	9	18	19	19	7	6	41	1	4	7	24	17
MAY 25	10	20	21	21	7	6	41	1	4	7	24	17
MAY 26	10	22	23	23	8	6	41	1	4	7	24	17
MAY 27	10	24	24	25	8	6	41	1	4	7	24	17
MAY 28	10	26	26	27	8	6	41	1	5	7	24	17
MAY 29	10	27	28	29	8	6	41	1	5	7	24	17
MAY 30	10	29	30	30	9	7	41	1	5	8	24	17
MAY 31	10	31	32	32	9	7	41	1	5	8	24	17

June

Date & Time	SUN	MOON 1	MOON 2	MOON 3	MERCURY	VENUS	MARS	JUPITER	SATURN	URANUS	NEPTUNE	PLUTO
JUN. 1	10	33	33	34	9	7	41	1	5	8	24	17
JUN. 2	10	35	35	36	10	7	41	1	5	8	24	17
JUN. 3	11	36	37	37	10	7	41	2	5	8	24	17
JUN. 4	11	38	38	39	10	7	41	2	5	8	24	17
JUN. 5	11	40	40	41	10	7	41	2	5	8	24	17
JUN. 6	11	41	42	42	11	8	41	2	5	8	24	17
JUN. 7	11	43	43	44	11	8	41	2	5	8	24	17
JUN. 8	11	44	45	45	11	8	41	2	5	8	24	17
JUN. 9	11	46	46	47	12	8	41	2	5	8	24	17
JUN. 10	11	47	48	1	12	8	41	2	5	8	24	17
JUN. 11	12	1	2	2	12	8	41	2	5	8	24	17
JUN. 12	12	3	3	4	12	9	42	2	5	8	24	17
JUN. 13	12	4	5	6	13	9	42	2	5	8	24	17
JUN. 14	12	6	7	7	13	9	42	2	5	8	24	17
JUN. 15	12	8	9	9	13	9	42	2	5	8	24	17
JUN. 16	12	10	10	11	14	9	42	2	5	8	24	17
JUN. 17	12	12	12	13	14	9	42	2	5	8	24	17
JUN. 18	12	14	14	15	14	10	42	2	5	8	24	17
JUN. 19	13	16	16	17	14	10	42	2	5	8	24	17
JUN. 20	13	18	18	19	15	10	42	2	5	8	24	17
JUN. 21	13	20	20	21	15	10	42	2	5	8	24	17
JUN. 22	13	21	22	23	15	10	42	2	5	8	24	17
JUN. 23	13	23	24	25	15	10	42	2	5	8	24	17
JUN. 24	13	25	26	26	16	11	42	2	5	8	24	17
JUN. 25	14	27	28	28	16	11	42	2	5	8	24	17
JUN. 26	14	29	29	30	16	11	42	2	5	8	24	17
JUN. 27	14	31	31	32	16	11	42	2	5	8	24	17
JUN. 28	14	32	33	33	17	11	42	2	5	8	24	17
JUN. 29	14	34	35	35	17	11	42	2	5	8	24	17
JUN. 30	14	36	36	37	17	12	42	2	5	8	24	17

MOON 1 ◐ 12:01 A.M. TO 8:00 A.M.   **MOON 2** ◑ 8:01 A.M. TO 4:00 P.M.   **MOON 3** ● 4:01 P.M. TO 12:00 A.M.
Use only one "moon" number. Choose the column closest to your time of birth. If your place of birth is not on Eastern Standard Time, be sure to read "How to Convert to Eastern Standard Time" at the beginning of this section.

1939

July

Date & Time	SUN	MOON 1	MOON 2	MOON 3	MERCURY	VENUS	MARS	JUPITER	SATURN	URANUS	NEPTUNE	PLUTO
JUL. 1	14	37	38	38	17	12	42	2	5	8	24	17
JUL. 2	14	39	40	40	17	12	42	2	5	8	24	17
JUL. 3	15	41	41	42	18	12	42	2	5	8	24	17
JUL. 4	15	42	43	43	18	12	41	2	5	8	24	17
JUL. 5	15	44	44	45	18	12	41	2	5	8	24	17
JUL. 6	15	45	46	46	18	12	41	2	5	8	24	17
JUL. 7	15	47	48	48	18	13	41	2	5	8	24	17
JUL. 8	15	1	1	2	18	13	41	2	5	8	24	17
JUL. 9	15	2	3	3	19	13	41	2	5	8	24	17
JUL. 10	15	4	4	5	19	13	41	2	5	8	24	17
JUL. 11	16	5	6	7	19	13	41	2	5	8	24	17
JUL. 12	16	7	8	8	19	13	41	2	5	8	24	17
JUL. 13	16	9	10	10	19	14	41	2	5	8	24	17
JUL. 14	16	11	12	12	19	14	41	2	5	8	24	17
JUL. 15	16	13	13	14	19	14	41	2	5	8	24	17
JUL. 16	16	15	15	16	19	14	41	2	5	8	24	17
JUL. 17	16	17	17	18	20	14	41	2	5	8	24	17
JUL. 18	16	19	19	20	20	14	41	2	5	8	24	17
JUL. 19	17	21	21	22	20	15	41	2	5	8	24	17
JUL. 20	17	23	23	24	20	15	41	2	5	8	24	17
JUL. 21	17	25	25	26	20	15	41	2	5	8	24	17
JUL. 22	17	27	27	28	20	15	41	2	5	8	24	17
JUL. 23	17	28	29	30	20	15	41	2	5	8	24	17
JUL. 24	17	30	31	31	20	15	41	2	5	8	24	17
JUL. 25	17	32	33	33	20	16	41	2	5	8	24	17
JUL. 26	18	34	34	35	20	16	41	2	5	8	24	17
JUL. 27	18	35	36	36	20	16	41	2	5	8	24	17
JUL. 28	18	37	38	38	20	16	41	2	5	8	24	17
JUL. 29	18	39	39	40	20	16	41	2	5	8	24	17
JUL. 30	18	40	41	41	20	16	41	2	5	8	24	17
JUL. 31	18	42	42	43	20	17	41	2	5	8	24	17

August

Date & Time	SUN	MOON 1	MOON 2	MOON 3	MERCURY	VENUS	MARS	JUPITER	SATURN	URANUS	NEPTUNE	PLUTO
AUG. 1	18	43	44	44	20	17	41	2	5	8	24	17
AUG. 2	18	45	46	46	20	17	41	2	5	8	24	17
AUG. 3	19	47	47	48	20	17	41	2	5	8	24	17
AUG. 4	19	48	1	1	20	17	40	2	5	8	24	17
AUG. 5	19	2	2	3	20	17	40	2	5	8	24	17
AUG. 6	19	3	4	4	20	18	40	2	5	8	24	17
AUG. 7	19	5	6	6	20	18	40	2	5	8	24	17
AUG. 8	19	7	7	8	20	18	40	2	5	8	24	17
AUG. 9	19	8	9	10	19	18	40	2	5	8	24	17
AUG. 10	19	10	11	11	19	18	40	2	5	8	24	17
AUG. 11	20	12	13	13	19	18	40	2	5	8	24	17
AUG. 12	20	14	15	15	19	19	40	2	5	8	24	17
AUG. 13	20	16	17	17	19	19	40	2	5	8	24	17
AUG. 14	20	18	19	19	19	19	40	2	5	8	24	17
AUG. 15	20	20	21	21	19	19	40	2	5	8	24	17
AUG. 16	20	22	23	23	19	19	40	2	5	8	24	17
AUG. 17	20	24	25	25	19	19	40	2	5	8	24	17
AUG. 18	20	26	27	27	19	20	40	2	5	8	24	17
AUG. 19	21	28	28	29	19	20	40	2	5	8	24	17
AUG. 20	21	30	30	31	19	20	40	2	5	8	24	17
AUG. 21	21	31	32	33	19	20	40	2	5	8	24	17
AUG. 22	21	33	34	34	19	20	40	2	5	8	24	17
AUG. 23	21	35	35	36	19	20	40	2	5	8	24	17
AUG. 24	21	37	37	38	19	21	40	2	5	8	24	17
AUG. 25	21	38	39	39	19	21	40	2	5	8	24	17
AUG. 26	22	40	40	41	19	21	40	2	5	8	24	17
AUG. 27	22	41	42	42	19	21	40	2	5	8	24	17
AUG. 28	22	43	44	44	19	21	40	2	5	8	24	17
AUG. 29	22	45	45	46	19	21	40	2	5	8	24	17
AUG. 30	22	46	47	47	19	22	40	2	5	8	24	17
AUG. 31	22	48	48	1	20	22	40	2	5	8	24	17

MOON 1 ◗ 12:01 A.M. TO 8:00 A.M.   **MOON 2** ◖ 8:01 A.M. TO 4:00 P.M.   **MOON 3** ● 4:01 P.M. TO 12:00 A.M.

Use only one "moon" number. Choose the column closest to your time of birth. If your place of birth is not on Eastern Standard Time, be sure to read "How to Convert to Eastern Standard Time" at the beginning of this section.

1939

September

October

Date & Time	SUN	MOON 1	MOON 2	MOON 3	MERCURY	VENUS	MARS	JUPITER	SATURN	URANUS	NEPTUNE	PLUTO
SEP. 1	22	1	2	2	20	22	40	2	5	8	24	17
SEP. 2	22	3	3	4	20	22	40	2	5	8	24	17
SEP. 3	23	5	5	6	20	22	40	2	5	8	24	17
SEP. 4	23	6	7	7	20	22	40	2	5	8	24	17
SEP. 5	23	8	8	9	21	23	40	2	5	8	24	17
SEP. 6	23	10	10	11	21	23	40	2	5	8	24	17
SEP. 7	23	11	12	13	21	23	40	2	5	8	24	17
SEP. 8	23	13	14	14	21	23	40	2	5	8	24	17
SEP. 9	23	15	16	16	21	23	40	2	5	8	24	17
SEP. 10	23	17	18	18	22	23	40	2	5	8	24	17
SEP. 11	24	19	20	20	22	24	40	2	5	8	24	17
SEP. 12	24	21	22	22	22	24	40	2	5	8	24	17
SEP. 13	24	23	24	24	22	24	41	2	5	8	24	17
SEP. 14	24	25	26	26	23	24	41	2	5	8	24	17
SEP. 15	24	27	28	28	23	24	41	2	5	8	24	17
SEP. 16	24	29	30	30	23	24	41	2	5	8	24	17
SEP. 17	24	31	31	32	23	24	41	2	5	8	24	17
SEP. 18	24	33	33	34	24	25	41	2	5	8	24	17
SEP. 19	25	34	35	24	24	25	41	2	5	8	24	17
SEP. 20	25	36	37	37	24	25	41	2	5	8	24	17
SEP. 21	25	38	38	39	24	25	41	2	5	8	24	17
SEP. 22	25	39	40	40	25	25	41	2	5	8	24	17
SEP. 23	25	41	42	42	25	25	41	2	5	8	24	17
SEP. 24	25	43	43	44	25	26	41	2	5	8	24	17
SEP. 25	26	44	45	45	25	26	41	2	5	8	24	17
SEP. 26	26	46	46	47	26	26	41	1	5	8	24	17
SEP. 27	26	47	48	48	26	26	41	1	5	8	24	17
SEP. 28	26	1	1	2	26	26	41	1	5	8	24	17
SEP. 29	26	3	3	4	26	26	41	1	5	8	24	17
SEP. 30	26	4	5	5	27	27	41	1	5	8	24	17

Date & Time	SUN	MOON 1	MOON 2	MOON 3	MERCURY	VENUS	MARS	JUPITER	SATURN	URANUS	NEPTUNE	PLUTO
OCT. 1	26	6	6	7	27	27	41	1	5	8	24	17
OCT. 2	26	8	8	9	27	27	41	1	5	8	24	17
OCT. 3	27	9	10	10	27	27	41	1	5	8	24	17
OCT. 4	27	11	12	12	27	27	42	1	5	8	24	17
OCT. 5	27	13	13	14	28	27	42	1	5	8	24	17
OCT. 6	27	15	15	16	28	28	42	1	5	8	24	17
OCT. 7	27	16	17	18	28	28	42	1	5	8	24	17
OCT. 8	27	18	19	20	28	28	42	1	5	8	24	17
OCT. 9	27	20	21	22	29	28	42	1	5	8	24	17
OCT. 10	27	22	23	24	29	28	42	1	5	8	24	17
OCT. 11	28	24	25	26	29	28	42	1	5	8	24	17
OCT. 12	28	26	27	27	29	29	42	1	5	8	24	17
OCT. 13	28	28	29	29	29	29	42	1	5	8	24	17
OCT. 14	28	30	31	31	30	29	42	1	5	8	24	17
OCT. 15	28	32	33	33	30	29	42	1	5	8	24	17
OCT. 16	28	34	34	35	30	29	42	1	5	8	24	17
OCT. 17	28	36	36	37	30	29	42	1	5	8	24	17
OCT. 18	28	37	38	38	30	30	42	1	5	8	24	17
OCT. 19	29	39	39	40	31	30	42	1	5	8	24	17
OCT. 20	29	41	41	42	31	30	43	1	5	8	24	17
OCT. 21	29	42	43	43	31	30	43	1	5	8	24	17
OCT. 22	29	44	44	45	31	30	43	1	5	8	24	17
OCT. 23	29	45	46	46	31	30	43	1	5	8	24	17
OCT. 24	29	47	47	48	32	31	43	1	5	8	24	17
OCT. 25	29	48	1	2	32	31	43	1	5	8	24	17
OCT. 26	30	2	3	3	32	31	43	1	5	8	24	17
OCT. 27	30	4	4	5	32	31	43	1	5	8	24	17
OCT. 28	30	5	6	6	32	31	43	1	5	8	24	17
OCT. 29	30	7	8	8	32	31	43	1	5	8	24	17
OCT. 30	30	9	9	10	33	32	43	1	5	8	24	17
OCT. 31	30	11	11	12	33	32	43	1	5	8	24	17

MOON 1 ◐ 12:01 A.M. TO 8:00 A.M.   **MOON 2** ◑ 8:01 A.M. TO 4:00 P.M.   **MOON 3** ● 4:01 P.M. TO 12:00 A.M.

Use only one "moon" number. Choose the column closest to your time of birth. If your place of birth is not on Eastern Standard Time, be sure to read "How to Convert to Eastern Standard Time" at the beginning of this section.

1939

November

Date & Time	SUN	MOON 1	MOON 2	MOON 3	MERCURY	VENUS	MARS	JUPITER	SATURN	URANUS	NEPTUNE	PLUTO
NOV. 1	30	12	13	14	33	32	43	1	5	8	24	17
NOV. 2	30	14	15	15	33	32	44	1	5	8	24	17
NOV. 3	31	16	17	17	33	32	44	1	5	8	24	17
NOV. 4	31	18	18	19	33	32	44	1	5	8	24	17
NOV. 5	31	20	20	21	34	33	44	1	5	8	24	17
NOV. 6	31	22	22	23	34	33	44	1	5	8	24	17
NOV. 7	31	24	24	25	34	33	44	1	5	8	24	17
NOV. 8	31	25	26	27	34	33	44	1	4	8	24	17
NOV. 9	31	27	28	29	34	33	44	1	4	8	24	17
NOV. 10	31	29	30	31	34	33	44	1	4	8	24	17
NOV. 11	31	31	32	32	34	34	44	1	4	8	24	17
NOV. 12	32	33	34	34	34	34	44	1	4	8	24	17
NOV. 13	32	35	35	36	35	34	44	1	4	8	24	17
NOV. 14	32	37	37	38	35	34	45	1	4	8	24	17
NOV. 15	32	38	39	39	35	34	45	1	4	8	24	17
NOV. 16	32	40	40	41	35	34	45	1	4	8	24	17
NOV. 17	32	42	42	43	35	35	45	1	4	8	24	17
NOV. 18	32	43	44	44	35	35	45	1	4	8	24	17
NOV. 19	33	45	45	46	35	35	45	1	4	8	24	17
NOV. 20	33	46	47	47	35	35	45	1	4	8	24	17
NOV. 21	33	48	48	1	35	35	45	1	4	8	24	17
NOV. 22	33	2	2	3	35	35	45	1	4	8	24	17
NOV. 23	33	3	4	4	35	36	45	1	4	8	24	17
NOV. 24	33	5	5	6	34	36	45	1	4	8	24	17
NOV. 25	34	6	7	8	34	36	45	1	4	8	24	17
NOV. 26	34	8	9	9	34	36	46	1	4	8	24	17
NOV. 27	34	10	11	11	34	36	46	1	4	8	24	17
NOV. 28	34	12	12	13	34	36	46	1	4	8	24	17
NOV. 29	34	14	14	15	34	37	46	1	4	8	24	17
NOV. 30	34	16	16	17	33	37	46	1	4	8	24	17

December

Date & Time	SUN	MOON 1	MOON 2	MOON 3	MERCURY	VENUS	MARS	JUPITER	SATURN	URANUS	NEPTUNE	PLUTO
DEC. 1	34	17	18	19	33	37	46	1	4	8	24	17
DEC. 2	34	19	20	21	33	37	46	1	4	8	24	17
DEC. 3	35	21	22	22	33	37	46	1	4	8	24	17
DEC. 4	35	23	24	24	33	37	46	1	4	8	24	17
DEC. 5	35	25	26	26	33	38	46	1	4	8	24	17
DEC. 6	35	27	27	28	33	38	46	1	4	8	24	17
DEC. 7	35	29	29	30	33	38	46	1	4	7	24	17
DEC. 8	35	31	31	32	33	38	47	1	4	7	24	17
DEC. 9	35	32	33	34	33	38	47	1	4	7	24	17
DEC. 10	35	34	35	35	33	38	47	1	4	7	24	17
DEC. 11	36	36	36	37	33	39	47	1	4	7	24	17
DEC. 12	36	38	38	39	33	39	47	1	4	7	24	17
DEC. 13	36	39	40	40	33	39	47	1	4	7	24	17
DEC. 14	36	41	42	42	33	39	47	1	4	7	24	17
DEC. 15	36	43	43	44	33	39	47	1	4	7	24	17
DEC. 16	36	44	45	45	33	39	47	1	4	7	24	17
DEC. 17	36	46	46	47	33	40	47	1	4	7	24	17
DEC. 18	36	47	48	48	34	40	47	1	4	7	24	17
DEC. 19	37	1	1	2	34	40	48	1	4	7	24	17
DEC. 20	37	3	3	4	34	40	48	1	4	7	24	17
DEC. 21	37	4	5	5	34	40	48	1	4	7	24	17
DEC. 22	37	6	6	7	34	40	48	1	4	7	24	17
DEC. 23	37	8	8	9	34	41	48	1	4	7	24	17
DEC. 24	37	9	10	10	34	41	48	1	4	7	24	17
DEC. 25	37	11	12	12	35	41	48	1	4	7	24	17
DEC. 26	38	13	14	14	35	41	48	1	4	7	24	17
DEC. 27	38	15	16	16	35	41	48	1	4	7	24	17
DEC. 28	38	17	17	18	35	41	48	1	4	7	24	17
DEC. 29	38	19	19	20	35	42	48	1	4	7	24	17
DEC. 30	38	21	21	22	36	42	1	1	4	7	24	17
DEC. 31	38	23	23	24	36	42	1	1	4	7	24	17

MOON 1 ☾ 12:01 A.M. TO 8:00 A.M.   **MOON 2** ☽ 8:01 A.M. TO 4:00 P.M.   **MOON 3** ● 4:01 P.M. TO 12:00 A.M.

Use only one "moon" number. Choose the column closest to your time of birth. If your place of birth is not on Eastern Standard Time, be sure to read "How to Convert to Eastern Standard Time" at the beginning of this section.

1940-1949

1940s

William Jefferson Clinton

* * * BORN AUGUST 19, 1946 * * *

Brief Bio: Born in Hope, Arkansas, William Jefferson Clinton is a statesman and Rhodes scholar who was the first Democratic President since Franklin Roosevelt to win a second term.

Personology Profile:

SUN ON THE CUSP OF EXPOSURE
(LEO-VIRGO CUSP) AUGUST 19-25

✳

Hard to know at a deep level, these secretive individuals seem to reveal a lot but in fact keep even more hidden. Like the tip of an iceberg, there is a lot which doesn't meet the eye. Moreover, they only choose to reveal themselves at the right time and place, and only to very few people. Their trust factor is not high, making them very discriminating.

MOON IN THE WEEK OF THE NATURAL
(TAURUS III)

✳

The moon in this position can make an individual astonishingly frank. Blurting out whatever is on their mind is typical here. Often they have no thought for how such remarks may push the buttons of those around them. We can admire such individuals for their lack of inhibition, but they really must learn something about tact and consideration for others.

MERCURY IN THE WEEK OF AUTHORITY
(LEO I)

✳

Giving others the impression that you know what you are talking about can prove a strength here, but also leave one open to blame when things don't go well. It is best to abandon an omniscient attitude in favor of simply giving advice in a straightforward and humble manner. Telling others to take it or leave it is better than promising the moon.

VENUS IN THE WEEK OF THE PERFECTIONIST
(LIBRA I)

✳

Standards for one's mate, partner or friend may be impossibly high. Judgmental attitudes, standards and even checklists can abound, making it sometimes difficult to relate to these demands. Those with this Venus position should aim to accept people as they are and not to subject them to such evaluations. Remembering that we are all only human is vitally important.

MARS IN THE WEEK OF THE PERFECTIONIST
(LIBRA I)

✳

Being aggressive in one's perfectionistic demands does not usually earn friends. This stressful position can drive everyone concerned a bit crazy, unless they can learn to be a bit more laid back. In dealing with technical matters, Mars in this period does guarantee perseverance and usually produces results. Great care must be taken to avoid neglecting the emotional and social spheres. Scheduling regular yoga, meditation or prayer sessions is advised.

JUPITER IN THE WEEK OF THEATER
(LIBRA III)

✳

The more dramatic aspects of life exert a strong pull here, favoring colorful behavior and even an interest in betting and gambling. A daredevil aspect of Jupiter surfaces here, granting luck through risk-taking and daring to fail. Those who crash from lofty positions with this aspect are able to get up, dust themselves off and start anew.

SATURN ON THE CUSP OF SCILLATION
(CANCER-LEO CUSP)

✳

Saturn can have a positive effect here, evening out the swings of this cusp and granting the power to put both introvert and extrovert tendencies to good use. Thus, episodes of depression can serve as a window to self-knowledge; more manic phases can bring fun and vibrancy to one's life if modulated and not allowed to get out of control. Thus, more stability can be granted.

URANUS IN THE WEEK OF THE SEEKER
(GEMINI III)

✳

Penetrating into the unknown, those with this Uranus position expect to come up against barriers and obstacles, and to smash them out of their way. Easy tasks do not really interest such individuals much. It is the big challenge and even the impossibilities lying ahead which lure them on. The will to overcome is strong here and with it a desire to achieve significant breakthroughs.

NEPTUNE IN THE WEEK OF THE PERFECTIONIST
(LIBRA I)

✳

A preoccupation with computer software, technical intricacies, cars and web sites is characteristic here. Such individuals do well as consultants and troubleshooters, ferreting out problems and solving them. Usually strong in design concepts, they are never happier than when dreaming up a new plan for any group or organization. Being appreciated for their services is important to them in all aspects of life.

PLUTO IN THE WEEK OF BALANCED STRENGTH
(LEO II)

✳

Somber moods and depressions should be guarded against here. A tendency to take things too seriously demands a mate or friend who can keep things light and provide the opportunity to have fun. Also, being able to let off steam in physical or athletic pursuits will help them avoid negativity. Prone to worry, these folks need to learn to forget their troubles and to smile at life's ironies.

Some Highlights of the Decade 1940-1949

- THE HOUSE UN-AMERICAN ACTIVITIES COMMITTEE, LED BY JOSEPH McCARTHY, BEGINS HEARINGS; A GROUP OF SCREENWRITERS KNOWN AS THE "HOLLYWOOD TEN" IS SENTENCED FOR "CONTEMPT OF CONGRESS" AND LATER BLACKLISTED.

- AN ESTIMATED 20 MILLION VIEWERS WATCH THE CORONATION OF QUEEN ELIZABETH II IN WESTMINSTER ABBEY, THE FIRST TIME TELEVISION CAMERAS HAVE BEEN PERMITTED IN THE ABBEY.

- JEANNETTE RANKIN, THE FIRST WOMAN EVER ELECTED AS A US SENATOR, CREATES A FUROR WHEN SHE BECOMES THE ONLY LEGISLATOR TO VOTE AGAINST DECLARING WAR ON JAPAN AFTER THE PEARL HARBOR RAID.

- BASEBALL GREAT JACKIE ROBINSON BREAKS THE COLOR BARRIER WHEN HE BEGINS PLAYING FOR THE DODGERS IN THE MAJOR LEAGUES.

- BETTY CROCKER CAKE MIXES HIT AMERICA'S SHELVES, WITH A PRODUCT LABELED GINGERBREAD CAKE AND COOKIE MIX AND ONE CALLED DEVIL'S FOOD LAYER CAKE AND PARTY LAYER CAKE.

January

Date & Time	SUN	MOON 1	MOON 2	MOON 3	MERCURY	VENUS	MARS	JUPITER	SATURN	URANUS	NEPTUNE	PLUTO
JAN. 1	38	25	25	26	36	42	1	1	4	7	24	17
JAN. 2	38	26	27	28	36	42	1	1	4	7	24	17
JAN. 3	39	28	29	29	36	42	1	1	4	7	24	17
JAN. 4	39	30	31	31	37	43	1	1	4	7	24	17
JAN. 5	39	32	32	33	37	43	1	1	4	7	24	17
JAN. 6	39	34	34	35	37	43	1	1	4	7	24	17
JAN. 7	39	35	36	37	37	43	1	1	4	7	24	17
JAN. 8	39	37	38	38	37	43	1	1	4	7	24	17
JAN. 9	39	39	39	40	38	43	1	1	4	7	24	17
JAN. 10	40	40	41	42	38	44	2	1	4	7	24	17
JAN. 11	40	42	43	43	38	44	2	1	4	7	24	17
JAN. 12	40	44	44	45	38	44	2	1	4	7	24	17
JAN. 13	40	45	46	46	38	44	2	1	4	7	24	17
JAN. 14	40	47	47	48	39	44	2	1	4	7	24	17
JAN. 15	40	48	1	1	39	44	2	1	4	7	24	17
JAN. 16	40	2	3	3	39	45	2	1	4	7	24	17
JAN. 17	41	4	4	5	39	45	2	1	4	7	24	17
JAN. 18	41	5	6	6	39	45	2	1	4	7	24	17
JAN. 19	41	7	7	8	40	45	2	1	4	7	24	17
JAN. 20	41	9	9	10	40	45	2	1	4	7	24	17
JAN. 21	41	10	11	12	40	45	3	2	4	7	24	17
JAN. 22	41	12	13	13	40	46	3	2	4	7	24	17
JAN. 23	42	14	15	15	40	46	3	2	4	7	24	17
JAN. 24	42	16	17	17	41	46	3	2	4	7	24	17
JAN. 25	42	18	19	19	41	46	3	2	4	7	24	17
JAN. 26	42	20	21	21	41	46	3	2	4	7	24	17
JAN. 27	42	22	23	23	41	47	3	2	4	7	24	17
JAN. 28	42	24	25	25	42	47	3	2	4	7	24	17
JAN. 29	42	26	27	27	42	47	3	2	4	7	24	17
JAN. 30	42	28	28	29	42	47	3	2	4	7	24	17
JAN. 31	43	30	30	31	42	47	3	2	4	7	24	17

February

Date & Time	SUN	MOON 1	MOON 2	MOON 3	MERCURY	VENUS	MARS	JUPITER	SATURN	URANUS	NEPTUNE	PLUTO
FEB. 1	43	31	32	33	42	47	4	2	4	7	24	17
FEB. 2	43	33	34	34	43	47	4	2	4	7	24	17
FEB. 3	43	35	36	36	43	48	4	2	4	7	24	17
FEB. 4	43	37	37	38	43	48	4	2	4	7	24	17
FEB. 5	43	38	39	39	43	48	4	2	4	7	24	17
FEB. 6	43	40	41	41	44	48	4	2	4	7	24	17
FEB. 7	43	42	42	43	44	48	4	2	4	7	24	17
FEB. 8	44	43	44	44	44	48	4	2	4	7	24	17
FEB. 9	44	45	45	46	44	48	4	2	4	7	24	17
FEB. 10	44	46	47	47	45	1	4	2	4	7	24	17
FEB. 11	44	48	1	1	45	1	4	2	4	7	24	17
FEB. 12	44	2	2	3	45	1	5	2	4	7	24	17
FEB. 13	44	3	4	4	45	1	5	2	4	7	24	17
FEB. 14	44	5	5	6	46	1	5	2	4	7	24	17
FEB. 15	44	6	7	7	46	1	5	2	5	7	24	17
FEB. 16	45	8	8	9	46	2	5	2	5	7	24	17
FEB. 17	45	10	10	11	46	2	5	2	5	7	24	17
FEB. 18	45	11	12	13	47	2	5	2	5	7	24	17
FEB. 19	45	13	14	14	47	2	5	2	5	7	24	17
FEB. 20	45	15	16	16	47	2	5	2	5	7	24	17
FEB. 21	45	17	18	18	47	2	5	2	5	7	24	17
FEB. 22	45	19	20	20	47	3	5	2	5	7	24	17
FEB. 23	46	21	22	22	48	3	6	2	5	7	24	17
FEB. 24	46	23	24	24	48	3	6	2	5	7	24	17
FEB. 25	46	25	26	26	48	3	6	2	5	7	24	17
FEB. 26	46	27	28	28	48	3	6	2	5	7	24	17
FEB. 27	46	29	30	30	48	3	6	2	5	7	24	17
FEB. 28	46	31	32	32	1	3	6	3	5	7	24	17
FEB. 29	46	33	33	34	1	4	6	3	5	7	24	17

MOON 1 ◖ 12:01 A.M. TO 8:00 A.M.   **MOON 2** ◑ 8:01 A.M. TO 4:00 P.M.   **MOON 3** ● 4:01 P.M. TO 12:00 A.M.

Use only one "moon" number. Choose the column closest to your time of birth. If your place of birth is not on Eastern Standard Time, be sure to read "How to Convert to Eastern Standard Time" at the beginning of this section.

1940

March

April

Date & Time	SUN	MOON 1	MOON 2	MOON 3	MERCURY	VENUS	MARS	JUPITER	SATURN	URANUS	NEPTUNE	PLUTO
MAR. 1	46	35	35	36	1	4	6	3	5	7	24	17
MAR. 2	46	36	37	37	1	4	6	3	5	7	24	17
MAR. 3	47	38	38	39	1	4	6	3	5	7	24	17
MAR. 4	47	40	40	41	1	4	6	3	5	7	24	17
MAR. 5	47	41	42	42	1	4	7	3	5	7	24	17
MAR. 6	47	43	43	44	1	5	7	3	5	7	24	17
MAR. 7	47	44	45	45	1	5	7	3	5	7	24	17
MAR. 8	47	46	47	47	1	5	7	3	5	7	24	17
MAR. 9	47	48	48	1	1	5	7	3	5	7	24	17
MAR. 10	47	1	2	2	1	5	7	3	5	7	24	17
MAR. 11	48	3	3	4	1	5	7	3	5	7	24	17
MAR. 12	48	4	5	5	1	6	7	3	5	7	24	17
MAR. 13	48	6	6	7	1	6	7	3	5	7	24	17
MAR. 14	48	8	8	9	48	6	7	3	5	7	24	17
MAR. 15	48	9	10	10	48	6	7	3	5	7	24	17
MAR. 16	48	11	11	12	48	6	7	3	5	8	24	17
MAR. 17	48	13	13	14	48	6	8	3	5	8	24	17
MAR. 18	48	14	15	16	48	6	8	3	5	8	24	17
MAR. 19	1	16	17	18	48	7	8	3	5	8	24	17
MAR. 20	1	18	19	19	48	7	8	3	5	8	24	17
MAR. 21	1	20	21	21	48	7	8	3	5	8	24	17
MAR. 22	1	22	23	23	48	7	8	3	5	8	24	17
MAR. 23	1	24	25	25	47	7	8	3	5	8	24	17
MAR. 24	1	26	27	27	47	7	8	3	5	8	24	17
MAR. 25	2	28	29	29	47	7	8	3	5	8	24	17
MAR. 26	2	30	31	31	47	8	8	3	5	8	24	17
MAR. 27	2	32	33	33	47	8	8	3	5	8	24	17
MAR. 28	2	34	35	35	47	8	9	3	5	8	24	17
MAR. 29	2	36	36	37	47	8	9	3	5	8	24	17
MAR. 30	2	37	38	39	47	8	9	3	5	8	24	17
MAR. 31	2	39	40	40	47	8	9	4	5	8	24	17

Date & Time	SUN	MOON 1	MOON 2	MOON 3	MERCURY	VENUS	MARS	JUPITER	SATURN	URANUS	NEPTUNE	PLUTO
APR. 1	2	41	41	42	47	8	9	4	5	8	24	17
APR. 2	2	42	43	44	47	9	9	4	5	8	24	17
APR. 3	3	44	45	45	47	9	9	4	5	8	24	17
APR. 4	3	46	46	47	47	9	9	4	5	8	24	17
APR. 5	3	47	48	48	48	9	9	4	5	8	24	17
APR. 6	3	1	1	2	48	9	9	4	5	8	24	17
APR. 7	3	2	3	3	48	9	9	4	5	8	24	17
APR. 8	3	4	4	5	48	9	10	4	5	8	24	17
APR. 9	3	6	6	7	48	10	10	4	5	8	24	17
APR. 10	3	7	8	8	48	10	10	4	5	8	24	17
APR. 11	4	9	9	10	48	10	10	4	5	8	24	17
APR. 12	4	10	11	12	48	10	10	4	5	8	24	17
APR. 13	4	12	13	13	48	10	10	4	5	8	24	17
APR. 14	4	14	15	15	1	10	10	4	5	8	24	17
APR. 15	4	16	16	17	1	10	10	4	5	8	24	17
APR. 16	4	18	18	19	1	11	10	4	5	8	24	17
APR. 17	4	19	20	21	1	11	10	4	5	8	24	17
APR. 18	4	21	22	23	1	11	10	4	5	8	24	17
APR. 19	5	23	24	25	1	11	10	4	5	8	24	17
APR. 20	5	25	26	27	1	11	11	4	5	8	24	17
APR. 21	5	27	28	29	2	11	11	4	5	8	24	17
APR. 22	5	29	30	31	2	11	11	4	6	8	24	17
APR. 23	5	31	32	33	2	11	11	4	6	8	24	17
APR. 24	5	33	34	34	2	12	11	4	6	8	24	17
APR. 25	6	35	36	36	2	12	11	4	6	8	24	17
APR. 26	6	37	37	38	3	12	11	4	6	8	24	17
APR. 27	6	39	39	40	3	12	11	4	6	8	24	17
APR. 28	6	40	41	41	3	12	11	4	6	8	24	17
APR. 29	6	42	42	43	3	12	11	4	6	8	24	17
APR. 30	6	44	44	45	3	12	11	4	6	8	24	17

MOON 1 ☽ 12:01 A.M. TO 8:00 A.M.   **MOON 2** ☽ 8:01 A.M. TO 4:00 P.M.   **MOON 3** ● 4:01 P.M. TO 12:00 A.M.

Use only one "moon" number. Choose the column closest to your time of birth. If your place of birth is not on Eastern Standard Time, be sure to read "How to Convert to Eastern Standard Time" at the beginning of this section.

1940

May

June

Date & Time	SUN ☼	MOON 1 ◖	MOON 2 ◑	MOON 3 ●	MERCURY	VENUS	MARS	JUPITER	SATURN	URANUS	NEPTUNE	PLUTO
MAY 1	6	45	46	46	4	12	12	4	6	8	24	17
MAY 2	6	47	47	48	4	12	12	5	6	8	24	17
MAY 3	7	48	1	1	4	13	12	5	6	8	24	17
MAY 4	7	2	2	3	4	13	12	5	6	8	24	17
MAY 5	7	3	4	5	5	13	12	5	6	8	24	17
MAY 6	7	5	6	6	5	13	12	5	6	8	24	17
MAY 7	7	7	7	8	5	13	12	5	6	8	24	17
MAY 8	7	8	9	9	5	13	12	5	6	8	24	17
MAY 9	7	10	11	11	6	13	12	5	6	8	24	17
MAY 10	7	12	12	13	6	13	12	5	6	8	24	17
MAY 11	8	14	14	15	6	13	12	5	6	8	24	17
MAY 12	8	15	16	16	6	13	12	5	6	8	24	17
MAY 13	8	17	18	18	7	14	13	5	6	8	24	17
MAY 14	8	19	20	20	7	14	13	5	6	8	24	17
MAY 15	8	21	21	22	7	14	13	5	6	8	24	17
MAY 16	8	23	23	24	7	14	13	5	6	8	24	17
MAY 17	8	25	25	26	8	14	13	5	6	8	24	17
MAY 18	8	27	27	28	8	14	13	5	6	8	24	17
MAY 19	9	28	29	30	8	14	13	5	6	8	24	17
MAY 20	9	30	31	32	9	14	13	5	6	8	24	17
MAY 21	9	32	33	34	9	14	13	5	6	8	24	17
MAY 22	9	34	35	35	9	14	13	5	6	8	24	17
MAY 23	9	36	37	37	9	14	13	5	6	8	24	17
MAY 24	9	38	38	39	10	14	14	5	6	8	24	17
MAY 25	10	40	40	41	10	14	14	5	6	8	24	17
MAY 26	10	41	42	42	10	14	14	5	6	8	24	17
MAY 27	10	43	44	44	11	15	14	5	6	8	24	17
MAY 28	10	45	45	46	11	15	14	5	6	8	24	17
MAY 29	10	46	47	47	11	15	14	5	6	8	24	17
MAY 30	10	48	48	1	11	15	14	5	6	8	24	17
MAY 31	10	1	2	2	12	15	14	5	6	8	24	17

Date & Time	SUN ☼	MOON 1 ◖	MOON 2 ◑	MOON 3 ●	MERCURY	VENUS	MARS	JUPITER	SATURN	URANUS	NEPTUNE	PLUTO
JUN. 1	10	3	4	4	12	15	14	5	6	8	24	17
JUN. 2	10	5	5	6	12	15	14	5	6	8	24	17
JUN. 3	11	6	7	7	13	15	14	5	6	8	24	17
JUN. 4	11	8	8	9	13	15	14	6	6	8	24	17
JUN. 5	11	10	10	11	13	15	15	6	6	8	24	17
JUN. 6	11	11	12	12	13	15	15	6	6	8	24	17
JUN. 7	11	13	14	14	14	15	15	6	6	8	24	17
JUN. 8	11	15	15	16	14	15	15	6	6	8	24	17
JUN. 9	11	17	17	18	14	15	15	6	6	8	24	17
JUN. 10	11	19	19	20	14	15	15	6	6	8	24	17
JUN. 11	12	20	21	21	15	15	15	6	6	8	24	17
JUN. 12	12	22	23	23	15	15	15	6	6	8	24	17
JUN. 13	12	24	25	25	15	15	15	6	6	8	24	17
JUN. 14	12	26	27	27	15	15	15	6	6	8	24	17
JUN. 15	12	28	29	29	15	14	15	6	6	8	24	17
JUN. 16	12	30	30	31	15	14	16	6	6	8	24	17
JUN. 17	12	32	32	33	16	14	16	6	6	8	24	17
JUN. 18	12	34	34	35	16	14	16	6	6	8	24	17
JUN. 19	13	35	36	37	16	14	16	6	6	8	24	17
JUN. 20	13	37	38	38	16	14	16	6	6	8	24	17
JUN. 21	13	39	40	40	16	14	16	6	6	8	24	17
JUN. 22	13	41	41	42	16	14	16	6	6	8	24	17
JUN. 23	13	42	43	44	17	14	16	6	6	8	24	17
JUN. 24	13	44	45	45	17	14	16	6	6	8	24	17
JUN. 25	14	46	46	47	17	14	16	6	7	8	24	17
JUN. 26	14	47	48	48	17	14	16	6	7	8	24	17
JUN. 27	14	1	1	2	17	14	16	6	7	8	24	17
JUN. 28	14	2	3	4	17	14	17	6	7	8	24	17
JUN. 29	14	4	5	5	17	13	17	6	7	8	24	17
JUN. 30	14	6	6	7	17	13	17	6	7	8	24	17

MOON 1 ◖ 12:01 A.M. TO 8:00 A.M.   **MOON 2** ◑ 8:01 A.M. TO 4:00 P.M.   **MOON 3** ● 4:01 P.M. TO 12:00 A.M.
Use only one "moon" number. Choose the column closest to your time of birth. If your place of birth is not on Eastern Standard Time, be sure to read "How to Convert to Eastern Standard Time" at the beginning of this section.

Date & Time	SUN	MOON 1	MOON 2	MOON 3	MERCURY	VENUS	MARS	JUPITER	SATURN	URANUS	NEPTUNE	PLUTO
JUL. 1	14	7	8	8	17	13	17	6	7	8	24	17
JUL. 2	14	9	10	10	17	13	17	6	7	8	24	17
JUL. 3	15	11	11	12	18	13	17	6	7	8	24	17
JUL. 4	15	12	13	14	18	13	17	6	7	8	24	17
JUL. 5	15	14	15	15	18	13	17	6	7	8	24	17
JUL. 6	15	16	17	17	18	13	17	6	7	8	24	17
JUL. 7	15	18	19	19	18	13	17	6	7	8	24	17
JUL. 8	15	20	21	21	18	13	17	6	7	8	24	17
JUL. 9	15	22	22	23	18	13	17	6	7	8	24	17
JUL. 10	15	24	24	25	18	13	18	6	7	8	24	17
JUL. 11	16	26	26	27	18	13	18	6	7	8	24	17
JUL. 12	16	27	28	29	18	13	18	6	7	8	24	17
JUL. 13	16	29	30	31	18	13	18	6	7	8	24	17
JUL. 14	16	31	32	32	18	13	18	7	7	8	24	17
JUL. 15	16	33	34	34	17	13	18	7	7	8	24	17
JUL. 16	16	35	35	36	17	13	18	7	7	8	24	17
JUL. 17	16	37	37	38	17	13	18	7	7	8	24	17
JUL. 18	16	38	39	40	17	13	18	7	7	8	24	17
JUL. 19	17	40	41	41	17	13	18	7	7	8	24	17
JUL. 20	17	42	42	43	17	13	18	7	7	8	24	17
JUL. 21	17	44	44	45	17	13	18	7	7	8	24	17
JUL. 22	17	45	46	46	17	13	19	7	7	8	24	17
JUL. 23	17	47	47	48	17	13	19	7	7	8	24	17
JUL. 24	17	48	1	1	17	13	19	7	7	8	24	17
JUL. 25	17	2	2	3	17	13	19	7	7	8	24	17
JUL. 26	18	4	4	5	17	13	19	7	7	8	24	17
JUL. 27	18	5	6	6	16	13	19	7	7	8	24	17
JUL. 28	18	7	7	8	16	13	19	7	7	8	24	17
JUL. 29	18	8	9	9	16	13	19	7	7	8	24	17
JUL. 30	18	10	11	11	16	13	19	7	7	8	24	17
JUL. 31	18	12	12	13	16	13	19	7	7	8	24	17

Date & Time	SUN	MOON 1	MOON 2	MOON 3	MERCURY	VENUS	MARS	JUPITER	SATURN	URANUS	NEPTUNE	PLUTO
AUG. 1	18	14	14	15	16	13	19	7	7	8	24	17
AUG. 2	18	15	16	17	16	13	19	7	7	8	24	17
AUG. 3	19	17	18	19	16	13	20	7	7	8	24	17
AUG. 4	19	19	20	20	16	13	20	7	7	8	24	17
AUG. 5	19	21	22	22	16	13	20	7	7	8	24	17
AUG. 6	19	23	24	24	16	13	20	7	7	8	24	17
AUG. 7	19	25	26	26	17	13	20	7	7	8	24	17
AUG. 8	19	27	28	28	17	13	20	7	7	8	24	17
AUG. 9	19	29	30	30	17	14	20	7	7	8	24	17
AUG. 10	19	31	31	32	17	14	20	7	7	8	24	17
AUG. 11	20	33	33	34	17	14	20	7	7	8	24	17
AUG. 12	20	34	35	36	17	14	20	7	7	8	24	17
AUG. 13	20	36	37	37	17	14	20	7	7	8	24	17
AUG. 14	20	38	39	39	17	14	21	7	7	8	24	17
AUG. 15	20	40	40	41	18	14	21	7	7	8	24	17
AUG. 16	20	41	42	42	18	14	21	7	7	8	24	17
AUG. 17	20	43	44	44	18	14	21	7	7	8	24	17
AUG. 18	20	45	45	46	18	14	21	7	7	8	24	17
AUG. 19	21	46	47	47	18	15	21	7	7	8	24	17
AUG. 20	21	48	48	1	19	15	21	7	7	8	24	17
AUG. 21	21	1	2	3	19	15	21	7	7	8	24	17
AUG. 22	21	3	4	4	19	15	21	7	7	8	24	17
AUG. 23	21	5	5	6	19	15	21	7	7	8	24	17
AUG. 24	21	6	7	7	20	15	21	7	7	8	24	17
AUG. 25	21	8	8	9	20	15	21	7	7	8	24	17
AUG. 26	22	9	10	11	20	15	22	7	7	8	24	17
AUG. 27	22	11	12	12	20	15	22	7	7	8	24	17
AUG. 28	22	13	13	14	21	16	22	7	7	8	24	17
AUG. 29	22	15	15	16	21	16	22	7	7	8	24	17
AUG. 30	22	16	17	18	21	16	22	7	7	8	24	17
AUG. 31	22	18	19	20	21	16	22	7	7	8	24	17

MOON 1 ☽ 12:01 A.M. TO 8:00 A.M.   **MOON 2** ☽ 8:01 A.M. TO 4:00 P.M.   **MOON 3** ● 4:01 P.M. TO 12:00 A.M.
Use only one "moon" number. Choose the column closest to your time of birth. If your place of birth is not on Eastern Standard Time, be sure to read "How to Convert to Eastern Standard Time" at the beginning of this section.

September

Date & Time	SUN	MOON 1	MOON 2	MOON 3	MERCURY	VENUS	MARS	JUPITER	SATURN	URANUS	NEPTUNE	PLUTO
SEP. 1	22	20	21	22	22	16	22	7	7	8	24	17
SEP. 2	22	22	23	24	22	16	22	7	7	8	24	17
SEP. 3	23	24	25	26	22	16	22	7	7	8	24	17
SEP. 4	23	26	27	28	22	16	22	7	7	8	24	17
SEP. 5	23	28	29	30	23	17	22	7	7	8	24	17
SEP. 6	23	30	31	32	23	17	22	7	7	8	24	17
SEP. 7	23	32	33	33	23	17	22	7	7	8	24	17
SEP. 8	23	34	35	35	23	17	23	7	7	8	24	17
SEP. 9	23	36	36	37	24	17	23	7	7	8	24	17
SEP. 10	23	38	38	39	24	17	23	7	7	8	24	17
SEP. 11	24	39	40	40	24	17	23	7	7	8	24	17
SEP. 12	24	41	42	42	24	17	23	7	7	8	24	17
SEP. 13	24	43	43	44	25	18	23	7	7	8	24	17
SEP. 14	24	44	45	45	25	18	23	7	7	8	24	17
SEP. 15	24	46	46	47	25	18	23	7	7	8	24	17
SEP. 16	24	47	48	1	25	18	23	7	7	8	24	17
SEP. 17	24	1	2	2	26	18	23	7	7	8	24	17
SEP. 18	24	3	3	4	26	18	23	7	7	8	24	17
SEP. 19	25	4	5	5	26	18	24	7	7	8	24	17
SEP. 20	25	6	6	7	26	19	24	7	7	8	24	17
SEP. 21	25	7	8	8	26	19	24	7	7	8	24	17
SEP. 22	25	9	10	10	27	19	24	7	7	8	24	17
SEP. 23	25	11	11	12	27	19	24	7	7	8	24	17
SEP. 24	25	12	13	13	27	19	24	7	7	8	24	17
SEP. 25	26	14	15	15	27	19	24	7	7	8	24	17
SEP. 26	26	16	16	17	28	19	24	7	7	8	24	17
SEP. 27	26	18	18	19	28	20	24	7	7	8	24	18
SEP. 28	26	19	20	21	28	20	24	7	7	8	24	18
SEP. 29	26	21	22	23	28	20	24	7	7	8	24	18
SEP. 30	26	23	24	25	28	20	25	7	7	8	24	18

October

Date & Time	SUN	MOON 1	MOON 2	MOON 3	MERCURY	VENUS	MARS	JUPITER	SATURN	URANUS	NEPTUNE	PLUTO
OCT. 1	26	25	26	27	29	20	25	7	7	8	24	18
OCT. 2	26	27	28	29	29	20	25	7	7	8	24	18
OCT. 3	27	29	30	31	29	20	25	7	7	8	24	18
OCT. 4	27	31	32	33	29	21	25	7	7	8	24	18
OCT. 5	27	33	34	35	29	21	25	7	7	8	24	18
OCT. 6	27	35	36	36	29	21	25	7	7	8	24	18
OCT. 7	27	37	38	38	30	21	25	7	7	8	24	18
OCT. 8	27	39	39	40	30	21	25	7	7	8	24	18
OCT. 9	27	41	41	42	30	21	25	7	7	8	24	18
OCT. 10	27	42	43	43	30	21	25	7	7	8	24	18
OCT. 11	28	44	44	45	30	22	25	7	7	8	24	18
OCT. 12	28	45	46	47	31	22	26	7	7	8	24	18
OCT. 13	28	47	48	48	31	22	26	7	7	8	24	18
OCT. 14	28	1	1	2	31	22	26	7	7	8	24	18
OCT. 15	28	2	3	3	31	22	26	7	7	8	24	18
OCT. 16	28	4	4	5	31	22	26	7	7	8	24	18
OCT. 17	28	5	6	6	31	23	26	7	7	8	24	18
OCT. 18	28	7	7	8	31	23	26	7	7	8	24	18
OCT. 19	29	9	9	10	32	23	26	7	7	8	24	18
OCT. 20	29	10	11	11	32	23	26	7	7	8	24	18
OCT. 21	29	12	12	13	32	23	26	7	7	8	24	18
OCT. 22	29	14	14	15	32	23	26	7	7	8	24	18
OCT. 23	29	15	16	16	32	23	26	7	7	8	24	18
OCT. 24	29	17	18	18	32	24	27	7	7	8	25	18
OCT. 25	29	19	19	20	32	24	27	7	7	8	25	18
OCT. 26	30	21	21	22	32	24	27	7	7	8	25	18
OCT. 27	30	23	23	24	33	24	27	7	7	8	25	18
OCT. 28	30	25	25	26	33	24	6	7	8	8	25	18
OCT. 29	30	26	27	28	33	24	27	6	7	8	25	18
OCT. 30	30	29	29	30	33	25	27	6	7	8	25	18
OCT. 31	30	31	31	32	33	25	27	6	7	8	25	18

MOON 1 ☽ 12:01 A.M. TO 8:00 A.M. **MOON 2** ☽ 8:01 A.M. TO 4:00 P.M. **MOON 3** ● 4:01 P.M. TO 12:00 A.M.

Use only one "moon" number. Choose the column closest to your time of birth. If your place of birth is not on Eastern Standard Time, be sure to read "How to Convert to Eastern Standard Time" at the beginning of this section.

November

Date & Time	SUN	MOON 1	MOON 2	MOON 3	MERCURY	VENUS	MARS	JUPITER	SATURN	URANUS	NEPTUNE	PLUTO
NOV. 1	30	33	33	34	33	25	27	6	7	8	25	18
NOV. 2	30	34	35	36	33	25	27	6	6	8	25	18
NOV. 3	31	36	37	38	33	25	27	6	6	8	25	18
NOV. 4	31	38	39	39	33	25	28	6	6	8	25	18
NOV. 5	31	40	41	41	33	26	28	6	6	8	25	18
NOV. 6	31	42	42	43	32	26	28	6	6	8	25	18
NOV. 7	31	43	44	45	32	26	28	6	6	8	25	18
NOV. 8	31	45	46	46	32	26	28	6	6	8	25	18
NOV. 9	31	47	47	48	32	26	28	6	6	8	25	18
NOV. 10	31	48	1	1	32	26	28	6	6	8	25	18
NOV. 11	31	2	2	3	32	26	28	6	6	8	25	18
NOV. 12	32	3	4	4	32	27	28	6	6	8	25	18
NOV. 13	32	5	5	6	31	27	28	6	6	8	25	18
NOV. 14	32	7	7	8	31	27	28	6	6	8	25	18
NOV. 15	32	8	9	9	31	27	28	6	6	8	25	18
NOV. 16	32	10	10	11	31	27	29	6	6	8	25	18
NOV. 17	32	11	12	13	31	27	29	6	6	8	25	18
NOV. 18	32	13	14	14	31	28	29	6	6	8	25	18
NOV. 19	33	15	15	16	31	28	29	6	6	8	25	18
NOV. 20	33	17	17	18	31	28	29	6	6	8	25	18
NOV. 21	33	18	19	20	31	28	29	6	6	8	25	18
NOV. 22	33	20	21	21	31	28	29	6	6	8	25	18
NOV. 23	33	22	23	23	31	28	29	6	6	8	25	18
NOV. 24	33	24	24	25	31	29	29	6	6	8	25	18
NOV. 25	34	26	26	27	31	29	29	6	6	8	25	18
NOV. 26	34	28	28	29	31	29	29	6	6	8	25	18
NOV. 27	34	30	30	31	31	29	30	6	6	8	25	18
NOV. 28	34	32	32	33	31	29	30	6	6	8	25	18
NOV. 29	34	34	34	35	31	29	30	6	6	8	25	18
NOV. 30	34	36	36	37	31	30	30	6	6	8	25	18

December

Date & Time	SUN	MOON 1	MOON 2	MOON 3	MERCURY	VENUS	MARS	JUPITER	SATURN	URANUS	NEPTUNE	PLUTO
DEC. 1	34	37	38	39	31	30	30	6	6	8	25	18
DEC. 2	34	39	40	41	32	30	30	6	6	8	25	18
DEC. 3	35	41	42	42	32	30	30	6	6	8	25	18
DEC. 4	35	43	43	44	32	30	30	6	6	8	25	18
DEC. 5	35	45	45	46	32	30	30	6	6	8	25	18
DEC. 6	35	46	47	47	32	31	30	6	6	8	25	18
DEC. 7	35	48	48	1	33	31	30	6	6	8	25	18
DEC. 8	35	1	2	2	33	31	31	6	6	8	25	18
DEC. 9	35	3	3	4	33	31	31	6	6	8	25	18
DEC. 10	35	4	5	6	33	31	31	6	6	8	25	18
DEC. 11	36	6	7	7	33	31	31	6	6	8	25	18
DEC. 12	36	8	8	9	33	32	31	6	6	8	25	18
DEC. 13	36	9	10	10	34	32	31	6	6	8	25	18
DEC. 14	36	11	12	12	34	32	31	6	6	8	25	18
DEC. 15	36	13	13	14	34	32	31	6	6	8	25	18
DEC. 16	36	14	15	16	34	32	31	6	6	8	25	17
DEC. 17	36	16	17	17	34	32	31	6	6	8	25	17
DEC. 18	36	18	19	19	35	33	31	6	6	8	25	17
DEC. 19	37	20	20	21	35	33	31	6	6	8	25	17
DEC. 20	37	22	22	23	35	33	32	6	6	8	25	17
DEC. 21	37	23	24	25	35	33	32	6	6	8	25	17
DEC. 22	37	25	26	26	35	33	32	6	6	8	25	17
DEC. 23	37	27	28	28	36	33	32	6	6	8	25	17
DEC. 24	37	29	30	30	36	34	32	6	6	8	25	17
DEC. 25	37	31	32	32	36	34	32	6	6	8	25	17
DEC. 26	38	33	33	34	36	34	32	6	6	8	25	17
DEC. 27	38	35	35	36	37	34	32	6	6	8	25	17
DEC. 28	38	37	37	38	37	34	32	6	6	8	25	17
DEC. 29	38	39	39	40	37	34	32	6	6	8	25	17
DEC. 30	38	40	41	42	37	35	32	6	6	8	25	17
DEC. 31	38	42	43	43	37	35	33	6	6	8	25	17

MOON 1 ☽ 12:01 A.M. TO 8:00 A.M.   **MOON 2** ☽ 8:01 A.M. TO 4:00 P.M.   **MOON 3** ● 4:01 P.M. TO 12:00 A.M.
Use only one "moon" number. Choose the column closest to your time of birth. If your place of birth is not on Eastern Standard Time, be sure to read "How to Convert to Eastern Standard Time" at the beginning of this section.

1941

January   February

Date & Time	SUN	MOON 1	MOON 2	MOON 3	MERCURY	VENUS	MARS	JUPITER	SATURN	URANUS	NEPTUNE	PLUTO
JAN. 1	38	44	44	45	38	35	33	6	6	8	25	17
JAN. 2	38	46	46	47	38	35	33	6	6	8	25	17
JAN. 3	39	47	48	48	38	35	33	6	6	8	25	17
JAN. 4	39	1	1	2	38	35	33	6	6	8	25	17
JAN. 5	39	2	3	3	38	36	33	6	6	8	25	17
JAN. 6	39	4	4	5	39	36	33	6	6	8	25	17
JAN. 7	39	6	6	7	39	36	33	6	6	8	25	17
JAN. 8	39	7	8	8	39	36	33	6	6	8	25	17
JAN. 9	39	9	9	10	39	36	33	6	6	8	25	17
JAN. 10	40	10	11	12	39	36	33	6	6	8	25	17
JAN. 11	40	12	13	13	40	37	34	6	6	8	25	17
JAN. 12	40	14	14	15	40	37	34	6	6	8	25	17
JAN. 13	40	16	16	17	40	37	34	6	6	8	25	17
JAN. 14	40	17	18	19	40	37	34	6	6	8	25	17
JAN. 15	40	19	20	20	41	37	34	6	6	8	25	17
JAN. 16	40	21	22	22	41	37	34	6	6	8	25	17
JAN. 17	41	23	24	24	41	38	34	6	6	8	25	17
JAN. 18	41	25	25	26	41	38	34	6	6	8	25	17
JAN. 19	41	27	27	28	41	38	34	6	6	8	25	17
JAN. 20	41	29	29	30	42	38	34	6	6	8	25	17
JAN. 21	41	30	31	32	42	38	34	6	6	8	25	17
JAN. 22	41	32	33	34	42	38	35	6	6	8	25	17
JAN. 23	42	34	35	35	42	39	35	6	6	8	25	17
JAN. 24	42	36	37	37	43	39	35	6	6	8	25	17
JAN. 25	42	38	38	39	43	39	35	6	6	8	25	17
JAN. 26	42	40	40	41	43	39	35	6	6	8	25	17
JAN. 27	42	41	42	43	43	39	35	6	6	8	25	17
JAN. 28	42	43	44	44	44	39	35	6	6	8	25	17
JAN. 29	42	45	45	46	44	40	35	6	6	8	25	17
JAN. 30	42	47	47	48	44	40	35	6	6	8	25	17
JAN. 31	43	48	1	1	44	40	35	6	6	8	25	17

Date & Time	SUN	MOON 1	MOON 2	MOON 3	MERCURY	VENUS	MARS	JUPITER	SATURN	URANUS	NEPTUNE	PLUTO
FEB. 1	43	2	2	3	44	40	35	6	6	8	25	17
FEB. 2	43	3	4	4	45	40	36	6	6	8	25	17
FEB. 3	43	5	6	6	45	40	36	6	6	8	25	17
FEB. 4	43	7	7	8	45	41	36	6	6	8	25	17
FEB. 5	43	8	9	9	45	41	36	6	6	8	25	17
FEB. 6	43	10	10	11	46	41	36	6	6	8	25	17
FEB. 7	43	11	12	13	46	41	36	6	6	8	25	17
FEB. 8	44	13	14	14	46	41	36	6	6	8	25	17
FEB. 9	44	15	15	16	46	41	36	6	6	8	25	17
FEB. 10	44	17	17	18	46	42	36	6	6	8	25	17
FEB. 11	44	18	19	20	46	42	36	6	6	8	25	17
FEB. 12	44	20	21	22	46	42	36	6	6	8	25	17
FEB. 13	44	22	23	24	47	42	37	6	6	8	25	17
FEB. 14	44	24	25	26	47	42	37	6	6	8	25	17
FEB. 15	44	26	27	27	47	42	37	6	6	8	25	17
FEB. 16	45	28	29	29	47	43	37	6	6	8	25	17
FEB. 17	45	30	31	31	47	43	37	6	6	8	25	17
FEB. 18	45	32	33	33	47	43	37	6	6	8	25	17
FEB. 19	45	34	34	35	47	43	37	6	6	8	25	17
FEB. 20	45	36	36	37	47	43	37	6	6	8	25	17
FEB. 21	45	37	38	39	47	43	37	6	6	8	25	17
FEB. 22	45	39	40	40	47	44	37	6	6	8	25	17
FEB. 23	46	41	42	42	46	44	37	6	6	8	25	17
FEB. 24	46	43	43	44	46	44	38	6	6	8	25	17
FEB. 25	46	44	45	46	46	44	38	6	6	8	25	17
FEB. 26	46	46	47	47	46	44	38	6	6	8	25	17
FEB. 27	46	48	48	1	46	44	38	6	6	8	25	17
FEB. 28	46	1	2	2	46	45	38	6	6	8	25	17

MOON 1 ◖ 12:01 A.M. TO 8:00 A.M.   **MOON 2** ◐ 8:01 A.M. TO 4:00 P.M.   **MOON 3** ● 4:01 P.M. TO 12:00 A.M.

Use only one "moon" number. Choose the column closest to your time of birth. If your place of birth is not on Eastern Standard Time, be sure to read "How to Convert to Eastern Standard Time" at the beginning of this section.

1941

March   **April**

Date & Time	SUN	MOON 1	MOON 2	MOON 3	MERCURY	VENUS	MARS	JUPITER	SATURN	URANUS	NEPTUNE	PLUTO
MAR. 1	46	3	3	4	46	45	38	6	6	8	25	17
MAR. 2	46	4	5	6	45	45	38	6	6	8	25	17
MAR. 3	47	6	7	7	45	45	38	7	6	8	25	17
MAR. 4	47	8	8	9	45	45	38	7	6	8	25	17
MAR. 5	47	9	10	10	45	45	38	7	6	8	25	17
MAR. 6	47	11	11	12	45	45	38	7	6	8	25	17
MAR. 7	47	12	13	14	45	46	39	7	6	8	25	17
MAR. 8	47	14	15	15	45	46	39	7	6	8	25	17
MAR. 9	47	16	16	17	45	46	39	7	6	8	25	17
MAR. 10	47	18	18	19	45	46	39	7	6	8	25	17
MAR. 11	48	20	20	21	45	46	39	7	6	8	24	17
MAR. 12	48	21	22	23	45	47	39	7	6	8	24	17
MAR. 13	48	23	24	25	45	47	39	7	6	8	24	17
MAR. 14	48	25	26	27	45	47	39	7	6	8	24	17
MAR. 15	48	27	28	29	45	47	39	7	6	8	24	17
MAR. 16	48	29	30	31	45	47	39	7	7	8	24	17
MAR. 17	48	31	32	33	45	47	39	7	7	8	24	17
MAR. 18	48	33	34	35	45	48	40	7	7	8	24	17
MAR. 19	1	35	36	36	45	48	40	7	7	8	24	17
MAR. 20	1	37	38	38	45	48	40	7	7	8	24	17
MAR. 21	1	39	39	40	45	48	40	7	7	8	24	17
MAR. 22	1	41	41	42	45	48	40	7	7	8	24	17
MAR. 23	1	42	43	43	46	48	40	7	7	8	24	17
MAR. 24	1	44	45	45	46	48	40	7	7	8	24	17
MAR. 25	2	46	46	47	46	1	40	7	7	8	24	17
MAR. 26	2	47	48	48	46	1	40	7	7	8	24	17
MAR. 27	2	1	1	2	46	1	40	7	7	8	24	17
MAR. 28	2	2	3	4	46	1	40	7	7	8	24	17
MAR. 29	2	4	5	5	46	1	41	7	7	8	24	17
MAR. 30	2	6	6	7	47	1	41	7	7	8	24	17
MAR. 31	2	7	8	8	47	2	41	7	7	8	24	17

Date & Time	SUN	MOON 1	MOON 2	MOON 3	MERCURY	VENUS	MARS	JUPITER	SATURN	URANUS	NEPTUNE	PLUTO
APR. 1	2	9	9	10	47	2	41	7	7	8	24	17
APR. 2	2	10	11	11	47	2	41	7	7	8	24	17
APR. 3	3	12	13	13	47	2	41	7	7	8	24	17
APR. 4	3	14	14	15	47	2	41	7	7	8	24	17
APR. 5	3	15	16	16	48	2	41	7	7	8	24	17
APR. 6	3	17	18	18	48	3	41	7	7	8	24	17
APR. 7	3	19	19	20	48	3	41	7	7	8	24	17
APR. 8	3	21	21	22	48	3	41	7	7	8	24	17
APR. 9	3	23	23	24	48	3	42	8	7	8	24	17
APR. 10	3	24	25	26	1	3	42	8	7	8	24	17
APR. 11	4	26	27	28	1	3	42	8	7	8	24	17
APR. 12	4	28	29	30	1	4	42	8	7	8	24	17
APR. 13	4	31	31	32	1	4	42	8	7	8	24	17
APR. 14	4	33	33	34	1	4	42	8	7	8	24	17
APR. 15	4	35	35	36	2	4	42	8	7	8	24	17
APR. 16	4	36	37	38	2	4	42	8	7	8	24	17
APR. 17	4	38	39	40	2	4	42	8	7	8	24	17
APR. 18	4	40	41	41	2	5	42	8	7	8	24	17
APR. 19	5	42	42	43	3	5	43	8	7	8	24	17
APR. 20	5	44	44	45	3	5	43	8	7	8	24	17
APR. 21	5	45	46	46	3	5	43	8	7	8	24	17
APR. 22	5	47	47	48	3	5	43	8	7	8	24	17
APR. 23	5	48	1	2	3	5	43	8	7	8	24	17
APR. 24	5	2	3	3	4	6	43	8	7	8	24	17
APR. 25	6	4	4	5	4	6	43	8	7	8	24	17
APR. 26	6	5	6	6	4	6	43	8	7	8	24	17
APR. 27	6	7	7	8	4	6	43	8	7	8	24	17
APR. 28	6	8	9	9	4	6	43	8	7	8	24	17
APR. 29	6	10	10	11	5	6	43	8	7	8	24	17
APR. 30	6	12	12	13	5	7	44	8	7	8	24	17

MOON 1 ☽ 12:01 A.M. TO 8:00 A.M.   **MOON 2** ☽ 8:01 A.M. TO 4:00 P.M.   **MOON 3** ● 4:01 P.M. TO 12:00 A.M.

Use only one "moon" number. Choose the column closest to your time of birth. If your place of birth is not on Eastern Standard Time, be sure to read "How to Convert to Eastern Standard Time" at the beginning of this section.

1941

May

June

Date & Time	SUN	MOON 1	MOON 2	MOON 3	MERCURY	VENUS	MARS	JUPITER	SATURN	URANUS	NEPTUNE	PLUTO
MAY 1	6	13	14	14	6	7	44	8	7	8	24	17
MAY 2	6	15	15	16	6	7	44	8	7	8	24	17
MAY 3	7	17	17	18	6	7	44	8	7	8	24	17
MAY 4	7	18	19	19	6	7	44	8	7	8	24	17
MAY 5	7	20	21	21	7	7	44	8	7	8	24	17
MAY 6	7	22	22	23	7	8	44	8	7	8	24	17
MAY 7	7	24	24	25	7	8	44	8	7	8	24	17
MAY 8	7	26	26	27	8	8	44	8	7	8	24	17
MAY 9	7	28	28	29	8	8	44	8	7	8	24	17
MAY 10	7	30	30	31	8	8	44	8	7	8	24	17
MAY 11	8	32	32	33	8	8	45	8	7	8	24	17
MAY 12	8	34	34	35	9	9	45	9	7	8	24	17
MAY 13	8	36	36	37	9	9	45	9	7	8	24	17
MAY 14	8	38	38	39	9	9	45	9	7	8	24	17
MAY 15	8	39	40	41	10	9	45	9	7	8	24	17
MAY 16	8	41	42	43	10	9	45	9	7	8	24	17
MAY 17	8	43	44	44	10	9	45	9	8	8	24	17
MAY 18	8	45	45	46	10	10	45	9	8	8	24	17
MAY 19	9	46	47	48	11	10	45	9	8	8	24	17
MAY 20	9	48	1	1	11	10	45	9	8	8	24	17
MAY 21	9	2	2	3	11	10	45	9	8	8	24	17
MAY 22	9	3	4	4	11	10	46	9	8	8	24	17
MAY 23	9	5	5	6	12	10	46	9	8	9	24	17
MAY 24	9	6	7	7	12	11	46	9	8	9	24	17
MAY 25	10	8	8	9	12	11	46	9	8	9	24	17
MAY 26	10	10	10	11	12	11	46	9	8	9	24	17
MAY 27	10	11	12	12	13	11	46	9	8	9	24	17
MAY 28	10	13	13	14	13	11	46	9	8	9	24	17
MAY 29	10	14	15	16	13	11	46	9	8	9	24	17
MAY 30	10	16	17	17	13	12	46	9	8	9	24	17
MAY 31	10	18	18	19	13	12	46	9	8	9	24	17

Date & Time	SUN	MOON 1	MOON 2	MOON 3	MERCURY	VENUS	MARS	JUPITER	SATURN	URANUS	NEPTUNE	PLUTO
JUN. 1	10	20	20	21	13	12	46	9	8	9	24	17
JUN. 2	10	21	22	22	14	12	46	9	8	9	24	17
JUN. 3	11	23	24	24	14	12	47	9	8	9	24	17
JUN. 4	11	25	26	26	14	12	47	9	8	9	24	17
JUN. 5	11	27	27	28	14	13	47	9	8	9	24	17
JUN. 6	11	29	29	30	14	13	47	9	8	9	24	17
JUN. 7	11	31	31	32	14	13	47	9	8	9	24	17
JUN. 8	11	33	33	34	14	13	47	9	8	9	24	17
JUN. 9	11	35	35	36	14	13	47	9	8	9	24	17
JUN. 10	11	37	37	38	15	13	47	9	8	9	24	17
JUN. 11	12	39	39	40	15	13	47	9	8	9	24	17
JUN. 12	12	41	41	42	15	14	47	9	8	9	24	17
JUN. 13	12	42	43	44	15	14	47	10	8	9	24	17
JUN. 14	12	44	45	45	15	14	48	10	8	9	24	17
JUN. 15	12	46	46	47	15	14	48	10	8	9	24	17
JUN. 16	12	48	48	1	15	14	48	10	8	9	24	17
JUN. 17	12	1	2	2	15	14	48	10	8	9	24	17
JUN. 18	12	3	3	4	15	15	48	10	8	9	24	17
JUN. 19	13	4	5	5	15	15	48	10	8	9	24	17
JUN. 20	13	6	6	7	15	15	48	10	8	9	24	17
JUN. 21	13	8	8	9	15	15	48	10	8	9	24	17
JUN. 22	13	9	10	10	15	15	48	10	8	9	24	17
JUN. 23	13	11	11	12	15	15	48	10	8	9	24	17
JUN. 24	13	12	13	13	15	16	48	10	8	9	24	17
JUN. 25	14	14	15	15	15	16	48	10	8	9	24	17
JUN. 26	14	16	16	17	15	16	48	10	8	9	24	17
JUN. 27	14	17	18	19	15	16	1	10	8	9	24	17
JUN. 28	14	19	20	20	15	16	1	10	8	9	24	17
JUN. 29	14	21	21	22	15	16	1	10	8	9	24	17
JUN. 30	14	23	23	24	15	17	1	10	8	9	24	17

MOON 1 ◐ 12:01 A.M. TO 8:00 A.M.　**MOON 2** ◑ 8:01 A.M. TO 4:00 P.M.　**MOON 3** ● 4:01 P.M. TO 12:00 A.M.

Use only one "moon" number. Choose the column closest to your time of birth. If your place of birth is not on Eastern Standard Time, be sure to read "How to Convert to Eastern Standard Time" at the beginning of this section.

1941

July   August

Date & Time	SUN	MOON 1	MOON 2	MOON 3	MERCURY	VENUS	MARS	JUPITER	SATURN	URANUS	NEPTUNE	PLUTO
JUL. 1	14	24	25	26	15	17	1	10	8	9	24	17
JUL. 2	14	26	27	28	14	17	1	10	8	9	24	17
JUL. 3	15	28	29	29	14	17	1	10	8	9	24	17
JUL. 4	15	30	31	31	14	17	1	10	8	9	24	17
JUL. 5	15	32	33	33	14	17	1	10	8	9	24	17
JUL. 6	15	34	35	35	14	18	1	10	8	9	24	17
JUL. 7	15	36	37	37	14	18	1	10	8	9	24	17
JUL. 8	15	38	39	39	14	18	1	10	8	9	24	17
JUL. 9	15	40	40	41	14	18	1	10	8	9	24	17
JUL. 10	15	42	42	43	14	18	2	10	8	9	24	17
JUL. 11	16	44	44	45	14	18	2	10	8	9	24	17
JUL. 12	16	45	46	46	14	18	2	10	8	9	24	17
JUL. 13	16	47	48	48	14	19	2	10	8	9	24	17
JUL. 14	16	1	1	2	14	19	2	10	8	9	24	17
JUL. 15	16	2	3	3	14	19	2	10	8	9	24	17
JUL. 16	16	4	4	5	14	19	2	10	8	9	24	17
JUL. 17	16	5	6	7	14	19	2	11	8	9	24	17
JUL. 18	16	7	8	8	14	20	2	11	8	9	24	17
JUL. 19	17	9	9	10	14	20	2	11	8	9	24	17
JUL. 20	17	10	11	11	14	20	2	11	8	9	24	17
JUL. 21	17	12	12	13	14	20	2	11	8	9	24	17
JUL. 22	17	14	14	15	14	20	2	11	8	9	24	17
JUL. 23	17	15	16	16	14	20	2	11	8	9	24	17
JUL. 24	17	17	17	18	14	20	3	11	9	9	24	17
JUL. 25	17	19	19	20	15	21	3	11	9	9	24	17
JUL. 26	18	20	21	22	15	21	3	11	9	9	24	17
JUL. 27	18	22	23	23	15	21	3	11	9	9	24	17
JUL. 28	18	24	25	25	15	21	3	11	9	9	24	17
JUL. 29	18	26	27	27	15	21	3	11	9	9	24	17
JUL. 30	18	28	28	29	15	21	3	11	9	9	24	17
JUL. 31	18	30	30	31	16	22	3	11	9	9	24	18

Date & Time	SUN	MOON 1	MOON 2	MOON 3	MERCURY	VENUS	MARS	JUPITER	SATURN	URANUS	NEPTUNE	PLUTO
AUG. 1	18	32	32	33	16	22	3	11	9	9	24	18
AUG. 2	18	33	34	35	16	22	3	11	9	9	24	18
AUG. 3	19	35	36	37	16	22	3	11	9	9	24	18
AUG. 4	19	37	38	39	16	22	3	11	9	9	24	18
AUG. 5	19	39	40	40	17	22	3	11	9	9	24	18
AUG. 6	19	41	42	42	17	23	3	11	9	9	24	18
AUG. 7	19	43	43	44	17	23	3	11	9	9	24	18
AUG. 8	19	45	45	46	17	23	3	11	9	9	24	18
AUG. 9	19	46	47	47	18	23	3	11	9	9	24	18
AUG. 10	19	48	1	1	18	23	3	11	9	9	24	18
AUG. 11	20	2	2	3	18	23	4	11	9	9	24	18
AUG. 12	20	3	4	4	19	24	4	11	9	9	24	18
AUG. 13	20	5	5	6	19	24	4	11	9	9	24	18
AUG. 14	20	7	7	8	19	24	4	11	9	9	24	18
AUG. 15	20	8	9	9	19	24	4	11	9	9	24	18
AUG. 16	20	10	10	11	20	24	4	11	9	9	24	18
AUG. 17	20	11	12	12	20	24	4	11	9	9	24	18
AUG. 18	20	13	13	14	20	25	4	11	9	9	24	18
AUG. 19	21	15	15	16	20	25	4	11	9	9	24	18
AUG. 20	21	16	17	17	21	25	4	11	9	9	24	18
AUG. 21	21	18	19	19	21	25	4	11	9	9	24	18
AUG. 22	21	20	20	21	21	25	4	11	9	9	24	18
AUG. 23	21	22	22	23	22	25	4	11	9	9	24	18
AUG. 24	21	24	24	25	22	25	4	11	9	9	24	18
AUG. 25	21	25	26	27	22	26	4	11	9	9	24	18
AUG. 26	22	27	28	29	22	26	4	11	9	9	25	18
AUG. 27	22	29	30	30	22	26	4	11	9	9	25	18
AUG. 28	22	31	32	32	23	26	4	11	9	9	25	18
AUG. 29	22	33	34	34	23	26	4	11	9	9	25	18
AUG. 30	22	35	36	36	23	26	4	11	9	9	25	18
AUG. 31	22	37	37	38	23	27	4	11	9	9	25	18

MOON 1 ☽ 12:01 A.M. TO 8:00 A.M.   **MOON 2** ☽ 8:01 A.M. TO 4:00 P.M.   **MOON 3** ● 4:01 P.M. TO 12:00 A.M.
Use only one "moon" number. Choose the column closest to your time of birth. If your place of birth is not on Eastern Standard Time, be sure to read "How to Convert to Eastern Standard Time" at the beginning of this section.

1941

September   October

Date & Time	SUN	MOON 1	MOON 2	MOON 3	MERCURY	VENUS	MARS	JUPITER	SATURN	URANUS	NEPTUNE	PLUTO
SEP. 1	22	39	39	40	24	27	4	12	9	9	25	18
SEP. 2	22	40	41	42	24	27	4	12	9	9	25	18
SEP. 3	23	42	43	43	24	27	4	12	9	9	25	18
SEP. 4	23	44	45	45	24	27	4	12	9	9	25	18
SEP. 5	23	46	46	47	25	27	4	12	9	9	25	18
SEP. 6	23	47	48	1	25	28	4	12	9	9	25	18
SEP. 7	23	1	2	2	25	28	4	12	9	9	25	18
SEP. 8	23	3	3	4	25	28	4	12	9	9	25	18
SEP. 9	23	4	5	5	25	28	4	12	9	9	25	18
SEP. 10	23	6	7	7	26	28	4	12	9	9	25	18
SEP. 11	24	8	8	9	26	28	4	12	9	9	25	18
SEP. 12	24	9	10	10	26	28	4	12	9	9	25	18
SEP. 13	24	11	11	12	26	29	4	12	9	9	25	18
SEP. 14	24	12	13	13	26	29	4	12	9	9	25	18
SEP. 15	24	14	15	15	27	29	4	12	9	9	25	18
SEP. 16	24	16	16	17	27	29	4	12	9	9	25	18
SEP. 17	24	17	18	19	27	29	4	12	9	9	25	18
SEP. 18	24	19	20	20	27	29	4	12	9	9	25	18
SEP. 19	25	21	22	22	27	30	4	12	9	9	25	18
SEP. 20	25	23	23	24	28	30	4	12	9	9	25	18
SEP. 21	25	25	25	26	28	30	4	12	9	9	25	18
SEP. 22	25	27	27	28	28	30	4	12	9	9	25	18
SEP. 23	25	29	29	30	28	30	4	12	9	9	25	18
SEP. 24	25	31	31	32	28	30	4	12	9	9	25	18
SEP. 25	26	33	33	34	28	31	4	12	9	9	25	18
SEP. 26	26	34	35	36	29	31	4	12	9	9	25	18
SEP. 27	26	36	37	38	29	31	4	12	9	9	25	18
SEP. 28	26	38	39	39	29	31	4	12	9	9	25	18
SEP. 29	26	40	41	41	29	31	4	12	9	9	25	18
SEP. 30	26	42	42	43	29	31	4	12	9	9	25	18

Date & Time	SUN	MOON 1	MOON 2	MOON 3	MERCURY	VENUS	MARS	JUPITER	SATURN	URANUS	NEPTUNE	PLUTO
OCT. 1	26	44	44	45	29	31	4	12	9	9	25	18
OCT. 2	26	45	46	46	30	32	4	12	9	9	25	18
OCT. 3	27	47	48	48	30	32	4	12	9	9	25	18
OCT. 4	27	1	1	2	30	32	3	12	9	9	25	18
OCT. 5	27	2	3	3	30	32	3	12	9	9	25	18
OCT. 6	27	4	4	5	30	32	3	12	9	9	25	18
OCT. 7	27	6	6	7	30	32	3	12	9	9	25	18
OCT. 8	27	7	8	8	30	33	3	12	9	9	25	18
OCT. 9	27	9	9	10	30	33	3	12	9	9	25	18
OCT. 10	27	10	11	11	30	33	3	12	9	9	25	18
OCT. 11	28	12	12	13	30	33	3	12	9	9	25	18
OCT. 12	28	13	14	15	31	33	3	12	9	9	25	18
OCT. 13	28	15	16	16	31	33	3	12	9	9	25	18
OCT. 14	28	17	17	18	31	33	3	12	9	9	25	18
OCT. 15	28	18	19	20	31	34	3	12	9	9	25	18
OCT. 16	28	20	21	21	31	34	3	12	9	9	25	18
OCT. 17	28	22	23	23	31	34	3	12	9	9	25	18
OCT. 18	28	24	24	25	31	34	3	12	9	9	25	18
OCT. 19	29	26	26	27	30	34	3	12	9	9	25	18
OCT. 20	29	28	28	29	30	34	3	12	9	9	25	18
OCT. 21	29	30	30	31	30	35	3	12	9	9	25	18
OCT. 22	29	32	32	33	30	35	3	12	9	9	25	18
OCT. 23	29	34	34	35	30	35	3	12	9	9	25	18
OCT. 24	29	36	36	37	30	35	3	12	9	9	25	18
OCT. 25	29	38	38	39	30	35	3	12	9	9	25	18
OCT. 26	30	40	40	41	30	35	3	12	9	9	25	18
OCT. 27	30	41	42	43	29	35	3	12	9	9	25	18
OCT. 28	30	43	44	44	29	36	3	12	9	9	25	18
OCT. 29	30	45	45	46	29	36	3	12	9	9	25	18
OCT. 30	30	47	47	48	29	36	3	12	9	9	25	18
OCT. 31	30	48	1	1	29	36	3	12	8	9	25	18

MOON 1 ☽ 12:01 A.M. TO 8:00 A.M.   **MOON 2** ◑ 8:01 A.M. TO 4:00 P.M.   **MOON 3** ● 4:01 P.M. TO 12:00 A.M.
Use only one "moon" number. Choose the column closest to your time of birth. If your place of birth is not on Eastern Standard Time, be sure to read "How to Convert to Eastern Standard Time" at the beginning of this section.

1941

November

Date & Time	SUN	MOON 1	MOON 2	MOON 3	MERCURY	VENUS	MARS	JUPITER	SATURN	URANUS	NEPTUNE	PLUTO
NOV. 1	30	2	2	3	29	36	3	12	8	9	25	18
NOV. 2	30	3	4	5	29	36	3	12	8	9	25	18
NOV. 3	31	5	6	6	29	36	2	12	8	9	25	18
NOV. 4	31	7	7	8	28	37	2	12	8	9	25	18
NOV. 5	31	8	9	9	28	37	2	12	8	9	25	18
NOV. 6	31	10	10	11	28	37	2	12	8	9	25	18
NOV. 7	31	11	12	12	29	37	2	12	8	9	25	18
NOV. 8	31	13	14	14	29	37	2	12	8	9	25	18
NOV. 9	31	15	15	16	29	37	2	12	8	9	25	18
NOV. 10	31	16	17	17	29	38	2	12	8	9	25	18
NOV. 11	31	18	18	19	29	38	2	12	8	9	25	18
NOV. 12	32	20	20	21	29	38	2	12	8	9	25	18
NOV. 13	32	21	22	22	29	38	2	12	8	9	25	18
NOV. 14	32	23	24	24	29	38	2	12	8	9	25	18
NOV. 15	32	25	26	26	29	38	2	12	8	9	25	18
NOV. 16	32	27	28	28	30	38	2	12	8	9	25	18
NOV. 17	32	29	29	30	30	39	2	12	8	9	25	18
NOV. 18	32	31	32	32	30	39	2	12	8	9	25	18
NOV. 19	33	33	34	34	30	39	3	11	8	9	25	18
NOV. 20	33	35	36	36	30	39	3	11	8	9	25	18
NOV. 21	33	37	38	38	31	39	3	11	8	9	25	18
NOV. 22	33	39	40	40	31	39	3	11	8	9	25	18
NOV. 23	33	41	41	42	31	39	3	11	8	9	25	18
NOV. 24	33	43	43	44	31	39	3	11	8	9	25	18
NOV. 25	34	44	45	46	31	40	3	11	8	9	25	18
NOV. 26	34	46	47	47	32	40	3	11	8	9	25	18
NOV. 27	34	48	48	1	32	40	3	11	8	9	25	18
NOV. 28	34	1	2	3	32	40	3	11	8	9	25	18
NOV. 29	34	3	4	4	32	40	3	11	8	9	25	18
NOV. 30	34	5	5	6	32	40	3	11	8	9	25	18

December

Date & Time	SUN	MOON 1	MOON 2	MOON 3	MERCURY	VENUS	MARS	JUPITER	SATURN	URANUS	NEPTUNE	PLUTO
DEC. 1	34	6	7	7	33	40	3	11	8	9	25	18
DEC. 2	34	8	8	9	33	41	3	11	8	9	25	18
DEC. 3	35	9	10	10	33	41	3	11	8	9	25	18
DEC. 4	35	11	12	12	33	41	3	11	8	9	25	18
DEC. 5	35	13	13	14	33	41	3	11	8	9	25	18
DEC. 6	35	14	15	15	34	41	3	11	8	9	25	18
DEC. 7	35	16	16	17	34	41	3	11	8	9	25	18
DEC. 8	35	17	18	19	34	41	3	11	8	9	25	18
DEC. 9	35	19	20	20	34	41	3	11	8	9	25	18
DEC. 10	35	21	21	22	34	41	3	11	8	9	25	18
DEC. 11	36	23	23	24	35	42	3	11	8	9	25	18
DEC. 12	36	24	25	26	35	42	3	11	8	9	25	18
DEC. 13	36	26	27	27	35	42	3	11	8	9	25	18
DEC. 14	36	28	29	29	35	42	3	11	8	9	25	18
DEC. 15	36	30	31	31	36	42	3	11	8	9	25	18
DEC. 16	36	32	33	33	36	42	3	11	8	9	25	18
DEC. 17	36	34	35	35	36	42	3	11	8	9	25	18
DEC. 18	36	36	37	37	36	42	4	11	8	9	25	18
DEC. 19	37	38	39	39	36	42	4	11	8	9	25	18
DEC. 20	37	40	41	41	37	43	4	11	8	9	25	18
DEC. 21	37	42	43	43	37	43	4	11	8	9	25	18
DEC. 22	37	44	44	45	37	43	4	11	8	9	25	18
DEC. 23	37	46	46	47	37	43	4	11	8	9	25	18
DEC. 24	37	47	48	48	37	43	4	11	8	9	25	18
DEC. 25	37	1	2	2	38	43	4	11	8	9	25	18
DEC. 26	38	3	3	4	38	43	4	11	8	9	25	18
DEC. 27	38	4	5	5	38	43	4	11	8	9	25	18
DEC. 28	38	6	6	7	38	43	4	11	8	9	25	18
DEC. 29	38	7	8	8	38	43	4	11	8	9	25	18
DEC. 30	38	9	10	10	39	43	4	11	8	9	25	18
DEC. 31	38	11	11	12	39	43	4	11	8	9	25	18

MOON 1 ☽ 12:01 A.M. TO 8:00 A.M.　　**MOON 2** ☽ 8:01 A.M. TO 4:00 P.M.　　**MOON 3** ● 4:01 P.M. TO 12:00 A.M.

Use only one "moon" number. Choose the column closest to your time of birth. If your place of birth is not on Eastern Standard Time, be sure to read "How to Convert to Eastern Standard Time" at the beginning of this section.

1942

January

Date & Time	SUN	MOON 1	MOON 2	MOON 3	MERCURY	VENUS	MARS	JUPITER	SATURN	URANUS	NEPTUNE	PLUTO
JAN. 1	38	12	13	13	39	43	4	11	8	9	25	18
JAN. 2	38	14	14	15	39	43	4	11	8	9	25	18
JAN. 3	39	15	16	17	40	44	4	11	8	9	25	18
JAN. 4	39	17	18	18	40	44	4	11	8	9	25	18
JAN. 5	39	19	19	20	40	44	5	11	8	9	25	18
JAN. 6	39	20	21	22	40	44	5	11	8	9	25	18
JAN. 7	39	22	23	23	40	44	5	11	8	9	25	18
JAN. 8	39	24	24	25	41	44	5	11	8	9	25	18
JAN. 9	39	26	26	27	41	44	5	11	8	9	25	18
JAN. 10	40	27	28	29	41	44	5	11	8	9	25	18
JAN. 11	40	29	30	31	41	44	5	11	8	9	25	18
JAN. 12	40	31	32	33	42	44	5	11	8	9	25	18
JAN. 13	40	33	34	34	42	44	5	11	8	9	25	18
JAN. 14	40	35	36	36	42	44	5	11	8	9	25	18
JAN. 15	40	37	38	38	42	44	5	11	8	9	25	18
JAN. 16	40	39	40	40	42	44	5	11	8	8	25	18
JAN. 17	41	41	42	42	43	44	5	11	8	8	25	18
JAN. 18	41	43	44	44	43	44	5	11	8	8	25	18
JAN. 19	41	45	45	46	43	44	5	11	8	8	25	18
JAN. 20	41	47	47	48	43	44	6	11	8	8	25	18
JAN. 21	41	48	1	2	43	44	6	11	8	8	25	18
JAN. 22	41	2	3	3	44	44	6	11	8	8	25	18
JAN. 23	42	4	5	5	44	44	6	11	8	8	25	18
JAN. 24	42	5	6	6	44	44	6	11	8	8	25	18
JAN. 25	42	7	7	8	44	43	6	11	8	8	25	18
JAN. 26	42	9	9	10	44	43	6	11	8	8	25	18
JAN. 27	42	10	11	11	44	43	6	11	8	8	25	18
JAN. 28	42	12	12	13	44	43	6	10	8	8	25	18
JAN. 29	42	13	14	14	44	43	6	10	8	8	25	18
JAN. 30	42	15	15	16	45	43	6	10	8	8	25	18
JAN. 31	43	17	17	18	45	43	6	10	8	8	25	18

February

Date & Time	SUN	MOON 1	MOON 2	MOON 3	MERCURY	VENUS	MARS	JUPITER	SATURN	URANUS	NEPTUNE	PLUTO
FEB. 1	43	18	19	19	45	43	6	10	8	8	25	18
FEB. 2	43	20	21	21	45	43	6	10	8	8	25	18
FEB. 3	43	22	22	23	45	43	7	10	8	8	25	18
FEB. 4	43	23	24	25	44	43	7	10	8	8	25	18
FEB. 5	43	25	26	26	44	43	7	10	8	8	25	18
FEB. 6	43	27	28	28	44	42	7	10	8	8	25	18
FEB. 7	43	29	30	30	44	42	7	10	8	8	25	18
FEB. 8	44	31	31	32	44	42	7	10	8	8	25	18
FEB. 9	44	33	33	34	44	42	7	10	8	8	25	18
FEB. 10	44	35	35	36	44	42	7	10	8	8	25	18
FEB. 11	44	36	37	38	44	42	7	10	8	8	25	18
FEB. 12	44	38	39	40	43	42	7	10	8	8	25	18
FEB. 13	44	40	41	42	43	42	7	10	8	8	25	18
FEB. 14	44	42	43	43	43	42	7	11	8	8	25	18
FEB. 15	44	44	45	45	43	42	7	11	8	8	25	18
FEB. 16	45	46	46	47	43	42	7	11	8	8	25	18
FEB. 17	45	48	48	1	43	42	8	11	8	8	25	18
FEB. 18	45	1	2	3	43	42	8	11	8	8	25	18
FEB. 19	45	3	4	4	43	42	8	11	8	8	25	18
FEB. 20	45	5	5	6	43	42	8	11	8	8	25	18
FEB. 21	45	6	7	7	43	42	8	11	8	8	25	18
FEB. 22	45	8	9	9	43	42	8	11	8	9	25	18
FEB. 23	46	10	10	11	43	42	8	11	8	9	25	18
FEB. 24	46	11	12	12	43	42	8	11	8	9	25	17
FEB. 25	46	13	13	14	43	42	8	11	8	9	25	17
FEB. 26	46	14	15	15	43	42	8	11	8	9	25	17
FEB. 27	46	16	17	17	43	42	8	11	8	9	25	17
FEB. 28	46	18	18	19	43	42	8	11	8	9	25	17

MOON 1 ◐ 12:01 A.M. TO 8:00 A.M.　　**MOON 2** ◑ 8:01 A.M. TO 4:00 P.M.　　**MOON 3** ● 4:01 P.M. TO 12:00 A.M.
Use only one "moon" number. Choose the column closest to your time of birth. If your place of birth is not on Eastern Standard Time, be sure to read "How to Convert to Eastern Standard Time" at the beginning of this section.

March

Date & Time	SUN	MOON 1	MOON 2	MOON 3	MERCURY	VENUS	MARS	JUPITER	SATURN	URANUS	NEPTUNE	PLUTO
MAR. 1	46	19	20	21	43	42	8	11	8	9	25	17
MAR. 2	46	21	22	22	43	42	9	11	8	9	25	17
MAR. 3	47	23	23	24	43	42	9	11	8	9	25	17
MAR. 4	47	25	25	26	43	42	9	11	8	9	25	17
MAR. 5	47	27	27	28	43	42	9	11	8	9	25	17
MAR. 6	47	28	29	30	43	42	9	11	8	9	25	17
MAR. 7	47	30	31	32	43	42	9	11	8	9	25	17
MAR. 8	47	32	33	33	44	42	9	11	8	9	25	17
MAR. 9	47	34	35	35	44	42	9	11	8	9	25	17
MAR. 10	47	36	37	37	44	42	9	11	8	9	25	17
MAR. 11	48	38	39	39	44	42	9	11	8	9	25	17
MAR. 12	48	40	40	41	44	42	9	11	8	9	25	17
MAR. 13	48	42	42	43	44	42	9	11	8	9	25	17
MAR. 14	48	43	44	45	44	43	10	11	8	9	25	17
MAR. 15	48	45	46	46	45	43	10	11	8	9	25	17
MAR. 16	48	47	48	48	45	43	10	11	8	9	25	17
MAR. 17	48	1	1	2	45	43	10	11	8	9	25	17
MAR. 18	48	2	3	4	45	43	10	11	8	9	25	17
MAR. 19	1	4	5	5	45	43	10	11	8	9	25	17
MAR. 20	1	6	6	7	46	43	10	11	8	9	25	17
MAR. 21	1	7	8	9	46	43	10	11	8	9	25	17
MAR. 22	1	9	10	10	46	43	10	11	8	9	25	17
MAR. 23	1	11	11	12	46	43	10	11	8	9	25	17
MAR. 24	1	12	13	13	46	43	10	11	8	9	25	17
MAR. 25	2	14	14	15	47	44	10	11	8	9	25	17
MAR. 26	2	15	16	16	47	44	10	11	8	9	25	17
MAR. 27	2	17	18	18	47	44	11	11	8	9	25	17
MAR. 28	2	19	19	20	47	44	11	11	8	9	25	17
MAR. 29	2	20	21	22	47	44	11	11	8	9	25	17
MAR. 30	2	22	23	23	48	44	11	11	8	9	25	17
MAR. 31	2	24	25	25	48	44	11	11	8	9	25	17

April

Date & Time	SUN	MOON 1	MOON 2	MOON 3	MERCURY	VENUS	MARS	JUPITER	SATURN	URANUS	NEPTUNE	PLUTO
APR. 1	2	26	26	27	48	44	11	11	8	9	25	17
APR. 2	2	28	28	29	48	44	11	11	8	9	25	17
APR. 3	3	30	30	31	48	45	11	11	8	9	25	17
APR. 4	3	32	32	33	1	45	11	11	8	9	25	17
APR. 5	3	34	34	35	1	45	11	11	8	9	25	17
APR. 6	3	36	36	37	1	45	11	11	8	9	25	17
APR. 7	3	37	38	39	1	45	11	11	8	9	25	17
APR. 8	3	39	40	41	2	45	12	11	8	9	25	17
APR. 9	3	41	42	42	2	45	12	11	8	9	25	17
APR. 10	3	43	44	44	2	45	12	11	9	9	25	17
APR. 11	4	45	45	46	2	46	12	11	9	9	25	17
APR. 12	4	47	47	48	3	46	12	11	9	9	25	17
APR. 13	4	48	1	1	3	46	12	11	9	9	25	17
APR. 14	4	2	3	3	3	46	12	11	9	9	25	17
APR. 15	4	4	4	5	3	46	12	11	9	9	25	17
APR. 16	4	5	6	6	4	46	12	11	9	9	25	17
APR. 17	4	7	7	8	4	46	12	11	9	9	25	17
APR. 18	4	9	9	10	4	46	12	11	9	9	25	17
APR. 19	5	10	11	11	5	47	12	12	9	9	25	17
APR. 20	5	12	12	13	5	47	12	12	9	9	25	17
APR. 21	5	13	14	14	5	47	13	12	9	9	25	17
APR. 22	5	15	15	16	5	47	13	12	9	9	25	17
APR. 23	5	16	17	18	6	47	13	12	9	9	25	17
APR. 24	5	18	19	19	6	47	13	12	9	9	25	17
APR. 25	6	20	20	21	6	47	13	12	9	9	25	17
APR. 26	6	21	22	23	7	48	13	12	9	9	25	17
APR. 27	6	23	24	24	7	48	13	12	9	9	25	17
APR. 28	6	25	26	26	7	48	13	12	9	9	25	17
APR. 29	6	27	28	28	7	48	13	12	9	9	25	17
APR. 30	6	29	30	30	8	48	13	12	9	9	25	17

MOON 1 ◐ 12:01 A.M. TO 8:00 A.M.   **MOON 2** ◑ 8:01 A.M. TO 4:00 P.M.   **MOON 3** ● 4:01 P.M. TO 12:00 A.M.

Use only one "moon" number. Choose the column closest to your time of birth. If your place of birth is not on Eastern Standard Time, be sure to read "How to Convert to Eastern Standard Time" at the beginning of this section.

May

June

Date & Time	SUN	MOON 1	MOON 2	MOON 3	MERCURY	VENUS	MARS	JUPITER	SATURN	URANUS	NEPTUNE	PLUTO
MAY 1	6	31	32	32	8	48	13	12	9	9	25	17
MAY 2	6	33	34	34	8	48	13	12	9	9	25	17
MAY 3	7	35	36	36	8	1	14	12	9	9	25	17
MAY 4	7	37	38	38	9	1	14	12	9	9	25	17
MAY 5	7	39	39	40	9	1	14	12	9	9	25	17
MAY 6	7	41	41	42	9	1	14	12	9	9	25	17
MAY 7	7	43	43	44	9	1	14	12	9	9	25	17
MAY 8	7	44	45	46	10	1	14	12	9	9	25	17
MAY 9	7	46	47	47	10	1	14	12	9	9	25	17
MAY 10	7	48	48	1	10	2	14	12	9	9	25	17
MAY 11	8	2	2	3	10	2	14	12	9	9	25	17
MAY 12	8	3	4	4	10	2	14	12	9	9	25	17
MAY 13	8	5	5	6	11	2	14	12	9	9	25	17
MAY 14	8	6	7	8	11	2	14	12	9	9	25	17
MAY 15	8	8	9	9	11	2	15	12	9	9	25	17
MAY 16	8	10	10	11	11	2	15	12	9	9	25	17
MAY 17	8	11	12	12	11	3	15	12	9	9	25	17
MAY 18	8	13	13	14	11	3	15	12	9	9	25	17
MAY 19	9	14	15	15	12	3	15	12	9	9	25	17
MAY 20	9	16	17	17	12	3	15	12	9	9	25	17
MAY 21	9	18	18	19	12	3	15	12	9	9	25	17
MAY 22	9	19	20	20	12	3	15	12	9	9	25	17
MAY 23	9	21	21	22	12	3	15	12	9	9	25	17
MAY 24	9	23	23	24	12	4	15	12	9	9	25	17
MAY 25	10	24	25	26	12	4	15	12	9	9	25	17
MAY 26	10	26	27	27	12	4	15	13	9	9	25	17
MAY 27	10	28	29	29	12	4	15	13	9	9	25	17
MAY 28	10	30	31	31	12	4	16	13	9	9	25	17
MAY 29	10	32	33	33	12	4	16	13	9	9	25	17
MAY 30	10	34	35	35	12	5	16	13	9	9	25	17
MAY 31	10	36	37	37	12	5	16	13	9	9	25	17

Date & Time	SUN	MOON 1	MOON 2	MOON 3	MERCURY	VENUS	MARS	JUPITER	SATURN	URANUS	NEPTUNE	PLUTO
JUN. 1	10	38	39	39	12	5	16	13	9	9	25	17
JUN. 2	10	40	41	41	12	5	16	13	9	9	25	17
JUN. 3	11	42	43	43	12	5	16	13	9	9	25	17
JUN. 4	11	44	44	45	12	5	16	13	9	9	25	17
JUN. 5	11	46	46	47	12	5	16	13	9	9	25	17
JUN. 6	11	47	48	1	12	6	16	13	9	9	25	18
JUN. 7	11	1	2	2	12	6	16	13	9	9	25	18
JUN. 8	11	3	3	4	12	6	16	13	9	9	25	18
JUN. 9	11	4	5	6	12	6	17	13	10	9	25	18
JUN. 10	11	6	7	7	12	6	17	13	10	9	25	18
JUN. 11	12	8	9	9	12	6	17	13	10	9	25	18
JUN. 12	12	9	10	10	12	7	17	13	10	9	25	18
JUN. 13	12	11	11	12	12	7	17	13	10	9	25	18
JUN. 14	12	12	13	14	12	7	17	13	10	9	25	18
JUN. 15	12	14	15	15	12	7	17	13	10	9	25	18
JUN. 16	12	16	16	17	12	7	17	13	10	9	25	18
JUN. 17	12	17	18	18	11	7	17	13	10	9	25	18
JUN. 18	12	19	19	20	11	7	17	13	10	9	25	18
JUN. 19	13	20	21	22	11	8	17	13	10	9	25	18
JUN. 20	13	22	23	23	11	8	17	13	10	9	25	18
JUN. 21	13	24	24	25	11	8	18	13	10	9	25	18
JUN. 22	13	26	26	27	11	8	18	13	10	9	25	18
JUN. 23	13	27	28	29	11	8	18	13	10	9	25	18
JUN. 24	13	29	30	30	11	8	18	13	10	9	25	18
JUN. 25	14	31	32	32	11	9	18	13	10	9	25	18
JUN. 26	14	33	34	34	11	9	18	13	10	9	25	18
JUN. 27	14	35	36	36	11	9	18	13	10	9	25	18
JUN. 28	14	37	38	39	11	9	18	14	10	9	25	18
JUN. 29	14	39	40	41	11	9	18	14	10	9	25	18
JUN. 30	14	41	42	43	11	9	18	14	10	9	25	18

MOON 1 ◖ 12:01 A.M. TO 8:00 A.M.   **MOON 2** ◑ 8:01 A.M. TO 4:00 P.M.   **MOON 3** ● 4:01 P.M. TO 12:00 A.M.
Use only one "moon" number. Choose the column closest to your time of birth. If your place of birth is not on Eastern Standard Time, be sure to read "How to Convert to Eastern Standard Time" at the beginning of this section.

1942

July

August

Date & Time	SUN	MOON 1	MOON 2	MOON 3	MERCURY	VENUS	MARS	JUPITER	SATURN	URANUS	NEPTUNE	PLUTO
JUL. 1	14	43	44	44	11	9	18	14	10	9	25	18
JUL. 2	14	45	46	46	12	10	18	14	10	9	25	18
JUL. 3	15	47	47	48	12	10	19	14	10	9	25	18
JUL. 4	15	1	1	2	12	10	19	14	10	9	25	18
JUL. 5	15	2	3	3	12	10	19	14	10	9	25	18
JUL. 6	15	4	5	5	12	10	19	14	10	9	25	18
JUL. 7	15	6	6	7	12	10	19	14	10	9	25	18
JUL. 8	15	7	8	8	12	11	19	14	10	9	25	18
JUL. 9	15	9	9	10	12	11	19	14	10	9	25	18
JUL. 10	15	10	11	12	13	11	19	14	10	9	25	18
JUL. 11	16	12	13	13	13	11	19	14	10	9	25	18
JUL. 12	16	14	14	15	13	11	19	14	10	9	25	18
JUL. 13	16	15	16	16	13	11	19	14	10	9	25	18
JUL. 14	16	17	17	18	13	12	19	14	10	9	25	18
JUL. 15	16	18	19	20	13	12	20	14	10	9	25	18
JUL. 16	16	20	21	21	14	12	20	14	10	9	25	18
JUL. 17	16	22	22	23	14	12	20	14	10	9	25	18
JUL. 18	16	23	24	25	14	12	20	14	10	9	25	18
JUL. 19	17	25	26	26	14	12	20	14	10	9	25	18
JUL. 20	17	27	27	28	15	12	20	14	10	9	25	18
JUL. 21	17	29	29	30	15	13	20	14	10	9	25	18
JUL. 22	17	31	31	32	15	13	20	14	10	9	25	18
JUL. 23	17	32	33	34	15	13	20	14	10	9	25	18
JUL. 24	17	34	35	36	15	13	20	14	10	9	25	18
JUL. 25	17	36	37	38	16	13	20	14	10	9	25	18
JUL. 26	18	38	39	40	16	13	20	14	10	9	25	18
JUL. 27	18	40	41	42	16	14	21	14	10	9	25	18
JUL. 28	18	42	43	44	17	14	21	14	10	9	25	18
JUL. 29	18	44	45	46	17	14	21	14	10	9	25	18
JUL. 30	18	46	47	47	17	14	21	14	10	9	25	18
JUL. 31	18	48	1	1	18	14	21	14	10	9	25	18

Date & Time	SUN	MOON 1	MOON 2	MOON 3	MERCURY	VENUS	MARS	JUPITER	SATURN	URANUS	NEPTUNE	PLUTO
AUG. 1	18	2	2	3	18	14	21	15	10	9	25	18
AUG. 2	18	4	4	5	18	15	21	15	10	9	25	18
AUG. 3	19	5	6	6	18	15	21	15	10	9	25	18
AUG. 4	19	7	7	8	19	15	21	15	10	10	25	18
AUG. 5	19	8	9	10	19	15	21	15	10	10	25	18
AUG. 6	19	10	11	11	19	15	21	15	10	10	25	18
AUG. 7	19	12	12	13	19	15	21	15	10	10	25	18
AUG. 8	19	13	14	14	20	16	22	15	10	10	25	18
AUG. 9	19	15	15	16	20	16	22	15	10	10	25	18
AUG. 10	19	16	17	17	20	16	22	15	10	10	25	18
AUG. 11	20	18	19	19	20	16	22	15	10	10	25	18
AUG. 12	20	20	20	21	21	16	22	15	10	10	25	18
AUG. 13	20	21	22	22	21	16	22	15	10	10	25	18
AUG. 14	20	23	24	24	21	16	22	15	10	10	25	18
AUG. 15	20	25	25	26	21	17	22	15	10	10	25	18
AUG. 16	20	26	27	28	22	17	22	15	10	10	25	18
AUG. 17	20	28	29	29	22	17	22	15	10	10	25	18
AUG. 18	20	30	31	31	22	17	22	15	10	10	25	18
AUG. 19	21	32	33	33	22	17	22	15	10	10	25	18
AUG. 20	21	34	34	35	23	17	23	15	10	10	25	18
AUG. 21	21	36	36	37	23	18	23	15	10	10	25	18
AUG. 22	21	38	38	39	23	18	23	15	10	10	25	18
AUG. 23	21	40	40	41	23	18	23	15	11	10	25	18
AUG. 24	21	42	42	43	24	18	23	15	11	10	25	18
AUG. 25	21	43	44	45	24	18	23	15	11	10	25	18
AUG. 26	22	45	46	47	24	18	23	15	11	10	25	18
AUG. 27	22	47	48	48	24	19	23	15	11	10	25	18
AUG. 28	22	1	2	2	24	19	23	15	11	10	25	18
AUG. 29	22	3	3	4	25	19	23	15	11	10	25	18
AUG. 30	22	5	5	6	25	19	23	15	11	10	25	18
AUG. 31	22	6	7	7	25	19	23	15	11	10	25	18

MOON 1 ◐ 12:01 A.M. TO 8:00 A.M.   **MOON 2** ◑ 8:01 A.M. TO 4:00 P.M.   **MOON 3** ● 4:01 P.M. TO 12:00 A.M.

Use only one "moon" number. Choose the column closest to your time of birth. If your place of birth is not on Eastern Standard Time, be sure to read "How to Convert to Eastern Standard Time" at the beginning of this section.

Date & Time	SUN	MOON 1	MOON 2	MOON 3	MERCURY	VENUS	MARS	JUPITER	SATURN	URANUS	NEPTUNE	PLUTO
SEP. 1	22	8	8	9	25	19	24	15	11	10	25	18
SEP. 2	22	10	10	11	25	20	24	15	11	10	25	18
SEP. 3	23	11	12	12	25	20	24	15	11	10	25	18
SEP. 4	23	13	13	14	26	20	24	15	11	10	25	18
SEP. 5	23	14	15	15	26	20	24	15	11	10	25	18
SEP. 6	23	16	16	17	26	20	24	15	11	10	25	18
SEP. 7	23	17	18	19	26	20	24	15	11	10	25	18
SEP. 8	23	19	20	20	26	21	24	16	11	10	25	18
SEP. 9	23	21	21	22	27	21	24	16	11	10	25	18
SEP. 10	23	22	23	24	27	21	24	16	11	10	25	18
SEP. 11	24	24	25	25	27	21	24	16	11	10	25	18
SEP. 12	24	26	27	27	27	21	25	16	11	10	25	18
SEP. 13	24	28	28	29	27	21	25	16	11	10	25	18
SEP. 14	24	30	30	31	27	22	25	16	11	10	25	18
SEP. 15	24	31	32	33	27	22	25	16	11	10	25	18
SEP. 16	24	33	34	35	28	22	25	16	11	10	25	18
SEP. 17	24	35	36	37	28	22	25	16	11	10	25	18
SEP. 18	24	37	38	38	28	22	25	16	11	10	25	18
SEP. 19	25	39	40	40	28	22	25	16	11	10	25	18
SEP. 20	25	41	42	42	28	23	25	16	11	10	25	18
SEP. 21	25	43	43	44	28	23	25	16	11	10	25	18
SEP. 22	25	45	45	46	28	23	25	16	11	10	25	18
SEP. 23	25	47	47	48	28	23	25	16	11	10	25	18
SEP. 24	25	48	1	2	28	23	26	16	11	10	25	18
SEP. 25	26	2	3	3	28	23	26	16	11	10	25	18
SEP. 26	26	4	4	5	28	24	26	16	11	10	25	18
SEP. 27	26	6	6	7	28	24	26	16	11	10	25	18
SEP. 28	26	7	8	8	28	24	26	16	11	10	25	18
SEP. 29	26	9	10	10	28	24	26	16	11	10	25	18
SEP. 30	26	11	11	12	28	24	26	16	11	10	25	18

Date & Time	SUN	MOON 1	MOON 2	MOON 3	MERCURY	VENUS	MARS	JUPITER	SATURN	URANUS	NEPTUNE	PLUTO
OCT. 1	26	12	13	13	28	24	26	16	11	10	25	18
OCT. 2	26	14	14	15	28	25	26	16	11	10	25	18
OCT. 3	27	15	16	16	28	25	26	16	11	10	25	18
OCT. 4	27	17	17	18	28	25	26	16	11	10	25	18
OCT. 5	27	19	19	20	28	25	27	16	11	10	25	18
OCT. 6	27	20	21	21	28	25	27	16	11	10	25	18
OCT. 7	27	22	22	23	28	25	27	16	11	10	25	18
OCT. 8	27	24	24	25	28	26	27	16	11	10	25	18
OCT. 9	27	25	26	27	28	26	27	16	11	10	25	18
OCT. 10	27	27	28	28	27	26	27	16	11	10	25	18
OCT. 11	28	29	30	30	27	26	27	16	11	10	25	18
OCT. 12	28	31	32	32	27	26	27	16	11	10	25	18
OCT. 13	28	33	34	34	27	26	27	16	11	10	25	18
OCT. 14	28	35	35	36	27	27	27	16	11	10	25	18
OCT. 15	28	37	37	38	27	27	27	16	11	10	25	18
OCT. 16	28	39	39	40	27	27	28	16	11	10	25	18
OCT. 17	28	40	41	42	26	27	28	16	11	10	25	18
OCT. 18	28	42	43	44	26	27	28	16	11	10	25	18
OCT. 19	29	44	45	45	26	27	28	16	11	9	25	18
OCT. 20	29	46	47	47	26	28	28	16	11	9	25	18
OCT. 21	29	48	48	1	26	28	28	16	11	9	25	18
OCT. 22	29	2	2	3	26	28	28	16	11	9	25	18
OCT. 23	29	3	4	4	27	28	28	16	11	9	25	18
OCT. 24	29	5	6	6	27	28	28	16	11	9	25	18
OCT. 25	29	7	7	8	27	28	28	16	11	9	25	18
OCT. 26	30	8	9	9	27	29	29	16	11	9	25	18
OCT. 27	30	10	11	11	27	29	29	16	11	9	25	18
OCT. 28	30	12	12	13	27	29	29	16	11	9	25	18
OCT. 29	30	13	14	14	27	29	29	16	11	9	25	18
OCT. 30	30	15	15	16	27	29	29	16	11	9	25	18
OCT. 31	30	16	17	17	28	29	29	16	10	9	25	18

MOON 1 ◗ 12:01 A.M. TO 8:00 A.M.   **MOON 2** ◑ 8:01 A.M. TO 4:00 P.M.   **MOON 3** ● 4:01 P.M. TO 12:00 A.M.

Use only one "moon" number. Choose the column closest to your time of birth. If your place of birth is not on Eastern Standard Time, be sure to read "How to Convert to Eastern Standard Time" at the beginning of this section.

1942

November

Date & Time	SUN	MOON 1	MOON 2	MOON 3	MERCURY	VENUS	MARS	JUPITER	SATURN	URANUS	NEPTUNE	PLUTO
NOV. 1	30	18	19	19	28	30	29	16	10	9	25	18
NOV. 2	30	20	20	21	28	30	29	16	10	9	25	18
NOV. 3	31	21	22	22	28	30	29	16	10	9	25	18
NOV. 4	31	23	23	24	28	30	29	16	10	9	25	18
NOV. 5	31	25	25	26	29	30	29	16	10	9	25	18
NOV. 6	31	26	27	28	29	30	29	16	10	9	25	18
NOV. 7	31	28	29	30	29	31	29	16	10	9	25	18
NOV. 8	31	30	31	32	29	31	30	16	10	9	25	18
NOV. 9	31	32	33	33	29	31	30	16	10	9	25	18
NOV. 10	31	34	35	35	30	31	30	16	10	9	25	18
NOV. 11	31	36	37	37	30	31	30	16	10	9	25	18
NOV. 12	32	38	39	39	30	31	30	16	10	9	25	18
NOV. 13	32	40	41	41	30	32	30	16	10	9	25	18
NOV. 14	32	42	43	43	30	32	30	16	10	9	25	18
NOV. 15	32	44	44	45	31	32	30	16	10	9	25	18
NOV. 16	32	46	46	47	31	32	30	16	10	9	25	18
NOV. 17	32	47	48	1	31	32	30	16	10	9	25	18
NOV. 18	32	1	2	2	31	32	30	16	10	9	25	18
NOV. 19	33	3	3	4	32	33	31	16	10	9	25	18
NOV. 20	33	5	5	6	32	33	31	16	10	9	25	18
NOV. 21	33	6	7	7	32	33	31	16	10	9	25	18
NOV. 22	33	8	8	9	32	33	31	16	10	9	25	18
NOV. 23	33	10	10	11	32	33	31	16	10	9	25	18
NOV. 24	33	11	12	12	33	33	31	16	10	9	25	18
NOV. 25	34	13	13	14	33	34	31	16	10	9	25	18
NOV. 26	34	14	15	15	33	34	31	16	10	9	25	18
NOV. 27	34	16	16	17	33	34	31	16	10	9	25	18
NOV. 28	34	17	18	19	33	34	31	16	10	9	25	18
NOV. 29	34	19	20	20	34	34	31	16	10	9	25	18
NOV. 30	34	21	21	22	34	34	32	16	10	9	25	18

December

Date & Time	SUN	MOON 1	MOON 2	MOON 3	MERCURY	VENUS	MARS	JUPITER	SATURN	URANUS	NEPTUNE	PLUTO
DEC. 1	34	22	23	23	34	35	32	16	10	9	25	18
DEC. 2	34	24	25	25	34	35	32	16	10	9	25	18
DEC. 3	35	26	26	27	35	35	32	16	10	9	25	18
DEC. 4	35	27	28	29	35	35	32	16	10	9	25	18
DEC. 5	35	29	30	31	35	35	32	16	10	9	25	18
DEC. 6	35	31	32	33	35	35	32	16	10	9	25	18
DEC. 7	35	33	34	35	35	36	32	16	10	9	25	18
DEC. 8	35	35	36	37	36	36	32	16	10	9	25	18
DEC. 9	35	37	38	39	36	36	32	16	10	9	25	18
DEC. 10	35	39	40	41	36	36	32	16	10	9	25	18
DEC. 11	36	41	42	43	36	36	33	16	10	9	25	18
DEC. 12	36	43	44	45	36	36	33	16	10	9	25	18
DEC. 13	36	45	46	46	37	37	33	16	10	9	25	18
DEC. 14	36	47	48	48	37	37	33	16	10	9	25	18
DEC. 15	36	1	1	2	37	37	33	16	10	9	25	18
DEC. 16	36	2	3	4	37	37	33	16	10	9	25	18
DEC. 17	36	4	5	5	37	37	33	16	10	9	25	18
DEC. 18	36	6	6	7	38	37	33	16	10	9	25	18
DEC. 19	37	7	8	9	38	38	33	16	10	9	25	18
DEC. 20	37	9	10	10	38	38	33	16	10	9	25	18
DEC. 21	37	11	11	12	38	38	33	16	10	9	25	18
DEC. 22	37	12	13	13	38	38	34	16	10	9	25	18
DEC. 23	37	14	14	15	39	38	34	16	10	9	25	18
DEC. 24	37	15	16	17	39	38	34	16	10	9	25	18
DEC. 25	37	17	18	18	39	39	34	16	10	9	25	18
DEC. 26	38	19	19	20	39	39	34	16	10	9	25	18
DEC. 27	38	20	21	21	40	39	34	16	10	9	25	18
DEC. 28	38	22	22	23	40	39	34	16	10	9	25	18
DEC. 29	38	23	24	25	40	39	34	16	10	9	25	18
DEC. 30	38	25	26	26	40	39	34	16	10	9	25	18
DEC. 31	38	27	27	28	40	40	34	16	10	9	25	18

MOON 1 ◐ 12:01 A.M. TO 8:00 A.M.   **MOON 2** ◑ 8:01 A.M. TO 4:00 P.M.   **MOON 3** ● 4:01 P.M. TO 12:00 A.M.

Use only one "moon" number. Choose the column closest to your time of birth. If your place of birth is not on Eastern Standard Time, be sure to read "How to Convert to Eastern Standard Time" at the beginning of this section.

1943

January

Date & Time	SUN ☉	MOON 1 ☽	MOON 2 ☽	MOON 3 ●	MERCURY	VENUS	MARS	JUPITER	SATURN	URANUS	NEPTUNE	PLUTO
JAN. 1	38	29	29	30	41	40	35	16	10	9	25	18
JAN. 2	38	30	31	32	41	40	35	16	10	9	25	18
JAN. 3	39	32	33	34	41	40	35	16	10	9	25	18
JAN. 4	39	34	35	36	41	40	35	16	10	9	25	18
JAN. 5	39	36	37	38	41	40	35	16	10	9	25	18
JAN. 6	39	38	39	40	41	41	35	16	10	9	25	18
JAN. 7	39	40	41	42	42	41	35	16	10	9	25	18
JAN. 8	39	42	43	44	42	41	35	16	10	9	25	18
JAN. 9	39	44	45	46	42	41	35	16	10	9	25	18
JAN. 10	40	46	47	48	42	41	35	16	10	9	25	18
JAN. 11	40	48	1	1	42	41	35	16	10	9	25	18
JAN. 12	40	2	3	3	42	42	36	16	10	9	25	18
JAN. 13	40	4	4	5	42	42	36	16	10	9	25	18
JAN. 14	40	5	6	7	42	42	36	16	10	9	25	18
JAN. 15	40	7	8	8	42	42	36	16	10	9	25	18
JAN. 16	40	9	9	10	42	42	36	16	10	9	25	18
JAN. 17	41	10	11	11	42	42	36	16	10	9	25	18
JAN. 18	41	12	12	13	42	43	36	16	10	9	25	18
JAN. 19	41	14	14	15	42	43	36	16	10	9	25	18
JAN. 20	41	15	16	16	42	43	36	16	10	9	25	18
JAN. 21	41	17	17	18	42	43	36	15	10	9	25	18
JAN. 22	41	18	19	19	42	43	37	15	10	9	25	18
JAN. 23	42	20	20	21	42	43	37	15	10	9	25	18
JAN. 24	42	21	22	23	42	44	37	15	10	9	25	18
JAN. 25	42	23	24	24	41	44	37	15	10	9	25	18
JAN. 26	42	25	25	26	41	44	37	15	10	9	25	18
JAN. 27	42	26	27	27	41	44	37	15	10	9	25	18
JAN. 28	42	28	29	29	41	44	37	15	10	9	25	18
JAN. 29	42	30	30	31	41	44	37	15	10	9	25	18
JAN. 30	42	32	32	33	41	45	37	15	10	9	25	18
JAN. 31	43	34	34	35	41	45	37	15	10	9	25	18

February

Date & Time	SUN ☉	MOON 1 ☽	MOON 2 ☽	MOON 3 ●	MERCURY	VENUS	MARS	JUPITER	SATURN	URANUS	NEPTUNE	PLUTO
FEB. 1	43	35	36	37	40	45	37	15	10	9	25	18
FEB. 2	43	37	38	39	40	45	38	15	10	9	25	18
FEB. 3	43	39	40	41	40	45	38	15	10	9	25	18
FEB. 4	43	41	42	43	40	45	38	15	10	9	25	18
FEB. 5	43	43	44	45	40	46	38	15	10	9	25	18
FEB. 6	43	45	46	47	40	46	38	15	10	9	25	18
FEB. 7	43	47	48	1	40	46	38	15	10	9	25	18
FEB. 8	44	1	2	3	40	46	38	15	10	9	25	18
FEB. 9	44	3	4	4	40	46	38	15	10	9	25	18
FEB. 10	44	5	5	6	40	46	38	15	10	9	25	18
FEB. 11	44	7	7	8	41	47	38	15	10	9	25	18
FEB. 12	44	8	9	9	41	47	39	15	10	9	25	18
FEB. 13	44	10	10	11	41	47	39	15	10	9	25	18
FEB. 14	44	11	12	13	41	47	39	15	10	9	25	18
FEB. 15	44	13	14	14	41	47	39	15	10	9	25	18
FEB. 16	45	15	15	16	41	47	39	15	10	9	25	18
FEB. 17	45	16	17	17	41	48	39	15	10	9	25	18
FEB. 18	45	18	18	19	41	48	39	15	10	9	25	18
FEB. 19	45	19	20	20	41	48	39	15	10	9	25	18
FEB. 20	45	21	22	22	42	48	39	15	10	9	25	18
FEB. 21	45	23	23	24	42	48	39	15	10	9	25	18
FEB. 22	45	24	25	25	42	48	40	15	10	9	25	18
FEB. 23	46	26	27	27	42	1	40	15	10	9	25	18
FEB. 24	46	28	28	29	42	1	40	15	10	9	25	18
FEB. 25	46	29	30	31	42	1	40	15	10	9	25	18
FEB. 26	46	31	32	32	42	1	40	15	10	9	25	18
FEB. 27	46	33	34	34	43	1	40	15	10	9	25	18
FEB. 28	46	35	36	36	43	1	40	15	10	9	25	18

MOON 1 ☽ 12:01 A.M. TO 8:00 A.M.　　**MOON 2** ☽ 8:01 A.M. TO 4:00 P.M.　　**MOON 3** ● 4:01 P.M. TO 12:00 A.M.

Use only one "moon" number. Choose the column closest to your time of birth. If your place of birth is not on Eastern Standard Time, be sure to read "How to Convert to Eastern Standard Time" at the beginning of this section.

1943

March

Date & Time	SUN	MOON 1	MOON 2	MOON 3	MERCURY	VENUS	MARS	JUPITER	SATURN	URANUS	NEPTUNE	PLUTO
MAR. 1	46	37	37	38	43	2	40	15	10	9	25	18
MAR. 2	46	39	39	40	43	2	40	15	10	9	25	18
MAR. 3	47	41	41	42	43	2	40	15	10	9	25	18
MAR. 4	47	43	43	44	44	2	41	15	10	9	25	18
MAR. 5	47	45	45	46	44	2	41	15	10	9	25	18
MAR. 6	47	47	47	48	44	2	41	15	10	9	25	18
MAR. 7	47	48	1	2	44	3	41	15	10	9	25	18
MAR. 8	47	2	3	4	44	3	41	15	10	9	25	18
MAR. 9	47	4	5	5	45	3	41	15	10	9	25	18
MAR. 10	47	6	7	7	45	3	41	15	10	9	25	18
MAR. 11	48	8	9	9	45	3	41	15	10	9	25	18
MAR. 12	48	9	10	10	45	3	41	15	10	9	25	18
MAR. 13	48	11	12	12	45	4	41	15	10	9	25	18
MAR. 14	48	13	13	14	46	4	42	15	10	9	25	18
MAR. 15	48	14	15	15	46	4	42	15	10	9	25	18
MAR. 16	48	16	16	17	46	4	42	15	10	9	25	18
MAR. 17	48	17	18	18	46	4	42	15	10	9	25	18
MAR. 18	48	19	19	20	46	4	42	15	10	9	25	18
MAR. 19	1	21	21	22	47	5	42	15	10	9	25	18
MAR. 20	1	22	23	23	47	5	42	15	10	9	25	18
MAR. 21	1	24	24	25	47	5	42	15	10	9	25	18
MAR. 22	1	26	26	27	47	5	42	15	10	9	25	18
MAR. 23	1	27	28	28	48	5	42	15	10	9	25	18
MAR. 24	1	29	30	30	48	5	43	15	10	9	25	18
MAR. 25	2	31	31	32	48	5	43	15	10	9	25	18
MAR. 26	2	33	33	34	48	6	43	15	10	9	25	18
MAR. 27	2	34	35	36	1	6	43	15	10	9	25	18
MAR. 28	2	36	37	38	1	6	43	15	10	9	25	18
MAR. 29	2	38	39	39	1	6	43	15	10	9	25	18
MAR. 30	2	40	41	41	1	6	43	15	10	9	25	18
MAR. 31	2	42	43	43	2	6	43	15	10	9	25	18

April

Date & Time	SUN	MOON 1	MOON 2	MOON 3	MERCURY	VENUS	MARS	JUPITER	SATURN	URANUS	NEPTUNE	PLUTO
APR. 1	2	44	45	45	2	7	43	15	10	9	25	18
APR. 2	2	46	46	47	2	7	43	15	10	9	25	18
APR. 3	3	48	48	1	2	7	44	15	10	9	25	18
APR. 4	3	2	2	3	3	7	44	15	10	9	25	18
APR. 5	3	3	4	5	3	7	44	15	10	9	25	18
APR. 6	3	5	6	6	3	7	44	15	10	9	25	18
APR. 7	3	7	8	8	4	8	44	15	10	9	25	18
APR. 8	3	9	9	10	4	8	44	15	10	9	25	18
APR. 9	3	10	11	11	4	8	44	15	10	9	25	18
APR. 10	3	12	13	13	4	8	44	15	10	9	25	18
APR. 11	4	14	14	15	5	8	44	15	10	9	25	18
APR. 12	4	15	16	16	5	8	44	15	10	9	25	18
APR. 13	4	17	17	18	5	9	45	15	10	9	25	18
APR. 14	4	18	19	19	6	9	45	15	10	9	25	18
APR. 15	4	20	20	21	6	9	45	15	10	9	25	18
APR. 16	4	22	22	23	6	9	45	15	10	9	25	18
APR. 17	4	23	24	24	6	9	45	15	10	9	25	18
APR. 18	4	25	25	26	7	9	45	15	10	9	25	18
APR. 19	5	27	27	28	7	9	45	15	10	9	25	18
APR. 20	5	28	29	30	7	10	45	15	10	9	25	18
APR. 21	5	30	31	31	7	10	45	15	10	9	25	18
APR. 22	5	32	33	33	7	10	45	15	10	9	25	18
APR. 23	5	34	35	35	8	10	46	15	10	9	25	18
APR. 24	5	36	37	37	8	10	46	15	10	9	25	18
APR. 25	6	38	38	39	8	10	46	15	10	9	25	18
APR. 26	6	40	40	41	8	11	46	15	10	9	25	18
APR. 27	6	42	42	43	8	11	46	15	10	9	25	18
APR. 28	6	43	44	45	9	11	46	15	10	9	25	18
APR. 29	6	45	46	47	9	11	46	15	10	9	25	18
APR. 30	6	47	48	48	9	11	46	15	10	9	25	18

MOON 1 ☽ 12:01 A.M. TO 8:00 A.M. **MOON 2** ☽ 8:01 A.M. TO 4:00 P.M. **MOON 3** ● 4:01 P.M. TO 12:00 A.M.

Use only one "moon" number. Choose the column closest to your time of birth. If your place of birth is not on Eastern Standard Time, be sure to read "How to Convert to Eastern Standard Time" at the beginning of this section.

1943

May

June

Date & Time	SUN ☉	MOON 1 ◗	MOON 2 ◑	MOON 3 ●	MERCURY	VENUS	MARS	JUPITER	SATURN	URANUS	NEPTUNE	PLUTO
MAY 1	6	1	2	2	9	11	46	15	10	9	25	18
MAY 2	6	3	3	4	9	12	46	16	10	9	25	18
MAY 3	7	5	5	6	9	12	47	16	11	9	25	18
MAY 4	7	6	7	8	9	12	47	16	11	9	25	18
MAY 5	7	8	9	9	9	12	47	16	11	9	25	18
MAY 6	7	10	10	11	10	12	47	16	11	9	25	18
MAY 7	7	11	12	13	10	12	47	16	11	9	25	18
MAY 8	7	13	14	14	10	12	47	16	11	9	25	18
MAY 9	7	15	15	16	10	13	47	16	11	9	25	18
MAY 10	7	16	17	17	10	13	47	16	11	9	25	18
MAY 11	8	18	18	19	10	13	47	16	11	9	25	18
MAY 12	8	19	20	20	10	13	47	16	11	9	25	18
MAY 13	8	21	22	22	10	13	48	16	11	9	25	18
MAY 14	8	23	23	24	10	13	48	16	11	9	25	18
MAY 15	8	24	25	25	10	14	48	16	11	9	25	18
MAY 16	8	26	27	27	10	14	48	16	11	10	25	18
MAY 17	8	28	28	29	10	14	48	16	11	10	25	18
MAY 18	8	30	30	31	10	14	48	16	11	10	25	18
MAY 19	9	31	32	33	9	14	48	16	11	10	25	18
MAY 20	9	33	34	35	9	14	48	16	11	10	25	18
MAY 21	9	35	36	37	9	14	48	16	11	10	25	18
MAY 22	9	37	38	39	9	15	48	16	11	10	25	18
MAY 23	9	39	40	40	9	15	1	16	11	10	25	18
MAY 24	9	41	42	42	9	15	1	16	11	10	25	18
MAY 25	10	43	44	44	9	15	1	16	11	10	25	18
MAY 26	10	45	46	46	9	15	1	16	11	10	25	18
MAY 27	10	47	47	48	9	15	1	16	11	10	25	18
MAY 28	10	1	1	2	9	15	1	16	11	10	25	18
MAY 29	10	2	3	4	9	16	1	16	11	10	25	18
MAY 30	10	4	5	5	9	16	1	16	11	10	25	18
MAY 31	10	6	6	7	9	16	1	16	11	10	25	18

Date & Time	SUN ☉	MOON 1 ◗	MOON 2 ◑	MOON 3 ●	MERCURY	VENUS	MARS	JUPITER	SATURN	URANUS	NEPTUNE	PLUTO
JUN. 1	10	8	8	9	9	16	1	16	11	10	25	18
JUN. 2	10	9	10	10	9	16	2	16	11	10	25	18
JUN. 3	11	11	11	12	9	16	2	16	11	10	25	18
JUN. 4	11	13	13	14	9	16	2	16	11	10	25	18
JUN. 5	11	14	15	15	9	17	2	16	11	10	25	18
JUN. 6	11	16	16	17	9	17	2	16	11	10	25	18
JUN. 7	11	17	18	18	9	17	2	16	11	10	25	18
JUN. 8	11	19	19	20	9	17	2	16	11	10	25	18
JUN. 9	11	21	21	22	9	17	2	16	11	10	25	18
JUN. 10	11	22	23	23	9	17	2	16	11	10	25	18
JUN. 11	12	24	24	25	9	17	2	16	11	10	25	18
JUN. 12	12	25	26	26	9	18	3	16	11	10	25	18
JUN. 13	12	27	28	28	9	18	3	16	11	10	25	18
JUN. 14	12	29	29	30	9	18	3	17	11	10	25	18
JUN. 15	12	31	31	32	9	18	3	17	11	10	25	18
JUN. 16	12	33	33	34	9	18	3	17	11	10	25	18
JUN. 17	12	34	35	36	9	18	3	17	11	10	25	18
JUN. 18	12	36	37	38	9	18	3	17	11	10	25	18
JUN. 19	13	38	39	40	10	19	3	17	11	10	25	18
JUN. 20	13	40	41	42	10	19	3	17	11	10	25	18
JUN. 21	13	42	43	44	10	19	3	17	11	10	25	18
JUN. 22	13	44	45	46	10	19	3	17	11	10	25	18
JUN. 23	13	46	47	48	10	19	4	17	11	10	25	18
JUN. 24	13	48	1	1	10	19	4	17	11	10	25	18
JUN. 25	14	2	3	3	10	19	4	17	11	10	25	18
JUN. 26	14	4	4	5	11	20	4	17	11	10	25	18
JUN. 27	14	5	6	7	11	20	4	17	11	10	25	18
JUN. 28	14	7	8	8	11	20	4	17	11	10	25	18
JUN. 29	14	9	9	10	11	20	4	17	11	10	25	18
JUN. 30	14	11	11	12	11	20	4	17	11	10	25	18

MOON 1 ◗ 12:01 A.M. TO 8:00 A.M.   **MOON 2 ◑ 8:01 A.M. TO 4:00 P.M.**   **MOON 3 ● 4:01 P.M. TO 12:00 A.M.**

Use only one "moon" number. Choose the column closest to your time of birth. If your place of birth is not on Eastern Standard Time, be sure to read "How to Convert to Eastern Standard Time" at the beginning of this section.

1943

July

August

Date & Time	SUN	MOON 1	MOON 2	MOON 3	MERCURY	VENUS	MARS	JUPITER	SATURN	URANUS	NEPTUNE	PLUTO
JUL. 1	14	12	13	13	12	20	4	17	12	10	25	18
JUL. 2	14	14	14	15	12	20	4	17	12	10	25	18
JUL. 3	15	15	16	16	12	20	5	17	12	10	25	18
JUL. 4	15	17	17	18	12	21	5	17	12	10	25	18
JUL. 5	15	18	19	20	13	21	5	17	12	10	25	18
JUL. 6	15	20	21	21	13	21	5	17	12	10	25	18
JUL. 7	15	22	22	23	13	21	5	17	12	10	25	18
JUL. 8	15	23	24	24	13	21	5	17	12	10	25	18
JUL. 9	15	25	25	26	14	21	5	17	12	10	25	18
JUL. 10	15	26	27	28	14	21	5	17	12	10	25	18
JUL. 11	16	28	29	29	14	21	5	17	12	10	25	18
JUL. 12	16	30	31	31	15	21	5	17	12	10	25	18
JUL. 13	16	32	32	33	15	22	5	17	12	10	25	18
JUL. 14	16	34	34	35	15	22	6	17	12	10	25	18
JUL. 15	16	36	36	37	15	22	6	17	12	10	25	18
JUL. 16	16	38	38	39	16	22	6	17	12	10	25	18
JUL. 17	16	40	40	41	16	22	6	17	12	10	25	18
JUL. 18	16	42	42	43	16	22	6	17	12	10	25	18
JUL. 19	17	44	44	45	17	22	6	17	12	10	25	18
JUL. 20	17	46	46	47	17	22	6	18	12	10	25	18
JUL. 21	17	48	48	1	17	22	6	18	12	10	25	18
JUL. 22	17	1	2	3	17	22	6	18	12	10	25	18
JUL. 23	17	3	4	4	18	23	6	18	12	10	25	18
JUL. 24	17	5	6	6	18	23	6	18	12	10	25	18
JUL. 25	17	7	7	8	18	23	7	18	12	10	25	18
JUL. 26	18	8	9	10	18	23	7	18	12	10	25	18
JUL. 27	18	10	11	11	19	23	7	18	12	10	25	18
JUL. 28	18	12	12	13	19	23	7	18	12	10	25	18
JUL. 29	18	13	14	14	19	23	7	18	12	10	25	18
JUL. 30	18	15	15	16	19	23	7	18	12	10	25	18
JUL. 31	18	17	17	18	20	23	7	18	12	10	25	18

Date & Time	SUN	MOON 1	MOON 2	MOON 3	MERCURY	VENUS	MARS	JUPITER	SATURN	URANUS	NEPTUNE	PLUTO
AUG. 1	18	18	19	19	20	23	7	18	12	10	25	18
AUG. 2	18	20	20	21	20	23	7	18	12	10	25	18
AUG. 3	19	21	22	22	20	23	7	18	12	10	25	18
AUG. 4	19	23	23	24	21	23	7	18	12	10	25	18
AUG. 5	19	24	25	26	21	23	7	18	12	10	25	18
AUG. 6	19	26	27	27	21	23	8	18	12	10	25	18
AUG. 7	19	28	28	29	21	24	8	18	12	10	25	18
AUG. 8	19	29	30	31	22	24	8	18	12	10	25	18
AUG. 9	19	31	32	32	22	24	8	18	12	10	25	18
AUG. 10	19	33	34	34	22	24	8	18	12	10	25	18
AUG. 11	20	35	35	36	22	24	8	18	12	10	25	18
AUG. 12	20	37	37	38	22	24	8	18	12	10	25	18
AUG. 13	20	39	39	40	23	24	8	18	12	10	25	18
AUG. 14	20	41	41	42	23	24	8	18	12	10	25	18
AUG. 15	20	43	43	44	23	24	8	18	12	10	25	18
AUG. 16	20	45	45	46	23	24	8	18	12	10	25	18
AUG. 17	20	47	47	48	23	24	8	18	12	10	25	18
AUG. 18	20	1	1	2	24	24	9	18	12	10	25	18
AUG. 19	21	3	3	4	24	24	9	18	12	10	25	18
AUG. 20	21	4	5	6	24	24	9	18	12	10	25	18
AUG. 21	21	6	7	7	24	24	9	18	12	10	25	18
AUG. 22	21	8	9	9	24	24	9	18	12	10	25	18
AUG. 23	21	10	10	11	24	24	9	19	12	10	25	18
AUG. 24	21	11	12	12	24	24	9	19	12	10	25	18
AUG. 25	21	13	13	14	25	23	9	19	12	10	25	18
AUG. 26	22	15	15	16	25	23	9	19	12	10	25	18
AUG. 27	22	16	17	17	25	23	9	19	12	10	25	18
AUG. 28	22	18	18	19	25	23	9	19	12	10	25	18
AUG. 29	22	19	20	20	25	23	9	19	12	10	25	18
AUG. 30	22	21	21	22	25	23	9	19	12	10	25	18
AUG. 31	22	22	23	24	26	23	9	19	12	10	25	18

MOON 1 ◗ 12:01 A.M. TO 8:00 A.M.   **MOON 2** ◑ 8:01 A.M. TO 4:00 P.M.   **MOON 3** ● 4:01 P.M. TO 12:00 A.M.

Use only one "moon" number. Choose the column closest to your time of birth. If your place of birth is not on Eastern Standard Time, be sure to read "How to Convert to Eastern Standard Time" at the beginning of this section.

1943

September

October

Date & Time	SUN ☉	MOON 1 ◗	MOON 2 ◑	MOON 3 ●	MERCURY	VENUS	MARS	JUPITER	SATURN	URANUS	NEPTUNE	PLUTO
SEP. 1	22	24	25	25	26	23	10	19	12	10	25	18
SEP. 2	22	26	26	27	26	23	10	19	12	10	25	18
SEP. 3	23	27	28	28	26	23	10	19	12	10	25	18
SEP. 4	23	29	30	30	26	23	10	19	12	10	25	18
SEP. 5	23	31	31	32	26	23	10	19	12	10	25	18
SEP. 6	23	32	33	34	26	23	10	19	12	10	25	18
SEP. 7	23	34	35	35	26	23	10	19	12	10	25	18
SEP. 8	23	36	37	37	26	22	10	19	12	10	25	18
SEP. 9	23	38	39	39	26	22	10	19	12	10	25	18
SEP. 10	23	40	41	41	26	22	10	19	12	10	25	18
SEP. 11	24	42	42	43	26	22	10	19	12	10	25	18
SEP. 12	24	44	44	45	26	22	10	19	12	10	25	18
SEP. 13	24	46	46	47	26	22	10	19	12	10	25	18
SEP. 14	24	48	48	1	26	22	10	19	12	10	25	18
SEP. 15	24	2	2	3	26	22	10	19	12	10	25	18
SEP. 16	24	4	4	5	26	22	11	19	12	10	25	18
SEP. 17	24	6	6	7	26	22	11	19	12	10	25	18
SEP. 18	24	7	8	9	26	22	11	19	12	10	25	18
SEP. 19	25	9	10	10	26	22	11	19	12	10	25	18
SEP. 20	25	11	11	12	26	22	11	19	12	10	25	18
SEP. 21	25	12	13	14	26	22	11	19	12	10	25	18
SEP. 22	25	14	15	15	25	22	11	19	12	10	25	18
SEP. 23	25	16	16	17	25	22	11	19	12	10	25	18
SEP. 24	25	17	18	18	25	22	11	19	12	10	25	18
SEP. 25	26	19	19	20	25	22	11	19	12	10	25	18
SEP. 26	26	20	21	21	25	22	11	19	12	10	25	18
SEP. 27	26	22	23	23	25	22	11	19	12	10	25	18
SEP. 28	26	24	24	25	25	22	11	19	13	10	25	18
SEP. 29	26	25	26	26	24	22	11	20	13	10	25	18
SEP. 30	26	27	27	28	24	22	11	20	13	10	25	18

Date & Time	SUN ☉	MOON 1 ◗	MOON 2 ◑	MOON 3 ●	MERCURY	VENUS	MARS	JUPITER	SATURN	URANUS	NEPTUNE	PLUTO
OCT. 1	26	29	29	30	24	22	11	20	13	10	25	18
OCT. 2	26	30	31	31	24	22	11	20	13	10	25	18
OCT. 3	27	32	33	33	24	22	11	20	13	10	25	18
OCT. 4	27	34	34	35	24	22	11	20	13	10	25	18
OCT. 5	27	36	36	37	24	22	11	20	13	10	25	18
OCT. 6	27	37	38	39	24	22	12	20	13	10	25	18
OCT. 7	27	39	40	41	24	22	12	20	13	10	25	18
OCT. 8	27	41	42	43	24	22	12	20	13	10	25	18
OCT. 9	27	43	44	44	25	22	12	20	13	10	25	18
OCT. 10	27	45	46	46	25	22	12	20	13	10	25	18
OCT. 11	28	47	48	48	25	22	12	20	13	10	25	18
OCT. 12	28	1	2	2	25	22	12	20	13	10	25	18
OCT. 13	28	3	4	4	25	22	12	20	13	10	25	18
OCT. 14	28	5	5	6	25	22	12	20	13	10	25	18
OCT. 15	28	7	7	8	26	22	12	20	13	10	25	18
OCT. 16	28	8	9	10	26	22	12	20	13	10	25	18
OCT. 17	28	10	11	11	26	22	12	20	13	10	25	18
OCT. 18	28	12	12	13	26	23	12	20	13	10	25	18
OCT. 19	29	14	14	15	26	23	12	20	13	10	25	18
OCT. 20	29	15	16	16	27	23	12	20	13	10	25	18
OCT. 21	29	17	17	18	27	23	12	20	13	10	25	18
OCT. 22	29	18	19	19	27	23	12	20	12	10	25	18
OCT. 23	29	20	20	21	27	23	12	20	12	10	25	18
OCT. 24	29	21	22	23	27	23	12	20	12	10	25	18
OCT. 25	29	23	24	24	28	23	12	20	12	10	25	18
OCT. 26	30	25	25	26	28	23	12	20	12	10	25	18
OCT. 27	30	26	27	28	28	23	12	20	12	10	25	18
OCT. 28	30	28	29	29	28	23	12	20	12	10	25	18
OCT. 29	30	30	30	31	29	24	12	20	12	10	25	18
OCT. 30	30	32	32	33	29	24	12	20	12	10	25	18
OCT. 31	30	33	34	35	29	24	12	20	12	10	25	18

MOON 1 ◗ 12:01 A.M. TO 8:00 A.M.   **MOON 2** ◑ 8:01 A.M. TO 4:00 P.M.   **MOON 3** ● 4:01 P.M. TO 12:00 A.M.

Use only one "moon" number. Choose the column closest to your time of birth. If your place of birth is not on Eastern Standard Time, be sure to read "How to Convert to Eastern Standard Time" at the beginning of this section.

November

Date & Time	SUN	MOON 1	MOON 2	MOON 3	MERCURY	VENUS	MARS	JUPITER	SATURN	URANUS	NEPTUNE	PLUTO
NOV. 1	30	35	36	36	29	24	12	20	12	10	25	18
NOV. 2	30	37	38	38	29	24	12	20	12	10	25	18
NOV. 3	31	39	40	40	30	24	12	20	12	10	25	18
NOV. 4	31	41	41	42	30	24	12	20	12	10	25	18
NOV. 5	31	43	43	44	30	24	12	20	12	10	25	18
NOV. 6	31	45	45	46	30	25	12	20	12	10	25	18
NOV. 7	31	46	47	48	31	25	12	20	12	10	25	18
NOV. 8	31	48	1	2	31	25	12	20	12	10	25	18
NOV. 9	31	2	3	3	31	25	12	20	12	10	25	18
NOV. 10	31	4	5	5	31	25	12	20	12	10	25	18
NOV. 11	31	6	7	7	31	25	12	20	12	10	25	18
NOV. 12	32	8	8	9	32	25	12	20	12	10	25	18
NOV. 13	32	10	10	11	32	25	12	20	12	10	25	18
NOV. 14	32	11	12	12	32	26	12	20	12	10	25	18
NOV. 15	32	13	13	14	32	26	12	20	12	10	25	18
NOV. 16	32	15	15	16	32	26	12	20	12	10	25	18
NOV. 17	32	16	17	17	33	26	12	20	12	10	25	18
NOV. 18	32	18	18	19	33	26	12	20	12	10	25	18
NOV. 19	33	19	20	20	33	26	11	20	12	10	25	18
NOV. 20	33	21	21	22	33	26	11	20	12	10	25	18
NOV. 21	33	23	23	24	34	26	11	20	12	10	25	18
NOV. 22	33	24	25	25	34	27	11	20	12	10	25	18
NOV. 23	33	26	26	27	34	27	11	20	12	10	25	18
NOV. 24	33	27	28	29	34	27	11	20	12	10	25	18
NOV. 25	34	29	30	30	34	27	11	20	12	10	25	18
NOV. 26	34	31	32	32	35	27	11	21	12	10	25	18
NOV. 27	34	33	33	34	35	27	11	21	12	10	25	18
NOV. 28	34	35	35	36	35	27	11	21	12	10	25	18
NOV. 29	34	37	37	38	35	28	11	21	12	10	25	18
NOV. 30	34	38	39	40	35	28	11	21	12	10	25	18

December

Date & Time	SUN	MOON 1	MOON 2	MOON 3	MERCURY	VENUS	MARS	JUPITER	SATURN	URANUS	NEPTUNE	PLUTO
DEC. 1	34	40	41	42	36	28	11	21	12	10	25	18
DEC. 2	34	42	43	44	36	28	11	21	12	10	25	18
DEC. 3	35	44	45	45	36	28	11	21	12	10	25	18
DEC. 4	35	46	47	47	36	28	11	21	12	10	25	18
DEC. 5	35	48	1	1	36	29	11	21	12	10	25	18
DEC. 6	35	2	2	3	37	29	11	21	12	10	25	18
DEC. 7	35	4	4	5	37	29	11	21	12	10	25	18
DEC. 8	35	5	6	7	37	29	11	21	12	10	26	18
DEC. 9	35	7	8	8	37	29	10	21	12	10	26	18
DEC. 10	35	9	10	10	37	29	10	21	12	10	26	18
DEC. 11	36	11	11	12	38	29	10	21	12	10	26	18
DEC. 12	36	12	13	13	38	30	10	21	12	10	26	18
DEC. 13	36	14	15	15	38	30	10	21	12	10	26	18
DEC. 14	36	16	16	17	38	30	10	21	12	10	26	18
DEC. 15	36	17	18	18	38	30	10	21	12	10	26	18
DEC. 16	36	19	19	20	39	30	10	21	12	10	26	18
DEC. 17	36	20	21	21	39	30	10	21	12	10	26	18
DEC. 18	36	22	23	23	39	30	10	21	12	10	26	18
DEC. 19	37	24	24	25	39	31	10	21	12	10	26	18
DEC. 20	37	25	26	26	39	31	10	21	12	10	26	18
DEC. 21	37	27	27	28	39	31	10	21	12	10	26	18
DEC. 22	37	28	29	30	40	31	10	21	12	10	26	18
DEC. 23	37	30	31	31	40	31	10	21	12	10	26	18
DEC. 24	37	32	33	33	40	31	10	21	12	10	26	18
DEC. 25	37	34	34	35	40	32	10	21	12	10	26	18
DEC. 26	38	36	36	37	40	32	10	21	12	10	26	18
DEC. 27	38	38	38	39	40	32	10	21	12	10	26	18
DEC. 28	38	40	40	41	40	32	10	21	12	10	26	18
DEC. 29	38	42	42	43	40	32	10	21	12	10	26	18
DEC. 30	38	44	44	45	40	32	10	21	12	10	26	18
DEC. 31	38	46	46	47	40	32	10	21	12	10	26	18

MOON 1 ☽ 12:01 A.M. TO 8:00 A.M.   **MOON 2** ☽ 8:01 A.M. TO 4:00 P.M.   **MOON 3** ● 4:01 P.M. TO 12:00 A.M.
Use only one "moon" number. Choose the column closest to your time of birth. If your place of birth is not on
Eastern Standard Time, be sure to read "How to Convert to Eastern Standard Time" at the beginning of this section.

1944

January

Date & Time	SUN	MOON 1	MOON 2	MOON 3	MERCURY	VENUS	MARS	JUPITER	SATURN	URANUS	NEPTUNE	PLUTO
JAN. 1	38	47	48	1	40	33	10	21	12	10	26	18
JAN. 2	38	1	2	3	40	33	10	20	12	10	26	18
JAN. 3	39	3	4	4	40	33	10	20	12	10	26	18
JAN. 4	39	5	6	6	40	33	10	20	12	10	26	18
JAN. 5	39	7	7	8	40	33	10	20	12	10	26	18
JAN. 6	39	8	9	10	40	33	10	20	12	10	26	18
JAN. 7	39	10	11	11	40	34	10	20	12	10	26	18
JAN. 8	39	12	12	13	39	34	10	20	12	10	26	18
JAN. 9	39	14	14	15	39	34	10	20	12	10	26	18
JAN. 10	40	15	16	16	39	34	10	20	12	10	26	18
JAN. 11	40	17	17	18	39	34	10	20	12	10	26	18
JAN. 12	40	18	19	19	39	34	10	20	12	10	26	18
JAN. 13	40	20	20	21	39	35	10	20	12	10	26	18
JAN. 14	40	22	22	23	38	35	10	20	12	10	26	18
JAN. 15	40	23	24	24	38	35	10	20	12	10	26	18
JAN. 16	40	25	25	26	38	35	10	20	12	10	26	18
JAN. 17	41	26	27	27	38	35	10	20	12	10	26	18
JAN. 18	41	28	28	29	38	35	10	20	12	10	26	18
JAN. 19	41	30	30	31	38	36	10	20	12	10	26	18
JAN. 20	41	31	32	32	38	36	10	20	12	10	26	18
JAN. 21	41	33	34	34	38	36	10	20	12	10	26	18
JAN. 22	41	35	36	36	38	36	10	20	12	10	26	18
JAN. 23	42	37	37	38	38	36	10	20	12	10	26	18
JAN. 24	42	39	39	40	38	36	10	20	12	10	26	18
JAN. 25	42	41	41	41	38	36	10	20	12	10	26	18
JAN. 26	42	43	43	44	38	37	10	20	12	10	26	18
JAN. 27	42	45	45	46	39	37	10	20	12	10	26	18
JAN. 28	42	47	47	48	39	37	10	20	12	10	26	18
JAN. 29	42	1	1	2	39	37	10	20	12	10	26	18
JAN. 30	42	3	3	4	39	37	10	20	12	10	26	18
JAN. 31	43	4	5	6	39	37	10	20	12	10	26	18

February

Date & Time	SUN	MOON 1	MOON 2	MOON 3	MERCURY	VENUS	MARS	JUPITER	SATURN	URANUS	NEPTUNE	PLUTO
FEB. 1	43	6	7	7	39	38	10	20	12	10	26	18
FEB. 2	43	8	9	9	39	38	10	20	12	10	26	18
FEB. 3	43	10	10	11	39	38	10	20	12	10	26	18
FEB. 4	43	11	12	13	40	38	10	20	12	10	26	18
FEB. 5	43	13	14	14	40	38	10	20	12	10	26	18
FEB. 6	43	15	15	16	40	38	10	20	12	10	25	18
FEB. 7	43	16	17	17	40	39	10	20	12	10	25	18
FEB. 8	44	18	18	19	40	39	10	20	12	10	25	18
FEB. 9	44	20	20	21	40	39	10	20	12	10	25	18
FEB. 10	44	21	22	22	41	39	10	20	12	10	25	18
FEB. 11	44	23	24	24	41	39	10	20	12	10	25	18
FEB. 12	44	24	25	25	41	39	10	20	12	10	25	18
FEB. 13	44	26	26	27	41	40	10	20	12	10	25	18
FEB. 14	44	27	28	29	41	40	10	20	12	10	25	18
FEB. 15	44	29	30	30	41	40	11	20	12	10	25	18
FEB. 16	45	31	31	32	41	40	11	20	12	10	25	18
FEB. 17	45	32	33	34	41	40	11	20	12	10	25	18
FEB. 18	45	34	35	35	42	40	11	20	12	10	25	18
FEB. 19	45	36	37	37	42	41	11	20	12	10	25	18
FEB. 20	45	38	38	39	42	41	11	20	12	10	25	18
FEB. 21	45	40	40	41	43	41	11	20	12	10	25	18
FEB. 22	45	42	42	43	43	41	11	20	12	10	25	18
FEB. 23	46	44	44	45	43	41	11	20	12	10	25	18
FEB. 24	46	46	46	47	43	41	11	20	12	10	25	18
FEB. 25	46	48	1	1	43	42	11	20	12	10	25	18
FEB. 26	46	2	2	3	44	42	11	20	12	10	25	18
FEB. 27	46	4	4	5	44	42	11	20	12	10	25	18
FEB. 28	46	6	6	7	44	42	11	20	12	10	25	18
FEB. 29	46	8	8	9	44	42	11	20	12	10	25	18

MOON 1 ◗ 12:01 A.M. TO 8:00 A.M.   **MOON 2** ◑ 8:01 A.M. TO 4:00 P.M.   **MOON 3** ● 4:01 P.M. TO 12:00 A.M.
Use only one "moon" number. Choose the column closest to your time of birth. If your place of birth is not on Eastern Standard Time, be sure to read "How to Convert to Eastern Standard Time" at the beginning of this section.

1944

March

April

Date & Time	SUN	MOON 1	MOON 2	MOON 3	MERCURY	VENUS	MARS	JUPITER	SATURN	URANUS	NEPTUNE	PLUTO
MAR. 1	46	9	10	10	45	42	11	20	12	10	25	18
MAR. 2	46	11	12	12	45	43	11	20	12	10	25	18
MAR. 3	47	13	13	14	45	43	11	20	12	10	25	18
MAR. 4	47	14	15	15	45	43	11	20	12	10	25	18
MAR. 5	47	16	16	17	45	43	12	20	12	10	25	18
MAR. 6	47	18	18	19	46	43	12	20	12	10	25	18
MAR. 7	47	19	20	20	46	43	12	20	12	10	25	18
MAR. 8	47	21	21	22	46	44	12	19	12	10	25	18
MAR. 9	47	22	23	23	46	44	12	19	12	10	25	18
MAR. 10	47	24	24	25	47	44	12	19	12	10	25	18
MAR. 11	48	25	26	27	47	44	12	19	12	10	25	18
MAR. 12	48	27	28	28	47	44	12	19	12	10	25	18
MAR. 13	48	29	29	30	47	44	12	19	12	10	25	18
MAR. 14	48	30	31	31	48	44	12	19	12	10	25	18
MAR. 15	48	32	33	33	48	45	12	19	12	10	25	18
MAR. 16	48	34	34	35	48	45	12	19	12	10	25	18
MAR. 17	48	35	36	37	48	45	12	19	12	10	25	18
MAR. 18	48	37	38	38	1	45	12	19	12	10	25	18
MAR. 19	1	39	40	40	1	45	12	19	12	10	25	18
MAR. 20	1	41	42	42	1	45	12	19	12	10	25	18
MAR. 21	1	43	44	44	1	46	12	19	12	10	25	18
MAR. 22	1	45	46	46	2	46	13	19	12	10	25	18
MAR. 23	1	47	48	48	2	46	13	19	12	10	25	18
MAR. 24	1	1	2	2	2	46	13	19	12	10	25	18
MAR. 25	2	3	4	4	3	46	13	19	12	10	25	18
MAR. 26	2	5	6	6	3	46	13	19	12	10	25	18
MAR. 27	2	7	7	8	3	47	13	19	12	10	25	18
MAR. 28	2	9	9	10	3	47	13	19	12	10	25	18
MAR. 29	2	10	11	12	4	47	13	19	12	10	25	18
MAR. 30	2	12	13	13	4	47	13	19	12	10	25	18
MAR. 31	2	14	14	15	4	47	13	19	12	10	25	18

Date & Time	SUN	MOON 1	MOON 2	MOON 3	MERCURY	VENUS	MARS	JUPITER	SATURN	URANUS	NEPTUNE	PLUTO
APR. 1	2	16	16	17	4	47	13	19	12	10	25	18
APR. 2	2	17	18	18	5	48	13	19	12	10	25	18
APR. 3	3	19	19	20	5	48	13	19	12	10	25	18
APR. 4	3	20	21	21	5	48	13	19	12	10	25	18
APR. 5	3	22	22	23	5	48	13	19	12	10	25	18
APR. 6	3	23	24	24	5	48	14	19	12	10	25	18
APR. 7	3	25	26	26	6	48	14	19	12	10	25	18
APR. 8	3	27	27	28	6	1	14	19	12	10	25	18
APR. 9	3	28	29	29	6	1	14	19	12	10	25	18
APR. 10	3	30	30	31	6	1	14	19	12	10	25	18
APR. 11	4	32	32	33	6	1	14	19	12	10	25	18
APR. 12	4	33	34	34	7	1	14	19	12	10	25	18
APR. 13	4	35	36	36	7	1	14	19	12	10	25	18
APR. 14	4	37	37	38	7	2	14	19	12	10	25	18
APR. 15	4	39	39	40	7	2	14	19	12	10	25	18
APR. 16	4	40	41	42	7	2	14	19	12	10	25	18
APR. 17	4	42	43	44	7	2	14	19	12	10	25	18
APR. 18	4	44	45	45	7	2	14	19	12	10	25	18
APR. 19	5	46	47	47	7	2	14	19	12	10	25	18
APR. 20	5	48	1	1	7	3	15	19	12	10	25	18
APR. 21	5	2	3	3	7	3	15	19	12	10	25	18
APR. 22	5	4	5	5	7	3	15	19	12	10	25	18
APR. 23	5	6	7	7	7	3	15	19	12	10	25	18
APR. 24	5	8	9	9	7	3	15	19	12	10	25	18
APR. 25	6	10	10	11	7	3	15	19	12	10	25	18
APR. 26	6	12	12	13	7	4	15	19	12	10	25	18
APR. 27	6	13	14	14	7	4	15	19	12	10	25	18
APR. 28	6	15	16	16	7	4	15	19	12	10	25	18
APR. 29	6	17	17	18	7	4	15	19	12	10	25	18
APR. 30	6	18	19	19	7	4	15	19	12	10	25	18

MOON 1 ◖ 12:01 A.M. TO 8:00 A.M.   **MOON 2** ◗ 8:01 A.M. TO 4:00 P.M.   **MOON 3** ● 4:01 P.M. TO 12:00 A.M.
Use only one "moon" number. Choose the column closest to your time of birth. If your place of birth is not on
Eastern Standard Time, be sure to read "How to Convert to Eastern Standard Time" at the beginning of this section.

1944

May

Date & Time	SUN	MOON 1	MOON 2	MOON 3	MERCURY	VENUS	MARS	JUPITER	SATURN	URANUS	NEPTUNE	PLUTO
MAY 1	6	20	20	21	7	4	15	19	12	10	25	18
MAY 2	6	21	22	22	7	5	15	19	12	10	25	18
MAY 3	7	23	23	24	7	5	16	19	12	10	25	18
MAY 4	7	25	25	26	6	5	16	19	12	10	25	18
MAY 5	7	26	27	27	6	5	16	19	12	10	25	18
MAY 6	7	28	28	29	6	5	16	19	12	10	25	18
MAY 7	7	29	30	31	6	5	16	19	12	10	25	18
MAY 8	7	31	32	32	6	6	16	19	12	10	25	18
MAY 9	7	33	33	34	6	6	16	19	12	10	25	18
MAY 10	7	35	35	36	6	6	16	19	12	10	25	18
MAY 11	8	36	37	38	6	6	16	19	12	10	25	18
MAY 12	8	38	39	39	6	6	16	19	12	10	25	18
MAY 13	8	40	41	41	6	6	16	19	12	10	25	18
MAY 14	8	42	42	43	6	6	16	19	12	10	25	18
MAY 15	8	44	44	45	7	6	16	19	12	10	25	18
MAY 16	8	46	46	47	7	6	16	19	12	10	25	18
MAY 17	8	48	48	1	6	7	17	19	12	10	25	18
MAY 18	8	1	2	3	6	7	17	19	12	10	25	18
MAY 19	9	3	4	5	6	7	17	19	12	10	25	18
MAY 20	9	5	6	7	6	7	17	20	12	10	25	18
MAY 21	9	7	8	8	6	8	17	20	12	10	25	18
MAY 22	9	9	10	10	6	8	17	20	12	10	25	18
MAY 23	9	11	11	12	6	8	17	20	12	10	25	18
MAY 24	9	13	13	14	6	8	17	20	13	10	25	18
MAY 25	10	14	15	15	6	8	17	20	13	10	25	18
MAY 26	10	16	17	17	6	8	17	20	13	10	25	18
MAY 27	10	18	18	19	7	9	17	20	13	10	25	18
MAY 28	10	19	20	20	7	9	17	20	13	10	25	18
MAY 29	10	21	21	22	7	9	17	20	13	10	25	18
MAY 30	10	22	23	23	7	9	18	20	13	10	25	18
MAY 31	10	24	25	25	7	9	18	20	13	10	25	18

June

Date & Time	SUN	MOON 1	MOON 2	MOON 3	MERCURY	VENUS	MARS	JUPITER	SATURN	URANUS	NEPTUNE	PLUTO
JUN. 1	10	26	26	27	7	9	18	20	13	10	25	18
JUN. 2	10	27	28	28	7	10	18	20	13	10	25	18
JUN. 3	11	29	29	30	7	10	18	20	13	10	25	18
JUN. 4	11	31	31	32	8	10	18	20	13	10	25	18
JUN. 5	11	32	33	33	8	10	18	20	13	10	25	18
JUN. 6	11	34	35	35	8	10	18	20	13	10	25	18
JUN. 7	11	36	36	37	8	10	18	20	13	10	25	18
JUN. 8	11	38	38	39	8	11	18	20	13	10	25	18
JUN. 9	11	40	40	41	9	11	18	20	13	10	25	18
JUN. 10	11	41	42	43	9	11	18	20	13	10	25	18
JUN. 11	12	43	44	45	9	11	18	20	13	10	25	18
JUN. 12	12	45	46	46	9	11	19	20	13	10	25	18
JUN. 13	12	47	48	48	9	11	19	20	13	10	25	18
JUN. 14	12	1	2	2	10	12	19	20	13	10	25	18
JUN. 15	12	3	3	4	10	12	19	20	13	10	25	18
JUN. 16	12	5	5	6	10	12	19	20	13	10	25	18
JUN. 17	12	7	7	8	10	12	19	20	13	10	25	18
JUN. 18	12	8	9	10	11	12	19	20	13	10	25	18
JUN. 19	13	10	11	11	11	12	19	20	13	10	25	18
JUN. 20	13	12	13	13	11	12	19	20	13	10	25	18
JUN. 21	13	14	14	15	11	13	19	20	13	10	25	18
JUN. 22	13	15	16	17	12	13	20	20	13	10	25	18
JUN. 23	13	17	18	18	12	13	20	20	13	10	25	18
JUN. 24	13	19	19	20	12	13	20	20	13	10	25	18
JUN. 25	14	20	21	21	12	13	20	20	13	10	25	18
JUN. 26	14	22	22	23	13	14	20	20	13	10	25	18
JUN. 27	14	23	24	25	13	14	20	20	13	10	25	18
JUN. 28	14	25	26	26	13	14	20	20	13	10	25	18
JUN. 29	14	27	27	28	14	14	20	20	13	10	25	18
JUN. 30	14	28	29	29	14	14	20	20	13	10	25	18

MOON 1 ◖ 12:01 A.M. TO 8:00 A.M.   **MOON 2** ◑ 8:01 A.M. TO 4:00 P.M.   **MOON 3** ● 4:01 P.M. TO 12:00 A.M.

Use only one "moon" number. Choose the column closest to your time of birth. If your place of birth is not on Eastern Standard Time, be sure to read "How to Convert to Eastern Standard Time" at the beginning of this section.

1944

July

Date & Time	SUN	MOON 1	MOON 2	MOON 3	MERCURY	VENUS	MARS	JUPITER	SATURN	URANUS	NEPTUNE	PLUTO
JUL. 1	14	30	30	31	14	14	20	20	13	10	25	18
JUL. 2	14	32	32	33	14	15	20	20	13	10	25	18
JUL. 3	15	33	34	35	15	15	20	20	13	10	25	18
JUL. 4	15	35	36	36	15	15	20	20	13	10	25	18
JUL. 5	15	37	38	38	15	15	20	20	13	10	25	18
JUL. 6	15	39	40	40	16	15	20	20	13	10	25	18
JUL. 7	15	41	41	42	16	15	21	20	13	10	25	18
JUL. 8	15	43	43	44	16	15	21	20	13	10	25	18
JUL. 9	15	45	45	46	16	16	21	21	13	10	25	18
JUL. 10	15	47	47	48	17	16	21	21	13	10	25	18
JUL. 11	16	1	1	2	17	16	21	21	13	10	25	18
JUL. 12	16	2	3	4	17	16	21	21	13	10	25	18
JUL. 13	16	4	5	6	17	16	21	21	13	10	25	18
JUL. 14	16	6	7	7	18	16	21	21	13	10	25	18
JUL. 15	16	8	9	9	18	17	21	21	13	10	25	18
JUL. 16	16	10	10	11	18	17	21	21	13	10	25	18
JUL. 17	16	12	12	13	18	17	21	21	13	11	25	18
JUL. 18	16	13	14	14	19	17	21	21	13	11	25	18
JUL. 19	17	15	15	16	19	17	22	21	13	11	25	18
JUL. 20	17	17	17	18	19	17	22	21	13	11	25	18
JUL. 21	17	18	19	19	19	18	22	21	13	11	25	18
JUL. 22	17	20	20	21	20	18	22	21	14	11	25	18
JUL. 23	17	21	22	22	20	18	22	21	14	11	25	18
JUL. 24	17	23	24	24	20	18	22	21	14	11	25	18
JUL. 25	17	25	25	26	20	18	22	21	14	11	25	18
JUL. 26	18	26	27	27	20	18	22	21	14	11	25	18
JUL. 27	18	28	28	29	21	19	22	21	14	11	25	18
JUL. 28	18	29	30	30	21	19	22	21	14	11	25	18
JUL. 29	18	31	32	32	21	19	22	21	14	11	25	18
JUL. 30	18	33	33	34	21	19	22	21	14	11	25	18
JUL. 31	18	34	35	36	21	19	23	21	14	11	25	18

August

Date & Time	SUN	MOON 1	MOON 2	MOON 3	MERCURY	VENUS	MARS	JUPITER	SATURN	URANUS	NEPTUNE	PLUTO
AUG. 1	18	36	37	37	22	19	23	21	14	11	25	18
AUG. 2	18	38	39	39	22	20	23	21	14	11	25	18
AUG. 3	19	40	41	41	22	20	23	21	14	11	25	18
AUG. 4	19	42	43	43	22	20	23	21	14	11	25	18
AUG. 5	19	44	45	45	22	20	23	21	14	11	25	18
AUG. 6	19	46	47	47	22	20	23	21	14	11	25	18
AUG. 7	19	48	1	1	23	20	23	21	14	11	25	18
AUG. 8	19	2	3	3	23	21	23	21	14	11	25	18
AUG. 9	19	4	4	5	23	21	23	21	14	11	25	18
AUG. 10	19	6	6	7	23	21	23	21	14	11	25	18
AUG. 11	20	8	8	9	23	21	23	21	14	11	25	18
AUG. 12	20	9	10	11	23	21	24	21	14	11	25	18
AUG. 13	20	11	12	12	23	21	24	21	14	11	25	18
AUG. 14	20	13	13	14	23	22	24	22	14	11	25	18
AUG. 15	20	14	15	16	24	22	24	22	14	11	25	18
AUG. 16	20	16	17	17	24	22	24	22	14	11	25	18
AUG. 17	20	18	18	19	24	22	24	22	14	11	25	18
AUG. 18	20	19	20	20	24	22	24	22	14	11	25	18
AUG. 19	21	21	21	22	24	22	24	22	14	11	25	18
AUG. 20	21	23	23	24	24	23	24	22	14	11	25	18
AUG. 21	21	24	25	25	24	23	24	22	14	11	25	18
AUG. 22	21	26	26	27	24	23	24	22	14	11	25	18
AUG. 23	21	27	28	28	24	23	24	22	14	11	25	18
AUG. 24	21	29	29	30	24	23	25	22	14	11	25	18
AUG. 25	21	30	31	32	24	23	25	22	14	11	25	18
AUG. 26	22	32	33	33	24	24	25	22	14	11	25	18
AUG. 27	22	34	34	35	24	24	25	22	14	11	25	18
AUG. 28	22	36	36	37	24	24	25	22	14	11	25	18
AUG. 29	22	37	38	39	24	24	25	22	14	11	25	18
AUG. 30	22	39	40	40	24	24	25	22	14	11	25	18
AUG. 31	22	41	42	42	24	24	25	22	14	11	25	18

MOON 1 ◑ 12:01 A.M. TO 8:00 A.M.   **MOON 2** ◑ 8:01 A.M. TO 4:00 P.M.   **MOON 3** ● 4:01 P.M. TO 12:00 A.M.
Use only one "moon" number. Choose the column closest to your time of birth. If your place of birth is not on
Eastern Standard Time, be sure to read "How to Convert to Eastern Standard Time" at the beginning of this section.

1944

September

Date & Time	SUN	MOON 1	MOON 2	MOON 3	MERCURY	VENUS	MARS	JUPITER	SATURN	URANUS	NEPTUNE	PLUTO
SEP. 1	22	43	44	44	24	25	25	22	14	11	25	18
SEP. 2	22	45	46	46	23	25	25	22	14	11	25	18
SEP. 3	23	47	48	48	23	25	25	22	14	11	25	18
SEP. 4	23	1	2	2	23	25	25	22	14	11	25	18
SEP. 5	23	3	4	4	23	25	26	22	14	11	25	18
SEP. 6	23	5	6	6	23	25	26	22	14	11	25	18
SEP. 7	23	7	8	8	23	26	26	22	14	11	25	18
SEP. 8	23	9	9	10	23	26	26	22	14	11	25	18
SEP. 9	23	11	11	12	23	26	26	22	14	11	25	18
SEP. 10	23	12	13	14	22	26	26	22	14	11	25	18
SEP. 11	24	14	15	15	22	26	26	22	14	11	25	18
SEP. 12	24	16	16	17	22	26	26	22	14	11	25	18
SEP. 13	24	17	18	18	22	26	26	22	14	11	25	18
SEP. 14	24	19	20	20	22	27	26	22	14	11	25	18
SEP. 15	24	21	21	22	22	27	26	22	14	11	25	18
SEP. 16	24	22	23	23	22	27	27	22	14	11	25	18
SEP. 17	24	24	24	25	22	27	27	22	14	11	25	18
SEP. 18	24	25	26	26	22	27	27	23	14	11	25	18
SEP. 19	25	27	27	28	22	27	27	23	14	11	25	18
SEP. 20	25	28	29	30	22	28	27	23	14	11	25	18
SEP. 21	25	30	31	31	22	28	27	23	14	11	25	18
SEP. 22	25	32	32	33	22	28	27	23	14	11	25	18
SEP. 23	25	33	34	34	23	28	27	23	14	11	25	18
SEP. 24	25	35	36	36	23	28	27	23	14	11	25	18
SEP. 25	26	37	37	38	23	28	27	23	14	11	25	18
SEP. 26	26	39	39	40	23	29	27	23	14	11	25	18
SEP. 27	26	40	41	42	23	29	28	23	14	11	25	18
SEP. 28	26	42	43	43	23	29	28	23	14	11	26	18
SEP. 29	26	44	45	45	24	29	28	23	14	11	26	18
SEP. 30	26	46	47	47	24	29	28	23	14	11	26	18

October

Date & Time	SUN	MOON 1	MOON 2	MOON 3	MERCURY	VENUS	MARS	JUPITER	SATURN	URANUS	NEPTUNE	PLUTO
OCT. 1	26	48	1	2	24	29	28	23	14	11	26	18
OCT. 2	26	2	3	4	24	30	28	23	14	11	26	18
OCT. 3	27	4	5	6	25	30	28	23	14	11	26	18
OCT. 4	27	6	7	8	25	30	28	23	14	11	26	18
OCT. 5	27	8	9	9	25	30	28	23	14	11	26	18
OCT. 6	27	10	11	11	25	30	28	23	14	11	26	18
OCT. 7	27	12	12	13	25	30	28	23	14	11	26	18
OCT. 8	27	14	14	15	26	31	28	23	14	11	26	18
OCT. 9	27	15	16	16	26	31	29	23	14	11	26	18
OCT. 10	27	17	18	18	26	31	29	23	14	11	26	18
OCT. 11	28	19	19	20	26	31	29	23	14	11	26	18
OCT. 12	28	20	21	21	27	31	29	23	14	11	26	18
OCT. 13	28	22	22	23	27	31	29	23	14	11	26	18
OCT. 14	28	23	24	24	27	32	29	23	14	11	26	18
OCT. 15	28	25	25	26	27	32	29	23	14	11	26	18
OCT. 16	28	26	27	28	27	32	29	23	14	11	26	18
OCT. 17	28	28	29	29	28	32	29	23	14	11	26	18
OCT. 18	28	30	30	31	28	32	29	23	14	11	26	18
OCT. 19	29	31	32	32	28	32	29	23	14	11	26	18
OCT. 20	29	33	34	34	28	33	30	23	14	11	26	18
OCT. 21	29	35	35	36	29	33	30	23	14	11	26	18
OCT. 22	29	36	37	37	29	33	30	23	14	11	26	18
OCT. 23	29	38	39	39	29	33	30	23	14	11	26	18
OCT. 24	29	40	40	41	29	33	30	23	14	11	26	18
OCT. 25	29	42	42	43	30	33	30	24	14	11	26	18
OCT. 26	30	43	44	45	30	34	30	24	14	11	26	18
OCT. 27	30	45	46	47	30	34	30	24	14	11	26	18
OCT. 28	30	47	48	1	30	34	30	24	14	11	26	18
OCT. 29	30	1	2	3	30	34	30	24	14	11	26	18
OCT. 30	30	3	4	5	31	34	30	24	14	11	26	18
OCT. 31	30	5	6	7	31	34	31	24	14	11	26	18

MOON 1 ☽ 12:01 A.M. TO 8:00 A.M. **MOON 2** ☽ 8:01 A.M. TO 4:00 P.M. **MOON 3** ● 4:01 P.M. TO 12:00 A.M.
Use only one "moon" number. Choose the column closest to your time of birth. If your place of birth is not on Eastern Standard Time, be sure to read "How to Convert to Eastern Standard Time" at the beginning of this section.

Date & Time	SUN ☉	MOON 1 ☽	MOON 2 ◑	MOON 3 ●	MERCURY	VENUS	MARS	JUPITER	SATURN	URANUS	NEPTUNE	PLUTO
NOV. 1	30	7	8	9	31	35	31	24	14	11	26	18
NOV. 2	30	9	10	11	31	35	31	24	14	11	26	18
NOV. 3	31	11	12	12	31	35	31	24	14	11	26	18
NOV. 4	31	13	14	14	32	35	31	24	14	11	26	18
NOV. 5	31	15	15	16	32	35	31	24	14	11	26	18
NOV. 6	31	16	17	18	32	35	31	24	14	11	26	18
NOV. 7	31	18	19	19	32	35	31	24	14	11	26	18
NOV. 8	31	20	20	21	33	36	31	24	14	11	26	18
NOV. 9	31	21	22	22	33	36	31	24	14	11	26	18
NOV. 10	31	23	23	24	33	36	32	24	14	11	26	18
NOV. 11	31	24	25	26	33	36	32	24	14	11	26	18
NOV. 12	32	26	27	27	33	36	32	24	14	11	26	18
NOV. 13	32	28	28	29	34	36	32	24	14	11	26	18
NOV. 14	32	29	30	30	34	37	32	24	14	11	26	18
NOV. 15	32	31	31	32	34	37	32	24	14	11	26	18
NOV. 16	32	33	33	34	34	37	32	24	14	11	26	18
NOV. 17	32	34	35	35	34	37	32	24	14	11	26	18
NOV. 18	32	36	37	37	35	37	32	24	14	11	26	18
NOV. 19	33	38	38	39	35	37	32	24	14	11	26	18
NOV. 20	33	39	40	41	35	38	32	24	14	11	26	18
NOV. 21	33	41	42	42	35	38	33	24	14	11	26	18
NOV. 22	33	43	44	44	35	38	33	24	14	11	26	18
NOV. 23	33	45	45	46	35	38	33	24	14	11	26	18
NOV. 24	33	47	47	48	36	38	33	24	14	10	26	18
NOV. 25	34	1	1	2	36	38	33	24	14	10	26	18
NOV. 26	34	3	3	4	36	39	33	24	14	10	26	18
NOV. 27	34	5	5	6	36	39	33	24	14	10	26	18
NOV. 28	34	6	7	8	36	39	33	24	14	10	26	18
NOV. 29	34	8	9	10	37	39	33	24	14	10	26	18
NOV. 30	34	10	11	12	37	39	33	24	14	10	26	18

Date & Time	SUN ☉	MOON 1 ☽	MOON 2 ◑	MOON 3 ●	MERCURY	VENUS	MARS	JUPITER	SATURN	URANUS	NEPTUNE	PLUTO
DEC. 1	34	12	13	13	37	39	33	24	14	10	26	18
DEC. 2	34	14	15	15	37	40	34	24	14	10	26	18
DEC. 3	35	16	16	17	37	40	34	24	14	10	26	18
DEC. 4	35	17	18	19	37	40	34	24	14	10	26	18
DEC. 5	35	19	20	20	37	40	34	24	14	10	26	18
DEC. 6	35	21	21	22	38	40	34	24	14	10	26	18
DEC. 7	35	22	23	23	38	40	34	24	14	10	26	18
DEC. 8	35	24	24	25	38	40	34	24	14	10	26	18
DEC. 9	35	26	26	27	38	41	34	24	14	10	26	18
DEC. 10	35	27	28	28	38	41	34	24	14	10	26	18
DEC. 11	36	29	29	30	38	41	34	24	14	10	26	18
DEC. 12	36	30	31	31	38	41	35	24	14	10	26	18
DEC. 13	36	32	33	33	38	41	35	24	14	10	26	18
DEC. 14	36	34	34	35	38	41	35	24	14	10	26	18
DEC. 15	36	35	36	37	38	42	35	24	14	10	26	18
DEC. 16	36	37	38	38	38	42	35	24	14	10	26	18
DEC. 17	36	39	40	40	38	42	35	24	14	10	26	18
DEC. 18	36	41	41	42	38	42	35	25	14	10	26	18
DEC. 19	37	43	43	44	38	42	35	25	14	10	26	18
DEC. 20	37	44	45	46	38	42	35	25	14	10	26	18
DEC. 21	37	46	47	48	37	43	35	25	14	10	26	18
DEC. 22	37	48	1	1	37	43	36	25	14	10	26	18
DEC. 23	37	2	3	3	37	43	36	25	14	10	26	18
DEC. 24	37	4	5	5	37	43	36	25	14	10	26	18
DEC. 25	37	6	7	7	37	43	36	25	14	10	26	18
DEC. 26	38	8	8	9	37	43	36	25	14	10	26	18
DEC. 27	38	10	10	11	36	43	36	25	14	10	26	18
DEC. 28	38	11	12	13	36	44	36	25	14	10	26	18
DEC. 29	38	13	14	14	36	44	36	25	14	10	26	18
DEC. 30	38	15	16	16	36	44	36	25	14	10	26	18
DEC. 31	38	17	17	18	36	44	36	25	14	10	26	18

MOON 1 ☽ 12:01 A.M. TO 8:00 A.M.   **MOON 2** ◑ 8:01 A.M. TO 4:00 P.M.   **MOON 3** ● 4:01 P.M. TO 12:00 A.M.
Use only one "moon" number. Choose the column closest to your time of birth. If your place of birth is not on
Eastern Standard Time, be sure to read "How to Convert to Eastern Standard Time" at the beginning of this section.

1945

January

Date & Time	SUN	MOON 1	MOON 2	MOON 3	MERCURY	VENUS	MARS	JUPITER	SATURN	URANUS	NEPTUNE	PLUTO
JAN. 1	38	18	19	20	36	44	37	25	14	10	26	18
JAN. 2	38	20	21	21	36	44	37	25	14	10	26	18
JAN. 3	39	22	22	23	36	45	37	25	14	10	26	18
JAN. 4	39	23	24	24	36	45	37	25	14	10	26	18
JAN. 5	39	25	26	26	36	45	37	25	14	10	26	18
JAN. 6	39	27	27	28	36	45	37	25	14	10	26	18
JAN. 7	39	28	29	29	36	45	37	25	14	10	26	18
JAN. 8	39	30	30	31	36	45	37	25	14	10	26	18
JAN. 9	39	31	32	32	36	45	37	25	14	10	26	18
JAN. 10	40	33	34	34	36	46	37	25	14	10	26	18
JAN. 11	40	35	35	36	37	46	38	25	14	10	26	18
JAN. 12	40	36	37	38	37	46	38	25	14	10	26	18
JAN. 13	40	38	39	39	37	46	38	25	14	10	26	18
JAN. 14	40	40	41	41	37	46	38	25	14	10	26	18
JAN. 15	40	42	43	43	37	46	38	25	14	10	26	18
JAN. 16	40	44	45	45	37	47	38	25	14	10	26	18
JAN. 17	41	46	46	47	37	47	38	25	14	10	26	18
JAN. 18	41	48	48	1	38	47	38	25	14	10	26	18
JAN. 19	41	2	2	3	38	47	38	25	14	10	26	18
JAN. 20	41	4	4	5	38	47	38	25	14	10	26	18
JAN. 21	41	5	6	7	38	47	39	25	14	10	26	18
JAN. 22	41	7	8	9	38	47	39	25	14	10	26	18
JAN. 23	42	9	10	10	38	48	39	25	14	10	26	18
JAN. 24	42	11	12	12	39	48	39	25	14	10	26	18
JAN. 25	42	13	13	14	39	48	39	25	14	10	26	18
JAN. 26	42	14	15	16	39	48	39	25	14	10	26	18
JAN. 27	42	16	17	17	39	48	39	25	14	10	26	18
JAN. 28	42	18	18	19	39	48	39	25	14	10	26	18
JAN. 29	42	20	20	21	40	48	39	25	14	10	26	18
JAN. 30	42	21	22	22	40	1	39	25	14	10	26	18
JAN. 31	43	23	23	24	40	1	40	25	14	10	26	18

February

Date & Time	SUN	MOON 1	MOON 2	MOON 3	MERCURY	VENUS	MARS	JUPITER	SATURN	URANUS	NEPTUNE	PLUTO
FEB. 1	43	24	25	26	40	1	40	25	14	10	26	18
FEB. 2	43	26	27	27	40	1	40	25	14	10	26	18
FEB. 3	43	28	28	29	41	1	40	25	14	10	26	18
FEB. 4	43	29	30	30	41	1	40	25	14	10	26	18
FEB. 5	43	31	31	32	41	1	40	25	14	10	26	18
FEB. 6	43	32	33	34	41	1	40	25	14	10	26	18
FEB. 7	43	34	35	35	41	2	40	25	14	10	26	18
FEB. 8	44	36	36	37	42	2	40	24	14	10	26	18
FEB. 9	44	38	38	39	42	2	40	24	14	10	26	18
FEB. 10	44	39	40	41	42	2	41	24	14	10	26	18
FEB. 11	44	41	42	42	42	2	41	24	14	10	26	18
FEB. 12	44	43	44	44	42	2	41	24	14	10	26	18
FEB. 13	44	45	46	46	43	2	41	24	14	10	26	18
FEB. 14	44	47	48	48	43	3	41	24	14	10	26	18
FEB. 15	44	1	2	2	43	3	41	24	14	10	26	18
FEB. 16	45	3	4	4	43	3	41	24	14	10	26	18
FEB. 17	45	5	6	6	43	3	41	24	14	10	26	18
FEB. 18	45	7	7	8	44	3	41	24	14	10	26	18
FEB. 19	45	9	9	10	44	3	41	24	14	10	26	18
FEB. 20	45	11	11	12	44	3	42	24	14	10	26	18
FEB. 21	45	12	13	13	44	3	42	24	13	10	26	18
FEB. 22	45	14	15	15	45	3	42	24	13	10	26	18
FEB. 23	46	16	16	17	45	4	42	24	13	10	26	18
FEB. 24	46	17	18	19	45	4	42	24	13	10	26	18
FEB. 25	46	19	20	20	45	4	42	24	13	10	26	18
FEB. 26	46	21	21	22	46	4	42	24	13	10	26	18
FEB. 27	46	22	23	23	46	4	42	24	13	10	26	18
FEB. 28	46	24	25	25	46	4	42	24	13	10	26	18

MOON 1 ◑ 12:01 A.M. TO 8:00 A.M.   **MOON 2** ◐ 8:01 A.M. TO 4:00 P.M.   **MOON 3** ● 4:01 P.M. TO 12:00 A.M.
Use only one "moon" number. Choose the column closest to your time of birth. If your place of birth is not on
Eastern Standard Time, be sure to read "How to Convert to Eastern Standard Time" at the beginning of this section.

1945

March

April

Date & Time	SUN	MOON 1 ◐	MOON 2 ◑	MOON 3 ●	MERCURY	VENUS	MARS	JUPITER	SATURN	URANUS	NEPTUNE	PLUTO
MAR. 1	46	26	26	27	46	4	42	24	13	10	26	18
MAR. 2	46	27	28	28	47	4	43	24	13	10	26	18
MAR. 3	47	29	29	30	47	4	43	24	13	10	26	18
MAR. 4	47	30	31	31	47	4	43	24	13	10	26	18
MAR. 5	47	32	32	33	47	5	43	24	13	10	26	18
MAR. 6	47	34	34	35	48	5	43	24	13	10	26	18
MAR. 7	47	35	36	36	48	5	43	24	13	10	26	18
MAR. 8	47	37	37	38	48	5	43	24	13	10	26	18
MAR. 9	47	39	39	40	48	5	43	24	13	10	26	18
MAR. 10	47	40	41	42	1	5	43	24	13	10	26	18
MAR. 11	48	42	43	44	1	5	44	24	13	10	26	18
MAR. 12	48	44	45	45	1	5	44	24	13	10	26	18
MAR. 13	48	46	47	47	1	5	44	24	13	10	26	18
MAR. 14	48	48	1	2	2	5	44	24	13	10	26	18
MAR. 15	48	2	3	2	5	44	24	13	10	26	18	
MAR. 16	48	4	5	6	2	5	44	24	13	10	26	18
MAR. 17	48	6	7	8	2	5	44	24	13	10	26	18
MAR. 18	48	8	9	9	3	5	44	24	13	10	26	18
MAR. 19	1	10	11	11	3	5	44	24	13	10	26	18
MAR. 20	1	12	12	13	3	5	44	24	14	10	26	18
MAR. 21	1	14	14	15	3	5	45	24	14	10	26	18
MAR. 22	1	15	16	17	3	5	45	24	14	10	26	18
MAR. 23	1	17	18	18	4	5	45	24	14	10	26	18
MAR. 24	1	19	19	20	4	5	45	24	14	10	26	18
MAR. 25	2	20	21	21	4	5	45	24	14	10	26	18
MAR. 26	2	22	22	22	4	5	45	24	14	10	26	18
MAR. 27	2	24	24	25	4	5	45	24	14	10	26	18
MAR. 28	2	25	26	26	4	5	45	24	14	10	26	18
MAR. 29	2	27	27	28	4	5	45	24	14	10	26	18
MAR. 30	2	28	29	29	5	5	45	24	14	10	26	18
MAR. 31	2	30	30	31	5	5	46	24	14	10	26	18

Date & Time	SUN	MOON 1 ◐	MOON 2 ◑	MOON 3 ●	MERCURY	VENUS	MARS	JUPITER	SATURN	URANUS	NEPTUNE	PLUTO
APR. 1	2	31	32	33	5	5	46	24	14	10	26	18
APR. 2	2	33	34	34	5	5	46	24	14	10	26	18
APR. 3	3	35	35	36	5	5	46	24	14	10	26	18
APR. 4	3	36	37	37	5	5	46	24	14	10	26	18
APR. 5	3	38	39	39	5	5	46	24	14	10	26	18
APR. 6	3	40	40	41	5	5	46	24	14	10	26	18
APR. 7	3	42	42	43	5	5	46	24	14	10	26	18
APR. 8	3	43	44	45	5	5	46	24	14	10	26	18
APR. 9	3	45	46	47	4	5	47	24	14	10	26	18
APR. 10	3	47	48	1	4	5	47	24	14	10	26	18
APR. 11	4	1	2	3	4	5	47	24	14	10	26	18
APR. 12	4	3	4	5	4	5	47	24	14	10	26	18
APR. 13	4	5	6	7	4	5	47	24	14	10	26	18
APR. 14	4	7	8	9	4	4	47	23	14	10	26	18
APR. 15	4	9	10	11	4	4	47	23	14	10	26	18
APR. 16	4	11	12	12	4	4	47	23	14	10	26	18
APR. 17	4	13	14	14	4	4	47	23	14	10	26	18
APR. 18	4	15	15	16	4	4	47	23	14	10	26	18
APR. 19	5	17	17	18	4	4	48	23	14	10	26	18
APR. 20	5	18	19	19	3	4	48	23	14	10	26	18
APR. 21	5	20	20	21	3	4	48	23	14	10	26	18
APR. 22	5	22	22	23	3	4	48	23	14	10	26	18
APR. 23	5	23	24	24	3	4	48	23	14	10	26	18
APR. 24	5	25	25	26	3	4	48	23	14	10	26	18
APR. 25	6	26	27	27	3	4	48	23	14	10	26	18
APR. 26	6	28	28	29	3	4	48	23	14	10	26	18
APR. 27	6	30	30	31	3	4	48	23	14	10	26	18
APR. 28	6	31	32	32	3	3	48	23	14	10	26	18
APR. 29	6	33	33	34	3	3	1	23	14	10	26	18
APR. 30	6	34	35	35	3	3	1	23	14	10	26	18

MOON 1 ◐ 12:01 A.M. TO 8:00 A.M.   **MOON 2** ◑ 8:01 A.M. TO 4:00 P.M.   **MOON 3** ● 4:01 P.M. TO 12:00 A.M.
Use only one "moon" number. Choose the column closest to your time of birth. If your place of birth is not on
Eastern Standard Time, be sure to read "How to Convert to Eastern Standard Time" at the beginning of this section.

1945

May

Date & Time	SUN	MOON 1	MOON 2	MOON 3	MERCURY	VENUS	MARS	JUPITER	SATURN	URANUS	NEPTUNE	PLUTO
MAY 1	6	36	37	37	3	3	1	23	14	10	26	18
MAY 2	6	38	38	39	3	3	1	23	14	10	26	18
MAY 3	7	39	40	40	3	3	1	23	14	10	26	18
MAY 4	7	41	42	42	3	3	1	23	14	10	26	18
MAY 5	7	43	43	44	4	3	1	23	14	11	26	18
MAY 6	7	45	45	46	4	3	1	23	14	11	26	18
MAY 7	7	47	47	48	4	3	1	23	14	11	26	18
MAY 8	7	48	1	2	4	3	2	23	14	11	26	18
MAY 9	7	2	3	4	4	3	2	23	14	11	25	18
MAY 10	7	4	5	6	4	3	2	23	14	11	25	18
MAY 11	8	6	7	8	4	3	2	23	14	11	25	18
MAY 12	8	8	9	10	4	3	2	23	14	11	25	18
MAY 13	8	10	11	12	4	3	2	23	14	11	25	18
MAY 14	8	12	13	14	5	3	2	23	14	11	25	18
MAY 15	8	14	15	15	5	3	2	23	14	11	25	18
MAY 16	8	16	17	17	5	3	2	23	14	11	25	18
MAY 17	8	18	18	19	5	4	2	23	14	11	25	18
MAY 18	8	19	20	21	5	4	3	23	14	11	25	18
MAY 19	9	21	22	22	5	4	3	23	14	11	25	18
MAY 20	9	23	23	24	6	4	3	23	14	11	25	18
MAY 21	9	24	25	25	6	4	3	23	14	11	25	18
MAY 22	9	26	26	27	6	4	3	23	14	11	25	18
MAY 23	9	27	28	29	6	4	3	23	14	11	25	18
MAY 24	9	29	30	30	6	4	3	23	14	11	25	18
MAY 25	10	31	31	32	7	4	3	23	14	11	25	18
MAY 26	10	32	33	33	7	4	3	23	14	11	25	18
MAY 27	10	34	34	35	7	4	3	23	14	11	25	18
MAY 28	10	36	36	37	7	4	4	23	14	11	25	18
MAY 29	10	37	38	38	7	4	4	23	14	11	25	18
MAY 30	10	39	39	40	8	4	4	23	14	11	25	18
MAY 31	10	41	41	42	8	5	4	23	14	11	25	18

June

Date & Time	SUN	MOON 1	MOON 2	MOON 3	MERCURY	VENUS	MARS	JUPITER	SATURN	URANUS	NEPTUNE	PLUTO
JUN. 1	10	42	43	44	8	5	4	23	14	11	25	18
JUN. 2	10	44	45	45	8	5	4	23	14	11	25	18
JUN. 3	11	46	47	47	9	5	4	23	14	11	25	18
JUN. 4	11	48	1	1	9	5	4	23	14	11	25	18
JUN. 5	11	2	3	3	9	5	4	23	14	11	25	18
JUN. 6	11	4	4	5	9	5	4	23	14	11	25	18
JUN. 7	11	6	6	7	10	5	5	23	14	11	25	18
JUN. 8	11	8	8	9	10	5	5	23	14	11	25	18
JUN. 9	11	10	10	11	10	5	5	23	14	11	25	18
JUN. 10	11	12	12	13	11	6	5	23	14	11	25	18
JUN. 11	12	13	14	15	11	6	5	23	14	11	25	18
JUN. 12	12	15	16	16	11	6	5	23	14	11	25	18
JUN. 13	12	17	18	18	11	6	5	23	14	11	25	18
JUN. 14	12	19	19	20	12	6	5	23	14	11	25	18
JUN. 15	12	21	21	22	12	6	5	23	15	11	25	18
JUN. 16	12	22	23	23	12	6	5	24	15	11	25	18
JUN. 17	12	24	24	25	13	6	6	24	15	11	25	18
JUN. 18	12	25	26	26	13	6	6	24	15	11	25	18
JUN. 19	13	27	28	28	13	7	6	24	15	11	25	18
JUN. 20	13	29	29	30	13	7	6	24	15	11	25	18
JUN. 21	13	30	31	31	14	7	6	24	15	11	25	18
JUN. 22	13	32	32	33	14	7	6	24	15	11	25	18
JUN. 23	13	33	34	35	14	7	6	24	15	11	25	18
JUN. 24	13	35	36	36	15	7	6	24	15	11	25	18
JUN. 25	14	37	37	38	15	7	6	24	15	11	25	18
JUN. 26	14	38	39	40	15	7	6	24	15	11	25	18
JUN. 27	14	40	41	41	15	8	7	24	15	11	25	18
JUN. 28	14	42	43	43	16	8	7	24	15	11	25	18
JUN. 29	14	44	44	45	16	8	7	24	15	11	25	18
JUN. 30	14	46	46	47	16	8	7	24	15	11	25	18

MOON 1 ☽ 12:01 A.M. TO 8:00 A.M.   **MOON 2** ◑ 8:01 A.M. TO 4:00 P.M.   **MOON 3** ● 4:01 P.M. TO 12:00 A.M.
Use only one "moon" number. Choose the column closest to your time of birth. If your place of birth is not on Eastern Standard Time, be sure to read "How to Convert to Eastern Standard Time" at the beginning of this section.

1945

July

August

Date & Time	SUN	MOON 1	MOON 2	MOON 3	MERCURY	VENUS	MARS	JUPITER	SATURN	URANUS	NEPTUNE	PLUTO
JUL. 1	14	47	48	1	16	8	7	24	15	11	25	18
JUL. 2	14	1	2	3	17	8	7	24	15	11	25	18
JUL. 3	15	3	4	4	17	8	7	24	15	11	25	18
JUL. 4	15	5	6	6	17	8	7	24	15	11	25	18
JUL. 5	15	7	8	8	17	9	7	24	15	11	25	18
JUL. 6	15	9	10	10	18	9	7	24	15	11	25	18
JUL. 7	15	11	11	12	18	9	7	24	15	11	25	18
JUL. 8	15	13	13	14	18	9	8	24	15	11	25	18
JUL. 9	15	15	15	16	18	9	8	24	15	11	25	18
JUL. 10	15	16	17	18	18	9	8	24	15	11	25	18
JUL. 11	16	18	19	19	19	9	8	24	15	11	25	18
JUL. 12	16	20	20	21	19	10	8	24	15	11	25	18
JUL. 13	16	22	22	23	19	10	8	24	15	11	25	18
JUL. 14	16	23	24	24	19	10	8	24	15	11	25	18
JUL. 15	16	25	25	26	19	10	8	24	15	11	25	18
JUL. 16	16	26	27	28	20	10	8	24	15	11	25	18
JUL. 17	16	28	29	29	20	10	8	24	15	11	25	18
JUL. 18	16	30	30	31	20	10	8	24	15	11	25	18
JUL. 19	17	31	32	32	20	11	9	24	15	11	25	18
JUL. 20	17	33	33	34	20	11	9	24	15	11	25	18
JUL. 21	17	34	35	36	20	11	9	24	15	11	26	18
JUL. 22	17	36	37	37	20	11	9	24	15	11	26	18
JUL. 23	17	38	38	39	21	11	9	24	15	11	26	18
JUL. 24	17	40	40	41	21	11	9	24	15	11	26	18
JUL. 25	17	41	42	43	21	11	9	24	15	11	26	18
JUL. 26	18	43	44	44	21	12	9	24	15	11	26	18
JUL. 27	18	45	46	46	21	12	9	24	15	11	26	18
JUL. 28	18	47	48	48	21	12	9	24	15	11	26	18
JUL. 29	18	1	2	2	21	12	9	24	15	11	26	18
JUL. 30	18	3	3	4	21	12	10	24	15	11	26	18
JUL. 31	18	5	5	6	21	12	10	24	15	11	26	18

Date & Time	SUN	MOON 1	MOON 2	MOON 3	MERCURY	VENUS	MARS	JUPITER	SATURN	URANUS	NEPTUNE	PLUTO
AUG. 1	18	7	7	8	21	12	10	24	15	11	26	18
AUG. 2	18	8	9	10	21	13	10	24	15	11	26	18
AUG. 3	19	10	11	12	22	13	10	24	15	11	26	18
AUG. 4	19	12	13	13	22	13	10	24	15	11	26	18
AUG. 5	19	14	15	15	22	13	10	24	15	11	26	18
AUG. 6	19	16	16	17	22	13	10	24	15	11	26	18
AUG. 7	19	18	18	19	22	13	10	25	15	11	26	18
AUG. 8	19	19	20	22	22	14	10	25	15	11	26	18
AUG. 9	19	21	22	22	22	14	10	25	15	11	26	18
AUG. 10	19	23	23	24	22	14	11	25	15	11	26	18
AUG. 11	20	24	25	25	21	14	11	25	15	11	26	18
AUG. 12	20	26	26	27	21	14	11	25	15	11	26	18
AUG. 13	20	28	28	29	21	14	11	25	15	11	26	18
AUG. 14	20	29	30	30	21	14	11	25	16	11	26	18
AUG. 15	20	31	31	32	21	15	11	25	16	11	26	18
AUG. 16	20	32	33	33	21	15	11	25	16	11	26	18
AUG. 17	20	34	34	35	21	15	11	25	16	11	26	18
AUG. 18	20	36	36	37	21	15	11	25	16	11	26	18
AUG. 19	21	37	38	38	21	15	11	25	16	11	26	18
AUG. 20	21	39	40	40	21	15	11	25	16	11	26	18
AUG. 21	21	41	41	42	21	16	12	25	16	11	26	18
AUG. 22	21	43	43	44	20	16	12	25	16	11	26	18
AUG. 23	21	44	45	46	20	16	12	25	16	11	26	18
AUG. 24	21	46	47	48	20	16	12	25	16	11	26	18
AUG. 25	21	48	1	2	20	16	12	25	16	11	26	18
AUG. 26	22	2	3	4	20	16	12	25	16	11	26	18
AUG. 27	22	4	5	5	20	16	12	25	16	11	26	18
AUG. 28	22	6	7	7	20	17	12	25	16	11	26	18
AUG. 29	22	8	9	9	20	17	12	25	16	11	26	18
AUG. 30	22	10	11	11	20	17	12	25	16	11	26	18
AUG. 31	22	12	12	13	20	17	12	25	16	11	26	18

MOON 1 ☽ 12:01 A.M. TO 8:00 A.M.   **MOON 2** ☽ 8:01 A.M. TO 4:00 P.M.   **MOON 3** ● 4:01 P.M. TO 12:00 A.M.
Use only one "moon" number. Choose the column closest to your time of birth. If your place of birth is not on
Eastern Standard Time, be sure to read "How to Convert to Eastern Standard Time" at the beginning of this section.

1945

September

Date & Time	SUN ☉	MOON 1 ◐	MOON 2 ◑	MOON 3 ●	MERCURY	VENUS	MARS	JUPITER	SATURN	URANUS	NEPTUNE	PLUTO
SEP. 1	22	14	14	15	20	17	12	25	16	11	26	18
SEP. 2	22	15	16	17	20	17	13	25	16	11	26	18
SEP. 3	23	17	18	18	20	18	13	25	16	11	26	18
SEP. 4	23	19	19	20	20	18	13	25	16	11	26	18
SEP. 5	23	21	21	22	20	18	13	25	16	11	26	18
SEP. 6	23	22	23	23	20	18	13	25	16	11	26	18
SEP. 7	23	24	24	25	20	18	13	25	16	11	26	18
SEP. 8	23	25	26	27	21	18	13	25	16	11	26	18
SEP. 9	23	27	28	28	21	18	13	25	16	11	26	18
SEP. 10	23	29	29	30	21	19	13	25	16	11	26	18
SEP. 11	24	30	31	31	21	19	13	25	16	11	26	18
SEP. 12	24	32	32	33	21	19	13	25	16	11	26	18
SEP. 13	24	33	34	34	22	19	13	25	16	11	26	18
SEP. 14	24	35	36	36	22	19	13	26	16	11	26	18
SEP. 15	24	37	37	38	22	19	14	26	16	11	26	18
SEP. 16	24	38	39	39	22	20	14	26	16	11	26	18
SEP. 17	24	40	41	41	22	20	14	26	16	11	26	18
SEP. 18	24	42	42	43	23	20	14	26	16	11	26	18
SEP. 19	25	44	44	45	23	20	14	26	16	11	26	18
SEP. 20	25	46	46	47	23	20	14	26	16	11	26	18
SEP. 21	25	47	48	1	23	20	14	26	16	11	26	18
SEP. 22	25	1	2	3	24	21	14	26	16	11	26	18
SEP. 23	25	3	4	5	24	21	14	26	16	11	26	18
SEP. 24	25	5	6	7	24	21	14	26	16	11	26	18
SEP. 25	26	7	8	9	24	21	14	26	16	11	26	18
SEP. 26	26	9	10	11	25	21	14	26	16	11	26	18
SEP. 27	26	11	12	13	25	21	14	26	16	11	26	18
SEP. 28	26	13	14	14	25	22	15	26	16	11	26	18
SEP. 29	26	15	16	16	25	22	15	26	16	11	26	18
SEP. 30	26	17	17	18	26	22	15	26	16	11	26	18

October

Date & Time	SUN ☉	MOON 1 ◐	MOON 2 ◑	MOON 3 ●	MERCURY	VENUS	MARS	JUPITER	SATURN	URANUS	NEPTUNE	PLUTO
OCT. 1	26	18	19	20	26	22	15	26	16	11	26	18
OCT. 2	26	20	21	21	26	22	15	26	16	11	26	18
OCT. 3	27	22	22	23	26	22	15	26	16	11	26	18
OCT. 4	27	23	24	24	27	23	15	26	16	11	26	18
OCT. 5	27	25	26	26	27	23	15	26	16	11	26	18
OCT. 6	27	27	27	29	27	23	15	26	16	11	26	18
OCT. 7	27	28	29	29	27	23	15	26	16	11	26	19
OCT. 8	27	30	30	31	27	23	15	26	16	11	26	19
OCT. 9	27	31	32	32	28	23	15	26	16	11	26	19
OCT. 10	27	33	33	34	28	23	15	26	16	11	26	19
OCT. 11	28	35	35	36	28	24	15	26	16	11	26	19
OCT. 12	28	36	37	37	28	24	15	26	16	11	26	19
OCT. 13	28	38	38	39	29	24	15	26	16	11	26	19
OCT. 14	28	39	40	41	29	24	16	26	16	11	26	19
OCT. 15	28	41	42	42	29	24	16	26	16	11	26	19
OCT. 16	28	43	43	44	29	24	16	26	16	11	26	19
OCT. 17	28	45	45	46	29	25	16	26	16	11	26	19
OCT. 18	28	47	47	48	30	25	16	26	16	11	26	19
OCT. 19	29	1	1	2	30	25	16	27	16	11	26	19
OCT. 20	29	3	3	4	30	25	16	27	16	11	26	19
OCT. 21	29	5	5	6	30	25	16	27	16	11	26	19
OCT. 22	29	7	7	8	30	25	16	27	16	11	26	19
OCT. 23	29	9	9	10	31	26	16	27	16	11	26	19
OCT. 24	29	11	11	12	31	26	16	27	16	11	26	19
OCT. 25	29	13	13	14	31	26	16	27	16	11	26	19
OCT. 26	30	14	15	16	31	26	16	27	16	11	26	19
OCT. 27	30	16	17	17	31	26	16	27	16	11	26	19
OCT. 28	30	18	19	19	32	26	16	27	16	11	26	19
OCT. 29	30	20	20	21	32	27	16	27	16	11	26	19
OCT. 30	30	21	22	22	32	27	16	27	16	11	26	19
OCT. 31	30	23	24	24	32	27	16	27	16	11	26	19

MOON 1 ◐ 12:01 A.M. TO 8:00 A.M.　　**MOON 2** ◑ 8:01 A.M. TO 4:00 P.M.　　**MOON 3** ● 4:01 P.M. TO 12:00 A.M.

Use only one "moon" number. Choose the column closest to your time of birth. If your place of birth is not on Eastern Standard Time, be sure to read "How to Convert to Eastern Standard Time" at the beginning of this section.

1945

November

Date & Time	SUN ☉	MOON 1 ☽	MOON 2 ☽	MOON 3 ●	MERCURY	VENUS	MARS	JUPITER	SATURN	URANUS	NEPTUNE	PLUTO
NOV. 1	30	25	25	26	32	27	17	27	16	11	26	19
NOV. 2	30	26	27	27	33	27	17	27	16	11	26	19
NOV. 3	31	28	28	29	33	27	17	27	16	11	26	19
NOV. 4	31	29	30	30	33	28	17	27	16	11	26	19
NOV. 5	31	31	31	32	33	28	17	27	16	11	26	19
NOV. 6	31	33	33	34	33	28	17	27	16	11	26	19
NOV. 7	31	34	35	35	34	28	17	27	16	11	26	19
NOV. 8	31	36	36	37	34	28	17	27	16	11	26	19
NOV. 9	31	37	38	38	34	28	17	27	16	11	26	19
NOV. 10	31	39	40	40	34	29	17	27	16	11	26	19
NOV. 11	31	41	41	42	34	29	17	27	16	11	26	19
NOV. 12	32	42	43	43	34	29	17	27	16	11	26	19
NOV. 13	32	44	45	45	35	29	17	27	16	11	26	19
NOV. 14	32	46	46	47	35	29	17	27	16	11	26	19
NOV. 15	32	48	48	1	35	29	17	27	16	11	26	19
NOV. 16	32	2	2	3	35	30	17	27	16	11	26	19
NOV. 17	32	4	4	5	35	30	17	27	16	11	26	19
NOV. 18	32	6	6	7	35	30	17	27	16	11	26	19
NOV. 19	33	8	8	9	35	30	17	27	16	11	26	19
NOV. 20	33	10	10	11	36	30	17	27	16	11	26	19
NOV. 21	33	12	12	13	36	30	17	27	16	11	26	19
NOV. 22	33	14	14	15	36	31	17	27	16	11	26	19
NOV. 23	33	16	16	17	36	31	17	27	16	11	26	19
NOV. 24	33	17	18	19	36	31	17	27	16	11	26	19
NOV. 25	34	19	20	20	36	31	17	28	16	11	26	19
NOV. 26	34	21	21	22	36	31	17	28	16	11	26	19
NOV. 27	34	23	23	24	36	31	17	28	16	11	26	19
NOV. 28	34	24	25	25	36	32	17	28	16	11	26	19
NOV. 29	34	26	26	27	36	32	17	28	16	11	26	19
NOV. 30	34	27	28	28	36	32	17	28	16	11	26	19

December

Date & Time	SUN ☉	MOON 1 ☽	MOON 2 ☽	MOON 3 ●	MERCURY	VENUS	MARS	JUPITER	SATURN	URANUS	NEPTUNE	PLUTO
DEC. 1	34	29	30	30	36	32	17	28	16	11	26	19
DEC. 2	34	31	31	32	36	32	17	28	16	11	26	19
DEC. 3	35	32	33	33	36	32	17	28	16	11	26	19
DEC. 4	35	34	34	35	36	33	17	28	16	11	26	19
DEC. 5	35	35	36	36	35	33	17	28	16	11	26	19
DEC. 6	35	37	37	38	35	33	17	28	16	11	26	19
DEC. 7	35	39	39	40	35	33	17	28	16	11	26	19
DEC. 8	35	40	41	41	35	33	17	28	16	11	26	19
DEC. 9	35	42	42	43	35	33	17	28	16	11	26	19
DEC. 10	35	44	44	45	34	34	17	28	16	11	26	19
DEC. 11	36	45	46	47	34	34	17	28	16	11	26	19
DEC. 12	36	47	48	48	34	34	17	28	16	11	26	19
DEC. 13	36	1	2	2	34	34	17	28	16	11	26	19
DEC. 14	36	3	4	4	34	34	17	28	16	11	26	19
DEC. 15	36	5	5	6	34	34	17	28	16	11	26	19
DEC. 16	36	7	7	8	34	35	17	28	16	11	26	19
DEC. 17	36	9	9	10	34	35	17	28	16	11	26	19
DEC. 18	36	11	11	12	34	35	17	28	16	11	26	19
DEC. 19	37	13	13	14	34	35	17	28	16	11	26	19
DEC. 20	37	15	15	16	34	35	17	28	16	11	26	19
DEC. 21	37	17	17	18	34	35	17	28	16	11	26	18
DEC. 22	37	18	19	20	34	36	17	28	16	11	26	18
DEC. 23	37	20	21	21	34	36	17	28	16	11	26	18
DEC. 24	37	22	23	23	34	36	17	28	16	11	26	18
DEC. 25	37	24	24	25	34	36	17	28	16	11	26	18
DEC. 26	38	25	26	26	35	36	17	28	16	11	26	18
DEC. 27	38	27	27	28	35	36	17	28	16	11	26	18
DEC. 28	38	29	29	30	35	37	17	28	16	11	26	18
DEC. 29	38	30	31	31	35	37	17	28	16	11	26	18
DEC. 30	38	32	32	33	35	37	17	28	16	11	26	18
DEC. 31	38	33	34	34	35	37	17	28	16	11	26	18

MOON 1 ☽ 12:01 A.M. TO 8:00 A.M. **MOON 2** ☽ 8:01 A.M. TO 4:00 P.M. **MOON 3** ● 4:01 P.M. TO 12:00 A.M.
Use only one "moon" number. Choose the column closest to your time of birth. If your place of birth is not on Eastern Standard Time, be sure to read "How to Convert to Eastern Standard Time" at the beginning of this section.

1946

January

Date & Time	SUN	MOON 1	MOON 2	MOON 3	MERCURY	VENUS	MARS	JUPITER	SATURN	URANUS	NEPTUNE	PLUTO
JAN. 1	38	35	35	36	35	37	17	28	16	11	26	18
JAN. 2	38	36	37	38	36	37	17	28	16	11	26	18
JAN. 3	39	38	39	39	36	38	17	28	16	11	26	18
JAN. 4	39	40	40	41	36	38	17	28	16	11	26	18
JAN. 5	39	41	42	43	36	38	17	28	16	11	26	18
JAN. 6	39	43	44	44	36	38	16	28	16	11	26	18
JAN. 7	39	45	46	46	37	38	16	28	16	11	26	18
JAN. 8	39	47	47	48	37	38	16	28	16	11	26	18
JAN. 9	39	1	1	2	37	39	16	28	16	11	26	18
JAN. 10	40	2	3	4	37	39	16	28	16	11	26	18
JAN. 11	40	4	5	6	37	39	16	28	16	11	26	18
JAN. 12	40	6	7	7	37	39	16	28	16	11	26	18
JAN. 13	40	8	9	9	38	39	16	28	16	11	26	18
JAN. 14	40	10	11	11	38	40	16	28	16	11	26	18
JAN. 15	40	12	13	13	38	40	16	28	16	11	26	18
JAN. 16	40	14	15	15	38	40	16	28	16	11	26	18
JAN. 17	41	16	16	16	38	40	16	28	16	11	26	18
JAN. 18	41	18	18	19	39	40	16	28	16	11	26	18
JAN. 19	41	19	20	21	39	40	16	29	16	11	26	18
JAN. 20	41	21	22	22	39	41	16	29	16	11	26	18
JAN. 21	41	23	24	24	39	41	16	29	16	11	26	18
JAN. 22	41	25	25	26	39	41	16	29	16	11	26	18
JAN. 23	42	26	27	27	40	41	16	29	16	11	26	18
JAN. 24	42	28	29	29	40	41	16	29	16	11	26	18
JAN. 25	42	30	30	31	40	41	16	29	16	11	26	18
JAN. 26	42	31	32	32	40	42	15	29	16	11	26	18
JAN. 27	42	33	33	34	41	42	15	29	16	11	26	18
JAN. 28	42	34	35	35	41	42	15	29	16	11	26	18
JAN. 29	42	36	36	37	41	42	15	29	16	11	26	18
JAN. 30	42	38	38	39	41	42	15	29	16	11	26	18
JAN. 31	43	39	40	40	41	42	15	29	16	11	26	18

February

Date & Time	SUN	MOON 1	MOON 2	MOON 3	MERCURY	VENUS	MARS	JUPITER	SATURN	URANUS	NEPTUNE	PLUTO
FEB. 1	43	41	42	42	42	43	15	29	16	11	26	18
FEB. 2	43	43	43	44	42	43	15	29	16	11	26	18
FEB. 3	43	44	45	46	42	43	15	29	16	11	26	18
FEB. 4	43	46	47	48	42	43	15	29	16	11	26	18
FEB. 5	43	48	1	1	42	43	15	29	16	11	26	18
FEB. 6	43	2	3	3	42	43	15	29	16	11	26	18
FEB. 7	43	4	5	5	43	44	15	29	16	11	26	18
FEB. 8	44	6	6	7	43	44	15	29	16	11	26	18
FEB. 9	44	8	8	9	43	44	15	29	16	11	26	18
FEB. 10	44	10	10	11	44	44	15	29	16	11	26	18
FEB. 11	44	11	12	13	44	44	15	29	16	11	26	18
FEB. 12	44	13	14	15	44	44	15	29	16	11	26	18
FEB. 13	44	15	16	16	44	45	15	29	16	11	26	18
FEB. 14	44	17	18	18	45	45	15	29	15	11	26	18
FEB. 15	44	19	19	20	45	45	15	29	15	11	26	18
FEB. 16	45	21	21	22	45	45	15	29	15	11	26	18
FEB. 17	45	22	23	24	45	45	15	29	15	11	26	18
FEB. 18	45	24	25	25	46	45	15	29	15	11	26	18
FEB. 19	45	26	26	27	46	46	15	29	15	11	26	18
FEB. 20	45	27	28	28	46	46	15	29	15	11	26	18
FEB. 21	45	29	30	30	46	46	15	29	15	11	26	18
FEB. 22	45	31	31	32	47	46	15	29	15	11	26	18
FEB. 23	46	32	33	33	47	46	15	29	15	11	26	18
FEB. 24	46	34	34	35	47	46	15	29	15	11	26	18
FEB. 25	46	35	36	36	47	47	15	29	15	11	26	18
FEB. 26	46	37	38	38	48	47	15	29	15	11	26	18
FEB. 27	46	39	39	40	48	47	15	29	15	11	26	18
FEB. 28	46	40	41	41	48	47	15	29	15	11	26	18

MOON 1 ☽ 12:01 A.M. TO 8:00 A.M.   **MOON 2** ☽ 8:01 A.M. TO 4:00 P.M.   **MOON 3** ● 4:01 P.M. TO 12:00 A.M.

Use only one "moon" number. Choose the column closest to your time of birth. If your place of birth is not on Eastern Standard Time, be sure to read "How to Convert to Eastern Standard Time" at the beginning of this section.

1946

March

Date & Time	SUN	MOON 1	MOON 2	MOON 3	MERCURY	VENUS	MARS	JUPITER	SATURN	URANUS	NEPTUNE	PLUTO
MAR. 1	46	42	43	43	48	47	15	29	15	11	26	18
MAR. 2	46	44	44	45	1	47	15	29	15	11	26	18
MAR. 3	47	46	46	47	1	48	15	29	15	11	26	18
MAR. 4	47	48	48	1	1	48	15	29	15	11	26	18
MAR. 5	47	1	2	3	1	48	15	29	15	11	26	18
MAR. 6	47	3	4	5	1	48	15	29	15	11	26	18
MAR. 7	47	5	6	7	1	48	15	28	15	11	26	18
MAR. 8	47	7	8	8	2	48	15	28	15	11	26	18
MAR. 9	47	9	10	10	2	1	15	28	15	11	26	18
MAR. 10	47	11	12	12	2	1	15	28	15	11	26	18
MAR. 11	48	13	13	14	2	1	15	28	15	11	26	18
MAR. 12	48	15	15	16	2	1	15	28	15	11	26	18
MAR. 13	48	16	17	18	2	1	15	28	15	11	26	18
MAR. 14	48	18	19	19	2	1	15	28	15	11	26	18
MAR. 15	48	20	21	21	2	2	15	28	15	11	26	18
MAR. 16	48	22	22	23	2	2	15	28	15	11	26	18
MAR. 17	48	24	24	25	2	2	15	28	15	11	26	18
MAR. 18	48	25	26	26	2	2	15	28	15	11	26	18
MAR. 19	1	27	27	28	2	2	15	28	15	11	26	18
MAR. 20	1	28	29	30	2	2	15	28	15	11	26	18
MAR. 21	1	30	31	31	2	3	15	28	15	11	26	18
MAR. 22	1	32	32	33	2	3	15	28	15	11	26	18
MAR. 23	1	33	34	34	2	3	15	28	15	11	26	18
MAR. 24	1	35	35	36	2	3	15	28	15	11	26	18
MAR. 25	2	36	37	37	2	3	16	28	15	11	26	18
MAR. 26	2	38	39	39	2	3	16	28	15	11	26	18
MAR. 27	2	40	40	41	2	4	16	28	15	11	26	18
MAR. 28	2	41	42	42	1	4	16	28	15	11	26	18
MAR. 29	2	43	44	44	1	4	16	28	15	11	26	18
MAR. 30	2	45	45	46	1	4	16	28	15	11	26	18
MAR. 31	2	47	47	48	1	4	16	28	15	11	26	18

April

Date & Time	SUN	MOON 1	MOON 2	MOON 3	MERCURY	VENUS	MARS	JUPITER	SATURN	URANUS	NEPTUNE	PLUTO
APR. 1	2	1	1	2	1	4	16	28	15	11	26	18
APR. 2	2	3	3	4	1	4	16	28	15	11	26	18
APR. 3	3	5	5	6	1	5	16	28	15	11	26	18
APR. 4	3	7	7	8	1	5	16	28	15	11	26	18
APR. 5	3	9	9	10	1	5	16	28	15	11	26	18
APR. 6	3	10	11	12	1	5	16	28	15	11	26	18
APR. 7	3	12	13	14	1	5	16	28	15	11	26	18
APR. 8	3	14	15	15	1	5	16	28	15	11	26	18
APR. 9	3	16	17	17	1	6	16	28	15	11	26	18
APR. 10	3	18	18	19	1	6	16	28	15	11	26	18
APR. 11	4	20	20	21	1	6	16	28	15	11	26	18
APR. 12	4	21	22	23	1	6	16	28	15	11	26	18
APR. 13	4	23	24	24	1	6	16	28	15	11	26	18
APR. 14	4	25	25	26	1	6	16	28	15	11	26	18
APR. 15	4	26	27	27	1	7	17	28	15	11	26	18
APR. 16	4	28	29	29	1	7	17	28	15	11	26	18
APR. 17	4	30	30	31	1	7	17	28	15	11	26	18
APR. 18	4	31	32	32	1	7	17	28	15	11	26	18
APR. 19	5	33	33	34	1	7	17	28	15	11	26	18
APR. 20	5	34	35	35	1	7	17	28	15	11	26	18
APR. 21	5	36	36	37	1	8	17	28	15	11	26	18
APR. 22	5	38	38	39	2	8	17	28	15	11	26	18
APR. 23	5	39	40	40	2	8	17	28	15	11	26	18
APR. 24	5	41	41	42	2	8	17	28	16	11	26	18
APR. 25	6	42	43	44	2	8	17	28	16	11	26	18
APR. 26	6	44	45	45	2	8	17	28	16	11	26	18
APR. 27	6	46	47	47	2	9	17	28	16	11	26	18
APR. 28	6	48	48	1	2	9	17	28	16	11	26	18
APR. 29	6	2	2	3	3	9	17	28	16	11	26	18
APR. 30	6	4	4	5	3	9	17	28	16	11	26	18

MOON 1 ◗ 12:01 A.M. TO 8:00 A.M.   **MOON 2** ◑ 8:01 A.M. TO 4:00 P.M.   **MOON 3** ● 4:01 P.M. TO 12:00 A.M.

Use only one "moon" number. Choose the column closest to your time of birth. If your place of birth is not on Eastern Standard Time, be sure to read "How to Convert to Eastern Standard Time" at the beginning of this section.

1946

May

June

Date & Time	SUN	MOON 1	MOON 2	MOON 3	MERCURY	VENUS	MARS	JUPITER	SATURN	URANUS	NEPTUNE	PLUTO
MAY 1	6	6	6	7	3	9	17	28	16	11	26	18
MAY 2	6	8	8	9	3	9	18	28	16	11	26	18
MAY 3	7	10	10	11	3	10	18	28	16	11	26	18
MAY 4	7	12	12	13	3	10	18	28	16	11	26	18
MAY 5	7	14	14	15	4	10	18	28	16	11	26	18
MAY 6	7	16	16	17	4	10	18	28	16	11	26	18
MAY 7	7	17	18	19	4	10	18	28	16	11	26	18
MAY 8	7	19	20	20	4	10	18	28	16	11	26	18
MAY 9	7	21	22	22	4	11	18	28	16	11	26	18
MAY 10	7	23	23	24	5	11	18	28	16	11	26	18
MAY 11	8	24	25	25	5	11	18	28	16	11	26	18
MAY 12	8	26	27	27	5	11	18	28	16	11	26	18
MAY 13	8	28	28	29	5	11	18	27	16	11	26	18
MAY 14	8	29	30	30	6	11	18	27	16	11	26	18
MAY 15	8	31	31	32	6	12	18	27	16	11	26	18
MAY 16	8	32	33	33	6	12	18	27	16	11	26	18
MAY 17	8	34	34	35	6	12	19	27	16	11	26	18
MAY 18	8	36	36	37	7	12	19	27	16	11	26	18
MAY 19	9	37	38	38	7	12	19	27	16	11	26	18
MAY 20	9	39	39	40	7	12	19	27	16	11	26	18
MAY 21	9	40	41	41	7	12	19	27	16	11	26	18
MAY 22	9	42	43	43	8	13	19	27	16	11	26	18
MAY 23	9	44	44	45	8	13	19	27	16	11	26	18
MAY 24	9	45	46	47	8	13	19	27	16	11	26	18
MAY 25	10	47	48	48	8	13	19	27	16	11	26	18
MAY 26	10	1	2	2	9	13	19	27	16	11	26	18
MAY 27	10	3	3	4	9	13	19	27	16	11	26	18
MAY 28	10	5	5	6	9	14	19	27	16	11	26	18
MAY 29	10	7	7	8	10	14	19	27	16	11	26	18
MAY 30	10	9	9	10	10	14	19	27	16	11	26	18
MAY 31	10	11	12	12	10	14	19	27	16	11	26	18

Date & Time	SUN	MOON 1	MOON 2	MOON 3	MERCURY	VENUS	MARS	JUPITER	SATURN	URANUS	NEPTUNE	PLUTO
JUN. 1	10	13	14	14	10	14	20	27	16	11	26	18
JUN. 2	10	15	15	16	11	14	20	27	16	11	26	18
JUN. 3	11	17	17	18	11	15	20	27	16	11	26	18
JUN. 4	11	19	19	20	11	15	20	27	16	11	26	18
JUN. 5	11	20	21	22	11	15	20	27	16	11	26	18
JUN. 6	11	22	23	23	12	15	20	27	16	11	26	18
JUN. 7	11	24	24	25	12	15	20	27	16	11	26	18
JUN. 8	11	26	26	27	12	15	20	27	16	11	26	18
JUN. 9	11	27	28	28	13	16	20	27	16	11	26	18
JUN. 10	11	29	29	30	13	16	20	27	16	11	26	18
JUN. 11	12	30	31	31	13	16	20	27	16	11	26	18
JUN. 12	12	32	33	33	14	16	20	27	16	11	26	18
JUN. 13	12	34	34	35	14	16	20	27	16	11	26	18
JUN. 14	12	35	36	36	14	16	21	27	16	11	26	18
JUN. 15	12	37	37	38	14	16	21	27	16	11	26	18
JUN. 16	12	38	39	39	15	17	21	27	16	11	26	18
JUN. 17	12	40	40	41	15	17	21	27	16	11	26	18
JUN. 18	12	42	42	43	15	17	21	27	16	11	26	18
JUN. 19	13	43	44	44	15	17	21	27	16	11	26	18
JUN. 20	13	45	45	46	15	17	21	27	16	11	26	18
JUN. 21	13	47	47	48	16	17	21	27	16	11	26	18
JUN. 22	13	48	1	2	16	18	21	27	16	11	26	18
JUN. 23	13	2	3	3	16	18	21	27	16	11	26	18
JUN. 24	13	4	5	5	16	18	21	27	16	11	26	18
JUN. 25	14	6	7	7	16	18	21	27	16	11	26	18
JUN. 26	14	8	9	9	17	18	22	27	16	11	26	18
JUN. 27	14	10	11	11	17	18	21	27	16	11	26	18
JUN. 28	14	12	13	13	17	19	22	27	16	11	26	18
JUN. 29	14	14	15	15	17	19	22	27	16	11	26	18
JUN. 30	14	16	17	17	17	19	22	27	16	11	26	18

MOON 1 ◗ 12:01 A.M. TO 8:00 A.M.　　**MOON 2** ◖ 8:01 A.M. TO 4:00 P.M.　　**MOON 3** ● 4:01 P.M. TO 12:00 A.M.

Use only one "moon" number. Choose the column closest to your time of birth. If your place of birth is not on Eastern Standard Time, be sure to read "How to Convert to Eastern Standard Time" at the beginning of this section.

1946

July   August

Date & Time	SUN	MOON 1	MOON 2	MOON 3	MERCURY	VENUS	MARS	JUPITER	SATURN	URANUS	NEPTUNE	PLUTO
JUL. 1	14	18	19	19	18	19	22	27	16	11	26	18
JUL. 2	14	20	20	21	18	19	22	27	16	11	26	18
JUL. 3	15	22	22	23	18	19	22	27	16	11	26	18
JUL. 4	15	23	24	25	18	19	22	27	16	12	26	18
JUL. 5	15	25	26	26	18	20	22	27	16	12	26	18
JUL. 6	15	27	27	28	18	20	22	27	16	12	26	18
JUL. 7	15	28	29	29	18	20	22	27	17	12	26	18
JUL. 8	15	30	31	31	18	20	22	27	17	12	26	18
JUL. 9	15	32	32	33	19	20	22	27	17	12	26	18
JUL. 10	15	33	34	34	19	20	23	27	17	12	26	18
JUL. 11	16	35	35	36	19	21	23	27	17	12	26	18
JUL. 12	16	36	37	37	19	21	23	27	17	12	26	18
JUL. 13	16	38	38	39	19	21	23	27	17	12	26	18
JUL. 14	16	40	40	41	19	21	23	27	17	12	26	18
JUL. 15	16	41	42	42	19	21	23	27	17	12	26	18
JUL. 16	16	43	43	44	19	21	23	27	17	12	26	18
JUL. 17	16	45	45	46	19	21	23	27	17	12	26	18
JUL. 18	16	46	47	47	19	22	23	28	17	12	26	18
JUL. 19	17	48	1	1	19	22	23	28	17	12	26	18
JUL. 20	17	2	2	3	19	22	23	28	17	12	26	18
JUL. 21	17	4	4	5	19	22	23	28	17	12	26	18
JUL. 22	17	5	6	7	19	22	23	28	17	12	26	18
JUL. 23	17	7	8	9	19	22	24	28	17	12	26	18
JUL. 24	17	9	10	11	19	23	24	28	17	12	26	18
JUL. 25	17	11	12	13	19	23	24	28	17	12	26	18
JUL. 26	18	13	14	14	19	23	24	28	17	12	26	18
JUL. 27	18	15	16	16	19	23	24	28	17	12	26	18
JUL. 28	18	17	18	18	19	23	24	28	17	12	26	18
JUL. 29	18	19	20	20	19	23	24	28	17	12	26	18
JUL. 30	18	21	21	22	19	23	24	28	17	12	26	18
JUL. 31	18	23	23	24	18	24	24	28	17	12	26	18

Date & Time	SUN	MOON 1	MOON 2	MOON 3	MERCURY	VENUS	MARS	JUPITER	SATURN	URANUS	NEPTUNE	PLUTO
AUG. 1	18	24	25	26	18	24	24	28	17	12	26	18
AUG. 2	18	26	27	27	18	24	24	28	17	12	26	18
AUG. 3	19	28	28	29	18	24	24	28	17	12	26	18
AUG. 4	19	29	30	31	18	24	25	28	17	12	26	18
AUG. 5	19	31	32	32	18	24	25	28	17	12	26	18
AUG. 6	19	33	33	34	18	25	25	28	17	12	26	18
AUG. 7	19	34	35	35	18	25	25	28	17	12	26	18
AUG. 8	19	36	36	37	18	25	25	28	17	12	26	19
AUG. 9	19	37	38	38	18	25	25	28	17	12	26	19
AUG. 10	19	39	40	40	18	25	25	28	17	12	26	19
AUG. 11	20	41	41	42	18	25	25	28	17	12	26	19
AUG. 12	20	42	43	43	18	26	25	28	17	12	26	19
AUG. 13	20	44	45	45	18	26	25	28	17	12	26	19
AUG. 14	20	46	46	47	18	26	25	28	17	12	26	19
AUG. 15	20	48	48	1	18	26	25	28	17	12	26	19
AUG. 16	20	1	2	3	18	26	26	28	17	12	26	19
AUG. 17	20	3	4	4	18	26	26	28	17	12	26	19
AUG. 18	20	5	6	6	18	26	26	28	17	12	26	19
AUG. 19	21	7	8	8	18	26	26	28	17	12	26	19
AUG. 20	21	9	9	10	18	27	26	28	17	12	26	19
AUG. 21	21	11	11	12	18	27	26	28	17	12	26	19
AUG. 22	21	13	13	14	18	27	26	28	17	12	26	19
AUG. 23	21	14	15	16	18	27	26	28	17	12	26	19
AUG. 24	21	16	17	18	19	27	26	28	17	12	26	19
AUG. 25	21	18	19	20	19	27	26	28	17	12	26	19
AUG. 26	22	20	21	21	19	27	26	28	17	12	26	19
AUG. 27	22	22	23	23	19	28	27	28	17	12	26	19
AUG. 28	22	24	24	25	19	28	27	28	17	12	26	19
AUG. 29	22	26	26	27	20	28	27	28	17	12	26	19
AUG. 30	22	27	28	28	20	28	27	28	17	12	26	19
AUG. 31	22	29	29	30	20	28	27	28	17	12	26	19

MOON 1 ◖ 12:01 A.M. TO 8:00 A.M.   **MOON 2** ◑ 8:01 A.M. TO 4:00 P.M.   **MOON 3** ● 4:01 P.M. TO 12:00 A.M.

Use only one "moon" number. Choose the column closest to your time of birth. If your place of birth is not on Eastern Standard Time, be sure to read "How to Convert to Eastern Standard Time" at the beginning of this section.

Date & Time	SUN	MOON 1	MOON 2	MOON 3	MERCURY	VENUS	MARS	JUPITER	SATURN	URANUS	NEPTUNE	PLUTO
SEP. 1	22	31	31	32	20	28	27	28	17	12	26	19
SEP. 2	22	32	33	33	21	28	27	28	17	12	26	19
SEP. 3	23	34	34	35	21	28	27	28	17	12	26	19
SEP. 4	23	35	36	36	21	29	27	28	17	12	26	19
SEP. 5	23	37	37	38	21	29	27	28	18	12	26	19
SEP. 6	23	38	39	40	22	29	27	28	18	12	26	19
SEP. 7	23	40	41	41	22	29	27	28	18	12	26	19
SEP. 8	23	42	42	43	22	29	28	29	18	12	26	19
SEP. 9	23	43	44	45	22	29	28	29	18	12	26	19
SEP. 10	23	45	46	46	23	29	28	29	18	12	26	19
SEP. 11	24	47	48	48	23	30	28	29	18	12	26	19
SEP. 12	24	1	1	2	23	30	28	29	18	12	26	19
SEP. 13	24	3	3	4	23	30	28	29	18	12	26	19
SEP. 14	24	5	5	6	24	30	28	29	18	12	26	19
SEP. 15	24	6	7	8	24	30	28	29	18	12	26	19
SEP. 16	24	8	9	10	24	30	28	29	18	12	26	19
SEP. 17	24	10	11	12	24	30	28	29	18	12	26	19
SEP. 18	24	12	13	13	25	30	28	29	18	12	26	19
SEP. 19	25	14	15	15	25	30	28	29	18	12	26	19
SEP. 20	25	16	16	17	25	31	29	29	18	12	26	19
SEP. 21	25	18	18	19	25	31	29	29	18	12	26	19
SEP. 22	25	20	20	21	26	31	29	29	18	12	26	19
SEP. 23	25	21	22	23	26	31	29	29	18	12	26	19
SEP. 24	25	23	24	24	26	31	29	29	18	12	26	19
SEP. 25	26	25	25	26	26	31	29	29	18	12	26	19
SEP. 26	26	27	27	28	26	31	29	29	18	12	26	19
SEP. 27	26	28	29	29	27	31	29	29	18	12	26	19
SEP. 28	26	30	31	31	27	31	29	29	18	12	26	19
SEP. 29	26	32	32	33	27	32	29	29	18	12	26	19
SEP. 30	26	33	34	34	27	32	29	29	18	12	26	19

Date & Time	SUN	MOON 1	MOON 2	MOON 3	MERCURY	VENUS	MARS	JUPITER	SATURN	URANUS	NEPTUNE	PLUTO
OCT. 1	26	35	35	36	28	32	30	29	18	12	26	19
OCT. 2	26	36	37	37	28	32	30	29	18	12	26	19
OCT. 3	27	38	38	39	28	32	30	29	18	12	26	19
OCT. 4	27	40	40	41	28	32	30	29	18	12	26	19
OCT. 5	27	41	42	42	28	32	30	29	18	12	26	19
OCT. 6	27	43	43	44	29	32	30	29	18	12	26	19
OCT. 7	27	45	45	46	29	32	30	29	18	12	26	19
OCT. 8	27	46	47	47	29	32	30	29	18	12	26	19
OCT. 9	27	48	1	1	29	32	30	29	18	12	26	19
OCT. 10	27	2	3	4	29	33	30	29	18	12	26	19
OCT. 11	28	4	5	5	30	33	30	29	18	12	26	19
OCT. 12	28	6	6	7	30	33	31	29	18	12	26	19
OCT. 13	28	8	8	9	30	33	31	29	18	12	26	19
OCT. 14	28	10	10	11	30	33	31	29	18	12	26	19
OCT. 15	28	12	12	13	30	33	31	30	18	12	26	19
OCT. 16	28	14	14	15	31	33	31	30	18	12	26	19
OCT. 17	28	15	16	17	31	33	31	30	18	12	26	19
OCT. 18	28	17	18	19	31	33	31	30	18	12	26	19
OCT. 19	29	19	20	20	31	33	31	30	18	12	26	19
OCT. 20	29	21	22	22	31	33	31	30	18	12	26	19
OCT. 21	29	23	23	24	31	33	31	30	18	12	26	19
OCT. 22	29	24	25	26	32	33	31	30	18	12	26	19
OCT. 23	29	26	27	27	32	33	32	30	18	12	26	19
OCT. 24	29	28	28	29	32	33	32	30	18	12	26	19
OCT. 25	29	29	30	31	32	33	32	30	18	12	26	19
OCT. 26	30	31	32	32	32	33	32	30	18	12	26	19
OCT. 27	30	33	33	34	32	33	32	30	18	12	26	19
OCT. 28	30	34	35	35	33	33	32	30	18	12	26	19
OCT. 29	30	36	36	37	33	33	32	30	18	12	26	19
OCT. 30	30	37	38	38	33	33	32	30	18	12	26	19
OCT. 31	30	39	40	40	33	33	32	30	18	12	26	19

MOON 1 ◐ 12:01 A.M. TO 8:00 A.M.   **MOON 2** ◑ 8:01 A.M. TO 4:00 P.M.   **MOON 3** ● 4:01 P.M. TO 12:00 A.M.

Use only one "moon" number. Choose the column closest to your time of birth. If your place of birth is not on Eastern Standard Time, be sure to read "How to Convert to Eastern Standard Time" at the beginning of this section.

November

Date & Time	SUN	MOON 1	MOON 2	MOON 3	MERCURY	VENUS	MARS	JUPITER	SATURN	URANUS	NEPTUNE	PLUTO
NOV. 1	30	41	41	42	33	33	32	30	18	12	26	19
NOV. 2	30	42	43	43	33	33	33	30	18	12	26	19
NOV. 3	31	44	44	45	33	33	33	30	18	12	26	19
NOV. 4	31	46	46	47	34	33	33	30	18	12	26	19
NOV. 5	31	47	48	1	34	33	33	30	18	12	26	19
NOV. 6	31	1	2	2	34	33	33	30	18	12	26	19
NOV. 7	31	3	4	4	34	33	33	30	18	12	26	19
NOV. 8	31	5	6	6	34	33	33	30	18	12	26	19
NOV. 9	31	7	8	8	34	33	33	30	18	12	26	19
NOV. 10	31	9	10	10	34	33	33	30	18	12	26	19
NOV. 11	31	11	12	12	34	33	33	30	18	12	26	19
NOV. 12	32	13	14	14	34	33	33	30	18	12	26	19
NOV. 13	32	15	16	16	34	33	34	30	18	12	26	19
NOV. 14	32	17	17	18	34	33	34	30	18	12	26	19
NOV. 15	32	19	19	20	34	32	34	30	18	12	26	19
NOV. 16	32	21	21	22	34	32	34	30	18	12	26	19
NOV. 17	32	22	23	23	34	32	34	30	18	12	26	19
NOV. 18	32	24	25	25	33	32	34	31	18	12	26	19
NOV. 19	33	26	26	27	33	32	34	31	18	12	26	19
NOV. 20	33	27	28	28	33	32	34	31	18	12	26	19
NOV. 21	33	29	30	30	33	32	34	31	18	12	26	19
NOV. 22	33	31	31	32	33	32	34	31	18	12	26	19
NOV. 23	33	32	33	33	33	32	35	31	18	12	26	19
NOV. 24	33	34	34	35	32	32	35	31	18	12	26	19
NOV. 25	34	35	36	36	32	32	35	31	18	12	26	19
NOV. 26	34	37	38	38	32	32	35	31	18	12	26	19
NOV. 27	34	39	39	40	32	32	35	31	18	12	26	19
NOV. 28	34	40	41	41	32	32	35	31	18	12	26	19
NOV. 29	34	42	42	43	32	31	35	31	18	12	26	19
NOV. 30	34	43	44	44	32	31	35	31	18	12	26	19

December

Date & Time	SUN	MOON 1	MOON 2	MOON 3	MERCURY	VENUS	MARS	JUPITER	SATURN	URANUS	NEPTUNE	PLUTO
DEC. 1	34	45	46	46	32	31	35	31	18	12	26	19
DEC. 2	34	47	47	48	32	31	35	31	18	12	26	19
DEC. 3	35	48	1	2	32	31	36	31	18	12	26	19
DEC. 4	35	2	3	3	32	31	36	31	18	12	26	19
DEC. 5	35	4	5	5	32	31	36	31	18	12	26	19
DEC. 6	35	6	7	7	32	31	36	31	18	12	26	19
DEC. 7	35	8	9	9	32	31	36	31	18	12	26	19
DEC. 8	35	10	11	11	32	31	36	31	18	12	26	19
DEC. 9	35	12	13	13	32	31	36	31	18	12	26	19
DEC. 10	35	14	15	15	33	31	36	31	18	12	26	19
DEC. 11	36	16	17	17	33	31	36	31	18	12	26	19
DEC. 12	36	18	19	19	33	31	36	31	18	12	26	19
DEC. 13	36	20	21	21	33	31	37	31	18	12	26	19
DEC. 14	36	22	22	23	33	31	37	31	18	12	26	19
DEC. 15	36	24	24	25	33	31	37	31	18	12	26	19
DEC. 16	36	25	26	26	34	31	37	31	18	12	26	19
DEC. 17	36	27	28	28	34	31	37	31	18	12	26	19
DEC. 18	36	29	29	30	34	31	37	31	18	12	26	19
DEC. 19	37	30	31	31	34	32	37	31	18	12	26	19
DEC. 20	37	32	32	33	34	32	37	31	18	12	26	19
DEC. 21	37	33	34	34	34	32	37	31	18	12	26	19
DEC. 22	37	35	36	36	35	32	37	31	18	12	26	19
DEC. 23	37	37	37	38	35	32	38	31	18	12	26	19
DEC. 24	37	38	39	39	35	32	38	31	18	12	26	19
DEC. 25	37	40	40	41	35	32	38	32	18	12	26	19
DEC. 26	38	41	42	42	35	32	38	32	18	12	26	19
DEC. 27	38	43	44	44	36	32	38	32	18	12	26	19
DEC. 28	38	45	45	46	36	32	38	32	18	12	26	19
DEC. 29	38	46	47	47	36	32	38	32	18	12	26	19
DEC. 30	38	48	48	1	36	32	38	32	18	12	26	19
DEC. 31	38	2	2	3	36	32	38	32	18	11	26	19

MOON 1 ☽ 12:01 A.M. TO 8:00 A.M.   **MOON 2** ◑ 8:01 A.M. TO 4:00 P.M.   **MOON 3** ● 4:01 P.M. TO 12:00 A.M.
Use only one "moon" number. Choose the column closest to your time of birth. If your place of birth is not on
Eastern Standard Time, be sure to read "How to Convert to Eastern Standard Time" at the beginning of this section.

1947

January

Date & Time	SUN	MOON 1	MOON 2	MOON 3	MERCURY	VENUS	MARS	JUPITER	SATURN	URANUS	NEPTUNE	PLUTO
JAN. 1	38	3	4	5	37	33	38	32	18	11	26	19
JAN. 2	38	5	6	7	37	33	39	32	18	11	26	19
JAN. 3	39	7	8	8	37	33	39	32	18	11	26	19
JAN. 4	39	9	10	10	37	33	39	32	18	11	26	19
JAN. 5	39	11	12	12	37	33	39	32	18	11	26	19
JAN. 6	39	13	14	14	38	33	39	32	18	11	26	19
JAN. 7	39	15	16	16	38	33	39	32	18	11	26	19
JAN. 8	39	17	18	18	38	33	39	32	18	11	26	19
JAN. 9	39	19	20	20	38	33	39	32	18	11	26	19
JAN. 10	40	21	22	22	38	33	39	32	18	11	26	19
JAN. 11	40	23	24	24	39	34	39	32	18	11	26	19
JAN. 12	40	25	25	26	39	34	40	32	18	11	26	19
JAN. 13	40	26	27	28	39	34	40	32	18	11	26	19
JAN. 14	40	28	29	29	39	34	40	32	18	11	26	19
JAN. 15	40	30	30	31	40	34	40	32	18	11	26	19
JAN. 16	40	31	32	33	40	34	40	32	18	11	26	19
JAN. 17	41	33	34	34	40	34	40	32	18	11	26	19
JAN. 18	41	35	35	36	40	34	40	32	18	11	26	19
JAN. 19	41	36	37	37	40	35	40	32	18	11	26	19
JAN. 20	41	38	38	39	41	35	40	32	18	11	26	19
JAN. 21	41	39	40	40	41	35	41	32	18	11	26	19
JAN. 22	41	41	41	42	41	35	41	32	18	11	26	19
JAN. 23	42	43	43	44	41	35	41	32	18	11	26	19
JAN. 24	42	44	45	45	41	35	41	32	18	11	26	19
JAN. 25	42	46	46	47	42	35	41	32	18	11	26	19
JAN. 26	42	48	48	1	42	35	41	32	18	11	26	19
JAN. 27	42	1	2	2	42	36	41	32	18	11	26	19
JAN. 28	42	3	4	4	42	36	41	32	18	11	26	19
JAN. 29	42	5	5	6	43	36	41	32	18	11	26	19
JAN. 30	42	7	7	8	43	36	41	32	18	11	26	19
JAN. 31	43	8	9	10	43	36	42	32	18	11	26	19

February

Date & Time	SUN	MOON 1	MOON 2	MOON 3	MERCURY	VENUS	MARS	JUPITER	SATURN	URANUS	NEPTUNE	PLUTO
FEB. 1	43	10	11	12	43	36	42	32	18	11	26	19
FEB. 2	43	12	13	14	44	36	42	32	18	11	26	19
FEB. 3	43	14	15	16	44	37	42	32	18	11	26	19
FEB. 4	43	16	17	18	44	37	42	32	18	11	26	19
FEB. 5	43	18	19	20	44	37	42	32	18	11	26	19
FEB. 6	43	20	21	21	45	37	42	32	18	11	26	19
FEB. 7	43	22	23	23	45	37	42	32	18	11	26	19
FEB. 8	44	24	25	25	45	37	42	32	18	11	26	19
FEB. 9	44	26	26	27	45	37	43	32	18	11	26	19
FEB. 10	44	28	28	29	45	38	43	32	18	11	26	19
FEB. 11	44	29	30	30	46	38	43	32	18	11	26	19
FEB. 12	44	31	31	32	46	38	43	32	18	11	26	19
FEB. 13	44	33	33	34	46	38	43	32	18	11	26	19
FEB. 14	44	34	35	35	46	38	43	32	17	11	26	19
FEB. 15	44	36	36	37	47	38	43	32	17	11	26	19
FEB. 16	45	37	38	38	47	38	43	33	17	11	26	19
FEB. 17	45	39	39	40	47	39	43	33	17	11	26	19
FEB. 18	45	40	41	42	47	39	43	33	17	11	26	19
FEB. 19	45	42	43	43	47	39	44	33	17	11	26	19
FEB. 20	45	44	44	45	47	39	44	33	17	11	26	19
FEB. 21	45	45	46	47	48	39	44	33	17	11	26	19
FEB. 22	45	47	48	48	48	39	44	33	17	11	26	19
FEB. 23	46	1	1	2	48	39	44	33	17	11	26	19
FEB. 24	46	3	3	4	48	40	44	33	17	11	26	19
FEB. 25	46	4	5	6	48	40	44	33	17	11	26	19
FEB. 26	46	6	7	7	48	40	44	33	17	11	26	19
FEB. 27	46	8	9	9	48	40	44	33	17	11	26	19
FEB. 28	46	10	10	11	48	40	44	33	17	11	26	19

MOON 1 ◐ 12:01 A.M. TO 8:00 A.M.   **MOON 2** ◑ 8:01 A.M. TO 4:00 P.M.   **MOON 3** ● 4:01 P.M. TO 12:00 A.M.
Use only one "moon" number. Choose the column closest to your time of birth. If your place of birth is not on Eastern Standard Time, be sure to read "How to Convert to Eastern Standard Time" at the beginning of this section.

1947

March

Date & Time	SUN	MOON 1	MOON 2	MOON 3	MERCURY	VENUS	MARS	JUPITER	SATURN	URANUS	NEPTUNE	PLUTO
MAR. 1	46	12	12	13	48	40	45	33	17	11	26	19
MAR. 2	46	14	14	15	48	41	45	33	17	11	26	19
MAR. 3	47	16	16	17	48	41	45	33	17	11	26	19
MAR. 4	47	17	18	19	48	41	45	33	17	11	26	19
MAR. 5	47	19	20	21	48	41	45	33	17	11	26	19
MAR. 6	47	21	22	23	48	41	45	33	17	11	26	18
MAR. 7	47	23	24	24	48	41	45	33	17	11	26	18
MAR. 8	47	25	26	26	47	41	45	33	17	11	26	18
MAR. 9	47	27	27	28	47	42	45	33	17	11	26	18
MAR. 10	47	29	29	30	47	42	46	33	17	11	26	18
MAR. 11	48	30	31	31	47	42	46	33	17	11	26	18
MAR. 12	48	32	33	33	47	42	46	33	17	11	26	18
MAR. 13	48	34	34	35	47	42	46	33	17	11	26	18
MAR. 14	48	35	36	36	47	42	46	33	17	11	26	18
MAR. 15	48	37	37	38	47	43	46	33	17	11	26	18
MAR. 16	48	38	39	39	47	43	46	33	17	11	26	18
MAR. 17	48	40	40	41	46	43	46	33	17	11	26	18
MAR. 18	48	42	42	43	46	43	46	33	17	11	26	18
MAR. 19	1	43	44	44	46	43	46	33	17	11	26	18
MAR. 20	1	45	45	46	46	43	47	33	17	11	26	18
MAR. 21	1	47	47	48	46	44	47	33	17	11	26	18
MAR. 22	1	48	1	1	46	44	47	33	17	11	26	18
MAR. 23	1	2	3	3	46	44	47	33	17	11	26	18
MAR. 24	1	4	4	5	46	44	47	33	17	11	26	18
MAR. 25	2	6	6	7	46	44	47	33	17	11	26	18
MAR. 26	2	8	8	9	46	44	47	33	17	11	26	18
MAR. 27	2	9	10	11	46	44	47	33	17	11	26	18
MAR. 28	2	11	12	13	46	45	47	33	17	11	26	18
MAR. 29	2	13	14	14	46	45	48	33	17	11	26	18
MAR. 30	2	15	16	16	47	45	48	33	17	11	26	18
MAR. 31	2	17	18	18	47	45	48	33	17	11	26	18

April

Date & Time	SUN	MOON 1	MOON 2	MOON 3	MERCURY	VENUS	MARS	JUPITER	SATURN	URANUS	NEPTUNE	PLUTO
APR. 1	2	19	19	20	47	45	48	33	17	11	26	18
APR. 2	2	21	21	22	47	45	48	33	17	11	26	18
APR. 3	3	23	23	24	47	45	48	33	17	11	26	18
APR. 4	3	24	25	26	47	46	48	33	17	11	26	18
APR. 5	3	26	27	27	47	46	48	33	17	11	26	18
APR. 6	3	28	29	29	47	46	48	33	17	11	26	18
APR. 7	3	30	30	31	47	46	48	33	17	11	26	18
APR. 8	3	31	32	32	48	46	1	33	17	11	26	18
APR. 9	3	33	34	34	48	46	1	33	17	11	26	18
APR. 10	3	35	35	36	48	47	1	32	17	11	26	18
APR. 11	4	36	37	37	48	47	1	32	17	11	26	18
APR. 12	4	38	38	39	48	47	1	32	17	11	26	18
APR. 13	4	39	40	40	48	47	1	32	17	11	26	18
APR. 14	4	41	42	42	1	47	1	32	17	11	26	18
APR. 15	4	43	43	44	1	47	1	32	17	11	26	18
APR. 16	4	44	45	45	1	48	1	32	17	11	26	18
APR. 17	4	46	46	47	1	48	2	32	17	11	26	18
APR. 18	4	48	48	1	1	48	2	32	17	11	26	18
APR. 19	5	1	2	3	2	48	2	32	17	11	26	18
APR. 20	5	3	4	4	2	48	2	32	17	11	26	18
APR. 21	5	5	6	6	2	48	2	32	17	12	26	18
APR. 22	5	7	8	8	2	1	2	32	17	12	26	18
APR. 23	5	9	9	10	2	1	2	32	17	12	26	18
APR. 24	5	11	11	12	3	1	2	32	17	12	26	18
APR. 25	6	13	13	14	3	1	2	32	17	12	26	18
APR. 26	6	15	15	16	3	1	2	32	17	12	26	18
APR. 27	6	17	17	18	3	1	3	32	17	12	26	18
APR. 28	6	18	19	20	3	1	3	32	17	12	26	18
APR. 29	6	20	21	21	4	2	3	32	17	12	26	18
APR. 30	6	22	23	23	4	2	3	32	17	12	26	18

MOON 1 ☽ 12:01 A.M. TO 8:00 A.M. **MOON 2** ◑ 8:01 A.M. TO 4:00 P.M. **MOON 3** ● 4:01 P.M. TO 12:00 A.M.
Use only one "moon" number. Choose the column closest to your time of birth. If your place of birth is not on Eastern Standard Time, be sure to read "How to Convert to Eastern Standard Time" at the beginning of this section.

1947

May

June

Date & Time	SUN	MOON 1	MOON 2	MOON 3	MERCURY	VENUS	MARS	JUPITER	SATURN	URANUS	NEPTUNE	PLUTO
MAY 1	6	24	24	25	4	2	3	32	17	12	26	18
MAY 2	6	26	26	27	4	2	3	32	17	12	26	18
MAY 3	7	27	28	29	5	2	3	32	17	12	26	18
MAY 4	7	29	30	30	5	2	3	32	17	12	26	18
MAY 5	7	31	31	32	5	3	3	32	17	12	26	18
MAY 6	7	32	33	34	5	3	3	32	17	12	26	18
MAY 7	7	34	35	35	6	3	4	32	17	12	26	18
MAY 8	7	36	36	37	6	3	4	32	17	12	26	18
MAY 9	7	37	38	38	6	3	4	32	17	12	26	18
MAY 10	7	39	39	40	7	3	4	32	17	12	26	18
MAY 11	8	40	41	42	7	4	4	32	17	12	26	18
MAY 12	8	42	43	43	7	4	4	32	17	12	26	18
MAY 13	8	44	44	45	7	4	4	32	17	12	26	18
MAY 14	8	45	46	46	8	4	4	32	17	12	26	18
MAY 15	8	47	48	48	8	4	4	32	17	12	26	18
MAY 16	8	1	1	2	8	4	4	32	17	12	26	18
MAY 17	8	2	3	4	9	5	5	32	17	12	26	18
MAY 18	8	4	5	6	9	5	5	32	17	12	26	18
MAY 19	9	6	7	9	9	5	5	32	17	12	26	18
MAY 20	9	8	9	9	9	5	5	32	17	12	26	18
MAY 21	9	10	11	11	10	5	5	32	17	12	26	18
MAY 22	9	12	13	13	10	5	5	32	17	12	26	18
MAY 23	9	14	15	15	10	5	5	32	18	12	26	18
MAY 24	9	16	17	17	11	6	5	32	18	12	26	18
MAY 25	10	18	19	19	11	6	5	32	18	12	26	18
MAY 26	10	20	20	21	11	6	5	32	18	12	26	18
MAY 27	10	22	22	23	11	6	6	32	18	12	26	18
MAY 28	10	23	24	25	12	6	6	32	18	12	26	18
MAY 29	10	25	26	26	12	6	6	32	18	12	26	18
MAY 30	10	27	28	28	12	7	6	32	18	12	26	18
MAY 31	10	29	29	30	12	7	6	32	18	12	26	18

Date & Time	SUN	MOON 1	MOON 2	MOON 3	MERCURY	VENUS	MARS	JUPITER	SATURN	URANUS	NEPTUNE	PLUTO
JUN. 1	10	30	31	31	13	7	6	32	18	12	26	18
JUN. 2	10	32	33	33	13	7	6	32	18	12	26	18
JUN. 3	11	34	34	35	13	7	6	32	18	12	26	18
JUN. 4	11	35	36	36	13	7	6	32	18	12	26	18
JUN. 5	11	37	37	38	14	8	6	32	18	12	26	18
JUN. 6	11	38	39	39	14	8	7	32	18	12	26	18
JUN. 7	11	40	41	41	14	8	7	32	18	12	26	18
JUN. 8	11	42	42	43	14	8	7	32	18	12	26	18
JUN. 9	11	43	44	44	14	8	7	32	18	12	26	18
JUN. 10	11	45	45	46	15	8	7	32	18	12	26	18
JUN. 11	12	46	47	48	15	9	7	32	18	12	26	18
JUN. 12	12	48	1	1	15	9	7	32	18	12	26	19
JUN. 13	12	2	2	3	15	9	7	32	18	12	26	19
JUN. 14	12	4	4	5	15	9	7	32	18	12	26	19
JUN. 15	12	5	6	7	15	9	7	32	18	12	26	19
JUN. 16	12	7	8	9	15	9	8	31	18	12	26	19
JUN. 17	12	9	10	10	16	10	8	31	18	12	26	19
JUN. 18	12	11	12	13	16	10	8	31	18	12	26	19
JUN. 19	13	13	14	15	16	10	8	31	18	12	26	19
JUN. 20	13	15	16	17	16	10	8	31	18	12	26	19
JUN. 21	13	17	18	19	16	10	8	31	18	12	26	19
JUN. 22	13	19	20	20	16	10	8	31	18	12	26	19
JUN. 23	13	21	22	22	16	10	8	31	18	12	26	19
JUN. 24	13	23	24	24	16	11	8	31	18	12	26	19
JUN. 25	14	25	25	26	16	11	8	31	18	12	26	19
JUN. 26	14	27	27	28	16	11	8	31	18	12	26	19
JUN. 27	14	28	29	29	16	11	9	31	18	12	26	19
JUN. 28	14	30	31	31	17	11	9	31	18	12	26	19
JUN. 29	14	32	32	33	17	11	9	31	18	12	26	19
JUN. 30	14	33	34	34	17	12	9	31	18	12	26	19

MOON 1 ◐ 12:01 A.M. TO 8:00 A.M.   **MOON 2** ◑ 8:01 A.M. TO 4:00 P.M.   **MOON 3** ● 4:01 P.M. TO 12:00 A.M.

Use only one "moon" number. Choose the column closest to your time of birth. If your place of birth is not on Eastern Standard Time, be sure to read "How to Convert to Eastern Standard Time" at the beginning of this section.

Date & Time	SUN	MOON 1	MOON 2	MOON 3	MERCURY	VENUS	MARS	JUPITER	SATURN	URANUS	NEPTUNE	PLUTO
JUL. 1	14	35	35	36	17	12	9	31	18	12	26	19
JUL. 2	14	36	37	37	17	12	9	31	18	12	26	19
JUL. 3	15	38	39	39	17	12	9	31	18	12	26	19
JUL. 4	15	40	40	41	17	12	9	31	18	12	26	19
JUL. 5	15	41	42	42	17	12	9	31	18	12	26	19
JUL. 6	15	43	43	44	16	13	9	31	18	12	26	19
JUL. 7	15	44	45	45	16	13	10	31	18	12	26	19
JUL. 8	15	46	47	47	16	13	10	31	18	12	26	19
JUL. 9	15	48	48	1	16	13	10	31	18	12	26	19
JUL. 10	15	1	2	2	16	13	10	31	18	12	26	19
JUL. 11	16	3	4	4	16	13	10	31	18	12	26	19
JUL. 12	16	5	5	6	16	14	10	31	18	12	26	19
JUL. 13	16	7	7	8	16	14	10	31	18	12	26	19
JUL. 14	16	8	9	10	16	14	10	31	18	12	26	19
JUL. 15	16	10	11	12	16	14	10	31	18	12	26	19
JUL. 16	16	12	13	14	16	14	10	31	18	12	26	19
JUL. 17	16	14	15	16	16	14	10	31	18	12	26	19
JUL. 18	16	16	17	18	16	15	11	31	18	12	26	19
JUL. 19	17	18	19	20	15	15	11	31	18	12	26	19
JUL. 20	17	20	21	22	15	15	11	31	18	12	26	19
JUL. 21	17	22	23	24	15	15	11	31	18	12	26	19
JUL. 22	17	24	25	25	15	15	11	31	18	12	26	19
JUL. 23	17	26	27	27	15	15	11	31	18	12	26	19
JUL. 24	17	28	28	29	15	16	11	31	18	12	26	19
JUL. 25	17	30	30	31	15	16	11	31	18	12	26	19
JUL. 26	18	31	32	32	15	16	11	31	18	12	26	19
JUL. 27	18	33	33	34	15	16	11	31	18	12	26	19
JUL. 28	18	34	35	36	15	16	11	31	18	12	26	19
JUL. 29	18	36	37	37	15	16	12	31	18	12	26	19
JUL. 30	18	38	38	39	15	17	12	31	19	12	26	19
JUL. 31	18	39	40	40	15	17	12	31	19	12	26	19

Date & Time	SUN	MOON 1	MOON 2	MOON 3	MERCURY	VENUS	MARS	JUPITER	SATURN	URANUS	NEPTUNE	PLUTO
AUG. 1	18	41	41	42	16	17	12	31	19	12	26	19
AUG. 2	18	42	43	43	16	17	12	31	19	12	26	19
AUG. 3	19	44	45	45	16	17	12	31	19	12	26	19
AUG. 4	19	46	46	47	16	17	12	31	19	12	26	19
AUG. 5	19	47	48	48	16	17	12	31	19	12	26	19
AUG. 6	19	1	1	2	16	18	12	31	19	12	26	19
AUG. 7	19	3	3	4	16	18	12	31	19	12	26	19
AUG. 8	19	4	5	5	16	18	12	31	19	12	26	19
AUG. 9	19	6	7	7	17	18	13	31	19	12	26	19
AUG. 10	19	8	8	9	17	18	13	31	19	12	26	19
AUG. 11	20	10	10	11	17	18	13	31	19	12	26	19
AUG. 12	20	12	12	13	17	19	13	31	19	12	26	19
AUG. 13	20	13	14	15	18	19	13	31	19	12	26	19
AUG. 14	20	15	16	17	18	19	13	31	19	12	26	19
AUG. 15	20	17	18	19	18	19	13	32	19	12	26	19
AUG. 16	20	19	20	21	18	19	13	32	19	12	26	19
AUG. 17	20	21	22	23	18	19	13	32	19	12	26	19
AUG. 18	20	23	24	25	18	20	13	32	19	12	26	19
AUG. 19	21	25	26	27	18	20	13	32	19	12	26	19
AUG. 20	21	27	28	28	19	20	14	32	19	12	26	19
AUG. 21	21	29	30	30	20	20	14	32	19	12	26	19
AUG. 22	21	31	31	32	20	20	14	32	19	12	26	19
AUG. 23	21	32	33	33	20	20	14	32	19	12	26	19
AUG. 24	21	34	35	35	20	21	14	32	19	12	26	19
AUG. 25	21	36	36	37	21	21	14	32	19	12	26	19
AUG. 26	22	37	38	38	21	21	14	32	19	12	26	19
AUG. 27	22	39	39	40	21	21	14	32	19	12	26	19
AUG. 28	22	40	41	41	21	21	14	32	19	12	26	19
AUG. 29	22	42	42	43	22	21	14	32	19	12	26	19
AUG. 30	22	44	44	45	22	22	14	32	19	12	26	19
AUG. 31	22	45	46	46	22	22	14	32	19	12	26	19

MOON 1 ☽ 12:01 A.M. TO 8:00 A.M.   **MOON 2** ☽ 8:01 A.M. TO 4:00 P.M.   **MOON 3** ● 4:01 P.M. TO 12:00 A.M.

Use only one "moon" number. Choose the column closest to your time of birth. If your place of birth is not on Eastern Standard Time, be sure to read "How to Convert to Eastern Standard Time" at the beginning of this section.

1947

September

Date & Time	SUN	MOON 1	MOON 2	MOON 3	MERCURY	VENUS	MARS	JUPITER	SATURN	URANUS	NEPTUNE	PLUTO
SEP. 1	22	47	47	48	22	22	15	32	19	12	26	19
SEP. 2	22	48	1	2	23	22	15	32	19	12	26	19
SEP. 3	23	2	3	3	23	22	15	32	19	12	26	19
SEP. 4	23	4	4	5	23	22	15	32	19	12	26	19
SEP. 5	23	6	6	7	23	23	15	32	19	12	26	19
SEP. 6	23	7	8	9	24	23	15	32	19	12	26	19
SEP. 7	23	9	10	10	24	23	15	32	19	12	26	19
SEP. 8	23	11	12	12	24	23	15	32	19	12	26	19
SEP. 9	23	13	14	14	24	23	15	32	19	12	26	19
SEP. 10	23	15	15	16	25	23	15	32	19	12	26	19
SEP. 11	24	17	17	18	25	24	15	32	19	12	26	19
SEP. 12	24	19	19	20	25	24	15	32	19	12	26	19
SEP. 13	24	21	21	22	25	24	16	32	19	12	26	19
SEP. 14	24	23	23	24	25	24	16	32	19	12	26	19
SEP. 15	24	25	25	26	26	24	16	32	19	12	26	19
SEP. 16	24	26	27	28	26	24	16	32	19	12	26	19
SEP. 17	24	28	29	29	26	25	16	32	19	12	26	19
SEP. 18	24	30	31	31	26	25	16	32	19	12	26	19
SEP. 19	25	32	32	33	27	25	16	32	19	12	26	19
SEP. 20	25	33	34	35	27	25	16	32	19	12	26	19
SEP. 21	25	35	36	36	27	25	16	32	19	12	26	19
SEP. 22	25	37	37	38	27	25	16	32	19	12	26	19
SEP. 23	25	38	39	39	27	26	16	32	19	12	26	19
SEP. 24	25	40	40	41	28	26	16	32	19	12	26	19
SEP. 25	26	41	42	43	28	26	17	32	19	12	26	19
SEP. 26	26	43	44	44	28	26	17	32	19	12	26	19
SEP. 27	26	45	45	46	28	26	17	32	19	12	26	19
SEP. 28	26	46	47	47	28	26	17	32	19	12	26	19
SEP. 29	26	48	1	1	29	27	17	32	19	12	26	19
SEP. 30	26	2	2	3	29	27	17	32	20	12	26	19

October

Date & Time	SUN	MOON 1	MOON 2	MOON 3	MERCURY	VENUS	MARS	JUPITER	SATURN	URANUS	NEPTUNE	PLUTO
OCT. 1	26	3	4	5	29	27	17	32	20	12	26	19
OCT. 2	26	5	6	6	29	27	17	32	20	12	26	19
OCT. 3	27	7	8	8	29	27	17	32	20	12	26	19
OCT. 4	27	9	9	10	29	27	17	32	20	12	26	19
OCT. 5	27	11	11	12	30	28	17	32	20	12	26	19
OCT. 6	27	12	13	14	30	28	17	32	20	12	26	19
OCT. 7	27	14	15	16	30	28	17	33	20	12	26	19
OCT. 8	27	16	17	17	30	28	18	33	20	12	26	19
OCT. 9	27	18	19	19	30	28	18	33	20	12	26	19
OCT. 10	27	20	21	21	30	28	18	33	20	12	26	19
OCT. 11	28	22	23	23	31	29	18	33	20	12	26	19
OCT. 12	28	24	24	25	31	29	18	33	20	12	26	19
OCT. 13	28	26	26	27	31	29	18	33	20	12	26	19
OCT. 14	28	28	28	29	31	29	18	33	20	12	26	19
OCT. 15	28	29	30	31	31	29	18	33	20	12	26	19
OCT. 16	28	31	32	32	31	29	18	33	20	12	26	19
OCT. 17	28	33	33	34	31	30	19	33	20	12	26	19
OCT. 18	28	35	35	36	31	30	18	33	20	12	26	19
OCT. 19	29	36	37	37	32	30	18	33	20	12	26	19
OCT. 20	29	38	38	39	32	30	18	33	20	12	26	19
OCT. 21	29	39	40	40	32	30	18	33	20	12	26	19
OCT. 22	29	41	41	42	32	30	19	33	20	12	26	19
OCT. 23	29	43	43	44	32	31	19	33	20	12	26	19
OCT. 24	29	44	45	45	32	31	19	33	20	12	26	19
OCT. 25	29	46	46	47	32	31	19	33	20	12	26	19
OCT. 26	30	47	48	1	32	31	19	33	20	12	26	19
OCT. 27	30	1	2	2	32	31	19	33	20	12	26	19
OCT. 28	30	3	3	4	32	31	19	33	20	12	26	19
OCT. 29	30	5	5	6	32	32	19	33	20	12	26	19
OCT. 30	30	6	7	8	32	32	19	33	20	12	26	19
OCT. 31	30	8	9	9	32	32	19	33	20	12	27	19

MOON 1 ◖ 12:01 A.M. TO 8:00 A.M.   **MOON 2** ◑ 8:01 A.M. TO 4:00 P.M.   **MOON 3** ● 4:01 P.M. TO 12:00 A.M.
Use only one "moon" number. Choose the column closest to your time of birth. If your place of birth is not on
Eastern Standard Time, be sure to read "How to Convert to Eastern Standard Time" at the beginning of this section.

1947

November

Date & Time	SUN	MOON 1	MOON 2	MOON 3	MERCURY	VENUS	MARS	JUPITER	SATURN	URANUS	NEPTUNE	PLUTO
NOV. 1	30	10	11	11	31	32	19	33	20	12	27	19
NOV. 2	30	12	13	13	31	32	19	33	20	12	27	19
NOV. 3	31	14	15	15	31	32	19	33	20	12	27	19
NOV. 4	31	16	16	17	31	33	19	33	20	12	27	19
NOV. 5	31	18	18	19	31	33	19	33	20	12	27	19
NOV. 6	31	20	20	21	31	33	20	33	20	12	27	19
NOV. 7	31	21	22	23	30	33	20	33	20	12	27	19
NOV. 8	31	23	24	25	30	33	20	33	20	12	27	19
NOV. 9	31	25	26	26	30	33	20	33	20	12	27	19
NOV. 10	31	27	28	28	30	34	20	33	20	12	27	19
NOV. 11	31	29	29	30	30	34	20	33	20	12	27	19
NOV. 12	32	30	31	32	30	34	20	34	20	12	27	19
NOV. 13	32	32	33	33	30	34	20	34	20	12	27	19
NOV. 14	32	34	34	35	30	34	20	34	20	12	27	19
NOV. 15	32	36	36	37	30	34	20	34	20	12	27	19
NOV. 16	32	37	38	38	30	35	20	34	20	12	27	19
NOV. 17	32	39	39	40	30	35	20	34	20	12	27	19
NOV. 18	32	40	41	41	30	35	20	34	20	12	27	19
NOV. 19	33	42	42	43	30	35	20	34	20	12	27	19
NOV. 20	33	44	44	45	30	35	20	34	20	12	27	19
NOV. 21	33	45	46	46	30	35	20	34	20	12	27	19
NOV. 22	33	47	47	48	30	36	20	34	20	12	27	19
NOV. 23	33	48	1	2	30	36	21	34	20	12	27	19
NOV. 24	33	2	3	3	31	36	21	34	20	12	27	19
NOV. 25	34	4	4	5	31	36	21	34	20	12	27	19
NOV. 26	34	6	6	7	31	36	21	34	20	12	27	19
NOV. 27	34	7	8	9	31	36	21	34	20	12	27	19
NOV. 28	34	9	10	11	31	37	21	34	20	12	27	19
NOV. 29	34	11	12	13	31	37	21	34	20	12	27	19
NOV. 30	34	13	14	15	32	37	21	34	20	12	27	19

December

Date & Time	SUN	MOON 1	MOON 2	MOON 3	MERCURY	VENUS	MARS	JUPITER	SATURN	URANUS	NEPTUNE	PLUTO
DEC. 1	34	15	16	17	32	37	21	34	20	12	27	19
DEC. 2	34	17	18	18	32	37	21	34	20	12	27	19
DEC. 3	35	19	20	20	32	37	21	34	20	12	27	19
DEC. 4	35	21	22	22	32	38	21	34	20	12	27	19
DEC. 5	35	23	24	24	33	38	21	34	20	12	27	19
DEC. 6	35	25	25	26	33	38	21	34	20	12	27	19
DEC. 7	35	27	27	28	33	38	21	34	20	12	27	19
DEC. 8	35	28	29	29	33	38	21	34	20	12	27	19
DEC. 9	35	30	31	31	33	38	21	34	20	12	27	19
DEC. 10	35	32	32	33	34	39	21	34	20	12	27	19
DEC. 11	36	33	34	35	34	39	21	34	20	12	27	19
DEC. 12	36	35	36	36	34	39	21	34	20	12	27	19
DEC. 13	36	37	37	38	34	39	21	34	20	12	27	19
DEC. 14	36	38	39	39	34	39	21	34	20	12	27	19
DEC. 15	36	40	40	41	35	39	22	34	20	12	27	19
DEC. 16	36	41	42	43	35	40	22	35	20	12	27	19
DEC. 17	36	43	44	44	35	40	22	35	20	12	27	19
DEC. 18	36	45	45	46	35	40	22	35	20	12	27	19
DEC. 19	37	46	47	47	35	40	22	35	20	12	27	19
DEC. 20	37	48	48	1	36	40	22	35	20	12	27	19
DEC. 21	37	1	2	3	36	40	22	35	20	12	27	19
DEC. 22	37	3	4	4	36	41	22	35	20	12	27	19
DEC. 23	37	5	5	6	36	41	22	35	20	12	27	19
DEC. 24	37	7	7	8	36	41	22	35	20	12	27	19
DEC. 25	37	9	9	10	37	41	22	35	20	12	27	19
DEC. 26	38	10	11	12	37	41	22	35	20	12	27	19
DEC. 27	38	12	13	14	37	41	22	35	20	12	27	19
DEC. 28	38	14	15	16	37	42	22	35	20	12	27	19
DEC. 29	38	16	17	18	37	42	22	35	20	12	27	19
DEC. 30	38	18	19	20	38	42	22	35	20	12	27	19
DEC. 31	38	20	21	22	38	42	22	35	20	12	27	19

MOON 1 ☽ 12:01 A.M. TO 8:00 A.M.   **MOON 2** ☾ 8:01 A.M. TO 4:00 P.M.   **MOON 3** ● 4:01 P.M. TO 12:00 A.M.

Use only one "moon" number. Choose the column closest to your time of birth. If your place of birth is not on Eastern Standard Time, be sure to read "How to Convert to Eastern Standard Time" at the beginning of this section.

1948

January

Date & Time	SUN	MOON 1	MOON 2	MOON 3	MERCURY	VENUS	MARS	JUPITER	SATURN	URANUS	NEPTUNE	PLUTO
JAN. 1	38	22	23	24	38	42	22	35	20	12	27	19
JAN. 2	38	24	25	25	38	42	22	35	20	12	27	19
JAN. 3	39	26	27	27	39	43	22	35	20	12	27	19
JAN. 4	39	28	28	29	39	43	22	35	20	12	27	19
JAN. 5	39	30	30	31	39	43	22	35	20	12	27	19
JAN. 6	39	31	32	32	39	43	22	35	20	12	27	19
JAN. 7	39	33	34	34	39	43	22	35	20	12	27	19
JAN. 8	39	35	35	36	40	43	22	35	20	12	27	19
JAN. 9	39	36	37	37	40	44	22	35	20	12	27	19
JAN. 10	40	38	38	39	40	44	22	35	20	12	27	19
JAN. 11	40	39	40	41	40	44	22	35	20	12	27	19
JAN. 12	40	41	42	42	40	44	22	35	20	12	27	19
JAN. 13	40	43	43	44	41	44	22	35	20	12	27	19
JAN. 14	40	44	45	45	41	44	22	35	20	12	27	19
JAN. 15	40	46	46	47	41	44	22	35	20	12	27	19
JAN. 16	40	47	48	48	41	45	22	35	20	12	27	19
JAN. 17	41	1	2	2	42	45	22	35	20	12	27	19
JAN. 18	41	3	3	4	42	45	22	35	20	12	27	19
JAN. 19	41	4	5	5	42	45	22	35	20	12	27	19
JAN. 20	41	6	7	7	42	45	22	36	20	12	27	19
JAN. 21	41	8	8	9	42	45	22	36	20	12	27	19
JAN. 22	41	10	10	11	43	46	22	36	20	12	27	19
JAN. 23	42	11	12	13	43	46	22	36	20	12	27	19
JAN. 24	42	13	14	15	43	46	22	36	20	12	27	19
JAN. 25	42	15	16	17	43	46	22	36	20	12	27	19
JAN. 26	42	17	18	19	44	46	22	36	20	12	27	19
JAN. 27	42	20	20	21	44	46	22	36	20	12	27	19
JAN. 28	42	22	22	23	44	47	22	36	20	12	27	19
JAN. 29	42	24	24	25	44	47	22	36	20	12	27	19
JAN. 30	42	25	26	27	44	47	22	36	20	12	27	19
JAN. 31	43	27	28	29	45	47	22	36	20	12	27	19

February

Date & Time	SUN	MOON 1	MOON 2	MOON 3	MERCURY	VENUS	MARS	JUPITER	SATURN	URANUS	NEPTUNE	PLUTO
FEB. 1	43	29	30	30	45	47	21	36	20	12	27	19
FEB. 2	43	31	31	32	45	47	21	36	20	12	27	19
FEB. 3	43	33	33	34	45	48	21	36	20	12	27	19
FEB. 4	43	34	35	35	45	48	21	36	20	12	27	19
FEB. 5	43	36	36	37	45	48	21	36	20	12	27	19
FEB. 6	43	37	38	39	46	48	21	36	20	12	27	19
FEB. 7	43	39	40	40	46	48	21	36	20	12	27	19
FEB. 8	44	41	41	42	46	48	21	36	20	12	27	19
FEB. 9	44	42	43	43	46	1	21	36	20	12	27	19
FEB. 10	44	44	44	45	46	1	21	36	20	12	27	19
FEB. 11	44	45	46	46	46	1	21	36	20	12	27	19
FEB. 12	44	47	48	48	46	1	21	36	19	12	27	19
FEB. 13	44	1	1	2	46	1	21	36	19	12	27	19
FEB. 14	44	2	3	3	46	1	21	36	19	12	27	19
FEB. 15	44	4	4	5	46	2	21	36	19	12	27	19
FEB. 16	45	6	6	7	46	2	21	36	19	12	27	19
FEB. 17	45	7	8	8	45	2	21	36	19	12	27	19
FEB. 18	45	9	10	10	45	2	21	36	19	12	27	19
FEB. 19	45	11	11	12	45	2	21	36	19	12	27	19
FEB. 20	45	13	13	14	45	2	21	36	19	12	27	19
FEB. 21	45	15	15	16	45	2	21	36	19	12	27	19
FEB. 22	45	17	17	18	45	3	20	36	19	12	27	19
FEB. 23	46	19	19	20	45	3	20	36	19	12	27	19
FEB. 24	46	21	21	22	44	3	20	36	19	12	27	19
FEB. 25	46	23	23	24	44	3	20	36	19	12	27	19
FEB. 26	46	25	25	26	44	3	20	36	19	12	27	19
FEB. 27	46	27	27	28	44	3	20	36	19	12	27	19
FEB. 28	46	28	29	30	44	4	20	36	19	12	27	19
FEB. 29	46	30	31	31	44	4	20	36	19	12	27	19

MOON 1 ◔ 12:01 A.M. TO 8:00 A.M.   **MOON 2** ◑ 8:01 A.M. TO 4:00 P.M.   **MOON 3** ● 4:01 P.M. TO 12:00 A.M.
Use only one "moon" number. Choose the column closest to your time of birth. If your place of birth is not on Eastern Standard Time, be sure to read "How to Convert to Eastern Standard Time" at the beginning of this section.

1948

March

Date & Time	SUN	MOON 1	MOON 2	MOON 3	MERCURY	VENUS	MARS	JUPITER	SATURN	URANUS	NEPTUNE	PLUTO
MAR. 1	46	32	33	33	44	4	20	36	19	12	27	19
MAR. 2	46	34	34	35	44	4	20	36	19	12	27	19
MAR. 3	47	35	36	37	44	4	20	36	19	12	27	19
MAR. 4	47	37	38	38	44	4	20	36	19	12	27	19
MAR. 5	47	39	39	40	44	4	20	36	19	12	27	19
MAR. 6	47	40	41	41	44	5	20	37	19	12	27	19
MAR. 7	47	42	42	43	44	5	20	37	19	12	27	19
MAR. 8	47	43	44	44	44	5	20	37	19	12	27	19
MAR. 9	47	45	46	46	44	5	20	37	19	12	27	19
MAR. 10	47	47	47	48	44	5	20	37	19	12	27	19
MAR. 11	48	48	1	1	44	5	20	37	19	12	27	19
MAR. 12	48	2	2	3	44	6	20	37	19	12	27	19
MAR. 13	48	3	4	5	44	6	20	37	19	12	27	19
MAR. 14	48	5	6	6	44	6	20	37	19	12	27	19
MAR. 15	48	7	7	8	45	6	20	37	19	12	27	19
MAR. 16	48	9	9	10	45	6	20	37	19	12	27	19
MAR. 17	48	10	11	12	45	6	20	37	19	12	27	19
MAR. 18	48	12	13	13	45	6	19	37	19	12	27	19
MAR. 19	1	14	15	15	45	7	19	37	19	12	27	19
MAR. 20	1	16	16	17	45	7	19	37	19	12	27	19
MAR. 21	1	18	18	19	45	7	19	37	19	12	27	19
MAR. 22	1	20	20	21	46	7	19	37	19	12	27	19
MAR. 23	1	22	22	23	46	7	19	37	19	12	27	19
MAR. 24	1	24	24	25	46	7	19	37	19	12	27	19
MAR. 25	2	26	26	27	46	7	19	37	19	12	27	19
MAR. 26	2	28	28	29	46	8	19	37	19	12	27	19
MAR. 27	2	30	30	31	46	8	19	37	19	12	27	19
MAR. 28	2	31	32	33	47	8	19	37	19	12	27	19
MAR. 29	2	33	34	34	47	8	19	37	19	12	27	19
MAR. 30	2	35	35	36	47	8	19	37	19	12	27	19
MAR. 31	2	37	37	38	47	8	19	37	19	12	27	19

April

Date & Time	SUN	MOON 1	MOON 2	MOON 3	MERCURY	VENUS	MARS	JUPITER	SATURN	URANUS	NEPTUNE	PLUTO
APR. 1	2	38	39	39	47	9	19	37	19	12	27	19
APR. 2	2	40	40	41	48	9	19	37	19	12	27	19
APR. 3	3	41	42	42	48	9	19	37	19	12	27	19
APR. 4	3	43	43	44	48	9	19	37	19	12	27	19
APR. 5	3	45	45	46	48	9	19	37	19	12	27	19
APR. 6	3	46	47	47	48	9	19	37	19	12	26	19
APR. 7	3	48	48	1	1	9	19	37	19	12	26	19
APR. 8	3	1	2	2	1	9	19	37	19	12	26	19
APR. 9	3	3	4	4	1	10	19	37	19	12	26	19
APR. 10	3	5	5	6	1	10	19	37	19	12	26	19
APR. 11	4	6	7	8	1	10	20	37	19	12	26	19
APR. 12	4	8	9	9	2	10	20	37	19	12	26	19
APR. 13	4	10	10	11	2	10	20	37	19	12	26	19
APR. 14	4	12	12	13	2	10	20	37	19	12	26	19
APR. 15	4	14	14	15	2	10	20	37	19	12	26	19
APR. 16	4	15	16	17	3	11	20	37	19	12	26	19
APR. 17	4	17	18	19	3	11	20	37	19	12	26	19
APR. 18	4	19	20	20	3	11	20	37	19	12	26	19
APR. 19	5	21	22	22	3	11	20	37	19	12	26	19
APR. 20	5	23	24	24	4	11	20	37	19	12	26	19
APR. 21	5	25	26	26	4	11	20	37	19	12	26	19
APR. 22	5	27	27	28	4	11	20	37	19	12	26	19
APR. 23	5	29	29	30	4	11	20	37	19	12	26	19
APR. 24	5	31	31	32	5	12	20	37	19	12	26	19
APR. 25	6	32	33	34	5	12	20	37	19	12	26	19
APR. 26	6	34	35	35	5	12	20	37	19	12	26	19
APR. 27	6	36	36	37	5	12	20	37	19	12	26	19
APR. 28	6	38	38	39	6	12	20	37	19	12	26	19
APR. 29	6	39	40	40	6	12	20	37	19	12	26	19
APR. 30	6	41	41	42	6	12	20	37	19	12	26	19

MOON 1 ◐ 12:01 A.M. TO 8:00 A.M.   **MOON 2** ◑ 8:01 A.M. TO 4:00 P.M.   **MOON 3** ● 4:01 P.M. TO 12:00 A.M.

Use only one "moon" number. Choose the column closest to your time of birth. If your place of birth is not on Eastern Standard Time, be sure to read "How to Convert to Eastern Standard Time" at the beginning of this section.

1948

May

June

Date & Time	SUN ☉	MOON 1 ◔	MOON 2 ◑	MOON 3 ●	MERCURY	VENUS	MARS	JUPITER	SATURN	URANUS	NEPTUNE	PLUTO
MAY 1	6	42	43	43	7	12	20	37	19	12	26	19
MAY 2	6	44	45	45	7	12	20	37	19	12	26	19
MAY 3	7	46	46	47	7	13	20	37	19	12	26	19
MAY 4	7	47	48	48	8	13	20	37	19	12	26	19
MAY 5	7	1	1	2	8	13	20	37	19	12	26	19
MAY 6	7	2	3	4	8	13	20	37	19	12	26	19
MAY 7	7	4	5	5	8	13	20	37	19	12	26	19
MAY 8	7	6	6	7	9	13	20	37	19	12	26	19
MAY 9	7	8	8	9	9	13	20	37	19	12	26	19
MAY 10	7	9	10	11	9	13	21	37	19	12	26	19
MAY 11	8	11	12	12	9	13	21	37	19	12	26	19
MAY 12	8	13	14	14	10	13	21	37	19	12	26	19
MAY 13	8	15	16	16	10	13	21	37	19	12	26	19
MAY 14	8	17	17	18	10	14	21	37	19	12	26	19
MAY 15	8	19	19	20	10	14	21	37	19	12	26	19
MAY 16	8	21	21	22	11	14	21	37	19	12	26	19
MAY 17	8	23	23	24	11	14	21	37	19	12	26	19
MAY 18	8	24	25	26	11	14	21	37	19	12	26	19
MAY 19	9	26	27	28	11	14	21	37	19	12	26	19
MAY 20	9	28	29	29	12	14	21	37	19	12	26	19
MAY 21	9	30	31	31	12	14	21	37	19	12	26	19
MAY 22	9	32	32	33	12	14	21	37	19	12	26	19
MAY 23	9	34	34	35	12	14	21	37	19	12	26	19
MAY 24	9	35	36	36	12	14	21	37	19	12	26	19
MAY 25	10	37	38	38	12	14	21	37	19	12	26	19
MAY 26	10	39	39	40	13	14	21	37	19	12	26	19
MAY 27	10	40	41	41	13	14	21	36	19	12	26	19
MAY 28	10	42	42	43	13	14	21	36	19	12	26	19
MAY 29	10	43	44	45	13	14	22	36	19	12	26	19
MAY 30	10	45	46	46	13	14	22	36	19	12	26	19
MAY 31	10	47	47	48	13	14	22	36	19	12	26	19

Date & Time	SUN ☉	MOON 1 ◔	MOON 2 ◑	MOON 3 ●	MERCURY	VENUS	MARS	JUPITER	SATURN	URANUS	NEPTUNE	PLUTO
JUN. 1	10	48	1	1	13	14	22	36	19	12	26	19
JUN. 2	10	2	2	3	14	14	22	36	19	12	26	19
JUN. 3	11	4	4	5	14	14	22	36	19	12	26	19
JUN. 4	11	5	6	6	14	14	22	36	19	12	26	19
JUN. 5	11	7	8	8	14	14	22	36	19	12	26	19
JUN. 6	11	9	9	10	14	14	22	36	19	12	26	19
JUN. 7	11	11	11	12	14	14	22	36	19	12	26	19
JUN. 8	11	12	13	14	14	14	22	36	19	12	26	19
JUN. 9	11	14	15	16	14	14	22	36	19	12	26	19
JUN. 10	11	16	17	18	14	14	22	36	19	12	26	19
JUN. 11	12	18	19	20	14	14	22	36	19	12	26	19
JUN. 12	12	20	21	21	14	14	22	36	19	12	26	19
JUN. 13	12	22	23	23	14	14	23	36	19	12	26	19
JUN. 14	12	24	25	25	14	14	23	36	19	12	26	19
JUN. 15	12	26	26	27	14	14	23	36	19	12	26	19
JUN. 16	12	28	28	29	14	14	23	36	19	12	26	19
JUN. 17	12	29	30	31	14	14	23	36	19	12	26	19
JUN. 18	12	31	32	32	14	14	23	36	19	12	26	19
JUN. 19	13	33	34	34	14	14	23	36	20	12	26	19
JUN. 20	13	35	35	36	14	14	23	36	20	12	26	19
JUN. 21	13	36	37	38	14	14	23	36	20	13	26	19
JUN. 22	13	38	39	39	13	14	23	36	20	13	26	19
JUN. 23	13	40	40	41	13	13	23	36	20	13	26	19
JUN. 24	13	41	42	42	13	13	23	36	20	13	26	19
JUN. 25	14	43	43	44	13	13	23	36	20	13	26	19
JUN. 26	14	45	45	46	13	13	23	36	20	13	26	19
JUN. 27	14	46	47	47	13	13	23	36	20	13	26	19
JUN. 28	14	48	48	1	13	13	24	36	20	13	26	19
JUN. 29	14	1	2	2	13	13	24	36	20	13	26	19
JUN. 30	14	3	3	4	13	13	24	36	20	13	26	19

MOON 1 ◔ 12:01 A.M. TO 8:00 A.M.   **MOON 2** ◑ 8:01 A.M. TO 4:00 P.M.   **MOON 3** ● 4:01 P.M. TO 12:00 A.M.
Use only one "moon" number. Choose the column closest to your time of birth. If your place of birth is not on
Eastern Standard Time, be sure to read "How to Convert to Eastern Standard Time" at the beginning of this section.

1948

July

Date & Time	SUN	MOON 1	MOON 2	MOON 3	MERCURY	VENUS	MARS	JUPITER	SATURN	URANUS	NEPTUNE	PLUTO
JUL. 1	14	5	5	6	13	13	24	36	20	13	26	19
JUL. 2	14	6	7	7	13	13	24	36	20	13	26	19
JUL. 3	15	8	9	9	13	13	24	36	20	13	26	19
JUL. 4	15	10	10	11	13	13	24	36	20	13	26	19
JUL. 5	15	12	12	13	13	13	24	36	20	13	26	19
JUL. 6	15	14	14	15	13	12	24	36	20	13	26	19
JUL. 7	15	16	16	17	13	12	24	36	20	13	26	19
JUL. 8	15	18	18	19	13	12	24	36	20	13	26	19
JUL. 9	15	20	20	21	13	12	24	36	20	13	26	19
JUL. 10	15	22	22	23	13	12	24	36	20	13	26	19
JUL. 11	16	23	24	25	13	12	25	36	20	13	26	19
JUL. 12	16	25	26	27	13	12	25	36	20	13	26	19
JUL. 13	16	27	28	28	13	12	25	36	20	13	26	19
JUL. 14	16	29	30	30	13	12	25	36	20	13	26	19
JUL. 15	16	31	31	32	13	12	25	36	20	13	26	19
JUL. 16	16	33	33	34	13	12	25	36	20	13	26	19
JUL. 17	16	34	35	35	14	12	25	36	20	13	26	19
JUL. 18	16	36	37	37	14	12	25	36	20	13	26	19
JUL. 19	17	38	38	39	14	12	25	36	20	13	26	19
JUL. 20	17	39	40	40	14	12	25	36	20	13	26	19
JUL. 21	17	41	41	42	14	12	25	36	20	13	26	19
JUL. 22	17	43	43	44	14	12	25	36	20	13	26	19
JUL. 23	17	44	45	45	15	12	25	36	20	13	26	19
JUL. 24	17	46	46	47	15	12	25	36	20	13	26	19
JUL. 25	17	47	48	48	15	12	26	36	20	13	26	19
JUL. 26	18	1	1	2	15	13	26	36	20	13	26	19
JUL. 27	18	2	3	4	15	13	26	36	20	13	26	19
JUL. 28	18	4	5	5	16	13	26	36	20	13	26	19
JUL. 29	18	6	6	7	16	13	26	36	20	13	26	19
JUL. 30	18	7	8	9	16	13	26	36	20	13	26	19
JUL. 31	18	9	10	10	16	13	26	36	20	13	26	19

August

Date & Time	SUN	MOON 1	MOON 2	MOON 3	MERCURY	VENUS	MARS	JUPITER	SATURN	URANUS	NEPTUNE	PLUTO
AUG. 1	18	11	12	12	17	13	26	36	20	13	26	19
AUG. 2	18	13	13	14	17	13	26	36	20	13	26	19
AUG. 3	19	15	15	16	17	13	26	36	20	13	26	19
AUG. 4	19	17	17	18	17	13	26	36	20	13	26	19
AUG. 5	19	19	19	20	18	13	26	36	20	13	26	19
AUG. 6	19	21	21	22	18	13	27	36	20	13	26	19
AUG. 7	19	23	23	24	18	13	27	36	20	13	26	19
AUG. 8	19	25	25	26	19	13	27	36	20	13	26	19
AUG. 9	19	27	27	28	19	13	27	36	20	13	26	19
AUG. 10	19	29	29	30	19	14	27	36	20	13	26	19
AUG. 11	20	30	31	32	19	14	27	36	20	13	26	19
AUG. 12	20	32	33	33	20	14	27	36	20	13	26	19
AUG. 13	20	34	34	35	20	14	27	36	20	13	26	19
AUG. 14	20	36	36	37	20	14	27	36	20	13	26	19
AUG. 15	20	37	38	38	20	14	27	36	20	13	26	19
AUG. 16	20	39	39	40	21	14	27	36	20	13	26	19
AUG. 17	20	40	41	42	21	14	27	36	20	13	26	19
AUG. 18	20	42	43	43	21	14	28	36	20	13	26	19
AUG. 19	21	44	44	45	21	14	28	36	20	13	26	19
AUG. 20	21	45	46	46	22	15	28	36	20	13	26	19
AUG. 21	21	47	47	48	22	15	28	36	20	13	26	19
AUG. 22	21	48	1	1	22	15	28	36	21	13	26	19
AUG. 23	21	2	3	3	22	15	28	36	21	13	26	19
AUG. 24	21	4	5	5	23	15	28	36	21	13	26	19
AUG. 25	21	5	6	6	23	15	28	36	21	13	26	19
AUG. 26	22	7	7	8	23	15	28	36	21	13	26	19
AUG. 27	22	9	10	10	23	15	28	36	21	13	26	19
AUG. 28	22	10	11	11	24	16	28	36	21	13	26	19
AUG. 29	22	12	13	13	24	16	28	36	21	13	26	19
AUG. 30	22	14	15	15	24	16	29	36	21	13	26	19
AUG. 31	22	16	17	17	24	16	29	36	21	13	26	19

MOON 1 ◗ 12:01 A.M. TO 8:00 A.M.   **MOON 2** ◑ 8:01 A.M. TO 4:00 P.M.   **MOON 3** ● 4:01 P.M. TO 12:00 A.M.

Use only one "moon" number. Choose the column closest to your time of birth. If your place of birth is not on Eastern Standard Time, be sure to read "How to Convert to Eastern Standard Time" at the beginning of this section.

1948

September

Date & Time	SUN	MOON 1	MOON 2	MOON 3	MERCURY	VENUS	MARS	JUPITER	SATURN	URANUS	NEPTUNE	PLUTO
SEP. 1	22	18	18	19	24	16	29	36	21	13	26	19
SEP. 2	22	20	21	21	25	16	29	36	21	13	27	19
SEP. 3	23	22	23	23	25	16	29	36	21	13	27	19
SEP. 4	23	24	25	25	25	16	29	36	21	13	27	19
SEP. 5	23	26	27	27	25	17	29	36	21	13	27	19
SEP. 6	23	28	29	29	25	17	29	36	21	13	27	19
SEP. 7	23	30	30	31	26	17	29	36	21	13	27	19
SEP. 8	23	32	32	33	26	17	29	36	21	13	27	19
SEP. 9	23	33	34	35	26	17	29	36	21	13	27	19
SEP. 10	23	35	36	36	26	17	30	36	21	13	27	19
SEP. 11	24	37	37	38	26	17	30	36	21	13	27	19
SEP. 12	24	38	39	40	27	17	30	36	21	13	27	19
SEP. 13	24	40	41	41	27	18	30	36	21	13	27	19
SEP. 14	24	42	42	43	27	18	30	36	21	13	27	19
SEP. 15	24	43	44	44	27	18	30	36	21	13	27	19
SEP. 16	24	45	45	46	27	18	30	36	21	13	27	19
SEP. 17	24	46	47	48	28	18	30	36	21	13	27	19
SEP. 18	24	48	1	1	28	18	30	36	21	13	27	19
SEP. 19	25	2	2	3	28	18	30	36	21	13	27	19
SEP. 20	25	3	4	4	28	19	30	36	21	13	27	19
SEP. 21	25	5	5	6	28	19	31	36	21	13	27	19
SEP. 22	25	6	7	8	28	19	31	36	21	13	27	19
SEP. 23	25	8	9	9	28	19	31	36	21	13	27	19
SEP. 24	25	10	10	11	29	19	31	36	21	13	27	19
SEP. 25	26	12	12	13	29	19	31	36	21	13	27	19
SEP. 26	26	13	14	15	29	19	31	36	21	13	27	19
SEP. 27	26	15	16	16	29	20	31	36	21	13	27	19
SEP. 28	26	17	18	18	29	20	31	36	21	13	27	19
SEP. 29	26	19	20	20	29	20	31	36	21	13	27	19
SEP. 30	26	21	22	22	29	20	31	36	21	13	27	19

October

Date & Time	SUN	MOON 1	MOON 2	MOON 3	MERCURY	VENUS	MARS	JUPITER	SATURN	URANUS	NEPTUNE	PLUTO
OCT. 1	26	23	24	24	29	20	31	36	21	13	27	19
OCT. 2	26	25	26	26	29	20	32	36	21	13	27	19
OCT. 3	27	27	28	28	30	20	32	36	21	13	27	19
OCT. 4	27	29	30	30	30	21	32	36	21	13	27	19
OCT. 5	27	31	32	32	30	21	32	36	21	13	27	19
OCT. 6	27	33	33	34	30	21	32	36	21	13	27	19
OCT. 7	27	35	35	36	30	21	32	36	21	13	27	19
OCT. 8	27	36	37	37	30	21	32	36	21	13	27	19
OCT. 9	27	38	39	39	30	21	32	36	21	13	27	19
OCT. 10	27	40	40	41	30	22	32	36	21	13	27	19
OCT. 11	28	41	42	42	30	22	32	36	21	13	27	19
OCT. 12	28	43	43	44	30	22	32	36	21	13	27	19
OCT. 13	28	44	45	45	29	22	33	36	21	13	27	19
OCT. 14	28	46	47	47	29	22	33	36	21	13	27	19
OCT. 15	28	48	48	1	29	22	33	36	21	13	27	19
OCT. 16	28	1	2	2	29	22	33	36	21	13	27	19
OCT. 17	28	3	3	4	29	23	33	36	21	13	27	19
OCT. 18	28	4	5	6	29	23	33	36	21	13	27	19
OCT. 19	29	6	7	7	28	23	33	36	21	13	27	19
OCT. 20	29	8	8	9	28	23	33	36	21	13	27	19
OCT. 21	29	9	10	11	28	23	33	36	21	13	27	19
OCT. 22	29	11	12	12	28	23	33	36	21	13	27	19
OCT. 23	29	13	14	14	28	24	34	36	21	13	27	19
OCT. 24	29	15	15	16	28	24	34	36	21	13	27	19
OCT. 25	29	17	17	18	28	24	34	36	21	13	27	19
OCT. 26	30	18	19	20	28	24	34	36	21	13	27	19
OCT. 27	30	20	21	22	28	24	34	36	21	13	27	19
OCT. 28	30	22	23	24	28	24	34	36	22	13	27	19
OCT. 29	30	24	25	26	28	24	34	37	22	13	27	19
OCT. 30	30	26	27	27	28	25	34	37	22	13	27	19
OCT. 31	30	28	29	29	28	25	34	37	22	13	27	19

MOON 1 ◗ 12:01 A.M. TO 8:00 A.M.   **MOON 2** ◑ 8:01 A.M. TO 4:00 P.M.   **MOON 3** ● 4:01 P.M. TO 12:00 A.M.

Use only one "moon" number. Choose the column closest to your time of birth. If your place of birth is not on Eastern Standard Time, be sure to read "How to Convert to Eastern Standard Time" at the beginning of this section.

1948

November

Date & Time	SUN	MOON 1	MOON 2	MOON 3	MERCURY	VENUS	MARS	JUPITER	SATURN	URANUS	NEPTUNE	PLUTO
NOV. 1	30	30	31	31	28	25	34	37	22	13	27	19
NOV. 2	30	32	33	33	28	25	35	37	22	13	27	19
NOV. 3	31	34	34	35	28	25	35	37	22	13	27	19
NOV. 4	31	36	36	37	28	25	35	37	22	13	27	19
NOV. 5	31	37	38	38	28	26	35	37	22	13	27	19
NOV. 6	31	39	40	40	28	26	35	37	22	13	27	19
NOV. 7	31	41	41	42	28	26	35	37	22	13	27	19
NOV. 8	31	42	43	43	29	26	35	37	22	13	27	19
NOV. 9	31	44	44	45	29	26	35	37	22	13	27	19
NOV. 10	31	46	46	47	29	26	35	37	22	13	27	19
NOV. 11	31	47	48	48	29	27	35	37	22	13	27	19
NOV. 12	32	1	1	2	29	27	35	37	22	13	27	19
NOV. 13	32	2	3	3	30	27	36	37	22	13	27	19
NOV. 14	32	4	4	5	30	27	36	37	22	13	27	19
NOV. 15	32	6	6	7	30	27	36	37	22	13	27	19
NOV. 16	32	7	8	8	30	27	36	37	22	13	27	19
NOV. 17	32	9	10	10	30	28	36	37	22	13	27	19
NOV. 18	32	11	11	12	31	28	36	37	22	13	27	19
NOV. 19	33	13	13	14	31	28	36	37	22	13	27	19
NOV. 20	33	14	15	16	31	28	36	37	22	13	27	19
NOV. 21	33	16	17	17	31	28	36	37	22	13	27	19
NOV. 22	33	18	19	19	31	28	36	37	22	13	27	19
NOV. 23	33	20	21	21	32	29	37	37	22	13	27	19
NOV. 24	33	22	22	23	32	29	37	37	22	13	27	19
NOV. 25	34	24	24	25	32	29	37	37	22	13	27	19
NOV. 26	34	26	26	27	32	29	37	37	22	13	27	19
NOV. 27	34	27	28	29	32	29	37	37	22	13	27	19
NOV. 28	34	29	30	31	33	29	37	37	22	13	27	19
NOV. 29	34	31	32	32	33	29	37	37	22	13	27	19
NOV. 30	34	33	34	34	33	30	37	37	22	13	27	19

December

Date & Time	SUN	MOON 1	MOON 2	MOON 3	MERCURY	VENUS	MARS	JUPITER	SATURN	URANUS	NEPTUNE	PLUTO
DEC. 1	34	35	35	36	33	30	37	37	22	13	27	19
DEC. 2	34	37	37	38	34	30	38	37	22	13	27	19
DEC. 3	35	38	39	40	34	30	38	37	22	13	27	19
DEC. 4	35	40	41	41	34	30	38	38	22	13	27	19
DEC. 5	35	42	42	43	34	30	38	38	22	13	27	19
DEC. 6	35	43	44	44	34	31	38	38	22	13	27	19
DEC. 7	35	45	46	46	35	31	38	38	22	13	27	19
DEC. 8	35	47	47	48	35	31	38	38	22	13	27	19
DEC. 9	35	48	1	1	35	31	38	38	22	13	27	19
DEC. 10	35	2	2	3	35	31	38	38	22	13	27	19
DEC. 11	36	3	4	4	35	31	38	38	22	13	27	19
DEC. 12	36	5	6	6	36	32	39	38	22	13	27	19
DEC. 13	36	7	7	8	36	32	39	38	22	13	27	19
DEC. 14	36	8	9	9	36	32	39	38	22	13	27	19
DEC. 15	36	10	11	11	36	32	39	38	22	13	27	19
DEC. 16	36	12	13	13	36	32	39	38	22	13	27	19
DEC. 17	36	14	14	15	37	32	39	38	22	13	27	19
DEC. 18	36	16	16	17	37	33	39	38	22	13	27	19
DEC. 19	37	18	18	19	37	33	39	38	22	13	27	19
DEC. 20	37	19	20	21	37	33	39	38	22	13	27	19
DEC. 21	37	21	22	23	37	33	39	38	22	13	27	19
DEC. 22	37	23	24	24	38	33	40	38	22	13	27	19
DEC. 23	37	25	26	26	38	33	40	38	22	13	27	19
DEC. 24	37	27	28	28	38	34	40	38	22	13	27	19
DEC. 25	37	29	29	30	38	34	40	38	22	13	27	19
DEC. 26	38	31	31	32	39	34	40	38	22	13	27	19
DEC. 27	38	32	33	34	39	34	40	38	22	13	27	19
DEC. 28	38	34	35	35	39	34	40	38	22	13	27	19
DEC. 29	38	36	37	37	39	34	40	38	22	13	27	19
DEC. 30	38	38	38	39	39	35	40	38	22	13	27	19
DEC. 31	38	39	40	41	40	35	40	38	22	13	27	19

MOON 1 ☽ 12:01 A.M. TO 8:00 A.M.   **MOON 2** ◑ 8:01 A.M. TO 4:00 P.M.   **MOON 3** ● 4:01 P.M. TO 12:00 A.M.
Use only one "moon" number. Choose the column closest to your time of birth. If your place of birth is not on Eastern Standard Time, be sure to read "How to Convert to Eastern Standard Time" at the beginning of this section.

1949

January

Date & Time	SUN	MOON 1	MOON 2	MOON 3	MERCURY	VENUS	MARS	JUPITER	SATURN	URANUS	NEPTUNE	PLUTO
JAN. 1	38	41	42	42	40	35	41	38	22	13	27	19
JAN. 2	38	43	43	44	40	35	41	38	22	13	27	19
JAN. 3	39	44	45	46	40	35	41	38	22	13	27	19
JAN. 4	39	46	47	47	41	35	41	38	22	13	27	19
JAN. 5	39	48	48	1	41	36	41	38	22	13	27	19
JAN. 6	39	1	2	2	41	36	41	38	22	13	27	19
JAN. 7	39	3	3	4	41	36	41	38	22	13	27	19
JAN. 8	39	4	5	5	41	36	41	39	22	13	27	19
JAN. 9	39	6	7	7	42	36	41	39	22	13	27	19
JAN. 10	40	8	8	9	42	36	42	39	22	13	27	19
JAN. 11	40	9	10	11	42	37	42	39	22	13	27	19
JAN. 12	40	11	12	12	42	37	42	39	22	13	27	19
JAN. 13	40	13	14	14	42	37	42	39	22	13	27	19
JAN. 14	40	15	16	16	43	37	42	39	22	13	27	19
JAN. 15	40	17	17	18	43	37	42	39	22	13	27	19
JAN. 16	40	19	19	20	43	37	42	39	22	13	27	19
JAN. 17	41	21	21	22	43	38	42	39	22	13	27	19
JAN. 18	41	23	23	24	43	38	42	39	22	13	27	19
JAN. 19	41	25	25	26	43	38	42	39	22	13	27	19
JAN. 20	41	27	27	28	43	38	43	39	22	13	27	19
JAN. 21	41	28	29	30	44	38	43	39	22	13	27	19
JAN. 22	41	30	31	31	44	38	43	39	22	13	27	19
JAN. 23	42	32	33	33	44	39	43	39	22	13	27	19
JAN. 24	42	34	34	35	44	39	43	39	22	13	27	19
JAN. 25	42	36	36	37	44	39	43	39	22	13	27	19
JAN. 26	42	37	38	38	44	39	43	39	22	13	27	19
JAN. 27	42	39	40	40	44	39	43	39	22	13	27	19
JAN. 28	42	41	41	42	44	39	43	39	22	13	27	19
JAN. 29	42	42	43	43	43	40	44	39	22	13	27	19
JAN. 30	42	44	44	45	43	40	44	39	22	13	27	19
JAN. 31	43	46	46	47	43	40	44	39	22	13	27	19

February

Date & Time	SUN	MOON 1	MOON 2	MOON 3	MERCURY	VENUS	MARS	JUPITER	SATURN	URANUS	NEPTUNE	PLUTO
FEB. 1	43	47	48	48	43	40	44	39	22	13	27	19
FEB. 2	43	1	1	2	43	40	44	39	22	13	27	19
FEB. 3	43	2	3	3	43	40	44	39	22	13	27	19
FEB. 4	43	4	4	5	43	41	44	39	22	13	27	19
FEB. 5	43	5	6	7	42	41	44	39	22	13	27	19
FEB. 6	43	7	8	8	42	41	44	39	22	13	27	19
FEB. 7	43	9	9	10	42	41	44	39	21	13	27	19
FEB. 8	44	10	11	12	42	41	45	40	21	13	27	19
FEB. 9	44	12	13	13	42	41	45	40	21	13	27	19
FEB. 10	44	14	15	15	42	42	45	40	21	13	27	19
FEB. 11	44	16	17	17	42	42	45	40	21	13	27	19
FEB. 12	44	18	19	19	42	42	45	40	21	13	27	19
FEB. 13	44	20	21	21	42	42	45	40	21	13	27	19
FEB. 14	44	22	23	23	42	42	45	40	21	13	27	19
FEB. 15	44	24	25	25	42	42	45	40	21	13	27	19
FEB. 16	45	26	27	27	43	43	45	40	21	13	27	19
FEB. 17	45	28	28	29	42	43	46	40	21	13	27	19
FEB. 18	45	30	30	31	42	43	46	40	21	13	27	19
FEB. 19	45	32	32	33	42	43	46	40	21	13	27	19
FEB. 20	45	33	34	35	42	43	46	40	21	13	27	19
FEB. 21	45	35	36	36	42	43	46	40	21	13	27	19
FEB. 22	45	37	37	38	42	44	46	40	21	13	27	19
FEB. 23	46	39	39	40	42	44	46	40	21	13	27	19
FEB. 24	46	40	41	41	42	44	46	40	21	13	27	19
FEB. 25	46	42	42	43	42	44	46	40	21	13	27	19
FEB. 26	46	44	44	45	42	44	46	40	21	13	27	19
FEB. 27	46	45	46	46	42	44	47	40	21	13	27	19
FEB. 28	46	47	47	48	43	45	47	40	21	13	27	19

MOON 1 ☽ 12:01 A.M. TO 8:00 A.M. **MOON 2** ◑ 8:01 A.M. TO 4:00 P.M. **MOON 3** ● 4:01 P.M. TO 12:00 A.M.
Use only one "moon" number. Choose the column closest to your time of birth. If your place of birth is not on Eastern Standard Time, be sure to read "How to Convert to Eastern Standard Time" at the beginning of this section.

1949

March

April

Date & Time	SUN	MOON 1	MOON 2	MOON 3	MERCURY	VENUS	MARS	JUPITER	SATURN	URANUS	NEPTUNE	PLUTO
MAR. 1	46	48	1	1	43	45	47	40	21	13	27	19
MAR. 2	46	2	2	3	43	45	47	40	21	13	27	19
MAR. 3	47	3	4	4	43	45	47	40	21	13	27	19
MAR. 4	47	5	6	6	43	45	47	40	21	13	27	19
MAR. 5	47	7	7	8	43	45	47	40	21	13	27	19
MAR. 6	47	8	9	9	44	46	47	40	21	13	27	19
MAR. 7	47	10	10	11	44	46	47	40	21	13	27	19
MAR. 8	47	12	12	13	44	46	48	40	21	13	27	19
MAR. 9	47	13	14	15	44	46	48	40	21	13	27	19
MAR. 10	47	15	16	16	44	46	48	40	21	13	27	19
MAR. 11	48	17	18	18	44	46	48	40	21	13	27	19
MAR. 12	48	19	20	20	45	47	48	40	21	13	27	19
MAR. 13	48	21	22	22	45	47	48	40	21	13	27	19
MAR. 14	48	23	24	24	45	47	48	40	21	13	27	19
MAR. 15	48	25	26	26	45	47	48	40	21	13	27	19
MAR. 16	48	27	28	28	45	47	48	40	21	13	27	19
MAR. 17	48	29	30	30	46	47	48	40	21	13	27	19
MAR. 18	48	31	32	32	46	48	1	40	21	13	27	19
MAR. 19	1	33	33	34	46	48	1	41	21	13	27	19
MAR. 20	1	35	35	36	46	48	1	41	21	13	27	19
MAR. 21	1	36	37	38	46	48	1	41	21	13	27	19
MAR. 22	1	38	39	39	47	48	1	41	21	13	27	19
MAR. 23	1	40	40	41	47	48	1	41	21	13	27	19
MAR. 24	1	41	42	43	47	1	1	41	21	13	27	19
MAR. 25	2	43	44	44	47	1	1	41	21	13	27	19
MAR. 26	2	45	45	46	47	1	1	41	21	13	27	19
MAR. 27	2	46	47	47	48	1	2	41	21	13	27	19
MAR. 28	2	48	48	1	48	1	2	41	21	13	27	19
MAR. 29	2	1	2	2	48	1	2	41	21	13	27	19
MAR. 30	2	3	4	4	48	2	2	41	21	13	27	19
MAR. 31	2	5	5	6	1	2	2	41	21	13	27	19

Date & Time	SUN	MOON 1	MOON 2	MOON 3	MERCURY	VENUS	MARS	JUPITER	SATURN	URANUS	NEPTUNE	PLUTO
APR. 1	2	6	7	7	1	2	2	41	21	13	27	19
APR. 2	2	8	8	9	1	2	2	41	21	13	27	19
APR. 3	3	9	10	11	2	2	2	41	21	13	27	19
APR. 4	3	11	12	12	2	2	2	41	21	13	27	19
APR. 5	3	13	13	14	2	3	2	41	21	13	27	19
APR. 6	3	15	15	16	2	3	3	41	21	13	27	19
APR. 7	3	16	17	18	2	3	3	41	21	13	27	19
APR. 8	3	18	19	19	3	3	3	41	21	13	27	19
APR. 9	3	20	21	21	3	3	3	41	21	13	27	19
APR. 10	3	22	23	23	3	3	3	41	21	13	27	19
APR. 11	4	24	25	25	3	4	3	41	21	13	27	19
APR. 12	4	26	27	27	4	4	3	41	21	13	27	19
APR. 13	4	28	29	29	4	4	3	41	21	13	27	19
APR. 14	4	30	31	31	4	4	3	41	21	13	27	19
APR. 15	4	32	33	33	5	4	3	41	21	13	27	19
APR. 16	4	34	35	35	5	4	4	41	21	13	27	19
APR. 17	4	36	36	37	5	5	4	41	21	13	27	19
APR. 18	4	38	38	39	5	5	4	41	21	13	27	19
APR. 19	5	39	40	40	6	5	4	41	21	13	27	19
APR. 20	5	41	42	42	6	5	4	41	21	13	27	19
APR. 21	5	43	43	44	6	5	4	41	21	13	27	19
APR. 22	5	44	45	45	7	5	4	41	21	13	27	19
APR. 23	5	46	46	47	7	6	4	41	21	13	27	19
APR. 24	5	47	48	1	7	6	4	41	21	13	27	19
APR. 25	6	1	2	2	7	6	4	41	21	13	27	19
APR. 26	6	3	3	4	8	6	5	41	21	13	27	19
APR. 27	6	4	5	5	8	6	5	41	21	13	27	19
APR. 28	6	6	6	7	8	6	5	41	21	13	27	19
APR. 29	6	7	8	8	8	7	5	41	21	13	27	19
APR. 30	6	9	10	10	9	7	5	41	21	13	27	19

MOON 1 ☽ 12:01 A.M. TO 8:00 A.M. **MOON 2** ◗ 8:01 A.M. TO 4:00 P.M. **MOON 3** ● 4:01 P.M. TO 12:00 A.M.
Use only one "moon" number. Choose the column closest to your time of birth. If your place of birth is not on Eastern Standard Time, be sure to read "How to Convert to Eastern Standard Time" at the beginning of this section.

May

June

Date & Time	SUN	MOON 1	MOON 2	MOON 3	MERCURY	VENUS	MARS	JUPITER	SATURN	URANUS	NEPTUNE	PLUTO
MAY 1	6	11	11	12	9	7	5	41	21	13	27	19
MAY 2	6	12	13	14	9	7	5	41	21	13	27	19
MAY 3	7	14	15	15	9	7	5	41	21	13	27	19
MAY 4	7	16	17	17	9	7	5	41	21	13	27	19
MAY 5	7	18	18	19	10	8	5	41	21	13	27	19
MAY 6	7	20	20	21	10	8	6	41	21	13	27	19
MAY 7	7	21	22	23	10	8	6	41	21	13	27	19
MAY 8	7	23	24	25	10	8	6	41	21	13	27	19
MAY 9	7	25	26	27	10	8	6	41	21	13	27	19
MAY 10	7	27	28	29	10	8	6	41	21	13	27	19
MAY 11	8	29	30	31	11	9	6	41	21	13	27	19
MAY 12	8	31	32	32	11	9	6	41	21	13	27	19
MAY 13	8	33	34	34	11	9	6	41	21	13	27	19
MAY 14	8	35	36	36	11	9	6	41	21	13	27	19
MAY 15	8	37	38	38	11	9	6	41	21	13	27	19
MAY 16	8	39	39	40	11	9	7	41	21	13	27	19
MAY 17	8	40	41	42	11	9	7	41	21	13	27	19
MAY 18	8	42	43	43	11	10	7	41	21	13	27	19
MAY 19	9	44	44	45	11	10	7	41	21	13	27	19
MAY 20	9	45	46	46	11	10	7	41	21	13	27	19
MAY 21	9	47	48	48	11	10	7	41	21	13	27	19
MAY 22	9	1	1	2	11	10	7	41	21	13	27	19
MAY 23	9	2	3	3	11	10	7	41	21	13	27	19
MAY 24	9	4	4	5	11	7	7	41	21	13	27	19
MAY 25	10	5	6	6	11	11	7	41	21	13	27	19
MAY 26	10	7	7	8	11	11	8	41	21	13	27	19
MAY 27	10	9	9	10	11	11	8	41	21	13	27	19
MAY 28	10	10	11	11	11	11	8	41	21	13	27	19
MAY 29	10	12	13	13	11	11	8	41	21	13	27	19
MAY 30	10	14	14	15	11	12	8	41	21	13	27	19
MAY 31	10	15	16	17	11	12	8	41	21	13	27	19

Date & Time	SUN	MOON 1	MOON 2	MOON 3	MERCURY	VENUS	MARS	JUPITER	SATURN	URANUS	NEPTUNE	PLUTO
JUN. 1	10	17	18	19	11	12	8	41	21	13	27	19
JUN. 2	10	19	20	20	11	12	8	41	21	13	27	19
JUN. 3	11	21	22	22	11	12	8	41	21	13	27	19
JUN. 4	11	23	23	24	11	12	8	41	21	13	27	19
JUN. 5	11	25	25	26	11	13	9	41	21	13	27	19
JUN. 6	11	27	27	28	10	13	9	41	21	13	27	19
JUN. 7	11	29	29	30	10	13	9	41	21	13	27	19
JUN. 8	11	30	31	32	10	13	9	41	21	13	27	19
JUN. 9	11	32	33	34	10	13	9	41	21	13	27	19
JUN. 10	11	34	35	36	10	13	9	41	21	13	27	19
JUN. 11	12	36	37	37	10	14	9	41	21	13	27	19
JUN. 12	12	38	39	39	10	14	9	41	21	13	27	19
JUN. 13	12	40	40	41	10	14	9	41	21	13	27	19
JUN. 14	12	42	42	43	10	14	9	41	21	13	27	19
JUN. 15	12	43	44	44	10	14	9	41	21	13	27	19
JUN. 16	12	45	45	46	10	14	10	41	21	13	27	19
JUN. 17	12	46	47	48	10	15	10	41	21	13	27	19
JUN. 18	12	48	1	1	10	15	10	41	21	13	27	19
JUN. 19	13	2	2	3	10	15	10	41	21	13	27	19
JUN. 20	13	3	4	4	10	15	10	41	21	13	27	19
JUN. 21	13	5	5	6	10	15	10	41	21	13	27	19
JUN. 22	13	6	7	7	10	15	10	41	21	13	27	19
JUN. 23	13	8	9	9	10	16	10	41	21	13	27	19
JUN. 24	13	10	10	11	10	16	10	41	21	13	27	19
JUN. 25	14	11	12	13	11	16	10	41	21	13	27	19
JUN. 26	14	13	14	14	11	16	10	41	21	13	27	19
JUN. 27	14	15	16	16	11	16	11	41	21	13	27	19
JUN. 28	14	17	17	18	11	16	11	41	21	13	27	19
JUN. 29	14	19	19	20	11	17	11	41	21	13	27	19
JUN. 30	14	21	21	22	11	17	11	41	21	13	27	19

MOON 1 ◗ 12:01 A.M. TO 8:00 A.M.   **MOON 2** ◖ 8:01 A.M. TO 4:00 P.M.   **MOON 3** ● 4:01 P.M. TO 12:00 A.M.
Use only one "moon" number. Choose the column closest to your time of birth. If your place of birth is not on Eastern Standard Time, be sure to read "How to Convert to Eastern Standard Time" at the beginning of this section.

Date & Time	SUN	MOON 1 ◗	MOON 2 ◖	MOON 3 ●	MERCURY	VENUS	MARS	JUPITER	SATURN	URANUS	NEPTUNE	PLUTO
JUL. 1	14	22	23	24	11	17	11	41	21	13	27	19
JUL. 2	14	24	25	26	11	17	11	41	21	13	27	19
JUL. 3	15	26	27	27	12	17	11	41	21	13	27	19
JUL. 4	15	28	29	29	12	17	11	41	21	13	27	19
JUL. 5	15	30	31	31	12	17	11	41	21	13	27	19
JUL. 6	15	32	32	33	12	18	11	41	21	13	27	19
JUL. 7	15	34	34	35	12	18	12	41	21	13	27	19
JUL. 8	15	36	36	37	13	18	12	41	21	13	27	19
JUL. 9	15	37	38	39	13	18	12	41	21	13	27	19
JUL. 10	15	39	40	40	13	18	12	41	21	13	27	19
JUL. 11	16	41	41	42	13	18	12	41	21	13	27	19
JUL. 12	16	43	43	44	13	19	12	41	21	13	27	19
JUL. 13	16	44	45	45	14	19	12	41	21	13	27	19
JUL. 14	16	46	46	47	14	19	12	41	21	13	27	19
JUL. 15	16	48	48	1	14	19	12	41	21	13	27	19
JUL. 16	16	1	2	2	14	19	12	41	21	13	27	19
JUL. 17	16	3	3	4	15	19	12	41	21	13	27	19
JUL. 18	16	4	5	5	15	20	13	41	22	13	27	19
JUL. 19	17	6	6	7	15	20	13	41	22	13	27	19
JUL. 20	17	7	8	9	16	20	13	41	22	13	27	19
JUL. 21	17	9	10	10	16	20	13	41	22	13	27	19
JUL. 22	17	11	11	12	16	20	13	41	22	13	27	19
JUL. 23	17	13	13	14	17	20	13	41	22	13	27	19
JUL. 24	17	14	15	16	17	21	13	41	22	13	27	19
JUL. 25	17	16	17	17	17	21	13	41	22	13	27	19
JUL. 26	18	18	19	19	17	21	13	41	22	13	27	19
JUL. 27	18	20	21	21	18	21	13	40	22	13	27	19
JUL. 28	18	22	23	23	18	21	13	40	22	13	27	19
JUL. 29	18	24	24	25	18	21	14	40	22	13	27	19
JUL. 30	18	26	26	27	18	22	14	40	22	13	27	19
JUL. 31	18	28	28	29	18	22	14	40	22	13	27	19

Date & Time	SUN	MOON 1 ◗	MOON 2 ◖	MOON 3 ●	MERCURY	VENUS	MARS	JUPITER	SATURN	URANUS	NEPTUNE	PLUTO
AUG. 1	18	30	30	31	19	22	14	40	22	13	27	19
AUG. 2	18	31	32	33	19	22	14	40	22	13	27	19
AUG. 3	19	33	34	34	19	22	14	40	22	13	27	19
AUG. 4	19	35	36	36	20	22	14	40	22	13	27	19
AUG. 5	19	37	37	38	20	23	14	40	22	13	27	19
AUG. 6	19	39	39	40	20	23	14	40	22	13	27	19
AUG. 7	19	40	41	41	20	23	14	40	22	13	27	19
AUG. 8	19	42	43	43	21	23	14	40	22	13	27	19
AUG. 9	19	44	44	45	21	23	14	40	22	13	27	19
AUG. 10	19	45	46	46	21	23	15	40	22	13	27	19
AUG. 11	20	47	48	48	21	23	15	40	22	13	27	19
AUG. 12	20	1	1	2	22	24	15	40	22	13	27	19
AUG. 13	20	2	3	3	22	24	15	40	22	13	27	19
AUG. 14	20	4	4	5	22	24	15	40	22	13	27	19
AUG. 15	20	5	6	6	22	24	15	40	22	13	27	19
AUG. 16	20	7	7	8	23	24	15	40	22	13	27	19
AUG. 17	20	9	9	10	23	24	15	40	22	13	27	19
AUG. 18	20	10	11	11	23	25	15	40	22	13	27	19
AUG. 19	21	12	12	13	23	25	15	40	22	13	27	19
AUG. 20	21	14	14	15	23	25	15	40	22	13	27	19
AUG. 21	21	15	16	17	24	25	16	40	22	13	27	19
AUG. 22	21	17	18	19	24	25	16	40	22	13	27	19
AUG. 23	21	19	20	20	24	25	16	40	22	14	27	19
AUG. 24	21	21	22	22	24	26	16	40	22	14	27	19
AUG. 25	21	23	24	24	24	26	16	40	22	14	27	19
AUG. 26	22	25	26	26	25	26	16	40	22	14	27	19
AUG. 27	22	27	28	28	25	26	16	40	22	14	27	19
AUG. 28	22	29	30	30	25	26	16	40	22	14	27	19
AUG. 29	22	31	32	32	25	26	16	40	22	14	27	19
AUG. 30	22	33	33	34	25	27	16	40	22	14	27	19
AUG. 31	22	35	35	36	25	27	16	40	22	14	27	19

MOON 1 ◗ 12:01 A.M. TO 8:00 A.M.   **MOON 2** ◖ 8:01 A.M. TO 4:00 P.M.   **MOON 3** ● 4:01 P.M. TO 12:00 A.M.

Use only one "moon" number. Choose the column closest to your time of birth. If your place of birth is not on Eastern Standard Time, be sure to read "How to Convert to Eastern Standard Time" at the beginning of this section.

1949

September

October

Date & Time	SUN	MOON 1	MOON 2	MOON 3	MERCURY	VENUS	MARS	JUPITER	SATURN	URANUS	NEPTUNE	PLUTO
SEP. 1	22	36	37	38	26	27	16	40	22	14	27	19
SEP. 2	22	38	39	39	26	27	17	40	22	14	27	19
SEP. 3	23	40	40	41	26	27	17	40	22	14	27	19
SEP. 4	23	42	42	43	26	27	17	40	22	14	27	19
SEP. 5	23	43	44	44	26	27	17	40	22	14	27	19
SEP. 6	23	45	45	46	26	28	17	40	22	14	27	19
SEP. 7	23	47	47	48	26	28	17	40	22	14	27	19
SEP. 8	23	48	1	1	27	28	17	40	22	14	27	19
SEP. 9	23	2	2	3	27	28	17	40	22	14	27	19
SEP. 10	23	3	4	4	27	28	17	40	22	14	27	19
SEP. 11	24	5	5	6	27	28	17	40	22	14	27	19
SEP. 12	24	6	7	8	27	29	17	40	22	14	27	19
SEP. 13	24	8	9	9	27	29	17	40	22	14	27	19
SEP. 14	24	10	10	11	27	29	18	40	22	14	27	19
SEP. 15	24	11	12	12	27	29	18	40	22	14	27	19
SEP. 16	24	13	14	14	27	29	18	40	22	14	27	19
SEP. 17	24	15	15	16	27	29	18	40	22	14	27	19
SEP. 18	24	17	17	18	27	30	18	40	23	14	27	19
SEP. 19	25	18	19	20	27	30	18	40	23	14	27	19
SEP. 20	25	20	21	22	28	30	18	40	23	14	27	19
SEP. 21	25	22	23	24	28	30	18	40	23	14	27	19
SEP. 22	25	24	25	26	28	30	18	40	23	14	27	19
SEP. 23	25	26	27	28	27	30	18	40	23	14	27	19
SEP. 24	25	28	29	30	27	30	18	40	23	14	27	19
SEP. 25	26	30	31	32	27	31	18	40	23	14	27	19
SEP. 26	26	32	33	33	27	31	19	40	23	14	27	19
SEP. 27	26	34	35	35	27	31	19	40	23	14	27	19
SEP. 28	26	36	37	37	27	31	19	40	23	14	27	19
SEP. 29	26	38	38	39	27	31	19	40	23	14	27	19
SEP. 30	26	40	40	41	27	31	19	40	23	14	27	19

Date & Time	SUN	MOON 1	MOON 2	MOON 3	MERCURY	VENUS	MARS	JUPITER	SATURN	URANUS	NEPTUNE	PLUTO
OCT. 1	26	41	42	42	27	32	19	40	23	14	27	19
OCT. 2	26	43	43	44	27	32	19	40	23	14	27	19
OCT. 3	27	45	45	46	26	32	19	40	23	14	27	19
OCT. 4	27	46	47	47	26	32	19	40	23	14	27	19
OCT. 5	27	48	48	1	26	32	19	40	23	14	27	19
OCT. 6	27	1	2	2	26	32	19	40	23	14	27	19
OCT. 7	27	3	3	4	26	32	19	40	23	14	27	19
OCT. 8	27	4	5	6	26	33	20	40	23	14	27	19
OCT. 9	27	6	7	7	26	33	20	40	23	14	27	19
OCT. 10	27	8	8	9	26	33	20	40	23	14	27	19
OCT. 11	28	9	10	10	26	33	20	40	23	14	27	19
OCT. 12	28	11	11	12	25	33	20	40	23	14	27	19
OCT. 13	28	12	13	14	25	33	20	40	23	14	27	19
OCT. 14	28	14	15	15	26	34	20	40	23	14	27	19
OCT. 15	28	16	16	17	26	34	20	40	23	14	27	19
OCT. 16	28	18	18	19	26	34	20	40	23	14	27	19
OCT. 17	28	20	20	21	26	34	20	40	23	14	27	19
OCT. 18	28	21	22	23	26	34	20	40	23	14	27	19
OCT. 19	29	23	24	25	26	34	20	40	23	14	27	19
OCT. 20	29	25	26	27	26	34	20	40	23	14	27	19
OCT. 21	29	27	28	29	26	35	21	40	23	14	27	19
OCT. 22	29	29	30	31	26	35	21	40	23	14	27	19
OCT. 23	29	31	32	33	27	35	21	40	23	14	27	19
OCT. 24	29	33	34	35	27	35	21	40	23	14	27	19
OCT. 25	29	35	36	37	27	35	21	40	23	14	27	19
OCT. 26	30	37	38	38	27	35	21	40	23	14	27	19
OCT. 27	30	39	40	40	27	36	21	40	23	14	27	19
OCT. 28	30	41	41	42	28	36	21	40	23	14	27	19
OCT. 29	30	42	43	44	28	36	21	40	23	14	27	19
OCT. 30	30	44	45	45	28	36	21	40	23	14	27	19
OCT. 31	30	46	46	47	28	36	21	40	23	14	27	19

MOON 1 ◐ 12:01 A.M. TO 8:00 A.M.   **MOON 2** ◑ 8:01 A.M. TO 4:00 P.M.   **MOON 3** ● 4:01 P.M. TO 12:00 A.M.

Use only one "moon" number. Choose the column closest to your time of birth. If your place of birth is not on Eastern Standard Time, be sure to read "How to Convert to Eastern Standard Time" at the beginning of this section.

1949

November — December

Date & Time	SUN	MOON 1	MOON 2	MOON 3	MERCURY	VENUS	MARS	JUPITER	SATURN	URANUS	NEPTUNE	PLUTO
NOV. 1	30	47	48	48	28	36	21	40	23	14	27	19
NOV. 2	30	1	1	2	29	36	21	40	23	14	27	19
NOV. 3	31	3	3	4	29	37	22	40	23	14	27	19
NOV. 4	31	4	5	5	29	37	22	40	23	14	27	19
NOV. 5	31	6	6	7	29	37	22	40	23	14	27	19
NOV. 6	31	7	8	8	29	37	22	40	23	14	27	19
NOV. 7	31	9	9	10	30	37	22	40	23	14	27	19
NOV. 8	31	10	11	12	30	37	22	40	23	14	27	19
NOV. 9	31	12	13	13	30	37	22	40	23	14	27	19
NOV. 10	31	14	14	15	30	38	22	41	23	14	27	19
NOV. 11	31	15	16	17	31	38	22	41	23	14	27	19
NOV. 12	32	17	18	18	31	38	22	41	23	14	27	19
NOV. 13	32	19	20	20	31	38	22	41	23	14	27	19
NOV. 14	32	21	21	22	31	38	22	41	23	14	27	19
NOV. 15	32	23	23	24	31	38	22	41	23	14	27	19
NOV. 16	32	25	25	26	32	38	22	41	23	14	27	19
NOV. 17	32	26	27	28	32	39	23	41	23	14	27	19
NOV. 18	32	28	29	30	32	39	23	41	23	14	27	19
NOV. 19	33	30	31	32	32	39	23	41	23	14	27	19
NOV. 20	33	32	33	34	33	39	23	41	23	14	27	19
NOV. 21	33	34	35	36	33	39	23	41	23	14	27	19
NOV. 22	33	36	37	38	33	39	23	41	23	14	27	19
NOV. 23	33	38	39	40	33	39	23	41	23	14	27	19
NOV. 24	33	40	41	41	33	39	23	41	23	14	27	19
NOV. 25	34	42	42	43	34	40	23	41	23	14	27	19
NOV. 26	34	44	44	45	34	40	23	41	23	14	27	19
NOV. 27	34	45	46	46	34	40	23	41	23	14	27	19
NOV. 28	34	47	47	48	34	40	23	41	23	14	27	19
NOV. 29	34	48	1	2	34	40	23	41	23	14	27	19
NOV. 30	34	2	3	3	35	40	23	41	23	14	27	19
DEC. 1	34	4	4	5	35	40	23	41	23	13	27	19
DEC. 2	34	5	6	6	35	40	24	41	23	13	27	19
DEC. 3	35	7	7	8	35	41	24	41	23	13	27	19
DEC. 4	35	8	9	9	35	41	24	41	23	13	27	19
DEC. 5	35	10	11	11	36	41	24	41	23	13	27	19
DEC. 6	35	12	12	13	36	41	24	41	23	13	27	19
DEC. 7	35	13	14	14	36	41	24	41	23	13	27	19
DEC. 8	35	15	16	16	36	41	24	41	23	13	27	19
DEC. 9	35	17	17	18	36	41	24	41	24	13	27	19
DEC. 10	35	19	19	20	37	41	24	41	24	13	27	19
DEC. 11	36	20	21	22	37	42	24	41	24	13	27	19
DEC. 12	36	22	23	23	37	42	24	41	24	13	27	19
DEC. 13	36	24	25	25	37	42	24	41	24	13	27	19
DEC. 14	36	26	26	27	38	42	24	41	24	13	27	19
DEC. 15	36	28	28	29	38	42	24	41	24	13	27	19
DEC. 16	36	30	30	31	38	42	24	41	24	13	27	19
DEC. 17	36	32	32	33	38	42	24	41	24	13	27	19
DEC. 18	36	34	34	35	38	42	25	41	24	13	27	19
DEC. 19	37	36	36	37	39	42	25	41	24	13	27	19
DEC. 20	37	37	38	39	39	42	25	41	24	13	27	19
DEC. 21	37	39	40	41	39	43	25	42	24	13	27	19
DEC. 22	37	41	42	42	39	43	25	42	24	13	27	19
DEC. 23	37	43	44	44	39	43	25	42	24	13	27	19
DEC. 24	37	45	45	46	40	43	25	42	24	13	27	19
DEC. 25	37	46	47	47	40	43	25	42	24	13	27	19
DEC. 26	38	48	48	1	40	43	25	42	24	13	27	19
DEC. 27	38	2	2	3	40	43	25	42	24	13	27	19
DEC. 28	38	3	4	4	40	43	25	42	24	13	27	19
DEC. 29	38	5	5	6	40	43	25	42	24	13	27	19
DEC. 30	38	6	7	7	41	43	25	42	24	13	27	19
DEC. 31	38	8	8	9	41	43	25	42	24	13	27	19

MOON 1 ☽ 12:01 A.M. TO 8:00 A.M.   **MOON 2** ☽ 8:01 A.M. TO 4:00 P.M.   **MOON 3** ● 4:01 P.M. TO 12:00 A.M.

Use only one "moon" number. Choose the column closest to your time of birth. If your place of birth is not on Eastern Standard Time, be sure to read "How to Convert to Eastern Standard Time" at the beginning of this section.

1950-1959

1950s

Oprah Winfrey

★ ★ ★ BORN JANUARY 29, 1954 ★ ★ ★

Brief Bio: Oprah Winfrey is the influential talk show host of the "Oprah Winfrey Show," editor of *O Magazine* and the first African-American woman to become a billionaire.

Personology Profile:

SUN IN THE WEEK OF GENIUS
(AQUARIUS I)

✳

Those born in this week are extremely quick in picking things up. Often precocious in their early youth, they are often highly perceptive and mentally gifted. In order to avoid superficiality, they are advised to dig a bit deeper and indeed often seek out more profound partners in relationships. Learning to listen to what others have to say is an important lesson for them to learn.

MOON IN THE WEEK OF INDEPENDENCE
(SAGITTARIUS I)

✳

A rather nervous setting for the Moon. Emotional change and, in some cases, instability and unreliability is likely to accompany these individuals. Even though their feelings are so subject to change—and sometimes even because of it—they can hold out a fascinating lure for many. Magnetic individuals, they can be heartbreakers, but rarely intentionally.

MERCURY IN THE WEEK OF YOUTH AND EASE
(AQUARIUS II)

✳

Worry is anathema to those with Mercury in this week. It can cause enormous stress, leading to illness. The mind needs to be constantly reassured that everything is all right and will turn out for the best. These individuals should harness their abundant mental skills to more productive endeavors than endlessly ruminating on things. Puzzles, games and riddles are good outlets for these active minds.

VENUS IN THE WEEK OF GENIUS
(AQUARIUS I)

✳

Intelligent people are not necessarily all brain power. Exuding an interest in sexuality in all forms, those with this Venus position use their fertile minds to explore all aspects of sex and even to try out as many as they can. Open to almost any form of experimentation, they are likely to prove exciting and inventive lovers.

MARS IN THE WEEK OF CHARM
(SCORPIO III)

✳

Mars is given an extra seductive attraction in this position. If encouraged, these folks are likely to take over the lives of weaker family members and friends. Thus they are capable of making most or even all of the important decisions for the other person. In doing so they create dependencies which might not be so healthy for either party in the future.

JUPITER IN THE WEEK OF NEW LANGUAGE
(GEMINI II)

✳

Telling tall stories and spinning yarns is characteristic of this Jupiter position. Such individuals find it easier to embellish the truth than to blandly state it as it is. Trust is an important issue here, for many refuse to believe what these expressive individuals have to say, not wanting to get burned a second time. Building a trustworthy persona can be a major challenge.

SATURN IN THE WEEK OF INTENSITY
(SCORPIO I)

*

Saturn can have a negative effect on the ability to concentrate one's efforts on what is most important. In fact, attention can get fixated on certain areas which are not really relevant and divert one's energy from necessary pursuits. Moreover, if attitudes become too serious they may make matters too heavy for anyone to handle.

URANUS IN THE WEEK OF THE PERSUADER
(CANCER III)

*

It is less in the nature of Uranus to persuade and more to simply blast opponents out of the way. Therefore, Uranus is made nervous by the tact and diplomacy required here. This can result in an inability or unwillingness to win others over through patiently seductive tactics and a kind of gruff impatience which just doesn't work to convince them.

NEPTUNE IN THE WEEK OF THEATER
(LIBRA III)

*

Neptune can lead these folks to live in an unreal world, populated by film and TV stars, and with dramatic public figures. They see a connection between themselves and such notables, frequently fantasizing about possible relationships, sexual or otherwise. Their real challenge is to discover the true drama in everyday life and to invest more real energy in events around them.

PLUTO IN THE WEEK OF LEADERSHIP
(LEO III)

*

Strongly dictatorial tendencies can surface here. Those with this Pluto position are frequently at the mercy of their ambitious drives and too likely to sacrifice the well-being of their friends and colleagues to their desire for recognition. At the same time, they are able to hide their true feelings and have difficulty accessing or understanding them.

Some Highlights of the Decade 1950-1959

- ELVIS PRESLEY RECORDS "HEARTBREAK HOTEL," THE FIRST OF HIS RECORDS TO SELL OVER A MILLION COPIES.

- MATTEL DEBUTS THE FIRST BARBIE DOLL AT THE AMERICAN TOY FAIR IN NEW YORK CITY.

- US SUPREME COURT ENDS RACIAL SEGREGATION ON BUSES.

- AMERICAN ACTRESS GRACE KELLY MARRIES PRINCE RAINIER III OF MONACO AND BECOMES PRINCESS GRACE.

- ALASKA BECOMES THE 49TH US STATE.

- CHUBBY CHECKER RECORDS "THE TWIST," WHICH LATER BECOMES A DANCE SENSATION.

1950

January

Date & Time	SUN	MOON 1	MOON 2	MOON 3	MERCURY	VENUS	MARS	JUPITER	SATURN	URANUS	NEPTUNE	PLUTO
JAN. 1	38	9	10	11	41	43	25	42	24	13	27	19
JAN. 2	38	11	12	12	41	43	25	42	24	13	27	19
JAN. 3	39	13	13	14	41	43	25	42	24	13	27	19
JAN. 4	39	15	15	16	41	43	25	42	24	13	27	19
JAN. 5	39	16	17	17	41	43	25	42	24	13	27	19
JAN. 6	39	18	19	19	41	43	25	42	24	13	27	19
JAN. 7	39	20	21	21	41	43	26	42	24	13	27	19
JAN. 8	39	22	22	23	42	43	26	42	24	13	27	19
JAN. 9	39	24	24	25	42	43	26	42	24	13	27	19
JAN. 10	40	25	26	27	41	43	26	42	24	13	27	19
JAN. 11	40	27	28	29	41	43	26	42	24	13	27	19
JAN. 12	40	29	30	30	41	43	26	42	24	13	27	19
JAN. 13	40	31	32	32	41	43	26	42	24	13	27	19
JAN. 14	40	33	34	34	41	43	26	42	24	13	27	19
JAN. 15	40	35	35	36	41	43	26	42	24	13	27	19
JAN. 16	40	37	37	38	41	43	26	42	24	13	27	19
JAN. 17	41	39	39	40	41	43	26	42	24	13	27	19
JAN. 18	41	40	41	42	40	43	26	42	24	13	27	19
JAN. 19	41	42	43	43	40	43	26	42	24	13	27	19
JAN. 20	41	44	45	45	40	43	26	42	24	13	27	19
JAN. 21	41	46	46	47	40	43	26	42	24	13	27	19
JAN. 22	41	47	48	48	40	43	26	43	23	13	27	19
JAN. 23	42	1	2	2	40	43	26	43	23	13	27	19
JAN. 24	42	3	3	4	40	43	26	43	23	13	27	19
JAN. 25	42	4	5	5	40	43	26	43	23	13	27	19
JAN. 26	42	6	6	7	39	43	26	43	23	13	27	19
JAN. 27	42	7	8	8	39	43	26	43	23	13	27	19
JAN. 28	42	9	9	10	39	43	26	43	23	13	27	19
JAN. 29	42	11	11	12	39	43	26	43	23	13	27	19
JAN. 30	42	12	13	13	39	42	26	43	23	13	27	19
JAN. 31	43	14	14	15	39	42	26	43	23	13	27	19

February

Date & Time	SUN	MOON 1	MOON 2	MOON 3	MERCURY	VENUS	MARS	JUPITER	SATURN	URANUS	NEPTUNE	PLUTO
FEB. 1	43	16	16	17	39	42	26	43	23	13	27	19
FEB. 2	43	17	18	19	40	42	26	43	23	13	27	19
FEB. 3	43	19	20	21	40	42	26	43	23	13	27	19
FEB. 4	43	21	22	22	40	42	26	43	23	13	27	19
FEB. 5	43	23	24	24	40	42	26	43	23	13	27	19
FEB. 6	43	25	26	26	40	42	26	43	23	13	27	19
FEB. 7	43	27	27	28	40	42	26	43	23	13	27	19
FEB. 8	44	29	29	30	40	42	26	43	23	13	27	19
FEB. 9	44	31	31	32	40	42	26	43	23	13	27	19
FEB. 10	44	33	33	34	40	42	26	43	23	13	27	19
FEB. 11	44	34	35	36	40	42	26	43	23	13	27	19
FEB. 12	44	36	37	37	41	42	26	43	23	13	27	19
FEB. 13	44	38	39	39	41	42	26	43	23	13	27	19
FEB. 14	44	40	40	41	41	41	26	43	23	13	27	19
FEB. 15	44	42	42	43	41	41	26	43	23	13	27	19
FEB. 16	45	43	44	45	41	41	26	43	23	13	27	19
FEB. 17	45	45	46	46	41	41	26	43	23	13	27	19
FEB. 18	45	47	47	48	42	41	26	43	23	13	27	19
FEB. 19	45	48	1	2	42	41	26	43	23	13	27	19
FEB. 20	45	2	3	3	42	41	26	43	23	13	27	19
FEB. 21	45	4	4	5	42	41	26	43	23	13	27	19
FEB. 22	45	5	6	6	42	41	26	43	23	13	27	19
FEB. 23	46	7	7	8	42	41	26	44	23	13	27	19
FEB. 24	46	8	9	9	43	41	26	44	23	13	27	19
FEB. 25	46	10	10	11	43	41	26	44	23	13	27	19
FEB. 26	46	12	12	13	43	41	26	44	23	13	27	19
FEB. 27	46	13	14	14	43	41	26	44	23	13	27	19
FEB. 28	46	15	16	16	43	42	26	44	23	13	27	19

MOON 1 ☽ 12:01 A.M. TO 8:00 A.M.   **MOON 2** ◐ 8:01 A.M. TO 4:00 P.M.   **MOON 3** ● 4:01 P.M. TO 12:00 A.M.
Use only one "moon" number. Choose the column closest to your time of birth. If your place of birth is not on Eastern Standard Time, be sure to read "How to Convert to Eastern Standard Time" at the beginning of this section.

March

April

Date & Time	SUN	MOON 1	MOON 2	MOON 3	MERCURY	VENUS	MARS	JUPITER	SATURN	URANUS	NEPTUNE	PLUTO
MAR. 1	46	17	17	18	44	42	26	44	23	13	27	19
MAR. 2	46	19	19	20	44	42	26	44	23	13	27	19
MAR. 3	47	20	21	22	44	42	26	44	23	13	27	19
MAR. 4	47	22	23	24	44	42	26	44	23	13	27	19
MAR. 5	47	24	25	26	44	42	26	44	23	13	27	19
MAR. 6	47	26	27	28	45	42	26	44	23	13	27	19
MAR. 7	47	28	29	29	45	42	26	44	23	13	27	19
MAR. 8	47	30	31	31	45	42	26	44	23	13	27	19
MAR. 9	47	32	33	33	45	42	26	44	23	13	27	19
MAR. 10	47	34	35	35	45	42	26	44	23	13	27	19
MAR. 11	48	36	36	37	46	42	26	44	23	13	27	19
MAR. 12	48	38	38	39	46	42	26	44	23	13	27	19
MAR. 13	48	39	40	41	46	42	26	44	23	13	27	19
MAR. 14	48	41	42	42	46	42	26	44	23	13	27	19
MAR. 15	48	43	43	44	47	42	26	44	23	13	27	19
MAR. 16	48	45	45	46	47	43	26	44	23	13	27	19
MAR. 17	48	46	47	47	47	43	26	44	23	13	27	19
MAR. 18	48	48	48	1	47	43	25	44	23	13	27	19
MAR. 19	1	2	2	3	48	43	25	44	23	13	27	19
MAR. 20	1	3	4	4	48	43	25	44	23	13	27	19
MAR. 21	1	5	5	6	48	43	25	44	23	13	27	19
MAR. 22	1	6	7	7	48	43	25	44	23	13	27	19
MAR. 23	1	8	8	9	1	43	25	44	23	13	27	19
MAR. 24	1	9	10	11	1	43	25	44	23	13	27	19
MAR. 25	2	11	12	12	1	43	25	44	23	13	27	19
MAR. 26	2	13	13	14	1	44	25	44	23	13	27	19
MAR. 27	2	14	15	15	2	44	25	44	23	13	27	19
MAR. 28	2	16	17	17	2	44	25	44	23	13	27	19
MAR. 29	2	18	18	19	2	44	25	45	23	13	27	19
MAR. 30	2	20	20	21	2	44	25	45	23	13	27	19
MAR. 31	2	21	22	23	3	44	25	45	23	13	27	19

Date & Time	SUN	MOON 1	MOON 2	MOON 3	MERCURY	VENUS	MARS	JUPITER	SATURN	URANUS	NEPTUNE	PLUTO
APR. 1	2	23	24	25	3	44	25	45	23	13	27	19
APR. 2	2	25	26	27	3	44	25	45	23	13	27	19
APR. 3	3	27	28	29	4	45	25	45	23	13	27	19
APR. 4	3	29	30	31	4	45	25	45	23	13	27	19
APR. 5	3	31	32	33	4	45	25	45	23	13	27	19
APR. 6	3	33	34	35	4	45	25	45	23	13	27	19
APR. 7	3	35	36	37	5	45	24	45	23	13	27	19
APR. 8	3	37	38	38	5	45	24	45	23	13	27	19
APR. 9	3	39	40	40	5	45	24	45	23	13	27	19
APR. 10	3	41	41	42	5	45	24	45	23	13	27	19
APR. 11	4	43	43	44	6	46	24	45	23	13	27	19
APR. 12	4	44	45	45	6	46	24	45	23	13	27	19
APR. 13	4	46	46	47	6	46	24	45	23	13	27	19
APR. 14	4	48	48	1	6	46	24	45	23	13	27	19
APR. 15	4	1	2	2	7	46	24	45	23	13	27	19
APR. 16	4	3	3	4	7	46	24	45	23	13	27	19
APR. 17	4	4	5	5	7	46	24	45	23	13	27	19
APR. 18	4	6	6	7	7	46	24	45	23	13	27	19
APR. 19	5	7	8	9	7	47	24	45	23	13	27	19
APR. 20	5	9	10	10	8	47	24	45	23	13	27	19
APR. 21	5	11	11	12	8	47	24	45	23	13	27	19
APR. 22	5	12	13	13	8	47	24	45	23	13	27	19
APR. 23	5	14	14	15	8	47	24	45	23	13	27	19
APR. 24	5	15	16	17	8	47	24	45	23	13	27	19
APR. 25	6	17	18	18	8	47	24	45	23	13	27	19
APR. 26	6	19	20	20	8	48	24	45	23	13	27	19
APR. 27	6	21	21	22	8	48	24	45	23	13	27	19
APR. 28	6	23	23	24	8	48	24	45	23	13	27	19
APR. 29	6	24	25	26	9	48	24	45	23	13	27	19
APR. 30	6	26	27	28	9	48	24	45	23	13	27	19

MOON 1 ☽ 12:01 A.M. TO 8:00 A.M.   **MOON 2** ☽ 8:01 A.M. TO 4:00 P.M.   **MOON 3** ● 4:01 P.M. TO 12:00 A.M.
Use only one "moon" number. Choose the column closest to your time of birth. If your place of birth is not on Eastern Standard Time, be sure to read "How to Convert to Eastern Standard Time" at the beginning of this section.

1950

May

June

Date & Time	SUN	MOON 1	MOON 2	MOON 3	MERCURY	VENUS	MARS	JUPITER	SATURN	URANUS	NEPTUNE	PLUTO
MAY 1	6	28	29	30	9	48	24	45	23	13	27	19
MAY 2	6	30	31	32	9	48	24	45	23	13	27	19
MAY 3	7	32	33	34	9	1	24	45	23	13	27	19
MAY 4	7	34	35	36	9	1	24	45	23	13	27	19
MAY 5	7	36	37	38	9	1	24	45	23	13	27	19
MAY 6	7	38	39	40	9	1	24	45	23	13	27	19
MAY 7	7	40	41	41	9	1	24	45	23	13	27	19
MAY 8	7	42	43	43	9	1	24	45	23	13	27	19
MAY 9	7	44	44	45	8	1	24	45	23	13	27	19
MAY 10	7	45	46	47	8	2	24	45	23	13	27	19
MAY 11	8	47	48	48	8	2	24	46	23	13	27	19
MAY 12	8	1	1	2	8	2	24	46	23	13	27	19
MAY 13	8	2	3	3	8	2	24	46	23	13	27	19
MAY 14	8	4	4	5	8	2	24	46	23	13	27	19
MAY 15	8	5	6	7	8	2	24	46	23	13	27	19
MAY 16	8	7	8	8	8	2	24	46	23	13	27	19
MAY 17	8	9	9	10	8	3	24	46	23	13	27	19
MAY 18	8	10	11	11	8	3	24	46	23	13	27	19
MAY 19	9	12	12	13	8	3	24	46	23	13	27	19
MAY 20	9	13	14	15	8	3	24	46	23	13	27	19
MAY 21	9	15	16	16	8	3	24	46	23	13	27	19
MAY 22	9	17	17	18	8	3	24	46	23	13	27	19
MAY 23	9	18	19	20	8	4	24	46	23	13	27	19
MAY 24	9	20	21	21	8	4	24	46	23	13	27	19
MAY 25	10	22	23	23	7	4	24	46	23	13	27	19
MAY 26	10	24	24	25	7	4	24	46	23	13	27	19
MAY 27	10	26	26	27	7	4	24	46	23	13	27	19
MAY 28	10	28	28	29	7	4	24	46	23	13	27	19
MAY 29	10	30	30	31	7	4	24	46	23	13	27	19
MAY 30	10	32	32	33	7	5	24	46	23	13	27	19
MAY 31	10	34	34	35	8	5	24	46	23	13	27	19

Date & Time	SUN	MOON 1	MOON 2	MOON 3	MERCURY	VENUS	MARS	JUPITER	SATURN	URANUS	NEPTUNE	PLUTO
JUN. 1	10	36	36	37	8	5	24	46	23	13	27	19
JUN. 2	10	38	38	39	8	5	25	46	23	13	27	19
JUN. 3	11	40	40	41	8	5	25	46	23	13	27	19
JUN. 4	11	41	42	43	8	5	25	46	23	13	27	19
JUN. 5	11	43	44	44	8	6	25	46	23	13	27	19
JUN. 6	11	45	46	46	8	6	25	46	23	13	27	19
JUN. 7	11	47	47	48	8	6	25	46	23	13	27	19
JUN. 8	11	48	1	1	8	6	25	46	23	14	27	19
JUN. 9	11	2	2	3	8	6	25	46	23	14	27	19
JUN. 10	11	4	4	5	8	6	25	46	23	14	27	19
JUN. 11	12	5	6	6	8	6	25	46	23	14	27	19
JUN. 12	12	7	7	8	9	7	25	46	23	14	27	19
JUN. 13	12	8	9	9	9	7	25	46	23	14	27	19
JUN. 14	12	10	10	11	9	7	25	46	23	14	27	19
JUN. 15	12	11	12	13	9	7	25	46	23	14	27	19
JUN. 16	12	13	14	14	9	7	25	46	23	14	27	19
JUN. 17	12	15	15	16	9	7	25	46	23	14	27	19
JUN. 18	12	16	17	17	10	8	25	46	23	14	27	19
JUN. 19	13	18	19	19	10	8	25	46	23	14	27	19
JUN. 20	13	20	20	21	10	8	25	46	23	14	27	19
JUN. 21	13	22	22	23	10	8	25	46	23	14	27	19
JUN. 22	13	23	24	24	10	8	26	46	23	14	27	19
JUN. 23	13	25	26	26	11	8	26	46	23	14	27	19
JUN. 24	13	27	28	28	11	8	26	46	23	14	27	19
JUN. 25	14	29	30	30	11	9	26	46	23	14	27	19
JUN. 26	14	31	31	32	11	9	26	46	23	14	27	19
JUN. 27	14	33	33	34	12	9	26	46	23	14	27	19
JUN. 28	14	35	35	36	12	9	26	46	23	14	27	19
JUN. 29	14	37	37	38	12	9	26	46	23	14	27	19
JUN. 30	14	39	39	40	12	9	26	46	23	14	27	19

MOON 1 ◐ 12:01 A.M. TO 8:00 A.M.   **MOON 2** ◐ 8:01 A.M. TO 4:00 P.M.   **MOON 3** ● 4:01 P.M. TO 12:00 A.M.

Use only one "moon" number. Choose the column closest to your time of birth. If your place of birth is not on Eastern Standard Time, be sure to read "How to Convert to Eastern Standard Time" at the beginning of this section.

1950

July

August

Date & Time	SUN	MOON 1	MOON 2	MOON 3	MERCURY	VENUS	MARS	JUPITER	SATURN	URANUS	NEPTUNE	PLUTO
JUL. 1	14	41	41	42	13	10	26	46	23	14	27	19
JUL. 2	14	42	43	44	13	10	26	46	23	14	27	19
JUL. 3	15	44	45	45	13	10	26	46	23	14	27	19
JUL. 4	15	46	47	47	13	10	26	46	23	14	27	19
JUL. 5	15	48	48	1	14	10	26	46	23	14	27	19
JUL. 6	15	1	2	2	14	10	26	46	23	14	27	19
JUL. 7	15	3	4	4	14	11	26	46	23	14	27	19
JUL. 8	15	5	5	6	15	11	26	46	23	14	27	19
JUL. 9	15	6	7	7	15	11	27	46	23	14	27	19
JUL. 10	15	8	8	9	15	11	27	46	23	14	27	19
JUL. 11	16	9	10	10	15	11	27	46	23	14	27	19
JUL. 12	16	11	12	12	16	11	27	46	23	14	27	19
JUL. 13	16	13	13	14	16	11	27	46	23	14	27	19
JUL. 14	16	14	15	15	16	12	27	46	23	14	27	19
JUL. 15	16	16	16	17	17	12	27	46	23	14	27	19
JUL. 16	16	18	18	19	17	12	27	46	23	14	27	19
JUL. 17	16	19	20	21	17	12	27	46	23	14	27	19
JUL. 18	16	21	22	22	17	12	27	46	23	14	27	19
JUL. 19	17	23	23	24	18	12	27	46	23	14	27	19
JUL. 20	17	25	25	26	18	13	27	46	23	14	27	19
JUL. 21	17	27	27	28	18	13	27	46	23	14	27	19
JUL. 22	17	28	29	30	18	13	27	46	23	14	27	19
JUL. 23	17	30	31	32	19	13	28	46	23	14	27	19
JUL. 24	17	32	33	33	19	13	28	46	23	14	27	19
JUL. 25	17	34	35	35	19	13	28	46	23	14	27	19
JUL. 26	18	36	37	37	19	14	28	46	23	14	27	19
JUL. 27	18	38	39	39	20	14	28	46	23	14	27	19
JUL. 28	18	40	41	41	20	14	28	46	23	14	27	19
JUL. 29	18	42	42	43	20	14	28	46	23	14	27	19
JUL. 30	18	44	44	45	20	14	28	46	23	14	27	19
JUL. 31	18	45	46	47	21	14	28	46	23	14	27	19

Date & Time	SUN	MOON 1	MOON 2	MOON 3	MERCURY	VENUS	MARS	JUPITER	SATURN	URANUS	NEPTUNE	PLUTO
AUG. 1	18	47	48	48	21	14	28	46	23	14	27	19
AUG. 2	18	1	1	2	21	15	28	46	23	14	27	19
AUG. 3	19	2	3	4	21	15	28	46	23	14	27	19
AUG. 4	19	4	5	5	21	15	28	46	23	14	27	19
AUG. 5	19	6	6	7	22	15	29	46	23	14	27	19
AUG. 6	19	7	8	8	22	15	29	46	23	14	27	19
AUG. 7	19	9	9	10	22	15	29	46	23	14	27	19
AUG. 8	19	10	11	12	22	16	29	46	23	14	27	19
AUG. 9	19	12	13	13	22	16	29	46	23	14	27	19
AUG. 10	19	14	14	15	23	16	29	46	23	14	27	19
AUG. 11	20	15	16	16	23	16	29	46	23	14	27	19
AUG. 12	20	17	18	18	23	16	29	46	23	14	27	19
AUG. 13	20	19	19	20	23	16	29	46	23	14	27	19
AUG. 14	20	21	21	22	23	17	29	46	23	14	27	19
AUG. 15	20	22	23	24	23	17	29	45	23	14	27	19
AUG. 16	20	24	25	25	24	17	29	45	23	14	27	19
AUG. 17	20	26	27	27	24	17	29	45	24	14	27	19
AUG. 18	20	28	29	29	24	17	30	45	24	14	27	19
AUG. 19	21	30	30	31	24	17	30	45	24	14	27	19
AUG. 20	21	32	32	33	24	18	30	45	24	14	27	19
AUG. 21	21	34	34	35	24	18	30	45	24	14	27	19
AUG. 22	21	36	36	37	24	18	30	45	24	14	27	19
AUG. 23	21	37	38	39	25	18	30	45	24	14	27	19
AUG. 24	21	39	40	41	25	18	30	45	24	14	27	19
AUG. 25	21	41	42	42	25	18	30	45	24	14	27	19
AUG. 26	22	43	44	44	25	19	30	45	24	14	27	19
AUG. 27	22	45	45	46	25	19	30	45	24	14	27	19
AUG. 28	22	46	47	48	25	19	30	45	24	14	27	19
AUG. 29	22	48	1	1	25	19	31	45	24	14	27	19
AUG. 30	22	2	2	3	25	19	31	45	24	14	27	19
AUG. 31	22	4	4	5	25	19	31	45	24	14	27	19

MOON 1 ☽ 12:01 A.M. TO 8:00 A.M.   **MOON 2** ◑ 8:01 A.M. TO 4:00 P.M.   **MOON 3** ● 4:01 P.M. TO 12:00 A.M.

Use only one "moon" number. Choose the column closest to your time of birth. If your place of birth is not on Eastern Standard Time, be sure to read "How to Convert to Eastern Standard Time" at the beginning of this section.

1950

September

October

Date & Time	SUN	MOON 1	MOON 2	MOON 3	MERCURY	VENUS	MARS	JUPITER	SATURN	URANUS	NEPTUNE	PLUTO
SEP. 1	22	5	6	6	25	20	31	45	24	14	27	19
SEP. 2	22	7	7	8	25	20	31	45	24	14	27	19
SEP. 3	23	8	9	9	25	20	31	45	24	14	27	19
SEP. 4	23	10	10	11	25	20	31	45	24	14	27	19
SEP. 5	23	11	12	13	25	20	31	45	24	14	27	19
SEP. 6	23	13	14	14	25	20	31	45	24	14	27	19
SEP. 7	23	15	15	16	25	20	31	45	24	14	27	19
SEP. 8	23	16	17	18	25	21	31	45	24	14	27	19
SEP. 9	23	18	19	19	25	21	31	45	24	14	27	19
SEP. 10	23	20	21	21	25	21	32	45	24	14	27	19
SEP. 11	24	22	22	23	25	21	32	45	24	14	27	19
SEP. 12	24	24	24	25	25	21	32	45	24	14	27	19
SEP. 13	24	25	26	27	25	21	32	45	24	14	27	19
SEP. 14	24	27	28	29	25	22	32	45	24	14	27	19
SEP. 15	24	29	30	31	24	22	32	45	24	14	27	19
SEP. 16	24	31	32	33	24	22	32	45	24	14	27	19
SEP. 17	24	33	34	34	24	22	32	45	24	14	27	19
SEP. 18	24	35	36	36	24	22	32	45	24	14	27	19
SEP. 19	25	37	38	38	24	22	32	45	24	14	27	19
SEP. 20	25	39	39	40	24	23	32	45	24	14	27	19
SEP. 21	25	41	41	42	24	23	33	45	24	14	27	20
SEP. 22	25	42	43	44	24	23	33	45	24	14	27	20
SEP. 23	25	44	45	45	23	23	33	45	24	14	27	20
SEP. 24	25	46	47	47	23	23	33	45	24	14	27	20
SEP. 25	26	48	48	1	23	23	33	45	24	14	27	20
SEP. 26	26	1	2	2	23	24	33	45	24	14	27	20
SEP. 27	26	3	4	4	23	24	33	45	24	14	27	20
SEP. 28	26	5	6	6	23	24	33	45	24	14	27	20
SEP. 29	26	6	7	7	23	24	33	45	24	14	27	20
SEP. 30	26	8	8	9	24	24	33	45	24	14	27	20

Date & Time	SUN	MOON 1	MOON 2	MOON 3	MERCURY	VENUS	MARS	JUPITER	SATURN	URANUS	NEPTUNE	PLUTO
OCT. 1	26	9	10	10	24	24	33	45	24	14	27	20
OCT. 2	26	11	12	12	24	25	34	45	24	14	27	20
OCT. 3	27	13	13	14	24	25	34	45	24	14	27	20
OCT. 4	27	14	15	15	24	25	34	45	24	14	27	20
OCT. 5	27	16	16	17	24	25	34	45	24	14	27	20
OCT. 6	27	17	18	19	24	25	34	45	24	14	27	20
OCT. 7	27	19	20	20	24	25	34	45	24	14	27	20
OCT. 8	27	21	22	22	25	26	34	45	24	14	27	20
OCT. 9	27	23	23	24	25	26	34	45	24	14	27	20
OCT. 10	27	25	25	26	25	26	34	45	24	14	27	20
OCT. 11	28	27	27	28	25	26	34	45	24	14	27	20
OCT. 12	28	29	29	30	26	26	35	45	24	14	27	20
OCT. 13	28	31	31	32	26	26	35	45	24	14	27	20
OCT. 14	28	33	33	34	26	27	35	45	24	14	27	20
OCT. 15	28	35	35	36	26	27	35	45	24	14	27	20
OCT. 16	28	36	37	38	26	27	35	45	24	14	27	20
OCT. 17	28	38	39	40	27	27	35	45	24	14	27	20
OCT. 18	28	40	41	41	27	27	35	45	25	14	27	20
OCT. 19	29	42	43	43	27	27	35	45	25	14	27	20
OCT. 20	29	44	44	45	27	28	35	45	25	14	27	20
OCT. 21	29	46	46	47	28	28	35	45	25	14	27	20
OCT. 22	29	47	48	48	28	28	35	45	25	14	27	20
OCT. 23	29	1	1	2	28	28	36	45	25	14	27	20
OCT. 24	29	3	3	4	28	28	36	45	25	14	27	20
OCT. 25	29	4	5	5	28	28	36	45	25	14	27	20
OCT. 26	30	6	6	7	29	29	36	45	25	14	27	20
OCT. 27	30	7	8	8	29	29	36	45	25	14	27	20
OCT. 28	30	9	9	10	29	29	36	45	25	14	27	20
OCT. 29	30	11	11	12	29	29	36	45	25	14	27	20
OCT. 30	30	12	13	13	30	29	36	45	25	14	27	20
OCT. 31	30	14	14	15	30	29	36	45	25	14	27	20

MOON 1 ◖ 12:01 A.M. TO 8:00 A.M.   **MOON 2** ◐ 8:01 A.M. TO 4:00 P.M.   **MOON 3** ● 4:01 P.M. TO 12:00 A.M.
Use only one "moon" number. Choose the column closest to your time of birth. If your place of birth is not on Eastern Standard Time, be sure to read "How to Convert to Eastern Standard Time" at the beginning of this section.

November

December

Date & Time	SUN	MOON 1	MOON 2	MOON 3	MERCURY	VENUS	MARS	JUPITER	SATURN	URANUS	NEPTUNE	PLUTO
NOV. 1	30	15	16	16	30	30	36	45	25	14	27	20
NOV. 2	30	17	17	18	30	30	37	45	25	14	27	20
NOV. 3	31	19	19	20	30	30	37	45	25	14	27	20
NOV. 4	31	20	21	21	31	30	37	45	25	14	27	20
NOV. 5	31	22	23	23	31	30	37	45	25	14	27	20
NOV. 6	31	24	24	25	31	30	37	45	25	14	27	20
NOV. 7	31	26	26	27	31	31	37	45	25	14	27	20
NOV. 8	31	28	28	29	32	31	37	45	25	14	27	20
NOV. 9	31	30	30	31	32	31	37	45	25	14	27	20
NOV. 10	31	32	32	33	32	31	37	45	25	14	27	20
NOV. 11	31	34	34	35	32	31	37	45	25	14	27	20
NOV. 12	32	36	36	37	32	31	38	45	25	14	27	20
NOV. 13	32	38	38	39	33	32	38	45	25	14	27	20
NOV. 14	32	40	40	41	33	32	38	45	25	14	27	20
NOV. 15	32	42	42	43	33	32	38	45	25	14	27	20
NOV. 16	32	43	44	45	33	32	38	45	25	14	27	20
NOV. 17	32	45	46	46	33	32	38	45	25	14	27	20
NOV. 18	32	47	47	48	34	32	38	45	25	14	27	20
NOV. 19	33	1	1	2	34	33	38	45	25	14	27	20
NOV. 20	33	2	3	3	34	33	38	45	25	14	27	20
NOV. 21	33	4	4	5	34	33	38	45	25	14	27	20
NOV. 22	33	5	6	6	34	33	39	45	25	14	27	20
NOV. 23	33	7	7	8	35	33	39	45	25	14	27	20
NOV. 24	33	9	9	10	35	33	39	45	25	14	27	20
NOV. 25	34	10	11	11	35	34	39	45	25	14	27	20
NOV. 26	34	12	12	13	35	34	39	45	25	14	27	20
NOV. 27	34	13	14	14	35	34	39	45	25	14	27	20
NOV. 28	34	15	15	16	36	34	39	45	25	14	27	20
NOV. 29	34	16	17	18	36	34	39	45	25	14	27	20
NOV. 30	34	18	19	19	36	34	39	45	25	14	27	20

Date & Time	SUN	MOON 1	MOON 2	MOON 3	MERCURY	VENUS	MARS	JUPITER	SATURN	URANUS	NEPTUNE	PLUTO
DEC. 1	34	20	20	21	36	35	39	45	25	14	27	20
DEC. 2	34	21	22	23	36	35	40	45	25	14	27	20
DEC. 3	35	23	24	24	37	35	40	45	25	14	27	20
DEC. 4	35	25	26	26	37	35	40	45	25	14	27	20
DEC. 5	35	27	27	28	37	35	40	45	25	14	27	20
DEC. 6	35	29	29	30	37	35	40	45	25	14	27	20
DEC. 7	35	31	31	32	37	36	40	45	25	14	27	20
DEC. 8	35	33	33	34	38	36	40	45	25	14	27	20
DEC. 9	35	35	35	36	38	36	40	45	25	14	28	20
DEC. 10	35	37	38	38	38	36	40	45	25	14	28	20
DEC. 11	36	39	40	40	38	36	41	45	25	14	28	20
DEC. 12	36	41	41	42	38	36	41	45	25	14	28	20
DEC. 13	36	43	43	44	38	37	41	45	25	14	28	20
DEC. 14	36	45	45	46	39	37	41	45	25	14	28	20
DEC. 15	36	46	47	47	39	37	41	45	25	14	28	20
DEC. 16	36	48	1	1	39	37	41	45	25	14	28	20
DEC. 17	36	2	2	3	39	37	41	45	25	14	28	20
DEC. 18	36	3	4	4	39	38	41	45	25	14	28	20
DEC. 19	37	5	5	6	39	38	41	45	25	14	28	20
DEC. 20	37	7	7	8	39	38	41	45	25	14	28	20
DEC. 21	37	8	9	9	39	38	42	45	25	14	28	20
DEC. 22	37	10	10	11	39	38	42	45	25	14	28	20
DEC. 23	37	11	12	12	39	38	42	45	25	14	28	20
DEC. 24	37	13	13	14	39	39	42	45	25	14	28	20
DEC. 25	37	14	15	16	39	39	42	45	25	14	28	20
DEC. 26	38	16	17	17	39	39	42	45	25	14	28	20
DEC. 27	38	18	18	19	39	39	42	45	25	14	28	20
DEC. 28	38	19	20	20	39	39	42	45	25	14	28	20
DEC. 29	38	21	22	22	39	39	42	46	25	14	28	20
DEC. 30	38	23	23	24	39	40	43	46	25	14	28	20
DEC. 31	38	25	25	26	39	40	43	46	25	14	28	20

MOON 1 ☽ 12:01 A.M. TO 8:00 A.M.　　**MOON 2** ◑ 8:01 A.M. TO 4:00 P.M.　　**MOON 3** ● 4:01 P.M. TO 12:00 A.M.
Use only one "moon" number. Choose the column closest to your time of birth. If your place of birth is not on
Eastern Standard Time, be sure to read "How to Convert to Eastern Standard Time" at the beginning of this section.

1951

January

Date & Time	SUN	MOON 1	MOON 2	MOON 3	MERCURY	VENUS	MARS	JUPITER	SATURN	URANUS	NEPTUNE	PLUTO
JAN. 1	38	26	27	27	39	40	43	46	25	14	28	20
JAN. 2	38	28	29	29	38	40	43	46	25	14	28	20
JAN. 3	39	30	31	31	38	40	43	46	25	14	28	20
JAN. 4	39	32	33	33	38	40	43	46	25	14	28	20
JAN. 5	39	34	35	35	38	41	43	46	25	14	28	20
JAN. 6	39	36	37	37	38	41	43	46	25	14	28	20
JAN. 7	39	38	39	39	38	41	43	46	25	14	28	20
JAN. 8	39	40	41	41	37	41	43	46	25	14	28	20
JAN. 9	39	42	43	43	37	41	44	46	25	14	28	20
JAN. 10	40	44	44	45	37	41	44	46	25	14	28	20
JAN. 11	40	46	46	47	37	42	44	46	25	14	28	20
JAN. 12	40	47	48	1	37	42	44	46	25	14	28	20
JAN. 13	40	1	2	2	37	42	44	46	25	14	28	20
JAN. 14	40	3	3	4	37	42	44	46	25	14	28	20
JAN. 15	40	4	5	6	37	42	44	46	25	14	28	20
JAN. 16	40	6	7	7	37	42	44	46	25	14	28	20
JAN. 17	41	8	8	9	37	43	44	46	25	14	28	20
JAN. 18	41	9	10	10	37	43	45	46	25	14	28	20
JAN. 19	41	11	11	12	38	43	45	46	25	14	28	20
JAN. 20	41	12	13	13	38	43	45	46	25	14	28	20
JAN. 21	41	14	15	15	38	43	45	46	25	14	28	20
JAN. 22	41	16	16	17	38	43	45	46	25	14	28	20
JAN. 23	42	17	18	18	38	44	45	46	25	14	28	20
JAN. 24	42	19	20	20	38	44	45	46	25	14	28	20
JAN. 25	42	21	21	22	38	44	45	46	25	14	28	19
JAN. 26	42	22	23	24	38	44	45	46	25	14	28	19
JAN. 27	42	24	25	25	39	44	45	46	25	14	28	19
JAN. 28	42	26	26	27	39	44	46	46	25	14	28	19
JAN. 29	42	28	28	29	39	45	46	46	25	14	28	19
JAN. 30	42	29	30	31	39	45	46	46	25	14	28	19
JAN. 31	43	31	32	33	39	45	46	46	25	14	28	19

February

Date & Time	SUN	MOON 1	MOON 2	MOON 3	MERCURY	VENUS	MARS	JUPITER	SATURN	URANUS	NEPTUNE	PLUTO
FEB. 1	43	33	34	35	39	45	46	46	25	14	28	19
FEB. 2	43	35	36	36	40	45	46	46	25	14	28	19
FEB. 3	43	37	38	38	40	45	46	47	25	14	28	19
FEB. 4	43	39	40	40	40	46	46	47	25	14	28	19
FEB. 5	43	41	42	42	40	46	46	47	25	14	28	19
FEB. 6	43	43	44	44	40	46	47	47	25	14	28	19
FEB. 7	43	45	45	46	40	46	47	47	25	14	28	19
FEB. 8	44	47	47	48	41	46	47	47	25	14	28	19
FEB. 9	44	48	1	2	41	46	47	47	25	14	28	19
FEB. 10	44	2	3	3	41	47	47	47	25	14	28	19
FEB. 11	44	4	4	5	41	47	47	47	25	14	28	19
FEB. 12	44	6	6	7	41	47	47	47	25	14	28	19
FEB. 13	44	7	8	8	42	47	47	47	25	14	28	19
FEB. 14	44	9	9	10	42	47	47	47	25	14	28	19
FEB. 15	44	10	11	11	42	47	47	47	25	14	28	19
FEB. 16	45	12	12	13	42	48	48	47	25	14	28	19
FEB. 17	45	14	14	15	42	48	48	47	25	14	28	19
FEB. 18	45	15	16	16	43	48	48	47	25	14	28	19
FEB. 19	45	17	17	18	43	48	48	47	25	14	28	19
FEB. 20	45	18	19	20	43	48	48	47	25	14	28	19
FEB. 21	45	20	21	21	43	48	48	47	25	14	28	19
FEB. 22	45	22	22	23	44	1	48	47	25	14	28	19
FEB. 23	46	24	24	25	44	1	48	47	25	14	28	19
FEB. 24	46	25	26	27	44	1	48	47	25	14	28	19
FEB. 25	46	27	28	28	44	1	48	47	25	14	28	19
FEB. 26	46	29	30	30	44	1	1	47	25	14	28	19
FEB. 27	46	31	32	32	45	1	1	47	25	14	28	19
FEB. 28	46	33	33	34	45	1	1	47	25	14	28	19

MOON 1 ☽ 12:01 A.M. TO 8:00 A.M.   **MOON 2** ◑ 8:01 A.M. TO 4:00 P.M.   **MOON 3** ● 4:01 P.M. TO 12:00 A.M.
Use only one "moon" number. Choose the column closest to your time of birth. If your place of birth is not on Eastern Standard Time, be sure to read "How to Convert to Eastern Standard Time" at the beginning of this section.

Date & Time	SUN ☉	MOON 1 ◐	MOON 2 ◑	MOON 3 ●	MERCURY	VENUS	MARS	JUPITER	SATURN	URANUS	NEPTUNE	PLUTO
MAR. 1	46	35	35	36	45	2	1	47	25	14	28	19
MAR. 2	46	37	37	38	45	2	1	47	25	14	28	19
MAR. 3	47	39	39	40	46	2	1	47	25	14	28	19
MAR. 4	47	40	41	42	46	2	1	47	25	14	28	19
MAR. 5	47	42	43	44	46	2	1	47	25	14	28	19
MAR. 6	47	44	45	45	46	2	1	47	25	14	28	19
MAR. 7	47	46	47	47	47	3	2	48	25	14	28	19
MAR. 8	47	48	48	1	47	3	2	48	25	14	27	19
MAR. 9	47	2	2	3	47	3	2	48	25	14	27	19
MAR. 10	47	3	4	4	47	3	2	48	25	14	27	19
MAR. 11	48	5	5	6	48	3	2	48	25	14	27	19
MAR. 12	48	7	7	8	48	3	2	48	25	14	27	19
MAR. 13	48	8	9	9	48	4	2	48	25	14	27	19
MAR. 14	48	10	10	11	48	4	2	48	25	14	27	19
MAR. 15	48	11	12	12	1	4	2	48	25	14	27	19
MAR. 16	48	13	13	14	1	4	2	48	25	14	27	19
MAR. 17	48	15	15	16	1	4	3	48	25	14	27	19
MAR. 18	48	16	17	17	1	4	3	48	25	14	27	19
MAR. 19	1	18	18	19	2	5	3	48	25	14	27	19
MAR. 20	1	19	20	21	2	5	3	48	25	14	27	19
MAR. 21	1	21	22	22	2	5	3	48	25	14	27	19
MAR. 22	1	23	24	24	2	5	3	48	25	14	27	19
MAR. 23	1	25	25	26	3	5	3	48	25	14	27	19
MAR. 24	1	27	27	28	3	5	4	48	25	14	27	19
MAR. 25	2	29	29	30	3	6	4	48	25	14	27	19
MAR. 26	2	30	31	32	3	6	4	48	25	14	27	19
MAR. 27	2	32	33	34	4	6	4	48	25	14	27	19
MAR. 28	2	34	35	36	4	6	4	48	25	14	27	19
MAR. 29	2	36	37	37	4	6	4	48	25	14	27	19
MAR. 30	2	38	39	39	4	6	4	48	25	14	27	19
MAR. 31	2	40	41	41	5	7	4	48	25	14	27	19

Date & Time	SUN ☉	MOON 1 ◐	MOON 2 ◑	MOON 3 ●	MERCURY	VENUS	MARS	JUPITER	SATURN	URANUS	NEPTUNE	PLUTO
APR. 1	2	42	42	43	5	7	4	48	25	14	27	19
APR. 2	2	44	44	45	5	7	4	48	25	14	27	19
APR. 3	3	45	46	47	5	7	4	48	25	14	27	19
APR. 4	3	47	48	48	5	7	4	48	25	14	27	19
APR. 5	3	1	2	2	5	7	4	48	25	14	27	19
APR. 6	3	3	3	4	6	8	5	48	25	14	27	19
APR. 7	3	4	5	5	6	8	5	1	25	14	27	19
APR. 8	3	6	7	7	6	8	5	1	25	14	27	19
APR. 9	3	8	8	9	6	8	5	1	25	14	27	19
APR. 10	3	9	10	10	6	8	5	1	25	14	27	19
APR. 11	4	11	11	12	6	8	5	1	25	14	27	19
APR. 12	4	12	13	13	6	8	5	1	25	14	27	19
APR. 13	4	14	15	15	6	9	5	1	25	14	27	19
APR. 14	4	16	16	17	6	9	5	1	25	14	27	19
APR. 15	4	17	18	18	6	9	5	1	25	14	27	19
APR. 16	4	19	19	20	6	9	6	1	25	14	27	19
APR. 17	4	21	21	22	6	9	6	1	25	14	27	19
APR. 18	4	22	23	23	6	9	6	1	25	14	27	19
APR. 19	5	24	25	25	6	10	6	1	25	14	27	19
APR. 20	5	26	27	27	6	10	6	1	25	14	27	19
APR. 21	5	28	28	29	6	10	6	1	25	14	27	19
APR. 22	5	30	30	31	6	10	6	1	25	14	27	19
APR. 23	5	32	32	33	6	10	6	1	25	14	27	19
APR. 24	5	34	34	35	6	10	6	1	25	14	27	19
APR. 25	6	36	36	37	6	11	6	1	24	14	27	19
APR. 26	6	38	38	39	5	11	7	1	24	14	27	19
APR. 27	6	40	40	41	5	11	7	1	24	14	27	19
APR. 28	6	41	42	43	5	11	7	1	24	14	27	19
APR. 29	6	43	44	44	5	11	7	1	24	14	27	19
APR. 30	6	45	46	46	5	11	7	1	24	14	27	19

MOON 1 ◐ 12:01 A.M. TO 8:00 A.M.   **MOON 2 ◑ 8:01 A.M. TO 4:00 P.M.**   **MOON 3 ● 4:01 P.M. TO 12:00 A.M.**
Use only one "moon" number. Choose the column closest to your time of birth. If your place of birth is not on Eastern Standard Time, be sure to read "How to Convert to Eastern Standard Time" at the beginning of this section.

1951

May

Date & Time	SUN	MOON 1	MOON 2	MOON 3	MERCURY	VENUS	MARS	JUPITER	SATURN	URANUS	NEPTUNE	PLUTO
MAY 1	6	47	47	48	5	11	7	1	24	14	27	19
MAY 2	6	1	1	2	5	12	7	1	24	14	27	19
MAY 3	7	2	3	3	5	12	7	1	24	14	27	19
MAY 4	7	4	4	5	5	12	7	1	24	14	27	19
MAY 5	7	6	6	7	5	12	7	1	24	14	27	19
MAY 6	7	7	8	8	5	12	7	1	24	14	27	19
MAY 7	7	9	9	10	5	12	8	1	24	14	27	19
MAY 8	7	10	11	11	5	13	8	1	24	14	27	19
MAY 9	7	12	12	13	5	13	8	1	24	14	27	19
MAY 10	7	14	14	15	5	13	8	2	24	14	27	19
MAY 11	8	15	16	16	5	13	8	2	24	14	27	19
MAY 12	8	17	17	18	5	13	8	2	24	14	27	19
MAY 13	8	18	19	19	5	13	8	2	24	14	27	19
MAY 14	8	20	20	21	5	13	8	2	24	14	27	19
MAY 15	8	22	22	23	5	14	8	2	24	14	27	19
MAY 16	8	23	24	25	5	14	8	2	24	14	27	19
MAY 17	8	25	26	26	5	14	9	2	24	14	27	19
MAY 18	8	27	28	28	5	14	9	2	24	14	27	19
MAY 19	9	29	30	30	5	14	9	2	24	14	27	19
MAY 20	9	31	31	32	5	14	9	2	24	14	27	19
MAY 21	9	33	33	34	6	14	9	2	24	14	27	19
MAY 22	9	35	36	36	6	15	9	2	24	14	27	19
MAY 23	9	37	38	38	6	15	9	2	24	14	27	19
MAY 24	9	39	40	40	6	15	9	2	24	14	27	19
MAY 25	10	41	41	42	6	15	9	2	24	14	27	19
MAY 26	10	43	43	44	6	15	9	2	24	14	27	19
MAY 27	10	45	45	46	6	15	9	2	24	14	27	19
MAY 28	10	46	47	48	7	16	10	2	24	14	27	19
MAY 29	10	48	1	1	7	16	10	2	24	14	27	19
MAY 30	10	2	2	3	7	16	10	2	24	14	27	19
MAY 31	10	3	4	5	7	16	10	2	24	14	27	19

June

Date & Time	SUN	MOON 1	MOON 2	MOON 3	MERCURY	VENUS	MARS	JUPITER	SATURN	URANUS	NEPTUNE	PLUTO
JUN. 1	10	5	6	6	7	16	10	2	24	14	27	19
JUN. 2	10	7	7	8	7	16	10	2	24	14	27	19
JUN. 3	11	8	9	9	8	16	10	2	24	14	27	19
JUN. 4	11	10	10	11	8	17	10	2	24	14	27	19
JUN. 5	11	12	12	13	8	17	10	2	24	14	27	19
JUN. 6	11	13	14	14	8	17	10	2	24	14	27	19
JUN. 7	11	15	15	16	8	17	11	2	24	14	27	19
JUN. 8	11	16	17	17	9	17	11	2	24	14	27	19
JUN. 9	11	18	18	19	9	17	11	2	24	14	27	19
JUN. 10	11	19	20	21	9	17	11	2	24	14	27	19
JUN. 11	12	21	22	22	9	18	11	2	24	14	27	19
JUN. 12	12	23	23	24	10	18	11	2	24	14	27	19
JUN. 13	12	24	25	26	10	18	11	2	24	14	27	19
JUN. 14	12	26	27	27	10	18	11	2	24	14	27	19
JUN. 15	12	28	29	29	10	18	11	2	24	14	27	19
JUN. 16	12	30	31	31	11	18	11	2	24	14	27	19
JUN. 17	12	32	33	33	11	18	11	2	24	14	27	19
JUN. 18	12	34	35	35	11	18	12	2	24	14	27	19
JUN. 19	13	36	37	37	12	19	12	2	24	14	27	19
JUN. 20	13	38	39	39	12	19	12	2	24	14	27	19
JUN. 21	13	40	41	41	12	19	12	2	24	14	27	19
JUN. 22	13	42	43	43	12	19	12	2	24	14	27	19
JUN. 23	13	44	45	45	13	19	12	2	24	14	27	19
JUN. 24	13	46	46	47	13	19	12	3	24	14	27	19
JUN. 25	14	48	48	1	13	19	12	3	24	14	27	19
JUN. 26	14	1	2	3	14	20	12	3	24	14	27	19
JUN. 27	14	3	4	4	14	20	12	3	24	14	27	19
JUN. 28	14	5	5	6	14	20	12	3	24	14	27	19
JUN. 29	14	6	7	7	14	20	13	3	24	14	27	19
JUN. 30	14	8	9	15	14	20	13	3	24	14	27	19

MOON 1 ◐ 12:01 A.M. TO 8:00 A.M.   **MOON 2** ◑ 8:01 A.M. TO 4:00 P.M.   **MOON 3** ● 4:01 P.M. TO 12:00 A.M.
Use only one "moon" number. Choose the column closest to your time of birth. If your place of birth is not on
Eastern Standard Time, be sure to read "How to Convert to Eastern Standard Time" at the beginning of this section.

1951

July · August

Date & Time	SUN	MOON 1	MOON 2	MOON 3	MERCURY	VENUS	MARS	JUPITER	SATURN	URANUS	NEPTUNE	PLUTO
JUL. 1	14	10	10	11	15	20	13	3	24	14	27	19
JUL. 2	14	11	12	12	15	20	13	3	25	14	27	19
JUL. 3	15	13	13	14	16	20	13	3	25	14	27	19
JUL. 4	15	14	15	15	16	21	13	3	25	14	27	19
JUL. 5	15	16	16	17	16	21	13	3	25	14	27	19
JUL. 6	15	17	18	18	17	21	13	3	25	14	27	19
JUL. 7	15	19	20	20	17	21	13	3	25	14	27	19
JUL. 8	15	21	21	22	17	21	13	3	25	14	27	19
JUL. 9	15	22	23	23	17	21	13	3	25	14	27	19
JUL. 10	15	24	25	25	17	21	14	3	25	14	27	19
JUL. 11	16	26	26	27	18	21	14	3	25	14	27	19
JUL. 12	16	28	28	29	18	21	14	3	25	14	27	19
JUL. 13	16	29	30	31	18	22	14	3	25	14	27	19
JUL. 14	16	31	32	32	18	22	14	3	25	14	27	19
JUL. 15	16	33	34	34	19	22	14	3	25	14	27	19
JUL. 16	16	35	36	36	19	22	14	3	25	14	27	19
JUL. 17	16	37	38	38	19	22	14	3	25	14	27	19
JUL. 18	16	39	40	40	19	22	14	3	25	14	27	19
JUL. 19	17	41	42	42	19	22	14	3	25	14	27	19
JUL. 20	17	43	44	44	20	22	14	3	25	14	27	19
JUL. 21	17	45	46	46	20	22	15	3	25	14	27	19
JUL. 22	17	47	48	48	20	22	15	3	25	14	27	19
JUL. 23	17	1	1	2	20	22	15	3	25	14	27	19
JUL. 24	17	3	3	4	20	23	15	3	25	14	27	19
JUL. 25	17	4	5	5	21	23	15	3	25	14	27	19
JUL. 26	18	6	6	7	21	23	15	3	25	14	27	19
JUL. 27	18	8	8	8	21	23	15	3	25	14	27	19
JUL. 28	18	9	10	10	21	23	15	3	25	14	27	20
JUL. 29	18	11	11	12	21	23	15	3	25	14	27	20
JUL. 30	18	12	13	13	21	23	15	3	25	14	27	20
JUL. 31	18	14	14	15	22	23	15	3	25	14	27	20
AUG. 1	18	15	16	17	22	23	15	3	25	14	27	20
AUG. 2	18	17	18	18	22	23	16	3	25	14	27	20
AUG. 3	19	19	19	20	22	23	16	3	25	15	27	20
AUG. 4	19	20	21	21	22	23	16	3	25	15	27	20
AUG. 5	19	22	23	23	22	23	16	3	25	15	27	20
AUG. 6	19	24	24	25	22	23	16	3	25	15	27	20
AUG. 7	19	25	26	27	22	23	16	3	25	15	27	20
AUG. 8	19	27	28	28	23	23	16	3	25	15	27	20
AUG. 9	19	29	29	30	23	23	16	3	25	15	27	20
AUG. 10	19	31	31	32	23	23	16	3	25	15	27	20
AUG. 11	20	33	33	34	23	23	16	3	25	15	27	20
AUG. 12	20	34	35	36	23	23	16	3	25	15	27	20
AUG. 13	20	36	37	38	23	23	17	3	25	15	27	20
AUG. 14	20	38	39	40	23	23	17	3	25	15	27	20
AUG. 15	20	40	41	42	23	23	17	3	25	15	27	20
AUG. 16	20	42	43	44	23	23	17	3	25	15	27	20
AUG. 17	20	44	45	46	23	23	17	3	25	15	27	20
AUG. 18	20	46	47	47	23	23	17	3	25	15	27	20
AUG. 19	21	48	1	1	23	23	17	3	25	15	27	20
AUG. 20	21	2	2	3	23	23	17	3	25	15	27	20
AUG. 21	21	4	4	5	23	23	17	3	25	15	27	20
AUG. 22	21	5	6	6	23	23	17	3	25	15	27	20
AUG. 23	21	7	8	8	23	23	17	3	25	15	27	20
AUG. 24	21	9	9	10	23	23	17	3	25	15	27	20
AUG. 25	21	10	11	11	23	23	18	3	25	15	27	20
AUG. 26	22	12	12	13	23	23	18	3	25	15	27	20
AUG. 27	22	13	14	15	22	23	18	3	25	15	27	20
AUG. 28	22	15	16	16	22	23	18	3	25	15	27	20
AUG. 29	22	17	17	18	22	23	18	3	25	15	27	20
AUG. 30	22	18	19	19	22	23	18	3	25	15	27	20
AUG. 31	22	20	20	21	22	23	18	3	25	15	27	20

MOON 1 ☽ 12:01 A.M. TO 8:00 A.M.　　**MOON 2** ☽ 8:01 A.M. TO 4:00 P.M.　　**MOON 3** ● 4:01 P.M. TO 12:00 A.M.

Use only one "moon" number. Choose the column closest to your time of birth. If your place of birth is not on Eastern Standard Time, be sure to read "How to Convert to Eastern Standard Time" at the beginning of this section.

1951

September

Date & Time	SUN ☉	MOON 1 ◗	MOON 2 ◑	MOON 3 ●	MERCURY	VENUS	MARS	JUPITER	SATURN	URANUS	NEPTUNE	PLUTO
SEP. 1	22	22	22	23	22	23	18	3	25	15	27	20
SEP. 2	22	23	24	24	22	22	18	3	25	15	27	20
SEP. 3	23	25	26	26	22	22	18	3	25	15	27	20
SEP. 4	23	27	27	28	21	22	18	3	25	15	27	20
SEP. 5	23	28	29	30	21	22	18	3	25	15	27	20
SEP. 6	23	30	31	31	21	22	19	3	25	15	27	20
SEP. 7	23	32	33	33	21	22	19	3	25	15	27	20
SEP. 8	23	34	35	35	21	22	19	3	25	15	27	20
SEP. 9	23	36	36	37	21	22	19	3	25	15	27	20
SEP. 10	23	38	38	39	21	22	19	3	25	15	27	20
SEP. 11	24	40	40	41	21	22	19	3	25	15	27	20
SEP. 12	24	42	42	43	21	22	19	3	25	15	27	20
SEP. 13	24	44	44	45	21	22	19	3	25	15	27	20
SEP. 14	24	45	46	47	21	22	19	3	25	15	27	20
SEP. 15	24	47	48	1	21	22	19	2	25	15	27	20
SEP. 16	24	1	2	2	22	21	19	2	25	15	27	20
SEP. 17	24	3	4	4	22	21	19	2	25	15	27	20
SEP. 18	24	5	5	6	22	21	20	2	26	15	27	20
SEP. 19	25	6	7	8	22	21	20	2	26	15	27	20
SEP. 20	25	8	9	9	22	21	20	2	26	15	27	20
SEP. 21	25	10	10	11	22	21	20	2	26	15	27	20
SEP. 22	25	11	12	13	23	21	20	2	26	15	27	20
SEP. 23	25	13	13	14	23	21	20	2	26	15	27	20
SEP. 24	25	15	15	16	23	21	20	2	26	15	27	20
SEP. 25	26	16	17	17	23	21	20	2	26	15	27	20
SEP. 26	26	18	18	19	23	21	20	2	26	15	27	20
SEP. 27	26	19	20	20	24	21	20	2	26	15	27	20
SEP. 28	26	21	22	22	24	21	20	2	26	15	27	20
SEP. 29	26	23	23	24	24	21	20	2	26	15	27	20
SEP. 30	26	24	25	26	24	21	21	2	26	15	27	20

October

Date & Time	SUN ☉	MOON 1 ◗	MOON 2 ◑	MOON 3 ●	MERCURY	VENUS	MARS	JUPITER	SATURN	URANUS	NEPTUNE	PLUTO
OCT. 1	26	26	27	27	25	21	21	2	26	15	27	20
OCT. 2	26	28	29	29	25	21	21	2	26	15	27	20
OCT. 3	27	30	30	31	25	21	21	2	26	15	27	20
OCT. 4	27	32	32	33	25	21	21	2	26	15	27	20
OCT. 5	27	34	34	35	26	22	21	2	26	15	27	20
OCT. 6	27	35	36	37	26	22	21	2	26	15	28	20
OCT. 7	27	37	38	39	26	22	21	2	26	15	28	20
OCT. 8	27	39	40	40	26	22	21	2	26	15	28	20
OCT. 9	27	41	42	42	27	22	21	2	26	15	28	20
OCT. 10	27	43	44	44	27	22	21	2	26	15	28	20
OCT. 11	28	45	45	46	27	22	21	2	26	15	28	20
OCT. 12	28	47	47	48	27	22	22	2	26	15	28	20
OCT. 13	28	48	1	2	27	22	22	2	26	15	28	20
OCT. 14	28	2	3	3	28	22	22	2	26	15	28	20
OCT. 15	28	4	5	5	28	22	22	2	26	15	28	20
OCT. 16	28	6	6	7	28	22	22	2	26	15	28	20
OCT. 17	28	7	8	9	28	22	22	2	26	15	28	20
OCT. 18	28	9	10	10	29	22	22	2	26	15	28	20
OCT. 19	29	11	11	12	29	23	22	2	26	15	28	20
OCT. 20	29	12	13	13	29	23	22	2	26	15	28	20
OCT. 21	29	14	15	15	29	23	22	2	26	15	28	20
OCT. 22	29	16	16	17	29	23	22	2	26	15	28	20
OCT. 23	29	17	18	18	30	23	22	2	26	15	28	20
OCT. 24	29	19	19	20	30	23	23	2	26	15	28	20
OCT. 25	29	20	21	21	30	23	23	2	26	15	28	20
OCT. 26	30	22	23	23	30	23	23	2	26	15	28	20
OCT. 27	30	24	24	25	31	23	23	2	26	15	28	20
OCT. 28	30	25	26	27	31	23	23	2	26	15	28	20
OCT. 29	30	27	28	28	31	24	23	2	26	15	28	20
OCT. 30	30	29	30	30	31	24	23	2	26	15	28	20
OCT. 31	30	31	32	32	31	24	23	2	26	15	28	20

MOON 1 ◗ 12:01 A.M. TO 8:00 A.M. **MOON 2** ◑ 8:01 A.M. TO 4:00 P.M. **MOON 3** ● 4:01 P.M. TO 12:00 A.M.

Use only one "moon" number. Choose the column closest to your time of birth. If your place of birth is not on Eastern Standard Time, be sure to read "How to Convert to Eastern Standard Time" at the beginning of this section.

November

December

Date & Time	SUN	MOON 1	MOON 2	MOON 3	MERCURY	VENUS	MARS	JUPITER	SATURN	URANUS	NEPTUNE	PLUTO
NOV. 1	30	33	34	34	32	24	23	2	26	15	28	20
NOV. 2	30	35	36	36	32	24	23	2	26	15	28	20
NOV. 3	31	37	37	38	32	24	23	2	26	15	28	20
NOV. 4	31	39	39	40	32	24	23	2	26	15	28	20
NOV. 5	31	41	41	42	32	24	23	2	26	15	28	20
NOV. 6	31	43	43	44	33	25	24	2	26	15	28	20
NOV. 7	31	44	45	46	33	25	24	2	26	15	28	20
NOV. 8	31	46	47	47	33	25	24	2	26	15	28	20
NOV. 9	31	48	1	1	33	25	24	2	26	15	28	20
NOV. 10	31	2	2	3	33	25	24	2	26	15	28	20
NOV. 11	31	4	5	5	34	25	24	2	26	15	28	20
NOV. 12	32	5	6	6	34	25	24	2	26	15	28	20
NOV. 13	32	7	7	8	34	25	24	2	26	15	28	20
NOV. 14	32	9	9	10	34	26	24	2	26	15	28	20
NOV. 15	32	10	11	11	34	26	24	2	26	15	28	20
NOV. 16	32	12	12	13	35	26	24	2	26	15	28	20
NOV. 17	32	13	14	15	35	26	24	2	26	15	28	20
NOV. 18	32	15	16	16	35	26	25	2	26	15	28	20
NOV. 19	33	17	17	18	35	26	25	2	26	15	28	20
NOV. 20	33	18	19	19	35	26	25	2	26	15	28	20
NOV. 21	33	20	20	21	35	27	25	2	27	15	28	20
NOV. 22	33	21	22	22	36	27	25	2	27	15	28	20
NOV. 23	33	23	24	24	36	27	25	2	27	15	28	20
NOV. 24	33	25	25	26	36	27	25	2	27	15	28	20
NOV. 25	34	26	27	28	36	27	25	2	27	15	28	20
NOV. 26	34	28	29	30	36	27	25	2	27	15	28	20
NOV. 27	34	30	31	31	36	27	25	2	27	15	28	20
NOV. 28	34	32	33	33	37	28	25	2	27	15	28	20
NOV. 29	34	34	35	35	37	28	25	2	27	15	28	20
NOV. 30	34	36	37	37	37	28	25	2	27	15	28	20

Date & Time	SUN	MOON 1	MOON 2	MOON 3	MERCURY	VENUS	MARS	JUPITER	SATURN	URANUS	NEPTUNE	PLUTO
DEC. 1	34	38	39	39	37	28	25	2	27	15	28	20
DEC. 2	34	40	41	41	37	28	26	2	27	15	28	20
DEC. 3	35	42	43	43	37	28	26	2	27	15	28	20
DEC. 4	35	44	45	45	37	28	26	2	27	15	28	20
DEC. 5	35	46	46	47	37	29	26	2	27	15	28	20
DEC. 6	35	48	48	1	37	29	26	2	27	15	28	20
DEC. 7	35	1	2	3	37	29	26	2	27	15	28	20
DEC. 8	35	3	4	4	37	29	26	2	27	15	28	20
DEC. 9	35	5	5	6	37	29	26	2	27	15	28	20
DEC. 10	35	6	7	8	37	29	26	2	27	15	28	20
DEC. 11	36	8	9	9	37	29	26	2	27	15	28	20
DEC. 12	36	10	10	11	37	30	26	2	27	15	28	20
DEC. 13	36	11	12	12	37	30	26	2	27	15	28	20
DEC. 14	36	13	14	14	37	30	26	2	27	15	28	20
DEC. 15	36	15	15	16	37	30	27	2	27	15	28	20
DEC. 16	36	16	17	17	36	30	27	2	27	15	28	20
DEC. 17	36	18	18	19	36	30	27	2	27	15	28	20
DEC. 18	36	19	20	20	36	31	27	2	27	15	28	20
DEC. 19	37	21	21	22	36	31	27	2	27	15	28	20
DEC. 20	37	23	23	24	36	31	27	2	27	15	28	20
DEC. 21	37	24	25	25	36	31	27	2	27	15	28	20
DEC. 22	37	26	26	27	35	31	27	2	27	15	28	20
DEC. 23	37	28	28	29	35	31	27	2	27	15	28	20
DEC. 24	37	29	30	31	35	31	27	2	27	15	28	20
DEC. 25	37	31	32	33	35	32	27	2	27	15	28	20
DEC. 26	38	33	34	34	35	32	27	2	27	15	28	20
DEC. 27	38	35	36	37	35	32	27	2	27	15	28	20
DEC. 28	38	37	38	39	35	32	27	2	27	15	28	20
DEC. 29	38	39	40	41	35	32	28	2	27	15	28	20
DEC. 30	38	41	42	43	35	32	28	2	27	15	28	20
DEC. 31	38	43	44	45	35	33	28	2	27	15	28	20

MOON 1 ◐ **12:01 A.M. TO 8:00 A.M.**   **MOON 2** ◑ **8:01 A.M. TO 4:00 P.M.**   **MOON 3** ● **4:01 P.M. TO 12:00 A.M.**
Use only one "moon" number. Choose the column closest to your time of birth. If your place of birth is not on
Eastern Standard Time, be sure to read "How to Convert to Eastern Standard Time" at the beginning of this section.

1952

January

Date & Time	SUN ☉	MOON 1 ◐	MOON 2 ◑	MOON 3 ●	MERCURY	VENUS	MARS	JUPITER	SATURN	URANUS	NEPTUNE	PLUTO
JAN. 1	38	45	46	46	35	33	28	2	27	15	28	20
JAN. 2	38	47	48	48	35	33	28	2	27	15	28	20
JAN. 3	39	1	2	2	36	33	28	2	27	15	28	20
JAN. 4	39	3	3	4	36	33	28	2	27	15	28	20
JAN. 5	39	4	5	6	36	33	28	2	27	15	28	20
JAN. 6	39	6	7	7	36	34	28	2	27	15	28	20
JAN. 7	39	8	8	9	36	34	28	2	27	15	28	20
JAN. 8	39	9	10	10	36	34	28	2	27	15	28	20
JAN. 9	39	11	12	12	36	34	28	2	27	15	28	20
JAN. 10	40	13	13	14	36	34	28	2	27	15	28	20
JAN. 11	40	14	15	15	37	34	28	2	27	15	28	20
JAN. 12	40	16	16	17	37	34	28	2	27	15	28	20
JAN. 13	40	17	18	18	37	35	28	2	27	15	28	20
JAN. 14	40	19	19	20	37	35	29	2	27	14	28	20
JAN. 15	40	21	21	22	37	35	29	2	27	14	28	20
JAN. 16	40	22	23	23	37	35	29	2	27	14	28	20
JAN. 17	41	24	24	25	38	35	29	2	27	14	28	20
JAN. 18	41	25	26	26	38	35	29	2	27	14	28	20
JAN. 19	41	27	28	28	38	36	29	2	27	14	28	20
JAN. 20	41	29	29	30	38	36	29	2	27	14	28	20
JAN. 21	41	31	31	32	38	36	29	2	27	14	28	20
JAN. 22	41	32	33	34	38	36	29	2	27	14	28	20
JAN. 23	42	34	35	36	39	36	29	2	27	14	28	20
JAN. 24	42	36	37	38	39	36	29	2	27	14	28	20
JAN. 25	42	38	39	40	39	37	29	2	27	14	28	20
JAN. 26	42	40	41	42	39	37	29	2	27	14	28	20
JAN. 27	42	42	43	44	40	37	29	2	27	14	28	20
JAN. 28	42	44	45	46	40	37	29	2	27	14	28	20
JAN. 29	42	46	47	48	40	37	30	2	27	14	28	20
JAN. 30	42	48	1	1	40	37	30	2	27	14	28	20
JAN. 31	43	2	3	3	40	38	30	2	27	14	28	20

February

Date & Time	SUN ☉	MOON 1 ◐	MOON 2 ◑	MOON 3 ●	MERCURY	VENUS	MARS	JUPITER	SATURN	URANUS	NEPTUNE	PLUTO
FEB. 1	43	4	4	5	41	38	30	2	27	14	28	20
FEB. 2	43	6	6	7	41	38	30	2	27	14	28	20
FEB. 3	43	7	8	8	41	38	30	2	27	14	28	20
FEB. 4	43	9	10	10	41	38	30	2	27	14	28	20
FEB. 5	43	11	11	12	41	38	30	2	27	14	28	20
FEB. 6	43	12	13	13	42	39	30	3	27	14	28	20
FEB. 7	43	14	14	15	42	39	30	3	27	14	28	20
FEB. 8	44	15	16	16	42	39	30	3	27	14	28	20
FEB. 9	44	17	17	18	42	39	30	3	27	14	28	20
FEB. 10	44	19	19	20	43	39	30	3	27	14	28	20
FEB. 11	44	20	21	21	43	39	30	3	27	14	28	20
FEB. 12	44	22	22	23	43	39	30	3	27	14	28	20
FEB. 13	44	23	24	24	43	40	30	3	27	14	28	20
FEB. 14	44	25	26	26	43	40	30	3	27	14	28	20
FEB. 15	44	27	27	28	44	40	30	3	27	14	28	20
FEB. 16	45	28	29	29	44	40	30	3	27	14	28	20
FEB. 17	45	30	31	31	44	40	30	3	27	14	28	20
FEB. 18	45	32	32	33	44	40	31	3	27	14	28	20
FEB. 19	45	34	34	35	45	41	31	3	27	14	28	20
FEB. 20	45	36	36	37	45	41	31	3	27	14	28	20
FEB. 21	45	37	38	39	45	41	31	3	27	14	28	20
FEB. 22	45	39	40	41	45	41	31	3	27	14	28	20
FEB. 23	46	41	42	43	46	41	31	3	27	14	28	20
FEB. 24	46	43	44	45	46	41	31	3	27	14	28	20
FEB. 25	46	45	46	47	46	42	31	3	27	14	28	20
FEB. 26	46	47	48	1	46	42	31	3	27	14	28	20
FEB. 27	46	1	2	3	47	42	31	3	27	14	28	20
FEB. 28	46	3	4	4	47	42	31	3	27	14	28	20
FEB. 29	46	5	6	6	47	42	31	3	27	14	28	20

MOON 1 ◐ 12:01 A.M. TO 8:00 A.M. **MOON 2** ◑ 8:01 A.M. TO 4:00 P.M. **MOON 3** ● 4:01 P.M. TO 12:00 A.M.

Use only one "moon" number. Choose the column closest to your time of birth. If your place of birth is not on Eastern Standard Time, be sure to read "How to Convert to Eastern Standard Time" at the beginning of this section.

Date & Time	SUN ☉	MOON 1 ◗	MOON 2 ◑	MOON 3 ●	MERCURY	VENUS	MARS	JUPITER	SATURN	URANUS	NEPTUNE	PLUTO
MAR. 1	46	7	7	8	47	42	31	3	27	14	28	20
MAR. 2	46	8	9	10	48	43	31	3	27	14	28	20
MAR. 3	47	10	11	11	48	43	31	3	27	14	28	20
MAR. 4	47	12	12	13	48	43	31	3	27	14	28	20
MAR. 5	47	13	14	14	48	43	31	3	27	14	28	20
MAR. 6	47	15	15	16	1	43	31	3	27	14	28	20
MAR. 7	47	16	17	18	1	43	31	3	27	14	28	20
MAR. 8	47	18	19	19	1	44	31	3	27	14	28	20
MAR. 9	47	20	20	21	1	44	31	3	27	14	28	20
MAR. 10	47	21	22	22	2	44	31	3	27	14	28	20
MAR. 11	48	23	23	24	2	44	31	3	27	14	28	20
MAR. 12	48	25	25	26	2	44	31	3	27	14	28	20
MAR. 13	48	26	27	27	2	44	31	3	27	14	28	20
MAR. 14	48	28	29	29	2	45	31	4	27	14	28	20
MAR. 15	48	30	30	31	3	45	31	4	27	14	28	20
MAR. 16	48	31	32	33	3	45	31	4	27	14	28	20
MAR. 17	48	33	34	34	3	45	31	4	27	14	28	20
MAR. 18	48	35	36	36	3	45	31	4	27	14	28	20
MAR. 19	1	37	38	38	3	45	31	4	27	14	28	20
MAR. 20	1	39	39	40	3	46	31	4	27	14	28	20
MAR. 21	1	41	41	42	3	46	31	4	27	14	28	20
MAR. 22	1	43	43	44	4	46	31	4	27	14	28	20
MAR. 23	1	45	45	46	4	46	31	4	27	14	28	20
MAR. 24	1	47	47	48	4	46	31	4	27	14	28	20
MAR. 25	2	48	1	2	4	46	31	4	27	14	28	20
MAR. 26	2	2	3	4	4	47	31	4	27	14	28	20
MAR. 27	2	4	5	5	4	47	31	4	27	14	28	20
MAR. 28	2	6	7	7	4	47	31	4	27	14	28	20
MAR. 29	2	8	8	9	4	47	31	4	27	14	28	20
MAR. 30	2	9	10	11	4	47	31	4	27	14	28	20
MAR. 31	2	11	12	12	4	47	31	4	27	14	28	20

Date & Time	SUN ☉	MOON 1 ◗	MOON 2 ◑	MOON 3 ●	MERCURY	VENUS	MARS	JUPITER	SATURN	URANUS	NEPTUNE	PLUTO
APR. 1	2	13	13	14	3	48	31	4	27	14	28	20
APR. 2	2	14	15	15	3	48	31	4	27	14	28	20
APR. 3	3	16	16	17	3	48	31	4	26	14	28	20
APR. 4	3	18	18	19	3	48	31	4	26	14	28	20
APR. 5	3	19	20	20	3	48	31	4	26	14	28	20
APR. 6	3	21	21	22	3	48	31	4	26	14	28	20
APR. 7	3	22	23	23	3	1	31	4	26	14	28	20
APR. 8	3	24	25	25	3	1	31	4	26	14	28	20
APR. 9	3	26	26	27	3	1	31	4	26	14	28	20
APR. 10	3	27	28	29	3	1	31	4	26	14	28	20
APR. 11	4	29	30	30	2	1	31	4	26	14	28	20
APR. 12	4	31	32	32	2	1	31	4	26	14	28	20
APR. 13	4	33	33	34	2	1	31	4	26	14	28	20
APR. 14	4	35	35	36	2	2	31	4	26	14	28	20
APR. 15	4	37	37	38	2	2	31	5	26	14	28	20
APR. 16	4	38	39	40	2	2	31	5	26	14	28	20
APR. 17	4	40	41	42	2	2	31	5	26	14	28	20
APR. 18	4	42	43	43	2	2	31	5	26	14	28	20
APR. 19	5	44	45	45	2	2	31	5	26	14	28	20
APR. 20	5	46	47	47	2	3	31	5	26	14	28	20
APR. 21	5	48	48	1	2	3	31	5	26	14	28	20
APR. 22	5	2	2	3	2	3	31	5	26	14	28	20
APR. 23	5	4	4	5	2	3	31	5	26	14	28	20
APR. 24	5	5	6	7	2	3	31	5	26	14	28	20
APR. 25	6	7	8	8	2	3	31	5	26	14	28	20
APR. 26	6	9	9	10	2	4	31	5	26	14	28	20
APR. 27	6	11	11	12	2	4	31	5	26	14	28	20
APR. 28	6	12	13	13	3	4	31	5	26	14	28	20
APR. 29	6	14	14	15	3	4	30	5	26	14	28	20
APR. 30	6	15	16	16	3	4	30	5	26	14	28	20

MOON 1 ◗ 12:01 A.M. TO 8:00 A.M.　　**MOON 2** ◑ 8:01 A.M. TO 4:00 P.M.　　**MOON 3** ● 4:01 P.M. TO 12:00 A.M.

Use only one "moon" number. Choose the column closest to your time of birth. If your place of birth is not on Eastern Standard Time, be sure to read "How to Convert to Eastern Standard Time" at the beginning of this section.

Date & Time	SUN ☉	MOON 1 ☽	MOON 2 ☽	MOON 3 ●	MERCURY	VENUS	MARS	JUPITER	SATURN	URANUS	NEPTUNE	PLUTO
MAY 1	6	17	18	18	3	4	30	5	26	14	28	20
MAY 2	6	19	19	20	3	5	30	5	26	14	28	20
MAY 3	7	20	21	21	3	5	30	5	26	14	28	20
MAY 4	7	22	22	23	3	5	30	5	26	14	28	20
MAY 5	7	23	24	25	3	5	30	5	26	14	28	20
MAY 6	7	25	26	26	4	5	30	5	26	14	28	20
MAY 7	7	27	27	28	4	6	30	5	26	14	28	20
MAY 8	7	29	29	30	4	6	30	5	26	14	28	20
MAY 9	7	30	31	32	4	6	30	5	26	14	28	20
MAY 10	7	32	33	33	4	6	30	5	26	14	28	20
MAY 11	8	34	35	35	4	6	30	5	26	14	28	20
MAY 12	8	36	37	37	5	6	30	5	26	14	28	20
MAY 13	8	38	39	39	5	6	30	5	26	14	28	20
MAY 14	8	40	40	41	5	7	30	5	26	14	28	20
MAY 15	8	42	42	43	5	7	30	5	26	14	28	20
MAY 16	8	44	44	45	5	7	30	6	26	14	28	20
MAY 17	8	46	46	47	5	7	30	6	26	14	28	20
MAY 18	8	47	48	1	6	7	30	6	26	14	28	20
MAY 19	9	1	2	2	6	7	30	6	26	15	28	20
MAY 20	9	3	4	4	6	8	30	6	26	15	28	20
MAY 21	9	5	5	6	6	8	29	6	26	15	28	20
MAY 22	9	7	7	8	7	8	29	6	26	15	28	20
MAY 23	9	8	9	9	7	8	29	6	26	15	28	20
MAY 24	9	10	11	11	7	8	29	6	26	15	28	20
MAY 25	10	12	12	13	7	8	29	6	26	15	28	20
MAY 26	10	13	14	14	8	9	29	6	26	15	28	20
MAY 27	10	15	15	16	8	9	29	6	26	15	28	20
MAY 28	10	17	17	18	8	9	29	6	26	15	28	20
MAY 29	10	18	19	19	8	9	29	6	26	15	28	20
MAY 30	10	20	20	21	9	9	29	6	26	15	28	20
MAY 31	10	21	22	22	9	9	29	6	26	15	28	20

Date & Time	SUN ☉	MOON 1 ☽	MOON 2 ☽	MOON 3 ●	MERCURY	VENUS	MARS	JUPITER	SATURN	URANUS	NEPTUNE	PLUTO
JUN. 1	10	23	23	24	9	10	29	6	26	15	28	20
JUN. 2	10	24	25	26	9	10	29	6	26	15	28	20
JUN. 3	11	26	27	27	10	10	29	6	26	15	28	20
JUN. 4	11	28	28	29	10	10	29	6	26	15	28	20
JUN. 5	11	30	30	31	10	10	29	6	26	15	28	20
JUN. 6	11	31	32	33	10	10	29	6	26	15	28	20
JUN. 7	11	33	34	35	11	11	29	6	26	15	28	20
JUN. 8	11	35	36	37	11	11	29	6	26	15	28	20
JUN. 9	11	37	38	39	11	11	29	6	26	15	28	20
JUN. 10	11	39	40	41	12	11	29	6	26	15	28	20
JUN. 11	12	41	42	42	12	11	29	6	26	15	28	20
JUN. 12	12	43	44	44	12	11	29	6	26	15	28	20
JUN. 13	12	45	46	46	13	11	29	6	26	15	28	20
JUN. 14	12	47	48	48	13	12	29	6	26	15	28	20
JUN. 15	12	1	1	2	13	12	29	6	26	15	27	20
JUN. 16	12	3	3	4	13	12	29	6	26	15	27	20
JUN. 17	12	4	5	6	14	12	29	6	26	15	27	20
JUN. 18	12	6	7	7	14	12	29	6	26	15	27	20
JUN. 19	13	8	9	9	14	12	29	7	26	15	27	20
JUN. 20	13	10	10	11	15	13	29	7	26	15	27	20
JUN. 21	13	11	12	12	15	13	29	7	26	15	27	20
JUN. 22	13	13	13	14	15	13	29	7	26	15	27	20
JUN. 23	13	14	15	16	15	13	29	7	26	15	27	20
JUN. 24	13	16	17	17	16	13	29	7	26	15	27	20
JUN. 25	14	18	18	19	16	13	29	7	26	15	27	20
JUN. 26	14	19	20	20	16	14	29	7	26	15	27	20
JUN. 27	14	21	21	22	16	14	29	7	26	15	27	20
JUN. 28	14	22	23	23	16	14	29	7	26	15	27	20
JUN. 29	14	24	24	25	17	14	29	7	26	15	27	20
JUN. 30	14	26	26	27	17	14	29	7	26	15	27	20

MOON 1 ☽ 12:01 A.M. TO 8:00 A.M.   **MOON 2** ☽ 8:01 A.M. TO 4:00 P.M.   **MOON 3** ● 4:01 P.M. TO 12:00 A.M.
Use only one "moon" number. Choose the column closest to your time of birth. If your place of birth is not on
Eastern Standard Time, be sure to read "How to Convert to Eastern Standard Time" at the beginning of this section.

1952

July

August

Date & Time	SUN	MOON 1	MOON 2	MOON 3	MERCURY	VENUS	MARS	JUPITER	SATURN	URANUS	NEPTUNE	PLUTO
JUL. 1	14	27	28	28	17	14	29	7	26	15	27	20
JUL. 2	14	29	30	30	17	15	30	7	26	15	27	20
JUL. 3	15	31	31	32	18	15	30	7	26	15	27	20
JUL. 4	15	33	33	34	18	15	30	7	26	15	27	20
JUL. 5	15	34	35	36	18	15	30	7	26	15	27	20
JUL. 6	15	36	37	38	18	15	30	7	26	15	27	20
JUL. 7	15	38	39	40	18	15	30	7	26	15	27	20
JUL. 8	15	40	41	42	18	16	30	7	26	15	27	20
JUL. 9	15	42	43	44	19	16	30	7	26	15	27	20
JUL. 10	15	44	45	46	19	16	30	7	26	15	27	20
JUL. 11	16	46	47	48	19	16	30	7	26	15	27	20
JUL. 12	16	48	1	2	19	16	30	7	26	15	27	20
JUL. 13	16	2	3	3	19	16	30	7	26	15	27	20
JUL. 14	16	4	5	5	19	17	30	7	26	15	27	20
JUL. 15	16	6	6	7	20	17	30	7	26	15	27	20
JUL. 16	16	7	8	9	20	17	30	7	26	15	27	20
JUL. 17	16	9	10	10	20	17	30	7	26	15	28	20
JUL. 18	16	11	11	12	20	17	30	7	26	15	28	20
JUL. 19	17	12	13	13	20	17	30	7	26	15	28	20
JUL. 20	17	14	15	15	20	18	30	7	26	15	28	20
JUL. 21	17	16	16	17	20	18	30	7	26	15	28	20
JUL. 22	17	17	18	18	20	18	30	7	26	15	28	20
JUL. 23	17	19	19	20	20	18	30	7	26	15	28	20
JUL. 24	17	20	21	21	20	18	31	7	26	15	28	20
JUL. 25	17	22	22	23	20	18	31	7	26	15	28	20
JUL. 26	18	24	24	25	21	19	31	7	26	15	28	20
JUL. 27	18	25	26	26	21	19	31	7	26	15	28	20
JUL. 28	18	27	27	28	21	19	31	7	26	15	28	20
JUL. 29	18	28	29	30	21	19	31	7	26	15	28	20
JUL. 30	18	30	31	31	21	19	31	7	26	15	28	20
JUL. 31	18	32	32	33	21	19	31	7	26	15	28	20

Date & Time	SUN	MOON 1	MOON 2	MOON 3	MERCURY	VENUS	MARS	JUPITER	SATURN	URANUS	NEPTUNE	PLUTO
AUG. 1	18	34	34	35	21	20	31	7	26	15	28	20
AUG. 2	18	36	36	37	21	20	31	7	26	15	28	20
AUG. 3	19	37	38	39	20	20	31	7	26	15	28	20
AUG. 4	19	39	40	41	20	20	31	7	26	15	28	20
AUG. 5	19	41	42	43	20	20	31	7	26	15	28	20
AUG. 6	19	44	44	45	20	20	31	8	26	15	28	20
AUG. 7	19	46	46	47	20	21	31	8	26	15	28	20
AUG. 8	19	48	48	1	20	21	32	8	26	15	28	20
AUG. 9	19	1	2	3	20	21	32	8	26	15	28	20
AUG. 10	19	3	4	5	20	21	32	8	26	15	28	20
AUG. 11	20	5	6	5	20	21	32	8	26	15	28	20
AUG. 12	20	7	8	8	20	21	32	8	26	15	28	20
AUG. 13	20	9	9	10	20	21	32	8	26	15	28	20
AUG. 14	20	10	11	11	19	22	32	8	26	15	28	20
AUG. 15	20	12	13	13	19	22	32	8	27	15	28	20
AUG. 16	20	14	14	14	19	22	32	8	27	15	28	20
AUG. 17	20	15	16	16	19	22	32	8	27	15	28	20
AUG. 18	20	17	17	18	19	22	32	8	27	15	28	20
AUG. 19	21	18	19	19	19	22	32	8	27	15	28	20
AUG. 20	21	20	20	21	19	23	32	8	27	15	28	20
AUG. 21	21	22	22	23	19	23	32	8	27	15	28	20
AUG. 22	21	23	24	24	19	23	33	8	27	15	28	20
AUG. 23	21	25	25	26	19	23	33	8	27	15	28	20
AUG. 24	21	26	27	27	19	23	33	8	27	15	28	20
AUG. 25	21	28	29	29	19	23	33	8	27	15	28	20
AUG. 26	22	30	30	31	19	24	33	8	27	15	28	20
AUG. 27	22	31	32	33	19	24	33	8	27	15	28	20
AUG. 28	22	33	34	34	19	24	33	8	27	15	28	20
AUG. 29	22	35	36	36	19	24	33	8	27	15	28	20
AUG. 30	22	37	37	38	19	24	33	8	27	15	28	20
AUG. 31	22	39	39	40	20	24	33	8	27	15	28	20

MOON 1 ◗ 12:01 A.M. TO 8:00 A.M.   **MOON 2** ◖ 8:01 A.M. TO 4:00 P.M.   **MOON 3** ● 4:01 P.M. TO 12:00 A.M.
Use only one "moon" number. Choose the column closest to your time of birth. If your place of birth is not on Eastern Standard Time, be sure to read "How to Convert to Eastern Standard Time" at the beginning of this section.

1952

September

Date & Time	SUN	MOON 1	MOON 2	MOON 3	MERCURY	VENUS	MARS	JUPITER	SATURN	URANUS	NEPTUNE	PLUTO
SEP. 1	22	41	41	42	20	25	33	8	27	15	28	20
SEP. 2	22	43	43	44	20	25	33	8	27	15	28	20
SEP. 3	23	45	45	46	20	25	33	8	27	15	28	20
SEP. 4	23	47	47	48	20	25	34	8	27	15	28	20
SEP. 5	23	1	1	2	20	25	34	8	27	15	28	20
SEP. 6	23	3	3	4	21	25	34	8	27	15	28	20
SEP. 7	23	5	5	6	21	26	34	8	27	15	28	20
SEP. 8	23	6	7	8	21	26	34	8	27	15	28	20
SEP. 9	23	8	9	9	21	26	34	8	27	15	28	20
SEP. 10	23	10	10	11	22	26	34	8	27	15	28	20
SEP. 11	24	12	12	13	22	26	34	8	27	15	28	20
SEP. 12	24	13	14	14	22	26	34	8	27	15	28	20
SEP. 13	24	15	15	16	22	27	34	8	27	15	28	20
SEP. 14	24	16	17	17	23	27	34	8	27	15	28	20
SEP. 15	24	18	18	19	23	27	35	8	27	15	28	20
SEP. 16	24	20	20	21	23	27	35	8	27	15	28	20
SEP. 17	24	21	22	22	23	27	35	8	27	15	28	20
SEP. 18	24	23	23	24	24	27	35	8	27	15	28	20
SEP. 19	25	24	25	25	24	28	35	8	27	15	28	20
SEP. 20	25	26	26	27	24	28	35	8	27	15	28	20
SEP. 21	25	28	28	29	24	28	35	8	27	15	28	20
SEP. 22	25	29	30	30	25	28	35	8	27	15	28	20
SEP. 23	25	31	32	32	25	28	35	8	27	15	28	20
SEP. 24	25	33	33	34	25	28	35	8	27	15	28	20
SEP. 25	26	34	35	36	25	29	35	8	27	15	28	20
SEP. 26	26	36	37	37	26	29	35	8	27	15	28	20
SEP. 27	26	38	39	39	26	29	36	8	27	15	28	20
SEP. 28	26	40	41	41	26	29	36	8	27	15	28	20
SEP. 29	26	42	43	43	26	29	36	8	27	15	28	20
SEP. 30	26	44	44	45	26	29	36	8	27	15	28	20

October

Date & Time	SUN	MOON 1	MOON 2	MOON 3	MERCURY	VENUS	MARS	JUPITER	SATURN	URANUS	NEPTUNE	PLUTO
OCT. 1	26	46	46	47	27	30	36	8	27	15	28	20
OCT. 2	26	48	48	1	27	30	36	8	27	15	28	20
OCT. 3	27	2	2	3	27	30	36	8	27	15	28	20
OCT. 4	27	4	4	5	27	30	36	8	27	15	28	20
OCT. 5	27	6	6	7	28	30	36	8	27	15	28	20
OCT. 6	27	7	8	9	28	30	36	8	27	15	28	20
OCT. 7	27	9	10	10	28	31	36	8	27	15	28	20
OCT. 8	27	11	12	12	28	31	37	8	27	15	28	20
OCT. 9	27	13	13	14	28	31	37	8	27	15	28	20
OCT. 10	27	14	15	15	29	31	37	8	27	15	28	20
OCT. 11	28	16	16	17	29	31	37	8	27	15	28	20
OCT. 12	28	18	18	19	29	31	37	8	27	15	28	20
OCT. 13	28	19	20	20	29	31	37	8	27	15	28	20
OCT. 14	28	21	21	22	30	32	37	8	27	15	28	20
OCT. 15	28	22	23	23	30	32	37	7	27	15	28	20
OCT. 16	28	24	24	25	30	32	37	7	27	15	28	20
OCT. 17	28	25	26	27	30	32	37	7	27	15	28	20
OCT. 18	28	27	28	28	30	32	38	7	27	15	28	20
OCT. 19	29	29	29	30	31	32	38	7	27	15	28	20
OCT. 20	29	31	31	32	31	33	38	7	28	15	28	20
OCT. 21	29	32	33	33	31	33	38	7	28	15	28	20
OCT. 22	29	34	35	35	31	33	38	7	28	15	28	20
OCT. 23	29	36	36	37	31	33	38	7	28	15	28	20
OCT. 24	29	38	38	39	31	33	38	7	28	15	28	20
OCT. 25	29	40	40	41	32	33	38	7	28	15	28	20
OCT. 26	30	41	42	43	32	34	38	7	28	15	28	20
OCT. 27	30	43	44	45	32	34	38	7	28	15	28	20
OCT. 28	30	45	46	46	32	34	39	7	28	15	28	20
OCT. 29	30	47	48	48	32	34	39	7	28	15	28	20
OCT. 30	30	1	2	2	33	34	39	7	28	15	28	20
OCT. 31	30	3	4	4	33	34	39	7	28	15	28	20

MOON 1 ◗ 12:01 A.M. TO 8:00 A.M.　　**MOON 2** ◖ 8:01 A.M. TO 4:00 P.M.　　**MOON 3** ● 4:01 P.M. TO 12:00 A.M.
Use only one "moon" number. Choose the column closest to your time of birth. If your place of birth is not on
Eastern Standard Time, be sure to read "How to Convert to Eastern Standard Time" at the beginning of this section.

1952

November

Date & Time	SUN	MOON 1	MOON 2	MOON 3	MERCURY	VENUS	MARS	JUPITER	SATURN	URANUS	NEPTUNE	PLUTO
NOV. 1	30	5	5	6	33	35	39	7	28	15	28	20
NOV. 2	30	7	7	8	33	35	39	7	28	15	28	20
NOV. 3	31	9	9	10	33	35	39	7	28	15	28	20
NOV. 4	31	10	11	11	33	35	39	7	28	15	28	20
NOV. 5	31	12	13	13	34	35	39	7	28	15	28	20
NOV. 6	31	14	14	15	34	35	39	7	28	15	28	20
NOV. 7	31	15	16	16	34	35	39	7	28	15	28	20
NOV. 8	31	17	18	18	34	36	40	7	28	15	28	20
NOV. 9	31	19	19	20	34	36	40	7	28	15	28	20
NOV. 10	31	20	21	21	34	36	40	7	28	15	28	20
NOV. 11	31	22	22	23	35	36	40	7	28	15	28	20
NOV. 12	32	23	24	24	35	36	40	7	28	15	28	20
NOV. 13	32	25	25	26	35	37	40	7	28	15	28	20
NOV. 14	32	27	27	28	35	37	40	7	28	15	28	20
NOV. 15	32	28	29	29	35	37	40	7	28	15	28	20
NOV. 16	32	30	31	31	35	37	40	7	28	15	28	20
NOV. 17	32	32	32	33	35	37	41	7	28	15	28	20
NOV. 18	32	34	34	35	35	37	41	7	28	15	28	20
NOV. 19	33	35	36	37	35	38	41	7	28	15	28	20
NOV. 20	33	37	38	38	35	38	41	7	28	15	28	20
NOV. 21	33	39	40	40	35	38	41	7	28	15	28	20
NOV. 22	33	41	42	42	35	38	41	7	28	15	28	20
NOV. 23	33	43	43	44	35	38	41	7	28	15	28	20
NOV. 24	33	45	45	46	35	38	41	7	28	15	28	20
NOV. 25	34	47	47	48	35	38	41	7	28	15	28	20
NOV. 26	34	48	1	2	35	39	41	7	28	15	28	20
NOV. 27	34	2	3	4	35	39	42	7	28	15	28	20
NOV. 28	34	4	5	5	34	39	42	7	28	15	28	20
NOV. 29	34	6	7	7	34	39	42	7	28	15	28	20
NOV. 30	34	8	8	9	34	39	42	7	28	15	28	20

December

Date & Time	SUN	MOON 1	MOON 2	MOON 3	MERCURY	VENUS	MARS	JUPITER	SATURN	URANUS	NEPTUNE	PLUTO
DEC. 1	34	10	10	11	34	39	42	7	28	15	28	20
DEC. 2	34	11	12	13	34	40	42	7	28	15	28	20
DEC. 3	35	13	14	14	34	40	42	7	28	15	28	20
DEC. 4	35	15	15	16	33	40	42	7	28	15	28	20
DEC. 5	35	16	17	17	33	40	42	7	28	15	28	20
DEC. 6	35	18	19	19	33	40	42	7	28	15	28	20
DEC. 7	35	20	20	21	33	40	43	7	28	15	28	20
DEC. 8	35	21	22	22	33	41	43	7	28	15	28	20
DEC. 9	35	23	23	24	33	41	43	7	28	15	28	20
DEC. 10	35	24	25	25	33	41	43	7	28	15	28	20
DEC. 11	36	26	26	27	33	41	43	7	28	15	28	20
DEC. 12	36	28	28	29	33	41	43	7	28	15	28	20
DEC. 13	36	29	30	30	33	41	43	7	28	15	28	20
DEC. 14	36	31	32	32	33	42	43	7	28	15	28	20
DEC. 15	36	33	33	34	33	42	43	7	28	15	28	20
DEC. 16	36	35	35	36	33	42	43	7	28	15	28	20
DEC. 17	36	37	37	38	33	42	44	7	28	15	28	20
DEC. 18	36	38	39	40	34	42	44	7	28	15	28	20
DEC. 19	37	40	41	42	34	42	44	6	28	15	28	20
DEC. 20	37	42	43	44	34	42	44	6	28	15	28	20
DEC. 21	37	44	45	46	34	43	44	6	28	15	28	20
DEC. 22	37	46	47	47	34	43	44	6	28	15	28	20
DEC. 23	37	48	1	1	34	43	44	6	28	15	28	20
DEC. 24	37	2	3	3	34	43	44	6	28	15	28	20
DEC. 25	37	4	4	5	35	43	44	6	28	15	28	20
DEC. 26	38	6	6	7	35	43	44	6	28	15	28	20
DEC. 27	38	7	8	9	35	44	45	6	28	15	28	20
DEC. 28	38	9	10	10	35	44	45	6	28	15	28	20
DEC. 29	38	11	11	12	35	44	45	6	28	15	28	20
DEC. 30	38	13	13	14	36	44	45	6	28	15	28	20
DEC. 31	38	14	15	15	36	44	45	6	28	15	28	20

MOON 1 ☾ 12:01 A.M. TO 8:00 A.M.   **MOON 2** ◑ 8:01 A.M. TO 4:00 P.M.   **MOON 3** ● 4:01 P.M. TO 12:00 A.M.
Use only one "moon" number. Choose the column closest to your time of birth. If your place of birth is not on
Eastern Standard Time, be sure to read "How to Convert to Eastern Standard Time" at the beginning of this section.

1953

January

Date & Time	SUN	MOON 1	MOON 2	MOON 3	MERCURY	VENUS	MARS	JUPITER	SATURN	URANUS	NEPTUNE	PLUTO
JAN. 1	38	16	16	17	36	44	45	6	28	15	28	20
JAN. 2	38	17	18	19	36	44	45	6	28	15	28	20
JAN. 3	39	19	20	20	36	45	45	6	28	15	28	20
JAN. 4	39	21	21	22	37	45	45	6	28	15	28	20
JAN. 5	39	22	23	23	37	45	46	6	28	15	28	20
JAN. 6	39	24	24	25	37	45	46	6	29	15	28	20
JAN. 7	39	25	26	26	37	45	46	6	29	15	28	20
JAN. 8	39	27	28	28	37	45	46	6	29	15	28	20
JAN. 9	39	29	29	30	37	46	46	6	29	15	28	20
JAN. 10	40	30	31	31	38	46	46	6	29	15	28	20
JAN. 11	40	32	33	33	38	46	46	6	29	15	28	20
JAN. 12	40	34	34	35	38	46	46	6	29	15	28	20
JAN. 13	40	36	36	37	38	46	46	6	29	15	28	20
JAN. 14	40	38	38	39	39	46	46	6	29	15	28	20
JAN. 15	40	40	40	41	39	46	47	6	29	15	28	20
JAN. 16	40	42	42	43	39	47	47	6	29	15	28	20
JAN. 17	41	44	44	45	39	47	47	6	29	15	28	20
JAN. 18	41	46	46	47	39	47	47	6	29	15	28	20
JAN. 19	41	48	48	1	40	47	47	6	29	15	28	20
JAN. 20	41	1	2	3	40	47	47	6	29	15	28	20
JAN. 21	41	3	4	5	40	47	47	6	29	15	28	20
JAN. 22	41	5	6	6	40	47	47	6	29	15	28	20
JAN. 23	42	7	8	8	40	48	47	7	29	15	28	20
JAN. 24	42	9	9	10	41	48	47	7	29	15	28	20
JAN. 25	42	10	11	12	41	48	48	7	29	15	28	20
JAN. 26	42	12	13	13	41	48	48	7	29	15	28	20
JAN. 27	42	14	14	15	41	48	48	7	29	15	28	20
JAN. 28	42	15	16	16	42	48	48	7	29	15	28	20
JAN. 29	42	17	18	18	42	48	48	7	29	15	28	20
JAN. 30	42	19	19	20	42	1	48	7	29	15	28	20
JAN. 31	43	20	21	21	42	1	48	7	29	15	28	20

February

Date & Time	SUN	MOON 1	MOON 2	MOON 3	MERCURY	VENUS	MARS	JUPITER	SATURN	URANUS	NEPTUNE	PLUTO
FEB. 1	43	22	22	23	42	1	48	7	29	15	28	20
FEB. 2	43	23	24	24	43	1	48	7	29	15	28	20
FEB. 3	43	25	25	26	43	1	48	7	29	15	28	20
FEB. 4	43	27	27	28	43	1	1	7	29	15	28	20
FEB. 5	43	28	29	29	43	1	1	7	29	15	28	20
FEB. 6	43	30	30	31	44	1	1	7	29	15	28	20
FEB. 7	43	31	32	33	44	2	1	7	29	15	28	20
FEB. 8	44	33	34	34	44	2	1	7	29	15	28	20
FEB. 9	44	35	36	36	44	2	1	7	29	15	28	20
FEB. 10	44	37	37	38	45	2	1	7	29	15	28	20
FEB. 11	44	39	39	40	45	2	1	7	29	15	28	20
FEB. 12	44	41	41	42	45	2	1	7	29	15	28	20
FEB. 13	44	43	43	44	45	2	1	7	29	15	28	20
FEB. 14	44	45	45	46	46	2	2	7	29	15	28	20
FEB. 15	44	47	47	48	46	3	2	7	29	15	28	20
FEB. 16	45	1	1	2	46	3	2	7	29	15	28	20
FEB. 17	45	3	3	4	46	3	2	7	29	15	28	20
FEB. 18	45	5	5	6	46	3	2	7	29	15	28	20
FEB. 19	45	6	7	8	47	3	2	7	29	15	28	20
FEB. 20	45	8	9	9	47	3	2	7	29	15	28	20
FEB. 21	45	10	11	11	47	3	2	7	29	15	28	20
FEB. 22	45	12	12	13	47	3	2	7	29	15	28	20
FEB. 23	46	13	14	14	48	3	2	7	29	15	28	20
FEB. 24	46	15	16	16	48	4	3	7	29	15	28	20
FEB. 25	46	17	17	18	48	4	3	7	29	15	28	20
FEB. 26	46	18	19	19	48	4	3	7	29	15	28	20
FEB. 27	46	20	20	21	48	4	3	7	29	15	28	20
FEB. 28	46	21	22	22	1	4	3	7	29	15	28	20

MOON 1 ☽ 12:01 A.M. TO 8:00 A.M.   **MOON 2** ☽ 8:01 A.M. TO 4:00 P.M.   **MOON 3** ● 4:01 P.M. TO 12:00 A.M.
Use only one "moon" number. Choose the column closest to your time of birth. If your place of birth is not on Eastern Standard Time, be sure to read "How to Convert to Eastern Standard Time" at the beginning of this section.

1953

March

Date & Time	SUN ☉	MOON 1 ◖	MOON 2 ◑	MOON 3 ●	MERCURY	VENUS	MARS	JUPITER	SATURN	URANUS	NEPTUNE	PLUTO
MAR. 1	46	23	23	24	1	4	3	7	29	15	28	20
MAR. 2	46	25	25	26	1	4	3	7	29	15	28	20
MAR. 3	47	26	27	27	1	4	3	7	29	15	28	20
MAR. 4	47	28	28	29	1	4	3	7	29	15	28	20
MAR. 5	47	29	30	30	1	4	3	7	29	15	28	20
MAR. 6	47	31	32	32	1	4	4	7	29	15	28	20
MAR. 7	47	33	33	34	1	5	4	7	29	15	28	20
MAR. 8	47	34	35	36	1	5	4	7	28	15	28	20
MAR. 9	47	36	37	37	1	5	4	7	28	15	28	20
MAR. 10	47	38	39	39	1	5	4	7	28	15	28	20
MAR. 11	48	40	40	41	1	5	4	7	28	15	28	20
MAR. 12	48	42	42	43	1	5	4	7	28	15	28	20
MAR. 13	48	44	44	45	1	5	4	7	28	15	28	20
MAR. 14	48	46	46	47	1	5	4	7	28	15	28	20
MAR. 15	48	48	48	1	1	5	4	7	28	15	28	20
MAR. 16	48	2	2	3	1	5	5	7	28	15	28	20
MAR. 17	48	4	4	5	1	5	5	7	28	15	28	20
MAR. 18	48	6	6	7	1	5	5	7	28	15	28	20
MAR. 19	1	8	8	9	1	5	5	7	28	15	28	20
MAR. 20	1	9	10	11	48	5	5	8	28	15	28	20
MAR. 21	1	11	12	12	48	5	5	8	28	15	28	20
MAR. 22	1	13	13	14	48	5	5	8	28	15	28	20
MAR. 23	1	15	15	16	48	5	5	8	28	15	28	20
MAR. 24	1	16	17	17	48	5	5	8	28	15	28	20
MAR. 25	2	18	18	19	48	5	5	8	28	15	28	20
MAR. 26	2	19	20	20	48	5	6	8	28	15	28	20
MAR. 27	2	21	21	22	48	5	6	8	28	15	28	20
MAR. 28	2	23	23	24	48	5	6	8	28	15	28	20
MAR. 29	2	24	25	25	48	5	6	8	28	15	28	20
MAR. 30	2	26	26	27	48	5	6	8	28	15	28	20
MAR. 31	2	27	28	28	48	5	6	8	28	15	28	20

April

Date & Time	SUN ☉	MOON 1 ◖	MOON 2 ◑	MOON 3 ●	MERCURY	VENUS	MARS	JUPITER	SATURN	URANUS	NEPTUNE	PLUTO
APR. 1	2	29	29	30	48	5	6	8	28	15	28	20
APR. 2	2	31	31	32	48	5	6	8	28	15	28	20
APR. 3	3	32	33	33	48	5	6	8	28	15	28	20
APR. 4	3	34	35	35	48	5	6	8	28	15	28	20
APR. 5	3	36	36	37	48	5	7	8	28	15	28	20
APR. 6	3	37	38	39	48	5	7	8	28	15	28	20
APR. 7	3	39	40	40	48	5	7	8	28	15	28	20
APR. 8	3	41	42	42	48	4	7	8	28	15	28	20
APR. 9	3	43	44	44	48	4	7	8	28	15	28	20
APR. 10	3	45	46	46	48	4	7	8	28	15	28	20
APR. 11	4	47	48	48	48	4	7	8	28	15	28	20
APR. 12	4	1	2	2	48	4	7	8	28	15	28	20
APR. 13	4	3	4	4	48	4	7	8	28	15	28	20
APR. 14	4	5	5	6	48	4	7	8	28	15	28	20
APR. 15	4	7	7	8	1	4	7	8	28	15	28	20
APR. 16	4	9	9	10	1	4	8	8	28	15	28	20
APR. 17	4	11	11	12	1	4	8	8	28	15	28	20
APR. 18	4	12	13	13	1	4	8	8	28	15	28	20
APR. 19	5	14	15	15	1	4	8	8	28	15	28	20
APR. 20	5	16	16	17	1	4	8	8	28	15	28	20
APR. 21	5	17	18	18	2	3	8	8	28	15	28	20
APR. 22	5	19	19	20	2	3	8	8	28	15	28	20
APR. 23	5	21	21	22	2	3	8	8	28	15	28	20
APR. 24	5	22	23	23	2	3	8	8	28	15	28	20
APR. 25	6	24	24	25	2	3	8	9	28	15	28	20
APR. 26	6	25	26	26	2	3	8	9	28	15	28	20
APR. 27	6	27	27	28	2	3	8	9	28	15	28	20
APR. 28	6	28	29	30	2	3	9	9	28	15	28	20
APR. 29	6	30	31	31	3	3	9	9	28	15	28	20
APR. 30	6	32	32	33	3	3	9	9	28	15	28	20

MOON 1 ◖ 12:01 A.M. TO 8:00 A.M.   **MOON 2** ◑ 8:01 A.M. TO 4:00 P.M.   **MOON 3** ● 4:01 P.M. TO 12:00 A.M.
Use only one "moon" number. Choose the column closest to your time of birth. If your place of birth is not on Eastern Standard Time, be sure to read "How to Convert to Eastern Standard Time" at the beginning of this section.

1953

May

June

Date & Time	SUN	MOON 1	MOON 2	MOON 3	MERCURY	VENUS	MARS	JUPITER	SATURN	URANUS	NEPTUNE	PLUTO
MAY 1	6	34	34	35	3	3	9	9	28	15	28	20
MAY 2	6	35	36	36	4	3	9	9	28	15	28	20
MAY 3	7	37	38	38	4	3	9	9	28	15	28	20
MAY 4	7	39	39	40	4	3	9	9	28	15	28	20
MAY 5	7	41	41	42	4	3	9	9	28	15	28	20
MAY 6	7	42	43	44	4	3	9	9	28	15	28	20
MAY 7	7	44	45	46	5	3	10	9	28	15	28	20
MAY 8	7	46	47	48	5	3	10	9	28	15	28	20
MAY 9	7	48	1	1	5	3	10	9	28	15	28	20
MAY 10	7	2	3	3	5	3	10	9	28	15	28	20
MAY 11	8	4	5	5	6	3	10	9	28	15	28	20
MAY 12	8	6	7	7	6	3	10	9	28	15	28	20
MAY 13	8	8	9	9	6	3	10	9	28	15	28	20
MAY 14	8	10	10	11	6	3	10	9	28	15	28	20
MAY 15	8	12	12	13	7	3	10	9	28	15	28	20
MAY 16	8	13	14	15	7	3	10	9	28	15	28	20
MAY 17	8	15	16	17	7	3	10	9	28	15	28	20
MAY 18	8	17	17	18	8	3	11	9	28	15	28	20
MAY 19	9	18	19	19	8	3	11	9	28	15	28	20
MAY 20	9	20	21	21	8	4	11	9	28	15	28	20
MAY 21	9	22	22	23	8	4	11	9	28	15	28	20
MAY 22	9	23	24	24	9	4	11	9	28	15	28	20
MAY 23	9	25	25	26	9	4	11	9	28	15	28	20
MAY 24	9	26	27	27	9	4	11	9	28	15	28	20
MAY 25	10	28	29	29	10	4	11	9	28	15	28	20
MAY 26	10	30	30	31	10	4	11	9	28	15	28	20
MAY 27	10	31	32	32	10	4	11	10	28	15	28	20
MAY 28	10	33	34	34	10	4	11	10	28	15	28	20
MAY 29	10	35	35	36	11	4	12	10	28	15	28	20
MAY 30	10	37	37	38	11	4	12	10	28	15	28	20
MAY 31	10	38	39	40	11	4	12	10	28	15	28	20

Date & Time	SUN	MOON 1	MOON 2	MOON 3	MERCURY	VENUS	MARS	JUPITER	SATURN	URANUS	NEPTUNE	PLUTO
JUN. 1	10	40	41	41	12	5	12	10	28	15	28	20
JUN. 2	10	42	43	43	12	5	12	10	28	15	28	20
JUN. 3	11	44	45	45	12	5	12	10	28	15	28	20
JUN. 4	11	46	46	47	12	5	12	10	28	15	28	20
JUN. 5	11	48	48	1	13	5	12	10	28	15	28	20
JUN. 6	11	2	2	3	13	5	12	10	28	15	28	20
JUN. 7	11	3	4	5	13	5	12	10	28	15	28	20
JUN. 8	11	5	6	7	13	5	12	10	28	15	28	20
JUN. 9	11	7	8	9	14	5	13	10	28	15	28	20
JUN. 10	11	9	10	10	14	5	13	10	28	15	28	20
JUN. 11	12	11	12	12	14	6	13	10	28	15	28	20
JUN. 12	12	13	13	14	14	6	13	10	28	15	28	20
JUN. 13	12	14	15	16	15	6	13	10	28	15	28	20
JUN. 14	12	16	17	17	15	6	13	10	28	15	28	20
JUN. 15	12	18	18	19	15	6	13	10	28	15	28	20
JUN. 16	12	19	20	21	15	6	13	10	28	15	28	20
JUN. 17	12	21	22	22	15	6	13	10	28	15	28	20
JUN. 18	12	23	23	24	16	6	13	10	28	15	28	20
JUN. 19	13	24	25	25	16	7	13	10	28	15	28	20
JUN. 20	13	26	26	27	16	7	14	10	28	15	28	20
JUN. 21	13	27	28	28	16	7	14	10	28	15	28	20
JUN. 22	13	29	30	30	16	7	14	10	28	15	28	20
JUN. 23	13	31	31	32	16	7	14	10	28	15	28	20
JUN. 24	13	32	33	34	17	7	14	10	28	15	28	20
JUN. 25	14	34	35	35	17	7	14	10	28	15	28	20
JUN. 26	14	36	37	37	17	7	14	10	28	15	28	20
JUN. 27	14	38	38	39	17	8	14	10	28	15	28	20
JUN. 28	14	40	40	41	17	8	14	10	28	15	28	20
JUN. 29	14	42	42	43	17	8	14	11	28	15	28	20
JUN. 30	14	43	44	45	17	8	14	11	28	15	28	20

MOON 1 ◗ 12:01 A.M. TO 8:00 A.M.   **MOON 2** ◖ 8:01 A.M. TO 4:00 P.M.   **MOON 3** ● 4:01 P.M. TO 12:00 A.M.

Use only one "moon" number. Choose the column closest to your time of birth. If your place of birth is not on Eastern Standard Time, be sure to read "How to Convert to Eastern Standard Time" at the beginning of this section.

1953

July

August

Date & Time	SUN	MOON 1	MOON 2	MOON 3	MERCURY	VENUS	MARS	JUPITER	SATURN	URANUS	NEPTUNE	PLUTO
JUL. 1	14	45	46	47	18	8	14	11	28	15	28	20
JUL. 2	14	47	48	1	18	8	15	11	28	15	28	20
JUL. 3	15	1	2	2	18	8	15	11	28	15	28	20
JUL. 4	15	3	4	4	18	9	15	11	28	15	28	20
JUL. 5	15	5	6	6	18	9	15	11	28	15	28	20
JUL. 6	15	7	7	8	18	9	15	11	28	15	28	20
JUL. 7	15	9	9	10	18	9	15	11	28	15	28	20
JUL. 8	15	10	11	12	18	9	15	11	28	15	28	20
JUL. 9	15	12	13	13	18	9	15	11	28	15	28	20
JUL. 10	15	14	14	15	18	9	15	11	28	15	28	20
JUL. 11	16	16	16	17	18	9	15	11	28	15	28	20
JUL. 12	16	17	18	18	18	10	16	11	28	15	28	20
JUL. 13	16	19	19	20	18	10	16	11	28	15	28	20
JUL. 14	16	21	21	22	18	10	16	11	28	15	28	20
JUL. 15	16	22	23	23	18	10	16	11	28	16	28	20
JUL. 16	16	24	24	25	18	10	16	11	28	16	28	20
JUL. 17	16	25	26	26	18	10	16	11	28	16	28	20
JUL. 18	16	27	27	28	18	10	16	11	28	16	28	20
JUL. 19	17	28	29	30	18	11	16	11	28	16	28	20
JUL. 20	17	30	31	31	18	11	16	11	28	16	28	20
JUL. 21	17	32	32	33	18	11	16	11	28	16	28	20
JUL. 22	17	33	34	35	18	11	16	11	28	16	28	20
JUL. 23	17	35	36	36	17	11	16	11	28	16	28	20
JUL. 24	17	37	38	38	17	11	16	11	28	16	28	20
JUL. 25	17	39	40	40	17	12	17	11	28	16	28	20
JUL. 26	18	41	41	42	17	12	17	11	28	16	28	20
JUL. 27	18	43	43	44	17	12	17	11	28	16	28	20
JUL. 28	18	45	45	46	17	12	17	11	28	16	28	20
JUL. 29	18	47	47	48	17	12	17	11	28	16	28	20
JUL. 30	18	1	1	2	17	12	17	11	28	16	28	20
JUL. 31	18	3	3	4	17	12	17	11	28	16	28	20

Date & Time	SUN	MOON 1	MOON 2	MOON 3	MERCURY	VENUS	MARS	JUPITER	SATURN	URANUS	NEPTUNE	PLUTO
AUG. 1	18	4	5	6	17	13	17	11	28	16	28	20
AUG. 2	18	6	7	8	17	13	17	11	28	16	28	20
AUG. 3	19	8	9	9	17	13	17	11	28	16	28	20
AUG. 4	19	10	11	11	17	13	17	12	28	16	28	20
AUG. 5	19	12	12	13	17	13	18	12	28	16	28	20
AUG. 6	19	13	14	15	17	13	18	12	28	16	28	20
AUG. 7	19	15	16	16	17	13	18	12	28	16	28	20
AUG. 8	19	17	17	18	17	14	18	12	28	16	28	20
AUG. 9	19	18	19	20	17	14	18	12	28	16	28	20
AUG. 10	19	20	21	21	17	14	18	12	28	16	28	20
AUG. 11	20	22	22	22	17	14	18	12	28	16	28	20
AUG. 12	20	23	24	24	17	14	18	12	28	16	28	20
AUG. 13	20	25	25	26	17	14	18	12	28	16	28	20
AUG. 14	20	26	27	27	17	15	18	12	28	16	28	20
AUG. 15	20	28	29	29	17	15	18	12	28	16	28	20
AUG. 16	20	30	30	31	18	15	18	12	28	16	28	20
AUG. 17	20	31	32	32	18	15	19	12	28	16	28	20
AUG. 18	20	33	33	34	18	15	19	12	28	16	28	20
AUG. 19	21	35	35	36	18	15	19	12	28	16	28	20
AUG. 20	21	36	37	38	18	15	19	12	28	16	28	20
AUG. 21	21	38	39	39	19	16	19	12	28	16	28	20
AUG. 22	21	40	41	41	19	16	19	12	28	16	28	20
AUG. 23	21	42	43	43	19	16	19	12	28	16	28	20
AUG. 24	21	44	45	45	19	16	19	12	28	16	28	20
AUG. 25	21	46	47	47	19	16	19	12	28	16	28	20
AUG. 26	22	48	1	1	20	16	19	12	28	16	28	20
AUG. 27	22	2	3	3	20	17	19	12	28	16	28	20
AUG. 28	22	4	5	5	20	17	19	12	28	16	28	20
AUG. 29	22	6	6	7	21	17	20	12	28	16	28	20
AUG. 30	22	8	8	9	21	17	20	12	28	16	28	20
AUG. 31	22	10	10	11	21	17	20	12	28	16	28	20

MOON 1 ◐ 12:01 A.M. TO 8:00 A.M.   **MOON 2** ◑ 8:01 A.M. TO 4:00 P.M.   **MOON 3** ● 4:01 P.M. TO 12:00 A.M.

Use only one "moon" number. Choose the column closest to your time of birth. If your place of birth is not on Eastern Standard Time, be sure to read "How to Convert to Eastern Standard Time" at the beginning of this section.

1953

September

Date & Time	SUN	MOON 1	MOON 2	MOON 3	MERCURY	VENUS	MARS	JUPITER	SATURN	URANUS	NEPTUNE	PLUTO
SEP. 1	22	11	12	13	21	17	20	12	28	16	28	20
SEP. 2	22	13	14	14	22	17	20	12	28	16	28	20
SEP. 3	23	15	15	16	22	18	20	12	28	16	28	20
SEP. 4	23	16	17	18	22	18	20	12	28	16	28	20
SEP. 5	23	18	19	19	22	18	20	12	28	16	28	20
SEP. 6	23	20	20	21	23	18	20	12	28	16	28	20
SEP. 7	23	21	22	22	23	18	20	12	28	16	28	20
SEP. 8	23	23	23	24	23	18	20	12	28	16	28	20
SEP. 9	23	24	25	25	23	19	20	12	28	16	28	20
SEP. 10	23	26	27	27	24	19	21	12	28	16	28	20
SEP. 11	24	28	28	29	24	19	21	12	28	16	28	20
SEP. 12	24	29	30	30	24	19	21	12	28	16	28	20
SEP. 13	24	31	31	32	24	19	21	12	28	16	28	20
SEP. 14	24	32	33	33	25	19	21	12	28	16	28	20
SEP. 15	24	34	35	35	25	20	21	12	28	16	28	20
SEP. 16	24	36	36	37	25	20	21	12	28	16	28	20
SEP. 17	24	37	38	39	25	20	21	12	28	16	28	20
SEP. 18	24	39	40	40	25	20	21	12	28	16	28	20
SEP. 19	25	41	42	42	26	20	21	12	28	16	28	20
SEP. 20	25	43	44	44	26	20	21	12	28	16	28	20
SEP. 21	25	45	46	46	26	20	22	12	28	16	28	20
SEP. 22	25	47	48	48	26	21	22	12	28	16	28	20
SEP. 23	25	1	2	2	27	21	22	12	29	16	28	20
SEP. 24	25	3	4	4	27	21	22	12	29	16	28	20
SEP. 25	26	5	6	6	27	21	22	12	29	16	28	20
SEP. 26	26	7	8	8	27	21	22	12	29	16	28	20
SEP. 27	26	9	10	10	27	21	22	12	29	16	28	20
SEP. 28	26	11	11	12	28	22	22	12	29	16	28	20
SEP. 29	26	13	13	14	28	22	22	12	29	16	28	20
SEP. 30	26	14	15	15	28	22	22	12	29	16	28	20

October

Date & Time	SUN	MOON 1	MOON 2	MOON 3	MERCURY	VENUS	MARS	JUPITER	SATURN	URANUS	NEPTUNE	PLUTO
OCT. 1	26	16	17	17	28	22	22	12	29	16	28	20
OCT. 2	26	18	18	19	28	22	22	12	29	16	28	20
OCT. 3	27	19	20	20	29	22	23	12	29	16	28	20
OCT. 4	27	21	21	22	29	23	23	12	29	16	28	20
OCT. 5	27	22	23	23	29	23	23	12	29	16	28	20
OCT. 6	27	24	25	25	29	23	23	12	29	16	28	20
OCT. 7	27	26	26	27	29	23	23	12	29	16	28	20
OCT. 8	27	27	28	28	30	23	23	12	29	16	28	20
OCT. 9	27	29	29	30	30	23	23	12	29	16	28	20
OCT. 10	27	30	31	31	30	24	23	12	29	16	28	20
OCT. 11	28	32	33	33	30	24	23	12	29	16	28	20
OCT. 12	28	34	34	35	30	24	23	12	29	16	28	20
OCT. 13	28	35	36	36	31	24	23	12	29	16	28	20
OCT. 14	28	37	38	38	31	24	23	12	29	16	28	20
OCT. 15	28	39	39	40	31	24	24	12	29	16	28	20
OCT. 16	28	40	41	42	31	25	24	12	29	16	28	20
OCT. 17	28	42	43	44	31	25	24	12	29	16	28	20
OCT. 18	28	44	45	45	31	25	24	12	29	16	28	20
OCT. 19	29	46	47	47	32	25	24	12	29	16	28	20
OCT. 20	29	48	1	1	32	25	24	12	29	16	28	20
OCT. 21	29	2	3	3	32	25	24	12	29	16	28	20
OCT. 22	29	4	5	5	32	26	24	12	29	16	28	20
OCT. 23	29	6	7	7	32	26	24	12	29	16	28	20
OCT. 24	29	8	9	9	32	26	24	12	29	16	28	20
OCT. 25	29	10	11	11	32	26	24	12	29	16	28	20
OCT. 26	30	12	13	13	32	26	24	12	29	16	28	20
OCT. 27	30	14	14	15	33	26	25	12	29	16	28	20
OCT. 28	30	15	16	17	33	27	25	12	29	16	28	20
OCT. 29	30	17	18	18	33	27	25	12	29	16	28	20
OCT. 30	30	19	19	20	33	27	25	12	29	16	28	20
OCT. 31	30	20	21	21	33	27	25	12	29	16	28	20

MOON 1 ◗ 12:01 A.M. TO 8:00 A.M.   **MOON 2** ◑ 8:01 A.M. TO 4:00 P.M.   **MOON 3** ● 4:01 P.M. TO 12:00 A.M.

Use only one "moon" number. Choose the column closest to your time of birth. If your place of birth is not on Eastern Standard Time, be sure to read "How to Convert to Eastern Standard Time" at the beginning of this section.

1953

November

Date & Time	SUN	MOON 1	MOON 2	MOON 3	MERCURY	VENUS	MARS	JUPITER	SATURN	URANUS	NEPTUNE	PLUTO
NOV. 1	30	22	23	23	33	27	25	12	29	16	28	20
NOV. 2	30	24	24	25	33	27	25	12	29	16	28	20
NOV. 3	31	25	26	26	33	28	25	12	29	16	28	20
NOV. 4	31	27	27	28	33	28	25	12	29	16	28	20
NOV. 5	31	28	29	29	33	28	25	12	29	16	28	20
NOV. 6	31	30	31	31	33	28	25	12	29	16	28	20
NOV. 7	31	32	32	33	33	28	25	12	29	16	28	20
NOV. 8	31	33	34	34	33	28	26	12	29	16	28	20
NOV. 9	31	35	35	36	33	29	26	12	29	16	28	20
NOV. 10	31	37	37	38	33	29	26	12	29	16	28	20
NOV. 11	31	38	39	39	33	29	26	12	29	16	28	20
NOV. 12	32	40	41	41	32	29	26	12	29	16	28	20
NOV. 13	32	42	42	43	32	29	26	12	29	16	28	20
NOV. 14	32	44	44	45	32	29	26	12	29	16	28	20
NOV. 15	32	45	46	47	32	30	26	12	29	16	28	20
NOV. 16	32	47	48	1	32	30	26	12	29	16	28	20
NOV. 17	32	1	2	3	31	30	26	12	29	16	28	20
NOV. 18	32	3	4	5	31	30	26	12	29	16	28	20
NOV. 19	33	5	6	7	31	30	26	12	29	16	28	20
NOV. 20	33	7	8	9	31	30	27	12	29	16	28	20
NOV. 21	33	9	10	11	31	31	27	12	29	16	28	20
NOV. 22	33	11	12	12	31	31	27	12	29	16	28	20
NOV. 23	33	13	14	14	31	31	27	12	29	16	28	20
NOV. 24	33	15	15	16	31	31	27	12	29	16	28	20
NOV. 25	34	17	17	18	31	31	27	12	29	16	28	20
NOV. 26	34	18	19	19	31	31	27	12	30	16	28	20
NOV. 27	34	20	20	21	31	32	27	12	30	16	28	20
NOV. 28	34	22	22	23	31	32	27	12	30	16	28	20
NOV. 29	34	23	24	24	31	32	27	12	30	16	28	20
NOV. 30	34	25	25	26	31	32	27	12	30	16	28	20

December

Date & Time	SUN	MOON 1	MOON 2	MOON 3	MERCURY	VENUS	MARS	JUPITER	SATURN	URANUS	NEPTUNE	PLUTO
DEC. 1	34	26	27	27	31	32	27	12	30	16	28	20
DEC. 2	34	28	28	29	32	32	27	12	30	16	28	20
DEC. 3	35	29	30	31	32	33	28	12	30	16	28	20
DEC. 4	35	31	32	32	32	33	28	12	30	16	28	20
DEC. 5	35	33	33	34	32	33	28	12	30	16	28	20
DEC. 6	35	34	35	36	32	33	28	12	30	16	28	20
DEC. 7	35	36	37	37	32	33	28	12	30	16	28	20
DEC. 8	35	38	38	39	33	33	28	12	30	16	28	20
DEC. 9	35	40	40	41	33	34	28	12	30	16	28	20
DEC. 10	35	41	42	43	33	34	28	12	30	16	28	20
DEC. 11	36	43	44	44	33	34	28	12	30	16	28	20
DEC. 12	36	45	46	46	33	34	28	12	30	16	28	20
DEC. 13	36	47	48	48	33	34	28	12	30	16	28	20
DEC. 14	36	1	1	2	34	34	28	12	30	16	28	20
DEC. 15	36	3	3	4	34	35	29	12	30	16	28	20
DEC. 16	36	5	5	6	34	35	29	12	30	16	28	20
DEC. 17	36	7	7	8	34	35	29	12	30	16	28	20
DEC. 18	36	8	9	10	34	35	29	12	30	16	28	20
DEC. 19	37	10	11	12	35	35	29	12	30	16	28	20
DEC. 20	37	12	13	13	35	35	29	12	30	16	28	20
DEC. 21	37	14	15	15	35	36	29	12	30	16	28	20
DEC. 22	37	16	16	17	35	36	29	12	30	16	28	20
DEC. 23	37	18	18	19	35	36	29	12	30	16	28	20
DEC. 24	37	19	20	20	36	36	29	12	30	16	28	20
DEC. 25	37	21	21	22	36	36	29	12	30	16	28	20
DEC. 26	38	23	23	24	36	36	29	12	30	16	28	20
DEC. 27	38	24	25	25	36	37	30	12	30	16	28	20
DEC. 28	38	26	26	27	36	37	30	12	30	16	28	20
DEC. 29	38	27	28	28	37	37	30	12	30	16	28	20
DEC. 30	38	29	29	30	37	37	30	12	30	16	28	20
DEC. 31	38	31	31	32	37	37	30	12	30	16	28	20

MOON 1 ☽ 12:01 A.M. TO 8:00 A.M. **MOON 2** ☽ 8:01 A.M. TO 4:00 P.M. **MOON 3** ● 4:01 P.M. TO 12:00 A.M.
Use only one "moon" number. Choose the column closest to your time of birth. If your place of birth is not on Eastern Standard Time, be sure to read "How to Convert to Eastern Standard Time" at the beginning of this section.

1954

January

Date & Time	SUN	MOON 1	MOON 2	MOON 3	MERCURY	VENUS	MARS	JUPITER	SATURN	URANUS	NEPTUNE	PLUTO
JAN. 1	38	32	33	33	37	37	30	11	30	16	28	20
JAN. 2	38	34	34	35	37	38	30	11	30	16	28	20
JAN. 3	39	36	36	37	38	38	30	11	30	16	28	20
JAN. 4	39	37	38	38	38	38	30	11	30	16	28	20
JAN. 5	39	39	40	40	38	38	30	11	30	16	28	20
JAN. 6	39	41	41	42	38	38	30	11	30	16	28	20
JAN. 7	39	43	43	44	39	38	30	11	30	16	28	20
JAN. 8	39	45	45	46	39	39	30	11	30	16	28	20
JAN. 9	39	46	47	48	39	39	31	11	30	16	28	20
JAN. 10	40	48	1	2	39	39	31	11	30	16	28	20
JAN. 11	40	2	3	4	39	39	31	11	30	16	28	20
JAN. 12	40	4	5	5	40	39	31	11	30	16	28	20
JAN. 13	40	6	7	7	40	39	31	11	30	16	28	20
JAN. 14	40	8	9	9	40	40	31	11	30	16	28	20
JAN. 15	40	10	10	11	40	40	31	11	30	16	28	20
JAN. 16	40	12	12	13	40	40	31	11	30	16	28	20
JAN. 17	41	13	14	15	41	40	31	11	30	16	28	20
JAN. 18	41	15	16	16	41	40	31	11	30	16	28	20
JAN. 19	41	17	18	18	41	40	31	11	30	16	28	20
JAN. 20	41	19	19	20	41	41	31	11	30	16	28	20
JAN. 21	41	20	21	21	42	41	31	11	30	16	28	20
JAN. 22	41	22	23	23	42	41	32	11	30	16	28	20
JAN. 23	42	24	24	25	42	41	32	11	30	16	28	20
JAN. 24	42	25	26	27	42	41	32	11	30	16	28	20
JAN. 25	42	27	27	28	43	41	32	11	30	16	28	20
JAN. 26	42	28	29	29	43	42	32	11	30	16	28	20
JAN. 27	42	30	30	31	43	42	32	11	30	16	28	20
JAN. 28	42	32	32	33	43	42	32	11	30	16	28	20
JAN. 29	42	33	34	34	43	42	32	11	30	16	28	20
JAN. 30	42	35	35	36	44	42	32	11	30	16	28	20
JAN. 31	43	37	37	38	44	42	32	11	30	16	28	20

February

Date & Time	SUN	MOON 1	MOON 2	MOON 3	MERCURY	VENUS	MARS	JUPITER	SATURN	URANUS	NEPTUNE	PLUTO
FEB. 1	43	38	39	40	44	43	32	11	30	16	28	20
FEB. 2	43	40	41	41	44	43	32	11	30	16	28	20
FEB. 3	43	42	43	43	45	43	32	11	30	16	28	20
FEB. 4	43	44	45	45	45	43	33	11	30	16	28	20
FEB. 5	43	46	47	47	45	43	33	11	30	16	28	20
FEB. 6	43	48	48	1	45	43	33	11	30	16	28	20
FEB. 7	43	2	2	3	45	44	33	11	30	16	28	20
FEB. 8	44	4	4	5	46	44	33	11	30	16	28	20
FEB. 9	44	6	6	7	46	44	33	11	30	16	28	20
FEB. 10	44	8	8	9	46	44	33	11	30	16	28	20
FEB. 11	44	9	10	11	46	44	33	11	30	16	28	20
FEB. 12	44	11	12	12	46	44	33	11	30	16	28	20
FEB. 13	44	13	14	14	47	45	33	11	30	16	28	20
FEB. 14	44	15	15	16	47	45	33	11	30	16	28	20
FEB. 15	44	16	17	18	47	45	33	11	30	16	28	20
FEB. 16	45	18	19	19	47	45	33	11	30	16	28	20
FEB. 17	45	20	20	21	47	45	34	11	30	16	28	20
FEB. 18	45	21	22	23	47	45	34	11	30	16	28	20
FEB. 19	45	23	24	24	47	46	34	11	30	16	28	20
FEB. 20	45	25	25	26	47	46	34	11	30	16	28	20
FEB. 21	45	26	27	27	47	46	34	11	30	16	28	20
FEB. 22	45	28	28	29	47	46	34	11	30	16	28	20
FEB. 23	46	29	30	31	47	46	34	11	30	16	28	20
FEB. 24	46	31	32	32	47	46	34	11	30	16	28	20
FEB. 25	46	33	33	34	47	47	34	11	30	16	28	20
FEB. 26	46	34	35	35	47	47	34	11	30	16	28	20
FEB. 27	46	36	36	37	47	47	34	11	30	16	28	20
FEB. 28	46	38	38	39	47	47	34	11	30	16	28	20

MOON 1 ◗ 12:01 A.M. TO 8:00 A.M.   **MOON 2** ◑ 8:01 A.M. TO 4:00 P.M.   **MOON 3** ● 4:01 P.M. TO 12:00 A.M.

Use only one "moon" number. Choose the column closest to your time of birth. If your place of birth is not on Eastern Standard Time, be sure to read "How to Convert to Eastern Standard Time" at the beginning of this section.

1954

March

April

Date & Time	SUN	MOON 1	MOON 2	MOON 3	MERCURY	VENUS	MARS	JUPITER	SATURN	URANUS	NEPTUNE	PLUTO
MAR. 1	46	39	40	41	46	47	34	11	30	16	28	20
MAR. 2	46	41	42	42	46	47	34	11	30	16	28	20
MAR. 3	47	43	44	44	46	48	35	11	30	16	28	20
MAR. 4	47	45	46	46	46	48	35	11	30	16	28	20
MAR. 5	47	47	48	48	46	48	35	11	30	16	28	20
MAR. 6	47	1	2	2	46	48	35	11	30	16	28	20
MAR. 7	47	3	4	4	46	48	35	11	30	16	28	20
MAR. 8	47	5	6	6	45	48	35	11	30	16	28	20
MAR. 9	47	7	8	8	45	1	35	11	30	16	28	20
MAR. 10	47	9	10	10	45	1	35	11	30	16	28	20
MAR. 11	48	11	11	12	45	1	35	11	30	16	28	20
MAR. 12	48	13	13	14	45	1	35	11	30	16	28	20
MAR. 13	48	14	15	15	45	1	35	11	30	16	28	20
MAR. 14	48	16	17	17	45	1	35	11	30	16	28	20
MAR. 15	48	18	18	19	45	2	35	11	30	16	28	20
MAR. 16	48	19	20	20	45	2	35	11	30	16	28	20
MAR. 17	48	21	22	22	45	2	35	11	30	16	28	20
MAR. 18	48	23	23	24	45	2	36	11	30	16	28	20
MAR. 19	1	24	25	25	45	2	36	11	30	16	28	20
MAR. 20	1	26	26	27	45	2	36	11	30	16	28	20
MAR. 21	1	27	28	28	45	3	36	11	30	16	28	20
MAR. 22	1	29	30	30	46	3	36	11	30	16	28	20
MAR. 23	1	31	31	32	46	3	36	12	30	16	28	20
MAR. 24	1	32	33	33	46	3	36	12	30	16	28	20
MAR. 25	2	34	34	35	46	3	36	12	30	16	28	20
MAR. 26	2	35	36	36	46	3	36	12	30	16	28	20
MAR. 27	2	37	38	38	46	4	36	12	30	15	28	20
MAR. 28	2	39	39	40	46	4	36	12	30	15	28	20
MAR. 29	2	40	41	42	46	4	36	12	30	16	28	20
MAR. 30	2	42	43	44	46	4	36	12	30	16	28	20
MAR. 31	2	44	45	45	47	4	36	12	30	16	28	20

Date & Time	SUN	MOON 1	MOON 2	MOON 3	MERCURY	VENUS	MARS	JUPITER	SATURN	URANUS	NEPTUNE	PLUTO
APR. 1	2	46	47	47	47	4	36	12	30	16	28	20
APR. 2	2	48	1	1	47	5	36	12	30	16	28	20
APR. 3	3	2	3	3	47	5	36	12	30	16	28	20
APR. 4	3	4	5	5	47	5	37	12	30	16	28	20
APR. 5	3	6	7	8	47	5	37	12	30	16	28	20
APR. 6	3	8	9	9	48	5	37	12	30	16	28	20
APR. 7	3	10	11	11	48	5	37	12	30	16	28	20
APR. 8	3	12	13	13	48	6	37	12	30	16	28	20
APR. 9	3	14	14	15	48	6	37	12	30	16	28	20
APR. 10	3	16	16	17	48	6	37	12	30	16	28	20
APR. 11	4	17	18	18	1	6	37	12	30	16	28	20
APR. 12	4	19	20	20	1	6	37	12	30	16	28	20
APR. 13	4	21	21	22	1	6	37	12	30	16	28	20
APR. 14	4	22	23	23	1	7	37	12	30	16	28	20
APR. 15	4	24	24	25	1	7	37	12	30	16	28	20
APR. 16	4	25	26	26	2	7	37	12	30	16	28	20
APR. 17	4	27	28	28	2	7	37	12	30	16	28	20
APR. 18	4	29	29	30	2	7	37	12	30	16	28	20
APR. 19	5	30	31	31	2	7	37	12	30	16	28	20
APR. 20	5	32	32	33	2	8	37	12	30	16	28	20
APR. 21	5	33	34	34	3	8	37	12	30	16	28	20
APR. 22	5	35	36	36	3	8	37	12	30	16	28	20
APR. 23	5	37	37	38	3	8	37	12	30	16	28	20
APR. 24	5	38	39	39	3	8	37	12	30	16	28	20
APR. 25	6	40	41	41	4	8	38	12	30	16	28	20
APR. 26	6	42	42	43	4	9	38	12	30	16	28	20
APR. 27	6	43	44	45	4	9	38	12	30	16	28	20
APR. 28	6	45	46	47	4	9	38	12	30	16	28	20
APR. 29	6	47	48	1	5	9	38	12	30	16	28	20
APR. 30	6	1	2	3	5	9	38	12	30	16	28	20

MOON 1 ◔ **12:01** A.M. **TO 8:00** A.M.   **MOON 2** ◑ **8:01** A.M. **TO 4:00** P.M.   **MOON 3** ● **4:01** P.M. **TO 12:00** A.M.

Use only one "moon" number. Choose the column closest to your time of birth. If your place of birth is not on Eastern Standard Time, be sure to read "How to Convert to Eastern Standard Time" at the beginning of this section.

1954

May | June

Date & Time	SUN	MOON 1	MOON 2	MOON 3	MERCURY	VENUS	MARS	JUPITER	SATURN	URANUS	NEPTUNE	PLUTO
MAY 1	6	3	4	5	5	9	38	12	30	16	28	20
MAY 2	6	5	6	7	5	10	38	12	30	16	28	20
MAY 3	7	7	8	9	6	10	38	12	30	16	28	20
MAY 4	7	9	10	11	6	10	38	12	30	16	28	20
MAY 5	7	11	12	13	6	10	38	12	30	16	28	20
MAY 6	7	13	14	14	7	10	38	12	30	16	28	20
MAY 7	7	15	16	16	7	10	38	12	30	16	28	20
MAY 8	7	17	17	18	7	10	38	13	30	16	28	20
MAY 9	7	19	19	20	7	11	38	13	30	16	28	20
MAY 10	7	20	21	21	8	11	38	13	30	16	28	20
MAY 11	8	22	22	23	8	11	38	13	30	16	28	20
MAY 12	8	23	24	24	8	11	38	13	30	16	28	20
MAY 13	8	25	26	26	9	11	38	13	30	16	28	20
MAY 14	8	27	27	28	9	11	38	13	30	16	28	20
MAY 15	8	28	29	29	9	12	38	13	30	16	28	20
MAY 16	8	30	30	31	9	12	38	13	30	16	28	20
MAY 17	8	31	32	32	10	12	38	13	30	16	28	20
MAY 18	8	33	34	34	10	12	38	13	30	16	28	20
MAY 19	9	35	35	36	10	12	38	13	30	16	28	20
MAY 20	9	36	37	37	11	12	38	13	30	16	28	20
MAY 21	9	38	38	39	11	13	38	13	30	16	28	20
MAY 22	9	40	40	41	11	13	38	13	30	16	28	20
MAY 23	9	41	42	42	11	13	38	13	30	16	28	20
MAY 24	9	43	44	44	12	13	38	13	30	16	28	20
MAY 25	10	45	45	46	12	13	38	13	30	16	28	20
MAY 26	10	47	47	48	12	13	38	13	29	16	28	20
MAY 27	10	1	1	2	12	14	38	13	29	16	28	20
MAY 28	10	2	3	4	12	14	38	13	29	16	28	20
MAY 29	10	4	5	6	13	14	38	13	29	16	28	20
MAY 30	10	6	7	8	13	14	38	13	29	16	28	20
MAY 31	10	8	9	10	13	14	38	13	29	16	28	20

Date & Time	SUN	MOON 1	MOON 2	MOON 3	MERCURY	VENUS	MARS	JUPITER	SATURN	URANUS	NEPTUNE	PLUTO
JUN. 1	10	10	11	12	13	14	38	13	29	16	28	20
JUN. 2	10	12	13	14	13	15	38	13	29	16	28	20
JUN. 3	11	14	15	15	14	15	38	13	29	16	28	20
JUN. 4	11	16	17	17	14	15	38	13	29	16	28	20
JUN. 5	11	18	18	19	14	15	38	13	29	16	28	20
JUN. 6	11	20	20	21	14	15	38	13	29	16	28	20
JUN. 7	11	21	22	22	14	15	38	13	29	16	28	20
JUN. 8	11	23	23	24	14	15	38	13	29	16	28	20
JUN. 9	11	25	25	26	15	16	38	13	29	16	28	20
JUN. 10	11	26	27	27	15	16	38	13	29	16	28	20
JUN. 11	12	28	28	29	15	16	38	14	29	16	28	20
JUN. 12	12	29	30	30	15	16	38	14	29	16	28	20
JUN. 13	12	31	31	32	15	16	38	14	29	16	28	20
JUN. 14	12	33	33	34	15	16	38	14	29	16	28	20
JUN. 15	12	34	35	35	15	17	38	14	29	16	28	20
JUN. 16	12	36	36	37	15	17	38	14	29	16	28	20
JUN. 17	12	37	38	39	15	17	38	14	29	16	28	20
JUN. 18	12	39	40	40	15	17	38	14	29	16	28	20
JUN. 19	13	41	41	42	15	17	38	14	29	16	28	20
JUN. 20	13	43	43	44	15	17	38	14	29	16	28	20
JUN. 21	13	44	45	46	15	18	37	14	29	16	28	20
JUN. 22	13	46	47	47	15	18	37	14	29	16	28	20
JUN. 23	13	48	1	1	15	18	37	14	29	16	28	20
JUN. 24	13	2	3	3	15	18	37	14	29	16	28	20
JUN. 25	14	4	4	5	15	18	37	14	29	16	28	20
JUN. 26	14	6	6	7	15	18	37	14	29	16	28	20
JUN. 27	14	8	9	9	15	18	37	14	29	16	28	20
JUN. 28	14	10	10	11	15	19	37	14	29	16	28	20
JUN. 29	14	12	12	13	15	19	37	14	29	16	28	20
JUN. 30	14	13	14	15	15	19	37	14	29	16	28	20

MOON 1 ☽ 12:01 A.M. TO 8:00 A.M.   **MOON 2** ◑ 8:01 A.M. TO 4:00 P.M.   **MOON 3** ● 4:01 P.M. TO 12:00 A.M.
Use only one "moon" number. Choose the column closest to your time of birth. If your place of birth is not on Eastern Standard Time, be sure to read "How to Convert to Eastern Standard Time" at the beginning of this section.

July

August

Date & Time	SUN	MOON 1	MOON 2	MOON 3	MERCURY	VENUS	MARS	JUPITER	SATURN	URANUS	NEPTUNE	PLUTO
JUL. 1	14	15	16	17	15	19	37	14	29	16	28	20
JUL. 2	14	17	18	18	15	19	37	14	29	16	28	20
JUL. 3	15	19	20	20	15	19	37	14	29	16	28	20
JUL. 4	15	21	21	22	15	20	37	14	29	16	28	20
JUL. 5	15	22	23	23	15	20	37	14	29	16	28	20
JUL. 6	15	24	25	25	15	20	37	14	29	16	28	20
JUL. 7	15	26	26	27	15	20	37	14	29	16	28	20
JUL. 8	15	27	28	28	15	20	37	14	29	16	28	20
JUL. 9	15	29	29	30	15	20	37	14	29	16	28	20
JUL. 10	15	30	31	31	14	20	37	14	29	16	28	20
JUL. 11	16	32	33	33	14	21	37	14	29	16	28	20
JUL. 12	16	34	34	35	14	21	37	14	29	16	28	20
JUL. 13	16	35	36	36	14	21	37	14	29	16	28	20
JUL. 14	16	37	37	38	14	21	37	14	29	16	28	20
JUL. 15	16	39	39	40	14	21	37	15	29	16	28	20
JUL. 16	16	40	41	42	14	21	37	15	29	16	28	20
JUL. 17	16	42	43	43	14	22	37	15	29	16	28	20
JUL. 18	16	44	45	45	14	22	36	15	29	16	28	20
JUL. 19	17	46	46	47	14	22	36	15	29	16	28	20
JUL. 20	17	48	48	1	14	22	36	15	29	16	28	20
JUL. 21	17	2	2	3	14	22	36	15	29	16	28	20
JUL. 22	17	3	4	5	14	22	36	15	29	16	28	20
JUL. 23	17	5	6	7	14	22	36	15	29	16	28	20
JUL. 24	17	7	8	8	15	23	36	15	29	16	28	20
JUL. 25	17	9	10	10	15	23	36	15	29	16	28	20
JUL. 26	18	11	12	12	15	23	36	15	29	16	28	20
JUL. 27	18	13	13	14	15	23	36	15	29	16	28	20
JUL. 28	18	15	15	16	15	23	36	15	29	16	28	20
JUL. 29	18	17	17	18	15	23	36	15	29	16	28	20
JUL. 30	18	18	19	19	15	24	36	15	29	16	28	20
JUL. 31	18	20	21	21	15	24	36	15	29	16	28	20

Date & Time	SUN	MOON 1	MOON 2	MOON 3	MERCURY	VENUS	MARS	JUPITER	SATURN	URANUS	NEPTUNE	PLUTO
AUG. 1	18	22	22	23	16	24	36	15	29	16	28	20
AUG. 2	18	23	24	25	16	24	36	15	29	16	28	20
AUG. 3	19	25	26	26	16	24	36	15	29	16	28	20
AUG. 4	19	27	27	28	16	24	36	15	29	16	28	20
AUG. 5	19	28	29	29	16	24	36	15	29	16	28	20
AUG. 6	19	30	30	31	17	25	36	15	29	16	28	20
AUG. 7	19	31	32	33	17	25	36	15	29	16	28	20
AUG. 8	19	33	34	34	17	25	36	15	29	16	28	20
AUG. 9	19	35	35	36	17	25	36	15	29	16	28	20
AUG. 10	19	36	37	37	18	25	37	15	29	16	28	20
AUG. 11	20	38	39	39	18	25	37	15	29	16	28	20
AUG. 12	20	40	40	41	18	25	37	15	29	16	28	20
AUG. 13	20	41	42	43	18	26	37	15	29	16	28	20
AUG. 14	20	43	44	45	19	26	37	15	29	16	28	20
AUG. 15	20	45	46	46	19	26	37	15	29	16	28	20
AUG. 16	20	47	48	48	19	26	37	15	29	16	28	20
AUG. 17	20	1	2	2	19	26	37	15	30	16	28	20
AUG. 18	20	3	4	4	20	26	37	15	30	16	28	20
AUG. 19	21	5	5	6	20	26	37	16	30	16	28	20
AUG. 20	21	7	7	8	20	27	37	16	30	16	28	20
AUG. 21	21	9	9	10	21	27	37	16	30	16	28	20
AUG. 22	21	11	11	12	21	27	37	16	30	16	28	20
AUG. 23	21	12	13	14	21	27	37	16	30	16	28	20
AUG. 24	21	14	15	15	21	27	37	16	30	16	28	20
AUG. 25	21	16	17	17	22	27	37	16	30	16	28	20
AUG. 26	22	18	18	19	22	27	37	16	30	16	28	20
AUG. 27	22	19	20	21	22	28	37	16	30	16	28	20
AUG. 28	22	21	22	22	22	28	37	16	30	16	28	20
AUG. 29	22	23	23	24	23	28	37	16	30	16	28	20
AUG. 30	22	25	25	26	23	28	37	16	30	16	28	20
AUG. 31	22	26	27	27	23	28	37	16	30	16	28	20

MOON 1 ◗ 12:01 A.M. TO 8:00 A.M.   **MOON 2** ◑ 8:01 A.M. TO 4:00 P.M.   **MOON 3** ● 4:01 P.M. TO 12:00 A.M.

Use only one "moon" number. Choose the column closest to your time of birth. If your place of birth is not on Eastern Standard Time, be sure to read "How to Convert to Eastern Standard Time" at the beginning of this section.

1954

September

Date & Time	SUN	MOON 1	MOON 2	MOON 3	MERCURY	VENUS	MARS	JUPITER	SATURN	URANUS	NEPTUNE	PLUTO
SEP. 1	22	28	28	29	23	28	37	16	30	16	28	20
SEP. 2	22	29	30	30	24	28	37	16	30	16	28	20
SEP. 3	23	31	31	32	24	28	37	16	30	16	28	20
SEP. 4	23	33	33	34	24	29	37	16	30	16	28	20
SEP. 5	23	34	35	35	24	29	38	16	30	16	28	20
SEP. 6	23	36	36	37	24	29	38	16	30	16	28	20
SEP. 7	23	37	38	38	25	29	38	16	30	16	28	20
SEP. 8	23	39	40	40	25	29	38	16	30	16	28	20
SEP. 9	23	41	41	42	25	29	38	16	30	16	28	20
SEP. 10	23	43	43	44	25	29	38	16	30	16	28	20
SEP. 11	24	44	45	46	26	29	38	16	30	16	28	20
SEP. 12	24	46	47	48	26	30	38	16	30	17	28	20
SEP. 13	24	48	1	2	26	30	38	16	30	17	28	20
SEP. 14	24	2	3	4	26	30	38	16	30	17	28	20
SEP. 15	24	4	5	6	26	30	38	16	30	17	28	20
SEP. 16	24	6	7	8	27	30	38	16	30	17	28	20
SEP. 17	24	8	9	9	27	30	38	16	30	17	28	20
SEP. 18	24	10	11	11	27	30	38	16	30	17	28	20
SEP. 19	25	12	13	13	27	30	38	16	30	17	28	20
SEP. 20	25	14	14	15	27	31	38	16	30	17	28	20
SEP. 21	25	16	16	17	28	31	39	16	30	17	28	20
SEP. 22	25	17	18	18	28	31	39	16	30	17	28	20
SEP. 23	25	19	20	20	28	31	39	16	30	17	28	20
SEP. 24	25	21	21	22	28	31	39	16	30	17	28	20
SEP. 25	26	22	23	24	28	31	39	16	30	17	28	20
SEP. 26	26	24	25	25	28	31	39	16	30	17	28	20
SEP. 27	26	26	26	27	29	31	39	16	30	17	28	20
SEP. 28	26	27	28	28	29	31	39	16	30	17	28	20
SEP. 29	26	29	29	30	29	32	39	16	30	17	28	20
SEP. 30	26	30	31	32	29	32	39	16	30	17	28	20

October

Date & Time	SUN	MOON 1	MOON 2	MOON 3	MERCURY	VENUS	MARS	JUPITER	SATURN	URANUS	NEPTUNE	PLUTO
OCT. 1	26	32	33	33	29	32	39	17	30	17	28	20
OCT. 2	26	34	34	35	29	32	39	17	30	17	28	20
OCT. 3	27	35	36	36	30	32	39	17	30	17	28	20
OCT. 4	27	37	37	38	30	32	40	17	30	17	28	20
OCT. 5	27	38	39	40	30	32	40	17	30	17	28	20
OCT. 6	27	40	41	41	30	32	40	17	30	17	28	20
OCT. 7	27	42	42	43	30	32	40	17	30	17	28	20
OCT. 8	27	44	44	45	30	32	40	17	30	17	28	20
OCT. 9	27	45	46	47	30	32	40	17	30	17	28	20
OCT. 10	27	47	48	1	30	32	40	17	30	17	28	20
OCT. 11	28	1	2	3	31	32	40	17	30	17	28	20
OCT. 12	28	3	4	5	31	33	40	17	30	17	28	20
OCT. 13	28	5	6	7	31	33	40	17	30	17	28	20
OCT. 14	28	7	8	9	31	33	40	17	30	17	28	20
OCT. 15	28	9	10	11	31	33	40	17	30	17	28	20
OCT. 16	28	11	12	13	31	33	41	17	30	17	28	20
OCT. 17	28	13	14	15	31	33	41	17	30	17	28	20
OCT. 18	28	15	16	16	31	33	41	17	30	17	28	20
OCT. 19	29	17	18	18	31	33	41	17	30	17	28	20
OCT. 20	29	19	19	20	31	33	41	17	30	17	28	20
OCT. 21	29	20	21	21	31	33	41	17	30	17	28	20
OCT. 22	29	22	23	23	31	33	41	17	30	17	28	20
OCT. 23	29	24	24	25	31	33	41	17	30	17	28	20
OCT. 24	29	25	26	26	31	33	41	17	30	17	28	20
OCT. 25	29	27	27	28	30	33	41	17	30	17	28	21
OCT. 26	30	28	29	30	30	33	41	17	30	17	28	21
OCT. 27	30	30	31	31	30	33	41	17	30	17	28	21
OCT. 28	30	32	32	33	30	33	42	17	30	17	28	21
OCT. 29	30	33	34	34	30	32	42	17	30	17	28	21
OCT. 30	30	35	35	36	30	33	42	17	30	17	28	21
OCT. 31	30	36	37	37	30	33	42	17	31	17	28	21

MOON 1 ◖ 12:01 A.M. TO 8:00 A.M.   **MOON 2** ◑ 8:01 A.M. TO 4:00 P.M.   **MOON 3** ● 4:01 P.M. TO 12:00 A.M.
Use only one "moon" number. Choose the column closest to your time of birth. If your place of birth is not on
Eastern Standard Time, be sure to read "How to Convert to Eastern Standard Time" at the beginning of this section.

1954

November

Date & Time	SUN	MOON 1	MOON 2	MOON 3	MERCURY	VENUS	MARS	JUPITER	SATURN	URANUS	NEPTUNE	PLUTO
NOV. 1	30	38	39	39	29	33	42	17	31	17	28	21
NOV. 2	30	40	40	41	29	33	42	17	31	17	28	21
NOV. 3	31	41	42	42	29	33	42	17	31	17	28	21
NOV. 4	31	43	44	44	29	33	42	17	31	17	28	21
NOV. 5	31	45	45	46	29	33	42	17	31	17	28	21
NOV. 6	31	47	47	48	29	33	42	17	31	17	28	21
NOV. 7	31	1	1	2	29	33	42	17	31	17	28	21
NOV. 8	31	2	3	4	29	32	43	17	31	17	29	21
NOV. 9	31	4	5	6	29	32	43	17	31	17	29	21
NOV. 10	31	7	7	8	29	32	43	17	31	17	29	21
NOV. 11	31	9	9	10	29	32	43	17	31	17	29	21
NOV. 12	32	11	11	12	29	32	43	17	31	17	29	21
NOV. 13	32	13	13	14	29	32	43	17	31	17	29	21
NOV. 14	32	14	15	16	29	32	43	17	31	17	29	21
NOV. 15	32	16	17	18	29	32	43	17	31	17	29	21
NOV. 16	32	18	19	19	30	32	43	17	31	17	29	21
NOV. 17	32	20	20	21	30	32	43	17	31	17	29	21
NOV. 18	32	22	22	23	30	32	43	17	31	17	29	21
NOV. 19	33	23	24	24	30	32	44	17	31	17	29	21
NOV. 20	33	25	25	26	30	32	44	17	31	17	29	21
NOV. 21	33	27	27	28	30	31	44	17	31	17	29	21
NOV. 22	33	28	29	29	31	31	44	17	31	17	29	21
NOV. 23	33	30	30	31	31	31	44	17	31	17	29	21
NOV. 24	33	31	32	32	31	31	44	17	31	17	29	21
NOV. 25	34	33	33	34	31	31	44	17	31	17	29	21
NOV. 26	34	34	35	35	31	31	44	17	31	17	29	21
NOV. 27	34	36	37	37	31	31	44	17	31	17	29	21
NOV. 28	34	38	38	39	32	31	44	17	31	17	29	21
NOV. 29	34	39	40	40	32	31	44	17	31	17	29	21
NOV. 30	34	41	41	42	32	31	45	17	31	17	29	21

December

Date & Time	SUN	MOON 1	MOON 2	MOON 3	MERCURY	VENUS	MARS	JUPITER	SATURN	URANUS	NEPTUNE	PLUTO
DEC. 1	34	43	43	44	32	31	45	17	31	17	29	21
DEC. 2	34	44	45	45	33	31	45	17	31	17	29	21
DEC. 3	35	46	47	47	33	31	45	17	31	17	29	21
DEC. 4	35	48	48	1	33	31	45	17	31	17	29	21
DEC. 5	35	2	2	3	33	31	45	17	31	17	29	21
DEC. 6	35	4	4	5	33	31	45	17	31	17	29	21
DEC. 7	35	6	6	7	34	31	45	17	31	17	29	21
DEC. 8	35	8	8	9	34	31	45	17	31	17	29	21
DEC. 9	35	10	10	11	34	31	45	17	31	17	29	21
DEC. 10	35	12	12	13	34	31	46	17	31	17	29	21
DEC. 11	36	14	14	15	34	31	46	17	31	17	29	21
DEC. 12	36	16	16	17	35	31	46	17	31	17	29	21
DEC. 13	36	17	18	19	35	31	46	17	31	17	29	21
DEC. 14	36	19	20	20	35	31	46	17	31	17	29	21
DEC. 15	36	21	22	22	35	31	46	17	31	17	29	21
DEC. 16	36	23	23	24	35	31	46	17	31	17	29	21
DEC. 17	36	24	25	26	36	31	46	17	31	17	29	21
DEC. 18	36	26	27	27	36	31	46	17	31	17	29	21
DEC. 19	37	28	28	29	36	31	46	17	31	17	29	21
DEC. 20	37	29	30	30	36	31	46	17	31	17	29	21
DEC. 21	37	31	31	32	36	31	47	17	31	17	29	21
DEC. 22	37	32	33	33	37	32	47	17	31	17	29	21
DEC. 23	37	34	35	35	37	32	47	17	31	17	29	21
DEC. 24	37	36	36	37	37	32	47	17	31	17	29	21
DEC. 25	37	37	38	38	37	32	47	17	31	17	29	21
DEC. 26	38	39	39	40	38	32	47	17	31	17	29	21
DEC. 27	38	40	41	42	38	32	47	17	31	17	29	21
DEC. 28	38	42	43	43	38	32	47	17	31	16	29	21
DEC. 29	38	44	44	45	38	32	47	17	31	16	29	21
DEC. 30	38	46	46	47	38	32	47	17	31	16	29	21
DEC. 31	38	47	48	1	39	32	48	17	31	16	29	21

MOON 1 ☽ 12:01 A.M. TO 8:00 A.M.　　**MOON 2** ◑ 8:01 A.M. TO 4:00 P.M.　　**MOON 3** ● 4:01 P.M. TO 12:00 A.M.

Use only one "moon" number. Choose the column closest to your time of birth. If your place of birth is not on Eastern Standard Time, be sure to read "How to Convert to Eastern Standard Time" at the beginning of this section.

1955

January

February

Date & Time	SUN	MOON 1	MOON 2	MOON 3	MERCURY	VENUS	MARS	JUPITER	SATURN	URANUS	NEPTUNE	PLUTO
JAN. 1	38	1	2	2	39	32	48	17	31	16	29	21
JAN. 2	38	3	4	4	39	33	48	17	31	16	29	21
JAN. 3	39	5	6	6	39	33	48	17	31	16	29	21
JAN. 4	39	7	7	8	39	33	48	16	31	16	29	20
JAN. 5	39	9	9	10	40	33	48	16	31	16	29	20
JAN. 6	39	11	11	12	40	33	48	16	31	16	29	20
JAN. 7	39	13	13	14	40	33	48	16	31	16	29	20
JAN. 8	39	15	15	16	40	33	48	16	31	16	29	20
JAN. 9	39	17	17	18	41	33	48	16	32	16	29	20
JAN. 10	40	18	19	20	41	33	48	16	32	16	29	20
JAN. 11	40	20	21	22	41	34	1	16	32	16	29	20
JAN. 12	40	22	23	23	41	34	1	16	32	16	29	20
JAN. 13	40	24	24	25	41	34	1	16	32	16	29	20
JAN. 14	40	26	26	27	42	34	1	16	32	16	29	20
JAN. 15	40	27	28	28	42	34	1	16	32	16	29	20
JAN. 16	40	29	29	30	42	34	1	16	32	16	29	20
JAN. 17	41	30	31	31	42	34	1	16	32	16	29	20
JAN. 18	41	32	32	33	42	34	1	16	32	16	29	20
JAN. 19	41	33	34	35	43	35	1	16	32	16	29	20
JAN. 20	41	35	36	36	43	35	1	16	32	16	29	20
JAN. 21	41	37	37	38	43	35	2	16	32	16	29	20
JAN. 22	41	38	39	39	43	35	2	16	32	16	29	20
JAN. 23	42	40	41	41	44	35	2	16	32	16	29	20
JAN. 24	42	42	42	43	44	35	2	16	32	16	29	20
JAN. 25	42	43	44	45	44	35	2	16	32	16	29	20
JAN. 26	42	45	46	46	44	35	2	16	32	16	29	20
JAN. 27	42	47	48	48	44	36	2	16	32	16	29	20
JAN. 28	42	1	1	2	44	36	2	16	32	16	29	20
JAN. 29	42	3	3	4	45	36	2	16	32	16	29	20
JAN. 30	42	4	5	6	45	36	2	16	32	16	29	20
JAN. 31	43	6	7	8	45	36	2	16	32	16	29	20

Date & Time	SUN	MOON 1	MOON 2	MOON 3	MERCURY	VENUS	MARS	JUPITER	SATURN	URANUS	NEPTUNE	PLUTO
FEB. 1	43	8	9	10	45	36	3	16	32	16	29	20
FEB. 2	43	10	11	11	45	36	3	16	32	16	29	20
FEB. 3	43	12	13	13	45	37	3	16	32	16	29	20
FEB. 4	43	14	15	15	45	37	3	16	32	16	29	20
FEB. 5	43	16	16	17	45	37	3	16	32	16	29	20
FEB. 6	43	18	18	19	45	37	3	16	32	16	29	20
FEB. 7	43	20	20	21	45	37	3	16	32	16	29	20
FEB. 8	44	21	22	23	45	37	3	16	32	16	29	20
FEB. 9	44	23	24	24	45	37	3	16	32	16	29	20
FEB. 10	44	25	25	26	44	38	3	16	32	16	29	20
FEB. 11	44	27	27	28	44	38	4	16	32	16	29	20
FEB. 12	44	28	29	29	44	38	4	16	32	16	29	20
FEB. 13	44	30	30	31	44	38	4	16	32	16	29	20
FEB. 14	44	31	32	32	44	38	4	16	32	16	29	20
FEB. 15	44	33	33	34	44	38	4	16	32	16	29	20
FEB. 16	45	35	35	36	44	38	4	16	32	16	29	20
FEB. 17	45	36	37	37	43	39	4	16	32	16	29	20
FEB. 18	45	38	38	39	43	39	4	16	32	16	29	20
FEB. 19	45	39	40	41	43	39	4	16	32	16	29	20
FEB. 20	45	41	42	42	43	39	4	16	32	16	29	20
FEB. 21	45	43	43	44	43	39	4	16	32	16	29	20
FEB. 22	45	45	45	46	43	39	5	16	32	16	29	20
FEB. 23	46	46	47	48	43	39	5	16	32	16	29	20
FEB. 24	46	48	1	2	43	40	5	16	32	16	29	20
FEB. 25	46	2	3	3	43	40	5	16	32	16	29	20
FEB. 26	46	4	5	5	43	40	5	16	32	16	29	20
FEB. 27	46	6	7	7	43	40	5	16	32	16	29	20
FEB. 28	46	8	8	9	43	40	5	16	32	16	29	20

MOON 1 ◐ 12:01 A.M. TO 8:00 A.M.   **MOON 2** ◑ 8:01 A.M. TO 4:00 P.M.   **MOON 3** ● 4:01 P.M. TO 12:00 A.M.

Use only one "moon" number. Choose the column closest to your time of birth. If your place of birth is not on Eastern Standard Time, be sure to read "How to Convert to Eastern Standard Time" at the beginning of this section.

March

Date & Time	SUN	MOON 1	MOON 2	MOON 3	MERCURY	VENUS	MARS	JUPITER	SATURN	URANUS	NEPTUNE	PLUTO
MAR. 1	46	10	10	11	43	40	5	16	32	16	29	20
MAR. 2	46	12	12	13	43	41	5	16	32	16	29	20
MAR. 3	47	13	14	15	43	41	5	16	32	16	29	20
MAR. 4	47	15	16	17	43	41	6	16	32	16	29	20
MAR. 5	47	17	18	18	43	41	6	16	32	16	29	20
MAR. 6	47	19	20	20	43	41	6	16	32	16	29	20
MAR. 7	47	21	21	22	43	41	6	16	32	16	29	20
MAR. 8	47	22	23	24	44	41	6	16	32	16	29	20
MAR. 9	47	24	25	25	44	42	6	16	32	16	29	20
MAR. 10	47	26	26	27	44	42	6	16	32	16	29	20
MAR. 11	48	28	28	29	44	42	6	16	32	16	29	20
MAR. 12	48	29	30	30	44	42	6	16	32	16	29	20
MAR. 13	48	31	31	32	44	42	6	16	32	16	29	20
MAR. 14	48	32	33	33	44	42	6	16	32	16	29	20
MAR. 15	48	34	35	35	45	43	7	16	32	16	29	20
MAR. 16	48	36	36	37	45	43	7	16	32	16	29	20
MAR. 17	48	37	38	38	45	43	7	16	32	16	29	20
MAR. 18	48	39	39	40	45	43	7	16	32	16	29	20
MAR. 19	1	40	41	42	45	43	7	16	32	16	29	20
MAR. 20	1	42	43	43	45	43	7	16	32	16	29	20
MAR. 21	1	44	44	45	46	44	7	16	32	16	29	20
MAR. 22	1	46	46	47	46	44	7	16	32	16	29	20
MAR. 23	1	48	48	1	46	44	7	16	32	16	29	20
MAR. 24	1	1	2	3	46	44	7	16	32	16	29	20
MAR. 25	2	3	4	5	46	44	7	16	32	16	29	20
MAR. 26	2	5	6	7	46	44	8	16	32	16	29	20
MAR. 27	2	7	8	9	47	44	8	16	32	16	29	20
MAR. 28	2	9	10	11	47	45	8	16	32	16	29	20
MAR. 29	2	11	12	12	47	45	8	16	32	16	29	20
MAR. 30	2	13	14	14	47	45	8	16	32	16	29	20
MAR. 31	2	15	16	16	48	45	8	16	32	16	29	20

April

Date & Time	SUN	MOON 1	MOON 2	MOON 3	MERCURY	VENUS	MARS	JUPITER	SATURN	URANUS	NEPTUNE	PLUTO
APR. 1	2	17	17	18	48	45	8	16	32	16	29	20
APR. 2	2	19	19	20	48	45	8	16	32	16	29	20
APR. 3	3	20	21	21	48	46	8	16	32	16	29	20
APR. 4	3	22	23	23	48	46	8	16	32	16	29	20
APR. 5	3	24	24	25	1	46	8	16	32	16	29	20
APR. 6	3	25	26	27	1	46	9	16	32	16	29	20
APR. 7	3	27	28	28	1	46	9	16	32	16	29	20
APR. 8	3	29	29	30	1	46	9	16	32	16	29	20
APR. 9	3	30	31	31	2	47	9	16	32	16	29	20
APR. 10	3	32	32	33	2	47	9	16	32	16	29	20
APR. 11	4	34	34	35	2	47	9	16	32	16	29	20
APR. 12	4	35	36	36	2	47	9	16	32	16	29	20
APR. 13	4	37	37	38	3	47	9	16	32	16	29	20
APR. 14	4	38	39	39	3	47	9	16	32	16	29	20
APR. 15	4	40	40	41	3	47	9	16	32	16	29	20
APR. 16	4	41	42	43	3	48	9	16	32	16	29	20
APR. 17	4	43	44	44	4	48	10	16	32	16	29	20
APR. 18	4	45	46	46	4	48	10	16	32	16	29	20
APR. 19	5	47	47	48	4	48	10	16	32	16	29	20
APR. 20	5	1	1	2	4	48	10	16	32	16	29	20
APR. 21	5	3	3	4	5	48	10	16	32	16	29	20
APR. 22	5	5	5	6	5	1	10	16	32	16	29	20
APR. 23	5	7	7	8	5	1	10	16	32	16	29	20
APR. 24	5	9	9	10	6	1	10	16	31	16	29	20
APR. 25	6	11	11	12	6	1	10	16	31	16	29	20
APR. 26	6	12	13	14	6	1	10	16	31	16	29	20
APR. 27	6	14	15	16	6	1	10	16	31	16	29	20
APR. 28	6	16	17	17	7	2	11	16	31	16	29	20
APR. 29	6	18	19	19	7	2	11	16	31	16	29	20
APR. 30	6	20	20	21	7	2	11	16	31	16	29	20

MOON 1 ◗ 12:01 A.M. TO 8:00 A.M.   **MOON 2** ◑ 8:01 A.M. TO 4:00 P.M.   **MOON 3** ● 4:01 P.M. TO 12:00 A.M.
Use only one "moon" number. Choose the column closest to your time of birth. If your place of birth is not on Eastern Standard Time, be sure to read "How to Convert to Eastern Standard Time" at the beginning of this section.

1955

May

June

Date & Time	SUN	MOON 1	MOON 2	MOON 3	MERCURY	VENUS	MARS	JUPITER	SATURN	URANUS	NEPTUNE	PLUTO
MAY 1	6	22	22	23	8	2	11	16	31	16	29	20
MAY 2	6	23	24	24	8	2	11	16	31	16	28	20
MAY 3	7	25	26	26	8	2	11	16	31	16	28	20
MAY 4	7	27	27	28	8	2	11	16	31	16	28	20
MAY 5	7	28	29	29	9	3	11	16	31	16	28	20
MAY 6	7	30	30	31	9	3	11	16	31	16	28	20
MAY 7	7	31	32	33	9	3	11	16	31	16	28	20
MAY 8	7	33	34	34	9	3	11	16	31	16	28	20
MAY 9	7	35	35	36	10	3	11	16	31	16	28	20
MAY 10	7	36	37	37	10	3	12	16	31	16	28	20
MAY 11	8	38	38	39	10	4	12	16	31	16	28	20
MAY 12	8	39	40	40	10	4	12	16	31	16	28	20
MAY 13	8	41	42	42	10	4	12	16	31	16	28	20
MAY 14	8	43	43	44	11	4	12	16	31	16	28	20
MAY 15	8	44	45	45	11	4	12	16	31	16	28	20
MAY 16	8	46	47	47	11	4	12	16	31	16	28	20
MAY 17	8	48	48	1	11	5	12	16	31	16	28	20
MAY 18	8	2	2	3	11	5	12	16	31	16	28	20
MAY 19	9	4	4	5	12	5	12	16	31	16	28	20
MAY 20	9	6	6	7	12	5	12	16	31	16	28	20
MAY 21	9	8	8	9	12	5	13	16	31	16	28	20
MAY 22	9	10	10	11	12	5	13	16	31	16	28	20
MAY 23	9	12	12	13	12	6	13	16	31	16	28	20
MAY 24	9	14	14	15	12	6	13	16	31	16	28	20
MAY 25	10	16	16	17	12	6	13	17	31	16	28	20
MAY 26	10	18	18	19	12	6	13	17	31	16	28	20
MAY 27	10	19	20	21	13	6	13	17	31	16	28	20
MAY 28	10	21	22	22	13	6	13	17	31	16	28	20
MAY 29	10	23	23	24	13	7	13	17	31	16	28	20
MAY 30	10	25	25	26	13	7	13	17	31	16	28	20
MAY 31	10	26	27	27	13	7	13	17	31	16	28	20

Date & Time	SUN	MOON 1	MOON 2	MOON 3	MERCURY	VENUS	MARS	JUPITER	SATURN	URANUS	NEPTUNE	PLUTO
JUN. 1	10	28	28	29	13	7	14	17	31	16	28	20
JUN. 2	10	30	30	31	13	7	14	17	31	16	28	20
JUN. 3	11	31	32	32	13	7	14	17	31	16	28	20
JUN. 4	11	33	33	34	13	7	14	17	31	16	28	20
JUN. 5	11	34	35	35	8	8	14	17	31	16	28	20
JUN. 6	11	36	36	37	13	8	14	17	31	16	28	20
JUN. 7	11	37	38	38	13	8	14	17	31	16	28	20
JUN. 8	11	39	40	40	13	8	14	17	31	16	28	20
JUN. 9	11	41	41	42	13	8	14	17	31	16	28	20
JUN. 10	11	42	43	43	8	8	14	17	31	16	28	20
JUN. 11	12	44	44	45	13	9	14	17	31	16	28	20
JUN. 12	12	46	46	47	13	9	14	17	31	16	28	20
JUN. 13	12	47	48	48	12	9	15	17	31	16	28	20
JUN. 14	12	1	2	2	12	9	15	17	31	16	28	20
JUN. 15	12	3	4	4	12	9	15	17	31	16	28	20
JUN. 16	12	5	5	6	12	9	15	17	31	16	28	20
JUN. 17	12	7	7	8	12	10	15	17	31	16	28	20
JUN. 18	12	9	9	10	12	10	15	17	31	16	28	20
JUN. 19	13	11	11	12	12	10	15	17	31	16	28	20
JUN. 20	13	13	13	14	12	10	15	17	31	16	28	20
JUN. 21	13	15	15	16	12	10	15	17	31	16	28	20
JUN. 22	13	17	17	18	12	10	15	17	31	16	28	20
JUN. 23	13	19	19	20	12	11	15	17	31	16	28	20
JUN. 24	13	21	21	22	12	11	15	17	31	16	28	20
JUN. 25	14	22	23	24	12	11	15	17	31	16	28	20
JUN. 26	14	24	25	25	11	11	16	17	31	16	28	20
JUN. 27	14	26	26	27	11	11	16	17	31	17	28	20
JUN. 28	14	27	28	29	11	11	16	17	31	17	28	20
JUN. 29	14	29	30	30	12	12	16	17	31	17	28	20
JUN. 30	14	31	31	32	12	12	16	17	31	17	28	20

MOON 1 ☽ 12:01 A.M. TO 8:00 A.M.   **MOON 2** ☽ 8:01 A.M. TO 4:00 P.M.   **MOON 3** ● 4:01 P.M. TO 12:00 A.M.
Use only one "moon" number. Choose the column closest to your time of birth. If your place of birth is not on
Eastern Standard Time, be sure to read "How to Convert to Eastern Standard Time" at the beginning of this section.

July

August

Date & Time	SUN	MOON 1	MOON 2	MOON 3	MERCURY	VENUS	MARS	JUPITER	SATURN	URANUS	NEPTUNE	PLUTO
JUL. 1	14	32	33	33	12	12	16	17	31	17	28	20
JUL. 2	14	34	34	35	12	12	16	17	31	17	28	20
JUL. 3	15	35	36	36	12	12	16	18	31	17	28	20
JUL. 4	15	37	38	38	12	12	16	18	31	17	28	20
JUL. 5	15	39	39	40	12	13	16	18	31	17	28	20
JUL. 6	15	40	41	41	12	13	17	18	31	17	28	20
JUL. 7	15	42	42	43	12	13	17	18	31	17	28	20
JUL. 8	15	43	44	45	12	13	17	18	31	17	28	20
JUL. 9	15	45	46	46	12	13	17	18	31	17	28	20
JUL. 10	15	47	47	48	12	13	17	18	31	17	28	20
JUL. 11	16	1	1	2	13	13	17	18	31	17	28	20
JUL. 12	16	2	3	4	13	14	17	18	31	17	28	20
JUL. 13	16	4	5	5	13	14	17	18	31	17	28	20
JUL. 14	16	6	7	7	13	14	17	18	31	17	28	20
JUL. 15	16	8	9	9	13	14	17	18	31	17	28	20
JUL. 16	16	10	11	11	14	14	17	18	31	17	28	20
JUL. 17	16	12	13	13	14	14	17	18	31	17	28	20
JUL. 18	16	14	15	15	14	15	18	18	31	17	28	20
JUL. 19	17	16	17	17	14	15	18	18	31	17	28	20
JUL. 20	17	18	19	19	14	15	18	18	31	17	28	20
JUL. 21	17	20	20	21	14	15	18	18	31	17	28	20
JUL. 22	17	22	22	23	15	15	18	18	31	17	28	20
JUL. 23	17	23	24	25	15	15	18	18	31	17	28	20
JUL. 24	17	25	26	26	15	16	18	18	31	17	28	20
JUL. 25	17	27	28	28	15	16	18	18	31	17	28	20
JUL. 26	18	29	29	30	16	16	18	18	31	17	28	20
JUL. 27	18	30	31	31	16	16	18	18	31	17	28	20
JUL. 28	18	32	32	33	16	16	18	18	31	17	28	20
JUL. 29	18	33	34	34	17	16	18	18	31	17	28	20
JUL. 30	18	35	35	36	17	17	19	18	31	17	28	20
JUL. 31	18	37	37	38	17	17	19	18	31	17	28	20

Date & Time	SUN	MOON 1	MOON 2	MOON 3	MERCURY	VENUS	MARS	JUPITER	SATURN	URANUS	NEPTUNE	PLUTO
AUG. 1	18	38	39	39	17	17	19	18	31	17	28	20
AUG. 2	18	40	40	41	18	17	19	18	31	17	28	20
AUG. 3	19	41	42	42	18	17	19	18	31	17	28	20
AUG. 4	19	43	44	44	18	17	19	18	31	17	28	20
AUG. 5	19	45	45	46	18	18	19	18	31	17	28	20
AUG. 6	19	46	47	48	18	18	19	19	31	17	28	20
AUG. 7	19	48	1	1	19	18	19	19	31	17	28	20
AUG. 8	19	2	3	3	19	18	19	19	31	17	28	20
AUG. 9	19	4	4	5	20	18	19	19	31	17	28	20
AUG. 10	19	6	6	7	20	18	20	19	31	17	28	20
AUG. 11	20	8	8	9	20	19	20	19	31	17	28	20
AUG. 12	20	9	10	11	20	19	20	19	31	17	28	20
AUG. 13	20	11	12	13	21	19	20	19	31	17	28	20
AUG. 14	20	13	14	15	21	19	20	19	31	17	28	20
AUG. 15	20	15	16	16	21	19	20	19	31	17	28	20
AUG. 16	20	17	18	18	21	19	20	19	31	17	28	20
AUG. 17	20	19	20	20	22	20	20	19	31	17	28	20
AUG. 18	20	21	22	22	22	20	20	19	31	17	28	20
AUG. 19	21	23	23	24	22	20	20	19	31	17	28	20
AUG. 20	21	25	25	26	22	20	20	19	31	17	28	20
AUG. 21	21	26	27	27	23	20	20	19	31	17	28	21
AUG. 22	21	28	29	29	23	20	21	19	31	17	28	21
AUG. 23	21	30	30	31	23	21	21	19	31	17	28	21
AUG. 24	21	31	32	32	23	21	21	19	31	17	28	21
AUG. 25	21	33	33	34	23	21	21	19	31	17	28	21
AUG. 26	22	34	35	36	24	21	21	19	31	17	28	21
AUG. 27	22	36	37	37	24	21	21	19	31	17	28	21
AUG. 28	22	38	38	39	24	21	21	19	31	17	28	21
AUG. 29	22	39	40	40	24	22	21	19	31	17	28	21
AUG. 30	22	41	41	42	25	22	21	19	31	17	28	21
AUG. 31	22	43	43	44	25	22	21	19	31	17	28	21

MOON 1 ☽ 12:01 A.M. TO 8:00 A.M.   **MOON 2** ☽ 8:01 A.M. TO 4:00 P.M.   **MOON 3** ● 4:01 P.M. TO 12:00 A.M.
Use only one "moon" number. Choose the column closest to your time of birth. If your place of birth is not on
Eastern Standard Time, be sure to read "How to Convert to Eastern Standard Time" at the beginning of this section.

September

October

Date & Time	SUN	MOON 1	MOON 2	MOON 3	MERCURY	VENUS	MARS	JUPITER	SATURN	URANUS	NEPTUNE	PLUTO
SEP. 1	22	44	45	45	25	22	21	19	31	17	28	21
SEP. 2	22	46	47	47	25	22	21	19	31	17	28	21
SEP. 3	23	48	48	1	25	22	22	19	31	17	28	21
SEP. 4	23	2	2	3	25	23	22	19	31	17	28	21
SEP. 5	23	3	4	5	26	23	22	19	31	17	28	21
SEP. 6	23	5	6	6	26	23	22	19	31	17	28	21
SEP. 7	23	7	8	8	26	23	22	19	31	17	28	21
SEP. 8	23	9	10	10	26	23	22	19	31	17	28	21
SEP. 9	23	11	11	12	26	23	22	19	31	17	28	21
SEP. 10	23	13	13	14	27	24	22	20	31	17	29	21
SEP. 11	24	15	15	16	27	24	22	20	31	17	29	21
SEP. 12	24	16	17	18	27	24	22	20	31	17	29	21
SEP. 13	24	18	19	20	27	24	22	20	31	17	29	21
SEP. 14	24	20	21	21	27	24	22	20	31	17	29	21
SEP. 15	24	22	23	23	27	24	23	20	31	17	29	21
SEP. 16	24	24	24	25	27	25	23	20	31	17	29	21
SEP. 17	24	26	26	27	28	25	23	20	31	17	29	21
SEP. 18	24	27	28	29	28	25	23	20	31	17	29	21
SEP. 19	25	29	30	30	28	25	23	20	31	17	29	21
SEP. 20	25	31	31	32	28	25	23	20	31	17	29	21
SEP. 21	25	32	33	33	28	25	23	20	31	17	29	21
SEP. 22	25	34	34	35	28	26	23	20	31	17	29	21
SEP. 23	25	36	36	37	28	26	23	20	31	17	29	21
SEP. 24	25	37	38	38	29	26	23	20	31	17	29	21
SEP. 25	26	39	39	40	29	26	23	20	31	17	29	21
SEP. 26	26	40	41	41	29	26	23	20	31	17	29	21
SEP. 27	26	42	42	43	29	26	24	20	31	17	29	21
SEP. 28	26	44	44	45	29	27	24	20	31	17	29	21
SEP. 29	26	45	46	46	29	27	24	20	31	17	29	21
SEP. 30	26	47	48	48	29	27	24	20	31	17	29	21

Date & Time	SUN	MOON 1	MOON 2	MOON 3	MERCURY	VENUS	MARS	JUPITER	SATURN	URANUS	NEPTUNE	PLUTO
OCT. 1	26	1	2	2	29	27	24	20	31	17	29	21
OCT. 2	26	3	3	4	29	27	24	20	31	17	29	21
OCT. 3	27	5	5	6	29	27	24	20	31	17	29	21
OCT. 4	27	7	7	8	29	28	24	20	31	17	29	21
OCT. 5	27	8	9	10	29	28	24	20	31	17	29	21
OCT. 6	27	10	11	12	28	28	24	20	32	17	29	21
OCT. 7	27	12	13	14	28	28	24	20	32	17	29	21
OCT. 8	27	14	15	15	28	28	25	20	32	17	29	21
OCT. 9	27	16	17	17	28	28	25	20	32	17	29	21
OCT. 10	27	18	19	19	28	28	25	20	32	17	29	21
OCT. 11	28	20	20	21	28	29	25	20	32	17	29	21
OCT. 12	28	22	22	23	28	29	25	20	32	17	29	21
OCT. 13	28	23	24	25	28	29	25	20	32	17	29	21
OCT. 14	28	25	26	26	28	29	25	20	32	17	29	21
OCT. 15	28	27	27	28	27	29	25	20	32	17	29	21
OCT. 16	28	29	29	30	27	29	25	20	32	17	29	21
OCT. 17	28	30	31	31	27	30	25	20	32	17	29	21
OCT. 18	28	32	32	33	27	30	25	20	32	17	29	21
OCT. 19	29	33	34	34	27	30	25	20	32	17	29	21
OCT. 20	29	35	36	36	27	30	26	20	32	17	29	21
OCT. 21	29	37	37	38	27	30	26	21	32	17	29	21
OCT. 22	29	38	39	39	27	30	26	21	32	17	29	21
OCT. 23	29	40	40	41	27	31	26	21	32	17	29	21
OCT. 24	29	41	42	42	27	31	26	21	32	17	29	21
OCT. 25	29	43	44	44	27	31	26	21	32	17	29	21
OCT. 26	30	45	45	46	27	31	26	21	32	17	29	21
OCT. 27	30	46	47	48	27	31	26	21	32	17	29	21
OCT. 28	30	48	1	1	27	31	26	21	32	17	29	21
OCT. 29	30	2	3	3	27	32	26	21	32	17	29	21
OCT. 30	30	4	5	5	27	32	26	21	32	17	29	21
OCT. 31	30	6	6	7	27	32	26	21	32	17	29	21

MOON 1 ◐ 12:01 A.M. TO 8:00 A.M.   **MOON 2** ◑ 8:01 A.M. TO 4:00 P.M.   **MOON 3** ● 4:01 P.M. TO 12:00 A.M.
Use only one "moon" number. Choose the column closest to your time of birth. If your place of birth is not on Eastern Standard Time, be sure to read "How to Convert to Eastern Standard Time" at the beginning of this section.

1955

November

Date & Time	SUN	MOON 1	MOON 2	MOON 3	MERCURY	VENUS	MARS	JUPITER	SATURN	URANUS	NEPTUNE	PLUTO
NOV. 1	30	8	8	9	28	32	27	21	32	17	29	21
NOV. 2	30	10	10	11	28	32	27	21	32	17	29	21
NOV. 3	31	12	12	13	28	32	27	21	32	17	29	21
NOV. 4	31	14	14	15	28	33	27	21	32	17	29	21
NOV. 5	31	16	16	17	28	33	27	21	32	17	29	21
NOV. 6	31	17	18	19	29	33	27	21	32	17	29	21
NOV. 7	31	19	20	21	29	33	27	21	32	17	29	21
NOV. 8	31	21	22	22	29	33	27	21	32	17	29	21
NOV. 9	31	23	24	24	29	33	27	21	32	17	29	21
NOV. 10	31	25	25	26	29	34	27	21	32	17	29	21
NOV. 11	31	26	27	27	30	34	27	21	32	17	29	21
NOV. 12	32	28	29	29	30	34	28	21	32	17	29	21
NOV. 13	32	30	30	31	30	34	28	21	32	17	29	21
NOV. 14	32	31	32	32	30	34	28	21	32	17	29	21
NOV. 15	32	33	33	34	30	34	28	21	32	17	29	21
NOV. 16	32	35	35	36	31	35	28	21	32	17	29	21
NOV. 17	32	36	37	37	31	35	28	21	32	17	29	21
NOV. 18	32	38	38	39	31	35	28	21	32	17	29	21
NOV. 19	33	39	40	40	31	35	28	21	32	17	29	21
NOV. 20	33	41	41	42	31	35	28	21	32	17	29	21
NOV. 21	33	42	43	44	32	35	28	21	32	17	29	21
NOV. 22	33	44	45	45	32	36	28	21	32	17	29	21
NOV. 23	33	46	46	47	32	36	28	21	32	17	29	21
NOV. 24	33	47	48	1	32	36	29	21	32	17	29	21
NOV. 25	34	1	2	2	33	36	29	21	32	17	29	21
NOV. 26	34	3	4	4	33	36	29	21	32	17	29	21
NOV. 27	34	5	6	6	33	36	29	21	32	17	29	21
NOV. 28	34	7	8	8	33	37	29	21	32	17	29	21
NOV. 29	34	9	10	10	33	37	29	21	32	17	29	21
NOV. 30	34	11	12	12	34	37	29	21	32	17	29	21

December

Date & Time	SUN	MOON 1	MOON 2	MOON 3	MERCURY	VENUS	MARS	JUPITER	SATURN	URANUS	NEPTUNE	PLUTO
DEC. 1	34	13	14	14	34	37	29	21	32	17	29	21
DEC. 2	34	15	16	16	34	37	29	21	32	17	29	21
DEC. 3	35	17	18	18	34	37	29	21	32	17	29	21
DEC. 4	35	19	19	20	34	38	29	21	32	17	29	21
DEC. 5	35	21	21	22	35	38	29	21	32	17	29	21
DEC. 6	35	22	23	24	35	38	30	21	32	17	29	21
DEC. 7	35	24	25	25	35	38	30	21	32	17	29	21
DEC. 8	35	26	27	27	35	38	30	21	32	17	29	21
DEC. 9	35	28	28	29	35	38	30	21	32	17	29	21
DEC. 10	35	29	30	30	36	39	30	21	33	17	29	21
DEC. 11	36	31	31	32	36	39	30	21	33	17	29	21
DEC. 12	36	33	33	34	36	39	30	21	33	17	29	21
DEC. 13	36	34	35	35	36	39	30	21	33	17	29	21
DEC. 14	36	36	36	37	37	39	30	21	33	17	29	21
DEC. 15	36	37	38	38	37	39	30	21	33	17	29	21
DEC. 16	36	39	39	40	37	40	30	21	33	17	29	21
DEC. 17	36	40	41	41	37	40	31	21	33	17	29	21
DEC. 18	36	42	43	43	37	40	31	21	33	17	29	21
DEC. 19	37	44	44	45	38	40	31	21	33	17	29	21
DEC. 20	37	45	46	46	38	40	31	21	33	17	29	21
DEC. 21	37	47	47	48	38	40	31	21	33	17	29	21
DEC. 22	37	1	1	1	38	41	31	21	33	17	29	21
DEC. 23	37	2	3	4	38	41	31	21	33	17	29	21
DEC. 24	37	4	5	5	39	41	31	21	33	17	29	21
DEC. 25	37	6	7	7	39	41	31	21	33	17	29	21
DEC. 26	38	8	9	9	39	41	31	21	33	17	29	21
DEC. 27	38	10	11	11	39	41	31	21	33	17	29	21
DEC. 28	38	12	13	13	39	42	31	21	33	17	29	21
DEC. 29	38	14	15	15	40	42	32	21	33	17	29	21
DEC. 30	38	16	17	17	40	42	32	21	33	17	29	21
DEC. 31	38	18	19	19	40	42	32	21	33	17	29	21

MOON 1 ◗ 12:01 A.M. TO 8:00 A.M.   **MOON 2** ◑ 8:01 A.M. TO 4:00 P.M.   **MOON 3** ● 4:01 P.M. TO 12:00 A.M.

Use only one "moon" number. Choose the column closest to your time of birth. If your place of birth is not on Eastern Standard Time, be sure to read "How to Convert to Eastern Standard Time" at the beginning of this section.

1956

January

February

Date & Time	SUN	MOON 1	MOON 2	MOON 3	MERCURY	VENUS	MARS	JUPITER	SATURN	URANUS	NEPTUNE	PLUTO
JAN. 1	38	20	21	21	40	42	32	21	33	17	29	21
JAN. 2	38	22	22	23	41	42	32	21	33	17	29	21
JAN. 3	39	24	24	25	41	43	32	21	33	17	29	21
JAN. 4	39	25	26	27	41	43	32	21	33	17	29	21
JAN. 5	39	27	28	28	41	43	32	21	33	17	29	21
JAN. 6	39	29	29	30	41	43	32	21	33	17	29	21
JAN. 7	39	31	31	32	42	43	32	21	33	17	29	21
JAN. 8	39	32	33	33	42	43	32	21	33	17	29	21
JAN. 9	39	34	34	35	42	44	33	21	33	17	29	21
JAN. 10	40	35	36	36	42	44	33	21	33	17	29	21
JAN. 11	40	37	37	38	42	44	33	21	33	17	29	21
JAN. 12	40	38	39	39	42	44	33	21	33	17	29	21
JAN. 13	40	40	41	41	42	44	33	21	33	17	29	21
JAN. 14	40	42	42	43	43	44	33	21	33	17	29	21
JAN. 15	40	43	44	44	43	45	33	21	33	17	29	21
JAN. 16	40	45	45	46	43	45	33	21	33	17	29	21
JAN. 17	41	46	47	48	43	45	33	21	33	17	29	21
JAN. 18	41	48	1	1	43	45	33	21	33	17	29	21
JAN. 19	41	2	2	3	43	45	33	21	33	17	29	21
JAN. 20	41	4	4	5	43	45	33	21	33	17	29	21
JAN. 21	41	5	6	7	43	46	34	21	33	17	29	21
JAN. 22	41	7	8	8	43	46	34	21	33	17	29	21
JAN. 23	42	9	10	10	42	46	34	21	33	17	29	21
JAN. 24	42	11	12	12	42	46	34	21	33	17	29	21
JAN. 25	42	13	14	14	42	46	34	21	33	17	29	21
JAN. 26	42	15	16	16	42	46	34	21	33	17	29	21
JAN. 27	42	17	18	18	42	47	34	21	33	17	29	21
JAN. 28	42	19	20	20	42	47	34	21	33	17	29	21
JAN. 29	42	21	22	22	42	47	34	21	33	17	29	21
JAN. 30	42	23	24	24	41	47	34	21	33	17	29	21
JAN. 31	43	25	25	26	41	47	34	21	33	17	29	21

Date & Time	SUN	MOON 1	MOON 2	MOON 3	MERCURY	VENUS	MARS	JUPITER	SATURN	URANUS	NEPTUNE	PLUTO
FEB. 1	43	27	27	28	41	47	35	21	33	17	29	21
FEB. 2	43	28	29	29	41	48	35	21	33	17	29	21
FEB. 3	43	30	31	31	41	48	35	21	33	17	29	21
FEB. 4	43	32	32	33	41	48	35	21	33	17	29	21
FEB. 5	43	33	34	34	41	48	35	21	33	17	29	21
FEB. 6	43	35	35	36	41	48	35	21	33	17	29	21
FEB. 7	43	36	37	37	41	48	35	21	33	17	29	21
FEB. 8	44	38	39	39	41	48	35	21	33	17	29	21
FEB. 9	44	40	40	41	41	1	35	21	33	17	29	21
FEB. 10	44	41	42	42	41	1	35	21	33	17	29	21
FEB. 11	44	43	43	44	41	1	35	21	33	17	29	21
FEB. 12	44	44	45	46	41	1	36	21	33	17	29	21
FEB. 13	44	46	47	47	41	1	36	21	33	17	29	21
FEB. 14	44	48	48	1	41	1	36	21	33	17	29	21
FEB. 15	44	1	2	3	41	2	36	21	33	17	29	21
FEB. 16	45	3	4	4	41	2	36	21	33	17	29	21
FEB. 17	45	5	6	6	41	2	36	20	33	17	29	21
FEB. 18	45	7	7	8	41	2	36	20	33	17	29	21
FEB. 19	45	9	9	10	41	2	36	20	33	17	29	21
FEB. 20	45	10	11	12	42	2	36	20	33	17	29	21
FEB. 21	45	12	13	14	42	3	36	20	33	17	29	21
FEB. 22	45	14	15	16	42	3	36	20	33	17	29	21
FEB. 23	46	16	17	18	42	3	36	20	33	17	29	21
FEB. 24	46	18	19	19	42	3	37	20	33	17	29	21
FEB. 25	46	20	21	21	42	3	37	20	33	17	29	21
FEB. 26	46	22	23	23	42	3	37	20	33	17	29	21
FEB. 27	46	24	25	25	43	3	37	20	33	17	29	21
FEB. 28	46	26	26	27	43	4	37	20	33	17	29	21
FEB. 29	46	28	28	29	43	4	37	20	33	17	29	21

MOON 1 ☽ 12:01 A.M. TO 8:00 A.M.   **MOON 2** ☾ 8:01 A.M. TO 4:00 P.M.   **MOON 3** ● 4:01 P.M. TO 12:00 A.M.
Use only one "moon" number. Choose the column closest to your time of birth. If your place of birth is not on Eastern Standard Time, be sure to read "How to Convert to Eastern Standard Time" at the beginning of this section.

1956

March

Date & Time	SUN	MOON 1	MOON 2	MOON 3	MERCURY	VENUS	MARS	JUPITER	SATURN	URANUS	NEPTUNE	PLUTO
MAR. 1	46	29	30	31	43	4	37	20	33	17	29	21
MAR. 2	46	31	32	32	43	4	37	20	33	17	29	21
MAR. 3	47	33	33	34	43	4	37	20	33	17	29	21
MAR. 4	47	34	35	35	44	4	37	20	33	17	29	21
MAR. 5	47	36	36	37	44	5	37	20	33	17	29	21
MAR. 6	47	38	38	39	44	5	38	20	33	17	29	21
MAR. 7	47	39	40	40	44	5	38	20	33	17	29	21
MAR. 8	47	41	41	42	44	5	38	20	33	17	29	21
MAR. 9	47	42	43	43	45	5	38	20	33	17	29	21
MAR. 10	47	44	44	45	45	5	38	20	33	17	29	21
MAR. 11	48	46	46	46	45	5	38	20	33	17	29	21
MAR. 12	48	47	48	48	45	6	38	20	33	17	29	21
MAR. 13	48	1	2	2	45	6	38	20	33	17	29	21
MAR. 14	48	3	3	4	46	6	38	20	33	17	29	21
MAR. 15	48	5	5	6	46	6	38	20	33	17	29	21
MAR. 16	48	6	7	8	46	6	38	20	33	17	29	21
MAR. 17	48	8	9	9	46	6	38	20	33	17	29	21
MAR. 18	48	10	11	11	46	7	39	20	33	17	29	21
MAR. 19	1	12	13	13	47	7	39	20	33	17	29	21
MAR. 20	1	14	14	15	47	7	39	20	33	17	29	21
MAR. 21	1	16	16	17	47	7	39	20	33	17	29	21
MAR. 22	1	18	18	19	47	7	39	20	33	17	29	21
MAR. 23	1	19	20	21	48	7	39	20	33	17	29	21
MAR. 24	1	21	22	23	48	7	39	20	33	17	29	21
MAR. 25	2	23	24	25	48	8	39	20	33	17	29	21
MAR. 26	2	25	26	26	48	8	39	20	33	17	29	21
MAR. 27	2	27	28	28	1	8	39	20	33	17	29	20
MAR. 28	2	29	29	30	1	8	39	20	33	17	29	20
MAR. 29	2	30	31	32	1	8	40	20	33	17	29	20
MAR. 30	2	32	33	33	1	8	40	20	33	17	29	20
MAR. 31	2	34	34	35	2	8	40	20	33	17	29	20

April

Date & Time	SUN	MOON 1	MOON 2	MOON 3	MERCURY	VENUS	MARS	JUPITER	SATURN	URANUS	NEPTUNE	PLUTO
APR. 1	2	35	36	36	2	9	40	20	33	17	29	20
APR. 2	2	37	38	38	2	9	40	20	33	17	29	20
APR. 3	3	39	39	40	2	9	40	20	33	17	29	20
APR. 4	3	40	41	41	3	9	40	20	33	17	29	20
APR. 5	3	42	42	43	3	9	40	20	33	17	29	20
APR. 6	3	43	44	44	3	9	40	20	33	17	29	20
APR. 7	3	45	46	46	3	9	40	20	33	17	29	20
APR. 8	3	47	47	48	4	9	40	20	33	17	29	20
APR. 9	3	48	1	2	4	10	40	20	33	17	29	20
APR. 10	3	2	3	4	4	10	41	20	33	17	29	20
APR. 11	4	4	5	5	5	10	41	20	33	17	29	20
APR. 12	4	6	6	7	5	10	41	20	33	17	29	20
APR. 13	4	8	8	9	5	10	41	20	33	17	29	20
APR. 14	4	10	10	11	5	10	41	20	33	17	29	20
APR. 15	4	11	12	13	5	10	41	20	33	17	29	20
APR. 16	4	13	14	15	6	11	41	20	33	17	29	20
APR. 17	4	15	16	16	6	11	41	20	33	17	29	20
APR. 18	4	17	18	18	6	11	41	20	33	17	29	20
APR. 19	5	19	20	20	7	11	41	20	33	17	29	20
APR. 20	5	21	21	22	7	11	41	20	33	17	29	20
APR. 21	5	23	23	24	7	11	41	20	33	17	29	20
APR. 22	5	25	25	26	7	11	42	20	33	17	29	20
APR. 23	5	26	27	28	8	11	42	20	33	17	29	20
APR. 24	5	28	29	29	8	12	42	20	33	17	29	20
APR. 25	6	30	30	31	8	12	42	20	33	17	29	20
APR. 26	6	32	32	33	8	12	42	20	33	17	29	20
APR. 27	6	33	34	34	8	12	42	20	33	17	29	20
APR. 28	6	35	35	36	9	12	42	20	33	17	29	20
APR. 29	6	36	37	38	9	12	42	20	33	17	29	20
APR. 30	6	38	39	39	9	12	42	20	33	17	29	20

MOON 1 ○ 12:01 A.M. TO 8:00 A.M.   **MOON 2** ◖ 8:01 A.M. TO 4:00 P.M.   **MOON 3** ● 4:01 P.M. TO 12:00 A.M.
Use only one "moon" number. Choose the column closest to your time of birth. If your place of birth is not on Eastern Standard Time, be sure to read "How to Convert to Eastern Standard Time" at the beginning of this section.

May

June

Date & Time	SUN	MOON 1	MOON 2	MOON 3	MERCURY	VENUS	MARS	JUPITER	SATURN	URANUS	NEPTUNE	PLUTO
MAY 1	6	40	40	41	9	12	42	20	33	17	29	20
MAY 2	6	41	42	42	9	12	42	20	33	17	29	20
MAY 3	7	43	43	44	9	12	43	20	33	17	29	20
MAY 4	7	44	45	45	10	13	43	20	33	17	29	20
MAY 5	7	46	47	47	10	13	43	20	33	17	29	20
MAY 6	7	48	48	1	10	13	43	20	33	17	29	20
MAY 7	7	1	2	3	10	13	43	20	33	17	29	20
MAY 8	7	3	4	4	10	13	43	20	33	17	29	20
MAY 9	7	5	6	6	10	13	43	20	33	17	29	20
MAY 10	7	7	8	8	10	13	43	20	33	17	29	20
MAY 11	8	9	10	10	10	13	43	20	33	17	29	20
MAY 12	8	11	11	12	10	13	43	20	33	17	29	20
MAY 13	8	13	13	14	10	13	43	20	33	17	29	20
MAY 14	8	15	15	16	10	13	43	20	33	17	29	20
MAY 15	8	17	17	18	10	14	43	20	33	17	29	20
MAY 16	8	19	19	20	10	14	44	20	33	17	29	20
MAY 17	8	20	21	22	10	14	44	20	33	17	29	20
MAY 18	8	22	23	24	10	14	44	20	33	17	29	20
MAY 19	9	24	25	25	10	14	44	20	33	17	29	20
MAY 20	9	26	26	27	10	14	44	20	33	17	29	20
MAY 21	9	28	28	29	10	14	44	20	33	17	29	20
MAY 22	9	29	30	30	10	14	44	20	33	17	29	20
MAY 23	9	31	32	32	10	14	44	20	33	17	29	20
MAY 24	9	33	33	34	10	14	44	20	33	17	29	20
MAY 25	10	34	35	35	10	14	44	20	33	17	29	20
MAY 26	10	36	36	37	10	14	44	20	33	17	29	20
MAY 27	10	38	38	39	10	14	44	20	33	17	29	20
MAY 28	10	39	40	40	9	14	45	20	33	17	29	20
MAY 29	10	41	41	42	9	14	45	20	33	17	29	20
MAY 30	10	42	43	43	9	14	45	20	33	17	29	20
MAY 31	10	44	44	45	9	14	45	20	33	17	29	20

Date & Time	SUN	MOON 1	MOON 2	MOON 3	MERCURY	VENUS	MARS	JUPITER	SATURN	URANUS	NEPTUNE	PLUTO
JUN. 1	10	45	46	47	9	14	45	20	33	17	29	20
JUN. 2	10	47	48	48	9	14	45	20	33	17	29	20
JUN. 3	11	1	1	2	9	14	45	20	33	17	29	20
JUN. 4	11	3	3	4	9	14	45	20	33	17	29	20
JUN. 5	11	4	5	6	9	14	45	20	33	17	29	20
JUN. 6	11	6	7	7	9	14	45	20	33	17	29	20
JUN. 7	11	8	9	9	9	14	45	20	33	17	29	20
JUN. 8	11	10	11	11	9	14	45	20	33	17	29	20
JUN. 9	11	12	13	13	9	14	45	20	33	17	29	20
JUN. 10	11	14	15	15	9	14	45	20	33	17	29	20
JUN. 11	12	16	17	17	9	14	46	20	33	17	29	20
JUN. 12	12	18	19	19	9	14	46	20	33	17	29	20
JUN. 13	12	20	21	21	9	14	46	20	33	17	29	20
JUN. 14	12	22	22	23	9	14	46	20	33	17	29	20
JUN. 15	12	24	24	25	9	14	46	20	33	17	29	20
JUN. 16	12	25	26	27	9	14	46	20	33	17	29	20
JUN. 17	12	27	28	28	9	13	46	21	33	17	29	20
JUN. 18	12	29	30	30	10	13	46	21	33	17	29	21
JUN. 19	13	31	31	32	10	13	46	21	33	17	29	21
JUN. 20	13	32	33	33	10	13	46	21	33	17	29	21
JUN. 21	13	34	34	35	10	13	46	21	33	17	29	21
JUN. 22	13	36	36	37	10	13	46	21	33	17	29	21
JUN. 23	13	37	38	38	10	13	46	21	33	17	29	21
JUN. 24	13	39	39	40	10	13	46	21	33	17	29	21
JUN. 25	14	40	41	41	11	13	46	21	33	17	29	21
JUN. 26	14	42	42	43	11	13	47	21	33	17	29	21
JUN. 27	14	43	44	45	11	13	47	21	33	17	29	21
JUN. 28	14	45	46	46	11	13	47	21	33	17	29	21
JUN. 29	14	47	47	48	11	13	47	21	33	17	29	21
JUN. 30	14	48	1	1	11	12	47	21	33	17	29	21

MOON 1 ◐ 12:01 A.M. TO 8:00 A.M.   **MOON 2** ◑ 8:01 A.M. TO 4:00 P.M.   **MOON 3** ● 4:01 P.M. TO 12:00 A.M.

Use only one "moon" number. Choose the column closest to your time of birth. If your place of birth is not on Eastern Standard Time, be sure to read "How to Convert to Eastern Standard Time" at the beginning of this section.

1956

July

August

Date & Time	SUN ☀	MOON 1 ◖	MOON 2 ◐	MOON 3 ●	MERCURY	VENUS	MARS	JUPITER	SATURN	URANUS	NEPTUNE	PLUTO
JUL. 1	14	2	3	3	12	12	47	21	33	17	29	21
JUL. 2	14	4	4	5	12	12	47	21	33	17	29	21
JUL. 3	15	5	6	7	12	12	47	21	33	17	29	21
JUL. 4	15	7	8	9	12	12	47	21	33	17	29	21
JUL. 5	15	9	10	10	13	12	47	21	33	17	29	21
JUL. 6	15	11	12	12	13	12	47	21	33	17	29	21
JUL. 7	15	13	14	14	13	12	47	21	33	17	29	21
JUL. 8	15	15	16	16	13	12	47	21	33	17	29	21
JUL. 9	15	17	18	19	14	12	47	21	33	17	29	21
JUL. 10	15	19	20	21	14	12	47	21	33	17	29	21
JUL. 11	16	21	22	22	14	12	47	21	32	17	29	21
JUL. 12	16	23	24	24	14	12	47	21	32	17	29	21
JUL. 13	16	25	26	26	15	12	47	21	32	17	29	21
JUL. 14	16	27	27	28	15	12	47	21	32	17	29	21
JUL. 15	16	29	29	30	15	12	48	21	32	17	29	21
JUL. 16	16	30	31	31	16	12	48	21	32	17	29	21
JUL. 17	16	32	32	33	16	12	48	21	32	17	29	21
JUL. 18	16	34	34	35	16	12	48	21	32	17	29	21
JUL. 19	17	35	36	36	16	12	48	21	32	17	29	21
JUL. 20	17	37	37	38	17	12	48	21	32	17	29	21
JUL. 21	17	38	39	39	17	12	48	21	32	17	29	21
JUL. 22	17	40	40	41	17	12	48	21	32	17	29	21
JUL. 23	17	41	42	43	18	12	48	21	32	17	29	21
JUL. 24	17	43	44	44	18	12	48	21	32	17	29	21
JUL. 25	17	45	45	46	18	12	48	21	32	17	29	21
JUL. 26	18	46	47	47	18	12	48	21	32	17	29	21
JUL. 27	18	48	48	1	19	12	48	21	32	17	29	21
JUL. 28	18	2	2	3	19	12	48	21	32	17	29	21
JUL. 29	18	3	4	4	19	13	48	22	32	17	29	21
JUL. 30	18	5	5	6	19	13	48	22	32	17	29	21
JUL. 31	18	7	7	8	20	13	48	22	32	17	29	21

Date & Time	SUN ☀	MOON 1 ◖	MOON 2 ◐	MOON 3 ●	MERCURY	VENUS	MARS	JUPITER	SATURN	URANUS	NEPTUNE	PLUTO
AUG. 1	18	8	9	10	20	13	48	22	32	17	29	21
AUG. 2	18	10	11	12	20	13	48	22	32	17	29	21
AUG. 3	19	12	13	14	20	13	48	22	32	17	29	21
AUG. 4	19	14	15	16	21	13	48	22	32	17	29	21
AUG. 5	19	16	17	18	21	13	48	22	32	17	29	21
AUG. 6	19	18	19	20	21	13	48	22	32	17	29	21
AUG. 7	19	20	21	22	21	13	48	22	32	17	29	21
AUG. 8	19	22	23	24	22	13	48	22	32	17	29	21
AUG. 9	19	24	25	26	22	13	48	22	32	17	29	21
AUG. 10	19	26	27	27	22	13	48	22	32	17	29	21
AUG. 11	20	28	29	29	22	14	48	22	32	17	29	21
AUG. 12	20	30	30	31	22	14	48	22	32	17	29	21
AUG. 13	20	31	32	33	23	14	48	22	32	17	29	21
AUG. 14	20	33	34	34	23	14	48	22	32	17	29	21
AUG. 15	20	35	35	36	23	14	48	22	32	17	29	21
AUG. 16	20	36	37	37	23	14	48	22	32	17	29	21
AUG. 17	20	38	38	39	23	14	48	22	32	17	29	21
AUG. 18	20	39	40	41	24	14	48	22	32	18	29	21
AUG. 19	21	41	42	42	24	14	48	22	32	18	29	21
AUG. 20	21	43	43	44	24	15	48	22	33	18	29	21
AUG. 21	21	44	45	45	24	15	48	22	33	18	29	21
AUG. 22	21	46	46	47	24	15	48	22	33	18	29	21
AUG. 23	21	47	48	1	24	15	48	22	33	18	29	21
AUG. 24	21	1	2	2	25	15	48	22	33	18	29	21
AUG. 25	21	3	3	4	25	15	48	22	33	18	29	21
AUG. 26	22	5	5	6	25	15	48	22	33	18	29	21
AUG. 27	22	6	7	7	25	15	48	22	33	18	29	21
AUG. 28	22	8	9	9	25	16	48	22	33	18	29	21
AUG. 29	22	10	10	11	25	16	48	22	33	18	29	21
AUG. 30	22	12	12	13	25	16	48	22	33	18	29	21
AUG. 31	22	14	14	15	26	16	48	22	33	18	29	21

MOON 1 ◖ 12:01 A.M. TO 8:00 A.M.　　**MOON 2** ◐ 8:01 A.M. TO 4:00 P.M.　　**MOON 3** ● 4:01 P.M. TO 12:00 A.M.
Use only one "moon" number. Choose the column closest to your time of birth. If your place of birth is not on
Eastern Standard Time, be sure to read "How to Convert to Eastern Standard Time" at the beginning of this section.

1956

September

Date & Time	SUN	MOON 1	MOON 2	MOON 3	MERCURY	VENUS	MARS	JUPITER	SATURN	URANUS	NEPTUNE	PLUTO
SEP. 1	22	15	16	17	26	16	48	22	33	18	29	21
SEP. 2	22	17	18	19	26	16	48	23	33	18	29	21
SEP. 3	23	19	20	21	26	16	48	23	33	18	29	21
SEP. 4	23	21	22	23	26	16	48	23	33	18	29	21
SEP. 5	23	23	24	25	26	17	48	23	33	18	29	21
SEP. 6	23	25	26	27	26	17	48	23	33	18	29	21
SEP. 7	23	27	28	28	26	17	48	23	33	18	29	21
SEP. 8	23	29	30	30	26	17	47	23	33	18	29	21
SEP. 9	23	31	31	32	26	17	47	23	33	18	29	21
SEP. 10	23	33	33	34	27	17	47	23	33	18	29	21
SEP. 11	24	34	35	35	27	17	47	23	33	18	29	21
SEP. 12	24	36	36	37	27	17	47	23	33	18	29	21
SEP. 13	24	37	38	39	27	18	47	23	33	18	29	21
SEP. 14	24	39	40	40	27	18	47	23	33	18	29	21
SEP. 15	24	41	41	42	27	18	47	23	33	18	29	21
SEP. 16	24	42	43	43	27	18	47	23	33	18	29	21
SEP. 17	24	44	44	45	26	18	47	23	33	18	29	21
SEP. 18	24	45	46	46	26	18	47	23	33	18	29	21
SEP. 19	25	47	48	48	26	18	47	23	33	18	29	21
SEP. 20	25	1	1	2	26	19	47	23	33	18	29	21
SEP. 21	25	2	3	4	26	19	47	23	33	18	29	21
SEP. 22	25	4	5	5	26	19	47	23	33	18	29	21
SEP. 23	25	6	6	7	26	19	47	23	33	18	29	21
SEP. 24	25	8	8	9	26	19	47	23	33	18	29	21
SEP. 25	26	9	10	11	26	19	47	23	33	18	29	21
SEP. 26	26	11	12	12	25	19	47	23	33	18	29	21
SEP. 27	26	13	14	14	25	20	47	23	33	18	29	21
SEP. 28	26	15	16	16	25	20	47	23	33	18	29	21
SEP. 29	26	17	17	18	25	20	47	23	33	18	29	21
SEP. 30	26	19	19	20	25	20	47	23	33	18	29	21

October

Date & Time	SUN	MOON 1	MOON 2	MOON 3	MERCURY	VENUS	MARS	JUPITER	SATURN	URANUS	NEPTUNE	PLUTO
OCT. 1	26	21	21	22	25	20	47	23	33	18	29	21
OCT. 2	26	23	23	24	25	20	47	23	33	18	29	21
OCT. 3	27	25	25	26	25	21	47	23	33	18	29	21
OCT. 4	27	26	27	28	25	21	47	23	33	18	29	21
OCT. 5	27	28	29	30	25	21	47	23	33	18	29	21
OCT. 6	27	30	31	31	25	21	47	23	33	18	29	21
OCT. 7	27	32	32	33	25	21	47	24	33	18	29	21
OCT. 8	27	34	34	35	25	21	47	24	33	18	29	21
OCT. 9	27	35	36	36	25	21	47	24	33	18	29	21
OCT. 10	27	37	37	38	25	22	47	24	33	18	29	21
OCT. 11	28	39	39	40	25	22	47	24	33	18	29	21
OCT. 12	28	40	41	41	25	22	47	24	33	18	29	21
OCT. 13	28	42	42	43	25	22	47	24	33	18	29	21
OCT. 14	28	43	44	44	25	22	47	24	33	18	29	21
OCT. 15	28	45	45	46	26	22	47	24	33	18	29	21
OCT. 16	28	46	47	48	26	23	47	24	33	18	29	21
OCT. 17	28	48	1	1	26	23	47	24	33	18	29	21
OCT. 18	28	2	2	3	26	23	47	24	33	18	29	21
OCT. 19	29	4	4	5	26	23	47	24	33	18	29	21
OCT. 20	29	5	6	7	27	23	47	24	33	18	29	21
OCT. 21	29	7	8	8	27	23	47	24	33	18	29	21
OCT. 22	29	9	10	10	27	23	47	24	33	18	29	21
OCT. 23	29	11	11	12	27	24	47	24	33	18	29	21
OCT. 24	29	13	13	14	27	24	47	24	33	18	29	21
OCT. 25	29	14	15	16	28	24	47	24	33	18	29	21
OCT. 26	30	16	17	18	28	24	47	24	33	18	29	21
OCT. 27	30	18	19	20	28	24	47	24	33	18	29	21
OCT. 28	30	20	21	21	28	24	47	24	33	18	29	21
OCT. 29	30	22	23	23	28	25	47	24	33	18	29	21
OCT. 30	30	24	25	25	29	25	47	24	33	18	29	21
OCT. 31	30	26	26	27	29	25	47	24	33	18	29	21

MOON 1 ◑ 12:01 A.M. TO 8:00 A.M.   **MOON 2** ◐ 8:01 A.M. TO 4:00 P.M.   **MOON 3** ● 4:01 P.M. TO 12:00 A.M.
Use only one "moon" number. Choose the column closest to your time of birth. If your place of birth is not on Eastern Standard Time, be sure to read "How to Convert to Eastern Standard Time" at the beginning of this section.

November

Date & Time	SUN	MOON 1	MOON 2	MOON 3	MERCURY	VENUS	MARS	JUPITER	SATURN	URANUS	NEPTUNE	PLUTO
NOV. 1	30	28	28	29	29	25	47	24	33	18	29	21
NOV. 2	30	29	30	31	29	25	47	24	33	18	29	21
NOV. 3	31	31	32	32	30	25	47	24	33	18	29	21
NOV. 4	31	33	34	34	30	26	47	24	33	18	29	21
NOV. 5	31	35	35	36	30	26	47	24	33	18	29	21
NOV. 6	31	36	37	37	30	26	47	24	33	18	29	21
NOV. 7	31	38	38	39	30	26	47	24	33	18	29	21
NOV. 8	31	40	40	41	31	26	47	24	33	18	29	21
NOV. 9	31	41	42	42	31	26	47	24	33	18	29	21
NOV. 10	31	43	43	44	31	26	47	24	33	18	29	21
NOV. 11	31	44	45	45	31	27	48	24	33	18	29	21
NOV. 12	32	46	46	47	32	27	48	24	33	18	29	21
NOV. 13	32	48	48	1	32	27	48	24	33	18	29	21
NOV. 14	32	1	2	2	32	27	48	24	33	18	29	21
NOV. 15	32	3	3	4	32	27	48	24	33	18	29	21
NOV. 16	32	5	5	6	32	27	48	24	33	18	29	21
NOV. 17	32	6	7	8	33	28	48	25	34	18	29	21
NOV. 18	32	8	9	10	33	28	48	25	34	18	29	21
NOV. 19	33	10	11	11	33	28	48	25	34	18	29	21
NOV. 20	33	12	13	13	33	28	48	25	34	18	29	21
NOV. 21	33	14	15	15	33	28	48	25	34	18	29	21
NOV. 22	33	16	17	17	34	28	48	25	34	18	29	21
NOV. 23	33	18	18	19	34	29	48	25	34	18	29	21
NOV. 24	33	20	20	21	34	29	48	25	34	18	29	21
NOV. 25	34	22	22	23	34	29	48	25	34	18	29	21
NOV. 26	34	23	24	25	34	29	48	25	34	18	29	21
NOV. 27	34	25	26	27	35	29	48	25	34	18	29	21
NOV. 28	34	27	28	28	35	29	48	25	34	18	29	21
NOV. 29	34	29	30	30	35	30	1	25	34	18	29	21
NOV. 30	34	31	31	32	35	30	1	25	34	18	29	21

December

Date & Time	SUN	MOON 1	MOON 2	MOON 3	MERCURY	VENUS	MARS	JUPITER	SATURN	URANUS	NEPTUNE	PLUTO
DEC. 1	34	32	33	34	36	30	1	25	34	18	29	21
DEC. 2	34	34	35	35	36	30	1	25	34	18	29	21
DEC. 3	35	36	36	37	36	30	1	25	34	18	29	21
DEC. 4	35	37	38	38	36	30	1	25	34	18	29	21
DEC. 5	35	39	40	40	36	31	1	25	34	18	29	21
DEC. 6	35	41	41	42	37	31	1	25	34	18	29	21
DEC. 7	35	42	43	43	37	31	1	25	34	18	29	21
DEC. 8	35	44	44	45	37	31	1	25	34	18	29	21
DEC. 9	35	45	46	46	37	31	1	25	34	18	29	21
DEC. 10	35	47	48	48	37	31	1	25	34	18	29	21
DEC. 11	36	1	1	2	38	32	1	25	34	18	29	21
DEC. 12	36	2	3	3	38	32	1	25	34	18	29	21
DEC. 13	36	4	5	5	38	32	1	25	34	18	29	21
DEC. 14	36	6	6	7	38	32	1	25	34	18	29	21
DEC. 15	36	7	8	9	38	32	2	25	34	18	29	21
DEC. 16	36	9	10	11	39	32	2	25	34	18	29	21
DEC. 17	36	11	12	13	39	33	2	25	34	18	29	21
DEC. 18	36	13	14	15	39	33	2	25	34	18	29	21
DEC. 19	37	15	16	17	39	33	2	25	34	18	29	21
DEC. 20	37	17	18	19	39	33	2	25	34	18	29	21
DEC. 21	37	19	20	20	39	33	2	25	34	18	29	21
DEC. 22	37	21	22	22	40	33	2	25	34	18	29	21
DEC. 23	37	23	24	24	40	34	2	25	34	18	29	21
DEC. 24	37	25	26	26	40	34	2	25	34	18	29	21
DEC. 25	37	27	27	28	40	34	2	25	34	18	29	21
DEC. 26	38	29	29	30	40	34	2	25	34	18	29	21
DEC. 27	38	30	31	31	40	34	2	25	34	18	29	21
DEC. 28	38	32	33	33	40	34	3	25	34	18	29	21
DEC. 29	38	34	34	35	40	35	3	25	34	18	29	21
DEC. 30	38	35	36	36	41	35	3	25	34	18	29	21
DEC. 31	38	37	37	38	41	35	3	25	34	18	29	21

MOON 1 ◗ 12:01 A.M. TO 8:00 A.M.   **MOON 2 ◑ 8:01 A.M. TO 4:00 P.M.**   **MOON 3 ● 4:01 P.M. TO 12:00 A.M.**

Use only one "moon" number. Choose the column closest to your time of birth. If your place of birth is not on Eastern Standard Time, be sure to read "How to Convert to Eastern Standard Time" at the beginning of this section.

1957

January

Date & Time	SUN ☉	MOON 1 ◖	MOON 2 ◑	MOON 3 ●	MERCURY	VENUS	MARS	JUPITER	SATURN	URANUS	NEPTUNE	PLUTO
JAN. 1	38	39	39	40	41	35	3	25	34	18	29	21
JAN. 2	38	40	41	41	41	35	3	25	34	18	29	21
JAN. 3	39	42	42	43	41	35	3	25	34	18	29	21
JAN. 4	39	43	44	44	41	36	3	25	34	18	29	21
JAN. 5	39	45	45	46	40	36	3	25	34	18	29	21
JAN. 6	39	46	47	48	40	36	3	25	34	18	29	21
JAN. 7	39	48	1	1	40	36	3	25	34	18	29	21
JAN. 8	39	2	2	3	40	36	3	25	34	18	29	21
JAN. 9	39	3	4	4	40	36	3	25	34	18	29	21
JAN. 10	40	5	6	6	40	37	4	25	34	18	29	21
JAN. 11	40	7	7	8	40	37	4	25	34	18	29	21
JAN. 12	40	9	9	10	39	37	4	25	34	18	29	21
JAN. 13	40	10	11	12	39	37	4	25	34	18	29	21
JAN. 14	40	12	13	14	39	37	4	25	34	18	29	21
JAN. 15	40	14	15	16	39	37	4	25	34	18	29	21
JAN. 16	40	16	17	18	39	38	4	25	34	18	29	21
JAN. 17	41	18	19	20	39	38	4	25	34	18	29	21
JAN. 18	41	20	21	22	39	38	4	25	34	18	29	21
JAN. 19	41	22	23	24	39	38	4	25	34	18	29	21
JAN. 20	41	24	25	26	38	38	4	25	34	18	29	21
JAN. 21	41	26	27	27	38	38	4	25	34	18	29	21
JAN. 22	41	28	29	29	38	38	4	25	34	18	29	21
JAN. 23	42	30	30	31	38	39	5	25	34	18	29	21
JAN. 24	42	32	32	33	38	39	5	25	35	18	29	21
JAN. 25	42	33	34	34	39	39	5	25	35	18	29	21
JAN. 26	42	35	35	36	39	39	5	25	35	18	29	21
JAN. 27	42	37	37	38	39	39	5	25	35	18	29	21
JAN. 28	42	38	39	39	39	40	5	25	35	18	29	21
JAN. 29	42	40	40	41	39	40	5	25	35	18	29	21
JAN. 30	42	41	42	42	39	40	5	25	35	18	29	21
JAN. 31	43	43	43	44	39	40	5	25	35	18	29	21

February

Date & Time	SUN ☉	MOON 1 ◖	MOON 2 ◑	MOON 3 ●	MERCURY	VENUS	MARS	JUPITER	SATURN	URANUS	NEPTUNE	PLUTO
FEB. 1	43	44	45	46	39	40	5	25	35	18	29	21
FEB. 2	43	46	47	47	39	40	5	25	35	18	29	21
FEB. 3	43	48	48	1	39	41	5	25	35	18	29	21
FEB. 4	43	1	2	2	40	41	6	25	35	18	29	21
FEB. 5	43	3	4	4	40	41	6	25	35	18	29	21
FEB. 6	43	5	5	6	40	41	6	25	35	18	29	21
FEB. 7	43	6	7	7	40	41	6	25	35	18	29	21
FEB. 8	44	8	8	9	40	41	6	25	35	18	29	21
FEB. 9	44	10	10	11	40	42	6	25	35	18	29	21
FEB. 10	44	11	12	13	41	42	6	25	35	18	29	21
FEB. 11	44	13	14	15	41	42	6	25	35	18	29	21
FEB. 12	44	15	16	17	41	42	6	25	35	18	29	21
FEB. 13	44	17	18	19	41	42	6	25	35	18	29	21
FEB. 14	44	19	20	21	41	42	6	25	35	18	29	21
FEB. 15	44	21	22	23	41	43	6	25	35	18	29	21
FEB. 16	45	23	24	25	42	43	6	25	35	18	29	21
FEB. 17	45	25	26	27	42	43	7	25	35	17	29	21
FEB. 18	45	27	28	29	42	43	7	25	35	17	29	21
FEB. 19	45	29	30	30	42	43	7	25	35	17	29	21
FEB. 20	45	31	32	32	42	43	7	25	35	17	29	21
FEB. 21	45	33	33	34	43	44	7	25	35	17	29	21
FEB. 22	45	34	35	36	43	44	7	25	35	17	29	21
FEB. 23	46	36	37	37	43	44	7	25	35	17	29	21
FEB. 24	46	38	38	39	43	44	7	25	35	17	29	21
FEB. 25	46	39	40	40	43	44	7	25	35	17	29	21
FEB. 26	46	41	41	42	44	44	7	25	35	17	29	21
FEB. 27	46	43	43	44	44	45	7	25	35	17	29	21
FEB. 28	46	44	45	45	44	45	7	25	35	17	29	21

MOON 1 ◖ 12:01 A.M. TO 8:00 A.M.   **MOON 2 ◑** 8:01 A.M. TO 4:00 P.M.   **MOON 3 ●** 4:01 P.M. TO 12:00 A.M.

Use only one "moon" number. Choose the column closest to your time of birth. If your place of birth is not on Eastern Standard Time, be sure to read "How to Convert to Eastern Standard Time" at the beginning of this section.

1957

March

April

Date & Time	SUN ☉	MOON 1 ◐	MOON 2 ◑	MOON 3 ●	MERCURY	VENUS	MARS	JUPITER	SATURN	URANUS	NEPTUNE	PLUTO
MAR. 1	46	46	46	47	44	45	8	25	35	17	29	21
MAR. 2	46	47	48	48	44	45	8	25	35	17	29	21
MAR. 3	47	1	1	2	45	45	8	25	35	17	29	21
MAR. 4	47	2	3	4	45	45	8	25	35	17	29	21
MAR. 5	47	4	5	5	45	46	8	25	35	17	29	21
MAR. 6	47	6	6	7	46	46	8	25	35	17	29	21
MAR. 7	47	7	8	9	46	46	8	25	35	17	29	21
MAR. 8	47	9	10	10	46	46	8	25	35	17	29	21
MAR. 9	47	11	12	12	46	46	8	25	35	17	29	21
MAR. 10	47	13	13	14	46	46	8	25	35	17	29	21
MAR. 11	48	15	15	16	47	47	8	25	35	17	29	21
MAR. 12	48	17	17	18	47	47	8	25	35	17	29	21
MAR. 13	48	19	19	20	47	47	9	25	35	17	29	21
MAR. 14	48	21	21	22	47	47	9	25	35	17	29	21
MAR. 15	48	23	23	24	48	47	9	25	35	17	29	21
MAR. 16	48	25	25	26	48	47	9	25	35	17	29	21
MAR. 17	48	27	27	28	48	48	9	25	35	17	29	21
MAR. 18	48	28	29	30	48	48	9	25	35	17	29	21
MAR. 19	1	30	31	32	1	48	9	25	35	17	29	21
MAR. 20	1	32	33	33	1	48	9	25	35	17	29	21
MAR. 21	1	34	34	35	1	48	9	24	35	17	29	21
MAR. 22	1	36	36	37	1	48	9	24	35	17	29	21
MAR. 23	1	37	38	38	2	1	9	24	35	17	29	21
MAR. 24	1	39	39	40	2	1	9	24	35	17	29	21
MAR. 25	2	40	41	42	2	1	10	24	35	17	29	21
MAR. 26	2	42	43	43	2	1	10	24	35	17	29	21
MAR. 27	2	44	44	45	1	1	10	24	35	17	29	21
MAR. 28	2	45	46	46	3	1	10	24	35	17	29	21
MAR. 29	2	47	47	48	3	2	10	24	35	17	29	21
MAR. 30	2	48	1	2	3	2	10	24	35	17	29	21
MAR. 31	2	2	3	3	4	2	10	24	35	17	29	21

Date & Time	SUN ☉	MOON 1 ◐	MOON 2 ◑	MOON 3 ●	MERCURY	VENUS	MARS	JUPITER	SATURN	URANUS	NEPTUNE	PLUTO
APR. 1	2	4	4	5	4	2	10	24	35	17	29	21
APR. 2	2	5	6	6	4	2	10	24	35	17	29	21
APR. 3	3	7	8	8	5	2	10	24	35	17	29	21
APR. 4	3	9	9	10	5	2	10	24	35	17	29	21
APR. 5	3	11	11	12	5	3	11	24	35	17	29	21
APR. 6	3	12	13	14	5	3	11	24	35	17	29	21
APR. 7	3	14	15	15	5	3	11	24	35	17	29	21
APR. 8	3	16	17	17	6	3	11	24	35	17	29	21
APR. 9	3	18	19	19	6	3	11	24	35	17	29	21
APR. 10	3	20	20	21	6	3	11	24	35	17	29	21
APR. 11	4	22	22	23	6	4	11	24	35	17	29	21
APR. 12	4	24	24	25	6	4	11	24	35	17	29	21
APR. 13	4	26	26	27	7	4	11	24	35	17	29	21
APR. 14	4	28	28	29	7	4	11	24	35	17	29	21
APR. 15	4	30	30	31	7	4	11	24	35	17	29	21
APR. 16	4	31	32	32	7	4	11	24	35	17	29	21
APR. 17	4	33	34	34	7	5	12	24	35	17	29	21
APR. 18	4	35	36	36	7	5	12	24	35	17	29	21
APR. 19	5	37	37	38	7	5	12	24	35	17	29	21
APR. 20	5	38	39	39	7	5	12	24	35	17	29	21
APR. 21	5	40	41	41	7	5	12	24	35	17	29	21
APR. 22	5	42	42	43	8	5	12	24	35	17	29	21
APR. 23	5	43	44	44	8	6	12	24	35	17	29	21
APR. 24	5	45	45	46	8	6	12	24	35	17	29	21
APR. 25	6	46	47	47	8	6	12	24	35	17	29	21
APR. 26	6	48	48	1	8	6	12	24	35	17	29	21
APR. 27	6	2	2	3	8	6	12	24	35	17	29	21
APR. 28	6	3	4	4	8	6	12	24	35	17	29	21
APR. 29	6	5	5	6	7	7	13	24	35	17	29	21
APR. 30	6	7	7	8	7	7	13	24	35	17	29	21

MOON 1 ◐ 12:01 A.M. TO 8:00 A.M.   **MOON 2** ◑ 8:01 A.M. TO 4:00 P.M.   **MOON 3** ● 4:01 P.M. TO 12:00 A.M.
Use only one "moon" number. Choose the column closest to your time of birth. If your place of birth is not on
Eastern Standard Time, be sure to read "How to Convert to Eastern Standard Time" at the beginning of this section.

1957

May

June

Date & Time	SUN	MOON 1	MOON 2	MOON 3	MERCURY	VENUS	MARS	JUPITER	SATURN	URANUS	NEPTUNE	PLUTO
MAY 1	6	8	9	9	7	7	13	24	35	17	29	21
MAY 2	6	10	11	11	7	7	13	24	35	17	29	21
MAY 3	7	12	12	13	7	7	13	24	35	17	29	21
MAY 4	7	14	14	15	7	7	13	24	35	17	29	21
MAY 5	7	16	16	17	7	8	13	24	35	17	29	21
MAY 6	7	17	18	19	7	8	13	24	35	17	29	21
MAY 7	7	19	20	21	7	8	13	24	35	17	29	21
MAY 8	7	21	22	23	7	8	13	24	35	17	29	21
MAY 9	7	23	24	24	7	8	13	24	35	17	29	21
MAY 10	7	25	26	26	7	8	13	24	35	17	29	21
MAY 11	8	27	28	28	7	9	14	24	35	17	29	21
MAY 12	8	29	29	30	7	9	14	24	35	17	29	21
MAY 13	8	31	31	32	6	9	14	24	35	17	29	21
MAY 14	8	33	33	34	6	9	14	24	35	17	29	21
MAY 15	8	34	35	35	6	9	14	24	35	17	29	21
MAY 16	8	36	37	37	6	9	14	24	35	17	29	21
MAY 17	8	38	38	39	6	10	14	24	35	17	29	21
MAY 18	8	39	40	40	6	10	14	24	35	17	29	21
MAY 19	9	41	42	42	6	10	14	24	35	17	29	21
MAY 20	9	43	43	44	6	10	14	24	35	17	29	21
MAY 21	9	44	45	45	6	10	14	24	35	17	29	21
MAY 22	9	46	46	47	6	10	14	24	35	17	29	21
MAY 23	9	47	48	48	6	11	15	24	35	17	29	21
MAY 24	9	1	2	2	6	11	15	24	35	17	29	21
MAY 25	10	3	3	4	6	11	15	24	35	17	29	21
MAY 26	10	4	5	5	7	11	15	24	35	17	29	21
MAY 27	10	6	7	7	7	11	15	24	34	17	29	21
MAY 28	10	8	8	9	7	11	15	24	34	17	29	21
MAY 29	10	10	10	11	7	12	15	24	34	17	29	21
MAY 30	10	11	12	13	7	12	15	24	34	17	29	21
MAY 31	10	13	14	14	7	12	15	24	34	17	29	21

Date & Time	SUN	MOON 1	MOON 2	MOON 3	MERCURY	VENUS	MARS	JUPITER	SATURN	URANUS	NEPTUNE	PLUTO
JUN. 1	10	15	16	16	7	12	15	24	34	18	29	21
JUN. 2	10	17	18	18	7	12	15	24	34	18	29	21
JUN. 3	11	19	20	20	7	12	15	24	34	18	29	21
JUN. 4	11	21	21	22	8	13	16	24	34	18	29	21
JUN. 5	11	23	23	24	8	13	16	24	34	18	29	21
JUN. 6	11	25	25	26	8	13	16	24	34	18	29	21
JUN. 7	11	26	27	28	8	13	16	24	34	18	29	21
JUN. 8	11	28	29	30	8	13	16	24	34	18	29	21
JUN. 9	11	30	31	31	8	13	16	24	34	18	29	21
JUN. 10	11	32	33	33	9	14	16	24	34	18	29	21
JUN. 11	12	34	34	35	9	14	16	24	34	18	29	21
JUN. 12	12	35	36	37	9	14	16	24	34	18	29	21
JUN. 13	12	37	38	38	9	14	16	24	34	18	29	21
JUN. 14	12	39	39	40	9	14	16	24	34	18	29	21
JUN. 15	12	40	41	42	10	14	16	24	34	18	29	21
JUN. 16	12	42	43	43	10	14	17	24	34	18	29	21
JUN. 17	12	44	44	45	10	15	17	24	34	18	29	21
JUN. 18	12	45	46	46	10	15	17	24	34	18	29	21
JUN. 19	13	47	47	48	10	15	17	24	34	18	29	21
JUN. 20	13	48	1	2	11	15	17	24	34	18	29	21
JUN. 21	13	2	3	3	11	15	17	24	34	18	29	21
JUN. 22	13	4	4	5	11	15	17	24	34	18	29	21
JUN. 23	13	5	6	6	11	16	17	24	34	18	29	21
JUN. 24	13	7	8	8	12	16	17	24	34	18	29	21
JUN. 25	14	9	9	10	12	16	17	24	34	18	29	21
JUN. 26	14	11	11	12	12	16	17	24	34	18	29	21
JUN. 27	14	12	13	14	12	16	17	24	34	18	29	21
JUN. 28	14	14	15	16	13	16	18	24	34	18	29	21
JUN. 29	14	16	17	18	13	17	18	24	34	18	29	21
JUN. 30	14	18	19	20	13	17	18	24	34	18	29	21

MOON 1 12:01 A.M. TO 8:00 A.M.   **MOON 2** 8:01 A.M. TO 4:00 P.M.   **MOON 3** 4:01 P.M. TO 12:00 A.M.

Use only one "moon" number. Choose the column closest to your time of birth. If your place of birth is not on Eastern Standard Time, be sure to read "How to Convert to Eastern Standard Time" at the beginning of this section.

1957

July

Date & Time	SUN	MOON 1	MOON 2	MOON 3	MERCURY	VENUS	MARS	JUPITER	SATURN	URANUS	NEPTUNE	PLUTO
JUL. 1	14	20	21	22	14	17	18	24	34	18	29	21
JUL. 2	14	22	23	24	14	17	18	24	34	18	29	21
JUL. 3	15	24	25	25	14	17	18	24	34	18	29	21
JUL. 4	15	26	27	27	15	17	18	24	34	18	29	21
JUL. 5	15	28	29	29	15	18	18	24	34	18	29	21
JUL. 6	15	30	30	31	15	18	18	24	34	18	29	21
JUL. 7	15	31	32	33	15	18	18	24	34	18	29	21
JUL. 8	15	33	34	34	16	18	18	24	34	18	29	21
JUL. 9	15	35	36	36	16	18	18	24	34	18	29	21
JUL. 10	15	37	37	38	16	18	19	24	34	18	29	21
JUL. 11	16	38	39	39	17	19	19	24	34	18	29	21
JUL. 12	16	40	41	41	17	19	19	24	34	18	29	21
JUL. 13	16	42	42	43	17	19	19	24	34	18	29	21
JUL. 14	16	43	44	44	17	19	19	24	34	18	29	21
JUL. 15	16	45	45	46	18	19	19	24	34	18	29	21
JUL. 16	16	46	47	47	18	19	19	24	34	18	29	21
JUL. 17	16	48	48	1	18	20	19	25	34	18	29	21
JUL. 18	16	2	2	3	18	20	19	25	34	18	29	21
JUL. 19	17	3	4	4	19	20	19	25	34	18	29	21
JUL. 20	17	5	5	6	19	20	19	25	34	18	29	21
JUL. 21	17	6	7	8	19	20	19	25	34	18	29	21
JUL. 22	17	8	9	9	20	20	20	25	34	18	29	21
JUL. 23	17	10	10	11	20	20	20	25	34	18	29	21
JUL. 24	17	12	12	13	20	21	20	25	34	18	29	21
JUL. 25	17	14	14	15	20	21	20	25	34	18	29	21
JUL. 26	18	16	16	17	20	21	20	25	34	18	29	21
JUL. 27	18	18	18	19	20	21	20	25	34	18	29	21
JUL. 28	18	20	20	21	21	21	20	25	34	18	29	21
JUL. 29	18	22	22	23	21	21	20	25	34	18	29	21
JUL. 30	18	24	24	25	21	22	20	25	34	18	29	21
JUL. 31	18	26	26	27	21	22	20	25	34	18	29	21

August

Date & Time	SUN	MOON 1	MOON 2	MOON 3	MERCURY	VENUS	MARS	JUPITER	SATURN	URANUS	NEPTUNE	PLUTO
AUG. 1	18	27	28	29	21	22	20	25	34	18	29	21
AUG. 2	18	29	30	30	22	22	20	25	34	18	29	21
AUG. 3	19	31	32	32	22	22	21	25	34	18	29	21
AUG. 4	19	33	33	34	22	22	21	25	34	18	29	21
AUG. 5	19	35	35	36	22	23	21	25	34	18	29	21
AUG. 6	19	36	37	37	22	23	21	25	34	18	29	21
AUG. 7	19	38	38	39	22	23	21	25	34	18	29	21
AUG. 8	19	40	40	41	23	23	21	25	34	18	29	21
AUG. 9	19	41	42	42	23	23	21	25	34	18	29	21
AUG. 10	19	43	43	44	23	23	21	25	34	18	29	21
AUG. 11	20	44	45	45	23	24	21	25	34	18	29	21
AUG. 12	20	46	46	47	23	24	21	25	34	18	29	21
AUG. 13	20	48	48	1	23	24	21	25	34	18	29	21
AUG. 14	20	1	2	2	23	24	21	25	34	18	29	21
AUG. 15	20	3	3	4	24	24	22	25	34	18	29	21
AUG. 16	20	4	5	5	24	24	22	25	34	18	29	21
AUG. 17	20	6	6	7	24	25	22	25	34	18	29	21
AUG. 18	20	8	8	9	24	25	22	25	34	18	29	21
AUG. 19	21	9	10	10	24	25	22	25	34	18	29	21
AUG. 20	21	11	12	12	24	25	22	25	34	18	29	21
AUG. 21	21	13	13	14	24	25	22	25	34	18	29	21
AUG. 22	21	15	15	16	24	25	22	25	34	18	29	21
AUG. 23	21	17	17	18	24	25	22	25	34	18	29	21
AUG. 24	21	19	19	20	24	26	22	25	34	18	29	21
AUG. 25	21	21	21	22	24	26	22	25	34	18	29	21
AUG. 26	22	23	23	24	24	26	22	25	34	18	29	21
AUG. 27	22	25	25	26	24	26	23	26	34	18	29	21
AUG. 28	22	27	27	28	24	26	23	26	34	18	29	21
AUG. 29	22	29	29	30	24	26	23	26	34	18	29	21
AUG. 30	22	31	31	32	24	27	23	26	34	18	29	21
AUG. 31	22	32	33	34	24	27	23	26	34	18	29	21

MOON 1 ◐ 12:01 A.M. TO 8:00 A.M.   **MOON 2** ◑ 8:01 A.M. TO 4:00 P.M.   **MOON 3** ● 4:01 P.M. TO 12:00 A.M.

Use only one "moon" number. Choose the column closest to your time of birth. If your place of birth is not on Eastern Standard Time, be sure to read "How to Convert to Eastern Standard Time" at the beginning of this section.

1957

September — October

Date & Time	SUN	MOON 1	MOON 2	MOON 3	MERCURY	VENUS	MARS	JUPITER	SATURN	URANUS	NEPTUNE	PLUTO
SEP. 1	22	34	35	35	24	27	23	26	34	18	29	21
SEP. 2	22	36	36	37	24	27	23	26	34	18	29	21
SEP. 3	23	38	38	39	24	27	23	26	34	18	29	21
SEP. 4	23	39	40	40	24	27	23	26	34	18	29	21
SEP. 5	23	41	41	42	24	28	23	26	34	18	29	21
SEP. 6	23	42	43	43	24	28	23	26	34	18	29	21
SEP. 7	23	44	45	45	24	28	23	26	34	18	29	21
SEP. 8	23	46	46	47	23	28	24	26	34	18	29	21
SEP. 9	23	47	48	48	23	28	24	26	34	18	29	21
SEP. 10	23	1	1	2	23	28	24	26	34	18	29	21
SEP. 11	24	2	3	3	23	28	24	26	34	18	29	21
SEP. 12	24	4	4	5	23	29	24	26	34	18	29	21
SEP. 13	24	6	6	7	23	29	24	26	34	18	29	21
SEP. 14	24	7	8	8	23	29	24	26	34	18	29	21
SEP. 15	24	9	9	10	23	29	24	26	34	18	29	21
SEP. 16	24	10	11	12	23	29	24	26	34	18	29	21
SEP. 17	24	12	13	13	22	29	24	26	34	18	29	21
SEP. 18	24	14	15	15	22	30	24	26	34	18	29	21
SEP. 19	25	16	17	17	22	30	25	26	34	18	29	21
SEP. 20	25	18	18	19	22	30	25	26	34	18	29	21
SEP. 21	25	20	20	21	22	30	25	26	34	18	29	21
SEP. 22	25	22	22	23	23	30	25	26	34	18	29	21
SEP. 23	25	24	24	25	23	30	25	26	34	18	29	21
SEP. 24	25	26	27	27	23	31	25	26	34	18	29	21
SEP. 25	26	28	29	29	23	31	25	26	34	18	29	21
SEP. 26	26	30	30	31	23	31	25	26	34	18	29	21
SEP. 27	26	32	32	33	23	31	25	26	34	18	29	21
SEP. 28	26	34	34	35	23	31	25	26	34	18	29	21
SEP. 29	26	35	36	36	23	31	25	26	34	18	29	21
SEP. 30	26	37	38	38	24	31	25	26	34	18	29	21
OCT. 1	26	39	39	40	24	32	26	26	34	18	29	21
OCT. 2	26	40	41	41	24	32	26	26	34	18	29	21
OCT. 3	27	42	43	43	24	32	26	27	34	18	29	21
OCT. 4	27	44	44	45	24	32	26	27	34	18	29	21
OCT. 5	27	45	46	46	25	32	26	27	34	18	29	21
OCT. 6	27	47	47	48	25	32	26	27	34	18	29	21
OCT. 7	27	48	1	1	25	33	26	27	34	18	29	21
OCT. 8	27	2	2	3	25	33	26	27	34	18	29	21
OCT. 9	27	3	4	5	26	33	26	27	34	18	29	21
OCT. 10	27	5	6	6	26	33	26	27	34	18	29	21
OCT. 11	28	7	7	8	26	33	26	27	34	18	29	21
OCT. 12	28	8	9	10	26	33	27	27	34	18	29	21
OCT. 13	28	10	11	11	27	33	27	27	34	18	29	21
OCT. 14	28	12	12	13	27	34	27	27	34	18	29	21
OCT. 15	28	14	14	15	27	34	27	27	34	18	29	21
OCT. 16	28	15	16	17	27	34	27	27	34	18	29	21
OCT. 17	28	17	18	18	27	34	27	27	34	18	29	21
OCT. 18	28	19	20	20	28	34	27	27	34	18	29	21
OCT. 19	29	21	22	22	28	34	27	27	34	18	29	21
OCT. 20	29	23	24	24	28	35	27	27	34	18	29	21
OCT. 21	29	25	26	26	28	35	27	27	34	18	29	21
OCT. 22	29	27	28	28	29	35	27	27	34	18	29	21
OCT. 23	29	29	30	30	29	35	27	27	35	18	29	21
OCT. 24	29	31	32	32	29	35	28	27	35	18	29	21
OCT. 25	29	33	33	34	29	35	28	27	35	18	29	21
OCT. 26	30	35	35	36	29	35	28	27	35	18	29	21
OCT. 27	30	36	37	38	30	36	28	27	35	18	29	21
OCT. 28	30	38	39	39	30	36	28	27	35	18	29	21
OCT. 29	30	40	40	41	30	36	28	27	35	18	29	21
OCT. 30	30	41	42	43	30	36	28	27	35	19	29	21
OCT. 31	30	43	44	44	31	36	28	27	35	19	29	21

MOON 1 ☽ 12:01 A.M. TO 8:00 A.M.   **MOON 2** ◑ 8:01 A.M. TO 4:00 P.M.   **MOON 3** ● 4:01 P.M. TO 12:00 A.M.

Use only one "moon" number. Choose the column closest to your time of birth. If your place of birth is not on Eastern Standard Time, be sure to read "How to Convert to Eastern Standard Time" at the beginning of this section.

November

Date & Time	SUN	MOON 1	MOON 2	MOON 3	MERCURY	VENUS	MARS	JUPITER	SATURN	URANUS	NEPTUNE	PLUTO
NOV. 1	30	45	45	46	31	36	28	27	35	19	29	21
NOV. 2	30	46	47	47	31	36	28	27	35	19	29	21
NOV. 3	31	48	48	1	31	37	28	27	35	19	29	21
NOV. 4	31	1	2	2	31	37	29	27	35	19	29	21
NOV. 5	31	3	4	4	32	37	29	27	35	19	29	21
NOV. 6	31	5	5	6	32	37	29	27	35	19	29	21
NOV. 7	31	6	7	7	32	37	29	28	35	19	29	21
NOV. 8	31	8	9	9	32	37	29	28	35	19	29	21
NOV. 9	31	10	10	11	32	37	29	28	35	19	29	21
NOV. 10	31	11	12	13	33	38	29	28	35	19	29	21
NOV. 11	31	13	14	14	33	38	29	28	35	19	29	21
NOV. 12	32	15	16	16	33	38	29	28	35	19	29	21
NOV. 13	32	17	17	18	33	38	29	28	35	19	29	21
NOV. 14	32	19	19	20	33	38	29	28	35	19	29	21
NOV. 15	32	20	21	22	34	38	30	28	35	19	29	21
NOV. 16	32	22	23	24	34	38	30	28	35	19	29	21
NOV. 17	32	24	25	26	34	39	30	28	35	19	29	21
NOV. 18	32	26	27	28	34	39	30	28	35	19	29	21
NOV. 19	33	28	29	29	34	39	30	28	35	19	29	21
NOV. 20	33	30	31	31	35	39	30	28	35	19	29	21
NOV. 21	33	32	33	33	35	39	30	28	35	19	29	21
NOV. 22	33	34	34	35	35	39	30	28	35	19	29	21
NOV. 23	33	36	36	37	35	39	30	28	35	19	29	21
NOV. 24	33	37	38	39	35	39	30	28	35	19	29	21
NOV. 25	34	39	40	40	36	40	30	28	35	19	29	21
NOV. 26	34	41	41	42	36	40	31	28	35	19	29	21
NOV. 27	34	43	43	44	36	40	31	28	35	19	29	21
NOV. 28	34	44	45	45	36	40	31	28	35	19	29	21
NOV. 29	34	46	46	47	36	40	31	28	35	19	29	21
NOV. 30	34	47	48	48	37	40	31	28	35	19	29	21

December

Date & Time	SUN	MOON 1	MOON 2	MOON 3	MERCURY	VENUS	MARS	JUPITER	SATURN	URANUS	NEPTUNE	PLUTO
DEC. 1	34	1	1	2	37	40	31	28	35	19	29	21
DEC. 2	34	2	3	4	37	40	31	28	35	19	29	21
DEC. 3	35	4	5	5	37	41	31	28	35	19	29	21
DEC. 4	35	6	6	7	37	41	31	28	35	19	29	21
DEC. 5	35	7	8	9	37	41	31	28	35	19	29	21
DEC. 6	35	9	10	10	38	41	31	28	35	19	29	21
DEC. 7	35	11	11	12	38	41	32	28	35	18	29	21
DEC. 8	35	13	13	14	38	41	32	28	35	18	29	21
DEC. 9	35	14	15	16	38	41	32	28	35	18	29	21
DEC. 10	35	16	17	18	38	41	32	28	35	18	29	21
DEC. 11	36	18	19	19	38	41	32	28	35	18	29	21
DEC. 12	36	20	21	21	38	42	32	28	35	18	29	21
DEC. 13	36	22	23	23	38	42	32	28	35	18	29	21
DEC. 14	36	24	24	25	38	42	32	28	35	18	30	21
DEC. 15	36	26	26	27	38	42	32	28	35	18	30	21
DEC. 16	36	28	28	29	39	42	32	28	35	18	30	21
DEC. 17	36	29	30	31	38	42	32	28	35	18	30	21
DEC. 18	36	31	32	33	38	42	33	29	35	18	30	21
DEC. 19	37	33	34	34	38	42	33	29	35	18	30	21
DEC. 20	37	35	36	36	38	42	33	29	35	18	30	21
DEC. 21	37	37	37	38	38	42	33	29	35	18	30	21
DEC. 22	37	39	39	40	38	42	33	29	35	18	30	21
DEC. 23	37	40	41	41	38	43	33	29	35	18	30	21
DEC. 24	37	42	42	43	38	43	33	29	35	18	30	21
DEC. 25	37	44	44	45	38	43	33	29	35	18	30	21
DEC. 26	38	45	46	46	37	43	33	29	35	18	30	21
DEC. 27	38	47	47	48	37	43	33	29	35	18	30	21
DEC. 28	38	48	1	1	37	43	33	29	36	18	30	21
DEC. 29	38	2	2	3	37	43	34	29	36	18	30	21
DEC. 30	38	4	4	5	37	43	34	29	36	18	30	21
DEC. 31	38	5	6	6	37	43	34	29	36	18	30	21

MOON 1 ☽ 12:01 A.M. TO 8:00 A.M.   **MOON 2** ☽ 8:01 A.M. TO 4:00 P.M.   **MOON 3** ● 4:01 P.M. TO 12:00 A.M.

Use only one "moon" number. Choose the column closest to your time of birth. If your place of birth is not on Eastern Standard Time, be sure to read "How to Convert to Eastern Standard Time" at the beginning of this section.

1958

January

Date & Time	SUN	MOON 1	MOON 2	MOON 3	MERCURY	VENUS	MARS	JUPITER	SATURN	URANUS	NEPTUNE	PLUTO
JAN. 1	38	7	7	8	37	43	34	29	36	18	30	21
JAN. 2	38	8	9	10	36	43	34	29	36	18	30	21
JAN. 3	39	10	11	11	36	43	34	29	36	18	30	21
JAN. 4	39	12	13	13	36	43	34	29	36	18	30	21
JAN. 5	39	14	14	15	36	43	34	29	36	18	30	21
JAN. 6	39	16	16	17	36	43	34	29	36	18	30	21
JAN. 7	39	18	18	19	36	43	34	29	36	18	30	21
JAN. 8	39	20	20	21	36	43	34	29	36	18	30	21
JAN. 9	39	21	22	23	36	43	35	29	36	18	30	21
JAN. 10	40	23	24	25	37	43	35	29	36	18	30	21
JAN. 11	40	25	26	27	37	43	35	29	36	18	30	21
JAN. 12	40	27	28	28	37	43	35	29	36	18	30	21
JAN. 13	40	29	30	30	37	43	35	29	36	18	30	21
JAN. 14	40	31	31	32	37	43	35	29	36	18	30	21
JAN. 15	40	33	33	34	37	43	35	29	36	18	30	21
JAN. 16	40	34	35	36	37	43	35	29	36	18	30	21
JAN. 17	41	36	37	37	37	43	35	29	36	18	30	21
JAN. 18	41	38	39	39	37	43	35	29	36	18	30	21
JAN. 19	41	40	40	41	38	43	35	29	36	18	30	21
JAN. 20	41	41	42	42	38	43	36	29	36	18	30	21
JAN. 21	41	43	44	44	38	43	36	29	36	18	30	21
JAN. 22	41	45	45	46	38	43	36	29	36	18	30	21
JAN. 23	42	46	47	47	38	43	36	29	36	18	30	21
JAN. 24	42	48	48	1	38	42	36	29	36	18	30	21
JAN. 25	42	1	2	2	39	42	36	29	36	18	30	21
JAN. 26	42	3	4	4	39	42	36	29	36	18	30	21
JAN. 27	42	5	5	6	39	42	36	29	36	18	30	21
JAN. 28	42	6	7	7	39	42	36	29	36	18	30	21
JAN. 29	42	8	8	9	39	42	36	29	36	18	30	21
JAN. 30	42	9	10	11	40	42	37	29	36	18	30	21
JAN. 31	43	11	12	12	40	42	37	29	36	18	30	21

February

Date & Time	SUN	MOON 1	MOON 2	MOON 3	MERCURY	VENUS	MARS	JUPITER	SATURN	URANUS	NEPTUNE	PLUTO
FEB. 1	43	13	14	14	40	42	37	29	36	18	30	21
FEB. 2	43	15	15	16	40	42	37	29	36	18	30	21
FEB. 3	43	17	17	18	40	42	37	29	36	18	30	21
FEB. 4	43	19	19	20	40	42	37	29	36	18	30	21
FEB. 5	43	21	21	22	41	42	37	29	36	18	30	21
FEB. 6	43	23	23	24	41	41	37	29	36	18	30	21
FEB. 7	43	25	25	26	41	41	37	29	36	18	30	21
FEB. 8	44	27	27	28	41	41	37	29	36	18	30	21
FEB. 9	44	29	29	30	41	41	37	29	36	18	30	21
FEB. 10	44	30	31	32	42	41	38	29	36	18	30	21
FEB. 11	44	32	33	33	42	41	38	29	36	18	30	21
FEB. 12	44	34	35	35	42	41	38	29	36	18	30	21
FEB. 13	44	36	36	37	42	41	38	29	36	18	30	21
FEB. 14	44	38	38	39	43	41	38	29	36	18	30	21
FEB. 15	44	39	40	40	43	41	38	29	36	18	30	21
FEB. 16	45	41	41	42	43	41	38	29	36	18	30	21
FEB. 17	45	43	43	44	43	41	38	29	36	18	30	21
FEB. 18	45	44	45	45	43	41	38	29	36	18	30	21
FEB. 19	45	46	46	47	44	41	38	29	36	18	30	21
FEB. 20	45	47	48	48	44	41	39	29	36	18	30	21
FEB. 21	45	1	1	2	44	41	39	29	36	18	30	21
FEB. 22	45	3	3	4	44	41	39	29	36	18	30	21
FEB. 23	46	4	5	5	45	41	39	29	36	18	30	21
FEB. 24	46	6	6	7	45	41	39	29	36	18	30	21
FEB. 25	46	7	8	8	45	41	39	29	36	18	30	21
FEB. 26	46	9	9	10	45	41	39	29	36	18	30	21
FEB. 27	46	11	11	12	45	41	39	29	36	18	30	21
FEB. 28	46	12	13	13	46	41	39	29	36	18	30	21

MOON 1 ◑ 12:01 A.M. TO 8:00 A.M.   **MOON 2** ◐ 8:01 A.M. TO 4:00 P.M.   **MOON 3** ● 4:01 P.M. TO 12:00 A.M.

Use only one "moon" number. Choose the column closest to your time of birth. If your place of birth is not on Eastern Standard Time, be sure to read "How to Convert to Eastern Standard Time" at the beginning of this section.

Date & Time	SUN	MOON 1	MOON 2	MOON 3	MERCURY	VENUS	MARS	JUPITER	SATURN	URANUS	NEPTUNE	PLUTO
MAR. 1	46	14	15	15	46	41	39	29	36	18	30	21
MAR. 2	46	16	17	17	46	41	40	29	36	18	30	21
MAR. 3	47	18	18	19	47	41	40	29	36	18	30	21
MAR. 4	47	20	20	21	47	42	40	29	36	18	30	21
MAR. 5	47	22	22	23	47	42	40	29	36	18	30	21
MAR. 6	47	24	24	25	47	42	40	29	36	18	30	21
MAR. 7	47	26	27	27	48	42	40	29	36	18	30	21
MAR. 8	47	28	29	29	48	42	40	29	36	18	30	21
MAR. 9	47	30	30	31	48	42	40	29	36	18	30	21
MAR. 10	47	32	32	33	48	42	40	29	36	18	30	21
MAR. 11	48	34	34	35	1	42	40	29	36	18	30	21
MAR. 12	48	35	36	37	1	42	40	29	36	18	30	21
MAR. 13	48	37	38	38	1	42	41	29	36	18	30	21
MAR. 14	48	39	39	40	1	42	41	29	36	18	30	21
MAR. 15	48	41	41	42	2	42	41	29	36	18	30	21
MAR. 16	48	42	43	43	2	43	41	29	36	18	30	21
MAR. 17	48	44	44	45	2	43	41	29	36	18	30	21
MAR. 18	48	45	46	46	2	43	41	29	36	18	30	21
MAR. 19	1	47	48	48	3	43	41	29	36	18	30	21
MAR. 20	1	1	1	2	3	43	41	29	36	18	30	21
MAR. 21	1	2	3	3	3	43	41	29	36	18	30	21
MAR. 22	1	4	5	5	3	43	41	29	36	18	30	21
MAR. 23	1	5	6	6	4	43	42	29	36	18	30	21
MAR. 24	1	7	7	8	4	43	42	29	36	18	30	21
MAR. 25	2	8	9	10	4	43	42	29	36	18	30	21
MAR. 26	2	10	11	11	4	44	42	29	36	18	30	21
MAR. 27	2	12	12	13	4	44	42	29	36	18	30	21
MAR. 28	2	13	14	15	4	44	42	29	36	18	30	21
MAR. 29	2	15	16	16	5	44	42	29	36	18	30	21
MAR. 30	2	17	18	18	5	44	42	29	36	18	30	21
MAR. 31	2	19	20	20	5	44	42	29	36	18	30	21

Date & Time	SUN	MOON 1	MOON 2	MOON 3	MERCURY	VENUS	MARS	JUPITER	SATURN	URANUS	NEPTUNE	PLUTO
APR. 1	2	21	22	22	5	44	42	29	36	18	30	21
APR. 2	2	23	24	24	5	44	43	29	36	18	29	21
APR. 3	3	25	26	26	5	45	43	29	36	18	29	21
APR. 4	3	27	28	28	5	45	43	29	36	18	29	21
APR. 5	3	29	30	30	5	45	43	29	36	18	29	21
APR. 6	3	31	32	32	5	45	43	29	36	18	29	21
APR. 7	3	33	34	34	5	45	43	29	36	18	29	21
APR. 8	3	35	35	36	5	45	43	29	36	18	29	21
APR. 9	3	37	37	38	5	45	43	29	36	18	29	21
APR. 10	3	38	39	40	5	45	43	29	36	18	29	21
APR. 11	4	40	41	41	5	46	43	29	36	18	29	21
APR. 12	4	42	42	43	5	46	44	29	36	18	29	21
APR. 13	4	43	44	44	5	46	44	29	36	18	29	21
APR. 14	4	45	46	46	5	46	44	29	36	18	29	21
APR. 15	4	47	47	48	5	46	44	29	36	18	29	21
APR. 16	4	48	1	1	5	46	44	29	36	18	29	21
APR. 17	4	2	2	3	4	46	44	29	36	18	29	21
APR. 18	4	3	4	4	4	47	44	29	36	18	29	21
APR. 19	5	5	5	5	4	47	44	29	36	18	29	21
APR. 20	5	6	7	8	4	47	44	28	36	18	29	21
APR. 21	5	8	9	9	4	47	44	28	36	18	29	21
APR. 22	5	10	10	11	4	47	44	28	36	18	29	21
APR. 23	5	11	12	12	4	47	45	28	36	18	29	21
APR. 24	5	13	14	14	4	47	45	28	36	18	29	21
APR. 25	6	15	15	16	4	47	45	28	36	18	29	21
APR. 26	6	17	17	18	4	48	45	28	36	18	29	21
APR. 27	6	18	19	20	4	48	45	28	36	18	29	21
APR. 28	6	20	21	21	4	48	45	28	36	18	29	21
APR. 29	6	22	23	23	4	48	45	28	36	18	29	21
APR. 30	6	24	25	25	4	48	45	28	36	18	29	21

MOON 1 ☽ 12:01 A.M. TO 8:00 A.M.   **MOON 2** ☽ 8:01 A.M. TO 4:00 P.M.   **MOON 3** ● 4:01 P.M. TO 12:00 A.M.

Use only one "moon" number. Choose the column closest to your time of birth. If your place of birth is not on Eastern Standard Time, be sure to read "How to Convert to Eastern Standard Time" at the beginning of this section.

1958

May

June

Date & Time	SUN	MOON 1	MOON 2	MOON 3	MERCURY	VENUS	MARS	JUPITER	SATURN	URANUS	NEPTUNE	PLUTO
MAY 1	6	26	27	27	4	48	45	28	36	18	29	21
MAY 2	6	28	29	29	4	48	45	28	36	18	29	21
MAY 3	7	30	31	31	4	1	46	28	36	18	29	21
MAY 4	7	32	33	33	4	1	46	28	36	18	29	21
MAY 5	7	34	35	35	4	1	46	28	36	18	29	21
MAY 6	7	36	36	37	4	1	46	28	36	18	29	21
MAY 7	7	38	38	39	4	1	46	28	36	18	29	21
MAY 8	7	39	40	41	4	1	46	28	36	18	29	21
MAY 9	7	41	42	42	4	2	46	28	36	18	29	21
MAY 10	7	43	43	44	4	2	46	28	36	18	29	21
MAY 11	8	45	45	46	4	2	46	28	36	18	29	21
MAY 12	8	46	47	47	4	2	46	28	36	18	29	21
MAY 13	8	48	48	1	4	2	47	28	36	18	29	21
MAY 14	8	1	2	2	5	2	47	28	36	18	29	21
MAY 15	8	3	3	4	5	2	47	28	36	18	29	21
MAY 16	8	4	5	6	5	3	47	28	36	18	29	21
MAY 17	8	6	7	7	5	3	47	28	36	18	29	21
MAY 18	8	8	8	9	5	3	47	28	36	18	29	21
MAY 19	9	9	10	10	5	3	47	28	36	18	29	21
MAY 20	9	11	12	12	5	3	47	28	36	18	29	21
MAY 21	9	13	13	14	7	3	47	28	36	18	29	21
MAY 22	9	14	15	16	7	3	47	28	36	18	29	21
MAY 23	9	16	17	17	6	4	48	28	36	18	29	21
MAY 24	9	18	19	19	6	4	48	28	36	18	29	21
MAY 25	10	20	20	21	6	4	48	28	36	18	29	21
MAY 26	10	22	22	23	7	4	48	28	36	18	29	21
MAY 27	10	23	24	25	7	4	48	28	36	18	29	21
MAY 28	10	25	26	27	7	4	48	28	36	18	29	21
MAY 29	10	27	28	29	7	5	48	28	36	18	29	21
MAY 30	10	29	30	31	7	5	48	28	36	18	29	21
MAY 31	10	31	32	32	8	5	48	28	36	18	29	21

Date & Time	SUN	MOON 1	MOON 2	MOON 3	MERCURY	VENUS	MARS	JUPITER	SATURN	URANUS	NEPTUNE	PLUTO
JUN. 1	10	33	34	34	8	5	48	28	36	18	29	21
JUN. 2	10	35	36	36	8	5	48	28	36	18	29	21
JUN. 3	11	37	38	38	8	5	1	28	36	18	29	21
JUN. 4	11	39	39	40	9	5	1	28	36	18	29	21
JUN. 5	11	41	41	42	9	5	1	28	36	18	29	21
JUN. 6	11	42	43	43	9	6	1	28	36	18	29	21
JUN. 7	11	44	45	45	9	6	1	28	36	18	29	21
JUN. 8	11	46	46	47	10	6	1	28	36	18	29	21
JUN. 9	11	47	48	48	10	6	1	28	36	18	29	21
JUN. 10	11	1	1	2	10	6	1	28	36	18	29	21
JUN. 11	12	2	3	3	10	7	1	28	36	18	29	21
JUN. 12	12	4	4	5	11	7	1	28	36	18	29	21
JUN. 13	12	6	6	7	11	7	2	28	36	18	29	21
JUN. 14	12	7	8	8	11	7	2	28	36	18	29	21
JUN. 15	12	9	9	10	12	7	2	28	36	18	29	21
JUN. 16	12	10	11	12	12	7	2	28	36	18	29	21
JUN. 17	12	12	13	13	12	7	2	28	36	18	29	21
JUN. 18	12	14	14	15	12	8	2	28	36	18	29	21
JUN. 19	13	16	16	17	13	8	2	28	36	18	29	21
JUN. 20	13	17	18	19	13	8	2	28	36	18	29	21
JUN. 21	13	19	20	21	13	8	2	28	36	18	29	21
JUN. 22	13	21	22	22	14	8	2	28	36	18	29	21
JUN. 23	13	23	24	24	14	8	2	28	36	18	29	21
JUN. 24	13	25	26	26	14	9	3	28	36	18	29	21
JUN. 25	14	27	27	28	14	9	3	28	36	18	29	21
JUN. 26	14	29	29	30	15	9	3	28	36	18	29	21
JUN. 27	14	31	31	32	15	9	3	28	36	18	29	21
JUN. 28	14	32	33	34	15	9	3	28	36	18	29	21
JUN. 29	14	34	35	36	16	9	3	28	36	18	29	21
JUN. 30	14	36	37	37	16	9	3	28	36	18	29	21

MOON 1 ◑ 12:01 A.M. TO 8:00 A.M.   **MOON 2** ◑ 8:01 A.M. TO 4:00 P.M.   **MOON 3** ● 4:01 P.M. TO 12:00 A.M.
Use only one "moon" number. Choose the column closest to your time of birth. If your place of birth is not on Eastern Standard Time, be sure to read "How to Convert to Eastern Standard Time" at the beginning of this section.

1958

July

Date & Time	SUN ☀	MOON 1 ◖	MOON 2 ◐	MOON 3 ●	MERCURY	VENUS	MARS	JUPITER	SATURN	URANUS	NEPTUNE	PLUTO
JUL. 1	14	38	39	39	16	10	3	28	36	18	29	21
JUL. 2	14	40	40	41	16	10	3	28	36	18	29	21
JUL. 3	15	42	42	43	17	10	3	28	36	18	29	21
JUL. 4	15	43	44	44	17	10	3	28	36	18	29	21
JUL. 5	15	45	46	46	17	10	4	28	36	18	29	21
JUL. 6	15	47	47	48	17	10	4	28	36	18	29	21
JUL. 7	15	48	1	1	17	11	4	28	36	18	29	21
JUL. 8	15	2	2	3	18	11	4	28	36	18	29	21
JUL. 9	15	3	4	4	18	11	4	28	36	18	29	21
JUL. 10	15	5	6	6	18	11	4	28	36	18	29	21
JUL. 11	16	7	7	8	18	11	4	28	36	18	29	21
JUL. 12	16	8	9	9	19	11	4	28	36	18	29	21
JUL. 13	16	10	10	11	19	12	4	28	36	18	29	21
JUL. 14	16	12	12	13	19	12	4	28	36	18	29	21
JUL. 15	16	13	14	14	19	12	4	28	36	18	29	21
JUL. 16	16	15	16	16	19	12	5	28	36	18	29	21
JUL. 17	16	17	18	18	20	12	5	28	36	18	29	21
JUL. 18	16	19	19	20	20	12	5	28	36	18	29	21
JUL. 19	17	21	21	22	20	12	5	28	36	18	29	21
JUL. 20	17	23	23	24	20	13	5	28	36	18	29	21
JUL. 21	17	24	25	26	20	13	5	28	36	18	29	21
JUL. 22	17	26	27	28	20	13	5	28	36	18	29	21
JUL. 23	17	28	29	30	21	13	5	28	36	18	29	21
JUL. 24	17	30	31	31	21	13	5	28	36	18	29	21
JUL. 25	17	32	33	33	21	13	5	28	36	18	29	21
JUL. 26	18	34	34	35	21	14	5	28	36	18	29	21
JUL. 27	18	36	36	37	21	14	5	28	36	18	29	21
JUL. 28	18	38	38	39	21	14	6	28	36	19	29	21
JUL. 29	18	39	40	40	21	14	6	28	36	19	29	21
JUL. 30	18	41	42	42	21	14	6	28	36	19	29	21
JUL. 31	18	43	43	44	22	14	6	28	36	19	29	21

August

Date & Time	SUN ☀	MOON 1 ◖	MOON 2 ◐	MOON 3 ●	MERCURY	VENUS	MARS	JUPITER	SATURN	URANUS	NEPTUNE	PLUTO
AUG. 1	18	44	45	46	22	15	6	28	36	19	29	21
AUG. 2	18	46	47	47	22	15	6	28	36	19	29	21
AUG. 3	19	48	48	1	22	15	6	28	36	19	29	21
AUG. 4	19	1	2	2	22	15	6	28	36	19	29	21
AUG. 5	19	3	3	4	22	15	6	28	36	19	29	21
AUG. 6	19	5	5	6	22	15	6	28	36	19	29	21
AUG. 7	19	6	7	7	22	15	6	28	36	19	29	21
AUG. 8	19	8	8	9	22	16	6	28	36	19	29	21
AUG. 9	19	9	10	10	22	16	6	28	36	19	29	21
AUG. 10	19	11	12	12	22	16	7	28	36	19	29	21
AUG. 11	20	13	13	14	22	16	7	28	36	19	29	21
AUG. 12	20	14	15	16	22	16	7	28	36	19	29	21
AUG. 13	20	16	17	17	22	17	7	28	36	19	29	21
AUG. 14	20	18	19	19	22	17	7	28	36	19	29	21
AUG. 15	20	20	21	21	22	17	7	28	36	19	29	21
AUG. 16	20	22	23	23	22	17	7	28	36	19	29	21
AUG. 17	20	24	25	25	22	17	7	29	36	19	29	21
AUG. 18	20	26	26	27	22	17	7	29	36	19	29	21
AUG. 19	21	28	28	29	21	17	7	29	36	19	29	21
AUG. 20	21	30	30	31	21	18	7	29	36	19	29	21
AUG. 21	21	32	32	33	21	18	7	29	36	19	29	21
AUG. 22	21	33	34	35	21	18	7	29	36	19	29	21
AUG. 23	21	35	36	36	21	18	7	29	36	19	29	21
AUG. 24	21	37	38	38	21	18	8	29	36	19	29	21
AUG. 25	21	39	39	40	21	18	8	29	36	19	29	21
AUG. 26	22	41	41	42	21	19	8	29	36	19	29	21
AUG. 27	22	42	43	43	21	19	8	29	36	19	29	21
AUG. 28	22	44	45	45	20	19	8	29	36	19	29	21
AUG. 29	22	46	46	47	20	19	8	29	36	19	29	21
AUG. 30	22	47	48	48	20	19	8	29	36	19	29	21
AUG. 31	22	1	1	2	20	19	8	29	36	19	29	21

MOON 1 ◖ 12:01 A.M. TO 8:00 A.M.   **MOON 2** ◐ 8:01 A.M. TO 4:00 P.M.   **MOON 3** ● 4:01 P.M. TO 12:00 A.M.

Use only one "moon" number. Choose the column closest to your time of birth. If your place of birth is not on Eastern Standard Time, be sure to read "How to Convert to Eastern Standard Time" at the beginning of this section.

1958

September

October

Date & Time	SUN	MOON 1	MOON 2	MOON 3	MERCURY	VENUS	MARS	JUPITER	SATURN	URANUS	NEPTUNE	PLUTO
SEP. 1	22	2	3	4	20	20	8	29	36	19	29	21
SEP. 2	22	4	5	5	20	20	8	29	36	19	29	21
SEP. 3	23	6	6	7	20	20	8	29	36	19	29	21
SEP. 4	23	7	8	8	20	20	8	29	36	19	29	21
SEP. 5	23	9	9	10	20	20	8	29	36	19	29	21
SEP. 6	23	10	11	11	20	20	8	29	36	19	29	21
SEP. 7	23	12	13	13	20	20	8	29	36	19	29	21
SEP. 8	23	14	14	15	21	21	8	29	36	19	29	21
SEP. 9	23	15	16	17	21	21	8	29	36	19	29	21
SEP. 10	23	17	18	19	21	21	9	29	36	19	29	21
SEP. 11	24	19	20	20	21	21	9	29	36	19	29	21
SEP. 12	24	21	22	22	21	21	9	29	36	19	29	21
SEP. 13	24	23	24	24	21	22	9	29	36	19	29	21
SEP. 14	24	25	26	26	22	22	9	29	36	19	29	21
SEP. 15	24	27	28	28	22	22	9	29	36	19	29	21
SEP. 16	24	29	30	30	22	22	9	29	36	19	29	21
SEP. 17	24	31	32	32	22	22	9	29	36	19	29	21
SEP. 18	24	33	34	34	22	22	9	29	36	19	29	21
SEP. 19	25	35	35	36	23	23	9	29	36	19	29	21
SEP. 20	25	37	37	38	23	23	9	29	36	19	29	21
SEP. 21	25	38	39	40	23	23	9	29	36	19	29	21
SEP. 22	25	40	41	41	23	23	9	29	36	19	29	21
SEP. 23	25	42	42	43	24	23	9	29	36	19	29	21
SEP. 24	25	44	44	45	24	23	9	29	36	19	29	21
SEP. 25	26	45	46	46	24	24	9	29	36	19	29	21
SEP. 26	26	47	47	48	24	24	9	29	36	19	29	21
SEP. 27	26	48	1	1	25	24	9	29	36	19	29	21
SEP. 28	26	2	3	3	25	24	9	30	36	19	29	21
SEP. 29	26	4	4	5	25	24	9	30	36	19	29	21
SEP. 30	26	5	6	6	25	24	9	30	36	19	29	21

Date & Time	SUN	MOON 1	MOON 2	MOON 3	MERCURY	VENUS	MARS	JUPITER	SATURN	URANUS	NEPTUNE	PLUTO
OCT. 1	26	7	7	8	26	25	9	30	36	19	29	21
OCT. 2	26	8	9	9	26	25	9	30	36	19	29	21
OCT. 3	27	10	10	11	26	25	9	30	36	19	29	21
OCT. 4	27	12	12	13	26	25	9	30	36	19	29	21
OCT. 5	27	13	14	14	26	25	9	30	36	19	29	21
OCT. 6	27	15	15	16	26	25	9	30	36	19	29	21
OCT. 7	27	17	17	18	27	26	9	30	36	19	29	21
OCT. 8	27	18	19	20	27	26	9	30	36	19	29	21
OCT. 9	27	20	21	22	27	26	9	30	36	19	29	21
OCT. 10	27	22	23	23	28	26	9	30	36	19	29	21
OCT. 11	28	24	25	25	28	26	9	30	36	19	29	21
OCT. 12	28	26	27	28	28	26	9	30	36	19	29	21
OCT. 13	28	28	29	30	28	27	9	30	36	19	29	21
OCT. 14	28	30	31	32	28	27	9	30	36	19	29	21
OCT. 15	28	32	33	34	29	27	9	30	36	19	30	21
OCT. 16	28	34	35	35	29	27	9	30	36	19	30	21
OCT. 17	28	36	37	37	29	27	9	30	36	19	30	21
OCT. 18	28	38	39	39	29	27	9	30	36	19	30	21
OCT. 19	29	40	40	41	30	28	9	30	36	19	30	21
OCT. 20	29	41	42	43	30	28	9	30	36	19	30	21
OCT. 21	29	43	44	44	30	28	9	30	36	19	30	21
OCT. 22	29	45	45	46	30	28	9	30	36	19	30	21
OCT. 23	29	46	47	47	30	28	9	30	36	19	30	21
OCT. 24	29	48	1	1	31	28	9	30	36	19	30	21
OCT. 25	29	2	2	3	31	29	9	30	36	19	30	21
OCT. 26	30	3	4	4	31	29	9	30	36	19	30	21
OCT. 27	30	5	5	6	31	29	9	30	36	19	30	21
OCT. 28	30	6	7	7	31	29	9	30	36	19	30	21
OCT. 29	30	8	8	9	32	29	9	30	36	19	30	21
OCT. 30	30	10	10	11	32	29	9	30	36	19	30	21
OCT. 31	30	11	12	12	32	30	9	30	36	19	30	21

MOON 1 ◗ 12:01 A.M. TO 8:00 A.M.   **MOON 2** ◖ 8:01 A.M. TO 4:00 P.M.   **MOON 3** ● 4:01 P.M. TO 12:00 A.M.
Use only one "moon" number. Choose the column closest to your time of birth. If your place of birth is not on Eastern Standard Time, be sure to read "How to Convert to Eastern Standard Time" at the beginning of this section.

1958

November

Date & Time	SUN	MOON 1	MOON 2	MOON 3	MERCURY	VENUS	MARS	JUPITER	SATURN	URANUS	NEPTUNE	PLUTO
NOV. 1	30	13	13	14	32	30	9	30	36	19	30	21
NOV. 2	30	14	15	16	32	30	9	30	36	19	30	21
NOV. 3	31	16	17	17	33	30	9	31	36	19	30	21
NOV. 4	31	18	18	19	33	30	9	31	36	19	30	21
NOV. 5	31	20	20	21	33	30	9	31	36	19	30	21
NOV. 6	31	21	22	23	33	31	9	31	36	19	30	21
NOV. 7	31	23	24	25	33	31	9	31	36	19	30	22
NOV. 8	31	25	26	27	34	31	9	31	36	19	30	22
NOV. 9	31	27	28	29	34	31	8	31	36	19	30	22
NOV. 10	31	29	30	31	34	31	8	31	36	19	30	22
NOV. 11	31	31	32	33	34	31	8	31	36	19	30	22
NOV. 12	32	33	34	35	34	32	8	31	36	19	30	22
NOV. 13	32	35	36	37	34	32	8	31	36	19	30	22
NOV. 14	32	37	38	38	35	32	8	31	36	19	30	22
NOV. 15	32	39	40	40	35	32	8	31	36	19	30	22
NOV. 16	32	41	41	42	35	32	8	31	36	19	30	22
NOV. 17	32	43	43	44	35	32	8	31	36	19	30	22
NOV. 18	32	44	45	45	35	33	8	31	36	19	30	22
NOV. 19	33	46	47	47	35	33	8	31	36	19	30	22
NOV. 20	33	48	48	1	36	33	8	31	36	19	30	22
NOV. 21	33	1	2	2	36	33	8	31	36	19	30	22
NOV. 22	33	3	3	4	36	33	8	31	36	19	30	22
NOV. 23	33	4	5	5	36	33	8	31	36	19	30	22
NOV. 24	33	6	6	7	36	34	8	31	36	19	30	22
NOV. 25	34	8	8	9	36	34	8	31	36	19	30	22
NOV. 26	34	9	10	10	36	34	8	31	36	19	30	22
NOV. 27	34	11	11	12	36	34	8	31	36	19	30	22
NOV. 28	34	12	13	13	36	34	8	31	36	19	30	22
NOV. 29	34	14	15	15	36	34	8	31	36	19	30	22
NOV. 30	34	16	16	17	36	35	8	31	36	19	30	22

December

Date & Time	SUN	MOON 1	MOON 2	MOON 3	MERCURY	VENUS	MARS	JUPITER	SATURN	URANUS	NEPTUNE	PLUTO
DEC. 1	34	17	18	19	36	35	8	31	36	19	30	22
DEC. 2	34	19	20	20	36	35	7	31	36	19	30	22
DEC. 3	35	21	22	22	36	35	7	31	36	19	30	22
DEC. 4	35	23	23	24	36	35	7	31	36	19	30	22
DEC. 5	35	25	25	26	36	35	7	31	36	19	30	22
DEC. 6	35	27	27	28	36	36	7	32	37	19	30	22
DEC. 7	35	28	29	30	36	36	7	32	37	19	30	22
DEC. 8	35	30	31	32	36	36	7	32	37	19	30	22
DEC. 9	35	32	33	34	35	36	7	32	37	19	30	22
DEC. 10	35	34	35	36	35	36	7	32	37	19	30	22
DEC. 11	36	36	37	38	35	36	7	32	37	19	30	22
DEC. 12	36	38	39	40	35	37	7	32	37	19	30	22
DEC. 13	36	40	41	41	35	37	7	32	37	19	30	22
DEC. 14	36	42	43	43	35	37	7	32	37	19	30	22
DEC. 15	36	44	44	45	34	37	7	32	37	19	30	22
DEC. 16	36	45	46	47	34	37	7	32	37	19	30	22
DEC. 17	36	47	48	48	34	37	7	32	37	19	30	22
DEC. 18	36	1	1	2	34	38	7	32	37	19	30	22
DEC. 19	37	2	3	3	34	38	7	32	37	19	30	22
DEC. 20	37	4	4	5	34	38	7	32	37	19	30	22
DEC. 21	37	5	6	7	34	38	7	32	37	19	30	22
DEC. 22	37	7	7	8	34	38	7	32	37	19	30	22
DEC. 23	37	9	9	10	34	38	7	32	37	19	30	22
DEC. 24	37	10	11	11	34	39	7	32	37	19	30	22
DEC. 25	37	12	12	13	34	39	7	32	37	19	30	22
DEC. 26	38	14	14	15	35	39	7	32	37	19	30	22
DEC. 27	38	15	16	16	35	39	7	32	37	19	30	22
DEC. 28	38	17	18	18	35	39	7	32	37	19	30	22
DEC. 29	38	19	19	20	35	39	7	32	37	19	30	22
DEC. 30	38	21	21	22	35	40	7	32	37	19	30	22
DEC. 31	38	22	23	24	35	40	7	32	37	19	30	22

MOON 1 ☽ 12:01 A.M. TO 8:00 A.M.   **MOON 2** ◑ 8:01 A.M. TO 4:00 P.M.   **MOON 3** ● 4:01 P.M. TO 12:00 A.M.
Use only one "moon" number. Choose the column closest to your time of birth. If your place of birth is not on Eastern Standard Time, be sure to read "How to Convert to Eastern Standard Time" at the beginning of this section.

1959

January

Date & Time	SUN	MOON 1	MOON 2	MOON 3	MERCURY	VENUS	MARS	JUPITER	SATURN	URANUS	NEPTUNE	PLUTO
JAN. 1	38	24	25	25	35	40	7	32	37	19	30	22
JAN. 2	38	26	27	27	36	40	7	32	37	19	30	22
JAN. 3	39	28	29	29	36	40	7	32	37	19	30	22
JAN. 4	39	30	30	31	36	40	7	32	37	19	30	22
JAN. 5	39	32	32	33	36	41	7	32	37	19	30	22
JAN. 6	39	34	34	35	36	41	7	32	37	19	30	21
JAN. 7	39	36	36	37	36	41	7	32	37	19	30	21
JAN. 8	39	37	38	39	37	41	7	32	37	19	30	21
JAN. 9	39	39	40	41	37	41	7	32	37	19	30	21
JAN. 10	40	41	42	42	37	41	8	32	37	19	30	21
JAN. 11	40	43	44	44	37	42	8	32	37	19	30	21
JAN. 12	40	45	45	46	37	42	8	32	37	19	30	21
JAN. 13	40	46	47	48	37	42	8	32	37	19	30	21
JAN. 14	40	48	1	1	38	42	8	32	37	19	30	21
JAN. 15	40	2	2	3	38	42	8	32	37	19	30	21
JAN. 16	40	3	4	4	38	42	8	33	37	19	30	21
JAN. 17	41	5	5	6	38	43	8	33	37	19	30	21
JAN. 18	41	7	7	8	38	43	8	33	37	19	30	21
JAN. 19	41	8	9	9	39	43	8	33	37	19	30	21
JAN. 20	41	10	10	11	39	43	8	33	37	19	30	21
JAN. 21	41	11	12	12	39	43	8	33	37	19	30	21
JAN. 22	41	13	14	14	39	43	8	33	37	19	30	21
JAN. 23	42	15	15	16	39	44	8	33	37	19	30	21
JAN. 24	42	16	17	18	40	44	8	33	37	19	30	21
JAN. 25	42	18	19	20	40	44	8	33	37	19	30	21
JAN. 26	42	20	21	21	40	44	8	33	37	19	30	21
JAN. 27	42	22	22	23	40	44	8	33	37	19	30	21
JAN. 28	42	24	24	25	40	44	8	33	37	19	30	21
JAN. 29	42	26	26	27	41	45	8	33	37	19	30	21
JAN. 30	42	27	28	29	41	45	8	33	37	19	30	21
JAN. 31	43	29	30	31	41	45	8	33	37	19	30	21

February

Date & Time	SUN	MOON 1	MOON 2	MOON 3	MERCURY	VENUS	MARS	JUPITER	SATURN	URANUS	NEPTUNE	PLUTO
FEB. 1	43	31	32	32	41	45	8	33	37	19	30	21
FEB. 2	43	33	34	34	42	45	9	33	37	19	30	21
FEB. 3	43	35	36	36	42	45	9	33	37	19	30	21
FEB. 4	43	37	37	38	42	46	9	33	37	19	30	21
FEB. 5	43	39	39	40	42	46	9	33	37	19	30	21
FEB. 6	43	41	41	42	43	46	9	33	37	19	30	21
FEB. 7	43	42	43	44	43	46	9	33	37	19	30	21
FEB. 8	44	44	45	45	43	46	9	33	37	19	30	21
FEB. 9	44	46	46	47	43	46	9	33	37	19	30	21
FEB. 10	44	48	48	1	43	47	9	33	37	19	30	21
FEB. 11	44	1	2	2	44	47	9	33	37	19	30	21
FEB. 12	44	3	3	4	44	47	9	33	37	19	30	21
FEB. 13	44	4	5	5	44	47	9	33	38	19	30	21
FEB. 14	44	6	6	7	44	47	9	33	38	19	30	21
FEB. 15	44	8	8	9	45	47	9	33	38	19	30	21
FEB. 16	45	9	10	10	45	48	9	33	38	19	30	21
FEB. 17	45	11	11	12	45	48	9	33	38	19	30	21
FEB. 18	45	12	13	13	45	48	9	33	38	19	30	21
FEB. 19	45	14	15	15	45	48	9	33	38	19	30	21
FEB. 20	45	16	16	17	46	48	10	33	38	19	30	21
FEB. 21	45	18	18	19	46	48	10	33	38	19	30	21
FEB. 22	45	19	20	21	46	1	10	33	38	19	30	21
FEB. 23	46	21	22	22	46	1	10	33	38	19	30	21
FEB. 24	46	23	24	24	47	1	10	33	38	19	30	21
FEB. 25	46	25	26	26	47	1	10	33	38	19	30	21
FEB. 26	46	27	28	28	47	1	10	33	38	19	30	21
FEB. 27	46	29	30	30	47	1	10	33	38	19	30	21
FEB. 28	46	31	31	32	48	2	10	33	38	19	30	21

MOON 1 ☽ 12:01 A.M. TO 8:00 A.M.   **MOON 2** ☾ 8:01 A.M. TO 4:00 P.M.   **MOON 3** ● 4:01 P.M. TO 12:00 A.M.
Use only one "moon" number. Choose the column closest to your time of birth. If your place of birth is not on Eastern Standard Time, be sure to read "How to Convert to Eastern Standard Time" at the beginning of this section.

March

Date & Time	SUN	MOON 1	MOON 2	MOON 3	MERCURY	VENUS	MARS	JUPITER	SATURN	URANUS	NEPTUNE	PLUTO
MAR. 1	46	33	33	34	48	2	10	33	38	19	30	21
MAR. 2	46	35	35	36	48	2	10	33	38	19	30	21
MAR. 3	47	36	37	38	48	2	10	33	38	19	30	21
MAR. 4	47	38	39	39	1	2	10	33	38	19	30	21
MAR. 5	47	40	41	41	1	2	10	33	38	19	30	21
MAR. 6	47	42	42	43	1	3	10	33	38	19	30	21
MAR. 7	47	44	44	45	1	3	11	33	38	19	30	21
MAR. 8	47	45	46	46	2	3	11	33	38	19	30	21
MAR. 9	47	47	48	48	2	3	11	33	38	19	30	21
MAR. 10	47	1	1	2	2	3	11	33	38	19	30	21
MAR. 11	48	2	3	3	2	3	11	33	38	19	30	21
MAR. 12	48	4	4	5	2	4	11	33	38	19	30	21
MAR. 13	48	5	6	7	2	4	11	33	38	19	30	21
MAR. 14	48	7	8	8	2	4	11	33	38	19	30	21
MAR. 15	48	9	9	10	3	4	11	33	38	19	30	21
MAR. 16	48	10	11	11	3	4	11	33	38	19	30	21
MAR. 17	48	12	12	13	3	4	11	33	38	19	30	21
MAR. 18	48	13	14	15	3	5	11	33	38	19	30	21
MAR. 19	1	15	16	16	3	5	11	33	38	19	30	21
MAR. 20	1	17	17	18	3	5	11	33	38	19	30	21
MAR. 21	1	19	19	20	3	5	11	33	38	19	30	21
MAR. 22	1	20	21	22	3	5	12	33	38	19	30	21
MAR. 23	1	22	23	24	3	5	12	33	38	19	30	21
MAR. 24	1	24	25	26	3	5	12	33	38	19	30	21
MAR. 25	2	26	27	27	2	6	12	33	38	19	30	21
MAR. 26	2	28	29	29	2	6	12	33	38	19	30	21
MAR. 27	2	30	31	31	2	6	12	33	38	19	30	21
MAR. 28	2	32	33	33	2	6	12	33	38	19	30	21
MAR. 29	2	34	35	35	2	6	12	33	38	19	30	21
MAR. 30	2	36	37	37	2	6	12	33	38	19	30	21
MAR. 31	2	38	38	39	2	7	12	33	38	19	30	21

April

Date & Time	SUN	MOON 1	MOON 2	MOON 3	MERCURY	VENUS	MARS	JUPITER	SATURN	URANUS	NEPTUNE	PLUTO
APR. 1	2	40	40	41	2	7	12	33	38	19	30	21
APR. 2	2	41	42	43	2	7	12	33	38	19	30	21
APR. 3	3	43	44	44	2	7	12	33	38	19	30	21
APR. 4	3	45	45	46	1	7	13	33	38	19	30	21
APR. 5	3	47	47	48	1	7	13	33	38	19	30	21
APR. 6	3	48	1	1	1	8	13	33	38	19	30	21
APR. 7	3	2	2	3	1	8	13	33	38	19	30	21
APR. 8	3	3	4	4	1	8	13	33	38	19	30	21
APR. 9	3	5	6	6	1	8	13	33	38	19	30	21
APR. 10	3	7	7	8	1	8	13	33	38	19	30	21
APR. 11	4	8	9	9	1	8	13	33	38	19	30	21
APR. 12	4	10	10	11	1	9	13	33	38	19	30	21
APR. 13	4	11	12	12	1	9	13	33	38	19	30	21
APR. 14	4	13	13	14	1	9	13	33	38	19	30	21
APR. 15	4	15	15	16	1	9	13	33	38	19	30	21
APR. 16	4	16	17	17	1	9	13	33	38	19	30	21
APR. 17	4	18	18	19	1	9	13	33	38	19	30	21
APR. 18	4	20	20	21	1	9	14	33	38	19	30	21
APR. 19	5	21	22	23	1	10	14	33	38	19	30	21
APR. 20	5	23	24	25	1	10	14	33	38	19	30	21
APR. 21	5	25	26	27	1	10	14	33	38	19	30	21
APR. 22	5	27	28	29	2	10	14	33	38	19	30	21
APR. 23	5	29	30	31	2	10	14	33	38	19	30	21
APR. 24	5	31	32	33	2	10	14	33	38	19	30	21
APR. 25	6	33	34	35	2	11	14	33	38	19	30	21
APR. 26	6	35	36	37	2	11	14	33	38	19	30	21
APR. 27	6	37	38	39	2	11	14	33	38	19	30	21
APR. 28	6	39	40	40	2	11	14	33	38	19	30	21
APR. 29	6	41	42	42	2	11	14	33	38	19	30	21
APR. 30	6	43	43	44	3	11	14	33	38	19	30	21

MOON 1 ☽ 12:01 A.M. TO 8:00 A.M. **MOON 2** ◐ 8:01 A.M. TO 4:00 P.M. **MOON 3** ● 4:01 P.M. TO 12:00 A.M.
Use only one "moon" number. Choose the column closest to your time of birth. If your place of birth is not on Eastern Standard Time, be sure to read "How to Convert to Eastern Standard Time" at the beginning of this section.

1959

May

June

Date & Time	SUN	MOON 1	MOON 2	MOON 3	MERCURY	VENUS	MARS	JUPITER	SATURN	URANUS	NEPTUNE	PLUTO
MAY 1	6	44	45	46	3	12	15	33	38	19	30	21
MAY 2	6	46	47	47	3	12	15	33	38	19	30	21
MAY 3	7	48	48	1	3	12	15	33	38	19	30	21
MAY 4	7	1	2	2	3	12	15	33	38	19	30	21
MAY 5	7	3	4	4	3	12	15	33	38	19	30	21
MAY 6	7	5	5	6	4	12	15	33	38	19	30	21
MAY 7	7	6	7	7	4	12	15	33	38	19	30	21
MAY 8	7	8	8	9	4	13	15	33	38	19	30	21
MAY 9	7	9	10	10	4	13	15	33	38	19	30	21
MAY 10	7	11	11	12	4	13	15	33	38	19	30	21
MAY 11	8	13	13	14	5	13	15	33	38	19	30	21
MAY 12	8	14	15	15	5	13	15	33	38	19	30	21
MAY 13	8	16	16	17	5	13	15	33	38	19	30	21
MAY 14	8	17	18	19	5	14	16	33	38	19	30	21
MAY 15	8	19	20	20	5	14	16	33	38	19	30	21
MAY 16	8	21	21	22	6	14	16	33	38	19	30	21
MAY 17	8	23	23	24	6	14	16	33	38	19	30	21
MAY 18	8	24	25	26	6	14	16	33	38	19	30	21
MAY 19	9	26	27	28	6	14	16	33	38	19	30	21
MAY 20	9	28	29	30	7	14	16	33	38	19	30	21
MAY 21	9	30	31	32	7	15	16	33	38	19	30	21
MAY 22	9	32	33	34	7	15	16	33	38	19	30	21
MAY 23	9	34	35	36	7	15	16	33	38	19	30	21
MAY 24	9	36	37	38	8	15	16	32	38	19	30	21
MAY 25	10	38	39	40	8	15	16	32	38	19	30	21
MAY 26	10	40	41	42	8	15	16	32	38	19	30	21
MAY 27	10	42	43	43	9	15	16	32	38	19	30	21
MAY 28	10	44	45	45	9	16	17	32	38	19	30	21
MAY 29	10	46	46	47	9	16	17	32	38	19	30	21
MAY 30	10	47	48	48	9	16	17	32	38	19	30	21
MAY 31	10	1	2	2	10	16	17	32	38	19	30	21

Date & Time	SUN	MOON 1	MOON 2	MOON 3	MERCURY	VENUS	MARS	JUPITER	SATURN	URANUS	NEPTUNE	PLUTO
JUN. 1	10	3	3	4	10	16	17	32	38	19	30	21
JUN. 2	10	4	5	5	10	16	17	32	38	19	30	21
JUN. 3	11	6	6	7	11	16	17	32	38	19	30	21
JUN. 4	11	7	8	8	11	17	17	32	38	19	30	21
JUN. 5	11	9	9	10	11	17	17	32	38	19	30	21
JUN. 6	11	11	11	12	11	17	17	32	38	19	30	21
JUN. 7	11	12	13	13	12	17	17	32	38	19	30	21
JUN. 8	11	14	14	15	12	17	18	32	38	19	30	21
JUN. 9	11	15	16	16	12	17	18	32	38	19	30	21
JUN. 10	11	17	18	18	13	17	18	32	38	19	30	21
JUN. 11	12	19	19	20	13	18	18	32	38	19	30	21
JUN. 12	12	20	21	22	13	18	18	32	38	19	30	21
JUN. 13	12	22	23	23	13	18	18	32	38	19	30	21
JUN. 14	12	24	25	25	14	18	18	32	38	19	30	21
JUN. 15	12	26	26	27	14	18	18	32	38	19	30	21
JUN. 16	12	28	28	29	14	18	18	32	38	19	30	21
JUN. 17	12	30	30	31	14	18	18	32	38	19	30	21
JUN. 18	12	32	32	33	15	19	18	32	38	19	30	21
JUN. 19	13	34	34	35	15	19	18	32	38	19	30	21
JUN. 20	13	36	36	37	15	19	18	32	38	19	30	21
JUN. 21	13	38	38	39	15	19	19	32	38	19	30	21
JUN. 22	13	40	40	41	16	19	19	32	38	19	30	21
JUN. 23	13	41	42	43	16	19	19	32	37	19	30	21
JUN. 24	13	43	44	45	16	19	19	32	37	19	30	21
JUN. 25	14	45	46	46	16	19	19	32	37	19	30	21
JUN. 26	14	47	47	48	16	20	19	32	37	19	30	21
JUN. 27	14	1	1	2	17	20	19	32	37	19	30	21
JUN. 28	14	2	3	3	17	20	19	32	37	19	30	21
JUN. 29	14	4	4	5	17	20	19	32	37	19	30	21
JUN. 30	14	5	6	6	17	20	19	32	37	19	30	21

MOON 1 ◐ 12:01 A.M. TO 8:00 A.M.   **MOON 2** ◑ 8:01 A.M. TO 4:00 P.M.   **MOON 3** ● 4:01 P.M. TO 12:00 A.M.
Use only one "moon" number. Choose the column closest to your time of birth. If your place of birth is not on Eastern Standard Time, be sure to read "How to Convert to Eastern Standard Time" at the beginning of this section.

1959

July

August

Date & Time	SUN	MOON 1 ◗	MOON 2 ◖	MOON 3 ●	MERCURY	VENUS	MARS	JUPITER	SATURN	URANUS	NEPTUNE	PLUTO
JUL. 1	14	7	7	8	17	20	19	32	37	19	30	21
JUL. 2	14	8	9	10	18	20	19	32	37	19	30	21
JUL. 3	15	10	11	11	18	20	20	32	37	19	30	21
JUL. 4	15	12	12	13	18	20	20	32	37	19	30	21
JUL. 5	15	13	14	14	18	21	20	32	37	19	30	21
JUL. 6	15	15	15	16	18	21	20	32	37	19	30	21
JUL. 7	15	17	17	18	18	21	20	32	37	19	30	21
JUL. 8	15	18	19	19	19	21	20	32	37	19	30	21
JUL. 9	15	20	21	21	19	21	20	32	37	19	30	21
JUL. 10	15	22	22	23	19	21	20	32	37	19	30	21
JUL. 11	16	24	24	25	19	21	20	32	37	19	30	21
JUL. 12	16	25	26	27	19	21	20	32	37	19	30	21
JUL. 13	16	27	28	28	19	21	20	32	37	19	30	21
JUL. 14	16	29	30	30	19	22	20	32	37	19	30	21
JUL. 15	16	31	32	32	19	22	21	32	37	19	30	21
JUL. 16	16	33	33	34	19	22	21	32	37	19	30	21
JUL. 17	16	35	35	36	19	22	21	32	37	19	30	21
JUL. 18	16	37	37	38	19	22	21	32	37	19	30	21
JUL. 19	17	39	39	40	19	22	21	32	37	19	30	21
JUL. 20	17	41	41	42	20	22	21	32	37	19	30	21
JUL. 21	17	43	43	44	20	22	21	32	37	19	30	21
JUL. 22	17	44	45	46	20	22	21	32	37	19	30	21
JUL. 23	17	46	47	47	20	22	21	32	37	19	30	21
JUL. 24	17	48	48	1	20	22	21	32	37	19	30	21
JUL. 25	17	2	2	3	20	22	21	32	37	19	30	21
JUL. 26	18	3	4	4	19	23	21	32	37	19	30	21
JUL. 27	18	5	5	6	19	23	22	32	37	19	30	21
JUL. 28	18	6	7	7	19	23	22	32	37	19	30	21
JUL. 29	18	8	9	9	19	23	22	32	37	19	30	21
JUL. 30	18	10	10	11	19	23	22	32	37	19	30	21
JUL. 31	18	11	12	12	19	23	22	32	37	19	30	21

Date & Time	SUN	MOON 1 ◗	MOON 2 ◖	MOON 3 ●	MERCURY	VENUS	MARS	JUPITER	SATURN	URANUS	NEPTUNE	PLUTO
AUG. 1	18	13	13	14	19	23	22	32	37	19	30	21
AUG. 2	18	14	15	16	19	23	22	32	37	19	30	21
AUG. 3	19	16	17	17	19	23	22	32	37	19	30	21
AUG. 4	19	18	18	19	19	23	22	32	37	19	30	21
AUG. 5	19	20	20	21	19	23	22	32	37	19	30	21
AUG. 6	19	21	22	22	19	23	22	32	37	19	30	21
AUG. 7	19	23	24	24	18	23	22	32	37	19	30	21
AUG. 8	19	25	26	26	18	23	23	32	37	19	30	21
AUG. 9	19	27	27	28	18	23	23	32	37	19	30	21
AUG. 10	19	29	29	30	18	23	23	32	37	19	30	21
AUG. 11	20	30	31	32	18	23	23	32	37	19	30	21
AUG. 12	20	32	33	34	18	23	23	32	37	19	30	21
AUG. 13	20	34	35	36	18	23	23	32	37	19	30	21
AUG. 14	20	36	37	37	18	23	23	32	37	19	30	21
AUG. 15	20	38	39	39	18	23	23	32	37	19	30	21
AUG. 16	20	40	41	41	18	23	23	32	37	19	30	21
AUG. 17	20	42	42	43	18	23	23	32	37	19	30	21
AUG. 18	20	44	44	45	18	23	23	32	37	19	30	21
AUG. 19	21	45	46	47	18	23	23	32	37	19	30	21
AUG. 20	21	47	48	48	18	23	24	32	37	19	30	21
AUG. 21	21	1	2	2	18	23	24	32	37	19	30	21
AUG. 22	21	3	3	4	18	23	24	32	37	19	30	21
AUG. 23	21	4	5	5	18	23	24	32	37	19	30	21
AUG. 24	21	6	6	7	19	23	24	32	37	19	30	21
AUG. 25	21	7	8	9	19	23	24	32	37	19	30	21
AUG. 26	22	9	10	10	19	23	24	32	37	19	30	21
AUG. 27	22	11	11	12	19	22	24	32	37	19	30	21
AUG. 28	22	12	13	13	19	22	24	32	37	19	30	21
AUG. 29	22	14	14	15	19	22	24	32	37	19	30	21
AUG. 30	22	16	16	17	20	22	24	32	37	19	30	22
AUG. 31	22	17	18	18	20	22	24	32	37	19	30	22

MOON 1 ◗ 12:01 A.M. TO 8:00 A.M.   **MOON 2** ◖ 8:01 A.M. TO 4:00 P.M.   **MOON 3** ● 4:01 P.M. TO 12:00 A.M.
Use only one "moon" number. Choose the column closest to your time of birth. If your place of birth is not on
Eastern Standard Time, be sure to read "How to Convert to Eastern Standard Time" at the beginning of this section.

1959

September   October

Date & Time	SUN	MOON 1	MOON 2	MOON 3	MERCURY	VENUS	MARS	JUPITER	SATURN	URANUS	NEPTUNE	PLUTO
SEP. 1	22	19	20	20	20	22	25	32	37	19	30	22
SEP. 2	22	21	21	22	20	22	25	32	37	19	30	22
SEP. 3	23	23	23	24	21	22	25	32	37	19	30	22
SEP. 4	23	24	25	26	21	22	25	32	37	19	30	22
SEP. 5	23	26	27	27	21	22	25	32	37	19	30	22
SEP. 6	23	28	29	29	21	22	25	32	37	19	30	22
SEP. 7	23	30	31	31	21	22	25	32	37	19	30	22
SEP. 8	23	32	33	33	22	21	25	32	37	19	30	22
SEP. 9	23	34	34	35	22	21	25	32	37	19	30	22
SEP. 10	23	36	36	37	22	21	25	32	37	19	30	22
SEP. 11	24	38	38	39	23	21	25	32	37	19	30	22
SEP. 12	24	39	40	41	23	21	25	32	37	19	30	22
SEP. 13	24	41	42	43	23	21	26	32	37	19	30	22
SEP. 14	24	43	44	44	23	21	26	32	37	19	30	22
SEP. 15	24	45	45	46	24	21	26	33	37	19	30	22
SEP. 16	24	47	47	48	24	21	26	33	37	19	30	22
SEP. 17	24	48	1	2	24	21	26	33	37	19	30	22
SEP. 18	24	2	3	3	24	21	26	33	37	20	30	22
SEP. 19	25	4	4	5	25	21	26	33	37	20	30	22
SEP. 20	25	5	6	6	25	21	26	33	37	20	30	22
SEP. 21	25	7	7	8	25	21	26	33	37	20	30	22
SEP. 22	25	9	9	10	25	21	26	33	37	20	30	22
SEP. 23	25	10	11	11	25	21	26	33	37	20	30	22
SEP. 24	25	12	12	13	26	21	27	33	37	20	30	22
SEP. 25	26	13	14	14	26	21	27	33	37	20	30	22
SEP. 26	26	15	15	16	26	21	27	33	37	20	30	22
SEP. 27	26	17	17	18	26	21	27	33	37	20	30	22
SEP. 28	26	18	19	19	27	21	27	33	37	20	30	22
SEP. 29	26	20	21	21	27	21	27	33	37	20	30	22
SEP. 30	26	22	22	23	27	21	27	33	37	20	30	22

Date & Time	SUN	MOON 1	MOON 2	MOON 3	MERCURY	VENUS	MARS	JUPITER	SATURN	URANUS	NEPTUNE	PLUTO
OCT. 1	26	24	24	25	27	21	27	33	37	20	30	22
OCT. 2	26	26	26	27	28	21	27	33	37	20	30	22
OCT. 3	27	27	28	29	28	21	27	33	37	20	30	22
OCT. 4	27	29	30	31	28	21	27	33	37	20	30	22
OCT. 5	27	31	32	33	28	21	28	33	37	20	30	22
OCT. 6	27	33	34	35	28	21	28	33	37	20	30	22
OCT. 7	27	35	36	37	29	21	28	33	37	20	30	22
OCT. 8	27	37	38	38	29	22	28	33	37	20	30	22
OCT. 9	27	39	40	40	29	22	28	33	37	20	30	22
OCT. 10	27	41	41	42	29	22	28	33	37	20	30	22
OCT. 11	28	43	43	44	29	22	28	33	37	20	30	22
OCT. 12	28	44	45	46	30	22	28	33	37	20	30	22
OCT. 13	28	46	47	47	30	22	28	33	37	20	30	22
OCT. 14	28	48	48	1	30	22	28	33	37	20	30	22
OCT. 15	28	2	2	3	30	22	28	33	37	20	30	22
OCT. 16	28	3	4	4	30	22	28	33	37	20	30	22
OCT. 17	28	5	5	6	31	22	29	33	37	20	30	22
OCT. 18	28	6	7	8	31	22	29	33	37	20	30	22
OCT. 19	29	8	9	9	31	22	29	33	37	20	30	22
OCT. 20	29	10	10	11	31	22	29	33	37	20	30	22
OCT. 21	29	11	12	12	31	23	29	33	37	20	30	22
OCT. 22	29	13	13	14	31	23	29	33	37	20	30	22
OCT. 23	29	14	15	15	32	23	29	33	37	20	30	22
OCT. 24	29	16	17	17	32	23	29	33	37	20	30	22
OCT. 25	29	18	18	19	32	23	29	33	37	20	30	22
OCT. 26	30	19	20	20	32	23	29	34	37	20	30	22
OCT. 27	30	21	22	22	32	23	29	34	37	20	30	22
OCT. 28	30	23	23	24	33	23	30	34	37	20	30	22
OCT. 29	30	25	25	26	33	24	30	34	37	20	30	22
OCT. 30	30	27	27	28	33	24	30	34	37	20	30	22
OCT. 31	30	29	29	30	33	24	30	34	37	20	30	22

MOON 1 ◐ 12:01 A.M. TO 8:00 A.M. **MOON 2** ◑ 8:01 A.M. TO 4:00 P.M. **MOON 3** ● 4:01 P.M. TO 12:00 A.M.
Use only one "moon" number. Choose the column closest to your time of birth. If your place of birth is not on Eastern Standard Time, be sure to read "How to Convert to Eastern Standard Time" at the beginning of this section.

1959

November

December

Date & Time	SUN	MOON 1	MOON 2	MOON 3	MERCURY	VENUS	MARS	JUPITER	SATURN	URANUS	NEPTUNE	PLUTO
NOV. 1	30	31	31	32	33	24	30	34	37	20	30	22
NOV. 2	30	33	33	34	33	24	30	34	37	20	30	22
NOV. 3	31	35	35	36	33	24	30	34	37	20	30	22
NOV. 4	31	37	37	38	34	24	30	34	37	20	30	22
NOV. 5	31	39	39	40	34	24	30	34	37	20	30	22
NOV. 6	31	40	41	42	34	25	30	34	37	20	30	22
NOV. 7	31	42	43	43	34	25	30	34	37	20	30	22
NOV. 8	31	44	45	45	34	25	31	34	37	20	30	22
NOV. 9	31	46	46	47	34	25	31	34	37	20	30	22
NOV. 10	31	47	48	1	34	25	31	34	37	20	30	22
NOV. 11	31	1	2	2	34	25	31	34	37	20	30	22
NOV. 12	32	3	3	4	34	25	31	34	37	20	30	22
NOV. 13	32	4	5	5	34	25	31	34	38	20	30	22
NOV. 14	32	6	7	7	34	26	31	34	38	20	30	22
NOV. 15	32	8	8	9	34	26	31	34	38	20	30	22
NOV. 16	32	9	10	10	34	26	31	34	38	20	30	22
NOV. 17	32	11	11	12	34	26	31	34	38	20	30	22
NOV. 18	32	12	13	13	34	26	32	34	38	20	30	22
NOV. 19	33	14	14	15	34	26	32	34	38	20	30	22
NOV. 20	33	16	16	17	34	26	32	34	38	20	30	22
NOV. 21	33	17	18	18	34	27	32	34	38	20	30	22
NOV. 22	33	19	19	20	34	27	32	34	38	20	30	22
NOV. 23	33	20	21	22	33	27	32	34	38	20	30	22
NOV. 24	33	22	23	23	33	27	32	34	38	20	30	22
NOV. 25	34	24	25	25	33	27	32	34	38	20	30	22
NOV. 26	34	26	26	27	33	27	32	34	38	20	30	22
NOV. 27	34	28	28	29	33	28	32	34	38	20	30	22
NOV. 28	34	30	30	31	32	28	32	34	38	20	30	22
NOV. 29	34	32	32	33	32	28	33	34	38	20	30	22
NOV. 30	34	34	34	35	32	28	33	35	38	20	30	22

Date & Time	SUN	MOON 1	MOON 2	MOON 3	MERCURY	VENUS	MARS	JUPITER	SATURN	URANUS	NEPTUNE	PLUTO
DEC. 1	34	36	36	37	32	28	33	35	38	20	30	22
DEC. 2	34	38	38	39	32	28	33	35	38	20	30	22
DEC. 3	35	40	40	41	32	28	33	35	38	20	30	22
DEC. 4	35	42	42	43	32	28	33	35	38	20	30	22
DEC. 5	35	44	44	45	32	29	33	35	38	20	30	22
DEC. 6	35	45	46	46	32	29	33	35	38	20	30	22
DEC. 7	35	47	48	48	32	29	33	35	38	20	30	22
DEC. 8	35	1	1	2	32	29	33	35	38	20	30	22
DEC. 9	35	2	3	3	32	29	33	35	38	20	30	22
DEC. 10	35	4	5	5	33	29	34	35	38	20	30	22
DEC. 11	36	6	6	7	33	30	34	35	38	20	30	22
DEC. 12	36	7	8	8	33	30	34	35	38	20	30	22
DEC. 13	36	9	9	10	33	30	34	35	38	20	30	22
DEC. 14	36	10	11	11	33	30	34	35	38	20	30	22
DEC. 15	36	12	13	13	33	30	34	35	38	20	30	22
DEC. 16	36	14	14	15	33	30	34	35	38	20	30	22
DEC. 17	36	15	16	16	34	30	34	35	38	20	30	22
DEC. 18	36	17	17	18	34	31	34	35	38	20	30	22
DEC. 19	37	18	19	19	34	31	34	35	38	20	30	22
DEC. 20	37	20	21	21	34	31	35	35	38	20	30	22
DEC. 21	37	22	22	23	34	31	35	35	38	20	30	22
DEC. 22	37	23	24	25	34	31	35	35	38	20	30	22
DEC. 23	37	25	26	26	35	31	35	35	38	20	30	22
DEC. 24	37	27	28	28	35	32	35	35	38	20	30	22
DEC. 25	37	29	29	30	35	32	35	35	38	20	30	22
DEC. 26	38	31	31	32	35	32	35	35	38	20	30	22
DEC. 27	38	33	33	34	35	32	35	35	38	20	30	22
DEC. 28	38	35	35	36	36	32	35	35	38	20	30	22
DEC. 29	38	37	37	38	36	32	35	35	38	20	30	22
DEC. 30	38	39	39	40	36	32	36	35	38	20	30	22
DEC. 31	38	41	41	42	36	33	36	35	38	20	30	22

MOON 1 ☽ 12:01 A.M. TO 8:00 A.M.   **MOON 2** ☽ 8:01 A.M. TO 4:00 P.M.   **MOON 3** ● 4:01 P.M. TO 12:00 A.M.

Use only one "moon" number. Choose the column closest to your time of birth. If your place of birth is not on Eastern Standard Time, be sure to read "How to Convert to Eastern Standard Time" at the beginning of this section.

1960-1969

1960s

Princess Diana

✱ ✱ ✱ BORN JULY 1, 1961 ✱ ✱ ✱

Brief Bio: Born Diana Spencer, she became a celebrity royal and icon; in later years, she turned to humanitarian causes, especially the fight against AIDS and the campaign to increase awareness of landmine dangers.

Personology Profile:

SUN IN THE WEEK OF THE EMPATH
(CANCER I)

✱

Those born in this week arouse strong feelings in others. Also, they are so tuned in to the emotional state of those they meet, often at an unconscious level, that they tend to experience feelings of other people. True psychological mirrors, they must realize when they are picking up on what the other guy is projecting.

MOON IN THE WEEK OF ACCEPTANCE
(AQUARIUS III)

✱

Peculiar likes and dislikes and idiosyncrasy in general may be the bane of those with this Moon position. Irrational prejudices can surface, causing difficulties for all in their immediate environment. If they can become more emotionally accepting, they will have accomplished one of their chief tasks in life. However, they must still remember to maintain ego boundaries and not go overboard in giving their feelings away.

MERCURY ON THE CUSP OF MAGIC
(GEMINI-CANCER CUSP)

✱

This position grants the charisma to attract others and bewitch them with your verbal expression. Of course, attracting unstable individuals can have a deleterious effect and undermine the stability of any given situation. Best to harness this energy for positive ends and not to abuse it. Also, to learn to be selective when choosing lasting friendships.

VENUS IN THE WEEK OF THE NATURAL
(TAURUS III)

✱

A shamelessly honest approach to love characterizes Venus in Taurus III. They are not only outwardly demonstrative but also refuse to fake it or appear to have feelings or attitudes which are not true. These individuals hate pretense above all. Their approach is so straightforward that they can be accused occasionally of being too rough in their refusal to coddle their sweethearts.

MARS ON THE CUSP OF EXPOSURE
(LEO-VIRGO CUSP)

✱

This is an internalized and highly personal position for the Red Planet. These folks are likely to try to hide their light under a bushel, often in vain. Their standout energies will usually attract attention anyway, in spite of their efforts to conceal them. Because they may appear to be strong silent types, their enormous energies can be hidden at times but are accessible when needed.

JUPITER IN THE WEEK OF GENIUS
(AQUARIUS I)

✱

A quick mind allows immediate comprehension of the matter at hand. Although problems can be encountered in the emotional sphere, a grasp of logic and the ability to order one's thinking will give an advantage to those with this Jupiter position. Although long-term memory can suffer later on in life, an alert and highly conscious orientation to everyday affairs can bring good luck.

SATURN ON THE CUSP OF MYSTERY AND IMAGINATION
(CAPRICORN-AQUARIUS CUSP)

✳

This Saturn position can work out well by grounding some of this cusp's imaginative qualities. Actually, the combination of fantasy and practicality which results can lead to success or, at the very least, supply a more pragmatic base for both plans and implementation. In extreme cases, Saturn may inhibit the creative process here and its critical and restrictive faculties will have to be controlled.

URANUS IN THE WEEK OF LEADERSHIP
(LEO III)

✳

Although Uranus may fancy himself a leader, he really isn't. His attempts to take the reins of power are not likely to succeed, therefore. If he can reconcile himself to a secondary role, which is unlikely, the group to which this individual belongs will be spared a lot of agony. Incompatible energies here are likely to upset the old apple cart.

NEPTUNE IN THE WEEK OF INTENSITY
(SCORPIO I)

✳

Sexual fantasies may periodically overcome those with this Neptune placement. If there are real outlets for this energy, involving a loving person, many good results can be expected both in the relationship and in other aspects of daily life. However, should narcissism or other extreme forms of self-stimulation result, frustration can build to intolerable levels. Frequent reality checks are advised.

PLUTO IN THE WEEK OF SYSTEM BUILDERS
(VIRGO I)

✳

Investments often thrive in the hands of these individuals. If they are inclined to save rather than spend, they are capable of making outstanding decisions as to what to do with their money. They can also give good advice on this subject to others, both as amateurs and professionals. Because they recognize the importance of sound finances, they make realistic plans for the future.

Some Highlights of the Decade 1960-1969

- SHIRLEY CHISHOLM IS THE FIRST AFRICAN-AMERICAN WOMAN ELECTED TO THE US CONGRESS.
- MORE THAN 6000 PEOPLE A DAY FLOCK TO CARTIER'S NEW YORK STORE TO SEE THE TAYLOR-BURTON, A 69.42 CARAT, PEAR-SHAPED DIAMOND WHICH RICHARD BURTON BOUGHT FOR $1,100,000 AS A GIFT FOR ELIZABETH TAYLOR.
- NEIL ARMSTRONG BECOMES THE FIRST MAN TO WALK ON THE MOON.
- THE BEATLES TAKE AMERICA BY STORM WITH THEIR HIT "I WANNA HOLD YOUR HAND" AND A US TOUR.
- MARTIN LUTHER KING DELIVERS HIS "I HAVE A DREAM" SPEECH ON THE STEPS OF THE LINCOLN MEMORIAL IN WASHINGTON, D.C.

January

Date & Time	SUN	MOON 1	MOON 2	MOON 3	MERCURY	VENUS	MARS	JUPITER	SATURN	URANUS	NEPTUNE	PLUTO
JAN. 1	38	43	43	44	36	33	36	35	38	20	30	22
JAN. 2	38	45	45	46	37	33	36	36	38	20	30	22
JAN. 3	39	46	47	48	37	33	36	36	38	20	30	22
JAN. 4	39	48	1	1	37	33	36	36	38	20	30	22
JAN. 5	39	2	2	3	37	33	36	36	38	20	30	22
JAN. 6	39	4	4	5	37	34	36	36	38	20	30	22
JAN. 7	39	5	6	6	37	34	36	36	38	20	30	22
JAN. 8	39	7	7	8	38	34	36	36	38	20	30	22
JAN. 9	39	8	9	9	38	34	36	36	38	20	30	22
JAN. 10	40	10	10	11	38	34	37	36	38	20	30	22
JAN. 11	40	12	12	13	38	34	37	36	38	20	30	22
JAN. 12	40	13	14	14	39	35	37	36	38	20	30	22
JAN. 13	40	15	15	16	39	35	37	36	38	20	30	22
JAN. 14	40	16	17	17	39	35	37	36	38	20	30	22
JAN. 15	40	18	19	19	39	35	37	36	38	20	30	22
JAN. 16	40	20	20	21	39	35	37	36	38	20	30	22
JAN. 17	41	21	22	22	40	35	37	36	38	20	30	22
JAN. 18	41	23	24	24	40	36	37	36	38	20	30	22
JAN. 19	41	25	25	26	40	36	37	36	39	20	30	22
JAN. 20	41	26	27	28	40	36	38	36	39	20	30	22
JAN. 21	41	28	29	30	41	36	38	36	39	20	30	22
JAN. 22	41	30	31	31	41	36	38	36	39	20	30	22
JAN. 23	42	32	33	33	41	36	38	36	39	20	30	22
JAN. 24	42	34	35	35	41	36	38	36	39	20	30	22
JAN. 25	42	36	37	37	41	37	38	36	39	20	30	22
JAN. 26	42	38	39	39	42	37	38	36	39	20	30	22
JAN. 27	42	40	41	41	42	37	38	36	39	20	30	22
JAN. 28	42	42	42	43	42	37	38	36	39	20	30	22
JAN. 29	42	44	44	45	42	37	38	36	39	20	30	22
JAN. 30	42	46	46	47	43	37	39	36	39	20	30	22
JAN. 31	43	48	48	1	43	38	39	36	39	20	30	22

February

Date & Time	SUN	MOON 1	MOON 2	MOON 3	MERCURY	VENUS	MARS	JUPITER	SATURN	URANUS	NEPTUNE	PLUTO
FEB. 1	43	1	2	2	43	38	39	36	39	20	30	22
FEB. 2	43	3	4	4	43	38	39	36	39	20	30	22
FEB. 3	43	5	5	6	43	38	39	36	39	20	30	22
FEB. 4	43	6	7	7	44	38	39	36	39	20	30	22
FEB. 5	43	8	9	9	44	39	39	36	39	20	30	22
FEB. 6	43	9	10	11	44	39	39	36	39	20	30	22
FEB. 7	43	11	12	12	44	39	39	36	39	20	30	22
FEB. 8	44	13	13	14	45	39	39	36	39	20	30	22
FEB. 9	44	14	15	15	45	39	40	37	39	20	30	22
FEB. 10	44	16	16	17	45	39	40	37	39	19	30	22
FEB. 11	44	18	18	19	45	39	40	37	39	19	30	22
FEB. 12	44	19	20	20	46	40	40	37	39	19	30	22
FEB. 13	44	21	21	22	46	40	40	37	39	19	30	22
FEB. 14	44	23	23	24	46	40	40	37	39	19	30	22
FEB. 15	44	24	25	25	46	40	40	37	39	19	30	22
FEB. 16	45	26	26	27	47	40	40	37	39	19	30	22
FEB. 17	45	28	28	29	47	40	40	37	39	19	30	22
FEB. 18	45	30	30	31	47	41	40	37	39	19	30	22
FEB. 19	45	32	32	33	47	41	41	37	39	19	30	22
FEB. 20	45	33	34	35	47	41	41	37	39	19	30	22
FEB. 21	45	35	36	37	48	41	41	37	39	19	30	22
FEB. 22	45	37	38	39	48	41	41	37	39	19	30	22
FEB. 23	46	39	40	40	48	41	41	37	39	19	30	22
FEB. 24	46	41	42	42	48	42	41	37	39	19	30	22
FEB. 25	46	43	44	44	48	42	41	37	39	19	30	22
FEB. 26	46	45	46	46	48	42	41	37	39	19	30	22
FEB. 27	46	47	47	48	48	42	41	37	39	19	30	22
FEB. 28	46	1	1	2	48	42	41	37	39	19	30	22
FEB. 29	46	2	3	3	48	42	42	37	39	19	30	22

MOON 1 ☽ 12:01 A.M. TO 8:00 A.M.   **MOON 2** ☽ 8:01 A.M. TO 4:00 P.M.   **MOON 3** ● 4:01 P.M. TO 12:00 A.M.

Use only one "moon" number. Choose the column closest to your time of birth. If your place of birth is not on Eastern Standard Time, be sure to read "How to Convert to Eastern Standard Time" at the beginning of this section.

1960

March   April

Date & Time	SUN	MOON 1	MOON 2	MOON 3	MERCURY	VENUS	MARS	JUPITER	SATURN	URANUS	NEPTUNE	PLUTO
MAR. 1	46	4	5	5	48	43	42	37	39	19	30	22
MAR. 2	46	6	6	7	48	43	42	37	39	19	30	22
MAR. 3	47	7	8	8	48	43	42	37	39	19	30	22
MAR. 4	47	9	9	10	48	43	42	37	39	19	30	22
MAR. 5	47	11	11	12	48	43	42	37	39	19	30	22
MAR. 6	47	12	13	13	48	43	42	37	39	19	30	22
MAR. 7	47	14	14	15	48	43	42	37	39	19	30	22
MAR. 8	47	15	16	16	48	44	42	37	39	19	30	22
MAR. 9	47	17	17	18	48	44	42	37	39	19	30	22
MAR. 10	47	19	19	20	48	44	43	37	39	19	30	22
MAR. 11	48	20	21	21	48	44	43	37	39	19	30	22
MAR. 12	48	22	23	23	48	44	43	37	39	19	30	22
MAR. 13	48	24	24	25	47	44	43	37	39	19	30	22
MAR. 14	48	26	26	27	47	45	43	37	39	19	30	22
MAR. 15	48	27	28	29	47	45	43	37	39	19	30	22
MAR. 16	48	29	30	30	47	45	43	37	39	19	30	22
MAR. 17	48	31	32	32	47	45	43	37	39	19	30	22
MAR. 18	48	33	34	34	47	45	43	37	39	19	30	22
MAR. 19	1	35	36	36	47	45	44	37	39	19	30	22
MAR. 20	1	37	37	38	47	46	44	37	39	19	30	22
MAR. 21	1	39	39	40	47	46	44	37	39	19	30	22
MAR. 22	1	41	41	42	47	46	44	37	39	19	30	22
MAR. 23	1	42	43	44	47	46	44	37	39	19	30	22
MAR. 24	1	44	45	45	47	46	44	37	39	19	30	22
MAR. 25	2	46	47	47	47	46	44	37	39	19	30	22
MAR. 26	2	48	48	1	47	47	44	37	39	19	30	22
MAR. 27	2	2	2	3	47	47	44	37	39	19	30	22
MAR. 28	2	3	4	5	47	47	44	37	39	19	30	22
MAR. 29	2	5	6	6	47	47	45	37	39	19	30	22
MAR. 30	2	7	7	8	47	47	45	37	39	19	30	22
MAR. 31	2	8	9	9	47	47	45	37	39	19	30	22
APR. 1	2	10	11	11	47	48	45	37	39	19	30	22
APR. 2	2	12	12	13	47	48	45	37	39	19	30	22
APR. 3	3	13	14	14	47	48	45	37	39	19	30	22
APR. 4	3	15	15	16	47	48	45	37	39	19	30	21
APR. 5	3	16	17	17	47	48	45	37	39	19	30	21
APR. 6	3	18	19	19	47	48	45	37	39	19	30	21
APR. 7	3	20	20	21	48	1	45	37	39	19	30	21
APR. 8	3	21	22	22	48	1	46	37	39	19	30	21
APR. 9	3	23	24	24	48	1	46	37	39	19	30	21
APR. 10	3	25	25	26	48	1	46	37	39	19	30	21
APR. 11	4	27	27	28	48	1	46	37	39	19	30	21
APR. 12	4	29	29	30	48	1	46	37	39	19	30	21
APR. 13	4	30	31	32	48	2	46	37	39	19	30	21
APR. 14	4	32	33	34	1	2	46	37	39	19	30	21
APR. 15	4	34	35	36	1	2	46	37	39	19	30	21
APR. 16	4	36	37	38	1	2	46	37	39	19	30	21
APR. 17	4	38	39	40	1	2	47	37	39	19	30	21
APR. 18	4	40	41	41	1	2	47	37	39	19	30	21
APR. 19	5	42	43	43	2	3	47	37	39	19	30	21
APR. 20	5	44	44	45	2	3	47	37	39	19	30	21
APR. 21	5	46	46	47	2	3	47	37	39	19	30	21
APR. 22	5	47	48	1	2	3	47	37	39	19	30	21
APR. 23	5	1	2	2	3	3	47	37	39	19	30	21
APR. 24	5	3	3	4	3	3	47	37	39	19	30	21
APR. 25	6	5	5	6	3	4	47	37	39	19	30	21
APR. 26	6	6	7	7	3	4	47	37	39	19	30	21
APR. 27	6	8	8	9	3	4	48	37	39	19	30	21
APR. 28	6	9	10	11	3	4	48	37	39	19	30	21
APR. 29	6	11	12	12	4	4	48	37	39	19	30	21
APR. 30	6	13	13	14	4	4	48	37	39	19	30	21

MOON 1 ◗ 12:01 A.M. TO 8:00 A.M.   **MOON 2** ◑ 8:01 A.M. TO 4:00 P.M.   **MOON 3** ● 4:01 P.M. TO 12:00 A.M.
Use only one "moon" number. Choose the column closest to your time of birth. If your place of birth is not on Eastern Standard Time, be sure to read "How to Convert to Eastern Standard Time" at the beginning of this section.

1960

May   June

Date & Time	SUN	MOON 1	MOON 2	MOON 3	MERCURY	VENUS	MARS	JUPITER	SATURN	URANUS	NEPTUNE	PLUTO
MAY 1	6	14	15	15	4	5	48	37	39	19	30	21
MAY 2	6	16	16	17	4	5	48	37	39	19	30	21
MAY 3	7	17	18	19	5	5	48	37	39	19	30	21
MAY 4	7	19	20	20	5	5	48	37	39	19	30	21
MAY 5	7	21	21	22	5	5	48	37	39	19	30	21
MAY 6	7	22	23	24	5	5	48	37	39	19	30	21
MAY 7	7	24	25	25	6	6	1	37	39	19	30	21
MAY 8	7	26	27	27	6	6	1	37	39	19	30	21
MAY 9	7	28	28	29	6	6	1	37	39	19	30	21
MAY 10	7	30	30	31	6	6	1	37	39	19	30	21
MAY 11	8	32	32	33	7	6	1	37	39	19	30	21
MAY 12	8	34	34	35	7	6	1	37	39	19	30	21
MAY 13	8	36	36	37	7	7	1	37	39	19	30	21
MAY 14	8	38	38	39	8	7	1	37	39	19	30	21
MAY 15	8	40	40	41	8	7	1	37	39	19	30	21
MAY 16	8	42	42	43	8	7	1	37	39	19	30	21
MAY 17	8	43	44	45	8	7	2	37	39	19	30	21
MAY 18	8	45	46	46	9	7	2	37	39	19	30	21
MAY 19	9	47	48	48	9	7	2	37	39	19	30	21
MAY 20	9	1	1	2	9	8	2	37	39	19	30	21
MAY 21	9	2	3	4	10	8	2	37	39	19	30	21
MAY 22	9	4	5	5	10	8	2	37	39	19	30	21
MAY 23	9	6	6	7	10	8	2	37	39	19	30	21
MAY 24	9	7	8	9	10	8	2	37	39	19	30	21
MAY 25	10	9	10	10	11	8	2	37	39	19	30	21
MAY 26	10	11	11	12	11	9	2	37	39	19	30	21
MAY 27	10	12	13	13	11	9	3	37	39	19	30	21
MAY 28	10	14	14	15	12	9	3	37	39	19	30	21
MAY 29	10	15	16	16	12	9	3	37	39	19	30	21
MAY 30	10	17	18	18	12	9	3	37	39	19	30	21
MAY 31	10	19	19	20	12	9	3	37	39	19	30	21
JUN. 1	10	20	21	21	13	10	3	37	39	19	30	21
JUN. 2	10	22	22	23	13	10	3	37	39	19	30	21
JUN. 3	11	23	24	25	13	10	3	37	39	19	30	21
JUN. 4	11	25	26	26	13	10	3	37	39	19	30	21
JUN. 5	11	27	28	28	14	10	3	37	39	19	30	21
JUN. 6	11	29	29	30	14	10	4	37	39	19	30	21
JUN. 7	11	31	31	32	14	11	4	37	39	19	30	21
JUN. 8	11	33	33	34	14	11	4	37	39	19	30	21
JUN. 9	11	35	35	36	14	11	4	37	39	19	30	21
JUN. 10	11	37	37	38	15	11	4	37	39	19	30	21
JUN. 11	12	39	40	40	15	11	4	37	39	19	30	21
JUN. 12	12	41	42	42	15	11	4	37	39	19	30	21
JUN. 13	12	43	43	44	15	12	4	37	39	19	30	21
JUN. 14	12	45	45	46	15	12	4	37	39	19	30	21
JUN. 15	12	47	47	48	15	12	4	37	39	19	30	21
JUN. 16	12	48	1	1	16	12	5	37	39	19	30	21
JUN. 17	12	2	3	3	16	12	5	37	39	19	30	21
JUN. 18	12	4	4	5	16	12	5	37	39	19	30	21
JUN. 19	13	5	6	6	16	13	5	37	39	19	30	21
JUN. 20	13	7	8	8	16	13	5	37	39	19	30	21
JUN. 21	13	9	9	10	16	13	5	37	39	19	30	21
JUN. 22	13	10	11	11	16	13	5	37	39	19	30	21
JUN. 23	13	12	12	13	16	13	5	37	39	19	30	21
JUN. 24	13	13	14	14	17	13	5	37	39	19	30	21
JUN. 25	14	15	16	16	17	14	5	37	39	19	30	22
JUN. 26	14	17	17	18	17	14	6	37	39	19	30	22
JUN. 27	14	18	19	19	17	14	6	37	39	19	30	22
JUN. 28	14	20	20	21	17	14	6	37	39	19	30	22
JUN. 29	14	21	22	22	17	14	6	37	39	19	30	22
JUN. 30	14	23	24	24	17	14	6	37	39	19	30	22

MOON 1 ☽ 12:01 A.M. TO 8:00 A.M.   **MOON 2** ◐ 8:01 A.M. TO 4:00 P.M.   **MOON 3** ● 4:01 P.M. TO 12:00 A.M.

Use only one "moon" number. Choose the column closest to your time of birth. If your place of birth is not on Eastern Standard Time, be sure to read "How to Convert to Eastern Standard Time" at the beginning of this section.

July

August

Date & Time	SUN ☀	MOON 1 ◗	MOON 2 ◖	MOON 3 ●	MERCURY	VENUS	MARS	JUPITER	SATURN	URANUS	NEPTUNE	PLUTO
JUL. 1	14	25	25	26	17	15	6	37	39	19	30	22
JUL. 2	14	26	27	28	17	15	6	37	39	19	30	22
JUL. 3	15	28	29	29	17	15	6	37	39	19	30	22
JUL. 4	15	30	31	31	17	15	6	37	39	19	30	22
JUL. 5	15	32	33	33	17	15	6	37	39	20	30	22
JUL. 6	15	34	35	35	17	15	6	37	39	20	30	22
JUL. 7	15	36	37	37	17	15	7	37	39	20	30	22
JUL. 8	15	38	39	39	17	16	7	37	39	20	30	22
JUL. 9	15	40	41	41	17	16	7	36	39	20	30	22
JUL. 10	15	42	43	43	17	16	7	36	39	20	30	22
JUL. 11	16	44	45	45	17	16	7	36	39	20	30	22
JUL. 12	16	46	47	47	17	16	7	36	39	20	30	22
JUL. 13	16	48	48	1	17	16	7	36	39	20	30	22
JUL. 14	16	2	2	3	16	17	7	36	39	20	30	22
JUL. 15	16	3	4	4	16	17	7	36	39	20	30	22
JUL. 16	16	5	6	6	16	17	7	36	39	20	30	22
JUL. 17	16	7	7	8	16	17	8	36	39	20	30	22
JUL. 18	16	8	9	9	16	17	8	36	39	20	30	22
JUL. 19	17	10	10	11	16	17	8	36	39	20	30	22
JUL. 20	17	11	12	12	16	18	8	36	39	20	30	22
JUL. 21	17	13	14	14	16	18	8	36	39	20	30	22
JUL. 22	17	15	15	16	16	18	8	36	39	20	30	22
JUL. 23	17	16	17	17	16	18	8	36	39	20	30	22
JUL. 24	17	18	18	19	16	18	8	36	39	20	30	22
JUL. 25	17	19	20	20	16	18	8	36	39	20	30	22
JUL. 26	18	21	22	22	16	19	8	36	39	20	30	22
JUL. 27	18	23	23	24	16	19	9	36	39	20	30	22
JUL. 28	18	24	25	25	16	19	9	36	39	20	30	22
JUL. 29	18	26	27	27	16	19	9	36	39	20	30	22
JUL. 30	18	28	28	29	16	19	9	36	39	20	30	22
JUL. 31	18	29	30	31	16	19	9	36	39	20	30	22

Date & Time	SUN ☀	MOON 1 ◗	MOON 2 ◖	MOON 3 ●	MERCURY	VENUS	MARS	JUPITER	SATURN	URANUS	NEPTUNE	PLUTO
AUG. 1	18	31	32	33	16	20	9	36	39	20	30	22
AUG. 2	18	33	34	34	16	20	9	36	39	20	30	22
AUG. 3	19	35	36	36	16	20	9	36	39	20	30	22
AUG. 4	19	37	38	38	16	20	9	36	39	20	30	22
AUG. 5	19	39	40	40	16	20	9	36	39	20	30	22
AUG. 6	19	41	42	42	16	20	9	36	39	20	30	22
AUG. 7	19	43	44	44	16	21	9	36	39	20	30	22
AUG. 8	19	45	46	46	17	21	9	36	39	20	30	22
AUG. 9	19	47	48	48	17	21	10	36	39	20	30	22
AUG. 10	19	1	1	2	17	21	10	36	39	20	30	22
AUG. 11	20	3	3	4	17	21	10	36	39	20	30	22
AUG. 12	20	4	5	6	17	21	10	36	39	20	30	22
AUG. 13	20	6	7	7	17	22	10	36	39	20	30	22
AUG. 14	20	8	8	9	18	22	10	36	39	20	30	22
AUG. 15	20	9	10	10	18	22	10	36	39	20	30	22
AUG. 16	20	11	12	12	18	22	10	36	39	20	30	22
AUG. 17	20	13	13	14	18	22	10	36	39	20	30	22
AUG. 18	20	14	15	15	19	22	10	36	39	20	30	22
AUG. 19	21	16	16	17	19	23	10	36	39	20	30	22
AUG. 20	21	17	18	18	19	23	11	36	39	20	30	22
AUG. 21	21	19	19	20	19	23	11	36	39	20	30	22
AUG. 22	21	21	21	22	20	23	11	36	39	20	30	22
AUG. 23	21	22	23	23	20	23	11	36	39	20	30	22
AUG. 24	21	24	24	25	20	23	11	36	39	20	30	22
AUG. 25	21	26	26	27	20	24	11	36	39	20	30	22
AUG. 26	22	27	28	28	21	24	11	36	39	20	30	22
AUG. 27	22	29	30	30	21	24	11	36	39	20	30	22
AUG. 28	22	31	31	32	21	24	11	36	39	20	30	22
AUG. 29	22	33	33	34	22	24	11	36	39	20	30	22
AUG. 30	22	35	35	36	22	24	11	36	39	20	30	22
AUG. 31	22	36	37	38	22	25	11	36	39	20	30	22

MOON 1 ◗ 12:01 A.M. TO 8:00 A.M.   **MOON 2** ◖ 8:01 A.M. TO 4:00 P.M.   **MOON 3** ● 4:01 P.M. TO 12:00 A.M.

Use only one "moon" number. Choose the column closest to your time of birth. If your place of birth is not on Eastern Standard Time, be sure to read "How to Convert to Eastern Standard Time" at the beginning of this section.

Date & Time	SUN	MOON 1	MOON 2	MOON 3	MERCURY	VENUS	MARS	JUPITER	SATURN	URANUS	NEPTUNE	PLUTO
SEP. 1	22	38	39	40	22	25	11	36	39	20	30	22
SEP. 2	22	40	41	42	23	25	12	36	39	20	30	22
SEP. 3	23	42	43	44	23	25	12	36	39	20	30	22
SEP. 4	23	44	45	46	23	25	12	36	39	20	30	22
SEP. 5	23	46	47	47	23	25	12	36	39	20	30	22
SEP. 6	23	48	1	1	24	26	12	36	39	20	30	22
SEP. 7	23	2	3	3	24	26	12	36	39	20	30	22
SEP. 8	23	4	4	5	24	26	12	36	39	20	30	22
SEP. 9	23	5	6	7	24	26	12	36	39	20	30	22
SEP. 10	23	7	8	8	24	26	12	36	39	20	30	22
SEP. 11	24	9	9	10	25	26	12	36	39	20	30	22
SEP. 12	24	10	11	12	25	27	12	36	39	20	30	22
SEP. 13	24	12	13	13	25	27	12	36	39	20	30	22
SEP. 14	24	14	14	15	25	27	12	36	39	20	30	22
SEP. 15	24	15	16	16	26	27	13	36	39	20	30	22
SEP. 16	24	17	17	18	26	27	13	36	39	20	30	22
SEP. 17	24	18	19	20	26	27	13	36	39	20	30	22
SEP. 18	24	20	21	21	26	27	13	36	39	20	30	22
SEP. 19	25	22	22	23	26	28	13	36	39	20	30	22
SEP. 20	25	23	24	25	27	28	13	36	39	20	30	22
SEP. 21	25	25	26	26	27	28	13	36	39	20	30	22
SEP. 22	25	27	27	28	27	28	13	36	39	20	30	22
SEP. 23	25	29	29	30	27	28	13	36	39	20	30	22
SEP. 24	25	30	31	32	28	28	13	36	39	20	30	22
SEP. 25	26	32	33	34	28	29	13	36	39	20	30	22
SEP. 26	26	34	35	35	28	29	13	36	39	20	30	22
SEP. 27	26	36	37	37	28	29	13	36	39	20	30	22
SEP. 28	26	38	39	39	28	29	13	36	39	20	30	22
SEP. 29	26	40	40	41	28	29	13	36	39	20	30	22
SEP. 30	26	42	42	43	29	29	14	36	39	20	30	22

Date & Time	SUN	MOON 1	MOON 2	MOON 3	MERCURY	VENUS	MARS	JUPITER	SATURN	URANUS	NEPTUNE	PLUTO
OCT. 1	26	44	44	45	29	30	14	36	39	20	30	22
OCT. 2	26	45	46	47	29	30	14	36	39	20	30	22
OCT. 3	27	47	48	1	29	30	14	37	39	20	30	22
OCT. 4	27	1	2	2	29	30	14	37	39	20	30	22
OCT. 5	27	3	4	4	30	30	14	37	39	20	30	22
OCT. 6	27	5	5	6	30	30	14	37	39	20	30	22
OCT. 7	27	7	7	8	30	31	14	37	39	20	30	22
OCT. 8	27	8	9	9	30	31	14	37	39	20	30	22
OCT. 9	27	10	10	11	30	31	14	37	39	20	30	22
OCT. 10	27	12	12	13	30	31	14	37	39	20	30	22
OCT. 11	28	13	14	14	31	31	14	37	39	20	30	22
OCT. 12	28	15	15	16	31	31	14	37	39	20	30	22
OCT. 13	28	16	17	17	31	32	14	37	39	20	30	22
OCT. 14	28	18	18	19	31	32	14	37	39	20	30	22
OCT. 15	28	19	20	21	31	32	14	37	39	20	30	22
OCT. 16	28	21	22	22	31	32	14	37	39	20	30	22
OCT. 17	28	23	23	24	31	32	15	37	39	20	30	22
OCT. 18	28	24	25	26	32	32	15	37	39	20	30	22
OCT. 19	29	26	27	27	32	33	15	37	39	20	30	22
OCT. 20	29	28	29	29	32	33	15	37	39	20	30	22
OCT. 21	29	30	31	31	32	33	15	37	39	20	30	22
OCT. 22	29	32	32	33	32	33	15	37	39	20	30	22
OCT. 23	29	34	34	35	32	33	15	37	39	20	30	22
OCT. 24	29	36	36	37	32	33	15	37	39	20	30	22
OCT. 25	29	37	38	39	32	34	15	37	39	20	30	22
OCT. 26	30	39	40	41	32	34	15	37	39	20	30	22
OCT. 27	30	41	42	43	32	34	15	37	39	20	30	22
OCT. 28	30	43	44	44	32	34	15	37	39	20	30	22
OCT. 29	30	45	46	46	32	34	15	37	39	20	30	22
OCT. 30	30	47	47	48	32	34	15	37	39	20	30	22
OCT. 31	30	1	1	2	32	35	15	37	39	20	30	22

MOON 1 ◗ 12:01 A.M. TO 8:00 A.M.　　**MOON 2** ◑ 8:01 A.M. TO 4:00 P.M.　　**MOON 3** ● 4:01 P.M. TO 12:00 A.M.
Use only one "moon" number. Choose the column closest to your time of birth. If your place of birth is not on Eastern Standard Time, be sure to read "How to Convert to Eastern Standard Time" at the beginning of this section.

1960

November

Date & Time	SUN ☉	MOON 1 ◗	MOON 2 ◑	MOON 3 ●	MERCURY	VENUS	MARS	JUPITER	SATURN	URANUS	NEPTUNE	PLUTO
NOV. 1	30	2	3	4	32	35	15	37	39	20	30	22
NOV. 2	30	4	5	5	32	35	15	37	39	20	30	22
NOV. 3	31	6	7	7	32	35	15	37	39	20	30	22
NOV. 4	31	8	8	9	32	35	15	37	39	20	30	22
NOV. 5	31	9	10	10	31	35	15	37	39	20	30	22
NOV. 6	31	11	12	12	31	35	15	37	39	20	30	22
NOV. 7	31	13	13	14	31	36	15	37	39	20	30	22
NOV. 8	31	14	15	15	31	36	15	37	39	20	30	22
NOV. 9	31	16	16	17	31	36	15	37	39	20	30	22
NOV. 10	31	17	18	18	31	36	15	37	39	20	30	22
NOV. 11	31	19	19	20	30	36	15	37	39	20	30	22
NOV. 12	32	21	21	22	30	36	15	37	39	20	30	22
NOV. 13	32	22	23	23	30	37	15	37	39	20	30	22
NOV. 14	32	24	24	25	30	37	15	37	39	20	30	22
NOV. 15	32	26	26	27	30	37	15	37	39	20	30	22
NOV. 16	32	27	28	29	30	37	15	37	39	20	30	22
NOV. 17	32	29	30	30	30	37	15	38	39	20	30	22
NOV. 18	32	31	32	32	30	37	15	38	39	20	30	22
NOV. 19	33	33	34	34	30	38	15	38	39	20	30	22
NOV. 20	33	35	36	36	30	38	15	38	39	20	30	22
NOV. 21	33	37	38	38	30	38	15	38	39	20	30	22
NOV. 22	33	39	40	40	30	38	15	38	39	20	30	22
NOV. 23	33	41	41	42	30	38	15	38	39	20	30	22
NOV. 24	33	43	43	44	31	38	15	38	39	20	30	22
NOV. 25	34	45	45	46	31	39	15	38	39	20	30	22
NOV. 26	34	46	47	48	31	39	15	38	39	20	30	22
NOV. 27	34	48	1	1	31	39	15	38	39	20	30	22
NOV. 28	34	2	3	3	31	39	15	38	39	20	30	22
NOV. 29	34	4	4	5	31	39	15	38	39	20	30	22
NOV. 30	34	5	6	7	32	39	15	38	39	20	30	22

December

Date & Time	SUN ☉	MOON 1 ◗	MOON 2 ◑	MOON 3 ●	MERCURY	VENUS	MARS	JUPITER	SATURN	URANUS	NEPTUNE	PLUTO
DEC. 1	34	7	8	8	32	40	15	38	39	20	30	22
DEC. 2	34	9	9	10	32	40	15	38	39	20	30	22
DEC. 3	35	10	11	12	32	40	15	38	39	20	30	22
DEC. 4	35	12	13	13	32	40	15	38	39	20	30	22
DEC. 5	35	14	14	15	32	40	15	38	39	20	30	22
DEC. 6	35	15	16	16	33	40	15	38	39	20	30	22
DEC. 7	35	17	17	18	33	40	15	38	39	20	30	22
DEC. 8	35	18	19	20	33	41	15	38	39	20	30	22
DEC. 9	35	20	21	21	33	41	15	38	39	20	30	22
DEC. 10	35	22	22	23	33	41	15	38	39	20	30	22
DEC. 11	36	23	24	24	34	41	15	38	39	20	30	22
DEC. 12	36	25	25	26	34	41	15	38	39	20	30	22
DEC. 13	36	27	27	28	34	41	15	38	39	20	30	22
DEC. 14	36	28	29	30	34	42	15	38	39	20	30	22
DEC. 15	36	30	31	31	34	42	15	38	39	20	30	22
DEC. 16	36	32	33	33	35	42	15	38	39	20	30	22
DEC. 17	36	34	35	35	35	42	15	38	39	20	30	22
DEC. 18	36	36	37	37	35	42	15	38	39	20	30	22
DEC. 19	37	38	39	39	35	42	15	38	39	20	30	22
DEC. 20	37	40	41	41	35	43	15	38	39	20	30	22
DEC. 21	37	42	43	43	36	43	15	39	39	20	30	22
DEC. 22	37	44	45	45	36	43	15	39	39	20	30	22
DEC. 23	37	46	47	47	36	43	15	39	39	20	30	22
DEC. 24	37	48	48	1	36	43	14	39	39	20	30	22
DEC. 25	37	2	2	3	37	43	14	39	39	20	30	22
DEC. 26	38	3	4	5	37	43	14	39	39	20	30	22
DEC. 27	38	5	6	6	37	44	14	39	40	20	30	22
DEC. 28	38	7	7	8	37	44	14	39	40	20	30	22
DEC. 29	38	8	9	10	37	44	14	39	40	20	30	22
DEC. 30	38	10	11	11	38	44	14	39	40	20	30	22
DEC. 31	38	12	12	13	38	44	14	39	40	20	30	22

MOON 1 ◗ 12:01 A.M. TO 8:00 A.M.   **MOON 2** ◑ 8:01 A.M. TO 4:00 P.M.   **MOON 3** ● 4:01 P.M. TO 12:00 A.M.

Use only one "moon" number. Choose the column closest to your time of birth. If your place of birth is not on Eastern Standard Time, be sure to read "How to Convert to Eastern Standard Time" at the beginning of this section.

1961

January

Date & Time	SUN	MOON 1	MOON 2	MOON 3	MERCURY	VENUS	MARS	JUPITER	SATURN	URANUS	NEPTUNE	PLUTO
JAN. 1	38	13	14	14	38	44	14	39	40	20	30	22
JAN. 2	38	15	15	16	38	45	14	39	40	20	30	22
JAN. 3	39	16	17	17	38	45	14	39	40	20	30	22
JAN. 4	39	18	19	19	39	45	14	39	40	20	30	22
JAN. 5	39	20	20	21	39	45	14	39	40	20	30	22
JAN. 6	39	21	22	22	39	46	14	39	40	20	30	22
JAN. 7	39	23	23	24	39	45	14	39	40	20	30	22
JAN. 8	39	24	25	25	40	45	14	39	40	20	30	22
JAN. 9	39	26	27	27	40	46	14	39	40	20	30	22
JAN. 10	40	28	28	29	40	46	14	39	40	20	30	22
JAN. 11	40	29	30	31	40	46	14	39	40	20	30	22
JAN. 12	40	31	32	33	40	46	14	39	40	20	30	22
JAN. 13	40	33	34	34	41	46	13	39	40	20	30	22
JAN. 14	40	35	36	36	41	46	13	39	40	20	30	22
JAN. 15	40	37	38	38	41	46	13	39	40	20	30	22
JAN. 16	40	39	40	40	41	47	13	39	40	20	30	22
JAN. 17	41	41	42	42	42	47	13	39	40	20	30	22
JAN. 18	41	43	44	45	42	47	13	39	40	20	30	22
JAN. 19	41	45	46	46	42	47	13	39	40	20	30	22
JAN. 20	41	47	48	48	42	47	13	39	40	20	30	22
JAN. 21	41	1	2	2	42	47	13	39	40	20	30	22
JAN. 22	41	3	3	4	43	47	13	40	40	20	30	22
JAN. 23	42	5	5	6	43	48	13	40	40	20	30	22
JAN. 24	42	6	7	7	43	48	13	40	40	20	30	22
JAN. 25	42	8	9	9	43	48	13	40	40	20	30	22
JAN. 26	42	10	10	11	44	48	13	40	40	20	30	22
JAN. 27	42	11	12	12	44	48	13	40	40	20	30	22
JAN. 28	42	13	13	14	44	48	13	40	40	20	30	22
JAN. 29	42	14	15	16	44	48	13	40	40	20	30	22
JAN. 30	42	16	17	17	44	1	13	40	40	20	30	22
JAN. 31	43	18	18	19	45	1	13	40	40	20	30	22

February

Date & Time	SUN	MOON 1	MOON 2	MOON 3	MERCURY	VENUS	MARS	JUPITER	SATURN	URANUS	NEPTUNE	PLUTO
FEB. 1	43	19	20	20	45	1	13	40	40	20	30	22
FEB. 2	43	21	21	22	45	1	13	40	40	20	30	22
FEB. 3	43	22	23	23	45	1	13	40	40	20	30	22
FEB. 4	43	24	25	25	45	1	13	40	40	20	30	22
FEB. 5	43	26	26	27	46	1	13	40	40	20	30	22
FEB. 6	43	27	28	28	46	1	13	40	40	20	30	22
FEB. 7	43	29	30	30	46	2	13	40	40	20	30	22
FEB. 8	44	31	31	32	46	2	13	40	40	20	30	22
FEB. 9	44	33	33	34	46	2	13	40	40	20	30	22
FEB. 10	44	34	35	36	46	2	13	40	40	20	30	22
FEB. 11	44	36	37	38	46	2	13	40	40	20	30	22
FEB. 12	44	38	39	40	46	2	13	40	40	20	30	22
FEB. 13	44	40	41	42	46	2	13	40	40	20	30	22
FEB. 14	44	42	43	44	46	2	13	40	40	20	30	22
FEB. 15	44	44	45	46	46	3	13	40	40	20	30	22
FEB. 16	45	46	47	48	46	3	13	40	40	20	30	22
FEB. 17	45	48	1	1	46	3	13	40	40	20	30	22
FEB. 18	45	2	3	3	46	3	13	40	40	20	30	22
FEB. 19	45	4	5	5	46	3	13	40	40	20	30	22
FEB. 20	45	6	6	7	46	3	13	40	40	20	30	22
FEB. 21	45	7	8	9	45	3	13	40	40	20	30	22
FEB. 22	45	9	10	10	45	3	13	40	40	20	30	22
FEB. 23	46	11	11	12	45	3	13	40	40	20	30	22
FEB. 24	46	12	13	14	45	4	13	40	40	20	30	22
FEB. 25	46	14	15	15	45	4	13	40	40	20	30	22
FEB. 26	46	16	16	17	45	4	13	41	40	20	30	22
FEB. 27	46	17	18	18	45	4	13	41	40	20	30	22
FEB. 28	46	19	19	20	45	4	13	41	40	20	30	22

MOON 1 ◑ 12:01 A.M. TO 8:00 A.M.   **MOON 2** ◑ 8:01 A.M. TO 4:00 P.M.   **MOON 3** ● 4:01 P.M. TO 12:00 A.M.

Use only one "moon" number. Choose the column closest to your time of birth. If your place of birth is not on Eastern Standard Time, be sure to read "How to Convert to Eastern Standard Time" at the beginning of this section.

1961

March

April

Date & Time	SUN	MOON 1	MOON 2	MOON 3	MERCURY	VENUS	MARS	JUPITER	SATURN	URANUS	NEPTUNE	PLUTO
MAR. 1	46	20	21	21	44	4	13	41	40	20	30	22
MAR. 2	46	22	22	23	44	4	13	41	40	20	30	22
MAR. 3	47	24	24	25	44	4	13	41	40	20	30	22
MAR. 4	47	25	26	26	44	4	13	41	41	20	30	22
MAR. 5	47	27	27	28	44	4	13	41	41	20	30	22
MAR. 6	47	29	29	30	44	4	14	41	41	20	30	22
MAR. 7	47	30	31	31	44	4	14	41	41	20	30	22
MAR. 8	47	32	33	33	44	4	14	41	41	20	30	22
MAR. 9	47	34	34	35	44	5	14	41	41	20	30	22
MAR. 10	47	36	36	37	44	5	14	41	41	20	30	22
MAR. 11	48	38	38	39	44	5	14	41	41	20	30	22
MAR. 12	48	39	40	41	44	5	14	41	41	20	30	22
MAR. 13	48	41	42	43	44	5	14	41	41	20	30	22
MAR. 14	48	43	44	45	45	5	14	41	41	20	30	22
MAR. 15	48	45	46	47	45	5	14	41	41	20	30	22
MAR. 16	48	47	48	1	45	5	14	41	41	20	30	22
MAR. 17	48	1	2	3	45	5	14	41	41	20	30	22
MAR. 18	48	3	4	4	45	5	14	41	41	20	30	22
MAR. 19	1	5	6	6	45	5	14	41	41	20	30	22
MAR. 20	1	7	7	8	45	5	14	41	41	20	30	22
MAR. 21	1	9	9	10	45	5	14	41	41	20	30	22
MAR. 22	1	10	11	11	45	5	14	41	41	20	30	22
MAR. 23	1	12	12	13	46	5	14	41	41	20	30	22
MAR. 24	1	14	14	15	46	5	14	41	41	20	30	22
MAR. 25	2	15	16	16	46	5	14	41	41	20	30	22
MAR. 26	2	17	17	18	46	5	14	41	41	20	30	22
MAR. 27	2	18	19	19	46	5	14	41	41	20	30	22
MAR. 28	2	20	20	21	46	5	15	41	41	20	30	22
MAR. 29	2	21	22	23	47	5	15	41	41	20	30	22
MAR. 30	2	23	24	24	47	5	15	41	41	20	30	22
MAR. 31	2	25	25	26	47	5	15	41	41	20	30	22

Date & Time	SUN	MOON 1	MOON 2	MOON 3	MERCURY	VENUS	MARS	JUPITER	SATURN	URANUS	NEPTUNE	PLUTO
APR. 1	2	26	27	28	47	4	15	41	41	20	30	22
APR. 2	2	28	29	29	47	4	15	41	41	20	30	22
APR. 3	3	30	30	31	47	4	15	41	41	20	30	22
APR. 4	3	32	32	33	48	4	15	41	41	20	30	22
APR. 5	3	33	34	35	48	4	15	41	41	20	30	22
APR. 6	3	35	36	37	48	4	15	41	41	20	30	22
APR. 7	3	37	38	38	48	4	15	41	41	20	30	22
APR. 8	3	39	40	40	48	4	15	41	41	20	30	22
APR. 9	3	41	42	42	1	4	15	41	41	20	30	22
APR. 10	3	43	43	44	1	4	15	42	41	20	30	22
APR. 11	4	45	45	46	1	4	15	42	41	20	30	22
APR. 12	4	47	47	48	1	4	15	42	41	20	30	22
APR. 13	4	48	1	2	2	4	15	42	41	20	30	22
APR. 14	4	2	3	4	2	3	16	42	41	20	30	22
APR. 15	4	4	5	5	2	3	16	42	41	20	30	22
APR. 16	4	6	7	7	2	3	16	42	41	20	30	22
APR. 17	4	8	8	9	3	3	16	42	41	20	30	22
APR. 18	4	10	10	11	3	3	16	42	41	20	30	22
APR. 19	5	11	12	12	3	3	16	42	41	20	30	22
APR. 20	5	13	14	14	3	3	16	42	41	20	30	22
APR. 21	5	15	15	16	4	3	16	42	41	20	30	22
APR. 22	5	16	17	17	4	3	16	42	41	20	30	22
APR. 23	5	18	18	19	4	3	16	42	41	20	30	22
APR. 24	5	19	20	20	4	3	16	42	41	20	30	22
APR. 25	6	21	21	22	5	3	16	42	41	20	30	22
APR. 26	6	23	23	24	5	3	16	42	41	20	30	22
APR. 27	6	24	25	25	5	3	16	42	41	20	30	22
APR. 28	6	26	26	27	5	3	16	42	41	20	30	22
APR. 29	6	28	28	29	6	3	17	42	41	20	30	22
APR. 30	6	29	30	30	6	3	17	42	41	20	30	22

MOON 1 ◐ 12:01 A.M. TO 8:00 A.M.   **MOON 2** ◑ 8:01 A.M. TO 4:00 P.M.   **MOON 3** ● 4:01 P.M. TO 12:00 A.M.

Use only one "moon" number. Choose the column closest to your time of birth. If your place of birth is not on Eastern Standard Time, be sure to read "How to Convert to Eastern Standard Time" at the beginning of this section.

1961

May

June

Date & Time	SUN ☉	MOON 1 ◗	MOON 2 ◑	MOON 3 ●	MERCURY	VENUS	MARS	JUPITER	SATURN	URANUS	NEPTUNE	PLUTO
MAY 1	6	31	32	32	6	3	17	42	41	20	30	22
MAY 2	6	33	34	34	7	3	17	42	41	20	30	22
MAY 3	7	35	35	36	7	3	17	42	41	20	30	22
MAY 4	7	37	37	38	7	3	17	42	41	20	30	22
MAY 5	7	39	39	40	7	3	17	42	41	20	30	22
MAY 6	7	40	41	42	8	3	17	42	41	20	30	22
MAY 7	7	42	43	44	8	3	17	42	41	20	30	22
MAY 8	7	44	45	45	8	3	17	42	41	20	30	22
MAY 9	7	46	47	47	9	3	17	42	41	20	30	22
MAY 10	7	48	1	1	9	3	17	42	41	20	30	22
MAY 11	8	2	2	3	9	3	17	42	41	20	30	22
MAY 12	8	4	4	5	9	3	17	42	41	20	30	22
MAY 13	8	5	6	7	10	3	17	42	41	20	30	22
MAY 14	8	7	8	8	10	3	18	42	41	20	30	22
MAY 15	8	9	10	10	10	3	18	42	41	20	30	22
MAY 16	8	11	11	12	10	3	18	42	41	20	30	22
MAY 17	8	12	13	13	11	3	18	42	41	20	30	22
MAY 18	8	14	15	15	11	3	18	42	41	20	30	22
MAY 19	9	16	16	17	11	3	18	42	41	20	30	22
MAY 20	9	17	18	18	11	3	18	42	41	20	30	22
MAY 21	9	19	19	20	12	3	18	42	41	20	30	22
MAY 22	9	20	21	21	12	4	18	42	41	20	30	22
MAY 23	9	22	23	23	12	4	18	42	41	20	30	22
MAY 24	9	24	24	25	12	4	18	42	41	20	30	22
MAY 25	10	25	26	26	12	4	18	42	41	20	30	22
MAY 26	10	27	27	28	13	4	18	42	41	20	30	22
MAY 27	10	29	29	30	13	4	18	42	41	20	30	22
MAY 28	10	30	31	32	13	4	19	42	41	20	30	22
MAY 29	10	32	33	34	13	4	19	42	41	20	30	22
MAY 30	10	34	35	35	13	4	19	42	41	20	30	22
MAY 31	10	36	37	37	13	4	19	42	41	20	30	22

Date & Time	SUN ☉	MOON 1 ◗	MOON 2 ◑	MOON 3 ●	MERCURY	VENUS	MARS	JUPITER	SATURN	URANUS	NEPTUNE	PLUTO
JUN. 1	10	38	39	39	13	4	19	42	41	20	30	22
JUN. 2	10	40	41	41	14	5	19	42	41	20	30	22
JUN. 3	11	42	43	43	14	5	19	42	41	20	30	22
JUN. 4	11	44	44	45	14	5	19	42	41	20	30	22
JUN. 5	11	46	46	47	14	5	19	42	41	20	30	22
JUN. 6	11	48	48	1	14	5	19	42	41	20	30	22
JUN. 7	11	1	2	3	14	5	19	42	41	20	30	22
JUN. 8	11	3	4	4	14	5	19	42	41	20	30	22
JUN. 9	11	5	6	6	14	5	19	42	41	20	30	22
JUN. 10	11	7	7	8	14	5	20	42	41	20	30	22
JUN. 11	12	8	9	9	14	6	20	42	41	20	30	22
JUN. 12	12	10	11	11	14	6	20	42	41	20	30	22
JUN. 13	12	12	12	13	14	6	20	42	41	20	30	22
JUN. 14	12	14	14	15	14	6	20	42	41	20	30	22
JUN. 15	12	15	16	16	14	6	20	42	41	20	30	22
JUN. 16	12	17	17	19	14	6	20	42	41	20	30	22
JUN. 17	12	18	19	19	14	6	20	42	41	20	30	22
JUN. 18	12	20	20	21	14	6	20	42	41	20	30	22
JUN. 19	13	21	22	23	14	7	20	42	41	20	30	22
JUN. 20	13	23	24	24	14	7	20	42	41	20	30	22
JUN. 21	13	25	25	26	14	7	20	42	41	20	30	22
JUN. 22	13	26	27	27	14	7	20	42	41	20	30	22
JUN. 23	13	28	29	29	14	7	21	42	41	20	30	22
JUN. 24	13	30	30	31	14	7	21	42	41	20	30	22
JUN. 25	14	31	32	33	14	7	21	42	41	20	30	22
JUN. 26	14	33	34	35	14	7	21	42	41	20	30	22
JUN. 27	14	35	36	37	14	8	21	42	41	20	30	22
JUN. 28	14	37	38	39	14	8	21	42	41	20	30	22
JUN. 29	14	39	40	41	14	8	21	42	41	20	30	22
JUN. 30	14	41	42	43	14	8	21	42	41	20	30	22

MOON 1 ◗ 12:01 A.M. TO 8:00 A.M.   **MOON 2** ◑ 8:01 A.M. TO 4:00 P.M.   **MOON 3** ● 4:01 P.M. TO 12:00 A.M.
Use only one "moon" number. Choose the column closest to your time of birth. If your place of birth is not on
Eastern Standard Time, be sure to read "How to Convert to Eastern Standard Time" at the beginning of this section.

1961 — July / August

Date & Time	SUN	MOON 1	MOON 2	MOON 3	MERCURY	VENUS	MARS	JUPITER	SATURN	URANUS	NEPTUNE	PLUTO
JUL. 1	14	43	44	44	13	8	21	42	41	20	30	22
JUL. 2	14	45	46	46	13	8	21	42	41	20	30	22
JUL. 3	15	47	48	48	13	8	21	42	41	20	30	22
JUL. 4	15	1	2	2	13	9	21	42	41	20	30	22
JUL. 5	15	3	3	4	13	9	21	42	41	20	30	22
JUL. 6	15	5	5	6	13	9	22	42	41	20	30	22
JUL. 7	15	6	7	8	13	9	22	42	41	20	30	22
JUL. 8	15	8	9	9	13	9	22	42	41	20	30	22
JUL. 9	15	10	10	11	13	9	22	42	41	20	30	22
JUL. 10	15	11	12	13	13	9	22	42	41	20	30	22
JUL. 11	16	13	14	14	13	10	22	42	41	20	30	22
JUL. 12	16	15	15	16	13	10	22	41	41	20	30	22
JUL. 13	16	16	17	17	13	10	22	41	41	20	30	22
JUL. 14	16	18	18	19	13	10	22	41	41	20	30	22
JUL. 15	16	19	20	21	13	10	22	41	41	20	30	22
JUL. 16	16	21	22	22	13	10	22	41	41	20	30	22
JUL. 17	16	23	23	24	14	10	22	41	41	20	30	22
JUL. 18	16	24	25	25	14	11	22	41	41	20	30	22
JUL. 19	17	26	26	27	14	11	23	41	41	20	30	22
JUL. 20	17	27	28	29	14	11	23	41	40	20	30	22
JUL. 21	17	29	30	30	14	11	23	41	40	20	30	22
JUL. 22	17	31	31	32	14	11	23	41	40	20	30	22
JUL. 23	17	33	33	34	14	11	23	41	40	20	30	22
JUL. 24	17	34	35	36	15	11	23	41	40	20	30	22
JUL. 25	17	36	37	38	15	12	23	41	40	20	30	22
JUL. 26	18	38	39	40	15	12	23	41	40	20	30	22
JUL. 27	18	40	41	42	15	12	23	41	40	20	30	22
JUL. 28	18	42	43	44	15	12	23	41	40	20	30	22
JUL. 29	18	44	45	46	16	12	23	40	40	20	30	22
JUL. 30	18	46	47	48	16	12	23	41	40	20	30	22
JUL. 31	18	48	1	2	16	12	24	41	40	20	30	22

Date & Time	SUN	MOON 1	MOON 2	MOON 3	MERCURY	VENUS	MARS	JUPITER	SATURN	URANUS	NEPTUNE	PLUTO
AUG. 1	18	2	3	3	16	13	24	41	40	20	30	22
AUG. 2	18	4	5	5	16	13	24	41	40	20	30	22
AUG. 3	19	6	7	7	17	13	24	41	40	20	30	22
AUG. 4	19	8	8	9	17	13	24	41	40	20	30	22
AUG. 5	19	9	10	11	17	13	24	41	40	20	30	22
AUG. 6	19	11	12	12	18	13	24	41	40	20	30	22
AUG. 7	19	13	13	14	18	14	24	41	40	20	30	22
AUG. 8	19	14	15	15	18	14	24	41	40	20	30	22
AUG. 9	19	16	16	17	18	14	24	41	40	20	30	22
AUG. 10	19	17	18	19	19	14	24	41	40	20	30	22
AUG. 11	20	19	20	19	19	14	24	41	40	20	30	22
AUG. 12	20	21	21	22	19	14	25	41	40	20	30	22
AUG. 13	20	22	23	23	19	14	25	41	40	20	30	22
AUG. 14	20	24	24	25	20	15	25	41	40	20	30	22
AUG. 15	20	25	26	26	20	15	25	41	40	20	30	22
AUG. 16	20	27	28	28	20	15	25	41	40	20	30	22
AUG. 17	20	29	29	30	21	15	25	41	40	20	30	22
AUG. 18	20	30	31	31	21	15	25	41	40	20	30	22
AUG. 19	21	32	33	33	21	15	25	41	40	20	30	22
AUG. 20	21	34	34	35	21	16	25	41	40	20	30	22
AUG. 21	21	36	36	37	22	16	25	41	40	20	30	22
AUG. 22	21	38	38	39	22	16	25	41	40	20	30	22
AUG. 23	21	39	40	41	22	16	25	41	40	20	30	22
AUG. 24	21	41	42	43	22	16	26	41	40	20	30	22
AUG. 25	21	43	44	45	23	16	26	41	40	21	30	22
AUG. 26	22	45	46	47	23	16	26	41	40	21	30	22
AUG. 27	22	47	48	1	23	17	26	41	40	21	30	22
AUG. 28	22	1	2	3	23	17	26	41	40	21	30	22
AUG. 29	22	3	4	5	23	17	26	41	40	21	30	22
AUG. 30	22	5	6	7	24	17	26	41	40	21	30	22
AUG. 31	22	7	8	8	24	17	26	41	40	21	30	22

MOON 1 ◗ 12:01 A.M. TO 8:00 A.M.   **MOON 2** ◑ 8:01 A.M. TO 4:00 P.M.   **MOON 3** ● 4:01 P.M. TO 12:00 A.M.

Use only one "moon" number. Choose the column closest to your time of birth. If your place of birth is not on Eastern Standard Time, be sure to read "How to Convert to Eastern Standard Time" at the beginning of this section.

1961

September

Date & Time	SUN	MOON 1	MOON 2	MOON 3	MERCURY	VENUS	MARS	JUPITER	SATURN	URANUS	NEPTUNE	PLUTO
SEP. 1	22	9	9	10	24	17	26	41	40	21	30	22
SEP. 2	22	11	11	12	24	18	26	41	40	21	30	22
SEP. 3	23	12	13	13	25	18	26	41	40	21	30	22
SEP. 4	23	14	14	15	25	18	27	41	40	21	30	22
SEP. 5	23	16	16	17	25	18	27	41	40	21	30	22
SEP. 6	23	17	18	18	25	18	27	41	40	21	30	22
SEP. 7	23	19	19	20	25	18	27	41	40	21	30	22
SEP. 8	23	20	21	21	26	18	27	41	40	21	30	22
SEP. 9	23	22	22	23	26	19	27	41	40	21	30	22
SEP. 10	23	23	24	24	26	19	27	41	40	21	30	22
SEP. 11	24	25	26	26	26	19	27	41	40	21	30	22
SEP. 12	24	27	27	28	26	19	27	41	40	21	30	22
SEP. 13	24	28	29	29	27	19	27	41	40	21	30	22
SEP. 14	24	30	30	31	27	19	27	41	40	21	30	22
SEP. 15	24	32	32	33	27	20	27	41	40	21	30	22
SEP. 16	24	33	34	35	27	20	28	41	40	21	30	22
SEP. 17	24	35	36	36	27	20	28	41	40	21	30	22
SEP. 18	24	37	38	38	28	20	28	41	40	21	30	22
SEP. 19	25	39	39	40	28	20	28	41	40	21	30	22
SEP. 20	25	41	41	42	28	20	28	41	40	21	30	22
SEP. 21	25	43	43	44	28	21	28	41	40	21	30	22
SEP. 22	25	45	45	46	28	21	28	41	40	21	30	22
SEP. 23	25	47	47	48	28	21	28	41	40	21	30	22
SEP. 24	25	1	1	2	28	21	28	41	40	21	30	22
SEP. 25	26	3	3	4	29	21	28	41	40	21	30	22
SEP. 26	26	5	5	6	29	21	28	41	40	21	30	22
SEP. 27	26	6	7	8	29	21	29	41	40	21	30	22
SEP. 28	26	8	9	9	29	22	29	41	40	21	30	22
SEP. 29	26	10	11	11	29	22	29	41	40	21	30	22
SEP. 30	26	12	12	13	29	22	29	41	40	21	30	22

October

Date & Time	SUN	MOON 1	MOON 2	MOON 3	MERCURY	VENUS	MARS	JUPITER	SATURN	URANUS	NEPTUNE	PLUTO
OCT. 1	26	13	14	15	29	22	29	41	40	21	30	22
OCT. 2	26	15	16	16	30	22	29	41	40	21	30	22
OCT. 3	27	17	17	18	30	23	29	41	40	21	30	22
OCT. 4	27	18	19	19	30	23	29	41	40	21	30	22
OCT. 5	27	20	20	21	30	23	29	41	40	21	30	22
OCT. 6	27	21	22	22	30	23	29	41	40	21	30	22
OCT. 7	27	23	23	24	30	23	29	41	40	21	30	22
OCT. 8	27	25	25	26	30	23	30	41	40	21	30	22
OCT. 9	27	26	27	27	30	24	30	41	40	21	30	22
OCT. 10	27	28	28	29	30	24	30	41	40	21	30	22
OCT. 11	28	30	30	31	30	24	30	41	40	21	30	22
OCT. 12	28	31	32	32	30	24	30	41	40	21	30	22
OCT. 13	28	33	34	34	30	24	30	41	40	21	30	22
OCT. 14	28	35	35	36	30	24	30	41	40	21	30	22
OCT. 15	28	36	37	38	30	24	30	41	40	21	30	22
OCT. 16	28	38	39	40	30	25	30	41	40	21	30	22
OCT. 17	28	40	41	41	30	25	30	41	40	21	30	22
OCT. 18	28	42	43	43	30	25	30	41	40	21	30	22
OCT. 19	29	44	45	45	29	25	31	41	40	21	30	22
OCT. 20	29	46	46	47	29	25	31	41	40	21	30	22
OCT. 21	29	48	48	1	29	25	31	41	40	21	30	22
OCT. 22	29	2	2	3	29	26	31	41	40	21	30	22
OCT. 23	29	4	4	5	29	26	31	41	40	21	30	22
OCT. 24	29	6	6	7	29	26	31	41	40	21	30	22
OCT. 25	29	7	8	9	28	26	31	41	40	21	30	22
OCT. 26	30	9	10	11	28	26	31	41	40	21	30	22
OCT. 27	30	11	12	12	28	26	31	41	40	21	30	22
OCT. 28	30	13	13	14	28	27	31	41	40	21	30	22
OCT. 29	30	14	15	16	28	27	31	41	40	21	30	22
OCT. 30	30	16	17	17	28	27	32	41	40	21	30	22
OCT. 31	30	18	18	19	28	27	32	41	40	21	30	22

MOON 1 ☽ 12:01 A.M. TO 8:00 A.M.　　**MOON 2** ☽ 8:01 A.M. TO 4:00 P.M.　　**MOON 3** ● 4:01 P.M. TO 12:00 A.M.
Use only one "moon" number. Choose the column closest to your time of birth. If your place of birth is not on
Eastern Standard Time, be sure to read "How to Convert to Eastern Standard Time" at the beginning of this section.

1961

November

December

Date & Time	SUN ☉	MOON 1 ◐	MOON 2 ◑	MOON 3 ●	MERCURY	VENUS	MARS	JUPITER	SATURN	URANUS	NEPTUNE	PLUTO
NOV. 1	30	19	20	20	28	27	32	41	40	21	30	22
NOV. 2	30	21	21	22	28	27	32	41	40	21	30	22
NOV. 3	31	22	23	24	28	28	32	41	40	21	30	22
NOV. 4	31	24	25	25	28	28	32	41	40	21	30	22
NOV. 5	31	26	26	27	28	28	32	41	40	21	30	22
NOV. 6	31	27	28	28	28	28	32	41	40	21	30	22
NOV. 7	31	29	30	30	28	28	32	41	40	21	30	22
NOV. 8	31	31	31	32	29	28	32	41	40	21	30	22
NOV. 9	31	32	33	34	29	29	33	41	40	21	30	22
NOV. 10	31	34	35	35	29	29	33	41	40	21	30	22
NOV. 11	31	36	37	37	29	29	33	41	40	21	30	22
NOV. 12	32	38	38	39	29	29	33	41	40	21	30	22
NOV. 13	32	40	40	41	29	29	33	41	40	21	30	22
NOV. 14	32	42	42	43	30	29	33	41	40	21	30	22
NOV. 15	32	43	44	45	30	30	33	41	40	21	30	22
NOV. 16	32	45	46	47	30	30	33	41	40	21	31	22
NOV. 17	32	47	48	48	30	30	33	41	40	21	31	22
NOV. 18	32	1	2	2	30	30	33	41	40	21	31	22
NOV. 19	33	3	4	4	31	30	33	41	40	21	31	22
NOV. 20	33	5	6	6	31	30	34	41	40	21	31	22
NOV. 21	33	7	7	8	31	31	34	41	40	21	31	22
NOV. 22	33	9	9	10	31	31	34	41	40	21	31	22
NOV. 23	33	10	11	12	31	31	34	41	40	21	31	22
NOV. 24	33	12	13	13	32	31	34	41	40	21	31	22
NOV. 25	34	14	14	15	32	31	34	41	40	21	31	22
NOV. 26	34	16	16	17	32	31	34	41	40	21	31	22
NOV. 27	34	17	18	18	32	32	34	41	40	21	31	22
NOV. 28	34	19	19	20	32	32	34	41	40	21	31	22
NOV. 29	34	20	21	21	33	32	34	41	40	21	31	22
NOV. 30	34	22	22	23	33	32	35	42	40	21	31	22

Date & Time	SUN ☉	MOON 1 ◐	MOON 2 ◑	MOON 3 ●	MERCURY	VENUS	MARS	JUPITER	SATURN	URANUS	NEPTUNE	PLUTO
DEC. 1	34	23	24	25	33	32	35	42	40	21	31	22
DEC. 2	34	25	26	26	33	32	35	42	41	21	31	22
DEC. 3	35	27	27	28	33	33	35	42	41	21	31	22
DEC. 4	35	28	29	29	34	33	35	42	41	21	31	22
DEC. 5	35	30	31	31	34	33	35	42	41	21	31	22
DEC. 6	35	32	32	33	34	33	35	42	41	21	31	22
DEC. 7	35	34	34	35	34	33	35	42	41	21	31	22
DEC. 8	35	35	36	37	34	33	35	42	41	21	31	22
DEC. 9	35	37	38	39	35	34	35	42	41	21	31	22
DEC. 10	35	39	40	40	35	34	36	42	41	21	31	22
DEC. 11	36	41	42	42	35	34	36	42	41	21	31	22
DEC. 12	36	43	44	44	35	34	36	42	41	21	31	22
DEC. 13	36	45	46	46	36	34	36	42	41	21	31	22
DEC. 14	36	47	47	48	36	34	36	42	41	21	31	22
DEC. 15	36	1	1	2	36	35	36	42	41	21	31	22
DEC. 16	36	3	3	4	36	35	36	42	41	21	31	22
DEC. 17	36	4	5	6	36	35	36	42	41	21	31	22
DEC. 18	36	6	7	7	37	35	36	42	41	21	31	22
DEC. 19	37	8	9	9	37	35	36	42	41	21	31	22
DEC. 20	37	10	10	11	37	35	37	42	41	21	31	22
DEC. 21	37	12	12	13	37	36	37	42	41	21	31	22
DEC. 22	37	13	14	14	37	36	37	42	41	21	31	22
DEC. 23	37	15	16	16	38	36	37	42	41	21	31	22
DEC. 24	37	17	17	18	38	36	37	42	41	21	31	22
DEC. 25	37	18	19	19	38	36	37	42	41	21	31	22
DEC. 26	38	20	20	21	38	36	37	42	41	21	31	22
DEC. 27	38	21	22	22	38	37	37	42	41	21	31	22
DEC. 28	38	23	23	24	39	37	37	42	41	21	31	22
DEC. 29	38	25	25	26	39	37	37	42	41	21	31	22
DEC. 30	38	26	27	27	39	37	38	42	41	21	31	22
DEC. 31	38	28	28	29	39	37	38	42	41	21	31	22

MOON 1 ◐ 12:01 A.M. TO 8:00 A.M.   **MOON 2** ◑ 8:01 A.M. TO 4:00 P.M.   **MOON 3** ● 4:01 P.M. TO 12:00 A.M.

Use only one "moon" number. Choose the column closest to your time of birth. If your place of birth is not on Eastern Standard Time, be sure to read "How to Convert to Eastern Standard Time" at the beginning of this section.

1962

January

Date & Time	SUN ☉	MOON 1 ◖	MOON 2 ◑	MOON 3 ●	MERCURY	VENUS	MARS	JUPITER	SATURN	URANUS	NEPTUNE	PLUTO
JAN. 1	38	29	30	31	40	38	38	42	41	21	31	22
JAN. 2	38	31	32	32	40	38	38	42	41	21	31	22
JAN. 3	39	33	33	34	40	38	38	42	41	21	31	22
JAN. 4	39	35	35	36	40	38	38	42	41	21	31	22
JAN. 5	39	37	37	38	40	38	38	42	41	21	31	22
JAN. 6	39	38	39	40	41	38	38	42	41	21	31	22
JAN. 7	39	40	41	42	41	39	38	42	41	21	31	22
JAN. 8	39	42	43	44	41	39	38	43	41	21	31	22
JAN. 9	39	44	45	46	41	39	39	43	41	21	31	22
JAN. 10	40	46	47	48	42	39	39	43	41	21	31	22
JAN. 11	40	48	1	1	42	39	39	43	41	21	31	22
JAN. 12	40	2	3	3	42	39	39	43	41	21	31	22
JAN. 13	40	4	5	5	42	40	39	43	41	21	31	22
JAN. 14	40	6	6	7	42	40	39	43	41	21	31	22
JAN. 15	40	8	8	9	43	40	39	43	41	21	31	22
JAN. 16	40	9	10	11	43	40	39	43	41	21	31	22
JAN. 17	41	11	12	12	43	40	39	43	41	21	31	22
JAN. 18	41	13	13	14	43	40	39	43	41	21	31	22
JAN. 19	41	14	15	16	43	41	40	43	41	21	31	22
JAN. 20	41	16	17	17	43	41	40	43	41	21	31	22
JAN. 21	41	18	18	19	44	41	40	43	41	21	31	22
JAN. 22	41	19	20	20	44	41	40	43	41	21	31	22
JAN. 23	42	21	21	22	44	41	40	43	41	21	31	22
JAN. 24	42	22	23	24	44	41	40	43	41	21	31	22
JAN. 25	42	24	25	25	44	42	40	43	41	21	31	22
JAN. 26	42	26	26	27	44	42	40	43	41	21	31	22
JAN. 27	42	27	28	28	44	42	40	43	41	21	31	22
JAN. 28	42	29	29	30	44	42	41	43	41	21	31	22
JAN. 29	42	30	31	32	44	42	41	43	41	21	31	22
JAN. 30	42	32	33	33	44	42	41	43	41	21	31	22
JAN. 31	43	34	35	35	44	43	41	43	41	21	31	22

February

Date & Time	SUN ☉	MOON 1 ◖	MOON 2 ◑	MOON 3 ●	MERCURY	VENUS	MARS	JUPITER	SATURN	URANUS	NEPTUNE	PLUTO
FEB. 1	43	36	36	37	44	43	41	43	41	21	31	22
FEB. 2	43	38	38	39	44	43	41	43	41	21	31	22
FEB. 3	43	40	40	41	43	43	41	43	41	21	31	22
FEB. 4	43	41	42	43	43	43	41	43	41	21	31	22
FEB. 5	43	43	44	45	43	43	41	43	41	21	31	22
FEB. 6	43	45	46	47	43	44	41	43	41	21	31	22
FEB. 7	43	47	48	1	43	44	42	44	42	21	31	22
FEB. 8	44	1	2	3	43	44	42	44	42	21	31	22
FEB. 9	44	3	4	5	43	44	42	44	42	21	31	22
FEB. 10	44	5	6	7	42	44	42	44	42	21	31	22
FEB. 11	44	7	8	8	42	44	42	44	42	21	31	22
FEB. 12	44	9	10	10	42	45	42	44	42	21	31	22
FEB. 13	44	11	11	12	42	45	42	44	42	21	31	22
FEB. 14	44	12	13	13	42	45	42	44	42	21	31	22
FEB. 15	44	14	15	15	42	45	42	44	42	21	31	22
FEB. 16	45	16	16	17	42	45	42	44	42	21	31	22
FEB. 17	45	17	18	18	42	45	43	44	42	21	31	22
FEB. 18	45	19	19	20	42	46	43	44	42	21	31	22
FEB. 19	45	20	21	22	42	46	43	44	42	21	31	22
FEB. 20	45	22	23	23	42	46	43	44	42	21	31	22
FEB. 21	45	24	24	25	42	46	43	44	42	21	31	22
FEB. 22	45	25	26	26	42	46	43	44	42	21	31	22
FEB. 23	46	27	27	28	42	46	43	44	42	21	31	22
FEB. 24	46	28	29	29	42	47	43	44	42	21	31	22
FEB. 25	46	30	31	31	42	47	43	44	42	21	31	22
FEB. 26	46	32	32	33	42	47	43	44	42	21	31	22
FEB. 27	46	33	34	34	42	47	44	44	42	21	31	22
FEB. 28	46	35	36	36	43	47	44	44	42	21	31	22

MOON 1 ◖ 12:01 A.M. TO 8:00 A.M.　　**MOON 2** ◑ 8:01 A.M. TO 4:00 P.M.　　**MOON 3** ● 4:01 P.M. TO 12:00 A.M.

Use only one "moon" number. Choose the column closest to your time of birth. If your place of birth is not on Eastern Standard Time, be sure to read "How to Convert to Eastern Standard Time" at the beginning of this section.

March

April

Date & Time	SUN	MOON 1	MOON 2	MOON 3	MERCURY	VENUS	MARS	JUPITER	SATURN	URANUS	NEPTUNE	PLUTO
MAR. 1	46	37	37	38	43	47	44	44	42	21	31	22
MAR. 2	46	39	39	40	43	48	44	44	42	21	31	22
MAR. 3	47	41	41	42	43	48	44	44	42	21	31	22
MAR. 4	47	43	43	44	43	48	44	44	42	21	31	22
MAR. 5	47	45	45	46	43	48	44	44	42	21	31	22
MAR. 6	47	47	47	48	43	48	44	44	42	21	31	22
MAR. 7	47	1	1	2	44	48	44	44	42	21	31	22
MAR. 8	47	3	3	4	44	1	45	44	42	21	31	22
MAR. 9	47	5	5	6	44	1	45	44	42	21	31	22
MAR. 10	47	7	7	8	44	1	45	44	42	21	31	22
MAR. 11	48	8	9	10	44	1	45	45	42	21	31	22
MAR. 12	48	10	11	11	44	1	45	45	42	21	31	22
MAR. 13	48	12	13	13	45	1	45	45	42	21	31	22
MAR. 14	48	14	14	15	45	2	45	45	42	21	31	22
MAR. 15	48	15	16	16	45	2	45	45	42	21	31	22
MAR. 16	48	17	17	18	45	2	45	45	42	21	31	22
MAR. 17	48	18	19	20	45	2	45	45	42	21	31	22
MAR. 18	48	20	21	21	45	2	46	45	42	21	31	22
MAR. 19	1	22	22	23	46	2	46	45	42	21	31	22
MAR. 20	1	23	24	24	46	3	46	45	42	21	31	22
MAR. 21	1	25	25	26	46	3	46	45	42	21	31	22
MAR. 22	1	26	27	27	46	3	46	45	42	21	31	22
MAR. 23	1	28	29	29	46	3	46	45	42	21	31	22
MAR. 24	1	30	30	31	47	3	46	45	42	21	31	22
MAR. 25	2	31	32	32	47	3	46	45	42	21	31	22
MAR. 26	2	33	33	34	47	4	46	45	42	21	31	22
MAR. 27	2	35	35	36	47	4	47	45	42	21	31	22
MAR. 28	2	36	37	37	48	4	47	45	42	21	31	22
MAR. 29	2	38	39	39	48	4	47	45	42	21	31	22
MAR. 30	2	40	41	41	48	4	47	45	42	21	31	22
MAR. 31	2	42	42	43	48	4	47	45	42	21	31	22

Date & Time	SUN	MOON 1	MOON 2	MOON 3	MERCURY	VENUS	MARS	JUPITER	SATURN	URANUS	NEPTUNE	PLUTO
APR. 1	2	44	44	45	1	5	47	45	42	21	31	22
APR. 2	2	46	46	47	1	5	47	45	42	21	31	22
APR. 3	3	48	48	1	1	5	47	45	42	21	31	22
APR. 4	3	2	2	3	1	5	47	45	42	21	31	22
APR. 5	3	4	4	5	1	5	47	45	42	21	31	22
APR. 6	3	6	6	7	2	5	48	45	42	21	31	22
APR. 7	3	8	8	9	2	6	48	45	42	21	31	22
APR. 8	3	10	10	11	2	6	48	45	42	21	31	22
APR. 9	3	11	12	13	3	6	48	45	42	21	31	22
APR. 10	3	13	14	14	3	6	48	45	42	21	31	22
APR. 11	4	15	15	16	3	6	48	45	42	21	31	22
APR. 12	4	16	17	18	3	6	48	45	42	21	31	22
APR. 13	4	18	19	19	4	6	48	45	42	21	31	22
APR. 14	4	20	20	21	4	7	48	45	42	21	31	22
APR. 15	4	21	22	22	4	7	1	46	42	21	31	22
APR. 16	4	23	23	24	4	7	1	46	42	21	31	22
APR. 17	4	24	25	25	5	7	1	46	42	21	31	22
APR. 18	4	26	27	27	5	7	1	46	42	21	31	22
APR. 19	5	28	28	29	5	7	1	46	42	20	31	22
APR. 20	5	29	30	30	6	8	1	46	42	20	31	22
APR. 21	5	31	31	32	6	8	1	46	42	20	31	22
APR. 22	5	33	33	34	6	8	1	46	42	20	31	22
APR. 23	5	34	35	35	6	8	1	46	42	20	31	22
APR. 24	5	36	37	37	7	8	1	46	42	20	31	22
APR. 25	6	38	38	39	7	8	2	46	42	20	31	22
APR. 26	6	39	40	41	7	9	2	46	42	20	31	22
APR. 27	6	41	42	42	7	9	2	46	42	20	31	22
APR. 28	6	43	44	44	8	9	2	46	42	20	31	22
APR. 29	6	45	46	46	8	9	2	46	42	20	31	22
APR. 30	6	47	48	48	8	9	2	46	42	20	31	22

MOON 1 ☽ 12:01 A.M. TO 8:00 A.M.   **MOON 2** ◑ 8:01 A.M. TO 4:00 P.M.   **MOON 3** ● 4:01 P.M. TO 12:00 A.M.
Use only one "moon" number. Choose the column closest to your time of birth. If your place of birth is not on
Eastern Standard Time, be sure to read "How to Convert to Eastern Standard Time" at the beginning of this section.

1962

May

June

Date & Time	SUN ☉	MOON 1 ☽	MOON 2 ◗	MOON 3 ●	MERCURY	VENUS	MARS	JUPITER	SATURN	URANUS	NEPTUNE	PLUTO
MAY 1	6	1	2	2	8	9	2	46	42	20	31	22
MAY 2	6	3	4	4	9	10	2	46	42	20	31	22
MAY 3	7	5	5	6	9	10	2	46	42	20	31	22
MAY 4	7	7	7	8	9	10	2	46	42	20	31	22
MAY 5	7	9	9	10	9	10	3	46	42	20	31	22
MAY 6	7	11	11	12	10	10	3	46	42	20	31	22
MAY 7	7	12	13	14	10	10	3	46	42	20	31	22
MAY 8	7	14	15	15	10	11	3	46	42	20	31	22
MAY 9	7	16	16	17	10	11	3	46	42	20	31	22
MAY 10	7	18	18	19	10	11	3	46	42	20	31	22
MAY 11	8	19	20	20	10	11	3	46	42	20	31	22
MAY 12	8	21	21	22	11	11	3	46	42	20	31	22
MAY 13	8	22	23	23	11	11	3	46	42	20	31	22
MAY 14	8	24	24	25	11	12	3	46	42	20	31	22
MAY 15	8	25	26	27	11	12	4	46	42	20	31	22
MAY 16	8	27	28	28	11	12	4	46	42	20	31	22
MAY 17	8	29	29	30	11	12	4	46	42	20	31	22
MAY 18	8	30	31	31	11	12	4	46	42	20	31	22
MAY 19	9	32	33	33	11	12	4	46	42	20	31	22
MAY 20	9	34	34	35	11	12	4	46	42	21	31	22
MAY 21	9	35	36	37	12	13	4	46	42	21	31	22
MAY 22	9	37	38	38	12	13	4	46	42	21	31	22
MAY 23	9	39	40	40	12	13	4	46	42	21	31	22
MAY 24	9	41	41	42	12	13	4	46	42	21	31	22
MAY 25	10	43	43	44	12	13	5	46	42	21	31	22
MAY 26	10	45	45	46	12	13	5	46	42	21	31	22
MAY 27	10	46	47	48	12	14	5	46	42	21	30	22
MAY 28	10	48	1	2	12	14	5	46	42	21	30	22
MAY 29	10	2	3	4	12	14	5	46	42	21	30	22
MAY 30	10	4	5	5	12	14	5	46	42	21	30	22
MAY 31	10	6	7	7	12	14	5	46	42	21	30	22

Date & Time	SUN ☉	MOON 1 ☽	MOON 2 ◗	MOON 3 ●	MERCURY	VENUS	MARS	JUPITER	SATURN	URANUS	NEPTUNE	PLUTO
JUN. 1	10	8	9	9	12	14	5	46	42	21	30	22
JUN. 2	10	10	10	11	11	15	5	46	42	21	30	22
JUN. 3	11	12	12	13	11	15	5	46	42	21	30	22
JUN. 4	11	13	14	15	11	15	6	46	42	21	30	22
JUN. 5	11	15	16	16	11	15	6	47	42	21	30	22
JUN. 6	11	17	17	18	11	15	6	47	42	21	30	22
JUN. 7	11	19	19	20	11	15	6	47	42	21	30	22
JUN. 8	11	20	21	21	11	16	6	47	42	21	30	22
JUN. 9	11	22	22	23	11	16	6	47	42	21	30	22
JUN. 10	11	23	24	24	11	16	6	47	42	21	30	22
JUN. 11	12	25	26	26	11	16	6	47	42	21	30	22
JUN. 12	12	27	27	28	11	16	6	47	42	21	30	22
JUN. 13	12	28	29	29	11	16	6	47	42	21	30	22
JUN. 14	12	30	30	31	11	16	7	47	42	21	30	22
JUN. 15	12	31	32	33	11	17	7	47	42	21	30	22
JUN. 16	12	33	34	34	11	17	7	47	42	21	30	22
JUN. 17	12	35	36	36	11	17	7	47	42	21	30	22
JUN. 18	12	37	37	38	11	17	7	47	42	21	30	22
JUN. 19	13	39	39	40	11	17	7	47	42	21	30	22
JUN. 20	13	40	41	42	11	17	7	47	42	21	30	22
JUN. 21	13	42	43	43	11	18	7	47	42	21	30	22
JUN. 22	13	44	45	45	11	18	7	47	42	21	30	22
JUN. 23	13	46	47	47	11	18	7	47	42	21	30	22
JUN. 24	13	48	1	1	11	18	8	47	42	21	30	22
JUN. 25	14	2	2	3	11	18	8	47	42	21	30	22
JUN. 26	14	4	4	5	11	18	8	47	42	21	30	22
JUN. 27	14	6	6	7	11	19	8	47	42	21	30	22
JUN. 28	14	7	8	9	11	19	8	47	42	21	30	22
JUN. 29	14	9	10	10	11	19	8	47	42	21	30	22
JUN. 30	14	11	12	12	11	19	8	47	42	21	30	22

MOON 1 ☽ 12:01 A.M. TO 8:00 A.M.　　**MOON 2** ◗ 8:01 A.M. TO 4:00 P.M.　　**MOON 3** ● 4:01 P.M. TO 12:00 A.M.
Use only one "moon" number. Choose the column closest to your time of birth. If your place of birth is not on Eastern Standard Time, be sure to read "How to Convert to Eastern Standard Time" at the beginning of this section.

1962

July

August

Date & Time	SUN	MOON 1	MOON 2	MOON 3	MERCURY	VENUS	MARS	JUPITER	SATURN	URANUS	NEPTUNE	PLUTO
JUL. 1	14	13	13	14	11	19	8	47	42	21	30	22
JUL. 2	14	15	15	16	11	19	8	47	42	21	30	22
JUL. 3	15	16	17	17	12	19	8	47	42	21	30	22
JUL. 4	15	18	19	19	12	20	8	47	42	21	30	22
JUL. 5	15	20	20	21	12	20	9	47	42	21	30	22
JUL. 6	15	21	22	22	12	20	9	47	42	21	30	22
JUL. 7	15	23	23	24	12	20	9	47	42	21	30	22
JUL. 8	15	24	25	26	12	20	9	47	42	21	30	22
JUL. 9	15	26	27	27	13	20	9	47	42	21	30	22
JUL. 10	15	28	28	29	13	21	9	47	42	21	30	22
JUL. 11	16	29	30	30	13	21	9	47	42	21	30	22
JUL. 12	16	31	31	32	13	21	9	47	42	21	30	22
JUL. 13	16	33	33	34	13	21	9	47	42	21	30	22
JUL. 14	16	34	35	35	14	21	9	47	42	21	30	22
JUL. 15	16	36	37	37	14	21	10	47	42	21	30	22
JUL. 16	16	38	38	39	14	21	10	47	42	21	30	22
JUL. 17	16	40	40	41	14	22	10	47	42	21	30	22
JUL. 18	16	42	42	43	15	22	10	47	42	21	30	22
JUL. 19	17	44	44	45	15	22	10	47	42	21	30	22
JUL. 20	17	45	46	47	15	22	10	47	42	21	30	22
JUL. 21	17	47	48	1	15	22	10	47	42	21	30	22
JUL. 22	17	1	2	3	16	22	10	47	42	21	30	22
JUL. 23	17	3	4	5	16	23	10	47	42	21	30	22
JUL. 24	17	5	6	6	16	23	10	47	42	21	30	22
JUL. 25	17	7	8	8	17	23	10	47	42	21	30	22
JUL. 26	18	9	9	10	17	23	11	47	42	21	30	22
JUL. 27	18	11	11	12	17	23	11	47	42	21	30	22
JUL. 28	18	12	13	14	17	23	11	47	42	21	30	22
JUL. 29	18	14	15	15	18	23	11	47	42	21	30	22
JUL. 30	18	16	16	17	18	24	11	46	42	21	30	22
JUL. 31	18	17	18	19	18	24	11	46	42	21	30	22

Date & Time	SUN	MOON 1	MOON 2	MOON 3	MERCURY	VENUS	MARS	JUPITER	SATURN	URANUS	NEPTUNE	PLUTO
AUG. 1	18	19	20	20	18	24	11	46	42	21	30	22
AUG. 2	18	21	21	22	19	24	11	46	42	21	30	22
AUG. 3	19	22	23	23	19	24	11	46	42	21	30	22
AUG. 4	19	24	24	25	19	24	11	46	42	21	30	22
AUG. 5	19	26	26	27	20	24	11	46	42	21	30	22
AUG. 6	19	27	28	28	20	25	12	46	42	21	30	22
AUG. 7	19	29	29	30	20	25	12	46	42	21	30	22
AUG. 8	19	30	31	31	20	25	12	46	42	21	30	22
AUG. 9	19	32	32	33	21	25	12	46	42	21	30	22
AUG. 10	19	34	34	35	21	25	12	46	42	21	30	22
AUG. 11	20	35	36	36	21	25	12	46	42	21	30	22
AUG. 12	20	37	38	38	21	25	12	46	42	21	30	22
AUG. 13	20	39	40	40	21	26	12	46	42	21	30	22
AUG. 14	20	41	41	42	22	26	12	46	42	21	30	22
AUG. 15	20	43	43	44	22	26	12	46	42	21	30	22
AUG. 16	20	45	45	46	22	26	12	46	42	21	30	22
AUG. 17	20	47	47	48	22	26	13	46	42	21	30	22
AUG. 18	20	1	1	2	23	26	13	46	42	21	30	22
AUG. 19	21	3	3	4	23	26	13	46	42	21	30	22
AUG. 20	21	5	5	6	23	27	13	46	42	21	30	22
AUG. 21	21	7	7	8	23	27	13	46	42	21	30	22
AUG. 22	21	8	9	10	24	27	13	46	42	21	30	22
AUG. 23	21	10	11	11	24	27	13	46	42	21	30	22
AUG. 24	21	12	13	13	24	27	13	46	42	21	30	22
AUG. 25	21	14	14	15	24	27	13	46	42	21	30	22
AUG. 26	22	15	16	17	24	27	13	46	42	21	30	22
AUG. 27	22	17	18	18	25	28	13	46	42	21	30	22
AUG. 28	22	19	19	20	25	28	13	46	42	21	30	22
AUG. 29	22	20	21	21	25	28	14	46	42	21	30	22
AUG. 30	22	22	22	23	25	28	14	46	42	21	30	22
AUG. 31	22	24	24	25	25	28	14	46	42	21	30	22

MOON 1 ◖ 12:01 A.M. TO 8:00 A.M. **MOON 2** ◐ 8:01 A.M. TO 4:00 P.M. **MOON 3** ● 4:01 P.M. TO 12:00 A.M.
Use only one "moon" number. Choose the column closest to your time of birth. If your place of birth is not on Eastern Standard Time, be sure to read "How to Convert to Eastern Standard Time" at the beginning of this section.

1962

September

Date & Time	SUN ☉	MOON 1 ☽	MOON 2 ☽	MOON 3 ●	MERCURY	VENUS	MARS	JUPITER	SATURN	URANUS	NEPTUNE	PLUTO
SEP. 1	22	25	26	26	25	28	14	46	42	21	30	22
SEP. 2	22	27	27	28	26	28	14	46	42	21	30	22
SEP. 3	23	28	29	29	26	28	14	46	42	21	30	22
SEP. 4	23	30	30	31	26	29	14	46	42	21	30	22
SEP. 5	23	31	32	33	26	29	14	46	42	21	30	22
SEP. 6	23	33	34	34	26	29	14	46	42	21	30	22
SEP. 7	23	35	35	36	26	29	14	46	42	21	30	22
SEP. 8	23	36	37	38	27	29	14	46	42	21	30	22
SEP. 9	23	38	39	39	27	29	14	46	42	21	30	22
SEP. 10	23	40	41	41	27	29	15	46	42	21	30	22
SEP. 11	24	42	43	43	27	29	15	46	42	21	30	22
SEP. 12	24	44	44	45	27	30	15	46	42	21	30	22
SEP. 13	24	46	46	47	27	30	15	46	42	21	30	22
SEP. 14	24	48	48	1	27	30	15	46	42	21	30	22
SEP. 15	24	2	3	3	27	30	15	46	42	21	30	22
SEP. 16	24	4	5	5	27	30	15	46	42	21	30	22
SEP. 17	24	6	7	7	28	30	15	46	42	21	31	22
SEP. 18	24	8	8	9	28	30	15	46	42	21	31	22
SEP. 19	25	10	10	11	28	30	15	46	42	21	31	22
SEP. 20	25	12	12	13	28	31	15	46	42	21	31	22
SEP. 21	25	13	14	14	28	31	15	46	42	21	31	22
SEP. 22	25	15	16	16	28	31	15	46	42	21	31	22
SEP. 23	25	17	17	18	28	31	16	46	42	21	31	22
SEP. 24	25	18	19	19	28	31	16	46	42	21	31	22
SEP. 25	26	20	20	21	28	31	16	46	42	21	31	22
SEP. 26	26	22	22	23	28	31	16	46	42	21	31	22
SEP. 27	26	23	24	24	28	31	16	46	42	21	31	22
SEP. 28	26	25	25	26	28	31	16	46	42	21	31	22
SEP. 29	26	26	27	27	28	31	16	46	42	21	31	22
SEP. 30	26	28	28	29	28	32	16	46	42	21	31	22

October

Date & Time	SUN ☉	MOON 1 ☽	MOON 2 ☽	MOON 3 ●	MERCURY	VENUS	MARS	JUPITER	SATURN	URANUS	NEPTUNE	PLUTO
OCT. 1	26	29	30	31	27	32	16	46	42	21	31	22
OCT. 2	26	31	32	32	27	32	16	46	42	21	31	22
OCT. 3	27	33	33	34	27	32	16	45	42	21	31	22
OCT. 4	27	34	35	35	27	32	16	45	42	21	31	22
OCT. 5	27	36	37	37	27	32	16	45	42	21	31	22
OCT. 6	27	38	38	39	27	32	17	45	42	21	31	22
OCT. 7	27	39	40	41	27	32	17	45	42	21	31	22
OCT. 8	27	41	42	42	26	32	17	45	42	21	31	22
OCT. 9	27	43	44	44	26	32	17	45	42	21	31	22
OCT. 10	27	45	46	46	26	32	17	45	42	21	31	22
OCT. 11	28	47	48	48	26	32	17	45	42	21	31	22
OCT. 12	28	1	2	2	26	32	17	45	42	21	31	22
OCT. 13	28	3	4	4	26	32	17	45	42	21	31	22
OCT. 14	28	5	6	6	26	32	17	45	42	21	31	22
OCT. 15	28	7	8	8	26	32	17	45	42	21	31	22
OCT. 16	28	9	10	10	26	33	17	45	42	21	31	22
OCT. 17	28	11	12	12	26	33	17	45	42	21	31	22
OCT. 18	28	13	13	14	26	33	17	45	42	22	31	22
OCT. 19	29	15	15	16	26	33	17	45	42	22	31	22
OCT. 20	29	16	17	17	26	33	18	45	42	22	31	22
OCT. 21	29	18	18	19	26	33	18	45	42	22	31	22
OCT. 22	29	20	20	21	26	33	18	45	42	22	31	22
OCT. 23	29	21	22	22	26	33	18	45	42	22	31	22
OCT. 24	29	23	23	24	27	33	18	45	42	22	31	22
OCT. 25	29	24	25	25	27	33	18	45	42	22	31	23
OCT. 26	30	26	26	27	27	33	18	45	42	22	31	23
OCT. 27	30	27	28	29	27	33	18	45	42	22	31	23
OCT. 28	30	29	30	30	27	33	18	45	42	22	31	23
OCT. 29	30	31	31	32	28	33	18	45	42	22	31	23
OCT. 30	30	32	33	33	28	33	18	45	42	22	31	23
OCT. 31	30	34	34	35	28	32	18	45	42	22	31	23

MOON 1 ☽ 12:01 A.M. TO 8:00 A.M.　　**MOON 2** ☽ 8:01 A.M. TO 4:00 P.M.　　**MOON 3** ● 4:01 P.M. TO 12:00 A.M.
Use only one "moon" number. Choose the column closest to your time of birth. If your place of birth is not on Eastern Standard Time, be sure to read "How to Convert to Eastern Standard Time" at the beginning of this section.

1963

November

Date & Time	SUN	MOON 1	MOON 2	MOON 3	MERCURY	VENUS	MARS	JUPITER	SATURN	URANUS	NEPTUNE	PLUTO
NOV. 1	30	5	6	7	30	32	34	2	43	22	31	23
NOV. 2	30	7	8	9	30	32	34	2	43	22	31	23
NOV. 3	31	9	10	11	30	33	34	2	43	22	31	23
NOV. 4	31	11	12	13	30	33	34	2	43	22	31	23
NOV. 5	31	13	14	15	31	33	34	2	43	22	31	23
NOV. 6	31	15	16	16	31	33	34	2	43	22	31	23
NOV. 7	31	17	18	18	31	33	34	2	43	22	31	23
NOV. 8	31	19	19	20	31	33	34	2	43	22	31	23
NOV. 9	31	21	21	22	31	34	34	2	43	22	31	23
NOV. 10	31	22	23	23	32	34	34	2	43	22	31	23
NOV. 11	31	24	24	25	32	34	35	2	43	22	31	23
NOV. 12	32	26	26	27	32	34	35	2	43	22	31	23
NOV. 13	32	27	28	28	32	34	35	2	43	22	31	23
NOV. 14	32	29	29	30	32	34	35	2	43	22	31	23
NOV. 15	32	30	31	31	33	35	35	2	43	22	31	23
NOV. 16	32	32	32	33	33	35	35	2	43	22	31	23
NOV. 17	32	34	34	35	33	35	35	2	43	22	31	23
NOV. 18	32	35	36	36	33	35	35	2	43	22	31	23
NOV. 19	33	37	37	38	34	35	35	2	43	22	31	23
NOV. 20	33	38	39	39	34	35	35	2	43	22	31	23
NOV. 21	33	40	40	41	34	36	36	2	43	22	31	23
NOV. 22	33	42	42	43	34	36	36	2	43	22	31	23
NOV. 23	33	43	44	44	34	36	36	2	43	22	31	23
NOV. 24	33	45	46	46	35	36	36	2	43	22	31	23
NOV. 25	34	47	47	48	35	36	36	2	43	22	31	23
NOV. 26	34	1	1	2	35	36	36	2	43	22	31	23
NOV. 27	34	2	3	4	35	37	36	2	43	22	31	23
NOV. 28	34	4	5	6	35	37	36	2	43	22	31	23
NOV. 29	34	6	7	8	36	37	36	2	43	22	31	23
NOV. 30	34	8	9	10	36	37	36	2	43	22	31	23

December

Date & Time	SUN	MOON 1	MOON 2	MOON 3	MERCURY	VENUS	MARS	JUPITER	SATURN	URANUS	NEPTUNE	PLUTO
DEC. 1	34	10	11	12	36	37	37	2	43	22	31	23
DEC. 2	34	12	13	14	36	37	37	2	43	22	31	23
DEC. 3	35	14	15	16	36	38	37	2	43	22	31	23
DEC. 4	35	16	17	18	37	38	37	2	43	22	31	23
DEC. 5	35	18	19	19	37	38	37	2	43	22	31	23
DEC. 6	35	20	21	21	37	38	37	2	43	22	31	23
DEC. 7	35	22	22	23	37	38	37	2	43	22	31	23
DEC. 8	35	23	24	25	37	38	37	2	43	22	31	23
DEC. 9	35	25	26	26	38	39	37	2	43	22	31	23
DEC. 10	35	27	27	28	38	39	37	2	43	22	31	23
DEC. 11	36	28	29	29	38	39	38	2	43	22	31	23
DEC. 12	36	30	30	31	38	39	38	2	43	22	31	23
DEC. 13	36	32	32	33	38	39	38	2	43	22	31	23
DEC. 14	36	33	34	34	38	39	38	2	43	22	31	23
DEC. 15	36	35	35	36	39	40	38	2	43	22	31	23
DEC. 16	36	36	37	37	39	40	38	2	43	22	31	23
DEC. 17	36	38	38	39	39	40	38	2	44	22	31	23
DEC. 18	36	39	40	41	39	40	38	2	44	22	31	23
DEC. 19	37	41	42	42	39	40	38	2	44	22	31	23
DEC. 20	37	43	43	44	39	40	38	2	44	22	31	23
DEC. 21	37	45	45	46	39	41	39	2	44	22	31	23
DEC. 22	37	46	47	47	40	41	39	2	44	22	31	23
DEC. 23	37	48	1	1	40	41	39	2	44	22	31	23
DEC. 24	37	2	2	3	40	41	39	2	44	22	31	23
DEC. 25	37	4	4	5	40	41	39	2	44	22	31	23
DEC. 26	38	6	6	7	40	41	39	2	44	22	31	23
DEC. 27	38	8	8	9	40	42	39	2	44	22	31	23
DEC. 28	38	10	10	11	40	42	39	2	44	22	31	23
DEC. 29	38	12	12	13	40	42	39	2	44	22	31	23
DEC. 30	38	14	14	15	40	42	40	2	44	22	31	23
DEC. 31	38	16	16	17	39	42	40	2	44	22	31	23

MOON 1 ☽ 12:01 A.M. TO 8:00 A.M.   **MOON 2** ☽ 8:01 A.M. TO 4:00 P.M.   **MOON 3** ● 4:01 P.M. TO 12:00 A.M.

Use only one "moon" number. Choose the column closest to your time of birth. If your place of birth is not on Eastern Standard Time, be sure to read "How to Convert to Eastern Standard Time" at the beginning of this section.

1963

January

Date & Time	SUN	MOON 1	MOON 2	MOON 3	MERCURY	VENUS	MARS	JUPITER	SATURN	URANUS	NEPTUNE	PLUTO
JAN. 1	38	47	48	48	41	32	20	46	42	22	31	23
JAN. 2	38	1	2	2	41	32	20	46	42	22	31	23
JAN. 3	39	3	4	4	41	33	20	46	42	22	31	23
JAN. 4	39	5	5	6	41	33	20	46	42	22	31	23
JAN. 5	39	7	7	8	41	33	20	46	42	22	31	23
JAN. 6	39	9	9	10	42	33	20	46	42	22	31	23
JAN. 7	39	10	11	12	42	33	20	46	42	22	31	23
JAN. 8	39	12	13	14	42	33	20	46	42	22	31	23
JAN. 9	39	14	15	15	42	33	20	46	42	22	31	23
JAN. 10	40	16	17	17	42	33	20	46	42	22	31	23
JAN. 11	40	18	18	19	42	33	20	46	42	22	31	23
JAN. 12	40	19	20	21	42	34	20	46	42	22	31	23
JAN. 13	40	21	22	22	42	34	20	46	42	22	31	23
JAN. 14	40	23	23	24	42	34	20	47	42	22	31	23
JAN. 15	40	24	25	25	42	34	20	47	43	22	31	23
JAN. 16	40	26	26	27	42	34	20	47	43	22	31	23
JAN. 17	41	28	28	29	41	34	20	47	43	22	31	23
JAN. 18	41	29	30	30	41	34	20	47	43	22	31	23
JAN. 19	41	31	31	32	41	35	20	47	43	22	31	23
JAN. 20	41	32	33	33	41	35	20	47	43	22	31	23
JAN. 21	41	34	35	35	41	35	20	47	43	22	31	23
JAN. 22	41	36	36	37	41	35	20	47	43	22	31	23
JAN. 23	42	37	38	39	40	35	20	47	43	22	31	23
JAN. 24	42	39	40	41	40	35	20	47	43	22	31	23
JAN. 25	42	41	42	42	40	35	19	47	43	22	31	23
JAN. 26	42	43	43	44	40	35	19	47	43	22	31	23
JAN. 27	42	45	45	46	40	36	19	47	43	22	31	23
JAN. 28	42	47	47	48	40	36	19	47	43	22	31	23
JAN. 29	42	1	1	2	40	36	19	47	43	22	31	23
JAN. 30	42	2	3	4	40	36	19	47	43	22	31	23
JAN. 31	43	4	5	6	40	36	19	47	43	22	31	23

February

Date & Time	SUN	MOON 1	MOON 2	MOON 3	MERCURY	VENUS	MARS	JUPITER	SATURN	URANUS	NEPTUNE	PLUTO
FEB. 1	43	6	7	7	40	36	19	47	43	22	31	23
FEB. 2	43	8	9	9	40	36	19	47	43	22	31	23
FEB. 3	43	10	11	11	40	37	19	47	43	22	31	23
FEB. 4	43	12	12	13	40	37	19	47	43	22	31	23
FEB. 5	43	14	14	15	40	37	19	47	43	22	31	22
FEB. 6	43	15	16	17	40	37	19	47	43	21	31	22
FEB. 7	43	17	18	18	40	37	19	47	43	21	31	22
FEB. 8	44	19	19	20	40	37	19	47	43	21	31	22
FEB. 9	44	21	21	22	40	37	19	47	43	21	31	22
FEB. 10	44	22	23	23	40	38	19	47	43	21	31	22
FEB. 11	44	24	24	25	40	38	19	47	43	21	31	22
FEB. 12	44	25	26	26	41	38	19	47	43	21	31	22
FEB. 13	44	27	28	28	41	38	19	47	43	21	31	22
FEB. 14	44	29	29	30	41	38	18	47	43	21	31	22
FEB. 15	44	30	31	31	41	38	18	47	43	21	31	22
FEB. 16	45	32	32	33	41	38	18	47	43	21	31	22
FEB. 17	45	33	34	34	41	39	18	47	43	21	31	22
FEB. 18	45	35	36	36	41	39	18	48	43	21	31	22
FEB. 19	45	37	37	38	42	39	18	48	43	21	31	22
FEB. 20	45	38	39	40	42	39	18	48	43	21	31	22
FEB. 21	45	40	41	41	42	39	18	48	43	21	31	22
FEB. 22	45	42	43	43	42	39	18	48	43	21	31	22
FEB. 23	46	44	45	45	42	40	18	48	43	21	31	22
FEB. 24	46	46	46	47	42	40	18	48	43	21	31	22
FEB. 25	46	48	48	1	43	40	18	48	43	21	31	22
FEB. 26	46	2	2	3	43	40	18	48	43	21	31	22
FEB. 27	46	4	4	5	43	40	18	48	43	21	31	22
FEB. 28	46	6	6	7	43	40	18	48	43	21	31	22

MOON 1 ☽ 12:01 A.M. TO 8:00 A.M.   **MOON 2** ☽ 8:01 A.M. TO 4:00 P.M.   **MOON 3** ● 4:01 P.M. TO 12:00 A.M.
Use only one "moon" number. Choose the column closest to your time of birth. If your place of birth is not on
Eastern Standard Time, be sure to read "How to Convert to Eastern Standard Time" at the beginning of this section.

1963

March

Date & Time	SUN	MOON 1	MOON 2	MOON 3	MERCURY	VENUS	MARS	JUPITER	SATURN	URANUS	NEPTUNE	PLUTO
MAR. 1	46	8	8	9	43	40	18	48	43	21	31	22
MAR. 2	46	10	10	11	44	41	18	48	43	21	31	22
MAR. 3	47	11	12	13	44	41	18	48	43	21	31	22
MAR. 4	47	13	14	14	44	41	18	48	43	21	31	22
MAR. 5	47	15	16	16	44	41	18	48	43	21	31	22
MAR. 6	47	17	17	18	44	41	18	48	43	21	31	22
MAR. 7	47	18	19	19	45	41	18	48	43	21	31	22
MAR. 8	47	20	21	21	45	41	18	48	43	21	31	22
MAR. 9	47	22	22	23	45	42	18	48	43	21	31	22
MAR. 10	47	23	24	24	45	42	18	48	43	21	31	22
MAR. 11	48	25	25	26	45	42	18	48	43	21	31	22
MAR. 12	48	27	27	28	46	42	18	48	43	21	31	22
MAR. 13	48	28	29	29	46	42	18	48	43	21	31	22
MAR. 14	48	30	30	31	46	42	18	48	43	21	31	22
MAR. 15	48	31	32	32	46	43	18	48	43	21	31	22
MAR. 16	48	33	33	34	47	43	18	48	43	21	31	22
MAR. 17	48	34	35	36	47	43	18	48	43	21	31	22
MAR. 18	48	36	37	37	47	43	18	48	43	21	31	22
MAR. 19	1	38	38	39	47	43	18	48	43	21	31	22
MAR. 20	1	39	40	41	47	43	18	48	43	21	31	22
MAR. 21	1	41	42	42	48	44	18	1	44	21	31	22
MAR. 22	1	43	44	44	48	44	18	1	44	21	31	22
MAR. 23	1	45	46	46	48	44	18	1	44	21	31	22
MAR. 24	1	47	48	48	48	44	18	1	44	21	31	22
MAR. 25	2	1	2	2	1	44	18	1	44	21	31	22
MAR. 26	2	3	4	4	1	44	18	1	44	21	31	22
MAR. 27	2	5	6	6	1	45	18	1	44	21	31	22
MAR. 28	2	7	8	8	2	45	18	1	44	21	31	22
MAR. 29	2	9	10	10	2	45	18	1	44	21	31	22
MAR. 30	2	11	11	12	2	45	18	1	44	21	31	22
MAR. 31	2	13	13	14	2	45	18	1	44	21	31	22

April

Date & Time	SUN	MOON 1	MOON 2	MOON 3	MERCURY	VENUS	MARS	JUPITER	SATURN	URANUS	NEPTUNE	PLUTO
APR. 1	2	15	15	16	3	45	18	1	44	21	31	22
APR. 2	2	16	17	17	3	45	18	1	44	21	31	22
APR. 3	3	18	19	19	3	46	18	1	44	21	31	22
APR. 4	3	20	20	21	3	46	18	1	44	21	31	22
APR. 5	3	21	22	22	4	46	18	1	44	21	31	22
APR. 6	3	23	23	24	4	46	18	1	44	21	31	22
APR. 7	3	25	25	26	4	46	18	1	44	21	31	22
APR. 8	3	26	27	27	5	46	18	1	44	21	31	22
APR. 9	3	28	28	29	5	47	18	1	44	21	31	22
APR. 10	3	29	30	30	5	47	18	1	44	21	31	22
APR. 11	4	31	31	32	5	47	18	1	44	21	31	22
APR. 12	4	32	33	34	6	47	18	1	44	21	31	22
APR. 13	4	34	35	35	6	47	18	1	44	21	31	22
APR. 14	4	36	36	37	6	47	18	1	44	21	31	22
APR. 15	4	37	38	38	6	48	18	1	44	21	31	22
APR. 16	4	39	39	40	7	48	18	1	44	21	31	22
APR. 17	4	41	41	42	7	48	18	1	44	21	31	22
APR. 18	4	42	43	44	7	48	18	1	44	21	31	22
APR. 19	5	44	45	45	7	48	18	1	44	21	31	22
APR. 20	5	46	47	47	7	48	18	1	44	21	31	22
APR. 21	5	48	1	1	8	48	19	2	44	21	31	22
APR. 22	5	2	3	3	8	1	19	2	44	21	31	22
APR. 23	5	4	5	5	8	1	19	2	44	21	31	22
APR. 24	5	6	7	7	8	1	19	2	44	21	31	22
APR. 25	6	8	9	9	8	1	19	2	44	21	31	22
APR. 26	6	10	11	11	8	1	19	2	44	21	31	22
APR. 27	6	12	13	13	8	1	19	2	44	21	31	22
APR. 28	6	14	15	15	9	1	19	2	44	21	31	22
APR. 29	6	16	16	17	9	2	19	2	44	21	31	22
APR. 30	6	18	18	19	9	2	19	2	44	21	31	22

MOON 1 ☽ 12:01 A.M. TO 8:00 A.M.　　**MOON 2** ◑ 8:01 A.M. TO 4:00 P.M.　　**MOON 3** ● 4:01 P.M. TO 12:00 A.M.

Use only one "moon" number. Choose the column closest to your time of birth. If your place of birth is not on Eastern Standard Time, be sure to read "How to Convert to Eastern Standard Time" at the beginning of this section.

1963

May   June

Date & Time	SUN	MOON 1	MOON 2	MOON 3	MERCURY	VENUS	MARS	JUPITER	SATURN	URANUS	NEPTUNE	PLUTO
MAY 1	6	19	20	20	9	2	19	2	44	21	31	22
MAY 2	6	21	21	22	9	2	19	2	44	21	31	22
MAY 3	7	23	23	24	9	2	19	2	44	21	31	22
MAY 4	7	24	25	25	9	3	19	2	44	21	31	22
MAY 5	7	26	26	27	9	3	19	2	44	21	31	22
MAY 6	7	27	28	28	9	3	19	2	44	21	31	22
MAY 7	7	29	29	30	9	3	19	2	44	21	31	22
MAY 8	7	30	31	32	9	3	19	2	44	21	31	22
MAY 9	7	32	33	33	9	3	19	2	44	21	31	22
MAY 10	7	34	34	35	9	4	19	2	44	21	31	22
MAY 11	8	35	36	36	9	4	20	2	44	21	31	22
MAY 12	8	37	37	38	9	4	20	2	44	21	31	22
MAY 13	8	39	39	40	9	4	20	2	44	21	31	22
MAY 14	8	40	41	41	9	4	20	2	44	21	31	22
MAY 15	8	42	42	43	9	4	20	2	44	21	31	22
MAY 16	8	44	44	45	9	5	20	2	44	21	31	22
MAY 17	8	45	46	47	9	5	20	2	44	21	31	22
MAY 18	8	47	48	1	8	5	20	2	44	21	31	22
MAY 19	9	1	2	3	8	5	20	2	44	21	31	22
MAY 20	9	3	4	5	8	5	20	2	44	21	31	22
MAY 21	9	5	6	7	8	5	20	2	44	21	31	22
MAY 22	9	7	8	9	8	5	20	2	44	21	31	22
MAY 23	9	9	10	11	8	6	20	2	44	21	31	22
MAY 24	9	11	12	13	8	6	20	2	44	21	31	22
MAY 25	10	13	14	14	8	6	20	2	44	21	31	22
MAY 26	10	15	16	16	8	6	20	2	44	21	31	22
MAY 27	10	17	17	18	8	6	21	2	44	21	31	22
MAY 28	10	19	19	20	8	6	21	3	44	21	31	22
MAY 29	10	20	21	21	8	7	21	3	44	21	31	22
MAY 30	10	22	23	23	8	7	21	3	44	21	31	22
MAY 31	10	24	24	25	8	7	21	3	44	21	31	22

Date & Time	SUN	MOON 1	MOON 2	MOON 3	MERCURY	VENUS	MARS	JUPITER	SATURN	URANUS	NEPTUNE	PLUTO
JUN. 1	10	25	26	26	8	7	21	3	44	21	31	22
JUN. 2	10	27	27	28	8	7	21	3	44	21	31	22
JUN. 3	11	28	29	30	8	7	21	3	44	21	31	22
JUN. 4	11	30	31	31	8	8	21	3	44	21	31	22
JUN. 5	11	32	32	33	8	8	21	3	44	21	31	22
JUN. 6	11	33	34	34	8	8	21	3	44	21	31	22
JUN. 7	11	35	35	36	8	8	21	3	44	21	31	22
JUN. 8	11	36	37	38	8	8	21	3	44	21	31	22
JUN. 9	11	38	39	39	8	8	21	3	44	21	31	22
JUN. 10	11	40	40	41	8	9	21	3	44	21	31	22
JUN. 11	12	42	42	43	9	9	22	3	44	21	31	22
JUN. 12	12	43	44	44	9	9	22	3	44	21	31	22
JUN. 13	12	45	46	46	9	9	22	3	44	21	31	22
JUN. 14	12	47	47	48	9	9	22	3	44	21	31	22
JUN. 15	12	1	1	2	9	9	22	3	44	21	31	22
JUN. 16	12	3	3	4	9	10	22	3	44	21	31	22
JUN. 17	12	4	5	6	9	10	22	3	44	21	31	22
JUN. 18	12	6	7	8	9	10	22	3	44	21	31	22
JUN. 19	13	8	9	10	9	10	22	3	44	21	31	22
JUN. 20	13	10	11	12	10	10	22	3	44	21	31	22
JUN. 21	13	12	13	14	10	10	22	3	44	21	31	22
JUN. 22	13	14	15	16	10	10	22	3	44	21	31	22
JUN. 23	13	16	17	17	10	11	22	3	44	21	31	22
JUN. 24	13	18	19	19	11	11	22	3	44	21	31	22
JUN. 25	14	20	20	21	11	11	23	3	44	21	31	22
JUN. 26	14	21	22	23	11	11	23	3	44	21	31	22
JUN. 27	14	23	24	24	11	11	23	3	44	21	31	22
JUN. 28	14	25	25	26	11	11	23	3	44	21	31	22
JUN. 29	14	26	27	27	12	12	23	3	44	21	31	22
JUN. 30	14	28	29	29	12	12	23	3	44	21	31	22

MOON 1 ☽ 12:01 A.M. TO 8:00 A.M.   **MOON 2** ◑ 8:01 A.M. TO 4:00 P.M.   **MOON 3** ● 4:01 P.M. TO 12:00 A.M.
Use only one "moon" number. Choose the column closest to your time of birth. If your place of birth is not on Eastern Standard Time, be sure to read "How to Convert to Eastern Standard Time" at the beginning of this section.

July

August

Date & Time	SUN	MOON 1	MOON 2	MOON 3	MERCURY	VENUS	MARS	JUPITER	SATURN	URANUS	NEPTUNE	PLUTO
JUL. 1	14	30	30	31	12	12	23	3	44	21	31	22
JUL. 2	14	31	32	32	12	12	23	3	44	21	31	22
JUL. 3	15	33	33	34	13	12	23	3	44	21	31	22
JUL. 4	15	34	35	35	13	12	23	3	44	21	31	22
JUL. 5	15	36	37	37	13	13	23	3	44	21	31	22
JUL. 6	15	38	38	39	14	13	23	3	44	21	31	22
JUL. 7	15	39	40	40	14	13	23	3	44	21	31	22
JUL. 8	15	41	42	42	14	13	23	3	44	21	31	22
JUL. 9	15	43	43	44	14	13	24	3	44	21	31	22
JUL. 10	15	45	45	46	15	13	24	3	44	21	31	22
JUL. 11	16	46	47	48	15	14	24	3	44	21	31	22
JUL. 12	16	48	1	1	15	14	24	3	44	21	31	22
JUL. 13	16	2	3	3	15	14	24	3	44	21	31	22
JUL. 14	16	4	5	5	16	14	24	3	44	21	31	22
JUL. 15	16	6	7	7	16	14	24	3	44	21	31	22
JUL. 16	16	8	8	9	16	14	24	3	44	21	31	22
JUL. 17	16	10	10	11	17	15	24	3	44	21	31	22
JUL. 18	16	12	12	13	17	15	24	3	44	21	31	22
JUL. 19	17	14	14	15	17	15	24	3	44	21	31	22
JUL. 20	17	15	16	17	17	15	24	3	44	21	31	22
JUL. 21	17	17	18	18	18	15	24	3	44	21	31	22
JUL. 22	17	19	20	20	18	15	25	3	44	21	31	22
JUL. 23	17	21	21	22	18	16	25	3	44	21	31	22
JUL. 24	17	23	23	24	19	16	25	4	44	21	31	22
JUL. 25	17	24	25	25	19	16	25	4	44	21	31	22
JUL. 26	18	26	26	27	19	16	25	4	44	21	31	22
JUL. 27	18	27	28	29	19	16	25	4	44	21	31	22
JUL. 28	18	29	30	30	20	16	25	4	44	21	31	22
JUL. 29	18	31	31	32	20	17	25	4	44	21	31	22
JUL. 30	18	32	33	33	20	17	25	4	44	21	31	22
JUL. 31	18	34	34	35	20	17	25	4	44	21	31	22

Date & Time	SUN	MOON 1	MOON 2	MOON 3	MERCURY	VENUS	MARS	JUPITER	SATURN	URANUS	NEPTUNE	PLUTO
AUG. 1	18	35	36	37	20	17	25	4	44	21	31	22
AUG. 2	18	37	38	38	21	17	25	4	44	21	31	22
AUG. 3	19	39	39	40	21	17	26	4	44	22	31	22
AUG. 4	19	40	41	42	21	18	26	4	44	22	31	22
AUG. 5	19	42	43	43	21	18	26	4	44	22	31	22
AUG. 6	19	44	45	45	22	18	26	4	44	22	31	22
AUG. 7	19	46	47	47	22	18	26	4	44	22	31	22
AUG. 8	19	48	48	1	22	18	26	4	44	22	31	22
AUG. 9	19	2	2	3	22	18	26	4	44	22	31	22
AUG. 10	19	4	4	5	22	18	26	4	44	22	31	22
AUG. 11	20	5	6	7	23	19	26	4	44	22	31	22
AUG. 12	20	7	8	9	23	19	26	4	44	22	31	22
AUG. 13	20	9	10	11	23	19	26	4	44	22	31	22
AUG. 14	20	11	12	12	23	19	26	4	44	22	31	22
AUG. 15	20	13	14	14	23	19	27	4	44	22	31	22
AUG. 16	20	15	15	16	23	19	27	4	44	22	31	22
AUG. 17	20	17	17	18	24	20	27	4	44	22	31	22
AUG. 18	20	18	19	20	24	20	27	4	44	22	31	22
AUG. 19	21	20	21	21	24	20	27	4	44	22	31	22
AUG. 20	21	22	22	23	24	20	27	4	44	22	31	22
AUG. 21	21	24	24	25	24	20	27	4	44	22	31	22
AUG. 22	21	25	26	26	24	20	27	4	44	22	31	22
AUG. 23	21	27	27	28	25	21	27	4	44	22	31	22
AUG. 24	21	29	29	30	25	21	27	4	43	22	31	22
AUG. 25	21	30	31	31	25	21	27	4	43	22	31	23
AUG. 26	22	32	32	33	25	21	27	4	43	22	31	23
AUG. 27	22	33	34	34	25	21	28	3	43	22	31	23
AUG. 28	22	35	35	36	25	21	28	3	43	22	31	23
AUG. 29	22	36	37	38	25	22	28	3	43	22	31	23
AUG. 30	22	38	39	39	25	22	28	3	43	22	31	23
AUG. 31	22	40	40	41	25	22	28	3	43	22	31	23

MOON 1 ☽ 12:01 A.M. TO 8:00 A.M. **MOON 2** ☽ 8:01 A.M. TO 4:00 P.M. **MOON 3** ● 4:01 P.M. TO 12:00 A.M.
Use only one "moon" number. Choose the column closest to your time of birth. If your place of birth is not on Eastern Standard Time, be sure to read "How to Convert to Eastern Standard Time" at the beginning of this section.

1963

September

Date & Time	SUN	MOON 1	MOON 2	MOON 3	MERCURY	VENUS	MARS	JUPITER	SATURN	URANUS	NEPTUNE	PLUTO
SEP. 1	22	42	42	43	25	22	28	3	43	22	31	23
SEP. 2	22	43	44	45	26	22	28	3	43	22	31	23
SEP. 3	23	45	46	46	26	22	28	3	43	22	31	23
SEP. 4	23	47	48	48	26	23	28	3	43	22	31	23
SEP. 5	23	1	2	2	26	23	28	3	43	22	31	23
SEP. 6	23	3	4	4	26	23	28	3	43	22	31	23
SEP. 7	23	5	6	6	26	23	28	3	43	22	31	23
SEP. 8	23	7	8	8	26	23	29	3	43	22	31	23
SEP. 9	23	9	9	10	26	23	29	3	43	22	31	23
SEP. 10	23	11	11	12	26	24	29	3	43	22	31	23
SEP. 11	24	13	13	14	26	24	29	3	43	22	31	23
SEP. 12	24	14	15	16	26	24	29	3	43	22	31	23
SEP. 13	24	16	17	17	25	24	29	3	43	22	31	23
SEP. 14	24	18	19	19	25	24	29	3	43	22	31	23
SEP. 15	24	20	20	21	25	24	29	3	43	22	31	23
SEP. 16	24	21	22	23	25	25	29	3	43	22	31	23
SEP. 17	24	23	24	24	25	25	29	3	43	22	31	23
SEP. 18	24	25	25	26	25	25	29	3	43	22	31	23
SEP. 19	25	26	27	27	25	25	30	3	43	22	31	23
SEP. 20	25	28	29	29	25	25	30	3	43	22	31	23
SEP. 21	25	30	30	31	24	25	30	3	43	22	31	23
SEP. 22	25	31	32	32	24	26	30	3	43	22	31	23
SEP. 23	25	33	33	34	24	26	30	3	43	22	31	23
SEP. 24	25	34	35	35	24	26	30	3	43	22	31	23
SEP. 25	26	36	36	37	24	26	30	3	43	22	31	23
SEP. 26	26	38	38	39	24	26	30	3	43	22	31	23
SEP. 27	26	39	40	40	24	26	30	3	43	22	31	23
SEP. 28	26	41	41	42	24	27	30	3	43	22	31	23
SEP. 29	26	43	43	44	24	27	30	3	43	22	31	23
SEP. 30	26	44	45	46	24	27	31	3	43	22	31	23

October

Date & Time	SUN	MOON 1	MOON 2	MOON 3	MERCURY	VENUS	MARS	JUPITER	SATURN	URANUS	NEPTUNE	PLUTO
OCT. 1	26	46	47	48	24	27	31	3	43	22	31	23
OCT. 2	26	48	1	2	24	27	31	3	43	22	31	23
OCT. 3	27	2	3	4	24	27	31	3	43	22	31	23
OCT. 4	27	4	5	6	24	28	31	3	43	22	31	23
OCT. 5	27	6	7	8	24	28	31	3	43	22	31	23
OCT. 6	27	8	9	10	24	28	31	3	43	22	31	23
OCT. 7	27	10	11	11	24	28	31	3	43	22	31	23
OCT. 8	27	12	13	13	25	28	31	3	43	22	31	23
OCT. 9	27	14	15	15	25	28	31	3	43	22	31	23
OCT. 10	27	16	16	17	25	29	32	3	43	22	31	23
OCT. 11	28	18	18	19	25	29	32	3	43	22	31	23
OCT. 12	28	19	20	20	25	29	32	3	43	22	31	23
OCT. 13	28	21	22	22	25	29	32	3	43	22	31	23
OCT. 14	28	23	23	24	26	29	32	3	43	22	31	23
OCT. 15	28	24	25	25	26	29	32	3	43	22	31	23
OCT. 16	28	26	26	27	26	30	32	3	43	22	31	23
OCT. 17	28	28	28	29	26	30	32	3	43	22	31	23
OCT. 18	28	29	30	30	27	30	32	3	43	22	31	23
OCT. 19	29	31	31	32	27	30	32	3	43	22	31	23
OCT. 20	29	32	33	33	27	30	32	3	43	22	31	23
OCT. 21	29	34	34	35	27	30	33	3	43	22	31	23
OCT. 22	29	35	36	37	27	31	33	3	43	22	31	23
OCT. 23	29	37	38	38	28	31	33	3	43	22	31	23
OCT. 24	29	39	39	40	28	31	33	3	43	22	31	23
OCT. 25	29	40	41	41	28	31	33	3	43	22	31	23
OCT. 26	30	42	43	43	28	31	33	3	43	22	31	23
OCT. 27	30	44	44	45	29	31	33	3	43	22	31	23
OCT. 28	30	46	46	47	29	32	33	3	43	22	31	23
OCT. 29	30	47	48	1	29	32	33	3	43	22	31	23
OCT. 30	30	1	2	3	29	32	33	3	43	22	31	23
OCT. 31	30	3	4	5	29	32	33	3	43	22	31	23

MOON 1 ☽ 12:01 A.M. TO 8:00 A.M. **MOON 2** ◑ 8:01 A.M. TO 4:00 P.M. **MOON 3** ● 4:01 P.M. TO 12:00 A.M.

Use only one "moon" number. Choose the column closest to your time of birth. If your place of birth is not on Eastern Standard Time, be sure to read "How to Convert to Eastern Standard Time" at the beginning of this section.

1963

November

Date & Time	SUN	MOON 1	MOON 2	MOON 3	MERCURY	VENUS	MARS	JUPITER	SATURN	URANUS	NEPTUNE	PLUTO
NOV. 1	30	5	6	7	30	32	34	2	43	22	31	23
NOV. 2	30	7	8	9	30	32	34	2	43	22	31	23
NOV. 3	31	9	10	11	30	33	34	2	43	22	31	23
NOV. 4	31	11	12	13	30	33	34	2	43	22	31	23
NOV. 5	31	13	14	15	31	33	34	2	43	22	31	23
NOV. 6	31	15	16	16	31	33	34	2	43	22	31	23
NOV. 7	31	17	18	18	31	33	34	2	43	22	31	23
NOV. 8	31	19	19	20	31	33	34	2	43	22	31	23
NOV. 9	31	21	21	22	31	34	34	2	43	22	31	23
NOV. 10	31	22	23	23	32	34	34	2	43	22	31	23
NOV. 11	31	24	24	25	32	34	35	2	43	22	31	23
NOV. 12	32	26	26	27	32	34	35	2	43	22	31	23
NOV. 13	32	27	28	28	32	34	35	2	43	22	31	23
NOV. 14	32	29	29	30	32	34	35	2	43	22	31	23
NOV. 15	32	30	31	31	33	35	35	2	43	22	31	23
NOV. 16	32	32	32	33	33	35	35	2	43	22	31	23
NOV. 17	32	34	34	35	33	35	35	2	43	22	31	23
NOV. 18	32	35	36	36	33	35	35	2	43	22	31	23
NOV. 19	33	37	37	38	34	35	35	2	43	22	31	23
NOV. 20	33	38	39	39	34	35	35	2	43	22	31	23
NOV. 21	33	40	40	41	34	36	36	2	43	22	31	23
NOV. 22	33	42	42	43	34	36	36	2	43	22	31	23
NOV. 23	33	43	44	44	34	36	36	2	43	22	31	23
NOV. 24	33	45	46	46	35	36	36	2	43	22	31	23
NOV. 25	34	47	47	48	35	36	36	2	43	22	31	23
NOV. 26	34	1	1	2	35	36	36	2	43	22	31	23
NOV. 27	34	2	3	4	35	37	36	2	43	22	31	23
NOV. 28	34	4	5	6	35	37	36	2	43	22	31	23
NOV. 29	34	6	7	8	36	37	36	2	43	22	31	23
NOV. 30	34	8	9	10	36	37	36	2	43	22	31	23

December

Date & Time	SUN	MOON 1	MOON 2	MOON 3	MERCURY	VENUS	MARS	JUPITER	SATURN	URANUS	NEPTUNE	PLUTO
DEC. 1	34	10	11	12	36	37	37	2	43	22	31	23
DEC. 2	34	12	13	14	36	37	37	2	43	22	31	23
DEC. 3	35	14	15	16	36	38	37	2	43	22	31	23
DEC. 4	35	16	17	18	37	38	37	2	43	22	31	23
DEC. 5	35	18	19	19	37	38	37	2	43	22	31	23
DEC. 6	35	20	21	21	37	38	37	2	43	22	31	23
DEC. 7	35	22	22	23	37	38	37	2	43	22	31	23
DEC. 8	35	23	24	25	37	38	37	2	43	22	31	23
DEC. 9	35	25	26	26	38	39	37	2	43	22	31	23
DEC. 10	35	27	27	28	38	39	37	2	43	22	31	23
DEC. 11	36	28	29	29	38	39	38	2	43	22	31	23
DEC. 12	36	30	30	31	38	39	38	2	43	22	31	23
DEC. 13	36	32	32	33	38	39	38	2	43	22	31	23
DEC. 14	36	33	34	34	38	39	38	2	43	22	31	23
DEC. 15	36	35	35	36	39	40	38	2	43	22	31	23
DEC. 16	36	36	37	37	39	40	38	2	43	22	31	23
DEC. 17	36	38	38	39	39	40	38	2	44	22	31	23
DEC. 18	36	39	40	41	39	40	38	2	44	22	31	23
DEC. 19	37	41	42	42	39	40	38	2	44	22	31	23
DEC. 20	37	43	43	44	39	40	38	2	44	22	31	23
DEC. 21	37	45	45	46	39	41	39	2	44	22	31	23
DEC. 22	37	46	47	47	40	41	39	2	44	22	31	23
DEC. 23	37	48	1	1	40	41	39	2	44	22	31	23
DEC. 24	37	2	2	3	40	41	39	2	44	22	31	23
DEC. 25	37	4	4	5	40	41	39	2	44	22	31	23
DEC. 26	38	6	6	7	40	41	39	2	44	22	31	23
DEC. 27	38	8	8	9	40	42	39	2	44	22	31	23
DEC. 28	38	10	10	11	40	42	39	2	44	22	31	23
DEC. 29	38	12	12	13	40	42	39	2	44	22	31	23
DEC. 30	38	14	14	15	40	42	40	2	44	22	31	23
DEC. 31	38	16	16	17	39	42	40	2	44	22	31	23

MOON 1 ◔ 12:01 A.M. TO 8:00 A.M.　　**MOON 2** ◑ 8:01 A.M. TO 4:00 P.M.　　**MOON 3** ● 4:01 P.M. TO 12:00 A.M.

Use only one "moon" number. Choose the column closest to your time of birth. If your place of birth is not on Eastern Standard Time, be sure to read "How to Convert to Eastern Standard Time" at the beginning of this section.

1964

January

Date & Time	SUN	MOON 1	MOON 2	MOON 3	MERCURY	VENUS	MARS	JUPITER	SATURN	URANUS	NEPTUNE	PLUTO
JAN. 1	38	17	18	19	39	42	40	2	44	22	31	23
JAN. 2	38	19	20	21	39	43	40	2	44	22	31	23
JAN. 3	39	21	22	22	39	43	40	2	44	22	31	23
JAN. 4	39	23	23	24	39	43	40	2	44	22	31	23
JAN. 5	39	25	25	26	39	43	40	2	44	22	31	23
JAN. 6	39	26	27	27	38	43	40	2	44	22	31	23
JAN. 7	39	28	28	29	38	44	40	2	44	22	31	23
JAN. 8	39	29	30	31	38	44	40	2	44	22	31	23
JAN. 9	39	31	32	32	38	44	41	3	44	22	31	23
JAN. 10	40	33	33	34	38	44	41	3	44	22	31	23
JAN. 11	40	34	35	35	38	44	41	3	44	22	31	23
JAN. 12	40	36	36	37	38	44	41	3	44	22	31	23
JAN. 13	40	37	38	39	38	44	41	3	44	22	31	23
JAN. 14	40	39	40	40	38	44	41	3	44	22	31	23
JAN. 15	40	41	41	42	38	45	41	3	44	22	31	23
JAN. 16	40	42	43	44	38	45	41	3	44	22	31	23
JAN. 17	41	44	45	45	38	45	41	3	44	22	31	23
JAN. 18	41	46	46	47	38	45	41	3	44	22	31	23
JAN. 19	41	48	48	1	38	45	42	3	44	22	31	23
JAN. 20	41	1	2	3	38	45	42	3	44	22	31	23
JAN. 21	41	3	4	4	38	46	42	3	44	22	31	23
JAN. 22	41	5	6	6	38	46	42	3	44	22	31	23
JAN. 23	42	7	8	8	38	46	42	3	44	22	31	23
JAN. 24	42	9	10	10	38	46	42	3	44	22	31	23
JAN. 25	42	11	11	12	38	46	42	3	44	22	31	23
JAN. 26	42	13	13	14	38	46	42	3	44	22	31	23
JAN. 27	42	15	15	16	39	47	42	3	44	22	31	23
JAN. 28	42	17	17	18	39	47	43	3	44	22	31	23
JAN. 29	42	18	19	20	39	47	43	3	44	22	31	23
JAN. 30	42	20	21	22	39	47	43	3	44	22	31	23
JAN. 31	43	22	23	23	39	47	43	3	44	22	31	23

February

Date & Time	SUN	MOON 1	MOON 2	MOON 3	MERCURY	VENUS	MARS	JUPITER	SATURN	URANUS	NEPTUNE	PLUTO
FEB. 1	43	24	25	25	39	47	43	3	44	22	31	23
FEB. 2	43	26	26	27	39	48	43	3	44	22	31	23
FEB. 3	43	27	28	28	40	48	43	3	44	22	31	23
FEB. 4	43	29	29	30	40	48	43	3	44	22	31	23
FEB. 5	43	31	31	32	40	48	43	3	44	22	31	23
FEB. 6	43	32	33	33	40	48	43	3	44	22	31	23
FEB. 7	43	34	34	35	40	48	44	3	44	22	31	23
FEB. 8	44	35	36	36	40	1	44	3	44	22	31	23
FEB. 9	44	37	37	38	41	1	44	3	44	22	31	23
FEB. 10	44	39	39	40	41	1	44	3	44	22	31	23
FEB. 11	44	40	41	41	41	1	44	3	44	22	31	23
FEB. 12	44	42	42	43	41	1	44	3	44	22	31	23
FEB. 13	44	44	44	45	41	1	44	3	44	22	31	23
FEB. 14	44	45	46	47	42	1	44	3	44	22	31	23
FEB. 15	44	47	48	48	42	2	44	3	44	22	31	23
FEB. 16	45	1	2	2	42	2	45	3	44	22	31	23
FEB. 17	45	3	3	4	42	2	45	3	44	22	31	23
FEB. 18	45	5	5	6	42	2	45	3	44	22	31	23
FEB. 19	45	7	7	8	43	2	45	3	44	22	31	23
FEB. 20	45	8	9	10	43	2	45	3	44	22	31	23
FEB. 21	45	10	11	12	43	3	45	3	44	22	31	23
FEB. 22	45	12	13	13	43	3	45	3	44	22	31	23
FEB. 23	46	14	15	15	43	3	45	3	45	22	31	23
FEB. 24	46	16	17	17	44	3	45	4	45	22	31	23
FEB. 25	46	18	18	19	44	3	45	4	45	22	31	23
FEB. 26	46	20	20	21	44	3	46	4	45	22	31	23
FEB. 27	46	21	22	23	44	4	46	4	45	22	31	23
FEB. 28	46	23	24	24	45	4	46	4	45	22	31	23
FEB. 29	46	25	26	26	45	4	46	4	45	22	31	23

MOON 1 ◖ 12:01 A.M. TO 8:00 A.M.   **MOON 2** ◑ 8:01 A.M. TO 4:00 P.M.   **MOON 3** ● 4:01 P.M. TO 12:00 A.M.
Use only one "moon" number. Choose the column closest to your time of birth. If your place of birth is not on Eastern Standard Time, be sure to read "How to Convert to Eastern Standard Time" at the beginning of this section.

1964

March

April

Date & Time	SUN ☀	MOON 1 ◐	MOON 2 ◑	MOON 3 ●	MERCURY	VENUS	MARS	JUPITER	SATURN	URANUS	NEPTUNE	PLUTO
MAR. 1	46	27	27	28	45	4	46	4	45	22	31	23
MAR. 2	46	28	29	29	45	4	46	4	45	22	31	23
MAR. 3	47	30	31	31	45	4	46	4	45	22	31	23
MAR. 4	47	32	32	33	46	4	46	4	45	22	31	23
MAR. 5	47	33	34	34	46	5	46	4	45	22	31	23
MAR. 6	47	35	35	36	46	5	47	4	45	22	31	23
MAR. 7	47	36	37	37	46	5	47	4	45	22	31	23
MAR. 8	47	38	38	39	47	5	47	4	45	22	31	23
MAR. 9	47	40	40	41	47	5	47	4	45	22	31	23
MAR. 10	47	41	42	42	47	5	47	4	45	22	31	23
MAR. 11	48	43	43	45	47	6	47	4	45	22	31	23
MAR. 12	48	45	45	46	48	6	47	4	45	22	31	23
MAR. 13	48	46	47	48	48	6	47	4	45	22	31	23
MAR. 14	48	48	1	2	48	6	47	4	45	22	31	23
MAR. 15	48	2	3	3	48	6	47	4	45	22	31	23
MAR. 16	48	4	5	5	1	6	48	4	45	22	31	23
MAR. 17	48	6	7	7	1	6	48	4	45	22	31	23
MAR. 18	48	8	9	9	1	7	48	4	45	22	31	23
MAR. 19	1	10	11	11	2	7	48	4	45	22	31	23
MAR. 20	1	12	12	13	2	7	48	4	45	22	31	23
MAR. 21	1	14	14	15	2	7	48	4	45	22	31	23
MAR. 22	1	15	16	17	2	7	48	4	45	22	31	23
MAR. 23	1	17	18	19	3	7	48	4	45	22	31	23
MAR. 24	1	19	20	20	3	7	48	4	45	22	31	23
MAR. 25	2	21	22	22	3	8	1	4	45	22	31	23
MAR. 26	2	23	23	24	3	8	1	4	45	22	31	23
MAR. 27	2	24	25	26	4	8	1	4	45	22	31	23
MAR. 28	2	26	27	27	4	8	1	4	45	22	31	23
MAR. 29	2	28	28	29	4	8	1	5	45	22	31	23
MAR. 30	2	29	30	31	4	8	1	5	45	22	31	23
MAR. 31	2	31	32	32	5	8	1	5	45	22	31	23

Date & Time	SUN ☀	MOON 1 ◐	MOON 2 ◑	MOON 3 ●	MERCURY	VENUS	MARS	JUPITER	SATURN	URANUS	NEPTUNE	PLUTO
APR. 1	2	33	33	34	5	9	1	5	45	22	31	23
APR. 2	2	34	35	35	5	9	1	5	45	22	31	23
APR. 3	3	36	36	37	5	9	1	5	45	22	31	23
APR. 4	3	37	38	38	5	9	2	5	45	22	31	23
APR. 5	3	39	40	40	6	9	2	5	45	22	31	23
APR. 6	3	41	41	42	6	9	2	5	45	22	31	23
APR. 7	3	42	43	43	6	9	2	5	45	22	31	23
APR. 8	3	44	45	45	6	10	2	5	45	22	31	23
APR. 9	3	46	46	47	6	10	2	5	45	22	31	23
APR. 10	3	48	48	1	6	10	2	5	45	22	31	23
APR. 11	4	1	2	3	6	10	2	5	45	22	31	23
APR. 12	4	3	4	5	6	10	2	5	45	22	31	23
APR. 13	4	5	6	7	6	10	2	5	45	22	31	23
APR. 14	4	7	8	9	6	10	3	5	45	22	31	23
APR. 15	4	9	10	11	6	10	3	5	45	22	31	23
APR. 16	4	11	12	13	6	11	3	5	45	22	31	23
APR. 17	4	13	14	14	7	11	3	5	45	22	31	23
APR. 18	4	15	16	16	6	11	3	5	45	22	31	23
APR. 19	5	17	18	18	6	11	3	5	45	22	31	23
APR. 20	5	19	19	20	6	11	3	5	45	22	31	23
APR. 21	5	21	21	22	6	11	3	5	45	22	31	23
APR. 22	5	22	23	23	6	11	3	5	45	22	31	23
APR. 23	5	24	25	25	6	11	4	5	45	22	31	23
APR. 24	5	26	26	27	6	11	4	5	45	22	31	23
APR. 25	6	27	28	28	6	12	4	5	45	22	31	23
APR. 26	6	29	30	30	6	12	4	5	45	22	31	23
APR. 27	6	31	31	32	6	12	4	5	45	22	31	23
APR. 28	6	32	33	33	6	12	4	5	45	22	31	23
APR. 29	6	34	34	35	6	12	4	6	45	22	31	23
APR. 30	6	35	36	36	6	12	4	6	45	22	31	23

MOON 1 ◐ **12:01 A.M. TO 8:00 A.M.**   **MOON 2** ◑ **8:01 A.M. TO 4:00 P.M.**   **MOON 3** ● **4:01 P.M. TO 12:00 A.M.**
Use only one "moon" number. Choose the column closest to your time of birth. If your place of birth is not on
Eastern Standard Time, be sure to read "How to Convert to Eastern Standard Time" at the beginning of this section.

May

June

Date & Time	SUN	MOON 1	MOON 2	MOON 3	MERCURY	VENUS	MARS	JUPITER	SATURN	URANUS	NEPTUNE	PLUTO
MAY 1	6	37	37	38	6	12	4	6	45	22	31	23
MAY 2	6	38	39	40	6	12	4	6	45	22	31	23
MAY 3	7	40	41	41	5	12	5	6	45	22	31	23
MAY 4	7	42	42	43	5	13	5	6	45	22	31	23
MAY 5	7	43	44	44	5	13	5	6	45	22	31	23
MAY 6	7	45	46	46	5	13	5	6	45	22	31	23
MAY 7	7	47	47	48	5	13	5	6	45	22	31	23
MAY 8	7	1	1	2	5	13	5	6	45	22	31	23
MAY 9	7	3	3	4	5	13	5	6	45	22	31	23
MAY 10	7	4	5	6	5	13	5	6	45	22	31	23
MAY 11	8	6	7	8	5	13	5	6	46	22	31	23
MAY 12	8	8	9	10	5	13	5	6	46	22	31	23
MAY 13	8	10	11	12	5	13	6	6	46	22	31	23
MAY 14	8	12	13	14	5	13	6	6	46	22	31	23
MAY 15	8	14	15	16	5	13	6	6	46	22	31	23
MAY 16	8	16	17	18	5	13	6	6	46	22	31	23
MAY 17	8	18	19	19	5	14	6	6	46	22	31	23
MAY 18	8	20	21	21	5	14	6	6	46	22	31	23
MAY 19	9	22	22	23	6	14	6	6	46	22	31	23
MAY 20	9	24	24	25	6	14	6	6	46	22	31	23
MAY 21	9	25	26	26	6	14	6	6	46	22	31	23
MAY 22	9	27	27	28	6	14	6	6	46	22	31	23
MAY 23	9	29	29	30	6	14	7	6	46	22	31	23
MAY 24	9	30	31	31	6	14	7	6	46	22	31	23
MAY 25	10	32	32	33	6	14	7	6	46	22	31	23
MAY 26	10	33	34	34	6	14	7	6	46	22	31	23
MAY 27	10	35	35	36	7	14	7	6	46	22	31	23
MAY 28	10	37	37	38	7	14	7	6	46	22	31	23
MAY 29	10	38	39	39	7	14	7	6	46	22	31	23
MAY 30	10	40	40	41	7	14	7	6	46	22	31	23
MAY 31	10	41	42	42	7	14	7	7	46	22	31	23

Date & Time	SUN	MOON 1	MOON 2	MOON 3	MERCURY	VENUS	MARS	JUPITER	SATURN	URANUS	NEPTUNE	PLUTO
JUN. 1	10	43	43	44	7	14	7	7	46	22	31	23
JUN. 2	10	45	45	46	7	14	7	7	46	22	31	23
JUN. 3	11	46	47	47	8	14	8	7	46	22	31	23
JUN. 4	11	48	1	1	8	14	8	7	46	22	31	23
JUN. 5	11	2	2	3	8	14	8	7	46	22	31	23
JUN. 6	11	4	4	5	8	14	8	7	46	22	31	23
JUN. 7	11	6	6	7	8	14	8	7	46	22	31	23
JUN. 8	11	8	9	9	9	14	8	7	46	22	31	23
JUN. 9	11	10	10	11	9	14	8	7	46	22	31	23
JUN. 10	11	12	12	13	9	14	8	7	46	22	31	23
JUN. 11	12	14	14	15	9	13	8	7	46	22	31	23
JUN. 12	12	16	16	17	10	13	8	7	46	22	31	23
JUN. 13	12	18	18	19	10	13	9	7	46	22	31	23
JUN. 14	12	19	20	21	10	13	9	7	46	22	31	23
JUN. 15	12	21	22	23	10	13	9	7	46	22	31	23
JUN. 16	12	23	24	24	11	13	9	7	46	22	31	23
JUN. 17	12	25	25	26	11	13	9	7	46	22	31	23
JUN. 18	12	27	27	28	11	13	9	7	46	22	31	23
JUN. 19	13	28	29	29	11	13	9	7	46	22	31	23
JUN. 20	13	30	30	31	12	13	9	7	46	22	31	23
JUN. 21	13	31	32	32	12	13	9	7	46	22	31	23
JUN. 22	13	33	33	34	12	13	9	7	46	22	31	23
JUN. 23	13	35	35	36	13	13	10	7	46	22	31	23
JUN. 24	13	36	37	37	13	12	10	7	46	22	31	23
JUN. 25	14	38	38	39	13	12	10	7	46	22	31	23
JUN. 26	14	39	40	40	13	12	10	7	46	22	31	23
JUN. 27	14	41	41	42	14	12	10	7	46	22	31	23
JUN. 28	14	42	43	44	14	12	10	7	46	22	31	23
JUN. 29	14	44	45	45	14	12	10	7	46	22	31	23
JUN. 30	14	46	46	47	15	12	10	7	46	22	31	23

MOON 1 ◐ 12:01 A.M. TO 8:00 A.M.   **MOON 2** ◑ 8:01 A.M. TO 4:00 P.M.   **MOON 3** ● 4:01 P.M. TO 12:00 A.M.
Use only one "moon" number. Choose the column closest to your time of birth. If your place of birth is not on Eastern Standard Time, be sure to read "How to Convert to Eastern Standard Time" at the beginning of this section.

July   August

Date & Time	SUN	MOON 1	MOON 2	MOON 3	MERCURY	VENUS	MARS	JUPITER	SATURN	URANUS	NEPTUNE	PLUTO
JUL. 1	14	48	48	1	15	12	10	7	46	22	31	23
JUL. 2	14	1	2	2	15	12	10	7	46	22	31	23
JUL. 3	15	3	4	4	15	12	10	7	46	22	31	23
JUL. 4	15	5	6	6	16	12	11	7	46	22	31	23
JUL. 5	15	7	7	8	16	12	11	7	46	22	31	23
JUL. 6	15	9	9	10	16	12	11	7	46	22	31	23
JUL. 7	15	11	11	12	16	12	11	8	46	22	31	23
JUL. 8	15	13	13	14	17	12	11	8	46	22	31	23
JUL. 9	15	15	15	16	17	12	11	8	46	22	31	23
JUL. 10	15	17	17	18	17	12	11	8	46	22	31	23
JUL. 11	16	19	19	20	18	12	11	8	46	22	31	23
JUL. 12	16	21	21	22	18	12	11	8	46	22	31	23
JUL. 13	16	22	23	24	18	12	11	8	46	22	31	23
JUL. 14	16	24	25	25	18	12	11	8	46	22	31	23
JUL. 15	16	26	27	27	18	12	12	8	46	22	31	23
JUL. 16	16	28	28	29	19	12	12	8	46	22	31	23
JUL. 17	16	29	30	30	19	12	12	8	46	22	31	23
JUL. 18	16	31	31	32	19	12	12	8	46	22	31	23
JUL. 19	17	33	33	34	19	12	12	8	46	22	31	23
JUL. 20	17	34	35	35	20	12	12	8	46	22	31	23
JUL. 21	17	36	36	37	20	12	12	8	46	22	31	23
JUL. 22	17	37	38	38	20	12	12	8	45	22	31	23
JUL. 23	17	39	39	40	20	12	12	8	45	22	31	23
JUL. 24	17	40	41	42	20	12	12	8	45	22	31	23
JUL. 25	17	42	43	43	21	12	12	8	45	22	31	23
JUL. 26	18	44	44	45	21	12	13	8	45	22	31	23
JUL. 27	18	45	46	47	21	12	13	8	45	22	31	23
JUL. 28	18	47	48	48	21	12	13	8	45	22	31	23
JUL. 29	18	1	1	2	21	12	13	8	45	22	31	23
JUL. 30	18	3	3	4	21	12	13	8	45	22	31	23
JUL. 31	18	4	5	6	22	13	13	8	45	22	31	23

Date & Time	SUN	MOON 1	MOON 2	MOON 3	MERCURY	VENUS	MARS	JUPITER	SATURN	URANUS	NEPTUNE	PLUTO
AUG. 1	18	6	7	8	22	13	13	8	45	22	31	23
AUG. 2	18	8	9	9	22	13	13	8	45	22	31	23
AUG. 3	19	10	11	11	22	13	13	8	45	22	31	23
AUG. 4	19	12	13	13	22	13	13	8	45	22	31	23
AUG. 5	19	14	15	15	22	13	13	8	45	22	31	23
AUG. 6	19	16	17	17	22	13	14	8	45	22	31	23
AUG. 7	19	18	18	19	23	13	14	8	45	22	31	23
AUG. 8	19	20	20	21	23	13	14	8	45	22	31	23
AUG. 9	19	22	22	23	23	13	14	8	45	22	31	23
AUG. 10	19	24	24	25	23	13	14	8	45	22	31	23
AUG. 11	20	25	26	27	23	14	14	8	45	22	31	23
AUG. 12	20	27	28	28	23	14	14	8	45	22	31	23
AUG. 13	20	29	29	30	23	14	14	8	45	22	31	23
AUG. 14	20	30	31	32	23	14	14	8	45	22	31	23
AUG. 15	20	32	33	33	23	14	14	8	45	22	31	23
AUG. 16	20	34	34	35	23	14	14	8	45	22	31	23
AUG. 17	20	35	36	36	23	14	15	8	45	22	31	23
AUG. 18	20	37	37	38	23	14	15	8	45	22	31	23
AUG. 19	21	38	39	39	23	14	15	8	45	22	31	23
AUG. 20	21	40	41	41	23	15	15	8	45	22	31	23
AUG. 21	21	42	42	43	23	15	15	8	45	22	31	23
AUG. 22	21	43	44	44	23	15	15	8	45	22	31	23
AUG. 23	21	45	46	46	23	15	15	8	45	22	31	23
AUG. 24	21	47	47	48	23	15	15	8	45	22	31	23
AUG. 25	21	48	1	2	23	15	15	8	45	22	31	23
AUG. 26	22	2	3	3	23	15	15	8	45	22	31	23
AUG. 27	22	4	5	5	23	15	15	8	45	22	31	23
AUG. 28	22	6	6	7	23	15	15	8	45	22	31	23
AUG. 29	22	8	8	9	23	16	16	8	45	22	31	23
AUG. 30	22	10	10	11	23	16	16	8	45	22	31	23
AUG. 31	22	11	12	13	23	16	16	8	45	22	31	23

MOON 1 ☽ 12:01 A.M. TO 8:00 A.M.   **MOON 2** ☽ 8:01 A.M. TO 4:00 P.M.   **MOON 3** ● 4:01 P.M. TO 12:00 A.M.

Use only one "moon" number. Choose the column closest to your time of birth. If your place of birth is not on Eastern Standard Time, be sure to read "How to Convert to Eastern Standard Time" at the beginning of this section.

1964

September

Date & Time	SUN	MOON 1	MOON 2	MOON 3	MERCURY	VENUS	MARS	JUPITER	SATURN	URANUS	NEPTUNE	PLUTO
SEP. 1	22	13	14	15	22	16	16	8	45	22	31	23
SEP. 2	22	15	16	17	22	16	16	8	45	22	31	23
SEP. 3	23	17	18	18	22	16	16	8	45	22	31	23
SEP. 4	23	19	20	20	22	16	16	8	45	22	31	23
SEP. 5	23	21	22	22	22	17	16	8	45	22	31	23
SEP. 6	23	23	23	24	22	17	16	8	45	22	31	23
SEP. 7	23	25	25	26	22	17	16	8	45	22	31	23
SEP. 8	23	26	27	28	22	17	16	8	45	22	31	23
SEP. 9	23	28	29	29	22	17	16	8	45	22	31	23
SEP. 10	23	30	30	31	22	17	17	8	45	22	31	23
SEP. 11	24	32	32	33	22	17	17	8	45	22	31	23
SEP. 12	24	33	34	34	22	18	17	8	45	22	31	23
SEP. 13	24	35	35	36	22	18	17	8	45	22	31	23
SEP. 14	24	36	37	37	22	18	17	8	45	22	31	23
SEP. 15	24	38	38	39	22	18	17	8	45	22	31	23
SEP. 16	24	39	40	41	22	18	17	8	45	22	31	23
SEP. 17	24	41	42	42	22	18	17	8	45	22	31	23
SEP. 18	24	43	43	44	22	18	17	8	45	22	31	23
SEP. 19	25	44	45	46	22	19	17	8	45	22	31	23
SEP. 20	25	46	47	47	22	19	17	8	45	23	31	23
SEP. 21	25	48	48	1	22	19	17	8	45	23	31	23
SEP. 22	25	2	2	3	23	19	18	8	45	23	31	23
SEP. 23	25	4	4	5	23	19	18	8	45	23	31	23
SEP. 24	25	5	6	7	23	19	18	8	45	23	31	23
SEP. 25	26	7	8	9	23	19	18	8	45	23	31	23
SEP. 26	26	9	10	10	23	20	18	8	45	23	31	23
SEP. 27	26	11	12	12	24	20	18	8	45	23	31	23
SEP. 28	26	13	14	14	24	20	18	8	45	23	31	23
SEP. 29	26	15	15	16	24	20	18	8	45	23	31	23
SEP. 30	26	17	17	18	24	20	18	8	45	23	31	23

October

Date & Time	SUN	MOON 1	MOON 2	MOON 3	MERCURY	VENUS	MARS	JUPITER	SATURN	URANUS	NEPTUNE	PLUTO
OCT. 1	26	19	19	20	25	20	18	8	45	23	31	23
OCT. 2	26	20	21	22	25	20	18	8	45	23	31	23
OCT. 3	27	22	23	23	25	21	18	8	45	23	31	23
OCT. 4	27	24	25	25	25	21	18	8	45	23	31	23
OCT. 5	27	26	26	27	25	21	19	8	45	23	31	23
OCT. 6	27	28	28	29	26	21	19	8	45	23	31	23
OCT. 7	27	29	30	30	26	21	19	8	45	23	31	23
OCT. 8	27	31	31	32	26	21	19	8	45	23	31	23
OCT. 9	27	33	33	34	26	21	19	8	45	23	31	23
OCT. 10	27	34	35	35	27	22	19	8	45	23	31	23
OCT. 11	28	36	36	37	27	22	19	8	45	23	31	23
OCT. 12	28	37	38	38	27	22	19	8	45	23	31	23
OCT. 13	28	39	39	40	27	22	19	8	45	23	31	23
OCT. 14	28	40	41	42	28	22	19	8	45	23	31	23
OCT. 15	28	42	43	43	28	22	19	8	45	23	31	23
OCT. 16	28	44	44	45	28	23	19	8	45	23	31	23
OCT. 17	28	45	46	47	28	23	20	8	45	23	31	23
OCT. 18	28	47	48	48	29	23	20	8	45	23	31	23
OCT. 19	29	1	2	2	29	23	20	8	45	23	31	23
OCT. 20	29	3	3	4	29	23	20	8	45	23	31	23
OCT. 21	29	5	5	6	29	23	20	8	45	23	31	23
OCT. 22	29	7	7	8	29	24	20	8	45	23	31	23
OCT. 23	29	9	9	10	30	24	20	8	45	23	31	23
OCT. 24	29	11	11	12	30	24	20	8	45	23	31	23
OCT. 25	29	12	13	14	30	24	20	8	45	23	31	23
OCT. 26	30	14	15	16	30	24	20	8	45	23	31	23
OCT. 27	30	16	17	17	30	24	20	8	45	23	31	23
OCT. 28	30	18	19	19	31	24	20	8	45	23	31	23
OCT. 29	30	20	21	21	31	25	20	8	45	23	31	23
OCT. 30	30	22	22	23	31	25	20	8	45	23	31	23
OCT. 31	30	24	24	25	31	25	21	8	45	23	31	23

MOON 1 ☽ 12:01 A.M. TO 8:00 A.M.   **MOON 2** ◑ 8:01 A.M. TO 4:00 P.M.   **MOON 3** ● 4:01 P.M. TO 12:00 A.M.
Use only one "moon" number. Choose the column closest to your time of birth. If your place of birth is not on Eastern Standard Time, be sure to read "How to Convert to Eastern Standard Time" at the beginning of this section.

1965

November

Date & Time	SUN	MOON 1	MOON 2	MOON 3	MERCURY	VENUS	MARS	JUPITER	SATURN	URANUS	NEPTUNE	PLUTO
NOV. 1	30	25	26	26	31	25	21	8	45	23	31	23
NOV. 2	30	27	28	28	32	25	21	8	45	23	31	23
NOV. 3	31	29	29	30	32	25	21	8	45	23	31	23
NOV. 4	31	30	31	31	32	26	21	8	45	23	31	23
NOV. 5	31	32	33	33	32	26	21	8	45	23	31	23
NOV. 6	31	34	34	35	33	26	21	8	45	23	31	23
NOV. 7	31	35	36	36	33	26	21	8	45	23	31	23
NOV. 8	31	37	37	38	33	26	21	8	45	23	31	23
NOV. 9	31	38	39	39	33	26	21	8	45	23	31	23
NOV. 10	31	40	40	41	33	27	21	8	45	23	31	23
NOV. 11	31	42	42	43	34	27	21	8	45	23	31	23
NOV. 12	32	43	44	44	34	27	21	8	45	23	31	23
NOV. 13	32	45	45	46	34	27	21	8	45	23	31	23
NOV. 14	32	46	47	48	34	27	22	8	45	23	31	23
NOV. 15	32	48	1	1	34	27	22	8	45	23	31	23
NOV. 16	32	2	3	3	34	28	22	8	45	23	31	23
NOV. 17	32	4	4	5	35	28	22	8	45	23	31	23
NOV. 18	32	6	6	7	35	28	22	8	45	23	31	23
NOV. 19	33	8	8	9	35	28	22	8	45	23	31	23
NOV. 20	33	10	10	11	35	28	22	8	45	23	31	23
NOV. 21	33	12	12	13	35	28	22	8	45	23	31	23
NOV. 22	33	14	14	15	36	28	22	8	45	23	31	23
NOV. 23	33	16	16	17	36	29	22	8	45	23	31	23
NOV. 24	33	18	18	19	36	29	22	8	45	23	31	23
NOV. 25	34	19	20	21	36	29	22	8	45	23	31	23
NOV. 26	34	21	22	23	36	29	22	8	45	23	31	23
NOV. 27	34	23	24	24	36	29	22	8	45	23	31	23
NOV. 28	34	25	25	26	37	29	22	8	45	23	31	23
NOV. 29	34	27	27	28	37	30	22	7	45	23	31	23
NOV. 30	34	28	29	29	37	30	23	7	45	23	31	23

December

Date & Time	SUN	MOON 1	MOON 2	MOON 3	MERCURY	VENUS	MARS	JUPITER	SATURN	URANUS	NEPTUNE	PLUTO
DEC. 1	34	30	31	31	37	30	23	7	45	23	31	23
DEC. 2	34	32	32	33	37	30	23	7	45	23	31	23
DEC. 3	35	33	34	34	37	30	23	7	45	23	31	23
DEC. 4	35	35	35	36	37	30	23	7	45	23	31	23
DEC. 5	35	36	37	37	37	31	23	7	45	23	31	23
DEC. 6	35	38	38	39	38	31	23	7	45	23	31	23
DEC. 7	35	40	40	41	38	31	23	7	45	23	31	23
DEC. 8	35	41	42	42	38	31	23	7	45	23	31	23
DEC. 9	35	43	43	44	38	31	23	7	45	23	31	23
DEC. 10	35	44	45	45	38	31	23	7	45	23	31	23
DEC. 11	36	46	46	47	38	32	23	7	45	23	31	23
DEC. 12	36	48	48	1	38	32	23	7	45	23	31	23
DEC. 13	36	1	2	2	37	32	23	7	45	23	31	23
DEC. 14	36	3	4	4	37	32	23	7	45	23	31	23
DEC. 15	36	5	6	6	37	32	23	7	45	23	31	23
DEC. 16	36	7	7	8	37	32	23	7	45	23	31	23
DEC. 17	36	9	9	10	37	33	23	7	45	23	31	23
DEC. 18	36	11	11	12	37	33	24	7	45	23	31	23
DEC. 19	37	13	13	14	36	33	24	7	45	23	31	23
DEC. 20	37	15	15	16	36	33	24	7	45	23	31	23
DEC. 21	37	17	18	18	36	33	24	7	45	23	32	23
DEC. 22	37	19	19	20	36	33	24	7	45	23	32	23
DEC. 23	37	21	21	22	36	34	24	7	45	23	32	23
DEC. 24	37	23	23	24	36	34	24	7	45	23	32	23
DEC. 25	37	24	25	26	36	34	24	7	45	23	32	23
DEC. 26	38	26	27	27	36	34	24	7	45	23	32	23
DEC. 27	38	28	28	29	36	34	24	7	45	23	32	23
DEC. 28	38	30	30	31	35	34	24	7	45	23	32	23
DEC. 29	38	31	32	32	35	35	24	7	45	23	32	23
DEC. 30	38	33	33	34	35	35	24	7	45	23	32	23
DEC. 31	38	34	35	35	35	35	24	7	45	23	32	23

MOON 1 ☽ 12:01 A.M. TO 8:00 A.M.   **MOON 2** ☽ 8:01 A.M. TO 4:00 P.M.   **MOON 3** ● 4:01 P.M. TO 12:00 A.M.

Use only one "moon" number. Choose the column closest to your time of birth. If your place of birth is not on Eastern Standard Time, be sure to read "How to Convert to Eastern Standard Time" at the beginning of this section.

January

Date & Time	SUN	MOON 1	MOON 2	MOON 3	MERCURY	VENUS	MARS	JUPITER	SATURN	URANUS	NEPTUNE	PLUTO
JAN. 1	38	36	37	37	36	35	24	7	45	23	32	23
JAN. 2	38	38	38	39	36	35	24	7	45	23	32	23
JAN. 3	39	39	40	40	36	35	24	7	45	23	32	23
JAN. 4	39	41	41	42	36	36	24	7	45	23	32	23
JAN. 5	39	42	43	43	36	36	24	7	45	23	32	23
JAN. 6	39	44	44	45	36	36	24	7	45	23	32	23
JAN. 7	39	46	46	47	36	36	24	7	45	23	32	23
JAN. 8	39	47	48	48	36	36	24	7	45	23	32	23
JAN. 9	39	1	1	2	36	36	24	7	45	23	32	23
JAN. 10	40	3	3	4	37	37	24	7	45	23	32	23
JAN. 11	40	4	5	5	37	37	24	7	45	23	32	23
JAN. 12	40	6	7	7	37	37	24	7	45	23	32	23
JAN. 13	40	8	9	9	37	37	25	7	45	23	32	23
JAN. 14	40	10	11	11	37	37	25	7	45	23	32	23
JAN. 15	40	12	13	13	37	37	25	7	45	23	32	23
JAN. 16	40	14	15	15	37	38	25	7	45	23	32	23
JAN. 17	41	16	17	17	38	38	25	7	45	23	32	23
JAN. 18	41	18	19	19	38	38	25	7	45	23	32	23
JAN. 19	41	20	21	21	38	38	25	7	45	23	32	23
JAN. 20	41	22	23	23	38	38	25	7	45	23	32	23
JAN. 21	41	24	24	25	38	38	25	7	45	23	32	23
JAN. 22	41	26	26	27	39	39	25	7	45	23	32	23
JAN. 23	42	27	28	29	39	39	25	7	45	23	32	23
JAN. 24	42	29	30	30	39	39	25	7	45	23	32	23
JAN. 25	42	31	31	32	39	39	25	7	45	23	32	23
JAN. 26	42	32	33	33	39	39	25	7	45	23	32	23
JAN. 27	42	34	35	35	40	39	25	7	45	23	32	23
JAN. 28	42	36	36	37	40	40	25	7	46	23	32	23
JAN. 29	42	37	38	38	40	40	25	7	46	23	32	23
JAN. 30	42	39	39	40	40	40	25	7	46	23	32	23
JAN. 31	43	40	41	41	40	40	25	7	46	23	32	23

February

Date & Time	SUN	MOON 1	MOON 2	MOON 3	MERCURY	VENUS	MARS	JUPITER	SATURN	URANUS	NEPTUNE	PLUTO
FEB. 1	43	42	42	43	41	40	25	7	46	23	32	23
FEB. 2	43	43	44	45	41	40	25	7	46	23	32	23
FEB. 3	43	45	46	46	41	41	25	7	46	23	32	23
FEB. 4	43	47	47	48	41	41	25	7	46	23	32	23
FEB. 5	43	48	1	2	41	41	25	7	46	23	32	23
FEB. 6	43	2	3	3	42	41	25	7	46	23	32	23
FEB. 7	43	4	4	5	42	41	25	7	46	23	32	23
FEB. 8	44	6	6	7	42	41	25	7	46	23	32	23
FEB. 9	44	7	8	9	42	42	25	7	46	23	32	23
FEB. 10	44	9	10	10	42	42	25	7	46	23	32	23
FEB. 11	44	11	12	12	43	42	25	7	46	23	32	23
FEB. 12	44	13	14	14	43	42	25	7	46	23	32	23
FEB. 13	44	15	16	16	43	42	25	7	46	23	32	23
FEB. 14	44	17	18	18	43	42	24	7	46	23	32	23
FEB. 15	44	19	20	20	44	43	24	7	46	23	32	23
FEB. 16	45	21	22	22	44	43	24	7	46	23	32	23
FEB. 17	45	23	24	24	44	43	24	7	46	23	32	23
FEB. 18	45	25	25	26	44	43	24	7	46	23	32	23
FEB. 19	45	27	27	28	44	43	24	7	46	23	32	23
FEB. 20	45	28	29	30	45	43	24	7	46	23	32	23
FEB. 21	45	30	31	31	45	44	24	7	46	23	32	23
FEB. 22	45	32	32	33	45	44	24	8	46	23	32	23
FEB. 23	46	34	34	35	45	44	24	8	46	23	32	23
FEB. 24	46	35	36	36	46	44	24	8	46	23	32	23
FEB. 25	46	37	37	38	46	44	24	8	46	23	32	23
FEB. 26	46	38	39	39	46	44	24	8	46	23	32	23
FEB. 27	46	40	40	41	46	45	24	8	46	23	32	23
FEB. 28	46	41	42	42	47	45	24	8	46	23	32	23

MOON 1 ◖ 12:01 A.M. TO 8:00 A.M.　**MOON 2** ◑ 8:01 A.M. TO 4:00 P.M.　**MOON 3** ● 4:01 P.M. TO 12:00 A.M.
Use only one "moon" number. Choose the column closest to your time of birth. If your place of birth is not on
Eastern Standard Time, be sure to read "How to Convert to Eastern Standard Time" at the beginning of this section.

1965

March

April

Date & Time	SUN	MOON 1	MOON 2	MOON 3	MERCURY	VENUS	MARS	JUPITER	SATURN	URANUS	NEPTUNE	PLUTO
MAR. 1	46	43	44	44	47	45	24	8	46	23	32	23
MAR. 2	46	45	45	46	47	45	24	8	46	23	32	23
MAR. 3	47	46	47	47	47	45	24	8	46	23	32	23
MAR. 4	47	48	1	1	48	45	24	8	46	23	32	23
MAR. 5	47	2	2	3	48	46	24	8	46	23	32	23
MAR. 6	47	3	4	5	48	46	24	8	46	23	32	23
MAR. 7	47	5	6	6	48	46	24	8	46	23	32	23
MAR. 8	47	7	8	8	1	46	24	8	46	23	32	23
MAR. 9	47	9	9	10	1	46	23	8	46	23	32	23
MAR. 10	47	11	11	12	1	46	23	8	46	23	32	23
MAR. 11	48	12	13	14	1	47	23	8	46	23	32	23
MAR. 12	48	14	15	16	2	47	23	8	46	23	32	23
MAR. 13	48	16	17	18	2	47	23	8	46	23	32	23
MAR. 14	48	18	19	20	2	47	23	8	46	23	32	23
MAR. 15	48	20	21	21	2	47	23	8	46	23	32	23
MAR. 16	48	22	23	23	3	47	23	8	46	23	32	23
MAR. 17	48	24	25	25	3	48	23	8	46	23	32	23
MAR. 18	48	26	27	27	3	48	23	8	46	23	32	23
MAR. 19	1	28	28	29	3	48	23	8	46	23	32	23
MAR. 20	1	30	30	31	3	48	23	8	46	23	32	23
MAR. 21	1	31	32	32	3	48	23	8	46	23	32	23
MAR. 22	1	33	33	34	4	48	23	8	46	23	32	23
MAR. 23	1	35	35	36	4	1	23	8	46	23	32	23
MAR. 24	1	36	37	37	4	1	23	8	46	23	32	23
MAR. 25	2	38	38	39	4	1	23	8	46	23	32	23
MAR. 26	2	39	40	40	4	1	23	8	46	23	32	23
MAR. 27	2	41	41	42	4	1	23	8	46	23	32	23
MAR. 28	2	42	43	44	4	1	23	8	46	23	32	23
MAR. 29	2	44	45	45	4	2	23	8	46	23	32	23
MAR. 30	2	46	46	47	4	2	22	8	46	23	32	23
MAR. 31	2	47	48	1	4	2	22	8	46	23	32	23

Date & Time	SUN	MOON 1	MOON 2	MOON 3	MERCURY	VENUS	MARS	JUPITER	SATURN	URANUS	NEPTUNE	PLUTO
APR. 1	2	1	2	2	4	2	22	8	47	23	32	23
APR. 2	2	3	4	4	4	2	22	8	47	23	32	23
APR. 3	3	5	5	6	4	2	22	8	47	23	32	23
APR. 4	3	7	7	8	4	3	22	8	47	23	32	23
APR. 5	3	8	9	10	4	3	22	8	47	22	32	23
APR. 6	3	10	11	11	4	3	22	8	47	22	32	23
APR. 7	3	12	13	13	4	3	22	9	47	22	32	23
APR. 8	3	14	15	15	3	3	22	9	47	22	32	23
APR. 9	3	16	16	17	3	3	22	9	47	22	32	23
APR. 10	3	18	18	19	3	4	22	9	47	22	32	23
APR. 11	4	20	20	21	3	4	22	9	47	22	32	23
APR. 12	4	21	22	23	3	4	22	9	47	22	32	23
APR. 13	4	23	24	25	3	4	22	9	47	22	32	23
APR. 14	4	25	26	26	3	4	22	9	47	22	32	23
APR. 15	4	27	28	28	3	4	22	9	47	22	32	23
APR. 16	4	29	29	30	3	5	22	9	47	22	32	23
APR. 17	4	31	31	32	3	5	22	9	47	22	32	23
APR. 18	4	32	33	33	3	5	22	9	47	22	32	23
APR. 19	5	34	35	35	3	5	22	9	47	22	32	23
APR. 20	5	36	36	37	3	5	22	9	47	22	32	23
APR. 21	5	37	38	38	3	5	22	9	47	22	32	23
APR. 22	5	39	39	40	3	6	22	9	47	22	32	23
APR. 23	5	40	41	41	3	6	22	9	47	22	32	23
APR. 24	5	42	42	43	3	6	22	9	47	22	32	23
APR. 25	6	44	44	45	3	6	22	9	47	22	32	23
APR. 26	6	45	46	46	3	6	22	9	47	22	31	23
APR. 27	6	47	47	48	3	6	22	9	47	22	31	23
APR. 28	6	1	1	2	3	7	22	9	47	22	31	23
APR. 29	6	2	3	3	3	7	22	9	47	22	31	23
APR. 30	6	4	5	5	3	7	22	9	47	22	31	23

MOON 1 ◗ 12:01 A.M. TO 8:00 A.M.　　**MOON 2** ◐ 8:01 A.M. TO 4:00 P.M.　　**MOON 3** ● 4:01 P.M. TO 12:00 A.M.

Use only one "moon" number. Choose the column closest to your time of birth. If your place of birth is not on
Eastern Standard Time, be sure to read "How to Convert to Eastern Standard Time" at the beginning of this section.

1965

May

Date & Time	SUN	MOON 1	MOON 2	MOON 3	MERCURY	VENUS	MARS	JUPITER	SATURN	URANUS	NEPTUNE	PLUTO
MAY 1	6	6	7	7	3	7	22	9	47	22	31	23
MAY 2	6	8	8	9	3	7	22	9	47	22	31	23
MAY 3	7	10	10	11	3	7	22	9	47	22	31	23
MAY 4	7	12	12	13	3	8	22	9	47	22	31	23
MAY 5	7	13	14	15	3	8	22	9	47	22	31	23
MAY 6	7	15	16	17	4	8	22	9	47	22	31	23
MAY 7	7	17	18	19	4	8	22	9	47	22	31	23
MAY 8	7	19	20	20	4	8	22	9	47	22	31	23
MAY 9	7	21	22	22	4	8	22	9	47	22	31	23
MAY 10	7	23	24	24	4	9	22	9	47	22	31	23
MAY 11	8	25	25	26	4	9	22	10	47	22	31	23
MAY 12	8	27	27	28	4	9	22	10	47	22	31	23
MAY 13	8	28	29	29	5	9	23	10	47	22	31	23
MAY 14	8	30	31	31	5	9	23	10	47	22	31	23
MAY 15	8	32	32	33	5	9	23	10	47	22	31	23
MAY 16	8	33	34	35	5	10	23	10	47	22	31	23
MAY 17	8	35	36	36	5	10	23	10	47	22	31	23
MAY 18	8	37	37	38	5	10	23	10	47	22	31	23
MAY 19	9	38	39	39	6	10	23	10	47	22	31	23
MAY 20	9	40	40	41	6	10	23	10	47	22	31	23
MAY 21	9	41	42	42	6	10	23	10	47	22	31	23
MAY 22	9	43	44	44	6	10	23	10	47	22	31	23
MAY 23	9	45	45	46	7	11	23	10	47	22	31	23
MAY 24	9	46	47	47	7	11	23	10	47	22	31	23
MAY 25	10	48	48	1	7	11	23	10	47	22	31	23
MAY 26	10	2	2	3	7	11	23	10	47	22	31	23
MAY 27	10	3	4	5	7	11	23	10	47	22	31	23
MAY 28	10	5	6	6	8	11	23	10	47	22	31	23
MAY 29	10	7	8	8	8	12	23	10	47	22	31	23
MAY 30	10	9	10	10	8	12	23	10	47	22	31	23
MAY 31	10	11	11	12	8	12	23	10	47	22	31	23

June

Date & Time	SUN	MOON 1	MOON 2	MOON 3	MERCURY	VENUS	MARS	JUPITER	SATURN	URANUS	NEPTUNE	PLUTO
JUN. 1	10	13	13	14	9	12	23	10	47	22	31	23
JUN. 2	10	15	15	16	9	12	23	10	47	22	31	23
JUN. 3	11	17	17	18	9	12	23	10	47	22	31	23
JUN. 4	11	19	19	20	10	13	23	10	47	22	31	23
JUN. 5	11	21	21	22	10	13	24	10	47	22	31	23
JUN. 6	11	22	23	24	10	13	24	10	47	22	31	23
JUN. 7	11	24	25	26	10	13	24	10	47	22	31	23
JUN. 8	11	26	27	27	11	13	24	10	47	22	31	23
JUN. 9	11	28	28	29	11	13	24	10	47	22	31	23
JUN. 10	11	30	30	31	11	14	24	10	47	22	31	23
JUN. 11	12	31	32	32	12	14	24	10	47	22	31	23
JUN. 12	12	33	34	34	12	14	24	11	47	22	31	23
JUN. 13	12	35	35	36	12	14	24	11	47	22	31	23
JUN. 14	12	36	37	37	12	14	24	11	47	22	31	23
JUN. 15	12	38	38	39	13	14	24	11	47	22	31	23
JUN. 16	12	39	40	40	13	15	24	11	47	22	31	23
JUN. 17	12	41	42	42	13	15	24	11	47	22	31	23
JUN. 18	12	43	43	44	14	15	24	11	47	22	31	23
JUN. 19	13	44	45	45	14	15	24	11	47	22	31	23
JUN. 20	13	46	46	47	14	15	24	11	47	22	31	23
JUN. 21	13	47	48	48	14	15	24	11	47	22	31	23
JUN. 22	13	1	2	2	15	16	25	11	47	22	31	23
JUN. 23	13	3	3	4	15	16	25	11	47	22	31	23
JUN. 24	13	4	5	6	15	16	25	11	47	22	31	23
JUN. 25	14	6	7	7	15	16	25	11	47	22	31	23
JUN. 26	14	8	9	9	16	16	25	11	47	22	31	23
JUN. 27	14	10	11	11	16	16	25	11	47	22	31	23
JUN. 28	14	12	13	13	16	17	25	11	47	22	31	23
JUN. 29	14	14	15	15	16	17	25	11	47	22	31	23
JUN. 30	14	16	17	17	17	17	25	11	47	22	31	23

MOON 1 ☽ 12:01 A.M. TO 8:00 A.M.   **MOON 2** ☽ 8:01 A.M. TO 4:00 P.M.   **MOON 3** ● 4:01 P.M. TO 12:00 A.M.
Use only one "moon" number. Choose the column closest to your time of birth. If your place of birth is not on Eastern Standard Time, be sure to read "How to Convert to Eastern Standard Time" at the beginning of this section.

1965

July

August

Date & Time	SUN	MOON 1	MOON 2	MOON 3	MERCURY	VENUS	MARS	JUPITER	SATURN	URANUS	NEPTUNE	PLUTO
JUL. 1	14	18	19	19	17	17	25	11	47	23	31	23
JUL. 2	14	20	21	21	17	17	25	11	47	23	31	23
JUL. 3	15	22	23	23	17	17	25	11	47	23	31	23
JUL. 4	15	24	24	25	18	18	25	11	47	23	31	23
JUL. 5	15	26	26	27	18	18	25	11	47	23	31	23
JUL. 6	15	27	28	29	18	18	25	11	47	23	31	23
JUL. 7	15	29	30	30	18	18	26	11	47	23	31	23
JUL. 8	15	31	31	32	18	18	26	11	47	23	31	23
JUL. 9	15	33	33	34	18	18	26	11	47	23	31	23
JUL. 10	15	34	35	35	19	18	26	11	47	23	31	23
JUL. 11	16	36	36	37	19	18	26	11	47	23	31	23
JUL. 12	16	37	38	38	19	19	26	11	47	23	31	23
JUL. 13	16	39	40	40	19	19	26	11	47	23	31	23
JUL. 14	16	41	41	42	19	19	26	11	47	23	31	23
JUL. 15	16	42	43	43	19	19	26	12	47	23	31	23
JUL. 16	16	44	44	45	20	19	26	12	47	23	31	23
JUL. 17	16	45	46	46	20	20	26	12	47	23	31	23
JUL. 18	16	47	47	48	20	20	26	12	47	23	31	23
JUL. 19	17	1	1	2	20	20	26	12	47	23	31	23
JUL. 20	17	2	3	3	20	20	26	12	47	23	31	23
JUL. 21	17	4	4	5	20	20	27	12	47	23	31	23
JUL. 22	17	6	6	7	20	20	27	12	47	23	31	23
JUL. 23	17	7	8	9	20	21	27	12	47	23	31	23
JUL. 24	17	9	10	10	21	21	27	12	47	23	31	23
JUL. 25	17	11	12	12	21	21	27	12	47	23	31	23
JUL. 26	18	13	14	14	21	21	27	12	47	23	31	23
JUL. 27	18	15	16	16	21	21	27	12	47	23	31	23
JUL. 28	18	17	18	18	21	21	27	12	47	23	31	23
JUL. 29	18	19	20	20	21	22	27	12	47	23	31	23
JUL. 30	18	21	22	22	21	22	27	12	47	23	31	23
JUL. 31	18	23	24	24	21	22	27	12	47	23	31	23

Date & Time	SUN	MOON 1	MOON 2	MOON 3	MERCURY	VENUS	MARS	JUPITER	SATURN	URANUS	NEPTUNE	PLUTO
AUG. 1	18	25	26	26	21	22	27	12	47	23	31	23
AUG. 2	18	27	28	28	21	22	27	12	47	23	31	23
AUG. 3	19	29	29	30	21	22	28	12	47	23	31	23
AUG. 4	19	30	31	32	21	23	28	12	47	23	31	23
AUG. 5	19	32	33	33	21	23	28	12	47	23	31	23
AUG. 6	19	34	34	35	21	23	28	12	47	23	31	23
AUG. 7	19	35	36	36	21	23	28	12	47	23	31	23
AUG. 8	19	37	38	38	21	23	28	12	47	23	31	23
AUG. 9	19	39	39	40	21	23	28	12	47	23	31	23
AUG. 10	19	40	41	41	21	23	28	12	47	23	31	23
AUG. 11	20	42	42	43	20	24	28	12	47	23	31	23
AUG. 12	20	43	44	44	20	24	28	12	47	23	31	23
AUG. 13	20	45	45	46	20	24	28	12	47	23	31	23
AUG. 14	20	47	47	48	20	24	28	12	47	23	31	23
AUG. 15	20	48	1	1	20	24	29	12	47	23	31	23
AUG. 16	20	2	2	3	20	24	29	12	47	23	31	23
AUG. 17	20	3	4	5	20	25	29	12	47	23	31	23
AUG. 18	20	5	6	6	20	25	29	12	47	23	31	23
AUG. 19	21	7	7	8	20	25	29	12	47	23	31	23
AUG. 20	21	9	9	10	20	25	29	12	47	23	31	23
AUG. 21	21	10	11	12	19	25	29	12	47	23	31	23
AUG. 22	21	12	13	14	19	25	29	12	47	23	31	23
AUG. 23	21	14	15	16	19	26	29	12	47	23	31	23
AUG. 24	21	16	17	18	19	26	29	13	47	23	31	23
AUG. 25	21	18	19	20	19	26	29	13	47	23	31	23
AUG. 26	22	20	21	22	19	26	29	13	47	23	31	23
AUG. 27	22	22	23	24	19	26	30	13	47	23	31	23
AUG. 28	22	24	25	26	19	26	30	13	47	23	31	23
AUG. 29	22	26	27	27	19	27	30	13	47	23	31	23
AUG. 30	22	28	29	29	19	27	30	13	47	23	31	23
AUG. 31	22	30	30	31	20	27	30	13	47	23	31	23

MOON 1 ☽ 12:01 A.M. TO 8:00 A.M.   **MOON 2** ☽ 8:01 A.M. TO 4:00 P.M.   **MOON 3** ● 4:01 P.M. TO 12:00 A.M.
Use only one "moon" number. Choose the column closest to your time of birth. If your place of birth is not on
Eastern Standard Time, be sure to read "How to Convert to Eastern Standard Time" at the beginning of this section.

1965

September

Date & Time	SUN ☉	MOON 1 ◖	MOON 2 ◑	MOON 3 ●	MERCURY	VENUS	MARS	JUPITER	SATURN	URANUS	NEPTUNE	PLUTO
SEP. 1	22	32	32	33	20	27	30	13	47	23	31	23
SEP. 2	22	33	34	34	20	27	30	13	47	23	31	23
SEP. 3	23	35	36	36	20	27	30	13	47	23	31	23
SEP. 4	23	37	37	38	20	27	30	13	47	23	31	23
SEP. 5	23	38	39	39	20	28	30	13	47	23	31	23
SEP. 6	23	40	40	41	20	28	30	13	47	23	31	23
SEP. 7	23	41	42	42	21	28	30	13	47	23	31	23
SEP. 8	23	43	43	44	21	28	31	13	47	23	31	23
SEP. 9	23	45	45	46	21	28	31	13	47	23	31	23
SEP. 10	23	46	47	47	21	28	31	13	47	23	31	23
SEP. 11	24	48	48	1	22	29	31	13	47	23	31	23
SEP. 12	24	1	2	3	22	29	31	13	47	23	31	23
SEP. 13	24	3	4	4	22	29	31	13	47	23	31	23
SEP. 14	24	5	5	6	22	29	31	13	47	23	31	23
SEP. 15	24	6	7	8	22	29	31	13	47	23	31	23
SEP. 16	24	8	9	9	23	29	31	13	47	23	31	23
SEP. 17	24	10	11	11	23	29	31	13	47	23	31	23
SEP. 18	24	12	12	13	23	30	31	13	47	23	31	23
SEP. 19	25	14	14	15	23	30	32	13	47	23	31	23
SEP. 20	25	16	16	17	24	30	32	13	47	23	31	23
SEP. 21	25	17	18	19	24	30	32	13	47	23	31	23
SEP. 22	25	19	20	21	24	30	32	13	47	23	31	23
SEP. 23	25	21	22	23	24	30	32	13	47	23	31	23
SEP. 24	25	23	24	25	25	31	32	13	47	23	31	23
SEP. 25	26	25	26	27	25	31	32	13	47	23	31	23
SEP. 26	26	27	28	29	25	31	32	13	47	23	31	23
SEP. 27	26	29	30	30	25	31	32	13	47	23	31	23
SEP. 28	26	31	32	32	26	31	32	13	47	23	31	23
SEP. 29	26	33	33	34	26	31	32	13	47	23	31	23
SEP. 30	26	34	35	36	26	32	33	13	47	23	31	23

October

Date & Time	SUN ☉	MOON 1 ◖	MOON 2 ◑	MOON 3 ●	MERCURY	VENUS	MARS	JUPITER	SATURN	URANUS	NEPTUNE	PLUTO
OCT. 1	26	36	37	37	26	32	33	13	47	23	31	23
OCT. 2	26	38	38	39	27	32	33	13	47	23	31	23
OCT. 3	27	39	40	40	27	32	33	13	47	23	31	23
OCT. 4	27	41	41	42	27	32	33	13	47	23	31	23
OCT. 5	27	42	43	43	27	32	33	13	47	23	31	23
OCT. 6	27	44	45	45	28	32	33	13	47	23	31	23
OCT. 7	27	46	46	47	28	33	33	13	47	23	31	23
OCT. 8	27	47	48	48	28	33	33	13	47	23	31	23
OCT. 9	27	1	1	2	28	33	33	13	47	23	31	23
OCT. 10	27	3	3	4	28	33	34	13	46	23	31	23
OCT. 11	28	4	5	5	29	33	34	13	46	23	31	23
OCT. 12	28	6	7	7	29	33	34	13	46	23	31	23
OCT. 13	28	8	8	9	29	33	34	13	46	23	31	23
OCT. 14	28	10	10	11	29	34	34	13	46	23	31	23
OCT. 15	28	11	12	13	29	34	34	13	46	23	31	23
OCT. 16	28	13	14	14	30	34	34	13	46	23	31	23
OCT. 17	28	15	16	16	30	34	34	13	46	23	31	23
OCT. 18	28	17	18	18	30	34	34	13	46	23	31	23
OCT. 19	29	19	20	20	30	34	34	13	46	23	31	23
OCT. 20	29	21	21	22	30	35	34	13	46	23	31	23
OCT. 21	29	23	23	24	31	35	35	13	46	23	31	23
OCT. 22	29	25	25	26	31	35	35	13	46	23	31	23
OCT. 23	29	27	27	28	31	35	35	13	46	23	31	23
OCT. 24	29	28	29	30	31	35	35	13	46	23	32	23
OCT. 25	29	30	31	31	31	35	35	13	46	23	32	23
OCT. 26	30	32	33	33	32	35	35	13	46	23	32	23
OCT. 27	30	34	34	35	32	36	35	13	46	23	32	23
OCT. 28	30	35	36	37	32	36	35	13	46	23	32	23
OCT. 29	30	37	38	38	32	36	35	13	46	23	32	23
OCT. 30	30	39	39	40	32	36	35	13	46	23	32	23
OCT. 31	30	40	41	41	33	36	36	13	46	23	32	23

MOON 1 ◖ 12:01 A.M. TO 8:00 A.M.   **MOON 2** ◑ 8:01 A.M. TO 4:00 P.M.   **MOON 3** ● 4:01 P.M. TO 12:00 A.M.
Use only one "moon" number. Choose the column closest to your time of birth. If your place of birth is not on Eastern Standard Time, be sure to read "How to Convert to Eastern Standard Time" at the beginning of this section.

1965

November

Date & Time	SUN	MOON 1	MOON 2	MOON 3	MERCURY	VENUS	MARS	JUPITER	SATURN	URANUS	NEPTUNE	PLUTO
NOV. 1	30	42	42	43	33	36	36	13	46	23	32	23
NOV. 2	30	43	44	45	33	36	36	13	46	23	32	23
NOV. 3	31	45	46	46	33	37	36	13	46	23	32	23
NOV. 4	31	47	47	48	33	37	36	13	46	23	32	23
NOV. 5	31	48	1	1	33	37	36	13	46	23	32	23
NOV. 6	31	2	3	3	34	37	36	13	46	23	32	23
NOV. 7	31	4	4	5	34	37	36	13	46	23	32	23
NOV. 8	31	5	6	7	34	37	36	13	46	23	32	23
NOV. 9	31	7	8	8	34	37	36	13	46	23	32	23
NOV. 10	31	9	10	10	34	38	37	13	46	23	32	23
NOV. 11	31	11	12	12	34	38	37	13	46	23	32	23
NOV. 12	32	13	13	14	35	38	37	13	46	23	32	23
NOV. 13	32	15	15	16	35	38	37	13	46	23	32	23
NOV. 14	32	17	17	18	35	38	37	13	46	23	32	23
NOV. 15	32	18	19	20	35	38	37	13	46	23	32	23
NOV. 16	32	20	21	22	35	38	37	13	46	23	32	23
NOV. 17	32	22	23	23	35	39	37	13	46	23	32	23
NOV. 18	32	24	25	25	35	39	37	13	46	23	32	23
NOV. 19	33	26	27	27	35	39	37	13	46	24	32	23
NOV. 20	33	28	28	29	35	39	38	13	46	24	32	23
NOV. 21	33	30	30	31	35	39	38	13	46	24	32	23
NOV. 22	33	31	32	33	36	39	38	13	46	24	32	23
NOV. 23	33	33	34	34	36	39	38	13	46	24	32	23
NOV. 24	33	35	35	36	35	39	38	13	46	24	32	23
NOV. 25	34	37	37	38	35	40	38	13	46	24	32	23
NOV. 26	34	38	39	39	35	40	38	13	46	24	32	23
NOV. 27	34	40	40	41	35	40	38	13	46	24	32	23
NOV. 28	34	41	42	42	35	40	38	13	46	24	32	23
NOV. 29	34	43	43	44	35	40	38	13	46	24	32	23
NOV. 30	34	45	45	46	35	40	39	13	46	24	32	23

December

Date & Time	SUN	MOON 1	MOON 2	MOON 3	MERCURY	VENUS	MARS	JUPITER	SATURN	URANUS	NEPTUNE	PLUTO
DEC. 1	34	46	47	47	35	40	39	13	46	24	32	23
DEC. 2	34	48	48	1	35	40	39	13	46	24	32	23
DEC. 3	35	1	2	2	34	41	39	13	46	24	32	23
DEC. 4	35	3	4	4	34	41	39	13	46	24	32	23
DEC. 5	35	5	5	6	34	41	39	13	46	24	32	23
DEC. 6	35	6	7	8	34	41	39	13	46	24	32	23
DEC. 7	35	8	9	10	34	41	39	13	46	24	32	23
DEC. 8	35	10	11	11	34	41	39	13	46	24	32	23
DEC. 9	35	12	13	13	34	41	40	13	46	24	32	23
DEC. 10	35	14	15	15	33	41	40	13	46	24	32	23
DEC. 11	36	16	17	17	33	41	40	13	46	24	32	23
DEC. 12	36	18	19	19	33	41	40	13	46	24	32	23
DEC. 13	36	20	21	21	33	42	40	13	46	24	32	23
DEC. 14	36	22	22	23	33	42	40	13	46	24	32	23
DEC. 15	36	24	24	25	33	42	40	13	46	24	32	23
DEC. 16	36	26	26	27	33	42	40	13	46	24	32	23
DEC. 17	36	27	28	29	34	42	40	12	46	24	32	23
DEC. 18	36	29	30	30	34	42	40	12	46	24	32	23
DEC. 19	37	31	31	32	34	42	41	12	47	24	32	23
DEC. 20	37	33	33	34	34	42	41	12	47	24	32	23
DEC. 21	37	34	35	35	34	42	41	12	47	24	32	23
DEC. 22	37	36	37	37	34	42	41	12	47	24	32	23
DEC. 23	37	38	38	39	34	42	41	12	47	24	32	23
DEC. 24	37	39	40	40	34	42	41	12	47	24	32	23
DEC. 25	37	41	41	42	35	42	41	12	47	24	32	23
DEC. 26	38	42	43	43	35	43	41	12	47	24	32	23
DEC. 27	38	44	45	45	35	43	41	12	47	24	32	23
DEC. 28	38	46	46	47	35	43	41	12	47	24	32	23
DEC. 29	38	47	48	48	35	43	42	12	47	24	32	23
DEC. 30	38	1	1	2	35	43	42	12	47	24	32	23
DEC. 31	38	2	3	4	36	43	42	12	47	24	32	23

MOON 1 ☽ 12:01 A.M. TO 8:00 A.M.   **MOON 2** ◑ 8:01 A.M. TO 4:00 P.M.   **MOON 3** ● 4:01 P.M. TO 12:00 A.M.
Use only one "moon" number. Choose the column closest to your time of birth. If your place of birth is not on Eastern Standard Time, be sure to read "How to Convert to Eastern Standard Time" at the beginning of this section.

1966

January

Date & Time	SUN	MOON 1	MOON 2	MOON 3	MERCURY	VENUS	MARS	JUPITER	SATURN	URANUS	NEPTUNE	PLUTO
JAN. 1	38	4	5	5	36	43	42	12	47	24	32	23
JAN. 2	38	6	6	7	36	43	42	12	47	24	32	23
JAN. 3	39	8	8	9	36	43	42	12	47	24	32	23
JAN. 4	39	9	10	11	36	43	42	12	47	24	32	23
JAN. 5	39	11	12	13	36	43	42	12	47	24	32	23
JAN. 6	39	13	14	14	37	43	42	12	47	24	32	23
JAN. 7	39	15	16	16	37	43	43	12	47	24	32	23
JAN. 8	39	17	18	18	37	43	43	12	47	24	32	23
JAN. 9	39	19	20	21	37	43	43	12	47	24	32	23
JAN. 10	40	21	22	22	37	43	43	12	47	24	32	23
JAN. 11	40	23	24	24	38	43	43	12	47	24	32	23
JAN. 12	40	25	26	26	38	43	43	12	47	24	32	23
JAN. 13	40	27	28	28	38	43	43	12	47	24	32	23
JAN. 14	40	29	29	30	38	43	43	12	47	24	32	23
JAN. 15	40	30	31	32	38	43	43	12	47	24	32	23
JAN. 16	40	32	33	33	39	43	43	12	47	24	32	23
JAN. 17	41	34	34	35	39	42	44	12	47	24	32	23
JAN. 18	41	36	36	37	39	42	44	12	47	24	32	23
JAN. 19	41	37	38	38	39	42	44	12	47	24	32	23
JAN. 20	41	39	39	40	39	42	44	12	47	24	32	23
JAN. 21	41	40	41	41	40	42	44	12	47	24	32	23
JAN. 22	41	42	43	43	40	42	44	12	47	24	32	23
JAN. 23	42	44	44	45	40	42	44	12	47	24	32	23
JAN. 24	42	45	46	46	40	42	44	12	47	24	32	23
JAN. 25	42	47	47	48	41	42	44	12	47	24	32	23
JAN. 26	42	48	1	1	41	42	45	12	47	24	32	23
JAN. 27	42	2	2	3	41	42	45	12	47	24	32	23
JAN. 28	42	4	4	5	41	42	45	12	47	24	32	23
JAN. 29	42	5	6	6	41	42	45	12	47	24	32	23
JAN. 30	42	7	7	8	42	41	45	12	47	24	32	23
JAN. 31	43	9	9	10	42	41	45	12	47	24	32	23

February

Date & Time	SUN	MOON 1	MOON 2	MOON 3	MERCURY	VENUS	MARS	JUPITER	SATURN	URANUS	NEPTUNE	PLUTO
FEB. 1	43	10	11	12	42	41	45	12	47	23	32	23
FEB. 2	43	12	13	14	42	41	45	12	47	23	32	23
FEB. 3	43	14	15	16	43	41	45	12	47	23	32	23
FEB. 4	43	16	17	18	43	41	45	12	47	23	32	23
FEB. 5	43	18	19	20	43	41	46	12	47	23	32	23
FEB. 6	43	20	21	22	43	41	46	12	47	23	32	23
FEB. 7	43	22	23	24	43	41	46	12	47	23	32	23
FEB. 8	44	24	25	26	44	41	46	12	47	23	32	23
FEB. 9	44	26	27	28	44	41	46	12	47	23	32	23
FEB. 10	44	28	29	29	44	41	46	12	47	23	32	23
FEB. 11	44	30	31	31	44	41	46	12	47	23	32	23
FEB. 12	44	32	32	33	45	41	46	12	47	23	32	23
FEB. 13	44	33	34	35	45	41	46	12	47	23	32	23
FEB. 14	44	35	36	36	45	41	47	12	47	23	32	23
FEB. 15	44	37	37	38	45	41	47	12	47	23	32	23
FEB. 16	45	38	39	39	46	41	47	12	47	23	32	23
FEB. 17	45	40	41	41	46	41	47	12	47	23	32	23
FEB. 18	45	42	42	43	46	41	47	12	47	23	32	23
FEB. 19	45	43	44	44	46	41	47	12	47	23	32	23
FEB. 20	45	45	45	46	47	41	47	12	47	23	32	23
FEB. 21	45	46	47	47	47	41	47	12	47	23	32	23
FEB. 22	45	48	48	1	47	41	47	12	47	23	32	23
FEB. 23	46	2	2	3	47	41	47	12	47	23	32	23
FEB. 24	46	3	4	4	48	41	48	12	47	23	32	23
FEB. 25	46	5	5	6	48	41	48	12	47	23	32	23
FEB. 26	46	6	7	8	48	41	48	12	47	23	32	23
FEB. 27	46	8	9	9	48	41	48	12	47	23	32	23
FEB. 28	46	10	10	11	48	41	48	12	47	23	32	23

MOON 1 ◐ 12:01 A.M. TO 8:00 A.M.　　**MOON 2** ◑ 8:01 A.M. TO 4:00 P.M.　　**MOON 3** ● 4:01 P.M. TO 12:00 A.M.

Use only one "moon" number. Choose the column closest to your time of birth. If your place of birth is not on Eastern Standard Time, be sure to read "How to Convert to Eastern Standard Time" at the beginning of this section.

Date & Time	SUN ☉	MOON 1 ◗	MOON 2 ◑	MOON 3 ●	MERCURY	VENUS	MARS	JUPITER	SATURN	URANUS	NEPTUNE	PLUTO
MAR. 1	46	12	12	13	1	41	48	12	47	23	32	23
MAR. 2	46	13	14	15	1	41	48	12	47	23	32	23
MAR. 3	47	15	16	17	1	41	48	12	47	23	32	23
MAR. 4	47	17	18	19	1	41	48	12	48	23	32	23
MAR. 5	47	19	20	21	1	41	1	12	48	23	32	23
MAR. 6	47	21	22	23	1	42	1	12	48	23	32	23
MAR. 7	47	23	24	25	1	42	1	12	48	23	32	23
MAR. 8	47	25	26	27	2	42	1	12	48	23	32	23
MAR. 9	47	27	28	29	2	42	1	12	48	23	32	23
MAR. 10	47	29	30	31	2	42	1	12	48	23	32	23
MAR. 11	48	31	32	32	2	42	1	12	48	23	32	23
MAR. 12	48	33	34	34	2	42	1	12	48	23	32	23
MAR. 13	48	35	35	36	2	42	1	12	48	23	32	23
MAR. 14	48	36	37	37	2	42	1	12	48	23	32	23
MAR. 15	48	38	39	39	2	42	2	12	48	23	32	23
MAR. 16	48	40	40	41	2	42	2	12	48	23	32	23
MAR. 17	48	41	42	42	1	43	2	12	48	23	32	23
MAR. 18	48	43	43	44	1	43	2	12	48	23	32	23
MAR. 19	1	44	45	45	1	43	2	12	48	23	32	23
MAR. 20	1	46	46	47	1	43	2	12	48	23	32	23
MAR. 21	1	48	48	1	1	43	2	12	48	23	32	23
MAR. 22	1	1	2	2	1	43	2	12	48	23	32	23
MAR. 23	1	3	3	4	1	43	2	12	48	23	32	23
MAR. 24	1	4	5	5	1	43	2	12	48	23	32	23
MAR. 25	2	6	7	7	1	43	3	12	48	23	32	23
MAR. 26	2	8	8	9	48	44	3	12	48	23	32	23
MAR. 27	2	9	10	11	48	44	3	12	48	23	32	23
MAR. 28	2	11	12	12	48	44	3	12	48	23	32	23
MAR. 29	2	13	14	14	48	44	3	12	48	23	32	23
MAR. 30	2	15	15	16	48	44	3	12	48	23	32	23
MAR. 31	2	17	17	18	48	44	3	12	48	23	32	23

Date & Time	SUN ☉	MOON 1 ◗	MOON 2 ◑	MOON 3 ●	MERCURY	VENUS	MARS	JUPITER	SATURN	URANUS	NEPTUNE	PLUTO
APR. 1	2	19	19	20	48	44	3	12	48	23	32	23
APR. 2	2	21	21	22	48	44	3	12	48	23	32	23
APR. 3	3	22	23	24	48	45	3	12	48	23	32	23
APR. 4	3	24	25	26	48	45	4	12	48	23	32	23
APR. 5	3	26	27	28	48	45	4	12	48	23	32	23
APR. 6	3	28	29	30	48	45	4	12	48	23	32	23
APR. 7	3	30	31	32	48	45	4	12	48	23	32	23
APR. 8	3	32	33	33	48	45	4	12	48	23	32	23
APR. 9	3	34	35	35	48	45	4	12	48	23	32	23
APR. 10	3	36	36	37	48	45	4	12	48	23	32	23
APR. 11	4	37	38	39	48	46	4	12	48	23	32	23
APR. 12	4	39	40	40	48	46	4	12	48	23	32	23
APR. 13	4	41	41	42	48	46	5	12	48	23	32	23
APR. 14	4	42	43	43	1	46	5	12	48	23	32	23
APR. 15	4	44	44	45	1	46	5	12	48	23	32	23
APR. 16	4	45	46	47	1	46	5	13	48	23	32	23
APR. 17	4	47	48	48	1	46	5	13	48	23	32	23
APR. 18	4	1	1	2	1	47	5	13	48	23	32	23
APR. 19	5	2	3	3	1	47	5	13	48	23	32	23
APR. 20	5	4	4	5	1	47	5	13	48	23	32	23
APR. 21	5	6	6	7	1	47	5	13	48	23	32	23
APR. 22	5	7	8	8	2	47	5	13	48	23	32	23
APR. 23	5	9	10	10	2	47	5	13	48	23	32	23
APR. 24	5	11	11	12	2	47	6	13	48	23	32	23
APR. 25	6	13	13	14	2	48	6	13	48	23	32	23
APR. 26	6	14	15	16	2	48	6	13	48	23	32	23
APR. 27	6	16	17	17	2	48	6	13	48	23	32	23
APR. 28	6	18	19	19	2	48	6	13	48	23	32	23
APR. 29	6	20	21	21	3	48	6	13	48	23	32	23
APR. 30	6	22	23	23	3	48	6	13	48	23	32	23

MOON 1 ◗ 12:01 A.M. TO 8:00 A.M.   **MOON 2** ◑ 8:01 A.M. TO 4:00 P.M.   **MOON 3** ● 4:01 P.M. TO 12:00 A.M.

Use only one "moon" number. Choose the column closest to your time of birth. If your place of birth is not on Eastern Standard Time, be sure to read "How to Convert to Eastern Standard Time" at the beginning of this section.

1966

May   June

Date & Time	SUN	MOON 1	MOON 2	MOON 3	MERCURY	VENUS	MARS	JUPITER	SATURN	URANUS	NEPTUNE	PLUTO
MAY 1	6	24	24	25	3	48	6	13	48	23	32	23
MAY 2	6	26	26	27	3	1	6	13	48	23	32	23
MAY 3	7	28	28	29	4	1	6	13	48	23	32	23
MAY 4	7	30	30	31	4	1	7	13	48	23	32	23
MAY 5	7	31	32	33	4	1	7	13	48	23	32	23
MAY 6	7	33	34	34	4	1	7	13	48	23	32	23
MAY 7	7	35	36	36	4	1	7	13	48	23	32	23
MAY 8	7	37	37	38	5	1	7	13	48	23	32	23
MAY 9	7	39	39	40	5	2	7	13	1	23	32	23
MAY 10	7	40	41	41	5	2	7	13	1	23	32	23
MAY 11	8	42	42	43	5	2	7	13	1	23	32	23
MAY 12	8	43	44	44	6	2	7	13	1	23	32	23
MAY 13	8	45	46	46	6	2	7	13	1	23	32	23
MAY 14	8	47	47	48	6	2	8	13	1	23	32	23
MAY 15	8	48	1	1	6	2	8	13	1	23	32	23
MAY 16	8	2	2	3	7	3	8	13	1	23	32	23
MAY 17	8	3	4	4	7	3	8	13	1	23	32	23
MAY 18	8	5	6	6	7	3	8	13	1	23	32	23
MAY 19	9	7	7	8	7	3	8	13	1	23	32	23
MAY 20	9	8	9	10	8	3	8	13	1	23	32	23
MAY 21	9	10	11	11	8	3	8	13	1	23	32	23
MAY 22	9	12	13	13	8	4	8	13	1	23	32	23
MAY 23	9	14	15	15	9	4	8	13	1	23	32	23
MAY 24	9	16	16	17	9	4	9	13	1	23	32	23
MAY 25	10	18	18	19	9	4	9	13	1	23	32	23
MAY 26	10	20	20	21	9	4	9	14	1	23	32	23
MAY 27	10	21	23	23	10	4	9	14	1	23	32	23
MAY 28	10	23	24	25	10	4	9	14	1	23	32	23
MAY 29	10	25	26	26	10	5	9	14	1	23	32	23
MAY 30	10	27	28	28	11	5	9	14	1	23	32	23
MAY 31	10	29	30	30	11	5	9	14	1	23	32	23

Date & Time	SUN	MOON 1	MOON 2	MOON 3	MERCURY	VENUS	MARS	JUPITER	SATURN	URANUS	NEPTUNE	PLUTO
JUN. 1	10	31	31	32	11	5	9	14	1	23	32	23
JUN. 2	10	33	33	34	11	5	9	14	1	23	32	23
JUN. 3	11	34	35	36	12	5	9	14	1	23	32	23
JUN. 4	11	36	37	37	12	5	10	14	1	23	32	23
JUN. 5	11	38	38	39	12	6	10	14	1	23	32	23
JUN. 6	11	40	40	41	13	6	10	14	1	23	32	23
JUN. 7	11	41	42	42	13	6	10	14	1	23	32	23
JUN. 8	11	43	43	44	13	6	10	14	1	23	32	23
JUN. 9	11	44	45	45	13	6	10	14	1	23	32	23
JUN. 10	11	46	47	47	14	6	10	14	1	23	32	23
JUN. 11	12	48	48	1	14	7	10	14	1	23	32	23
JUN. 12	12	1	2	2	14	7	10	14	1	23	32	23
JUN. 13	12	3	3	4	14	7	10	14	1	23	32	23
JUN. 14	12	4	5	6	15	7	10	14	1	23	32	23
JUN. 15	12	6	7	7	15	7	11	14	1	23	32	23
JUN. 16	12	8	8	9	15	7	11	14	1	23	32	23
JUN. 17	12	10	10	11	15	8	11	14	1	23	32	23
JUN. 18	12	11	12	13	15	8	11	14	1	23	32	23
JUN. 19	13	13	14	15	16	8	11	14	1	23	32	23
JUN. 20	13	15	16	16	16	8	11	14	1	23	32	23
JUN. 21	13	17	18	18	16	8	11	14	1	23	32	23
JUN. 22	13	19	20	20	16	8	11	14	1	23	32	23
JUN. 23	13	21	22	22	16	8	11	14	1	23	32	23
JUN. 24	13	23	24	24	17	9	11	14	1	23	32	23
JUN. 25	14	25	25	26	17	9	12	14	1	23	32	23
JUN. 26	14	27	27	28	17	9	12	14	1	23	32	23
JUN. 27	14	29	29	30	17	9	12	14	1	23	32	23
JUN. 28	14	30	31	32	17	9	12	14	1	23	32	23
JUN. 29	14	32	33	33	17	9	12	15	1	23	32	23
JUN. 30	14	34	34	35	17	10	12	15	1	23	32	23

MOON 1 ◗ 12:01 A.M. TO 8:00 A.M.   **MOON 2** ◑ 8:01 A.M. TO 4:00 P.M.   **MOON 3** ● 4:01 P.M. TO 12:00 A.M.
Use only one "moon" number. Choose the column closest to your time of birth. If your place of birth is not on
Eastern Standard Time, be sure to read "How to Convert to Eastern Standard Time" at the beginning of this section.

Date & Time	SUN ☉	MOON 1 ◗	MOON 2 ◐	MOON 3 ●	MERCURY	VENUS	MARS	JUPITER	SATURN	URANUS	NEPTUNE	PLUTO
JUL. 1	14	36	36	37	18	10	12	15	1	23	32	23
JUL. 2	14	37	38	38	18	10	12	15	1	23	32	23
JUL. 3	15	39	40	40	18	10	12	15	1	23	32	23
JUL. 4	15	41	41	42	18	10	12	15	1	23	32	23
JUL. 5	15	42	43	43	18	10	12	15	1	23	32	23
JUL. 6	15	44	44	45	18	10	13	15	1	23	32	23
JUL. 7	15	46	46	47	18	11	13	15	1	23	32	23
JUL. 8	15	47	48	48	18	11	13	15	1	23	32	23
JUL. 9	15	1	1	2	18	11	13	15	1	23	32	23
JUL. 10	15	2	3	3	18	11	13	15	1	23	32	23
JUL. 11	16	4	4	5	18	11	13	15	1	23	32	23
JUL. 12	16	6	6	7	18	11	13	15	1	23	32	23
JUL. 13	16	7	8	8	18	12	13	15	1	23	32	23
JUL. 14	16	9	9	10	18	12	13	15	1	23	32	23
JUL. 15	16	11	11	12	18	12	13	15	1	23	32	23
JUL. 16	16	13	13	14	18	12	13	15	1	23	32	23
JUL. 17	16	14	15	16	18	12	14	15	1	23	32	23
JUL. 18	16	16	17	18	18	12	14	15	1	23	32	23
JUL. 19	17	18	19	20	18	13	14	15	1	23	32	23
JUL. 20	17	20	21	22	18	13	14	15	1	23	32	23
JUL. 21	17	22	23	24	18	13	14	15	1	23	32	23
JUL. 22	17	24	25	26	18	13	14	15	1	23	32	23
JUL. 23	17	26	27	27	18	13	14	15	1	23	32	23
JUL. 24	17	28	29	29	18	13	14	15	1	23	32	23
JUL. 25	17	30	31	31	18	14	14	15	1	23	32	23
JUL. 26	18	32	32	33	18	14	14	15	1	23	32	23
JUL. 27	18	33	34	35	18	14	14	15	1	23	32	23
JUL. 28	18	35	36	36	18	14	14	15	1	23	32	23
JUL. 29	18	37	37	38	18	14	15	15	1	23	32	23
JUL. 30	18	39	39	40	17	14	15	15	1	23	32	23
JUL. 31	18	40	41	41	17	14	15	15	1	23	32	23

Date & Time	SUN ☉	MOON 1 ◗	MOON 2 ◐	MOON 3 ●	MERCURY	VENUS	MARS	JUPITER	SATURN	URANUS	NEPTUNE	PLUTO
AUG. 1	18	42	42	43	17	15	15	16	1	23	32	23
AUG. 2	18	43	44	45	17	15	15	16	1	23	32	23
AUG. 3	19	45	46	46	17	15	15	16	1	23	32	23
AUG. 4	19	47	47	48	17	15	15	16	1	23	32	23
AUG. 5	19	48	1	1	17	15	15	16	1	23	32	23
AUG. 6	19	2	2	3	17	15	15	16	1	23	32	23
AUG. 7	19	3	4	4	17	15	15	16	1	23	32	23
AUG. 8	19	5	6	6	17	15	15	16	1	23	32	23
AUG. 9	19	7	7	8	17	16	16	16	1	23	32	23
AUG. 10	19	8	9	9	17	16	16	16	1	23	32	23
AUG. 11	20	10	11	11	16	16	16	16	1	23	32	23
AUG. 12	20	12	12	13	16	16	16	16	1	23	32	23
AUG. 13	20	14	14	15	17	17	16	16	1	23	32	23
AUG. 14	20	16	16	17	17	17	16	16	1	23	32	23
AUG. 15	20	17	18	19	17	17	16	16	1	23	32	23
AUG. 16	20	19	20	21	18	17	16	16	1	23	32	23
AUG. 17	20	22	22	23	18	17	16	16	1	23	32	23
AUG. 18	20	24	24	25	18	17	16	16	1	23	32	23
AUG. 19	21	26	26	27	18	18	16	16	1	23	32	23
AUG. 20	21	27	28	29	18	18	16	16	1	23	32	23
AUG. 21	21	29	30	31	18	18	17	16	1	23	32	23
AUG. 22	21	31	32	32	19	18	17	16	1	23	32	23
AUG. 23	21	33	34	34	18	18	17	16	1	23	32	23
AUG. 24	21	35	35	36	19	18	17	16	1	23	32	23
AUG. 25	21	37	37	38	19	19	17	16	1	23	32	23
AUG. 26	22	38	39	39	19	19	17	16	1	23	32	23
AUG. 27	22	40	40	41	20	19	17	16	1	23	32	23
AUG. 28	22	41	42	43	20	19	17	16	1	24	32	23
AUG. 29	22	43	44	44	20	19	17	16	1	24	32	23
AUG. 30	22	45	45	46	20	19	17	16	1	24	32	23
AUG. 31	22	46	47	47	21	20	17	16	1	24	32	23

MOON 1 ◗ 12:01 A.M. TO 8:00 A.M.　　**MOON 2** ◐ 8:01 A.M. TO 4:00 P.M.　　**MOON 3** ● 4:01 P.M. TO 12:00 A.M.

Use only one "moon" number. Choose the column closest to your time of birth. If your place of birth is not on Eastern Standard Time, be sure to read "How to Convert to Eastern Standard Time" at the beginning of this section.

1966

September

Date & Time	SUN	MOON 1	MOON 2	MOON 3	MERCURY	VENUS	MARS	JUPITER	SATURN	URANUS	NEPTUNE	PLUTO
SEP. 1	22	48	48	1	21	20	18	16	1	24	32	23
SEP. 2	22	1	2	2	21	20	18	16	1	24	32	23
SEP. 3	23	3	4	4	21	20	18	16	1	24	32	23
SEP. 4	23	5	5	6	22	20	18	16	1	24	32	23
SEP. 5	23	6	7	7	22	20	18	16	1	24	32	23
SEP. 6	23	8	8	9	22	21	18	16	1	24	32	23
SEP. 7	23	9	10	11	22	21	18	17	1	24	32	23
SEP. 8	23	11	12	12	23	21	18	17	1	24	32	23
SEP. 9	23	13	14	14	23	21	18	17	1	24	32	23
SEP. 10	23	15	15	16	23	21	18	17	1	24	32	23
SEP. 11	24	17	17	18	23	21	18	17	1	24	32	23
SEP. 12	24	19	19	20	24	21	18	17	1	24	32	23
SEP. 13	24	21	21	22	24	22	19	17	1	24	32	23
SEP. 14	24	23	23	24	24	22	19	17	1	24	32	23
SEP. 15	24	25	25	26	24	22	19	17	1	24	32	23
SEP. 16	24	27	27	28	25	22	19	17	1	24	32	23
SEP. 17	24	29	29	30	25	22	19	17	48	24	32	23
SEP. 18	24	31	31	32	25	22	19	17	48	24	32	23
SEP. 19	25	32	33	34	25	23	19	17	48	24	32	23
SEP. 20	25	34	35	35	26	23	19	17	48	24	32	23
SEP. 21	25	36	37	37	26	23	19	17	48	24	32	23
SEP. 22	25	38	38	39	26	23	19	17	48	24	32	23
SEP. 23	25	39	40	41	26	23	19	17	48	24	32	23
SEP. 24	25	41	42	42	27	23	19	17	48	24	32	23
SEP. 25	26	43	43	44	27	24	20	17	48	24	32	23
SEP. 26	26	44	45	45	27	24	20	17	48	24	32	23
SEP. 27	26	46	46	47	27	24	20	17	48	24	32	23
SEP. 28	26	47	48	48	27	24	20	17	48	24	32	23
SEP. 29	26	1	2	2	28	24	20	17	48	24	32	23
SEP. 30	26	3	3	4	28	24	20	17	48	24	32	23

October

Date & Time	SUN	MOON 1	MOON 2	MOON 3	MERCURY	VENUS	MARS	JUPITER	SATURN	URANUS	NEPTUNE	PLUTO
OCT. 1	26	4	5	5	28	25	20	17	48	24	32	23
OCT. 2	26	6	6	7	28	25	20	17	48	24	32	23
OCT. 3	27	7	8	9	28	25	20	17	48	24	32	24
OCT. 4	27	9	10	10	29	25	20	17	48	24	32	24
OCT. 5	27	11	11	12	29	25	20	17	48	24	32	24
OCT. 6	27	12	13	14	29	25	20	17	48	24	32	24
OCT. 7	27	14	15	15	29	26	21	17	48	24	32	24
OCT. 8	27	16	17	17	29	26	21	17	48	24	32	24
OCT. 9	27	18	19	19	30	26	21	17	48	24	32	24
OCT. 10	27	20	20	21	30	26	21	17	48	24	32	24
OCT. 11	28	22	22	23	30	26	21	17	48	24	32	24
OCT. 12	28	24	24	25	30	26	21	17	48	24	32	24
OCT. 13	28	26	26	27	30	27	21	17	48	24	32	24
OCT. 14	28	28	28	29	31	27	21	17	48	24	32	24
OCT. 15	28	30	30	31	31	27	21	17	48	24	32	24
OCT. 16	28	32	32	33	31	27	21	17	48	24	32	24
OCT. 17	28	34	34	35	31	27	21	17	48	24	32	24
OCT. 18	28	35	36	37	31	27	21	17	48	24	32	24
OCT. 19	29	37	38	38	31	28	21	17	48	24	32	24
OCT. 20	29	39	39	40	32	28	22	17	48	24	32	24
OCT. 21	29	41	41	42	32	28	22	17	48	24	32	24
OCT. 22	29	42	43	43	32	28	22	17	48	24	32	24
OCT. 23	29	44	44	45	32	28	22	17	48	24	32	24
OCT. 24	29	45	46	46	32	28	22	17	48	24	32	24
OCT. 25	29	47	48	48	32	29	22	17	48	24	32	24
OCT. 26	30	1	1	2	32	29	22	17	48	24	32	24
OCT. 27	30	2	3	3	33	29	22	17	48	24	32	24
OCT. 28	30	4	4	5	33	29	22	17	48	24	32	24
OCT. 29	30	5	6	6	33	29	22	17	48	24	32	24
OCT. 30	30	7	8	8	33	29	22	17	48	24	32	24
OCT. 31	30	9	9	10	33	30	22	17	48	24	32	24

MOON 1 ◐ 12:01 A.M. TO 8:00 A.M.   **MOON 2** ◑ 8:01 A.M. TO 4:00 P.M.   **MOON 3** ● 4:01 P.M. TO 12:00 A.M.

Use only one "moon" number. Choose the column closest to your time of birth. If your place of birth is not on Eastern Standard Time, be sure to read "How to Convert to Eastern Standard Time" at the beginning of this section.

November

December

Date & Time	SUN	MOON 1	MOON 2	MOON 3	MERCURY	VENUS	MARS	JUPITER	SATURN	URANUS	NEPTUNE	PLUTO
NOV. 1	30	10	11	11	33	30	23	17	48	24	32	24
NOV. 2	30	12	13	13	33	30	23	17	48	24	32	24
NOV. 3	31	14	14	15	33	30	23	17	48	24	32	24
NOV. 4	31	16	16	17	33	30	23	17	48	24	32	24
NOV. 5	31	17	18	19	33	30	23	18	48	24	32	24
NOV. 6	31	19	20	20	33	31	23	18	48	24	32	24
NOV. 7	31	21	22	22	33	31	23	18	48	24	32	24
NOV. 8	31	23	24	24	33	31	23	18	48	24	32	24
NOV. 9	31	25	26	26	33	31	23	18	48	24	32	24
NOV. 10	31	27	28	28	33	31	23	18	48	24	32	24
NOV. 11	31	29	30	30	33	31	23	18	48	24	32	24
NOV. 12	32	31	31	32	33	32	23	18	48	24	32	24
NOV. 13	32	33	33	34	33	32	23	18	48	24	32	24
NOV. 14	32	35	35	36	33	32	24	18	48	24	32	24
NOV. 15	32	36	37	38	33	32	24	18	48	24	32	24
NOV. 16	32	38	39	39	32	32	24	18	48	24	32	24
NOV. 17	32	40	41	41	32	32	24	18	48	24	32	24
NOV. 18	32	42	42	43	32	33	24	18	48	24	32	24
NOV. 19	33	43	44	44	32	33	24	18	48	24	32	24
NOV. 20	33	45	45	46	32	33	24	18	48	24	32	24
NOV. 21	33	46	47	48	32	33	24	18	48	24	32	24
NOV. 22	33	48	1	1	32	33	24	18	48	24	32	24
NOV. 23	33	2	2	3	31	33	24	18	48	24	32	24
NOV. 24	33	3	4	4	31	34	24	18	48	24	32	24
NOV. 25	34	5	5	6	31	34	24	18	48	24	32	24
NOV. 26	34	6	7	8	31	34	24	18	48	24	32	24
NOV. 27	34	8	9	9	31	34	24	18	48	24	32	24
NOV. 28	34	10	10	11	31	34	25	18	48	24	32	24
NOV. 29	34	12	12	13	31	35	25	18	48	24	32	24
NOV. 30	34	13	14	15	31	35	25	18	48	24	32	24

Date & Time	SUN	MOON 1	MOON 2	MOON 3	MERCURY	VENUS	MARS	JUPITER	SATURN	URANUS	NEPTUNE	PLUTO
DEC. 1	34	15	16	16	31	35	25	18	48	24	32	24
DEC. 2	34	17	18	18	32	35	25	18	48	24	32	24
DEC. 3	35	19	19	20	32	35	25	18	48	24	32	24
DEC. 4	35	21	21	22	32	35	25	18	48	24	32	24
DEC. 5	35	23	23	24	32	36	25	18	48	24	32	24
DEC. 6	35	24	25	26	32	36	25	18	48	24	32	24
DEC. 7	35	26	27	28	32	36	25	18	48	24	32	24
DEC. 8	35	28	29	29	32	36	25	18	48	24	32	24
DEC. 9	35	30	31	31	33	36	25	17	48	24	32	24
DEC. 10	35	32	33	33	33	36	25	17	48	24	32	24
DEC. 11	36	34	34	35	33	37	25	17	48	24	32	24
DEC. 12	36	36	36	37	33	37	26	17	48	24	32	24
DEC. 13	36	38	38	39	33	37	26	17	48	24	32	24
DEC. 14	36	39	40	40	33	37	26	17	48	24	32	24
DEC. 15	36	41	42	42	34	37	26	17	48	24	32	24
DEC. 16	36	43	43	44	34	37	26	17	48	24	32	24
DEC. 17	36	44	45	45	34	38	26	17	48	24	32	24
DEC. 18	36	46	46	47	34	38	26	17	48	24	32	24
DEC. 19	37	48	48	1	34	38	26	17	48	24	32	24
DEC. 20	37	1	2	2	35	38	26	17	48	24	32	24
DEC. 21	37	3	3	4	35	38	26	17	48	24	32	24
DEC. 22	37	4	5	5	35	38	26	17	48	24	32	24
DEC. 23	37	6	6	7	35	39	26	17	48	24	32	24
DEC. 24	37	8	8	9	35	39	26	17	48	24	32	24
DEC. 25	37	9	10	10	36	39	26	17	48	24	32	24
DEC. 26	38	11	12	12	36	39	26	17	48	24	32	24
DEC. 27	38	13	13	14	36	39	27	17	48	24	32	24
DEC. 28	38	15	15	16	36	39	27	17	48	24	32	24
DEC. 29	38	16	17	18	36	40	27	17	48	24	32	24
DEC. 30	38	18	19	20	37	40	27	17	48	24	32	24
DEC. 31	38	20	21	21	37	40	27	17	48	24	32	24

MOON 1 ◗ 12:01 A.M. TO 8:00 A.M.   **MOON 2** ◖ 8:01 A.M. TO 4:00 P.M.   **MOON 3** ● 4:01 P.M. TO 12:00 A.M.

Use only one "moon" number. Choose the column closest to your time of birth. If your place of birth is not on Eastern Standard Time, be sure to read "How to Convert to Eastern Standard Time" at the beginning of this section.

1967

January

Date & Time	SUN	MOON 1	MOON 2	MOON 3	MERCURY	VENUS	MARS	JUPITER	SATURN	URANUS	NEPTUNE	PLUTO
JAN. 1	38	22	23	23	37	40	27	17	48	24	32	24
JAN. 2	38	24	25	25	37	40	27	17	48	24	32	24
JAN. 3	39	26	27	27	37	40	27	17	48	24	32	24
JAN. 4	39	28	28	29	38	41	27	17	48	24	32	24
JAN. 5	39	30	30	31	38	41	27	17	48	24	32	24
JAN. 6	39	31	32	33	38	41	27	17	48	24	32	24
JAN. 7	39	33	34	35	38	41	27	17	48	24	32	24
JAN. 8	39	35	36	36	38	41	27	17	48	24	32	24
JAN. 9	39	37	37	38	39	41	27	17	48	24	32	24
JAN. 10	40	39	39	40	39	42	27	17	48	24	32	24
JAN. 11	40	40	41	42	39	42	27	17	48	24	32	24
JAN. 12	40	42	43	43	39	42	28	17	48	24	32	24
JAN. 13	40	44	44	45	40	42	28	17	48	24	32	24
JAN. 14	40	45	46	46	40	42	28	17	48	24	32	24
JAN. 15	40	47	48	48	40	42	28	17	48	24	32	24
JAN. 16	40	1	1	2	40	43	28	17	48	24	32	24
JAN. 17	41	2	3	3	40	43	28	17	48	24	32	24
JAN. 18	41	4	4	5	41	43	28	17	48	24	32	24
JAN. 19	41	5	6	6	41	43	28	17	48	24	32	24
JAN. 20	41	7	7	8	41	43	28	17	48	24	32	24
JAN. 21	41	9	9	10	41	43	28	17	48	24	32	24
JAN. 22	41	10	11	11	42	43	28	17	48	24	32	24
JAN. 23	42	12	13	13	42	44	28	17	48	24	32	24
JAN. 24	42	14	14	15	42	44	28	17	48	24	32	24
JAN. 25	42	16	16	17	42	44	28	17	48	24	32	24
JAN. 26	42	18	18	19	42	44	28	17	48	24	32	24
JAN. 27	42	20	20	21	43	44	28	17	48	24	32	24
JAN. 28	42	21	22	23	43	45	28	17	48	24	32	24
JAN. 29	42	23	24	25	43	45	28	17	48	24	32	24
JAN. 30	42	25	26	27	43	45	28	17	48	24	32	24
JAN. 31	43	27	28	29	44	45	28	17	48	24	32	24

February

Date & Time	SUN	MOON 1	MOON 2	MOON 3	MERCURY	VENUS	MARS	JUPITER	SATURN	URANUS	NEPTUNE	PLUTO
FEB. 1	43	29	30	30	44	45	29	17	1	24	32	24
FEB. 2	43	31	32	32	44	45	29	17	1	24	32	24
FEB. 3	43	33	33	34	44	46	29	17	1	24	32	24
FEB. 4	43	35	35	36	45	46	29	17	1	24	32	24
FEB. 5	43	36	37	38	45	46	29	17	1	24	32	24
FEB. 6	43	38	39	39	45	46	29	17	1	24	32	24
FEB. 7	43	40	40	41	45	46	29	17	1	24	32	24
FEB. 8	44	42	42	43	45	46	29	17	1	24	32	24
FEB. 9	44	43	44	44	46	47	29	17	1	24	32	24
FEB. 10	44	45	45	46	46	47	29	17	1	24	32	24
FEB. 11	44	46	47	48	46	47	29	17	1	24	32	24
FEB. 12	44	48	1	1	46	47	29	17	1	24	32	24
FEB. 13	44	2	2	3	46	47	29	16	1	24	32	24
FEB. 14	44	3	4	4	47	47	29	16	1	24	32	24
FEB. 15	44	5	5	6	47	48	29	16	1	24	32	24
FEB. 16	45	6	7	7	47	48	29	16	1	24	32	24
FEB. 17	45	8	9	9	47	48	29	16	1	24	32	24
FEB. 18	45	10	10	11	47	48	29	16	1	24	32	24
FEB. 19	45	11	12	12	47	48	29	16	1	24	32	24
FEB. 20	45	13	14	14	47	48	29	16	1	24	32	24
FEB. 21	45	15	15	16	47	1	29	16	1	24	32	24
FEB. 22	45	17	17	18	47	1	29	16	1	24	32	24
FEB. 23	46	19	19	20	47	1	29	16	1	24	32	24
FEB. 24	46	21	21	22	47	1	29	16	1	24	32	24
FEB. 25	46	23	23	24	47	1	29	16	1	24	32	24
FEB. 26	46	25	25	26	47	1	29	16	1	24	32	24
FEB. 27	46	27	27	28	47	2	29	16	1	24	32	24
FEB. 28	46	29	29	30	47	2	29	16	1	24	32	24

MOON 1 ◖ 12:01 A.M. TO 8:00 A.M.   **MOON 2** ◗ 8:01 A.M. TO 4:00 P.M.   **MOON 3** ● 4:01 P.M. TO 12:00 A.M.
Use only one "moon" number. Choose the column closest to your time of birth. If your place of birth is not on Eastern Standard Time, be sure to read "How to Convert to Eastern Standard Time" at the beginning of this section.

1967

March

Date & Time	SUN	MOON 1	MOON 2	MOON 3	MERCURY	VENUS	MARS	JUPITER	SATURN	URANUS	NEPTUNE	PLUTO
MAR. 1	46	31	31	32	47	2	29	16	1	24	32	24
MAR. 2	46	32	33	34	47	2	29	16	1	24	32	24
MAR. 3	47	34	35	35	47	2	29	16	1	24	32	24
MAR. 4	47	36	37	37	47	2	29	16	1	24	32	24
MAR. 5	47	38	38	39	47	2	29	16	1	24	32	24
MAR. 6	47	39	40	41	46	3	29	16	1	24	32	24
MAR. 7	47	41	42	42	46	3	29	16	1	24	32	24
MAR. 8	47	43	43	44	46	3	29	16	1	24	32	24
MAR. 9	47	44	45	46	46	3	29	16	1	24	32	24
MAR. 10	47	46	47	47	46	3	29	16	1	24	32	24
MAR. 11	48	48	48	1	46	3	29	16	1	24	32	24
MAR. 12	48	1	2	2	46	4	29	16	1	24	32	24
MAR. 13	48	3	3	4	46	4	29	16	1	24	32	24
MAR. 14	48	4	5	5	46	4	29	16	1	24	32	24
MAR. 15	48	6	6	7	46	4	29	16	1	24	32	24
MAR. 16	48	8	8	9	46	4	29	16	1	24	32	24
MAR. 17	48	9	10	10	46	4	29	16	1	24	32	24
MAR. 18	48	11	11	12	46	5	29	16	1	24	32	24
MAR. 19	1	12	13	14	46	5	29	16	1	24	32	24
MAR. 20	1	14	15	15	46	5	29	16	1	24	32	24
MAR. 21	1	16	17	17	46	5	29	16	1	24	32	24
MAR. 22	1	18	18	19	46	5	29	16	1	24	32	24
MAR. 23	1	20	20	21	46	5	29	16	1	24	32	24
MAR. 24	1	22	22	23	46	6	29	16	1	24	32	23
MAR. 25	2	24	24	25	46	6	29	16	1	24	32	23
MAR. 26	2	26	26	27	46	6	29	16	1	24	32	23
MAR. 27	2	28	28	29	46	6	29	16	1	24	32	23
MAR. 28	2	30	30	31	46	6	29	16	1	24	32	23
MAR. 29	2	32	32	33	46	6	29	16	1	24	32	23
MAR. 30	2	34	34	35	46	7	29	16	1	24	32	23
MAR. 31	2	36	36	37	47	7	29	16	1	24	32	23

April

Date & Time	SUN	MOON 1	MOON 2	MOON 3	MERCURY	VENUS	MARS	JUPITER	SATURN	URANUS	NEPTUNE	PLUTO
APR. 1	2	37	38	38	47	7	29	16	1	24	32	23
APR. 2	2	39	40	40	47	7	29	16	1	24	32	23
APR. 3	3	41	41	42	47	7	29	16	1	24	32	23
APR. 4	3	42	43	44	47	7	29	16	1	24	32	23
APR. 5	3	44	45	45	47	8	29	16	1	24	32	23
APR. 6	3	46	46	47	47	8	29	16	2	24	32	23
APR. 7	3	47	48	48	48	8	29	16	2	24	32	23
APR. 8	3	1	1	2	48	8	29	16	2	24	32	23
APR. 9	3	2	3	3	48	8	29	16	2	24	32	23
APR. 10	3	4	5	5	48	8	29	16	2	24	32	23
APR. 11	4	6	6	7	48	8	28	16	2	24	32	23
APR. 12	4	7	8	8	1	9	28	16	2	24	32	23
APR. 13	4	9	9	10	1	9	28	16	2	24	32	23
APR. 14	4	10	11	11	1	9	28	16	2	24	32	23
APR. 15	4	12	13	13	1	9	28	16	2	24	32	23
APR. 16	4	14	14	15	1	9	28	16	2	24	32	23
APR. 17	4	15	16	17	1	9	28	16	2	24	32	23
APR. 18	4	17	18	18	2	10	28	16	2	24	32	23
APR. 19	5	19	20	20	2	10	28	16	2	24	32	23
APR. 20	5	21	22	22	2	10	28	16	2	24	32	23
APR. 21	5	23	24	24	2	10	28	16	2	24	32	23
APR. 22	5	25	25	26	3	10	28	16	2	24	32	23
APR. 23	5	27	28	28	3	10	28	16	2	24	32	23
APR. 24	5	29	30	30	3	11	28	16	2	24	32	23
APR. 25	6	31	32	32	3	11	28	16	2	24	32	23
APR. 26	6	33	33	34	4	11	28	16	2	24	32	23
APR. 27	6	35	35	36	4	11	28	16	2	24	32	23
APR. 28	6	37	37	38	4	11	28	17	2	24	32	23
APR. 29	6	38	39	40	4	11	28	17	2	24	32	23
APR. 30	6	40	41	41	5	11	28	17	2	24	32	23

MOON 1 ☽ 12:01 A.M. TO 8:00 A.M.   **MOON 2** ◑ 8:01 A.M. TO 4:00 P.M.   **MOON 3** ● 4:01 P.M. TO 12:00 A.M.

Use only one "moon" number. Choose the column closest to your time of birth. If your place of birth is not on Eastern Standard Time, be sure to read "How to Convert to Eastern Standard Time" at the beginning of this section.

May

June

Date & Time	SUN	MOON 1	MOON 2	MOON 3	MERCURY	VENUS	MARS	JUPITER	SATURN	URANUS	NEPTUNE	PLUTO
MAY 1	6	42	43	43	5	12	28	17	2	24	32	23
MAY 2	6	44	44	45	5	12	27	17	2	24	32	23
MAY 3	7	45	46	46	5	12	27	17	2	24	32	23
MAY 4	7	47	47	48	6	12	27	17	2	24	32	23
MAY 5	7	48	1	1	6	12	27	17	2	24	32	23
MAY 6	7	2	3	3	6	12	27	17	2	24	32	23
MAY 7	7	4	4	5	6	13	27	17	2	24	32	23
MAY 8	7	5	6	6	7	13	27	17	2	24	32	23
MAY 9	7	7	7	8	7	13	27	17	2	24	32	23
MAY 10	7	8	9	9	7	13	27	17	2	24	32	23
MAY 11	8	10	11	11	8	13	27	17	2	24	32	23
MAY 12	8	12	12	13	8	13	27	17	2	24	32	23
MAY 13	8	13	14	14	8	13	27	17	2	24	32	23
MAY 14	8	15	16	16	8	14	27	17	2	24	32	23
MAY 15	8	17	17	18	9	14	27	17	2	24	32	23
MAY 16	8	19	19	20	9	14	27	17	2	24	32	23
MAY 17	8	20	21	22	9	14	27	17	2	24	32	23
MAY 18	8	22	23	23	10	14	27	17	2	24	32	23
MAY 19	9	24	25	25	10	14	27	17	2	24	32	23
MAY 20	9	26	27	27	10	14	27	17	2	24	32	23
MAY 21	9	28	29	29	10	15	27	17	2	24	32	23
MAY 22	9	30	31	31	11	15	27	17	2	24	32	23
MAY 23	9	32	33	33	11	15	27	17	2	24	32	23
MAY 24	9	34	35	35	11	15	27	17	2	24	32	23
MAY 25	10	36	36	37	11	15	27	17	2	24	32	23
MAY 26	10	38	38	39	12	15	27	17	2	24	32	23
MAY 27	10	40	40	41	12	15	27	17	2	24	32	23
MAY 28	10	41	42	43	12	15	27	17	2	24	32	23
MAY 29	10	43	44	44	12	16	27	17	2	24	32	23
MAY 30	10	45	45	46	13	16	27	17	2	24	32	23
MAY 31	10	46	47	47	13	16	27	17	2	24	32	23

Date & Time	SUN	MOON 1	MOON 2	MOON 3	MERCURY	VENUS	MARS	JUPITER	SATURN	URANUS	NEPTUNE	PLUTO
JUN. 1	10	48	48	1	13	16	27	17	2	24	32	23
JUN. 2	10	2	2	3	13	16	27	17	2	24	32	23
JUN. 3	11	3	4	4	13	16	27	17	2	24	32	23
JUN. 4	11	5	5	6	14	17	27	17	2	24	32	23
JUN. 5	11	6	7	7	14	17	27	17	2	24	32	23
JUN. 6	11	8	9	9	14	17	27	17	2	24	32	23
JUN. 7	11	10	10	11	14	17	27	17	2	24	32	23
JUN. 8	11	11	12	12	14	17	27	17	2	24	32	23
JUN. 9	11	13	13	14	15	17	27	17	2	24	32	23
JUN. 10	11	15	15	16	15	17	27	17	2	24	32	23
JUN. 11	12	16	17	17	15	18	27	17	2	24	32	23
JUN. 12	12	18	19	19	15	18	27	17	2	24	32	23
JUN. 13	12	20	21	21	15	18	27	17	2	24	32	23
JUN. 14	12	22	22	23	15	18	27	17	2	24	32	23
JUN. 15	12	24	24	25	15	18	27	18	2	24	32	23
JUN. 16	12	26	26	27	15	18	27	18	2	24	32	23
JUN. 17	12	27	28	29	15	18	27	18	2	24	32	23
JUN. 18	12	29	30	31	16	19	27	18	2	24	32	23
JUN. 19	13	31	32	33	16	19	27	18	2	24	32	23
JUN. 20	13	33	34	34	16	19	27	18	2	24	32	23
JUN. 21	13	35	36	36	16	19	27	18	2	24	32	23
JUN. 22	13	37	38	38	16	19	28	18	3	24	32	23
JUN. 23	13	39	39	40	16	19	28	18	3	24	32	23
JUN. 24	13	41	41	42	16	19	28	18	3	24	32	23
JUN. 25	14	42	43	44	16	19	28	18	3	24	32	23
JUN. 26	14	44	45	45	16	20	28	18	3	24	32	23
JUN. 27	14	46	46	47	16	20	28	18	3	24	32	23
JUN. 28	14	47	48	1	16	20	28	18	3	24	32	23
JUN. 29	14	1	2	2	16	20	28	18	3	24	32	23
JUN. 30	14	3	3	4	16	20	28	18	3	24	32	23

MOON 1 ◗ 12:01 A.M. TO 8:00 A.M. **MOON 2** ◑ 8:01 A.M. TO 4:00 P.M. **MOON 3** ● 4:01 P.M. TO 12:00 A.M.

Use only one "moon" number. Choose the column closest to your time of birth. If your place of birth is not on Eastern Standard Time, be sure to read "How to Convert to Eastern Standard Time" at the beginning of this section.

1967

July

Date & Time	SUN	MOON 1	MOON 2	MOON 3	MERCURY	VENUS	MARS	JUPITER	SATURN	URANUS	NEPTUNE	PLUTO
JUL. 1	14	4	5	5	16	20	28	18	3	24	32	23
JUL. 2	14	6	6	7	16	20	28	18	3	24	32	23
JUL. 3	15	7	8	8	16	20	28	18	3	24	32	23
JUL. 4	15	9	10	10	16	20	28	18	3	24	32	23
JUL. 5	15	11	11	12	16	21	28	18	3	24	32	23
JUL. 6	15	12	13	13	15	21	28	18	3	24	32	23
JUL. 7	15	14	15	15	15	21	28	18	3	24	32	23
JUL. 8	15	16	16	17	15	21	28	18	3	24	32	23
JUL. 9	15	18	18	19	15	21	28	18	3	24	32	23
JUL. 10	15	19	20	21	15	21	28	18	3	24	32	23
JUL. 11	16	21	22	23	15	21	28	18	3	24	32	23
JUL. 12	16	23	24	24	15	21	28	18	3	24	32	23
JUL. 13	16	25	26	26	15	21	29	18	3	24	32	23
JUL. 14	16	27	28	28	15	21	29	18	3	24	32	23
JUL. 15	16	29	29	30	15	22	29	18	3	24	32	23
JUL. 16	16	31	31	32	15	22	29	18	3	24	32	23
JUL. 17	16	33	33	34	15	22	29	18	3	24	32	23
JUL. 18	16	34	35	36	15	22	29	18	3	24	32	23
JUL. 19	17	36	37	38	15	22	29	18	3	24	32	23
JUL. 20	17	38	39	39	15	22	29	18	3	24	32	23
JUL. 21	17	40	41	41	15	22	29	18	3	24	32	23
JUL. 22	17	42	42	43	15	22	29	19	3	24	32	23
JUL. 23	17	44	44	45	15	22	29	19	3	24	32	23
JUL. 24	17	45	46	46	15	22	29	19	3	24	32	23
JUL. 25	17	47	47	48	15	22	29	19	3	24	32	23
JUL. 26	18	48	1	2	15	22	29	19	3	24	32	23
JUL. 27	18	2	3	3	15	22	29	19	3	24	32	23
JUL. 28	18	4	4	5	15	23	30	19	3	24	32	23
JUL. 29	18	5	6	6	15	23	30	19	3	24	32	23
JUL. 30	18	7	7	8	15	23	30	19	3	24	32	23
JUL. 31	18	8	9	10	15	23	30	19	3	24	32	23

August

Date & Time	SUN	MOON 1	MOON 2	MOON 3	MERCURY	VENUS	MARS	JUPITER	SATURN	URANUS	NEPTUNE	PLUTO
AUG. 1	18	10	11	11	15	23	30	19	3	24	32	23
AUG. 2	18	12	12	13	16	23	30	19	3	24	32	23
AUG. 3	19	13	14	15	16	23	30	19	3	24	32	24
AUG. 4	19	15	16	16	16	23	30	19	3	24	32	24
AUG. 5	19	17	18	18	16	23	30	19	3	24	32	24
AUG. 6	19	19	19	20	16	23	30	19	3	24	32	24
AUG. 7	19	21	21	22	17	23	30	19	3	24	32	24
AUG. 8	19	23	23	24	17	23	30	19	3	24	32	24
AUG. 9	19	25	25	26	17	23	30	19	3	24	32	24
AUG. 10	19	27	27	28	17	23	30	19	3	24	32	24
AUG. 11	20	28	29	30	18	23	31	19	3	24	32	24
AUG. 12	20	30	31	32	18	23	31	19	3	24	32	24
AUG. 13	20	32	33	33	18	23	31	19	3	24	32	24
AUG. 14	20	34	35	35	18	23	31	19	3	24	32	24
AUG. 15	20	36	36	37	19	23	31	19	3	24	32	24
AUG. 16	20	38	38	39	19	23	31	19	3	24	32	24
AUG. 17	20	39	40	41	19	23	31	19	3	24	32	24
AUG. 18	20	41	42	42	19	23	31	19	3	24	32	24
AUG. 19	21	43	44	44	20	23	31	19	3	24	32	24
AUG. 20	21	45	45	46	20	22	31	19	3	24	32	24
AUG. 21	21	46	47	47	20	22	31	19	3	24	32	24
AUG. 22	21	48	1	1	20	22	31	19	3	24	32	24
AUG. 23	21	2	2	3	21	22	31	19	3	24	32	24
AUG. 24	21	3	4	4	21	22	32	19	3	24	32	24
AUG. 25	21	5	5	6	21	22	32	20	3	24	32	24
AUG. 26	22	6	7	7	21	22	32	20	3	24	32	24
AUG. 27	22	8	8	9	22	22	32	20	3	24	32	24
AUG. 28	22	9	10	11	22	22	32	20	3	24	32	24
AUG. 29	22	11	12	12	22	22	32	20	2	24	32	24
AUG. 30	22	13	13	14	22	22	32	20	2	24	32	24
AUG. 31	22	15	15	16	23	22	32	20	2	24	32	24

MOON 1 ◗ 12:01 A.M. TO 8:00 A.M.   **MOON 2** ◖ 8:01 A.M. TO 4:00 P.M.   **MOON 3** ● 4:01 P.M. TO 12:00 A.M.

Use only one "moon" number. Choose the column closest to your time of birth. If your place of birth is not on Eastern Standard Time, be sure to read "How to Convert to Eastern Standard Time" at the beginning of this section.

September

October

Date & Time	SUN	MOON 1 ◖	MOON 2 ◑	MOON 3 ●	MERCURY	VENUS	MARS	JUPITER	SATURN	URANUS	NEPTUNE	PLUTO
SEP. 1	22	16	17	17	23	22	32	20	2	24	32	24
SEP. 2	22	18	19	19	23	21	32	20	2	24	32	24
SEP. 3	23	20	21	21	23	21	32	20	2	24	32	24
SEP. 4	23	22	23	23	24	21	32	20	2	24	32	24
SEP. 5	23	24	25	25	24	21	33	20	2	24	32	24
SEP. 6	23	26	27	27	24	21	33	20	2	24	32	24
SEP. 7	23	28	28	29	24	21	33	20	2	24	32	24
SEP. 8	23	30	30	31	25	21	33	20	2	24	32	24
SEP. 9	23	32	32	33	25	21	33	20	2	24	32	24
SEP. 10	23	34	34	35	25	21	33	20	2	24	32	24
SEP. 11	24	35	36	37	25	21	33	20	2	24	32	24
SEP. 12	24	37	38	38	25	21	33	20	2	24	32	24
SEP. 13	24	39	40	40	26	21	33	20	2	24	32	24
SEP. 14	24	41	41	42	26	21	33	20	2	24	32	24
SEP. 15	24	43	43	44	26	21	33	20	2	24	32	24
SEP. 16	24	44	45	45	26	21	34	20	2	24	32	24
SEP. 17	24	46	46	47	27	21	34	20	2	24	32	24
SEP. 18	24	48	48	1	27	21	34	20	2	24	32	24
SEP. 19	25	1	2	2	27	21	34	20	2	24	32	24
SEP. 20	25	3	3	4	27	21	34	20	2	24	32	24
SEP. 21	25	4	5	5	27	21	34	20	2	24	32	24
SEP. 22	25	6	6	7	28	21	34	20	2	24	32	24
SEP. 23	25	7	8	8	28	21	34	20	2	24	32	24
SEP. 24	25	9	10	10	28	21	34	20	2	24	32	24
SEP. 25	26	11	11	12	28	21	34	20	2	24	32	24
SEP. 26	26	12	13	13	28	21	34	20	2	24	32	24
SEP. 27	26	14	14	15	28	21	35	20	2	24	32	24
SEP. 28	26	16	16	17	29	21	35	20	2	24	32	24
SEP. 29	26	17	18	19	29	21	35	20	2	24	32	24
SEP. 30	26	19	20	20	29	21	35	21	2	24	32	24

Date & Time	SUN	MOON 1 ◖	MOON 2 ◑	MOON 3 ●	MERCURY	VENUS	MARS	JUPITER	SATURN	URANUS	NEPTUNE	PLUTO
OCT. 1	26	21	22	22	29	21	35	21	2	24	32	24
OCT. 2	26	23	24	24	29	21	35	21	2	24	32	24
OCT. 3	27	25	26	26	29	21	35	21	2	24	32	24
OCT. 4	27	27	28	28	30	21	35	21	2	24	32	24
OCT. 5	27	29	30	30	30	21	35	21	2	24	32	24
OCT. 6	27	31	32	32	30	21	35	21	2	24	32	24
OCT. 7	27	33	34	34	30	21	35	21	2	24	32	24
OCT. 8	27	35	36	36	30	21	36	21	2	24	32	24
OCT. 9	27	37	37	38	30	21	36	21	2	24	32	24
OCT. 10	27	39	39	40	30	22	36	21	2	24	32	24
OCT. 11	28	40	41	42	31	22	36	21	2	24	32	24
OCT. 12	28	42	43	43	31	22	36	21	2	24	32	24
OCT. 13	28	44	44	45	31	22	36	21	2	24	32	24
OCT. 14	28	45	46	47	31	22	36	21	2	24	32	24
OCT. 15	28	47	48	48	31	22	36	21	2	24	32	24
OCT. 16	28	1	1	2	31	22	36	21	2	25	32	24
OCT. 17	28	2	3	3	31	22	36	21	2	25	32	24
OCT. 18	28	4	4	5	31	22	36	21	2	25	32	24
OCT. 19	29	5	6	6	31	22	37	21	2	25	32	24
OCT. 20	29	7	8	8	31	22	37	21	2	25	32	24
OCT. 21	29	9	9	10	31	23	37	21	2	25	32	24
OCT. 22	29	10	11	11	31	23	37	21	2	25	32	24
OCT. 23	29	12	12	13	31	23	37	21	2	25	32	24
OCT. 24	29	13	14	15	31	23	37	21	2	25	32	24
OCT. 25	29	15	16	16	31	23	37	21	2	25	32	24
OCT. 26	30	17	17	18	31	23	37	21	2	25	32	24
OCT. 27	30	19	19	20	31	23	37	21	2	25	32	24
OCT. 28	30	20	21	22	31	23	37	21	2	25	32	24
OCT. 29	30	22	23	23	31	23	38	21	2	25	32	24
OCT. 30	30	24	25	25	31	24	38	21	2	25	32	24
OCT. 31	30	26	27	27	30	24	38	21	2	25	32	24

MOON 1 ◖ 12:01 A.M. TO 8:00 A.M.   **MOON 2** ◑ 8:01 A.M. TO 4:00 P.M.   **MOON 3** ● 4:01 P.M. TO 12:00 A.M.
Use only one "moon" number. Choose the column closest to your time of birth. If your place of birth is not on Eastern Standard Time, be sure to read "How to Convert to Eastern Standard Time" at the beginning of this section.

1967

November

Date & Time	SUN	MOON 1	MOON 2	MOON 3	MERCURY	VENUS	MARS	JUPITER	SATURN	URANUS	NEPTUNE	PLUTO
NOV. 1	30	28	29	29	30	24	38	21	2	25	32	24
NOV. 2	30	30	31	31	30	24	38	21	2	25	32	24
NOV. 3	31	32	33	33	30	24	38	21	2	25	32	24
NOV. 4	31	34	35	35	30	24	38	21	2	25	32	24
NOV. 5	31	36	37	37	30	24	38	21	2	25	32	24
NOV. 6	31	38	39	39	29	25	38	21	2	25	32	24
NOV. 7	31	40	40	41	29	25	38	21	2	25	32	24
NOV. 8	31	42	42	43	29	25	39	21	2	25	32	24
NOV. 9	31	43	44	45	29	25	39	21	2	25	32	24
NOV. 10	31	45	46	46	29	25	39	21	2	25	32	24
NOV. 11	31	47	47	48	29	25	39	21	2	25	32	24
NOV. 12	32	48	1	1	29	25	39	21	2	25	32	24
NOV. 13	32	2	2	3	29	25	39	21	2	25	32	24
NOV. 14	32	3	4	5	29	26	39	21	2	25	32	24
NOV. 15	32	5	6	6	29	26	39	21	2	25	32	24
NOV. 16	32	7	7	8	29	26	39	21	2	25	32	24
NOV. 17	32	8	9	9	30	26	39	21	2	25	32	24
NOV. 18	32	10	10	11	30	26	40	22	2	25	32	24
NOV. 19	33	11	12	12	30	26	40	22	2	25	32	24
NOV. 20	33	13	14	14	30	26	40	22	2	25	32	24
NOV. 21	33	15	15	16	30	27	40	22	2	25	32	24
NOV. 22	33	16	17	17	30	27	40	22	2	25	32	24
NOV. 23	33	18	19	19	31	27	40	22	2	25	32	24
NOV. 24	33	20	20	21	31	27	40	22	2	25	32	24
NOV. 25	34	22	22	23	31	27	40	22	2	25	32	24
NOV. 26	34	23	24	25	31	27	40	22	2	25	32	24
NOV. 27	34	25	26	27	31	27	40	22	2	25	32	24
NOV. 28	34	27	28	29	31	28	41	22	2	25	32	24
NOV. 29	34	29	30	31	32	28	41	22	2	25	32	24
NOV. 30	34	31	32	33	32	28	41	22	2	25	32	24

December

Date & Time	SUN	MOON 1	MOON 2	MOON 3	MERCURY	VENUS	MARS	JUPITER	SATURN	URANUS	NEPTUNE	PLUTO
DEC. 1	34	33	34	35	32	28	41	22	2	25	32	24
DEC. 2	34	35	36	37	32	28	41	22	2	25	32	24
DEC. 3	35	37	38	38	32	28	41	22	2	25	32	24
DEC. 4	35	39	40	40	33	28	41	22	2	25	32	24
DEC. 5	35	41	42	42	33	29	41	22	2	25	32	24
DEC. 6	35	43	43	44	33	29	41	22	2	25	32	24
DEC. 7	35	45	45	46	33	29	42	22	2	25	32	24
DEC. 8	35	46	47	47	34	29	42	22	2	25	32	24
DEC. 9	35	48	48	1	34	29	42	22	2	25	32	24
DEC. 10	35	1	2	3	34	29	42	22	2	25	32	24
DEC. 11	36	3	4	4	34	30	42	22	2	25	32	24
DEC. 12	36	5	5	6	34	30	42	22	2	25	32	24
DEC. 13	36	6	7	7	35	30	42	22	2	25	32	24
DEC. 14	36	8	8	9	35	30	42	22	2	25	32	24
DEC. 15	36	9	10	10	35	30	42	22	2	25	32	24
DEC. 16	36	11	12	12	35	30	42	22	2	25	32	24
DEC. 17	36	13	13	14	35	30	43	22	2	25	32	24
DEC. 18	36	14	15	15	36	31	43	22	2	25	32	24
DEC. 19	37	16	17	17	36	31	43	22	2	25	32	24
DEC. 20	37	18	18	19	36	31	43	22	2	25	32	24
DEC. 21	37	19	20	21	36	31	43	22	2	25	32	24
DEC. 22	37	21	22	22	36	31	43	22	2	25	32	24
DEC. 23	37	23	24	24	37	31	43	22	2	25	32	24
DEC. 24	37	25	25	26	37	32	43	22	2	25	32	24
DEC. 25	37	27	27	28	37	32	43	22	2	25	32	24
DEC. 26	38	29	29	30	37	32	43	22	2	25	32	24
DEC. 27	38	30	31	32	37	32	44	22	2	25	32	24
DEC. 28	38	32	33	34	38	32	44	22	2	25	32	24
DEC. 29	38	34	35	36	38	32	44	22	2	25	32	24
DEC. 30	38	36	37	38	38	33	44	22	2	25	32	24
DEC. 31	38	38	39	40	38	33	44	22	2	25	32	24

MOON 1 ◗ 12:01 A.M. TO 8:00 A.M.   **MOON 2** ◖ 8:01 A.M. TO 4:00 P.M.   **MOON 3** ● 4:01 P.M. TO 12:00 A.M.
Use only one "moon" number. Choose the column closest to your time of birth. If your place of birth is not on
Eastern Standard Time, be sure to read "How to Convert to Eastern Standard Time" at the beginning of this section.

1968

January

Date & Time	SUN ☉	MOON 1 ☽	MOON 2 ◑	MOON 3 ●	MERCURY	VENUS	MARS	JUPITER	SATURN	URANUS	NEPTUNE	PLUTO
JAN. 1	38	40	41	41	39	33	44	22	2	25	32	24
JAN. 2	38	42	43	43	39	33	44	22	2	25	32	24
JAN. 3	39	44	44	45	39	33	44	22	2	25	32	24
JAN. 4	39	46	46	47	39	33	44	22	2	25	32	24
JAN. 5	39	47	48	48	39	33	45	22	2	25	32	24
JAN. 6	39	1	1	2	40	34	45	22	2	25	32	24
JAN. 7	39	3	3	4	40	34	45	22	2	25	32	24
JAN. 8	39	4	5	5	40	34	45	22	2	25	32	24
JAN. 9	39	6	6	7	40	34	45	22	2	25	32	24
JAN. 10	40	7	8	8	41	34	45	22	2	25	32	24
JAN. 11	40	9	10	10	41	34	45	22	2	25	32	24
JAN. 12	40	10	11	12	41	35	45	22	2	25	32	24
JAN. 13	40	12	13	13	41	35	45	22	2	25	32	24
JAN. 14	40	14	14	15	41	35	45	22	2	25	32	24
JAN. 15	40	15	16	17	42	35	46	22	2	25	32	24
JAN. 16	40	17	18	18	42	35	46	22	2	25	32	24
JAN. 17	41	19	20	20	42	35	46	22	2	25	32	24
JAN. 18	41	21	21	22	42	36	46	22	2	25	32	24
JAN. 19	41	23	23	24	43	36	46	22	2	25	32	24
JAN. 20	41	24	25	26	43	36	46	22	2	25	32	24
JAN. 21	41	26	27	27	43	36	46	22	2	25	32	24
JAN. 22	41	28	29	29	43	36	46	22	2	25	32	24
JAN. 23	42	30	31	31	43	36	46	22	2	25	32	24
JAN. 24	42	32	32	33	44	37	47	22	2	25	32	24
JAN. 25	42	34	34	35	44	37	47	22	2	25	32	24
JAN. 26	42	36	36	37	44	37	47	21	2	25	32	24
JAN. 27	42	38	38	39	44	37	47	21	2	25	32	24
JAN. 28	42	39	40	41	44	37	47	21	2	25	32	24
JAN. 29	42	41	42	42	45	37	47	21	2	25	32	24
JAN. 30	42	43	44	44	45	38	47	21	2	25	32	24
JAN. 31	43	45	45	46	45	38	47	21	2	25	32	24

February

Date & Time	SUN ☉	MOON 1 ☽	MOON 2 ◑	MOON 3 ●	MERCURY	VENUS	MARS	JUPITER	SATURN	URANUS	NEPTUNE	PLUTO
FEB. 1	43	47	47	48	45	38	47	21	2	25	32	24
FEB. 2	43	48	1	1	45	38	47	21	2	25	32	24
FEB. 3	43	2	2	3	45	38	48	21	2	25	32	24
FEB. 4	43	4	4	5	45	38	48	21	2	25	32	24
FEB. 5	43	5	6	6	45	39	48	21	2	25	32	24
FEB. 6	43	7	7	8	45	39	48	21	2	25	32	24
FEB. 7	43	8	9	9	45	39	48	21	2	25	32	24
FEB. 8	44	10	10	11	45	39	48	21	2	25	32	24
FEB. 9	44	11	12	13	45	39	48	21	2	25	32	24
FEB. 10	44	13	14	14	45	39	48	21	2	25	32	24
FEB. 11	44	15	15	16	45	39	48	21	2	25	32	24
FEB. 12	44	17	17	18	45	40	48	21	2	25	32	24
FEB. 13	44	18	19	20	45	40	1	21	2	25	32	24
FEB. 14	44	20	21	21	45	40	1	21	2	25	32	24
FEB. 15	44	22	23	23	44	40	1	21	2	25	32	24
FEB. 16	45	24	24	25	44	40	1	21	2	25	32	24
FEB. 17	45	26	26	27	44	40	1	21	2	25	33	24
FEB. 18	45	28	28	29	44	41	1	21	2	25	33	24
FEB. 19	45	30	30	31	44	41	1	21	2	25	33	24
FEB. 20	45	31	32	33	44	41	1	21	2	25	33	24
FEB. 21	45	33	34	35	44	41	1	21	2	25	33	24
FEB. 22	45	35	36	36	44	41	1	21	2	25	33	24
FEB. 23	46	37	38	38	43	41	2	21	2	25	33	24
FEB. 24	46	39	39	40	43	42	2	21	2	25	33	24
FEB. 25	46	41	41	42	43	42	2	21	2	25	33	24
FEB. 26	46	42	43	44	43	42	2	21	2	25	33	24
FEB. 27	46	44	45	45	43	42	2	21	2	25	33	24
FEB. 28	46	46	47	47	43	42	2	21	2	25	33	24
FEB. 29	46	48	48	1	43	42	2	21	2	25	33	24

MOON 1 ☽ 12:01 A.M. TO 8:00 A.M.   **MOON 2** ◑ 8:01 A.M. TO 4:00 P.M.   **MOON 3** ● 4:01 P.M. TO 12:00 A.M.
Use only one "moon" number. Choose the column closest to your time of birth. If your place of birth is not on Eastern Standard Time, be sure to read "How to Convert to Eastern Standard Time" at the beginning of this section.

March

April

Date & Time	SUN	MOON 1	MOON 2	MOON 3	MERCURY	VENUS	MARS	JUPITER	SATURN	URANUS	NEPTUNE	PLUTO
MAR. 1	46	1	2	2	43	43	2	21	2	25	33	24
MAR. 2	46	3	4	4	43	43	2	21	2	25	33	24
MAR. 3	47	5	5	6	43	43	2	21	2	25	33	24
MAR. 4	47	6	7	7	43	43	3	21	2	25	33	24
MAR. 5	47	8	8	9	43	43	3	21	3	25	33	24
MAR. 6	47	9	10	10	44	43	3	21	3	25	33	24
MAR. 7	47	11	11	12	44	44	3	21	3	25	33	24
MAR. 8	47	13	13	14	44	44	3	21	3	25	33	24
MAR. 9	47	14	15	15	44	44	3	21	3	25	32	24
MAR. 10	47	16	16	17	44	44	3	21	3	25	32	24
MAR. 11	48	18	18	19	44	44	3	21	3	25	32	24
MAR. 12	48	19	20	21	44	44	3	21	3	25	32	24
MAR. 13	48	21	22	22	44	45	4	21	3	25	32	24
MAR. 14	48	23	24	24	44	45	4	21	3	25	32	24
MAR. 15	48	25	26	26	45	45	4	21	3	25	32	24
MAR. 16	48	27	28	28	45	45	4	21	3	25	32	24
MAR. 17	48	29	30	30	45	45	4	21	3	25	32	24
MAR. 18	48	31	32	32	45	45	4	21	3	25	32	24
MAR. 19	1	33	33	34	45	46	4	21	3	25	32	24
MAR. 20	1	35	35	36	45	46	4	21	3	25	32	24
MAR. 21	1	37	37	38	46	46	4	21	3	25	32	24
MAR. 22	1	38	39	40	46	46	4	21	3	25	32	24
MAR. 23	1	40	41	41	46	46	4	21	3	25	32	24
MAR. 24	1	42	43	43	46	46	5	21	3	25	32	24
MAR. 25	2	44	44	45	46	47	5	21	3	25	32	24
MAR. 26	2	46	46	47	46	47	5	21	3	25	32	24
MAR. 27	2	47	48	48	47	47	5	21	3	25	32	24
MAR. 28	2	1	1	2	47	47	5	21	3	25	32	24
MAR. 29	2	2	3	4	47	47	5	21	3	25	32	24
MAR. 30	2	4	5	5	47	47	5	21	3	25	32	24
MAR. 31	2	6	6	7	47	48	5	21	3	25	32	24

Date & Time	SUN	MOON 1	MOON 2	MOON 3	MERCURY	VENUS	MARS	JUPITER	SATURN	URANUS	NEPTUNE	PLUTO
APR. 1	2	7	8	8	48	48	5	20	3	25	32	24
APR. 2	2	9	9	10	48	48	5	20	3	25	32	24
APR. 3	3	10	11	11	48	48	6	20	3	24	32	24
APR. 4	3	12	13	13	48	48	6	20	3	24	32	24
APR. 5	3	14	14	15	1	48	6	20	3	24	32	24
APR. 6	3	15	16	16	1	1	6	20	3	24	32	24
APR. 7	3	17	18	18	1	1	6	20	3	24	32	24
APR. 8	3	19	19	20	1	1	6	20	3	24	32	24
APR. 9	3	20	21	22	1	1	6	20	3	24	32	24
APR. 10	3	22	23	24	2	1	6	20	3	24	32	24
APR. 11	4	24	25	25	2	1	6	20	3	24	32	24
APR. 12	4	26	27	27	2	2	6	20	3	24	32	24
APR. 13	4	28	29	29	2	2	7	20	3	24	32	24
APR. 14	4	30	31	31	3	2	7	20	3	24	32	24
APR. 15	4	32	33	33	3	2	7	20	3	24	32	24
APR. 16	4	34	35	35	3	2	7	20	3	24	32	24
APR. 17	4	36	37	37	3	2	7	20	3	24	32	24
APR. 18	4	38	39	39	4	2	7	20	3	24	32	24
APR. 19	5	40	40	41	4	3	7	20	3	24	32	24
APR. 20	5	42	42	43	4	3	7	20	3	24	32	24
APR. 21	5	43	44	45	5	3	7	20	3	24	32	24
APR. 22	5	45	46	46	5	3	8	20	3	24	32	24
APR. 23	5	47	47	48	5	3	8	20	3	24	32	24
APR. 24	5	48	1	2	5	3	8	20	3	24	32	24
APR. 25	6	2	3	3	6	4	8	20	3	24	32	24
APR. 26	6	4	4	5	6	4	8	20	3	24	32	24
APR. 27	6	5	6	6	6	4	8	20	3	24	32	24
APR. 28	6	7	7	8	7	4	8	20	3	24	32	24
APR. 29	6	8	9	9	7	4	8	20	3	24	32	24
APR. 30	6	10	11	11	7	4	8	20	3	24	32	24

MOON 1 ☽ 12:01 A.M. TO 8:00 A.M.   **MOON 2** ◑ 8:01 A.M. TO 4:00 P.M.   **MOON 3** ● 4:01 P.M. TO 12:00 A.M.

Use only one "moon" number. Choose the column closest to your time of birth. If your place of birth is not on
Eastern Standard Time, be sure to read "How to Convert to Eastern Standard Time" at the beginning of this section.

1968

May

Date & Time	SUN	MOON 1	MOON 2	MOON 3	MERCURY	VENUS	MARS	JUPITER	SATURN	URANUS	NEPTUNE	PLUTO
MAY 1	6	12	12	13	7	5	8	20	3	24	32	24
MAY 2	6	13	14	14	8	5	8	20	3	24	32	24
MAY 3	7	15	15	16	8	5	8	20	3	24	32	24
MAY 4	7	16	17	18	8	5	9	20	3	24	32	24
MAY 5	7	18	19	19	9	5	9	20	4	24	32	24
MAY 6	7	20	20	21	9	5	9	20	4	24	32	24
MAY 7	7	22	22	23	9	6	9	20	4	24	32	24
MAY 8	7	23	24	25	9	6	9	20	4	24	32	24
MAY 9	7	25	26	27	10	6	9	20	4	24	32	24
MAY 10	7	27	28	29	10	6	9	20	4	24	32	24
MAY 11	8	29	30	31	10	6	9	20	4	24	32	24
MAY 12	8	31	32	33	10	6	9	20	4	24	32	24
MAY 13	8	33	34	35	10	7	9	21	4	24	32	24
MAY 14	8	35	36	37	11	7	9	21	4	24	32	24
MAY 15	8	37	38	39	11	7	10	21	4	24	32	24
MAY 16	8	39	40	40	11	7	10	21	4	24	32	24
MAY 17	8	41	42	42	11	7	10	21	4	24	32	24
MAY 18	8	43	44	44	11	7	10	21	4	24	32	24
MAY 19	9	45	45	46	12	8	10	21	4	24	32	24
MAY 20	9	46	47	48	12	8	10	21	4	24	32	24
MAY 21	9	48	1	1	12	8	10	21	4	24	32	24
MAY 22	9	2	2	3	12	8	10	21	4	24	32	24
MAY 23	9	3	4	4	12	8	10	21	4	24	32	24
MAY 24	9	5	5	6	12	8	10	21	4	24	32	24
MAY 25	10	6	7	8	13	9	11	21	4	24	32	24
MAY 26	10	8	9	9	13	9	11	21	4	24	32	24
MAY 27	10	10	10	11	13	9	11	21	4	24	32	24
MAY 28	10	11	12	12	13	9	11	21	4	24	32	24
MAY 29	10	13	13	14	13	9	11	21	4	24	32	24
MAY 30	10	14	15	15	13	9	11	21	4	24	32	24
MAY 31	10	16	17	17	13	10	11	21	4	24	32	24

June

Date & Time	SUN	MOON 1	MOON 2	MOON 3	MERCURY	VENUS	MARS	JUPITER	SATURN	URANUS	NEPTUNE	PLUTO
JUN. 1	10	18	18	19	13	10	11	21	4	24	32	24
JUN. 2	10	19	20	20	13	10	11	21	4	24	32	24
JUN. 3	11	21	22	22	13	10	11	21	4	24	32	24
JUN. 4	11	23	23	24	13	10	11	21	4	24	32	24
JUN. 5	11	25	25	26	13	10	12	21	4	24	32	24
JUN. 6	11	26	27	28	13	11	12	21	4	24	32	24
JUN. 7	11	28	29	30	13	11	12	21	4	24	32	24
JUN. 8	11	30	31	32	13	11	12	21	4	24	32	24
JUN. 9	11	32	33	34	13	11	12	21	4	24	32	24
JUN. 10	11	34	35	36	13	11	12	21	4	24	32	24
JUN. 11	12	36	37	38	13	11	12	21	4	24	32	24
JUN. 12	12	38	39	40	13	12	12	21	4	24	32	24
JUN. 13	12	40	41	42	13	12	12	21	4	24	32	24
JUN. 14	12	42	43	43	13	12	12	21	4	24	32	24
JUN. 15	12	44	45	45	13	12	12	21	4	24	32	24
JUN. 16	12	46	46	47	13	12	13	21	4	24	32	24
JUN. 17	12	48	48	1	13	12	13	21	4	24	32	24
JUN. 18	12	1	2	2	13	12	13	21	4	24	32	24
JUN. 19	13	3	3	4	13	13	13	21	4	24	32	24
JUN. 20	13	4	5	6	13	13	13	21	4	24	32	24
JUN. 21	13	6	7	7	12	13	13	21	4	24	32	24
JUN. 22	13	8	8	9	12	13	13	21	4	24	32	24
JUN. 23	13	9	10	10	12	13	13	21	4	24	32	24
JUN. 24	13	11	11	12	12	13	13	21	4	24	32	24
JUN. 25	14	12	13	13	12	14	13	21	4	24	32	24
JUN. 26	14	14	15	15	12	14	13	21	4	24	32	24
JUN. 27	14	16	16	17	12	14	14	21	4	24	32	24
JUN. 28	14	17	18	18	12	14	14	21	4	24	32	24
JUN. 29	14	19	20	20	12	14	14	21	4	24	32	24
JUN. 30	14	21	21	22	12	14	14	21	4	24	32	24

MOON 1 ◗ 12:01 A.M. TO 8:00 A.M.   **MOON 2** ◑ 8:01 A.M. TO 4:00 P.M.   **MOON 3** ● 4:01 P.M. TO 12:00 A.M.
Use only one "moon" number. Choose the column closest to your time of birth. If your place of birth is not on Eastern Standard Time, be sure to read "How to Convert to Eastern Standard Time" at the beginning of this section.

July

Date & Time	SUN	MOON 1	MOON 2	MOON 3	MERCURY	VENUS	MARS	JUPITER	SATURN	URANUS	NEPTUNE	PLUTO
JUL. 1	14	22	23	24	12	15	14	21	4	24	32	24
JUL. 2	14	24	25	25	12	15	14	21	4	24	32	24
JUL. 3	15	26	27	27	12	15	14	21	4	24	32	24
JUL. 4	15	28	28	29	12	15	14	21	4	24	32	24
JUL. 5	15	30	30	31	12	15	14	21	4	24	32	24
JUL. 6	15	32	32	33	12	15	14	21	4	24	32	24
JUL. 7	15	34	34	35	12	16	14	21	4	24	32	24
JUL. 8	15	36	36	37	12	16	14	21	4	24	32	24
JUL. 9	15	38	38	39	13	16	15	21	4	24	32	24
JUL. 10	15	39	40	41	13	16	15	21	4	24	32	24
JUL. 11	16	41	42	43	13	16	15	22	4	24	32	24
JUL. 12	16	43	44	45	13	16	15	22	4	24	32	24
JUL. 13	16	45	46	46	13	17	15	22	4	24	32	24
JUL. 14	16	47	48	48	13	17	15	22	4	24	32	24
JUL. 15	16	1	1	2	13	17	15	22	4	24	32	24
JUL. 16	16	2	3	3	13	17	15	22	4	24	32	24
JUL. 17	16	4	5	5	14	17	15	22	4	24	32	24
JUL. 18	16	6	6	7	14	17	15	22	4	24	32	24
JUL. 19	17	7	8	8	14	18	15	22	4	24	32	24
JUL. 20	17	9	9	10	14	18	16	22	4	24	32	24
JUL. 21	17	10	11	11	14	18	16	22	4	24	32	24
JUL. 22	17	12	12	13	15	18	16	22	4	24	32	24
JUL. 23	17	14	14	15	15	18	16	22	4	24	32	24
JUL. 24	17	15	16	16	15	18	16	22	4	24	32	24
JUL. 25	17	17	17	18	15	19	16	22	4	24	32	24
JUL. 26	18	19	19	20	16	19	16	22	4	24	32	24
JUL. 27	18	20	21	21	16	19	16	22	4	24	32	24
JUL. 28	18	22	23	23	16	19	16	22	4	24	32	24
JUL. 29	18	24	24	25	16	19	16	22	4	24	32	24
JUL. 30	18	26	26	27	17	19	16	22	4	24	32	24
JUL. 31	18	27	28	29	17	20	16	22	4	25	32	24

August

Date & Time	SUN	MOON 1	MOON 2	MOON 3	MERCURY	VENUS	MARS	JUPITER	SATURN	URANUS	NEPTUNE	PLUTO
AUG. 1	18	29	30	30	17	20	17	22	4	25	32	24
AUG. 2	18	31	32	32	18	20	17	22	4	25	32	24
AUG. 3	19	33	34	34	18	20	17	22	4	25	32	24
AUG. 4	19	35	36	36	18	20	17	22	4	25	32	24
AUG. 5	19	37	37	38	18	20	17	22	4	25	32	24
AUG. 6	19	39	39	40	19	21	17	22	4	25	32	24
AUG. 7	19	41	41	42	19	21	17	22	4	25	32	24
AUG. 8	19	43	43	44	19	21	17	22	4	25	32	24
AUG. 9	19	44	45	46	19	21	17	22	4	25	32	24
AUG. 10	19	46	47	47	20	21	17	22	4	25	32	24
AUG. 11	20	48	1	1	20	21	17	22	4	25	32	24
AUG. 12	20	2	2	3	20	22	18	22	4	25	32	24
AUG. 13	20	3	4	5	20	22	18	22	4	25	32	24
AUG. 14	20	5	6	6	21	22	18	22	4	25	32	24
AUG. 15	20	7	7	8	21	22	18	22	4	25	32	24
AUG. 16	20	8	8	9	21	22	18	22	4	25	32	24
AUG. 17	20	10	10	11	22	22	18	22	4	25	32	24
AUG. 18	20	11	12	12	22	22	18	23	4	25	32	24
AUG. 19	21	13	14	14	22	23	18	23	4	25	32	24
AUG. 20	21	15	15	16	22	23	18	23	4	25	32	24
AUG. 21	21	16	17	17	22	23	18	23	4	25	32	24
AUG. 22	21	18	19	19	23	23	18	23	4	25	32	24
AUG. 23	21	20	20	21	23	23	18	23	4	25	32	24
AUG. 24	21	21	22	23	23	23	19	23	4	25	32	24
AUG. 25	21	23	24	24	23	24	19	23	4	25	32	24
AUG. 26	22	25	26	26	24	24	19	23	4	25	32	24
AUG. 27	22	27	28	28	24	24	19	23	4	25	32	24
AUG. 28	22	29	29	30	24	24	19	23	4	25	32	24
AUG. 29	22	31	31	32	24	24	19	23	4	25	32	24
AUG. 30	22	33	33	34	24	24	19	23	4	25	32	24
AUG. 31	22	34	35	36	25	25	19	23	4	25	32	24

MOON 1 ◗ 12:01 A.M. TO 8:00 A.M.   **MOON 2** ◖ 8:01 A.M. TO 4:00 P.M.   **MOON 3** ● 4:01 P.M. TO 12:00 A.M.
Use only one "moon" number. Choose the column closest to your time of birth. If your place of birth is not on Eastern Standard Time, be sure to read "How to Convert to Eastern Standard Time" at the beginning of this section.

1968

September

Date & Time	SUN	MOON 1	MOON 2	MOON 3	MERCURY	VENUS	MARS	JUPITER	SATURN	URANUS	NEPTUNE	PLUTO
SEP. 1	22	36	37	38	25	25	19	23	4	25	32	24
SEP. 2	22	38	39	39	25	25	19	23	4	25	32	24
SEP. 3	23	40	41	41	25	25	19	23	4	25	32	24
SEP. 4	23	42	43	43	25	25	19	23	4	25	32	24
SEP. 5	23	44	44	45	26	25	20	23	4	25	32	24
SEP. 6	23	46	46	47	26	26	20	23	4	25	32	24
SEP. 7	23	47	48	1	26	26	20	23	4	25	32	24
SEP. 8	23	1	2	2	26	26	20	23	4	25	32	24
SEP. 9	23	3	3	4	26	26	20	23	4	25	32	24
SEP. 10	23	4	5	6	27	26	20	23	4	25	32	24
SEP. 11	24	6	7	7	27	26	20	23	4	25	32	24
SEP. 12	24	8	8	9	27	27	20	23	4	25	32	24
SEP. 13	24	9	10	10	27	27	20	23	4	25	32	24
SEP. 14	24	11	11	12	27	27	20	23	4	25	32	24
SEP. 15	24	12	13	14	27	27	20	23	4	25	32	24
SEP. 16	24	14	15	15	28	27	20	23	4	25	32	24
SEP. 17	24	16	16	17	28	27	21	23	4	25	32	24
SEP. 18	24	17	18	18	28	28	21	23	4	25	32	24
SEP. 19	25	19	20	20	28	28	21	23	4	25	32	24
SEP. 20	25	21	21	22	28	28	21	24	4	25	32	24
SEP. 21	25	23	23	24	28	28	21	24	4	25	32	24
SEP. 22	25	24	25	26	28	28	21	24	4	25	32	24
SEP. 23	25	26	27	28	28	28	21	24	4	25	32	24
SEP. 24	25	28	29	29	29	29	21	24	4	25	32	24
SEP. 25	26	30	31	31	29	29	21	24	4	25	32	24
SEP. 26	26	32	33	33	29	29	21	24	4	25	32	24
SEP. 27	26	34	35	35	29	29	21	24	4	25	32	24
SEP. 28	26	36	37	37	29	29	22	24	4	25	32	24
SEP. 29	26	38	38	39	29	29	22	24	4	25	32	24
SEP. 30	26	40	40	41	29	30	22	24	4	25	32	24

October

Date & Time	SUN	MOON 1	MOON 2	MOON 3	MERCURY	VENUS	MARS	JUPITER	SATURN	URANUS	NEPTUNE	PLUTO
OCT. 1	26	41	42	43	29	30	22	24	4	25	32	24
OCT. 2	26	43	44	44	29	30	22	24	4	25	32	24
OCT. 3	27	45	46	46	29	30	22	24	4	25	32	24
OCT. 4	27	47	47	48	29	30	22	24	4	25	32	24
OCT. 5	27	1	1	2	29	30	22	24	4	25	32	24
OCT. 6	27	2	3	3	29	31	22	24	4	25	32	24
OCT. 7	27	4	4	5	29	31	22	24	4	25	32	24
OCT. 8	27	6	6	7	29	31	22	24	4	25	32	24
OCT. 9	27	7	8	8	29	31	22	24	4	25	32	24
OCT. 10	27	9	9	10	29	31	23	24	4	25	32	24
OCT. 11	28	10	11	11	29	31	23	24	4	25	32	24
OCT. 12	28	12	12	13	28	31	23	24	4	25	32	24
OCT. 13	28	14	14	15	28	32	23	24	4	25	32	24
OCT. 14	28	15	16	16	28	32	23	24	4	25	32	24
OCT. 15	28	17	17	18	28	32	23	24	4	25	32	24
OCT. 16	28	18	19	20	28	32	23	24	4	25	32	24
OCT. 17	28	20	21	21	28	32	23	24	4	25	32	24
OCT. 18	28	22	22	23	28	32	23	24	4	25	32	24
OCT. 19	29	24	24	25	27	33	23	24	4	25	32	24
OCT. 20	29	26	26	27	27	33	23	24	4	25	32	24
OCT. 21	29	27	28	29	27	33	23	24	4	25	32	24
OCT. 22	29	29	30	31	27	33	23	24	4	25	32	24
OCT. 23	29	31	32	33	27	33	24	24	4	25	32	24
OCT. 24	29	33	34	35	27	33	24	24	4	25	32	24
OCT. 25	29	35	36	37	27	34	24	24	4	25	32	24
OCT. 26	30	37	38	39	27	34	24	24	4	25	32	24
OCT. 27	30	39	40	40	27	34	24	24	4	25	32	24
OCT. 28	30	41	42	42	27	34	24	25	4	25	32	24
OCT. 29	30	43	43	44	27	34	24	25	4	25	32	24
OCT. 30	30	45	45	46	27	34	24	25	4	25	32	24
OCT. 31	30	46	47	48	28	35	24	25	4	25	32	24

MOON 1 ◐ 12:01 A.M. TO 8:00 A.M.　　**MOON 2** ◑ 8:01 A.M. TO 4:00 P.M.　　**MOON 3** ● 4:01 P.M. TO 12:00 A.M.

Use only one "moon" number. Choose the column closest to your time of birth. If your place of birth is not on Eastern Standard Time, be sure to read "How to Convert to Eastern Standard Time" at the beginning of this section.

1968

November

Date & Time	SUN	MOON 1	MOON 2	MOON 3	MERCURY	VENUS	MARS	JUPITER	SATURN	URANUS	NEPTUNE	PLUTO
NOV. 1	30	48	1	1	28	35	24	25	4	25	32	24
NOV. 2	30	2	2	3	28	35	24	25	4	25	32	24
NOV. 3	31	3	4	5	28	35	24	25	4	25	32	24
NOV. 4	31	5	6	6	28	35	25	25	4	25	32	24
NOV. 5	31	7	7	8	28	35	25	25	4	25	32	24
NOV. 6	31	8	9	9	29	36	25	25	4	25	32	24
NOV. 7	31	10	10	11	29	36	25	25	4	25	32	24
NOV. 8	31	11	12	13	29	36	25	25	4	25	32	24
NOV. 9	31	13	14	14	29	36	25	25	4	25	32	24
NOV. 10	31	15	15	16	29	36	25	25	4	25	32	24
NOV. 11	31	16	17	17	30	36	25	25	4	25	32	24
NOV. 12	32	18	18	19	30	37	25	25	4	25	32	24
NOV. 13	32	20	20	21	30	37	25	25	4	25	32	24
NOV. 14	32	21	22	22	30	37	25	25	4	25	32	24
NOV. 15	32	23	24	24	30	37	25	25	4	25	32	24
NOV. 16	32	25	25	26	31	37	26	25	4	25	32	24
NOV. 17	32	27	27	28	31	37	26	25	4	25	32	24
NOV. 18	32	28	29	30	31	37	26	25	4	25	32	24
NOV. 19	33	30	31	32	31	38	26	25	4	25	32	24
NOV. 20	33	32	33	34	31	38	26	25	4	25	32	24
NOV. 21	33	34	35	36	32	38	26	25	4	25	32	24
NOV. 22	33	37	37	38	32	38	26	25	4	25	32	24
NOV. 23	33	39	39	40	32	38	26	25	4	25	32	24
NOV. 24	33	40	41	42	32	38	26	25	4	25	32	24
NOV. 25	34	42	43	44	32	38	26	25	4	25	33	24
NOV. 26	34	44	45	45	33	39	26	25	4	25	33	24
NOV. 27	34	46	47	47	33	39	26	25	4	25	33	24
NOV. 28	34	48	48	1	33	39	26	25	4	25	33	24
NOV. 29	34	1	2	3	33	39	27	25	4	25	33	24
NOV. 30	34	3	4	4	34	39	27	25	4	25	33	24

December

Date & Time	SUN	MOON 1	MOON 2	MOON 3	MERCURY	VENUS	MARS	JUPITER	SATURN	URANUS	NEPTUNE	PLUTO
DEC. 1	34	5	5	6	34	40	27	25	4	25	33	24
DEC. 2	34	6	7	7	34	40	27	25	4	25	33	24
DEC. 3	35	8	8	9	34	40	27	25	3	25	33	24
DEC. 4	35	9	10	11	34	40	27	25	3	25	33	24
DEC. 5	35	11	12	12	35	40	27	25	3	25	33	24
DEC. 6	35	13	13	14	35	40	27	25	3	25	33	24
DEC. 7	35	14	15	15	35	41	27	25	3	25	33	24
DEC. 8	35	16	16	17	35	41	27	25	3	25	33	24
DEC. 9	35	17	18	19	35	41	27	25	3	25	33	24
DEC. 10	35	19	20	20	36	41	27	25	3	25	33	24
DEC. 11	36	21	21	22	36	41	28	25	3	25	33	24
DEC. 12	36	22	23	24	36	41	28	25	3	25	33	24
DEC. 13	36	24	25	25	36	41	28	25	3	25	33	24
DEC. 14	36	26	26	27	36	42	28	25	3	25	33	24
DEC. 15	36	28	28	29	37	42	28	26	3	25	33	24
DEC. 16	36	30	30	31	37	42	28	26	3	25	33	24
DEC. 17	36	32	32	33	37	42	28	26	3	25	33	24
DEC. 18	36	34	34	35	37	42	28	26	3	25	33	24
DEC. 19	37	36	36	37	38	42	28	26	3	25	33	24
DEC. 20	37	38	38	39	38	43	28	26	3	25	33	24
DEC. 21	37	40	40	41	38	43	28	26	3	25	33	24
DEC. 22	37	42	42	43	38	43	28	26	3	25	33	24
DEC. 23	37	44	44	45	38	43	28	26	3	25	33	24
DEC. 24	37	45	46	47	39	43	29	26	3	25	33	24
DEC. 25	37	47	48	48	39	43	29	26	3	25	33	24
DEC. 26	38	1	2	2	39	44	29	26	3	25	33	24
DEC. 27	38	3	3	4	39	44	29	26	3	25	33	24
DEC. 28	38	4	5	5	39	44	29	26	3	25	33	24
DEC. 29	38	6	6	7	40	44	29	26	3	25	33	24
DEC. 30	38	8	8	9	40	44	29	26	3	25	33	24
DEC. 31	38	9	10	10	40	44	29	26	3	25	33	24

MOON 1 ☽ **12:01 A.M. TO 8:00 A.M.**   **MOON 2** ☽ **8:01 A.M. TO 4:00 P.M.**   **MOON 3** ● **4:01 P.M. TO 12:00 A.M.**
Use only one "moon" number. Choose the column closest to your time of birth. If your place of birth is not on
Eastern Standard Time, be sure to read "How to Convert to Eastern Standard Time" at the beginning of this section.

1969

January

Date & Time	SUN	MOON 1	MOON 2	MOON 3	MERCURY	VENUS	MARS	JUPITER	SATURN	URANUS	NEPTUNE	PLUTO
JAN. 1	38	11	11	12	40	44	29	26	3	25	33	24
JAN. 2	38	12	13	13	40	45	29	26	3	25	33	24
JAN. 3	39	14	14	15	41	45	29	26	3	25	33	24
JAN. 4	39	15	16	17	41	45	29	26	3	26	33	24
JAN. 5	39	17	18	18	41	45	29	26	3	26	33	24
JAN. 6	39	19	19	20	41	45	30	26	3	26	33	24
JAN. 7	39	20	21	21	42	45	30	26	3	26	33	24
JAN. 8	39	22	23	23	42	45	30	26	3	26	33	24
JAN. 9	39	24	24	25	42	46	30	26	4	26	33	24
JAN. 10	40	25	26	27	42	46	30	26	4	26	33	24
JAN. 11	40	27	28	28	42	46	30	26	4	26	33	24
JAN. 12	40	29	30	30	42	46	30	26	4	26	33	24
JAN. 13	40	31	31	32	43	46	30	26	4	25	33	24
JAN. 14	40	33	33	34	43	46	30	26	4	25	33	24
JAN. 15	40	35	35	36	43	46	30	26	4	25	33	24
JAN. 16	40	37	37	38	43	47	30	26	4	25	33	24
JAN. 17	41	39	39	40	43	47	30	26	4	25	33	24
JAN. 18	41	41	41	42	43	47	30	26	4	25	33	24
JAN. 19	41	43	43	44	43	47	30	26	4	25	33	24
JAN. 20	41	45	45	46	43	47	31	26	4	25	33	24
JAN. 21	41	47	47	48	43	47	31	26	4	25	33	24
JAN. 22	41	48	1	1	43	47	31	26	4	25	33	24
JAN. 23	42	2	3	3	43	48	31	26	4	25	33	24
JAN. 24	42	4	4	5	43	48	31	26	4	25	33	24
JAN. 25	42	5	6	7	43	48	31	26	4	25	33	24
JAN. 26	42	7	8	8	43	48	31	26	4	25	33	24
JAN. 27	42	9	9	10	43	48	31	26	4	25	33	24
JAN. 28	42	10	11	11	42	48	31	26	4	25	33	24
JAN. 29	42	12	12	13	42	48	31	26	4	25	33	24
JAN. 30	42	13	14	14	42	1	31	26	4	25	33	24
JAN. 31	43	15	16	16	42	1	31	26	4	25	33	24

February

Date & Time	SUN	MOON 1	MOON 2	MOON 3	MERCURY	VENUS	MARS	JUPITER	SATURN	URANUS	NEPTUNE	PLUTO
FEB. 1	43	17	17	18	42	1	31	26	4	25	33	24
FEB. 2	43	18	19	19	42	1	31	26	4	25	33	24
FEB. 3	43	20	20	21	41	1	32	26	4	25	33	24
FEB. 4	43	22	22	23	41	1	32	26	4	25	33	24
FEB. 5	43	23	24	24	41	1	32	26	4	25	33	24
FEB. 6	43	25	26	26	41	1	32	26	4	25	33	24
FEB. 7	43	27	27	28	41	2	32	26	4	25	33	24
FEB. 8	44	28	29	30	41	2	32	26	4	25	33	24
FEB. 9	44	30	31	32	41	2	32	26	4	25	33	24
FEB. 10	44	32	33	33	41	2	32	26	4	25	33	24
FEB. 11	44	34	35	35	41	2	32	26	4	25	33	24
FEB. 12	44	36	37	37	41	2	32	26	4	25	33	24
FEB. 13	44	38	39	39	41	2	32	26	4	25	33	24
FEB. 14	44	40	41	41	41	2	32	26	4	25	33	24
FEB. 15	44	42	42	43	41	3	32	26	4	25	33	24
FEB. 16	45	44	44	45	41	3	32	26	4	25	33	24
FEB. 17	45	46	46	47	41	3	32	26	4	25	33	24
FEB. 18	45	48	48	1	41	3	33	26	4	25	33	24
FEB. 19	45	1	2	3	42	3	33	26	4	25	33	24
FEB. 20	45	3	4	4	42	3	33	26	4	25	33	24
FEB. 21	45	5	5	6	42	3	33	26	4	25	33	24
FEB. 22	45	6	7	8	42	3	33	26	4	25	33	24
FEB. 23	46	8	9	9	42	3	33	26	4	25	33	24
FEB. 24	46	10	10	11	42	3	33	26	4	25	33	24
FEB. 25	46	11	12	12	42	4	33	26	4	25	33	24
FEB. 26	46	13	13	14	42	4	33	26	4	25	33	24
FEB. 27	46	14	15	16	43	4	33	25	4	25	33	24
FEB. 28	46	16	17	17	43	4	33	25	4	25	33	24

MOON 1 ◐ 12:01 A.M. TO 8:00 A.M.   **MOON 2** ◑ 8:01 A.M. TO 4:00 P.M.   **MOON 3** ● 4:01 P.M. TO 12:00 A.M.
Use only one "moon" number. Choose the column closest to your time of birth. If your place of birth is not on Eastern Standard Time, be sure to read "How to Convert to Eastern Standard Time" at the beginning of this section.

1969

March

Date & Time	SUN	MOON 1	MOON 2	MOON 3	MERCURY	VENUS	MARS	JUPITER	SATURN	URANUS	NEPTUNE	PLUTO
MAR. 1	46	18	18	19	43	4	33	25	4	25	33	24
MAR. 2	46	19	20	20	43	4	33	25	4	25	33	24
MAR. 3	47	21	22	22	43	4	33	25	4	25	33	24
MAR. 4	47	23	23	24	43	4	33	25	4	25	33	24
MAR. 5	47	24	25	26	44	4	33	25	4	25	33	24
MAR. 6	47	26	27	27	44	4	33	25	4	25	33	24
MAR. 7	47	28	29	29	44	4	34	25	4	25	33	24
MAR. 8	47	30	31	31	44	4	34	25	4	25	33	24
MAR. 9	47	32	32	33	44	4	34	25	4	25	33	24
MAR. 10	47	34	34	35	44	4	34	25	4	25	33	24
MAR. 11	48	35	36	37	45	4	34	25	4	25	33	24
MAR. 12	48	37	38	39	45	4	34	25	4	25	33	24
MAR. 13	48	39	40	41	45	4	34	25	4	25	33	24
MAR. 14	48	41	42	42	45	4	34	25	4	25	33	24
MAR. 15	48	43	44	44	45	5	34	25	4	25	33	24
MAR. 16	48	45	46	46	46	5	34	25	4	25	33	24
MAR. 17	48	47	47	48	46	5	34	25	4	25	33	24
MAR. 18	48	1	1	2	46	5	34	25	4	25	33	24
MAR. 19	1	2	3	4	46	5	34	25	4	25	33	24
MAR. 20	1	4	5	5	47	5	34	25	4	25	33	24
MAR. 21	1	6	6	7	47	5	34	25	4	25	33	24
MAR. 22	1	8	8	9	47	5	34	25	4	25	33	24
MAR. 23	1	9	10	10	47	4	34	25	4	25	33	24
MAR. 24	1	11	11	12	47	4	34	25	4	25	33	24
MAR. 25	2	12	13	13	48	4	34	25	4	25	33	24
MAR. 26	2	14	14	15	48	4	34	25	4	25	33	24
MAR. 27	2	16	16	17	48	4	35	25	4	25	33	24
MAR. 28	2	17	18	18	48	4	35	25	4	25	33	24
MAR. 29	2	19	19	20	1	4	35	25	4	25	33	24
MAR. 30	2	20	21	22	1	4	35	25	4	25	33	24
MAR. 31	2	22	23	23	1	4	35	25	4	25	33	24

April

Date & Time	SUN	MOON 1	MOON 2	MOON 3	MERCURY	VENUS	MARS	JUPITER	SATURN	URANUS	NEPTUNE	PLUTO
APR. 1	2	24	24	25	1	4	35	25	4	25	33	24
APR. 2	2	26	26	27	2	4	35	25	4	25	33	24
APR. 3	3	27	28	29	2	4	35	25	5	25	33	24
APR. 4	3	29	30	31	2	4	35	25	5	25	33	24
APR. 5	3	31	32	32	2	4	35	25	5	25	33	24
APR. 6	3	33	34	34	3	4	35	25	5	25	33	24
APR. 7	3	35	36	36	3	4	35	25	5	25	33	24
APR. 8	3	37	38	38	3	3	35	25	5	25	33	24
APR. 9	3	39	39	40	4	3	35	25	5	25	33	24
APR. 10	3	41	41	42	4	3	35	25	5	25	33	24
APR. 11	4	43	43	44	4	3	35	25	5	25	33	24
APR. 12	4	44	45	46	4	3	35	25	5	25	33	24
APR. 13	4	46	47	47	5	3	35	25	5	25	33	24
APR. 14	4	48	1	1	5	3	35	25	5	25	33	24
APR. 15	4	2	2	3	5	3	35	25	5	25	33	24
APR. 16	4	4	4	5	6	3	35	25	5	25	33	24
APR. 17	4	5	6	6	6	3	35	25	5	25	33	24
APR. 18	4	7	7	8	6	3	35	25	5	25	33	24
APR. 19	5	9	9	10	6	3	35	25	5	25	33	24
APR. 20	5	10	11	11	7	3	35	25	5	25	33	24
APR. 21	5	12	12	13	7	3	35	25	5	25	33	24
APR. 22	5	13	14	14	7	3	35	25	5	25	33	24
APR. 23	5	15	16	16	7	2	35	25	5	25	33	24
APR. 24	5	17	17	18	8	2	35	25	5	25	33	24
APR. 25	6	18	19	19	8	2	35	25	5	25	33	24
APR. 26	6	20	20	21	8	2	35	25	5	25	33	24
APR. 27	6	21	22	23	8	2	35	25	5	25	33	24
APR. 28	6	23	24	24	8	2	35	25	5	25	33	24
APR. 29	6	25	26	26	9	2	35	25	5	25	33	24
APR. 30	6	27	27	28	9	2	35	25	5	25	33	24

MOON 1 ☽ 12:01 A.M. TO 8:00 A.M. **MOON 2** ◑ 8:01 A.M. TO 4:00 P.M. **MOON 3** ● 4:01 P.M. TO 12:00 A.M.

Use only one "moon" number. Choose the column closest to your time of birth. If your place of birth is not on Eastern Standard Time, be sure to read "How to Convert to Eastern Standard Time" at the beginning of this section.

1969

May

June

Date & Time	SUN	MOON 1	MOON 2	MOON 3	MERCURY	VENUS	MARS	JUPITER	SATURN	URANUS	NEPTUNE	PLUTO
MAY 1	6	29	29	30	9	2	35	25	5	25	33	24
MAY 2	6	30	31	32	9	2	35	25	5	25	33	24
MAY 3	7	32	33	34	9	2	35	25	5	25	33	24
MAY 4	7	34	35	36	10	2	35	25	5	25	33	24
MAY 5	7	36	37	38	10	2	35	25	5	25	33	24
MAY 6	7	38	39	40	10	2	35	25	5	25	33	24
MAY 7	7	40	41	42	10	2	35	24	5	25	33	24
MAY 8	7	42	43	43	10	3	35	24	5	25	33	24
MAY 9	7	44	45	45	10	3	35	24	5	25	33	24
MAY 10	7	46	46	47	10	3	35	24	5	25	33	24
MAY 11	8	48	48	1	10	3	35	24	5	25	33	24
MAY 12	8	1	2	3	10	3	35	24	5	25	33	24
MAY 13	8	3	4	4	10	3	35	24	5	25	33	24
MAY 14	8	5	5	6	10	3	35	24	5	25	33	24
MAY 15	8	6	7	8	11	3	35	24	5	25	33	24
MAY 16	8	8	9	9	11	3	35	24	5	25	33	24
MAY 17	8	10	10	11	11	3	35	24	5	25	33	24
MAY 18	8	11	12	12	11	3	35	24	5	25	33	24
MAY 19	9	13	13	14	11	3	35	24	5	25	33	24
MAY 20	9	15	15	16	11	3	35	24	5	25	33	24
MAY 21	9	16	17	17	11	3	35	24	5	25	33	24
MAY 22	9	18	18	19	10	3	35	24	5	25	33	24
MAY 23	9	19	20	20	10	4	35	24	5	25	33	24
MAY 24	9	21	21	22	10	4	35	24	5	25	33	24
MAY 25	10	23	23	24	10	4	35	24	5	25	33	24
MAY 26	10	24	25	25	10	4	35	24	5	25	33	24
MAY 27	10	26	27	27	10	4	34	24	5	25	33	24
MAY 28	10	28	28	29	10	4	34	24	5	25	33	24
MAY 29	10	30	30	31	10	4	34	24	5	25	33	24
MAY 30	10	32	32	33	10	4	34	24	5	25	33	24
MAY 31	10	34	34	35	10	4	34	24	5	25	33	24

Date & Time	SUN	MOON 1	MOON 2	MOON 3	MERCURY	VENUS	MARS	JUPITER	SATURN	URANUS	NEPTUNE	PLUTO
JUN. 1	10	36	36	37	10	4	34	24	5	25	33	24
JUN. 2	10	38	38	39	10	5	34	24	5	25	33	24
JUN. 3	11	40	40	41	10	5	34	24	5	25	33	24
JUN. 4	11	42	42	43	10	5	34	24	6	25	33	24
JUN. 5	11	44	44	45	10	5	34	24	6	25	33	24
JUN. 6	11	45	46	47	10	5	34	24	6	25	33	24
JUN. 7	11	47	48	48	9	5	34	24	6	25	33	24
JUN. 8	11	1	2	2	9	5	34	24	6	25	33	24
JUN. 9	11	3	3	4	9	5	34	25	6	25	33	24
JUN. 10	11	4	5	6	9	5	34	25	6	25	33	24
JUN. 11	12	6	7	7	9	6	34	25	6	25	33	24
JUN. 12	12	8	8	9	9	6	34	25	6	25	33	24
JUN. 13	12	9	10	10	9	6	34	25	6	25	33	24
JUN. 14	12	11	11	12	9	6	34	25	6	25	33	24
JUN. 15	12	13	13	14	10	6	34	25	6	25	33	24
JUN. 16	12	14	15	15	10	6	34	25	6	25	33	24
JUN. 17	12	16	16	17	10	6	34	25	6	25	33	24
JUN. 18	12	17	18	18	10	6	34	25	6	25	33	24
JUN. 19	13	19	19	20	10	7	34	25	6	25	33	24
JUN. 20	13	20	21	22	10	7	33	25	6	25	33	24
JUN. 21	13	22	23	23	10	7	33	25	6	25	32	24
JUN. 22	13	24	24	25	10	7	33	25	6	25	32	24
JUN. 23	13	25	26	27	10	7	33	25	6	25	32	24
JUN. 24	13	27	28	28	10	7	33	25	6	25	32	24
JUN. 25	14	29	30	30	10	7	33	25	6	25	32	24
JUN. 26	14	31	31	32	11	7	33	25	6	25	32	24
JUN. 27	14	33	33	34	11	8	33	25	6	25	32	24
JUN. 28	14	35	35	36	11	8	33	25	6	25	32	24
JUN. 29	14	37	37	38	11	8	33	25	6	25	32	24
JUN. 30	14	39	39	40	11	8	33	25	6	25	32	24

MOON 1 ☽ 12:01 A.M. TO 8:00 A.M.　　**MOON 2** ◑ 8:01 A.M. TO 4:00 P.M.　　**MOON 3** ● 4:01 P.M. TO 12:00 A.M.

Use only one "moon" number. Choose the column closest to your time of birth. If your place of birth is not on Eastern Standard Time, be sure to read "How to Convert to Eastern Standard Time" at the beginning of this section.

1969

July

August

Date & Time	SUN	MOON 1	MOON 2	MOON 3	MERCURY	VENUS	MARS	JUPITER	SATURN	URANUS	NEPTUNE	PLUTO
JUL. 1	14	41	41	42	11	8	33	25	6	25	32	24
JUL. 2	14	43	43	44	12	8	33	25	6	25	32	24
JUL. 3	15	45	45	46	12	8	33	25	6	25	32	24
JUL. 4	15	47	47	48	12	9	33	25	6	25	32	24
JUL. 5	15	48	1	2	12	9	33	25	6	25	32	24
JUL. 6	15	2	3	3	9	9	33	25	6	25	32	24
JUL. 7	15	4	5	5	13	9	33	25	6	25	32	24
JUL. 8	15	6	6	7	13	9	33	25	6	25	32	24
JUL. 9	15	7	8	8	13	9	33	25	6	25	32	24
JUL. 10	15	9	9	10	13	9	33	25	6	25	32	24
JUL. 11	16	11	11	12	14	10	33	25	6	25	32	24
JUL. 12	16	12	13	13	14	10	33	25	6	25	32	24
JUL. 13	16	14	14	15	14	10	33	25	6	25	32	24
JUL. 14	16	15	16	16	15	10	33	25	6	25	32	24
JUL. 15	16	17	17	18	15	10	33	25	6	25	32	24
JUL. 16	16	18	19	20	15	10	33	25	6	25	32	24
JUL. 17	16	20	21	21	15	10	33	25	6	25	32	24
JUL. 18	16	22	22	23	16	11	33	25	6	25	32	24
JUL. 19	17	23	24	24	16	11	33	25	6	25	32	24
JUL. 20	17	25	26	26	16	11	33	25	6	25	32	24
JUL. 21	17	27	27	28	17	11	33	25	6	25	32	24
JUL. 22	17	28	29	30	17	11	33	25	6	25	32	24
JUL. 23	17	30	31	31	17	11	33	25	6	25	32	24
JUL. 24	17	32	33	33	17	11	33	25	6	25	32	24
JUL. 25	17	34	35	35	18	12	33	25	6	25	32	24
JUL. 26	18	36	37	37	18	12	33	25	6	25	32	24
JUL. 27	18	38	39	39	18	12	34	25	6	25	32	24
JUL. 28	18	40	41	41	18	12	34	25	6	25	32	24
JUL. 29	18	42	43	43	19	12	34	25	6	25	32	24
JUL. 30	18	44	45	45	19	12	34	25	6	25	32	24
JUL. 31	18	46	47	47	19	13	34	25	6	25	32	24

Date & Time	SUN	MOON 1	MOON 2	MOON 3	MERCURY	VENUS	MARS	JUPITER	SATURN	URANUS	NEPTUNE	PLUTO
AUG. 1	18	48	48	1	20	13	34	25	6	25	32	24
AUG. 2	18	2	2	3	20	13	34	25	6	25	32	24
AUG. 3	19	3	4	5	20	13	34	25	6	25	32	24
AUG. 4	19	5	6	6	20	13	34	25	6	25	32	24
AUG. 5	19	7	7	8	20	13	34	25	6	25	32	24
AUG. 6	19	9	9	10	21	14	34	25	6	25	32	24
AUG. 7	19	10	11	11	21	14	34	25	6	25	32	24
AUG. 8	19	12	12	13	21	14	34	25	6	25	32	24
AUG. 9	19	13	14	14	21	14	34	25	6	25	32	24
AUG. 10	19	15	15	16	22	14	34	26	6	25	32	24
AUG. 11	20	16	17	18	22	14	34	26	6	25	32	24
AUG. 12	20	18	19	19	22	14	34	26	6	25	32	24
AUG. 13	20	20	20	21	22	14	34	26	6	25	32	24
AUG. 14	20	21	22	22	23	15	34	26	6	25	32	24
AUG. 15	20	23	23	24	23	15	34	26	6	25	32	24
AUG. 16	20	25	25	26	23	15	34	26	6	25	32	24
AUG. 17	20	26	27	27	23	15	34	26	6	25	32	24
AUG. 18	20	28	29	29	23	15	35	26	6	25	32	24
AUG. 19	21	30	30	31	24	15	35	26	6	25	32	24
AUG. 20	21	32	32	33	24	16	35	26	6	25	32	24
AUG. 21	21	33	34	35	24	16	35	26	6	25	32	24
AUG. 22	21	35	36	36	24	16	35	26	6	25	32	24
AUG. 23	21	37	38	38	24	16	35	26	6	25	32	24
AUG. 24	21	39	40	40	24	16	35	26	6	25	32	24
AUG. 25	21	41	42	42	25	16	35	26	6	25	32	24
AUG. 26	22	43	44	44	25	17	35	26	6	25	32	24
AUG. 27	22	45	46	46	25	17	35	26	6	25	32	24
AUG. 28	22	47	48	48	25	17	35	26	6	25	32	24
AUG. 29	22	1	2	2	25	17	35	26	6	25	32	24
AUG. 30	22	3	3	4	25	17	35	26	6	25	32	24
AUG. 31	22	5	5	6	26	17	35	26	6	25	32	24

MOON 1 ◑ 12:01 A.M. TO 8:00 A.M.   **MOON 2** ◐ 8:01 A.M. TO 4:00 P.M.   **MOON 3** ● 4:01 P.M. TO 12:00 A.M.

Use only one "moon" number. Choose the column closest to your time of birth. If your place of birth is not on Eastern Standard Time, be sure to read "How to Convert to Eastern Standard Time" at the beginning of this section.

Date & Time	SUN	MOON 1	MOON 2	MOON 3	MERCURY	VENUS	MARS	JUPITER	SATURN	URANUS	NEPTUNE	PLUTO
SEP. 1	22	6	7	7	26	17	35	26	6	25	32	24
SEP. 2	22	8	9	9	26	18	36	26	6	25	32	24
SEP. 3	23	10	10	11	26	18	36	26	6	25	32	24
SEP. 4	23	11	12	12	26	18	36	26	6	25	32	24
SEP. 5	23	13	13	14	26	18	36	26	6	25	32	24
SEP. 6	23	14	15	15	26	18	36	26	6	25	32	24
SEP. 7	23	16	17	17	26	18	36	26	6	25	32	24
SEP. 8	23	18	18	19	27	19	36	26	6	25	32	24
SEP. 9	23	19	20	20	27	19	36	26	6	25	32	24
SEP. 10	23	21	21	22	27	19	36	26	6	25	32	24
SEP. 11	24	22	23	24	27	19	36	26	6	25	32	24
SEP. 12	24	24	25	25	27	19	36	26	6	25	32	24
SEP. 13	24	26	26	27	27	19	36	26	6	25	32	24
SEP. 14	24	28	28	29	27	20	36	26	6	25	32	24
SEP. 15	24	29	30	30	27	20	36	26	6	25	32	24
SEP. 16	24	31	32	32	27	20	37	26	6	25	32	24
SEP. 17	24	33	34	34	27	20	37	27	6	25	32	24
SEP. 18	24	35	35	36	27	20	37	27	6	25	32	24
SEP. 19	25	37	37	38	27	20	37	27	6	25	32	24
SEP. 20	25	39	39	40	27	20	37	27	6	25	32	24
SEP. 21	25	40	41	42	27	21	37	27	6	25	32	24
SEP. 22	25	42	43	44	27	21	37	27	6	26	32	24
SEP. 23	25	44	45	46	27	21	37	27	6	26	33	24
SEP. 24	25	46	47	47	26	21	37	27	6	26	33	24
SEP. 25	26	48	1	1	26	21	37	27	6	26	33	24
SEP. 26	26	2	3	3	26	21	37	27	6	26	33	24
SEP. 27	26	4	4	5	26	22	37	27	6	26	33	24
SEP. 28	26	6	6	7	26	22	38	27	6	26	33	24
SEP. 29	26	7	8	8	26	22	38	27	6	26	33	24
SEP. 30	26	9	10	10	26	22	38	27	6	26	33	24

Date & Time	SUN	MOON 1	MOON 2	MOON 3	MERCURY	VENUS	MARS	JUPITER	SATURN	URANUS	NEPTUNE	PLUTO
OCT. 1	26	11	11	12	26	22	38	27	6	26	33	24
OCT. 2	26	12	13	13	25	22	38	27	6	26	33	24
OCT. 3	27	14	14	15	25	23	38	27	6	26	33	24
OCT. 4	27	15	16	17	25	23	38	27	6	26	33	24
OCT. 5	27	17	18	18	25	23	38	27	6	26	33	24
OCT. 6	27	19	19	20	25	23	38	27	6	26	33	24
OCT. 7	27	20	21	21	25	23	38	27	6	26	33	24
OCT. 8	27	22	22	23	25	23	38	27	6	26	33	24
OCT. 9	27	24	24	25	25	24	39	27	6	26	33	24
OCT. 10	27	25	26	26	25	24	39	27	6	26	33	24
OCT. 11	28	27	27	28	25	24	39	27	6	26	33	24
OCT. 12	28	29	29	30	25	24	39	27	6	26	33	24
OCT. 13	28	31	31	32	25	24	39	27	6	26	33	24
OCT. 14	28	32	33	34	25	24	39	27	6	26	33	24
OCT. 15	28	34	35	36	25	25	39	27	6	26	33	24
OCT. 16	28	36	37	37	25	25	39	27	6	26	33	24
OCT. 17	28	38	39	39	25	25	39	27	6	26	33	24
OCT. 18	28	40	41	41	26	25	39	27	6	26	33	24
OCT. 19	29	42	43	43	26	25	39	27	6	26	33	24
OCT. 20	29	44	44	45	26	25	40	27	6	26	33	24
OCT. 21	29	46	46	47	26	26	40	27	6	26	33	24
OCT. 22	29	47	48	1	27	26	40	28	6	26	33	24
OCT. 23	29	1	2	3	27	26	40	28	6	26	33	24
OCT. 24	29	3	4	4	27	26	40	28	6	26	33	24
OCT. 25	29	5	6	6	27	26	40	28	6	26	33	24
OCT. 26	30	7	7	8	28	26	40	28	6	26	33	24
OCT. 27	30	8	9	10	28	27	40	28	6	26	33	24
OCT. 28	30	10	11	11	28	27	40	28	6	26	33	24
OCT. 29	30	12	12	13	28	27	40	28	6	26	33	24
OCT. 30	30	13	14	14	28	27	40	28	6	26	33	24
OCT. 31	30	15	15	16	29	27	41	28	6	26	33	24

MOON 1 ◑ 12:01 A.M. TO 8:00 A.M.   **MOON 2** ◐ 8:01 A.M. TO 4:00 P.M.   **MOON 3** ● 4:01 P.M. TO 12:00 A.M.
Use only one "moon" number. Choose the column closest to your time of birth. If your place of birth is not on Eastern Standard Time, be sure to read "How to Convert to Eastern Standard Time" at the beginning of this section.

Date & Time	SUN ☉	MOON 1 ◑	MOON 2 ◐	MOON 3 ●	MERCURY	VENUS	MARS	JUPITER	SATURN	URANUS	NEPTUNE	PLUTO
SEP. 1	22	6	7	7	26	17	35	26	6	25	32	24
SEP. 2	22	8	9	9	26	18	36	26	6	25	32	24
SEP. 3	23	10	10	11	26	18	36	26	6	25	32	24
SEP. 4	23	11	12	12	26	18	36	26	6	25	32	24
SEP. 5	23	13	13	14	26	18	36	26	6	25	32	24
SEP. 6	23	14	15	15	26	18	36	26	6	25	32	24
SEP. 7	23	16	17	17	26	18	36	26	6	25	32	24
SEP. 8	23	18	18	19	27	19	36	26	6	25	32	24
SEP. 9	23	19	20	20	27	19	36	26	6	25	32	24
SEP. 10	23	21	21	22	27	19	36	26	6	25	32	24
SEP. 11	24	22	23	24	27	19	36	26	6	25	32	24
SEP. 12	24	24	25	25	27	19	36	26	6	25	32	24
SEP. 13	24	26	26	27	27	19	36	26	6	25	32	24
SEP. 14	24	28	28	29	27	20	36	26	6	25	32	24
SEP. 15	24	29	30	30	27	20	36	26	6	25	32	24
SEP. 16	24	31	32	32	27	20	37	26	6	25	32	24
SEP. 17	24	33	34	34	27	20	37	27	6	25	32	24
SEP. 18	24	35	35	36	27	20	37	27	6	25	32	24
SEP. 19	25	37	37	38	27	20	37	27	6	25	32	24
SEP. 20	25	39	39	40	27	20	37	27	6	25	32	24
SEP. 21	25	40	41	42	27	21	37	27	6	25	32	24
SEP. 22	25	42	43	44	27	21	37	27	6	26	32	24
SEP. 23	25	44	45	46	27	21	37	27	6	26	33	24
SEP. 24	25	46	47	47	26	21	37	27	6	26	33	24
SEP. 25	26	48	1	1	26	21	37	27	6	26	33	24
SEP. 26	26	2	3	3	26	21	37	27	6	26	33	24
SEP. 27	26	4	4	5	26	22	37	27	6	26	33	24
SEP. 28	26	6	6	7	26	22	38	27	6	26	33	24
SEP. 29	26	7	8	8	26	22	38	27	6	26	33	24
SEP. 30	26	9	10	10	26	22	38	27	6	26	33	24

Date & Time	SUN ☉	MOON 1 ◑	MOON 2 ◐	MOON 3 ●	MERCURY	VENUS	MARS	JUPITER	SATURN	URANUS	NEPTUNE	PLUTO
OCT. 1	26	11	11	12	26	22	38	27	6	26	33	24
OCT. 2	26	12	13	13	25	22	38	27	6	26	33	24
OCT. 3	27	14	14	15	25	23	38	27	6	26	33	24
OCT. 4	27	15	16	17	25	23	38	27	6	26	33	24
OCT. 5	27	17	18	18	25	23	38	27	6	26	33	24
OCT. 6	27	19	19	20	25	23	38	27	6	26	33	24
OCT. 7	27	20	21	21	25	23	38	27	6	26	33	24
OCT. 8	27	22	22	23	25	23	38	27	6	26	33	24
OCT. 9	27	24	24	25	25	24	39	27	6	26	33	24
OCT. 10	27	25	26	26	25	24	39	27	6	26	33	24
OCT. 11	28	27	28	28	25	24	39	27	6	26	33	24
OCT. 12	28	29	29	30	25	24	39	27	6	26	33	24
OCT. 13	28	31	31	32	25	24	39	27	6	26	33	24
OCT. 14	28	32	33	34	25	24	39	27	6	26	33	24
OCT. 15	28	34	35	36	25	25	39	27	6	26	33	24
OCT. 16	28	36	37	37	26	25	39	27	6	26	33	24
OCT. 17	28	38	39	39	26	25	39	27	6	26	33	24
OCT. 18	28	40	41	41	26	25	39	27	6	26	33	24
OCT. 19	29	42	43	43	26	25	39	27	6	26	33	24
OCT. 20	29	44	44	45	26	25	40	27	6	26	33	24
OCT. 21	29	46	46	47	26	26	40	27	6	26	33	24
OCT. 22	29	47	48	1	27	26	40	28	6	26	33	24
OCT. 23	29	1	2	3	27	26	40	28	6	26	33	24
OCT. 24	29	3	4	4	27	26	40	28	6	26	33	24
OCT. 25	29	5	6	6	27	26	40	28	6	26	33	24
OCT. 26	30	7	7	8	28	26	40	28	6	26	33	24
OCT. 27	30	8	9	10	28	27	40	28	6	26	33	24
OCT. 28	30	10	11	11	28	27	40	28	6	26	33	24
OCT. 29	30	12	12	13	28	27	40	28	6	26	33	24
OCT. 30	30	13	14	14	28	27	40	28	6	26	33	24
OCT. 31	30	15	15	16	29	27	41	28	6	26	33	24

MOON 1 ◑ 12:01 A.M. TO 8:00 A.M. **MOON 2** ◐ 8:01 A.M. TO 4:00 P.M. **MOON 3** ● 4:01 P.M. TO 12:00 A.M.
Use only one "moon" number. Choose the column closest to your time of birth. If your place of birth is not on
Eastern Standard Time, be sure to read "How to Convert to Eastern Standard Time" at the beginning of this section.

1970-1979

1970s

Tiger Woods

★ ★ ★ BORN DECEMBER 30, 1975 ★ ★ ★

Brief Bio: This golf prodigy began playing the game at age two. He became the, biggest moneymaker in golf and the very first to win all four major tournaments at the same time.

Personology Profile:

SUN IN THE WEEK OF THE RULER
(CAPRICORN I)

※

Those born in this week know how to control their living and working situations. True rulers, they regard their home as their castle and like to see it running smoothly. Allergic to chaos, they run the risk of becoming control freaks. Unless they give up their tendency to make up other people's minds for them, they are likely to arouse resentments.

MOON IN THE WEEK OF THE ORIGINATOR
(SAGITTARIUS II)

※

Too often these individuals can isolate themselves in a fantasy world. Difficult to fathom, they are likely to spend long periods of time alone with their own thoughts and feelings. Because they do not easily fit into a category, they can be misunderstood and be seen to send out mixed signals. Knowing when to approach and when to avoid them is key to gaining their friendship.

MERCURY IN THE WEEK OF DOMINANCE
(CAPRICORN III)

※

Mercury can serve the purpose of this week by bringing structure and logic to the activities of daily life. With this position, the intellect is easily put in the service of pragmatism, allowing a high degree of control. Dominance here usually means dominating one's material rather than one's friends. In the workplace, it could denote a tidy agenda and an orderly work flow; at home, a spotless kitchen and everything in its place.

VENUS ON THE CUSP OF REVOLUTION
(SCORPIO-SAGITTARIUS CUSP)

※

Stormy scenes frequently punctuate the love lives of those with this Venus position. Very outspoken in their views about their partners, they are not long-suffering types and will not allow themselves to be trodden upon without protest and, ultimately, without separation and even divorce. Not unlike a combination of nitroglycerine and dynamite, their package bears the words "Handle with Extreme Care."

MARS IN THE WEEK OF NEW LANGUAGE
(GEMINI II)

※

Aggressive in speech, those with this Mars position will have to learn to tone down the rhetoric. Born salespeople and promoters, whether pushing a product or a person, even themselves, they are likely to make a strong impression. However, they can also alienate others with their pitch, particularly those who misunderstand where they are coming from.

JUPITER IN THE WEEK OF THE STAR
(ARIES II)

※

Self-expression is demanded here, even if the personality involved is a quiet one. Working behind the scenes will achieve as much success as being in the spotlight. The important thing is maintaining the central position, whether the principal player or not. Good luck comes easily here and cannot really be earned with hard work. Serendipity plays an important role.

SATURN ON THE CUSP OF OSCILLATION
(CANCER-LEO CUSP)

*

Saturn can have a positive effect here, evening out the swings of this cusp and granting the power to put both introvert and extrovert tendencies to good use. Thus, episodes of depression can serve as a window to self-knowledge; more manic phases can bring fun and vibrancy to one's life if modulated and not allowed to get out of control. Thus, more stability can be granted.

URANUS IN THE WEEK OF INTENSITY
(SCORPIO I)

*

The normally acute focus of this week can be undermined by Uranus's unpredictability and need for sudden, extreme change. An inability to concentrate can surface here, often during the most stressful of times. The result may be pursuing detours and byways which only take attention away from the principal matter at hand. An unexciting, methodical approach should be employed whenever this occurs.

NEPTUNE IN THE WEEK OF ORIGINALITY
(SAGITTARIUS II)

*

Few people outdo Sagittarius II in the scope of their imagination and depth of fantasy. These colorful individuals definitely dream in Technicolor. Those who are able to bring unconscious elements into their work are likely to achieve recognition for their highly idiosyncratic world view and for their artistic vision. Giving structure to such vision is usually their greatest challenge.

PLUTO IN THE WEEK OF SOCIETY
(LIBRA II)

*

The need of these individuals to isolate themselves should be countered by an attempt to become more socially active. A conscious effort will have to be made, however, because if given their preference, such people might just as soon decide to stay home. Joining community organizations and taking an active role in school, church and sporting activities is recommended.

Some Highlights of the Decade 1970-1979

- MAO TSE-TUNG PROCLAIMS A "CULTURAL REVOLUTION" IN CHINA.

- ISABEL PERON SUCCEEDS HER HUSBAND JUAN AS PRESIDENT OF ARGENTINA.

- THE WATERGATE INVESTIGATIONS AND OTHER CONVICTIONS ON TAX EVASION EVENTUALLY BRING DOWN THE NIXON PRESIDENCY, AND PRESIDENT RICHARD NIXON RESIGNS.

- AFTER RULING ETHIOPIA FOR 58 YEARS, EMPEROR HAILE SELASSIE IS DEPOSED BY THAT COUNTRY'S MILITARY.

- THE "RUMBLE IN THE JUNGLE," A BOXING MATCH BETWEEN MUHAMMAD ALI AND GEORGE FOREMAN, IS HELD IN KINSHASA, ZAIRE.

- IN THE WAKE OF THE WATERGATE SCANDAL, THE FREEDOM OF INFORMATION ACT IS PASSED, ALLOWING US CITIZENS TO HOLD THE GOVERNMENT ACCOUNTABLE BY REQUESTING PUBLIC DOCUMENTS AND RECORDS.

1970

January

Date & Time	SUN	MOON 1 ◗	MOON 2 ◖	MOON 3 ●	MERCURY	VENUS	MARS	JUPITER	SATURN	URANUS	NEPTUNE	PLUTO
JAN. 1	38	27	27	28	41	38	47	29	5	26	33	25
JAN. 2	38	28	29	30	41	38	47	29	5	26	33	25
JAN. 3	39	30	31	31	41	38	47	29	5	26	33	25
JAN. 4	39	32	33	33	41	38	47	29	5	26	33	25
JAN. 5	39	34	35	35	41	38	47	29	5	26	33	25
JAN. 6	39	36	37	37	41	38	47	29	5	26	33	25
JAN. 7	39	38	39	39	41	39	47	29	5	26	33	25
JAN. 8	39	40	41	41	41	39	47	29	5	26	33	25
JAN. 9	39	42	43	43	41	39	47	29	5	26	33	25
JAN. 10	40	44	45	45	41	39	48	29	5	26	33	25
JAN. 11	40	46	47	47	40	39	48	29	5	26	33	25
JAN. 12	40	48	1	1	40	39	48	29	5	26	33	25
JAN. 13	40	2	2	3	40	40	48	29	5	26	33	25
JAN. 14	40	4	4	5	40	40	48	29	5	26	33	25
JAN. 15	40	5	6	6	40	40	48	30	5	26	33	25
JAN. 16	40	7	8	8	40	40	48	30	5	26	33	25
JAN. 17	41	9	9	10	39	40	48	30	5	26	33	25
JAN. 18	41	10	11	11	39	40	48	30	5	26	33	25
JAN. 19	41	12	12	13	39	41	48	30	5	26	33	25
JAN. 20	41	14	14	15	39	41	1	30	5	26	33	25
JAN. 21	41	15	16	16	39	41	1	30	5	26	33	25
JAN. 22	41	17	17	18	39	41	1	30	5	26	33	25
JAN. 23	42	18	19	19	39	41	1	30	5	26	33	25
JAN. 24	42	20	20	21	39	41	1	30	5	26	33	25
JAN. 25	42	21	22	23	39	42	1	30	5	26	33	25
JAN. 26	42	23	24	24	39	42	1	30	5	26	33	25
JAN. 27	42	25	25	26	39	42	1	30	5	26	33	25
JAN. 28	42	26	27	27	39	42	1	30	5	26	33	25
JAN. 29	42	28	29	29	39	42	1	30	5	26	33	25
JAN. 30	42	30	30	31	39	42	1	30	5	26	33	25
JAN. 31	43	31	32	33	39	43	2	30	5	26	33	25

February

Date & Time	SUN	MOON 1 ◗	MOON 2 ◖	MOON 3 ●	MERCURY	VENUS	MARS	JUPITER	SATURN	URANUS	NEPTUNE	PLUTO
FEB. 1	43	33	34	34	39	43	2	30	5	26	33	25
FEB. 2	43	35	36	36	39	43	2	30	5	26	33	25
FEB. 3	43	37	38	38	39	43	2	30	5	26	33	25
FEB. 4	43	39	40	40	40	43	2	30	5	26	33	25
FEB. 5	43	41	42	42	40	43	2	30	5	26	33	25
FEB. 6	43	43	44	44	40	44	2	30	5	26	33	25
FEB. 7	43	45	46	46	40	44	2	30	5	26	33	25
FEB. 8	44	47	48	48	40	44	2	30	5	26	33	25
FEB. 9	44	1	2	2	40	44	2	30	5	26	33	25
FEB. 10	44	3	4	4	40	44	3	30	5	26	33	25
FEB. 11	44	5	5	6	41	44	3	30	5	26	33	25
FEB. 12	44	7	7	8	41	45	3	30	5	26	33	25
FEB. 13	44	8	9	9	41	45	3	30	5	26	33	25
FEB. 14	44	10	10	11	41	45	3	30	5	26	33	25
FEB. 15	44	12	12	13	41	45	3	30	5	26	33	25
FEB. 16	45	13	14	14	41	45	3	30	5	26	33	25
FEB. 17	45	15	15	16	42	45	3	30	5	26	33	25
FEB. 18	45	16	17	17	42	46	3	30	5	26	33	25
FEB. 19	45	18	18	19	42	46	3	30	5	26	33	25
FEB. 20	45	19	20	21	42	46	4	30	6	26	33	25
FEB. 21	45	21	22	22	42	46	4	30	6	26	33	25
FEB. 22	45	23	23	24	43	46	4	30	6	26	33	25
FEB. 23	46	24	25	25	43	46	4	30	6	26	33	25
FEB. 24	46	26	26	27	43	47	4	30	6	26	33	25
FEB. 25	46	28	28	29	43	47	4	30	6	26	33	25
FEB. 26	46	29	30	30	43	47	4	30	6	26	33	25
FEB. 27	46	31	32	32	44	47	4	30	6	26	33	25
FEB. 28	46	33	33	34	44	47	4	30	6	26	33	25

MOON 1 ◗ 12:01 A.M. TO 8:00 A.M.   **MOON 2** ◖ 8:01 A.M. TO 4:00 P.M.   **MOON 3** ● 4:01 P.M. TO 12:00 A.M.
Use only one "moon" number. Choose the column closest to your time of birth. If your place of birth is not on
Eastern Standard Time, be sure to read "How to Convert to Eastern Standard Time" at the beginning of this section.

1970

March

Date & Time	SUN	MOON 1	MOON 2	MOON 3	MERCURY	VENUS	MARS	JUPITER	SATURN	URANUS	NEPTUNE	PLUTO
MAR. 1	46	34	35	36	44	47	4	30	6	26	33	24
MAR. 2	46	36	37	38	44	48	5	30	6	26	33	24
MAR. 3	47	38	39	40	44	48	5	30	6	26	33	24
MAR. 4	47	40	41	41	45	48	5	30	6	26	33	24
MAR. 5	47	42	43	43	45	48	5	30	6	26	33	24
MAR. 6	47	44	45	45	45	48	5	30	6	26	33	24
MAR. 7	47	46	47	47	45	48	5	30	6	26	33	24
MAR. 8	47	48	1	1	45	1	5	30	6	26	33	24
MAR. 9	47	2	3	3	46	1	5	30	6	26	33	24
MAR. 10	47	4	5	5	46	1	5	30	6	26	33	24
MAR. 11	48	6	6	7	46	1	5	30	6	26	33	24
MAR. 12	48	8	8	9	46	1	5	30	6	26	33	24
MAR. 13	48	9	10	10	47	1	6	30	6	26	33	24
MAR. 14	48	11	12	12	47	2	6	30	6	26	33	24
MAR. 15	48	13	13	14	47	2	6	30	6	26	33	24
MAR. 16	48	14	15	15	47	2	6	30	6	26	33	24
MAR. 17	48	16	16	17	48	2	6	30	6	26	33	24
MAR. 18	48	17	18	18	48	2	6	30	6	26	33	24
MAR. 19	1	19	20	20	48	2	6	30	6	26	33	24
MAR. 20	1	21	21	22	48	3	6	30	6	26	33	24
MAR. 21	1	22	23	23	1	3	6	30	6	26	33	24
MAR. 22	1	24	24	25	1	3	6	30	6	26	33	24
MAR. 23	1	25	26	27	1	3	6	30	6	26	33	24
MAR. 24	1	27	28	28	1	3	7	30	6	26	33	24
MAR. 25	2	29	29	30	2	3	7	30	6	26	33	24
MAR. 26	2	31	31	32	2	4	7	30	6	26	33	24
MAR. 27	2	32	33	33	2	4	7	30	6	26	33	24
MAR. 28	2	34	35	35	3	4	7	30	6	26	33	24
MAR. 29	2	36	37	37	3	4	7	29	6	26	33	24
MAR. 30	2	38	38	39	3	4	7	29	6	26	33	24
MAR. 31	2	40	40	41	3	4	7	29	6	26	33	24

April

Date & Time	SUN	MOON 1	MOON 2	MOON 3	MERCURY	VENUS	MARS	JUPITER	SATURN	URANUS	NEPTUNE	PLUTO
APR. 1	2	42	42	43	4	5	7	29	6	26	33	24
APR. 2	2	43	44	45	4	5	7	29	6	26	33	24
APR. 3	3	45	46	47	4	5	8	29	6	26	33	24
APR. 4	3	47	48	1	4	5	8	29	6	26	33	24
APR. 5	3	1	2	3	5	5	8	29	6	26	33	24
APR. 6	3	3	4	4	5	5	8	29	6	26	33	24
APR. 7	3	5	6	6	5	6	8	29	6	26	33	24
APR. 8	3	7	7	8	5	6	8	29	6	26	33	24
APR. 9	3	9	9	10	6	6	8	29	6	26	33	24
APR. 10	3	10	11	12	6	6	8	29	6	26	33	24
APR. 11	4	12	13	13	6	6	8	29	6	26	33	24
APR. 12	4	14	14	15	6	6	8	29	6	26	33	24
APR. 13	4	15	16	16	6	7	8	29	6	26	33	24
APR. 14	4	17	17	18	7	7	9	29	6	26	33	24
APR. 15	4	19	19	20	7	7	9	29	6	26	33	24
APR. 16	4	20	21	21	7	7	9	29	6	26	33	24
APR. 17	4	22	22	23	7	7	9	29	6	26	33	24
APR. 18	4	23	24	24	7	7	9	29	6	26	33	24
APR. 19	5	25	25	26	7	8	9	29	6	26	33	24
APR. 20	5	27	27	28	8	8	9	29	6	26	33	24
APR. 21	5	28	29	29	8	8	9	29	6	26	33	24
APR. 22	5	30	31	31	8	8	9	29	6	26	33	24
APR. 23	5	32	32	33	8	8	9	29	6	26	33	24
APR. 24	5	34	34	35	8	8	9	29	6	26	33	24
APR. 25	6	35	36	37	8	9	10	29	6	26	33	24
APR. 26	6	37	38	39	8	9	10	29	6	26	33	24
APR. 27	6	39	40	40	8	9	10	29	6	26	33	24
APR. 28	6	41	42	42	8	9	10	29	7	26	33	24
APR. 29	6	43	44	44	8	9	10	29	7	26	33	24
APR. 30	6	45	45	46	8	9	10	29	7	26	33	24

MOON 1 ◐ 12:01 A.M. TO 8:00 A.M. **MOON 2** ◑ 8:01 A.M. TO 4:00 P.M. **MOON 3** ● 4:01 P.M. TO 12:00 A.M.
Use only one "moon" number. Choose the column closest to your time of birth. If your place of birth is not on Eastern Standard Time, be sure to read "How to Convert to Eastern Standard Time" at the beginning of this section.

1970

May   June

Date & Time	SUN	MOON 1	MOON 2	MOON 3	MERCURY	VENUS	MARS	JUPITER	SATURN	URANUS	NEPTUNE	PLUTO
MAY 1	6	47	47	48	8	10	10	29	7	26	33	24
MAY 2	6	1	1	2	8	10	10	29	7	26	33	24
MAY 3	7	2	3	4	8	10	10	29	7	26	33	24
MAY 4	7	4	5	6	8	10	10	29	7	26	33	24
MAY 5	7	6	7	7	8	10	10	29	7	26	33	24
MAY 6	7	8	9	9	8	10	11	29	7	26	33	24
MAY 7	7	10	10	11	8	10	11	29	7	26	33	24
MAY 8	7	11	12	13	7	11	11	29	7	26	33	24
MAY 9	7	13	14	14	7	11	11	29	7	26	33	24
MAY 10	7	15	15	16	7	11	11	29	7	26	33	24
MAY 11	8	16	17	17	7	11	11	29	7	26	33	24
MAY 12	8	18	19	19	7	11	11	29	7	26	33	24
MAY 13	8	20	20	21	7	11	11	29	7	26	33	24
MAY 14	8	21	22	22	7	12	11	29	7	26	33	24
MAY 15	8	23	23	24	7	12	11	29	7	26	33	24
MAY 16	8	24	25	25	7	12	11	29	7	26	33	24
MAY 17	8	26	27	27	7	12	12	29	7	26	33	24
MAY 18	8	28	28	29	7	12	12	29	7	26	33	24
MAY 19	9	29	30	31	7	12	12	29	7	26	33	24
MAY 20	9	31	32	32	7	13	12	29	7	26	33	24
MAY 21	9	33	34	34	7	13	12	29	7	26	33	24
MAY 22	9	35	36	36	7	13	12	29	7	26	33	24
MAY 23	9	37	37	38	7	13	12	29	7	26	33	24
MAY 24	9	39	39	40	7	13	12	29	7	26	33	24
MAY 25	10	41	41	42	7	13	12	29	7	26	33	24
MAY 26	10	43	43	44	7	14	12	29	7	26	33	24
MAY 27	10	44	45	46	7	14	12	29	7	26	33	24
MAY 28	10	46	47	48	7	14	13	29	7	26	33	24
MAY 29	10	48	1	1	7	14	13	29	7	26	33	24
MAY 30	10	2	3	3	7	14	13	29	7	26	33	24
MAY 31	10	4	4	5	7	14	13	29	7	26	33	24
JUN. 1	10	6	6	7	7	15	13	29	7	26	33	24
JUN. 2	10	7	8	9	7	15	13	29	7	26	33	24
JUN. 3	11	9	10	10	7	15	13	29	7	26	33	24
JUN. 4	11	11	11	12	8	15	13	29	7	26	33	24
JUN. 5	11	13	13	14	8	15	13	29	7	26	33	24
JUN. 6	11	14	15	15	8	15	13	29	7	26	33	24
JUN. 7	11	16	16	17	8	15	13	29	7	26	33	24
JUN. 8	11	17	18	19	8	16	13	28	7	26	33	24
JUN. 9	11	19	20	20	8	16	14	28	7	26	33	24
JUN. 10	11	21	21	22	8	16	14	28	7	26	33	24
JUN. 11	12	22	23	23	9	16	14	28	7	26	33	24
JUN. 12	12	24	24	25	9	16	14	28	7	26	33	24
JUN. 13	12	25	26	27	9	16	14	28	7	26	33	24
JUN. 14	12	27	28	28	9	17	14	28	7	26	33	24
JUN. 15	12	29	29	30	9	17	14	28	7	26	33	24
JUN. 16	12	30	31	32	9	17	14	28	7	26	33	24
JUN. 17	12	32	33	34	10	17	14	28	7	26	33	24
JUN. 18	12	34	35	35	10	17	14	28	7	26	33	24
JUN. 19	13	36	37	37	10	17	14	28	7	26	33	24
JUN. 20	13	38	39	39	10	18	15	28	7	26	33	24
JUN. 21	13	40	41	41	11	18	15	28	7	26	33	24
JUN. 22	13	42	43	43	11	18	15	28	7	26	33	24
JUN. 23	13	44	45	45	11	18	15	28	7	26	33	24
JUN. 24	13	46	46	47	11	18	15	28	7	26	33	24
JUN. 25	14	48	48	1	12	18	15	28	7	26	33	24
JUN. 26	14	2	2	3	12	18	15	28	7	26	33	24
JUN. 27	14	3	4	5	12	19	15	28	7	26	33	24
JUN. 28	14	5	6	6	12	19	15	28	7	26	33	24
JUN. 29	14	7	8	8	13	19	15	28	7	26	33	24
JUN. 30	14	9	9	10	13	19	15	28	8	26	33	24

MOON 1 ☽ 12:01 A.M. TO 8:00 A.M.   **MOON 2** ◑ 8:01 A.M. TO 4:00 P.M.   **MOON 3** ● 4:01 P.M. TO 12:00 A.M.
Use only one "moon" number. Choose the column closest to your time of birth. If your place of birth is not on Eastern Standard Time, be sure to read "How to Convert to Eastern Standard Time" at the beginning of this section.

1970

July

August

Date & Time	SUN ☉	MOON 1 ◐	MOON 2 ◑	MOON 3 ●	MERCURY	VENUS	MARS	JUPITER	SATURN	URANUS	NEPTUNE	PLUTO
JUL. 1	14	10	11	12	13	19	15	28	8	26	33	24
JUL. 2	14	12	13	13	14	19	16	28	8	26	33	24
JUL. 3	15	14	14	15	14	20	16	28	8	26	33	24
JUL. 4	15	15	16	16	14	20	16	28	8	26	33	24
JUL. 5	15	17	18	18	14	20	16	28	8	26	33	24
JUL. 6	15	19	19	20	15	20	16	28	8	26	33	24
JUL. 7	15	20	21	21	15	20	16	28	8	26	33	24
JUL. 8	15	22	22	23	15	20	16	28	8	26	33	24
JUL. 9	15	23	24	24	16	20	16	28	8	26	33	24
JUL. 10	15	25	25	26	16	21	16	28	8	26	33	24
JUL. 11	16	27	27	28	16	21	16	29	8	26	33	24
JUL. 12	16	28	29	29	16	21	16	29	8	26	33	24
JUL. 13	16	30	30	31	17	21	17	29	8	26	33	24
JUL. 14	16	32	32	33	17	21	17	29	8	26	33	24
JUL. 15	16	33	34	35	17	21	17	29	8	26	33	24
JUL. 16	16	35	36	37	17	22	17	29	8	26	33	24
JUL. 17	16	37	38	38	17	22	17	29	8	26	33	24
JUL. 18	16	39	40	40	18	22	17	29	8	26	33	24
JUL. 19	17	41	42	42	18	22	17	29	8	26	33	24
JUL. 20	17	43	44	45	18	22	17	29	8	26	33	24
JUL. 21	17	45	46	46	19	22	17	29	8	26	33	24
JUL. 22	17	47	48	48	19	22	17	29	8	26	33	24
JUL. 23	17	1	2	2	19	23	17	29	8	26	33	24
JUL. 24	17	3	4	4	19	23	17	29	8	26	33	24
JUL. 25	17	5	5	6	20	23	18	29	8	26	33	24
JUL. 26	18	7	7	8	20	23	18	29	8	26	33	24
JUL. 27	18	8	9	9	20	23	18	29	8	26	33	24
JUL. 28	18	10	11	11	20	23	18	29	8	26	33	24
JUL. 29	18	12	12	13	21	23	18	29	8	26	33	24
JUL. 30	18	13	14	14	21	24	18	29	8	26	33	24
JUL. 31	18	15	16	16	21	24	18	29	8	26	33	24

Date & Time	SUN ☉	MOON 1 ◐	MOON 2 ◑	MOON 3 ●	MERCURY	VENUS	MARS	JUPITER	SATURN	URANUS	NEPTUNE	PLUTO
AUG. 1	18	17	17	18	21	24	18	29	8	26	33	24
AUG. 2	18	18	19	19	21	24	18	29	8	26	33	24
AUG. 3	19	20	20	21	22	24	18	29	8	26	33	24
AUG. 4	19	21	22	22	22	24	18	29	8	26	33	24
AUG. 5	19	23	23	24	22	25	19	29	8	26	33	24
AUG. 6	19	24	25	26	22	25	19	29	8	26	33	24
AUG. 7	19	26	27	27	22	25	19	29	8	26	33	24
AUG. 8	19	28	28	29	22	25	19	29	8	26	33	24
AUG. 9	19	29	30	30	23	25	19	29	8	26	33	24
AUG. 10	19	31	32	32	23	25	19	29	8	26	33	24
AUG. 11	20	33	34	34	23	25	19	29	8	26	33	24
AUG. 12	20	35	35	36	23	26	19	29	8	26	33	24
AUG. 13	20	36	37	38	23	26	19	29	8	26	33	24
AUG. 14	20	38	39	40	23	26	19	29	8	26	33	24
AUG. 15	20	40	41	42	24	26	19	29	8	26	33	24
AUG. 16	20	42	43	44	24	26	19	29	8	26	33	24
AUG. 17	20	44	45	46	24	26	20	29	8	26	33	24
AUG. 18	20	46	47	48	24	26	20	29	8	26	33	24
AUG. 19	21	48	1	2	24	26	20	29	8	26	33	24
AUG. 20	21	2	3	4	24	27	20	29	8	26	33	24
AUG. 21	21	4	5	5	24	27	20	29	8	26	33	24
AUG. 22	21	6	7	7	24	27	20	29	8	26	33	24
AUG. 23	21	8	8	9	24	27	20	29	8	26	33	24
AUG. 24	21	10	10	11	24	27	20	29	8	26	33	24
AUG. 25	21	11	12	12	25	27	20	29	8	26	33	24
AUG. 26	22	13	14	14	25	27	20	29	8	26	33	24
AUG. 27	22	15	15	16	25	28	20	29	8	26	33	24
AUG. 28	22	16	17	17	25	28	20	29	8	26	33	24
AUG. 29	22	18	18	19	25	28	21	29	8	26	33	24
AUG. 30	22	19	20	20	25	28	21	29	8	26	33	24
AUG. 31	22	21	21	22	25	28	21	29	8	26	33	24

MOON 1 ◐ 12:01 A.M. TO 8:00 A.M.   **MOON 2** ◑ 8:01 A.M. TO 4:00 P.M.   **MOON 3** ● 4:01 P.M. TO 12:00 A.M.
Use only one "moon" number. Choose the column closest to your time of birth. If your place of birth is not on Eastern Standard Time, be sure to read "How to Convert to Eastern Standard Time" at the beginning of this section.

1970

September

Date & Time	SUN ☉	MOON 1 ☽	MOON 2 ☽	MOON 3 ●	MERCURY	VENUS	MARS	JUPITER	SATURN	URANUS	NEPTUNE	PLUTO
SEP. 1	22	23	23	24	25	28	21	29	8	26	33	25
SEP. 2	22	24	25	25	25	28	21	29	8	26	33	25
SEP. 3	23	26	26	27	25	28	21	29	8	26	33	25
SEP. 4	23	27	28	28	25	29	21	29	8	26	33	25
SEP. 5	23	29	29	30	24	29	21	29	8	26	33	25
SEP. 6	23	31	31	32	24	29	21	29	8	26	33	25
SEP. 7	23	32	33	33	24	29	21	29	8	26	33	25
SEP. 8	23	34	35	35	24	29	21	29	8	26	33	25
SEP. 9	23	36	36	37	24	29	21	29	8	26	33	25
SEP. 10	23	38	38	39	24	29	22	30	8	26	33	25
SEP. 11	24	39	40	41	24	29	22	30	8	26	33	25
SEP. 12	24	41	42	43	24	30	22	30	8	26	33	25
SEP. 13	24	43	44	45	24	30	22	30	8	26	33	25
SEP. 14	24	45	46	47	23	30	22	30	8	26	33	25
SEP. 15	24	47	48	1	23	30	22	30	8	26	33	25
SEP. 16	24	1	2	3	23	30	22	30	8	26	33	25
SEP. 17	24	3	4	5	23	30	22	30	8	26	33	25
SEP. 18	24	5	6	7	23	30	22	30	8	26	33	25
SEP. 19	25	7	8	8	23	30	22	30	8	26	33	25
SEP. 20	25	9	10	10	23	30	22	30	8	26	33	25
SEP. 21	25	11	11	12	23	31	22	30	8	26	33	25
SEP. 22	25	13	13	14	23	31	23	30	8	26	33	25
SEP. 23	25	14	15	15	23	31	23	30	8	26	33	25
SEP. 24	25	16	16	17	23	31	23	30	8	26	33	25
SEP. 25	26	17	18	18	23	31	23	30	8	26	33	25
SEP. 26	26	19	19	20	23	31	23	30	8	26	33	25
SEP. 27	26	21	21	22	23	31	23	30	8	26	33	25
SEP. 28	26	22	23	23	23	31	23	30	8	26	33	25
SEP. 29	26	24	24	25	23	31	23	30	8	26	33	25
SEP. 30	26	25	26	26	23	31	23	30	8	26	33	25

October

Date & Time	SUN ☉	MOON 1 ☽	MOON 2 ☽	MOON 3 ●	MERCURY	VENUS	MARS	JUPITER	SATURN	URANUS	NEPTUNE	PLUTO
OCT. 1	26	27	27	28	24	31	23	30	8	26	33	25
OCT. 2	26	29	29	30	24	32	23	30	8	26	33	25
OCT. 3	27	30	31	31	24	32	24	30	8	26	33	25
OCT. 4	27	32	32	33	24	32	24	30	8	26	33	25
OCT. 5	27	34	34	35	24	32	24	30	8	26	33	25
OCT. 6	27	35	36	37	25	32	24	30	8	26	33	25
OCT. 7	27	37	38	38	25	32	24	30	8	26	33	25
OCT. 8	27	39	40	40	25	32	24	30	8	26	33	25
OCT. 9	27	41	41	42	25	32	24	30	8	26	33	25
OCT. 10	27	43	43	44	26	32	24	30	8	26	33	25
OCT. 11	28	45	45	46	26	32	24	30	8	26	33	25
OCT. 12	28	47	47	48	26	32	24	30	8	26	33	25
OCT. 13	28	1	1	2	26	32	24	30	8	26	33	25
OCT. 14	28	3	3	4	26	32	24	30	8	26	33	25
OCT. 15	28	4	5	6	27	32	25	30	8	26	33	25
OCT. 16	28	6	7	7	27	32	25	30	8	26	33	25
OCT. 17	28	8	9	10	27	32	25	30	8	26	33	25
OCT. 18	28	10	11	11	27	32	25	31	8	26	33	25
OCT. 19	29	12	12	13	28	32	25	31	8	26	33	25
OCT. 20	29	14	14	15	28	32	25	31	8	26	33	25
OCT. 21	29	15	16	16	28	32	25	31	8	26	33	25
OCT. 22	29	17	17	18	28	32	25	31	8	26	33	25
OCT. 23	29	18	19	20	29	32	25	31	8	26	33	25
OCT. 24	29	20	21	21	29	32	25	31	8	26	33	25
OCT. 25	29	22	22	23	29	32	25	31	8	26	33	25
OCT. 26	30	23	24	24	29	32	25	31	8	26	33	25
OCT. 27	30	25	25	26	29	32	26	31	8	26	33	25
OCT. 28	30	26	27	27	30	32	26	31	8	26	33	25
OCT. 29	30	28	29	29	30	32	26	31	8	26	33	25
OCT. 30	30	30	30	31	30	32	26	31	8	26	33	25
OCT. 31	30	31	32	33	30	32	26	31	8	26	33	25

MOON 1 ☽ 12:01 A.M. TO 8:00 A.M.   **MOON 2 ☽ 8:01 A.M. TO 4:00 P.M.**   **MOON 3 ● 4:01 P.M. TO 12:00 A.M.**
Use only one "moon" number. Choose the column closest to your time of birth. If your place of birth is not on
Eastern Standard Time, be sure to read "How to Convert to Eastern Standard Time" at the beginning of this section.

Date & Time	SUN	MOON 1 ◖	MOON 2 ◑	MOON 3 ●	MERCURY	VENUS	MARS	JUPITER	SATURN	URANUS	NEPTUNE	PLUTO
NOV. 1	30	33	34	34	30	32	26	31	8	26	33	25
NOV. 2	30	35	36	36	31	32	26	31	8	26	33	25
NOV. 3	31	37	37	38	31	32	26	31	8	26	33	25
NOV. 4	31	39	39	40	31	32	26	31	8	26	33	25
NOV. 5	31	40	41	42	31	32	26	31	8	26	33	25
NOV. 6	31	42	43	43	32	32	26	31	8	26	33	25
NOV. 7	31	44	45	45	32	32	26	31	8	26	33	25
NOV. 8	31	46	47	47	32	31	27	31	8	26	33	25
NOV. 9	31	48	48	1	32	31	27	31	8	26	33	25
NOV. 10	31	2	2	3	32	31	27	31	8	26	33	25
NOV. 11	31	4	4	5	33	31	27	31	8	27	33	25
NOV. 12	32	6	6	7	33	31	27	31	8	27	33	25
NOV. 13	32	8	8	9	33	31	27	31	8	27	33	25
NOV. 14	32	9	10	11	33	31	27	31	7	27	33	25
NOV. 15	32	11	12	12	33	31	27	31	7	27	33	25
NOV. 16	32	13	14	14	34	31	27	31	7	27	33	25
NOV. 17	32	15	15	16	34	31	27	31	7	27	33	25
NOV. 18	32	16	17	17	34	31	27	31	7	27	33	25
NOV. 19	33	18	18	19	34	31	27	31	7	27	33	25
NOV. 20	33	20	20	21	34	31	28	31	7	27	33	25
NOV. 21	33	21	22	22	35	31	28	32	7	27	33	25
NOV. 22	33	23	23	24	35	30	28	32	7	27	33	25
NOV. 23	33	24	25	25	35	30	28	32	7	27	33	25
NOV. 24	33	26	26	27	35	30	28	32	7	27	33	25
NOV. 25	34	27	28	29	35	30	28	32	7	27	33	25
NOV. 26	34	29	30	30	36	30	28	32	7	27	33	25
NOV. 27	34	31	31	32	36	30	28	32	7	27	33	25
NOV. 28	34	33	33	34	36	30	28	32	7	27	33	25
NOV. 29	34	34	35	36	36	30	28	32	7	27	33	25
NOV. 30	34	36	37	37	36	30	28	32	7	27	33	25

Date & Time	SUN	MOON 1 ◖	MOON 2 ◑	MOON 3 ●	MERCURY	VENUS	MARS	JUPITER	SATURN	URANUS	NEPTUNE	PLUTO
DEC. 1	34	38	39	39	37	30	29	32	7	27	33	25
DEC. 2	34	40	41	41	37	30	29	32	7	27	33	25
DEC. 3	35	42	42	43	37	30	29	32	7	27	33	25
DEC. 4	35	44	44	45	37	30	29	32	7	27	33	25
DEC. 5	35	46	46	47	37	30	29	32	7	27	33	25
DEC. 6	35	47	48	1	37	30	29	32	7	27	33	25
DEC. 7	35	1	2	3	38	30	29	32	7	27	33	25
DEC. 8	35	3	4	4	38	30	29	32	7	27	33	25
DEC. 9	35	5	6	6	38	30	29	32	7	27	33	25
DEC. 10	35	7	7	8	38	30	29	32	7	27	33	25
DEC. 11	36	9	9	10	38	31	29	32	7	27	33	25
DEC. 12	36	11	11	12	38	31	29	32	7	27	33	25
DEC. 13	36	12	13	13	38	31	30	32	7	27	33	25
DEC. 14	36	14	15	15	39	31	30	32	7	27	33	25
DEC. 15	36	16	16	17	39	31	30	32	7	27	33	25
DEC. 16	36	17	18	18	39	31	30	32	7	27	33	25
DEC. 17	36	19	20	20	39	31	30	32	7	27	33	25
DEC. 18	36	21	21	22	39	31	30	32	7	27	33	25
DEC. 19	37	22	23	23	39	31	30	32	7	27	33	25
DEC. 20	37	24	24	25	39	31	30	32	7	27	33	25
DEC. 21	37	25	26	26	39	31	30	32	7	27	33	25
DEC. 22	37	27	27	28	39	31	30	33	7	27	33	25
DEC. 23	37	29	29	30	39	31	30	33	7	27	33	25
DEC. 24	37	30	31	31	39	31	30	33	7	27	33	25
DEC. 25	37	32	32	33	38	32	31	33	7	27	33	25
DEC. 26	38	34	34	35	38	32	31	33	7	27	33	25
DEC. 27	38	35	36	37	38	32	31	33	7	27	33	25
DEC. 28	38	37	38	39	38	32	31	33	7	27	33	25
DEC. 29	38	39	40	41	38	32	31	33	7	27	33	25
DEC. 30	38	41	42	42	38	32	31	33	7	27	33	25
DEC. 31	38	43	44	44	37	32	31	33	7	27	33	25

MOON 1 ◖ 12:01 A.M. TO 8:00 A.M.   **MOON 2** ◑ 8:01 A.M. TO 4:00 P.M.   **MOON 3** ● 4:01 P.M. TO 12:00 A.M.

Use only one "moon" number. Choose the column closest to your time of birth. If your place of birth is not on Eastern Standard Time, be sure to read "How to Convert to Eastern Standard Time" at the beginning of this section.

January

February

Date & Time	SUN ☉	MOON 1 ◗	MOON 2 ◖	MOON 3 ●	MERCURY	VENUS	MARS	JUPITER	SATURN	URANUS	NEPTUNE	PLUTO
JAN. 1	38	45	46	46	37	32	31	33	7	27	33	25
JAN. 2	38	47	48	48	37	32	31	33	7	27	33	25
JAN. 3	39	1	1	2	37	33	31	33	7	27	33	25
JAN. 4	39	3	3	4	37	33	31	33	7	27	33	25
JAN. 5	39	5	5	6	37	33	31	33	7	27	33	25
JAN. 6	39	6	7	8	37	33	31	33	7	27	33	25
JAN. 7	39	8	9	9	37	33	31	33	7	27	33	25
JAN. 8	39	10	11	11	37	33	32	33	7	27	33	25
JAN. 9	39	12	12	13	37	33	32	33	7	27	33	25
JAN. 10	40	13	14	15	37	33	32	33	7	27	33	25
JAN. 11	40	15	16	16	37	33	32	33	7	27	33	25
JAN. 12	40	17	17	18	37	34	32	33	7	27	33	25
JAN. 13	40	18	19	20	37	34	32	33	7	27	33	25
JAN. 14	40	20	21	21	37	34	32	33	7	27	33	25
JAN. 15	40	22	22	23	37	34	32	33	7	27	33	25
JAN. 16	40	23	24	24	37	34	32	33	7	27	33	25
JAN. 17	41	25	25	26	37	34	32	33	7	27	33	25
JAN. 18	41	26	27	27	37	34	33	33	7	27	33	25
JAN. 19	41	28	28	29	38	35	33	33	7	27	33	25
JAN. 20	41	30	30	31	38	35	33	33	7	27	33	25
JAN. 21	41	31	32	32	38	35	33	33	7	27	33	25
JAN. 22	41	33	34	35	38	35	33	33	7	27	33	25
JAN. 23	42	35	35	36	38	35	33	33	7	27	33	25
JAN. 24	42	37	37	38	38	35	33	33	7	27	33	25
JAN. 25	42	38	39	40	38	35	33	33	7	27	33	25
JAN. 26	42	40	41	42	39	35	33	33	7	27	33	25
JAN. 27	42	42	43	44	39	36	33	33	7	27	33	25
JAN. 28	42	44	45	46	39	36	33	33	7	27	33	25
JAN. 29	42	46	47	48	39	36	33	33	7	27	33	25
JAN. 30	42	48	1	2	39	36	34	33	7	27	33	25
JAN. 31	43	2	3	3	40	36	34	33	7	27	33	25

Date & Time	SUN ☉	MOON 1 ◗	MOON 2 ◖	MOON 3 ●	MERCURY	VENUS	MARS	JUPITER	SATURN	URANUS	NEPTUNE	PLUTO
FEB. 1	43	4	5	5	40	36	34	33	7	27	33	25
FEB. 2	43	6	7	7	40	36	34	33	7	27	33	25
FEB. 3	43	8	8	9	40	37	34	33	7	27	33	25
FEB. 4	43	10	10	11	40	37	34	33	7	27	33	25
FEB. 5	43	11	12	12	40	37	34	33	7	27	33	25
FEB. 6	43	13	14	14	41	37	34	33	7	27	33	25
FEB. 7	43	15	15	16	41	37	34	33	7	27	33	25
FEB. 8	44	16	17	17	41	37	34	33	7	27	33	25
FEB. 9	44	18	19	19	41	37	34	33	7	27	33	25
FEB. 10	44	20	20	21	41	38	35	34	7	27	33	25
FEB. 11	44	21	22	22	42	38	35	34	7	27	33	25
FEB. 12	44	23	23	24	42	38	35	34	7	27	33	25
FEB. 13	44	24	25	25	42	38	35	34	7	27	33	25
FEB. 14	44	26	26	27	42	38	35	34	7	27	33	25
FEB. 15	44	27	28	29	42	38	35	34	7	27	33	25
FEB. 16	45	29	30	30	43	39	35	34	7	27	33	25
FEB. 17	45	31	31	32	43	39	35	34	7	27	33	25
FEB. 18	45	32	33	33	43	39	35	34	7	27	33	25
FEB. 19	45	34	35	35	43	39	35	34	7	27	33	25
FEB. 20	45	36	36	37	44	39	35	34	7	27	33	25
FEB. 21	45	38	38	39	44	39	35	34	7	27	33	25
FEB. 22	45	39	40	41	44	39	35	34	7	27	33	25
FEB. 23	46	41	42	43	44	40	36	34	7	27	33	25
FEB. 24	46	43	44	45	44	40	36	34	7	27	33	25
FEB. 25	46	45	46	47	45	40	36	34	7	27	33	25
FEB. 26	46	47	48	1	45	40	36	34	7	27	33	25
FEB. 27	46	1	2	3	45	40	36	34	7	27	33	25
FEB. 28	46	3	4	5	45	40	36	34	7	27	33	25

MOON 1 ◗ 12:01 A.M. TO 8:00 A.M.   **MOON 2** ◖ 8:01 A.M. TO 4:00 P.M.   **MOON 3** ● 4:01 P.M. TO 12:00 A.M.
Use only one "moon" number. Choose the column closest to your time of birth. If your place of birth is not on Eastern Standard Time, be sure to read "How to Convert to Eastern Standard Time" at the beginning of this section.

Date & Time	SUN ☉	MOON 1 ◐	MOON 2 ◑	MOON 3 ●	MERCURY	VENUS	MARS	JUPITER	SATURN	URANUS	NEPTUNE	PLUTO
MAR. 1	46	5	6	7	46	41	36	34	7	27	33	25
MAR. 2	46	7	8	9	46	41	36	34	7	27	33	25
MAR. 3	47	9	10	10	46	41	36	34	7	27	33	25
MAR. 4	47	11	11	12	46	41	36	34	7	27	33	25
MAR. 5	47	13	13	14	47	41	36	34	7	27	33	25
MAR. 6	47	14	15	15	47	41	36	34	7	27	33	25
MAR. 7	47	16	16	17	47	41	37	34	7	27	33	25
MAR. 8	47	18	18	19	47	42	37	34	7	27	33	25
MAR. 9	47	19	20	20	48	42	37	34	7	27	33	25
MAR. 10	47	21	21	22	48	42	37	34	7	27	33	25
MAR. 11	48	22	23	23	48	42	37	34	7	27	33	25
MAR. 12	48	24	24	25	48	42	37	34	7	27	33	25
MAR. 13	48	25	26	27	1	42	37	34	7	27	33	25
MAR. 14	48	27	28	28	1	43	37	34	7	27	33	25
MAR. 15	48	29	29	30	1	43	37	34	7	27	33	25
MAR. 16	48	30	31	31	1	43	37	34	7	27	33	25
MAR. 17	48	32	32	33	2	43	37	34	7	27	33	25
MAR. 18	48	34	34	35	2	43	37	34	7	27	33	25
MAR. 19	1	35	36	36	2	43	38	34	7	27	33	25
MAR. 20	1	37	38	38	3	43	38	34	7	27	33	25
MAR. 21	1	39	39	40	3	44	38	34	8	27	33	25
MAR. 22	1	41	41	42	3	44	38	34	8	27	33	25
MAR. 23	1	43	43	44	3	44	38	34	8	27	33	25
MAR. 24	1	44	45	46	3	44	38	34	8	27	33	25
MAR. 25	2	46	47	48	4	44	38	34	8	27	33	25
MAR. 26	2	48	1	2	4	44	38	34	8	27	33	25
MAR. 27	2	3	3	4	4	45	38	34	8	27	33	25
MAR. 28	2	5	5	6	4	45	38	34	8	27	33	25
MAR. 29	2	7	7	8	4	45	38	34	8	27	33	25
MAR. 30	2	8	9	10	5	45	38	34	8	27	33	25
MAR. 31	2	10	11	12	5	45	38	34	8	27	33	25

Date & Time	SUN ☉	MOON 1 ◐	MOON 2 ◑	MOON 3 ●	MERCURY	VENUS	MARS	JUPITER	SATURN	URANUS	NEPTUNE	PLUTO
APR. 1	2	12	13	13	5	45	39	34	8	27	33	25
APR. 2	2	14	14	15	5	46	39	34	8	27	33	25
APR. 3	3	16	16	17	5	46	39	34	8	26	33	25
APR. 4	3	17	18	18	5	46	39	34	8	26	33	25
APR. 5	3	19	19	20	5	46	39	34	8	26	33	25
APR. 6	3	20	21	21	5	46	39	34	8	26	33	25
APR. 7	3	22	22	23	5	46	39	34	8	26	33	25
APR. 8	3	24	24	25	5	46	39	34	8	26	33	25
APR. 9	3	25	26	26	5	47	39	34	8	26	33	25
APR. 10	3	27	27	28	5	47	39	34	8	26	33	25
APR. 11	4	28	29	29	5	47	39	34	8	26	33	25
APR. 12	4	30	30	31	5	47	39	34	8	26	33	25
APR. 13	4	32	32	33	5	47	39	34	8	26	33	25
APR. 14	4	33	34	34	5	47	40	34	8	26	33	25
APR. 15	4	35	35	36	5	48	40	34	8	26	33	25
APR. 16	4	37	37	38	5	48	40	34	8	26	33	25
APR. 17	4	38	39	39	5	48	40	34	8	26	33	25
APR. 18	4	40	41	41	5	48	40	34	8	26	33	25
APR. 19	5	42	43	43	5	48	40	34	8	26	33	25
APR. 20	5	44	44	45	5	48	40	34	8	26	33	25
APR. 21	5	46	46	47	5	1	40	34	8	26	33	25
APR. 22	5	48	48	1	5	1	40	34	8	26	33	25
APR. 23	5	2	2	3	5	1	40	34	8	26	33	25
APR. 24	5	4	4	5	4	1	40	34	8	26	33	25
APR. 25	6	6	6	7	4	1	40	34	8	26	33	25
APR. 26	6	8	8	9	4	1	40	34	8	26	33	25
APR. 27	6	10	10	11	4	2	40	34	8	26	33	25
APR. 28	6	11	12	13	4	2	41	34	8	26	33	25
APR. 29	6	13	14	14	4	2	41	34	8	26	33	25
APR. 30	6	15	16	16	4	2	41	34	8	26	33	25

MOON 1 ◐ 12:01 A.M. TO 8:00 A.M.   **MOON 2 ◑ 8:01 A.M. TO 4:00 P.M.**   **MOON 3 ● 4:01 P.M. TO 12:00 A.M.**

Use only one "moon" number. Choose the column closest to your time of birth. If your place of birth is not on Eastern Standard Time, be sure to read "How to Convert to Eastern Standard Time" at the beginning of this section.

1971

May

Date & Time	SUN	MOON 1	MOON 2	MOON 3	MERCURY	VENUS	MARS	JUPITER	SATURN	URANUS	NEPTUNE	PLUTO
MAY 1	6	17	17	18	4	2	41	34	8	26	33	25
MAY 2	6	18	19	19	4	2	41	34	8	26	33	25
MAY 3	7	20	20	21	4	3	41	34	8	26	33	25
MAY 4	7	21	22	23	4	3	41	33	8	26	33	25
MAY 5	7	23	24	24	4	3	41	33	8	26	33	25
MAY 6	7	25	25	26	4	3	41	33	8	26	33	25
MAY 7	7	26	27	27	4	3	41	33	8	26	33	25
MAY 8	7	28	28	29	4	3	41	33	8	26	33	25
MAY 9	7	29	30	31	4	3	41	33	8	26	33	25
MAY 10	7	31	32	32	4	4	41	33	8	26	33	25
MAY 11	8	33	33	34	4	4	41	33	8	26	33	25
MAY 12	8	34	35	36	4	4	42	33	8	26	33	25
MAY 13	8	36	37	37	5	4	42	33	8	26	33	25
MAY 14	8	38	38	39	4	4	42	33	8	26	33	25
MAY 15	8	40	40	41	4	4	42	33	8	26	33	25
MAY 16	8	41	42	43	5	5	42	33	8	26	33	25
MAY 17	8	43	44	45	5	5	42	33	8	26	33	25
MAY 18	8	45	46	46	5	5	42	33	8	26	33	25
MAY 19	9	47	48	48	5	5	42	33	8	26	33	25
MAY 20	9	1	2	2	5	5	42	33	8	26	33	25
MAY 21	9	3	4	4	5	6	42	33	8	26	33	25
MAY 22	9	5	5	6	6	6	42	33	9	26	33	25
MAY 23	9	7	7	8	6	6	42	33	9	26	33	25
MAY 24	9	9	9	10	6	6	42	33	9	26	33	25
MAY 25	10	11	11	12	6	6	42	33	9	26	33	25
MAY 26	10	12	13	14	6	6	42	33	9	26	33	25
MAY 27	10	14	15	15	6	6	43	33	9	26	33	25
MAY 28	10	16	17	17	7	7	43	33	9	26	33	25
MAY 29	10	18	18	19	7	7	43	33	9	26	33	25
MAY 30	10	19	20	20	7	7	43	33	9	26	33	25
MAY 31	10	21	22	22	7	7	43	33	9	26	33	25

June

Date & Time	SUN	MOON 1	MOON 2	MOON 3	MERCURY	VENUS	MARS	JUPITER	SATURN	URANUS	NEPTUNE	PLUTO
JUN. 1	10	23	23	24	8	7	43	33	9	26	33	25
JUN. 2	10	24	25	25	8	7	43	33	9	26	33	25
JUN. 3	11	26	26	27	8	7	43	33	9	26	33	25
JUN. 4	11	27	28	28	8	8	43	33	9	26	33	25
JUN. 5	11	29	29	30	8	8	43	33	9	26	33	25
JUN. 6	11	31	31	32	9	8	43	33	9	26	33	25
JUN. 7	11	32	33	33	9	8	43	33	9	26	33	25
JUN. 8	11	34	35	35	9	8	43	33	9	26	33	25
JUN. 9	11	36	36	37	9	8	43	33	9	26	33	25
JUN. 10	11	37	38	39	10	9	43	33	9	26	33	25
JUN. 11	12	39	40	40	10	9	43	33	9	26	33	25
JUN. 12	12	41	42	42	10	9	43	33	9	26	33	25
JUN. 13	12	43	43	44	11	9	43	33	9	26	33	25
JUN. 14	12	45	45	46	11	9	43	33	9	26	33	25
JUN. 15	12	47	47	48	11	10	43	33	9	26	33	25
JUN. 16	12	48	1	2	11	10	43	33	9	26	33	25
JUN. 17	12	2	3	4	12	10	43	33	9	26	33	25
JUN. 18	12	4	5	6	12	10	43	33	9	26	33	25
JUN. 19	13	6	7	7	12	10	44	33	9	26	33	25
JUN. 20	13	8	9	9	13	10	44	33	9	26	33	25
JUN. 21	13	10	11	11	13	10	44	33	9	26	33	25
JUN. 22	13	12	12	13	13	11	44	33	9	26	33	25
JUN. 23	13	14	14	15	13	11	44	33	9	26	33	25
JUN. 24	13	15	16	17	14	11	44	33	9	26	33	25
JUN. 25	14	17	18	18	14	11	44	33	9	26	33	25
JUN. 26	14	19	19	20	14	11	44	33	9	26	33	25
JUN. 27	14	20	21	21	15	11	44	33	9	26	33	25
JUN. 28	14	22	23	23	15	12	44	33	9	26	33	25
JUN. 29	14	24	24	25	15	12	44	33	9	26	33	25
JUN. 30	14	25	26	26	15	12	44	33	9	26	33	25

MOON 1 ◖ 12:01 A.M. TO 8:00 A.M.　**MOON 2** ◐ 8:01 A.M. TO 4:00 P.M.　**MOON 3** ● 4:01 P.M. TO 12:00 A.M.
Use only one "moon" number. Choose the column closest to your time of birth. If your place of birth is not on Eastern Standard Time, be sure to read "How to Convert to Eastern Standard Time" at the beginning of this section.

1971

July

Date & Time	SUN	MOON 1	MOON 2	MOON 3	MERCURY	VENUS	MARS	JUPITER	SATURN	URANUS	NEPTUNE	PLUTO
JUL. 1	14	27	27	28	16	12	44	33	9	26	33	25
JUL. 2	14	28	29	29	16	12	44	33	9	26	33	25
JUL. 3	15	30	31	31	16	12	44	33	9	26	33	25
JUL. 4	15	32	32	33	16	13	44	33	9	26	33	25
JUL. 5	15	33	34	34	17	13	44	33	9	26	33	25
JUL. 6	15	35	36	36	17	13	44	33	9	26	33	25
JUL. 7	15	37	37	38	17	13	44	33	9	26	33	25
JUL. 8	15	39	39	40	17	13	44	33	9	26	33	25
JUL. 9	15	40	41	42	18	13	44	33	9	26	33	25
JUL. 10	15	42	43	44	18	14	44	33	9	26	33	25
JUL. 11	16	44	45	46	18	14	44	33	9	26	33	25
JUL. 12	16	46	47	47	18	14	44	33	9	26	33	25
JUL. 13	16	48	1	1	19	14	44	33	9	26	33	25
JUL. 14	16	2	3	3	19	14	44	33	9	26	33	25
JUL. 15	16	4	4	5	19	14	44	33	9	26	33	25
JUL. 16	16	6	6	7	19	14	44	33	9	26	33	25
JUL. 17	16	8	8	9	19	15	44	33	9	26	33	25
JUL. 18	16	9	10	11	20	15	44	33	9	26	33	25
JUL. 19	17	11	12	12	20	15	44	33	9	26	33	25
JUL. 20	17	13	14	14	20	15	44	33	9	26	33	25
JUL. 21	17	15	15	16	20	15	44	33	9	26	33	25
JUL. 22	17	17	17	18	20	15	44	33	9	26	33	25
JUL. 23	17	18	19	19	20	16	44	33	9	26	33	25
JUL. 24	17	20	20	21	21	16	44	33	9	26	33	25
JUL. 25	17	21	22	23	21	16	44	33	9	26	33	25
JUL. 26	18	23	24	24	21	16	44	33	9	26	33	25
JUL. 27	18	25	25	26	21	16	44	33	10	26	33	25
JUL. 28	18	26	27	27	21	16	44	33	10	26	33	25
JUL. 29	18	28	28	29	21	17	44	33	10	26	33	25
JUL. 30	18	29	30	31	21	17	44	33	10	26	33	25
JUL. 31	18	31	32	32	22	17	44	33	10	26	33	25

August

Date & Time	SUN	MOON 1	MOON 2	MOON 3	MERCURY	VENUS	MARS	JUPITER	SATURN	URANUS	NEPTUNE	PLUTO
AUG. 1	18	33	33	34	22	17	44	33	10	26	33	25
AUG. 2	18	34	35	36	22	17	44	33	10	26	33	25
AUG. 3	19	36	37	37	22	17	43	33	10	26	33	25
AUG. 4	19	38	39	39	22	18	43	33	10	26	33	25
AUG. 5	19	40	40	41	22	18	43	33	10	26	33	25
AUG. 6	19	42	42	43	22	18	43	33	10	26	33	25
AUG. 7	19	44	44	45	22	18	43	33	10	26	33	25
AUG. 8	19	45	46	47	22	18	43	33	10	26	33	25
AUG. 9	19	47	48	1	22	18	43	33	10	26	33	25
AUG. 10	19	1	2	3	22	19	43	33	10	26	33	25
AUG. 11	20	3	4	5	22	19	43	33	10	26	33	25
AUG. 12	20	5	6	7	22	19	43	33	10	26	33	25
AUG. 13	20	7	8	8	22	19	43	33	10	26	33	25
AUG. 14	20	9	10	10	22	19	43	33	10	26	33	25
AUG. 15	20	11	11	12	22	19	43	33	10	26	33	25
AUG. 16	20	13	13	14	22	20	43	33	10	26	33	25
AUG. 17	20	14	15	15	22	20	43	33	10	26	33	25
AUG. 18	20	16	17	17	22	20	43	33	10	26	33	25
AUG. 19	21	18	18	19	22	20	43	33	10	26	33	25
AUG. 20	21	19	20	20	22	20	43	33	10	26	33	25
AUG. 21	21	21	22	22	22	20	43	33	10	26	33	25
AUG. 22	21	23	23	24	22	21	43	33	10	26	33	25
AUG. 23	21	25	25	25	22	21	43	33	10	26	33	25
AUG. 24	21	26	26	27	22	21	43	33	10	26	33	25
AUG. 25	21	27	28	28	22	21	43	33	10	26	33	25
AUG. 26	22	29	29	30	21	21	43	33	10	26	33	25
AUG. 27	22	31	31	32	21	21	43	33	10	27	33	25
AUG. 28	22	32	33	33	21	22	43	33	10	27	33	25
AUG. 29	22	34	34	35	21	22	43	33	10	27	33	25
AUG. 30	22	35	36	37	21	22	43	33	10	27	33	25
AUG. 31	22	37	38	38	21	22	43	33	10	27	33	25

MOON 1 ◔ 12:01 A.M. TO 8:00 A.M.   **MOON 2** ◑ 8:01 A.M. TO 4:00 P.M.   **MOON 3** ● 4:01 P.M. TO 12:00 A.M.

Use only one "moon" number. Choose the column closest to your time of birth. If your place of birth is not on Eastern Standard Time, be sure to read "How to Convert to Eastern Standard Time" at the beginning of this section.

1971

September / October

Date & Time	☼ SUN	◖ MOON 1	◑ MOON 2	● MOON 3	MERCURY	VENUS	MARS	JUPITER	SATURN	URANUS	NEPTUNE	PLUTO
SEP. 1	22	39	40	40	21	22	43	33	10	27	33	25
SEP. 2	22	41	41	42	21	22	43	33	10	27	33	25
SEP. 3	23	43	43	44	21	23	43	33	10	27	33	25
SEP. 4	23	45	45	46	21	23	43	33	10	27	33	25
SEP. 5	23	47	47	48	21	23	43	33	10	27	33	25
SEP. 6	23	1	1	2	21	23	43	33	10	27	33	25
SEP. 7	23	3	3	4	21	23	43	33	10	27	33	25
SEP. 8	23	5	5	6	21	23	43	33	10	27	33	25
SEP. 9	23	7	7	8	21	24	43	33	10	27	33	25
SEP. 10	23	9	9	10	21	24	43	33	10	27	33	25
SEP. 11	24	10	11	12	21	24	43	33	10	27	33	25
SEP. 12	24	12	13	13	21	24	43	33	10	27	33	25
SEP. 13	24	14	15	15	21	24	43	33	10	27	33	25
SEP. 14	24	16	16	17	21	24	43	33	10	27	33	25
SEP. 15	24	17	18	18	22	25	43	33	10	27	33	25
SEP. 16	24	19	20	20	22	25	43	33	10	27	33	25
SEP. 17	24	21	21	22	22	25	43	33	10	27	33	25
SEP. 18	24	22	23	23	22	25	43	33	10	27	33	25
SEP. 19	25	24	24	25	22	25	43	33	10	27	33	25
SEP. 20	25	25	26	26	23	25	43	33	10	27	33	25
SEP. 21	25	27	27	28	23	26	43	33	10	27	33	25
SEP. 22	25	29	29	30	23	26	43	33	10	27	33	25
SEP. 23	25	30	31	31	23	26	43	33	10	27	33	25
SEP. 24	25	32	32	33	23	26	43	33	10	27	33	25
SEP. 25	26	33	34	34	24	26	43	33	10	27	33	25
SEP. 26	26	35	36	36	24	26	43	33	10	27	33	25
SEP. 27	26	37	37	38	24	27	43	33	10	27	33	25
SEP. 28	26	38	39	39	24	27	43	33	10	27	33	25
SEP. 29	26	40	41	41	25	27	43	33	10	27	33	25
SEP. 30	26	42	43	43	25	27	43	33	10	27	33	25
OCT. 1	26	44	44	45	25	27	43	33	10	27	33	25
OCT. 2	26	46	46	47	25	27	43	33	10	27	33	25
OCT. 3	27	48	48	1	26	28	43	33	10	27	33	25
OCT. 4	27	2	2	3	26	28	43	33	10	27	33	25
OCT. 5	27	4	4	5	26	28	43	33	10	27	33	25
OCT. 6	27	6	7	7	26	28	43	33	10	27	33	25
OCT. 7	27	8	8	9	27	28	43	33	10	27	33	25
OCT. 8	27	10	10	11	27	28	43	34	10	27	33	25
OCT. 9	27	12	12	13	27	29	43	34	10	27	33	25
OCT. 10	27	13	14	15	27	29	43	34	10	27	33	25
OCT. 11	28	15	16	16	28	29	43	34	10	27	33	25
OCT. 12	28	17	17	18	28	29	43	34	10	27	33	25
OCT. 13	28	19	19	20	28	29	43	34	10	27	33	25
OCT. 14	28	20	21	21	28	29	44	34	10	27	33	25
OCT. 15	28	22	22	23	28	30	44	34	10	27	33	25
OCT. 16	28	23	24	24	29	30	44	34	10	27	33	25
OCT. 17	28	25	26	26	29	30	44	34	10	27	33	25
OCT. 18	28	27	27	28	29	30	44	34	10	27	33	25
OCT. 19	29	28	29	29	29	30	44	34	10	27	33	25
OCT. 20	29	30	30	31	29	30	44	34	10	27	33	25
OCT. 21	29	31	32	32	30	31	44	34	10	27	33	25
OCT. 22	29	33	33	34	30	31	44	34	10	27	33	25
OCT. 23	29	35	35	36	30	31	44	34	10	27	33	25
OCT. 24	29	36	37	37	30	31	44	34	10	27	33	25
OCT. 25	29	38	38	39	31	31	44	34	10	27	33	25
OCT. 26	30	40	40	41	31	31	44	34	10	27	33	25
OCT. 27	30	41	42	43	31	32	44	34	10	27	33	25
OCT. 28	30	43	44	44	31	32	44	34	10	27	33	25
OCT. 29	30	45	46	46	31	32	44	34	10	27	33	25
OCT. 30	30	47	48	48	32	32	44	34	10	27	33	25
OCT. 31	30	1	2	2	32	32	45	34	10	27	33	25

MOON 1 ◖ 12:01 A.M. TO 8:00 A.M.   **MOON 2** ◑ 8:01 A.M. TO 4:00 P.M.   **MOON 3** ● 4:01 P.M. TO 12:00 A.M.

Use only one "moon" number. Choose the column closest to your time of birth. If your place of birth is not on Eastern Standard Time, be sure to read "How to Convert to Eastern Standard Time" at the beginning of this section.

Date & Time	SUN ☉	MOON 1 ◗	MOON 2 ◑	MOON 3 ●	MERCURY	VENUS	MARS	JUPITER	SATURN	URANUS	NEPTUNE	PLUTO
NOV. 1	30	3	4	4	32	32	45	34	10	27	33	25
NOV. 2	30	5	6	6	32	32	45	34	10	27	33	25
NOV. 3	31	7	8	8	32	33	45	34	10	27	33	25
NOV. 4	31	9	10	10	33	33	45	34	10	27	33	25
NOV. 5	31	11	12	12	33	33	45	34	10	27	33	25
NOV. 6	31	13	13	14	33	33	45	34	10	27	33	25
NOV. 7	31	15	15	16	33	33	45	34	10	27	33	25
NOV. 8	31	16	17	18	33	33	45	34	10	27	33	25
NOV. 9	31	18	19	19	34	34	45	34	10	27	33	25
NOV. 10	31	20	20	21	34	34	45	34	10	27	33	25
NOV. 11	31	21	22	22	34	34	45	34	10	27	33	25
NOV. 12	32	23	24	24	34	34	45	34	10	27	33	25
NOV. 13	32	25	25	26	34	34	45	34	10	27	33	25
NOV. 14	32	26	27	27	34	34	46	35	9	27	33	25
NOV. 15	32	28	28	29	35	35	46	35	9	27	33	25
NOV. 16	32	29	30	30	35	35	46	35	9	27	33	25
NOV. 17	32	31	31	32	35	35	46	35	9	27	33	25
NOV. 18	32	33	33	34	35	35	46	35	9	27	33	25
NOV. 19	33	34	35	35	35	35	46	35	9	27	33	25
NOV. 20	33	36	36	37	35	35	46	35	9	27	33	25
NOV. 21	33	37	38	39	36	36	46	35	9	27	33	25
NOV. 22	33	39	40	40	36	36	46	35	9	27	33	25
NOV. 23	33	41	41	42	36	36	46	35	9	27	33	25
NOV. 24	33	43	44	44	36	36	46	35	9	27	33	25
NOV. 25	34	44	45	46	36	36	46	35	9	27	33	25
NOV. 26	34	46	47	48	36	36	46	35	9	27	33	25
NOV. 27	34	48	1	1	36	37	47	35	9	27	33	25
NOV. 28	34	2	3	3	37	37	47	35	9	27	33	25
NOV. 29	34	4	5	5	37	37	47	35	9	27	33	25
NOV. 30	34	6	7	7	37	37	47	35	9	27	33	25

Date & Time	SUN ☉	MOON 1 ◗	MOON 2 ◑	MOON 3 ●	MERCURY	VENUS	MARS	JUPITER	SATURN	URANUS	NEPTUNE	PLUTO
DEC. 1	34	8	9	9	37	37	47	35	9	27	33	25
DEC. 2	34	10	11	11	37	37	47	35	9	27	33	25
DEC. 3	35	12	13	13	37	38	47	35	9	27	33	25
DEC. 4	35	14	14	15	37	38	47	35	9	27	33	25
DEC. 5	35	16	16	17	37	38	47	35	9	27	33	25
DEC. 6	35	17	18	19	37	38	47	35	9	27	33	25
DEC. 7	35	19	20	20	37	38	47	35	9	27	33	25
DEC. 8	35	21	21	22	36	38	47	35	9	27	33	25
DEC. 9	35	22	23	24	36	39	47	35	9	27	33	25
DEC. 10	35	24	25	25	36	39	48	35	9	27	33	25
DEC. 11	36	26	26	27	36	39	48	35	9	27	33	25
DEC. 12	36	27	28	28	36	39	48	35	9	27	33	25
DEC. 13	36	29	29	30	36	39	48	35	9	27	33	25
DEC. 14	36	30	31	32	35	39	48	35	9	27	33	25
DEC. 15	36	32	33	33	35	40	48	35	9	27	33	25
DEC. 16	36	34	34	35	35	40	48	35	9	27	33	25
DEC. 17	36	35	36	36	35	40	48	36	9	27	33	25
DEC. 18	36	37	38	38	35	40	48	36	9	27	33	25
DEC. 19	37	39	39	40	35	40	48	36	9	27	33	25
DEC. 20	37	40	41	42	35	40	48	36	9	27	33	25
DEC. 21	37	42	43	43	35	41	48	36	9	27	33	25
DEC. 22	37	44	45	45	35	41	1	36	9	27	33	25
DEC. 23	37	46	46	47	35	41	1	36	9	27	33	25
DEC. 24	37	48	48	1	35	41	1	36	9	27	33	25
DEC. 25	37	2	2	3	35	41	1	36	9	27	33	25
DEC. 26	38	3	4	5	35	41	1	36	9	27	33	25
DEC. 27	38	5	6	7	35	42	1	36	9	27	33	25
DEC. 28	38	7	8	9	35	42	1	36	9	27	33	25
DEC. 29	38	9	10	11	35	42	1	36	9	27	34	25
DEC. 30	38	11	12	12	35	42	1	36	9	27	34	25
DEC. 31	38	13	14	14	35	42	1	36	9	27	34	25

MOON 1 ◗ 12:01 A.M. TO 8:00 A.M.   **MOON 2** ◑ 8:01 A.M. TO 4:00 P.M.   **MOON 3** ● 4:01 P.M. TO 12:00 A.M.

Use only one "moon" number. Choose the column closest to your time of birth. If your place of birth is not on Eastern Standard Time, be sure to read "How to Convert to Eastern Standard Time" at the beginning of this section.

1972

January

Date & Time	SUN	MOON 1	MOON 2	MOON 3	MERCURY	VENUS	MARS	JUPITER	SATURN	URANUS	NEPTUNE	PLUTO
JAN. 1	38	15	16	16	35	42	1	36	9	27	34	25
JAN. 2	38	17	17	18	35	43	2	36	9	27	34	25
JAN. 3	39	18	19	20	36	43	2	36	9	27	34	25
JAN. 4	39	20	21	21	36	43	2	36	9	27	34	25
JAN. 5	39	22	22	23	36	43	2	36	9	27	34	25
JAN. 6	39	24	24	25	36	43	2	36	9	27	34	25
JAN. 7	39	25	26	26	36	43	2	36	9	27	34	25
JAN. 8	39	27	27	28	36	44	2	36	9	27	34	25
JAN. 9	39	28	29	29	37	44	2	36	9	27	34	25
JAN. 10	40	30	30	31	37	44	2	36	9	27	34	25
JAN. 11	40	31	32	33	37	44	2	36	9	27	34	25
JAN. 12	40	33	34	34	37	44	2	36	9	27	34	25
JAN. 13	40	35	35	36	37	44	2	36	9	27	34	25
JAN. 14	40	36	37	38	37	45	3	36	9	27	34	25
JAN. 15	40	38	39	39	38	45	3	36	9	27	34	25
JAN. 16	40	40	41	41	38	45	3	36	9	27	34	25
JAN. 17	41	42	42	43	38	45	3	36	9	27	34	25
JAN. 18	41	44	44	45	38	45	3	36	9	27	34	25
JAN. 19	41	45	46	47	38	45	3	36	9	27	34	25
JAN. 20	41	47	48	1	39	46	3	36	9	27	34	25
JAN. 21	41	1	2	2	39	46	3	37	9	27	34	25
JAN. 22	41	3	4	4	39	46	3	37	9	27	34	25
JAN. 23	42	5	6	6	39	46	3	37	9	27	34	25
JAN. 24	42	7	7	8	39	46	3	37	9	27	34	25
JAN. 25	42	9	9	10	40	46	4	37	9	27	34	25
JAN. 26	42	11	11	12	40	47	4	37	9	27	34	25
JAN. 27	42	12	13	14	40	47	4	37	9	27	34	25
JAN. 28	42	14	15	15	40	47	4	37	9	27	34	25
JAN. 29	42	16	17	17	40	47	4	37	9	27	34	25
JAN. 30	42	18	18	19	41	47	4	37	9	27	34	25
JAN. 31	43	20	20	21	41	47	4	37	9	27	34	25

February

Date & Time	SUN	MOON 1	MOON 2	MOON 3	MERCURY	VENUS	MARS	JUPITER	SATURN	URANUS	NEPTUNE	PLUTO
FEB. 1	43	21	22	22	41	47	4	37	9	27	34	25
FEB. 2	43	23	23	24	41	48	4	37	9	27	34	25
FEB. 3	43	25	25	26	41	48	4	37	9	27	34	25
FEB. 4	43	26	27	27	42	48	4	37	9	27	34	25
FEB. 5	43	28	28	29	42	48	4	37	9	27	34	25
FEB. 6	43	29	30	30	42	48	5	37	9	27	34	25
FEB. 7	43	31	31	32	42	48	5	37	9	27	34	25
FEB. 8	44	33	33	34	43	1	5	37	9	27	34	25
FEB. 9	44	34	35	35	43	1	5	37	9	27	34	25
FEB. 10	44	36	36	37	43	1	5	37	9	27	34	25
FEB. 11	44	37	38	39	43	1	5	37	9	27	34	25
FEB. 12	44	39	40	40	43	1	5	37	9	27	34	25
FEB. 13	44	41	42	42	44	1	5	37	9	27	34	25
FEB. 14	44	43	43	44	44	2	5	37	9	27	34	25
FEB. 15	44	45	45	46	44	2	5	37	9	27	34	25
FEB. 16	45	47	47	48	44	2	5	37	9	27	34	25
FEB. 17	45	1	1	2	45	2	6	37	9	27	34	25
FEB. 18	45	3	3	4	45	2	6	37	9	27	34	25
FEB. 19	45	4	5	6	45	2	6	37	9	27	34	25
FEB. 20	45	6	7	8	45	3	6	37	9	27	34	25
FEB. 21	45	8	9	10	46	3	6	37	9	27	34	25
FEB. 22	45	10	11	11	46	3	6	37	9	27	34	25
FEB. 23	46	12	13	13	46	3	6	37	9	27	34	25
FEB. 24	46	14	14	15	46	3	6	37	9	27	34	25
FEB. 25	46	16	16	17	47	3	6	37	9	27	34	25
FEB. 26	46	17	18	18	47	3	6	37	9	27	34	25
FEB. 27	46	19	20	20	47	4	6	37	9	27	34	25
FEB. 28	46	21	21	22	47	4	7	37	9	27	34	25
FEB. 29	46	22	23	23	48	4	7	37	9	27	34	25

MOON 1 ◗ 12:01 A.M. TO 8:00 A.M.   **MOON 2** ◑ 8:01 A.M. TO 4:00 P.M.   **MOON 3** ● 4:01 P.M. TO 12:00 A.M.
Use only one "moon" number. Choose the column closest to your time of birth. If your place of birth is not on Eastern Standard Time, be sure to read "How to Convert to Eastern Standard Time" at the beginning of this section.

1972

March

Date & Time	SUN	MOON 1	MOON 2	MOON 3	MERCURY	VENUS	MARS	JUPITER	SATURN	URANUS	NEPTUNE	PLUTO
MAR. 1	46	24	25	25	48	4	7	37	9	27	34	25
MAR. 2	46	26	26	27	48	4	7	38	9	27	34	25
MAR. 3	47	27	28	28	48	4	7	38	9	27	34	25
MAR. 4	47	29	29	30	1	5	7	38	9	27	34	25
MAR. 5	47	30	31	31	1	5	7	38	9	27	34	25
MAR. 6	47	32	33	33	1	5	7	38	9	27	34	25
MAR. 7	47	34	34	35	1	5	7	38	9	27	34	25
MAR. 8	47	35	36	36	2	5	7	38	9	27	34	25
MAR. 9	47	37	37	38	2	5	7	38	9	27	34	25
MAR. 10	47	39	39	40	2	5	7	38	9	27	34	25
MAR. 11	48	40	41	41	2	6	8	38	9	27	34	25
MAR. 12	48	42	43	43	2	6	8	38	9	27	34	25
MAR. 13	48	44	45	45	2	6	8	38	9	27	34	25
MAR. 14	48	46	46	47	3	6	8	38	9	27	34	25
MAR. 15	48	48	48	1	3	6	8	38	9	27	34	25
MAR. 16	48	2	2	3	3	6	8	38	9	27	34	25
MAR. 17	48	4	4	5	3	6	8	38	9	27	34	25
MAR. 18	48	6	6	7	3	7	8	38	9	27	34	25
MAR. 19	1	8	8	9	3	7	8	38	9	27	34	25
MAR. 20	1	10	10	11	3	7	8	38	9	27	34	25
MAR. 21	1	12	12	13	3	7	8	38	9	27	34	25
MAR. 22	1	13	14	15	3	7	8	38	9	27	34	25
MAR. 23	1	15	16	16	3	7	9	38	9	27	34	25
MAR. 24	1	17	17	18	3	7	9	38	9	27	34	25
MAR. 25	2	19	19	20	3	8	9	38	9	27	34	25
MAR. 26	2	20	21	21	3	8	9	38	9	27	34	25
MAR. 27	2	22	22	23	3	8	9	38	9	27	34	25
MAR. 28	2	24	24	25	3	8	9	38	9	27	34	25
MAR. 29	2	25	26	26	3	8	9	38	9	27	34	25
MAR. 30	2	27	27	28	3	8	9	38	9	27	34	25
MAR. 31	2	28	29	29	2	8	9	38	9	27	34	25

April

Date & Time	SUN	MOON 1	MOON 2	MOON 3	MERCURY	VENUS	MARS	JUPITER	SATURN	URANUS	NEPTUNE	PLUTO
APR. 1	2	30	30	31	2	9	9	38	9	27	34	25
APR. 2	2	32	32	33	2	9	9	38	9	27	34	25
APR. 3	3	33	34	34	2	9	10	38	9	27	34	25
APR. 4	3	35	35	36	2	9	10	38	9	27	34	25
APR. 5	3	36	37	37	2	9	10	38	9	27	34	25
APR. 6	3	38	39	39	2	9	10	38	9	27	34	25
APR. 7	3	40	40	41	2	9	10	38	9	27	34	25
APR. 8	3	41	42	43	2	10	10	38	9	27	34	25
APR. 9	3	43	44	44	2	10	10	38	9	27	34	25
APR. 10	3	45	46	46	2	10	10	38	9	27	34	25
APR. 11	4	47	48	48	2	10	10	38	9	27	34	25
APR. 12	4	1	2	2	1	10	10	38	9	27	34	25
APR. 13	4	3	4	4	1	10	10	38	10	27	34	25
APR. 14	4	5	6	6	1	10	11	38	10	27	34	25
APR. 15	4	7	8	8	1	10	11	38	10	27	34	25
APR. 16	4	9	10	10	1	11	11	38	10	27	34	25
APR. 17	4	11	12	12	2	11	11	38	10	27	34	25
APR. 18	4	13	14	14	2	11	11	38	10	27	34	25
APR. 19	5	15	15	16	2	11	11	38	10	27	34	25
APR. 20	5	16	17	18	2	11	11	38	10	27	34	25
APR. 21	5	18	19	19	2	11	11	38	10	27	34	25
APR. 22	5	20	20	21	2	11	11	38	10	27	34	25
APR. 23	5	22	22	23	2	11	11	38	10	27	34	25
APR. 24	5	23	24	24	2	11	11	38	10	27	34	25
APR. 25	6	25	25	26	2	12	11	38	10	27	34	25
APR. 26	6	26	27	27	2	12	12	38	10	27	34	25
APR. 27	6	28	29	29	2	12	12	38	10	27	34	25
APR. 28	6	30	30	31	2	12	12	38	10	27	34	25
APR. 29	6	31	32	32	3	12	12	38	10	27	34	25
APR. 30	6	33	33	34	3	12	12	38	10	27	34	25

MOON 1 ☽ 12:01 A.M. TO 8:00 A.M. **MOON 2** ☾ 8:01 A.M. TO 4:00 P.M. **MOON 3** ● 4:01 P.M. TO 12:00 A.M.

Use only one "moon" number. Choose the column closest to your time of birth. If your place of birth is not on Eastern Standard Time, be sure to read "How to Convert to Eastern Standard Time" at the beginning of this section.

1972

May

June

Date & Time	SUN	MOON 1	MOON 2	MOON 3	MERCURY	VENUS	MARS	JUPITER	SATURN	URANUS	NEPTUNE	PLUTO
MAY 1	6	34	35	35	3	12	12	38	10	27	34	25
MAY 2	6	36	36	37	3	12	12	38	10	27	34	25
MAY 3	7	38	38	39	3	12	12	38	10	27	34	25
MAY 4	7	39	40	40	3	12	12	38	10	27	34	25
MAY 5	7	41	41	42	3	13	12	38	10	27	34	25
MAY 6	7	43	43	44	4	13	12	38	10	27	34	25
MAY 7	7	44	45	46	4	13	12	38	10	27	34	25
MAY 8	7	46	47	47	4	13	13	38	10	27	34	25
MAY 9	7	48	1	1	4	13	13	38	10	27	34	25
MAY 10	7	2	3	3	4	13	13	38	10	27	34	25
MAY 11	8	4	5	5	5	13	13	38	10	27	34	25
MAY 12	8	6	7	7	5	13	13	38	10	27	34	25
MAY 13	8	8	9	9	5	13	13	38	10	27	34	25
MAY 14	8	10	11	11	5	13	13	38	10	27	34	25
MAY 15	8	12	13	13	5	13	13	38	10	27	34	25
MAY 16	8	14	15	15	6	13	13	38	10	27	34	25
MAY 17	8	16	16	17	6	13	13	38	10	27	34	25
MAY 18	8	18	18	19	6	13	13	38	10	27	34	25
MAY 19	9	19	20	21	6	13	14	38	10	27	34	25
MAY 20	9	21	22	22	7	13	14	38	10	27	34	25
MAY 21	9	23	23	24	7	14	14	38	10	27	33	25
MAY 22	9	24	25	25	7	14	14	38	10	27	33	25
MAY 23	9	26	27	27	7	14	14	38	10	27	33	25
MAY 24	9	28	28	29	7	14	14	38	10	27	33	25
MAY 25	10	29	30	30	8	14	14	38	10	27	33	25
MAY 26	10	31	31	32	8	14	14	38	10	27	33	25
MAY 27	10	32	33	33	8	14	14	38	10	27	33	25
MAY 28	10	34	34	35	9	14	14	38	10	27	33	25
MAY 29	10	36	36	37	9	14	14	38	10	27	33	25
MAY 30	10	37	38	38	9	14	14	38	10	27	33	25
MAY 31	10	39	39	40	10	14	15	38	10	27	33	25

Date & Time	SUN	MOON 1	MOON 2	MOON 3	MERCURY	VENUS	MARS	JUPITER	SATURN	URANUS	NEPTUNE	PLUTO
JUN. 1	10	40	41	42	10	14	15	38	10	27	33	25
JUN. 2	10	42	43	43	10	14	15	38	10	27	33	25
JUN. 3	11	44	44	45	10	13	15	38	10	27	33	25
JUN. 4	11	46	46	47	11	13	15	38	10	27	33	25
JUN. 5	11	47	48	1	11	13	15	38	10	27	33	25
JUN. 6	11	1	2	3	11	13	15	38	10	27	33	25
JUN. 7	11	3	4	5	12	13	15	38	10	27	33	25
JUN. 8	11	5	6	7	12	13	15	38	10	27	33	25
JUN. 9	11	7	8	9	12	13	15	38	10	27	33	25
JUN. 10	11	9	10	11	12	13	15	38	10	27	33	25
JUN. 11	12	11	12	12	13	13	15	38	10	27	33	25
JUN. 12	12	13	14	14	13	13	15	38	10	27	33	25
JUN. 13	12	15	16	16	13	13	16	38	11	27	33	25
JUN. 14	12	17	18	18	14	13	16	38	11	27	33	25
JUN. 15	12	19	19	20	14	13	16	38	11	27	33	25
JUN. 16	12	21	21	22	14	13	16	38	11	27	33	25
JUN. 17	12	22	23	23	14	13	16	38	11	27	33	25
JUN. 18	12	24	24	25	15	12	16	38	11	27	33	25
JUN. 19	13	26	26	27	15	12	16	38	11	27	33	25
JUN. 20	13	27	28	28	15	12	16	38	11	27	33	25
JUN. 21	13	29	29	30	15	12	16	37	11	27	33	25
JUN. 22	13	30	31	31	16	12	16	37	11	27	33	25
JUN. 23	13	32	32	33	16	12	17	37	11	27	33	25
JUN. 24	13	33	34	35	16	12	17	37	11	27	33	25
JUN. 25	14	35	36	36	16	12	17	37	11	27	33	25
JUN. 26	14	37	37	38	16	12	17	37	11	27	33	25
JUN. 27	14	38	39	39	17	12	17	37	11	27	33	25
JUN. 28	14	40	41	41	17	12	17	37	11	27	33	25
JUN. 29	14	42	42	43	17	12	17	37	11	27	33	25
JUN. 30	14	43	44	45	17	12	17	37	11	27	33	25

MOON 1 ◗ 12:01 A.M. TO 8:00 A.M.   **MOON 2** ◑ 8:01 A.M. TO 4:00 P.M.   **MOON 3** ● 4:01 P.M. TO 12:00 A.M.

Use only one "moon" number. Choose the column closest to your time of birth. If your place of birth is not on Eastern Standard Time, be sure to read "How to Convert to Eastern Standard Time" at the beginning of this section.

1972

July

August

Date & Time	SUN	MOON 1	MOON 2	MOON 3	MERCURY	VENUS	MARS	JUPITER	SATURN	URANUS	NEPTUNE	PLUTO
JUL. 1	14	45	46	46	17	12	17	37	11	27	33	25
JUL. 2	14	47	48	48	18	12	17	37	11	27	33	25
JUL. 3	15	1	1	2	18	11	17	37	11	27	33	25
JUL. 4	15	3	3	4	18	11	17	37	11	27	33	25
JUL. 5	15	5	5	6	18	11	18	37	11	27	33	25
JUL. 6	15	7	7	8	18	11	18	37	11	27	33	25
JUL. 7	15	8	9	10	18	11	18	37	11	27	33	25
JUL. 8	15	10	11	12	19	11	18	37	11	27	33	25
JUL. 9	15	12	13	14	19	11	18	37	11	27	33	25
JUL. 10	15	14	15	16	19	11	18	37	11	27	33	25
JUL. 11	16	16	17	17	19	11	18	37	11	27	33	25
JUL. 12	16	18	19	19	19	11	18	37	11	27	33	25
JUL. 13	16	20	20	21	19	11	18	37	11	27	33	25
JUL. 14	16	22	22	23	19	11	18	37	11	27	33	25
JUL. 15	16	23	24	24	19	11	18	37	11	27	33	25
JUL. 16	16	25	26	26	20	12	18	37	11	27	33	25
JUL. 17	16	27	27	28	20	12	19	37	11	27	33	25
JUL. 18	16	28	29	29	20	12	19	37	11	27	33	25
JUL. 19	17	30	30	31	20	12	19	37	11	27	33	25
JUL. 20	17	31	32	32	20	12	19	37	11	27	33	25
JUL. 21	17	33	34	34	20	12	19	37	11	27	33	25
JUL. 22	17	35	35	36	20	12	19	37	11	27	33	25
JUL. 23	17	36	37	37	20	12	19	37	11	27	33	25
JUL. 24	17	38	38	39	20	12	19	37	11	27	33	25
JUL. 25	17	40	40	41	20	12	19	37	11	27	33	25
JUL. 26	18	41	42	42	20	12	19	37	11	27	33	25
JUL. 27	18	43	44	44	20	12	19	37	11	27	33	25
JUL. 28	18	45	45	46	20	12	19	37	11	27	33	25
JUL. 29	18	47	47	48	20	12	20	37	11	27	33	25
JUL. 30	18	48	1	2	20	12	20	37	11	27	33	25
JUL. 31	18	2	3	4	20	12	20	37	11	27	33	25

Date & Time	SUN	MOON 1	MOON 2	MOON 3	MERCURY	VENUS	MARS	JUPITER	SATURN	URANUS	NEPTUNE	PLUTO
AUG. 1	18	4	5	5	20	13	20	37	11	27	33	25
AUG. 2	18	6	7	7	20	13	20	37	11	27	33	25
AUG. 3	19	8	9	9	19	13	20	37	11	27	33	25
AUG. 4	19	10	11	11	19	13	20	37	11	27	33	25
AUG. 5	19	12	12	13	19	13	20	37	11	27	33	25
AUG. 6	19	14	14	15	19	13	20	37	11	27	33	25
AUG. 7	19	16	16	17	19	13	20	37	11	27	33	25
AUG. 8	19	17	18	19	19	13	20	37	11	27	33	25
AUG. 9	19	19	20	20	19	13	20	37	11	27	33	25
AUG. 10	19	21	22	22	19	13	21	37	11	27	33	25
AUG. 11	20	23	23	24	19	13	21	37	11	27	33	25
AUG. 12	20	24	25	25	19	14	21	37	11	27	33	25
AUG. 13	20	26	27	27	19	14	21	37	11	27	33	25
AUG. 14	20	28	28	29	18	14	21	37	11	27	33	25
AUG. 15	20	29	30	30	18	14	21	37	11	27	33	25
AUG. 16	20	31	31	32	18	14	21	37	11	27	33	25
AUG. 17	20	32	33	34	18	14	21	37	11	27	33	25
AUG. 18	20	34	35	35	18	14	21	37	11	27	33	25
AUG. 19	21	36	36	37	18	14	21	37	11	27	33	25
AUG. 20	21	37	38	38	18	15	21	37	11	27	33	25
AUG. 21	21	39	39	40	18	15	21	37	12	27	33	25
AUG. 22	21	41	41	42	19	15	22	37	12	27	33	25
AUG. 23	21	42	43	44	19	15	22	37	12	27	33	25
AUG. 24	21	44	45	45	19	15	22	37	12	27	33	25
AUG. 25	21	46	47	47	19	15	22	37	12	27	33	25
AUG. 26	22	48	1	1	19	15	22	37	12	27	33	25
AUG. 27	22	2	2	3	19	15	22	37	12	27	33	25
AUG. 28	22	4	4	5	19	16	22	37	12	27	33	25
AUG. 29	22	6	6	7	19	16	22	37	12	27	33	25
AUG. 30	22	8	8	9	20	16	22	37	12	27	33	25
AUG. 31	22	9	10	11	20	16	22	37	12	27	33	25

MOON 1 ◐ 12:01 A.M. TO 8:00 A.M.　　**MOON 2** ◑ 8:01 A.M. TO 4:00 P.M.　　**MOON 3** ● 4:01 P.M. TO 12:00 A.M.

Use only one "moon" number. Choose the column closest to your time of birth. If your place of birth is not on Eastern Standard Time, be sure to read "How to Convert to Eastern Standard Time" at the beginning of this section.

September

Date & Time	SUN	MOON 1	MOON 2	MOON 3	MERCURY	VENUS	MARS	JUPITER	SATURN	URANUS	NEPTUNE	PLUTO
SEP. 1	22	11	12	13	20	16	22	37	12	27	33	25
SEP. 2	22	13	14	14	20	16	23	37	12	27	33	25
SEP. 3	23	15	16	16	20	16	23	37	12	27	33	25
SEP. 4	23	17	17	18	21	16	23	37	12	27	33	25
SEP. 5	23	19	19	20	21	17	23	37	12	27	33	25
SEP. 6	23	20	21	22	21	17	23	37	12	27	33	25
SEP. 7	23	22	23	23	21	17	23	37	12	27	33	25
SEP. 8	23	24	24	25	22	17	23	37	12	27	33	25
SEP. 9	23	25	26	27	22	17	23	37	12	27	33	25
SEP. 10	23	27	28	28	22	17	23	37	12	27	33	25
SEP. 11	24	29	29	30	22	17	23	37	12	27	33	25
SEP. 12	24	30	31	31	23	18	23	37	12	27	33	25
SEP. 13	24	32	32	33	23	18	23	37	12	27	33	25
SEP. 14	24	34	34	35	23	18	24	37	12	27	33	25
SEP. 15	24	35	36	36	23	18	24	37	12	27	33	25
SEP. 16	24	37	37	38	24	18	24	37	12	27	33	25
SEP. 17	24	38	39	39	24	18	24	37	12	27	33	25
SEP. 18	24	40	41	41	24	18	24	37	12	27	33	25
SEP. 19	25	42	42	43	24	18	24	37	12	27	33	25
SEP. 20	25	43	44	45	25	19	24	37	12	27	33	25
SEP. 21	25	45	46	47	25	19	24	37	12	27	33	25
SEP. 22	25	47	48	48	25	19	24	37	12	27	33	25
SEP. 23	25	1	2	2	25	19	24	37	12	27	33	25
SEP. 24	25	3	4	4	26	19	24	37	12	27	33	25
SEP. 25	26	5	6	6	26	19	24	37	12	27	33	25
SEP. 26	26	7	8	8	26	20	25	37	12	27	33	25
SEP. 27	26	9	10	10	26	20	25	37	12	27	33	25
SEP. 28	26	11	12	12	27	20	25	37	12	27	33	25
SEP. 29	26	13	13	14	27	20	25	37	12	27	33	25
SEP. 30	26	15	15	16	27	20	25	37	12	27	33	25

October

Date & Time	SUN	MOON 1	MOON 2	MOON 3	MERCURY	VENUS	MARS	JUPITER	SATURN	URANUS	NEPTUNE	PLUTO
OCT. 1	26	16	17	18	27	20	25	37	12	27	33	25
OCT. 2	26	18	19	19	27	20	25	37	12	27	33	25
OCT. 3	27	20	21	21	28	21	25	37	12	27	33	25
OCT. 4	27	22	22	23	28	21	25	37	12	27	33	25
OCT. 5	27	23	24	24	28	21	25	37	12	27	33	25
OCT. 6	27	25	26	26	28	21	25	37	12	27	33	25
OCT. 7	27	27	27	28	28	21	25	37	12	27	33	25
OCT. 8	27	28	29	29	29	21	26	37	12	27	33	25
OCT. 9	27	30	30	31	29	22	26	37	12	27	33	25
OCT. 10	27	31	32	33	29	22	26	37	12	27	33	25
OCT. 11	28	33	34	34	29	22	26	37	12	27	33	25
OCT. 12	28	35	35	36	30	22	26	37	12	27	33	25
OCT. 13	28	36	37	37	30	22	26	37	12	27	33	25
OCT. 14	28	38	38	39	30	22	26	37	12	27	33	25
OCT. 15	28	39	40	40	30	22	26	37	12	27	33	25
OCT. 16	28	41	42	42	30	23	26	37	12	27	33	25
OCT. 17	28	43	43	44	31	23	26	37	12	28	33	25
OCT. 18	28	45	45	46	31	23	26	37	12	28	33	25
OCT. 19	29	46	47	48	31	23	27	37	12	28	33	25
OCT. 20	29	48	1	2	31	23	27	37	12	28	33	25
OCT. 21	29	2	3	3	31	23	27	37	12	28	33	25
OCT. 22	29	4	5	6	31	24	27	37	12	28	33	25
OCT. 23	29	6	7	8	32	24	27	37	12	28	33	25
OCT. 24	29	8	9	10	32	24	27	37	12	28	33	25
OCT. 25	29	10	11	12	32	24	27	37	12	28	33	25
OCT. 26	30	12	13	13	32	24	27	37	12	28	33	25
OCT. 27	30	14	15	15	32	24	27	38	12	28	33	25
OCT. 28	30	16	17	17	33	25	27	38	12	28	33	25
OCT. 29	30	18	18	19	33	25	27	38	12	28	33	25
OCT. 30	30	20	20	21	33	25	27	38	12	28	33	25
OCT. 31	30	21	22	22	33	25	28	38	12	28	33	25

MOON 1 ☽ 12:01 A.M. TO 8:00 A.M.   **MOON 2** ◑ 8:01 A.M. TO 4:00 P.M.   **MOON 3** ● 4:01 P.M. TO 12:00 A.M.
Use only one "moon" number. Choose the column closest to your time of birth. If your place of birth is not on Eastern Standard Time, be sure to read "How to Convert to Eastern Standard Time" at the beginning of this section.

1972

November

Date & Time	SUN	MOON 1	MOON 2	MOON 3	MERCURY	VENUS	MARS	JUPITER	SATURN	URANUS	NEPTUNE	PLUTO
NOV. 1	30	23	23	24	33	25	28	38	12	28	34	25
NOV. 2	30	25	25	26	33	25	28	38	12	28	34	25
NOV. 3	31	26	27	27	33	25	28	38	12	28	34	25
NOV. 4	31	28	28	29	34	26	28	38	12	28	34	25
NOV. 5	31	29	30	31	34	26	28	38	12	28	34	25
NOV. 6	31	31	32	32	34	26	28	38	12	28	34	25
NOV. 7	31	33	33	34	34	26	28	38	12	28	34	25
NOV. 8	31	34	35	35	34	26	28	38	12	28	34	25
NOV. 9	31	36	36	37	34	26	28	38	12	28	34	25
NOV. 10	31	37	38	38	34	27	28	38	12	28	34	25
NOV. 11	31	39	39	40	34	27	29	38	12	28	34	25
NOV. 12	32	41	41	42	35	27	29	38	12	28	34	25
NOV. 13	32	42	43	43	35	27	29	38	12	28	34	25
NOV. 14	32	44	44	45	35	27	29	38	12	28	34	25
NOV. 15	32	46	46	47	35	27	29	38	11	28	34	25
NOV. 16	32	47	48	1	35	28	29	38	11	28	34	25
NOV. 17	32	1	2	3	35	28	29	38	11	28	34	25
NOV. 18	32	3	4	5	35	28	29	38	11	28	34	25
NOV. 19	33	5	6	7	35	28	29	38	11	28	34	25
NOV. 20	33	7	8	9	34	28	29	38	11	28	34	25
NOV. 21	33	9	10	11	34	28	29	38	11	28	34	25
NOV. 22	33	11	12	13	34	29	30	38	11	28	34	25
NOV. 23	33	13	14	15	34	29	30	38	11	28	34	25
NOV. 24	33	15	16	17	34	29	30	38	11	28	34	25
NOV. 25	34	17	18	18	34	29	30	38	11	28	34	25
NOV. 26	34	19	20	20	33	29	30	38	11	28	34	25
NOV. 27	34	21	21	22	33	29	30	38	11	28	34	25
NOV. 28	34	23	23	24	33	30	30	38	11	28	34	25
NOV. 29	34	24	25	25	33	30	30	38	11	28	34	26
NOV. 30	34	26	26	27	33	30	30	38	11	28	34	26

December

Date & Time	SUN	MOON 1	MOON 2	MOON 3	MERCURY	VENUS	MARS	JUPITER	SATURN	URANUS	NEPTUNE	PLUTO
DEC. 1	34	27	28	29	33	30	30	38	11	28	34	26
DEC. 2	34	29	30	30	33	30	30	38	11	28	34	26
DEC. 3	35	31	31	32	33	30	30	38	11	28	34	26
DEC. 4	35	32	33	33	32	31	31	39	11	28	34	26
DEC. 5	35	34	34	35	32	31	31	39	11	28	34	26
DEC. 6	35	35	36	36	32	31	31	39	11	28	34	26
DEC. 7	35	37	37	38	33	31	31	39	11	28	34	26
DEC. 8	35	39	39	40	33	31	31	39	11	28	34	26
DEC. 9	35	40	41	41	33	31	31	39	11	28	34	26
DEC. 10	35	42	42	43	33	32	31	39	11	28	34	26
DEC. 11	36	43	44	45	33	32	31	39	11	28	34	26
DEC. 12	36	45	46	46	33	32	31	39	11	28	34	26
DEC. 13	36	47	47	48	33	32	31	39	11	28	34	26
DEC. 14	36	1	1	2	33	32	31	39	11	28	34	26
DEC. 15	36	3	3	4	33	32	32	39	11	28	34	26
DEC. 16	36	4	5	6	33	33	32	39	11	28	34	26
DEC. 17	36	6	7	8	34	33	32	39	11	28	34	26
DEC. 18	36	8	9	10	34	33	32	39	11	28	34	26
DEC. 19	37	10	11	12	34	33	32	39	11	28	34	26
DEC. 20	37	12	13	14	34	33	32	39	11	28	34	26
DEC. 21	37	14	15	16	34	33	32	39	11	28	34	26
DEC. 22	37	16	17	18	34	34	32	39	11	28	34	26
DEC. 23	37	18	19	20	35	34	32	39	11	28	34	26
DEC. 24	37	20	21	21	35	34	32	39	11	28	34	26
DEC. 25	37	22	23	23	35	34	32	39	11	28	34	26
DEC. 26	38	24	24	25	35	34	33	39	11	28	34	26
DEC. 27	38	25	26	26	35	34	33	39	11	28	34	26
DEC. 28	38	27	28	28	35	35	33	39	11	28	34	26
DEC. 29	38	29	29	30	36	35	33	39	11	28	34	26
DEC. 30	38	30	31	31	36	35	33	39	11	28	34	26
DEC. 31	38	32	32	33	36	35	33	39	11	28	34	26

MOON 1 ☽ 12:01 A.M. TO 8:00 A.M.　　**MOON 2** ◑ 8:01 A.M. TO 4:00 P.M.　　**MOON 3** ● 4:01 P.M. TO 12:00 A.M.

Use only one "moon" number. Choose the column closest to your time of birth. If your place of birth is not on Eastern Standard Time, be sure to read "How to Convert to Eastern Standard Time" at the beginning of this section.

1973

January

Date & Time	SUN	MOON 1	MOON 2	MOON 3	MERCURY	VENUS	MARS	JUPITER	SATURN	URANUS	NEPTUNE	PLUTO
JAN. 1	38	33	34	34	36	35	33	39	11	28	34	26
JAN. 2	38	35	35	36	36	35	33	39	11	28	34	26
JAN. 3	39	37	37	38	37	36	33	39	11	28	34	26
JAN. 4	39	38	39	39	37	36	33	39	11	28	34	26
JAN. 5	39	40	40	41	37	36	33	39	11	28	34	26
JAN. 6	39	41	42	43	37	36	34	39	11	28	34	26
JAN. 7	39	43	44	44	37	36	34	40	11	28	34	26
JAN. 8	39	45	45	46	38	36	34	40	11	28	34	26
JAN. 9	39	46	47	48	38	37	34	40	11	28	34	26
JAN. 10	40	48	1	1	38	37	34	40	11	28	34	26
JAN. 11	40	2	3	3	38	37	34	40	11	28	34	26
JAN. 12	40	4	4	5	39	37	34	40	11	28	34	26
JAN. 13	40	6	6	7	39	37	34	40	11	28	34	26
JAN. 14	40	8	8	9	39	37	34	40	11	28	34	26
JAN. 15	40	10	10	11	39	38	34	40	11	28	34	26
JAN. 16	40	12	12	13	39	38	34	40	11	28	34	26
JAN. 17	41	13	14	15	40	38	35	40	11	28	34	26
JAN. 18	41	15	16	17	40	38	35	40	11	28	34	26
JAN. 19	41	17	18	19	40	38	35	40	11	28	34	26
JAN. 20	41	19	20	21	40	38	35	40	11	28	34	26
JAN. 21	41	21	22	22	40	39	35	40	11	28	34	26
JAN. 22	41	23	24	24	41	39	35	40	11	28	34	26
JAN. 23	42	25	25	26	41	39	35	40	11	28	34	26
JAN. 24	42	26	27	28	41	39	35	40	11	28	34	26
JAN. 25	42	28	29	29	41	39	35	40	11	28	34	26
JAN. 26	42	30	30	31	42	39	35	40	11	28	34	26
JAN. 27	42	31	32	32	42	40	35	40	11	28	34	26
JAN. 28	42	33	33	34	42	40	36	40	11	28	34	26
JAN. 29	42	34	35	36	42	40	36	40	11	28	34	26
JAN. 30	42	36	37	37	42	40	36	40	11	28	34	26
JAN. 31	43	38	38	39	43	40	36	40	11	28	34	26

February

Date & Time	SUN	MOON 1	MOON 2	MOON 3	MERCURY	VENUS	MARS	JUPITER	SATURN	URANUS	NEPTUNE	PLUTO
FEB. 1	43	39	40	40	43	40	36	40	11	28	34	26
FEB. 2	43	41	41	42	43	41	36	40	11	28	34	26
FEB. 3	43	43	43	44	43	41	36	40	11	28	34	26
FEB. 4	43	44	45	45	44	41	36	40	11	28	34	26
FEB. 5	43	46	47	47	44	41	36	40	11	28	34	26
FEB. 6	43	48	48	1	44	41	36	40	11	28	34	26
FEB. 7	43	2	2	3	44	41	36	40	11	28	34	26
FEB. 8	44	3	4	5	45	42	37	41	11	28	34	26
FEB. 9	44	5	6	7	45	42	37	41	11	28	34	26
FEB. 10	44	7	8	8	45	42	37	41	11	28	34	26
FEB. 11	44	9	10	10	45	42	37	41	11	28	34	26
FEB. 12	44	11	12	12	46	42	37	41	11	28	34	26
FEB. 13	44	13	13	14	46	42	37	41	11	28	34	26
FEB. 14	44	15	15	16	46	43	37	41	11	28	34	26
FEB. 15	44	17	17	18	46	43	37	41	11	28	34	25
FEB. 16	45	19	19	20	46	43	37	41	11	28	34	25
FEB. 17	45	20	21	22	47	43	37	41	11	28	34	25
FEB. 18	45	22	23	23	47	43	38	41	11	28	34	25
FEB. 19	45	24	25	25	47	43	38	41	11	28	34	25
FEB. 20	45	26	26	27	47	44	38	41	11	28	34	25
FEB. 21	45	27	28	29	48	44	38	41	11	28	34	25
FEB. 22	45	29	30	30	48	44	38	41	11	28	34	25
FEB. 23	46	31	31	32	48	44	38	41	11	28	34	25
FEB. 24	46	32	33	33	48	44	38	41	11	28	34	25
FEB. 25	46	34	34	35	48	44	38	41	11	28	34	25
FEB. 26	46	36	36	37	48	45	38	41	11	28	34	25
FEB. 27	46	37	38	38	48	45	38	41	11	28	34	25
FEB. 28	46	39	39	40	1	45	38	41	11	28	34	25

MOON 1 ◐ 12:01 A.M. TO 8:00 A.M.   **MOON 2** ◑ 8:01 A.M. TO 4:00 P.M.   **MOON 3** ● 4:01 P.M. TO 12:00 A.M.
Use only one "moon" number. Choose the column closest to your time of birth. If your place of birth is not on
Eastern Standard Time, be sure to read "How to Convert to Eastern Standard Time" at the beginning of this section.

1973

March

Date & Time	SUN	MOON 1	MOON 2	MOON 3	MERCURY	VENUS	MARS	JUPITER	SATURN	URANUS	NEPTUNE	PLUTO
MAR. 1	46	40	41	41	1	45	39	41	11	28	34	25
MAR. 2	46	42	43	43	1	45	39	41	11	28	34	25
MAR. 3	47	44	44	45	1	45	39	41	11	28	34	25
MAR. 4	47	45	46	47	1	46	39	41	11	28	34	25
MAR. 5	47	47	48	48	1	46	39	41	11	28	34	25
MAR. 6	47	1	2	2	1	46	39	41	11	28	34	25
MAR. 7	47	3	4	4	1	46	39	41	11	28	34	25
MAR. 8	47	5	5	6	1	46	39	41	11	28	34	25
MAR. 9	47	7	7	8	1	46	39	41	11	28	34	25
MAR. 10	47	9	9	10	48	47	39	41	11	28	34	25
MAR. 11	48	11	11	12	48	47	39	41	11	28	34	25
MAR. 12	48	12	13	14	48	47	40	41	11	28	34	25
MAR. 13	48	14	15	15	48	47	40	41	11	28	34	25
MAR. 14	48	16	17	17	48	47	40	41	11	28	34	25
MAR. 15	48	18	19	19	48	47	40	41	11	28	34	25
MAR. 16	48	20	20	21	48	48	40	42	11	28	34	25
MAR. 17	48	22	22	23	48	48	40	42	11	28	34	25
MAR. 18	48	23	24	25	48	48	40	42	11	28	34	25
MAR. 19	1	25	26	26	47	48	40	42	11	28	34	25
MAR. 20	1	27	27	28	47	48	40	42	11	28	34	25
MAR. 21	1	29	29	30	47	48	40	42	11	28	34	25
MAR. 22	1	30	31	31	47	1	41	42	11	28	34	25
MAR. 23	1	32	32	33	47	1	41	42	11	28	34	25
MAR. 24	1	33	34	34	47	1	41	42	11	28	34	25
MAR. 25	2	35	36	36	47	1	41	42	11	28	34	25
MAR. 26	2	37	37	38	47	1	41	42	11	28	34	25
MAR. 27	2	38	39	39	47	1	41	42	11	28	34	25
MAR. 28	2	40	40	41	47	2	41	42	11	28	34	25
MAR. 29	2	41	42	42	47	2	41	42	11	28	34	25
MAR. 30	2	43	44	44	47	2	41	42	11	28	34	25
MAR. 31	2	45	45	46	47	2	41	42	11	28	34	25

April

Date & Time	SUN	MOON 1	MOON 2	MOON 3	MERCURY	VENUS	MARS	JUPITER	SATURN	URANUS	NEPTUNE	PLUTO
APR. 1	2	47	47	48	47	2	41	42	11	28	34	25
APR. 2	2	48	1	2	47	2	42	42	11	28	34	25
APR. 3	3	2	3	4	47	3	42	42	11	28	34	25
APR. 4	3	4	5	5	47	3	42	42	11	28	34	25
APR. 5	3	6	7	7	47	3	42	42	11	28	34	25
APR. 6	3	8	9	9	48	3	42	42	11	28	34	25
APR. 7	3	10	11	11	48	3	42	42	11	28	34	25
APR. 8	3	12	13	13	48	3	42	42	11	28	34	25
APR. 9	3	14	14	15	48	4	42	42	11	28	34	25
APR. 10	3	16	16	17	48	4	42	42	11	28	34	25
APR. 11	4	18	18	19	48	4	42	42	11	28	34	25
APR. 12	4	19	20	21	48	4	43	42	11	28	34	25
APR. 13	4	21	22	22	48	4	43	42	11	28	34	25
APR. 14	4	23	23	24	1	4	43	42	11	28	34	25
APR. 15	4	25	25	26	1	4	43	42	11	28	34	25
APR. 16	4	26	27	27	1	5	43	42	11	28	34	25
APR. 17	4	28	29	29	1	5	43	42	11	28	34	25
APR. 18	4	30	30	31	1	5	43	42	11	28	34	25
APR. 19	5	31	32	32	1	5	43	42	11	28	34	25
APR. 20	5	33	33	34	2	5	43	42	11	28	34	25
APR. 21	5	34	35	36	2	5	43	42	11	28	34	25
APR. 22	5	36	37	37	2	6	43	42	11	28	34	25
APR. 23	5	38	38	39	2	6	44	42	11	28	34	25
APR. 24	5	39	40	40	2	6	44	42	11	28	34	25
APR. 25	6	41	41	42	3	6	44	42	11	28	34	25
APR. 26	6	42	43	44	3	6	44	42	11	28	34	25
APR. 27	6	44	45	45	3	6	44	42	11	28	34	25
APR. 28	6	46	46	47	3	6	44	42	11	28	34	25
APR. 29	6	48	48	1	3	7	44	42	11	28	34	25
APR. 30	6	1	2	3	4	7	44	42	11	28	34	25

MOON 1 ◗ 12:01 A.M. TO 8:00 A.M.   **MOON 2** ◖ 8:01 A.M. TO 4:00 P.M.   **MOON 3** ● 4:01 P.M. TO 12:00 A.M.

Use only one "moon" number. Choose the column closest to your time of birth. If your place of birth is not on Eastern Standard Time, be sure to read "How to Convert to Eastern Standard Time" at the beginning of this section.

1973

May

Date & Time	SUN	MOON 1	MOON 2	MOON 3	MERCURY	VENUS	MARS	JUPITER	SATURN	URANUS	NEPTUNE	PLUTO
MAY 1	6	3	4	5	4	7	44	42	11	28	34	25
MAY 2	6	5	6	7	4	7	44	42	11	28	34	25
MAY 3	7	7	8	9	4	7	44	42	11	28	34	25
MAY 4	7	9	10	11	5	8	45	42	11	28	34	25
MAY 5	7	11	12	13	5	8	45	42	11	28	34	25
MAY 6	7	13	14	15	5	8	45	42	11	28	34	25
MAY 7	7	15	16	16	5	8	45	42	11	28	34	25
MAY 8	7	17	18	18	5	8	45	42	12	28	34	25
MAY 9	7	19	20	20	6	8	45	42	12	28	34	25
MAY 10	7	21	21	22	6	9	45	42	12	28	34	25
MAY 11	8	22	23	24	6	9	45	43	12	28	34	25
MAY 12	8	24	25	25	7	9	45	43	12	28	34	25
MAY 13	8	26	26	27	7	9	45	43	12	28	34	25
MAY 14	8	28	28	29	7	9	46	43	12	28	34	25
MAY 15	8	29	30	30	7	9	46	43	12	28	34	25
MAY 16	8	31	31	32	8	10	46	43	12	28	34	25
MAY 17	8	32	33	34	8	10	46	43	12	28	34	25
MAY 18	8	34	35	35	8	10	46	43	12	28	34	25
MAY 19	9	36	36	37	9	10	46	43	12	28	34	25
MAY 20	9	37	38	38	9	10	46	43	12	28	34	25
MAY 21	9	39	39	40	9	10	46	43	12	28	34	25
MAY 22	9	40	41	41	9	11	46	43	12	28	34	25
MAY 23	9	42	42	43	10	11	46	43	12	28	34	25
MAY 24	9	44	44	45	10	11	46	43	12	28	34	25
MAY 25	10	45	46	46	11	11	47	43	12	28	34	25
MAY 26	10	47	48	48	11	11	47	43	12	28	34	25
MAY 27	10	1	1	2	11	11	47	43	12	28	34	25
MAY 28	10	3	3	4	11	12	47	43	12	28	34	25
MAY 29	10	4	5	6	11	12	47	43	12	28	34	25
MAY 30	10	6	7	8	12	12	47	43	12	28	34	25
MAY 31	10	8	9	10	12	12	47	43	12	28	34	25

June

Date & Time	SUN	MOON 1	MOON 2	MOON 3	MERCURY	VENUS	MARS	JUPITER	SATURN	URANUS	NEPTUNE	PLUTO
JUN. 1	10	10	11	12	12	12	47	43	12	28	34	25
JUN. 2	10	12	13	14	12	12	47	43	12	28	34	25
JUN. 3	11	14	15	16	13	13	47	43	12	28	34	25
JUN. 4	11	16	17	18	13	13	47	43	12	28	34	25
JUN. 5	11	18	19	20	13	13	48	43	12	28	34	25
JUN. 6	11	20	21	21	13	13	48	43	12	28	34	25
JUN. 7	11	22	23	23	14	13	48	43	12	28	34	25
JUN. 8	11	24	24	25	14	13	48	43	12	28	34	25
JUN. 9	11	26	26	27	14	14	48	43	12	28	34	25
JUN. 10	11	27	28	28	14	14	48	43	12	28	34	25
JUN. 11	12	29	29	30	15	14	48	43	12	28	34	25
JUN. 12	12	30	31	32	15	14	48	43	12	28	34	25
JUN. 13	12	32	33	33	15	14	48	43	12	28	34	25
JUN. 14	12	34	34	35	15	14	48	43	12	28	34	25
JUN. 15	12	35	36	36	15	15	48	43	12	27	34	25
JUN. 16	12	37	37	38	15	15	1	43	12	27	34	25
JUN. 17	12	38	39	39	16	15	1	43	12	27	34	25
JUN. 18	12	40	40	41	16	15	1	43	12	27	34	25
JUN. 19	13	42	42	43	16	15	1	43	12	27	34	25
JUN. 20	13	43	44	44	16	15	1	42	12	27	34	25
JUN. 21	13	45	45	46	16	15	1	42	12	27	34	25
JUN. 22	13	46	47	48	16	16	1	42	12	27	34	25
JUN. 23	13	48	1	1	17	16	1	42	12	27	34	25
JUN. 24	13	2	3	3	17	16	1	42	12	27	34	25
JUN. 25	14	4	4	5	17	16	1	42	12	27	34	25
JUN. 26	14	6	6	7	17	16	1	42	12	27	34	25
JUN. 27	14	8	8	9	17	16	2	42	12	27	34	25
JUN. 28	14	10	10	11	17	17	2	42	12	27	34	25
JUN. 29	14	12	12	13	17	17	2	42	12	27	34	25
JUN. 30	14	14	14	15	17	17	2	42	12	27	34	25

MOON 1 ☽ 12:01 A.M. TO 8:00 A.M. **MOON 2** ☽ 8:01 A.M. TO 4:00 P.M. **MOON 3** ● 4:01 P.M. TO 12:00 A.M.

Use only one "moon" number. Choose the column closest to your time of birth. If your place of birth is not on Eastern Standard Time, be sure to read "How to Convert to Eastern Standard Time" at the beginning of this section.

1973

July

August

Date & Time	SUN	MOON 1	MOON 2	MOON 3	MERCURY	VENUS	MARS	JUPITER	SATURN	URANUS	NEPTUNE	PLUTO
JUL. 1	14	16	16	17	17	17	2	42	12	27	34	25
JUL. 2	14	18	18	19	17	17	2	42	12	27	34	25
JUL. 3	15	19	20	21	17	17	2	42	12	27	34	25
JUL. 4	15	21	22	23	17	18	2	42	13	27	34	25
JUL. 5	15	23	24	24	17	18	2	42	13	27	34	25
JUL. 6	15	25	26	26	17	18	2	42	13	27	34	25
JUL. 7	15	27	27	28	17	18	2	42	13	27	34	25
JUL. 8	15	28	29	30	17	18	2	42	13	27	34	25
JUL. 9	15	30	31	31	17	18	3	42	13	28	34	25
JUL. 10	15	32	32	33	17	19	3	42	13	28	34	25
JUL. 11	16	33	34	34	17	19	3	42	13	28	34	25
JUL. 12	16	35	35	36	17	19	3	42	13	28	34	25
JUL. 13	16	36	37	37	17	19	3	42	13	28	34	25
JUL. 14	16	38	38	39	17	19	3	42	13	28	34	25
JUL. 15	16	40	40	41	17	19	3	42	13	28	34	25
JUL. 16	16	41	42	42	17	20	3	42	13	28	34	25
JUL. 17	16	43	43	44	17	20	3	42	13	28	34	25
JUL. 18	16	44	45	46	17	20	3	42	13	28	34	25
JUL. 19	17	46	47	47	17	20	3	42	13	28	34	25
JUL. 20	17	48	48	1	17	20	3	42	13	28	34	25
JUL. 21	17	1	2	3	17	20	3	42	13	28	34	25
JUL. 22	17	3	4	4	16	21	4	42	13	28	34	25
JUL. 23	17	5	6	6	16	21	4	42	13	28	34	25
JUL. 24	17	7	8	8	16	21	4	42	13	28	34	25
JUL. 25	17	9	9	10	16	21	4	42	13	28	34	25
JUL. 26	18	11	11	12	16	21	4	42	13	28	34	25
JUL. 27	18	13	13	14	16	21	4	42	13	28	34	25
JUL. 28	18	15	15	16	16	21	4	42	13	28	34	25
JUL. 29	18	17	17	18	16	22	4	42	13	28	34	25
JUL. 30	18	19	19	20	16	22	4	42	13	28	34	25
JUL. 31	18	21	21	22	16	22	4	42	13	28	34	25

Date & Time	SUN	MOON 1	MOON 2	MOON 3	MERCURY	VENUS	MARS	JUPITER	SATURN	URANUS	NEPTUNE	PLUTO
AUG. 1	18	23	23	24	16	22	4	42	13	28	34	25
AUG. 2	18	24	25	26	16	22	4	42	13	28	34	25
AUG. 3	19	26	27	27	16	22	4	42	13	28	34	25
AUG. 4	19	28	28	29	16	23	4	42	13	28	34	25
AUG. 5	19	30	30	31	16	23	5	42	13	28	34	25
AUG. 6	19	31	32	32	16	23	5	42	13	28	34	25
AUG. 7	19	33	33	34	16	23	5	42	13	28	34	25
AUG. 8	19	34	35	35	17	23	5	42	13	28	34	25
AUG. 9	19	36	36	37	17	23	5	42	13	28	34	25
AUG. 10	19	38	38	39	17	24	5	42	13	28	34	25
AUG. 11	20	39	40	40	17	24	5	42	13	28	34	25
AUG. 12	20	41	41	42	17	24	5	42	13	28	34	25
AUG. 13	20	42	43	43	17	24	5	42	13	28	34	25
AUG. 14	20	44	45	45	17	24	5	42	13	28	34	25
AUG. 15	20	46	46	47	18	24	5	42	13	28	34	25
AUG. 16	20	47	48	1	18	25	5	42	13	28	34	25
AUG. 17	20	1	2	2	18	25	5	42	13	28	34	25
AUG. 18	20	3	3	3	18	25	5	42	13	28	34	25
AUG. 19	21	5	5	6	19	25	5	42	13	28	34	25
AUG. 20	21	6	7	8	19	25	5	42	13	28	34	25
AUG. 21	21	8	9	10	19	25	5	42	13	28	34	25
AUG. 22	21	10	11	11	19	25	5	42	13	28	34	25
AUG. 23	21	12	13	13	20	26	6	42	13	28	34	25
AUG. 24	21	14	15	15	20	26	6	42	13	28	34	25
AUG. 25	21	16	17	17	20	26	6	42	13	28	34	25
AUG. 26	22	18	19	19	20	26	6	42	13	28	34	25
AUG. 27	22	20	20	21	21	26	6	41	13	28	34	25
AUG. 28	22	22	22	23	21	26	6	41	13	28	34	25
AUG. 29	22	24	24	25	21	27	6	41	13	28	34	25
AUG. 30	22	25	26	27	21	27	6	41	13	28	34	25
AUG. 31	22	27	28	28	22	27	6	41	13	28	34	25

MOON 1 ☽ 12:01 A.M. TO 8:00 A.M.   **MOON 2** ☽ 8:01 A.M. TO 4:00 P.M.   **MOON 3** ● 4:01 P.M. TO 12:00 A.M.

Use only one "moon" number. Choose the column closest to your time of birth. If your place of birth is not on Eastern Standard Time, be sure to read "How to Convert to Eastern Standard Time" at the beginning of this section.

1973

September — October

Date & Time	SUN	MOON 1	MOON 2	MOON 3	MERCURY	VENUS	MARS	JUPITER	SATURN	URANUS	NEPTUNE	PLUTO
SEP. 1	22	29	30	30	22	27	6	41	13	28	34	25
SEP. 2	22	31	31	32	22	27	6	41	13	28	34	25
SEP. 3	23	32	33	33	22	27	6	41	13	28	34	25
SEP. 4	23	34	34	35	23	28	6	41	13	28	34	25
SEP. 5	23	35	36	37	23	28	6	41	13	28	34	25
SEP. 6	23	37	38	38	23	28	6	41	13	28	34	25
SEP. 7	23	39	39	40	23	28	6	41	13	28	34	25
SEP. 8	23	40	41	41	24	28	6	41	13	28	34	25
SEP. 9	23	42	42	43	24	28	6	41	13	28	34	25
SEP. 10	23	43	44	45	24	28	6	41	13	28	34	25
SEP. 11	24	45	46	46	24	29	6	41	13	28	34	25
SEP. 12	24	47	47	48	25	29	6	41	13	28	34	25
SEP. 13	24	1	1	2	25	29	6	41	13	28	34	25
SEP. 14	24	2	3	4	25	29	6	41	13	28	34	25
SEP. 15	24	4	5	5	25	29	6	41	13	28	34	25
SEP. 16	24	6	7	7	26	29	6	41	13	28	34	25
SEP. 17	24	8	9	9	26	30	6	41	13	28	34	25
SEP. 18	24	10	10	11	26	30	6	41	13	28	34	25
SEP. 19	25	12	12	13	26	30	6	41	14	28	34	25
SEP. 20	25	14	14	15	26	30	6	41	14	28	34	26
SEP. 21	25	15	16	17	27	30	6	41	14	28	34	26
SEP. 22	25	17	18	19	27	30	6	41	14	28	34	26
SEP. 23	25	19	20	20	27	30	6	41	14	28	34	26
SEP. 24	25	21	22	22	27	31	6	41	14	28	34	26
SEP. 25	26	23	24	24	27	31	6	41	14	28	34	26
SEP. 26	26	25	25	26	28	31	6	41	14	28	34	26
SEP. 27	26	27	27	28	28	31	6	41	14	28	34	26
SEP. 28	26	28	29	29	28	31	6	41	14	28	34	26
SEP. 29	26	30	31	31	28	31	6	41	14	28	34	26
SEP. 30	26	32	32	33	28	32	6	41	14	28	34	26
OCT. 1	26	33	34	34	29	32	6	41	14	28	34	26
OCT. 2	26	35	35	36	29	32	6	41	14	28	34	26
OCT. 3	27	37	37	38	29	32	6	41	14	28	34	26
OCT. 4	27	38	39	39	29	32	6	41	14	28	34	26
OCT. 5	27	40	40	41	29	32	6	41	14	28	34	26
OCT. 6	27	41	42	42	30	32	6	41	14	28	34	26
OCT. 7	27	43	43	44	30	33	6	41	14	28	34	26
OCT. 8	27	45	45	46	30	33	6	41	14	28	34	26
OCT. 9	27	46	47	47	30	33	6	41	14	28	34	26
OCT. 10	27	48	1	1	30	33	6	41	14	28	34	26
OCT. 11	28	2	2	3	30	33	6	41	14	28	34	26
OCT. 12	28	4	4	5	31	33	6	41	14	28	34	26
OCT. 13	28	5	6	7	31	34	6	41	14	28	34	26
OCT. 14	28	7	8	9	31	34	6	41	14	28	34	26
OCT. 15	28	9	10	11	31	34	6	41	14	28	34	26
OCT. 16	28	11	12	12	31	34	6	41	14	28	34	26
OCT. 17	28	13	14	14	31	34	6	41	14	28	34	26
OCT. 18	28	15	16	16	32	34	5	41	14	28	34	26
OCT. 19	29	17	17	18	32	34	5	41	14	28	34	26
OCT. 20	29	19	19	20	32	35	5	41	14	28	34	26
OCT. 21	29	21	21	22	32	35	5	41	14	28	34	26
OCT. 22	29	22	23	24	32	35	5	41	14	28	34	26
OCT. 23	29	24	25	25	32	35	5	41	14	28	34	26
OCT. 24	29	26	27	27	32	35	5	41	14	28	34	26
OCT. 25	29	28	28	29	32	35	5	41	14	28	34	26
OCT. 26	30	29	30	31	32	35	5	41	14	28	34	26
OCT. 27	30	31	32	32	32	36	5	41	14	28	34	26
OCT. 28	30	33	33	34	32	36	5	41	14	28	34	26
OCT. 29	30	34	35	35	33	36	5	41	14	28	34	26
OCT. 30	30	36	37	37	33	36	5	41	14	28	34	26
OCT. 31	30	38	38	39	33	36	5	41	14	28	34	26

MOON 1 ☽ 12:01 A.M. TO 8:00 A.M.   **MOON 2** ◑ 8:01 A.M. TO 4:00 P.M.   **MOON 3** ● 4:01 P.M. TO 12:00 A.M.

Use only one "moon" number. Choose the column closest to your time of birth. If your place of birth is not on Eastern Standard Time, be sure to read "How to Convert to Eastern Standard Time" at the beginning of this section.

1973

November

Date & Time	SUN	MOON 1	MOON 2	MOON 3	MERCURY	VENUS	MARS	JUPITER	SATURN	URANUS	NEPTUNE	PLUTO
NOV. 1	30	5	6	7	30	32	34	2	43	22	31	23
NOV. 2	30	7	8	9	30	32	34	2	43	22	31	23
NOV. 3	31	9	10	11	30	33	34	2	43	22	31	23
NOV. 4	31	11	12	13	30	33	34	2	43	22	31	23
NOV. 5	31	13	14	15	31	33	34	2	43	22	31	23
NOV. 6	31	15	16	16	31	33	34	2	43	22	31	23
NOV. 7	31	17	18	18	31	33	34	2	43	22	31	23
NOV. 8	31	19	19	20	31	33	34	2	43	22	31	23
NOV. 9	31	21	21	22	31	34	34	2	43	22	31	23
NOV. 10	31	22	23	23	32	34	34	2	43	22	31	23
NOV. 11	31	24	24	25	32	34	35	2	43	22	31	23
NOV. 12	32	26	26	27	32	34	35	2	43	22	31	23
NOV. 13	32	27	28	28	32	34	35	2	43	22	31	23
NOV. 14	32	29	29	30	32	34	35	2	43	22	31	23
NOV. 15	32	30	31	31	33	35	35	2	43	22	31	23
NOV. 16	32	32	32	33	33	35	35	2	43	22	31	23
NOV. 17	32	34	34	35	33	35	35	2	43	22	31	23
NOV. 18	32	35	36	36	33	35	35	2	43	22	31	23
NOV. 19	33	37	37	38	34	35	35	2	43	22	31	23
NOV. 20	33	38	39	39	34	35	35	2	43	22	31	23
NOV. 21	33	40	40	41	34	36	36	2	43	22	31	23
NOV. 22	33	42	42	43	34	36	36	2	43	22	31	23
NOV. 23	33	43	44	44	34	36	36	2	43	22	31	23
NOV. 24	33	45	46	46	35	36	36	2	43	22	31	23
NOV. 25	34	47	47	48	35	36	36	2	43	22	31	23
NOV. 26	34	1	1	2	35	36	36	2	43	22	31	23
NOV. 27	34	2	3	4	35	37	36	2	43	22	31	23
NOV. 28	34	4	5	6	35	37	36	2	43	22	31	23
NOV. 29	34	6	7	8	36	37	36	2	43	22	31	23
NOV. 30	34	8	9	10	36	37	36	2	43	22	31	23

December

Date & Time	SUN	MOON 1	MOON 2	MOON 3	MERCURY	VENUS	MARS	JUPITER	SATURN	URANUS	NEPTUNE	PLUTO
DEC. 1	34	10	11	12	36	37	37	2	43	22	31	23
DEC. 2	34	12	13	14	36	37	37	2	43	22	31	23
DEC. 3	35	14	15	16	36	38	37	2	43	22	31	23
DEC. 4	35	16	17	18	37	38	37	2	43	22	31	23
DEC. 5	35	18	19	19	37	38	37	2	43	22	31	23
DEC. 6	35	20	21	21	37	38	37	2	43	22	31	23
DEC. 7	35	22	22	23	37	38	37	2	43	22	31	23
DEC. 8	35	23	24	25	37	38	37	2	43	22	31	23
DEC. 9	35	25	26	26	38	39	37	2	43	22	31	23
DEC. 10	35	27	27	28	38	39	37	2	43	22	31	23
DEC. 11	36	28	29	29	38	39	38	2	43	22	31	23
DEC. 12	36	30	30	31	38	39	38	2	43	22	31	23
DEC. 13	36	32	32	33	38	39	38	2	43	22	31	23
DEC. 14	36	33	34	34	38	39	38	2	43	22	31	23
DEC. 15	36	35	35	36	39	40	38	2	43	22	31	23
DEC. 16	36	36	37	37	39	40	38	2	43	22	31	23
DEC. 17	36	38	38	39	39	40	38	2	44	22	31	23
DEC. 18	36	39	40	41	39	40	38	2	44	22	31	23
DEC. 19	37	41	42	42	39	40	38	2	44	22	31	23
DEC. 20	37	43	43	44	39	40	38	2	44	22	31	23
DEC. 21	37	45	45	46	39	41	39	2	44	22	31	23
DEC. 22	37	46	47	47	40	41	39	2	44	22	31	23
DEC. 23	37	48	1	1	40	41	39	2	44	22	31	23
DEC. 24	37	2	2	3	40	41	39	2	44	22	31	23
DEC. 25	37	4	4	5	40	41	39	2	44	22	31	23
DEC. 26	38	6	6	7	40	41	39	2	44	22	31	23
DEC. 27	38	8	8	9	40	42	39	2	44	22	31	23
DEC. 28	38	10	10	11	40	42	39	2	44	22	31	23
DEC. 29	38	12	12	13	40	42	39	2	44	22	31	23
DEC. 30	38	14	14	15	40	42	40	2	44	22	31	23
DEC. 31	38	16	16	17	39	42	40	2	44	22	31	23

MOON 1 ◑ 12:01 A.M. TO 8:00 A.M.　　**MOON 2** ◑ 8:01 A.M. TO 4:00 P.M.　　**MOON 3** ● 4:01 P.M. TO 12:00 A.M.

Use only one "moon" number. Choose the column closest to your time of birth. If your place of birth is not on Eastern Standard Time, be sure to read "How to Convert to Eastern Standard Time" at the beginning of this section.

1974

January

February

Date & Time	SUN	MOON 1	MOON 2	MOON 3	MERCURY	VENUS	MARS	JUPITER	SATURN	URANUS	NEPTUNE	PLUTO
JAN. 1	38	1	2	3	38	42	5	43	13	29	34	26
JAN. 2	38	3	4	4	38	42	5	43	13	29	34	26
JAN. 3	39	5	6	6	38	42	5	43	13	29	34	26
JAN. 4	39	7	7	8	38	42	5	43	13	29	34	26
JAN. 5	39	9	9	10	39	42	6	43	13	29	34	26
JAN. 6	39	11	11	12	39	42	6	43	13	29	34	26
JAN. 7	39	13	13	14	39	42	6	43	13	29	34	26
JAN. 8	39	15	15	16	39	42	6	43	13	29	34	26
JAN. 9	39	17	17	18	39	42	6	43	13	29	34	26
JAN. 10	40	19	19	20	40	42	6	43	13	29	34	26
JAN. 11	40	21	21	22	40	42	6	43	13	29	34	26
JAN. 12	40	23	23	24	40	42	6	43	13	29	34	26
JAN. 13	40	25	25	26	40	42	6	43	13	29	34	26
JAN. 14	40	26	27	28	41	42	6	43	13	29	34	26
JAN. 15	40	28	29	29	41	42	6	43	13	29	34	26
JAN. 16	40	30	30	31	41	42	6	43	13	29	34	26
JAN. 17	41	31	32	33	41	42	6	43	13	29	34	26
JAN. 18	41	33	34	34	41	42	6	43	13	29	34	26
JAN. 19	41	35	35	36	42	42	6	43	13	29	34	26
JAN. 20	41	36	37	37	42	42	6	43	13	29	34	26
JAN. 21	41	38	38	39	42	42	6	43	13	29	34	26
JAN. 22	41	39	40	40	42	42	6	44	13	29	34	26
JAN. 23	42	41	42	42	43	41	7	44	13	29	34	26
JAN. 24	42	43	43	44	43	41	7	44	13	29	34	26
JAN. 25	42	44	45	45	43	41	7	44	13	29	34	26
JAN. 26	42	46	46	47	43	41	7	44	13	29	34	26
JAN. 27	42	47	48	1	43	41	7	44	13	29	34	26
JAN. 28	42	1	2	2	44	41	7	44	13	29	34	26
JAN. 29	42	3	3	4	44	41	7	44	13	29	34	26
JAN. 30	42	4	5	6	44	41	7	44	13	29	34	26
JAN. 31	43	6	7	7	44	41	7	44	13	29	34	26

Date & Time	SUN	MOON 1	MOON 2	MOON 3	MERCURY	VENUS	MARS	JUPITER	SATURN	URANUS	NEPTUNE	PLUTO
FEB. 1	43	8	9	9	45	41	7	44	13	29	34	26
FEB. 2	43	10	11	11	45	41	7	44	13	29	34	26
FEB. 3	43	12	12	13	45	41	7	44	13	29	34	26
FEB. 4	43	14	14	15	45	41	7	44	13	29	34	26
FEB. 5	43	16	16	17	45	41	7	44	13	29	34	26
FEB. 6	43	18	18	19	46	41	7	44	13	29	34	26
FEB. 7	43	20	20	21	46	41	8	44	13	29	34	26
FEB. 8	44	22	22	23	46	40	8	44	13	29	34	26
FEB. 9	44	24	24	25	46	40	8	44	13	29	34	26
FEB. 10	44	26	26	27	46	40	8	44	13	29	34	26
FEB. 11	44	27	28	29	46	40	8	44	13	29	34	26
FEB. 12	44	29	30	30	46	40	8	44	13	29	34	26
FEB. 13	44	31	32	32	46	40	8	44	13	29	34	26
FEB. 14	44	33	33	34	47	40	8	44	13	29	34	26
FEB. 15	44	34	35	35	47	40	8	44	13	29	34	26
FEB. 16	45	36	36	37	47	40	8	44	13	29	34	26
FEB. 17	45	37	38	38	47	40	8	44	13	29	34	26
FEB. 18	45	39	39	40	47	40	8	44	13	29	34	26
FEB. 19	45	41	41	42	46	40	8	44	13	29	34	26
FEB. 20	45	42	43	43	46	41	8	44	13	29	34	26
FEB. 21	45	44	44	45	46	41	9	44	13	29	34	26
FEB. 22	45	45	46	46	46	41	9	45	13	29	34	26
FEB. 23	46	47	48	48	46	41	9	45	13	29	34	26
FEB. 24	46	1	1	2	46	41	9	45	13	29	34	26
FEB. 25	46	2	3	4	46	41	9	45	13	29	34	26
FEB. 26	46	4	5	5	46	41	9	45	13	29	34	26
FEB. 27	46	6	6	7	45	41	9	45	13	29	34	26
FEB. 28	46	8	8	9	45	41	9	45	13	29	34	26

MOON 1 ☽ 12:01 A.M. TO 8:00 A.M. **MOON 2** ☽ 8:01 A.M. TO 4:00 P.M. **MOON 3** ● 4:01 P.M. TO 12:00 A.M.

Use only one "moon" number. Choose the column closest to your time of birth. If your place of birth is not on Eastern Standard Time, be sure to read "How to Convert to Eastern Standard Time" at the beginning of this section.

Date & Time	SUN	MOON 1 ◗	MOON 2 ◖	MOON 3 ●	MERCURY	VENUS	MARS	JUPITER	SATURN	URANUS	NEPTUNE	PLUTO
MAY 1	6	22	22	23	6	48	14	46	13	28	34	26
MAY 2	6	24	24	25	6	1	14	47	13	28	34	26
MAY 3	7	25	26	27	6	1	14	47	13	28	34	26
MAY 4	7	27	28	28	7	1	14	47	13	28	34	26
MAY 5	7	29	30	30	7	1	14	47	13	28	34	26
MAY 6	7	31	31	32	7	1	14	47	13	28	34	26
MAY 7	7	32	33	34	8	1	14	47	13	28	34	26
MAY 8	7	34	35	35	8	1	14	47	13	28	34	26
MAY 9	7	36	36	37	8	2	14	47	13	28	34	26
MAY 10	7	37	38	38	8	2	15	47	13	28	34	26
MAY 11	8	39	40	40	9	2	15	47	13	28	34	26
MAY 12	8	41	41	42	9	2	15	47	13	28	34	26
MAY 13	8	42	43	43	9	2	15	47	13	28	34	26
MAY 14	8	44	44	45	10	2	15	47	13	28	34	26
MAY 15	8	45	46	46	10	3	15	47	13	28	34	26
MAY 16	8	47	48	48	10	3	15	47	13	28	34	26
MAY 17	8	1	1	2	10	3	15	47	13	28	34	26
MAY 18	8	2	3	4	11	3	15	47	13	28	34	26
MAY 19	9	4	5	5	11	3	15	47	13	28	34	26
MAY 20	9	6	7	7	11	3	15	47	13	28	34	26
MAY 21	9	8	8	9	11	3	15	47	13	28	34	26
MAY 22	9	10	10	11	12	4	16	47	13	28	34	26
MAY 23	9	12	12	13	12	4	16	47	13	28	34	26
MAY 24	9	14	14	15	12	4	16	47	13	28	34	26
MAY 25	10	15	16	17	12	4	16	47	13	28	34	26
MAY 26	10	17	18	19	12	4	16	47	13	28	34	26
MAY 27	10	19	20	21	13	4	16	47	13	28	34	26
MAY 28	10	21	22	22	13	4	16	47	14	28	34	26
MAY 29	10	23	24	24	13	5	16	47	14	28	34	26
MAY 30	10	25	26	26	13	5	16	47	14	28	34	26
MAY 31	10	27	27	28	13	5	16	47	14	28	34	26

Date & Time	SUN	MOON 1 ◗	MOON 2 ◖	MOON 3 ●	MERCURY	VENUS	MARS	JUPITER	SATURN	URANUS	NEPTUNE	PLUTO
JUN. 1	10	29	29	30	13	5	16	47	14	28	34	26
JUN. 2	10	30	31	31	14	5	16	47	14	28	34	26
JUN. 3	11	32	33	33	14	5	16	47	14	28	34	26
JUN. 4	11	34	34	35	14	6	17	47	14	28	34	26
JUN. 5	11	35	36	36	14	6	17	47	14	28	34	26
JUN. 6	11	37	37	38	14	6	17	47	14	28	34	26
JUN. 7	11	39	39	40	14	6	17	47	14	28	34	26
JUN. 8	11	40	41	41	14	6	17	47	14	28	34	26
JUN. 9	11	42	42	43	14	6	17	47	14	28	34	26
JUN. 10	11	43	44	44	14	6	17	47	14	28	34	26
JUN. 11	12	45	45	46	15	7	17	47	14	28	34	26
JUN. 12	12	46	47	48	15	7	17	47	14	28	34	26
JUN. 13	12	48	1	1	15	7	17	47	14	28	34	26
JUN. 14	12	2	2	3	15	7	17	47	14	28	34	26
JUN. 15	12	3	4	5	15	7	17	47	14	28	34	26
JUN. 16	12	5	6	6	15	7	18	47	14	28	34	26
JUN. 17	12	7	8	8	15	8	18	47	14	28	34	26
JUN. 18	12	9	10	10	15	8	18	47	14	28	34	26
JUN. 19	13	11	11	12	15	8	18	47	14	28	34	26
JUN. 20	13	13	13	14	15	8	18	47	14	28	34	26
JUN. 21	13	15	15	16	15	8	18	47	14	28	34	26
JUN. 22	13	17	17	18	15	8	18	47	14	28	34	26
JUN. 23	13	19	19	20	15	9	18	47	14	28	34	26
JUN. 24	13	21	21	22	15	9	18	47	14	28	34	26
JUN. 25	14	23	23	24	15	9	18	47	14	28	34	26
JUN. 26	14	25	25	26	14	9	18	47	14	28	34	26
JUN. 27	14	26	27	28	14	9	18	47	14	28	34	26
JUN. 28	14	28	29	29	14	9	19	47	14	28	34	26
JUN. 29	14	30	30	31	14	9	19	47	14	28	34	26
JUN. 30	14	32	32	33	14	10	19	47	14	28	34	26

MOON 1 ◗ 12:01 A.M. TO 8:00 A.M.   **MOON 2** ◖ 8:01 A.M. TO 4:00 P.M.   **MOON 3** ● 4:01 P.M. TO 12:00 A.M.

Use only one "moon" number. Choose the column closest to your time of birth. If your place of birth is not on Eastern Standard Time, be sure to read "How to Convert to Eastern Standard Time" at the beginning of this section.

Date & Time	SUN	MOON 1	MOON 2	MOON 3	MERCURY	VENUS	MARS	JUPITER	SATURN	URANUS	NEPTUNE	PLUTO
MAY 1	6	22	22	23	6	48	14	46	13	28	34	26
MAY 2	6	24	24	25	6	1	14	47	13	28	34	26
MAY 3	7	25	26	27	6	1	14	47	13	28	34	26
MAY 4	7	27	28	28	7	1	14	47	13	28	34	26
MAY 5	7	29	30	30	7	1	14	47	13	28	34	26
MAY 6	7	31	31	32	7	1	14	47	13	28	34	26
MAY 7	7	32	33	34	8	1	14	47	13	28	34	26
MAY 8	7	34	35	35	8	1	14	47	13	28	34	26
MAY 9	7	36	36	37	8	2	14	47	13	28	34	26
MAY 10	7	37	38	38	8	2	15	47	13	28	34	26
MAY 11	8	39	40	40	9	2	15	47	13	28	34	26
MAY 12	8	41	41	42	9	2	15	47	13	28	34	26
MAY 13	8	42	43	43	9	2	15	47	13	28	34	26
MAY 14	8	44	44	45	10	2	15	47	13	28	34	26
MAY 15	8	45	46	46	10	3	15	47	13	28	34	26
MAY 16	8	47	48	48	10	3	15	47	13	28	34	26
MAY 17	8	1	1	2	10	3	15	47	13	28	34	26
MAY 18	8	2	3	4	11	3	15	47	13	28	34	26
MAY 19	9	4	5	5	11	3	15	47	13	28	34	26
MAY 20	9	6	7	7	11	3	15	47	13	28	34	26
MAY 21	9	8	8	9	11	3	15	47	13	28	34	26
MAY 22	9	10	10	11	12	4	16	47	13	28	34	26
MAY 23	9	12	12	13	12	4	16	47	13	28	34	26
MAY 24	9	14	14	15	12	4	16	47	13	28	34	26
MAY 25	10	15	16	17	12	4	16	47	13	28	34	26
MAY 26	10	17	18	19	12	4	16	47	13	28	34	26
MAY 27	10	19	20	21	13	4	16	47	14	28	34	26
MAY 28	10	21	22	22	13	4	16	47	14	28	34	26
MAY 29	10	23	24	24	13	5	16	47	14	28	34	26
MAY 30	10	25	26	26	13	5	16	47	14	28	34	26
MAY 31	10	27	27	28	13	5	16	47	14	28	34	26

Date & Time	SUN	MOON 1	MOON 2	MOON 3	MERCURY	VENUS	MARS	JUPITER	SATURN	URANUS	NEPTUNE	PLUTO
JUN. 1	10	29	29	30	13	5	16	47	14	28	34	26
JUN. 2	10	30	31	31	14	5	16	47	14	28	34	26
JUN. 3	11	32	33	33	14	5	16	47	14	28	34	26
JUN. 4	11	34	34	35	14	6	17	47	14	28	34	26
JUN. 5	11	35	36	36	14	6	17	47	14	28	34	26
JUN. 6	11	37	37	38	14	6	17	47	14	28	34	26
JUN. 7	11	39	39	40	14	6	17	47	14	28	34	26
JUN. 8	11	40	41	41	14	6	17	47	14	28	34	26
JUN. 9	11	42	42	43	14	6	17	47	14	28	34	26
JUN. 10	11	43	44	44	14	6	17	47	14	28	34	26
JUN. 11	12	45	45	46	15	7	17	47	14	28	34	26
JUN. 12	12	46	47	48	15	7	17	47	14	28	34	26
JUN. 13	12	48	1	1	15	7	17	47	14	28	34	26
JUN. 14	12	2	2	3	15	7	17	47	14	28	34	26
JUN. 15	12	3	4	5	15	7	17	47	14	28	34	26
JUN. 16	12	5	6	6	15	7	18	47	14	28	34	26
JUN. 17	12	7	8	8	15	8	18	47	14	28	34	26
JUN. 18	12	9	10	10	15	8	18	47	14	28	34	26
JUN. 19	13	11	11	12	15	8	18	47	14	28	34	26
JUN. 20	13	13	13	14	15	8	18	47	14	28	34	26
JUN. 21	13	15	15	16	15	8	18	47	14	28	34	26
JUN. 22	13	17	17	18	15	8	18	47	14	28	34	26
JUN. 23	13	19	19	20	15	9	18	47	14	28	34	26
JUN. 24	13	21	21	22	15	9	18	47	14	28	34	26
JUN. 25	14	23	23	24	15	9	18	47	14	28	34	26
JUN. 26	14	25	25	26	14	9	18	47	14	28	34	26
JUN. 27	14	26	27	28	14	9	18	47	14	28	34	26
JUN. 28	14	28	29	29	14	9	19	47	14	28	34	26
JUN. 29	14	30	30	31	14	9	19	47	14	28	34	26
JUN. 30	14	32	32	33	14	10	19	47	14	28	34	26

MOON 1 ◑ 12:01 A.M. TO 8:00 A.M.   **MOON 2** ◑ 8:01 A.M. TO 4:00 P.M.   **MOON 3** ● 4:01 P.M. TO 12:00 A.M.
Use only one "moon" number. Choose the column closest to your time of birth. If your place of birth is not on Eastern Standard Time, be sure to read "How to Convert to Eastern Standard Time" at the beginning of this section.

1974

July   August

Date & Time	SUN	MOON 1	MOON 2	MOON 3	MERCURY	VENUS	MARS	JUPITER	SATURN	URANUS	NEPTUNE	PLUTO
JUL. 1	14	33	34	34	14	10	19	47	14	28	34	26
JUL. 2	14	35	35	36	14	10	19	47	14	28	34	26
JUL. 3	15	36	37	38	14	10	19	47	14	28	34	26
JUL. 4	15	38	39	39	14	10	19	47	14	28	34	26
JUL. 5	15	40	40	41	14	10	19	47	14	28	34	26
JUL. 6	15	41	42	42	14	11	19	47	14	28	34	26
JUL. 7	15	43	44	44	14	11	19	47	14	28	34	26
JUL. 8	15	44	45	45	14	11	19	47	14	28	34	26
JUL. 9	15	46	47	47	14	11	19	47	14	28	34	26
JUL. 10	15	48	48	1	14	11	20	47	14	28	34	26
JUL. 11	16	1	2	2	14	11	20	47	14	28	34	26
JUL. 12	16	3	3	4	14	12	20	47	14	28	34	26
JUL. 13	16	5	5	6	14	12	20	47	14	28	34	26
JUL. 14	16	6	7	8	14	12	20	47	14	28	34	26
JUL. 15	16	8	9	9	14	12	20	47	14	28	34	26
JUL. 16	16	10	11	11	14	12	20	47	14	28	34	26
JUL. 17	16	12	13	13	14	12	20	47	14	28	34	26
JUL. 18	16	14	15	15	14	12	20	47	14	28	34	26
JUL. 19	17	16	17	17	14	13	20	47	14	28	34	26
JUL. 20	17	18	19	19	14	13	20	47	14	28	34	26
JUL. 21	17	20	21	21	14	13	20	47	14	28	34	26
JUL. 22	17	22	23	23	14	13	21	47	14	28	34	26
JUL. 23	17	24	25	25	14	13	21	47	14	28	34	26
JUL. 24	17	26	26	27	14	13	21	47	14	28	34	26
JUL. 25	17	28	28	29	15	14	21	47	15	28	34	26
JUL. 26	18	29	30	31	15	14	21	47	15	28	34	26
JUL. 27	18	31	32	32	15	14	21	47	15	28	34	26
JUL. 28	18	33	33	34	15	14	21	47	15	28	34	26
JUL. 29	18	34	35	36	15	14	21	47	15	28	34	26
JUL. 30	18	36	37	37	15	14	21	47	15	28	34	26
JUL. 31	18	38	38	39	16	15	21	47	15	28	34	26

Date & Time	SUN	MOON 1	MOON 2	MOON 3	MERCURY	VENUS	MARS	JUPITER	SATURN	URANUS	NEPTUNE	PLUTO
AUG. 1	18	39	40	40	16	15	21	47	15	28	34	26
AUG. 2	18	41	41	42	16	15	21	47	15	28	34	26
AUG. 3	19	42	43	43	16	15	22	47	15	28	34	26
AUG. 4	19	44	45	45	17	15	22	47	15	28	34	26
AUG. 5	19	46	46	47	17	15	22	47	15	28	34	26
AUG. 6	19	47	48	48	17	16	22	47	15	28	34	26
AUG. 7	19	1	1	2	17	16	22	47	15	28	34	26
AUG. 8	19	2	3	4	18	16	22	47	15	28	34	26
AUG. 9	19	4	5	5	18	16	22	47	15	28	34	26
AUG. 10	19	6	6	7	18	16	22	47	15	28	34	26
AUG. 11	20	8	8	9	18	16	22	47	15	28	34	26
AUG. 12	20	9	10	11	19	17	22	47	15	28	34	26
AUG. 13	20	11	12	12	19	17	22	47	15	28	34	26
AUG. 14	20	13	14	14	19	17	22	47	15	28	34	26
AUG. 15	20	15	16	16	20	17	23	47	15	28	34	26
AUG. 16	20	17	18	18	20	17	23	47	15	28	34	26
AUG. 17	20	19	20	20	20	17	23	47	15	28	34	26
AUG. 18	20	21	22	22	20	17	23	47	15	28	34	26
AUG. 19	21	23	24	24	21	18	23	47	15	28	34	26
AUG. 20	21	25	26	26	21	18	23	47	15	28	34	26
AUG. 21	21	27	28	28	21	18	23	47	15	28	34	26
AUG. 22	21	29	29	30	21	18	23	47	15	28	34	26
AUG. 23	21	31	31	32	22	18	23	47	15	28	34	26
AUG. 24	21	32	33	33	22	18	23	47	15	28	34	26
AUG. 25	21	34	35	35	22	19	23	47	15	28	34	26
AUG. 26	22	36	36	37	22	19	23	47	15	28	34	26
AUG. 27	22	37	38	38	23	19	24	47	15	28	34	26
AUG. 28	22	39	39	40	23	19	24	47	15	28	34	26
AUG. 29	22	40	41	42	23	19	24	47	15	28	34	26
AUG. 30	22	42	43	43	23	19	24	47	15	28	34	26
AUG. 31	22	44	44	45	24	20	24	47	15	28	34	26

MOON 1 ◐ 12:01 A.M. TO 8:00 A.M.   **MOON 2** ◑ 8:01 A.M. TO 4:00 P.M.   **MOON 3** ● 4:01 P.M. TO 12:00 A.M.
Use only one "moon" number. Choose the column closest to your time of birth. If your place of birth is not on Eastern Standard Time, be sure to read "How to Convert to Eastern Standard Time" at the beginning of this section.

1974

September

Date & Time	SUN ☉	MOON 1 ◗	MOON 2 ◑	MOON 3 ●	MERCURY	VENUS	MARS	JUPITER	SATURN	URANUS	NEPTUNE	PLUTO
SEP. 1	22	45	46	46	24	20	24	47	15	28	34	26
SEP. 2	22	47	47	48	24	20	24	47	15	28	34	26
SEP. 3	23	48	1	2	24	20	24	47	15	28	34	26
SEP. 4	23	2	3	3	25	20	24	47	15	28	34	26
SEP. 5	23	4	4	5	25	20	24	47	15	28	34	26
SEP. 6	23	5	6	7	25	21	24	47	15	28	34	26
SEP. 7	23	7	8	8	25	21	24	47	15	28	34	26
SEP. 8	23	9	9	10	25	21	25	47	15	28	34	26
SEP. 9	23	11	11	12	26	21	25	47	15	28	34	26
SEP. 10	23	12	13	14	26	21	25	47	15	28	34	26
SEP. 11	24	14	15	16	26	21	25	47	15	28	34	26
SEP. 12	24	16	17	18	26	22	25	47	15	28	34	26
SEP. 13	24	18	19	20	26	22	25	47	15	28	34	26
SEP. 14	24	20	21	22	27	22	25	47	15	28	34	26
SEP. 15	24	22	23	24	27	22	25	47	15	28	34	26
SEP. 16	24	24	25	26	27	22	25	47	15	28	34	26
SEP. 17	24	26	27	27	27	22	25	46	15	28	34	26
SEP. 18	24	28	29	29	27	23	25	46	15	28	34	26
SEP. 19	25	30	31	31	28	23	26	46	15	28	34	26
SEP. 20	25	32	32	33	28	23	26	46	15	28	34	26
SEP. 21	25	33	34	35	28	23	26	46	15	28	34	26
SEP. 22	25	35	36	36	28	23	26	46	15	28	34	26
SEP. 23	25	37	37	38	28	23	26	46	15	28	34	26
SEP. 24	25	38	39	39	28	24	26	46	15	28	34	26
SEP. 25	26	40	41	41	29	24	26	46	15	28	34	26
SEP. 26	26	42	42	43	29	24	26	46	15	29	34	26
SEP. 27	26	43	44	44	29	24	26	46	15	29	34	26
SEP. 28	26	45	45	46	29	24	26	46	15	29	34	26
SEP. 29	26	46	47	47	29	24	26	46	15	29	34	26
SEP. 30	26	48	1	1	29	25	26	46	15	29	34	26

October

Date & Time	SUN ☉	MOON 1 ◗	MOON 2 ◑	MOON 3 ●	MERCURY	VENUS	MARS	JUPITER	SATURN	URANUS	NEPTUNE	PLUTO
OCT. 1	26	2	2	3	29	25	27	46	15	29	34	26
OCT. 2	26	3	4	4	30	25	27	46	15	29	34	26
OCT. 3	27	5	6	6	30	25	27	46	15	29	34	26
OCT. 4	27	7	7	8	30	25	27	46	15	29	34	26
OCT. 5	27	8	9	10	30	25	27	46	15	29	34	26
OCT. 6	27	10	11	11	30	26	27	46	15	29	34	26
OCT. 7	27	12	13	13	30	26	27	46	15	29	34	26
OCT. 8	27	14	14	15	30	26	27	46	15	29	34	26
OCT. 9	27	16	16	17	30	26	27	46	15	29	34	26
OCT. 10	27	18	18	19	30	26	27	46	15	29	34	26
OCT. 11	28	20	20	21	30	26	27	46	15	29	34	26
OCT. 12	28	21	22	23	30	27	28	46	15	29	34	26
OCT. 13	28	23	24	25	30	27	28	46	15	29	34	26
OCT. 14	28	25	26	27	30	27	28	46	15	29	34	26
OCT. 15	28	27	28	29	30	27	28	46	15	29	34	26
OCT. 16	28	29	30	30	30	27	28	46	15	29	34	26
OCT. 17	28	31	32	32	30	27	28	46	15	29	34	26
OCT. 18	28	33	33	34	30	28	28	46	15	29	34	26
OCT. 19	29	35	35	36	30	28	28	46	15	29	34	26
OCT. 20	29	36	37	37	30	28	28	46	15	29	34	26
OCT. 21	29	38	38	39	30	28	28	46	15	29	34	26
OCT. 22	29	39	40	41	30	28	29	46	15	29	34	26
OCT. 23	29	41	42	42	30	28	29	46	15	29	34	26
OCT. 24	29	43	43	44	29	29	29	46	15	29	34	26
OCT. 25	29	44	45	45	29	29	29	46	15	29	34	26
OCT. 26	30	46	46	47	29	29	29	46	15	29	34	26
OCT. 27	30	47	48	1	29	29	29	46	15	29	34	26
OCT. 28	30	1	2	2	29	29	29	46	15	29	34	26
OCT. 29	30	3	3	4	29	29	29	46	15	29	34	26
OCT. 30	30	4	5	6	29	30	29	46	15	29	34	26
OCT. 31	30	6	7	7	28	30	29	46	15	29	34	26

MOON 1 ◗ 12:01 A.M. TO 8:00 A.M.   **MOON 2** ◑ 8:01 A.M. TO 4:00 P.M.   **MOON 3** ● 4:01 P.M. TO 12:00 A.M.

Use only one "moon" number. Choose the column closest to your time of birth. If your place of birth is not on Eastern Standard Time, be sure to read "How to Convert to Eastern Standard Time" at the beginning of this section.

1974

November

December

Date & Time	SUN	MOON 1	MOON 2	MOON 3	MERCURY	VENUS	MARS	JUPITER	SATURN	URANUS	NEPTUNE	PLUTO
NOV. 1	30	8	9	9	28	30	29	46	15	29	34	26
NOV. 2	30	10	10	11	28	30	29	46	15	29	34	26
NOV. 3	31	12	12	13	28	30	29	46	15	29	34	26
NOV. 4	31	13	14	15	28	30	30	46	15	29	34	26
NOV. 5	31	15	16	17	28	31	30	46	15	29	34	26
NOV. 6	31	17	18	18	28	31	30	46	15	29	34	26
NOV. 7	31	19	20	20	28	31	30	46	15	29	34	26
NOV. 8	31	21	22	22	29	31	30	46	15	29	34	26
NOV. 9	31	23	23	24	29	31	30	46	15	29	34	26
NOV. 10	31	25	25	26	29	31	30	46	15	29	34	26
NOV. 11	31	27	27	28	29	32	30	46	15	29	34	26
NOV. 12	32	28	29	30	29	32	30	46	15	29	34	26
NOV. 13	32	30	31	32	29	32	30	46	15	29	34	26
NOV. 14	32	32	33	33	29	32	30	46	15	29	34	26
NOV. 15	32	34	34	35	30	32	31	46	15	29	34	26
NOV. 16	32	36	36	37	30	32	31	46	15	29	34	26
NOV. 17	32	37	38	38	30	33	31	46	15	29	34	26
NOV. 18	32	39	39	40	30	33	31	46	15	29	34	26
NOV. 19	33	41	41	42	30	33	31	46	15	29	34	26
NOV. 20	33	42	43	43	30	33	31	46	15	29	34	26
NOV. 21	33	44	44	45	31	33	31	46	15	29	34	26
NOV. 22	33	45	46	46	31	33	31	46	15	29	34	26
NOV. 23	33	47	47	48	31	34	31	46	15	29	34	26
NOV. 24	33	48	1	2	31	34	31	46	15	29	34	26
NOV. 25	34	2	3	3	32	34	32	46	15	29	34	26
NOV. 26	34	4	4	5	32	34	32	46	15	29	34	26
NOV. 27	34	6	6	7	32	34	32	46	15	29	34	26
NOV. 28	34	7	8	9	32	34	32	46	15	29	34	26
NOV. 29	34	9	10	10	32	35	32	46	15	29	34	26
NOV. 30	34	11	12	12	33	35	32	46	15	29	34	26

Date & Time	SUN	MOON 1	MOON 2	MOON 3	MERCURY	VENUS	MARS	JUPITER	SATURN	URANUS	NEPTUNE	PLUTO
DEC. 1	34	13	13	14	33	35	32	46	15	29	34	26
DEC. 2	34	15	15	16	33	35	32	46	15	29	34	26
DEC. 3	35	17	17	18	33	35	32	46	15	29	34	26
DEC. 4	35	19	19	20	33	35	32	46	15	29	34	26
DEC. 5	35	21	21	22	34	36	32	46	15	29	34	26
DEC. 6	35	22	23	24	34	36	33	46	15	29	34	26
DEC. 7	35	24	25	26	34	36	33	46	15	29	34	26
DEC. 8	35	26	27	27	34	36	33	46	15	29	34	26
DEC. 9	35	28	29	29	34	36	33	46	15	29	34	26
DEC. 10	35	30	30	31	35	36	33	46	15	29	34	26
DEC. 11	36	32	32	33	35	37	33	46	15	29	34	26
DEC. 12	36	33	34	34	35	37	33	46	15	29	34	26
DEC. 13	36	35	36	36	35	37	33	46	15	29	34	26
DEC. 14	36	37	37	38	35	37	33	46	15	29	34	26
DEC. 15	36	38	39	39	36	37	33	46	15	29	34	26
DEC. 16	36	40	41	41	36	37	33	46	15	29	34	26
DEC. 17	36	42	42	43	36	38	34	46	15	29	34	26
DEC. 18	36	43	44	44	36	38	34	46	15	29	34	26
DEC. 19	37	45	45	46	36	38	34	46	15	29	34	26
DEC. 20	37	46	47	47	37	38	34	46	15	29	34	26
DEC. 21	37	48	48	1	37	38	34	47	15	29	34	26
DEC. 22	37	2	2	3	37	38	34	47	15	29	34	26
DEC. 23	37	3	4	4	37	39	34	47	15	29	34	26
DEC. 24	37	5	5	6	38	39	34	47	15	29	34	26
DEC. 25	37	7	7	8	38	39	34	47	15	29	34	26
DEC. 26	38	8	9	10	38	39	34	47	15	29	34	26
DEC. 27	38	10	11	11	38	39	35	47	15	29	34	26
DEC. 28	38	12	13	13	38	39	35	47	15	29	34	26
DEC. 29	38	14	15	15	39	40	35	47	15	29	34	26
DEC. 30	38	16	17	17	39	40	35	47	15	29	34	26
DEC. 31	38	18	19	19	39	40	35	47	15	29	34	26

MOON 1 ☽ 12:01 A.M. TO 8:00 A.M.   **MOON 2** ☽ 8:01 A.M. TO 4:00 P.M.   **MOON 3** ● 4:01 P.M. TO 12:00 A.M.

Use only one "moon" number. Choose the column closest to your time of birth. If your place of birth is not on Eastern Standard Time, be sure to read "How to Convert to Eastern Standard Time" at the beginning of this section.

1975

January

Date & Time	SUN	MOON 1	MOON 2	MOON 3	MERCURY	VENUS	MARS	JUPITER	SATURN	URANUS	NEPTUNE	PLUTO
JAN. 1	38	20	21	21	39	40	35	47	15	29	34	26
JAN. 2	38	22	23	23	40	40	35	47	15	29	34	26
JAN. 3	39	24	24	25	40	40	35	47	15	29	34	26
JAN. 4	39	26	26	27	40	41	35	47	15	29	34	26
JAN. 5	39	28	28	29	40	41	35	47	15	29	34	26
JAN. 6	39	29	30	31	40	41	35	47	15	29	34	26
JAN. 7	39	31	32	32	41	41	36	47	15	29	34	26
JAN. 8	39	33	33	34	41	41	36	47	15	29	34	26
JAN. 9	39	35	35	36	41	41	36	47	15	29	34	26
JAN. 10	40	36	37	37	41	42	36	47	15	29	34	26
JAN. 11	40	38	38	39	41	42	36	47	15	29	34	26
JAN. 12	40	39	40	41	42	42	36	47	15	29	34	26
JAN. 13	40	41	42	42	42	42	36	47	15	29	34	26
JAN. 14	40	43	43	44	42	42	36	47	15	29	34	26
JAN. 15	40	44	45	45	42	42	36	47	15	29	34	26
JAN. 16	40	46	46	47	43	43	36	47	15	29	34	26
JAN. 17	41	47	48	48	43	43	37	47	15	29	34	26
JAN. 18	41	1	2	2	43	43	37	47	15	29	34	26
JAN. 19	41	3	3	4	43	43	37	47	15	29	34	26
JAN. 20	41	4	5	5	43	43	37	47	15	29	34	26
JAN. 21	41	6	6	7	43	43	37	47	15	29	34	26
JAN. 22	41	8	8	9	44	44	37	47	15	29	34	26
JAN. 23	42	9	10	11	44	44	37	47	15	29	34	26
JAN. 24	42	11	12	12	44	44	37	47	15	29	34	26
JAN. 25	42	13	14	14	44	44	37	47	15	29	34	26
JAN. 26	42	15	16	16	44	44	37	47	15	29	34	26
JAN. 27	42	17	18	18	44	44	37	47	15	29	34	26
JAN. 28	42	19	20	20	44	44	38	47	15	29	34	26
JAN. 29	42	21	22	22	44	45	38	47	15	29	34	26
JAN. 30	42	23	24	24	44	45	38	47	15	29	34	26
JAN. 31	43	25	26	26	44	45	38	48	15	29	34	26

February

Date & Time	SUN	MOON 1	MOON 2	MOON 3	MERCURY	VENUS	MARS	JUPITER	SATURN	URANUS	NEPTUNE	PLUTO
FEB. 1	43	27	28	28	44	45	38	48	15	29	34	26
FEB. 2	43	29	30	30	44	45	38	48	15	29	34	26
FEB. 3	43	31	31	32	44	46	38	48	15	29	34	26
FEB. 4	43	32	33	34	44	46	38	48	15	29	34	26
FEB. 5	43	34	35	35	44	46	38	48	15	29	34	26
FEB. 6	43	36	36	37	44	46	38	48	15	29	34	26
FEB. 7	43	37	38	39	44	46	39	48	15	29	34	26
FEB. 8	44	39	40	40	44	46	39	48	15	29	34	26
FEB. 9	44	41	41	42	43	47	39	48	15	29	34	26
FEB. 10	44	42	43	43	43	47	39	48	15	29	35	26
FEB. 11	44	44	44	45	43	47	39	48	15	29	35	26
FEB. 12	44	45	46	46	43	47	39	48	15	29	35	26
FEB. 13	44	47	48	48	43	47	39	48	15	29	35	26
FEB. 14	44	1	1	2	43	47	39	48	15	29	35	26
FEB. 15	44	2	3	3	43	48	39	48	15	29	35	26
FEB. 16	45	4	4	5	42	48	39	48	15	29	35	26
FEB. 17	45	5	6	7	42	48	40	48	15	29	35	26
FEB. 18	45	7	8	8	42	48	40	48	15	29	35	26
FEB. 19	45	9	9	10	42	48	40	48	15	29	35	26
FEB. 20	45	11	11	12	42	48	40	48	15	29	35	26
FEB. 21	45	12	13	14	42	1	40	48	15	29	35	26
FEB. 22	45	14	15	15	42	1	40	48	15	29	35	26
FEB. 23	46	16	17	17	42	1	40	48	15	29	35	26
FEB. 24	46	18	19	19	42	1	40	48	15	29	35	26
FEB. 25	46	20	21	22	42	1	40	48	15	29	35	26
FEB. 26	46	22	23	24	42	1	40	48	15	29	35	26
FEB. 27	46	24	25	26	43	2	41	48	15	29	35	26
FEB. 28	46	26	27	28	43	2	41	48	15	29	35	26

MOON 1 ◯ 12:01 A.M. TO 8:00 A.M.   **MOON 2** ◑ 8:01 A.M. TO 4:00 P.M.   **MOON 3** ● 4:01 P.M. TO 12:00 A.M.
Use only one "moon" number. Choose the column closest to your time of birth. If your place of birth is not on
Eastern Standard Time, be sure to read "How to Convert to Eastern Standard Time" at the beginning of this section.

Date & Time	SUN	MOON 1	MOON 2	MOON 3	MERCURY	VENUS	MARS	JUPITER	SATURN	URANUS	NEPTUNE	PLUTO
MAR. 1	46	28	29	29	43	2	41	48	15	29	35	26
MAR. 2	46	30	31	31	43	2	41	48	15	29	35	26
MAR. 3	47	32	33	33	43	2	41	48	15	29	35	26
MAR. 4	47	34	34	35	43	2	41	1	15	29	35	26
MAR. 5	47	35	36	37	43	3	41	1	15	29	35	26
MAR. 6	47	37	38	38	43	3	41	1	15	29	35	26
MAR. 7	47	39	39	40	43	3	41	1	15	29	35	26
MAR. 8	47	40	41	41	44	3	41	1	15	29	35	26
MAR. 9	47	42	42	43	44	3	42	1	15	29	35	26
MAR. 10	47	43	44	45	44	3	42	1	15	29	35	26
MAR. 11	48	45	46	46	44	4	42	1	15	29	35	26
MAR. 12	48	47	47	48	44	4	42	1	15	29	35	26
MAR. 13	48	48	1	1	44	4	42	1	15	29	35	26
MAR. 14	48	2	2	3	45	4	42	1	15	29	35	26
MAR. 15	48	3	4	5	45	4	42	1	15	29	35	26
MAR. 16	48	5	6	6	45	4	42	1	15	29	35	26
MAR. 17	48	7	7	8	45	5	42	1	15	29	35	26
MAR. 18	48	8	9	9	45	5	42	1	15	29	35	26
MAR. 19	1	10	11	11	45	5	43	1	15	29	35	26
MAR. 20	1	12	12	13	46	5	43	1	15	29	35	26
MAR. 21	1	14	14	15	46	5	43	1	15	29	35	26
MAR. 22	1	15	16	17	46	5	43	1	15	29	35	26
MAR. 23	1	17	18	19	46	6	43	1	15	29	35	26
MAR. 24	1	19	20	21	46	6	43	1	15	29	35	26
MAR. 25	2	21	22	23	47	6	43	1	15	29	35	26
MAR. 26	2	23	24	25	47	6	43	1	15	29	35	26
MAR. 27	2	25	26	27	47	6	43	1	15	29	35	26
MAR. 28	2	27	28	29	47	6	43	1	15	29	35	26
MAR. 29	2	29	30	31	48	6	44	1	15	29	35	26
MAR. 30	2	31	32	32	48	7	44	1	15	29	35	26
MAR. 31	2	33	34	34	48	7	44	1	15	29	35	26

Date & Time	SUN	MOON 1	MOON 2	MOON 3	MERCURY	VENUS	MARS	JUPITER	SATURN	URANUS	NEPTUNE	PLUTO
APR. 1	2	35	35	36	48	7	44	1	15	29	35	26
APR. 2	2	37	37	38	48	7	44	1	15	29	35	26
APR. 3	3	38	39	39	1	7	44	1	15	29	35	26
APR. 4	3	40	40	41	1	7	44	1	15	29	35	26
APR. 5	3	41	42	43	1	8	44	2	15	29	35	26
APR. 6	3	43	44	44	1	8	44	2	15	29	35	26
APR. 7	3	45	45	46	2	8	45	2	15	29	35	26
APR. 8	3	46	47	47	2	8	45	2	15	29	35	26
APR. 9	3	48	48	1	2	8	45	2	15	29	35	26
APR. 10	3	1	2	2	2	8	45	2	15	29	35	26
APR. 11	4	3	4	4	3	9	45	2	15	29	35	26
APR. 12	4	5	5	6	3	9	45	2	15	29	35	26
APR. 13	4	6	7	7	3	9	45	2	15	29	35	26
APR. 14	4	8	9	9	3	9	45	2	15	29	35	26
APR. 15	4	10	10	11	4	9	45	2	15	29	35	26
APR. 16	4	11	12	13	4	9	45	2	15	29	35	26
APR. 17	4	13	14	14	4	9	46	2	15	29	34	26
APR. 18	4	15	16	16	5	10	46	2	15	29	34	26
APR. 19	5	17	17	18	5	10	46	2	15	29	34	26
APR. 20	5	19	19	20	5	10	46	2	15	29	34	26
APR. 21	5	21	21	22	5	10	46	2	15	29	34	26
APR. 22	5	23	23	24	6	10	46	2	15	29	34	26
APR. 23	5	24	25	26	6	10	46	2	15	29	34	26
APR. 24	5	26	27	28	6	11	46	2	15	29	34	26
APR. 25	6	28	29	30	7	11	46	2	15	29	34	26
APR. 26	6	30	31	32	7	11	46	2	15	29	34	26
APR. 27	6	32	33	33	7	11	47	2	15	29	34	26
APR. 28	6	34	35	35	7	11	47	2	15	29	34	26
APR. 29	6	36	36	37	8	11	47	2	15	29	34	26
APR. 30	6	38	38	39	8	12	47	2	15	29	34	26

MOON 1 ☽ 12:01 A.M. TO 8:00 A.M.   **MOON 2** ☽ 8:01 A.M. TO 4:00 P.M.   **MOON 3** ● 4:01 P.M. TO 12:00 A.M.

Use only one "moon" number. Choose the column closest to your time of birth. If your place of birth is not on Eastern Standard Time, be sure to read "How to Convert to Eastern Standard Time" at the beginning of this section.

1975

May

June

Date & Time	SUN	MOON 1	MOON 2	MOON 3	MERCURY	VENUS	MARS	JUPITER	SATURN	URANUS	NEPTUNE	PLUTO
MAY 1	6	39	40	40	8	12	47	2	15	29	34	26
MAY 2	6	41	41	42	8	12	47	2	15	29	34	26
MAY 3	7	43	43	44	8	12	47	2	15	29	34	26
MAY 4	7	44	45	45	9	12	47	2	15	29	34	26
MAY 5	7	46	46	47	9	12	47	2	15	29	34	26
MAY 6	7	47	48	48	9	12	47	2	15	29	34	26
MAY 7	7	1	1	2	10	13	48	3	15	29	34	26
MAY 8	7	3	3	4	10	13	48	3	15	29	34	26
MAY 9	7	4	5	5	10	13	48	3	15	29	34	26
MAY 10	7	6	6	7	10	13	48	3	15	29	34	26
MAY 11	8	7	8	9	10	13	48	3	15	29	34	26
MAY 12	8	9	10	10	11	13	48	3	15	29	34	26
MAY 13	8	11	12	12	11	13	48	3	15	29	34	26
MAY 14	8	13	13	14	11	14	48	3	15	29	34	26
MAY 15	8	15	15	16	11	14	48	3	15	29	34	26
MAY 16	8	16	17	18	11	14	48	3	15	29	34	26
MAY 17	8	18	19	19	11	14	1	3	15	29	34	26
MAY 18	8	20	21	21	11	14	1	3	15	29	34	26
MAY 19	9	22	23	23	12	14	1	3	15	29	34	26
MAY 20	9	24	25	25	12	15	1	3	15	29	34	26
MAY 21	9	26	26	27	12	15	1	3	15	29	34	26
MAY 22	9	28	28	29	12	15	1	3	15	29	34	26
MAY 23	9	30	30	31	12	15	1	3	15	29	34	26
MAY 24	9	32	32	33	12	15	1	3	15	29	34	26
MAY 25	10	33	34	35	12	15	1	3	15	29	34	26
MAY 26	10	35	36	36	12	15	1	3	15	29	34	26
MAY 27	10	37	38	38	12	16	2	3	15	29	34	26
MAY 28	10	39	39	40	12	16	2	3	15	29	34	26
MAY 29	10	40	41	42	12	16	2	3	15	29	34	26
MAY 30	10	42	43	43	12	16	2	3	15	29	34	26
MAY 31	10	44	44	45	12	16	2	3	15	29	34	26

Date & Time	SUN	MOON 1	MOON 2	MOON 3	MERCURY	VENUS	MARS	JUPITER	SATURN	URANUS	NEPTUNE	PLUTO
JUN. 1	10	45	46	46	12	16	2	3	15	29	34	26
JUN. 2	10	47	47	48	12	16	2	3	15	29	34	26
JUN. 3	11	48	1	1	12	17	2	3	15	29	34	26
JUN. 4	11	2	2	3	12	17	2	3	15	29	34	26
JUN. 5	11	4	4	5	12	17	2	3	15	29	34	26
JUN. 6	11	5	6	6	12	17	3	3	15	29	34	26
JUN. 7	11	7	7	8	12	17	3	3	15	29	34	26
JUN. 8	11	9	9	10	12	17	3	3	15	29	34	26
JUN. 9	11	10	11	12	12	17	3	3	15	29	34	26
JUN. 10	11	12	13	13	12	17	3	3	15	29	34	26
JUN. 11	12	14	15	15	11	18	3	3	15	29	34	26
JUN. 12	12	16	17	17	11	18	3	3	15	29	34	26
JUN. 13	12	18	18	19	11	18	3	3	15	29	34	26
JUN. 14	12	20	20	21	11	18	3	4	15	29	34	26
JUN. 15	12	22	22	23	11	18	3	4	15	29	34	26
JUN. 16	12	23	24	25	11	18	4	4	15	29	34	26
JUN. 17	12	25	26	27	11	18	4	4	15	29	34	26
JUN. 18	12	27	28	29	11	19	4	4	16	29	34	26
JUN. 19	13	29	30	30	11	19	4	4	16	29	34	26
JUN. 20	13	31	32	32	11	19	4	4	16	29	34	26
JUN. 21	13	33	33	34	11	19	4	4	16	29	34	26
JUN. 22	13	35	35	36	11	19	4	4	16	29	34	26
JUN. 23	13	36	37	37	11	19	4	4	16	29	34	26
JUN. 24	13	38	39	39	11	19	4	4	16	29	34	26
JUN. 25	14	40	40	41	11	19	4	4	16	29	34	26
JUN. 26	14	41	42	43	11	20	4	4	16	29	34	26
JUN. 27	14	43	44	44	11	20	5	4	16	29	34	26
JUN. 28	14	45	45	46	11	20	5	4	16	29	34	26
JUN. 29	14	46	47	47	11	20	5	4	16	29	34	26
JUN. 30	14	48	48	1	11	20	5	4	16	29	34	26

MOON 1 ☽ 12:01 A.M. TO 8:00 A.M.   **MOON 2** ☽ 8:01 A.M. TO 4:00 P.M.   **MOON 3** ● 4:01 P.M. TO 12:00 A.M.
Use only one "moon" number. Choose the column closest to your time of birth. If your place of birth is not on
Eastern Standard Time, be sure to read "How to Convert to Eastern Standard Time" at the beginning of this section.

1975

July

August

Date & Time	SUN	MOON 1	MOON 2	MOON 3	MERCURY	VENUS	MARS	JUPITER	SATURN	URANUS	NEPTUNE	PLUTO
JUL. 1	14	1	2	2	11	20	5	4	16	29	34	26
JUL. 2	14	3	4	4	11	20	5	4	16	29	34	26
JUL. 3	15	5	5	6	12	20	5	4	16	29	34	26
JUL. 4	15	6	7	7	12	20	5	4	16	29	34	26
JUL. 5	15	8	9	9	12	21	5	4	16	29	34	26
JUL. 6	15	10	10	11	12	21	5	4	16	29	34	26
JUL. 7	15	11	12	13	12	21	6	4	16	29	34	26
JUL. 8	15	13	14	15	12	21	6	4	16	29	34	26
JUL. 9	15	15	16	16	12	21	6	4	16	29	34	26
JUL. 10	15	17	18	18	13	21	6	4	16	29	34	26
JUL. 11	16	19	20	20	13	21	6	4	16	29	34	26
JUL. 12	16	21	22	22	13	21	6	4	16	29	34	26
JUL. 13	16	23	24	24	13	21	6	4	16	29	34	26
JUL. 14	16	25	26	26	13	21	6	4	16	29	34	26
JUL. 15	16	27	27	28	14	21	6	4	16	29	34	26
JUL. 16	16	29	29	30	14	22	6	4	16	29	34	26
JUL. 17	16	31	31	32	14	22	6	4	16	29	34	26
JUL. 18	16	32	33	34	14	22	7	4	16	29	34	26
JUL. 19	17	34	35	35	14	22	7	4	16	29	34	26
JUL. 20	17	36	36	37	15	22	7	4	16	29	34	26
JUL. 21	17	38	38	39	15	22	7	4	16	29	34	26
JUL. 22	17	39	40	40	15	22	7	4	16	29	34	26
JUL. 23	17	41	41	42	16	22	7	4	16	29	34	26
JUL. 24	17	43	43	44	16	22	7	4	16	29	34	26
JUL. 25	17	44	45	45	16	22	7	4	16	29	34	26
JUL. 26	18	46	46	47	16	22	7	4	16	29	34	26
JUL. 27	18	47	48	48	17	22	7	4	16	29	34	26
JUL. 28	18	1	1	2	17	22	7	4	16	29	34	26
JUL. 29	18	3	3	4	17	22	8	4	16	29	34	26
JUL. 30	18	4	5	5	17	22	8	4	16	29	34	26
JUL. 31	18	6	6	7	18	22	8	4	16	29	34	26

Date & Time	SUN	MOON 1	MOON 2	MOON 3	MERCURY	VENUS	MARS	JUPITER	SATURN	URANUS	NEPTUNE	PLUTO
AUG. 1	18	7	8	8	18	22	8	4	16	29	34	26
AUG. 2	18	9	10	10	18	22	8	4	16	29	34	26
AUG. 3	19	11	11	12	19	23	8	4	16	29	34	26
AUG. 4	19	13	13	14	19	23	8	4	16	29	34	26
AUG. 5	19	14	15	16	19	23	8	4	16	29	34	26
AUG. 6	19	16	17	18	19	23	8	4	16	29	34	26
AUG. 7	19	18	19	20	20	23	8	4	16	29	34	26
AUG. 8	19	20	21	22	20	23	8	4	16	29	34	26
AUG. 9	19	22	23	24	20	23	8	4	16	29	34	26
AUG. 10	19	24	25	26	20	22	9	4	16	29	34	26
AUG. 11	20	26	27	28	21	22	9	4	16	29	34	26
AUG. 12	20	28	29	29	21	22	9	4	16	29	34	26
AUG. 13	20	30	31	31	21	22	9	4	16	29	34	26
AUG. 14	20	32	33	33	21	22	9	4	16	29	34	26
AUG. 15	20	34	34	35	22	22	9	4	16	29	34	26
AUG. 16	20	35	36	37	22	22	9	4	17	29	34	26
AUG. 17	20	37	38	38	22	22	9	4	17	29	34	26
AUG. 18	20	39	39	40	22	22	9	4	17	29	34	26
AUG. 19	21	40	41	42	23	22	9	4	17	29	34	26
AUG. 20	21	42	43	43	23	22	9	4	17	29	34	26
AUG. 21	21	44	44	45	23	22	9	4	17	29	34	26
AUG. 22	21	45	46	46	23	22	10	4	17	29	34	26
AUG. 23	21	47	47	48	23	22	10	4	17	29	34	26
AUG. 24	21	1	1	2	24	22	10	4	17	29	34	26
AUG. 25	21	2	3	3	24	22	10	4	17	29	34	26
AUG. 26	22	4	4	5	24	22	10	4	17	29	34	26
AUG. 27	22	5	6	6	24	21	10	4	17	29	34	26
AUG. 28	22	7	7	8	24	21	10	4	17	29	34	26
AUG. 29	22	8	9	10	25	21	10	4	17	29	34	26
AUG. 30	22	10	11	11	25	21	10	4	17	29	34	26
AUG. 31	22	12	12	13	25	21	10	4	17	29	34	26

MOON 1 ◗ 12:01 A.M. TO 8:00 A.M.   **MOON 2** ◗ 8:01 A.M. TO 4:00 P.M.   **MOON 3** ● 4:01 P.M. TO 12:00 A.M.

Use only one "moon" number. Choose the column closest to your time of birth. If your place of birth is not on Eastern Standard Time, be sure to read "How to Convert to Eastern Standard Time" at the beginning of this section.

1975

September

Date & Time	SUN	MOON 1	MOON 2	MOON 3	MERCURY	VENUS	MARS	JUPITER	SATURN	URANUS	NEPTUNE	PLUTO
SEP. 1	22	14	14	15	25	21	10	4	17	29	34	26
SEP. 2	22	16	16	17	25	21	10	4	17	29	34	26
SEP. 3	23	17	18	19	26	21	10	4	17	29	34	26
SEP. 4	23	19	20	21	26	21	11	4	17	29	34	26
SEP. 5	23	21	22	23	26	21	11	4	17	29	34	26
SEP. 6	23	23	24	25	27	21	11	4	17	29	34	26
SEP. 7	23	26	26	27	27	21	11	4	17	29	34	26
SEP. 8	23	28	28	29	26	21	11	4	17	29	34	26
SEP. 9	23	29	30	31	27	21	11	4	17	29	34	26
SEP. 10	23	31	32	33	27	21	11	4	17	29	34	26
SEP. 11	24	33	34	34	27	20	11	4	17	29	34	26
SEP. 12	24	35	36	36	27	20	11	4	17	29	34	26
SEP. 13	24	37	37	38	27	20	11	4	17	29	34	26
SEP. 14	24	38	39	40	27	20	11	4	17	29	34	26
SEP. 15	24	40	41	41	27	20	11	4	17	29	34	26
SEP. 16	24	42	42	43	28	20	11	4	17	29	34	26
SEP. 17	24	43	44	44	28	20	11	4	17	29	34	26
SEP. 18	24	45	45	46	28	20	12	4	17	29	34	26
SEP. 19	25	47	47	48	28	20	12	4	17	29	34	26
SEP. 20	25	48	1	1	28	20	12	4	17	29	34	26
SEP. 21	25	2	2	3	28	20	12	4	17	29	34	26
SEP. 22	25	3	4	4	28	20	12	4	17	29	34	26
SEP. 23	25	5	5	6	28	20	12	4	17	29	34	26
SEP. 24	25	6	7	8	28	20	12	4	17	29	34	26
SEP. 25	26	8	9	9	28	20	12	4	17	29	34	26
SEP. 26	26	10	10	11	28	21	12	4	17	29	34	26
SEP. 27	26	11	12	13	28	21	12	4	17	29	34	26
SEP. 28	26	13	14	14	28	21	12	4	17	29	34	26
SEP. 29	26	15	15	16	28	21	12	4	17	29	34	26
SEP. 30	26	17	17	18	28	21	12	4	17	29	34	26

October

Date & Time	SUN	MOON 1	MOON 2	MOON 3	MERCURY	VENUS	MARS	JUPITER	SATURN	URANUS	NEPTUNE	PLUTO
OCT. 1	26	19	19	20	28	21	12	4	17	29	34	26
OCT. 2	26	21	21	22	28	21	12	4	17	29	34	26
OCT. 3	27	23	23	24	28	21	12	4	17	29	34	26
OCT. 4	27	25	25	26	28	21	12	4	17	29	34	26
OCT. 5	27	27	27	28	28	21	12	4	17	29	34	26
OCT. 6	27	29	29	30	28	21	13	4	17	29	34	26
OCT. 7	27	31	31	32	27	21	13	4	17	29	34	26
OCT. 8	27	33	33	34	27	21	13	4	17	29	34	26
OCT. 9	27	34	35	36	27	21	13	4	17	29	34	26
OCT. 10	27	36	37	37	27	21	13	4	17	29	34	26
OCT. 11	28	38	39	39	27	22	13	4	17	29	34	26
OCT. 12	28	40	40	41	27	22	13	4	17	29	34	26
OCT. 13	28	41	42	42	27	22	13	4	17	29	34	26
OCT. 14	28	43	43	44	26	22	13	4	17	29	34	26
OCT. 15	28	45	45	46	26	22	13	4	17	29	34	26
OCT. 16	28	46	47	47	26	22	13	4	17	29	34	26
OCT. 17	28	48	48	1	26	22	13	4	17	29	34	26
OCT. 18	28	1	2	2	26	22	13	4	17	29	34	26
OCT. 19	29	3	3	4	26	22	13	3	17	29	34	26
OCT. 20	29	4	5	6	26	22	13	3	17	29	34	26
OCT. 21	29	6	7	7	26	23	13	3	17	29	34	26
OCT. 22	29	8	8	9	26	23	13	3	17	29	34	26
OCT. 23	29	9	10	10	26	23	13	3	17	29	34	26
OCT. 24	29	11	12	12	27	23	13	3	17	29	34	26
OCT. 25	29	13	13	14	27	23	13	3	17	29	34	26
OCT. 26	30	14	15	16	27	23	13	3	17	29	34	26
OCT. 27	30	16	17	17	27	23	13	3	17	29	34	26
OCT. 28	30	18	19	19	27	23	13	3	17	29	34	26
OCT. 29	30	20	21	21	27	23	13	3	17	29	34	26
OCT. 30	30	22	22	23	24	24	13	3	17	29	34	26
OCT. 31	30	24	24	25	28	24	13	3	17	29	34	26

MOON 1 ☽ 12:01 A.M. TO 8:00 A.M.   **MOON 2** ◐ 8:01 A.M. TO 4:00 P.M.   **MOON 3** ● 4:01 P.M. TO 12:00 A.M.
Use only one "moon" number. Choose the column closest to your time of birth. If your place of birth is not on
Eastern Standard Time, be sure to read "How to Convert to Eastern Standard Time" at the beginning of this section.

November

Date & Time	☉ SUN	◐ MOON 1	◑ MOON 2	● MOON 3	MERCURY	VENUS	MARS	JUPITER	SATURN	URANUS	NEPTUNE	PLUTO
NOV. 1	30	26	26	27	28	24	13	3	17	29	34	26
NOV. 2	30	28	28	29	28	24	13	3	17	29	34	26
NOV. 3	31	30	30	31	28	24	13	3	17	29	34	26
NOV. 4	31	32	32	33	29	24	13	3	17	29	34	26
NOV. 5	31	34	34	35	29	24	13	3	17	29	34	26
NOV. 6	31	35	36	37	29	25	13	3	17	29	34	26
NOV. 7	31	37	38	38	29	25	13	3	17	29	34	26
NOV. 8	31	39	40	40	29	25	13	3	17	29	34	26
NOV. 9	31	41	41	42	30	25	13	3	17	29	34	26
NOV. 10	31	42	43	44	30	25	13	3	17	29	34	26
NOV. 11	31	44	45	45	30	25	13	3	17	29	34	26
NOV. 12	32	46	46	47	30	25	13	3	17	29	34	26
NOV. 13	32	47	48	48	30	25	13	3	17	29	34	26
NOV. 14	32	1	1	2	31	26	13	3	17	29	34	26
NOV. 15	32	2	3	3	31	26	13	3	17	30	34	26
NOV. 16	32	4	5	5	31	26	13	3	17	30	34	26
NOV. 17	32	6	6	7	31	26	13	3	17	30	34	26
NOV. 18	32	7	8	8	32	26	13	3	17	30	34	26
NOV. 19	33	9	9	10	32	26	13	3	17	30	34	26
NOV. 20	33	11	11	12	32	26	13	3	17	30	34	26
NOV. 21	33	12	13	13	32	27	13	3	17	30	34	26
NOV. 22	33	14	15	15	32	27	13	3	17	30	34	26
NOV. 23	33	16	16	17	33	27	13	3	17	30	34	26
NOV. 24	33	18	18	19	33	27	13	3	17	30	34	26
NOV. 25	34	19	20	21	33	27	13	3	17	30	34	26
NOV. 26	34	21	22	23	33	27	13	3	17	30	34	26
NOV. 27	34	23	24	24	33	27	13	3	17	30	34	26
NOV. 28	34	25	26	26	34	28	13	3	17	30	34	26
NOV. 29	34	27	28	28	34	28	13	3	17	30	34	26
NOV. 30	34	29	30	30	34	28	13	3	17	30	34	26

December

Date & Time	☉ SUN	◐ MOON 1	◑ MOON 2	● MOON 3	MERCURY	VENUS	MARS	JUPITER	SATURN	URANUS	NEPTUNE	PLUTO
DEC. 1	34	31	31	32	34	28	13	3	17	30	34	26
DEC. 2	34	33	33	34	34	28	13	3	17	30	34	26
DEC. 3	35	35	35	36	35	28	13	3	17	30	34	26
DEC. 4	35	37	37	38	35	29	13	3	17	30	35	26
DEC. 5	35	38	39	40	35	29	13	3	17	30	35	26
DEC. 6	35	40	41	41	35	29	13	3	17	30	35	26
DEC. 7	35	42	42	43	36	29	12	3	17	30	35	26
DEC. 8	35	43	44	45	36	29	12	3	17	30	35	26
DEC. 9	35	45	46	46	36	29	12	3	17	30	35	26
DEC. 10	35	47	47	48	36	29	12	3	17	30	35	26
DEC. 11	36	48	1	1	36	30	12	3	17	30	35	26
DEC. 12	36	2	2	3	37	30	12	3	17	30	35	26
DEC. 13	36	3	4	5	37	30	12	3	17	30	35	26
DEC. 14	36	5	6	6	37	30	12	3	17	30	35	26
DEC. 15	36	7	7	8	37	30	12	3	17	30	35	26
DEC. 16	36	8	9	9	37	30	12	3	17	30	35	26
DEC. 17	36	10	11	11	38	31	12	3	17	30	35	26
DEC. 18	36	12	12	13	38	31	12	3	17	30	35	26
DEC. 19	37	13	14	15	38	31	12	3	17	30	35	27
DEC. 20	37	15	16	17	38	31	12	3	17	30	35	27
DEC. 21	37	17	18	18	38	31	12	3	17	30	35	27
DEC. 22	37	19	20	20	39	31	12	3	17	30	35	27
DEC. 23	37	21	21	22	39	31	12	3	17	30	35	27
DEC. 24	37	23	23	24	39	32	12	3	17	30	35	27
DEC. 25	37	25	25	26	39	32	12	3	17	30	35	27
DEC. 26	38	27	27	28	39	32	12	3	17	30	35	27
DEC. 27	38	28	29	30	40	32	11	3	17	30	35	27
DEC. 28	38	30	31	32	40	32	11	3	17	30	35	27
DEC. 29	38	32	33	33	40	32	11	3	17	30	35	27
DEC. 30	38	34	35	35	40	33	11	3	17	30	35	27
DEC. 31	38	36	36	37	40	33	11	3	17	30	35	27

MOON 1 ◐ 12:01 A.M. TO 8:00 A.M.   **MOON 2** ◑ 8:01 A.M. TO 4:00 P.M.   **MOON 3** ● 4:01 P.M. TO 12:00 A.M.
Use only one "moon" number. Choose the column closest to your time of birth. If your place of birth is not on Eastern Standard Time, be sure to read "How to Convert to Eastern Standard Time" at the beginning of this section.

1976

January

Date & Time	SUN	MOON 1	MOON 2	MOON 3	MERCURY	VENUS	MARS	JUPITER	SATURN	URANUS	NEPTUNE	PLUTO
JAN. 1	38	38	38	39	41	33	11	3	17	30	35	27
JAN. 2	38	39	40	41	41	33	11	3	17	30	35	27
JAN. 3	39	41	42	42	41	33	11	3	17	30	35	27
JAN. 4	39	43	43	44	41	33	11	3	17	30	35	27
JAN. 5	39	45	45	46	41	34	11	3	17	30	35	27
JAN. 6	39	46	47	47	42	34	11	3	17	30	35	27
JAN. 7	39	48	48	1	42	34	11	3	17	30	35	27
JAN. 8	39	1	2	2	42	34	11	3	17	30	35	27
JAN. 9	39	3	3	4	42	34	11	3	17	30	35	27
JAN. 10	40	4	5	6	42	34	11	3	17	30	35	27
JAN. 11	40	6	7	7	42	35	11	3	17	30	35	27
JAN. 12	40	8	8	9	42	35	11	3	17	30	35	27
JAN. 13	40	9	10	10	42	35	11	3	17	30	35	27
JAN. 14	40	11	12	12	42	35	11	3	17	30	35	27
JAN. 15	40	13	13	14	42	35	11	3	17	30	35	27
JAN. 16	40	15	15	16	42	35	11	3	17	30	35	27
JAN. 17	41	16	17	18	42	35	11	3	17	30	35	27
JAN. 18	41	18	19	20	42	36	11	3	17	30	35	27
JAN. 19	41	20	21	22	42	36	11	3	17	30	35	27
JAN. 20	41	22	23	24	42	36	11	3	17	30	35	27
JAN. 21	41	24	25	25	42	36	11	3	17	30	35	27
JAN. 22	41	26	27	27	41	36	11	3	17	30	35	27
JAN. 23	42	28	29	29	41	36	11	3	17	30	35	27
JAN. 24	42	30	30	31	41	37	11	3	17	30	35	27
JAN. 25	42	32	32	33	41	37	11	3	17	30	35	27
JAN. 26	42	34	34	35	41	37	11	3	17	30	35	27
JAN. 27	42	35	36	36	41	37	11	3	17	30	35	27
JAN. 28	42	37	38	38	41	37	11	3	17	30	35	27
JAN. 29	42	39	39	40	40	37	11	3	17	30	35	27
JAN. 30	42	41	41	42	40	38	11	3	17	30	35	27
JAN. 31	43	42	43	43	40	38	11	4	17	30	35	27

February

Date & Time	SUN	MOON 1	MOON 2	MOON 3	MERCURY	VENUS	MARS	JUPITER	SATURN	URANUS	NEPTUNE	PLUTO
FEB. 1	43	44	45	45	40	38	11	4	17	30	35	27
FEB. 2	43	46	46	47	40	38	11	4	17	30	35	27
FEB. 3	43	47	48	48	40	38	11	4	17	30	35	27
FEB. 4	43	1	1	2	40	38	11	4	17	30	35	27
FEB. 5	43	2	3	3	40	39	11	4	17	30	35	27
FEB. 6	43	4	4	5	40	39	11	4	17	30	35	27
FEB. 7	43	6	6	7	40	39	11	4	17	30	35	27
FEB. 8	44	7	8	8	40	39	11	4	17	30	35	27
FEB. 9	44	9	9	10	40	39	11	4	17	30	35	27
FEB. 10	44	10	11	12	40	39	11	4	17	30	35	27
FEB. 11	44	12	13	13	40	40	11	4	17	30	35	26
FEB. 12	44	14	14	15	41	40	11	4	17	30	35	26
FEB. 13	44	16	16	17	41	40	11	4	17	30	35	26
FEB. 14	44	18	18	19	41	40	11	4	17	30	35	26
FEB. 15	44	19	20	21	41	40	11	4	17	30	35	26
FEB. 16	45	21	22	23	41	40	11	4	17	30	35	26
FEB. 17	45	23	24	25	41	41	11	4	17	30	35	26
FEB. 18	45	25	26	27	41	41	12	4	17	30	35	26
FEB. 19	45	27	28	29	41	41	12	4	17	30	35	26
FEB. 20	45	29	30	31	42	41	12	4	17	30	35	26
FEB. 21	45	31	32	32	42	41	12	4	17	30	35	26
FEB. 22	45	33	34	34	42	41	12	4	17	30	35	26
FEB. 23	46	35	36	36	42	42	12	4	17	30	35	26
FEB. 24	46	37	37	38	42	42	12	4	17	30	35	26
FEB. 25	46	38	39	40	42	42	12	4	17	30	35	26
FEB. 26	46	40	41	41	43	42	12	4	17	30	35	26
FEB. 27	46	42	42	43	42	42	12	4	17	30	35	26
FEB. 28	46	44	44	45	43	42	12	4	17	30	35	26
FEB. 29	46	45	46	46	43	43	12	4	17	30	35	26

MOON 1 ◗ 12:01 A.M. TO 8:00 A.M.   **MOON 2** ◑ 8:01 A.M. TO 4:00 P.M.   **MOON 3** ● 4:01 P.M. TO 12:00 A.M.
Use only one "moon" number. Choose the column closest to your time of birth. If your place of birth is not on Eastern Standard Time, be sure to read "How to Convert to Eastern Standard Time" at the beginning of this section.

March

Date & Time	SUN ☉	MOON 1 ◗	MOON 2 ◑	MOON 3 ●	MERCURY	VENUS	MARS	JUPITER	SATURN	URANUS	NEPTUNE	PLUTO
MAR. 1	46	47	47	48	43	43	12	4	17	30	35	26
MAR. 2	46	48	1	1	44	43	12	4	17	30	35	26
MAR. 3	47	2	2	3	44	43	12	4	17	30	35	26
MAR. 4	47	4	4	5	44	43	12	4	17	30	35	26
MAR. 5	47	5	6	6	44	43	12	4	16	30	35	26
MAR. 6	47	7	7	8	44	44	12	4	16	30	35	26
MAR. 7	47	8	9	9	44	44	12	4	16	30	35	26
MAR. 8	47	10	10	11	45	44	12	4	16	30	35	26
MAR. 9	47	11	12	13	45	44	12	4	16	30	35	26
MAR. 10	47	13	14	14	45	44	12	4	16	30	35	26
MAR. 11	48	15	16	16	45	44	13	5	16	30	35	26
MAR. 12	48	17	17	18	46	45	13	5	16	30	35	26
MAR. 13	48	19	19	20	46	45	13	5	16	30	35	26
MAR. 14	48	21	21	22	46	45	13	5	16	30	35	26
MAR. 15	48	23	23	24	46	45	13	5	16	30	35	26
MAR. 16	48	25	25	26	46	45	13	5	16	30	35	26
MAR. 17	48	27	27	28	47	45	13	5	16	30	35	26
MAR. 18	48	29	29	30	47	45	13	5	16	30	35	26
MAR. 19	1	31	31	32	47	46	13	5	16	30	35	26
MAR. 20	1	33	33	34	47	46	13	5	16	30	35	26
MAR. 21	1	34	35	36	48	46	13	5	16	30	35	26
MAR. 22	1	36	37	37	48	46	13	5	16	30	35	26
MAR. 23	1	38	39	39	48	46	13	5	16	30	35	26
MAR. 24	1	40	40	41	48	46	13	5	16	30	35	26
MAR. 25	2	41	42	43	1	47	13	5	16	30	35	26
MAR. 26	2	43	44	44	1	47	13	5	16	30	35	26
MAR. 27	2	45	45	46	1	47	13	5	16	30	35	26
MAR. 28	2	46	47	47	1	47	14	5	16	30	35	26
MAR. 29	2	48	48	1	2	47	14	5	16	30	35	26
MAR. 30	2	2	2	3	2	47	14	5	16	30	35	26
MAR. 31	2	3	4	4	2	48	14	5	16	30	35	26

April

Date & Time	SUN ☉	MOON 1 ◗	MOON 2 ◑	MOON 3 ●	MERCURY	VENUS	MARS	JUPITER	SATURN	URANUS	NEPTUNE	PLUTO
APR. 1	2	5	5	6	2	48	14	5	16	30	35	26
APR. 2	2	6	7	7	3	48	14	5	16	30	35	26
APR. 3	3	8	8	9	3	48	14	5	16	30	35	26
APR. 4	3	9	10	10	3	48	14	5	16	30	35	26
APR. 5	3	11	12	12	4	48	14	5	16	30	35	26
APR. 6	3	13	13	14	4	1	14	5	16	30	35	26
APR. 7	3	14	15	16	4	1	14	5	16	30	35	26
APR. 8	3	16	17	17	4	1	14	5	16	30	35	26
APR. 9	3	18	19	19	5	1	14	5	16	30	35	26
APR. 10	3	20	20	21	5	1	14	5	16	30	35	26
APR. 11	4	22	22	23	5	1	14	5	16	30	35	26
APR. 12	4	24	24	25	5	2	15	5	16	30	35	26
APR. 13	4	26	26	27	6	2	15	6	16	30	35	26
APR. 14	4	28	28	29	6	2	15	6	16	30	35	26
APR. 15	4	30	30	31	6	2	15	6	16	30	35	26
APR. 16	4	32	32	33	6	2	15	6	16	30	35	26
APR. 17	4	34	34	35	7	2	15	6	16	30	35	26
APR. 18	4	36	36	37	7	3	15	6	16	30	35	26
APR. 19	5	37	38	39	7	3	15	6	16	30	35	26
APR. 20	5	39	40	40	7	3	15	6	17	30	35	26
APR. 21	5	41	42	42	8	3	15	6	17	30	35	26
APR. 22	5	43	43	44	8	3	15	6	17	30	35	26
APR. 23	5	44	45	45	8	3	15	6	17	30	35	26
APR. 24	5	46	46	47	8	4	15	6	17	30	35	26
APR. 25	6	48	48	1	8	4	15	6	17	30	35	26
APR. 26	6	1	2	2	8	4	15	6	17	30	35	26
APR. 27	6	3	3	4	9	4	16	6	17	30	35	26
APR. 28	6	4	5	5	9	4	16	6	17	30	35	26
APR. 29	6	6	6	7	9	4	16	6	17	30	35	26
APR. 30	6	7	8	8	9	5	16	6	17	30	35	26

MOON 1 ◗ 12:01 A.M. TO 8:00 A.M.   **MOON 2** ◑ 8:01 A.M. TO 4:00 P.M.   **MOON 3** ● 4:01 P.M. TO 12:00 A.M.
Use only one "moon" number. Choose the column closest to your time of birth. If your place of birth is not on Eastern Standard Time, be sure to read "How to Convert to Eastern Standard Time" at the beginning of this section.

1976

May ★★★ **June** ★★★

Date & Time	SUN ☉	MOON 1 ◗	MOON 2 ◖	MOON 3 ●	MERCURY	VENUS	MARS	JUPITER	SATURN	URANUS	NEPTUNE	PLUTO
MAY 1	6	9	10	10	9	5	16	6	17	30	35	26
MAY 2	6	11	11	12	9	5	16	6	17	30	35	26
MAY 3	7	12	13	13	9	5	16	6	17	30	35	26
MAY 4	7	14	15	15	9	5	16	6	17	30	35	26
MAY 5	7	16	16	17	9	5	16	6	17	30	35	26
MAY 6	7	17	18	19	9	6	16	6	17	30	35	26
MAY 7	7	19	20	20	9	6	16	6	17	30	35	26
MAY 8	7	21	22	22	9	6	16	6	17	30	35	26
MAY 9	7	23	24	24	9	6	16	6	17	30	35	26
MAY 10	7	25	25	26	9	6	17	6	17	30	35	26
MAY 11	8	27	27	28	9	6	17	6	17	30	35	26
MAY 12	8	29	29	30	7	6	17	6	17	30	35	26
MAY 13	8	31	31	32	9	7	17	6	17	30	35	26
MAY 14	8	33	33	34	9	7	17	7	17	30	35	26
MAY 15	8	35	35	36	9	7	17	7	17	30	35	26
MAY 16	8	37	37	38	9	7	17	7	17	30	35	26
MAY 17	8	39	39	40	9	7	17	7	17	30	35	26
MAY 18	8	40	41	42	9	7	17	7	17	30	35	26
MAY 19	9	42	43	43	9	8	17	7	17	30	35	26
MAY 20	9	44	44	45	9	8	17	7	17	30	35	26
MAY 21	9	45	46	47	9	8	17	7	17	30	35	26
MAY 22	9	47	48	48	9	8	17	7	17	30	35	26
MAY 23	9	1	1	2	9	8	17	7	17	29	35	26
MAY 24	9	2	3	3	9	8	18	7	17	29	35	26
MAY 25	10	4	4	5	9	9	18	7	17	29	35	26
MAY 26	10	5	6	6	9	9	18	7	17	29	35	26
MAY 27	10	7	8	8	9	9	18	7	17	29	35	26
MAY 28	10	9	9	10	8	9	18	7	17	29	35	26
MAY 29	10	10	11	11	8	9	18	7	17	29	35	26
MAY 30	10	12	12	13	8	9	18	7	17	29	35	26
MAY 31	10	14	14	15	8	10	18	7	17	29	35	26

Date & Time	SUN ☉	MOON 1 ◗	MOON 2 ◖	MOON 3 ●	MERCURY	VENUS	MARS	JUPITER	SATURN	URANUS	NEPTUNE	PLUTO
JUN. 1	10	15	16	16	8	10	18	7	17	29	35	26
JUN. 2	10	17	18	18	8	10	18	7	17	29	35	26
JUN. 3	11	19	19	20	8	10	18	7	17	29	35	26
JUN. 4	11	21	21	22	8	10	18	7	17	29	35	26
JUN. 5	11	22	23	24	8	10	18	7	17	29	35	26
JUN. 6	11	24	25	26	8	11	19	7	17	29	35	26
JUN. 7	11	26	27	27	8	11	19	7	17	29	35	26
JUN. 8	11	28	29	29	8	11	19	7	17	29	35	26
JUN. 9	11	30	31	31	9	11	19	7	17	29	35	26
JUN. 10	11	32	33	33	9	11	19	7	17	29	35	26
JUN. 11	12	34	35	35	9	11	19	7	17	29	35	26
JUN. 12	12	36	37	37	9	12	19	7	17	29	35	26
JUN. 13	12	38	38	39	9	12	19	7	17	29	35	26
JUN. 14	12	40	40	41	9	12	19	7	17	29	35	26
JUN. 15	12	41	42	43	9	12	19	7	17	29	35	26
JUN. 16	12	43	44	44	9	12	19	8	17	29	35	26
JUN. 17	12	45	45	46	9	12	19	8	17	29	35	26
JUN. 18	12	47	47	48	10	13	19	8	17	29	35	26
JUN. 19	13	48	1	1	10	13	20	8	17	29	35	26
JUN. 20	13	2	2	3	10	13	20	8	17	29	35	26
JUN. 21	13	3	4	4	10	13	20	8	17	29	35	26
JUN. 22	13	5	5	6	10	13	20	8	17	29	35	26
JUN. 23	13	7	7	8	10	13	20	8	17	29	35	26
JUN. 24	13	8	9	10	11	14	20	8	17	29	35	26
JUN. 25	14	10	10	11	11	14	20	8	17	29	35	26
JUN. 26	14	11	12	13	11	14	20	8	17	29	35	26
JUN. 27	14	13	14	14	11	14	20	8	17	29	35	26
JUN. 28	14	15	15	16	11	14	20	8	17	29	35	26
JUN. 29	14	17	17	18	12	14	20	8	17	29	35	26
JUN. 30	14	18	19	20	12	15	20	8	17	29	35	26

MOON 1 ◗ 12:01 A.M. TO 8:00 A.M.   **MOON 2** ◖ 8:01 A.M. TO 4:00 P.M.   **MOON 3** ● 4:01 P.M. TO 12:00 A.M.

Use only one "moon" number. Choose the column closest to your time of birth. If your place of birth is not on Eastern Standard Time, be sure to read "How to Convert to Eastern Standard Time" at the beginning of this section.

1976

July

August

Date & Time	SUN	MOON 1	MOON 2	MOON 3	MERCURY	VENUS	MARS	JUPITER	SATURN	URANUS	NEPTUNE	PLUTO
JUL. 1	14	20	21	21	12	15	21	8	17	29	35	26
JUL. 2	14	22	23	23	12	15	21	8	17	29	35	26
JUL. 3	15	24	24	25	13	15	21	8	17	29	35	26
JUL. 4	15	26	26	27	13	15	21	8	17	29	35	26
JUL. 5	15	28	28	29	13	15	21	8	17	29	35	26
JUL. 6	15	29	30	31	13	16	21	8	17	29	35	26
JUL. 7	15	31	32	33	14	16	21	8	17	29	35	26
JUL. 8	15	33	34	35	14	16	21	8	17	29	35	26
JUL. 9	15	35	36	36	14	16	21	8	17	29	35	26
JUL. 10	15	37	38	38	15	16	21	8	18	29	35	26
JUL. 11	16	39	40	40	15	16	21	8	18	29	35	26
JUL. 12	16	41	41	42	15	17	21	8	18	29	35	26
JUL. 13	16	43	43	44	15	17	21	8	18	29	35	26
JUL. 14	16	44	45	45	16	17	22	8	18	29	35	26
JUL. 15	16	46	47	47	16	17	22	8	18	29	35	26
JUL. 16	16	48	48	1	16	17	22	8	18	29	35	26
JUL. 17	16	1	2	2	17	17	22	8	18	29	35	26
JUL. 18	16	3	3	4	17	17	22	8	18	29	35	26
JUL. 19	17	4	5	5	17	18	22	8	18	29	35	26
JUL. 20	17	6	7	7	17	18	22	8	18	29	34	26
JUL. 21	17	8	9	9	18	18	22	8	18	29	34	26
JUL. 22	17	9	10	10	18	18	22	8	18	29	34	26
JUL. 23	17	11	11	12	18	18	22	8	18	29	34	26
JUL. 24	17	12	13	14	18	18	22	8	18	29	34	26
JUL. 25	17	14	15	15	19	19	22	8	18	29	34	26
JUL. 26	18	16	17	17	19	19	23	9	18	29	34	26
JUL. 27	18	18	18	19	19	19	23	9	18	29	34	26
JUL. 28	18	20	20	21	19	19	23	9	18	29	34	26
JUL. 29	18	21	22	23	20	19	23	9	18	29	34	26
JUL. 30	18	23	24	25	20	19	23	9	18	29	34	26
JUL. 31	18	25	26	27	20	20	23	9	18	29	34	26

Date & Time	SUN	MOON 1	MOON 2	MOON 3	MERCURY	VENUS	MARS	JUPITER	SATURN	URANUS	NEPTUNE	PLUTO
AUG. 1	18	27	28	28	20	20	23	9	18	29	34	26
AUG. 2	18	29	30	30	21	20	23	9	18	29	34	26
AUG. 3	19	31	32	32	21	20	23	9	18	29	34	26
AUG. 4	19	33	33	34	21	20	23	9	18	29	34	26
AUG. 5	19	35	35	36	21	20	23	9	18	29	34	26
AUG. 6	19	37	37	38	22	21	23	9	18	29	34	26
AUG. 7	19	38	39	40	22	21	24	9	18	29	34	26
AUG. 8	19	40	41	41	22	21	24	9	18	29	34	26
AUG. 9	19	42	43	43	22	21	24	9	18	29	34	26
AUG. 10	19	44	44	45	22	21	24	9	18	29	34	26
AUG. 11	20	45	46	47	23	21	24	9	18	29	34	26
AUG. 12	20	47	48	48	23	22	24	9	18	29	34	26
AUG. 13	20	1	1	2	23	22	24	9	18	29	34	26
AUG. 14	20	2	3	3	23	22	24	9	18	29	34	26
AUG. 15	20	4	4	5	23	22	24	9	18	29	34	26
AUG. 16	20	5	6	7	23	22	24	9	18	29	34	26
AUG. 17	20	7	8	8	24	22	24	9	18	29	34	26
AUG. 18	20	9	9	10	24	23	24	9	18	29	34	26
AUG. 19	21	10	11	11	24	23	25	9	18	29	34	26
AUG. 20	21	12	12	13	24	23	25	9	18	29	34	26
AUG. 21	21	14	14	15	24	23	25	9	18	29	34	26
AUG. 22	21	15	16	16	24	23	25	9	18	29	34	26
AUG. 23	21	17	18	18	25	23	25	9	18	29	34	26
AUG. 24	21	19	20	20	25	24	25	9	18	29	34	26
AUG. 25	21	21	21	22	25	24	25	9	18	29	34	26
AUG. 26	22	23	23	24	25	24	25	9	18	29	34	26
AUG. 27	22	25	25	26	25	24	25	9	18	29	34	26
AUG. 28	22	27	27	28	25	24	25	9	18	30	34	26
AUG. 29	22	29	29	30	25	24	25	9	18	30	34	26
AUG. 30	22	30	31	32	25	25	25	9	18	30	34	26
AUG. 31	22	32	33	34	26	25	26	9	18	30	34	26

MOON 1 ◐ 12:01 A.M. TO 8:00 A.M.   **MOON 2** ◑ 8:01 A.M. TO 4:00 P.M.   **MOON 3** ● 4:01 P.M. TO 12:00 A.M.

Use only one "moon" number. Choose the column closest to your time of birth. If your place of birth is not on Eastern Standard Time, be sure to read "How to Convert to Eastern Standard Time" at the beginning of this section.

1976

September

Date & Time	SUN	MOON 1	MOON 2	MOON 3	MERCURY	VENUS	MARS	JUPITER	SATURN	URANUS	NEPTUNE	PLUTO
SEP. 1	22	34	35	35	26	25	26	9	18	30	34	26
SEP. 2	22	36	37	37	26	25	26	9	18	30	34	26
SEP. 3	23	38	39	39	26	25	26	9	18	30	34	26
SEP. 4	23	40	40	41	26	25	26	9	18	30	34	26
SEP. 5	23	41	42	43	26	26	26	9	18	30	34	26
SEP. 6	23	43	44	44	26	26	26	9	18	30	34	26
SEP. 7	23	45	45	46	26	26	26	9	18	30	34	26
SEP. 8	23	47	47	48	26	26	26	9	19	30	34	26
SEP. 9	23	48	1	1	26	26	26	9	19	30	34	26
SEP. 10	23	2	2	3	26	26	26	9	19	30	34	26
SEP. 11	24	3	4	4	26	27	27	9	19	30	34	26
SEP. 12	24	5	6	6	26	27	27	9	19	30	34	26
SEP. 13	24	7	7	8	26	27	27	9	19	30	34	26
SEP. 14	24	8	9	9	26	27	27	9	19	30	34	26
SEP. 15	24	10	10	11	26	27	27	9	19	30	34	26
SEP. 16	24	11	12	12	26	27	27	9	19	30	34	26
SEP. 17	24	13	14	14	26	27	27	9	19	30	34	26
SEP. 18	24	15	15	16	25	28	27	9	19	30	34	26
SEP. 19	25	16	17	18	25	28	27	9	19	30	34	26
SEP. 20	25	18	19	19	25	28	27	9	19	30	34	26
SEP. 21	25	20	21	21	25	28	27	9	19	30	34	26
SEP. 22	25	22	23	23	25	28	27	9	19	30	34	26
SEP. 23	25	24	25	25	25	28	28	9	19	30	34	26
SEP. 24	25	26	27	27	24	29	28	9	19	30	34	26
SEP. 25	26	28	29	29	24	29	28	9	19	30	34	26
SEP. 26	26	30	30	31	24	29	28	9	19	30	35	26
SEP. 27	26	32	32	33	24	29	28	9	19	30	35	26
SEP. 28	26	34	34	35	24	29	28	9	19	30	35	26
SEP. 29	26	36	36	37	24	29	28	9	19	30	35	26
SEP. 30	26	37	38	39	24	30	28	9	19	30	35	26

October

Date & Time	SUN	MOON 1	MOON 2	MOON 3	MERCURY	VENUS	MARS	JUPITER	SATURN	URANUS	NEPTUNE	PLUTO
OCT. 1	26	39	40	40	24	30	28	9	19	30	35	26
OCT. 2	26	41	42	42	24	30	28	9	19	30	35	26
OCT. 3	27	43	43	44	24	30	28	9	19	30	35	27
OCT. 4	27	44	45	46	24	30	29	9	19	30	35	27
OCT. 5	27	46	47	47	24	30	29	9	19	30	35	27
OCT. 6	27	48	48	1	24	31	29	9	19	30	35	27
OCT. 7	27	1	2	2	24	31	29	9	19	30	35	27
OCT. 8	27	3	4	4	25	31	29	9	19	30	35	27
OCT. 9	27	5	5	6	25	31	29	9	19	30	35	27
OCT. 10	27	6	7	7	25	31	29	9	19	30	35	27
OCT. 11	28	8	8	9	25	31	29	9	19	30	35	27
OCT. 12	28	9	10	10	25	32	29	9	19	30	35	27
OCT. 13	28	11	11	12	25	32	29	9	19	30	35	27
OCT. 14	28	12	13	14	26	32	29	9	19	30	35	27
OCT. 15	28	14	15	15	26	32	30	9	19	30	35	27
OCT. 16	28	16	16	17	26	32	30	9	19	30	35	27
OCT. 17	28	17	18	19	26	32	30	9	19	30	35	27
OCT. 18	28	19	20	20	26	33	30	9	19	30	35	27
OCT. 19	29	21	22	22	27	33	30	9	19	30	35	27
OCT. 20	29	23	24	24	27	33	30	9	19	30	35	27
OCT. 21	29	25	26	26	27	33	30	9	19	30	35	27
OCT. 22	29	27	28	28	27	33	30	9	19	30	35	27
OCT. 23	29	29	30	30	28	33	30	9	19	30	35	27
OCT. 24	29	31	32	32	28	34	30	9	19	30	35	27
OCT. 25	29	33	34	34	28	34	30	9	19	30	35	27
OCT. 26	30	35	36	36	28	34	31	9	19	30	35	27
OCT. 27	30	37	38	38	29	34	31	9	19	30	35	27
OCT. 28	30	39	39	40	29	34	31	9	19	30	35	27
OCT. 29	30	41	41	42	29	34	31	9	19	30	35	27
OCT. 30	30	42	43	43	29	35	31	9	19	30	35	27
OCT. 31	30	44	45	45	29	35	31	9	19	30	35	27

MOON 1 ☽ 12:01 A.M. TO 8:00 A.M.　**MOON 2** ◐ 8:01 A.M. TO 4:00 P.M.　**MOON 3** ● 4:01 P.M. TO 12:00 A.M.
Use only one "moon" number. Choose the column closest to your time of birth. If your place of birth is not on Eastern Standard Time, be sure to read "How to Convert to Eastern Standard Time" at the beginning of this section.

1976

November

Date & Time	SUN	MOON 1	MOON 2	MOON 3	MERCURY	VENUS	MARS	JUPITER	SATURN	URANUS	NEPTUNE	PLUTO
NOV. 1	30	46	46	47	30	35	31	9	19	30	35	27
NOV. 2	30	47	48	48	30	35	31	9	19	30	35	27
NOV. 3	31	1	2	2	30	35	31	9	19	30	35	27
NOV. 4	31	3	3	4	30	35	31	9	19	30	35	27
NOV. 5	31	4	5	5	31	35	31	9	19	30	35	27
NOV. 6	31	6	6	7	31	36	32	9	19	30	35	27
NOV. 7	31	7	8	8	31	36	32	9	19	30	35	27
NOV. 8	31	9	9	10	31	36	32	9	19	30	35	27
NOV. 9	31	10	11	12	31	36	32	9	19	30	35	27
NOV. 10	31	12	13	13	32	36	32	9	19	30	35	27
NOV. 11	31	14	14	15	32	36	32	9	19	30	35	27
NOV. 12	32	15	16	16	32	37	32	9	19	30	35	27
NOV. 13	32	17	18	18	32	37	32	9	19	30	35	27
NOV. 14	32	19	19	20	32	37	32	9	19	30	35	27
NOV. 15	32	20	21	22	33	37	32	9	19	30	35	27
NOV. 16	32	22	23	24	33	37	33	8	19	30	35	27
NOV. 17	32	24	25	25	33	37	33	8	19	30	35	27
NOV. 18	32	26	27	27	33	38	33	8	19	30	35	27
NOV. 19	33	28	29	29	33	38	33	8	19	30	35	27
NOV. 20	33	30	31	31	34	38	33	8	19	30	35	27
NOV. 21	33	32	33	33	34	38	33	8	19	30	35	27
NOV. 22	33	34	35	35	34	38	33	8	19	30	35	27
NOV. 23	33	36	37	37	34	38	33	8	19	30	35	27
NOV. 24	33	38	39	39	34	39	33	8	19	30	35	27
NOV. 25	34	40	41	41	35	39	33	8	19	30	35	27
NOV. 26	34	42	42	43	35	39	33	8	19	30	35	27
NOV. 27	34	44	44	45	35	39	34	8	19	30	35	27
NOV. 28	34	45	46	46	35	39	34	8	19	30	35	27
NOV. 29	34	47	47	48	36	39	34	8	19	30	35	27
NOV. 30	34	1	1	2	36	39	34	8	19	30	35	27

December

Date & Time	SUN	MOON 1	MOON 2	MOON 3	MERCURY	VENUS	MARS	JUPITER	SATURN	URANUS	NEPTUNE	PLUTO
DEC. 1	34	2	3	3	36	40	34	8	19	30	35	27
DEC. 2	34	4	4	5	36	40	34	8	19	30	35	27
DEC. 3	35	5	5	6	36	40	34	8	19	30	35	27
DEC. 4	35	7	7	8	37	40	34	8	19	30	35	27
DEC. 5	35	8	9	10	37	40	34	8	19	30	35	27
DEC. 6	35	10	11	11	37	40	34	8	19	30	35	27
DEC. 7	35	12	12	13	37	41	35	8	19	30	35	27
DEC. 8	35	13	14	14	37	41	35	8	19	30	35	27
DEC. 9	35	15	15	16	38	41	35	8	19	30	35	27
DEC. 10	35	17	17	18	38	41	35	8	19	30	35	27
DEC. 11	36	18	19	19	38	41	35	8	19	30	35	27
DEC. 12	36	20	21	21	38	41	35	8	19	30	35	27
DEC. 13	36	22	22	23	38	42	35	8	19	30	35	27
DEC. 14	36	24	24	25	38	42	35	8	19	30	35	27
DEC. 15	36	25	26	27	39	42	35	8	19	30	35	27
DEC. 16	36	27	28	29	39	42	35	8	19	30	35	27
DEC. 17	36	29	30	31	39	42	36	8	19	30	35	27
DEC. 18	36	31	32	32	39	42	36	8	19	30	35	27
DEC. 19	37	33	34	34	39	42	36	8	19	30	35	27
DEC. 20	37	35	36	36	39	43	36	8	19	30	35	27
DEC. 21	37	37	38	38	40	43	36	8	19	30	35	27
DEC. 22	37	39	40	40	40	43	36	8	19	30	35	27
DEC. 23	37	41	42	42	40	43	36	8	19	30	35	27
DEC. 24	37	43	43	44	40	43	36	8	19	30	35	27
DEC. 25	37	45	45	46	40	43	36	8	19	30	35	27
DEC. 26	38	46	47	47	40	44	36	8	19	30	35	27
DEC. 27	38	48	1	1	40	44	36	8	19	30	35	27
DEC. 28	38	2	2	3	40	44	37	8	19	30	35	27
DEC. 29	38	3	4	4	40	44	37	8	19	30	35	27
DEC. 30	38	5	5	6	40	44	37	8	19	30	35	27
DEC. 31	38	6	7	7	40	44	37	8	19	30	35	27

MOON 1 ◖ 12:01 A.M. TO 8:00 A.M.   **MOON 2** ◑ 8:01 A.M. TO 4:00 P.M.   **MOON 3** ● 4:01 P.M. TO 12:00 A.M.

Use only one "moon" number. Choose the column closest to your time of birth. If your place of birth is not on Eastern Standard Time, be sure to read "How to Convert to Eastern Standard Time" at the beginning of this section.

1977

January

Date & Time	SUN	MOON 1	MOON 2	MOON 3	MERCURY	VENUS	MARS	JUPITER	SATURN	URANUS	NEPTUNE	PLUTO
JAN. 1	38	8	9	9	40	44	37	8	19	30	35	27
JAN. 2	38	10	10	11	40	45	37	8	19	30	35	27
JAN. 3	39	11	12	12	40	45	37	8	19	30	35	27
JAN. 4	39	13	13	14	39	45	37	8	19	30	35	27
JAN. 5	39	14	15	16	39	45	37	8	19	30	35	27
JAN. 6	39	16	17	17	39	45	37	8	19	30	35	27
JAN. 7	39	18	18	19	39	45	38	8	19	30	35	27
JAN. 8	39	20	20	21	39	46	38	8	19	30	35	27
JAN. 9	39	21	22	23	39	46	38	8	19	30	35	27
JAN. 10	40	23	24	24	38	46	38	8	19	30	35	27
JAN. 11	40	25	26	26	38	46	38	8	19	30	35	27
JAN. 12	40	27	27	28	38	46	38	8	19	30	35	27
JAN. 13	40	29	29	30	38	46	38	8	19	30	35	27
JAN. 14	40	31	31	32	38	46	38	8	19	30	35	27
JAN. 15	40	32	33	34	38	47	38	8	19	30	35	27
JAN. 16	40	34	35	36	38	47	38	8	19	30	35	27
JAN. 17	41	36	37	38	38	47	39	8	19	30	35	27
JAN. 18	41	38	39	40	38	47	39	8	19	30	35	27
JAN. 19	41	40	41	41	38	47	39	8	19	30	35	27
JAN. 20	41	42	43	43	38	47	39	8	19	30	35	27
JAN. 21	41	44	44	45	38	47	39	8	19	31	35	27
JAN. 22	41	46	46	47	38	48	39	8	19	31	35	27
JAN. 23	42	47	48	1	38	48	39	8	19	31	35	27
JAN. 24	42	1	2	2	38	48	39	8	19	31	35	27
JAN. 25	42	3	3	4	38	48	39	8	19	31	35	27
JAN. 26	42	4	5	5	38	48	40	8	19	31	35	27
JAN. 27	42	6	6	7	39	48	40	8	19	31	35	27
JAN. 28	42	7	8	8	39	48	40	8	19	31	35	27
JAN. 29	42	9	10	10	39	48	40	8	19	31	35	27
JAN. 30	42	11	11	12	39	1	40	8	19	31	35	27
JAN. 31	43	12	13	13	39	1	40	8	19	31	35	27

February

Date & Time	SUN	MOON 1	MOON 2	MOON 3	MERCURY	VENUS	MARS	JUPITER	SATURN	URANUS	NEPTUNE	PLUTO
FEB. 1	43	14	14	15	39	1	40	8	19	31	35	27
FEB. 2	43	16	16	17	39	1	40	8	19	31	35	27
FEB. 3	43	17	18	18	40	1	40	8	19	31	35	27
FEB. 4	43	19	20	20	40	1	40	8	19	31	35	27
FEB. 5	43	21	21	22	40	1	41	8	19	31	35	27
FEB. 6	43	23	23	24	40	1	41	8	19	31	35	27
FEB. 7	43	25	25	26	40	2	41	8	19	31	35	27
FEB. 8	44	26	27	28	40	2	41	8	19	31	35	27
FEB. 9	44	28	29	30	41	2	41	8	19	31	35	27
FEB. 10	44	30	31	31	41	2	41	8	19	31	35	27
FEB. 11	44	32	33	33	41	2	41	8	19	31	35	27
FEB. 12	44	34	35	35	41	2	41	8	19	31	35	27
FEB. 13	44	36	36	37	41	2	41	8	19	31	35	27
FEB. 14	44	38	38	39	42	2	41	8	19	31	35	27
FEB. 15	44	40	40	41	42	2	42	8	19	31	35	27
FEB. 16	45	41	42	43	42	3	42	8	19	31	35	27
FEB. 17	45	43	44	44	42	3	42	8	19	31	35	27
FEB. 18	45	45	46	46	42	3	42	8	19	31	35	27
FEB. 19	45	47	47	48	43	3	42	8	19	31	35	27
FEB. 20	45	48	1	2	43	3	42	8	19	31	35	27
FEB. 21	45	2	3	3	43	3	42	8	19	31	35	27
FEB. 22	45	4	4	5	43	3	42	8	19	31	35	27
FEB. 23	46	5	6	6	43	3	42	8	19	31	35	27
FEB. 24	46	7	7	8	44	3	42	8	19	31	35	27
FEB. 25	46	9	9	10	44	3	43	8	19	31	35	27
FEB. 26	46	10	11	11	44	3	43	8	19	31	35	27
FEB. 27	46	12	12	13	44	4	43	8	19	31	35	27
FEB. 28	46	13	14	14	44	4	43	8	18	31	35	27

MOON 1 ◐ 12:01 A.M. TO 8:00 A.M.   **MOON 2** ◑ 8:01 A.M. TO 4:00 P.M.   **MOON 3** ● 4:01 P.M. TO 12:00 A.M.

Use only one "moon" number. Choose the column closest to your time of birth. If your place of birth is not on Eastern Standard Time, be sure to read "How to Convert to Eastern Standard Time" at the beginning of this section.

Date & Time	SUN	MOON 1	MOON 2	MOON 3	MERCURY	VENUS	MARS	JUPITER	SATURN	URANUS	NEPTUNE	PLUTO
MAR. 1	46	15	16	16	45	4	43	8	18	31	35	27
MAR. 2	46	17	17	18	45	4	43	8	18	31	35	27
MAR. 3	47	18	19	20	45	4	43	8	18	31	35	27
MAR. 4	47	20	21	21	45	4	43	8	18	31	35	27
MAR. 5	47	22	23	23	46	4	43	8	18	31	35	27
MAR. 6	47	24	25	25	46	4	44	8	18	31	35	27
MAR. 7	47	26	26	27	46	4	44	8	18	31	35	27
MAR. 8	47	28	28	29	46	4	44	8	18	31	35	27
MAR. 9	47	30	30	31	47	4	44	8	18	31	35	27
MAR. 10	47	32	32	33	47	4	44	8	18	31	35	27
MAR. 11	48	33	34	35	47	4	44	8	18	31	35	27
MAR. 12	48	35	36	37	47	4	44	8	18	31	35	27
MAR. 13	48	37	38	38	48	4	44	8	18	30	35	27
MAR. 14	48	39	40	40	48	4	44	8	18	30	35	27
MAR. 15	48	41	41	42	48	4	44	8	18	30	35	27
MAR. 16	48	43	43	44	48	4	45	9	18	30	35	27
MAR. 17	48	44	45	46	1	4	45	9	18	30	35	27
MAR. 18	48	46	47	47	1	4	45	9	18	30	35	27
MAR. 19	1	48	48	1	1	4	45	9	18	30	35	27
MAR. 20	1	2	2	3	1	4	45	9	18	30	35	27
MAR. 21	1	3	4	4	2	4	45	9	18	30	35	27
MAR. 22	1	5	6	6	2	4	45	9	18	30	35	27
MAR. 23	1	6	7	7	2	4	45	9	18	30	35	27
MAR. 24	1	8	9	9	2	4	45	9	18	30	35	27
MAR. 25	2	10	10	11	3	4	45	9	18	30	35	27
MAR. 26	2	11	12	12	3	4	46	9	18	30	35	27
MAR. 27	2	13	13	14	3	4	46	9	18	30	35	27
MAR. 28	2	14	15	15	4	4	46	9	18	30	35	27
MAR. 29	2	16	17	17	4	4	46	9	18	30	35	27
MAR. 30	2	18	18	19	4	4	46	9	18	30	35	27
MAR. 31	2	19	20	21	4	4	46	9	18	30	35	27

Date & Time	SUN	MOON 1	MOON 2	MOON 3	MERCURY	VENUS	MARS	JUPITER	SATURN	URANUS	NEPTUNE	PLUTO
APR. 1	2	21	22	22	5	4	46	9	18	30	35	27
APR. 2	2	23	24	24	5	3	46	9	18	30	35	27
APR. 3	3	25	26	26	5	3	46	9	18	30	35	27
APR. 4	3	27	28	28	5	3	47	9	18	30	35	27
APR. 5	3	29	30	30	5	3	47	9	18	30	35	27
APR. 6	3	31	32	32	6	3	47	9	18	30	35	27
APR. 7	3	33	34	34	6	3	47	9	18	30	35	27
APR. 8	3	35	35	36	6	3	47	9	18	30	35	27
APR. 9	3	37	37	38	6	3	47	9	18	30	35	27
APR. 10	3	39	39	40	6	3	47	9	18	30	35	27
APR. 11	4	40	41	42	6	3	47	9	18	30	35	27
APR. 12	4	42	43	43	6	3	47	9	18	30	35	27
APR. 13	4	44	45	45	7	3	47	9	18	30	35	27
APR. 14	4	46	46	47	7	3	48	9	18	30	35	27
APR. 15	4	47	48	1	7	2	48	9	18	30	35	27
APR. 16	4	1	2	2	7	2	48	9	18	30	35	27
APR. 17	4	3	3	4	7	2	48	9	18	30	35	27
APR. 18	4	4	5	5	7	2	48	9	18	30	35	27
APR. 19	5	6	6	7	7	2	48	9	18	30	35	27
APR. 20	5	8	8	9	7	2	48	9	18	30	35	27
APR. 21	5	9	10	10	7	2	48	9	18	30	35	27
APR. 22	5	11	11	12	7	2	48	9	18	30	35	27
APR. 23	5	12	13	13	7	2	1	10	18	30	35	27
APR. 24	5	14	14	15	7	2	1	10	18	30	35	27
APR. 25	6	15	16	17	7	2	1	10	18	30	35	27
APR. 26	6	17	18	18	7	2	1	10	18	30	35	27
APR. 27	6	19	19	20	7	2	1	10	18	30	35	27
APR. 28	6	21	21	22	7	2	1	10	18	30	35	27
APR. 29	6	22	23	24	6	2	1	10	18	30	35	27
APR. 30	6	24	25	25	6	2	1	10	18	30	35	27

MOON 1 ◐ 12:01 A.M. TO 8:00 A.M.　　**MOON 2** ◐ 8:01 A.M. TO 4:00 P.M.　　**MOON 3** ● 4:01 P.M. TO 12:00 A.M.
Use only one "moon" number. Choose the column closest to your time of birth. If your place of birth is not on
Eastern Standard Time, be sure to read "How to Convert to Eastern Standard Time" at the beginning of this section.

May

June

Date & Time	SUN	MOON 1	MOON 2	MOON 3	MERCURY	VENUS	MARS	JUPITER	SATURN	URANUS	NEPTUNE	PLUTO
MAY 1	6	26	27	27	6	2	1	10	18	30	35	27
MAY 2	6	28	29	29	6	2	1	10	18	30	35	27
MAY 3	7	30	31	31	6	2	2	10	18	30	35	27
MAY 4	7	32	33	33	6	2	2	10	18	30	35	27
MAY 5	7	34	35	35	6	2	2	10	18	30	35	27
MAY 6	7	36	37	37	6	2	2	10	18	30	35	27
MAY 7	7	38	39	39	6	2	2	10	18	30	35	27
MAY 8	7	40	41	41	6	2	2	10	18	30	35	27
MAY 9	7	42	42	43	6	2	2	10	18	30	35	27
MAY 10	7	44	44	45	6	2	2	10	18	30	35	27
MAY 11	8	45	46	47	6	3	2	10	18	30	35	27
MAY 12	8	47	48	48	6	3	2	10	18	30	35	27
MAY 13	8	1	1	2	6	3	3	10	18	30	35	27
MAY 14	8	2	3	3	6	3	3	10	18	30	35	27
MAY 15	8	4	4	5	6	3	3	10	18	30	35	27
MAY 16	8	6	6	7	6	3	3	10	18	30	35	27
MAY 17	8	7	8	8	6	3	3	10	18	30	35	27
MAY 18	8	9	9	10	6	3	3	10	18	30	35	27
MAY 19	9	10	11	11	6	3	3	10	18	30	35	27
MAY 20	9	12	12	13	6	3	3	10	18	30	35	27
MAY 21	9	13	14	15	6	3	3	10	18	30	35	27
MAY 22	9	15	16	16	6	3	3	10	18	30	35	27
MAY 23	9	17	17	18	6	3	4	10	18	30	35	27
MAY 24	9	18	19	19	6	4	4	10	19	30	35	27
MAY 25	10	20	21	21	6	4	4	10	19	30	35	27
MAY 26	10	22	22	23	6	4	4	11	19	30	35	27
MAY 27	10	23	24	25	6	4	4	11	19	30	35	27
MAY 28	10	25	26	27	7	4	4	11	19	30	35	27
MAY 29	10	27	28	28	7	4	4	11	19	30	35	27
MAY 30	10	29	30	30	7	4	4	11	19	30	35	27
MAY 31	10	31	32	32	7	4	4	11	19	30	35	27

Date & Time	SUN	MOON 1	MOON 2	MOON 3	MERCURY	VENUS	MARS	JUPITER	SATURN	URANUS	NEPTUNE	PLUTO
JUN. 1	10	33	34	35	7	4	4	11	19	30	35	27
JUN. 2	10	35	36	37	7	5	5	11	19	30	35	27
JUN. 3	11	37	38	39	7	5	5	11	19	30	35	26
JUN. 4	11	39	40	41	8	5	5	11	19	30	35	26
JUN. 5	11	41	42	42	8	5	5	11	19	30	35	26
JUN. 6	11	43	44	44	8	5	5	11	19	30	35	26
JUN. 7	11	45	45	46	8	5	5	11	19	30	35	26
JUN. 8	11	47	47	48	8	5	5	11	19	30	35	26
JUN. 9	11	48	1	1	9	5	5	11	19	30	35	26
JUN. 10	11	2	2	3	9	5	5	11	19	30	35	26
JUN. 11	12	4	4	5	9	6	5	11	19	30	35	26
JUN. 12	12	5	6	6	9	6	5	11	19	30	35	26
JUN. 13	12	7	7	8	9	6	6	11	19	30	35	26
JUN. 14	12	8	9	9	10	6	6	11	19	30	35	26
JUN. 15	12	10	10	11	10	6	6	11	19	30	35	26
JUN. 16	12	11	12	13	10	6	6	11	19	30	35	26
JUN. 17	12	13	14	14	10	6	6	11	19	30	35	26
JUN. 18	12	15	15	16	11	6	6	11	19	30	35	26
JUN. 19	13	16	17	17	11	7	6	11	19	30	35	26
JUN. 20	13	18	18	19	11	7	6	11	19	30	35	26
JUN. 21	13	20	20	21	12	7	6	11	19	30	35	26
JUN. 22	13	21	22	22	12	7	7	11	19	30	35	26
JUN. 23	13	23	24	24	12	7	7	11	19	30	35	26
JUN. 24	13	25	25	26	12	7	7	11	19	30	35	26
JUN. 25	14	27	27	28	13	7	7	11	19	30	35	26
JUN. 26	14	28	29	30	13	8	7	11	19	30	35	26
JUN. 27	14	30	31	32	13	8	7	11	19	30	35	26
JUN. 28	14	32	33	34	14	8	7	12	19	30	35	26
JUN. 29	14	34	35	36	14	8	7	12	19	30	35	26
JUN. 30	14	36	37	38	14	8	7	12	19	30	35	26

MOON 1 ◐ 12:01 A.M. TO 8:00 A.M.   **MOON 2** ◑ 8:01 A.M. TO 4:00 P.M.   **MOON 3** ● 4:01 P.M. TO 12:00 A.M.
Use only one "moon" number. Choose the column closest to your time of birth. If your place of birth is not on Eastern Standard Time, be sure to read "How to Convert to Eastern Standard Time" at the beginning of this section.

1977

July

August

Date & Time	SUN	MOON 1	MOON 2	MOON 3	MERCURY	VENUS	MARS	JUPITER	SATURN	URANUS	NEPTUNE	PLUTO
JUL. 1	14	4	5	5	16	20	28	18	3	24	32	23
JUL. 2	14	6	6	7	16	20	28	18	3	24	32	23
JUL. 3	15	7	8	8	16	20	28	18	3	24	32	23
JUL. 4	15	9	10	10	16	20	28	18	3	24	32	23
JUL. 5	15	11	11	12	16	21	28	18	3	24	32	23
JUL. 6	15	12	13	13	15	21	28	18	3	24	32	23
JUL. 7	15	14	15	15	15	21	28	18	3	24	32	23
JUL. 8	15	16	16	17	15	21	28	18	3	24	32	23
JUL. 9	15	18	18	19	15	21	28	18	3	24	32	23
JUL. 10	15	19	20	21	15	21	28	18	3	24	32	23
JUL. 11	16	21	22	23	15	21	28	18	3	24	32	23
JUL. 12	16	23	24	24	15	21	28	18	3	24	32	23
JUL. 13	16	25	26	26	15	21	29	18	3	24	32	23
JUL. 14	16	27	28	28	15	21	29	18	3	24	32	23
JUL. 15	16	29	29	30	15	22	29	18	3	24	32	23
JUL. 16	16	31	31	32	15	22	29	18	3	24	32	23
JUL. 17	16	33	33	34	15	22	29	18	3	24	32	23
JUL. 18	16	34	35	36	15	22	29	18	3	24	32	23
JUL. 19	17	36	37	38	15	22	29	18	3	24	32	23
JUL. 20	17	38	39	39	15	22	29	18	3	24	32	23
JUL. 21	17	40	41	41	15	22	29	18	3	24	32	23
JUL. 22	17	42	42	43	15	22	29	19	3	24	32	23
JUL. 23	17	44	44	45	15	22	29	19	3	24	32	23
JUL. 24	17	45	46	46	15	22	29	19	3	24	32	23
JUL. 25	17	47	47	48	15	22	29	19	3	24	32	23
JUL. 26	18	48	1	2	15	22	29	19	3	24	32	23
JUL. 27	18	2	3	3	15	22	29	19	3	24	32	23
JUL. 28	18	4	4	5	15	23	30	19	3	24	32	23
JUL. 29	18	5	6	6	15	23	30	19	3	24	32	23
JUL. 30	18	7	7	8	15	23	30	19	3	24	32	23
JUL. 31	18	8	9	10	15	23	30	19	3	24	32	23

Date & Time	SUN	MOON 1	MOON 2	MOON 3	MERCURY	VENUS	MARS	JUPITER	SATURN	URANUS	NEPTUNE	PLUTO
AUG. 1	18	10	11	11	15	23	30	19	3	24	32	23
AUG. 2	18	12	12	13	16	23	30	19	3	24	32	23
AUG. 3	19	13	14	15	16	23	30	19	3	24	32	24
AUG. 4	19	15	16	16	16	23	30	19	3	24	32	24
AUG. 5	19	17	18	18	16	23	30	19	3	24	32	24
AUG. 6	19	19	19	20	16	23	30	19	3	24	32	24
AUG. 7	19	21	21	22	17	23	30	19	3	24	32	24
AUG. 8	19	23	23	24	17	23	30	19	3	24	32	24
AUG. 9	19	25	25	26	17	23	30	19	3	24	32	24
AUG. 10	19	27	27	28	17	23	30	19	3	24	32	24
AUG. 11	20	28	29	30	18	23	31	19	3	24	32	24
AUG. 12	20	30	31	32	18	23	31	19	3	24	32	24
AUG. 13	20	32	33	33	18	23	31	19	3	24	32	24
AUG. 14	20	34	35	35	18	23	31	19	3	24	32	24
AUG. 15	20	36	36	37	19	23	31	19	3	24	32	24
AUG. 16	20	38	38	39	19	23	31	19	3	24	32	24
AUG. 17	20	39	40	41	19	23	31	19	3	24	32	24
AUG. 18	20	41	42	42	19	23	31	19	3	24	32	24
AUG. 19	21	43	44	44	20	23	31	19	3	24	32	24
AUG. 20	21	45	45	46	20	22	31	19	3	24	32	24
AUG. 21	21	46	47	47	20	22	31	19	3	24	32	24
AUG. 22	21	48	1	1	20	22	31	19	3	24	32	24
AUG. 23	21	2	2	3	21	22	31	19	3	24	32	24
AUG. 24	21	3	4	4	21	22	32	19	3	24	32	24
AUG. 25	21	5	5	6	21	22	32	20	3	24	32	24
AUG. 26	22	6	7	7	21	22	32	20	3	24	32	24
AUG. 27	22	8	8	9	22	22	32	20	3	24	32	24
AUG. 28	22	9	10	11	22	22	32	20	3	24	32	24
AUG. 29	22	11	12	12	22	22	32	20	2	24	32	24
AUG. 30	22	13	13	14	22	22	32	20	2	24	32	24
AUG. 31	22	15	15	16	23	22	32	20	2	24	32	24

MOON 1 ☽ 12:01 A.M. TO 8:00 A.M.   **MOON 2** ☽ 8:01 A.M. TO 4:00 P.M.   **MOON 3** ● 4:01 P.M. TO 12:00 A.M.
Use only one "moon" number. Choose the column closest to your time of birth. If your place of birth is not on
Eastern Standard Time, be sure to read "How to Convert to Eastern Standard Time" at the beginning of this section.

1977

September | October

Date & Time	SUN	MOON 1	MOON 2	MOON 3	MERCURY	VENUS	MARS	JUPITER	SATURN	URANUS	NEPTUNE	PLUTO
SEP. 1	22	4	4	5	23	18	13	13	20	30	35	27
SEP. 2	22	5	6	6	23	18	13	13	20	30	35	27
SEP. 3	23	7	7	8	23	18	13	13	20	30	35	27
SEP. 4	23	8	9	10	23	18	13	13	20	30	35	27
SEP. 5	23	10	11	11	23	18	13	13	20	30	35	27
SEP. 6	23	12	12	13	23	18	13	13	20	30	35	27
SEP. 7	23	13	14	14	22	18	13	13	20	30	35	27
SEP. 8	23	15	15	16	22	19	14	13	20	30	35	27
SEP. 9	23	16	17	18	22	19	14	13	20	30	35	27
SEP. 10	23	18	19	19	22	19	14	13	20	30	35	27
SEP. 11	24	20	20	21	22	19	14	13	20	30	35	27
SEP. 12	24	22	22	23	22	19	14	13	20	30	35	27
SEP. 13	24	23	24	25	22	19	14	13	20	30	35	27
SEP. 14	24	25	26	26	22	20	14	13	20	30	35	27
SEP. 15	24	27	28	28	22	20	14	13	20	30	35	27
SEP. 16	24	29	30	30	22	20	14	13	20	30	35	27
SEP. 17	24	31	31	32	22	20	14	13	20	30	35	27
SEP. 18	24	33	33	34	22	20	14	14	20	30	35	27
SEP. 19	25	35	35	36	22	20	14	14	20	30	35	27
SEP. 20	25	36	37	38	22	21	14	14	20	30	35	27
SEP. 21	25	38	39	40	22	21	15	14	20	30	35	27
SEP. 22	25	40	41	41	22	21	15	14	20	30	35	27
SEP. 23	25	42	43	43	23	21	15	14	20	30	35	27
SEP. 24	25	44	45	45	23	21	15	14	20	30	35	27
SEP. 25	26	46	46	47	23	21	15	14	20	30	35	27
SEP. 26	26	48	48	1	23	22	15	14	20	30	35	27
SEP. 27	26	1	2	2	23	22	15	14	20	30	35	27
SEP. 28	26	3	4	4	24	22	15	14	20	30	35	27
SEP. 29	26	5	5	6	24	22	15	14	20	30	35	27
SEP. 30	26	6	7	7	24	22	15	14	20	30	35	27
OCT. 1	26	8	8	9	24	22	15	14	20	30	35	27
OCT. 2	26	10	10	11	24	23	15	14	20	30	35	27
OCT. 3	27	11	12	12	25	23	15	14	21	30	35	27
OCT. 4	27	13	13	14	25	23	16	14	21	30	35	27
OCT. 5	27	14	15	15	25	23	16	14	21	30	35	27
OCT. 6	27	16	16	17	25	23	16	14	21	30	35	27
OCT. 7	27	18	18	19	26	23	16	14	21	30	35	27
OCT. 8	27	19	20	20	26	24	16	14	21	30	35	27
OCT. 9	27	21	21	22	26	24	16	14	21	30	35	27
OCT. 10	27	23	23	24	26	24	16	14	21	30	35	27
OCT. 11	28	24	25	26	27	24	16	14	21	30	35	27
OCT. 12	28	26	27	28	27	24	16	14	21	30	35	27
OCT. 13	28	28	29	30	27	24	16	14	21	30	35	27
OCT. 14	28	30	31	31	27	24	16	14	21	30	35	27
OCT. 15	28	32	33	33	28	25	16	14	21	30	35	27
OCT. 16	28	34	35	35	28	25	16	14	21	30	35	27
OCT. 17	28	36	37	37	28	25	16	14	21	30	35	27
OCT. 18	28	38	39	39	28	25	16	14	21	30	35	27
OCT. 19	29	40	40	41	28	25	17	14	21	30	35	27
OCT. 20	29	42	42	43	29	25	17	14	21	30	35	27
OCT. 21	29	44	44	45	29	26	17	14	21	30	35	27
OCT. 22	29	45	46	46	29	26	17	14	21	30	35	27
OCT. 23	29	47	48	48	29	26	17	14	21	30	35	27
OCT. 24	29	1	1	2	30	26	17	14	21	30	35	27
OCT. 25	29	2	3	4	30	26	17	14	21	30	35	27
OCT. 26	30	4	5	5	30	26	17	14	21	31	35	27
OCT. 27	30	6	6	7	30	27	17	14	21	31	35	27
OCT. 28	30	7	8	8	30	27	17	14	21	31	35	27
OCT. 29	30	9	10	10	31	27	17	14	21	31	35	27
OCT. 30	30	11	11	12	31	27	17	14	21	31	35	27
OCT. 31	30	12	13	13	31	27	17	14	21	31	35	27

MOON 1 ◐ 12:01 A.M. TO 8:00 A.M.   **MOON 2** ◑ 8:01 A.M. TO 4:00 P.M.   **MOON 3** ● 4:01 P.M. TO 12:00 A.M.

Use only one "moon" number. Choose the column closest to your time of birth. If your place of birth is not on Eastern Standard Time, be sure to read "How to Convert to Eastern Standard Time" at the beginning of this section.

Date & Time	SUN	MOON 1	MOON 2	MOON 3	MERCURY	VENUS	MARS	JUPITER	SATURN	URANUS	NEPTUNE	PLUTO
NOV. 1	30	14	14	15	31	27	17	14	21	31	35	27
NOV. 2	30	15	16	16	31	28	17	14	21	31	35	27
NOV. 3	31	17	18	18	32	28	17	14	21	31	35	27
NOV. 4	31	19	19	20	32	28	17	14	21	31	35	27
NOV. 5	31	20	21	21	32	28	17	14	21	31	35	27
NOV. 6	31	22	23	23	32	28	18	14	21	31	35	27
NOV. 7	31	24	24	25	32	28	18	14	21	31	35	27
NOV. 8	31	26	26	27	33	29	18	14	21	31	35	27
NOV. 9	31	27	28	29	33	29	18	14	21	31	35	27
NOV. 10	31	29	30	31	33	29	18	14	21	31	35	27
NOV. 11	31	31	32	33	33	29	18	14	21	31	35	27
NOV. 12	32	33	34	35	33	29	18	14	21	31	35	27
NOV. 13	32	35	36	37	34	29	18	14	21	31	35	27
NOV. 14	32	37	38	39	34	30	18	14	21	31	35	27
NOV. 15	32	39	40	41	34	30	18	14	21	31	35	27
NOV. 16	32	41	42	42	34	30	18	14	21	31	35	27
NOV. 17	32	43	44	44	34	30	18	14	21	31	35	27
NOV. 18	32	45	45	46	35	30	18	14	21	31	35	27
NOV. 19	33	47	47	48	35	30	18	14	21	31	35	27
NOV. 20	33	48	1	2	35	31	18	14	21	31	35	27
NOV. 21	33	2	3	3	35	31	18	14	21	31	35	27
NOV. 22	33	4	4	5	35	31	18	14	21	31	35	27
NOV. 23	33	5	6	6	36	31	18	14	21	31	35	27
NOV. 24	33	7	8	8	36	31	18	14	21	31	35	27
NOV. 25	34	9	9	10	36	31	18	14	21	31	35	27
NOV. 26	34	10	11	11	36	32	18	14	21	31	35	27
NOV. 27	34	12	12	13	36	32	18	14	21	31	35	27
NOV. 28	34	13	14	14	36	32	18	14	21	31	35	27
NOV. 29	34	15	15	16	37	32	18	14	21	31	35	27
NOV. 30	34	17	17	18	37	32	18	13	21	31	35	27

Date & Time	SUN	MOON 1	MOON 2	MOON 3	MERCURY	VENUS	MARS	JUPITER	SATURN	URANUS	NEPTUNE	PLUTO
DEC. 1	34	18	19	19	37	32	18	13	21	31	35	27
DEC. 2	34	20	20	21	37	33	18	13	21	31	35	27
DEC. 3	35	21	22	22	37	33	18	13	21	31	35	27
DEC. 4	35	23	24	24	37	33	18	13	21	31	35	27
DEC. 5	35	25	25	26	38	33	18	13	21	31	35	27
DEC. 6	35	27	27	28	38	33	18	13	21	31	35	27
DEC. 7	35	28	29	30	38	34	18	13	21	31	35	27
DEC. 8	35	30	31	32	38	34	18	13	21	31	35	27
DEC. 9	35	32	33	34	38	34	18	13	21	31	35	27
DEC. 10	35	34	35	36	38	34	19	13	21	31	35	27
DEC. 11	36	36	37	38	38	34	19	13	21	31	35	27
DEC. 12	36	38	39	40	38	34	19	13	21	31	35	27
DEC. 13	36	40	41	42	38	34	19	13	21	31	35	27
DEC. 14	36	42	43	44	38	35	19	13	21	31	35	27
DEC. 15	36	44	45	46	38	35	19	13	21	31	35	27
DEC. 16	36	46	47	47	38	35	18	13	21	31	35	27
DEC. 17	36	48	1	1	38	35	18	13	21	31	35	27
DEC. 18	36	2	2	3	37	35	18	13	21	31	35	27
DEC. 19	37	3	4	4	37	36	18	13	21	31	35	27
DEC. 20	37	5	6	6	37	36	18	13	21	31	35	27
DEC. 21	37	7	7	8	37	36	18	13	21	31	35	27
DEC. 22	37	8	9	9	37	36	18	13	21	31	35	27
DEC. 23	37	10	10	11	37	36	18	13	21	31	35	27
DEC. 24	37	11	12	12	36	36	18	13	21	31	35	27
DEC. 25	37	13	13	14	36	37	18	13	21	31	35	27
DEC. 26	38	15	15	16	36	37	18	13	21	31	35	27
DEC. 27	38	16	17	17	36	37	18	13	21	31	35	27
DEC. 28	38	18	18	19	36	37	18	13	21	31	35	27
DEC. 29	38	19	20	20	36	37	18	13	21	31	35	27
DEC. 30	38	21	21	22	36	37	18	13	21	31	35	27
DEC. 31	38	23	23	24	36	38	18	13	21	31	35	27

MOON 1 ◐ 12:01 A.M. TO 8:00 A.M.   **MOON 2** ◑ 8:01 A.M. TO 4:00 P.M.   **MOON 3** ● 4:01 P.M. TO 12:00 A.M.

Use only one "moon" number. Choose the column closest to your time of birth. If your place of birth is not on Eastern Standard Time, be sure to read "How to Convert to Eastern Standard Time" at the beginning of this section.

1978

January

Date & Time	SUN	MOON 1	MOON 2	MOON 3	MERCURY	VENUS	MARS	JUPITER	SATURN	URANUS	NEPTUNE	PLUTO
JAN. 1	38	24	25	25	36	38	18	13	21	31	35	27
JAN. 2	38	26	27	27	36	38	18	13	21	31	35	27
JAN. 3	39	28	28	29	36	38	18	13	21	31	35	27
JAN. 4	39	30	30	31	36	38	18	13	21	31	35	27
JAN. 5	39	32	32	33	36	38	18	13	21	31	35	27
JAN. 6	39	33	34	34	36	38	18	13	21	31	35	27
JAN. 7	39	35	36	37	36	38	18	13	21	31	35	27
JAN. 8	39	37	38	39	36	39	18	13	21	31	35	27
JAN. 9	39	40	40	41	36	39	18	13	21	31	35	27
JAN. 10	40	42	42	43	36	39	18	13	21	31	35	27
JAN. 11	40	44	44	45	37	39	18	13	21	31	35	27
JAN. 12	40	45	46	47	37	40	18	13	21	31	35	27
JAN. 13	40	47	48	1	37	40	18	13	21	31	35	27
JAN. 14	40	1	2	2	37	40	18	13	21	31	35	27
JAN. 15	40	3	3	4	37	40	18	13	21	31	35	27
JAN. 16	40	5	5	6	37	40	17	13	21	31	35	27
JAN. 17	41	6	7	7	37	40	17	13	21	31	35	27
JAN. 18	41	8	8	9	38	41	17	13	21	31	35	27
JAN. 19	41	9	10	10	38	41	17	13	21	31	35	27
JAN. 20	41	11	11	12	38	41	17	13	21	31	35	27
JAN. 21	41	13	13	14	38	41	17	13	21	31	35	27
JAN. 22	41	14	14	15	38	41	17	13	21	31	35	27
JAN. 23	42	16	16	17	39	41	17	13	21	31	35	27
JAN. 24	42	17	18	18	39	42	17	13	21	31	35	27
JAN. 25	42	19	19	20	39	42	17	13	21	31	35	27
JAN. 26	42	21	21	22	39	42	17	13	21	31	35	27
JAN. 27	42	22	23	23	39	42	17	13	21	31	35	27
JAN. 28	42	24	24	25	39	42	17	13	21	31	35	27
JAN. 29	42	26	26	27	40	42	17	13	21	31	35	27
JAN. 30	42	27	28	29	40	43	17	13	21	31	35	27
JAN. 31	43	29	30	30	40	43	17	13	21	31	35	27

February

Date & Time	SUN	MOON 1	MOON 2	MOON 3	MERCURY	VENUS	MARS	JUPITER	SATURN	URANUS	NEPTUNE	PLUTO
FEB. 1	43	31	32	32	40	43	17	13	21	31	35	27
FEB. 2	43	33	33	34	40	43	17	13	21	31	35	27
FEB. 3	43	35	35	36	41	43	17	13	21	31	35	27
FEB. 4	43	37	37	38	41	43	17	12	21	31	35	27
FEB. 5	43	39	39	40	41	44	16	12	21	31	35	27
FEB. 6	43	41	41	42	41	44	16	12	21	31	35	27
FEB. 7	43	43	43	44	41	44	16	12	21	31	35	27
FEB. 8	44	45	45	46	42	44	16	12	21	31	35	27
FEB. 9	44	46	47	48	42	44	16	12	21	31	35	27
FEB. 10	44	48	1	2	42	44	16	12	21	31	35	27
FEB. 11	44	2	3	3	42	45	16	12	21	31	35	27
FEB. 12	44	4	4	5	43	45	16	12	21	31	35	27
FEB. 13	44	6	6	7	43	45	16	12	21	31	35	27
FEB. 14	44	7	8	8	43	45	16	12	21	31	35	27
FEB. 15	44	9	9	10	43	45	16	12	21	31	35	27
FEB. 16	45	10	11	12	43	45	16	12	21	31	35	27
FEB. 17	45	12	13	13	44	45	16	12	21	31	35	27
FEB. 18	45	14	14	15	44	46	16	12	21	31	35	27
FEB. 19	45	15	16	16	44	46	16	12	21	31	35	27
FEB. 20	45	17	17	18	44	46	16	12	21	31	35	27
FEB. 21	45	18	19	20	45	46	16	12	21	31	35	27
FEB. 22	45	20	21	21	45	46	16	12	21	31	35	27
FEB. 23	46	22	22	23	45	47	16	12	21	31	35	27
FEB. 24	46	23	24	25	45	47	16	12	20	31	35	27
FEB. 25	46	25	26	26	46	47	16	12	20	31	35	27
FEB. 26	46	27	28	28	46	47	16	12	20	31	35	27
FEB. 27	46	29	29	30	46	47	16	12	20	31	35	27
FEB. 28	46	31	31	32	46	47	16	12	20	31	35	27

MOON 1 ○ 12:01 A.M. TO 8:00 A.M.　　**MOON 2** ◑ 8:01 A.M. TO 4:00 P.M.　　**MOON 3** ● 4:01 P.M. TO 12:00 A.M.

Use only one "moon" number. Choose the column closest to your time of birth. If your place of birth is not on Eastern Standard Time, be sure to read "How to Convert to Eastern Standard Time" at the beginning of this section.

1978

March

Date & Time	SUN	MOON 1	MOON 2	MOON 3	MERCURY	VENUS	MARS	JUPITER	SATURN	URANUS	NEPTUNE	PLUTO
MAR. 1	46	32	33	34	47	48	16	12	20	31	35	27
MAR. 2	46	34	35	35	47	48	16	12	20	31	35	27
MAR. 3	47	36	37	37	47	48	16	12	20	31	35	27
MAR. 4	47	38	39	39	47	48	16	12	20	31	35	27
MAR. 5	47	40	41	41	48	48	16	12	20	31	35	27
MAR. 6	47	42	43	43	48	48	16	12	20	31	35	27
MAR. 7	47	44	44	45	48	1	16	12	20	31	35	27
MAR. 8	47	46	46	47	48	1	16	12	20	31	35	27
MAR. 9	47	48	48	1	1	1	16	13	20	31	35	27
MAR. 10	47	1	2	3	1	1	16	13	20	31	35	27
MAR. 11	48	3	4	4	1	1	16	13	20	31	35	27
MAR. 12	48	5	6	6	1	1	16	13	20	31	35	27
MAR. 13	48	7	7	8	2	2	16	13	20	31	35	27
MAR. 14	48	8	9	9	2	2	16	13	20	31	35	27
MAR. 15	48	10	10	11	2	2	16	13	20	31	35	27
MAR. 16	48	12	12	13	2	2	16	13	20	31	35	27
MAR. 17	48	13	14	14	3	2	16	13	20	31	35	27
MAR. 18	48	15	15	16	3	2	16	13	20	31	35	27
MAR. 19	1	16	17	17	3	3	16	13	20	31	35	27
MAR. 20	1	18	18	19	3	3	16	13	20	31	35	27
MAR. 21	1	20	20	21	3	3	16	13	20	31	35	27
MAR. 22	1	21	22	22	4	3	16	13	20	31	35	27
MAR. 23	1	23	23	24	4	3	16	13	20	31	35	27
MAR. 24	1	25	25	26	4	3	16	13	20	31	35	27
MAR. 25	2	26	27	28	4	4	16	13	20	31	35	27
MAR. 26	2	28	29	29	4	4	16	13	20	31	35	27
MAR. 27	2	30	31	31	4	4	16	13	20	31	35	27
MAR. 28	2	32	33	33	4	4	16	13	20	31	35	27
MAR. 29	2	34	34	35	4	4	16	13	20	31	35	27
MAR. 30	2	36	36	37	4	4	16	13	20	31	35	27
MAR. 31	2	38	38	39	4	5	17	13	20	31	35	27

April

Date & Time	SUN	MOON 1	MOON 2	MOON 3	MERCURY	VENUS	MARS	JUPITER	SATURN	URANUS	NEPTUNE	PLUTO
APR. 1	2	39	40	41	4	5	17	13	20	31	35	27
APR. 2	2	41	42	43	4	5	17	13	20	31	35	27
APR. 3	3	43	44	44	4	5	17	13	20	31	35	27
APR. 4	3	45	46	46	4	5	17	13	20	31	35	27
APR. 5	3	47	48	48	4	5	17	13	20	31	35	27
APR. 6	3	1	1	2	4	6	17	13	20	31	35	27
APR. 7	3	3	3	4	4	6	17	13	20	31	35	27
APR. 8	3	4	5	5	4	6	17	13	20	31	35	27
APR. 9	3	6	7	7	4	6	17	13	20	31	35	27
APR. 10	3	8	8	9	4	6	17	13	20	31	35	27
APR. 11	4	9	10	10	4	6	17	13	20	31	35	27
APR. 12	4	11	12	12	4	6	17	13	20	31	35	27
APR. 13	4	13	13	14	4	7	17	13	20	31	35	27
APR. 14	4	14	15	15	4	7	17	13	20	31	35	27
APR. 15	4	16	16	17	3	7	17	13	20	31	35	27
APR. 16	4	17	18	18	3	7	17	13	20	31	35	27
APR. 17	4	19	19	20	3	7	17	13	20	31	35	27
APR. 18	4	21	21	22	3	7	17	13	20	31	35	27
APR. 19	5	22	23	23	3	8	17	13	20	31	35	27
APR. 20	5	24	25	25	3	8	17	13	20	31	35	27
APR. 21	5	26	26	27	3	8	17	13	20	31	35	27
APR. 22	5	28	28	29	3	8	18	13	20	31	35	27
APR. 23	5	29	30	31	3	8	18	13	20	31	35	27
APR. 24	5	31	32	33	3	8	18	13	20	31	35	27
APR. 25	6	33	34	35	3	9	18	13	20	31	35	27
APR. 26	6	35	36	36	3	9	18	13	20	31	35	27
APR. 27	6	37	38	38	3	9	18	13	20	31	35	27
APR. 28	6	39	40	40	3	9	18	13	20	31	35	27
APR. 29	6	41	42	42	3	9	18	13	20	31	35	27
APR. 30	6	43	43	44	3	9	18	13	20	31	35	27

MOON 1 ◗ 12:01 A.M. TO 8:00 A.M.   **MOON 2** ◗ 8:01 A.M. TO 4:00 P.M.   **MOON 3** ● 4:01 P.M. TO 12:00 A.M.

Use only one "moon" number. Choose the column closest to your time of birth. If your place of birth is not on Eastern Standard Time, be sure to read "How to Convert to Eastern Standard Time" at the beginning of this section.

1978

May

Date & Time	SUN	MOON 1	MOON 2	MOON 3	MERCURY	VENUS	MARS	JUPITER	SATURN	URANUS	NEPTUNE	PLUTO
MAY 1	6	45	45	46	3	10	18	13	20	31	35	27
MAY 2	6	46	47	48	3	10	18	13	20	31	35	27
MAY 3	7	48	1	1	3	10	18	13	20	31	35	27
MAY 4	7	2	3	3	3	10	18	13	20	31	35	27
MAY 5	7	4	4	5	3	10	18	13	20	31	35	27
MAY 6	7	5	6	7	4	10	18	13	20	31	35	27
MAY 7	7	7	8	8	4	11	18	14	20	31	35	27
MAY 8	7	9	9	10	4	11	18	14	20	31	35	27
MAY 9	7	10	11	12	4	11	19	14	20	31	35	27
MAY 10	7	12	13	13	4	11	19	14	20	31	35	27
MAY 11	8	14	14	15	4	11	19	14	20	31	35	27
MAY 12	8	15	16	16	4	11	19	14	20	31	35	27
MAY 13	8	17	17	18	4	12	19	14	20	31	35	27
MAY 14	8	18	19	19	5	12	19	14	20	31	35	27
MAY 15	8	20	21	21	5	12	19	14	20	31	35	27
MAY 16	8	22	22	23	5	12	19	14	20	31	35	27
MAY 17	8	23	24	24	5	12	19	14	20	31	35	27
MAY 18	8	25	26	26	5	12	19	14	20	31	35	27
MAY 19	9	27	27	28	5	13	19	14	20	31	35	27
MAY 20	9	29	29	30	6	13	19	14	20	31	35	27
MAY 21	9	30	31	32	6	13	19	14	20	31	35	27
MAY 22	9	32	33	34	6	13	19	14	20	31	35	27
MAY 23	9	34	35	36	6	13	19	14	20	31	35	27
MAY 24	9	36	37	38	6	13	19	14	20	31	35	27
MAY 25	10	38	39	40	7	13	20	14	20	31	35	27
MAY 26	10	40	41	42	7	14	20	14	20	31	35	27
MAY 27	10	42	43	44	7	14	20	14	20	31	35	27
MAY 28	10	44	45	45	7	14	20	14	20	31	35	27
MAY 29	10	46	47	47	8	14	20	14	20	31	35	27
MAY 30	10	48	48	1	8	14	20	14	20	31	35	27
MAY 31	10	2	2	3	8	14	20	14	20	31	35	27

June

Date & Time	SUN	MOON 1	MOON 2	MOON 3	MERCURY	VENUS	MARS	JUPITER	SATURN	URANUS	NEPTUNE	PLUTO
JUN. 1	10	3	4	4	8	15	20	14	20	31	35	27
JUN. 2	10	5	6	6	9	15	20	14	20	31	35	27
JUN. 3	11	7	7	8	9	15	20	14	20	31	35	27
JUN. 4	11	8	9	9	9	15	20	14	20	31	35	27
JUN. 5	11	10	11	11	9	15	20	14	20	31	35	27
JUN. 6	11	12	12	13	10	15	20	14	20	31	35	27
JUN. 7	11	13	14	14	10	16	20	14	20	31	35	27
JUN. 8	11	15	15	16	10	16	21	14	20	31	35	27
JUN. 9	11	16	17	17	11	16	21	14	20	31	35	27
JUN. 10	11	18	18	19	11	16	21	14	20	31	35	27
JUN. 11	12	20	20	21	11	16	21	14	20	31	35	27
JUN. 12	12	21	22	22	11	16	21	15	20	31	35	27
JUN. 13	12	23	23	24	12	16	21	15	20	31	35	27
JUN. 14	12	24	25	26	12	17	21	15	20	31	35	27
JUN. 15	12	26	27	27	12	17	21	15	20	31	35	27
JUN. 16	12	28	28	29	13	17	21	15	20	31	35	27
JUN. 17	12	30	30	31	13	17	21	15	20	31	35	27
JUN. 18	12	32	32	33	13	17	21	15	20	31	35	27
JUN. 19	13	34	34	35	13	17	21	15	20	31	35	27
JUN. 20	13	36	36	37	14	18	21	15	20	31	35	27
JUN. 21	13	38	38	39	14	18	21	15	20	31	35	27
JUN. 22	13	40	40	41	14	18	22	15	20	31	35	27
JUN. 23	13	42	42	43	15	18	22	15	20	31	35	27
JUN. 24	13	44	44	45	15	18	22	15	21	31	35	27
JUN. 25	14	46	46	47	15	18	22	15	21	31	35	27
JUN. 26	14	47	48	1	15	19	22	15	21	31	35	27
JUN. 27	14	1	2	2	16	19	22	15	21	31	35	27
JUN. 28	14	3	4	4	16	19	22	15	21	31	35	27
JUN. 29	14	5	5	6	16	19	22	15	21	31	35	27
JUN. 30	14	6	7	7	16	19	22	15	21	31	35	27

MOON 1 ☽ 12:01 A.M. TO 8:00 A.M.   **MOON 2** ☽ 8:01 A.M. TO 4:00 P.M.   **MOON 3** ● 4:01 P.M. TO 12:00 A.M.
Use only one "moon" number. Choose the column closest to your time of birth. If your place of birth is not on Eastern Standard Time, be sure to read "How to Convert to Eastern Standard Time" at the beginning of this section.

July

Date & Time	SUN ☼	MOON 1 ◗	MOON 2 ◖	MOON 3 ●	MERCURY	VENUS	MARS	JUPITER	SATURN	URANUS	NEPTUNE	PLUTO
JUL. 1	14	8	9	9	17	19	22	15	21	31	35	27
JUL. 2	14	10	10	11	17	19	22	15	21	31	35	27
JUL. 3	15	11	12	12	17	20	22	15	21	31	35	27
JUL. 4	15	13	13	14	17	20	22	15	21	31	35	27
JUL. 5	15	14	15	15	17	20	23	15	21	31	35	27
JUL. 6	15	16	16	17	18	20	23	15	21	31	35	27
JUL. 7	15	18	18	19	18	20	23	15	21	31	35	27
JUL. 8	15	19	20	20	18	20	23	15	21	31	35	27
JUL. 9	15	21	21	22	18	21	23	15	21	31	35	27
JUL. 10	15	22	23	23	18	21	23	15	21	31	35	27
JUL. 11	16	24	24	25	19	21	23	15	21	31	35	27
JUL. 12	16	26	26	27	19	21	23	15	21	31	35	27
JUL. 13	16	27	28	28	19	21	23	15	21	31	35	27
JUL. 14	16	29	30	30	19	21	23	15	21	31	35	27
JUL. 15	16	31	31	32	19	21	23	15	21	31	35	27
JUL. 16	16	33	33	34	20	22	23	16	21	31	35	27
JUL. 17	16	35	35	36	20	22	23	16	21	31	35	27
JUL. 18	16	37	37	38	20	22	24	16	21	31	35	27
JUL. 19	17	39	39	40	20	22	24	16	21	31	35	27
JUL. 20	17	41	41	42	20	22	24	16	21	31	35	27
JUL. 21	17	43	43	44	20	22	24	16	21	31	35	27
JUL. 22	17	45	45	46	20	22	24	16	21	31	35	27
JUL. 23	17	47	47	48	21	23	24	16	21	31	35	27
JUL. 24	17	1	1	2	21	23	24	16	21	31	35	27
JUL. 25	17	2	3	4	21	23	24	16	21	31	35	27
JUL. 26	18	4	5	5	21	23	24	16	21	31	35	27
JUL. 27	18	6	6	7	21	23	24	16	21	31	35	27
JUL. 28	18	8	8	9	21	23	24	16	21	31	35	27
JUL. 29	18	9	10	10	21	24	24	16	21	31	35	27
JUL. 30	18	11	11	12	21	24	25	16	21	31	35	27
JUL. 31	18	12	13	13	21	24	25	16	21	31	35	27

August

Date & Time	SUN ☼	MOON 1 ◗	MOON 2 ◖	MOON 3 ●	MERCURY	VENUS	MARS	JUPITER	SATURN	URANUS	NEPTUNE	PLUTO
AUG. 1	18	14	15	15	21	24	25	16	21	31	35	27
AUG. 2	18	16	16	17	21	24	25	16	21	31	35	27
AUG. 3	19	17	18	18	21	24	25	16	21	31	35	27
AUG. 4	19	19	19	20	21	24	25	16	21	31	35	27
AUG. 5	19	20	21	21	21	25	25	16	21	31	35	27
AUG. 6	19	22	22	23	21	25	25	16	21	31	35	27
AUG. 7	19	24	24	25	21	25	25	16	21	31	35	27
AUG. 8	19	25	26	26	21	25	25	16	21	31	35	27
AUG. 9	19	27	27	28	21	25	25	16	21	31	35	27
AUG. 10	19	29	29	30	21	25	25	16	21	31	35	27
AUG. 11	20	30	31	32	21	25	26	16	21	31	35	27
AUG. 12	20	32	33	33	21	26	26	16	21	31	35	27
AUG. 13	20	34	35	35	21	26	26	16	21	31	35	27
AUG. 14	20	36	37	37	21	26	26	16	21	31	35	27
AUG. 15	20	38	39	39	21	26	26	16	21	31	35	27
AUG. 16	20	40	41	41	21	26	26	16	21	31	35	27
AUG. 17	20	42	43	43	21	26	26	16	21	31	35	27
AUG. 18	20	44	45	45	20	26	26	16	21	31	35	27
AUG. 19	21	46	47	47	20	27	26	17	21	31	35	27
AUG. 20	21	48	48	1	20	27	26	17	21	31	35	27
AUG. 21	21	2	2	3	20	27	26	17	21	31	35	27
AUG. 22	21	4	4	5	20	27	26	17	21	31	35	27
AUG. 23	21	5	6	6	20	27	27	17	21	31	35	27
AUG. 24	21	7	7	8	20	27	27	17	21	31	35	27
AUG. 25	21	9	9	10	20	27	27	17	21	31	35	27
AUG. 26	22	10	11	11	20	27	27	17	21	31	35	27
AUG. 27	22	12	13	13	20	28	27	17	21	31	35	27
AUG. 28	22	14	14	15	20	28	27	17	22	31	35	27
AUG. 29	22	15	16	16	20	28	27	17	22	31	35	27
AUG. 30	22	17	17	18	20	28	27	17	22	31	35	27
AUG. 31	22	18	19	19	20	28	27	17	22	31	35	27

MOON 1 ◗ 12:01 A.M. TO 8:00 A.M.   **MOON 2** ◖ 8:01 A.M. TO 4:00 P.M.   **MOON 3** ● 4:01 P.M. TO 12:00 A.M.
Use only one "moon" number. Choose the column closest to your time of birth. If your place of birth is not on
Eastern Standard Time, be sure to read "How to Convert to Eastern Standard Time" at the beginning of this section.

1978

September   October

Date & Time	SUN	MOON 1	MOON 2	MOON 3	MERCURY	VENUS	MARS	JUPITER	SATURN	URANUS	NEPTUNE	PLUTO
SEP. 1	22	20	20	21	20	28	27	17	22	31	35	27
SEP. 2	22	22	22	23	20	28	27	17	22	31	35	27
SEP. 3	23	23	24	24	20	28	27	17	22	31	35	27
SEP. 4	23	25	25	26	20	29	28	17	22	31	35	27
SEP. 5	23	26	27	28	20	29	28	17	22	31	35	27
SEP. 6	23	28	29	29	20	29	28	17	22	31	35	27
SEP. 7	23	30	31	31	20	29	28	17	22	31	35	27
SEP. 8	23	32	32	33	21	29	28	17	22	31	35	27
SEP. 9	23	34	34	35	21	29	28	17	22	31	35	27
SEP. 10	23	35	36	37	21	29	28	17	22	31	35	27
SEP. 11	24	37	38	39	21	29	28	17	22	31	35	27
SEP. 12	24	39	40	40	21	30	28	17	22	31	35	27
SEP. 13	24	41	42	42	22	30	28	17	22	31	35	27
SEP. 14	24	43	44	44	22	30	28	17	22	31	35	27
SEP. 15	24	45	46	46	22	30	29	17	22	31	35	27
SEP. 16	24	47	48	48	22	30	29	17	22	31	35	27
SEP. 17	24	1	2	2	23	30	29	17	22	31	35	27
SEP. 18	24	3	3	4	23	30	29	17	22	31	35	27
SEP. 19	25	5	5	6	23	30	29	17	22	31	35	27
SEP. 20	25	6	7	8	23	30	29	17	22	31	35	27
SEP. 21	25	8	9	9	24	30	29	17	22	31	35	27
SEP. 22	25	10	10	11	24	31	29	17	22	31	35	27
SEP. 23	25	11	12	13	24	31	29	17	22	31	35	27
SEP. 24	25	13	14	14	24	31	29	17	22	31	35	27
SEP. 25	26	15	15	16	25	31	29	17	22	31	35	27
SEP. 26	26	16	17	17	25	31	30	17	22	31	35	27
SEP. 27	26	18	18	19	25	31	30	17	22	31	35	27
SEP. 28	26	19	20	20	25	31	30	18	22	31	35	27
SEP. 29	26	21	22	22	26	31	30	18	22	31	35	27
SEP. 30	26	23	23	24	26	31	30	18	22	31	35	27

Date & Time	SUN	MOON 1	MOON 2	MOON 3	MERCURY	VENUS	MARS	JUPITER	SATURN	URANUS	NEPTUNE	PLUTO
OCT. 1	26	24	25	25	26	31	30	18	22	31	35	27
OCT. 2	26	26	27	27	26	31	30	18	22	31	35	27
OCT. 3	27	28	28	29	27	31	30	18	22	31	35	27
OCT. 4	27	29	30	31	27	32	30	18	22	31	35	27
OCT. 5	27	31	32	33	27	32	30	18	22	31	35	27
OCT. 6	27	33	34	34	27	32	30	18	22	31	35	27
OCT. 7	27	35	36	36	27	32	31	18	22	31	35	27
OCT. 8	27	37	37	38	28	32	31	18	22	31	35	27
OCT. 9	27	39	39	40	28	32	31	18	22	31	35	27
OCT. 10	27	41	41	42	28	32	31	18	22	31	35	27
OCT. 11	28	42	43	44	28	32	31	18	22	31	35	27
OCT. 12	28	44	45	46	29	32	31	18	22	31	35	27
OCT. 13	28	46	47	48	29	32	31	18	22	31	35	27
OCT. 14	28	48	1	1	29	32	31	18	22	31	35	27
OCT. 15	28	2	3	3	29	32	31	18	22	31	35	27
OCT. 16	28	4	4	5	29	32	31	18	22	31	35	27
OCT. 17	28	6	6	7	30	32	31	18	22	31	35	27
OCT. 18	28	7	8	9	30	32	32	18	22	31	35	27
OCT. 19	29	9	10	10	30	32	32	18	22	31	35	27
OCT. 20	29	11	11	12	30	32	32	18	22	31	35	27
OCT. 21	29	13	13	14	30	32	32	18	22	31	35	27
OCT. 22	29	14	15	16	31	32	32	18	22	31	35	27
OCT. 23	29	16	16	17	31	32	32	18	22	31	35	27
OCT. 24	29	17	18	18	31	32	32	18	22	31	35	27
OCT. 25	29	19	19	20	31	32	32	18	22	31	35	27
OCT. 26	30	20	21	22	31	32	32	18	22	31	35	27
OCT. 27	30	22	23	23	32	32	32	18	22	31	35	27
OCT. 28	30	24	24	25	32	33	32	18	22	31	35	27
OCT. 29	30	25	26	27	32	32	33	18	22	31	35	27
OCT. 30	30	27	28	28	32	32	33	18	22	31	35	27
OCT. 31	30	29	30	30	32	32	33	18	22	31	35	27

MOON 1 ☽ 12:01 A.M. TO 8:00 A.M.   **MOON 2** ☾ 8:01 A.M. TO 4:00 P.M.   **MOON 3** ● 4:01 P.M. TO 12:00 A.M.

Use only one "moon" number. Choose the column closest to your time of birth. If your place of birth is not on Eastern Standard Time, be sure to read "How to Convert to Eastern Standard Time" at the beginning of this section.

1978

November

December

Date & Time	SUN	MOON 1	MOON 2	MOON 3	MERCURY	VENUS	MARS	JUPITER	SATURN	URANUS	NEPTUNE	PLUTO
NOV. 1	30	31	31	32	33	31	33	18	22	31	35	27
NOV. 2	30	33	33	34	33	31	33	18	23	31	35	27
NOV. 3	31	34	35	36	33	31	33	18	23	31	35	27
NOV. 4	31	36	37	38	33	31	33	18	23	31	35	27
NOV. 5	31	38	39	40	33	31	33	18	23	31	35	27
NOV. 6	31	40	41	41	33	31	33	18	23	31	35	27
NOV. 7	31	42	43	43	34	31	33	18	23	31	35	27
NOV. 8	31	44	45	45	34	31	34	18	23	31	35	27
NOV. 9	31	46	46	47	34	31	34	18	23	31	35	27
NOV. 10	31	48	48	1	34	31	34	18	23	31	35	27
NOV. 11	31	1	2	3	34	31	34	18	23	31	35	27
NOV. 12	32	3	4	4	35	31	34	18	23	31	35	27
NOV. 13	32	5	6	6	35	31	34	18	23	31	35	27
NOV. 14	32	7	7	8	35	30	34	18	23	31	35	27
NOV. 15	32	9	9	10	35	30	34	18	23	31	35	27
NOV. 16	32	10	11	11	35	30	34	18	23	31	35	27
NOV. 17	32	12	12	13	35	30	34	18	23	31	35	27
NOV. 18	32	14	14	15	35	30	35	18	23	31	35	27
NOV. 19	33	15	16	16	35	30	35	18	23	31	35	27
NOV. 20	33	17	17	18	36	30	35	18	23	31	35	27
NOV. 21	33	18	19	19	36	30	35	18	23	31	35	27
NOV. 22	33	20	20	21	36	30	35	18	23	31	35	27
NOV. 23	33	22	22	23	36	30	35	18	23	31	35	27
NOV. 24	33	23	24	24	36	30	35	18	23	31	35	27
NOV. 25	34	25	25	26	36	30	35	18	23	31	35	27
NOV. 26	34	26	27	28	36	30	35	18	23	31	35	27
NOV. 27	34	28	29	29	36	30	35	18	23	31	35	27
NOV. 28	34	30	31	31	36	30	36	18	23	31	35	27
NOV. 29	34	32	32	33	36	30	36	18	23	31	35	27
NOV. 30	34	34	34	35	36	30	36	18	23	31	35	27

Date & Time	SUN	MOON 1	MOON 2	MOON 3	MERCURY	VENUS	MARS	JUPITER	SATURN	URANUS	NEPTUNE	PLUTO
DEC. 1	34	36	36	37	36	30	36	18	23	31	35	27
DEC. 2	34	38	38	39	35	30	36	18	23	31	35	27
DEC. 3	35	40	40	41	35	30	36	18	23	31	35	27
DEC. 4	35	42	42	43	35	30	36	18	23	31	35	27
DEC. 5	35	43	44	45	35	30	36	18	23	31	35	27
DEC. 6	35	45	46	47	35	30	36	18	23	31	35	27
DEC. 7	35	47	48	48	35	30	36	18	23	31	35	27
DEC. 8	35	1	2	2	34	30	37	18	23	31	35	27
DEC. 9	35	3	3	4	34	30	37	18	23	31	35	27
DEC. 10	35	5	5	6	34	30	37	18	23	31	35	27
DEC. 11	36	6	7	7	34	30	37	18	23	31	35	27
DEC. 12	36	8	9	9	34	30	37	18	23	31	35	27
DEC. 13	36	10	10	11	34	30	37	18	23	31	35	27
DEC. 14	36	11	12	13	34	31	37	18	23	31	35	27
DEC. 15	36	13	14	14	34	31	37	18	23	31	35	27
DEC. 16	36	15	15	16	34	31	37	18	23	31	35	27
DEC. 17	36	16	17	17	34	31	37	18	23	31	35	27
DEC. 18	36	18	18	19	34	31	38	18	23	32	35	27
DEC. 19	37	19	20	20	34	31	38	18	23	32	35	27
DEC. 20	37	21	22	22	34	31	38	18	23	32	35	27
DEC. 21	37	23	23	24	34	31	38	18	23	32	35	27
DEC. 22	37	24	25	25	34	31	38	18	23	32	35	27
DEC. 23	37	26	26	27	34	31	38	18	23	32	35	27
DEC. 24	37	27	28	29	34	31	38	18	23	32	35	27
DEC. 25	37	29	30	30	34	31	38	18	23	32	35	27
DEC. 26	38	31	32	32	35	32	38	18	23	32	35	28
DEC. 27	38	33	34	34	35	32	38	18	23	32	35	28
DEC. 28	38	35	35	36	35	32	39	18	23	32	35	28
DEC. 29	38	37	37	38	35	32	39	18	23	32	35	28
DEC. 30	38	39	39	40	35	32	39	18	23	32	35	28
DEC. 31	38	41	41	42	35	32	39	18	23	32	35	28

MOON 1 ◐ 12:01 A.M. TO 8:00 A.M.　　**MOON 2** ◑ 8:01 A.M. TO 4:00 P.M.　　**MOON 3** ● 4:01 P.M. TO 12:00 A.M.

Use only one "moon" number. Choose the column closest to your time of birth. If your place of birth is not on Eastern Standard Time, be sure to read "How to Convert to Eastern Standard Time" at the beginning of this section.

1979

January

Date & Time	SUN	MOON 1	MOON 2	MOON 3	MERCURY	VENUS	MARS	JUPITER	SATURN	URANUS	NEPTUNE	PLUTO
JAN. 1	38	43	43	44	36	32	39	18	23	32	35	28
JAN. 2	38	45	45	46	36	32	39	18	23	32	35	28
JAN. 3	39	47	47	48	36	32	39	18	23	32	35	28
JAN. 4	39	1	1	2	36	33	39	18	23	32	35	28
JAN. 5	39	2	3	4	36	33	39	18	23	32	35	28
JAN. 6	39	4	5	5	36	33	39	18	23	32	35	28
JAN. 7	39	6	7	7	37	33	40	18	23	32	36	28
JAN. 8	39	8	8	9	37	33	40	18	23	32	36	28
JAN. 9	39	9	10	10	37	33	40	18	23	32	36	28
JAN. 10	40	11	12	12	37	33	40	18	23	32	36	28
JAN. 11	40	13	13	14	37	33	40	18	23	32	36	28
JAN. 12	40	14	15	15	38	34	40	18	23	32	36	28
JAN. 13	40	16	16	17	38	34	40	18	23	32	36	28
JAN. 14	40	17	18	18	38	34	40	18	23	32	36	28
JAN. 15	40	19	20	20	38	34	40	18	23	32	36	28
JAN. 16	40	21	21	22	38	34	40	18	23	32	36	28
JAN. 17	41	22	23	23	39	34	41	18	23	32	36	28
JAN. 18	41	24	24	25	39	34	41	18	23	32	36	28
JAN. 19	41	25	26	26	39	35	41	18	23	32	36	28
JAN. 20	41	27	28	28	39	35	41	18	23	32	36	28
JAN. 21	41	29	29	30	39	35	41	18	23	32	36	28
JAN. 22	41	30	31	32	40	35	41	18	23	32	36	28
JAN. 23	42	32	33	33	40	35	41	18	23	32	36	28
JAN. 24	42	34	35	35	40	35	41	18	23	32	36	28
JAN. 25	42	36	37	37	40	35	41	17	23	32	36	28
JAN. 26	42	38	39	39	40	35	42	17	23	32	36	28
JAN. 27	42	40	41	41	41	36	42	17	23	32	36	28
JAN. 28	42	42	43	43	41	36	42	17	23	32	36	28
JAN. 29	42	44	45	45	41	36	42	17	23	32	36	28
JAN. 30	42	46	47	47	41	36	42	17	23	32	36	28
JAN. 31	43	48	1	1	42	36	42	17	23	32	36	28

February

Date & Time	SUN	MOON 1	MOON 2	MOON 3	MERCURY	VENUS	MARS	JUPITER	SATURN	URANUS	NEPTUNE	PLUTO
FEB. 1	43	2	2	3	42	36	42	17	23	32	36	28
FEB. 2	43	4	4	5	42	37	42	17	23	32	36	28
FEB. 3	43	5	6	7	42	37	42	17	23	32	36	28
FEB. 4	43	7	8	8	42	37	42	17	23	32	36	28
FEB. 5	43	9	9	10	43	37	43	17	23	32	36	28
FEB. 6	43	11	11	12	43	37	43	17	23	32	36	28
FEB. 7	43	12	13	13	43	37	43	17	23	32	36	28
FEB. 8	44	14	14	15	43	37	43	17	23	32	36	28
FEB. 9	44	15	16	16	44	38	43	17	23	32	36	28
FEB. 10	44	17	18	18	44	38	43	17	23	32	36	28
FEB. 11	44	19	19	20	44	38	43	17	23	32	36	28
FEB. 12	44	20	21	21	44	38	43	17	23	32	36	28
FEB. 13	44	22	22	23	45	38	43	17	23	32	36	28
FEB. 14	44	23	24	24	45	38	44	17	23	32	36	28
FEB. 15	44	25	25	26	45	38	44	17	23	32	36	28
FEB. 16	45	27	27	28	45	39	44	17	23	32	36	28
FEB. 17	45	28	29	29	46	39	44	17	23	32	36	28
FEB. 18	45	30	30	31	46	39	44	17	22	32	36	28
FEB. 19	45	32	32	33	46	39	44	17	22	32	36	27
FEB. 20	45	33	34	35	46	39	44	17	22	32	36	27
FEB. 21	45	35	36	36	47	39	44	17	22	32	36	27
FEB. 22	45	37	38	38	47	39	44	17	22	32	36	27
FEB. 23	46	39	40	40	47	40	44	17	22	32	36	27
FEB. 24	46	41	42	42	47	40	45	17	22	32	36	27
FEB. 25	46	43	44	44	48	40	45	17	22	32	36	27
FEB. 26	46	45	46	46	48	40	45	17	22	32	36	27
FEB. 27	46	47	48	48	48	40	45	17	22	32	36	27
FEB. 28	46	1	2	2	48	40	45	17	22	32	36	27

MOON 1 ◔ 12:01 A.M. TO 8:00 A.M.   **MOON 2** ◑ 8:01 A.M. TO 4:00 P.M.   **MOON 3** ● 4:01 P.M. TO 12:00 A.M.

Use only one "moon" number. Choose the column closest to your time of birth. If your place of birth is not on Eastern Standard Time, be sure to read "How to Convert to Eastern Standard Time" at the beginning of this section.

March | April

Date & Time	SUN	MOON 1	MOON 2	MOON 3	MERCURY	VENUS	MARS	JUPITER	SATURN	URANUS	NEPTUNE	PLUTO
MAR. 1	46	3	4	4	48	41	45	17	22	32	36	27
MAR. 2	46	5	5	6	1	41	45	17	22	32	36	27
MAR. 3	47	7	7	8	1	41	45	17	22	32	36	27
MAR. 4	47	8	9	10	1	41	45	17	22	32	36	27
MAR. 5	47	10	11	11	1	41	46	17	22	32	36	27
MAR. 6	47	12	12	13	1	41	46	17	22	32	36	27
MAR. 7	47	13	14	14	2	42	46	17	22	32	36	27
MAR. 8	47	15	16	16	2	42	46	17	22	32	36	27
MAR. 9	47	17	17	18	2	42	46	17	22	32	36	27
MAR. 10	47	18	19	19	2	42	46	17	22	32	36	27
MAR. 11	48	20	20	21	2	42	46	17	22	32	36	27
MAR. 12	48	21	22	22	2	42	46	17	22	32	36	27
MAR. 13	48	23	23	24	2	42	46	17	22	32	36	27
MAR. 14	48	25	25	26	2	43	46	17	22	32	36	27
MAR. 15	48	26	27	27	2	43	47	17	22	32	36	27
MAR. 16	48	28	28	29	2	43	47	17	22	32	36	27
MAR. 17	48	29	30	31	2	43	47	17	22	32	36	27
MAR. 18	48	31	32	32	2	43	47	17	22	32	36	27
MAR. 19	1	33	34	34	2	43	47	17	22	32	36	27
MAR. 20	1	35	35	36	2	44	47	17	22	32	36	27
MAR. 21	1	37	37	38	2	44	47	17	22	32	36	27
MAR. 22	1	38	39	40	2	44	47	17	22	32	36	27
MAR. 23	1	40	41	42	2	44	47	17	22	32	36	27
MAR. 24	1	42	43	43	1	44	48	17	22	32	36	27
MAR. 25	2	44	45	45	1	44	48	17	22	32	36	27
MAR. 26	2	46	47	47	1	45	48	17	22	32	36	27
MAR. 27	2	48	1	1	1	45	48	17	22	32	36	27
MAR. 28	2	2	3	3	1	45	48	17	22	32	36	27
MAR. 29	2	4	5	5	1	45	48	17	22	32	36	27
MAR. 30	2	6	6	7	1	45	48	17	22	32	36	27
MAR. 31	2	8	8	9	1	45	48	17	22	32	36	27

Date & Time	SUN	MOON 1	MOON 2	MOON 3	MERCURY	VENUS	MARS	JUPITER	SATURN	URANUS	NEPTUNE	PLUTO
APR. 1	2	9	10	11	1	45	48	17	22	32	36	27
APR. 2	2	11	12	12	1	46	48	17	22	32	36	27
APR. 3	3	13	13	14	48	46	1	17	22	32	36	27
APR. 4	3	15	15	16	48	46	1	17	22	32	36	27
APR. 5	3	16	17	17	48	46	1	17	22	32	36	27
APR. 6	3	18	18	18	48	46	1	17	22	32	36	27
APR. 7	3	19	20	20	48	46	1	17	22	32	36	27
APR. 8	3	21	21	22	48	47	1	17	22	32	36	27
APR. 9	3	22	23	23	48	47	1	17	22	32	36	27
APR. 10	3	24	25	25	48	47	1	17	22	32	36	27
APR. 11	4	26	26	27	48	47	1	17	22	32	36	27
APR. 12	4	27	28	28	1	47	2	17	22	32	36	27
APR. 13	4	29	30	30	1	47	2	17	22	32	36	27
APR. 14	4	31	31	32	1	48	2	17	22	32	36	27
APR. 15	4	33	33	34	1	48	2	17	22	32	36	27
APR. 16	4	34	35	35	1	48	2	17	22	32	36	27
APR. 17	4	36	37	37	1	48	2	17	22	32	36	27
APR. 18	4	38	39	39	1	48	2	17	22	32	36	27
APR. 19	5	40	40	41	1	48	2	17	22	32	36	27
APR. 20	5	42	42	43	1	48	2	17	22	32	36	27
APR. 21	5	44	44	45	1	1	2	17	22	32	36	27
APR. 22	5	45	46	47	2	1	3	17	22	32	36	27
APR. 23	5	47	48	1	2	1	3	17	22	32	36	27
APR. 24	5	1	2	3	2	1	3	17	22	32	36	27
APR. 25	6	3	4	4	2	1	3	17	22	32	36	27
APR. 26	6	5	6	6	2	1	3	17	22	32	36	27
APR. 27	6	7	8	8	2	2	3	17	22	32	36	27
APR. 28	6	9	9	10	2	2	3	17	22	32	36	27
APR. 29	6	11	11	12	3	2	3	17	22	32	36	27
APR. 30	6	12	13	13	3	2	3	17	22	32	36	27

MOON 1 ◐ 12:01 A.M. TO 8:00 A.M.   **MOON 2 ◑ 8:01 A.M. TO 4:00 P.M.**   **MOON 3 ● 4:01 P.M. TO 12:00 A.M.**

Use only one "moon" number. Choose the column closest to your time of birth. If your place of birth is not on Eastern Standard Time, be sure to read "How to Convert to Eastern Standard Time" at the beginning of this section.

1979

May

Date & Time	SUN	MOON 1	MOON 2	MOON 3	MERCURY	VENUS	MARS	JUPITER	SATURN	URANUS	NEPTUNE	PLUTO
MAY 1	6	14	14	15	3	2	3	17	22	32	36	27
MAY 2	6	16	16	17	3	2	4	17	22	32	36	27
MAY 3	7	17	18	18	3	3	4	17	22	32	36	27
MAY 4	7	19	19	20	4	3	4	17	22	32	36	27
MAY 5	7	20	21	21	4	3	4	17	22	32	36	27
MAY 6	7	22	22	23	4	3	4	17	22	32	36	27
MAY 7	7	24	24	25	4	3	4	17	22	32	36	27
MAY 8	7	25	26	26	4	3	4	17	22	32	36	27
MAY 9	7	27	27	28	5	4	4	17	22	32	36	27
MAY 10	7	28	29	30	5	4	4	17	22	31	36	27
MAY 11	8	30	31	31	5	4	4	17	22	31	36	27
MAY 12	8	32	33	33	5	4	5	17	22	31	36	27
MAY 13	8	34	34	35	5	4	5	17	22	31	36	27
MAY 14	8	36	36	37	6	4	5	17	22	31	36	27
MAY 15	8	37	38	39	6	5	5	17	22	31	36	27
MAY 16	8	39	40	41	6	5	5	17	22	31	36	27
MAY 17	8	41	42	43	6	5	5	17	22	31	36	27
MAY 18	8	43	44	44	7	5	5	17	22	31	36	27
MAY 19	9	45	46	46	7	5	5	17	22	31	36	27
MAY 20	9	47	48	48	7	5	5	17	22	31	36	27
MAY 21	9	1	1	2	8	5	5	17	22	31	36	27
MAY 22	9	3	3	4	8	6	6	17	22	31	36	27
MAY 23	9	4	5	6	8	6	6	17	22	31	36	27
MAY 24	9	6	7	8	8	6	6	17	22	31	36	27
MAY 25	10	8	9	9	9	6	6	18	22	31	36	27
MAY 26	10	10	10	11	9	6	6	18	22	31	36	27
MAY 27	10	12	12	13	9	6	6	18	22	31	36	27
MAY 28	10	13	14	14	10	7	6	18	22	31	36	27
MAY 29	10	15	16	16	10	7	6	18	22	31	36	27
MAY 30	10	17	17	18	10	7	6	18	22	31	36	27
MAY 31	10	18	19	19	10	7	6	18	22	31	36	27

June

Date & Time	SUN	MOON 1	MOON 2	MOON 3	MERCURY	VENUS	MARS	JUPITER	SATURN	URANUS	NEPTUNE	PLUTO
JUN. 1	10	20	20	21	11	7	7	18	22	31	36	27
JUN. 2	10	21	22	22	11	7	7	18	22	31	36	27
JUN. 3	11	23	23	24	11	8	7	18	22	31	36	27
JUN. 4	11	25	25	26	12	8	7	18	22	31	36	27
JUN. 5	11	26	26	27	12	8	7	18	22	31	36	27
JUN. 6	11	28	28	29	12	8	7	18	22	31	36	27
JUN. 7	11	30	30	31	12	8	7	18	22	31	36	27
JUN. 8	11	31	32	32	13	8	7	18	22	31	36	27
JUN. 9	11	33	34	34	13	9	7	18	22	31	36	27
JUN. 10	11	35	36	36	13	9	7	18	22	31	36	27
JUN. 11	12	37	37	38	13	9	8	18	22	31	36	27
JUN. 12	12	39	39	40	14	9	8	18	22	31	36	27
JUN. 13	12	41	41	42	14	9	8	18	22	31	36	27
JUN. 14	12	43	43	44	14	9	8	18	22	31	36	27
JUN. 15	12	45	45	46	14	10	8	18	22	31	36	27
JUN. 16	12	46	47	48	15	10	8	18	22	31	35	27
JUN. 17	12	48	1	2	15	10	8	18	22	31	35	27
JUN. 18	12	2	3	3	15	10	8	18	22	31	35	27
JUN. 19	13	4	5	5	15	10	8	18	22	31	35	27
JUN. 20	13	6	6	7	16	10	8	18	22	31	35	27
JUN. 21	13	8	8	9	16	10	9	18	22	31	35	27
JUN. 22	13	9	10	11	16	11	9	18	22	31	35	27
JUN. 23	13	11	12	12	16	11	9	18	22	31	35	27
JUN. 24	13	13	13	14	16	11	9	18	22	31	35	27
JUN. 25	14	14	15	16	17	11	9	18	22	31	35	27
JUN. 26	14	16	17	17	17	11	9	18	22	31	35	27
JUN. 27	14	18	18	19	17	11	9	18	22	31	35	27
JUN. 28	14	19	20	20	17	12	9	18	22	31	35	27
JUN. 29	14	21	21	22	17	12	9	18	22	31	35	27
JUN. 30	14	22	23	24	17	12	9	18	22	31	35	27

MOON 1 ☽ 12:01 A.M. TO 8:00 A.M.　　**MOON 2** ☽ 8:01 A.M. TO 4:00 P.M.　　**MOON 3** ● 4:01 P.M. TO 12:00 A.M.
Use only one "moon" number. Choose the column closest to your time of birth. If your place of birth is not on Eastern Standard Time, be sure to read "How to Convert to Eastern Standard Time" at the beginning of this section.

1979

July

Date & Time	SUN	MOON 1	MOON 2	MOON 3	MERCURY	VENUS	MARS	JUPITER	SATURN	URANUS	NEPTUNE	PLUTO
JUL. 1	14	24	25	25	18	12	9	18	22	31	35	27
JUL. 2	14	26	26	27	18	12	10	18	22	31	35	27
JUL. 3	15	27	28	28	18	12	10	18	22	31	35	27
JUL. 4	15	29	29	30	18	13	10	18	22	31	35	27
JUL. 5	15	31	31	32	18	13	10	19	22	31	35	27
JUL. 6	15	32	33	34	18	13	10	19	22	31	35	27
JUL. 7	15	34	35	35	18	13	10	19	22	31	35	27
JUL. 8	15	36	37	37	18	13	10	19	22	31	35	27
JUL. 9	15	38	39	39	19	13	10	19	22	31	35	27
JUL. 10	15	40	41	41	19	14	10	19	22	31	35	27
JUL. 11	16	42	43	43	19	14	10	19	22	31	35	27
JUL. 12	16	44	45	45	19	14	10	19	22	31	35	27
JUL. 13	16	46	47	47	19	14	11	19	22	31	35	27
JUL. 14	16	48	48	1	19	14	11	19	22	31	35	27
JUL. 15	16	2	2	3	19	14	11	19	22	31	35	27
JUL. 16	16	4	4	5	19	15	11	19	22	31	35	27
JUL. 17	16	5	6	7	19	15	11	19	22	31	35	27
JUL. 18	16	7	8	8	19	15	11	19	22	31	35	27
JUL. 19	17	9	10	10	19	15	11	19	22	31	35	27
JUL. 20	17	11	11	12	19	15	11	19	22	31	35	27
JUL. 21	17	12	13	13	19	15	11	19	22	31	35	27
JUL. 22	17	14	15	15	19	16	11	19	22	31	35	27
JUL. 23	17	16	16	17	19	16	11	19	22	31	35	27
JUL. 24	17	17	18	18	19	16	12	19	23	31	35	27
JUL. 25	17	19	19	20	19	16	12	19	23	31	35	27
JUL. 26	18	20	21	21	19	16	12	19	23	31	35	27
JUL. 27	18	22	23	23	18	16	12	19	23	31	35	27
JUL. 28	18	24	24	25	18	17	12	19	23	31	35	27
JUL. 29	18	25	26	26	18	17	12	19	23	31	35	27
JUL. 30	18	27	27	28	18	17	12	19	23	31	35	27
JUL. 31	18	28	29	29	18	17	12	19	23	31	35	27

August

Date & Time	SUN	MOON 1	MOON 2	MOON 3	MERCURY	VENUS	MARS	JUPITER	SATURN	URANUS	NEPTUNE	PLUTO
AUG. 1	18	30	31	31	18	17	12	19	23	31	35	27
AUG. 2	18	32	32	33	18	17	12	19	23	31	35	27
AUG. 3	19	33	34	35	18	18	12	19	23	31	35	27
AUG. 4	19	35	36	37	18	18	13	19	23	31	35	27
AUG. 5	19	37	38	38	18	18	13	19	23	31	35	27
AUG. 6	19	39	40	40	18	18	13	19	23	31	35	27
AUG. 7	19	41	42	42	17	18	13	19	23	31	35	27
AUG. 8	19	43	44	44	17	18	13	19	23	31	35	27
AUG. 9	19	45	46	46	17	19	13	20	23	31	35	27
AUG. 10	19	47	48	48	17	19	13	20	23	31	35	27
AUG. 11	20	1	2	2	17	19	13	20	23	31	35	27
AUG. 12	20	3	4	4	17	19	13	20	23	31	35	27
AUG. 13	20	5	6	6	17	19	13	20	23	31	35	27
AUG. 14	20	7	7	8	17	19	13	20	23	31	35	27
AUG. 15	20	9	9	10	18	19	14	20	23	31	35	27
AUG. 16	20	10	11	11	18	20	14	20	23	31	35	27
AUG. 17	20	12	13	13	18	20	14	20	23	31	35	27
AUG. 18	20	14	14	15	18	20	14	20	23	31	35	27
AUG. 19	21	15	16	16	18	20	14	20	23	31	35	27
AUG. 20	21	17	17	18	18	20	14	20	23	31	35	27
AUG. 21	21	18	19	20	18	20	14	20	23	31	35	27
AUG. 22	21	20	21	21	18	21	14	20	23	31	35	27
AUG. 23	21	22	22	23	19	21	14	20	23	31	35	27
AUG. 24	21	23	24	24	19	21	14	20	23	31	35	27
AUG. 25	21	25	25	26	19	21	14	20	23	31	35	27
AUG. 26	22	26	27	27	19	21	15	20	23	31	35	27
AUG. 27	22	28	28	29	19	21	15	20	23	31	35	27
AUG. 28	22	30	30	31	20	22	15	20	23	31	35	27
AUG. 29	22	31	32	32	20	22	15	20	23	31	35	27
AUG. 30	22	33	33	34	20	22	15	20	23	31	35	27
AUG. 31	22	35	35	36	20	22	15	20	23	31	35	27

MOON 1 ☽ 12:01 A.M. TO 8:00 A.M.   **MOON 2** ☽ 8:01 A.M. TO 4:00 P.M.   **MOON 3** ● 4:01 P.M. TO 12:00 A.M.

Use only one "moon" number. Choose the column closest to your time of birth. If your place of birth is not on Eastern Standard Time, be sure to read "How to Convert to Eastern Standard Time" at the beginning of this section.

Date & Time	SUN	MOON 1	MOON 2	MOON 3	MERCURY	VENUS	MARS	JUPITER	SATURN	URANUS	NEPTUNE	PLUTO
SEP. 1	22	36	37	38	21	22	15	20	23	31	35	27
SEP. 2	22	38	39	40	21	22	15	20	23	31	35	27
SEP. 3	23	40	41	42	21	23	15	20	23	31	35	27
SEP. 4	23	42	43	44	21	23	15	20	23	31	35	27
SEP. 5	23	44	45	46	22	23	15	20	23	31	35	27
SEP. 6	23	46	47	48	22	23	15	20	23	31	35	27
SEP. 7	23	48	1	2	22	23	16	20	23	31	35	27
SEP. 8	23	2	3	4	22	23	16	20	23	31	35	27
SEP. 9	23	4	5	6	23	24	16	20	23	31	35	27
SEP. 10	23	6	7	7	23	24	16	20	23	31	35	27
SEP. 11	24	8	9	9	23	24	16	20	23	31	35	27
SEP. 12	24	10	10	11	23	24	16	20	23	31	35	27
SEP. 13	24	12	12	13	24	24	16	21	23	31	35	27
SEP. 14	24	13	14	14	24	24	16	21	23	31	35	27
SEP. 15	24	15	15	16	24	25	16	21	23	31	35	27
SEP. 16	24	16	17	18	24	25	16	21	23	31	35	27
SEP. 17	24	18	19	19	25	25	16	21	23	31	35	27
SEP. 18	24	20	20	21	25	25	16	21	23	31	35	27
SEP. 19	25	21	22	22	25	25	17	21	23	31	35	27
SEP. 20	25	23	23	24	25	25	17	21	23	31	35	27
SEP. 21	25	24	25	25	26	26	17	21	23	31	35	27
SEP. 22	25	26	26	27	26	26	17	21	23	31	35	27
SEP. 23	25	28	28	29	26	26	17	21	23	31	35	27
SEP. 24	25	29	30	30	26	26	17	21	23	31	35	27
SEP. 25	26	31	31	32	26	26	17	21	24	31	35	27
SEP. 26	26	33	33	34	27	26	17	21	24	31	35	27
SEP. 27	26	34	35	35	27	27	17	21	24	31	35	27
SEP. 28	26	36	37	37	27	27	17	21	24	31	35	27
SEP. 29	26	38	38	39	27	27	17	21	24	31	35	27
SEP. 30	26	40	40	41	28	27	17	21	24	31	35	27

Date & Time	SUN	MOON 1	MOON 2	MOON 3	MERCURY	VENUS	MARS	JUPITER	SATURN	URANUS	NEPTUNE	PLUTO
OCT. 1	26	41	42	43	28	27	17	21	24	31	35	27
OCT. 2	26	43	44	45	28	27	18	21	24	31	35	27
OCT. 3	27	45	46	47	28	28	18	21	24	31	35	27
OCT. 4	27	47	48	1	28	28	18	21	24	31	35	27
OCT. 5	27	1	2	3	29	28	18	21	24	31	35	27
OCT. 6	27	3	4	5	29	28	18	21	24	31	35	27
OCT. 7	27	5	6	7	29	28	18	21	24	32	35	27
OCT. 8	27	7	8	8	29	28	18	21	24	32	35	27
OCT. 9	27	9	10	10	29	29	18	21	24	32	35	27
OCT. 10	27	11	12	12	30	29	18	21	24	32	35	28
OCT. 11	28	13	13	14	30	29	18	21	24	32	35	28
OCT. 12	28	14	15	15	30	29	18	21	24	32	35	28
OCT. 13	28	16	17	17	30	29	18	21	24	32	35	28
OCT. 14	28	18	18	19	30	29	18	21	24	32	35	28
OCT. 15	28	19	20	20	31	30	19	21	24	32	35	28
OCT. 16	28	21	21	22	31	30	19	21	24	32	35	28
OCT. 17	28	22	23	23	31	30	19	21	24	32	35	28
OCT. 18	28	24	24	25	31	30	19	21	24	32	35	28
OCT. 19	29	26	26	27	31	30	19	21	24	32	35	28
OCT. 20	29	27	28	28	31	30	19	21	24	32	35	28
OCT. 21	29	29	29	30	32	31	19	21	24	32	35	28
OCT. 22	29	30	31	32	32	31	19	22	24	32	35	28
OCT. 23	29	32	33	33	32	31	19	22	24	32	35	28
OCT. 24	29	34	34	35	32	31	19	22	24	32	35	28
OCT. 25	29	36	36	37	32	31	19	22	24	32	35	28
OCT. 26	30	37	38	39	32	31	19	22	24	32	35	28
OCT. 27	30	39	40	40	33	32	19	22	24	32	35	28
OCT. 28	30	41	42	42	33	32	19	22	24	32	35	28
OCT. 29	30	43	43	44	33	32	20	22	24	32	35	28
OCT. 30	30	45	45	46	33	32	20	22	24	32	35	28
OCT. 31	30	47	47	48	33	32	20	22	24	32	35	28

MOON 1 ◗ 12:01 A.M. TO 8:00 A.M.   **MOON 2** ◑ 8:01 A.M. TO 4:00 P.M.   **MOON 3** ● 4:01 P.M. TO 12:00 A.M.
Use only one "moon" number. Choose the column closest to your time of birth. If your place of birth is not on
Eastern Standard Time, be sure to read "How to Convert to Eastern Standard Time" at the beginning of this section.

1979

November

December

Date & Time	SUN	MOON 1	MOON 2	MOON 3	MERCURY	VENUS	MARS	JUPITER	SATURN	URANUS	NEPTUNE	PLUTO
NOV. 1	30	1	1	2	33	32	20	22	24	32	35	28
NOV. 2	30	3	3	4	33	33	20	22	24	32	35	28
NOV. 3	31	4	5	6	33	33	20	22	24	32	35	28
NOV. 4	31	6	7	8	33	33	20	22	24	32	35	28
NOV. 5	31	8	9	10	34	33	20	22	24	32	35	28
NOV. 6	31	10	11	11	34	33	20	22	24	32	35	28
NOV. 7	31	12	13	13	34	33	20	22	24	32	35	28
NOV. 8	31	14	14	15	34	34	20	22	24	32	35	28
NOV. 9	31	15	16	17	34	34	20	22	24	32	35	28
NOV. 10	31	17	18	18	34	34	20	22	24	32	36	28
NOV. 11	31	19	19	20	34	34	20	22	24	32	36	28
NOV. 12	32	20	21	21	34	34	20	22	24	32	36	28
NOV. 13	32	22	22	23	34	34	21	22	24	32	36	28
NOV. 14	32	23	24	24	34	35	21	22	24	32	36	28
NOV. 15	32	25	26	26	33	35	21	22	24	32	36	28
NOV. 16	32	27	27	28	33	35	21	22	24	32	36	28
NOV. 17	32	28	29	29	33	35	21	22	24	32	36	28
NOV. 18	32	30	30	31	33	35	21	22	24	32	36	28
NOV. 19	33	32	32	33	33	35	21	22	24	32	36	28
NOV. 20	33	33	34	35	33	36	21	22	24	32	36	28
NOV. 21	33	35	36	36	32	36	21	22	24	32	36	28
NOV. 22	33	37	37	38	32	36	21	22	24	32	36	28
NOV. 23	33	39	39	40	32	36	21	22	24	32	36	28
NOV. 24	33	41	41	42	32	36	21	22	24	32	36	28
NOV. 25	34	42	43	44	32	36	21	22	24	32	36	28
NOV. 26	34	44	45	45	32	37	21	22	24	32	36	28
NOV. 27	34	46	47	47	32	37	21	22	24	32	36	28
NOV. 28	34	48	1	1	32	37	21	22	24	32	36	28
NOV. 29	34	2	3	3	32	37	22	22	24	32	36	28
NOV. 30	34	4	4	5	32	37	22	22	24	32	36	28

Date & Time	SUN	MOON 1	MOON 2	MOON 3	MERCURY	VENUS	MARS	JUPITER	SATURN	URANUS	NEPTUNE	PLUTO
DEC. 1	34	6	6	7	32	37	22	22	24	32	36	28
DEC. 2	34	8	8	9	32	38	22	22	24	32	36	28
DEC. 3	35	9	10	11	32	38	22	22	24	32	36	28
DEC. 4	35	11	12	12	32	38	22	22	24	32	36	28
DEC. 5	35	13	14	14	32	38	22	22	24	32	36	28
DEC. 6	35	15	15	16	32	38	22	22	24	32	36	28
DEC. 7	35	16	17	18	32	38	22	22	24	32	36	28
DEC. 8	35	18	19	19	32	39	22	22	24	32	36	28
DEC. 9	35	20	20	21	32	39	22	22	24	32	36	28
DEC. 10	35	21	22	22	33	39	22	22	24	32	36	28
DEC. 11	36	23	23	24	33	39	22	22	24	32	36	28
DEC. 12	36	24	25	26	33	39	22	22	24	32	36	28
DEC. 13	36	26	27	27	33	39	22	22	24	32	36	28
DEC. 14	36	28	28	29	33	40	22	22	25	32	36	28
DEC. 15	36	29	30	30	33	40	22	22	25	32	36	28
DEC. 16	36	31	32	32	34	40	22	22	25	32	36	28
DEC. 17	36	33	33	34	34	40	22	22	25	32	36	28
DEC. 18	36	34	35	36	34	40	22	22	25	32	36	28
DEC. 19	37	36	37	38	34	40	22	22	25	32	36	28
DEC. 20	37	38	39	39	34	41	22	22	25	32	36	28
DEC. 21	37	40	41	41	35	41	23	22	25	32	36	28
DEC. 22	37	42	43	43	35	41	23	22	25	32	36	28
DEC. 23	37	44	44	45	35	41	23	22	25	32	36	28
DEC. 24	37	46	46	47	35	41	23	22	25	32	36	28
DEC. 25	37	48	48	1	35	41	23	22	25	32	36	28
DEC. 26	38	1	2	3	36	42	23	22	25	32	36	28
DEC. 27	38	3	4	5	36	42	23	22	25	32	36	28
DEC. 28	38	5	6	6	36	42	23	22	25	32	36	28
DEC. 29	38	7	8	8	36	42	23	22	25	32	36	28
DEC. 30	38	9	9	10	36	42	23	22	25	32	36	28
DEC. 31	38	11	11	12	37	42	23	22	25	32	36	28

MOON 1 ◐ 12:01 A.M. TO 8:00 A.M.   **MOON 2** ◑ 8:01 A.M. TO 4:00 P.M.   **MOON 3** ● 4:01 P.M. TO 12:00 A.M.

Use only one "moon" number. Choose the column closest to your time of birth. If your place of birth is not on Eastern Standard Time, be sure to read "How to Convert to Eastern Standard Time" at the beginning of this section.

1980-1989

1980s

Prince William

★ ★ ★ BORN JUNE 21, 1982 ★ ★ ★

Brief Bio: Prince William is the first-born son of the Prince of Wales and the late Princess Diana, and second in line of succession to the British throne.

Personology Profile:

SUN ON THE CUSP OF MAGIC
(GEMINI-CANCER CUSP)

*

The most romantic of all Personology periods, this magical cusp lends a compelling intimacy to contacts with these individuals. Private, but not shy, they are likely to lead a life hidden from the prying eyes of the world in which love plays an important role. Summer solstice people, they radiate conscious energies and can be highly developed both mentally and emotionally.

MOON IN THE WEEK OF
THE SEEKER
(GEMINI III)

*

When it comes to new emotional experiences, these folks are up for almost anything. Challenged by an unattainable love, they are likely to be led astray by their desires and left with a whole lot of unhappiness. Until they get a grip on their feelings, they will continue to make poor partner choices. Falling in love with love will provide continual ecstatic highs, but inevitably depressions also.

MERCURY IN THE WEEK
OF FREEDOM
(GEMINI I)

*

Frequently branded as troublemakers, those born in this week usually work to undermine authority and encourage others to think as freely as they themselves do. Since they often lack structure in their lives, it will be useful to work in circumstances where limits are put on their thinking and demands are made to support their ideas with hard facts.

MARS IN THE WEEK OF
THE PERFECTIONIST
(LIBRA I)

*

Being aggressive in one's perfectionistic demands does not usually earn friends. This stressful position can drive everyone concerned a bit crazy, unless they can learn to be a bit more laid back. In dealing with technical matters, Mars in this period does guarantee perseverance and usually produces results. Great care must be taken to avoid neglecting the emotional and social spheres. Scheduling regular yoga, meditation or prayer sessions is advised.

VENUS IN THE WEEK OF
THE NATURAL
(TAURUS III)

*

A shamelessly honest approach to love characterizes Venus in Taurus III. They are not only outwardly demonstrative but also refuse to fake it or appear to have feelings or attitudes which are not true. These individuals hate pretense above all. Their approach is so straightforward that they can be accused occasionally of being too rough in their refusal to coddle their sweethearts.

JUPITER ON THE CUSP OF
DRAMA AND CRITICISM
(LIBRA-SCORPIO CUSP)

*

Although Jupiter does not feel comfortable with criticism, this position tends to make success more a matter of diligent attention to detail than to sheer luck. This position of the jovial planet favors the use of mental powers and concise expression. By conserving energy rather than spreading it too thin, success can be achieved in a conservative, straightforward fashion.

SATURN IN THE WEEK OF SOCIETY
(LIBRA II)

✳

This Saturn position can impair one's social skills and in extreme cases make the individual a bit reclusive or antisocial. The upside of this is a strong sense of social responsibility, making for a personality which can be trusted with putting the good of the group first. However, such altruism can lead to neglect of one's own personal development, and this must be guarded against.

URANUS ON THE CUSP OF REVOLUTION
(SCORPIO-SAGITTARIUS CUSP)

✳

Revolution is something that is close to the very essence of the planet Uranus. Conceived and discovered at the time of the French Revolution, it carries an energy which opposes established systems and seeks to overthrow them. These energies should not be allowed to get out of control here or this individual may become very unpopular with those around them.

NEPTUNE IN THE WEEK OF THE TITAN
(SAGITTARIUS III)

✳

Because of their expansiveness of thought, these individuals are likely to get out of touch with reality easily. Those with this Neptune position do not acknowledge boundaries nor heed warning signals of having gone too far. Grounding and actualizing their ideas is their major problem, since these individuals often prefer to enjoy their latest fantasy. A touch of pragmatism will help implement their ideas.

PLUTO IN THE WEEK OF THEATER
(LIBRA III)

✳

An interest in the darker aspects of life, particularly those connected with conflicts, wars and battles of all sorts is evident in these individuals. They can even encounter problems that do not exist by summoning them up with their active imaginations. Expectation of excitement is characteristic here and does not allow for a dull moment in their lives.

Some Highlights of the Decade 1980-1989

- DIANA SPENCER MARRIES THE PRINCE OF WALES IN A LAVISH CEREMONY AT ST. PAUL'S CATHEDRAL.

- AFTER A QUARTER CENTURY OF CONFINEMENT ON ROBBEN ISLAND, NELSON MANDELA IS RELEASED FROM PRISON AND BECOMES THE FIRST BLACK PRESIDENT OF SOUTH AFRICA.

- JOHN LENNON IS MURDERED BY A DERANGED FAN IN FRONT OF THE DAKOTA APARTMENT BUILDING IN NEW YORK CITY.

- PRESIDENT REAGAN AND SOVIET LEADER MIKHAIL S. GORBACHEV SIGN THE INTERMEDIATE-RANGE NUCLEAR FORCES (INF) TREATY, UNDER WHICH THE SUPERPOWERS AGREE TO DESTROY THEIR ARSENALS OF INTERMEDIATE-RANGE NUCLEAR MISSILES.

- AMID GREAT EUPHORIA, THE BERLIN WALL THAT SEPARATES EAST AND WEST BERLIN COMES DOWN, SYMBOLIZING THE END OF THE COLD WAR.

1980

January   February

Date & Time	SUN	MOON 1	MOON 2	MOON 3	MERCURY	VENUS	MARS	JUPITER	SATURN	URANUS	NEPTUNE	PLUTO
JAN. 1	38	12	13	14	37	43	23	22	25	32	36	28
JAN. 2	38	14	15	15	37	43	23	22	25	32	36	28
JAN. 3	39	16	16	17	37	43	23	22	25	32	36	28
JAN. 4	39	18	18	19	37	43	23	22	25	32	36	28
JAN. 5	39	19	20	20	38	43	23	22	25	32	36	28
JAN. 6	39	21	21	22	38	43	23	22	25	32	36	28
JAN. 7	39	22	23	23	38	44	23	22	25	32	36	28
JAN. 8	39	24	24	25	38	44	23	22	25	32	36	28
JAN. 9	39	26	26	27	38	44	23	22	25	32	36	28
JAN. 10	40	27	28	28	39	44	23	22	25	32	36	28
JAN. 11	40	29	29	30	39	44	23	22	25	32	36	28
JAN. 12	40	30	31	31	39	44	23	22	25	32	36	28
JAN. 13	40	32	33	33	39	44	23	22	25	32	36	28
JAN. 14	40	34	34	35	39	45	23	22	25	32	36	28
JAN. 15	40	36	36	37	40	45	23	22	25	32	36	28
JAN. 16	40	37	38	39	40	45	23	22	25	32	36	28
JAN. 17	41	39	40	41	40	45	23	22	25	32	36	28
JAN. 18	41	41	42	42	40	45	23	22	25	32	36	28
JAN. 19	41	43	44	44	41	45	23	22	25	32	36	28
JAN. 20	41	45	46	46	41	46	23	22	25	32	36	28
JAN. 21	41	47	48	48	41	46	23	22	25	32	36	28
JAN. 22	41	1	2	2	41	46	23	22	25	32	36	28
JAN. 23	42	3	4	4	41	46	23	22	25	32	36	28
JAN. 24	42	5	5	6	42	46	23	22	25	32	36	28
JAN. 25	42	7	7	8	42	46	23	22	25	32	36	28
JAN. 26	42	8	9	10	42	47	23	22	25	32	36	28
JAN. 27	42	10	11	11	42	47	23	22	25	32	36	28
JAN. 28	42	12	13	13	43	47	23	22	25	32	36	28
JAN. 29	42	14	14	15	43	47	23	22	25	32	36	28
JAN. 30	42	15	16	16	43	47	23	22	25	32	36	28
JAN. 31	43	17	18	18	43	47	23	22	24	32	36	28

Date & Time	SUN	MOON 1	MOON 2	MOON 3	MERCURY	VENUS	MARS	JUPITER	SATURN	URANUS	NEPTUNE	PLUTO
FEB. 1	43	19	19	20	44	48	23	22	24	32	36	28
FEB. 2	43	20	21	21	44	48	23	22	24	32	36	28
FEB. 3	43	22	22	23	44	48	23	22	24	32	36	28
FEB. 4	43	23	24	25	44	48	23	22	24	32	36	28
FEB. 5	43	25	26	26	44	48	23	22	24	32	36	28
FEB. 6	43	27	27	28	45	48	23	22	24	32	36	28
FEB. 7	43	28	29	29	45	1	23	22	24	32	36	28
FEB. 8	44	30	30	31	45	1	23	22	24	32	36	28
FEB. 9	44	31	32	33	45	1	23	22	24	32	36	28
FEB. 10	44	33	34	34	46	1	22	22	24	32	36	28
FEB. 11	44	35	35	36	46	1	22	22	24	32	36	28
FEB. 12	44	37	37	38	46	1	22	22	24	32	36	28
FEB. 13	44	38	39	40	46	1	22	22	24	32	36	28
FEB. 14	44	40	41	42	46	2	22	22	24	32	36	28
FEB. 15	44	42	43	44	47	2	22	22	24	32	36	28
FEB. 16	45	44	45	46	47	2	22	22	24	32	36	28
FEB. 17	45	46	47	48	47	2	22	22	24	32	36	28
FEB. 18	45	48	1	2	47	2	22	22	24	32	36	28
FEB. 19	45	2	3	4	47	2	22	22	24	32	36	28
FEB. 20	45	4	5	5	47	3	22	22	24	32	36	28
FEB. 21	45	6	7	7	48	3	22	22	24	32	36	28
FEB. 22	45	8	9	9	48	3	22	22	24	32	36	28
FEB. 23	46	10	10	11	48	3	22	22	24	32	36	28
FEB. 24	46	12	12	13	48	3	22	22	24	32	36	28
FEB. 25	46	13	14	14	48	3	22	22	24	32	36	28
FEB. 26	46	15	16	16	48	4	22	22	24	32	36	28
FEB. 27	46	17	17	18	48	4	22	22	24	32	36	28
FEB. 28	46	18	19	19	48	4	22	22	24	32	36	28
FEB. 29	46	20	20	21	48	4	22	22	24	32	36	28

MOON 1 ◗ 12:01 A.M. TO 8:00 A.M.   **MOON 2** ◖ 8:01 A.M. TO 4:00 P.M.   **MOON 3** ● 4:01 P.M. TO 12:00 A.M.

Use only one "moon" number. Choose the column closest to your time of birth. If your place of birth is not on Eastern Standard Time, be sure to read "How to Convert to Eastern Standard Time" at the beginning of this section.

Date & Time	SUN	MOON 1	MOON 2	MOON 3	MERCURY	VENUS	MARS	JUPITER	SATURN	URANUS	NEPTUNE	PLUTO
MAR. 1	46	21	22	22	48	4	21	22	24	32	36	28
MAR. 2	46	23	24	24	48	4	21	22	24	32	36	28
MAR. 3	47	25	25	26	47	4	21	22	24	32	36	28
MAR. 4	47	26	27	27	47	5	21	22	24	32	36	28
MAR. 5	47	28	28	29	47	5	21	22	24	32	36	28
MAR. 6	47	29	30	30	47	5	21	21	24	32	36	28
MAR. 7	47	31	31	32	47	5	21	21	24	32	36	28
MAR. 8	47	33	33	34	47	5	21	21	24	32	36	28
MAR. 9	47	34	35	35	47	5	21	21	24	32	36	28
MAR. 10	47	36	37	37	47	5	21	21	24	32	36	28
MAR. 11	48	38	38	39	46	6	21	21	24	32	36	28
MAR. 12	48	40	40	41	46	6	21	21	24	32	36	28
MAR. 13	48	41	42	43	46	6	21	21	24	32	36	28
MAR. 14	48	43	44	45	46	6	21	21	24	32	36	28
MAR. 15	48	45	46	47	46	6	21	21	24	32	36	28
MAR. 16	48	47	48	1	46	6	21	21	24	32	36	28
MAR. 17	48	1	2	3	46	7	21	21	24	32	36	28
MAR. 18	48	3	4	5	46	7	21	21	24	32	36	28
MAR. 19	1	5	6	7	46	7	21	21	24	32	36	28
MAR. 20	1	7	8	9	46	7	21	21	24	32	36	28
MAR. 21	1	9	10	10	46	7	21	21	24	32	36	28
MAR. 22	1	11	12	12	46	7	21	21	24	32	36	28
MAR. 23	1	13	13	14	46	7	21	21	24	32	36	28
MAR. 24	1	15	15	16	46	8	21	21	24	32	36	28
MAR. 25	2	16	17	17	46	8	21	21	24	32	36	28
MAR. 26	2	18	18	19	46	8	21	21	24	32	36	28
MAR. 27	2	19	20	21	46	8	21	21	24	32	36	28
MAR. 28	2	21	22	22	46	8	20	21	24	32	36	28
MAR. 29	2	23	23	24	46	8	20	21	24	32	36	28
MAR. 30	2	24	25	25	47	8	20	21	24	32	36	28
MAR. 31	2	26	26	27	47	8	20	21	24	32	36	28

Date & Time	SUN	MOON 1	MOON 2	MOON 3	MERCURY	VENUS	MARS	JUPITER	SATURN	URANUS	NEPTUNE	PLUTO
APR. 1	2	27	28	28	47	9	20	21	24	32	36	28
APR. 2	2	29	29	30	47	9	20	21	24	32	36	28
APR. 3	3	31	31	32	47	9	20	21	24	32	36	28
APR. 4	3	32	33	33	47	9	20	21	24	32	36	28
APR. 5	3	34	34	35	47	9	20	21	24	32	36	28
APR. 6	3	35	36	37	48	9	20	21	24	32	36	28
APR. 7	3	37	38	38	48	9	20	21	24	32	36	28
APR. 8	3	39	40	40	48	10	20	21	24	32	36	28
APR. 9	3	41	41	42	48	10	20	21	24	32	36	28
APR. 10	3	43	43	44	48	10	20	21	24	32	36	28
APR. 11	4	44	45	46	48	10	20	21	24	32	36	28
APR. 12	4	46	47	48	1	10	20	21	24	32	36	28
APR. 13	4	48	1	2	1	10	20	21	24	32	36	28
APR. 14	4	2	3	4	1	10	20	21	24	32	36	28
APR. 15	4	4	5	6	1	10	20	21	24	32	36	28
APR. 16	4	6	7	8	1	11	20	21	24	32	36	28
APR. 17	4	8	9	10	1	11	21	21	24	32	36	28
APR. 18	4	10	11	12	2	11	21	21	24	32	36	28
APR. 19	5	12	13	13	2	11	21	21	24	32	36	28
APR. 20	5	14	15	15	2	11	21	21	24	32	36	28
APR. 21	5	16	16	17	2	11	21	21	24	32	36	28
APR. 22	5	17	18	18	3	11	21	21	24	32	36	28
APR. 23	5	19	20	20	3	11	21	21	24	32	36	28
APR. 24	5	21	21	22	3	11	21	21	24	32	36	28
APR. 25	6	22	23	23	3	12	21	21	24	32	36	28
APR. 26	6	24	24	25	3	12	21	21	24	32	36	28
APR. 27	6	25	26	26	4	12	21	21	24	32	36	28
APR. 28	6	27	27	28	4	12	21	21	24	32	36	28
APR. 29	6	29	29	30	4	12	21	21	24	32	36	28
APR. 30	6	30	31	31	4	12	21	21	24	32	36	28

MOON 1 ☽ 12:01 A.M. TO 8:00 A.M.   **MOON 2** ◑ 8:01 A.M. TO 4:00 P.M.   **MOON 3** ● 4:01 P.M. TO 12:00 A.M.
Use only one "moon" number. Choose the column closest to your time of birth. If your place of birth is not on Eastern Standard Time, be sure to read "How to Convert to Eastern Standard Time" at the beginning of this section.

Date & Time	SUN	MOON 1	MOON 2	MOON 3	MERCURY	VENUS	MARS	JUPITER	SATURN	URANUS	NEPTUNE	PLUTO
MAY 1	6	32	32	33	5	12	21	21	24	32	36	28
MAY 2	6	33	34	35	5	12	21	21	24	32	36	28
MAY 3	7	35	36	36	5	12	21	21	24	32	36	28
MAY 4	7	37	37	38	5	12	21	21	24	32	36	28
MAY 5	7	39	39	40	6	12	21	21	24	32	36	28
MAY 6	7	40	41	41	6	13	21	21	24	32	36	28
MAY 7	7	42	43	43	6	13	21	21	24	32	36	28
MAY 8	7	44	45	45	7	13	21	21	24	32	36	28
MAY 9	7	46	46	47	7	13	21	21	24	32	36	28
MAY 10	7	48	48	1	7	13	21	21	24	32	36	28
MAY 11	8	2	2	3	7	13	21	21	24	32	36	28
MAY 12	8	4	4	5	8	13	21	21	24	32	36	28
MAY 13	8	6	6	7	8	13	21	21	24	32	36	28
MAY 14	8	8	8	9	8	13	21	21	24	32	36	28
MAY 15	8	10	10	11	9	13	21	21	24	32	36	28
MAY 16	8	11	12	13	9	13	21	21	24	32	36	28
MAY 17	8	13	14	14	9	13	22	21	24	32	36	28
MAY 18	8	15	16	16	9	13	22	21	24	32	36	28
MAY 19	9	17	17	18	10	13	22	21	24	32	36	28
MAY 20	9	18	19	20	10	13	22	21	24	32	36	28
MAY 21	9	20	21	21	10	13	22	21	24	32	36	28
MAY 22	9	22	22	23	11	13	22	21	24	32	36	28
MAY 23	9	23	24	24	11	13	22	21	24	32	36	28
MAY 24	9	25	25	26	11	13	22	21	24	32	36	28
MAY 25	10	26	27	28	11	13	22	21	24	32	36	28
MAY 26	10	28	29	29	12	13	22	21	24	32	36	28
MAY 27	10	30	30	31	12	13	22	21	24	32	36	28
MAY 28	10	31	32	32	12	13	22	21	24	32	36	28
MAY 29	10	33	34	34	12	13	22	21	24	32	36	28
MAY 30	10	35	35	36	13	13	22	21	24	32	36	28
MAY 31	10	36	37	38	13	13	22	21	24	32	36	28

Date & Time	SUN	MOON 1	MOON 2	MOON 3	MERCURY	VENUS	MARS	JUPITER	SATURN	URANUS	NEPTUNE	PLUTO
JUN. 1	10	38	39	39	13	13	22	21	24	32	36	28
JUN. 2	10	40	40	41	13	13	22	21	24	32	36	28
JUN. 3	11	42	42	43	13	13	22	21	24	32	36	28
JUN. 4	11	43	44	45	14	13	22	21	24	32	36	28
JUN. 5	11	45	46	47	14	13	23	21	24	32	36	28
JUN. 6	11	47	48	48	14	13	23	21	24	32	36	28
JUN. 7	11	1	2	2	14	13	23	21	24	32	36	28
JUN. 8	11	3	4	4	14	13	23	21	24	32	36	28
JUN. 9	11	5	6	6	15	13	23	21	24	32	36	28
JUN. 10	11	7	7	8	15	13	23	21	24	32	36	28
JUN. 11	12	9	9	10	15	13	23	21	24	32	36	28
JUN. 12	12	11	11	12	15	12	23	21	24	32	36	28
JUN. 13	12	13	13	14	15	12	23	21	24	32	36	28
JUN. 14	12	14	15	16	15	12	23	21	24	32	36	28
JUN. 15	12	16	17	17	15	12	23	21	24	32	36	28
JUN. 16	12	18	18	19	16	12	23	21	24	32	36	28
JUN. 17	12	20	20	21	16	12	23	22	24	32	36	28
JUN. 18	12	21	22	22	16	12	23	22	24	32	36	27
JUN. 19	13	23	23	24	16	12	23	22	24	32	36	27
JUN. 20	13	24	25	25	16	12	24	22	24	32	36	27
JUN. 21	13	26	26	27	16	12	24	22	24	32	36	27
JUN. 22	13	28	28	29	16	12	24	22	24	32	36	27
JUN. 23	13	29	30	30	16	12	24	22	24	32	36	27
JUN. 24	13	31	31	32	16	12	24	22	24	32	36	27
JUN. 25	14	32	33	34	16	11	24	22	24	32	36	27
JUN. 26	14	34	35	35	16	11	24	22	24	32	36	27
JUN. 27	14	36	36	37	16	11	24	22	24	32	36	27
JUN. 28	14	38	38	39	16	11	24	22	24	32	36	27
JUN. 29	14	39	40	41	16	11	24	22	24	32	36	27
JUN. 30	14	41	42	42	16	11	24	22	24	32	36	27

MOON 1 ◖ 12:01 A.M. TO 8:00 A.M.   **MOON 2** ◑ 8:01 A.M. TO 4:00 P.M.   **MOON 3** ● 4:01 P.M. TO 12:00 A.M.

Use only one "moon" number. Choose the column closest to your time of birth. If your place of birth is not on Eastern Standard Time, be sure to read "How to Convert to Eastern Standard Time" at the beginning of this section.

1980

July

August

Date & Time	SUN	MOON 1	MOON 2	MOON 3	MERCURY	VENUS	MARS	JUPITER	SATURN	URANUS	NEPTUNE	PLUTO
JUL. 1	14	43	44	44	16	11	24	22	24	32	36	27
JUL. 2	14	45	46	46	16	11	24	22	24	32	36	27
JUL. 3	15	47	47	48	16	11	24	22	24	32	36	27
JUL. 4	15	1	1	2	16	11	24	22	24	32	36	27
JUL. 5	15	3	3	4	16	11	25	22	24	32	36	27
JUL. 6	15	4	5	6	16	11	25	22	24	32	36	27
JUL. 7	15	6	7	8	16	11	25	22	24	32	36	27
JUL. 8	15	8	9	9	16	11	25	22	24	32	36	27
JUL. 9	15	10	11	11	16	11	25	22	24	32	36	27
JUL. 10	15	12	13	13	16	11	25	22	24	32	36	28
JUL. 11	16	14	14	15	16	11	25	22	24	32	36	28
JUL. 12	16	16	16	17	16	11	25	22	24	32	36	28
JUL. 13	16	17	18	18	15	11	25	22	24	32	36	28
JUL. 14	16	19	20	20	15	11	25	22	24	32	36	28
JUL. 15	16	21	21	22	15	11	25	22	24	32	36	28
JUL. 16	16	22	23	23	15	11	25	22	24	32	36	28
JUL. 17	16	24	24	25	15	11	26	22	24	32	36	28
JUL. 18	16	25	26	26	15	11	26	22	24	32	36	28
JUL. 19	17	27	28	28	15	11	26	22	24	32	36	28
JUL. 20	17	29	29	30	15	12	26	22	24	32	36	28
JUL. 21	17	30	31	31	15	12	26	22	24	32	36	28
JUL. 22	17	32	32	33	15	12	26	22	24	32	36	28
JUL. 23	17	33	34	35	15	12	26	22	24	32	36	28
JUL. 24	17	35	36	36	15	12	26	22	24	32	36	28
JUL. 25	17	37	38	38	15	12	26	22	24	32	36	28
JUL. 26	18	39	39	40	15	12	26	22	24	32	36	28
JUL. 27	18	41	41	42	15	12	26	22	24	32	36	28
JUL. 28	18	42	43	44	15	12	26	22	24	32	36	28
JUL. 29	18	44	45	46	15	12	26	22	24	32	36	28
JUL. 30	18	46	47	48	15	12	26	22	24	32	36	28
JUL. 31	18	48	1	1	15	12	27	22	24	32	36	28

Date & Time	SUN	MOON 1	MOON 2	MOON 3	MERCURY	VENUS	MARS	JUPITER	SATURN	URANUS	NEPTUNE	PLUTO
AUG. 1	18	2	3	3	16	12	27	23	24	32	36	28
AUG. 2	18	4	5	5	16	13	27	23	24	32	36	28
AUG. 3	19	6	7	7	16	13	27	23	24	32	36	28
AUG. 4	19	8	8	9	16	13	27	23	24	32	36	28
AUG. 5	19	10	10	11	16	13	27	23	24	32	36	28
AUG. 6	19	11	12	13	16	13	27	23	24	32	36	28
AUG. 7	19	13	14	14	17	13	27	23	24	32	36	28
AUG. 8	19	15	16	16	17	13	27	23	24	32	36	28
AUG. 9	19	17	17	18	17	13	27	23	24	32	36	28
AUG. 10	19	18	19	20	17	13	27	23	24	32	36	28
AUG. 11	20	20	21	21	17	13	27	23	24	32	36	28
AUG. 12	20	22	22	23	18	14	28	23	24	32	36	28
AUG. 13	20	23	24	24	18	14	28	23	24	32	36	28
AUG. 14	20	25	25	26	18	14	28	23	24	32	36	28
AUG. 15	20	27	27	28	18	14	28	23	24	32	36	28
AUG. 16	20	28	29	29	19	14	28	23	24	32	36	28
AUG. 17	20	30	30	31	19	14	28	23	24	32	36	28
AUG. 18	20	31	32	32	19	14	28	23	24	32	36	28
AUG. 19	21	33	33	34	19	14	28	23	24	32	36	28
AUG. 20	21	35	35	36	20	15	28	23	24	32	36	28
AUG. 21	21	36	37	37	20	15	28	23	24	32	36	28
AUG. 22	21	38	39	39	20	15	28	23	24	32	36	28
AUG. 23	21	40	40	41	21	15	28	23	24	32	36	28
AUG. 24	21	42	42	43	21	15	29	23	25	32	36	28
AUG. 25	21	44	44	45	21	15	29	23	25	32	36	28
AUG. 26	22	45	46	47	21	15	29	23	25	32	36	28
AUG. 27	22	47	48	1	22	15	29	23	25	32	36	28
AUG. 28	22	1	2	3	22	16	29	23	25	32	36	28
AUG. 29	22	3	4	5	22	16	29	23	25	32	36	28
AUG. 30	22	5	6	7	22	16	29	23	25	32	36	28
AUG. 31	22	7	8	9	23	16	29	23	25	32	36	28

MOON 1 ☽ 12:01 A.M. TO 8:00 A.M.   **MOON 2** ☽ 8:01 A.M. TO 4:00 P.M.   **MOON 3** ● 4:01 P.M. TO 12:00 A.M.
Use only one "moon" number. Choose the column closest to your time of birth. If your place of birth is not on
Eastern Standard Time, be sure to read "How to Convert to Eastern Standard Time" at the beginning of this section.

September

Date & Time	SUN	MOON 1	MOON 2	MOON 3	MERCURY	VENUS	MARS	JUPITER	SATURN	URANUS	NEPTUNE	PLUTO
SEP. 1	22	9	10	10	23	16	29	23	25	32	36	28
SEP. 2	22	11	12	12	23	16	29	23	25	32	36	28
SEP. 3	23	13	13	14	23	16	29	23	25	32	36	28
SEP. 4	23	15	15	16	24	16	29	23	25	32	36	28
SEP. 5	23	16	17	17	24	17	30	23	25	32	36	28
SEP. 6	23	18	19	19	24	17	30	24	25	32	36	28
SEP. 7	23	20	20	21	24	17	30	24	25	32	36	28
SEP. 8	23	21	22	22	25	17	30	24	25	32	36	28
SEP. 9	23	23	23	24	25	17	30	24	25	32	36	28
SEP. 10	23	24	25	26	25	17	30	24	25	32	36	28
SEP. 11	24	26	27	27	25	17	30	24	25	32	36	28
SEP. 12	24	28	28	29	25	18	30	24	25	32	36	28
SEP. 13	24	29	30	30	26	18	30	24	25	32	36	28
SEP. 14	24	31	31	32	26	18	30	24	25	32	36	28
SEP. 15	24	32	33	33	26	18	30	24	25	32	36	28
SEP. 16	24	34	35	35	26	18	31	24	25	32	36	28
SEP. 17	24	36	36	37	27	18	31	24	25	32	36	28
SEP. 18	24	37	38	38	27	18	31	24	25	32	36	28
SEP. 19	25	39	40	40	27	19	31	24	25	32	36	28
SEP. 20	25	41	41	42	27	19	31	24	25	32	36	28
SEP. 21	25	43	43	44	27	19	31	24	25	32	36	28
SEP. 22	25	45	45	46	28	19	31	24	25	32	36	28
SEP. 23	25	47	47	48	28	19	31	24	25	32	36	28
SEP. 24	25	1	1	2	28	19	31	24	25	32	36	28
SEP. 25	26	3	3	4	28	19	31	24	25	32	36	28
SEP. 26	26	5	5	6	28	20	31	24	25	32	36	28
SEP. 27	26	7	7	8	28	20	32	24	25	32	36	28
SEP. 28	26	9	9	10	29	20	32	24	25	32	36	28
SEP. 29	26	11	11	12	29	20	32	24	25	32	36	28
SEP. 30	26	12	13	14	29	20	32	24	25	32	36	28

October

Date & Time	SUN	MOON 1	MOON 2	MOON 3	MERCURY	VENUS	MARS	JUPITER	SATURN	URANUS	NEPTUNE	PLUTO
OCT. 1	26	14	15	15	29	20	32	24	25	32	36	28
OCT. 2	26	16	16	17	29	21	32	24	25	32	36	28
OCT. 3	27	18	18	19	30	21	32	24	25	32	36	28
OCT. 4	27	19	20	20	30	21	32	24	25	32	36	28
OCT. 5	27	21	21	22	30	21	32	24	25	32	36	28
OCT. 6	27	22	23	24	30	21	32	24	25	32	36	28
OCT. 7	27	24	25	25	30	21	32	24	25	32	36	28
OCT. 8	27	26	26	27	30	21	33	24	25	32	36	28
OCT. 9	27	27	28	28	30	22	33	24	25	32	36	28
OCT. 10	27	29	29	30	31	22	33	24	25	32	36	28
OCT. 11	28	30	31	31	31	22	33	25	25	32	36	28
OCT. 12	28	32	33	33	31	22	33	25	25	32	36	28
OCT. 13	28	34	34	35	31	22	33	25	25	32	36	28
OCT. 14	28	35	36	36	31	22	33	25	25	32	36	28
OCT. 15	28	37	37	38	31	23	33	25	25	32	36	28
OCT. 16	28	39	39	40	31	23	33	25	25	32	36	28
OCT. 17	28	40	41	41	31	23	33	25	25	32	36	28
OCT. 18	28	42	43	43	31	23	34	25	25	32	36	28
OCT. 19	29	44	44	45	32	23	34	25	25	32	36	28
OCT. 20	29	46	46	47	32	23	34	25	25	32	36	28
OCT. 21	29	48	48	1	32	23	34	25	25	32	36	28
OCT. 22	29	2	2	3	32	24	34	25	25	32	36	28
OCT. 23	29	4	4	5	32	24	34	25	25	32	36	28
OCT. 24	29	6	6	7	32	24	34	25	25	32	36	28
OCT. 25	29	8	8	9	32	24	34	25	26	32	36	28
OCT. 26	30	10	10	11	32	24	34	25	26	32	36	28
OCT. 27	30	12	12	13	31	24	34	25	26	32	36	28
OCT. 28	30	14	14	15	31	25	34	25	26	32	36	28
OCT. 29	30	15	16	17	31	25	35	25	26	32	36	28
OCT. 30	30	17	18	18	31	25	35	25	26	32	36	28
OCT. 31	30	19	19	20	31	25	35	25	26	32	36	28

MOON 1 ☾ 12:01 A.M. TO 8:00 A.M.   **MOON 2** ☽ 8:01 A.M. TO 4:00 P.M.   **MOON 3** ● 4:01 P.M. TO 12:00 A.M.
Use only one "moon" number. Choose the column closest to your time of birth. If your place of birth is not on Eastern Standard Time, be sure to read "How to Convert to Eastern Standard Time" at the beginning of this section.

1980

November

Date & Time	SUN ☉	MOON 1 ☽	MOON 2 ☽	MOON 3 ●	MERCURY	VENUS	MARS	JUPITER	SATURN	URANUS	NEPTUNE	PLUTO
NOV. 1	30	20	21	22	31	25	35	25	26	32	36	28
NOV. 2	30	22	23	23	31	25	35	25	26	32	36	28
NOV. 3	31	24	24	25	30	26	35	25	26	32	36	28
NOV. 4	31	25	26	26	30	26	35	25	26	32	36	28
NOV. 5	31	27	27	28	30	26	35	25	26	32	36	28
NOV. 6	31	28	29	29	30	26	35	25	26	32	36	28
NOV. 7	31	30	31	31	30	26	35	25	26	32	36	28
NOV. 8	31	32	32	33	30	26	35	25	26	32	36	28
NOV. 9	31	33	34	34	30	27	36	25	26	32	36	28
NOV. 10	31	35	35	36	30	27	36	25	26	32	36	28
NOV. 11	31	36	37	38	30	27	36	25	26	32	36	28
NOV. 12	32	38	39	39	29	27	36	25	26	32	36	28
NOV. 13	32	40	40	41	30	27	36	25	26	32	36	28
NOV. 14	32	42	42	43	30	27	36	25	26	32	36	28
NOV. 15	32	43	44	44	30	28	36	25	26	32	36	28
NOV. 16	32	45	46	46	30	28	36	25	26	32	36	28
NOV. 17	32	47	48	48	30	28	36	25	26	32	36	28
NOV. 18	32	1	2	2	30	28	37	26	26	32	36	28
NOV. 19	33	3	3	4	30	28	37	26	26	32	36	28
NOV. 20	33	5	5	6	30	28	37	26	26	32	36	28
NOV. 21	33	7	8	8	30	28	37	26	26	32	36	28
NOV. 22	33	9	10	10	30	29	37	26	26	32	36	28
NOV. 23	33	11	11	12	31	29	37	26	26	32	36	28
NOV. 24	33	13	13	14	31	29	37	26	26	32	36	28
NOV. 25	34	15	15	16	31	29	37	26	26	32	36	28
NOV. 26	34	16	17	18	31	29	37	26	26	32	36	28
NOV. 27	34	18	19	19	31	29	37	26	26	32	36	28
NOV. 28	34	20	21	21	31	30	38	26	26	32	36	28
NOV. 29	34	22	22	23	32	30	38	26	26	33	36	28
NOV. 30	34	23	24	24	32	30	38	26	26	33	36	28

December

Date & Time	SUN ☉	MOON 1 ☽	MOON 2 ☽	MOON 3 ●	MERCURY	VENUS	MARS	JUPITER	SATURN	URANUS	NEPTUNE	PLUTO
DEC. 1	34	25	25	26	32	30	38	26	26	33	36	28
DEC. 2	34	26	27	27	32	30	38	26	26	33	36	28
DEC. 3	35	28	29	29	32	30	38	26	26	33	36	28
DEC. 4	35	30	30	31	33	31	38	26	26	33	36	28
DEC. 5	35	31	32	32	33	31	38	26	26	33	36	28
DEC. 6	35	33	33	34	33	31	38	26	26	33	36	28
DEC. 7	35	34	35	35	33	31	39	26	26	33	36	28
DEC. 8	35	36	37	37	33	31	39	26	26	33	36	28
DEC. 9	35	38	38	39	34	31	39	26	26	33	36	28
DEC. 10	35	39	40	41	34	32	39	26	26	33	36	28
DEC. 11	36	41	42	42	34	32	39	26	26	33	36	28
DEC. 12	36	43	43	44	34	32	39	26	26	33	36	28
DEC. 13	36	45	45	46	34	32	39	26	26	33	36	28
DEC. 14	36	46	47	48	35	32	39	26	26	33	36	28
DEC. 15	36	48	1	2	35	32	39	26	26	33	36	28
DEC. 16	36	2	3	3	35	33	39	26	26	33	36	28
DEC. 17	36	4	5	5	35	33	40	26	26	33	36	28
DEC. 18	36	6	7	7	35	33	40	26	26	33	36	28
DEC. 19	37	8	9	9	35	33	40	26	26	33	36	28
DEC. 20	37	10	11	11	36	33	40	26	26	33	36	28
DEC. 21	37	12	13	13	36	33	40	26	26	33	36	28
DEC. 22	37	14	14	15	36	34	40	26	26	33	36	28
DEC. 23	37	16	16	17	37	34	40	26	26	33	36	28
DEC. 24	37	18	18	19	37	34	40	26	26	33	36	28
DEC. 25	37	19	20	20	37	34	40	26	26	33	36	28
DEC. 26	38	21	22	22	37	34	40	26	26	33	36	28
DEC. 27	38	23	23	24	37	34	41	26	26	33	36	28
DEC. 28	38	24	25	25	38	35	41	26	26	33	36	28
DEC. 29	38	26	26	27	38	35	41	26	26	33	36	28
DEC. 30	38	27	28	29	38	35	41	26	26	33	36	28
DEC. 31	38	29	30	30	38	35	41	26	26	33	36	28

MOON 1 ☽ 12:01 A.M. TO 8:00 A.M.　　**MOON 2** ☽ 8:01 A.M. TO 4:00 P.M.　　**MOON 3** ● 4:01 P.M. TO 12:00 A.M.

Use only one "moon" number. Choose the column closest to your time of birth. If your place of birth is not on Eastern Standard Time, be sure to read "How to Convert to Eastern Standard Time" at the beginning of this section.

January

Date & Time	SUN	MOON 1 ☽	MOON 2 ◐	MOON 3 ●	MERCURY	VENUS	MARS	JUPITER	SATURN	URANUS	NEPTUNE	PLUTO
JAN. 1	38	31	31	32	38	35	41	26	26	33	36	28
JAN. 2	38	32	33	33	39	35	41	26	26	33	36	28
JAN. 3	39	34	34	35	39	36	41	26	26	33	36	28
JAN. 4	39	36	36	37	39	36	41	26	26	33	36	28
JAN. 5	39	37	38	38	39	36	42	26	26	33	36	28
JAN. 6	39	39	39	40	40	36	42	26	26	33	36	28
JAN. 7	39	41	41	42	40	36	42	26	26	33	36	28
JAN. 8	39	42	43	44	40	36	42	26	26	33	36	28
JAN. 9	39	44	45	45	40	37	42	26	26	33	36	28
JAN. 10	40	46	47	47	40	37	42	26	26	33	36	28
JAN. 11	40	48	1	1	41	37	42	26	26	33	36	28
JAN. 12	40	2	2	3	41	37	42	26	26	33	36	28
JAN. 13	40	4	4	5	41	37	42	26	26	33	36	28
JAN. 14	40	6	6	7	41	37	42	26	26	33	36	28
JAN. 15	40	7	8	9	42	38	43	26	26	33	36	28
JAN. 16	40	9	10	11	42	38	43	26	26	33	36	28
JAN. 17	41	11	12	12	42	38	43	26	26	33	36	28
JAN. 18	41	13	14	14	42	38	43	26	26	33	36	28
JAN. 19	41	15	16	16	42	38	43	26	26	33	36	28
JAN. 20	41	17	17	18	43	38	43	26	26	33	36	28
JAN. 21	41	19	19	20	43	39	43	26	26	33	36	28
JAN. 22	41	20	21	21	43	39	43	26	26	33	36	28
JAN. 23	42	22	23	23	43	39	43	26	26	33	36	28
JAN. 24	42	24	24	44	44	39	44	26	26	33	36	28
JAN. 25	42	25	26	26	44	39	44	26	26	33	36	28
JAN. 26	42	27	27	28	44	39	44	26	26	33	36	28
JAN. 27	42	29	29	30	44	40	44	26	26	33	36	28
JAN. 28	42	30	31	31	44	40	44	26	26	33	36	28
JAN. 29	42	32	32	33	45	40	44	26	26	33	36	28
JAN. 30	42	33	34	34	45	40	44	26	26	33	36	28
JAN. 31	43	35	35	36	45	40	44	26	26	33	36	28

February

Date & Time	SUN	MOON 1 ☽	MOON 2 ◐	MOON 3 ●	MERCURY	VENUS	MARS	JUPITER	SATURN	URANUS	NEPTUNE	PLUTO
FEB. 1	43	37	37	38	45	40	44	26	26	33	36	28
FEB. 2	43	38	39	39	45	41	44	26	26	33	36	28
FEB. 3	43	40	41	41	45	41	45	26	26	33	36	28
FEB. 4	43	42	42	43	45	41	45	26	26	33	36	28
FEB. 5	43	44	44	45	45	41	45	26	26	33	36	28
FEB. 6	43	45	46	47	46	41	45	26	26	33	36	28
FEB. 7	43	47	48	1	46	41	45	26	26	33	36	28
FEB. 8	44	1	2	3	46	42	45	26	26	33	36	28
FEB. 9	44	3	4	4	46	42	45	26	26	33	36	28
FEB. 10	44	5	6	6	46	42	45	26	26	33	36	28
FEB. 11	44	7	8	8	46	42	45	26	26	33	36	28
FEB. 12	44	9	10	10	45	42	46	26	26	33	36	28
FEB. 13	44	11	11	12	45	42	46	26	26	33	36	28
FEB. 14	44	13	13	14	45	43	46	26	26	33	36	28
FEB. 15	44	14	15	16	45	43	46	26	26	33	36	28
FEB. 16	45	16	17	17	45	43	46	26	26	33	36	28
FEB. 17	45	18	19	19	45	43	46	26	26	33	36	28
FEB. 18	45	20	20	21	45	43	46	26	26	33	36	28
FEB. 19	45	21	22	23	45	43	46	26	26	33	36	28
FEB. 20	45	23	24	24	44	44	46	26	26	33	36	28
FEB. 21	45	25	25	26	44	44	46	26	26	33	36	28
FEB. 22	45	26	27	27	44	44	47	26	26	33	36	28
FEB. 23	46	28	29	29	44	44	47	26	26	33	36	28
FEB. 24	46	30	30	31	44	44	47	26	26	33	36	28
FEB. 25	46	31	32	32	44	44	47	26	26	33	36	28
FEB. 26	46	33	33	34	44	45	47	26	26	33	36	28
FEB. 27	46	34	35	35	44	45	47	26	26	33	36	28
FEB. 28	46	36	37	37	44	45	47	26	26	33	36	28

MOON 1 ☽ 12:01 A.M. TO 8:00 A.M.　　**MOON 2** ◐ 8:01 A.M. TO 4:00 P.M.　　**MOON 3** ● 4:01 P.M. TO 12:00 A.M.
Use only one "moon" number. Choose the column closest to your time of birth. If your place of birth is not on Eastern Standard Time, be sure to read "How to Convert to Eastern Standard Time" at the beginning of this section.

1981

March — April

Date & Time	SUN	MOON 1	MOON 2	MOON 3	MERCURY	VENUS	MARS	JUPITER	SATURN	URANUS	NEPTUNE	PLUTO
MAY 1	6	1	1	2	7	7	6	25	25	33	36	28
MAY 2	6	3	3	4	7	7	6	25	25	33	36	28
MAY 3	7	5	5	6	8	8	6	25	25	33	36	28
MAY 4	7	7	8	8	8	8	6	25	25	33	36	28
MAY 5	7	9	10	10	8	8	6	25	25	33	36	28
MAY 6	7	11	12	12	8	8	6	25	25	33	36	28
MAY 7	7	13	14	14	9	8	6	25	25	33	36	28
MAY 8	7	15	15	16	9	8	6	25	25	33	36	28
MAY 9	7	17	17	18	9	8	6	25	25	33	36	28
MAY 10	7	18	19	20	9	9	6	25	25	33	36	28
MAY 11	8	20	21	21	10	9	7	25	25	33	36	28
MAY 12	8	22	22	23	10	9	7	25	25	33	36	28
MAY 13	8	23	24	25	10	9	7	25	25	33	36	28
MAY 14	8	25	26	26	10	9	7	25	25	33	36	28
MAY 15	8	27	27	28	11	10	7	25	25	33	36	28
MAY 16	8	28	29	29	11	10	7	25	25	33	36	28
MAY 17	8	30	30	31	11	10	7	25	25	33	36	28
MAY 18	8	31	32	32	11	10	7	25	25	33	36	28
MAY 19	9	33	34	34	11	10	7	25	25	33	36	28
MAY 20	9	35	35	36	12	10	7	25	25	33	36	28
MAY 21	9	36	37	37	12	11	8	25	25	33	36	28
MAY 22	9	38	38	39	12	11	8	25	25	33	36	28
MAY 23	9	39	40	41	12	11	8	25	25	33	36	28
MAY 24	9	41	42	42	12	11	8	25	25	33	36	28
MAY 25	10	43	43	44	13	11	8	25	25	33	36	28
MAY 26	10	45	45	46	13	11	8	25	25	33	36	28
MAY 27	10	46	47	48	13	11	8	25	25	33	36	28
MAY 28	10	48	1	1	13	12	8	25	25	33	36	28
MAY 29	10	2	3	3	13	12	8	25	25	33	36	28
MAY 30	10	4	5	5	13	12	8	25	25	33	36	28
MAY 31	10	6	7	7	13	12	8	25	25	33	36	28

Date & Time	SUN	MOON 1	MOON 2	MOON 3	MERCURY	VENUS	MARS	JUPITER	SATURN	URANUS	NEPTUNE	PLUTO
JUN. 1	10	8	9	9	13	12	9	25	25	33	36	28
JUN. 2	10	10	11	11	13	12	9	25	25	33	36	28
JUN. 3	11	12	13	13	13	13	9	25	25	33	36	28
JUN. 4	11	14	15	15	14	13	9	25	25	33	36	28
JUN. 5	11	16	17	17	14	13	9	25	25	33	36	28
JUN. 6	11	18	18	19	14	13	9	25	25	33	36	28
JUN. 7	11	20	20	21	14	13	9	25	25	33	36	28
JUN. 8	11	21	22	22	14	13	9	25	25	33	36	28
JUN. 9	11	23	24	24	14	14	9	25	25	33	36	28
JUN. 10	11	25	25	26	14	14	9	25	25	33	36	28
JUN. 11	12	26	27	27	14	14	10	25	25	33	36	28
JUN. 12	12	28	28	29	14	14	10	25	25	33	36	28
JUN. 13	12	29	30	30	14	14	10	25	25	33	36	28
JUN. 14	12	31	32	32	14	14	10	25	25	33	36	28
JUN. 15	12	33	33	34	14	15	10	25	25	33	36	28
JUN. 16	12	34	35	35	13	15	10	25	25	33	36	28
JUN. 17	12	36	36	37	13	15	10	25	25	33	36	28
JUN. 18	12	37	38	39	13	15	10	25	25	33	36	28
JUN. 19	13	39	40	40	13	15	10	25	25	33	36	28
JUN. 20	13	41	41	42	13	15	10	25	25	33	36	28
JUN. 21	13	42	43	44	13	16	10	25	25	33	36	28
JUN. 22	13	44	45	45	13	16	11	25	25	33	36	28
JUN. 23	13	46	46	47	13	16	11	25	25	33	36	28
JUN. 24	13	48	48	1	13	16	11	25	25	33	36	28
JUN. 25	14	1	2	3	13	16	11	25	25	33	36	28
JUN. 26	14	3	4	5	13	16	11	25	25	33	36	28
JUN. 27	14	5	6	7	13	17	11	25	25	33	36	28
JUN. 28	14	7	8	9	13	17	11	25	25	33	36	28
JUN. 29	14	9	10	11	13	17	11	25	25	33	36	28
JUN. 30	14	11	12	12	13	17	11	25	25	33	36	28

MOON 1 ☽ 12:01 A.M. TO 8:00 A.M.   **MOON 2** ◑ 8:01 A.M. TO 4:00 P.M.   **MOON 3** ● 4:01 P.M. TO 12:00 A.M.

Use only one "moon" number. Choose the column closest to your time of birth. If your place of birth is not on Eastern Standard Time, be sure to read "How to Convert to Eastern Standard Time" at the beginning of this section.

1981

May

June

Date & Time	SUN ☉	MOON 1 ☽	MOON 2 ◑	MOON 3 ●	MERCURY	VENUS	MARS	JUPITER	SATURN	URANUS	NEPTUNE	PLUTO
MAY 1	6	1	1	2	7	7	6	25	25	33	36	28
MAY 2	6	3	3	4	7	7	6	25	25	33	36	28
MAY 3	7	5	5	6	8	8	6	25	25	33	36	28
MAY 4	7	7	8	8	8	8	6	25	25	33	36	28
MAY 5	7	9	10	10	8	8	6	25	25	33	36	28
MAY 6	7	11	12	12	8	8	6	25	25	33	36	28
MAY 7	7	13	14	14	9	8	6	25	25	33	36	28
MAY 8	7	15	15	16	9	8	6	25	25	33	36	28
MAY 9	7	17	17	18	9	9	6	25	25	33	36	28
MAY 10	7	18	19	20	9	9	6	25	25	33	36	28
MAY 11	8	20	21	21	10	9	7	25	25	33	36	28
MAY 12	8	22	22	23	10	9	7	25	25	33	36	28
MAY 13	8	23	24	25	10	9	7	25	25	33	36	28
MAY 14	8	25	26	26	10	9	7	25	25	33	36	28
MAY 15	8	27	27	28	11	10	7	25	25	33	36	28
MAY 16	8	28	29	29	11	10	7	25	25	33	36	28
MAY 17	8	30	30	31	11	10	7	25	25	33	36	28
MAY 18	8	31	32	32	11	10	7	25	25	33	36	28
MAY 19	9	33	34	34	11	10	7	25	25	33	36	28
MAY 20	9	35	35	36	12	10	7	25	25	33	36	28
MAY 21	9	36	37	37	12	11	8	25	25	33	36	28
MAY 22	9	38	38	39	12	11	8	25	25	33	36	28
MAY 23	9	39	40	41	12	11	8	25	25	33	36	28
MAY 24	9	41	42	42	12	11	8	25	25	33	36	28
MAY 25	10	43	43	44	13	11	8	25	25	33	36	28
MAY 26	10	45	45	46	13	11	8	25	25	33	36	28
MAY 27	10	46	47	48	13	11	8	25	25	33	36	28
MAY 28	10	48	1	1	13	12	8	25	25	33	36	28
MAY 29	10	2	3	3	13	12	8	25	25	33	36	28
MAY 30	10	4	5	5	13	12	8	25	25	33	36	28
MAY 31	10	6	7	7	13	12	8	25	25	33	36	28

Date & Time	SUN ☉	MOON 1 ☽	MOON 2 ◑	MOON 3 ●	MERCURY	VENUS	MARS	JUPITER	SATURN	URANUS	NEPTUNE	PLUTO
JUN. 1	10	8	9	9	13	12	9	25	25	33	36	28
JUN. 2	10	10	11	11	13	12	9	25	25	33	36	28
JUN. 3	11	12	13	13	13	13	9	25	25	33	36	28
JUN. 4	11	14	15	15	14	13	9	25	25	33	36	28
JUN. 5	11	16	17	17	14	13	9	25	25	33	36	28
JUN. 6	11	18	18	19	14	13	9	25	25	33	36	28
JUN. 7	11	20	20	21	14	13	9	25	25	33	36	28
JUN. 8	11	21	22	22	14	13	9	25	25	33	36	28
JUN. 9	11	23	24	24	14	14	9	25	25	33	36	28
JUN. 10	11	25	25	26	14	14	9	25	25	33	36	28
JUN. 11	12	26	27	27	14	14	10	25	25	33	36	28
JUN. 12	12	28	28	29	14	14	10	25	25	33	36	28
JUN. 13	12	29	30	30	14	14	10	25	25	33	36	28
JUN. 14	12	31	32	32	14	14	10	25	25	33	36	28
JUN. 15	12	33	33	34	14	15	10	25	25	33	36	28
JUN. 16	12	34	35	35	13	15	10	25	25	33	36	28
JUN. 17	12	36	36	37	13	15	10	25	25	33	36	28
JUN. 18	12	37	38	39	13	15	10	25	25	33	36	28
JUN. 19	13	39	40	40	13	15	10	25	25	33	36	28
JUN. 20	13	41	41	42	13	15	10	25	25	33	36	28
JUN. 21	13	42	43	44	13	16	10	25	25	33	36	28
JUN. 22	13	44	45	45	13	16	11	25	25	33	36	28
JUN. 23	13	46	46	47	13	16	11	25	25	33	36	28
JUN. 24	13	48	48	1	13	16	11	25	25	33	36	28
JUN. 25	14	1	2	3	13	16	11	25	25	33	36	28
JUN. 26	14	3	4	5	13	16	11	25	25	33	36	28
JUN. 27	14	5	6	7	13	17	11	25	25	33	36	28
JUN. 28	14	7	8	9	13	17	11	25	25	33	36	28
JUN. 29	14	9	10	11	13	17	11	25	25	33	36	28
JUN. 30	14	11	12	12	13	17	11	25	25	33	36	28

MOON 1 ☽ 12:01 A.M. TO 8:00 A.M.   **MOON 2** ◑ 8:01 A.M. TO 4:00 P.M.   **MOON 3** ● 4:01 P.M. TO 12:00 A.M.

Use only one "moon" number. Choose the column closest to your time of birth. If your place of birth is not on Eastern Standard Time, be sure to read "How to Convert to Eastern Standard Time" at the beginning of this section.

1981

July   August

Date & Time	SUN	MOON 1	MOON 2	MOON 3	MERCURY	VENUS	MARS	JUPITER	SATURN	URANUS	NEPTUNE	PLUTO
JUL. 1	14	13	14	14	13	17	11	25	25	33	36	28
JUL. 2	14	15	16	16	12	17	11	25	25	33	36	28
JUL. 3	15	17	18	18	12	18	12	25	25	32	36	28
JUL. 4	15	19	19	20	12	18	12	25	25	32	36	28
JUL. 5	15	21	21	22	12	18	12	25	25	32	36	28
JUL. 6	15	22	23	24	13	18	12	25	25	32	36	28
JUL. 7	15	24	25	25	13	18	12	25	25	32	36	28
JUL. 8	15	26	26	27	13	18	12	25	25	32	36	28
JUL. 9	15	27	28	28	13	18	12	25	25	32	36	28
JUL. 10	15	29	29	30	13	19	12	25	26	32	36	28
JUL. 11	16	31	31	32	13	19	12	25	26	32	36	28
JUL. 12	16	32	33	33	13	19	12	25	26	32	36	28
JUL. 13	16	34	34	35	13	19	12	25	26	32	36	28
JUL. 14	16	35	36	36	13	19	13	25	26	32	36	28
JUL. 15	16	37	37	38	13	19	13	25	26	32	36	28
JUL. 16	16	39	39	40	13	20	13	25	26	32	36	28
JUL. 17	16	40	41	41	14	20	13	25	26	32	36	28
JUL. 18	16	42	43	43	14	20	13	26	26	32	36	28
JUL. 19	17	44	44	45	14	20	13	26	26	32	36	28
JUL. 20	17	45	46	47	14	20	13	26	26	32	36	28
JUL. 21	17	47	48	48	14	20	13	26	26	32	36	28
JUL. 22	17	1	2	2	14	21	13	26	26	32	36	28
JUL. 23	17	3	4	4	15	21	13	26	26	32	36	28
JUL. 24	17	5	5	6	15	21	13	26	26	32	36	28
JUL. 25	17	7	7	8	15	21	14	26	26	32	36	28
JUL. 26	18	9	9	10	15	21	14	26	26	32	36	28
JUL. 27	18	11	11	12	16	21	14	26	26	32	36	28
JUL. 28	18	12	13	14	16	22	14	26	26	32	36	28
JUL. 29	18	14	15	16	16	22	14	26	26	32	36	28
JUL. 30	18	16	17	17	16	22	14	26	26	32	36	28
JUL. 31	18	18	19	19	17	22	14	26	26	32	36	28
AUG. 1	18	20	21	21	17	22	14	26	26	32	36	28
AUG. 2	18	22	22	23	17	22	14	26	26	32	36	28
AUG. 3	19	23	24	25	17	23	14	26	26	32	36	28
AUG. 4	19	25	26	26	18	23	14	26	26	32	36	28
AUG. 5	19	27	27	28	18	23	15	26	26	32	36	28
AUG. 6	19	28	29	30	18	23	15	26	26	32	36	28
AUG. 7	19	30	31	31	18	23	15	26	26	32	36	28
AUG. 8	19	32	32	33	19	23	15	26	26	32	36	28
AUG. 9	19	33	34	34	19	23	15	26	26	32	36	28
AUG. 10	19	35	35	36	19	24	15	26	26	32	36	28
AUG. 11	20	36	36	37	20	24	15	26	26	32	36	28
AUG. 12	20	38	39	39	20	24	15	26	26	32	36	28
AUG. 13	20	40	40	41	20	24	15	26	26	32	36	28
AUG. 14	20	41	42	43	20	24	15	26	26	32	36	28
AUG. 15	20	43	44	44	21	24	15	26	26	32	36	28
AUG. 16	20	45	46	46	21	25	16	26	26	32	36	28
AUG. 17	20	47	47	48	21	25	16	26	26	32	36	28
AUG. 18	20	1	1	2	21	25	16	26	26	32	36	28
AUG. 19	21	2	3	4	22	25	16	26	26	32	36	28
AUG. 20	21	4	5	6	22	25	16	26	26	32	36	28
AUG. 21	21	6	7	8	22	25	16	26	26	32	36	28
AUG. 22	21	8	9	9	22	26	16	26	26	32	36	28
AUG. 23	21	10	11	11	23	26	16	26	26	32	36	28
AUG. 24	21	12	13	13	23	26	16	26	26	32	36	28
AUG. 25	21	14	14	15	23	26	16	26	26	32	36	28
AUG. 26	22	16	16	17	23	26	16	26	26	32	36	28
AUG. 27	22	17	18	19	24	26	16	26	26	32	36	28
AUG. 28	22	19	20	20	24	26	17	26	26	32	36	28
AUG. 29	22	21	22	22	24	27	17	26	26	32	36	28
AUG. 30	22	23	23	24	24	27	17	26	26	32	36	28
AUG. 31	22	25	25	26	24	27	17	27	26	32	36	28

MOON 1 ◐ 12:01 A.M. TO 8:00 A.M.   **MOON 2** ◑ 8:01 A.M. TO 4:00 P.M.   **MOON 3** ● 4:01 P.M. TO 12:00 A.M.

Use only one "moon" number. Choose the column closest to your time of birth. If your place of birth is not on Eastern Standard Time, be sure to read "How to Convert to Eastern Standard Time" at the beginning of this section.

Date & Time	SUN ☉	MOON 1 ◗	MOON 2 ◑	MOON 3 ●	MERCURY	VENUS	MARS	JUPITER	SATURN	URANUS	NEPTUNE	PLUTO
SEP. 1	22	26	27	27	25	27	17	27	26	32	36	28
SEP. 2	22	28	28	29	25	27	17	27	26	32	36	28
SEP. 3	23	29	30	31	25	27	17	27	26	32	36	28
SEP. 4	23	31	32	32	25	28	17	27	26	32	36	28
SEP. 5	23	33	33	34	25	28	17	27	26	32	36	28
SEP. 6	23	34	35	35	26	28	17	27	26	33	36	28
SEP. 7	23	36	36	37	26	28	17	27	26	33	36	28
SEP. 8	23	37	38	39	26	28	17	27	26	33	36	28
SEP. 9	23	39	40	40	26	28	18	27	26	33	36	28
SEP. 10	23	41	41	42	26	29	18	27	26	33	36	28
SEP. 11	24	42	43	44	27	29	18	27	26	33	36	28
SEP. 12	24	44	45	45	27	29	18	27	26	33	36	28
SEP. 13	24	46	47	47	27	29	18	27	26	33	36	28
SEP. 14	24	48	1	1	27	29	18	27	26	33	36	28
SEP. 15	24	2	2	3	27	29	18	27	26	33	36	28
SEP. 16	24	4	4	5	27	29	18	27	26	33	36	28
SEP. 17	24	6	6	7	28	30	18	27	26	33	36	28
SEP. 18	24	8	8	9	28	30	18	27	26	33	36	28
SEP. 19	25	10	10	11	28	30	18	27	26	33	36	28
SEP. 20	25	12	12	13	28	30	18	27	26	33	36	28
SEP. 21	25	13	14	15	28	30	19	27	26	33	36	28
SEP. 22	25	15	16	16	28	30	19	27	26	33	36	28
SEP. 23	25	17	18	18	28	31	19	27	26	33	36	28
SEP. 24	25	19	19	20	29	31	19	27	26	33	36	28
SEP. 25	26	21	21	22	29	31	19	27	26	33	36	28
SEP. 26	26	22	23	23	29	31	19	27	27	33	36	28
SEP. 27	26	24	25	25	29	31	19	27	27	33	36	28
SEP. 28	26	26	26	27	29	31	19	27	27	33	36	28
SEP. 29	26	27	28	28	29	31	19	27	27	33	36	28
SEP. 30	26	29	30	30	29	32	19	27	27	33	36	28
OCT. 1	26	31	31	32	29	32	19	27	27	33	36	28
OCT. 2	26	32	33	33	29	32	19	27	27	33	36	28
OCT. 3	27	34	34	35	29	32	20	27	27	33	36	28
OCT. 4	27	35	36	36	29	32	20	27	27	33	36	28
OCT. 5	27	37	37	38	29	32	20	27	27	33	36	28
OCT. 6	27	39	39	40	29	33	20	27	27	33	36	28
OCT. 7	27	40	41	41	29	33	20	27	27	33	36	28
OCT. 8	27	42	42	43	29	33	20	28	27	33	36	28
OCT. 9	27	44	44	45	29	33	20	28	27	33	36	28
OCT. 10	27	45	46	47	29	33	20	28	27	33	36	28
OCT. 11	28	47	48	48	29	33	20	28	27	33	36	28
OCT. 12	28	1	2	2	29	33	20	28	27	33	36	28
OCT. 13	28	3	4	4	29	34	20	28	27	33	36	28
OCT. 14	28	5	6	6	29	34	20	28	27	33	36	28
OCT. 15	28	7	8	8	29	34	21	28	27	33	36	28
OCT. 16	28	9	10	10	29	34	21	28	27	33	36	28
OCT. 17	28	11	12	12	28	34	21	28	27	33	36	28
OCT. 18	28	13	14	14	28	34	21	28	27	33	36	28
OCT. 19	29	15	15	16	28	34	21	28	27	33	36	28
OCT. 20	29	17	17	18	28	35	21	28	27	33	36	28
OCT. 21	29	18	19	20	28	35	21	28	27	33	36	28
OCT. 22	29	20	21	21	28	35	21	28	27	33	36	28
OCT. 23	29	22	22	23	28	35	21	28	27	33	36	28
OCT. 24	29	24	24	25	28	35	21	28	27	33	36	28
OCT. 25	29	25	26	27	27	35	21	28	27	33	36	28
OCT. 26	30	27	27	28	27	36	21	28	27	33	36	28
OCT. 27	30	29	29	30	27	36	21	28	27	33	36	28
OCT. 28	30	30	31	31	27	36	22	28	27	33	36	28
OCT. 29	30	32	32	33	27	36	22	28	27	33	36	28
OCT. 30	30	33	34	34	27	36	22	28	27	33	36	28
OCT. 31	30	35	35	36	28	36	22	28	27	33	36	28

MOON 1 ◗ 12:01 A.M. TO 8:00 A.M.   **MOON 2** ◑ 8:01 A.M. TO 4:00 P.M.   **MOON 3** ● 4:01 P.M. TO 12:00 A.M.
Use only one "moon" number. Choose the column closest to your time of birth. If your place of birth is not on Eastern Standard Time, be sure to read "How to Convert to Eastern Standard Time" at the beginning of this section.

1981

November | December

Date & Time	SUN	MOON 1	MOON 2	MOON 3	MERCURY	VENUS	MARS	JUPITER	SATURN	URANUS	NEPTUNE	PLUTO
NOV. 1	30	36	37	38	28	36	22	28	27	33	36	28
NOV. 2	30	38	39	39	28	37	22	28	27	33	36	28
NOV. 3	31	40	40	41	28	37	22	28	27	33	36	28
NOV. 4	31	41	42	42	28	37	22	28	27	33	36	28
NOV. 5	31	43	43	44	28	37	22	28	27	33	36	28
NOV. 6	31	45	45	46	28	37	22	28	27	33	36	28
NOV. 7	31	46	47	48	29	37	22	28	27	33	36	28
NOV. 8	31	48	1	1	29	37	22	28	27	33	36	28
NOV. 9	31	2	3	3	29	37	22	28	27	33	36	28
NOV. 10	31	4	5	5	29	38	22	29	27	33	36	28
NOV. 11	31	6	7	7	29	38	23	29	27	33	36	28
NOV. 12	32	8	9	9	29	38	23	29	27	33	36	28
NOV. 13	32	10	11	12	30	38	23	29	27	33	36	28
NOV. 14	32	12	13	13	30	38	23	29	27	33	36	28
NOV. 15	32	14	15	15	30	38	23	29	27	33	36	28
NOV. 16	32	16	17	17	30	38	23	29	27	33	36	28
NOV. 17	32	18	19	19	31	39	23	29	27	33	36	28
NOV. 18	32	20	20	21	31	39	23	29	27	33	36	28
NOV. 19	33	21	22	23	31	39	23	29	27	33	36	28
NOV. 20	33	23	24	24	31	39	23	29	27	33	36	28
NOV. 21	33	25	25	26	31	39	23	29	27	33	36	28
NOV. 22	33	27	27	28	32	39	23	29	27	33	36	28
NOV. 23	33	28	29	32	32	39	23	29	27	33	36	28
NOV. 24	33	30	30	31	32	39	24	29	27	33	36	28
NOV. 25	34	31	32	32	32	40	24	29	27	33	36	28
NOV. 26	34	33	33	34	32	40	24	29	27	33	36	28
NOV. 27	34	34	35	36	33	40	24	29	27	33	36	28
NOV. 28	34	36	37	37	33	40	24	29	27	33	36	28
NOV. 29	34	38	38	39	33	40	24	29	27	33	36	28
NOV. 30	34	39	40	40	33	40	24	29	28	33	36	28
DEC. 1	34	41	41	42	33	40	24	29	28	33	36	28
DEC. 2	34	42	43	44	34	40	24	29	28	33	36	28
DEC. 3	35	44	45	45	34	40	24	29	28	33	36	28
DEC. 4	35	46	46	47	34	41	24	29	28	33	36	28
DEC. 5	35	48	48	1	34	41	24	29	28	33	36	28
DEC. 6	35	1	2	3	35	41	24	29	28	33	36	28
DEC. 7	35	3	4	5	35	41	24	29	28	33	36	28
DEC. 8	35	5	6	6	35	41	24	29	28	33	36	28
DEC. 9	35	7	8	9	35	41	25	29	28	33	36	28
DEC. 10	35	9	10	11	35	41	25	29	28	33	36	28
DEC. 11	36	11	12	13	36	41	25	29	28	33	36	28
DEC. 12	36	13	14	15	36	41	25	29	28	33	36	28
DEC. 13	36	15	16	17	36	41	25	29	28	33	36	28
DEC. 14	36	17	18	18	36	41	25	29	28	33	36	28
DEC. 15	36	19	20	20	36	41	25	29	28	33	36	28
DEC. 16	36	21	22	22	37	42	25	29	28	33	36	28
DEC. 17	36	23	23	24	37	42	25	29	28	33	36	28
DEC. 18	36	24	25	26	37	42	25	29	28	33	36	28
DEC. 19	37	26	27	27	37	42	25	30	28	33	36	28
DEC. 20	37	28	28	29	37	42	25	30	28	33	36	28
DEC. 21	37	29	30	30	38	42	25	30	28	33	36	28
DEC. 22	37	31	31	32	38	42	25	30	28	33	36	28
DEC. 23	37	32	33	34	38	42	25	30	28	33	36	29
DEC. 24	37	34	35	35	38	42	25	30	28	33	36	29
DEC. 25	37	36	36	37	39	42	26	30	28	33	36	29
DEC. 26	38	37	38	38	39	42	26	30	28	33	36	29
DEC. 27	38	39	39	40	39	42	26	30	28	33	36	29
DEC. 28	38	40	41	42	39	42	26	30	28	33	36	29
DEC. 29	38	42	43	43	39	42	26	30	28	33	36	29
DEC. 30	38	44	44	45	40	42	26	30	28	33	36	29
DEC. 31	38	45	46	47	40	42	26	30	28	33	36	29

MOON 1 ☽ 12:01 A.M. TO 8:00 A.M.   **MOON 2** ◑ 8:01 A.M. TO 4:00 P.M.   **MOON 3** ● 4:01 P.M. TO 12:00 A.M.
Use only one "moon" number. Choose the column closest to your time of birth. If your place of birth is not on Eastern Standard Time, be sure to read "How to Convert to Eastern Standard Time" at the beginning of this section.

January

Date & Time	SUN	MOON 1	MOON 2	MOON 3	MERCURY	VENUS	MARS	JUPITER	SATURN	URANUS	NEPTUNE	PLUTO
JAN. 1	38	47	48	48	40	42	26	30	28	33	36	29
JAN. 2	38	1	1	2	40	42	26	30	28	33	36	29
JAN. 3	39	3	3	4	40	42	26	30	28	33	36	29
JAN. 4	39	4	5	6	41	42	26	30	28	33	36	29
JAN. 5	39	6	7	8	41	42	26	30	28	33	36	29
JAN. 6	39	8	9	10	41	42	26	30	28	33	36	29
JAN. 7	39	10	11	12	41	42	26	30	28	33	36	29
JAN. 8	39	12	13	14	41	42	26	30	28	33	36	29
JAN. 9	39	14	15	16	42	42	26	30	28	33	36	29
JAN. 10	40	16	17	18	42	42	26	30	28	33	36	29
JAN. 11	40	18	19	20	42	42	26	30	28	33	36	29
JAN. 12	40	20	21	21	42	42	26	30	28	33	36	29
JAN. 13	40	22	23	23	42	42	27	30	28	33	36	29
JAN. 14	40	24	24	25	43	42	27	30	28	33	36	29
JAN. 15	40	26	26	27	43	42	27	30	28	33	36	29
JAN. 16	40	27	28	28	43	42	27	30	28	33	36	29
JAN. 17	41	29	29	30	43	41	27	30	28	33	36	29
JAN. 18	41	30	31	32	43	41	27	30	28	33	36	29
JAN. 19	41	32	33	33	43	41	27	30	28	33	36	29
JAN. 20	41	34	34	35	43	41	27	30	28	33	36	29
JAN. 21	41	35	36	36	43	41	27	30	28	33	36	29
JAN. 22	41	37	37	38	43	41	27	30	28	33	36	29
JAN. 23	42	38	39	39	43	41	27	30	28	33	36	29
JAN. 24	42	40	41	41	43	41	27	30	28	33	36	29
JAN. 25	42	42	42	43	43	41	27	30	28	33	36	29
JAN. 26	42	43	44	44	43	41	27	30	28	33	36	29
JAN. 27	42	45	46	46	43	41	27	30	28	33	36	29
JAN. 28	42	47	47	48	43	41	27	30	28	33	36	29
JAN. 29	42	48	1	2	43	41	27	30	28	33	36	29
JAN. 30	42	2	3	3	43	40	27	30	28	33	36	29
JAN. 31	43	4	5	5	43	40	27	30	28	33	36	29

February

Date & Time	SUN	MOON 1	MOON 2	MOON 3	MERCURY	VENUS	MARS	JUPITER	SATURN	URANUS	NEPTUNE	PLUTO
FEB. 1	43	6	7	7	43	40	27	30	28	34	36	29
FEB. 2	43	8	8	9	42	40	27	30	28	34	36	29
FEB. 3	43	10	10	11	42	40	27	30	28	34	36	29
FEB. 4	43	12	12	13	42	40	27	30	28	34	36	29
FEB. 5	43	14	14	15	42	40	27	30	28	34	36	29
FEB. 6	43	15	16	17	42	40	27	30	28	34	36	29
FEB. 7	43	17	18	19	42	40	27	30	28	34	36	29
FEB. 8	44	19	20	21	42	40	27	30	28	34	36	29
FEB. 9	44	21	22	22	41	40	27	30	28	34	36	29
FEB. 10	44	23	24	24	41	40	27	30	28	34	36	29
FEB. 11	44	25	25	26	41	40	27	30	28	34	36	29
FEB. 12	44	27	27	28	41	40	27	30	28	34	36	29
FEB. 13	44	28	29	29	41	40	27	30	28	34	37	29
FEB. 14	44	30	30	31	41	40	27	30	28	34	37	29
FEB. 15	44	32	32	33	41	40	27	30	28	34	37	29
FEB. 16	45	33	34	34	41	40	28	30	28	34	37	29
FEB. 17	45	35	35	36	41	40	28	30	28	34	37	29
FEB. 18	45	36	37	37	42	40	28	30	28	34	37	29
FEB. 19	45	38	38	39	42	40	28	30	28	34	37	29
FEB. 20	45	39	40	41	42	40	28	30	28	34	37	29
FEB. 21	45	41	42	42	42	40	28	30	28	34	37	29
FEB. 22	45	43	43	44	42	40	28	30	28	34	37	29
FEB. 23	46	44	45	46	42	40	28	30	28	34	37	29
FEB. 24	46	46	47	47	42	41	28	30	28	34	37	29
FEB. 25	46	48	1	1	42	41	28	30	28	34	37	29
FEB. 26	46	2	2	3	42	41	27	30	28	34	37	29
FEB. 27	46	4	4	5	42	41	27	30	28	34	37	29
FEB. 28	46	5	6	7	43	41	27	30	28	34	37	29

MOON 1 ☽ 12:01 A.M. TO 8:00 A.M.   **MOON 2** ☽ 8:01 A.M. TO 4:00 P.M.   **MOON 3** ● 4:01 P.M. TO 12:00 A.M.
Use only one "moon" number. Choose the column closest to your time of birth. If your place of birth is not on Eastern Standard Time, be sure to read "How to Convert to Eastern Standard Time" at the beginning of this section.

1982

March

April

Date & Time	SUN	MOON 1	MOON 2	MOON 3	MERCURY	VENUS	MARS	JUPITER	SATURN	URANUS	NEPTUNE	PLUTO
MAR. 1	46	7	8	9	43	41	27	30	28	34	37	29
MAR. 2	46	9	10	10	43	41	27	30	28	34	37	29
MAR. 3	47	11	12	12	43	41	27	30	28	34	37	29
MAR. 4	47	13	14	14	43	41	27	30	28	34	37	29
MAR. 5	47	15	15	16	43	41	27	30	28	34	37	29
MAR. 6	47	17	17	18	44	41	27	30	28	34	37	29
MAR. 7	47	19	19	20	44	41	27	30	28	34	37	29
MAR. 8	47	20	21	22	44	41	27	30	28	34	37	29
MAR. 9	47	22	23	24	44	42	27	30	28	34	37	29
MAR. 10	47	24	25	25	44	42	27	30	28	34	37	28
MAR. 11	48	26	26	27	44	42	27	30	28	34	37	28
MAR. 12	48	28	28	29	45	42	27	30	28	34	37	28
MAR. 13	48	29	30	30	45	42	27	30	28	34	37	28
MAR. 14	48	31	31	32	45	42	27	30	28	34	37	28
MAR. 15	48	33	33	34	45	42	27	30	28	34	37	28
MAR. 16	48	34	35	35	45	42	27	30	28	34	37	28
MAR. 17	48	36	36	37	46	42	27	30	28	34	37	28
MAR. 18	48	37	38	38	46	43	27	30	28	34	37	28
MAR. 19	1	39	39	40	46	43	27	30	28	34	37	28
MAR. 20	1	41	41	42	46	43	27	30	28	34	37	28
MAR. 21	1	42	43	43	46	43	27	30	28	34	37	28
MAR. 22	1	44	44	45	47	43	27	30	28	34	37	28
MAR. 23	1	46	46	47	47	43	27	30	28	34	37	28
MAR. 24	1	47	48	1	47	43	27	30	28	34	37	28
MAR. 25	2	1	2	2	47	43	27	30	28	34	37	28
MAR. 26	2	3	4	4	48	43	27	30	28	34	37	28
MAR. 27	2	5	6	6	48	44	27	30	28	34	37	28
MAR. 28	2	7	7	8	48	44	27	30	28	34	37	28
MAR. 29	2	9	9	10	48	44	26	30	28	34	37	28
MAR. 30	2	11	11	12	1	44	26	30	28	34	37	28
MAR. 31	2	13	13	14	1	44	26	30	28	34	37	28

Date & Time	SUN	MOON 1	MOON 2	MOON 3	MERCURY	VENUS	MARS	JUPITER	SATURN	URANUS	NEPTUNE	PLUTO
APR. 1	2	14	15	16	1	44	26	30	28	34	37	28
APR. 2	2	16	17	18	1	44	26	30	28	34	37	28
APR. 3	3	18	19	19	2	45	26	30	28	34	37	28
APR. 4	3	20	21	21	2	45	26	30	28	34	37	28
APR. 5	3	22	22	23	2	45	26	30	28	34	37	28
APR. 6	3	24	24	25	2	45	26	30	28	34	37	28
APR. 7	3	25	26	26	3	45	26	30	28	34	37	28
APR. 8	3	27	28	28	3	45	26	30	27	34	37	28
APR. 9	3	29	29	30	3	45	26	30	27	34	37	28
APR. 10	3	30	31	31	3	45	26	30	27	34	37	28
APR. 11	4	32	33	33	4	46	26	30	27	34	37	28
APR. 12	4	34	34	35	4	46	26	30	27	34	37	28
APR. 13	4	35	36	36	4	46	26	30	27	34	37	28
APR. 14	4	37	37	38	5	46	26	30	27	34	37	28
APR. 15	4	38	39	39	5	46	26	30	27	34	37	28
APR. 16	4	40	40	41	5	46	26	30	27	34	37	28
APR. 17	4	42	42	43	5	46	26	30	27	34	37	28
APR. 18	4	43	44	44	6	47	25	30	27	33	37	28
APR. 19	5	45	45	46	6	47	25	30	27	33	37	28
APR. 20	5	47	47	48	6	47	25	30	27	33	37	28
APR. 21	5	48	1	2	6	47	25	30	27	33	37	28
APR. 22	5	2	3	4	7	47	25	30	27	33	37	28
APR. 23	5	4	5	5	7	47	25	30	27	33	37	28
APR. 24	5	6	7	7	7	47	25	30	27	33	37	28
APR. 25	6	8	9	9	8	48	25	30	27	33	37	28
APR. 26	6	10	11	11	8	48	25	30	27	33	37	28
APR. 27	6	12	13	13	8	48	25	30	27	33	37	28
APR. 28	6	14	15	15	8	48	25	30	27	33	37	28
APR. 29	6	16	16	17	9	48	25	30	27	33	37	28
APR. 30	6	18	18	19	9	48	25	30	27	33	37	28

MOON 1 ◗ 12:01 A.M. TO 8:00 A.M. **MOON 2** ◐ 8:01 A.M. TO 4:00 P.M. **MOON 3** ● 4:01 P.M. TO 12:00 A.M.
Use only one "moon" number. Choose the column closest to your time of birth. If your place of birth is not on
Eastern Standard Time, be sure to read "How to Convert to Eastern Standard Time" at the beginning of this section.

1982

May

June

Date & Time	SUN	MOON 1	MOON 2	MOON 3	MERCURY	VENUS	MARS	JUPITER	SATURN	URANUS	NEPTUNE	PLUTO
MAY 1	6	20	20	21	9	48	25	30	27	33	37	28
MAY 2	6	21	22	23	9	1	25	30	27	33	37	28
MAY 3	7	23	24	24	9	1	25	30	27	33	37	28
MAY 4	7	25	25	26	9	1	25	30	27	33	37	28
MAY 5	7	27	27	28	10	1	25	30	27	33	37	28
MAY 6	7	28	29	29	10	1	25	30	27	33	37	28
MAY 7	7	30	30	31	10	1	25	30	27	33	37	28
MAY 8	7	32	32	33	10	2	25	29	27	33	37	28
MAY 9	7	33	34	34	10	2	25	29	27	33	37	28
MAY 10	7	35	35	36	10	2	25	29	27	33	37	28
MAY 11	8	36	37	37	10	2	25	29	27	33	37	28
MAY 12	8	38	38	39	11	2	25	29	27	33	37	28
MAY 13	8	39	40	41	11	2	25	29	27	33	37	28
MAY 14	8	41	42	42	11	2	25	29	27	33	37	28
MAY 15	8	43	43	44	11	3	25	29	27	33	37	28
MAY 16	8	44	45	45	11	3	25	29	27	33	36	28
MAY 17	8	46	47	47	11	3	25	29	27	33	36	28
MAY 18	8	48	48	1	11	3	25	29	27	33	36	28
MAY 19	9	1	2	3	11	3	25	29	27	33	36	28
MAY 20	9	3	4	5	11	3	25	29	27	33	36	28
MAY 21	9	5	6	7	11	3	25	29	27	33	36	28
MAY 22	9	7	8	9	11	4	25	29	27	33	36	28
MAY 23	9	9	10	11	11	4	25	29	27	33	36	28
MAY 24	9	11	12	13	11	4	25	29	27	33	36	28
MAY 25	10	13	14	15	11	4	25	29	27	33	36	28
MAY 26	10	15	16	17	11	4	25	29	27	33	36	28
MAY 27	10	17	18	18	11	4	25	29	27	33	36	28
MAY 28	10	19	20	20	11	5	25	29	27	33	36	28
MAY 29	10	21	22	22	11	5	25	29	27	33	36	28
MAY 30	10	23	23	24	11	5	25	29	27	33	36	28
MAY 31	10	24	25	26	11	5	25	29	27	33	36	28
JUN. 1	10	26	27	27	10	5	25	29	27	33	36	28
JUN. 2	10	28	28	29	10	5	25	29	27	33	36	28
JUN. 3	11	30	30	31	10	5	25	29	27	33	36	28
JUN. 4	11	31	32	32	10	6	25	29	27	33	36	28
JUN. 5	11	33	33	34	10	6	25	29	27	33	36	28
JUN. 6	11	34	35	35	10	6	26	29	27	33	36	28
JUN. 7	11	36	36	37	10	6	26	29	27	33	36	28
JUN. 8	11	37	38	39	10	6	26	29	27	33	36	28
JUN. 9	11	39	40	40	10	6	26	29	27	33	36	28
JUN. 10	11	41	41	42	10	7	26	29	27	33	36	28
JUN. 11	12	42	43	43	10	7	26	29	27	33	36	28
JUN. 12	12	44	44	45	10	7	26	29	27	33	36	28
JUN. 13	12	45	46	47	10	7	26	29	27	33	36	28
JUN. 14	12	47	48	48	10	7	26	29	27	33	36	28
JUN. 15	12	1	1	2	10	7	26	29	27	33	36	28
JUN. 16	12	3	3	4	10	8	26	29	27	33	36	28
JUN. 17	12	4	5	6	10	8	26	29	27	33	36	28
JUN. 18	12	6	7	8	10	8	26	29	27	33	36	28
JUN. 19	13	8	9	10	10	8	26	29	27	33	36	28
JUN. 20	13	10	11	12	10	8	26	29	27	33	36	28
JUN. 21	13	12	13	14	10	8	26	29	27	33	36	28
JUN. 22	13	14	15	16	10	8	26	29	27	33	36	28
JUN. 23	13	16	17	18	9	9	26	29	27	33	36	28
JUN. 24	13	18	19	20	9	9	26	29	27	33	36	28
JUN. 25	14	20	21	22	10	9	26	29	27	33	36	28
JUN. 26	14	22	23	23	11	9	26	29	27	33	36	28
JUN. 27	14	24	25	25	11	9	26	29	27	33	36	28
JUN. 28	14	26	26	27	11	9	27	29	27	33	36	28
JUN. 29	14	27	28	29	11	10	27	29	27	33	36	28
JUN. 30	14	29	30	30	11	10	27	29	27	33	36	28

MOON 1 ◗ 12:01 A.M. TO 8:00 A.M.   **MOON 2** ◖ 8:01 A.M. TO 4:00 P.M.   **MOON 3** ● 4:01 P.M. TO 12:00 A.M.
Use only one "moon" number. Choose the column closest to your time of birth. If your place of birth is not on Eastern Standard Time, be sure to read "How to Convert to Eastern Standard Time" at the beginning of this section.

1982

July

August

Date & Time	SUN	MOON 1	MOON 2	MOON 3	MERCURY	VENUS	MARS	JUPITER	SATURN	URANUS	NEPTUNE	PLUTO
JUL. 1	14	31	31	32	11	10	27	29	27	33	36	28
JUL. 2	14	32	33	33	11	10	27	29	27	33	36	28
JUL. 3	15	34	34	35	12	10	27	29	27	33	36	28
JUL. 4	15	36	36	37	12	10	27	29	27	33	36	28
JUL. 5	15	37	38	38	12	10	27	29	27	33	36	28
JUL. 6	15	39	39	40	12	11	27	29	27	33	36	28
JUL. 7	15	40	41	41	12	11	27	29	27	33	36	28
JUL. 8	15	42	42	43	13	11	27	29	27	33	36	28
JUL. 9	15	43	44	45	13	11	27	29	27	33	36	28
JUL. 10	15	45	46	46	13	11	27	29	27	33	36	28
JUL. 11	16	47	47	48	13	11	27	29	27	33	36	28
JUL. 12	16	48	1	2	14	12	27	29	27	33	36	28
JUL. 13	16	2	3	3	14	12	27	29	27	33	36	28
JUL. 14	16	4	5	5	14	12	28	29	27	33	36	28
JUL. 15	16	6	6	7	14	12	28	29	27	33	36	28
JUL. 16	16	8	8	9	15	12	28	29	27	33	36	28
JUL. 17	16	10	10	11	15	12	28	29	27	33	36	28
JUL. 18	16	11	12	13	15	13	28	29	27	33	36	28
JUL. 19	17	13	14	15	16	13	28	29	27	33	36	28
JUL. 20	17	15	16	17	16	13	28	29	27	33	36	28
JUL. 21	17	18	18	19	16	13	28	29	27	33	36	28
JUL. 22	17	19	20	21	16	13	28	29	27	33	36	28
JUL. 23	17	21	22	23	17	13	28	29	27	33	36	28
JUL. 24	17	23	24	25	17	14	28	29	27	33	36	28
JUL. 25	17	25	26	26	17	14	28	29	27	33	36	28
JUL. 26	18	27	27	28	17	14	28	29	27	33	36	28
JUL. 27	18	29	29	30	18	14	28	29	27	33	36	28
JUL. 28	18	30	31	31	18	14	28	29	27	33	36	28
JUL. 29	18	32	32	33	18	14	29	29	27	33	36	28
JUL. 30	18	34	34	35	19	14	29	29	27	33	36	28
JUL. 31	18	35	36	36	19	15	29	29	27	33	36	28

Date & Time	SUN	MOON 1	MOON 2	MOON 3	MERCURY	VENUS	MARS	JUPITER	SATURN	URANUS	NEPTUNE	PLUTO
AUG. 1	18	37	37	38	19	15	29	29	27	33	36	28
AUG. 2	18	38	39	39	19	15	29	29	27	33	36	28
AUG. 3	19	40	40	41	20	15	29	29	27	33	36	28
AUG. 4	19	41	42	42	20	15	29	29	27	33	36	28
AUG. 5	19	43	44	44	20	15	29	29	27	33	36	28
AUG. 6	19	45	45	46	20	16	29	29	27	33	36	28
AUG. 7	19	46	47	47	21	16	29	29	27	33	36	28
AUG. 8	19	48	1	1	21	16	29	29	27	33	36	28
AUG. 9	19	2	2	3	21	16	29	29	27	33	36	28
AUG. 10	19	3	4	5	21	16	29	29	27	33	36	28
AUG. 11	20	5	6	6	22	16	30	29	27	33	36	28
AUG. 12	20	7	8	8	22	17	30	29	27	33	36	28
AUG. 13	20	9	10	10	22	17	30	29	27	33	36	28
AUG. 14	20	11	11	12	22	17	30	29	27	33	36	28
AUG. 15	20	13	13	14	22	17	30	29	27	33	36	28
AUG. 16	20	15	15	16	23	17	30	29	27	33	36	28
AUG. 17	20	17	17	18	23	17	30	29	27	33	36	28
AUG. 18	20	19	19	20	23	18	30	30	27	33	36	28
AUG. 19	21	21	21	22	23	18	30	30	27	33	36	28
AUG. 20	21	23	23	24	23	18	30	30	27	33	36	28
AUG. 21	21	24	25	26	24	18	30	30	27	33	36	28
AUG. 22	21	26	27	27	24	18	30	30	27	33	36	28
AUG. 23	21	28	29	29	24	18	31	30	27	33	36	28
AUG. 24	21	30	30	31	24	19	31	30	27	33	36	28
AUG. 25	21	31	32	32	24	19	31	30	28	33	36	28
AUG. 26	22	33	34	34	25	19	31	30	28	33	36	28
AUG. 27	22	35	35	36	25	19	31	30	28	33	36	28
AUG. 28	22	36	37	37	25	19	31	30	28	33	36	28
AUG. 29	22	38	38	39	25	19	31	30	28	33	36	28
AUG. 30	22	39	40	40	25	20	31	30	28	33	36	28
AUG. 31	22	41	41	42	25	20	31	30	28	33	36	28

MOON 1 ☽ 12:01 A.M. TO 8:00 A.M.   **MOON 2** ☽ 8:01 A.M. TO 4:00 P.M.   **MOON 3** ● 4:01 P.M. TO 12:00 A.M.

Use only one "moon" number. Choose the column closest to your time of birth. If your place of birth is not on Eastern Standard Time, be sure to read "How to Convert to Eastern Standard Time" at the beginning of this section.

Date & Time	SUN	MOON 1	MOON 2	MOON 3	MERCURY	VENUS	MARS	JUPITER	SATURN	URANUS	NEPTUNE	PLUTO
SEP. 1	22	43	43	44	26	20	31	30	28	33	36	28
SEP. 2	22	44	45	45	26	20	31	30	28	33	36	28
SEP. 3	23	46	46	47	26	20	31	30	28	33	36	28
SEP. 4	23	48	48	1	26	20	32	30	28	33	36	28
SEP. 5	23	1	2	2	26	21	32	30	28	33	36	28
SEP. 6	23	3	4	4	26	21	32	30	28	33	36	28
SEP. 7	23	5	5	6	26	21	32	30	28	33	36	28
SEP. 8	23	7	7	8	27	21	32	30	28	33	36	28
SEP. 9	23	9	9	10	27	21	32	30	28	33	36	28
SEP. 10	23	10	11	12	27	21	32	30	28	33	36	28
SEP. 11	24	12	13	13	27	22	32	30	28	33	36	28
SEP. 12	24	14	15	15	27	22	32	30	28	33	36	28
SEP. 13	24	16	17	17	27	22	32	30	28	33	36	28
SEP. 14	24	18	19	19	27	22	32	30	28	33	36	28
SEP. 15	24	20	20	21	27	22	33	30	28	33	36	28
SEP. 16	24	22	22	23	27	22	33	30	28	33	36	28
SEP. 17	24	24	24	25	27	23	33	30	28	33	36	28
SEP. 18	24	25	26	27	27	23	33	30	28	33	36	28
SEP. 19	25	27	28	28	27	23	33	30	28	33	36	28
SEP. 20	25	29	30	30	27	23	33	30	28	33	36	28
SEP. 21	25	31	31	32	27	23	33	30	28	33	36	28
SEP. 22	25	32	33	34	27	23	33	30	28	33	36	28
SEP. 23	25	34	35	35	27	23	33	30	28	33	36	28
SEP. 24	25	36	36	37	27	24	33	30	28	33	36	28
SEP. 25	26	37	38	38	27	24	33	30	28	33	36	28
SEP. 26	26	39	39	40	27	24	34	30	28	33	36	28
SEP. 27	26	40	41	41	27	24	34	30	28	33	36	28
SEP. 28	26	42	43	43	27	24	34	30	28	33	36	28
SEP. 29	26	44	44	45	27	24	34	30	28	33	36	28
SEP. 30	26	45	46	46	26	25	34	30	28	33	36	28

Date & Time	SUN	MOON 1	MOON 2	MOON 3	MERCURY	VENUS	MARS	JUPITER	SATURN	URANUS	NEPTUNE	PLUTO
OCT. 1	26	47	48	48	26	25	34	31	28	33	36	28
OCT. 2	26	1	1	2	26	25	34	31	28	33	36	28
OCT. 3	27	3	3	4	26	25	34	31	28	33	36	28
OCT. 4	27	4	5	6	26	25	34	31	28	33	36	28
OCT. 5	27	6	7	7	26	25	34	31	28	33	36	28
OCT. 6	27	8	9	9	26	26	34	31	28	33	36	28
OCT. 7	27	10	11	11	25	26	35	31	28	33	36	28
OCT. 8	27	12	12	13	25	26	35	31	28	33	36	28
OCT. 9	27	14	14	15	25	26	35	31	28	33	36	28
OCT. 10	27	16	16	17	25	26	35	31	28	33	36	28
OCT. 11	28	17	18	19	25	26	35	31	28	33	36	28
OCT. 12	28	19	20	21	25	27	35	31	28	33	36	29
OCT. 13	28	21	22	22	25	27	35	31	28	33	36	29
OCT. 14	28	23	24	24	25	27	35	31	28	33	36	29
OCT. 15	28	25	25	26	25	27	35	31	28	33	36	29
OCT. 16	28	27	27	28	25	27	35	31	28	33	36	29
OCT. 17	28	28	29	30	26	27	36	31	28	33	36	29
OCT. 18	28	30	31	31	26	28	36	31	28	33	36	29
OCT. 19	29	32	32	33	26	28	36	31	28	33	36	29
OCT. 20	29	34	34	35	26	28	36	31	28	33	36	29
OCT. 21	29	35	36	36	26	28	36	31	28	33	36	29
OCT. 22	29	37	37	38	26	28	36	31	28	33	36	29
OCT. 23	29	38	39	39	27	28	36	31	28	33	36	29
OCT. 24	29	40	40	41	27	29	36	31	28	33	36	29
OCT. 25	29	41	42	43	27	29	36	31	28	33	36	29
OCT. 26	30	43	44	44	27	29	36	31	28	33	36	29
OCT. 27	30	45	45	46	27	29	36	31	28	33	36	29
OCT. 28	30	46	47	47	27	29	37	31	28	33	36	29
OCT. 29	30	48	1	1	28	29	37	31	28	33	36	29
OCT. 30	30	2	2	3	28	30	37	31	29	33	36	29
OCT. 31	30	4	4	5	28	30	37	31	29	33	36	29

MOON 1 ☽ 12:01 A.M. TO 8:00 A.M.   **MOON 2** ☽ 8:01 A.M. TO 4:00 P.M.   **MOON 3** ● 4:01 P.M. TO 12:00 A.M.
Use only one "moon" number. Choose the column closest to your time of birth. If your place of birth is not on Eastern Standard Time, be sure to read "How to Convert to Eastern Standard Time" at the beginning of this section.

1982

November — December

Date & Time	SUN	MOON 1	MOON 2	MOON 3	MERCURY	VENUS	MARS	JUPITER	SATURN	URANUS	NEPTUNE	PLUTO
NOV. 1	30	6	6	7	29	30	37	31	29	33	36	29
NOV. 2	30	7	8	9	29	30	37	31	29	33	36	29
NOV. 3	31	9	10	11	29	30	37	31	29	33	36	29
NOV. 4	31	11	12	13	29	30	37	31	29	33	36	29
NOV. 5	31	13	14	14	29	31	37	32	29	33	36	29
NOV. 6	31	15	16	16	30	31	37	32	29	33	36	29
NOV. 7	31	17	18	18	30	31	38	32	29	33	36	29
NOV. 8	31	19	20	20	30	31	38	32	29	33	36	29
NOV. 9	31	21	21	22	30	31	38	32	29	33	36	29
NOV. 10	31	23	23	24	31	32	38	32	29	33	36	29
NOV. 11	31	24	25	26	31	32	38	32	29	33	36	29
NOV. 12	32	26	27	27	31	32	38	32	29	33	36	29
NOV. 13	32	28	28	29	31	32	38	32	29	34	36	29
NOV. 14	32	30	30	31	31	32	38	32	29	34	36	29
NOV. 15	32	31	32	32	32	32	38	32	29	34	36	29
NOV. 16	32	33	34	34	32	33	38	32	29	34	36	29
NOV. 17	32	35	35	36	32	33	39	32	29	34	36	29
NOV. 18	32	36	37	37	32	33	39	32	29	34	36	29
NOV. 19	33	38	38	39	32	33	39	32	29	34	36	29
NOV. 20	33	39	40	40	33	33	39	32	29	34	36	29
NOV. 21	33	41	41	42	33	33	39	32	29	34	36	29
NOV. 22	33	43	43	44	33	34	39	32	29	34	36	29
NOV. 23	33	44	45	45	33	34	39	32	29	34	36	29
NOV. 24	33	46	46	47	34	34	39	32	29	34	36	29
NOV. 25	34	47	48	1	34	34	39	32	29	34	36	29
NOV. 26	34	1	2	2	34	34	40	32	29	34	36	29
NOV. 27	34	3	3	4	34	34	40	32	29	34	36	29
NOV. 28	34	5	5	6	34	35	40	32	29	34	36	29
NOV. 29	34	7	7	8	35	35	40	32	29	34	36	29
NOV. 30	34	9	9	10	35	35	40	32	29	34	36	29

Date & Time	SUN	MOON 1	MOON 2	MOON 3	MERCURY	VENUS	MARS	JUPITER	SATURN	URANUS	NEPTUNE	PLUTO
DEC. 1	34	10	11	12	35	35	40	32	29	34	36	29
DEC. 2	34	12	13	14	35	35	40	32	29	34	36	29
DEC. 3	35	14	15	16	35	35	40	32	29	34	36	29
DEC. 4	35	16	17	18	36	36	40	32	29	34	36	29
DEC. 5	35	18	19	20	36	36	40	32	29	34	36	29
DEC. 6	35	20	21	22	36	36	41	32	29	34	36	29
DEC. 7	35	22	23	23	36	36	41	32	29	34	36	29
DEC. 8	35	24	25	25	36	36	41	32	29	34	36	29
DEC. 9	35	26	26	27	37	36	41	32	29	34	36	29
DEC. 10	35	28	28	29	37	37	41	33	29	34	36	29
DEC. 11	36	29	30	30	37	37	41	33	29	34	36	29
DEC. 12	36	31	31	32	37	37	41	33	29	34	37	29
DEC. 13	36	33	33	34	37	37	41	33	29	34	37	29
DEC. 14	36	34	35	35	38	37	41	33	29	34	37	29
DEC. 15	36	36	36	37	38	37	41	33	29	34	37	29
DEC. 16	36	37	38	38	38	38	42	33	29	34	37	29
DEC. 17	36	39	39	40	38	38	42	33	29	34	37	29
DEC. 18	36	40	41	42	38	38	42	33	29	34	37	29
DEC. 19	37	42	43	43	39	38	42	33	29	34	37	29
DEC. 20	37	44	44	45	39	38	42	33	29	34	37	29
DEC. 21	37	45	46	46	39	38	42	33	29	34	37	29
DEC. 22	37	47	47	48	39	39	42	33	29	34	37	29
DEC. 23	37	1	1	2	39	39	42	33	29	34	37	29
DEC. 24	37	2	3	3	40	39	42	33	29	34	37	29
DEC. 25	37	4	5	5	40	39	43	33	29	34	37	29
DEC. 26	38	6	6	7	40	39	43	33	29	34	37	29
DEC. 27	38	8	8	9	40	39	43	33	29	34	37	29
DEC. 28	38	10	10	11	40	40	43	33	29	34	37	29
DEC. 29	38	12	12	13	41	40	43	33	29	34	37	29
DEC. 30	38	14	14	15	41	40	43	33	29	34	37	29
DEC. 31	38	16	16	17	41	40	43	33	29	34	37	29

MOON 1 ☽ 12:01 A.M. TO 8:00 A.M.　　**MOON 2** ◑ 8:01 A.M. TO 4:00 P.M.　　**MOON 3** ● 4:01 P.M. TO 12:00 A.M.

Use only one "moon" number. Choose the column closest to your time of birth. If your place of birth is not on Eastern Standard Time, be sure to read "How to Convert to Eastern Standard Time" at the beginning of this section.

1983

January

Date & Time	SUN	MOON 1	MOON 2	MOON 3	MERCURY	VENUS	MARS	JUPITER	SATURN	URANUS	NEPTUNE	PLUTO
JAN. 1	38	18	18	19	41	40	43	33	29	34	37	29
JAN. 2	38	20	20	21	41	40	43	33	29	34	37	29
JAN. 3	39	22	22	23	41	41	43	33	29	34	37	29
JAN. 4	39	23	24	25	41	41	44	33	29	34	37	29
JAN. 5	39	25	26	26	41	41	44	33	29	34	37	29
JAN. 6	39	27	28	28	41	41	44	33	29	34	37	29
JAN. 7	39	29	29	30	41	41	44	33	29	34	37	29
JAN. 8	39	30	31	32	41	41	44	33	29	34	37	29
JAN. 9	39	32	33	33	41	42	44	33	29	34	37	29
JAN. 10	40	34	34	35	41	42	44	33	29	34	37	29
JAN. 11	40	35	36	36	41	42	44	33	29	34	37	29
JAN. 12	40	37	37	38	41	42	44	33	29	34	37	29
JAN. 13	40	39	39	40	41	42	45	33	29	34	37	29
JAN. 14	40	40	41	41	41	42	45	33	29	34	37	29
JAN. 15	40	42	42	43	41	43	45	33	29	34	37	29
JAN. 16	40	43	44	44	40	43	45	34	29	34	37	29
JAN. 17	41	45	45	46	40	43	45	34	29	34	37	29
JAN. 18	41	46	47	48	40	43	45	34	29	34	37	29
JAN. 19	41	48	1	1	40	43	45	34	29	34	37	29
JAN. 20	41	2	2	3	40	43	45	34	29	34	37	29
JAN. 21	41	3	4	5	40	44	45	34	30	34	37	29
JAN. 22	41	5	6	6	39	44	45	34	30	34	37	29
JAN. 23	42	7	8	8	39	44	46	34	30	34	37	29
JAN. 24	42	9	9	10	39	44	46	34	30	34	37	29
JAN. 25	42	11	11	12	39	44	46	34	30	34	37	29
JAN. 26	42	13	13	14	39	44	46	34	30	34	37	29
JAN. 27	42	15	15	16	39	45	46	34	30	34	37	29
JAN. 28	42	17	17	18	39	45	46	34	30	34	37	29
JAN. 29	42	19	19	20	39	45	46	34	30	34	37	29
JAN. 30	42	21	21	22	39	45	46	34	30	34	37	29
JAN. 31	43	23	23	24	39	45	46	34	30	34	37	29

February

Date & Time	SUN	MOON 1	MOON 2	MOON 3	MERCURY	VENUS	MARS	JUPITER	SATURN	URANUS	NEPTUNE	PLUTO
FEB. 1	43	25	25	26	39	45	46	34	30	34	37	29
FEB. 2	43	26	27	28	39	46	47	34	30	34	37	29
FEB. 3	43	28	29	29	39	46	47	34	30	34	37	29
FEB. 4	43	30	31	31	40	46	47	34	30	34	37	29
FEB. 5	43	32	32	33	40	46	47	34	30	34	37	29
FEB. 6	43	33	34	34	40	46	47	34	30	34	37	29
FEB. 7	43	35	35	36	40	46	47	34	30	34	37	29
FEB. 8	44	37	37	38	40	47	47	34	30	34	37	29
FEB. 9	44	38	39	39	40	47	47	34	30	34	37	29
FEB. 10	44	40	40	41	40	47	47	34	30	34	37	29
FEB. 11	44	41	42	42	40	47	48	34	30	34	37	29
FEB. 12	44	43	43	44	41	47	48	34	30	34	37	29
FEB. 13	44	44	45	46	41	47	48	34	30	34	37	29
FEB. 14	44	46	47	47	41	48	48	34	30	34	37	29
FEB. 15	44	48	48	1	41	48	48	34	30	34	37	29
FEB. 16	45	1	2	2	41	48	48	34	30	34	37	29
FEB. 17	45	3	4	4	41	48	48	34	30	34	37	29
FEB. 18	45	5	5	6	42	48	48	34	30	34	37	29
FEB. 19	45	6	7	8	42	48	48	34	30	34	37	29
FEB. 20	45	8	9	9	42	1	48	34	30	34	37	29
FEB. 21	45	10	11	11	42	1	1	34	30	34	37	29
FEB. 22	45	12	13	13	42	1	1	34	30	34	37	29
FEB. 23	46	14	14	15	43	1	1	34	30	34	37	29
FEB. 24	46	16	16	17	43	1	1	34	30	34	37	29
FEB. 25	46	18	18	19	43	1	1	34	30	34	37	29
FEB. 26	46	20	20	21	43	2	1	34	30	34	37	29
FEB. 27	46	22	22	23	43	2	1	34	30	34	37	29
FEB. 28	46	24	24	25	43	2	1	34	30	34	37	29

MOON 1 ☽ 12:01 A.M. TO 8:00 A.M.　　**MOON 2** ◐ 8:01 A.M. TO 4:00 P.M.　　**MOON 3** ● 4:01 P.M. TO 12:00 A.M.

Use only one "moon" number. Choose the column closest to your time of birth. If your place of birth is not on Eastern Standard Time, be sure to read "How to Convert to Eastern Standard Time" at the beginning of this section.

1983

March

April

Date & Time	SUN	MOON 1	MOON 2	MOON 3	MERCURY	VENUS	MARS	JUPITER	SATURN	URANUS	NEPTUNE	PLUTO
MAR. 1	46	26	26	27	44	2	1	34	30	34	37	29
MAR. 2	46	28	28	29	44	2	1	34	30	34	37	29
MAR. 3	47	29	30	31	44	2	2	34	30	34	37	29
MAR. 4	47	31	32	32	44	2	2	34	30	34	37	29
MAR. 5	47	33	33	34	45	3	2	34	30	34	37	29
MAR. 6	47	34	35	36	45	3	2	34	30	34	37	29
MAR. 7	47	36	37	37	45	3	2	34	29	34	37	29
MAR. 8	47	38	38	39	45	3	2	34	29	34	37	29
MAR. 9	47	39	40	40	45	3	2	34	29	34	37	29
MAR. 10	47	41	41	42	46	3	2	34	29	34	37	29
MAR. 11	48	42	43	43	46	4	2	34	29	34	37	29
MAR. 12	48	44	45	45	46	4	3	34	29	34	37	29
MAR. 13	48	46	46	47	46	4	3	34	29	34	37	29
MAR. 14	48	47	48	48	47	4	3	34	29	34	37	29
MAR. 15	48	1	1	2	47	4	3	34	29	34	37	29
MAR. 16	48	3	3	4	47	4	3	34	29	34	37	29
MAR. 17	48	4	5	5	47	5	3	34	29	34	37	29
MAR. 18	48	6	7	7	48	5	3	34	29	34	37	29
MAR. 19	1	8	8	9	48	5	3	34	29	34	37	29
MAR. 20	1	10	10	11	48	5	3	34	29	34	37	29
MAR. 21	1	11	12	13	48	5	3	34	29	34	37	29
MAR. 22	1	13	14	15	1	5	4	34	29	34	37	29
MAR. 23	1	15	16	16	1	6	4	34	29	34	37	29
MAR. 24	1	17	18	17	1	6	4	34	29	34	37	29
MAR. 25	2	19	20	20	1	6	4	34	29	34	37	29
MAR. 26	2	21	22	22	2	6	4	34	29	34	37	29
MAR. 27	2	23	24	24	2	6	4	34	29	34	37	29
MAR. 28	2	25	25	26	2	6	4	34	29	34	37	29
MAR. 29	2	27	27	28	2	7	4	34	29	34	37	29
MAR. 30	2	29	29	30	3	7	4	34	29	34	37	29
MAR. 31	2	30	31	32	3	7	4	34	29	34	37	29

Date & Time	SUN	MOON 1	MOON 2	MOON 3	MERCURY	VENUS	MARS	JUPITER	SATURN	URANUS	NEPTUNE	PLUTO
APR. 1	2	32	33	33	3	7	5	34	29	34	37	29
APR. 2	2	34	34	35	3	7	5	34	29	34	37	29
APR. 3	3	36	36	37	4	7	5	34	29	34	37	29
APR. 4	3	37	38	38	4	8	5	34	29	34	37	29
APR. 5	3	39	39	40	4	8	5	34	29	34	37	29
APR. 6	3	40	41	41	5	8	5	34	29	34	37	29
APR. 7	3	42	42	43	5	8	5	34	29	34	37	29
APR. 8	3	43	44	45	5	8	5	34	29	34	37	29
APR. 9	3	45	46	46	5	8	5	34	29	34	37	29
APR. 10	3	47	47	48	6	8	5	34	29	34	37	29
APR. 11	4	48	1	1	6	9	6	34	29	34	37	29
APR. 12	4	2	3	3	6	9	6	34	29	34	37	29
APR. 13	4	4	4	5	6	9	6	34	29	34	37	29
APR. 14	4	6	6	7	6	9	6	34	29	34	37	29
APR. 15	4	7	8	9	7	9	6	34	29	34	37	29
APR. 16	4	9	10	10	7	9	6	34	29	34	37	29
APR. 17	4	11	12	12	7	10	6	34	29	34	37	29
APR. 18	4	13	13	14	7	10	6	34	29	34	37	29
APR. 19	5	15	15	16	7	10	6	34	29	34	37	29
APR. 20	5	17	17	18	8	10	6	34	29	34	37	29
APR. 21	5	19	19	20	8	10	7	34	29	34	37	29
APR. 22	5	20	21	22	8	10	7	34	29	34	37	29
APR. 23	5	22	23	24	8	10	7	34	29	34	37	29
APR. 24	5	24	25	25	8	11	7	34	29	34	37	29
APR. 25	6	26	27	27	8	11	7	34	29	34	37	29
APR. 26	6	28	29	29	8	11	7	34	29	34	37	29
APR. 27	6	30	30	31	8	11	7	34	29	34	37	29
APR. 28	6	31	32	33	8	11	7	34	29	34	37	29
APR. 29	6	33	34	34	8	11	7	34	29	34	37	29
APR. 30	6	35	35	36	8	12	7	34	29	34	37	29

MOON 1 ☽ 12:01 A.M. TO 8:00 A.M.   **MOON 2** ◑ 8:01 A.M. TO 4:00 P.M.   **MOON 3** ● 4:01 P.M. TO 12:00 A.M.

Use only one "moon" number. Choose the column closest to your time of birth. If your place of birth is not on Eastern Standard Time, be sure to read "How to Convert to Eastern Standard Time" at the beginning of this section.

1983

May

June

Date & Time	SUN ☉	MOON 1 ☽	MOON 2 ☽	MOON 3 ●	MERCURY	VENUS	MARS	JUPITER	SATURN	URANUS	NEPTUNE	PLUTO
MAY 1	6	37	37	38	8	12	7	34	29	34	37	29
MAY 2	6	38	39	39	8	12	8	34	29	34	37	29
MAY 3	7	40	40	41	8	12	8	34	29	34	37	29
MAY 4	7	41	42	42	8	12	8	34	29	34	37	29
MAY 5	7	43	43	44	8	12	8	34	29	34	37	29
MAY 6	7	45	45	46	8	12	8	34	29	34	37	29
MAY 7	7	46	47	47	8	13	8	34	29	34	37	29
MAY 8	7	48	48	1	8	13	8	34	29	34	37	29
MAY 9	7	1	2	3	8	13	8	34	29	34	37	29
MAY 10	7	3	4	4	8	13	8	34	29	34	37	29
MAY 11	8	5	6	6	8	13	8	34	29	34	37	29
MAY 12	8	7	7	8	8	13	9	34	29	34	37	29
MAY 13	8	9	9	10	8	14	9	34	29	34	37	29
MAY 14	8	10	11	12	8	14	9	34	29	34	37	29
MAY 15	8	12	13	14	8	14	9	34	29	34	37	29
MAY 16	8	14	15	16	8	14	9	34	29	34	37	29
MAY 17	8	16	17	17	7	14	9	34	29	34	37	29
MAY 18	8	18	19	19	7	14	9	34	29	34	37	29
MAY 19	9	20	21	21	7	14	9	34	29	34	37	29
MAY 20	9	22	22	23	7	15	9	34	29	34	37	29
MAY 21	9	24	24	25	7	15	9	34	29	34	37	29
MAY 22	9	26	26	27	7	15	9	34	29	34	37	29
MAY 23	9	27	28	29	7	15	10	34	29	34	37	29
MAY 24	9	29	30	30	7	15	10	34	29	34	37	29
MAY 25	10	31	32	32	7	15	10	34	29	34	37	29
MAY 26	10	33	33	34	7	15	10	34	29	34	37	29
MAY 27	10	34	35	35	7	16	10	34	29	34	37	29
MAY 28	10	36	37	37	7	16	10	34	29	34	37	29
MAY 29	10	38	38	39	7	16	10	34	29	34	37	29
MAY 30	10	39	40	40	7	16	10	34	29	34	37	29
MAY 31	10	41	41	42	7	16	10	34	29	34	37	29

Date & Time	SUN ☉	MOON 1 ☽	MOON 2 ☽	MOON 3 ●	MERCURY	VENUS	MARS	JUPITER	SATURN	URANUS	NEPTUNE	PLUTO
JUN. 1	10	42	43	43	7	16	10	34	29	34	37	29
JUN. 2	10	44	45	45	7	16	10	34	29	34	37	29
JUN. 3	11	46	46	47	8	17	11	34	29	34	37	29
JUN. 4	11	47	48	48	8	17	11	34	29	34	37	29
JUN. 5	11	1	1	2	8	17	11	34	29	34	37	29
JUN. 6	11	3	3	4	8	17	11	34	29	34	37	29
JUN. 7	11	4	5	5	8	17	11	34	29	34	37	29
JUN. 8	11	6	7	7	8	17	11	34	29	34	37	29
JUN. 9	11	8	8	9	8	17	11	34	29	34	37	29
JUN. 10	11	10	10	11	8	17	11	34	29	34	37	29
JUN. 11	12	12	12	13	8	18	11	34	29	34	37	29
JUN. 12	12	14	14	15	9	18	11	34	29	34	37	29
JUN. 13	12	16	16	17	9	18	12	34	29	34	37	29
JUN. 14	12	18	18	19	9	18	12	33	29	34	37	29
JUN. 15	12	19	20	21	9	18	12	33	29	34	37	29
JUN. 16	12	21	22	23	9	18	12	33	29	34	37	29
JUN. 17	12	23	24	25	9	18	12	33	29	34	37	29
JUN. 18	12	25	26	26	10	19	12	33	29	34	37	29
JUN. 19	13	27	28	28	10	19	12	33	29	34	37	29
JUN. 20	13	29	29	30	10	19	12	33	29	34	37	29
JUN. 21	13	30	31	32	10	19	12	33	29	34	37	29
JUN. 22	13	32	33	33	11	19	12	33	29	34	37	29
JUN. 23	13	34	34	35	11	19	12	33	29	34	37	29
JUN. 24	13	36	36	37	11	19	13	33	29	34	37	29
JUN. 25	14	37	38	38	11	19	13	33	29	34	37	29
JUN. 26	14	39	39	40	11	20	13	33	29	34	37	29
JUN. 27	14	40	41	41	12	20	13	33	29	34	37	29
JUN. 28	14	42	42	43	12	20	13	33	29	34	37	29
JUN. 29	14	44	44	45	12	20	13	33	29	34	37	29
JUN. 30	14	45	46	46	13	20	13	33	29	34	37	29

MOON 1 ☽ 12:01 A.M. TO 8:00 A.M.   **MOON 2** ☽ 8:01 A.M. TO 4:00 P.M.   **MOON 3** ● 4:01 P.M. TO 12:00 A.M.

Use only one "moon" number. Choose the column closest to your time of birth. If your place of birth is not on Eastern Standard Time, be sure to read "How to Convert to Eastern Standard Time" at the beginning of this section.

1983

July

August

Date & Time	SUN	MOON 1	MOON 2	MOON 3	MERCURY	VENUS	MARS	JUPITER	SATURN	URANUS	NEPTUNE	PLUTO
JUL. 1	14	47	47	48	13	20	13	33	29	34	37	29
JUL. 2	14	48	1	1	13	20	13	33	29	34	37	29
JUL. 3	15	2	2	3	13	20	13	33	29	34	37	29
JUL. 4	15	4	4	5	14	20	13	33	29	34	37	29
JUL. 5	15	5	6	6	14	20	13	33	29	34	37	29
JUL. 6	15	7	8	8	14	21	14	33	29	34	37	29
JUL. 7	15	9	10	10	15	21	14	33	29	34	37	29
JUL. 8	15	11	11	12	15	21	14	33	29	34	37	29
JUL. 9	15	13	13	14	15	21	14	33	29	34	37	29
JUL. 10	15	15	15	16	15	21	14	33	29	34	37	29
JUL. 11	16	17	17	18	16	21	14	33	29	34	37	29
JUL. 12	16	19	19	20	16	21	14	33	29	34	37	29
JUL. 13	16	21	21	22	16	21	14	33	29	34	37	29
JUL. 14	16	23	23	24	17	21	14	33	29	34	37	29
JUL. 15	16	25	25	26	17	21	14	33	29	34	37	29
JUL. 16	16	27	27	28	17	21	14	33	29	34	37	29
JUL. 17	16	28	29	30	17	22	15	33	29	34	37	29
JUL. 18	16	30	31	31	18	22	15	33	29	34	37	29
JUL. 19	17	32	32	33	18	22	15	33	29	34	37	29
JUL. 20	17	33	34	35	18	22	15	33	29	34	37	29
JUL. 21	17	35	36	36	18	22	15	33	29	34	37	29
JUL. 22	17	37	37	38	19	22	15	33	29	34	37	29
JUL. 23	17	38	39	39	19	22	15	33	29	34	37	29
JUL. 24	17	40	40	41	19	22	15	33	29	34	37	29
JUL. 25	17	42	42	43	19	22	15	33	29	34	37	29
JUL. 26	18	43	44	44	20	22	15	33	29	34	37	29
JUL. 27	18	45	45	46	20	22	15	33	29	34	37	29
JUL. 28	18	46	47	47	20	22	16	33	29	34	37	29
JUL. 29	18	48	48	1	20	22	16	33	29	34	37	29
JUL. 30	18	1	2	3	20	22	16	33	29	34	37	29
JUL. 31	18	3	4	4	21	22	16	33	29	34	37	29

Date & Time	SUN	MOON 1	MOON 2	MOON 3	MERCURY	VENUS	MARS	JUPITER	SATURN	URANUS	NEPTUNE	PLUTO
AUG. 1	18	5	5	6	21	22	16	33	29	34	37	29
AUG. 2	18	6	7	8	21	22	16	33	29	34	37	29
AUG. 3	19	8	9	9	21	22	16	33	29	34	37	29
AUG. 4	19	10	11	11	22	22	16	33	29	34	37	29
AUG. 5	19	12	13	13	22	22	16	33	29	34	37	29
AUG. 6	19	14	14	15	22	22	16	33	29	34	37	29
AUG. 7	19	16	16	17	22	22	16	33	29	34	37	29
AUG. 8	19	18	19	19	22	22	16	33	29	34	37	29
AUG. 9	19	20	21	21	22	22	17	33	29	34	37	29
AUG. 10	19	22	23	23	23	22	17	33	29	34	37	29
AUG. 11	20	24	25	25	23	22	17	33	29	34	37	29
AUG. 12	20	26	27	27	23	22	17	33	29	34	37	29
AUG. 13	20	28	28	29	23	22	17	33	29	34	37	29
AUG. 14	20	30	30	31	23	22	17	33	29	34	37	29
AUG. 15	20	31	32	33	23	22	17	33	29	34	37	29
AUG. 16	20	33	34	34	24	22	17	33	29	34	37	29
AUG. 17	20	35	35	36	24	22	17	33	29	34	37	29
AUG. 18	20	36	37	37	24	22	17	33	29	34	37	29
AUG. 19	21	38	38	39	24	22	17	33	29	34	37	29
AUG. 20	21	40	40	41	24	22	18	33	29	34	37	29
AUG. 21	21	41	42	42	24	21	18	33	29	34	37	29
AUG. 22	21	43	43	44	24	21	18	33	29	34	37	29
AUG. 23	21	44	45	45	25	21	18	33	29	34	37	29
AUG. 24	21	46	46	47	25	21	18	33	29	34	37	29
AUG. 25	21	47	48	1	25	21	18	33	29	34	37	29
AUG. 26	22	1	2	2	25	21	18	33	29	34	37	29
AUG. 27	22	3	3	4	25	21	18	33	29	34	37	29
AUG. 28	22	4	5	5	25	21	18	33	29	34	36	29
AUG. 29	22	6	7	7	25	21	18	33	29	34	36	29
AUG. 30	22	8	8	9	25	21	18	33	29	34	36	29
AUG. 31	22	9	10	11	25	21	18	33	29	34	36	29

MOON 1 ◖ 12:01 A.M. TO 8:00 A.M.   **MOON 2** ◑ 8:01 A.M. TO 4:00 P.M.   **MOON 3** ● 4:01 P.M. TO 12:00 A.M.
Use only one "moon" number. Choose the column closest to your time of birth. If your place of birth is not on Eastern Standard Time, be sure to read "How to Convert to Eastern Standard Time" at the beginning of this section.

1983

September

October

Date & Time	SUN	MOON 1	MOON 2	MOON 3	MERCURY	VENUS	MARS	JUPITER	SATURN	URANUS	NEPTUNE	PLUTO
SEP. 1	22	11	12	13	25	21	19	33	29	34	36	29
SEP. 2	22	13	14	14	25	21	19	33	29	34	36	29
SEP. 3	23	15	16	16	25	20	19	33	29	34	36	29
SEP. 4	23	17	18	18	25	20	19	33	29	34	36	29
SEP. 5	23	19	20	20	25	20	19	33	29	34	36	29
SEP. 6	23	21	22	22	25	20	19	33	29	34	36	29
SEP. 7	23	23	24	24	25	20	19	33	29	34	36	29
SEP. 8	23	25	26	26	25	20	19	33	29	34	36	29
SEP. 9	23	27	28	28	25	20	19	33	29	34	36	29
SEP. 10	23	29	30	30	25	20	19	33	29	34	36	29
SEP. 11	24	31	31	32	25	20	19	33	29	34	36	29
SEP. 12	24	33	33	34	24	20	19	33	29	34	36	29
SEP. 13	24	34	35	35	24	20	20	34	29	34	36	29
SEP. 14	24	36	36	37	24	20	20	34	29	34	36	29
SEP. 15	24	38	38	39	24	20	20	34	29	34	36	29
SEP. 16	24	39	40	40	24	20	20	34	29	34	36	29
SEP. 17	24	41	41	42	24	20	20	34	29	34	36	29
SEP. 18	24	42	43	43	24	20	20	34	29	34	36	29
SEP. 19	25	44	44	45	23	20	20	34	29	34	36	29
SEP. 20	25	45	46	47	23	20	20	34	29	34	37	29
SEP. 21	25	47	48	48	23	20	20	34	29	34	37	29
SEP. 22	25	1	1	2	23	20	20	34	29	34	37	29
SEP. 23	25	2	3	3	23	20	20	34	29	34	37	29
SEP. 24	25	4	5	5	23	20	20	34	29	34	37	29
SEP. 25	26	6	6	7	23	20	21	34	29	34	37	29
SEP. 26	26	7	8	9	23	20	21	34	29	34	37	29
SEP. 27	26	9	10	10	23	20	21	34	29	34	37	29
SEP. 28	26	11	11	12	23	20	21	34	29	34	37	29
SEP. 29	26	13	13	14	23	20	21	34	29	34	37	29
SEP. 30	26	14	15	16	23	21	21	34	29	34	37	29

Date & Time	SUN	MOON 1	MOON 2	MOON 3	MERCURY	VENUS	MARS	JUPITER	SATURN	URANUS	NEPTUNE	PLUTO
OCT. 1	26	16	17	18	24	21	21	34	29	34	37	29
OCT. 2	26	18	19	20	24	21	21	34	29	34	37	29
OCT. 3	27	20	21	22	24	21	21	34	29	34	37	29
OCT. 4	27	22	23	24	24	21	21	34	30	34	37	29
OCT. 5	27	24	25	25	24	21	21	34	30	34	37	29
OCT. 6	27	26	27	27	24	21	21	34	30	34	37	29
OCT. 7	27	28	29	29	25	21	22	34	30	34	37	29
OCT. 8	27	30	31	31	25	21	22	34	30	34	37	29
OCT. 9	27	32	32	33	25	21	22	34	30	34	37	29
OCT. 10	27	34	34	35	25	21	22	34	30	34	37	29
OCT. 11	28	35	36	36	25	21	22	34	30	34	37	29
OCT. 12	28	37	38	38	26	22	22	34	30	34	37	29
OCT. 13	28	39	39	40	26	22	22	34	30	34	37	29
OCT. 14	28	40	41	41	26	22	22	34	30	34	37	29
OCT. 15	28	42	42	43	26	22	22	34	30	34	37	29
OCT. 16	28	43	44	44	27	22	22	34	30	34	37	29
OCT. 17	28	45	46	46	27	22	22	34	30	34	37	29
OCT. 18	28	47	47	48	27	22	22	34	30	34	37	29
OCT. 19	29	48	1	1	27	22	23	34	30	34	37	29
OCT. 20	29	2	2	3	28	22	23	34	30	34	37	29
OCT. 21	29	4	4	5	28	23	23	34	30	34	37	29
OCT. 22	29	5	6	6	28	23	23	34	30	34	37	29
OCT. 23	29	7	7	8	28	23	23	34	30	34	37	29
OCT. 24	29	9	9	10	28	23	23	34	30	34	37	29
OCT. 25	29	10	11	12	29	23	23	34	30	34	37	29
OCT. 26	30	12	13	13	29	23	23	34	30	34	37	29
OCT. 27	30	14	15	15	29	23	23	34	30	34	37	29
OCT. 28	30	16	17	17	29	23	23	35	30	34	37	29
OCT. 29	30	18	18	19	30	23	23	35	30	34	37	29
OCT. 30	30	20	20	21	30	24	23	35	30	34	37	29
OCT. 31	30	22	22	23	30	24	24	35	30	34	37	29

MOON 1 ◗ 12:01 A.M. TO 8:00 A.M.   **MOON 2** ◑ 8:01 A.M. TO 4:00 P.M.   **MOON 3** ● 4:01 P.M. TO 12:00 A.M.

Use only one "moon" number. Choose the column closest to your time of birth. If your place of birth is not on Eastern Standard Time, be sure to read "How to Convert to Eastern Standard Time" at the beginning of this section.

1983

November

Date & Time	SUN	MOON 1	MOON 2	MOON 3	MERCURY	VENUS	MARS	JUPITER	SATURN	URANUS	NEPTUNE	PLUTO
NOV. 1	30	23	24	25	30	24	24	35	30	34	37	29
NOV. 2	30	25	26	27	30	24	24	35	30	34	37	29
NOV. 3	31	27	28	29	31	24	24	35	30	34	37	29
NOV. 4	31	29	30	30	31	24	24	35	30	34	37	29
NOV. 5	31	31	32	32	31	24	24	35	30	34	37	29
NOV. 6	31	33	33	34	31	25	24	35	30	34	37	29
NOV. 7	31	35	35	36	31	25	24	35	30	34	37	29
NOV. 8	31	36	37	37	32	25	24	35	30	34	37	29
NOV. 9	31	38	39	39	32	25	24	35	30	34	37	29
NOV. 10	31	40	40	41	32	25	24	35	30	34	37	29
NOV. 11	31	41	42	42	32	25	24	35	30	34	37	29
NOV. 12	32	43	43	44	33	25	24	35	30	34	37	29
NOV. 13	32	44	45	46	33	25	25	35	30	34	37	29
NOV. 14	32	46	47	47	33	26	25	35	30	34	37	29
NOV. 15	32	48	48	1	33	26	25	35	30	34	37	29
NOV. 16	32	1	2	2	33	26	25	35	30	34	37	29
NOV. 17	32	3	3	4	34	26	25	35	30	34	37	29
NOV. 18	32	5	5	6	34	26	25	35	30	34	37	29
NOV. 19	33	6	7	7	34	26	25	35	30	34	37	29
NOV. 20	33	8	9	9	34	26	25	35	30	34	37	29
NOV. 21	33	10	10	11	34	27	25	35	30	34	37	29
NOV. 22	33	12	12	13	35	27	25	35	30	34	37	29
NOV. 23	33	14	14	15	35	27	25	35	30	34	37	29
NOV. 24	33	15	16	17	35	27	25	35	30	34	37	29
NOV. 25	34	17	18	19	35	27	25	35	30	34	37	29
NOV. 26	34	19	20	20	35	27	26	35	30	34	37	29
NOV. 27	34	21	22	22	36	28	26	35	30	34	37	29
NOV. 28	34	23	24	24	36	28	26	35	30	34	37	29
NOV. 29	34	25	26	26	36	28	26	35	30	34	37	29
NOV. 30	34	27	27	28	36	28	26	35	30	34	37	29

December

Date & Time	SUN	MOON 1	MOON 2	MOON 3	MERCURY	VENUS	MARS	JUPITER	SATURN	URANUS	NEPTUNE	PLUTO
DEC. 1	34	29	29	30	36	28	26	35	30	34	37	29
DEC. 2	34	30	31	32	37	28	26	36	30	34	37	29
DEC. 3	35	32	33	33	37	28	26	36	30	34	37	29
DEC. 4	35	34	35	35	37	29	26	36	30	34	37	29
DEC. 5	35	36	36	37	37	29	26	36	30	34	37	29
DEC. 6	35	37	38	39	37	29	26	36	30	34	37	29
DEC. 7	35	39	40	40	37	29	26	36	31	34	37	29
DEC. 8	35	41	41	42	38	29	26	36	31	34	37	29
DEC. 9	35	42	43	43	38	29	27	36	31	34	37	29
DEC. 10	35	44	44	45	38	30	27	36	31	34	37	29
DEC. 11	36	46	46	47	38	30	27	36	31	34	37	29
DEC. 12	36	47	48	48	38	30	27	36	31	34	37	29
DEC. 13	36	1	1	2	38	30	27	36	31	34	37	29
DEC. 14	36	2	3	3	39	30	27	36	31	34	37	29
DEC. 15	36	4	5	5	39	30	27	36	31	34	37	29
DEC. 16	36	6	6	7	39	30	27	36	31	34	37	29
DEC. 17	36	7	8	9	39	31	27	36	31	34	37	29
DEC. 18	36	9	10	10	39	31	27	36	31	34	37	29
DEC. 19	37	11	12	12	39	31	27	36	31	34	37	29
DEC. 20	37	13	14	14	39	31	27	36	31	34	37	29
DEC. 21	37	15	15	16	39	31	27	36	31	34	37	29
DEC. 22	37	17	17	18	39	31	28	36	31	34	37	29
DEC. 23	37	19	19	20	39	32	28	36	31	34	37	29
DEC. 24	37	21	21	22	39	32	28	36	31	34	37	29
DEC. 25	37	23	23	24	39	32	28	36	31	34	37	29
DEC. 26	38	24	25	26	39	32	28	36	31	34	37	29
DEC. 27	38	26	27	28	39	32	28	36	31	34	37	29
DEC. 28	38	28	29	29	39	32	28	36	31	34	37	29
DEC. 29	38	30	31	31	39	33	28	36	31	34	37	29
DEC. 30	38	32	32	33	38	33	28	36	31	34	37	29
DEC. 31	38	33	34	35	38	33	28	36	31	34	37	29

MOON 1 ◗ 12:01 A.M. TO 8:00 A.M. **MOON 2** ◗ 8:01 A.M. TO 4:00 P.M. **MOON 3** ● 4:01 P.M. TO 12:00 A.M.
Use only one "moon" number. Choose the column closest to your time of birth. If your place of birth is not on Eastern Standard Time, be sure to read "How to Convert to Eastern Standard Time" at the beginning of this section.

1984

January

Date & Time	SUN	MOON 1	MOON 2	MOON 3	MERCURY	VENUS	MARS	JUPITER	SATURN	URANUS	NEPTUNE	PLUTO
JAN. 1	38	35	36	36	38	33	28	36	31	34	37	29
JAN. 2	38	37	37	38	38	33	28	36	31	34	37	29
JAN. 3	39	39	39	40	38	33	28	36	31	34	37	29
JAN. 4	39	40	41	41	38	33	28	37	31	34	37	29
JAN. 5	39	42	42	43	37	34	29	37	31	34	37	29
JAN. 6	39	43	44	44	37	34	29	37	31	34	37	29
JAN. 7	39	45	46	46	37	34	29	37	31	34	37	29
JAN. 8	39	47	47	48	37	34	29	37	31	35	37	29
JAN. 9	39	48	1	1	37	34	29	37	31	35	37	29
JAN. 10	40	2	2	3	37	34	29	37	31	35	37	29
JAN. 11	40	3	4	4	37	35	29	37	31	35	37	29
JAN. 12	40	5	6	6	37	35	29	37	31	35	37	29
JAN. 13	40	7	7	8	37	35	29	37	31	35	37	29
JAN. 14	40	8	9	10	37	35	29	37	31	35	37	29
JAN. 15	40	10	11	11	37	35	29	37	31	35	37	29
JAN. 16	40	12	13	13	37	35	29	37	31	35	37	29
JAN. 17	41	14	15	15	37	36	29	37	31	35	37	29
JAN. 18	41	16	17	17	37	36	29	37	31	35	37	29
JAN. 19	41	18	19	19	38	36	30	37	31	35	37	29
JAN. 20	41	20	21	21	38	36	30	37	31	35	37	29
JAN. 21	41	22	23	23	38	36	30	37	31	35	37	29
JAN. 22	41	24	25	25	38	36	30	37	31	35	37	29
JAN. 23	42	26	26	27	38	37	30	37	31	35	37	29
JAN. 24	42	28	28	29	38	37	30	37	31	35	37	29
JAN. 25	42	30	30	31	38	37	30	37	31	35	37	29
JAN. 26	42	31	32	33	38	37	30	37	31	35	37	29
JAN. 27	42	33	34	34	39	37	30	37	31	35	37	29
JAN. 28	42	35	35	36	39	37	30	37	31	35	37	29
JAN. 29	42	36	37	38	39	38	30	37	31	35	37	29
JAN. 30	42	38	39	39	39	38	30	37	31	35	37	29
JAN. 31	43	40	40	41	39	38	30	37	31	35	37	29

February

Date & Time	SUN	MOON 1	MOON 2	MOON 3	MERCURY	VENUS	MARS	JUPITER	SATURN	URANUS	NEPTUNE	PLUTO
FEB. 1	43	41	42	42	39	38	30	37	31	35	37	29
FEB. 2	43	43	43	44	40	38	30	37	31	35	37	29
FEB. 3	43	45	45	46	40	38	30	37	31	35	37	29
FEB. 4	43	46	47	47	40	39	31	37	31	35	37	29
FEB. 5	43	48	48	1	40	39	31	37	31	35	37	29
FEB. 6	43	1	2	2	40	39	31	37	31	35	37	29
FEB. 7	43	3	3	4	41	39	31	37	31	35	37	29
FEB. 8	44	4	5	6	41	39	31	37	31	35	37	29
FEB. 9	44	6	7	7	41	39	31	38	31	35	37	29
FEB. 10	44	8	8	9	41	39	31	38	31	35	37	29
FEB. 11	44	9	10	11	41	40	31	38	31	35	37	29
FEB. 12	44	11	12	12	42	40	31	38	31	35	37	29
FEB. 13	44	13	14	14	42	40	31	38	31	35	37	29
FEB. 14	44	15	16	16	42	40	31	38	31	35	37	29
FEB. 15	44	17	18	18	42	40	31	38	31	35	37	29
FEB. 16	45	19	20	20	42	40	31	38	31	35	37	29
FEB. 17	45	21	22	22	43	41	31	38	31	35	37	29
FEB. 18	45	23	24	24	43	41	31	38	31	35	37	29
FEB. 19	45	25	26	26	43	41	31	38	31	35	37	29
FEB. 20	45	27	28	28	43	41	31	38	31	35	37	29
FEB. 21	45	29	30	30	43	41	31	38	31	35	37	29
FEB. 22	45	31	31	32	44	41	32	38	31	35	37	29
FEB. 23	46	33	33	34	44	42	32	38	31	35	37	29
FEB. 24	46	34	35	36	44	42	32	38	31	35	37	29
FEB. 25	46	36	37	37	44	42	32	38	31	35	37	29
FEB. 26	46	38	38	39	45	42	32	38	31	35	37	29
FEB. 27	46	39	40	40	45	42	32	38	31	35	37	29
FEB. 28	46	41	41	42	45	42	32	38	31	35	37	29
FEB. 29	46	43	43	44	45	43	32	38	31	35	37	29

MOON 1 ☽ 12:01 A.M. TO 8:00 A.M.   **MOON 2** ☽ 8:01 A.M. TO 4:00 P.M.   **MOON 3** ● 4:01 P.M. TO 12:00 A.M.
Use only one "moon" number. Choose the column closest to your time of birth. If your place of birth is not on
Eastern Standard Time, be sure to read "How to Convert to Eastern Standard Time" at the beginning of this section.

Date & Time	SUN ○	MOON 1 ◐	MOON 2 ◑	MOON 3 ●	MERCURY	VENUS	MARS	JUPITER	SATURN	URANUS	NEPTUNE	PLUTO
MAR. 1	46	44	45	45	46	43	32	38	31	35	37	29
MAR. 2	46	46	46	47	46	43	32	38	31	35	37	29
MAR. 3	47	47	48	48	46	43	32	38	31	35	37	29
MAR. 4	47	1	1	2	46	43	32	38	31	35	37	29
MAR. 5	47	2	3	4	47	43	32	38	31	35	37	29
MAR. 6	47	4	5	5	47	44	32	38	31	35	37	29
MAR. 7	47	6	6	7	47	44	32	38	31	35	37	29
MAR. 8	47	7	8	8	47	44	32	38	31	35	37	29
MAR. 9	47	9	10	10	48	44	32	38	31	35	37	29
MAR. 10	47	11	11	12	48	44	32	38	31	35	37	29
MAR. 11	48	12	13	14	48	44	32	38	31	35	37	29
MAR. 12	48	14	15	16	48	45	32	38	31	35	37	29
MAR. 13	48	16	17	17	1	45	32	38	31	35	37	29
MAR. 14	48	18	19	19	1	45	32	38	31	35	37	29
MAR. 15	48	20	21	21	1	45	32	38	31	35	37	29
MAR. 16	48	22	23	23	1	45	32	38	31	35	37	29
MAR. 17	48	24	25	25	2	45	32	38	31	35	37	29
MAR. 18	48	26	27	28	2	46	32	38	31	35	37	29
MAR. 19	1	28	29	29	2	46	33	38	31	35	37	29
MAR. 20	1	30	31	31	2	46	33	38	31	35	37	29
MAR. 21	1	32	33	33	3	46	33	38	31	35	37	29
MAR. 22	1	34	34	35	3	46	33	38	31	35	37	29
MAR. 23	1	36	36	37	3	46	33	38	31	35	37	29
MAR. 24	1	37	38	38	3	47	33	38	31	35	37	29
MAR. 25	2	39	39	40	4	47	33	38	31	35	37	29
MAR. 26	2	41	41	42	4	47	33	38	31	35	37	29
MAR. 27	2	42	43	43	4	47	33	38	31	35	37	29
MAR. 28	2	44	44	45	4	47	33	38	31	35	37	29
MAR. 29	2	45	46	46	5	47	33	38	31	35	37	29
MAR. 30	2	47	47	48	5	48	33	39	31	35	37	29
MAR. 31	2	48	1	2	5	48	33	39	31	35	37	29

Date & Time	SUN ○	MOON 1 ◐	MOON 2 ◑	MOON 3 ●	MERCURY	VENUS	MARS	JUPITER	SATURN	URANUS	NEPTUNE	PLUTO
APR. 1	2	2	3	3	5	48	33	39	31	35	37	29
APR. 2	2	4	4	5	5	48	33	39	31	35	37	29
APR. 3	3	5	6	6	5	48	33	39	31	35	37	29
APR. 4	3	7	8	8	5	48	33	39	31	35	37	29
APR. 5	3	9	9	10	6	1	33	39	31	35	37	29
APR. 6	3	10	11	11	6	1	33	39	31	35	37	29
APR. 7	3	12	13	13	6	1	33	39	31	35	37	29
APR. 8	3	14	14	15	6	1	33	39	31	35	37	29
APR. 9	3	16	16	17	6	1	33	39	31	35	37	29
APR. 10	3	17	18	19	6	1	33	39	31	35	37	29
APR. 11	4	19	20	21	6	2	33	39	31	35	37	29
APR. 12	4	21	22	23	6	2	33	39	31	35	37	29
APR. 13	4	23	24	25	6	2	33	39	31	35	37	29
APR. 14	4	25	26	27	6	2	33	39	31	35	37	29
APR. 15	4	27	28	29	6	2	33	39	31	35	37	29
APR. 16	4	29	30	31	6	2	33	39	31	35	37	29
APR. 17	4	31	32	32	6	3	33	39	31	35	37	29
APR. 18	4	33	34	34	6	3	33	39	31	35	37	29
APR. 19	5	35	35	36	6	3	33	39	31	35	37	29
APR. 20	5	37	37	38	5	3	33	39	31	35	37	29
APR. 21	5	38	39	39	5	3	33	39	31	35	37	29
APR. 22	5	40	41	41	5	3	33	39	31	35	37	29
APR. 23	5	42	42	43	5	3	32	39	31	35	37	29
APR. 24	5	43	44	44	4	4	32	39	31	35	37	29
APR. 25	6	45	45	46	5	4	32	39	31	35	37	29
APR. 26	6	46	47	48	5	4	32	39	31	35	37	29
APR. 27	6	48	1	1	5	4	32	39	31	35	37	29
APR. 28	6	2	2	3	5	4	32	39	31	35	37	29
APR. 29	6	3	4	4	5	4	32	39	31	35	37	29
APR. 30	6	5	5	6	5	5	32	39	31	35	37	29

MOON 1 ◐ 12:01 A.M. TO 8:00 A.M.   **MOON 2 ◑** 8:01 A.M. TO 4:00 P.M.   **MOON 3 ●** 4:01 P.M. TO 12:00 A.M.
Use only one "moon" number. Choose the column closest to your time of birth. If your place of birth is not on
Eastern Standard Time, be sure to read "How to Convert to Eastern Standard Time" at the beginning of this section.

May

Date & Time	SUN ☉	MOON 1 ☽	MOON 2 ☽	MOON 3 ●	MERCURY	VENUS	MARS	JUPITER	SATURN	URANUS	NEPTUNE	PLUTO
MAY 1	6	7	7	8	5	5	32	39	31	35	37	29
MAY 2	6	8	9	9	5	5	32	39	31	35	37	29
MAY 3	7	10	10	11	5	5	32	39	31	35	37	29
MAY 4	7	12	12	13	4	5	32	39	31	35	37	29
MAY 5	7	13	14	15	4	5	32	39	31	35	37	29
MAY 6	7	15	16	16	4	6	32	39	31	35	37	29
MAY 7	7	17	18	18	4	6	32	39	31	35	37	29
MAY 8	7	19	19	20	5	6	32	39	31	35	37	29
MAY 9	7	21	21	22	5	6	32	39	31	35	37	29
MAY 10	7	23	23	24	5	6	32	39	31	35	37	29
MAY 11	8	25	25	26	5	6	32	39	31	35	37	29
MAY 12	8	27	27	28	5	7	32	39	31	35	37	29
MAY 13	8	28	29	30	5	7	32	39	31	35	37	29
MAY 14	8	30	31	32	5	7	32	39	31	35	37	29
MAY 15	8	32	33	34	5	7	32	39	31	35	37	29
MAY 16	8	34	35	35	5	7	32	39	31	35	37	29
MAY 17	8	36	37	37	5	7	31	39	31	35	37	29
MAY 18	8	38	38	39	5	8	31	39	31	35	37	29
MAY 19	9	39	40	41	5	8	31	39	31	35	37	29
MAY 20	9	41	42	42	5	8	31	39	31	35	37	29
MAY 21	9	43	43	44	6	8	31	39	31	35	37	29
MAY 22	9	44	45	45	6	8	31	39	31	35	37	29
MAY 23	9	46	46	47	6	8	31	39	31	35	37	29
MAY 24	9	48	48	1	6	9	31	39	31	35	37	29
MAY 25	10	1	2	2	6	9	31	39	30	35	37	29
MAY 26	10	3	3	4	6	9	31	39	30	35	37	29
MAY 27	10	4	5	5	7	9	31	39	30	35	37	29
MAY 28	10	6	7	7	7	9	31	39	30	35	37	29
MAY 29	10	8	8	9	7	9	31	39	30	35	37	29
MAY 30	10	9	10	11	7	10	31	39	30	35	37	29
MAY 31	10	11	12	12	7	10	31	38	30	35	37	29

June

Date & Time	SUN ☉	MOON 1 ☽	MOON 2 ☽	MOON 3 ●	MERCURY	VENUS	MARS	JUPITER	SATURN	URANUS	NEPTUNE	PLUTO
JUN. 1	10	13	14	14	8	10	31	38	30	35	37	29
JUN. 2	10	15	15	16	8	10	31	38	30	35	37	29
JUN. 3	11	17	17	18	8	10	31	38	30	35	37	29
JUN. 4	11	18	19	20	8	10	31	38	30	34	37	29
JUN. 5	11	20	21	22	8	11	31	38	30	34	37	29
JUN. 6	11	22	23	23	9	11	31	38	30	34	37	29
JUN. 7	11	24	25	25	9	11	31	38	30	34	37	29
JUN. 8	11	26	27	27	9	11	31	38	30	34	37	29
JUN. 9	11	28	29	29	9	11	31	38	30	34	37	29
JUN. 10	11	30	30	31	10	11	31	38	30	34	37	29
JUN. 11	12	32	32	33	10	12	31	38	30	34	37	29
JUN. 12	12	33	34	35	10	12	31	38	30	34	37	29
JUN. 13	12	35	36	36	10	12	31	38	30	34	37	29
JUN. 14	12	37	38	38	11	12	31	38	30	34	37	29
JUN. 15	12	39	39	40	11	12	31	38	30	34	37	29
JUN. 16	12	40	41	42	11	12	31	38	30	34	37	29
JUN. 17	12	42	43	43	11	13	31	38	30	34	37	29
JUN. 18	12	44	44	45	12	13	31	38	30	34	37	29
JUN. 19	13	45	46	46	12	13	31	38	30	34	37	29
JUN. 20	13	47	48	48	12	13	31	38	30	34	37	29
JUN. 21	13	1	1	2	13	13	31	38	30	34	37	29
JUN. 22	13	2	3	3	13	13	31	38	30	34	37	29
JUN. 23	13	4	5	5	13	13	31	38	30	34	37	29
JUN. 24	13	5	6	6	14	14	31	38	30	34	37	29
JUN. 25	14	7	8	8	14	14	31	38	30	34	37	29
JUN. 26	14	9	9	10	14	14	31	38	30	34	37	29
JUN. 27	14	10	11	12	14	14	31	38	30	34	37	29
JUN. 28	14	12	13	13	15	14	31	38	30	34	37	29
JUN. 29	14	14	15	15	15	14	31	38	30	34	37	29
JUN. 30	14	16	17	17	15	15	31	38	30	34	37	29

MOON 1 ☽ 12:01 A.M. TO 8:00 A.M.　　**MOON 2** ☽ 8:01 A.M. TO 4:00 P.M.　　**MOON 3** ● 4:01 P.M. TO 12:00 A.M.
Use only one "moon" number. Choose the column closest to your time of birth. If your place of birth is not on Eastern Standard Time, be sure to read "How to Convert to Eastern Standard Time" at the beginning of this section.

1984

July

Date & Time	SUN	MOON 1	MOON 2	MOON 3	MERCURY	VENUS	MARS	JUPITER	SATURN	URANUS	NEPTUNE	PLUTO
JUL. 1	14	18	19	19	16	15	31	38	30	34	37	29
JUL. 2	14	20	20	21	16	15	31	38	30	34	37	29
JUL. 3	15	22	22	23	16	15	31	38	30	34	37	29
JUL. 4	15	24	24	25	16	15	31	38	30	34	37	29
JUL. 5	15	26	26	27	17	15	31	38	30	34	37	29
JUL. 6	15	27	28	29	17	16	31	38	30	34	37	29
JUL. 7	15	29	30	31	17	16	31	38	30	34	37	29
JUL. 8	15	31	32	32	17	16	31	38	30	34	37	29
JUL. 9	15	33	34	34	18	16	31	38	30	34	37	29
JUL. 10	15	35	35	36	18	16	31	38	30	34	37	29
JUL. 11	16	37	37	38	18	16	31	38	30	34	37	29
JUL. 12	16	38	39	39	18	17	31	38	30	34	37	29
JUL. 13	16	40	40	41	18	17	31	38	30	34	37	29
JUL. 14	16	42	42	43	19	17	31	38	30	34	37	29
JUL. 15	16	43	44	44	19	17	31	38	30	34	37	29
JUL. 16	16	45	45	46	19	17	31	38	30	34	37	29
JUL. 17	16	46	47	48	19	17	31	38	30	34	37	29
JUL. 18	16	48	1	1	20	18	31	38	30	34	37	29
JUL. 19	17	2	2	3	20	18	31	38	30	34	37	29
JUL. 20	17	3	4	4	20	18	31	38	30	34	37	29
JUL. 21	17	5	5	6	20	18	31	38	30	34	37	29
JUL. 22	17	6	7	8	20	18	31	38	30	34	37	29
JUL. 23	17	8	9	9	20	18	31	38	30	34	37	29
JUL. 24	17	10	10	11	21	19	31	38	30	34	37	29
JUL. 25	17	12	12	13	21	19	32	38	30	34	37	29
JUL. 26	18	13	14	15	21	19	32	38	30	34	37	29
JUL. 27	18	15	16	17	21	19	32	38	30	34	37	29
JUL. 28	18	17	18	18	21	19	32	38	30	34	37	29
JUL. 29	18	19	20	20	21	19	32	38	30	34	37	29
JUL. 30	18	21	22	22	22	20	32	38	30	34	37	29
JUL. 31	18	23	24	24	22	20	32	38	30	34	37	29

August

Date & Time	SUN	MOON 1	MOON 2	MOON 3	MERCURY	VENUS	MARS	JUPITER	SATURN	URANUS	NEPTUNE	PLUTO
AUG. 1	18	25	26	26	22	20	32	38	30	34	37	29
AUG. 2	18	27	28	28	22	20	32	38	30	34	37	29
AUG. 3	19	29	30	30	22	20	32	38	30	34	37	29
AUG. 4	19	31	31	32	22	20	32	38	30	34	37	29
AUG. 5	19	33	33	34	22	21	32	38	30	34	37	29
AUG. 6	19	34	35	35	22	21	32	37	30	34	37	29
AUG. 7	19	36	37	37	22	21	32	37	30	34	37	29
AUG. 8	19	38	38	39	23	21	32	37	30	34	37	29
AUG. 9	19	39	40	41	23	21	32	37	30	34	37	29
AUG. 10	19	41	42	42	23	21	32	37	30	34	37	29
AUG. 11	20	43	43	44	23	22	33	37	30	34	37	29
AUG. 12	20	44	45	45	23	22	33	37	30	34	37	29
AUG. 13	20	46	47	47	23	22	33	37	30	34	37	29
AUG. 14	20	48	48	1	23	22	33	37	30	34	37	29
AUG. 15	20	1	2	2	23	22	33	37	30	34	37	29
AUG. 16	20	3	3	4	23	22	33	37	30	34	37	29
AUG. 17	20	4	5	5	23	23	33	37	30	34	37	29
AUG. 18	20	6	6	7	23	23	33	37	30	34	37	29
AUG. 19	21	8	8	9	23	23	33	37	30	34	37	29
AUG. 20	21	9	10	10	23	23	33	37	30	34	37	29
AUG. 21	21	11	11	12	22	23	33	37	30	34	37	29
AUG. 22	21	13	13	14	22	23	33	37	30	34	37	29
AUG. 23	21	14	15	16	22	23	33	37	30	34	37	29
AUG. 24	21	16	17	18		24	33	37	30	34	37	29
AUG. 25	21	18	19	20	22	24	34	37	30	34	37	29
AUG. 26	22	20	21	22	22	24	34	37	30	34	37	29
AUG. 27	22	22	23	24	22	24	34	37	30	34	37	29
AUG. 28	22	24	25	26	22	24	34	37	30	34	37	29
AUG. 29	22	26	27	28	22	24	34	37	30	34	37	29
AUG. 30	22	28	29	30	22	25	34	37	31	34	37	29
AUG. 31	22	30	31	31	21	25	34	37	31	34	37	29

MOON 1 ◐ 12:01 A.M. TO 8:00 A.M.   **MOON 2** ◑ 8:01 A.M. TO 4:00 P.M.   **MOON 3** ● 4:01 P.M. TO 12:00 A.M.

Use only one "moon" number. Choose the column closest to your time of birth. If your place of birth is not on Eastern Standard Time, be sure to read "How to Convert to Eastern Standard Time" at the beginning of this section.

September

Date & Time	SUN	MOON 1	MOON 2	MOON 3	MERCURY	VENUS	MARS	JUPITER	SATURN	URANUS	NEPTUNE	PLUTO
SEP. 1	22	32	33	33	21	25	34	37	31	34	37	29
SEP. 2	22	34	35	35	21	25	34	37	31	34	37	29
SEP. 3	23	36	36	37	21	25	34	37	31	34	37	29
SEP. 4	23	37	38	39	21	25	34	37	31	34	37	29
SEP. 5	23	39	40	40	21	26	34	37	31	34	37	29
SEP. 6	23	41	41	42	21	26	34	37	31	34	37	29
SEP. 7	23	42	43	43	21	26	35	37	31	34	37	29
SEP. 8	23	44	45	45	21	26	35	37	31	34	37	29
SEP. 9	23	46	46	47	21	26	35	37	31	34	37	29
SEP. 10	23	47	48	48	21	26	35	37	31	34	37	29
SEP. 11	24	1	1	2	21	27	35	37	31	34	37	29
SEP. 12	24	2	3	3	21	27	35	37	31	34	37	29
SEP. 13	24	4	4	5	21	27	35	37	31	34	37	29
SEP. 14	24	6	6	7	21	27	35	37	31	34	37	29
SEP. 15	24	7	8	8	22	27	35	37	31	34	37	29
SEP. 16	24	9	9	10	22	27	35	37	31	34	37	29
SEP. 17	24	10	11	11	22	28	35	37	31	34	37	29
SEP. 18	24	12	13	13	22	28	35	37	31	34	37	29
SEP. 19	25	14	14	15	22	28	36	37	31	34	37	29
SEP. 20	25	16	16	17	23	28	36	37	31	34	37	29
SEP. 21	25	17	18	19	23	28	36	37	31	34	37	29
SEP. 22	25	19	20	21	23	28	36	37	31	34	37	29
SEP. 23	25	21	22	23	23	29	36	38	31	34	37	29
SEP. 24	25	23	24	25	23	29	36	38	31	34	37	29
SEP. 25	26	25	26	27	24	29	36	38	31	34	37	29
SEP. 26	26	27	28	29	24	29	36	38	31	34	37	29
SEP. 27	26	29	30	31	24	29	36	38	31	34	37	29
SEP. 28	26	31	32	33	24	29	36	38	31	34	37	29
SEP. 29	26	33	34	35	25	30	36	38	31	34	37	29
SEP. 30	26	35	36	36	25	30	37	38	31	34	37	29

October

Date & Time	SUN	MOON 1	MOON 2	MOON 3	MERCURY	VENUS	MARS	JUPITER	SATURN	URANUS	NEPTUNE	PLUTO
OCT. 1	26	37	38	38	25	30	37	38	31	34	37	29
OCT. 2	26	39	39	40	25	30	37	38	31	34	37	29
OCT. 3	27	40	41	41	26	30	37	38	31	34	37	29
OCT. 4	27	42	43	43	26	30	37	38	31	34	37	29
OCT. 5	27	44	44	45	26	31	37	38	31	34	37	29
OCT. 6	27	45	46	46	26	31	37	38	31	34	37	29
OCT. 7	27	47	47	48	26	31	37	38	31	34	37	29
OCT. 8	27	48	1	1	27	31	37	38	31	34	37	29
OCT. 9	27	2	2	3	27	31	37	38	31	34	37	29
OCT. 10	27	4	4	5	27	31	37	38	31	34	37	29
OCT. 11	28	5	6	6	27	31	38	38	31	34	37	29
OCT. 12	28	7	7	8	28	32	38	38	31	34	37	29
OCT. 13	28	8	9	9	28	32	38	38	31	34	37	29
OCT. 14	28	10	11	11	28	32	38	38	31	34	37	29
OCT. 15	28	12	12	13	28	32	38	38	31	34	37	29
OCT. 16	28	13	14	14	29	32	38	38	31	34	37	29
OCT. 17	28	15	16	16	29	32	38	38	31	34	37	29
OCT. 18	28	17	17	18	29	33	38	38	31	34	37	29
OCT. 19	29	19	19	20	29	33	38	38	31	34	37	29
OCT. 20	29	21	21	22	29	33	38	38	31	34	37	29
OCT. 21	29	23	23	24	30	33	38	38	31	34	37	29
OCT. 22	29	25	25	26	30	33	39	38	31	34	37	29
OCT. 23	29	27	27	28	30	34	39	38	31	34	37	29
OCT. 24	29	29	29	30	30	34	39	38	31	34	37	29
OCT. 25	29	31	31	32	30	34	39	38	31	34	37	29
OCT. 26	30	33	33	34	31	34	39	38	31	34	37	29
OCT. 27	30	34	35	36	31	34	39	38	31	34	37	29
OCT. 28	30	36	37	37	31	34	39	38	31	34	37	29
OCT. 29	30	38	39	39	31	34	39	38	31	35	37	29
OCT. 30	30	40	40	41	32	35	39	38	31	35	37	29
OCT. 31	30	42	42	43	32	35	39	38	31	35	37	29

MOON 1 ◔ 12:01 A.M. TO 8:00 A.M.　　**MOON 2** ◑ 8:01 A.M. TO 4:00 P.M.　　**MOON 3** ● 4:01 P.M. TO 12:00 A.M.

Use only one "moon" number. Choose the column closest to your time of birth. If your place of birth is not on Eastern Standard Time, be sure to read "How to Convert to Eastern Standard Time" at the beginning of this section.

1984

November

Date & Time	SUN ☉	MOON 1 ☽	MOON 2 ☽	MOON 3 ●	MERCURY	VENUS	MARS	JUPITER	SATURN	URANUS	NEPTUNE	PLUTO
NOV. 1	30	43	44	44	32	35	40	38	31	35	37	29
NOV. 2	30	45	45	46	32	35	40	38	31	35	37	29
NOV. 3	31	46	47	47	32	35	40	38	31	35	37	29
NOV. 4	31	48	48	1	33	35	40	38	31	35	37	29
NOV. 5	31	2	2	3	33	36	40	38	31	35	37	29
NOV. 6	31	3	4	4	33	36	40	38	31	35	37	29
NOV. 7	31	5	5	6	33	36	40	38	31	35	37	29
NOV. 8	31	6	7	7	33	36	40	38	31	35	37	29
NOV. 9	31	8	8	9	33	36	40	38	31	35	37	29
NOV. 10	31	10	10	11	34	36	40	38	31	35	37	29
NOV. 11	31	11	12	12	34	37	41	38	32	35	37	29
NOV. 12	32	13	14	14	34	37	41	38	32	35	37	29
NOV. 13	32	15	15	16	34	37	41	38	32	35	37	29
NOV. 14	32	16	17	18	34	37	41	38	32	35	37	29
NOV. 15	32	18	19	19	35	37	41	38	32	35	37	29
NOV. 16	32	20	21	21	35	37	41	39	32	35	37	29
NOV. 17	32	22	23	23	35	37	41	39	32	35	37	29
NOV. 18	32	24	24	25	38	41	41	39	32	35	37	29
NOV. 19	33	26	26	27	35	38	41	39	32	35	37	29
NOV. 20	33	28	28	29	35	38	41	39	32	35	37	29
NOV. 21	33	30	30	31	36	38	42	39	32	35	37	29
NOV. 22	33	32	32	33	36	38	42	39	32	35	37	29
NOV. 23	33	34	34	35	36	38	42	39	32	35	37	29
NOV. 24	33	35	36	37	36	39	42	39	32	35	37	29
NOV. 25	34	37	38	39	36	39	42	39	32	35	37	29
NOV. 26	34	39	40	40	36	39	42	39	32	35	37	29
NOV. 27	34	41	41	42	37	39	42	39	32	35	37	29
NOV. 28	34	43	43	44	37	39	42	39	32	35	37	29
NOV. 29	34	44	45	45	37	39	42	39	32	35	37	29
NOV. 30	34	46	46	47	37	40	42	39	32	35	37	29

December

Date & Time	SUN ☉	MOON 1 ☽	MOON 2 ☽	MOON 3 ●	MERCURY	VENUS	MARS	JUPITER	SATURN	URANUS	NEPTUNE	PLUTO
DEC. 1	34	47	48	1	37	40	43	39	32	35	37	29
DEC. 2	34	1	2	2	37	40	43	39	32	35	37	29
DEC. 3	35	3	3	4	37	40	43	39	32	35	37	29
DEC. 4	35	4	5	5	37	40	43	39	32	35	37	29
DEC. 5	35	6	6	7	37	40	43	39	32	35	37	29
DEC. 6	35	7	8	9	37	41	43	39	32	35	37	29
DEC. 7	35	9	10	10	37	41	43	39	32	35	37	29
DEC. 8	35	11	11	12	37	41	43	39	32	35	37	29
DEC. 9	35	12	13	14	37	41	43	39	32	35	37	29
DEC. 10	35	14	15	15	37	41	43	39	32	35	37	29
DEC. 11	36	16	17	17	37	41	44	39	32	35	37	29
DEC. 12	36	18	18	19	36	41	44	39	32	35	37	29
DEC. 13	36	20	20	21	36	42	44	39	32	35	37	29
DEC. 14	36	21	22	23	36	42	44	39	32	35	37	29
DEC. 15	36	23	24	25	36	42	44	39	32	35	37	29
DEC. 16	36	25	26	26	36	42	44	39	32	35	37	29
DEC. 17	36	27	28	28	36	42	44	39	32	35	37	29
DEC. 18	36	29	30	30	35	42	44	39	32	35	37	30
DEC. 19	37	31	32	32	35	43	44	39	32	35	37	30
DEC. 20	37	33	33	34	35	43	44	39	32	35	37	30
DEC. 21	37	35	35	36	35	43	45	39	32	35	37	30
DEC. 22	37	37	37	38	35	43	45	40	32	35	37	30
DEC. 23	37	38	39	40	35	43	45	40	32	35	37	30
DEC. 24	37	40	41	41	35	43	45	40	32	35	37	30
DEC. 25	37	42	42	43	35	43	45	40	32	35	37	30
DEC. 26	38	44	44	45	35	44	45	40	32	35	37	30
DEC. 27	38	45	46	46	35	44	45	40	32	35	37	30
DEC. 28	38	47	47	48	35	44	45	40	32	35	37	30
DEC. 29	38	1	1	2	35	44	45	40	32	35	37	30
DEC. 30	38	2	3	3	35	44	45	40	32	35	37	30
DEC. 31	38	4	4	5	35	44	46	40	32	35	37	30

MOON 1 ☽ 12:01 A.M. TO 8:00 A.M.   **MOON 2** ☽ 8:01 A.M. TO 4:00 P.M.   **MOON 3** ● 4:01 P.M. TO 12:00 A.M.

Use only one "moon" number. Choose the column closest to your time of birth. If your place of birth is not on Eastern Standard Time, be sure to read "How to Convert to Eastern Standard Time" at the beginning of this section.

January

Date & Time	SUN ☉	MOON 1 ◗	MOON 2 ◖	MOON 3 ●	MERCURY	VENUS	MARS	JUPITER	SATURN	URANUS	NEPTUNE	PLUTO
JAN. 1	38	5	6	6	35	45	46	40	32	35	37	30
JAN. 2	38	7	7	8	36	45	46	40	32	35	37	30
JAN. 3	39	8	9	10	36	45	46	40	32	35	37	30
JAN. 4	39	10	11	11	36	45	46	40	32	35	37	30
JAN. 5	39	12	12	13	36	45	46	40	32	35	37	30
JAN. 6	39	14	14	15	36	45	46	40	32	35	37	30
JAN. 7	39	15	16	17	36	45	46	40	32	35	37	30
JAN. 8	39	17	18	18	36	46	46	40	32	35	37	30
JAN. 9	39	19	20	20	37	46	46	40	32	35	37	30
JAN. 10	40	21	22	22	37	46	47	40	32	35	37	30
JAN. 11	40	23	24	24	37	46	47	40	32	35	37	30
JAN. 12	40	25	25	26	37	46	47	40	32	35	37	30
JAN. 13	40	27	27	28	37	46	47	40	32	35	37	30
JAN. 14	40	29	29	30	37	46	47	40	32	35	37	30
JAN. 15	40	30	31	32	38	47	47	40	32	35	37	30
JAN. 16	40	32	33	34	38	47	47	40	32	35	37	30
JAN. 17	41	34	35	35	38	47	47	40	32	35	37	30
JAN. 18	41	36	37	37	38	47	47	40	32	35	37	30
JAN. 19	41	38	38	39	38	47	48	40	32	35	37	30
JAN. 20	41	40	40	41	39	47	48	40	32	35	37	30
JAN. 21	41	41	42	42	39	47	48	40	32	35	37	30
JAN. 22	41	43	44	44	39	48	48	40	33	35	37	30
JAN. 23	42	45	45	46	39	48	48	41	33	35	37	30
JAN. 24	42	46	47	47	39	48	48	41	33	35	37	30
JAN. 25	42	48	48	1	40	48	48	41	33	35	37	30
JAN. 26	42	2	2	3	40	48	48	41	33	35	37	30
JAN. 27	42	3	4	4	40	48	48	41	33	35	37	30
JAN. 28	42	5	5	6	40	48	48	41	33	35	37	30
JAN. 29	42	6	7	7	40	48	1	41	33	35	37	30
JAN. 30	42	8	8	9	41	1	1	41	33	35	37	30
JAN. 31	43	10	10	11	41	1	1	41	33	35	37	30

February

Date & Time	SUN ☉	MOON 1 ◗	MOON 2 ◖	MOON 3 ●	MERCURY	VENUS	MARS	JUPITER	SATURN	URANUS	NEPTUNE	PLUTO
FEB. 1	43	11	12	12	41	1	1	41	33	35	37	30
FEB. 2	43	13	13	14	41	1	1	41	33	35	37	30
FEB. 3	43	15	15	16	41	1	1	41	33	35	37	30
FEB. 4	43	16	17	18	42	1	1	41	33	35	37	30
FEB. 5	43	18	19	20	42	1	1	41	33	35	37	30
FEB. 6	43	20	21	22	42	1	1	41	33	35	37	30
FEB. 7	43	22	23	24	42	2	1	41	33	35	37	30
FEB. 8	44	24	25	26	42	2	2	41	33	35	37	30
FEB. 9	44	26	27	27	43	2	2	41	33	35	37	30
FEB. 10	44	28	29	29	43	2	2	41	33	35	37	30
FEB. 11	44	30	31	31	43	2	2	41	33	35	37	30
FEB. 12	44	32	32	33	43	2	2	41	33	35	37	30
FEB. 13	44	34	34	35	44	2	2	41	33	35	37	30
FEB. 14	44	36	36	37	44	2	2	41	33	35	37	30
FEB. 15	44	37	38	38	44	2	2	41	33	35	37	30
FEB. 16	45	39	40	40	44	3	2	41	33	35	37	30
FEB. 17	45	41	41	42	45	3	2	41	33	35	37	30
FEB. 18	45	42	43	44	45	3	3	41	33	35	37	30
FEB. 19	45	44	45	45	45	3	3	41	33	35	37	30
FEB. 20	45	46	46	47	45	3	3	41	33	35	37	30
FEB. 21	45	47	48	1	46	3	3	41	33	35	37	30
FEB. 22	45	1	2	2	46	3	3	41	33	35	37	30
FEB. 23	46	3	3	4	46	3	3	41	33	35	37	30
FEB. 24	46	4	5	5	46	3	3	41	33	35	37	30
FEB. 25	46	6	6	7	47	3	3	42	33	35	37	30
FEB. 26	46	7	8	8	47	3	3	42	33	35	37	30
FEB. 27	46	9	9	10	47	3	3	42	33	35	37	30
FEB. 28	46	11	11	12	47	3	4	42	33	35	37	30

MOON 1 ◗ 12:01 A.M. TO 8:00 A.M. **MOON 2** ◖ 8:01 A.M. TO 4:00 P.M. **MOON 3** ● 4:01 P.M. TO 12:00 A.M.
Use only one "moon" number. Choose the column closest to your time of birth. If your place of birth is not on Eastern Standard Time, be sure to read "How to Convert to Eastern Standard Time" at the beginning of this section.

1985

March
April

Date & Time	SUN	MOON 1	MOON 2	MOON 3	MERCURY	VENUS	MARS	JUPITER	SATURN	URANUS	NEPTUNE	PLUTO
MAR. 1	46	12	13	13	48	4	4	42	33	35	37	30
MAR. 2	46	14	15	15	48	4	4	42	33	35	37	30
MAR. 3	47	16	16	17	48	4	4	42	33	35	37	30
MAR. 4	47	18	18	19	48	4	4	42	33	35	37	30
MAR. 5	47	19	20	21	1	4	4	42	33	35	37	30
MAR. 6	47	21	22	23	1	4	4	42	33	35	37	30
MAR. 7	47	23	24	25	1	4	4	42	33	35	37	30
MAR. 8	47	25	26	27	1	4	4	42	33	35	37	30
MAR. 9	47	27	28	29	1	4	4	42	33	35	37	30
MAR. 10	47	29	30	31	2	4	4	42	33	35	37	30
MAR. 11	48	31	32	33	2	4	5	42	33	35	37	30
MAR. 12	48	33	34	34	2	4	5	42	33	35	37	30
MAR. 13	48	35	36	36	2	4	5	42	33	35	37	30
MAR. 14	48	37	37	38	2	4	5	42	33	35	37	30
MAR. 15	48	39	39	40	3	4	5	42	33	35	37	30
MAR. 16	48	40	41	42	3	4	5	42	33	35	37	30
MAR. 17	48	42	43	43	3	4	5	42	33	35	37	30
MAR. 18	48	44	44	45	3	4	5	42	33	35	37	30
MAR. 19	1	45	46	46	3	4	5	42	33	35	37	30
MAR. 20	1	47	48	48	3	4	5	42	33	35	37	30
MAR. 21	1	1	1	2	3	4	6	42	33	35	37	30
MAR. 22	1	2	3	3	3	4	6	42	33	35	37	30
MAR. 23	1	4	4	5	3	4	6	42	33	35	37	30
MAR. 24	1	5	6	6	3	4	6	42	33	35	37	30
MAR. 25	2	7	7	8	3	4	6	42	33	35	37	30
MAR. 26	2	9	9	10	3	4	6	42	33	35	37	30
MAR. 27	2	10	11	11	3	3	6	42	33	35	37	30
MAR. 28	2	12	12	13	3	3	6	42	33	35	37	30
MAR. 29	2	13	14	14	3	3	6	42	33	35	37	30
MAR. 30	2	15	16	16	3	3	6	42	33	35	37	30
MAR. 31	2	17	17	18	3	3	7	42	33	35	37	29
APR. 1	2	19	19	20	3	3	7	42	33	35	37	29
APR. 2	2	21	21	22	3	3	7	42	33	35	37	29
APR. 3	3	22	23	24	3	3	7	42	33	35	37	29
APR. 4	3	24	25	26	3	3	7	42	33	35	37	29
APR. 5	3	26	27	28	3	3	7	43	33	35	37	29
APR. 6	3	29	29	30	3	3	7	43	33	35	37	29
APR. 7	3	31	31	32	2	3	7	43	33	35	37	29
APR. 8	3	33	33	34	2	2	7	43	33	35	37	29
APR. 9	3	34	35	36	2	2	7	43	33	35	37	29
APR. 10	3	36	37	38	2	2	7	43	33	35	37	29
APR. 11	4	38	39	39	2	2	8	43	33	35	37	29
APR. 12	4	40	41	41	2	2	8	43	33	35	37	29
APR. 13	4	42	42	43	2	2	8	43	33	35	37	29
APR. 14	4	43	44	44	2	2	8	43	33	35	37	29
APR. 15	4	45	46	46	2	2	8	43	33	35	37	29
APR. 16	4	47	47	48	2	2	8	43	33	35	37	29
APR. 17	4	48	1	1	2	2	8	43	33	35	37	29
APR. 18	4	2	2	2	2	2	8	43	33	35	37	29
APR. 19	5	3	4	4	2	2	8	43	33	35	37	29
APR. 20	5	5	5	6	2	2	8	43	33	35	37	29
APR. 21	5	7	7	8	2	2	8	43	33	35	37	29
APR. 22	5	8	9	9	2	2	9	43	33	35	37	29
APR. 23	5	10	10	11	2	2	9	43	32	35	37	29
APR. 24	5	11	12	12	2	2	9	43	32	35	37	29
APR. 25	6	13	13	14	2	2	9	43	32	35	37	29
APR. 26	6	15	15	16	2	2	9	43	32	35	37	29
APR. 27	6	16	17	17	2	2	9	43	32	35	37	29
APR. 28	6	18	19	19	2	2	9	43	32	35	37	29
APR. 29	6	20	20	21	3	2	9	43	32	35	37	29
APR. 30	6	22	22	23	3	2	9	43	32	35	37	29

MOON 1 ◖ 12:01 A.M. TO 8:00 A.M.   **MOON 2** ◑ 8:01 A.M. TO 4:00 P.M.   **MOON 3** ● 4:01 P.M. TO 12:00 A.M.

Use only one "moon" number. Choose the column closest to your time of birth. If your place of birth is not on Eastern Standard Time, be sure to read "How to Convert to Eastern Standard Time" at the beginning of this section.

May

Date & Time	SUN ☼	MOON 1 ☽	MOON 2 ◗	MOON 3 ●	MERCURY	VENUS	MARS	JUPITER	SATURN	URANUS	NEPTUNE	PLUTO
MAR. 1	46	12	13	13	48	4	4	42	33	35	37	30
MAR. 2	46	14	15	15	48	4	4	42	33	35	37	30
MAR. 3	47	16	16	17	48	4	4	42	33	35	37	30
MAR. 4	47	18	18	19	48	4	4	42	33	35	37	30
MAR. 5	47	19	20	21	1	4	4	42	33	35	37	30
MAR. 6	47	21	22	23	1	4	4	42	33	35	37	30
MAR. 7	47	23	24	25	1	4	4	42	33	35	37	30
MAR. 8	47	25	26	27	1	4	4	42	33	35	37	30
MAR. 9	47	27	28	29	1	4	4	42	33	35	37	30
MAR. 10	47	29	30	31	2	4	4	42	33	35	37	30
MAR. 11	48	31	32	33	2	4	5	42	33	35	37	30
MAR. 12	48	33	34	34	2	4	5	42	33	35	37	30
MAR. 13	48	35	36	36	2	4	5	42	33	35	37	30
MAR. 14	48	37	37	38	2	4	5	42	33	35	37	30
MAR. 15	48	39	39	40	3	4	5	42	33	35	37	30
MAR. 16	48	40	41	42	3	4	5	42	33	35	37	30
MAR. 17	48	42	43	43	3	4	5	42	33	35	37	30
MAR. 18	48	44	44	45	3	4	5	42	33	35	37	30
MAR. 19	1	45	46	46	3	4	5	42	33	35	37	30
MAR. 20	1	47	48	48	3	4	5	42	33	35	37	30
MAR. 21	1	1	1	2	3	4	6	42	33	35	37	30
MAR. 22	1	2	3	3	3	4	6	42	33	35	37	30
MAR. 23	1	4	5	5	3	4	6	42	33	35	37	30
MAR. 24	1	5	6	6	3	4	6	42	33	35	37	30
MAR. 25	2	7	7	8	3	4	6	42	33	35	37	30
MAR. 26	2	9	9	10	3	4	6	42	33	35	37	30
MAR. 27	2	10	11	11	3	3	6	42	33	35	37	30
MAR. 28	2	12	12	13	3	3	6	42	33	35	37	30
MAR. 29	2	13	14	14	3	3	6	42	33	35	37	30
MAR. 30	2	15	16	16	3	3	6	42	33	35	37	30
MAR. 31	2	17	17	18	3	3	7	42	33	35	37	29

June

Date & Time	SUN ☼	MOON 1 ☽	MOON 2 ◗	MOON 3 ●	MERCURY	VENUS	MARS	JUPITER	SATURN	URANUS	NEPTUNE	PLUTO
APR. 1	2	19	19	20	3	3	7	42	33	35	37	29
APR. 2	2	21	21	22	3	3	7	42	33	35	37	29
APR. 3	3	22	23	24	3	3	7	42	33	35	37	29
APR. 4	3	24	25	26	3	3	7	42	33	35	37	29
APR. 5	3	26	27	28	3	3	7	43	33	35	37	29
APR. 6	3	29	29	30	3	3	7	43	33	35	37	29
APR. 7	3	31	31	32	2	3	7	43	33	35	37	29
APR. 8	3	33	33	34	2	2	7	43	33	35	37	29
APR. 9	3	34	35	36	2	2	7	43	33	35	37	29
APR. 10	3	36	37	38	2	2	7	43	33	35	37	29
APR. 11	4	38	39	39	2	2	8	43	33	35	37	29
APR. 12	4	40	41	41	2	2	8	43	33	35	37	29
APR. 13	4	42	42	43	2	2	8	43	33	35	37	29
APR. 14	4	43	44	44	2	2	8	43	33	35	37	29
APR. 15	4	45	46	46	2	2	8	43	33	35	37	29
APR. 16	4	47	47	48	2	2	8	43	33	35	37	29
APR. 17	4	48	1	1	2	2	8	43	33	35	37	29
APR. 18	4	2	2	3	2	2	8	43	33	35	37	29
APR. 19	5	3	4	4	2	2	8	43	33	35	37	29
APR. 20	5	5	5	6	2	2	8	43	33	35	37	29
APR. 21	5	7	7	8	2	2	8	43	33	35	37	29
APR. 22	5	8	9	9	2	2	9	43	33	35	37	29
APR. 23	5	10	10	11	2	2	9	43	32	35	37	29
APR. 24	5	11	12	12	2	2	9	43	32	35	37	29
APR. 25	6	13	13	14	2	2	9	43	32	35	37	29
APR. 26	6	15	15	16	2	2	9	43	32	35	37	29
APR. 27	6	16	17	17	2	2	9	43	32	35	37	29
APR. 28	6	18	19	19	2	2	9	43	32	35	37	29
APR. 29	6	20	20	21	3	2	9	43	32	35	37	29
APR. 30	6	22	22	23	3	2	9	43	32	35	37	29

MOON 1 ☽ 12:01 A.M. TO 8:00 A.M.   **MOON 2** ◗ 8:01 A.M. TO 4:00 P.M.   **MOON 3** ● 4:01 P.M. TO 12:00 A.M.
Use only one "moon" number. Choose the column closest to your time of birth. If your place of birth is not on Eastern Standard Time, be sure to read "How to Convert to Eastern Standard Time" at the beginning of this section.

1985

July

Date & Time	SUN	MOON 1	MOON 2	MOON 3	MERCURY	VENUS	MARS	JUPITER	SATURN	URANUS	NEPTUNE	PLUTO
JUL. 1	14	36	37	37	17	8	15	43	32	35	37	29
JUL. 2	14	38	38	39	17	8	15	43	32	35	37	29
JUL. 3	15	40	40	41	18	9	15	43	32	35	37	29
JUL. 4	15	42	42	43	18	9	15	43	32	35	37	29
JUL. 5	15	43	44	44	18	9	15	43	32	35	37	29
JUL. 6	15	45	46	46	18	9	15	43	32	35	37	29
JUL. 7	15	47	47	48	18	9	15	43	32	35	37	29
JUL. 8	15	48	1	1	19	9	15	43	32	35	37	29
JUL. 9	15	2	3	3	19	9	16	43	32	35	37	29
JUL. 10	15	4	4	5	19	10	16	43	32	35	37	29
JUL. 11	16	5	6	6	19	10	16	43	32	35	37	29
JUL. 12	16	7	7	8	19	10	16	43	32	35	37	29
JUL. 13	16	8	9	9	19	10	16	43	32	35	37	29
JUL. 14	16	10	10	11	19	10	16	43	32	35	37	29
JUL. 15	16	12	12	13	20	10	16	43	32	35	37	29
JUL. 16	16	13	14	14	20	10	16	43	32	35	37	29
JUL. 17	16	15	16	16	20	11	16	43	32	35	37	29
JUL. 18	16	17	17	18	20	11	16	43	32	35	37	29
JUL. 19	17	19	19	20	20	11	16	43	32	35	37	29
JUL. 20	17	20	21	22	20	11	17	43	32	35	37	29
JUL. 21	17	22	23	23	20	11	17	43	32	35	37	29
JUL. 22	17	24	25	25	20	11	17	43	32	35	37	29
JUL. 23	17	26	27	27	20	11	17	43	32	35	37	29
JUL. 24	17	28	28	29	20	12	17	43	32	35	37	29
JUL. 25	17	30	30	31	20	12	17	43	32	35	37	29
JUL. 26	18	32	32	33	20	12	17	43	32	35	37	29
JUL. 27	18	33	34	35	20	12	17	43	32	35	37	29
JUL. 28	18	35	36	37	20	12	17	43	32	35	37	29
JUL. 29	18	37	38	38	20	12	17	43	32	35	37	29
JUL. 30	18	39	40	40	20	12	17	43	32	35	37	29
JUL. 31	18	41	41	42	20	13	17	43	32	35	37	29

August

Date & Time	SUN	MOON 1	MOON 2	MOON 3	MERCURY	VENUS	MARS	JUPITER	SATURN	URANUS	NEPTUNE	PLUTO
AUG. 1	18	43	43	44	20	13	18	43	32	35	37	29
AUG. 2	18	44	45	46	20	13	18	43	32	35	37	29
AUG. 3	19	46	47	47	20	13	18	43	32	35	37	29
AUG. 4	19	48	48	1	20	13	18	43	32	35	37	29
AUG. 5	19	1	2	3	20	13	18	43	32	35	37	29
AUG. 6	19	3	4	4	20	14	18	43	32	35	37	29
AUG. 7	19	5	5	6	20	14	18	43	32	35	37	29
AUG. 8	19	6	7	7	20	14	18	43	32	35	37	29
AUG. 9	19	8	8	9	20	14	18	42	32	35	37	29
AUG. 10	19	9	10	10	19	14	18	42	32	35	37	29
AUG. 11	20	11	12	12	19	14	18	42	32	35	37	29
AUG. 12	20	13	13	14	19	14	19	42	32	35	37	29
AUG. 13	20	14	15	15	19	15	19	42	32	35	37	29
AUG. 14	20	16	17	17	19	15	19	42	32	35	37	29
AUG. 15	20	18	18	19	19	15	19	42	32	35	37	29
AUG. 16	20	20	20	21	19	15	19	42	32	35	37	29
AUG. 17	20	22	22	23	19	15	19	42	32	35	37	29
AUG. 18	20	23	24	25	19	15	19	42	32	35	37	29
AUG. 19	21	25	26	27	19	16	19	42	32	35	37	29
AUG. 20	21	27	28	29	19	16	19	42	32	35	37	29
AUG. 21	21	29	30	30	19	16	19	42	32	35	37	29
AUG. 22	21	31	32	32	19	16	19	42	32	35	37	29
AUG. 23	21	33	34	34	19	16	19	42	32	35	37	29
AUG. 24	21	35	36	36	19	16	20	42	32	35	37	29
AUG. 25	21	37	37	38	19	17	20	42	32	35	37	29
AUG. 26	22	39	39	40	19	17	20	42	32	35	37	29
AUG. 27	22	40	41	42	19	17	20	42	32	35	37	29
AUG. 28	22	42	43	43	19	17	20	42	32	35	37	29
AUG. 29	22	44	44	45	19	17	20	42	32	35	37	29
AUG. 30	22	46	46	47	19	17	20	42	32	35	37	29
AUG. 31	22	47	48	48	20	17	20	42	32	35	37	29

MOON 1 ◗ 12:01 A.M. TO 8:00 A.M.   **MOON 2** ◑ 8:01 A.M. TO 4:00 P.M.   **MOON 3** ● 4:01 P.M. TO 12:00 A.M.

Use only one "moon" number. Choose the column closest to your time of birth. If your place of birth is not on Eastern Standard Time, be sure to read "How to Convert to Eastern Standard Time" at the beginning of this section.

1985

September

Date & Time	SUN	MOON 1	MOON 2	MOON 3	MERCURY	VENUS	MARS	JUPITER	SATURN	URANUS	NEPTUNE	PLUTO
SEP. 1	22	1	1	2	20	18	20	42	32	35	37	29
SEP. 2	22	3	3	4	20	18	20	42	32	35	37	29
SEP. 3	23	4	5	5	20	18	20	42	32	35	37	29
SEP. 4	23	6	6	7	20	18	20	42	32	35	37	29
SEP. 5	23	7	8	8	21	18	21	42	32	35	37	29
SEP. 6	23	9	9	10	21	18	21	42	32	35	37	29
SEP. 7	23	10	11	12	21	19	21	42	32	35	37	29
SEP. 8	23	12	13	13	21	19	21	42	32	35	37	29
SEP. 9	23	14	14	15	22	19	21	42	32	35	37	29
SEP. 10	23	15	16	17	22	19	21	42	32	35	37	29
SEP. 11	24	17	18	18	22	19	21	42	32	35	37	29
SEP. 12	24	19	20	20	22	19	21	42	32	35	37	29
SEP. 13	24	21	21	22	23	20	21	42	32	35	37	29
SEP. 14	24	23	23	24	23	20	21	42	32	35	37	29
SEP. 15	24	25	25	26	23	20	21	42	32	35	37	29
SEP. 16	24	27	27	28	23	20	21	42	32	35	37	29
SEP. 17	24	29	29	30	24	20	22	42	32	35	37	29
SEP. 18	24	31	31	32	24	20	22	42	32	35	37	29
SEP. 19	25	33	33	34	24	20	22	42	32	35	37	29
SEP. 20	25	34	35	36	24	21	22	42	32	35	37	29
SEP. 21	25	36	37	38	25	21	22	42	32	35	37	29
SEP. 22	25	38	39	39	25	21	22	42	32	35	37	29
SEP. 23	25	40	41	41	25	21	22	42	32	35	37	29
SEP. 24	25	42	42	43	25	21	22	42	32	35	37	29
SEP. 25	26	43	44	45	26	21	22	42	32	35	37	29
SEP. 26	26	45	46	46	26	22	22	42	32	35	37	29
SEP. 27	26	47	47	48	26	22	22	42	32	35	37	29
SEP. 28	26	48	1	2	26	22	22	42	32	35	37	29
SEP. 29	26	2	3	3	26	22	23	42	32	35	37	29
SEP. 30	26	4	4	5	27	22	23	42	32	35	37	29

October

Date & Time	SUN	MOON 1	MOON 2	MOON 3	MERCURY	VENUS	MARS	JUPITER	SATURN	URANUS	NEPTUNE	PLUTO
OCT. 1	26	5	6	6	27	22	23	42	32	35	37	29
OCT. 2	26	7	7	8	27	23	23	42	32	35	37	29
OCT. 3	27	8	9	9	27	23	23	42	32	35	37	29
OCT. 4	27	10	11	11	28	23	23	42	32	35	37	29
OCT. 5	27	12	12	13	28	23	23	42	32	35	37	29
OCT. 6	27	13	14	14	28	23	23	42	32	35	37	29
OCT. 7	27	15	15	16	28	23	23	42	32	35	37	29
OCT. 8	27	16	17	18	28	24	23	42	32	35	37	29
OCT. 9	27	18	19	19	29	24	23	42	32	35	37	29
OCT. 10	27	20	21	21	29	24	24	42	32	35	37	29
OCT. 11	28	22	23	23	29	24	24	42	32	35	37	30
OCT. 12	28	24	24	25	29	24	24	42	32	35	37	30
OCT. 13	28	26	26	27	29	24	24	42	32	35	37	30
OCT. 14	28	28	28	29	30	25	24	42	32	35	37	30
OCT. 15	28	30	30	31	30	25	24	42	32	35	37	30
OCT. 16	28	32	32	33	30	25	24	42	32	35	37	30
OCT. 17	28	34	34	35	30	25	24	42	32	35	37	30
OCT. 18	28	36	36	37	30	25	24	42	33	35	37	30
OCT. 19	29	38	38	39	31	25	24	42	33	35	37	30
OCT. 20	29	39	40	41	31	26	24	42	33	35	37	30
OCT. 21	29	41	42	42	31	26	24	42	33	35	37	30
OCT. 22	29	43	44	44	31	26	25	42	33	35	37	30
OCT. 23	29	45	45	46	31	26	25	42	33	35	37	30
OCT. 24	29	46	47	47	32	26	25	42	33	35	37	30
OCT. 25	29	48	1	1	32	26	25	42	33	35	37	30
OCT. 26	30	2	2	3	32	27	25	42	33	35	37	30
OCT. 27	30	3	4	4	32	27	25	42	33	35	37	30
OCT. 28	30	5	5	6	32	27	25	42	33	35	37	30
OCT. 29	30	6	7	7	33	27	25	42	33	35	37	30
OCT. 30	30	8	9	9	33	27	25	42	33	35	37	30
OCT. 31	30	10	10	11	33	27	25	42	33	35	37	30

MOON 1 ☽ 12:01 A.M. TO 8:00 A.M.   **MOON 2** ☾ 8:01 A.M. TO 4:00 P.M.   **MOON 3** ● 4:01 P.M. TO 12:00 A.M.

Use only one "moon" number. Choose the column closest to your time of birth. If your place of birth is not on Eastern Standard Time, be sure to read "How to Convert to Eastern Standard Time" at the beginning of this section.

Date & Time	SUN	MOON 1	MOON 2	MOON 3	MERCURY	VENUS	MARS	JUPITER	SATURN	URANUS	NEPTUNE	PLUTO
NOV. 1	30	11	12	12	33	28	25	42	33	35	37	30
NOV. 2	30	13	13	14	33	28	25	42	33	35	37	30
NOV. 3	31	14	15	15	33	28	26	42	33	35	37	30
NOV. 4	31	16	17	17	34	28	26	42	33	35	37	30
NOV. 5	31	18	18	19	34	28	26	42	33	35	37	30
NOV. 6	31	19	20	21	34	28	26	42	33	35	37	30
NOV. 7	31	21	22	22	34	28	26	42	33	35	37	30
NOV. 8	31	23	24	24	34	29	26	42	33	35	37	30
NOV. 9	31	25	26	26	34	29	26	42	33	35	37	30
NOV. 10	31	27	28	28	34	29	26	42	33	35	37	30
NOV. 11	31	29	30	30	35	29	26	42	33	35	37	30
NOV. 12	32	31	32	32	35	29	26	42	33	35	37	30
NOV. 13	32	33	34	34	35	30	26	42	33	35	37	30
NOV. 14	32	35	36	36	35	30	26	42	33	35	37	30
NOV. 15	32	37	38	38	35	30	27	42	33	35	37	30
NOV. 16	32	39	39	40	35	30	27	42	33	35	37	30
NOV. 17	32	41	41	42	35	30	27	42	33	35	37	30
NOV. 18	32	43	43	44	35	30	27	42	33	35	37	30
NOV. 19	33	44	45	45	35	31	27	42	33	35	37	30
NOV. 20	33	46	47	47	35	31	27	42	33	35	37	30
NOV. 21	33	48	48	1	35	31	27	42	33	35	37	30
NOV. 22	33	1	2	2	35	31	27	42	33	35	37	30
NOV. 23	33	3	3	4	35	31	27	42	33	35	37	30
NOV. 24	33	4	5	5	35	31	27	42	33	35	37	30
NOV. 25	34	6	7	7	34	32	27	42	33	35	37	30
NOV. 26	34	8	8	9	34	32	27	43	33	35	37	30
NOV. 27	34	9	10	10	34	32	28	43	33	35	37	30
NOV. 28	34	11	11	12	34	32	28	43	33	35	37	30
NOV. 29	34	12	13	13	34	32	28	43	33	35	37	30
NOV. 30	34	14	14	15	34	32	28	43	33	35	37	30

Date & Time	SUN	MOON 1	MOON 2	MOON 3	MERCURY	VENUS	MARS	JUPITER	SATURN	URANUS	NEPTUNE	PLUTO
DEC. 1	34	16	16	17	33	33	28	43	33	35	37	30
DEC. 2	34	17	18	18	33	33	28	43	33	35	37	30
DEC. 3	35	19	20	20	33	33	28	43	33	35	37	30
DEC. 4	35	21	21	22	33	33	28	43	33	35	37	30
DEC. 5	35	22	23	24	33	33	28	43	33	35	37	30
DEC. 6	35	24	25	25	33	33	28	43	33	35	37	30
DEC. 7	35	26	27	27	33	34	28	43	33	35	37	30
DEC. 8	35	28	29	29	33	34	28	43	33	35	37	30
DEC. 9	35	30	31	31	33	34	29	43	33	35	37	30
DEC. 10	35	32	33	33	33	34	29	43	33	35	37	30
DEC. 11	36	34	35	35	33	34	29	43	33	35	37	30
DEC. 12	36	36	37	37	33	34	29	43	33	35	37	30
DEC. 13	36	38	39	39	33	35	29	43	33	35	37	30
DEC. 14	36	40	41	41	33	35	29	43	33	35	37	30
DEC. 15	36	42	42	43	33	35	29	43	33	35	37	30
DEC. 16	36	44	44	45	33	35	29	43	33	35	37	30
DEC. 17	36	45	46	47	33	35	29	43	33	35	37	30
DEC. 18	36	47	48	48	34	35	29	43	33	35	37	30
DEC. 19	37	1	1	2	34	36	29	43	33	35	37	30
DEC. 20	37	2	3	3	34	36	29	43	33	35	37	30
DEC. 21	37	4	5	5	34	36	29	43	33	35	37	30
DEC. 22	37	6	6	7	34	36	30	43	34	35	37	30
DEC. 23	37	7	8	8	34	36	30	43	34	35	37	30
DEC. 24	37	9	9	10	35	36	30	43	34	36	37	30
DEC. 25	37	10	11	11	35	37	30	43	34	36	37	30
DEC. 26	38	12	12	13	35	37	30	43	34	36	37	30
DEC. 27	38	14	14	15	35	37	30	43	34	36	37	30
DEC. 28	38	15	16	16	35	37	30	43	34	36	37	30
DEC. 29	38	17	17	18	35	37	30	43	34	36	37	30
DEC. 30	38	19	19	20	36	37	30	43	34	36	37	30
DEC. 31	38	20	21	21	36	38	30	43	34	36	37	30

MOON 1 ◗ 12:01 A.M. TO 8:00 A.M.   **MOON 2** ◗ 8:01 A.M. TO 4:00 P.M.   **MOON 3** ● 4:01 P.M. TO 12:00 A.M.
Use only one "moon" number. Choose the column closest to your time of birth. If your place of birth is not on Eastern Standard Time, be sure to read "How to Convert to Eastern Standard Time" at the beginning of this section.

1986

January

Date & Time	SUN	MOON 1	MOON 2	MOON 3	MERCURY	VENUS	MARS	JUPITER	SATURN	URANUS	NEPTUNE	PLUTO
JAN. 1	38	22	23	23	36	38	30	43	34	36	37	30
JAN. 2	38	24	24	25	36	38	30	43	34	36	37	30
JAN. 3	39	26	26	27	36	38	31	43	34	36	37	30
JAN. 4	39	27	28	29	37	38	31	43	34	36	37	30
JAN. 5	39	29	30	31	37	38	31	44	34	36	37	30
JAN. 6	39	31	32	32	37	39	31	44	34	36	37	30
JAN. 7	39	33	34	34	37	39	31	44	34	36	37	30
JAN. 8	39	35	36	36	37	39	31	44	34	36	37	30
JAN. 9	39	37	38	38	38	39	31	44	34	36	37	30
JAN. 10	40	39	40	40	38	39	31	44	34	36	37	30
JAN. 11	40	41	42	42	38	39	31	44	34	36	37	30
JAN. 12	40	43	43	44	38	40	31	44	34	36	38	30
JAN. 13	40	45	45	46	38	40	31	44	34	36	38	30
JAN. 14	40	46	47	48	39	40	31	44	34	36	38	30
JAN. 15	40	48	1	1	39	40	32	44	34	36	38	30
JAN. 16	40	2	2	3	39	40	32	44	34	36	38	30
JAN. 17	41	3	4	5	39	40	32	44	34	36	38	30
JAN. 18	41	5	6	6	39	41	32	44	34	36	38	30
JAN. 19	41	7	7	8	40	41	32	44	34	36	38	30
JAN. 20	41	8	9	9	40	41	32	44	34	36	38	30
JAN. 21	41	10	10	11	40	41	32	44	34	36	38	30
JAN. 22	41	11	12	12	40	41	32	44	34	36	38	30
JAN. 23	42	13	14	14	41	41	32	44	34	36	38	30
JAN. 24	42	15	15	16	41	42	32	44	34	36	38	30
JAN. 25	42	16	17	17	41	42	32	44	34	36	38	30
JAN. 26	42	18	19	19	41	42	32	44	34	36	38	30
JAN. 27	42	20	20	21	41	42	32	44	34	36	38	30
JAN. 28	42	22	22	23	42	42	33	44	34	36	38	30
JAN. 29	42	23	24	25	42	42	33	44	34	36	38	30
JAN. 30	42	25	26	26	42	43	33	44	34	36	38	30
JAN. 31	43	27	28	28	42	43	33	44	34	36	38	30

February

Date & Time	SUN	MOON 1	MOON 2	MOON 3	MERCURY	VENUS	MARS	JUPITER	SATURN	URANUS	NEPTUNE	PLUTO
FEB. 1	43	29	29	30	43	43	33	44	34	36	38	30
FEB. 2	43	31	31	32	43	43	33	44	34	36	38	30
FEB. 3	43	33	33	34	43	43	33	44	34	36	38	30
FEB. 4	43	35	35	36	43	43	33	44	34	36	38	30
FEB. 5	43	36	37	38	44	44	33	45	34	36	38	30
FEB. 6	43	38	39	40	44	44	33	45	34	36	38	30
FEB. 7	43	40	41	41	44	44	33	45	34	36	38	30
FEB. 8	44	42	43	43	44	44	33	45	34	36	38	30
FEB. 9	44	44	45	45	44	44	34	45	34	36	38	30
FEB. 10	44	46	46	47	45	44	34	45	34	36	38	30
FEB. 11	44	48	48	1	45	45	34	45	34	36	38	30
FEB. 12	44	1	2	2	45	45	34	45	34	36	38	30
FEB. 13	44	3	3	4	45	45	34	45	34	36	38	30
FEB. 14	44	5	5	6	46	45	34	45	34	36	38	30
FEB. 15	44	6	7	7	46	45	34	45	34	36	38	30
FEB. 16	45	8	8	9	46	45	34	45	34	36	38	30
FEB. 17	45	9	10	10	46	46	34	45	34	36	38	30
FEB. 18	45	11	11	12	47	46	34	45	34	36	38	30
FEB. 19	45	12	13	14	47	46	34	45	34	36	38	30
FEB. 20	45	14	15	15	47	46	34	45	34	36	38	30
FEB. 21	45	16	16	17	47	46	34	45	34	36	38	30
FEB. 22	45	17	18	19	48	46	35	45	34	36	38	30
FEB. 23	46	19	20	20	48	47	35	45	34	36	38	30
FEB. 24	46	21	22	22	48	47	35	45	34	36	38	30
FEB. 25	46	23	23	24	48	47	35	45	34	36	38	30
FEB. 26	46	25	25	26	48	47	35	45	34	36	38	30
FEB. 27	46	27	27	28	48	47	35	45	34	36	38	30
FEB. 28	46	28	29	30	1	47	35	45	34	36	38	30

MOON 1 ◗ 12:01 A.M. TO 8:00 A.M.　**MOON 2** ◖ 8:01 A.M. TO 4:00 P.M.　**MOON 3** ● 4:01 P.M. TO 12:00 A.M.

Use only one "moon" number. Choose the column closest to your time of birth. If your place of birth is not on Eastern Standard Time, be sure to read "How to Convert to Eastern Standard Time" at the beginning of this section.

1986

March / April

Date & Time	SUN	MOON 1	MOON 2	MOON 3	MERCURY	VENUS	MARS	JUPITER	SATURN	URANUS	NEPTUNE	PLUTO
MAR. 1	46	30	31	32	1	48	35	45	34	36	38	30
MAR. 2	46	32	33	33	1	48	35	45	34	36	38	30
MAR. 3	47	34	35	35	1	48	35	45	34	36	38	30
MAR. 4	47	36	37	37	1	48	35	45	34	36	38	30
MAR. 5	47	38	38	39	1	48	35	45	34	36	38	30
MAR. 6	47	40	40	41	1	48	35	45	34	36	38	30
MAR. 7	47	42	42	43	1	1	35	45	34	36	38	30
MAR. 8	47	43	44	45	1	1	36	45	34	36	38	30
MAR. 9	47	45	46	46	1	1	36	45	34	36	38	30
MAR. 10	47	47	47	48	1	1	36	45	34	36	38	30
MAR. 11	48	1	1	2	1	1	36	46	34	36	38	30
MAR. 12	48	2	3	3	1	1	36	46	34	36	38	30
MAR. 13	48	4	4	5	1	2	36	46	34	36	38	30
MAR. 14	48	6	6	7	1	2	36	46	34	36	38	30
MAR. 15	48	7	8	8	1	2	36	46	34	36	38	30
MAR. 16	48	9	9	10	48	2	36	46	34	36	38	30
MAR. 17	48	10	11	11	48	2	36	46	34	36	38	30
MAR. 18	48	12	12	13	48	2	36	46	34	36	38	30
MAR. 19	1	13	14	15	48	3	36	46	34	36	38	30
MAR. 20	1	15	16	16	48	3	36	46	34	36	38	30
MAR. 21	1	17	17	18	48	3	36	46	34	36	38	30
MAR. 22	1	18	19	20	48	3	37	46	34	36	38	30
MAR. 23	1	20	21	21	48	3	37	46	34	36	38	30
MAR. 24	1	22	23	23	48	3	37	46	34	36	38	30
MAR. 25	2	24	25	25	48	4	37	46	34	36	38	30
MAR. 26	2	26	26	27	47	4	37	46	34	36	38	30
MAR. 27	2	28	28	29	47	4	37	46	34	36	38	30
MAR. 28	2	30	30	31	47	4	37	46	34	36	38	30
MAR. 29	2	32	32	33	47	4	37	46	34	36	38	30
MAR. 30	2	34	34	35	47	4	37	46	34	36	38	30
MAR. 31	2	36	36	37	47	5	37	46	34	36	38	30
APR. 1	2	37	38	39	47	5	37	46	34	36	38	30
APR. 2	2	39	40	40	47	5	37	46	34	36	38	30
APR. 3	3	41	42	42	47	5	37	46	34	36	38	30
APR. 4	3	43	43	44	47	5	37	46	34	36	38	30
APR. 5	3	45	45	46	48	5	37	46	34	36	38	30
APR. 6	3	46	47	48	48	6	38	46	34	36	38	30
APR. 7	3	48	1	1	48	6	38	46	34	36	38	30
APR. 8	3	2	2	3	48	6	38	46	34	36	38	30
APR. 9	3	3	4	5	48	6	38	46	34	36	38	30
APR. 10	3	5	6	6	48	6	38	46	34	36	38	30
APR. 11	4	7	7	8	48	6	38	46	34	36	38	30
APR. 12	4	8	9	9	48	7	38	47	34	36	38	30
APR. 13	4	10	10	11	48	7	38	47	34	36	38	30
APR. 14	4	11	12	12	48	7	38	47	34	36	38	30
APR. 15	4	13	14	14	1	7	38	47	34	36	38	30
APR. 16	4	15	15	16	1	7	38	47	34	36	38	30
APR. 17	4	16	17	17	1	7	38	47	34	36	38	30
APR. 18	4	18	18	19	1	8	38	47	34	36	38	30
APR. 19	5	20	20	21	1	8	38	47	34	36	38	30
APR. 20	5	21	22	23	1	8	38	47	34	36	38	30
APR. 21	5	23	24	24	2	8	38	47	34	36	38	30
APR. 22	5	25	26	26	2	8	39	47	34	36	38	30
APR. 23	5	27	28	28	2	8	39	47	34	36	38	30
APR. 24	5	29	30	30	2	9	39	47	34	36	38	30
APR. 25	6	31	32	32	2	9	39	47	34	36	38	30
APR. 26	6	33	34	34	2	9	39	47	34	36	38	30
APR. 27	6	35	36	36	3	9	39	47	34	36	38	30
APR. 28	6	37	37	38	3	9	39	47	34	36	38	30
APR. 29	6	39	39	40	3	9	39	47	34	36	38	30
APR. 30	6	41	41	42	3	10	39	47	34	36	38	30

MOON 1 ◐ 12:01 A.M. TO 8:00 A.M.   **MOON 2** ◑ 8:01 A.M. TO 4:00 P.M.   **MOON 3** ● 4:01 P.M. TO 12:00 A.M.

Use only one "moon" number. Choose the column closest to your time of birth. If your place of birth is not on Eastern Standard Time, be sure to read "How to Convert to Eastern Standard Time" at the beginning of this section.

1986

May

Date & Time	SUN	MOON 1	MOON 2	MOON 3	MERCURY	VENUS	MARS	JUPITER	SATURN	URANUS	NEPTUNE	PLUTO
MAY 1	6	42	43	44	4	10	39	47	34	36	38	30
MAY 2	6	44	45	45	4	10	39	47	34	36	38	30
MAY 3	7	46	47	47	4	10	39	47	34	36	38	30
MAY 4	7	48	48	1	4	10	39	47	34	36	38	30
MAY 5	7	1	2	2	4	10	39	47	34	36	38	30
MAY 6	7	3	4	4	5	10	39	47	34	36	38	30
MAY 7	7	5	5	6	5	11	39	47	34	36	38	30
MAY 8	7	6	7	7	5	11	39	47	34	36	38	30
MAY 9	7	8	9	9	5	11	39	47	34	36	38	30
MAY 10	7	9	10	10	6	11	39	47	34	36	38	30
MAY 11	8	11	11	12	6	11	39	47	34	36	38	30
MAY 12	8	13	13	14	6	11	39	47	34	36	38	30
MAY 13	8	14	15	15	6	12	40	47	34	36	38	30
MAY 14	8	16	16	17	7	12	40	47	34	36	38	30
MAY 15	8	17	18	18	7	12	40	47	34	36	38	30
MAY 16	8	19	20	20	7	12	40	47	34	36	38	30
MAY 17	8	21	21	22	8	12	40	47	34	36	38	30
MAY 18	8	22	23	24	8	12	40	47	34	36	38	30
MAY 19	9	24	25	25	8	13	40	47	34	36	38	30
MAY 20	9	26	27	27	8	13	40	47	34	36	38	30
MAY 21	9	28	29	29	9	13	40	47	34	36	38	30
MAY 22	9	30	31	31	9	13	40	47	34	36	38	30
MAY 23	9	32	33	33	9	13	40	48	34	36	38	30
MAY 24	9	34	35	35	9	14	40	48	34	36	38	30
MAY 25	10	36	37	37	10	14	40	48	34	36	38	30
MAY 26	10	38	39	39	10	14	40	48	34	36	38	30
MAY 27	10	40	41	41	10	14	40	48	34	36	38	30
MAY 28	10	42	43	43	11	14	40	48	34	36	38	30
MAY 29	10	44	44	45	11	14	40	48	34	36	38	30
MAY 30	10	46	46	47	11	14	40	48	34	36	38	30
MAY 31	10	47	48	48	12	15	40	48	34	36	38	30

June

Date & Time	SUN	MOON 1	MOON 2	MOON 3	MERCURY	VENUS	MARS	JUPITER	SATURN	URANUS	NEPTUNE	PLUTO
JUN. 1	10	1	2	2	12	15	40	48	34	36	38	30
JUN. 2	10	3	3	4	12	15	40	48	34	36	38	30
JUN. 3	11	4	5	5	12	15	40	48	34	36	38	30
JUN. 4	11	6	6	7	13	15	40	48	34	36	38	30
JUN. 5	11	7	8	8	13	15	40	48	34	36	38	30
JUN. 6	11	9	10	10	13	15	40	48	34	36	38	30
JUN. 7	11	11	11	12	13	16	40	48	34	36	38	30
JUN. 8	11	12	13	13	14	16	40	48	34	36	38	30
JUN. 9	11	14	14	15	14	16	40	48	34	36	38	30
JUN. 10	11	15	16	16	14	16	40	48	34	36	38	30
JUN. 11	12	17	17	18	14	16	40	48	34	36	38	30
JUN. 12	12	19	19	20	15	16	40	48	34	36	38	30
JUN. 13	12	20	21	21	15	17	40	48	34	36	38	30
JUN. 14	12	22	23	23	15	17	40	48	34	36	38	30
JUN. 15	12	24	24	25	15	17	40	48	34	36	38	30
JUN. 16	12	25	26	27	15	17	40	48	34	36	38	30
JUN. 17	12	27	28	29	16	17	40	48	34	36	38	30
JUN. 18	12	29	30	30	16	17	40	48	34	36	38	30
JUN. 19	13	31	32	32	16	18	40	48	34	36	38	30
JUN. 20	13	33	34	34	16	18	40	48	34	36	38	30
JUN. 21	13	35	36	36	16	18	40	48	34	36	38	30
JUN. 22	13	37	38	38	16	18	40	48	34	36	38	30
JUN. 23	13	39	40	40	17	18	40	48	34	36	38	30
JUN. 24	13	41	42	42	17	18	40	48	34	36	38	30
JUN. 25	14	43	44	44	17	18	40	48	34	36	38	30
JUN. 26	14	45	46	46	17	19	40	48	34	36	38	30
JUN. 27	14	47	47	48	17	19	40	48	34	36	38	30
JUN. 28	14	48	1	2	17	19	40	48	34	36	38	30
JUN. 29	14	2	3	3	17	19	40	48	34	36	38	30
JUN. 30	14	4	4	5	17	19	40	48	34	36	38	30

MOON 1 ◖ 12:01 A.M. TO 8:00 A.M.   **MOON 2** ◑ 8:01 A.M. TO 4:00 P.M.   **MOON 3** ● 4:01 P.M. TO 12:00 A.M.

Use only one "moon" number. Choose the column closest to your time of birth. If your place of birth is not on Eastern Standard Time, be sure to read "How to Convert to Eastern Standard Time" at the beginning of this section.

1986

July

Date & Time	SUN	MOON 1	MOON 2	MOON 3	MERCURY	VENUS	MARS	JUPITER	SATURN	URANUS	NEPTUNE	PLUTO
JUL. 1	14	5	6	7	17	19	40	48	34	36	38	30
JUL. 2	14	7	8	8	18	20	40	48	34	36	38	30
JUL. 3	15	9	9	10	18	20	40	48	34	36	38	30
JUL. 4	15	10	11	11	18	20	40	48	33	36	38	30
JUL. 5	15	12	12	13	18	20	40	48	33	36	38	30
JUL. 6	15	13	14	14	18	20	39	48	33	36	38	30
JUL. 7	15	15	15	16	18	20	39	48	33	36	38	30
JUL. 8	15	17	17	18	18	20	39	48	33	36	38	30
JUL. 9	15	18	19	19	18	21	39	48	33	36	38	30
JUL. 10	15	20	20	21	18	21	39	48	33	36	38	30
JUL. 11	16	22	22	23	18	21	39	48	33	36	38	30
JUL. 12	16	23	24	24	18	21	39	48	33	36	38	30
JUL. 13	16	25	26	26	18	21	39	48	33	36	37	30
JUL. 14	16	27	27	28	18	21	39	48	33	36	37	30
JUL. 15	16	29	29	30	18	21	39	48	33	36	37	30
JUL. 16	16	30	31	32	18	22	39	48	33	36	37	30
JUL. 17	16	32	33	34	18	22	39	48	33	36	37	30
JUL. 18	16	34	35	36	17	22	39	48	33	36	37	30
JUL. 19	17	36	37	38	17	22	39	48	33	35	37	30
JUL. 20	17	38	39	40	17	22	39	48	33	35	37	30
JUL. 21	17	40	41	42	17	22	39	48	33	35	37	30
JUL. 22	17	42	43	44	17	23	39	48	33	35	37	30
JUL. 23	17	44	45	45	17	23	39	48	33	35	37	30
JUL. 24	17	46	47	47	17	23	39	48	33	35	37	30
JUL. 25	17	48	48	1	17	23	39	48	33	35	37	30
JUL. 26	18	2	2	3	17	23	39	48	33	35	37	30
JUL. 27	18	3	4	4	17	23	39	48	33	35	37	30
JUL. 28	18	5	5	6	17	23	39	48	33	35	37	30
JUL. 29	18	7	7	8	17	24	39	48	33	35	37	30
JUL. 30	18	8	9	9	16	24	39	48	33	35	37	30
JUL. 31	18	10	10	11	16	24	39	48	33	35	37	30

August

Date & Time	SUN	MOON 1	MOON 2	MOON 3	MERCURY	VENUS	MARS	JUPITER	SATURN	URANUS	NEPTUNE	PLUTO
AUG. 1	18	11	12	12	16	24	39	48	33	35	37	30
AUG. 2	18	13	13	14	16	24	39	48	33	35	37	30
AUG. 3	19	14	15	16	16	24	39	48	33	35	37	30
AUG. 4	19	16	17	17	16	24	39	48	33	35	37	30
AUG. 5	19	18	18	19	16	25	39	48	33	35	37	30
AUG. 6	19	19	20	21	16	25	39	48	33	35	37	30
AUG. 7	19	21	22	22	17	25	39	48	33	35	37	30
AUG. 8	19	23	23	24	17	25	39	48	33	35	37	30
AUG. 9	19	25	25	26	17	25	38	48	33	35	37	30
AUG. 10	19	26	27	28	17	25	38	48	33	35	37	30
AUG. 11	20	28	29	29	17	25	38	48	33	35	37	30
AUG. 12	20	30	31	31	17	26	38	48	33	35	37	30
AUG. 13	20	32	32	33	17	26	38	48	33	35	37	30
AUG. 14	20	34	34	35	17	26	38	48	33	35	37	30
AUG. 15	20	36	36	37	17	26	38	48	33	35	37	30
AUG. 16	20	38	38	39	18	26	39	48	33	35	37	30
AUG. 17	20	40	40	41	18	26	39	48	33	35	37	30
AUG. 18	20	41	42	43	18	26	39	48	33	35	37	30
AUG. 19	21	43	44	45	18	27	39	48	33	35	37	30
AUG. 20	21	45	46	47	18	27	39	48	33	35	37	30
AUG. 21	21	47	48	48	19	27	39	48	33	35	37	30
AUG. 22	21	1	2	2	19	27	39	48	33	35	37	30
AUG. 23	21	3	3	4	19	27	39	48	33	35	37	30
AUG. 24	21	4	5	5	19	27	39	48	33	35	37	30
AUG. 25	21	6	7	7	20	27	39	48	33	35	37	30
AUG. 26	22	8	8	9	20	27	39	48	33	35	37	30
AUG. 27	22	9	10	10	20	28	39	48	33	35	37	30
AUG. 28	22	11	11	12	20	28	39	48	33	35	37	30
AUG. 29	22	12	13	13	21	28	39	48	33	35	37	30
AUG. 30	22	14	15	15	21	28	39	48	33	35	37	30
AUG. 31	22	16	16	17	21	28	39	48	33	35	37	30

MOON 1 ☽ 12:01 A.M. TO 8:00 A.M.   **MOON 2** ☽ 8:01 A.M. TO 4:00 P.M.   **MOON 3** ● 4:01 P.M. TO 12:00 A.M.

Use only one "moon" number. Choose the column closest to your time of birth. If your place of birth is not on Eastern Standard Time, be sure to read "How to Convert to Eastern Standard Time" at the beginning of this section.

1986

September

Date & Time	SUN ☉	MOON 1 ☽	MOON 2 ☽	MOON 3 ●	MERCURY	VENUS	MARS	JUPITER	SATURN	URANUS	NEPTUNE	PLUTO
SEP. 1	22	17	18	18	22	28	39	48	33	35	37	30
SEP. 2	22	19	19	20	22	28	39	48	33	35	37	30
SEP. 3	23	21	21	22	22	28	39	47	33	35	37	30
SEP. 4	23	22	23	24	22	29	39	47	33	35	37	30
SEP. 5	23	24	25	25	23	29	39	47	33	35	37	30
SEP. 6	23	26	27	27	23	29	39	47	33	35	37	30
SEP. 7	23	28	28	29	23	29	39	47	33	35	37	30
SEP. 8	23	30	30	31	23	29	39	47	33	35	37	30
SEP. 9	23	31	32	33	24	29	39	47	33	35	37	30
SEP. 10	23	33	34	35	24	29	39	47	33	35	37	30
SEP. 11	24	35	36	36	24	29	39	47	34	35	37	30
SEP. 12	24	37	38	38	24	30	39	47	34	35	37	30
SEP. 13	24	39	40	40	25	30	39	47	34	35	37	30
SEP. 14	24	41	42	42	25	30	39	47	34	35	37	30
SEP. 15	24	43	43	44	25	30	39	47	34	35	37	30
SEP. 16	24	45	45	46	25	30	40	47	34	35	37	30
SEP. 17	24	46	47	48	25	30	40	47	34	35	37	30
SEP. 18	24	48	1	1	26	30	40	47	34	35	37	30
SEP. 19	25	2	3	3	26	30	40	47	34	35	37	30
SEP. 20	25	4	4	5	26	30	40	47	34	35	37	30
SEP. 21	25	5	6	7	26	30	40	47	34	35	37	30
SEP. 22	25	7	8	8	26	31	40	47	34	35	37	30
SEP. 23	25	9	9	10	27	31	40	47	34	35	37	30
SEP. 24	25	10	11	11	27	31	40	47	34	35	37	30
SEP. 25	26	12	12	13	27	31	40	47	34	35	37	30
SEP. 26	26	13	14	15	27	31	40	47	34	35	37	30
SEP. 27	26	15	16	16	28	31	40	47	34	35	37	30
SEP. 28	26	17	17	18	28	31	40	47	34	35	37	30
SEP. 29	26	18	19	19	28	31	40	47	34	35	37	30
SEP. 30	26	20	21	21	28	31	40	47	34	35	37	30

October

Date & Time	SUN ☉	MOON 1 ☽	MOON 2 ☽	MOON 3 ●	MERCURY	VENUS	MARS	JUPITER	SATURN	URANUS	NEPTUNE	PLUTO
OCT. 1	26	22	22	23	28	31	40	47	34	35	37	30
OCT. 2	26	23	24	25	29	31	40	47	34	35	37	30
OCT. 3	27	25	26	26	29	31	41	47	34	35	37	30
OCT. 4	27	27	28	28	29	31	41	47	34	35	37	30
OCT. 5	27	29	30	30	29	31	41	47	34	35	37	30
OCT. 6	27	31	32	32	29	31	41	47	34	36	37	30
OCT. 7	27	33	33	34	30	32	41	47	34	36	37	30
OCT. 8	27	35	35	36	30	32	41	47	34	36	37	30
OCT. 9	27	37	37	38	30	32	41	47	34	36	37	30
OCT. 10	27	39	39	40	30	32	41	47	34	36	37	30
OCT. 11	28	40	41	42	30	32	41	47	34	36	37	30
OCT. 12	28	42	43	44	30	32	41	47	34	36	37	30
OCT. 13	28	44	45	45	31	32	41	47	34	36	37	30
OCT. 14	28	46	47	47	31	32	41	47	34	36	37	30
OCT. 15	28	48	48	1	31	32	41	47	34	36	37	30
OCT. 16	28	1	2	3	31	32	42	47	34	36	37	30
OCT. 17	28	3	4	4	31	32	42	47	34	36	37	30
OCT. 18	28	5	5	6	31	32	42	47	34	36	37	30
OCT. 19	29	7	7	8	32	32	42	47	34	36	37	30
OCT. 20	29	8	9	9	32	32	42	47	34	36	37	30
OCT. 21	29	10	10	11	32	32	42	47	34	36	37	30
OCT. 22	29	11	12	12	32	32	42	47	34	36	37	30
OCT. 23	29	13	13	14	32	32	42	47	34	36	37	30
OCT. 24	29	15	15	16	32	31	42	47	34	36	37	30
OCT. 25	29	16	17	17	32	31	42	47	34	36	37	30
OCT. 26	30	18	18	19	32	31	42	47	34	36	37	30
OCT. 27	30	19	20	20	33	31	42	47	34	36	37	30
OCT. 28	30	21	22	22	33	31	42	47	34	36	37	30
OCT. 29	30	23	23	24	33	31	43	47	34	36	37	30
OCT. 30	30	25	25	26	33	31	43	47	34	36	37	30
OCT. 31	30	26	27	28	33	31	43	47	34	36	37	30

MOON 1 ☽ 12:01 A.M. TO 8:00 A.M.   **MOON 2** ☽ 8:01 A.M. TO 4:00 P.M.   **MOON 3** ● 4:01 P.M. TO 12:00 A.M.

Use only one "moon" number. Choose the column closest to your time of birth. If your place of birth is not on Eastern Standard Time, be sure to read "How to Convert to Eastern Standard Time" at the beginning of this section.

1986

November

Date & Time	SUN	MOON 1	MOON 2	MOON 3	MERCURY	VENUS	MARS	JUPITER	SATURN	URANUS	NEPTUNE	PLUTO
NOV. 1	30	28	29	30	33	31	43	47	34	36	37	30
NOV. 2	30	30	31	31	33	31	43	47	34	36	37	30
NOV. 3	31	32	33	33	33	31	43	47	34	36	37	30
NOV. 4	31	34	35	35	33	31	43	47	34	36	37	30
NOV. 5	31	36	37	37	33	31	43	47	34	36	37	30
NOV. 6	31	38	39	39	33	31	43	47	34	36	37	30
NOV. 7	31	40	41	41	33	31	43	47	34	36	37	30
NOV. 8	31	42	42	43	32	30	43	47	34	36	37	30
NOV. 9	31	44	44	45	32	30	43	47	34	36	37	30
NOV. 10	31	46	46	47	32	30	44	47	34	36	37	30
NOV. 11	31	47	48	48	32	30	44	47	34	36	37	30
NOV. 12	32	1	2	2	32	30	44	47	34	36	37	30
NOV. 13	32	3	3	4	32	30	44	47	34	36	37	30
NOV. 14	32	4	5	5	32	30	44	47	34	36	37	30
NOV. 15	32	6	7	7	31	30	44	47	34	36	38	30
NOV. 16	32	8	8	9	31	30	44	47	34	36	38	30
NOV. 17	32	9	10	10	31	30	44	47	34	36	38	30
NOV. 18	32	11	11	12	31	30	44	47	34	36	38	30
NOV. 19	33	12	13	14	31	30	44	47	34	36	38	30
NOV. 20	33	14	15	15	31	30	44	47	34	36	38	30
NOV. 21	33	16	16	17	31	30	45	47	34	36	38	30
NOV. 22	33	17	18	18	31	30	45	47	34	36	38	30
NOV. 23	33	19	19	20	31	30	45	47	34	36	38	30
NOV. 24	33	20	21	22	31	30	45	47	34	36	38	30
NOV. 25	34	22	23	23	31	30	45	47	34	36	38	30
NOV. 26	34	24	24	25	31	30	45	47	34	36	38	30
NOV. 27	34	26	26	27	31	30	45	47	34	36	38	30
NOV. 28	34	27	28	29	31	30	45	47	34	36	38	30
NOV. 29	34	29	30	31	31	30	45	47	35	36	38	30
NOV. 30	34	31	32	33	31	30	45	47	35	36	38	30

December

Date & Time	SUN	MOON 1	MOON 2	MOON 3	MERCURY	VENUS	MARS	JUPITER	SATURN	URANUS	NEPTUNE	PLUTO
DEC. 1	34	33	34	35	31	30	45	47	35	36	38	30
DEC. 2	34	35	36	37	32	30	46	47	35	36	38	30
DEC. 3	35	37	38	39	32	30	46	47	35	36	38	30
DEC. 4	35	39	40	41	32	30	46	47	35	36	38	30
DEC. 5	35	41	42	43	32	30	46	47	35	36	38	30
DEC. 6	35	43	44	44	32	30	46	47	35	36	38	30
DEC. 7	35	45	46	46	32	30	46	47	35	36	38	30
DEC. 8	35	47	47	48	33	30	46	47	35	36	38	30
DEC. 9	35	1	1	2	33	30	46	47	35	36	38	30
DEC. 10	35	2	3	3	33	30	46	47	35	36	38	30
DEC. 11	36	4	5	5	33	30	46	47	35	36	38	30
DEC. 12	36	6	6	7	33	30	46	47	35	36	38	30
DEC. 13	36	7	8	8	34	30	47	47	35	36	38	30
DEC. 14	36	9	9	10	34	30	47	47	35	36	38	30
DEC. 15	36	10	11	12	34	30	47	47	35	36	38	30
DEC. 16	36	12	13	13	34	31	47	47	35	36	38	30
DEC. 17	36	14	14	15	34	31	47	47	35	36	38	30
DEC. 18	36	15	16	16	35	31	47	47	35	36	38	30
DEC. 19	37	17	17	18	35	31	47	47	35	36	38	30
DEC. 20	37	18	19	19	35	31	47	47	35	36	38	30
DEC. 21	37	20	21	21	35	31	47	47	35	36	38	30
DEC. 22	37	22	22	23	35	31	47	47	35	36	38	30
DEC. 23	37	23	24	24	36	31	47	47	35	36	38	30
DEC. 24	37	25	26	26	36	31	48	47	35	36	38	30
DEC. 25	37	27	27	28	36	31	48	47	35	36	38	30
DEC. 26	38	28	29	30	36	32	48	47	35	36	38	30
DEC. 27	38	30	31	32	36	32	48	47	35	36	38	30
DEC. 28	38	32	33	34	37	32	48	47	35	36	38	30
DEC. 29	38	34	35	36	37	32	48	47	35	36	38	30
DEC. 30	38	36	37	38	37	32	48	47	35	36	38	30
DEC. 31	38	38	39	40	37	32	48	47	35	36	38	30

MOON 1 ☽ 12:01 A.M. TO 8:00 A.M.   **MOON 2** ☽ 8:01 A.M. TO 4:00 P.M.   **MOON 3** ● 4:01 P.M. TO 12:00 A.M.

Use only one "moon" number. Choose the column closest to your time of birth. If your place of birth is not on Eastern Standard Time, be sure to read "How to Convert to Eastern Standard Time" at the beginning of this section.

1987

January

Date & Time	SUN	MOON 1	MOON 2	MOON 3	MERCURY	VENUS	MARS	JUPITER	SATURN	URANUS	NEPTUNE	PLUTO
JAN. 1	38	40	41	42	37	32	48	47	35	36	38	30
JAN. 2	38	42	43	44	38	32	48	47	35	36	38	30
JAN. 3	39	44	45	46	38	32	48	47	35	36	38	30
JAN. 4	39	46	47	47	38	33	1	47	35	36	38	30
JAN. 5	39	48	1	1	38	33	1	47	35	36	38	30
JAN. 6	39	2	2	3	38	33	1	47	35	36	38	30
JAN. 7	39	4	4	5	39	33	1	47	35	36	38	30
JAN. 8	39	5	6	6	39	33	1	47	35	36	38	30
JAN. 9	39	7	7	8	39	33	1	47	35	36	38	30
JAN. 10	40	8	9	10	39	33	1	48	35	36	38	30
JAN. 11	40	10	11	11	40	33	1	48	35	36	38	30
JAN. 12	40	12	12	13	40	34	1	48	35	36	38	30
JAN. 13	40	13	14	14	40	34	1	48	35	36	38	30
JAN. 14	40	15	15	16	40	34	1	48	35	36	38	30
JAN. 15	40	16	17	17	40	34	2	48	35	36	38	30
JAN. 16	40	18	19	19	41	34	2	48	35	36	38	30
JAN. 17	41	20	20	21	41	34	2	48	35	36	38	30
JAN. 18	41	21	22	22	41	34	2	48	35	36	38	30
JAN. 19	41	23	23	24	41	35	2	48	35	36	38	30
JAN. 20	41	25	25	26	42	35	2	48	35	36	38	30
JAN. 21	41	26	27	27	42	35	2	48	35	36	38	30
JAN. 22	41	28	29	29	42	35	2	48	35	36	38	30
JAN. 23	42	30	30	31	42	35	2	48	35	36	38	30
JAN. 24	42	32	32	33	42	35	2	48	35	36	38	30
JAN. 25	42	33	34	35	43	35	3	48	35	36	38	30
JAN. 26	42	35	36	37	43	36	3	48	35	36	38	30
JAN. 27	42	37	38	39	43	36	3	48	35	36	38	30
JAN. 28	42	39	40	41	43	36	3	48	35	36	38	30
JAN. 29	42	41	42	43	44	36	3	48	35	36	38	30
JAN. 30	42	43	44	45	44	36	3	48	35	36	38	30
JAN. 31	43	45	46	47	44	36	3	48	35	36	38	30

February

Date & Time	SUN	MOON 1	MOON 2	MOON 3	MERCURY	VENUS	MARS	JUPITER	SATURN	URANUS	NEPTUNE	PLUTO
FEB. 1	43	47	48	1	44	36	3	48	35	36	38	30
FEB. 2	43	1	2	2	45	37	3	48	35	36	38	30
FEB. 3	43	3	4	4	45	37	3	48	35	36	38	30
FEB. 4	43	5	5	6	45	37	3	48	35	36	38	30
FEB. 5	43	6	7	7	45	37	4	48	35	36	38	30
FEB. 6	43	8	9	9	45	37	4	48	35	36	38	30
FEB. 7	43	10	10	11	46	37	4	48	35	36	38	30
FEB. 8	44	11	12	12	46	37	4	48	36	36	38	30
FEB. 9	44	13	13	14	46	38	4	48	36	36	38	30
FEB. 10	44	14	15	15	46	38	4	48	36	36	38	30
FEB. 11	44	16	16	17	46	38	4	48	36	36	38	30
FEB. 12	44	18	18	19	46	38	4	48	36	36	38	30
FEB. 13	44	19	20	20	47	38	4	48	36	36	38	30
FEB. 14	44	21	21	22	47	38	4	48	36	36	38	30
FEB. 15	44	22	23	24	47	38	4	48	36	36	38	30
FEB. 16	45	24	25	25	47	39	5	1	36	36	38	30
FEB. 17	45	26	26	27	47	39	5	1	36	36	38	30
FEB. 18	45	28	28	29	47	39	5	1	36	36	38	30
FEB. 19	45	29	30	31	47	39	5	1	36	36	38	30
FEB. 20	45	31	32	32	47	39	5	1	36	36	38	30
FEB. 21	45	33	34	34	47	39	5	1	36	36	38	30
FEB. 22	45	35	35	36	47	40	5	1	36	36	38	30
FEB. 23	46	37	37	38	47	40	5	1	36	36	38	30
FEB. 24	46	39	39	40	47	40	5	1	36	36	38	30
FEB. 25	46	41	41	42	46	40	5	1	36	36	38	30
FEB. 26	46	43	43	44	46	40	5	1	36	36	38	30
FEB. 27	46	45	45	46	46	40	6	1	36	36	38	30
FEB. 28	46	46	47	48	46	40	6	1	36	36	38	30

MOON 1 ◐ 12:01 A.M. TO 8:00 A.M.   **MOON 2** ◑ 8:01 A.M. TO 4:00 P.M.   **MOON 3** ● 4:01 P.M. TO 12:00 A.M.

Use only one "moon" number. Choose the column closest to your time of birth. If your place of birth is not on Eastern Standard Time, be sure to read "How to Convert to Eastern Standard Time" at the beginning of this section.

1987

March

Date & Time	SUN	MOON 1	MOON 2	MOON 3	MERCURY	VENUS	MARS	JUPITER	SATURN	URANUS	NEPTUNE	PLUTO
MAR. 1	46	48	1	2	46	41	6	1	36	36	38	30
MAR. 2	46	2	3	3	46	41	6	1	36	36	38	30
MAR. 3	47	4	5	5	46	41	6	1	36	36	38	30
MAR. 4	47	6	6	7	46	41	6	1	36	36	38	30
MAR. 5	47	7	8	9	45	41	6	1	36	36	38	30
MAR. 6	47	9	10	10	45	41	6	1	36	36	38	30
MAR. 7	47	11	11	12	45	42	6	1	36	36	38	30
MAR. 8	47	12	13	13	45	42	6	1	36	36	38	30
MAR. 9	47	14	14	15	45	42	6	1	36	36	38	30
MAR. 10	47	15	16	17	45	42	7	1	36	37	38	30
MAR. 11	48	17	18	18	45	42	7	1	36	37	38	30
MAR. 12	48	19	19	20	45	42	7	1	36	37	38	30
MAR. 13	48	20	21	21	45	43	7	1	36	37	38	30
MAR. 14	48	22	23	23	45	43	7	1	36	37	38	30
MAR. 15	48	24	24	25	45	43	7	1	36	37	38	30
MAR. 16	48	25	26	26	45	43	7	1	36	37	38	30
MAR. 17	48	27	28	28	45	43	7	1	36	37	38	30
MAR. 18	48	29	29	30	45	43	7	1	36	37	38	30
MAR. 19	1	31	31	32	45	43	7	1	36	37	38	30
MAR. 20	1	33	33	34	45	44	7	2	36	37	38	30
MAR. 21	1	34	35	36	45	44	8	2	36	37	38	30
MAR. 22	1	36	37	38	45	44	8	2	36	37	38	30
MAR. 23	1	38	39	39	46	44	8	2	36	37	38	30
MAR. 24	1	40	41	41	46	44	8	2	36	37	38	30
MAR. 25	2	42	43	43	46	44	8	2	36	37	38	30
MAR. 26	2	44	45	45	46	45	8	2	36	37	38	30
MAR. 27	2	46	46	47	46	45	8	2	36	37	38	30
MAR. 28	2	48	48	1	46	45	8	2	36	37	38	30
MAR. 29	2	1	2	3	46	45	8	2	36	37	38	30
MAR. 30	2	3	4	4	46	45	8	2	36	37	38	30
MAR. 31	2	5	6	6	47	45	8	2	36	37	38	30

April

Date & Time	SUN	MOON 1	MOON 2	MOON 3	MERCURY	VENUS	MARS	JUPITER	SATURN	URANUS	NEPTUNE	PLUTO
APR. 1	2	7	7	8	47	46	9	2	36	37	38	30
APR. 2	2	8	9	10	47	46	9	2	36	37	38	30
APR. 3	3	10	11	11	47	46	9	2	36	37	38	30
APR. 4	3	12	12	13	47	46	9	2	36	37	38	30
APR. 5	3	13	14	14	47	46	9	2	36	37	38	30
APR. 6	3	15	15	16	48	46	9	2	36	37	38	30
APR. 7	3	16	17	18	48	46	9	2	36	37	38	30
APR. 8	3	18	19	19	48	47	9	2	36	37	38	30
APR. 9	3	20	20	21	48	47	9	2	36	37	38	30
APR. 10	3	21	22	22	48	47	9	2	36	37	38	30
APR. 11	4	23	24	24	1	47	9	2	36	37	38	30
APR. 12	4	25	25	26	1	47	10	2	36	37	38	30
APR. 13	4	27	27	28	1	47	10	2	36	37	38	30
APR. 14	4	28	29	30	1	48	10	2	36	37	38	30
APR. 15	4	30	31	31	1	48	10	2	36	37	38	30
APR. 16	4	32	33	33	2	48	10	2	36	37	38	30
APR. 17	4	34	35	35	2	48	10	2	36	37	38	30
APR. 18	4	36	36	37	2	48	10	2	36	37	38	30
APR. 19	5	38	38	39	2	48	10	2	36	37	38	30
APR. 20	5	40	40	41	3	1	10	3	36	37	38	30
APR. 21	5	42	42	43	3	1	10	3	36	37	38	30
APR. 22	5	43	44	45	3	1	10	3	36	37	38	30
APR. 23	5	45	46	46	3	1	11	3	36	37	38	30
APR. 24	5	47	48	48	4	1	11	3	36	37	38	30
APR. 25	6	1	2	2	4	1	11	3	36	36	38	30
APR. 26	6	3	3	4	4	2	11	3	36	36	38	30
APR. 27	6	4	5	6	4	2	11	3	36	36	38	30
APR. 28	6	6	7	7	5	2	11	3	36	36	38	30
APR. 29	6	8	8	9	5	2	11	3	36	36	38	30
APR. 30	6	10	10	11	5	2	11	3	36	36	38	30

MOON 1 ◐ 12:01 A.M. TO 8:00 A.M.   **MOON 2** ◑ 8:01 A.M. TO 4:00 P.M.   **MOON 3** ● 4:01 P.M. TO 12:00 A.M.

Use only one "moon" number. Choose the column closest to your time of birth. If your place of birth is not on Eastern Standard Time, be sure to read "How to Convert to Eastern Standard Time" at the beginning of this section.

1987

May

June

Date & Time	SUN	MOON 1	MOON 2	MOON 3	MERCURY	VENUS	MARS	JUPITER	SATURN	URANUS	NEPTUNE	PLUTO
JAN. 1	38	40	41	42	37	32	48	47	35	36	38	30
JAN. 2	38	42	43	44	38	32	48	47	35	36	38	30
JAN. 3	39	44	45	46	38	32	48	47	35	36	38	30
JAN. 4	39	46	47	47	38	33	1	47	35	36	38	30
JAN. 5	39	48	1	1	38	33	1	47	35	36	38	30
JAN. 6	39	2	2	3	38	33	1	47	35	36	38	30
JAN. 7	39	4	4	5	39	33	1	47	35	36	38	30
JAN. 8	39	5	6	6	39	33	1	47	35	36	38	30
JAN. 9	39	7	7	8	39	33	1	47	35	36	38	30
JAN. 10	40	8	9	10	39	33	1	48	35	36	38	30
JAN. 11	40	10	11	11	40	33	1	48	35	36	38	30
JAN. 12	40	12	12	13	40	34	1	48	35	36	38	30
JAN. 13	40	13	14	14	40	34	1	48	35	36	38	30
JAN. 14	40	15	15	16	40	34	1	48	35	36	38	30
JAN. 15	40	16	17	17	40	34	2	48	35	36	38	30
JAN. 16	40	18	19	19	41	34	2	48	35	36	38	30
JAN. 17	41	20	20	21	41	34	2	48	35	36	38	30
JAN. 18	41	21	22	22	41	34	2	48	35	36	38	30
JAN. 19	41	23	23	24	41	35	2	48	35	36	38	30
JAN. 20	41	25	25	26	42	35	2	48	35	36	38	30
JAN. 21	41	26	27	27	42	35	2	48	35	36	38	30
JAN. 22	41	28	29	29	42	35	2	48	36	36	38	30
JAN. 23	42	30	30	31	42	35	2	48	35	36	38	30
JAN. 24	42	32	32	33	42	35	2	48	35	36	38	30
JAN. 25	42	33	34	35	43	35	3	48	35	36	38	30
JAN. 26	42	35	36	37	43	36	3	48	35	36	38	30
JAN. 27	42	37	38	39	43	36	3	48	35	36	38	30
JAN. 28	42	39	40	41	43	36	3	48	35	36	38	30
JAN. 29	42	41	42	43	44	36	3	48	35	36	38	30
JAN. 30	42	43	44	45	44	36	3	48	35	36	38	30
JAN. 31	43	45	46	47	44	36	3	48	35	36	38	30
FEB. 1	43	47	48	1	44	36	3	48	35	36	38	30
FEB. 2	43	1	2	2	45	37	3	48	35	36	38	30
FEB. 3	43	3	4	4	45	37	3	48	35	36	38	30
FEB. 4	43	5	5	6	45	37	3	48	35	36	38	30
FEB. 5	43	6	7	7	45	37	4	48	35	36	38	30
FEB. 6	43	8	9	9	45	37	4	48	35	36	38	30
FEB. 7	43	10	10	11	46	37	4	48	35	36	38	30
FEB. 8	44	11	12	12	46	37	4	48	36	36	38	30
FEB. 9	44	13	13	14	46	38	4	48	36	36	38	30
FEB. 10	44	14	15	15	46	38	4	48	36	36	38	30
FEB. 11	44	16	16	17	46	38	4	48	36	36	38	30
FEB. 12	44	18	18	19	46	38	4	48	36	36	38	30
FEB. 13	44	19	20	20	47	38	4	48	36	36	38	30
FEB. 14	44	21	21	22	47	38	4	48	36	36	38	30
FEB. 15	44	22	23	24	47	38	4	48	36	36	38	30
FEB. 16	45	24	25	25	47	39	5	1	36	36	38	30
FEB. 17	45	26	26	27	47	39	5	1	36	36	38	30
FEB. 18	45	28	28	29	47	39	5	1	36	36	38	30
FEB. 19	45	29	30	31	47	39	5	1	36	36	38	30
FEB. 20	45	31	32	32	47	39	5	1	36	36	38	30
FEB. 21	45	33	34	34	47	39	5	1	36	36	38	30
FEB. 22	45	35	35	36	47	40	5	1	36	36	38	30
FEB. 23	46	37	37	38	47	40	5	1	36	36	38	30
FEB. 24	46	39	39	40	47	40	5	1	36	36	38	30
FEB. 25	46	41	41	42	46	40	5	1	36	36	38	30
FEB. 26	46	43	43	44	46	40	5	1	36	36	38	30
FEB. 27	46	45	45	46	46	40	6	1	36	36	38	30
FEB. 28	46	46	47	48	46	40	6	1	36	36	38	30

MOON 1 ◗ 12:01 A.M. TO 8:00 A.M.   **MOON 2** ◑ 8:01 A.M. TO 4:00 P.M.   **MOON 3** ● 4:01 P.M. TO 12:00 A.M.
Use only one "moon" number. Choose the column closest to your time of birth. If your place of birth is not on Eastern Standard Time, be sure to read "How to Convert to Eastern Standard Time" at the beginning of this section.

1987

July

August

Date & Time	SUN	MOON 1	MOON 2	MOON 3	MERCURY	VENUS	MARS	JUPITER	SATURN	URANUS	NEPTUNE	PLUTO
JUL. 1	14	21	22	22	15	12	16	4	35	36	38	30
JUL. 2	14	23	24	24	15	12	17	4	35	36	38	30
JUL. 3	15	25	25	26	15	13	17	4	35	36	38	30
JUL. 4	15	26	27	27	15	13	17	4	35	36	38	30
JUL. 5	15	28	29	29	14	13	17	5	35	36	38	30
JUL. 6	15	30	30	31	14	13	17	5	35	36	38	30
JUL. 7	15	32	32	33	14	13	17	5	35	36	38	30
JUL. 8	15	34	34	35	14	13	17	5	35	36	38	30
JUL. 9	15	35	36	37	14	14	17	5	35	36	38	30
JUL. 10	15	37	38	39	14	14	17	5	35	36	38	30
JUL. 11	16	40	40	41	14	14	17	5	35	36	38	30
JUL. 12	16	42	42	43	14	14	17	5	35	36	38	30
JUL. 13	16	44	44	45	14	14	18	5	35	36	38	30
JUL. 14	16	46	46	47	14	14	18	5	35	36	38	30
JUL. 15	16	47	48	1	14	14	18	5	35	36	38	30
JUL. 16	16	1	2	3	14	15	18	5	35	36	38	30
JUL. 17	16	3	4	4	14	15	18	5	35	36	38	30
JUL. 18	16	5	5	6	14	15	18	5	35	36	38	30
JUL. 19	17	7	7	8	14	15	18	5	35	36	38	30
JUL. 20	17	8	9	9	14	15	18	5	35	36	38	30
JUL. 21	17	10	10	11	14	15	18	5	35	36	38	30
JUL. 22	17	11	12	13	14	15	18	5	35	36	38	30
JUL. 23	17	13	14	14	14	16	18	5	35	36	38	30
JUL. 24	17	15	15	16	14	16	18	5	35	36	38	30
JUL. 25	17	16	17	17	15	16	19	5	35	36	38	30
JUL. 26	18	18	18	19	15	16	19	5	35	36	38	30
JUL. 27	18	19	20	20	15	16	19	5	35	36	38	30
JUL. 28	18	21	22	22	15	17	19	5	35	36	38	30
JUL. 29	18	23	23	24	15	17	19	5	35	36	38	30
JUL. 30	18	24	25	25	15	17	19	5	35	36	38	30
JUL. 31	18	26	26	27	15	17	19	5	35	36	38	30

Date & Time	SUN	MOON 1	MOON 2	MOON 3	MERCURY	VENUS	MARS	JUPITER	SATURN	URANUS	NEPTUNE	PLUTO
AUG. 1	18	28	28	29	16	17	19	5	35	36	38	30
AUG. 2	18	29	30	30	16	17	19	5	35	36	38	30
AUG. 3	19	31	32	32	16	18	19	5	35	36	38	30
AUG. 4	19	33	33	34	16	18	19	5	35	36	38	30
AUG. 5	19	35	35	36	17	18	19	5	35	36	38	30
AUG. 6	19	37	37	38	17	18	20	5	35	36	38	30
AUG. 7	19	39	39	40	17	18	20	5	35	36	38	30
AUG. 8	19	41	41	42	17	18	20	5	35	36	38	30
AUG. 9	19	43	43	44	18	19	20	5	35	36	38	30
AUG. 10	19	45	45	46	18	19	20	5	35	36	38	30
AUG. 11	20	47	47	48	18	19	20	5	35	36	38	30
AUG. 12	20	1	1	2	18	19	20	5	35	36	38	30
AUG. 13	20	3	3	4	19	19	20	5	35	36	38	30
AUG. 14	20	4	5	6	19	19	20	5	35	36	38	30
AUG. 15	20	6	7	7	19	20	20	5	35	36	38	30
AUG. 16	20	8	8	9	19	20	20	5	35	36	38	30
AUG. 17	20	9	10	11	20	20	20	5	35	36	38	30
AUG. 18	20	11	12	12	20	20	21	5	35	36	38	30
AUG. 19	21	13	13	14	20	20	21	5	35	36	38	30
AUG. 20	21	14	15	15	21	20	21	5	35	36	38	30
AUG. 21	21	16	16	17	21	21	21	5	35	36	38	30
AUG. 22	21	17	18	18	21	21	21	5	35	36	38	30
AUG. 23	21	19	20	20	21	21	21	5	35	36	38	30
AUG. 24	21	21	21	22	22	21	21	5	35	36	38	30
AUG. 25	21	22	23	23	22	21	21	5	35	36	38	30
AUG. 26	22	24	24	25	22	21	21	5	35	36	38	30
AUG. 27	22	25	26	27	22	22	21	5	35	36	38	30
AUG. 28	22	27	28	28	23	22	21	5	35	36	38	30
AUG. 29	22	29	29	30	23	22	22	5	35	36	38	30
AUG. 30	22	31	31	32	23	22	22	5	35	36	38	30
AUG. 31	22	32	33	34	23	22	22	5	35	36	38	30

MOON 1 ☽ 12:01 A.M. TO 8:00 A.M.   **MOON 2** ☽ 8:01 A.M. TO 4:00 P.M.   **MOON 3** ● 4:01 P.M. TO 12:00 A.M.

Use only one "moon" number. Choose the column closest to your time of birth. If your place of birth is not on Eastern Standard Time, be sure to read "How to Convert to Eastern Standard Time" at the beginning of this section.

Date & Time	SUN	MOON 1	MOON 2	MOON 3	MERCURY	VENUS	MARS	JUPITER	SATURN	URANUS	NEPTUNE	PLUTO
SEP. 1	22	34	35	35	24	22	22	5	35	36	38	30
SEP. 2	22	36	37	37	24	23	22	5	35	36	38	30
SEP. 3	23	38	39	39	24	23	22	5	35	36	38	30
SEP. 4	23	40	41	41	24	23	22	5	35	36	38	30
SEP. 5	23	42	43	43	24	23	22	5	35	36	38	30
SEP. 6	23	44	45	45	25	23	22	5	35	36	38	30
SEP. 7	23	46	46	47	25	23	22	5	35	36	38	30
SEP. 8	23	48	48	1	25	24	22	5	35	36	38	30
SEP. 9	23	2	2	3	25	24	22	5	35	36	38	30
SEP. 10	23	4	4	5	26	24	23	5	35	36	38	30
SEP. 11	24	5	6	7	26	24	23	5	35	36	38	30
SEP. 12	24	7	8	8	26	24	23	5	35	36	38	30
SEP. 13	24	9	9	10	26	24	23	5	35	36	38	30
SEP. 14	24	11	11	12	26	25	23	5	35	36	38	30
SEP. 15	24	12	13	13	27	25	23	5	35	36	38	30
SEP. 16	24	14	14	15	27	25	23	5	35	36	38	30
SEP. 17	24	15	16	16	27	25	23	5	35	36	38	30
SEP. 18	24	17	18	18	27	25	23	5	35	36	38	30
SEP. 19	25	19	19	20	27	25	23	5	35	36	38	30
SEP. 20	25	20	21	21	28	26	23	5	35	36	38	30
SEP. 21	25	22	22	23	28	26	23	5	35	36	38	30
SEP. 22	25	23	24	24	28	26	24	5	35	36	38	30
SEP. 23	25	25	26	26	28	26	24	5	35	36	38	30
SEP. 24	25	27	27	28	28	26	24	5	35	36	38	30
SEP. 25	26	28	29	30	28	26	24	5	35	36	38	30
SEP. 26	26	30	31	31	29	27	24	5	35	36	38	30
SEP. 27	26	32	33	33	29	27	24	5	35	36	38	30
SEP. 28	26	34	34	35	29	27	24	5	35	36	38	30
SEP. 29	26	36	36	37	29	27	24	5	35	36	38	30
SEP. 30	26	37	38	39	29	27	24	5	35	36	38	30

Date & Time	SUN	MOON 1	MOON 2	MOON 3	MERCURY	VENUS	MARS	JUPITER	SATURN	URANUS	NEPTUNE	PLUTO
OCT. 1	26	39	40	41	29	27	24	5	35	36	38	30
OCT. 2	26	41	42	42	29	28	24	5	35	36	38	30
OCT. 3	27	43	44	44	30	28	24	5	35	36	38	30
OCT. 4	27	45	46	46	30	28	25	5	35	36	38	30
OCT. 5	27	47	48	48	30	28	25	4	35	36	38	30
OCT. 6	27	1	2	2	30	28	25	4	35	36	38	30
OCT. 7	27	3	3	4	30	28	25	4	35	36	38	30
OCT. 8	27	5	5	6	30	29	25	4	35	36	38	30
OCT. 9	27	6	7	8	30	29	25	4	35	36	38	30
OCT. 10	27	8	9	9	30	29	25	4	35	36	38	30
OCT. 11	28	10	11	11	31	29	25	4	35	36	38	30
OCT. 12	28	12	12	13	31	29	25	4	35	36	38	30
OCT. 13	28	13	14	14	31	29	25	4	35	36	38	30
OCT. 14	28	15	15	16	31	30	25	4	35	36	38	30
OCT. 15	28	16	17	18	31	30	26	4	35	36	38	30
OCT. 16	28	18	19	19	31	30	26	4	35	36	38	30
OCT. 17	28	20	20	21	31	30	26	4	35	36	38	30
OCT. 18	28	21	22	22	31	30	26	4	35	36	38	30
OCT. 19	29	23	23	24	31	30	26	4	35	36	38	30
OCT. 20	29	24	25	26	31	31	26	4	35	36	38	30
OCT. 21	29	26	27	27	31	31	26	4	35	36	38	30
OCT. 22	29	28	28	29	30	31	26	4	35	36	38	30
OCT. 23	29	30	30	31	30	31	26	4	35	36	38	30
OCT. 24	29	31	32	33	30	31	26	4	35	36	38	30
OCT. 25	29	33	34	35	30	31	26	4	35	36	38	30
OCT. 26	30	35	36	36	30	32	26	4	35	36	38	30
OCT. 27	30	37	38	38	30	32	27	4	35	36	38	30
OCT. 28	30	39	40	40	30	32	27	4	35	36	38	30
OCT. 29	30	41	41	42	29	32	27	4	35	36	38	30
OCT. 30	30	43	43	44	29	32	27	4	35	36	38	30
OCT. 31	30	45	45	46	29	32	27	4	35	36	38	30

MOON 1 ☽ 12:01 A.M. TO 8:00 A.M. **MOON 2** ☽ 8:01 A.M. TO 4:00 P.M. **MOON 3** ● 4:01 P.M. TO 12:00 A.M.

Use only one "moon" number. Choose the column closest to your time of birth. If your place of birth is not on Eastern Standard Time, be sure to read "How to Convert to Eastern Standard Time" at the beginning of this section.

Date & Time	SUN	MOON 1	MOON 2	MOON 3	MERCURY	VENUS	MARS	JUPITER	SATURN	URANUS	NEPTUNE	PLUTO
NOV. 1	30	46	47	48	29	33	27	4	35	36	38	30
NOV. 2	30	48	1	2	29	33	27	4	35	36	38	30
NOV. 3	31	2	3	3	29	33	27	4	35	36	38	30
NOV. 4	31	4	5	5	29	33	27	4	35	36	38	30
NOV. 5	31	6	6	7	29	33	27	4	35	36	38	30
NOV. 6	31	8	8	9	29	33	27	4	35	36	38	30
NOV. 7	31	9	10	10	29	34	27	4	35	36	38	30
NOV. 8	31	11	12	12	29	34	28	4	36	36	38	30
NOV. 9	31	13	13	14	29	34	28	4	36	36	38	30
NOV. 10	31	14	15	15	29	34	28	4	36	36	38	30
NOV. 11	31	16	16	17	29	34	28	4	36	36	38	30
NOV. 12	32	18	18	19	29	34	28	4	36	36	38	30
NOV. 13	32	19	20	20	29	35	28	4	36	36	38	30
NOV. 14	32	21	21	22	29	35	28	4	36	36	38	30
NOV. 15	32	22	23	23	29	35	28	4	36	36	38	30
NOV. 16	32	24	24	25	30	35	28	4	36	36	38	30
NOV. 17	32	26	26	27	30	35	28	4	36	36	38	30
NOV. 18	32	27	28	28	30	35	28	4	36	36	38	30
NOV. 19	33	29	30	30	30	35	29	4	36	36	38	30
NOV. 20	33	31	31	32	30	36	29	4	36	36	38	30
NOV. 21	33	33	33	34	30	36	29	4	36	36	38	30
NOV. 22	33	35	35	36	31	36	29	4	36	36	38	30
NOV. 23	33	36	37	38	31	36	29	4	36	36	38	30
NOV. 24	33	38	39	40	31	36	29	4	36	36	38	30
NOV. 25	34	40	41	42	31	36	29	4	36	36	38	30
NOV. 26	34	42	43	43	31	37	29	4	36	36	38	30
NOV. 27	34	44	45	45	32	37	29	4	36	36	38	30
NOV. 28	34	46	47	47	32	37	29	4	36	36	38	30
NOV. 29	34	48	48	1	32	37	29	4	36	36	38	30
NOV. 30	34	2	2	3	32	37	29	4	36	36	38	30

Date & Time	SUN	MOON 1	MOON 2	MOON 3	MERCURY	VENUS	MARS	JUPITER	SATURN	URANUS	NEPTUNE	PLUTO
DEC. 1	34	3	4	5	32	37	30	4	36	36	38	30
DEC. 2	34	5	6	6	33	38	30	4	36	36	38	30
DEC. 3	35	7	8	8	33	38	30	4	36	36	38	30
DEC. 4	35	9	9	10	33	38	30	4	36	36	38	30
DEC. 5	35	10	11	12	33	38	30	4	36	36	38	30
DEC. 6	35	12	13	13	34	38	30	4	36	36	38	30
DEC. 7	35	14	14	15	34	38	30	4	36	36	38	30
DEC. 8	35	15	16	16	34	39	30	4	36	36	38	30
DEC. 9	35	17	18	18	34	39	30	4	36	36	38	30
DEC. 10	35	19	19	20	34	39	30	4	36	36	38	30
DEC. 11	36	20	21	21	35	39	30	4	36	36	38	30
DEC. 12	36	22	22	23	35	39	31	4	36	36	38	30
DEC. 13	36	23	24	24	35	39	31	4	36	37	38	30
DEC. 14	36	25	25	26	35	40	31	4	36	37	38	30
DEC. 15	36	27	27	28	35	40	31	4	36	37	38	31
DEC. 16	36	28	29	29	36	40	31	4	36	37	38	31
DEC. 17	36	30	31	31	36	40	31	4	36	37	38	31
DEC. 18	36	32	32	33	36	40	31	4	36	37	38	31
DEC. 19	37	34	34	35	36	40	31	4	36	37	38	31
DEC. 20	37	36	36	37	36	41	31	4	36	37	38	31
DEC. 21	37	38	38	39	37	41	31	4	36	37	38	31
DEC. 22	37	40	40	41	37	41	31	4	36	37	38	31
DEC. 23	37	42	42	43	37	41	32	4	36	37	38	31
DEC. 24	37	44	44	45	37	41	32	4	36	37	38	31
DEC. 25	37	46	46	47	37	41	32	4	36	37	38	31
DEC. 26	38	47	48	1	38	42	32	4	36	37	38	31
DEC. 27	38	1	2	2	38	42	32	4	36	37	38	31
DEC. 28	38	3	4	4	38	42	32	4	36	37	38	31
DEC. 29	38	5	5	6	38	42	32	4	36	37	38	31
DEC. 30	38	7	7	8	39	42	32	4	36	37	38	31
DEC. 31	38	8	9	9	39	42	32	4	36	37	38	31

MOON 1 ◐ 12:01 A.M. TO 8:00 A.M.   **MOON 2** ◑ 8:01 A.M. TO 4:00 P.M.   **MOON 3** ● 4:01 P.M. TO 12:00 A.M.

Use only one "moon" number. Choose the column closest to your time of birth. If your place of birth is not on Eastern Standard Time, be sure to read "How to Convert to Eastern Standard Time" at the beginning of this section.

1988

January

Date & Time	SUN	MOON 1	MOON 2	MOON 3	MERCURY	VENUS	MARS	JUPITER	SATURN	URANUS	NEPTUNE	PLUTO
JAN. 1	38	10	11	11	39	43	32	4	36	37	38	31
JAN. 2	38	12	12	13	39	43	32	4	36	37	38	31
JAN. 3	39	13	14	14	39	43	32	4	36	37	38	31
JAN. 4	39	15	15	16	40	43	33	4	36	37	38	31
JAN. 5	39	17	17	18	40	43	33	4	36	37	38	31
JAN. 6	39	18	19	19	40	43	33	4	36	37	38	31
JAN. 7	39	20	20	21	40	44	33	4	36	37	38	31
JAN. 8	39	21	22	22	41	44	33	4	36	37	38	31
JAN. 9	39	23	23	24	41	44	33	4	36	37	38	31
JAN. 10	40	24	25	25	41	44	33	4	37	37	38	31
JAN. 11	40	26	27	27	41	44	33	4	37	37	38	31
JAN. 12	40	28	28	29	41	44	33	4	37	37	38	31
JAN. 13	40	29	30	31	42	45	33	4	37	37	38	31
JAN. 14	40	31	32	32	42	45	33	4	37	37	38	31
JAN. 15	40	33	34	34	42	45	34	4	37	37	38	31
JAN. 16	40	35	35	36	42	45	34	4	37	37	38	31
JAN. 17	41	37	37	38	42	45	34	4	37	37	38	31
JAN. 18	41	39	39	40	43	45	34	4	37	37	38	31
JAN. 19	41	41	41	42	43	46	34	4	37	37	38	31
JAN. 20	41	43	43	44	43	46	34	4	37	37	38	31
JAN. 21	41	45	45	46	43	46	34	4	37	37	38	31
JAN. 22	41	47	47	48	43	46	34	4	37	37	38	31
JAN. 23	42	1	1	2	44	46	34	4	37	37	38	31
JAN. 24	42	3	3	4	44	46	34	4	37	37	38	31
JAN. 25	42	4	5	6	44	47	34	4	37	37	38	31
JAN. 26	42	6	7	7	44	47	35	4	37	37	38	31
JAN. 27	42	8	8	9	44	47	35	4	37	37	38	31
JAN. 28	42	10	10	11	44	47	35	4	37	37	38	31
JAN. 29	42	11	12	12	45	47	35	4	37	37	38	31
JAN. 30	42	13	13	14	45	47	35	4	37	37	38	31
JAN. 31	43	15	15	16	45	47	35	4	37	37	38	31

February

Date & Time	SUN	MOON 1	MOON 2	MOON 3	MERCURY	VENUS	MARS	JUPITER	SATURN	URANUS	NEPTUNE	PLUTO
FEB. 1	43	16	17	17	45	48	35	4	37	37	38	31
FEB. 2	43	18	18	19	45	48	35	4	37	37	38	31
FEB. 3	43	19	20	20	45	48	35	4	37	37	38	31
FEB. 4	43	21	21	22	45	48	35	4	37	37	38	31
FEB. 5	43	22	23	23	45	48	35	4	37	37	38	31
FEB. 6	43	24	25	25	45	48	36	4	37	37	38	31
FEB. 7	43	26	26	27	44	1	36	4	37	37	38	31
FEB. 8	44	27	28	28	44	1	36	4	37	37	38	31
FEB. 9	44	29	29	30	44	1	36	4	37	37	38	31
FEB. 10	44	31	31	32	44	1	36	4	37	37	38	31
FEB. 11	44	32	33	33	44	1	36	4	37	37	38	31
FEB. 12	44	34	35	35	44	1	36	4	37	37	38	31
FEB. 13	44	36	37	37	44	2	36	4	37	37	38	31
FEB. 14	44	38	38	39	43	2	36	4	37	37	38	31
FEB. 15	44	40	40	41	43	2	36	4	37	37	38	31
FEB. 16	45	42	42	43	43	2	36	4	37	37	38	31
FEB. 17	45	44	44	45	43	2	36	4	37	37	38	31
FEB. 18	45	46	47	47	43	2	37	4	37	37	38	31
FEB. 19	45	48	1	1	43	2	37	4	37	37	38	31
FEB. 20	45	2	2	3	43	3	37	5	37	37	38	31
FEB. 21	45	4	4	5	43	3	37	5	37	37	38	31
FEB. 22	45	6	6	7	43	3	37	5	37	37	38	31
FEB. 23	46	7	8	9	43	3	37	5	37	37	38	31
FEB. 24	46	9	10	10	43	3	37	5	37	37	38	31
FEB. 25	46	11	11	12	43	3	37	5	37	37	38	31
FEB. 26	46	12	13	14	43	4	37	5	37	37	38	31
FEB. 27	46	14	15	15	43	4	37	5	37	37	38	31
FEB. 28	46	16	16	17	43	4	37	5	37	37	38	31
FEB. 29	46	17	18	18	43	4	38	5	37	37	38	31

MOON 1 ◗ 12:01 A.M. TO 8:00 A.M.   **MOON 2** ◖ 8:01 A.M. TO 4:00 P.M.   **MOON 3** ● 4:01 P.M. TO 12:00 A.M.
Use only one "moon" number. Choose the column closest to your time of birth. If your place of birth is not on
Eastern Standard Time, be sure to read "How to Convert to Eastern Standard Time" at the beginning of this section.

1988

March

April

Date & Time	SUN ☉	MOON 1 ◗	MOON 2 ◑	MOON 3 ●	MERCURY	VENUS	MARS	JUPITER	SATURN	URANUS	NEPTUNE	PLUTO
MAR. 1	46	19	19	20	43	4	38	5	37	37	38	31
MAR. 2	46	20	21	21	43	4	38	5	37	37	38	31
MAR. 3	47	22	23	23	43	4	38	5	37	37	38	31
MAR. 4	47	24	24	25	43	5	38	5	37	37	38	31
MAR. 5	47	25	26	26	43	5	38	5	37	37	38	31
MAR. 6	47	27	27	28	43	5	38	5	37	37	38	31
MAR. 7	47	28	29	30	44	5	38	5	37	37	38	31
MAR. 8	47	30	31	31	44	5	38	5	37	37	38	31
MAR. 9	47	32	32	33	44	5	38	5	37	37	38	31
MAR. 10	47	34	34	35	44	6	38	5	37	37	38	31
MAR. 11	48	35	36	37	44	6	39	5	37	37	38	31
MAR. 12	48	37	38	38	44	6	39	5	37	37	38	31
MAR. 13	48	39	40	40	44	6	39	5	37	37	38	31
MAR. 14	48	41	42	42	45	6	39	5	37	37	38	31
MAR. 15	48	43	44	44	45	6	39	5	37	37	38	31
MAR. 16	48	45	46	46	45	6	39	5	37	37	38	31
MAR. 17	48	47	48	48	45	7	39	5	37	37	38	31
MAR. 18	48	1	2	2	45	7	39	5	37	37	38	31
MAR. 19	1	3	4	4	45	7	39	5	37	37	38	31
MAR. 20	1	5	5	6	46	7	39	5	37	37	38	31
MAR. 21	1	7	7	8	46	7	39	5	37	37	38	31
MAR. 22	1	8	9	10	46	7	40	5	37	37	38	31
MAR. 23	1	10	11	11	46	7	40	5	37	37	38	31
MAR. 24	1	12	13	13	46	8	40	5	37	37	38	31
MAR. 25	2	14	14	15	47	8	40	5	37	37	38	31
MAR. 26	2	15	16	16	47	8	40	5	37	37	38	31
MAR. 27	2	17	17	18	47	8	40	6	37	37	38	31
MAR. 28	2	18	19	19	47	8	40	6	37	37	38	31
MAR. 29	2	20	21	21	47	8	40	6	37	37	38	31
MAR. 30	2	22	22	23	48	8	40	6	37	37	38	31
MAR. 31	2	23	24	24	48	9	40	6	37	37	38	31

Date & Time	SUN ☉	MOON 1 ◗	MOON 2 ◑	MOON 3 ●	MERCURY	VENUS	MARS	JUPITER	SATURN	URANUS	NEPTUNE	PLUTO
APR. 1	2	25	25	26	48	9	40	6	37	37	38	31
APR. 2	2	26	27	27	48	9	41	6	37	37	38	31
APR. 3	3	28	29	29	1	9	41	6	37	37	38	31
APR. 4	3	30	30	31	1	9	41	6	37	37	38	31
APR. 5	3	31	32	33	1	9	41	6	37	37	38	31
APR. 6	3	33	34	34	1	9	41	6	37	37	38	31
APR. 7	3	35	36	36	1	9	41	6	37	37	38	31
APR. 8	3	37	37	38	2	10	41	6	37	37	38	31
APR. 9	3	39	39	40	2	10	41	6	37	37	38	31
APR. 10	3	40	41	42	2	10	41	6	37	37	38	31
APR. 11	4	42	43	44	3	10	41	6	37	37	38	31
APR. 12	4	44	45	45	3	10	41	6	37	37	38	31
APR. 13	4	46	47	47	3	10	42	6	37	37	38	31
APR. 14	4	48	1	1	3	10	42	6	37	37	38	31
APR. 15	4	2	3	3	4	10	42	6	37	37	38	31
APR. 16	4	4	5	5	4	11	42	6	37	37	38	31
APR. 17	4	6	7	7	4	11	42	6	37	37	38	31
APR. 18	4	8	8	9	4	11	42	6	37	37	38	31
APR. 19	5	10	10	11	5	11	42	6	37	37	38	31
APR. 20	5	11	12	12	5	11	42	6	37	37	38	31
APR. 21	5	13	14	14	5	11	42	6	37	37	38	30
APR. 22	5	15	15	16	5	11	42	6	37	37	38	30
APR. 23	5	16	17	17	6	11	42	6	37	37	38	30
APR. 24	5	18	18	19	6	11	43	6	37	37	38	30
APR. 25	6	20	20	21	6	11	43	6	37	37	38	30
APR. 26	6	21	22	22	7	12	43	6	37	37	38	30
APR. 27	6	23	23	24	7	12	43	6	37	37	38	30
APR. 28	6	24	25	25	7	12	43	7	37	37	38	30
APR. 29	6	26	26	27	7	12	43	7	37	37	38	30
APR. 30	6	28	28	29	8	12	43	7	37	37	38	30

MOON 1 ◗ **12:01 A.M. TO 8:00 A.M.**　　**MOON 2** ◑ **8:01 A.M. TO 4:00 P.M.**　　**MOON 3** ● **4:01 P.M. TO 12:00 A.M.**

Use only one "moon" number. Choose the column closest to your time of birth. If your place of birth is not on
Eastern Standard Time, be sure to read "How to Convert to Eastern Standard Time" at the beginning of this section.

1988

May

June

Date & Time	SUN	MOON 1	MOON 2	MOON 3	MERCURY	VENUS	MARS	JUPITER	SATURN	URANUS	NEPTUNE	PLUTO
MAY 1	6	29	30	30	8	12	43	7	37	37	38	30
MAY 2	6	31	32	32	8	12	43	7	37	37	38	30
MAY 3	7	33	33	34	9	12	43	7	37	37	38	30
MAY 4	7	34	35	36	9	12	43	7	37	37	38	30
MAY 5	7	36	37	38	9	12	43	7	37	37	38	30
MAY 6	7	38	39	39	9	12	44	7	37	37	38	30
MAY 7	7	40	41	41	10	12	44	7	37	37	38	30
MAY 8	7	42	42	43	10	13	44	7	37	37	38	30
MAY 9	7	44	44	45	10	13	44	7	37	37	38	30
MAY 10	7	46	46	47	10	13	44	7	37	37	38	30
MAY 11	8	48	48	1	10	13	44	7	37	37	38	30
MAY 12	8	1	2	3	11	13	44	7	37	37	38	30
MAY 13	8	3	4	5	11	13	44	7	37	37	38	30
MAY 14	8	5	6	6	11	13	44	7	37	37	38	30
MAY 15	8	7	8	8	11	13	44	7	37	37	38	30
MAY 16	8	9	9	10	11	13	44	7	37	37	38	30
MAY 17	8	11	11	12	11	13	45	7	37	37	38	30
MAY 18	8	12	13	14	12	13	45	7	37	37	38	30
MAY 19	9	14	15	15	12	13	45	7	37	37	38	30
MAY 20	9	16	16	17	12	13	45	7	37	37	38	30
MAY 21	9	17	18	18	12	13	45	7	37	37	38	30
MAY 22	9	19	20	20	12	13	45	7	37	37	38	30
MAY 23	9	21	21	22	12	13	45	7	37	37	38	30
MAY 24	9	22	23	23	12	13	45	7	37	37	38	30
MAY 25	10	24	24	25	12	13	45	7	37	37	38	30
MAY 26	10	25	26	26	12	13	45	7	37	37	38	30
MAY 27	10	27	27	28	12	13	45	7	37	37	38	30
MAY 28	10	29	29	30	12	13	45	7	37	37	38	30
MAY 29	10	30	31	31	12	13	46	7	37	37	38	30
MAY 30	10	32	33	33	13	13	46	8	37	37	38	30
MAY 31	10	34	34	35	13	13	46	8	37	37	38	30

Date & Time	SUN	MOON 1	MOON 2	MOON 3	MERCURY	VENUS	MARS	JUPITER	SATURN	URANUS	NEPTUNE	PLUTO
JUN. 1	10	36	36	37	13	13	46	8	37	37	38	30
JUN. 2	10	38	38	39	13	13	46	8	37	37	38	30
JUN. 3	11	39	40	41	13	13	46	8	37	37	38	30
JUN. 4	11	41	42	43	12	13	46	8	37	37	38	30
JUN. 5	11	43	44	45	12	13	46	8	37	37	38	30
JUN. 6	11	45	46	46	12	12	46	8	37	37	38	30
JUN. 7	11	47	48	48	12	12	46	8	37	37	38	30
JUN. 8	11	1	2	2	12	12	46	8	37	37	38	30
JUN. 9	11	3	3	4	12	12	46	8	37	37	38	30
JUN. 10	11	5	5	6	12	12	47	8	37	37	38	30
JUN. 11	12	6	7	6	12	12	47	8	37	37	38	30
JUN. 12	12	8	9	9	12	12	47	8	37	37	38	30
JUN. 13	12	10	11	11	12	12	47	8	37	37	38	30
JUN. 14	12	12	12	13	12	12	47	8	37	37	38	30
JUN. 15	12	14	14	15	12	12	47	8	37	37	38	30
JUN. 16	12	15	16	16	12	12	47	8	37	37	38	30
JUN. 17	12	17	17	18	12	12	47	8	37	37	38	30
JUN. 18	12	18	19	20	12	12	47	8	37	37	38	30
JUN. 19	13	20	21	21	12	11	47	8	37	37	38	30
JUN. 20	13	22	22	23	11	11	47	8	37	37	38	30
JUN. 21	13	23	24	24	11	11	47	8	37	37	38	30
JUN. 22	13	25	25	26	11	11	47	8	37	37	38	30
JUN. 23	13	26	27	27	11	11	48	8	37	37	38	30
JUN. 24	13	28	29	29	11	11	48	8	37	37	38	30
JUN. 25	14	30	30	31	11	11	48	8	37	37	38	30
JUN. 26	14	31	32	33	11	11	48	8	37	37	38	30
JUN. 27	14	33	34	34	11	11	48	8	37	37	38	30
JUN. 28	14	35	36	36	11	11	48	8	37	37	38	30
JUN. 29	14	37	38	38	11	11	48	8	37	37	38	30
JUN. 30	14	39	39	40	12	11	48	8	37	37	38	30

MOON 1 ☽ 12:01 A.M. TO 8:00 A.M.   **MOON 2** ☾ 8:01 A.M. TO 4:00 P.M.   **MOON 3** ● 4:01 P.M. TO 12:00 A.M.
Use only one "moon" number. Choose the column closest to your time of birth. If your place of birth is not on Eastern Standard Time, be sure to read "How to Convert to Eastern Standard Time" at the beginning of this section.

July

Date & Time	SUN ☉	MOON 1 ◐	MOON 2 ◑	MOON 3 ●	MERCURY	VENUS	MARS	JUPITER	SATURN	URANUS	NEPTUNE	PLUTO
JUL. 1	14	41	41	42	12	11	48	8	37	37	38	30
JUL. 2	14	43	43	44	12	11	48	8	37	37	38	30
JUL. 3	15	45	45	46	12	11	48	8	37	37	38	30
JUL. 4	15	47	47	48	12	11	48	9	37	37	38	30
JUL. 5	15	1	1	2	12	11	48	9	37	37	38	30
JUL. 6	15	2	3	4	12	11	48	9	37	37	38	30
JUL. 7	15	4	5	5	12	11	1	9	37	37	38	30
JUL. 8	15	6	7	7	12	11	1	9	37	37	38	30
JUL. 9	15	8	8	9	12	11	1	9	37	37	38	30
JUL. 10	15	10	10	11	13	11	1	9	37	37	38	30
JUL. 11	16	11	12	12	13	11	1	9	37	37	38	30
JUL. 12	16	13	14	14	13	11	1	9	37	37	38	30
JUL. 13	16	15	15	16	13	11	1	9	37	37	38	30
JUL. 14	16	16	17	17	13	11	1	9	37	37	38	30
JUL. 15	16	18	18	19	14	11	1	9	37	37	38	30
JUL. 16	16	20	20	21	14	11	1	9	37	37	38	30
JUL. 17	16	21	22	22	14	11	1	9	37	37	38	30
JUL. 18	16	23	23	24	14	11	1	9	37	37	38	30
JUL. 19	17	24	25	25	14	11	1	9	37	37	38	30
JUL. 20	17	26	26	27	15	11	1	9	37	37	38	30
JUL. 21	17	27	28	29	15	11	1	9	37	37	38	30
JUL. 22	17	29	30	30	15	12	1	9	37	37	38	30
JUL. 23	17	31	31	32	15	12	2	9	37	37	38	30
JUL. 24	17	32	33	34	16	12	2	9	37	37	38	30
JUL. 25	17	34	35	35	16	12	2	9	37	37	38	30
JUL. 26	18	36	37	37	16	12	2	9	37	37	38	30
JUL. 27	18	38	39	39	16	12	2	9	37	37	38	30
JUL. 28	18	40	41	41	17	12	2	9	37	37	38	30
JUL. 29	18	42	43	43	17	12	2	9	37	37	38	30
JUL. 30	18	44	45	45	17	12	2	9	37	37	38	30
JUL. 31	18	46	47	47	18	12	2	9	37	37	38	30

August

Date & Time	SUN ☉	MOON 1 ◐	MOON 2 ◑	MOON 3 ●	MERCURY	VENUS	MARS	JUPITER	SATURN	URANUS	NEPTUNE	PLUTO
AUG. 1	18	48	1	1	18	12	2	9	37	37	38	30
AUG. 2	18	2	3	3	18	12	2	9	37	37	38	30
AUG. 3	19	4	4	5	18	13	2	9	37	37	38	30
AUG. 4	19	6	6	7	19	13	2	9	36	37	38	30
AUG. 5	19	7	8	9	19	13	2	9	36	37	38	30
AUG. 6	19	9	10	10	19	13	2	9	36	37	38	30
AUG. 7	19	11	12	12	20	13	2	9	36	37	38	30
AUG. 8	19	13	13	14	20	13	2	9	36	37	38	30
AUG. 9	19	14	15	15	20	13	2	9	36	37	38	30
AUG. 10	19	16	16	17	20	13	2	9	36	37	38	30
AUG. 11	20	18	18	19	21	13	2	9	36	37	38	30
AUG. 12	20	19	20	20	21	14	2	9	36	37	38	30
AUG. 13	20	21	21	22	21	14	2	9	36	37	38	30
AUG. 14	20	22	23	23	21	14	2	9	36	37	38	30
AUG. 15	20	24	24	25	22	14	2	9	36	37	38	30
AUG. 16	20	25	26	26	22	14	2	9	36	37	38	30
AUG. 17	20	27	28	28	22	14	2	9	36	37	38	30
AUG. 18	20	29	29	30	22	14	2	9	36	37	38	30
AUG. 19	21	30	31	31	23	14	2	10	36	37	38	30
AUG. 20	21	32	32	33	23	15	2	10	36	37	38	30
AUG. 21	21	34	34	35	23	15	2	10	36	37	38	30
AUG. 22	21	35	36	37	23	15	2	10	36	37	38	30
AUG. 23	21	37	38	38	23	15	2	10	36	37	38	30
AUG. 24	21	39	40	40	24	15	2	10	36	37	38	30
AUG. 25	21	41	42	42	24	15	2	10	36	37	38	30
AUG. 26	22	43	44	44	24	15	2	10	36	37	38	30
AUG. 27	22	45	46	46	24	15	2	10	36	37	38	30
AUG. 28	22	47	48	48	24	16	2	10	36	37	38	30
AUG. 29	22	1	2	2	25	16	2	10	36	37	38	30
AUG. 30	22	3	4	4	25	16	2	10	36	37	38	30
AUG. 31	22	5	6	6	25	16	2	10	36	37	38	30

MOON 1 ◐ 12:01 A.M. TO 8:00 A.M.　　**MOON 2** ◑ 8:01 A.M. TO 4:00 P.M.　　**MOON 3** ● 4:01 P.M. TO 12:00 A.M.

Use only one "moon" number. Choose the column closest to your time of birth. If your place of birth is not on Eastern Standard Time, be sure to read "How to Convert to Eastern Standard Time" at the beginning of this section.

1988

September

Date & Time	SUN	MOON 1	MOON 2	MOON 3	MERCURY	VENUS	MARS	JUPITER	SATURN	URANUS	NEPTUNE	PLUTO
SEP. 1	22	7	8	8	25	16	2	10	36	37	38	30
SEP. 2	22	9	9	10	25	16	2	10	36	37	38	30
SEP. 3	23	10	11	12	26	16	2	10	36	37	38	30
SEP. 4	23	12	13	13	26	17	2	10	36	37	38	30
SEP. 5	23	14	14	15	26	17	2	10	36	37	38	30
SEP. 6	23	16	16	17	26	17	2	10	36	37	38	30
SEP. 7	23	17	18	18	26	17	2	10	36	37	38	30
SEP. 8	23	19	19	20	26	17	2	10	36	37	38	30
SEP. 9	23	20	21	21	27	17	2	10	36	37	38	30
SEP. 10	23	22	22	23	27	17	2	10	36	37	38	30
SEP. 11	24	23	24	25	27	17	2	10	36	37	38	30
SEP. 12	24	25	26	26	27	18	2	10	36	37	38	30
SEP. 13	24	27	27	28	27	18	2	10	36	37	38	30
SEP. 14	24	28	29	29	27	18	2	10	36	37	38	30
SEP. 15	24	30	30	31	28	18	2	10	36	37	38	30
SEP. 16	24	31	32	33	28	18	2	10	36	37	38	30
SEP. 17	24	33	34	34	28	18	2	10	36	37	38	30
SEP. 18	24	35	35	36	28	19	2	10	36	37	38	30
SEP. 19	25	37	37	38	28	19	2	10	36	37	38	30
SEP. 20	25	38	39	40	28	19	2	10	36	37	38	30
SEP. 21	25	40	41	42	28	19	2	10	36	37	38	30
SEP. 22	25	42	43	43	28	19	2	10	36	37	38	30
SEP. 23	25	44	45	45	28	19	2	10	36	37	38	30
SEP. 24	25	46	47	47	28	19	2	10	36	37	38	30
SEP. 25	26	48	1	2	28	20	2	10	36	37	38	30
SEP. 26	26	2	3	4	29	20	2	10	37	37	38	30
SEP. 27	26	4	5	5	29	20	2	10	37	37	38	30
SEP. 28	26	6	7	7	29	20	2	10	37	37	38	30
SEP. 29	26	8	9	9	29	20	2	10	37	37	38	30
SEP. 30	26	10	11	11	29	20	2	10	37	37	38	30

October

Date & Time	SUN	MOON 1	MOON 2	MOON 3	MERCURY	VENUS	MARS	JUPITER	SATURN	URANUS	NEPTUNE	PLUTO
OCT. 1	26	12	12	13	29	20	2	10	37	37	38	30
OCT. 2	26	13	14	15	28	21	2	10	37	37	38	30
OCT. 3	27	15	16	16	28	21	1	10	37	37	38	30
OCT. 4	27	17	17	18	28	21	1	10	37	37	38	30
OCT. 5	27	18	19	19	28	21	1	10	37	37	38	30
OCT. 6	27	20	20	21	28	21	1	10	37	37	38	30
OCT. 7	27	21	22	23	28	21	1	10	37	37	38	30
OCT. 8	27	23	24	24	28	22	1	10	37	37	38	30
OCT. 9	27	25	25	26	28	22	1	10	37	37	38	30
OCT. 10	27	26	27	27	28	22	1	10	37	37	38	31
OCT. 11	28	28	28	29	27	22	1	10	37	37	38	31
OCT. 12	28	29	30	31	27	22	1	10	37	37	38	31
OCT. 13	28	31	32	32	27	22	1	10	37	37	38	31
OCT. 14	28	33	33	34	27	22	1	10	37	37	38	31
OCT. 15	28	34	35	36	27	23	1	10	37	37	38	31
OCT. 16	28	36	37	37	27	23	1	10	37	37	38	31
OCT. 17	28	38	39	39	27	23	1	10	37	37	38	31
OCT. 18	28	40	40	41	27	23	1	10	37	37	38	31
OCT. 19	29	42	42	43	27	23	1	10	37	37	38	31
OCT. 20	29	43	44	45	27	23	1	10	37	37	38	31
OCT. 21	29	45	46	47	27	24	1	10	37	37	38	31
OCT. 22	29	47	48	1	27	24	1	10	37	37	38	31
OCT. 23	29	1	2	3	27	24	1	10	37	37	38	31
OCT. 24	29	3	4	5	27	24	1	10	37	37	38	31
OCT. 25	29	5	6	7	27	24	1	10	37	37	38	31
OCT. 26	30	7	8	8	27	24	1	10	37	37	38	31
OCT. 27	30	9	10	10	27	25	1	10	37	37	38	31
OCT. 28	30	11	12	12	27	25	1	10	37	37	38	31
OCT. 29	30	13	13	14	27	25	1	10	37	37	38	31
OCT. 30	30	15	15	16	28	25	1	10	37	37	38	31
OCT. 31	30	16	17	17	28	25	1	9	37	37	38	31

MOON 1 ◑ 12:01 A.M. TO 8:00 A.M.　　**MOON 2** ◐ 8:01 A.M. TO 4:00 P.M.　　**MOON 3** ● 4:01 P.M. TO 12:00 A.M.

Use only one "moon" number. Choose the column closest to your time of birth. If your place of birth is not on Eastern Standard Time, be sure to read "How to Convert to Eastern Standard Time" at the beginning of this section.

November

Date & Time	SUN ☉	MOON 1 ◐	MOON 2 ◑	MOON 3 ●	MERCURY	VENUS	MARS	JUPITER	SATURN	URANUS	NEPTUNE	PLUTO
NOV. 1	30	18	18	19	28	25	1	9	37	37	38	31
NOV. 2	30	19	20	21	28	25	1	9	37	37	38	31
NOV. 3	31	21	22	22	28	26	1	9	37	37	38	31
NOV. 4	31	23	23	24	28	26	1	9	37	37	38	31
NOV. 5	31	24	25	25	29	26	1	9	37	37	38	31
NOV. 6	31	26	26	27	29	26	1	9	37	37	38	31
NOV. 7	31	27	28	28	29	26	1	9	37	37	38	31
NOV. 8	31	29	30	30	29	26	1	9	37	37	38	31
NOV. 9	31	31	31	32	30	27	1	9	37	37	38	31
NOV. 10	31	32	33	33	30	27	1	9	37	37	38	31
NOV. 11	31	34	35	35	30	27	1	9	37	37	38	31
NOV. 12	32	36	36	37	30	27	1	9	37	37	38	31
NOV. 13	32	38	38	39	30	27	1	9	37	37	38	31
NOV. 14	32	39	40	41	31	27	1	9	37	37	38	31
NOV. 15	32	41	42	42	31	28	1	9	37	37	38	31
NOV. 16	32	43	44	44	31	28	1	9	37	37	38	31
NOV. 17	32	45	45	46	31	28	1	9	37	37	38	31
NOV. 18	32	47	47	48	31	28	1	9	37	37	38	31
NOV. 19	33	1	1	2	32	28	1	9	37	37	38	31
NOV. 20	33	3	3	4	32	28	1	9	37	37	38	31
NOV. 21	33	4	5	6	32	29	1	9	37	37	38	31
NOV. 22	33	6	7	8	32	29	1	9	37	37	38	31
NOV. 23	33	8	9	10	32	29	1	9	37	37	38	31
NOV. 24	33	10	11	11	33	29	2	9	37	37	38	31
NOV. 25	34	12	13	13	33	29	2	9	37	37	38	31
NOV. 26	34	14	14	15	33	29	2	9	37	37	38	31
NOV. 27	34	16	16	17	33	30	2	9	37	37	38	31
NOV. 28	34	17	18	18	34	30	2	9	37	37	38	31
NOV. 29	34	19	19	20	34	30	2	9	37	37	38	31
NOV. 30	34	21	21	22	34	30	2	9	37	37	38	31

December

Date & Time	SUN ☉	MOON 1 ◐	MOON 2 ◑	MOON 3 ●	MERCURY	VENUS	MARS	JUPITER	SATURN	URANUS	NEPTUNE	PLUTO
DEC. 1	34	22	23	23	34	30	2	9	37	37	38	31
DEC. 2	34	24	24	25	34	30	2	9	37	37	38	31
DEC. 3	35	25	26	26	35	31	2	9	37	37	38	31
DEC. 4	35	27	27	28	35	31	2	9	37	37	38	31
DEC. 5	35	28	29	30	35	31	2	9	37	37	38	31
DEC. 6	35	30	31	31	35	31	2	9	37	37	38	31
DEC. 7	35	32	32	33	35	31	2	9	37	37	38	31
DEC. 8	35	33	34	35	36	31	2	9	37	37	38	31
DEC. 9	35	35	36	36	36	32	2	9	37	37	38	31
DEC. 10	35	37	38	38	36	32	2	9	37	37	38	31
DEC. 11	36	39	39	40	36	32	2	9	37	37	38	31
DEC. 12	36	41	41	42	36	32	2	9	37	37	38	31
DEC. 13	36	43	43	44	37	32	2	9	37	37	38	31
DEC. 14	36	44	45	46	37	32	3	9	37	37	38	31
DEC. 15	36	46	47	48	37	33	3	9	37	37	38	31
DEC. 16	36	48	1	1	37	33	3	9	37	37	38	31
DEC. 17	36	2	3	3	38	33	3	9	37	37	38	31
DEC. 18	36	4	5	5	38	33	3	9	37	37	38	31
DEC. 19	37	6	6	7	38	33	3	9	38	37	38	31
DEC. 20	37	8	8	9	38	33	3	9	38	37	38	31
DEC. 21	37	10	10	11	38	34	3	9	38	37	38	31
DEC. 22	37	11	12	13	39	34	3	9	38	37	38	31
DEC. 23	37	13	14	14	39	34	3	9	38	37	38	31
DEC. 24	37	15	15	16	39	34	3	9	38	37	38	31
DEC. 25	37	17	17	18	39	34	3	9	38	37	38	31
DEC. 26	38	18	19	19	39	34	3	9	38	37	38	31
DEC. 27	38	20	20	21	40	35	3	9	38	37	38	31
DEC. 28	38	22	22	23	40	35	3	9	38	37	38	31
DEC. 29	38	23	24	24	40	35	3	9	38	37	38	31
DEC. 30	38	25	25	26	40	35	4	9	38	37	38	31
DEC. 31	38	26	27	27	40	35	4	9	38	37	38	31

MOON 1 ◐ 12:01 A.M. TO 8:00 A.M.　　**MOON 2** ◑ 8:01 A.M. TO 4:00 P.M.　　**MOON 3** ● 4:01 P.M. TO 12:00 A.M.

Use only one "moon" number. Choose the column closest to your time of birth. If your place of birth is not on Eastern Standard Time, be sure to read "How to Convert to Eastern Standard Time" at the beginning of this section.

1989

January

Date & Time	SUN	MOON 1	MOON 2	MOON 3	MERCURY	VENUS	MARS	JUPITER	SATURN	URANUS	NEPTUNE	PLUTO
JAN. 1	38	28	28	29	41	35	4	9	38	37	38	31
JAN. 2	38	29	30	31	41	36	4	9	38	37	38	31
JAN. 3	39	31	32	32	41	36	4	9	38	37	38	31
JAN. 4	39	33	33	34	41	36	4	9	38	37	38	31
JAN. 5	39	35	35	36	41	36	4	8	38	37	38	31
JAN. 6	39	36	37	38	42	36	4	8	38	37	38	31
JAN. 7	39	38	39	39	42	36	4	8	38	37	38	31
JAN. 8	39	40	41	41	42	37	4	8	38	37	38	31
JAN. 9	39	42	43	43	42	37	4	8	38	37	38	31
JAN. 10	40	44	45	45	42	37	4	8	38	37	38	31
JAN. 11	40	46	46	47	42	37	4	8	38	37	38	31
JAN. 12	40	48	48	1	42	37	4	8	38	37	38	31
JAN. 13	40	2	2	3	42	37	5	8	38	37	38	31
JAN. 14	40	4	4	5	43	38	5	8	38	37	38	31
JAN. 15	40	5	6	7	43	38	5	8	38	37	38	31
JAN. 16	40	7	8	8	43	38	5	8	38	37	38	31
JAN. 17	41	9	10	10	43	38	5	8	38	37	38	31
JAN. 18	41	11	11	12	42	38	5	8	38	37	38	31
JAN. 19	41	13	13	14	42	38	5	8	38	37	38	31
JAN. 20	41	14	15	15	42	39	5	8	38	37	38	31
JAN. 21	41	16	17	17	42	39	5	8	38	37	38	31
JAN. 22	41	18	18	19	42	39	5	8	38	37	38	31
JAN. 23	42	19	20	20	42	39	5	8	38	37	38	31
JAN. 24	42	21	22	22	42	39	5	8	38	37	38	31
JAN. 25	42	23	23	24	42	39	5	8	38	37	38	31
JAN. 26	42	24	25	25	41	40	5	8	38	37	38	31
JAN. 27	42	26	26	27	41	40	6	8	38	37	38	31
JAN. 28	42	27	28	28	41	40	6	8	38	37	38	31
JAN. 29	42	29	29	30	41	40	6	8	38	37	38	31
JAN. 30	42	31	31	32	41	40	6	8	38	37	38	31
JAN. 31	43	32	33	33	41	40	6	8	38	37	38	31

February

Date & Time	SUN	MOON 1	MOON 2	MOON 3	MERCURY	VENUS	MARS	JUPITER	SATURN	URANUS	NEPTUNE	PLUTO
FEB. 1	43	34	34	35	41	41	6	8	38	37	38	31
FEB. 2	43	36	36	37	41	41	6	8	38	37	38	31
FEB. 3	43	37	38	39	40	41	6	8	38	37	38	31
FEB. 4	43	39	40	40	40	41	6	8	38	37	38	31
FEB. 5	43	41	42	42	40	41	6	9	38	37	38	31
FEB. 6	43	43	44	44	40	41	6	9	38	37	38	31
FEB. 7	43	45	46	46	40	42	6	9	38	37	38	31
FEB. 8	44	47	48	48	40	42	6	9	38	37	38	31
FEB. 9	44	1	2	2	41	42	7	9	38	37	38	31
FEB. 10	44	3	4	4	41	42	7	9	38	37	38	31
FEB. 11	44	5	6	6	41	42	7	9	38	38	38	31
FEB. 12	44	7	7	8	41	42	7	9	38	38	38	31
FEB. 13	44	9	9	10	41	43	7	9	38	38	38	31
FEB. 14	44	10	11	12	41	43	7	9	38	38	38	31
FEB. 15	44	12	13	13	41	43	7	9	38	38	38	31
FEB. 16	45	14	14	15	41	43	7	9	38	38	39	31
FEB. 17	45	16	16	17	41	43	7	9	38	38	39	31
FEB. 18	45	17	18	18	41	43	7	9	38	38	39	31
FEB. 19	45	19	19	20	42	44	7	9	38	38	39	31
FEB. 20	45	21	21	22	42	44	7	9	38	38	39	31
FEB. 21	45	22	23	23	42	44	8	9	38	38	39	31
FEB. 22	45	24	24	25	42	44	8	9	38	38	39	31
FEB. 23	46	25	26	26	42	44	8	9	38	38	39	31
FEB. 24	46	27	27	28	42	44	8	9	38	38	39	31
FEB. 25	46	28	29	29	42	45	8	9	38	38	39	31
FEB. 26	46	30	31	31	43	45	8	9	38	38	39	31
FEB. 27	46	32	32	33	43	45	8	9	39	38	39	31
FEB. 28	46	33	34	34	43	45	8	9	39	38	39	31

MOON 1 ☽ 12:01 A.M. TO 8:00 A.M.   **MOON 2** ◗ 8:01 A.M. TO 4:00 P.M.   **MOON 3** ● 4:01 P.M. TO 12:00 A.M.
Use only one "moon" number. Choose the column closest to your time of birth. If your place of birth is not on
Eastern Standard Time, be sure to read "How to Convert to Eastern Standard Time" at the beginning of this section.

1989

March   April

Date & Time	SUN	MOON 1	MOON 2	MOON 3	MERCURY	VENUS	MARS	JUPITER	SATURN	URANUS	NEPTUNE	PLUTO
MAR. 1	46	35	36	36	43	45	8	9	39	38	39	31
MAR. 2	46	37	37	38	43	45	8	9	39	38	39	31
MAR. 3	47	38	39	40	43	46	8	9	39	38	39	31
MAR. 4	47	40	41	42	44	46	8	9	39	38	39	31
MAR. 5	47	42	43	43	44	46	8	9	39	38	39	31
MAR. 6	47	44	45	45	44	46	8	9	39	38	39	31
MAR. 7	47	46	47	47	44	46	9	9	39	38	39	31
MAR. 8	47	48	1	2	44	46	9	9	39	38	39	31
MAR. 9	47	2	3	4	45	47	9	9	39	38	39	31
MAR. 10	47	4	5	6	45	47	9	9	39	38	39	31
MAR. 11	48	6	7	7	45	47	9	9	39	38	39	31
MAR. 12	48	8	9	9	45	47	9	9	39	38	39	31
MAR. 13	48	10	11	11	45	47	9	9	39	38	39	31
MAR. 14	48	12	12	13	46	47	9	9	39	38	39	31
MAR. 15	48	14	14	15	46	48	9	9	39	38	39	31
MAR. 16	48	15	16	16	46	48	9	9	39	38	39	31
MAR. 17	48	17	17	18	46	48	9	9	39	38	39	31
MAR. 18	48	19	19	20	47	48	10	9	39	38	39	31
MAR. 19	1	20	21	21	47	48	10	9	39	38	39	31
MAR. 20	1	22	22	23	47	48	10	9	39	38	39	31
MAR. 21	1	23	24	24	47	1	10	9	39	38	39	31
MAR. 22	1	25	25	26	48	1	10	9	39	38	39	31
MAR. 23	1	26	27	28	48	1	10	9	39	38	39	31
MAR. 24	1	28	29	29	48	1	10	9	39	38	39	31
MAR. 25	2	30	30	31	48	1	10	9	39	38	39	31
MAR. 26	2	31	32	32	48	1	10	9	39	38	39	31
MAR. 27	2	33	33	34	1	2	10	9	39	38	39	31
MAR. 28	2	34	35	36	1	2	10	9	39	38	39	31
MAR. 29	2	36	37	37	1	2	10	9	39	38	39	31
MAR. 30	2	38	38	39	2	2	11	9	39	38	39	31
MAR. 31	2	40	40	41	2	2	11	9	39	38	39	31
APR. 1	2	41	42	43	2	2	11	9	39	38	39	31
APR. 2	2	43	44	45	2	3	11	9	39	38	39	31
APR. 3	3	45	46	47	3	3	11	9	39	38	39	31
APR. 4	3	47	48	1	3	3	11	10	39	38	39	31
APR. 5	3	1	2	3	3	3	11	10	39	38	39	31
APR. 6	3	3	4	5	3	3	11	10	39	38	39	31
APR. 7	3	5	6	7	4	3	11	10	39	38	39	31
APR. 8	3	7	8	9	4	4	11	10	39	38	39	31
APR. 9	3	9	10	11	4	4	11	10	39	38	39	31
APR. 10	3	11	12	12	4	4	11	10	39	38	39	31
APR. 11	4	13	14	14	5	4	11	10	39	38	39	31
APR. 12	4	15	15	16	5	4	12	10	39	38	39	31
APR. 13	4	16	17	18	5	4	12	10	39	38	39	31
APR. 14	4	18	19	19	6	5	12	10	39	38	39	31
APR. 15	4	20	20	21	6	5	12	10	39	38	39	31
APR. 16	4	21	22	22	6	5	12	10	39	38	39	31
APR. 17	4	23	23	24	6	5	12	10	39	38	39	31
APR. 18	4	24	25	26	7	5	12	10	39	38	39	31
APR. 19	5	26	27	27	7	5	12	10	39	38	39	31
APR. 20	5	28	28	29	7	6	12	10	39	38	39	31
APR. 21	5	29	30	30	7	6	12	10	39	38	39	31
APR. 22	5	31	31	32	8	6	12	10	39	38	39	31
APR. 23	5	32	33	34	8	6	12	10	39	38	39	31
APR. 24	5	34	35	35	8	6	13	10	39	38	39	31
APR. 25	6	36	36	37	8	6	13	10	39	38	39	31
APR. 26	6	37	38	39	8	6	13	10	39	38	39	31
APR. 27	6	39	40	40	9	7	13	10	39	38	39	31
APR. 28	6	41	42	42	9	7	13	10	39	38	39	31
APR. 29	6	43	43	44	9	7	13	10	39	38	39	31
APR. 30	6	45	45	46	9	7	13	10	39	38	39	31

MOON 1 ◖ 12:01 A.M. TO 8:00 A.M.   **MOON 2** ◑ 8:01 A.M. TO 4:00 P.M.   **MOON 3** ● 4:01 P.M. TO 12:00 A.M.

Use only one "moon" number. Choose the column closest to your time of birth. If your place of birth is not on Eastern Standard Time, be sure to read "How to Convert to Eastern Standard Time" at the beginning of this section.

1989

May

Date & Time	SUN ☉	MOON 1 ◐	MOON 2 ◑	MOON 3 ●	MERCURY	VENUS	MARS	JUPITER	SATURN	URANUS	NEPTUNE	PLUTO
MAY 1	6	46	47	48	9	7	13	10	39	38	39	31
MAY 2	6	48	1	2	9	7	13	10	39	38	39	31
MAY 3	7	2	3	4	9	8	13	10	39	38	39	31
MAY 4	7	4	5	6	9	8	13	10	39	38	39	31
MAY 5	7	6	7	8	10	8	13	10	39	38	39	31
MAY 6	7	8	9	10	10	8	14	10	39	38	39	31
MAY 7	7	10	11	12	10	8	14	10	39	38	39	31
MAY 8	7	12	13	13	10	8	14	10	39	38	39	31
MAY 9	7	14	15	15	10	9	14	10	39	38	39	31
MAY 10	7	16	16	17	10	9	14	11	39	38	39	31
MAY 11	8	18	18	19	10	9	14	11	39	38	39	31
MAY 12	8	19	20	20	10	9	14	11	39	38	39	31
MAY 13	8	21	21	22	10	9	14	11	39	38	39	31
MAY 14	8	22	23	24	10	9	14	11	39	38	39	31
MAY 15	8	24	25	25	10	10	14	11	39	38	39	31
MAY 16	8	26	26	27	10	10	14	11	39	38	39	31
MAY 17	8	27	28	28	10	10	14	11	39	38	39	31
MAY 18	8	29	29	30	10	10	15	11	39	38	39	31
MAY 19	9	30	31	31	10	10	15	11	39	38	39	31
MAY 20	9	32	33	33	10	10	15	11	39	38	39	31
MAY 21	9	34	34	35	10	11	15	11	39	38	39	31
MAY 22	9	35	36	36	9	11	15	11	39	38	39	31
MAY 23	9	37	38	38	9	11	15	11	39	38	39	31
MAY 24	9	39	39	40	9	11	15	11	39	38	39	31
MAY 25	10	41	41	42	9	11	15	11	39	38	39	31
MAY 26	10	42	43	44	9	11	15	11	39	38	39	31
MAY 27	10	44	45	45	9	12	15	11	39	38	39	31
MAY 28	10	46	47	47	9	12	15	11	39	38	39	31
MAY 29	10	48	48	1	9	12	15	11	39	38	39	31
MAY 30	10	2	2	3	9	12	16	11	39	38	39	31
MAY 31	10	4	4	5	9	12	16	11	39	38	39	31

June

Date & Time	SUN ☉	MOON 1 ◐	MOON 2 ◑	MOON 3 ●	MERCURY	VENUS	MARS	JUPITER	SATURN	URANUS	NEPTUNE	PLUTO
JUN. 1	10	6	6	7	9	12	16	11	39	38	39	31
JUN. 2	10	8	8	9	9	13	16	11	39	38	39	31
JUN. 3	11	10	10	11	9	13	16	11	39	38	39	31
JUN. 4	11	11	12	13	9	13	16	11	39	38	39	31
JUN. 5	11	13	14	15	9	13	16	11	39	38	39	31
JUN. 6	11	15	16	16	9	13	16	11	39	38	39	31
JUN. 7	11	17	18	18	9	13	16	11	39	38	39	31
JUN. 8	11	19	19	20	9	14	16	11	39	38	39	31
JUN. 9	11	20	21	21	9	14	16	11	39	37	39	31
JUN. 10	11	22	22	23	9	14	16	11	39	37	39	31
JUN. 11	12	24	24	25	9	14	17	11	39	37	39	31
JUN. 12	12	25	26	26	9	14	17	12	39	37	39	31
JUN. 13	12	27	27	28	9	14	17	12	39	37	39	31
JUN. 14	12	28	29	29	9	15	17	12	39	37	38	31
JUN. 15	12	30	30	31	9	15	17	12	39	37	38	31
JUN. 16	12	32	32	33	9	15	17	12	39	37	38	31
JUN. 17	12	33	34	34	9	15	17	12	39	37	38	31
JUN. 18	12	35	35	36	10	15	17	12	39	37	38	31
JUN. 19	13	37	37	38	10	15	17	12	39	37	38	31
JUN. 20	13	38	39	39	10	15	17	12	39	37	38	31
JUN. 21	13	40	41	41	10	16	17	12	38	37	38	31
JUN. 22	13	42	42	43	10	16	17	12	38	37	38	31
JUN. 23	13	44	44	45	10	16	18	12	38	37	38	31
JUN. 24	13	46	46	47	10	16	18	12	38	37	38	31
JUN. 25	14	47	48	1	11	16	18	12	38	37	38	31
JUN. 26	14	1	2	3	11	16	18	12	38	37	38	31
JUN. 27	14	3	4	4	11	17	18	12	38	37	38	31
JUN. 28	14	5	6	6	11	17	18	12	38	37	38	31
JUN. 29	14	7	8	8	11	17	18	12	38	37	38	31
JUN. 30	14	9	10	10	12	17	18	12	38	37	38	31

MOON 1 ◐ 12:01 A.M. TO 8:00 A.M.   **MOON 2** ◑ 8:01 A.M. TO 4:00 P.M.   **MOON 3** ● 4:01 P.M. TO 12:00 A.M.

Use only one "moon" number. Choose the column closest to your time of birth. If your place of birth is not on Eastern Standard Time, be sure to read "How to Convert to Eastern Standard Time" at the beginning of this section.

1989

July

Date & Time	SUN	MOON 1	MOON 2	MOON 3	MERCURY	VENUS	MARS	JUPITER	SATURN	URANUS	NEPTUNE	PLUTO
JUL. 1	14	11	11	12	12	17	18	12	38	37	38	31
JUL. 2	14	13	13	14	12	17	18	12	38	37	38	31
JUL. 3	15	14	15	16	12	18	18	12	38	37	38	31
JUL. 4	15	16	17	17	13	18	18	12	38	37	38	31
JUL. 5	15	18	19	19	13	18	19	12	38	37	38	31
JUL. 6	15	20	20	21	13	18	19	12	38	37	38	31
JUL. 7	15	21	22	22	13	18	19	12	38	37	38	31
JUL. 8	15	23	24	24	14	18	19	12	38	37	38	31
JUL. 9	15	25	25	26	14	19	19	12	38	37	38	31
JUL. 10	15	26	27	27	14	19	19	12	38	37	38	31
JUL. 11	16	28	28	29	14	19	19	12	38	37	38	31
JUL. 12	16	29	30	30	15	19	19	12	38	37	38	31
JUL. 13	16	31	31	32	15	19	19	12	38	37	38	31
JUL. 14	16	33	33	34	15	19	19	12	38	37	38	31
JUL. 15	16	34	35	35	15	20	19	13	38	37	38	31
JUL. 16	16	36	37	37	16	20	19	13	38	37	38	31
JUL. 17	16	38	38	39	16	20	20	13	38	37	38	31
JUL. 18	16	39	40	41	16	20	20	13	38	37	38	31
JUL. 19	17	41	42	43	17	20	20	13	38	37	38	31
JUL. 20	17	43	44	44	17	20	20	13	38	37	38	31
JUL. 21	17	45	46	46	17	21	20	13	38	37	38	31
JUL. 22	17	47	48	48	17	21	20	13	38	37	38	31
JUL. 23	17	1	1	2	18	21	20	13	38	37	38	31
JUL. 24	17	3	3	4	18	21	20	13	38	37	38	31
JUL. 25	17	5	5	6	18	21	20	13	38	37	38	31
JUL. 26	18	7	7	8	19	21	20	13	38	37	38	31
JUL. 27	18	8	9	10	19	21	20	13	38	37	38	31
JUL. 28	18	10	11	11	19	22	20	13	38	37	38	31
JUL. 29	18	12	13	13	19	22	21	13	38	37	38	31
JUL. 30	18	14	14	15	20	22	21	13	38	37	38	31
JUL. 31	18	16	16	17	20	22	21	13	38	37	38	31

August

Date & Time	SUN	MOON 1	MOON 2	MOON 3	MERCURY	VENUS	MARS	JUPITER	SATURN	URANUS	NEPTUNE	PLUTO
AUG. 1	18	17	18	19	20	22	21	13	38	37	38	31
AUG. 2	18	19	20	20	20	22	21	13	38	37	38	31
AUG. 3	19	21	21	22	21	23	21	13	38	37	38	31
AUG. 4	19	22	23	24	21	23	21	13	38	37	38	31
AUG. 5	19	24	25	25	21	23	21	13	38	37	38	31
AUG. 6	19	26	26	27	21	23	21	13	38	37	38	31
AUG. 7	19	27	28	28	21	23	21	13	38	37	38	31
AUG. 8	19	29	29	30	22	23	21	13	38	37	38	31
AUG. 9	19	30	31	31	22	24	21	13	38	37	38	31
AUG. 10	19	32	33	33	22	24	22	13	38	37	38	31
AUG. 11	20	34	34	35	22	24	22	13	38	37	38	31
AUG. 12	20	35	36	36	23	24	22	13	38	37	38	31
AUG. 13	20	37	38	38	23	24	22	13	38	37	38	31
AUG. 14	20	39	39	40	23	24	22	13	38	37	38	31
AUG. 15	20	41	41	42	23	25	22	13	38	37	38	31
AUG. 16	20	42	43	44	23	25	22	13	38	37	38	31
AUG. 17	20	44	45	46	23	25	22	13	38	37	38	31
AUG. 18	20	46	47	48	24	25	22	13	38	37	38	31
AUG. 19	21	48	1	2	24	25	22	13	38	37	38	31
AUG. 20	21	2	3	3	24	25	22	13	38	37	38	31
AUG. 21	21	4	5	5	24	25	22	14	38	37	38	31
AUG. 22	21	6	7	7	24	26	23	14	38	37	38	31
AUG. 23	21	8	9	9	25	26	23	14	38	37	38	31
AUG. 24	21	10	10	11	25	26	23	14	38	37	38	31
AUG. 25	21	12	12	13	25	26	23	14	38	37	38	31
AUG. 26	22	13	14	15	25	26	23	14	38	37	38	31
AUG. 27	22	15	16	16	25	26	23	14	38	37	38	31
AUG. 28	22	17	18	18	25	27	23	14	38	37	38	31
AUG. 29	22	19	19	20	25	27	23	14	38	37	38	31
AUG. 30	22	20	21	21	25	27	23	14	38	37	38	31
AUG. 31	22	22	22	23	26	27	23	14	38	37	38	31

MOON 1 ☽ 12:01 A.M. TO 8:00 A.M.   **MOON 2** ◑ 8:01 A.M. TO 4:00 P.M.   **MOON 3** ● 4:01 P.M. TO 12:00 A.M.

Use only one "moon" number. Choose the column closest to your time of birth. If your place of birth is not on Eastern Standard Time, be sure to read "How to Convert to Eastern Standard Time" at the beginning of this section.

Date & Time	SUN	MOON 1	MOON 2	MOON 3	MERCURY	VENUS	MARS	JUPITER	SATURN	URANUS	NEPTUNE	PLUTO
SEP. 1	22	24	24	25	26	27	23	14	38	37	38	31
SEP. 2	22	25	26	26	26	27	23	14	38	37	38	31
SEP. 3	23	27	27	28	26	28	24	14	38	37	38	31
SEP. 4	23	28	29	29	26	28	24	14	38	37	38	31
SEP. 5	23	30	30	31	26	28	24	14	38	37	38	31
SEP. 6	23	32	32	33	26	28	24	14	38	37	38	31
SEP. 7	23	33	34	34	26	28	24	14	38	37	38	31
SEP. 8	23	35	35	36	26	28	24	14	38	37	38	31
SEP. 9	23	36	37	38	26	28	24	14	38	37	38	31
SEP. 10	23	38	39	39	26	29	24	14	38	37	38	31
SEP. 11	24	40	40	41	26	29	24	14	38	37	38	31
SEP. 12	24	42	42	43	26	29	24	14	38	37	38	31
SEP. 13	24	44	44	45	26	29	24	14	38	37	38	31
SEP. 14	24	45	46	47	26	29	25	14	38	37	38	31
SEP. 15	24	47	48	1	26	29	25	14	38	37	38	31
SEP. 16	24	1	2	3	26	30	25	14	38	37	38	31
SEP. 17	24	3	4	5	26	30	25	14	38	37	38	31
SEP. 18	24	5	6	7	26	30	25	14	38	37	38	31
SEP. 19	25	7	8	9	26	30	25	14	38	37	38	31
SEP. 20	25	9	10	11	26	30	25	14	38	37	38	31
SEP. 21	25	11	12	12	26	30	25	14	38	37	38	31
SEP. 22	25	13	14	14	26	30	25	14	38	37	38	31
SEP. 23	25	15	15	16	25	31	25	14	38	37	38	31
SEP. 24	25	17	17	18	25	31	25	14	38	37	38	31
SEP. 25	26	18	19	19	25	31	25	14	38	37	38	31
SEP. 26	26	20	20	21	25	31	26	14	38	37	38	31
SEP. 27	26	22	22	23	25	31	26	14	38	37	38	31
SEP. 28	26	23	24	24	25	31	26	14	38	37	38	31
SEP. 29	26	25	25	26	25	32	26	14	38	37	38	31
SEP. 30	26	26	27	27	25	32	26	14	38	37	38	31

Date & Time	SUN	MOON 1	MOON 2	MOON 3	MERCURY	VENUS	MARS	JUPITER	SATURN	URANUS	NEPTUNE	PLUTO
OCT. 1	26	28	28	29	24	32	26	14	38	37	38	31
OCT. 2	26	30	30	31	24	32	26	14	38	37	38	31
OCT. 3	27	31	32	32	24	32	26	14	38	37	38	31
OCT. 4	27	33	33	34	24	32	26	14	38	37	38	31
OCT. 5	27	34	35	35	24	32	26	14	38	37	38	31
OCT. 6	27	36	36	37	24	33	26	14	38	37	38	31
OCT. 7	27	38	38	39	25	33	26	14	38	37	38	31
OCT. 8	27	39	40	40	25	33	27	14	38	37	38	31
OCT. 9	27	41	42	42	25	33	27	14	38	37	38	31
OCT. 10	27	43	43	44	25	33	27	14	38	37	38	31
OCT. 11	28	45	45	46	25	33	27	14	38	37	38	31
OCT. 12	28	47	47	48	25	33	27	14	38	37	38	31
OCT. 13	28	48	1	2	25	34	27	14	38	37	38	31
OCT. 14	28	3	3	4	25	34	27	14	38	37	38	31
OCT. 15	28	5	5	6	26	34	27	14	38	37	38	31
OCT. 16	28	7	7	8	26	34	27	14	38	37	38	31
OCT. 17	28	9	9	10	26	34	27	14	38	37	38	31
OCT. 18	28	11	11	12	26	34	27	14	38	37	38	31
OCT. 19	29	12	13	14	26	35	28	14	38	37	38	31
OCT. 20	29	14	15	16	27	35	28	14	38	37	38	31
OCT. 21	29	16	17	17	27	35	28	14	38	37	38	31
OCT. 22	29	18	18	19	27	35	28	14	38	37	38	31
OCT. 23	29	20	20	21	27	35	28	14	38	37	38	31
OCT. 24	29	21	22	22	28	35	28	14	38	37	38	31
OCT. 25	29	23	23	24	28	35	28	14	38	37	38	31
OCT. 26	30	24	25	25	28	36	28	14	38	37	38	31
OCT. 27	30	26	26	27	28	36	28	14	38	37	38	31
OCT. 28	30	28	28	29	28	36	28	14	38	37	38	31
OCT. 29	30	29	30	30	29	36	28	14	38	37	38	31
OCT. 30	30	31	31	32	29	36	29	14	38	37	38	31
OCT. 31	30	32	33	33	29	36	29	14	38	37	38	31

MOON 1 ◐ 12:01 A.M. TO 8:00 A.M.   **MOON 2** ◑ 8:01 A.M. TO 4:00 P.M.   **MOON 3** ● 4:01 P.M. TO 12:00 A.M.

Use only one "moon" number. Choose the column closest to your time of birth. If your place of birth is not on Eastern Standard Time, be sure to read "How to Convert to Eastern Standard Time" at the beginning of this section.

November

December

Date & Time	SUN	MOON 1	MOON 2	MOON 3	MERCURY	VENUS	MARS	JUPITER	SATURN	URANUS	NEPTUNE	PLUTO
NOV. 1	30	34	34	35	29	36	29	14	38	37	38	31
NOV. 2	30	35	36	37	30	37	29	14	38	37	38	31
NOV. 3	31	37	38	38	30	37	29	14	38	37	38	31
NOV. 4	31	39	39	40	30	37	29	14	38	37	38	31
NOV. 5	31	40	41	42	30	37	29	14	38	37	38	31
NOV. 6	31	42	43	43	30	37	29	14	38	37	38	31
NOV. 7	31	44	45	45	31	37	29	14	38	37	38	31
NOV. 8	31	46	46	47	31	37	29	14	38	37	38	31
NOV. 9	31	48	48	1	31	37	29	14	38	37	38	31
NOV. 10	31	2	2	3	31	38	30	14	38	37	38	31
NOV. 11	31	4	4	5	32	38	30	14	38	37	38	31
NOV. 12	32	6	6	7	32	38	30	14	38	37	38	31
NOV. 13	32	8	8	9	32	38	30	14	38	37	38	31
NOV. 14	32	10	10	11	32	38	30	14	38	37	38	31
NOV. 15	32	12	12	13	32	38	30	14	38	37	38	31
NOV. 16	32	14	14	15	33	38	30	14	38	37	38	31
NOV. 17	32	15	16	17	33	39	30	14	38	37	38	31
NOV. 18	32	17	18	18	33	39	30	14	38	37	38	31
NOV. 19	33	19	20	20	33	39	30	14	38	37	38	31
NOV. 20	33	21	21	22	33	39	30	14	38	37	38	31
NOV. 21	33	22	23	23	34	39	30	14	38	37	38	31
NOV. 22	33	24	24	25	34	39	31	14	38	37	38	31
NOV. 23	33	26	26	27	34	39	31	14	38	37	38	31
NOV. 24	33	27	28	28	34	39	31	14	38	37	38	31
NOV. 25	34	29	29	30	34	39	31	14	38	37	38	31
NOV. 26	34	30	31	31	35	40	31	14	39	37	38	31
NOV. 27	34	32	32	33	35	40	31	14	39	37	38	31
NOV. 28	34	33	34	35	35	40	31	14	39	37	38	31
NOV. 29	34	35	36	36	35	40	31	14	39	37	38	31
NOV. 30	34	37	37	38	35	40	31	14	39	37	38	31

Date & Time	SUN	MOON 1	MOON 2	MOON 3	MERCURY	VENUS	MARS	JUPITER	SATURN	URANUS	NEPTUNE	PLUTO
DEC. 1	34	38	39	40	36	40	31	14	39	37	38	31
DEC. 2	34	40	41	41	36	40	31	14	39	37	38	31
DEC. 3	35	42	42	43	36	40	32	14	39	38	38	31
DEC. 4	35	44	44	45	36	40	32	14	39	38	38	31
DEC. 5	35	45	46	46	36	41	32	14	39	38	38	31
DEC. 6	35	47	48	48	37	41	32	14	39	38	38	31
DEC. 7	35	1	2	2	37	41	32	14	39	38	38	31
DEC. 8	35	3	4	4	37	41	32	14	39	38	38	31
DEC. 9	35	5	5	6	37	41	32	14	39	38	38	31
DEC. 10	35	7	7	8	37	41	32	14	39	38	38	31
DEC. 11	36	9	9	10	38	41	32	14	39	38	38	31
DEC. 12	36	11	11	12	38	41	32	14	39	38	38	31
DEC. 13	36	13	13	14	38	41	33	14	39	38	38	31
DEC. 14	36	15	15	16	38	41	33	14	39	38	38	31
DEC. 15	36	17	17	18	38	41	33	14	39	38	38	31
DEC. 16	36	18	19	20	39	41	33	14	39	38	38	31
DEC. 17	36	20	21	21	39	41	33	14	39	38	38	31
DEC. 18	36	22	22	23	39	42	33	14	39	38	39	31
DEC. 19	37	23	24	25	39	42	33	14	39	38	39	31
DEC. 20	37	25	26	26	39	42	33	14	39	38	39	31
DEC. 21	37	27	27	28	40	42	33	14	39	38	39	31
DEC. 22	37	28	29	29	40	42	33	14	39	38	39	31
DEC. 23	37	30	30	31	40	42	33	14	39	38	39	31
DEC. 24	37	31	32	32	40	42	34	14	39	38	39	31
DEC. 25	37	33	34	34	40	42	34	14	39	38	39	31
DEC. 26	38	35	35	36	40	42	34	14	39	38	39	31
DEC. 27	38	36	37	37	40	42	34	14	39	38	39	31
DEC. 28	38	38	38	39	40	42	34	14	39	38	39	31
DEC. 29	38	40	40	41	40	42	34	14	39	38	39	31
DEC. 30	38	41	42	43	40	42	34	14	39	38	39	31
DEC. 31	38	43	44	44	40	42	34	14	39	38	39	31

MOON 1 ☾ 12:01 A.M. TO 8:00 A.M.   **MOON 2** ☽ 8:01 A.M. TO 4:00 P.M.   **MOON 3** ● 4:01 P.M. TO 12:00 A.M.

Use only one "moon" number. Choose the column closest to your time of birth. If your place of birth is not on Eastern Standard Time, be sure to read "How to Convert to Eastern Standard Time" at the beginning of this section.

1990-1999

1990s

The McCaughey Septuplets

Natalie, Joel, Brandon, Nathan, Alexis, Kelsey and Michele

✳ ✳ ✳ BORN NOVEMBER 19, 1997 ✳ ✳ ✳

Brief Bio: Born to parents Bobbi and Kenny in Carlisle, Iowa, the septuplets Natalie, Joel, Brandon, Nathan, Alexis, Kelsey and Michele make history.

Personology Profile:

SUN ON THE CUSP OF REVOLUTION
(SCORPIO-SAGITTARIUS CUSP)

✳

Scorpio-Sagittarians must learn to keep their combative instincts under control. Feisty individuals, they will rarely back down from a fight. Moreover, they will discover sooner or later that by allowing others to push their buttons at will they are buying into such people controlling them. These are wonderful individuals to work with on projects—highly energetic, dependable, creative.

MERCURY IN THE WEEK OF ORIGINALITY
(SAGITTARIUS II)

✳

A creative and at times bizarre use of language characterizes these individuals. Because of this idiosyncratic way of expressing themselves, their original verbal style is easily recognizable. Indeed, it can become their hallmark and serve to identify them more than their appearance or their actions. Those who truly understand them occupy a special place in their heart.

MARS IN THE WEEK OF THE RULER
(CAPRICORN I)

✳

Mars is at his most regal here. Happy with taking command at the head of any team, such individuals can put all of their energies in constructive service of the group. Usually not so interested in furthering their own personal ambitions, they often nevertheless succeed in enhancing their social standing through the success of group endeavors which they lead.

MOON ON THE CUSP OF OSCILLATION
CANCER-LEO CUSP)

✳

The moon feels a bit unbalanced in this position and so imparts a restless instability to its natives. Moreover, since emotions can take a nosedive at almost any moment, those with their moon here tend to suffer periodically from bouts of depression. Manic phases can also arise, giving a see-saw effect to the feelings. Stimulants should be avoided by these folks.

VENUS IN THE WEEK OF DETERMINATION
(CAPRICORN II)

✳

"I'll make you love me" is too often the thought or spoken intention of these individuals. However, sooner or later they usually learn that if they begin to give up their need to control and go with the flow they can achieve much greater happiness and contentment. They will fight for the one they love against all comers and do not run away from pitched battles.

JUPITER IN THE WEEK OF YOUTH AND EASE
(AQUARIUS II)

✳

Jupiter is at its most relaxed in this position—perhaps too relaxed. Thus, a real threat posed to one's drive toward success may be feeling too comfortable with where one is in life. Although this attitude reduces stress, it can also promote lethargy, leading to overweight and a contentment which undermines one's chances to succeed in personal or career matters.

SATURN IN THE WEEK OF THE STAR
(ARIES II)

*

Saturn can lend approval to more responsible behavior here, i.e., being at the center of a group or project and providing solid and practical support to such groups and endeavors. This is particularly true in the family sphere. However, any sign of being a show-off or having an ego in need of excessive attention will meet with sharp disapproval. In extreme cases, Saturn here can produce an introverted and fearful individual.

URANUS IN THE WEEK OF GENIUS
(AQUARIUS I)

*

A mental predominance manifests here, which can cause problems to emerge in the emotional and physical spheres. Brain power is accentuated by this Uranus position, but not necessarily that of logic or even common sense. It is the kind of blinding and brilliant thought patterns which are likely to emerge from time to time, often at the most unexpected moments.

NEPTUNE ON THE CUSP OF MYSTERY AND IMAGINATION
(CAPRICORN-AQUARIUS CUSP)

*

One of the most imaginative and far-reaching positions of the year for Neptune. Those with this position have extremely vivid dream and fantasy lives, which usually spill over into their day-to-day existence. It may be difficult for those they live with to accept their often bizarre and strange points of view. Violent tendencies, when opposed or misunderstood, must be kept under control.

PLUTO IN THE WEEK OF INDEPENDENCE
(SAGITTARIUS I)

*

A feeling of optimism is pervasive here and with it the energy needed to accomplish great tasks. The more explosive aspects of Pluto are tempered and his energies can be effectively harnessed. Still there is a feeling that forces beyond one's control are operating here and that respect should be given to the mighty impersonal forces operating in the universe.

Some Highlights of the Decade 1990-1999

- THE FIRST INTERNATIONAL WAR CRIMES PROCEEDING SINCE NUREMBERG OPENS AT THE HAGUE IN THE NETHERLANDS.

- TIMOTHY MCVEIGH AND TERRY NICHOLS ENGINEER THE BOMBING OF THE MURRAY FEDERAL BUILDING IN OKLAHOMA CITY, KILLING 168 PEOPLE.

- OJ SIMPSON IS ACQUITTED OF THE BRUTAL STABBING MURDERS OF HIS EX-WIFE, NICOLE, AND HER FRIEND, RONALD GOLDMAN; THE TRIAL IS AN UNPRECEDENTED MEDIA SENSATION THAT POLARIZES RACIAL TENSION IN THE US.

- THE US IS GRIPPED BY "Y2K" HYSTERIA AT THE TURN OF THE CENTURY; DESPITE ALL THE BALLYHOO, COMPUTER PROGRAMS CONTINUE TO FUNCTION IN THE NEW MILLENNIUM.

- OPRAH WINFREY, TALK SHOW HOST AND MEDIA MAGNATE, SUGGESTS ON THE *OPRAH* SHOW THAT EATING BEEF MAY HAVE DELETERIOUS HEALTH CONSEQUENCES. SHE IS SUED BY THE TEXAS CATTLE INDUSTRY.

- AFTER THE MONICA LEWINSKY AFFAIR, CONGRESS MOVES TO IMPEACH BILL CLINTON, THE SECOND PRESIDENT IN AMERICAN HISTORY TO BE IMPEACHED.

1990

January

Date & Time	SUN	MOON 1	MOON 2	MOON 3	MERCURY	VENUS	MARS	JUPITER	SATURN	URANUS	NEPTUNE	PLUTO
JAN. 1	38	45	45	46	40	42	34	14	39	38	39	31
JAN. 2	38	47	47	48	40	42	34	14	39	38	39	31
JAN. 3	39	1	1	2	40	42	34	14	39	38	39	31
JAN. 4	39	2	3	4	40	42	35	14	39	38	39	31
JAN. 5	39	4	5	6	40	42	35	14	39	38	39	31
JAN. 6	39	6	7	7	40	42	35	14	39	38	39	31
JAN. 7	39	8	9	9	40	42	35	14	39	38	39	31
JAN. 8	39	10	11	11	40	42	35	14	39	38	39	31
JAN. 9	39	12	13	13	39	41	35	14	39	38	39	31
JAN. 10	40	14	14	15	39	41	35	14	39	38	39	31
JAN. 11	40	16	16	17	39	41	35	13	39	38	39	31
JAN. 12	40	18	18	19	39	41	35	13	39	38	39	31
JAN. 13	40	19	20	21	39	41	35	13	39	38	39	31
JAN. 14	40	21	22	22	39	41	35	13	39	38	39	31
JAN. 15	40	23	23	24	39	41	36	13	39	38	39	31
JAN. 16	40	24	25	26	38	41	36	13	39	38	39	31
JAN. 17	41	26	27	27	38	41	36	13	39	38	39	31
JAN. 18	41	28	28	28	38	41	36	13	39	38	39	31
JAN. 19	41	29	30	30	38	41	36	13	39	38	39	31
JAN. 20	41	31	31	32	38	41	36	13	39	38	39	31
JAN. 21	41	32	33	34	38	41	36	13	39	38	39	31
JAN. 22	41	34	35	35	38	41	36	13	39	38	39	31
JAN. 23	42	36	36	37	38	40	36	13	39	38	39	31
JAN. 24	42	37	38	38	38	40	36	13	39	38	39	31
JAN. 25	42	39	40	40	38	40	37	13	39	38	39	31
JAN. 26	42	41	41	42	39	40	37	13	39	38	39	31
JAN. 27	42	43	43	44	39	40	37	13	39	38	39	31
JAN. 28	42	44	45	46	39	40	37	13	39	38	39	31
JAN. 29	42	46	47	47	39	40	37	13	39	38	39	31
JAN. 30	42	48	1	1	39	40	37	13	40	38	39	31
JAN. 31	43	2	3	3	39	40	37	13	40	38	39	31

February

Date & Time	SUN	MOON 1	MOON 2	MOON 3	MERCURY	VENUS	MARS	JUPITER	SATURN	URANUS	NEPTUNE	PLUTO
FEB. 1	43	4	4	5	39	40	37	13	40	38	39	31
FEB. 2	43	6	6	7	39	40	37	13	40	38	39	31
FEB. 3	43	8	8	9	40	40	37	13	40	38	39	31
FEB. 4	43	10	10	11	40	40	38	13	40	38	39	31
FEB. 5	43	11	12	13	40	40	38	13	40	38	39	31
FEB. 6	43	13	14	14	40	40	38	13	40	38	39	31
FEB. 7	43	15	16	16	40	40	38	13	40	38	39	31
FEB. 8	44	17	18	18	40	40	38	13	40	38	39	31
FEB. 9	44	19	19	20	40	40	38	13	40	38	39	31
FEB. 10	44	20	21	22	41	40	38	13	40	38	39	31
FEB. 11	44	22	23	23	41	40	38	13	40	38	39	31
FEB. 12	44	24	24	25	41	40	38	13	40	38	39	31
FEB. 13	44	26	26	27	41	40	38	13	40	38	39	31
FEB. 14	44	27	28	28	41	40	38	13	40	38	39	31
FEB. 15	44	29	29	30	42	40	39	13	40	38	39	31
FEB. 16	45	30	31	31	42	40	39	13	40	38	39	31
FEB. 17	45	32	32	33	42	40	39	13	40	38	39	31
FEB. 18	45	33	34	35	42	40	39	13	40	38	39	31
FEB. 19	45	35	36	36	42	40	39	13	40	38	39	31
FEB. 20	45	37	37	38	43	40	39	13	40	38	39	31
FEB. 21	45	38	39	40	43	40	39	13	40	38	39	31
FEB. 22	45	40	41	41	43	40	39	13	40	38	39	31
FEB. 23	46	42	42	43	43	40	39	13	40	38	39	31
FEB. 24	46	44	44	45	43	40	39	13	40	38	39	31
FEB. 25	46	46	46	47	44	40	40	13	40	38	39	31
FEB. 26	46	47	48	1	44	41	40	13	40	38	39	31
FEB. 27	46	1	2	3	44	41	40	13	40	38	39	31
FEB. 28	46	3	4	5	44	41	40	13	40	38	39	31

MOON 1 ☾ 12:01 A.M. TO 8:00 A.M.   **MOON 2** ☽ 8:01 A.M. TO 4:00 P.M.   **MOON 3** ● 4:01 P.M. TO 12:00 A.M.
Use only one "moon" number. Choose the column closest to your time of birth. If your place of birth is not on Eastern Standard Time, be sure to read "How to Convert to Eastern Standard Time" at the beginning of this section.

1990

March / April

Date & Time	SUN	MOON 1	MOON 2	MOON 3	MERCURY	VENUS	MARS	JUPITER	SATURN	URANUS	NEPTUNE	PLUTO
MAR. 1	46	5	6	7	44	41	40	13	40	38	39	31
MAR. 2	46	7	8	8	45	41	40	13	40	38	39	31
MAR. 3	47	9	10	10	45	41	40	13	40	38	39	31
MAR. 4	47	11	12	12	45	41	40	13	40	38	39	31
MAR. 5	47	13	13	14	45	41	40	13	40	38	39	31
MAR. 6	47	15	15	16	46	41	40	13	40	38	39	31
MAR. 7	47	16	17	18	46	41	41	13	40	38	39	31
MAR. 8	47	18	19	19	46	41	41	13	40	38	39	31
MAR. 9	47	20	20	21	46	41	41	13	40	38	39	31
MAR. 10	47	22	22	23	46	42	41	13	40	38	39	31
MAR. 11	48	23	24	24	47	42	41	13	40	38	39	31
MAR. 12	48	25	26	26	47	42	41	13	40	38	39	31
MAR. 13	48	27	27	28	47	42	41	13	40	38	39	31
MAR. 14	48	28	29	29	47	42	41	13	40	38	39	31
MAR. 15	48	30	30	31	48	42	41	13	40	38	39	31
MAR. 16	48	31	32	32	48	42	41	13	40	38	39	31
MAR. 17	48	33	33	34	48	42	42	13	40	38	39	31
MAR. 18	48	35	35	36	48	42	42	13	40	38	39	31
MAR. 19	1	36	37	37	1	43	42	13	40	38	39	31
MAR. 20	1	38	38	39	1	43	42	13	40	38	39	31
MAR. 21	1	39	40	41	1	43	42	13	40	38	39	31
MAR. 22	1	41	42	42	2	43	42	13	40	38	39	31
MAR. 23	1	43	44	44	2	43	42	13	40	38	39	31
MAR. 24	1	45	45	46	2	43	42	13	40	38	39	31
MAR. 25	2	47	47	48	2	43	42	13	40	38	39	31
MAR. 26	2	1	1	2	3	43	42	13	40	38	39	31
MAR. 27	2	3	3	4	3	44	43	13	40	38	39	31
MAR. 28	2	5	5	6	3	44	43	13	40	38	39	31
MAR. 29	2	7	7	8	3	44	43	13	40	38	39	31
MAR. 30	2	8	9	10	4	44	43	13	40	38	39	31
MAR. 31	2	10	11	12	4	44	43	13	40	38	39	31
APR. 1	2	12	13	14	4	44	43	13	40	38	39	31
APR. 2	2	14	15	15	4	44	43	13	40	38	39	31
APR. 3	3	16	17	17	5	45	43	13	40	38	39	31
APR. 4	3	18	18	19	5	45	43	13	40	38	39	31
APR. 5	3	20	20	21	5	45	43	13	40	38	39	31
APR. 6	3	21	22	22	5	45	44	13	40	38	39	31
APR. 7	3	23	23	24	6	45	44	13	40	38	39	31
APR. 8	3	25	25	26	6	45	44	13	40	38	39	31
APR. 9	3	26	27	27	6	45	44	13	40	38	39	31
APR. 10	3	28	28	29	6	45	44	13	40	38	39	31
APR. 11	4	29	30	30	6	46	44	13	40	38	39	31
APR. 12	4	31	31	32	6	46	44	14	40	38	39	31
APR. 13	4	33	33	34	7	46	44	14	40	38	39	31
APR. 14	4	34	35	35	7	46	44	14	40	38	39	31
APR. 15	4	36	36	37	7	46	44	14	40	38	39	31
APR. 16	4	37	38	38	7	46	44	14	40	38	39	31
APR. 17	4	39	39	40	7	46	45	14	40	38	39	31
APR. 18	4	41	41	42	7	47	45	14	40	38	39	31
APR. 19	5	42	43	43	7	47	45	14	40	38	39	31
APR. 20	5	44	45	45	7	47	45	14	40	38	39	31
APR. 21	5	46	46	47	7	47	45	14	40	38	39	31
APR. 22	5	48	48	1	7	47	45	14	40	38	39	31
APR. 23	5	2	2	3	7	47	45	14	40	38	39	31
APR. 24	5	4	4	5	7	47	45	14	40	38	39	31
APR. 25	6	6	6	7	7	48	45	14	40	38	39	31
APR. 26	6	8	8	9	7	48	45	14	40	38	39	31
APR. 27	6	10	10	11	7	48	46	14	40	38	39	31
APR. 28	6	12	12	13	7	48	46	14	40	38	39	31
APR. 29	6	14	14	15	7	48	46	14	40	38	39	31
APR. 30	6	16	16	17	7	48	46	14	40	38	39	31

MOON 1 ☽ 12:01 A.M. TO 8:00 A.M.   **MOON 2** ☽ 8:01 A.M. TO 4:00 P.M.   **MOON 3** ● 4:01 P.M. TO 12:00 A.M.

Use only one "moon" number. Choose the column closest to your time of birth. If your place of birth is not on Eastern Standard Time, be sure to read "How to Convert to Eastern Standard Time" at the beginning of this section.

1990

May

Date & Time	SUN	MOON 1	MOON 2	MOON 3	MERCURY	VENUS	MARS	JUPITER	SATURN	URANUS	NEPTUNE	PLUTO
MAY 1	6	17	18	19	7	1	46	14	40	38	39	31
MAY 2	6	19	20	20	7	1	46	14	40	38	39	31
MAY 3	7	21	21	22	7	1	46	14	40	38	39	31
MAY 4	7	22	23	24	7	1	46	14	40	38	39	31
MAY 5	7	24	25	25	7	1	46	14	40	38	39	31
MAY 6	7	26	26	27	7	1	46	14	40	38	39	31
MAY 7	7	27	28	28	6	1	47	14	40	38	39	31
MAY 8	7	29	29	30	6	2	47	14	40	38	39	31
MAY 9	7	31	31	32	6	2	47	14	40	38	39	31
MAY 10	7	32	33	33	6	2	47	14	40	38	39	31
MAY 11	8	34	34	35	6	2	47	14	40	38	39	31
MAY 12	8	35	36	36	6	2	47	14	40	38	39	31
MAY 13	8	37	37	38	6	2	47	14	40	38	39	31
MAY 14	8	38	39	40	6	2	47	14	40	38	39	31
MAY 15	8	40	41	41	6	3	47	14	40	38	39	31
MAY 16	8	42	42	43	6	3	47	14	40	38	39	31
MAY 17	8	43	44	45	6	3	48	14	40	38	39	31
MAY 18	8	45	46	46	6	3	48	14	40	38	39	31
MAY 19	9	47	48	48	6	3	48	14	40	38	39	31
MAY 20	9	1	1	2	6	3	48	14	40	38	39	31
MAY 21	9	3	3	4	6	4	48	14	40	38	39	31
MAY 22	9	5	5	6	6	4	48	14	40	38	39	31
MAY 23	9	7	7	8	6	4	48	14	40	38	39	31
MAY 24	9	9	9	10	6	4	48	14	40	38	39	31
MAY 25	10	11	12	12	6	4	48	14	40	38	39	31
MAY 26	10	13	13	14	6	4	48	15	40	38	39	31
MAY 27	10	15	15	16	7	4	1	15	40	38	39	31
MAY 28	10	17	17	18	7	5	1	15	40	38	39	31
MAY 29	10	19	19	20	7	5	1	15	40	38	39	31
MAY 30	10	20	21	21	7	5	1	15	40	38	39	31
MAY 31	10	22	23	23	7	5	1	15	40	38	39	31

June

Date & Time	SUN	MOON 1	MOON 2	MOON 3	MERCURY	VENUS	MARS	JUPITER	SATURN	URANUS	NEPTUNE	PLUTO
JUN. 1	10	24	24	25	7	5	1	15	40	38	39	31
JUN. 2	10	25	26	26	7	5	1	15	40	38	39	31
JUN. 3	11	27	27	28	7	6	1	15	40	38	39	31
JUN. 4	11	29	29	30	8	6	1	15	40	38	39	31
JUN. 5	11	30	31	31	8	6	1	15	40	38	39	31
JUN. 6	11	32	32	33	8	6	2	15	40	38	39	31
JUN. 7	11	33	34	34	8	6	2	15	40	38	39	31
JUN. 8	11	35	35	36	8	6	2	15	40	38	39	31
JUN. 9	11	36	37	38	8	6	2	15	40	38	39	31
JUN. 10	11	38	39	39	9	7	2	15	40	38	39	31
JUN. 11	12	40	40	41	9	7	2	15	40	38	39	31
JUN. 12	12	41	42	42	9	7	2	15	40	38	39	31
JUN. 13	12	43	44	44	9	7	2	15	40	38	39	31
JUN. 14	12	45	45	46	9	7	2	15	40	38	39	31
JUN. 15	12	46	47	48	10	7	2	15	40	38	39	31
JUN. 16	12	48	1	2	10	8	3	15	40	38	39	31
JUN. 17	12	2	3	3	10	8	3	15	40	38	39	31
JUN. 18	12	4	5	5	10	8	3	15	40	38	39	31
JUN. 19	13	6	7	7	11	8	3	15	40	38	39	31
JUN. 20	13	8	9	9	11	8	3	15	40	38	39	31
JUN. 21	13	10	11	11	11	8	3	15	40	38	39	31
JUN. 22	13	12	13	13	11	9	3	15	40	38	39	31
JUN. 23	13	14	15	15	12	9	3	15	40	38	39	31
JUN. 24	13	16	17	17	12	9	3	15	40	38	39	31
JUN. 25	14	18	18	19	12	9	3	15	40	38	39	31
JUN. 26	14	20	20	21	12	9	3	15	40	38	39	31
JUN. 27	14	21	22	23	13	9	4	15	40	38	39	31
JUN. 28	14	23	24	24	13	9	4	15	40	38	39	31
JUN. 29	14	25	25	26	13	10	4	15	40	38	39	31
JUN. 30	14	26	27	28	14	10	4	16	40	38	39	31

MOON 1 ◐ 12:01 A.M. TO 8:00 A.M.   **MOON 2** ◑ 8:01 A.M. TO 4:00 P.M.   **MOON 3** ● 4:01 P.M. TO 12:00 A.M.

Use only one "moon" number. Choose the column closest to your time of birth. If your place of birth is not on Eastern Standard Time, be sure to read "How to Convert to Eastern Standard Time" at the beginning of this section.

Date & Time	SUN	MOON 1	MOON 2	MOON 3	MERCURY	VENUS	MARS	JUPITER	SATURN	URANUS	NEPTUNE	PLUTO
JUL. 1	14	28	29	29	14	10	4	16	40	38	39	31
JUL. 2	14	30	30	31	14	10	4	16	40	38	39	31
JUL. 3	15	31	32	32	15	10	4	16	40	38	39	31
JUL. 4	15	33	33	34	15	10	4	16	40	38	39	31
JUL. 5	15	34	35	36	15	11	4	16	40	38	39	31
JUL. 6	15	36	37	37	15	11	4	16	40	38	39	31
JUL. 7	15	38	38	39	16	11	4	16	40	38	39	31
JUL. 8	15	39	40	40	16	11	5	16	40	38	39	31
JUL. 9	15	41	42	42	16	11	5	16	40	38	39	31
JUL. 10	15	43	43	44	16	11	5	16	40	38	39	31
JUL. 11	16	44	45	46	17	12	5	16	40	38	39	31
JUL. 12	16	46	47	47	17	12	5	16	40	38	39	31
JUL. 13	16	48	48	1	17	12	5	16	40	38	39	31
JUL. 14	16	2	2	3	18	12	5	16	40	38	39	31
JUL. 15	16	4	4	5	18	12	5	16	40	38	39	31
JUL. 16	16	5	6	7	18	12	5	16	40	38	39	31
JUL. 17	16	7	8	9	18	12	5	16	40	38	39	31
JUL. 18	16	9	10	11	19	13	5	16	40	38	39	31
JUL. 19	17	11	12	13	19	13	6	16	40	38	39	31
JUL. 20	17	13	14	14	19	13	6	16	40	38	39	31
JUL. 21	17	15	16	16	19	13	6	16	40	38	39	31
JUL. 22	17	17	18	18	19	13	6	16	40	38	39	31
JUL. 23	17	19	20	20	20	13	6	16	40	38	39	31
JUL. 24	17	21	21	22	20	14	6	16	40	38	39	31
JUL. 25	17	23	23	24	20	14	6	16	40	38	39	31
JUL. 26	18	24	25	25	20	14	6	16	40	38	39	31
JUL. 27	18	26	26	27	21	14	6	16	40	38	39	31
JUL. 28	18	28	28	29	21	14	6	16	40	38	39	31
JUL. 29	18	29	30	30	21	14	6	16	40	38	39	31
JUL. 30	18	31	31	32	21	15	7	16	40	38	39	31
JUL. 31	18	32	33	33	21	15	7	16	40	38	39	31

Date & Time	SUN	MOON 1	MOON 2	MOON 3	MERCURY	VENUS	MARS	JUPITER	SATURN	URANUS	NEPTUNE	PLUTO
AUG. 1	18	34	34	35	21	15	7	16	40	38	39	31
AUG. 2	18	36	36	37	22	15	7	17	40	38	39	31
AUG. 3	19	37	38	38	22	15	7	17	40	38	39	31
AUG. 4	19	39	39	40	22	15	7	17	40	38	39	31
AUG. 5	19	40	41	42	22	16	7	17	40	38	39	31
AUG. 6	19	42	43	43	22	16	7	17	40	38	39	31
AUG. 7	19	44	44	45	22	16	7	17	40	38	39	31
AUG. 8	19	46	46	47	23	16	7	17	40	38	39	31
AUG. 9	19	47	48	1	23	16	7	17	40	38	39	31
AUG. 10	19	1	2	2	23	16	7	17	40	38	39	31
AUG. 11	20	3	4	4	23	17	7	17	40	38	39	31
AUG. 12	20	5	6	6	23	17	8	17	40	38	39	31
AUG. 13	20	7	7	8	23	17	8	17	40	38	39	31
AUG. 14	20	9	9	10	23	17	8	17	40	38	39	31
AUG. 15	20	11	11	12	24	17	8	17	40	38	39	31
AUG. 16	20	13	13	14	24	17	8	17	40	38	39	31
AUG. 17	20	14	15	16	24	18	8	17	40	38	39	31
AUG. 18	20	16	17	18	24	18	8	17	40	38	39	31
AUG. 19	21	18	19	19	24	18	8	17	40	38	39	31
AUG. 20	21	20	21	21	24	18	8	17	40	38	39	31
AUG. 21	21	22	22	23	24	18	8	17	40	38	39	31
AUG. 22	21	24	24	25	24	18	8	17	40	38	39	31
AUG. 23	21	25	26	26	24	18	8	17	40	38	39	31
AUG. 24	21	27	28	28	24	19	8	17	40	38	39	31
AUG. 25	21	29	29	30	24	19	9	17	40	38	39	31
AUG. 26	22	30	31	31	24	19	9	17	40	38	39	31
AUG. 27	22	32	32	33	24	19	9	17	40	38	39	31
AUG. 28	22	33	34	34	24	19	9	17	40	38	39	31
AUG. 29	22	35	36	36	24	19	9	17	40	38	39	31
AUG. 30	22	37	37	38	24	20	9	17	40	38	39	31
AUG. 31	22	38	39	39	24	20	9	17	40	38	39	31

MOON 1 ◖ 12:01 A.M. TO 8:00 A.M.   **MOON 2** ◐ 8:01 A.M. TO 4:00 P.M.   **MOON 3** ● 4:01 P.M. TO 12:00 A.M.
Use only one "moon" number. Choose the column closest to your time of birth. If your place of birth is not on
Eastern Standard Time, be sure to read "How to Convert to Eastern Standard Time" at the beginning of this section.

1990

September

Date & Time	SUN	MOON 1	MOON 2	MOON 3	MERCURY	VENUS	MARS	JUPITER	SATURN	URANUS	NEPTUNE	PLUTO
SEP. 1	22	40	40	41	24	20	9	17	40	38	39	31
SEP. 2	22	42	42	43	24	20	9	17	40	38	39	31
SEP. 3	23	43	44	44	24	20	9	17	40	38	39	31
SEP. 4	23	45	46	46	24	20	9	17	39	38	39	31
SEP. 5	23	47	47	48	23	21	9	17	39	38	39	31
SEP. 6	23	1	1	2	23	21	9	17	39	38	39	31
SEP. 7	23	3	3	4	23	21	9	18	39	38	39	31
SEP. 8	23	4	5	6	23	21	9	18	39	38	39	31
SEP. 9	23	6	7	8	23	21	10	18	39	38	39	31
SEP. 10	23	8	9	10	23	21	10	18	39	38	39	31
SEP. 11	24	10	11	11	23	22	10	18	39	38	39	31
SEP. 12	24	12	13	13	23	22	10	18	39	38	39	31
SEP. 13	24	14	15	15	22	22	10	18	39	38	39	31
SEP. 14	24	16	16	17	22	22	10	18	39	38	39	31
SEP. 15	24	18	18	19	22	22	10	18	39	38	39	31
SEP. 16	24	19	20	21	22	22	10	18	39	38	39	31
SEP. 17	24	21	22	22	22	23	10	18	39	38	39	31
SEP. 18	24	23	24	24	22	23	10	18	39	38	39	31
SEP. 19	25	25	25	26	22	23	10	18	39	38	39	31
SEP. 20	25	26	27	28	22	23	10	18	39	38	39	31
SEP. 21	25	28	29	29	22	23	10	18	39	38	39	31
SEP. 22	25	30	30	31	22	23	10	18	39	38	39	31
SEP. 23	25	31	32	32	23	24	10	18	39	38	39	31
SEP. 24	25	33	33	34	23	24	10	18	39	38	39	31
SEP. 25	26	34	35	36	23	24	10	18	39	38	39	31
SEP. 26	26	36	37	37	23	24	10	18	39	38	39	31
SEP. 27	26	38	38	39	23	24	10	18	39	38	39	31
SEP. 28	26	39	40	40	23	24	10	18	39	38	39	31
SEP. 29	26	41	41	42	24	25	10	18	39	38	39	31
SEP. 30	26	43	43	44	24	25	11	18	39	38	39	31

October

Date & Time	SUN	MOON 1	MOON 2	MOON 3	MERCURY	VENUS	MARS	JUPITER	SATURN	URANUS	NEPTUNE	PLUTO
OCT. 1	26	44	45	46	24	25	11	18	39	38	39	31
OCT. 2	26	46	47	47	24	25	11	18	39	38	39	31
OCT. 3	27	48	1	1	24	25	11	18	39	38	39	31
OCT. 4	27	2	3	3	25	25	11	18	39	38	39	31
OCT. 5	27	4	4	5	25	26	11	18	39	38	39	31
OCT. 6	27	6	6	7	25	26	11	18	39	38	39	31
OCT. 7	27	8	8	9	25	26	11	18	39	38	39	31
OCT. 8	27	10	10	11	26	26	11	18	39	38	39	31
OCT. 9	27	12	12	13	26	26	11	18	39	38	39	31
OCT. 10	27	14	14	15	26	26	11	18	39	38	39	31
OCT. 11	28	15	16	17	26	27	11	18	39	38	39	31
OCT. 12	28	17	18	18	26	27	11	18	40	38	39	31
OCT. 13	28	19	20	20	27	27	11	18	40	38	39	31
OCT. 14	28	21	21	22	27	27	11	18	40	38	39	31
OCT. 15	28	23	23	24	27	27	11	18	40	38	39	31
OCT. 16	28	24	25	25	27	27	11	18	40	38	39	31
OCT. 17	28	26	26	27	28	28	11	18	40	38	39	31
OCT. 18	28	28	28	29	28	28	11	18	40	38	39	31
OCT. 19	29	29	30	30	28	28	11	18	40	38	39	31
OCT. 20	29	31	31	32	28	28	11	18	40	38	39	31
OCT. 21	29	32	33	33	29	28	11	18	40	38	39	31
OCT. 22	29	34	35	35	29	28	11	18	40	38	39	31
OCT. 23	29	36	36	37	29	29	11	18	40	38	39	31
OCT. 24	29	37	38	38	29	29	11	18	40	38	39	31
OCT. 25	29	39	39	40	29	29	11	19	40	38	39	31
OCT. 26	30	40	41	41	30	29	11	19	40	38	39	31
OCT. 27	30	42	43	43	30	29	11	19	40	38	39	31
OCT. 28	30	44	44	45	30	29	11	19	40	38	39	31
OCT. 29	30	45	46	47	30	30	11	19	40	38	39	31
OCT. 30	30	47	48	48	31	30	11	19	40	38	39	31
OCT. 31	30	1	2	2	31	30	11	19	40	38	39	31

MOON 1 12:01 A.M. TO 8:00 A.M.   **MOON 2** 8:01 A.M. TO 4:00 P.M.   **MOON 3** 4:01 P.M. TO 12:00 A.M.

Use only one "moon" number. Choose the column closest to your time of birth. If your place of birth is not on Eastern Standard Time, be sure to read "How to Convert to Eastern Standard Time" at the beginning of this section.

1990

November

Date & Time	SUN	MOON 1	MOON 2	MOON 3	MERCURY	VENUS	MARS	JUPITER	SATURN	URANUS	NEPTUNE	PLUTO
NOV. 1	30	3	4	4	31	30	11	19	40	38	39	31
NOV. 2	30	5	6	6	31	30	11	19	40	38	39	31
NOV. 3	31	7	8	8	31	30	11	19	40	38	39	31
NOV. 4	31	9	10	10	32	31	11	19	40	38	39	31
NOV. 5	31	11	12	12	32	31	11	19	40	38	39	31
NOV. 6	31	13	14	14	32	31	11	19	40	38	39	31
NOV. 7	31	15	16	16	32	31	11	19	40	38	39	31
NOV. 8	31	17	17	18	32	31	11	19	40	38	39	31
NOV. 9	31	19	19	20	33	31	11	19	40	38	39	31
NOV. 10	31	20	21	22	33	32	11	19	40	38	39	31
NOV. 11	31	22	23	23	33	32	10	19	40	38	39	31
NOV. 12	32	24	24	25	33	32	10	19	40	38	39	31
NOV. 13	32	26	26	27	33	32	10	19	40	38	39	31
NOV. 14	32	27	28	28	34	32	10	19	40	38	39	31
NOV. 15	32	29	29	30	34	32	10	19	40	38	39	31
NOV. 16	32	30	31	31	34	33	10	19	40	38	39	31
NOV. 17	32	32	33	33	34	33	10	19	40	38	39	31
NOV. 18	32	34	34	35	34	33	10	19	40	38	39	31
NOV. 19	33	35	36	36	35	33	10	19	40	38	39	31
NOV. 20	33	37	37	38	35	33	10	19	40	38	39	31
NOV. 21	33	38	39	39	35	33	10	19	40	38	39	31
NOV. 22	33	40	40	41	35	34	10	19	40	38	39	31
NOV. 23	33	41	42	43	35	34	10	19	40	38	39	31
NOV. 24	33	43	44	44	36	34	10	19	40	38	39	31
NOV. 25	34	45	45	46	36	34	10	19	40	38	39	31
NOV. 26	34	47	47	48	36	34	10	19	40	38	39	31
NOV. 27	34	48	1	1	36	34	10	19	40	38	39	31
NOV. 28	34	2	3	3	36	35	10	19	40	38	39	31
NOV. 29	34	4	5	5	36	35	10	19	40	38	39	31
NOV. 30	34	6	7	7	37	35	10	19	40	38	39	31

December

Date & Time	SUN	MOON 1	MOON 2	MOON 3	MERCURY	VENUS	MARS	JUPITER	SATURN	URANUS	NEPTUNE	PLUTO
DEC. 1	34	8	9	9	37	35	10	19	40	38	39	31
DEC. 2	34	10	11	11	37	35	9	19	40	38	39	31
DEC. 3	35	12	13	13	37	35	9	19	40	38	39	31
DEC. 4	35	14	15	15	37	36	9	19	40	38	39	31
DEC. 5	35	16	17	17	37	36	9	19	40	38	39	31
DEC. 6	35	18	19	19	38	36	9	19	40	38	39	31
DEC. 7	35	20	20	21	38	36	9	19	40	38	39	31
DEC. 8	35	22	22	23	38	36	9	19	40	38	39	31
DEC. 9	35	23	24	25	38	36	9	19	40	38	39	31
DEC. 10	35	25	26	26	38	37	9	19	40	38	39	31
DEC. 11	36	27	27	28	38	37	9	19	40	38	39	31
DEC. 12	36	28	29	29	38	37	9	19	40	38	39	31
DEC. 13	36	30	31	31	38	37	9	19	40	38	39	31
DEC. 14	36	32	32	33	38	37	9	19	40	38	39	32
DEC. 15	36	33	34	34	38	37	9	19	40	38	39	32
DEC. 16	36	35	35	36	38	38	9	19	40	38	39	32
DEC. 17	36	36	37	37	38	38	9	19	40	38	39	32
DEC. 18	36	38	38	39	38	38	9	19	40	38	39	32
DEC. 19	37	40	40	41	38	38	9	19	40	38	39	32
DEC. 20	37	41	42	42	38	38	9	19	40	38	39	32
DEC. 21	37	43	43	44	38	38	9	19	40	38	39	32
DEC. 22	37	44	45	45	38	39	9	19	40	38	39	32
DEC. 23	37	46	47	47	37	39	9	19	40	38	39	32
DEC. 24	37	48	48	1	37	39	9	19	40	38	39	32
DEC. 25	37	2	2	3	37	39	9	19	40	38	39	32
DEC. 26	38	3	4	5	37	39	9	19	40	38	39	32
DEC. 27	38	5	6	6	37	39	9	19	40	38	39	32
DEC. 28	38	7	8	8	37	40	9	19	40	38	39	32
DEC. 29	38	9	10	10	36	40	9	19	40	38	39	32
DEC. 30	38	11	12	12	36	40	9	19	40	38	39	32
DEC. 31	38	13	14	14	36	40	9	19	40	38	39	32

MOON 1 ◐ 12:01 A.M. TO 8:00 A.M.   **MOON 2** ◑ 8:01 A.M. TO 4:00 P.M.   **MOON 3** ● 4:01 P.M. TO 12:00 A.M.

Use only one "moon" number. Choose the column closest to your time of birth. If your place of birth is not on Eastern Standard Time, be sure to read "How to Convert to Eastern Standard Time" at the beginning of this section.

1991

January

Date & Time	SUN	MOON 1	MOON 2	MOON 3	MERCURY	VENUS	MARS	JUPITER	SATURN	URANUS	NEPTUNE	PLUTO
JAN. 1	38	15	16	16	36	40	9	19	40	38	39	32
JAN. 2	38	17	18	18	36	40	9	19	40	38	39	32
JAN. 3	39	19	20	20	36	41	9	19	40	38	39	32
JAN. 4	39	21	22	22	36	41	9	19	40	38	39	32
JAN. 5	39	23	23	24	36	41	9	19	40	38	39	32
JAN. 6	39	25	25	26	36	41	9	18	40	38	39	32
JAN. 7	39	26	27	27	36	41	9	18	40	38	39	32
JAN. 8	39	28	28	29	36	41	9	18	41	38	39	32
JAN. 9	39	30	30	31	36	42	9	18	41	38	39	32
JAN. 10	40	31	32	32	36	42	9	18	41	38	39	32
JAN. 11	40	33	33	34	37	42	9	18	41	38	39	32
JAN. 12	40	34	35	35	37	42	9	18	41	38	39	32
JAN. 13	40	36	36	37	37	42	9	18	41	38	39	32
JAN. 14	40	37	38	39	37	42	9	18	41	38	39	32
JAN. 15	40	39	40	40	37	43	9	18	41	38	39	32
JAN. 16	40	41	41	42	37	43	9	18	41	38	39	32
JAN. 17	41	42	43	43	37	43	9	18	41	38	39	32
JAN. 18	41	44	45	45	38	43	9	18	41	38	39	32
JAN. 19	41	46	46	47	38	43	9	18	41	38	39	32
JAN. 20	41	47	48	48	38	43	9	18	41	38	39	32
JAN. 21	41	1	2	2	38	44	9	18	41	38	39	32
JAN. 22	41	3	3	4	38	44	9	18	41	38	39	32
JAN. 23	42	5	5	6	38	44	9	18	41	38	39	32
JAN. 24	42	7	7	8	39	44	9	18	41	38	39	32
JAN. 25	42	8	9	10	39	44	9	18	41	38	39	32
JAN. 26	42	10	11	12	39	44	9	18	41	38	39	32
JAN. 27	42	12	13	14	39	45	9	18	41	38	39	32
JAN. 28	42	14	15	16	39	45	9	18	41	38	39	32
JAN. 29	42	16	17	18	39	45	9	18	41	38	39	32
JAN. 30	42	18	19	19	40	45	9	18	41	38	39	32
JAN. 31	43	20	21	21	40	45	9	18	41	38	39	32

February

Date & Time	SUN	MOON 1	MOON 2	MOON 3	MERCURY	VENUS	MARS	JUPITER	SATURN	URANUS	NEPTUNE	PLUTO
FEB. 1	43	22	23	23	40	45	9	18	41	39	39	32
FEB. 2	43	24	24	25	40	46	9	18	41	39	39	32
FEB. 3	43	26	26	27	40	46	9	18	41	39	39	32
FEB. 4	43	27	28	28	41	46	9	18	41	39	39	32
FEB. 5	43	29	30	30	41	46	10	18	41	39	39	32
FEB. 6	43	31	31	32	41	46	10	18	41	39	39	32
FEB. 7	43	32	33	33	41	46	10	18	41	39	39	32
FEB. 8	44	34	34	35	41	47	10	18	41	39	39	32
FEB. 9	44	35	36	36	42	47	10	18	41	39	39	32
FEB. 10	44	37	38	38	42	47	10	18	41	39	39	32
FEB. 11	44	39	39	40	42	47	10	18	41	39	39	32
FEB. 12	44	40	41	41	42	47	10	18	41	39	39	32
FEB. 13	44	42	42	43	42	47	10	18	41	39	39	32
FEB. 14	44	43	44	45	43	48	10	18	41	39	39	32
FEB. 15	44	45	46	46	43	48	10	18	41	39	39	32
FEB. 16	45	47	48	48	43	48	10	18	41	39	39	32
FEB. 17	45	1	1	2	43	48	10	18	41	39	39	32
FEB. 18	45	2	3	4	44	48	10	18	41	39	39	32
FEB. 19	45	4	5	5	44	48	10	18	41	39	39	32
FEB. 20	45	6	7	7	44	1	10	18	41	39	39	32
FEB. 21	45	8	9	9	44	1	10	18	41	39	39	32
FEB. 22	45	10	10	11	45	1	10	18	41	39	39	32
FEB. 23	46	12	12	13	45	1	10	18	41	39	39	32
FEB. 24	46	14	14	15	1	11	18	41	39	39	32
FEB. 25	46	16	16	17	45	1	11	18	41	39	39	32
FEB. 26	46	17	18	19	45	2	11	18	41	39	39	32
FEB. 27	46	19	20	21	46	2	11	18	41	39	39	32
FEB. 28	46	21	22	22	46	2	11	18	41	39	39	32

MOON 1 12:01 A.M. TO 8:00 A.M.   **MOON 2** 8:01 A.M. TO 4:00 P.M.   **MOON 3** 4:01 P.M. TO 12:00 A.M.
Use only one "moon" number. Choose the column closest to your time of birth. If your place of birth is not on Eastern Standard Time, be sure to read "How to Convert to Eastern Standard Time" at the beginning of this section.

1991

March

Date & Time	SUN	MOON 1	MOON 2	MOON 3	MERCURY	VENUS	MARS	JUPITER	SATURN	URANUS	NEPTUNE	PLUTO
MAR. 1	46	23	24	24	46	2	11	18	41	39	39	32
MAR. 2	46	25	25	26	46	2	11	18	41	39	39	32
MAR. 3	47	27	27	28	47	2	11	18	41	39	39	32
MAR. 4	47	28	29	30	47	3	11	18	41	39	39	32
MAR. 5	47	30	31	31	47	3	11	18	41	39	39	32
MAR. 6	47	32	32	33	47	3	11	18	41	39	39	32
MAR. 7	47	33	34	34	48	3	11	18	41	39	39	32
MAR. 8	47	35	35	36	48	3	11	18	41	39	39	32
MAR. 9	47	36	37	38	48	3	11	18	41	39	39	32
MAR. 10	47	38	39	39	1	4	11	18	41	39	39	32
MAR. 11	48	40	40	41	1	4	11	18	41	39	39	32
MAR. 12	48	41	42	42	1	4	11	18	41	39	39	32
MAR. 13	48	43	43	44	1	4	12	18	41	39	39	32
MAR. 14	48	45	45	46	2	4	12	17	41	39	39	32
MAR. 15	48	46	47	47	2	4	12	17	41	39	39	32
MAR. 16	48	48	1	1	2	5	12	17	41	39	39	32
MAR. 17	48	2	3	3	2	5	12	17	41	39	39	32
MAR. 18	48	4	4	5	3	5	12	17	42	39	39	32
MAR. 19	1	6	6	7	3	5	12	17	42	39	39	32
MAR. 20	1	8	8	9	3	5	12	17	42	39	39	32
MAR. 21	1	9	10	11	3	5	12	17	42	39	39	32
MAR. 22	1	11	12	13	3	5	12	17	42	39	39	32
MAR. 23	1	13	14	14	4	6	12	17	42	39	39	32
MAR. 24	1	15	16	16	4	6	12	17	42	39	39	32
MAR. 25	2	17	18	18	4	6	12	17	42	39	39	32
MAR. 26	2	19	19	20	4	6	12	17	42	39	39	32
MAR. 27	2	21	21	22	4	6	12	17	42	39	39	32
MAR. 28	2	22	23	24	4	6	13	17	42	39	39	32
MAR. 29	2	24	25	25	4	7	13	17	42	39	39	32
MAR. 30	2	26	27	27	5	7	13	17	42	39	39	32
MAR. 31	2	28	28	29	5	7	13	17	42	39	39	32

April

Date & Time	SUN	MOON 1	MOON 2	MOON 3	MERCURY	VENUS	MARS	JUPITER	SATURN	URANUS	NEPTUNE	PLUTO
APR. 1	2	29	30	31	5	7	13	17	42	39	39	32
APR. 2	2	31	32	32	5	7	13	17	42	39	39	32
APR. 3	3	33	33	34	5	7	13	17	42	39	39	32
APR. 4	3	34	35	35	5	8	13	17	42	39	39	32
APR. 5	3	36	36	37	5	8	13	17	42	39	39	32
APR. 6	3	38	38	39	5	8	13	17	42	39	39	32
APR. 7	3	39	40	40	5	8	13	17	42	39	39	32
APR. 8	3	41	41	42	5	8	13	17	42	39	39	32
APR. 9	3	42	43	43	5	8	13	17	42	39	39	32
APR. 10	3	44	45	45	5	9	13	17	42	39	39	32
APR. 11	4	46	46	47	9	14	17	42	39	39	32	
APR. 12	4	47	48	1	4	9	14	17	42	39	39	32
APR. 13	4	1	2	2	4	9	14	17	42	39	39	32
APR. 14	4	3	4	4	4	9	14	17	42	39	39	32
APR. 15	4	5	6	6	4	9	14	17	42	39	39	32
APR. 16	4	7	8	8	4	9	14	17	42	39	39	32
APR. 17	4	9	9	10	4	10	14	18	42	39	39	32
APR. 18	4	11	11	12	4	10	14	18	42	39	39	32
APR. 19	5	13	13	14	4	10	14	18	42	39	39	32
APR. 20	5	15	15	16	4	10	14	18	42	39	39	32
APR. 21	5	16	17	18	4	10	14	18	42	39	39	32
APR. 22	5	18	19	20	4	10	14	18	42	39	39	32
APR. 23	5	20	21	21	4	11	14	18	42	39	39	32
APR. 24	5	22	23	23	3	11	15	18	42	39	39	32
APR. 25	6	24	24	25	3	11	15	18	42	39	39	32
APR. 26	6	26	26	27	3	11	15	18	42	39	39	32
APR. 27	6	27	28	28	3	11	15	18	42	39	39	32
APR. 28	6	29	29	30	3	11	15	18	42	39	39	32
APR. 29	6	31	31	32	3	11	15	18	42	39	39	32
APR. 30	6	32	33	33	3	12	15	18	42	39	39	32

MOON 1 ☽ 12:01 A.M. TO 8:00 A.M.   **MOON 2** ☽ 8:01 A.M. TO 4:00 P.M.   **MOON 3** ● 4:01 P.M. TO 12:00 A.M.
Use only one "moon" number. Choose the column closest to your time of birth. If your place of birth is not on
Eastern Standard Time, be sure to read "How to Convert to Eastern Standard Time" at the beginning of this section.

1991

May

Date & Time	SUN	MOON 1	MOON 2	MOON 3	MERCURY	VENUS	MARS	JUPITER	SATURN	URANUS	NEPTUNE	PLUTO
MAY 1	6	34	34	35	3	12	15	18	42	39	39	32
MAY 2	6	35	36	37	3	12	15	18	42	39	39	32
MAY 3	7	37	38	38	3	12	15	18	42	39	39	32
MAY 4	7	39	39	40	4	12	15	18	42	39	39	32
MAY 5	7	40	41	41	4	12	15	18	42	39	39	32
MAY 6	7	42	42	43	4	13	15	18	42	39	39	32
MAY 7	7	43	44	44	4	13	15	18	42	39	39	32
MAY 8	7	45	46	46	4	13	16	18	42	39	39	32
MAY 9	7	47	47	48	4	13	16	18	42	39	39	32
MAY 10	7	48	1	2	4	13	16	18	42	39	39	31
MAY 11	8	2	3	4	4	13	16	18	42	39	39	31
MAY 12	8	4	5	5	4	13	16	18	42	39	39	31
MAY 13	8	6	7	7	4	14	16	18	42	39	39	31
MAY 14	8	8	9	9	5	14	16	18	42	39	39	31
MAY 15	8	10	11	11	5	14	16	18	42	39	39	31
MAY 16	8	12	13	13	5	14	16	18	42	39	39	31
MAY 17	8	14	15	15	5	14	16	18	42	39	39	31
MAY 18	8	16	17	17	5	14	16	18	42	39	39	31
MAY 19	9	18	19	19	5	14	16	18	42	39	39	31
MAY 20	9	20	20	21	6	15	16	18	42	39	39	31
MAY 21	9	22	22	23	6	15	17	18	42	39	39	31
MAY 22	9	23	24	25	6	15	17	18	42	39	39	31
MAY 23	9	25	26	26	6	15	17	18	42	39	39	31
MAY 24	9	27	27	28	6	15	17	18	42	39	39	31
MAY 25	10	29	29	30	6	15	17	18	42	39	39	31
MAY 26	10	30	31	31	7	15	17	18	42	39	39	31
MAY 27	10	32	32	33	7	16	17	18	42	39	39	31
MAY 28	10	33	34	34	7	16	17	18	42	39	39	31
MAY 29	10	35	36	36	7	16	17	18	42	39	39	31
MAY 30	10	37	37	38	8	16	17	18	42	39	39	31
MAY 31	10	38	39	39	8	16	17	18	42	39	39	31

June

Date & Time	SUN	MOON 1	MOON 2	MOON 3	MERCURY	VENUS	MARS	JUPITER	SATURN	URANUS	NEPTUNE	PLUTO
JUN. 1	10	40	40	41	8	16	17	18	42	39	39	31
JUN. 2	10	41	42	42	8	16	17	18	42	39	39	31
JUN. 3	11	43	43	44	8	17	18	18	42	39	39	31
JUN. 4	11	45	45	46	9	17	18	18	42	39	39	31
JUN. 5	11	46	47	47	9	17	18	18	42	39	39	31
JUN. 6	11	48	48	1	9	17	18	18	42	39	39	31
JUN. 7	11	2	2	3	10	17	18	18	42	39	39	31
JUN. 8	11	3	4	5	10	17	18	18	42	39	39	31
JUN. 9	11	5	6	7	10	17	18	18	42	39	39	31
JUN. 10	11	7	8	9	10	18	18	18	42	39	39	31
JUN. 11	12	9	10	11	11	18	18	18	42	39	39	31
JUN. 12	12	11	12	13	11	18	18	18	42	39	39	31
JUN. 13	12	13	14	15	11	18	18	18	42	39	39	31
JUN. 14	12	15	16	17	11	18	18	18	42	39	39	31
JUN. 15	12	17	18	19	12	18	19	18	42	39	39	31
JUN. 16	12	19	20	20	12	18	19	18	42	39	39	31
JUN. 17	12	21	22	22	12	18	19	18	42	39	39	31
JUN. 18	12	23	23	24	13	19	19	19	42	39	39	31
JUN. 19	13	25	25	26	13	19	19	19	42	39	39	31
JUN. 20	13	26	27	28	13	19	19	19	42	39	39	31
JUN. 21	13	28	29	29	14	19	19	19	42	39	39	31
JUN. 22	13	30	30	31	14	19	19	19	42	39	39	31
JUN. 23	13	31	32	32	14	19	19	19	42	39	39	31
JUN. 24	13	33	34	34	14	19	19	19	42	39	39	31
JUN. 25	14	35	35	36	15	19	19	19	42	39	39	31
JUN. 26	14	36	37	37	15	19	19	19	42	39	39	31
JUN. 27	14	38	38	39	15	20	19	19	42	39	39	31
JUN. 28	14	39	40	40	15	20	20	19	42	39	39	31
JUN. 29	14	41	41	42	16	20	20	19	42	39	39	31
JUN. 30	14	43	43	44	16	20	20	19	42	39	39	31

MOON 1 ☽ 12:01 A.M. TO 8:00 A.M.   **MOON 2** ◑ 8:01 A.M. TO 4:00 P.M.   **MOON 3** ● 4:01 P.M. TO 12:00 A.M.
Use only one "moon" number. Choose the column closest to your time of birth. If your place of birth is not on
Eastern Standard Time, be sure to read "How to Convert to Eastern Standard Time" at the beginning of this section.

1991

July

August

Date & Time	SUN	MOON 1	MOON 2	MOON 3	MERCURY	VENUS	MARS	JUPITER	SATURN	URANUS	NEPTUNE	PLUTO
JUL. 1	14	44	45	45	16	20	20	19	42	39	39	31
JUL. 2	14	46	46	47	16	20	20	19	42	39	39	31
JUL. 3	15	47	48	1	17	20	20	19	42	39	39	31
JUL. 4	15	1	2	2	17	20	20	19	42	39	39	31
JUL. 5	15	3	3	4	17	20	20	19	42	39	39	31
JUL. 6	15	5	5	6	17	21	20	19	42	39	39	31
JUL. 7	15	6	7	8	18	21	20	19	42	39	39	31
JUL. 8	15	8	9	10	18	21	20	19	42	39	39	31
JUL. 9	15	10	11	12	18	21	20	19	42	39	39	31
JUL. 10	15	12	13	14	18	21	21	19	42	39	39	31
JUL. 11	16	14	15	16	18	21	21	19	42	39	39	31
JUL. 12	16	16	17	18	19	21	21	19	42	39	39	31
JUL. 13	16	18	19	20	19	21	21	19	42	38	39	31
JUL. 14	16	20	21	22	19	21	21	19	42	38	39	31
JUL. 15	16	22	23	23	19	21	21	19	42	38	39	31
JUL. 16	16	24	25	25	19	21	21	19	42	38	39	31
JUL. 17	16	26	26	27	20	21	21	19	42	38	39	31
JUL. 18	16	28	28	29	20	21	21	19	42	38	39	31
JUL. 19	17	29	30	30	20	22	21	19	42	38	39	31
JUL. 20	17	31	32	32	20	22	21	19	42	38	39	31
JUL. 21	17	33	33	34	20	22	21	19	41	38	39	31
JUL. 22	17	34	35	35	20	22	22	19	41	38	39	31
JUL. 23	17	36	36	37	21	22	22	19	41	38	39	31
JUL. 24	17	37	38	38	21	22	22	20	41	38	39	31
JUL. 25	17	39	39	40	21	22	22	20	41	38	39	31
JUL. 26	18	41	41	42	21	22	22	20	41	38	39	31
JUL. 27	18	42	43	43	21	22	22	20	41	38	39	31
JUL. 28	18	44	44	45	21	22	22	20	41	38	39	31
JUL. 29	18	45	46	46	21	22	22	20	41	38	39	31
JUL. 30	18	47	48	48	21	22	22	20	41	38	39	31
JUL. 31	18	1	1	2	21	22	22	20	41	38	39	31

Date & Time	SUN	MOON 1	MOON 2	MOON 3	MERCURY	VENUS	MARS	JUPITER	SATURN	URANUS	NEPTUNE	PLUTO
AUG. 1	18	2	3	4	22	22	22	20	41	38	39	31
AUG. 2	18	4	5	5	22	22	22	20	41	38	39	31
AUG. 3	19	6	7	7	22	22	23	20	41	38	39	31
AUG. 4	19	8	8	9	22	22	23	20	41	38	39	31
AUG. 5	19	10	10	11	22	22	23	20	41	38	39	31
AUG. 6	19	12	12	13	22	22	23	20	41	38	39	31
AUG. 7	19	13	14	15	22	22	23	20	41	38	39	31
AUG. 8	19	15	16	17	22	22	23	20	41	38	39	31
AUG. 9	19	17	18	19	22	22	23	20	41	38	39	31
AUG. 10	19	19	20	21	22	22	23	20	41	38	39	31
AUG. 11	20	21	22	23	22	22	23	20	41	38	39	31
AUG. 12	20	23	24	25	22	22	23	20	41	38	39	31
AUG. 13	20	25	26	26	22	22	23	20	41	38	39	31
AUG. 14	20	27	28	28	22	22	23	20	41	38	39	31
AUG. 15	20	29	29	30	21	21	24	20	41	38	39	31
AUG. 16	20	30	31	32	21	21	24	20	41	38	39	31
AUG. 17	20	32	33	33	21	21	24	20	41	38	39	31
AUG. 18	20	34	34	35	21	21	24	20	41	38	39	31
AUG. 19	21	35	36	36	21	21	24	20	41	38	39	31
AUG. 20	21	37	37	38	21	21	24	20	41	38	39	31
AUG. 21	21	39	39	40	21	21	24	20	41	38	39	31
AUG. 22	21	40	41	41	21	21	24	20	41	38	39	31
AUG. 23	21	42	42	43	21	21	24	20	41	38	39	31
AUG. 24	21	43	44	44	20	21	24	20	41	38	39	31
AUG. 25	21	45	45	46	20	21	24	20	41	38	39	31
AUG. 26	22	47	47	48	20	21	24	20	41	38	39	31
AUG. 27	22	48	1	1	20	20	25	21	41	38	39	31
AUG. 28	22	2	3	3	20	20	25	21	41	38	39	31
AUG. 29	22	4	4	5	20	20	25	21	41	38	39	31
AUG. 30	22	5	6	7	20	20	25	21	41	38	39	31
AUG. 31	22	7	8	9	20	20	25	21	41	38	39	31

MOON 1 ◐ 12:01 A.M. TO 8:00 A.M.   **MOON 2** ◑ 8:01 A.M. TO 4:00 P.M.   **MOON 3** ● 4:01 P.M. TO 12:00 A.M.
Use only one "moon" number. Choose the column closest to your time of birth. If your place of birth is not on
Eastern Standard Time, be sure to read "How to Convert to Eastern Standard Time" at the beginning of this section.

Date & Time	SUN	MOON 1	MOON 2	MOON 3	MERCURY	VENUS	MARS	JUPITER	SATURN	URANUS	NEPTUNE	PLUTO
SEP. 1	22	9	10	10	20	20	25	21	41	38	39	31
SEP. 2	22	11	12	12	20	20	25	21	41	38	39	31
SEP. 3	23	13	13	14	20	20	25	21	41	38	39	31
SEP. 4	23	15	15	16	20	20	25	21	41	38	39	31
SEP. 5	23	17	17	18	20	20	25	21	41	38	39	31
SEP. 6	23	19	19	20	20	20	25	21	41	38	39	31
SEP. 7	23	21	21	22	20	20	25	21	41	38	39	31
SEP. 8	23	23	23	24	21	20	26	21	41	38	39	31
SEP. 9	23	24	25	26	21	20	26	21	41	38	39	31
SEP. 10	23	26	27	28	21	20	26	21	41	38	39	31
SEP. 11	24	28	29	29	21	20	26	21	41	38	39	31
SEP. 12	24	30	30	31	21	20	26	21	41	38	39	31
SEP. 13	24	32	32	33	21	20	26	21	41	38	39	31
SEP. 14	24	33	34	34	22	20	26	21	41	38	39	31
SEP. 15	24	35	35	36	22	20	26	21	41	38	39	31
SEP. 16	24	36	37	37	22	20	26	21	41	38	39	31
SEP. 17	24	38	39	39	22	20	26	21	41	38	39	31
SEP. 18	24	40	40	41	23	20	26	21	41	38	39	31
SEP. 19	25	41	42	42	23	20	27	21	41	38	39	31
SEP. 20	25	43	43	44	23	20	27	21	41	38	39	31
SEP. 21	25	44	45	45	23	20	27	21	41	38	39	31
SEP. 22	25	46	47	47	24	20	27	21	41	38	39	31
SEP. 23	25	48	48	1	24	20	27	21	41	38	39	31
SEP. 24	25	1	2	3	24	20	27	21	41	38	39	31
SEP. 25	26	3	4	4	24	20	27	21	41	38	39	31
SEP. 26	26	5	6	6	24	20	27	21	41	38	39	31
SEP. 27	26	7	7	8	25	20	27	21	41	38	39	31
SEP. 28	26	9	9	10	25	20	27	21	41	38	39	31
SEP. 29	26	11	11	12	25	20	27	21	41	38	39	31
SEP. 30	26	12	13	14	25	20	27	21	41	38	39	31

Date & Time	SUN	MOON 1	MOON 2	MOON 3	MERCURY	VENUS	MARS	JUPITER	SATURN	URANUS	NEPTUNE	PLUTO
OCT. 1	26	14	15	16	26	20	28	21	41	38	39	31
OCT. 2	26	16	17	17	26	21	28	22	41	38	39	31
OCT. 3	27	18	19	19	26	21	28	22	41	38	39	31
OCT. 4	27	20	21	21	26	21	28	22	41	38	39	31
OCT. 5	27	22	22	23	27	21	28	22	41	38	39	31
OCT. 6	27	24	24	25	27	21	28	22	41	38	39	31
OCT. 7	27	26	26	27	27	21	28	22	41	38	39	31
OCT. 8	27	27	28	29	27	21	28	22	41	38	39	31
OCT. 9	27	29	30	30	28	21	28	22	41	38	39	31
OCT. 10	27	31	31	32	28	21	28	22	41	38	39	31
OCT. 11	28	33	33	34	28	21	28	22	41	38	39	32
OCT. 12	28	34	35	35	28	21	29	22	41	38	39	32
OCT. 13	28	36	36	37	28	22	29	22	41	38	39	32
OCT. 14	28	37	38	39	29	22	29	22	41	38	39	32
OCT. 15	28	39	40	40	29	22	29	22	41	38	39	32
OCT. 16	28	41	41	42	29	22	29	22	41	38	39	32
OCT. 17	28	42	43	43	29	22	29	22	41	38	39	32
OCT. 18	28	44	44	45	30	22	29	22	41	38	39	32
OCT. 19	29	45	46	47	30	22	29	22	41	38	39	32
OCT. 20	29	47	48	48	30	22	29	22	41	38	39	32
OCT. 21	29	1	1	2	30	22	29	22	41	38	39	32
OCT. 22	29	3	3	4	30	23	29	22	41	38	39	32
OCT. 23	29	4	5	6	31	23	30	22	41	38	39	32
OCT. 24	29	6	7	8	31	23	30	22	41	38	39	32
OCT. 25	29	8	9	9	31	23	30	22	41	38	39	32
OCT. 26	30	10	11	11	31	23	30	22	41	38	39	32
OCT. 27	30	12	13	13	31	23	30	22	41	38	39	32
OCT. 28	30	14	15	15	32	23	30	22	41	38	39	32
OCT. 29	30	16	16	17	32	23	30	22	41	38	39	32
OCT. 30	30	18	18	19	32	24	30	22	41	38	39	32
OCT. 31	30	20	20	21	32	24	30	22	41	38	39	32

MOON 1 ◗ 12:01 A.M. TO 8:00 A.M.   **MOON 2** ◗ 8:01 A.M. TO 4:00 P.M.   **MOON 3** ● 4:01 P.M. TO 12:00 A.M.

Use only one "moon" number. Choose the column closest to your time of birth. If your place of birth is not on Eastern Standard Time, be sure to read "How to Convert to Eastern Standard Time" at the beginning of this section.

1991

November

Date & Time	SUN ☉	MOON 1 ◗	MOON 2 ◖	MOON 3 ●	MERCURY	VENUS	MARS	JUPITER	SATURN	URANUS	NEPTUNE	PLUTO
NOV. 1	30	21	22	23	32	24	30	22	41	38	39	32
NOV. 2	30	23	24	24	33	24	30	22	41	38	39	32
NOV. 3	31	25	26	26	33	24	31	22	41	38	39	32
NOV. 4	31	27	27	28	33	24	31	22	41	38	39	32
NOV. 5	31	29	29	30	33	24	31	22	41	38	39	32
NOV. 6	31	30	31	31	33	25	31	22	41	38	39	32
NOV. 7	31	32	33	33	33	25	31	22	41	38	39	32
NOV. 8	31	34	34	35	34	25	31	22	41	38	39	32
NOV. 9	31	35	36	36	34	25	31	22	41	38	39	32
NOV. 10	31	37	37	38	34	25	31	22	41	38	39	32
NOV. 11	31	39	39	40	34	25	31	22	41	38	39	32
NOV. 12	32	40	41	41	34	25	31	22	41	38	39	32
NOV. 13	32	42	42	43	35	26	31	22	41	38	39	32
NOV. 14	32	43	44	44	35	26	32	22	41	38	39	32
NOV. 15	32	45	45	46	35	26	32	22	41	38	39	32
NOV. 16	32	46	47	48	35	26	32	23	41	38	39	32
NOV. 17	32	48	1	1	35	26	32	23	41	38	39	32
NOV. 18	32	2	2	3	35	26	32	23	41	38	39	32
NOV. 19	33	4	4	5	35	26	32	23	41	38	39	32
NOV. 20	33	6	6	7	36	27	32	23	41	38	39	32
NOV. 21	33	7	8	9	36	27	32	23	41	38	39	32
NOV. 22	33	9	10	11	36	27	32	23	41	38	39	32
NOV. 23	33	11	12	13	36	27	33	23	41	39	39	32
NOV. 24	33	13	14	15	36	27	33	23	41	39	39	32
NOV. 25	34	15	16	17	36	27	33	23	41	39	39	32
NOV. 26	34	17	18	18	36	27	33	23	41	39	39	32
NOV. 27	34	19	20	20	36	28	33	23	41	39	39	32
NOV. 28	34	21	22	22	36	28	33	23	41	39	39	32
NOV. 29	34	23	23	24	36	28	33	23	41	39	39	32
NOV. 30	34	25	25	26	36	28	33	23	41	39	39	32

December

Date & Time	SUN ☉	MOON 1 ◗	MOON 2 ◖	MOON 3 ●	MERCURY	VENUS	MARS	JUPITER	SATURN	URANUS	NEPTUNE	PLUTO
DEC. 1	34	26	27	28	36	28	33	23	41	39	39	32
DEC. 2	34	28	29	29	36	28	33	23	41	39	39	32
DEC. 3	35	30	30	31	36	28	33	23	41	39	39	32
DEC. 4	35	32	32	33	36	29	33	23	41	39	39	32
DEC. 5	35	33	34	34	36	29	34	23	41	39	39	32
DEC. 6	35	35	35	36	36	29	34	23	41	39	39	32
DEC. 7	35	36	37	38	35	29	34	23	41	39	39	32
DEC. 8	35	38	39	39	35	29	34	23	41	39	39	32
DEC. 9	35	40	40	41	35	29	34	23	41	39	39	32
DEC. 10	35	41	42	42	35	30	34	23	41	39	39	32
DEC. 11	36	43	43	44	35	30	34	23	41	39	39	32
DEC. 12	36	44	45	45	34	30	34	23	41	39	39	32.
DEC. 13	36	46	46	47	34	30	34	23	41	39	39	32
DEC. 14	36	48	48	1	34	30	34	23	41	39	39	32
DEC. 15	36	1	2	2	34	30	35	23	42	39	39	32
DEC. 16	36	3	4	4	34	31	35	23	42	39	39	32
DEC. 17	36	5	5	6	34	31	35	23	42	39	39	32
DEC. 18	36	7	7	8	34	31	35	23	42	39	39	32
DEC. 19	37	8	9	10	34	31	35	23	42	39	39	32
DEC. 20	37	10	11	12	34	31	35	23	42	39	39	32
DEC. 21	37	12	13	14	34	31	35	23	42	39	39	32
DEC. 22	37	14	15	16	34	31	35	23	42	39	39	32
DEC. 23	37	16	17	18	34	32	35	23	42	39	39	32
DEC. 24	37	18	19	20	34	32	35	23	42	39	39	32
DEC. 25	37	20	21	22	34	32	35	23	42	39	39	32
DEC. 26	38	22	23	24	35	32	36	23	42	39	39	32
DEC. 27	38	24	25	25	35	32	36	23	42	39	39	32
DEC. 28	38	26	27	27	35	32	36	23	42	39	39	32
DEC. 29	38	28	28	29	35	33	36	23	42	39	39	32
DEC. 30	38	29	30	31	35	33	36	23	42	39	39	32
DEC. 31	38	31	32	32	35	33	36	23	42	39	39	32

MOON 1 ◗ 12:01 A.M. TO 8:00 A.M.   **MOON 2** ◖ 8:01 A.M. TO 4:00 P.M.   **MOON 3** ● 4:01 P.M. TO 12:00 A.M.
Use only one "moon" number. Choose the column closest to your time of birth. If your place of birth is not on
Eastern Standard Time, be sure to read "How to Convert to Eastern Standard Time" at the beginning of this section.

1992

January

Date & Time	SUN	MOON 1	MOON 2	MOON 3	MERCURY	VENUS	MARS	JUPITER	SATURN	URANUS	NEPTUNE	PLUTO
JAN. 1	38	33	33	34	35	33	36	23	42	39	39	32
JAN. 2	38	34	35	35	36	33	36	23	42	39	39	32
JAN. 3	39	36	37	37	36	33	36	23	42	39	39	32
JAN. 4	39	38	38	39	36	34	36	23	42	39	39	32
JAN. 5	39	39	40	40	36	34	37	23	42	39	39	32
JAN. 6	39	41	41	42	36	34	37	23	42	39	39	32
JAN. 7	39	42	43	43	36	34	37	23	42	39	39	32
JAN. 8	39	44	44	45	37	34	37	23	42	39	39	32
JAN. 9	39	46	46	47	37	34	37	23	42	39	39	32
JAN. 10	40	47	48	48	37	35	37	23	42	39	39	32
JAN. 11	40	1	1	2	37	35	37	23	42	39	39	32
JAN. 12	40	2	3	4	37	35	37	23	42	39	39	32
JAN. 13	40	4	5	5	38	35	37	23	42	39	39	32
JAN. 14	40	6	6	7	38	35	37	23	42	39	39	32
JAN. 15	40	8	8	9	38	35	38	23	42	39	39	32
JAN. 16	40	10	10	11	38	35	38	23	42	39	39	32
JAN. 17	41	11	12	13	38	36	38	23	42	39	39	32
JAN. 18	41	13	14	15	39	36	38	23	42	39	39	32
JAN. 19	41	15	16	17	39	36	38	23	42	39	39	32
JAN. 20	41	17	18	19	39	36	38	23	42	39	39	32
JAN. 21	41	20	20	21	39	36	38	23	42	39	39	32
JAN. 22	41	22	22	23	39	36	38	23	42	39	39	32
JAN. 23	42	23	24	25	40	37	38	23	42	39	39	32
JAN. 24	42	25	26	27	40	37	38	23	42	39	39	32
JAN. 25	42	27	28	28	40	37	39	23	42	39	39	32
JAN. 26	42	29	30	30	40	37	39	23	42	39	39	32
JAN. 27	42	31	31	32	40	37	39	23	42	39	39	32
JAN. 28	42	32	33	33	41	37	39	23	42	39	39	32
JAN. 29	42	34	35	35	41	38	39	23	42	39	39	32
JAN. 30	42	36	36	37	41	38	39	23	42	39	39	32
JAN. 31	43	37	38	38	41	38	39	23	42	39	39	32

February

Date & Time	SUN	MOON 1	MOON 2	MOON 3	MERCURY	VENUS	MARS	JUPITER	SATURN	URANUS	NEPTUNE	PLUTO
FEB. 1	43	39	39	40	41	38	39	23	42	39	39	32
FEB. 2	43	40	41	41	42	38	39	23	42	39	39	32
FEB. 3	43	42	42	43	42	38	39	23	42	39	39	32
FEB. 4	43	44	44	45	42	39	40	23	42	39	39	32
FEB. 5	43	45	46	46	42	39	40	23	42	39	39	32
FEB. 6	43	47	47	48	43	39	40	23	42	39	39	32
FEB. 7	43	48	1	1	43	39	40	23	42	39	39	32
FEB. 8	44	2	3	3	43	39	40	23	42	39	39	32
FEB. 9	44	4	4	5	43	39	40	23	42	39	39	32
FEB. 10	44	5	6	7	44	40	40	23	42	39	39	32
FEB. 11	44	7	8	8	44	40	40	23	42	39	39	32
FEB. 12	44	9	9	10	44	40	40	23	42	39	39	32
FEB. 13	44	11	11	12	44	40	40	23	42	39	39	32
FEB. 14	44	13	13	14	44	40	41	23	42	39	39	32
FEB. 15	44	15	15	16	45	40	41	22	42	39	39	32
FEB. 16	45	17	17	18	45	41	41	22	42	39	39	32
FEB. 17	45	19	19	20	45	41	41	22	42	39	39	32
FEB. 18	45	21	21	22	45	41	41	22	43	39	39	32
FEB. 19	45	23	23	24	46	41	41	22	43	39	39	32
FEB. 20	45	25	25	26	46	41	41	22	43	39	39	32
FEB. 21	45	26	27	28	46	41	41	22	43	39	39	32
FEB. 22	45	28	29	30	46	42	41	22	43	39	39	32
FEB. 23	46	30	31	31	47	42	41	22	43	39	39	32
FEB. 24	46	32	32	33	47	42	42	22	43	39	39	32
FEB. 25	46	34	34	35	47	42	42	22	43	39	39	32
FEB. 26	46	35	36	36	47	42	42	22	43	39	39	32
FEB. 27	46	37	37	38	48	42	42	22	43	39	39	32
FEB. 28	46	38	39	39	48	43	42	22	43	39	39	32
FEB. 29	46	40	40	41	48	43	42	22	43	39	39	32

MOON 1 ◗ 12:01 A.M. TO 8:00 A.M.   **MOON 2** ◖ 8:01 A.M. TO 4:00 P.M.   **MOON 3** ● 4:01 P.M. TO 12:00 A.M.
Use only one "moon" number. Choose the column closest to your time of birth. If your place of birth is not on
Eastern Standard Time, be sure to read "How to Convert to Eastern Standard Time" at the beginning of this section.

1992

March

April

Date & Time	SUN	MOON 1	MOON 2	MOON 3	MERCURY	VENUS	MARS	JUPITER	SATURN	URANUS	NEPTUNE	PLUTO
MAR. 1	46	42	42	43	48	43	42	22	43	39	39	32
MAR. 2	46	43	44	44	1	43	42	22	43	39	39	32
MAR. 3	47	45	45	46	1	43	42	22	43	39	39	32
MAR. 4	47	46	47	47	1	43	43	22	43	39	39	32
MAR. 5	47	48	48	1	1	44	43	22	43	39	39	32
MAR. 6	47	2	2	3	1	44	43	22	43	39	39	32
MAR. 7	47	3	4	4	2	44	43	22	43	39	39	32
MAR. 8	47	5	6	6	2	44	43	22	43	39	39	32
MAR. 9	47	7	7	8	2	44	43	22	43	39	39	32
MAR. 10	47	8	9	10	2	44	43	22	43	39	39	32
MAR. 11	48	10	11	11	2	45	43	22	43	39	39	32
MAR. 12	48	12	13	13	2	45	43	22	43	39	39	32
MAR. 13	48	14	15	15	2	45	43	22	43	39	39	32
MAR. 14	48	16	16	17	2	45	44	22	43	39	39	32
MAR. 15	48	18	18	19	2	45	44	22	43	39	39	32
MAR. 16	48	20	20	21	2	45	44	22	43	39	39	32
MAR. 17	48	22	22	23	2	45	44	22	43	39	39	32
MAR. 18	48	24	24	25	2	46	44	22	43	39	39	32
MAR. 19	1	26	26	27	2	46	44	22	43	39	39	32
MAR. 20	1	28	28	29	2	46	44	22	43	39	39	32
MAR. 21	1	29	30	31	2	46	44	22	43	39	39	32
MAR. 22	1	31	32	32	2	46	44	22	43	39	39	32
MAR. 23	1	33	34	34	2	46	44	22	43	39	39	32
MAR. 24	1	35	35	36	2	47	45	22	43	39	39	32
MAR. 25	2	36	37	37	2	47	45	22	43	39	39	32
MAR. 26	2	38	38	39	2	47	45	22	43	39	39	32
MAR. 27	2	39	40	41	2	47	45	22	43	39	39	32
MAR. 28	2	41	42	42	2	47	45	22	43	39	39	32
MAR. 29	2	43	43	44	1	47	45	22	43	39	39	32
MAR. 30	2	44	45	45	1	48	45	22	43	39	39	32
MAR. 31	2	46	46	47	1	48	45	22	43	39	39	32

Date & Time	SUN	MOON 1	MOON 2	MOON 3	MERCURY	VENUS	MARS	JUPITER	SATURN	URANUS	NEPTUNE	PLUTO
APR. 1	2	47	48	1	1	48	45	22	43	39	39	32
APR. 2	2	1	2	2	1	48	45	22	43	39	39	32
APR. 3	3	3	3	4	1	48	46	22	43	39	39	32
APR. 4	3	5	5	6	1	48	46	22	43	39	39	32
APR. 5	3	6	7	7	1	1	46	22	43	39	39	32
APR. 6	3	8	9	9	1	1	46	22	43	39	39	32
APR. 7	3	10	10	11	1	1	46	22	43	39	39	32
APR. 8	3	12	12	13	1	1	46	22	43	39	39	32
APR. 9	3	13	14	15	1	1	46	22	43	39	39	32
APR. 10	3	15	16	17	1	1	46	22	43	39	39	32
APR. 11	4	17	18	18	1	2	46	22	43	39	39	32
APR. 12	4	19	20	20	1	2	47	22	43	39	39	32
APR. 13	4	21	22	22	1	2	47	22	43	39	39	32
APR. 14	4	23	24	24	1	2	47	22	43	39	39	32
APR. 15	4	25	26	26	1	2	47	22	43	39	39	32
APR. 16	4	27	27	28	1	2	47	22	43	39	39	32
APR. 17	4	29	29	30	1	3	47	22	43	39	39	32
APR. 18	4	30	31	32	1	3	47	22	43	39	39	32
APR. 19	5	32	33	33	1	3	47	22	43	39	39	32
APR. 20	5	34	35	35	1	3	47	22	43	39	39	32
APR. 21	5	36	36	37	2	3	47	22	43	39	39	32
APR. 22	5	37	38	38	2	3	48	22	43	39	39	32
APR. 23	5	39	39	40	2	4	48	22	43	39	39	32
APR. 24	5	41	41	42	2	4	48	22	43	39	39	32
APR. 25	6	42	43	43	2	4	48	22	43	39	39	32
APR. 26	6	44	44	45	2	4	48	22	43	39	39	32
APR. 27	6	45	46	46	2	4	48	22	43	39	39	32
APR. 28	6	47	47	48	3	4	48	22	43	39	39	32
APR. 29	6	1	1	2	3	5	48	22	43	39	39	32
APR. 30	6	2	3	3	3	5	48	22	43	39	39	32

MOON 1 ☽ 12:01 A.M. TO 8:00 A.M. **MOON 2** ◑ 8:01 A.M. TO 4:00 P.M. **MOON 3** ● 4:01 P.M. TO 12:00 A.M.

Use only one "moon" number. Choose the column closest to your time of birth. If your place of birth is not on Eastern Standard Time, be sure to read "How to Convert to Eastern Standard Time" at the beginning of this section.

1992

May

June

Date & Time	SUN	MOON 1	MOON 2	MOON 3	MERCURY	VENUS	MARS	JUPITER	SATURN	URANUS	NEPTUNE	PLUTO
MAY 1	6	4	5	5	3	5	48	22	43	39	39	32
MAY 2	6	6	6	7	3	5	1	22	43	39	39	32
MAY 3	7	7	8	9	3	5	1	22	43	39	39	32
MAY 4	7	9	10	11	4	5	1	22	43	39	39	32
MAY 5	7	11	12	12	4	6	1	22	43	39	39	32
MAY 6	7	13	14	14	4	6	1	22	43	39	39	32
MAY 7	7	15	16	16	4	6	1	22	43	39	39	32
MAY 8	7	17	17	18	4	6	1	22	43	39	39	32
MAY 9	7	19	19	20	5	6	1	22	43	39	39	32
MAY 10	7	21	21	22	5	6	1	22	43	39	39	32
MAY 11	8	22	23	24	5	7	2	22	43	39	39	32
MAY 12	8	24	25	26	5	7	2	22	43	39	39	32
MAY 13	8	26	27	27	5	7	2	22	43	39	39	32
MAY 14	8	28	29	29	6	7	2	22	43	39	39	32
MAY 15	8	30	30	31	6	7	2	22	43	39	39	32
MAY 16	8	32	32	33	6	7	2	22	43	39	39	32
MAY 17	8	33	34	35	6	8	2	22	43	39	39	32
MAY 18	8	35	36	36	7	8	2	22	43	39	39	32
MAY 19	9	37	37	38	7	8	2	22	43	39	39	32
MAY 20	9	38	39	39	7	8	2	22	43	39	39	32
MAY 21	9	40	41	41	7	8	3	22	43	39	39	32
MAY 22	9	42	42	43	8	8	3	22	43	39	39	32
MAY 23	9	43	44	44	8	9	3	22	43	39	39	32
MAY 24	9	45	45	46	8	9	3	22	43	39	39	32
MAY 25	10	46	47	47	8	9	3	22	43	39	39	32
MAY 26	10	48	48	1	9	9	3	22	43	39	39	32
MAY 27	10	2	2	3	9	9	3	22	43	39	39	32
MAY 28	10	3	4	4	9	9	3	22	43	39	39	32
MAY 29	10	5	6	6	10	9	3	22	43	39	39	32
MAY 30	10	7	7	8	10	10	3	22	43	39	39	32
MAY 31	10	9	9	10	10	10	4	22	43	39	39	32

Date & Time	SUN	MOON 1	MOON 2	MOON 3	MERCURY	VENUS	MARS	JUPITER	SATURN	URANUS	NEPTUNE	PLUTO
JUN. 1	10	11	11	12	11	10	4	22	43	39	39	32
JUN. 2	10	12	13	14	11	10	4	22	43	39	39	32
JUN. 3	11	14	15	16	11	10	4	22	43	39	39	32
JUN. 4	11	16	17	18	11	10	4	22	43	39	39	32
JUN. 5	11	18	19	19	12	11	4	22	43	39	39	32
JUN. 6	11	20	21	21	12	11	4	22	43	39	39	32
JUN. 7	11	22	23	23	12	11	4	22	43	39	39	32
JUN. 8	11	24	25	25	13	11	4	22	43	39	39	32
JUN. 9	11	26	26	27	13	11	4	22	43	39	39	32
JUN. 10	11	28	28	29	13	11	5	22	43	39	39	32
JUN. 11	12	29	30	31	13	12	5	22	43	39	39	32
JUN. 12	12	31	32	32	14	12	5	22	43	39	39	32
JUN. 13	12	33	33	34	14	12	5	22	43	39	39	32
JUN. 14	12	35	35	36	14	12	5	22	43	39	39	32
JUN. 15	12	36	37	37	14	12	5	22	43	39	39	32
JUN. 16	12	38	38	39	15	12	5	22	43	39	39	32
JUN. 17	12	39	40	41	15	13	5	22	43	39	39	32
JUN. 18	12	41	42	42	15	13	5	22	43	39	39	32
JUN. 19	13	43	43	44	15	13	5	22	43	39	39	32
JUN. 20	13	44	45	45	16	13	6	22	43	39	39	32
JUN. 21	13	46	46	47	16	13	6	22	43	39	39	32
JUN. 22	13	47	48	48	16	13	6	22	43	39	39	32
JUN. 23	13	1	2	2	16	14	6	22	43	39	39	32
JUN. 24	13	3	3	4	16	14	6	22	43	39	39	32
JUN. 25	14	4	5	6	17	14	6	22	43	39	39	32
JUN. 26	14	6	7	7	17	14	6	22	43	39	39	32
JUN. 27	14	8	9	9	17	14	6	22	43	39	39	32
JUN. 28	14	10	10	11	17	14	6	22	43	39	39	32
JUN. 29	14	12	12	13	17	15	6	22	43	39	39	32
JUN. 30	14	14	14	15	17	15	6	22	43	39	39	32

MOON 1 ☽ 12:01 A.M. TO 8:00 A.M.   **MOON 2** ☾ 8:01 A.M. TO 4:00 P.M.   **MOON 3** ● 4:01 P.M. TO 12:00 A.M.
Use only one "moon" number. Choose the column closest to your time of birth. If your place of birth is not on Eastern Standard Time, be sure to read "How to Convert to Eastern Standard Time" at the beginning of this section.

1992

July

August

Date & Time	SUN	MOON 1	MOON 2	MOON 3	MERCURY	VENUS	MARS	JUPITER	SATURN	URANUS	NEPTUNE	PLUTO
JUL. 1	14	16	16	17	18	15	7	22	43	39	39	32
JUL. 2	14	18	18	19	18	15	7	22	43	39	39	32
JUL. 3	15	20	20	21	18	15	7	22	43	39	39	32
JUL. 4	15	21	22	23	18	15	7	22	43	39	39	32
JUL. 5	15	23	24	25	18	16	7	22	43	39	39	32
JUL. 6	15	25	26	27	18	16	7	22	43	39	39	32
JUL. 7	15	27	28	28	18	16	7	22	43	39	39	32
JUL. 8	15	29	30	30	18	16	7	22	43	39	39	32
JUL. 9	15	31	31	32	19	16	7	22	43	39	39	32
JUL. 10	15	32	33	34	19	16	7	22	43	39	39	32
JUL. 11	16	34	35	35	19	17	8	22	43	39	39	32
JUL. 12	16	36	36	37	19	17	8	23	43	39	39	32
JUL. 13	16	37	38	38	19	17	8	23	43	39	39	32
JUL. 14	16	39	40	40	19	17	8	23	43	39	39	32
JUL. 15	16	41	41	42	19	17	8	23	43	39	39	32
JUL. 16	16	42	43	43	19	17	8	23	43	39	39	32
JUL. 17	16	44	44	45	19	18	8	23	43	39	39	32
JUL. 18	16	45	46	46	19	18	8	23	43	39	39	32
JUL. 19	17	47	47	48	19	18	8	23	43	39	39	32
JUL. 20	17	1	1	2	19	18	8	23	43	39	39	32
JUL. 21	17	2	3	3	19	18	8	23	43	39	39	32
JUL. 22	17	4	4	5	19	18	9	23	43	39	39	32
JUL. 23	17	5	6	7	19	18	9	23	43	39	39	32
JUL. 24	17	7	8	8	19	19	9	23	43	39	39	32
JUL. 25	17	9	10	10	19	19	9	23	43	39	39	32
JUL. 26	18	11	11	12	19	19	9	23	43	39	39	32
JUL. 27	18	13	13	14	19	19	9	23	43	39	39	32
JUL. 28	18	15	15	16	19	19	9	23	43	39	39	32
JUL. 29	18	17	17	18	19	19	9	23	43	39	39	32
JUL. 30	18	19	19	20	19	20	9	23	43	39	39	32
JUL. 31	18	21	21	22	19	20	9	23	43	39	39	32
AUG. 1	18	23	23	24	19	20	9	23	43	39	39	32
AUG. 2	18	25	25	26	18	20	10	23	43	39	39	32
AUG. 3	19	27	27	28	18	20	10	23	43	39	39	32
AUG. 4	19	28	29	30	18	20	10	23	43	39	39	32
AUG. 5	19	30	31	31	18	21	10	23	43	39	39	32
AUG. 6	19	32	33	33	18	21	10	23	43	39	39	32
AUG. 7	19	34	34	35	18	21	10	23	43	39	39	32
AUG. 8	19	35	36	36	18	21	10	23	43	39	39	32
AUG. 9	19	37	38	38	18	21	10	23	43	39	39	32
AUG. 10	19	39	39	40	18	21	10	23	43	39	39	32
AUG. 11	20	40	41	41	18	22	10	23	43	39	39	32
AUG. 12	20	42	42	43	18	22	10	23	43	39	39	32
AUG. 13	20	43	44	44	18	22	11	23	43	39	39	32
AUG. 14	20	45	46	46	18	22	11	23	43	39	39	32
AUG. 15	20	47	47	48	18	22	11	23	43	39	39	32
AUG. 16	20	48	1	1	18	22	11	23	43	39	39	32
AUG. 17	20	2	2	3	18	23	11	23	43	39	39	32
AUG. 18	20	3	4	4	18	23	11	23	43	39	39	32
AUG. 19	21	5	6	6	18	23	11	23	43	39	39	32
AUG. 20	21	7	7	8	18	23	11	24	43	39	39	32
AUG. 21	21	8	9	10	18	23	11	24	43	39	39	32
AUG. 22	21	10	11	11	18	23	11	24	43	39	39	32
AUG. 23	21	12	13	13	19	24	11	24	43	39	39	32
AUG. 24	21	14	15	15	19	24	11	24	43	39	39	32
AUG. 25	21	16	16	17	19	24	12	24	43	39	39	32
AUG. 26	22	18	18	19	19	24	12	24	43	39	39	32
AUG. 27	22	20	20	21	19	24	12	24	43	39	39	32
AUG. 28	22	22	23	23	20	24	12	24	43	39	39	32
AUG. 29	22	24	25	25	20	25	12	24	43	39	39	32
AUG. 30	22	26	27	27	20	25	12	24	43	39	39	32
AUG. 31	22	28	28	29	20	25	12	24	43	39	39	32

MOON 1 ◗ 12:01 A.M. TO 8:00 A.M.   **MOON 2** ◑ 8:01 A.M. TO 4:00 P.M.   **MOON 3** ● 4:01 P.M. TO 12:00 A.M.
Use only one "moon" number. Choose the column closest to your time of birth. If your place of birth is not on Eastern Standard Time, be sure to read "How to Convert to Eastern Standard Time" at the beginning of this section.

Date & Time	SUN	MOON 1	MOON 2	MOON 3	MERCURY	VENUS	MARS	JUPITER	SATURN	URANUS	NEPTUNE	PLUTO
SEP. 1	22	30	30	31	20	25	12	24	43	39	39	32
SEP. 2	22	32	32	33	21	25	12	24	43	39	39	32
SEP. 3	23	33	34	34	21	25	12	24	43	39	39	32
SEP. 4	23	35	36	36	21	26	12	24	43	39	39	32
SEP. 5	23	37	37	38	21	26	12	24	43	39	39	32
SEP. 6	23	38	39	39	22	26	12	24	43	39	39	32
SEP. 7	23	40	40	41	22	26	13	24	43	39	39	32
SEP. 8	23	41	42	42	22	26	13	24	43	39	39	32
SEP. 9	23	43	44	44	22	26	13	24	43	39	39	32
SEP. 10	23	45	45	46	23	27	13	24	43	39	39	32
SEP. 11	24	46	47	47	23	27	13	24	43	39	39	32
SEP. 12	24	48	48	1	23	27	13	24	43	39	39	32
SEP. 13	24	1	2	2	23	27	13	24	43	39	39	32
SEP. 14	24	3	4	4	24	27	13	24	43	39	39	32
SEP. 15	24	5	5	6	24	27	13	24	43	39	39	32
SEP. 16	24	6	7	7	24	28	13	24	43	39	39	32
SEP. 17	24	8	9	9	24	28	13	24	43	39	39	32
SEP. 18	24	10	10	11	25	28	13	24	43	39	39	32
SEP. 19	25	11	12	13	25	28	13	24	43	39	39	32
SEP. 20	25	13	14	14	25	28	14	24	43	39	39	32
SEP. 21	25	15	16	16	25	28	14	24	43	39	39	32
SEP. 22	25	17	18	18	26	28	14	24	43	39	39	32
SEP. 23	25	19	20	20	26	29	14	24	43	39	39	32
SEP. 24	25	21	22	22	26	29	14	24	43	39	39	32
SEP. 25	26	23	24	24	26	29	14	25	43	39	39	32
SEP. 26	26	25	26	26	27	29	14	25	43	39	39	32
SEP. 27	26	27	28	28	27	29	14	25	43	39	39	32
SEP. 28	26	29	30	30	27	29	14	25	43	39	39	32
SEP. 29	26	31	31	32	27	30	14	25	43	39	39	32
SEP. 30	26	33	33	34	27	30	14	25	43	39	39	32

Date & Time	SUN	MOON 1	MOON 2	MOON 3	MERCURY	VENUS	MARS	JUPITER	SATURN	URANUS	NEPTUNE	PLUTO
OCT. 1	26	34	35	36	28	30	14	25	43	39	39	32
OCT. 2	26	36	37	37	28	30	14	25	43	39	39	32
OCT. 3	27	38	38	39	28	30	14	25	43	39	39	32
OCT. 4	27	39	40	40	28	30	15	25	43	39	39	32
OCT. 5	27	41	42	42	29	31	15	25	43	39	39	32
OCT. 6	27	43	43	44	29	31	15	25	43	39	39	32
OCT. 7	27	44	45	45	29	31	15	25	43	39	39	32
OCT. 8	27	46	46	47	29	31	15	25	43	39	39	32
OCT. 9	27	47	48	48	29	31	15	25	43	39	39	32
OCT. 10	27	1	1	2	30	31	15	25	43	39	39	32
OCT. 11	28	3	3	4	30	32	15	25	43	39	39	32
OCT. 12	28	4	5	5	30	32	15	25	43	39	39	32
OCT. 13	28	6	6	7	30	32	15	25	43	39	39	32
OCT. 14	28	8	8	9	30	32	15	25	43	39	39	32
OCT. 15	28	9	10	10	30	32	15	25	43	39	39	32
OCT. 16	28	11	12	12	31	32	15	25	43	39	39	32
OCT. 17	28	13	13	14	31	33	15	25	43	39	39	32
OCT. 18	28	15	15	16	31	33	15	25	43	39	39	32
OCT. 19	29	16	17	18	31	33	15	25	43	39	39	32
OCT. 20	29	18	19	20	31	33	15	25	43	39	39	32
OCT. 21	29	20	21	22	32	33	16	25	43	39	39	32
OCT. 22	29	22	23	24	32	33	16	25	43	39	39	32
OCT. 23	29	24	25	25	32	34	16	25	43	39	39	32
OCT. 24	29	26	27	27	32	34	16	25	43	39	39	32
OCT. 25	29	28	29	29	32	34	16	25	43	39	39	32
OCT. 26	30	30	31	31	32	34	16	25	43	39	39	32
OCT. 27	30	32	32	33	33	34	16	25	43	39	39	32
OCT. 28	30	34	34	35	33	34	16	25	43	39	39	32
OCT. 29	30	35	36	37	33	35	16	25	43	39	39	32
OCT. 30	30	37	38	38	33	35	16	26	43	39	39	32
OCT. 31	30	39	39	40	33	35	16	26	43	39	39	32

MOON 1 ◐ 12:01 A.M. TO 8:00 A.M.   **MOON 2** ◐ 8:01 A.M. TO 4:00 P.M.   **MOON 3** ● 4:01 P.M. TO 12:00 A.M.
Use only one "moon" number. Choose the column closest to your time of birth. If your place of birth is not on Eastern Standard Time, be sure to read "How to Convert to Eastern Standard Time" at the beginning of this section.

1992

November   December

Date & Time	SUN	MOON 1	MOON 2	MOON 3	MERCURY	VENUS	MARS	JUPITER	SATURN	URANUS	NEPTUNE	PLUTO
NOV. 1	30	40	41	42	33	35	16	26	43	39	39	32
NOV. 2	30	42	43	43	33	35	16	26	43	39	39	32
NOV. 3	31	44	44	45	34	35	16	26	43	39	39	32
NOV. 4	31	45	46	46	34	35	16	26	43	39	39	32
NOV. 5	31	47	47	48	34	36	16	26	43	39	39	32
NOV. 6	31	48	1	1	34	36	16	26	43	39	39	32
NOV. 7	31	2	3	3	34	36	16	26	43	39	39	32
NOV. 8	31	4	4	5	34	36	16	26	43	39	39	32
NOV. 9	31	5	6	7	34	36	16	26	43	39	39	32
NOV. 10	31	7	8	8	34	36	16	26	43	39	39	32
NOV. 11	31	9	9	10	34	37	16	26	43	39	39	32
NOV. 12	32	11	11	12	34	37	16	26	43	39	39	32
NOV. 13	32	12	13	14	34	37	16	26	43	39	39	32
NOV. 14	32	14	15	15	34	37	16	26	43	39	39	32
NOV. 15	32	16	17	17	34	37	16	26	43	39	39	32
NOV. 16	32	18	19	19	34	37	17	26	43	39	39	32
NOV. 17	32	20	20	21	34	38	17	26	43	39	39	32
NOV. 18	32	22	22	23	34	38	17	26	43	39	39	32
NOV. 19	33	24	24	25	33	38	17	26	43	39	39	32
NOV. 20	33	26	26	27	33	38	17	26	43	39	39	32
NOV. 21	33	27	28	29	33	38	17	26	43	39	39	32
NOV. 22	33	29	30	31	33	38	17	26	43	39	39	32
NOV. 23	33	31	32	32	33	39	17	26	43	39	39	32
NOV. 24	33	33	34	34	33	39	17	26	43	39	39	32
NOV. 25	34	35	35	36	32	39	17	26	43	39	39	32
NOV. 26	34	36	37	38	32	39	17	26	43	39	39	32
NOV. 27	34	38	39	39	32	39	17	26	43	39	39	32
NOV. 28	34	40	40	41	32	39	17	26	43	39	39	32
NOV. 29	34	41	42	43	32	39	17	26	43	39	39	32
NOV. 30	34	43	44	44	32	40	17	26	43	39	39	32

Date & Time	SUN	MOON 1	MOON 2	MOON 3	MERCURY	VENUS	MARS	JUPITER	SATURN	URANUS	NEPTUNE	PLUTO
DEC. 1	34	45	45	46	32	40	17	26	43	39	39	32
DEC. 2	34	46	47	47	32	40	17	26	43	39	39	32
DEC. 3	35	48	48	1	32	40	17	26	43	39	39	32
DEC. 4	35	1	2	3	32	40	17	26	43	39	39	32
DEC. 5	35	3	4	4	32	40	17	26	43	39	39	32
DEC. 6	35	5	5	6	32	41	17	26	43	39	39	32
DEC. 7	35	6	7	8	32	41	17	26	43	39	39	32
DEC. 8	35	8	9	9	32	41	17	26	43	39	39	32
DEC. 9	35	10	11	11	33	41	17	26	43	39	39	32
DEC. 10	35	12	12	13	33	41	17	26	43	39	39	32
DEC. 11	36	14	14	15	33	41	17	26	43	39	39	32
DEC. 12	36	16	16	17	33	42	16	26	43	39	39	32
DEC. 13	36	17	18	19	33	42	16	26	43	39	39	32
DEC. 14	36	19	20	21	33	42	16	27	43	39	39	32
DEC. 15	36	21	22	23	33	42	16	27	43	39	39	32
DEC. 16	36	23	24	24	34	42	16	27	43	39	39	32
DEC. 17	36	25	26	26	34	42	16	27	43	39	39	32
DEC. 18	36	27	28	28	34	42	16	27	43	39	39	32
DEC. 19	37	29	29	30	34	43	16	27	43	39	39	32
DEC. 20	37	31	31	32	34	43	16	27	43	39	39	32
DEC. 21	37	32	33	34	35	43	16	27	43	39	39	32
DEC. 22	37	34	35	35	35	43	16	27	43	39	39	32
DEC. 23	37	36	36	37	35	43	16	27	43	39	39	32
DEC. 24	37	38	38	39	35	43	16	27	43	39	39	32
DEC. 25	37	39	40	40	35	44	16	27	43	39	39	32
DEC. 26	38	41	41	42	35	44	16	27	43	39	39	32
DEC. 27	38	43	43	44	36	44	16	27	43	39	39	32
DEC. 28	38	44	45	45	36	44	16	27	43	39	39	32
DEC. 29	38	46	46	47	36	44	16	27	43	39	39	32
DEC. 30	38	47	48	48	36	44	16	27	43	39	39	32
DEC. 31	38	1	1	2	36	44	16	27	43	39	39	32

MOON 1 ◖ 12:01 A.M. TO 8:00 A.M.   **MOON 2** ◑ 8:01 A.M. TO 4:00 P.M.   **MOON 3** ● 4:01 P.M. TO 12:00 A.M.

Use only one "moon" number. Choose the column closest to your time of birth. If your place of birth is not on Eastern Standard Time, be sure to read "How to Convert to Eastern Standard Time" at the beginning of this section.

1993

January

Date & Time	SUN	MOON 1	MOON 2	MOON 3	MERCURY	VENUS	MARS	JUPITER	SATURN	URANUS	NEPTUNE	PLUTO
JAN. 1	38	2	3	4	37	45	16	27	43	39	39	32
JAN. 2	38	4	5	5	37	45	16	27	43	39	39	32
JAN. 3	39	6	6	7	37	45	16	27	43	39	39	32
JAN. 4	39	7	8	9	37	45	16	27	43	39	39	32
JAN. 5	39	9	10	10	37	45	15	27	43	39	39	32
JAN. 6	39	11	12	12	38	45	15	27	43	39	39	32
JAN. 7	39	13	14	14	38	45	15	27	43	39	39	32
JAN. 8	39	15	15	16	38	46	15	27	43	39	39	32
JAN. 9	39	17	17	18	38	46	15	27	43	39	39	32
JAN. 10	40	19	19	20	39	46	15	27	43	39	39	32
JAN. 11	40	21	21	22	39	46	15	27	43	39	39	32
JAN. 12	40	23	23	24	39	46	15	27	43	39	39	32
JAN. 13	40	25	25	26	39	46	15	27	43	39	39	32
JAN. 14	40	27	27	28	39	46	15	27	43	39	39	32
JAN. 15	40	28	29	30	40	47	15	27	43	39	39	32
JAN. 16	40	30	31	31	40	47	15	27	43	39	39	32
JAN. 17	41	32	33	33	40	47	15	27	43	39	39	32
JAN. 18	41	34	34	35	40	47	15	27	43	39	40	32
JAN. 19	41	35	36	37	40	47	15	27	43	39	40	32
JAN. 20	41	37	38	38	41	47	15	27	43	39	40	32
JAN. 21	41	39	39	40	41	47	15	27	43	39	40	32
JAN. 22	41	40	41	42	41	48	15	27	43	39	40	32
JAN. 23	42	42	43	43	41	48	15	27	43	39	40	32
JAN. 24	42	44	44	45	42	48	15	27	43	40	40	32
JAN. 25	42	45	46	46	42	48	15	27	44	40	40	32
JAN. 26	42	47	47	48	42	48	14	27	44	40	40	32
JAN. 27	42	48	1	1	42	48	14	27	44	40	40	32
JAN. 28	42	2	3	3	42	48	14	27	44	40	40	32
JAN. 29	42	4	4	5	43	48	14	27	44	40	40	32
JAN. 30	42	5	6	6	43	1	14	27	44	40	40	32
JAN. 31	43	7	7	8	43	1	14	27	44	40	40	32

February

Date & Time	SUN	MOON 1	MOON 2	MOON 3	MERCURY	VENUS	MARS	JUPITER	SATURN	URANUS	NEPTUNE	PLUTO
FEB. 1	43	9	9	10	43	1	14	27	44	40	40	32
FEB. 2	43	10	11	11	44	1	14	27	44	40	40	32
FEB. 3	43	12	13	13	44	1	14	27	44	40	40	32
FEB. 4	43	14	15	15	44	1	14	27	44	40	40	32
FEB. 5	43	16	16	17	44	1	14	27	44	40	40	32
FEB. 6	43	18	18	19	45	1	14	27	44	40	40	32
FEB. 7	43	20	21	21	45	2	14	27	44	40	40	32
FEB. 8	44	22	23	23	45	2	14	27	44	40	40	32
FEB. 9	44	24	25	25	45	2	14	27	44	40	40	32
FEB. 10	44	26	27	27	46	2	14	27	44	40	40	32
FEB. 11	44	28	28	29	46	2	14	27	44	40	40	32
FEB. 12	44	30	30	31	46	2	14	27	44	40	40	32
FEB. 13	44	32	32	33	46	2	14	27	44	40	40	32
FEB. 14	44	33	34	34	46	2	14	27	44	40	40	32
FEB. 15	44	35	36	36	47	2	14	27	44	40	40	32
FEB. 16	45	37	37	38	47	2	14	27	44	40	40	32
FEB. 17	45	38	39	39	47	3	14	27	44	40	40	32
FEB. 18	45	40	41	41	47	3	14	27	44	40	40	32
FEB. 19	45	42	42	43	47	3	14	27	44	40	40	32
FEB. 20	45	43	44	44	48	3	14	27	44	40	40	32
FEB. 21	45	45	45	46	48	3	14	27	44	40	40	32
FEB. 22	45	46	47	47	48	3	14	27	44	40	40	32
FEB. 23	46	48	1	1	48	3	14	27	44	40	40	32
FEB. 24	46	2	2	3	48	3	14	27	44	40	40	32
FEB. 25	46	3	4	4	48	3	14	27	44	40	40	32
FEB. 26	46	5	5	6	48	3	14	27	44	40	40	32
FEB. 27	46	6	7	7	48	3	14	27	44	40	40	32
FEB. 28	46	8	9	9	48	3	14	27	44	40	40	32

MOON 1 ☽ 12:01 A.M. TO 8:00 A.M.   **MOON 2** ☽ 8:01 A.M. TO 4:00 P.M.   **MOON 3** ● 4:01 P.M. TO 12:00 A.M.
Use only one "moon" number. Choose the column closest to your time of birth. If your place of birth is not on Eastern Standard Time, be sure to read "How to Convert to Eastern Standard Time" at the beginning of this section.

March

Date & Time	SUN	MOON 1	MOON 2	MOON 3	MERCURY	VENUS	MARS	JUPITER	SATURN	URANUS	NEPTUNE	PLUTO
MAR. 1	46	10	10	11	48	3	14	27	44	40	40	32
MAR. 2	46	11	12	13	48	3	14	27	44	40	40	32
MAR. 3	47	13	14	14	48	3	14	27	44	40	40	32
MAR. 4	47	15	16	16	48	4	14	27	44	40	40	32
MAR. 5	47	17	18	18	48	4	14	27	44	40	40	32
MAR. 6	47	19	20	20	48	4	14	27	44	40	40	32
MAR. 7	47	21	22	22	48	4	14	27	44	40	40	32
MAR. 8	47	23	24	24	48	4	14	27	44	40	40	32
MAR. 9	47	25	26	26	47	4	14	27	44	40	40	32
MAR. 10	47	27	28	28	47	4	15	27	44	40	40	32
MAR. 11	48	29	30	30	47	4	15	27	44	40	40	32
MAR. 12	48	31	32	32	47	4	15	27	44	40	40	32
MAR. 13	48	33	33	34	47	4	15	27	44	40	40	32
MAR. 14	48	35	35	36	47	4	15	27	44	40	40	32
MAR. 15	48	36	37	37	47	4	15	27	44	40	40	32
MAR. 16	48	38	39	39	47	4	15	27	44	40	40	32
MAR. 17	48	40	40	41	47	4	15	26	44	40	40	32
MAR. 18	48	41	42	42	46	4	15	26	44	40	40	32
MAR. 19	1	43	43	44	46	3	15	26	44	40	40	32
MAR. 20	1	44	45	45	46	3	15	26	44	40	40	32
MAR. 21	1	46	47	47	46	3	15	26	44	40	40	32
MAR. 22	1	48	48	1	46	3	15	26	44	40	40	32
MAR. 23	1	1	2	2	46	3	15	26	44	40	40	32
MAR. 24	1	3	3	4	46	3	15	26	44	40	40	32
MAR. 25	2	4	5	5	46	3	15	26	44	40	40	32
MAR. 26	2	6	7	7	46	3	15	26	44	40	40	32
MAR. 27	2	8	8	9	47	3	15	26	44	40	40	32
MAR. 28	2	9	10	10	47	3	15	26	44	40	40	32
MAR. 29	2	11	12	12	47	3	15	26	44	40	40	32
MAR. 30	2	13	13	14	47	3	15	26	44	40	40	32
MAR. 31	2	14	15	16	47	3	15	26	45	40	40	32

April

Date & Time	SUN	MOON 1	MOON 2	MOON 3	MERCURY	VENUS	MARS	JUPITER	SATURN	URANUS	NEPTUNE	PLUTO
APR. 1	2	16	17	17	47	3	15	26	45	40	40	32
APR. 2	2	18	19	19	47	2	15	26	45	40	40	32
APR. 3	3	20	21	21	47	2	16	26	45	40	40	32
APR. 4	3	22	23	23	47	2	16	26	45	40	40	32
APR. 5	3	24	25	25	47	2	16	26	45	40	40	32
APR. 6	3	26	27	27	47	2	16	26	45	40	40	32
APR. 7	3	28	29	29	48	2	16	26	45	40	40	32
APR. 8	3	30	31	31	48	2	16	26	45	40	40	32
APR. 9	3	32	33	33	48	2	16	26	45	40	40	32
APR. 10	3	34	34	35	48	2	16	26	45	40	40	32
APR. 11	4	36	36	37	48	2	16	26	45	40	40	32
APR. 12	4	37	38	39	48	2	16	26	45	40	40	32
APR. 13	4	39	40	40	1	2	16	26	45	40	40	32
APR. 14	4	41	41	42	1	2	16	26	45	40	40	32
APR. 15	4	42	43	43	1	2	16	26	45	40	40	32
APR. 16	4	44	45	45	1	2	16	26	45	40	40	32
APR. 17	4	46	46	47	1	2	16	26	45	40	40	32
APR. 18	4	47	48	48	1	2	16	26	45	40	40	32
APR. 19	5	1	1	2	2	1	16	26	45	40	40	32
APR. 20	5	2	3	3	2	1	16	26	45	40	40	32
APR. 21	5	4	4	5	2	1	17	26	45	40	40	32
APR. 22	5	6	6	7	2	1	17	26	45	40	40	32
APR. 23	5	7	8	8	2	1	17	26	45	40	40	32
APR. 24	5	9	9	10	2	1	17	26	45	40	40	32
APR. 25	6	11	11	12	3	1	17	26	45	40	40	32
APR. 26	6	12	13	13	3	1	17	26	45	40	40	32
APR. 27	6	14	15	15	3	2	17	26	45	40	40	32
APR. 28	6	16	16	17	3	2	17	26	45	40	40	32
APR. 29	6	18	18	19	3	2	17	26	45	40	40	32
APR. 30	6	19	20	21	4	2	17	26	45	40	40	32

MOON 1 ◗ 12:01 A.M. TO 8:00 A.M.   **MOON 2** ◗ 8:01 A.M. TO 4:00 P.M.   **MOON 3** ● 4:01 P.M. TO 12:00 A.M.

Use only one "moon" number. Choose the column closest to your time of birth. If your place of birth is not on Eastern Standard Time, be sure to read "How to Convert to Eastern Standard Time" at the beginning of this section.

1993

May

Date & Time	SUN	MOON 1	MOON 2	MOON 3	MERCURY	VENUS	MARS	JUPITER	SATURN	URANUS	NEPTUNE	PLUTO
MAY 1	6	21	22	23	4	2	17	26	45	40	40	32
MAY 2	6	23	24	25	5	2	17	26	45	40	40	32
MAY 3	7	25	26	27	5	2	17	26	45	40	40	32
MAY 4	7	27	28	29	5	2	17	26	45	40	40	32
MAY 5	7	29	30	31	5	2	17	26	45	40	40	32
MAY 6	7	31	32	32	6	2	17	26	45	40	40	32
MAY 7	7	33	34	34	6	2	18	26	45	40	40	32
MAY 8	7	35	36	36	6	2	18	26	45	40	40	32
MAY 9	7	37	37	38	6	2	18	26	45	40	40	32
MAY 10	7	39	39	40	7	2	18	26	45	40	40	32
MAY 11	8	40	41	41	7	2	18	26	45	40	40	32
MAY 12	8	42	42	43	7	2	18	26	45	40	40	32
MAY 13	8	44	44	45	7	2	18	26	45	40	40	32
MAY 14	8	45	46	46	8	2	18	26	45	40	40	32
MAY 15	8	47	47	48	8	3	18	26	45	40	40	32
MAY 16	8	48	1	1	8	3	18	26	45	40	40	32
MAY 17	8	2	2	3	9	3	18	26	45	40	40	32
MAY 18	8	3	4	5	9	3	18	26	45	40	40	32
MAY 19	9	5	6	6	9	3	18	26	45	40	40	32
MAY 20	9	7	7	8	10	3	18	26	45	40	40	32
MAY 21	9	8	9	10	10	3	19	26	45	40	40	32
MAY 22	9	10	11	11	10	3	19	26	45	40	40	32
MAY 23	9	12	12	13	10	3	19	26	45	40	40	32
MAY 24	9	14	14	15	11	3	19	26	45	40	40	32
MAY 25	10	15	16	17	11	4	19	26	45	40	40	32
MAY 26	10	17	18	18	11	4	19	26	45	40	40	32
MAY 27	10	19	20	20	11	4	19	26	45	40	40	32
MAY 28	10	21	22	22	12	4	19	26	45	40	40	32
MAY 29	10	23	23	24	12	4	19	26	45	40	40	32
MAY 30	10	25	25	26	12	4	19	26	45	40	40	32
MAY 31	10	27	27	28	13	4	19	26	45	40	40	32

June

Date & Time	SUN	MOON 1	MOON 2	MOON 3	MERCURY	VENUS	MARS	JUPITER	SATURN	URANUS	NEPTUNE	PLUTO
JUN. 1	10	29	29	30	13	4	19	26	45	40	40	32
JUN. 2	10	30	31	32	13	4	19	26	45	40	40	32
JUN. 3	11	32	33	34	13	5	19	26	45	40	40	32
JUN. 4	11	34	35	35	13	5	20	26	45	40	40	32
JUN. 5	11	36	37	37	14	5	20	26	45	40	40	32
JUN. 6	11	38	38	39	14	5	20	26	45	40	40	32
JUN. 7	11	40	40	41	14	5	20	26	45	40	40	32
JUN. 8	11	41	42	42	14	5	20	26	45	40	40	32
JUN. 9	11	43	43	44	14	5	20	26	45	40	40	32
JUN. 10	11	45	45	46	15	5	20	26	45	40	40	32
JUN. 11	12	46	47	47	15	6	20	26	45	40	40	32
JUN. 12	12	48	48	1	15	6	20	26	45	40	40	32
JUN. 13	12	1	2	2	15	6	20	26	45	40	40	32
JUN. 14	12	3	3	4	15	6	20	26	45	40	40	32
JUN. 15	12	5	5	6	15	6	20	26	45	40	40	32
JUN. 16	12	6	7	7	16	6	20	26	45	40	40	32
JUN. 17	12	8	8	9	16	6	21	26	45	40	40	32
JUN. 18	12	10	10	11	16	6	21	26	45	40	40	32
JUN. 19	13	11	12	12	16	7	21	26	45	40	40	32
JUN. 20	13	13	14	14	16	7	21	26	45	40	40	32
JUN. 21	13	15	15	16	16	7	21	26	45	40	40	32
JUN. 22	13	17	17	18	16	7	21	26	45	40	40	32
JUN. 23	13	19	19	20	17	7	21	26	45	40	40	32
JUN. 24	13	20	21	22	17	7	21	26	45	40	40	32
JUN. 25	14	22	23	24	17	7	21	26	45	40	40	32
JUN. 26	14	24	25	26	17	8	21	26	45	40	40	32
JUN. 27	14	26	27	27	17	8	21	26	45	40	40	32
JUN. 28	14	28	29	29	17	8	21	26	45	40	40	32
JUN. 29	14	30	31	31	17	8	21	26	45	40	40	32
JUN. 30	14	32	32	33	17	8	21	26	45	40	40	32

MOON 1 ☽ 12:01 A.M. TO 8:00 A.M. **MOON 2** ☽ 8:01 A.M. TO 4:00 P.M. **MOON 3** ● 4:01 P.M. TO 12:00 A.M.
Use only one "moon" number. Choose the column closest to your time of birth. If your place of birth is not on Eastern Standard Time, be sure to read "How to Convert to Eastern Standard Time" at the beginning of this section.

Date & Time	SUN ☉	MOON 1 ◖	MOON 2 ◑	MOON 3 ●	MERCURY	VENUS	MARS	JUPITER	SATURN	URANUS	NEPTUNE	PLUTO
JUL. 1	14	34	34	35	17	8	22	26	45	40	40	32
JUL. 2	14	35	36	37	17	8	22	26	45	40	40	32
JUL. 3	15	37	38	38	17	9	22	26	45	40	40	32
JUL. 4	15	39	40	40	17	9	22	26	45	40	40	32
JUL. 5	15	41	41	42	17	9	22	26	45	40	40	32
JUL. 6	15	42	43	43	17	9	22	26	45	40	40	32
JUL. 7	15	44	45	45	17	9	22	26	45	40	40	32
JUL. 8	15	46	46	47	17	9	22	26	45	40	40	32
JUL. 9	15	47	48	48	16	9	22	26	45	40	40	32
JUL. 10	15	1	1	2	16	10	22	26	45	40	40	32
JUL. 11	16	2	3	3	16	10	22	26	45	40	40	32
JUL. 12	16	4	5	5	16	10	22	26	45	40	40	32
JUL. 13	16	6	6	7	16	10	23	26	45	40	40	32
JUL. 14	16	7	8	8	16	10	23	26	45	40	40	32
JUL. 15	16	9	9	10	16	10	23	26	45	40	40	32
JUL. 16	16	11	11	12	16	10	23	26	45	40	40	32
JUL. 17	16	12	13	14	16	11	23	26	45	40	40	32
JUL. 18	16	14	15	15	16	11	23	26	45	40	40	32
JUL. 19	17	16	17	17	16	11	23	26	45	40	40	32
JUL. 20	17	18	19	19	16	11	23	26	45	40	40	32
JUL. 21	17	20	21	21	16	11	23	26	45	40	40	32
JUL. 22	17	22	22	23	15	11	23	26	45	40	40	32
JUL. 23	17	24	24	25	15	11	23	26	45	40	40	32
JUL. 24	17	26	26	27	15	12	23	26	45	40	40	32
JUL. 25	17	28	28	29	15	12	23	26	45	40	40	32
JUL. 26	18	30	30	31	15	12	24	26	45	40	40	32
JUL. 27	18	31	32	33	15	12	24	26	45	40	40	32
JUL. 28	18	33	34	34	15	12	24	26	45	40	40	32
JUL. 29	18	35	36	36	15	12	24	26	45	40	40	32
JUL. 30	18	37	37	38	16	13	24	26	45	40	40	32
JUL. 31	18	38	39	40	16	13	24	26	45	40	40	32

Date & Time	SUN ☉	MOON 1 ◖	MOON 2 ◑	MOON 3 ●	MERCURY	VENUS	MARS	JUPITER	SATURN	URANUS	NEPTUNE	PLUTO
AUG. 1	18	40	41	41	16	13	24	26	45	40	40	32
AUG. 2	18	42	42	43	16	13	24	26	45	40	40	32
AUG. 3	19	43	44	45	16	13	24	26	45	40	40	32
AUG. 4	19	45	46	46	16	13	24	26	45	40	40	32
AUG. 5	19	47	47	48	16	13	24	26	45	40	40	32
AUG. 6	19	48	1	1	16	14	24	26	45	40	40	32
AUG. 7	19	2	2	3	16	14	25	26	45	40	40	32
AUG. 8	19	3	4	5	17	14	25	26	45	40	40	32
AUG. 9	19	5	6	6	17	14	25	26	45	40	40	32
AUG. 10	19	7	7	8	17	14	25	26	45	40	40	32
AUG. 11	20	8	9	9	17	14	25	26	45	40	40	32
AUG. 12	20	10	11	11	17	15	25	27	45	40	39	32
AUG. 13	20	12	12	13	18	15	25	27	45	40	39	32
AUG. 14	20	13	14	15	18	15	25	27	45	39	39	32
AUG. 15	20	15	16	17	18	15	25	27	45	39	39	32
AUG. 16	20	17	18	18	18	15	25	27	45	39	39	32
AUG. 17	20	19	20	20	19	15	25	27	45	39	39	32
AUG. 18	20	21	22	22	19	15	25	27	45	39	39	32
AUG. 19	21	23	24	24	19	16	26	27	45	39	39	32
AUG. 20	21	25	26	26	19	16	26	27	45	39	39	32
AUG. 21	21	27	28	28	20	16	26	27	45	39	39	32
AUG. 22	21	29	30	30	20	16	26	27	45	39	39	32
AUG. 23	21	31	32	32	20	16	26	27	45	39	39	32
AUG. 24	21	33	33	34	20	16	26	27	45	39	39	32
AUG. 25	21	35	35	36	21	17	26	27	45	39	39	32
AUG. 26	22	36	37	37	21	17	26	27	44	39	39	32
AUG. 27	22	38	39	39	21	17	26	27	44	39	39	32
AUG. 28	22	40	40	41	21	17	26	27	44	39	39	32
AUG. 29	22	41	42	43	22	17	26	27	44	39	39	32
AUG. 30	22	43	44	44	22	17	27	27	44	39	39	32
AUG. 31	22	45	45	46	22	18	27	27	44	39	39	32

MOON 1 ◖ 12:01 A.M. TO 8:00 A.M.   **MOON 2** ◑ 8:01 A.M. TO 4:00 P.M.   **MOON 3** ● 4:01 P.M. TO 12:00 A.M.
Use only one "moon" number. Choose the column closest to your time of birth. If your place of birth is not on Eastern Standard Time, be sure to read "How to Convert to Eastern Standard Time" at the beginning of this section.

Date & Time	SUN ☀	MOON 1 ◔	MOON 2 ◑	MOON 3 ●	MERCURY	VENUS	MARS	JUPITER	SATURN	URANUS	NEPTUNE	PLUTO
SEP. 1	22	46	47	47	23	18	27	27	44	39	39	32
SEP. 2	22	48	48	1	23	18	27	27	44	39	39	32
SEP. 3	23	1	2	3	23	18	27	27	44	39	39	32
SEP. 4	23	3	4	4	23	18	27	27	44	39	39	32
SEP. 5	23	5	5	6	23	18	27	27	44	39	39	32
SEP. 6	23	6	7	7	24	18	27	27	44	39	39	32
SEP. 7	23	8	8	9	24	19	27	27	44	39	39	32
SEP. 8	23	9	10	11	24	19	27	27	44	39	39	32
SEP. 9	23	11	12	12	24	19	27	27	44	39	39	32
SEP. 10	23	13	13	14	25	19	27	27	44	39	39	32
SEP. 11	24	15	15	16	25	19	28	27	44	39	39	32
SEP. 12	24	16	17	18	25	19	28	27	44	39	39	32
SEP. 13	24	18	19	20	25	20	28	27	44	39	39	32
SEP. 14	24	20	21	22	26	20	28	27	44	39	39	32
SEP. 15	24	22	23	24	26	20	28	27	44	39	39	32
SEP. 16	24	24	25	26	26	20	28	27	44	39	39	32
SEP. 17	24	26	27	28	26	20	28	27	44	39	39	32
SEP. 18	24	28	29	30	26	20	28	27	44	39	39	32
SEP. 19	25	30	31	32	27	21	28	27	44	39	39	32
SEP. 20	25	32	33	33	27	21	28	28	44	39	39	32
SEP. 21	25	34	35	35	27	21	28	28	44	39	39	32
SEP. 22	25	36	36	37	27	21	29	28	44	39	39	32
SEP. 23	25	38	38	39	27	21	29	28	44	39	39	32
SEP. 24	25	39	40	40	28	21	29	28	44	39	39	32
SEP. 25	26	41	42	42	28	22	29	28	44	39	39	32
SEP. 26	26	43	43	44	28	22	29	28	44	39	39	32
SEP. 27	26	44	45	45	28	22	29	28	44	39	39	32
SEP. 28	26	46	46	47	28	22	29	28	44	39	39	32
SEP. 29	26	47	48	1	29	22	29	28	44	39	39	32
SEP. 30	26	1	2	2	29	22	29	28	44	39	39	32

Date & Time	SUN ☀	MOON 1 ◔	MOON 2 ◑	MOON 3 ●	MERCURY	VENUS	MARS	JUPITER	SATURN	URANUS	NEPTUNE	PLUTO
OCT. 1	26	3	3	4	29	23	29	28	44	39	39	32
OCT. 2	26	4	5	5	29	23	29	28	44	39	39	32
OCT. 3	27	6	6	7	29	23	30	28	44	39	39	32
OCT. 4	27	7	8	8	30	23	30	28	44	39	39	32
OCT. 5	27	9	10	10	30	23	30	28	44	39	39	32
OCT. 6	27	11	11	12	30	23	30	28	44	39	39	32
OCT. 7	27	12	13	13	30	24	30	28	44	39	39	32
OCT. 8	27	14	15	15	30	24	30	28	44	39	39	32
OCT. 9	27	16	16	17	30	24	30	28	44	39	39	32
OCT. 10	27	18	18	19	30	24	30	28	44	39	39	32
OCT. 11	28	19	20	21	31	24	30	28	44	39	39	32
OCT. 12	28	21	22	23	31	24	30	28	44	39	39	32
OCT. 13	28	23	24	25	31	25	30	28	44	39	39	32
OCT. 14	28	25	26	27	31	25	31	28	44	39	39	32
OCT. 15	28	27	28	29	31	25	31	28	44	39	39	32
OCT. 16	28	29	30	31	31	25	31	28	44	39	39	32
OCT. 17	28	31	32	33	31	25	31	28	44	39	39	32
OCT. 18	28	33	34	35	32	25	31	28	44	39	39	32
OCT. 19	29	35	36	36	32	25	31	28	44	39	39	32
OCT. 20	29	37	38	38	32	26	31	28	44	39	39	32
OCT. 21	29	39	39	40	32	26	31	28	44	39	39	32
OCT. 22	29	41	41	42	32	26	31	28	44	39	39	32
OCT. 23	29	42	43	43	32	26	31	28	44	39	39	32
OCT. 24	29	44	44	45	32	26	31	28	44	39	39	32
OCT. 25	29	45	46	47	32	26	32	29	44	39	39	32
OCT. 26	30	47	48	48	32	27	32	29	44	39	39	32
OCT. 27	30	1	1	2	32	27	32	29	44	39	39	32
OCT. 28	30	2	3	3	32	27	32	29	44	39	39	32
OCT. 29	30	4	4	5	32	27	32	29	44	39	39	32
OCT. 30	30	5	6	6	32	27	32	29	44	39	39	32
OCT. 31	30	7	8	8	32	27	32	29	44	39	39	32

MOON 1 ◔ 12:01 A.M. TO 8:00 A.M.   **MOON 2** ◑ 8:01 A.M. TO 4:00 P.M.   **MOON 3** ● 4:01 P.M. TO 12:00 A.M.
Use only one "moon" number. Choose the column closest to your time of birth. If your place of birth is not on Eastern Standard Time, be sure to read "How to Convert to Eastern Standard Time" at the beginning of this section.

1993

November

Date & Time	SUN	MOON 1	MOON 2	MOON 3	MERCURY	VENUS	MARS	JUPITER	SATURN	URANUS	NEPTUNE	PLUTO
NOV. 1	30	9	9	10	32	28	32	29	44	39	39	32
NOV. 2	30	10	11	11	31	28	32	29	44	39	39	32
NOV. 3	31	12	12	13	31	28	32	29	44	39	39	32
NOV. 4	31	14	14	15	31	28	32	29	44	39	39	32
NOV. 5	31	15	16	16	31	28	33	29	44	39	39	32
NOV. 6	31	17	18	18	31	28	33	29	44	39	39	32
NOV. 7	31	19	19	20	31	29	33	29	44	39	39	32
NOV. 8	31	21	21	22	30	29	33	29	44	39	39	32
NOV. 9	31	23	23	24	30	29	33	29	44	39	39	32
NOV. 10	31	25	25	26	30	29	33	29	44	40	39	32
NOV. 11	31	26	27	28	30	29	33	29	44	40	39	32
NOV. 12	32	28	29	30	30	29	33	29	44	40	39	32
NOV. 13	32	30	31	32	30	29	33	29	44	40	39	32
NOV. 14	32	32	33	34	30	29	33	29	44	40	39	32
NOV. 15	32	34	35	36	30	30	34	29	44	40	39	32
NOV. 16	32	36	37	38	30	30	34	29	44	40	39	32
NOV. 17	32	38	39	39	30	30	34	29	44	40	40	32
NOV. 18	32	40	41	41	30	30	34	29	44	40	40	32
NOV. 19	33	42	42	43	30	31	34	29	44	40	40	32
NOV. 20	33	43	44	44	30	31	34	29	44	40	40	32
NOV. 21	33	45	46	46	30	31	34	29	44	40	40	32
NOV. 22	33	47	47	48	30	31	34	29	44	40	40	32
NOV. 23	33	48	1	1	30	31	34	29	44	40	40	32
NOV. 24	33	2	2	3	31	31	34	29	44	40	40	32
NOV. 25	34	3	4	4	31	32	35	29	44	40	40	32
NOV. 26	34	5	5	6	31	32	35	29	44	40	40	32
NOV. 27	34	7	7	8	31	32	35	29	44	40	40	32
NOV. 28	34	8	9	9	31	32	35	29	44	40	40	32
NOV. 29	34	10	10	11	31	32	35	29	44	40	40	32
NOV. 30	34	11	12	13	32	32	35	30	44	40	40	32

December

Date & Time	SUN	MOON 1	MOON 2	MOON 3	MERCURY	VENUS	MARS	JUPITER	SATURN	URANUS	NEPTUNE	PLUTO
DEC. 1	34	13	14	14	32	33	35	30	44	40	40	32
DEC. 2	34	15	15	16	32	33	35	30	44	40	40	32
DEC. 3	35	17	17	18	32	33	35	30	44	40	40	32
DEC. 4	35	18	19	20	32	33	35	30	44	40	40	32
DEC. 5	35	20	21	21	33	33	35	30	44	40	40	32
DEC. 6	35	22	23	23	33	34	36	30	44	40	40	32
DEC. 7	35	24	25	25	33	34	36	30	44	40	40	32
DEC. 8	35	26	26	27	33	34	36	30	44	40	40	32
DEC. 9	35	28	28	29	33	34	36	30	44	40	40	32
DEC. 10	35	30	30	31	34	34	36	30	44	40	40	32
DEC. 11	36	32	32	33	34	34	36	30	44	40	40	32
DEC. 12	36	34	34	35	34	35	36	30	44	40	40	32
DEC. 13	36	35	36	37	34	35	36	30	44	40	40	32
DEC. 14	36	37	38	39	34	35	36	30	44	40	40	32
DEC. 15	36	39	40	40	35	35	36	30	44	40	40	32
DEC. 16	36	41	42	42	35	35	37	30	44	40	40	33
DEC. 17	36	43	43	44	35	35	37	30	44	40	40	33
DEC. 18	36	44	45	46	35	36	37	30	44	40	40	33
DEC. 19	37	46	47	47	35	36	37	30	44	40	40	33
DEC. 20	37	48	48	1	36	36	37	30	44	40	40	33
DEC. 21	37	1	2	2	36	36	37	30	44	40	40	33
DEC. 22	37	3	3	4	36	36	37	30	44	40	40	33
DEC. 23	37	4	5	5	36	36	37	30	44	40	40	33
DEC. 24	37	6	7	7	36	37	37	30	44	40	40	33
DEC. 25	37	8	8	9	37	37	37	30	44	40	40	33
DEC. 26	38	9	10	10	37	37	38	30	44	40	40	33
DEC. 27	38	11	11	12	37	37	38	30	45	40	40	33
DEC. 28	38	13	13	14	37	37	38	30	45	40	40	33
DEC. 29	38	14	15	16	38	37	38	30	45	40	40	33
DEC. 30	38	16	17	17	38	38	38	30	45	40	40	33
DEC. 31	38	18	19	19	38	38	38	30	45	40	40	33

MOON 1 ◗ 12:01 A.M. TO 8:00 A.M.   **MOON 2** ◑ 8:01 A.M. TO 4:00 P.M.   **MOON 3** ● 4:01 P.M. TO 12:00 A.M.
Use only one "moon" number. Choose the column closest to your time of birth. If your place of birth is not on
Eastern Standard Time, be sure to read "How to Convert to Eastern Standard Time" at the beginning of this section.

1994

January

Date & Time	SUN	MOON 1	MOON 2	MOON 3	MERCURY	VENUS	MARS	JUPITER	SATURN	URANUS	NEPTUNE	PLUTO
JAN. 1	38	20	20	21	38	38	38	30	45	40	40	33
JAN. 2	38	22	22	23	38	38	38	30	45	40	40	33
JAN. 3	39	24	24	25	39	38	38	30	45	40	40	33
JAN. 4	39	25	26	27	39	38	39	30	45	40	40	33
JAN. 5	39	27	28	29	39	39	39	30	45	40	40	33
JAN. 6	39	29	30	30	39	39	39	30	45	40	40	33
JAN. 7	39	31	32	32	39	39	39	30	45	40	40	33
JAN. 8	39	33	34	34	40	39	39	30	45	40	40	33
JAN. 9	39	35	35	36	40	39	39	30	45	40	40	33
JAN. 10	40	37	37	38	40	39	39	30	45	40	40	33
JAN. 11	40	38	39	40	40	40	39	30	45	40	40	33
JAN. 12	40	40	41	41	41	40	39	30	45	40	40	33
JAN. 13	40	42	43	43	41	40	39	30	45	40	40	33
JAN. 14	40	44	44	45	41	40	40	31	45	40	40	33
JAN. 15	40	45	46	47	41	40	40	31	45	40	40	33
JAN. 16	40	47	48	48	41	40	40	31	45	40	40	33
JAN. 17	41	1	1	2	42	41	40	31	45	40	40	33
JAN. 18	41	2	3	3	42	41	40	31	45	40	40	33
JAN. 19	41	4	4	5	42	41	40	31	45	40	40	33
JAN. 20	41	5	6	7	42	41	40	31	45	40	40	33
JAN. 21	41	7	8	8	43	41	40	31	45	40	40	33
JAN. 22	41	9	9	10	43	41	40	31	45	40	40	33
JAN. 23	42	10	11	11	43	42	40	31	45	40	40	33
JAN. 24	42	12	13	13	43	42	41	31	45	40	40	33
JAN. 25	42	14	14	15	43	42	41	31	45	40	40	33
JAN. 26	42	15	16	17	44	42	41	31	45	40	40	33
JAN. 27	42	17	18	19	44	42	41	31	45	40	40	33
JAN. 28	42	19	20	20	44	42	41	31	45	40	40	33
JAN. 29	42	21	22	22	44	43	41	31	45	40	40	33
JAN. 30	42	23	24	24	45	43	41	31	45	40	40	33
JAN. 31	43	25	26	26	45	43	41	31	45	40	40	33

February

Date & Time	SUN	MOON 1	MOON 2	MOON 3	MERCURY	VENUS	MARS	JUPITER	SATURN	URANUS	NEPTUNE	PLUTO
FEB. 1	43	27	27	28	45	43	41	31	45	40	40	33
FEB. 2	43	29	29	30	45	43	41	31	45	40	40	33
FEB. 3	43	31	31	32	45	43	42	31	45	40	40	33
FEB. 4	43	32	33	34	45	44	42	31	45	40	40	33
FEB. 5	43	34	35	36	46	44	42	31	45	40	40	33
FEB. 6	43	36	37	37	46	44	42	31	45	40	40	33
FEB. 7	43	38	39	39	46	44	42	31	45	40	40	33
FEB. 8	44	40	40	41	46	44	42	31	45	40	40	33
FEB. 9	44	41	42	43	46	44	42	31	45	40	40	33
FEB. 10	44	43	44	44	46	45	42	31	45	40	40	33
FEB. 11	44	45	45	46	46	45	42	31	45	40	40	33
FEB. 12	44	47	47	48	46	45	43	31	45	40	40	33
FEB. 13	44	48	1	1	46	45	43	31	45	40	40	33
FEB. 14	44	2	2	3	46	45	43	31	45	40	40	33
FEB. 15	44	3	4	4	46	45	43	31	45	40	40	33
FEB. 16	45	5	5	6	46	46	43	31	45	40	40	33
FEB. 17	45	7	7	8	46	46	43	31	45	40	40	33
FEB. 18	45	8	9	9	45	46	43	31	45	40	40	33
FEB. 19	45	10	10	11	45	46	43	31	45	40	40	33
FEB. 20	45	11	12	12	45	46	43	31	45	40	40	33
FEB. 21	45	13	14	14	45	46	43	31	45	40	40	33
FEB. 22	45	15	15	16	45	47	44	31	45	40	40	33
FEB. 23	46	17	17	18	45	47	44	31	45	40	40	33
FEB. 24	46	18	19	20	45	47	44	31	45	40	40	33
FEB. 25	46	20	21	22	44	47	44	31	45	40	40	33
FEB. 26	46	22	23	24	44	47	44	31	45	40	40	33
FEB. 27	46	24	25	26	44	47	44	31	45	40	40	33
FEB. 28	46	26	27	28	44	48	44	31	45	40	40	33

MOON 1 ◗ 12:01 A.M. TO 8:00 A.M.　　**MOON 2** ◐ 8:01 A.M. TO 4:00 P.M.　　**MOON 3** ● 4:01 P.M. TO 12:00 A.M.

Use only one "moon" number. Choose the column closest to your time of birth. If your place of birth is not on Eastern Standard Time, be sure to read "How to Convert to Eastern Standard Time" at the beginning of this section.

1994

March ★★★

Date & Time	SUN	MOON 1	MOON 2	MOON 3	MERCURY	VENUS	MARS	JUPITER	SATURN	URANUS	NEPTUNE	PLUTO
MAR. 1	46	28	29	29	44	48	44	31	45	40	40	33
MAR. 2	46	30	31	31	44	48	44	31	45	40	40	33
MAR. 3	47	32	33	33	44	48	45	31	45	40	40	33
MAR. 4	47	34	35	35	44	48	45	31	46	40	40	33
MAR. 5	47	36	36	37	44	48	45	31	46	40	40	33
MAR. 6	47	38	38	39	44	1	45	31	46	40	40	33
MAR. 7	47	39	40	40	44	1	45	31	46	40	40	33
MAR. 8	47	41	42	42	44	1	45	31	46	40	40	33
MAR. 9	47	43	43	44	44	1	45	31	46	40	40	33
MAR. 10	47	44	45	46	44	1	45	31	46	40	40	33
MAR. 11	48	46	47	47	44	1	45	31	46	40	40	33
MAR. 12	48	48	48	1	44	2	45	31	46	40	40	33
MAR. 13	48	1	2	2	44	2	46	31	46	40	40	33
MAR. 14	48	3	3	4	44	2	46	31	46	40	40	33
MAR. 15	48	4	5	6	45	2	46	31	46	40	40	33
MAR. 16	48	6	7	7	45	2	46	31	46	40	40	33
MAR. 17	48	8	8	9	45	2	46	31	46	40	40	33
MAR. 18	48	9	10	10	45	3	46	31	46	40	40	33
MAR. 19	1	11	11	12	45	3	46	31	46	40	40	33
MAR. 20	1	12	13	14	45	3	46	31	46	40	40	33
MAR. 21	1	14	15	15	45	3	46	31	46	40	40	33
MAR. 22	1	16	16	17	45	3	47	31	46	40	40	33
MAR. 23	1	18	18	19	46	3	47	31	46	40	40	33
MAR. 24	1	19	20	21	46	4	47	31	46	40	40	33
MAR. 25	2	21	22	23	46	4	47	31	46	40	40	33
MAR. 26	2	23	24	25	46	4	47	31	46	40	40	33
MAR. 27	2	25	26	27	46	4	47	31	46	40	40	33
MAR. 28	2	27	28	29	46	4	47	31	46	40	40	33
MAR. 29	2	29	30	31	47	4	47	31	46	40	40	33
MAR. 30	2	31	32	33	47	5	47	31	46	40	40	33
MAR. 31	2	33	34	35	47	5	47	31	46	40	40	33

April ★★★

Date & Time	SUN	MOON 1	MOON 2	MOON 3	MERCURY	VENUS	MARS	JUPITER	SATURN	URANUS	NEPTUNE	PLUTO
APR. 1	2	35	36	36	47	5	48	31	46	40	40	33
APR. 2	2	37	38	38	47	5	48	31	46	40	40	33
APR. 3	3	39	39	40	48	5	48	31	46	40	40	33
APR. 4	3	41	41	42	48	5	48	31	46	40	40	33
APR. 5	3	42	43	43	48	6	48	31	46	40	40	33
APR. 6	3	44	45	45	48	6	48	31	46	40	40	33
APR. 7	3	46	46	47	48	6	48	31	46	40	40	33
APR. 8	3	47	48	48	1	6	48	31	46	40	40	33
APR. 9	3	1	1	2	1	6	48	31	46	40	40	33
APR. 10	3	2	3	4	1	6	48	31	46	40	40	33
APR. 11	4	4	5	5	1	7	1	31	46	40	40	33
APR. 12	4	6	6	7	2	7	1	31	46	40	40	33
APR. 13	4	7	8	8	2	7	1	31	46	40	40	33
APR. 14	4	9	9	10	2	7	1	31	46	40	40	33
APR. 15	4	10	11	11	2	7	1	31	46	40	40	33
APR. 16	4	12	13	13	2	7	1	31	46	40	40	33
APR. 17	4	14	14	15	3	7	1	30	46	40	40	33
APR. 18	4	15	16	16	3	8	1	30	46	40	40	33
APR. 19	5	17	18	18	3	8	1	30	46	40	40	33
APR. 20	5	19	19	20	3	8	2	30	46	40	40	33
APR. 21	5	21	21	22	4	8	2	30	46	40	40	33
APR. 22	5	22	23	24	4	8	2	30	46	40	40	33
APR. 23	5	24	25	26	4	8	2	30	46	40	40	33
APR. 24	5	26	27	28	5	9	2	30	46	40	40	33
APR. 25	6	28	29	30	5	9	2	30	46	40	40	33
APR. 26	6	30	31	32	5	9	2	30	46	40	40	33
APR. 27	6	32	33	34	5	9	2	30	46	40	40	33
APR. 28	6	34	35	36	6	9	2	30	46	40	40	33
APR. 29	6	36	37	38	6	9	2	30	46	40	40	33
APR. 30	6	38	39	40	6	10	3	30	46	40	40	33

MOON 1 ◐ 12:01 A.M. TO 8:00 A.M.   **MOON 2** ◑ 8:01 A.M. TO 4:00 P.M.   **MOON 3** ● 4:01 P.M. TO 12:00 A.M.

Use only one "moon" number. Choose the column closest to your time of birth. If your place of birth is not on Eastern Standard Time, be sure to read "How to Convert to Eastern Standard Time" at the beginning of this section.

May

June

Date & Time	SUN	MOON 1	MOON 2	MOON 3	MERCURY	VENUS	MARS	JUPITER	SATURN	URANUS	NEPTUNE	PLUTO
MAY 1	6	40	41	41	7	10	3	30	46	40	40	33
MAY 2	6	42	42	43	7	10	3	30	46	40	40	33
MAY 3	7	44	44	45	7	10	3	30	46	40	40	33
MAY 4	7	45	46	46	7	10	3	30	46	40	40	33
MAY 5	7	47	47	48	8	10	3	30	46	40	40	33
MAY 6	7	1	1	2	8	11	3	30	46	40	40	33
MAY 7	7	2	3	3	8	11	3	30	46	40	40	33
MAY 8	7	4	4	5	9	11	3	30	46	40	40	33
MAY 9	7	5	6	6	9	11	3	30	46	40	40	33
MAY 10	7	7	7	8	9	11	4	30	46	40	40	33
MAY 11	8	8	9	9	9	11	4	30	46	40	40	33
MAY 12	8	10	11	11	10	12	4	30	46	40	40	33
MAY 13	8	12	12	13	10	12	4	30	46	40	40	33
MAY 14	8	13	14	14	10	12	4	30	46	40	40	33
MAY 15	8	15	15	16	10	12	4	30	46	40	40	33
MAY 16	8	17	17	18	11	12	4	30	46	40	40	33
MAY 17	8	18	19	19	11	12	4	30	46	40	40	33
MAY 18	8	20	21	21	11	13	4	30	46	40	40	33
MAY 19	9	22	22	23	11	13	4	30	46	40	40	33
MAY 20	9	24	24	25	11	13	5	30	46	40	40	33
MAY 21	9	26	26	27	12	13	5	30	47	40	40	33
MAY 22	9	28	28	29	12	13	5	30	47	40	40	33
MAY 23	9	30	30	31	12	13	5	30	47	40	40	33
MAY 24	9	32	32	33	12	14	5	30	47	40	40	33
MAY 25	10	34	34	35	12	14	5	30	47	40	40	32
MAY 26	10	36	36	37	13	14	5	30	47	40	40	32
MAY 27	10	38	38	39	13	14	5	30	47	40	40	32
MAY 28	10	39	40	41	13	14	5	30	47	40	40	32
MAY 29	10	41	42	42	13	14	5	30	47	40	40	32
MAY 30	10	43	44	44	13	14	6	30	47	40	40	32
MAY 31	10	45	45	46	13	15	6	30	47	40	40	32

Date & Time	SUN	MOON 1	MOON 2	MOON 3	MERCURY	VENUS	MARS	JUPITER	SATURN	URANUS	NEPTUNE	PLUTO
JUN. 1	10	46	47	48	13	15	6	30	47	40	40	32
JUN. 2	10	48	1	1	14	15	6	30	47	40	40	32
JUN. 3	11	2	2	3	14	15	6	30	47	40	40	32
JUN. 4	11	3	4	4	14	15	6	30	47	40	40	32
JUN. 5	11	5	5	6	14	15	6	30	47	40	40	32
JUN. 6	11	6	7	7	14	16	6	30	47	40	40	32
JUN. 7	11	8	8	9	14	16	6	30	47	40	40	32
JUN. 8	11	10	10	11	14	16	6	30	47	40	40	32
JUN. 9	11	11	12	12	14	16	7	30	47	40	40	32
JUN. 10	11	13	13	14	14	16	7	30	47	40	40	32
JUN. 11	12	14	15	16	14	16	7	30	47	40	40	32
JUN. 12	12	16	17	17	14	16	7	30	47	40	40	32
JUN. 13	12	18	18	19	14	17	7	30	47	40	40	32
JUN. 14	12	20	20	21	14	17	7	30	47	40	40	32
JUN. 15	12	21	22	23	14	17	7	30	47	40	40	32
JUN. 16	12	23	24	24	14	17	7	30	47	40	40	32
JUN. 17	12	25	26	26	14	17	7	30	47	40	40	32
JUN. 18	12	27	28	28	14	17	7	30	47	40	40	32
JUN. 19	13	29	30	30	14	18	8	30	47	40	40	32
JUN. 20	13	31	31	32	14	18	8	30	47	40	40	32
JUN. 21	13	33	33	34	14	18	8	30	47	40	40	32
JUN. 22	13	35	35	36	14	18	8	30	47	40	40	32
JUN. 23	13	37	37	38	14	18	8	30	47	40	40	32
JUN. 24	13	39	39	40	14	18	8	30	47	40	40	32
JUN. 25	14	40	41	42	13	19	8	30	47	40	40	32
JUN. 26	14	42	43	44	13	19	8	30	47	40	40	32
JUN. 27	14	44	45	45	13	19	8	30	47	40	40	32
JUN. 28	14	46	46	47	13	19	8	30	47	40	40	32
JUN. 29	14	48	48	1	13	19	9	30	47	40	40	32
JUN. 30	14	1	2	2	13	19	9	30	47	40	40	32

MOON 1 ☽ 12:01 A.M. TO 8:00 A.M.   **MOON 2** ◗ 8:01 A.M. TO 4:00 P.M.   **MOON 3** ● 4:01 P.M. TO 12:00 A.M.
Use only one "moon" number. Choose the column closest to your time of birth. If your place of birth is not on
Eastern Standard Time, be sure to read "How to Convert to Eastern Standard Time" at the beginning of this section.

1994

July   August

Date & Time	SUN	MOON 1	MOON 2	MOON 3	MERCURY	VENUS	MARS	JUPITER	SATURN	URANUS	NEPTUNE	PLUTO
JUL. 1	14	3	3	4	13	19	9	30	47	40	40	32
JUL. 2	14	4	5	5	13	20	9	30	47	40	40	32
JUL. 3	15	6	6	7	13	20	9	30	47	40	40	32
JUL. 4	15	7	8	9	13	20	9	30	47	40	40	32
JUL. 5	15	9	10	10	13	20	9	30	47	40	40	32
JUL. 6	15	11	11	12	13	20	9	30	47	40	40	32
JUL. 7	15	12	13	13	13	20	9	30	47	40	40	32
JUL. 8	15	14	15	15	13	21	9	30	47	40	40	32
JUL. 9	15	16	16	17	13	21	9	30	47	40	40	32
JUL. 10	15	17	18	19	13	21	10	30	47	40	40	32
JUL. 11	16	19	20	20	13	21	10	30	47	40	40	32
JUL. 12	16	21	22	22	13	21	10	30	47	40	40	32
JUL. 13	16	23	23	24	13	21	10	30	47	40	40	32
JUL. 14	16	25	25	26	13	21	10	30	47	40	40	32
JUL. 15	16	26	27	28	13	22	10	30	47	40	40	32
JUL. 16	16	28	29	30	13	22	10	30	47	40	40	32
JUL. 17	16	30	31	32	14	22	10	30	47	40	40	32
JUL. 18	16	32	33	33	14	22	10	30	47	40	40	32
JUL. 19	17	34	35	35	14	22	10	30	47	40	40	32
JUL. 20	17	36	37	37	14	22	10	30	47	40	40	32
JUL. 21	17	38	39	39	14	22	11	30	47	40	40	32
JUL. 22	17	40	40	41	14	23	11	30	47	40	40	32
JUL. 23	17	42	42	43	14	23	11	30	47	40	40	32
JUL. 24	17	43	44	45	15	23	11	30	47	40	40	32
JUL. 25	17	45	46	46	15	23	11	30	47	40	40	32
JUL. 26	18	47	47	48	15	23	11	30	47	40	40	32
JUL. 27	18	1	1	2	15	23	11	30	46	40	40	32
JUL. 28	18	2	3	3	15	23	11	30	46	40	40	32
JUL. 29	18	4	4	5	16	24	11	30	46	40	40	32
JUL. 30	18	5	6	6	16	24	11	30	46	40	40	32
JUL. 31	18	7	8	8	16	24	11	30	46	40	40	32

Date & Time	SUN	MOON 1	MOON 2	MOON 3	MERCURY	VENUS	MARS	JUPITER	SATURN	URANUS	NEPTUNE	PLUTO
AUG. 1	18	9	9	10	16	24	12	30	46	40	40	32
AUG. 2	18	10	11	11	17	24	12	30	46	40	40	32
AUG. 3	19	12	12	13	17	24	12	30	46	40	40	32
AUG. 4	19	13	14	15	17	24	12	30	46	40	40	32
AUG. 5	19	15	16	16	17	25	12	30	46	40	40	32
AUG. 6	19	17	17	18	18	25	12	30	46	40	40	32
AUG. 7	19	19	19	20	18	25	12	30	46	40	40	32
AUG. 8	19	20	21	22	18	25	12	30	46	40	40	32
AUG. 9	19	22	23	24	19	25	12	30	46	40	40	32
AUG. 10	19	24	25	25	19	25	12	30	46	40	40	32
AUG. 11	20	26	27	27	19	25	12	30	46	40	40	32
AUG. 12	20	28	29	29	19	26	13	30	46	40	40	32
AUG. 13	20	30	30	31	20	26	13	30	46	40	40	32
AUG. 14	20	32	32	33	20	26	13	30	46	40	40	32
AUG. 15	20	34	34	35	20	26	13	30	46	40	40	32
AUG. 16	20	35	36	37	20	26	13	30	46	40	40	32
AUG. 17	20	37	38	39	21	26	13	30	46	40	40	32
AUG. 18	20	39	40	40	21	26	13	30	46	40	40	32
AUG. 19	21	41	42	42	21	27	13	30	46	40	40	32
AUG. 20	21	43	43	44	22	27	13	30	46	40	40	32
AUG. 21	21	45	45	46	22	27	13	30	46	40	40	32
AUG. 22	21	46	47	47	22	27	13	30	46	40	40	32
AUG. 23	21	48	1	1	22	27	14	30	46	40	40	32
AUG. 24	21	2	2	3	23	27	14	30	46	40	40	32
AUG. 25	21	3	4	4	23	27	14	30	46	40	40	32
AUG. 26	22	5	5	6	23	27	14	30	46	40	40	32
AUG. 27	22	6	7	8	23	28	14	30	46	40	40	32
AUG. 28	22	8	9	9	23	28	14	30	46	40	40	32
AUG. 29	22	10	10	11	24	28	14	30	46	40	40	32
AUG. 30	22	11	12	12	24	28	14	30	46	40	40	32
AUG. 31	22	13	13	14	24	28	14	30	46	40	40	32

MOON 1 ◗ 12:01 A.M. TO 8:00 A.M.   **MOON 2** ◑ 8:01 A.M. TO 4:00 P.M.   **MOON 3** ● 4:01 P.M. TO 12:00 A.M.

Use only one "moon" number. Choose the column closest to your time of birth. If your place of birth is not on Eastern Standard Time, be sure to read "How to Convert to Eastern Standard Time" at the beginning of this section.

1994

September

Date & Time	SUN	MOON 1	MOON 2	MOON 3	MERCURY	VENUS	MARS	JUPITER	SATURN	URANUS	NEPTUNE	PLUTO
SEP. 1	22	14	15	16	24	28	14	30	46	40	40	32
SEP. 2	22	16	17	17	25	28	14	30	46	40	40	32
SEP. 3	23	18	19	19	25	28	14	30	46	40	40	32
SEP. 4	23	20	20	21	25	29	15	30	46	40	40	32
SEP. 5	23	22	22	23	25	29	15	30	46	40	40	32
SEP. 6	23	24	24	25	25	29	15	30	46	40	40	32
SEP. 7	23	25	26	27	26	29	15	30	46	40	40	32
SEP. 8	23	27	28	29	26	29	15	30	46	40	40	32
SEP. 9	23	29	30	31	26	29	15	30	46	40	40	32
SEP. 10	23	31	32	33	26	29	15	30	46	40	40	32
SEP. 11	24	33	34	34	26	29	15	30	46	40	40	32
SEP. 12	24	35	36	36	27	29	15	31	46	40	40	32
SEP. 13	24	37	38	38	27	30	15	31	46	40	40	32
SEP. 14	24	39	39	40	27	30	15	31	46	40	40	32
SEP. 15	24	41	41	42	27	30	15	31	46	40	40	32
SEP. 16	24	42	43	43	27	30	16	31	46	40	40	32
SEP. 17	24	44	45	45	27	30	16	31	46	40	40	32
SEP. 18	24	46	46	47	28	30	16	31	46	40	40	32
SEP. 19	25	47	48	1	28	30	16	31	46	40	40	32
SEP. 20	25	1	2	2	28	30	16	31	46	40	40	32
SEP. 21	25	3	3	4	28	30	16	31	46	40	40	32
SEP. 22	25	4	5	5	28	30	16	31	46	40	40	32
SEP. 23	25	6	6	7	28	30	16	31	46	40	40	32
SEP. 24	25	8	8	9	29	31	16	31	46	40	40	32
SEP. 25	26	9	10	10	29	31	16	31	46	40	40	32
SEP. 26	26	11	11	12	29	31	16	31	46	40	40	32
SEP. 27	26	12	13	13	29	31	16	31	46	40	40	32
SEP. 28	26	14	14	15	29	31	16	31	46	40	40	32
SEP. 29	26	16	16	17	29	31	17	31	46	40	40	32
SEP. 30	26	17	18	18	29	31	17	31	46	40	40	32

October

Date & Time	SUN	MOON 1	MOON 2	MOON 3	MERCURY	VENUS	MARS	JUPITER	SATURN	URANUS	NEPTUNE	PLUTO
OCT. 1	26	19	20	20	29	31	17	31	46	40	40	32
OCT. 2	26	21	21	22	29	31	17	31	46	40	40	32
OCT. 3	27	23	23	24	30	31	17	31	46	40	40	32
OCT. 4	27	25	25	26	30	31	17	31	46	40	40	32
OCT. 5	27	27	27	28	30	31	17	31	46	40	40	32
OCT. 6	27	29	29	30	30	31	17	31	46	40	40	32
OCT. 7	27	31	31	32	30	31	17	31	46	40	40	32
OCT. 8	27	33	33	34	30	31	17	31	46	40	40	32
OCT. 9	27	35	35	36	30	31	17	31	46	40	40	32
OCT. 10	27	36	37	38	30	31	17	31	46	40	40	32
OCT. 11	28	38	39	40	30	31	17	31	46	40	40	32
OCT. 12	28	40	41	41	30	31	18	31	46	40	40	32
OCT. 13	28	42	43	43	30	31	18	31	46	40	40	33
OCT. 14	28	44	44	45	30	31	18	31	46	40	40	33
OCT. 15	28	45	46	46	30	31	18	31	46	40	40	33
OCT. 16	28	47	48	48	29	31	18	31	46	40	40	33
OCT. 17	28	1	1	2	29	31	18	31	46	40	40	33
OCT. 18	28	2	3	3	29	31	18	31	46	40	40	33
OCT. 19	29	4	4	5	29	31	18	31	46	40	40	33
OCT. 20	29	6	6	7	29	31	18	31	46	40	40	33
OCT. 21	29	7	8	8	29	31	18	32	46	40	40	33
OCT. 22	29	9	9	10	29	31	18	32	46	40	40	33
OCT. 23	29	10	11	11	28	31	18	32	46	40	40	33
OCT. 24	29	12	12	13	28	31	18	32	46	40	40	33
OCT. 25	29	13	14	14	28	31	18	32	46	40	40	33
OCT. 26	30	15	16	16	28	31	19	32	46	40	40	33
OCT. 27	30	17	17	18	28	31	19	32	46	40	40	33
OCT. 28	30	18	19	20	28	31	19	32	46	40	40	33
OCT. 29	30	20	21	21	28	31	19	32	46	40	40	33
OCT. 30	30	22	23	23	28	31	19	32	46	40	40	33
OCT. 31	30	24	24	25	28	31	19	32	46	40	40	33

MOON 1 ◐ 12:01 A.M. TO 8:00 A.M.   **MOON 2** ◑ 8:01 A.M. TO 4:00 P.M.   **MOON 3** ● 4:01 P.M. TO 12:00 A.M.

Use only one "moon" number. Choose the column closest to your time of birth. If your place of birth is not on Eastern Standard Time, be sure to read "How to Convert to Eastern Standard Time" at the beginning of this section.

Date & Time	SUN ☉	MOON 1 ◐	MOON 2 ◑	MOON 3 ●	MERCURY	VENUS	MARS	JUPITER	SATURN	URANUS	NEPTUNE	PLUTO
NOV. 1	30	26	26	27	28	30	19	32	46	40	40	33
NOV. 2	30	28	28	29	28	30	19	32	46	40	40	33
NOV. 3	31	30	30	31	28	30	19	32	46	40	40	33
NOV. 4	31	32	32	33	28	30	19	32	46	40	40	33
NOV. 5	31	34	34	35	28	30	19	32	46	40	40	33
NOV. 6	31	36	36	37	28	30	19	32	46	40	40	33
NOV. 7	31	38	38	39	28	30	19	32	46	40	40	33
NOV. 8	31	40	40	41	29	30	19	32	46	40	40	33
NOV. 9	31	41	42	43	29	30	19	32	46	40	40	33
NOV. 10	31	43	44	44	29	30	19	32	46	40	40	33
NOV. 11	31	45	46	46	29	30	20	32	46	40	40	33
NOV. 12	32	47	47	48	29	30	20	32	46	40	40	33
NOV. 13	32	48	1	1	29	30	20	32	46	40	40	33
NOV. 14	32	2	2	3	30	30	20	32	46	40	40	33
NOV. 15	32	4	4	5	30	29	20	32	46	40	40	33
NOV. 16	32	5	6	6	30	29	20	32	46	40	40	33
NOV. 17	32	7	7	8	30	29	20	32	46	40	40	33
NOV. 18	32	8	9	9	30	29	20	32	46	40	40	33
NOV. 19	33	10	10	11	31	29	20	32	46	40	40	33
NOV. 20	33	11	12	12	31	29	20	32	46	40	40	33
NOV. 21	33	13	14	14	31	29	20	32	46	40	40	33
NOV. 22	33	15	15	16	31	29	20	32	46	40	40	33
NOV. 23	33	16	17	17	32	29	20	32	46	40	40	33
NOV. 24	33	18	18	19	32	29	20	32	46	40	40	33
NOV. 25	34	20	20	21	32	29	20	33	46	40	40	33
NOV. 26	34	21	22	23	32	29	20	33	46	40	40	33
NOV. 27	34	23	24	24	32	29	20	33	46	40	40	33
NOV. 28	34	25	26	26	33	29	20	33	46	40	40	33
NOV. 29	34	27	27	28	33	29	20	33	46	40	40	33
NOV. 30	34	29	29	30	33	29	21	33	46	40	40	33

Date & Time	SUN ☉	MOON 1 ◐	MOON 2 ◑	MOON 3 ●	MERCURY	VENUS	MARS	JUPITER	SATURN	URANUS	NEPTUNE	PLUTO
DEC. 1	34	31	31	32	33	29	21	33	46	40	40	33
DEC. 2	34	33	33	34	33	29	21	33	46	40	40	33
DEC. 3	35	35	35	36	34	30	21	33	46	40	40	33
DEC. 4	35	37	37	38	34	30	21	33	46	40	40	33
DEC. 5	35	39	39	40	34	30	21	33	46	40	40	33
DEC. 6	35	41	41	42	34	30	21	33	46	40	40	33
DEC. 7	35	43	43	44	34	30	21	33	46	40	40	33
DEC. 8	35	44	45	46	35	30	21	33	46	40	40	33
DEC. 9	35	46	47	47	35	30	21	33	46	40	40	33
DEC. 10	35	48	48	1	35	30	21	33	46	40	40	33
DEC. 11	36	2	2	3	35	30	21	33	46	40	40	33
DEC. 12	36	3	4	4	35	30	21	33	46	40	40	33
DEC. 13	36	5	5	6	36	30	21	33	46	40	40	33
DEC. 14	36	6	7	7	36	30	21	33	46	40	40	33
DEC. 15	36	8	8	9	36	30	21	33	46	40	40	33
DEC. 16	36	9	10	10	36	30	21	33	46	40	40	33
DEC. 17	36	11	12	12	37	31	21	33	46	40	40	33
DEC. 18	36	13	13	14	37	31	21	33	46	40	40	33
DEC. 19	37	14	15	15	37	31	21	33	46	40	40	33
DEC. 20	37	16	16	17	37	31	21	33	46	40	40	33
DEC. 21	37	18	18	19	37	31	21	33	46	40	40	33
DEC. 22	37	19	20	20	38	31	21	33	46	40	40	33
DEC. 23	37	21	21	22	38	31	21	33	46	40	40	33
DEC. 24	37	23	23	24	38	31	21	33	46	40	40	33
DEC. 25	37	24	25	26	38	31	21	33	46	40	40	33
DEC. 26	38	26	27	27	38	31	21	33	46	40	40	33
DEC. 27	38	28	29	29	39	32	21	33	46	40	40	33
DEC. 28	38	30	31	31	39	32	21	33	46	40	40	33
DEC. 29	38	32	33	33	39	32	21	34	46	40	40	33
DEC. 30	38	34	35	35	39	32	21	34	46	40	40	33
DEC. 31	38	36	37	37	40	32	21	34	46	40	40	33

MOON 1 ◐ 12:01 A.M. TO 8:00 A.M.   **MOON 2** ◑ 8:01 A.M. TO 4:00 P.M.   **MOON 3** ● 4:01 P.M. TO 12:00 A.M.
Use only one "moon" number. Choose the column closest to your time of birth. If your place of birth is not on
Eastern Standard Time, be sure to read "How to Convert to Eastern Standard Time" at the beginning of this section.

Date & Time	SUN ☉	MOON 1 ◐	MOON 2 ◑	MOON 3 ●	MERCURY	VENUS	MARS	JUPITER	SATURN	URANUS	NEPTUNE	PLUTO
JAN. 1	38	38	39	39	40	32	21	34	46	40	40	33
JAN. 2	38	40	41	41	40	32	21	34	46	40	40	33
JAN. 3	39	42	42	43	40	32	21	34	46	40	40	33
JAN. 4	39	44	44	45	40	33	21	34	46	40	40	33
JAN. 5	39	46	46	47	41	33	21	34	46	40	40	33
JAN. 6	39	47	48	48	41	33	21	34	46	40	40	33
JAN. 7	39	1	2	2	41	33	21	34	46	40	40	33
JAN. 8	39	3	3	4	41	33	21	34	46	40	40	33
JAN. 9	39	4	5	5	41	33	21	34	46	40	40	33
JAN. 10	40	6	6	7	42	33	21	34	46	40	40	33
JAN. 11	40	7	8	8	42	33	21	34	46	40	40	33
JAN. 12	40	9	9	10	42	34	21	34	46	40	40	33
JAN. 13	40	11	11	12	42	34	21	34	46	40	40	33
JAN. 14	40	12	13	13	42	34	21	34	46	40	40	33
JAN. 15	40	14	14	15	43	34	21	34	46	40	40	33
JAN. 16	40	15	16	17	43	34	21	34	46	40	40	33
JAN. 17	41	17	18	18	43	34	21	34	46	40	40	33
JAN. 18	41	19	20	20	43	34	21	34	46	40	40	33
JAN. 19	41	20	21	22	43	35	21	34	46	41	40	33
JAN. 20	41	22	23	23	43	35	21	34	46	41	40	33
JAN. 21	41	24	25	25	44	35	21	34	46	41	40	33
JAN. 22	41	26	26	27	44	35	21	34	46	41	40	33
JAN. 23	42	28	28	29	44	35	21	34	46	41	40	33
JAN. 24	42	29	30	31	44	35	21	34	46	41	40	33
JAN. 25	42	31	32	33	44	35	21	34	46	41	40	33
JAN. 26	42	33	34	35	44	36	21	34	46	41	40	33
JAN. 27	42	35	36	36	44	36	21	34	46	41	40	33
JAN. 28	42	37	38	38	44	36	21	34	46	41	40	33
JAN. 29	42	39	40	40	44	36	21	34	46	41	40	33
JAN. 30	42	41	42	42	44	36	21	34	46	41	40	33
JAN. 31	43	43	43	44	43	36	21	34	46	41	40	33

Date & Time	SUN ☉	MOON 1 ◐	MOON 2 ◑	MOON 3 ●	MERCURY	VENUS	MARS	JUPITER	SATURN	URANUS	NEPTUNE	PLUTO
FEB. 1	43	45	45	46	43	36	21	34	46	41	40	33
FEB. 2	43	47	47	48	43	37	21	34	46	41	40	33
FEB. 3	43	48	1	1	43	37	20	34	46	41	40	33
FEB. 4	43	2	3	3	43	37	20	34	46	41	40	33
FEB. 5	43	4	4	5	43	37	20	34	47	41	40	33
FEB. 6	43	5	6	6	43	37	20	34	47	41	40	33
FEB. 7	43	7	7	8	42	37	20	34	47	41	40	33
FEB. 8	44	8	9	10	42	37	20	34	47	41	40	33
FEB. 9	44	10	11	11	42	38	20	35	47	41	40	33
FEB. 10	44	12	12	13	42	38	20	35	47	41	40	33
FEB. 11	44	13	14	14	42	38	20	35	47	41	40	33
FEB. 12	44	15	15	16	42	38	20	35	47	41	40	33
FEB. 13	44	17	17	18	42	38	20	35	47	41	40	33
FEB. 14	44	18	19	19	42	38	20	35	47	41	40	33
FEB. 15	44	20	21	21	42	39	20	35	47	41	40	33
FEB. 16	45	22	22	23	42	39	20	35	47	41	40	33
FEB. 17	45	24	24	25	42	39	20	35	47	41	40	33
FEB. 18	45	25	26	27	42	39	20	35	47	41	40	33
FEB. 19	45	27	28	28	42	39	20	35	47	41	40	33
FEB. 20	45	29	30	30	42	39	20	35	47	41	40	33
FEB. 21	45	31	32	32	42	39	20	35	47	41	40	33
FEB. 22	45	33	33	34	42	40	19	35	47	41	40	33
FEB. 23	46	35	35	36	42	40	19	35	47	41	40	33
FEB. 24	46	37	37	38	42	40	19	35	47	41	40	33
FEB. 25	46	38	39	40	42	40	19	35	47	41	40	33
FEB. 26	46	40	41	42	42	40	19	35	47	41	40	33
FEB. 27	46	42	43	43	42	40	19	35	47	41	40	33
FEB. 28	46	44	45	45	43	41	19	35	47	41	40	33

MOON 1 ◐ 12:01 A.M. TO 8:00 A.M. **MOON 2** ◑ 8:01 A.M. TO 4:00 P.M. **MOON 3** ● 4:01 P.M. TO 12:00 A.M.
Use only one "moon" number. Choose the column closest to your time of birth. If your place of birth is not on Eastern Standard Time, be sure to read "How to Convert to Eastern Standard Time" at the beginning of this section.

1995

March

April

Date & Time	SUN ☉	MOON 1 ☽	MOON 2 ◑	MOON 3 ●	MERCURY	VENUS	MARS	JUPITER	SATURN	URANUS	NEPTUNE	PLUTO
MAR. 1	46	46	46	47	43	41	19	35	47	41	40	33
MAR. 2	46	48	48	1	43	41	19	35	47	41	40	33
MAR. 3	47	1	2	2	43	41	19	35	47	41	40	33
MAR. 4	47	3	4	4	43	41	19	35	47	41	40	33
MAR. 5	47	5	5	6	43	41	19	35	47	41	40	33
MAR. 6	47	6	7	7	43	41	19	35	47	41	40	33
MAR. 7	47	8	8	9	44	42	19	35	47	41	40	33
MAR. 8	47	9	10	11	44	42	19	35	47	41	40	33
MAR. 9	47	11	12	12	44	42	19	35	47	41	40	33
MAR. 10	47	13	13	14	44	42	19	35	47	41	40	33
MAR. 11	48	14	15	15	44	42	19	35	47	41	40	33
MAR. 12	48	16	16	17	44	42	19	35	47	41	40	33
MAR. 13	48	18	18	19	45	43	19	35	47	41	40	33
MAR. 14	48	19	20	20	45	43	19	35	47	41	40	33
MAR. 15	48	21	22	22	45	43	19	35	47	41	40	33
MAR. 16	48	23	23	24	45	43	19	35	47	41	40	33
MAR. 17	48	25	25	26	45	43	19	35	47	41	40	33
MAR. 18	48	27	27	28	46	43	19	35	47	41	40	33
MAR. 19	1	28	29	30	46	44	19	35	47	41	40	33
MAR. 20	1	30	31	32	46	44	19	35	47	41	40	33
MAR. 21	1	32	33	34	46	44	19	35	47	41	40	33
MAR. 22	1	34	35	36	46	44	19	35	47	41	40	33
MAR. 23	1	36	37	37	47	44	19	35	47	41	40	33
MAR. 24	1	38	39	39	47	44	19	35	47	41	40	33
MAR. 25	2	40	40	41	47	44	19	35	47	41	40	33
MAR. 26	2	42	42	43	47	45	19	35	47	41	40	33
MAR. 27	2	44	44	45	48	45	19	35	47	41	40	33
MAR. 28	2	45	46	46	48	45	19	35	47	41	40	33
MAR. 29	2	47	48	48	48	45	19	35	47	41	40	33
MAR. 30	2	1	1	2	48	45	19	35	47	41	40	33
MAR. 31	2	2	3	4	48	45	19	35	47	41	40	33

Date & Time	SUN ☉	MOON 1 ☽	MOON 2 ◑	MOON 3 ●	MERCURY	VENUS	MARS	JUPITER	SATURN	URANUS	NEPTUNE	PLUTO
APR. 1	2	4	5	5	1	46	19	35	47	41	40	33
APR. 2	2	6	6	7	1	46	19	35	47	41	40	33
APR. 3	3	7	8	8	1	46	19	35	47	41	40	33
APR. 4	3	9	10	10	1	46	19	35	47	41	40	33
APR. 5	3	11	11	12	2	46	19	35	47	41	40	33
APR. 6	3	12	13	13	2	46	19	35	47	41	40	33
APR. 7	3	14	14	15	2	47	19	35	47	41	40	33
APR. 8	3	15	16	16	2	47	19	35	47	41	40	33
APR. 9	3	17	18	18	3	47	19	35	48	41	40	33
APR. 10	3	19	19	20	3	47	19	35	48	41	40	33
APR. 11	4	20	21	22	3	47	19	35	48	41	40	33
APR. 12	4	22	23	23	4	47	19	35	48	41	40	33
APR. 13	4	24	25	25	4	48	19	35	48	41	40	33
APR. 14	4	26	26	27	4	48	19	35	48	41	40	33
APR. 15	4	28	28	29	4	48	19	35	48	41	40	33
APR. 16	4	30	30	31	5	48	19	35	48	41	40	33
APR. 17	4	32	32	33	5	48	19	35	48	41	40	33
APR. 18	4	34	34	35	5	48	19	35	48	41	40	33
APR. 19	5	36	36	37	5	48	19	35	48	41	40	33
APR. 20	5	38	38	39	6	1	19	35	48	41	40	33
APR. 21	5	39	40	41	6	1	19	35	48	41	40	33
APR. 22	5	41	42	43	6	1	19	35	48	41	40	33
APR. 23	5	43	44	44	7	1	19	35	48	41	40	33
APR. 24	5	45	45	46	7	1	19	35	48	41	40	33
APR. 25	6	47	47	48	7	1	19	35	48	41	40	33
APR. 26	6	48	1	1	7	2	19	35	48	41	40	33
APR. 27	6	2	3	3	8	2	19	35	48	41	40	33
APR. 28	6	4	4	5	8	2	20	35	48	41	40	33
APR. 29	6	5	6	6	8	2	20	35	48	41	40	33
APR. 30	6	7	7	8	8	2	20	35	48	41	40	33

MOON 1 ☽ 12:01 A.M. TO 8:00 A.M.　　**MOON 2** ◑ 8:01 A.M. TO 4:00 P.M.　　**MOON 3** ● 4:01 P.M. TO 12:00 A.M.

Use only one "moon" number. Choose the column closest to your time of birth. If your place of birth is not on Eastern Standard Time, be sure to read "How to Convert to Eastern Standard Time" at the beginning of this section.

1995

May

Date & Time	SUN ☉	MOON 1 ◖	MOON 2 ◑	MOON 3 ●	MERCURY	VENUS	MARS	JUPITER	SATURN	URANUS	NEPTUNE	PLUTO
MAY 1	6	9	9	10	9	2	20	35	48	41	40	33
MAY 2	6	10	11	11	9	3	20	35	48	41	40	33
MAY 3	7	12	12	13	9	3	20	35	48	41	40	33
MAY 4	7	13	14	14	9	3	20	35	48	41	40	33
MAY 5	7	15	15	16	9	3	20	35	48	41	40	33
MAY 6	7	16	17	18	10	3	20	35	48	41	40	33
MAY 7	7	18	19	19	10	3	20	35	48	41	40	33
MAY 8	7	20	20	21	10	4	20	35	48	41	40	33
MAY 9	7	21	22	23	10	4	20	35	48	41	40	33
MAY 10	7	23	24	24	10	4	20	35	48	41	40	33
MAY 11	8	25	26	26	11	4	20	35	48	41	40	33
MAY 12	8	27	28	28	11	4	20	35	48	41	40	33
MAY 13	8	29	29	30	11	4	20	35	48	41	40	33
MAY 14	8	31	31	32	11	5	20	35	48	41	40	33
MAY 15	8	33	33	34	11	5	20	35	48	41	40	33
MAY 16	8	35	35	36	11	5	20	35	48	41	40	33
MAY 17	8	37	37	38	11	5	20	35	48	41	40	33
MAY 18	8	39	39	40	11	5	21	35	48	41	40	33
MAY 19	9	41	41	42	11	5	21	35	48	41	40	33
MAY 20	9	43	43	44	11	5	21	35	48	41	40	33
MAY 21	9	44	45	46	11	6	21	35	48	41	40	33
MAY 22	9	46	47	47	11	6	21	35	48	41	40	33
MAY 23	9	48	1	1	11	6	21	35	48	41	40	33
MAY 24	9	2	2	3	11	6	21	35	48	41	40	33
MAY 25	10	3	4	4	11	6	21	34	48	41	40	33
MAY 26	10	5	5	6	11	6	21	34	48	41	40	33
MAY 27	10	7	7	8	11	7	21	34	48	41	40	33
MAY 28	10	8	9	9	11	7	21	34	48	41	40	33
MAY 29	10	10	10	11	11	7	21	34	48	41	40	33
MAY 30	10	11	12	12	11	7	21	34	48	41	40	33
MAY 31	10	13	13	14	11	7	21	34	48	41	40	33

June

Date & Time	SUN ☉	MOON 1 ◖	MOON 2 ◑	MOON 3 ●	MERCURY	VENUS	MARS	JUPITER	SATURN	URANUS	NEPTUNE	PLUTO
JUN. 1	10	14	15	15	11	7	21	34	48	41	40	33
JUN. 2	10	16	17	17	11	8	21	34	48	41	40	33
JUN. 3	11	18	18	19	11	8	21	34	48	41	40	33
JUN. 4	11	19	20	20	11	8	22	34	48	41	40	33
JUN. 5	11	21	21	22	11	8	22	34	48	41	40	33
JUN. 6	11	23	23	24	11	8	22	34	48	41	40	33
JUN. 7	11	24	25	26	11	8	22	34	48	41	40	33
JUN. 8	11	26	27	27	11	9	22	34	48	41	40	33
JUN. 9	11	28	29	29	11	9	22	34	48	41	40	33
JUN. 10	11	30	31	31	11	9	22	34	48	41	40	33
JUN. 11	12	32	33	33	10	9	22	34	48	41	40	33
JUN. 12	12	34	35	35	10	9	22	34	48	41	40	33
JUN. 13	12	36	37	37	10	9	22	34	48	41	40	33
JUN. 14	12	38	39	39	10	10	22	34	48	41	40	33
JUN. 15	12	40	41	41	10	10	22	34	48	41	40	33
JUN. 16	12	42	43	43	10	10	22	34	48	41	40	33
JUN. 17	12	44	44	45	10	10	22	34	48	41	40	33
JUN. 18	12	46	46	47	10	10	23	34	48	41	40	33
JUN. 19	13	47	48	1	10	10	23	34	48	41	40	33
JUN. 20	13	1	2	2	10	11	23	34	48	41	40	33
JUN. 21	13	3	3	4	10	11	23	34	48	41	40	33
JUN. 22	13	5	5	6	10	11	23	34	48	41	40	33
JUN. 23	13	6	7	7	10	11	23	34	48	41	40	33
JUN. 24	13	8	8	9	11	11	23	34	48	41	40	33
JUN. 25	14	9	10	10	11	11	23	34	48	41	40	33
JUN. 26	14	11	11	12	11	11	23	34	48	41	40	33
JUN. 27	14	12	13	13	11	12	23	34	48	41	40	33
JUN. 28	14	14	15	15	11	12	23	34	48	41	40	33
JUN. 29	14	16	16	17	11	12	23	34	48	41	40	33
JUN. 30	14	17	18	18	11	12	23	34	48	41	40	33

MOON 1 ◖ 12:01 A.M. TO 8:00 A.M.   **MOON 2** ◑ 8:01 A.M. TO 4:00 P.M.   **MOON 3** ● 4:01 P.M. TO 12:00 A.M.
Use only one "moon" number. Choose the column closest to your time of birth. If your place of birth is not on
Eastern Standard Time, be sure to read "How to Convert to Eastern Standard Time" at the beginning of this section.

Date & Time	SUN ☉	MOON 1 ◗	MOON 2 ◑	MOON 3 ●	MERCURY	VENUS	MARS	JUPITER	SATURN	URANUS	NEPTUNE	PLUTO
JUL. 1	14	19	19	20	11	12	23	34	48	41	40	33
JUL. 2	14	21	21	22	11	12	24	34	48	41	40	33
JUL. 3	15	22	23	23	12	13	24	34	48	41	40	33
JUL. 4	15	24	24	25	12	13	24	34	48	41	40	33
JUL. 5	15	26	26	27	12	13	24	34	48	41	40	33
JUL. 6	15	27	28	29	12	13	24	34	48	41	40	33
JUL. 7	15	29	30	31	12	13	24	34	48	41	40	33
JUL. 8	15	31	32	32	12	13	24	34	48	41	40	33
JUL. 9	15	33	34	34	13	14	24	34	48	41	40	33
JUL. 10	15	35	36	36	13	14	24	34	48	41	40	33
JUL. 11	16	37	38	38	13	14	24	34	48	41	40	33
JUL. 12	16	39	40	40	13	14	24	34	48	41	40	33
JUL. 13	16	41	42	42	14	14	24	34	48	41	40	33
JUL. 14	16	43	44	44	14	14	24	34	48	41	40	33
JUL. 15	16	45	46	46	14	15	24	34	48	41	40	33
JUL. 16	16	47	47	48	14	15	25	34	48	41	40	33
JUL. 17	16	1	1	2	15	15	25	34	48	41	40	33
JUL. 18	16	2	3	4	15	15	25	34	48	41	40	33
JUL. 19	17	4	5	5	15	15	25	34	48	41	40	33
JUL. 20	17	6	6	7	15	15	25	34	48	41	40	33
JUL. 21	17	7	8	8	16	16	25	34	48	41	40	33
JUL. 22	17	9	9	10	16	16	25	34	48	41	40	33
JUL. 23	17	10	11	12	16	16	25	34	48	41	40	33
JUL. 24	17	12	13	13	16	16	25	34	48	41	40	33
JUL. 25	17	14	14	15	17	16	25	34	48	41	40	33
JUL. 26	18	15	16	17	17	16	25	34	48	41	40	33
JUL. 27	18	17	17	18	17	17	25	34	48	41	40	33
JUL. 28	18	18	19	20	18	17	26	34	48	41	40	33
JUL. 29	18	20	21	21	18	17	26	34	48	41	40	33
JUL. 30	18	22	22	23	18	17	26	34	48	41	40	33
JUL. 31	18	23	24	25	18	17	26	34	48	41	40	33

Date & Time	SUN ☉	MOON 1 ◗	MOON 2 ◑	MOON 3 ●	MERCURY	VENUS	MARS	JUPITER	SATURN	URANUS	NEPTUNE	PLUTO
AUG. 1	18	25	26	26	19	17	26	34	48	41	40	33
AUG. 2	18	27	28	28	19	18	26	34	48	41	40	33
AUG. 3	19	29	29	30	19	18	26	34	48	41	40	33
AUG. 4	19	31	31	32	20	18	26	34	48	41	40	33
AUG. 5	19	32	33	34	20	18	26	34	48	41	40	33
AUG. 6	19	34	35	36	20	18	26	34	48	41	40	33
AUG. 7	19	36	37	38	20	18	26	34	48	41	40	33
AUG. 8	19	38	39	40	21	19	26	34	48	41	40	33
AUG. 9	19	40	41	42	21	19	26	34	48	41	40	33
AUG. 10	19	42	43	44	21	19	27	34	48	41	40	33
AUG. 11	20	44	45	45	21	19	27	34	48	41	40	33
AUG. 12	20	46	47	47	21	19	27	34	48	41	40	33
AUG. 13	20	48	1	1	22	19	27	34	48	41	40	33
AUG. 14	20	2	2	3	22	20	27	34	48	41	40	33
AUG. 15	20	3	4	5	22	20	27	34	48	41	40	33
AUG. 16	20	5	6	6	22	20	27	34	48	41	40	33
AUG. 17	20	7	7	8	23	20	27	34	48	41	40	33
AUG. 18	20	8	9	9	23	20	27	34	48	41	40	33
AUG. 19	21	10	11	11	23	20	27	34	48	41	40	33
AUG. 20	21	12	12	13	23	21	27	34	48	41	40	33
AUG. 21	21	13	14	14	23	21	27	34	48	41	40	33
AUG. 22	21	15	15	16	24	21	28	34	48	41	40	33
AUG. 23	21	16	17	17	24	21	28	34	48	41	40	33
AUG. 24	21	18	19	19	24	21	28	34	48	41	40	33
AUG. 25	21	20	20	21	24	21	28	34	48	41	40	33
AUG. 26	22	21	22	22	24	21	28	34	48	41	40	33
AUG. 27	22	23	24	24	25	22	28	34	48	41	40	33
AUG. 28	22	25	25	26	25	22	28	34	48	41	40	33
AUG. 29	22	27	27	28	25	22	28	34	48	41	40	33
AUG. 30	22	28	29	30	25	22	28	34	48	41	40	33
AUG. 31	22	30	31	31	25	22	28	34	48	41	40	33

MOON 1 ◗ 12:01 A.M. TO 8:00 A.M.　**MOON 2** ◑ 8:01 A.M. TO 4:00 P.M.　**MOON 3** ● 4:01 P.M. TO 12:00 A.M.

Use only one "moon" number. Choose the column closest to your time of birth. If your place of birth is not on Eastern Standard Time, be sure to read "How to Convert to Eastern Standard Time" at the beginning of this section.

1995

September

October

Date & Time	SUN ☉	MOON 1 ◗	MOON 2 ◑	MOON 3 ●	MERCURY	VENUS	MARS	JUPITER	SATURN	URANUS	NEPTUNE	PLUTO
SEP. 1	22	32	33	33	26	22	28	34	48	41	40	33
SEP. 2	22	34	35	35	26	23	29	34	48	41	40	33
SEP. 3	23	36	36	37	26	23	29	34	48	41	40	33
SEP. 4	23	38	38	39	26	23	29	34	48	41	40	33
SEP. 5	23	40	40	41	26	23	29	34	48	41	40	33
SEP. 6	23	42	42	43	26	23	29	34	48	41	40	33
SEP. 7	23	43	44	45	26	23	29	34	48	41	40	33
SEP. 8	23	45	46	47	27	24	29	34	48	41	40	33
SEP. 9	23	47	48	48	27	24	29	34	48	41	40	33
SEP. 10	23	1	2	2	27	24	29	34	48	41	40	33
SEP. 11	24	3	3	4	27	24	29	34	48	41	40	33
SEP. 12	24	5	5	6	27	24	29	34	48	41	40	33
SEP. 13	24	6	7	7	27	24	29	34	48	41	40	33
SEP. 14	24	8	8	9	27	25	30	34	48	41	40	33
SEP. 15	24	9	10	11	27	25	30	34	48	41	40	33
SEP. 16	24	11	12	12	27	25	30	34	48	41	40	33
SEP. 17	24	13	13	14	27	25	30	34	48	41	40	33
SEP. 18	24	14	15	15	28	25	30	34	48	41	40	33
SEP. 19	25	16	16	17	28	25	30	34	48	41	40	33
SEP. 20	25	17	18	19	28	26	30	34	48	41	40	33
SEP. 21	25	19	20	20	28	26	30	34	48	41	40	33
SEP. 22	25	21	21	22	28	26	30	34	48	41	40	33
SEP. 23	25	22	23	24	28	26	30	34	48	41	40	33
SEP. 24	25	24	25	25	28	26	30	34	48	41	40	33
SEP. 25	26	26	27	27	28	26	31	34	48	41	40	33
SEP. 26	26	28	28	29	28	27	31	34	48	41	40	33
SEP. 27	26	30	30	31	27	27	31	34	48	41	40	33
SEP. 28	26	32	32	33	27	27	31	34	48	41	40	33
SEP. 29	26	33	34	35	27	27	31	34	48	41	40	33
SEP. 30	26	35	36	37	27	27	31	34	48	41	40	33

Date & Time	SUN ☉	MOON 1 ◗	MOON 2 ◑	MOON 3 ●	MERCURY	VENUS	MARS	JUPITER	SATURN	URANUS	NEPTUNE	PLUTO
OCT. 1	26	37	38	39	27	27	31	34	48	41	40	33
OCT. 2	26	39	40	40	27	28	31	34	48	41	40	33
OCT. 3	27	41	42	42	27	28	31	34	48	41	40	33
OCT. 4	27	43	44	44	27	28	31	34	48	41	40	33
OCT. 5	27	45	45	46	26	28	31	34	48	41	40	33
OCT. 6	27	47	47	48	26	28	32	34	48	41	40	33
OCT. 7	27	48	1	2	26	28	32	34	48	41	40	33
OCT. 8	27	2	3	3	26	29	32	35	48	41	40	33
OCT. 9	27	4	4	5	26	29	32	35	48	41	40	33
OCT. 10	27	6	6	7	26	29	32	35	48	41	40	33
OCT. 11	28	7	8	8	26	29	32	35	48	41	40	33
OCT. 12	28	9	9	10	26	29	32	35	48	41	40	33
OCT. 13	28	10	11	12	26	29	32	35	48	41	40	33
OCT. 14	28	12	13	13	26	30	32	35	48	41	40	33
OCT. 15	28	14	14	15	26	30	32	35	48	41	40	33
OCT. 16	28	15	16	16	26	30	33	35	48	41	40	33
OCT. 17	28	17	17	18	26	30	33	35	48	41	40	33
OCT. 18	28	18	19	20	26	30	33	35	48	41	40	33
OCT. 19	29	20	21	21	26	30	33	35	47	41	40	33
OCT. 20	29	22	22	23	26	31	33	35	47	41	40	33
OCT. 21	29	24	24	25	26	31	33	35	47	41	40	33
OCT. 22	29	25	26	26	26	31	33	35	47	41	40	33
OCT. 23	29	27	28	27	26	31	33	35	47	41	40	33
OCT. 24	29	29	30	30	27	31	33	35	47	41	40	33
OCT. 25	29	31	32	32	27	31	33	35	47	41	40	33
OCT. 26	30	33	34	34	27	32	33	35	47	41	40	33
OCT. 27	30	35	35	36	27	32	34	35	47	41	40	33
OCT. 28	30	37	37	38	27	32	34	35	47	41	40	33
OCT. 29	30	39	39	40	28	32	34	35	47	41	40	33
OCT. 30	30	41	41	42	28	32	34	35	47	41	40	33
OCT. 31	30	42	43	44	28	32	34	35	47	41	40	33

MOON 1 ◗ 12:01 A.M. TO 8:00 A.M.   **MOON 2** ◑ 8:01 A.M. TO 4:00 P.M.   **MOON 3** ● 4:01 P.M. TO 12:00 A.M.
Use only one "moon" number. Choose the column closest to your time of birth. If your place of birth is not on
Eastern Standard Time, be sure to read "How to Convert to Eastern Standard Time" at the beginning of this section.

Date & Time	SUN	MOON 1	MOON 2	MOON 3	MERCURY	VENUS	MARS	JUPITER	SATURN	URANUS	NEPTUNE	PLUTO
NOV. 1	30	44	45	46	28	33	34	35	47	41	40	33
NOV. 2	30	46	47	47	28	33	34	35	47	41	40	33
NOV. 3	31	48	1	1	29	33	34	35	47	41	40	33
NOV. 4	31	2	2	3	29	33	34	35	47	41	40	33
NOV. 5	31	3	4	5	29	33	34	35	47	41	40	33
NOV. 6	31	5	6	6	29	33	35	35	47	41	40	33
NOV. 7	31	7	7	8	30	34	35	35	47	41	40	33
NOV. 8	31	8	9	9	30	34	35	35	47	41	40	33
NOV. 9	31	10	11	11	30	34	35	35	47	41	40	33
NOV. 10	31	12	12	13	30	34	35	35	47	41	40	33
NOV. 11	31	13	14	14	30	34	35	35	47	41	40	33
NOV. 12	32	15	15	16	31	34	35	35	47	41	40	33
NOV. 13	32	16	17	17	31	35	35	35	47	41	40	33
NOV. 14	32	18	18	19	31	35	35	35	47	41	40	33
NOV. 15	32	20	20	21	31	35	35	35	47	41	40	33
NOV. 16	32	21	22	22	32	35	36	36	47	41	40	33
NOV. 17	32	23	23	24	32	35	36	36	47	41	40	33
NOV. 18	32	25	25	26	32	35	36	36	47	41	40	33
NOV. 19	33	26	27	28	32	36	36	36	47	41	40	33
NOV. 20	33	28	29	29	32	36	36	36	47	41	40	33
NOV. 21	33	30	31	31	33	36	36	36	47	41	40	33
NOV. 22	33	32	33	33	33	36	36	36	47	41	40	33
NOV. 23	33	34	35	35	33	36	36	36	47	41	40	33
NOV. 24	33	36	37	37	33	36	36	36	47	41	40	33
NOV. 25	34	38	39	39	33	37	36	36	47	41	40	33
NOV. 26	34	40	41	41	34	37	37	36	47	41	40	33
NOV. 27	34	42	43	43	34	37	37	36	47	41	40	33
NOV. 28	34	44	45	45	34	37	37	36	47	41	40	33
NOV. 29	34	46	46	47	34	37	37	36	47	41	40	33
NOV. 30	34	48	48	1	34	37	37	36	47	41	40	33

Date & Time	SUN	MOON 1	MOON 2	MOON 3	MERCURY	VENUS	MARS	JUPITER	SATURN	URANUS	NEPTUNE	PLUTO
DEC. 1	34	1	2	2	35	38	37	36	47	41	40	33
DEC. 2	34	3	4	4	35	38	37	36	47	41	40	33
DEC. 3	35	5	5	6	35	38	37	36	47	41	40	33
DEC. 4	35	6	7	7	35	38	37	36	47	41	40	33
DEC. 5	35	8	8	9	36	38	37	36	47	41	40	33
DEC. 6	35	10	10	11	36	38	38	36	47	41	40	33
DEC. 7	35	11	12	12	36	39	38	36	47	41	40	33
DEC. 8	35	13	13	14	36	39	38	36	47	41	40	33
DEC. 9	35	14	15	15	36	39	38	36	47	41	40	33
DEC. 10	35	16	16	17	37	39	38	36	47	41	40	33
DEC. 11	36	17	18	19	37	39	38	36	47	41	40	33
DEC. 12	36	19	20	20	37	39	38	36	47	41	40	33
DEC. 13	36	21	21	22	37	40	38	36	47	41	40	33
DEC. 14	36	22	23	23	37	40	38	36	47	41	40	33
DEC. 15	36	24	25	25	38	40	38	36	47	41	40	33
DEC. 16	36	26	26	27	38	40	39	36	47	41	40	33
DEC. 17	36	27	28	29	38	40	39	36	47	41	40	33
DEC. 18	36	29	30	31	38	40	39	36	47	41	40	33
DEC. 19	37	31	32	32	38	41	39	37	47	41	40	33
DEC. 20	37	33	34	34	39	41	39	37	47	41	40	33
DEC. 21	37	35	36	36	39	41	39	37	47	41	40	33
DEC. 22	37	37	38	39	39	41	39	37	47	41	40	33
DEC. 23	37	39	40	41	39	41	39	37	47	41	40	33
DEC. 24	37	41	42	43	39	41	39	37	47	41	40	33
DEC. 25	37	43	44	45	40	42	39	37	47	41	40	33
DEC. 26	38	45	46	46	40	42	40	37	48	41	40	33
DEC. 27	38	47	48	48	40	42	40	37	48	41	40	33
DEC. 28	38	1	1	2	40	42	40	37	48	41	40	33
DEC. 29	38	3	3	4	40	42	40	37	48	41	40	33
DEC. 30	38	4	5	5	41	42	40	37	48	41	40	33
DEC. 31	38	6	6	7	41	43	40	37	48	41	40	33

MOON 1 ◗ 12:01 A.M. TO 8:00 A.M.　　**MOON 2** ◑ 8:01 A.M. TO 4:00 P.M.　　**MOON 3** ● 4:01 P.M. TO 12:00 A.M.

Use only one "moon" number. Choose the column closest to your time of birth. If your place of birth is not on Eastern Standard Time, be sure to read "How to Convert to Eastern Standard Time" at the beginning of this section.

1996

January

Date & Time	SUN	MOON 1	MOON 2	MOON 3	MERCURY	VENUS	MARS	JUPITER	SATURN	URANUS	NEPTUNE	PLUTO
JAN. 1	38	8	8	9	41	43	40	37	48	41	40	33
JAN. 2	38	9	10	10	41	43	40	37	48	41	40	33
JAN. 3	39	11	11	12	41	43	40	37	48	41	40	33
JAN. 4	39	12	13	13	41	43	41	37	48	41	40	33
JAN. 5	39	14	14	15	41	43	41	37	48	41	40	33
JAN. 6	39	15	16	17	41	44	41	37	48	41	40	33
JAN. 7	39	17	18	18	42	44	41	37	48	41	40	33
JAN. 8	39	19	19	20	42	44	41	37	48	41	40	33
JAN. 9	39	20	21	21	42	44	41	37	48	41	40	33
JAN. 10	40	22	22	23	42	44	41	37	48	41	40	33
JAN. 11	40	24	24	25	42	44	41	37	48	41	40	33
JAN. 12	40	25	26	26	42	44	41	37	48	41	40	33
JAN. 13	40	27	27	28	42	45	41	37	48	41	40	33
JAN. 14	40	29	29	30	41	45	42	37	48	41	40	33
JAN. 15	40	30	31	32	41	45	42	37	48	41	40	33
JAN. 16	40	32	33	34	41	45	42	37	48	41	40	33
JAN. 17	41	34	35	36	41	45	42	37	48	41	40	33
JAN. 18	41	36	37	38	41	45	42	37	48	41	40	33
JAN. 19	41	38	39	40	41	46	42	37	48	41	40	33
JAN. 20	41	40	41	42	40	46	42	37	48	41	40	33
JAN. 21	41	42	43	44	40	46	42	37	48	41	40	33
JAN. 22	41	44	45	46	40	46	42	38	48	41	40	33
JAN. 23	42	46	47	48	40	46	43	38	48	41	40	33
JAN. 24	42	48	1	2	40	46	43	38	48	41	40	33
JAN. 25	42	2	3	3	40	47	43	38	48	41	40	33
JAN. 26	42	4	4	5	40	47	43	38	48	41	40	33
JAN. 27	42	5	6	7	40	47	43	38	48	41	40	33
JAN. 28	42	7	8	8	40	47	43	38	48	41	40	33
JAN. 29	42	9	9	10	40	47	43	38	48	41	40	33
JAN. 30	42	10	11	11	40	47	43	38	48	41	40	33
JAN. 31	43	12	12	13	40	48	43	38	48	41	40	33

February

Date & Time	SUN	MOON 1	MOON 2	MOON 3	MERCURY	VENUS	MARS	JUPITER	SATURN	URANUS	NEPTUNE	PLUTO
FEB. 1	43	13	14	15	40	48	43	38	48	41	40	33
FEB. 2	43	15	16	16	40	48	44	38	48	41	40	33
FEB. 3	43	17	17	18	40	48	44	38	48	41	40	33
FEB. 4	43	18	19	19	40	48	44	38	48	41	40	33
FEB. 5	43	20	20	21	40	48	44	38	48	41	40	33
FEB. 6	43	21	22	23	40	1	44	38	48	41	40	33
FEB. 7	43	23	24	24	40	1	44	38	48	41	40	33
FEB. 8	44	25	25	26	40	1	44	38	48	41	40	33
FEB. 9	44	26	27	28	40	1	44	38	48	41	40	33
FEB. 10	44	28	29	29	40	1	44	38	48	41	40	33
FEB. 11	44	30	31	31	40	1	45	38	48	41	40	33
FEB. 12	44	32	32	33	41	1	45	38	48	41	40	33
FEB. 13	44	34	34	35	41	2	45	38	48	41	40	33
FEB. 14	44	35	36	37	41	2	45	38	48	41	40	33
FEB. 15	44	37	38	39	41	2	45	38	48	41	40	33
FEB. 16	45	39	40	41	41	2	45	38	48	41	40	33
FEB. 17	45	41	42	43	41	2	45	38	48	41	40	33
FEB. 18	45	43	44	45	41	2	45	38	48	41	40	33
FEB. 19	45	45	46	47	42	3	45	38	48	41	40	33
FEB. 20	45	47	48	1	42	3	45	38	48	41	41	33
FEB. 21	45	1	2	2	42	3	46	38	48	41	41	33
FEB. 22	45	3	4	4	42	3	46	38	48	41	41	33
FEB. 23	46	5	5	6	42	3	46	38	48	41	41	33
FEB. 24	46	7	7	8	43	3	46	38	48	41	41	33
FEB. 25	46	8	9	9	43	3	46	38	48	41	41	33
FEB. 26	46	10	10	11	43	4	46	38	48	41	41	33
FEB. 27	46	11	12	12	43	4	46	38	48	41	41	33
FEB. 28	46	13	14	14	43	4	46	38	48	41	41	33
FEB. 29	46	15	15	16	43	4	46	39	48	41	41	33

MOON 1 ☽ 12:01 A.M. TO 8:00 A.M.   **MOON 2** ◑ 8:01 A.M. TO 4:00 P.M.   **MOON 3** ● 4:01 P.M. TO 12:00 A.M.

Use only one "moon" number. Choose the column closest to your time of birth. If your place of birth is not on Eastern Standard Time, be sure to read "How to Convert to Eastern Standard Time" at the beginning of this section.

1996

March   April

Date & Time	SUN	MOON 1	MOON 2	MOON 3	MERCURY	VENUS	MARS	JUPITER	SATURN	URANUS	NEPTUNE	PLUTO
MAR. 1	46	16	17	17	44	4	47	39	48	41	41	33
MAR. 2	46	18	18	19	44	4	47	39	48	41	41	33
MAR. 3	47	19	20	20	44	5	47	39	48	41	41	33
MAR. 4	47	21	22	22	44	5	47	39	48	41	41	33
MAR. 5	47	23	23	24	44	5	47	39	48	41	41	33
MAR. 6	47	24	25	25	45	5	47	39	48	41	41	33
MAR. 7	47	26	27	27	45	5	47	39	48	41	41	33
MAR. 8	47	28	28	29	45	5	47	39	48	41	41	33
MAR. 9	47	30	30	31	45	5	47	39	48	41	41	33
MAR. 10	47	31	32	33	46	6	47	39	1	41	41	33
MAR. 11	48	33	34	34	46	6	48	39	1	41	41	33
MAR. 12	48	35	36	36	46	6	48	39	1	41	41	33
MAR. 13	48	37	38	38	46	6	48	39	1	41	41	33
MAR. 14	48	39	39	40	46	6	48	39	1	41	41	33
MAR. 15	48	41	41	42	47	6	48	39	1	41	41	33
MAR. 16	48	43	43	44	47	6	48	39	1	41	41	33
MAR. 17	48	45	45	46	47	7	48	39	1	41	41	33
MAR. 18	48	47	47	48	47	7	48	39	1	41	41	33
MAR. 19	1	48	1	2	48	7	48	39	1	41	41	33
MAR. 20	1	2	3	3	48	7	1	39	1	41	41	33
MAR. 21	1	4	5	5	48	7	1	39	1	41	41	33
MAR. 22	1	6	6	7	48	7	1	39	1	41	41	33
MAR. 23	1	8	8	9	1	7	1	39	1	41	41	33
MAR. 24	1	9	10	10	1	8	1	39	1	41	41	33
MAR. 25	2	11	11	12	1	8	1	39	1	41	41	33
MAR. 26	2	12	13	14	1	8	1	39	1	41	41	33
MAR. 27	2	14	15	15	2	8	1	39	1	41	41	33
MAR. 28	2	16	16	17	2	8	1	39	1	41	41	33
MAR. 29	2	17	18	18	2	8	1	39	1	41	41	33
MAR. 30	2	19	19	20	3	8	2	39	1	41	41	33
MAR. 31	2	20	21	22	3	9	2	39	1	41	41	33

Date & Time	SUN	MOON 1	MOON 2	MOON 3	MERCURY	VENUS	MARS	JUPITER	SATURN	URANUS	NEPTUNE	PLUTO
APR. 1	2	22	23	23	3	9	2	39	1	42	41	33
APR. 2	2	24	24	25	3	9	2	39	1	42	41	33
APR. 3	3	26	26	27	4	9	2	39	1	42	41	33
APR. 4	3	27	28	28	4	9	2	39	1	42	41	33
APR. 5	3	29	30	30	4	9	2	39	1	42	41	33
APR. 6	3	31	31	32	4	9	2	39	1	42	41	33
APR. 7	3	33	33	34	5	9	2	39	1	42	41	33
APR. 8	3	35	35	36	5	10	2	39	1	42	41	33
APR. 9	3	36	37	38	5	10	3	39	1	42	41	33
APR. 10	3	38	39	40	6	10	3	39	1	42	41	33
APR. 11	4	40	41	42	6	10	3	39	1	42	41	33
APR. 12	4	42	43	43	6	10	3	39	1	42	41	33
APR. 13	4	44	45	45	6	10	3	39	1	42	41	33
APR. 14	4	46	47	47	6	10	3	39	1	42	41	33
APR. 15	4	48	48	1	7	10	3	39	1	42	41	33
APR. 16	4	2	2	3	7	10	3	39	1	42	41	33
APR. 17	4	3	4	5	7	11	3	39	1	42	41	33
APR. 18	4	5	6	6	7	11	3	39	1	42	41	33
APR. 19	5	7	7	8	7	11	4	39	1	42	41	33
APR. 20	5	9	9	10	8	11	4	39	1	42	41	33
APR. 21	5	10	11	11	8	11	4	39	1	42	41	33
APR. 22	5	12	12	13	8	11	4	39	1	42	41	33
APR. 23	5	14	14	15	8	11	4	39	1	42	41	33
APR. 24	5	15	16	16	8	11	4	39	1	42	41	33
APR. 25	6	17	17	18	8	11	4	39	1	42	41	33
APR. 26	6	18	19	19	8	12	4	39	1	42	41	33
APR. 27	6	20	20	21	9	12	4	39	1	42	41	33
APR. 28	6	22	22	23	9	12	5	39	1	42	41	33
APR. 29	6	23	24	24	9	12	5	39	1	42	41	33
APR. 30	6	25	25	26	9	12	5	39	1	42	41	33

MOON 1 ☽ 12:01 A.M. TO 8:00 A.M.   **MOON 2** ☽ 8:01 A.M. TO 4:00 P.M.   **MOON 3** ● 4:01 P.M. TO 12:00 A.M.

Use only one "moon" number. Choose the column closest to your time of birth. If your place of birth is not on Eastern Standard Time, be sure to read "How to Convert to Eastern Standard Time" at the beginning of this section.

Date & Time	☉ SUN	☽ MOON 1	◐ MOON 2	● MOON 3	MERCURY	VENUS	MARS	JUPITER	SATURN	URANUS	NEPTUNE	PLUTO
MAY 1	6	27	27	28	9	12	5	39	1	42	41	33
MAY 2	6	28	29	30	9	12	5	39	1	42	41	33
MAY 3	7	30	31	31	9	12	5	39	1	42	41	33
MAY 4	7	32	33	33	9	12	5	39	1	42	41	33
MAY 5	7	34	35	35	9	12	5	39	1	42	41	33
MAY 6	7	36	37	37	9	12	5	39	1	42	41	33
MAY 7	7	38	39	39	9	12	5	39	1	42	41	33
MAY 8	7	40	40	41	9	12	6	39	1	42	41	33
MAY 9	7	42	42	43	9	12	6	39	1	42	41	33
MAY 10	7	44	44	45	9	12	6	39	1	42	41	33
MAY 11	8	45	46	47	13	6	39	1	42	41	33	
MAY 12	8	47	48	1	8	13	6	39	1	42	41	33
MAY 13	8	1	2	2	8	13	6	39	1	42	41	33
MAY 14	8	3	3	4	8	13	6	39	2	42	41	33
MAY 15	8	5	5	6	8	13	6	39	2	42	41	33
MAY 16	8	6	7	8	8	13	6	39	2	42	41	33
MAY 17	8	8	9	9	8	13	6	39	2	42	41	33
MAY 18	8	10	10	11	8	13	7	39	2	42	41	33
MAY 19	9	11	12	12	8	13	7	39	2	42	41	33
MAY 20	9	13	14	14	8	13	7	39	2	42	41	33
MAY 21	9	15	15	16	8	13	7	39	2	42	41	33
MAY 22	9	16	17	17	8	13	7	39	2	42	41	33
MAY 23	9	18	18	19	8	13	7	39	2	42	41	33
MAY 24	9	19	20	20	8	13	7	39	2	42	41	33
MAY 25	10	21	22	22	8	13	7	39	2	42	41	33
MAY 26	10	23	23	24	8	13	7	39	2	42	41	33
MAY 27	10	24	25	25	8	13	7	39	2	42	41	33
MAY 28	10	26	26	27	8	13	7	39	2	42	41	33
MAY 29	10	28	28	29	8	13	8	39	2	42	41	33
MAY 30	10	29	30	31	8	12	8	39	2	42	41	33
MAY 31	10	31	32	33	8	12	8	39	2	42	41	33

Date & Time	☉ SUN	☽ MOON 1	◐ MOON 2	● MOON 3	MERCURY	VENUS	MARS	JUPITER	SATURN	URANUS	NEPTUNE	PLUTO
JUN. 1	10	33	34	35	8	12	8	39	2	42	41	33
JUN. 2	10	35	36	37	8	12	8	39	2	42	41	33
JUN. 3	11	37	38	39	8	12	8	39	2	42	41	33
JUN. 4	11	39	40	40	8	12	8	39	2	42	41	33
JUN. 5	11	41	42	42	8	12	8	39	2	42	41	33
JUN. 6	11	43	44	44	8	12	8	39	2	42	41	33
JUN. 7	11	45	46	46	8	12	8	39	2	42	41	33
JUN. 8	11	47	48	48	8	12	9	39	2	42	41	33
JUN. 9	11	1	1	2	8	12	9	39	2	42	41	33
JUN. 10	11	2	3	4	8	12	9	39	2	42	41	33
JUN. 11	12	4	5	5	9	12	9	39	2	42	41	33
JUN. 12	12	6	7	7	9	12	9	39	2	42	41	33
JUN. 13	12	8	8	9	9	11	9	39	2	42	41	33
JUN. 14	12	9	10	10	9	11	9	39	2	42	41	33
JUN. 15	12	11	11	12	9	11	9	39	2	42	41	33
JUN. 16	12	13	13	14	9	11	9	39	2	42	41	33
JUN. 17	12	14	15	15	10	11	9	39	2	41	41	33
JUN. 18	12	16	16	17	10	11	9	39	2	41	41	33
JUN. 19	13	17	18	18	10	11	10	39	2	41	41	33
JUN. 20	13	19	19	20	10	11	10	39	2	41	41	33
JUN. 21	13	20	21	22	10	11	10	39	2	41	41	33
JUN. 22	13	22	23	23	10	11	10	39	2	41	41	33
JUN. 23	13	24	24	25	11	11	10	39	2	41	41	33
JUN. 24	13	25	26	26	11	11	10	39	2	41	41	33
JUN. 25	14	27	28	28	11	11	10	39	2	41	41	33
JUN. 26	14	29	29	30	11	11	10	39	2	41	41	33
JUN. 27	14	31	31	32	12	11	10	39	2	41	41	33
JUN. 28	14	32	33	34	12	11	10	39	2	41	41	33
JUN. 29	14	34	35	36	12	11	11	39	2	41	41	33
JUN. 30	14	36	37	38	12	11	11	39	2	41	41	33

MOON 1 ☽ 12:01 A.M. TO 8:00 A.M. **MOON 2** ◐ 8:01 A.M. TO 4:00 P.M. **MOON 3** ● 4:01 P.M. TO 12:00 A.M.

Use only one "moon" number. Choose the column closest to your time of birth. If your place of birth is not on Eastern Standard Time, be sure to read "How to Convert to Eastern Standard Time" at the beginning of this section.

Date & Time	SUN	MOON 1	MOON 2	MOON 3	MERCURY	VENUS	MARS	JUPITER	SATURN	URANUS	NEPTUNE	PLUTO
JUL. 1	14	38	39	40	13	11	11	39	2	41	41	33
JUL. 2	14	40	41	42	13	11	11	39	2	41	41	33
JUL. 3	15	42	43	44	13	11	11	39	2	41	41	33
JUL. 4	15	44	45	46	13	11	11	39	2	41	41	33
JUL. 5	15	46	47	48	14	11	11	39	2	41	41	33
JUL. 6	15	48	1	1	14	11	11	39	2	41	41	33
JUL. 7	15	2	3	3	14	11	11	39	2	41	41	33
JUL. 8	15	4	4	5	15	11	11	39	2	41	41	33
JUL. 9	15	6	6	7	15	11	11	39	2	41	41	33
JUL. 10	15	7	8	8	15	11	12	39	2	41	41	33
JUL. 11	16	9	9	10	15	11	12	39	2	41	41	33
JUL. 12	16	11	11	12	16	11	12	39	2	41	41	33
JUL. 13	16	12	13	13	16	11	12	39	2	41	41	33
JUL. 14	16	14	14	15	16	11	12	39	2	41	40	33
JUL. 15	16	15	16	16	17	11	12	38	2	41	40	33
JUL. 16	16	17	17	18	17	11	12	38	2	41	40	33
JUL. 17	16	19	19	20	17	11	12	38	2	41	40	33
JUL. 18	16	20	21	21	17	11	12	38	2	41	40	33
JUL. 19	17	22	22	23	18	11	12	38	2	41	40	33
JUL. 20	17	23	24	24	18	11	12	38	2	41	40	33
JUL. 21	17	25	25	26	18	11	13	38	2	41	40	33
JUL. 22	17	27	27	28	19	11	13	38	2	41	40	33
JUL. 23	17	28	29	29	19	11	13	38	2	41	40	33
JUL. 24	17	30	31	31	19	12	13	38	2	41	40	33
JUL. 25	17	32	32	33	19	12	13	38	2	41	40	33
JUL. 26	18	34	34	35	19	12	13	38	2	41	40	33
JUL. 27	18	35	36	37	20	12	13	38	2	41	40	33
JUL. 28	18	37	38	39	20	12	13	38	2	41	40	33
JUL. 29	18	39	40	41	20	12	13	38	2	41	40	33
JUL. 30	18	41	42	43	20	12	13	38	2	41	40	33
JUL. 31	18	44	44	45	21	12	13	38	2	41	40	33

Date & Time	SUN	MOON 1	MOON 2	MOON 3	MERCURY	VENUS	MARS	JUPITER	SATURN	URANUS	NEPTUNE	PLUTO
AUG. 1	18	46	46	47	21	12	14	38	2	41	40	33
AUG. 2	18	48	48	1	21	12	14	38	2	41	40	33
AUG. 3	19	1	2	3	21	13	14	38	2	41	40	33
AUG. 4	19	3	4	4	21	13	14	38	2	41	40	33
AUG. 5	19	5	6	6	22	13	14	38	2	41	40	33
AUG. 6	19	7	7	8	22	13	14	38	2	41	40	33
AUG. 7	19	8	9	10	22	13	14	38	2	41	40	33
AUG. 8	19	10	11	11	22	13	14	38	2	41	40	33
AUG. 9	19	12	12	13	22	13	14	38	2	41	40	33
AUG. 10	19	13	14	14	23	13	14	38	2	41	40	33
AUG. 11	20	15	15	16	23	13	14	38	2	41	40	33
AUG. 12	20	17	17	18	23	14	15	38	2	41	40	33
AUG. 13	20	18	19	19	23	14	15	38	2	41	40	33
AUG. 14	20	20	20	21	23	14	15	38	2	41	40	33
AUG. 15	20	21	22	22	24	14	15	38	2	41	40	33
AUG. 16	20	23	23	24	24	14	15	38	2	41	40	33
AUG. 17	20	24	25	26	24	14	15	38	2	41	40	33
AUG. 18	20	26	26	27	24	14	15	38	2	41	40	33
AUG. 19	21	28	28	29	24	14	15	38	2	41	40	33
AUG. 20	21	29	30	31	24	15	15	38	2	41	40	33
AUG. 21	21	31	32	32	24	15	15	38	2	41	40	33
AUG. 22	21	33	34	34	25	15	15	38	2	41	40	33
AUG. 23	21	35	35	36	25	15	15	38	2	41	40	33
AUG. 24	21	37	37	38	25	16	15	38	2	41	40	33
AUG. 25	21	39	39	40	25	15	16	38	2	41	40	33
AUG. 26	22	41	41	42	25	15	16	38	2	41	40	33
AUG. 27	22	43	43	44	25	15	16	38	2	41	40	33
AUG. 28	22	45	45	46	25	16	16	38	2	41	40	33
AUG. 29	22	47	47	48	25	16	16	38	2	41	40	33
AUG. 30	22	1	1	2	25	16	16	38	2	41	40	33
AUG. 31	22	3	3	4	25	16	16	38	2	41	40	33

MOON 1 ☽ 12:01 A.M. TO 8:00 A.M. **MOON 2** ☽ 8:01 A.M. TO 4:00 P.M. **MOON 3** ● 4:01 P.M. TO 12:00 A.M.
Use only one "moon" number. Choose the column closest to your time of birth. If your place of birth is not on
Eastern Standard Time, be sure to read "How to Convert to Eastern Standard Time" at the beginning of this section.

1996

September

October

Date & Time	☉ SUN	☽ MOON 1	☽ MOON 2	● MOON 3	MERCURY	VENUS	MARS	JUPITER	SATURN	URANUS	NEPTUNE	PLUTO
SEP. 1	22	4	5	6	25	16	16	38	2	41	40	33
SEP. 2	22	6	7	7	25	16	16	38	2	41	40	33
SEP. 3	23	8	9	9	25	16	16	38	2	41	40	33
SEP. 4	23	10	10	11	25	17	16	38	2	41	40	33
SEP. 5	23	11	12	12	25	17	17	38	2	41	40	33
SEP. 6	23	13	13	14	25	17	17	38	2	41	40	33
SEP. 7	23	15	15	16	25	17	17	38	2	41	40	33
SEP. 8	23	16	17	17	25	17	17	38	2	41	40	33
SEP. 9	23	18	18	19	25	17	17	38	2	41	40	33
SEP. 10	23	19	20	20	25	17	17	38	2	41	40	33
SEP. 11	24	21	21	22	25	18	17	38	2	41	40	33
SEP. 12	24	22	23	24	25	18	17	38	2	41	40	33
SEP. 13	24	24	25	25	25	18	17	38	2	41	40	33
SEP. 14	24	26	26	27	25	18	17	38	2	41	40	33
SEP. 15	24	27	28	29	25	18	17	38	2	41	40	33
SEP. 16	24	29	30	30	24	18	17	38	2	41	40	33
SEP. 17	24	31	31	32	24	18	18	38	2	41	40	33
SEP. 18	24	33	33	34	24	19	18	38	2	41	40	33
SEP. 19	25	34	35	36	24	19	18	38	2	41	40	33
SEP. 20	25	36	37	37	24	19	18	38	2	41	40	33
SEP. 21	25	38	39	39	24	19	18	38	2	41	40	33
SEP. 22	25	40	41	41	24	19	18	38	2	41	40	33
SEP. 23	25	42	43	43	24	19	18	38	2	41	40	33
SEP. 24	25	44	44	45	24	19	18	38	2	41	40	33
SEP. 25	26	46	46	47	24	20	18	38	2	41	40	33
SEP. 26	26	48	48	1	24	20	18	38	2	41	40	33
SEP. 27	26	2	2	3	24	20	18	38	1	41	40	33
SEP. 28	26	4	4	5	24	20	19	38	1	41	40	33
SEP. 29	26	5	6	7	24	20	19	38	1	41	40	33
SEP. 30	26	7	8	8	24	20	19	38	1	41	40	33

Date & Time	☉ SUN	☽ MOON 1	☽ MOON 2	● MOON 3	MERCURY	VENUS	MARS	JUPITER	SATURN	URANUS	NEPTUNE	PLUTO
OCT. 1	26	9	10	10	24	21	19	38	1	41	40	33
OCT. 2	26	11	11	12	24	21	19	38	1	41	40	33
OCT. 3	27	12	13	13	24	21	19	38	1	41	40	33
OCT. 4	27	14	15	15	24	21	19	38	1	41	40	33
OCT. 5	27	16	16	17	24	21	19	38	1	41	40	33
OCT. 6	27	17	18	18	24	21	19	38	1	41	40	33
OCT. 7	27	19	19	20	25	21	19	38	1	41	40	33
OCT. 8	27	20	21	21	25	22	19	38	1	41	40	33
OCT. 9	27	22	23	23	25	22	19	38	1	41	40	33
OCT. 10	27	24	24	25	25	22	19	38	1	41	40	33
OCT. 11	28	25	26	26	25	22	20	38	1	41	40	33
OCT. 12	28	27	27	28	25	22	20	38	1	41	40	33
OCT. 13	28	29	29	30	25	22	20	38	1	41	40	33
OCT. 14	28	30	31	32	26	23	20	38	1	41	40	33
OCT. 15	28	32	33	33	26	23	20	38	1	41	40	33
OCT. 16	28	34	35	35	27	23	20	38	1	41	40	33
OCT. 17	28	36	36	37	27	23	20	38	1	41	40	33
OCT. 18	28	38	38	39	27	23	20	38	1	41	40	33
OCT. 19	29	39	40	41	27	23	20	38	1	41	40	33
OCT. 20	29	41	42	43	27	23	20	38	1	41	40	33
OCT. 21	29	43	44	45	28	24	20	38	1	41	40	33
OCT. 22	29	45	46	46	28	24	20	38	1	41	40	33
OCT. 23	29	47	48	48	28	24	20	38	1	41	40	33
OCT. 24	29	1	2	2	28	24	21	39	1	41	40	33
OCT. 25	29	3	3	4	29	24	21	39	1	41	40	33
OCT. 26	30	5	5	6	29	24	21	39	1	41	40	33
OCT. 27	30	7	7	8	29	25	21	39	1	41	40	33
OCT. 28	30	8	9	10	29	25	21	39	1	41	40	33
OCT. 29	30	10	11	11	29	25	21	39	1	41	40	33
OCT. 30	30	12	12	13	30	25	21	39	1	41	40	33
OCT. 31	30	13	14	15	30	25	21	39	1	41	40	33

MOON 1 ☽ 12:01 A.M. TO 8:00 A.M.   **MOON 2** ◐ 8:01 A.M. TO 4:00 P.M.   **MOON 3** ● 4:01 P.M. TO 12:00 A.M.
Use only one "moon" number. Choose the column closest to your time of birth. If your place of birth is not on Eastern Standard Time, be sure to read "How to Convert to Eastern Standard Time" at the beginning of this section.

1996

November · December

Date & Time	SUN	MOON 1	MOON 2	MOON 3	MERCURY	VENUS	MARS	JUPITER	SATURN	URANUS	NEPTUNE	PLUTO
NOV. 1	30	15	16	16	30	25	21	39	1	41	40	33
NOV. 2	30	17	17	18	30	26	21	39	1	41	40	33
NOV. 3	31	18	19	19	31	26	21	39	1	41	40	33
NOV. 4	31	20	20	21	31	26	21	39	1	41	40	33
NOV. 5	31	21	22	22	31	26	21	39	1	41	40	33
NOV. 6	31	23	24	24	31	26	21	39	1	41	40	33
NOV. 7	31	25	25	26	31	26	21	39	1	41	40	33
NOV. 8	31	26	27	27	32	27	22	39	1	41	40	33
NOV. 9	31	28	29	29	32	27	22	39	1	41	40	33
NOV. 10	31	30	30	31	32	27	22	39	1	41	40	33
NOV. 11	31	32	32	33	32	27	22	39	1	41	40	33
NOV. 12	32	33	34	35	32	27	22	39	1	41	40	33
NOV. 13	32	35	36	37	33	27	22	39	1	41	40	33
NOV. 14	32	37	38	38	33	28	22	39	1	41	40	33
NOV. 15	32	39	40	40	33	28	22	39	1	41	40	33
NOV. 16	32	41	42	42	33	28	22	39	1	41	40	33
NOV. 17	32	43	43	44	33	28	22	39	1	41	40	33
NOV. 18	32	45	45	46	34	28	22	39	1	41	40	33
NOV. 19	33	47	47	48	34	28	22	39	1	41	40	33
NOV. 20	33	48	1	2	34	28	23	39	1	41	40	33
NOV. 21	33	2	3	4	34	28	23	39	1	41	40	33
NOV. 22	33	4	5	5	35	29	23	39	1	41	40	33
NOV. 23	33	6	7	7	35	29	23	39	1	41	40	33
NOV. 24	33	8	8	9	35	29	23	39	1	41	40	33
NOV. 25	34	9	10	11	35	29	23	39	1	41	40	33
NOV. 26	34	11	12	12	35	29	23	39	1	41	40	33
NOV. 27	34	13	13	14	36	30	23	39	1	41	40	33
NOV. 28	34	15	15	16	36	30	23	39	1	41	40	33
NOV. 29	34	16	17	17	36	30	23	39	1	41	40	33
NOV. 30	34	18	18	19	36	30	23	39	1	41	40	33

Date & Time	SUN	MOON 1	MOON 2	MOON 3	MERCURY	VENUS	MARS	JUPITER	SATURN	URANUS	NEPTUNE	PLUTO
DEC. 1	34	19	20	20	36	30	23	39	1	41	40	33
DEC. 2	34	21	21	22	37	30	23	39	1	41	40	33
DEC. 3	35	22	23	24	37	31	23	39	1	41	40	33
DEC. 4	35	24	25	25	37	31	23	40	1	41	40	33
DEC. 5	35	26	26	27	37	31	23	40	1	41	40	33
DEC. 6	35	27	28	28	37	31	23	40	1	41	40	33
DEC. 7	35	29	30	30	37	31	24	40	1	41	40	33
DEC. 8	35	31	31	32	38	31	24	40	1	41	40	33
DEC. 9	35	33	33	34	38	32	24	40	1	41	40	33
DEC. 10	35	35	35	36	38	32	24	40	1	41	40	33
DEC. 11	36	36	37	38	38	32	24	40	1	41	40	33
DEC. 12	36	38	39	40	38	32	24	40	1	41	40	33
DEC. 13	36	40	41	42	39	32	24	40	1	41	40	33
DEC. 14	36	42	43	44	39	32	24	40	1	41	40	33
DEC. 15	36	44	45	46	39	33	24	40	1	41	40	33
DEC. 16	36	46	47	47	39	33	24	40	1	41	40	33
DEC. 17	36	48	1	1	39	33	24	40	1	41	40	33
DEC. 18	36	2	2	3	39	33	24	40	1	41	40	33
DEC. 19	37	4	4	5	39	33	24	40	1	41	40	33
DEC. 20	37	5	6	7	39	33	24	40	1	41	40	33
DEC. 21	37	7	8	8	39	34	24	40	1	41	40	34
DEC. 22	37	9	10	10	39	34	24	40	1	41	40	34
DEC. 23	37	11	11	12	40	34	24	40	1	41	41	34
DEC. 24	37	12	13	13	40	34	24	40	1	41	41	34
DEC. 25	37	14	15	15	40	34	25	40	1	41	41	34
DEC. 26	38	16	16	17	39	34	25	40	1	41	41	34
DEC. 27	38	17	18	18	39	35	25	40	1	41	41	34
DEC. 28	38	19	19	20	39	35	25	40	1	41	41	34
DEC. 29	38	20	21	21	39	35	25	40	1	41	41	34
DEC. 30	38	22	22	23	39	35	25	40	1	41	41	34
DEC. 31	38	24	24	25	39	35	25	40	1	41	41	34

MOON 1 ◔ 12:01 A.M. TO 8:00 A.M.   **MOON 2** ◑ 8:01 A.M. TO 4:00 P.M.   **MOON 3** ● 4:01 P.M. TO 12:00 A.M.

Use only one "moon" number. Choose the column closest to your time of birth. If your place of birth is not on Eastern Standard Time, be sure to read "How to Convert to Eastern Standard Time" at the beginning of this section.

January

Date & Time	SUN	MOON 1	MOON 2	MOON 3	MERCURY	VENUS	MARS	JUPITER	SATURN	URANUS	NEPTUNE	PLUTO
JAN. 1	38	25	26	26	39	35	25	40	1	41	41	34
JAN. 2	38	27	27	28	38	36	25	40	1	41	41	34
JAN. 3	39	28	29	30	38	36	25	40	1	41	41	34
JAN. 4	39	30	31	31	38	36	25	40	1	41	41	34
JAN. 5	39	32	32	33	38	36	25	40	1	41	41	34
JAN. 6	39	34	34	35	38	36	25	40	1	41	41	34
JAN. 7	39	36	36	37	38	36	25	41	1	41	41	34
JAN. 8	39	38	38	39	38	37	25	41	1	41	41	34
JAN. 9	39	40	40	41	37	37	25	41	1	41	41	34
JAN. 10	40	42	42	43	37	37	25	41	1	41	41	34
JAN. 11	40	44	44	45	37	37	25	41	1	41	41	34
JAN. 12	40	46	46	47	37	37	25	41	1	41	41	34
JAN. 13	40	48	48	1	37	37	25	41	1	41	41	34
JAN. 14	40	1	2	3	37	38	25	41	1	42	41	34
JAN. 15	40	3	4	4	37	38	25	41	1	42	41	34
JAN. 16	40	5	6	6	37	38	25	41	1	42	41	34
JAN. 17	41	7	7	8	38	38	25	41	1	42	41	34
JAN. 18	41	9	9	10	38	38	25	41	1	42	41	34
JAN. 19	41	10	11	11	38	38	26	41	1	42	41	34
JAN. 20	41	12	12	13	38	39	26	41	1	42	41	34
JAN. 21	41	14	14	15	38	39	26	41	1	42	41	34
JAN. 22	41	15	16	17	38	39	26	41	1	42	41	34
JAN. 23	42	17	17	18	38	39	26	41	1	42	41	34
JAN. 24	42	18	19	19	38	39	26	41	1	42	41	34
JAN. 25	42	20	20	21	38	39	26	41	1	42	41	34
JAN. 26	42	22	22	23	39	40	26	41	1	42	41	34
JAN. 27	42	23	24	24	39	40	26	41	1	42	41	34
JAN. 28	42	25	25	26	39	40	26	41	1	42	41	34
JAN. 29	42	26	27	27	39	40	26	41	1	42	41	34
JAN. 30	42	28	28	29	39	40	26	41	1	42	41	34
JAN. 31	43	30	30	31	39	40	26	41	1	42	41	34

February

Date & Time	SUN	MOON 1	MOON 2	MOON 3	MERCURY	VENUS	MARS	JUPITER	SATURN	URANUS	NEPTUNE	PLUTO
FEB. 1	43	31	32	32	40	41	26	41	1	42	41	34
FEB. 2	43	33	34	34	40	41	26	41	1	42	41	34
FEB. 3	43	35	35	36	40	41	26	41	1	42	41	34
FEB. 4	43	37	37	38	40	41	26	41	1	42	41	34
FEB. 5	43	39	39	40	40	41	26	41	2	42	41	34
FEB. 6	43	41	41	42	40	41	26	41	2	42	41	34
FEB. 7	43	43	43	44	41	42	26	41	2	42	41	34
FEB. 8	44	45	45	46	41	42	26	42	2	42	41	34
FEB. 9	44	47	47	48	41	42	26	42	2	42	41	34
FEB. 10	44	1	1	2	41	42	26	42	2	42	41	34
FEB. 11	44	3	3	4	41	42	26	42	2	42	41	34
FEB. 12	44	5	5	6	42	42	26	42	2	42	41	34
FEB. 13	44	6	7	8	42	43	26	42	2	42	41	34
FEB. 14	44	8	9	9	42	43	26	42	2	42	41	34
FEB. 15	44	10	10	11	42	43	26	42	2	42	41	34
FEB. 16	45	12	12	13	42	43	26	42	2	42	41	34
FEB. 17	45	13	14	14	43	43	26	42	2	42	41	34
FEB. 18	45	15	15	16	43	43	26	42	2	42	41	34
FEB. 19	45	16	17	17	44	44	26	42	2	42	41	34
FEB. 20	45	18	18	19	44	44	26	42	2	42	41	34
FEB. 21	45	20	20	21	43	44	26	42	2	42	41	34
FEB. 22	45	21	22	22	44	44	26	42	2	42	41	34
FEB. 23	46	23	23	24	44	44	26	42	2	42	41	34
FEB. 24	46	24	25	25	44	44	25	42	2	42	41	34
FEB. 25	46	26	26	27	44	45	25	42	2	42	41	34
FEB. 26	46	27	28	29	45	45	25	42	2	42	41	34
FEB. 27	46	29	30	30	45	45	25	42	2	42	41	34
FEB. 28	46	31	31	32	45	45	25	42	2	42	41	34

MOON 1 ◗ 12:01 A.M. TO 8:00 A.M.   **MOON 2** ◖ 8:01 A.M. TO 4:00 P.M.   **MOON 3** ● 4:01 P.M. TO 12:00 A.M.

Use only one "moon" number. Choose the column closest to your time of birth. If your place of birth is not on Eastern Standard Time, be sure to read "How to Convert to Eastern Standard Time" at the beginning of this section.

Date & Time	SUN ☉	MOON 1 ◑	MOON 2 ◐	MOON 3 ●	MERCURY	VENUS	MARS	JUPITER	SATURN	URANUS	NEPTUNE	PLUTO
MAR. 1	46	32	33	34	45	45	25	42	2	42	41	34
MAR. 2	46	34	35	35	45	45	25	42	2	42	41	34
MAR. 3	47	36	37	37	46	46	25	42	2	42	41	34
MAR. 4	47	38	38	39	46	46	25	42	2	42	41	34
MAR. 5	47	40	40	41	46	46	25	42	2	42	41	34
MAR. 6	47	42	42	43	46	46	25	42	2	42	41	34
MAR. 7	47	44	44	45	47	46	25	42	2	42	41	34
MAR. 8	47	46	46	47	47	46	25	42	2	42	41	34
MAR. 9	47	48	48	1	47	47	25	42	2	42	41	34
MAR. 10	47	2	2	3	47	47	25	42	2	42	41	34
MAR. 11	48	4	4	5	48	47	25	42	2	42	41	34
MAR. 12	48	6	6	7	48	47	25	42	2	42	41	34
MAR. 13	48	7	8	9	48	47	25	42	2	42	41	34
MAR. 14	48	9	10	10	48	47	25	43	2	42	41	34
MAR. 15	48	11	12	12	1	48	25	43	2	42	41	34
MAR. 16	48	13	13	14	1	48	25	43	2	42	41	34
MAR. 17	48	14	15	15	1	48	25	43	2	42	41	34
MAR. 18	48	16	16	17	2	48	24	43	2	42	41	34
MAR. 19	1	18	18	19	2	48	24	43	2	42	41	34
MAR. 20	1	19	20	20	2	48	24	43	2	42	41	34
MAR. 21	1	21	21	22	2	1	24	43	2	42	41	34
MAR. 22	1	22	23	23	3	1	24	43	2	42	41	34
MAR. 23	1	24	24	25	3	1	24	43	2	42	41	34
MAR. 24	1	25	26	27	3	1	24	43	2	42	41	34
MAR. 25	2	27	28	28	3	1	24	43	2	42	41	34
MAR. 26	2	29	29	30	4	1	24	43	2	42	41	34
MAR. 27	2	30	31	31	4	2	24	43	2	42	41	34
MAR. 28	2	32	33	33	4	2	24	43	2	42	41	34
MAR. 29	2	34	34	35	4	2	24	43	2	42	41	34
MAR. 30	2	36	36	37	4	2	24	43	2	42	41	34
MAR. 31	2	37	38	39	5	2	24	43	2	42	41	34

Date & Time	SUN ☉	MOON 1 ◑	MOON 2 ◐	MOON 3 ●	MERCURY	VENUS	MARS	JUPITER	SATURN	URANUS	NEPTUNE	PLUTO
APR. 1	2	39	40	40	5	2	24	43	2	42	41	34
APR. 2	2	41	42	42	5	3	24	43	2	42	41	34
APR. 3	3	43	44	44	5	3	24	43	2	42	41	34
APR. 4	3	45	46	46	5	3	24	43	2	42	41	34
APR. 5	3	47	48	48	6	3	24	43	2	42	41	34
APR. 6	3	1	2	2	6	3	24	43	2	42	41	34
APR. 7	3	3	3	4	6	3	24	43	2	42	41	34
APR. 8	3	5	5	6	6	4	24	43	2	42	41	34
APR. 9	3	7	7	8	6	4	23	43	2	42	41	34
APR. 10	3	9	9	10	6	4	23	43	3	42	41	34
APR. 11	4	10	11	12	6	4	23	43	3	42	41	34
APR. 12	4	12	13	13	6	4	23	43	3	42	41	34
APR. 13	4	14	14	15	6	4	23	43	3	42	41	34
APR. 14	4	15	16	17	6	5	23	43	3	42	41	34
APR. 15	4	17	18	18	6	5	23	43	3	42	41	34
APR. 16	4	19	19	20	6	5	23	43	3	42	41	34
APR. 17	4	20	21	21	6	5	23	43	3	42	41	34
APR. 18	4	22	22	23	6	5	23	43	3	42	41	34
APR. 19	5	23	24	24	6	5	23	43	3	42	41	34
APR. 20	5	25	26	26	6	6	23	43	3	42	41	34
APR. 21	5	27	27	28	6	6	23	43	3	42	41	34
APR. 22	5	28	29	29	6	6	23	43	3	42	41	34
APR. 23	5	30	30	31	6	6	23	43	3	42	41	34
APR. 24	5	32	32	33	6	6	23	43	3	42	41	34
APR. 25	6	33	34	35	6	6	23	43	3	42	41	34
APR. 26	6	35	36	36	6	7	23	43	3	42	41	34
APR. 27	6	37	38	38	6	7	23	44	3	42	41	34
APR. 28	6	39	39	40	5	7	23	44	3	42	41	34
APR. 29	6	41	41	42	5	7	23	44	3	42	41	34
APR. 30	6	42	43	44	5	7	23	44	3	42	41	34

MOON 1 ◑ 12:01 A.M. TO 8:00 A.M.   **MOON 2** ◐ 8:01 A.M. TO 4:00 P.M.   **MOON 3** ● 4:01 P.M. TO 12:00 A.M.

Use only one "moon" number. Choose the column closest to your time of birth. If your place of birth is not on Eastern Standard Time, be sure to read "How to Convert to Eastern Standard Time" at the beginning of this section.

1997

May

Date & Time	SUN	MOON 1	MOON 2	MOON 3	MERCURY	VENUS	MARS	JUPITER	SATURN	URANUS	NEPTUNE	PLUTO
MAY 1	6	44	45	46	5	7	23	44	3	42	41	34
MAY 2	6	46	47	48	5	8	23	44	3	42	41	34
MAY 3	7	48	1	1	5	8	23	44	3	42	41	34
MAY 4	7	2	3	3	5	8	23	44	3	42	41	34
MAY 5	7	4	5	5	5	8	23	44	3	42	41	34
MAY 6	7	6	7	7	5	8	23	44	3	42	41	34
MAY 7	8	8	9	9	5	8	23	44	3	42	41	34
MAY 8	7	10	10	11	5	9	23	44	3	42	41	34
MAY 9	7	11	12	13	5	9	23	44	3	42	41	34
MAY 10	7	13	14	14	5	9	23	44	3	42	41	34
MAY 11	8	15	15	16	5	9	23	44	3	42	41	34
MAY 12	8	17	17	18	5	9	23	44	3	42	41	34
MAY 13	8	18	19	19	5	9	23	44	3	42	41	34
MAY 14	8	20	20	21	5	10	23	44	3	42	41	34
MAY 15	8	21	22	22	5	10	23	44	3	42	41	34
MAY 16	8	23	23	24	5	10	23	44	3	42	41	34
MAY 17	8	24	25	26	5	10	23	44	3	42	41	34
MAY 18	8	26	27	27	5	10	24	44	3	42	41	34
MAY 19	9	28	28	29	5	10	24	44	3	42	41	34
MAY 20	9	29	30	31	6	11	24	44	3	42	41	34
MAY 21	9	31	32	32	6	11	24	44	3	42	41	34
MAY 22	9	33	33	34	6	11	24	44	3	42	41	34
MAY 23	9	35	35	36	6	11	24	44	3	42	41	34
MAY 24	9	36	37	38	6	11	24	44	3	42	41	34
MAY 25	10	38	39	40	6	11	24	44	3	42	41	34
MAY 26	10	40	41	41	6	12	24	44	3	42	41	34
MAY 27	10	42	43	43	6	12	24	44	3	42	41	34
MAY 28	10	44	45	45	7	12	24	44	3	42	41	34
MAY 29	10	46	46	47	7	12	24	44	3	42	41	34
MAY 30	10	48	48	1	7	12	24	44	3	42	41	34
MAY 31	10	2	2	3	7	12	24	44	3	42	41	34

June

Date & Time	SUN	MOON 1	MOON 2	MOON 3	MERCURY	VENUS	MARS	JUPITER	SATURN	URANUS	NEPTUNE	PLUTO
JUN. 1	10	3	4	5	7	12	24	44	3	42	41	34
JUN. 2	10	5	6	7	8	13	24	44	3	42	41	34
JUN. 3	11	7	8	8	8	13	24	44	3	42	41	33
JUN. 4	11	9	10	10	8	13	24	44	3	42	41	33
JUN. 5	11	11	11	12	8	13	24	44	3	42	41	33
JUN. 6	11	13	13	14	8	13	24	44	3	42	41	33
JUN. 7	11	14	15	15	9	13	24	44	3	42	41	33
JUN. 8	11	16	16	17	9	14	24	44	3	42	41	33
JUN. 9	11	18	18	19	9	14	24	44	3	42	41	33
JUN. 10	11	19	20	20	9	14	24	44	3	42	41	33
JUN. 11	12	21	21	22	10	14	25	44	3	42	41	33
JUN. 12	12	22	23	23	10	14	25	44	3	42	41	33
JUN. 13	12	24	24	25	10	14	25	44	3	42	41	33
JUN. 14	12	26	26	27	10	15	25	44	3	42	41	33
JUN. 15	12	27	28	28	11	15	25	44	3	42	41	33
JUN. 16	12	29	29	30	11	15	25	44	3	42	41	33
JUN. 17	12	30	31	32	11	15	25	44	3	42	41	33
JUN. 18	12	32	33	33	11	15	25	44	3	42	41	33
JUN. 19	13	34	35	35	12	15	25	44	3	42	41	33
JUN. 20	13	36	36	37	12	16	25	44	3	42	41	33
JUN. 21	13	38	38	39	12	16	25	44	3	42	41	33
JUN. 22	13	40	40	41	12	16	25	44	3	42	41	33
JUN. 23	13	42	42	43	13	16	25	44	4	42	41	33
JUN. 24	13	43	44	45	13	16	25	44	4	42	41	33
JUN. 25	14	45	46	47	13	16	25	44	4	42	41	33
JUN. 26	14	47	48	1	14	17	25	44	4	42	41	33
JUN. 27	14	1	2	2	14	17	25	44	4	42	41	33
JUN. 28	14	3	4	4	14	17	26	44	4	42	41	33
JUN. 29	14	5	5	6	15	17	26	44	4	42	41	33
JUN. 30	14	7	7	8	15	17	26	44	4	42	41	33

MOON 1 ◖ 12:01 A.M. TO 8:00 A.M.   **MOON 2** ◗ 8:01 A.M. TO 4:00 P.M.   **MOON 3** ● 4:01 P.M. TO 12:00 A.M.
Use only one "moon" number. Choose the column closest to your time of birth. If your place of birth is not on Eastern Standard Time, be sure to read "How to Convert to Eastern Standard Time" at the beginning of this section.

1997

July ★★★ **August** ★★★

Date & Time	SUN ☉	MOON 1 ◑	MOON 2 ◐	MOON 3 ●	MERCURY	VENUS	MARS	JUPITER	SATURN	URANUS	NEPTUNE	PLUTO
JUL. 1	14	8	9	10	15	17	26	44	4	42	41	33
JUL. 2	14	10	11	11	15	18	26	44	4	42	41	33
JUL. 3	15	12	13	13	16	18	26	44	4	42	41	33
JUL. 4	15	14	14	15	16	18	26	44	4	42	41	33
JUL. 5	15	15	16	17	16	18	26	44	4	42	41	33
JUL. 6	15	17	18	18	16	18	26	44	4	42	41	33
JUL. 7	15	19	19	20	17	18	26	44	4	42	41	33
JUL. 8	15	20	21	21	17	18	26	44	4	42	41	33
JUL. 9	15	22	22	23	17	19	26	44	4	42	41	33
JUL. 10	15	23	24	24	17	19	26	44	4	42	41	33
JUL. 11	16	25	26	26	18	19	26	44	4	42	41	33
JUL. 12	16	27	27	28	18	19	26	44	4	42	41	33
JUL. 13	16	28	29	29	18	19	27	44	4	42	41	33
JUL. 14	16	30	30	31	18	19	27	44	4	42	41	33
JUL. 15	16	32	32	33	19	20	27	44	4	42	41	33
JUL. 16	16	33	34	34	19	20	27	44	4	42	41	33
JUL. 17	16	35	36	36	19	20	27	44	4	42	41	33
JUL. 18	16	37	38	38	19	20	27	44	4	42	41	33
JUL. 19	17	39	39	40	19	20	27	44	4	42	41	33
JUL. 20	17	41	41	42	20	20	27	44	4	42	41	33
JUL. 21	17	43	43	44	20	21	27	44	4	42	41	33
JUL. 22	17	45	45	46	20	21	27	44	4	42	41	33
JUL. 23	17	47	47	48	20	21	27	44	4	42	41	33
JUL. 24	17	1	1	2	20	21	27	44	4	42	41	33
JUL. 25	17	3	3	4	21	21	27	43	4	42	41	33
JUL. 26	18	4	5	6	21	21	27	43	4	42	41	33
JUL. 27	18	6	7	7	21	22	28	43	4	42	41	33
JUL. 28	18	8	9	9	21	22	28	43	4	42	41	33
JUL. 29	18	10	10	11	21	22	28	43	4	42	41	33
JUL. 30	18	12	12	13	21	22	28	43	4	42	41	33
JUL. 31	18	13	14	14	22	22	28	43	4	42	41	33

Date & Time	SUN ☉	MOON 1 ◑	MOON 2 ◐	MOON 3 ●	MERCURY	VENUS	MARS	JUPITER	SATURN	URANUS	NEPTUNE	PLUTO
AUG. 1	18	15	16	16	22	22	28	43	4	42	41	33
AUG. 2	18	17	17	18	22	23	28	43	4	42	41	33
AUG. 3	19	18	19	19	22	23	28	43	4	42	41	33
AUG. 4	19	20	20	21	22	23	28	43	4	42	41	33
AUG. 5	19	21	22	22	22	23	28	43	4	42	41	33
AUG. 6	19	23	24	24	22	23	28	43	4	42	41	33
AUG. 7	19	25	25	26	23	23	28	43	4	42	41	33
AUG. 8	19	26	27	27	23	23	28	43	4	42	41	33
AUG. 9	19	28	28	29	23	24	29	43	4	42	41	33
AUG. 10	19	29	30	30	23	24	29	43	4	42	41	33
AUG. 11	20	31	32	32	23	24	29	43	4	42	41	33
AUG. 12	20	33	33	34	23	24	29	43	4	42	41	33
AUG. 13	20	34	35	36	23	24	29	43	4	42	41	33
AUG. 14	20	36	37	37	23	24	29	43	4	42	41	33
AUG. 15	20	38	39	39	23	25	29	43	4	42	41	33
AUG. 16	20	40	41	41	23	25	29	43	4	42	41	33
AUG. 17	20	42	43	43	23	25	29	43	4	42	41	33
AUG. 18	20	44	45	45	23	25	29	43	4	42	41	33
AUG. 19	21	46	47	47	23	25	29	43	4	42	41	33
AUG. 20	21	48	1	1	23	25	29	43	4	42	41	33
AUG. 21	21	2	3	3	23	26	30	43	4	42	41	33
AUG. 22	21	4	4	5	23	26	30	43	4	42	41	33
AUG. 23	21	6	6	7	23	26	30	43	4	42	41	33
AUG. 24	21	8	8	9	23	26	30	43	4	42	41	33
AUG. 25	21	9	10	11	23	26	30	43	4	42	41	33
AUG. 26	22	11	12	12	23	26	30	43	4	42	41	33
AUG. 27	22	13	13	14	23	26	30	43	4	42	41	33
AUG. 28	22	15	15	16	22	27	30	43	4	42	41	33
AUG. 29	22	16	17	17	22	27	30	43	4	42	41	33
AUG. 30	22	18	18	19	22	27	30	43	4	42	41	33
AUG. 31	22	19	20	20	22	27	30	43	4	42	41	33

MOON 1 ◑ 12:01 A.M. TO 8:00 A.M.   **MOON 2** ◐ 8:01 A.M. TO 4:00 P.M.   **MOON 3** ● 4:01 P.M. TO 12:00 A.M.

Use only one "moon" number. Choose the column closest to your time of birth. If your place of birth is not on Eastern Standard Time, be sure to read "How to Convert to Eastern Standard Time" at the beginning of this section.

1997

September

October

Date & Time	SUN	MOON 1	MOON 2	MOON 3	MERCURY	VENUS	MARS	JUPITER	SATURN	URANUS	NEPTUNE	PLUTO
SEP. 1	22	21	22	22	22	27	30	43	4	42	41	33
SEP. 2	22	23	23	24	22	27	31	43	4	42	41	33
SEP. 3	23	24	25	25	22	28	31	43	4	42	41	33
SEP. 4	23	26	26	27	22	28	31	43	4	42	41	33
SEP. 5	23	27	28	28	22	28	31	43	4	42	41	33
SEP. 6	23	29	29	30	21	28	31	43	4	42	41	33
SEP. 7	23	31	31	32	21	28	31	43	4	42	41	33
SEP. 8	23	32	33	33	21	28	31	43	4	42	41	33
SEP. 9	23	34	34	35	21	29	31	43	4	42	41	33
SEP. 10	23	36	36	37	21	29	31	43	4	42	41	33
SEP. 11	24	37	38	39	21	29	31	43	4	42	41	33
SEP. 12	24	39	40	40	21	29	31	43	3	42	41	33
SEP. 13	24	41	42	42	21	29	32	43	3	42	41	33
SEP. 14	24	43	44	44	21	29	32	43	3	42	41	33
SEP. 15	24	45	46	46	22	29	32	43	3	42	41	33
SEP. 16	24	47	48	48	22	30	32	43	3	42	41	33
SEP. 17	24	1	2	2	22	30	32	43	3	42	41	33
SEP. 18	24	3	4	4	22	30	32	43	3	42	41	33
SEP. 19	25	5	6	6	22	30	32	43	3	42	41	33
SEP. 20	25	7	8	8	22	30	32	43	3	42	41	33
SEP. 21	25	9	9	10	22	30	32	43	3	42	41	33
SEP. 22	25	11	11	12	23	31	32	43	3	42	41	33
SEP. 23	25	12	13	14	23	31	32	43	3	42	41	33
SEP. 24	25	14	15	15	23	31	33	43	3	42	41	33
SEP. 25	26	16	16	17	23	31	33	43	3	42	41	33
SEP. 26	26	17	18	18	24	31	33	43	3	42	41	33
SEP. 27	26	19	20	20	24	31	33	43	3	42	41	33
SEP. 28	26	21	21	22	24	31	33	43	3	42	41	33
SEP. 29	26	22	23	23	24	32	33	43	3	42	41	33
SEP. 30	26	24	24	25	24	32	33	43	3	42	41	33

Date & Time	SUN	MOON 1	MOON 2	MOON 3	MERCURY	VENUS	MARS	JUPITER	SATURN	URANUS	NEPTUNE	PLUTO
OCT. 1	26	25	26	26	25	32	33	43	3	42	41	33
OCT. 2	26	27	27	28	25	32	33	43	3	42	41	33
OCT. 3	27	29	29	30	25	32	33	43	3	42	41	33
OCT. 4	27	30	31	31	25	32	33	43	3	42	41	33
OCT. 5	27	32	32	33	26	32	34	43	3	42	41	33
OCT. 6	27	33	34	35	26	33	34	43	3	42	41	33
OCT. 7	27	35	36	36	26	33	34	43	3	42	41	33
OCT. 8	27	37	37	38	26	33	34	43	3	42	41	33
OCT. 9	27	39	39	40	27	33	34	43	3	42	41	33
OCT. 10	27	40	41	42	27	33	34	43	3	42	41	33
OCT. 11	28	42	43	44	27	33	34	43	3	42	41	33
OCT. 12	28	44	45	45	27	34	34	43	3	42	41	33
OCT. 13	28	46	47	47	28	34	34	43	3	42	41	33
OCT. 14	28	48	1	1	28	34	34	43	3	42	41	33
OCT. 15	28	2	3	3	28	34	35	43	3	42	41	33
OCT. 16	28	4	5	5	28	34	35	43	3	42	41	33
OCT. 17	28	6	7	7	28	34	35	43	3	42	41	33
OCT. 18	28	8	9	9	29	34	35	43	3	42	41	33
OCT. 19	29	10	11	11	29	35	35	43	3	42	41	34
OCT. 20	29	12	12	13	29	35	35	43	3	42	41	34
OCT. 21	29	14	14	15	29	35	35	43	3	42	41	34
OCT. 22	29	15	16	16	30	35	35	43	3	42	41	34
OCT. 23	29	17	18	18	30	35	35	43	3	42	41	34
OCT. 24	29	19	19	20	30	35	35	43	3	42	41	34
OCT. 25	29	20	21	21	30	35	35	43	3	42	41	34
OCT. 26	30	22	22	23	30	36	36	43	3	42	41	34
OCT. 27	30	23	24	24	31	36	36	43	3	42	41	34
OCT. 28	30	25	25	26	31	36	36	43	3	42	41	34
OCT. 29	30	26	27	28	31	36	36	43	3	42	41	34
OCT. 30	30	28	29	29	31	36	36	43	3	42	41	34
OCT. 31	30	30	30	31	31	36	36	43	3	42	41	34

MOON 1 ◗ 12:01 A.M. TO 8:00 A.M.   **MOON 2** ◑ 8:01 A.M. TO 4:00 P.M.   **MOON 3** ● 4:01 P.M. TO 12:00 A.M.

Use only one "moon" number. Choose the column closest to your time of birth. If your place of birth is not on Eastern Standard Time, be sure to read "How to Convert to Eastern Standard Time" at the beginning of this section.

1997

November

December

Date & Time	SUN	MOON 1	MOON 2	MOON 3	MERCURY	VENUS	MARS	JUPITER	SATURN	URANUS	NEPTUNE	PLUTO
NOV. 1	30	31	32	32	32	36	36	43	3	42	41	34
NOV. 2	30	33	34	34	32	37	36	43	3	42	41	34
NOV. 3	31	35	35	36	32	37	36	43	3	42	41	34
NOV. 4	31	36	37	38	32	37	36	43	3	42	41	34
NOV. 5	31	38	39	39	32	37	37	43	3	42	41	34
NOV. 6	31	40	41	41	33	37	37	43	3	42	41	34
NOV. 7	31	42	42	43	33	37	37	43	3	42	41	34
NOV. 8	31	44	44	45	33	37	37	43	3	42	41	34
NOV. 9	31	45	46	47	33	37	37	43	3	42	41	34
NOV. 10	31	47	48	1	33	38	37	43	3	42	41	34
NOV. 11	31	1	2	3	34	38	37	43	3	42	41	34
NOV. 12	32	3	4	5	34	38	37	43	3	42	41	34
NOV. 13	32	5	6	7	34	38	37	43	3	42	41	34
NOV. 14	32	7	8	8	34	38	37	43	3	42	41	34
NOV. 15	32	9	10	10	34	38	38	43	3	42	41	34
NOV. 16	32	11	12	12	35	38	38	43	3	42	41	34
NOV. 17	32	13	13	14	35	38	38	43	3	42	41	34
NOV. 18	32	15	15	16	35	39	38	43	3	42	41	34
NOV. 19	33	16	17	17	35	39	38	43	3	42	41	34
NOV. 20	33	18	19	19	35	39	38	43	3	42	41	34
NOV. 21	33	20	20	21	36	39	38	43	3	42	41	34
NOV. 22	33	21	22	22	36	39	38	43	3	42	41	34
NOV. 23	33	23	23	24	36	39	38	43	3	42	41	34
NOV. 24	33	24	25	25	36	39	38	43	3	42	41	34
NOV. 25	34	26	27	27	36	39	39	43	3	42	41	34
NOV. 26	34	28	28	29	36	40	39	43	3	42	41	34
NOV. 27	34	29	30	30	36	40	39	43	3	42	41	34
NOV. 28	34	31	31	32	37	40	39	43	3	42	41	34
NOV. 29	34	33	33	34	37	40	39	43	3	42	41	34
NOV. 30	34	34	35	35	37	40	39	43	3	42	41	34

Date & Time	SUN	MOON 1	MOON 2	MOON 3	MERCURY	VENUS	MARS	JUPITER	SATURN	URANUS	NEPTUNE	PLUTO
DEC. 1	34	36	37	37	37	40	39	43	3	42	41	34
DEC. 2	34	38	38	39	37	40	39	43	3	42	41	34
DEC. 3	35	40	40	41	37	40	39	43	3	42	41	34
DEC. 4	35	41	42	43	37	40	40	43	3	42	41	34
DEC. 5	35	43	44	44	37	40	40	43	3	42	41	34
DEC. 6	35	45	46	46	37	41	40	43	3	42	41	34
DEC. 7	35	47	48	48	37	41	40	43	3	42	41	34
DEC. 8	35	1	1	2	37	41	40	43	3	42	41	34
DEC. 9	35	3	3	4	37	41	40	43	3	42	41	34
DEC. 10	35	5	5	6	37	41	40	43	3	42	41	34
DEC. 11	36	6	7	8	37	41	40	43	3	42	41	34
DEC. 12	36	8	9	10	37	41	40	43	3	42	41	34
DEC. 13	36	10	11	11	37	41	40	43	3	42	41	34
DEC. 14	36	12	13	13	37	41	41	43	3	42	41	34
DEC. 15	36	14	15	15	37	41	41	43	3	42	41	34
DEC. 16	36	16	16	17	37	41	41	44	3	42	41	34
DEC. 17	36	17	18	19	36	41	41	44	3	42	41	34
DEC. 18	36	19	20	20	36	41	41	44	3	42	41	34
DEC. 19	37	21	21	22	36	41	41	44	3	42	41	34
DEC. 20	37	22	23	23	36	41	41	44	3	42	41	34
DEC. 21	37	24	24	25	36	41	41	44	3	42	41	34
DEC. 22	37	25	26	27	36	41	41	44	3	42	41	34
DEC. 23	37	27	28	28	35	41	41	44	3	42	41	34
DEC. 24	37	29	29	30	35	41	42	44	3	42	41	34
DEC. 25	37	30	31	31	35	41	42	44	3	42	41	34
DEC. 26	38	32	32	33	35	41	42	44	3	42	41	34
DEC. 27	38	34	34	35	35	41	42	44	3	42	41	34
DEC. 28	38	35	36	37	35	41	42	44	3	42	41	34
DEC. 29	38	37	38	38	35	41	42	44	3	42	41	34
DEC. 30	38	39	40	40	35	41	42	44	3	42	41	34
DEC. 31	38	41	41	42	35	41	42	44	3	42	41	34

MOON 1 ☽ 12:01 A.M. TO 8:00 A.M.　　**MOON 2** ☽ 8:01 A.M. TO 4:00 P.M.　　**MOON 3** ● 4:01 P.M. TO 12:00 A.M.
Use only one "moon" number. Choose the column closest to your time of birth. If your place of birth is not on Eastern Standard Time, be sure to read "How to Convert to Eastern Standard Time" at the beginning of this section.

1998

January

Date & Time	SUN	MOON 1	MOON 2	MOON 3	MERCURY	VENUS	MARS	JUPITER	SATURN	URANUS	NEPTUNE	PLUTO
JAN. 1	38	43	43	44	35	41	42	44	3	42	41	34
JAN. 2	38	45	45	46	36	41	43	44	3	42	41	34
JAN. 3	39	46	47	48	36	41	43	44	3	42	41	34
JAN. 4	39	48	1	2	36	41	43	44	3	42	41	34
JAN. 5	39	2	3	3	36	41	43	44	3	42	41	34
JAN. 6	39	4	5	5	36	41	43	44	3	42	41	34
JAN. 7	39	6	7	7	36	41	43	44	3	42	41	34
JAN. 8	39	8	8	9	36	41	43	44	3	42	41	34
JAN. 9	39	10	10	11	36	41	43	44	3	42	41	34
JAN. 10	40	11	12	13	37	41	43	44	3	42	41	34
JAN. 11	40	13	14	14	37	41	43	44	3	42	41	34
JAN. 12	40	15	16	16	37	41	44	44	3	42	41	34
JAN. 13	40	17	17	18	37	41	44	44	3	42	41	34
JAN. 14	40	18	19	20	37	41	44	44	3	42	41	34
JAN. 15	40	20	21	21	37	41	44	44	3	42	41	34
JAN. 16	40	22	22	23	38	40	44	44	3	42	41	34
JAN. 17	41	23	24	24	38	40	44	44	3	42	41	34
JAN. 18	41	25	25	26	38	40	44	44	3	42	41	34
JAN. 19	41	26	27	28	38	40	44	44	3	42	41	34
JAN. 20	41	28	29	29	38	40	44	44	3	42	41	34
JAN. 21	41	30	30	31	38	40	45	45	3	42	41	34
JAN. 22	41	31	32	32	38	40	45	45	3	42	41	34
JAN. 23	42	33	33	34	39	40	45	45	3	42	41	34
JAN. 24	42	35	35	36	39	40	45	45	3	42	41	34
JAN. 25	42	36	37	38	39	40	45	45	3	42	41	34
JAN. 26	42	38	39	39	39	40	45	45	3	42	41	34
JAN. 27	42	40	41	41	40	40	45	45	3	42	41	34
JAN. 28	42	42	43	43	40	40	45	45	3	42	41	34
JAN. 29	42	44	45	45	40	40	45	45	3	42	41	34
JAN. 30	42	46	47	47	40	40	45	45	3	42	41	34
JAN. 31	43	48	48	1	40	40	46	45	3	42	41	34

February

Date & Time	SUN	MOON 1	MOON 2	MOON 3	MERCURY	VENUS	MARS	JUPITER	SATURN	URANUS	NEPTUNE	PLUTO
FEB. 1	43	2	2	3	41	39	46	45	3	42	41	34
FEB. 2	43	4	4	5	41	39	46	45	3	42	41	34
FEB. 3	43	6	6	7	41	39	46	45	3	42	41	34
FEB. 4	43	7	8	9	41	39	46	45	3	42	41	34
FEB. 5	43	9	10	10	42	39	46	45	3	42	41	34
FEB. 6	43	11	12	12	42	39	46	45	3	42	41	34
FEB. 7	43	13	13	14	42	39	46	45	3	42	41	34
FEB. 8	44	15	15	16	42	39	46	45	3	42	41	34
FEB. 9	44	16	17	17	42	39	47	45	3	42	41	34
FEB. 10	44	18	18	19	43	39	47	45	3	42	41	34
FEB. 11	44	20	20	21	43	40	47	45	3	42	41	34
FEB. 12	44	21	22	22	43	40	47	45	3	42	41	34
FEB. 13	44	23	23	24	43	40	47	45	3	42	41	34
FEB. 14	44	24	25	25	44	40	47	45	3	42	41	34
FEB. 15	44	26	27	27	44	40	47	45	3	42	41	34
FEB. 16	45	28	28	29	44	40	47	45	3	42	41	34
FEB. 17	45	29	30	30	44	40	47	45	3	42	41	34
FEB. 18	45	31	31	32	44	40	47	45	3	42	41	34
FEB. 19	45	32	33	33	45	40	48	45	3	42	41	34
FEB. 20	45	34	35	35	45	40	48	45	3	42	41	34
FEB. 21	45	36	36	37	45	40	48	45	3	42	41	34
FEB. 22	45	37	38	39	45	40	48	45	3	42	41	34
FEB. 23	46	39	40	40	46	40	48	46	3	42	41	34
FEB. 24	46	41	42	42	46	40	48	46	3	42	41	34
FEB. 25	46	43	44	44	46	40	48	46	3	42	41	34
FEB. 26	46	45	46	46	46	40	48	46	3	42	41	34
FEB. 27	46	47	48	48	47	40	48	46	3	42	41	34
FEB. 28	46	1	2	2	47	41	1	46	3	42	41	34

MOON 1 ◗ 12:01 A.M. TO 8:00 A.M.   **MOON 2** ◖ 8:01 A.M. TO 4:00 P.M.   **MOON 3** ● 4:01 P.M. TO 12:00 A.M.

Use only one "moon" number. Choose the column closest to your time of birth. If your place of birth is not on Eastern Standard Time, be sure to read "How to Convert to Eastern Standard Time" at the beginning of this section.

1998

March

April

Date & Time	SUN ☉	MOON 1 ◗	MOON 2 ◖	MOON 3 ●	MERCURY	VENUS	MARS	JUPITER	SATURN	URANUS	NEPTUNE	PLUTO
MAR. 1	46	3	4	4	47	41	1	46	3	42	41	34
MAR. 2	46	5	6	6	47	41	1	46	3	42	41	34
MAR. 3	47	7	8	8	48	41	1	46	3	42	41	34
MAR. 4	47	9	9	10	48	41	1	46	3	42	41	34
MAR. 5	47	11	11	12	48	41	1	46	3	42	41	34
MAR. 6	47	12	13	14	48	41	1	46	3	42	41	34
MAR. 7	47	14	15	15	1	41	1	46	3	42	41	34
MAR. 8	47	16	16	17	1	41	1	46	3	42	41	34
MAR. 9	47	18	18	19	1	41	1	46	4	42	41	34
MAR. 10	47	19	20	20	1	42	2	46	4	42	41	34
MAR. 11	48	21	21	22	2	42	2	46	4	42	41	34
MAR. 12	48	22	23	23	2	42	2	46	4	42	41	34
MAR. 13	48	24	25	25	2	42	2	46	4	42	41	34
MAR. 14	48	26	26	27	2	42	2	46	4	42	41	34
MAR. 15	48	27	28	28	3	42	2	46	4	42	41	34
MAR. 16	48	29	29	30	3	42	2	46	4	42	41	34
MAR. 17	48	30	31	31	3	42	2	46	4	42	41	34
MAR. 18	48	32	32	33	3	42	2	46	4	42	41	34
MAR. 19	1	34	34	35	3	43	2	46	4	42	41	34
MAR. 20	1	35	36	36	3	43	3	46	4	42	41	34
MAR. 21	1	37	37	38	3	43	3	46	4	42	41	34
MAR. 22	1	39	39	40	4	43	3	46	4	42	41	34
MAR. 23	1	40	41	42	4	43	3	46	4	43	41	34
MAR. 24	1	42	43	43	4	43	3	46	4	43	41	34
MAR. 25	2	44	45	45	4	43	3	47	4	43	41	34
MAR. 26	2	46	47	47	4	43	3	47	4	43	41	34
MAR. 27	2	48	1	1	4	44	3	47	4	43	41	34
MAR. 28	2	2	3	3	4	44	4	47	4	43	41	34
MAR. 29	2	4	5	5	4	44	3	47	4	43	41	34
MAR. 30	2	6	7	7	4	44	4	47	4	43	41	34
MAR. 31	2	8	9	9	4	44	4	47	4	43	41	34

Date & Time	SUN ☉	MOON 1 ◗	MOON 2 ◖	MOON 3 ●	MERCURY	VENUS	MARS	JUPITER	SATURN	URANUS	NEPTUNE	PLUTO
APR. 1	2	10	11	11	4	44	4	47	4	43	41	34
APR. 2	2	12	13	13	4	44	4	47	4	43	41	34
APR. 3	3	14	14	15	4	45	4	47	4	43	41	34
APR. 4	3	15	16	17	3	45	4	47	4	43	41	34
APR. 5	3	17	18	18	3	45	4	47	4	43	41	34
APR. 6	3	19	19	20	3	45	4	47	4	43	41	34
APR. 7	3	20	21	21	3	45	4	47	4	43	41	34
APR. 8	3	22	23	23	3	45	4	47	4	43	41	34
APR. 9	3	24	24	25	3	45	5	47	4	43	41	34
APR. 10	3	25	26	26	3	46	5	47	4	43	41	34
APR. 11	4	27	27	28	3	46	5	47	4	43	41	34
APR. 12	4	28	29	29	3	46	5	47	4	43	41	34
APR. 13	4	30	30	31	3	46	5	47	4	43	41	34
APR. 14	4	31	32	33	2	46	5	47	4	43	41	34
APR. 15	4	33	34	34	2	46	5	47	4	43	41	34
APR. 16	4	35	35	36	2	46	5	47	4	43	41	34
APR. 17	4	36	37	38	2	47	5	47	4	43	41	34
APR. 18	4	38	39	39	2	47	5	47	4	43	41	34
APR. 19	5	40	40	41	2	47	6	47	4	43	41	34
APR. 20	5	42	42	43	2	47	6	47	4	43	41	34
APR. 21	5	43	44	45	2	47	6	47	4	43	41	34
APR. 22	5	45	46	47	2	47	6	47	4	43	41	34
APR. 23	5	47	48	1	2	47	6	47	4	43	41	34
APR. 24	5	1	2	2	2	48	6	47	4	43	41	34
APR. 25	6	3	4	5	2	48	6	47	4	43	41	34
APR. 26	6	5	6	7	2	48	6	47	4	43	41	34
APR. 27	6	7	8	9	3	48	6	47	4	43	41	34
APR. 28	6	9	10	11	3	48	6	47	4	43	41	34
APR. 29	6	11	12	12	3	48	7	48	4	43	41	34
APR. 30	6	13	14	14	3	48	7	48	4	43	41	34

MOON 1 ◗ 12:01 A.M. TO 8:00 A.M.   **MOON 2** ◖ 8:01 A.M. TO 4:00 P.M.   **MOON 3** ● 4:01 P.M. TO 12:00 A.M.

Use only one "moon" number. Choose the column closest to your time of birth. If your place of birth is not on Eastern Standard Time, be sure to read "How to Convert to Eastern Standard Time" at the beginning of this section.

1998

May

June

Date & Time	SUN	MOON 1	MOON 2	MOON 3	MERCURY	VENUS	MARS	JUPITER	SATURN	URANUS	NEPTUNE	PLUTO
MAY 1	6	15	15	16	3	1	7	48	4	43	41	34
MAY 2	6	17	17	18	3	1	7	48	4	43	41	34
MAY 3	7	18	19	19	3	1	7	48	4	43	41	34
MAY 4	7	20	21	21	3	1	7	48	4	43	41	34
MAY 5	7	22	22	23	3	1	7	48	4	43	41	34
MAY 6	7	23	24	24	3	1	7	48	4	43	41	34
MAY 7	7	25	25	26	4	1	7	48	4	43	41	34
MAY 8	7	26	27	27	4	2	7	48	4	43	41	34
MAY 9	7	28	28	29	4	2	8	48	5	43	41	34
MAY 10	7	29	30	31	4	2	8	48	5	43	41	34
MAY 11	8	31	32	32	4	2	8	48	5	43	41	34
MAY 12	8	33	33	34	4	2	8	48	5	43	41	34
MAY 13	8	34	35	35	5	2	8	48	5	43	41	34
MAY 14	8	36	37	37	5	3	8	48	5	43	41	34
MAY 15	8	38	38	39	5	3	8	48	5	43	41	34
MAY 16	8	39	40	41	5	3	8	48	5	43	41	34
MAY 17	8	41	42	42	5	3	8	48	5	43	41	34
MAY 18	8	43	44	44	6	3	8	48	5	43	41	34
MAY 19	9	45	45	46	6	3	8	48	5	43	41	34
MAY 20	9	47	47	48	6	3	9	48	5	43	41	34
MAY 21	9	48	1	2	6	4	9	48	5	43	41	34
MAY 22	9	2	3	4	6	4	9	48	5	43	41	34
MAY 23	9	4	5	6	7	4	9	48	5	43	41	34
MAY 24	9	6	7	8	7	4	9	48	5	43	41	34
MAY 25	10	8	9	10	7	4	9	48	5	43	41	34
MAY 26	10	10	11	12	7	4	9	48	5	43	41	34
MAY 27	10	12	13	14	8	5	9	48	5	43	41	34
MAY 28	10	14	15	15	8	5	9	48	5	43	41	34
MAY 29	10	16	17	17	8	5	9	48	5	43	41	34
MAY 30	10	18	18	19	8	5	10	48	5	43	41	34
MAY 31	10	19	20	21	9	5	10	48	5	43	41	34

Date & Time	SUN	MOON 1	MOON 2	MOON 3	MERCURY	VENUS	MARS	JUPITER	SATURN	URANUS	NEPTUNE	PLUTO
JUN. 1	10	21	22	22	9	5	10	48	5	43	41	34
JUN. 2	10	23	23	24	9	5	10	48	5	43	41	34
JUN. 3	11	24	25	26	9	6	10	48	5	43	41	34
JUN. 4	11	26	26	27	10	6	10	48	5	43	41	34
JUN. 5	11	27	28	28	10	6	10	48	5	43	41	34
JUN. 6	11	29	30	30	10	6	10	48	5	43	41	34
JUN. 7	11	31	31	32	11	6	10	48	5	43	41	34
JUN. 8	11	32	33	33	11	6	10	48	5	43	41	34
JUN. 9	11	34	34	35	11	7	10	48	5	43	41	34
JUN. 10	11	36	36	37	12	7	11	48	5	43	41	34
JUN. 11	12	37	38	38	12	7	11	48	5	43	41	34
JUN. 12	12	39	40	40	12	7	11	48	5	43	41	34
JUN. 13	12	41	41	42	12	7	11	48	5	43	41	34
JUN. 14	12	43	43	44	13	7	11	48	5	43	41	34
JUN. 15	12	44	45	46	13	7	11	48	5	43	41	34
JUN. 16	12	46	47	47	13	8	11	48	5	43	41	34
JUN. 17	12	48	1	1	14	8	11	5	5	43	41	34
JUN. 18	12	2	3	3	14	8	11	1	5	43	41	34
JUN. 19	13	4	4	5	14	8	11	1	5	43	41	34
JUN. 20	13	6	6	7	14	8	11	1	5	43	41	34
JUN. 21	13	8	8	9	15	8	12	1	5	43	41	34
JUN. 22	13	10	10	11	15	9	12	1	5	43	41	34
JUN. 23	13	11	12	13	15	9	12	1	5	43	41	34
JUN. 24	13	13	14	15	15	9	12	1	5	43	41	34
JUN. 25	14	15	16	16	16	9	12	1	5	43	41	34
JUN. 26	14	17	18	18	16	9	12	1	5	43	41	34
JUN. 27	14	19	19	20	16	9	12	1	5	43	41	34
JUN. 28	14	20	21	22	16	10	12	1	5	43	41	34
JUN. 29	14	22	23	23	17	10	12	1	5	43	41	34
JUN. 30	14	24	24	25	17	10	12	1	5	43	41	34

MOON 1 ◔ 12:01 A.M. TO 8:00 A.M.   **MOON 2** ◑ 8:01 A.M. TO 4:00 P.M.   **MOON 3** ● 4:01 P.M. TO 12:00 A.M.

Use only one "moon" number. Choose the column closest to your time of birth. If your place of birth is not on Eastern Standard Time, be sure to read "How to Convert to Eastern Standard Time" at the beginning of this section.

Date & Time	SUN	MOON 1	MOON 2	MOON 3	MERCURY	VENUS	MARS	JUPITER	SATURN	URANUS	NEPTUNE	PLUTO
JUL. 1	14	25	26	26	17	10	12	1	5	43	41	34
JUL. 2	14	27	27	28	17	10	13	1	5	43	41	34
JUL. 3	15	29	29	30	17	10	13	1	5	43	41	34
JUL. 4	15	30	31	31	18	11	13	1	5	43	41	34
JUL. 5	15	32	32	33	18	11	13	1	5	43	41	34
JUL. 6	15	33	34	34	18	11	13	1	5	43	41	34
JUL. 7	15	35	36	36	18	11	13	1	5	43	41	34
JUL. 8	15	37	37	38	18	11	13	1	5	43	41	34
JUL. 9	15	38	39	40	19	11	13	1	5	43	41	34
JUL. 10	15	40	41	41	19	11	13	1	5	43	41	34
JUL. 11	16	42	43	43	19	12	13	1	5	43	41	34
JUL. 12	16	44	44	45	19	12	13	1	5	43	41	34
JUL. 13	16	46	46	47	19	12	14	1	5	43	41	34
JUL. 14	16	48	48	1	19	12	14	1	5	43	41	34
JUL. 15	16	1	2	3	20	12	14	1	5	43	41	34
JUL. 16	16	3	4	5	20	12	14	1	5	42	41	34
JUL. 17	16	5	6	7	20	13	14	1	5	42	41	34
JUL. 18	16	7	8	8	20	13	14	1	5	42	41	34
JUL. 19	17	9	10	10	20	13	14	1	5	42	41	34
JUL. 20	17	11	12	12	20	13	14	1	5	42	41	34
JUL. 21	17	13	13	14	20	13	14	1	5	42	41	34
JUL. 22	17	15	16	16	20	13	14	1	5	42	41	34
JUL. 23	17	16	17	19	20	14	14	1	5	42	41	34
JUL. 24	17	18	19	19	20	14	15	1	5	42	41	34
JUL. 25	17	20	20	21	21	14	15	1	5	42	41	34
JUL. 26	18	22	22	23	21	14	15	1	5	42	41	34
JUL. 27	18	23	24	24	21	14	15	1	5	42	41	34
JUL. 28	18	25	25	26	21	14	15	1	5	42	41	34
JUL. 29	18	26	27	27	21	15	15	1	5	42	41	34
JUL. 30	18	28	29	29	21	15	15	1	5	42	41	34
JUL. 31	18	30	30	31	21	15	15	1	5	42	41	34

Date & Time	SUN	MOON 1	MOON 2	MOON 3	MERCURY	VENUS	MARS	JUPITER	SATURN	URANUS	NEPTUNE	PLUTO
AUG. 1	18	31	32	32	21	15	15	1	5	42	41	34
AUG. 2	18	33	33	34	21	15	15	1	5	42	41	34
AUG. 3	19	34	35	36	21	15	15	1	5	42	41	34
AUG. 4	19	36	37	37	21	15	16	1	5	42	41	34
AUG. 5	19	38	38	39	21	16	16	1	5	42	41	34
AUG. 6	19	40	40	41	21	16	16	1	5	42	41	34
AUG. 7	19	41	42	43	20	16	16	1	5	42	41	34
AUG. 8	19	43	44	44	20	16	16	1	5	42	41	34
AUG. 9	19	45	46	46	20	16	16	1	5	42	41	34
AUG. 10	19	47	48	48	20	16	16	1	5	42	41	34
AUG. 11	20	1	2	2	20	17	16	1	5	42	41	34
AUG. 12	20	3	4	4	20	17	16	1	5	42	41	34
AUG. 13	20	5	5	6	20	17	16	1	5	42	41	34
AUG. 14	20	7	7	8	20	17	16	1	5	42	41	34
AUG. 15	20	9	9	10	20	17	16	1	5	42	41	34
AUG. 16	20	10	11	12	20	17	17	1	5	42	41	34
AUG. 17	20	12	13	13	19	18	17	1	5	42	41	34
AUG. 18	20	14	15	15	19	18	17	1	5	42	41	34
AUG. 19	21	16	16	17	19	18	17	48	5	42	41	34
AUG. 20	21	18	18	19	19	18	17	48	5	42	41	34
AUG. 21	21	19	20	20	19	18	17	48	5	42	41	34
AUG. 22	21	21	22	22	19	18	17	48	5	42	41	34
AUG. 23	21	23	23	24	19	19	17	48	5	42	41	34
AUG. 24	21	24	25	25	19	19	17	48	5	42	41	34
AUG. 25	21	26	26	27	19	19	17	48	5	42	41	34
AUG. 26	22	27	28	29	19	19	17	48	5	42	41	34
AUG. 27	22	29	30	30	19	19	18	48	5	42	41	34
AUG. 28	22	31	31	32	19	19	18	48	5	42	41	34
AUG. 29	22	32	33	33	19	20	18	48	5	42	41	34
AUG. 30	22	34	34	35	19	20	18	48	5	42	41	34
AUG. 31	22	35	36	37	20	20	18	48	5	42	41	34

MOON 1 ☽ 12:01 A.M. TO 8:00 A.M.   **MOON 2** ◑ 8:01 A.M. TO 4:00 P.M.   **MOON 3** ● 4:01 P.M. TO 12:00 A.M.
Use only one "moon" number. Choose the column closest to your time of birth. If your place of birth is not on Eastern Standard Time, be sure to read "How to Convert to Eastern Standard Time" at the beginning of this section.

1998

September

Date & Time	SUN	MOON 1	MOON 2	MOON 3	MERCURY	VENUS	MARS	JUPITER	SATURN	URANUS	NEPTUNE	PLUTO
SEP. 1	22	37	38	38	20	20	18	48	5	42	41	34
SEP. 2	22	39	39	40	20	20	18	48	5	42	41	34
SEP. 3	23	41	41	42	20	20	18	48	5	42	41	34
SEP. 4	23	42	43	44	20	21	18	48	5	42	41	34
SEP. 5	23	44	45	46	20	21	18	48	5	42	41	34
SEP. 6	23	46	47	48	21	21	18	48	5	42	41	34
SEP. 7	23	48	1	2	21	21	18	48	5	42	41	34
SEP. 8	23	2	3	4	21	21	19	48	5	42	41	34
SEP. 9	23	4	5	6	21	21	19	48	5	42	41	34
SEP. 10	23	6	7	7	21	22	19	48	5	42	41	34
SEP. 11	24	8	9	9	22	22	19	48	5	42	41	34
SEP. 12	24	10	11	11	22	22	19	48	5	42	41	34
SEP. 13	24	12	12	13	22	22	19	48	5	42	41	34
SEP. 14	24	14	14	15	22	22	19	48	5	42	41	34
SEP. 15	24	15	16	17	23	22	19	48	5	42	41	34
SEP. 16	24	17	18	18	23	23	19	48	5	42	41	34
SEP. 17	24	19	19	20	23	23	19	48	5	42	41	34
SEP. 18	24	21	21	22	23	23	19	48	5	42	41	34
SEP. 19	25	22	23	23	24	23	19	48	5	42	41	34
SEP. 20	25	24	24	25	24	23	20	48	5	42	41	34
SEP. 21	25	25	26	27	24	23	20	48	5	42	41	34
SEP. 22	25	27	28	28	24	24	20	48	5	42	41	34
SEP. 23	25	29	29	30	25	24	20	48	5	42	41	34
SEP. 24	25	30	31	31	25	24	20	48	5	42	41	34
SEP. 25	26	32	32	33	25	24	20	48	5	42	41	34
SEP. 26	26	33	34	34	25	24	20	48	5	42	41	34
SEP. 27	26	35	36	36	26	24	20	48	5	42	41	34
SEP. 28	26	37	37	38	26	25	20	48	5	42	41	34
SEP. 29	26	38	39	39	26	25	20	48	5	42	41	34
SEP. 30	26	40	41	41	26	25	20	48	5	42	41	34

October

Date & Time	SUN	MOON 1	MOON 2	MOON 3	MERCURY	VENUS	MARS	JUPITER	SATURN	URANUS	NEPTUNE	PLUTO
OCT. 1	26	42	42	43	27	25	20	48	5	42	41	34
OCT. 2	26	44	44	45	27	25	21	48	5	42	41	34
OCT. 3	27	45	46	47	27	25	21	48	5	42	41	34
OCT. 4	27	47	48	1	27	26	21	48	5	42	41	34
OCT. 5	27	1	2	3	27	26	21	48	5	42	41	34
OCT. 6	27	3	4	5	28	26	21	48	5	42	41	34
OCT. 7	27	5	6	7	28	26	21	48	5	42	41	34
OCT. 8	27	7	8	9	28	26	21	48	5	42	41	34
OCT. 9	27	9	10	11	28	26	21	48	5	42	41	34
OCT. 10	27	11	12	13	29	27	21	48	5	42	41	34
OCT. 11	28	13	14	14	29	27	21	48	5	42	41	34
OCT. 12	28	15	16	16	29	27	21	48	5	42	41	34
OCT. 13	28	17	17	18	29	27	21	48	5	42	41	34
OCT. 14	28	19	19	20	29	27	22	48	5	42	41	34
OCT. 15	28	20	21	21	30	27	22	48	5	42	41	34
OCT. 16	28	22	22	23	30	28	22	48	5	42	41	34
OCT. 17	28	23	24	24	30	28	22	48	5	42	41	34
OCT. 18	28	25	26	26	30	28	22	48	5	42	41	34
OCT. 19	29	27	27	28	30	28	22	48	5	42	41	34
OCT. 20	29	28	29	29	31	28	22	48	5	42	41	34
OCT. 21	29	30	30	31	31	28	22	48	5	42	41	34
OCT. 22	29	31	32	32	31	29	22	47	5	42	41	34
OCT. 23	29	33	33	34	31	29	22	47	5	42	41	34
OCT. 24	29	35	35	36	31	29	22	47	5	42	41	34
OCT. 25	29	36	37	37	32	29	22	47	5	42	41	34
OCT. 26	30	38	38	39	32	29	22	47	5	42	41	34
OCT. 27	30	39	40	41	32	29	23	47	5	42	41	34
OCT. 28	30	41	42	42	32	30	23	47	5	42	41	34
OCT. 29	30	43	43	44	32	30	23	47	5	42	41	34
OCT. 30	30	45	45	46	33	30	23	47	5	42	41	34
OCT. 31	30	47	47	48	33	30	23	47	5	42	41	34

MOON 1 ◗ 12:01 A.M. TO 8:00 A.M.   **MOON 2** ◐ 8:01 A.M. TO 4:00 P.M.   **MOON 3** ● 4:01 P.M. TO 12:00 A.M.

Use only one "moon" number. Choose the column closest to your time of birth. If your place of birth is not on Eastern Standard Time, be sure to read "How to Convert to Eastern Standard Time" at the beginning of this section.

1998

November

Date & Time	SUN	MOON 1	MOON 2	MOON 3	MERCURY	VENUS	MARS	JUPITER	SATURN	URANUS	NEPTUNE	PLUTO
NOV. 1	30	48	1	2	33	30	23	47	5	42	41	34
NOV. 2	30	2	3	4	33	30	23	47	5	42	41	34
NOV. 3	31	4	5	6	33	31	23	47	5	42	41	34
NOV. 4	31	6	7	8	33	31	23	47	5	42	41	34
NOV. 5	31	9	9	10	34	31	23	47	5	42	41	34
NOV. 6	31	11	11	12	34	31	23	47	5	42	41	34
NOV. 7	31	13	13	14	34	31	23	47	5	42	41	34
NOV. 8	31	14	15	16	34	31	23	47	5	42	41	34
NOV. 9	31	16	17	17	34	32	24	47	5	42	41	34
NOV. 10	31	18	19	19	34	32	24	47	5	42	41	34
NOV. 11	31	20	20	21	34	32	24	47	5	42	41	34
NOV. 12	32	21	22	22	35	32	24	47	5	42	41	34
NOV. 13	32	23	24	24	35	32	24	47	5	42	41	34
NOV. 14	32	25	25	26	35	32	24	47	5	42	41	34
NOV. 15	32	26	27	27	35	33	24	47	5	42	41	34
NOV. 16	32	28	28	29	35	33	24	47	5	42	41	34
NOV. 17	32	29	30	30	35	33	24	47	5	42	41	34
NOV. 18	32	31	31	32	35	33	24	47	5	42	41	34
NOV. 19	33	33	33	34	35	33	24	47	5	42	41	34
NOV. 20	33	34	35	35	35	33	24	47	5	42	41	34
NOV. 21	33	36	36	37	35	34	24	47	5	42	41	34
NOV. 22	33	37	38	38	35	34	25	47	5	42	41	34
NOV. 23	33	39	40	40	35	34	25	47	5	42	41	34
NOV. 24	33	41	41	42	35	34	25	47	5	42	41	34
NOV. 25	34	42	43	44	35	34	25	47	5	42	41	34
NOV. 26	34	44	45	45	35	34	25	47	5	42	41	34
NOV. 27	34	46	47	47	35	35	25	47	5	42	41	34
NOV. 28	34	48	48	1	35	35	25	47	5	42	41	34
NOV. 29	34	2	2	3	35	35	25	47	5	42	41	34
NOV. 30	34	4	4	5	34	35	25	47	5	42	41	34

December

Date & Time	SUN	MOON 1	MOON 2	MOON 3	MERCURY	VENUS	MARS	JUPITER	SATURN	URANUS	NEPTUNE	PLUTO
DEC. 1	34	6	6	7	34	35	25	47	5	42	41	34
DEC. 2	34	8	8	9	34	35	25	47	5	42	41	34
DEC. 3	35	10	10	11	34	36	25	47	5	42	41	34
DEC. 4	35	12	12	13	34	36	25	47	5	42	41	34
DEC. 5	35	14	14	15	34	36	26	47	5	42	41	34
DEC. 6	35	15	16	17	33	36	26	48	5	42	41	34
DEC. 7	35	17	18	19	33	36	26	48	5	42	41	34
DEC. 8	35	19	20	20	33	36	26	48	5	42	41	34
DEC. 9	35	21	21	22	33	37	26	48	5	42	41	34
DEC. 10	35	23	23	24	33	37	26	48	5	42	41	34
DEC. 11	36	24	25	25	33	37	26	48	5	42	41	34
DEC. 12	36	26	26	27	33	37	26	48	5	42	41	34
DEC. 13	36	27	28	28	33	37	26	48	5	42	41	34
DEC. 14	36	29	29	30	33	37	26	48	5	42	41	34
DEC. 15	36	31	31	32	33	38	26	48	5	42	41	34
DEC. 16	36	32	33	33	33	38	26	48	5	42	41	34
DEC. 17	36	34	34	35	33	38	26	48	5	42	41	34
DEC. 18	36	35	36	36	33	38	26	48	5	42	41	34
DEC. 19	37	37	38	38	34	38	27	48	5	42	41	34
DEC. 20	37	39	39	40	34	38	27	48	5	42	41	34
DEC. 21	37	40	41	41	34	39	27	48	5	42	41	34
DEC. 22	37	42	43	43	34	39	27	48	5	42	41	34
DEC. 23	37	44	44	45	34	39	27	48	5	42	41	34
DEC. 24	37	46	46	47	34	39	27	48	5	42	41	34
DEC. 25	37	47	48	1	35	39	27	48	5	42	41	34
DEC. 26	38	1	2	2	35	39	27	48	5	42	41	34
DEC. 27	38	3	4	4	35	40	27	48	5	42	41	34
DEC. 28	38	5	6	6	35	40	27	48	5	42	41	34
DEC. 29	38	7	7	8	35	40	27	48	5	42	41	34
DEC. 30	38	9	9	10	35	40	27	48	5	42	41	34
DEC. 31	38	11	11	12	36	40	27	48	5	42	41	34

MOON 1 ☽ 12:01 A.M. TO 8:00 A.M.　　**MOON 2** ◑ 8:01 A.M. TO 4:00 P.M.　　**MOON 3** ● 4:01 P.M. TO 12:00 A.M.

Use only one "moon" number. Choose the column closest to your time of birth. If your place of birth is not on Eastern Standard Time, be sure to read "How to Convert to Eastern Standard Time" at the beginning of this section.

1999

January

February

Date & Time	SUN	MOON 1	MOON 2	MOON 3	MERCURY	VENUS	MARS	JUPITER	SATURN	URANUS	NEPTUNE	PLUTO
JAN. 1	38	13	13	14	36	40	27	48	5	42	41	34
JAN. 2	38	15	15	16	36	41	27	48	5	42	41	34
JAN. 3	39	17	17	18	36	41	28	48	5	42	41	34
JAN. 4	39	18	19	20	36	41	28	48	5	42	41	34
JAN. 5	39	20	21	21	37	41	28	48	5	42	41	34
JAN. 6	39	22	22	23	37	41	28	48	5	42	41	34
JAN. 7	39	24	24	25	37	41	28	48	5	42	41	34
JAN. 8	39	25	26	26	37	42	28	48	5	42	41	34
JAN. 9	39	27	27	28	37	42	28	48	5	42	41	34
JAN. 10	40	28	29	30	38	42	28	48	5	42	41	34
JAN. 11	40	30	31	31	38	42	28	48	5	43	41	34
JAN. 12	40	32	32	33	38	42	28	48	5	43	41	34
JAN. 13	40	33	34	34	38	42	28	48	5	43	41	34
JAN. 14	40	35	35	36	38	43	28	48	5	43	41	34
JAN. 15	40	36	37	38	39	43	28	48	5	43	41	34
JAN. 16	40	38	39	39	39	43	28	48	5	43	41	34
JAN. 17	41	40	40	41	39	43	28	48	5	43	41	34
JAN. 18	41	42	42	43	39	43	28	48	5	43	41	34
JAN. 19	41	43	44	44	39	43	29	48	5	43	41	34
JAN. 20	41	45	46	46	40	44	29	48	5	43	41	34
JAN. 21	41	47	47	48	40	44	29	48	5	43	41	34
JAN. 22	41	1	1	2	40	44	29	48	5	43	41	34
JAN. 23	42	3	3	4	40	44	29	48	5	43	41	34
JAN. 24	42	4	5	6	40	44	29	48	5	43	41	34
JAN. 25	42	6	7	8	41	44	29	48	5	43	41	34
JAN. 26	42	8	9	9	41	45	29	48	5	43	41	34
JAN. 27	42	10	11	11	41	45	29	48	5	43	41	34
JAN. 28	42	12	13	13	41	45	29	1	5	43	41	34
JAN. 29	42	14	15	15	42	45	29	1	5	43	41	34
JAN. 30	42	16	16	17	42	45	29	1	5	43	41	34
JAN. 31	43	18	18	19	42	45	29	1	5	43	41	34

Date & Time	SUN	MOON 1	MOON 2	MOON 3	MERCURY	VENUS	MARS	JUPITER	SATURN	URANUS	NEPTUNE	PLUTO
FEB. 1	43	19	20	21	42	46	29	1	5	43	41	34
FEB. 2	43	21	22	22	42	46	29	1	5	43	41	34
FEB. 3	43	23	24	24	43	46	29	1	5	43	41	34
FEB. 4	43	25	25	26	43	46	29	1	5	43	41	34
FEB. 5	43	26	27	27	43	46	29	1	5	43	41	34
FEB. 6	43	28	28	29	43	46	30	1	5	43	41	34
FEB. 7	43	29	30	31	44	47	30	1	5	43	41	34
FEB. 8	44	31	32	32	44	47	30	1	5	43	41	34
FEB. 9	44	33	33	34	44	47	30	1	5	43	41	34
FEB. 10	44	34	35	35	44	47	30	1	5	43	41	34
FEB. 11	44	36	36	37	45	47	30	1	5	43	41	34
FEB. 12	44	38	38	39	45	47	30	1	5	43	41	34
FEB. 13	44	39	40	40	45	48	30	1	5	43	41	34
FEB. 14	44	41	41	42	45	48	30	1	5	43	41	34
FEB. 15	44	43	43	44	46	48	30	1	5	43	41	34
FEB. 16	45	44	45	46	46	48	30	1	5	43	41	34
FEB. 17	45	46	47	48	46	48	30	1	5	43	41	34
FEB. 18	45	48	1	1	46	48	30	1	5	43	41	34
FEB. 19	45	2	3	3	47	1	30	1	5	43	41	34
FEB. 20	45	4	5	5	47	1	30	1	5	43	41	34
FEB. 21	45	6	7	7	47	1	30	1	5	43	41	34
FEB. 22	45	8	8	9	47	1	30	1	5	43	41	34
FEB. 23	46	10	10	11	48	1	30	1	5	43	41	34
FEB. 24	46	12	12	13	48	1	30	1	5	43	41	34
FEB. 25	46	13	14	15	48	2	30	1	5	43	41	34
FEB. 26	46	15	16	16	48	2	30	1	5	43	41	34
FEB. 27	46	17	18	18	48	2	30	1	5	43	41	34
FEB. 28	46	19	19	20	1	2	30	1	5	43	41	34

MOON 1 ◗ 12:01 A.M. TO 8:00 A.M.   **MOON 2** ◑ 8:01 A.M. TO 4:00 P.M.   **MOON 3** ● 4:01 P.M. TO 12:00 A.M.

Use only one "moon" number. Choose the column closest to your time of birth. If your place of birth is not on Eastern Standard Time, be sure to read "How to Convert to Eastern Standard Time" at the beginning of this section.

March

Date & Time	SUN	MOON 1	MOON 2	MOON 3	MERCURY	VENUS	MARS	JUPITER	SATURN	URANUS	NEPTUNE	PLUTO
MAR. 1	46	21	21	22	1	2	30	1	5	43	41	34
MAR. 2	46	22	23	23	1	2	30	1	5	43	41	34
MAR. 3	47	24	25	25	1	2	30	2	5	43	41	34
MAR. 4	47	26	26	27	1	3	30	2	5	43	41	34
MAR. 5	47	27	28	28	1	3	30	2	5	43	41	34
MAR. 6	47	29	29	30	1	3	30	2	5	43	41	34
MAR. 7	47	31	31	32	1	3	30	2	5	43	41	34
MAR. 8	47	32	33	33	1	3	31	2	5	43	41	34
MAR. 9	47	34	34	35	1	3	31	2	5	43	41	34
MAR. 10	47	35	36	36	2	4	31	2	5	43	41	34
MAR. 11	48	37	37	38	2	4	31	2	5	43	41	34
MAR. 12	48	39	39	40	1	4	31	2	5	43	41	34
MAR. 13	48	40	41	41	1	4	31	2	5	43	41	34
MAR. 14	48	42	43	43	1	4	31	2	5	43	41	34
MAR. 15	48	44	44	45	1	4	31	2	5	43	41	34
MAR. 16	48	46	46	47	1	5	31	2	5	43	41	34
MAR. 17	48	47	48	1	1	5	31	2	5	43	41	34
MAR. 18	48	1	2	3	1	5	31	2	5	43	41	34
MAR. 19	1	3	4	5	1	5	31	2	5	43	41	34
MAR. 20	1	5	6	7	1	5	31	2	5	43	41	34
MAR. 21	1	7	8	9	1	5	31	2	5	43	41	34
MAR. 22	1	9	10	10	1	6	31	2	5	43	41	34
MAR. 23	1	11	12	12	48	6	31	2	5	43	41	34
MAR. 24	1	13	14	14	48	6	31	2	5	43	41	34
MAR. 25	2	15	15	16	48	6	31	2	5	43	41	34
MAR. 26	2	17	17	18	48	6	31	2	5	43	41	34
MAR. 27	2	18	19	20	48	6	31	2	5	43	41	34
MAR. 28	2	20	21	21	48	7	31	2	5	43	41	34
MAR. 29	2	22	22	23	48	7	30	2	5	43	41	34
MAR. 30	2	24	24	25	48	7	30	2	5	43	41	34
MAR. 31	2	25	26	26	48	7	30	2	5	43	42	34

April

Date & Time	SUN	MOON 1	MOON 2	MOON 3	MERCURY	VENUS	MARS	JUPITER	SATURN	URANUS	NEPTUNE	PLUTO
APR. 1	2	27	27	28	48	7	30	2	5	43	42	34
APR. 2	2	28	29	30	48	7	30	2	5	43	42	34
APR. 3	3	30	31	31	48	7	30	3	5	43	42	34
APR. 4	3	32	32	33	48	8	30	3	5	43	42	34
APR. 5	3	33	34	34	48	8	30	3	5	43	42	34
APR. 6	3	35	35	36	48	8	30	3	6	43	42	34
APR. 7	3	36	37	37	48	8	30	3	6	43	42	34
APR. 8	3	38	39	39	48	8	30	3	6	43	42	34
APR. 9	3	40	40	41	48	8	30	3	6	43	42	34
APR. 10	3	41	42	42	48	9	30	3	6	43	42	34
APR. 11	4	43	44	44	48	9	30	3	6	43	42	34
APR. 12	4	45	45	46	48	9	30	3	6	43	42	34
APR. 13	4	47	47	48	48	9	30	3	6	43	42	34
APR. 14	4	1	1	2	48	9	30	3	6	43	42	34
APR. 15	4	2	3	4	1	9	30	3	6	43	42	34
APR. 16	4	4	5	6	1	10	30	3	6	43	42	34
APR. 17	4	6	7	8	1	10	30	3	6	43	42	34
APR. 18	4	8	9	10	1	10	30	3	6	43	42	34
APR. 19	5	10	11	12	1	10	30	3	6	43	42	34
APR. 20	5	12	13	14	1	10	30	3	6	43	42	34
APR. 21	5	14	15	16	1	10	30	3	6	43	42	34
APR. 22	5	16	17	17	2	10	30	3	6	43	42	34
APR. 23	5	18	19	19	2	11	30	3	6	43	42	34
APR. 24	5	20	20	21	2	11	30	3	6	43	42	34
APR. 25	6	21	22	23	2	11	29	3	6	43	42	34
APR. 26	6	23	24	24	2	11	29	3	6	43	42	34
APR. 27	6	25	25	26	2	11	29	3	6	43	42	34
APR. 28	6	26	27	27	3	11	29	3	6	43	42	34
APR. 29	6	28	29	29	3	12	29	3	6	43	42	34
APR. 30	6	30	30	31	3	12	29	3	6	43	42	34

MOON 1 ◐ 12:01 A.M. TO 8:00 A.M. **MOON 2** ◑ 8:01 A.M. TO 4:00 P.M. **MOON 3** ● 4:01 P.M. TO 12:00 A.M.

Use only one "moon" number. Choose the column closest to your time of birth. If your place of birth is not on Eastern Standard Time, be sure to read "How to Convert to Eastern Standard Time" at the beginning of this section.

1999

May

Date & Time	SUN	MOON 1	MOON 2	MOON 3	MERCURY	VENUS	MARS	JUPITER	SATURN	URANUS	NEPTUNE	PLUTO
MAY 1	6	31	32	32	3	12	29	3	6	43	42	34
MAY 2	6	33	33	34	3	12	29	3	6	43	42	34
MAY 3	7	34	35	35	4	12	29	3	6	43	42	34
MAY 4	7	36	36	37	4	12	29	3	6	43	42	34
MAY 5	7	38	38	39	4	12	29	4	6	43	42	34
MAY 6	7	39	40	40	4	12	29	4	6	43	42	34
MAY 7	7	41	41	42	5	13	29	4	6	43	42	34
MAY 8	7	42	43	44	5	13	29	4	6	43	42	34
MAY 9	7	44	45	45	5	13	29	4	6	43	42	34
MAY 10	7	46	47	47	5	13	29	4	6	43	42	34
MAY 11	8	48	48	1	6	13	29	4	6	43	42	34
MAY 12	8	2	2	3	6	13	29	4	6	43	42	34
MAY 13	8	4	4	5	6	14	29	4	6	43	42	34
MAY 14	8	6	6	7	6	14	29	4	6	43	42	34
MAY 15	8	8	8	9	7	14	29	4	6	43	42	34
MAY 16	8	10	10	11	7	14	29	4	6	43	42	34
MAY 17	8	12	12	13	7	14	29	4	6	43	42	34
MAY 18	8	14	14	15	7	14	28	4	6	43	42	34
MAY 19	9	16	16	17	8	15	28	4	6	43	42	34
MAY 20	9	17	18	19	8	15	28	4	6	43	42	34
MAY 21	9	19	20	20	8	15	28	4	6	43	42	34
MAY 22	9	21	22	22	8	15	28	4	6	43	42	34
MAY 23	9	23	23	24	9	15	28	4	6	43	42	34
MAY 24	9	24	25	25	9	15	28	4	6	43	42	34
MAY 25	10	26	27	27	9	15	28	4	6	43	42	34
MAY 26	10	28	28	29	10	16	28	4	6	43	42	34
MAY 27	10	29	30	30	10	16	28	4	6	43	42	34
MAY 28	10	31	31	32	10	16	28	4	6	43	42	34
MAY 29	10	32	33	33	11	16	28	4	6	43	42	34
MAY 30	10	34	35	35	11	16	28	4	6	43	42	34
MAY 31	10	36	36	37	11	16	28	4	6	43	42	34

June

Date & Time	SUN	MOON 1	MOON 2	MOON 3	MERCURY	VENUS	MARS	JUPITER	SATURN	URANUS	NEPTUNE	PLUTO
JUN. 1	10	37	38	38	11	16	28	4	6	43	42	34
JUN. 2	10	39	39	40	12	16	28	4	6	43	42	34
JUN. 3	11	40	41	41	12	17	28	4	6	43	42	34
JUN. 4	11	42	43	43	12	17	28	4	6	43	42	34
JUN. 5	11	44	44	45	12	17	28	4	7	43	42	34
JUN. 6	11	45	46	46	13	17	28	4	7	43	42	34
JUN. 7	11	47	48	48	13	17	28	4	7	43	42	34
JUN. 8	11	1	2	2	13	17	28	4	7	43	42	34
JUN. 9	11	3	3	4	14	17	28	5	7	43	42	34
JUN. 10	11	5	5	6	14	18	28	5	7	43	42	34
JUN. 11	12	7	7	8	14	18	28	5	7	43	42	34
JUN. 12	12	9	9	10	14	18	28	5	7	43	42	34
JUN. 13	12	11	11	12	14	18	28	5	7	43	42	34
JUN. 14	12	13	13	14	15	18	28	5	7	43	41	34
JUN. 15	12	15	15	16	15	18	28	5	7	43	41	34
JUN. 16	12	17	17	18	15	18	28	5	7	43	41	34
JUN. 17	12	19	19	20	15	18	28	5	7	43	41	34
JUN. 18	12	20	21	22	16	19	28	5	7	43	41	34
JUN. 19	13	22	23	23	16	19	28	5	7	43	41	34
JUN. 20	13	24	24	25	16	19	28	5	7	43	41	34
JUN. 21	13	26	26	27	16	19	28	5	7	43	41	34
JUN. 22	13	27	28	29	16	19	28	5	7	43	41	34
JUN. 23	13	29	29	30	16	19	29	5	7	43	41	34
JUN. 24	13	30	31	31	17	19	29	5	7	43	41	34
JUN. 25	14	32	33	33	17	19	29	5	7	43	41	34
JUN. 26	14	34	34	35	17	19	29	5	7	43	41	34
JUN. 27	14	35	36	36	17	20	29	5	7	43	41	34
JUN. 28	14	37	37	38	17	20	29	5	7	43	41	34
JUN. 29	14	38	39	39	17	20	29	5	7	43	41	34
JUN. 30	14	40	41	41	17	20	29	5	7	43	41	34

MOON 1 ◐ 12:01 A.M. TO 8:00 A.M.   **MOON 2** ◑ 8:01 A.M. TO 4:00 P.M.   **MOON 3** ● 4:01 P.M. TO 12:00 A.M.

Use only one "moon" number. Choose the column closest to your time of birth. If your place of birth is not on Eastern Standard Time, be sure to read "How to Convert to Eastern Standard Time" at the beginning of this section.

1999

July

Date & Time	SUN	MOON 1	MOON 2	MOON 3	MERCURY	VENUS	MARS	JUPITER	SATURN	URANUS	NEPTUNE	PLUTO
JUL. 1	14	42	42	43	18	20	29	5	7	43	41	34
JUL. 2	14	43	44	44	18	20	29	5	7	43	41	34
JUL. 3	15	45	46	46	18	20	29	5	7	43	41	34
JUL. 4	15	47	47	48	18	20	29	5	7	43	41	34
JUL. 5	15	48	1	2	18	20	29	5	7	43	41	34
JUL. 6	15	2	3	4	18	20	29	5	7	43	41	34
JUL. 7	15	4	5	5	18	21	29	5	7	43	41	34
JUL. 8	15	6	7	7	18	21	29	5	7	43	41	34
JUL. 9	15	8	9	9	18	21	29	5	7	43	41	34
JUL. 10	15	10	11	11	18	21	29	5	7	43	41	34
JUL. 11	16	12	13	13	18	21	29	5	7	43	41	34
JUL. 12	16	14	15	15	18	21	29	5	7	43	41	34
JUL. 13	16	16	17	17	18	21	29	5	7	43	41	34
JUL. 14	16	18	18	19	18	21	29	5	7	43	41	34
JUL. 15	16	20	20	21	18	21	29	5	7	43	41	34
JUL. 16	16	22	22	23	18	21	30	5	7	43	41	34
JUL. 17	16	23	24	24	18	21	30	5	7	43	41	34
JUL. 18	16	25	26	26	18	21	30	5	7	43	41	34
JUL. 19	17	27	27	28	18	21	30	5	7	43	41	34
JUL. 20	17	28	29	29	18	21	30	5	7	43	41	34
JUL. 21	17	30	30	31	18	21	30	5	7	43	41	34
JUL. 22	17	32	32	33	18	21	30	5	7	43	41	34
JUL. 23	17	33	34	34	18	22	30	5	7	43	41	34
JUL. 24	17	35	35	36	18	22	30	5	7	43	41	34
JUL. 25	17	36	37	37	18	22	30	5	7	43	41	34
JUL. 26	18	38	38	39	17	22	30	5	7	43	41	34
JUL. 27	18	40	40	41	17	22	30	5	7	43	41	34
JUL. 28	18	41	42	42	17	22	30	5	7	43	41	34
JUL. 29	18	43	43	44	17	22	30	5	7	43	41	34
JUL. 30	18	45	45	46	17	22	30	5	7	43	41	34
JUL. 31	18	46	47	47	17	22	30	5	7	43	41	34

August

Date & Time	SUN	MOON 1	MOON 2	MOON 3	MERCURY	VENUS	MARS	JUPITER	SATURN	URANUS	NEPTUNE	PLUTO
AUG. 1	18	48	1	1	17	22	30	6	7	43	41	34
AUG. 2	18	2	2	3	17	22	31	6	7	43	41	34
AUG. 3	19	4	4	5	17	22	31	6	7	43	41	34
AUG. 4	19	6	6	7	17	22	31	6	7	43	41	34
AUG. 5	19	7	8	9	17	22	31	6	7	43	41	34
AUG. 6	19	9	10	11	17	22	31	6	7	43	41	34
AUG. 7	19	11	12	13	17	21	31	6	7	43	41	34
AUG. 8	19	13	14	15	17	21	31	6	7	43	41	34
AUG. 9	19	15	16	16	17	21	31	6	7	43	41	34
AUG. 10	19	17	18	18	17	21	31	6	7	43	41	34
AUG. 11	20	19	20	20	17	21	31	6	7	43	41	34
AUG. 12	20	21	21	22	17	21	31	6	7	43	41	34
AUG. 13	20	23	23	24	17	21	31	6	7	43	41	34
AUG. 14	20	24	25	26	17	21	31	6	7	43	41	34
AUG. 15	20	26	27	27	17	21	31	6	7	43	41	34
AUG. 16	20	28	28	29	18	21	32	6	7	43	41	34
AUG. 17	20	29	30	30	18	21	32	6	7	43	41	34
AUG. 18	20	31	32	32	18	21	32	6	7	43	41	34
AUG. 19	21	33	33	34	18	21	32	6	7	43	41	34
AUG. 20	21	34	35	35	18	21	32	6	7	43	41	34
AUG. 21	21	36	36	37	18	21	32	6	7	43	41	34
AUG. 22	21	37	38	38	19	20	32	6	7	43	41	34
AUG. 23	21	39	40	40	19	20	32	6	7	43	41	34
AUG. 24	21	41	41	42	19	20	32	6	7	43	41	34
AUG. 25	21	42	43	43	19	20	32	6	7	43	41	34
AUG. 26	22	44	45	45	20	20	32	6	7	43	41	34
AUG. 27	22	46	46	47	20	20	32	6	7	43	41	34
AUG. 28	22	48	48	1	20	20	33	6	7	43	41	34
AUG. 29	22	1	2	3	20	20	33	6	7	43	41	34
AUG. 30	22	3	4	5	21	20	33	6	7	43	41	34
AUG. 31	22	5	6	6	21	20	33	6	7	43	41	34

MOON 1 ◗ 12:01 A.M. TO 8:00 A.M. **MOON 2** ◖ 8:01 A.M. TO 4:00 P.M. **MOON 3** ● 4:01 P.M. TO 12:00 A.M.

Use only one "moon" number. Choose the column closest to your time of birth. If your place of birth is not on Eastern Standard Time, be sure to read "How to Convert to Eastern Standard Time" at the beginning of this section.

1999

September

Date & Time	SUN	MOON 1	MOON 2	MOON 3	MERCURY	VENUS	MARS	JUPITER	SATURN	URANUS	NEPTUNE	PLUTO
SEP. 1	22	7	8	8	21	20	33	6	7	43	41	34
SEP. 2	22	9	10	10	21	20	33	6	7	43	41	34
SEP. 3	23	11	11	12	22	20	33	6	7	43	41	34
SEP. 4	23	13	13	14	22	20	33	6	7	43	41	34
SEP. 5	23	15	15	16	22	20	33	6	7	43	41	34
SEP. 6	23	16	17	18	22	20	33	6	7	43	41	34
SEP. 7	23	18	19	20	23	20	33	6	7	43	41	34
SEP. 8	23	20	21	21	23	19	33	6	7	43	41	34
SEP. 9	23	22	23	23	23	19	34	6	7	43	41	34
SEP. 10	23	24	24	25	23	19	34	6	7	43	41	34
SEP. 11	24	25	26	27	24	19	34	6	7	43	41	34
SEP. 12	24	27	28	28	24	19	34	6	7	43	41	34
SEP. 13	24	29	29	30	24	19	34	6	7	43	41	34
SEP. 14	24	30	31	32	24	19	34	6	7	43	41	34
SEP. 15	24	32	33	33	25	20	34	6	7	43	41	34
SEP. 16	24	34	34	35	25	20	34	6	7	43	41	34
SEP. 17	24	35	36	36	25	20	34	6	7	43	41	34
SEP. 18	24	37	37	38	25	20	34	6	7	43	41	34
SEP. 19	25	38	39	39	26	20	34	5	7	43	41	34
SEP. 20	25	40	41	41	26	20	34	5	7	43	41	34
SEP. 21	25	42	42	43	26	20	35	5	7	43	41	34
SEP. 22	25	43	44	45	26	20	35	5	7	43	41	34
SEP. 23	25	45	46	46	26	20	35	5	7	43	41	34
SEP. 24	25	47	48	48	27	20	35	5	7	43	41	34
SEP. 25	26	1	1	2	27	20	35	5	7	43	41	34
SEP. 26	26	3	3	4	27	20	35	5	7	43	41	34
SEP. 27	26	5	5	6	27	20	35	5	7	43	41	34
SEP. 28	26	7	7	8	28	20	35	5	7	43	41	34
SEP. 29	26	8	9	10	28	20	35	5	7	43	41	34
SEP. 30	26	10	11	12	28	20	35	5	7	43	41	34

October

Date & Time	SUN	MOON 1	MOON 2	MOON 3	MERCURY	VENUS	MARS	JUPITER	SATURN	URANUS	NEPTUNE	PLUTO
OCT. 1	26	12	13	14	28	20	35	5	7	43	41	34
OCT. 2	26	14	15	15	28	20	36	5	7	43	41	34
OCT. 3	27	16	17	17	29	21	36	5	7	43	41	34
OCT. 4	27	18	18	19	29	21	36	5	7	43	41	34
OCT. 5	27	20	20	21	29	21	36	5	7	43	41	34
OCT. 6	27	21	22	22	29	21	36	5	7	43	41	34
OCT. 7	27	23	24	24	29	21	36	5	7	43	41	34
OCT. 8	27	25	25	26	30	21	36	5	7	43	41	34
OCT. 9	27	27	27	28	30	21	36	5	7	43	41	34
OCT. 10	27	28	29	29	30	21	36	5	7	43	41	34
OCT. 11	28	30	30	31	30	21	36	5	7	43	41	34
OCT. 12	28	32	32	33	30	21	37	5	7	43	41	34
OCT. 13	28	33	34	34	30	22	37	5	7	43	41	34
OCT. 14	28	35	35	36	31	22	37	5	7	43	41	34
OCT. 15	28	36	37	37	31	22	37	5	7	43	41	34
OCT. 16	28	38	38	39	31	22	37	5	7	43	41	34
OCT. 17	28	39	40	41	31	22	37	5	7	43	41	34
OCT. 18	28	41	42	42	31	22	37	5	7	43	41	34
OCT. 19	29	43	43	44	31	22	37	5	7	43	41	34
OCT. 20	29	44	45	46	32	22	37	5	7	43	41	34
OCT. 21	29	46	47	47	32	22	37	5	7	43	41	34
OCT. 22	29	48	1	1	32	23	37	5	7	43	41	34
OCT. 23	29	2	2	3	32	23	38	5	7	43	41	34
OCT. 24	29	4	4	5	32	23	38	5	7	43	41	34
OCT. 25	29	6	6	7	32	23	38	5	7	43	41	34
OCT. 26	30	8	8	9	32	23	38	5	7	43	41	34
OCT. 27	30	10	10	11	33	23	38	5	7	43	41	34
OCT. 28	30	12	12	13	33	23	38	5	7	43	41	34
OCT. 29	30	14	14	15	33	23	38	5	7	43	41	34
OCT. 30	30	16	16	17	33	24	38	5	7	43	41	34
OCT. 31	30	17	18	19	33	24	38	5	7	43	41	34

MOON 1 ◗ 12:01 A.M. TO 8:00 A.M.　　**MOON 2** ◑ 8:01 A.M. TO 4:00 P.M.　　**MOON 3** ● 4:01 P.M. TO 12:00 A.M.

Use only one "moon" number. Choose the column closest to your time of birth. If your place of birth is not on Eastern Standard Time, be sure to read "How to Convert to Eastern Standard Time" at the beginning of this section.

Date & Time	SUN	MOON 1	MOON 2	MOON 3	MERCURY	VENUS	MARS	JUPITER	SATURN	URANUS	NEPTUNE	PLUTO
NOV. 1	30	19	20	20	33	24	38	5	7	43	41	34
NOV. 2	30	21	22	22	33	24	39	5	7	43	41	34
NOV. 3	31	23	23	24	33	24	39	5	7	43	41	34
NOV. 4	31	24	25	26	33	24	39	5	7	43	41	34
NOV. 5	31	26	27	27	33	24	39	5	7	43	41	34
NOV. 6	31	28	28	29	33	25	39	5	7	43	41	34
NOV. 7	31	29	30	31	33	25	39	5	7	43	41	34
NOV. 8	31	31	32	32	33	25	39	5	7	43	41	34
NOV. 9	31	33	33	34	33	25	39	5	7	43	41	34
NOV. 10	31	34	35	35	33	25	39	5	7	43	41	34
NOV. 11	31	36	36	37	33	25	39	5	7	43	41	34
NOV. 12	32	37	38	38	33	25	40	5	7	43	41	34
NOV. 13	32	39	40	40	33	26	40	5	7	43	41	34
NOV. 14	32	41	41	42	32	26	40	5	7	43	41	34
NOV. 15	32	42	43	43	32	26	40	5	7	43	41	34
NOV. 16	32	44	44	45	32	26	40	5	7	43	41	34
NOV. 17	32	46	46	47	32	26	40	5	7	43	41	34
NOV. 18	32	47	48	48	32	26	40	5	7	43	41	34
NOV. 19	33	1	2	2	31	26	40	5	7	43	41	34
NOV. 20	33	3	4	4	31	27	40	5	7	43	41	34
NOV. 21	33	5	6	6	31	27	40	4	7	43	41	34
NOV. 22	33	7	8	8	31	27	41	4	7	43	41	34
NOV. 23	33	9	10	10	31	27	41	4	7	43	41	34
NOV. 24	33	11	12	12	31	27	41	4	7	43	41	34
NOV. 25	34	13	14	14	31	27	41	4	7	43	41	34
NOV. 26	34	15	16	16	31	27	41	4	7	43	41	34
NOV. 27	34	17	17	18	31	28	41	4	7	43	41	34
NOV. 28	34	19	19	20	31	28	41	4	7	43	41	34
NOV. 29	34	21	21	22	31	28	41	4	7	43	41	34
NOV. 30	34	22	23	24	31	28	41	4	7	43	41	34

Date & Time	SUN	MOON 1	MOON 2	MOON 3	MERCURY	VENUS	MARS	JUPITER	SATURN	URANUS	NEPTUNE	PLUTO
DEC. 1	34	24	25	25	31	28	41	4	7	43	41	34
DEC. 2	34	26	26	27	32	28	42	4	7	43	41	34
DEC. 3	35	27	28	29	32	29	42	4	7	43	41	34
DEC. 4	35	29	30	30	32	29	42	4	7	43	41	34
DEC. 5	35	31	31	32	32	29	42	4	7	43	41	34
DEC. 6	35	32	33	33	32	29	42	4	6	43	41	34
DEC. 7	35	34	34	35	32	29	42	4	6	43	41	34
DEC. 8	35	35	36	36	32	29	42	4	6	43	41	34
DEC. 9	35	37	38	38	33	29	42	4	6	43	41	34
DEC. 10	35	39	39	40	33	30	42	4	6	43	41	34
DEC. 11	36	40	41	41	33	30	42	4	6	43	41	34
DEC. 12	36	42	42	43	33	30	43	4	6	43	41	34
DEC. 13	36	43	44	44	33	30	43	4	6	43	41	34
DEC. 14	36	45	46	46	34	30	43	4	6	43	41	34
DEC. 15	36	47	47	48	34	30	43	4	6	43	41	34
DEC. 16	36	48	1	2	34	31	43	4	6	43	41	34
DEC. 17	36	2	3	3	34	31	43	4	6	43	41	34
DEC. 18	36	4	5	5	34	31	43	4	6	43	41	34
DEC. 19	37	6	7	7	35	31	43	4	6	43	41	34
DEC. 20	37	8	9	9	35	31	43	4	6	43	41	34
DEC. 21	37	10	11	11	35	31	44	4	6	43	41	34
DEC. 22	37	12	13	13	35	32	44	4	6	43	41	34
DEC. 23	37	14	15	15	35	32	44	4	6	43	41	34
DEC. 24	37	16	17	17	36	32	44	4	6	43	41	34
DEC. 25	37	18	19	19	36	32	44	4	6	43	41	34
DEC. 26	38	20	21	21	36	32	44	4	6	43	41	34
DEC. 27	38	22	22	23	36	32	44	4	6	43	41	34
DEC. 28	38	24	24	25	36	32	44	4	6	43	41	34
DEC. 29	38	25	26	26	37	33	44	4	6	43	41	34
DEC. 30	38	27	28	28	37	33	44	4	6	43	41	34
DEC. 31	38	29	29	30	37	33	45	4	6	43	41	34

MOON 1 ◐ 12:01 A.M. TO 8:00 A.M.   **MOON 2** ◑ 8:01 A.M. TO 4:00 P.M.   **MOON 3** ● 4:01 P.M. TO 12:00 A.M.

Use only one "moon" number. Choose the column closest to your time of birth. If your place of birth is not on Eastern Standard Time, be sure to read "How to Convert to Eastern Standard Time" at the beginning of this section.

2000-2009

2000s

Kala Sosefina Mileniume Kauvaka

★ ★ ★ BORN JANUARY 1, 2000 ★ ★ ★

Brief Bio: Kala Sosefina Mileniume Kauvaka was the first baby born in the new millennium.

Personology Profile:

SUN IN THE WEEK OF THE RULER
(CAPRICORN I)

*

Those born in this week know how to control their living and working situations. True rulers, they regard their home as their castle and like to see it running smoothly. Allergic to chaos, they run the risk of becoming control freaks. Unless they give up their tendency to make up other people's minds for them, they are likely to arouse resentments.

MOON IN THE WEEK OF DEPTH
(SCORPIO II)

*

A very profound position for the moon. Deep thoughts and feelings, however, should not turn to endless rumination and worry. A tendency to withdraw and brood is all too apparent here. Also, a suspicion of anything too glib or superficial. Such individuals must not undervalue love and happiness or ignore their need for it on a regular basis.

MERCURY ON THE CUSP OF PROPHECY
(SAGITTARIUS-CAPRICORN CUSP)

*

A deep and probing mind which is able to see in the life of things is usually denoted by this Mercury position. Not necessarily intelligent, but highly intuitive, such individuals use their mind power to best advantage. They are able to convince others through the focus and intensity of their arguments. Others often rely on them for sage advice.

VENUS ON THE CUSP OF REVOLUTION
(SCORPIO-SAGITTARIUS CUSP)

*

Stormy scenes frequently punctuate the love lives of those with this Venus position. Very outspoken in their views about their partners, they are not long-suffering types and will not allow themselves to be trodden upon without protest and, ultimately, without separation and even divorce. Not unlike a combination of nitroglycerine and dynamite, their package bears the words "Handle with Extreme Care."

MARS ON THE CUSP OF SENSITIVITY
(AQUARIUS-PISCES CUSP)

*

Overreactive, these folks must not let people push their buttons so easily. Moreover, they must learn that there is not so much to be afraid of and to modify or even drop their sometimes paranoid stance. By toughening up a bit and being more sure of themselves they won't get so upset by the attitudes of others toward them.

JUPITER IN THE WEEK OF THE PIONEER
(ARIES III)

*

Taking the lead in one's family or social group, at least ideologically, is favored here. Professional endeavors, however, can be tainted with financial difficulties by someone with this Jupiter position, through lack of good business sense. However, impulse and initiative are bestowed, which can get many a favorable domestic or neighborhood project up and running, with a successful outcome.

SATURN IN THE WEEK OF MANIFESTATION
(TAURUS I)

✳

The ability to manifest ideas is impaired here by Saturn's presence. Consequently, plans can be aborted and many jobs left unfinished. Derailment of work in progress is common, often through a self-destructive impulse which is unrecognized by the individuals themselves. Working carefully, step by step, is advised here, with frequent checks and a realistic goal kept in sight.

URANUS IN THE WEEK OF YOUTH AND EASE
(AQUARIUS II)

✳

Uranus is perhaps at his most relaxed point in the Zodiac here. Even his dynamic and electric energies enjoy a rest from time to time, and here he can fully stretch out, kick back and enjoy himself. During such periods of enjoyment he is quite likely to become inspired to new feats of daring. With fully charged batteries he is ready to leap into the fray once more.

NEPTUNE ON THE CUSP OF MYSTERY AND IMAGINATION
(CAPRICORN-AQUARIUS CUSP)

✳

One of the most imaginative and far-reaching positions of the year for Neptune. Those with this position have extremely vivid dream and fantasy lives, which usually spill over into their day-to-day existence. It may be difficult for those they live with to accept their often bizarre and strange points of view. Violent tendencies, when opposed or misunderstood, must be kept under control.

PLUTO IN THE WEEK OF INDEPENDENCE
(SAGITTARIUS I)

✳

A feeling of optimism is pervasive here and with it the energy needed to accomplish great tasks. The more explosive aspects of Pluto are tempered and his energies can be effectively harnessed. Still there is a feeling that forces beyond one's control are operating here and that respect should be given to the mighty impersonal forces operating in the universe.

Some Highlights of the Decade 2000-2009

- IN CHINA, AT LEAST 100 FALUN GONG SECT MEMBERS ARE DRAGGED FROM TIANANMEN SQUARE FOLLOWING A PROTEST OF THE YEAR ANNIVERSARY OF A GOVERNMENT BAN OF THE CULT.

- ON SEPTEMBER 11, 2001, SUICIDE BOMBERS ATTACK THE WORLD TRADE TOWERS IN NEW YORK CITY, KILLING THOUSANDS AND DEVASTATING THE CITY; THE US LAUNCHES A "WAR ON TERROR."

- HALLE BERRY BECOMES THE FIRST AFRICAN-AMERICAN WOMAN TO WIN AN ACADEMY AWARD FOR BEST ACTRESS.

- AGATHA CHRISTIE'S *THE MOUSETRAP* OPENS IN LONDON IN 1952 AND RUNS FOR 50 YEARS WITHOUT CLOSING, MAKING IT "THE WORLD'S LONGEST RUNNING PLAY."

- A HUGE EARTHQUAKE HITS ASIA IN THE INDIAN OCEAN, RESULTING IN A TSUNAMI THAT DEVASTATES INDONESIA AND OTHER COUNTRIES, KILLING THOUSANDS AND LEAVING MANY MORE HOMELESS.

2000

January / February

Date & Time	☉ SUN	◐ MOON 1	◑ MOON 2	● MOON 3	MERCURY	VENUS	MARS	JUPITER	SATURN	URANUS	NEPTUNE	PLUTO
JAN. 1	38	30	31	31	37	33	45	4	6	43	41	34
JAN. 2	38	32	32	33	37	33	45	4	6	43	41	34
JAN. 3	39	33	34	35	38	33	45	4	6	43	41	35
JAN. 4	39	35	36	36	38	34	45	4	6	43	41	35
JAN. 5	39	37	37	38	38	34	45	4	6	43	41	35
JAN. 6	39	38	39	39	38	34	45	4	6	43	41	35
JAN. 7	39	40	40	41	38	34	45	4	6	43	41	35
JAN. 8	39	41	42	42	39	34	45	4	6	43	41	35
JAN. 9	39	43	44	44	39	34	45	4	6	43	41	35
JAN. 10	40	45	45	46	39	35	46	4	6	43	41	35
JAN. 11	40	46	47	47	39	35	46	4	6	43	41	35
JAN. 12	40	48	1	1	39	35	46	4	6	43	41	35
JAN. 13	40	2	2	3	40	35	46	4	6	43	41	35
JAN. 14	40	3	4	5	40	35	46	4	6	43	41	35
JAN. 15	40	5	6	7	40	35	46	4	6	43	41	35
JAN. 16	40	7	8	8	40	36	46	4	6	43	41	35
JAN. 17	41	9	10	10	41	36	46	4	6	43	41	35
JAN. 18	41	11	12	12	41	36	46	4	6	43	41	35
JAN. 19	41	13	14	14	41	36	47	4	6	43	41	35
JAN. 20	41	15	16	16	41	36	47	5	6	43	41	35
JAN. 21	41	17	18	18	41	36	47	5	6	43	41	35
JAN. 22	41	19	20	20	42	37	47	5	6	43	41	35
JAN. 23	42	21	22	22	42	37	47	5	6	43	42	35
JAN. 24	42	23	23	24	42	37	47	5	6	43	42	35
JAN. 25	42	25	25	26	42	37	47	5	6	43	42	35
JAN. 26	42	26	27	28	43	37	47	5	6	43	42	35
JAN. 27	42	28	29	29	43	37	47	5	6	43	42	35
JAN. 28	42	30	30	31	43	38	47	5	6	43	42	35
JAN. 29	42	31	32	32	43	38	48	5	6	43	42	35
JAN. 30	42	33	34	34	44	38	48	5	6	43	42	35
JAN. 31	43	35	35	36	44	38	48	5	6	43	42	35
FEB. 1	43	36	37	37	44	38	48	5	6	43	42	35
FEB. 2	43	38	38	39	44	38	48	5	6	43	42	35
FEB. 3	43	39	40	40	44	39	48	5	6	43	42	35
FEB. 4	43	41	41	42	45	39	48	5	6	43	42	35
FEB. 5	43	43	43	44	45	39	48	5	6	43	42	35
FEB. 6	43	44	45	45	45	39	48	5	6	43	42	35
FEB. 7	43	46	46	47	45	39	48	5	6	43	42	35
FEB. 8	44	48	48	1	46	39	1	5	6	43	42	35
FEB. 9	44	1	2	2	46	39	1	5	6	43	42	35
FEB. 10	44	3	4	4	46	40	1	5	6	43	42	35
FEB. 11	44	5	5	6	46	40	1	5	6	43	42	35
FEB. 12	44	7	7	8	46	40	1	5	6	43	42	35
FEB. 13	44	9	9	10	47	40	1	5	6	43	42	35
FEB. 14	44	10	11	12	47	40	1	5	6	43	42	35
FEB. 15	44	12	13	14	47	40	1	5	6	43	42	35
FEB. 16	45	14	15	16	47	41	1	5	6	43	42	35
FEB. 17	45	16	17	18	47	41	1	5	6	43	42	35
FEB. 18	45	18	19	19	47	41	2	5	7	43	42	35
FEB. 19	45	20	21	21	47	41	2	5	7	43	42	35
FEB. 20	45	22	23	23	47	41	2	5	7	43	42	35
FEB. 21	45	24	24	25	47	41	2	5	7	43	42	35
FEB. 22	45	26	26	27	47	42	2	5	7	43	42	35
FEB. 23	46	27	28	29	47	42	2	5	7	43	42	35
FEB. 24	46	29	30	30	47	42	2	5	7	43	42	35
FEB. 25	46	31	31	32	47	42	2	5	7	43	42	35
FEB. 26	46	32	33	34	47	42	2	5	7	43	42	35
FEB. 27	46	34	35	35	47	42	2	5	7	43	42	35
FEB. 28	46	36	36	37	47	43	3	5	7	43	42	35
FEB. 29	46	37	38	38	47	43	3	5	7	43	42	35

MOON 1 ◐ 12:01 A.M. TO 8:00 A.M.   **MOON 2** ◑ 8:01 A.M. TO 4:00 P.M.   **MOON 3** ● 4:01 P.M. TO 12:00 A.M.

Use only one "moon" number. Choose the column closest to your time of birth. If your place of birth is not on Eastern Standard Time, be sure to read "How to Convert to Eastern Standard Time" at the beginning of this section.

Date & Time	SUN ☀	MOON 1 ◐	MOON 2 ◑	MOON 3 ●	MERCURY	VENUS	MARS	JUPITER	SATURN	URANUS	NEPTUNE	PLUTO
MAR. 1	46	39	39	40	47	43	3	5	7	43	42	35
MAR. 2	46	40	41	41	46	43	3	5	7	43	42	35
MAR. 3	47	42	43	43	46	43	3	5	7	43	42	35
MAR. 4	47	44	44	45	46	43	3	5	7	43	42	35
MAR. 5	47	45	46	46	46	44	3	5	7	43	42	35
MAR. 6	47	47	48	48	46	44	3	5	7	43	42	35
MAR. 7	47	1	1	2	46	44	3	6	7	43	42	35
MAR. 8	47	3	3	4	46	44	3	6	7	43	42	35
MAR. 9	47	4	5	6	46	44	4	6	7	43	42	35
MAR. 10	47	6	7	8	45	44	4	6	7	43	42	35
MAR. 11	48	8	9	9	45	45	4	6	7	43	42	35
MAR. 12	48	10	11	11	45	45	4	6	7	43	42	35
MAR. 13	48	12	13	13	45	45	4	6	7	43	42	35
MAR. 14	48	14	14	15	45	45	4	6	7	43	42	35
MAR. 15	48	16	16	17	45	45	4	6	7	43	42	35
MAR. 16	48	18	18	19	45	45	4	6	7	43	42	35
MAR. 17	48	19	20	21	45	45	4	6	7	43	42	35
MAR. 18	48	21	22	23	45	46	4	6	7	44	42	35
MAR. 19	1	23	24	24	45	46	5	6	7	44	42	35
MAR. 20	1	25	26	26	46	46	5	6	7	44	42	35
MAR. 21	1	27	27	28	46	46	5	6	7	44	42	35
MAR. 22	1	29	29	30	46	46	5	6	7	44	42	35
MAR. 23	1	30	31	31	46	47	5	6	7	44	42	35
MAR. 24	1	32	32	33	46	47	5	6	7	44	42	35
MAR. 25	2	34	34	35	46	47	5	6	7	44	42	35
MAR. 26	2	35	36	36	46	47	5	6	7	44	42	35
MAR. 27	2	37	37	38	46	47	6	6	7	44	42	35
MAR. 28	2	38	39	39	46	47	6	6	7	44	42	35
MAR. 29	2	40	40	41	46	48	6	6	7	44	42	35
MAR. 30	2	41	42	43	47	48	6	6	7	44	42	35
MAR. 31	2	43	44	44	47	48	6	6	7	44	42	35

Date & Time	SUN ☀	MOON 1 ◐	MOON 2 ◑	MOON 3 ●	MERCURY	VENUS	MARS	JUPITER	SATURN	URANUS	NEPTUNE	PLUTO
APR. 1	2	45	45	46	47	48	6	6	7	44	42	35
APR. 2	2	46	47	48	47	48	6	6	7	44	42	35
APR. 3	3	48	1	1	47	48	6	6	7	44	42	35
APR. 4	3	2	3	3	47	1	6	6	7	44	42	35
APR. 5	3	4	4	5	48	1	6	6	7	44	42	35
APR. 6	3	6	6	7	48	1	6	6	7	44	42	35
APR. 7	3	8	8	9	48	1	6	6	7	44	42	35
APR. 8	3	10	10	11	48	1	7	6	7	44	42	35
APR. 9	3	11	12	13	48	1	7	6	7	44	42	35
APR. 10	3	13	14	15	48	2	7	6	7	44	42	35
APR. 11	4	15	16	16	1	2	7	7	7	44	42	35
APR. 12	4	17	18	18	1	2	7	7	7	44	42	35
APR. 13	4	19	20	20	1	2	7	7	7	44	42	35
APR. 14	4	21	21	22	1	2	7	7	7	44	42	35
APR. 15	4	23	23	24	1	2	7	7	7	44	42	35
APR. 16	4	24	25	26	2	3	7	7	7	44	42	35
APR. 17	4	26	27	27	2	3	7	7	7	44	42	35
APR. 18	4	28	28	29	2	3	7	7	7	44	42	35
APR. 19	5	30	30	31	2	3	8	7	7	44	42	35
APR. 20	5	31	32	32	3	3	8	7	7	44	42	35
APR. 21	5	33	34	34	3	3	8	7	7	44	42	35
APR. 22	5	35	35	36	3	4	8	7	7	44	42	35
APR. 23	5	36	37	37	3	4	8	7	7	44	42	35
APR. 24	5	38	38	39	3	4	8	7	7	44	42	35
APR. 25	6	39	40	40	4	4	8	7	7	44	42	35
APR. 26	6	41	41	42	4	4	8	7	7	44	42	35
APR. 27	6	43	43	44	4	4	8	7	7	44	42	35
APR. 28	6	44	45	45	4	4	8	7	7	44	42	35
APR. 29	6	46	46	47	5	5	9	7	7	44	42	35
APR. 30	6	48	48	1	5	5	9	7	8	44	42	35

MOON 1 ◐ 12:01 A.M. TO 8:00 A.M. **MOON 2** ◑ 8:01 A.M. TO 4:00 P.M. **MOON 3** ● 4:01 P.M. TO 12:00 A.M.
Use only one "moon" number. Choose the column closest to your time of birth. If your place of birth is not on
Eastern Standard Time, be sure to read "How to Convert to Eastern Standard Time" at the beginning of this section.

2000

May / June

Date & Time	SUN	MOON 1	MOON 2	MOON 3	MERCURY	VENUS	MARS	JUPITER	SATURN	URANUS	NEPTUNE	PLUTO
MAY 1	6	1	2	2	5	5	9	7	8	44	42	35
MAY 2	6	3	4	4	6	5	9	7	8	44	42	35
MAY 3	7	5	6	6	6	5	9	7	8	44	42	35
MAY 4	7	7	8	8	6	5	9	7	8	44	42	35
MAY 5	7	9	10	10	6	6	9	7	8	44	42	35
MAY 6	7	11	11	12	6	6	9	7	8	44	42	35
MAY 7	7	13	13	14	7	6	9	7	8	44	42	35
MAY 8	7	15	15	16	7	6	9	7	8	44	42	35
MAY 9	7	17	17	18	7	6	9	7	8	44	42	35
MAY 10	7	19	19	20	8	6	10	7	8	44	42	35
MAY 11	8	20	21	22	8	7	10	7	8	44	42	35
MAY 12	8	22	23	23	8	7	10	7	8	44	42	35
MAY 13	8	24	25	25	9	7	10	8	8	44	42	35
MAY 14	8	26	26	27	9	7	10	8	8	44	42	35
MAY 15	8	27	28	29	9	7	10	8	8	44	42	35
MAY 16	8	29	30	30	9	7	10	8	8	44	42	35
MAY 17	8	31	31	32	10	7	10	8	8	44	42	35
MAY 18	8	32	33	34	10	8	10	8	8	44	42	35
MAY 19	9	34	35	35	10	8	10	8	8	44	42	35
MAY 20	9	36	36	37	11	8	10	8	8	44	42	35
MAY 21	9	37	38	38	11	8	11	8	8	44	42	35
MAY 22	9	39	39	40	11	8	11	8	8	44	42	35
MAY 23	9	40	41	41	11	9	11	8	8	44	42	35
MAY 24	9	42	43	43	12	9	11	8	8	44	42	35
MAY 25	10	44	44	45	12	9	11	8	8	44	42	35
MAY 26	10	45	46	46	12	9	11	8	8	44	42	35
MAY 27	10	47	47	48	12	9	11	8	8	44	42	35
MAY 28	10	1	1	2	13	9	11	8	8	44	42	35
MAY 29	10	2	3	4	13	10	11	8	8	44	42	35
MAY 30	10	4	5	5	13	10	11	8	8	44	42	35
MAY 31	10	6	7	7	13	10	11	8	8	44	42	35

Date & Time	SUN	MOON 1	MOON 2	MOON 3	MERCURY	VENUS	MARS	JUPITER	SATURN	URANUS	NEPTUNE	PLUTO
JUN. 1	10	8	9	9	13	10	12	8	8	44	42	35
JUN. 2	10	10	11	11	14	10	12	8	8	44	42	35
JUN. 3	11	12	13	13	14	10	12	8	8	44	42	34
JUN. 4	11	14	15	15	14	11	12	8	8	44	42	34
JUN. 5	11	16	17	17	14	11	12	8	8	44	42	34
JUN. 6	11	18	19	19	14	11	12	8	8	44	42	34
JUN. 7	11	20	21	21	14	11	12	8	8	44	42	34
JUN. 8	11	22	22	23	15	11	12	8	8	44	42	34
JUN. 9	11	24	24	25	15	11	12	8	8	44	42	34
JUN. 10	11	25	26	26	15	12	12	8	8	44	42	34
JUN. 11	12	27	28	28	15	12	12	8	8	44	42	34
JUN. 12	12	29	29	30	15	12	13	8	8	44	42	34
JUN. 13	12	30	31	32	15	12	13	8	8	44	42	34
JUN. 14	12	32	33	33	15	12	13	9	8	44	42	34
JUN. 15	12	34	34	35	15	12	13	9	8	44	42	34
JUN. 16	12	35	36	36	15	13	13	9	8	44	42	34
JUN. 17	12	37	37	38	15	13	13	9	8	44	42	34
JUN. 18	12	38	39	39	15	13	13	9	8	44	42	34
JUN. 19	13	40	41	41	16	13	13	9	8	44	42	34
JUN. 20	13	42	42	43	16	13	13	9	8	44	42	34
JUN. 21	13	43	44	44	16	13	13	9	8	44	42	34
JUN. 22	13	45	45	46	16	14	13	9	8	44	42	34
JUN. 23	13	46	47	47	16	14	14	9	8	44	42	34
JUN. 24	13	48	1	1	16	14	14	9	8	44	42	34
JUN. 25	14	2	2	3	16	14	14	9	8	44	42	34
JUN. 26	14	4	4	5	16	14	14	9	8	44	42	34
JUN. 27	14	5	6	7	16	14	14	9	8	44	42	34
JUN. 28	14	7	8	8	16	14	14	9	8	44	42	34
JUN. 29	14	9	10	10	15	15	14	9	8	44	42	34
JUN. 30	14	11	12	12	15	15	14	9	9	44	42	34

MOON 1 ◐ 12:01 A.M. TO 8:00 A.M.   **MOON 2** ◑ 8:01 A.M. TO 4:00 P.M.   **MOON 3** ● 4:01 P.M. TO 12:00 A.M.

Use only one "moon" number. Choose the column closest to your time of birth. If your place of birth is not on Eastern Standard Time, be sure to read "How to Convert to Eastern Standard Time" at the beginning of this section.

2000

July   August

Date & Time	SUN ☉	MOON 1 ☽	MOON 2 ◑	MOON 3 ●	MERCURY	VENUS	MARS	JUPITER	SATURN	URANUS	NEPTUNE	PLUTO
JUL. 1	14	13	14	14	15	15	14	9	9	44	42	34
JUL. 2	14	15	16	16	15	15	14	9	9	44	42	34
JUL. 3	15	17	18	18	15	15	14	9	9	44	42	34
JUL. 4	15	19	20	20	15	15	15	9	9	44	42	34
JUL. 5	15	21	22	22	15	16	15	9	9	44	42	34
JUL. 6	15	23	24	24	15	16	15	9	9	44	42	34
JUL. 7	15	25	25	26	15	16	15	9	9	44	42	34
JUL. 8	15	27	27	28	15	16	15	9	9	44	42	34
JUL. 9	15	28	29	29	15	16	15	9	9	44	42	34
JUL. 10	15	30	31	31	15	16	15	9	9	44	42	34
JUL. 11	16	32	32	33	15	17	15	9	9	44	42	34
JUL. 12	16	33	34	34	15	17	15	9	9	44	42	34
JUL. 13	16	35	35	36	14	17	15	9	9	44	42	34
JUL. 14	16	36	37	38	14	17	15	9	9	44	42	34
JUL. 15	16	38	39	39	14	17	16	9	9	44	42	34
JUL. 16	16	40	40	41	14	17	16	9	9	44	42	34
JUL. 17	16	41	42	42	14	18	16	9	9	44	42	34
JUL. 18	16	43	43	44	14	18	16	9	9	44	42	34
JUL. 19	17	44	45	45	14	18	16	9	9	44	42	34
JUL. 20	17	46	47	47	14	18	16	9	9	44	42	34
JUL. 21	17	48	48	1	14	18	16	10	9	44	42	34
JUL. 22	17	1	2	2	14	18	16	10	9	44	42	34
JUL. 23	17	3	4	4	15	19	16	10	9	44	42	34
JUL. 24	17	5	5	6	15	19	16	10	9	44	42	34
JUL. 25	17	7	7	8	15	19	16	10	9	44	42	34
JUL. 26	18	8	9	10	15	19	16	10	9	44	42	34
JUL. 27	18	10	11	12	15	19	17	10	9	44	42	34
JUL. 28	18	12	13	14	15	19	17	10	9	44	42	34
JUL. 29	18	14	15	16	15	20	17	10	9	44	42	34
JUL. 30	18	16	17	18	15	20	17	10	9	44	42	34
JUL. 31	18	18	19	20	16	20	17	10	9	44	42	34
AUG. 1	18	20	21	22	16	20	17	10	9	44	42	34
AUG. 2	18	22	23	24	16	20	17	10	9	44	42	34
AUG. 3	19	24	25	25	16	20	17	10	9	44	42	34
AUG. 4	19	26	27	27	16	21	17	10	9	44	42	34
AUG. 5	19	28	28	29	17	21	17	10	9	44	42	34
AUG. 6	19	30	30	31	17	21	17	10	9	44	42	34
AUG. 7	19	31	32	32	17	21	17	10	9	44	42	34
AUG. 8	19	33	33	34	17	21	18	10	9	43	42	34
AUG. 9	19	34	35	36	17	21	18	10	9	43	42	34
AUG. 10	19	36	37	37	18	22	18	10	9	43	42	34
AUG. 11	20	38	38	39	18	22	18	10	9	43	42	34
AUG. 12	20	39	40	40	18	22	18	10	9	43	42	34
AUG. 13	20	41	41	42	18	22	18	10	9	43	42	34
AUG. 14	20	42	43	43	19	22	18	10	9	43	42	34
AUG. 15	20	44	45	45	19	22	18	10	9	43	42	34
AUG. 16	20	46	46	47	19	23	18	10	9	43	42	34
AUG. 17	20	47	48	48	20	23	18	10	9	43	42	34
AUG. 18	20	1	1	2	20	23	18	10	9	43	42	34
AUG. 19	21	3	3	4	20	23	19	10	9	43	42	34
AUG. 20	21	4	5	6	20	23	19	10	9	43	42	34
AUG. 21	21	6	7	7	21	23	19	10	9	43	42	34
AUG. 22	21	8	9	9	21	24	19	10	9	43	42	34
AUG. 23	21	10	10	11	21	24	19	10	9	43	42	34
AUG. 24	21	12	12	13	21	24	19	10	9	43	42	34
AUG. 25	21	14	14	15	22	24	19	10	9	43	42	34
AUG. 26	22	15	16	17	22	24	19	10	9	43	42	34
AUG. 27	22	17	18	19	22	24	19	10	9	43	42	34
AUG. 28	22	19	20	21	22	24	19	10	9	43	42	34
AUG. 29	22	21	22	23	23	25	19	10	9	43	42	34
AUG. 30	22	23	24	25	23	25	19	10	9	43	42	34
AUG. 31	22	25	26	26	23	25	20	10	9	43	42	34

MOON 1 ☽ 12:01 A.M. TO 8:00 A.M.   **MOON 2** ◑ 8:01 A.M. TO 4:00 P.M.   **MOON 3** ● 4:01 P.M. TO 12:00 A.M.

Use only one "moon" number. Choose the column closest to your time of birth. If your place of birth is not on Eastern Standard Time, be sure to read "How to Convert to Eastern Standard Time" at the beginning of this section.

September

October

Date & Time	SUN	MOON 1	MOON 2	MOON 3	MERCURY	VENUS	MARS	JUPITER	SATURN	URANUS	NEPTUNE	PLUTO
SEP. 1	22	27	28	28	23	25	20	10	9	43	42	34
SEP. 2	22	29	29	30	24	25	20	10	9	43	42	34
SEP. 3	23	31	31	32	24	25	20	10	9	43	42	34
SEP. 4	23	32	33	33	24	26	20	10	9	43	42	34
SEP. 5	23	34	35	35	24	26	20	10	9	43	42	34
SEP. 6	23	36	36	37	25	26	20	10	9	43	42	34
SEP. 7	23	37	38	38	25	26	20	10	9	43	42	34
SEP. 8	23	39	39	40	25	26	20	10	9	43	42	34
SEP. 9	23	40	41	41	25	26	20	10	9	43	42	34
SEP. 10	23	42	42	43	25	27	20	10	9	43	42	34
SEP. 11	24	44	44	45	26	27	20	10	9	43	42	34
SEP. 12	24	45	46	46	26	27	21	10	9	43	42	34
SEP. 13	24	47	47	48	26	27	21	10	9	43	42	34
SEP. 14	24	48	1	2	26	27	21	10	9	43	42	34
SEP. 15	24	2	3	3	27	27	21	10	9	43	42	34
SEP. 16	24	4	5	5	27	28	21	10	9	43	42	34
SEP. 17	24	6	6	7	27	28	21	10	9	43	42	34
SEP. 18	24	7	8	9	27	28	21	10	9	43	41	34
SEP. 19	25	9	10	11	27	28	21	10	9	43	41	34
SEP. 20	25	11	12	12	27	28	21	10	9	43	41	34
SEP. 21	25	13	14	14	28	28	21	10	9	43	41	34
SEP. 22	25	15	16	16	28	29	21	10	9	43	41	34
SEP. 23	25	17	17	18	28	29	21	10	9	43	41	34
SEP. 24	25	19	19	20	28	29	22	10	9	43	41	34
SEP. 25	26	21	21	22	28	29	22	10	9	43	41	34
SEP. 26	26	23	23	24	29	29	22	10	9	43	41	34
SEP. 27	26	24	25	26	29	29	22	10	9	43	41	34
SEP. 28	26	26	27	28	29	29	22	10	9	43	41	34
SEP. 29	26	28	29	29	29	30	22	10	9	43	41	34
SEP. 30	26	30	31	31	29	30	22	10	9	43	41	34

Date & Time	SUN	MOON 1	MOON 2	MOON 3	MERCURY	VENUS	MARS	JUPITER	SATURN	URANUS	NEPTUNE	PLUTO
OCT. 1	26	32	32	33	29	30	22	10	9	43	41	34
OCT. 2	26	33	34	34	30	30	22	10	9	43	41	34
OCT. 3	27	35	36	36	30	30	22	10	9	43	41	34
OCT. 4	27	37	37	38	30	31	22	10	9	43	41	34
OCT. 5	27	38	39	39	30	31	22	10	9	43	41	34
OCT. 6	27	40	40	41	30	31	23	10	9	43	41	34
OCT. 7	27	41	42	42	30	31	23	10	9	43	41	34
OCT. 8	27	43	44	44	30	31	23	10	9	43	41	34
OCT. 9	27	45	45	46	30	31	23	10	9	43	41	34
OCT. 10	27	46	47	47	31	31	23	10	9	43	41	34
OCT. 11	28	48	48	1	31	32	23	10	9	43	41	34
OCT. 12	28	2	2	3	31	32	23	10	9	43	41	34
OCT. 13	28	3	4	5	31	32	23	10	9	43	41	34
OCT. 14	28	5	6	6	31	32	23	10	9	43	41	34
OCT. 15	28	7	8	8	31	32	23	10	9	43	41	34
OCT. 16	28	9	9	10	31	32	23	10	9	43	41	34
OCT. 17	28	11	11	12	31	33	23	10	9	43	41	34
OCT. 18	28	13	13	14	31	33	24	10	9	43	41	34
OCT. 19	29	14	15	16	31	33	24	10	9	43	41	34
OCT. 20	29	16	17	18	31	33	24	10	9	43	41	34
OCT. 21	29	18	19	19	31	33	24	10	9	43	41	34
OCT. 22	29	20	21	21	31	33	24	10	9	43	41	34
OCT. 23	29	22	23	23	31	34	24	10	9	43	41	34
OCT. 24	29	24	24	25	31	34	24	10	9	43	41	34
OCT. 25	29	26	26	27	31	34	24	10	9	43	41	34
OCT. 26	30	28	28	29	31	34	24	10	9	43	41	34
OCT. 27	30	29	30	30	30	34	24	10	9	43	41	34
OCT. 28	30	31	32	32	30	34	24	10	9	43	41	34
OCT. 29	30	33	33	34	30	35	24	10	9	43	41	34
OCT. 30	30	34	35	36	30	35	25	10	9	43	41	34
OCT. 31	30	36	37	37	30	35	25	10	9	43	41	34

MOON 1 ◐ 12:01 A.M. TO 8:00 A.M. **MOON 2** ◑ 8:01 A.M. TO 4:00 P.M. **MOON 3** ● 4:01 P.M. TO 12:00 A.M.
Use only one "moon" number. Choose the column closest to your time of birth. If your place of birth is not on
Eastern Standard Time, be sure to read "How to Convert to Eastern Standard Time" at the beginning of this section.

2000

November

Date & Time	SUN ☉	MOON 1 ☽	MOON 2 ◑	MOON 3 ●	MERCURY	VENUS	MARS	JUPITER	SATURN	URANUS	NEPTUNE	PLUTO
NOV. 1	30	38	38	39	30	35	25	10	9	43	41	34
NOV. 2	30	39	40	40	29	35	25	10	9	43	41	35
NOV. 3	31	41	41	42	29	35	25	10	9	43	41	35
NOV. 4	31	42	43	43	29	36	25	10	9	43	41	35
NOV. 5	31	44	45	45	29	36	25	10	9	43	41	35
NOV. 6	31	46	46	47	29	36	25	10	9	43	41	35
NOV. 7	31	47	48	48	29	36	25	10	9	43	41	35
NOV. 8	31	1	2	2	29	36	25	10	9	43	41	35
NOV. 9	31	3	3	4	29	36	25	10	9	43	41	35
NOV. 10	31	4	5	6	29	37	25	10	9	43	41	35
NOV. 11	31	6	7	8	29	37	26	10	9	43	41	35
NOV. 12	32	8	9	9	29	37	26	10	9	43	42	35
NOV. 13	32	10	11	11	29	37	26	10	9	43	42	35
NOV. 14	32	12	13	13	29	37	26	10	9	43	42	35
NOV. 15	32	14	15	15	29	37	26	10	9	43	42	35
NOV. 16	32	16	17	17	30	37	26	10	9	43	42	35
NOV. 17	32	18	18	19	30	38	26	10	9	43	42	35
NOV. 18	32	20	20	21	30	38	26	10	9	43	42	35
NOV. 19	33	22	22	23	30	38	26	10	9	43	42	35
NOV. 20	33	23	24	25	30	38	26	10	9	43	42	35
NOV. 21	33	25	26	26	30	38	26	10	9	43	42	35
NOV. 22	33	27	28	28	31	38	26	10	9	43	42	35
NOV. 23	33	29	29	30	31	39	27	10	9	43	42	35
NOV. 24	33	31	31	32	31	39	27	10	9	43	42	35
NOV. 25	34	32	33	33	31	39	27	10	9	43	42	35
NOV. 26	34	34	34	35	31	39	27	10	9	43	42	35
NOV. 27	34	36	36	37	32	39	27	10	9	43	42	35
NOV. 28	34	37	38	38	32	39	27	10	9	43	42	35
NOV. 29	34	39	39	40	32	40	27	10	9	43	42	35
NOV. 30	34	40	41	41	32	40	27	10	9	43	42	35

December

Date & Time	SUN ☉	MOON 1 ☽	MOON 2 ◑	MOON 3 ●	MERCURY	VENUS	MARS	JUPITER	SATURN	URANUS	NEPTUNE	PLUTO
DEC. 1	34	42	42	43	32	40	27	10	9	43	42	35
DEC. 2	34	43	44	45	33	40	27	10	8	43	42	35
DEC. 3	35	45	46	46	33	40	27	10	8	43	42	35
DEC. 4	35	47	47	48	33	40	27	10	8	43	42	35
DEC. 5	35	48	1	1	33	40	27	10	8	43	42	35
DEC. 6	35	2	2	3	33	41	28	10	8	43	42	35
DEC. 7	35	4	4	5	34	41	28	10	8	43	42	35
DEC. 8	35	6	6	7	34	41	28	10	8	43	42	35
DEC. 9	35	7	8	9	34	41	28	10	8	43	42	35
DEC. 10	35	9	10	11	34	41	28	10	8	43	42	35
DEC. 11	36	11	12	13	34	41	28	10	8	43	42	35
DEC. 12	36	13	14	15	35	42	28	10	8	43	42	35
DEC. 13	36	15	16	17	35	42	28	10	8	43	42	35
DEC. 14	36	17	18	19	35	42	28	10	8	43	42	35
DEC. 15	36	19	20	20	35	42	28	9	8	43	42	35
DEC. 16	36	21	22	22	36	42	28	9	8	43	42	35
DEC. 17	36	23	24	24	36	42	28	9	8	43	42	35
DEC. 18	36	25	25	26	36	42	29	9	8	43	42	35
DEC. 19	37	27	27	28	36	43	29	9	8	43	42	35
DEC. 20	37	28	29	30	36	43	29	9	8	43	42	35
DEC. 21	37	30	31	31	37	43	29	9	8	43	42	35
DEC. 22	37	32	32	33	37	43	29	9	8	43	42	35
DEC. 23	37	33	34	35	37	43	29	9	8	43	42	35
DEC. 24	37	35	36	36	37	43	29	9	8	43	42	35
DEC. 25	37	37	37	38	37	44	29	9	8	43	42	35
DEC. 26	38	38	39	39	38	44	29	9	8	43	42	35
DEC. 27	38	40	40	41	38	44	29	9	8	43	42	35
DEC. 28	38	41	42	43	38	44	29	9	8	43	42	35
DEC. 29	38	43	44	44	38	44	29	9	8	43	42	35
DEC. 30	38	45	45	46	38	44	29	9	8	43	42	35
DEC. 31	38	46	47	47	39	44	30	9	8	43	42	35

MOON 1 ☽ 12:01 A.M. TO 8:00 A.M.   **MOON 2** ◑ 8:01 A.M. TO 4:00 P.M.   **MOON 3** ● 4:01 P.M. TO 12:00 A.M.
Use only one "moon" number. Choose the column closest to your time of birth. If your place of birth is not on
Eastern Standard Time, be sure to read "How to Convert to Eastern Standard Time" at the beginning of this section.

2001

January

Date & Time	SUN	MOON 1	MOON 2	MOON 3	MERCURY	VENUS	MARS	JUPITER	SATURN	URANUS	NEPTUNE	PLUTO
JAN. 1	38	48	48	1	39	45	30	9	8	43	42	35
JAN. 2	38	1	2	3	39	45	30	9	8	43	42	35
JAN. 3	39	3	4	4	39	45	30	9	8	43	42	35
JAN. 4	39	5	5	6	40	45	30	9	8	43	42	35
JAN. 5	39	7	7	8	40	45	30	9	8	43	42	35
JAN. 6	39	8	9	10	40	45	30	9	8	43	42	35
JAN. 7	39	10	11	12	40	45	30	9	8	43	42	35
JAN. 8	39	12	13	14	40	45	30	9	8	44	42	35
JAN. 9	39	14	15	16	41	46	30	9	8	44	42	35
JAN. 10	40	16	17	18	41	46	30	9	8	44	42	35
JAN. 11	40	18	19	20	41	46	30	9	8	44	42	35
JAN. 12	40	20	21	22	41	46	30	9	8	44	42	35
JAN. 13	40	22	23	24	42	46	31	9	8	44	42	35
JAN. 14	40	24	25	26	42	46	31	9	8	44	42	35
JAN. 15	40	26	27	27	42	47	31	9	8	44	42	35
JAN. 16	40	28	29	29	42	47	31	9	8	44	42	35
JAN. 17	41	30	30	31	42	47	31	9	8	44	42	35
JAN. 18	41	31	32	33	43	47	31	9	8	44	42	35
JAN. 19	41	33	34	34	43	47	31	9	8	44	42	35
JAN. 20	41	35	35	36	43	47	31	9	8	44	42	35
JAN. 21	41	36	37	37	43	47	31	9	8	44	42	35
JAN. 22	41	38	38	39	43	48	31	9	8	44	42	35
JAN. 23	42	39	40	41	44	48	31	9	8	44	42	35
JAN. 24	42	41	42	42	44	48	31	9	8	44	42	35
JAN. 25	42	43	43	44	44	48	31	9	8	44	42	35
JAN. 26	42	44	45	45	44	48	32	9	8	44	42	35
JAN. 27	42	46	46	47	44	48	32	9	8	44	42	35
JAN. 28	42	47	48	48	45	48	32	9	8	44	42	35
JAN. 29	42	1	2	2	45	48	32	9	8	44	42	35
JAN. 30	42	3	3	4	45	1	32	9	8	44	42	35
JAN. 31	43	4	5	5	45	1	32	9	8	44	42	35

February

Date & Time	SUN	MOON 1	MOON 2	MOON 3	MERCURY	VENUS	MARS	JUPITER	SATURN	URANUS	NEPTUNE	PLUTO
FEB. 1	43	6	7	7	45	1	32	9	8	44	42	35
FEB. 2	43	8	8	9	45	1	32	9	8	44	42	35
FEB. 3	43	10	10	11	45	1	32	9	8	44	42	35
FEB. 4	43	11	12	13	45	1	32	9	8	44	42	35
FEB. 5	43	13	14	15	45	1	32	9	8	44	42	35
FEB. 6	43	15	16	17	45	1	32	9	8	44	42	35
FEB. 7	43	17	18	19	45	1	32	9	8	44	42	35
FEB. 8	44	19	20	21	45	2	32	9	8	44	42	35
FEB. 9	44	21	22	23	45	2	33	9	8	44	42	35
FEB. 10	44	23	24	25	45	2	33	9	8	44	42	35
FEB. 11	44	25	26	27	44	2	33	9	8	44	42	35
FEB. 12	44	27	28	29	44	2	33	9	8	44	42	35
FEB. 13	44	29	30	30	44	2	33	9	8	44	42	35
FEB. 14	44	31	31	32	44	2	33	9	8	44	42	35
FEB. 15	44	33	33	34	44	2	33	9	8	44	42	35
FEB. 16	45	34	35	35	44	2	33	9	8	44	42	35
FEB. 17	45	36	36	37	44	2	33	9	8	44	42	35
FEB. 18	45	37	38	39	43	2	33	9	8	44	42	35
FEB. 19	45	39	40	40	43	3	33	9	8	44	42	35
FEB. 20	45	41	41	42	43	3	33	9	8	44	42	35
FEB. 21	45	42	43	43	43	3	33	9	8	44	42	35
FEB. 22	45	44	44	45	43	3	33	9	8	44	42	35
FEB. 23	46	45	46	46	43	3	34	9	8	44	42	35
FEB. 24	46	47	48	48	43	3	34	9	8	44	42	35
FEB. 25	46	1	1	2	43	3	34	9	8	44	42	35
FEB. 26	46	2	3	3	43	3	34	9	8	44	42	35
FEB. 27	46	4	4	5	43	3	34	9	8	44	42	35
FEB. 28	46	6	6	7	43	3	34	9	8	44	42	35

MOON 1 ☽ 12:01 A.M. TO 8:00 A.M.   **MOON 2** ☽ 8:01 A.M. TO 4:00 P.M.   **MOON 3** ● 4:01 P.M. TO 12:00 A.M.
Use only one "moon" number. Choose the column closest to your time of birth. If your place of birth is not on Eastern Standard Time, be sure to read "How to Convert to Eastern Standard Time" at the beginning of this section.

2001

March

April

Date & Time	SUN	MOON 1	MOON 2	MOON 3	MERCURY	VENUS	MARS	JUPITER	SATURN	URANUS	NEPTUNE	PLUTO
MAR. 1	46	7	8	8	43	3	34	9	8	44	42	35
MAR. 2	46	9	10	10	43	3	34	9	8	44	42	35
MAR. 3	47	11	11	12	43	3	34	9	8	44	42	35
MAR. 4	47	13	13	14	43	3	34	9	8	44	42	35
MAR. 5	47	15	15	16	43	3	34	9	8	44	42	35
MAR. 6	47	17	17	18	43	3	34	9	8	44	42	35
MAR. 7	47	18	19	20	44	3	34	9	8	44	42	35
MAR. 8	47	20	21	22	44	3	34	9	8	44	42	35
MAR. 9	47	22	23	24	44	3	34	10	8	44	42	35
MAR. 10	47	24	25	26	44	3	35	10	8	44	42	35
MAR. 11	48	26	27	28	44	3	35	10	8	44	42	35
MAR. 12	48	28	29	30	44	3	35	10	8	44	42	35
MAR. 13	48	30	31	31	44	3	35	10	8	44	42	35
MAR. 14	48	32	33	33	44	3	35	10	8	44	42	35
MAR. 15	48	34	34	35	45	3	35	10	8	44	42	35
MAR. 16	48	35	36	36	45	3	35	10	8	44	42	35
MAR. 17	48	37	38	38	45	3	35	10	8	44	42	35
MAR. 18	48	39	39	40	45	3	35	10	8	44	42	35
MAR. 19	1	40	41	41	45	3	35	10	9	44	42	35
MAR. 20	1	42	42	43	45	3	35	10	9	44	42	35
MAR. 21	1	43	44	44	46	3	35	10	9	44	42	35
MAR. 22	1	45	45	46	46	3	35	10	9	44	42	35
MAR. 23	1	47	47	48	46	3	35	10	9	44	42	35
MAR. 24	1	48	1	1	46	3	35	10	9	44	42	35
MAR. 25	2	2	3	3	46	3	35	10	9	44	42	35
MAR. 26	2	3	4	5	47	3	35	10	9	44	42	35
MAR. 27	2	5	6	6	47	2	35	10	9	44	42	35
MAR. 28	2	7	8	8	47	2	35	10	9	44	42	35
MAR. 29	2	9	9	10	47	2	36	10	9	44	42	35
MAR. 30	2	10	11	12	47	2	36	10	9	44	42	35
MAR. 31	2	12	13	13	48	2	36	10	9	44	42	35

Date & Time	SUN	MOON 1	MOON 2	MOON 3	MERCURY	VENUS	MARS	JUPITER	SATURN	URANUS	NEPTUNE	PLUTO
APR. 1	2	14	15	15	48	2	36	10	9	44	42	35
APR. 2	2	16	17	17	48	2	36	10	9	44	42	35
APR. 3	3	18	18	19	48	2	36	10	9	44	42	35
APR. 4	3	20	20	21	48	2	36	10	9	44	42	35
APR. 5	3	22	22	23	1	2	36	10	9	44	42	35
APR. 6	3	24	24	25	1	2	36	10	9	44	42	35
APR. 7	3	26	26	27	1	2	36	10	9	44	42	35
APR. 8	3	28	28	29	1	2	36	10	9	44	42	35
APR. 9	3	29	30	31	2	1	36	10	9	44	42	35
APR. 10	3	31	32	32	2	1	36	10	9	44	42	35
APR. 11	4	33	34	34	2	1	36	10	9	44	42	35
APR. 12	4	35	35	36	2	1	36	10	9	44	42	35
APR. 13	4	36	37	38	3	1	36	10	9	44	42	35
APR. 14	4	38	39	39	3	1	36	10	9	44	42	35
APR. 15	4	40	40	41	3	1	36	10	9	44	42	35
APR. 16	4	41	42	42	3	1	36	10	9	44	42	35
APR. 17	4	43	43	44	4	1	36	10	9	44	42	35
APR. 18	4	44	45	45	4	1	36	10	9	44	42	35
APR. 19	5	46	47	47	4	1	36	10	9	44	42	35
APR. 20	5	48	48	1	5	1	36	10	9	44	42	35
APR. 21	5	1	2	2	5	1	37	10	9	44	42	35
APR. 22	5	3	4	4	5	1	37	11	9	44	42	35
APR. 23	5	5	5	6	5	1	37	11	9	44	42	35
APR. 24	5	6	7	8	6	1	37	11	9	44	42	35
APR. 25	6	8	9	9	6	1	37	11	9	44	42	35
APR. 26	6	10	11	11	6	1	37	11	9	44	42	35
APR. 27	6	12	12	13	6	1	37	11	9	44	42	35
APR. 28	6	14	14	15	7	1	37	11	9	44	42	35
APR. 29	6	16	16	17	7	1	37	11	9	44	42	35
APR. 30	6	17	18	19	7	1	37	11	9	44	42	35

MOON 1 ☾ 12:01 A.M. TO 8:00 A.M.   **MOON 2** ☽ 8:01 A.M. TO 4:00 P.M.   **MOON 3** ● 4:01 P.M. TO 12:00 A.M.

Use only one "moon" number. Choose the column closest to your time of birth. If your place of birth is not on Eastern Standard Time, be sure to read "How to Convert to Eastern Standard Time" at the beginning of this section.

2001

May

June

Date & Time	SUN	MOON 1	MOON 2	MOON 3	MERCURY	VENUS	MARS	JUPITER	SATURN	URANUS	NEPTUNE	PLUTO
MAY 1	6	19	20	21	8	1	37	11	9	44	42	35
MAY 2	6	21	22	22	8	2	37	11	9	44	42	35
MAY 3	7	23	24	24	8	2	37	11	9	44	42	35
MAY 4	7	25	26	26	8	2	37	11	9	44	42	35
MAY 5	7	27	27	28	9	2	37	11	9	44	42	35
MAY 6	7	29	29	30	9	2	37	11	9	44	42	35
MAY 7	7	31	31	32	9	2	37	11	9	44	42	35
MAY 8	7	32	33	34	9	2	37	11	9	44	42	35
MAY 9	7	34	35	35	10	2	37	11	9	44	42	35
MAY 10	7	36	36	37	10	2	37	11	9	44	42	35
MAY 11	8	38	38	39	10	2	37	11	9	44	42	35
MAY 12	8	39	40	40	10	2	37	11	9	44	42	35
MAY 13	8	41	41	42	11	2	37	11	9	44	42	35
MAY 14	8	42	43	43	11	2	37	11	9	44	42	35
MAY 15	8	44	44	45	11	2	37	11	9	44	42	35
MAY 16	8	45	46	47	11	3	37	11	9	44	42	35
MAY 17	8	47	48	48	11	3	37	11	9	44	42	35
MAY 18	8	1	1	2	12	3	37	11	9	44	42	35
MAY 19	9	2	3	3	12	3	37	11	9	44	42	35
MAY 20	9	4	5	5	12	3	37	11	9	44	42	35
MAY 21	9	6	6	7	12	3	37	11	9	44	42	35
MAY 22	9	8	8	9	12	3	37	11	9	44	42	35
MAY 23	9	9	10	11	12	3	37	11	10	44	42	35
MAY 24	9	11	12	13	12	3	37	11	10	44	42	35
MAY 25	10	13	14	14	12	4	37	11	10	44	42	35
MAY 26	10	15	16	16	13	4	37	12	10	44	42	35
MAY 27	10	17	18	18	13	4	37	12	10	44	42	35
MAY 28	10	19	19	20	13	4	37	12	10	44	42	35
MAY 29	10	21	21	22	13	4	37	12	10	44	42	35
MAY 30	10	23	23	24	13	4	37	12	10	44	42	35
MAY 31	10	25	25	26	13	4	37	12	10	44	42	35

Date & Time	SUN	MOON 1	MOON 2	MOON 3	MERCURY	VENUS	MARS	JUPITER	SATURN	URANUS	NEPTUNE	PLUTO
JUN. 1	10	26	27	28	13	4	36	12	10	44	42	35
JUN. 2	10	28	29	29	13	4	36	12	10	44	42	35
JUN. 3	11	30	31	31	13	5	36	12	10	44	42	35
JUN. 4	11	32	32	33	13	5	36	12	10	44	42	35
JUN. 5	11	34	34	35	13	5	36	12	10	44	42	35
JUN. 6	11	35	36	36	13	5	36	12	10	44	42	35
JUN. 7	11	37	37	38	13	5	36	12	10	44	42	35
JUN. 8	11	39	39	40	13	5	36	12	10	44	42	35
JUN. 9	11	40	41	41	13	5	36	12	10	44	42	35
JUN. 10	11	42	42	43	13	5	36	12	10	44	42	35
JUN. 11	12	43	44	44	13	6	36	12	10	44	42	35
JUN. 12	12	45	46	46	13	6	36	12	10	44	42	35
JUN. 13	12	47	47	48	13	6	36	12	10	44	42	35
JUN. 14	12	48	1	1	13	6	36	12	10	44	42	35
JUN. 15	12	2	2	3	12	6	36	12	10	44	42	35
JUN. 16	12	3	4	5	12	6	36	12	10	44	42	35
JUN. 17	12	5	6	6	12	6	36	12	10	44	42	35
JUN. 18	12	7	7	8	12	7	36	12	10	44	42	35
JUN. 19	13	9	9	10	12	7	36	12	10	44	42	35
JUN. 20	13	11	11	12	12	7	36	12	10	44	42	35
JUN. 21	13	12	13	14	12	7	36	12	10	44	42	35
JUN. 22	13	14	15	16	12	7	36	12	10	44	42	35
JUN. 23	13	16	17	18	12	7	36	12	10	44	42	35
JUN. 24	13	18	19	20	12	7	36	12	10	44	42	35
JUN. 25	14	20	21	22	12	7	36	12	10	44	42	35
JUN. 26	14	22	23	23	12	8	35	12	10	44	42	35
JUN. 27	14	24	25	25	12	8	35	12	10	44	42	35
JUN. 28	14	26	27	27	12	8	35	13	10	44	42	35
JUN. 29	14	28	28	29	12	8	35	13	10	44	42	35
JUN. 30	14	30	30	31	12	8	35	13	10	44	42	35

MOON 1 ☽ 12:01 A.M. TO 8:00 A.M.   **MOON 2** ☽ 8:01 A.M. TO 4:00 P.M.   **MOON 3** ● 4:01 P.M. TO 12:00 A.M.
Use only one "moon" number. Choose the column closest to your time of birth. If your place of birth is not on Eastern Standard Time, be sure to read "How to Convert to Eastern Standard Time" at the beginning of this section.

2001

July   August

Date & Time	SUN	MOON 1	MOON 2	MOON 3	MERCURY	VENUS	MARS	JUPITER	SATURN	URANUS	NEPTUNE	PLUTO
JUL. 1	14	31	32	33	12	8	35	13	10	44	42	35
JUL. 2	14	33	34	34	12	8	35	13	10	44	42	35
JUL. 3	15	35	35	36	12	9	35	13	10	44	42	35
JUL. 4	15	36	37	38	12	9	35	13	10	44	42	35
JUL. 5	15	38	39	39	12	9	35	13	10	44	42	35
JUL. 6	15	40	40	41	12	9	35	13	10	44	42	35
JUL. 7	15	41	42	42	12	9	35	13	10	44	42	35
JUL. 8	15	43	43	44	12	9	35	13	10	44	42	35
JUL. 9	15	45	45	46	12	9	35	13	10	44	42	35
JUL. 10	15	46	47	47	13	10	35	13	10	44	42	35
JUL. 11	16	48	48	1	13	10	35	13	10	44	42	35
JUL. 12	16	1	2	2	13	10	35	13	10	44	42	35
JUL. 13	16	3	3	4	13	10	35	13	10	44	42	35
JUL. 14	16	5	5	6	13	10	35	13	10	44	42	35
JUL. 15	16	6	7	7	13	10	35	13	10	44	42	35
JUL. 16	16	8	9	9	14	11	35	13	10	44	42	35
JUL. 17	16	10	10	11	14	11	35	13	10	44	42	35
JUL. 18	16	12	12	13	14	11	35	13	10	44	42	35
JUL. 19	17	14	14	15	14	11	35	13	10	44	42	35
JUL. 20	17	15	16	17	14	11	35	13	10	44	42	35
JUL. 21	17	17	18	19	15	11	35	13	10	44	42	35
JUL. 22	17	20	20	21	15	11	35	13	10	44	42	35
JUL. 23	17	22	22	23	15	12	35	13	10	44	42	35
JUL. 24	17	23	24	25	15	12	35	13	10	44	42	35
JUL. 25	17	25	26	27	16	12	35	13	11	44	42	35
JUL. 26	18	27	28	29	16	12	35	13	11	44	42	35
JUL. 27	18	29	30	30	16	12	35	13	11	44	42	35
JUL. 28	18	31	32	32	16	12	35	13	11	44	42	35
JUL. 29	18	33	33	34	17	12	35	13	11	44	42	35
JUL. 30	18	34	35	36	17	13	35	13	11	44	42	35
JUL. 31	18	36	37	37	17	13	35	13	11	44	42	35

Date & Time	SUN	MOON 1	MOON 2	MOON 3	MERCURY	VENUS	MARS	JUPITER	SATURN	URANUS	NEPTUNE	PLUTO
AUG. 1	18	38	38	39	17	13	35	14	11	44	42	35
AUG. 2	18	39	40	40	18	13	35	14	11	44	42	35
AUG. 3	19	41	41	42	18	13	35	14	11	44	42	35
AUG. 4	19	42	43	44	18	13	35	14	11	44	42	35
AUG. 5	19	44	45	45	19	14	35	14	11	44	42	35
AUG. 6	19	46	46	47	19	14	35	14	11	44	42	35
AUG. 7	19	47	48	48	19	14	35	14	11	44	42	35
AUG. 8	19	1	1	2	19	14	35	14	11	44	42	35
AUG. 9	19	2	3	4	20	14	35	14	11	44	42	35
AUG. 10	19	4	5	5	20	14	35	14	11	44	42	35
AUG. 11	20	6	6	7	20	14	35	14	11	44	42	35
AUG. 12	20	7	8	9	20	15	35	14	11	44	42	35
AUG. 13	20	9	10	10	21	15	35	14	11	44	42	35
AUG. 14	20	11	12	12	21	15	36	14	11	44	42	35
AUG. 15	20	13	13	14	21	15	36	14	11	44	42	35
AUG. 16	20	15	15	16	21	15	36	14	11	44	42	35
AUG. 17	20	17	17	18	22	15	36	14	11	44	42	35
AUG. 18	20	19	19	20	22	16	36	14	11	44	42	35
AUG. 19	21	21	21	22	22	16	36	14	11	44	42	35
AUG. 20	21	23	23	24	22	16	36	14	11	44	42	35
AUG. 21	21	25	25	26	23	16	36	14	11	44	42	35
AUG. 22	21	27	27	28	23	16	36	14	11	44	42	35
AUG. 23	21	29	29	30	23	16	36	14	11	44	42	35
AUG. 24	21	30	31	32	23	16	36	14	11	44	42	35
AUG. 25	21	32	33	33	24	17	36	14	11	44	42	35
AUG. 26	22	34	35	35	24	17	36	14	11	44	42	35
AUG. 27	22	36	36	37	24	17	36	14	11	44	42	35
AUG. 28	22	37	38	38	24	17	36	14	11	44	42	35
AUG. 29	22	39	39	40	24	17	36	14	11	44	42	35
AUG. 30	22	41	41	42	25	17	36	14	11	44	42	35
AUG. 31	22	42	43	43	25	18	36	14	11	44	42	35

MOON 1 ☽ 12:01 A.M. TO 8:00 A.M.   **MOON 2** ☾ 8:01 A.M. TO 4:00 P.M.   **MOON 3** ● 4:01 P.M. TO 12:00 A.M.

Use only one "moon" number. Choose the column closest to your time of birth. If your place of birth is not on Eastern Standard Time, be sure to read "How to Convert to Eastern Standard Time" at the beginning of this section.

2001

September

Date & Time	SUN	MOON 1	MOON 2	MOON 3	MERCURY	VENUS	MARS	JUPITER	SATURN	URANUS	NEPTUNE	PLUTO
SEP. 1	22	44	44	45	25	18	36	14	11	44	42	35
SEP. 2	22	45	46	46	25	18	37	14	11	44	42	35
SEP. 3	23	47	47	48	25	18	37	14	11	44	42	35
SEP. 4	23	48	1	2	26	18	37	14	11	44	42	35
SEP. 5	23	2	3	3	26	18	37	14	11	44	42	35
SEP. 6	23	4	4	5	26	19	37	14	11	44	42	35
SEP. 7	23	5	6	6	26	19	37	14	11	44	42	35
SEP. 8	23	7	8	8	26	19	37	14	11	44	42	35
SEP. 9	23	9	9	10	26	19	37	14	11	44	42	35
SEP. 10	23	10	11	12	27	19	37	14	11	44	42	35
SEP. 11	24	12	13	13	27	19	37	15	11	44	42	35
SEP. 12	24	14	15	15	27	20	37	15	11	44	42	35
SEP. 13	24	16	16	17	27	20	37	15	11	44	42	35
SEP. 14	24	18	18	19	27	20	37	15	11	44	42	35
SEP. 15	24	20	20	21	27	20	37	15	11	44	42	35
SEP. 16	24	22	22	23	28	20	37	15	11	44	42	35
SEP. 17	24	24	24	25	28	20	38	15	11	44	42	35
SEP. 18	24	26	26	28	28	20	38	15	11	44	42	35
SEP. 19	25	28	28	29	28	21	38	15	11	44	42	35
SEP. 20	25	30	30	31	28	21	38	15	11	44	42	35
SEP. 21	25	32	32	33	28	21	38	15	11	44	42	35
SEP. 22	25	33	34	35	28	21	38	15	11	44	42	35
SEP. 23	25	35	36	36	28	21	38	15	11	44	42	35
SEP. 24	25	37	37	38	29	21	38	15	11	44	42	35
SEP. 25	26	38	39	40	29	22	38	15	11	44	42	35
SEP. 26	26	40	41	41	29	22	38	15	11	44	42	35
SEP. 27	26	42	42	43	29	22	38	15	11	44	42	35
SEP. 28	26	43	44	44	29	22	38	15	11	44	42	35
SEP. 29	26	45	45	46	29	22	38	15	11	44	42	35
SEP. 30	26	46	47	47	29	22	39	15	11	44	42	35

October

Date & Time	SUN	MOON 1	MOON 2	MOON 3	MERCURY	VENUS	MARS	JUPITER	SATURN	URANUS	NEPTUNE	PLUTO
OCT. 1	26	48	1	1	29	23	39	15	11	44	42	35
OCT. 2	26	2	2	3	29	23	39	15	11	44	42	35
OCT. 3	27	3	4	4	29	23	39	15	11	44	42	35
OCT. 4	27	5	5	6	29	23	39	15	11	44	42	35
OCT. 5	27	7	7	8	29	23	39	15	11	44	42	35
OCT. 6	27	8	9	9	29	23	39	15	11	44	42	35
OCT. 7	27	10	11	11	29	24	39	15	11	44	42	35
OCT. 8	27	12	12	13	29	24	39	15	11	44	42	35
OCT. 9	27	13	14	15	28	24	39	15	11	44	42	35
OCT. 10	27	15	16	17	28	24	39	15	11	44	42	35
OCT. 11	28	17	18	18	28	24	40	15	11	44	42	35
OCT. 12	28	19	20	20	28	24	40	15	11	44	42	35
OCT. 13	28	21	22	22	28	25	40	15	11	44	42	35
OCT. 14	28	23	24	24	28	25	40	15	11	44	42	35
OCT. 15	28	25	26	26	28	25	40	15	11	44	42	35
OCT. 16	28	27	28	28	27	25	40	15	11	44	42	35
OCT. 17	28	29	30	30	27	25	40	15	11	44	42	35
OCT. 18	28	31	31	32	27	25	40	15	11	44	42	35
OCT. 19	29	33	33	34	27	26	40	15	11	44	42	35
OCT. 20	29	34	35	36	27	26	40	15	11	44	42	35
OCT. 21	29	36	37	37	27	26	40	15	11	44	42	35
OCT. 22	29	38	38	39	27	26	40	15	11	44	42	35
OCT. 23	29	40	40	41	27	26	41	15	11	44	42	35
OCT. 24	29	41	42	42	27	26	41	15	11	44	42	35
OCT. 25	29	43	43	44	27	27	41	15	11	44	42	35
OCT. 26	30	44	45	45	27	27	41	15	11	44	42	35
OCT. 27	30	46	46	47	27	27	41	15	11	44	42	35
OCT. 28	30	48	48	1	27	27	41	15	11	44	42	35
OCT. 29	30	1	2	2	27	27	41	15	11	44	42	35
OCT. 30	30	3	3	4	27	27	41	15	11	44	42	35
OCT. 31	30	4	5	6	28	28	41	15	11	44	42	35

MOON 1 ◖ 12:01 A.M. TO 8:00 A.M.   **MOON 2** ◑ 8:01 A.M. TO 4:00 P.M.   **MOON 3** ● 4:01 P.M. TO 12:00 A.M.

Use only one "moon" number. Choose the column closest to your time of birth. If your place of birth is not on Eastern Standard Time, be sure to read "How to Convert to Eastern Standard Time" at the beginning of this section.

2001

November · December

Date & Time	SUN	MOON 1	MOON 2	MOON 3	MERCURY	VENUS	MARS	JUPITER	SATURN	URANUS	NEPTUNE	PLUTO
NOV. 1	30	6	7	7	28	28	41	15	11	44	42	35
NOV. 2	30	8	8	9	28	28	41	15	11	44	42	35
NOV. 3	31	10	10	11	28	28	42	15	11	44	42	35
NOV. 4	31	11	12	12	28	28	42	15	11	44	42	35
NOV. 5	31	13	14	14	28	28	42	15	11	44	42	35
NOV. 6	31	15	15	16	29	29	42	15	11	44	42	35
NOV. 7	31	17	17	18	29	29	42	15	11	44	42	35
NOV. 8	31	19	19	20	29	29	42	15	11	44	42	35
NOV. 9	31	20	21	22	29	29	42	15	11	44	42	35
NOV. 10	31	22	23	24	29	29	42	15	11	44	42	35
NOV. 11	31	24	25	26	30	29	42	15	11	44	42	35
NOV. 12	32	26	27	27	30	30	42	15	11	44	42	35
NOV. 13	32	28	29	29	30	30	42	15	11	44	42	35
NOV. 14	32	30	31	31	30	30	43	15	11	44	42	35
NOV. 15	32	32	33	33	31	30	43	15	11	44	42	35
NOV. 16	32	34	34	35	31	30	43	15	11	44	42	35
NOV. 17	32	36	36	37	31	30	43	15	11	44	42	35
NOV. 18	32	37	38	38	31	31	43	15	11	44	42	35
NOV. 19	33	39	40	40	31	31	43	15	11	44	42	35
NOV. 20	33	41	41	42	32	31	43	15	11	44	42	35
NOV. 21	33	42	43	43	32	31	43	15	11	44	42	35
NOV. 22	33	44	44	45	32	31	43	15	11	44	42	35
NOV. 23	33	45	46	46	32	31	44	15	11	44	42	35
NOV. 24	33	47	48	48	32	32	44	15	11	44	42	35
NOV. 25	34	1	1	2	33	32	44	15	11	44	42	35
NOV. 26	34	2	3	3	33	32	44	15	11	44	42	35
NOV. 27	34	4	4	5	33	32	44	15	11	44	42	35
NOV. 28	34	6	6	7	33	32	44	15	11	44	42	35
NOV. 29	34	7	8	8	33	32	44	15	11	44	42	35
NOV. 30	34	9	10	10	34	33	44	15	11	44	42	35
DEC. 1	34	11	11	12	34	33	44	15	11	44	42	35
DEC. 2	34	13	13	14	34	33	44	15	11	44	42	35
DEC. 3	35	14	15	16	34	33	44	15	11	44	42	35
DEC. 4	35	16	17	17	35	33	45	15	10	44	42	35
DEC. 5	35	18	19	19	35	33	45	15	10	44	42	35
DEC. 6	35	20	21	21	35	34	45	15	10	44	42	35
DEC. 7	35	22	23	23	35	34	45	15	10	44	42	35
DEC. 8	35	24	24	25	35	34	45	15	10	44	42	35
DEC. 9	35	26	26	27	36	34	45	15	10	44	42	35
DEC. 10	35	28	28	29	36	34	45	15	10	44	42	35
DEC. 11	36	29	30	31	36	34	45	15	10	44	42	35
DEC. 12	36	31	32	32	36	35	45	15	10	44	42	35
DEC. 13	36	33	34	34	36	35	45	15	10	44	42	35
DEC. 14	36	35	35	36	37	35	45	15	10	44	42	35
DEC. 15	36	37	37	38	37	35	46	15	10	44	42	35
DEC. 16	36	38	39	39	37	35	46	15	10	44	42	35
DEC. 17	36	40	41	41	37	35	46	15	10	44	42	35
DEC. 18	36	42	42	43	37	36	46	15	10	44	42	35
DEC. 19	37	43	44	44	38	36	46	15	10	44	42	35
DEC. 20	37	45	45	46	38	36	46	15	10	44	42	35
DEC. 21	37	46	47	48	38	36	46	15	10	44	42	35
DEC. 22	37	48	1	1	38	36	46	15	10	44	42	35
DEC. 23	37	2	2	3	39	36	46	15	10	44	42	35
DEC. 24	37	3	3	4	39	37	46	15	10	44	42	35
DEC. 25	37	5	5	6	39	37	47	15	10	44	42	35
DEC. 26	38	7	7	8	39	37	47	14	10	44	42	35
DEC. 27	38	8	9	9	39	37	47	14	10	44	42	35
DEC. 28	38	10	11	11	40	37	47	14	10	44	42	35
DEC. 29	38	12	12	13	40	37	47	14	10	44	42	35
DEC. 30	38	14	14	15	40	38	47	14	10	44	42	35
DEC. 31	38	16	16	17	40	38	47	14	10	44	42	35

MOON 1 ◗ 12:01 A.M. TO 8:00 A.M.   **MOON 2** ◑ 8:01 A.M. TO 4:00 P.M.   **MOON 3** ● 4:01 P.M. TO 12:00 A.M.

Use only one "moon" number. Choose the column closest to your time of birth. If your place of birth is not on Eastern Standard Time, be sure to read "How to Convert to Eastern Standard Time" at the beginning of this section.

2002

January

Date & Time	SUN	MOON 1	MOON 2	MOON 3	MERCURY	VENUS	MARS	JUPITER	SATURN	URANUS	NEPTUNE	PLUTO
JAN. 1	38	18	18	19	40	38	47	14	10	44	42	35
JAN. 2	38	19	20	21	41	38	47	14	10	44	42	35
JAN. 3	39	21	22	23	41	38	47	14	10	44	42	35
JAN. 4	39	23	24	25	41	38	48	14	10	44	42	35
JAN. 5	39	25	26	27	41	39	48	14	10	44	42	35
JAN. 6	39	27	28	28	41	39	48	14	10	44	42	35
JAN. 7	39	29	30	30	42	39	48	14	10	44	42	35
JAN. 8	39	31	31	32	42	39	48	14	10	44	42	35
JAN. 9	39	33	33	34	42	39	48	14	10	44	42	35
JAN. 10	40	34	35	36	42	39	48	14	10	44	42	35
JAN. 11	40	36	37	37	42	40	48	14	10	44	42	35
JAN. 12	40	38	38	39	42	40	48	14	10	44	42	35
JAN. 13	40	39	40	41	43	40	48	14	10	44	42	35
JAN. 14	40	41	42	42	43	40	1	14	10	44	42	35
JAN. 15	40	43	43	44	43	40	1	14	10	44	42	35
JAN. 16	40	44	45	45	43	40	1	14	10	44	42	35
JAN. 17	41	46	46	47	43	41	1	14	10	44	42	35
JAN. 18	41	48	48	1	43	41	1	14	10	44	42	35
JAN. 19	41	1	2	2	43	41	1	14	10	44	42	35
JAN. 20	41	3	3	4	43	41	1	14	10	44	42	35
JAN. 21	41	4	5	5	43	41	1	14	10	44	42	35
JAN. 22	41	6	6	7	43	41	1	14	10	44	42	35
JAN. 23	42	8	8	9	43	42	1	14	10	44	42	35
JAN. 24	42	9	10	10	43	42	1	14	10	44	42	35
JAN. 25	42	11	12	12	42	42	2	14	10	44	42	35
JAN. 26	42	13	13	14	42	42	2	14	10	44	42	35
JAN. 27	42	15	15	16	42	42	2	14	10	44	42	35
JAN. 28	42	17	17	18	42	42	2	14	10	44	42	35
JAN. 29	42	19	19	20	42	43	2	14	10	44	42	35
JAN. 30	42	21	21	22	42	43	2	14	10	44	42	35
JAN. 31	43	23	23	24	41	43	2	14	10	44	42	35

February

Date & Time	SUN	MOON 1	MOON 2	MOON 3	MERCURY	VENUS	MARS	JUPITER	SATURN	URANUS	NEPTUNE	PLUTO
FEB. 1	43	25	25	26	41	43	2	14	10	44	42	35
FEB. 2	43	27	27	28	41	43	2	14	10	44	42	35
FEB. 3	43	29	29	30	41	43	2	14	10	44	42	35
FEB. 4	43	30	31	32	41	44	3	14	10	44	42	35
FEB. 5	43	32	33	33	41	44	3	14	10	44	42	35
FEB. 6	43	34	35	35	41	44	3	14	10	44	42	35
FEB. 7	43	36	36	37	41	44	3	14	10	44	42	35
FEB. 8	44	37	38	38	41	44	3	14	10	44	42	35
FEB. 9	44	39	40	40	41	44	3	14	10	44	42	35
FEB. 10	44	41	41	42	41	45	3	14	10	44	42	35
FEB. 11	44	42	43	43	41	45	3	14	10	44	42	35
FEB. 12	44	44	44	45	41	45	3	14	10	44	42	35
FEB. 13	44	46	46	47	41	45	3	14	10	44	42	35
FEB. 14	44	47	48	48	41	45	3	14	10	44	42	35
FEB. 15	44	1	1	2	41	45	4	14	10	44	42	35
FEB. 16	45	2	3	3	41	46	4	14	10	44	42	35
FEB. 17	45	4	4	5	41	46	4	14	10	44	42	35
FEB. 18	45	5	6	7	41	46	4	14	10	44	42	35
FEB. 19	45	7	8	8	41	46	4	14	10	44	42	35
FEB. 20	45	9	9	10	42	46	4	14	10	44	42	35
FEB. 21	45	10	11	12	42	46	4	14	10	44	42	35
FEB. 22	45	12	13	13	42	47	4	14	10	44	42	35
FEB. 23	46	14	15	15	42	47	4	14	10	44	42	35
FEB. 24	46	16	16	17	42	47	4	14	10	44	42	35
FEB. 25	46	18	18	19	42	47	5	14	10	44	42	35
FEB. 26	46	20	20	21	42	47	5	14	10	44	42	35
FEB. 27	46	22	22	23	43	47	5	14	10	44	42	35
FEB. 28	46	24	24	25	43	48	5	14	10	44	42	35

MOON 1 ☽ 12:01 A.M. TO 8:00 A.M.   **MOON 2** ☽ 8:01 A.M. TO 4:00 P.M.   **MOON 3** ● 4:01 P.M. TO 12:00 A.M.
Use only one "moon" number. Choose the column closest to your time of birth. If your place of birth is not on Eastern Standard Time, be sure to read "How to Convert to Eastern Standard Time" at the beginning of this section.

2002

March

Date & Time	SUN	MOON 1	MOON 2	MOON 3	MERCURY	VENUS	MARS	JUPITER	SATURN	URANUS	NEPTUNE	PLUTO
MAR. 1	46	26	27	27	43	48	5	14	10	44	42	35
MAR. 2	46	28	28	29	43	48	5	14	10	44	42	35
MAR. 3	47	30	30	31	43	48	5	14	10	44	42	35
MAR. 4	47	32	32	33	43	48	5	14	10	44	42	35
MAR. 5	47	33	34	35	44	48	5	14	10	44	42	35
MAR. 6	47	35	36	36	44	1	5	14	10	44	42	35
MAR. 7	47	37	38	38	44	1	5	14	10	44	42	35
MAR. 8	47	39	39	40	44	1	6	14	10	44	42	35
MAR. 9	47	40	41	41	44	1	6	14	10	44	42	35
MAR. 10	47	42	42	43	45	1	6	14	10	44	42	35
MAR. 11	48	44	44	45	45	1	6	14	10	44	42	35
MAR. 12	48	45	46	46	45	2	6	14	10	44	42	35
MAR. 13	48	47	47	48	45	2	6	14	10	44	42	35
MAR. 14	48	48	1	1	45	2	6	14	10	44	42	35
MAR. 15	48	2	2	3	46	2	6	14	10	44	42	35
MAR. 16	48	3	4	5	46	2	6	14	10	45	42	35
MAR. 17	48	5	6	6	46	2	6	14	10	45	42	35
MAR. 18	48	7	7	8	46	3	7	14	10	45	42	35
MAR. 19	1	8	9	9	47	3	7	14	10	45	42	35
MAR. 20	1	10	10	11	47	3	7	14	10	45	42	35
MAR. 21	1	12	12	13	47	3	7	14	10	45	42	35
MAR. 22	1	13	14	15	47	3	7	14	10	45	42	35
MAR. 23	1	15	16	16	47	3	7	14	10	45	42	35
MAR. 24	1	17	18	18	48	4	7	14	10	45	42	35
MAR. 25	2	19	20	20	48	4	7	14	10	45	42	35
MAR. 26	2	21	21	22	48	4	7	14	10	45	42	35
MAR. 27	2	23	24	24	48	4	7	14	10	45	42	35
MAR. 28	2	25	26	26	1	4	7	14	10	45	42	35
MAR. 29	2	27	28	28	1	4	8	14	10	45	42	35
MAR. 30	2	29	30	30	1	5	8	14	10	45	42	35
MAR. 31	2	31	32	32	1	5	8	14	10	45	42	35

April

Date & Time	SUN	MOON 1	MOON 2	MOON 3	MERCURY	VENUS	MARS	JUPITER	SATURN	URANUS	NEPTUNE	PLUTO
APR. 1	2	33	33	34	2	5	8	14	10	45	42	35
APR. 2	2	35	35	36	2	5	8	14	10	45	42	35
APR. 3	3	36	37	38	2	5	8	14	10	45	42	35
APR. 4	3	38	39	39	2	5	8	14	10	45	42	35
APR. 5	3	40	40	41	3	6	8	14	10	45	42	35
APR. 6	3	42	42	43	3	6	8	14	10	45	42	35
APR. 7	3	43	44	44	3	6	8	14	10	45	42	35
APR. 8	3	45	45	46	4	6	8	14	10	45	42	35
APR. 9	3	46	47	47	4	6	9	14	10	45	42	35
APR. 10	3	48	48	1	4	6	9	14	10	45	42	35
APR. 11	4	1	2	3	4	7	9	14	10	45	42	35
APR. 12	4	3	4	4	4	7	9	14	10	45	42	35
APR. 13	4	5	5	6	5	7	9	14	11	45	42	35
APR. 14	4	6	7	7	5	7	9	14	11	45	42	35
APR. 15	4	8	8	9	5	7	9	14	11	45	42	35
APR. 16	4	10	10	11	6	7	9	14	11	45	42	35
APR. 17	4	11	12	12	6	8	9	14	11	45	42	35
APR. 18	4	13	13	14	6	8	9	14	11	45	42	35
APR. 19	5	15	15	16	7	8	9	14	11	45	42	35
APR. 20	5	16	17	18	7	8	10	14	11	45	42	35
APR. 21	5	18	19	19	7	8	10	14	11	45	42	35
APR. 22	5	20	21	21	7	8	10	14	11	45	42	35
APR. 23	5	22	23	23	8	9	10	14	11	45	42	35
APR. 24	5	24	25	25	8	9	10	14	11	45	42	35
APR. 25	6	26	27	27	8	9	10	14	11	45	42	35
APR. 26	6	28	29	29	8	9	10	14	11	45	42	35
APR. 27	6	30	31	31	8	9	10	14	11	45	42	35
APR. 28	6	32	33	33	9	9	10	14	11	45	42	35
APR. 29	6	34	35	35	9	10	10	14	11	45	42	35
APR. 30	6	36	36	37	9	10	10	14	11	45	42	35

MOON 1 ◐ 12:01 A.M. TO 8:00 A.M.   **MOON 2** ◑ 8:01 A.M. TO 4:00 P.M.   **MOON 3** ● 4:01 P.M. TO 12:00 A.M.

Use only one "moon" number. Choose the column closest to your time of birth. If your place of birth is not on Eastern Standard Time, be sure to read "How to Convert to Eastern Standard Time" at the beginning of this section.

Date & Time	SUN	MOON 1	MOON 2	MOON 3	MERCURY	VENUS	MARS	JUPITER	SATURN	URANUS	NEPTUNE	PLUTO
MAY 1	6	38	38	39	9	10	11	14	11	45	42	35
MAY 2	6	39	40	40	9	10	11	14	11	45	42	35
MAY 3	7	41	42	42	9	10	11	14	11	45	42	35
MAY 4	7	43	43	44	10	10	11	14	11	45	42	35
MAY 5	7	44	45	45	10	10	11	15	11	45	42	35
MAY 6	7	46	46	47	10	11	11	15	11	45	42	35
MAY 7	7	47	48	48	10	11	11	15	11	45	42	35
MAY 8	7	1	2	2	10	11	11	15	11	45	42	35
MAY 9	7	3	3	4	10	11	11	15	11	45	42	35
MAY 10	7	4	5	5	10	11	11	15	11	45	42	35
MAY 11	8	6	6	7	10	11	11	15	11	45	42	35
MAY 12	8	7	8	9	10	12	12	15	11	45	42	35
MAY 13	8	9	10	10	10	12	12	15	11	45	42	35
MAY 14	8	11	11	12	10	12	12	15	11	45	42	35
MAY 15	8	12	13	14	10	12	12	15	11	45	42	35
MAY 16	8	14	15	15	10	12	12	15	11	45	42	35
MAY 17	8	16	17	17	10	12	12	15	11	45	42	35
MAY 18	8	18	18	19	10	13	12	15	11	45	42	35
MAY 19	9	20	20	21	10	13	12	15	11	45	42	35
MAY 20	9	22	22	23	10	13	12	15	11	45	42	35
MAY 21	9	23	24	25	10	13	12	15	11	45	42	35
MAY 22	9	25	26	27	10	13	12	15	11	45	42	35
MAY 23	9	27	28	29	10	13	12	15	11	45	42	35
MAY 24	9	29	30	31	10	14	13	15	11	45	42	35
MAY 25	10	31	32	32	10	14	13	15	11	45	42	35
MAY 26	10	33	34	34	10	14	13	15	11	45	42	35
MAY 27	10	35	36	36	10	14	13	15	11	45	42	35
MAY 28	10	37	37	38	10	14	13	15	11	45	42	35
MAY 29	10	39	39	40	10	14	13	15	11	45	42	35
MAY 30	10	40	41	41	10	15	13	15	11	45	42	35
MAY 31	10	42	43	43	9	15	13	15	11	45	42	35

Date & Time	SUN	MOON 1	MOON 2	MOON 3	MERCURY	VENUS	MARS	JUPITER	SATURN	URANUS	NEPTUNE	PLUTO
JUN. 1	10	44	44	45	9	15	13	15	11	45	42	35
JUN. 2	10	45	46	46	9	15	13	15	11	45	42	35
JUN. 3	11	47	47	48	9	15	13	15	11	45	42	35
JUN. 4	11	1	1	2	9	15	14	15	11	45	42	35
JUN. 5	11	2	3	3	9	15	14	15	11	45	42	35
JUN. 6	11	4	5	5	9	16	14	15	11	45	42	35
JUN. 7	11	5	6	6	9	16	14	15	11	45	42	35
JUN. 8	11	7	7	8	9	16	14	15	11	45	42	35
JUN. 9	11	9	9	10	9	16	14	15	11	45	42	35
JUN. 10	11	10	11	11	9	16	14	15	11	45	42	35
JUN. 11	12	12	13	13	9	16	14	15	11	45	42	35
JUN. 12	12	14	14	15	9	17	14	15	11	45	42	35
JUN. 13	12	16	16	17	9	17	14	15	11	45	42	35
JUN. 14	12	17	18	19	9	17	14	16	12	45	42	35
JUN. 15	12	19	20	20	9	17	15	16	12	45	42	35
JUN. 16	12	21	22	22	9	17	15	16	12	45	42	35
JUN. 17	12	23	24	24	10	17	15	16	12	45	42	35
JUN. 18	12	25	26	26	10	17	15	16	12	45	42	35
JUN. 19	13	27	27	28	10	18	15	16	12	45	42	35
JUN. 20	13	29	29	30	10	18	15	16	12	45	42	35
JUN. 21	13	31	31	32	10	18	15	16	12	45	42	35
JUN. 22	13	32	33	34	10	18	15	16	12	45	42	35
JUN. 23	13	34	35	36	10	18	15	16	12	45	42	35
JUN. 24	13	36	37	37	10	18	15	16	12	45	42	35
JUN. 25	14	38	39	39	10	19	15	16	12	45	42	35
JUN. 26	14	40	40	41	11	19	15	16	12	45	42	35
JUN. 27	14	41	42	43	11	19	16	16	12	45	42	35
JUN. 28	14	43	44	44	11	19	16	16	12	45	42	35
JUN. 29	14	45	45	46	11	19	16	16	12	45	42	35
JUN. 30	14	46	47	47	11	19	16	16	12	45	42	35

MOON 1 ☾ 12:01 A.M. TO 8:00 A.M.   **MOON 2** ☽ 8:01 A.M. TO 4:00 P.M.   **MOON 3** ● 4:01 P.M. TO 12:00 A.M.
Use only one "moon" number. Choose the column closest to your time of birth. If your place of birth is not on Eastern Standard Time, be sure to read "How to Convert to Eastern Standard Time" at the beginning of this section.

Date & Time	SUN	MOON 1	MOON 2	MOON 3	MERCURY	VENUS	MARS	JUPITER	SATURN	URANUS	NEPTUNE	PLUTO
JUL. 1	14	48	1	1	12	19	16	16	12	45	42	35
JUL. 2	14	2	2	3	12	20	16	16	12	45	42	35
JUL. 3	15	3	4	4	12	20	16	16	12	45	42	35
JUL. 4	15	5	5	6	12	20	16	16	12	45	42	35
JUL. 5	15	6	7	7	12	20	16	16	12	45	42	35
JUL. 6	15	8	9	9	13	20	16	16	12	45	42	35
JUL. 7	15	10	10	11	13	20	16	16	12	45	42	35
JUL. 8	15	11	12	13	13	21	17	16	12	45	42	35
JUL. 9	15	13	14	14	13	21	17	16	12	45	42	35
JUL. 10	15	15	16	16	14	21	17	16	12	45	42	35
JUL. 11	16	17	17	18	14	21	17	16	12	45	42	35
JUL. 12	16	19	19	20	14	21	17	16	12	45	42	35
JUL. 13	16	21	21	22	14	21	17	16	12	45	42	35
JUL. 14	16	23	23	24	15	21	17	16	12	45	42	35
JUL. 15	16	24	25	26	15	22	17	16	12	45	42	35
JUL. 16	16	26	27	28	15	22	17	16	12	45	42	35
JUL. 17	16	28	29	29	16	22	17	17	12	45	42	35
JUL. 18	16	30	31	16	16	22	17	17	12	45	42	35
JUL. 19	17	32	33	33	16	22	17	17	12	45	42	35
JUL. 20	17	34	34	35	16	22	18	17	12	45	42	35
JUL. 21	17	36	36	37	17	23	18	17	12	45	42	35
JUL. 22	17	37	38	39	17	23	18	17	12	45	42	35
JUL. 23	17	39	40	40	17	23	18	17	12	45	42	35
JUL. 24	17	41	41	18	18	23	18	17	12	45	42	35
JUL. 25	17	43	43	44	18	23	18	17	12	45	42	35
JUL. 26	18	44	45	45	18	23	18	17	12	45	42	35
JUL. 27	18	46	46	47	18	23	18	17	12	45	42	35
JUL. 28	18	47	48	1	19	24	18	17	12	45	42	35
JUL. 29	18	1	2	2	19	24	18	17	12	45	42	35
JUL. 30	18	3	3	4	19	24	18	17	12	45	42	35
JUL. 31	18	4	5	5	19	24	18	17	12	45	42	35

Date & Time	SUN	MOON 1	MOON 2	MOON 3	MERCURY	VENUS	MARS	JUPITER	SATURN	URANUS	NEPTUNE	PLUTO
AUG. 1	18	6	6	7	20	24	19	17	12	45	42	35
AUG. 2	18	7	8	9	20	24	19	17	12	45	42	35
AUG. 3	19	9	10	10	20	24	19	17	12	45	42	35
AUG. 4	19	11	11	12	20	25	19	17	12	45	42	35
AUG. 5	19	12	13	14	21	25	19	17	12	45	42	35
AUG. 6	19	14	15	15	21	25	19	17	12	45	42	35
AUG. 7	19	16	17	17	21	25	19	17	12	45	42	35
AUG. 8	19	18	19	19	21	25	19	17	12	45	42	35
AUG. 9	19	20	21	21	22	25	19	17	12	45	42	35
AUG. 10	19	22	23	23	22	25	19	17	12	45	42	35
AUG. 11	20	24	25	25	22	25	19	17	12	45	42	35
AUG. 12	20	26	26	27	22	26	19	17	12	45	42	35
AUG. 13	20	28	28	29	22	26	20	17	12	45	42	35
AUG. 14	20	30	30	31	23	26	20	17	12	45	42	35
AUG. 15	20	32	32	33	23	26	20	17	12	45	42	35
AUG. 16	20	33	34	35	23	26	20	17	12	45	42	35
AUG. 17	20	35	36	36	23	26	20	17	13	45	42	35
AUG. 18	20	37	38	38	23	26	20	17	13	45	42	35
AUG. 19	21	39	39	40	24	27	20	17	13	45	42	35
AUG. 20	21	40	41	42	24	27	20	18	13	45	42	35
AUG. 21	21	42	43	43	24	27	20	18	13	45	42	35
AUG. 22	21	44	44	45	24	27	20	18	13	45	42	35
AUG. 23	21	45	46	46	24	27	20	18	13	45	42	35
AUG. 24	21	47	48	48	25	27	21	18	13	45	42	35
AUG. 25	21	1	1	2	25	27	21	18	13	45	42	35
AUG. 26	22	2	3	3	25	27	21	18	13	45	42	35
AUG. 27	22	4	4	5	25	28	21	18	13	45	42	35
AUG. 28	22	5	6	7	25	28	21	18	13	45	42	35
AUG. 29	22	7	7	8	25	28	21	18	13	44	42	35
AUG. 30	22	9	9	10	25	28	21	18	13	44	42	35
AUG. 31	22	10	11	11	26	28	21	18	13	44	42	35

MOON 1 ☽ 12:01 A.M. TO 8:00 A.M.   **MOON 2** ◑ 8:01 A.M. TO 4:00 P.M.   **MOON 3** ● 4:01 P.M. TO 12:00 A.M.
Use only one "moon" number. Choose the column closest to your time of birth. If your place of birth is not on
Eastern Standard Time, be sure to read "How to Convert to Eastern Standard Time" at the beginning of this section.

2002

September — October

Date & Time	SUN	MOON 1	MOON 2	MOON 3	MERCURY	VENUS	MARS	JUPITER	SATURN	URANUS	NEPTUNE	PLUTO
SEP. 1	22	12	12	13	26	28	21	18	13	44	42	35
SEP. 2	22	14	14	15	26	28	21	18	13	44	42	35
SEP. 3	23	15	16	17	26	28	21	18	13	44	42	35
SEP. 4	23	17	18	18	26	29	21	18	13	44	42	35
SEP. 5	23	19	20	20	26	29	22	18	13	44	42	35
SEP. 6	23	21	22	22	26	29	22	18	13	44	42	35
SEP. 7	23	23	24	24	26	29	22	18	13	44	42	35
SEP. 8	23	25	26	26	26	29	22	18	13	44	42	35
SEP. 9	23	27	28	28	27	29	22	18	13	44	42	35
SEP. 10	23	29	30	30	27	29	22	18	13	44	42	35
SEP. 11	24	31	32	32	27	29	22	18	13	44	42	35
SEP. 12	24	33	34	34	27	29	22	18	13	44	42	35
SEP. 13	24	35	35	36	27	29	22	18	13	44	42	35
SEP. 14	24	37	37	38	27	30	22	18	13	44	42	35
SEP. 15	24	38	39	39	27	30	22	18	13	44	42	35
SEP. 16	24	40	41	41	27	30	22	18	13	44	42	35
SEP. 17	24	42	42	43	27	30	23	18	13	44	42	35
SEP. 18	24	43	44	44	27	30	23	18	13	44	42	35
SEP. 19	25	45	45	46	27	30	23	18	13	44	42	35
SEP. 20	25	47	47	48	27	30	23	18	13	44	42	35
SEP. 21	25	48	1	1	26	30	23	18	13	44	42	35
SEP. 22	25	2	2	3	26	30	23	18	13	44	42	35
SEP. 23	25	3	4	4	26	30	23	18	13	44	42	35
SEP. 24	25	5	5	6	26	30	23	18	13	44	42	35
SEP. 25	26	6	7	8	26	30	23	18	13	44	42	35
SEP. 26	26	8	9	9	26	31	23	18	13	44	42	35
SEP. 27	26	10	10	11	26	31	23	18	13	44	42	35
SEP. 28	26	11	12	12	25	31	23	19	13	44	42	35
SEP. 29	26	13	14	14	25	31	24	19	13	44	42	35
SEP. 30	26	15	15	16	25	31	24	19	13	44	42	35

Date & Time	SUN	MOON 1	MOON 2	MOON 3	MERCURY	VENUS	MARS	JUPITER	SATURN	URANUS	NEPTUNE	PLUTO
OCT. 1	26	16	17	18	25	31	24	19	13	44	42	35
OCT. 2	26	18	19	20	25	31	24	19	13	44	42	35
OCT. 3	27	20	21	21	25	31	24	19	13	44	42	35
OCT. 4	27	22	23	23	25	31	24	19	13	44	42	35
OCT. 5	27	24	25	25	25	31	24	19	13	44	42	35
OCT. 6	27	26	27	27	25	31	24	19	13	44	42	35
OCT. 7	27	28	29	30	25	31	24	19	13	44	42	35
OCT. 8	27	30	31	32	25	31	24	19	13	44	42	35
OCT. 9	27	32	33	34	25	31	24	19	13	44	42	35
OCT. 10	27	34	35	35	25	31	24	19	13	44	42	35
OCT. 11	28	36	37	37	25	31	25	19	13	44	42	35
OCT. 12	28	38	38	39	25	31	25	19	13	44	42	35
OCT. 13	28	40	40	41	25	31	25	19	13	44	42	35
OCT. 14	28	41	42	42	25	31	25	19	13	44	42	35
OCT. 15	28	43	43	44	25	31	25	19	13	44	42	35
OCT. 16	28	45	45	46	26	31	25	19	13	44	42	35
OCT. 17	28	46	47	47	26	31	25	19	13	44	42	35
OCT. 18	28	48	48	1	26	31	25	19	13	44	42	35
OCT. 19	29	1	2	2	26	31	25	19	13	44	42	35
OCT. 20	29	3	3	4	26	31	25	19	13	44	42	35
OCT. 21	29	5	5	6	27	31	25	19	13	44	42	35
OCT. 22	29	6	7	7	27	31	26	19	13	44	42	35
OCT. 23	29	8	8	9	27	31	26	19	13	44	42	35
OCT. 24	29	9	10	10	27	31	26	19	13	44	42	35
OCT. 25	29	11	11	12	27	31	26	19	13	44	42	35
OCT. 26	30	13	13	14	28	30	26	19	13	44	42	35
OCT. 27	30	14	15	15	28	30	26	19	13	44	42	35
OCT. 28	30	16	17	17	28	30	26	19	13	44	42	35
OCT. 29	30	18	18	19	28	30	26	19	13	44	42	35
OCT. 30	30	19	20	21	29	30	26	19	13	44	42	35
OCT. 31	30	21	22	23	29	30	26	19	13	44	42	35

MOON 1 ☽ 12:01 A.M. TO 8:00 A.M.   **MOON 2** ◐ 8:01 A.M. TO 4:00 P.M.   **MOON 3** ● 4:01 P.M. TO 12:00 A.M.

Use only one "moon" number. Choose the column closest to your time of birth. If your place of birth is not on Eastern Standard Time, be sure to read "How to Convert to Eastern Standard Time" at the beginning of this section.

2002

November

Date & Time	SUN	MOON 1	MOON 2	MOON 3	MERCURY	VENUS	MARS	JUPITER	SATURN	URANUS	NEPTUNE	PLUTO
NOV. 1	30	23	24	25	29	30	26	19	13	44	42	35
NOV. 2	30	25	26	27	29	30	26	19	13	44	42	35
NOV. 3	31	27	28	29	29	30	27	19	13	44	42	35
NOV. 4	31	29	30	31	30	30	27	19	13	44	42	35
NOV. 5	31	31	32	33	30	30	27	19	13	44	42	35
NOV. 6	31	33	34	35	30	30	27	19	13	44	42	35
NOV. 7	31	35	36	37	30	30	27	19	13	44	42	35
NOV. 8	31	37	38	38	31	29	27	19	13	44	42	35
NOV. 9	31	39	40	40	31	29	27	19	13	44	42	35
NOV. 10	31	41	41	42	31	29	27	19	13	44	42	35
NOV. 11	31	42	43	44	31	29	27	19	13	44	42	35
NOV. 12	32	44	45	45	31	29	27	19	13	44	42	35
NOV. 13	32	46	46	47	32	29	27	19	13	44	42	35
NOV. 14	32	47	48	48	32	29	27	19	13	44	42	35
NOV. 15	32	1	1	2	32	29	28	19	13	44	42	35
NOV. 16	32	3	3	4	32	29	28	19	13	44	42	35
NOV. 17	32	4	5	5	32	29	28	19	13	44	42	35
NOV. 18	32	6	6	7	33	29	28	19	13	44	42	35
NOV. 19	33	7	8	8	33	29	28	19	13	44	42	35
NOV. 20	33	9	9	10	33	29	28	19	13	44	42	35
NOV. 21	33	10	11	12	33	29	28	19	13	44	42	35
NOV. 22	33	12	13	13	34	29	28	19	13	44	42	35
NOV. 23	33	14	14	15	34	29	28	19	13	44	42	35
NOV. 24	33	16	16	17	34	29	28	19	13	44	42	35
NOV. 25	34	17	18	18	34	29	28	19	13	44	42	35
NOV. 26	34	19	20	20	34	29	29	19	13	44	42	35
NOV. 27	34	21	21	22	35	29	29	19	13	44	42	35
NOV. 28	34	23	23	24	35	29	29	19	13	44	42	35
NOV. 29	34	25	25	26	35	29	29	19	13	44	42	35
NOV. 30	34	27	27	28	35	29	29	19	13	44	42	35

December

Date & Time	SUN	MOON 1	MOON 2	MOON 3	MERCURY	VENUS	MARS	JUPITER	SATURN	URANUS	NEPTUNE	PLUTO
DEC. 1	34	28	29	30	35	29	29	19	13	44	42	35
DEC. 2	34	30	31	32	36	29	29	19	13	44	42	35
DEC. 3	35	32	33	34	36	29	29	19	13	44	42	35
DEC. 4	35	34	35	36	36	29	29	19	13	44	42	35
DEC. 5	35	36	37	38	36	29	29	19	13	44	42	35
DEC. 6	35	38	39	39	36	30	29	19	13	44	42	35
DEC. 7	35	40	41	41	37	30	29	19	12	44	42	35
DEC. 8	35	42	42	43	37	30	30	19	12	44	42	35
DEC. 9	35	44	44	45	37	30	30	19	12	44	42	35
DEC. 10	35	45	46	46	37	30	30	19	12	44	42	35
DEC. 11	36	47	47	48	37	30	30	19	12	44	42	35
DEC. 12	36	48	1	1	38	30	30	19	12	44	42	35
DEC. 13	36	2	3	3	38	30	30	19	12	44	42	35
DEC. 14	36	4	4	5	38	30	30	19	12	44	42	35
DEC. 15	36	5	6	6	38	30	30	19	12	44	42	35
DEC. 16	36	7	7	8	38	30	30	19	12	44	42	35
DEC. 17	36	8	9	9	39	30	30	19	12	44	42	35
DEC. 18	36	10	11	11	39	31	30	19	12	44	42	35
DEC. 19	37	12	12	13	39	31	30	19	12	44	42	35
DEC. 20	37	13	14	15	39	31	31	19	12	44	42	35
DEC. 21	37	15	16	16	39	31	31	19	12	44	42	35
DEC. 22	37	17	17	18	40	31	31	19	12	44	42	35
DEC. 23	37	19	19	20	40	31	31	19	12	44	42	35
DEC. 24	37	20	21	22	40	31	31	19	12	44	42	35
DEC. 25	37	22	23	23	40	31	31	19	12	44	42	35
DEC. 26	38	24	25	25	40	31	31	19	12	44	42	35
DEC. 27	38	26	27	27	40	32	31	19	12	44	42	35
DEC. 28	38	28	29	29	40	32	31	19	12	44	42	35
DEC. 29	38	30	30	31	41	32	31	19	12	44	42	35
DEC. 30	38	32	32	33	41	32	31	19	12	44	42	35
DEC. 31	38	34	34	35	41	32	32	19	12	44	42	35

MOON 1 ☽ 12:01 A.M. TO 8:00 A.M.   **MOON 2** ☽ 8:01 A.M. TO 4:00 P.M.   **MOON 3** ● 4:01 P.M. TO 12:00 A.M.

Use only one "moon" number. Choose the column closest to your time of birth. If your place of birth is not on Eastern Standard Time, be sure to read "How to Convert to Eastern Standard Time" at the beginning of this section.

2003

January

February

Date & Time	SUN	MOON 1	MOON 2	MOON 3	MERCURY	VENUS	MARS	JUPITER	SATURN	URANUS	NEPTUNE	PLUTO
JAN. 1	38	35	36	37	41	32	32	19	12	44	42	35
JAN. 2	38	37	38	39	41	32	32	19	12	44	42	35
JAN. 3	39	39	40	40	41	32	32	19	12	44	42	35
JAN. 4	39	41	42	42	41	33	32	19	12	44	42	35
JAN. 5	39	43	43	44	41	33	32	19	12	44	42	35
JAN. 6	39	45	45	46	41	33	32	19	12	44	42	35
JAN. 7	39	46	47	47	41	33	32	19	12	45	42	35
JAN. 8	39	48	48	1	40	33	32	19	12	45	42	35
JAN. 9	39	1	2	3	40	33	32	19	12	44	42	35
JAN. 10	40	3	4	4	40	33	32	19	12	44	42	35
JAN. 11	40	5	5	6	40	33	32	19	12	45	42	35
JAN. 12	40	6	7	7	40	34	33	19	12	45	42	35
JAN. 13	40	8	8	9	40	34	33	19	12	45	42	35
JAN. 14	40	9	10	11	39	34	33	19	12	45	42	35
JAN. 15	40	11	12	12	39	34	33	19	12	45	42	35
JAN. 16	40	13	13	14	39	34	33	19	12	45	42	35
JAN. 17	41	14	15	16	39	34	33	19	12	45	42	35
JAN. 18	41	16	17	17	39	34	33	19	12	45	42	35
JAN. 19	41	18	19	19	39	35	33	19	12	45	42	35
JAN. 20	41	20	21	21	39	35	33	19	12	45	42	35
JAN. 21	41	22	22	23	39	35	33	19	12	45	42	35
JAN. 22	41	24	24	25	39	35	33	19	12	45	42	35
JAN. 23	42	26	26	27	39	35	33	19	12	45	42	35
JAN. 24	42	27	28	29	39	35	34	19	12	45	42	36
JAN. 25	42	29	30	31	39	35	34	19	12	45	42	36
JAN. 26	42	31	32	32	39	36	34	19	12	45	42	36
JAN. 27	42	33	34	34	39	36	34	19	12	45	42	36
JAN. 28	42	35	36	36	39	36	34	19	12	45	42	36
JAN. 29	42	37	37	38	39	36	34	19	12	45	42	36
JAN. 30	42	39	39	40	39	36	34	19	12	45	42	36
JAN. 31	43	40	41	42	39	36	34	19	12	45	42	36

Date & Time	SUN	MOON 1	MOON 2	MOON 3	MERCURY	VENUS	MARS	JUPITER	SATURN	URANUS	NEPTUNE	PLUTO
FEB. 1	43	42	43	43	39	36	34	19	12	45	42	36
FEB. 2	43	44	44	45	39	37	34	19	12	45	42	36
FEB. 3	43	46	46	47	39	37	34	19	12	45	42	36
FEB. 4	43	47	48	48	40	37	35	19	12	45	42	36
FEB. 5	43	1	1	2	40	37	35	19	12	45	42	36
FEB. 6	43	3	3	4	40	37	35	19	12	45	42	36
FEB. 7	43	4	5	5	40	37	35	19	12	45	42	36
FEB. 8	44	6	6	7	40	38	35	19	12	45	42	36
FEB. 9	44	7	8	8	40	38	35	19	12	45	42	36
FEB. 10	44	9	9	10	40	38	35	19	12	45	42	36
FEB. 11	44	10	11	12	41	38	35	19	12	45	42	36
FEB. 12	44	12	13	13	41	38	35	19	12	45	42	36
FEB. 13	44	14	14	15	41	38	35	19	12	45	42	36
FEB. 14	44	16	16	17	41	38	35	19	12	45	42	36
FEB. 15	44	17	18	19	41	39	35	18	12	45	42	36
FEB. 16	45	19	20	20	42	39	36	18	12	45	42	36
FEB. 17	45	21	22	22	42	39	36	18	12	45	42	36
FEB. 18	45	23	24	24	42	39	36	18	12	45	42	36
FEB. 19	45	25	26	26	42	39	36	18	12	45	42	36
FEB. 20	45	27	28	28	42	39	36	18	12	45	42	36
FEB. 21	45	29	30	30	42	40	36	18	12	45	42	36
FEB. 22	45	31	31	32	43	40	36	18	12	45	42	36
FEB. 23	46	33	33	34	43	40	36	18	12	45	43	36
FEB. 24	46	35	35	36	43	40	36	18	12	45	43	36
FEB. 25	46	36	37	38	43	40	36	18	12	45	43	36
FEB. 26	46	38	39	39	44	40	36	18	12	45	43	36
FEB. 27	46	40	41	41	44	40	36	18	12	45	43	36
FEB. 28	46	42	42	43	44	41	37	18	12	45	43	36

MOON 1 ◗ 12:01 A.M. TO 8:00 A.M.　　**MOON 2 ◖ 8:01 A.M. TO 4:00 P.M.**　　**MOON 3 ● 4:01 P.M. TO 12:00 A.M.**
Use only one "moon" number. Choose the column closest to your time of birth. If your place of birth is not on Eastern Standard Time, be sure to read "How to Convert to Eastern Standard Time" at the beginning of this section.

2003

March — April

Date & Time	SUN	MOON 1	MOON 2	MOON 3	MERCURY	VENUS	MARS	JUPITER	SATURN	URANUS	NEPTUNE	PLUTO
MAR. 1	46	43	44	45	44	41	37	18	12	45	43	36
MAR. 2	46	45	46	46	44	41	37	18	12	45	43	36
MAR. 3	47	47	47	48	44	41	37	18	12	45	43	36
MAR. 4	47	48	1	1	45	41	37	18	12	45	43	36
MAR. 5	47	2	3	3	45	41	37	18	12	45	43	36
MAR. 6	47	4	4	5	45	42	37	18	12	45	43	36
MAR. 7	47	5	6	6	45	42	37	18	12	45	43	36
MAR. 8	47	7	7	8	46	42	37	18	12	45	43	36
MAR. 9	47	8	9	9	46	42	37	18	12	45	43	36
MAR. 10	47	10	10	11	46	42	37	18	12	45	43	36
MAR. 11	48	12	12	13	46	42	38	18	12	45	43	36
MAR. 12	48	13	14	14	47	42	38	18	12	45	43	36
MAR. 13	48	15	15	16	47	43	38	18	12	45	43	36
MAR. 14	48	17	17	18	47	43	38	18	12	45	43	36
MAR. 15	48	18	19	20	47	43	38	18	12	45	43	36
MAR. 16	48	20	21	22	48	43	38	18	12	45	43	36
MAR. 17	48	22	23	23	48	43	38	18	12	45	43	36
MAR. 18	48	24	25	25	48	43	38	18	12	45	43	36
MAR. 19	1	26	27	27	48	44	38	18	12	45	43	36
MAR. 20	1	28	29	29	1	44	38	18	12	45	43	36
MAR. 21	1	30	31	31	1	44	38	18	12	45	43	36
MAR. 22	1	32	33	33	1	44	38	18	12	45	43	36
MAR. 23	1	34	35	35	1	44	39	18	12	45	43	36
MAR. 24	1	36	37	37	2	44	39	18	12	45	43	36
MAR. 25	2	38	38	39	2	45	39	18	12	45	43	36
MAR. 26	2	40	40	41	2	45	39	18	12	45	43	36
MAR. 27	2	41	42	42	2	45	39	18	12	45	43	36
MAR. 28	2	43	44	44	3	45	39	18	12	45	43	36
MAR. 29	2	45	45	46	3	45	39	18	12	45	43	36
MAR. 30	2	46	47	47	3	45	39	18	12	45	43	36
MAR. 31	2	48	48	1	4	46	39	18	12	45	43	36
APR. 1	2	2	2	3	4	46	39	18	12	45	43	36
APR. 2	2	3	4	4	4	46	39	18	12	45	43	36
APR. 3	3	5	5	6	4	46	39	18	12	45	43	36
APR. 4	3	6	7	7	5	46	40	18	12	45	43	36
APR. 5	3	8	8	9	5	46	40	18	12	45	43	36
APR. 6	3	9	10	11	5	46	40	18	12	45	43	36
APR. 7	3	11	12	12	5	47	40	18	12	45	43	36
APR. 8	3	13	13	14	6	47	40	18	12	45	43	36
APR. 9	3	14	15	15	6	47	40	18	12	45	43	36
APR. 10	3	16	17	17	6	47	40	18	12	45	43	36
APR. 11	4	18	18	19	6	47	40	18	12	45	43	36
APR. 12	4	19	20	21	6	47	40	18	12	45	43	36
APR. 13	4	21	22	23	7	48	40	18	12	45	43	36
APR. 14	4	23	24	25	7	48	40	18	12	45	43	36
APR. 15	4	25	26	27	7	48	40	18	12	45	43	36
APR. 16	4	27	28	29	7	48	40	18	12	45	43	36
APR. 17	4	29	30	31	7	48	41	18	12	45	43	36
APR. 18	4	31	32	33	7	48	41	18	12	45	43	36
APR. 19	5	33	34	35	7	1	41	18	12	45	43	36
APR. 20	5	35	36	37	7	1	41	18	12	45	43	36
APR. 21	5	37	38	38	8	1	41	18	12	45	43	36
APR. 22	5	39	40	40	8	1	41	18	12	45	43	36
APR. 23	5	41	41	42	8	1	41	18	12	45	43	36
APR. 24	5	43	43	44	8	1	41	18	12	45	43	36
APR. 25	6	44	45	45	8	2	41	18	12	45	43	36
APR. 26	6	46	46	47	8	2	41	18	12	45	43	36
APR. 27	6	48	48	1	8	2	41	18	12	45	43	36
APR. 28	6	1	2	2	8	2	41	18	12	45	43	36
APR. 29	6	3	3	4	8	2	42	18	12	45	43	36
APR. 30	6	4	5	5	8	2	42	18	12	45	43	36

MOON 1 ◑ 12:01 A.M. TO 8:00 A.M.   **MOON 2** ◑ 8:01 A.M. TO 4:00 P.M.   **MOON 3** ● 4:01 P.M. TO 12:00 A.M.

Use only one "moon" number. Choose the column closest to your time of birth. If your place of birth is not on Eastern Standard Time, be sure to read "How to Convert to Eastern Standard Time" at the beginning of this section.

2003

May   **June**

Date & Time	SUN	MOON 1	MOON 2	MOON 3	MERCURY	VENUS	MARS	JUPITER	SATURN	URANUS	NEPTUNE	PLUTO
MAY 1	6	6	6	7	8	3	42	18	12	45	43	36
MAY 2	6	7	8	9	8	3	42	18	12	45	43	36
MAY 3	7	9	10	10	7	3	42	18	12	45	43	36
MAY 4	7	11	11	12	7	3	42	18	12	45	43	36
MAY 5	7	12	13	13	7	3	42	18	12	45	43	36
MAY 6	7	14	14	15	7	3	42	18	13	45	43	36
MAY 7	7	16	16	17	7	3	42	18	13	45	43	36
MAY 8	7	17	18	18	7	4	42	18	13	45	43	36
MAY 9	7	19	20	20	7	4	42	18	13	45	43	36
MAY 10	7	21	21	22	7	4	42	18	13	45	43	36
MAY 11	8	23	23	24	7	4	42	18	13	45	43	36
MAY 12	8	24	25	26	7	4	43	18	13	45	43	36
MAY 13	8	26	27	28	7	4	43	18	13	45	43	36
MAY 14	8	28	29	30	7	5	43	18	13	45	43	36
MAY 15	8	30	31	32	7	5	43	18	13	45	43	36
MAY 16	8	32	33	34	7	5	43	18	13	45	43	36
MAY 17	8	34	35	36	7	5	43	18	13	45	43	36
MAY 18	8	36	37	38	6	5	43	18	13	45	43	36
MAY 19	9	38	39	40	6	5	43	18	13	45	43	36
MAY 20	9	40	41	41	6	6	43	18	13	45	43	36
MAY 21	9	42	43	43	6	6	43	18	13	45	43	36
MAY 22	9	44	44	45	6	6	43	18	13	45	43	36
MAY 23	9	45	46	47	6	6	43	19	13	45	43	36
MAY 24	9	47	48	48	6	6	43	19	13	45	43	36
MAY 25	10	1	1	2	6	6	43	19	13	45	43	36
MAY 26	10	2	3	3	7	7	44	19	13	45	43	35
MAY 27	10	4	4	5	7	7	44	19	13	45	43	35
MAY 28	10	6	6	7	7	7	44	19	13	45	43	35
MAY 29	10	7	8	8	7	7	44	19	13	45	43	35
MAY 30	10	9	9	10	7	7	44	19	13	45	43	35
MAY 31	10	10	11	11	7	7	44	19	13	45	43	35
JUN. 1	10	12	12	13	7	8	44	19	13	45	43	35
JUN. 2	10	13	14	15	7	8	44	19	13	45	43	35
JUN. 3	11	15	16	16	7	8	44	19	13	45	43	35
JUN. 4	11	17	17	18	8	8	44	19	13	45	43	35
JUN. 5	11	19	19	20	8	8	44	19	13	45	43	35
JUN. 6	11	20	21	21	8	8	44	19	13	45	43	35
JUN. 7	11	22	23	23	8	8	44	19	13	45	43	35
JUN. 8	11	24	24	25	8	9	44	19	13	45	43	35
JUN. 9	11	26	26	27	8	9	44	19	13	45	43	35
JUN. 10	11	28	28	29	8	9	45	19	13	45	43	35
JUN. 11	12	30	30	31	9	9	45	19	13	45	43	35
JUN. 12	12	32	32	33	9	9	45	19	13	45	43	35
JUN. 13	12	34	34	35	9	9	45	19	13	45	43	35
JUN. 14	12	36	36	37	9	10	45	19	13	45	43	35
JUN. 15	12	37	38	39	9	10	45	19	13	45	43	35
JUN. 16	12	39	40	41	10	10	45	19	13	45	43	35
JUN. 17	12	41	42	43	10	10	45	19	13	45	43	35
JUN. 18	12	43	44	44	10	10	45	19	13	45	43	35
JUN. 19	13	45	45	46	10	10	45	19	13	45	43	35
JUN. 20	13	47	47	48	11	11	45	19	13	45	43	35
JUN. 21	13	48	1	1	11	11	45	19	13	45	43	35
JUN. 22	13	2	2	3	11	11	45	19	13	45	43	35
JUN. 23	13	4	4	5	11	11	45	19	13	45	43	35
JUN. 24	13	5	6	6	12	11	45	19	13	45	43	35
JUN. 25	14	7	7	8	12	11	45	19	13	45	43	35
JUN. 26	14	8	9	9	12	12	45	19	13	45	43	35
JUN. 27	14	10	10	11	12	12	45	19	13	45	43	35
JUN. 28	14	11	12	12	13	12	46	19	13	45	43	35
JUN. 29	14	13	14	14	13	12	46	19	13	45	43	35
JUN. 30	14	15	15	16	13	12	46	19	13	45	43	35

MOON 1 ☽ 12:01 A.M. TO 8:00 A.M.   **MOON 2** ☽ 8:01 A.M. TO 4:00 P.M.   **MOON 3** ● 4:01 P.M. TO 12:00 A.M.
Use only one "moon" number. Choose the column closest to your time of birth. If your place of birth is not on Eastern Standard Time, be sure to read "How to Convert to Eastern Standard Time" at the beginning of this section.

2003

July

Date & Time	SUN	MOON 1	MOON 2	MOON 3	MERCURY	VENUS	MARS	JUPITER	SATURN	URANUS	NEPTUNE	PLUTO
JUL. 1	14	16	17	18	13	12	46	19	13	45	43	35
JUL. 2	14	18	19	19	14	13	46	19	13	45	43	35
JUL. 3	15	20	20	21	14	13	46	19	13	45	43	35
JUL. 4	15	22	22	23	14	13	46	19	13	45	43	35
JUL. 5	15	23	24	25	15	13	46	19	14	45	43	35
JUL. 6	15	25	26	26	15	13	46	19	14	45	43	35
JUL. 7	15	27	28	28	15	13	46	20	14	45	43	35
JUL. 8	15	29	30	30	15	14	46	20	14	45	43	35
JUL. 9	15	31	32	32	16	14	46	20	14	45	43	35
JUL. 10	15	33	33	34	16	14	46	20	14	45	43	35
JUL. 11	16	35	35	36	16	14	46	20	14	45	43	35
JUL. 12	16	37	37	38	17	14	46	20	14	45	43	35
JUL. 13	16	39	39	40	17	14	46	20	14	45	43	35
JUL. 14	16	41	41	42	17	14	46	20	14	45	43	35
JUL. 15	16	42	43	44	17	15	46	20	14	45	43	35
JUL. 16	16	44	45	45	18	15	46	20	14	45	43	35
JUL. 17	16	46	47	47	18	15	46	20	14	45	43	35
JUL. 18	16	48	48	1	18	15	46	20	14	45	43	35
JUL. 19	17	1	2	2	18	15	46	20	14	45	43	35
JUL. 20	17	3	4	4	19	15	46	20	14	45	43	35
JUL. 21	17	5	5	6	19	16	46	20	14	45	43	35
JUL. 22	17	6	7	7	19	16	46	20	14	45	43	35
JUL. 23	17	8	9	9	19	16	46	20	14	45	43	35
JUL. 24	17	9	10	10	20	16	46	20	14	45	43	35
JUL. 25	17	11	11	12	20	16	46	20	14	45	43	35
JUL. 26	18	13	13	14	20	16	46	20	14	45	43	35
JUL. 27	18	14	15	15	20	17	46	20	14	45	43	35
JUL. 28	18	16	16	17	20	17	46	20	14	45	43	35
JUL. 29	18	18	18	19	21	17	46	20	14	45	43	35
JUL. 30	18	19	20	21	21	17	46	20	14	45	43	35
JUL. 31	18	21	22	22	21	17	46	20	14	45	43	35

August

Date & Time	SUN	MOON 1	MOON 2	MOON 3	MERCURY	VENUS	MARS	JUPITER	SATURN	URANUS	NEPTUNE	PLUTO
AUG. 1	18	23	24	24	21	17	46	20	14	45	43	35
AUG. 2	18	25	25	26	21	18	46	20	14	45	43	35
AUG. 3	19	27	27	28	22	18	46	20	14	45	43	35
AUG. 4	19	29	29	30	22	18	46	20	14	45	43	35
AUG. 5	19	30	31	32	22	18	46	20	14	45	43	35
AUG. 6	19	32	33	34	22	18	46	20	14	45	43	35
AUG. 7	19	34	35	35	22	18	46	20	14	45	43	35
AUG. 8	19	36	37	37	23	19	46	20	14	45	43	35
AUG. 9	19	38	39	39	23	19	46	20	14	45	43	35
AUG. 10	19	40	40	41	23	19	46	20	14	45	43	35
AUG. 11	20	42	42	43	23	19	46	20	14	45	43	35
AUG. 12	20	44	44	45	23	19	46	21	14	45	43	35
AUG. 13	20	45	46	46	23	19	46	21	14	45	43	35
AUG. 14	20	47	48	48	23	20	46	21	14	45	43	35
AUG. 15	20	1	1	2	24	20	46	21	14	45	43	35
AUG. 16	20	2	3	4	24	20	46	21	14	45	42	35
AUG. 17	20	4	5	5	24	20	46	21	14	45	42	35
AUG. 18	20	6	6	7	24	20	46	21	14	45	42	35
AUG. 19	21	7	8	8	24	20	46	21	14	45	42	35
AUG. 20	21	9	10	10	24	21	46	21	14	45	42	35
AUG. 21	21	10	11	11	24	21	46	21	14	45	42	35
AUG. 22	21	12	13	13	24	21	46	21	14	45	42	35
AUG. 23	21	14	14	15	24	21	46	21	14	45	42	35
AUG. 24	21	15	16	16	24	21	46	21	14	45	42	35
AUG. 25	21	17	18	18	24	21	46	21	14	45	42	35
AUG. 26	22	19	19	20	24	22	46	21	14	45	42	35
AUG. 27	22	21	21	22	24	22	46	21	14	45	42	35
AUG. 28	22	22	23	24	24	22	46	21	14	45	42	35
AUG. 29	22	24	25	26	24	22	46	21	14	45	42	35
AUG. 30	22	26	27	27	24	22	46	21	14	45	42	35
AUG. 31	22	28	29	29	24	22	46	21	14	45	42	35

MOON 1 ☽ 12:01 A.M. TO 8:00 A.M.   **MOON 2** ☽ 8:01 A.M. TO 4:00 P.M.   **MOON 3** ● 4:01 P.M. TO 12:00 A.M.

Use only one "moon" number. Choose the column closest to your time of birth. If your place of birth is not on Eastern Standard Time, be sure to read "How to Convert to Eastern Standard Time" at the beginning of this section.

2003

September

Date & Time	SUN	MOON 1	MOON 2	MOON 3	MERCURY	VENUS	MARS	JUPITER	SATURN	URANUS	NEPTUNE	PLUTO
SEP. 1	22	30	31	31	24	23	46	21	14	45	42	35
SEP. 2	22	32	33	33	24	23	45	21	14	45	42	35
SEP. 3	23	34	34	35	24	23	45	21	14	45	42	35
SEP. 4	23	36	36	37	24	23	45	21	14	45	42	35
SEP. 5	23	38	38	39	24	23	45	21	14	45	42	35
SEP. 6	23	39	40	41	24	23	45	21	14	45	42	35
SEP. 7	23	41	42	42	24	24	45	21	14	45	42	35
SEP. 8	23	43	44	44	24	24	45	21	14	45	42	35
SEP. 9	23	45	45	46	24	24	45	21	14	45	42	35
SEP. 10	23	46	47	48	23	24	45	21	14	45	42	35
SEP. 11	24	48	1	1	23	24	45	21	14	45	42	35
SEP. 12	24	2	2	3	23	24	45	21	15	45	42	35
SEP. 13	24	3	4	5	23	25	45	21	15	45	42	35
SEP. 14	24	5	6	6	23	25	45	21	15	45	42	35
SEP. 15	24	7	7	8	23	25	45	22	15	45	42	35
SEP. 16	24	8	9	9	23	25	45	22	15	45	42	35
SEP. 17	24	10	10	11	23	25	45	22	15	45	42	35
SEP. 18	24	11	12	12	23	25	45	22	15	45	42	35
SEP. 19	25	13	14	14	23	26	45	22	15	45	42	35
SEP. 20	25	15	15	16	23	26	45	22	15	45	42	35
SEP. 21	25	16	17	17	23	26	45	22	15	45	42	35
SEP. 22	25	18	19	19	23	26	45	22	15	45	42	35
SEP. 23	25	20	20	21	23	26	45	22	15	45	42	35
SEP. 24	25	22	22	23	23	26	45	22	15	45	42	35
SEP. 25	26	24	24	25	23	27	45	22	15	45	42	35
SEP. 26	26	25	26	27	23	27	45	22	15	45	42	35
SEP. 27	26	27	28	29	23	27	45	22	15	45	42	35
SEP. 28	26	29	30	31	23	27	45	22	15	45	42	35
SEP. 29	26	31	32	33	23	27	45	22	15	45	42	35
SEP. 30	26	33	34	35	24	27	45	22	15	45	42	35

October

Date & Time	SUN	MOON 1	MOON 2	MOON 3	MERCURY	VENUS	MARS	JUPITER	SATURN	URANUS	NEPTUNE	PLUTO
OCT. 1	26	35	36	36	24	28	45	22	15	45	42	35
OCT. 2	26	37	38	38	24	28	45	22	15	45	42	35
OCT. 3	27	39	40	40	24	28	45	22	15	45	42	35
OCT. 4	27	41	41	42	24	28	45	22	15	45	42	35
OCT. 5	27	43	43	44	25	28	45	22	15	45	42	35
OCT. 6	27	44	45	45	25	28	45	22	15	45	42	35
OCT. 7	27	46	47	47	25	29	45	22	15	45	42	35
OCT. 8	27	48	48	1	25	29	45	22	15	45	42	35
OCT. 9	27	1	2	2	25	29	45	22	15	45	42	35
OCT. 10	27	3	4	4	26	29	45	22	15	45	42	35
OCT. 11	28	5	5	6	26	29	45	22	15	45	42	35
OCT. 12	28	6	7	7	26	29	45	22	15	45	42	35
OCT. 13	28	8	8	9	26	30	45	22	15	45	42	35
OCT. 14	28	9	10	10	27	30	45	22	15	45	42	35
OCT. 15	28	11	11	12	27	30	45	22	15	45	42	35
OCT. 16	28	13	13	14	27	30	45	22	15	45	42	35
OCT. 17	28	14	15	15	27	30	45	22	15	45	42	35
OCT. 18	28	16	16	17	28	30	45	22	15	45	42	35
OCT. 19	29	17	18	19	28	31	45	22	15	45	42	35
OCT. 20	29	19	20	20	28	31	45	22	15	45	42	35
OCT. 21	29	21	21	22	28	31	45	22	15	45	42	35
OCT. 22	29	23	23	24	28	31	45	22	15	45	42	35
OCT. 23	29	25	25	26	29	31	46	23	15	45	42	35
OCT. 24	29	27	27	28	29	31	46	23	15	45	42	35
OCT. 25	29	29	29	30	29	32	46	23	15	45	42	35
OCT. 26	30	31	31	32	29	32	46	23	15	45	42	35
OCT. 27	30	33	33	34	30	32	46	23	15	45	42	35
OCT. 28	30	35	35	36	30	32	46	23	15	45	42	35
OCT. 29	30	37	37	38	30	32	46	23	15	45	42	35
OCT. 30	30	38	39	40	30	32	46	23	15	45	42	35
OCT. 31	30	40	41	42	30	33	46	23	15	45	42	35

MOON 1 ☽ 12:01 A.M. TO 8:00 A.M.   **MOON 2** ☽ 8:01 A.M. TO 4:00 P.M.   **MOON 3** ● 4:01 P.M. TO 12:00 A.M.

Use only one "moon" number. Choose the column closest to your time of birth. If your place of birth is not on Eastern Standard Time, be sure to read "How to Convert to Eastern Standard Time" at the beginning of this section.

2003

November

Date & Time	SUN	MOON 1	MOON 2	MOON 3	MERCURY	VENUS	MARS	JUPITER	SATURN	URANUS	NEPTUNE	PLUTO
NOV. 1	30	42	43	43	31	33	46	23	15	45	42	35
NOV. 2	30	44	44	45	31	33	46	23	15	45	42	35
NOV. 3	31	46	46	47	31	33	46	23	15	45	42	35
NOV. 4	31	47	48	48	31	33	46	23	15	45	42	35
NOV. 5	31	1	2	2	31	33	46	23	15	45	42	35
NOV. 6	31	3	3	4	32	34	46	23	15	45	42	35
NOV. 7	31	4	5	5	32	34	46	23	15	45	42	35
NOV. 8	31	6	6	7	32	34	46	23	15	45	42	35
NOV. 9	31	7	8	8	32	34	46	23	15	45	42	35
NOV. 10	31	9	9	10	33	34	46	23	15	45	42	35
NOV. 11	31	11	11	12	33	34	47	23	15	45	42	35
NOV. 12	32	12	13	13	33	35	47	23	15	45	42	35
NOV. 13	32	14	14	15	33	35	47	23	15	45	42	35
NOV. 14	32	15	16	16	33	35	47	23	15	45	42	35
NOV. 15	32	17	17	18	34	35	47	23	15	45	42	35
NOV. 16	32	19	19	20	34	35	47	23	15	45	42	35
NOV. 17	32	20	21	21	34	35	47	23	15	45	42	35
NOV. 18	32	22	23	23	34	35	47	23	15	45	42	35
NOV. 19	33	24	24	25	34	35	47	23	15	45	42	35
NOV. 20	33	26	26	27	35	35	47	23	15	45	42	35
NOV. 21	33	28	28	29	35	35	47	23	15	45	42	35
NOV. 22	33	30	30	31	35	35	47	23	15	45	42	36
NOV. 23	33	32	32	33	35	35	47	23	15	45	42	36
NOV. 24	33	34	34	35	35	35	47	23	15	45	42	36
NOV. 25	34	36	36	37	36	37	47	23	15	45	42	36
NOV. 26	34	38	38	39	36	37	47	23	15	45	42	36
NOV. 27	34	40	40	41	36	37	48	23	15	45	42	36
NOV. 28	34	42	42	43	36	37	48	23	15	45	42	36
NOV. 29	34	43	44	45	36	37	48	23	15	45	42	36
NOV. 30	34	45	46	46	36	37	48	23	15	45	42	36

December

Date & Time	SUN	MOON 1	MOON 2	MOON 3	MERCURY	VENUS	MARS	JUPITER	SATURN	URANUS	NEPTUNE	PLUTO
DEC. 1	34	47	47	48	37	38	48	23	15	45	42	36
DEC. 2	34	1	1	2	37	38	48	23	15	45	42	36
DEC. 3	35	2	3	3	37	38	48	23	15	45	42	36
DEC. 4	35	4	4	5	37	38	48	23	15	45	42	36
DEC. 5	35	5	6	6	37	38	48	23	15	45	42	36
DEC. 6	35	7	7	8	38	38	48	23	15	45	42	36
DEC. 7	35	9	9	10	38	39	48	23	15	45	42	36
DEC. 8	35	10	11	11	38	39	48	23	15	45	42	36
DEC. 9	35	12	12	13	38	39	48	23	15	45	42	36
DEC. 10	35	13	14	14	38	39	48	23	14	45	42	36
DEC. 11	36	15	15	16	38	39	1	23	14	45	42	36
DEC. 12	36	17	17	18	38	39	1	23	14	45	42	36
DEC. 13	36	18	19	19	38	40	1	23	14	45	42	36
DEC. 14	36	20	20	21	39	40	1	23	14	45	42	36
DEC. 15	36	22	22	23	39	40	1	23	14	45	42	36
DEC. 16	36	23	24	24	39	40	1	23	14	45	42	36
DEC. 17	36	25	26	26	39	40	1	23	14	45	42	36
DEC. 18	36	27	28	28	39	40	1	23	14	45	42	36
DEC. 19	37	29	29	30	39	41	1	23	14	45	42	36
DEC. 20	37	31	31	32	39	41	1	23	14	45	42	36
DEC. 21	37	33	33	34	38	41	1	23	14	45	42	36
DEC. 22	37	35	35	36	38	41	1	23	14	45	42	36
DEC. 23	37	37	37	38	38	41	1	23	14	45	42	36
DEC. 24	37	39	39	40	38	41	2	23	14	45	42	36
DEC. 25	37	41	41	42	38	42	2	23	14	45	42	36
DEC. 26	38	43	43	44	38	42	2	23	14	45	43	36
DEC. 27	38	44	45	46	38	42	2	23	14	45	43	36
DEC. 28	38	46	47	47	37	42	2	23	14	45	43	36
DEC. 29	38	48	1	1	37	42	2	23	14	45	43	36
DEC. 30	38	2	2	3	37	42	2	23	14	45	43	36
DEC. 31	38	3	4	4	37	43	2	23	14	45	43	36

MOON 1 ☽ 12:01 A.M. TO 8:00 A.M.   **MOON 2** ☽ 8:01 A.M. TO 4:00 P.M.   **MOON 3** ● 4:01 P.M. TO 12:00 A.M.

Use only one "moon" number. Choose the column closest to your time of birth. If your place of birth is not on Eastern Standard Time, be sure to read "How to Convert to Eastern Standard Time" at the beginning of this section.

2004

January

Date & Time	SUN ☀	MOON 1 ☽	MOON 2 ◑	MOON 3 ●	MERCURY	VENUS	MARS	JUPITER	SATURN	URANUS	NEPTUNE	PLUTO
JAN. 1	38	5	5	6	37	43	2	23	14	45	43	36
JAN. 2	38	7	7	8	37	43	2	23	14	45	43	36
JAN. 3	39	8	9	9	37	43	2	23	14	45	43	36
JAN. 4	39	10	10	11	37	43	2	23	14	45	43	36
JAN. 5	39	11	12	12	36	43	3	23	14	45	43	36
JAN. 6	39	13	13	14	36	44	3	23	14	45	43	36
JAN. 7	39	14	15	16	36	44	3	23	14	45	43	36
JAN. 8	39	16	17	17	36	44	3	23	14	45	43	36
JAN. 9	39	18	18	19	37	44	3	23	14	45	43	36
JAN. 10	40	19	20	21	37	44	3	23	14	45	43	36
JAN. 11	40	21	22	22	37	45	3	23	14	45	43	36
JAN. 12	40	23	23	24	37	45	3	23	14	45	43	36
JAN. 13	40	25	25	26	37	45	3	23	14	45	43	36
JAN. 14	40	26	27	28	37	45	3	23	14	45	43	36
JAN. 15	40	28	29	29	37	45	3	23	14	45	43	36
JAN. 16	40	30	31	31	37	45	3	23	14	45	43	36
JAN. 17	41	32	33	33	37	45	4	23	14	45	43	36
JAN. 18	41	34	35	35	37	46	4	23	14	45	43	36
JAN. 19	41	36	37	37	38	46	4	23	14	45	43	36
JAN. 20	41	38	38	39	38	46	4	23	14	45	43	36
JAN. 21	41	40	40	41	38	46	4	23	14	45	43	36
JAN. 22	41	42	42	43	38	46	4	23	14	45	43	36
JAN. 23	42	44	44	45	38	46	4	23	14	45	43	36
JAN. 24	42	46	46	47	38	47	4	23	14	45	43	36
JAN. 25	42	47	48	1	39	47	4	23	14	45	43	36
JAN. 26	42	1	2	2	39	47	4	23	14	45	43	36
JAN. 27	42	3	4	4	39	47	4	23	14	45	43	36
JAN. 28	42	4	5	6	39	47	4	23	14	45	43	36
JAN. 29	42	6	7	7	39	47	5	23	14	45	43	36
JAN. 30	42	8	8	9	39	47	5	23	14	45	43	36
JAN. 31	43	9	10	10	40	48	5	23	14	45	43	36

February

Date & Time	SUN ☀	MOON 1 ☽	MOON 2 ◑	MOON 3 ●	MERCURY	VENUS	MARS	JUPITER	SATURN	URANUS	NEPTUNE	PLUTO
FEB. 1	43	11	11	12	40	48	5	23	14	45	43	36
FEB. 2	43	12	13	13	40	48	5	23	14	45	43	36
FEB. 3	43	14	15	15	40	48	5	23	14	45	43	36
FEB. 4	43	16	16	17	40	48	5	23	14	45	43	36
FEB. 5	43	17	18	18	41	48	5	23	14	45	43	36
FEB. 6	43	19	20	20	41	1	5	23	14	45	43	36
FEB. 7	43	21	21	22	41	1	5	23	14	45	43	36
FEB. 8	44	22	23	24	41	1	5	23	14	45	43	36
FEB. 9	44	24	25	25	41	1	5	23	14	45	43	36
FEB. 10	44	26	27	27	42	1	6	23	14	45	43	36
FEB. 11	44	28	28	29	42	1	6	23	14	45	43	36
FEB. 12	44	30	30	31	42	2	6	23	14	45	43	36
FEB. 13	44	32	32	33	42	2	6	23	14	45	43	36
FEB. 14	44	33	34	35	42	2	6	23	14	45	43	36
FEB. 15	44	35	36	37	43	2	6	23	14	45	43	36
FEB. 16	45	37	38	38	43	2	6	23	14	45	43	36
FEB. 17	45	39	40	40	43	2	6	23	14	45	43	36
FEB. 18	45	41	42	42	43	2	6	23	14	45	43	36
FEB. 19	45	43	44	44	44	3	6	23	14	45	43	36
FEB. 20	45	45	45	46	44	3	6	23	14	45	43	36
FEB. 21	45	47	47	48	44	3	6	23	14	45	43	36
FEB. 22	45	48	1	2	44	3	7	23	14	45	43	36
FEB. 23	46	2	3	3	44	3	7	23	14	45	43	36
FEB. 24	46	4	4	5	45	3	7	23	14	45	43	36
FEB. 25	46	5	6	7	45	4	7	23	14	45	43	36
FEB. 26	46	7	8	8	45	4	7	23	14	45	43	36
FEB. 27	46	9	9	10	45	4	7	23	14	45	43	36
FEB. 28	46	10	11	11	46	4	7	23	14	45	43	36
FEB. 29	46	12	12	13	46	4	7	23	14	45	43	36

MOON 1 ☽ 12:01 A.M. TO 8:00 A.M.   **MOON 2 ◑ 8:01 A.M. TO 4:00 P.M.**   **MOON 3 ● 4:01 P.M. TO 12:00 A.M.**
Use only one "moon" number. Choose the column closest to your time of birth. If your place of birth is not on
Eastern Standard Time, be sure to read "How to Convert to Eastern Standard Time" at the beginning of this section.

2004

March

April

Date & Time	SUN	MOON 1	MOON 2	MOON 3	MERCURY	VENUS	MARS	JUPITER	SATURN	URANUS	NEPTUNE	PLUTO
MAR. 1	46	13	14	14	46	4	7	23	14	45	43	36
MAR. 2	46	15	16	16	46	4	7	23	14	45	43	36
MAR. 3	47	17	17	18	47	5	7	23	14	45	43	36
MAR. 4	47	18	19	19	47	5	8	23	14	45	43	36
MAR. 5	47	20	21	21	47	5	8	23	14	45	43	36
MAR. 6	47	22	22	23	47	5	8	23	14	45	43	36
MAR. 7	47	24	24	25	48	5	8	23	14	45	43	36
MAR. 8	47	25	26	27	48	5	8	23	14	45	43	36
MAR. 9	47	27	28	29	48	5	8	23	14	45	43	36
MAR. 10	47	29	30	30	48	6	8	23	14	45	43	36
MAR. 11	48	31	32	32	1	6	8	23	14	45	43	36
MAR. 12	48	33	34	34	1	6	8	23	14	45	43	36
MAR. 13	48	35	35	36	1	6	8	23	14	45	43	36
MAR. 14	48	37	37	38	1	6	8	23	14	45	43	36
MAR. 15	48	39	39	40	2	6	8	23	14	46	43	36
MAR. 16	48	40	41	42	2	6	9	23	14	46	43	36
MAR. 17	48	42	43	44	2	7	9	23	14	46	43	36
MAR. 18	48	44	45	45	2	7	9	23	14	46	43	36
MAR. 19	1	46	47	47	3	7	9	23	14	46	43	36
MAR. 20	1	48	48	1	3	7	9	23	14	46	43	36
MAR. 21	1	2	2	3	3	7	9	23	14	46	43	36
MAR. 22	1	3	4	4	3	7	9	23	14	46	43	36
MAR. 23	1	5	5	6	4	7	9	23	14	46	43	36
MAR. 24	1	7	7	8	4	8	9	22	14	46	43	36
MAR. 25	2	8	9	9	4	8	9	22	14	46	43	36
MAR. 26	2	10	10	11	4	8	9	22	14	46	43	36
MAR. 27	2	11	12	12	4	8	9	22	14	46	43	36
MAR. 28	2	13	13	14	5	8	10	22	14	46	43	36
MAR. 29	2	14	15	16	5	8	10	22	14	46	43	36
MAR. 30	2	16	17	17	5	8	10	22	14	46	43	36
MAR. 31	2	18	18	19	5	9	10	22	14	46	43	36

Date & Time	SUN	MOON 1	MOON 2	MOON 3	MERCURY	VENUS	MARS	JUPITER	SATURN	URANUS	NEPTUNE	PLUTO
APR. 1	2	19	20	21	5	9	10	22	14	46	43	36
APR. 2	2	21	22	22	5	9	10	22	14	46	43	36
APR. 3	3	23	24	24	5	9	10	22	14	46	43	36
APR. 4	3	25	25	26	5	9	10	22	14	46	43	36
APR. 5	3	27	27	28	5	9	10	22	14	46	43	36
APR. 6	3	29	29	30	5	9	10	22	14	46	43	36
APR. 7	3	30	31	32	5	9	10	22	14	46	43	36
APR. 8	3	32	33	34	5	10	10	22	14	46	43	36
APR. 9	3	34	35	36	5	10	11	22	14	46	43	36
APR. 10	3	36	37	38	5	10	11	22	14	46	43	36
APR. 11	4	38	39	39	5	10	11	22	14	46	43	36
APR. 12	4	40	41	41	5	10	11	22	14	46	43	36
APR. 13	4	42	43	43	5	10	11	22	14	46	43	36
APR. 14	4	44	44	45	5	10	11	22	14	46	43	36
APR. 15	4	46	46	47	5	10	11	22	14	46	43	36
APR. 16	4	47	48	48	5	10	11	22	14	46	43	36
APR. 17	4	1	2	2	5	11	11	22	14	46	43	36
APR. 18	4	3	3	4	5	11	11	22	14	46	43	36
APR. 19	5	4	5	5	4	11	11	22	14	46	43	36
APR. 20	5	6	7	7	4	11	12	22	14	46	43	36
APR. 21	5	8	8	9	4	11	12	22	14	46	43	36
APR. 22	5	9	10	10	4	11	12	22	14	46	43	36
APR. 23	5	11	11	12	4	11	12	22	14	46	43	36
APR. 24	5	12	13	13	4	11	12	22	14	46	43	36
APR. 25	6	14	14	15	4	11	12	22	14	46	43	36
APR. 26	6	16	16	17	4	11	12	22	14	46	43	36
APR. 27	6	17	18	18	4	12	12	22	14	46	43	36
APR. 28	6	19	19	20	4	12	12	22	14	46	43	36
APR. 29	6	20	21	22	4	12	12	22	14	46	43	36
APR. 30	6	22	23	23	4	12	12	22	14	46	43	36

MOON 1 ☽ 12:01 A.M. TO 8:00 A.M. **MOON 2** ☽ 8:01 A.M. TO 4:00 P.M. **MOON 3** ● 4:01 P.M. TO 12:00 A.M.
Use only one "moon" number. Choose the column closest to your time of birth. If your place of birth is not on Eastern Standard Time, be sure to read "How to Convert to Eastern Standard Time" at the beginning of this section.

Date & Time	SUN ☉	MOON 1 ◐	MOON 2 ◑	MOON 3 ●	MERCURY	VENUS	MARS	JUPITER	SATURN	URANUS	NEPTUNE	PLUTO
MAY 1	6	24	25	25	4	12	12	22	14	46	43	36
MAY 2	6	26	26	27	4	12	13	22	14	46	43	36
MAY 3	7	28	28	29	4	12	13	22	14	46	43	36
MAY 4	7	30	30	31	4	12	13	22	14	46	43	36
MAY 5	7	32	32	33	4	12	13	22	14	46	43	36
MAY 6	7	34	34	35	4	12	13	22	14	46	43	36
MAY 7	7	36	36	37	4	12	13	22	14	46	43	36
MAY 8	7	38	38	39	4	12	13	22	14	46	43	36
MAY 9	7	40	40	41	4	12	13	22	14	46	43	36
MAY 10	7	41	42	43	4	12	13	22	14	46	43	36
MAY 11	8	43	44	45	4	12	13	22	14	46	43	36
MAY 12	8	45	46	46	4	12	13	22	14	46	43	36
MAY 13	8	47	47	48	5	12	13	22	14	46	43	36
MAY 14	8	1	1	2	5	12	14	22	14	46	43	36
MAY 15	8	2	3	3	5	12	14	22	14	46	43	36
MAY 16	8	4	4	5	5	12	14	22	14	46	43	36
MAY 17	8	6	6	7	5	12	14	22	14	46	43	36
MAY 18	8	7	8	8	5	12	14	22	14	46	43	36
MAY 19	9	9	9	10	5	12	14	22	14	46	43	36
MAY 20	9	10	11	11	6	12	14	22	14	46	43	36
MAY 21	9	12	12	13	6	12	14	22	14	46	43	36
MAY 22	9	14	14	15	6	12	14	22	14	46	43	36
MAY 23	9	15	16	16	6	12	14	22	14	46	43	36
MAY 24	9	17	17	18	6	12	14	22	14	46	43	36
MAY 25	10	18	19	19	6	12	14	22	14	46	43	36
MAY 26	10	20	20	21	7	12	15	22	14	46	43	36
MAY 27	10	22	22	23	7	12	15	22	15	46	43	36
MAY 28	10	23	24	24	7	12	15	22	15	46	43	36
MAY 29	10	25	26	26	7	12	15	22	15	46	43	36
MAY 30	10	27	28	28	7	12	15	22	15	46	43	36
MAY 31	10	29	29	30	8	12	15	22	15	46	43	36

Date & Time	SUN ☉	MOON 1 ◐	MOON 2 ◑	MOON 3 ●	MERCURY	VENUS	MARS	JUPITER	SATURN	URANUS	NEPTUNE	PLUTO
JUN. 1	10	31	31	32	8	12	15	22	15	46	43	36
JUN. 2	10	33	33	34	8	12	15	22	15	46	43	36
JUN. 3	11	35	35	36	8	12	15	22	15	46	43	36
JUN. 4	11	37	37	38	9	12	15	22	15	46	43	36
JUN. 5	11	39	39	40	9	12	15	22	15	46	43	36
JUN. 6	11	41	41	42	9	12	15	22	15	46	43	36
JUN. 7	11	43	43	44	9	11	15	22	15	46	43	36
JUN. 8	11	45	45	46	10	11	16	22	15	46	43	36
JUN. 9	11	46	47	48	10	11	16	22	15	46	43	36
JUN. 10	11	48	1	1	10	11	16	22	15	46	43	36
JUN. 11	12	2	2	3	10	11	16	22	15	46	43	36
JUN. 12	12	4	4	5	11	11	16	22	15	46	43	36
JUN. 13	12	5	6	6	11	11	16	22	15	46	43	36
JUN. 14	12	7	7	8	11	11	16	22	15	46	43	36
JUN. 15	12	8	9	9	12	11	16	22	15	46	43	36
JUN. 16	12	10	10	11	12	11	16	22	15	46	43	36
JUN. 17	12	12	12	13	12	11	16	23	15	46	43	36
JUN. 18	12	13	14	14	12	11	16	23	15	46	43	36
JUN. 19	13	15	15	16	13	11	17	23	15	46	43	36
JUN. 20	13	16	17	17	13	10	17	23	15	46	43	36
JUN. 21	13	18	18	19	13	10	17	23	15	46	43	36
JUN. 22	13	20	20	21	14	10	17	23	15	46	43	36
JUN. 23	13	21	22	22	14	10	17	23	15	46	43	36
JUN. 24	13	23	23	24	14	10	17	23	15	46	43	36
JUN. 25	14	25	25	26	15	10	17	23	15	46	43	36
JUN. 26	14	26	27	27	15	10	17	23	15	46	43	36
JUN. 27	14	28	29	29	15	10	17	23	15	46	43	36
JUN. 28	14	30	31	31	15	10	17	23	15	46	43	36
JUN. 29	14	32	33	33	16	10	17	23	15	46	43	36
JUN. 30	14	34	35	35	16	10	17	23	15	46	43	36

MOON 1 ◐ 12:01 A.M. TO 8:00 A.M.   **MOON 2** ◑ 8:01 A.M. TO 4:00 P.M.   **MOON 3** ● 4:01 P.M. TO 12:00 A.M.
Use only one "moon" number. Choose the column closest to your time of birth. If your place of birth is not on Eastern Standard Time, be sure to read "How to Convert to Eastern Standard Time" at the beginning of this section.

2004

July   August

Date & Time	SUN	MOON 1	MOON 2	MOON 3	MERCURY	VENUS	MARS	JUPITER	SATURN	URANUS	NEPTUNE	PLUTO
JUL. 1	14	36	37	37	16	10	18	23	15	46	43	36
JUL. 2	14	38	39	39	16	10	18	23	15	46	43	36
JUL. 3	15	40	41	41	17	10	18	23	15	46	43	36
JUL. 4	15	42	43	43	17	10	18	23	15	46	43	36
JUL. 5	15	44	45	45	17	10	18	23	15	46	43	36
JUL. 6	15	46	46	47	17	10	18	23	15	46	43	36
JUL. 7	15	48	48	1	18	10	18	23	15	46	43	36
JUL. 8	15	1	2	3	18	10	18	23	15	46	43	36
JUL. 9	15	3	4	4	18	10	18	23	15	46	43	36
JUL. 10	15	5	5	6	18	11	18	23	15	46	43	36
JUL. 11	16	6	7	7	18	11	18	23	15	46	43	36
JUL. 12	16	8	9	9	18	11	18	23	15	46	43	36
JUL. 13	16	10	10	11	19	11	19	23	15	46	43	36
JUL. 14	16	11	12	12	19	11	19	23	15	46	43	36
JUL. 15	16	13	13	14	19	11	19	23	15	46	43	36
JUL. 16	16	14	15	15	19	11	19	23	15	46	43	36
JUL. 17	16	16	16	17	20	11	19	23	15	46	43	36
JUL. 18	16	18	18	19	20	11	19	23	15	46	43	36
JUL. 19	17	19	20	20	20	11	19	23	15	46	43	36
JUL. 20	17	21	21	22	20	11	19	23	15	46	43	36
JUL. 21	17	22	23	24	20	11	19	23	15	46	43	36
JUL. 22	17	24	25	25	20	11	19	23	15	46	43	36
JUL. 23	17	26	26	27	21	11	19	23	15	46	43	36
JUL. 24	17	28	28	29	21	11	20	23	15	46	43	36
JUL. 25	17	29	30	31	21	12	20	23	15	46	43	36
JUL. 26	18	31	32	33	21	12	20	23	16	46	43	36
JUL. 27	18	33	34	34	21	12	20	23	16	46	43	36
JUL. 28	18	35	36	36	21	12	20	23	16	46	43	36
JUL. 29	18	37	38	38	21	12	20	23	16	46	43	36
JUL. 30	18	39	40	40	22	12	20	23	16	46	43	36
JUL. 31	18	41	42	42	22	12	20	23	16	46	43	36

Date & Time	SUN	MOON 1	MOON 2	MOON 3	MERCURY	VENUS	MARS	JUPITER	SATURN	URANUS	NEPTUNE	PLUTO
AUG. 1	18	43	44	44	22	12	20	23	16	46	43	36
AUG. 2	18	45	46	46	22	12	20	23	16	46	43	36
AUG. 3	19	47	48	48	22	12	20	23	16	46	43	36
AUG. 4	19	1	1	2	22	13	20	24	16	46	43	36
AUG. 5	19	3	3	4	22	13	21	24	16	46	43	36
AUG. 6	19	4	5	5	22	13	21	24	16	46	43	36
AUG. 7	19	6	6	7	22	13	21	24	16	46	43	36
AUG. 8	19	8	8	9	22	13	21	24	16	46	43	36
AUG. 9	19	9	10	10	22	13	21	24	16	46	43	36
AUG. 10	19	11	11	12	22	13	21	24	16	46	43	36
AUG. 11	20	12	13	13	22	13	21	24	16	46	43	36
AUG. 12	20	14	14	15	22	14	21	24	16	46	43	36
AUG. 13	20	15	16	17	22	14	21	24	16	46	43	36
AUG. 14	20	17	18	18	22	14	21	24	16	46	43	36
AUG. 15	20	19	19	20	22	14	21	24	16	46	43	36
AUG. 16	20	20	21	21	22	14	21	24	16	46	43	36
AUG. 17	20	22	23	23	22	14	22	24	16	46	43	36
AUG. 18	20	24	24	25	22	14	22	24	16	46	43	36
AUG. 19	21	25	26	27	22	14	22	24	16	46	43	36
AUG. 20	21	27	28	28	22	15	22	24	16	46	43	36
AUG. 21	21	29	30	30	21	15	22	24	16	46	43	36
AUG. 22	21	31	31	32	21	15	22	24	16	46	43	36
AUG. 23	21	33	33	34	21	15	22	24	16	46	43	36
AUG. 24	21	35	35	36	21	15	22	24	16	46	43	36
AUG. 25	21	36	37	38	21	15	22	24	16	46	43	36
AUG. 26	22	38	39	40	21	15	22	24	16	46	43	36
AUG. 27	22	40	41	42	21	15	22	24	16	46	43	36
AUG. 28	22	42	43	44	21	16	23	24	16	46	43	36
AUG. 29	22	44	45	45	21	16	23	24	16	46	43	36
AUG. 30	22	46	47	47	20	16	23	24	16	46	43	36
AUG. 31	22	48	1	1	20	16	23	24	16	46	43	36

MOON 1 ◔ 12:01 A.M. TO 8:00 A.M.   **MOON 2** ◑ 8:01 A.M. TO 4:00 P.M.   **MOON 3** ● 4:01 P.M. TO 12:00 A.M.

Use only one "moon" number. Choose the column closest to your time of birth. If your place of birth is not on Eastern Standard Time, be sure to read "How to Convert to Eastern Standard Time" at the beginning of this section.

2004

September   ## October

Date & Time	SUN	MOON 1	MOON 2	MOON 3	MERCURY	VENUS	MARS	JUPITER	SATURN	URANUS	NEPTUNE	PLUTO
SEP. 1	22	2	2	3	20	16	23	24	16	46	43	36
SEP. 2	22	4	4	5	20	16	23	24	16	46	43	36
SEP. 3	23	5	6	6	20	16	23	24	16	46	43	36
SEP. 4	23	7	8	8	20	17	23	24	16	46	43	36
SEP. 5	23	9	9	10	20	17	23	24	16	46	43	36
SEP. 6	23	10	11	11	21	17	23	24	16	46	43	36
SEP. 7	23	12	12	13	21	17	23	24	16	46	43	36
SEP. 8	23	13	14	14	21	17	23	24	16	46	43	36
SEP. 9	23	15	15	16	21	17	23	25	16	46	43	36
SEP. 10	23	17	17	18	21	17	24	25	16	46	43	36
SEP. 11	24	18	19	19	21	18	24	25	16	46	43	36
SEP. 12	24	20	20	21	21	18	24	25	16	46	43	36
SEP. 13	24	22	22	23	21	18	24	25	16	46	43	36
SEP. 14	24	23	24	24	22	18	24	25	16	46	43	36
SEP. 15	24	25	26	26	22	18	24	25	16	46	43	36
SEP. 16	24	27	27	28	22	18	24	25	16	46	43	36
SEP. 17	24	29	29	30	22	18	24	25	16	46	43	36
SEP. 18	24	30	31	32	22	19	24	25	16	45	43	36
SEP. 19	25	32	33	33	23	19	24	25	16	45	43	36
SEP. 20	25	34	35	35	23	19	24	25	16	45	43	36
SEP. 21	25	36	37	37	23	19	25	25	16	45	43	36
SEP. 22	25	38	38	39	23	19	25	25	16	45	43	36
SEP. 23	25	40	40	41	24	19	25	25	16	45	43	36
SEP. 24	25	42	42	43	24	20	25	25	16	45	43	36
SEP. 25	26	44	44	45	24	20	25	25	16	45	43	36
SEP. 26	26	45	46	47	24	20	25	25	16	45	43	36
SEP. 27	26	47	48	1	25	20	25	25	16	45	43	36
SEP. 28	26	1	2	2	25	20	25	25	16	45	43	36
SEP. 29	26	3	3	4	25	20	25	25	16	45	43	36
SEP. 30	26	5	5	6	25	20	25	25	16	45	43	36

Date & Time	SUN	MOON 1	MOON 2	MOON 3	MERCURY	VENUS	MARS	JUPITER	SATURN	URANUS	NEPTUNE	PLUTO
OCT. 1	26	6	7	7	26	21	25	25	16	45	43	36
OCT. 2	26	8	9	9	26	21	25	25	16	45	43	36
OCT. 3	27	10	10	11	26	21	26	25	16	45	43	36
OCT. 4	27	11	12	12	26	21	26	25	16	45	43	36
OCT. 5	27	13	13	14	27	21	26	25	16	45	43	36
OCT. 6	27	14	15	15	27	21	26	25	16	45	43	36
OCT. 7	27	16	17	17	27	22	26	25	16	45	43	36
OCT. 8	27	18	18	19	27	22	26	26	16	45	43	36
OCT. 9	27	19	20	20	27	22	26	25	17	45	43	36
OCT. 10	27	21	21	22	28	22	26	25	17	45	43	36
OCT. 11	28	23	23	24	28	22	26	25	17	45	43	36
OCT. 12	28	24	25	25	28	22	26	25	17	45	43	36
OCT. 13	28	26	27	27	28	22	27	26	17	45	43	36
OCT. 14	28	28	29	29	29	23	27	26	17	45	43	36
OCT. 15	28	30	30	31	29	23	27	26	17	45	43	36
OCT. 16	28	32	32	33	29	23	27	26	17	45	43	36
OCT. 17	28	34	34	35	29	23	27	26	17	45	43	36
OCT. 18	28	36	36	37	29	23	27	26	17	45	43	36
OCT. 19	29	37	38	39	30	23	27	26	17	45	43	36
OCT. 20	29	39	40	41	30	24	27	26	17	45	43	36
OCT. 21	29	41	42	42	30	24	27	26	17	45	43	36
OCT. 22	29	43	44	44	30	24	27	26	17	45	43	36
OCT. 23	29	45	46	46	30	24	27	26	17	45	43	36
OCT. 24	29	47	47	48	31	24	27	26	17	45	43	36
OCT. 25	29	1	1	2	31	24	27	26	17	45	43	36
OCT. 26	30	2	3	3	31	25	28	26	17	45	43	36
OCT. 27	30	4	5	5	31	25	28	26	17	45	43	36
OCT. 28	30	6	6	7	32	25	28	26	17	45	43	36
OCT. 29	30	7	8	9	32	25	28	26	17	45	43	36
OCT. 30	30	9	10	10	32	25	28	26	17	45	43	36
OCT. 31	30	11	11	12	32	25	28	26	17	45	43	36

MOON 1 ◐ 12:01 A.M. TO 8:00 A.M.   **MOON 2** ◑ 8:01 A.M. TO 4:00 P.M.   **MOON 3** ● 4:01 P.M. TO 12:00 A.M.

Use only one "moon" number. Choose the column closest to your time of birth. If your place of birth is not on Eastern Standard Time, be sure to read "How to Convert to Eastern Standard Time" at the beginning of this section.

Date & Time	SUN	MOON 1	MOON 2	MOON 3	MERCURY	VENUS	MARS	JUPITER	SATURN	URANUS	NEPTUNE	PLUTO
NOV. 1	30	12	13	13	32	25	28	26	17	45	43	36
NOV. 2	30	14	14	15	33	26	28	26	17	45	43	36
NOV. 3	31	15	16	17	33	26	28	26	17	45	43	36
NOV. 4	31	17	18	18	33	26	28	26	17	45	43	36
NOV. 5	31	19	19	20	33	26	28	26	17	45	43	36
NOV. 6	31	20	21	21	33	26	29	26	17	45	43	36
NOV. 7	31	22	22	23	33	26	29	26	17	45	43	36
NOV. 8	31	24	24	25	34	27	29	26	17	45	43	36
NOV. 9	31	25	26	27	34	27	29	26	17	45	43	36
NOV. 10	31	27	28	28	34	27	29	26	17	45	43	36
NOV. 11	31	29	30	30	34	27	29	26	17	45	43	36
NOV. 12	32	31	32	32	34	27	29	26	17	45	43	36
NOV. 13	32	33	34	34	35	27	29	26	17	45	43	36
NOV. 14	32	35	36	36	35	28	29	26	17	45	43	36
NOV. 15	32	37	37	38	35	28	29	26	17	45	43	36
NOV. 16	32	39	39	40	35	28	29	26	17	45	43	36
NOV. 17	32	41	41	42	35	28	29	26	17	45	43	36
NOV. 18	32	43	43	44	35	28	30	26	17	45	43	36
NOV. 19	33	45	45	46	36	28	30	26	17	45	43	36
NOV. 20	33	46	47	48	36	29	30	26	17	45	43	36
NOV. 21	33	48	1	1	36	29	30	27	17	45	43	36
NOV. 22	33	2	2	3	36	29	30	27	17	45	43	36
NOV. 23	33	4	4	5	36	29	30	27	17	45	43	36
NOV. 24	33	5	6	6	36	29	30	27	17	45	43	36
NOV. 25	34	7	8	8	36	29	30	27	17	45	43	36
NOV. 26	34	9	9	10	36	30	30	27	17	45	43	36
NOV. 27	34	10	11	11	36	30	30	27	17	45	43	36
NOV. 28	34	12	12	13	36	30	30	27	17	45	43	36
NOV. 29	34	13	14	14	37	30	31	27	17	45	43	36
NOV. 30	34	15	16	16	37	30	31	27	17	45	43	36

Date & Time	SUN	MOON 1	MOON 2	MOON 3	MERCURY	VENUS	MARS	JUPITER	SATURN	URANUS	NEPTUNE	PLUTO
DEC. 1	34	17	17	18	37	30	31	27	17	45	43	36
DEC. 2	34	18	19	19	36	31	31	27	17	45	43	36
DEC. 3	35	20	20	21	36	31	31	27	17	45	43	36
DEC. 4	35	21	22	22	36	31	31	27	17	45	43	36
DEC. 5	35	23	24	24	36	31	31	27	17	45	43	36
DEC. 6	35	25	25	26	36	31	31	27	17	45	43	36
DEC. 7	35	26	27	28	36	31	31	27	17	45	43	36
DEC. 8	35	28	29	29	36	32	31	27	17	45	43	36
DEC. 9	35	30	31	31	36	32	31	27	16	45	43	36
DEC. 10	35	32	33	33	35	32	32	27	16	45	43	36
DEC. 11	36	34	35	35	35	32	32	27	16	45	43	36
DEC. 12	36	36	37	37	35	32	32	27	16	45	43	36
DEC. 13	36	38	39	39	35	32	32	27	16	45	43	36
DEC. 14	36	40	41	41	35	33	32	27	16	45	43	36
DEC. 15	36	42	43	43	35	33	32	27	16	45	43	36
DEC. 16	36	44	45	45	35	33	32	27	16	45	43	36
DEC. 17	36	46	46	47	34	33	32	27	16	45	43	36
DEC. 18	36	48	48	1	34	33	32	27	16	45	43	36
DEC. 19	37	1	2	3	34	33	32	27	16	45	43	36
DEC. 20	37	3	4	4	34	34	32	27	16	45	43	36
DEC. 21	37	5	5	6	34	34	33	27	16	45	43	36
DEC. 22	37	7	7	8	34	34	33	27	16	45	43	36
DEC. 23	37	8	9	9	34	34	33	27	16	45	43	36
DEC. 24	37	10	10	11	35	34	33	27	16	45	43	36
DEC. 25	37	11	12	12	35	34	33	27	16	45	43	36
DEC. 26	38	13	14	14	35	35	33	27	16	45	43	36
DEC. 27	38	15	15	16	35	35	33	27	16	45	43	36
DEC. 28	38	16	17	17	35	35	33	27	16	45	43	36
DEC. 29	38	18	18	19	35	35	33	27	16	45	43	36
DEC. 30	38	19	20	20	35	35	33	27	16	45	43	36
DEC. 31	38	21	21	22	35	35	33	27	16	45	43	36

MOON 1 ☽ 12:01 A.M. TO 8:00 A.M. **MOON 2** ◑ 8:01 A.M. TO 4:00 P.M. **MOON 3** ● 4:01 P.M. TO 12:00 A.M.

Use only one "moon" number. Choose the column closest to your time of birth. If your place of birth is not on Eastern Standard Time, be sure to read "How to Convert to Eastern Standard Time" at the beginning of this section.

January

Date & Time	SUN	MOON 1	MOON 2	MOON 3	MERCURY	VENUS	MARS	JUPITER	SATURN	URANUS	NEPTUNE	PLUTO
JAN. 1	38	23	23	24	35	36	34	27	16	45	43	36
JAN. 2	38	24	25	25	36	36	34	27	16	45	43	36
JAN. 3	39	26	26	27	36	36	34	27	16	45	43	36
JAN. 4	39	28	28	29	36	36	34	27	16	46	43	36
JAN. 5	39	29	30	31	36	36	34	27	16	46	43	36
JAN. 6	39	31	32	32	36	36	34	27	16	46	43	36
JAN. 7	39	33	34	34	36	37	34	27	16	46	43	36
JAN. 8	39	35	36	36	37	37	34	27	16	46	43	36
JAN. 9	39	37	38	38	37	37	34	27	16	46	43	36
JAN. 10	40	39	40	40	37	37	34	27	16	46	43	36
JAN. 11	40	41	42	42	37	37	34	27	16	46	43	36
JAN. 12	40	43	44	44	37	37	35	27	16	46	43	36
JAN. 13	40	45	46	46	38	38	35	27	16	46	43	36
JAN. 14	40	47	48	48	38	38	35	27	16	46	43	36
JAN. 15	40	1	2	2	38	38	35	27	16	46	43	36
JAN. 16	40	3	3	4	38	38	35	27	16	46	43	36
JAN. 17	41	4	5	6	38	38	35	27	16	46	43	36
JAN. 18	41	6	7	7	38	38	35	27	16	46	43	36
JAN. 19	41	8	8	9	39	39	35	27	16	46	43	36
JAN. 20	41	9	10	10	39	39	35	27	16	46	43	36
JAN. 21	41	11	12	12	39	39	35	27	16	46	43	36
JAN. 22	41	13	13	14	39	39	36	27	16	46	43	36
JAN. 23	42	14	15	15	39	39	36	27	16	46	43	36
JAN. 24	42	16	16	17	40	39	36	27	16	46	43	36
JAN. 25	42	17	18	18	40	40	36	27	16	46	43	36
JAN. 26	42	19	19	20	40	40	36	27	16	46	43	36
JAN. 27	42	21	21	22	40	40	36	27	16	46	43	36
JAN. 28	42	22	23	23	41	40	36	27	16	46	43	36
JAN. 29	42	24	24	25	41	40	36	27	16	46	43	36
JAN. 30	42	25	26	27	41	40	36	27	16	46	43	36
JAN. 31	43	27	28	28	41	41	36	27	16	46	43	36

February

Date & Time	SUN	MOON 1	MOON 2	MOON 3	MERCURY	VENUS	MARS	JUPITER	SATURN	URANUS	NEPTUNE	PLUTO
FEB. 1	43	29	29	30	41	41	36	27	16	46	43	36
FEB. 2	43	31	31	32	42	41	37	27	16	46	43	36
FEB. 3	43	32	33	34	42	41	37	27	16	46	43	36
FEB. 4	43	34	35	36	42	41	37	27	16	46	43	36
FEB. 5	43	36	37	37	42	41	37	27	16	46	43	36
FEB. 6	43	38	39	39	42	42	37	27	16	46	43	36
FEB. 7	43	40	41	42	43	42	37	27	16	46	43	36
FEB. 8	44	42	43	44	43	42	37	27	16	46	43	36
FEB. 9	44	44	45	46	43	42	37	27	16	46	43	36
FEB. 10	44	46	47	48	43	42	37	27	16	46	43	36
FEB. 11	44	48	1	1	44	42	37	27	16	46	43	36
FEB. 12	44	2	3	3	44	43	37	27	16	46	43	36
FEB. 13	44	4	4	5	44	43	38	27	16	46	43	36
FEB. 14	44	6	6	7	44	43	38	27	16	46	43	36
FEB. 15	44	7	8	8	45	43	38	27	16	46	43	36
FEB. 16	45	9	9	10	45	43	38	27	16	46	43	36
FEB. 17	45	11	11	12	45	43	38	27	16	46	43	36
FEB. 18	45	12	13	13	45	44	38	27	16	46	43	36
FEB. 19	45	14	14	15	46	44	38	27	16	46	43	36
FEB. 20	45	15	16	16	46	44	38	27	16	46	43	36
FEB. 21	45	17	17	18	46	44	38	27	16	46	43	36
FEB. 22	45	18	19	20	46	44	39	27	16	46	43	36
FEB. 23	46	20	21	21	47	44	39	27	16	46	43	36
FEB. 24	46	22	22	23	47	45	39	27	16	46	43	36
FEB. 25	46	23	24	24	47	45	39	27	16	46	43	36
FEB. 26	46	25	26	26	47	45	39	27	16	46	43	36
FEB. 27	46	27	27	28	48	45	39	27	16	46	43	36
FEB. 28	46	28	29	30	48	45	39	27	16	46	43	36

MOON 1 ◐ 12:01 A.M. TO 8:00 A.M.   **MOON 2** ◑ 8:01 A.M. TO 4:00 P.M.   **MOON 3** ● 4:01 P.M. TO 12:00 A.M.
Use only one "moon" number. Choose the column closest to your time of birth. If your place of birth is not on Eastern Standard Time, be sure to read "How to Convert to Eastern Standard Time" at the beginning of this section.

March

April

Date & Time	SUN	MOON 1	MOON 2	MOON 3	MERCURY	VENUS	MARS	JUPITER	SATURN	URANUS	NEPTUNE	PLUTO
MAR. 1	46	30	31	31	48	45	39	27	16	46	43	36
MAR. 2	46	32	33	33	48	46	39	27	16	46	43	36
MAR. 3	47	34	34	35	1	46	39	27	16	46	43	36
MAR. 4	47	36	36	37	1	46	39	27	16	46	43	36
MAR. 5	47	38	38	39	1	46	39	27	16	46	43	36
MAR. 6	47	39	40	41	1	46	40	27	16	46	43	36
MAR. 7	47	41	42	43	1	46	40	27	16	46	43	36
MAR. 8	47	43	44	45	2	47	40	27	16	46	43	36
MAR. 9	47	45	46	47	2	47	40	27	16	46	43	36
MAR. 10	47	47	48	1	2	47	40	27	16	46	43	36
MAR. 11	48	1	2	2	2	47	40	27	16	46	43	36
MAR. 12	48	3	4	4	2	47	40	27	16	46	43	36
MAR. 13	48	5	5	6	2	47	40	27	16	46	43	36
MAR. 14	48	7	7	8	3	48	40	27	16	46	43	36
MAR. 15	48	8	9	9	3	48	40	27	16	46	43	36
MAR. 16	48	10	11	11	3	48	41	27	16	46	43	36
MAR. 17	48	12	12	13	3	48	41	27	16	46	43	36
MAR. 18	48	13	14	14	3	48	41	27	16	46	43	36
MAR. 19	1	15	15	16	3	48	41	27	16	46	43	36
MAR. 20	1	16	17	17	3	1	41	27	16	46	43	36
MAR. 21	1	18	19	19	3	1	41	27	16	46	43	36
MAR. 22	1	20	20	21	3	1	41	27	16	46	43	36
MAR. 23	1	21	22	22	3	1	41	27	16	46	43	36
MAR. 24	1	23	23	24	3	1	41	27	16	46	43	36
MAR. 25	2	25	25	26	3	1	41	27	16	46	43	36
MAR. 26	2	26	27	27	3	2	41	27	16	46	43	36
MAR. 27	2	28	29	29	2	2	42	27	16	46	43	36
MAR. 28	2	30	30	31	2	2	42	27	16	46	43	36
MAR. 29	2	32	32	33	2	2	42	27	16	46	43	36
MAR. 30	2	33	34	35	2	2	42	27	16	46	43	36
MAR. 31	2	35	36	36	2	2	42	27	16	46	43	36

Date & Time	SUN	MOON 1	MOON 2	MOON 3	MERCURY	VENUS	MARS	JUPITER	SATURN	URANUS	NEPTUNE	PLUTO
APR. 1	2	37	38	38	2	3	42	27	16	46	43	36
APR. 2	2	39	40	40	2	3	42	27	16	46	43	36
APR. 3	3	41	41	42	2	3	42	27	16	46	43	36
APR. 4	3	43	43	44	2	3	42	27	16	46	43	36
APR. 5	3	45	45	46	1	3	42	27	16	46	43	36
APR. 6	3	47	47	48	1	3	43	27	16	46	43	36
APR. 7	3	48	1	2	1	4	43	27	16	46	43	36
APR. 8	3	2	3	4	1	4	43	27	16	46	43	36
APR. 9	3	4	5	5	1	4	43	27	16	46	43	36
APR. 10	3	6	7	7	1	4	43	27	16	46	43	36
APR. 11	4	8	8	9	1	4	43	27	16	46	43	36
APR. 12	4	9	10	11	1	4	43	27	16	46	43	36
APR. 13	4	11	12	12	1	5	43	27	16	46	43	36
APR. 14	4	13	13	14	1	5	43	27	16	46	43	36
APR. 15	4	14	15	15	1	5	43	27	16	46	43	36
APR. 16	4	16	16	17	1	5	44	27	16	46	43	36
APR. 17	4	17	18	19	1	5	44	27	16	46	43	36
APR. 18	4	19	20	20	1	5	44	27	16	46	43	36
APR. 19	5	21	21	22	1	6	44	27	16	46	43	36
APR. 20	5	22	23	23	2	6	44	27	16	46	43	36
APR. 21	5	24	25	25	2	6	44	27	16	46	43	36
APR. 22	5	26	26	27	2	6	44	27	16	46	43	36
APR. 23	5	27	28	29	2	6	44	27	16	46	43	36
APR. 24	5	29	30	30	2	6	44	26	16	46	43	36
APR. 25	6	31	32	32	2	7	44	26	16	46	43	36
APR. 26	6	33	33	34	2	7	44	26	16	46	43	36
APR. 27	6	35	35	36	2	7	45	26	16	46	43	36
APR. 28	6	37	37	38	2	7	45	26	16	46	43	36
APR. 29	6	39	39	40	3	7	45	26	16	46	43	36
APR. 30	6	40	41	42	3	7	45	26	16	46	43	36

MOON 1 ◗ 12:01 A.M. TO 8:00 A.M.   **MOON 2** ◑ 8:01 A.M. TO 4:00 P.M.   **MOON 3** ● 4:01 P.M. TO 12:00 A.M.
Use only one "moon" number. Choose the column closest to your time of birth. If your place of birth is not on Eastern Standard Time, be sure to read "How to Convert to Eastern Standard Time" at the beginning of this section.

2005

May

Date & Time	SUN	MOON 1	MOON 2	MOON 3	MERCURY	VENUS	MARS	JUPITER	SATURN	URANUS	NEPTUNE	PLUTO
MAY 1	6	42	43	44	3	7	45	26	16	46	43	36
MAY 2	6	44	45	45	3	8	45	26	16	46	43	36
MAY 3	7	46	47	47	3	8	45	26	16	46	43	36
MAY 4	7	48	1	1	3	8	45	26	16	46	43	36
MAY 5	7	2	2	3	4	8	45	26	16	46	43	36
MAY 6	7	4	4	5	4	8	45	26	16	46	43	36
MAY 7	7	5	6	6	4	8	46	26	16	46	43	36
MAY 8	7	7	8	8	4	9	46	26	16	46	43	36
MAY 9	7	9	9	10	4	9	46	26	16	46	43	36
MAY 10	7	10	11	12	5	9	46	26	16	46	43	36
MAY 11	8	12	13	13	5	9	46	26	16	46	43	36
MAY 12	8	14	14	15	5	9	46	26	16	46	43	36
MAY 13	8	15	16	16	5	9	46	26	16	46	43	36
MAY 14	8	17	17	18	5	10	46	26	16	46	43	36
MAY 15	8	19	19	20	6	10	46	26	16	46	43	36
MAY 16	8	20	21	21	6	10	46	26	16	46	43	36
MAY 17	8	22	22	23	6	10	47	26	16	46	43	36
MAY 18	8	23	24	24	6	10	47	26	16	46	43	36
MAY 19	9	25	26	26	7	10	47	26	16	46	43	36
MAY 20	9	27	27	28	7	11	47	26	16	46	43	36
MAY 21	9	28	29	30	7	11	47	26	16	46	43	36
MAY 22	9	30	31	32	7	11	47	26	16	46	43	36
MAY 23	9	32	33	33	8	11	47	26	16	46	43	36
MAY 24	9	34	35	35	8	11	47	26	16	46	43	36
MAY 25	10	36	37	37	8	11	47	26	16	46	43	36
MAY 26	10	38	39	39	8	12	47	26	16	46	43	36
MAY 27	10	40	41	41	9	12	47	26	16	46	43	36
MAY 28	10	42	42	43	9	12	48	26	16	46	43	36
MAY 29	10	44	44	45	9	12	48	26	16	46	43	36
MAY 30	10	46	46	47	9	12	48	26	16	46	43	36
MAY 31	10	48	48	1	10	12	48	26	16	46	43	36

June

Date & Time	SUN	MOON 1	MOON 2	MOON 3	MERCURY	VENUS	MARS	JUPITER	SATURN	URANUS	NEPTUNE	PLUTO
JUN. 1	10	1	2	3	10	13	48	26	16	46	43	36
JUN. 2	10	3	4	4	10	13	48	26	16	46	43	36
JUN. 3	11	5	5	6	11	13	48	26	16	46	43	36
JUN. 4	11	7	7	8	11	13	48	26	16	46	43	36
JUN. 5	11	8	9	9	11	13	48	26	16	46	43	36
JUN. 6	11	10	11	11	12	13	48	26	16	46	43	36
JUN. 7	11	12	12	13	12	14	1	26	16	46	43	36
JUN. 8	11	13	14	14	12	14	1	26	16	46	43	36
JUN. 9	11	15	15	16	12	14	1	26	16	46	43	36
JUN. 10	11	16	17	18	13	14	1	26	16	46	43	36
JUN. 11	12	18	19	19	13	14	1	26	16	46	43	36
JUN. 12	12	20	20	21	13	14	1	26	16	46	43	36
JUN. 13	12	21	22	22	13	15	1	26	16	46	43	36
JUN. 14	12	23	23	24	14	15	1	26	16	46	43	36
JUN. 15	12	24	25	26	14	15	1	26	16	46	43	36
JUN. 16	12	26	27	27	14	15	1	26	16	46	43	36
JUN. 17	12	28	28	29	15	15	1	26	16	46	43	36
JUN. 18	12	30	30	31	15	15	2	26	16	46	43	36
JUN. 19	13	31	32	33	15	16	2	26	17	46	43	36
JUN. 20	13	33	34	35	15	16	2	26	17	46	43	36
JUN. 21	13	35	36	36	15	16	2	26	17	46	43	36
JUN. 22	13	37	38	38	16	16	2	26	17	46	43	36
JUN. 23	13	39	40	40	16	16	2	26	17	46	43	36
JUN. 24	13	41	42	43	16	16	2	26	17	46	43	36
JUN. 25	14	43	44	44	16	16	2	26	17	46	43	36
JUN. 26	14	45	46	46	17	17	2	26	17	46	43	36
JUN. 27	14	47	48	48	17	17	2	26	17	46	43	36
JUN. 28	14	1	2	2	17	17	2	26	17	46	43	36
JUN. 29	14	3	3	4	17	17	3	26	17	46	43	36
JUN. 30	14	4	5	6	17	17	3	26	17	46	43	36

MOON 1 ☽ 12:01 A.M. TO 8:00 A.M.   **MOON 2** ☽ 8:01 A.M. TO 4:00 P.M.   **MOON 3** ● 4:01 P.M. TO 12:00 A.M.

Use only one "moon" number. Choose the column closest to your time of birth. If your place of birth is not on Eastern Standard Time, be sure to read "How to Convert to Eastern Standard Time" at the beginning of this section.

2005

July

August

Date & Time	SUN	MOON 1	MOON 2	MOON 3	MERCURY	VENUS	MARS	JUPITER	SATURN	URANUS	NEPTUNE	PLUTO
JUL. 1	14	6	7	7	18	17	3	26	17	46	43	36
JUL. 2	14	8	8	9	18	18	3	26	17	46	43	36
JUL. 3	15	10	10	11	18	18	3	26	17	46	43	36
JUL. 4	15	11	12	12	18	18	3	26	17	46	43	36
JUL. 5	15	13	13	14	18	18	3	26	17	46	43	36
JUL. 6	15	14	15	15	18	18	3	26	17	46	43	36
JUL. 7	15	16	17	17	18	18	3	26	17	46	43	36
JUL. 8	15	18	18	19	19	19	3	26	17	46	43	36
JUL. 9	15	19	20	20	19	19	3	26	17	46	43	36
JUL. 10	15	21	21	22	19	19	3	26	17	46	43	36
JUL. 11	16	22	23	23	19	19	4	26	17	46	43	36
JUL. 12	16	24	24	25	19	19	4	26	17	46	43	36
JUL. 13	16	26	26	27	19	19	4	26	17	46	43	36
JUL. 14	16	27	28	28	19	20	4	26	17	46	43	36
JUL. 15	16	29	29	30	19	20	4	26	17	46	43	36
JUL. 16	16	31	31	32	19	20	4	26	17	46	43	36
JUL. 17	16	32	33	34	20	20	4	26	17	46	43	36
JUL. 18	16	34	35	36	20	20	4	27	17	46	43	36
JUL. 19	17	36	37	38	20	20	4	27	17	46	43	36
JUL. 20	17	38	39	40	20	21	4	27	17	46	43	36
JUL. 21	17	40	41	42	20	21	4	27	17	46	43	36
JUL. 22	17	42	43	44	20	21	4	27	17	46	43	36
JUL. 23	17	44	45	46	20	21	5	27	17	46	43	36
JUL. 24	17	46	47	48	20	21	5	27	17	46	43	36
JUL. 25	17	48	1	2	20	21	5	27	17	46	43	36
JUL. 26	18	2	3	3	20	21	5	27	17	46	43	36
JUL. 27	18	4	5	5	20	21	5	27	17	46	43	36
JUL. 28	18	6	6	7	20	22	5	27	17	46	43	36
JUL. 29	18	7	8	9	19	22	5	27	17	46	43	36
JUL. 30	18	9	10	10	19	22	5	27	17	46	43	36
JUL. 31	18	11	11	12	19	22	5	27	17	46	43	36

Date & Time	SUN	MOON 1	MOON 2	MOON 3	MERCURY	VENUS	MARS	JUPITER	SATURN	URANUS	NEPTUNE	PLUTO
AUG. 1	18	12	13	14	19	22	5	27	17	46	43	36
AUG. 2	18	14	15	15	19	23	5	27	17	46	43	36
AUG. 3	19	16	16	17	19	23	5	27	17	46	43	36
AUG. 4	19	17	18	18	19	23	5	27	17	46	43	36
AUG. 5	19	19	19	20	19	23	6	27	17	46	43	36
AUG. 6	19	20	21	21	19	23	6	27	17	46	43	36
AUG. 7	19	22	22	23	19	23	6	27	17	46	43	36
AUG. 8	19	24	24	25	19	24	6	27	17	46	43	36
AUG. 9	19	25	26	26	18	24	6	27	17	46	43	36
AUG. 10	19	27	27	28	18	24	6	27	17	46	43	36
AUG. 11	20	28	29	30	18	24	6	27	17	46	43	36
AUG. 12	20	30	31	31	18	24	6	27	17	46	43	36
AUG. 13	20	32	32	33	18	24	6	27	17	46	43	36
AUG. 14	20	34	34	35	18	25	6	27	17	46	43	36
AUG. 15	20	36	36	37	18	25	6	27	17	46	43	36
AUG. 16	20	37	38	39	18	25	6	27	17	46	43	36
AUG. 17	20	39	40	41	18	25	6	27	18	46	43	36
AUG. 18	20	41	42	43	18	25	6	27	18	46	43	36
AUG. 19	21	43	44	45	18	25	7	27	18	46	43	36
AUG. 20	21	45	46	47	18	25	7	27	18	46	43	36
AUG. 21	21	47	48	1	18	26	7	27	18	46	43	36
AUG. 22	21	1	2	3	18	26	7	27	18	46	43	36
AUG. 23	21	3	4	5	19	26	7	27	18	46	43	36
AUG. 24	21	5	6	6	19	26	7	27	18	46	43	36
AUG. 25	21	7	8	8	19	26	7	27	18	46	43	36
AUG. 26	22	9	9	10	19	26	7	27	18	46	43	36
AUG. 27	22	10	11	11	19	27	7	27	18	46	43	36
AUG. 28	22	12	13	13	19	27	7	27	18	46	43	36
AUG. 29	22	14	14	15	19	27	7	27	18	46	43	36
AUG. 30	22	15	16	16	20	27	7	27	18	46	43	36
AUG. 31	22	17	17	18	20	27	7	27	18	46	43	36

MOON 1 ◐ 12:01 A.M. TO 8:00 A.M.　　**MOON 2** ◑ 8:01 A.M. TO 4:00 P.M.　　**MOON 3** ● 4:01 P.M. TO 12:00 A.M.

Use only one "moon" number. Choose the column closest to your time of birth. If your place of birth is not on Eastern Standard Time, be sure to read "How to Convert to Eastern Standard Time" at the beginning of this section.

2005

September

Date & Time	SUN	MOON 1	MOON 2	MOON 3	MERCURY	VENUS	MARS	JUPITER	SATURN	URANUS	NEPTUNE	PLUTO
SEP. 1	22	18	19	19	20	27	7	27	18	46	43	36
SEP. 2	22	20	21	21	20	27	7	27	18	46	43	36
SEP. 3	23	22	22	23	21	28	7	27	18	46	43	36
SEP. 4	23	23	24	24	21	28	7	28	18	46	43	36
SEP. 5	23	25	25	26	21	28	7	28	18	46	43	36
SEP. 6	23	26	27	27	21	28	7	28	18	46	43	36
SEP. 7	23	28	29	29	22	28	8	28	18	46	43	36
SEP. 8	23	30	30	31	22	28	8	28	18	46	43	36
SEP. 9	23	31	32	33	22	29	8	28	18	46	43	36
SEP. 10	23	33	34	34	22	29	8	28	18	46	43	36
SEP. 11	24	35	36	36	23	29	8	28	18	46	43	36
SEP. 12	24	37	37	38	23	29	8	28	18	46	43	36
SEP. 13	24	39	39	40	23	29	8	28	18	46	43	36
SEP. 14	24	41	41	42	23	29	8	28	18	46	43	36
SEP. 15	24	43	43	44	24	30	8	28	18	46	43	36
SEP. 16	24	45	45	46	24	30	8	28	18	46	43	36
SEP. 17	24	47	47	48	24	30	8	28	18	46	43	36
SEP. 18	24	1	1	2	24	30	8	28	18	46	43	36
SEP. 19	25	3	3	4	25	30	8	28	18	46	43	36
SEP. 20	25	4	5	6	25	30	8	28	18	46	43	36
SEP. 21	25	6	7	7	25	30	8	28	18	46	43	36
SEP. 22	25	8	9	9	25	31	8	28	18	46	43	36
SEP. 23	25	10	10	11	25	31	8	28	18	46	43	36
SEP. 24	25	12	12	13	26	31	8	28	18	46	43	36
SEP. 25	26	13	14	14	26	31	8	28	18	46	43	36
SEP. 26	26	15	15	16	26	31	8	28	18	46	43	36
SEP. 27	26	16	17	17	26	31	8	28	18	46	43	36
SEP. 28	26	18	18	19	26	31	8	28	18	46	43	36
SEP. 29	26	20	20	21	27	32	8	28	18	46	43	36
SEP. 30	26	21	22	22	27	32	8	28	18	46	43	36

October

Date & Time	SUN	MOON 1	MOON 2	MOON 3	MERCURY	VENUS	MARS	JUPITER	SATURN	URANUS	NEPTUNE	PLUTO
OCT. 1	26	23	23	24	27	32	8	28	18	46	43	36
OCT. 2	26	24	25	25	28	32	8	28	18	46	43	36
OCT. 3	27	26	27	27	28	32	8	28	18	46	43	36
OCT. 4	27	28	28	29	28	32	8	28	18	46	43	36
OCT. 5	27	29	30	30	28	33	8	28	18	46	43	36
OCT. 6	27	31	32	32	28	33	8	28	18	46	43	36
OCT. 7	27	33	33	34	29	33	8	28	18	46	43	36
OCT. 8	27	35	35	36	29	33	8	28	18	46	43	36
OCT. 9	27	36	37	38	29	33	8	28	18	46	43	36
OCT. 10	27	38	39	39	29	33	8	29	18	46	43	36
OCT. 11	28	40	41	41	29	33	8	29	18	46	43	36
OCT. 12	28	42	43	43	30	34	8	29	18	46	43	36
OCT. 13	28	44	45	45	30	34	8	29	18	46	43	36
OCT. 14	28	46	46	47	30	34	8	29	18	46	43	36
OCT. 15	28	48	48	1	30	34	8	29	18	46	43	36
OCT. 16	28	2	2	3	30	34	8	29	18	46	43	36
OCT. 17	28	4	4	5	31	34	8	29	18	46	43	36
OCT. 18	28	6	6	7	31	34	8	29	18	46	43	36
OCT. 19	29	7	8	9	31	35	8	29	18	46	43	36
OCT. 20	29	9	10	10	31	35	8	29	18	46	43	36
OCT. 21	29	11	11	12	31	35	8	29	18	46	43	36
OCT. 22	29	13	13	14	32	35	8	29	18	46	43	36
OCT. 23	29	14	15	15	32	35	8	29	18	46	43	36
OCT. 24	29	16	16	17	32	35	8	29	18	46	43	36
OCT. 25	29	17	18	18	32	35	8	29	18	46	43	36
OCT. 26	30	19	20	20	32	36	8	29	18	46	43	36
OCT. 27	30	21	21	22	32	36	7	29	18	46	43	36
OCT. 28	30	22	23	23	33	36	7	29	18	46	43	36
OCT. 29	30	24	24	25	33	36	7	29	18	46	43	36
OCT. 30	30	25	26	27	33	36	7	29	18	46	43	36
OCT. 31	30	27	28	28	33	36	7	29	18	46	43	36

MOON 1 ◐ 12:01 A.M. TO 8:00 A.M.   **MOON 2** ◑ 8:01 A.M. TO 4:00 P.M.   **MOON 3** ● 4:01 P.M. TO 12:00 A.M.
Use only one "moon" number. Choose the column closest to your time of birth. If your place of birth is not on Eastern Standard Time, be sure to read "How to Convert to Eastern Standard Time" at the beginning of this section.

2005

November   December

Date & Time	SUN	MOON 1	MOON 2	MOON 3	MERCURY	VENUS	MARS	JUPITER	SATURN	URANUS	NEPTUNE	PLUTO
NOV. 1	30	29	29	30	33	36	7	29	18	46	43	36
NOV. 2	30	31	31	32	33	37	7	29	18	46	43	36
NOV. 3	31	32	33	34	34	37	7	29	18	46	43	36
NOV. 4	31	34	35	35	34	37	7	29	18	46	43	36
NOV. 5	31	36	37	37	34	37	7	29	18	46	43	36
NOV. 6	31	38	38	39	34	37	7	29	18	46	43	36
NOV. 7	31	40	40	41	34	37	7	29	18	46	43	36
NOV. 8	31	42	42	43	34	37	7	29	18	46	43	36
NOV. 9	31	43	44	45	34	37	7	29	18	46	43	36
NOV. 10	31	45	46	47	34	38	7	29	18	46	43	36
NOV. 11	31	47	48	48	34	38	7	29	18	46	43	36
NOV. 12	32	1	2	2	34	38	7	29	18	46	43	36
NOV. 13	32	3	4	4	34	38	7	29	18	46	43	36
NOV. 14	32	5	5	6	34	38	7	30	18	46	43	36
NOV. 15	32	7	7	8	34	38	7	30	18	46	43	36
NOV. 16	32	8	9	10	34	38	7	30	18	46	43	36
NOV. 17	32	10	11	11	34	38	7	30	18	46	43	36
NOV. 18	32	12	12	13	34	39	6	30	18	46	43	36
NOV. 19	33	14	14	15	34	39	6	30	18	46	43	36
NOV. 20	33	15	16	16	34	39	6	30	18	46	43	36
NOV. 21	33	17	17	18	34	39	6	30	18	46	43	36
NOV. 22	33	18	19	20	34	39	6	30	18	46	43	36
NOV. 23	33	20	21	21	34	39	6	30	18	46	43	36
NOV. 24	33	22	22	23	33	39	6	30	18	46	43	36
NOV. 25	34	23	24	24	33	39	6	30	18	46	43	36
NOV. 26	34	25	25	26	33	39	6	30	18	46	43	36
NOV. 27	34	26	27	28	33	40	6	30	18	46	43	36
NOV. 28	34	28	29	29	33	40	6	30	18	46	43	36
NOV. 29	34	30	30	31	33	40	6	30	18	46	43	36
NOV. 30	34	32	32	33	32	40	6	30	18	46	43	36
DEC. 1	34	33	34	35	32	40	6	30	18	46	43	36
DEC. 2	34	35	36	37	32	40	6	30	18	46	43	36
DEC. 3	35	37	38	39	32	40	6	30	18	46	43	36
DEC. 4	35	39	40	40	32	40	6	30	18	46	43	36
DEC. 5	35	41	42	42	32	40	6	30	18	46	43	36
DEC. 6	35	43	44	44	32	40	6	30	18	46	43	36
DEC. 7	35	45	46	46	32	40	6	30	18	46	43	36
DEC. 8	35	47	47	48	32	41	6	30	18	46	43	36
DEC. 9	35	1	1	2	33	41	6	30	18	46	43	36
DEC. 10	35	2	3	4	33	41	6	30	18	46	43	36
DEC. 11	36	4	5	6	33	41	6	30	18	46	43	36
DEC. 12	36	6	7	7	33	41	6	30	18	46	43	36
DEC. 13	36	8	8	9	33	41	6	30	18	46	43	36
DEC. 14	36	10	10	11	33	41	6	30	18	46	43	36
DEC. 15	36	11	12	12	33	41	6	30	18	46	43	36
DEC. 16	36	13	14	14	33	41	6	30	18	46	43	36
DEC. 17	36	15	15	16	34	41	6	30	18	46	43	36
DEC. 18	36	16	17	17	34	41	6	30	18	46	43	36
DEC. 19	37	18	18	19	34	41	6	30	18	46	43	36
DEC. 20	37	20	20	21	34	41	6	30	18	46	43	36
DEC. 21	37	21	22	22	34	41	6	30	18	46	43	36
DEC. 22	37	23	23	24	35	41	6	31	18	46	43	36
DEC. 23	37	24	25	25	35	41	6	31	18	46	43	36
DEC. 24	37	26	26	27	35	41	6	31	18	46	43	36
DEC. 25	37	28	28	29	35	41	6	31	18	46	43	36
DEC. 26	38	29	30	30	35	41	6	31	18	46	43	36
DEC. 27	38	31	31	32	35	41	6	31	18	46	43	36
DEC. 28	38	33	33	34	36	41	6	31	18	46	43	36
DEC. 29	38	35	35	36	36	41	6	31	18	46	43	36
DEC. 30	38	36	37	38	36	41	6	31	18	46	43	36
DEC. 31	38	38	39	40	36	41	6	31	18	46	43	36

MOON 1 ☽ 12:01 A.M. TO 8:00 A.M.   **MOON 2** ◗ 8:01 A.M. TO 4:00 P.M.   **MOON 3** ● 4:01 P.M. TO 12:00 A.M.

Use only one "moon" number. Choose the column closest to your time of birth. If your place of birth is not on Eastern Standard Time, be sure to read "How to Convert to Eastern Standard Time" at the beginning of this section.

2006

January

Date & Time	SUN ☉	MOON 1 ◗	MOON 2 ◑	MOON 3 ●	MERCURY	VENUS	MARS	JUPITER	SATURN	URANUS	NEPTUNE	PLUTO
JAN. 1	38	40	41	42	36	41	6	31	18	46	43	36
JAN. 2	38	42	43	44	37	41	6	31	18	46	43	36
JAN. 3	39	44	45	46	37	41	7	31	18	46	43	36
JAN. 4	39	46	47	48	37	41	7	31	18	46	43	36
JAN. 5	39	48	1	1	37	41	7	31	18	46	43	36
JAN. 6	39	2	3	3	37	41	7	31	18	46	43	36
JAN. 7	39	4	5	5	38	41	7	31	18	46	43	36
JAN. 8	39	6	6	7	38	41	7	31	18	46	43	36
JAN. 9	39	7	8	9	38	41	7	31	18	46	43	36
JAN. 10	40	9	10	10	38	40	7	31	18	46	43	36
JAN. 11	40	11	11	12	38	40	7	31	18	46	43	36
JAN. 12	40	13	13	14	39	40	7	31	18	46	43	36
JAN. 13	40	14	15	15	39	40	7	31	18	46	43	36
JAN. 14	40	16	16	17	39	40	7	31	18	46	43	36
JAN. 15	40	17	18	19	39	40	7	31	18	46	43	36
JAN. 16	40	19	20	20	40	40	7	31	18	46	43	36
JAN. 17	41	21	21	22	40	40	7	31	18	46	43	36
JAN. 18	41	22	23	23	40	40	7	31	18	46	43	36
JAN. 19	41	24	24	25	40	40	7	31	18	46	43	36
JAN. 20	41	25	26	26	40	40	7	31	18	46	43	36
JAN. 21	41	27	28	28	41	40	7	31	18	46	43	36
JAN. 22	41	29	29	30	41	40	7	31	18	46	43	36
JAN. 23	42	30	31	31	41	39	7	31	18	46	43	36
JAN. 24	42	32	33	33	41	39	7	31	18	46	43	36
JAN. 25	42	34	34	35	41	39	8	31	18	46	43	36
JAN. 26	42	36	36	37	42	39	8	31	18	46	43	36
JAN. 27	42	37	38	39	42	39	8	31	18	46	43	36
JAN. 28	42	39	40	41	42	39	8	31	18	46	43	36
JAN. 29	42	41	42	43	42	39	8	31	18	46	43	36
JAN. 30	42	43	44	45	43	39	8	31	18	46	43	36
JAN. 31	43	46	46	47	43	39	8	31	18	46	43	36

February

Date & Time	SUN ☉	MOON 1 ◗	MOON 2 ◑	MOON 3 ●	MERCURY	VENUS	MARS	JUPITER	SATURN	URANUS	NEPTUNE	PLUTO
FEB. 1	43	48	48	1	43	39	8	31	18	46	43	36
FEB. 2	43	1	2	3	43	39	8	31	18	46	43	36
FEB. 3	43	3	4	5	44	39	8	31	18	46	43	36
FEB. 4	43	5	6	6	44	39	8	31	18	46	43	36
FEB. 5	43	7	8	8	44	39	8	31	18	46	43	36
FEB. 6	43	9	9	10	44	39	8	31	18	46	43	36
FEB. 7	43	10	11	12	45	39	8	31	18	46	43	36
FEB. 8	44	12	13	13	45	39	8	31	18	46	43	36
FEB. 9	44	14	14	15	45	39	8	31	18	46	43	36
FEB. 10	44	15	16	17	45	39	8	31	18	46	43	36
FEB. 11	44	17	18	18	45	39	9	31	18	46	43	36
FEB. 12	44	19	19	20	46	39	9	31	18	46	43	36
FEB. 13	44	20	21	21	46	39	9	31	18	46	43	36
FEB. 14	44	22	22	23	46	39	9	31	18	46	43	36
FEB. 15	44	23	24	24	46	39	9	31	18	46	43	36
FEB. 16	45	25	25	26	47	40	9	31	18	46	43	36
FEB. 17	45	27	27	28	47	40	9	31	18	46	43	36
FEB. 18	45	28	29	29	47	40	9	31	18	46	43	36
FEB. 19	45	30	30	31	47	40	9	31	18	46	43	36
FEB. 20	45	31	32	33	47	40	9	31	18	46	43	36
FEB. 21	45	33	34	34	48	40	9	31	18	46	43	36
FEB. 22	45	35	35	36	48	40	9	31	18	46	43	36
FEB. 23	46	37	37	38	48	40	9	31	18	46	43	36
FEB. 24	46	39	39	40	48	40	9	31	18	46	43	36
FEB. 25	46	41	41	42	48	40	9	31	18	46	43	36
FEB. 26	46	43	43	44	48	40	10	31	18	46	43	36
FEB. 27	46	45	45	46	48	40	10	31	18	46	43	37
FEB. 28	46	47	47	48	48	40	10	31	18	46	43	37

MOON 1 ◗ 12:01 A.M. TO 8:00 A.M.   **MOON 2** ◑ 8:01 A.M. TO 4:00 P.M.   **MOON 3** ● 4:01 P.M. TO 12:00 A.M.

Use only one "moon" number. Choose the column closest to your time of birth. If your place of birth is not on Eastern Standard Time, be sure to read "How to Convert to Eastern Standard Time" at the beginning of this section.

2006

March

April

Date & Time	SUN	MOON 1	MOON 2	MOON 3	MERCURY	VENUS	MARS	JUPITER	SATURN	URANUS	NEPTUNE	PLUTO
MAR. 1	46	1	1	2	1	41	10	31	18	46	43	37
MAR. 2	46	3	3	4	1	41	10	31	18	46	43	37
MAR. 3	47	5	5	6	1	41	10	31	18	46	43	37
MAR. 4	47	6	7	8	1	41	10	31	18	46	43	37
MAR. 5	47	8	9	9	48	41	10	31	18	46	43	37
MAR. 6	47	10	11	11	48	41	10	31	18	46	43	37
MAR. 7	47	12	12	13	48	41	10	31	18	46	43	37
MAR. 8	47	13	14	15	48	41	10	31	18	46	43	37
MAR. 9	47	15	16	16	48	41	10	31	18	46	43	37
MAR. 10	47	17	17	18	48	41	10	31	18	46	43	37
MAR. 11	48	18	19	19	48	42	10	31	18	46	43	37
MAR. 12	48	20	20	21	48	42	11	31	18	46	43	37
MAR. 13	48	21	22	22	48	42	11	31	18	46	43	37
MAR. 14	48	23	24	24	48	42	11	31	18	46	43	37
MAR. 15	48	25	25	26	47	42	11	31	18	47	43	37
MAR. 16	48	26	27	27	47	42	11	31	18	47	43	37
MAR. 17	48	28	28	29	47	42	11	31	18	47	43	37
MAR. 18	48	29	30	30	47	42	11	31	18	47	43	37
MAR. 19	1	31	32	32	47	43	11	31	18	47	43	37
MAR. 20	1	33	33	34	47	43	11	31	18	47	43	37
MAR. 21	1	34	35	36	47	43	11	31	18	47	43	37
MAR. 22	1	36	37	37	47	43	11	31	18	47	43	37
MAR. 23	1	38	39	39	47	43	11	31	18	47	43	37
MAR. 24	1	40	40	41	47	43	11	31	18	47	43	37
MAR. 25	2	42	42	43	47	43	11	31	18	47	43	37
MAR. 26	2	44	44	45	47	43	12	31	18	47	43	37
MAR. 27	2	46	46	47	47	44	12	31	18	47	43	37
MAR. 28	2	48	48	1	47	44	12	31	18	47	44	37
MAR. 29	2	2	2	3	47	44	12	31	18	47	44	37
MAR. 30	2	4	4	5	47	44	12	31	18	47	44	37
MAR. 31	2	6	6	7	47	44	12	31	18	47	44	37

Date & Time	SUN	MOON 1	MOON 2	MOON 3	MERCURY	VENUS	MARS	JUPITER	SATURN	URANUS	NEPTUNE	PLUTO
APR. 1	2	8	8	9	47	44	12	31	18	47	44	37
APR. 2	2	9	10	11	47	44	12	31	18	47	44	37
APR. 3	3	11	12	12	47	45	12	31	18	47	44	37
APR. 4	3	13	13	14	47	45	12	31	18	47	44	37
APR. 5	3	15	15	16	47	45	12	31	18	47	44	37
APR. 6	3	16	17	17	47	45	12	31	18	47	44	37
APR. 7	3	18	18	19	48	45	12	31	18	47	44	37
APR. 8	3	19	20	20	48	45	13	31	18	47	44	37
APR. 9	3	21	21	22	48	45	13	31	18	47	44	37
APR. 10	3	23	23	24	48	46	13	31	18	47	44	37
APR. 11	4	24	25	25	48	46	13	31	18	47	44	37
APR. 12	4	26	26	27	48	46	13	31	18	47	44	37
APR. 13	4	27	28	28	48	46	13	31	18	47	44	37
APR. 14	4	29	30	30	1	46	13	31	18	47	44	37
APR. 15	4	31	31	32	1	46	13	31	18	47	44	37
APR. 16	4	32	33	33	1	46	13	31	18	47	44	37
APR. 17	4	34	35	35	1	47	13	31	18	47	44	37
APR. 18	4	36	36	37	1	47	13	31	18	47	44	37
APR. 19	5	38	38	39	1	47	13	31	18	47	44	37
APR. 20	5	39	40	41	2	47	13	31	18	47	44	37
APR. 21	5	41	42	42	2	47	14	31	18	47	44	37
APR. 22	5	43	44	44	2	47	14	31	18	47	44	37
APR. 23	5	45	46	46	2	47	14	31	18	47	44	37
APR. 24	5	47	48	2	48	14	31	18	47	44	37
APR. 25	6	1	2	2	3	48	14	31	18	47	44	37
APR. 26	6	3	3	4	3	48	14	31	18	47	44	37
APR. 27	6	5	5	6	3	48	14	31	18	47	44	37
APR. 28	6	7	7	8	3	48	14	31	18	47	44	37
APR. 29	6	9	9	10	4	48	14	31	18	47	44	37
APR. 30	6	10	11	12	4	48	14	31	18	47	44	36

MOON 1 ☽ 12:01 A.M. TO 8:00 A.M.   **MOON 2** ☽ 8:01 A.M. TO 4:00 P.M.   **MOON 3** ● 4:01 P.M. TO 12:00 A.M.
Use only one "moon" number. Choose the column closest to your time of birth. If your place of birth is not on
Eastern Standard Time, be sure to read "How to Convert to Eastern Standard Time" at the beginning of this section.

2006

May   June

Date & Time	SUN ☉	MOON 1 ◖	MOON 2 ◑	MOON 3 ●	MERCURY	VENUS	MARS	JUPITER	SATURN	URANUS	NEPTUNE	PLUTO
MAY 1	6	12	13	13	4	1	14	31	18	47	44	36
MAY 2	6	14	15	15	4	1	14	31	18	47	44	36
MAY 3	7	16	16	17	4	1	14	31	18	47	44	36
MAY 4	7	17	18	18	5	1	15	31	18	47	44	36
MAY 5	7	19	19	20	5	1	15	31	18	47	44	36
MAY 6	7	20	21	22	5	1	15	31	18	47	44	36
MAY 7	7	22	23	23	5	2	15	31	18	47	44	36
MAY 8	7	24	24	25	6	2	15	31	18	47	44	36
MAY 9	7	25	26	26	6	2	15	31	18	47	44	36
MAY 10	7	27	27	28	6	2	15	31	18	47	44	36
MAY 11	8	28	29	30	6	2	15	31	18	47	44	36
MAY 12	8	30	31	31	7	2	15	31	18	47	44	36
MAY 13	8	32	32	33	7	2	15	31	18	47	44	36
MAY 14	8	34	34	35	7	3	15	31	18	47	44	36
MAY 15	8	35	36	37	8	3	15	31	18	47	44	36
MAY 16	8	37	38	38	8	3	15	31	18	47	44	36
MAY 17	8	39	40	40	8	3	16	31	18	47	44	36
MAY 18	8	41	41	42	8	3	16	31	18	47	44	36
MAY 19	9	43	43	44	9	3	16	31	18	47	44	36
MAY 20	9	45	45	46	9	4	16	31	18	47	44	36
MAY 21	9	46	47	48	9	4	16	31	18	47	44	36
MAY 22	9	48	1	2	10	4	16	31	18	47	44	36
MAY 23	9	2	3	3	10	4	16	31	18	47	44	36
MAY 24	9	4	5	5	10	4	16	31	18	47	44	36
MAY 25	10	6	7	7	11	4	16	30	18	47	44	36
MAY 26	10	8	8	9	11	4	16	30	18	47	44	36
MAY 27	10	10	10	11	11	5	16	30	18	47	44	36
MAY 28	10	12	12	13	11	5	16	30	18	47	44	36
MAY 29	10	13	14	14	12	5	17	30	18	47	44	36
MAY 30	10	15	16	16	12	5	17	30	18	47	44	36
MAY 31	10	17	17	18	12	5	17	30	18	47	44	36

Date & Time	SUN ☉	MOON 1 ◖	MOON 2 ◑	MOON 3 ●	MERCURY	VENUS	MARS	JUPITER	SATURN	URANUS	NEPTUNE	PLUTO
JUN. 1	10	18	19	19	12	5	17	30	18	47	44	36
JUN. 2	10	20	20	21	13	6	17	30	18	47	44	36
JUN. 3	11	22	22	23	13	6	17	30	18	47	44	36
JUN. 4	11	23	24	24	13	6	17	30	18	47	44	36
JUN. 5	11	25	25	26	13	6	17	30	18	47	44	36
JUN. 6	11	26	27	27	14	6	17	30	18	47	44	36
JUN. 7	11	28	28	29	14	6	17	30	18	47	44	36
JUN. 8	11	30	30	31	14	6	17	30	18	47	44	36
JUN. 9	11	31	32	32	14	7	17	30	18	47	44	36
JUN. 10	11	33	34	34	14	7	17	30	18	47	44	36
JUN. 11	12	35	35	36	15	7	18	30	18	47	44	36
JUN. 12	12	37	37	38	15	7	18	30	18	47	44	36
JUN. 13	12	38	39	40	15	7	18	30	18	47	44	36
JUN. 14	12	40	41	42	15	7	18	30	18	47	44	36
JUN. 15	12	42	43	43	15	8	18	30	18	47	44	36
JUN. 16	12	44	45	45	16	8	18	30	18	47	44	36
JUN. 17	12	46	47	47	16	8	18	30	18	47	44	36
JUN. 18	12	48	1	1	16	8	18	30	18	47	44	36
JUN. 19	13	2	2	3	16	8	18	30	18	47	44	36
JUN. 20	13	4	4	5	16	8	18	30	18	47	44	36
JUN. 21	13	5	6	7	16	8	18	30	18	47	44	36
JUN. 22	13	7	8	9	16	9	19	30	18	47	44	36
JUN. 23	13	9	10	10	17	9	19	30	18	47	44	36
JUN. 24	13	11	12	12	17	9	19	30	18	47	44	36
JUN. 25	14	13	13	14	17	9	19	30	18	47	44	36
JUN. 26	14	14	15	16	17	9	19	30	18	47	44	36
JUN. 27	14	16	17	17	17	9	19	30	18	47	44	36
JUN. 28	14	18	18	19	17	10	19	30	18	47	44	36
JUN. 29	14	19	20	20	17	10	19	30	18	47	44	36
JUN. 30	14	21	22	22	17	10	19	30	18	47	44	36

MOON 1 ◖ 12:01 A.M. TO 8:00 A.M.   **MOON 2** ◑ 8:01 A.M. TO 4:00 P.M.   **MOON 3** ● 4:01 P.M. TO 12:00 A.M.
Use only one "moon" number. Choose the column closest to your time of birth. If your place of birth is not on Eastern Standard Time, be sure to read "How to Convert to Eastern Standard Time" at the beginning of this section.

2006

July

Date & Time	SUN	MOON 1	MOON 2	MOON 3	MERCURY	VENUS	MARS	JUPITER	SATURN	URANUS	NEPTUNE	PLUTO
JUL. 1	14	23	23	24	17	10	19	30	18	47	44	36
JUL. 2	14	24	25	25	17	10	19	30	18	47	44	36
JUL. 3	15	26	26	27	17	10	19	30	18	47	44	36
JUL. 4	15	27	28	28	17	11	19	30	18	47	44	36
JUL. 5	15	29	29	30	17	11	20	30	18	47	44	36
JUL. 6	15	31	31	32	17	11	20	30	18	47	44	36
JUL. 7	15	32	33	33	17	11	20	30	18	47	44	36
JUL. 8	15	34	35	35	17	11	20	30	18	47	44	36
JUL. 9	15	36	36	37	17	11	20	30	18	47	44	36
JUL. 10	15	38	38	39	17	12	20	30	18	47	44	36
JUL. 11	16	40	40	41	17	12	20	30	18	47	44	36
JUL. 12	16	42	42	43	17	12	20	30	18	47	44	36
JUL. 13	16	44	44	45	17	12	20	30	19	47	44	36
JUL. 14	16	45	46	47	17	12	20	30	19	47	44	36
JUL. 15	16	47	48	1	17	12	20	30	19	47	44	36
JUL. 16	16	1	2	3	17	13	20	30	19	47	44	36
JUL. 17	16	3	4	4	16	13	21	30	19	47	44	36
JUL. 18	16	5	6	6	16	13	21	30	19	47	44	36
JUL. 19	17	7	7	8	16	13	21	30	19	47	44	36
JUL. 20	17	9	9	10	16	13	21	30	19	47	44	36
JUL. 21	17	10	11	12	16	13	21	30	19	47	43	36
JUL. 22	17	12	13	13	16	13	21	30	19	47	43	36
JUL. 23	17	14	14	15	16	14	21	30	19	47	43	36
JUL. 24	17	16	16	17	16	14	21	30	19	47	43	36
JUL. 25	17	17	18	18	16	14	21	30	19	47	43	36
JUL. 26	18	19	19	20	16	14	21	30	19	47	43	36
JUL. 27	18	21	21	22	16	14	21	30	19	47	43	36
JUL. 28	18	22	23	23	16	14	21	30	19	47	43	36
JUL. 29	18	24	24	25	16	15	22	30	19	47	43	36
JUL. 30	18	25	26	26	16	15	22	30	19	47	43	36
JUL. 31	18	27	27	28	16	15	22	30	19	47	43	36

August

Date & Time	SUN	MOON 1	MOON 2	MOON 3	MERCURY	VENUS	MARS	JUPITER	SATURN	URANUS	NEPTUNE	PLUTO
AUG. 1	18	28	29	29	16	15	22	30	19	47	43	36
AUG. 2	18	30	31	31	16	15	22	30	19	47	43	36
AUG. 3	19	32	32	33	16	15	22	30	19	47	43	36
AUG. 4	19	33	34	35	16	16	22	30	19	47	43	36
AUG. 5	19	35	36	36	16	16	22	30	19	47	43	36
AUG. 6	19	37	38	38	16	16	22	30	19	47	43	36
AUG. 7	19	39	39	40	16	16	22	30	19	47	43	36
AUG. 8	19	41	41	42	16	16	22	30	19	47	43	36
AUG. 9	19	43	43	44	17	16	22	30	19	47	43	36
AUG. 10	19	45	45	46	17	17	23	30	19	47	43	36
AUG. 11	20	47	47	48	17	17	23	30	19	47	43	36
AUG. 12	20	1	1	2	17	17	23	30	19	47	43	36
AUG. 13	20	3	3	4	17	17	23	30	19	47	43	36
AUG. 14	20	5	5	6	18	17	23	30	19	47	43	36
AUG. 15	20	6	7	8	18	17	23	30	19	47	43	36
AUG. 16	20	8	9	9	18	18	23	30	19	47	43	36
AUG. 17	20	10	11	11	18	18	23	30	19	47	43	36
AUG. 18	20	12	12	13	18	18	23	31	19	47	43	36
AUG. 19	21	14	14	15	19	18	23	31	19	47	43	36
AUG. 20	21	15	16	16	19	18	23	31	19	47	43	36
AUG. 21	21	17	17	18	19	18	23	31	19	47	43	36
AUG. 22	21	18	19	20	19	18	24	31	19	47	43	36
AUG. 23	21	20	21	21	20	19	24	31	19	47	43	36
AUG. 24	21	22	22	23	20	19	24	31	19	47	43	36
AUG. 25	21	23	24	24	20	19	24	31	19	47	43	36
AUG. 26	22	25	25	26	21	19	24	31	19	47	43	36
AUG. 27	22	26	27	27	21	19	24	31	19	47	43	36
AUG. 28	22	28	29	29	21	19	24	31	19	47	43	36
AUG. 29	22	30	30	31	21	20	24	31	19	47	43	36
AUG. 30	22	31	32	32	22	20	24	31	19	47	43	36
AUG. 31	22	33	33	34	22	20	24	31	19	47	43	36

MOON 1 ☽ 12:01 A.M. TO 8:00 A.M.   **MOON 2** ☽ 8:01 A.M. TO 4:00 P.M.   **MOON 3** ● 4:01 P.M. TO 12:00 A.M.

Use only one "moon" number. Choose the column closest to your time of birth. If your place of birth is not on Eastern Standard Time, be sure to read "How to Convert to Eastern Standard Time" at the beginning of this section.

2006

September

October

Date & Time	SUN	MOON 1 ◖	MOON 2 ◑	MOON 3 ●	MERCURY	VENUS	MARS	JUPITER	SATURN	URANUS	NEPTUNE	PLUTO
SEP. 1	22	35	35	36	22	20	24	31	19	47	43	36
SEP. 2	22	36	37	37	22	20	24	31	19	47	43	36
SEP. 3	23	38	39	39	23	20	25	31	19	47	43	36
SEP. 4	23	40	41	41	23	21	25	31	19	47	43	36
SEP. 5	23	42	42	43	23	21	25	31	19	47	43	36
SEP. 6	23	44	44	45	23	21	25	31	19	47	43	36
SEP. 7	23	46	46	47	24	21	25	31	19	47	43	36
SEP. 8	23	48	1	1	24	21	25	31	19	47	43	36
SEP. 9	23	2	3	3	24	21	25	31	19	47	43	36
SEP. 10	23	4	5	5	24	22	25	31	20	47	43	36
SEP. 11	24	6	6	7	25	22	25	31	20	47	43	36
SEP. 12	24	8	8	9	25	22	25	31	20	47	43	36
SEP. 13	24	10	10	11	25	22	25	31	20	47	43	36
SEP. 14	24	11	12	13	25	22	25	31	20	47	43	36
SEP. 15	24	13	14	14	25	22	26	31	20	47	43	36
SEP. 16	24	15	15	16	26	23	26	31	20	47	43	36
SEP. 17	24	16	17	18	26	23	26	31	20	47	43	36
SEP. 18	24	18	19	19	26	23	26	31	20	47	43	36
SEP. 19	25	20	20	21	26	23	26	31	20	47	43	36
SEP. 20	25	21	22	22	27	23	26	31	20	47	43	36
SEP. 21	25	23	23	24	27	23	26	31	20	47	43	36
SEP. 22	25	24	25	25	27	24	26	31	20	47	43	36
SEP. 23	25	26	27	27	27	24	26	31	20	47	43	36
SEP. 24	25	28	28	29	27	24	26	31	20	47	43	36
SEP. 25	26	29	30	30	28	24	26	31	20	47	43	36
SEP. 26	26	31	31	32	28	24	27	31	20	47	43	36
SEP. 27	26	32	33	33	28	24	27	31	20	47	43	36
SEP. 28	26	34	35	35	28	25	27	31	20	47	43	36
SEP. 29	26	36	36	37	28	25	27	31	20	47	43	36
SEP. 30	26	37	38	39	29	25	27	31	20	47	43	36

Date & Time	SUN	MOON 1 ◖	MOON 2 ◑	MOON 3 ●	MERCURY	VENUS	MARS	JUPITER	SATURN	URANUS	NEPTUNE	PLUTO
OCT. 1	26	39	40	40	29	25	27	31	20	47	43	36
OCT. 2	26	41	42	42	29	25	27	31	20	47	43	36
OCT. 3	27	43	44	44	29	25	27	31	20	47	43	36
OCT. 4	27	45	46	46	29	26	27	32	20	47	43	36
OCT. 5	27	47	48	48	30	26	27	32	20	47	43	36
OCT. 6	27	1	2	2	30	26	27	32	20	47	43	36
OCT. 7	27	3	4	4	30	26	27	32	20	47	43	36
OCT. 8	27	5	6	6	30	26	28	32	20	47	43	36
OCT. 9	27	7	8	8	30	26	28	32	20	47	43	36
OCT. 10	27	9	10	10	30	27	28	32	20	46	43	36
OCT. 11	28	11	11	12	31	27	28	32	20	46	43	36
OCT. 12	28	13	13	14	31	27	28	32	20	46	43	36
OCT. 13	28	14	15	15	31	27	28	32	20	46	43	36
OCT. 14	28	16	17	17	31	27	28	32	20	46	43	36
OCT. 15	28	18	18	19	31	27	28	32	20	46	43	36
OCT. 16	28	19	20	20	31	28	28	32	20	46	43	36
OCT. 17	28	21	21	22	31	28	28	32	20	46	43	36
OCT. 18	28	22	23	24	32	28	28	32	20	46	43	36
OCT. 19	29	24	25	25	32	28	29	32	20	46	43	36
OCT. 20	29	26	26	27	32	28	29	32	20	46	43	36
OCT. 21	29	27	28	28	32	28	29	32	20	46	43	36
OCT. 22	29	29	29	30	32	29	29	32	20	46	43	36
OCT. 23	29	30	31	31	32	29	29	32	20	46	43	36
OCT. 24	29	32	33	33	32	29	29	32	20	46	43	36
OCT. 25	29	34	34	35	32	29	29	32	20	46	43	36
OCT. 26	30	35	36	36	32	29	29	32	20	46	43	36
OCT. 27	30	37	38	38	32	29	29	32	20	46	43	36
OCT. 28	30	39	39	40	32	30	29	32	20	46	43	36
OCT. 29	30	41	41	42	32	30	29	32	20	46	43	36
OCT. 30	30	42	43	44	32	30	30	32	20	46	43	36
OCT. 31	30	44	45	46	32	30	30	32	20	46	43	36

MOON 1 ◖ 12:01 A.M. TO 8:00 A.M.   **MOON 2** ◑ 8:01 A.M. TO 4:00 P.M.   **MOON 3** ● 4:01 P.M. TO 12:00 A.M.
Use only one "moon" number. Choose the column closest to your time of birth. If your place of birth is not on
Eastern Standard Time, be sure to read "How to Convert to Eastern Standard Time" at the beginning of this section.

November

Date & Time	SUN	MOON 1	MOON 2	MOON 3	MERCURY	VENUS	MARS	JUPITER	SATURN	URANUS	NEPTUNE	PLUTO
NOV. 1	30	46	47	47	32	30	30	32	20	46	43	36
NOV. 2	30	48	1	1	32	30	30	32	20	46	43	36
NOV. 3	31	2	3	3	32	31	30	32	20	46	43	36
NOV. 4	31	4	5	5	32	31	30	32	20	46	43	36
NOV. 5	31	6	7	7	32	31	30	32	20	46	43	36
NOV. 6	31	8	9	9	32	31	30	32	20	46	43	36
NOV. 7	31	10	11	11	31	31	30	32	20	46	43	36
NOV. 8	31	12	12	13	31	31	30	32	20	46	43	36
NOV. 9	31	14	14	15	31	32	30	33	20	46	43	36
NOV. 10	31	15	16	17	31	32	31	33	20	46	43	36
NOV. 11	31	17	18	18	31	32	31	33	20	46	43	36
NOV. 12	32	19	19	20	31	32	31	33	20	46	43	36
NOV. 13	32	20	21	21	30	32	31	33	20	46	43	36
NOV. 14	32	22	23	23	30	32	31	33	20	46	43	36
NOV. 15	32	24	24	25	30	33	31	33	20	46	43	36
NOV. 16	32	25	26	26	30	33	31	33	20	46	43	36
NOV. 17	32	27	27	28	30	33	31	33	20	46	43	36
NOV. 18	32	28	29	29	30	33	31	33	20	46	43	36
NOV. 19	33	30	30	31	30	33	31	33	20	46	43	36
NOV. 20	33	32	32	33	30	33	31	33	20	46	43	36
NOV. 21	33	33	34	34	30	34	32	33	20	46	43	36
NOV. 22	33	35	35	36	30	34	32	33	20	46	43	36
NOV. 23	33	37	37	38	30	34	32	33	20	46	43	36
NOV. 24	33	38	39	40	31	34	32	33	20	46	43	36
NOV. 25	34	40	41	41	31	34	32	33	20	46	43	36
NOV. 26	34	42	43	43	31	34	32	33	20	46	43	36
NOV. 27	34	44	44	45	31	35	32	33	20	46	43	36
NOV. 28	34	46	46	47	31	35	32	33	20	46	43	36
NOV. 29	34	48	48	1	31	35	32	33	20	46	43	36
NOV. 30	34	1	2	3	31	35	32	33	20	46	43	36

December

Date & Time	SUN	MOON 1	MOON 2	MOON 3	MERCURY	VENUS	MARS	JUPITER	SATURN	URANUS	NEPTUNE	PLUTO
DEC. 1	34	3	4	5	32	35	32	33	20	46	43	36
DEC. 2	34	5	6	7	32	35	33	33	20	46	43	36
DEC. 3	35	7	8	8	32	36	33	33	20	46	43	36
DEC. 4	35	9	10	10	32	36	33	33	20	46	43	36
DEC. 5	35	11	12	12	32	36	33	33	20	46	43	36
DEC. 6	35	13	14	14	33	36	33	33	20	46	43	36
DEC. 7	35	15	15	16	33	36	33	33	20	46	43	36
DEC. 8	35	16	17	18	33	36	33	33	20	46	43	36
DEC. 9	35	18	19	19	33	37	33	33	20	46	43	36
DEC. 10	35	20	20	21	33	37	33	33	20	46	43	36
DEC. 11	36	21	22	23	34	37	33	33	20	46	43	36
DEC. 12	36	23	24	24	34	37	34	33	20	46	43	36
DEC. 13	36	25	25	26	34	37	34	34	20	46	43	36
DEC. 14	36	26	27	27	34	37	34	34	20	46	43	36
DEC. 15	36	28	28	29	34	38	34	34	20	46	43	36
DEC. 16	36	29	30	30	35	38	34	34	20	46	43	36
DEC. 17	36	31	32	32	35	38	34	34	20	46	43	36
DEC. 18	36	33	33	34	35	38	34	34	20	46	43	37
DEC. 19	37	34	35	36	35	38	34	34	20	46	43	37
DEC. 20	37	36	37	37	35	38	34	34	20	46	43	37
DEC. 21	37	38	38	39	36	38	34	34	20	46	43	37
DEC. 22	37	40	40	41	36	39	34	34	20	46	43	37
DEC. 23	37	42	42	43	36	39	35	34	20	46	43	37
DEC. 24	37	43	44	45	36	39	35	34	20	46	43	37
DEC. 25	37	45	46	46	36	39	35	34	20	46	43	37
DEC. 26	38	47	48	48	37	39	35	34	20	46	43	37
DEC. 27	38	1	2	2	37	40	35	34	20	46	43	37
DEC. 28	38	3	3	4	37	40	35	34	20	46	43	37
DEC. 29	38	5	5	6	37	40	35	34	20	46	43	37
DEC. 30	38	7	7	8	37	40	35	34	20	46	43	37
DEC. 31	38	8	9	10	38	40	35	34	20	47	43	37

MOON 1 ☽ 12:01 A.M. TO 8:00 A.M.   **MOON 2** ☽ 8:01 A.M. TO 4:00 P.M.   **MOON 3** ● 4:01 P.M. TO 12:00 A.M.
Use only one "moon" number. Choose the column closest to your time of birth. If your place of birth is not on Eastern Standard Time, be sure to read "How to Convert to Eastern Standard Time" at the beginning of this section.

2007

January

Date & Time	SUN	MOON 1	MOON 2	MOON 3	MERCURY	VENUS	MARS	JUPITER	SATURN	URANUS	NEPTUNE	PLUTO
JAN. 1	38	10	11	12	38	40	35	34	20	47	43	37
JAN. 2	38	12	13	13	38	41	36	34	20	47	43	37
JAN. 3	39	14	15	15	38	41	36	34	20	47	43	37
JAN. 4	39	16	16	17	39	41	36	34	20	47	43	37
JAN. 5	39	18	18	19	39	41	36	34	20	47	43	37
JAN. 6	39	19	20	20	39	41	36	34	20	47	43	37
JAN. 7	39	21	21	22	39	41	36	34	20	47	43	37
JAN. 8	39	22	23	24	39	42	36	34	20	47	43	37
JAN. 9	39	24	25	25	40	42	36	34	20	47	43	37
JAN. 10	40	26	26	27	40	42	36	34	20	47	43	37
JAN. 11	40	27	28	28	40	42	36	34	20	47	43	37
JAN. 12	40	29	29	30	40	42	37	34	20	47	43	37
JAN. 13	40	30	31	32	40	42	37	34	20	47	43	37
JAN. 14	40	32	33	33	41	43	37	34	20	47	43	37
JAN. 15	40	34	34	35	41	43	37	34	20	47	43	37
JAN. 16	40	35	36	37	41	43	37	34	20	47	43	37
JAN. 17	41	37	38	38	41	43	37	34	20	47	43	37
JAN. 18	41	39	40	40	42	43	37	35	20	47	43	37
JAN. 19	41	41	41	42	42	43	37	35	20	47	43	37
JAN. 20	41	43	43	44	42	44	37	35	20	47	43	37
JAN. 21	41	45	45	46	42	44	37	35	20	47	43	37
JAN. 22	41	47	47	48	43	44	38	35	20	47	43	37
JAN. 23	42	48	1	2	43	44	38	35	20	47	43	37
JAN. 24	42	2	3	4	43	44	38	35	20	47	43	37
JAN. 25	42	4	5	6	43	44	38	35	20	47	43	37
JAN. 26	42	6	7	7	43	45	38	35	20	47	43	37
JAN. 27	42	8	9	9	44	45	38	35	20	47	44	37
JAN. 28	42	10	10	11	44	45	38	35	20	47	44	37
JAN. 29	42	12	12	13	44	45	38	35	20	47	44	37
JAN. 30	42	13	14	15	44	45	38	35	20	47	44	37
JAN. 31	43	15	16	16	45	45	38	35	20	47	44	37

February

Date & Time	SUN	MOON 1	MOON 2	MOON 3	MERCURY	VENUS	MARS	JUPITER	SATURN	URANUS	NEPTUNE	PLUTO
FEB. 1	43	17	18	18	45	46	38	35	20	47	44	37
FEB. 2	43	19	19	20	45	46	39	35	20	47	44	37
FEB. 3	43	20	21	21	45	46	39	35	20	47	44	37
FEB. 4	43	22	22	23	45	46	39	35	20	47	44	37
FEB. 5	43	24	24	25	45	46	39	35	20	47	44	37
FEB. 6	43	25	26	26	46	46	39	35	20	47	44	37
FEB. 7	43	27	27	28	46	47	39	35	20	47	44	37
FEB. 8	44	28	29	29	46	47	39	35	20	47	44	37
FEB. 9	44	30	30	31	46	47	39	35	20	47	44	37
FEB. 10	44	31	32	33	46	47	39	35	20	47	44	37
FEB. 11	44	33	34	34	47	47	39	35	20	47	44	37
FEB. 12	44	35	35	36	46	47	40	35	20	47	44	37
FEB. 13	44	36	37	38	46	48	40	35	20	47	44	37
FEB. 14	44	38	39	39	46	48	40	35	20	47	44	37
FEB. 15	44	40	41	41	46	48	40	35	20	47	44	37
FEB. 16	45	42	43	43	46	48	40	35	20	47	44	37
FEB. 17	45	44	45	45	46	48	40	35	20	47	44	37
FEB. 18	45	46	46	47	46	48	40	35	20	47	44	37
FEB. 19	45	48	48	1	46	1	40	35	20	47	44	37
FEB. 20	45	2	2	3	46	1	40	35	20	47	44	37
FEB. 21	45	4	4	5	46	1	40	35	20	47	44	37
FEB. 22	45	6	6	7	46	1	41	35	20	47	44	37
FEB. 23	46	8	8	9	46	1	41	35	20	47	44	37
FEB. 24	46	9	10	11	45	1	41	35	20	47	44	37
FEB. 25	46	11	12	12	45	2	41	35	20	47	44	37
FEB. 26	46	13	14	14	45	2	41	35	20	47	44	37
FEB. 27	46	15	15	16	45	2	41	35	20	47	44	37
FEB. 28	46	17	17	18	45	2	41	35	20	47	44	37

MOON 1 ☽ 12:01 A.M. TO 8:00 A.M. **MOON 2** ◐ 8:01 A.M. TO 4:00 P.M. **MOON 3** ● 4:01 P.M. TO 12:00 A.M.
Use only one "moon" number. Choose the column closest to your time of birth. If your place of birth is not on Eastern Standard Time, be sure to read "How to Convert to Eastern Standard Time" at the beginning of this section.

Date & Time	SUN ☉	MOON 1 ☽	MOON 2 ☽	MOON 3 ●	MERCURY	VENUS	MARS	JUPITER	SATURN	URANUS	NEPTUNE	PLUTO
MAR. 1	46	18	19	19	45	2	41	35	20	47	44	37
MAR. 2	46	20	20	21	45	2	41	35	20	47	44	37
MAR. 3	47	21	22	23	45	3	41	35	20	47	44	37
MAR. 4	47	23	24	24	44	3	42	35	20	47	44	37
MAR. 5	47	25	25	26	44	3	42	35	20	47	44	37
MAR. 6	47	26	27	27	44	3	42	35	20	47	44	37
MAR. 7	47	28	28	29	44	3	42	35	20	47	44	37
MAR. 8	47	29	30	30	44	3	42	35	20	47	44	37
MAR. 9	47	31	32	32	44	4	42	35	20	47	44	37
MAR. 10	47	33	33	34	44	4	42	35	20	47	44	37
MAR. 11	48	34	35	35	44	4	42	35	20	47	44	37
MAR. 12	48	36	36	37	44	4	42	35	20	47	44	37
MAR. 13	48	38	38	39	45	4	43	35	20	47	44	37
MAR. 14	48	39	40	41	45	4	43	35	20	47	44	37
MAR. 15	48	41	42	42	45	5	43	36	20	47	44	37
MAR. 16	48	43	44	44	45	5	43	36	20	47	44	37
MAR. 17	48	45	46	46	45	5	43	36	20	47	44	37
MAR. 18	48	47	48	48	45	5	43	36	20	47	44	37
MAR. 19	1	1	2	2	45	5	43	36	20	47	44	37
MAR. 20	1	3	4	4	45	5	43	36	19	47	44	37
MAR. 21	1	5	6	6	45	5	43	36	19	47	44	37
MAR. 22	1	7	8	8	45	6	44	36	19	47	44	37
MAR. 23	1	9	10	10	46	6	44	36	19	47	44	37
MAR. 24	1	11	11	12	46	6	44	36	19	47	44	37
MAR. 25	2	13	13	14	46	6	44	36	19	47	44	37
MAR. 26	2	14	15	16	46	6	44	36	19	47	44	37
MAR. 27	2	16	17	17	46	6	44	36	19	47	44	37
MAR. 28	2	18	18	19	46	7	44	36	19	47	44	37
MAR. 29	2	19	20	21	46	7	44	36	19	47	44	37
MAR. 30	2	21	22	22	47	7	44	36	19	47	44	37
MAR. 31	2	23	23	24	47	7	44	36	19	47	44	37

Date & Time	SUN ☉	MOON 1 ☽	MOON 2 ☽	MOON 3 ●	MERCURY	VENUS	MARS	JUPITER	SATURN	URANUS	NEPTUNE	PLUTO
APR. 1	2	24	25	25	47	7	44	36	19	47	44	37
APR. 2	2	26	26	27	47	7	45	36	19	47	44	37
APR. 3	3	27	28	28	47	8	45	36	19	47	44	37
APR. 4	3	29	30	30	48	8	45	36	19	47	44	37
APR. 5	3	31	31	32	48	8	45	36	19	47	44	37
APR. 6	3	32	33	33	48	8	45	36	19	47	44	37
APR. 7	3	34	34	35	48	8	45	36	19	47	44	37
APR. 8	3	35	36	37	48	8	45	36	19	47	44	37
APR. 9	3	37	38	38	1	9	45	36	19	47	44	37
APR. 10	3	39	39	40	1	9	45	36	19	47	44	37
APR. 11	4	40	41	42	1	9	45	36	19	47	44	37
APR. 12	4	42	43	44	1	9	46	36	19	47	44	37
APR. 13	4	44	45	45	1	9	46	36	19	47	44	37
APR. 14	4	46	47	47	2	9	46	36	19	47	44	37
APR. 15	4	48	1	1	2	9	46	36	19	47	44	37
APR. 16	4	2	3	3	2	10	46	36	19	47	44	37
APR. 17	4	4	5	5	2	10	46	36	19	47	44	37
APR. 18	4	6	7	7	2	10	46	36	19	47	44	37
APR. 19	5	8	9	9	3	10	46	36	19	47	44	37
APR. 20	5	10	11	11	3	10	46	36	19	47	44	37
APR. 21	5	12	13	13	3	10	46	36	19	47	44	37
APR. 22	5	14	14	15	4	11	47	36	19	47	44	37
APR. 23	5	16	16	17	4	11	47	36	19	47	44	37
APR. 24	5	17	18	18	4	11	47	36	19	47	44	37
APR. 25	6	19	20	20	4	11	47	36	19	47	44	37
APR. 26	6	21	21	22	5	11	47	36	19	47	44	37
APR. 27	6	22	23	23	5	11	47	36	19	47	44	37
APR. 28	6	24	24	25	5	11	47	36	19	47	44	37
APR. 29	6	25	26	26	5	12	47	35	19	47	44	37
APR. 30	6	27	28	28	6	12	47	35	19	47	44	37

MOON 1 ☽ 12:01 A.M. TO 8:00 A.M.   **MOON 2** ☽ 8:01 A.M. TO 4:00 P.M.   **MOON 3** ● 4:01 P.M. TO 12:00 A.M.

Use only one "moon" number. Choose the column closest to your time of birth. If your place of birth is not on Eastern Standard Time, be sure to read "How to Convert to Eastern Standard Time" at the beginning of this section.

Date & Time	SUN	MOON 1	MOON 2	MOON 3	MERCURY	VENUS	MARS	JUPITER	SATURN	URANUS	NEPTUNE	PLUTO
MAY 1	6	29	29	30	6	12	48	35	19	47	44	37
MAY 2	6	30	31	31	6	12	48	35	19	47	44	37
MAY 3	7	32	32	33	7	12	48	35	19	47	44	37
MAY 4	7	33	34	34	7	12	48	35	19	47	44	37
MAY 5	7	35	36	36	7	13	48	35	19	47	44	37
MAY 6	7	37	37	38	7	13	48	35	19	47	44	37
MAY 7	7	38	39	39	8	13	48	35	19	47	44	37
MAY 8	7	40	41	41	8	13	48	35	19	47	44	37
MAY 9	7	42	42	43	8	13	48	35	19	47	44	37
MAY 10	7	44	44	45	9	13	48	35	19	47	44	37
MAY 11	8	45	46	47	9	14	1	35	19	47	44	37
MAY 12	8	47	48	1	9	14	1	35	19	47	44	37
MAY 13	8	1	2	2	9	14	1	35	19	47	44	37
MAY 14	8	3	4	4	10	14	1	35	19	47	44	37
MAY 15	8	5	6	6	10	14	1	35	19	47	44	37
MAY 16	8	7	8	9	10	14	1	35	19	47	44	37
MAY 17	8	9	10	11	11	14	1	35	19	47	44	37
MAY 18	8	11	12	12	11	14	1	35	19	47	44	37
MAY 19	9	13	14	14	11	15	1	35	19	47	44	37
MAY 20	9	15	16	16	11	15	1	35	19	47	44	37
MAY 21	9	17	17	18	11	15	2	35	20	47	44	37
MAY 22	9	18	19	20	12	15	2	35	20	47	44	37
MAY 23	9	20	21	21	12	15	2	35	20	47	44	37
MAY 24	9	22	22	23	12	15	2	35	20	47	44	37
MAY 25	10	23	24	24	12	15	2	35	20	47	44	37
MAY 26	10	25	26	26	12	16	2	35	20	47	44	37
MAY 27	10	27	27	28	13	16	2	35	20	47	44	37
MAY 28	10	28	29	29	13	16	2	35	20	47	44	37
MAY 29	10	30	30	31	13	16	2	35	20	47	44	37
MAY 30	10	31	32	32	13	16	2	35	20	47	44	37
MAY 31	10	33	34	34	13	16	3	35	20	47	44	37

Date & Time	SUN	MOON 1	MOON 2	MOON 3	MERCURY	VENUS	MARS	JUPITER	SATURN	URANUS	NEPTUNE	PLUTO
JUN. 1	10	35	35	36	13	16	3	35	20	47	44	37
JUN. 2	10	36	37	37	14	16	3	35	20	47	44	37
JUN. 3	11	38	39	39	14	17	3	35	20	47	44	37
JUN. 4	11	40	40	41	14	17	3	35	20	47	44	37
JUN. 5	11	41	42	43	14	17	3	35	20	47	44	37
JUN. 6	11	43	44	44	14	17	3	35	20	47	44	37
JUN. 7	11	45	46	46	14	17	3	35	20	47	44	37
JUN. 8	11	47	47	48	14	17	3	35	20	47	44	37
JUN. 9	11	1	1	2	14	17	3	35	20	47	44	37
JUN. 10	11	3	3	4	14	18	4	35	20	47	44	37
JUN. 11	12	4	5	5	14	18	4	35	20	47	44	37
JUN. 12	12	6	7	8	14	18	4	35	20	47	44	37
JUN. 13	12	8	9	10	14	18	4	35	20	47	44	37
JUN. 14	12	10	11	12	14	18	4	35	20	47	44	37
JUN. 15	12	12	13	14	15	18	4	35	20	47	44	37
JUN. 16	12	14	15	15	15	18	4	35	20	47	44	37
JUN. 17	12	16	17	17	15	18	4	35	20	47	44	37
JUN. 18	12	18	18	19	15	18	4	35	20	47	44	37
JUN. 19	13	20	20	21	14	18	4	35	20	47	44	37
JUN. 20	13	21	22	22	14	19	5	35	20	47	44	37
JUN. 21	13	23	23	24	14	19	5	35	20	47	44	37
JUN. 22	13	25	25	26	14	19	5	35	20	47	44	37
JUN. 23	13	26	27	27	14	19	5	35	20	47	44	37
JUN. 24	13	28	28	29	14	19	5	35	20	47	44	37
JUN. 25	14	29	30	30	14	19	5	35	20	47	44	37
JUN. 26	14	31	31	32	14	19	5	35	20	47	44	37
JUN. 27	14	32	33	34	14	20	5	35	20	47	44	37
JUN. 28	14	34	35	35	14	20	5	35	20	47	44	37
JUN. 29	14	36	36	37	14	20	5	35	20	47	44	37
JUN. 30	14	37	38	39	14	20	5	35	20	47	44	37

MOON 1 ☽ 12:01 A.M. TO 8:00 A.M.   **MOON 2** ◗ 8:01 A.M. TO 4:00 P.M.   **MOON 3** ● 4:01 P.M. TO 12:00 A.M.

Use only one "moon" number. Choose the column closest to your time of birth. If your place of birth is not on Eastern Standard Time, be sure to read "How to Convert to Eastern Standard Time" at the beginning of this section.

2007

July

August

Date & Time	SUN	MOON 1	MOON 2	MOON 3	MERCURY	VENUS	MARS	JUPITER	SATURN	URANUS	NEPTUNE	PLUTO
JUL. 1	14	39	40	40	14	20	6	35	20	47	44	37
JUL. 2	14	41	42	42	14	20	6	35	20	47	44	37
JUL. 3	15	43	43	44	14	20	6	35	20	47	44	37
JUL. 4	15	45	45	46	13	20	6	35	20	47	44	37
JUL. 5	15	46	47	48	13	20	6	35	20	47	44	37
JUL. 6	15	48	1	1	13	20	6	34	20	47	44	37
JUL. 7	15	2	3	3	13	20	6	34	20	47	44	37
JUL. 8	15	4	5	5	13	21	6	34	20	47	44	37
JUL. 9	15	6	6	7	13	21	6	34	20	47	44	37
JUL. 10	15	8	8	9	13	21	6	34	20	47	44	37
JUL. 11	16	10	10	11	13	21	7	34	20	47	44	37
JUL. 12	16	12	12	13	13	21	7	34	20	47	44	37
JUL. 13	16	13	14	15	13	21	7	34	20	47	44	37
JUL. 14	16	15	16	17	13	21	7	34	20	47	44	37
JUL. 15	16	17	18	18	13	21	7	34	20	47	44	37
JUL. 16	16	19	19	20	14	21	7	34	20	47	44	37
JUL. 17	16	21	21	22	14	21	7	34	20	47	44	37
JUL. 18	16	22	23	23	14	21	7	34	20	47	44	37
JUL. 19	17	24	25	25	14	21	7	34	20	47	44	37
JUL. 20	17	26	26	27	14	21	7	34	20	47	44	37
JUL. 21	17	27	28	28	14	21	7	34	20	47	44	37
JUL. 22	17	29	29	30	14	21	8	34	20	47	44	37
JUL. 23	17	30	31	31	14	21	8	34	20	47	44	37
JUL. 24	17	32	32	33	14	21	8	34	20	47	44	37
JUL. 25	17	34	34	35	15	21	8	34	20	47	44	37
JUL. 26	18	35	36	36	15	21	8	34	20	47	44	37
JUL. 27	18	37	37	38	15	21	8	34	20	47	44	37
JUL. 28	18	39	39	40	15	21	8	34	20	47	44	37
JUL. 29	18	40	41	42	15	21	8	34	20	47	44	37
JUL. 30	18	42	43	43	16	21	8	34	20	47	44	37
JUL. 31	18	44	45	45	16	21	8	34	20	47	44	37

Date & Time	SUN	MOON 1	MOON 2	MOON 3	MERCURY	VENUS	MARS	JUPITER	SATURN	URANUS	NEPTUNE	PLUTO
AUG. 1	18	46	46	47	16	21	8	34	20	47	44	37
AUG. 2	18	48	48	1	16	21	9	34	20	47	44	37
AUG. 3	19	2	2	3	17	21	9	34	20	47	44	37
AUG. 4	19	4	4	5	17	21	9	34	20	47	44	37
AUG. 5	19	5	6	7	17	21	9	34	20	47	44	37
AUG. 6	19	7	8	9	17	21	9	34	21	47	44	37
AUG. 7	19	9	10	10	18	21	9	34	21	47	44	37
AUG. 8	19	11	12	12	18	21	9	34	21	47	44	37
AUG. 9	19	13	14	14	18	21	9	34	21	47	44	37
AUG. 10	19	15	15	16	18	21	9	34	21	47	44	37
AUG. 11	20	17	17	18	19	21	9	34	21	47	44	36
AUG. 12	20	18	19	19	19	21	9	34	21	47	44	36
AUG. 13	20	20	21	21	19	21	9	34	21	47	44	36
AUG. 14	20	22	22	23	20	21	10	34	21	47	44	36
AUG. 15	20	23	24	24	20	21	10	34	21	47	44	36
AUG. 16	20	25	26	26	20	20	10	34	21	47	44	36
AUG. 17	20	27	27	28	20	20	10	34	21	47	44	36
AUG. 18	20	28	29	29	21	20	10	34	21	47	44	36
AUG. 19	21	30	30	31	21	20	10	34	21	47	44	36
AUG. 20	21	31	32	32	21	20	10	34	21	47	44	36
AUG. 21	21	33	34	34	21	20	10	34	21	47	44	36
AUG. 22	21	35	35	36	21	20	10	34	21	47	44	36
AUG. 23	21	36	37	37	22	20	10	34	21	47	44	36
AUG. 24	21	38	39	39	22	20	10	34	21	47	44	36
AUG. 25	21	40	40	41	22	20	10	34	21	47	44	36
AUG. 26	22	41	42	43	23	20	11	34	21	47	44	36
AUG. 27	22	43	44	45	23	20	11	34	21	47	44	36
AUG. 28	22	45	46	46	23	20	11	34	21	47	44	36
AUG. 29	22	47	48	48	23	19	11	34	21	47	44	36
AUG. 30	22	1	2	2	24	19	11	34	21	47	44	36
AUG. 31	22	3	4	4	24	19	11	34	21	47	44	36

MOON 1 ☽ 12:01 A.M. TO 8:00 A.M.   **MOON 2** ☽ 8:01 A.M. TO 4:00 P.M.   **MOON 3** ● 4:01 P.M. TO 12:00 A.M.
Use only one "moon" number. Choose the column closest to your time of birth. If your place of birth is not on Eastern Standard Time, be sure to read "How to Convert to Eastern Standard Time" at the beginning of this section.

2007

September

October

Date & Time	SUN	MOON 1	MOON 2	MOON 3	MERCURY	VENUS	MARS	JUPITER	SATURN	URANUS	NEPTUNE	PLUTO
SEP. 1	22	5	6	6	24	19	11	34	21	47	44	36
SEP. 2	22	7	7	8	24	19	11	34	21	47	44	36
SEP. 3	23	9	9	10	24	19	11	34	21	47	44	36
SEP. 4	23	11	11	12	25	19	11	34	21	47	44	36
SEP. 5	23	13	13	14	25	19	11	34	21	47	44	36
SEP. 6	23	14	15	16	25	19	11	34	21	47	44	36
SEP. 7	23	16	17	17	25	19	11	34	21	47	44	36
SEP. 8	23	18	18	19	26	19	12	34	21	47	44	36
SEP. 9	23	20	20	21	26	19	12	35	21	47	44	36
SEP. 10	23	21	22	22	26	19	12	35	21	47	44	36
SEP. 11	24	23	23	24	26	19	12	35	21	47	44	36
SEP. 12	24	25	25	26	26	19	12	35	21	47	44	36
SEP. 13	24	26	27	27	27	19	12	35	21	47	44	36
SEP. 14	24	28	28	29	27	19	12	35	21	47	44	36
SEP. 15	24	29	30	30	27	19	12	35	21	47	44	36
SEP. 16	24	31	31	32	27	19	12	35	21	47	44	36
SEP. 17	24	32	33	34	27	19	12	35	21	47	44	36
SEP. 18	24	34	35	35	27	19	12	35	21	47	44	36
SEP. 19	25	36	36	37	28	19	12	35	21	47	44	36
SEP. 20	25	37	38	38	28	19	12	35	21	47	44	36
SEP. 21	25	39	40	40	28	20	12	35	21	47	44	36
SEP. 22	25	41	41	42	28	20	13	35	21	47	44	36
SEP. 23	25	43	43	44	28	20	13	35	21	47	44	36
SEP. 24	25	44	45	46	28	20	13	35	21	47	44	36
SEP. 25	26	46	47	48	29	20	13	35	21	47	44	36
SEP. 26	26	48	1	2	29	20	13	35	21	47	44	36
SEP. 27	26	2	3	4	29	20	13	35	21	47	44	36
SEP. 28	26	4	5	6	29	20	13	35	21	47	44	36
SEP. 29	26	6	7	8	29	20	13	35	21	47	44	36
SEP. 30	26	8	9	9	29	20	13	35	21	47	44	36

Date & Time	SUN	MOON 1	MOON 2	MOON 3	MERCURY	VENUS	MARS	JUPITER	SATURN	URANUS	NEPTUNE	PLUTO
OCT. 1	26	10	11	11	29	20	13	35	21	47	44	36
OCT. 2	26	12	13	13	30	20	13	35	21	47	44	36
OCT. 3	27	14	14	15	30	20	13	35	21	47	44	36
OCT. 4	27	16	16	17	30	21	13	35	21	47	44	36
OCT. 5	27	17	18	19	30	21	13	35	21	47	44	37
OCT. 6	27	19	20	20	30	21	13	35	22	47	44	37
OCT. 7	27	21	21	22	30	21	13	35	22	47	44	37
OCT. 8	27	22	23	24	30	21	13	35	22	47	44	37
OCT. 9	27	24	25	25	30	21	14	35	22	47	44	37
OCT. 10	27	26	26	27	30	21	14	35	22	47	44	37
OCT. 11	28	27	28	28	30	21	14	35	22	47	44	37
OCT. 12	28	29	29	30	30	21	14	35	22	47	44	37
OCT. 13	28	30	31	32	30	22	14	35	22	47	44	37
OCT. 14	28	32	33	33	30	22	14	35	22	47	44	37
OCT. 15	28	34	34	35	30	22	14	35	22	47	44	37
OCT. 16	28	35	36	36	30	22	14	35	22	47	44	37
OCT. 17	28	37	37	38	30	22	14	35	22	47	44	37
OCT. 18	28	38	39	40	30	22	14	35	22	47	44	37
OCT. 19	29	40	41	41	30	22	14	35	22	47	44	37
OCT. 20	29	42	42	43	30	22	14	35	22	47	44	37
OCT. 21	29	44	44	45	29	22	14	35	22	47	44	37
OCT. 22	29	45	46	47	29	23	14	35	22	47	44	37
OCT. 23	29	47	48	1	29	23	14	35	22	47	44	37
OCT. 24	29	1	2	3	29	23	14	35	22	47	44	37
OCT. 25	29	3	4	5	29	23	14	35	22	47	44	37
OCT. 26	30	5	6	7	29	23	14	35	22	47	44	37
OCT. 27	30	7	8	9	28	23	14	35	22	47	44	37
OCT. 28	30	9	10	11	28	23	14	35	22	47	44	37
OCT. 29	30	11	12	13	28	23	14	36	22	47	44	37
OCT. 30	30	13	14	15	28	24	14	36	22	47	44	37
OCT. 31	30	15	16	16	28	24	14	36	22	47	44	37

MOON 1 ☽ 12:01 A.M. TO 8:00 A.M.　　**MOON 2** ☽ 8:01 A.M. TO 4:00 P.M.　　**MOON 3** ● 4:01 P.M. TO 12:00 A.M.

Use only one "moon" number. Choose the column closest to your time of birth. If your place of birth is not on Eastern Standard Time, be sure to read "How to Convert to Eastern Standard Time" at the beginning of this section.

November

Date & Time	SUN	MOON 1	MOON 2	MOON 3	MERCURY	VENUS	MARS	JUPITER	SATURN	URANUS	NEPTUNE	PLUTO
NOV. 1	30	17	18	18	28	24	14	36	22	47	44	37
NOV. 2	30	19	19	20	28	24	14	36	22	47	44	37
NOV. 3	31	20	21	22	28	24	14	36	22	47	44	37
NOV. 4	31	22	23	23	28	24	15	36	22	47	44	37
NOV. 5	31	24	24	25	28	24	15	36	22	47	44	37
NOV. 6	31	25	26	26	28	25	15	36	22	47	44	37
NOV. 7	31	27	27	28	28	25	15	36	22	47	44	37
NOV. 8	31	28	29	30	29	25	15	36	22	47	44	37
NOV. 9	31	30	31	31	29	25	15	36	22	47	44	37
NOV. 10	31	32	32	33	29	25	15	36	22	47	44	37
NOV. 11	31	33	34	34	29	25	15	36	22	47	44	37
NOV. 12	32	35	35	36	29	25	15	36	22	47	44	37
NOV. 13	32	36	37	38	29	26	15	36	22	47	44	37
NOV. 14	32	38	39	39	29	26	15	36	22	47	44	37
NOV. 15	32	40	40	41	30	26	15	36	22	47	44	37
NOV. 16	32	41	42	42	30	26	15	36	22	47	44	37
NOV. 17	32	43	44	44	30	26	15	36	22	47	44	37
NOV. 18	32	45	45	46	30	26	15	36	22	47	44	37
NOV. 19	33	47	47	48	30	26	15	36	22	47	44	37
NOV. 20	33	48	1	2	31	27	15	36	22	47	44	37
NOV. 21	33	2	3	4	31	27	15	36	22	47	44	37
NOV. 22	33	4	5	6	31	27	15	36	22	47	44	37
NOV. 23	33	6	7	8	31	27	15	36	22	47	44	37
NOV. 24	33	8	9	10	31	27	15	36	22	47	44	37
NOV. 25	34	10	11	12	32	27	15	36	22	47	44	37
NOV. 26	34	12	13	14	32	28	15	36	22	47	44	37
NOV. 27	34	14	15	16	32	28	15	36	22	47	44	37
NOV. 28	34	16	17	18	32	28	14	36	22	47	44	37
NOV. 29	34	18	19	19	32	28	14	36	22	47	44	37
NOV. 30	34	20	20	21	33	28	14	36	22	47	44	37

December

Date & Time	SUN	MOON 1	MOON 2	MOON 3	MERCURY	VENUS	MARS	JUPITER	SATURN	URANUS	NEPTUNE	PLUTO
DEC. 1	34	22	22	23	33	28	14	36	22	47	44	37
DEC. 2	34	23	24	24	33	28	14	36	22	47	44	37
DEC. 3	35	25	25	26	33	29	14	36	22	47	44	37
DEC. 4	35	26	27	28	34	29	14	37	22	47	44	37
DEC. 5	35	28	29	29	34	29	14	37	22	47	44	37
DEC. 6	35	30	30	31	34	29	14	37	22	47	44	37
DEC. 7	35	31	32	32	34	29	14	37	22	47	44	37
DEC. 8	35	33	33	34	34	29	14	37	22	47	44	37
DEC. 9	35	34	35	35	35	30	14	37	22	47	44	37
DEC. 10	35	36	37	37	35	30	14	37	22	47	44	37
DEC. 11	36	38	38	39	35	30	14	37	22	47	44	37
DEC. 12	36	39	40	40	35	30	14	37	22	47	44	37
DEC. 13	36	41	42	42	35	30	14	37	22	47	44	37
DEC. 14	36	43	43	44	36	30	14	37	22	47	44	37
DEC. 15	36	44	45	46	36	30	14	37	22	47	44	37
DEC. 16	36	46	47	47	36	31	14	37	22	47	44	37
DEC. 17	36	48	1	1	36	31	14	37	22	47	44	37
DEC. 18	36	2	2	3	36	31	14	37	22	47	44	37
DEC. 19	37	4	4	5	37	31	14	37	22	47	44	37
DEC. 20	37	6	6	7	37	31	14	37	22	47	44	37
DEC. 21	37	8	8	9	37	31	14	37	22	47	44	37
DEC. 22	37	10	10	11	37	32	13	37	22	47	44	37
DEC. 23	37	12	12	13	38	32	13	37	22	47	44	37
DEC. 24	37	14	14	15	38	32	13	37	22	47	44	37
DEC. 25	37	15	16	17	38	32	13	37	22	47	44	37
DEC. 26	38	17	18	19	38	32	13	37	22	47	44	37
DEC. 27	38	19	20	20	38	32	13	37	22	47	44	37
DEC. 28	38	21	22	22	39	33	13	37	22	47	44	37
DEC. 29	38	23	23	24	39	33	13	37	22	47	44	37
DEC. 30	38	24	25	25	39	33	13	37	22	47	44	37
DEC. 31	38	26	27	27	39	33	13	37	22	47	44	37

MOON 1 ☽ 12:01 A.M. TO 8:00 A.M.   **MOON 2** ☽ 8:01 A.M. TO 4:00 P.M.   **MOON 3** ● 4:01 P.M. TO 12:00 A.M.

Use only one "moon" number. Choose the column closest to your time of birth. If your place of birth is not on Eastern Standard Time, be sure to read "How to Convert to Eastern Standard Time" at the beginning of this section.

2008

January

Date & Time	SUN	MOON 1	MOON 2	MOON 3	MERCURY	VENUS	MARS	JUPITER	SATURN	URANUS	NEPTUNE	PLUTO
JAN. 1	38	28	28	29	39	33	13	37	22	47	44	37
JAN. 2	38	29	30	30	40	33	13	37	22	47	44	37
JAN. 3	39	31	31	32	40	34	13	37	22	47	44	37
JAN. 4	39	32	33	33	40	34	13	37	22	47	44	37
JAN. 5	39	34	34	35	40	34	13	37	22	47	44	37
JAN. 6	39	36	36	37	41	34	13	38	22	47	44	37
JAN. 7	39	37	38	38	41	34	13	38	22	47	44	37
JAN. 8	39	39	39	40	41	34	13	38	22	47	44	37
JAN. 9	39	41	41	42	41	34	13	38	22	47	44	37
JAN. 10	40	42	43	43	41	35	13	38	22	47	44	37
JAN. 11	40	44	45	45	42	35	13	38	22	47	44	37
JAN. 12	40	46	46	47	42	35	12	38	22	47	44	37
JAN. 13	40	48	48	1	42	35	12	38	22	47	44	37
JAN. 14	40	1	2	3	42	35	12	38	22	47	44	37
JAN. 15	40	3	4	4	42	35	12	38	22	47	44	37
JAN. 16	40	5	6	6	43	36	12	38	22	47	44	37
JAN. 17	41	7	8	8	43	36	12	38	22	47	44	37
JAN. 18	41	9	9	10	43	36	12	38	22	47	44	37
JAN. 19	41	11	11	12	43	36	12	38	22	47	44	37
JAN. 20	41	13	13	14	43	36	12	38	22	47	44	37
JAN. 21	41	15	15	16	44	36	12	38	22	47	44	37
JAN. 22	41	17	17	18	44	37	12	38	22	47	44	37
JAN. 23	42	18	19	20	44	37	12	38	22	47	44	37
JAN. 24	42	20	21	21	44	37	12	38	22	47	44	37
JAN. 25	42	22	23	23	44	37	12	38	22	47	44	37
JAN. 26	42	24	24	25	44	37	12	38	22	47	44	37
JAN. 27	42	25	26	27	44	37	12	38	22	47	44	37
JAN. 28	42	27	28	28	44	37	12	38	22	47	44	37
JAN. 29	42	29	29	30	44	38	12	38	22	47	44	37
JAN. 30	42	30	31	31	44	38	12	38	22	47	44	37
JAN. 31	43	32	32	33	44	38	12	38	22	47	44	37

February

Date & Time	SUN	MOON 1	MOON 2	MOON 3	MERCURY	VENUS	MARS	JUPITER	SATURN	URANUS	NEPTUNE	PLUTO
FEB. 1	43	33	34	34	44	38	12	38	22	47	44	37
FEB. 2	43	35	36	36	44	38	12	38	22	47	44	37
FEB. 3	43	37	37	38	44	39	12	38	22	47	44	37
FEB. 4	43	38	39	39	44	39	12	38	22	47	44	37
FEB. 5	43	40	41	41	44	39	12	38	22	47	44	37
FEB. 6	43	42	42	43	43	39	12	38	22	47	44	37
FEB. 7	43	43	44	45	43	39	12	38	22	47	44	37
FEB. 8	44	45	46	46	43	39	12	38	22	47	44	37
FEB. 9	44	47	48	48	43	40	12	39	22	47	44	37
FEB. 10	44	1	1	2	43	40	12	39	22	47	44	37
FEB. 11	44	3	3	4	43	40	12	39	22	47	44	37
FEB. 12	44	5	5	6	42	40	12	39	22	47	44	37
FEB. 13	44	6	7	8	42	40	12	39	22	47	44	37
FEB. 14	44	8	9	10	42	40	12	39	22	47	44	37
FEB. 15	44	10	11	12	42	41	12	39	22	47	44	37
FEB. 16	45	12	13	13	42	41	12	39	22	47	44	37
FEB. 17	45	14	15	15	42	41	12	39	22	47	44	37
FEB. 18	45	16	17	17	42	41	12	39	22	47	44	37
FEB. 19	45	18	18	19	42	41	12	39	22	47	44	37
FEB. 20	45	20	20	21	42	41	12	39	22	47	44	37
FEB. 21	45	21	22	22	42	42	13	39	22	47	44	37
FEB. 22	45	23	24	24	42	42	13	39	22	47	44	37
FEB. 23	46	25	25	26	42	42	13	39	22	47	44	37
FEB. 24	46	26	27	28	42	42	13	39	22	47	44	37
FEB. 25	46	28	29	29	42	42	13	39	22	47	44	37
FEB. 26	46	30	30	31	42	42	13	39	22	47	44	37
FEB. 27	46	31	32	32	43	43	13	39	22	47	44	37
FEB. 28	46	33	33	34	43	43	13	39	22	47	44	37
FEB. 29	46	34	35	36	43	43	13	39	22	47	44	37

MOON 1 ☽ 12:01 A.M. TO 8:00 A.M.   **MOON 2** ☽ 8:01 A.M. TO 4:00 P.M.   **MOON 3** ● 4:01 P.M. TO 12:00 A.M.

Use only one "moon" number. Choose the column closest to your time of birth. If your place of birth is not on Eastern Standard Time, be sure to read "How to Convert to Eastern Standard Time" at the beginning of this section.

March

April

Date & Time	SUN	MOON 1	MOON 2	MOON 3	MERCURY	VENUS	MARS	JUPITER	SATURN	URANUS	NEPTUNE	PLUTO
MAR. 1	46	36	37	37	43	43	13	39	22	47	44	37
MAR. 2	46	38	38	39	43	43	13	39	22	47	44	37
MAR. 3	47	39	40	40	43	43	13	39	22	47	44	37
MAR. 4	47	41	42	42	43	44	13	39	22	47	44	37
MAR. 5	47	43	43	44	43	44	13	39	22	47	44	37
MAR. 6	47	45	45	46	44	44	13	39	22	47	44	37
MAR. 7	47	46	47	48	44	44	13	39	22	47	44	37
MAR. 8	47	48	1	1	44	44	13	39	22	47	44	37
MAR. 9	47	2	3	3	44	44	13	39	22	47	44	37
MAR. 10	47	4	5	5	44	45	13	39	21	47	44	37
MAR. 11	48	6	7	7	44	45	13	39	21	47	44	37
MAR. 12	48	8	9	9	44	45	13	39	21	47	44	37
MAR. 13	48	10	10	11	45	45	13	39	21	47	44	37
MAR. 14	48	12	12	13	45	45	13	39	21	47	44	37
MAR. 15	48	14	14	15	45	45	13	39	21	48	44	37
MAR. 16	48	15	16	17	45	46	14	39	21	48	44	37
MAR. 17	48	17	18	18	45	46	14	39	21	48	44	37
MAR. 18	48	19	20	20	46	46	14	39	21	48	44	37
MAR. 19	1	21	21	22	46	46	14	39	21	48	44	37
MAR. 20	1	23	23	24	46	46	14	39	21	48	44	37
MAR. 21	1	24	25	25	46	46	14	39	21	48	44	37
MAR. 22	1	26	26	27	46	46	14	39	21	48	44	37
MAR. 23	1	28	28	29	47	47	14	40	21	48	44	37
MAR. 24	1	29	30	30	47	47	14	40	21	48	44	37
MAR. 25	2	31	31	32	47	47	14	40	21	48	44	37
MAR. 26	2	32	33	33	47	47	14	40	21	48	44	37
MAR. 27	2	34	34	35	47	47	14	40	21	48	44	37
MAR. 28	2	36	36	37	48	47	14	40	21	48	44	37
MAR. 29	2	37	38	38	48	48	14	40	21	48	44	37
MAR. 30	2	39	39	40	48	48	14	40	21	48	44	37
MAR. 31	2	40	41	41	48	48	14	40	21	48	44	37

Date & Time	SUN	MOON 1	MOON 2	MOON 3	MERCURY	VENUS	MARS	JUPITER	SATURN	URANUS	NEPTUNE	PLUTO
APR. 1	2	42	43	43	1	48	14	40	21	48	44	37
APR. 2	2	44	44	45	1	48	14	40	21	48	44	37
APR. 3	3	46	46	47	1	48	15	40	21	48	44	37
APR. 4	3	47	48	1	1	1	15	40	21	48	44	37
APR. 5	3	1	2	3	2	1	15	40	21	48	44	37
APR. 6	3	3	4	5	2	1	15	40	21	48	44	37
APR. 7	3	5	6	7	2	1	15	40	21	48	44	37
APR. 8	3	7	8	9	2	1	15	40	21	48	44	37
APR. 9	3	9	10	11	3	1	15	40	21	48	44	37
APR. 10	3	11	12	13	3	2	15	40	21	48	44	37
APR. 11	4	13	14	14	3	2	15	40	21	48	44	37
APR. 12	4	15	16	16	3	2	15	40	21	48	44	37
APR. 13	4	17	17	18	4	2	15	40	21	48	44	37
APR. 14	4	19	19	20	4	2	15	40	21	48	44	37
APR. 15	4	20	21	22	4	2	15	40	21	48	44	37
APR. 16	4	22	23	23	4	3	15	40	21	48	44	37
APR. 17	4	24	24	25	5	3	15	40	21	48	44	37
APR. 18	4	25	26	27	5	3	15	40	21	48	44	37
APR. 19	5	27	28	28	5	3	16	40	21	48	44	37
APR. 20	5	29	29	30	6	3	16	40	21	48	44	37
APR. 21	5	30	31	31	6	4	16	40	21	48	44	37
APR. 22	5	32	32	33	6	4	16	40	21	48	44	37
APR. 23	5	33	34	35	6	4	16	40	21	48	44	37
APR. 24	5	35	36	36	7	4	16	40	21	48	44	37
APR. 25	6	37	37	38	7	4	16	40	21	48	44	37
APR. 26	6	38	39	39	7	4	16	40	21	48	44	37
APR. 27	6	40	40	41	8	4	16	40	21	48	44	37
APR. 28	6	41	42	43	8	5	16	40	21	48	44	37
APR. 29	6	43	44	44	8	5	16	40	21	48	44	37
APR. 30	6	45	45	46	8	5	16	40	21	48	44	37

MOON 1 ☽ 12:01 A.M. TO 8:00 A.M.   **MOON 2** ☽ 8:01 A.M. TO 4:00 P.M.   **MOON 3** ● 4:01 P.M. TO 12:00 A.M.

Use only one "moon" number. Choose the column closest to your time of birth. If your place of birth is not on Eastern Standard Time, be sure to read "How to Convert to Eastern Standard Time" at the beginning of this section.

2008

May

Date & Time	SUN ☉	MOON 1 ◖	MOON 2 ◑	MOON 3 ●	MERCURY	VENUS	MARS	JUPITER	SATURN	URANUS	NEPTUNE	PLUTO
MAY 1	6	47	47	48	9	5	16	40	21	48	44	37
MAY 2	6	1	1	2	9	5	16	40	21	48	44	37
MAY 3	7	2	3	4	9	5	16	40	21	48	44	37
MAY 4	7	4	5	6	9	6	17	40	21	48	44	37
MAY 5	7	6	7	8	9	6	17	40	21	48	44	37
MAY 6	7	8	9	10	10	6	17	40	21	48	44	37
MAY 7	7	10	11	12	10	6	17	40	21	48	44	37
MAY 8	7	12	13	14	10	6	17	40	21	48	44	37
MAY 9	7	14	15	16	10	6	17	40	21	48	44	37
MAY 10	7	16	17	18	10	7	17	40	21	48	44	37
MAY 11	8	18	19	19	11	7	17	40	21	48	44	37
MAY 12	8	20	21	21	11	7	17	40	21	48	44	37
MAY 13	8	22	22	23	11	7	17	40	21	48	44	37
MAY 14	8	23	24	25	11	7	17	40	21	48	44	37
MAY 15	8	25	26	26	11	7	17	40	21	48	44	37
MAY 16	8	27	27	28	11	8	17	40	21	48	44	37
MAY 17	8	28	29	29	11	8	17	40	21	48	44	37
MAY 18	8	30	30	31	11	8	18	40	21	48	44	37
MAY 19	9	31	32	33	12	8	18	40	21	48	44	37
MAY 20	9	33	34	34	12	8	18	40	21	48	44	37
MAY 21	9	35	35	36	12	8	18	40	21	48	44	37
MAY 22	9	36	37	37	12	9	18	40	21	48	44	37
MAY 23	9	38	38	39	12	9	18	40	21	48	44	37
MAY 24	9	39	40	41	12	9	18	40	21	48	44	37
MAY 25	10	41	42	42	12	9	18	40	21	48	44	37
MAY 26	10	43	43	44	12	9	18	40	21	48	44	37
MAY 27	10	44	45	45	12	9	18	40	21	48	44	37
MAY 28	10	46	47	47	12	10	18	40	21	48	44	37
MAY 29	10	48	48	1	12	10	18	40	21	48	44	37
MAY 30	10	2	2	3	12	10	18	40	21	48	44	37
MAY 31	10	4	4	5	12	10	19	40	21	48	44	37

June

Date & Time	SUN ☉	MOON 1 ◖	MOON 2 ◑	MOON 3 ●	MERCURY	VENUS	MARS	JUPITER	SATURN	URANUS	NEPTUNE	PLUTO
JUN. 1	10	6	6	7	12	10	19	40	21	48	44	37
JUN. 2	10	8	8	9	12	10	19	40	21	48	44	37
JUN. 3	11	10	10	11	12	10	19	40	21	48	44	37
JUN. 4	11	12	12	13	12	11	19	40	21	48	44	37
JUN. 5	11	14	14	15	11	11	19	40	21	48	44	37
JUN. 6	11	16	16	17	11	11	19	40	21	48	44	37
JUN. 7	11	18	18	19	11	11	19	40	21	48	44	37
JUN. 8	11	19	20	21	11	11	19	40	21	48	44	37
JUN. 9	11	21	22	22	11	11	19	40	21	48	44	37
JUN. 10	11	23	24	24	11	12	19	40	21	48	44	37
JUN. 11	12	25	25	26	11	12	19	40	21	48	44	37
JUN. 12	12	26	27	27	11	12	19	40	21	48	44	37
JUN. 13	12	28	28	29	11	12	20	40	21	48	44	37
JUN. 14	12	30	30	31	11	12	20	40	21	48	44	37
JUN. 15	12	31	32	32	11	12	20	40	21	48	44	37
JUN. 16	12	33	33	34	11	13	20	40	21	48	44	37
JUN. 17	12	34	35	35	11	13	20	40	21	48	44	37
JUN. 18	12	36	36	37	11	13	20	40	21	48	44	37
JUN. 19	13	37	38	39	11	13	20	40	21	48	44	37
JUN. 20	13	39	40	40	11	13	20	40	21	48	44	37
JUN. 21	13	41	41	42	11	13	20	40	21	48	44	37
JUN. 22	13	42	43	43	11	14	20	40	21	48	44	37
JUN. 23	13	44	45	45	11	14	20	40	21	48	44	37
JUN. 24	13	46	46	47	11	14	20	40	21	48	44	37
JUN. 25	14	47	48	1	11	14	20	40	22	48	44	37
JUN. 26	14	1	2	2	11	14	21	40	22	48	44	37
JUN. 27	14	3	4	4	11	14	21	40	22	48	44	37
JUN. 28	14	5	5	6	11	15	21	39	22	48	44	37
JUN. 29	14	7	7	8	11	15	21	39	22	48	44	37
JUN. 30	14	9	9	10	11	15	21	39	22	48	44	37

MOON 1 ◖ 12:01 A.M. TO 8:00 A.M.   **MOON 2** ◑ 8:01 A.M. TO 4:00 P.M.   **MOON 3** ● 4:01 P.M. TO 12:00 A.M.
Use only one "moon" number. Choose the column closest to your time of birth. If your place of birth is not on
Eastern Standard Time, be sure to read "How to Convert to Eastern Standard Time" at the beginning of this section.

Date & Time	SUN	MOON 1	MOON 2	MOON 3	MERCURY	VENUS	MARS	JUPITER	SATURN	URANUS	NEPTUNE	PLUTO
JUL. 1	14	11	11	12	11	15	21	39	22	48	44	37
JUL. 2	14	13	13	14	12	15	21	39	22	48	44	37
JUL. 3	15	15	15	16	12	15	21	39	22	48	44	37
JUL. 4	15	17	17	18	12	16	21	39	22	48	44	37
JUL. 5	15	19	19	20	12	16	21	39	22	48	44	37
JUL. 6	15	21	21	22	12	16	21	39	22	48	44	37
JUL. 7	15	22	23	23	12	16	21	39	22	48	44	37
JUL. 8	15	24	25	25	12	16	21	39	22	48	44	37
JUL. 9	15	26	26	27	13	16	22	39	22	48	44	37
JUL. 10	15	27	28	29	13	17	22	39	22	48	44	37
JUL. 11	16	29	30	30	13	17	22	39	22	48	44	37
JUL. 12	16	31	31	32	13	17	22	39	22	48	44	37
JUL. 13	16	32	33	33	13	17	22	39	22	48	44	37
JUL. 14	16	34	34	35	14	17	22	39	22	48	44	37
JUL. 15	16	35	36	36	14	17	22	39	22	48	44	37
JUL. 16	16	37	38	38	14	18	22	39	22	48	44	37
JUL. 17	16	39	39	40	14	18	22	39	22	48	44	37
JUL. 18	16	40	41	41	15	18	22	39	22	48	44	37
JUL. 19	17	42	42	43	15	18	22	39	22	48	44	37
JUL. 20	17	44	44	45	15	18	22	39	22	48	44	37
JUL. 21	17	45	46	46	15	18	23	39	22	48	44	37
JUL. 22	17	47	48	48	16	19	23	39	22	48	44	37
JUL. 23	17	1	1	2	16	19	23	39	22	48	44	37
JUL. 24	17	3	3	4	16	19	23	39	22	48	44	37
JUL. 25	17	4	5	6	17	19	23	39	22	48	44	37
JUL. 26	18	6	7	7	17	19	23	39	22	48	44	37
JUL. 27	18	8	9	9	17	19	23	39	22	48	44	37
JUL. 28	18	10	11	11	17	19	23	39	22	48	44	37
JUL. 29	18	12	13	13	18	20	23	39	22	48	44	37
JUL. 30	18	14	15	15	18	20	23	39	22	48	44	37
JUL. 31	18	16	17	17	18	20	23	39	22	48	44	37

Date & Time	SUN	MOON 1	MOON 2	MOON 3	MERCURY	VENUS	MARS	JUPITER	SATURN	URANUS	NEPTUNE	PLUTO
AUG. 1	18	18	18	19	19	20	23	39	22	48	44	37
AUG. 2	18	20	20	21	19	20	24	39	22	48	44	37
AUG. 3	19	22	22	23	19	20	24	39	22	48	44	37
AUG. 4	19	23	24	25	19	21	24	39	22	48	44	37
AUG. 5	19	25	26	26	20	21	24	39	22	48	44	37
AUG. 6	19	27	27	28	20	21	24	39	22	48	44	37
AUG. 7	19	29	29	30	20	21	24	39	22	48	44	37
AUG. 8	19	30	31	31	20	21	24	39	22	48	44	37
AUG. 9	19	32	32	33	21	21	24	39	22	48	44	37
AUG. 10	19	33	34	34	21	22	24	39	22	48	44	37
AUG. 11	20	35	35	36	21	22	24	39	22	48	44	37
AUG. 12	20	37	37	38	21	22	24	39	22	48	44	37
AUG. 13	20	38	39	39	22	22	24	39	22	48	44	37
AUG. 14	20	40	40	41	22	22	25	39	22	48	44	37
AUG. 15	20	41	42	42	22	22	25	39	22	48	44	37
AUG. 16	20	43	44	44	22	23	25	39	22	48	44	37
AUG. 17	20	45	45	46	23	23	25	39	22	48	44	37
AUG. 18	20	47	47	48	23	23	25	39	22	48	44	37
AUG. 19	21	48	1	1	23	23	25	39	22	48	44	37
AUG. 20	21	2	3	3	23	23	25	39	22	48	44	37
AUG. 21	21	4	5	5	23	23	25	39	22	48	44	37
AUG. 22	21	6	6	7	24	24	25	39	22	48	44	37
AUG. 23	21	8	8	9	24	24	25	39	22	48	44	37
AUG. 24	21	10	10	11	24	24	25	39	22	48	44	37
AUG. 25	21	11	12	13	24	24	25	39	22	48	44	37
AUG. 26	22	13	14	15	24	24	26	39	22	48	44	37
AUG. 27	22	15	16	17	24	24	26	39	22	48	44	37
AUG. 28	22	17	18	18	25	25	26	39	22	48	44	37
AUG. 29	22	19	20	20	25	25	26	39	22	48	44	37
AUG. 30	22	21	21	22	25	25	26	39	22	48	44	37
AUG. 31	22	23	23	24	25	25	26	39	22	48	44	37

MOON 1 ◖ 12:01 A.M. TO 8:00 A.M.   **MOON 2** ◑ 8:01 A.M. TO 4:00 P.M.   **MOON 3** ● 4:01 P.M. TO 12:00 A.M.

Use only one "moon" number. Choose the column closest to your time of birth. If your place of birth is not on Eastern Standard Time, be sure to read "How to Convert to Eastern Standard Time" at the beginning of this section.

2008

September

Date & Time	SUN ☉	MOON 1 ☽	MOON 2 ◐	MOON 3 ●	MERCURY	VENUS	MARS	JUPITER	SATURN	URANUS	NEPTUNE	PLUTO
SEP. 1	22	24	25	26	26	25	26	39	23	48	44	37
SEP. 2	22	26	27	27	26	25	26	39	23	48	44	37
SEP. 3	23	28	28	29	26	26	26	39	23	48	44	37
SEP. 4	23	30	30	31	26	26	26	39	23	48	44	37
SEP. 5	23	31	32	32	26	26	26	39	23	48	44	37
SEP. 6	23	33	33	34	26	26	26	39	23	48	44	37
SEP. 7	23	34	35	35	26	26	27	39	23	48	44	37
SEP. 8	23	36	37	37	27	26	27	39	23	48	44	37
SEP. 9	23	38	38	39	27	27	27	39	23	48	44	37
SEP. 10	23	39	40	40	27	27	27	39	23	48	44	37
SEP. 11	24	41	41	42	27	27	27	39	23	48	44	37
SEP. 12	24	42	43	44	27	27	27	39	23	48	44	37
SEP. 13	24	44	45	45	27	27	27	39	23	48	44	37
SEP. 14	24	46	47	47	27	27	27	39	23	48	44	37
SEP. 15	24	48	48	1	28	28	27	39	23	48	44	37
SEP. 16	24	2	2	3	28	28	27	39	23	48	44	37
SEP. 17	24	3	4	5	28	28	27	39	23	48	44	37
SEP. 18	24	5	6	7	28	28	28	39	23	48	44	37
SEP. 19	25	7	8	8	28	28	28	39	23	48	44	37
SEP. 20	25	9	10	10	28	28	28	39	23	48	44	37
SEP. 21	25	11	12	12	28	28	28	39	23	48	44	37
SEP. 22	25	13	14	14	28	29	28	39	23	48	44	37
SEP. 23	25	15	15	16	28	29	28	39	23	48	44	37
SEP. 24	25	17	17	18	28	29	28	39	23	48	44	37
SEP. 25	26	18	19	20	28	29	28	39	23	48	44	37
SEP. 26	26	20	21	22	28	29	28	39	23	48	44	37
SEP. 27	26	22	23	23	28	29	28	39	23	48	44	37
SEP. 28	26	24	24	25	30	30	29	39	23	48	44	37
SEP. 29	26	26	26	27	28	30	29	39	23	48	44	37
SEP. 30	26	27	28	28	28	30	29	39	23	48	44	37

October

Date & Time	SUN ☉	MOON 1 ☽	MOON 2 ◐	MOON 3 ●	MERCURY	VENUS	MARS	JUPITER	SATURN	URANUS	NEPTUNE	PLUTO
OCT. 1	26	29	30	30	28	30	29	39	23	48	44	37
OCT. 2	26	31	31	32	28	30	29	39	23	48	44	37
OCT. 3	27	32	33	33	27	30	29	39	23	48	44	37
OCT. 4	27	34	34	35	27	31	29	39	23	48	44	37
OCT. 5	27	35	36	37	27	31	29	39	23	48	44	37
OCT. 6	27	37	38	38	27	31	29	39	23	48	44	37
OCT. 7	27	39	39	40	27	31	29	39	23	48	44	37
OCT. 8	27	40	41	41	27	31	29	39	23	48	44	37
OCT. 9	27	42	42	43	26	31	29	39	23	48	44	37
OCT. 10	27	44	44	45	26	32	30	39	23	48	44	37
OCT. 11	28	45	46	46	26	32	30	39	23	48	44	37
OCT. 12	28	47	48	48	26	32	30	39	23	48	44	37
OCT. 13	28	1	1	2	26	32	30	39	23	48	44	37
OCT. 14	28	3	3	4	26	32	30	39	23	48	44	37
OCT. 15	28	5	5	6	26	32	30	39	23	48	44	37
OCT. 16	28	7	7	8	26	33	30	39	23	48	44	37
OCT. 17	28	9	9	10	26	33	30	39	23	48	44	37
OCT. 18	28	10	11	12	26	33	30	39	23	48	44	37
OCT. 19	29	12	13	14	26	33	30	39	23	48	44	37
OCT. 20	29	14	15	16	26	33	30	39	23	48	44	37
OCT. 21	29	16	17	17	26	33	31	39	23	48	44	37
OCT. 22	29	18	19	19	26	34	31	39	23	48	44	37
OCT. 23	29	20	20	21	27	34	31	39	23	48	44	37
OCT. 24	29	22	22	23	27	34	31	39	23	48	44	37
OCT. 25	29	23	24	25	27	34	31	39	23	48	44	37
OCT. 26	30	25	26	26	27	34	31	39	23	48	44	37
OCT. 27	30	27	27	28	27	34	31	39	23	48	44	37
OCT. 28	30	28	29	30	27	34	31	39	23	48	44	37
OCT. 29	30	30	31	31	28	35	31	39	23	48	44	37
OCT. 30	30	32	32	33	28	35	31	39	23	48	44	37
OCT. 31	30	33	34	34	28	35	31	39	23	48	44	37

MOON 1 ☽ 12:01 A.M. TO 8:00 A.M.   **MOON 2** ◐ 8:01 A.M. TO 4:00 P.M.   **MOON 3** ● 4:01 P.M. TO 12:00 A.M.
Use only one "moon" number. Choose the column closest to your time of birth. If your place of birth is not on
Eastern Standard Time, be sure to read "How to Convert to Eastern Standard Time" at the beginning of this section.

2008

November — December

Date & Time	SUN	MOON 1	MOON 2	MOON 3	MERCURY	VENUS	MARS	JUPITER	SATURN	URANUS	NEPTUNE	PLUTO
NOV. 1	30	35	36	36	28	35	32	39	23	48	44	37
NOV. 2	30	37	37	38	28	35	32	39	23	48	44	37
NOV. 3	31	38	39	39	29	35	32	39	23	47	44	37
NOV. 4	31	40	40	41	29	36	32	39	23	47	44	37
NOV. 5	31	41	42	42	29	36	32	39	24	47	44	37
NOV. 6	31	43	43	44	29	36	32	39	24	47	44	37
NOV. 7	31	45	45	46	30	36	32	39	24	47	44	37
NOV. 8	31	46	47	47	30	36	32	39	24	47	44	37
NOV. 9	31	48	1	1	30	36	32	39	24	47	44	37
NOV. 10	31	2	2	3	30	37	32	39	24	47	44	37
NOV. 11	31	4	4	5	30	37	32	39	24	47	44	37
NOV. 12	32	6	6	7	31	37	33	39	24	47	44	37
NOV. 13	32	8	8	9	31	37	33	39	24	47	44	37
NOV. 14	32	10	10	11	31	37	33	39	24	47	44	37
NOV. 15	32	12	12	13	31	37	33	40	24	47	44	37
NOV. 16	32	14	14	15	31	38	33	40	24	47	44	37
NOV. 17	32	16	16	17	32	38	33	40	24	47	44	37
NOV. 18	32	18	18	19	32	38	33	40	24	47	44	37
NOV. 19	33	19	20	21	32	38	33	40	24	47	44	37
NOV. 20	33	21	22	22	32	38	33	40	24	47	44	37
NOV. 21	33	23	24	24	33	38	34	40	24	47	44	37
NOV. 22	33	25	25	26	33	38	34	40	24	47	44	37
NOV. 23	33	26	27	28	33	39	34	40	24	47	44	37
NOV. 24	33	28	29	29	33	39	34	40	24	47	44	37
NOV. 25	34	30	30	31	33	39	34	40	24	47	44	37
NOV. 26	34	31	32	32	34	39	34	40	24	47	44	37
NOV. 27	34	33	33	34	34	39	34	40	24	47	44	37
NOV. 28	34	35	35	36	34	39	34	40	24	47	44	37
NOV. 29	34	36	37	37	34	40	34	40	24	47	44	37
NOV. 30	34	38	38	39	34	40	34	40	24	47	44	37

Date & Time	SUN	MOON 1	MOON 2	MOON 3	MERCURY	VENUS	MARS	JUPITER	SATURN	URANUS	NEPTUNE	PLUTO
DEC. 1	34	39	40	40	35	40	34	40	24	47	44	37
DEC. 2	34	41	41	42	35	40	34	40	24	47	44	37
DEC. 3	35	42	43	44	35	40	35	40	24	47	44	37
DEC. 4	35	44	45	45	35	40	35	40	24	47	44	37
DEC. 5	35	46	46	47	35	41	35	40	24	47	44	37
DEC. 6	35	47	48	1	36	41	35	40	24	47	44	37
DEC. 7	35	1	2	2	36	41	35	40	24	47	44	37
DEC. 8	35	3	4	4	36	41	35	40	24	47	44	37
DEC. 9	35	5	5	6	36	41	35	40	24	47	44	37
DEC. 10	35	7	7	8	37	41	35	40	24	47	44	37
DEC. 11	36	9	9	10	37	41	35	40	24	47	44	37
DEC. 12	36	11	11	12	37	42	35	40	24	47	44	37
DEC. 13	36	13	14	14	37	42	36	40	24	47	44	37
DEC. 14	36	15	16	16	37	42	36	40	24	47	44	37
DEC. 15	36	17	18	18	38	42	36	40	24	47	44	37
DEC. 16	36	19	19	20	38	42	36	40	24	47	44	37
DEC. 17	36	21	21	22	38	42	36	40	24	47	44	37
DEC. 18	36	23	23	24	38	43	36	40	24	47	44	37
DEC. 19	37	24	25	25	38	43	36	40	24	47	44	37
DEC. 20	37	26	27	27	39	43	36	40	24	47	44	37
DEC. 21	37	28	28	29	39	43	36	40	24	47	44	37
DEC. 22	37	29	30	30	39	43	36	40	24	47	44	37
DEC. 23	37	31	31	32	39	43	37	41	24	48	44	37
DEC. 24	37	33	33	34	39	43	37	41	24	48	44	37
DEC. 25	37	34	35	35	40	44	37	41	24	48	44	37
DEC. 26	38	36	36	37	40	44	37	41	24	48	44	37
DEC. 27	38	37	38	38	40	44	37	41	24	48	44	37
DEC. 28	38	39	39	40	40	44	37	41	24	48	44	37
DEC. 29	38	40	41	42	40	44	37	41	24	48	44	37
DEC. 30	38	42	43	43	41	44	37	41	24	48	44	37
DEC. 31	38	44	44	45	41	44	37	41	24	48	44	37

MOON 1 ☽ 12:01 A.M. TO 8:00 A.M.   **MOON 2** ☾ 8:01 A.M. TO 4:00 P.M.   **MOON 3** ● 4:01 P.M. TO 12:00 A.M.
Use only one "moon" number. Choose the column closest to your time of birth. If your place of birth is not on Eastern Standard Time, be sure to read "How to Convert to Eastern Standard Time" at the beginning of this section.

2009

January

February

Date & Time	SUN ☀	MOON 1 ◔	MOON 2 ◑	MOON 3 ●	MERCURY	VENUS	MARS	JUPITER	SATURN	URANUS	NEPTUNE	PLUTO
JAN. 1	38	45	46	46	41	45	37	41	24	48	44	37
JAN. 2	38	47	47	48	41	45	38	41	24	48	44	37
JAN. 3	39	1	1	2	41	45	38	41	24	48	44	37
JAN. 4	39	2	3	4	41	45	38	41	24	48	44	37
JAN. 5	39	4	5	5	42	45	38	41	24	48	44	37
JAN. 6	39	6	7	7	42	45	38	41	24	48	44	37
JAN. 7	39	8	9	9	42	45	38	41	24	48	44	37
JAN. 8	39	10	11	11	42	46	38	41	24	48	44	37
JAN. 9	39	12	13	13	42	46	38	41	24	48	44	37
JAN. 10	40	14	15	15	42	46	38	41	24	48	44	37
JAN. 11	40	16	17	17	42	46	38	41	24	48	44	37
JAN. 12	40	18	19	19	42	46	39	41	24	48	44	37
JAN. 13	40	20	21	21	42	46	39	41	24	48	44	37
JAN. 14	40	22	22	23	42	46	39	41	24	48	44	37
JAN. 15	40	24	24	25	42	47	39	41	24	48	44	37
JAN. 16	40	25	26	27	42	47	39	41	24	48	44	37
JAN. 17	41	27	28	28	42	47	39	41	24	48	44	37
JAN. 18	41	29	29	30	41	47	39	41	24	48	44	37
JAN. 19	41	31	31	32	41	47	39	41	24	48	44	37
JAN. 20	41	32	33	33	41	47	39	41	24	48	44	37
JAN. 21	41	34	34	35	41	47	39	41	24	48	44	37
JAN. 22	41	35	36	36	41	48	40	41	24	48	44	37
JAN. 23	42	37	37	38	41	48	40	42	24	48	44	37
JAN. 24	42	38	39	40	40	48	40	42	24	48	44	37
JAN. 25	42	40	41	41	40	48	40	42	24	48	44	37
JAN. 26	42	42	42	43	40	48	40	42	24	48	44	37
JAN. 27	42	43	44	44	40	48	40	42	24	48	44	37
JAN. 28	42	45	45	46	40	48	40	42	24	48	44	37
JAN. 29	42	47	47	48	40	48	40	42	24	48	44	37
JAN. 30	42	48	1	1	40	1	40	42	24	48	44	37
JAN. 31	43	2	3	3	40	1	41	42	24	48	44	37

Date & Time	SUN ☀	MOON 1 ◔	MOON 2 ◑	MOON 3 ●	MERCURY	VENUS	MARS	JUPITER	SATURN	URANUS	NEPTUNE	PLUTO
FEB. 1	43	4	4	5	40	1	41	42	24	48	44	37
FEB. 2	43	5	6	7	40	1	41	42	24	48	44	37
FEB. 3	43	7	8	9	40	1	41	42	24	48	44	37
FEB. 4	43	9	10	10	40	1	41	42	24	48	44	37
FEB. 5	43	11	12	12	40	1	41	42	24	48	44	37
FEB. 6	43	13	14	14	40	1	41	42	24	48	44	37
FEB. 7	43	15	16	16	40	1	41	42	24	48	44	37
FEB. 8	44	17	18	18	40	2	41	42	24	48	44	37
FEB. 9	44	19	20	20	40	2	41	42	24	48	44	37
FEB. 10	44	21	22	22	40	2	42	42	24	48	44	37
FEB. 11	44	23	23	24	41	2	42	42	24	48	44	37
FEB. 12	44	25	25	26	41	2	42	42	24	48	44	37
FEB. 13	44	27	27	28	41	2	42	42	24	48	44	37
FEB. 14	44	28	29	29	41	2	42	42	24	48	44	37
FEB. 15	44	30	31	31	41	2	42	42	24	48	44	37
FEB. 16	45	32	32	33	41	2	42	42	24	48	44	37
FEB. 17	45	33	34	34	41	2	42	42	24	48	44	37
FEB. 18	45	35	35	36	41	2	42	42	24	48	44	37
FEB. 19	45	36	37	37	42	2	42	42	24	48	44	37
FEB. 20	45	38	39	39	42	3	43	42	24	48	44	37
FEB. 21	45	40	40	41	42	3	43	42	24	48	44	37
FEB. 22	45	41	42	42	43	3	43	42	24	48	44	37
FEB. 23	46	43	43	44	43	3	43	42	24	48	44	37
FEB. 24	46	44	45	46	43	3	43	43	24	48	44	37
FEB. 25	46	46	47	47	43	3	43	43	24	48	44	37
FEB. 26	46	48	48	1	43	3	43	43	24	48	44	37
FEB. 27	46	2	2	3	43	3	43	43	24	48	44	37
FEB. 28	46	3	4	4	43	3	43	43	24	48	44	37

MOON 1 ◔ 12:01 A.M. TO 8:00 A.M.   **MOON 2 ◑ 8:01 A.M. TO 4:00 P.M.**   **MOON 3 ● 4:01 P.M. TO 12:00 A.M.**
Use only one "moon" number. Choose the column closest to your time of birth. If your place of birth is not on Eastern Standard Time, be sure to read "How to Convert to Eastern Standard Time" at the beginning of this section.

2009

March

April

Date & Time	SUN ☉	MOON 1 ◔	MOON 2 ◑	MOON 3 ●	MERCURY	VENUS	MARS	JUPITER	SATURN	URANUS	NEPTUNE	PLUTO
MAR. 1	46	5	6	6	43	3	44	43	23	48	44	37
MAR. 2	46	7	8	8	44	3	44	43	23	48	44	37
MAR. 3	47	9	9	10	44	3	44	43	23	48	44	37
MAR. 4	47	11	11	12	44	3	44	43	23	48	44	37
MAR. 5	47	12	13	14	44	3	44	43	23	48	44	37
MAR. 6	47	14	15	16	44	3	44	43	23	48	44	37
MAR. 7	47	16	17	18	45	3	44	43	23	48	44	37
MAR. 8	47	18	19	19	45	3	44	43	23	48	44	37
MAR. 9	47	20	21	21	45	3	44	43	23	48	44	37
MAR. 10	47	22	23	23	45	3	44	43	23	48	44	37
MAR. 11	48	24	25	25	45	3	45	43	23	48	44	37
MAR. 12	48	26	26	27	46	3	45	43	23	48	44	37
MAR. 13	48	28	28	29	46	3	45	43	23	48	44	37
MAR. 14	48	29	30	30	46	3	45	43	23	48	44	37
MAR. 15	48	31	32	32	46	3	45	43	23	48	44	37
MAR. 16	48	33	33	34	47	3	45	43	23	48	44	37
MAR. 17	48	34	35	35	47	3	45	43	23	48	44	37
MAR. 18	48	36	36	37	47	3	45	43	23	48	44	37
MAR. 19	1	37	38	39	47	3	45	43	23	48	44	37
MAR. 20	1	39	40	40	48	3	45	43	23	48	44	37
MAR. 21	1	41	41	42	48	2	46	43	23	48	44	37
MAR. 22	1	42	43	43	48	2	46	43	23	48	44	37
MAR. 23	1	44	44	45	48	2	46	43	23	48	44	37
MAR. 24	1	46	46	47	1	2	46	43	23	48	44	37
MAR. 25	2	47	48	48	1	2	46	43	23	48	44	37
MAR. 26	2	1	2	2	1	2	46	43	23	48	44	37
MAR. 27	2	3	3	4	1	2	46	43	23	48	44	37
MAR. 28	2	5	5	6	2	2	46	43	23	48	44	37
MAR. 29	2	6	7	8	2	2	46	43	23	48	44	37
MAR. 30	2	8	9	10	2	2	47	43	23	48	44	37
MAR. 31	2	10	11	11	2	2	47	43	23	48	44	37

Date & Time	SUN ☉	MOON 1 ◔	MOON 2 ◑	MOON 3 ●	MERCURY	VENUS	MARS	JUPITER	SATURN	URANUS	NEPTUNE	PLUTO
APR. 1	2	12	13	13	3	2	47	44	23	48	44	37
APR. 2	2	14	15	15	3	1	47	44	23	48	44	37
APR. 3	3	16	16	17	3	1	47	44	23	48	44	37
APR. 4	3	18	18	19	3	1	47	44	23	48	44	37
APR. 5	3	20	20	21	4	1	47	44	23	48	44	37
APR. 6	3	21	22	23	4	1	47	44	23	48	44	37
APR. 7	3	23	24	24	4	1	47	44	23	48	44	37
APR. 8	3	25	26	26	5	1	47	44	23	48	44	37
APR. 9	3	27	27	28	5	1	48	44	23	48	44	37
APR. 10	3	29	29	30	5	1	48	44	23	48	44	37
APR. 11	4	30	31	32	5	1	48	44	23	48	44	37
APR. 12	4	32	33	33	6	1	48	44	23	48	44	37
APR. 13	4	34	34	35	6	1	48	44	23	48	44	37
APR. 14	4	35	36	36	6	1	48	44	23	48	44	37
APR. 15	4	37	37	38	6	1	48	44	23	48	44	37
APR. 16	4	39	39	40	7	1	48	44	23	48	44	37
APR. 17	4	40	41	41	7	1	48	44	23	48	44	37
APR. 18	4	42	42	43	7	1	1	44	23	48	44	37
APR. 19	5	43	44	44	7	1	1	44	23	48	44	37
APR. 20	5	45	45	46	7	1	1	44	23	48	44	37
APR. 21	5	47	47	48	8	1	1	44	23	48	44	37
APR. 22	5	48	1	1	8	1	1	44	23	48	44	37
APR. 23	5	2	3	3	8	1	1	44	23	48	44	37
APR. 24	5	4	5	5	8	1	1	44	23	48	44	37
APR. 25	6	6	6	7	8	1	1	44	23	48	44	37
APR. 26	6	8	8	9	8	1	1	44	23	48	44	37
APR. 27	6	10	10	11	9	1	1	44	23	48	44	37
APR. 28	6	12	12	13	9	1	2	44	23	48	44	37
APR. 29	6	13	14	15	9	1	2	44	23	48	44	37
APR. 30	6	15	16	17	9	1	2	44	23	48	44	37

MOON 1 ◔ 12:01 A.M. TO 8:00 A.M.   **MOON 2** ◑ 8:01 A.M. TO 4:00 P.M.   **MOON 3** ● 4:01 P.M. TO 12:00 A.M.

Use only one "moon" number. Choose the column closest to your time of birth. If your place of birth is not on Eastern Standard Time, be sure to read "How to Convert to Eastern Standard Time" at the beginning of this section.

2009

May

Date & Time	SUN	MOON 1	MOON 2	MOON 3	MERCURY	VENUS	MARS	JUPITER	SATURN	URANUS	NEPTUNE	PLUTO
MAY 1	6	17	18	19	9	1	2	44	23	48	44	37
MAY 2	6	19	20	20	9	1	2	44	23	48	44	37
MAY 3	7	21	22	22	9	1	2	44	23	48	44	37
MAY 4	7	23	23	24	9	1	2	44	23	48	44	37
MAY 5	7	25	25	26	9	2	2	44	23	48	44	37
MAY 6	7	26	27	28	9	2	2	44	23	48	44	37
MAY 7	7	28	29	29	9	2	2	44	23	48	44	37
MAY 8	7	30	30	31	9	2	3	44	23	48	44	37
MAY 9	7	32	32	33	9	2	3	44	23	48	44	37
MAY 10	7	33	34	34	9	2	3	44	23	48	44	37
MAY 11	8	35	35	36	9	2	3	44	23	48	44	37
MAY 12	8	36	37	37	9	2	3	44	23	48	44	37
MAY 13	8	38	39	39	9	2	3	44	23	48	44	37
MAY 14	8	40	40	41	9	2	3	44	23	48	44	37
MAY 15	8	41	42	42	9	2	3	44	23	48	44	37
MAY 16	8	43	43	44	9	3	3	44	23	48	44	37
MAY 17	8	44	45	45	9	3	3	44	23	48	44	37
MAY 18	8	46	47	47	9	3	4	44	23	48	44	37
MAY 19	9	48	48	1	9	3	4	44	23	48	44	37
MAY 20	9	1	2	3	9	3	4	44	23	48	44	37
MAY 21	9	3	4	4	8	3	4	44	23	48	44	37
MAY 22	9	5	6	6	8	3	4	44	23	48	44	37
MAY 23	9	7	8	8	8	3	4	44	23	48	44	37
MAY 24	9	9	9	10	8	3	4	44	23	48	44	37
MAY 25	10	11	11	12	8	3	4	44	23	48	44	37
MAY 26	10	13	13	14	8	4	4	44	23	48	44	37
MAY 27	10	15	15	16	8	4	4	44	23	48	44	37
MAY 28	10	17	17	18	8	4	5	44	23	48	44	37
MAY 29	10	19	19	20	8	4	5	45	23	48	44	37
MAY 30	10	21	21	22	8	4	5	45	23	48	44	37
MAY 31	10	22	23	24	8	4	5	45	23	48	44	37

June

Date & Time	SUN	MOON 1	MOON 2	MOON 3	MERCURY	VENUS	MARS	JUPITER	SATURN	URANUS	NEPTUNE	PLUTO
JUN. 1	10	24	25	25	8	4	5	45	23	48	44	37
JUN. 2	10	26	27	27	8	4	5	45	23	48	44	37
JUN. 3	11	28	28	29	8	5	5	45	23	48	44	37
JUN. 4	11	29	30	31	8	5	5	45	23	48	44	37
JUN. 5	11	31	32	32	8	5	5	45	23	48	44	37
JUN. 6	11	33	33	34	8	5	5	45	23	48	44	37
JUN. 7	11	34	35	35	8	5	5	45	23	48	44	37
JUN. 8	11	36	37	37	8	5	6	45	23	48	44	37
JUN. 9	11	38	38	39	8	5	6	45	23	48	44	37
JUN. 10	11	39	40	40	9	5	6	45	23	48	44	37
JUN. 11	12	41	41	42	9	6	6	45	23	48	44	37
JUN. 12	12	42	43	43	9	6	6	45	23	48	44	37
JUN. 13	12	44	44	45	9	6	6	45	23	48	44	37
JUN. 14	12	45	46	47	9	6	6	45	23	1	44	37
JUN. 15	12	47	48	48	9	6	6	45	23	1	44	37
JUN. 16	12	1	1	2	9	6	6	45	23	1	44	37
JUN. 17	12	2	3	4	9	6	7	45	23	1	44	37
JUN. 18	12	4	5	5	10	7	7	45	23	1	44	37
JUN. 19	13	6	7	7	10	7	7	45	23	1	44	37
JUN. 20	13	8	9	9	10	7	7	45	23	1	44	37
JUN. 21	13	10	11	11	10	7	7	45	23	1	44	37
JUN. 22	13	12	13	13	10	7	7	45	23	1	44	37
JUN. 23	13	14	15	15	10	7	7	45	23	1	44	37
JUN. 24	13	16	17	17	11	7	7	45	23	1	44	37
JUN. 25	14	18	19	19	11	8	7	45	23	1	44	37
JUN. 26	14	20	21	21	11	8	7	45	23	1	44	37
JUN. 27	14	22	22	23	11	8	8	45	23	1	44	37
JUN. 28	14	24	24	25	12	8	8	45	23	1	44	37
JUN. 29	14	26	26	27	12	8	8	45	23	1	44	37
JUN. 30	14	27	28	28	12	8	8	45	23	1	44	37

MOON 1 ◗ 12:01 A.M. TO 8:00 A.M.   **MOON 2** ◖ 8:01 A.M. TO 4:00 P.M.   **MOON 3** ● 4:01 P.M. TO 12:00 A.M.
Use only one "moon" number. Choose the column closest to your time of birth. If your place of birth is not on Eastern Standard Time, be sure to read "How to Convert to Eastern Standard Time" at the beginning of this section.

2009

July

August

Date & Time	SUN	MOON 1	MOON 2	MOON 3	MERCURY	VENUS	MARS	JUPITER	SATURN	URANUS	NEPTUNE	PLUTO
JUL. 1	14	29	30	30	12	8	8	45	23	1	44	37
JUL. 2	14	31	31	32	13	9	8	45	23	1	44	37
JUL. 3	15	32	33	33	13	9	8	45	23	1	44	37
JUL. 4	15	34	35	35	13	9	8	44	23	1	44	37
JUL. 5	15	36	36	37	13	9	8	44	23	1	44	37
JUL. 6	15	37	38	38	14	9	8	44	23	1	44	37
JUL. 7	15	39	39	40	14	9	9	44	23	1	44	37
JUL. 8	15	40	41	41	14	9	9	44	23	1	44	37
JUL. 9	15	42	42	43	14	10	9	44	23	1	44	37
JUL. 10	15	43	44	45	15	10	9	44	23	1	44	37
JUL. 11	16	45	46	46	15	10	9	44	23	1	44	37
JUL. 12	16	47	47	48	15	10	9	44	23	1	44	37
JUL. 13	16	48	1	1	16	10	9	44	23	1	44	37
JUL. 14	16	2	3	3	16	10	9	44	23	1	44	37
JUL. 15	16	4	4	5	16	10	9	44	23	1	44	37
JUL. 16	16	5	6	7	16	11	9	44	23	1	44	37
JUL. 17	16	7	8	9	17	11	9	44	23	1	44	37
JUL. 18	16	9	10	10	17	11	10	44	23	1	44	37
JUL. 19	17	11	12	12	17	11	10	44	23	48	44	37
JUL. 20	17	13	14	14	18	11	10	44	23	48	44	37
JUL. 21	17	15	16	16	18	11	10	44	23	48	44	37
JUL. 22	17	17	18	18	18	11	10	44	23	48	44	37
JUL. 23	17	19	20	20	18	12	10	44	23	48	44	37
JUL. 24	17	21	22	22	19	12	10	44	23	48	44	37
JUL. 25	17	23	24	24	19	12	10	44	23	48	44	37
JUL. 26	18	25	26	26	19	12	10	44	23	48	44	37
JUL. 27	18	27	27	28	19	12	10	44	23	48	44	37
JUL. 28	18	29	29	30	20	12	10	44	23	48	44	37
JUL. 29	18	30	31	31	20	13	11	44	24	48	44	37
JUL. 30	18	32	32	33	20	13	11	44	24	48	44	37
JUL. 31	18	34	34	35	20	13	11	44	24	48	44	37

Date & Time	SUN	MOON 1	MOON 2	MOON 3	MERCURY	VENUS	MARS	JUPITER	SATURN	URANUS	NEPTUNE	PLUTO
AUG. 1	18	35	36	36	21	13	11	44	24	48	44	37
AUG. 2	18	37	37	38	21	13	11	44	24	48	44	37
AUG. 3	19	38	39	39	21	13	11	44	24	48	44	37
AUG. 4	19	40	40	41	21	13	11	44	24	48	44	37
AUG. 5	19	41	42	43	21	14	11	44	24	48	44	37
AUG. 6	19	43	44	44	22	14	11	44	24	48	44	37
AUG. 7	19	45	45	46	22	14	11	44	24	48	44	37
AUG. 8	19	46	47	47	22	14	11	44	24	48	44	37
AUG. 9	19	48	48	1	22	14	12	44	24	48	44	37
AUG. 10	19	2	2	3	22	14	12	44	24	48	44	37
AUG. 11	20	3	4	4	23	15	12	44	24	48	44	37
AUG. 12	20	5	6	6	23	15	12	44	24	48	44	37
AUG. 13	20	7	7	8	23	15	12	44	24	48	44	37
AUG. 14	20	9	9	10	23	15	12	44	24	48	44	37
AUG. 15	20	10	11	12	23	15	12	44	24	48	44	37
AUG. 16	20	12	13	14	24	15	12	44	24	48	44	37
AUG. 17	20	14	15	16	24	15	12	44	24	48	44	37
AUG. 18	20	16	17	18	24	16	12	44	24	48	44	37
AUG. 19	21	18	19	20	24	16	12	44	24	48	44	37
AUG. 20	21	20	21	22	24	16	12	44	24	48	44	37
AUG. 21	21	22	23	24	24	16	13	44	24	48	44	37
AUG. 22	21	24	25	25	24	16	13	44	24	48	44	37
AUG. 23	21	26	27	27	25	16	13	44	24	48	44	37
AUG. 24	21	28	28	29	25	17	13	44	24	48	44	37
AUG. 25	21	30	30	31	25	17	13	44	24	48	44	37
AUG. 26	22	31	32	33	25	17	13	44	24	48	44	37
AUG. 27	22	33	34	34	25	17	13	44	24	48	44	37
AUG. 28	22	35	35	36	25	17	13	44	24	48	44	37
AUG. 29	22	36	37	37	25	17	13	44	24	48	44	37
AUG. 30	22	38	38	39	25	18	13	44	24	48	44	37
AUG. 31	22	39	40	41	26	18	13	44	24	48	44	37

MOON 1 ◗ 12:01 A.M. TO 8:00 A.M.　　**MOON 2** ◑ 8:01 A.M. TO 4:00 P.M.　　**MOON 3** ● 4:01 P.M. TO 12:00 A.M.

Use only one "moon" number. Choose the column closest to your time of birth. If your place of birth is not on Eastern Standard Time, be sure to read "How to Convert to Eastern Standard Time" at the beginning of this section.

2009

September

Date & Time	SUN	MOON 1	MOON 2	MOON 3	MERCURY	VENUS	MARS	JUPITER	SATURN	URANUS	NEPTUNE	PLUTO
SEP. 1	22	41	42	42	26	18	14	44	24	48	44	37
SEP. 2	22	43	43	44	26	18	14	44	24	48	44	37
SEP. 3	23	44	45	45	26	18	14	44	24	48	44	37
SEP. 4	23	46	46	47	26	18	14	44	24	48	44	37
SEP. 5	23	47	48	1	26	18	14	44	24	48	44	37
SEP. 6	23	1	2	2	26	19	14	44	24	48	44	37
SEP. 7	23	3	3	4	26	19	14	44	24	48	44	37
SEP. 8	23	5	5	6	26	19	14	44	24	48	44	37
SEP. 9	23	6	7	8	26	19	14	43	24	48	44	37
SEP. 10	23	8	9	9	26	19	14	43	24	48	44	37
SEP. 11	24	10	11	11	26	19	14	43	24	48	44	37
SEP. 12	24	12	12	13	26	20	14	43	24	48	44	37
SEP. 13	24	14	14	15	26	20	14	43	24	48	44	37
SEP. 14	24	16	16	17	25	20	15	43	24	48	44	37
SEP. 15	24	17	18	19	25	20	15	43	24	48	44	37
SEP. 16	24	19	20	21	25	20	15	43	24	48	44	37
SEP. 17	24	21	22	23	25	20	15	43	24	48	44	37
SEP. 18	24	23	24	25	25	21	15	43	24	48	44	37
SEP. 19	25	25	26	27	25	21	15	43	24	48	44	37
SEP. 20	25	27	28	28	25	21	15	43	24	48	44	37
SEP. 21	25	29	30	30	25	21	15	43	24	48	44	37
SEP. 22	25	31	31	32	24	21	15	43	24	48	44	37
SEP. 23	25	32	33	34	24	21	15	43	24	48	44	37
SEP. 24	25	34	35	35	24	22	15	43	24	48	44	37
SEP. 25	26	36	36	37	24	22	15	43	24	48	44	37
SEP. 26	26	37	38	38	24	22	16	43	24	48	44	37
SEP. 27	26	39	40	40	24	22	16	43	24	48	44	37
SEP. 28	26	41	41	42	24	22	16	43	24	48	44	37
SEP. 29	26	42	43	43	24	22	16	43	24	48	44	37
SEP. 30	26	44	44	45	24	23	16	43	25	48	44	37

October

Date & Time	SUN	MOON 1	MOON 2	MOON 3	MERCURY	VENUS	MARS	JUPITER	SATURN	URANUS	NEPTUNE	PLUTO
OCT. 1	26	45	46	46	24	23	16	43	25	48	44	37
OCT. 2	26	47	48	48	24	23	16	43	25	48	44	37
OCT. 3	27	1	1	2	24	23	16	43	25	48	44	37
OCT. 4	27	2	3	4	24	23	16	43	25	48	44	37
OCT. 5	27	4	5	5	24	23	16	43	25	48	44	37
OCT. 6	27	6	6	7	24	24	16	43	25	48	44	37
OCT. 7	27	8	8	9	24	24	16	43	25	48	44	37
OCT. 8	27	10	10	11	25	24	16	43	25	48	44	37
OCT. 9	27	11	12	13	25	24	16	43	25	48	44	37
OCT. 10	27	13	14	14	25	24	17	43	25	48	44	37
OCT. 11	28	15	16	16	25	24	17	43	25	48	44	37
OCT. 12	28	17	18	18	25	25	17	43	25	48	44	37
OCT. 13	28	19	19	20	26	25	17	43	25	48	44	37
OCT. 14	28	21	21	22	26	25	17	43	25	48	44	37
OCT. 15	28	23	23	24	26	25	17	43	25	48	44	37
OCT. 16	28	25	25	26	26	25	17	43	25	48	44	37
OCT. 17	28	26	27	28	26	25	17	43	25	48	44	37
OCT. 18	28	28	29	29	27	26	17	43	25	48	44	37
OCT. 19	29	30	31	31	27	26	17	43	25	48	44	37
OCT. 20	29	32	32	33	27	26	17	43	25	48	44	37
OCT. 21	29	34	34	35	27	26	17	43	25	48	44	37
OCT. 22	29	35	36	36	28	26	17	43	25	48	44	37
OCT. 23	29	37	37	38	28	26	17	43	25	48	44	37
OCT. 24	29	38	39	40	28	27	17	43	25	48	44	37
OCT. 25	29	40	41	41	28	27	18	43	25	48	44	37
OCT. 26	30	42	42	43	28	27	18	43	25	48	44	37
OCT. 27	30	43	44	44	29	27	18	43	25	48	44	37
OCT. 28	30	45	45	46	29	27	18	43	25	48	44	37
OCT. 29	30	46	47	48	29	27	18	43	25	48	44	37
OCT. 30	30	48	1	1	29	27	18	43	25	48	44	37
OCT. 31	30	2	2	3	30	28	18	43	25	48	44	37

MOON 1 ◐ 12:01 A.M. TO 8:00 A.M. **MOON 2** ◑ 8:01 A.M. TO 4:00 P.M. **MOON 3** ● 4:01 P.M. TO 12:00 A.M.
Use only one "moon" number. Choose the column closest to your time of birth. If your place of birth is not on Eastern Standard Time, be sure to read "How to Convert to Eastern Standard Time" at the beginning of this section.

2009

November

Date & Time	SUN	MOON 1	MOON 2	MOON 3	MERCURY	VENUS	MARS	JUPITER	SATURN	URANUS	NEPTUNE	PLUTO
NOV. 1	30	3	4	5	30	28	18	43	25	48	44	37
NOV. 2	30	5	6	7	30	28	18	43	25	48	44	37
NOV. 3	31	7	8	8	30	28	18	43	25	48	44	37
NOV. 4	31	9	10	10	30	28	18	43	25	48	44	37
NOV. 5	31	11	11	12	31	28	18	43	25	48	44	37
NOV. 6	31	13	13	14	31	29	18	43	25	48	44	37
NOV. 7	31	15	15	16	31	29	18	43	25	48	44	37
NOV. 8	31	17	17	18	31	29	18	43	25	48	44	37
NOV. 9	31	18	19	20	32	29	18	43	25	48	44	37
NOV. 10	31	20	21	22	32	29	18	43	25	48	44	37
NOV. 11	31	22	23	23	32	29	18	43	25	48	44	37
NOV. 12	32	24	25	25	32	30	19	43	25	48	44	37
NOV. 13	32	26	26	27	32	30	19	43	25	48	44	37
NOV. 14	32	28	28	29	33	30	19	43	25	48	44	37
NOV. 15	32	29	30	31	33	30	19	43	25	48	44	37
NOV. 16	32	31	32	32	33	30	19	44	25	48	44	37
NOV. 17	32	33	34	34	33	31	19	44	25	48	44	37
NOV. 18	32	35	35	36	33	31	19	44	25	48	44	37
NOV. 19	33	36	37	37	34	31	19	44	25	48	44	37
NOV. 20	33	38	38	39	34	31	19	44	25	48	44	37
NOV. 21	33	40	40	41	34	31	19	44	25	48	44	37
NOV. 22	33	41	42	42	34	31	19	44	25	48	44	37
NOV. 23	33	43	43	44	34	32	19	44	25	48	44	37
NOV. 24	33	44	45	45	35	32	19	44	25	48	44	37
NOV. 25	34	46	46	47	35	32	19	44	25	48	44	37
NOV. 26	34	47	48	1	35	32	19	44	25	48	44	37
NOV. 27	34	1	2	2	35	32	19	44	25	48	44	37
NOV. 28	34	3	3	4	35	32	19	44	25	48	44	37
NOV. 29	34	5	5	6	36	33	19	44	25	48	44	37
NOV. 30	34	6	7	8	36	33	19	44	25	48	44	37

December

Date & Time	SUN	MOON 1	MOON 2	MOON 3	MERCURY	VENUS	MARS	JUPITER	SATURN	URANUS	NEPTUNE	PLUTO
DEC. 1	34	8	9	9	36	33	19	44	25	48	44	37
DEC. 2	34	10	11	11	36	33	19	44	25	48	44	37
DEC. 3	35	12	13	13	36	33	19	44	25	48	44	37
DEC. 4	35	14	15	15	37	33	19	44	25	48	44	37
DEC. 5	35	16	17	17	37	34	19	44	25	48	44	37
DEC. 6	35	18	19	19	37	34	19	44	25	48	44	37
DEC. 7	35	20	20	21	37	34	19	44	25	48	44	37
DEC. 8	35	22	22	23	37	34	19	44	25	48	44	37
DEC. 9	35	24	24	25	38	34	19	44	25	48	44	37
DEC. 10	35	25	26	27	38	34	20	44	25	48	44	37
DEC. 11	36	27	28	28	38	35	20	44	25	48	44	37
DEC. 12	36	29	30	30	38	35	20	44	25	48	44	37
DEC. 13	36	31	31	32	38	35	20	44	25	48	44	37
DEC. 14	36	32	33	34	39	35	20	44	25	48	44	37
DEC. 15	36	34	35	35	39	35	20	44	25	48	44	37
DEC. 16	36	36	36	37	39	35	20	44	25	48	44	37
DEC. 17	36	37	38	38	39	36	20	44	25	48	44	37
DEC. 18	36	39	40	40	39	36	20	44	26	48	44	37
DEC. 19	37	41	41	42	39	36	20	44	26	48	44	37
DEC. 20	37	42	43	43	39	36	20	44	26	48	44	37
DEC. 21	37	44	44	45	40	36	20	44	26	48	44	37
DEC. 22	37	45	46	46	40	36	20	44	26	48	44	37
DEC. 23	37	47	47	48	40	37	20	44	26	48	44	37
DEC. 24	37	1	1	2	40	37	20	44	26	48	44	37
DEC. 25	37	2	3	3	40	37	20	44	26	48	44	37
DEC. 26	38	4	4	5	40	37	20	44	26	48	44	37
DEC. 27	38	6	6	7	40	37	20	44	26	48	44	37
DEC. 28	38	7	8	9	40	37	20	44	26	48	44	37
DEC. 29	38	9	10	11	40	38	20	44	26	48	44	37
DEC. 30	38	11	12	12	40	38	20	44	26	48	44	37
DEC. 31	38	13	14	14	40	38	19	44	26	48	44	37

MOON 1 ◗ 12:01 A.M. TO 8:00 A.M.   **MOON 2** ◑ 8:01 A.M. TO 4:00 P.M.   **MOON 3** ● 4:01 P.M. TO 12:00 A.M.

Use only one "moon" number. Choose the column closest to your time of birth. If your place of birth is not on Eastern Standard Time, be sure to read "How to Convert to Eastern Standard Time" at the beginning of this section.

2010-2019

2010s

January 1, 2015

* *

As you've seen, Personology is quite useful for creating natal portraits. But how good is it at predicting the future? You'll have to judge for yourself. Here is what the Personology forecasting system predicts—in terms of planetary influences—for January 1, 2015.

SUN IN THE WEEK OF THE RULER
(CAPRICORN I)

*

Those born in this week know how to control their living and working situations. True rulers, they regard their home as their castle and like to see it running smoothly. Allergic to chaos, they run the risk of becoming control freaks. Unless they give up their tendency to make up other people's minds for them, they are likely to arouse resentments.

MOON IN THE WEEK OF THE NATURAL
(TAURUS III)

*

The moon in this position can make an individual astonishingly frank. Blurting out whatever is on their mind is typical here. Often they have no thought for how such remarks may push the buttons of those around them. We can admire such individuals for their lack of inhibition, but they really must learn something about tact and consideration for others.

MERCURY IN THE WEEK OF DOMINANCE
(CAPRICORN III)

*

Mercury can serve the purpose of this week by bringing structure and logic to the activities of daily life. With this position, the intellect is easily put in the service of pragmatism, allowing a high degree of control. Dominance here usually means dominating one's material rather than one's friends. In the workplace, it could denote a tidy agenda and an orderly work flow; at home, a spotless kitchen and everything in its place.

VENUS ON THE CUSP OF MYSTERY AND IMAGINATION
(CAPRICORN-AQUARIUS CUSP)

*

Exciting love affairs and romantic infatuations are the order of the day here. Vivid imaginations can conjure up the wildest fantasies, rarely equaled in intensity by real life experiences. One might say that these individuals can go pretty far without even having a real-life love object. They must convince their lovers that they really care for them and not just their own fantasies.

MARS IN THE WEEK OF ACCEPTANCE
(AQUARIUS III)

*

Too often Mars here lends intolerance to one's outlook. The inability to accept things as they are often leads these folks to try to change people and, if that fails, to judge and reject them. Learning acceptance is obviously their most important lesson or, at the very least, they need to learn to back off and leave people alone.

JUPITER IN THE WEEK OF LEADERSHIP
(LEO III)

*

Even if this person is not a born leader, they can achieve great success at the helm of a family or professional group. This may very well be only a temporary leadership position, perhaps adopted in times of need and stress. Quiet individuals who are able to rise to the occasion are frequently found here. Once the crisis is past they can return to more humble activities.

SATURN ON THE CUSP OF REVOLUTION
(SCORPIO-SAGITTARIUS CUSP)

✳

A serious desire to change the status quo manifests itself here. The problem is that rebelliousness may be carried too far and Saturn, in reaction, can substitute repression in its place. Thus, these energies may arouse the very opposite of what they seem to portend. Instead of becoming freer, this individual may wind up more restricted through the reactions of others.

URANUS IN THE WEEK OF THE STAR
(ARIES II)

✳

Uranus strives for recognition and attention, sometimes using rather spectacular means to get it. If ignored, such individuals may use the element of surprise to garner attention, saving up their energy and unleashing it on a gathering at the most opportune, albeit awkward, moment. Such unforgettable and regrettable displays may earn them a reputation for theatrical behavior.

NEPTUNE IN THE WEEK OF SPIRIT
(PISCES I)

✳

One of the most spiritual positions of Neptune, the higher causes of humanity are usually espoused and the most noble truths followed. These individuals are more likely than most to see beyond the petty problems of everyday life and to look toward the high ideals and beliefs of mankind. Following a love of truth and compassion usually characterizes their life's work.

PLUTO IN THE WEEK OF DETERMINATION
(CAPRICORN II)

✳

It is not easy to oppose Pluto's pursuits in this position. Such individuals are very prone to the workings of fate and the more forceful of them are relentlessly advancing their own projects. Free will does not seem to play a part here, since such individuals are clearly driven by forces beyond their control. Kindness and sympathy must be achieved through struggle.

NOTE

If you were to chart this day on the Personology wheel, you'd find that Pluto, which is in Capricorn II, and Uranus, which is in Aries, II, form what is called a **SQUARE,** which defines the relationship whenever two planets are exactly three signs or three cusps apart. Generally speaking squares in astrology are thought of as dynamic and action-oriented. Because of Pluto's irresistible power in Capricorn II and Uranus' spectacular force in Aries II, this square between them could upset everyone's applecart, including your own. Care should be taken to tone things down and to remember to respect the feelings of others.

SQUARE

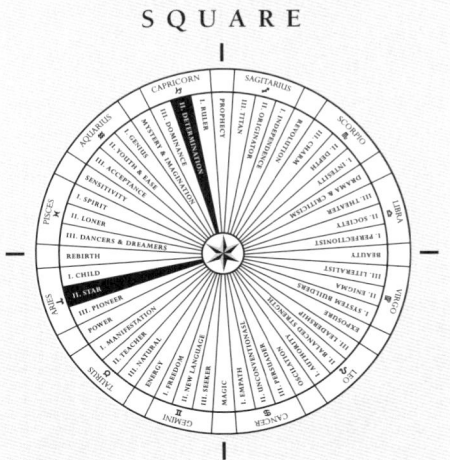

Meanwhile, Mars, which is in Aquarius III, and Jupiter, which is in Leo III, form what is called an **OPPOSITION,** which defines the relationship whenever the planets are directly 180 degrees opposite each other. Such oppositions are thought to create conflict, but they can also compliment each other through their differences. This opposition could be an invitation to step out in front and take a leadership role, but it requires being aware that intolerance or disrespect for one's subordinates can lead to resistance. Learning to guide one's family members, colleagues or other dependents with understanding and wisdom is the challenge here.

OPPOSITION

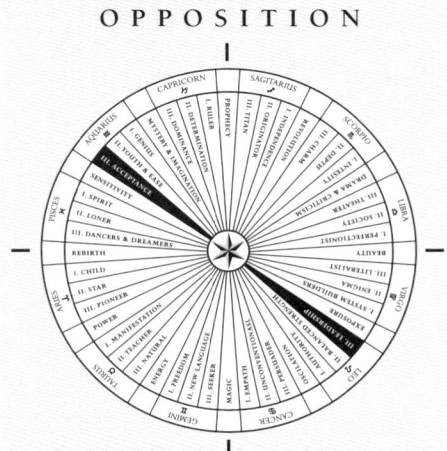

Finally, Mercury in Capricorn III is **TRINE** the Moon in Taurus III. Trines are operative when two planets are four signs or four cusps apart. They are easy aspects that promote relaxation and enjoyment. However, they can also lead to procrastination and laziness. In this case, the relaxed trine reduce the irritating exhibitionism of the Moon in Taurus III and help Mercury secure the pragmatic control it aspires to. Success in one's career is particularly favored.

TRINE

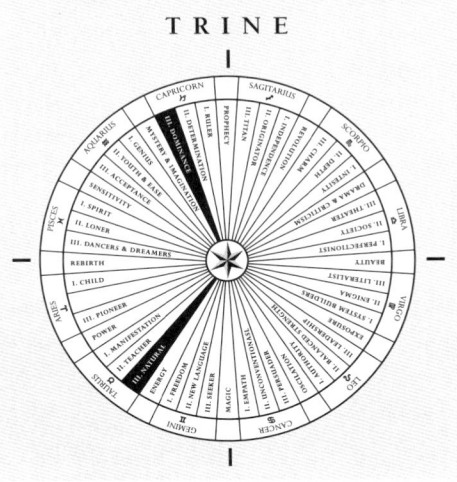

2010

January

Date & Time	SUN ☉	MOON 1 ◔	MOON 2 ◑	MOON 3 ●	MERCURY	VENUS	MARS	JUPITER	SATURN	URANUS	NEPTUNE	PLUTO
JAN. 1	38	15	16	16	39	38	19	44	26	48	44	37
JAN. 2	38	17	18	18	39	38	19	45	26	48	44	37
JAN. 3	39	19	20	20	39	38	19	45	26	48	44	37
JAN. 4	39	21	22	22	39	39	19	45	26	48	44	37
JAN. 5	39	23	24	24	39	39	19	45	26	48	44	37
JAN. 6	39	25	26	26	39	39	19	45	26	48	44	37
JAN. 7	39	27	27	28	38	39	19	45	26	48	44	37
JAN. 8	39	29	29	30	38	39	19	45	26	48	44	37
JAN. 9	39	30	31	31	38	39	19	45	26	48	44	37
JAN. 10	40	32	33	33	38	40	19	45	26	48	44	37
JAN. 11	40	34	34	35	38	40	19	45	26	48	44	37
JAN. 12	40	35	36	36	38	40	19	45	26	48	44	37
JAN. 13	40	37	38	38	38	40	19	45	26	48	44	37
JAN. 14	40	39	39	40	38	40	19	45	26	48	44	37
JAN. 15	40	40	41	41	38	40	19	45	26	48	44	37
JAN. 16	40	42	42	43	38	41	19	45	26	48	44	37
JAN. 17	41	43	44	44	38	41	19	45	26	48	44	37
JAN. 18	41	45	45	46	38	41	19	45	26	48	44	37
JAN. 19	41	46	47	48	38	41	19	45	26	48	44	37
JAN. 20	41	48	1	1	38	41	19	45	26	48	44	37
JAN. 21	41	2	3	3	38	41	19	45	26	48	44	38
JAN. 22	41	3	4	4	38	42	19	45	26	48	44	38
JAN. 23	42	5	6	6	38	42	19	45	26	48	44	38
JAN. 24	42	7	7	8	38	42	19	45	26	48	44	38
JAN. 25	42	8	9	10	38	42	19	45	26	48	44	38
JAN. 26	42	10	11	12	38	42	18	45	26	48	44	38
JAN. 27	42	12	13	14	39	42	18	45	26	48	44	38
JAN. 28	42	14	15	16	39	43	18	45	26	48	44	38
JAN. 29	42	16	17	18	39	43	18	45	26	48	44	38
JAN. 30	42	18	19	20	39	43	18	45	26	48	44	38
JAN. 31	43	20	21	22	39	43	18	45	26	48	44	38

February

Date & Time	SUN ☉	MOON 1 ◔	MOON 2 ◑	MOON 3 ●	MERCURY	VENUS	MARS	JUPITER	SATURN	URANUS	NEPTUNE	PLUTO
FEB. 1	43	22	23	24	39	43	18	45	26	48	44	38
FEB. 2	43	24	25	26	40	43	18	45	26	48	44	38
FEB. 3	43	26	27	27	40	44	18	45	26	48	44	38
FEB. 4	43	28	29	29	40	44	18	45	26	48	44	38
FEB. 5	43	30	30	31	40	44	18	46	26	48	44	38
FEB. 6	43	32	32	33	40	44	18	46	26	48	44	38
FEB. 7	43	33	34	34	40	44	18	46	26	48	44	38
FEB. 8	44	35	36	36	41	44	18	46	26	48	44	38
FEB. 9	44	37	37	38	41	45	18	46	26	48	44	38
FEB. 10	44	38	39	39	41	45	18	46	25	48	44	38
FEB. 11	44	40	40	41	41	45	18	46	25	48	44	38
FEB. 12	44	41	42	42	41	45	18	46	25	48	44	38
FEB. 13	44	43	43	44	42	45	18	46	25	48	44	38
FEB. 14	44	44	45	46	42	45	18	46	25	48	44	38
FEB. 15	44	46	47	47	42	46	17	46	25	48	44	38
FEB. 16	45	48	48	1	42	46	17	46	25	48	44	38
FEB. 17	45	1	2	2	42	46	17	46	25	48	44	38
FEB. 18	45	3	3	4	43	46	17	46	25	48	44	38
FEB. 19	45	5	5	6	43	46	17	46	25	48	44	38
FEB. 20	45	6	7	7	43	46	17	46	25	48	44	38
FEB. 21	45	8	9	9	43	47	17	46	25	48	44	38
FEB. 22	45	10	10	11	43	47	17	46	25	48	44	38
FEB. 23	46	12	12	13	44	47	17	46	25	48	44	38
FEB. 24	46	13	14	15	44	47	17	46	25	48	45	38
FEB. 25	46	15	16	17	44	47	17	46	25	48	45	38
FEB. 26	46	17	18	19	44	47	17	46	25	48	45	38
FEB. 27	46	19	20	21	44	48	17	46	25	48	45	38
FEB. 28	46	21	22	23	45	48	17	46	25	48	45	38

MOON 1 ◔ 12:01 A.M. TO 8:00 A.M. **MOON 2** ◑ 8:01 A.M. TO 4:00 P.M. **MOON 3** ● 4:01 P.M. TO 12:00 A.M.
Use only one "moon" number. Choose the column closest to your time of birth. If your place of birth is not on Eastern Standard Time, be sure to read "How to Convert to Eastern Standard Time" at the beginning of this section.

2010

March

April

Date & Time	SUN	MOON 1	MOON 2	MOON 3	MERCURY	VENUS	MARS	JUPITER	SATURN	URANUS	NEPTUNE	PLUTO
MAR. 1	46	23	24	25	45	48	17	46	25	48	45	38
MAR. 2	46	25	26	27	45	48	17	46	25	48	45	38
MAR. 3	47	27	28	29	45	48	17	46	25	48	45	38
MAR. 4	47	29	30	30	46	48	17	46	25	48	45	38
MAR. 5	47	31	32	32	46	1	17	46	25	48	45	38
MAR. 6	47	33	33	34	46	1	17	46	25	48	45	38
MAR. 7	47	34	35	36	46	1	17	46	25	48	45	38
MAR. 8	47	36	37	37	47	1	17	47	25	48	45	38
MAR. 9	47	38	38	39	47	1	17	47	25	48	45	38
MAR. 10	47	39	40	40	47	1	17	47	25	48	45	38
MAR. 11	48	41	41	42	47	2	17	47	25	48	45	38
MAR. 12	48	42	43	44	48	2	17	47	25	48	45	38
MAR. 13	48	44	45	45	48	2	17	47	25	48	45	38
MAR. 14	48	46	46	47	48	2	17	47	25	48	45	38
MAR. 15	48	47	48	48	48	2	17	47	25	48	45	38
MAR. 16	48	1	1	2	1	2	17	47	25	1	45	38
MAR. 17	48	3	3	4	1	3	17	47	25	1	45	38
MAR. 18	48	4	5	5	1	3	17	47	25	1	45	38
MAR. 19	1	6	6	7	1	3	17	47	25	1	45	38
MAR. 20	1	8	8	9	2	3	17	47	25	1	45	38
MAR. 21	1	9	10	10	2	3	17	47	25	1	45	38
MAR. 22	1	11	12	12	2	3	17	47	25	1	45	38
MAR. 23	1	13	13	14	2	4	17	47	25	1	45	38
MAR. 24	1	15	15	16	3	4	17	47	25	1	45	38
MAR. 25	2	17	17	18	3	4	17	47	25	1	45	38
MAR. 26	2	19	19	20	3	4	17	47	25	1	45	38
MAR. 27	2	20	21	22	3	4	17	47	25	1	45	38
MAR. 28	2	22	23	24	4	4	17	47	25	1	45	38
MAR. 29	2	24	25	26	4	5	17	47	25	1	45	38
MAR. 30	2	26	27	28	4	5	17	47	25	1	45	38
MAR. 31	2	28	29	30	4	5	17	47	25	1	45	38

Date & Time	SUN	MOON 1	MOON 2	MOON 3	MERCURY	VENUS	MARS	JUPITER	SATURN	URANUS	NEPTUNE	PLUTO
APR. 1	2	30	31	31	5	5	17	47	25	1	45	38
APR. 2	2	32	33	33	5	5	17	47	25	1	45	38
APR. 3	3	34	34	35	5	5	17	47	25	1	45	38
APR. 4	3	36	36	37	5	6	17	47	25	1	45	38
APR. 5	3	37	38	38	5	6	17	47	25	1	45	38
APR. 6	3	39	39	40	6	6	18	47	25	1	45	38
APR. 7	3	40	41	42	6	6	18	47	25	1	45	38
APR. 8	3	42	43	43	6	6	18	47	25	1	45	38
APR. 9	3	44	44	45	6	6	18	48	25	1	45	38
APR. 10	3	45	46	46	6	7	18	48	25	1	45	38
APR. 11	4	47	47	48	6	7	18	48	25	1	45	38
APR. 12	4	48	1	1	6	7	18	48	25	1	45	38
APR. 13	4	2	3	3	6	7	18	48	25	1	45	38
APR. 14	4	4	4	5	7	7	18	48	25	1	45	38
APR. 15	4	5	6	7	7	7	18	48	25	1	45	38
APR. 16	4	7	8	8	7	8	18	48	25	1	45	38
APR. 17	4	9	9	10	7	8	18	48	25	1	45	38
APR. 18	4	11	11	12	7	8	18	48	25	1	45	38
APR. 19	5	12	13	14	7	8	18	48	25	1	45	38
APR. 20	5	14	15	16	7	8	18	48	25	1	45	38
APR. 21	5	16	17	17	7	8	18	48	25	1	45	38
APR. 22	5	18	19	19	7	8	18	48	25	1	45	38
APR. 23	5	20	21	21	6	9	18	48	25	1	45	38
APR. 24	5	22	22	23	6	9	18	48	25	1	45	38
APR. 25	6	24	24	25	6	9	18	48	25	1	45	38
APR. 26	6	26	26	27	6	9	18	48	25	1	45	38
APR. 27	6	28	28	29	6	9	18	48	25	1	45	38
APR. 28	6	29	30	31	6	9	18	48	25	1	45	38
APR. 29	6	31	32	33	6	10	19	48	25	1	45	38
APR. 30	6	33	34	34	6	10	19	48	25	1	45	38

MOON 1 ◗ 12:01 A.M. TO 8:00 A.M.　　**MOON 2** ◖ 8:01 A.M. TO 4:00 P.M.　　**MOON 3** ● 4:01 P.M. TO 12:00 A.M.

Use only one "moon" number. Choose the column closest to your time of birth. If your place of birth is not on Eastern Standard Time, be sure to read "How to Convert to Eastern Standard Time" at the beginning of this section.

2010

May — June

Date & Time	SUN	MOON 1	MOON 2	MOON 3	MERCURY	VENUS	MARS	JUPITER	SATURN	URANUS	NEPTUNE	PLUTO
MAY 1	6	35	35	36	6	10	19	48	25	1	45	38
MAY 2	6	37	37	38	6	10	19	48	25	1	45	38
MAY 3	7	38	39	39	6	10	19	48	25	1	45	38
MAY 4	7	40	40	41	6	10	19	48	25	1	45	38
MAY 5	7	42	42	43	6	11	19	48	25	1	45	38
MAY 6	7	43	44	44	5	11	19	48	25	1	45	38
MAY 7	7	45	45	46	5	11	19	48	25	1	45	38
MAY 8	7	46	47	47	5	11	19	48	25	1	45	38
MAY 9	7	48	48	1	5	11	19	48	25	1	45	38
MAY 10	7	1	2	3	5	11	19	48	25	1	45	38
MAY 11	8	3	4	4	5	12	19	48	25	1	45	38
MAY 12	8	5	6	6	5	12	19	48	25	1	45	38
MAY 13	8	7	7	8	5	12	19	48	25	1	45	38
MAY 14	8	8	9	10	5	12	19	48	25	1	45	38
MAY 15	8	10	11	11	5	12	19	48	25	1	45	38
MAY 16	8	12	13	13	5	12	20	1	25	1	45	38
MAY 17	8	14	14	15	5	13	20	1	25	1	45	38
MAY 18	8	16	16	17	6	13	20	1	25	1	45	38
MAY 19	9	18	18	19	6	13	20	1	25	1	45	38
MAY 20	9	19	20	21	6	13	20	1	25	1	45	38
MAY 21	9	21	22	23	6	13	20	1	25	1	45	38
MAY 22	9	23	24	25	6	13	20	1	25	1	45	38
MAY 23	9	25	26	26	6	13	20	1	25	1	45	38
MAY 24	9	27	28	28	6	14	20	1	25	1	45	38
MAY 25	10	29	29	30	6	14	20	1	25	1	45	38
MAY 26	10	31	31	32	6	14	20	1	25	1	45	38
MAY 27	10	33	33	34	6	14	20	1	25	1	45	38
MAY 28	10	34	35	35	7	14	20	1	25	1	45	38
MAY 29	10	36	37	37	7	14	20	1	25	1	45	38
MAY 30	10	38	38	39	7	15	20	1	25	1	45	38
MAY 31	10	39	40	40	7	15	20	1	25	1	45	38

Date & Time	SUN	MOON 1	MOON 2	MOON 3	MERCURY	VENUS	MARS	JUPITER	SATURN	URANUS	NEPTUNE	PLUTO
JUN. 1	10	41	41	42	7	15	21	1	25	1	45	38
JUN. 2	10	43	43	44	7	15	21	1	25	1	45	38
JUN. 3	11	44	45	45	8	15	21	1	25	1	45	38
JUN. 4	11	46	46	47	8	15	21	1	25	1	45	38
JUN. 5	11	47	48	48	8	16	21	1	25	1	45	38
JUN. 6	11	1	1	2	8	16	21	1	25	1	45	38
JUN. 7	11	3	3	4	8	16	21	1	25	1	45	38
JUN. 8	11	4	5	5	9	16	21	1	25	1	45	38
JUN. 9	11	6	7	7	9	16	21	1	25	1	45	38
JUN. 10	11	8	8	9	9	16	21	1	25	1	45	38
JUN. 11	12	9	10	11	9	16	21	1	25	1	45	38
JUN. 12	12	11	12	13	9	17	21	1	25	1	45	38
JUN. 13	12	13	14	14	10	17	21	1	25	1	45	38
JUN. 14	12	15	16	16	10	17	21	1	25	1	45	38
JUN. 15	12	17	18	18	10	17	22	1	25	1	45	38
JUN. 16	12	19	20	20	10	17	22	1	25	1	45	38
JUN. 17	12	21	22	22	11	17	22	1	25	1	45	38
JUN. 18	12	23	23	24	11	18	22	1	25	1	45	38
JUN. 19	13	25	25	26	11	18	22	1	25	1	45	38
JUN. 20	13	27	27	28	11	18	22	1	25	1	45	38
JUN. 21	13	28	29	30	12	18	22	1	25	1	45	38
JUN. 22	13	30	31	31	12	18	22	1	25	1	45	38
JUN. 23	13	32	33	33	12	18	22	1	25	1	45	38
JUN. 24	13	34	34	35	13	18	22	1	25	1	45	38
JUN. 25	14	35	36	37	13	19	22	1	25	1	45	38
JUN. 26	14	37	38	38	13	19	22	1	25	1	45	38
JUN. 27	14	39	39	40	13	19	22	1	25	1	45	38
JUN. 28	14	40	41	42	14	19	22	1	25	1	45	38
JUN. 29	14	42	43	43	14	19	23	1	25	1	45	38
JUN. 30	14	44	44	45	14	19	23	1	25	1	45	37

MOON 1 ☽ 12:01 A.M. TO 8:00 A.M.   **MOON 2** ☾ 8:01 A.M. TO 4:00 P.M.   **MOON 3** ● 4:01 P.M. TO 12:00 A.M.
Use only one "moon" number. Choose the column closest to your time of birth. If your place of birth is not on Eastern Standard Time, be sure to read "How to Convert to Eastern Standard Time" at the beginning of this section.

2010

July

Date & Time	SUN	MOON 1	MOON 2	MOON 3	MERCURY	VENUS	MARS	JUPITER	SATURN	URANUS	NEPTUNE	PLUTO
JUL. 1	14	45	46	46	15	20	23	1	25	1	45	37
JUL. 2	14	47	47	48	15	20	23	1	25	1	45	37
JUL. 3	15	48	1	1	15	20	23	1	25	1	45	37
JUL. 4	15	2	3	3	15	20	23	1	25	1	45	37
JUL. 5	15	4	4	5	16	20	23	1	25	1	45	37
JUL. 6	15	5	6	6	16	20	23	1	25	1	45	37
JUL. 7	15	7	8	8	16	20	23	1	25	1	45	37
JUL. 8	15	9	9	10	17	21	23	1	25	1	45	37
JUL. 9	15	11	11	12	17	21	23	1	25	1	45	37
JUL. 10	15	12	13	14	17	21	23	1	25	1	45	37
JUL. 11	16	14	15	16	17	21	23	1	25	1	45	37
JUL. 12	16	16	17	18	18	21	24	1	25	1	45	37
JUL. 13	16	18	19	20	18	21	24	1	25	1	45	37
JUL. 14	16	20	21	22	18	22	24	1	25	1	45	37
JUL. 15	16	22	23	24	18	22	24	1	25	1	45	37
JUL. 16	16	24	25	25	19	22	24	1	25	1	45	37
JUL. 17	16	26	27	27	19	22	24	1	25	1	45	37
JUL. 18	16	28	29	29	19	22	24	1	25	1	45	37
JUL. 19	17	30	30	31	19	22	24	1	25	1	45	37
JUL. 20	17	32	32	33	19	22	24	1	25	1	45	37
JUL. 21	17	33	34	34	20	23	24	1	25	1	45	37
JUL. 22	17	35	36	36	20	23	24	1	25	1	45	37
JUL. 23	17	37	37	38	20	23	24	1	25	1	45	37
JUL. 24	17	38	39	39	20	23	25	1	25	1	45	37
JUL. 25	17	40	41	41	20	23	25	1	25	1	45	37
JUL. 26	18	42	42	43	21	23	25	1	25	1	45	37
JUL. 27	18	43	44	44	21	23	25	1	25	1	45	37
JUL. 28	18	45	45	46	21	23	25	1	25	1	45	37
JUL. 29	18	46	47	47	21	24	25	1	25	1	45	37
JUL. 30	18	48	48	1	21	24	25	1	25	1	45	37
JUL. 31	18	2	2	3	22	24	25	1	25	1	45	37

August

Date & Time	SUN	MOON 1	MOON 2	MOON 3	MERCURY	VENUS	MARS	JUPITER	SATURN	URANUS	NEPTUNE	PLUTO
AUG. 1	18	3	4	4	22	24	25	1	25	1	45	37
AUG. 2	18	5	5	6	22	24	25	1	25	1	45	37
AUG. 3	19	6	7	8	22	24	25	1	25	1	45	37
AUG. 4	19	8	9	9	22	25	25	1	25	1	45	37
AUG. 5	19	10	10	11	22	25	25	1	25	1	45	37
AUG. 6	19	12	12	13	22	25	26	1	25	1	45	37
AUG. 7	19	14	14	15	23	25	26	1	25	1	45	37
AUG. 8	19	15	16	17	23	25	26	1	25	1	45	37
AUG. 9	19	17	18	19	23	25	26	1	25	1	45	37
AUG. 10	19	19	20	21	23	25	26	1	25	1	45	37
AUG. 11	20	21	22	23	23	26	26	1	25	1	45	37
AUG. 12	20	23	24	25	23	26	26	1	25	1	45	37
AUG. 13	20	25	26	27	23	26	26	1	25	1	45	37
AUG. 14	20	27	28	29	23	26	26	1	25	1	45	37
AUG. 15	20	29	30	31	23	26	26	1	25	1	45	37
AUG. 16	20	31	32	32	23	26	26	1	25	1	45	37
AUG. 17	20	33	34	34	23	26	26	1	25	1	45	37
AUG. 18	20	35	35	36	23	26	27	1	25	1	45	37
AUG. 19	21	36	37	37	23	27	27	1	25	1	45	37
AUG. 20	21	38	39	39	24	27	27	1	25	1	45	37
AUG. 21	21	40	40	41	24	27	27	1	25	1	45	37
AUG. 22	21	41	42	42	23	27	27	1	25	1	45	37
AUG. 23	21	43	43	44	23	27	27	1	25	1	45	37
AUG. 24	21	44	45	45	23	27	27	1	25	1	45	37
AUG. 25	21	46	46	47	23	27	27	1	25	1	45	37
AUG. 26	22	48	48	1	23	27	27	1	25	1	45	37
AUG. 27	22	1	2	2	23	28	27	1	25	1	45	37
AUG. 28	22	3	3	4	23	28	27	1	25	1	45	37
AUG. 29	22	4	5	5	23	28	27	1	25	1	45	37
AUG. 30	22	6	6	7	23	28	28	1	25	1	45	37
AUG. 31	22	8	8	9	23	28	28	1	26	1	45	37

MOON 1 ☽ 12:01 A.M. TO 8:00 A.M.   **MOON 2** ☾ 8:01 A.M. TO 4:00 P.M.   **MOON 3** ● 4:01 P.M. TO 12:00 A.M.
Use only one "moon" number. Choose the column closest to your time of birth. If your place of birth is not on Eastern Standard Time, be sure to read "How to Convert to Eastern Standard Time" at the beginning of this section.

Date & Time	SUN	MOON 1	MOON 2	MOON 3	MERCURY	VENUS	MARS	JUPITER	SATURN	URANUS	NEPTUNE	PLUTO
SEP. 1	22	9	10	10	23	28	28	1	26	1	45	37
SEP. 2	22	11	12	12	23	28	28	1	26	1	45	37
SEP. 3	23	13	13	14	22	28	28	1	26	1	45	37
SEP. 4	23	15	15	16	22	28	28	1	26	1	45	37
SEP. 5	23	17	17	18	22	29	28	1	26	1	45	37
SEP. 6	23	19	19	20	22	29	28	1	26	1	45	37
SEP. 7	23	21	21	22	22	29	28	1	26	1	45	37
SEP. 8	23	23	23	24	22	29	28	1	26	1	45	37
SEP. 9	23	25	25	26	22	29	28	1	26	1	45	37
SEP. 10	23	27	27	28	22	29	29	1	26	1	45	37
SEP. 11	24	29	29	30	22	29	29	1	26	1	45	37
SEP. 12	24	31	31	32	22	29	29	1	26	1	45	37
SEP. 13	24	32	33	34	22	29	29	1	26	1	45	37
SEP. 14	24	34	35	35	22	30	29	1	26	1	45	37
SEP. 15	24	36	36	37	22	30	29	1	26	1	45	37
SEP. 16	24	38	38	39	22	30	29	1	26	1	45	37
SEP. 17	24	39	40	40	22	30	29	1	26	1	45	37
SEP. 18	24	41	41	42	22	30	29	1	26	1	45	37
SEP. 19	25	42	43	43	22	30	29	1	26	1	45	37
SEP. 20	25	44	44	45	22	30	29	1	26	1	45	37
SEP. 21	25	46	46	47	22	30	30	1	26	1	44	37
SEP. 22	25	47	48	48	23	30	30	1	26	1	44	37
SEP. 23	25	1	1	2	23	30	30	1	26	1	44	37
SEP. 24	25	2	3	3	23	30	30	1	26	1	44	37
SEP. 25	26	4	4	5	23	30	30	1	26	1	44	37
SEP. 26	26	6	6	7	23	30	30	1	26	1	44	37
SEP. 27	26	7	8	8	23	30	30	1	26	1	44	37
SEP. 28	26	9	9	10	24	30	30	1	26	1	44	37
SEP. 29	26	11	11	12	24	31	30	1	26	1	44	37
SEP. 30	26	12	13	14	24	31	30	1	26	1	44	37

Date & Time	SUN	MOON 1	MOON 2	MOON 3	MERCURY	VENUS	MARS	JUPITER	SATURN	URANUS	NEPTUNE	PLUTO
OCT. 1	26	14	15	15	24	31	30	1	26	1	44	37
OCT. 2	26	16	17	17	25	31	31	1	26	1	44	37
OCT. 3	27	18	18	19	25	31	31	1	26	1	44	37
OCT. 4	27	20	20	21	25	31	31	1	26	1	44	37
OCT. 5	27	22	22	23	25	31	31	1	26	1	44	37
OCT. 6	27	24	24	25	26	31	31	48	26	1	44	37
OCT. 7	27	26	26	27	26	31	31	48	26	1	44	37
OCT. 8	27	28	28	29	26	31	31	48	26	1	44	37
OCT. 9	27	30	30	31	26	31	31	48	26	1	44	37
OCT. 10	27	32	32	33	27	31	31	48	26	1	44	37
OCT. 11	28	33	34	35	27	31	31	48	26	1	44	37
OCT. 12	28	35	36	36	27	31	31	48	26	1	44	37
OCT. 13	28	37	38	38	27	31	32	48	26	1	44	37
OCT. 14	28	39	39	40	27	31	32	48	26	1	44	37
OCT. 15	28	40	41	41	28	31	32	48	26	1	44	37
OCT. 16	28	42	42	43	28	31	32	48	26	1	44	37
OCT. 17	28	44	44	45	28	31	32	48	26	1	44	37
OCT. 18	28	45	46	47	28	30	32	48	26	1	44	37
OCT. 19	29	47	47	48	29	30	32	48	26	1	44	37
OCT. 20	29	48	1	1	29	30	32	48	26	1	44	37
OCT. 21	29	2	2	3	29	30	32	48	26	1	44	37
OCT. 22	29	3	4	5	29	30	32	48	26	1	44	37
OCT. 23	29	5	6	6	29	30	32	48	26	1	44	37
OCT. 24	29	7	7	8	30	30	33	48	26	1	44	37
OCT. 25	29	8	9	10	30	30	33	48	26	1	44	37
OCT. 26	30	10	11	11	30	30	33	48	26	1	44	37
OCT. 27	30	12	13	13	30	30	33	48	26	1	44	37
OCT. 28	30	14	14	15	31	30	33	48	26	1	44	37
OCT. 29	30	15	16	17	31	30	33	48	26	1	44	37
OCT. 30	30	17	18	19	31	30	33	48	26	1	44	37
OCT. 31	30	19	20	20	31	30	33	48	26	1	44	37

MOON 1 ○ 12:01 A.M. TO 8:00 A.M.   **MOON 2** ◑ 8:01 A.M. TO 4:00 P.M.   **MOON 3** ● 4:01 P.M. TO 12:00 A.M.
Use only one "moon" number. Choose the column closest to your time of birth. If your place of birth is not on Eastern Standard Time, be sure to read "How to Convert to Eastern Standard Time" at the beginning of this section.

2010

November

Date & Time	SUN ☉	MOON 1 ◐	MOON 2 ◑	MOON 3 ●	MERCURY	VENUS	MARS	JUPITER	SATURN	URANUS	NEPTUNE	PLUTO
NOV. 1	30	21	22	22	31	29	33	48	26	1	44	37
NOV. 2	30	23	24	24	32	29	33	48	27	1	44	37
NOV. 3	31	25	26	26	32	29	34	48	27	1	44	37
NOV. 4	31	27	28	28	32	29	34	48	27	1	44	37
NOV. 5	31	29	30	30	32	29	34	48	27	1	44	37
NOV. 6	31	31	31	32	32	29	34	48	27	1	44	37
NOV. 7	31	33	33	34	33	29	34	48	27	1	44	37
NOV. 8	31	35	35	36	33	29	34	48	27	1	44	37
NOV. 9	31	36	37	38	33	29	34	48	27	1	44	37
NOV. 10	31	38	39	39	33	29	34	48	27	1	44	37
NOV. 11	31	40	40	41	33	29	34	48	27	1	44	37
NOV. 12	32	41	42	42	34	29	35	48	27	1	44	37
NOV. 13	32	43	44	44	34	29	35	48	27	1	44	37
NOV. 14	32	45	45	46	34	29	35	48	27	1	44	37
NOV. 15	32	46	47	47	34	29	35	48	27	1	44	37
NOV. 16	32	48	48	1	34	29	35	48	27	1	44	37
NOV. 17	32	1	2	2	35	29	35	48	27	1	44	37
NOV. 18	32	3	4	4	35	29	35	48	27	1	44	37
NOV. 19	33	5	5	6	35	29	35	48	27	1	44	37
NOV. 20	33	6	7	7	35	29	35	48	27	1	44	37
NOV. 21	33	8	9	9	35	29	35	48	27	1	44	37
NOV. 22	33	10	10	11	36	29	35	48	27	1	44	37
NOV. 23	33	11	12	13	36	29	35	48	27	1	44	37
NOV. 24	33	13	14	14	36	29	36	48	27	1	44	38
NOV. 25	34	15	16	16	36	29	36	48	27	1	44	38
NOV. 26	34	17	18	18	36	29	36	48	27	1	44	38
NOV. 27	34	19	19	20	36	29	36	48	27	1	44	38
NOV. 28	34	21	21	22	37	29	36	48	27	1	44	38
NOV. 29	34	22	23	24	37	29	36	48	27	1	44	38
NOV. 30	34	24	25	26	37	29	36	48	27	1	44	38

December

Date & Time	SUN ☉	MOON 1 ◐	MOON 2 ◑	MOON 3 ●	MERCURY	VENUS	MARS	JUPITER	SATURN	URANUS	NEPTUNE	PLUTO
DEC. 1	34	26	27	28	37	29	36	48	27	1	44	38
DEC. 2	34	28	29	29	37	29	36	48	27	1	44	38
DEC. 3	35	30	31	31	37	29	36	48	27	1	44	38
DEC. 4	35	32	33	33	37	29	37	48	27	1	44	38
DEC. 5	35	34	34	35	37	29	37	48	27	1	44	38
DEC. 6	35	36	36	37	38	29	37	48	27	1	44	38
DEC. 7	35	37	38	39	38	29	37	48	27	1	44	38
DEC. 8	35	39	40	40	38	30	37	48	27	1	44	38
DEC. 9	35	41	41	42	38	30	37	48	27	1	44	38
DEC. 10	35	42	43	44	38	30	37	48	27	1	44	38
DEC. 11	36	44	45	45	38	30	37	48	27	1	44	38
DEC. 12	36	46	46	47	38	30	37	48	27	1	44	38
DEC. 13	36	47	48	48	38	30	37	48	27	1	44	38
DEC. 14	36	1	1	2	38	30	38	48	27	1	44	38
DEC. 15	36	2	3	3	37	30	38	48	27	1	44	38
DEC. 16	36	4	5	5	37	30	38	48	27	1	44	38
DEC. 17	36	6	6	7	37	30	38	48	27	1	44	38
DEC. 18	36	7	8	8	37	30	38	48	27	1	44	38
DEC. 19	37	9	10	10	37	31	38	48	27	1	44	38
DEC. 20	37	11	11	12	37	31	38	48	27	1	44	38
DEC. 21	37	13	13	14	36	31	38	48	27	1	44	38
DEC. 22	37	14	15	16	36	31	38	48	27	1	44	38
DEC. 23	37	16	17	18	36	31	39	48	27	1	45	38
DEC. 24	37	18	19	20	36	31	39	48	27	1	45	38
DEC. 25	37	20	21	21	36	31	39	48	27	1	45	38
DEC. 26	38	22	23	23	36	31	39	48	27	1	45	38
DEC. 27	38	24	25	25	36	32	39	48	27	1	45	38
DEC. 28	38	26	26	27	36	32	39	48	27	1	45	38
DEC. 29	38	28	28	29	36	32	39	48	27	1	45	38
DEC. 30	38	30	30	31	36	32	39	48	27	1	45	38
DEC. 31	38	31	32	33	36	32	39	48	27	1	45	38

MOON 1 ◐ 12:01 A.M. TO 8:00 A.M.   **MOON 2** ◑ 8:01 A.M. TO 4:00 P.M.   **MOON 3** ● 4:01 P.M. TO 12:00 A.M.
Use only one "moon" number. Choose the column closest to your time of birth. If your place of birth is not on Eastern Standard Time, be sure to read "How to Convert to Eastern Standard Time" at the beginning of this section.

2011

January

Date & Time	SUN	MOON 1	MOON 2	MOON 3	MERCURY	VENUS	MARS	JUPITER	SATURN	URANUS	NEPTUNE	PLUTO
JAN. 1	38	33	34	34	36	32	39	1	27	1	45	38
JAN. 2	38	35	36	36	36	32	40	1	27	1	45	38
JAN. 3	39	37	37	38	36	32	40	1	27	1	45	38
JAN. 4	39	38	39	40	36	33	40	1	27	1	45	38
JAN. 5	39	40	41	41	36	33	40	1	27	1	45	38
JAN. 6	39	42	42	43	36	33	40	1	27	1	45	38
JAN. 7	39	43	44	45	36	33	40	1	27	1	45	38
JAN. 8	39	45	46	46	36	33	40	1	27	1	45	38
JAN. 9	39	47	47	48	36	33	40	1	27	1	45	38
JAN. 10	40	48	1	1	36	33	40	1	27	1	45	38
JAN. 11	40	2	3	3	37	33	40	1	27	1	45	38
JAN. 12	40	3	4	5	37	34	41	1	27	1	45	38
JAN. 13	40	5	6	6	37	34	41	1	27	1	45	38
JAN. 14	40	7	7	8	37	34	41	1	27	1	45	38
JAN. 15	40	8	9	10	37	34	41	1	27	1	45	38
JAN. 16	40	10	11	11	37	34	41	1	27	1	45	38
JAN. 17	41	12	12	13	38	34	41	1	27	1	45	38
JAN. 18	41	14	14	15	38	34	41	1	27	1	45	38
JAN. 19	41	16	16	17	38	35	41	1	27	1	45	38
JAN. 20	41	18	18	19	38	35	41	1	27	1	45	38
JAN. 21	41	19	20	21	38	35	42	1	27	1	45	38
JAN. 22	41	21	22	23	38	35	42	1	27	1	45	38
JAN. 23	42	23	24	25	39	35	42	1	27	1	45	38
JAN. 24	42	25	26	27	39	35	42	1	27	1	45	38
JAN. 25	42	27	28	29	39	35	42	1	27	1	45	38
JAN. 26	42	29	30	30	39	36	42	1	27	1	45	38
JAN. 27	42	31	32	32	39	36	42	1	27	1	45	38
JAN. 28	42	33	33	34	40	36	42	1	27	1	45	38
JAN. 29	42	35	35	36	40	36	42	1	27	1	45	38
JAN. 30	42	36	37	37	40	36	42	1	27	1	45	38
JAN. 31	43	38	39	39	40	36	43	1	27	1	45	38

February

Date & Time	SUN	MOON 1	MOON 2	MOON 3	MERCURY	VENUS	MARS	JUPITER	SATURN	URANUS	NEPTUNE	PLUTO
FEB. 1	43	40	40	41	40	37	43	1	27	1	45	38
FEB. 2	43	41	42	42	41	37	43	1	27	1	45	38
FEB. 3	43	43	44	44	41	37	43	1	27	1	45	38
FEB. 4	43	45	45	46	41	37	43	1	27	1	45	38
FEB. 5	43	46	47	47	41	37	43	1	27	1	45	38
FEB. 6	43	48	48	1	41	37	43	1	27	1	45	38
FEB. 7	43	1	2	2	42	37	43	1	27	1	45	38
FEB. 8	44	3	3	4	42	38	43	1	27	1	45	38
FEB. 9	44	5	5	6	42	38	44	1	27	1	45	38
FEB. 10	44	6	7	7	42	38	44	1	27	1	45	38
FEB. 11	44	8	8	9	43	38	44	1	27	1	45	38
FEB. 12	44	9	10	11	43	38	44	2	27	1	45	38
FEB. 13	44	11	12	12	43	38	44	2	27	1	45	38
FEB. 14	44	13	14	14	43	38	44	2	27	1	45	38
FEB. 15	44	15	15	16	43	39	44	2	27	1	45	38
FEB. 16	45	17	17	18	44	39	44	2	27	1	45	38
FEB. 17	45	19	19	20	44	39	44	2	27	1	45	38
FEB. 18	45	21	21	22	44	39	44	2	27	1	45	38
FEB. 19	45	23	23	24	44	39	45	2	27	1	45	38
FEB. 20	45	25	25	26	44	39	45	2	27	1	45	38
FEB. 21	45	27	27	28	45	40	45	2	27	1	45	38
FEB. 22	45	29	29	30	45	40	45	2	27	1	45	38
FEB. 23	46	31	31	32	45	40	45	2	27	1	45	38
FEB. 24	46	32	33	34	46	40	45	2	27	1	45	38
FEB. 25	46	34	35	35	46	40	45	2	27	1	45	38
FEB. 26	46	36	37	37	46	40	45	2	27	1	45	38
FEB. 27	46	38	38	39	46	41	45	2	27	1	45	38
FEB. 28	46	39	40	40	47	41	46	2	27	1	45	38

MOON 1 ○ 12:01 A.M. TO 8:00 A.M.   **MOON 2** ◑ 8:01 A.M. TO 4:00 P.M.   **MOON 3** ● 4:01 P.M. TO 12:00 A.M.

Use only one "moon" number. Choose the column closest to your time of birth. If your place of birth is not on Eastern Standard Time, be sure to read "How to Convert to Eastern Standard Time" at the beginning of this section.

2011

March — April

Date & Time	SUN ☉	MOON 1 ◐	MOON 2 ◑	MOON 3 ●	MERCURY	VENUS	MARS	JUPITER	SATURN	URANUS	NEPTUNE	PLUTO
MAR. 1	46	41	41	42	47	41	46	2	27	1	45	38
MAR. 2	46	43	43	44	47	41	46	2	27	1	45	38
MAR. 3	47	44	45	45	47	41	46	2	27	1	45	38
MAR. 4	47	46	46	47	48	41	46	2	27	1	45	38
MAR. 5	47	47	48	48	48	41	46	2	27	1	45	38
MAR. 6	47	1	1	2	48	42	46	2	27	1	45	38
MAR. 7	47	3	3	4	48	42	46	2	27	1	45	38
MAR. 8	47	4	5	5	1	42	46	2	27	1	45	38
MAR. 9	47	6	6	7	1	42	46	2	27	1	45	38
MAR. 10	47	7	8	8	1	42	47	2	27	1	45	38
MAR. 11	48	9	9	10	1	42	47	2	27	1	45	38
MAR. 12	48	11	11	12	2	43	47	2	27	1	45	38
MAR. 13	48	12	13	13	2	43	47	2	27	1	45	38
MAR. 14	48	14	15	15	2	43	47	2	27	1	45	38
MAR. 15	48	16	16	17	2	43	47	2	27	1	45	38
MAR. 16	48	18	18	19	3	43	47	2	27	1	45	38
MAR. 17	48	20	20	21	3	43	47	3	27	1	45	38
MAR. 18	48	22	22	23	3	44	47	3	27	1	45	38
MAR. 19	1	24	24	25	3	44	48	3	27	1	45	38
MAR. 20	1	26	26	27	3	44	48	3	27	1	45	38
MAR. 21	1	28	28	29	3	44	48	3	27	1	45	38
MAR. 22	1	30	30	31	4	44	48	3	27	1	45	38
MAR. 23	1	32	32	33	4	44	48	3	27	1	45	38
MAR. 24	1	34	34	35	4	44	48	3	27	1	45	38
MAR. 25	2	35	36	37	4	45	48	3	27	1	45	38
MAR. 26	2	37	38	38	4	45	48	3	27	1	45	38
MAR. 27	2	39	39	40	4	45	48	3	27	1	45	38
MAR. 28	2	41	41	42	4	45	48	3	27	1	45	38
MAR. 29	2	42	43	43	4	45	1	3	27	1	45	38
MAR. 30	2	44	44	45	4	45	1	3	27	1	45	38
MAR. 31	2	45	46	46	4	46	1	3	27	1	45	38
APR. 1	2	47	48	48	4	46	1	3	27	1	45	38
APR. 2	2	1	1	2	4	46	1	3	27	1	45	38
APR. 3	3	2	3	3	4	46	1	3	27	1	45	38
APR. 4	3	4	4	5	4	46	1	3	27	1	45	38
APR. 5	3	5	6	6	4	46	1	3	27	1	45	38
APR. 6	3	7	7	8	4	47	1	3	27	1	45	38
APR. 7	3	9	9	10	4	47	1	3	27	1	45	38
APR. 8	3	10	11	11	4	47	2	3	27	1	45	38
APR. 9	3	12	12	13	4	47	2	3	27	1	45	38
APR. 10	3	14	14	15	4	47	2	3	27	1	45	38
APR. 11	4	15	16	16	3	47	2	3	27	1	45	38
APR. 12	4	17	18	18	3	48	2	3	27	1	45	38
APR. 13	4	19	20	20	3	48	2	3	27	1	45	38
APR. 14	4	21	21	22	3	48	2	3	27	1	45	38
APR. 15	4	23	23	24	3	48	2	3	27	1	45	38
APR. 16	4	25	25	26	3	48	2	3	27	1	45	38
APR. 17	4	27	28	28	3	48	3	4	27	1	45	38
APR. 18	4	29	30	30	3	48	3	4	27	1	45	38
APR. 19	5	31	32	32		1	3	4	27	1	45	38
APR. 20	5	33	33	34		1	3	4	27	1	45	38
APR. 21	5	35	35	36		1	3	4	27	1	45	38
APR. 22	5	37	37	38		1	3	4	27	1	45	38
APR. 23	5	38	39	39		1	3	4	27	1	45	38
APR. 24	5	40	41	41	3	1	3	4	27	1	45	38
APR. 25	6	42	42	43	2	2	3	4	27	1	45	38
APR. 26	6	43	44	44	3	2	3	4	27	1	45	38
APR. 27	6	45	46	46	3	2	4	4	27	1	45	38
APR. 28	6	47	47	48	3	2	4	4	27	1	45	38
APR. 29	6	48	1	1	3	2	4	4	27	1	45	38
APR. 30	6	2	2	3	3	2	4	4	27	1	45	38

MOON 1 ◐ 12:01 A.M. TO 8:00 A.M.   **MOON 2** ◑ 8:01 A.M. TO 4:00 P.M.   **MOON 3** ● 4:01 P.M. TO 12:00 A.M.

Use only one "moon" number. Choose the column closest to your time of birth. If your place of birth is not on Eastern Standard Time, be sure to read "How to Convert to Eastern Standard Time" at the beginning of this section.

2011

May

June

Date & Time	SUN	MOON 1	MOON 2	MOON 3	MERCURY	VENUS	MARS	JUPITER	SATURN	URANUS	NEPTUNE	PLUTO
MAY 1	6	3	4	4	3	3	4	4	27	1	45	38
MAY 2	6	5	5	6	3	3	4	4	27	1	45	38
MAY 3	7	7	7	8	3	3	4	4	27	1	45	38
MAY 4	7	8	9	9	3	3	4	4	27	1	45	38
MAY 5	7	10	10	11	3	3	4	4	27	1	45	38
MAY 6	7	11	12	13	3	4	4	4	27	1	45	38
MAY 7	7	13	14	14	4	4	5	4	27	1	45	38
MAY 8	7	15	15	16	4	4	5	4	26	1	45	38
MAY 9	7	17	17	18	4	4	5	4	26	1	45	38
MAY 10	7	18	19	20	4	4	5	4	26	1	45	38
MAY 11	8	20	21	22	4	4	5	4	26	1	45	38
MAY 12	8	22	23	23	4	4	5	4	26	1	45	38
MAY 13	8	24	25	25	4	5	5	4	26	1	45	38
MAY 14	8	26	27	27	5	5	5	4	26	1	45	38
MAY 15	8	28	29	29	5	5	5	4	26	1	45	38
MAY 16	8	30	31	31	5	5	5	4	26	1	45	38
MAY 17	8	32	33	33	5	5	6	4	26	1	45	38
MAY 18	8	34	35	35	5	5	6	4	26	1	45	38
MAY 19	9	36	36	37	6	5	6	4	26	1	45	38
MAY 20	9	38	38	39	6	6	6	5	26	1	45	38
MAY 21	9	39	40	41	6	6	6	5	26	1	45	38
MAY 22	9	41	42	42	6	6	6	5	26	1	45	38
MAY 23	9	43	43	44	6	6	6	5	26	1	45	38
MAY 24	9	44	45	46	7	6	6	5	26	1	45	38
MAY 25	10	46	47	47	7	6	6	5	26	1	45	38
MAY 26	10	48	48	1	7	7	6	5	26	1	45	38
MAY 27	10	1	2	2	7	7	7	5	26	1	45	38
MAY 28	10	3	3	4	7	7	7	5	26	1	45	38
MAY 29	10	4	5	6	7	7	7	5	26	1	45	38
MAY 30	10	6	7	7	8	7	7	5	26	1	45	38
MAY 31	10	8	8	9	8	7	7	5	26	1	45	38

Date & Time	SUN	MOON 1	MOON 2	MOON 3	MERCURY	VENUS	MARS	JUPITER	SATURN	URANUS	NEPTUNE	PLUTO
JUN. 1	10	9	10	10	9	8	7	5	26	1	45	38
JUN. 2	10	11	12	12	9	8	7	5	26	1	45	38
JUN. 3	11	13	13	14	9	8	7	5	26	2	45	38
JUN. 4	11	14	15	16	9	8	7	5	26	2	45	38
JUN. 5	11	16	17	17	10	8	7	5	26	2	45	38
JUN. 6	11	18	19	19	10	8	8	5	26	2	45	38
JUN. 7	11	20	20	21	10	9	8	5	26	2	45	38
JUN. 8	11	22	22	23	10	9	8	5	26	2	45	38
JUN. 9	11	24	24	25	11	9	8	5	26	2	45	38
JUN. 10	11	25	26	27	11	9	8	5	26	2	45	38
JUN. 11	12	27	28	29	11	9	8	5	26	2	45	38
JUN. 12	12	29	30	31	12	9	8	5	26	2	45	38
JUN. 13	12	31	32	33	12	10	8	5	26	2	45	38
JUN. 14	12	33	34	34	12	10	8	5	26	2	45	38
JUN. 15	12	35	36	36	13	10	8	5	26	2	45	38
JUN. 16	12	37	38	38	13	10	9	5	26	2	45	38
JUN. 17	12	39	39	40	13	10	9	5	26	2	45	38
JUN. 18	12	40	41	42	13	10	9	5	26	2	45	38
JUN. 19	13	42	43	43	14	11	9	5	26	2	45	38
JUN. 20	13	44	44	45	14	11	9	5	26	2	45	38
JUN. 21	13	46	46	47	14	11	9	5	26	2	45	38
JUN. 22	13	47	48	48	14	11	9	5	26	2	45	38
JUN. 23	13	1	1	2	15	11	9	5	26	2	45	38
JUN. 24	13	2	3	3	15	11	9	5	26	2	45	38
JUN. 25	14	4	4	5	15	12	9	5	26	2	45	38
JUN. 26	14	6	6	7	16	12	9	6	26	2	45	38
JUN. 27	14	7	8	8	16	12	10	6	26	2	45	38
JUN. 28	14	9	9	10	16	12	10	6	26	2	45	38
JUN. 29	14	10	11	12	16	12	10	6	26	2	45	38
JUN. 30	14	12	13	13	17	12	10	6	26	2	45	38

MOON 1 ☽ 12:01 A.M. TO 8:00 A.M.   **MOON 2** ☽ 8:01 A.M. TO 4:00 P.M.   **MOON 3** ● 4:01 P.M. TO 12:00 A.M.

Use only one "moon" number. Choose the column closest to your time of birth. If your place of birth is not on Eastern Standard Time, be sure to read "How to Convert to Eastern Standard Time" at the beginning of this section.

2011

July   August

Date & Time	SUN	MOON 1	MOON 2	MOON 3	MERCURY	VENUS	MARS	JUPITER	SATURN	URANUS	NEPTUNE	PLUTO
JUL. 1	14	14	14	15	17	12	10	6	26	2	45	38
JUL. 2	14	16	16	17	17	13	10	6	26	2	45	38
JUL. 3	15	18	18	19	17	13	10	6	26	2	45	38
JUL. 4	15	19	20	21	17	13	10	6	26	2	45	38
JUL. 5	15	21	22	23	18	13	10	6	26	2	45	38
JUL. 6	15	23	24	24	18	13	10	6	26	2	45	38
JUL. 7	15	25	26	26	18	13	10	6	26	2	45	38
JUL. 8	15	27	28	28	18	14	11	6	26	2	45	38
JUL. 9	15	29	29	30	18	14	11	6	26	2	45	38
JUL. 10	15	31	31	32	19	14	11	6	26	2	45	38
JUL. 11	16	33	33	34	19	14	11	6	26	2	45	38
JUL. 12	16	34	35	36	19	14	11	6	26	2	45	38
JUL. 13	16	36	37	37	19	14	11	6	26	2	45	38
JUL. 14	16	38	39	39	19	15	11	6	26	2	45	38
JUL. 15	16	40	40	41	19	15	11	6	26	2	45	38
JUL. 16	16	42	42	43	20	15	11	6	26	2	45	38
JUL. 17	16	43	44	44	20	15	11	6	26	2	45	38
JUL. 18	16	45	46	46	20	15	12	6	26	2	45	38
JUL. 19	17	47	47	48	20	15	12	6	27	2	45	38
JUL. 20	17	48	1	1	20	16	12	6	27	2	45	38
JUL. 21	17	2	2	2	20	16	12	6	27	2	45	38
JUL. 22	17	3	4	4	20	16	12	6	27	2	45	38
JUL. 23	17	5	5	6	21	16	12	6	27	2	45	38
JUL. 24	17	7	7	8	21	16	12	6	27	2	45	38
JUL. 25	17	8	9	9	21	16	12	6	27	2	45	38
JUL. 26	18	10	10	11	21	17	12	6	27	2	45	38
JUL. 27	18	12	12	13	21	17	12	6	27	2	45	38
JUL. 28	18	13	14	14	21	17	12	6	27	2	45	38
JUL. 29	18	15	16	16	21	17	13	6	27	2	45	38
JUL. 30	18	17	17	18	21	17	13	6	27	2	45	38
JUL. 31	18	19	19	20	21	17	13	6	27	2	45	38

Date & Time	SUN	MOON 1	MOON 2	MOON 3	MERCURY	VENUS	MARS	JUPITER	SATURN	URANUS	NEPTUNE	PLUTO
AUG. 1	18	21	21	22	21	18	13	6	27	2	45	38
AUG. 2	18	23	23	24	21	18	13	6	27	2	45	38
AUG. 3	19	25	25	26	21	18	13	6	27	2	45	38
AUG. 4	19	26	27	28	21	18	13	6	27	2	45	38
AUG. 5	19	28	29	30	21	18	13	6	27	2	45	38
AUG. 6	19	30	31	32	21	18	13	6	27	2	45	38
AUG. 7	19	32	33	33	21	19	13	6	27	2	45	38
AUG. 8	19	34	35	35	21	19	13	6	27	2	45	38
AUG. 9	19	36	36	37	21	19	13	6	27	2	45	38
AUG. 10	19	38	38	39	21	19	14	6	27	2	45	38
AUG. 11	20	39	40	40	21	19	14	6	27	2	45	38
AUG. 12	20	41	42	42	21	19	14	6	27	2	45	38
AUG. 13	20	43	43	44	21	20	14	6	27	2	45	38
AUG. 14	20	44	45	46	20	20	14	6	27	2	45	38
AUG. 15	20	46	47	47	20	20	14	6	27	2	45	38
AUG. 16	20	48	48	1	20	20	14	6	27	2	45	38
AUG. 17	20	1	2	2	20	20	14	6	27	2	45	38
AUG. 18	20	3	3	4	20	20	14	6	27	1	45	38
AUG. 19	21	4	5	6	20	21	14	6	27	1	45	38
AUG. 20	21	6	7	7	20	21	14	6	27	1	45	38
AUG. 21	21	8	9	9	20	21	15	6	27	1	45	38
AUG. 22	21	9	10	10	20	21	15	6	27	1	45	38
AUG. 23	21	11	11	12	20	21	15	6	27	1	45	38
AUG. 24	21	13	13	14	20	21	15	6	27	1	45	38
AUG. 25	21	14	15	16	19	22	15	6	27	1	45	38
AUG. 26	22	16	17	17	19	22	15	6	27	1	45	38
AUG. 27	22	18	19	19	19	22	15	6	27	1	45	38
AUG. 28	22	20	21	21	19	22	15	6	27	1	45	38
AUG. 29	22	22	23	23	20	22	15	6	27	1	45	38
AUG. 30	22	24	25	25	20	22	15	6	27	1	45	38
AUG. 31	22	26	27	27	20	23	15	6	27	1	45	38

MOON 1 ◑ 12:01 A.M. TO 8:00 A.M.   **MOON 2** ◐ 8:01 A.M. TO 4:00 P.M.   **MOON 3** ● 4:01 P.M. TO 12:00 A.M.

Use only one "moon" number. Choose the column closest to your time of birth. If your place of birth is not on Eastern Standard Time, be sure to read "How to Convert to Eastern Standard Time" at the beginning of this section.

2011

September

Date & Time	SUN	MOON 1	MOON 2	MOON 3	MERCURY	VENUS	MARS	JUPITER	SATURN	URANUS	NEPTUNE	PLUTO
SEP. 1	22	28	28	29	20	23	15	6	27	1	45	38
SEP. 2	22	30	30	31	20	23	16	6	27	1	45	38
SEP. 3	23	32	32	33	20	23	16	6	27	1	45	38
SEP. 4	23	34	34	35	20	23	16	6	27	1	45	38
SEP. 5	23	35	36	37	20	23	16	6	27	1	45	38
SEP. 6	23	37	38	38	20	23	16	6	27	1	45	38
SEP. 7	23	39	39	40	21	24	16	6	27	1	45	38
SEP. 8	23	41	41	42	21	24	16	6	27	1	45	38
SEP. 9	23	42	43	43	21	24	16	6	27	1	45	38
SEP. 10	23	44	45	45	21	24	16	6	27	1	45	38
SEP. 11	24	46	46	47	21	24	16	6	27	1	45	38
SEP. 12	24	47	48	48	22	24	16	6	27	1	45	38
SEP. 13	24	1	1	2	22	25	16	6	27	1	45	38
SEP. 14	24	2	3	3	22	25	17	6	27	1	45	38
SEP. 15	24	4	5	5	22	25	17	6	27	1	45	38
SEP. 16	24	6	6	7	23	25	17	6	27	1	45	38
SEP. 17	24	7	8	8	23	25	17	6	27	1	45	38
SEP. 18	24	9	9	10	23	25	17	6	27	1	45	38
SEP. 19	25	10	11	11	23	26	17	6	27	1	45	38
SEP. 20	25	12	13	13	24	26	17	6	27	1	45	38
SEP. 21	25	14	14	15	24	26	17	6	27	1	45	38
SEP. 22	25	15	16	17	24	26	17	6	27	1	45	38
SEP. 23	25	17	18	18	24	26	17	6	27	1	45	38
SEP. 24	25	19	20	20	25	26	17	6	27	1	45	38
SEP. 25	26	21	22	22	25	27	17	6	27	1	45	38
SEP. 26	26	23	24	24	25	27	18	6	27	1	45	38
SEP. 27	26	25	26	26	25	27	18	6	27	1	45	38
SEP. 28	26	27	28	28	26	27	18	6	27	1	45	38
SEP. 29	26	29	30	30	26	27	18	6	27	1	45	38
SEP. 30	26	31	32	32	26	27	18	6	27	1	45	38

October

Date & Time	SUN	MOON 1	MOON 2	MOON 3	MERCURY	VENUS	MARS	JUPITER	SATURN	URANUS	NEPTUNE	PLUTO
OCT. 1	26	33	34	34	26	28	18	6	27	1	45	38
OCT. 2	26	35	36	36	26	28	18	6	27	1	45	38
OCT. 3	27	37	37	38	27	28	18	6	27	1	45	38
OCT. 4	27	39	39	40	27	28	18	6	28	1	45	38
OCT. 5	27	40	41	41	27	28	18	6	28	1	45	38
OCT. 6	27	42	42	43	27	28	18	6	28	1	45	38
OCT. 7	27	44	44	45	28	29	18	6	28	1	45	38
OCT. 8	27	45	46	46	28	29	18	6	28	1	45	38
OCT. 9	27	47	47	48	28	29	19	6	28	1	45	38
OCT. 10	27	48	1	2	28	29	19	6	28	1	45	38
OCT. 11	28	2	3	3	28	29	19	6	28	1	45	38
OCT. 12	28	4	4	5	29	29	19	6	28	1	45	38
OCT. 13	28	5	6	6	29	30	19	6	28	1	45	38
OCT. 14	28	7	7	8	29	30	19	6	28	1	45	38
OCT. 15	28	8	9	9	29	30	19	6	28	1	45	38
OCT. 16	28	10	10	11	30	30	19	6	28	1	45	38
OCT. 17	28	12	12	13	30	30	19	6	28	1	45	38
OCT. 18	28	13	14	14	30	30	19	6	28	1	45	38
OCT. 19	29	15	15	16	30	31	19	6	28	1	45	38
OCT. 20	29	17	17	18	30	31	19	6	28	1	45	38
OCT. 21	29	18	19	20	31	31	19	6	28	1	45	38
OCT. 22	29	20	21	21	31	31	20	6	28	1	45	38
OCT. 23	29	22	23	23	31	31	20	6	28	1	45	38
OCT. 24	29	24	25	25	31	31	20	6	28	1	45	38
OCT. 25	29	26	27	27	31	32	20	6	28	1	45	38
OCT. 26	30	28	29	29	32	32	20	6	28	1	45	38
OCT. 27	30	30	31	31	32	32	20	6	28	1	45	38
OCT. 28	30	32	33	33	32	32	20	6	28	1	45	38
OCT. 29	30	34	35	35	32	32	20	6	28	1	45	38
OCT. 30	30	36	37	37	32	32	20	6	28	1	45	38
OCT. 31	30	38	39	39	33	33	20	6	28	1	45	38

MOON 1 ☽ 12:01 A.M. TO 8:00 A.M.   **MOON 2** ☽ 8:01 A.M. TO 4:00 P.M.   **MOON 3** ● 4:01 P.M. TO 12:00 A.M.

Use only one "moon" number. Choose the column closest to your time of birth. If your place of birth is not on Eastern Standard Time, be sure to read "How to Convert to Eastern Standard Time" at the beginning of this section.

November

December

Date & Time	SUN	MOON 1	MOON 2	MOON 3	MERCURY	VENUS	MARS	JUPITER	SATURN	URANUS	NEPTUNE	PLUTO
NOV. 1	30	40	40	41	33	33	20	6	28	1	45	38
NOV. 2	30	41	42	43	33	33	20	6	28	1	45	38
NOV. 3	31	43	44	44	33	33	20	6	28	1	45	38
NOV. 4	31	45	45	46	33	33	20	6	28	1	45	38
NOV. 5	31	46	47	48	33	33	21	6	28	1	45	38
NOV. 6	31	48	1	1	34	34	21	6	28	1	45	38
NOV. 7	31	2	3	3	34	34	21	6	28	1	45	38
NOV. 8	31	3	4	4	34	34	21	5	28	1	45	38
NOV. 9	31	5	5	6	34	34	21	5	28	1	45	38
NOV. 10	31	6	7	7	34	34	21	5	28	1	45	38
NOV. 11	31	8	8	9	34	34	21	5	28	1	45	38
NOV. 12	32	10	10	11	35	35	21	5	28	1	45	38
NOV. 13	32	11	12	12	35	35	21	5	28	1	45	38
NOV. 14	32	13	13	14	35	35	21	5	28	1	45	38
NOV. 15	32	14	15	16	35	35	21	5	28	1	45	38
NOV. 16	32	16	17	17	35	35	21	5	28	1	45	38
NOV. 17	32	18	18	19	35	35	21	5	28	1	45	38
NOV. 18	32	20	20	21	35	36	21	5	28	1	45	38
NOV. 19	33	21	22	23	35	36	21	5	28	1	45	38
NOV. 20	33	23	24	25	35	36	22	5	28	1	45	38
NOV. 21	33	25	26	27	36	36	22	5	28	1	45	38
NOV. 22	33	27	28	29	36	36	22	5	28	1	45	38
NOV. 23	33	29	30	31	36	36	22	5	28	1	45	38
NOV. 24	33	31	32	33	36	37	22	5	28	1	45	38
NOV. 25	34	33	34	35	36	37	22	5	28	1	45	38
NOV. 26	34	35	36	36	36	37	22	5	28	1	45	38
NOV. 27	34	37	38	38	36	37	22	5	28	1	45	38
NOV. 28	34	39	40	40	35	37	22	5	28	1	45	38
NOV. 29	34	41	41	42	35	37	22	5	28	1	45	38
NOV. 30	34	43	43	44	35	38	22	5	28	1	45	38

Date & Time	SUN	MOON 1	MOON 2	MOON 3	MERCURY	VENUS	MARS	JUPITER	SATURN	URANUS	NEPTUNE	PLUTO
DEC. 1	34	44	45	45	35	38	22	5	28	1	45	38
DEC. 2	34	46	46	47	35	38	22	5	28	1	45	38
DEC. 3	35	48	48	1	35	38	22	5	28	1	45	38
DEC. 4	35	1	2	2	35	38	22	5	28	1	45	38
DEC. 5	35	3	3	4	34	38	22	5	28	1	45	38
DEC. 6	35	4	5	5	34	39	23	5	28	1	45	38
DEC. 7	35	6	6	7	34	39	23	5	28	1	45	38
DEC. 8	35	8	8	9	34	39	23	5	28	1	45	38
DEC. 9	35	9	10	10	34	39	23	5	29	1	45	38
DEC. 10	35	11	11	12	34	39	23	5	29	1	45	38
DEC. 11	36	12	13	13	34	39	23	5	29	1	45	38
DEC. 12	36	14	15	15	34	40	23	5	29	1	45	38
DEC. 13	36	16	16	17	33	40	23	5	29	1	45	38
DEC. 14	36	17	18	19	33	40	23	5	29	1	45	38
DEC. 15	36	19	20	20	33	40	23	5	29	1	45	38
DEC. 16	36	21	22	22	34	40	23	5	29	1	45	38
DEC. 17	36	23	23	24	34	40	23	5	29	1	45	38
DEC. 18	36	25	25	26	34	41	23	5	29	1	45	38
DEC. 19	37	27	27	28	34	41	23	5	29	1	45	38
DEC. 20	37	29	29	30	34	41	23	5	29	1	45	38
DEC. 21	37	30	31	32	34	41	23	5	29	1	45	38
DEC. 22	37	32	33	34	34	41	23	5	29	1	45	38
DEC. 23	37	34	35	36	34	41	23	5	29	1	45	38
DEC. 24	37	36	37	38	34	42	23	5	29	1	45	38
DEC. 25	37	38	39	39	34	42	23	5	29	1	45	38
DEC. 26	38	40	41	41	35	42	23	5	29	1	45	38
DEC. 27	38	42	42	43	35	42	23	5	29	1	45	38
DEC. 28	38	44	44	45	35	42	24	5	29	1	45	38
DEC. 29	38	45	46	46	35	42	24	5	29	1	45	38
DEC. 30	38	47	48	48	35	43	24	5	29	1	45	38
DEC. 31	38	1	1	2	35	43	24	5	29	1	45	38

MOON 1 ☽ 12:01 A.M. TO 8:00 A.M.   **MOON 2** ☽ 8:01 A.M. TO 4:00 P.M.   **MOON 3** ● 4:01 P.M. TO 12:00 A.M.

Use only one "moon" number. Choose the column closest to your time of birth. If your place of birth is not on Eastern Standard Time, be sure to read "How to Convert to Eastern Standard Time" at the beginning of this section.

2012

January / February

Date & Time	SUN	MOON 1	MOON 2	MOON 3	MERCURY	VENUS	MARS	JUPITER	SATURN	URANUS	NEPTUNE	PLUTO
JAN. 1	38	2	3	3	36	43	24	5	29	1	45	38
JAN. 2	38	4	4	5	36	43	24	5	29	1	45	38
JAN. 3	39	5	6	6	36	43	24	5	29	1	45	38
JAN. 4	39	7	8	8	36	43	24	5	29	1	45	38
JAN. 5	39	9	9	10	36	43	24	5	29	1	45	38
JAN. 6	39	10	11	11	37	44	24	5	29	1	45	38
JAN. 7	39	12	12	13	37	44	24	5	29	1	45	38
JAN. 8	39	14	14	15	37	44	24	5	29	1	45	38
JAN. 9	39	15	16	16	37	44	24	5	29	1	45	38
JAN. 10	40	17	18	18	37	44	24	5	29	1	45	38
JAN. 11	40	19	19	20	38	44	24	5	29	1	45	38
JAN. 12	40	21	21	22	38	45	24	5	29	1	45	38
JAN. 13	40	22	23	24	38	45	24	5	29	1	45	38
JAN. 14	40	24	25	26	38	45	24	5	29	1	45	38
JAN. 15	40	26	27	27	38	45	24	5	29	1	45	38
JAN. 16	40	28	29	29	39	45	24	5	29	1	45	38
JAN. 17	41	30	31	31	39	45	24	5	29	1	45	38
JAN. 18	41	32	32	33	39	46	24	5	29	1	45	38
JAN. 19	41	34	34	35	39	46	24	5	29	1	45	38
JAN. 20	41	36	36	37	39	46	24	5	29	1	45	38
JAN. 21	41	37	38	39	40	46	24	5	29	1	45	38
JAN. 22	41	39	40	41	40	46	24	5	29	1	45	38
JAN. 23	42	41	42	42	40	46	24	5	29	1	45	38
JAN. 24	42	43	44	44	40	47	24	5	29	1	45	38
JAN. 25	42	45	45	46	40	47	24	5	29	1	45	38
JAN. 26	42	46	47	47	41	47	24	5	29	1	45	38
JAN. 27	42	48	1	1	41	47	24	5	29	1	45	38
JAN. 28	42	2	2	3	41	47	24	5	29	1	45	38
JAN. 29	42	3	4	4	41	47	24	5	29	1	45	38
JAN. 30	42	5	5	6	42	48	24	5	29	1	45	38
JAN. 31	43	6	7	7	42	48	24	5	29	1	45	38

Date & Time	SUN	MOON 1	MOON 2	MOON 3	MERCURY	VENUS	MARS	JUPITER	SATURN	URANUS	NEPTUNE	PLUTO
FEB. 1	43	8	9	9	42	48	24	5	29	1	45	38
FEB. 2	43	10	10	11	42	48	24	5	29	1	45	38
FEB. 3	43	11	12	12	42	48	24	5	29	1	45	38
FEB. 4	43	13	13	14	43	48	24	5	29	1	45	38
FEB. 5	43	15	15	16	43	48	24	5	29	1	45	38
FEB. 6	43	16	17	18	43	1	24	5	29	1	45	38
FEB. 7	43	18	19	19	43	1	24	5	29	1	45	38
FEB. 8	44	20	21	21	44	1	24	5	29	1	45	38
FEB. 9	44	22	23	23	44	1	24	5	29	1	45	38
FEB. 10	44	24	24	25	44	1	24	5	29	1	45	38
FEB. 11	44	26	26	27	44	1	24	5	29	1	45	38
FEB. 12	44	28	28	29	45	2	24	6	29	1	45	38
FEB. 13	44	30	30	31	45	2	24	6	29	1	45	38
FEB. 14	44	31	32	33	45	2	24	6	29	1	45	38
FEB. 15	44	33	34	35	45	2	24	6	29	1	45	38
FEB. 16	45	35	36	36	45	2	24	6	29	1	45	38
FEB. 17	45	37	38	38	46	2	24	6	29	1	45	38
FEB. 18	45	39	39	40	46	3	24	6	29	1	45	38
FEB. 19	45	41	41	42	46	3	23	6	29	1	45	38
FEB. 20	45	42	43	43	46	3	23	6	29	1	45	38
FEB. 21	45	44	45	45	47	3	23	6	29	1	45	38
FEB. 22	45	46	46	47	47	3	23	6	29	1	45	38
FEB. 23	46	47	48	1	47	3	23	6	29	1	45	38
FEB. 24	46	1	2	2	47	3	23	6	29	1	45	38
FEB. 25	46	3	3	4	48	4	23	6	29	1	45	38
FEB. 26	46	4	5	5	48	4	23	6	29	1	45	38
FEB. 27	46	6	6	7	48	4	23	6	29	1	45	38
FEB. 28	46	7	8	9	48	4	23	6	29	1	45	38
FEB. 29	46	9	10	10	1	4	23	6	29	1	45	38

MOON 1 ◗ 12:01 A.M. TO 8:00 A.M.   **MOON 2** ◖ 8:01 A.M. TO 4:00 P.M.   **MOON 3** ● 4:01 P.M. TO 12:00 A.M.

Use only one "moon" number. Choose the column closest to your time of birth. If your place of birth is not on Eastern Standard Time, be sure to read "How to Convert to Eastern Standard Time" at the beginning of this section.

2012

March

Date & Time	SUN	MOON 1	MOON 2	MOON 3	MERCURY	VENUS	MARS	JUPITER	SATURN	URANUS	NEPTUNE	PLUTO
MAR. 1	46	11	11	12	1	4	23	6	29	1	45	38
MAR. 2	46	12	13	13	1	4	23	6	29	1	45	38
MAR. 3	47	14	14	15	1	5	23	6	29	1	45	38
MAR. 4	47	16	16	17	1	5	23	6	29	1	45	38
MAR. 5	47	17	18	19	1	5	23	6	29	1	45	38
MAR. 6	47	19	20	20	2	5	23	6	29	1	45	38
MAR. 7	47	21	22	22	2	5	23	6	29	1	45	38
MAR. 8	47	23	24	24	2	5	23	6	29	1	45	38
MAR. 9	47	25	26	26	2	6	23	6	29	1	45	38
MAR. 10	47	27	28	28	2	6	22	6	29	1	45	38
MAR. 11	48	29	30	30	2	6	22	6	29	1	45	38
MAR. 12	48	31	32	32	2	6	22	6	29	1	45	38
MAR. 13	48	33	33	34	2	6	22	6	29	1	45	38
MAR. 14	48	35	35	36	2	6	22	6	29	1	45	38
MAR. 15	48	37	37	38	2	6	22	6	29	1	45	38
MAR. 16	48	38	39	40	2	7	22	6	29	2	45	38
MAR. 17	48	40	41	41	2	7	22	6	29	2	45	38
MAR. 18	48	42	42	43	2	7	22	6	29	2	45	38
MAR. 19	1	44	44	45	1	7	22	6	29	2	45	38
MAR. 20	1	45	46	46	1	7	22	6	29	2	45	38
MAR. 21	1	47	48	48	1	7	22	6	29	2	45	38
MAR. 22	1	1	1	2	1	7	22	6	29	2	45	38
MAR. 23	1	2	3	3	1	7	22	6	29	2	45	38
MAR. 24	1	4	4	5	1	8	22	7	29	2	45	38
MAR. 25	2	5	6	6	1	8	22	7	29	2	45	38
MAR. 26	2	7	8	8	1	8	22	7	29	2	45	38
MAR. 27	2	9	9	10	1	8	22	7	29	2	45	38
MAR. 28	2	10	11	11	48	8	22	7	29	2	45	38
MAR. 29	2	12	12	13	48	8	22	7	29	2	45	38
MAR. 30	2	13	14	14	48	8	22	7	29	2	45	38
MAR. 31	2	15	16	16	48	9	22	7	29	2	45	38

April

Date & Time	SUN	MOON 1	MOON 2	MOON 3	MERCURY	VENUS	MARS	JUPITER	SATURN	URANUS	NEPTUNE	PLUTO
APR. 1	2	17	17	18	48	9	22	7	29	2	45	38
APR. 2	2	18	19	20	48	9	22	7	29	2	45	38
APR. 3	3	20	21	22	48	9	22	7	29	2	45	38
APR. 4	3	22	23	23	48	9	22	7	29	2	45	38
APR. 5	3	24	25	25	48	9	22	7	29	2	45	38
APR. 6	3	26	27	27	48	9	22	7	29	2	45	38
APR. 7	3	28	29	29	48	9	21	7	29	2	45	38
APR. 8	3	30	31	31	48	10	21	7	29	2	45	38
APR. 9	3	32	33	33	48	10	21	7	29	2	45	38
APR. 10	3	34	35	35	48	10	21	7	29	2	45	38
APR. 11	4	36	37	37	48	10	21	7	29	2	45	38
APR. 12	4	38	39	39	48	10	21	7	29	2	45	38
APR. 13	4	40	40	41	1	10	21	7	28	2	45	38
APR. 14	4	41	42	43	1	10	21	7	28	2	45	38
APR. 15	4	43	44	44	1	10	21	7	28	2	45	38
APR. 16	4	45	45	46	1	10	21	7	28	2	45	38
APR. 17	4	47	47	48	1	11	21	7	28	2	45	38
APR. 18	4	48	1	1	1	11	21	7	28	2	45	38
APR. 19	5	2	2	3	1	11	21	7	28	2	45	38
APR. 20	5	3	4	4	1	11	21	7	28	2	45	38
APR. 21	5	5	6	6	2	11	21	7	28	2	45	38
APR. 22	5	7	7	8	2	11	22	7	28	2	45	38
APR. 23	5	8	9	9	2	11	22	7	28	2	45	38
APR. 24	5	10	10	11	2	11	22	7	28	2	45	38
APR. 25	6	11	12	12	2	11	22	7	28	2	45	38
APR. 26	6	13	13	14	2	11	22	8	28	2	45	38
APR. 27	6	15	15	16	3	11	22	8	28	2	45	38
APR. 28	6	16	17	17	3	11	22	8	28	2	45	38
APR. 29	6	18	18	19	3	12	22	8	28	2	45	38
APR. 30	6	20	20	21	3	12	22	8	28	2	45	38

MOON 1 ☽ 12:01 A.M. TO 8:00 A.M.　　**MOON 2** ☽ 8:01 A.M. TO 4:00 P.M.　　**MOON 3** ● 4:01 P.M. TO 12:00 A.M.

Use only one "moon" number. Choose the column closest to your time of birth. If your place of birth is not on Eastern Standard Time, be sure to read "How to Convert to Eastern Standard Time" at the beginning of this section.

2012

May

Date & Time	SUN	MOON 1	MOON 2	MOON 3	MERCURY	VENUS	MARS	JUPITER	SATURN	URANUS	NEPTUNE	PLUTO
MAY 1	6	21	22	23	3	12	22	8	28	2	45	38
MAY 2	6	23	24	25	3	12	22	8	28	2	45	38
MAY 3	7	25	26	27	4	12	22	8	28	2	45	38
MAY 4	7	27	28	29	4	12	22	8	28	2	45	38
MAY 5	7	29	30	31	4	12	22	8	28	2	45	38
MAY 6	7	31	32	33	4	12	22	8	28	2	45	38
MAY 7	7	33	34	35	5	12	22	8	28	2	45	38
MAY 8	7	35	36	37	5	12	22	8	28	2	45	38
MAY 9	7	37	38	38	5	12	22	8	28	2	45	38
MAY 10	7	39	40	40	5	12	22	8	28	2	45	38
MAY 11	8	41	42	42	5	12	22	8	28	2	45	38
MAY 12	8	43	43	44	6	12	22	8	28	2	45	38
MAY 13	8	44	45	46	6	12	22	8	28	2	45	38
MAY 14	8	46	47	47	6	12	22	8	28	2	45	38
MAY 15	8	48	48	1	6	12	22	8	28	2	45	38
MAY 16	8	1	2	3	7	12	22	8	28	2	45	38
MAY 17	8	3	4	4	7	12	22	8	28	2	45	38
MAY 18	8	5	5	6	7	12	22	8	28	2	45	38
MAY 19	9	6	7	7	7	12	22	8	28	2	45	38
MAY 20	9	8	8	9	8	12	22	8	28	2	45	38
MAY 21	9	9	10	10	8	12	22	8	28	2	45	38
MAY 22	9	11	11	12	8	12	22	8	28	2	45	38
MAY 23	9	13	13	14	9	12	22	8	28	2	45	38
MAY 24	9	14	15	15	9	12	23	8	28	2	45	38
MAY 25	10	16	16	17	9	12	23	8	28	2	45	38
MAY 26	10	17	18	19	9	12	23	8	28	2	45	38
MAY 27	10	19	20	20	10	12	23	8	28	2	45	38
MAY 28	10	21	21	22	10	12	23	9	28	2	45	38
MAY 29	10	23	23	24	10	12	23	9	28	2	45	38
MAY 30	10	25	25	26	11	12	23	9	28	2	45	38
MAY 31	10	26	27	28	11	12	23	9	28	2	45	38

June

Date & Time	SUN	MOON 1	MOON 2	MOON 3	MERCURY	VENUS	MARS	JUPITER	SATURN	URANUS	NEPTUNE	PLUTO
JUN. 1	10	28	29	30	11	11	23	9	28	2	45	38
JUN. 2	10	30	31	32	12	11	23	9	28	2	45	38
JUN. 3	11	32	33	34	12	11	23	9	28	2	45	38
JUN. 4	11	34	35	36	12	11	23	9	28	2	45	38
JUN. 5	11	36	37	38	12	11	23	9	28	2	45	38
JUN. 6	11	38	39	40	13	11	23	9	28	2	45	38
JUN. 7	11	40	41	41	13	11	23	9	28	2	45	38
JUN. 8	11	42	43	43	13	11	23	9	28	2	45	38
JUN. 9	11	44	45	45	13	11	23	9	28	2	45	38
JUN. 10	11	46	46	47	14	11	23	9	28	2	45	38
JUN. 11	12	47	48	48	14	11	24	9	28	2	45	38
JUN. 12	12	1	2	2	14	11	24	9	28	2	45	38
JUN. 13	12	3	3	4	14	10	24	9	28	2	45	38
JUN. 14	12	4	5	5	15	10	24	9	28	2	45	38
JUN. 15	12	6	6	7	15	10	24	9	28	2	45	38
JUN. 16	12	7	8	8	15	10	24	9	28	2	45	38
JUN. 17	12	9	9	10	15	10	24	9	28	2	45	38
JUN. 18	12	11	11	12	16	10	24	9	28	2	45	38
JUN. 19	13	12	13	13	16	10	24	9	28	2	45	38
JUN. 20	13	14	14	15	16	10	24	9	28	2	45	38
JUN. 21	13	15	16	16	16	10	24	9	28	2	45	38
JUN. 22	13	17	18	18	16	10	24	9	28	2	45	38
JUN. 23	13	19	19	20	16	10	24	9	28	2	45	38
JUN. 24	13	20	21	22	17	10	24	9	28	2	45	38
JUN. 25	14	22	23	23	17	10	24	9	28	2	45	38
JUN. 26	14	24	25	25	17	10	24	9	28	2	45	38
JUN. 27	14	26	26	27	17	10	25	9	28	2	45	38
JUN. 28	14	28	28	29	17	10	25	9	28	2	45	38
JUN. 29	14	30	30	31	17	10	25	9	28	2	45	38
JUN. 30	14	32	32	33	18	10	25	10	28	2	45	38

MOON 1 ◐ 12:01 A.M. TO 8:00 A.M.   **MOON 2** ◑ 8:01 A.M. TO 4:00 P.M.   **MOON 3** ● 4:01 P.M. TO 12:00 A.M.
Use only one "moon" number. Choose the column closest to your time of birth. If your place of birth is not on Eastern Standard Time, be sure to read "How to Convert to Eastern Standard Time" at the beginning of this section.

2012

July

August

Date & Time	SUN ☉	MOON 1 ◗	MOON 2 ◖	MOON 3 ●	MERCURY	VENUS	MARS	JUPITER	SATURN	URANUS	NEPTUNE	PLUTO
JUL. 1	14	34	34	35	18	10	25	10	28	2	45	38
JUL. 2	14	36	36	37	18	10	25	10	28	2	45	38
JUL. 3	15	37	38	39	18	10	25	10	28	2	45	38
JUL. 4	15	39	40	41	18	10	25	10	28	2	45	38
JUL. 5	15	41	42	43	18	10	25	10	28	2	45	38
JUL. 6	15	43	44	44	18	10	25	10	28	2	45	38
JUL. 7	15	45	46	46	18	10	25	10	28	2	45	38
JUL. 8	15	47	47	48	18	10	25	10	28	2	45	38
JUL. 9	15	48	1	2	18	10	25	10	28	2	45	38
JUL. 10	15	2	3	3	19	10	25	10	28	2	45	38
JUL. 11	16	4	4	5	19	10	26	10	28	2	45	38
JUL. 12	16	5	6	6	19	10	26	10	28	2	45	38
JUL. 13	16	7	7	8	19	11	26	10	28	2	45	38
JUL. 14	16	8	9	10	19	11	26	10	28	2	45	38
JUL. 15	16	10	11	11	19	11	26	10	28	2	45	38
JUL. 16	16	12	12	13	19	11	26	10	28	2	45	38
JUL. 17	16	13	14	14	19	11	26	10	28	2	45	38
JUL. 18	16	15	15	16	19	11	26	10	28	2	45	38
JUL. 19	17	17	17	18	19	11	26	10	28	2	45	38
JUL. 20	17	18	19	19	19	11	26	10	28	2	45	38
JUL. 21	17	20	21	21	18	11	26	10	28	2	45	38
JUL. 22	17	22	22	23	18	11	26	10	28	2	45	38
JUL. 23	17	24	24	25	18	11	26	10	28	2	45	38
JUL. 24	17	25	26	27	18	11	26	10	28	2	45	38
JUL. 25	17	27	28	29	18	12	27	10	28	2	45	38
JUL. 26	18	29	30	30	18	12	27	10	28	2	45	38
JUL. 27	18	31	32	32	18	12	27	10	28	2	45	38
JUL. 28	18	33	34	34	18	12	27	10	28	2	45	38
JUL. 29	18	35	35	36	18	12	27	10	28	2	45	38
JUL. 30	18	37	37	38	18	12	27	10	28	2	45	38
JUL. 31	18	39	39	40	18	12	27	10	28	2	45	38

Date & Time	SUN ☉	MOON 1 ◗	MOON 2 ◖	MOON 3 ●	MERCURY	VENUS	MARS	JUPITER	SATURN	URANUS	NEPTUNE	PLUTO
AUG. 1	18	41	41	42	17	12	27	10	28	2	45	38
AUG. 2	18	42	43	44	17	12	27	10	28	2	45	38
AUG. 3	19	44	45	45	17	12	27	10	28	2	45	38
AUG. 4	19	46	47	47	17	13	27	10	28	2	45	38
AUG. 5	19	48	48	1	17	13	27	10	28	2	45	38
AUG. 6	19	2	2	3	17	13	28	10	28	2	45	38
AUG. 7	19	3	4	4	17	13	28	10	28	2	45	38
AUG. 8	19	5	5	6	17	13	28	10	28	2	45	38
AUG. 9	19	6	7	7	17	13	28	11	28	2	45	38
AUG. 10	19	8	8	9	17	13	28	11	28	2	45	38
AUG. 11	20	10	10	11	17	13	28	11	28	2	45	38
AUG. 12	20	11	12	12	17	14	28	11	28	2	45	38
AUG. 13	20	13	13	14	17	14	28	11	28	2	45	38
AUG. 14	20	14	15	15	17	14	28	11	28	2	45	38
AUG. 15	20	16	17	17	18	14	28	11	28	2	45	38
AUG. 16	20	18	18	19	18	14	28	11	28	2	45	38
AUG. 17	20	20	20	21	18	14	28	11	28	2	45	38
AUG. 18	20	21	22	23	18	14	29	11	28	2	45	38
AUG. 19	21	23	24	24	18	14	29	11	28	2	45	38
AUG. 20	21	25	26	26	18	15	29	11	28	2	45	38
AUG. 21	21	27	27	28	18	15	29	11	28	2	45	38
AUG. 22	21	29	29	30	19	15	29	11	28	2	45	38
AUG. 23	21	31	31	32	19	15	29	11	28	2	45	38
AUG. 24	21	33	33	34	19	15	29	11	28	2	45	38
AUG. 25	21	34	35	36	19	15	29	11	28	2	45	38
AUG. 26	22	36	37	38	19	15	29	11	28	2	45	38
AUG. 27	22	38	39	39	20	16	29	11	28	2	45	38
AUG. 28	22	40	41	41	20	16	29	11	28	2	45	38
AUG. 29	22	42	42	43	20	16	29	11	28	2	45	38
AUG. 30	22	44	44	45	20	16	30	11	28	2	45	38
AUG. 31	22	45	46	47	21	16	30	11	28	2	45	38

MOON 1 ◗ 12:01 A.M. TO 8:00 A.M.   **MOON 2** ◖ 8:01 A.M. TO 4:00 P.M.   **MOON 3** ● 4:01 P.M. TO 12:00 A.M.
Use only one "moon" number. Choose the column closest to your time of birth. If your place of birth is not on
Eastern Standard Time, be sure to read "How to Convert to Eastern Standard Time" at the beginning of this section.

2012

September

October

Date & Time	SUN	MOON 1	MOON 2	MOON 3	MERCURY	VENUS	MARS	JUPITER	SATURN	URANUS	NEPTUNE	PLUTO
SEP. 1	22	47	48	48	21	16	30	11	28	2	45	38
SEP. 2	22	1	1	2	21	16	30	11	28	2	45	38
SEP. 3	23	3	3	4	22	16	30	11	28	2	45	38
SEP. 4	23	4	5	5	22	17	30	11	29	2	45	38
SEP. 5	23	6	6	7	22	17	30	11	29	2	45	38
SEP. 6	23	7	8	8	22	17	30	11	29	2	45	38
SEP. 7	23	9	10	10	23	17	30	11	29	2	45	38
SEP. 8	23	11	11	12	23	17	30	11	29	2	45	38
SEP. 9	23	12	13	13	23	17	30	11	29	2	45	38
SEP. 10	23	14	14	15	23	17	30	11	29	2	45	38
SEP. 11	24	15	16	17	24	18	31	11	29	2	45	38
SEP. 12	24	17	18	18	24	18	31	11	29	2	45	38
SEP. 13	24	19	19	20	24	18	31	11	29	2	45	38
SEP. 14	24	21	21	22	24	18	31	11	29	2	45	38
SEP. 15	24	22	23	24	25	18	31	11	29	2	45	38
SEP. 16	24	24	25	26	25	18	31	11	29	2	45	38
SEP. 17	24	26	27	28	25	19	31	11	29	2	45	38
SEP. 18	24	28	29	29	25	19	31	11	29	2	45	38
SEP. 19	25	30	31	31	25	19	31	11	29	2	45	38
SEP. 20	25	32	33	33	26	19	31	11	29	2	45	38
SEP. 21	25	34	35	35	26	19	31	11	29	2	45	38
SEP. 22	25	36	36	37	26	19	32	11	29	2	45	38
SEP. 23	25	38	38	39	26	19	32	11	29	2	45	38
SEP. 24	25	40	40	41	27	20	32	11	29	2	45	38
SEP. 25	26	41	42	43	27	20	32	11	29	2	45	38
SEP. 26	26	43	44	44	27	20	32	11	29	2	45	38
SEP. 27	26	45	46	46	27	20	32	11	29	2	45	38
SEP. 28	26	47	47	48	27	20	32	11	29	2	45	38
SEP. 29	26	48	1	2	28	20	32	11	29	2	45	38
SEP. 30	26	2	3	3	28	20	32	11	29	2	45	38

Date & Time	SUN	MOON 1	MOON 2	MOON 3	MERCURY	VENUS	MARS	JUPITER	SATURN	URANUS	NEPTUNE	PLUTO
OCT. 1	26	4	4	5	28	21	32	11	29	2	45	38
OCT. 2	26	5	6	6	28	21	33	11	29	2	45	38
OCT. 3	27	7	7	8	29	21	33	11	29	2	45	38
OCT. 4	27	9	9	10	29	21	33	11	29	2	45	38
OCT. 5	27	10	11	11	29	21	33	11	29	2	45	38
OCT. 6	27	12	12	13	29	21	33	11	29	2	45	38
OCT. 7	27	13	14	14	29	22	33	11	29	2	45	38
OCT. 8	27	15	15	16	30	22	33	11	29	2	45	38
OCT. 9	27	16	17	18	30	22	33	11	29	2	45	38
OCT. 10	27	18	19	19	30	22	33	11	29	2	45	38
OCT. 11	28	20	20	21	30	22	33	11	29	2	45	38
OCT. 12	28	22	22	23	30	22	33	11	29	2	45	38
OCT. 13	28	24	24	25	30	23	34	11	29	2	45	38
OCT. 14	28	25	26	27	31	23	34	11	29	2	45	38
OCT. 15	28	27	28	29	31	23	34	11	29	2	45	38
OCT. 16	28	29	30	31	31	23	34	11	29	2	45	38
OCT. 17	28	31	32	33	31	23	34	11	29	2	45	38
OCT. 18	28	33	34	35	31	23	34	11	29	2	45	38
OCT. 19	29	35	36	37	32	23	34	11	29	2	45	38
OCT. 20	29	37	38	38	32	24	34	11	29	2	45	38
OCT. 21	29	39	40	40	32	24	34	11	29	2	45	38
OCT. 22	29	41	42	42	32	24	34	11	29	2	45	38
OCT. 23	29	43	43	44	32	24	35	11	29	2	45	38
OCT. 24	29	45	45	46	32	24	35	11	29	2	45	38
OCT. 25	29	46	47	47	32	24	35	11	29	2	45	38
OCT. 26	30	48	1	1	33	25	35	11	29	2	45	38
OCT. 27	30	2	2	3	33	25	35	11	29	2	45	38
OCT. 28	30	3	4	4	33	25	35	11	29	2	45	38
OCT. 29	30	5	5	6	33	25	35	11	29	2	45	38
OCT. 30	30	6	7	8	33	25	35	11	29	2	45	38
OCT. 31	30	8	9	9	33	25	35	11	29	2	45	38

MOON 1 ☽ 12:01 A.M. TO 8:00 A.M.   **MOON 2** ☽ 8:01 A.M. TO 4:00 P.M.   **MOON 3** ● 4:01 P.M. TO 12:00 A.M.
Use only one "moon" number. Choose the column closest to your time of birth. If your place of birth is not on Eastern Standard Time, be sure to read "How to Convert to Eastern Standard Time" at the beginning of this section.

2012

November — December

Date & Time	SUN	MOON 1	MOON 2	MOON 3	MERCURY	VENUS	MARS	JUPITER	SATURN	URANUS	NEPTUNE	PLUTO
NOV. 1	30	10	10	11	33	26	35	11	29	2	45	38
NOV. 2	30	11	12	12	33	26	35	11	29	2	45	38
NOV. 3	31	13	13	14	33	26	36	11	29	2	45	38
NOV. 4	31	14	15	15	33	26	36	11	29	2	45	38
NOV. 5	31	16	17	17	34	26	36	11	29	2	45	38
NOV. 6	31	18	18	19	34	26	36	11	29	2	45	38
NOV. 7	31	19	20	20	34	27	36	11	29	2	45	38
NOV. 8	31	21	22	22	34	27	36	11	30	2	45	38
NOV. 9	31	23	23	24	33	27	36	11	30	2	45	38
NOV. 10	31	25	25	26	33	27	36	11	30	2	45	38
NOV. 11	31	27	27	28	33	27	36	11	30	2	45	38
NOV. 12	32	28	29	30	33	27	36	11	30	2	45	38
NOV. 13	32	30	31	32	33	28	37	11	30	2	45	38
NOV. 14	32	32	33	34	33	28	37	11	30	2	45	38
NOV. 15	32	34	35	36	33	28	37	11	30	2	45	38
NOV. 16	32	37	37	38	33	28	37	11	30	2	45	38
NOV. 17	32	38	39	40	32	28	37	11	30	2	45	38
NOV. 18	32	40	41	42	32	28	37	11	30	2	45	38
NOV. 19	33	42	43	43	32	28	37	11	30	2	45	38
NOV. 20	33	44	45	45	32	29	37	11	30	2	45	38
NOV. 21	33	46	46	47	32	29	37	11	30	2	45	38
NOV. 22	33	48	48	1	32	29	37	11	30	2	45	38
NOV. 23	33	1	2	2	32	29	38	11	30	2	45	38
NOV. 24	33	3	3	4	31	29	38	11	30	2	45	38
NOV. 25	34	4	5	6	31	29	38	11	30	2	45	38
NOV. 26	34	6	7	7	31	30	38	11	30	2	45	38
NOV. 27	34	8	8	9	31	30	38	11	30	2	45	38
NOV. 28	34	9	10	10	31	30	38	11	30	2	45	38
NOV. 29	34	11	11	12	31	30	38	11	30	2	45	38
NOV. 30	34	12	13	13	32	30	38	11	30	2	45	38

Date & Time	SUN	MOON 1	MOON 2	MOON 3	MERCURY	VENUS	MARS	JUPITER	SATURN	URANUS	NEPTUNE	PLUTO
DEC. 1	34	14	14	15	32	30	38	11	30	2	45	38
DEC. 2	34	16	16	17	32	31	39	10	30	2	45	38
DEC. 3	35	17	18	18	32	31	39	10	30	2	45	38
DEC. 4	35	19	19	20	32	31	39	10	30	2	45	38
DEC. 5	35	20	21	22	32	31	39	10	30	2	45	38
DEC. 6	35	22	23	23	32	31	39	10	30	2	45	38
DEC. 7	35	24	25	25	32	31	39	10	30	2	45	38
DEC. 8	35	26	26	27	32	32	39	10	30	2	45	38
DEC. 9	35	28	28	29	33	32	39	10	30	2	45	38
DEC. 10	35	30	30	31	33	32	39	10	30	2	45	38
DEC. 11	36	32	32	33	33	32	39	10	30	2	45	38
DEC. 12	36	34	34	35	33	32	40	10	30	2	45	38
DEC. 13	36	36	36	37	33	32	40	10	30	2	45	38
DEC. 14	36	38	38	39	34	33	40	10	30	2	45	38
DEC. 15	36	40	40	41	34	33	40	10	30	2	45	38
DEC. 16	36	42	42	43	34	33	40	10	30	2	45	38
DEC. 17	36	43	44	45	34	33	40	10	30	2	45	38
DEC. 18	36	45	46	46	34	33	40	10	30	2	45	38
DEC. 19	37	47	48	48	34	33	40	10	30	2	45	38
DEC. 20	37	1	1	2	35	34	40	10	30	2	45	38
DEC. 21	37	2	3	4	35	34	40	10	30	2	45	38
DEC. 22	37	4	5	5	35	34	41	10	30	2	45	38
DEC. 23	37	6	6	7	35	34	41	10	30	2	45	38
DEC. 24	37	7	7	8	35	34	41	10	30	2	45	38
DEC. 25	37	9	9	10	36	34	41	10	30	2	45	38
DEC. 26	38	10	11	11	36	35	41	10	30	2	45	38
DEC. 27	38	12	12	13	36	35	41	10	30	2	45	38
DEC. 28	38	14	14	15	36	35	41	10	30	2	45	38
DEC. 29	38	15	16	16	36	35	41	10	30	2	45	38
DEC. 30	38	17	17	18	37	35	41	10	30	2	45	38
DEC. 31	38	18	19	20	37	35	42	10	30	2	45	38

MOON 1 ☽ 12:01 A.M. TO 8:00 A.M.   **MOON 2** ☽ 8:01 A.M. TO 4:00 P.M.   **MOON 3** ● 4:01 P.M. TO 12:00 A.M.
Use only one "moon" number. Choose the column closest to your time of birth. If your place of birth is not on Eastern Standard Time, be sure to read "How to Convert to Eastern Standard Time" at the beginning of this section.

2013

January

Date & Time	SUN ☉	MOON 1 ◗	MOON 2 ◑	MOON 3 ●	MERCURY	VENUS	MARS	JUPITER	SATURN	URANUS	NEPTUNE	PLUTO
JAN. 1	38	20	21	21	37	36	42	10	30	2	45	38
JAN. 2	38	22	22	23	37	36	42	10	30	2	45	38
JAN. 3	39	23	24	25	38	36	42	10	30	2	45	38
JAN. 4	39	25	26	26	38	36	42	10	30	2	45	38
JAN. 5	39	27	28	28	38	36	42	10	30	2	45	38
JAN. 6	39	29	29	29	38	36	42	10	30	2	45	38
JAN. 7	39	31	31	32	38	37	42	10	30	2	45	38
JAN. 8	39	33	33	34	39	37	42	10	30	2	45	38
JAN. 9	39	35	35	36	39	37	42	10	30	2	45	38
JAN. 10	40	37	37	38	39	37	43	10	30	2	45	38
JAN. 11	40	39	39	40	39	37	43	10	30	2	45	38
JAN. 12	40	41	41	42	39	37	43	10	30	2	45	38
JAN. 13	40	43	43	44	40	38	43	10	30	2	45	38
JAN. 14	40	45	45	46	40	38	43	10	30	2	45	38
JAN. 15	40	46	47	48	40	38	43	10	30	2	45	38
JAN. 16	40	48	1	1	40	38	43	10	30	2	45	38
JAN. 17	41	2	2	3	40	38	43	10	30	2	45	38
JAN. 18	41	4	4	5	41	38	43	10	30	2	45	38
JAN. 19	41	5	6	6	41	39	44	10	30	2	45	38
JAN. 20	41	7	7	8	41	39	44	10	30	2	45	38
JAN. 21	41	8	9	9	41	39	44	10	30	2	45	38
JAN. 22	41	10	10	11	42	39	44	10	30	2	45	38
JAN. 23	42	12	12	13	42	39	44	10	30	2	45	38
JAN. 24	42	13	14	14	42	39	44	10	30	2	45	38
JAN. 25	42	15	15	16	42	40	44	10	30	2	45	38
JAN. 26	42	16	17	17	43	40	44	10	30	2	45	38
JAN. 27	42	18	19	19	43	40	44	10	30	2	45	38
JAN. 28	42	20	20	21	43	40	44	10	30	2	45	38
JAN. 29	42	21	22	23	43	40	45	10	30	2	45	38
JAN. 30	42	23	24	24	43	40	45	10	30	2	45	38
JAN. 31	43	25	25	26	44	41	45	10	30	2	45	38

February

Date & Time	SUN ☉	MOON 1 ◗	MOON 2 ◑	MOON 3 ●	MERCURY	VENUS	MARS	JUPITER	SATURN	URANUS	NEPTUNE	PLUTO
FEB. 1	43	27	27	28	44	41	45	10	30	2	45	38
FEB. 2	43	28	29	30	44	41	45	10	30	2	45	38
FEB. 3	43	30	31	32	44	41	45	10	30	2	45	38
FEB. 4	43	32	33	33	45	41	45	10	30	2	45	38
FEB. 5	43	34	35	35	45	41	45	10	30	2	45	38
FEB. 6	43	36	37	37	45	42	45	10	30	2	45	38
FEB. 7	43	38	39	39	45	42	46	10	30	2	45	38
FEB. 8	44	40	40	41	46	42	46	10	30	2	45	38
FEB. 9	44	42	42	43	46	42	46	10	30	2	45	38
FEB. 10	44	44	44	45	46	42	46	10	30	2	45	38
FEB. 11	44	46	46	47	46	42	46	10	30	2	45	38
FEB. 12	44	47	48	1	46	43	46	10	30	2	45	38
FEB. 13	44	1	2	2	47	43	46	10	30	2	45	38
FEB. 14	44	3	3	4	47	43	46	10	31	2	45	38
FEB. 15	44	5	5	6	47	43	46	10	31	2	45	38
FEB. 16	45	6	7	7	47	43	46	10	31	2	45	38
FEB. 17	45	8	8	9	47	43	47	10	31	2	45	38
FEB. 18	45	9	10	10	47	44	47	10	31	2	45	38
FEB. 19	45	11	12	12	47	44	47	10	31	2	45	38
FEB. 20	45	13	13	14	48	44	47	10	31	2	45	38
FEB. 21	45	14	15	15	48	44	47	10	31	2	45	38
FEB. 22	45	16	16	17	48	44	47	10	31	2	45	38
FEB. 23	46	17	18	19	48	44	47	10	31	2	45	38
FEB. 24	46	19	20	20	48	45	47	10	30	2	45	38
FEB. 25	46	21	21	22	48	45	47	10	30	2	45	38
FEB. 26	46	23	23	24	48	45	48	10	30	2	45	38
FEB. 27	46	24	25	26	47	45	48	10	30	2	45	38
FEB. 28	46	26	27	27	47	45	48	10	30	2	45	38

MOON 1 ◗ 12:01 A.M. TO 8:00 A.M.   **MOON 2** ◑ 8:01 A.M. TO 4:00 P.M.   **MOON 3** ● 4:01 P.M. TO 12:00 A.M.

Use only one "moon" number. Choose the column closest to your time of birth. If your place of birth is not on Eastern Standard Time, be sure to read "How to Convert to Eastern Standard Time" at the beginning of this section.

2013

March

Date & Time	SUN	MOON 1	MOON 2	MOON 3	MERCURY	VENUS	MARS	JUPITER	SATURN	URANUS	NEPTUNE	PLUTO
MAR. 1	46	28	29	29	47	45	48	10	30	2	45	38
MAR. 2	46	30	30	31	47	46	48	10	30	2	45	38
MAR. 3	47	32	32	33	47	46	48	10	30	2	45	38
MAR. 4	47	34	34	35	47	46	48	10	30	2	45	38
MAR. 5	47	35	36	37	47	46	48	10	30	2	45	38
MAR. 6	47	37	38	39	47	46	48	10	30	2	45	38
MAR. 7	47	39	40	40	46	46	48	10	30	2	45	38
MAR. 8	47	41	42	42	46	47	1	10	30	2	45	38
MAR. 9	47	43	44	44	46	47	1	10	30	2	45	38
MAR. 10	47	45	45	46	46	47	1	10	30	2	45	38
MAR. 11	48	47	47	48	46	47	1	10	30	2	45	38
MAR. 12	48	1	1	2	46	47	1	10	30	2	45	38
MAR. 13	48	2	3	3	46	47	1	10	30	2	45	38
MAR. 14	48	4	5	5	46	48	1	10	30	2	45	38
MAR. 15	48	6	6	7	46	48	1	10	30	2	45	38
MAR. 16	48	7	8	8	46	48	1	10	30	2	45	38
MAR. 17	48	9	9	10	46	48	1	10	30	2	45	38
MAR. 18	48	10	11	12	46	48	2	10	30	2	45	38
MAR. 19	1	12	13	13	46	48	2	10	30	2	45	38
MAR. 20	1	14	14	15	46	1	2	10	30	2	45	38
MAR. 21	1	15	16	16	46	1	2	10	30	2	45	38
MAR. 22	1	17	17	18	46	1	2	10	30	2	45	38
MAR. 23	1	18	19	20	46	1	2	10	30	2	45	38
MAR. 24	1	20	21	21	46	1	2	10	30	2	45	38
MAR. 25	2	22	23	23	46	1	2	10	30	2	45	38
MAR. 26	2	24	24	25	46	2	2	10	30	2	46	39
MAR. 27	2	26	26	27	46	2	3	10	30	2	46	39
MAR. 28	2	27	28	29	46	2	3	10	30	2	46	39
MAR. 29	2	29	30	31	46	2	3	10	30	2	46	39
MAR. 30	2	31	32	32	47	2	3	11	30	2	46	39
MAR. 31	2	33	34	34	47	2	3	11	30	2	46	39

April

Date & Time	SUN	MOON 1	MOON 2	MOON 3	MERCURY	VENUS	MARS	JUPITER	SATURN	URANUS	NEPTUNE	PLUTO
APR. 1	2	35	36	36	47	3	3	11	30	2	46	39
APR. 2	2	37	38	38	47	3	3	11	30	2	46	39
APR. 3	3	39	39	40	47	3	3	11	30	2	46	39
APR. 4	3	41	41	42	47	3	3	11	30	2	46	39
APR. 5	3	43	43	44	47	3	3	11	30	2	46	39
APR. 6	3	44	45	46	48	3	3	11	30	2	46	39
APR. 7	3	46	47	47	48	4	4	11	30	2	46	39
APR. 8	3	48	1	1	48	4	4	11	30	2	46	39
APR. 9	3	2	2	3	48	4	4	11	30	2	46	39
APR. 10	3	3	4	5	48	4	4	11	30	2	46	39
APR. 11	4	5	6	7	48	4	4	11	30	2	46	39
APR. 12	4	7	7	8	1	4	4	11	30	2	46	39
APR. 13	4	8	9	9	1	5	4	11	30	2	46	39
APR. 14	4	10	10	11	1	5	4	11	30	2	46	39
APR. 15	4	12	12	13	1	5	4	11	30	2	46	39
APR. 16	4	13	14	14	1	5	5	11	30	2	46	39
APR. 17	4	15	15	16	2	5	5	11	30	2	46	39
APR. 18	4	16	17	17	2	5	5	11	30	2	46	39
APR. 19	5	18	18	19	2	6	5	11	30	2	46	39
APR. 20	5	20	20	21	2	6	5	11	30	2	46	39
APR. 21	5	21	22	22	2	6	5	11	30	2	46	39
APR. 22	5	23	24	24	2	6	5	11	30	2	46	39
APR. 23	5	25	25	26	2	6	5	11	30	2	46	39
APR. 24	5	27	27	28	3	6	5	11	30	2	46	39
APR. 25	6	29	29	30	3	7	5	11	30	2	46	39
APR. 26	6	30	31	32	4	7	6	11	30	2	46	39
APR. 27	6	32	33	34	4	7	6	11	30	2	46	39
APR. 28	6	34	35	36	4	7	6	11	30	2	46	39
APR. 29	6	36	37	38	4	7	6	11	30	2	46	39
APR. 30	6	38	39	40	5	7	6	11	30	2	46	39

MOON 1 ◗ 12:01 A.M. TO 8:00 A.M. **MOON 2** ◑ 8:01 A.M. TO 4:00 P.M. **MOON 3** ● 4:01 P.M. TO 12:00 A.M.

Use only one "moon" number. Choose the column closest to your time of birth. If your place of birth is not on Eastern Standard Time, be sure to read "How to Convert to Eastern Standard Time" at the beginning of this section.

2013

May   June

Date & Time	SUN	MOON 1	MOON 2	MOON 3	MERCURY	VENUS	MARS	JUPITER	SATURN	URANUS	NEPTUNE	PLUTO
MAY 1	6	40	41	41	5	8	6	11	30	2	46	38
MAY 2	6	42	43	43	5	8	6	11	30	2	46	38
MAY 3	7	44	45	45	5	8	6	11	30	2	46	38
MAY 4	7	46	46	47	6	8	6	11	30	2	46	38
MAY 5	7	48	48	1	6	8	6	11	30	2	46	38
MAY 6	7	1	2	2	6	8	7	11	30	2	46	38
MAY 7	7	3	4	4	6	9	7	11	30	2	46	38
MAY 8	7	5	5	6	7	9	7	12	30	2	46	38
MAY 9	7	6	7	7	7	9	7	12	30	2	46	38
MAY 10	7	8	8	9	7	9	7	12	30	2	46	38
MAY 11	8	9	10	11	8	9	7	12	30	2	46	38
MAY 12	8	11	12	12	8	9	7	12	30	2	46	38
MAY 13	8	13	13	14	8	10	7	12	30	2	46	38
MAY 14	8	14	15	15	8	10	7	12	30	2	46	38
MAY 15	8	16	16	17	9	10	7	12	30	2	46	38
MAY 16	8	17	18	19	9	10	8	12	30	2	46	38
MAY 17	8	19	20	20	9	10	8	12	30	2	46	38
MAY 18	8	21	21	22	10	10	8	12	30	2	46	38
MAY 19	9	22	23	23	10	11	8	12	30	2	46	38
MAY 20	9	24	25	25	10	11	8	12	30	2	46	38
MAY 21	9	26	26	27	10	11	8	12	30	2	46	38
MAY 22	9	28	28	29	11	11	8	12	30	2	46	38
MAY 23	9	30	30	31	11	11	8	12	30	2	46	38
MAY 24	9	32	32	33	11	11	8	12	30	2	46	38
MAY 25	10	34	34	35	12	12	8	12	30	2	46	38
MAY 26	10	36	36	37	12	12	8	12	30	2	46	38
MAY 27	10	38	38	39	12	12	9	12	30	2	46	38
MAY 28	10	40	40	41	12	12	9	12	30	3	46	38
MAY 29	10	42	42	43	13	12	9	12	30	3	46	38
MAY 30	10	43	44	45	13	12	9	12	30	3	46	38
MAY 31	10	45	46	47	13	12	9	12	30	3	46	38

Date & Time	SUN	MOON 1	MOON 2	MOON 3	MERCURY	VENUS	MARS	JUPITER	SATURN	URANUS	NEPTUNE	PLUTO
JUN. 1	10	47	48	48	13	13	9	12	30	3	46	38
JUN. 2	10	1	1	2	13	13	9	12	30	3	46	38
JUN. 3	11	3	3	4	14	13	9	12	30	3	46	38
JUN. 4	11	4	5	5	14	13	9	12	30	3	46	38
JUN. 5	11	6	6	7	14	13	9	12	30	3	46	38
JUN. 6	11	7	8	9	14	13	10	12	30	3	46	38
JUN. 7	11	9	10	10	14	14	10	12	30	3	46	38
JUN. 8	11	11	11	12	14	14	10	12	30	3	46	38
JUN. 9	11	12	13	13	15	14	10	12	30	3	46	38
JUN. 10	11	14	14	15	15	14	10	12	30	3	46	38
JUN. 11	12	15	16	16	15	14	10	13	30	3	46	38
JUN. 12	12	17	18	18	15	14	10	13	30	3	46	38
JUN. 13	12	19	19	20	15	15	10	13	30	3	46	38
JUN. 14	12	20	21	21	15	15	10	13	30	3	46	38
JUN. 15	12	22	22	23	15	15	10	13	30	3	46	38
JUN. 16	12	24	24	25	16	15	10	13	30	3	46	38
JUN. 17	12	25	26	26	16	15	11	13	30	3	46	38
JUN. 18	12	27	28	28	16	15	11	13	30	3	46	38
JUN. 19	13	29	29	30	16	16	11	13	30	3	46	38
JUN. 20	13	31	31	32	16	16	11	13	30	3	46	38
JUN. 21	13	33	33	34	16	16	11	13	30	3	46	38
JUN. 22	13	35	35	36	16	16	11	13	30	3	46	38
JUN. 23	13	37	37	38	16	16	11	13	30	3	46	38
JUN. 24	13	39	39	40	16	16	11	13	30	3	46	38
JUN. 25	14	41	41	42	16	17	11	13	30	3	46	38
JUN. 26	14	43	43	44	16	17	11	13	30	3	46	38
JUN. 27	14	45	45	46	16	17	11	13	30	3	46	38
JUN. 28	14	47	47	48	16	17	12	13	30	3	46	38
JUN. 29	14	48	1	2	16	17	12	13	30	3	46	38
JUN. 30	14	2	3	3	16	17	12	13	30	3	46	38

MOON 1 ☽ 12:01 A.M. TO 8:00 A.M.   **MOON 2** ☽ 8:01 A.M. TO 4:00 P.M.   **MOON 3** ● 4:01 P.M. TO 12:00 A.M.
Use only one "moon" number. Choose the column closest to your time of birth. If your place of birth is not on Eastern Standard Time, be sure to read "How to Convert to Eastern Standard Time" at the beginning of this section.

July

August

Date & Time	SUN	MOON 1	MOON 2	MOON 3	MERCURY	VENUS	MARS	JUPITER	SATURN	URANUS	NEPTUNE	PLUTO
JUL. 1	14	4	4	5	16	18	12	13	30	3	46	38
JUL. 2	14	5	6	7	16	18	12	13	30	3	46	38
JUL. 3	15	7	8	8	16	18	12	13	30	3	46	38
JUL. 4	15	9	9	10	16	18	12	13	30	3	46	38
JUL. 5	15	10	11	11	16	18	12	13	30	3	46	38
JUL. 6	15	12	12	13	16	18	12	13	30	3	46	38
JUL. 7	15	13	14	14	16	18	12	13	30	3	46	38
JUL. 8	15	15	16	16	15	19	12	13	30	3	46	38
JUL. 9	15	17	17	18	15	19	13	13	30	3	46	38
JUL. 10	15	18	19	19	15	19	13	13	30	3	46	38
JUL. 11	16	20	20	21	15	19	13	13	30	3	46	38
JUL. 12	16	21	22	23	15	19	13	13	30	3	46	38
JUL. 13	16	23	24	24	15	19	13	13	30	3	46	38
JUL. 14	16	25	25	26	15	20	13	14	30	3	46	38
JUL. 15	16	26	27	28	15	20	13	14	30	3	46	38
JUL. 16	16	28	29	29	15	20	13	14	30	3	46	38
JUL. 17	16	30	31	31	15	20	13	14	30	3	46	38
JUL. 18	16	32	33	33	15	20	13	14	30	3	46	38
JUL. 19	17	34	35	35	15	20	13	14	30	3	46	38
JUL. 20	17	36	36	37	15	21	14	14	30	3	46	38
JUL. 21	17	38	39	39	15	21	14	14	30	3	46	38
JUL. 22	17	40	41	41	15	21	14	14	30	3	46	38
JUL. 23	17	42	43	43	15	21	14	14	30	3	46	38
JUL. 24	17	44	45	45	15	21	14	14	30	3	46	38
JUL. 25	17	46	46	47	15	21	14	14	30	3	46	38
JUL. 26	18	48	48	1	15	22	14	14	30	3	46	38
JUL. 27	18	2	2	3	15	22	14	14	30	3	46	38
JUL. 28	18	3	4	4	15	22	14	14	30	3	46	38
JUL. 29	18	5	6	6	15	22	14	14	30	3	46	38
JUL. 30	18	7	7	8	15	22	14	14	30	3	46	38
JUL. 31	18	8	9	9	15	22	15	14	30	3	46	38

Date & Time	SUN	MOON 1	MOON 2	MOON 3	MERCURY	VENUS	MARS	JUPITER	SATURN	URANUS	NEPTUNE	PLUTO
AUG. 1	18	10	10	11	16	23	15	14	30	3	46	38
AUG. 2	18	11	12	12	16	23	15	14	30	3	46	38
AUG. 3	19	13	14	14	16	23	15	14	30	3	46	38
AUG. 4	19	15	15	16	16	23	15	14	30	3	46	38
AUG. 5	19	16	17	17	16	23	15	14	30	3	46	38
AUG. 6	19	18	18	19	16	23	15	14	30	3	46	38
AUG. 7	19	19	20	20	17	23	15	14	30	3	46	38
AUG. 8	19	21	22	22	17	24	15	14	30	3	46	38
AUG. 9	19	23	23	24	17	24	15	14	30	3	46	38
AUG. 10	19	24	25	26	17	24	15	14	30	3	46	38
AUG. 11	20	26	27	27	18	24	16	14	30	3	46	38
AUG. 12	20	28	28	29	18	24	16	14	30	3	46	38
AUG. 13	20	30	30	31	18	24	16	14	30	3	46	38
AUG. 14	20	31	32	33	18	25	16	14	30	3	46	38
AUG. 15	20	33	34	35	19	25	16	14	30	3	46	38
AUG. 16	20	35	36	36	19	25	16	14	30	3	46	38
AUG. 17	20	37	38	38	19	25	16	14	30	3	46	38
AUG. 18	20	39	40	40	19	25	16	14	30	3	46	38
AUG. 19	21	41	42	42	20	25	16	15	30	3	46	38
AUG. 20	21	43	44	44	20	26	16	15	30	3	46	38
AUG. 21	21	45	46	46	20	26	16	15	30	3	46	38
AUG. 22	21	47	48	48	21	26	16	15	30	3	46	38
AUG. 23	21	1	1	2	21	26	17	15	30	3	46	38
AUG. 24	21	3	3	4	21	26	17	15	30	3	46	38
AUG. 25	21	4	5	6	21	26	17	15	30	3	46	38
AUG. 26	22	6	7	7	22	26	17	15	30	3	45	38
AUG. 27	22	8	8	9	22	27	17	15	30	3	45	38
AUG. 28	22	9	10	10	22	27	17	15	30	3	45	38
AUG. 29	22	11	11	12	22	27	17	15	30	3	45	38
AUG. 30	22	13	13	14	23	27	17	15	30	3	45	38
AUG. 31	22	14	15	15	23	27	17	15	30	3	45	38

MOON 1 ◐ 12:01 A.M. TO 8:00 A.M.   **MOON 2** ◑ 8:01 A.M. TO 4:00 P.M.   **MOON 3** ● 4:01 P.M. TO 12:00 A.M.
Use only one "moon" number. Choose the column closest to your time of birth. If your place of birth is not on
Eastern Standard Time, be sure to read "How to Convert to Eastern Standard Time" at the beginning of this section.

2013

September

October

Date & Time	SUN	MOON 1	MOON 2	MOON 3	MERCURY	VENUS	MARS	JUPITER	SATURN	URANUS	NEPTUNE	PLUTO
SEP. 1	22	16	16	17	23	27	17	15	30	3	45	38
SEP. 2	22	17	18	18	23	28	17	15	30	3	45	38
SEP. 3	23	19	19	20	24	28	17	15	30	3	45	38
SEP. 4	23	21	21	22	24	28	18	15	30	3	45	38
SEP. 5	23	22	23	23	24	28	18	15	30	3	45	38
SEP. 6	23	24	25	25	24	28	18	15	30	3	45	38
SEP. 7	23	26	26	27	24	28	18	15	30	3	45	38
SEP. 8	23	27	28	29	25	28	18	15	30	3	45	38
SEP. 9	23	29	30	30	25	29	18	15	30	2	45	38
SEP. 10	23	31	32	32	25	29	18	15	30	2	45	38
SEP. 11	24	33	33	34	25	29	18	15	30	2	45	38
SEP. 12	24	35	35	36	26	29	18	15	30	2	45	38
SEP. 13	24	37	37	38	26	29	18	15	30	2	45	38
SEP. 14	24	38	39	40	26	29	18	15	30	2	45	38
SEP. 15	24	40	41	42	26	30	18	15	30	2	45	38
SEP. 16	24	42	43	44	26	30	19	15	30	2	45	38
SEP. 17	24	44	45	46	27	30	19	15	30	2	45	38
SEP. 18	24	46	47	47	27	30	19	15	30	2	45	38
SEP. 19	25	48	1	1	27	30	19	15	30	2	45	38
SEP. 20	25	2	2	3	27	30	19	15	30	2	45	38
SEP. 21	25	4	4	5	27	30	19	15	30	2	45	38
SEP. 22	25	5	6	7	28	31	19	15	30	2	45	38
SEP. 23	25	7	8	8	28	31	19	15	30	2	45	38
SEP. 24	25	9	9	10	28	31	19	15	30	2	45	38
SEP. 25	26	10	11	11	28	31	19	15	30	2	45	38
SEP. 26	26	12	13	13	28	31	19	15	30	2	45	38
SEP. 27	26	14	14	15	29	31	19	15	30	2	45	38
SEP. 28	26	15	16	16	29	32	20	15	30	2	45	38
SEP. 29	26	17	17	18	29	32	20	15	30	2	45	38
SEP. 30	26	18	19	19	29	32	20	15	30	2	45	38

Date & Time	SUN	MOON 1	MOON 2	MOON 3	MERCURY	VENUS	MARS	JUPITER	SATURN	URANUS	NEPTUNE	PLUTO
OCT. 1	26	20	21	21	29	32	20	15	30	2	45	38
OCT. 2	26	22	22	23	29	32	20	15	30	2	45	38
OCT. 3	27	23	24	25	30	32	20	15	30	2	45	38
OCT. 4	27	25	26	26	30	32	20	15	30	2	45	38
OCT. 5	27	27	27	28	30	33	20	15	30	2	45	38
OCT. 6	27	29	29	30	30	33	20	15	30	2	45	38
OCT. 7	27	31	31	32	30	33	20	15	30	2	45	38
OCT. 8	27	32	33	34	30	33	20	16	30	2	45	38
OCT. 9	27	34	35	36	30	33	20	16	30	2	45	38
OCT. 10	27	36	37	37	31	33	21	16	30	2	45	38
OCT. 11	28	38	39	39	31	33	21	16	30	2	45	38
OCT. 12	28	40	41	41	31	34	21	16	30	2	45	38
OCT. 13	28	42	42	43	31	34	21	16	30	2	45	38
OCT. 14	28	44	44	45	31	34	21	16	30	2	45	38
OCT. 15	28	46	46	47	31	34	21	16	31	2	45	38
OCT. 16	28	47	48	1	31	34	21	16	31	2	45	38
OCT. 17	28	1	2	2	31	34	21	16	31	2	45	38
OCT. 18	28	3	4	4	31	34	21	16	31	2	45	38
OCT. 19	29	5	5	6	31	35	21	16	31	2	45	38
OCT. 20	29	7	7	8	31	35	21	16	31	2	45	38
OCT. 21	29	8	9	9	31	35	21	16	31	2	45	38
OCT. 22	29	10	10	11	31	35	22	16	31	2	45	38
OCT. 23	29	11	12	13	31	35	22	16	31	2	45	38
OCT. 24	29	13	14	14	31	35	22	16	31	2	45	38
OCT. 25	29	15	15	16	31	35	22	16	31	2	45	38
OCT. 26	30	16	17	17	31	36	22	16	31	2	45	38
OCT. 27	30	18	18	19	31	36	22	16	31	2	45	38
OCT. 28	30	19	20	21	31	36	22	16	31	2	45	38
OCT. 29	30	21	22	22	31	36	22	16	31	2	45	38
OCT. 30	30	23	23	24	31	36	22	16	31	2	45	38
OCT. 31	30	24	25	26	31	36	22	16	31	2	45	38

MOON 1 ◖ 12:01 A.M. TO 8:00 A.M.   **MOON 2** ◗ 8:01 A.M. TO 4:00 P.M.   **MOON 3** ● 4:01 P.M. TO 12:00 A.M.
Use only one "moon" number. Choose the column closest to your time of birth. If your place of birth is not on Eastern Standard Time, be sure to read "How to Convert to Eastern Standard Time" at the beginning of this section.

2013

November

December

Date & Time	SUN	MOON 1	MOON 2	MOON 3	MERCURY	VENUS	MARS	JUPITER	SATURN	URANUS	NEPTUNE	PLUTO
NOV. 1	30	26	27	27	30	36	22	16	31	2	45	38
NOV. 2	30	28	29	29	30	37	22	16	31	2	45	38
NOV. 3	31	30	30	31	30	37	22	16	31	2	45	38
NOV. 4	31	32	32	33	30	37	23	16	31	2	45	38
NOV. 5	31	34	34	35	30	37	23	16	31	2	45	38
NOV. 6	31	36	36	37	30	37	23	16	31	2	45	38
NOV. 7	31	38	38	39	29	37	23	16	31	2	45	38
NOV. 8	31	39	40	41	29	37	23	16	31	2	45	38
NOV. 9	31	41	42	43	29	37	23	16	31	2	45	38
NOV. 10	31	43	44	45	29	38	23	16	31	2	45	38
NOV. 11	31	45	46	46	29	38	23	16	31	2	45	38
NOV. 12	32	47	48	48	29	38	23	16	31	2	45	38
NOV. 13	32	1	1	2	29	38	23	16	31	2	45	38
NOV. 14	32	3	3	4	29	38	23	16	31	2	45	38
NOV. 15	32	4	5	5	30	38	23	16	31	2	45	38
NOV. 16	32	6	7	7	30	38	23	16	31	2	45	38
NOV. 17	32	8	8	8	30	38	23	16	31	2	45	38
NOV. 18	32	9	10	10	30	39	24	16	31	2	45	38
NOV. 19	33	11	11	12	30	39	24	16	31	2	45	38
NOV. 20	33	13	13	14	30	39	24	16	31	2	45	38
NOV. 21	33	14	15	15	30	39	24	16	31	2	45	38
NOV. 22	33	16	16	16	30	39	24	16	31	2	45	38
NOV. 23	33	17	18	18	31	39	24	16	31	2	45	38
NOV. 24	33	19	19	20	31	39	24	16	31	2	45	38
NOV. 25	34	20	21	22	31	39	24	16	31	2	45	38
NOV. 26	34	22	23	23	31	39	24	16	31	2	45	38
NOV. 27	34	24	24	25	31	40	24	16	31	2	45	38
NOV. 28	34	25	26	27	32	40	24	16	31	2	45	38
NOV. 29	34	27	28	28	32	40	24	16	31	2	45	38
NOV. 30	34	29	30	30	32	40	24	16	31	2	45	38

Date & Time	SUN	MOON 1	MOON 2	MOON 3	MERCURY	VENUS	MARS	JUPITER	SATURN	URANUS	NEPTUNE	PLUTO
DEC. 1	34	31	32	32	32	40	25	16	31	2	45	38
DEC. 2	34	33	33	34	32	40	25	16	31	2	45	38
DEC. 3	35	35	35	36	33	40	25	16	31	2	45	38
DEC. 4	35	37	37	38	33	40	25	16	31	2	45	38
DEC. 5	35	39	39	40	33	40	25	16	31	2	45	38
DEC. 6	35	41	41	42	33	40	25	16	31	2	45	38
DEC. 7	35	43	43	44	33	40	25	16	31	2	45	38
DEC. 8	35	45	45	46	34	40	25	15	31	2	45	38
DEC. 9	35	47	47	48	34	40	25	15	31	2	45	38
DEC. 10	35	48	1	2	34	40	25	15	31	2	45	38
DEC. 11	36	2	3	3	34	41	25	15	31	2	45	38
DEC. 12	36	4	4	5	34	41	25	15	31	2	45	38
DEC. 13	36	6	6	7	35	41	25	15	31	2	45	38
DEC. 14	36	7	8	8	35	41	25	15	31	2	45	38
DEC. 15	36	9	9	10	35	41	25	15	31	2	45	38
DEC. 16	36	10	11	12	35	41	26	15	31	2	45	38
DEC. 17	36	12	13	13	35	41	26	15	31	2	45	38
DEC. 18	36	14	14	15	36	41	26	15	32	2	45	38
DEC. 19	37	15	16	16	36	41	26	15	32	2	45	38
DEC. 20	37	17	17	18	36	41	26	15	32	2	45	38
DEC. 21	37	18	19	19	36	41	26	15	32	2	45	38
DEC. 22	37	20	21	21	37	41	26	15	32	2	45	38
DEC. 23	37	22	22	23	37	41	26	15	32	2	45	38
DEC. 24	37	23	24	24	37	41	26	15	32	2	45	38
DEC. 25	37	25	25	26	37	41	26	15	32	2	45	38
DEC. 26	38	27	27	28	37	41	26	15	32	2	45	38
DEC. 27	38	28	29	29	38	41	26	15	32	2	45	38
DEC. 28	38	30	31	31	38	41	26	15	32	2	45	38
DEC. 29	38	32	33	33	38	41	26	15	32	2	45	38
DEC. 30	38	34	35	35	38	41	26	15	32	2	45	38
DEC. 31	38	36	37	37	38	41	26	15	32	2	45	38

MOON 1 ◖ 12:01 A.M. TO 8:00 A.M.   **MOON 2** ◑ 8:01 A.M. TO 4:00 P.M.   **MOON 3** ● 4:01 P.M. TO 12:00 A.M.

Use only one "moon" number. Choose the column closest to your time of birth. If your place of birth is not on Eastern Standard Time, be sure to read "How to Convert to Eastern Standard Time" at the beginning of this section.

2014

January

Date & Time	SUN	MOON 1	MOON 2	MOON 3	MERCURY	VENUS	MARS	JUPITER	SATURN	URANUS	NEPTUNE	PLUTO
JAN. 1	38	38	39	39	39	41	27	15	32	2	45	38
JAN. 2	38	40	41	41	39	40	27	15	32	2	45	38
JAN. 3	39	42	43	43	39	40	27	15	32	2	45	38
JAN. 4	39	44	45	45	39	40	27	15	32	2	45	38
JAN. 5	39	46	47	47	39	40	27	15	32	2	45	38
JAN. 6	39	48	48	1	40	40	27	15	32	2	45	38
JAN. 7	39	2	2	3	40	40	27	15	32	2	45	38
JAN. 8	39	3	4	5	40	40	27	15	32	2	45	39
JAN. 9	39	5	6	6	40	40	27	15	32	2	45	39
JAN. 10	40	7	7	8	41	40	27	15	32	2	45	39
JAN. 11	40	8	9	10	41	40	27	15	32	2	45	39
JAN. 12	40	10	11	11	41	40	27	15	32	2	45	39
JAN. 13	40	12	12	13	41	40	27	15	32	2	45	39
JAN. 14	40	13	14	14	41	40	27	15	32	2	45	39
JAN. 15	40	15	15	16	42	39	27	15	32	2	45	39
JAN. 16	40	16	17	17	42	39	27	15	32	2	45	39
JAN. 17	41	18	19	19	42	39	27	15	32	2	45	39
JAN. 18	41	20	20	21	42	39	27	15	32	2	45	39
JAN. 19	41	21	22	22	43	39	28	15	32	2	45	39
JAN. 20	41	23	23	24	43	39	28	15	32	2	45	39
JAN. 21	41	24	25	26	43	39	28	15	32	2	45	39
JAN. 22	41	26	27	27	43	39	28	15	32	2	45	39
JAN. 23	42	28	28	29	43	39	28	15	32	2	45	39
JAN. 24	42	29	30	31	44	39	28	15	32	2	45	39
JAN. 25	42	31	32	32	44	39	28	15	32	2	45	39
JAN. 26	42	33	34	34	44	39	28	15	32	2	46	39
JAN. 27	42	35	36	36	44	39	28	15	32	2	46	39
JAN. 28	42	37	38	38	44	39	28	15	32	2	46	39
JAN. 29	42	39	40	40	45	39	28	15	32	2	46	39
JAN. 30	42	41	42	42	45	39	28	15	32	2	46	39
JAN. 31	43	43	44	44	45	39	28	15	32	2	46	39

February

Date & Time	SUN	MOON 1	MOON 2	MOON 3	MERCURY	VENUS	MARS	JUPITER	SATURN	URANUS	NEPTUNE	PLUTO
FEB. 1	43	45	46	46	45	39	28	15	32	2	46	39
FEB. 2	43	47	48	48	45	39	28	15	32	2	46	39
FEB. 3	43	1	2	2	45	39	28	15	32	2	46	39
FEB. 4	43	3	3	4	45	39	28	15	32	2	46	39
FEB. 5	43	5	5	6	45	39	28	15	32	2	46	39
FEB. 6	43	6	7	7	45	39	28	15	32	2	46	39
FEB. 7	43	8	9	9	45	39	28	15	32	2	46	39
FEB. 8	44	10	10	11	45	39	28	15	32	2	46	39
FEB. 9	44	11	12	12	45	39	28	14	32	2	46	39
FEB. 10	44	13	13	14	45	39	28	14	32	2	46	39
FEB. 11	44	14	15	16	45	39	28	14	32	2	46	39
FEB. 12	44	16	17	17	45	39	28	14	32	2	46	39
FEB. 13	44	18	18	19	45	39	28	14	32	2	46	39
FEB. 14	44	19	20	20	45	39	28	14	32	2	46	39
FEB. 15	44	21	21	23	45	39	28	14	32	2	46	39
FEB. 16	45	22	23	24	45	39	28	14	32	2	46	39
FEB. 17	45	24	25	25	44	39	29	14	32	2	46	39
FEB. 18	45	26	26	27	44	39	29	14	32	2	46	39
FEB. 19	45	27	28	29	44	40	29	14	32	2	46	39
FEB. 20	45	29	30	30	44	40	29	14	32	2	46	39
FEB. 21	45	31	31	32	44	40	29	14	32	2	46	39
FEB. 22	45	33	33	34	44	40	29	14	32	2	46	39
FEB. 23	46	34	35	36	44	40	29	14	32	2	46	39
FEB. 24	46	36	37	38	44	40	29	14	32	2	46	39
FEB. 25	46	38	39	39	43	40	29	14	32	2	46	39
FEB. 26	46	40	41	41	43	40	29	14	32	2	46	39
FEB. 27	46	42	43	43	43	40	29	14	32	2	46	39
FEB. 28	46	44	45	45	43	40	29	14	32	2	46	39

MOON 1 ◖ 12:01 A.M. TO 8:00 A.M.   **MOON 2** ◗ 8:01 A.M. TO 4:00 P.M.   **MOON 3** ● 4:01 P.M. TO 12:00 A.M.
Use only one "moon" number. Choose the column closest to your time of birth. If your place of birth is not on Eastern Standard Time, be sure to read "How to Convert to Eastern Standard Time" at the beginning of this section.

2014

March

Date & Time	SUN	MOON 1	MOON 2	MOON 3	MERCURY	VENUS	MARS	JUPITER	SATURN	URANUS	NEPTUNE	PLUTO
MAR. 1	46	46	47	47	43	40	29	14	32	2	46	39
MAR. 2	46	48	1	1	43	41	29	14	32	2	46	39
MAR. 3	47	2	3	3	43	41	29	14	32	2	46	39
MAR. 4	47	4	5	5	43	41	29	14	32	2	46	39
MAR. 5	47	6	6	7	44	41	29	14	32	2	46	39
MAR. 6	47	7	8	9	44	41	29	14	32	2	46	39
MAR. 7	47	9	10	10	44	41	29	14	32	2	46	39
MAR. 8	47	11	11	12	44	41	29	14	32	2	46	39
MAR. 9	47	12	13	13	44	41	29	14	32	2	46	39
MAR. 10	47	14	15	14	44	41	29	14	32	2	46	39
MAR. 11	48	16	16	17	44	42	29	14	32	2	46	39
MAR. 12	48	17	18	18	44	42	29	14	32	2	46	39
MAR. 13	48	19	19	20	44	42	29	14	32	2	46	39
MAR. 14	48	20	21	21	44	42	29	14	32	2	46	39
MAR. 15	48	22	23	23	45	42	28	14	32	2	46	39
MAR. 16	48	24	24	25	45	42	28	14	32	2	46	39
MAR. 17	48	25	26	26	45	42	28	14	32	3	46	39
MAR. 18	48	27	28	28	45	42	28	14	32	3	46	39
MAR. 19	1	29	29	30	45	43	28	14	32	3	46	39
MAR. 20	1	30	31	32	45	43	28	14	32	3	46	39
MAR. 21	1	32	33	33	45	43	28	14	32	3	46	39
MAR. 22	1	34	35	35	46	43	28	14	32	3	46	39
MAR. 23	1	36	36	37	46	43	28	14	32	3	46	39
MAR. 24	1	38	38	39	46	43	28	14	32	3	46	39
MAR. 25	2	40	40	41	46	43	28	14	32	3	46	39
MAR. 26	2	41	42	43	46	43	28	14	32	3	46	39
MAR. 27	2	43	44	45	47	44	28	14	32	3	46	39
MAR. 28	2	45	46	47	47	44	28	14	32	3	46	39
MAR. 29	2	47	48	1	47	44	28	14	32	3	46	39
MAR. 30	2	1	2	2	47	44	28	14	32	3	46	39
MAR. 31	2	3	4	4	47	44	28	14	32	3	46	39

April

Date & Time	SUN	MOON 1	MOON 2	MOON 3	MERCURY	VENUS	MARS	JUPITER	SATURN	URANUS	NEPTUNE	PLUTO
APR. 1	2	5	6	6	48	44	28	14	32	3	46	39
APR. 2	2	7	7	8	48	44	28	15	32	3	46	39
APR. 3	3	8	9	10	48	45	28	15	32	3	46	39
APR. 4	3	10	11	11	48	45	28	15	32	3	46	39
APR. 5	3	12	12	13	48	45	28	15	32	3	46	39
APR. 6	3	13	14	15	1	45	28	15	32	3	46	39
APR. 7	3	15	16	16	1	45	28	15	32	3	46	39
APR. 8	3	17	17	18	1	45	28	15	32	3	46	39
APR. 9	3	18	19	19	1	45	27	15	32	3	46	39
APR. 10	3	20	20	21	2	46	27	15	32	3	46	39
APR. 11	4	21	22	23	2	46	27	15	32	3	46	39
APR. 12	4	23	24	24	2	46	27	15	32	3	46	39
APR. 13	4	25	25	26	2	46	27	15	32	3	46	39
APR. 14	4	26	27	28	3	46	27	15	32	3	46	39
APR. 15	4	28	29	29	3	46	27	15	32	3	46	39
APR. 16	4	30	30	31	3	46	27	15	32	3	46	39
APR. 17	4	32	32	33	3	47	27	15	32	3	46	39
APR. 18	4	34	34	35	4	47	27	15	32	3	46	39
APR. 19	5	35	36	37	4	47	27	15	32	3	46	39
APR. 20	5	37	38	38	4	47	27	15	32	3	46	39
APR. 21	5	39	40	40	4	47	27	15	32	3	46	39
APR. 22	5	41	42	42	5	47	27	15	32	3	46	39
APR. 23	5	43	44	44	5	47	27	15	32	3	46	39
APR. 24	5	45	45	46	5	48	27	15	32	3	46	39
APR. 25	6	47	47	48	5	48	27	15	32	3	46	39
APR. 26	6	1	1	2	6	48	27	15	32	3	46	39
APR. 27	6	2	3	4	6	48	27	15	32	3	46	39
APR. 28	6	4	5	5	6	48	27	15	32	3	46	39
APR. 29	6	6	7	7	7	48	27	15	32	3	46	39
APR. 30	6	8	8	9	7	1	27	15	32	3	46	39

MOON 1 ☽ 12:01 A.M. TO 8:00 A.M.   **MOON 2** ☽ 8:01 A.M. TO 4:00 P.M.   **MOON 3** ● 4:01 P.M. TO 12:00 A.M.

Use only one "moon" number. Choose the column closest to your time of birth. If your place of birth is not on Eastern Standard Time, be sure to read "How to Convert to Eastern Standard Time" at the beginning of this section.

2014

May

June

Date & Time	SUN	MOON 1	MOON 2	MOON 3	MERCURY	VENUS	MARS	JUPITER	SATURN	URANUS	NEPTUNE	PLUTO
MAY 1	6	10	10	11	7	1	26	15	32	3	46	39
MAY 2	6	11	12	12	7	1	26	15	32	3	46	39
MAY 3	7	13	13	14	8	1	26	15	32	3	46	39
MAY 4	7	15	15	16	8	1	26	15	32	3	46	39
MAY 5	7	16	17	17	8	1	26	15	32	3	46	39
MAY 6	7	18	18	19	9	1	26	15	32	3	46	39
MAY 7	7	19	20	20	9	2	26	15	32	3	46	39
MAY 8	7	21	21	22	9	2	26	15	32	3	46	39
MAY 9	7	22	23	24	9	2	26	15	32	3	46	39
MAY 10	7	24	25	25	10	2	26	15	32	3	46	39
MAY 11	8	26	26	27	10	2	26	15	32	3	46	39
MAY 12	8	27	28	29	10	2	26	15	32	3	46	39
MAY 13	8	29	30	30	10	3	26	15	32	3	46	39
MAY 14	8	31	32	32	11	3	26	15	32	3	46	39
MAY 15	8	33	34	34	11	3	26	15	32	3	46	39
MAY 16	8	35	35	36	11	3	26	15	32	3	46	39
MAY 17	8	37	37	38	11	3	26	15	32	3	46	39
MAY 18	8	39	39	40	11	3	26	15	32	3	46	39
MAY 19	9	41	41	42	12	3	26	15	32	3	46	39
MAY 20	9	42	43	44	12	4	26	15	32	3	46	39
MAY 21	9	44	45	46	12	4	26	15	32	3	46	39
MAY 22	9	46	47	48	12	4	26	15	32	3	46	39
MAY 23	9	48	1	1	12	4	26	15	32	3	46	39
MAY 24	9	2	3	3	12	4	26	15	32	3	46	39
MAY 25	10	4	4	5	13	4	26	16	31	3	46	39
MAY 26	10	6	6	6	13	5	26	16	31	3	46	39
MAY 27	10	7	8	8	13	5	26	16	31	3	46	39
MAY 28	10	9	10	10	13	5	26	16	31	3	46	39
MAY 29	10	11	11	12	13	5	26	16	31	3	46	39
MAY 30	10	12	13	13	13	5	26	16	31	3	46	39
MAY 31	10	14	15	15	13	5	26	16	31	3	46	39

Date & Time	SUN	MOON 1	MOON 2	MOON 3	MERCURY	VENUS	MARS	JUPITER	SATURN	URANUS	NEPTUNE	PLUTO
JUN. 1	10	16	16	17	13	5	26	16	31	3	46	39
JUN. 2	10	17	18	18	13	6	26	16	31	3	46	39
JUN. 3	11	19	19	20	13	6	26	16	31	3	46	39
JUN. 4	11	20	21	21	13	6	26	16	31	3	46	39
JUN. 5	11	22	22	23	13	6	26	16	31	3	46	39
JUN. 6	11	24	24	25	13	6	26	16	31	3	46	39
JUN. 7	11	25	26	26	13	6	26	16	31	3	46	39
JUN. 8	11	27	27	28	13	7	26	16	31	3	46	39
JUN. 9	11	29	29	30	13	7	26	16	31	3	46	39
JUN. 10	11	30	31	32	13	7	27	16	31	3	46	39
JUN. 11	12	32	33	33	13	7	27	16	31	3	46	39
JUN. 12	12	34	35	35	13	7	27	16	31	3	46	39
JUN. 13	12	36	37	37	13	7	27	16	31	3	46	39
JUN. 14	12	38	39	39	13	7	27	16	31	3	46	39
JUN. 15	12	40	41	41	13	8	27	16	31	3	46	39
JUN. 16	12	42	43	43	13	8	27	16	31	3	46	39
JUN. 17	12	44	45	45	13	8	27	16	31	3	46	39
JUN. 18	12	46	46	47	13	8	27	16	31	3	46	39
JUN. 19	13	48	48	1	13	8	27	16	31	3	46	39
JUN. 20	13	2	2	3	13	8	27	16	31	3	46	39
JUN. 21	13	3	4	5	13	9	27	16	31	3	46	39
JUN. 22	13	5	6	6	13	9	27	16	31	3	46	39
JUN. 23	13	7	7	8	13	9	27	16	31	3	46	39
JUN. 24	13	9	9	10	12	9	27	16	31	3	46	39
JUN. 25	14	10	11	11	12	9	27	16	31	3	46	39
JUN. 26	14	12	12	12	12	9	27	16	31	3	46	39
JUN. 27	14	14	14	15	12	10	27	16	31	3	46	39
JUN. 28	14	15	16	16	12	10	27	16	31	3	46	39
JUN. 29	14	17	17	18	12	10	27	16	31	3	46	39
JUN. 30	14	18	19	19	12	10	27	16	31	3	46	39

MOON 1 ◐ 12:01 A.M. TO 8:00 A.M.   **MOON 2** ◑ 8:01 A.M. TO 4:00 P.M.   **MOON 3** ● 4:01 P.M. TO 12:00 A.M.
Use only one "moon" number. Choose the column closest to your time of birth. If your place of birth is not on Eastern Standard Time, be sure to read "How to Convert to Eastern Standard Time" at the beginning of this section.

Date & Time	SUN	MOON 1	MOON 2	MOON 3	MERCURY	VENUS	MARS	JUPITER	SATURN	URANUS	NEPTUNE	PLUTO
JUL. 1	14	20	20	21	12	10	27	17	31	3	46	39
JUL. 2	14	21	22	23	12	10	27	17	31	3	46	39
JUL. 3	15	23	24	24	12	11	28	17	31	3	46	39
JUL. 4	15	25	25	26	12	11	28	17	31	3	46	39
JUL. 5	15	26	27	27	12	11	28	17	31	3	46	39
JUL. 6	15	28	29	29	12	11	28	17	31	3	46	39
JUL. 7	15	30	30	31	12	11	28	17	31	3	46	39
JUL. 8	15	31	32	33	12	11	28	17	31	3	46	39
JUL. 9	15	33	34	35	13	11	28	17	31	3	46	39
JUL. 10	15	35	36	36	13	12	28	17	31	3	46	39
JUL. 11	16	37	38	38	13	12	28	17	31	3	46	39
JUL. 12	16	39	40	40	13	12	28	17	31	3	46	39
JUL. 13	16	41	42	42	13	12	28	17	31	3	46	39
JUL. 14	16	43	44	44	13	12	28	17	31	3	46	39
JUL. 15	16	45	46	46	13	12	28	17	31	3	46	39
JUL. 16	16	47	48	48	13	13	28	17	31	3	46	39
JUL. 17	16	1	2	2	14	13	28	17	31	3	46	39
JUL. 18	16	3	3	4	14	13	28	17	31	3	46	39
JUL. 19	17	5	5	6	14	13	29	17	31	3	46	39
JUL. 20	17	6	7	8	14	13	29	17	31	3	46	39
JUL. 21	17	8	9	9	14	13	29	17	31	3	46	39
JUL. 22	17	10	10	11	15	14	29	17	31	3	46	39
JUL. 23	17	11	12	13	15	14	29	17	31	3	46	39
JUL. 24	17	13	14	14	15	14	29	17	31	3	46	39
JUL. 25	17	15	15	16	15	14	29	17	31	3	46	39
JUL. 26	18	16	17	17	15	14	29	17	31	3	46	39
JUL. 27	18	18	18	19	16	14	29	17	31	3	46	39
JUL. 28	18	19	20	21	16	15	29	17	31	3	46	39
JUL. 29	18	21	22	22	16	15	29	17	31	3	46	39
JUL. 30	18	23	23	24	16	15	29	17	31	3	46	39
JUL. 31	18	24	25	25	17	15	29	17	31	3	46	39

Date & Time	SUN	MOON 1	MOON 2	MOON 3	MERCURY	VENUS	MARS	JUPITER	SATURN	URANUS	NEPTUNE	PLUTO
AUG. 1	18	26	26	27	17	15	29	17	31	3	46	39
AUG. 2	18	27	28	29	17	15	29	17	31	3	46	39
AUG. 3	19	29	30	30	18	15	30	17	31	3	46	39
AUG. 4	19	31	31	32	18	16	30	18	31	3	46	39
AUG. 5	19	33	33	34	18	16	30	18	31	3	46	39
AUG. 6	19	34	35	36	18	16	30	18	31	3	46	38
AUG. 7	19	36	37	38	19	16	30	18	31	3	46	38
AUG. 8	19	38	39	40	19	16	30	18	31	3	46	38
AUG. 9	19	40	41	42	19	16	30	18	31	3	46	38
AUG. 10	19	42	43	44	20	17	30	18	31	3	46	38
AUG. 11	20	44	45	46	20	17	30	18	31	3	46	38
AUG. 12	20	46	47	48	20	17	30	18	31	3	46	38
AUG. 13	20	48	1	2	20	17	30	18	31	3	46	38
AUG. 14	20	2	3	4	21	17	30	18	31	3	46	38
AUG. 15	20	4	5	5	21	17	30	18	31	3	46	38
AUG. 16	20	6	7	7	21	18	31	18	31	3	46	38
AUG. 17	20	8	8	9	21	18	31	18	31	3	46	38
AUG. 18	20	9	10	11	22	18	31	18	31	3	46	38
AUG. 19	21	11	12	12	22	18	31	18	31	3	46	38
AUG. 20	21	13	13	14	22	18	31	18	31	3	46	38
AUG. 21	21	14	15	15	22	18	31	18	31	3	46	38
AUG. 22	21	16	16	17	23	19	31	18	31	3	46	38
AUG. 23	21	18	18	19	23	19	31	18	31	3	46	38
AUG. 24	21	19	20	21	23	19	31	18	31	3	46	38
AUG. 25	21	21	21	22	23	19	31	18	31	3	46	38
AUG. 26	22	22	23	23	23	19	31	18	31	3	46	38
AUG. 27	22	24	24	25	24	19	31	18	31	3	46	38
AUG. 28	22	25	26	27	24	20	32	18	31	3	46	38
AUG. 29	22	27	28	28	24	20	32	18	31	3	46	38
AUG. 30	22	29	29	30	24	20	32	18	31	3	46	38
AUG. 31	22	30	31	32	25	20	32	18	31	3	46	38

MOON 1 ☽ 12:01 A.M. TO 8:00 A.M.   **MOON 2** ☾ 8:01 A.M. TO 4:00 P.M.   **MOON 3** ● 4:01 P.M. TO 12:00 A.M.
Use only one "moon" number. Choose the column closest to your time of birth. If your place of birth is not on Eastern Standard Time, be sure to read "How to Convert to Eastern Standard Time" at the beginning of this section.

September

Date & Time	SUN	MOON 1	MOON 2	MOON 3	MERCURY	VENUS	MARS	JUPITER	SATURN	URANUS	NEPTUNE	PLUTO
SEP. 1	22	32	33	33	25	20	32	18	31	3	46	38
SEP. 2	22	34	34	35	25	20	32	18	31	3	46	38
SEP. 3	23	36	36	37	25	21	32	18	31	3	46	38
SEP. 4	23	37	38	39	25	21	32	18	31	3	46	38
SEP. 5	23	39	40	41	26	21	32	18	31	3	46	38
SEP. 6	23	41	42	43	26	21	32	18	31	3	46	38
SEP. 7	23	43	44	45	26	21	32	19	31	3	46	38
SEP. 8	23	45	46	47	26	21	32	19	31	3	46	38
SEP. 9	23	47	48	1	26	22	33	19	31	3	46	38
SEP. 10	23	1	2	3	26	22	33	19	31	3	46	38
SEP. 11	24	3	4	5	27	22	33	19	31	3	46	38
SEP. 12	24	5	6	6	27	22	33	19	31	3	46	38
SEP. 13	24	7	8	8	27	22	33	19	31	3	46	38
SEP. 14	24	9	9	10	27	22	33	19	32	3	46	38
SEP. 15	24	11	11	12	27	23	33	19	32	3	46	38
SEP. 16	24	12	13	13	27	23	33	19	32	3	46	38
SEP. 17	24	14	14	15	28	23	33	19	32	3	46	38
SEP. 18	24	15	16	17	28	23	33	19	32	3	46	38
SEP. 19	25	17	18	18	28	23	33	19	32	3	46	38
SEP. 20	25	19	19	20	28	23	34	19	32	3	46	38
SEP. 21	25	20	21	21	28	24	34	19	32	3	46	38
SEP. 22	25	22	22	23	28	24	34	19	32	3	46	38
SEP. 23	25	23	24	24	28	24	34	19	32	3	46	38
SEP. 24	25	25	26	26	29	24	34	19	32	3	46	38
SEP. 25	26	27	27	28	29	24	34	19	32	3	46	38
SEP. 26	26	28	29	29	29	24	34	19	32	3	46	38
SEP. 27	26	30	31	31	29	25	34	19	32	3	46	38
SEP. 28	26	32	32	33	29	25	34	19	32	3	46	38
SEP. 29	26	33	34	35	29	25	34	19	32	3	46	38
SEP. 30	26	35	36	36	29	25	34	19	32	3	46	38

October

Date & Time	SUN	MOON 1	MOON 2	MOON 3	MERCURY	VENUS	MARS	JUPITER	SATURN	URANUS	NEPTUNE	PLUTO
OCT. 1	26	37	38	38	29	25	35	19	32	3	46	38
OCT. 2	26	39	39	40	29	25	35	19	32	3	46	38
OCT. 3	27	41	41	42	29	26	35	19	32	3	46	38
OCT. 4	27	43	43	44	29	26	35	19	32	3	46	38
OCT. 5	27	45	45	46	29	26	35	19	32	3	46	38
OCT. 6	27	47	47	48	29	26	35	19	32	3	46	38
OCT. 7	27	1	1	2	29	26	35	19	32	3	46	38
OCT. 8	27	3	3	4	29	26	35	19	32	3	46	38
OCT. 9	27	4	5	6	29	27	35	19	32	3	46	38
OCT. 10	27	6	7	8	29	27	35	19	32	3	46	38
OCT. 11	28	8	9	9	29	27	35	19	32	3	46	38
OCT. 12	28	10	11	11	29	27	36	19	32	3	46	38
OCT. 13	28	12	12	13	29	27	36	19	32	3	46	38
OCT. 14	28	13	14	14	29	27	36	19	32	3	46	38
OCT. 15	28	15	16	16	28	28	36	19	32	3	46	38
OCT. 16	28	17	17	18	28	28	36	19	32	3	46	38
OCT. 17	28	18	19	19	28	28	36	19	32	3	46	38
OCT. 18	28	20	20	21	28	28	36	19	32	3	46	38
OCT. 19	29	21	22	22	28	28	36	19	32	3	46	38
OCT. 20	29	23	23	24	28	28	36	19	32	3	46	38
OCT. 21	29	25	25	26	27	29	36	20	32	3	46	38
OCT. 22	29	26	27	27	27	29	37	20	32	3	46	38
OCT. 23	29	28	28	29	27	29	37	20	32	3	46	38
OCT. 24	29	30	30	31	27	29	37	20	32	3	46	38
OCT. 25	29	31	32	32	27	29	37	20	32	3	46	38
OCT. 26	30	33	34	34	27	29	37	20	32	3	46	38
OCT. 27	30	35	35	36	27	30	37	20	32	3	46	38
OCT. 28	30	37	37	38	27	30	37	20	32	3	46	38
OCT. 29	30	38	39	40	27	30	37	20	32	3	46	38
OCT. 30	30	40	41	42	27	30	37	20	32	3	46	38
OCT. 31	30	42	43	43	28	30	37	20	32	3	46	38

MOON 1 ☽ 12:01 A.M. TO 8:00 A.M.   **MOON 2** ◑ 8:01 A.M. TO 4:00 P.M.   **MOON 3** ● 4:01 P.M. TO 12:00 A.M.

Use only one "moon" number. Choose the column closest to your time of birth. If your place of birth is not on Eastern Standard Time, be sure to read "How to Convert to Eastern Standard Time" at the beginning of this section.

November

Date & Time	SUN	MOON 1	MOON 2	MOON 3	MERCURY	VENUS	MARS	JUPITER	SATURN	URANUS	NEPTUNE	PLUTO
NOV. 1	30	44	45	45	28	30	38	20	32	3	46	38
NOV. 2	30	46	47	47	28	31	38	20	32	3	46	38
NOV. 3	31	48	48	1	28	31	38	20	32	3	46	38
NOV. 4	31	2	2	3	28	31	38	20	32	3	46	38
NOV. 5	31	4	4	5	28	31	38	20	32	3	46	38
NOV. 6	31	6	6	7	28	31	38	20	32	3	46	38
NOV. 7	31	7	8	9	29	31	38	20	32	3	46	39
NOV. 8	31	9	10	10	29	32	38	20	32	3	46	39
NOV. 9	31	11	12	12	29	32	38	20	32	3	46	39
NOV. 10	31	13	13	14	29	32	38	20	32	3	46	39
NOV. 11	31	14	15	15	29	32	39	20	32	3	46	39
NOV. 12	32	16	17	17	30	32	39	20	32	3	46	39
NOV. 13	32	18	18	19	30	32	39	20	32	3	46	39
NOV. 14	32	19	20	20	30	33	39	20	32	3	46	39
NOV. 15	32	21	21	22	30	33	39	20	32	3	46	39
NOV. 16	32	22	23	23	30	33	39	20	32	3	46	39
NOV. 17	32	24	25	25	31	33	39	20	32	3	46	39
NOV. 18	32	26	26	27	31	33	39	20	32	3	46	39
NOV. 19	33	27	28	28	31	33	39	20	32	3	46	39
NOV. 20	33	29	29	30	31	34	39	20	32	3	46	39
NOV. 21	33	31	31	32	32	34	40	20	32	3	46	39
NOV. 22	33	32	33	34	32	34	40	20	32	3	46	39
NOV. 23	33	34	35	35	32	34	40	20	32	3	46	39
NOV. 24	33	36	37	37	32	34	40	20	33	3	46	39
NOV. 25	34	38	39	39	32	34	40	20	33	3	46	39
NOV. 26	34	40	40	41	33	35	40	20	33	3	46	39
NOV. 27	34	42	42	43	33	35	40	20	33	3	46	39
NOV. 28	34	44	44	45	33	35	40	20	33	3	46	39
NOV. 29	34	46	46	47	33	35	40	20	33	3	46	39
NOV. 30	34	47	48	1	33	35	40	20	33	3	46	39

December

Date & Time	SUN	MOON 1	MOON 2	MOON 3	MERCURY	VENUS	MARS	JUPITER	SATURN	URANUS	NEPTUNE	PLUTO
DEC. 1	34	1	2	2	34	35	41	20	33	3	46	39
DEC. 2	34	3	4	4	34	36	41	20	33	3	46	39
DEC. 3	35	5	6	6	34	36	41	20	33	3	46	39
DEC. 4	35	7	7	8	34	36	41	20	33	3	46	39
DEC. 5	35	9	9	10	34	36	41	20	33	3	46	39
DEC. 6	35	10	11	11	35	36	41	20	33	3	46	39
DEC. 7	35	12	13	13	35	36	41	20	33	3	46	39
DEC. 8	35	14	14	15	35	37	41	20	33	3	46	39
DEC. 9	35	15	16	17	35	37	41	20	33	3	46	39
DEC. 10	35	17	18	18	36	37	42	20	33	3	46	39
DEC. 11	36	19	19	20	36	37	42	20	33	3	46	39
DEC. 12	36	20	21	21	36	37	42	20	33	3	46	39
DEC. 13	36	22	22	23	36	37	42	20	33	3	46	39
DEC. 14	36	23	24	24	36	38	42	20	33	3	46	39
DEC. 15	36	25	26	26	37	38	42	20	33	3	46	39
DEC. 16	36	27	27	28	37	38	42	20	33	3	46	39
DEC. 17	36	28	29	29	37	38	42	20	33	3	46	39
DEC. 18	36	30	31	31	37	38	42	20	33	3	46	39
DEC. 19	37	32	32	33	37	38	42	20	33	3	46	39
DEC. 20	37	34	34	35	38	39	43	20	33	3	46	39
DEC. 21	37	35	36	37	38	39	43	20	33	3	46	39
DEC. 22	37	37	38	39	38	39	43	20	33	3	46	39
DEC. 23	37	39	40	40	38	39	43	20	33	3	46	39
DEC. 24	37	41	42	42	38	39	43	20	33	3	46	39
DEC. 25	37	43	44	44	39	39	43	20	33	3	46	39
DEC. 26	38	45	46	46	39	40	43	20	33	3	46	39
DEC. 27	38	47	48	48	39	40	43	20	33	3	46	39
DEC. 28	38	1	1	2	39	40	43	20	33	3	46	39
DEC. 29	38	3	3	4	40	40	43	20	33	3	46	39
DEC. 30	38	5	5	6	40	40	44	20	33	3	46	39
DEC. 31	38	6	7	7	40	40	44	20	33	3	46	39

MOON 1 ◗ 12:01 A.M. TO 8:00 A.M.　　**MOON 2** ◖ 8:01 A.M. TO 4:00 P.M.　　**MOON 3** ● 4:01 P.M. TO 12:00 A.M.

Use only one "moon" number. Choose the column closest to your time of birth. If your place of birth is not on Eastern Standard Time, be sure to read "How to Convert to Eastern Standard Time" at the beginning of this section.

2015

January

Date & Time	SUN	MOON 1	MOON 2	MOON 3	MERCURY	VENUS	MARS	JUPITER	SATURN	URANUS	NEPTUNE	PLUTO
JAN. 1	38	8	9	9	40	41	44	20	33	3	46	39
JAN. 2	38	10	10	11	40	41	44	20	33	3	46	39
JAN. 3	39	12	12	13	41	41	44	20	33	3	46	39
JAN. 4	39	13	14	14	41	41	44	20	33	3	46	39
JAN. 5	39	15	15	16	41	41	44	20	33	3	46	39
JAN. 6	39	17	17	18	41	41	44	20	33	3	46	39
JAN. 7	39	18	19	19	41	42	44	20	33	3	46	39
JAN. 8	39	20	20	21	42	42	45	20	33	3	46	39
JAN. 9	39	21	22	22	42	42	45	20	33	3	46	39
JAN. 10	40	23	23	24	42	42	45	20	33	3	46	39
JAN. 11	40	25	25	26	42	42	45	20	33	3	46	39
JAN. 12	40	26	27	27	42	42	45	20	33	3	46	39
JAN. 13	40	28	28	29	42	43	45	20	33	3	46	39
JAN. 14	40	29	30	30	43	43	45	20	33	3	46	39
JAN. 15	40	31	32	32	43	43	45	20	33	3	46	39
JAN. 16	40	33	33	34	43	43	45	20	33	3	46	39
JAN. 17	41	35	35	36	43	43	45	20	33	3	46	39
JAN. 18	41	36	37	38	43	43	46	20	33	3	46	39
JAN. 19	41	38	39	40	43	44	46	20	33	3	46	39
JAN. 20	41	40	41	42	43	44	46	20	33	3	46	39
JAN. 21	41	42	43	44	43	44	46	20	33	3	46	39
JAN. 22	41	44	45	46	43	44	46	20	33	3	46	39
JAN. 23	42	46	47	48	43	44	46	20	33	3	46	39
JAN. 24	42	48	1	2	43	44	46	20	33	3	46	39
JAN. 25	42	2	3	3	43	45	46	20	33	3	46	39
JAN. 26	42	4	5	5	43	45	46	20	33	3	46	39
JAN. 27	42	6	7	7	43	45	47	20	33	3	46	39
JAN. 28	42	8	8	9	43	45	47	19	33	3	46	39
JAN. 29	42	9	10	11	43	45	47	19	33	3	46	39
JAN. 30	42	11	12	12	42	45	47	19	33	3	46	39
JAN. 31	43	13	13	14	42	46	47	19	33	3	46	39

February

Date & Time	SUN	MOON 1	MOON 2	MOON 3	MERCURY	VENUS	MARS	JUPITER	SATURN	URANUS	NEPTUNE	PLUTO
FEB. 1	43	14	15	16	42	46	47	19	33	3	46	39
FEB. 2	43	16	17	17	42	46	47	19	33	3	46	39
FEB. 3	43	18	18	19	42	46	47	19	33	3	46	39
FEB. 4	43	19	20	20	42	46	47	19	33	3	46	39
FEB. 5	43	21	21	22	42	46	47	19	33	3	46	39
FEB. 6	43	22	23	24	41	47	48	19	33	3	46	39
FEB. 7	43	24	25	25	41	47	48	19	33	3	46	39
FEB. 8	44	26	26	27	41	47	48	19	33	3	46	39
FEB. 9	44	27	28	28	41	47	48	19	33	3	46	39
FEB. 10	44	29	29	30	41	47	48	19	34	3	46	39
FEB. 11	44	30	31	32	41	47	48	19	34	3	46	39
FEB. 12	44	32	33	33	41	48	48	19	34	3	46	39
FEB. 13	44	34	34	35	41	48	48	19	34	3	46	39
FEB. 14	44	36	36	37	41	48	48	19	34	3	46	39
FEB. 15	44	37	38	39	41	48	48	19	34	3	46	39
FEB. 16	45	39	40	41	41	48	1	19	34	3	46	39
FEB. 17	45	41	42	43	41	48	1	19	34	3	46	39
FEB. 18	45	43	44	45	41	1	1	19	34	3	46	39
FEB. 19	45	45	46	47	42	1	1	19	34	3	46	39
FEB. 20	45	47	48	1	42	1	1	19	34	3	46	39
FEB. 21	45	1	2	3	42	1	1	19	34	3	46	39
FEB. 22	45	3	4	5	42	1	1	19	34	3	46	39
FEB. 23	46	5	6	7	42	1	1	19	34	3	46	39
FEB. 24	46	7	8	8	42	2	1	19	34	3	46	39
FEB. 25	46	9	10	10	42	2	1	19	34	3	46	39
FEB. 26	46	11	11	12	42	2	2	19	34	3	46	39
FEB. 27	46	12	13	14	43	2	2	19	34	3	46	39
FEB. 28	46	14	15	15	43	2	2	19	34	3	46	39

MOON 1 ◗ 12:01 A.M. TO 8:00 A.M.   **MOON 2** ◖ 8:01 A.M. TO 4:00 P.M.   **MOON 3** ● 4:01 P.M. TO 12:00 A.M.

Use only one "moon" number. Choose the column closest to your time of birth. If your place of birth is not on Eastern Standard Time, be sure to read "How to Convert to Eastern Standard Time" at the beginning of this section.

2015

March

April

Date & Time	SUN ☉	MOON 1 ◖	MOON 2 ◑	MOON 3 ●	MERCURY	VENUS	MARS	JUPITER	SATURN	URANUS	NEPTUNE	PLUTO
MAR. 1	46	16	16	17	43	2	2	19	34	3	46	39
MAR. 2	46	17	18	18	43	3	2	19	34	3	46	39
MAR. 3	47	19	19	20	43	3	2	19	34	3	46	39
MAR. 4	47	21	21	22	43	3	2	19	34	3	46	39
MAR. 5	47	22	23	23	43	3	2	19	34	3	46	39
MAR. 6	47	24	24	25	44	3	2	19	34	3	46	39
MAR. 7	47	25	26	26	44	3	3	19	34	3	46	39
MAR. 8	47	27	27	28	44	3	3	19	34	3	46	39
MAR. 9	47	28	29	29	44	4	3	19	34	3	46	39
MAR. 10	47	30	31	31	44	4	3	19	34	3	46	39
MAR. 11	48	32	32	33	45	4	3	19	34	3	46	39
MAR. 12	48	33	34	34	45	4	3	19	34	3	46	39
MAR. 13	48	35	36	36	45	4	3	19	34	3	46	39
MAR. 14	48	37	37	38	45	4	3	19	34	3	46	39
MAR. 15	48	39	39	40	45	5	3	19	34	3	46	39
MAR. 16	48	41	41	42	46	5	3	19	34	3	46	39
MAR. 17	48	42	43	44	46	5	4	19	34	3	46	39
MAR. 18	48	44	45	46	46	5	4	19	34	3	46	39
MAR. 19	1	46	47	48	46	5	4	19	34	3	46	39
MAR. 20	1	1	1	2	46	5	4	19	34	3	46	39
MAR. 21	1	3	3	4	47	6	4	19	34	3	46	39
MAR. 22	1	5	5	6	47	6	4	19	34	3	46	39
MAR. 23	1	6	7	8	47	6	4	19	34	3	46	39
MAR. 24	1	8	9	10	47	6	4	19	34	3	46	39
MAR. 25	2	10	11	11	48	6	4	19	34	3	46	39
MAR. 26	2	12	12	13	48	6	4	19	34	3	46	39
MAR. 27	2	14	14	15	48	7	5	19	34	3	46	39
MAR. 28	2	15	16	16	48	7	5	19	34	3	46	39
MAR. 29	2	17	17	18	1	7	5	19	34	3	46	39
MAR. 30	2	19	19	20	1	7	5	19	34	3	46	39
MAR. 31	2	20	21	21	1	7	5	19	34	3	46	39

Date & Time	SUN ☉	MOON 1 ◖	MOON 2 ◑	MOON 3 ●	MERCURY	VENUS	MARS	JUPITER	SATURN	URANUS	NEPTUNE	PLUTO
APR. 1	2	22	22	23	1	7	5	19	34	3	46	39
APR. 2	2	23	24	24	2	7	5	19	34	3	46	39
APR. 3	3	25	25	26	2	8	5	19	34	3	46	39
APR. 4	3	26	27	27	2	8	5	19	34	3	46	39
APR. 5	3	28	29	29	2	8	5	19	34	3	46	39
APR. 6	3	30	30	31	3	8	6	19	34	3	46	39
APR. 7	3	31	32	32	3	8	6	19	34	3	46	39
APR. 8	3	33	34	34	3	8	6	19	34	3	46	39
APR. 9	3	35	35	36	3	9	6	19	34	3	46	39
APR. 10	3	36	37	38	4	9	6	19	34	3	46	39
APR. 11	4	38	39	39	4	9	6	19	34	3	46	39
APR. 12	4	40	41	41	4	9	6	19	34	3	46	39
APR. 13	4	42	42	43	4	9	6	19	34	3	46	39
APR. 14	4	44	44	45	5	9	6	19	34	3	46	39
APR. 15	4	46	46	47	5	10	6	19	34	3	46	39
APR. 16	4	48	48	1	5	10	6	19	34	3	46	39
APR. 17	4	2	2	3	6	10	7	19	34	3	46	39
APR. 18	4	4	4	5	6	10	7	19	33	3	46	39
APR. 19	5	6	6	7	6	10	7	19	33	3	46	39
APR. 20	5	8	8	9	6	10	7	19	33	3	46	39
APR. 21	5	9	10	11	6	10	7	19	33	3	46	39
APR. 22	5	11	12	12	7	11	7	19	33	3	46	39
APR. 23	5	13	14	14	7	11	7	19	33	3	46	39
APR. 24	5	15	15	16	7	11	7	19	33	3	46	39
APR. 25	6	16	17	17	8	11	7	19	33	3	46	39
APR. 26	6	18	19	19	8	11	7	19	33	3	46	39
APR. 27	6	20	20	21	8	11	8	19	33	3	46	39
APR. 28	6	21	22	22	8	12	8	19	33	3	46	39
APR. 29	6	23	23	24	9	12	8	19	33	3	46	39
APR. 30	6	24	25	25	9	12	8	19	33	3	46	39

MOON 1 ◖ 12:01 A.M. TO 8:00 A.M.   **MOON 2** ◑ 8:01 A.M. TO 4:00 P.M.   **MOON 3** ● 4:01 P.M. TO 12:00 A.M.

Use only one "moon" number. Choose the column closest to your time of birth. If your place of birth is not on Eastern Standard Time, be sure to read "How to Convert to Eastern Standard Time" at the beginning of this section.

2015

May

Date & Time	SUN	MOON 1	MOON 2	MOON 3	MERCURY	VENUS	MARS	JUPITER	SATURN	URANUS	NEPTUNE	PLUTO
MAY 1	6	26	26	27	9	12	8	19	33	3	46	39
MAY 2	6	28	28	29	9	12	8	19	33	3	46	39
MAY 3	7	29	30	30	9	12	8	19	33	3	46	39
MAY 4	7	31	31	32	10	12	8	19	33	3	46	39
MAY 5	7	33	33	34	10	13	8	19	33	3	46	39
MAY 6	7	34	35	35	10	13	8	19	33	3	46	39
MAY 7	7	36	37	37	10	13	9	19	33	3	46	39
MAY 8	7	38	38	39	10	13	9	19	33	3	46	39
MAY 9	7	40	40	41	10	13	9	19	33	3	46	39
MAY 10	7	41	42	43	10	13	9	19	33	3	46	39
MAY 11	8	43	44	45	10	13	9	19	33	3	46	39
MAY 12	8	45	46	46	10	14	9	19	33	3	46	39
MAY 13	8	47	48	48	11	14	9	19	33	3	46	39
MAY 14	8	1	2	2	11	14	9	19	33	3	46	39
MAY 15	8	3	4	4	11	14	9	19	33	3	46	39
MAY 16	8	5	5	6	11	14	9	19	33	3	46	39
MAY 17	8	7	7	8	11	14	9	19	33	3	46	39
MAY 18	8	9	9	10	11	14	10	19	33	3	46	39
MAY 19	9	10	11	12	11	15	10	19	33	3	46	39
MAY 20	9	12	13	13	11	15	10	19	33	3	46	39
MAY 21	9	14	15	15	11	15	10	19	33	3	46	39
MAY 22	9	16	16	17	11	15	10	19	33	3	46	39
MAY 23	9	17	18	19	11	15	10	19	33	3	46	39
MAY 24	9	19	20	20	11	15	10	19	33	3	46	39
MAY 25	10	21	21	22	11	15	10	19	33	4	46	39
MAY 26	10	22	23	23	10	16	10	19	33	4	46	39
MAY 27	10	24	24	25	10	16	10	19	33	4	46	39
MAY 28	10	25	26	27	10	16	10	19	33	4	46	39
MAY 29	10	27	28	28	10	16	11	19	33	4	46	39
MAY 30	10	29	29	30	10	16	11	19	33	4	46	39
MAY 31	10	30	31	31	10	16	11	19	33	4	46	39

June

Date & Time	SUN	MOON 1	MOON 2	MOON 3	MERCURY	VENUS	MARS	JUPITER	SATURN	URANUS	NEPTUNE	PLUTO
JUN. 1	10	32	33	33	10	16	11	19	33	4	46	39
JUN. 2	10	34	34	35	10	17	11	19	33	4	46	39
JUN. 3	11	35	36	37	10	17	11	19	33	4	46	39
JUN. 4	11	37	38	38	10	17	11	19	33	4	46	39
JUN. 5	11	39	40	40	10	17	11	19	33	4	46	39
JUN. 6	11	41	42	42	10	17	11	19	33	4	46	39
JUN. 7	11	43	43	44	10	17	11	19	33	4	46	39
JUN. 8	11	45	45	46	10	17	11	19	33	4	46	39
JUN. 9	11	47	47	48	10	17	12	19	33	4	46	39
JUN. 10	11	48	1	2	10	18	12	19	33	4	46	39
JUN. 11	12	2	3	4	10	18	12	19	33	4	46	39
JUN. 12	12	4	5	5	10	18	12	19	33	4	46	39
JUN. 13	12	6	7	7	10	18	12	19	33	4	46	39
JUN. 14	12	8	9	9	10	18	12	19	33	4	46	39
JUN. 15	12	10	10	11	10	18	12	19	33	4	46	39
JUN. 16	12	12	12	13	10	18	12	19	33	4	46	39
JUN. 17	12	13	14	15	10	18	12	20	33	4	46	39
JUN. 18	12	15	16	16	10	18	12	20	33	4	46	39
JUN. 19	13	17	17	18	10	19	12	20	33	4	46	39
JUN. 20	13	19	19	20	10	19	13	20	33	4	46	39
JUN. 21	13	20	21	21	10	19	13	20	33	4	46	39
JUN. 22	13	22	22	23	10	19	13	20	33	4	46	39
JUN. 23	13	24	24	25	10	19	13	20	33	4	46	39
JUN. 24	13	25	25	26	10	19	13	20	33	4	46	39
JUN. 25	14	27	27	28	11	19	13	20	33	4	46	39
JUN. 26	14	28	29	29	11	19	13	20	33	4	46	39
JUN. 27	14	30	30	31	11	19	13	20	33	4	46	39
JUN. 28	14	31	32	33	11	20	13	20	33	4	46	39
JUN. 29	14	33	34	34	11	20	13	20	33	4	46	39
JUN. 30	14	35	35	36	11	20	13	20	33	4	46	39

MOON 1 ◐ 12:01 A.M. TO 8:00 A.M.   **MOON 2** ◑ 8:01 A.M. TO 4:00 P.M.   **MOON 3** ● 4:01 P.M. TO 12:00 A.M.
Use only one "moon" number. Choose the column closest to your time of birth. If your place of birth is not on Eastern Standard Time, be sure to read "How to Convert to Eastern Standard Time" at the beginning of this section.

2015

July

August

Date & Time	SUN	MOON 1	MOON 2	MOON 3	MERCURY	VENUS	MARS	JUPITER	SATURN	URANUS	NEPTUNE	PLUTO
JUL. 1	14	37	37	38	11	20	14	20	33	4	46	39
JUL. 2	14	38	39	40	12	20	14	20	33	4	46	39
JUL. 3	15	40	41	42	12	20	14	20	33	4	46	39
JUL. 4	15	42	43	44	12	20	14	20	33	4	46	39
JUL. 5	15	44	45	45	12	20	14	20	33	4	46	39
JUL. 6	15	46	47	47	12	20	14	20	33	4	46	39
JUL. 7	15	48	1	1	13	20	14	20	33	4	46	39
JUL. 8	15	2	3	3	13	20	14	20	33	4	46	39
JUL. 9	15	4	4	5	13	20	14	20	33	4	46	39
JUL. 10	15	6	6	7	13	21	14	20	33	4	46	39
JUL. 11	16	8	8	9	14	21	14	20	33	4	46	39
JUL. 12	16	9	10	11	14	21	15	20	33	4	46	39
JUL. 13	16	11	12	12	14	21	15	20	33	4	46	39
JUL. 14	16	13	13	14	14	21	15	20	33	4	46	39
JUL. 15	16	15	15	16	15	21	15	20	33	4	46	39
JUL. 16	16	16	17	17	15	21	15	20	33	4	46	39
JUL. 17	16	18	19	19	15	21	15	20	33	4	46	39
JUL. 18	16	20	20	21	15	21	15	20	33	4	46	39
JUL. 19	17	21	22	22	16	21	15	20	33	4	46	39
JUL. 20	17	23	23	24	16	21	15	20	33	4	46	39
JUL. 21	17	24	25	25	16	21	15	20	33	4	46	39
JUL. 22	17	26	27	27	17	21	15	20	33	4	46	39
JUL. 23	17	28	28	29	17	21	16	20	33	4	46	39
JUL. 24	17	29	30	30	17	21	16	20	33	4	46	39
JUL. 25	17	31	31	32	17	21	16	20	33	4	46	39
JUL. 26	18	32	33	34	18	21	16	21	33	4	46	39
JUL. 27	18	34	35	35	18	21	16	21	33	4	46	39
JUL. 28	18	36	37	37	18	21	16	21	33	4	46	39
JUL. 29	18	38	38	39	19	21	16	21	33	4	46	39
JUL. 30	18	40	40	41	19	21	16	21	33	4	46	39
JUL. 31	18	42	42	43	19	21	16	21	33	4	46	39

Date & Time	SUN	MOON 1	MOON 2	MOON 3	MERCURY	VENUS	MARS	JUPITER	SATURN	URANUS	NEPTUNE	PLUTO
AUG. 1	18	44	44	45	19	21	16	21	33	4	46	39
AUG. 2	18	45	46	47	20	21	16	21	33	4	46	39
AUG. 3	19	47	48	1	20	21	16	21	33	4	46	39
AUG. 4	19	1	2	3	20	21	17	21	33	4	46	39
AUG. 5	19	3	4	5	20	21	17	21	33	4	46	39
AUG. 6	19	5	6	6	21	21	17	21	33	4	46	39
AUG. 7	19	7	8	8	21	21	17	21	33	4	46	39
AUG. 8	19	9	10	10	21	21	17	21	33	4	46	39
AUG. 9	19	11	11	12	21	21	17	21	33	4	46	39
AUG. 10	19	12	13	14	22	20	17	21	33	4	46	39
AUG. 11	20	14	15	15	22	20	17	21	33	4	46	39
AUG. 12	20	16	16	17	22	20	17	21	33	4	46	39
AUG. 13	20	18	18	19	22	20	17	21	33	4	46	39
AUG. 14	20	19	20	20	22	20	17	21	33	4	46	39
AUG. 15	20	21	21	22	23	20	18	21	33	4	46	39
AUG. 16	20	22	23	23	23	20	18	21	33	4	46	39
AUG. 17	20	24	24	25	23	20	18	21	33	4	46	39
AUG. 18	20	26	26	27	23	20	18	21	33	4	46	39
AUG. 19	21	27	28	28	23	20	18	21	33	4	46	39
AUG. 20	21	29	29	30	24	20	18	21	33	4	46	39
AUG. 21	21	30	31	31	24	20	18	21	33	4	46	39
AUG. 22	21	32	32	33	24	19	18	21	33	4	46	39
AUG. 23	21	34	34	35	24	19	18	21	33	4	46	39
AUG. 24	21	35	36	36	24	19	18	21	33	4	46	39
AUG. 25	21	37	38	38	25	19	18	21	33	4	46	39
AUG. 26	22	39	39	40	25	19	18	21	33	4	46	39
AUG. 27	22	41	41	42	25	19	19	21	33	4	46	39
AUG. 28	22	43	43	44	25	19	19	21	33	4	46	39
AUG. 29	22	45	45	46	25	19	19	21	33	4	46	39
AUG. 30	22	47	47	48	25	19	19	22	33	4	46	39
AUG. 31	22	1	1	2	26	19	19	22	33	4	46	39

MOON 1 ◗ 12:01 A.M. TO 8:00 A.M.   **MOON 2** ◐ 8:01 A.M. TO 4:00 P.M.   **MOON 3** ● 4:01 P.M. TO 12:00 A.M.

Use only one "moon" number. Choose the column closest to your time of birth. If your place of birth is not on Eastern Standard Time, be sure to read "How to Convert to Eastern Standard Time" at the beginning of this section.

September

October

Date & Time	SUN	MOON 1 ◐	MOON 2 ◑	MOON 3 ●	MERCURY	VENUS	MARS	JUPITER	SATURN	URANUS	NEPTUNE	PLUTO
SEP. 1	22	3	3	4	26	19	19	22	33	4	46	39
SEP. 2	22	5	5	6	26	19	19	22	33	4	46	39
SEP. 3	23	7	7	8	26	19	19	22	33	4	46	39
SEP. 4	23	8	9	10	26	19	19	22	33	4	46	39
SEP. 5	23	10	11	11	26	19	19	22	33	4	46	39
SEP. 6	23	12	13	13	26	19	19	22	33	4	46	39
SEP. 7	23	14	14	15	26	19	19	22	33	4	46	39
SEP. 8	23	15	16	17	27	19	20	22	33	4	46	39
SEP. 9	23	17	18	18	27	19	20	22	33	4	46	39
SEP. 10	23	19	19	20	27	19	20	22	33	4	46	39
SEP. 11	24	20	21	21	27	19	20	22	33	4	46	39
SEP. 12	24	22	22	23	27	19	20	22	33	4	46	39
SEP. 13	24	24	24	25	27	19	20	22	33	4	46	39
SEP. 14	24	25	26	26	27	19	20	22	33	4	46	39
SEP. 15	24	27	27	28	27	19	20	22	33	4	46	39
SEP. 16	24	28	29	29	27	19	20	22	33	4	46	39
SEP. 17	24	30	30	31	27	19	20	22	33	4	46	39
SEP. 18	24	31	32	33	27	19	20	22	33	4	46	39
SEP. 19	25	33	34	34	27	19	20	22	33	4	46	39
SEP. 20	25	35	35	36	27	19	21	22	33	4	46	39
SEP. 21	25	36	37	38	27	19	21	22	33	4	46	39
SEP. 22	25	38	39	39	27	19	21	22	33	4	46	39
SEP. 23	25	40	41	41	27	20	21	22	33	4	46	39
SEP. 24	25	42	42	43	27	20	21	22	33	4	46	39
SEP. 25	26	44	44	45	27	20	21	22	33	4	46	39
SEP. 26	26	46	46	47	27	20	21	22	33	4	46	39
SEP. 27	26	48	48	1	26	20	21	22	33	4	46	39
SEP. 28	26	2	2	3	26	20	21	22	33	4	46	39
SEP. 29	26	4	4	5	26	20	21	22	33	4	46	39
SEP. 30	26	6	6	7	26	20	21	22	33	3	46	39

Date & Time	SUN	MOON 1 ◐	MOON 2 ◑	MOON 3 ●	MERCURY	VENUS	MARS	JUPITER	SATURN	URANUS	NEPTUNE	PLUTO
OCT. 1	26	8	8	9	26	20	21	22	33	3	46	39
OCT. 2	26	10	10	11	26	20	22	22	33	3	46	39
OCT. 3	27	12	12	13	26	20	22	22	33	3	46	39
OCT. 4	27	13	14	14	25	20	22	22	33	3	46	39
OCT. 5	27	15	16	16	25	21	22	23	33	3	46	39
OCT. 6	27	17	17	18	25	21	22	23	33	3	46	39
OCT. 7	27	18	19	19	25	21	22	23	33	3	46	39
OCT. 8	27	20	21	21	25	21	22	23	33	3	46	39
OCT. 9	27	22	22	23	25	21	23	23	33	3	46	39
OCT. 10	27	23	24	24	25	21	23	23	33	3	46	39
OCT. 11	28	25	25	26	25	21	22	23	33	3	46	39
OCT. 12	28	26	27	27	25	21	22	23	33	3	46	39
OCT. 13	28	28	28	29	25	21	22	23	33	3	46	39
OCT. 14	28	29	30	31	25	22	23	23	33	3	46	39
OCT. 15	28	31	32	32	25	22	23	23	33	3	46	39
OCT. 16	28	33	33	34	26	22	23	23	33	3	46	39
OCT. 17	28	34	35	35	26	22	23	23	33	3	46	39
OCT. 18	28	36	37	37	26	22	23	23	33	3	46	39
OCT. 19	29	38	38	39	26	22	23	23	33	3	46	39
OCT. 20	29	39	40	41	26	22	23	23	33	3	46	39
OCT. 21	29	41	42	42	26	22	23	23	33	3	46	39
OCT. 22	29	43	44	44	27	23	23	23	33	3	46	39
OCT. 23	29	45	46	46	27	23	23	23	33	3	46	39
OCT. 24	29	47	48	48	27	23	23	23	33	3	46	39
OCT. 25	29	1	2	2	27	23	23	23	33	3	46	39
OCT. 26	30	3	4	4	27	23	23	24	33	3	46	39
OCT. 27	30	5	6	6	28	23	24	23	33	3	46	39
OCT. 28	30	7	8	8	28	23	24	23	33	3	46	39
OCT. 29	30	9	10	10	28	24	24	23	33	3	46	39
OCT. 30	30	11	11	12	28	24	24	23	33	3	46	39
OCT. 31	30	13	13	14	29	24	24	23	34	3	46	39

MOON 1 ◐ 12:01 A.M. TO 8:00 A.M.   **MOON 2** ◑ 8:01 A.M. TO 4:00 P.M.   **MOON 3** ● 4:01 P.M. TO 12:00 A.M.
Use only one "moon" number. Choose the column closest to your time of birth. If your place of birth is not on
Eastern Standard Time, be sure to read "How to Convert to Eastern Standard Time" at the beginning of this section.

2015

November

Date & Time	SUN	MOON 1	MOON 2	MOON 3	MERCURY	VENUS	MARS	JUPITER	SATURN	URANUS	NEPTUNE	PLUTO
NOV. 1	30	14	15	16	29	24	24	23	34	3	46	39
NOV. 2	30	16	17	17	29	24	24	23	34	3	46	39
NOV. 3	31	18	18	19	29	24	24	23	34	3	46	39
NOV. 4	31	20	20	21	29	24	24	23	34	3	46	39
NOV. 5	31	21	22	22	30	24	24	23	34	3	46	39
NOV. 6	31	23	23	24	30	25	24	23	34	3	46	39
NOV. 7	31	24	25	25	30	25	25	23	34	3	46	39
NOV. 8	31	26	26	27	30	25	25	23	34	3	46	39
NOV. 9	31	27	28	28	30	25	25	23	34	3	46	39
NOV. 10	31	29	30	30	31	25	25	23	34	3	46	39
NOV. 11	31	31	31	32	31	25	25	23	34	3	46	39
NOV. 12	32	32	33	33	31	25	25	23	34	3	46	39
NOV. 13	32	34	34	35	31	25	25	23	34	3	46	39
NOV. 14	32	36	36	37	32	26	25	23	34	3	46	39
NOV. 15	32	37	38	38	32	26	25	23	34	3	46	39
NOV. 16	32	39	40	40	32	26	25	24	34	3	46	39
NOV. 17	32	41	41	42	32	26	25	24	34	3	46	39
NOV. 18	32	43	43	44	32	26	25	24	34	3	46	39
NOV. 19	33	44	45	46	33	27	25	24	34	3	46	39
NOV. 20	33	46	47	48	33	27	26	24	34	3	46	39
NOV. 21	33	48	1	1	33	27	26	24	34	3	46	39
NOV. 22	33	2	3	3	33	27	26	24	34	3	46	39
NOV. 23	33	4	5	5	33	27	26	24	34	3	46	39
NOV. 24	33	6	7	7	34	27	26	24	34	3	46	39
NOV. 25	34	8	9	9	34	27	26	24	34	3	46	39
NOV. 26	34	10	11	11	34	28	26	24	34	3	46	39
NOV. 27	34	12	12	13	34	28	26	24	34	3	46	39
NOV. 28	34	14	14	15	35	28	26	24	34	3	46	39
NOV. 29	34	16	16	17	35	28	26	24	34	3	46	39
NOV. 30	34	17	18	18	35	28	26	24	34	3	46	39

December

Date & Time	SUN	MOON 1	MOON 2	MOON 3	MERCURY	VENUS	MARS	JUPITER	SATURN	URANUS	NEPTUNE	PLUTO
DEC. 1	34	19	20	20	35	28	26	24	34	3	46	39
DEC. 2	34	21	21	22	35	29	26	24	34	3	46	39
DEC. 3	35	22	23	23	36	29	27	24	34	3	46	39
DEC. 4	35	24	24	25	36	29	27	24	34	3	46	39
DEC. 5	35	25	26	26	36	29	27	24	34	3	46	39
DEC. 6	35	27	27	28	36	29	27	24	34	3	46	39
DEC. 7	35	29	29	30	36	29	27	24	34	3	46	39
DEC. 8	35	30	31	31	37	29	27	24	34	3	46	39
DEC. 9	35	32	32	33	37	30	27	24	34	3	46	39
DEC. 10	35	33	34	35	37	30	27	24	34	3	46	39
DEC. 11	36	35	36	36	37	30	27	24	34	3	46	39
DEC. 12	36	37	37	38	37	30	27	24	34	3	46	39
DEC. 13	36	39	39	40	38	30	27	24	34	3	46	39
DEC. 14	36	40	41	42	38	30	27	24	34	3	46	39
DEC. 15	36	42	43	43	38	31	28	24	34	3	46	39
DEC. 16	36	44	45	45	38	31	28	24	34	3	46	39
DEC. 17	36	46	46	47	38	31	28	24	34	3	46	39
DEC. 18	36	48	48	1	39	31	28	24	34	3	46	39
DEC. 19	37	2	2	3	39	31	28	24	34	3	46	39
DEC. 20	37	3	4	5	39	31	28	24	34	3	46	39
DEC. 21	37	5	6	7	39	32	28	24	34	3	46	39
DEC. 22	37	7	8	9	39	32	28	24	34	3	46	39
DEC. 23	37	9	10	10	40	32	28	24	34	3	46	39
DEC. 24	37	11	12	12	40	32	28	24	34	3	46	39
DEC. 25	37	13	14	14	40	32	28	24	34	3	46	39
DEC. 26	38	15	15	16	40	32	28	24	34	3	46	39
DEC. 27	38	17	17	18	40	32	28	24	34	3	46	39
DEC. 28	38	18	19	19	40	33	28	24	34	3	46	39
DEC. 29	38	20	21	21	41	33	29	24	34	3	46	39
DEC. 30	38	22	22	23	41	33	29	24	34	3	46	39
DEC. 31	38	23	24	24	41	33	29	24	34	3	46	39

MOON 1 ☽ 12:01 A.M. TO 8:00 A.M.　　**MOON 2** ☽ 8:01 A.M. TO 4:00 P.M.　　**MOON 3** ● 4:01 P.M. TO 12:00 A.M.

Use only one "moon" number. Choose the column closest to your time of birth. If your place of birth is not on Eastern Standard Time, be sure to read "How to Convert to Eastern Standard Time" at the beginning of this section.

2016

January

Date & Time	SUN ☼	MOON 1 ◐	MOON 2 ◑	MOON 3 ●	MERCURY	VENUS	MARS	JUPITER	SATURN	URANUS	NEPTUNE	PLUTO
JAN. 1	38	25	25	26	41	33	29	24	34	3	46	39
JAN. 2	38	26	27	27	41	33	29	24	34	3	46	39
JAN. 3	39	28	29	29	41	34	29	24	34	3	46	39
JAN. 4	39	30	30	31	41	34	29	24	34	3	46	39
JAN. 5	39	31	32	32	41	34	29	24	35	3	46	39
JAN. 6	39	33	33	34	41	34	29	24	35	3	46	39
JAN. 7	39	35	35	36	41	34	29	24	35	3	46	39
JAN. 8	39	36	37	37	41	34	29	24	35	3	46	39
JAN. 9	39	38	39	39	41	35	29	24	35	3	46	39
JAN. 10	40	40	40	41	41	35	29	24	35	3	46	39
JAN. 11	40	42	42	43	41	35	30	24	35	3	46	39
JAN. 12	40	43	44	45	41	35	30	24	35	3	46	39
JAN. 13	40	45	46	47	40	35	30	24	35	3	46	39
JAN. 14	40	47	48	1	40	35	30	24	35	3	46	39
JAN. 15	40	1	2	2	40	36	30	24	35	3	46	39
JAN. 16	40	3	4	4	40	36	30	24	35	3	46	39
JAN. 17	41	5	6	6	40	36	30	24	35	3	46	39
JAN. 18	41	7	7	8	40	36	30	24	35	3	46	39
JAN. 19	41	9	9	10	39	36	30	24	35	3	46	39
JAN. 20	41	10	11	12	39	36	30	24	35	3	46	39
JAN. 21	41	12	13	14	39	37	30	24	35	3	46	39
JAN. 22	41	14	15	15	39	37	30	24	35	3	46	39
JAN. 23	42	16	17	17	39	37	30	24	35	3	46	39
JAN. 24	42	18	18	19	39	37	30	24	35	3	46	39
JAN. 25	42	19	20	20	39	37	31	24	35	3	46	39
JAN. 26	42	21	22	22	39	37	31	24	35	3	46	39
JAN. 27	42	23	23	24	39	38	31	24	35	3	46	39
JAN. 28	42	24	25	25	39	38	31	24	35	3	46	39
JAN. 29	42	26	26	27	39	38	31	24	35	3	46	39
JAN. 30	42	27	28	29	39	38	31	24	35	3	46	39
JAN. 31	43	29	30	30	39	38	31	24	35	3	46	39

February

Date & Time	SUN ☼	MOON 1 ◐	MOON 2 ◑	MOON 3 ●	MERCURY	VENUS	MARS	JUPITER	SATURN	URANUS	NEPTUNE	PLUTO
FEB. 1	43	31	31	32	39	38	31	24	35	3	46	39
FEB. 2	43	32	33	33	39	39	31	24	35	3	46	39
FEB. 3	43	34	34	35	39	39	31	24	35	3	46	39
FEB. 4	43	36	36	37	40	39	31	24	35	3	46	39
FEB. 5	43	37	38	38	40	39	31	24	35	3	46	39
FEB. 6	43	39	40	40	40	39	31	24	35	3	46	39
FEB. 7	43	41	42	42	40	39	31	24	35	3	46	39
FEB. 8	44	43	43	44	40	39	31	24	35	3	46	39
FEB. 9	44	45	45	46	40	40	31	24	35	3	46	39
FEB. 10	44	47	47	48	40	40	32	24	35	3	46	39
FEB. 11	44	1	1	2	41	40	32	24	35	3	46	39
FEB. 12	44	3	3	4	41	40	32	24	35	3	46	39
FEB. 13	44	4	5	6	41	40	32	24	35	3	46	39
FEB. 14	44	6	7	8	41	40	32	24	35	3	46	39
FEB. 15	44	8	9	9	41	41	32	24	35	3	46	39
FEB. 16	45	10	11	11	41	41	32	24	35	3	46	39
FEB. 17	45	12	12	13	42	41	32	24	35	3	46	39
FEB. 18	45	14	14	15	42	41	32	24	35	3	46	39
FEB. 19	45	15	16	17	42	41	32	24	35	3	46	39
FEB. 20	45	17	18	18	42	41	32	24	35	3	46	39
FEB. 21	45	19	19	20	42	42	32	24	35	3	46	39
FEB. 22	45	21	21	22	42	42	32	24	35	3	46	39
FEB. 23	46	22	23	23	43	42	32	24	35	3	46	39
FEB. 24	46	24	24	25	43	42	32	24	35	3	46	39
FEB. 25	46	25	26	26	43	42	32	24	35	3	46	39
FEB. 26	46	27	27	28	43	42	33	24	35	3	46	39
FEB. 27	46	29	29	30	43	43	33	24	35	3	46	39
FEB. 28	46	30	31	31	44	43	33	24	35	3	46	39
FEB. 29	46	32	32	33	44	43	33	24	35	3	46	39

MOON 1 ◐ 12:01 A.M. TO 8:00 A.M. **MOON 2** ◑ 8:01 A.M. TO 4:00 P.M. **MOON 3** ● 4:01 P.M. TO 12:00 A.M.

Use only one "moon" number. Choose the column closest to your time of birth. If your place of birth is not on Eastern Standard Time, be sure to read "How to Convert to Eastern Standard Time" at the beginning of this section.

Date & Time	SUN	MOON 1	MOON 2	MOON 3	MERCURY	VENUS	MARS	JUPITER	SATURN	URANUS	NEPTUNE	PLUTO
MAR. 1	46	33	34	34	44	43	33	24	35	3	46	39
MAR. 2	46	35	35	36	44	43	33	24	35	3	46	39
MAR. 3	47	37	37	38	44	43	33	23	35	3	46	39
MAR. 4	47	38	39	40	45	44	33	23	35	3	46	39
MAR. 5	47	40	41	41	45	44	33	23	35	3	46	39
MAR. 6	47	42	43	43	45	44	33	23	35	3	46	39
MAR. 7	47	44	44	45	45	44	33	23	35	3	46	39
MAR. 8	47	46	46	47	46	44	33	23	35	3	46	39
MAR. 9	47	48	48	1	46	44	33	23	35	3	46	39
MAR. 10	47	2	2	3	46	45	33	23	35	3	46	39
MAR. 11	48	4	4	5	46	45	33	23	35	3	46	39
MAR. 12	48	6	6	7	47	45	33	23	35	3	46	39
MAR. 13	48	8	8	9	47	45	33	23	35	3	46	39
MAR. 14	48	10	10	11	47	45	33	23	35	3	46	39
MAR. 15	48	11	12	13	47	45	33	23	35	4	46	39
MAR. 16	48	13	14	14	47	45	33	23	35	4	46	39
MAR. 17	48	15	16	16	48	45	33	23	35	4	46	39
MAR. 18	48	17	17	18	48	46	34	23	35	4	46	39
MAR. 19	1	18	19	20	48	46	34	23	35	4	46	39
MAR. 20	1	20	21	21	48	46	34	23	35	4	46	39
MAR. 21	1	22	22	23	1	46	34	23	35	4	46	39
MAR. 22	1	23	24	24	1	47	34	23	35	4	46	39
MAR. 23	1	25	25	26	1	47	34	23	35	4	46	39
MAR. 24	1	27	27	28	2	47	34	23	35	4	46	39
MAR. 25	2	28	29	29	2	47	34	23	35	4	46	39
MAR. 26	2	30	30	31	2	47	34	23	35	4	46	39
MAR. 27	2	31	32	32	2	47	34	23	35	4	46	39
MAR. 28	2	33	33	34	3	48	34	23	35	4	46	39
MAR. 29	2	34	35	36	3	48	34	23	35	4	46	39
MAR. 30	2	36	37	37	3	48	34	23	35	4	46	39
MAR. 31	2	38	38	39	3	48	34	23	35	4	46	39

Date & Time	SUN	MOON 1	MOON 2	MOON 3	MERCURY	VENUS	MARS	JUPITER	SATURN	URANUS	NEPTUNE	PLUTO
APR. 1	2	39	40	41	4	48	34	23	35	4	46	39
APR. 2	2	41	42	42	4	48	34	23	35	4	46	39
APR. 3	3	43	44	44	4	1	34	23	35	4	46	39
APR. 4	3	45	46	46	5	1	34	23	35	4	46	39
APR. 5	3	47	47	48	5	1	34	23	35	4	46	39
APR. 6	3	1	1	2	5	1	34	23	35	4	46	39
APR. 7	3	3	4	4	5	1	34	23	35	4	46	39
APR. 8	3	5	6	6	6	1	34	23	35	4	46	39
APR. 9	3	7	8	8	6	2	34	23	35	4	46	39
APR. 10	3	9	10	10	6	2	34	23	35	4	46	39
APR. 11	4	11	11	12	6	2	34	23	35	4	46	39
APR. 12	4	13	13	14	6	2	34	23	35	4	46	39
APR. 13	4	15	15	16	7	2	34	23	35	4	46	39
APR. 14	4	16	17	17	7	2	34	23	35	4	46	39
APR. 15	4	18	19	19	7	3	34	23	35	4	46	39
APR. 16	4	20	20	21	7	3	34	23	35	4	46	39
APR. 17	4	21	22	22	7	3	34	23	35	4	46	39
APR. 18	4	23	23	24	7	3	34	23	35	4	46	39
APR. 19	5	25	25	26	8	3	34	23	35	4	46	39
APR. 20	5	26	27	27	8	3	34	23	35	4	46	39
APR. 21	5	28	28	29	8	4	34	23	35	4	46	39
APR. 22	5	29	30	30	8	4	34	23	35	4	46	39
APR. 23	5	31	31	32	8	4	34	23	35	4	46	39
APR. 24	5	32	33	34	8	4	34	23	35	4	46	39
APR. 25	6	34	35	35	8	4	34	23	35	4	46	39
APR. 26	6	36	36	37	8	4	34	23	35	4	46	39
APR. 27	6	37	38	38	8	5	34	23	35	4	46	39
APR. 28	6	39	40	40	8	5	34	23	35	4	46	39
APR. 29	6	41	41	42	8	5	34	23	35	4	46	39
APR. 30	6	42	43	44	8	5	34	23	35	4	47	39

MOON 1 ◖ 12:01 A.M. TO 8:00 A.M.   **MOON 2** ◑ 8:01 A.M. TO 4:00 P.M.   **MOON 3** ● 4:01 P.M. TO 12:00 A.M.

Use only one "moon" number. Choose the column closest to your time of birth. If your place of birth is not on Eastern Standard Time, be sure to read "How to Convert to Eastern Standard Time" at the beginning of this section.

2016

May

June

Date & Time	SUN	MOON 1	MOON 2	MOON 3	MERCURY	VENUS	MARS	JUPITER	SATURN	URANUS	NEPTUNE	PLUTO
MAY 1	6	44	45	45	8	5	34	23	35	4	47	39
MAY 2	6	46	47	47	8	5	34	23	35	4	47	39
MAY 3	7	48	1	1	8	5	34	23	35	4	47	39
MAY 4	7	2	3	3	8	6	34	23	35	4	47	39
MAY 5	7	4	5	5	8	6	34	23	35	4	47	39
MAY 6	7	6	7	7	8	6	34	23	35	4	47	39
MAY 7	7	8	9	9	8	6	34	23	35	4	47	39
MAY 8	7	10	11	11	8	6	34	23	35	4	47	39
MAY 9	7	12	13	13	8	6	34	23	35	4	47	39
MAY 10	7	14	15	15	8	7	34	23	35	4	47	39
MAY 11	8	16	16	17	7	7	34	23	35	4	47	39
MAY 12	8	18	18	19	7	7	34	23	35	4	47	39
MAY 13	8	19	20	20	7	7	34	23	35	4	47	39
MAY 14	8	21	21	22	7	7	34	23	35	4	47	39
MAY 15	8	23	23	24	7	7	34	23	35	4	47	39
MAY 16	8	24	25	25	7	8	33	23	35	4	47	39
MAY 17	8	26	26	27	7	8	33	23	35	4	47	39
MAY 18	8	27	28	28	7	8	33	23	35	4	47	39
MAY 19	9	29	29	30	7	8	33	23	35	4	47	39
MAY 20	9	30	31	32	7	8	33	23	35	4	47	39
MAY 21	9	32	33	33	7	8	33	23	35	4	47	39
MAY 22	9	34	34	35	7	9	33	23	35	4	47	39
MAY 23	9	35	36	36	7	9	33	23	35	4	47	39
MAY 24	9	37	37	38	7	9	33	23	35	4	47	39
MAY 25	10	39	39	40	7	9	33	23	35	4	47	39
MAY 26	10	40	41	41	7	9	33	23	35	4	47	39
MAY 27	10	42	43	43	7	9	33	23	35	4	47	39
MAY 28	10	44	44	45	7	10	33	23	35	4	47	39
MAY 29	10	46	46	47	7	10	33	23	35	4	47	39
MAY 30	10	47	48	1	7	10	33	23	35	4	47	39
MAY 31	10	1	2	3	7	10	33	23	35	4	47	39

Date & Time	SUN	MOON 1	MOON 2	MOON 3	MERCURY	VENUS	MARS	JUPITER	SATURN	URANUS	NEPTUNE	PLUTO
JUN. 1	10	3	4	4	7	10	33	23	35	4	47	39
JUN. 2	10	5	6	6	7	10	33	23	35	4	47	39
JUN. 3	11	7	8	8	8	11	33	23	35	4	47	39
JUN. 4	11	9	10	10	8	11	33	23	35	4	47	39
JUN. 5	11	11	12	12	8	11	33	23	35	4	47	39
JUN. 6	11	13	14	14	8	11	33	23	35	4	47	39
JUN. 7	11	15	16	16	8	11	33	23	35	4	47	39
JUN. 8	11	17	17	18	8	11	32	23	35	4	47	39
JUN. 9	11	19	19	20	8	12	32	23	35	4	47	39
JUN. 10	11	20	21	21	8	12	32	23	35	4	47	39
JUN. 11	12	22	23	23	9	12	32	23	35	4	47	39
JUN. 12	12	24	24	25	9	12	32	23	35	4	47	39
JUN. 13	12	25	26	26	9	12	32	23	35	4	47	39
JUN. 14	12	27	27	28	9	12	32	23	35	4	47	39
JUN. 15	12	28	29	29	9	13	32	23	35	4	47	39
JUN. 16	12	30	31	31	10	13	32	23	35	4	47	39
JUN. 17	12	32	32	33	10	13	32	23	35	4	47	39
JUN. 18	12	33	34	34	10	13	32	23	35	4	47	39
JUN. 19	13	35	35	36	10	13	32	23	35	4	47	39
JUN. 20	13	36	37	38	10	13	32	23	35	4	47	39
JUN. 21	13	38	39	39	11	14	32	23	35	4	47	39
JUN. 22	13	40	40	41	11	14	32	23	35	4	47	39
JUN. 23	13	42	42	43	11	14	32	23	35	4	47	39
JUN. 24	13	43	44	45	11	14	32	23	35	4	47	39
JUN. 25	14	45	46	46	12	14	32	23	35	4	47	39
JUN. 26	14	47	48	48	12	14	32	23	34	4	47	39
JUN. 27	14	1	1	2	12	15	32	23	34	4	47	39
JUN. 28	14	3	3	4	12	15	32	23	34	4	47	39
JUN. 29	14	5	5	6	13	15	32	23	34	4	47	39
JUN. 30	14	6	7	8	13	15	32	23	34	4	47	39

MOON 1 ◐ 12:01 A.M. TO 8:00 A.M. **MOON 2** ◑ 8:01 A.M. TO 4:00 P.M. **MOON 3** ● 4:01 P.M. TO 12:00 A.M.

Use only one "moon" number. Choose the column closest to your time of birth. If your place of birth is not on Eastern Standard Time, be sure to read "How to Convert to Eastern Standard Time" at the beginning of this section.

2016

July ✦✦✦   **August** ✦✦✦

Date & Time	SUN	MOON 1	MOON 2	MOON 3	MERCURY	VENUS	MARS	JUPITER	SATURN	URANUS	NEPTUNE	PLUTO
JUL. 1	14	8	9	10	13	15	32	23	34	4	47	39
JUL. 2	14	10	11	12	14	15	32	23	34	4	47	39
JUL. 3	15	12	13	14	14	15	32	23	34	4	47	39
JUL. 4	15	14	15	15	14	16	32	23	34	4	47	39
JUL. 5	15	16	17	17	14	16	32	23	34	4	47	39
JUL. 6	15	18	19	19	15	16	32	23	34	4	47	39
JUL. 7	15	20	20	21	15	16	32	23	34	4	47	39
JUL. 8	15	21	22	23	15	16	32	23	34	4	47	39
JUL. 9	15	23	24	24	16	16	32	23	34	4	47	39
JUL. 10	15	25	25	26	16	17	32	23	34	4	47	39
JUL. 11	16	26	27	27	16	17	32	23	34	4	47	39
JUL. 12	16	28	28	29	16	17	32	23	34	4	47	39
JUL. 13	16	30	30	31	17	17	32	23	34	4	47	39
JUL. 14	16	31	32	32	17	17	32	24	34	4	47	39
JUL. 15	16	33	33	34	17	17	32	24	34	4	47	39
JUL. 16	16	34	35	35	18	18	32	24	34	4	47	39
JUL. 17	16	36	37	37	18	18	32	24	34	4	47	39
JUL. 18	16	38	38	39	18	18	32	24	34	4	47	39
JUL. 19	17	39	40	41	18	18	32	24	34	4	47	39
JUL. 20	17	41	42	42	19	18	32	24	34	4	47	39
JUL. 21	17	43	43	44	19	18	32	24	34	4	47	39
JUL. 22	17	45	45	46	19	18	32	24	34	4	47	39
JUL. 23	17	47	47	48	19	19	33	24	34	4	47	39
JUL. 24	17	48	1	2	20	19	33	24	34	4	47	39
JUL. 25	17	2	3	4	20	19	33	24	34	4	47	39
JUL. 26	18	4	5	5	20	19	33	24	34	4	47	39
JUL. 27	18	6	7	7	20	19	33	24	34	4	47	39
JUL. 28	18	8	9	9	20	20	33	24	34	4	47	39
JUL. 29	18	10	10	11	21	20	33	24	34	4	47	39
JUL. 30	18	12	12	13	21	20	33	24	34	4	47	39
JUL. 31	18	14	14	15	21	20	33	24	34	4	46	39

Date & Time	SUN	MOON 1	MOON 2	MOON 3	MERCURY	VENUS	MARS	JUPITER	SATURN	URANUS	NEPTUNE	PLUTO
AUG. 1	18	15	16	17	21	20	33	24	34	4	46	39
AUG. 2	18	17	18	18	21	20	33	24	34	4	46	39
AUG. 3	19	19	20	20	22	21	33	24	34	4	46	39
AUG. 4	19	21	21	22	22	21	33	24	34	4	46	39
AUG. 5	19	22	23	24	22	21	33	24	34	4	46	39
AUG. 6	19	24	25	25	22	21	33	24	34	4	46	39
AUG. 7	19	26	26	27	22	21	33	24	34	4	46	39
AUG. 8	19	27	28	28	23	21	33	24	34	4	46	39
AUG. 9	19	29	30	30	23	22	33	24	34	4	46	39
AUG. 10	19	31	31	32	23	22	33	24	34	4	46	39
AUG. 11	20	32	33	33	23	22	33	24	34	4	46	39
AUG. 12	20	34	34	35	23	22	33	24	34	4	46	39
AUG. 13	20	35	36	36	23	22	34	24	34	4	46	39
AUG. 14	20	37	38	38	24	22	34	24	34	4	46	39
AUG. 15	20	39	39	40	24	23	34	24	34	4	46	39
AUG. 16	20	40	41	42	24	23	34	24	34	4	46	39
AUG. 17	20	42	43	43	24	23	34	24	34	4	46	39
AUG. 18	20	44	45	45	24	23	34	24	34	4	46	39
AUG. 19	21	46	47	47	24	23	34	24	34	4	46	39
AUG. 20	21	48	48	1	24	23	34	24	34	4	46	39
AUG. 21	21	2	2	3	24	24	34	24	34	4	46	39
AUG. 22	21	4	4	5	24	24	34	24	34	4	46	39
AUG. 23	21	6	6	7	25	24	34	24	34	4	46	39
AUG. 24	21	7	8	9	25	24	34	25	34	4	46	39
AUG. 25	21	9	10	11	25	24	34	25	34	4	46	39
AUG. 26	22	11	12	12	25	24	34	25	34	4	46	39
AUG. 27	22	13	14	14	25	24	34	25	34	4	46	39
AUG. 28	22	15	16	16	25	25	35	25	34	4	46	39
AUG. 29	22	17	17	18	25	25	35	25	34	4	46	39
AUG. 30	22	18	19	20	25	25	35	25	34	4	46	39
AUG. 31	22	20	21	21	25	25	35	25	34	4	46	39

MOON 1 ◖ 12:01 A.M. TO 8:00 A.M.   **MOON 2** ◗ 8:01 A.M. TO 4:00 P.M.   **MOON 3** ● 4:01 P.M. TO 12:00 A.M.
Use only one "moon" number. Choose the column closest to your time of birth. If your place of birth is not on Eastern Standard Time, be sure to read "How to Convert to Eastern Standard Time" at the beginning of this section.

2016

September

Date & Time	SUN	MOON 1	MOON 2	MOON 3	MERCURY	VENUS	MARS	JUPITER	SATURN	URANUS	NEPTUNE	PLUTO
SEP. 1	22	22	22	23	25	25	35	25	34	4	46	39
SEP. 2	22	24	24	25	25	25	35	25	34	4	46	39
SEP. 3	23	25	26	26	25	26	35	25	34	4	46	39
SEP. 4	23	27	27	28	25	26	35	25	34	4	46	39
SEP. 5	23	28	29	30	25	26	35	25	34	4	46	39
SEP. 6	23	30	31	31	25	26	35	25	34	4	46	39
SEP. 7	23	32	32	33	24	26	35	25	34	4	46	39
SEP. 8	23	33	34	34	24	26	35	25	34	4	46	39
SEP. 9	23	35	35	36	24	27	35	25	34	4	46	39
SEP. 10	23	36	37	38	24	27	36	25	34	4	46	39
SEP. 11	24	38	39	39	24	27	36	25	34	4	46	39
SEP. 12	24	40	40	41	24	27	36	25	34	4	46	39
SEP. 13	24	42	42	43	24	27	36	25	34	4	46	39
SEP. 14	24	43	44	45	24	27	36	25	34	4	46	39
SEP. 15	24	45	46	46	23	28	36	25	34	4	46	39
SEP. 16	24	47	48	48	23	28	36	25	34	4	46	39
SEP. 17	24	1	2	2	23	28	36	25	34	4	46	39
SEP. 18	24	3	4	4	23	28	36	25	34	4	46	39
SEP. 19	25	5	6	6	23	28	36	25	34	4	46	39
SEP. 20	25	7	8	8	23	28	36	25	34	4	46	39
SEP. 21	25	9	10	10	23	29	36	25	34	4	46	39
SEP. 22	25	11	11	12	23	29	37	25	34	4	46	39
SEP. 23	25	13	13	14	23	29	37	25	34	4	46	39
SEP. 24	25	15	15	16	23	29	37	25	34	4	46	39
SEP. 25	26	16	17	17	23	29	37	25	34	4	46	39
SEP. 26	26	18	19	19	23	30	37	25	34	4	46	39
SEP. 27	26	20	20	21	23	30	37	25	34	4	46	39
SEP. 28	26	21	22	23	23	30	37	26	34	4	46	39
SEP. 29	26	23	24	24	23	30	37	26	34	4	46	39
SEP. 30	26	25	25	26	24	30	37	26	35	4	46	39

October

Date & Time	SUN	MOON 1	MOON 2	MOON 3	MERCURY	VENUS	MARS	JUPITER	SATURN	URANUS	NEPTUNE	PLUTO
OCT. 1	26	26	27	27	24	30	37	26	35	4	46	39
OCT. 2	26	28	29	29	24	30	37	26	35	4	46	39
OCT. 3	27	30	30	31	24	31	37	26	35	4	46	39
OCT. 4	27	31	32	32	24	31	38	26	35	4	46	39
OCT. 5	27	33	33	34	25	31	38	26	35	4	46	39
OCT. 6	27	34	35	35	25	31	38	26	35	4	46	39
OCT. 7	27	36	36	37	25	31	38	26	35	4	46	39
OCT. 8	27	38	38	39	25	31	38	26	35	4	46	39
OCT. 9	27	39	40	40	25	31	38	26	35	4	46	39
OCT. 10	27	41	41	42	26	32	38	26	35	4	46	39
OCT. 11	28	43	43	44	26	32	38	26	35	4	46	39
OCT. 12	28	44	45	46	26	32	38	26	35	4	46	39
OCT. 13	28	46	47	47	26	32	38	26	35	4	46	39
OCT. 14	28	48	1	1	27	32	38	26	35	4	46	39
OCT. 15	28	2	3	3	27	32	39	26	35	4	46	39
OCT. 16	28	4	5	5	27	33	39	26	35	4	46	39
OCT. 17	28	6	7	7	27	33	39	26	35	4	46	39
OCT. 18	28	8	9	10	27	33	39	26	35	4	46	39
OCT. 19	29	10	11	11	28	33	39	26	35	4	46	39
OCT. 20	29	12	13	13	28	33	39	26	35	4	46	39
OCT. 21	29	14	15	15	28	33	39	26	35	4	46	39
OCT. 22	29	16	16	17	28	34	39	26	35	4	46	39
OCT. 23	29	18	18	19	29	34	39	26	35	4	46	39
OCT. 24	29	19	20	21	29	34	39	26	35	4	46	39
OCT. 25	29	21	22	22	29	34	40	26	35	4	46	39
OCT. 26	30	23	23	23	29	34	40	26	35	4	46	39
OCT. 27	30	24	25	25	29	34	40	26	35	4	46	39
OCT. 28	30	26	27	27	30	35	40	26	35	4	46	39
OCT. 29	30	28	28	29	30	35	40	26	35	4	46	39
OCT. 30	30	29	30	30	30	35	40	26	35	4	46	39
OCT. 31	30	31	31	32	30	35	40	26	35	4	46	39

MOON 1 ◐ 12:01 A.M. TO 8:00 A.M.   **MOON 2** ◑ 8:01 A.M. TO 4:00 P.M.   **MOON 3** ● 4:01 P.M. TO 12:00 A.M.
Use only one "moon" number. Choose the column closest to your time of birth. If your place of birth is not on Eastern Standard Time, be sure to read "How to Convert to Eastern Standard Time" at the beginning of this section.

Date & Time	SUN ☼	MOON 1 ◗	MOON 2 ◑	MOON 3 ●	MERCURY	VENUS	MARS	JUPITER	SATURN	URANUS	NEPTUNE	PLUTO
NOV. 1	30	32	33	33	31	35	40	26	35	4	46	39
NOV. 2	30	34	34	35	31	35	40	26	35	4	46	39
NOV. 3	31	35	36	37	31	36	40	27	35	4	46	39
NOV. 4	31	37	38	38	31	36	40	27	35	4	46	39
NOV. 5	31	39	39	40	31	36	41	27	35	4	46	39
NOV. 6	31	40	41	41	32	36	41	27	35	4	46	39
NOV. 7	31	42	43	43	32	36	41	27	35	4	46	39
NOV. 8	31	44	44	45	32	36	41	27	35	4	46	39
NOV. 9	31	46	46	47	32	36	41	27	35	4	46	39
NOV. 10	31	47	48	1	32	37	41	27	35	4	46	39
NOV. 11	31	1	2	3	33	37	41	27	35	4	46	39
NOV. 12	32	3	4	5	33	37	41	27	35	4	46	39
NOV. 13	32	5	6	7	33	37	41	27	35	4	46	39
NOV. 14	32	7	8	9	33	37	41	27	35	4	46	39
NOV. 15	32	9	10	11	33	37	42	27	35	4	46	39
NOV. 16	32	11	12	13	34	38	42	27	35	4	46	39
NOV. 17	32	13	14	15	34	38	42	27	35	4	46	39
NOV. 18	32	15	16	16	34	38	42	27	35	4	46	39
NOV. 19	33	17	18	18	34	38	42	27	35	4	46	39
NOV. 20	33	19	19	20	35	38	42	27	35	4	46	39
NOV. 21	33	21	21	22	35	38	42	27	35	4	46	39
NOV. 22	33	22	23	23	35	39	42	27	35	4	46	39
NOV. 23	33	24	25	25	35	39	42	27	35	4	46	39
NOV. 24	33	26	26	27	35	39	42	27	35	4	46	39
NOV. 25	34	27	28	28	36	39	43	27	35	4	46	39
NOV. 26	34	29	29	30	36	39	43	27	35	4	46	39
NOV. 27	34	30	31	31	36	39	43	27	35	4	46	39
NOV. 28	34	32	32	33	36	39	43	27	35	4	46	39
NOV. 29	34	34	34	35	36	40	43	27	35	4	46	39
NOV. 30	34	35	36	36	36	40	43	27	35	4	46	39

Date & Time	SUN ☼	MOON 1 ◗	MOON 2 ◑	MOON 3 ●	MERCURY	VENUS	MARS	JUPITER	SATURN	URANUS	NEPTUNE	PLUTO
DEC. 1	34	37	37	38	37	40	43	27	35	4	46	39
DEC. 2	34	38	39	39	37	40	43	27	35	4	46	39
DEC. 3	35	40	41	41	37	40	43	27	35	4	46	39
DEC. 4	35	42	42	43	37	40	43	27	35	4	46	39
DEC. 5	35	43	44	44	37	41	44	27	35	4	46	39
DEC. 6	35	45	46	46	38	41	44	27	35	4	46	39
DEC. 7	35	47	47	48	38	41	44	27	35	4	46	39
DEC. 8	35	1	1	2	38	41	44	27	35	4	46	39
DEC. 9	35	2	3	4	38	41	44	27	35	4	46	39
DEC. 10	35	4	5	6	38	41	44	27	35	4	46	39
DEC. 11	36	6	7	8	38	42	44	27	35	4	46	39
DEC. 12	36	8	9	10	38	42	44	27	36	4	46	39
DEC. 13	36	10	11	12	39	42	44	27	36	4	46	39
DEC. 14	36	12	13	14	39	42	44	27	36	4	46	39
DEC. 15	36	14	15	16	39	42	45	28	36	4	46	39
DEC. 16	36	16	17	18	39	42	45	28	36	4	46	39
DEC. 17	36	18	19	19	39	42	45	28	36	4	46	39
DEC. 18	36	20	21	21	39	43	45	28	36	4	46	39
DEC. 19	37	22	22	23	39	43	45	28	36	4	46	39
DEC. 20	37	23	24	25	39	43	45	28	36	4	46	39
DEC. 21	37	25	26	26	39	43	45	28	36	4	46	39
DEC. 22	37	27	27	28	39	43	45	28	36	4	46	39
DEC. 23	37	28	29	29	39	43	45	28	36	4	46	39
DEC. 24	37	30	30	31	39	43	45	28	36	4	46	39
DEC. 25	37	31	32	33	39	44	46	28	36	4	46	39
DEC. 26	38	33	34	34	38	44	46	28	36	4	46	39
DEC. 27	38	35	35	36	38	44	46	28	36	4	46	39
DEC. 28	38	36	37	37	38	44	46	28	36	4	46	39
DEC. 29	38	38	38	39	38	44	46	28	36	4	46	39
DEC. 30	38	40	40	41	38	44	46	28	36	4	46	39
DEC. 31	38	41	42	42	38	45	46	28	36	4	46	39

MOON 1 ◗ 12:01 A.M. TO 8:00 A.M.   **MOON 2** ◑ 8:01 A.M. TO 4:00 P.M.   **MOON 3** ● 4:01 P.M. TO 12:00 A.M.

Use only one "moon" number. Choose the column closest to your time of birth. If your place of birth is not on Eastern Standard Time, be sure to read "How to Convert to Eastern Standard Time" at the beginning of this section.

2017

January

Date & Time	SUN	MOON 1	MOON 2	MOON 3	MERCURY	VENUS	MARS	JUPITER	SATURN	URANUS	NEPTUNE	PLUTO
JAN. 1	38	43	43	44	37	45	46	28	36	4	46	39
JAN. 2	38	45	45	46	37	45	46	28	36	4	46	39
JAN. 3	39	46	47	48	37	45	46	28	36	4	46	39
JAN. 4	39	48	1	1	37	45	47	28	36	4	46	39
JAN. 5	39	2	3	3	37	45	47	28	36	4	46	39
JAN. 6	39	4	4	5	37	45	47	28	36	4	46	39
JAN. 7	39	6	6	7	37	46	47	28	36	4	46	39
JAN. 8	39	8	8	9	37	46	47	28	36	4	46	39
JAN. 9	39	10	10	11	37	46	47	28	36	4	46	39
JAN. 10	40	12	12	13	37	46	47	28	36	4	46	39
JAN. 11	40	13	14	15	37	46	47	28	36	4	46	39
JAN. 12	40	15	16	17	37	46	47	28	36	4	46	39
JAN. 13	40	17	18	19	37	46	47	28	36	4	46	39
JAN. 14	40	19	20	20	37	46	48	28	36	4	46	39
JAN. 15	40	21	22	22	37	47	48	28	36	4	46	39
JAN. 16	40	23	23	24	37	47	48	28	36	4	46	39
JAN. 17	41	25	25	26	37	47	48	28	36	4	46	39
JAN. 18	41	26	27	27	38	47	48	28	36	4	46	39
JAN. 19	41	28	28	29	38	47	48	28	36	4	46	39
JAN. 20	41	29	30	30	38	47	48	28	36	4	46	39
JAN. 21	41	31	32	32	38	48	48	28	36	4	46	39
JAN. 22	41	33	33	34	38	48	48	28	36	4	46	39
JAN. 23	42	34	35	35	38	48	48	28	36	4	46	39
JAN. 24	42	36	36	37	38	48	1	28	36	4	46	39
JAN. 25	42	37	38	38	39	48	1	28	36	4	46	39
JAN. 26	42	39	40	40	39	48	1	28	36	4	46	39
JAN. 27	42	41	41	42	39	48	1	28	36	4	46	39
JAN. 28	42	42	43	44	39	48	1	28	36	4	46	39
JAN. 29	42	44	45	45	39	48	1	28	36	4	46	39
JAN. 30	42	46	47	47	39	48	1	28	36	4	46	39
JAN. 31	43	48	48	1	40	1	1	28	36	4	46	39

February

Date & Time	SUN	MOON 1	MOON 2	MOON 3	MERCURY	VENUS	MARS	JUPITER	SATURN	URANUS	NEPTUNE	PLUTO
FEB. 1	43	2	2	3	40	1	1	28	36	4	46	39
FEB. 2	43	3	4	5	40	1	1	28	36	4	46	39
FEB. 3	43	5	6	6	40	1	2	28	36	4	46	39
FEB. 4	43	7	8	8	40	1	2	28	36	4	46	39
FEB. 5	43	9	10	10	41	1	2	28	36	4	46	39
FEB. 6	43	11	12	12	41	1	2	28	36	4	46	39
FEB. 7	43	13	13	14	41	1	2	28	36	4	46	39
FEB. 8	44	15	15	16	41	1	2	28	36	4	46	39
FEB. 9	44	17	17	18	41	2	2	28	36	4	46	39
FEB. 10	44	18	19	20	42	2	2	28	36	4	46	39
FEB. 11	44	20	21	22	42	2	2	28	36	4	46	39
FEB. 12	44	22	23	23	42	2	2	28	36	4	46	39
FEB. 13	44	24	24	25	42	2	3	28	36	4	46	39
FEB. 14	44	26	26	27	42	2	3	28	36	4	46	39
FEB. 15	44	27	28	28	43	2	3	28	36	4	46	39
FEB. 16	45	29	29	30	43	2	3	28	36	4	46	39
FEB. 17	45	30	31	32	43	2	3	28	36	4	46	39
FEB. 18	45	32	33	33	43	2	3	28	36	4	46	39
FEB. 19	45	34	34	35	43	3	3	28	36	4	46	39
FEB. 20	45	35	36	36	44	3	3	28	36	4	46	39
FEB. 21	45	37	37	38	44	3	3	28	36	4	46	39
FEB. 22	45	38	39	40	44	3	3	28	36	4	46	39
FEB. 23	46	40	41	41	44	3	4	28	36	4	46	39
FEB. 24	46	42	42	43	45	3	4	28	36	4	46	39
FEB. 25	46	44	44	45	45	3	4	28	36	4	47	39
FEB. 26	46	45	46	47	45	3	4	28	37	4	47	39
FEB. 27	46	47	48	48	45	3	4	28	37	4	47	39
FEB. 28	46	1	2	2	45	3	4	28	37	4	47	39

MOON 1 ◖ 12:01 A.M. TO 8:00 A.M.   **MOON 2** ◑ 8:01 A.M. TO 4:00 P.M.   **MOON 3** ● 4:01 P.M. TO 12:00 A.M.
Use only one "moon" number. Choose the column closest to your time of birth. If your place of birth is not on
Eastern Standard Time, be sure to read "How to Convert to Eastern Standard Time" at the beginning of this section.

2017

March

April

Date & Time	SUN	MOON 1	MOON 2	MOON 3	MERCURY	VENUS	MARS	JUPITER	SATURN	URANUS	NEPTUNE	PLUTO
MAR. 1	46	3	3	4	46	3	4	28	37	4	47	39
MAR. 2	46	5	5	6	46	3	4	28	37	4	47	39
MAR. 3	47	7	7	8	46	3	4	28	37	4	47	39
MAR. 4	47	9	9	10	46	3	4	28	37	4	47	39
MAR. 5	47	10	11	12	47	3	5	28	37	4	47	39
MAR. 6	47	12	13	14	47	3	5	28	37	4	47	39
MAR. 7	47	14	15	15	47	3	5	28	37	4	47	39
MAR. 8	47	16	17	17	47	3	5	28	37	4	47	39
MAR. 9	47	18	18	19	48	3	5	28	37	4	47	39
MAR. 10	47	20	20	21	48	3	5	28	37	4	47	39
MAR. 11	48	21	22	23	48	3	5	28	37	4	47	39
MAR. 12	48	23	24	24	1	3	5	28	37	4	47	40
MAR. 13	48	25	25	26	1	3	5	28	37	4	47	40
MAR. 14	48	27	27	28	1	2	5	28	37	4	47	40
MAR. 15	48	28	29	29	1	2	5	28	37	4	47	40
MAR. 16	48	30	30	31	2	2	6	28	37	4	47	40
MAR. 17	48	32	32	33	2	2	6	28	37	4	47	40
MAR. 18	48	33	34	34	2	2	6	28	37	4	47	40
MAR. 19	1	35	35	36	2	2	6	28	37	4	47	40
MAR. 20	1	36	37	37	3	2	6	28	37	4	47	40
MAR. 21	1	38	38	39	3	2	6	28	37	4	47	40
MAR. 22	1	39	40	41	3	2	6	28	37	4	47	40
MAR. 23	1	41	42	42	3	2	6	28	37	4	47	40
MAR. 24	1	43	43	44	4	2	6	28	37	4	47	40
MAR. 25	2	45	45	46	4	2	6	28	37	4	47	40
MAR. 26	2	46	47	48	4	2	7	28	37	4	47	40
MAR. 27	2	48	1	2	4	1	7	28	37	4	47	40
MAR. 28	2	2	3	3	4	1	7	28	37	4	47	40
MAR. 29	2	4	5	5	5	1	7	28	37	4	47	40
MAR. 30	2	6	7	7	5	1	7	28	37	4	47	40
MAR. 31	2	8	9	9	5	1	7	28	37	4	47	40

Date & Time	SUN	MOON 1	MOON 2	MOON 3	MERCURY	VENUS	MARS	JUPITER	SATURN	URANUS	NEPTUNE	PLUTO
APR. 1	2	10	11	11	5	1	7	28	37	4	47	40
APR. 2	2	12	13	13	5	1	7	27	37	4	47	40
APR. 3	3	14	14	15	5	1	7	27	37	4	47	40
APR. 4	3	16	16	17	5	1	7	27	37	4	47	40
APR. 5	3	17	18	19	5	1	7	27	37	4	47	40
APR. 6	3	19	20	20	6	1	8	27	37	4	47	40
APR. 7	3	21	22	22	6	1	8	27	37	4	47	40
APR. 8	3	23	23	24	6	1	8	27	37	4	47	40
APR. 9	3	24	25	26	6	1	8	27	37	4	47	40
APR. 10	3	26	27	27	6	1	8	27	37	4	47	40
APR. 11	4	28	28	29	6	1	8	27	37	4	47	40
APR. 12	4	29	30	30	6	1	8	27	37	4	47	40
APR. 13	4	31	32	32	6	1	8	27	37	4	47	40
APR. 14	4	33	33	34	5	1	8	27	37	4	47	40
APR. 15	4	34	35	35	5	1	8	27	37	4	47	40
APR. 16	4	36	36	37	5	1	8	27	37	4	47	40
APR. 17	4	37	38	38	5	1	9	27	37	4	47	40
APR. 18	4	39	39	40	5	1	9	27	37	4	47	40
APR. 19	5	41	41	42	5	1	9	27	37	4	47	40
APR. 20	5	42	43	43	5	1	9	27	37	4	47	40
APR. 21	5	44	44	45	5	1	9	27	37	4	47	40
APR. 22	5	46	46	47	5	1	9	27	37	4	47	40
APR. 23	5	47	48	1	5	1	9	27	37	4	47	40
APR. 24	5	1	2	3	5	1	9	27	37	4	47	40
APR. 25	6	3	4	5	5	1	9	27	37	4	47	40
APR. 26	6	5	6	7	5	1	9	27	37	4	47	40
APR. 27	6	7	8	9	4	1	9	27	37	4	47	40
APR. 28	6	9	10	11	4	1	10	27	37	4	47	40
APR. 29	6	11	12	13	4	1	10	27	37	4	47	40
APR. 30	6	13	14	15	4	1	10	27	37	4	47	40

MOON 1 ☽ 12:01 A.M. TO 8:00 A.M.   **MOON 2** ☽ 8:01 A.M. TO 4:00 P.M.   **MOON 3** ● 4:01 P.M. TO 12:00 A.M.

Use only one "moon" number. Choose the column closest to your time of birth. If your place of birth is not on Eastern Standard Time, be sure to read "How to Convert to Eastern Standard Time" at the beginning of this section.

2017

May | June

Date & Time	SUN	MOON 1	MOON 2	MOON 3	MERCURY	VENUS	MARS	JUPITER	SATURN	URANUS	NEPTUNE	PLUTO
MAY 1	6	15	16	16	4	1	10	27	37	4	47	40
MAY 2	6	17	18	18	4	1	10	27	37	4	47	40
MAY 3	7	19	19	20	4	1	10	27	37	4	47	40
MAY 4	7	21	21	22	4	1	10	27	37	4	47	40
MAY 5	7	22	23	23	4	1	10	27	37	4	47	40
MAY 6	7	24	25	25	4	2	10	27	37	4	47	40
MAY 7	7	26	26	27	4	2	10	27	37	4	47	40
MAY 8	7	27	28	28	4	2	11	27	37	4	47	40
MAY 9	7	29	30	30	4	2	11	27	37	4	47	40
MAY 10	7	31	31	32	4	2	11	27	37	4	47	40
MAY 11	8	32	33	33	4	2	11	27	37	4	47	40
MAY 12	8	34	34	35	5	2	11	27	37	4	47	40
MAY 13	8	35	36	36	5	2	11	27	37	4	47	40
MAY 14	8	37	37	38	5	2	11	27	37	4	47	40
MAY 15	8	39	39	40	5	2	11	27	37	4	47	40
MAY 16	8	40	41	41	5	2	11	27	37	4	47	40
MAY 17	8	42	42	43	5	3	11	27	37	4	47	40
MAY 18	8	43	44	44	5	3	11	27	36	4	47	40
MAY 19	9	45	46	46	5	3	11	27	36	4	47	40
MAY 20	9	47	47	48	5	3	12	27	36	4	47	40
MAY 21	9	1	1	2	6	3	12	27	36	4	47	40
MAY 22	9	2	3	4	6	3	12	27	36	5	47	40
MAY 23	9	4	5	6	6	3	12	27	36	5	47	40
MAY 24	9	6	7	8	6	3	12	27	36	5	47	40
MAY 25	10	8	9	10	6	3	12	27	36	5	47	40
MAY 26	10	10	11	12	6	4	12	27	36	5	47	40
MAY 27	10	12	13	14	7	4	12	27	36	5	47	40
MAY 28	10	14	15	16	7	4	12	27	36	5	47	40
MAY 29	10	16	17	18	7	4	12	27	36	5	47	40
MAY 30	10	18	19	20	7	4	12	27	36	5	47	40
MAY 31	10	20	21	21	7	4	13	27	36	5	47	40

Date & Time	SUN	MOON 1	MOON 2	MOON 3	MERCURY	VENUS	MARS	JUPITER	SATURN	URANUS	NEPTUNE	PLUTO
JUN. 1	10	22	22	23	8	4	13	27	36	5	47	39
JUN. 2	10	24	24	25	8	4	13	27	36	5	47	39
JUN. 3	11	25	26	26	8	5	13	27	36	5	47	39
JUN. 4	11	27	28	28	8	5	13	27	36	5	47	39
JUN. 5	11	29	29	30	9	5	13	27	36	5	47	39
JUN. 6	11	30	31	31	9	5	13	27	36	5	47	39
JUN. 7	11	32	32	33	9	5	13	27	36	5	47	39
JUN. 8	11	33	34	34	9	5	13	27	36	5	47	39
JUN. 9	11	35	35	36	10	5	13	27	36	5	47	39
JUN. 10	11	37	37	38	10	5	13	27	36	5	47	39
JUN. 11	12	38	39	39	10	6	14	27	36	5	47	39
JUN. 12	12	40	40	41	10	6	14	27	36	5	47	39
JUN. 13	12	41	42	42	11	6	14	27	36	5	47	39
JUN. 14	12	43	43	44	11	6	14	27	36	5	47	39
JUN. 15	12	45	45	46	11	6	14	27	36	5	47	39
JUN. 16	12	46	47	47	11	6	14	27	36	5	47	39
JUN. 17	12	48	1	1	12	6	14	27	36	5	47	39
JUN. 18	12	2	2	3	12	7	14	27	36	5	47	39
JUN. 19	13	4	4	5	12	7	14	27	36	5	47	39
JUN. 20	13	6	6	7	13	7	14	27	36	5	47	39
JUN. 21	13	7	8	9	13	7	14	27	36	5	47	39
JUN. 22	13	9	10	11	13	7	15	27	36	5	47	39
JUN. 23	13	12	12	13	13	7	15	27	36	5	47	39
JUN. 24	13	14	14	15	14	7	15	27	36	5	47	39
JUN. 25	14	16	16	17	14	8	15	27	36	5	47	39
JUN. 26	14	18	18	19	14	8	15	27	36	5	47	39
JUN. 27	14	19	20	21	15	8	15	27	36	5	47	39
JUN. 28	14	21	22	22	15	8	15	27	36	5	47	39
JUN. 29	14	23	24	24	15	8	15	27	36	5	47	39
JUN. 30	14	25	25	26	15	8	15	27	36	5	47	39

MOON 1 ☽ 12:01 A.M. TO 8:00 A.M.   **MOON 2** ◑ 8:01 A.M. TO 4:00 P.M.   **MOON 3** ● 4:01 P.M. TO 12:00 A.M.
Use only one "moon" number. Choose the column closest to your time of birth. If your place of birth is not on Eastern Standard Time, be sure to read "How to Convert to Eastern Standard Time" at the beginning of this section.

2017

July

⭐⭐⭐

August

⭐⭐⭐

Date & Time	SUN ☀	MOON 1 ◗	MOON 2 ◐	MOON 3 ●	MERCURY	VENUS	MARS	JUPITER	SATURN	URANUS	NEPTUNE	PLUTO
JUL. 1	14	27	27	28	16	8	15	27	36	5	47	39
JUL. 2	14	28	29	29	16	9	15	27	36	5	47	39
JUL. 3	15	30	30	31	16	9	15	27	36	5	47	39
JUL. 4	15	31	32	32	17	9	16	27	36	5	47	39
JUL. 5	15	33	33	34	17	9	16	27	36	5	47	39
JUL. 6	15	35	35	36	17	9	16	27	36	5	47	39
JUL. 7	15	36	37	37	17	9	16	27	36	5	47	39
JUL. 8	15	38	38	39	17	9	16	27	36	5	47	39
JUL. 9	15	39	40	40	18	10	16	27	36	5	47	39
JUL. 10	15	41	41	42	18	10	16	27	36	5	47	39
JUL. 11	16	43	43	44	18	10	16	27	36	5	47	39
JUL. 12	16	44	45	45	18	10	16	27	36	5	47	39
JUL. 13	16	46	46	47	19	10	16	27	36	5	47	39
JUL. 14	16	48	48	1	19	10	16	27	36	5	47	39
JUL. 15	16	1	2	3	19	10	17	27	36	5	47	39
JUL. 16	16	3	4	4	19	11	17	27	36	5	47	39
JUL. 17	16	5	6	6	19	11	17	27	36	5	47	39
JUL. 18	16	7	7	8	20	11	17	27	36	5	47	39
JUL. 19	17	9	9	10	20	11	17	27	36	5	47	39
JUL. 20	17	11	11	12	20	11	17	27	36	5	47	39
JUL. 21	17	13	13	14	20	11	17	27	36	5	47	39
JUL. 22	17	15	15	16	20	12	17	27	36	5	47	39
JUL. 23	17	17	17	18	21	12	17	27	36	5	47	39
JUL. 24	17	19	19	20	21	12	17	27	36	5	47	39
JUL. 25	17	21	21	22	21	12	17	27	36	5	47	39
JUL. 26	18	22	23	24	21	12	17	27	36	5	47	39
JUL. 27	18	24	25	25	21	12	18	27	36	5	47	39
JUL. 28	18	26	27	27	21	12	18	27	36	5	47	39
JUL. 29	18	28	28	29	21	13	18	27	36	5	47	39
JUL. 30	18	29	30	30	22	13	18	27	36	5	47	39
JUL. 31	18	31	31	32	22	13	18	27	36	5	47	39

Date & Time	SUN ☀	MOON 1 ◗	MOON 2 ◐	MOON 3 ●	MERCURY	VENUS	MARS	JUPITER	SATURN	URANUS	NEPTUNE	PLUTO
AUG. 1	18	33	33	34	22	13	18	27	36	5	47	39
AUG. 2	18	34	35	35	22	13	18	27	36	5	47	39
AUG. 3	19	36	36	37	22	13	18	27	36	5	47	39
AUG. 4	19	37	38	38	22	14	18	27	36	5	47	39
AUG. 5	19	39	39	40	22	14	18	27	36	5	47	39
AUG. 6	19	40	41	42	22	14	18	27	36	5	47	39
AUG. 7	19	42	43	43	22	14	18	27	36	5	47	39
AUG. 8	19	44	44	45	22	14	19	27	36	5	47	39
AUG. 9	19	45	46	47	22	14	19	27	36	5	47	39
AUG. 10	19	47	48	48	22	14	19	27	36	5	47	39
AUG. 11	20	1	2	2	22	15	19	27	36	5	47	39
AUG. 12	20	3	3	4	23	15	19	27	36	5	47	39
AUG. 13	20	5	5	6	23	15	19	27	36	5	47	39
AUG. 14	20	6	7	8	23	15	19	27	36	5	47	39
AUG. 15	20	8	9	10	22	15	19	28	36	5	47	39
AUG. 16	20	10	11	11	22	15	19	28	36	5	47	39
AUG. 17	20	12	13	13	22	16	19	28	36	5	47	39
AUG. 18	20	14	15	15	22	16	19	28	36	5	47	39
AUG. 19	21	16	17	17	22	16	20	28	36	5	47	39
AUG. 20	21	18	18	19	22	16	20	28	36	5	47	39
AUG. 21	21	20	20	21	22	16	20	28	36	5	47	39
AUG. 22	21	22	22	23	22	16	20	28	36	5	47	39
AUG. 23	21	23	24	25	22	16	20	28	36	5	47	39
AUG. 24	21	25	26	26	22	17	20	28	36	5	47	39
AUG. 25	21	27	28	28	22	17	20	28	36	5	47	39
AUG. 26	22	29	29	30	22	17	20	28	36	5	47	39
AUG. 27	22	30	31	31	21	17	20	28	36	5	47	39
AUG. 28	22	32	33	33	21	17	20	28	36	5	47	39
AUG. 29	22	34	34	35	21	17	20	28	36	5	47	39
AUG. 30	22	35	36	36	21	18	20	28	36	5	47	39
AUG. 31	22	37	37	38	21	18	21	28	36	5	47	39

MOON 1 ◗ 12:01 A.M. TO 8:00 A.M.　　**MOON 2** ◐ 8:01 A.M. TO 4:00 P.M.　　**MOON 3** ● 4:01 P.M. TO 12:00 A.M.

Use only one "moon" number. Choose the column closest to your time of birth. If your place of birth is not on Eastern Standard Time, be sure to read "How to Convert to Eastern Standard Time" at the beginning of this section.

2017

September

October

Date & Time	SUN	MOON 1 ◐	MOON 2 ◑	MOON 3 ●	MERCURY	VENUS	MARS	JUPITER	SATURN	URANUS	NEPTUNE	PLUTO
SEP. 1	22	38	39	39	21	18	21	28	36	5	47	39
SEP. 2	22	40	40	41	21	18	21	28	36	5	47	39
SEP. 3	23	42	42	43	21	18	21	28	36	5	47	39
SEP. 4	23	43	44	44	21	18	21	28	36	5	47	39
SEP. 5	23	45	46	46	21	19	21	28	36	5	47	39
SEP. 6	23	47	47	48	21	19	21	28	36	5	47	39
SEP. 7	23	48	1	2	21	19	21	28	36	5	47	39
SEP. 8	23	2	3	3	21	19	21	28	36	5	47	39
SEP. 9	23	4	5	5	21	19	21	28	36	5	47	39
SEP. 10	23	6	7	7	21	19	21	28	36	5	47	39
SEP. 11	24	8	8	9	21	20	21	28	36	5	47	39
SEP. 12	24	10	10	11	21	20	22	28	36	5	47	39
SEP. 13	24	12	12	13	21	20	22	28	36	5	47	39
SEP. 14	24	14	14	15	21	20	22	28	36	5	47	39
SEP. 15	24	15	16	17	22	20	22	28	36	5	47	39
SEP. 16	24	17	18	19	22	20	22	28	36	5	47	39
SEP. 17	24	19	20	20	22	21	22	28	36	5	47	39
SEP. 18	24	21	22	22	22	21	22	28	36	5	47	39
SEP. 19	25	23	23	24	22	21	22	28	36	5	47	39
SEP. 20	25	25	25	26	23	21	22	28	36	5	47	39
SEP. 21	25	26	27	28	23	21	22	28	36	5	47	39
SEP. 22	25	28	29	29	23	21	22	28	36	5	47	39
SEP. 23	25	30	30	31	23	21	22	28	36	5	47	39
SEP. 24	25	31	32	32	24	22	23	29	36	5	47	39
SEP. 25	26	33	34	34	24	22	23	29	36	5	47	39
SEP. 26	26	35	35	36	24	22	23	29	36	5	47	39
SEP. 27	26	36	37	37	24	22	23	29	36	5	47	39
SEP. 28	26	38	38	39	25	22	23	29	36	5	47	39
SEP. 29	26	39	40	40	25	22	23	29	36	5	47	39
SEP. 30	26	41	42	42	25	23	23	29	36	5	47	39

Date & Time	SUN	MOON 1 ◐	MOON 2 ◑	MOON 3 ●	MERCURY	VENUS	MARS	JUPITER	SATURN	URANUS	NEPTUNE	PLUTO
OCT. 1	26	43	43	44	25	23	23	29	36	5	47	39
OCT. 2	26	44	45	45	25	23	23	29	36	5	47	39
OCT. 3	27	46	47	47	26	23	23	29	36	5	47	39
OCT. 4	27	48	48	1	26	23	23	29	36	5	47	39
OCT. 5	27	2	1	3	26	23	23	29	36	5	47	39
OCT. 6	27	3	4	5	26	24	24	29	36	5	47	39
OCT. 7	27	5	6	7	27	24	24	29	36	5	47	39
OCT. 8	27	7	8	9	27	24	24	29	36	5	47	39
OCT. 9	27	9	10	11	27	24	24	29	36	5	47	39
OCT. 10	27	11	12	12	27	24	24	29	36	5	47	39
OCT. 11	28	13	14	14	28	24	24	29	36	5	47	39
OCT. 12	28	15	16	16	28	25	24	29	36	5	47	39
OCT. 13	28	17	17	18	28	25	24	29	36	5	47	39
OCT. 14	28	19	19	20	28	25	24	29	36	5	47	39
OCT. 15	28	20	21	22	29	25	24	29	36	5	47	39
OCT. 16	28	22	23	23	29	25	24	29	36	5	47	39
OCT. 17	28	24	25	25	29	25	24	29	36	5	47	39
OCT. 18	28	26	26	27	29	26	25	29	36	5	47	39
OCT. 19	29	28	28	29	29	26	25	29	36	5	47	39
OCT. 20	29	29	30	30	30	26	25	29	36	5	47	39
OCT. 21	29	31	31	32	30	26	25	29	36	4	47	39
OCT. 22	29	32	33	34	30	26	25	29	36	4	47	39
OCT. 23	29	34	35	35	30	26	25	29	36	4	47	39
OCT. 24	29	36	36	37	30	27	25	29	36	4	47	39
OCT. 25	29	37	38	38	31	27	25	29	36	4	47	39
OCT. 26	30	39	39	40	31	27	25	29	36	4	47	39
OCT. 27	30	40	41	42	31	27	25	29	36	4	47	39
OCT. 28	30	42	43	43	31	27	25	29	36	4	47	39
OCT. 29	30	44	44	45	31	27	26	30	36	4	47	39
OCT. 30	30	45	46	46	32	28	26	30	36	4	47	39
OCT. 31	30	47	48	48	32	28	26	30	36	4	47	39

MOON 1 ◐ 12:01 A.M. TO 8:00 A.M.   **MOON 2 ◑ 8:01 A.M. TO 4:00 P.M.**   **MOON 3 ● 4:01 P.M. TO 12:00 A.M.**
Use only one "moon" number. Choose the column closest to your time of birth. If your place of birth is not on Eastern Standard Time, be sure to read "How to Convert to Eastern Standard Time" at the beginning of this section.

Date & Time	SUN	MOON 1	MOON 2	MOON 3	MERCURY	VENUS	MARS	JUPITER	SATURN	URANUS	NEPTUNE	PLUTO
NOV. 1	30	1	1	2	32	28	26	30	36	4	47	39
NOV. 2	30	3	3	4	32	28	26	30	36	4	47	39
NOV. 3	31	5	5	6	32	28	26	30	36	4	47	39
NOV. 4	31	7	7	8	33	28	26	30	36	4	47	39
NOV. 5	31	9	9	10	33	29	26	30	36	4	47	39
NOV. 6	31	11	11	12	33	29	26	30	36	4	47	39
NOV. 7	31	12	13	14	33	29	26	30	36	4	47	39
NOV. 8	31	14	15	16	33	29	26	30	36	4	47	39
NOV. 9	31	16	17	18	34	29	26	30	36	4	47	39
NOV. 10	31	18	19	19	34	29	27	30	36	4	47	39
NOV. 11	31	20	21	21	34	30	27	30	36	4	47	39
NOV. 12	32	22	22	23	34	30	27	30	36	4	47	39
NOV. 13	32	24	24	25	34	30	27	30	36	4	46	39
NOV. 14	32	25	26	26	35	30	27	30	36	4	46	39
NOV. 15	32	27	28	28	35	30	27	30	36	4	46	39
NOV. 16	32	29	29	30	35	30	27	30	36	4	46	39
NOV. 17	32	30	31	31	35	31	27	30	36	4	46	39
NOV. 18	32	32	33	33	35	31	27	30	36	4	46	39
NOV. 19	33	34	34	35	35	31	27	30	36	4	46	39
NOV. 20	33	35	36	36	35	31	27	30	37	4	46	39
NOV. 21	33	37	37	38	35	31	27	30	37	4	46	39
NOV. 22	33	38	39	39	36	31	28	30	37	4	46	39
NOV. 23	33	40	40	41	36	32	28	30	37	4	46	39
NOV. 24	33	42	42	43	36	32	28	30	37	4	46	39
NOV. 25	34	43	44	44	36	32	28	30	37	4	46	39
NOV. 26	34	45	45	46	36	32	28	30	37	4	46	39
NOV. 27	34	46	47	48	37	32	28	30	37	4	46	39
NOV. 28	34	48	1	1	37	32	28	30	37	4	46	39
NOV. 29	34	2	3	3	37	33	28	30	37	4	46	39
NOV. 30	34	4	4	5	37	33	28	30	37	4	46	39

Date & Time	SUN	MOON 1	MOON 2	MOON 3	MERCURY	VENUS	MARS	JUPITER	SATURN	URANUS	NEPTUNE	PLUTO
DEC. 1	34	6	6	7	37	33	28	30	37	4	46	39
DEC. 2	34	8	8	9	37	33	28	30	37	4	46	39
DEC. 3	35	10	10	11	37	33	28	31	37	4	47	39
DEC. 4	35	12	12	13	37	33	29	31	37	4	47	39
DEC. 5	35	14	14	15	37	34	29	31	37	4	47	39
DEC. 6	35	16	16	17	37	34	29	31	37	4	47	39
DEC. 7	35	18	18	19	37	34	29	31	37	4	47	39
DEC. 8	35	20	20	21	37	34	29	31	37	4	47	39
DEC. 9	35	21	22	23	36	34	29	31	37	4	47	39
DEC. 10	35	23	24	24	36	34	29	31	37	4	47	39
DEC. 11	36	25	26	26	36	35	29	31	37	4	47	39
DEC. 12	36	27	27	28	36	35	29	31	37	4	47	39
DEC. 13	36	28	29	29	36	35	29	31	37	4	47	39
DEC. 14	36	30	31	31	36	35	29	31	37	4	47	39
DEC. 15	36	32	32	33	35	35	29	31	37	4	47	39
DEC. 16	36	33	34	34	35	35	30	31	37	4	47	39
DEC. 17	36	35	35	36	35	36	30	31	37	4	47	39
DEC. 18	36	36	37	37	35	36	30	31	37	4	47	39
DEC. 19	37	38	39	39	35	36	30	31	37	4	47	39
DEC. 20	37	40	40	41	35	36	30	31	37	4	47	39
DEC. 21	37	41	42	42	35	36	30	31	37	4	47	39
DEC. 22	37	43	43	44	35	36	30	31	37	4	47	39
DEC. 23	37	44	45	45	35	37	30	31	37	4	47	39
DEC. 24	37	46	46	47	35	37	30	31	37	4	47	39
DEC. 25	37	48	48	1	35	37	30	31	37	4	47	39
DEC. 26	38	1	2	2	35	37	30	31	37	4	47	39
DEC. 27	38	3	4	4	35	37	30	31	37	4	47	39
DEC. 28	38	5	5	6	35	37	31	31	37	4	47	39
DEC. 29	38	7	7	8	35	38	31	31	37	4	47	39
DEC. 30	38	9	9	10	35	38	31	31	37	4	47	39
DEC. 31	38	11	11	12	35	38	31	31	37	4	47	39

MOON 1 ◑ 12:01 A.M. TO 8:00 A.M.   **MOON 2** ◐ 8:01 A.M. TO 4:00 P.M.   **MOON 3** ● 4:01 P.M. TO 12:00 A.M.
Use only one "moon" number. Choose the column closest to your time of birth. If your place of birth is not on Eastern Standard Time, be sure to read "How to Convert to Eastern Standard Time" at the beginning of this section.

2018

January

Date & Time	SUN	MOON 1	MOON 2	MOON 3	MERCURY	VENUS	MARS	JUPITER	SATURN	URANUS	NEPTUNE	PLUTO
JAN. 1	38	13	13	14	35	38	31	31	37	4	47	39
JAN. 2	38	15	15	16	36	38	31	31	37	4	47	39
JAN. 3	39	17	17	18	36	38	31	31	37	4	47	39
JAN. 4	39	19	19	20	36	39	31	31	37	4	47	39
JAN. 5	39	21	21	22	36	39	31	31	37	4	47	39
JAN. 6	39	23	23	24	36	39	31	31	37	4	47	39
JAN. 7	39	24	25	26	36	39	31	31	37	4	47	39
JAN. 8	39	26	27	27	36	39	31	31	37	4	47	40
JAN. 9	39	28	28	29	37	39	32	31	37	4	47	40
JAN. 10	40	30	30	31	37	40	32	31	37	4	47	40
JAN. 11	40	31	32	32	37	40	32	31	37	4	47	40
JAN. 12	40	33	33	34	37	40	32	31	37	4	47	40
JAN. 13	40	34	35	35	37	40	32	31	37	4	47	40
JAN. 14	40	36	37	37	38	40	32	32	37	4	47	40
JAN. 15	40	38	38	39	38	40	32	32	37	4	47	40
JAN. 16	40	39	40	40	38	41	32	32	37	4	47	40
JAN. 17	41	41	41	42	38	41	32	32	37	4	47	40
JAN. 18	41	42	43	43	38	41	32	32	37	4	47	40
JAN. 19	41	44	44	45	38	41	32	32	37	4	47	40
JAN. 20	41	46	46	47	39	41	32	32	37	4	47	40
JAN. 21	41	47	48	48	39	41	33	32	37	4	47	40
JAN. 22	41	1	1	2	39	42	33	32	37	4	47	40
JAN. 23	42	3	3	4	39	42	33	32	37	4	47	40
JAN. 24	42	4	5	6	39	42	33	32	38	4	47	40
JAN. 25	42	6	7	7	40	42	33	32	38	4	47	40
JAN. 26	42	8	9	9	40	42	33	32	38	4	47	40
JAN. 27	42	10	11	11	40	42	33	32	38	4	47	40
JAN. 28	42	12	12	13	40	43	33	32	38	4	47	40
JAN. 29	42	14	14	15	40	43	33	32	38	4	47	40
JAN. 30	42	16	16	17	41	43	33	32	38	4	47	40
JAN. 31	43	18	18	19	41	43	33	32	38	4	47	40

February

Date & Time	SUN	MOON 1	MOON 2	MOON 3	MERCURY	VENUS	MARS	JUPITER	SATURN	URANUS	NEPTUNE	PLUTO
FEB. 1	43	20	20	21	41	43	33	32	38	4	47	40
FEB. 2	43	22	22	23	41	44	34	32	38	4	47	40
FEB. 3	43	24	24	25	42	44	34	32	38	4	47	40
FEB. 4	43	26	26	27	42	44	34	32	38	4	47	40
FEB. 5	43	27	28	28	42	44	34	32	38	4	47	40
FEB. 6	43	29	30	30	42	44	34	32	38	4	47	40
FEB. 7	43	31	31	32	42	44	34	32	38	4	47	40
FEB. 8	44	32	33	33	43	45	34	32	38	4	47	40
FEB. 9	44	34	35	35	43	45	34	32	38	4	47	40
FEB. 10	44	36	36	37	43	45	34	32	38	4	47	40
FEB. 11	44	37	38	38	43	45	34	32	38	4	47	40
FEB. 12	44	39	39	40	44	45	34	32	38	4	47	40
FEB. 13	44	40	41	41	44	45	34	32	38	4	47	40
FEB. 14	44	42	42	43	44	46	34	32	38	4	47	40
FEB. 15	44	43	44	45	44	46	35	32	38	4	47	40
FEB. 16	45	45	46	46	44	46	35	32	38	4	47	40
FEB. 17	45	47	47	48	45	46	35	32	38	4	47	40
FEB. 18	45	48	1	2	45	46	35	32	38	4	47	40
FEB. 19	45	2	3	3	45	46	35	32	38	4	47	40
FEB. 20	45	4	5	5	45	47	35	32	38	4	47	40
FEB. 21	45	6	6	7	45	47	35	32	38	4	47	40
FEB. 22	45	8	8	9	46	47	35	32	38	4	47	40
FEB. 23	46	9	10	11	46	47	35	32	38	4	47	40
FEB. 24	46	11	12	12	46	47	35	32	38	4	47	40
FEB. 25	46	13	14	14	47	47	35	32	38	4	47	40
FEB. 26	46	15	16	16	47	48	35	32	38	4	47	40
FEB. 27	46	17	18	18	47	48	36	32	38	4	47	40
FEB. 28	46	19	20	20	47	48	36	32	38	4	47	40

MOON 1 ◗ 12:01 A.M. TO 8:00 A.M.   **MOON 2** ◖ 8:01 A.M. TO 4:00 P.M.   **MOON 3** ● 4:01 P.M. TO 12:00 A.M.

Use only one "moon" number. Choose the column closest to your time of birth. If your place of birth is not on Eastern Standard Time, be sure to read "How to Convert to Eastern Standard Time" at the beginning of this section.

March

April

Date & Time	SUN ☉	MOON 1 ◗	MOON 2 ◑	MOON 3 ●	MERCURY	VENUS	MARS	JUPITER	SATURN	URANUS	NEPTUNE	PLUTO
MAR. 1	46	21	22	22	48	48	36	32	38	4	47	40
MAR. 2	46	23	23	24	48	48	36	32	38	4	47	40
MAR. 3	47	25	25	26	48	48	36	32	38	4	47	40
MAR. 4	47	27	27	28	48	1	36	32	38	4	47	40
MAR. 5	47	28	29	30	1	1	36	32	38	4	47	40
MAR. 6	47	30	31	31	1	1	36	32	38	4	47	40
MAR. 7	47	32	32	33	1	1	36	32	38	4	47	40
MAR. 8	47	33	34	35	1	1	36	32	38	4	47	40
MAR. 9	47	35	36	36	2	1	36	32	38	4	47	40
MAR. 10	47	37	37	38	2	2	36	32	38	4	47	40
MAR. 11	48	38	39	39	2	2	36	32	38	4	47	40
MAR. 12	48	40	40	41	2	2	37	32	38	4	47	40
MAR. 13	48	41	42	42	2	2	37	32	38	4	47	40
MAR. 14	48	43	44	44	3	2	37	32	38	5	47	40
MAR. 15	48	45	45	46	3	2	37	32	38	5	47	40
MAR. 16	48	46	47	48	3	2	37	32	38	5	47	40
MAR. 17	48	48	1	1	3	3	37	32	38	5	47	40
MAR. 18	48	2	2	3	3	3	37	32	38	5	47	40
MAR. 19	1	3	4	5	3	3	37	32	38	5	47	40
MAR. 20	1	5	6	6	3	3	37	32	38	5	47	40
MAR. 21	1	7	8	8	3	3	37	32	38	5	47	40
MAR. 22	1	9	10	10	3	3	37	32	38	5	47	40
MAR. 23	1	11	11	12	3	4	37	32	38	5	47	40
MAR. 24	1	13	13	14	3	4	37	32	38	5	47	40
MAR. 25	2	15	15	16	3	4	38	32	38	5	47	40
MAR. 26	2	16	17	18	3	4	38	32	38	5	47	40
MAR. 27	2	18	19	20	3	4	38	32	38	5	47	40
MAR. 28	2	20	21	21	3	4	38	32	38	5	47	40
MAR. 29	2	22	23	23	3	5	38	32	38	5	47	40
MAR. 30	2	24	25	25	3	5	38	32	38	5	47	40
MAR. 31	2	26	26	27	3	5	38	32	38	5	47	40

Date & Time	SUN ☉	MOON 1 ◗	MOON 2 ◑	MOON 3 ●	MERCURY	VENUS	MARS	JUPITER	SATURN	URANUS	NEPTUNE	PLUTO
APR. 1	2	28	28	29	3	5	38	32	38	5	47	40
APR. 2	2	29	30	31	3	5	38	32	38	5	47	40
APR. 3	3	31	32	32	2	5	38	32	38	5	47	40
APR. 4	3	33	33	34	2	6	38	32	38	5	47	40
APR. 5	3	34	35	36	2	6	38	32	38	5	47	40
APR. 6	3	36	37	37	2	6	38	32	38	5	47	40
APR. 7	3	38	38	39	2	6	38	32	38	5	47	40
APR. 8	3	39	40	40	2	6	39	32	38	5	47	40
APR. 9	3	41	41	42	2	6	39	32	38	5	47	40
APR. 10	3	42	43	43	2	7	39	32	38	5	47	40
APR. 11	4	44	45	45	2	7	39	32	38	5	47	40
APR. 12	4	46	46	47	2	7	39	32	38	5	47	40
APR. 13	4	47	48	1	2	7	39	32	38	5	47	40
APR. 14	4	1	2	2	2	7	39	32	38	5	47	40
APR. 15	4	3	3	4	2	7	39	32	38	5	47	40
APR. 16	4	5	5	6	2	8	39	32	38	5	47	40
APR. 17	4	7	7	8	2	8	39	32	38	5	47	40
APR. 18	4	8	9	10	2	8	39	32	38	5	47	40
APR. 19	5	10	11	12	2	8	39	32	38	5	47	40
APR. 20	5	12	13	13	2	8	39	32	38	5	47	40
APR. 21	5	14	15	15	2	8	39	32	38	5	47	40
APR. 22	5	16	17	17	2	9	40	32	38	5	47	40
APR. 23	5	18	19	19	2	9	40	32	38	5	47	40
APR. 24	5	20	20	21	2	9	40	32	38	5	47	40
APR. 25	6	22	22	23	2	9	40	32	38	5	47	40
APR. 26	6	23	24	25	2	9	40	32	38	5	47	40
APR. 27	6	25	26	26	2	9	40	32	38	5	47	40
APR. 28	6	27	28	28	2	10	40	32	38	5	47	40
APR. 29	6	29	29	30	3	10	40	32	38	5	47	40
APR. 30	6	31	31	32	3	10	40	32	38	5	47	40

MOON 1 ◗ 12:01 A.M. TO 8:00 A.M.   **MOON 2** ◑ 8:01 A.M. TO 4:00 P.M.   **MOON 3** ● 4:01 P.M. TO 12:00 A.M.

Use only one "moon" number. Choose the column closest to your time of birth. If your place of birth is not on Eastern Standard Time, be sure to read "How to Convert to Eastern Standard Time" at the beginning of this section.

2018

May

June

Date & Time	SUN	MOON 1	MOON 2	MOON 3	MERCURY	VENUS	MARS	JUPITER	SATURN	URANUS	NEPTUNE	PLUTO
MAY 1	6	32	33	33	3	10	40	32	38	5	47	40
MAY 2	6	34	34	35	3	10	40	32	38	5	47	40
MAY 3	7	36	36	37	3	10	40	32	38	5	47	40
MAY 4	7	37	38	38	3	11	40	31	38	5	47	40
MAY 5	7	39	39	40	3	11	40	31	38	5	47	40
MAY 6	7	40	41	41	4	11	40	31	38	5	47	40
MAY 7	7	42	42	43	4	11	40	31	38	5	47	40
MAY 8	7	43	44	45	4	11	41	31	38	5	47	40
MAY 9	7	45	46	46	4	11	41	31	38	5	47	40
MAY 10	7	47	47	48	4	11	41	31	38	5	47	40
MAY 11	8	48	1	2	5	12	41	31	38	5	47	40
MAY 12	8	2	3	3	5	12	41	31	38	5	47	40
MAY 13	8	4	5	5	5	12	41	31	38	5	47	40
MAY 14	8	6	6	7	5	12	41	31	38	5	47	40
MAY 15	8	8	8	9	5	12	41	31	38	5	47	40
MAY 16	8	10	10	11	5	12	41	31	38	5	47	40
MAY 17	8	12	12	13	6	13	41	31	38	5	47	40
MAY 18	8	14	14	15	6	13	41	31	38	5	47	40
MAY 19	9	16	16	17	6	13	41	31	38	5	47	40
MAY 20	9	17	18	19	6	13	41	31	38	5	47	40
MAY 21	9	19	20	21	7	13	41	31	38	5	47	40
MAY 22	9	21	22	22	7	13	41	31	38	5	47	40
MAY 23	9	23	24	24	7	14	41	31	38	5	47	40
MAY 24	9	25	25	26	7	14	41	31	38	5	47	40
MAY 25	10	27	27	28	8	14	41	31	38	5	47	40
MAY 26	10	28	29	29	8	14	41	31	38	5	47	40
MAY 27	10	30	31	31	8	14	41	31	38	5	47	40
MAY 28	10	32	32	33	8	14	42	31	38	5	47	40
MAY 29	10	33	34	35	9	15	42	31	38	5	47	40
MAY 30	10	35	36	36	9	15	42	31	38	5	47	40
MAY 31	10	37	37	38	9	15	42	31	38	5	47	40

Date & Time	SUN	MOON 1	MOON 2	MOON 3	MERCURY	VENUS	MARS	JUPITER	SATURN	URANUS	NEPTUNE	PLUTO
JUN. 1	10	38	39	39	10	15	42	31	38	5	47	40
JUN. 2	10	40	40	41	10	15	42	31	38	5	47	40
JUN. 3	11	41	42	42	10	15	42	31	38	5	47	40
JUN. 4	11	43	44	44	10	15	42	31	38	5	47	40
JUN. 5	11	45	45	46	11	16	42	31	38	5	47	40
JUN. 6	11	46	47	47	11	16	42	31	38	5	47	40
JUN. 7	11	48	48	1	11	16	42	31	38	5	47	40
JUN. 8	11	2	2	3	12	16	42	31	38	5	47	40
JUN. 9	11	3	4	4	12	16	42	31	38	5	47	40
JUN. 10	11	5	6	6	12	16	42	31	38	5	47	40
JUN. 11	12	7	8	8	13	17	42	31	38	5	47	40
JUN. 12	12	9	9	10	13	17	42	31	38	5	47	40
JUN. 13	12	11	11	12	13	17	42	31	38	5	47	40
JUN. 14	12	13	13	14	13	17	42	31	38	5	47	40
JUN. 15	12	15	15	16	14	17	42	31	38	5	47	40
JUN. 16	12	17	17	18	14	17	42	31	38	5	47	40
JUN. 17	12	19	19	20	14	17	42	31	38	5	47	40
JUN. 18	12	21	21	22	14	18	42	31	38	5	47	40
JUN. 19	13	23	23	24	15	18	42	31	38	5	47	40
JUN. 20	13	24	25	26	15	18	42	31	38	5	47	40
JUN. 21	13	26	27	27	15	18	42	31	38	5	47	40
JUN. 22	13	28	29	29	15	18	42	31	38	5	47	40
JUN. 23	13	30	30	31	16	18	42	31	38	5	47	40
JUN. 24	13	31	32	32	16	19	42	31	38	5	47	40
JUN. 25	14	33	34	34	16	19	42	31	38	5	47	40
JUN. 26	14	35	35	36	16	19	42	31	38	5	47	40
JUN. 27	14	36	37	37	17	19	42	31	38	5	47	40
JUN. 28	14	38	38	39	17	19	42	31	38	5	47	40
JUN. 29	14	39	40	40	17	19	42	31	38	5	47	40
JUN. 30	14	41	42	42	17	19	42	31	38	5	47	40

MOON 1 ◐ 12:01 A.M. TO 8:00 A.M.   **MOON 2** ◑ 8:01 A.M. TO 4:00 P.M.   **MOON 3** ● 4:01 P.M. TO 12:00 A.M.

Use only one "moon" number. Choose the column closest to your time of birth. If your place of birth is not on Eastern Standard Time, be sure to read "How to Convert to Eastern Standard Time" at the beginning of this section.

2018

July   ## August

Date & Time	SUN ☉	MOON 1 ☽	MOON 2 ☽	MOON 3 ●	MERCURY	VENUS	MARS	JUPITER	SATURN	URANUS	NEPTUNE	PLUTO
JUL. 1	14	43	43	44	17	20	42	31	38	5	47	40
JUL. 2	14	44	45	45	18	20	42	31	38	5	47	40
JUL. 3	15	46	46	47	18	20	42	31	38	5	47	40
JUL. 4	15	47	48	48	18	20	42	31	38	5	47	40
JUL. 5	15	1	2	2	18	20	42	31	38	5	47	40
JUL. 6	15	3	3	4	18	20	42	31	38	5	47	40
JUL. 7	15	4	5	6	18	21	42	31	38	5	47	40
JUL. 8	15	6	7	7	19	21	42	31	38	5	47	40
JUL. 9	15	8	9	9	19	21	42	31	38	5	47	40
JUL. 10	15	10	11	11	19	21	42	31	38	5	47	40
JUL. 11	16	12	13	13	19	21	42	31	38	5	47	40
JUL. 12	16	14	15	15	19	21	42	31	38	5	47	40
JUL. 13	16	16	17	17	19	21	42	31	38	5	47	40
JUL. 14	16	18	19	19	19	22	42	31	38	5	47	40
JUL. 15	16	20	21	21	19	22	42	31	38	5	47	40
JUL. 16	16	22	23	23	20	22	42	31	38	5	47	40
JUL. 17	16	24	24	25	20	22	42	31	38	5	47	40
JUL. 18	16	26	26	27	20	22	42	31	38	5	47	40
JUL. 19	17	27	28	29	20	22	42	31	38	5	47	40
JUL. 20	17	29	30	30	20	22	42	31	38	5	47	40
JUL. 21	17	31	32	32	20	23	42	31	38	5	47	40
JUL. 22	17	33	33	34	20	23	42	31	38	5	47	40
JUL. 23	17	34	35	35	20	23	42	31	38	5	47	40
JUL. 24	17	36	36	37	20	23	42	31	38	5	47	40
JUL. 25	17	37	38	38	20	23	42	31	37	5	47	40
JUL. 26	18	39	40	40	20	23	42	31	37	5	47	40
JUL. 27	18	41	41	42	20	23	42	31	37	5	47	40
JUL. 28	18	42	43	43	20	24	41	31	37	5	47	40
JUL. 29	18	44	44	45	20	24	41	31	37	5	47	40
JUL. 30	18	45	46	46	20	24	41	31	37	5	47	40
JUL. 31	18	47	47	47	20	24	41	31	37	5	47	40

Date & Time	SUN ☉	MOON 1 ☽	MOON 2 ☽	MOON 3 ●	MERCURY	VENUS	MARS	JUPITER	SATURN	URANUS	NEPTUNE	PLUTO
AUG. 1	18	1	1	2	20	24	41	31	37	5	47	40
AUG. 2	18	2	3	3	20	24	41	31	37	5	47	40
AUG. 3	19	4	4	5	20	24	41	31	37	5	47	40
AUG. 4	19	6	6	7	20	25	41	31	37	5	47	40
AUG. 5	19	7	8	9	20	25	41	31	37	5	47	40
AUG. 6	19	10	10	10	19	25	41	31	37	5	47	40
AUG. 7	19	11	12	12	19	25	41	31	37	5	47	40
AUG. 8	19	13	14	14	19	25	41	31	37	5	47	40
AUG. 9	19	15	16	16	19	25	41	31	37	5	47	40
AUG. 10	19	17	18	18	19	25	41	31	37	5	47	40
AUG. 11	20	19	20	20	19	26	41	31	37	5	47	40
AUG. 12	20	21	22	22	19	26	41	31	37	5	47	40
AUG. 13	20	23	24	24	19	26	41	31	37	5	47	40
AUG. 14	20	25	26	26	19	26	41	31	37	5	47	40
AUG. 15	20	27	27	28	19	26	41	31	37	5	47	40
AUG. 16	20	29	29	30	19	26	41	31	37	5	47	40
AUG. 17	20	30	31	32	19	26	41	31	37	5	47	40
AUG. 18	20	32	33	33	19	26	41	31	37	5	47	40
AUG. 19	21	34	34	35	19	27	41	31	37	5	47	40
AUG. 20	21	35	36	37	19	27	41	31	37	5	47	40
AUG. 21	21	37	38	38	19	27	41	31	37	5	47	40
AUG. 22	21	39	39	40	19	27	41	31	37	5	47	40
AUG. 23	21	40	41	41	19	27	41	31	37	5	47	40
AUG. 24	21	42	42	43	19	27	41	31	37	5	47	40
AUG. 25	21	43	44	44	19	27	41	31	37	5	47	40
AUG. 26	22	45	45	46	19	27	41	31	37	5	47	40
AUG. 27	22	47	47	48	19	28	41	31	37	5	47	40
AUG. 28	22	48	1	1	19	28	41	31	37	5	47	40
AUG. 29	22	2	2	3	19	28	41	31	37	5	47	40
AUG. 30	22	4	4	5	20	28	41	31	37	5	47	39
AUG. 31	22	5	6	6	20	28	41	31	37	5	47	39

MOON 1 ☽ 12:01 A.M. TO 8:00 A.M.   **MOON 2** ☽ 8:01 A.M. TO 4:00 P.M.   **MOON 3** ● 4:01 P.M. TO 12:00 A.M.

Use only one "moon" number. Choose the column closest to your time of birth. If your place of birth is not on Eastern Standard Time, be sure to read "How to Convert to Eastern Standard Time" at the beginning of this section.

2018

September

Date & Time	SUN	MOON 1	MOON 2	MOON 3	MERCURY	VENUS	MARS	JUPITER	SATURN	URANUS	NEPTUNE	PLUTO
SEP. 1	22	7	8	8	20	28	41	31	37	5	47	39
SEP. 2	22	9	9	10	20	28	41	31	37	5	47	39
SEP. 3	23	11	11	12	20	28	41	31	37	5	47	39
SEP. 4	23	12	13	14	21	28	41	31	37	5	47	39
SEP. 5	23	14	15	16	21	29	41	31	37	5	47	39
SEP. 6	23	16	17	18	21	29	41	31	37	5	47	39
SEP. 7	23	18	19	20	21	29	41	31	37	5	47	39
SEP. 8	23	20	21	22	21	29	41	31	37	5	47	39
SEP. 9	23	22	23	23	22	29	41	31	37	5	47	39
SEP. 10	23	24	25	25	22	29	41	31	37	5	47	39
SEP. 11	24	26	27	27	22	29	41	31	37	5	47	39
SEP. 12	24	28	29	29	22	29	41	31	37	5	47	39
SEP. 13	24	30	30	31	23	29	41	31	37	5	47	39
SEP. 14	24	32	32	33	23	29	41	32	37	5	47	39
SEP. 15	24	33	34	34	23	29	41	32	37	5	47	39
SEP. 16	24	35	35	36	23	30	41	32	37	5	47	39
SEP. 17	24	37	37	38	24	30	41	32	37	5	47	39
SEP. 18	24	38	39	39	24	30	41	32	37	5	47	39
SEP. 19	25	40	40	41	24	30	41	32	37	5	47	39
SEP. 20	25	41	42	42	24	30	41	32	37	5	47	39
SEP. 21	25	43	43	44	25	30	41	32	37	5	47	39
SEP. 22	25	44	45	46	25	30	41	32	37	5	47	39
SEP. 23	25	46	47	47	25	30	41	32	37	5	47	39
SEP. 24	25	48	48	1	25	30	41	32	37	5	47	39
SEP. 25	26	1	2	3	26	30	41	32	37	5	47	39
SEP. 26	26	3	4	4	26	30	42	32	37	5	47	39
SEP. 27	26	5	5	6	26	30	42	32	37	5	47	39
SEP. 28	26	7	7	8	26	30	42	32	37	5	47	39
SEP. 29	26	8	9	10	27	30	42	32	37	5	47	39
SEP. 30	26	10	11	11	27	30	42	32	37	5	47	39

October

Date & Time	SUN	MOON 1	MOON 2	MOON 3	MERCURY	VENUS	MARS	JUPITER	SATURN	URANUS	NEPTUNE	PLUTO
OCT. 1	26	12	13	13	27	30	42	32	37	5	47	39
OCT. 2	26	14	14	15	27	30	42	32	37	5	47	39
OCT. 3	27	16	16	17	28	30	42	32	37	5	47	39
OCT. 4	27	18	18	19	28	30	42	32	37	5	47	39
OCT. 5	27	19	20	21	28	30	42	32	37	5	47	39
OCT. 6	27	21	22	23	28	30	42	32	37	5	47	39
OCT. 7	27	23	24	25	28	30	42	32	37	5	47	39
OCT. 8	27	25	26	27	29	30	42	32	37	5	47	39
OCT. 9	27	27	28	28	29	30	42	32	37	5	47	39
OCT. 10	27	29	30	30	29	30	42	32	37	5	47	39
OCT. 11	28	31	31	32	29	30	42	32	37	5	47	39
OCT. 12	28	33	33	34	29	30	42	32	37	5	47	39
OCT. 13	28	34	35	35	30	30	42	32	37	5	47	39
OCT. 14	28	36	37	37	30	30	43	32	37	5	47	39
OCT. 15	28	38	38	39	30	30	43	32	37	5	47	39
OCT. 16	28	39	40	40	30	30	43	32	37	5	47	39
OCT. 17	28	41	41	42	30	30	43	32	37	5	47	39
OCT. 18	28	42	43	43	31	30	43	32	37	5	47	39
OCT. 19	29	44	44	45	31	30	43	32	37	5	47	39
OCT. 20	29	46	46	47	31	30	43	32	38	5	47	39
OCT. 21	29	47	48	48	31	30	43	32	38	5	47	39
OCT. 22	29	1	1	2	31	30	43	32	38	5	47	39
OCT. 23	29	3	3	4	32	30	43	32	38	5	47	39
OCT. 24	29	4	4	5	32	30	43	33	38	5	47	39
OCT. 25	29	6	7	7	32	29	43	33	38	5	47	39
OCT. 26	30	8	8	9	32	29	43	33	38	5	47	39
OCT. 27	30	10	10	11	32	29	43	33	38	5	47	39
OCT. 28	30	12	12	13	32	29	44	33	38	5	47	39
OCT. 29	30	13	14	15	33	29	44	33	38	5	47	39
OCT. 30	30	15	16	17	33	29	44	33	38	5	47	39
OCT. 31	30	17	18	18	33	29	44	33	38	5	47	39

MOON 1 ◐ 12:01 A.M. TO 8:00 A.M.　　**MOON 2** ◑ 8:01 A.M. TO 4:00 P.M.　　**MOON 3** ● 4:01 P.M. TO 12:00 A.M.

Use only one "moon" number. Choose the column closest to your time of birth. If your place of birth is not on Eastern Standard Time, be sure to read "How to Convert to Eastern Standard Time" at the beginning of this section.

2018

November

Date & Time	SUN	MOON 1	MOON 2	MOON 3	MERCURY	VENUS	MARS	JUPITER	SATURN	URANUS	NEPTUNE	PLUTO
NOV. 1	30	19	20	20	33	29	44	33	38	5	47	39
NOV. 2	30	21	22	22	33	29	44	33	38	5	47	40
NOV. 3	31	23	23	24	33	29	44	33	38	5	47	40
NOV. 4	31	25	25	26	34	29	44	33	38	5	47	40
NOV. 5	31	27	27	28	34	29	44	33	38	5	47	40
NOV. 6	31	28	29	30	34	29	44	33	38	5	47	40
NOV. 7	31	30	31	31	34	29	44	33	38	5	47	40
NOV. 8	31	32	33	33	34	29	44	33	38	5	47	40
NOV. 9	31	34	34	35	34	29	44	33	38	5	47	40
NOV. 10	31	35	36	36	34	28	45	33	38	5	47	40
NOV. 11	31	37	38	38	34	28	45	33	38	5	47	40
NOV. 12	32	39	39	40	35	28	45	33	38	5	47	40
NOV. 13	32	40	41	41	35	28	45	33	38	5	47	40
NOV. 14	32	42	42	43	35	28	45	33	38	5	47	40
NOV. 15	32	43	44	44	35	28	45	33	38	5	47	40
NOV. 16	32	45	46	46	35	28	45	33	38	5	47	40
NOV. 17	32	47	47	48	35	28	45	33	38	5	47	40
NOV. 18	32	48	1	1	35	28	45	33	38	5	47	40
NOV. 19	33	2	2	3	35	28	45	33	38	5	47	40
NOV. 20	33	4	4	5	35	28	45	33	38	5	47	40
NOV. 21	33	5	6	7	35	28	45	33	38	5	47	40
NOV. 22	33	7	8	8	34	28	45	33	38	5	47	40
NOV. 23	33	9	10	10	34	28	46	33	38	5	47	40
NOV. 24	33	11	12	12	34	28	46	33	38	5	47	40
NOV. 25	34	13	13	14	34	29	46	33	38	5	47	40
NOV. 26	34	15	15	16	34	29	46	33	38	5	47	40
NOV. 27	34	17	17	18	34	29	46	34	38	5	47	40
NOV. 28	34	19	19	20	33	29	46	34	38	5	47	40
NOV. 29	34	20	21	22	33	29	46	34	38	5	47	40
NOV. 30	34	22	23	24	33	29	46	34	38	5	47	40

December

Date & Time	SUN	MOON 1	MOON 2	MOON 3	MERCURY	VENUS	MARS	JUPITER	SATURN	URANUS	NEPTUNE	PLUTO
DEC. 1	34	24	25	25	33	29	46	34	38	5	47	40
DEC. 2	34	26	27	27	33	29	46	34	38	5	47	40
DEC. 3	35	28	28	29	33	29	46	34	38	5	47	40
DEC. 4	35	30	30	31	33	29	47	34	38	5	47	40
DEC. 5	35	31	32	33	33	29	47	34	38	5	47	40
DEC. 6	35	33	34	34	33	29	47	34	38	5	47	40
DEC. 7	35	35	35	36	33	29	47	34	38	5	47	40
DEC. 8	35	36	37	38	33	29	47	34	38	5	47	40
DEC. 9	35	38	39	39	33	30	47	34	38	5	47	40
DEC. 10	35	40	40	41	33	30	47	34	38	5	47	40
DEC. 11	36	41	42	42	33	30	47	34	38	5	47	40
DEC. 12	36	43	43	44	33	30	47	34	38	5	47	40
DEC. 13	36	44	45	46	33	30	47	34	38	5	47	40
DEC. 14	36	46	47	47	33	30	47	34	38	5	47	40
DEC. 15	36	48	48	1	33	30	47	34	38	5	47	40
DEC. 16	36	1	2	2	33	30	48	34	38	5	47	40
DEC. 17	36	3	3	4	34	30	48	34	38	5	47	40
DEC. 18	36	5	5	6	34	30	48	34	38	5	47	40
DEC. 19	37	6	7	8	34	31	48	34	38	5	47	40
DEC. 20	37	8	9	9	34	31	48	34	38	5	47	40
DEC. 21	37	10	11	11	34	31	48	34	38	5	47	40
DEC. 22	37	12	13	13	34	31	48	34	38	5	47	40
DEC. 23	37	14	15	15	34	31	48	34	38	5	47	40
DEC. 24	37	16	17	17	35	31	48	34	38	5	47	40
DEC. 25	37	18	19	19	35	31	48	34	38	5	47	40
DEC. 26	38	20	21	21	35	31	48	34	38	5	47	40
DEC. 27	38	22	23	23	35	31	1	34	38	5	47	40
DEC. 28	38	24	24	25	35	32	1	34	38	5	47	40
DEC. 29	38	26	26	27	36	32	1	34	38	5	47	40
DEC. 30	38	27	28	29	36	32	1	34	38	5	47	40
DEC. 31	38	29	30	30	36	32	1	35	38	5	47	40

MOON 1 ◔ 12:01 A.M. TO 8:00 A.M.   **MOON 2** ◑ 8:01 A.M. TO 4:00 P.M.   **MOON 3** ● 4:01 P.M. TO 12:00 A.M.

Use only one "moon" number. Choose the column closest to your time of birth. If your place of birth is not on Eastern Standard Time, be sure to read "How to Convert to Eastern Standard Time" at the beginning of this section.

2019

January

Date & Time	SUN	MOON 1	MOON 2	MOON 3	MERCURY	VENUS	MARS	JUPITER	SATURN	URANUS	NEPTUNE	PLUTO
JAN. 1	38	31	32	32	36	32	1	35	38	5	47	40
JAN. 2	38	33	33	34	36	32	1	35	39	5	47	40
JAN. 3	39	34	35	35	37	32	1	35	39	5	47	40
JAN. 4	39	36	37	37	37	33	1	35	39	5	47	40
JAN. 5	39	38	38	39	37	33	1	35	39	5	47	40
JAN. 6	39	39	40	40	37	33	1	35	39	5	47	40
JAN. 7	39	41	41	42	37	33	2	35	39	5	47	40
JAN. 8	39	42	43	43	38	33	2	35	39	5	47	40
JAN. 9	39	44	45	45	38	33	2	35	39	5	47	40
JAN. 10	40	46	46	47	38	33	2	35	39	5	47	40
JAN. 11	40	47	48	48	38	33	2	35	39	5	47	40
JAN. 12	40	1	1	2	38	34	2	35	39	5	47	40
JAN. 13	40	2	3	3	39	34	2	35	39	5	47	40
JAN. 14	40	4	5	5	39	34	2	35	39	5	47	40
JAN. 15	40	6	6	7	39	34	2	35	39	5	47	40
JAN. 16	40	7	8	9	39	34	2	35	39	5	47	40
JAN. 17	41	9	10	11	39	34	2	35	39	5	47	40
JAN. 18	41	11	12	12	40	34	3	35	39	5	47	40
JAN. 19	41	13	14	14	40	34	3	35	39	5	47	40
JAN. 20	41	15	16	16	40	34	3	35	39	5	47	40
JAN. 21	41	17	18	18	40	35	3	35	39	5	47	40
JAN. 22	41	19	20	20	41	35	3	35	39	5	47	40
JAN. 23	42	21	22	22	41	35	3	35	39	5	47	40
JAN. 24	42	23	24	24	41	35	3	35	39	5	47	40
JAN. 25	42	25	26	26	41	35	3	35	39	5	47	40
JAN. 26	42	27	28	28	41	35	3	35	39	5	47	40
JAN. 27	42	29	29	30	41	36	3	35	39	5	47	40
JAN. 28	42	31	31	32	42	36	3	35	39	5	47	40
JAN. 29	42	32	33	33	42	36	4	35	39	5	47	40
JAN. 30	42	34	35	35	42	36	4	35	39	5	47	40
JAN. 31	43	36	36	37	43	36	4	35	39	5	47	40

February

Date & Time	SUN	MOON 1	MOON 2	MOON 3	MERCURY	VENUS	MARS	JUPITER	SATURN	URANUS	NEPTUNE	PLUTO
FEB. 1	43	37	38	38	43	37	4	35	39	5	47	40
FEB. 2	43	39	39	40	43	37	4	35	39	5	47	40
FEB. 3	43	40	41	41	43	37	4	35	39	5	47	40
FEB. 4	43	42	43	43	43	37	4	35	39	5	47	40
FEB. 5	43	44	44	45	44	37	4	35	39	5	47	40
FEB. 6	43	45	46	46	44	37	4	35	39	5	47	40
FEB. 7	43	47	47	48	44	37	4	35	39	5	47	40
FEB. 8	44	48	1	1	44	38	4	35	39	5	47	40
FEB. 9	44	2	2	3	45	38	4	36	39	5	47	40
FEB. 10	44	4	4	5	45	38	5	36	39	5	47	40
FEB. 11	44	5	6	6	45	38	5	36	39	5	47	40
FEB. 12	44	7	7	8	45	38	5	36	39	5	47	40
FEB. 13	44	9	9	10	46	38	5	36	39	5	47	40
FEB. 14	44	10	11	12	46	39	5	36	39	5	47	40
FEB. 15	44	12	13	14	46	39	5	36	39	5	47	40
FEB. 16	45	14	15	15	46	39	5	36	39	5	47	40
FEB. 17	45	16	17	17	47	39	5	36	39	5	47	40
FEB. 18	45	18	19	19	47	39	5	36	39	5	47	40
FEB. 19	45	20	21	21	47	39	5	36	39	5	47	40
FEB. 20	45	22	23	24	47	39	5	36	39	5	47	40
FEB. 21	45	24	25	26	47	40	6	36	39	5	47	40
FEB. 22	45	26	27	27	48	40	6	36	39	5	47	40
FEB. 23	46	28	29	29	48	40	6	36	39	5	47	40
FEB. 24	46	30	31	31	48	40	6	36	39	5	47	40
FEB. 25	46	32	32	33	48	40	6	36	39	5	47	40
FEB. 26	46	34	34	35	48	40	6	36	39	5	47	40
FEB. 27	46	35	36	36	48	41	6	36	39	5	47	40
FEB. 28	46	37	37	38	1	41	6	36	39	5	47	40

MOON 1 ☽ 12:01 A.M. TO 8:00 A.M.   **MOON 2** ☽ 8:01 A.M. TO 4:00 P.M.   **MOON 3** ● 4:01 P.M. TO 12:00 A.M.

Use only one "moon" number. Choose the column closest to your time of birth. If your place of birth is not on Eastern Standard Time, be sure to read "How to Convert to Eastern Standard Time" at the beginning of this section.

Date & Time	SUN ☉	MOON 1 ◖	MOON 2 ◑	MOON 3 ●	MERCURY	VENUS	MARS	JUPITER	SATURN	URANUS	NEPTUNE	PLUTO
MAR. 1	46	38	39	40	1	41	6	36	39	5	47	40
MAR. 2	46	40	41	41	1	41	6	36	39	5	47	40
MAR. 3	47	42	42	43	1	41	6	36	39	5	47	40
MAR. 4	47	43	44	44	1	41	7	36	39	5	47	40
MAR. 5	47	45	45	46	1	42	7	36	39	5	47	40
MAR. 6	47	46	47	47	1	42	7	36	39	5	47	40
MAR. 7	47	48	48	1	1	42	7	36	39	5	47	40
MAR. 8	47	2	2	3	1	42	7	36	39	5	47	40
MAR. 9	47	3	4	4	1	42	7	36	39	5	47	40
MAR. 10	47	5	5	6	1	42	7	36	39	5	47	40
MAR. 11	48	6	7	8	1	42	7	36	39	5	47	40
MAR. 12	48	8	9	9	1	43	7	36	39	5	47	40
MAR. 13	48	10	11	11	48	43	7	36	39	5	47	40
MAR. 14	48	12	12	13	48	43	7	36	39	5	47	40
MAR. 15	48	14	14	15	48	43	8	36	39	5	47	40
MAR. 16	48	15	16	17	48	43	8	36	39	5	47	40
MAR. 17	48	17	18	19	48	43	8	36	39	5	47	40
MAR. 18	48	19	20	21	48	44	8	36	40	5	47	40
MAR. 19	1	21	22	23	48	44	8	36	40	5	47	40
MAR. 20	1	23	24	25	48	44	8	36	40	5	47	40
MAR. 21	1	25	26	27	47	44	8	36	40	5	47	40
MAR. 22	1	27	28	29	47	44	8	36	40	5	47	40
MAR. 23	1	29	30	30	47	44	8	36	40	5	47	40
MAR. 24	1	31	32	32	47	45	8	36	40	5	47	40
MAR. 25	2	33	33	34	47	45	8	36	40	5	47	40
MAR. 26	2	35	35	36	47	45	9	36	40	5	47	40
MAR. 27	2	36	37	37	47	45	9	36	40	5	47	40
MAR. 28	2	38	39	39	47	45	9	36	40	5	47	40
MAR. 29	2	40	40	41	47	45	9	36	40	5	47	40
MAR. 30	2	41	42	42	47	46	9	36	40	5	47	40
MAR. 31	2	43	43	44	47	46	9	36	40	5	47	40

Date & Time	SUN ☉	MOON 1 ◖	MOON 2 ◑	MOON 3 ●	MERCURY	VENUS	MARS	JUPITER	SATURN	URANUS	NEPTUNE	PLUTO
APR. 1	2	44	45	45	47	46	9	36	40	5	47	40
APR. 2	2	46	46	47	47	46	9	36	40	5	47	40
APR. 3	3	47	48	1	47	46	9	36	40	5	47	40
APR. 4	3	1	2	2	47	46	9	36	40	5	47	40
APR. 5	3	3	3	4	47	46	9	36	40	5	47	40
APR. 6	3	4	5	6	48	47	9	36	40	5	47	40
APR. 7	3	6	7	7	48	47	10	36	40	5	47	40
APR. 8	3	8	8	9	48	47	10	36	40	5	47	40
APR. 9	3	10	10	11	48	47	10	36	40	5	47	40
APR. 10	3	11	12	12	48	47	10	36	40	5	47	40
APR. 11	4	13	14	14	48	47	10	36	40	5	47	40
APR. 12	4	15	16	16	48	48	10	36	40	5	47	40
APR. 13	4	17	17	18	48	48	10	36	40	5	47	40
APR. 14	4	19	19	20	48	48	10	36	40	5	47	40
APR. 15	4	21	21	22	1	48	10	36	40	5	47	40
APR. 16	4	22	23	24	1	48	10	36	40	5	47	40
APR. 17	4	24	25	26	1	48	10	36	40	5	47	40
APR. 18	4	26	27	28	1	1	11	36	40	5	47	40
APR. 19	5	28	29	30	1	1	11	36	40	5	47	40
APR. 20	5	30	31	32	1	1	11	36	40	5	47	40
APR. 21	5	32	33	33	2	1	11	36	40	5	47	40
APR. 22	5	34	35	35	2	1	11	36	40	5	47	40
APR. 23	5	36	36	37	2	1	11	36	40	5	47	40
APR. 24	5	37	38	39	2	2	11	36	40	5	47	40
APR. 25	6	39	40	40	2	2	11	36	40	5	47	40
APR. 26	6	41	41	42	3	2	11	36	40	5	47	40
APR. 27	6	42	43	43	3	2	11	36	40	5	47	40
APR. 28	6	44	44	45	3	2	11	36	40	5	47	40
APR. 29	6	45	46	46	3	2	12	36	40	5	47	40
APR. 30	6	47	48	48	3	3	12	36	40	5	47	40

MOON 1 ◖ 12:01 A.M. TO 8:00 A.M.　　**MOON 2** ◑ 8:01 A.M. TO 4:00 P.M.　　**MOON 3** ● 4:01 P.M. TO 12:00 A.M.

Use only one "moon" number. Choose the column closest to your time of birth. If your place of birth is not on Eastern Standard Time, be sure to read "How to Convert to Eastern Standard Time" at the beginning of this section.

2019

May   June

Date & Time	SUN	MOON 1	MOON 2	MOON 3	MERCURY	VENUS	MARS	JUPITER	SATURN	URANUS	NEPTUNE	PLUTO
MAY 1	6	1	1	2	4	3	12	36	40	5	47	40
MAY 2	6	2	3	3	4	3	12	36	40	5	47	40
MAY 3	7	4	4	5	4	3	12	36	40	5	47	40
MAY 4	7	6	6	7	4	3	12	36	40	5	47	40
MAY 5	7	7	8	8	5	3	12	36	40	5	47	40
MAY 6	7	9	10	10	5	3	12	36	40	5	47	40
MAY 7	7	11	11	12	4	3	12	36	40	5	47	40
MAY 8	7	13	13	14	5	4	12	36	40	5	47	40
MAY 9	7	14	15	16	6	4	12	36	40	5	47	40
MAY 10	7	16	17	18	6	4	12	36	40	5	47	40
MAY 11	8	18	19	19	6	4	13	36	40	5	47	40
MAY 12	8	20	21	21	6	4	13	36	40	5	47	40
MAY 13	8	22	23	23	7	5	13	36	40	5	47	40
MAY 14	8	24	25	25	7	5	13	36	40	5	47	40
MAY 15	8	26	26	27	7	5	13	36	40	5	47	40
MAY 16	8	28	28	29	7	5	13	36	40	5	47	40
MAY 17	8	30	30	31	8	5	13	36	40	5	47	40
MAY 18	8	31	32	33	8	5	13	36	40	5	47	40
MAY 19	9	33	34	34	8	6	13	36	40	6	47	40
MAY 20	9	35	36	36	9	6	13	36	40	6	47	40
MAY 21	9	37	37	38	9	6	13	36	40	6	47	40
MAY 22	9	38	39	40	9	6	13	36	40	6	47	40
MAY 23	9	40	41	41	9	6	14	36	40	6	47	40
MAY 24	9	42	42	43	10	6	14	36	40	6	47	40
MAY 25	10	43	44	44	10	7	14	36	40	6	47	40
MAY 26	10	45	45	46	10	7	14	36	40	6	47	40
MAY 27	10	46	47	48	11	7	14	36	40	6	47	40
MAY 28	10	48	1	1	11	7	14	36	40	6	47	40
MAY 29	10	2	2	3	11	7	14	36	40	6	47	40
MAY 30	10	3	4	4	11	7	14	36	40	6	47	40
MAY 31	10	5	6	6	12	8	14	36	40	6	47	40
JUN. 1	10	7	7	8	12	8	14	36	40	6	47	40
JUN. 2	10	8	9	10	12	8	14	36	40	6	47	40
JUN. 3	11	10	11	11	13	8	15	36	40	6	47	40
JUN. 4	11	12	13	13	13	8	15	36	40	6	47	40
JUN. 5	11	14	15	15	13	8	15	36	40	6	47	40
JUN. 6	11	16	16	17	13	9	15	36	40	6	47	40
JUN. 7	11	18	18	19	14	9	15	36	40	6	47	40
JUN. 8	11	20	20	21	14	9	15	36	40	6	47	40
JUN. 9	11	22	22	23	14	9	15	36	40	6	47	40
JUN. 10	11	23	24	25	14	9	15	36	40	6	47	40
JUN. 11	12	25	26	27	14	9	15	36	40	6	47	40
JUN. 12	12	27	28	28	15	9	15	36	40	6	47	40
JUN. 13	12	29	30	30	15	10	15	36	40	6	47	40
JUN. 14	12	31	31	32	15	10	15	36	39	6	47	40
JUN. 15	12	33	33	34	15	10	16	35	39	6	47	40
JUN. 16	12	34	35	36	15	10	16	35	39	6	47	40
JUN. 17	12	36	37	37	16	10	16	35	39	6	47	40
JUN. 18	12	38	38	39	16	10	16	35	39	6	47	40
JUN. 19	13	40	40	41	16	11	16	35	39	6	47	40
JUN. 20	13	41	42	42	16	11	16	35	39	6	47	40
JUN. 21	13	43	43	44	16	11	16	35	39	6	47	40
JUN. 22	13	44	45	45	16	11	16	35	39	6	47	40
JUN. 23	13	46	46	47	17	11	16	35	39	6	47	40
JUN. 24	13	48	48	1	17	11	16	35	39	6	47	40
JUN. 25	14	1	2	2	17	12	16	35	39	6	47	40
JUN. 26	14	3	3	4	17	12	16	35	39	6	47	40
JUN. 27	14	5	5	5	17	12	17	35	39	6	47	40
JUN. 28	14	6	7	7	17	12	17	35	39	6	47	40
JUN. 29	14	8	8	9	17	12	17	35	39	6	47	40
JUN. 30	14	10	10	11	17	12	17	35	39	6	47	40

MOON 1 ◐ 12:01 A.M. TO 8:00 A.M.   **MOON 2** ◑ 8:01 A.M. TO 4:00 P.M.   **MOON 3** ● 4:01 P.M. TO 12:00 A.M.

Use only one "moon" number. Choose the column closest to your time of birth. If your place of birth is not on Eastern Standard Time, be sure to read "How to Convert to Eastern Standard Time" at the beginning of this section.

Date & Time	SUN	MOON 1	MOON 2	MOON 3	MERCURY	VENUS	MARS	JUPITER	SATURN	URANUS	NEPTUNE	PLUTO
JUL. 1	14	11	12	13	17	13	17	35	39	6	47	40
JUL. 2	14	13	14	15	17	13	17	35	39	6	47	40
JUL. 3	15	15	16	16	17	13	17	35	39	6	47	40
JUL. 4	15	17	18	18	17	13	17	35	39	6	47	40
JUL. 5	15	19	20	20	18	13	17	35	39	6	47	40
JUL. 6	15	21	22	22	18	13	17	35	39	6	47	40
JUL. 7	15	23	24	24	18	14	17	35	39	6	47	40
JUL. 8	15	25	26	26	18	14	17	35	39	6	47	40
JUL. 9	15	27	27	28	18	14	18	35	39	6	47	40
JUL. 10	15	29	29	30	18	14	18	35	39	6	47	40
JUL. 11	16	30	31	32	18	14	18	35	39	6	47	40
JUL. 12	16	32	33	33	17	14	18	35	39	6	47	40
JUL. 13	16	34	35	35	17	15	18	35	39	6	47	40
JUL. 14	16	36	36	37	17	15	18	35	39	6	47	40
JUL. 15	16	37	38	38	17	15	18	35	39	6	47	40
JUL. 16	16	39	40	40	17	15	18	35	39	6	47	40
JUL. 17	16	41	41	42	17	15	18	35	39	6	47	40
JUL. 18	16	42	43	43	17	15	18	35	39	6	47	40
JUL. 19	17	44	44	45	17	16	18	35	39	6	47	40
JUL. 20	17	45	46	47	16	16	19	35	39	6	47	40
JUL. 21	17	47	48	48	17	16	19	35	39	6	47	40
JUL. 22	17	1	1	2	17	16	19	35	39	6	47	40
JUL. 23	17	2	3	3	17	16	19	35	39	6	47	40
JUL. 24	17	4	4	5	17	16	19	35	39	6	47	40
JUL. 25	17	5	6	7	16	16	19	35	39	6	47	40
JUL. 26	18	7	8	8	16	17	19	35	39	6	47	40
JUL. 27	18	9	9	10	16	17	19	35	39	6	47	40
JUL. 28	18	11	11	12	16	17	19	35	39	6	47	40
JUL. 29	18	12	13	14	16	17	19	35	39	6	47	40
JUL. 30	18	14	15	16	16	17	19	35	39	6	47	40
JUL. 31	18	16	17	18	16	17	19	35	39	6	47	40

Date & Time	SUN	MOON 1	MOON 2	MOON 3	MERCURY	VENUS	MARS	JUPITER	SATURN	URANUS	NEPTUNE	PLUTO
AUG. 1	18	18	19	20	16	18	20	35	39	6	47	40
AUG. 2	18	20	21	22	16	18	20	35	39	6	47	40
AUG. 3	19	22	23	24	16	18	20	35	39	6	47	40
AUG. 4	19	24	25	26	16	18	20	35	39	6	47	40
AUG. 5	19	26	27	28	16	18	20	35	39	6	47	40
AUG. 6	19	28	29	29	16	18	20	35	39	6	47	40
AUG. 7	19	30	31	31	16	19	20	35	39	6	47	40
AUG. 8	19	32	32	33	17	19	20	35	39	6	47	40
AUG. 9	19	34	34	35	17	19	20	35	39	6	47	40
AUG. 10	19	35	36	36	17	19	20	35	39	6	47	40
AUG. 11	20	37	38	38	17	19	20	35	39	6	47	40
AUG. 12	20	39	39	40	17	19	20	35	39	6	47	40
AUG. 13	20	40	41	41	17	20	21	35	39	6	47	40
AUG. 14	20	42	42	43	17	20	21	35	39	6	47	40
AUG. 15	20	43	44	45	18	20	21	35	39	6	47	40
AUG. 16	20	45	46	46	18	20	21	35	39	6	47	40
AUG. 17	20	47	47	48	18	20	21	35	39	6	47	40
AUG. 18	20	48	1	1	18	20	21	35	39	6	47	40
AUG. 19	21	2	2	3	18	21	21	35	39	6	47	40
AUG. 20	21	3	4	4	19	21	21	35	39	6	47	40
AUG. 21	21	5	6	6	19	21	21	35	39	6	47	40
AUG. 22	21	7	7	8	19	21	21	35	39	6	47	40
AUG. 23	21	8	9	9	19	21	21	35	39	6	47	40
AUG. 24	21	10	11	11	20	21	21	35	39	6	47	40
AUG. 25	21	12	12	13	20	22	22	35	39	6	47	40
AUG. 26	22	14	14	15	20	22	22	35	39	6	47	40
AUG. 27	22	15	16	17	20	22	22	35	39	6	47	40
AUG. 28	22	17	18	19	21	22	22	35	39	6	47	40
AUG. 29	22	19	20	21	21	22	22	35	39	6	47	40
AUG. 30	22	21	22	23	21	22	22	35	39	6	47	40
AUG. 31	22	23	24	25	21	23	22	35	39	6	47	40

MOON 1 ☽ 12:01 A.M. TO 8:00 A.M.　　**MOON 2** ◑ 8:01 A.M. TO 4:00 P.M.　　**MOON 3** ● 4:01 P.M. TO 12:00 A.M.

Use only one "moon" number. Choose the column closest to your time of birth. If your place of birth is not on Eastern Standard Time, be sure to read "How to Convert to Eastern Standard Time" at the beginning of this section.

September | October

Date & Time	SUN	MOON 1	MOON 2	MOON 3	MERCURY	VENUS	MARS	JUPITER	SATURN	URANUS	NEPTUNE	PLUTO
SEP. 1	22	25	26	27	22	23	22	35	39	6	47	40
SEP. 2	22	27	28	29	22	23	22	35	39	6	47	40
SEP. 3	23	29	30	31	22	23	22	35	39	6	47	40
SEP. 4	23	31	32	33	23	23	22	35	39	6	47	40
SEP. 5	23	33	34	34	23	23	22	35	39	6	47	40
SEP. 6	23	35	35	36	23	24	23	35	39	6	47	40
SEP. 7	23	37	37	38	23	24	23	35	39	6	47	40
SEP. 8	23	38	39	39	24	24	23	35	39	6	47	40
SEP. 9	23	40	40	41	24	24	23	35	39	6	47	40
SEP. 10	23	41	42	43	24	24	23	35	39	6	47	40
SEP. 11	24	43	44	44	24	24	23	35	39	6	47	40
SEP. 12	24	45	45	46	24	25	23	35	39	6	47	40
SEP. 13	24	46	47	47	25	25	23	35	39	6	47	40
SEP. 14	24	48	48	1	25	25	23	35	39	6	47	40
SEP. 15	24	1	2	2	25	25	23	35	39	6	47	40
SEP. 16	24	3	4	4	25	25	23	35	39	6	47	40
SEP. 17	24	5	5	6	26	25	24	35	39	6	47	40
SEP. 18	24	6	7	7	26	25	24	35	39	6	47	40
SEP. 19	25	8	8	9	26	26	24	35	39	6	47	40
SEP. 20	25	10	10	11	26	26	24	35	39	6	47	40
SEP. 21	25	11	12	12	27	26	24	35	39	6	47	40
SEP. 22	25	13	14	14	27	26	24	35	39	6	47	40
SEP. 23	25	15	15	16	27	26	24	35	39	6	47	40
SEP. 24	25	17	17	18	27	27	24	35	39	6	47	40
SEP. 25	26	19	19	20	27	27	24	35	39	6	47	40
SEP. 26	26	21	21	22	28	27	24	35	39	6	47	40
SEP. 27	26	23	23	24	28	27	24	35	39	6	47	40
SEP. 28	26	25	25	26	28	27	24	35	39	6	47	40
SEP. 29	26	27	27	28	28	27	25	35	39	6	47	40
SEP. 30	26	29	29	30	28	28	25	35	39	6	47	40

Date & Time	SUN	MOON 1	MOON 2	MOON 3	MERCURY	VENUS	MARS	JUPITER	SATURN	URANUS	NEPTUNE	PLUTO
OCT. 1	26	31	31	32	29	28	25	35	39	6	47	40
OCT. 2	26	32	33	34	29	28	25	35	39	6	47	40
OCT. 3	27	34	35	35	29	28	25	35	39	6	47	40
OCT. 4	27	36	37	37	29	28	25	35	39	6	47	40
OCT. 5	27	38	38	39	29	28	25	35	39	6	47	40
OCT. 6	27	39	40	41	30	29	25	36	39	6	47	40
OCT. 7	27	41	42	42	30	29	25	36	39	6	47	40
OCT. 8	27	43	43	44	30	29	25	36	39	6	47	40
OCT. 9	27	44	45	45	30	29	25	36	39	6	47	40
OCT. 10	27	46	46	47	30	29	25	36	39	6	47	40
OCT. 11	28	47	47	48	30	29	26	36	39	6	47	40
OCT. 12	28	1	2	2	31	30	26	36	39	6	47	40
OCT. 13	28	3	3	4	31	30	26	36	39	6	47	40
OCT. 14	28	4	5	5	31	30	26	36	39	6	47	40
OCT. 15	28	6	6	7	31	30	26	36	39	6	47	40
OCT. 16	28	7	8	9	31	30	26	36	39	6	47	40
OCT. 17	28	9	10	10	31	30	26	36	39	6	47	40
OCT. 18	28	11	11	12	31	31	26	36	39	6	47	40
OCT. 19	29	13	13	14	32	31	26	36	39	6	47	40
OCT. 20	29	14	15	15	32	31	26	36	39	6	47	40
OCT. 21	29	16	17	17	32	31	26	36	39	6	47	40
OCT. 22	29	18	19	19	32	31	26	36	39	6	47	40
OCT. 23	29	20	20	21	32	31	27	36	39	6	47	40
OCT. 24	29	22	22	23	32	32	27	36	39	6	47	40
OCT. 25	29	24	24	25	32	32	27	36	39	6	47	40
OCT. 26	30	26	26	27	32	32	27	36	39	6	47	40
OCT. 27	30	28	28	29	32	32	27	36	39	6	47	40
OCT. 28	30	30	30	31	33	32	27	36	39	6	47	40
OCT. 29	30	32	32	33	33	32	27	36	39	6	47	40
OCT. 30	30	34	34	35	33	33	27	36	39	6	47	40
OCT. 31	30	35	36	37	33	33	27	36	39	6	47	40

MOON 1 ☽ 12:01 A.M. TO 8:00 A.M.   **MOON 2** ◖ 8:01 A.M. TO 4:00 P.M.   **MOON 3** ● 4:01 P.M. TO 12:00 A.M.
Use only one "moon" number. Choose the column closest to your time of birth. If your place of birth is not on Eastern Standard Time, be sure to read "How to Convert to Eastern Standard Time" at the beginning of this section.

2019

November

Date & Time	SUN	MOON 1	MOON 2	MOON 3	MERCURY	VENUS	MARS	JUPITER	SATURN	URANUS	NEPTUNE	PLUTO
NOV. 1	30	37	38	38	33	33	27	36	39	6	47	40
NOV. 2	30	39	39	40	33	33	27	36	39	6	47	40
NOV. 3	31	41	41	42	33	33	28	36	39	6	47	40
NOV. 4	31	42	43	43	33	33	28	36	39	6	47	40
NOV. 5	31	44	44	45	32	34	28	36	39	6	47	40
NOV. 6	31	45	46	46	32	34	28	36	39	6	47	40
NOV. 7	31	47	47	48	32	34	28	36	39	6	47	40
NOV. 8	31	1	1	2	32	34	28	36	39	6	47	40
NOV. 9	31	2	3	3	32	34	28	36	39	6	47	40
NOV. 10	31	4	4	5	32	34	28	36	39	6	47	40
NOV. 11	31	5	6	6	32	35	28	36	39	6	47	40
NOV. 12	32	7	8	8	31	35	28	36	39	6	47	40
NOV. 13	32	9	9	10	31	35	28	36	39	5	47	40
NOV. 14	32	10	11	12	31	35	29	36	39	5	47	40
NOV. 15	32	12	13	13	31	35	29	36	39	5	47	40
NOV. 16	32	14	14	15	31	35	29	36	39	5	47	40
NOV. 17	32	16	16	17	31	36	29	37	39	5	47	40
NOV. 18	32	18	18	19	31	36	29	37	39	5	47	40
NOV. 19	33	19	20	21	31	36	29	37	39	5	47	40
NOV. 20	33	21	22	22	31	36	29	37	39	5	47	40
NOV. 21	33	23	24	24	31	36	29	37	39	5	47	40
NOV. 22	33	25	26	26	31	36	29	37	39	5	47	40
NOV. 23	33	27	28	28	31	37	29	37	39	5	47	40
NOV. 24	33	29	30	30	31	37	29	37	39	5	47	40
NOV. 25	34	31	31	32	31	37	29	37	39	5	47	40
NOV. 26	34	33	33	34	31	37	30	37	39	5	47	40
NOV. 27	34	35	35	36	31	37	30	37	39	5	47	40
NOV. 28	34	36	37	38	31	37	30	37	39	5	47	40
NOV. 29	34	38	39	39	31	37	30	37	39	5	47	40
NOV. 30	34	40	40	41	31	38	30	37	39	5	47	40

December

Date & Time	SUN	MOON 1	MOON 2	MOON 3	MERCURY	VENUS	MARS	JUPITER	SATURN	URANUS	NEPTUNE	PLUTO
DEC. 1	34	42	42	43	32	38	30	37	39	5	47	40
DEC. 2	34	43	44	44	32	38	30	37	39	5	47	40
DEC. 3	35	45	45	46	32	38	30	37	39	5	47	40
DEC. 4	35	46	47	47	32	38	30	37	39	5	47	40
DEC. 5	35	48	1	1	32	38	30	37	39	5	47	40
DEC. 6	35	2	2	3	32	39	30	37	39	5	47	40
DEC. 7	35	3	4	4	33	39	31	37	39	5	47	40
DEC. 8	35	5	5	6	33	39	31	37	39	5	47	40
DEC. 9	35	6	7	8	33	39	31	37	39	5	47	40
DEC. 10	35	8	9	9	33	39	31	37	39	5	47	40
DEC. 11	36	10	10	11	33	39	31	37	40	5	47	40
DEC. 12	36	12	12	13	34	39	31	37	40	5	47	40
DEC. 13	36	13	14	15	34	40	31	37	40	5	47	40
DEC. 14	36	15	16	16	34	40	31	37	40	5	47	40
DEC. 15	36	17	18	18	34	40	31	37	40	5	47	40
DEC. 16	36	19	20	20	34	40	31	37	40	5	47	40
DEC. 17	36	21	21	22	35	40	31	37	40	5	47	40
DEC. 18	36	23	23	24	35	41	32	37	40	5	47	40
DEC. 19	37	25	25	26	35	41	32	37	40	5	47	40
DEC. 20	37	26	27	28	35	41	32	37	40	5	47	40
DEC. 21	37	28	29	30	35	41	32	38	40	5	47	40
DEC. 22	37	30	31	31	36	41	32	38	40	5	47	40
DEC. 23	37	32	33	33	36	41	32	38	40	5	47	40
DEC. 24	37	34	35	35	36	42	32	38	40	5	47	40
DEC. 25	37	36	36	37	36	42	32	38	40	5	47	40
DEC. 26	38	37	38	39	36	42	32	38	40	5	47	40
DEC. 27	38	39	40	40	37	42	32	38	40	5	47	40
DEC. 28	38	41	42	42	37	42	32	38	40	5	47	40
DEC. 29	38	43	43	44	37	42	33	38	40	5	47	40
DEC. 30	38	44	45	45	37	43	33	38	40	5	47	40
DEC. 31	38	46	46	47	37	43	33	38	40	5	47	40

MOON 1 ○ 12:01 A.M. TO 8:00 A.M.　　**MOON 2** ◑ 8:01 A.M. TO 4:00 P.M.　　**MOON 3** ● 4:01 P.M. TO 12:00 A.M.

Use only one "moon" number. Choose the column closest to your time of birth. If your place of birth is not on Eastern Standard Time, be sure to read "How to Convert to Eastern Standard Time" at the beginning of this section.

2020-2025

2020s

January 1, 2025

* *

There's no limit to Personology's ability to predict the planetary influences on any given day, no matter how far out into the future. The prior section contained a forecast for January 1, 2015. Let's look out another 10 years now, to January 1, 2025.

SUN IN THE WEEK OF THE RULER
(CAPRICORN I)

*

Those born in this week know how to control their living and working situations. True rulers, they regard their home as their castle and like to see it running smoothly. Allergic to chaos, they run the risk of becoming control freaks. Unless they give up their tendency to make up other people's minds for them, they are likely to arouse resentments.

MOON ON THE CUSP OF MYSTERY AND IMAGINATION
(CAPRICORN-AQUARIUS CUSP)

*

A wealth of fantasies and dreams come crowding in on these people during both waking and sleeping hours. Often prey to such visions, they may at times be overwhelmed by the intensity of their inner life. Keeping their feet on the ground while tending to the normal tasks of everyday life can be quite challenging, but is essential to their mental health.

MERCURY IN THE WEEK OF THE TITAN
(SAGITTARIUS III)

*

Because expansive thought is already an important part of this Personology period, the presence of Mercury is doubly stimulating as far as seeing the big picture is concerned and communicating important ideas. Those with this Mercury position should be careful not to overlook the details or to trip over their shoelaces while taking in the panoramic view ahead.

VENUS ON THE CUSP OF SENSITIVITY
(AQUARIUS-PISCES CUSP)

*

Rejection is the hardest thing for these individuals to deal with. Often they go too far in acquiescing to their partner's demands in order to avoid rejection. It is perhaps their greatest challenge in life to learn to be honest about their feelings and to express them without fear of rejection. Building a stronger ego can improve the quality of their relationships.

MARS ON THE CUSP OF OSCILLATION
(CANCER-LEO CUSP)

*

Unbalanced energies can topple even the most stable structures and therefore it is important to keep things under control. An inability to follow through on plans and schedules accompanies this position, due to an erratic energy flow. Evening out highs and lows will result in forward motion. Above all, be objective. Aim for attainable goals.

JUPITER IN THE WEEK OF NEW LANGUAGE
(GEMINI II)

*

Telling tall stories and spinning yarns is characteristic of this Jupiter position. Such individuals find it easier to embellish the truth than to blandly state it as it is. Trust is an important issue here, for many refuse to believe what these expressive individuals have to say, not wanting to get burned a second time. Building a trustworthy persona can be a major challenge.

SATURN IN THE WEEK OF THE LONER
(PISCES II)

✳

A serious cast to one's inner thoughts is frequently the result here. Such an attitude enables the individual to work on themselves and proceed further in their self-development. Deep introversion can be a problem here in extreme cases. Often such an individual takes their few friendships seriously and makes an excellent companion or associate. Holding on to failed relationships can be a problem, however.

URANUS IN THE WEEK OF THE NATURAL
(TAURUS III)

✳

Free and open attitudes rule this week with Uranus here, but with them also a need to express somewhat outlandish behavior. Letting it all hang out is one thing, but such individuals revel in displaying themselves. Care should be taken not to insult more conservative minded individuals or drive them to take reprisals against this behavior. Enjoyment need not be at the cost of other people's feelings.

NEPTUNE ON THE CUSP OF REBIRTH
(PISCES-ARIES CUSP)

✳

The watery influence of Neptune is felt strongly on the Pisces-Aries Cusp. Hence, new beginnings are likely to be blunted or clouded in hopes and expectations rather than resulting in solid action. Undermining one's own efforts is the danger here. Great care must be taken that self-destructive energies do not spiral out of control. Start with small things and build slowly.

PLUTO ON THE CUSP OF MYSTERY AND IMAGINATION
(CAPRICORN-AQUARIUS CUSP)

✳

An exciting and vibrant position for Pluto, one which seeks out adventure and new opportunities. Sexual energies are high, but not necessarily leading to biological reproduction. If such energies are overpowering they can be sublimated in sports, martial-arts, body-building, running, swimming and other physical endeavors. Such individuals must find an outlet for their energies or else suffer major frustrations and depressions.

NOTE

If you were to chart this on the Personology wheel, you'd find that Pluto and the Moon form a **CONJUNCTION,** since both are found on the Capricorn-Aquarius Cusp. Conjunctions between two planets are found when both occupy the same Personology period and imply the yoking together of the energies of the planets concerned. In this case, the highly imaginative sides of the planets, which are enhanced on this cusp, can lead to overload and burnout. Frying your wires is a real danger with this position and keeping your feet on the ground is advised.

CONJUNCTION

Meanwhile, Neptune, which is on the Pisces-Aries Cusp, forms a **TRINE** with Mars on the Cancer-Leo Cusp, exactly four cusps apart. This easy aspect can have the effect of toning down the unbalanced energies of Mars but unfortunately also enhancing Neptune's tendency here to substitute dreamy expectations for solid work.

TRINE

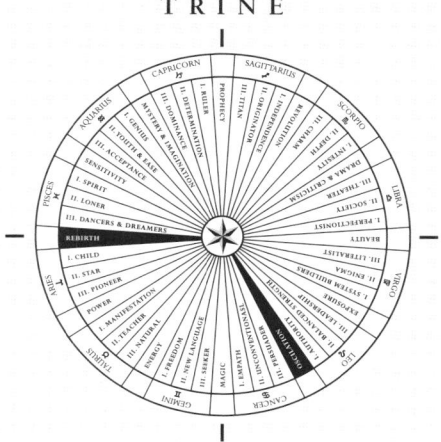

Finally, Pluto and the Moon, which are **CONJUNCT** on the Capricorn-Aquarius cusp, are in **OPPOSITION** to Mars, which is 180 degrees away on the Cancer-Leo Cusp. Since oppositions can create conflict, the Pluto-Moon burnout tendencies referred to above can become even more perilous under Mars' destabilizing influence. The only hope to avoid real disaster is to exert a stabilizing influence which seeks balance and control, taking things one step at a time without getting unduly carried away by fantasy.

CONJUNCTION
AND
OPPOSITION

January

February

Date & Time	SUN	MOON 1 ◗	MOON 2 ◑	MOON 3 ●	MERCURY	VENUS	MARS	JUPITER	SATURN	URANUS	NEPTUNE	PLUTO
JAN. 1	38	47	48	1	38	43	33	38	40	5	47	40
JAN. 2	38	1	2	2	38	43	33	38	40	5	47	40
JAN. 3	39	3	3	4	38	43	33	38	40	5	47	40
JAN. 4	39	4	5	5	38	43	33	38	40	5	47	40
JAN. 5	39	6	6	7	38	44	33	38	40	5	47	40
JAN. 6	39	7	8	9	39	44	33	38	40	5	47	40
JAN. 7	39	9	10	10	39	44	33	38	40	5	47	40
JAN. 8	39	11	11	12	39	44	33	38	40	5	47	40
JAN. 9	39	13	13	14	39	44	33	38	40	5	47	40
JAN. 10	40	15	15	16	40	44	34	38	40	5	47	40
JAN. 11	40	16	17	18	40	45	34	38	40	5	47	40
JAN. 12	40	18	19	20	40	45	34	38	40	5	47	40
JAN. 13	40	20	21	22	40	45	34	38	40	5	47	40
JAN. 14	40	22	23	23	40	45	34	38	40	5	47	40
JAN. 15	40	24	25	25	41	45	34	38	40	5	47	40
JAN. 16	40	26	27	27	41	45	34	38	40	5	47	40
JAN. 17	41	28	29	29	41	46	34	38	40	5	47	40
JAN. 18	41	30	30	31	41	46	34	38	40	5	47	40
JAN. 19	41	32	32	33	42	46	34	38	40	5	47	40
JAN. 20	41	33	34	35	42	46	34	38	40	5	47	40
JAN. 21	41	35	36	36	42	46	35	38	40	5	47	40
JAN. 22	41	37	38	38	42	46	35	39	40	5	47	40
JAN. 23	42	39	39	40	42	46	35	39	40	5	47	40
JAN. 24	42	40	41	41	43	47	35	39	40	5	47	40
JAN. 25	42	42	43	43	43	47	35	39	40	5	47	40
JAN. 26	42	44	44	45	43	47	35	39	40	5	47	40
JAN. 27	42	45	46	47	43	47	35	39	40	5	47	40
JAN. 28	42	47	47	48	44	47	35	39	40	5	47	40
JAN. 29	42	1	1	2	44	47	35	39	40	5	47	40
JAN. 30	42	2	3	3	44	48	35	39	40	5	47	40
JAN. 31	43	4	4	5	44	48	35	39	40	5	47	40

Date & Time	SUN	MOON 1 ◗	MOON 2 ◑	MOON 3 ●	MERCURY	VENUS	MARS	JUPITER	SATURN	URANUS	NEPTUNE	PLUTO
FEB. 1	43	5	6	6	44	48	36	39	40	5	47	40
FEB. 2	43	7	7	8	45	48	36	39	40	5	47	40
FEB. 3	43	9	9	10	45	48	36	39	40	5	47	40
FEB. 4	43	10	11	11	45	48	36	39	40	5	47	40
FEB. 5	43	12	13	13	45	1	36	39	40	5	47	40
FEB. 6	43	14	14	15	46	1	36	39	40	5	47	40
FEB. 7	43	16	16	17	46	1	36	39	40	5	47	40
FEB. 8	44	17	18	19	46	1	36	39	40	5	47	40
FEB. 9	44	19	20	21	46	1	36	39	40	5	47	40
FEB. 10	44	21	22	23	46	1	36	39	40	5	47	40
FEB. 11	44	23	24	25	46	1	36	39	40	5	47	40
FEB. 12	44	25	26	27	46	2	37	39	40	5	47	40
FEB. 13	44	27	28	29	47	2	37	39	40	5	47	40
FEB. 14	44	29	30	31	47	2	37	39	41	5	47	40
FEB. 15	44	31	32	32	47	2	37	39	41	5	47	40
FEB. 16	45	33	34	34	47	2	37	39	41	5	47	40
FEB. 17	45	35	35	36	47	2	37	39	41	5	47	40
FEB. 18	45	37	37	38	47	3	37	39	41	5	47	40
FEB. 19	45	38	39	39	47	3	37	39	41	5	47	40
FEB. 20	45	40	41	41	47	3	37	39	41	5	47	40
FEB. 21	45	42	42	43	46	3	37	39	41	5	47	40
FEB. 22	45	43	44	44	46	3	37	39	41	5	47	40
FEB. 23	46	45	45	46	46	3	38	39	41	5	47	40
FEB. 24	46	46	47	48	46	3	38	39	41	5	47	40
FEB. 25	46	48	1	1	46	4	38	39	41	5	47	40
FEB. 26	46	2	2	3	46	4	38	39	41	5	47	40
FEB. 27	46	3	3	4	46	4	38	40	41	5	47	40
FEB. 28	46	5	5	6	46	4	38	40	41	5	47	40
FEB. 29	46	6	7	7	45	4	38	40	41	5	47	40

MOON 1 ◗ 12:01 A.M. TO 8:00 A.M.   **MOON 2** ◑ 8:01 A.M. TO 4:00 P.M.   **MOON 3** ● 4:01 P.M. TO 12:00 A.M.

Use only one "moon" number. Choose the column closest to your time of birth. If your place of birth is not on Eastern Standard Time, be sure to read "How to Convert to Eastern Standard Time" at the beginning of this section.

Date & Time	SUN	MOON 1	MOON 2	MOON 3	MERCURY	VENUS	MARS	JUPITER	SATURN	URANUS	NEPTUNE	PLUTO
MAR. 1	46	8	9	9	45	4	38	40	41	5	47	40
MAR. 2	46	10	10	11	45	5	38	40	41	5	47	40
MAR. 3	47	11	12	12	45	5	38	40	41	5	47	40
MAR. 4	47	13	14	14	45	5	39	40	41	5	47	40
MAR. 5	47	15	15	16	45	5	39	40	41	5	47	40
MAR. 6	47	17	17	18	45	5	39	40	41	5	47	40
MAR. 7	47	19	19	20	45	5	39	40	41	5	47	40
MAR. 8	47	20	21	22	45	5	39	40	41	5	47	40
MAR. 9	47	22	23	24	45	6	39	40	41	6	47	40
MAR. 10	47	25	25	26	45	6	39	40	41	6	47	40
MAR. 11	48	27	27	28	45	6	39	40	41	6	47	40
MAR. 12	48	29	29	30	45	6	39	40	41	6	47	40
MAR. 13	48	31	31	32	45	6	39	40	41	6	47	40
MAR. 14	48	32	33	34	45	6	39	40	41	6	47	40
MAR. 15	48	34	35	36	45	6	40	40	41	6	47	40
MAR. 16	48	36	37	37	45	7	40	40	41	6	47	40
MAR. 17	48	38	38	39	45	7	40	40	41	6	47	40
MAR. 18	48	40	40	41	45	7	40	40	41	6	47	40
MAR. 19	1	41	42	42	45	7	40	40	41	6	47	40
MAR. 20	1	43	43	44	45	7	40	40	41	6	47	40
MAR. 21	1	44	45	46	45	7	40	40	41	6	47	40
MAR. 22	1	46	47	47	45	7	40	40	41	6	47	40
MAR. 23	1	48	48	1	46	8	40	40	41	6	47	40
MAR. 24	1	1	2	2	46	8	40	40	41	6	47	40
MAR. 25	2	3	3	4	46	8	40	40	41	6	48	40
MAR. 26	2	4	5	5	46	8	40	40	41	6	48	40
MAR. 27	2	6	7	7	46	8	41	40	41	6	48	40
MAR. 28	2	8	8	9	46	8	41	40	41	6	48	40
MAR. 29	2	9	10	10	47	8	41	40	41	6	48	40
MAR. 30	2	11	11	12	47	8	41	40	41	6	48	40
MAR. 31	2	12	13	14	47	9	41	40	41	6	48	40

Date & Time	SUN	MOON 1	MOON 2	MOON 3	MERCURY	VENUS	MARS	JUPITER	SATURN	URANUS	NEPTUNE	PLUTO
APR. 1	2	14	15	15	47	9	41	40	41	6	48	40
APR. 2	2	16	17	17	47	9	41	40	41	6	48	40
APR. 3	3	18	18	19	47	9	41	40	41	6	48	40
APR. 4	3	20	20	21	48	9	41	40	41	6	48	40
APR. 5	3	22	22	23	48	9	41	40	41	6	48	40
APR. 6	3	24	24	25	48	9	42	40	41	6	48	40
APR. 7	3	26	26	27	48	9	42	40	41	6	48	40
APR. 8	3	28	28	29	48	9	42	40	41	6	48	40
APR. 9	3	30	30	31	1	10	42	40	41	6	48	40
APR. 10	3	32	32	33	1	10	42	40	41	6	48	40
APR. 11	4	34	34	35	1	10	42	40	41	6	48	40
APR. 12	4	36	36	37	1	10	42	40	41	6	48	40
APR. 13	4	37	38	39	1	10	42	40	41	6	48	40
APR. 14	4	39	40	40	2	10	42	40	41	6	48	40
APR. 15	4	41	41	42	2	10	42	40	41	6	48	40
APR. 16	4	42	43	44	2	10	42	40	41	6	48	40
APR. 17	4	44	45	45	2	10	43	40	41	6	48	40
APR. 18	4	46	46	47	3	11	43	40	41	6	48	40
APR. 19	5	47	48	48	3	11	43	40	41	6	48	40
APR. 20	5	1	1	2	3	11	43	40	41	6	48	40
APR. 21	5	2	3	3	3	11	43	40	41	6	48	40
APR. 22	5	4	5	5	4	11	43	40	41	6	48	40
APR. 23	5	6	6	7	4	11	43	41	41	6	48	40
APR. 24	5	7	8	8	4	11	43	41	41	6	48	40
APR. 25	6	9	9	10	4	11	43	41	41	6	48	40
APR. 26	6	10	11	12	5	11	43	41	41	6	48	40
APR. 27	6	12	13	13	5	11	44	41	41	6	48	40
APR. 28	6	14	14	15	5	11	44	41	41	6	48	40
APR. 29	6	15	16	17	5	11	44	41	41	6	48	40
APR. 30	6	17	18	18	6	11	44	41	41	6	48	40

MOON 1 ☽ 12:01 A.M. TO 8:00 A.M.   **MOON 2** ☽ 8:01 A.M. TO 4:00 P.M.   **MOON 3** ● 4:01 P.M. TO 12:00 A.M.

Use only one "moon" number. Choose the column closest to your time of birth. If your place of birth is not on Eastern Standard Time, be sure to read "How to Convert to Eastern Standard Time" at the beginning of this section.

Date & Time	SUN	MOON 1	MOON 2	MOON 3	MERCURY	VENUS	MARS	JUPITER	SATURN	URANUS	NEPTUNE	PLUTO
MAY 1	6	19	20	20	6	12	44	41	41	6	48	40
MAY 2	6	21	22	22	6	12	44	41	41	6	48	40
MAY 3	7	23	23	24	6	12	44	41	41	6	48	40
MAY 4	7	25	25	26	7	12	44	41	41	6	48	40
MAY 5	7	27	27	28	7	12	44	41	41	6	48	40
MAY 6	7	29	29	30	7	12	44	41	41	6	48	40
MAY 7	7	31	31	32	8	12	44	41	41	6	48	40
MAY 8	7	33	33	34	8	12	45	41	41	6	48	40
MAY 9	7	35	35	36	8	12	45	41	41	6	48	40
MAY 10	7	37	37	38	8	12	45	41	41	6	48	40
MAY 11	8	38	39	40	8	12	45	41	41	6	48	40
MAY 12	8	40	41	41	9	12	45	41	41	6	48	40
MAY 13	8	42	42	43	9	12	45	41	41	6	48	40
MAY 14	8	44	44	45	10	12	45	41	41	6	48	40
MAY 15	8	45	46	46	10	12	45	41	41	6	48	40
MAY 16	8	47	47	48	10	12	45	41	41	6	48	40
MAY 17	8	48	1	1	10	12	45	41	41	6	48	40
MAY 18	8	2	3	3	11	12	45	41	41	6	48	40
MAY 19	9	4	4	5	11	12	46	41	41	6	48	40
MAY 20	9	5	6	6	11	12	46	41	41	6	48	40
MAY 21	9	7	7	8	11	12	46	41	41	6	48	40
MAY 22	9	8	8	9	11	12	46	41	41	6	48	40
MAY 23	9	10	11	11	12	12	46	41	41	6	48	40
MAY 24	9	12	12	13	12	12	46	41	41	6	48	40
MAY 25	10	13	14	15	12	12	46	41	41	6	48	40
MAY 26	10	15	16	16	12	11	46	41	41	6	48	40
MAY 27	10	17	17	18	12	11	46	41	41	6	48	40
MAY 28	10	19	19	20	13	11	46	41	41	6	48	40
MAY 29	10	20	21	22	13	11	46	41	41	6	48	40
MAY 30	10	22	23	24	13	11	47	41	41	6	48	40
MAY 31	10	24	25	25	13	11	47	41	41	6	48	40

Date & Time	SUN	MOON 1	MOON 2	MOON 3	MERCURY	VENUS	MARS	JUPITER	SATURN	URANUS	NEPTUNE	PLUTO
JUN. 1	10	26	27	27	14	11	47	41	41	6	48	40
JUN. 2	10	28	29	29	14	11	47	41	41	6	48	40
JUN. 3	11	30	31	31	14	11	47	41	41	6	48	40
JUN. 4	11	32	33	33	14	11	47	41	41	6	48	40
JUN. 5	11	34	35	35	14	11	47	41	41	6	48	40
JUN. 6	11	36	36	37	14	11	47	40	41	6	48	40
JUN. 7	11	38	38	39	14	10	47	40	41	6	48	40
JUN. 8	11	39	40	41	14	10	47	40	41	6	48	40
JUN. 9	11	41	42	42	15	10	47	40	41	6	48	40
JUN. 10	11	43	44	44	15	10	47	40	41	6	48	40
JUN. 11	12	45	45	46	15	10	48	40	41	6	48	40
JUN. 12	12	46	47	47	15	10	48	40	41	6	48	40
JUN. 13	12	48	48	1	15	10	48	40	41	6	48	40
JUN. 14	12	1	2	3	15	10	48	40	41	6	48	40
JUN. 15	12	3	4	4	15	10	48	40	41	6	48	40
JUN. 16	12	5	5	6	15	10	48	40	41	6	48	40
JUN. 17	12	6	7	7	15	10	48	40	41	6	48	40
JUN. 18	12	8	8	9	15	10	48	40	41	6	48	40
JUN. 19	13	10	10	11	15	10	48	40	41	6	48	40
JUN. 20	13	11	12	12	15	10	48	40	41	6	48	40
JUN. 21	13	13	13	14	15	10	48	40	41	6	48	40
JUN. 22	13	15	15	16	15	10	48	40	41	6	48	40
JUN. 23	13	16	17	18	15	10	1	40	41	6	48	40
JUN. 24	13	18	19	19	15	10	1	40	41	6	48	40
JUN. 25	14	20	21	21	15	10	1	40	41	6	48	40
JUN. 26	14	22	23	23	15	10	1	40	41	6	48	40
JUN. 27	14	24	24	25	15	10	1	40	41	6	48	40
JUN. 28	14	26	26	27	14	10	1	40	41	6	48	40
JUN. 29	14	28	28	29	14	10	1	40	41	6	48	40
JUN. 30	14	29	30	31	14	10	1	40	41	6	48	40

MOON 1 ◖ 12:01 A.M. TO 8:00 A.M.　　**MOON 2** ◑ 8:01 A.M. TO 4:00 P.M.　　**MOON 3** ● 4:01 P.M. TO 12:00 A.M.

Use only one "moon" number. Choose the column closest to your time of birth. If your place of birth is not on Eastern Standard Time, be sure to read "How to Convert to Eastern Standard Time" at the beginning of this section.

2020

July

August

Date & Time	SUN ☀	MOON 1 ◖	MOON 2 ◗	MOON 3 ●	MERCURY	VENUS	MARS	JUPITER	SATURN	URANUS	NEPTUNE	PLUTO
JUL. 1	14	31	32	33	14	10	1	40	41	6	48	40
JUL. 2	14	33	34	35	14	10	1	40	41	6	48	40
JUL. 3	15	35	36	36	14	10	1	40	41	6	48	40
JUL. 4	15	37	38	38	14	10	1	40	41	6	48	40
JUL. 5	15	39	39	40	14	10	2	40	41	6	48	40
JUL. 6	15	41	41	42	14	10	2	40	41	6	48	40
JUL. 7	15	42	43	43	14	10	2	40	41	6	48	40
JUL. 8	15	44	45	45	14	10	2	40	41	6	48	40
JUL. 9	15	46	46	47	14	10	2	40	41	6	48	40
JUL. 10	15	47	48	48	14	10	2	40	41	6	48	40
JUL. 11	16	1	1	2	14	10	2	40	41	6	48	40
JUL. 12	16	3	3	4	14	10	2	40	41	6	48	40
JUL. 13	16	4	5	5	14	10	2	40	41	6	48	40
JUL. 14	16	6	6	7	14	10	2	40	41	6	48	40
JUL. 15	16	7	8	8	14	10	2	40	41	6	48	40
JUL. 16	16	9	9	10	14	10	2	40	41	6	48	40
JUL. 17	16	11	11	12	14	10	2	40	41	6	48	40
JUL. 18	16	12	13	13	14	11	2	40	41	6	48	40
JUL. 19	17	14	15	15	14	11	3	40	41	6	48	40
JUL. 20	17	16	16	17	14	11	3	40	41	6	48	40
JUL. 21	17	18	18	19	14	11	3	40	41	6	48	40
JUL. 22	17	19	20	21	14	11	3	40	41	6	48	40
JUL. 23	17	21	22	23	14	11	3	40	41	6	48	40
JUL. 24	17	23	24	25	15	11	3	40	41	6	48	40
JUL. 25	17	25	26	26	15	11	3	40	41	6	48	40
JUL. 26	18	27	28	28	15	12	3	40	41	6	48	40
JUL. 27	18	29	30	30	15	12	3	40	41	6	48	40
JUL. 28	18	31	32	32	15	12	3	40	41	6	48	40
JUL. 29	18	33	33	34	15	12	3	40	41	6	48	40
JUL. 30	18	35	35	36	16	12	3	40	41	6	48	40
JUL. 31	18	36	37	38	16	12	3	40	41	6	48	40

Date & Time	SUN ☀	MOON 1 ◖	MOON 2 ◗	MOON 3 ●	MERCURY	VENUS	MARS	JUPITER	SATURN	URANUS	NEPTUNE	PLUTO
AUG. 1	18	38	39	39	16	12	3	40	41	6	48	40
AUG. 2	18	40	41	41	16	12	3	40	41	6	48	40
AUG. 3	19	42	42	43	16	12	4	40	41	6	48	40
AUG. 4	19	43	44	45	17	13	4	40	41	6	48	40
AUG. 5	19	45	46	46	17	13	4	40	41	6	48	40
AUG. 6	19	47	47	48	17	13	4	40	41	6	48	40
AUG. 7	19	48	1	1	17	13	4	40	41	6	48	40
AUG. 8	19	2	3	3	18	13	4	40	41	6	48	40
AUG. 9	19	4	4	5	18	13	4	40	41	6	48	40
AUG. 10	19	5	6	6	18	13	4	40	41	6	48	40
AUG. 11	20	7	7	8	19	13	4	40	41	6	48	40
AUG. 12	20	8	9	9	19	14	4	39	41	6	48	40
AUG. 13	20	10	11	11	19	14	4	39	41	6	48	40
AUG. 14	20	12	12	13	19	14	4	39	41	6	48	40
AUG. 15	20	13	14	15	20	14	4	39	41	6	48	40
AUG. 16	20	15	16	16	20	14	4	39	41	6	48	40
AUG. 17	20	17	18	18	20	14	4	39	41	6	48	40
AUG. 18	20	19	19	20	20	14	4	39	41	6	48	40
AUG. 19	21	21	21	22	21	14	4	39	41	6	48	40
AUG. 20	21	23	23	24	21	15	4	39	41	6	48	40
AUG. 21	21	25	25	26	21	15	4	39	41	6	48	40
AUG. 22	21	27	27	28	21	15	4	39	40	6	48	40
AUG. 23	21	29	29	30	22	15	4	39	40	6	48	40
AUG. 24	21	30	31	32	22	15	4	39	40	6	48	40
AUG. 25	21	32	33	34	22	15	4	39	40	6	48	40
AUG. 26	22	34	35	35	22	15	5	39	40	6	48	40
AUG. 27	22	36	37	37	23	16	5	39	40	6	48	40
AUG. 28	22	38	38	39	23	16	5	39	40	6	48	40
AUG. 29	22	40	40	41	23	16	5	39	40	6	48	40
AUG. 30	22	41	42	42	23	16	5	39	40	6	48	40
AUG. 31	22	43	44	44	24	16	5	39	40	6	48	40

MOON 1 ◖ 12:01 A.M. TO 8:00 A.M.   **MOON 2** ◗ 8:01 A.M. TO 4:00 P.M.   **MOON 3** ● 4:01 P.M. TO 12:00 A.M.

Use only one "moon" number. Choose the column closest to your time of birth. If your place of birth is not on Eastern Standard Time, be sure to read "How to Convert to Eastern Standard Time" at the beginning of this section.

September | October

Date & Time	SUN ☉	MOON 1 ◗	MOON 2 ◑	MOON 3 ●	MERCURY	VENUS	MARS	JUPITER	SATURN	URANUS	NEPTUNE	PLUTO
SEP. 1	22	45	45	46	24	16	5	39	40	6	48	40
SEP. 2	22	46	47	47	24	16	5	39	40	6	48	40
SEP. 3	23	48	48	1	24	17	5	39	40	6	48	40
SEP. 4	23	2	2	3	25	17	5	39	40	6	48	40
SEP. 5	23	3	4	4	25	17	5	39	40	6	48	40
SEP. 6	23	5	5	6	25	17	5	39	40	6	48	40
SEP. 7	23	6	7	7	25	17	5	39	40	6	48	40
SEP. 8	23	8	8	9	25	17	5	39	40	6	48	40
SEP. 9	23	9	10	11	26	17	5	39	40	6	48	40
SEP. 10	23	11	12	12	26	18	5	39	40	6	48	40
SEP. 11	24	13	13	14	26	18	5	39	40	6	48	40
SEP. 12	24	14	15	16	26	18	5	39	40	6	48	40
SEP. 13	24	16	17	17	26	18	5	39	40	6	48	40
SEP. 14	24	18	19	19	27	18	5	39	40	6	48	40
SEP. 15	24	20	21	21	27	18	5	39	40	6	48	40
SEP. 16	24	22	22	23	27	18	5	39	40	6	48	40
SEP. 17	24	24	24	25	27	19	5	39	40	6	48	40
SEP. 18	24	26	26	27	27	19	5	39	40	6	48	40
SEP. 19	25	28	29	29	28	19	5	39	40	6	48	40
SEP. 20	25	30	30	31	28	19	5	39	40	6	48	40
SEP. 21	25	32	32	33	28	19	5	39	40	6	48	40
SEP. 22	25	34	34	35	28	19	5	39	40	6	48	40
SEP. 23	25	36	36	37	28	19	5	39	40	6	48	40
SEP. 24	25	37	38	39	28	20	5	39	40	6	48	40
SEP. 25	26	39	40	40	29	20	4	39	40	6	48	40
SEP. 26	26	41	41	42	29	20	4	39	40	6	48	40
SEP. 27	26	43	43	44	29	20	4	39	40	6	48	40
SEP. 28	26	44	45	45	29	20	4	39	40	6	48	40
SEP. 29	26	46	46	47	29	20	4	39	40	6	48	40
SEP. 30	26	48	48	1	29	21	4	39	40	6	48	40

Date & Time	SUN ☉	MOON 1 ◗	MOON 2 ◑	MOON 3 ●	MERCURY	VENUS	MARS	JUPITER	SATURN	URANUS	NEPTUNE	PLUTO
OCT. 1	26	1	2	2	30	21	4	39	40	6	48	40
OCT. 2	26	3	3	4	30	21	4	39	40	6	48	40
OCT. 3	27	4	5	5	30	21	4	39	40	6	47	40
OCT. 4	27	6	6	7	30	21	4	39	40	6	47	40
OCT. 5	27	7	8	9	30	21	4	39	40	6	47	40
OCT. 6	27	9	10	10	30	21	4	39	40	6	47	40
OCT. 7	27	11	11	12	30	22	4	39	40	6	47	40
OCT. 8	27	12	13	13	30	22	4	39	40	6	47	40
OCT. 9	27	14	14	15	30	22	4	39	40	6	47	40
OCT. 10	27	16	16	17	30	22	4	39	40	6	47	40
OCT. 11	28	17	18	18	30	22	4	39	40	6	47	40
OCT. 12	28	19	20	20	30	22	4	39	40	6	47	40
OCT. 13	28	21	22	22	31	23	4	39	40	6	47	40
OCT. 14	28	23	24	24	31	23	4	39	40	6	47	40
OCT. 15	28	25	26	26	31	23	4	40	40	6	47	40
OCT. 16	28	27	28	28	30	23	4	40	40	6	47	40
OCT. 17	28	29	30	30	30	23	4	40	40	6	47	40
OCT. 18	28	31	32	32	30	23	4	40	40	6	47	40
OCT. 19	29	33	34	34	30	24	4	40	40	6	47	40
OCT. 20	29	35	36	36	30	24	4	40	40	6	47	40
OCT. 21	29	37	37	38	30	24	3	40	40	6	47	40
OCT. 22	29	39	39	40	30	24	3	40	40	6	47	40
OCT. 23	29	40	41	42	30	24	3	40	40	6	47	40
OCT. 24	29	42	43	43	30	24	3	40	40	6	47	40
OCT. 25	29	44	44	45	29	25	3	40	40	6	47	40
OCT. 26	30	45	46	47	29	25	3	40	40	6	47	40
OCT. 27	30	47	48	48	29	25	3	40	40	6	47	40
OCT. 28	30	1	1	2	29	25	3	40	40	6	47	40
OCT. 29	30	2	3	3	29	25	3	40	40	6	47	40
OCT. 30	30	4	4	5	29	25	3	40	40	6	47	40
OCT. 31	30	5	6	7	29	25	3	40	40	6	47	40

MOON 1 ◗ 12:01 A.M. TO 8:00 A.M.   **MOON 2** ◑ 8:01 A.M. TO 4:00 P.M.   **MOON 3** ● 4:01 P.M. TO 12:00 A.M.

Use only one "moon" number. Choose the column closest to your time of birth. If your place of birth is not on Eastern Standard Time, be sure to read "How to Convert to Eastern Standard Time" at the beginning of this section.

November

Date & Time	SUN ☉	MOON 1 ◐	MOON 2 ◑	MOON 3 ●	MERCURY	VENUS	MARS	JUPITER	SATURN	URANUS	NEPTUNE	PLUTO
NOV. 1	30	7	8	8	29	26	3	40	40	6	47	40
NOV. 2	30	9	9	10	28	26	3	40	40	6	47	40
NOV. 3	31	10	11	11	28	26	3	40	40	6	47	40
NOV. 4	31	12	12	13	28	26	3	40	40	6	47	40
NOV. 5	31	13	14	15	28	26	3	40	40	6	47	40
NOV. 6	31	15	16	16	28	26	3	40	41	6	47	40
NOV. 7	31	17	17	18	29	27	3	40	41	6	47	40
NOV. 8	31	19	19	20	29	27	3	40	41	6	47	40
NOV. 9	31	20	21	22	29	27	3	40	41	6	47	40
NOV. 10	31	22	23	23	29	27	3	40	41	6	47	40
NOV. 11	31	24	25	25	29	27	3	40	41	6	47	40
NOV. 12	32	26	27	27	29	27	3	40	41	6	47	40
NOV. 13	32	28	29	29	29	28	3	40	41	6	47	40
NOV. 14	32	30	31	31	29	28	3	40	41	6	47	40
NOV. 15	32	32	33	33	30	28	3	40	41	6	47	40
NOV. 16	32	34	35	35	30	28	3	40	41	6	47	40
NOV. 17	32	36	37	37	30	28	3	40	41	6	47	40
NOV. 18	32	38	39	39	30	28	3	40	41	6	47	40
NOV. 19	33	40	40	41	30	29	3	40	41	6	47	40
NOV. 20	33	42	42	43	31	29	3	40	41	6	47	40
NOV. 21	33	43	44	44	31	29	3	40	41	6	47	40
NOV. 22	33	45	46	46	31	29	3	40	41	6	47	40
NOV. 23	33	47	47	48	31	29	3	40	41	6	47	40
NOV. 24	33	48	1	1	31	29	3	40	41	6	47	40
NOV. 25	34	2	2	3	32	30	3	40	41	6	47	40
NOV. 26	34	3	4	5	32	30	3	40	41	6	47	40
NOV. 27	34	5	6	6	32	30	3	40	41	6	47	40
NOV. 28	34	7	7	8	32	30	3	40	41	6	47	40
NOV. 29	34	8	9	9	32	30	3	40	41	6	47	40
NOV. 30	34	10	10	11	33	30	3	40	41	6	47	40

December

Date & Time	SUN ☉	MOON 1 ◐	MOON 2 ◑	MOON 3 ●	MERCURY	VENUS	MARS	JUPITER	SATURN	URANUS	NEPTUNE	PLUTO
DEC. 1	34	11	12	13	33	31	3	40	41	6	47	40
DEC. 2	34	13	14	14	33	31	3	40	41	6	47	40
DEC. 3	35	15	15	16	33	31	3	41	41	6	47	40
DEC. 4	35	16	17	18	33	31	3	41	41	6	47	40
DEC. 5	35	18	19	19	34	31	3	41	41	6	47	40
DEC. 6	35	20	20	21	34	31	3	41	41	6	47	40
DEC. 7	35	22	22	23	34	32	3	41	41	6	47	40
DEC. 8	35	23	24	25	34	32	3	41	41	6	47	40
DEC. 9	35	25	26	27	35	32	4	41	41	6	47	40
DEC. 10	35	27	28	29	35	32	4	41	41	6	47	40
DEC. 11	36	29	30	31	35	32	4	41	41	6	47	40
DEC. 12	36	31	32	33	35	32	4	41	41	6	47	40
DEC. 13	36	33	34	34	35	33	4	41	41	6	47	40
DEC. 14	36	35	36	36	36	33	4	41	41	6	47	40
DEC. 15	36	37	38	38	36	33	4	41	41	6	47	40
DEC. 16	36	39	40	40	36	33	4	41	41	6	47	40
DEC. 17	36	41	41	42	36	33	4	41	41	6	47	40
DEC. 18	36	43	43	44	36	33	4	41	41	6	47	40
DEC. 19	37	44	45	46	37	34	4	41	41	6	47	40
DEC. 20	37	46	47	47	37	34	4	41	41	6	47	40
DEC. 21	37	48	48	1	37	34	4	41	41	6	47	40
DEC. 22	37	1	2	2	37	34	4	41	41	6	47	40
DEC. 23	37	3	4	4	37	34	4	41	41	6	47	40
DEC. 24	37	5	5	6	38	34	4	41	41	6	47	40
DEC. 25	37	6	7	7	38	35	4	41	41	6	47	40
DEC. 26	38	8	8	9	38	35	4	41	41	6	47	40
DEC. 27	38	9	10	10	38	35	4	41	41	6	47	40
DEC. 28	38	11	11	12	39	35	4	41	41	6	47	40
DEC. 29	38	13	13	14	39	35	4	41	41	6	47	40
DEC. 30	38	14	15	15	39	35	5	41	41	6	47	40
DEC. 31	38	16	17	17	39	36	5	41	41	6	47	40

MOON 1 ◐ 12:01 A.M. TO 8:00 A.M.   **MOON 2** ◑ 8:01 A.M. TO 4:00 P.M.   **MOON 3** ● 4:01 P.M. TO 12:00 A.M.

Use only one "moon" number. Choose the column closest to your time of birth. If your place of birth is not on Eastern Standard Time, be sure to read "How to Convert to Eastern Standard Time" at the beginning of this section.

Date & Time	SUN	MOON 1	MOON 2	MOON 3	MERCURY	VENUS	MARS	JUPITER	SATURN	URANUS	NEPTUNE	PLUTO
JAN. 1	38	18	18	19	39	36	5	41	41	6	47	40
JAN. 2	38	19	20	21	40	36	5	41	41	6	47	40
JAN. 3	39	21	22	22	40	36	5	41	41	6	47	40
JAN. 4	39	23	24	24	40	36	5	41	41	6	47	40
JAN. 5	39	25	26	26	40	36	5	41	41	6	47	40
JAN. 6	39	27	27	28	40	37	5	41	41	6	47	40
JAN. 7	39	29	29	30	41	37	5	42	41	6	47	40
JAN. 8	39	31	31	32	41	37	5	42	41	6	47	40
JAN. 9	39	32	33	34	41	37	5	42	41	6	47	40
JAN. 10	40	34	35	36	41	37	5	42	41	6	47	40
JAN. 11	40	36	37	38	42	37	5	42	41	6	47	40
JAN. 12	40	38	39	39	42	38	5	42	41	6	47	40
JAN. 13	40	40	41	41	42	38	5	42	41	6	47	40
JAN. 14	40	42	43	43	42	38	5	42	41	6	47	40
JAN. 15	40	44	44	45	42	38	5	42	41	6	47	40
JAN. 16	40	45	46	47	42	38	6	42	41	6	47	40
JAN. 17	41	47	48	48	43	38	6	42	41	6	47	40
JAN. 18	41	1	1	2	43	39	6	42	41	6	47	40
JAN. 19	41	2	3	4	43	39	6	42	41	6	47	40
JAN. 20	41	4	5	5	43	39	6	42	41	6	47	40
JAN. 21	41	6	6	7	44	39	6	42	41	6	47	40
JAN. 22	41	7	8	8	44	39	6	42	42	6	47	40
JAN. 23	42	9	9	10	44	39	6	42	42	6	48	40
JAN. 24	42	10	11	11	44	40	6	42	42	6	48	40
JAN. 25	42	12	13	13	44	40	6	42	42	6	48	40
JAN. 26	42	14	14	15	44	40	6	42	42	6	48	40
JAN. 27	42	15	16	17	44	40	6	42	42	6	48	40
JAN. 28	42	17	18	18	44	40	6	42	42	6	48	40
JAN. 29	42	19	20	20	44	40	6	42	42	6	48	40
JAN. 30	42	21	21	22	44	41	7	42	42	6	48	40
JAN. 31	43	23	23	24	44	41	7	42	42	6	48	40

Date & Time	SUN	MOON 1	MOON 2	MOON 3	MERCURY	VENUS	MARS	JUPITER	SATURN	URANUS	NEPTUNE	PLUTO
FEB. 1	43	24	25	26	44	41	7	42	42	6	48	40
FEB. 2	43	26	27	28	44	41	7	42	42	6	48	40
FEB. 3	43	28	29	29	44	41	7	42	42	6	48	40
FEB. 4	43	30	31	31	44	41	7	42	42	6	48	40
FEB. 5	43	32	33	33	44	42	7	42	42	6	48	40
FEB. 6	43	34	35	35	44	42	7	42	42	6	48	40
FEB. 7	43	36	36	37	44	42	7	43	42	6	48	40
FEB. 8	44	38	38	39	44	42	7	43	42	6	48	40
FEB. 9	44	39	40	41	44	42	7	43	42	6	48	40
FEB. 10	44	41	42	42	43	42	7	43	42	6	48	40
FEB. 11	44	43	44	44	43	43	7	43	42	6	48	40
FEB. 12	44	45	45	46	43	43	7	43	42	6	48	40
FEB. 13	44	47	47	48	43	43	8	43	42	6	48	40
FEB. 14	44	48	1	1	43	43	8	43	42	6	48	40
FEB. 15	44	2	2	3	43	43	8	43	42	6	48	40
FEB. 16	45	3	4	5	43	43	8	43	42	6	48	40
FEB. 17	45	5	6	6	43	44	8	43	42	6	48	40
FEB. 18	45	7	7	8	43	44	8	43	42	6	48	40
FEB. 19	45	8	9	9	42	44	8	43	42	6	48	40
FEB. 20	45	10	10	11	42	44	8	43	42	6	48	40
FEB. 21	45	11	12	12	42	44	8	43	42	6	48	40
FEB. 22	45	13	14	14	42	44	8	43	42	6	48	40
FEB. 23	46	15	15	16	42	45	8	43	42	6	48	40
FEB. 24	46	16	17	18	43	45	8	43	42	6	48	40
FEB. 25	46	18	19	19	43	45	8	43	42	6	48	40
FEB. 26	46	20	21	21	43	45	9	43	42	6	48	40
FEB. 27	46	22	23	23	43	45	9	43	42	6	48	40
FEB. 28	46	24	24	25	43	45	9	43	42	6	48	40

MOON 1 ◐ 12:01 A.M. TO 8:00 A.M.   **MOON 2** ◑ 8:01 A.M. TO 4:00 P.M.   **MOON 3** ● 4:01 P.M. TO 12:00 A.M.
Use only one "moon" number. Choose the column closest to your time of birth. If your place of birth is not on Eastern Standard Time, be sure to read "How to Convert to Eastern Standard Time" at the beginning of this section.

Date & Time	SUN	MOON 1	MOON 2	MOON 3	MERCURY	VENUS	MARS	JUPITER	SATURN	URANUS	NEPTUNE	PLUTO
MAR. 1	46	26	26	27	43	46	9	43	42	6	48	40
MAR. 2	46	28	28	29	43	46	9	43	42	6	48	40
MAR. 3	47	30	30	31	43	46	9	43	42	6	48	40
MAR. 4	47	32	32	33	43	46	9	43	42	6	48	40
MAR. 5	47	33	34	35	43	46	9	43	42	6	48	40
MAR. 6	47	35	36	37	43	46	9	43	42	6	48	40
MAR. 7	47	37	38	38	44	47	9	43	42	6	48	40
MAR. 8	47	39	40	40	44	47	9	43	42	6	48	40
MAR. 9	47	41	41	42	44	47	9	43	42	6	48	40
MAR. 10	47	43	43	44	44	47	9	43	42	6	48	40
MAR. 11	48	44	45	45	44	10	43	42	6	48	40
MAR. 12	48	46	47	47	44	10	44	42	6	48	40
MAR. 13	48	48	48	1	44	48	10	44	42	6	48	40
MAR. 14	48	1	2	2	45	48	10	44	42	6	48	40
MAR. 15	48	3	4	4	45	48	10	44	42	6	48	40
MAR. 16	48	5	5	6	45	48	10	44	42	6	48	40
MAR. 17	48	6	7	7	45	48	10	44	42	6	48	40
MAR. 18	48	8	8	9	45	48	10	44	42	6	48	40
MAR. 19	1	9	10	10	46	1	10	44	42	6	48	40
MAR. 20	1	11	11	12	46	1	10	44	42	6	48	40
MAR. 21	1	12	13	14	46	1	10	44	42	6	48	40
MAR. 22	1	14	15	15	46	1	10	44	42	6	48	40
MAR. 23	1	16	16	17	46	1	10	44	42	6	48	40
MAR. 24	1	17	18	19	47	1	11	44	42	6	48	41
MAR. 25	2	19	20	20	47	2	11	44	42	6	48	41
MAR. 26	2	21	22	22	47	2	11	44	42	6	48	41
MAR. 27	2	23	24	24	47	2	11	44	42	6	48	41
MAR. 28	2	25	26	26	47	2	11	44	42	6	48	41
MAR. 29	2	27	28	28	48	2	11	44	42	6	48	41
MAR. 30	2	29	30	30	48	2	11	44	42	6	48	41
MAR. 31	2	31	32	32	48	3	11	44	42	6	48	41

Date & Time	SUN	MOON 1	MOON 2	MOON 3	MERCURY	VENUS	MARS	JUPITER	SATURN	URANUS	NEPTUNE	PLUTO
APR. 1	2	33	34	34	48	3	11	44	42	6	48	41
APR. 2	2	35	35	36	1	3	11	44	42	6	48	41
APR. 3	3	37	37	38	1	3	11	44	43	6	48	41
APR. 4	3	39	39	40	1	3	11	44	43	6	48	41
APR. 5	3	40	41	42	1	3	11	44	43	6	48	41
APR. 6	3	42	43	43	1	4	12	44	43	6	48	41
APR. 7	3	44	44	45	2	4	12	44	43	6	48	41
APR. 8	3	46	46	47	2	4	12	44	43	6	48	41
APR. 9	3	47	48	48	2	4	12	44	43	6	48	41
APR. 10	3	1	1	2	2	4	12	44	43	6	48	41
APR. 11	4	3	3	4	3	4	12	44	43	6	48	41
APR. 12	4	4	5	5	3	5	12	44	43	6	48	41
APR. 13	4	6	6	7	3	5	12	44	43	6	48	41
APR. 14	4	7	8	8	4	5	12	44	43	6	48	41
APR. 15	4	9	9	10	4	5	12	44	43	6	48	41
APR. 16	4	10	11	11	4	5	12	44	43	6	48	41
APR. 17	4	12	13	13	4	5	12	44	43	6	48	41
APR. 18	4	14	14	15	5	6	13	44	43	6	48	41
APR. 19	5	15	16	16	5	6	13	45	43	6	48	41
APR. 20	5	17	17	18	5	6	13	45	43	6	48	41
APR. 21	5	19	19	20	5	6	13	45	43	6	48	41
APR. 22	5	20	21	22	6	6	13	45	43	6	48	41
APR. 23	5	22	23	23	6	6	13	45	43	6	48	41
APR. 24	5	24	25	25	6	7	13	45	43	6	48	41
APR. 25	6	26	27	27	7	7	13	45	43	6	48	41
APR. 26	6	28	29	29	7	7	13	45	43	6	48	41
APR. 27	6	30	31	31	7	7	13	45	43	6	48	41
APR. 28	6	32	33	33	7	7	13	45	43	6	48	41
APR. 29	6	34	35	35	8	7	13	45	43	6	48	41
APR. 30	6	36	37	37	8	8	14	45	43	6	48	41

MOON 1 ◐ 12:01 A.M. TO 8:00 A.M. **MOON 2** ◑ 8:01 A.M. TO 4:00 P.M. **MOON 3** ● 4:01 P.M. TO 12:00 A.M.

Use only one "moon" number. Choose the column closest to your time of birth. If your place of birth is not on Eastern Standard Time, be sure to read "How to Convert to Eastern Standard Time" at the beginning of this section.

2021 — May | June

Date & Time	SUN ☉	MOON 1 ◑	MOON 2 ◐	MOON 3 ●	MERCURY	VENUS	MARS	JUPITER	SATURN	URANUS	NEPTUNE	PLUTO
MAY 1	6	38	39	39	8	8	14	45	43	6	48	41
MAY 2	6	40	40	41	8	8	14	45	43	6	48	41
MAY 3	7	42	42	43	9	8	14	45	43	6	48	41
MAY 4	7	43	44	45	9	8	14	45	43	6	48	41
MAY 5	7	45	46	46	9	8	14	45	43	6	48	41
MAY 6	7	47	47	48	9	8	14	45	43	6	48	41
MAY 7	7	48	1	2	10	9	14	45	43	6	48	41
MAY 8	7	2	3	3	10	9	14	45	43	6	48	41
MAY 9	7	4	4	5	10	9	14	45	43	6	48	41
MAY 10	7	5	6	6	10	9	14	45	43	6	48	41
MAY 11	8	7	7	8	10	9	14	45	43	6	48	41
MAY 12	8	9	9	10	11	9	14	45	43	6	48	41
MAY 13	8	10	11	11	11	10	15	45	43	6	48	41
MAY 14	8	12	12	13	11	10	15	45	43	6	48	41
MAY 15	8	13	14	14	11	10	15	45	43	7	48	41
MAY 16	8	15	15	16	11	10	15	45	43	7	48	41
MAY 17	8	16	17	18	11	10	15	45	43	7	48	41
MAY 18	8	18	19	19	12	10	15	45	43	7	48	41
MAY 19	9	20	20	21	12	11	15	45	43	7	48	41
MAY 20	9	22	22	23	12	11	15	45	43	7	48	41
MAY 21	9	23	24	25	12	11	15	45	43	7	48	41
MAY 22	9	25	26	27	12	11	15	45	43	7	48	41
MAY 23	9	27	28	28	12	11	15	45	43	7	48	41
MAY 24	9	29	30	30	12	11	15	45	43	7	48	41
MAY 25	10	31	32	32	12	12	16	45	43	7	48	41
MAY 26	10	33	34	35	12	12	16	45	43	7	48	41
MAY 27	10	35	36	37	12	12	16	45	43	7	48	41
MAY 28	10	37	38	38	12	12	16	45	43	7	48	41
MAY 29	10	39	40	40	12	12	16	45	43	7	48	41
MAY 30	10	41	42	42	12	12	16	45	43	7	48	41
MAY 31	10	43	43	44	12	13	16	45	43	7	48	41

Date & Time	SUN ☉	MOON 1 ◑	MOON 2 ◐	MOON 3 ●	MERCURY	VENUS	MARS	JUPITER	SATURN	URANUS	NEPTUNE	PLUTO
JUN. 1	10	45	45	46	12	13	16	45	43	7	48	41
JUN. 2	10	46	47	48	12	13	16	45	43	7	48	41
JUN. 3	11	48	1	1	12	13	16	45	43	7	48	41
JUN. 4	11	2	2	3	12	13	16	45	43	7	48	40
JUN. 5	11	3	4	4	12	13	16	45	43	7	48	40
JUN. 6	11	5	5	5	12	14	17	45	43	7	48	40
JUN. 7	11	6	7	8	12	14	17	45	43	7	48	40
JUN. 8	11	8	9	9	12	14	17	45	43	7	48	40
JUN. 9	11	10	10	11	12	14	17	45	43	7	48	40
JUN. 10	11	11	12	12	12	14	17	45	43	7	48	40
JUN. 11	12	13	13	14	12	14	17	45	43	7	48	40
JUN. 12	12	14	15	16	12	15	17	45	43	7	48	40
JUN. 13	12	16	17	17	12	15	17	45	43	7	48	40
JUN. 14	12	18	18	19	11	15	17	45	43	7	48	40
JUN. 15	12	19	20	21	11	15	17	45	43	7	48	40
JUN. 16	12	21	22	23	11	15	17	45	43	7	48	40
JUN. 17	12	23	23	24	11	15	17	45	43	7	48	40
JUN. 18	12	25	25	26	11	16	18	45	43	7	48	40
JUN. 19	13	27	27	28	11	16	18	45	43	7	48	40
JUN. 20	13	28	29	30	11	16	18	45	43	7	48	40
JUN. 21	13	30	31	32	11	16	18	45	43	7	48	40
JUN. 22	13	32	33	34	11	16	18	45	43	7	48	40
JUN. 23	13	34	35	36	11	16	18	45	43	7	48	40
JUN. 24	13	36	37	38	11	16	18	45	43	7	48	40
JUN. 25	14	38	39	40	11	17	18	45	43	7	48	40
JUN. 26	14	40	41	42	11	17	18	45	43	7	48	40
JUN. 27	14	42	43	44	11	17	18	45	43	7	48	40
JUN. 28	14	44	45	45	11	17	18	45	43	7	48	40
JUN. 29	14	46	46	47	11	17	18	45	43	7	48	40
JUN. 30	14	48	48	1	11	17	19	45	43	7	48	40

MOON 1 ◑ 12:01 A.M. TO 8:00 A.M. **MOON 2** ◐ 8:01 A.M. TO 4:00 P.M. **MOON 3** ● 4:01 P.M. TO 12:00 A.M.
Use only one "moon" number. Choose the column closest to your time of birth. If your place of birth is not on Eastern Standard Time, be sure to read "How to Convert to Eastern Standard Time" at the beginning of this section.

2021

July

Date & Time	SUN	MOON 1	MOON 2	MOON 3	MERCURY	VENUS	MARS	JUPITER	SATURN	URANUS	NEPTUNE	PLUTO
JUL. 1	14	1	2	2	11	18	19	45	43	7	48	40
JUL. 2	14	3	3	4	12	18	19	45	43	7	48	40
JUL. 3	15	4	5	6	12	18	19	45	43	7	48	40
JUL. 4	15	6	7	7	12	18	19	45	43	7	48	40
JUL. 5	15	8	8	9	12	18	19	45	43	7	48	40
JUL. 6	15	9	10	10	12	18	19	45	43	7	48	40
JUL. 7	15	11	11	12	12	19	19	45	43	7	48	40
JUL. 8	15	12	13	13	12	19	19	45	43	7	48	40
JUL. 9	15	14	15	15	12	19	19	45	43	7	48	40
JUL. 10	15	16	16	17	13	19	19	45	43	7	48	40
JUL. 11	16	17	18	18	13	19	19	45	43	7	48	40
JUL. 12	16	19	20	20	13	19	19	45	43	7	48	40
JUL. 13	16	21	21	22	13	20	20	45	43	7	48	40
JUL. 14	16	22	23	24	13	20	20	45	43	7	48	40
JUL. 15	16	24	25	25	14	20	20	45	42	7	48	40
JUL. 16	16	26	27	27	14	20	20	45	42	7	48	40
JUL. 17	16	28	29	29	14	20	20	45	42	7	48	40
JUL. 18	16	30	30	31	14	20	20	45	42	7	48	40
JUL. 19	17	32	32	33	15	21	20	45	42	7	48	40
JUL. 20	17	34	34	35	15	21	20	45	42	7	48	40
JUL. 21	17	36	36	37	15	21	20	45	42	7	48	40
JUL. 22	17	37	38	39	15	21	20	45	42	7	48	40
JUL. 23	17	39	40	41	16	21	20	45	42	7	48	40
JUL. 24	17	41	42	43	16	21	20	45	42	7	48	40
JUL. 25	17	43	44	44	16	21	21	45	42	7	48	40
JUL. 26	18	45	46	46	16	22	21	45	42	7	48	40
JUL. 27	18	47	47	48	17	22	21	45	42	7	48	40
JUL. 28	18	1	1	2	17	22	21	45	42	7	48	40
JUL. 29	18	2	3	3	17	22	21	45	42	7	48	40
JUL. 30	18	4	4	5	18	22	21	45	42	7	48	40
JUL. 31	18	6	6	7	18	22	21	45	42	7	48	40

August

Date & Time	SUN	MOON 1	MOON 2	MOON 3	MERCURY	VENUS	MARS	JUPITER	SATURN	URANUS	NEPTUNE	PLUTO
AUG. 1	18	7	8	8	18	23	21	45	42	7	48	40
AUG. 2	18	9	9	10	18	23	21	45	42	7	48	40
AUG. 3	19	10	11	11	19	23	21	45	42	7	48	40
AUG. 4	19	12	12	13	19	23	21	45	42	7	48	40
AUG. 5	19	13	14	15	19	23	21	45	42	7	48	40
AUG. 6	19	15	16	16	19	23	22	45	42	7	48	40
AUG. 7	19	17	17	18	20	24	22	45	42	7	48	40
AUG. 8	19	18	19	20	20	24	22	45	42	7	48	40
AUG. 9	19	20	21	21	20	24	22	45	42	7	48	40
AUG. 10	19	22	23	23	21	24	22	45	42	7	48	40
AUG. 11	20	24	24	25	21	24	22	45	42	7	48	40
AUG. 12	20	26	26	27	21	24	22	45	42	7	48	40
AUG. 13	20	27	28	29	21	24	22	45	42	7	48	40
AUG. 14	20	29	30	31	22	25	22	45	42	7	48	40
AUG. 15	20	31	32	32	22	25	22	45	42	7	48	40
AUG. 16	20	33	34	34	22	25	22	45	42	7	48	40
AUG. 17	20	35	36	36	22	25	23	45	42	7	48	40
AUG. 18	20	37	38	38	22	25	23	45	42	7	48	40
AUG. 19	21	39	39	40	23	25	23	45	42	7	48	40
AUG. 20	21	41	41	42	23	26	23	45	42	7	48	40
AUG. 21	21	43	43	44	23	26	23	45	42	7	48	40
AUG. 22	21	44	45	46	23	26	23	45	42	7	48	40
AUG. 23	21	46	47	47	24	26	23	45	42	7	48	40
AUG. 24	21	48	1	1	24	26	23	45	42	7	48	40
AUG. 25	21	2	2	3	24	26	23	45	42	7	48	40
AUG. 26	22	3	4	4	24	27	23	44	42	7	48	40
AUG. 27	22	5	6	6	24	27	23	44	42	7	48	40
AUG. 28	22	7	7	8	25	27	23	44	42	7	48	40
AUG. 29	22	8	9	9	25	27	24	44	42	7	48	40
AUG. 30	22	10	10	11	25	27	24	44	42	7	48	40
AUG. 31	22	11	12	12	25	27	24	44	42	7	48	40

MOON 1 ◗ 12:01 A.M. TO 8:00 A.M.   **MOON 2** ◐ 8:01 A.M. TO 4:00 P.M.   **MOON 3** ● 4:01 P.M. TO 12:00 A.M.

Use only one "moon" number. Choose the column closest to your time of birth. If your place of birth is not on Eastern Standard Time, be sure to read "How to Convert to Eastern Standard Time" at the beginning of this section.

2021

September

Date & Time	SUN ☉	MOON 1 ◗	MOON 2 ◖	MOON 3 ●	MERCURY	VENUS	MARS	JUPITER	SATURN	URANUS	NEPTUNE	PLUTO
SEP. 1	22	13	13	14	25	27	24	44	42	7	48	40
SEP. 2	22	15	15	16	26	28	24	44	42	7	48	40
SEP. 3	23	16	17	17	26	28	24	44	42	7	48	40
SEP. 4	23	18	18	19	26	28	24	44	42	7	48	40
SEP. 5	23	20	20	21	26	28	24	44	42	7	48	40
SEP. 6	23	21	22	23	26	28	24	44	42	7	48	40
SEP. 7	23	23	24	24	26	28	24	44	42	7	48	40
SEP. 8	23	25	26	26	27	28	24	44	42	7	48	40
SEP. 9	23	27	28	28	27	29	24	44	42	7	48	40
SEP. 10	23	29	30	30	27	29	25	44	42	7	48	40
SEP. 11	24	31	31	32	27	29	25	44	42	7	48	40
SEP. 12	24	33	33	34	27	29	25	44	42	7	48	40
SEP. 13	24	35	35	36	27	29	25	44	42	7	48	40
SEP. 14	24	36	37	38	27	29	25	44	42	7	48	40
SEP. 15	24	38	39	40	28	30	25	44	42	7	48	40
SEP. 16	24	40	41	41	28	30	25	44	42	7	48	40
SEP. 17	24	42	43	43	28	30	25	44	42	7	48	40
SEP. 18	24	44	44	45	28	30	25	44	42	7	48	40
SEP. 19	25	46	46	47	28	30	25	44	42	7	48	40
SEP. 20	25	47	48	1	28	30	25	44	42	7	48	40
SEP. 21	25	1	2	2	28	31	26	44	42	7	48	40
SEP. 22	25	3	3	4	28	31	26	44	42	7	48	40
SEP. 23	25	4	5	6	28	31	26	44	42	7	48	40
SEP. 24	25	6	7	7	28	31	26	44	42	7	48	40
SEP. 25	26	8	8	9	28	31	26	44	42	7	48	40
SEP. 26	26	9	10	10	28	31	26	44	42	7	48	40
SEP. 27	26	11	11	12	28	31	26	44	42	7	48	40
SEP. 28	26	12	13	13	28	32	26	44	42	7	48	40
SEP. 29	26	14	15	15	28	32	26	44	42	7	48	40
SEP. 30	26	16	16	17	28	32	26	44	42	7	48	40

October

Date & Time	SUN ☉	MOON 1 ◗	MOON 2 ◖	MOON 3 ●	MERCURY	VENUS	MARS	JUPITER	SATURN	URANUS	NEPTUNE	PLUTO
OCT. 1	26	17	18	18	28	32	26	44	42	7	48	40
OCT. 2	26	19	20	20	28	32	26	44	42	7	48	40
OCT. 3	27	21	21	22	28	32	27	44	42	7	48	40
OCT. 4	27	23	23	24	28	32	27	44	42	7	48	40
OCT. 5	27	24	25	26	28	33	27	44	42	7	48	40
OCT. 6	27	26	27	28	28	33	27	44	42	7	48	40
OCT. 7	27	28	29	30	28	33	27	44	42	7	48	40
OCT. 8	27	30	31	31	27	33	27	44	42	7	48	40
OCT. 9	27	32	33	33	27	33	27	44	42	7	48	40
OCT. 10	27	34	35	35	27	33	27	44	42	7	48	40
OCT. 11	28	36	37	37	27	34	27	44	42	7	48	40
OCT. 12	28	38	39	39	27	34	27	44	42	7	48	40
OCT. 13	28	40	40	41	27	34	27	44	42	7	48	40
OCT. 14	28	42	42	43	27	34	28	44	42	7	48	40
OCT. 15	28	43	44	45	27	34	28	44	42	7	48	40
OCT. 16	28	45	46	46	26	34	28	44	42	7	48	40
OCT. 17	28	47	47	48	26	34	28	44	42	7	48	40
OCT. 18	28	1	1	2	26	35	28	44	42	7	48	40
OCT. 19	29	2	3	3	26	35	28	44	42	7	48	40
OCT. 20	29	4	4	5	26	35	28	44	42	7	48	40
OCT. 21	29	6	6	6	26	35	28	44	42	7	48	40
OCT. 22	29	7	8	8	26	35	28	44	42	7	48	40
OCT. 23	29	9	9	10	27	35	28	44	42	7	48	40
OCT. 24	29	10	11	11	27	35	28	44	42	7	48	40
OCT. 25	29	12	12	13	27	35	28	44	42	7	48	40
OCT. 26	30	13	14	15	27	36	29	44	42	7	48	40
OCT. 27	30	15	16	16	27	36	29	44	42	7	48	40
OCT. 28	30	17	17	18	27	36	29	44	42	7	48	40
OCT. 29	30	18	19	19	27	36	29	44	42	7	48	40
OCT. 30	30	20	21	21	28	36	29	44	42	7	48	40
OCT. 31	30	22	22	23	28	36	29	44	42	7	48	40

MOON 1 ◗ 12:01 A.M. TO 8:00 A.M.   **MOON 2** ◖ 8:01 A.M. TO 4:00 P.M.   **MOON 3** ● 4:01 P.M. TO 12:00 A.M.
Use only one "moon" number. Choose the column closest to your time of birth. If your place of birth is not on Eastern Standard Time, be sure to read "How to Convert to Eastern Standard Time" at the beginning of this section.

November

Date & Time	SUN	MOON 1	MOON 2	MOON 3	MERCURY	VENUS	MARS	JUPITER	SATURN	URANUS	NEPTUNE	PLUTO
NOV. 1	30	24	24	25	28	36	29	44	42	7	48	40
NOV. 2	30	25	26	27	28	37	29	44	42	7	48	40
NOV. 3	31	27	28	29	28	37	29	44	42	7	48	40
NOV. 4	31	29	30	31	29	37	29	44	42	7	48	40
NOV. 5	31	31	32	33	29	37	29	44	42	7	48	40
NOV. 6	31	33	34	35	29	37	30	44	42	7	48	40
NOV. 7	31	35	36	37	29	37	30	44	42	7	48	40
NOV. 8	31	37	38	39	29	37	30	44	42	7	48	40
NOV. 9	31	39	40	40	30	37	30	44	42	7	48	40
NOV. 10	31	41	42	42	30	38	30	44	42	7	48	40
NOV. 11	31	43	44	44	30	38	30	44	42	7	48	40
NOV. 12	32	45	45	46	30	38	30	44	42	7	48	40
NOV. 13	32	47	47	48	31	38	30	44	42	7	48	40
NOV. 14	32	48	1	1	31	38	30	44	42	7	48	40
NOV. 15	32	2	2	3	31	38	30	44	42	7	48	40
NOV. 16	32	4	4	5	31	38	30	44	42	7	48	40
NOV. 17	32	5	6	7	31	38	31	44	42	7	48	40
NOV. 18	32	7	7	8	32	38	31	44	42	7	48	40
NOV. 19	33	8	9	9	32	39	31	44	42	7	48	40
NOV. 20	33	10	10	11	32	39	31	44	42	7	48	40
NOV. 21	33	11	12	13	32	39	31	44	42	7	48	40
NOV. 22	33	13	14	14	32	39	31	44	42	7	48	40
NOV. 23	33	15	15	16	33	39	31	44	42	7	48	40
NOV. 24	33	16	17	17	33	39	31	44	42	7	48	40
NOV. 25	34	18	18	19	33	39	31	44	42	7	48	40
NOV. 26	34	19	20	21	33	39	31	44	42	7	48	40
NOV. 27	34	21	22	22	34	39	31	44	42	7	48	40
NOV. 28	34	23	23	24	34	39	32	44	42	7	48	40
NOV. 29	34	25	25	26	34	40	32	44	42	7	48	40
NOV. 30	34	27	27	28	34	40	32	44	42	7	48	40

December

Date & Time	SUN	MOON 1	MOON 2	MOON 3	MERCURY	VENUS	MARS	JUPITER	SATURN	URANUS	NEPTUNE	PLUTO
DEC. 1	34	28	29	30	34	40	32	44	42	7	48	40
DEC. 2	34	30	31	32	35	40	32	44	42	7	48	40
DEC. 3	35	32	33	34	35	40	32	44	42	7	48	40
DEC. 4	35	34	35	36	35	40	32	44	42	7	48	40
DEC. 5	35	36	37	38	35	40	32	44	42	7	48	40
DEC. 6	35	38	39	40	35	40	32	44	42	7	48	40
DEC. 7	35	40	41	42	36	40	32	44	42	7	48	40
DEC. 8	35	42	43	44	36	40	32	44	42	7	48	40
DEC. 9	35	44	45	45	36	40	33	45	42	6	48	40
DEC. 10	35	46	47	47	36	40	33	45	42	6	48	40
DEC. 11	36	48	48	1	36	40	33	45	42	6	48	40
DEC. 12	36	1	2	3	37	40	33	45	42	6	48	40
DEC. 13	36	3	4	4	37	40	33	45	42	6	48	40
DEC. 14	36	5	5	6	37	40	33	45	42	6	48	40
DEC. 15	36	6	7	7	37	40	33	45	42	6	48	40
DEC. 16	36	8	8	9	37	40	33	45	42	6	48	40
DEC. 17	36	10	10	11	38	40	33	45	42	6	48	40
DEC. 18	36	11	12	12	38	40	33	45	42	6	48	40
DEC. 19	37	13	13	14	38	40	34	45	42	6	48	40
DEC. 20	37	14	15	15	38	40	34	45	42	6	48	40
DEC. 21	37	16	16	17	39	40	34	45	42	6	48	40
DEC. 22	37	17	18	19	39	40	34	45	42	6	48	40
DEC. 23	37	19	20	20	39	40	34	45	42	6	48	40
DEC. 24	37	21	21	22	39	40	34	45	42	6	48	40
DEC. 25	37	22	23	24	39	40	34	45	42	6	48	40
DEC. 26	38	24	25	25	40	40	34	45	42	6	48	40
DEC. 27	38	26	26	27	40	40	34	45	42	6	48	40
DEC. 28	38	28	28	29	40	40	34	45	42	6	48	40
DEC. 29	38	30	30	31	40	40	34	45	43	6	48	40
DEC. 30	38	31	32	33	40	40	35	45	43	6	48	40
DEC. 31	38	33	34	35	41	40	35	45	43	6	48	40

MOON 1 ☽ 12:01 A.M. TO 8:00 A.M.　　**MOON 2** ◑ 8:01 A.M. TO 4:00 P.M.　　**MOON 3** ● 4:01 P.M. TO 12:00 A.M.

Use only one "moon" number. Choose the column closest to your time of birth. If your place of birth is not on Eastern Standard Time, be sure to read "How to Convert to Eastern Standard Time" at the beginning of this section.

2022

January

Date & Time	SUN	MOON 1	MOON 2	MOON 3	MERCURY	VENUS	MARS	JUPITER	SATURN	URANUS	NEPTUNE	PLUTO
JAN. 1	38	35	36	37	41	40	35	45	43	6	48	40
JAN. 2	38	37	38	39	41	40	35	45	43	6	48	40
JAN. 3	39	39	40	41	41	40	35	45	43	6	48	40
JAN. 4	39	41	42	43	41	40	35	45	43	6	48	40
JAN. 5	39	43	44	45	41	40	35	45	43	6	48	40
JAN. 6	39	45	46	47	42	40	35	45	43	6	48	40
JAN. 7	39	47	48	48	42	40	35	45	43	6	48	40
JAN. 8	39	1	2	2	42	40	35	45	43	6	48	40
JAN. 9	39	3	3	4	42	39	35	45	43	6	48	40
JAN. 10	40	4	5	5	42	39	36	45	43	6	48	40
JAN. 11	40	6	6	7	42	39	36	45	43	6	48	40
JAN. 12	40	8	8	9	42	39	36	45	43	6	48	40
JAN. 13	40	9	10	10	42	39	36	45	43	6	48	40
JAN. 14	40	11	11	12	42	39	36	45	43	6	48	40
JAN. 15	40	12	13	13	42	39	36	45	43	6	48	40
JAN. 16	40	14	14	15	42	39	36	45	43	6	48	40
JAN. 17	41	15	16	16	42	39	36	45	43	6	48	40
JAN. 18	41	17	18	18	42	39	36	46	43	6	48	40
JAN. 19	41	19	19	20	42	39	36	46	43	6	48	41
JAN. 20	41	20	21	21	42	39	37	46	43	6	48	41
JAN. 21	41	22	23	23	42	39	37	46	43	6	48	41
JAN. 22	41	24	24	25	42	39	37	46	43	6	48	41
JAN. 23	42	25	26	27	41	39	37	46	43	6	48	41
JAN. 24	42	27	28	28	41	39	37	46	43	6	48	41
JAN. 25	42	29	30	30	41	38	37	46	43	6	48	41
JAN. 26	42	31	32	32	41	38	37	46	43	6	48	41
JAN. 27	42	33	33	34	41	38	37	46	43	6	48	41
JAN. 28	42	35	35	36	41	38	37	46	43	6	48	41
JAN. 29	42	37	37	38	41	38	37	46	43	6	48	41
JAN. 30	42	39	39	40	40	38	38	46	43	6	48	41
JAN. 31	43	41	41	42	40	38	38	46	43	6	48	41

February

Date & Time	SUN	MOON 1	MOON 2	MOON 3	MERCURY	VENUS	MARS	JUPITER	SATURN	URANUS	NEPTUNE	PLUTO
FEB. 1	43	43	43	44	40	38	38	46	43	6	48	41
FEB. 2	43	44	45	46	40	38	38	46	43	6	48	41
FEB. 3	43	46	47	48	40	39	38	46	43	6	48	41
FEB. 4	43	48	1	1	40	39	38	46	43	6	48	41
FEB. 5	43	2	3	3	40	39	38	46	43	6	48	41
FEB. 6	43	4	4	5	40	39	38	46	43	6	48	41
FEB. 7	43	5	6	6	40	39	38	46	43	6	48	41
FEB. 8	44	7	8	8	40	39	38	46	43	6	48	41
FEB. 9	44	9	9	10	40	39	38	46	43	6	48	41
FEB. 10	44	10	11	11	40	39	39	46	43	6	48	41
FEB. 11	44	12	12	13	41	39	39	46	43	6	48	41
FEB. 12	44	13	14	14	41	39	39	46	43	6	48	41
FEB. 13	44	15	15	16	41	39	39	46	43	6	48	41
FEB. 14	44	17	17	18	41	39	39	46	43	6	48	41
FEB. 15	44	18	19	19	41	39	39	46	43	6	48	41
FEB. 16	45	20	20	21	41	39	39	46	43	6	48	41
FEB. 17	45	22	22	23	41	39	39	46	43	6	48	41
FEB. 18	45	23	24	24	41	39	39	46	43	6	48	41
FEB. 19	45	25	26	26	42	39	39	47	43	6	48	41
FEB. 20	45	27	27	28	42	40	40	47	43	6	48	41
FEB. 21	45	29	29	30	42	40	40	47	43	6	48	41
FEB. 22	45	30	31	32	42	40	40	47	43	6	48	41
FEB. 23	46	32	33	34	42	40	40	47	43	6	48	41
FEB. 24	46	34	35	35	42	40	40	47	43	6	48	41
FEB. 25	46	36	37	37	43	40	40	47	43	6	48	41
FEB. 26	46	38	39	39	43	40	40	47	43	6	48	41
FEB. 27	46	40	41	41	43	40	40	47	43	6	48	41
FEB. 28	46	42	42	43	43	40	40	47	43	7	48	41

MOON 1 ◑ 12:01 A.M. TO 8:00 A.M.   **MOON 2** ◑ 8:01 A.M. TO 4:00 P.M.   **MOON 3** ● 4:01 P.M. TO 12:00 A.M.
Use only one "moon" number. Choose the column closest to your time of birth. If your place of birth is not on Eastern Standard Time, be sure to read "How to Convert to Eastern Standard Time" at the beginning of this section.

Date & Time	SUN	MOON 1	MOON 2	MOON 3	MERCURY	VENUS	MARS	JUPITER	SATURN	URANUS	NEPTUNE	PLUTO
MAR. 1	46	44	44	45	43	40	40	47	43	7	48	41
MAR. 2	46	46	46	47	43	41	41	47	43	7	48	41
MAR. 3	47	47	48	1	44	41	41	47	44	7	48	41
MAR. 4	47	1	2	2	44	41	41	47	44	7	48	41
MAR. 5	47	3	4	4	44	41	41	47	44	7	48	41
MAR. 6	47	5	5	6	44	41	41	47	44	7	48	41
MAR. 7	47	6	7	8	44	41	41	47	44	7	48	41
MAR. 8	47	8	9	9	45	41	41	47	44	7	48	41
MAR. 9	47	10	10	11	45	41	41	47	44	7	48	41
MAR. 10	47	11	12	12	45	41	41	47	44	7	48	41
MAR. 11	48	13	13	14	45	42	41	47	44	7	48	41
MAR. 12	48	14	15	15	45	42	42	47	44	7	48	41
MAR. 13	48	16	17	17	46	42	42	47	44	7	48	41
MAR. 14	48	18	18	19	46	42	42	47	44	7	48	41
MAR. 15	48	19	20	20	46	42	42	47	44	7	48	41
MAR. 16	48	21	22	22	46	42	42	47	44	7	48	41
MAR. 17	48	23	23	24	47	42	42	47	44	7	48	41
MAR. 18	48	24	25	26	47	42	42	47	44	7	48	41
MAR. 19	1	26	27	28	47	43	42	47	44	7	48	41
MAR. 20	1	28	29	29	47	43	42	47	44	7	48	41
MAR. 21	1	30	31	31	47	43	42	47	44	7	48	41
MAR. 22	1	32	32	33	48	43	43	47	44	7	48	41
MAR. 23	1	34	34	35	48	43	43	48	44	7	48	41
MAR. 24	1	36	36	37	48	43	43	48	44	7	48	41
MAR. 25	2	38	38	39	48	43	43	48	44	7	48	41
MAR. 26	2	39	40	41	1	44	43	48	44	7	48	41
MAR. 27	2	41	42	43	1	44	43	48	44	7	48	41
MAR. 28	2	43	44	44	1	44	43	48	44	7	48	41
MAR. 29	2	45	46	46	1	44	43	48	44	7	48	41
MAR. 30	2	47	47	48	2	44	43	48	44	7	48	41
MAR. 31	2	1	1	2	2	44	43	48	44	7	48	41
APR. 1	2	2	3	4	2	44	44	48	44	7	48	41
APR. 2	2	4	5	5	3	44	44	48	44	7	48	41
APR. 3	3	6	6	7	3	45	44	48	44	7	48	41
APR. 4	3	7	8	9	3	45	44	48	44	7	48	41
APR. 5	3	9	10	10	3	45	44	48	44	7	48	41
APR. 6	3	11	11	12	4	45	44	48	44	7	48	41
APR. 7	3	12	13	13	4	45	44	48	44	7	48	41
APR. 8	3	14	14	15	4	45	44	48	44	7	48	41
APR. 9	3	15	16	16	4	45	44	48	44	7	48	41
APR. 10	3	17	18	18	5	46	44	48	44	7	48	41
APR. 11	4	19	19	20	5	46	45	48	44	7	48	41
APR. 12	4	20	21	21	5	46	45	48	44	7	48	41
APR. 13	4	22	23	23	6	46	45	48	44	7	48	41
APR. 14	4	24	24	25	6	46	45	48	44	7	48	41
APR. 15	4	26	26	27	6	46	45	48	44	7	48	41
APR. 16	4	27	28	29	6	47	45	48	44	7	48	41
APR. 17	4	29	30	31	7	47	45	48	44	7	48	41
APR. 18	4	31	32	33	7	47	45	48	44	7	48	41
APR. 19	5	33	34	34	7	47	45	48	44	7	48	41
APR. 20	5	35	36	36	7	47	45	48	44	7	48	41
APR. 21	5	37	38	38	7	47	46	48	44	7	48	41
APR. 22	5	39	40	40	8	47	46	48	44	7	48	41
APR. 23	5	41	41	42	8	48	46	48	44	7	48	41
APR. 24	5	43	43	44	8	48	46	1	44	7	48	41
APR. 25	6	45	45	46	8	48	46	1	44	7	48	41
APR. 26	6	46	47	48	8	48	46	1	44	7	48	41
APR. 27	6	48	1	1	9	48	46	1	44	7	48	41
APR. 28	6	2	2	3	9	48	46	1	44	7	48	41
APR. 29	6	4	4	5	9	48	46	1	44	7	48	41
APR. 30	6	5	6	6	9	1	46	1	44	7	48	41

MOON 1 ◑ 12:01 A.M. TO 8:00 A.M. **MOON 2** ◑ 8:01 A.M. TO 4:00 P.M. **MOON 3** ● 4:01 P.M. TO 12:00 A.M.
Use only one "moon" number. Choose the column closest to your time of birth. If your place of birth is not on Eastern Standard Time, be sure to read "How to Convert to Eastern Standard Time" at the beginning of this section.

2022

May

June

Date & Time	SUN	MOON 1	MOON 2	MOON 3	MERCURY	VENUS	MARS	JUPITER	SATURN	URANUS	NEPTUNE	PLUTO
MAY 1	6	7	7	8	9	1	47	1	44	7	48	41
MAY 2	6	9	9	10	9	1	47	1	44	7	48	41
MAY 3	7	10	11	11	9	1	47	1	44	7	48	41
MAY 4	7	12	12	13	9	1	47	1	44	7	48	41
MAY 5	7	13	14	14	9	1	47	1	44	7	48	41
MAY 6	7	15	15	16	10	2	47	1	44	7	48	41
MAY 7	7	17	17	18	10	2	47	1	44	7	48	41
MAY 8	7	18	19	19	10	2	47	1	44	7	48	41
MAY 9	7	20	20	21	10	2	47	1	44	7	48	41
MAY 10	7	21	22	23	10	2	47	1	44	7	48	41
MAY 11	8	23	24	24	10	2	48	1	44	7	48	41
MAY 12	8	25	25	26	10	2	48	1	44	7	48	41
MAY 13	8	27	27	28	10	3	48	1	44	7	48	41
MAY 14	8	29	29	30	10	3	48	1	44	7	48	41
MAY 15	8	30	31	32	9	3	48	1	44	7	48	41
MAY 16	8	32	33	34	9	3	48	1	44	7	48	41
MAY 17	8	34	35	36	9	3	48	1	44	7	48	41
MAY 18	8	36	37	38	9	3	48	1	44	7	48	41
MAY 19	9	38	39	40	9	4	48	1	44	7	48	41
MAY 20	9	40	41	42	9	4	48	1	44	7	48	41
MAY 21	9	42	43	44	9	4	1	1	44	7	48	41
MAY 22	9	44	45	45	9	4	1	1	44	7	48	41
MAY 23	9	46	47	47	9	4	1	1	44	7	48	41
MAY 24	9	48	48	1	9	4	1	1	44	7	48	41
MAY 25	10	1	2	3	9	4	1	1	44	7	48	41
MAY 26	10	3	4	4	9	5	1	1	44	7	48	41
MAY 27	10	5	5	6	9	5	1	1	44	7	48	41
MAY 28	10	7	7	8	9	5	1	1	44	7	48	41
MAY 29	10	8	9	9	9	5	1	1	44	7	48	41
MAY 30	10	10	10	11	9	5	1	1	44	7	48	41
MAY 31	10	11	12	12	8	5	2	1	44	7	48	41

Date & Time	SUN	MOON 1	MOON 2	MOON 3	MERCURY	VENUS	MARS	JUPITER	SATURN	URANUS	NEPTUNE	PLUTO
JUN. 1	10	13	13	14	8	6	2	1	44	7	48	41
JUN. 2	10	14	15	16	8	6	2	1	44	7	48	41
JUN. 3	11	16	17	17	8	6	2	2	44	7	48	41
JUN. 4	11	18	18	19	8	6	2	2	44	7	48	41
JUN. 5	11	19	20	20	8	6	2	2	44	7	48	41
JUN. 6	11	21	21	22	8	6	2	2	44	7	48	41
JUN. 7	11	23	23	24	9	6	2	2	44	7	48	41
JUN. 8	11	24	25	25	9	7	2	2	44	7	48	41
JUN. 9	11	26	27	27	9	7	2	2	44	7	48	41
JUN. 10	11	28	28	29	9	7	3	2	44	7	48	41
JUN. 11	12	30	30	31	9	7	3	2	44	7	48	41
JUN. 12	12	32	32	33	9	7	3	2	44	7	48	41
JUN. 13	12	34	34	35	9	7	3	2	44	7	48	41
JUN. 14	12	36	36	37	9	8	3	2	44	7	48	41
JUN. 15	12	38	38	39	9	8	3	2	44	7	48	41
JUN. 16	12	40	40	41	9	8	3	2	44	7	48	41
JUN. 17	12	42	42	43	9	8	3	2	44	7	48	41
JUN. 18	12	44	44	45	10	8	3	2	44	7	48	41
JUN. 19	13	45	46	47	10	8	3	2	44	7	48	41
JUN. 20	13	47	48	48	10	9	4	2	44	7	48	41
JUN. 21	13	1	2	2	10	9	4	2	44	7	48	41
JUN. 22	13	3	3	4	10	9	4	2	44	7	48	41
JUN. 23	13	4	5	6	10	9	4	2	44	7	48	41
JUN. 24	13	6	7	7	10	9	4	2	44	7	48	41
JUN. 25	14	8	8	9	11	9	4	2	44	7	48	41
JUN. 26	14	9	10	10	11	9	4	2	44	7	48	41
JUN. 27	14	11	11	12	11	10	4	2	44	7	48	41
JUN. 28	14	13	13	14	11	10	4	2	44	7	48	41
JUN. 29	14	14	15	15	12	10	4	2	44	7	48	41
JUN. 30	14	16	16	17	12	10	4	2	44	7	48	41

MOON 1 ◐ 12:01 A.M. TO 8:00 A.M.   **MOON 2** ◑ 8:01 A.M. TO 4:00 P.M.   **MOON 3** ● 4:01 P.M. TO 12:00 A.M.
Use only one "moon" number. Choose the column closest to your time of birth. If your place of birth is not on
Eastern Standard Time, be sure to read "How to Convert to Eastern Standard Time" at the beginning of this section.

July

August

Date & Time	SUN	MOON 1	MOON 2	MOON 3	MERCURY	VENUS	MARS	JUPITER	SATURN	URANUS	NEPTUNE	PLUTO
JUL. 1	14	17	18	18	12	10	5	2	44	7	48	41
JUL. 2	14	19	19	20	12	10	5	2	44	7	48	41
JUL. 3	15	20	21	22	12	11	5	2	44	7	48	41
JUL. 4	15	22	23	23	13	11	5	2	44	7	48	41
JUL. 5	15	24	24	25	13	11	5	2	44	7	48	41
JUL. 6	15	25	26	27	13	11	5	2	44	7	48	41
JUL. 7	15	27	28	28	13	11	5	2	44	7	48	41
JUL. 8	15	29	30	30	14	11	5	2	44	7	48	41
JUL. 9	15	31	31	32	14	12	5	2	44	7	48	41
JUL. 10	15	33	33	34	14	12	5	2	44	7	48	41
JUL. 11	16	35	35	36	15	12	6	2	44	7	48	41
JUL. 12	16	37	37	38	15	12	6	2	44	7	48	41
JUL. 13	16	39	39	40	15	12	6	2	44	7	48	41
JUL. 14	16	41	41	42	15	12	6	2	44	7	48	41
JUL. 15	16	43	43	44	16	13	6	2	44	7	48	41
JUL. 16	16	45	45	46	16	13	6	2	44	7	48	41
JUL. 17	16	47	47	48	16	13	6	2	44	7	48	41
JUL. 18	16	48	1	2	17	13	6	2	44	7	48	41
JUL. 19	17	2	3	3	17	13	6	2	44	7	48	41
JUL. 20	17	4	5	5	17	13	6	2	44	7	48	41
JUL. 21	17	6	6	7	17	13	6	2	44	7	48	41
JUL. 22	17	7	8	8	18	14	7	2	44	7	48	41
JUL. 23	17	9	9	10	18	14	7	2	44	7	48	41
JUL. 24	17	11	11	12	18	14	7	2	44	7	48	41
JUL. 25	17	12	13	13	19	14	7	2	44	7	48	41
JUL. 26	18	14	14	15	19	14	7	2	44	7	48	41
JUL. 27	18	15	16	16	19	14	7	2	44	7	48	41
JUL. 28	18	17	17	18	19	15	7	2	44	7	48	41
JUL. 29	18	18	19	20	20	15	7	2	44	7	48	41
JUL. 30	18	20	21	21	20	15	7	2	44	7	48	41
JUL. 31	18	22	22	23	20	15	7	2	44	7	48	41

Date & Time	SUN	MOON 1	MOON 2	MOON 3	MERCURY	VENUS	MARS	JUPITER	SATURN	URANUS	NEPTUNE	PLUTO
AUG. 1	18	23	24	24	20	15	7	2	44	7	48	41
AUG. 2	18	25	26	26	20	15	7	2	44	7	48	41
AUG. 3	19	27	27	28	21	16	8	2	44	7	48	41
AUG. 4	19	28	29	30	21	16	8	2	44	7	48	41
AUG. 5	19	30	31	31	21	16	8	2	44	7	48	41
AUG. 6	19	32	33	33	21	16	8	2	44	7	48	41
AUG. 7	19	34	35	35	22	16	8	2	44	7	48	41
AUG. 8	19	36	37	37	22	16	8	2	44	7	48	41
AUG. 9	19	38	38	39	22	17	8	2	44	7	48	41
AUG. 10	19	40	40	41	22	17	8	2	44	7	48	41
AUG. 11	20	42	42	43	22	17	8	2	44	7	48	41
AUG. 12	20	44	44	45	23	17	8	2	44	7	48	41
AUG. 13	20	46	46	47	23	17	8	2	44	7	48	41
AUG. 14	20	48	48	1	23	17	8	2	44	7	48	41
AUG. 15	20	2	2	3	23	18	9	2	44	7	48	41
AUG. 16	20	3	4	5	23	18	9	2	44	7	48	41
AUG. 17	20	5	6	6	24	18	9	2	44	7	48	41
AUG. 18	20	7	7	8	24	18	9	2	44	7	48	41
AUG. 19	21	8	9	10	24	18	9	2	44	7	48	41
AUG. 20	21	10	11	11	24	18	9	2	44	7	48	41
AUG. 21	21	12	12	13	24	19	9	2	44	7	48	41
AUG. 22	21	13	14	14	24	19	9	2	44	7	48	41
AUG. 23	21	15	15	16	25	19	9	2	44	7	48	41
AUG. 24	21	16	17	17	25	19	9	2	44	7	48	41
AUG. 25	21	18	19	19	25	19	9	2	44	7	48	41
AUG. 26	22	20	20	21	25	19	9	2	44	7	48	41
AUG. 27	22	21	22	22	25	19	9	2	44	7	48	41
AUG. 28	22	23	24	24	25	20	10	2	44	7	48	41
AUG. 29	22	25	25	26	25	20	10	2	44	7	48	40
AUG. 30	22	26	27	27	25	20	10	2	44	7	48	40
AUG. 31	22	28	29	29	26	20	10	2	44	7	48	40

MOON 1 ☽ 12:01 A.M. TO 8:00 A.M.   **MOON 2** ☾ 8:01 A.M. TO 4:00 P.M.   **MOON 3** ● 4:01 P.M. TO 12:00 A.M.
Use only one "moon" number. Choose the column closest to your time of birth. If your place of birth is not on Eastern Standard Time, be sure to read "How to Convert to Eastern Standard Time" at the beginning of this section.

September

October

Date & Time	SUN	MOON 1	MOON 2	MOON 3	MERCURY	VENUS	MARS	JUPITER	SATURN	URANUS	NEPTUNE	PLUTO
SEP. 1	22	30	30	31	26	20	10	2	44	7	48	40
SEP. 2	22	32	32	33	26	20	10	2	44	7	48	40
SEP. 3	23	33	34	35	26	21	10	2	44	7	48	40
SEP. 4	23	35	36	37	26	21	10	2	44	7	48	40
SEP. 5	23	37	38	38	26	21	10	2	44	7	48	40
SEP. 6	23	39	40	40	26	21	10	2	44	7	48	40
SEP. 7	23	41	42	42	26	21	10	2	44	7	48	40
SEP. 8	23	43	44	44	26	21	10	2	44	7	48	40
SEP. 9	23	45	46	46	26	22	10	2	44	7	48	40
SEP. 10	23	47	48	48	26	22	10	2	44	7	48	40
SEP. 11	24	1	1	2	26	22	11	2	44	7	48	40
SEP. 12	24	3	3	4	26	22	11	2	44	7	48	40
SEP. 13	24	4	5	6	26	22	11	2	44	7	48	40
SEP. 14	24	6	7	7	26	22	11	2	44	7	48	40
SEP. 15	24	8	8	9	26	23	11	2	44	7	48	40
SEP. 16	24	10	10	11	26	23	11	2	44	7	48	40
SEP. 17	24	11	12	12	26	23	11	2	44	7	48	40
SEP. 18	24	13	13	14	26	23	11	2	44	7	48	40
SEP. 19	25	14	15	15	26	23	11	2	44	7	48	40
SEP. 20	25	16	16	17	25	23	11	2	44	7	48	40
SEP. 21	25	18	18	19	25	24	11	2	44	7	48	40
SEP. 22	25	19	20	20	25	24	11	2	44	7	48	40
SEP. 23	25	21	21	22	25	24	11	2	44	7	48	40
SEP. 24	25	22	23	24	25	24	11	2	44	7	48	40
SEP. 25	26	24	25	25	25	24	11	1	44	7	48	40
SEP. 26	26	26	26	27	25	24	11	1	44	7	48	40
SEP. 27	26	28	28	29	24	25	11	1	44	7	48	40
SEP. 28	26	29	30	31	24	25	12	1	44	7	48	40
SEP. 29	26	31	32	32	24	25	12	1	44	7	48	40
SEP. 30	26	33	34	34	24	25	12	1	44	7	48	40

Date & Time	SUN	MOON 1	MOON 2	MOON 3	MERCURY	VENUS	MARS	JUPITER	SATURN	URANUS	NEPTUNE	PLUTO
OCT. 1	26	35	36	36	24	25	12	1	43	7	48	40
OCT. 2	26	37	37	38	24	25	12	1	43	7	48	40
OCT. 3	27	39	39	40	24	26	12	1	43	7	48	40
OCT. 4	27	41	41	42	24	26	12	1	43	7	48	40
OCT. 5	27	42	43	44	24	26	12	1	43	7	48	40
OCT. 6	27	44	45	46	24	26	12	1	43	7	48	40
OCT. 7	27	46	47	47	24	26	12	1	43	7	48	40
OCT. 8	27	48	1	1	25	26	12	1	43	7	48	40
OCT. 9	27	2	3	3	25	27	12	1	43	7	48	40
OCT. 10	27	4	4	5	25	27	12	1	43	7	48	40
OCT. 11	28	6	6	7	25	27	12	1	43	7	48	40
OCT. 12	28	7	8	8	25	27	12	1	43	7	48	40
OCT. 13	28	9	10	10	25	27	12	1	43	7	48	40
OCT. 14	28	11	11	12	26	27	12	1	43	7	48	40
OCT. 15	28	12	13	13	26	28	12	1	43	7	48	40
OCT. 16	28	14	14	15	26	28	12	1	43	7	48	40
OCT. 17	28	15	16	16	26	28	12	1	43	7	48	40
OCT. 18	28	17	18	18	26	28	12	1	43	7	48	40
OCT. 19	29	19	19	20	27	28	12	1	43	7	48	40
OCT. 20	29	20	21	21	27	28	12	1	43	7	48	40
OCT. 21	29	22	22	23	27	28	12	1	43	7	48	40
OCT. 22	29	24	24	25	27	29	12	1	43	7	48	40
OCT. 23	29	25	26	26	27	29	12	1	43	7	48	40
OCT. 24	29	27	28	28	28	29	12	1	43	7	48	40
OCT. 25	29	29	29	30	28	29	12	1	43	7	48	40
OCT. 26	30	31	31	32	28	29	12	1	43	7	48	40
OCT. 27	30	33	33	34	28	30	12	1	43	7	48	40
OCT. 28	30	34	35	36	29	30	12	1	43	7	48	40
OCT. 29	30	36	37	38	29	30	12	1	43	7	48	40
OCT. 30	30	38	39	39	29	30	12	1	43	7	48	40
OCT. 31	30	40	41	41	29	30	12	1	43	7	48	40

MOON 1 ◐ 12:01 A.M. TO 8:00 A.M.   **MOON 2** ◑ 8:01 A.M. TO 4:00 P.M.   **MOON 3** ● 4:01 P.M. TO 12:00 A.M.

Use only one "moon" number. Choose the column closest to your time of birth. If your place of birth is not on Eastern Standard Time, be sure to read "How to Convert to Eastern Standard Time" at the beginning of this section.

2022

November

Date & Time	SUN	MOON 1	MOON 2	MOON 3	MERCURY	VENUS	MARS	JUPITER	SATURN	URANUS	NEPTUNE	PLUTO
NOV. 1	30	42	43	43	30	30	12	1	43	7	48	40
NOV. 2	30	44	45	45	30	31	12	1	43	7	48	40
NOV. 3	31	46	46	47	30	31	12	1	43	7	48	40
NOV. 4	31	48	48	1	30	31	12	1	43	7	48	40
NOV. 5	31	1	2	3	30	31	12	1	43	7	48	40
NOV. 6	31	3	4	4	31	31	12	1	43	7	48	40
NOV. 7	31	5	6	6	31	31	12	1	43	7	48	40
NOV. 8	31	7	7	8	31	32	12	1	43	7	48	40
NOV. 9	31	8	9	9	31	32	12	1	43	7	48	40
NOV. 10	31	10	11	11	31	32	12	1	43	7	48	40
NOV. 11	31	12	12	13	32	32	12	1	43	7	48	40
NOV. 12	32	13	14	14	32	32	12	1	43	7	48	40
NOV. 13	32	15	15	16	32	32	12	1	43	7	48	40
NOV. 14	32	16	17	18	32	33	12	1	44	7	48	40
NOV. 15	32	18	19	19	33	33	12	1	44	7	48	40
NOV. 16	32	20	20	21	33	33	12	1	44	7	48	40
NOV. 17	32	21	22	22	33	33	12	1	44	7	48	40
NOV. 18	32	23	23	24	33	33	12	1	44	7	48	41
NOV. 19	33	25	25	26	33	33	12	1	44	7	48	41
NOV. 20	33	26	27	27	34	34	12	1	44	7	48	41
NOV. 21	33	28	29	29	34	34	12	1	44	7	48	41
NOV. 22	33	30	30	31	34	34	12	1	44	7	48	41
NOV. 23	33	32	32	33	34	34	12	1	44	7	48	41
NOV. 24	33	34	34	35	34	34	12	1	44	7	48	41
NOV. 25	34	36	36	37	35	34	12	1	44	7	48	41
NOV. 26	34	38	38	39	35	35	12	1	44	7	48	41
NOV. 27	34	40	40	41	35	35	12	1	44	7	48	41
NOV. 28	34	42	42	43	35	35	12	1	44	7	48	41
NOV. 29	34	43	44	45	35	35	12	1	44	7	48	41
NOV. 30	34	45	46	47	36	35	12	1	44	7	48	41

December

Date & Time	SUN	MOON 1	MOON 2	MOON 3	MERCURY	VENUS	MARS	JUPITER	SATURN	URANUS	NEPTUNE	PLUTO
DEC. 1	34	47	48	48	36	35	11	1	44	7	48	41
DEC. 2	34	1	2	2	36	36	11	1	44	7	48	41
DEC. 3	35	3	3	4	36	36	11	1	44	7	48	41
DEC. 4	35	4	5	6	36	36	11	1	44	7	48	41
DEC. 5	35	6	7	7	37	36	11	1	44	7	48	41
DEC. 6	35	8	9	9	37	36	11	1	44	7	48	41
DEC. 7	35	10	10	11	37	36	11	1	44	7	48	41
DEC. 8	35	11	12	12	37	37	11	1	44	7	48	41
DEC. 9	35	13	13	14	37	37	11	1	44	7	48	41
DEC. 10	35	14	15	15	38	37	11	1	44	7	48	41
DEC. 11	36	16	16	17	38	37	11	1	44	7	48	41
DEC. 12	36	18	18	19	38	37	11	1	44	7	48	41
DEC. 13	36	19	20	20	38	37	11	1	44	7	48	41
DEC. 14	36	21	21	22	38	38	11	1	44	7	48	41
DEC. 15	36	22	23	23	39	38	11	1	44	7	48	41
DEC. 16	36	24	24	25	39	38	11	1	44	7	48	41
DEC. 17	36	26	26	27	39	38	11	1	44	7	48	41
DEC. 18	36	27	28	28	39	38	11	1	44	7	48	41
DEC. 19	37	29	30	30	39	38	11	1	44	7	48	41
DEC. 20	37	31	32	32	39	39	11	1	44	7	48	41
DEC. 21	37	33	33	34	40	39	11	1	44	7	48	41
DEC. 22	37	35	35	36	40	39	10	1	44	7	48	41
DEC. 23	37	37	37	38	40	39	10	1	44	7	48	41
DEC. 24	37	39	39	40	40	39	10	1	44	7	48	41
DEC. 25	37	41	41	42	40	39	10	1	44	7	48	41
DEC. 26	38	43	43	44	40	40	10	1	44	7	48	41
DEC. 27	38	45	45	46	40	40	10	1	44	7	48	41
DEC. 28	38	47	47	48	40	40	10	1	44	7	48	41
DEC. 29	38	1	1	2	40	40	10	1	44	7	48	41
DEC. 30	38	2	3	4	40	40	10	1	44	7	48	41
DEC. 31	38	4	5	5	40	40	10	1	44	7	48	41

MOON 1 ◐ 12:01 A.M. TO 8:00 A.M.   **MOON 2** ◑ 8:01 A.M. TO 4:00 P.M.   **MOON 3** ● 4:01 P.M. TO 12:00 A.M.

Use only one "moon" number. Choose the column closest to your time of birth. If your place of birth is not on Eastern Standard Time, be sure to read "How to Convert to Eastern Standard Time" at the beginning of this section.

January

Date & Time	SUN ☼	MOON 1 ◐	MOON 2 ◑	MOON 3 ●	MERCURY	VENUS	MARS	JUPITER	SATURN	URANUS	NEPTUNE	PLUTO
JAN. 1	38	6	6	7	40	41	10	1	44	7	48	41
JAN. 2	38	7	8	9	40	41	10	1	44	7	48	41
JAN. 3	39	9	10	10	40	41	10	1	44	7	48	41
JAN. 4	39	11	11	12	40	41	10	1	44	7	48	41
JAN. 5	39	12	13	13	40	41	10	1	44	7	48	41
JAN. 6	39	14	14	15	39	41	10	1	44	7	48	41
JAN. 7	39	16	16	17	39	42	10	1	44	7	48	41
JAN. 8	39	17	18	18	39	42	10	1	44	7	48	41
JAN. 9	39	19	19	20	39	42	10	1	44	7	48	41
JAN. 10	40	20	21	21	39	42	10	1	44	7	48	41
JAN. 11	40	22	22	23	39	42	10	1	44	7	48	41
JAN. 12	40	23	24	25	38	42	10	1	44	7	48	41
JAN. 13	40	25	26	26	38	43	10	1	44	7	48	41
JAN. 14	40	27	27	28	38	43	10	1	44	7	48	41
JAN. 15	40	28	29	30	38	43	10	1	44	7	48	41
JAN. 16	40	30	31	31	38	43	10	1	44	7	48	41
JAN. 17	41	32	33	33	38	43	10	1	44	7	48	41
JAN. 18	41	34	35	35	38	43	10	1	44	7	48	41
JAN. 19	41	36	36	37	38	44	10	1	44	7	48	41
JAN. 20	41	38	38	39	38	44	10	1	44	7	48	41
JAN. 21	41	40	40	41	38	44	10	2	44	7	48	41
JAN. 22	41	42	43	43	38	44	10	2	44	7	48	41
JAN. 23	42	44	45	45	38	44	10	2	44	7	48	41
JAN. 24	42	46	47	47	38	44	10	2	44	7	48	41
JAN. 25	42	48	1	1	38	45	10	2	44	7	48	41
JAN. 26	42	2	2	3	38	45	10	2	44	7	48	41
JAN. 27	42	4	4	5	39	45	10	2	44	7	48	41
JAN. 28	42	5	6	6	39	45	10	2	44	7	48	41
JAN. 29	42	7	8	8	39	45	10	2	44	7	48	41
JAN. 30	42	9	9	10	39	45	10	2	44	7	48	41
JAN. 31	43	10	11	11	39	46	10	2	44	7	48	41

February

Date & Time	SUN ☼	MOON 1 ◐	MOON 2 ◑	MOON 3 ●	MERCURY	VENUS	MARS	JUPITER	SATURN	URANUS	NEPTUNE	PLUTO
FEB. 1	43	12	12	13	39	46	10	2	44	7	48	41
FEB. 2	43	14	14	15	39	46	10	2	44	7	48	41
FEB. 3	43	15	16	16	40	46	10	2	44	7	48	41
FEB. 4	43	17	17	18	40	46	10	2	44	7	48	41
FEB. 5	43	18	19	19	40	46	10	2	44	7	48	41
FEB. 6	43	20	20	21	40	47	11	2	44	7	48	41
FEB. 7	43	21	22	23	40	47	11	2	45	7	48	41
FEB. 8	44	23	24	24	40	47	11	2	45	7	48	41
FEB. 9	44	25	25	26	41	47	11	2	45	7	48	41
FEB. 10	44	26	27	27	41	47	11	2	45	7	48	41
FEB. 11	44	28	29	29	41	47	11	2	45	7	48	41
FEB. 12	44	30	30	31	41	48	11	2	45	7	48	41
FEB. 13	44	31	32	33	41	48	11	2	45	7	48	41
FEB. 14	44	33	34	34	41	48	11	2	45	7	48	41
FEB. 15	44	35	36	36	42	48	11	2	45	7	48	41
FEB. 16	45	37	38	38	42	48	11	2	45	7	48	41
FEB. 17	45	39	40	40	42	48	11	2	45	7	48	41
FEB. 18	45	41	42	42	42	1	11	2	45	7	48	41
FEB. 19	45	43	44	44	42	1	11	2	45	7	48	41
FEB. 20	45	45	46	46	43	1	11	2	45	7	48	41
FEB. 21	45	47	48	48	43	1	11	2	45	7	48	41
FEB. 22	45	1	2	2	43	1	11	2	45	7	48	41
FEB. 23	46	3	3	4	43	1	11	2	45	7	48	41
FEB. 24	46	5	6	6	43	2	11	2	45	7	48	41
FEB. 25	46	6	7	8	44	2	11	2	45	7	48	41
FEB. 26	46	8	9	9	44	2	11	2	45	7	48	41
FEB. 27	46	10	10	11	44	2	11	2	45	7	48	41
FEB. 28	46	12	12	13	44	2	11	3	45	7	48	41

MOON 1 ◐ 12:01 A.M. TO 8:00 A.M.   **MOON 2** ◑ 8:01 A.M. TO 4:00 P.M.   **MOON 3** ● 4:01 P.M. TO 12:00 A.M.

Use only one "moon" number. Choose the column closest to your time of birth. If your place of birth is not on Eastern Standard Time, be sure to read "How to Convert to Eastern Standard Time" at the beginning of this section.

Date & Time	SUN	MOON 1 ◗	MOON 2 ◖	MOON 3 ●	MERCURY	VENUS	MARS	JUPITER	SATURN	URANUS	NEPTUNE	PLUTO
MAR. 1	46	13	14	14	45	2	12	3	45	7	48	41
MAR. 2	46	15	15	16	45	3	12	3	45	7	48	41
MAR. 3	47	16	17	17	45	3	12	3	45	7	48	41
MAR. 4	47	18	18	19	45	3	12	3	45	7	48	41
MAR. 5	47	19	20	21	45	3	12	3	45	7	48	41
MAR. 6	47	21	22	22	46	3	12	3	45	7	48	41
MAR. 7	47	23	23	24	46	3	12	3	45	7	48	41
MAR. 8	47	24	25	25	46	4	12	3	45	7	48	41
MAR. 9	47	26	27	27	46	4	12	3	45	7	48	41
MAR. 10	47	28	28	29	47	4	12	3	45	7	48	41
MAR. 11	48	29	30	30	47	4	12	3	45	7	48	41
MAR. 12	48	31	32	32	47	4	12	3	45	7	48	41
MAR. 13	48	33	33	34	47	4	12	3	45	7	48	41
MAR. 14	48	35	35	36	48	5	12	3	45	7	48	41
MAR. 15	48	36	37	38	48	5	12	3	45	7	48	41
MAR. 16	48	38	39	40	48	5	12	3	45	7	48	41
MAR. 17	48	40	41	42	48	5	12	3	45	7	48	41
MAR. 18	48	42	43	43	1	5	13	3	45	7	48	41
MAR. 19	1	44	45	45	1	5	13	3	45	7	48	41
MAR. 20	1	46	47	47	1	5	13	3	45	7	48	41
MAR. 21	1	48	1	1	2	6	13	3	45	7	48	41
MAR. 22	1	2	3	3	2	6	13	3	45	7	48	41
MAR. 23	1	4	5	5	2	6	13	3	45	7	48	41
MAR. 24	1	6	6	7	2	6	13	3	45	7	48	41
MAR. 25	2	8	8	9	3	6	13	3	45	7	48	41
MAR. 26	2	9	10	10	3	6	13	3	45	7	48	41
MAR. 27	2	11	12	12	3	7	13	3	45	7	48	41
MAR. 28	2	13	13	14	3	7	13	3	45	7	48	41
MAR. 29	2	14	15	15	4	7	13	3	45	7	48	41
MAR. 30	2	16	16	17	4	7	13	3	45	7	48	41
MAR. 31	2	17	18	18	4	7	13	3	45	7	48	41

Date & Time	SUN	MOON 1 ◗	MOON 2 ◖	MOON 3 ●	MERCURY	VENUS	MARS	JUPITER	SATURN	URANUS	NEPTUNE	PLUTO
APR. 1	2	19	20	20	4	7	13	4	45	7	48	41
APR. 2	2	21	21	22	5	8	13	4	45	7	48	41
APR. 3	3	22	23	23	5	8	14	4	45	7	48	41
APR. 4	3	24	24	25	5	8	14	4	45	7	48	41
APR. 5	3	25	26	27	5	8	14	4	45	7	48	41
APR. 6	3	27	28	28	5	8	14	4	45	7	48	41
APR. 7	3	29	29	30	6	8	14	4	45	7	48	41
APR. 8	3	31	31	32	6	9	14	4	45	7	48	41
APR. 9	3	32	33	34	6	9	14	4	45	7	48	41
APR. 10	3	34	35	35	6	9	14	4	45	7	48	41
APR. 11	4	36	37	37	6	9	14	4	45	7	48	41
APR. 12	4	38	38	39	6	9	14	4	45	7	48	41
APR. 13	4	40	40	41	7	9	14	4	45	7	48	41
APR. 14	4	42	42	43	7	9	14	4	46	7	48	41
APR. 15	4	44	44	45	7	10	14	4	46	7	48	41
APR. 16	4	45	46	47	7	10	14	4	46	7	48	41
APR. 17	4	47	48	1	7	10	15	4	46	7	48	41
APR. 18	4	1	2	3	7	10	15	4	46	7	48	41
APR. 19	5	3	4	4	7	10	15	4	46	7	48	41
APR. 20	5	5	6	6	7	10	15	4	46	7	48	41
APR. 21	5	7	7	8	7	11	15	4	46	7	48	41
APR. 22	5	9	9	10	7	11	15	4	46	7	48	41
APR. 23	5	10	11	11	7	11	15	4	46	7	48	41
APR. 24	5	12	13	13	7	11	15	4	46	7	1	41
APR. 25	6	14	14	15	7	11	15	4	46	7	1	41
APR. 26	6	15	16	16	7	11	15	4	46	7	1	41
APR. 27	6	17	17	18	7	11	15	4	46	7	1	41
APR. 28	6	18	19	20	7	12	15	4	46	7	1	41
APR. 29	6	20	21	21	7	12	15	4	46	7	1	41
APR. 30	6	22	22	23	7	12	15	4	46	7	1	41

MOON 1 ◗ 12:01 A.M. TO 8:00 A.M.   **MOON 2** ◖ 8:01 A.M. TO 4:00 P.M.   **MOON 3** ● 4:01 P.M. TO 12:00 A.M.

Use only one "moon" number. Choose the column closest to your time of birth. If your place of birth is not on Eastern Standard Time, be sure to read "How to Convert to Eastern Standard Time" at the beginning of this section.

Date & Time	SUN	MOON 1	MOON 2	MOON 3	MERCURY	VENUS	MARS	JUPITER	SATURN	URANUS	NEPTUNE	PLUTO
MAY 1	6	23	24	24	7	12	16	4	46	7	1	41
MAY 2	6	25	25	26	6	12	16	5	46	7	1	41
MAY 3	7	27	27	28	6	12	16	5	46	7	1	41
MAY 4	7	28	29	29	6	12	16	5	46	7	1	41
MAY 5	7	30	31	31	6	13	16	5	46	7	1	41
MAY 6	7	32	32	33	6	13	16	5	46	7	1	41
MAY 7	7	34	34	35	6	13	16	5	46	7	1	41
MAY 8	7	36	36	37	6	13	16	5	46	7	1	41
MAY 9	7	37	38	39	6	13	16	5	46	7	1	41
MAY 10	7	39	40	41	6	13	16	5	46	7	1	41
MAY 11	8	41	42	42	6	13	16	5	46	8	1	41
MAY 12	8	43	44	44	6	14	16	5	46	8	1	41
MAY 13	8	45	46	46	6	14	16	5	46	8	1	41
MAY 14	8	47	47	48	6	14	16	5	46	8	1	41
MAY 15	8	1	1	2	6	14	17	5	46	8	1	41
MAY 16	8	3	3	4	6	14	17	5	46	8	1	41
MAY 17	8	4	5	6	6	14	17	5	46	8	1	41
MAY 18	8	6	7	7	6	14	17	5	46	8	1	41
MAY 19	9	8	9	9	6	15	17	5	46	8	1	41
MAY 20	9	10	10	11	6	15	17	5	46	8	1	41
MAY 21	9	11	12	13	6	15	17	5	46	8	1	41
MAY 22	9	13	14	14	6	15	17	5	46	8	1	41
MAY 23	9	15	15	16	6	15	17	5	46	8	1	41
MAY 24	9	16	17	17	6	15	17	5	46	8	1	41
MAY 25	10	18	18	19	6	15	17	5	46	8	1	41
MAY 26	10	20	20	21	6	16	17	5	46	8	1	41
MAY 27	10	21	22	22	6	16	17	5	46	8	1	41
MAY 28	10	23	23	24	7	16	18	5	46	8	1	41
MAY 29	10	24	25	25	7	16	18	5	46	8	1	41
MAY 30	10	26	26	27	7	16	18	5	46	8	1	41
MAY 31	10	28	28	29	7	16	18	5	46	8	1	41

Date & Time	SUN	MOON 1	MOON 2	MOON 3	MERCURY	VENUS	MARS	JUPITER	SATURN	URANUS	NEPTUNE	PLUTO
JUN. 1	10	29	30	31	7	16	18	5	46	8	1	41
JUN. 2	10	31	32	32	7	17	18	5	46	8	1	41
JUN. 3	11	33	34	34	7	17	18	5	46	8	1	41
JUN. 4	11	35	35	36	8	17	18	6	46	8	1	41
JUN. 5	11	37	37	38	8	17	18	6	46	8	1	41
JUN. 6	11	39	39	40	8	17	18	6	46	8	1	41
JUN. 7	11	41	41	42	8	17	18	6	46	8	1	41
JUN. 8	11	43	43	44	8	17	18	6	46	8	1	41
JUN. 9	11	45	45	46	9	17	18	6	46	8	1	41
JUN. 10	11	46	47	48	9	18	19	6	46	8	1	41
JUN. 11	12	48	1	2	9	18	19	6	46	8	1	41
JUN. 12	12	2	3	3	9	18	19	6	46	8	1	41
JUN. 13	12	4	5	5	9	18	19	6	46	8	1	41
JUN. 14	12	6	6	7	10	18	19	6	46	8	1	41
JUN. 15	12	7	8	9	10	18	19	6	46	8	1	41
JUN. 16	12	9	10	10	10	19	19	6	46	8	1	41
JUN. 17	12	11	11	12	10	19	19	6	46	8	1	41
JUN. 18	12	13	13	14	11	18	19	6	46	8	1	41
JUN. 19	13	14	15	15	11	19	19	6	46	8	1	41
JUN. 20	13	16	16	17	11	19	19	6	46	8	1	41
JUN. 21	13	17	18	18	11	19	19	6	46	8	1	41
JUN. 22	13	19	20	20	12	19	19	6	46	8	1	41
JUN. 23	13	21	21	22	12	19	20	6	46	8	1	41
JUN. 24	13	22	23	24	12	19	20	6	46	8	1	41
JUN. 25	14	24	24	25	12	19	20	6	46	8	1	41
JUN. 26	14	25	26	26	13	19	20	6	46	8	1	41
JUN. 27	14	27	28	28	13	19	20	6	46	8	1	41
JUN. 28	14	29	29	30	13	19	20	6	46	8	1	41
JUN. 29	14	30	31	32	14	20	20	6	46	8	1	41
JUN. 30	14	32	33	33	14	20	20	6	46	8	1	41

MOON 1 ◖ 12:01 A.M. TO 8:00 A.M.   **MOON 2** ◑ 8:01 A.M. TO 4:00 P.M.   **MOON 3** ● 4:01 P.M. TO 12:00 A.M.

Use only one "moon" number. Choose the column closest to your time of birth. If your place of birth is not on Eastern Standard Time, be sure to read "How to Convert to Eastern Standard Time" at the beginning of this section.

Date & Time	SUN	MOON 1	MOON 2	MOON 3	MERCURY	VENUS	MARS	JUPITER	SATURN	URANUS	NEPTUNE	PLUTO
JUL. 1	14	34	35	35	14	20	20	6	46	8	1	41
JUL. 2	14	36	37	37	14	20	20	6	46	8	1	41
JUL. 3	15	38	39	39	15	20	20	6	46	8	1	41
JUL. 4	15	40	41	41	15	20	20	6	46	8	1	41
JUL. 5	15	42	43	43	15	20	21	6	46	8	1	41
JUL. 6	15	44	45	45	16	20	21	6	46	8	1	41
JUL. 7	15	46	47	47	16	20	21	6	46	8	1	41
JUL. 8	15	48	48	1	16	20	21	6	46	8	1	41
JUL. 9	15	2	2	3	16	20	21	6	46	8	1	41
JUL. 10	15	4	4	5	17	20	21	6	46	8	1	41
JUL. 11	16	5	6	7	17	20	21	6	46	8	1	41
JUL. 12	16	7	8	8	17	21	21	6	46	8	1	41
JUL. 13	16	9	9	10	17	21	21	6	46	8	1	41
JUL. 14	16	10	11	12	18	21	21	6	46	8	1	41
JUL. 15	16	12	13	13	18	21	21	7	46	8	1	41
JUL. 16	16	14	14	15	18	21	21	7	46	8	1	41
JUL. 17	16	15	16	16	18	21	22	7	46	8	1	41
JUL. 18	16	17	18	18	19	21	22	7	46	8	1	41
JUL. 19	17	19	19	20	19	21	22	7	46	8	1	41
JUL. 20	17	20	21	21	19	21	22	7	46	8	1	41
JUL. 21	17	22	22	23	19	21	22	7	46	8	1	41
JUL. 22	17	23	24	24	20	21	22	7	46	8	1	41
JUL. 23	17	25	25	26	20	21	22	7	46	8	1	41
JUL. 24	17	27	27	28	20	21	22	7	46	8	1	41
JUL. 25	17	28	29	29	20	21	22	7	46	8	1	41
JUL. 26	18	30	30	31	20	21	22	7	46	8	1	41
JUL. 27	18	32	32	33	21	21	22	7	46	8	1	41
JUL. 28	18	33	34	35	21	21	23	7	46	8	1	41
JUL. 29	18	35	36	36	21	21	23	7	46	8	1	41
JUL. 30	18	37	38	38	21	21	23	7	46	8	1	41
JUL. 31	18	39	40	40	21	21	23	7	46	8	1	41

Date & Time	SUN	MOON 1	MOON 2	MOON 3	MERCURY	VENUS	MARS	JUPITER	SATURN	URANUS	NEPTUNE	PLUTO
AUG. 1	18	41	42	42	22	21	23	7	46	8	1	41
AUG. 2	18	43	44	44	22	21	23	7	46	8	1	41
AUG. 3	19	45	46	46	22	20	23	7	46	8	1	41
AUG. 4	19	47	48	48	22	20	23	7	46	8	1	41
AUG. 5	19	1	2	2	22	20	23	7	46	8	1	41
AUG. 6	19	3	4	4	22	20	23	7	46	8	1	41
AUG. 7	19	5	5	6	23	20	23	7	46	8	1	41
AUG. 8	19	7	7	8	23	20	23	7	46	8	1	41
AUG. 9	19	8	9	10	23	20	23	7	46	8	1	41
AUG. 10	19	10	11	11	23	20	23	7	46	8	1	41
AUG. 11	20	12	12	13	23	20	24	7	46	8	1	41
AUG. 12	20	13	14	14	23	20	24	7	46	8	1	41
AUG. 13	20	15	16	16	23	20	24	7	46	8	1	41
AUG. 14	20	17	17	18	23	20	24	7	46	8	1	41
AUG. 15	20	18	19	19	23	20	24	7	46	8	1	41
AUG. 16	20	20	20	21	24	19	24	7	46	8	1	41
AUG. 17	20	21	22	22	24	19	24	7	46	8	1	41
AUG. 18	20	23	23	24	24	19	24	7	46	8	1	41
AUG. 19	21	25	25	26	24	19	24	7	46	8	1	41
AUG. 20	21	26	27	27	24	19	24	7	46	8	1	41
AUG. 21	21	28	28	29	24	19	24	7	46	8	1	41
AUG. 22	21	29	30	30	24	19	25	7	46	8	1	41
AUG. 23	21	31	32	32	24	19	25	7	46	8	1	41
AUG. 24	21	33	33	34	24	19	25	7	46	8	1	41
AUG. 25	21	35	35	36	24	19	25	7	45	8	1	41
AUG. 26	22	36	37	38	24	19	25	7	45	8	1	41
AUG. 27	22	38	39	40	24	19	25	7	45	8	1	41
AUG. 28	22	40	41	42	24	19	25	7	45	8	1	41
AUG. 29	22	42	43	44	24	19	25	7	45	8	1	41
AUG. 30	22	44	45	46	24	19	25	7	45	8	1	41
AUG. 31	22	46	47	48	24	19	25	7	45	8	1	41

MOON 1 ☽ 12:01 A.M. TO 8:00 A.M.   **MOON 2** ◑ 8:01 A.M. TO 4:00 P.M.   **MOON 3** ● 4:01 P.M. TO 12:00 A.M.
Use only one "moon" number. Choose the column closest to your time of birth. If your place of birth is not on Eastern Standard Time, be sure to read "How to Convert to Eastern Standard Time" at the beginning of this section.

2023

September ✦ **October**

Date & Time	SUN	MOON 1	MOON 2	MOON 3	MERCURY	VENUS	MARS	JUPITER	SATURN	URANUS	NEPTUNE	PLUTO
SEP. 1	22	48	1	2	23	19	25	7	45	8	1	41
SEP. 2	22	2	3	4	23	19	25	7	45	8	1	41
SEP. 3	23	4	5	5	23	19	26	7	45	8	1	41
SEP. 4	23	6	7	7	23	19	26	7	45	8	1	41
SEP. 5	23	8	8	9	23	19	26	7	45	8	1	41
SEP. 6	23	10	10	11	23	19	26	7	45	8	1	41
SEP. 7	23	11	12	12	23	19	26	7	45	8	1	41
SEP. 8	23	13	14	14	23	19	26	7	45	8	1	41
SEP. 9	23	15	15	16	22	19	26	7	45	8	1	41
SEP. 10	23	16	17	17	22	19	26	7	45	8	1	41
SEP. 11	24	18	18	19	22	19	26	7	45	8	1	41
SEP. 12	24	19	20	20	22	19	26	7	45	8	48	41
SEP. 13	24	21	21	22	22	19	26	7	45	8	48	41
SEP. 14	24	23	23	24	22	19	26	7	45	8	48	41
SEP. 15	24	24	25	25	22	19	27	7	45	8	48	41
SEP. 16	24	26	26	27	22	19	27	7	45	8	48	41
SEP. 17	24	27	28	28	22	19	27	7	45	8	48	41
SEP. 18	24	29	30	30	22	19	27	7	45	8	48	41
SEP. 19	25	31	31	32	22	19	27	7	45	8	48	41
SEP. 20	25	32	33	33	22	19	27	7	45	8	48	41
SEP. 21	25	34	35	35	22	19	27	7	45	8	48	41
SEP. 22	25	36	36	37	22	19	27	7	45	8	48	41
SEP. 23	25	38	38	39	22	19	27	7	45	8	48	41
SEP. 24	25	39	40	41	23	19	27	7	45	8	48	41
SEP. 25	26	41	42	43	23	20	27	7	45	8	48	41
SEP. 26	26	43	44	45	23	20	28	7	45	8	48	41
SEP. 27	26	45	46	47	23	20	28	7	45	8	48	41
SEP. 28	26	47	48	1	23	20	28	7	45	8	48	41
SEP. 29	26	1	2	3	24	20	28	7	45	8	48	41
SEP. 30	26	3	4	5	24	20	28	7	45	8	48	41
OCT. 1	26	5	6	7	24	20	28	7	45	8	48	41
OCT. 2	26	7	8	8	24	20	28	7	45	8	48	41
OCT. 3	27	9	10	10	25	20	28	7	45	8	48	41
OCT. 4	27	11	11	12	25	20	28	7	45	8	48	41
OCT. 5	27	12	13	14	25	21	28	7	45	8	48	41
OCT. 6	27	14	15	15	25	21	28	7	45	8	48	41
OCT. 7	27	16	16	17	25	21	28	7	45	8	48	41
OCT. 8	27	17	18	18	26	21	29	7	45	8	48	41
OCT. 9	27	19	19	20	26	21	29	7	45	8	48	41
OCT. 10	27	21	21	22	26	21	29	7	45	8	48	41
OCT. 11	28	22	23	23	26	21	29	7	45	8	48	41
OCT. 12	28	24	24	25	27	21	29	7	45	8	48	41
OCT. 13	28	25	26	26	27	21	29	7	45	8	48	41
OCT. 14	28	27	27	28	27	22	29	7	45	8	48	41
OCT. 15	28	29	29	30	27	22	29	7	45	8	48	41
OCT. 16	28	30	31	31	28	22	29	7	45	8	48	41
OCT. 17	28	32	32	33	28	22	29	7	45	8	48	41
OCT. 18	28	34	34	35	28	22	30	7	45	8	48	41
OCT. 19	29	35	36	37	28	22	30	7	45	8	48	41
OCT. 20	29	37	38	38	29	22	30	7	45	8	48	41
OCT. 21	29	39	40	40	29	22	30	7	45	8	48	41
OCT. 22	29	41	42	42	29	23	30	7	45	8	48	41
OCT. 23	29	43	43	44	29	23	30	7	45	8	48	41
OCT. 24	29	45	45	46	29	23	30	7	45	8	48	41
OCT. 25	29	47	47	48	30	23	30	7	45	8	48	41
OCT. 26	30	1	1	2	30	23	30	7	45	8	48	41
OCT. 27	30	3	3	4	30	23	30	7	45	8	48	41
OCT. 28	30	4	5	6	30	23	30	6	45	8	48	41
OCT. 29	30	6	7	8	30	24	31	6	45	8	48	41
OCT. 30	30	8	9	9	31	24	31	6	45	8	48	41
OCT. 31	30	10	11	11	31	24	31	6	45	8	48	41

MOON 1 ◗ 12:01 A.M. TO 8:00 A.M. **MOON 2** ◑ 8:01 A.M. TO 4:00 P.M. **MOON 3** ● 4:01 P.M. TO 12:00 A.M.
Use only one "moon" number. Choose the column closest to your time of birth. If your place of birth is not on Eastern Standard Time, be sure to read "How to Convert to Eastern Standard Time" at the beginning of this section.

2023

November — December

Date & Time	SUN	MOON 1	MOON 2	MOON 3	MERCURY	VENUS	MARS	JUPITER	SATURN	URANUS	NEPTUNE	PLUTO
NOV. 1	30	12	12	13	31	24	31	6	45	8	48	41
NOV. 2	30	13	14	15	31	24	31	6	45	8	48	41
NOV. 3	31	15	16	16	32	24	31	6	45	8	48	41
NOV. 4	31	17	17	18	32	24	31	6	45	8	48	41
NOV. 5	31	18	19	19	32	25	31	6	45	8	48	41
NOV. 6	31	20	21	21	32	25	31	6	45	8	48	41
NOV. 7	31	22	22	23	32	25	31	6	45	8	48	41
NOV. 8	31	23	24	24	33	25	31	6	45	8	48	41
NOV. 9	31	25	25	26	33	25	32	6	45	8	48	41
NOV. 10	31	26	27	27	33	25	32	6	45	8	48	41
NOV. 11	31	28	29	29	33	25	32	6	45	8	48	41
NOV. 12	32	30	30	31	33	25	32	6	45	8	48	41
NOV. 13	32	31	32	33	34	26	32	6	45	8	48	41
NOV. 14	32	33	34	34	34	26	32	6	45	8	48	41
NOV. 15	32	35	36	36	34	26	32	6	45	8	48	41
NOV. 16	32	37	37	38	34	26	32	6	45	8	48	41
NOV. 17	32	39	39	40	34	26	32	6	45	8	48	41
NOV. 18	32	40	41	42	35	26	32	6	45	8	48	41
NOV. 19	33	42	43	44	35	27	32	6	45	8	48	41
NOV. 20	33	44	45	45	35	27	33	6	45	8	48	41
NOV. 21	33	46	47	47	35	27	33	6	45	8	48	41
NOV. 22	33	48	1	1	35	27	33	6	45	8	48	41
NOV. 23	33	2	3	3	35	27	33	6	45	8	48	41
NOV. 24	33	4	4	5	36	27	33	6	45	8	48	41
NOV. 25	34	6	6	7	36	27	33	6	45	8	48	41
NOV. 26	34	7	8	9	36	28	33	6	45	8	48	41
NOV. 27	34	9	10	10	36	28	33	6	45	8	48	41
NOV. 28	34	11	12	12	36	28	33	6	45	8	48	41
NOV. 29	34	13	13	14	37	28	33	6	45	8	48	41
NOV. 30	34	15	15	16	37	28	34	6	45	8	48	41

Date & Time	SUN	MOON 1	MOON 2	MOON 3	MERCURY	VENUS	MARS	JUPITER	SATURN	URANUS	NEPTUNE	PLUTO
DEC. 1	34	16	17	17	37	28	34	6	45	8	48	41
DEC. 2	34	18	18	19	37	29	34	6	45	8	48	41
DEC. 3	35	19	20	21	37	29	34	6	45	8	48	41
DEC. 4	35	21	22	22	37	29	34	6	45	8	48	41
DEC. 5	35	23	23	24	37	29	34	6	45	8	48	41
DEC. 6	35	24	25	25	38	29	34	6	45	8	48	41
DEC. 7	35	26	26	27	38	29	34	6	45	8	48	41
DEC. 8	35	27	28	29	38	30	34	6	45	8	48	41
DEC. 9	35	29	30	30	38	30	34	6	45	8	48	41
DEC. 10	35	31	31	32	38	30	34	6	45	8	48	41
DEC. 11	36	33	33	34	38	30	35	6	45	8	48	41
DEC. 12	36	34	35	36	38	30	35	6	45	8	48	41
DEC. 13	36	36	37	37	38	30	35	6	45	8	48	41
DEC. 14	36	38	39	39	38	30	35	6	45	8	48	41
DEC. 15	36	40	41	41	38	31	35	6	45	8	48	41
DEC. 16	36	42	42	43	38	31	35	6	45	8	48	41
DEC. 17	36	44	44	45	38	31	35	6	45	8	48	41
DEC. 18	36	46	46	47	38	31	35	6	45	8	48	41
DEC. 19	37	48	48	1	38	31	35	6	45	8	48	41
DEC. 20	37	1	2	3	38	31	35	6	45	8	48	41
DEC. 21	37	3	4	5	37	32	36	6	45	8	48	41
DEC. 22	37	5	6	6	37	32	36	6	45	8	48	41
DEC. 23	37	7	8	8	37	32	36	6	45	8	48	41
DEC. 24	37	9	9	10	37	32	36	6	45	8	48	41
DEC. 25	37	10	11	12	37	32	36	6	45	8	48	41
DEC. 26	38	12	13	13	36	32	36	6	45	8	48	41
DEC. 27	38	14	15	15	36	33	36	6	45	8	48	41
DEC. 28	38	16	16	17	36	33	36	6	45	8	48	41
DEC. 29	38	17	18	18	36	33	36	6	45	8	48	41
DEC. 30	38	19	19	20	36	33	36	6	45	8	48	41
DEC. 31	38	21	21	22	36	33	37	6	45	8	48	41

MOON 1 ◖ 12:01 A.M. TO 8:00 A.M.   **MOON 2** ◑ 8:01 A.M. TO 4:00 P.M.   **MOON 3** ● 4:01 P.M. TO 12:00 A.M.
Use only one "moon" number. Choose the column closest to your time of birth. If your place of birth is not on Eastern Standard Time, be sure to read "How to Convert to Eastern Standard Time" at the beginning of this section.

Date & Time	SUN	MOON 1	MOON 2	MOON 3	MERCURY	VENUS	MARS	JUPITER	SATURN	URANUS	NEPTUNE	PLUTO
JAN. 1	38	22	23	23	36	33	37	6	45	8	48	41
JAN. 2	38	24	24	25	36	34	37	6	45	8	48	41
JAN. 3	39	25	26	26	36	34	37	6	45	8	48	41
JAN. 4	39	27	27	28	36	34	37	6	45	8	48	41
JAN. 5	39	28	29	30	36	34	37	6	45	8	48	41
JAN. 6	39	30	31	31	36	34	37	6	45	8	48	41
JAN. 7	39	32	32	33	36	34	37	6	45	8	48	41
JAN. 8	39	34	34	35	36	34	37	6	45	8	48	41
JAN. 9	39	35	36	37	36	35	37	6	46	8	48	41
JAN. 10	40	37	38	39	36	35	38	6	46	8	48	41
JAN. 11	40	39	40	40	37	35	38	6	46	8	48	41
JAN. 12	40	41	42	42	37	35	38	6	46	8	48	41
JAN. 13	40	43	44	44	37	35	38	6	46	8	48	41
JAN. 14	40	45	46	46	37	35	38	6	46	8	48	41
JAN. 15	40	47	48	48	37	36	38	6	46	8	48	41
JAN. 16	40	1	2	2	37	36	38	6	46	8	48	41
JAN. 17	41	3	3	4	37	36	38	6	46	8	48	41
JAN. 18	41	5	5	6	38	36	38	6	46	8	48	41
JAN. 19	41	7	7	8	38	36	38	6	46	8	48	41
JAN. 20	41	8	9	9	38	36	39	6	46	8	48	41
JAN. 21	41	10	11	11	38	37	39	6	46	8	48	41
JAN. 22	41	12	12	13	38	37	39	6	46	8	48	41
JAN. 23	42	13	14	15	38	37	39	6	46	8	48	41
JAN. 24	42	15	16	16	39	37	39	6	46	8	48	41
JAN. 25	42	17	17	18	39	37	39	6	46	8	48	41
JAN. 26	42	18	19	19	39	37	39	6	46	8	48	41
JAN. 27	42	20	21	21	39	38	39	6	46	8	48	41
JAN. 28	42	22	22	23	39	38	39	6	46	8	48	41
JAN. 29	42	23	24	24	40	38	39	6	46	8	48	41
JAN. 30	42	25	25	26	40	38	40	6	46	8	48	41
JAN. 31	43	26	27	27	40	38	40	6	46	8	48	41

Date & Time	SUN	MOON 1	MOON 2	MOON 3	MERCURY	VENUS	MARS	JUPITER	SATURN	URANUS	NEPTUNE	PLUTO
FEB. 1	43	28	28	29	40	38	40	6	46	8	48	41
FEB. 2	43	30	30	31	40	39	40	6	46	8	48	41
FEB. 3	43	31	32	32	41	39	40	6	46	8	48	41
FEB. 4	43	33	33	34	41	39	40	6	46	8	48	41
FEB. 5	43	35	35	36	41	39	40	6	46	8	48	41
FEB. 6	43	36	37	38	41	39	40	6	46	8	48	41
FEB. 7	43	38	39	40	41	39	40	6	46	8	48	41
FEB. 8	44	40	41	42	42	40	40	6	46	8	48	41
FEB. 9	44	42	43	44	42	40	41	6	46	8	48	41
FEB. 10	44	44	45	46	42	40	41	6	46	8	48	41
FEB. 11	44	46	47	48	42	40	41	6	46	8	48	41
FEB. 12	44	48	1	2	42	40	41	6	46	8	48	41
FEB. 13	44	2	3	4	43	40	41	6	46	8	48	41
FEB. 14	44	4	5	5	43	41	41	6	46	8	48	41
FEB. 15	44	6	7	7	43	41	41	6	46	8	48	41
FEB. 16	45	8	8	9	43	41	41	6	46	8	48	41
FEB. 17	45	10	10	11	44	41	41	6	46	8	48	41
FEB. 18	45	11	12	13	44	41	41	6	46	8	48	41
FEB. 19	45	13	14	14	44	41	42	6	46	8	48	41
FEB. 20	45	15	15	16	44	42	42	6	46	8	48	41
FEB. 21	45	16	17	17	44	42	42	6	46	8	48	41
FEB. 22	45	18	19	19	45	42	42	6	46	8	48	41
FEB. 23	46	20	20	21	45	42	42	6	46	8	1	41
FEB. 24	46	21	22	22	45	42	42	6	46	8	1	41
FEB. 25	46	23	23	24	45	42	42	6	46	8	1	41
FEB. 26	46	24	25	25	46	43	42	6	46	8	1	41
FEB. 27	46	26	26	27	46	43	42	6	46	8	1	41
FEB. 28	46	27	28	29	46	43	43	6	46	8	1	41
FEB. 29	46	29	30	30	46	43	43	6	46	8	1	41

MOON 1 ◖ 12:01 A.M. TO 8:00 A.M.   **MOON 2 ◑ 8:01 A.M. TO 4:00 P.M.**   **MOON 3 ● 4:01 P.M. TO 12:00 A.M.**
Use only one "moon" number. Choose the column closest to your time of birth. If your place of birth is not on Eastern Standard Time, be sure to read "How to Convert to Eastern Standard Time" at the beginning of this section.

Date & Time	SUN ☉	MOON 1 ◗	MOON 2 ◑	MOON 3 ●	MERCURY	VENUS	MARS	JUPITER	SATURN	URANUS	NEPTUNE	PLUTO
MAR. 1	46	31	31	32	47	43	43	6	46	8	1	41
MAR. 2	46	32	33	33	47	43	43	7	46	8	1	41
MAR. 3	47	34	35	35	47	44	43	7	46	8	1	41
MAR. 4	47	36	36	37	47	44	43	7	46	8	1	41
MAR. 5	47	38	38	39	48	44	43	7	46	8	1	41
MAR. 6	47	39	40	41	48	44	43	7	46	8	1	41
MAR. 7	47	41	42	43	48	44	43	7	46	8	1	41
MAR. 8	47	43	44	45	48	44	43	7	46	8	1	41
MAR. 9	47	45	46	47	1	45	44	7	46	8	1	41
MAR. 10	47	47	48	1	1	45	44	7	46	8	1	41
MAR. 11	48	1	2	3	1	45	44	7	46	8	1	41
MAR. 12	48	3	4	5	1	45	44	7	46	8	1	41
MAR. 13	48	5	6	7	2	45	44	7	46	8	1	41
MAR. 14	48	7	8	8	2	45	44	7	47	8	1	41
MAR. 15	48	9	10	10	2	46	44	7	47	8	1	41
MAR. 16	48	11	11	12	2	46	44	7	47	8	1	41
MAR. 17	48	13	13	14	3	46	44	7	47	8	1	41
MAR. 18	48	14	15	15	3	46	44	7	47	8	1	41
MAR. 19	1	16	17	17	3	46	45	7	47	8	1	41
MAR. 20	1	18	18	19	3	46	45	7	47	8	1	41
MAR. 21	1	19	20	20	3	47	45	7	47	8	1	41
MAR. 22	1	21	21	22	4	47	45	7	47	8	1	41
MAR. 23	1	22	23	23	4	47	45	7	47	8	1	41
MAR. 24	1	24	24	25	4	47	45	7	47	8	1	41
MAR. 25	2	26	26	27	4	47	45	7	47	8	1	41
MAR. 26	2	27	28	28	4	47	45	7	47	8	1	41
MAR. 27	2	29	29	30	4	47	45	7	47	8	1	41
MAR. 28	2	30	31	31	4	48	46	7	47	8	1	41
MAR. 29	2	32	32	33	4	48	46	7	47	8	1	41
MAR. 30	2	34	34	35	5	48	46	7	47	8	1	41
MAR. 31	2	35	36	36	5	48	46	7	47	8	1	41

Date & Time	SUN ☉	MOON 1 ◗	MOON 2 ◑	MOON 3 ●	MERCURY	VENUS	MARS	JUPITER	SATURN	URANUS	NEPTUNE	PLUTO
APR. 1	2	37	38	38	5	48	46	7	47	8	1	41
APR. 2	2	39	39	40	5	48	46	7	47	8	1	41
APR. 3	3	41	41	42	5	1	46	7	47	8	1	41
APR. 4	3	43	43	44	5	1	46	7	47	8	1	41
APR. 5	3	44	45	46	5	1	46	7	47	8	1	41
APR. 6	3	46	47	48	4	1	46	7	47	8	1	41
APR. 7	3	48	1	2	4	1	47	7	47	8	1	41
APR. 8	3	2	3	4	4	1	47	7	47	8	1	41
APR. 9	3	4	5	6	4	2	47	8	47	8	1	41
APR. 10	3	6	7	8	4	2	47	8	47	8	1	41
APR. 11	4	8	9	10	4	2	47	8	47	8	1	41
APR. 12	4	10	11	11	4	2	47	8	47	8	1	41
APR. 13	4	12	13	13	4	2	47	8	47	8	1	41
APR. 14	4	14	14	15	4	2	47	8	47	8	1	41
APR. 15	4	15	16	17	4	3	47	8	47	8	1	41
APR. 16	4	17	18	18	4	3	47	8	47	8	1	41
APR. 17	4	19	19	20	3	3	48	8	47	8	1	41
APR. 18	4	20	21	21	3	3	48	8	47	8	1	41
APR. 19	5	22	22	23	3	3	48	8	47	8	1	41
APR. 20	5	24	24	25	3	3	48	8	47	8	1	41
APR. 21	5	25	26	26	3	4	48	8	47	8	1	41
APR. 22	5	27	27	28	3	4	48	8	47	8	1	41
APR. 23	5	28	29	29	3	4	48	8	47	8	1	41
APR. 24	5	30	30	31	3	4	48	8	47	8	1	41
APR. 25	6	32	32	33	3	4	48	8	47	8	1	41
APR. 26	6	33	34	34	3	4	1	8	47	8	1	41
APR. 27	6	35	35	36	3	5	1	8	47	8	1	41
APR. 28	6	37	37	38	3	5	1	8	47	8	1	41
APR. 29	6	38	39	40	3	5	1	8	47	8	1	41
APR. 30	6	40	41	41	3	5	1	8	47	8	1	41

MOON 1 ◗ 12:01 A.M. TO 8:00 A.M.   **MOON 2 ◑ 8:01 A.M. TO 4:00 P.M.**   **MOON 3 ● 4:01 P.M. TO 12:00 A.M.**
Use only one "moon" number. Choose the column closest to your time of birth. If your place of birth is not on Eastern Standard Time, be sure to read "How to Convert to Eastern Standard Time" at the beginning of this section.

2024

May

June

Date & Time	SUN	MOON 1	MOON 2	MOON 3	MERCURY	VENUS	MARS	JUPITER	SATURN	URANUS	NEPTUNE	PLUTO
MAY 1	6	42	43	43	3	5	1	8	47	8	1	41
MAY 2	6	44	45	45	3	5	1	8	47	8	1	41
MAY 3	7	46	46	47	3	6	1	8	47	8	1	41
MAY 4	7	48	48	1	3	6	1	8	47	8	1	41
MAY 5	7	2	2	3	4	6	1	8	47	8	1	41
MAY 6	7	4	4	5	4	6	2	8	47	8	1	41
MAY 7	7	6	6	7	4	6	2	8	47	8	1	41
MAY 8	7	8	8	9	4	6	2	8	47	8	1	41
MAY 9	7	9	10	11	4	7	2	8	47	8	1	41
MAY 10	7	11	12	13	4	7	2	8	47	8	1	41
MAY 11	8	13	14	14	4	7	2	9	47	8	1	41
MAY 12	8	15	15	16	4	7	2	9	47	8	1	41
MAY 13	8	17	17	18	5	7	2	9	47	8	1	41
MAY 14	8	18	19	19	5	7	2	9	47	8	1	41
MAY 15	8	20	20	21	5	8	2	9	47	8	1	41
MAY 16	8	21	22	23	5	8	3	9	47	8	1	41
MAY 17	8	23	24	24	5	8	3	9	47	8	1	41
MAY 18	8	25	25	26	5	8	3	9	47	8	1	41
MAY 19	9	26	27	27	6	8	3	9	47	8	1	41
MAY 20	9	28	28	29	6	8	3	9	47	8	1	41
MAY 21	9	29	30	30	6	9	3	9	47	8	1	41
MAY 22	9	31	32	32	6	9	3	9	47	8	1	41
MAY 23	9	33	33	34	6	9	3	9	47	8	1	41
MAY 24	9	34	35	36	7	9	3	9	47	8	1	41
MAY 25	10	36	37	37	7	9	3	9	47	8	1	41
MAY 26	10	38	39	39	7	9	4	9	47	8	1	41
MAY 27	10	40	40	41	7	10	4	9	47	8	1	41
MAY 28	10	42	42	43	7	10	4	9	47	8	1	41
MAY 29	10	43	44	45	8	10	4	9	47	8	1	41
MAY 30	10	45	46	47	8	10	4	9	47	8	1	41
MAY 31	10	47	48	48	8	10	4	9	47	8	1	41

Date & Time	SUN	MOON 1	MOON 2	MOON 3	MERCURY	VENUS	MARS	JUPITER	SATURN	URANUS	NEPTUNE	PLUTO
JUN. 1	10	1	2	2	8	10	4	9	47	8	1	41
JUN. 2	10	3	4	4	9	10	4	9	47	8	1	41
JUN. 3	11	5	6	6	9	11	4	9	47	8	1	41
JUN. 4	11	7	7	7	9	11	4	9	47	8	1	41
JUN. 5	11	9	9	10	9	11	5	9	47	8	1	41
JUN. 6	11	11	11	12	10	11	5	9	47	8	1	41
JUN. 7	11	12	13	14	10	11	5	9	48	8	1	41
JUN. 8	11	14	15	15	10	11	5	9	48	8	1	41
JUN. 9	11	16	17	17	11	12	5	9	48	8	1	41
JUN. 10	11	18	18	19	11	12	5	9	48	8	1	41
JUN. 11	12	19	20	20	11	12	5	9	48	8	1	41
JUN. 12	12	21	21	22	11	12	5	10	48	8	1	41
JUN. 13	12	23	23	24	12	12	5	10	48	8	1	41
JUN. 14	12	24	25	25	12	12	5	10	48	8	1	41
JUN. 15	12	26	26	27	12	13	6	10	48	8	1	41
JUN. 16	12	27	28	28	13	13	6	10	48	8	1	41
JUN. 17	12	29	29	30	13	13	6	10	48	8	1	41
JUN. 18	12	30	31	32	13	13	6	10	48	8	1	41
JUN. 19	13	32	33	33	13	13	6	10	48	8	1	41
JUN. 20	13	34	34	35	14	13	6	10	48	8	1	41
JUN. 21	13	36	36	37	14	14	6	10	48	8	1	41
JUN. 22	13	37	38	39	14	14	6	10	48	8	1	41
JUN. 23	13	39	40	40	15	14	6	10	48	8	1	41
JUN. 24	13	41	42	42	15	14	6	10	48	8	1	41
JUN. 25	14	43	44	44	15	14	7	10	48	8	1	41
JUN. 26	14	45	46	46	15	14	7	10	48	8	1	41
JUN. 27	14	47	47	48	16	15	7	10	48	8	1	41
JUN. 28	14	1	1	2	16	15	7	10	48	8	1	41
JUN. 29	14	3	3	4	16	15	7	10	48	8	1	41
JUN. 30	14	4	5	6	16	15	7	10	48	8	1	41

MOON 1 ☽ 12:01 A.M. TO 8:00 A.M.   **MOON 2** ☾ 8:01 A.M. TO 4:00 P.M.   **MOON 3** ● 4:01 P.M. TO 12:00 A.M.

Use only one "moon" number. Choose the column closest to your time of birth. If your place of birth is not on Eastern Standard Time, be sure to read "How to Convert to Eastern Standard Time" at the beginning of this section.

Date & Time	SUN	MOON 1	MOON 2	MOON 3	MERCURY	VENUS	MARS	JUPITER	SATURN	URANUS	NEPTUNE	PLUTO
JUL. 1	14	6	7	8	17	15	7	10	48	8	1	41
JUL. 2	14	8	9	9	17	15	7	10	48	8	1	41
JUL. 3	15	10	11	11	17	16	7	10	48	8	1	41
JUL. 4	15	12	12	13	17	16	7	10	48	8	1	41
JUL. 5	15	14	14	15	18	16	7	10	48	8	1	41
JUL. 6	15	15	16	16	18	16	8	10	48	8	1	41
JUL. 7	15	17	18	18	18	16	8	10	48	8	1	41
JUL. 8	15	19	19	20	18	16	8	10	48	8	1	41
JUL. 9	15	20	21	21	18	17	8	10	48	8	1	41
JUL. 10	15	22	23	23	19	17	8	10	48	8	1	41
JUL. 11	16	24	24	25	19	17	8	10	48	8	1	41
JUL. 12	16	25	26	26	19	17	8	10	48	8	1	41
JUL. 13	16	27	27	28	19	17	8	10	48	8	1	41
JUL. 14	16	28	29	29	19	17	8	10	48	8	1	41
JUL. 15	16	30	30	31	20	18	8	10	48	8	1	41
JUL. 16	16	32	32	33	20	18	9	10	48	8	1	41
JUL. 17	16	33	34	34	20	18	9	11	48	8	1	41
JUL. 18	16	35	36	36	20	18	9	11	48	8	1	41
JUL. 19	17	37	37	38	20	18	9	11	48	8	1	41
JUL. 20	17	39	39	40	20	18	9	11	48	8	1	41
JUL. 21	17	40	41	42	20	19	9	11	48	9	1	41
JUL. 22	17	42	43	44	21	19	9	11	48	9	1	41
JUL. 23	17	44	45	46	21	19	9	11	47	9	1	41
JUL. 24	17	46	47	48	21	19	9	11	47	9	1	41
JUL. 25	17	48	1	1	21	19	9	11	47	9	1	41
JUL. 26	18	2	3	3	21	19	9	11	47	9	1	41
JUL. 27	18	4	5	5	21	20	10	11	47	9	1	41
JUL. 28	18	6	6	7	21	20	10	11	47	9	1	41
JUL. 29	18	8	8	9	21	20	10	11	47	9	1	41
JUL. 30	18	10	10	11	21	20	10	11	47	9	1	41
JUL. 31	18	11	12	13	21	20	10	11	47	9	1	41

Date & Time	SUN	MOON 1	MOON 2	MOON 3	MERCURY	VENUS	MARS	JUPITER	SATURN	URANUS	NEPTUNE	PLUTO
AUG. 1	18	13	14	14	21	20	10	11	47	9	1	41
AUG. 2	18	15	15	16	21	20	10	11	47	9	1	41
AUG. 3	19	17	17	18	21	21	10	11	47	9	1	41
AUG. 4	19	18	19	19	22	21	10	11	47	9	1	41
AUG. 5	19	20	20	21	22	21	10	11	47	9	1	41
AUG. 6	19	21	22	23	22	21	10	11	47	9	1	41
AUG. 7	19	23	24	24	21	21	11	11	47	9	1	41
AUG. 8	19	25	25	26	21	21	11	11	47	9	1	41
AUG. 9	19	26	27	27	21	22	11	11	47	9	1	41
AUG. 10	19	28	28	29	21	22	11	11	47	9	1	41
AUG. 11	20	29	30	30	21	22	11	11	47	9	1	41
AUG. 12	20	31	32	32	21	22	11	11	47	9	1	41
AUG. 13	20	33	33	34	21	22	11	11	47	9	1	41
AUG. 14	20	34	35	35	21	22	11	11	47	9	1	41
AUG. 15	20	36	37	37	21	23	11	11	47	9	1	41
AUG. 16	20	38	38	39	21	23	11	11	47	9	1	41
AUG. 17	20	40	40	41	21	23	11	11	47	9	1	41
AUG. 18	20	42	42	43	21	23	11	11	47	9	1	41
AUG. 19	21	43	44	45	20	23	12	11	47	9	1	41
AUG. 20	21	45	46	47	20	23	12	11	47	9	1	41
AUG. 21	21	47	48	1	20	24	12	11	47	9	1	41
AUG. 22	21	1	2	3	20	24	12	11	47	9	1	41
AUG. 23	21	3	4	5	20	24	12	11	47	9	1	41
AUG. 24	21	5	6	7	20	24	12	11	47	9	1	41
AUG. 25	21	7	8	9	20	24	12	11	47	9	1	41
AUG. 26	22	9	10	10	20	24	12	11	47	9	1	41
AUG. 27	22	11	12	12	20	25	12	11	47	9	1	41
AUG. 28	22	13	13	14	20	25	12	11	47	9	1	41
AUG. 29	22	14	15	16	20	25	12	11	47	9	1	41
AUG. 30	22	16	17	17	20	25	13	11	47	9	1	41
AUG. 31	22	18	18	19	20	25	13	11	47	9	1	41

MOON 1 ☽ 12:01 A.M. TO 8:00 A.M.   **MOON 2** ☽ 8:01 A.M. TO 4:00 P.M.   **MOON 3** ● 4:01 P.M. TO 12:00 A.M.

Use only one "moon" number. Choose the column closest to your time of birth. If your place of birth is not on Eastern Standard Time, be sure to read "How to Convert to Eastern Standard Time" at the beginning of this section.

2024

September

October

Date & Time	SUN	MOON 1	MOON 2	MOON 3	MERCURY	VENUS	MARS	JUPITER	SATURN	URANUS	NEPTUNE	PLUTO
SEP. 1	22	19	20	21	20	25	13	12	47	9	1	41
SEP. 2	22	21	22	22	20	26	13	12	47	9	1	41
SEP. 3	23	23	23	24	20	26	13	12	47	9	1	41
SEP. 4	23	24	25	25	20	26	13	12	47	9	1	41
SEP. 5	23	26	26	27	20	26	13	12	47	9	1	41
SEP. 6	23	27	28	28	20	26	13	12	47	9	1	41
SEP. 7	23	29	29	30	21	26	13	12	47	9	1	41
SEP. 8	23	31	31	32	21	27	13	12	47	9	1	41
SEP. 9	23	32	33	33	21	27	13	12	47	9	1	41
SEP. 10	23	34	34	35	21	27	13	12	47	9	1	41
SEP. 11	24	35	36	37	21	27	13	12	47	9	1	41
SEP. 12	24	37	38	38	22	27	14	12	47	9	1	41
SEP. 13	24	39	40	40	22	27	14	12	47	9	1	41
SEP. 14	24	41	41	42	22	28	14	12	47	9	1	41
SEP. 15	24	43	43	44	22	28	14	12	47	9	1	41
SEP. 16	24	45	45	46	22	28	14	12	47	9	1	41
SEP. 17	24	47	47	48	23	28	14	12	47	9	1	41
SEP. 18	24	1	1	2	23	28	14	12	47	9	1	41
SEP. 19	25	3	3	4	23	28	14	12	47	9	1	41
SEP. 20	25	5	5	6	23	28	14	12	47	9	1	41
SEP. 21	25	7	7	8	24	29	14	12	47	9	1	41
SEP. 22	25	9	9	10	24	29	14	12	47	9	1	41
SEP. 23	25	10	11	12	24	29	14	12	47	9	1	41
SEP. 24	25	12	13	13	24	29	14	12	47	9	1	41
SEP. 25	26	14	15	15	25	29	15	12	47	9	1	41
SEP. 26	26	16	16	17	25	29	15	12	47	9	1	41
SEP. 27	26	17	18	18	25	30	15	12	47	9	1	41
SEP. 28	26	19	20	20	25	30	15	12	47	9	1	41
SEP. 29	26	21	21	22	26	30	15	12	47	9	1	41
SEP. 30	26	22	23	23	26	30	15	12	47	9	1	41

Date & Time	SUN	MOON 1	MOON 2	MOON 3	MERCURY	VENUS	MARS	JUPITER	SATURN	URANUS	NEPTUNE	PLUTO
OCT. 1	26	24	24	25	26	30	15	12	47	9	1	41
OCT. 2	26	25	26	26	26	30	15	12	47	9	1	41
OCT. 3	27	27	27	28	27	31	15	12	47	9	1	41
OCT. 4	27	29	29	30	27	31	15	12	47	9	1	41
OCT. 5	27	30	31	31	27	31	15	12	47	9	1	41
OCT. 6	27	32	32	33	27	31	15	12	47	9	1	41
OCT. 7	27	33	34	34	28	31	15	12	47	9	1	41
OCT. 8	27	35	36	36	28	31	15	12	47	9	1	41
OCT. 9	27	37	37	38	28	32	16	12	47	9	1	41
OCT. 10	27	38	39	40	28	32	16	12	47	9	1	41
OCT. 11	28	40	41	41	28	32	16	12	47	9	1	41
OCT. 12	28	42	43	43	29	32	16	12	47	9	1	41
OCT. 13	28	44	44	45	29	32	16	12	47	9	1	41
OCT. 14	28	46	46	47	29	32	16	12	47	9	1	41
OCT. 15	28	48	48	1	29	33	16	12	47	9	1	41
OCT. 16	28	2	2	3	29	33	16	12	47	8	1	41
OCT. 17	28	4	4	5	30	33	16	12	47	8	1	41
OCT. 18	28	6	6	7	30	33	16	12	47	8	1	41
OCT. 19	29	8	8	9	30	33	16	12	47	8	1	41
OCT. 20	29	10	10	11	30	33	16	12	47	8	1	41
OCT. 21	29	12	12	13	31	34	16	12	47	8	1	41
OCT. 22	29	13	14	15	31	34	16	12	47	8	1	41
OCT. 23	29	15	16	16	31	34	16	12	47	8	1	41
OCT. 24	29	17	18	18	31	34	16	12	47	8	1	41
OCT. 25	29	19	19	20	31	34	16	12	47	8	1	41
OCT. 26	30	20	21	21	32	34	17	12	47	8	1	41
OCT. 27	30	22	23	23	32	34	17	12	47	8	1	41
OCT. 28	30	23	24	24	32	35	17	12	47	8	1	41
OCT. 29	30	25	26	26	32	35	17	12	47	8	1	41
OCT. 30	30	27	27	28	32	35	17	12	47	8	1	41
OCT. 31	30	28	29	29	32	35	17	12	47	8	1	41

MOON 1 ◐ 12:01 A.M. TO 8:00 A.M.   **MOON 2** ◑ 8:01 A.M. TO 4:00 P.M.   **MOON 3** ● 4:01 P.M. TO 12:00 A.M.

Use only one "moon" number. Choose the column closest to your time of birth. If your place of birth is not on Eastern Standard Time, be sure to read "How to Convert to Eastern Standard Time" at the beginning of this section.

2024

November

Date & Time	SUN	MOON 1	MOON 2	MOON 3	MERCURY	VENUS	MARS	JUPITER	SATURN	URANUS	NEPTUNE	PLUTO
NOV. 1	30	30	30	31	33	35	17	12	47	8	1	41
NOV. 2	30	31	32	32	33	35	17	12	47	8	1	41
NOV. 3	31	33	33	34	33	36	17	12	47	8	1	41
NOV. 4	31	35	35	36	33	36	17	12	47	8	1	41
NOV. 5	31	36	37	37	33	36	17	12	47	8	1	41
NOV. 6	31	38	39	39	34	36	17	12	47	8	1	41
NOV. 7	31	40	40	41	34	36	17	12	47	8	1	41
NOV. 8	31	41	42	43	34	36	17	12	47	8	1	41
NOV. 9	31	43	44	44	34	37	17	12	47	8	1	41
NOV. 10	31	45	46	46	34	37	17	12	47	8	1	41
NOV. 11	31	47	48	48	34	37	17	12	47	8	1	41
NOV. 12	32	1	2	2	35	37	17	12	47	8	1	41
NOV. 13	32	3	3	4	35	37	17	12	47	8	1	41
NOV. 14	32	5	5	6	35	37	17	12	47	8	1	41
NOV. 15	32	7	7	8	35	38	17	12	47	8	1	41
NOV. 16	32	9	9	10	35	38	17	12	47	8	1	41
NOV. 17	32	11	11	12	35	38	17	11	47	8	1	41
NOV. 18	32	13	13	14	35	38	17	11	47	8	1	41
NOV. 19	33	15	15	16	36	38	18	11	47	8	1	41
NOV. 20	33	16	17	17	36	38	18	11	47	8	1	41
NOV. 21	33	18	19	19	36	38	18	11	47	8	1	41
NOV. 22	33	20	20	21	36	39	18	11	47	8	1	41
NOV. 23	33	21	22	22	36	39	18	11	47	8	1	41
NOV. 24	33	23	24	24	36	39	18	11	47	8	1	41
NOV. 25	34	25	25	26	36	39	18	11	47	8	1	41
NOV. 26	34	26	27	27	36	39	18	11	47	8	1	41
NOV. 27	34	28	28	29	36	39	18	11	47	8	1	41
NOV. 28	34	29	30	30	36	40	18	11	47	8	1	41
NOV. 29	34	31	31	32	36	40	18	11	47	8	1	41
NOV. 30	34	32	33	34	36	40	18	11	47	8	1	41

December

Date & Time	SUN	MOON 1	MOON 2	MOON 3	MERCURY	VENUS	MARS	JUPITER	SATURN	URANUS	NEPTUNE	PLUTO
DEC. 1	34	34	35	35	36	40	18	11	47	8	1	41
DEC. 2	34	36	36	37	36	40	18	11	47	8	1	41
DEC. 3	35	38	38	39	35	40	18	11	47	8	1	41
DEC. 4	35	39	40	40	35	40	18	11	47	8	1	41
DEC. 5	35	41	42	42	35	41	18	11	47	8	1	41
DEC. 6	35	43	43	44	35	41	18	11	47	8	1	41
DEC. 7	35	45	45	46	35	41	18	11	47	8	1	41
DEC. 8	35	46	47	48	35	41	18	11	47	8	1	41
DEC. 9	35	48	1	2	34	41	18	11	47	8	1	41
DEC. 10	35	2	3	3	34	41	18	11	47	8	1	41
DEC. 11	36	4	5	5	34	42	18	11	47	8	1	41
DEC. 12	36	6	7	7	34	42	18	11	47	8	1	41
DEC. 13	36	8	9	9	34	42	18	11	47	8	1	41
DEC. 14	36	10	11	11	34	42	18	11	47	8	1	41
DEC. 15	36	12	12	13	34	42	18	11	47	8	1	41
DEC. 16	36	14	14	15	34	42	18	11	47	8	1	41
DEC. 17	36	16	16	17	34	42	18	11	47	8	1	41
DEC. 18	36	17	18	19	34	43	18	11	47	8	1	41
DEC. 19	37	19	20	20	34	43	18	11	47	8	1	41
DEC. 20	37	21	21	22	34	43	18	11	47	8	1	41
DEC. 21	37	22	23	24	34	43	18	11	47	8	1	41
DEC. 22	37	24	25	25	34	43	18	11	47	8	1	41
DEC. 23	37	26	26	27	34	43	18	11	47	8	1	41
DEC. 24	37	27	28	28	34	44	18	11	47	8	1	41
DEC. 25	37	29	29	30	35	44	17	11	47	8	1	41
DEC. 26	38	30	31	31	35	44	17	11	47	8	1	41
DEC. 27	38	32	33	33	35	44	17	11	47	8	1	41
DEC. 28	38	34	34	35	35	44	17	11	47	8	1	41
DEC. 29	38	35	36	36	35	44	17	11	47	8	1	41
DEC. 30	38	37	38	38	35	44	17	11	47	8	1	41
DEC. 31	38	39	39	40	35	45	17	11	47	8	1	41

MOON 1 ◐ 12:01 A.M. TO 8:00 A.M.   **MOON 2** ◑ 8:01 A.M. TO 4:00 P.M.   **MOON 3** ● 4:01 P.M. TO 12:00 A.M.
Use only one "moon" number. Choose the column closest to your time of birth. If your place of birth is not on Eastern Standard Time, be sure to read "How to Convert to Eastern Standard Time" at the beginning of this section.

2025

January

⭐ ☆ ⭐

February

⭐ ☆ ⭐

Date & Time	SUN ☉	MOON 1 ◐	MOON 2 ◑	MOON 3 ●	MERCURY	VENUS	MARS	JUPITER	SATURN	URANUS	NEPTUNE	PLUTO
JAN. 1	38	41	41	42	36	45	17	11	47	8	1	41
JAN. 2	38	42	43	44	36	45	17	11	47	8	1	41
JAN. 3	39	44	45	45	36	45	17	11	47	8	1	41
JAN. 4	39	46	47	47	36	45	17	11	47	8	1	41
JAN. 5	39	48	48	1	36	45	17	11	47	8	1	41
JAN. 6	39	2	2	3	37	45	17	11	47	8	1	41
JAN. 7	39	4	4	5	37	46	17	11	47	8	1	41
JAN. 8	39	6	6	7	37	46	17	11	47	8	1	41
JAN. 9	39	7	8	9	37	46	17	11	47	8	1	41
JAN. 10	40	9	10	11	37	46	17	11	47	8	1	41
JAN. 11	40	11	12	12	37	46	17	11	47	8	1	41
JAN. 12	40	13	14	14	38	46	17	11	47	8	1	41
JAN. 13	40	15	15	16	38	46	17	11	47	8	1	41
JAN. 14	40	17	17	18	38	46	17	11	47	8	1	41
JAN. 15	40	18	19	20	38	47	17	11	47	8	1	41
JAN. 16	40	20	21	21	38	47	16	11	47	8	1	41
JAN. 17	41	22	22	23	39	47	16	11	47	8	1	41
JAN. 18	41	23	24	25	39	47	16	11	47	8	1	41
JAN. 19	41	25	26	26	39	47	16	11	47	8	1	41
JAN. 20	41	27	27	28	39	47	16	11	47	8	1	41
JAN. 21	41	28	29	29	40	47	16	11	47	8	1	41
JAN. 22	41	30	30	31	40	48	16	11	47	8	1	41
JAN. 23	42	31	32	32	40	48	16	11	47	8	1	41
JAN. 24	42	33	34	34	40	48	16	10	47	8	1	41
JAN. 25	42	35	35	36	40	48	16	10	47	8	1	41
JAN. 26	42	36	37	37	41	48	16	10	47	8	1	41
JAN. 27	42	38	39	39	41	48	16	10	47	8	1	41
JAN. 28	42	40	40	41	41	48	16	10	47	8	1	41
JAN. 29	42	42	42	43	41	48	16	10	47	8	1	41
JAN. 30	42	44	44	45	41	48	16	10	47	8	1	41
JAN. 31	43	45	46	47	42	1	16	10	47	8	1	41

Date & Time	SUN ☉	MOON 1 ◐	MOON 2 ◑	MOON 3 ●	MERCURY	VENUS	MARS	JUPITER	SATURN	URANUS	NEPTUNE	PLUTO
FEB. 1	43	47	48	1	42	1	16	10	47	8	1	41
FEB. 2	43	1	2	3	42	1	16	10	47	8	1	41
FEB. 3	43	3	4	4	42	1	16	10	47	8	1	41
FEB. 4	43	5	6	6	43	1	16	10	47	8	1	41
FEB. 5	43	7	8	8	43	1	16	10	47	8	1	41
FEB. 6	43	9	9	10	43	1	16	10	47	8	1	41
FEB. 7	43	11	11	12	43	1	15	10	47	8	1	41
FEB. 8	44	13	13	14	43	1	15	10	47	8	1	41
FEB. 9	44	14	15	15	44	1	15	10	47	8	1	41
FEB. 10	44	16	17	17	44	2	15	10	47	8	1	41
FEB. 11	44	18	18	19	44	2	15	10	47	8	1	41
FEB. 12	44	20	20	21	44	2	15	10	47	8	1	41
FEB. 13	44	21	22	22	45	2	15	10	47	8	1	41
FEB. 14	44	23	23	24	45	2	15	10	47	8	1	41
FEB. 15	44	25	25	26	45	2	15	10	48	8	1	41
FEB. 16	45	26	27	27	45	2	15	11	48	8	1	41
FEB. 17	45	28	28	29	46	2	15	11	48	8	1	41
FEB. 18	45	29	30	30	46	2	15	11	48	8	1	41
FEB. 19	45	31	31	32	46	2	15	11	48	8	1	41
FEB. 20	45	32	33	34	46	2	15	11	48	8	1	41
FEB. 21	45	34	35	35	47	2	15	11	48	8	1	41
FEB. 22	45	36	36	37	47	2	15	11	48	8	1	41
FEB. 23	46	37	38	39	47	2	15	11	48	8	1	41
FEB. 24	46	39	40	40	47	2	15	11	48	8	1	41
FEB. 25	46	41	42	42	48	2	15	11	48	8	1	41
FEB. 26	46	43	43	44	48	2	15	11	48	8	1	41
FEB. 27	46	45	45	46	48	2	15	11	48	8	1	41
FEB. 28	46	47	47	48	48	2	15	11	48	8	1	41

MOON 1 ◐ 12:01 A.M. TO 8:00 A.M.   **MOON 2** ◑ 8:01 A.M. TO 4:00 P.M.   **MOON 3** ● 4:01 P.M. TO 12:00 A.M.

Use only one "moon" number. Choose the column closest to your time of birth. If your place of birth is not on Eastern Standard Time, be sure to read "How to Convert to Eastern Standard Time" at the beginning of this section.

2025

March

April

Date & Time	SUN	MOON 1	MOON 2	MOON 3	MERCURY	VENUS	MARS	JUPITER	SATURN	URANUS	NEPTUNE	PLUTO
MAR. 1	46	1	1	2	1	2	15	11	48	8	1	41
MAR. 2	46	3	3	4	1	2	15	11	48	8	1	41
MAR. 3	47	5	5	6	1	2	15	11	48	8	1	41
MAR. 4	47	6	7	8	1	2	15	11	48	8	1	41
MAR. 5	47	8	9	10	1	2	15	11	48	8	1	41
MAR. 6	47	10	11	11	1	2	15	11	48	8	1	41
MAR. 7	47	12	13	13	2	2	15	11	48	8	1	41
MAR. 8	47	14	14	15	2	2	15	11	48	8	1	41
MAR. 9	47	16	16	17	2	2	15	11	48	8	1	41
MAR. 10	47	17	18	19	2	2	15	11	48	8	1	41
MAR. 11	48	19	20	20	2	2	15	11	48	8	1	41
MAR. 12	48	21	21	22	2	2	15	11	48	8	1	41
MAR. 13	48	22	23	23	2	2	15	11	48	8	1	41
MAR. 14	48	24	25	25	2	2	15	11	48	8	1	41
MAR. 15	48	26	26	27	2	2	16	11	48	8	1	41
MAR. 16	48	27	28	28	2	2	16	11	48	8	1	41
MAR. 17	48	29	29	30	2	2	16	11	48	8	1	41
MAR. 18	48	30	31	31	2	2	16	11	48	8	1	41
MAR. 19	1	32	32	33	2	2	16	11	48	8	1	41
MAR. 20	1	34	34	35	2	2	16	11	48	8	1	41
MAR. 21	1	35	36	36	2	1	16	11	48	8	1	41
MAR. 22	1	37	37	38	2	1	16	11	48	8	1	41
MAR. 23	1	38	39	40	2	1	16	11	48	8	1	41
MAR. 24	1	40	41	41	2	1	16	11	48	8	1	41
MAR. 25	2	42	43	43	2	1	16	11	48	8	1	41
MAR. 26	2	44	44	45	1	1	16	11	48	8	1	41
MAR. 27	2	46	46	47	1	1	16	11	48	8	1	41
MAR. 28	2	48	48	1	1	1	16	11	48	8	1	41
MAR. 29	2	2	2	3	1	1	16	11	48	8	1	41
MAR. 30	2	4	4	5	1	1	16	11	48	8	1	41
MAR. 31	2	6	6	7	1	1	16	11	48	8	1	41

Date & Time	SUN	MOON 1	MOON 2	MOON 3	MERCURY	VENUS	MARS	JUPITER	SATURN	URANUS	NEPTUNE	PLUTO
APR. 1	2	8	8	9	1	1	16	11	48	8	1	41
APR. 2	2	10	10	11	1	1	16	11	48	8	1	41
APR. 3	3	12	12	13	1	1	16	11	48	8	1	41
APR. 4	3	13	14	15	1	48	16	11	48	8	1	41
APR. 5	3	15	16	16	1	48	16	11	48	8	1	41
APR. 6	3	17	18	18	1	48	16	11	48	8	1	41
APR. 7	3	19	19	20	1	48	16	11	48	8	1	41
APR. 8	3	20	21	21	1	48	16	11	48	8	1	41
APR. 9	3	22	23	23	1	48	16	11	48	8	1	41
APR. 10	3	24	24	25	1	48	17	11	48	8	1	41
APR. 11	4	25	26	26	1	48	17	11	48	8	1	41
APR. 12	4	27	27	28	1	48	17	11	48	8	1	41
APR. 13	4	28	29	29	1	48	17	11	48	8	1	41
APR. 14	4	30	30	31	1	48	17	11	48	8	1	41
APR. 15	4	32	32	33	1	48	17	11	48	8	1	41
APR. 16	4	33	34	34	1	48	17	11	48	8	1	41
APR. 17	4	35	35	36	1	48	17	11	48	8	1	41
APR. 18	4	36	37	37	1	48	17	11	48	8	1	41
APR. 19	5	38	39	39	1	48	17	12	1	8	1	41
APR. 20	5	40	40	41	1	48	17	12	1	8	1	41
APR. 21	5	41	42	43	2	48	17	12	1	8	1	41
APR. 22	5	43	44	44	2	48	17	12	1	8	1	41
APR. 23	5	45	46	46	2	1	17	12	1	8	1	41
APR. 24	5	47	47	48	2	1	17	12	1	8	1	41
APR. 25	6	1	1	2	2	1	17	12	1	8	1	41
APR. 26	6	3	3	4	2	1	17	12	1	8	1	41
APR. 27	6	5	5	6	2	1	17	12	1	8	1	41
APR. 28	6	7	7	8	3	1	18	12	1	8	1	41
APR. 29	6	9	10	10	3	1	18	12	1	8	1	41
APR. 30	6	11	11	12	3	1	18	12	1	8	1	41

MOON 1 ◗ 12:01 A.M. TO 8:00 A.M.   **MOON 2** ◑ 8:01 A.M. TO 4:00 P.M.   **MOON 3** ● 4:01 P.M. TO 12:00 A.M.

Use only one "moon" number. Choose the column closest to your time of birth. If your place of birth is not on Eastern Standard Time, be sure to read "How to Convert to Eastern Standard Time" at the beginning of this section.

Date & Time	SUN	MOON 1	MOON 2	MOON 3	MERCURY	VENUS	MARS	JUPITER	SATURN	URANUS	NEPTUNE	PLUTO
MAY 1	6	13	13	14	3	1	18	12	1	8	1	41
MAY 2	6	15	15	16	3	1	18	12	1	8	1	41
MAY 3	7	16	17	18	3	1	18	12	1	8	1	41
MAY 4	7	18	19	19	4	1	18	12	1	8	1	41
MAY 5	7	20	21	21	4	1	18	12	1	8	1	41
MAY 6	7	22	22	23	4	1	18	12	1	8	1	41
MAY 7	7	23	24	24	4	2	18	12	1	8	1	41
MAY 8	7	25	25	26	4	2	18	12	1	9	1	41
MAY 9	7	26	27	27	5	2	18	12	1	9	1	41
MAY 10	7	28	29	29	5	2	18	12	1	9	1	41
MAY 11	8	30	30	31	5	2	18	12	1	9	1	41
MAY 12	8	31	32	32	5	2	18	12	1	9	1	41
MAY 13	8	33	33	34	5	2	18	12	1	9	1	41
MAY 14	8	34	35	35	6	2	19	12	1	9	1	41
MAY 15	8	36	36	37	6	2	19	12	1	9	1	41
MAY 16	8	38	38	39	6	2	19	12	1	9	1	41
MAY 17	8	39	40	40	7	3	19	12	1	9	1	41
MAY 18	8	41	42	42	7	3	19	12	1	9	1	41
MAY 19	9	43	43	44	7	3	19	12	1	9	1	41
MAY 20	9	44	45	46	7	3	19	12	1	9	1	41
MAY 21	9	46	47	47	8	3	19	12	1	9	1	41
MAY 22	9	48	1	1	8	3	19	12	1	9	1	41
MAY 23	9	2	3	3	8	3	19	12	1	9	1	41
MAY 24	9	4	5	5	8	3	19	12	1	9	1	41
MAY 25	10	6	7	7	9	3	19	12	1	9	1	41
MAY 26	10	8	9	9	9	4	19	13	1	9	1	41
MAY 27	10	10	11	11	9	4	19	13	1	9	1	41
MAY 28	10	12	13	13	10	4	20	13	1	9	1	41
MAY 29	10	14	15	15	10	4	20	13	1	9	1	41
MAY 30	10	16	16	17	10	4	20	13	1	9	1	41
MAY 31	10	18	18	19	10	4	20	13	1	9	1	41

Date & Time	SUN	MOON 1	MOON 2	MOON 3	MERCURY	VENUS	MARS	JUPITER	SATURN	URANUS	NEPTUNE	PLUTO
JUN. 1	10	19	20	21	11	4	20	13	1	9	1	41
JUN. 2	10	21	22	22	11	4	20	13	1	9	1	41
JUN. 3	11	23	23	24	11	5	20	13	1	9	1	41
JUN. 4	11	24	25	25	12	5	20	13	1	9	1	41
JUN. 5	11	26	27	27	12	5	20	13	1	9	1	41
JUN. 6	11	28	28	29	12	5	20	13	1	9	1	41
JUN. 7	11	29	30	30	12	5	20	13	1	9	1	41
JUN. 8	11	31	31	32	13	5	20	13	1	9	1	41
JUN. 9	11	32	33	33	13	5	20	13	1	9	1	41
JUN. 10	11	34	34	35	13	6	20	13	1	9	1	41
JUN. 11	12	36	36	37	14	6	21	13	1	9	1	41
JUN. 12	12	37	38	38	14	6	21	13	1	9	1	41
JUN. 13	12	39	39	40	14	6	21	13	1	9	1	41
JUN. 14	12	41	41	42	14	6	21	13	1	9	1	41
JUN. 15	12	42	43	43	15	6	21	13	1	9	1	41
JUN. 16	12	44	45	45	15	6	21	13	1	9	1	41
JUN. 17	12	46	46	47	15	6	21	13	1	9	1	41
JUN. 18	12	48	48	1	15	7	21	13	1	9	1	41
JUN. 19	13	1	2	3	15	7	21	13	1	9	1	41
JUN. 20	13	3	4	5	16	7	21	13	1	9	1	41
JUN. 21	13	5	6	7	16	7	21	13	1	9	1	41
JUN. 22	13	7	8	8	16	7	21	13	1	9	1	41
JUN. 23	13	9	10	10	16	7	21	13	1	9	1	41
JUN. 24	13	11	12	12	16	7	21	13	1	9	1	41
JUN. 25	14	13	14	14	17	8	22	13	1	9	1	41
JUN. 26	14	15	16	16	17	8	22	13	1	9	1	41
JUN. 27	14	17	17	18	17	8	22	14	1	9	1	41
JUN. 28	14	19	19	20	17	8	22	14	1	9	1	41
JUN. 29	14	20	21	22	17	8	22	14	1	9	1	41
JUN. 30	14	22	23	23	18	8	22	14	1	9	1	41

MOON 1 ☾ 12:01 A.M. TO 8:00 A.M.   **MOON 2** ☽ 8:01 A.M. TO 4:00 P.M.   **MOON 3** ● 4:01 P.M. TO 12:00 A.M.
Use only one "moon" number. Choose the column closest to your time of birth. If your place of birth is not on Eastern Standard Time, be sure to read "How to Convert to Eastern Standard Time" at the beginning of this section.

2025

July

August

Date & Time	SUN ☉	MOON 1 ◖	MOON 2 ◑	MOON 3 ●	MERCURY	VENUS	MARS	JUPITER	SATURN	URANUS	NEPTUNE	PLUTO
JUL. 1	14	24	24	25	18	8	22	14	1	9	1	41
JUL. 2	14	25	26	27	18	9	22	14	1	9	1	41
JUL. 3	15	27	28	28	18	9	22	14	1	9	1	41
JUL. 4	15	29	29	30	18	9	22	14	1	9	1	41
JUL. 5	15	30	31	31	18	9	22	14	1	9	1	41
JUL. 6	15	32	32	33	18	9	22	14	1	9	1	41
JUL. 7	15	33	34	35	18	9	22	14	1	9	1	41
JUL. 8	15	35	36	36	19	9	23	14	1	9	1	41
JUL. 9	15	37	37	38	19	10	23	14	1	9	1	41
JUL. 10	15	38	39	40	19	10	23	14	1	9	1	41
JUL. 11	16	40	41	41	19	10	23	14	1	9	1	41
JUL. 12	16	42	42	43	19	10	23	14	1	9	1	41
JUL. 13	16	44	44	45	19	10	23	14	1	9	1	41
JUL. 14	16	45	46	47	19	10	23	14	1	9	1	41
JUL. 15	16	47	48	48	19	11	23	14	1	9	1	41
JUL. 16	16	1	2	2	19	11	23	14	1	9	1	41
JUL. 17	16	3	3	4	19	11	23	14	1	9	1	41
JUL. 18	16	5	5	6	19	11	23	14	1	9	1	41
JUL. 19	17	7	7	8	19	11	23	14	1	9	1	41
JUL. 20	17	9	9	10	19	11	24	14	1	9	1	41
JUL. 21	17	10	11	12	19	11	24	14	1	9	1	41
JUL. 22	17	12	13	14	19	12	24	14	1	9	1	41
JUL. 23	17	14	15	16	19	12	24	14	1	9	1	41
JUL. 24	17	16	17	17	19	12	24	14	1	9	1	41
JUL. 25	17	18	19	19	19	12	24	14	1	9	1	41
JUL. 26	18	20	20	21	19	12	24	14	1	9	1	41
JUL. 27	18	22	22	23	19	12	24	14	1	9	1	41
JUL. 28	18	23	24	24	19	13	24	14	1	9	1	41
JUL. 29	18	25	25	26	18	13	24	14	1	9	1	41
JUL. 30	18	27	27	28	18	13	24	14	1	9	1	41
JUL. 31	18	28	29	29	18	13	24	15	1	9	1	41

Date & Time	SUN ☉	MOON 1 ◖	MOON 2 ◑	MOON 3 ●	MERCURY	VENUS	MARS	JUPITER	SATURN	URANUS	NEPTUNE	PLUTO
AUG. 1	18	30	30	31	18	13	24	15	1	9	1	41
AUG. 2	18	31	32	32	18	13	25	15	1	9	1	41
AUG. 3	19	33	33	34	18	13	25	15	1	9	1	41
AUG. 4	19	35	35	36	18	14	25	15	1	9	1	41
AUG. 5	19	36	37	37	18	14	25	15	1	9	1	41
AUG. 6	19	38	38	39	18	14	25	15	1	9	1	41
AUG. 7	19	39	40	41	18	14	25	15	1	9	1	41
AUG. 8	19	41	42	42	18	14	25	15	1	9	1	41
AUG. 9	19	43	44	44	18	14	25	15	1	9	1	41
AUG. 10	19	45	45	46	18	15	25	15	1	9	1	41
AUG. 11	20	47	47	48	18	15	25	15	1	9	1	41
AUG. 12	20	1	1	2	18	15	25	15	1	9	1	41
AUG. 13	20	2	3	4	18	15	25	15	1	9	1	41
AUG. 14	20	4	5	6	18	15	26	15	1	9	1	41
AUG. 15	20	6	7	7	18	15	26	15	1	9	1	41
AUG. 16	20	8	9	9	18	15	26	15	1	9	1	41
AUG. 17	20	10	11	11	18	16	26	15	1	9	1	41
AUG. 18	20	12	12	13	18	16	26	15	1	9	1	41
AUG. 19	21	14	14	15	18	16	26	15	1	9	1	41
AUG. 20	21	16	16	17	18	16	26	15	1	9	1	41
AUG. 21	21	17	18	19	18	16	26	15	1	9	1	41
AUG. 22	21	19	20	20	18	16	26	15	1	9	1	41
AUG. 23	21	21	22	22	19	17	26	15	1	9	1	41
AUG. 24	21	23	23	24	19	17	26	15	1	9	1	41
AUG. 25	21	24	25	25	19	17	27	15	1	9	1	41
AUG. 26	22	26	27	27	19	17	27	15	1	9	1	41
AUG. 27	22	28	28	29	19	17	27	15	1	9	1	41
AUG. 28	22	29	30	30	20	17	27	15	1	9	1	41
AUG. 29	22	31	31	32	20	18	27	15	1	9	1	41
AUG. 30	22	32	33	33	20	18	27	15	1	9	1	41
AUG. 31	22	34	34	35	20	18	27	15	1	9	1	41

MOON 1 ◖ 12:01 A.M. TO 8:00 A.M.   **MOON 2 ◑ 8:01 A.M. TO 4:00 P.M.**   **MOON 3 ● 4:01 P.M. TO 12:00 A.M.**

Use only one "moon" number. Choose the column closest to your time of birth. If your place of birth is not on Eastern Standard Time, be sure to read "How to Convert to Eastern Standard Time" at the beginning of this section.

September

Date & Time	SUN ☉	MOON 1 ☽	MOON 2 ☽	MOON 3 ●	MERCURY	VENUS	MARS	JUPITER	SATURN	URANUS	NEPTUNE	PLUTO
SEP. 1	22	36	36	37	21	18	27	15	1	9	1	41
SEP. 2	22	37	38	38	21	18	27	15	1	9	1	41
SEP. 3	23	39	39	40	21	18	27	15	1	9	1	41
SEP. 4	23	41	41	42	21	18	27	15	1	9	1	41
SEP. 5	23	42	43	44	22	19	27	15	1	9	1	41
SEP. 6	23	44	45	45	22	19	28	15	1	9	1	41
SEP. 7	23	46	47	47	22	19	28	15	1	9	1	41
SEP. 8	23	48	1	1	22	19	28	16	1	9	1	41
SEP. 9	23	2	2	3	23	19	28	16	1	9	1	41
SEP. 10	23	4	4	5	23	19	28	16	1	9	1	41
SEP. 11	24	6	6	7	23	20	28	16	1	9	1	41
SEP. 12	24	8	8	9	23	20	28	16	1	9	1	41
SEP. 13	24	10	10	11	24	20	28	16	1	9	1	41
SEP. 14	24	11	12	13	24	20	28	16	1	9	1	41
SEP. 15	24	13	14	15	24	20	28	16	1	9	1	41
SEP. 16	24	15	16	16	24	20	28	16	1	9	1	41
SEP. 17	24	17	18	18	25	21	29	16	1	9	1	41
SEP. 18	24	19	19	20	25	21	29	16	1	9	1	41
SEP. 19	25	20	21	22	25	21	29	16	1	9	1	41
SEP. 20	25	22	23	23	25	21	29	16	1	9	1	41
SEP. 21	25	24	24	25	26	21	29	16	1	9	1	41
SEP. 22	25	25	26	27	26	21	29	16	1	9	1	41
SEP. 23	25	27	28	28	26	22	29	16	1	9	1	41
SEP. 24	25	29	29	30	26	22	29	16	1	9	1	41
SEP. 25	26	30	31	31	27	22	29	16	1	9	1	41
SEP. 26	26	32	32	33	27	22	29	16	1	9	1	41
SEP. 27	26	33	34	35	27	22	29	16	1	9	1	41
SEP. 28	26	35	36	36	27	22	29	16	1	9	1	41
SEP. 29	26	37	37	38	27	23	30	16	1	9	1	41
SEP. 30	26	38	39	39	28	23	30	16	1	9	1	41

October

Date & Time	SUN ☉	MOON 1 ☽	MOON 2 ☽	MOON 3 ●	MERCURY	VENUS	MARS	JUPITER	SATURN	URANUS	NEPTUNE	PLUTO
OCT. 1	26	40	40	41	28	23	30	16	1	9	1	41
OCT. 2	26	42	42	43	28	23	30	16	1	9	1	41
OCT. 3	27	43	44	45	28	23	30	16	1	9	1	41
OCT. 4	27	45	46	46	28	23	30	16	1	9	1	41
OCT. 5	27	47	48	48	29	24	30	16	1	9	1	41
OCT. 6	27	1	2	2	29	24	30	16	1	9	1	41
OCT. 7	27	3	4	4	29	24	30	16	1	9	1	41
OCT. 8	27	5	6	6	29	24	30	16	1	9	1	41
OCT. 9	27	7	8	8	29	24	30	16	1	9	1	41
OCT. 10	27	9	10	10	30	24	31	16	1	9	1	41
OCT. 11	28	11	12	12	30	25	31	16	1	9	1	41
OCT. 12	28	13	13	14	30	25	31	16	1	9	1	41
OCT. 13	28	15	15	16	30	25	31	16	1	9	1	41
OCT. 14	28	17	17	18	30	25	31	16	1	9	1	41
OCT. 15	28	18	19	19	31	25	31	16	1	9	1	41
OCT. 16	28	20	21	21	31	25	31	16	1	9	1	41
OCT. 17	28	22	22	23	31	26	31	16	1	9	1	41
OCT. 18	28	23	24	24	31	26	31	16	1	9	1	41
OCT. 19	29	25	26	26	31	26	31	16	48	9	1	41
OCT. 20	29	27	27	28	32	26	32	16	48	9	1	41
OCT. 21	29	28	29	29	32	26	32	16	48	9	1	41
OCT. 22	29	30	30	31	32	26	32	16	48	9	1	41
OCT. 23	29	31	32	32	32	27	32	16	48	9	1	41
OCT. 24	29	33	34	34	32	27	32	16	48	9	1	41
OCT. 25	29	35	35	36	32	27	32	16	48	9	1	41
OCT. 26	30	36	37	37	32	27	32	16	48	9	1	41
OCT. 27	30	38	38	39	33	27	32	16	48	9	1	41
OCT. 28	30	39	40	40	33	27	32	16	48	9	1	41
OCT. 29	30	41	42	42	33	28	32	16	48	9	1	41
OCT. 30	30	43	43	44	33	28	32	16	48	9	1	41
OCT. 31	30	44	45	46	33	28	33	16	48	9	1	41

MOON 1 ☽ 12:01 A.M. TO 8:00 A.M.   **MOON 2 ☽ 8:01 A.M. TO 4:00 P.M.**   **MOON 3 ● 4:01 P.M. TO 12:00 A.M.**
Use only one "moon" number. Choose the column closest to your time of birth. If your place of birth is not on Eastern Standard Time, be sure to read "How to Convert to Eastern Standard Time" at the beginning of this section.

2025

November

December

Date & Time	SUN ☉	MOON 1 ☽	MOON 2 ☽	MOON 3 ●	MERCURY	VENUS	MARS	JUPITER	SATURN	URANUS	NEPTUNE	PLUTO
NOV. 1	30	14	15	16	29	24	24	23	34	3	46	39
NOV. 2	30	16	17	17	29	24	24	23	34	3	46	39
NOV. 3	31	18	18	19	29	24	24	23	34	3	46	39
NOV. 4	31	20	20	21	29	24	24	23	34	3	46	39
NOV. 5	31	21	22	22	30	24	24	23	34	3	46	39
NOV. 6	31	23	23	24	30	25	24	23	34	3	46	39
NOV. 7	31	24	25	25	30	25	25	23	34	3	46	39
NOV. 8	31	26	26	27	30	25	25	23	34	3	46	39
NOV. 9	31	27	28	28	30	25	25	23	34	3	46	39
NOV. 10	31	29	30	30	31	25	25	23	34	3	46	39
NOV. 11	31	31	31	32	31	25	25	23	34	3	46	39
NOV. 12	32	32	33	33	31	25	25	23	34	3	46	39
NOV. 13	32	34	34	35	31	26	25	23	34	3	46	39
NOV. 14	32	36	36	37	32	26	25	23	34	3	46	39
NOV. 15	32	37	38	38	32	26	25	23	34	3	46	39
NOV. 16	32	39	40	40	32	26	25	24	34	3	46	39
NOV. 17	32	41	41	42	32	26	25	24	34	3	46	39
NOV. 18	32	43	43	44	32	26	25	24	34	3	46	39
NOV. 19	33	44	45	46	33	27	25	24	34	3	46	39
NOV. 20	33	46	47	48	33	27	26	24	34	3	46	39
NOV. 21	33	48	1	1	33	27	26	24	34	3	46	39
NOV. 22	33	2	3	3	33	27	26	24	34	3	46	39
NOV. 23	33	4	5	5	33	27	26	24	34	3	46	39
NOV. 24	33	6	7	7	34	27	26	24	34	3	46	39
NOV. 25	34	8	9	9	34	27	26	24	34	3	46	39
NOV. 26	34	10	11	11	34	28	26	24	34	3	46	39
NOV. 27	34	12	12	13	34	28	26	24	34	3	46	39
NOV. 28	34	14	14	15	35	28	26	24	34	3	46	39
NOV. 29	34	16	16	17	35	28	26	24	34	3	46	39
NOV. 30	34	17	18	18	35	28	26	24	34	3	46	39

Date & Time	SUN ☉	MOON 1 ☽	MOON 2 ☽	MOON 3 ●	MERCURY	VENUS	MARS	JUPITER	SATURN	URANUS	NEPTUNE	PLUTO
DEC. 1	34	19	20	20	35	28	26	24	34	3	46	39
DEC. 2	34	21	21	22	35	29	26	24	34	3	46	39
DEC. 3	35	22	23	23	36	29	27	24	34	3	46	39
DEC. 4	35	24	24	25	36	29	27	24	34	3	46	39
DEC. 5	35	25	26	26	36	29	27	24	34	3	46	39
DEC. 6	35	27	27	28	36	29	27	24	34	3	46	39
DEC. 7	35	29	29	30	36	29	27	24	34	3	46	39
DEC. 8	35	30	31	31	37	29	27	24	34	3	46	39
DEC. 9	35	32	32	33	37	30	27	24	34	3	46	39
DEC. 10	35	33	34	35	37	30	27	24	34	3	46	39
DEC. 11	36	35	36	36	37	30	27	24	34	3	46	39
DEC. 12	36	37	37	38	37	30	27	24	34	3	46	39
DEC. 13	36	39	39	40	38	30	27	24	34	3	46	39
DEC. 14	36	40	41	42	38	30	27	24	34	3	46	39
DEC. 15	36	42	43	43	38	31	28	24	34	3	46	39
DEC. 16	36	44	45	45	38	31	28	24	34	3	46	39
DEC. 17	36	46	46	47	38	31	28	24	34	3	46	39
DEC. 18	36	48	1	1	39	31	28	24	34	3	46	39
DEC. 19	37	2	2	3	39	31	28	24	34	3	46	39
DEC. 20	37	3	4	5	39	31	28	24	34	3	46	39
DEC. 21	37	5	6	7	39	32	28	24	34	3	46	39
DEC. 22	37	7	8	9	39	32	28	24	34	3	46	39
DEC. 23	37	9	10	10	40	32	28	24	34	3	46	39
DEC. 24	37	11	12	12	40	32	28	24	34	3	46	39
DEC. 25	37	13	14	14	40	32	28	24	34	3	46	39
DEC. 26	38	15	15	16	40	32	28	24	34	3	46	39
DEC. 27	38	17	17	18	40	32	28	24	34	3	46	39
DEC. 28	38	18	19	19	40	33	28	24	34	3	46	39
DEC. 29	38	20	21	21	41	33	29	24	34	3	46	39
DEC. 30	38	22	22	23	41	33	29	24	34	3	46	39
DEC. 31	38	23	24	24	41	33	29	24	34	3	46	39

MOON 1 ☽ 12:01 A.M. TO 8:00 A.M.   **MOON 2 ☽ 8:01 A.M. TO 4:00 P.M.**   **MOON 3 ● 4:01 P.M. TO 12:00 A.M.**

Use only one "moon" number. Choose the column closest to your time of birth. If your place of birth is not on Eastern Standard Time, be sure to read "How to Convert to Eastern Standard Time" at the beginning of this section.

COMPARING CHARTS

Copy these side-by-side Fill-In Charts and Wheels and use any time you want to compare your birthday chart with the birthday chart of someone important to you, or to see how the planetary line up on an upcoming day compares with the alignment at your birth. Read page 18 for more information on comparing charts. Don't forget to check for conjunctions, trines, squares and/or oppositions.

FILL-IN CHART

Date & Time	SUN	MOON	MERCURY	VENUS	MARS	JUPITER	SATURN	URANUS	NEPTUNE	PLUTO

FILL-IN WHEEL

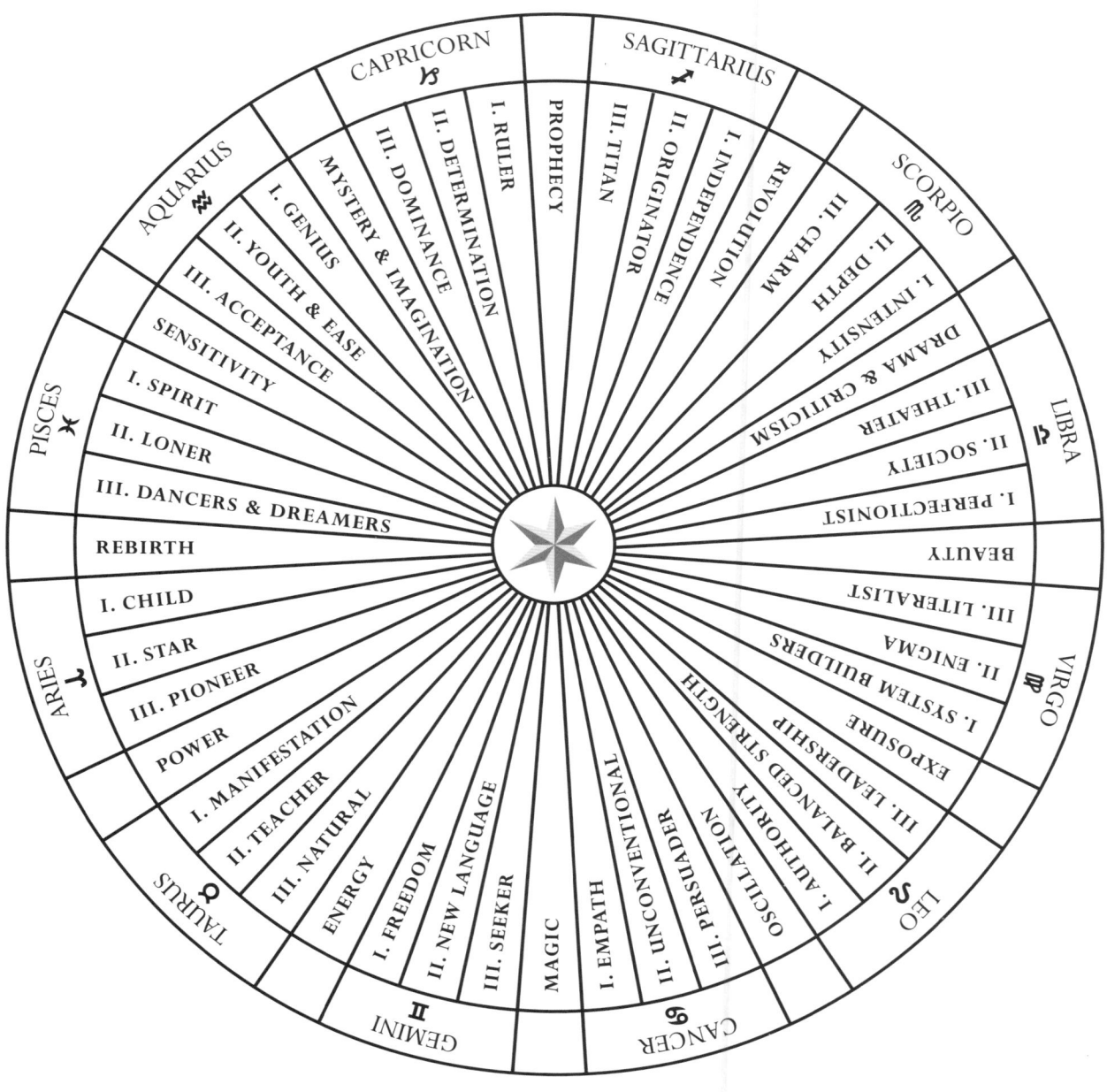

☉ Sun	♃ Jupiter		
☽ Moon	♄ Saturn		
☿ Mercury	♅ Uranus		
♀ Venus	♆ Neptune		
♂ Mars	♇ Pluto		

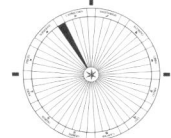

Conjunction:
Two planets
in the same
Personology period

Trine:
Two planets
exactly four signs
or cusps apart

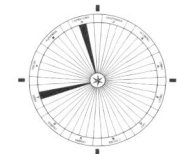

Square:
Two planets
exactly three signs
or cusps apart

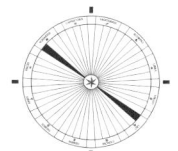

Opposition:
Two planets 180
degrees—or directly—
opposite each other

FILL-IN CHART

Date & Time	SUN	MOON	MERCURY	VENUS	MARS	JUPITER	SATURN	URANUS	NEPTUNE	PLUTO

FILL-IN WHEEL

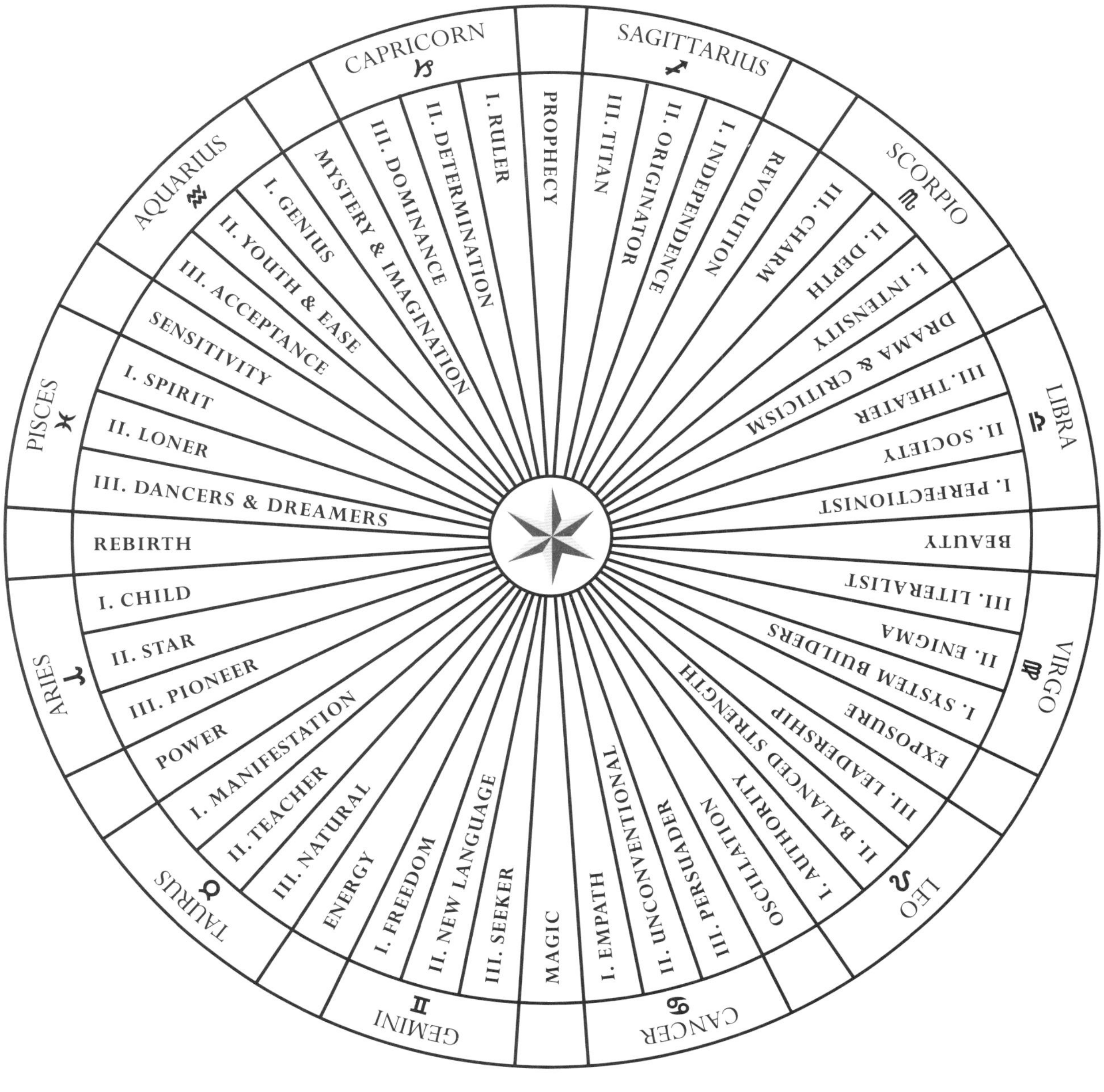

(Zodiac wheel with the following labels by sign)

CAPRICORN ♑: I. RULER; II. DETERMINATION; III. DOMINANCE; MYSTERY & IMAGINATION

SAGITTARIUS ♐: PROPHECY; I. INDEPENDENCE; II. ORIGINATOR; III. TITAN; REVOLUTION

AQUARIUS ♒: I. GENIUS; II. YOUTH & EASE; III. ACCEPTANCE; SENSITIVITY

SCORPIO ♏: III. CHARM; II. DEPTH; I. INTENSITY; DRAMA & CRITICISM

PISCES ♓: I. SPIRIT; II. LONER; III. DANCERS & DREAMERS; REBIRTH

LIBRA ♎: III. THEATER; II. SOCIETY; I. PERFECTIONIST; BEAUTY

ARIES ♈: I. CHILD; II. STAR; III. PIONEER; POWER

VIRGO ♍: III. LITERALIST; II. ENIGMA; I. SYSTEM BUILDERS; EXPOSURE

TAURUS ♉: I. MANIFESTATION; II. TEACHER; III. NATURAL; ENERGY

LEO ♌: III. LEADERSHIP; II. BALANCED STRENGTH; I. AUTHORITY; OSCILLATION

GEMINI ♊: I. FREEDOM; II. NEW LANGUAGE; III. SEEKER; MAGIC

CANCER ♋: I. EMPATH; II. UNCONVENTIONAL; III. PERSUADER

COMPARING CHARTS

Copy these side-by-side Fill-In Charts and Wheels and use any time you want to compare your birthday chart with the birthday chart of someone important to you, or to see how the planetary line up on an upcoming day compares with the alignment at your birth. Read page 18 for more information on comparing charts. Don't forget to check for conjunctions, trines, squares and/or oppositions.

FILL-IN CHART

Date & Time	SUN	MOON	MERCURY	VENUS	MARS	JUPITER	SATURN	URANUS	NEPTUNE	PLUTO

FILL-IN WHEEL

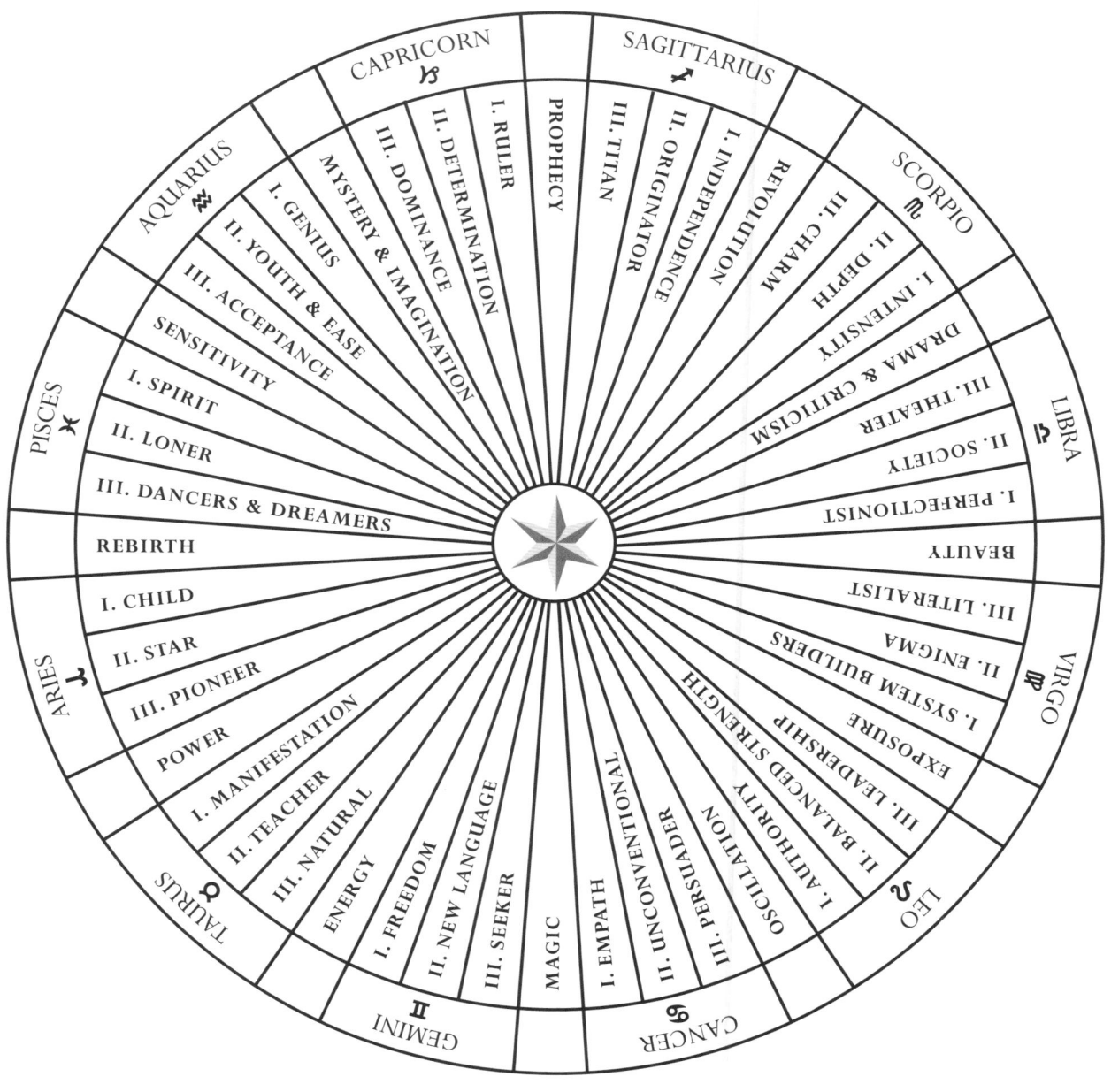

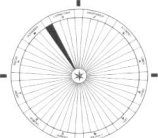

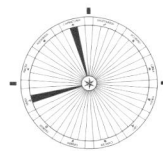
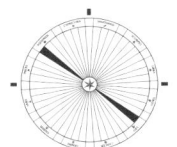
FILL-IN CHART

Date & Time	SUN	MOON	MERCURY	VENUS	MARS	JUPITER	SATURN	URANUS	NEPTUNE	PLUTO

FILL-IN WHEEL

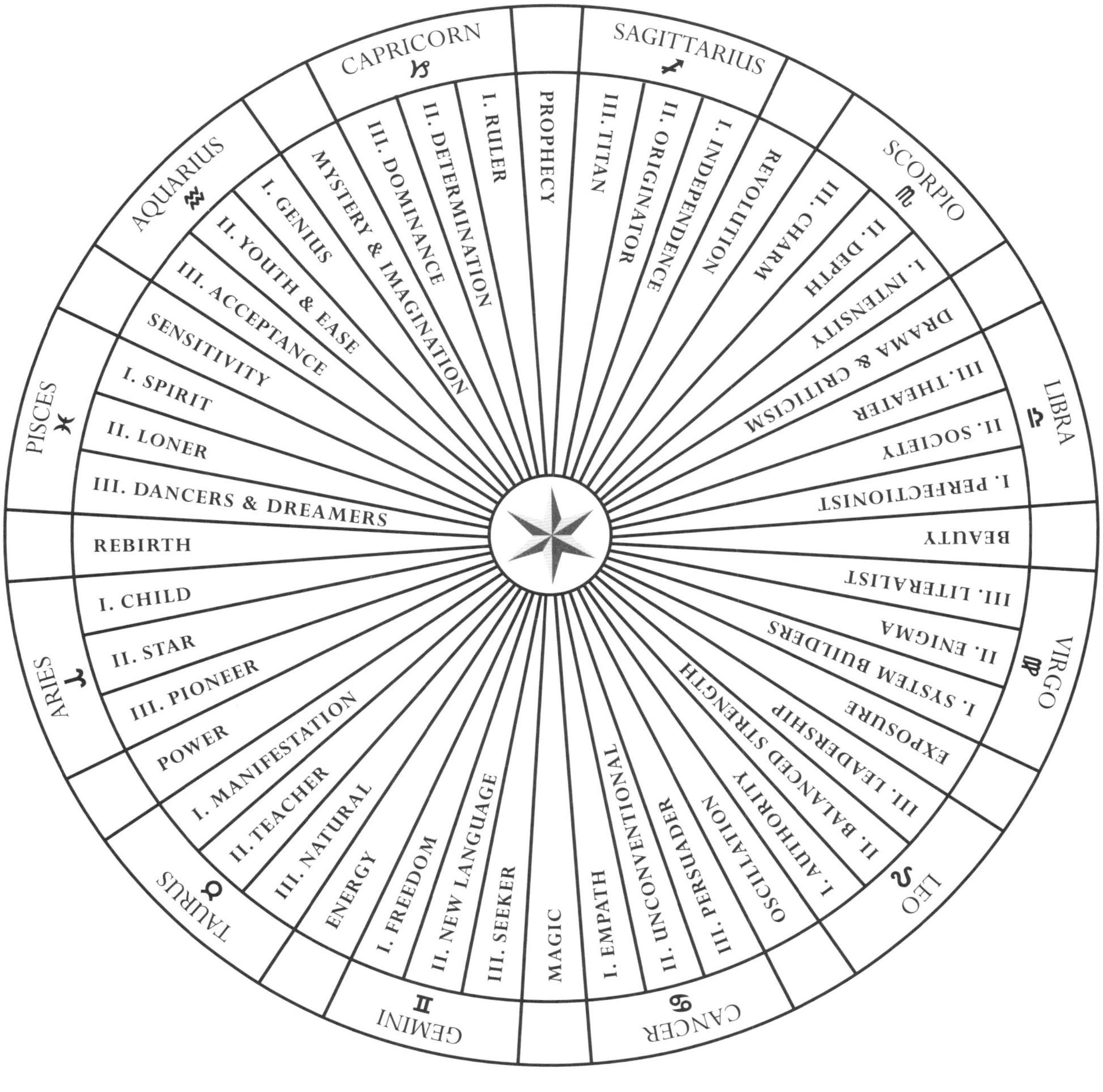

COMPARING CHARTS

Copy these side-by-side Fill-In Charts and Wheels and use any time you want to compare your birthday chart with the birthday chart of someone important to you, or to see how the planetary line up on an upcoming day compares with the alignment at your birth. Read page 18 for more information on comparing charts. Don't forget to check for conjunctions, trines, squares and/or oppositions.

FILL-IN CHART

Date & Time	SUN	MOON	MERCURY	VENUS	MARS	JUPITER	SATURN	URANUS	NEPTUNE	PLUTO

FILL-IN WHEEL

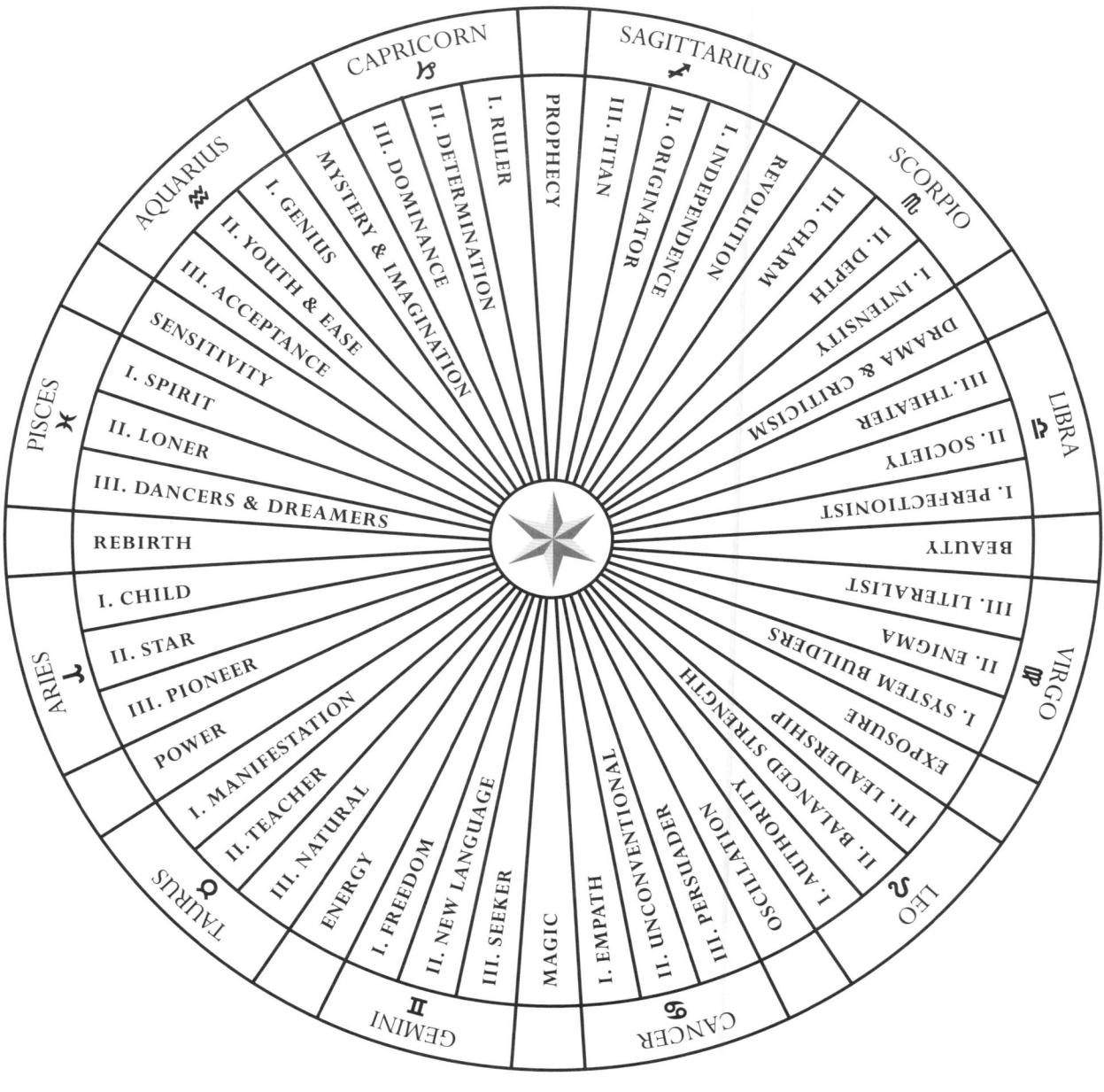

☉	Sun	♃	Jupiter
☽	Moon	♄	Saturn
☿	Mercury	♅	Uranus
♀	Venus	♆	Neptune
♂	Mars	♇	Pluto

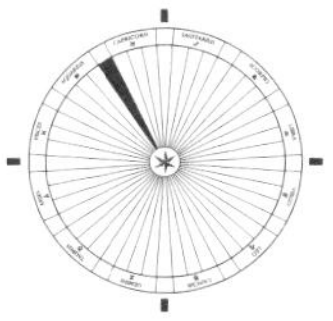

Conjunction:
Two planets
in the same
Personology period

Trine:
Two planets
exactly four signs
or cusps apart

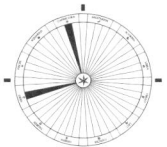

Square:
Two planets
exactly three signs
or cusps apart

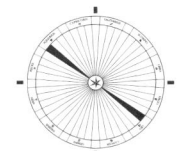

Opposition:
Two planets 180
degrees—or directly—
opposite each other

FILL-IN CHART

Date & Time	SUN	MOON	MERCURY	VENUS	MARS	JUPITER	SATURN	URANUS	NEPTUNE	PLUTO

FILL-IN WHEEL

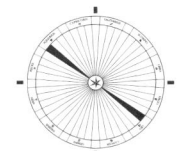

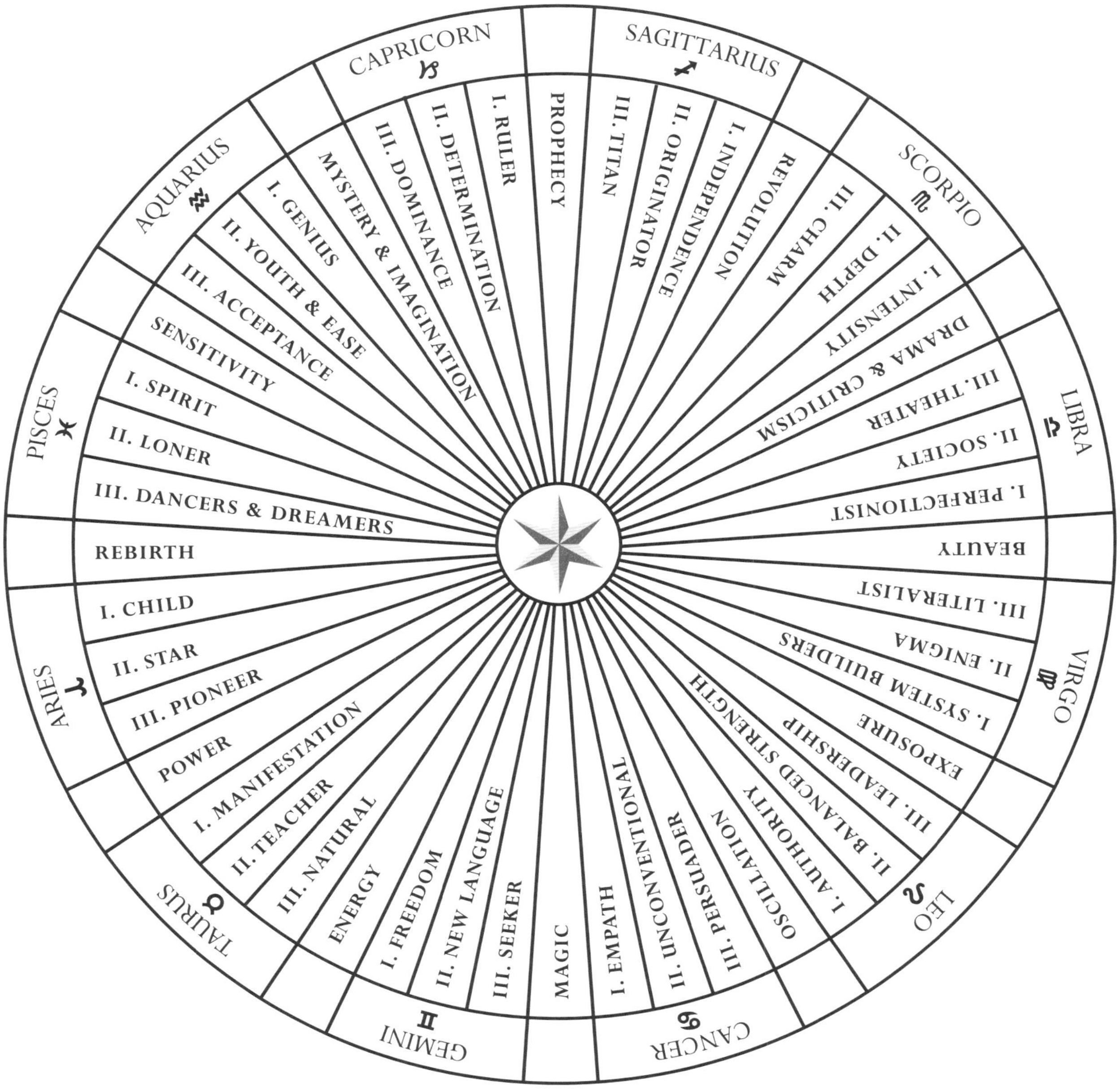

COMPARING CHARTS

Copy these side-by-side Fill-In Charts and Wheels and use any time you want to compare your birthday chart with the birthday chart of someone important to you, or to see how the planetary line up on an upcoming day compares with the alignment at your birth. Read page 18 for more information on comparing charts. Don't forget to check for conjunctions, trines, squares and/or oppositions.

FILL-IN CHART

Date & Time	SUN	MOON	MERCURY	VENUS	MARS	JUPITER	SATURN	URANUS	NEPTUNE	PLUTO

FILL-IN WHEEL

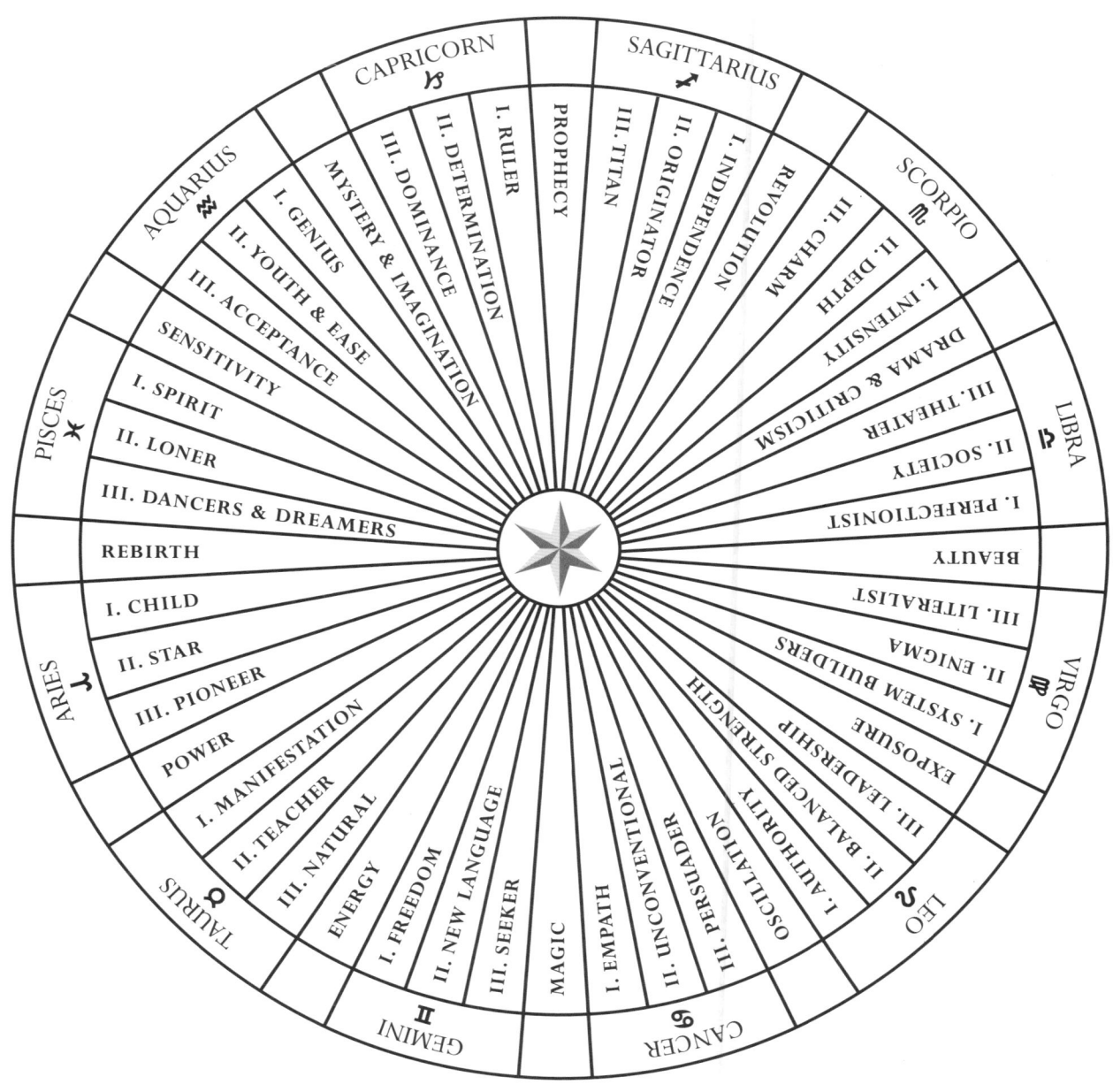

⊙ Sun	♃ Jupiter		
☽ Moon	♄ Saturn		
☿ Mercury	♅ Uranus		
♀ Venus	♆ Neptune		
♂ Mars	♇ Pluto		

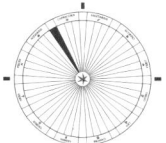

Conjunction:
Two planets
in the same
Personology period

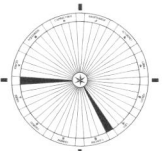

Trine:
Two planets
exactly four signs
or cusps apart

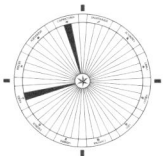

Square:
Two planets
exactly three signs
or cusps apart

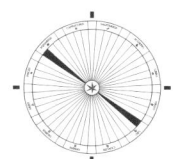

Opposition:
Two planets 180
degrees—or directly—
opposite each other

FILL-IN CHART

Date & Time | SUN | MOON | MERCURY | VENUS | MARS | JUPITER | SATURN | URANUS | NEPTUNE | PLUTO

FILL-IN WHEEL

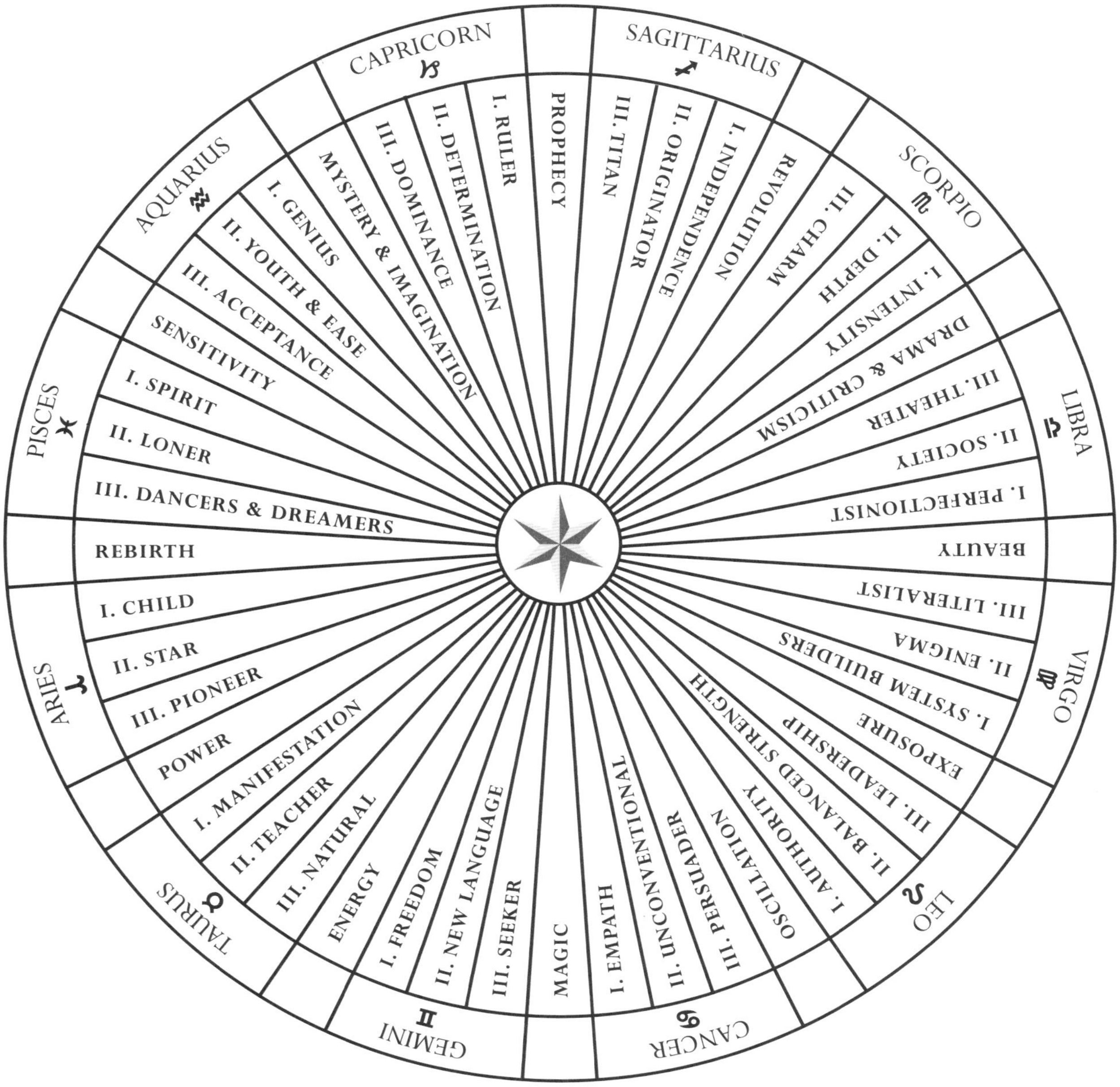

(astrological wheel chart with zodiac signs and their three decans/periods)

CAPRICORN ♑
- I. RULER
- II. DETERMINATION
- III. DOMINANCE
- MYSTERY & IMAGINATION

SAGITTARIUS ♐
- PROPHECY
- III. TITAN
- II. ORIGINATOR
- I. INDEPENDENCE

AQUARIUS ♒
- I. GENIUS
- II. YOUTH & EASE
- III. ACCEPTANCE
- SENSITIVITY

SCORPIO ♏
- REVOLUTION
- III. CHARM
- II. DEPTH
- I. INTENSITY
- DRAMA & CRITICISM

PISCES ♓
- I. SPIRIT
- II. LONER
- III. DANCERS & DREAMERS
- REBIRTH

LIBRA ♎
- III. THEATER
- II. SOCIETY
- I. PERFECTIONIST
- BEAUTY

ARIES ♈
- I. CHILD
- II. STAR
- III. PIONEER
- POWER

VIRGO ♍
- III. LITERALIST
- II. ENIGMA
- I. SYSTEM BUILDERS
- EXPOSURE

TAURUS ♉
- I. MANIFESTATION
- II. TEACHER
- III. NATURAL
- ENERGY

LEO ♌
- III. BALANCED STRENGTH
- II. LEADERSHIP
- I. AUTHORITY
- OSCILLATION

GEMINI ♊
- I. FREEDOM
- II. NEW LANGUAGE
- III. SEEKER
- MAGIC

CANCER ♋
- I. EMPATH
- II. UNCONVENTIONAL
- III. PERSUADER